...the House of the God of Jacob and He will teach us
...shall go forth the Law and the word of the Lord from
...em

ENCYCLOPAEDIA JUDAICA

VOLUME 12

MIN-O

ENCYCLOPAEDIA JUDAICA

ENCYCLOPAEDIA JUDAICA JERUSALEM

P.O.B. 7145, Jerusalem, Israel

Library of Congress Catalog Card Number: 72-90254

First printing 1972
Second printing 1973
Third printing 1974
Fourth printing 1978

Computerized typesetting, printing and binding by
Keterpress Enterprises, Jerusalem

Printed in Israel

A Clal Project

GLOSSARY

Asterisked terms have separate entries in the Encyclopaedia.

Actions Committee, early name of the Zionist General Council, the supreme institution of the World Zionist Organization in the interim between Congresses. The Zionist Executive's name was then the "Small Actions Committee."

***Adar,** twelfth month of the Jewish religious year, sixth of the civil, approximating to February-March.

***Aggadah,** name given to those sections of Talmud and Midrash containing homiletic expositions of the Bible, stories, legends, folklore, anecdotes, or maxims. In contradistinction to **halakhah*.

***Agunah,** woman unable to remarry according to Jewish law, because of desertion by her husband or inability to accept presumption of death.

***Aḥaronim,** later rabbinic authorities. In contradistinction to **rishonim* ("early ones").

Ahavah, liturgical poem inserted in the second benediction of the morning prayer *(*Ahavah Rabbah)* of the festivals and/or special Sabbaths.

Aktion (Ger.), operation involving the mass assembly, deportation, and murder of Jews by the Nazis during the *Holocaust.

***Aliyah,** (1) being called to Reading of the Law in synagogue; (2) immigration to Ereẓ Israel; (3) one of the waves of immigration to Ereẓ Israel from the early 1880s.

***Amidah,** main prayer recited at all services; also known as *Shemoneh Esreh* and *Tefillah*.

***Amora** (pl. **amoraim**), title given to the Jewish scholars in Ereẓ Israel and Babylonia in the third to sixth centuries who were responsible for the **Gemara*.

Aravah, the *willow; one of the *Four Species used on *Sukkot ("festival of Tabernacles") together with the **etrog, hadas,* and **lulav*.

***Arvit,** evening prayer.

Asarah be-Tevet, fast on the 10th of Tevet commemorating the commencement of the siege of Jerusalem by Nebuchadnezzar.

Asefat ha-Nivḥarim, representative assembly elected by Jews in Palestine during the period of the British Mandate (1920–48).

***Ashkenaz,** name applied generally in medieval rabbinical literature to Germany.

***Ashkenazi** (pl. **Ashkenazim**), German or West-, Central-, or East-European Jew(s), as contrasted with *Sephardi(m).

***Av,** fifth month of the Jewish religious year, eleventh of the civil, approximating to July-August.

***Av bet din,** vice-president of the supreme court *(bet din ha-gadol)* in Jerusalem during the Second Temple period; later, title given to communal rabbis as heads of the religious courts (see **bet din*).

***Badḥan,** jester, particularly at traditional Jewish weddings in Eastern Europe.

***Bakkashah** (Heb. "supplication"), type of petitionary prayer, mainly recited in the Sephardi rite on Rosh Ha-Shanah and the Day of Atonement.

Bar, "son of . . ."; frequently appearing in personal names.

***Baraita** (pl. **beraitot**), statement of **tanna* not found in *Mishnah.

***Bar mitzvah,** ceremony marking the initiation of a boy at the age of 13 into the Jewish religious community.

Ben, "son of . . ."; frequently appearing in personal names.

Berakhah (pl. **berakhot**), *benediction, blessing; formula of praise and thanksgiving.

***Bet din** (pl. **battei din**), rabbinic court of law.

***Bet ha-midrash,** school for higher rabbinic learning; often attached to or serving as a synagogue.

***Bilu,** first modern movement for pioneering and agricultural settlement in Ereẓ Israel, founded in 1882 at Kharkov, Russia.

***Bund,** Jewish socialist party founded in Vilna in 1897, supporting Jewish national rights; Yiddishist, and anti-Zionist.

Cohen (pl. **Cohanim**), see Kohen.

***Conservative Judaism,** trend in Judaism developed in the United States in the 20th century which, while opposing extreme changes in traditional observances, permits certain modifications of *halakhah* in response to the changing needs of the Jewish people.

***Consistory** (Fr. *consistoire*), governing body of a Jewish communal district in France and certain other countries.

***Converso(s),** term applied in Spain and Portugal to converted Jew(s), and sometimes more loosely to their descendants.

***Crypto-Jew,** term applied to a person who although observing outwardly Christianity (or some other religion) was at heart a Jew and maintained Jewish observances as far as possible (see Converso; Marrano; Neofiti; New Christian; Jadīd al-Islām).

***Dayyan,** member of rabbinic court.

Decisor, equivalent to the Hebrew *posek* (pl. **posekim*), the rabbi who gives the decision (*halakhah*) in Jewish law or practice.

***Devekut,** "devotion"; attachment or adhesion to God; communion with God.

***Diaspora,** Jews living in the "dispersion" outside Ereẓ Israel; area of Jewish settlement outside Ereẓ Israel.

Din, a law (both secular and religious), legal decision, or lawsuit.

Divan, diwan, collection of poems, especially in Hebrew, Arabic, or Persian.

Dunam, unit of land area (1,000 sq. m., c. 1/4 acre), used in Israel.

Einsatzgruppen, mobile units of Nazi S.S. and S.D.; in U.S.S.R. and Serbia, mobile killing units.

***Ein-Sof,** "without end"; "the infinite"; hidden, impersonal aspect of God; also used as a Divine Name.

***Elul,** sixth month of the Jewish religious calendar, 12th of the civil, precedes the High Holiday season in the fall.

Endloesung, see *Final Solution.

***Ereẓ Israel,** Land of Israel; Palestine.

***Eruv,** technical term for rabbinical provision permitting the alleviation of certain restrictions.

***Etrog,** citron; one of the *Four Species used on *Sukkot together with the **lulav, hadas,* and *aravah*.

Even ha-Ezer, see Shulḥan Arukh.

***Exilarch,** lay head of Jewish community in Babylonia (see also *resh galuta*), and elsewhere.

***Final Solution** (Ger. *Endloesung*), in Nazi terminology, the Nazi-planned mass murder and total annihilation of the Jews.

***Gabbai,** official of a Jewish congregation; originally a charity collector.

***Galut,** "exile"; the condition of the Jewish people in dispersion.
***Gaon** (pl. **geonim**), head of academy in post-talmudic period, especially in Babylonia.
Gaonate, office of *gaon.
***Gemara,** traditions, discussions, and rulings of the **amoraim*, commenting on and supplementing the *Mishnah, and forming part of the Babylonian and Palestinian Talmuds (see Talmud).
***Gematria,** interpretation of Hebrew word according to the numerical value of its letters.
General Government, territory in Poland administered by a German civilian governor-general with headquarters in Cracow after the German occupation in World War II.
***Genizah,** depository for sacred books. The best known was discovered in the synagogue of Fostat (old Cairo).
Get, bill of *divorce.
***Ge'ullah,** hymn inserted after the **Shema* into the benediction of the morning prayer of the festivals and special Sabbaths.
***Gilgul,** metempsychosis; transmigration of souls.
***Golem,** automaton, especially in human form, created by magical means and endowed with life.
***Ḥabad,** initials of *ḥokhmah, binah, da'at*: "wisdom, understanding, knowledge"; ḥasidic movement founded in Belorussia by *Shneur Zalman of Lyady.
Hadas, *myrtle; one of the *Four Species used on Sukkot together with the **etrog*, **lulav*, and *aravah*.
***Haftarah** (pl. **haftarot**), designation of the portion from the prophetical books of the Bible recited after the synagogue reading from the Pentateuch on Sabbaths and holidays.
***Haganah,** clandestine Jewish organization for armed self-defense in Ereẓ Israel under the British Mandate, which eventually evolved into a people's militia and became the basis for the Israel army.
***Haggadah,** ritual recited in the home on *Passover eve at *seder* table.
Haham, title of chief rabbi of the Spanish and Portuguese congregations in London, England.
***Ḥakham,** title of rabbi of *Sephardi congregation.
***Ḥakham bashi,** title in the 15th century and modern times of the chief rabbi in the Ottoman Empire, residing in Constantinople (Istanbul), also applied to principal rabbis in provincial towns.
Hakhsharah ("preparation"), organized training in the Diaspora of pioneers for agricultural settlement in Ereẓ Israel.
***Halakhah** (pl. **halakhot**), an accepted decision in rabbinic law. Also refers to those parts of the *Talmud concerned with legal matters. In contradistinction to **aggadah*.
Ḥaliẓah, biblically prescribed ceremony (Deut. 25:9–10) performed when a man refuses to marry his brother's childless widow, enabling her to remarry.
***Hallel,** term referring to Psalms 113–18 in liturgical use.
***Ḥalukkah,** system of financing the maintenance of Jewish communities in the holy cities of Ereẓ Israel by collections made abroad, mainly in the pre-Zionist era (see *kolel*).
Ḥalutz (pl. **ḥalutzim**), pioneer, especially in agriculture, in Ereẓ Israel.
Ḥalutziyyut, pioneering.
***Ḥanukkah,** eight-day celebration commemorating the victory of *Judah Maccabee over the Syrian king *Antiochus Epiphanes and the subsequent rededication of the Temple.
Ḥasid, adherent of *Ḥasidism.
***Ḥasidei Ashkenaz,** medieval pietist movement among the Jews of Germany.
***Ḥasidism,** (1) religious revivalist movement of popular mysticism among Jews of Germany in the Middle Ages; (2) religious movement founded by *Israel ben Eliezer Ba'al Shem Tov in the first half of the 18th century.
***Haskalah,** "Enlightenment"; movement for spreading modern European culture among Jews c. 1750–1880. See *maskil*.
***Havdalah,** ceremony marking the end of Sabbath or festival.
***Ḥazzan,** precentor who intones the liturgy and leads the prayers in synagogue; in earlier times a synagogue official.
***Ḥeder** (lit. "room"), school for teaching children Jewish religious observance.
Heikhalot, "palaces"; tradition in Jewish mysticism centering on mystical journeys through the heavenly spheres and palaces to the Divine Chariot (see Merkabah).
***Ḥerem,** excommunication, imposed by rabbinical authorities for purposes of religious and/or communal discipline; originally, in biblical times, that which is separated from common use either because it was an abomination or because it was consecrated to God.
Ḥeshvan, see Marḥeshvan.
***Ḥevra kaddisha,** title applied to charitable confraternity (**ḥevrah*), now generally limited to associations for burial of the dead.
***Ḥibbat Zion,** see Ḥovevei Zion.
***Histadrut** (abbr. for Heb. **Ha-Histadrut ha-Kelalit shel ha-Ovedim ha-Ivriyyim be-Ereẓ Israel).** Ereẓ Israel Jewish Labor Federation, founded in 1920; subsequently renamed Histadrut ha-Ovedim be-Ereẓ Israel.
***Holocaust,** the organized mass persecution and annihilation of European Jewry by the Nazis (1933–1945).
***Hoshana Rabba,** the seventh day of *Sukkot on which special observances are held.
Ḥoshen Mishpat, see Shulḥan Arukh.
Ḥovevei Zion, federation of *Ḥibbat Zion, early (pre-*Herzl) Zionist movement in Russia.
Illui, outstanding scholar or genius, especially a young prodigy in talmudic learning.
***Iyyar,** second month of the Jewish religious year, eighth of the civil, approximating to April-May.
I.Ẓ.L. (initials of Heb. ***Irgun Ẓeva'i Le'ummi;** "National Military Organization"), underground Jewish organization in Ereẓ Israel founded in 1931, which engaged from 1937 in retaliatory acts against Arab attacks and later against the British mandatory authorities.
***Jadīd al-Islām** (Ar.), a person practicing the Jewish religion in secret although outwardly observing Islam.
***Jewish Legion,** Jewish units in British army during World War I.
***Jihād** (Ar.), in Muslim religious law, holy war waged against infidels.
***Judenrat** (Ger. "Jewish council"), council set up in Jewish communities and ghettos under the Nazis to execute their instructions.
***Judenrein** (Ger. "clean of Jews"), in Nazi terminology the condition of a locality from which all Jews had been eliminated.
***Kabbalah,** the Jewish mystical tradition:
Kabbalah iyyunit, speculative Kabbalah;
Kabbalah ma'asit, practical Kabbalah;
Kabbalah nevu'it, prophetic Kabbalah.
Kabbalist, student of Kabbalah.
***Kaddish,** liturgical doxology.
Kahal, Jewish congregation; among Ashkenazim, *kehillah*.
***Kalām** (Ar.), science of Muslim theology; adherents of the Kalām are called *mutakallimūn*.
***Karaite,** member of a Jewish sect originating in the eighth century which rejected rabbinic (*Rabbanite) Judaism and claimed to accept only Scripture as authoritative.
***Kasher,** ritually permissible food.
Kashrut, Jewish *dietary laws.
***Kavvanah,** "intention"; term denoting the spiritual concentration accompanying prayer and the performance of ritual or of a commandment.
***Kedushah,** main addition to the third blessing in the reader's repetition of the *Amidah* in which the public responds to the precentor's introduction.
Kefar, village; first part of name of many settlements in Israel.
Kehillah, congregation; see *kahal*.
Kelippah (pl. **kelippot**), "husk(s)"; mystical term denoting force(s) of evil.
***Keneset Yisrael,** comprehensive communal organization of the Jews in Palestine during the British Mandate.
Keri, variants in the masoretic (*masorah) text of the Bible between the spelling (*ketiv*) and its pronunciation (*kerī*).
***Kerovah** (collective plural (corrupted) from **kerovez**), poem(s) incorporated into the **Amidah*.
Ketiv, see *keri*.
***Ketubbah,** marriage contract, stipulating husband's obligations to wife.
Kevuẓah, small commune of pioneers constituting an agricultural settlement in Ereẓ Israel (evolved later into *kibbutz).
***Kibbutz** (pl. **kibbutzim**), larger-size commune constituting a settlement in Ereẓ Israel based mainly on agriculture but engaging also in industry.
***Kiddush,** prayer of sanctification, recited over wine or bread on eve of Sabbaths and festivals.
***Kiddush ha-Shem,** term connoting martyrdom or act of strict integrity in support of Judaic principles.

***Kinah** (pl. **kinot**), lamentation dirge(s) for the Ninth of Av and other fast days.

***Kislev**, ninth month of the Jewish religious year, third of the civil, approximating to November-December.

Klaus, name given in Central and Eastern Europe to an institution, usually with synagogue attached, where *Talmud was studied perpetually by adults; applied by Ḥasidim to their synagogue (*"kloyz"*).

***Knesset**, parliament of the State of Israel.

K(c)ohen (pl. **K(c)ohanim**), Jew(s) of priestly (Aaronide) descent.

***Kolel**, (1) community in Ereẓ Israel of persons from a particular country or locality, often supported by their fellow countrymen in the Diaspora; (2) institution for higher Torah study.

Kosher, see *kasher*.

***Kristallnacht** (Ger. "crystal night," meaning "night of broken glass"), organized destruction of synagogues, Jewish houses, and shops, accompanied by mass arrests of Jews, which took place in Germany and Austria under the Nazis on the night of Nov. 9–10, 1938.

***Lag ba-Omer,** 33rd (Heb. **lag**) day of the **Omer* period falling on the 18th of *Iyyar; a semi-holiday.

Leḥi (abbr. for Heb. ***Loḥamei Ḥerut Israel,** "Fighters for the Freedom of Israel"), radically anti-British armed underground organization in Palestine, founded in 1940 by dissidents from *I.Ẓ.L.

Levir, husband's brother.

***Levirate marriage** (Heb. *yibbum*), marriage of childless widow *(yevamah)* by brother *(yavam)* of the deceased husband (in accordance with Deut. 25:5); release from such an obligation is effected through *ḥaliẓah*.

LHY, see Leḥi.

***Lulav,** palm branch; one of the *Four Species used on *Sukkot together with the **etrog, hadas,* and *aravah.*

***Ma'aravot,** hymns inserted into the evening prayer of the three festivals, Passover, Shavuot, and Sukkot.

Ma'ariv, evening prayer; also called **arvit.*

***Ma'barah,** transition camp; temporary settlement for newcomers in Israel during the period of mass immigration following 1948.

***Maftir,** reader of the concluding portion of the Pentateuchal section on Sabbaths and holidays in synagogue; reader of the portion of the prophetical books of the Bible (**haftarah*).

***Maggid,** popular preacher.

***Maḥzor** (pl. **maḥzorim**), festival prayer book.

***Mamzer,** bastard; according to Jewish law, the offspring of an incestuous relationship.

***Mandate, Palestine,** responsibility for the administration of Palestine conferred on Britain by the League of Nations in 1922; mandatory government: the British administration of Palestine.

***Maqāma** (Ar., pl. **maqamāt**), poetic form (rhymed prose) which, in its classical arrangement, has rigid rules of form and content.

***Marḥeshvan,** popularly called Ḥeshvan; eighth month of the Jewish religious year, second of the civil, approximating to October-November.

***Marrano(s),** descendant(s) of Jew(s) in Spain and Portugal whose ancestors had been converted to Christianity under pressure but who secretly observed Jewish rituals.

Maskil (pl. **maskilim**), adherent of *Haskalah ("Enlightenment") movement.

***Masorah,** body of traditions regarding the correct spelling, writing, and reading of the Hebrew Bible.

Masorete, scholar of the masoretic tradition.

Masoretic, in accordance with the masorah.

Meliẓah, in Middle Ages, elegant style; modern usage, florid style using biblical or talmudic phraseology.

Mellah, *Jewish quarter in North African towns.

***Menorah,** candelabrum; seven-branched oil lamp used in the Tabernacle and Temple; also eight-branched candelabrum used on *Ḥanukkah.

Me'orah, hymn inserted into the first benediction of the morning prayer (*Yoẓer ha-Me'orot*).

***Merkabah,** *merkavah,* "chariot"; mystical discipline associated with Ezekiel's vision of the Divine Throne-Chariot (Ezek. 1).

Meshullaḥ, emissary sent to conduct propaganda or raise funds for rabbinical academies or charitable institutions.

***Mezuzah** (pl. **mezuzot**), parchment scroll with selected Torah verses placed in container and affixed to gates and doorposts of houses occupied by Jews.

***Midrash,** method of interpreting Scripture to elucidate legal points (*Midrash Halakhah*) or to bring out lessons by stories or homiletics (*Midrash Aggadah*). Also the name for a collection of such rabbinic interpretations.

***Mikveh,** ritual bath.

***Minhag** (pl. **minhagim**), ritual custom(s); synagogal rite(s); especially of a specific sector of Jewry.

***Minḥah,** afternoon prayer; originally meal offering in Temple.

***Minyan,** group of ten male adult Jews, the minimum required for communal prayer.

***Mishnah,** earliest codification of Jewish Oral Law.

Mishnah (pl. **mishnayot**), subdivision of tractates of the Mishnah.

Mitnagged (pl. ***Mitnaggedim**), originally, opponents of *Ḥasidism in Eastern Europe.

***Mitzvah,** biblical or rabbinic injunction; applied also to good or charitable deeds.

Mohel, official performing circumcisions.

***Moshav,** smallholders' cooperative agricultural settlement in Israel, see moshav ovedim.

Moshavah, earliest type of Jewish village in modern Ereẓ Israel in which farming is conducted on individual farms mostly on privately owned land.

Moshav ovedim ("workers' moshav"), agricultural village in Israel whose inhabitants possess individual homes and holdings but cooperate in the purchase of equipment, sale of produce, mutual aid, etc.

***Moshav shittufi** ("collective moshav"), agricultural village in Israel whose members possess individual homesteads but where the agriculture and economy are conducted as a collective unit.

Mostegab (Ar.), poem with biblical verse at beginning of each stanza.

***Muqaddam** (Ar., pl. **muqaddamūn**), "leader," "head of the community."

***Musaf,** additional service on Sabbath and festivals; originally the additional sacrifice offered in the Temple.

Musar, traditional ethical literature.

***Musar movement,** ethical movement developing in the latter part of the 19th century among Orthodox Jewish groups in Lithuania; founded by R. Israel *Lipkin (Salanter).

***Nagid** (pl. **negidim**), title applied in Muslim (and some Christian) countries in the Middle Ages to a leader recognized by the state as head of the Jewish community.

Nakdan (pl. **nakdanim**), "punctuator"; scholar of the 9th to 14th centuries who provided biblical manuscripts with masoretic apparatus, vowels, and accents.

***Nasi** (pl. **nesi'im**), talmudic term for president of the Sanhedrin, who was also the spiritual head and, later, political representative of the Jewish people; from second century a descendant of Hillel recognized by the Roman authorities as patriarch of the Jews. Now applied to the president of the State of Israel.

***Negev,** the southern, mostly arid, area of Israel.

***Ne'ilah,** concluding service on the *Day of Atonement.

Neofiti, term applied in southern Italy to converts to Christianity from Judaism and their descendants who were suspected of maintaining secret allegiance to Judaism.

***Neology; Neolog; Neologism,** trend of *Reform Judaism in Hungary forming separate congregations after 1868.

***Nevelah** (lit. "carcass"), meat forbidden by the *dietary laws on account of the absence of, or defect in, the act of **sheḥitah* (ritual slaughter).

***New Christians,** term applied especially in Spain and Portugal to converts from Judaism (and from Islam) and their descendants; "Half New Christian" designated a person one of whose parents was of full Jewish blood.

***Niddah** ("menstruous woman"), woman during the period of menstruation.

***Nisan,** first month of the Jewish religious year, seventh of the civil, approximating to March-April.

Niẓoẓot, "sparks"; mystical term for sparks of the holy light imprisoned in all matter.

Nosaḥ (nusaḥ), "version"; (1) textual variant; (2) term applied to distinguish the various prayer rites, e.g., *nosaḥ Ashkenaz;* (3) the accepted tradition of synagogue melody.

***Notarikon,** method of abbreviating Hebrew words or phrases by acronym.

Novella(e) (Heb. **ḥiddush(im)*), commentary on talmudic and later rabbinic subjects that derives new facts or principles from the implications of the text.

***Nuremberg Laws,** Nazi laws excluding Jews from German citizenship, and imposing other restrictions.
Ofan, hymns inserted into a passage of the morning prayer.
***Omer,** first sheaf cut during the barley harvest, offered in the Temple on the second day of Passover.
Omer, Counting of (Heb. *Sefirat ha-Omer*), 49 days counted from the day on which the *omer* was first offered in the Temple (according to the rabbis the 16th of Nisan, i.e., the second day of Passover) until the festival of Shavuot; now a period of semi-mourning.
Oraḥ Ḥayyim, see Shulḥan Arukh.
***Orthodoxy** (Orthodox Judaism), modern term for the strictly traditional sector of Jewry.
***Pale of Settlement,** 25 provinces of czarist Russia where Jews were permitted permanent residence.
***Palmaḥ** (abbr. for Heb. *peluggot maḥaẓ;* "shock companies"), striking arm of the *Haganah.
***Pardes,** medieval biblical exegesis giving the literal, allegorical, homiletical, and esoteric interpretations.
***Parnas,** chief synagogue functionary, originally vested with both religious and administrative functions; subsequently an elected lay leader.
Partition plan(s), proposals for dividing Ereẓ Israel into autonomous areas.
Paytan, composer of **piyyut* (liturgical poetry).
***Peel Commission,** British Royal Commission appointed by the British government in 1936 to inquire into the Palestine problem and make recommendations for its solution.
Pesaḥ, *Passover.
***Pilpul,** in talmudic and rabbinic literature, a sharp dialectic used particularly by talmudists in Poland from the 16th century.
***Pinkas,** community register or minute-book.
***Piyyut** (pl. **piyyutim**), Hebrew liturgical poetry.
***Pizmon,** poem with refrain.
Posek (pl. ***posekim**), decisor; codifier or rabbinic scholar who pronounces decisions in disputes and on questions of Jewish law.
***Prosbul,** legal method of overcoming the cancelation of debts with the advent of the *sabbatical year.
***Purim,** festival held on Adar 14 or 15 in commemoration of the delivery of the Jews of Persia in the time of *Esther.
Rabban, honorific title higher than that of rabbi, applied to heads of the *Sanhedrin in mishnaic times.
***Rabbanite,** adherent of rabbinic Judaism. In contradistinction to *Karaite.
Reb, rebbe, Yiddish form for rabbi, applied generally to a teacher or ḥasidic rabbi.
***Reconstructionism,** trend in Jewish thought originating in the United States.
***Reform Judaism,** trend in Judaism advocating modification of *Orthodoxy in conformity with the exigencies of contemporary life and thought.
Resh galuta, lay head of Babylonian Jewry (see exilarch).
Responsum (pl. ***responsa**), written opinion (*teshuvah*) given to question (*she'elah*) on aspects of Jewish law by qualified authorities; pl. collection of such queries and opinions in book form *(she'elot u-teshuvot)*.
***Rishonim,** older rabbinical authorities. Distinguished from later authorities (**aḥaronim*).
***Rishon le-Zion,** title given to Sephardi chief rabbi of Ereẓ Israel.
***Rosh Ha-Shanah,** two-day holiday (one day in biblical and early mishnaic times) at the beginning of the month of *Tishri (September-October), traditionally the New Year.
Rosh Ḥodesh, *New Moon, marking the beginning of the Hebrew month.
Rosh Yeshivah, see *Yeshivah.
***R.S.H.A.** (initials of Ger. *Reichssicherheitshauptamt*: "Reich Security Main Office"), the central security department of the German Reich, formed in 1939, and combining the security police (Gestapo and Kripo) and the S.D.
***Sanhedrin,** the assembly of ordained scholars which functioned both as a supreme court and as a legislature before 70 C.E. In modern times the name was given to the body of representative Jews convoked by Napoleon in 1807.
***Savora** (pl. **savoraim**), name given to the Babylonian scholars of the period between the **amoraim* and the **geonim*, approximately 500–700 C.E.
S.D. (initials of Ger. *Sicherheitsdienst*: "security service"), security service of the *S.S. formed in 1932 as the sole intelligence organization of the Nazi party.
Seder, ceremony observed in the Jewish home on the first night of Passover (outside Ereẓ Israel first two nights), when the **Haggadah* is recited.
***Sefer Torah,** manuscript scroll of the Pentateuch for public reading in synagogue.
***Sefirot, the ten,** the ten "Numbers"; mystical term denoting the ten spheres or emanations through which the Divine manifests itself; elements of the world; dimensions, primordial numbers.
Selektion (Ger.), (1) in ghettos and other Jewish settlements, the drawing up by Nazis of lists of deportees; (2) separation of incoming victims to concentration camps into two categories—those destined for immediate killing and those to be sent for forced labor.
Seliḥah (pl. ***seliḥot**), penitential prayer.
***Semikhah,** ordination conferring the title "rabbi" and permission to give decisions in matters of ritual and law.
Sephardi (pl. ***Sephardim**), Jew(s) of Spain and Portugal and their descendants, wherever resident, as contrasted with *Ashkenazi(m).
Shabbatean, adherent of the pseudo-messiah *Shabbetai Ẓevi (17th century).
Shaddai, name of God found frequently in the Bible and commonly translated "Almighty."
***Shaḥarit,** morning service.
Shali'aḥ (pl. **sheliḥim**), in Jewish law, messenger, agent; in modern times, an emissary from Ereẓ Israel to Jewish communities or organizations abroad for the purpose of fund-raising, organizing pioneer immigrants, education, etc.
Shalmonit, poetic meter introduced by the liturgical poet *Solomon ha-Bavli.
***Shammash,** synagogue beadle.
***Shavuot,** Pentecost; Festival of Weeks; second of the three annual pilgrim festivals, commemorating the receiving of the Torah at Mt. Sinai.
***Sheḥitah,** ritual slaughtering of animals.
***Shekhinah,** Divine Presence.
Shelishit, poem with three-line stanzas.
***Sheluḥei Erez Israel** (or **shadarim**), emissaries from Ereẓ Israel.
***Shema** ([Yisrael]; "hear . . . [O Israel]," Deut. 6:4), Judaism's confession of faith, proclaiming the absolute unity of God.
Shemini Aẓeret, final festal day (in the Diaspora, final two days) at the conclusion of *Sukkot.
Shemittah, *Sabbatical year.
Sheniyyah, poem with two-line stanzas.
***Shephelah,** southern part of the coastal plain of Ereẓ Israel.
***Shevat,** eleventh month of the Jewish religious year, fifth of the civil, approximating to January-February.
***Shi'ur Komah,** Hebrew mystical work (c. eighth century) containing a physical description of God's dimensions; term denoting enormous spacial measurement used in speculations concerning the body of the **Shekhinah*.
Shivah, the "seven days" of *mourning following burial of a relative.
***Shofar,** horn of the ram (or any other ritually clean animal excepting the cow) sounded for the memorial blowing on *Rosh Ha-Shanah, and other occasions.
Shoḥet, person qualified to perform **sheḥitah*.
Shomer, *Ha-Shomer, organization of Jewish workers in Ereẓ Israel founded in 1909 to defend Jewish settlements.
***Shtadlan,** Jewish representative or negotiator with access to dignitaries of state, active at royal courts, etc.
***Shtetl,** Jewish small-town community in Eastern Europe.
***Shulḥan Arukh,** Joseph *Caro's code of Jewish law in four parts:
Oraḥ Ḥayyim, laws relating to prayers, Sabbath, festivals, and fasts;
Yoreh De'ah, dietary laws, etc;
Even ha-Ezer, laws dealing with women, marriage, etc;
Ḥoshen Mishpat, civil, criminal law, court procedure, etc.
Siddur, among Ashkenazim, the volume containing the daily prayers (in distinction to the **maḥzor* containing those for the festivals).
***Simḥat Torah,** holiday marking the completion in the synagogue of the annual cycle of reading the Pentateuch; in Ereẓ Israel observed on Shemini Aẓeret (outside Ereẓ Israel on the following day).
***Sinai Campaign,** brief campaign in October-November 1956

when Israel army reacted to Egyptian terrorist attacks and blockade by occupying the Sinai peninsula.

Sitra aḥra, "the other side" (of God); left side; the demoniac and satanic powers.

***Sivan,** third month of the Jewish religious year, ninth of the civil, approximating to May-June.

***Six-Day War,** rapid war in June 1967 when Israel reacted to Arab threats and blockade by defeating the Egyptian, Jordanian, and Syrian armies.

***S.S.** (initials of Ger. *Schutzstaffel*: "protection detachment"), Nazi formation established in 1925 which later became the "elite" organization of the Nazi Party and carried out central tasks in the "Final Solution."

***Status quo ante** community, community in Hungary retaining the status it had held before the convention of the General Jewish Congress there in 1868 and the resultant split in Hungarian Jewry.

***Sukkah,** booth or tabernacle erected for *Sukkot when, for seven days, religious Jews "dwell" or at least eat in the *sukkah* (Lev. 23:42).

***Sukkot,** festival of Tabernacles; last of the three pilgrim festivals, beginning on the 15th of Tishri.

Sūra (Ar.), chapter of the Koran.

Ta'anit Esther (Fast of *Esther), fast on the 13th of Adar, the day preceding Purim.

Takkanah (pl. ***takkanot**), regulation supplementing the law of the Torah; regulations governing the internal life of communities and congregations.

***Tallit (gadol),** four-cornered prayer shawl with fringes *(ẓiẓit)* at each corner.

***Tallit katan,** garment with fringes *(ẓiẓit)* appended, worn by observant male Jews under their outer garments.

***Talmud,** "teaching"; compendium of discussions on the Mishnah by generations of scholars and jurists in many academies over a period of several centuries. The Jerusalem (or Palestinian) Talmud mainly contains the discussions of the Palestinian sages. The Babylonian Talmud incorporates the parallel discussion in the Babylonian academies.

Talmud torah, term generally applied to Jewish religious (and ultimately to talmudic) study; also to traditional Jewish religious public schools.

***Tammuz,** fourth month of the Jewish religious year, tenth of the civil, approximating to June-July.

Tanna (pl. ***tannaim**), rabbinic teacher of mishnaic period.

***Targum,** Aramaic translation of the Bible.

***Tefillin,** phylacteries, small leather cases containing passages from Scripture and affixed on the forehead and arm by male Jews during the recital of morning prayers.

Tell (Ar. "mound," "hillock"), ancient mound in the Middle East composed of remains of successive settlements.

***Terefah,** food that is not **kasher*, owing to a defect in the animal.

***Territorialism,** 20th century movement supporting the creation of an autonomous territory for Jewish mass-settlement outside Ereẓ Israel.

***Tevet,** tenth month of the Jewish religious year, fourth of the civil, approximating to December-January.

Tikkun ("restitution," "reintegration"), (1) order of service for certain occasions, mostly recited at night; (2) mystical term denoting restoration of the right order and true unity after the spiritual "catastrophe" which occurred in the cosmos.

Tishah be-Av, Ninth of *Av, fast day commemorating the destruction of the First and Second Temples.

***Tishri,** seventh month of the Jewish religious year, first of the civil, approximating to September-October.

Tokheḥah, reproof sections of the Pentateuch (Lev. 26 and Deut. 28); poem of reproof.

***Torah,** Pentateuch or the Pentateuchal scroll for reading in synagogue; entire body of traditional Jewish teaching and literature.

Tosafist, talmudic glossator, mainly French (12th–14th centuries), bringing additions to the commentary by *Rashi.

***Tosafot,** glosses supplied by tosafist.

***Tosefta,** a collection of teachings and traditions of the *tannaim*, closely related to the Mishnah.

Tradent, person who hands down a talmudic statement in the name of his teacher or other earlier authority.

***Tu bi-Shevat,** the 15th day of Shevat, the New Year for Trees; date marking a dividing line for fruit tithing; in modern Israel celebrated as arbor day.

***Uganda Scheme,** plan suggested by the British government in 1903 to establish an autonomous Jewish settlement area in East Africa.

***Va'ad Le'ummi,** national council of the Jewish community in Ereẓ Israel during the period of the British *Mandate.

***Wannsee Conference,** Nazi conference held on Jan. 20, 1942, at which the planned annihilation of European Jewry was endorsed.

Waqf (Ar.), (1) a Muslim charitable pious foundation; (2) state lands and other property passed to the Muslim community for public welfare.

***War of Independence,** war of 1947–49 when the Jews of Israel fought off Arab invading armies and ensured the establishment of the new State.

***White Paper(s),** report(s) issued by British government, frequently statements of policy, as issued in connection with Palestine during the *Mandate period.

***Wissenschaft des Judentums** (Ger. "Science of Judaism"), movement in Europe beginning in the 19th century for scientific study of Jewish history, religion, and literature.

***Yad Vashem,** Israel official authority for commemorating the *Holocaust in the Nazi era and Jewish resistance and heroism at that time.

Yeshivah (pl. ***yeshivot**), Jewish traditional academy devoted primarily to study of rabbinic literature; *rosh yeshivah*, head of the yeshivah.

YHWH, the letters of the holy name of God, the Tetragrammaton.

Yibbum, see levirate marriage.

Yiḥud, "union"; mystical term for intention which causes the union of God with the **Shekhinah*.

Yishuv, settlement; more specifically, the Jewish community of Ereẓ Israel in the pre-State period. The pre-Zionist community is generally designated the "old yishuv" and the community evolving from 1880, the "new yishuv."

Yom Kippur, Yom ha-Kippurim, *Day of Atonement, solemn fast day observed on the 10th of Tishri.

Yoreh De'ah, see Shulḥan Arukh.

Yoẓer, hymns inserted in the first benediction *(Yoẓer Or)* of the morning **Shema*.

***Ẓaddik,** person outstanding for his faith and piety; especially a ḥasidic rabbi or leader.

Ẓimẓum, "contraction"; mystical term denoting the process whereby God withdraws or contracts within Himself so leaving a primordial vacuum in which creation can take place; primordial exile or self-limitation of God.

***Zionist Commission (1918),** commission appointed in 1918 by the British government to advise the British military authorities in Palestine on the implementation of the *Balfour Declaration.

Ẓiyyonei Zion, the organized opposition to Herzl in connection with the *Uganda Scheme.

***Ẓiẓit,** fringes attached to the **tallit* and **tallit katan*.

***Zohar,** mystical commentary on the Pentateuch; main textbook of *Kabbalah.

Zulat, hymn inserted after the **Shema* in the morning service.

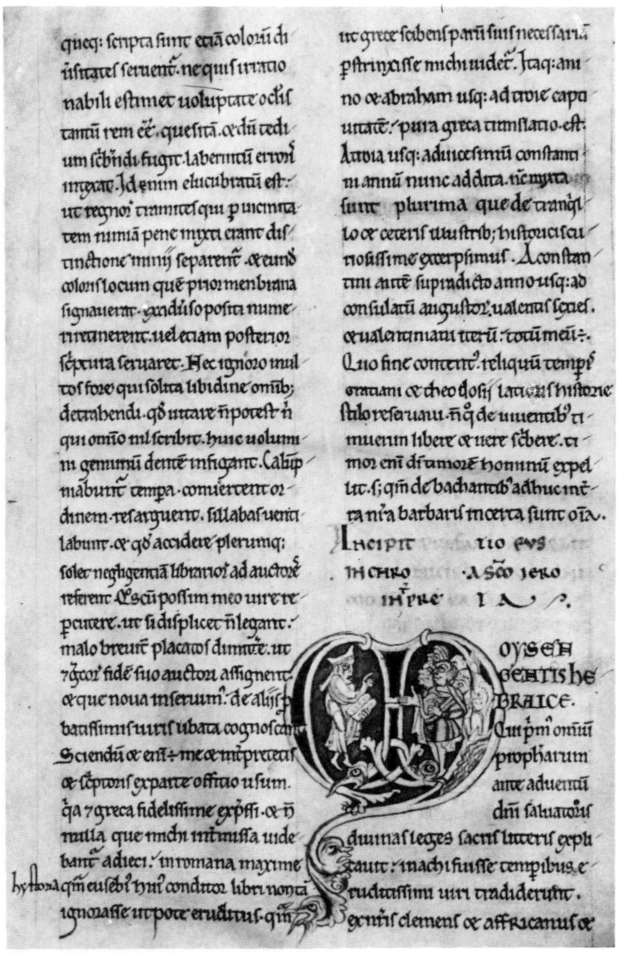

Illuminated initial letter "M" of the word *Moysen* (Moses) from the beginning of Eusebius' preface to the Book of Chronicles in a 12th-century manuscript of assorted Chronicles from southern France. Moses is depicted teaching the Ten Commandments to the Israelites. Avranches, Bibliothèque Municipale, Ms. 159, fol. 5.

MIN (Heb. מִין, pl. מִינִים, *minim;* "heretic," "sectarian"). The term *min* for which no truly convincing etymology has yet been found (see Talmudic Dictionaries; G. F. Moore, *Judaism,* 3 (1930), 68f.; S. Krauss, *Griechische und Lateinische Lehnwoerter,* 1 (1898), introd. 15, n. 2, etc.), occurs frequently in rabbinic literature, though in the printed texts, due to the censors, the terms *zedoki* and *kuti* ("Samaritan") have often been substituted. The term was widely applied to cover many different types of "heretics" or sectarians. From some halakhic definitions in the Talmud, it would appear the *min* was used to refer only to a Jewish sectarian (Ḥul. 13b; cf. Tosef., Shab. 13:5). Thus, for example, *Horayot* 11a states that a Jew who eats forbidden fat in a flaunting and defiant manner or (according to another opinion) worships idols is a *min.* The *minim* who ridiculed aggadic descriptions given by the rabbis (Git. 57a; BB 75a) were probably Jewish. However, there is also abundant evidence to show that the term was applied to non-Jews as well, as in *Pesaḥim* 87b where a Roman nationalist is called a *min* (see Ḥul. 13b; see also S. Lieberman, *Greek in Jewish Palestine* (1942), 141, n. 196; idem, *Hellenism in Jewish Palestine* (1950), 135, n. 69).

Any attempt to identify *minim* with one single sectarian group is thus doomed to failure. H. Hirschberg's discussion (in JBL, 67 (1948), 305–18) in which he defends his own earlier thesis that in talmudic literature the term denotes Pauline Christians is a case in point, since at various historical periods, the word *min* was applied to different kinds of "heretics." Thus the *min* who according to (the printed editions of) *Leviticus Rabbah* 13:5 upbraided Alexander the Great for standing up before Simeon the Just was probably a Samaritan, or even a member of Alexander's own retinue (cf. Mss. readings in M. Margalioth ed., 2 (1954), 294). The *minim* mentioned in *Berakhot* 9:5 (variant Sadducee, JQR, 6 (1915–16), 314, n. 86) who taught that there was but one world and who apparently had considerable influence in the Temple were undoubtedly Sadducees, who among other things, as is well-known, denied the existence of an afterlife. According to Johanan, the people of Israel did not go into exile until they had become 24 different groups of *minim* (TJ, Sanh. 10:6, 29c), i.e., Jewish schismatics. Johanan was probably referring to the situation in his own time, when there appears to have been a proliferation of Jewish schismatic groups, and there were numerous *minim* in most Galilean towns, with reference to whom the verse (Ps. 14:1) could be cited, "The fool hath said in his heart there is no God" (Sif. Deut. 320).

Sometimes the term *min* may apply to more than one kind of sectarian even within one text. Thus, in *Ḥullin* 87a, two *minim* are mentioned: The first puts forward a proof (from a biblical verse) for the existence of two deities, and was therefore in all probability either a heathen Christian (believing in God the Father and God the Son) or a Gnostic; but the second *min* was invited by Rabbi (Judah ha-Nasi) to pronounce the blessing over food, and must therefore have been a Jew. *Minim* appear as wonder-workers (TJ, Sanh. 7:19, 25d), but again it is not clear whether they were Gnostics (Ebionites?) or (Judeo-) Christians, such as the well-known Jacob of Kefar Sekhanya (fl. c. 80–110), the wonder healer (Av. Zar. 17a, 27b; Tosef., Ḥul. 2:22, 24; et al.). In some passages, however, it is fairly certain that Gnostics are being referred to. Thus, the *minim* who (according to Tanḥ. B., Num. 30, 41) believe that God does not revive the dead nor receive penitents, etc., were probably Marcionite Gnostics (A. Buechler, *Studies in Jewish History* (1956), 271). Similarly, those of *Megillah* 29b were, according to Lieberman, Gnostics believing in the demiurge (S. Lieberman, in *Biblical and Other Studies*, ed. by A. Altmann (1963), 140f.). However, it is very often difficult to know for certain whether heathen Christians or Gnostics are meant (e.g., Sanh. 4:5 and Gen. R. 8:8, where the plurality of gods may be either a Gnostic or a Christian notion; see Scholem, Mysticism, 359, n. 24). Now though it is true that the term *min* had a wide and ambiguous range of application, and that consequently in individual passages it is generally difficult to pinpoint exactly the schismatic group to which a *min* belongs, nonetheless, it is possible to distinguish historically two semantic phases in the use of the term. Thus according to Buechler (op. cit., 247, 271 etc.), until the early second century C.E. "it denoted heretic Jews," whereas "in Galilee in the second and third centuries *min* denoted in the first instance non-Jewish sectaries . . . Bible-reading heathens who oppose Judaism and its basic doctrines, antinomian Gnostics, or, in a few cases, heathen Christians who agree with them."

According to *Berakhot* 28b, Samuel ha-Katan (fl. c. 80–110), at the invitation of Gamaliel II of Jabneh, composed the "benediction against the *minim*," included in the *Amidah* as the twelfth benediction (see E. J. Bickerman, in HTR, 55 (1962), 171, n. 35). This was directed primarily against Judeo-Christians (specifically mentioned in one old text—see Schechter, JQR 10 (1897/98)), either to keep them out of the synagogue or to proclaim a definite breach between the two religions. This undoubtedly "represented the formal recognition by official Judaism of the severance of all ties between the Christian and other schismatic bodies, and the national body of Judaism" (Baron, Social[2], 2 (1952), 135, 381, n. 8, incl. bibl.). This severance of the *minim* from the national body of Judaism had obvious halakhic implications. Thus, meat slaughtered by a *min* was forbidden to a Jew (Ḥul. 13a). Likewise Torah scrolls, *tefillin*, and *mezuzot* written by him are barred from use (Git. 45b; cf. Tosef., Ḥul. 2:20). For Maimonides' five-fold classification of *minim* see *Mishneh Torah*, Teshuvah, 3:7. On the books of the *minim*, see **Sifrei ha-Minim*.

Bibliography: A. Buechler, *Studies in Jewish History* (1956), 245–74; G. F. Moore, *Judaism*, 3 (1930), 68f.; H. Hirschberg, in: JBL, 62 (1943), 73–87; 67 (1948), 305–18; Neusner, Babylonia, 3 (1968), 12–16; Allon, Meḥkarim, 1 (1957), 203–5. [D.S.]

MINC, HILARY (1905–), Polish Communist politician. Born in Kazimierz Dolny into an assimilated family, Minc joined the Communist youth movement in 1921. From 1925 to 1928, studying economics in France, he was a member of the French Communist Party. After his return to Poland, he worked in the chief statistical office in Warsaw and at the same time joined the illegal Communist Party, becoming secretary of its central editorial staff. During World War II Minc lived in the Soviet Union, and was one of the chief organizers of the Soviet-sponsored Union of Polish Patriots. He was also prominent in the formation of the Polish Army units organized in Russia. Following the liberation of Poland from the Germans (1945), Minc became minister for industry and commerce. He was made a vice-premier in 1949 and in the same year was appointed chairman of the State Planning Commission. In this capacity he was the chief author of Poland's economic policy; but in 1956, when Wladyslaw Gomulka came to power, he was removed from all his posts in the party and government, both as a Stalinist and as a Jew. [A.WE.]

MINCO, MARGA (1920–), Dutch author, born in Amsterdam. Her first book, *Het bittere kruid* (1957; *The Bitter Herb*, 1960), describes the deportation of her family and her own survival in hiding during World War II. It was translated into English, German, Swedish, and Italian. Some of the short stories in her collection, *De andere kant* ("The Other Side," 1959), also deal with Jewish themes relating to World War II. Her other works include a short story, *Terugkeer* ("Return," 1965), and *Een leeg huis* ("An Empty House," 1966), both of which describe the problems facing the Jew endeavoring to return to a normal life after the war. Marga Minco also wrote children's stories, notably *Kijk'ns in de la* ("Look into the Drawer," 1963). [G.A.-T.]

MINDEN, town in W. Germany. Jews are mentioned for the first time in 1270 as being under the bishop's protection. After 1336 the town agreed to recognize the bishop's prerogatives over the Jews provided that they paid municipal taxes as well as protection money to the bishop. Moneylending was the only authorized Jewish occupation at the time. The small community numbered no more than 12 families in 1318 and ten in 1340. They were expelled in 1350 following the *Black Death persecutions.

Jews did not settle in Minden again until the 16th century. In 1571 the council granted them residence permits of 12 years duration and allowed them to engage in commerce and moneylending and to hold religious services. From that time Jewish settlement was continuous, even after the town had come under the rule of Brandenburg, whose authorities claimed all prerogatives over the Jews. After 1652 no Jew was permitted to settle in Minden without permission from the elector; the numbers of "tolerated" Jews were ten in 1682 and 12 in 1700. In Prussian Minden the Jews engaged not only in moneylending but also in commerce and the slaughtering and sale of meat. Between 1806 and 1810 Minden belonged to the kingdom of *Westphalia, where the Jews received equal civil rights. After emancipation, when Minden reverted to Prussia, the small community grew steadily, from 65 in 1787 to 81 in 1810, 193 in 1840, and 267 in 1880. Their numbers later decreased to 192 in 1933 and 107 in 1939, when there were 228 Jews in the district of Minden. During World War II, 179 Jews were deported from the town and district. The **Memorbuch* of the synagogue from the 17th and 18th centuries has been preserved. The synagogue built in 1867 was destroyed in 1938. After World War II a small community was reconstituted, which had 44 members in 1962. A new synagogue was consecrated on June 15, 1958. The ethnologist Franz *Boas and the astronomer Philip S. Wolfers were born in Minden.

Bibliography: Germ Jud, 2 (1968), 542–3; B. Brilling and H. Richtering (eds.), *Westfalia Judaica* (1967), s.v.; M. Krieg, in: *Westfaelische Zeitschrift*, 93 (1937), 113ff.; L. Loewenstein, in: ZGJD, 1 (1887), 195ff. [B.BR.]

MINHAG (Heb. מִנְהָג; "custom," "usage") from the verb "to lead."

This entry is arranged according to the following outline:

Definition
General
In Jewish Law
- *Minhag* as a Source of Law
- Elucidation of Terms
- Scriptural Support for the Validity of *Minhag* as a Legal Source
- Functions and Categories of *Minhag*

DEFINITION

The word is found in the Bible (II Kings 9:2) meaning "the driving" (of a chariot) but it was taken by the rabbis to refer to "usage." As such, it is used in a wide variety of senses. It refers primarily: (1) to customs which, having been accepted in practice, became binding and assume the force of **halakhah* in all areas of Jewish law and practice (see below); (2) to local custom (*minhag ha-makom*) which obtains in one locality, whether a whole country or a single community, but not in another, and is binding upon the local community. The question of the extent to which the *minhag* is binding upon those who come from a place where it does not obtain is exhaustively debated in the Talmud and codes. The Mishnah already takes notice of this difference of local custom and its binding force (Pes. 4). These local *minhagim* have been collected in special **minhagim* books; (3) The word *minhag* is also employed to designate the various liturgical rites which have developed, e.g., *minhag Romania, minhag Polin, minhag Ashkenaz* (see *Liturgy). [ED.]

GENERAL

Custom is one of the most important foundations of the *halakhah*. It can be assumed that the Written Law (cf. *Oral Law) already takes for granted the continuation of some customs that were common practice before the giving of the law. This is probably the reason why the Torah makes no mention of laws which are fundamental in some domains, in spite of their importance and central position in life (such as the detailed laws of *betrothal and *marriage, modes of acquisition, *buying and selling). On the other hand, external customs entered the world of the precepts during later periods as a result of prevailing conditions, and were either temporarily integrated or remained permanently. An instructive example is that of the *New Moon, which the Torah only mentions with regard to the additional sacrifice and the blowing of the trumpets (and this too was probably only intended against those who believed it to be a festival to the god of the *Moon as was common in the ancient Middle East). During the days of the First Temple, however, as a result of Canaanite-Phoenician influence, the day became an accepted and important festival in Israel to such a degree that work and commerce were interrupted (with the difference that with the Jewish people the New Moon lost its pagan character and assumed a purified Jewish value of "a statute for Israel—a law of the God of Jacob" (Ps. 81:5)). Frequently, a particular matter of the *halakhah* is nothing but the consolidation of customs created among the people over the generations (e.g., see *Mourning, *Fasts). There are some customs which are as binding as legal regulations (see Tosef., Nid. 9:17) while others are no more than a consensus (أجماع with Muslims) which is accepted in cases where there is no fixed and decided *halakhah* ("Go out and see what the custom of the public is and act likewise" (TJ, Pe'ah 7:5, 20c); cf. "Go out and see how the people act" or "the people are accustomed" (TB, many times)). There are also individual customs in situations where there is no existing *halakhah;* these may be a local custom ("the custom of the country" (Suk. 3:11; Ket. 6:4; BM 7:1, 9:1; et al.), "in a place where the custom has been" (Pes. 4:1–5; Suk. 3:11; Av. Zar. 1:6; et al.), "the custom in Jerusalem" (BB 93b; Sof. 18:7)), or a custom of a section of the public ("the custom of those traveling with a caravan" (Tosef., BM 7:13); "the custom of the sailors" (*ibid.*), "the custom of women" (TJ, Pes. 4:1; 30c–d) "the custom of landlords" (Tosef., Pe'ah 2:21); "the custom of the priests" (*ibid.*, 4:3)), and even from one of these "there must be no deviation" (Tosef., BK 11:18; et al.). There are, however, also customs which are in opposition to the *halakhah*, and of these the sages said: "The custom annuls the *halakhah*" (TJ, Yev. 12:1, 12c; and cf.: "R. Judah said, the *halakhah* is according to the opinion of Bet Shammai, but the majority acts according to the opinion of Bet Hillel" Tosef., Ter. 3:12). It is obvious that "just as punishment is inflicted for transgression of the *halakhah*, so it is inflicted for transgression of a custom" (TJ, Pes. 4:3, 30d) and "permitted things [or actions] which the custom of others considers as prohibited, you are not authorized to permit them in their presence" (Pes. 50b–51a). It has also been prescribed many times that a man should deviate" neither from the custom of the place nor from that of his ancestors" (see TJ, Pes. 4:1, 30d; etc.), even though the reason for the custom has become obsolete. The following saying indicates the importance of the custom as a basis of the *halakhah:* "It has become accepted by the people that the *halakhah* cannot be fixed until a custom exists; and the saying, that a custom annuls the *halakhah*, applies to a custom of the earnest, while a custom for which there is no proof from the Torah is nothing but an error in reasoning" (Sof. 14:16).

Indeed, to prevent vain and foolish customs superseding the *halakhah*, the rabbis opposed following stupid customs which had their origin in error or even in periods of persecution. *Yehudai Gaon, who wrote to the population of Palestine in order to abolish the "custom of the persecution era" which they respected "against the *halakhah*" was unsuccessful. He received the reply that "A custom annuls the *halakhah*" (*Pirkoi b. Baboi*, L. Ginzberg, *Genizah Studies*, 2 (1929), 559–60). Maimonides violently attacked erroneous customs (see, e.g., Yad, Issurei Bi'ah 11:14–15, even in opposition to the opinion of the *geonim;* cf. responsa of Maimonides, ed. A. H. Freimann, §98–99), but even he stressed that there are certain cases which "depend on the custom" (see, e.g., Yad, Issurei Bi'ah 11:5–7). Customs arising from ignorance, however, and even those of which it was evident, not only from their origin but by their very nature, that they belonged to the "ways of the Amorites" and were to be suspected as idolatrous, often penetrated within the limits of the *halakhah* and secured a permanent place. It is significant that such customs often became so popular with the public, in spite of the opposition of the rabbis, that more importance was attached to them than to some of the strictest precepts of the Torah. There were instances where strange and doubtful customs became sanctified with the masses only because of the superstitious beliefs attaching to them. Such customs penetrated not only the text of the prayers but also the field of the prohibited and the permitted (see **Issur ve-Hetter*). They were especially tenacious in critical periods of human life (birth, marriage, death) or in the calendar (Day of Atonement, New Year). Thus, for example, some consider that the essentials of repentance and expiation can be found in the customs of **Kapparot* (expiation ceremony) and **Tashlikh*, and throughout the whole year do not visit the synagogue except for the *Kol Nidrei* ceremony. One common denominator of all these customs is their foreign origin and nature. However, they became so popular with the masses that even some of the rabbis attempted to find grounds to permit them, even through some kind of compromise. This was naturally even more true of customs which did not stem from a foreign origin, such as the recitation of *piyyutim* in the morning benedictions of *Shema* and during the repetition of the *Amidah* prayer by the *ḥazzan*, which became the accepted practice in many countries in spite of the opposition of many authorities. The same also applies to the foreign custom of addressing prayers to angels or mentioning their names in the *mezuzah*. This situation, whereby nonsensical customs found a home in Jewish life, still remains and has possibly even been strengthened in modern times. It is sufficient to mention the demonological customs connected with birth and circumcision (the night of vigil before the circumcision) or with death and burial, such as the strange custom current among Ashkenazim that a person whose parents are alive leaves the synagogue when the souls of the dead are remembered, or the "prohibition" of the sons from entering the cemetery during their fathers' funeral, which is widespread among the Ashkenazim of Jerusalem. Thus it can be said that the custom has been the most important channel through which external influences, even odd and unwanted ones, penetrated and still penetrate into the domain of *halakhah* (see also *Folklore). The general importance of customs is also reflected in literature (see **Minhagim* Books). [M.D.H.]

IN JEWISH LAW

Minhag as a Source of Law. Three possible meanings may be attributed to the term "source of law": a historical source of the law, i.e., a source which factually and historically speaking constitutes the origin of a particular legal norm; a legal source of the law, i.e., the source which lends the particular normative direction legal recognition and validity as part of the entire body of legal rules comprising the relevant legal system; and a literary source of the law, i.e., the informative source constituting the authentic repository for purposes of ascertaining the content of a particular legal direction (see **Mishpat Ivri*). *Minhag*, as does custom in other legal systems, sometimes serves as the historical source of a particular legal norm and sometimes as the legal source.

As a Historical Source. A study of the formative stages of any legal system will reveal that to some extent its directions originated from customs evolved in the practical life of the society concerned, and that only at a later stage was legal recognition conferred on such customs—by way of legislation or decision on the part of the legislator or judge. This phenomenon is also evidenced in Jewish law. Thus, for instance, certain legal usages which had been prevalent in pre-Mosaic Hebrew society later came to be affirmed in the Torah, as, for example, the law of the bailees' liability (see **Shomerim*), and sometimes also with material modifications, as with regard to the laws of *yibbum* (see *Levirate Marriage and *Ḥaliẓah*). The historical source of such directions is the pre-Mosaic usage, but their legal source is the Written Law, which gave them recognition and validity. Custom has fulfilled this historical function in all stages of the development of Jewish law, by serving to prepare a particular normative direction for acceptance into this legal system.

As a Legal Source. In Jewish law *minhag*, like custom in any other legal system, has also fulfilled an important function as a legal source, and it is with custom in this capacity that this article is concerned. Custom constitutes a legal source when the legal system, in certain circumstances and upon fulfillment of certain requirements, recognizes a consistently followed course of conduct as a binding legal norm. When custom serves merely as a historical source, it is only capable of preparing the normative course of conduct toward acquisition of legal recognition by means of a law-creating source, such as **takkanah;* however, when custom is a legal source, the normative usage already has legal force by virtue of such usage alone, without the affirmation of any law-creating source. As a legal source, the primary purpose of custom is like that of legislation (see **Takkanot ha-Kahal*), namely to fill a void in the existing *halakhah* when the latter offers no solution to new problems that arise, or in order to rectify or vary existing legal rules if and when the need arises. There is, however, a formal difference—which, as will be seen below, is also of substantive importance—between these two legal sources: legislation functions demonstratively and directly, at the direction of the competent authority, such as the halakhic scholars or the leaders of the people and of the community; custom, on the other hand, functions without preconceived intent and anonymously—at the hands of all or part of the people at large—and in order to ascertain it, it is necessary to "go and see what is the practice of the people" (Ber. 45a; Pes. 54a; in the TJ the version is, "go and see what is the practice of the public, and follow it" (TJ, Pe'ah 7:6, 20c; Ma'as. Sh. 5:3, 56b; Yev. 7:2, 8a). It is true that even in the case of a normative direction originating from custom there is the indirect influence of the halakhic scholars, by virtue of a certain control which they exercise over it (see below; see also Yad, Mamrim, 1:2–3); nevertheless it is the public as a whole that is the direct creative source of the legal direction. The public is invested with such creative authority on the presumption that, since its conduct is founded on the Torah, its creative authority will be directed in the spirit of the Torah, in accordance with the statement of Hillel the Elder made in affirmation of the binding force of a public custom in determining the *halakhah:* "Leave it to Israel. If they are not prophets, they are still the children of prophets" (Pes. 66a).

Substantiating the Validity of Minhag as a Legal Source. Some of the scholars apparently sought to explain the validity of a custom by saying that it had to be assumed that the earliest source of such a norm—now appearing in the form of custom—was ancient *halakhah* founded on transmitted tradition, *takkanah*, or other legal sources, but that the latter had become forgotten in the course of time, leaving the norm in the form of a custom only. This opinion finds expression in the Jerusalem Talmud: "Any Torah which has no source *(bet av)* is no Torah" (TJ, Shab. 19:1, 17a stated in relation to the *baraita* (Pes. 66a) in which Hillel recalls that the custom followed by the people concerning the paschal sacrifice on a Sabbath day he had heard mentioned by Shemaiah and Avtalyon (see below); the term *torah* is here used in the sense of custom). Elsewhere it is stated: "a custom which has no support in the Torah, is like the erroneous exercise of discretion" (Sof. 14:18; see also *Mordekhai* BM 366). According to this view custom has no independent creative force, but merely offers testimony to the existence of a rule created by one of the legal sources of the *halakhah*. In post-talmudic times some halakhic scholars expressly adopted this attitude toward custom (Resp. Rif no. 13; Nov. Ramban BB 144b s.v. *Ha de-Amrinan*). Some scholars explained the decisive power of custom, even when this was called forth only to decide between disputing scholarly opinions (see below), on the basis that a custom proves the existence of an ancient, deliberate determination of the law which has become forgotten, being preserved in this form only (Resp. Rosh 55:10). The source of authority of custom remained a matter of dispute among the *aḥaronim* (for particulars, see *Pitḥei Teshuvah* ḤM, 163, n. 16).

Certainly there are customs which have their source in ancient *halakhah*, as is evidenced by the Jerusalem Talmud in the matter of the paschal sacrifice on a Sabbath day (see above) and in other instances (see, e.g., Tosef., MK

2: 14–15; see also Pes. 51a and TJ, Pes. 4: 1, 30d). However, it transpires that the distinguishing feature of custom as a legal source lies not in its probative efficacy but in the law-creating authority of the public, whether the custom serves to decide between disputing opinions or to add to the existing *halakhah.* This is undoubtedly so as regards the validity of custom in matters of the civil law *(dinei mamonot),* where it is within the power of custom to operate even contrary to the existing law, in terms of the general principle of Jewish law which permits the parties to a transaction—and all the more so the public as a whole—to contract out of the Law of the Torah (see below). This is accepted by the majority of halakhic scholars as the explanation for the rule that custom overrides the law in matters of the civil law, which is certainly a classic illustration of the creative activity of custom.

Elucidation of Terms. At times, a particular halakhic direction which has its source in custom is also called *dat* (Beẓ. 25b and *Rashi* thereto) or *dat yehudit* (Ket 7:6 and *Rashi* to Ket. 72a; Tosef., Ket. 7:7). At other times the term *minhag* is used by the halakhic scholars to describe a normative direction having its source in *takkanah* (e.g., TJ, Ket. 1:5, 25c; Mid. Prov. to 22:28) and even the verb הנהיג is sometimes used to describe the enactment of a *takkanah* (cf. Tosef., RH 4:3 with RH 4:1 and Suk. 3:12). The use of a common term to describe both *takkanah* and custom (cf. further Yad, Mamrim 1:2–3; Resp. Rashba, vol. 2, no. 268) is attributable to their common function, namely legislative activity (each in its own different way, as already mentioned). Sometimes the term *minhag* is also used to describe *halakhah* which has its source in the Bible itself (see Sifra, Emor, 17:8, the law concerning habitation of a *sukkah* etc., described as *minhag le-dorot;* in Suk. 43a/b, the phrase is *mitzvah le-dorot*). Contrariwise, a normative direction having its source in custom is sometimes called *halakhah* (BM 7:8; Kid. 38b and see Samuel's interpretation, in TJ, Or. 3:8, 63b of the term *halakhah* appearing in Or. 3:9). Such use of common labels of *minhag, takkanah,* and *halakhah* for differing concepts not only calls for the exercise of great care in distinguishing the correct identity of each law appearing under such a name, but also offers proof of the legal efficacy of normative directions which have their source in custom and are integrated into the general halakhic system as a substantive part of it (even though there is a variance at times between the force of a direction originating from *takkanah* and one originating from custom; see below). Transgression against a direction decreed by custom is punishable by sanction: "Just as a fine is imposed in matters of *halakhah,* so a fine is imposed in matters of *minhag*" (TJ, Pes. 4:3, 30d) and R. Abbahu even sought to have punishment by flogging imposed on a person who transgressed a prohibition decreed by custom (TJ, Kid. 4:6, 66b; see also Kid. 77a).

At the same time, the scholars occasionally distinguished, primarily in the field of the ritual law, between a rule originating from custom and one originating from another legal source. Such distinctions, particularly from the amoraic period onward, are illustrated by the following examples: the majority of the *amoraim* held that the prohibition of **orlah* (eating the fruit of young trees) outside of Ereẓ Israel had its source in custom, and therefore they sought various legal ways in which to permit the fruit of *orlah* outside of Ereẓ Israel—something they would not have done had the prohibition belonged to the category of *halakhah le-Moshe mi-Sinai* (Kid. 38b–39a and see above). Similarly, there is recorded the talmudic dispute between R. Johanan and R. Joshua b. Levi as to whether the rite of taking the willow-branch on Sukkot (the branch that is raised and beaten on Hoshana Rabba) was an enactment of the prophets or a custom of the latter—i.e., a usage of the prophets but not enacted as a *takkanah* (Suk. 44a and *Rashi* ad loc.; see also *Sha'arei Teshuvah* no. 307); the answer to this question was relevant to the need (i.e., if it was an enactment) or otherwise (if it was a custom) for recital of a benediction at the time of beating the willow-branch (see Suk. 44a and see *takkanot* concerning benedictions in respect of matters instituted by the halakhic scholars). Even as regards deciding the *halakhah* in a matter under dispute, the *amoraim* distinguished between *halakhah* determined by way of open and deliberate decision, *halakhah* determined by custom introduced by the scholars, and *halakhah* determined by mere anonymous undirected custom (see TJ, Shek. 1:1, 46a, Meg. 1:6, 70d, Nid. 3:1, 50c, and Pes. 4:6, 31a; Av. Zar. 14b; Yev. 13b; Nid. 66a; et al.). Some of the Babylonian *amoraim* even laid down a further distinction, one relating to the nature of the custom. Thus three possibilities are distinguished: *nahagu ha-am* ("the practice followed by the people") was apparently interpreted by the Babylonian *amoraim* as referring to a usage not yet fully crystallized into an established custom, and therefore "we do not teach in this way initially, but should a person have done so, we allow the matter to stand"; *minhag,* to a crystallized custom which, although it has sufficient authority for the people to be taught to act from the start in accordance with it, nevertheless does not have the same force as a rule openly and expressly decided by the halakhic scholars—"we do not teach to act in this way in public, but we may teach (those who ask, to act according to the rule embodied in the custom)"; and that which is decided as *halakhah,* which must be published and made known to the public (Ta'an. 26b and see also Er. 62b and 72a). These distinctions relate primarily to the field of ritual law and not the the creative function of custom in civil law matters (see below, "Custom overrides the law").

Scriptural Support for the Validity of Minhag as a Legal Source. Halakhic scholars sought to rely on various scriptural passages as the source of the validity of custom. Simeon b. Yoḥai's statement, "Change not the custom set by your fathers!" is supported in the Midrash (Mid. Prov. 22:28, and see annotation there), by allusion to the scriptural injunction, "Remove not the ancient landmark, which thy fathers have set" (Prov. 22:28). R. Johanan found support for the validity of custom in another passage from the Book of Proverbs (1:8), "Hear, my son, the instruction of thy father, and forsake not the teaching of thy mother" (see Pes. 50b; Ḥul. 93b; cf. also *She'iltot,* Va-Yakhel, Sh. 67; *Halakhot Gedolot* end of Hil. Megillah). Sherira Gaon quotes the following tradition, which is not extant in the Talmuds: "Whence is it said that custom obliges? As it is said, 'Thou shalt not remove thy neighbor's landmark, which they of old time have set'" (Deut. 19:14; *Sha'arei Ẓedek,* 1:4, 20; Tur, ḤM 368). The discussion concerns an article stolen from its owner and sold to another; in law, if the owner has "despaired" (see *Ownership), the purchaser will not be required to return the article to him, but Sherira Gaon decided that there was in operation a custom to restore the article in such circumstance, from which there could be no departure. The factor which is common to all legal sources is that a norm which has been followed for some considerable time (see below) acquires for itself a fixed place in the *halakhah* and may not be overlooked nor "trespassed" upon (cf. the comment of Philo on the above scriptural passage, Spec. 4:149).

Functions and Categories of Minhag. Just as *takkanah*—the directed legislation of the halakhic scholars—has functioned in all fields of the *halakhah,* so custom—anonymous legislation—has also functioned in all its fields, although in some of them the measure of authority of custom is limited as compared with that of *takkanah*. Custom fulfills a number of functions in *halakhah* and is also divisible into several further *categories*.

FUNCTIONS. Custom serves three possible functions: (1) as the decisive factor in the case of disputing opinions as to a particular halakhic rule; in this event the custom operates even where the *halakhah*, but for such a custom, would be decided differently in accordance with the accepted rules of decision; (2) as adding to the existing *halakhah*, whenever the practical realities give rise to new problems to which the former has no available answer; and (3) as establishing new norms which stand in contradiction to the existing *halakhah*, i.e., norms which serve to vary the latter, or derogate therefrom. The latter two functions of custom parallel that of legislation (see *takkanot*), save that the last one (abrogation of an existing law) is of lesser efficacy than is the case with legislation (see below).

CATEGORIES OF MINHAG. *Custom (Minhag) and Usage (Nohag)*. At times *minhag* functions of its own inherent power, independently and directly, just as does a direction by express *takkanah;* at other times it functions by way of an inference that the parties to a particular matter acted as they did on the assumption that the decree of the *minhag* concerned would determine their relationship. This distinction is developed in other legal systems too, and in English law *minhag* of the first kind is termed "legal custom" or simply "custom," and *minhag* of the second kind "conventional custom" or "usage." In current Hebrew the latter is customarily termed *nohag*.

General Custom and Local Custom. A custom may be general in the sense of obliging the whole of the people or the public, or it may be local and obligatory only for the people of a particular place, in which case it is termed local custom, *mores civitatis* in Roman law. In the same way the operation of a custom may be confined to people of a particular class, occupation, etc., and further like subdivisions of custom may be made (see below).

Minhag as Deciding the Halakhah. In case of dispute between halakhic scholars as to the law, custom decides the issue—whether in circumstances where there are no established rules of decision concerning the particular matter, or in circumstances where the custom stands in contradiction to the accepted rules of decision. The matter is illustrated by the following examples: It is recorded that R. Tarfon differed from the majority opinion of the scholars with regard to the blessing to be recited over water (Ber. 6:8) and the *amoraim*, when asked how to decide the *halakhah*, replied: "go and see what is the practice of the people" (Ber. 45a; Eruv. 14b); this was also stated with regard to a similar question concerning the eating of **terumah* (TJ, Pe'ah 7:6, 20c, Ma'as. Sh. 5:3, 56b, and Yev. 7:2, 8a). In another case R. Judah and R. Yose held the view that just as the priests generally did not lift their hands when reciting the priestly benediction at the *Minḥah* (afternoon) service—because of the proximity of the service to the meal and the apprehension that a priest might lift his hands while intoxicated—so this was forbidden at the *Minḥah* service on the Day of Atonement (even though the above apprehension would not exist) lest this lead the priests to the erroneous practice of lifting their hands during weekday *Minḥah* services; however, R. Meir differed, holding that such lifting of the hands was permissible at the *Minḥah* service on the Day of Atonement (Ta'an. 26b). Although the accepted rules of decision required that the *halakhah* on the matter be decided according to R. Yose (see Eruv. 46b)—who in this case represented the stringent view—it was nevertheless decided according to the view of R. Meir—representing in this case the lenient view—for the reason that "the people followed the view of R. Meir" (Ta'an. 26b; see also Resp. Maharik no. 171).

According to some of the Babylonian *amoraim*, the power of determining the *halakhah* contrary to the accepted rules of decision was to be withheld from custom in matters concerning the ritual law *(dinei hetter ve-issur)*. Thus in response to R. Johanan's statement, "In regard to carob trees, it has become the custom of the people to follow the rule of R. Nehemiah" (RH 15b)—i.e., contrary to the majority of the scholars—the question is asked: "In a matter of prohibition, shall it be permitted to follow a custom?" *(ibid.)*. On the other hand, the *amoraim* of Ereẓ Israel—along with some Babylonian *amoraim*—conferred on custom the power of deciding the law in any case of dispute, even in matters of ritual law and even when it was contrary to the accepted rules of decision, for instance when decreeing in favor of an individual opinion against the majority opinion (TJ, Shev. 5:1, the opinion of R. Johanan quoted in RH 15b; cf. the statement of Rava, "The custom accords with the view of R. Meir" Ta'an. 26b; see also Pes. 103a and Ber. 52b, contrary to the unqualified statement of the law in the Mishnah).

In the 13th century, *Meir b. Baruch of Rothenburg stated, "For in all matters on which the great halakhic scholars are in dispute, I hold that a stringent approach must be followed, save . . . when the permissibility of a matter has spread in accordance with the custom of the scholars by whom we have been preceded" (Resp. Maharam of Rothenburg, ed. Berlin, no. 386). At this time too the dispute concerning the extent to which it was within the power of custom to determine the *halakhah* was continued. Thus Jacob *Moellin justified the custom of lending the money of orphans at fixed interest (*ribbit keẓuẓah*, see *Usury), contrary to the opinion of the majority of scholars, who held this to be prohibited; Moellin based his view on a solitary opinion (Resp. Maharil no. 37), which in fact only permitted such interest in respect of loans given from charitable funds (*Or Zaru'a*, Hil. Ẓedakah, no. 30), but Moellin extended the opinion to embrace also money lent by orphans, "for all matters concerning orphans are deemed to be matters of *mitzvah*, and this is truly so because they are alone and meek" (Maharil, loc. cit.). Other scholars contested this view: "There are places where it is customary for an **apotropos* [guardian] to lend orphans' money at fixed interest, but this is an erroneous custom and should not be followed" (Rema to YD 160:18; see also *Siftei Kohen* thereto, n. 27).

Minhag as Adding to Existing Halakhah. In its previously described function, custom serves to decide between two existing disputing opinions rather than to create a new rule. The latter effect is achieved by custom in fulfillment of its second function, namely that of establishing a new rule in relation to a question to which the existing *halakhah* offers no solution. For instance, as regards the paschal sacrifice, it is enjoined that it shall be brought on the 14th day of the month of Nisan (Num. 9:3), even when this falls on a Sabbath day (Pes. 6:1); when Hillel the Elder was asked what the law was in the event that it had been forgotten to prepare the knife on the eve of the Sabbath—i.e., whether it was also permissible to have the knife fetched on the Sabbath—he replied: "Leave it to Israel! If they are not prophets, they are still the children of prophets" (i.e., to await the morrow and see how the people would act); on the morrow, "he whose sacrifice was a lamb, stuck it [the knife] in its wool, and he whose sacrifice was a goat, stuck it between its horns; he [Hillel] saw the act and recalled the *halakhah*, saying, 'thus have I received the tradition from Shemaiah and Avtalyon'" (Pes. 66a). Hillel thus left the solution to the custom of the people, only later recalling that this custom had its source in ancient *halakhah.* A further illustration is to be found in the reply given in the Jerusalem Talmud to the question whether it was necessary or not to set aside tithes from the fruit of trees in their fourth year: "when there is no clearly established *halakhah* on any matter before the court and you do not know what its true nature is—go and ascertain the custom of the public and act accordingly, and we see that the public does not set aside tithes in this case" (TJ, Pe'ah 7:6, 20c and see Ma'as. Sh. 5:3, 56b). In this way custom served to decide the *halakhah* in a lenient manner (in TJ, Yev. 7:2, 8a—the above rule is quoted in connection with the function of custom as deciding between disputing opinions; see also Resp. Rosh 55:10).

"Custom Overrides the Law"—Minhag Mevattel Halakhah. Many halakhic scholars devoted a great deal of attention and research to the question whether it was within the power of custom, "concealed legislation," not only to add to existing *halakhah* but also to vary the latter and set aside any of its rules in certain circumstances—as it was within the power of *takkanah,* "open legislation," to do. This function, which in talmudic sources is termed *minhag mevattel halakhah* ("custom overrides the law"), has been the subject of much dispute—as in other legal systems in which custom is a recognized legal source. In Roman law, for instance, disputing opinions are found on the question whether custom *(mores, consuetudo)* has the power to create also a rule that is contrary to existing law (*contra legem,* see J. Salmond, *Jurisprudence* (1966[12]), 189–212; C. K. Allen, *Law in the Making* (1964[7]), 82f.).

DISTINCTION BETWEEN CIVIL AND RITUAL LAW. Jewish law distinguishes between civil and ritual law for purposes of the instant function of custom, recognizing the power of the latter to set aside the law in civil law matters but not in matters of the ritual law, where it cannot operate contrary to existing law in permitting that which has been prohibited. The explanation for this distinction lies in one of the substantive differences between these two fields of the law—one that relates to the freedom of stipulation (see *Contract; **Mishpat Ivri*). In matters of the civil law the rule is, "a person may contract out of the law of the Torah"—i.e., the law is *jus dispositivum,* since the premise is that halakhic rules of the civil law are laid down as a binding arrangement only as long as the parties do not disclose their preference for an alternative arrangement. On the other hand, the directions of the ritual law are *jus cogens,* obligatory and not variable at the will of the parties concerned. The logical conclusion is that just as the order in civil law matters is variable at the instance of the parties to a particular transaction, so it may be varied by the public as a whole, which, as it were, stipulates in advance that such and such an order, contrary to that laid down in the Torah, is convenient and desirable for each and every one of its members (see Resp. Rosh 64:4; Resp. Rashbash no. 562; Resp. Maharashdam ḤM no. 380). Thus custom, in expressing the collective will of the public, functions with power to change the *halakhah* in the civil law field—where the will to change the law has recognized authority—but not in the field of ritual law, in which a prohibition is obligatory and unchangeable whether at the will of the instant parties or of the public as a whole. In this function there is accordingly an important distinction between open legislation by way of *takkanah* and concealed legislation by way of custom. The Torah, in all fields, was entrusted to the authority of the halakhic scholars (see *Authority, Rabbinical), authority being delegated to them in the Torah itself to make legislation, whether to add to or derogate from the existing *halakhah* (see **Takkanot*). This is not the case as regards the authority of the public in relation to concealed legislation; the public may decide, by way of *minhag,* between disputing opinions of the halakhic scholars within the existing *halakhah,* may add to the *halakhah,* but may not set aside any rule of the existing *halakhah*—except when the abrogation of such a rule is rendered possible at the hands of individual members of that public by way of express stipulation, i.e., in the field of civil law.

COINAGE OF THE PHRASE MINHAG MEVATTEL HALAKHAH. The essential principle that in the field of civil law custom overrides the law is mentioned in various parts of talmudic and post-talmudic halakhic literature (see below). However, the characteristic phrase for this principle, *minhag mevattel halakhah,* is quoted in the Jerusalem Talmud in connection with the following two matters: The first relates to the determination in the Mishnah (BM 7:1) of the laborer's working hours in two different ways: one whereby he goes to work early in the morning and returns home late, these being the hours of work according to law (BM 83a–b); the other, whereby the laborer goes to work at a later hour and returns home earlier. The Mishnah lays down that local custom determines the hours of work even if this is contrary to the hours laid down by law; the comment of R. Hoshaiah is, "that is to say the custom overrides the *halakhah*" (TJ, BM 7:1, 11b), so that the employer may not withhold the wages of the worker by requiring that he abide by the legally prescribed working hours, but will himself have to abide by the working-hours decreed by custom—this without need for any proof that the parties had so intended (TJ, *ibid.*). The second matter in which the phrase is quoted relates to the laws of *ḥaliẓah* (see *Levirate Marriage); the fact that this forms part of ritual law does not affect the premise that in the latter field of the law the doctrine of *minhag mevattel halakhah* does not operate. In the Mishnah (Yev. 12:1) it is stated that the *ḥaliẓah* rite may be performed with a shoe or sandal (both of leather) but not with *anpilya* (sock or shoe made of cloth) since only the first two are included in the Pentateuchal term *na'al* (Deut. 25:9). In the Jerusalem Talmud (Yev. 12:1, 12c) it is stated: "If Elijah should come and state that *ḥaliẓah* may be performed with a shoe he would be obeyed; that *ḥaliẓah* may not be performed with a sandal he would not be obeyed, for it has been the practice of the public to perform *ḥaliẓah* with a sandal, and custom overrides the law." In this particular case custom supports the existing *halakhah,* since the Mishnah permits *ḥaliẓah* with a sandal and this is not prohibited by any extant talmudic source; accordingly, if Elijah were to come and forbid performance of *ḥaliẓah* with a sandal he would be determining a new rule, contradicting the existing *halakhah,* and in such an event custom—in supporting the existing *halakhah*—would serve to override the new *halakhah* being laid down by Elijah, a function of custom effective in the field of the ritual law. (It is also possible that the phrase *minhag mevattel halakhah* was originally stated in relation to the laborer's hours of work and its application extended to the case of *ḥaliẓah* by the redactor of the talmudic discussion. It may be noted that the above version of the doctrine does not occur in Yev. 102a, where the rule, "if Elijah should come . . ." is also found, nor in BM 83a–b; see also Men. 31b–32a).

The rule that it is not within the power of custom to render permissible an undisputed prohibition is stressed by the use, on several occasions, of the phrase, "Does the matter then depend on custom?" (Ḥul. 63a; BM 69b–70a). On the other hand, custom does have the power, even in the field of the ritual law, to render prohibited something that has been permitted, since the law is not abrogated thereby but only rendered more stringent: "Custom cannot set aside a prohibition, it can only prohibit that which has been permitted" (Yad, Shevitat Asor, 3:3; see also Resp. Rosh 55:10). According to some scholars, custom—even in civil law matters—only overrides *halakhah* when it has been accepted by way of a communal enactment (see *Takkanot ha-Kahal;* and see *Nimmukei Yosef* BB 144b; Nov. Ritba to Ket. 100a and *Shittah Mekubbezet* ad loc.; *Bedek ha-Bayit* ḤM 368:6, commentary on the statement of Sherira Gaon). This view seems to be in conflict with the plain meaning of a number of talmudic discussions, particularly as regards the rule of *sitomta* (affixing of a mark; see below), and was not accepted by the majority of the scholars. The matter was succinctly summarized by Solomon b. Simeon *Duran—after a detailed discussion of the two relevant talmudic references—as follows: "It will be seen that the doctrine of 'custom overrides *halakhah*' is true in matters of civil law, but erroneous when applied to a matter in which it has been the practice to permit something that is prohibited, for custom only has the power to prohibit something that has been permitted, and not to render permissible something that has been prohibited" (Resp. Rashbash no. 562).

Minhag as Varying the Law in Various Fields. The facility of custom to override the law in civil matters has lent Jewish law great flexibility in adapting to changing economic realities, and many rules—sometimes even entire branches of the law—have come to be based on the legal source of custom.

In the Talmudic Period. The following are some of the rules that were laid down: deeds that are not signed as required by law are valid if prepared in accordance with local custom (BB 10:1; BB 165a; Kid. 49a); debts which according to law may only be recovered from the debtor's immovable property (Ket. 51a, 69b) may also be recovered from his movable property when it is local custom to recover them in this way (TJ, Git. 5:3, 46d; in geonic times a special *takkanah* was enacted permitting the recovery of debts from the debtor's movable property since at that time most Jews had ceased to be landowners (see *Execution, Civil); this is an illustration of *halakhah* received first by way of custom and later by expressly enacted *takkanah*). Similarly, many illustrations of the rule that custom overrides the law are to be found in matters of the financial relationship between *husband and wife (see Ket. 6:3–4; Tosef., Ket. 6:5–6; see also *Beit ha-Beḥirah*, Nov. Rashba, and *Shitah Mekubbezet* to Ket. 68b).

In the Post-Talmudic Period. In this period too custom actively fulfilled the far-reaching function of changing the law, this phenomenon sometimes leading to sharp dispute—even in the case of one specific matter only—and at other times accepted by all scholars in relation to an entire branch of the law. Thus, as regards the authentication of deeds (see **Shetar*)—which according to law must be done by three judges and is ineffective if done by a single judge (Ket. 22a)—it was stated in the 15th century: "For the scholars of the yeshivot it is the accepted custom for deeds to be authenticated by the signature of one [judge], and this is a possible application of the doctrine that custom overrides the law in matters of the civil law" (*Terumat ha-Deshen*, Resp. no. 332). This custom was accepted by Moses Isserles (*Rema* ḤM 46:4), but others differed (see *Yam shel Shelomo*, BK 10:11; *Siftei Kohen* ḤM 46, n. 8). On the other hand, it is generally accepted that the extensive field of tax law is largely founded on the legal source of custom. This is due to the fact that halakhic principles stated in the Talmud in this field (including also the rule of **dina de-malkhuta dina* and the laws of *partnership) were unable to offer adequate solutions to the multiple legal problem that had arisen—commencing from the tenth century onward—in this field of the law (see *Taxation). At first a certain hesitation was expressed concerning the extent to which it was within the power of custom to create an obligation even when it was contrary to "established and known *halakhah*" of the Talmud concerning tax law matters (see statement of Baruch of Mainz, 12th-century author of the *Sefer ha-Ḥokhmah*, quoted in *Mordekhai* BB no. 477); later, however, this hesitation gave way to full recognition of the validity of any legal rule or usage sanctioned by custom, even when it was contrary to the existing *halakhah*:

> Nowhere are the tax laws founded on talmudic sanctity and everywhere there are to be found variations of such laws deriving from local usage and the consent of earlier scholars; and the town residents are entitled to establish fixed *takkanot* and uphold recognized customs as they please, even if these are not according to *halakhah*, this being a matter of civil law. Therefore if in this matter they have an established custom, it should be followed, since custom overrides the *halakhah* in matters of this kind (Resp. Rashba, vol. 4, nos. 177, 260 and see *Taxation for further particulars).

The preference for flexible custom above rule of *halakhah* as regards the legal order in all public matters was emphasized by Israel *Isserlein:

> In all matters affecting the public, their custom shall be followed in accordance with the order they set for themselves as dictated by their needs and the matter under consideration, for if they be required to follow the strict law in every matter, there will always be strife among themselves; furthermore, at the outset they allow each other to waive the strict law and make up their minds to follow the decree of their own custom (*Terumat ha-Deshen*, Resp. no. 342).

At the same time, the halakhic scholars made every effort to integrate the legal norm originating from custom into the pattern and spirit of the rules within the Jewish legal system, and in this regard Isserlein adds (*ibid.*):

> Even though it has been said that in tax matters custom overrides the law, it is at any rate desirable and proper to examine carefully whether we can reconcile all customs with the strict law and even if not entirely so, it is yet preferable that we find support and authority in the statements of the scholars and substantiate them with the aid of reason and legal logic (*ibid.*).

In this and in other ways—for instance by means of the control exercised by the halakhic scholars to ensure that rules originating from custom should not depart from the Jewish law principles of justice and equity—the rules of tax law, largely derived from custom, became an integral part of the Jewish legal system.

In Jewish Law in the State of Israel. The stated power of custom continues even in present times actively to assert itself in Jewish law, a fact that finds expression particularly in the decisions of the rabbinical courts in Israel. A notable example concerns the matter of severance pay, payable to the employee on his dismissal. The rabbinical courts have sought various legal ways of conferring binding legal force on the employer's duty to pay this (see **Ha'anakah*), and one of the principal ways has been reliance on the legal source of custom. Thus it was held, "since in our times there has spread this custom of paying compensation to employees . . . we have to enforce this as an obligation according to the law of the Torah, in terms of the rule stated in regard to the hire of workers: 'all in accordance with local custom'" (PDR, 1:330); moreover, by virtue of custom the claim for severance pay "is not a matter of grace, but a claim founded on law," for which the employer, even if a charitable institution, is liable (PDR, 3:286f.). Particular importance was held to attach to custom in this case, since "we have found support for it in the Torah and *halakhah* . . . this custom being based on the Pentateuchal law of the grant payable by the master to his Hebrew bound servant" (*ha'anakat eved Ivri*, PDR, 4:129; *Yam ha-Gadol* no. 22), and as such represented "a proper and just custom" (PDR, 1:330f.; cf. *Terumat ha-Deshen*, Resp. no. 342 concerning reliance on the Pentateuchal law on tax matters).

Minhag in the Development of the Modes of Acquisition and of Establishing Obligation. In the above field—one that is particularly sensitive to changing trends in commercial life, the nature and scope of which is subject to constant fluctuation—custom was destined to exercise a decisive influence. A transaction executed in a verbal manner alone attains no legal validity in Jewish law, which provides for the transfer of ownership and establishment of an obligation in prescribed ways, generally requiring much formality, as by way of *kinyan meshikhah* or *hagbahah*, etc. ("acquisition by pulling or lifting," etc.; see *Contract; *Acquisition). Such formality was not in keeping with the demands of developing commerce, which called for more convenient and flexible modes of acquisition. Custom, in the form of mercantile or trade usage, was instrumental in providing a large part of the forthcoming answer to the stated demands.

As early as talmudic times (BM 74a), it was laid down that where it was the custom of the merchants for a sale of wine to be concluded by the purchaser affixing a mark (*sitomta, Rashi* ad loc. and Targ. Jon., Gen. 38:18) on the barrel of wine, this action would complete the sale even though the purchaser had not yet "pulled" the barrel and it remained in the seller's possession. This is an illustration of law overridden by custom, since in law acquisition was not complete until the purchaser had "pulled" the barrel, and until then both the seller and the purchaser remained free to retract; thus, in law the barrel would still have remained in the ownership of the seller but custom decreed that ownership of the chattel would pass to the purchaser after it was marked in the customary manner and after this the parties might no longer retract. From this *halakhah* Solomon b. Abraham *Adret concluded: "From this we learn that custom overrides the law in all matters of the civil law, in which everything is acquired and transferred in accordance with custom; hence the merchants effect *kinyan* in any mode according with their own usage" (Nov. Rashba BM 73b; see also *Nimmukei Yosef* BM, loc. cit.; *Maggid Mishneh* Mekhirah 7:6; *Sma* ḤM 201, n. 2). In the course of time and on the basis of this principle, Jewish law came to recognize new modes of acquisition and of establishing obligation. Thus the fact that it was the trade custom to conclude a transaction by shaking hands, by making an advance on the purchase price (*Piskei ha-Rosh*, BM 5:72), or by delivering a key to the place where the goods were stored was held to be sufficient to confer full legal validity on a transaction concluded in any of these ways (Sh. Ar., ḤM 201:2).

The extent of the creative power of custom in relation to the modes of acquisition has been the subject of much discussion founded on halakhic and economic considerations. R. Joel *Sirkes held that custom served to create new modes of acquisition in respect of transactions of movables only, "as there is much trade in these and he [the purchaser] has not the time to pull all the goods into his possession" (*Baḥ* ḤM 201:2), but the majority of scholars took the view that custom also served to do so as regards various transactions of immovable property (*Yam shel Shelomo*, BK 5:36; *Sma* ḤM 201, n. 6; *Siftei Kohen* thereto, n. 1). Similarly, many scholars held that custom served to lend full legal validity to an acquisition of something not yet in existence (see *Acquisition, Modes of; *Contract; Resp. Rosh 13:20; other scholars differed—see *Keẓot ha-Ḥoshen* 201, n. 1; *Netivot ha-Mishpat, Mishpat ha-Urim*, 201, n. 1).

At times custom operated with such far-reaching effect that not only were new modes of acquisition added to those halakhically recognized but even certain substantive elements of the existing acquisitory modes as determined by the halakhic scholars were changed (see, e.g., Resp. Ribash no. 345 on the custom concerning acquisition incidental to four cubits of land (*kinyan aggav arba ammot karka*), without specification of the land, contrary to the opinion of Maimonides, when locally the latter's statement of the law was otherwise followed; similarly, in Resp. Rosh 79:4).

In the 13th century a question of principle arose whose answer was to be of great significance as regards the measure of the creative power attaching to custom in general. The fundamental idea underlying the need in Jewish law for acquisitory formalities in the formation of legal transaction is that in a such manner the parties demonstrate their absolute *gemirut ha-da'at* ("making up of their minds") to close the transaction (see *Contract). The modes of acquisition that came to be decreed by custom also served to demonstrate such *gemirut ha-da'at*, since these represented accepted trade customs; however, the question arose whether local custom to close a transaction in a verbal manner alone was capable, from the standpoint of Jewish law, of conferring full legal validity on such transaction. *Asher b. Jehiel took the view that no affirmative conclusion could be drawn from the rule of *sitomta* (see above), except with regard to the validity of a custom requiring the performance of some act such as those mentioned above (handshake, etc.), "but never by mere speech alone, and even when this is the practice it is a bad custom which is not to be followed" (Resp. Rosh 12:3). This view denied custom the power of contraverting the basic requirement of Jewish law for the performance of some act indicating the absolute *gemirut ha-da'at*; a custom of this kind was therefore not proper except when it served only to change the substance of the act, but when it was aimed at eliminating the need for any act at all it was a "bad custom" from which the scholars would withhold validity (see below).

Another view was that whenever custom decreed mere speech alone as sufficient for the conclusion of a legal transaction it had to be assumed that absolute *gemirut ha-da'at* would come about in such a way too (opinion of Meir of Rothenburg and of R. Jehiel, quoted in *Mordekhai*, Shab. nos. 472–3), and this was the opinion accepted by the majority of the *posekim*. Thus it was decided that a person who had promised his neighbor to be the *ba'al berit* ("sandek"; see *Circumcision) at a circumcision ceremony was not free to retract from such an undertaking and assign it to another "since it has long been the practice among all Israelites for the privilege of performing such a *mitzvah* to be conferred in mere verbal manner and it is already established that custom is an important tenet in all matters of this kind" (Resp. Radbaz no. 278). This is also the position as regards the formation of partnership. According to talmudic law a partnership is formed by performance on the part of each partner of an act of acquisition in relation to the share of the other partners (Ket. 10:4; Yad, Sheluḥin 4:1; and see *Partnership). However, it was held that "where it is local custom to become a partner even by speech alone—there will be a partnership; such is the custom in this country too . . . and so we decide in every case, for custom is an important matter in the field of the civil law" (Resp. Radbaz no. 380). This opinion came to be accepted as *halakhah* by the later *posekim*, "reason inclines to the view that whenever it is the custom to rely on speech alone, it is like the custom of *sitomta*" (*Kesef ha-Kedoshim* ḤM 201:1), in terms of which full recognition according to

Jewish law was given to public sales (*Mishpat u-Ẓedakah be-Ya'akov*, no. 33), to sales on the exchanges (Resp. Maharsham, pt. 3, no. 18), and to like legal transactions customarily concluded in mere verbal manner (see *Ohel Moshe* pt. 2, no. 138).

In cases before the rabbinical courts in the State of Israel reliance on custom (see above) is particularly evident in the field of the modes of *kinyan*. In several cases acquisition by way of registration in the registry in accordance with the state law is recognized as a valid *kinyan* according to Jewish law, by the force of custom (see, e.g., PDR 4:81). In another leading decision it was laid down that "in our times a signed contract between purchaser and seller constitutes a *kinyan* by virtue of the rule of *sitomta*, whether relating to immovable or to movable property, since this is a trade custom" (PDR 6:216, and see also the distinction drawn with regard to the text of the contract).

THE RULE OF MINHAG MEVATTEL HALAKHAH—IN THE CASE OF LOCAL CUSTOM. Custom overrides the law even when it is not general but customary with part of the public only. Thus in talmudic law it is laid down that when a desert caravan is attacked by robbers who demand a price for the release of the travelers, each must pay according to the amount of the property he carries and not on a per capita basis; in the case where a guide is taken to avert danger to life, payment of the guide is made according to a calculation based both on the amount of property carried by each and per capita; however, "the custom of caravan travelers must not be departed from" (i.e., if the custom decrees that the participation always be according to property and not per capita, it must be followed, Tosef., BM 7:13–14; see also BK 116b; TJ, BM 6:4, 11a). Similarly, it is laid down that "a shippers' custom *[minhag sappanin]* must not be departed from" in the case where cargo has to be jettisoned to lighten the load (Tosef., loc. cit.). Hence it follows that a local custom or trade usage overrides the *halakhah* for the people governed by such custom: "In matters of the civil law custom is followed, even the custom of ass drivers and shippers, for even if the strict law requires that participation must be according to money and the load carried, nevertheless the custom of ass drivers and of shippers overrides the law" (Resp. Maharik, no. 102).

Proof of the Existence of a Custom. Jewish law sets three requirements for the validity of a custom:

(1) It must be widespread over the whole country, or in the whole of a particular locality, or amidst the whole of a particular class of people, according to its purported field of operation: "In all such matters [of the financial relationship between spouses] custom is an important tenet and must be followed in deciding the law, provided, however, that the custom be widespread *(pashut)* over the whole country" (Yad, Ishut 23:12 and cf. with the matter of *takkanah, ibid.* 16:7–9). A custom which exists in most parts of a particular district must be presumed to exist in the whole of such a district (Resp. Rosh 79:4; *Beit Yosef* ḤM 42:21).

(2) A custom must be of frequent application: "It must be known that the custom is established and widespread, that the townspeople have followed it at least three times, for often the public adopt for themselves a practice to suit their immediate needs [i.e., in regard to a particular matter only] without intending to establish a custom at all" *(Terumat ha-Deshen*, Resp. no. 342; Resp. Maharashdam, ḤM no. 436). The time required for the evolution of a custom depends on the nature of the matter in each case: "This matter [whether or not there was a custom to exempt the communal cantor from tax payment] is not like a custom relating to the hire of workers, which happens every day so that everyone can see what the custom is; but as regards the cantor's tax immunity, since there is only one cantor in the town, how shall the fact that tax was not demanded from one or two cantors be called a custom unless it be public knowledge in the town that cantors had been exempted there on account of local custom to exempt them" (Resp. Ribash no. 475).

(3) The custom must be clear: "The custom must be clearly to exempt" (Resp. Ribash, loc. cit.). In another matter Samuel b. Moses *Medina held that the rule of custom overrides *halakhah* was applicable to that case, provided only that the instant custom was sufficiently clear, "there are two approaches to this matter: one according to the law of our holy Torah, the other according to the trade custom; for there is no doubt that in such matters custom is decisive, provided that the import of the custom be clear, but if there be any doubt about this then we have to revert to what is decreed by the law of the Torah" (Resp. Maharashdam, ḤM no. 33).

Jewish law dispenses with the formality of the laws of evidence for purposes of proving the establishment of a custom—a fact that has provided custom with wide creative opportunity. Thus hearsay evidence suffices and the testimony of normally disqualified witnesses is admitted (*Terumat ha-Deshen*, Resp. no. 342). The wide latitude which Jewish law allows to the creative power of custom is evidenced in a decision given by the rabbinical court in the State of Israel concerning the matter of severance pay due to an employee upon his dismissal (see above). In 1945 R. Ouziel (in a responsum quoted in M. Findling, *Teḥukat ha-Avodah*, p. 133f.) refrained from basing the law of severance pay on the legal source of custom (relying instead on an ethical-halakhic principle: see **Ha'anakah*), for the reason that a custom had no validity unless it was widespread, of frequent application, and clear: "and as far as I am aware this custom [of severance pay] is not widespread in the whole country nor of common application, but only followed in certain specific cases, and therefore the court is not ordering severance pay to be paid in terms thereof" *(ibid.)*. A mere ten years later the rabbinical court—seeking a full legal justification for the obligation of severance pay—held: "Now that this custom has spread and become accepted in the whole country, and is popular and of common, daily application, it must be followed and the statements mentioned above (i.e., of R. Ouziel), made in the year 1945, are no longer applicable or valid because the custom has become widespread and established." Recognition of such an accelerated spread of a custom within the short period of ten years is indicative of the special readiness of Jewish law to enrich itself by means of the legal source of custom.

Custom (Minhag) and Usage (Nohag). The customs so far discussed belong mainly to those in the category of a legal norm functioning of its own power and independently of the consent of the parties to a particular transaction. Thus, for instance, the validity of a mode of acquisition sanctioned by custom is not to be explained on the ground that the parties to a particular transaction intended, by implication, to confer legal validity thereon—since it is beyond the authority of the parties to pass on the validity of a *kinyan* even if they should expressly say so. In this case the new mode of acquisition draws its validity from the efficacy of custom to create new legal norms of selfstanding force. On the other hand, many customs operate in the *halakhah*—as in other legal systems—not from their own independent force but by virtue of a presumption that the parties intended, by implication, to introduce a particular usage as part of the transaction between themselves. An agreement between two parties is generally composed of two kinds of terms, those expressly stipulated and those imported by implication as an integral part of the agreement. Such implied terms may be inferred in two ways: either because they are decreed by factors of logic and reasonableness, or because they are usual and customary, since it may be presumed that the parties intended to include in the terms of their agreement the dictates of all the former factors (see J. Salmond, *Jurisprudence* (1966[12]), 193–7). The matter may be illustrated as follows: The Mishnah (BM 9: 1) lays down that a transaction of *arisut* or *ḥakhirah* (land tenancy and cultivation in return for a share of the crop, see *Lease and Hire) includes implied terms concerning cultivation of the land in accordance with local usage—*ke-minhag ha-medinah*—and that neither party to the transaction may contend, for instance, that he intended the crop to be reaped by scythe when it was local custom to reap by hand (BM 9: 1). The Talmud adds that a party's plea that he had not intended to abide by local custom will not be accepted even if it is supported by circumstantial evidence, such as higher or lower rental than usual (see BM 103b), because in the absence of any express stipulation to the contrary it will be presumed that both parties intended to embrace local custom in their agreement (see also Yad, Sekhirut 8:6; Sh. Ar., ḤM 320:4–5). Talmudic *halakhah* offers abundant examples, in most branches of the civil law, of usages which are imported by implication as part of the terms agreed upon between the parties to a transaction, e.g., in the laws of joint ownership (BB 1: 1 and 4a; TJ, BB 1:2, 12b) and partnership (BM 68b; 69b; Tosef., BM 5:6–7; TJ, BM 5:6, 10b; see also Yad, Sheluḥin 5: 1 and 8:4; and see Partnership); in the laws of *pledge (e.g., BM 67b–68a; Yad, Malveh 7:2–3); in the laws of master and servant (BM 7: 1: BM 83a concerning the hours of work; 86a concerning the worker's sustenance; 87a concerning the worker's wages; and see *Labor Law); in the laws concerning the pecuniary relationship between spouses (see above; see also *Husband and Wife), etc. Usages of the above kind also fulfill an important role as regards the interpretation of various deeds and documents, in which local usage in the particular matter is of decisive importance (BB 166b; Yad, Malveh 27: 15; and see *Interpretation).

The Rule of Doreshin Leshon Hedyot. This rule (Tosef., Ket. 4:9ff.; TJ, Ket. 4:8, 28d, TJ, Yev. 15:3, 14d; BM 104a) is of application in the interpretation of documents (for details, see *Interpretation). Many halakhic scholars regarded this rule as serving to give recognition to the implicit importation into the terms of a document of a usage followed by the people, on the presumption that the parties intended their transaction to be subject to such usage: "For whatever is customarily written by the people is deemed to have been written by the parties, even if they have not done so . . . and this is as if provided by an enactment" (*tenai bet din;* Resp. Rashba vol. 1, no. 662; vol. 3, nos. 17, 433, et al.; this is also the view of Hai Gaon and Ramban, in Nov. Ramban, Tos., *Beit ha-Beḥirah* Nov. Ritba and *Shitah Mekubbeẓet* BM 104a; Resp. Ran no. 54; Resp. Ritba no. 53). Just as scholars saw the need in matters of marriage and *ketubbah* to enact essential conditions for the good of all, these being applicable, *setaman ke-ferushan,* i.e., binding even if not expressly stipulated between the parties—so there are matters "which the scholars did not enact and which have not been accepted by all, but are usages which have been followed by the people in certain places, simply of their own accord without [communal] enactment, and this too is a matter of *setaman ke-ferushan,* which the scholars refer to as *derishat hedyotot*" (Resp. Rashba, vol. 4, no. 186). In this sense the rule of *derishat leshon hedyot* served the halakhic scholars as a means of solving many legal problems relating to the laws of marriage, property, and obligations (see Resp. Rashba, Ritba and Ran as cited above; for an interesting example in the field of obligations see Resp. Rashba, vol. 4, no. 125).

General and Local Custom. A general custom is created at the hands of the public as a whole and as such applies to the whole of that public, whereas a local custom is created at the hands of the people of a certain place, class, or some other group, and as such its application and validity is confined to the people of that place or group. Already mentioned above are the customs of various trade associations like those of shippers and caravan drivers, and the talmudic sources also mention customs relating to priests (Kid. 78b; TJ, Bik. 1:5, 64a and Kid. 4:6, 66b), women (Pes. 48b; TJ, Pes. 4:1, 30c), *ḥavurot* in Jerusalem (Tosef., Meg. 4: 10, 25c), the fair-minded (*nekiyyei ha-da'at*) of Jerusalem (Sanh. 30a), etc. Often a custom is referred to as *minhag ha-medinah* (i.e., custom of a particular area or district: BM 7: 1 and 9: 1; BB 1: 1 and 10: 1; Suk. 3: 11, et al.). Sometimes a custom is quoted as followed in Judea (Tosef. Ket. 1:4, 1:5 and 4: 12; BB 100b, et al.) in Galilee (Tosef. and Mishnah, *ibid.*), or in particular settlements, e.g., Tiberias, Acre, Kabul, (TJ, Pes. 4: 1, 30d, TJ, Ta'an. 1:6, 64c), also Jabneh, Sepphoris, etc. Such local or group customs relate to diverse fields of the *halakhah,* both the civil and the ritual law.

Many local customs render the law more severe by prohibiting matters which are permitted (see, e.g., Pes. 4: 1–4). Thus although the law permitted the performance of all labor on the 14th day of Nisan—i.e., on the eve of Passover—it became the general custom to refrain from labor from noon onward, since from that time the paschal sacrifice could properly be brought, so that the rest of the day was treated as a festival day; the Mishnah records that there were places where it was customary to perform labor until noon, and other places where it was customary not to do so lest the need for burning the leaven and other requirements of the festival be forgotten, and the Mishnah prescribes that the local inhabitants should follow their own custom. The halakhic validity of a custom that prohibited what was legally permissible was justified by regarding this as a form of vow undertaken by the public, and the sanction against breaking such a custom as akin to that of the prohibition against breaking a vow: "Matters which are permitted [in law] but prohibited by others by virtue of their custom may not be rendered permissible to the latter, as it is said (Num. 30:3), 'he shall not break his word'" (Ned. 15a; see also Ḥ. Albeck, *Shishah Sidrei Mishnah,* Nashim, p. 137f.). It seems however that the Babylonian *amoraim* restricted the operation of the prohibition deriving from the above rule, holding it as applicable only to a custom of the Cuthites (non-Jews), or of Jews amidst whom there were no scholars—out of apprehension that if the latter persons were permitted matters which their own custom prohibited, even though these were permissible in law, they would make light also of other prohibitions stemming from the law itself (Pes. 50b–51a).

These local customs were also discussed in relation to the biblical injunction, "you shall not cut yourselves" (Deut. 14: 1), interpreted by the halakhic scholars as a stringent prohibition against the formation of separate "societies" in relation to the rules of *halakhah,* so that the Torah "should not become like several Torot." In R. Johanan's opinion this prohibition only applied in circumstances where in one place a decision is given according to one opinion—for instance according to Bet Hillel, and in another place according to another opinion—for instance according to Bet Shammai, for in this way the *halakhah* itself would be divided; however, if from the standpoint of the law all decide according to the same opinion but part of the public renders the law additionally stringent for itself, this does not amount to a division of the *halakhah*, and it is permissible in the same way as any individual may take a vow and render prohibited for himself that which is permissible in law (TJ, Pes. 4:1, 30d; Yev. 13b; see also L. Ginzberg, *Perushim ve-Ḥiddushim ba-Yerushalmi*, 1 (1941), 152–60). Despite this theoretical distinction, the halakhic scholars maintained that in practice the diversity of customs might lead to division and strife and therefore laid down that a person should follow no custom but that of the place where he finds himself at any given time, if to do otherwise might lead to dispute (Pes. 4:1 and 51a; Yad, Yom Tov, 8:20; see also in detail *Peri Ḥadash*, OḤ 468 and 496).

Minhag and the Conflict of Laws (within Jewish Law). The multiplicity of customs, particularly local customs, inevitably gave rise to the phenomenon of varying laws on the same legal subject. At times it transpired that the law on the same subject differed in different places, and in this event—when the different stages of a legal obligation required performance in different places, in each of which there prevailed a different law concerning such an obligation—there arose the question of whether to apply the customary law at the time and place of establishment of the obligation, or the customary law at the time and place of its performance, or some other law. This and like questions, relating to the field of the conflict of laws, frequently arose in many fields of Jewish law against the background of differing customs on the same subject: e.g., as regards the laws of marriage, divorce, labor, partnership, and land tenancy. The result was the evolution of a proliferous body of case law on the subject of the *conflict of laws, constituting one of the important contributions made by custom to the development and creativity of Jewish law.

Control over Minhag by the Halakhic Scholars. Custom, because of its spontaneous and undirected nature, sometimes calls for a measure of supervision and control. At times a custom may be founded on error, or develop unreasonably or illogically in a certain direction, or may even be in conflict with substantive and fundamental principles of Jewish law in a manner leaving no room for its integration into this system. From time to time the halakhic scholars exercised such control in order to contain or discredit entirely a particular custom.

Custom Founded on Error. The Mishnah (Er. 10:10) mentions the case of a certain usage observed in Tiberias until the scholars came and set it aside; according to one opinion the usage of the people of Tiberias involved a prohibition which the scholars later permitted; according to another opinion, it involved a permission which the scholars later forbade (*ibid.*). Some commentators held that the usage was set aside because it was based on error (Tos. to Eruv. 101b, s.v. *"R. Yose omer"*; for a further illustration, see Ḥul. 6b concerning Rabbi's permissiveness regarding the eating of untithed fruit from Beth-Shean). In the Jerusalem Talmud a rule is laid down by R. Abun that a custom founded on error may be set aside: if the custom prohibits when it is clearly known that the relevant matter is permitted in law, the custom is valid and the matter must not be rendered permissible; however, if the custom prohibits as an outcome of an erroneous belief that the relevant matter is prohibited in law, when the error is discovered, the matter may be rendered permissible and the custom discredited (TJ, Pes. 4:1, 30d).

In post-talmudic literature frequent reference is made to customs discredited by the halakhic scholars on the ground of error. Thus Rabbenu Tam censured those who counted a minor as helping to make up a *minyan* as long as he held a Pentateuch in his hand: "This is a nonsensical custom . . . is a Pentateuch to be regarded as a man?" (Tos. to Ber. 48a). In another case Asher b. Jehiel examined the source of a custom concerning the testamentary disposition of property by a woman, concluding that "this is certainly an erroneous custom" and even if widespread, "it is not a custom that may properly be relied upon for purposes of the disposition of property . . . the custom is wrong and it must be invalidated" (Resp. Rosh 55:10). Similarly Mordecai *Jaffe opposed the custom of not reciting *birkat ha-mazon* (*Grace after Meals) in the home of a gentile, holding that the spread of "this nonsensical custom" originated from an erroneous understanding of a talmudic statement completely unconnected with such a custom (*Levush ha-Tekhelet*, 193:6). In another instance it became customary to take a stringent view and regard a woman as married in circumstances where—in the opinion of all scholars—there was no *kiddushin* at all in law; Simeon Duran strongly condemned this custom: "In circumstances where the whole world holds that there is no *kiddushin*, some people wish to impose on themselves such a stringent rendering of the law—this is a custom born in ignorance which the public must not be compelled to uphold" (*Tashbeẓ*, 1:154).

Unreasonable or Illogical Custom. At times the scholars examined a custom from the aspect of its reasonableness. Thus it was determined that a custom of the women not to do any work during the whole of the evening following the Sabbath was unreasonable and of no validity except insofar as it was restricted to the time of prayer on that evening (TJ, Pes. 4:1, 30d; Ta'an. 1:6, 64c); similarly invalid was a custom of the women not to do any work on Mondays and Thursdays, but their custom to do no work on a public fast-day or on Rosh Ḥodesh was reasonable and proper (*ibid.*). Some customs were condemned as imposing hardship on the public and contrary to the purpose of the actual law concerned. Thus the custom of those who prepared grits in Sepphoris and of the crushers of wheat in Acre not to work on *ḥol ha-mo'ed* was held to be a good custom since it was not likely to detract from the joy of the festival; however, the custom of the fishermen of Tiberias not to work on *ḥol ha-mo'ed* was opposed by the scholars, since it was impossible to prepare in advance fresh fish for the whole festival, and the custom was therefore likely to detract from the joy of the festival (TJ, *ibid.*).

Bad Custom. In post-talmudic times there was disputed the question of the extent to which a custom concerning a matter of civil law had to be accepted even when it appeared to be a "bad custom." On the dispute over a custom concerning the erection of a partition between two joint holders so that one might not observe the other (see below), Rabbenu Tam held that a custom of erecting a partition which fell short of the talmudic requirements was a bad custom and was not to be followed: "it may be concluded that some customs are not to be relied upon, even though it has been said, 'all in accordance with custom' " (Tos. to BB 2a). This opinion was followed by many scholars but others held that in civil law matters even a custom of this kind had to be followed when locally accepted (see *Piskei ha-Rosh* BB 1:1 and 5; Tur, ḤM 157:3–4, 16; Sh. Ar., ḤM 157:1 and commentaries; *Haggahot Maimuniyyot*, Shekhenim 2:20; *Mordekhai*, BM no. 366). Even those who took the former view conceded that in certain matters even a bad custom had to be followed—for instance in tax matters—if it was necessary for the good order of the public (*Terumat ha-Deshen*, Resp. no. 342; Sh. Ar., ḤM 163:3, *Rema* and commentaries).

Custom Contrary to Fundamental Rules and the Principles of Equity and Justice. The halakhic scholars were also at pains to ensure that custom did not contravert basic general rules as well as the principles of equity and justice in Jewish law. In so doing they rendered possible the integration of legal norms originating from custom into the general framework of the law, in the same way as their similar close control over communal enactments (see *Takkanot ha-Kahal*) rendered possible their integration. The matter is illustrated by the following examples:

(1) When Asher b. Jehiel decided that the custom of closing a transaction by verbal agreement alone contraverted the basic rule requiring demonstration of the absolute *gemirut ha-da'at* of the parties to a transaction, he laid down that this amounted to a bad custom which was not to be followed (see above).

(2) In law, on division of a courtyard between joint owners, "a partition must be built by both of them in the middle, so that neither may observe his neighbor in the enjoyment of his portions, since the injury of being observed is a real injury" (Yad, Shekhenim 2: 14, based on BB 3a); the width of the partition is determined by local custom "even when the custom is to build the partition of reeds and palm fronds" (BB 4a; Yad, Shekhenim 2:15). In this regard, Rashba decided that a custom not to erect any partition at all—leaving each neighbor free to observe the other—was of no legal validity, so that either partner could oblige the other to erect the partition: "If it has been the custom, as regards houses and courtyards, not to pay heed at all to the injury of observing one's neighbor, the custom is a bad one and no custom at all; for waiver may only be made in matters of civil law in which event a person may give of his own or tolerate damage to his property, but he is not free to breach the fences of Israel and to act immodestly in a manner causing the Divine Presence [*Shekhinah*] to depart from this people, as it is said, 'a person shall not make his windows to open onto his joint owner's courtyard' (BB 3:7)... Scripture relates, 'And Balaam lifted up his eyes, and he saw Israel abiding in his tents according to their tribes' (Num. 24:2). What did he see? That the openings to their tents were not made to face each other, and he said, 'These are worthy that the Divine Presence abide with them'" (BB 60a; Resp. Rashba, vol. 2, no. 268). Thus the custom in question stood in conflict with a material tract of the *halakhah* and could be given no legal recognition.

(3) A custom may not conflict with the Jewish law principles of justice and equity. Hence even in cases where a bad custom is given legal recognition, as in tax matters (see above), some way must be found for anchoring it within the general spirit of the *halakhah*. Hence a tax custom which did not adequately distinguish between rich and poor was held to have no legal validity: "The contention of the rich has no justification, for certainly according to the law of the Torah taxes must be shared according to financial means and there can be no greater injustice than to make the rich and the poor bear the tax burden in virtually equal measure, and even if the custom has been in existence for some years it must not be upheld" (Moses Rothenburg, quoted in *Pitḥei Teshuvah*, HM 163, n. 16). [M.E.]

Bibliography: GENERAL: S. Eisenstadt, *Ein Mishpat* (1931), 45–49; M. Higger, *Massekhet Soferim* (1937), 270–1; Weiss, Dor, index s.v. *Minhag;* Guedemann, Gesch Erz, index s.v.; Urbach, in: *Tarbiz*, 27 (1957/58), 169; B. De Vries, *Toledot ha-Halakhah ha-Talmudit* (1966²), 157–68; Dinary, in: *Benjamin De Vries Memorial Volume* (1968), 168–98. JEWISH LAW: *Naḥalat Shivah* no. 27, notes 6–16; S. A. Horodezky, in: *Ha-Shilo'aḥ*, 6 (1899), 417–20; Weiss, Dor, 2 (1904⁴), 62–65; Ha-Toseftai, in: *Ha-Shilo'aḥ*, 25 (1911), 600–8; A. Perls, in: *Festschrift... Israel Lewy* (1911), 66–75; J. Unna, in: *Jeschurun*, 10 (1923), 463–78; J. Carlebach, *ibid.*, 14 (1927), 329–51; Ch. Tchernowitz, *Toledot ha-Halakhah*, 1 pt. 1 (1934), 144–50; A. Guttmann, in: MGWJ, 83 (1939, repr. 1963), 226–38; J. L. Fischmann, in: *Sefer ha-Yovel... B. M. Lewin* (1939), 132–59; M. Vogelmann, in: *Ha-Zikkaron... le-ha-Rav... Cook* (1945), 366–77; Z. H. Chajes, *Darkhei ha-Hora'ah*, in his collected works: *Kol Sifrei Mahariẓ Ḥayyot*, 1 (1958), 207–80; T. Z. Kahana, in: *Mazkeret Kovez Torani... la-Rav Herzog* (1962), 554–64; M. Havatzelet, in: *Sinai*, 54 (1963/64), 155–63; idem, in: *Talpioth*, 9 (1964), 261–76; B. Z. Katz, *Mi-Zekenim Etbonen* (1964); Elon, Mafte'aḥ, 131f., 418–24; idem, in: ILR, 2 (1967), 547f.

MINHAGIM BOOKS. Variations in usage between various sections of Palestine are already recorded in the period of the *tannaim* and *amoraim*. Thus, customs of Jerusalem (Ket. 4b, 12b; BB 93b; TJ, Suk. 4: 14; Sem. 3:6), variations between Judah and Galilee (TJ, Pes. 4:5; Ket. 12b), differences between Sura and Pumbedita (Ḥul. 110a) are mentioned. Also mentioned are usages established by individual sages in certain localities (Shab. 130a, Yev. 14a, Ḥul. 116a). A tolerant attitude was obtained toward these variations but it was insisted that once established, the observance of the usage is obligatory (Pes. 4: 1, Ket. 6:4, BM 86b), sometimes even when it was contrary to a normative rule (TJ, Yev. 12: 1; BM 7: 1). De facto, the *minhag* assumed the force of law consisting of popular halakhic works, whose chief purpose was to record differences in religious custom as reflected in the daily life of their authors, in contrast to other *likkutim* ("anthologies"), which recorded similar—or at times the very same—differences culled from books or from the statements of rabbis but without personal acquaintance with them. By definition, a *minhag* is a prevalent religious practice or usage not enjoined by normative regulations, in contradistinction to *din*, which is a normative prescription. Often, however, such usages assumed the status of normative regulations (see *Minhag*).

Figure 1. Woodcut from the *Minhagim Book*, Venice 1601, showing the baking of *mazzah*. Jerusalem, J.N.U.L.

The first book of this nature to survive is the *Sefer ha-Ḥillukim bein Mizraḥ ve-Ereẓ Yisrael* (Variations in Customs Between the People of the East and of Israel; Jerusalem, 1938), which was apparently compiled in Ereẓ Israel in the eighth century. This early work summarizes some scores of major differences between the customs of Ereẓ Israel and Babylon actually in force, and seems to refer to the customs of Babylonian Jews living in Ereẓ Israel who preserved the customs of their country of origin. Many and varied suggestions have been made to explain the nature and purpose of this early work, but it is still not clear. Another work, *Ḥilluf Minhagim*, from the same period, of which not even a fragment has survived, gave the differences in custom between the academies of Sura and Pumbedita. It is certain, however, that such lists were in the possession of early scholars even though they may have been merely a collection from a variety of sources.

Minhagim books differ from one another in content, structure, purpose, and literary standard. Some describe the totality of customs peculiar to a certain area either on one topic only or covering a broader range—with the purpose of presenting "local custom" in its purity in order to preserve its existence and secure its uninterrupted continuation against penetration by external influences.

Middle Ages. *Sefer ha-Minhagot* of *Asher b. Saul of Lunel, which describes the customs of southern France over a very wide range of subjects and is apparently the earliest *minhagim* book to come down to us from Europe, belongs to this category. To this period also belongs *Ha-Manhig* of *Abraham b. Nathan ha-Yarḥi which is, however, of a different character. It limits itself mainly to the laws of prayer, Sabbath, and festival, but in it are described Spanish, Provençal, French, and German customs which the author himself saw while traveling in these countries. Consequently the aim of the two books also differs. While Asher of Lunel explicitly states that his purpose is to indicate the sources in rabbinical literature of the customs in order to prove their authenticity and prevent the disrespect for them which stems from lack of knowledge, the aim of *Ha-Manhig* was to show that all customs, even when contradicting one another, have a halakhic source, and that none of them should be rejected, but each locality should maintain its *minhag*. These two books were of great importance and played a prominent role in molding the *halakhah* in succeeding generations. A book, unique of its kind, though of the same type as the *Ha-Manhig*, discusses a collection of 25 variant customs between Catalonia and Provence. It was written by Menahem b. Solomon with the aim of proving that despite the great halakhic authority of *Naḥmanides, the ancient customs of Provence were not to be undermined because of him, and Menahem exerted himself to show their sources in the *halakhah* (see *Magen Avot*, London, 1909). In 12th-century Germany, halakhic compilations were known of the type of "*Minhagei Spira*," "*Kunteres Magenza*," and the like, which are mentioned for example in *Ha-Roke'aḥ* of *Eleazar b. Judah of Worms and the works of the school of Rashi. There are already allusions to it in *Sefer Rabban* of *Eliezer b. Nathan which was the first Hebrew book written in Germany. From the quotations it is recognizable that although these were not actually complete "books," like the Provençal and Spanish *minhag* books of the 13th century, they were nevertheless the first *minhag* books in this region, and some 300 years later they were to serve as the main source for the growth of a ramified and developed *minhagim* literature. These early Ashkenazi compilations committed to writing for the first time the great fragmentation in the sphere of custom that prevailed in Germany, each city, including even adjacent cities, having different customs.

Another type, much more rare, confines itself to the customs appertaining to one single theme, in most cases an actual professional sphere, like the book of *Jacob ha-Gozer which describes the comprehensive customs applying to the laws of circumcision, and was intended to serve as a handbook for those performing the ceremony. Despite the rarity of this type, it is of great importance, since through it the close connection which exists between *minhagim* literature and "professional" literature is well recognized, an affinity which became blurred in the course of time, but which is still apparent in one sphere of *halakhah*, **Issur ve-Hetter*. The various types of works of *Issur ve-Hetter* are in fact merely *minhagim* books intended to ease the burden of giving decisions from rabbis, and to a large extent they transmit different local customs in accordance with the different evidence they adduced, including visual evidence.

During the period of the *rishonim*, *minhagim* literature dealt mainly with the description of the customs of distinguished rabbis, with the avowed aim of establishing as the accepted norm their personal customs down to their last detail. The beginnings of this category are connected with the personality of *Meir b. Baruch of Rothenburg, who was the central figure in Germany in the 13th century and whose disciples created a complete *minhagim* literature, known as that "of the school of Maharam of Rothenburg," basing themselves on his customs and rulings. The first apparently was *Ḥayyim Paltiel, whose *minhagim* served as the foundation for the *Sefer ha-Minhagim* of Abraham *Klausner, regarded as "the father of the *minhag* Ashkenaz." In contrast to Ḥayyim Paltiel, who does not mention Meir of Rothenburg by name in his work, the *Ha-Parnes*, also compiled in conformity with the views and practices of Meir by his pupil Moses Parnes, in most cases refers to him by name. The personality of Meir is especially recognizable in the *Tashbeẓ* of his pupil *Samson b. Zadok, and in the anonymous *minhagim* book published by I. Elfenbein (New York, 1938). A century later this type of literature received powerful stimulus, chiefly in the Rhine region, and the description of the customs of outstanding rabbis became a widespread activity, in great demand by the public. It was engaged in by disciple-attendants who were in close personal contact with a certain scholar—at times living with him for decades—and these included in their descriptions

Figure 2. Woodcut from *Philologus Hebraeo-mixtus* by Leusden, Utrecht, 1663, showing merrymakers celebrating Purim. New York Public Library.

the actual minute-by-minute practice of their master, including the very smallest details even of the most intimate and private kind. They saw in each such detail a model worthy of emulation by every pious Jew. The best-known writers in this field are *Joseph b. Moses of Hochstadt who in his *Leket Yosher* described the customs of his distinguished teacher Israel *Isserlein, and *Zalman of St. Goar who recorded the customs of his teacher Jacob *Moellin ha-Levi. In this connection it is worth mentioning the *minhagim* book of Isaac *Tyrnau—incidentally the first rabbinic work to be written in Hungary—who in point of fact recorded the customs of his teachers, Abraham Klausner and R. *Sar Shalom of Vienna; but in contrast to the other two, who were not distinguished scholars, he was himself a renowned scholar who also devoted his energy to compiling a book of his teacher's customs. Together, these books constitute the well-known "*minhag* of Austria," and from them all important Ashkenazi customs developed—in particular the order of prayer and the festivals—down to the latest periods. Also deserving mention is the importance of the *Mordekhai* of *Mordecai b. Hillel which served as a primary work to which various Ashkenazi scholars, particularly in the 15th century, added their local customs, thus creating many different texts of the *Mordekhai*.

From the 15th century *minhagim* literature in Germany held an important place, without precedent in the world of *halakhah* and rabbinical literature. Moreover during this period the status of the *minhag* was raised to such a high level that great scholars and leading personalities of the period speak with great respect even about the customs of women and children and ascribe to custom a degree of authority exceeding that of the normative *halakhah* which is independent of custom. In opposition to the view of 19th-century Jewish historians, that the inordinate devotion to the writing of *minhagim* books in Germany in the 15th century testifies to the deterioration of intellectual creativity occasioned by the many persecutions with which this period was marked, it should be stressed that this tendency is evidence of a completely different process; namely, to a drawing near of the contemporary rabbis and leaders to the masses and their effort to transmit the practices of Judaism to the masses as a whole instead of to a mere handful of students. From the scholarly point of view, research into *minhagim* literature is very difficult, because these works have frequently been copied from one manuscript to another, and in the process sections of the halakhic discussions have been omitted, and glosses, supplements, **hassagot*, and corrections have been added by the various copyists, who tried to adjust the work to the local prevailing custom as it was known to them, or at least to interweave this custom into the earlier work. This feature is especially noticeable in the *minhag* book of Abraham Klausner, as it has been preserved in the printed edition (Riva di Trento, 1558) and in the manuscripts which are so completely surrounded by glosses and comments that it is no longer possible to distinguish the actual text from the additions.

[I.T.-S.]

Modern Period. In more recent times, the *minhagim* literature was enriched by works that sought to give reasons for each *minhag*. Among the more popular were *Ta'amei ha-Minhagim* (1896), by A. I. Sperling and *Oẓar kol Minhagei Yeshurun* (1917), by A. E. Hirshovitz. The reasons given are often far fetched and jarring to the modern ear. More recent works describe the *minhagim* lucidly and give reasons based on research and scholarship. Two examples are *Ziv ha-Minhagim* by J. D. Singer (1965), and *Sefer ha-Toda'ah* by Eliyahu Kitov, 2 vols. (1958–60; *Book of our Heritage*, 3 vols., 1968). Both follow the traditional pattern of the calendar.

Figure 3. Woodcut illustration for the *Amsterdam Minhagim Book*, 1662, showing the circumcision ceremony. Jerusalem, J.N.U.L.

The establishment of the State of Israel and the ingathering of the exiles has added impetus to the study of the *minhagim* of the various communities of the Diaspora, particularly of the oriental communities. The latter is pursued particularly by the Ben Zvi Institute in Jerusalem, which has already published a number of studies. Of the *minhagim* of other communities the following have been republished: *Sefer Ereẓ Ḥayyim*, by Ḥayyim Sithon (1968), and *Sefer Ereẓ Yisrael*, by Y. M. Tukazinsky (1966). Of special note is the exhaustive study of Jacob Gellis on *Minhagei Ereẓ Israel* (1968). [Is.Kl.]

Illustrations on Minhagim Books. A different kind of *minhagim* books were written for popular use, and, since they were designed also for women, many were written in Yiddish. They were usually arranged according to the order of the religious year and it was customary to add to their interest by the inclusion of illustrations. The anti-Semitic publications of the apostate J. *Pfefferkorn (*Judenbeichte*, 1508) contain illustrations of Jewish observances which may be based on an authentic prototype.

The Prague *Birkat ha-Mazon* ("Grace after Meals"), of which one copy has survived, is the first Hebrew work of the type known to contain such illustrations. The earliest published illustrated *minhagim* book is that of Venice of 1593. Its text was based on a similar work edited by one Simeon Ashkenazi in 1590. The 1593 edition, though printed in Italy, is in Yiddish. It was no doubt published partly for export and partly for the use of the Ashkenazi Jews then living in the north of Italy. It was accompanied by a series of woodcuts illustrating various observances and customs of Jewish religious life throughout the year, the participants dressed in the unmistakable German style. These illustrations became very popular. They were repeated but with growing indistinction in all manner of editions produced in Amsterdam and northern Europe from the second half of the 17th century onward. The same woodcut sometimes serves to illustrate two different subjects in different editions. Thus the Sabbath before Passover and the Day of Atonement is illustrated by a scene showing the delivery of the special sermon on that occasion. They are still reproduced to illustrate Dutch Jewish social life of the 17th–18th centuries, whereas they in fact belong to a much earlier period and in great part to another environment. In 1601 another *minhagim* book appeared in Venice with a series of remarkable woodcuts, far superior to the earlier edition and clearly illustrating the Italian Jewish environment.

A *minhagim* book produced in 1693 for the Sephardi community of Amsterdam but with illustrations in some cases showing typical Ashkenazi costume has some independent interest and attraction. Unfortunately this one was not imitated later. The imitative editions of Prague of 1665, of Frankfort c. 1674, and of Hamburg 1729 deserve cursory mention. That of Dyhernfurth of 1692, edited by S. Bass, has certain independent elements but like the earlier ones is poorly executed. The Frankfort edition of 1717 has half a dozen badly executed cuts (most of them repeated in the 1729 edition) reflecting tenth-century German Jewish customs and usages. The *minhagim* books as a whole, but particularly the hitherto neglected Venice edition of 1601, are of considerable importance for the study of Jewish social life. Of particular significance are the female costumes, the ritual details (e.g., the form of the Sabbath lamp and the **Havdalah* appurtenances), the interior of the synagogue and the separation of the sexes, the wedding ceremony, the Purim mummers, and even the barber's shop included to illustrate Lag ba-Omer. [C.R.]

Bibliography: Guedemann, Gesch Erz, 3 (1888), 12ff.; Weiss, Dor, 5 (1904[4]), index; Elbogen, Gottesdienst, 368ff., 565f.; S. Assaf, *Sifran shel Rishonim* (1935); I. Elfenbein (ed.), *Sefer Minhagim de-Rabbi Maharam b. Barukh mi-Rothenburg* (1938), 7–8; M. J. Sachs, *Kunteres Minhagei Ereẓ Yisrael* (1951); Baron, Social[2], 6 (1958), 129–30, 391–2; Zinberg, Sifrut, 3 (1958), 194ff.; D. Cassel, in: *Jubelschrift . . . Zunz* (1884), 122–37. ILLUSTRATIONS: Mayer, Art, nos. 60, 452; A. M. Habermann, in: Roth, Art, 478.

MINḤAH (Heb. מִנְחָה), the afternoon prayer service, one of the three daily services of the Jewish liturgy. The name of this prayer is derived from Elijah's devotions "at the time of the offering of the evening *(minḥah)* offering" (I Kings 18:36). One tradition ascribes the institution of this service to Isaac, who "went out to meditate in the field at eventide" (Gen. 24:63), while another attributes the formalization of the three daily prayer services to the men of the Great *Synagogue as substitutes for the daily sacrifices, with the *Minḥah* prayer taking the place of the lamb sacrificed in the Temple at dusk (Num. 28:8; Ber. 26b). The custom of three daily prayers is also implied by Daniel 6:11. The *Minḥah* prayer consists of **Ashrei* (Ps. 145, preceded by Ps. 84:5 and 144:15 and closed by Ps. 115:18) the **Amidah*, **Taḥanun*, and concludes with the **Aleinu*. On Sabbaths and fast days, a portion of the Torah is read before the *Amidah* (see *Torah, Reading of). In some rites, portions dealing with the daily sacrifices are read before *Ashrei*. The time for the recitation of the *Minḥah* prayer begins at the conclusion of six and one-half hours of the day. In calculating this time, an "hour" is one-twelfth of the length of the day. *Minḥah* prayed at this time is known as *Minḥah Gedolah* ("major"). *Minḥah* recited after nine and one-half hours of the day is called *Minḥah Ketannah* ("minor"). R. Judah set the final time for the *Minḥah* prayer until midway *(pelag)* through the time designated for the *Minḥah Ketannah*, or until one and one-quarter hours before sunset. The law is, however, in accordance with the opinion that the *Minḥah* may be recited until sunset, which is calculated to occur at the conclusion of the 12th hour of the day (Ber. 4:1; Ber. 26b–27a). As a precaution lest people forget to pray the afternoon prayer, the rabbis ruled that it is forbidden to commence a large business transaction or sit down to a banquet once the time has begun for the *Minḥah Gedolah*, without having previously recited the prayer. Likewise, it is forbidden to begin a minor transaction or partake of an ordinary meal after the time for the *Minḥah Ketannah* (Shab. 1:2; Shab. 9b). It seems that some made it a practice to pray both at *Minḥah Gedolah* and *Minḥah Ketannah*. However, *Asher b. Jehiel ruled that it is forbidden to do so (resp. 4:13). According to the Shulḥan Arukh (OḤ 234), it is permitted to recite the *Minḥah* prayer twice, provided one is recited as an obligatory prayer *(ḥovah)* and the other as a voluntary act *(reshut)*. This, however, is only allowed for the extremely pious who are certain that both their prayers will be recited with true devotion. Otherwise, the additional prayer will be considered an unwelcome addition in accordance with the exhortation of Isaiah: "To what purpose is the multitude of your sacrifices unto Me?" (Isa. 1:11). The third meal on the Sabbath (see **Se'udah Shelishit*) is usually eaten between *Minḥah* and *Ma'ariv*. During daily worship, the *Minḥah* prayer in the synagogue is usually delayed until near sunset in order that the congregation may assemble to pray *Ma'ariv* shortly after the *Minḥah* service is completed (see *Magen Avraham* to Sh. Ar., OḤ 233:1).

See also **Kedushah*.

Bibliography: Idelsohn, Liturgy, 118, 145; Elbogen, Gottesdienst, 98f., 117–20. [A.Ro.]

MINIS, family of original settlers of Savannah, Georgia. ABRAHAM MINIS (1694?–1757) arrived in Savannah with his wife ABIGAIL (1701–1794), two daughters, LEAH and ESTHER, and brother SIMON in 1733. Four sons and three daughters were born in Savannah. When fear of Florida's Spaniards drove Sephardi Jews from Georgia by 1741, only the Minis and Sheftall families, Ashkenazi in origin, remained. After trying farming unsuccessfully, Abraham began trading and shipping, and soon became an official supplier for General Oglethorpe. Upon Abraham's death, his widow Abigail, aided by her sons, continued his import business, and expanded their land holdings in Georgia to more than 2,500 acres. At the outbreak of the revolution, PHILIP MINIS (1734–1789), Abraham's only surviving son, was made acting paymaster and commissary general for Georgia, subsequently advancing $11,000 of his own funds to Virginia and North Carolina troops in Georgia. In 1779 he and Levi Sheftall guided Count d'Estaing and General Franklin in their unsuccessful attempt to recapture Savannah. The entire Minis family moved to Charleston, but Abigail secured agreement from the royal governor not to confiscate her property, and when the British left Savannah the family returned. Upon the reorganization of Savannah's Congregation Mikveh Israel in 1786, Philip was elected president. The following year he became a warden of the city, holding both posts until his death.

Bibliography: M. H. Stern, in: AJHSQ, 52 (1963), 169–99; 54 (1965), 243–77; J. R. Marcus, *Early American Jewry*, 2 (1953), passim; Rosenbloom, Biogr Dict, 113f., incl. bibl. [M.H.St.]

MINKIN, JACOB SAMUEL (1885–1962), U.S. rabbi and author. Born in Święciany, Russian Poland, Minkin went to the United States and was ordained by the Jewish Theological Seminary in 1910. He served congregations in Hamilton, Ont., and Rochester, N.Y., and for 25 years was the Jewish chaplain at Fordham Hospital in New York City. While in Hamilton he organized classes in English for immigrants and was active in many civic causes. Minkin devoted most of his later years to writing and published a number of popular scholarly works on Judaism. His *Romance of Hasidism* (1935) was one of the first books to introduce the ḥasidic movement to the English reader. He also wrote *Herod* (1936), *Abarbanel and the Expulsion of the Jews from Spain* (1938), *The World of Maimonides* (1957), *Shaping of the Modern Mind* (1963), and many articles on religious, philosophical, and historical subjects. [J.Ri.]

MINKOFF, NAHUM BARUCH (1893–1958), Yiddish poet, critic, literary historian. Born in Warsaw, he emigrated to the U.S. in 1914. He graduated from New York

Nahum Baruch Minkoff, Yiddish literary historian and poet. Courtesy H. Cooperman Minkoff, New York.

University's Law School in 1921, but instead of practicing law, taught at Jewish schools, at the Jewish Teachers' Seminary, and at the New School for Social Research. He edited the Yiddish literary monthly *Zukunft*. Together with the poets A. Glantz-*Leyeles and Jacob *Glatstein, he issued the first manifesto of the *In-Zikh group, emphasizing modernism, cosmopolitanism, and individualism.

In his five collections of poetry published between 1924 and 1952, Minkoff tried to analyze emotions and moods intellectually. He succeeded in his poems on the Holocaust, *Baym Rand* ("At the Edge," 1945). As a trained musician, he had an impeccable ear for tonal effects and for verse melodies. His critical essays and studies in literary history strengthened his position in Yiddish literature. He wrote studies on Elijah *Levita (1950), on *Glueckel of Hameln (1952), and a monumental work in three volumes on the pioneers of Yiddish poetry in America (*Pionern fun Yidisher Poezye in Amerike*, 1956). Regarding literary criticism as a scientific discipline, he attempted an intellectual, objective evaluation and classification of writers and their works—an approach which had found embodiment in his earlier works of criticism in the books *Yidishe Klasiker Poetn* (1939), *Zeks Yidishe Kritiker* (1954), and *Literarishe Vegn* (1955).

Bibliography: Rejzen, Leksikon, 2 (1927), 425ff.; LNYL, 5 (1963), 656–62; *N. B. Minkoff 1893–1958* (1959); A. Glantz-Leyeles, *Velt un Vort* (1958), 110–35; S. Bickel, *Shrayber fun Mayn Dor* (1958), 222–30; J. Glatstein, *In Tokh Genumen* (1960), 301–5.
[Sh.B.]

MINKOWSKI, EUGÈNE (1885–), French existentialist psychiatrist. Eugène Minkowski, born in St. Petersburg, studied medicine and was appointed psychiatrist at the Henri Rousselle Hospital in Paris from 1925. He had already come under the influence of the Zurich school of psychiatry led by Eugen Bleuler, which included Ludwig Binswanger the existentialist psychiatrist whom he met in 1922. In 1921 he wrote an analysis of Bleuler's conception of schizophrenia, *"La schizophrénie et la notion de la maladie mentale."* This was a precursor of his book *La Schizophrénie* (1927), in which Minkowski maintained that insanity was nothing more than an exaggeration of the individual's habitual character. The influence of Henri *Bergson is seen in his belief that the patient's impetus toward integration with reality was reduced and he existed in a world of his own. In the case of the schizophrenic, the dynamic functions of mental life were impaired and contact with reality lost. From Edmund *Husserl, he took his views on "phenomenology" as the study of immediate experiences in a living and concrete fashion of reality. Minkowski's existentialist views are in evidence generally in his writings. In *Les notions de distance vecue et d'ampleur de la vie* (*Journal de Psychologie*, 1930), he stated that the patient affirms his relation to a "becoming" around himself in which relationship he is able to grow and which contains all the vital dynamics of the human personality. In 1933 he published *Le Temps Vécu* and in 1936, *Vers une Cosmologie*. His many shorter works appeared regularly each year from 1921, except for the war years, in various medical journals. He served on the executive of the French *ORT and was honorary president of the world *OSE union. His wife Francoise Minkowski, a psychologist, carried out clinical work with the Rorschach test in the area of epilepsy, the typology of personality, and the rapport or detachment of the schizophrenic. In her book *Le Rorschach* (1956) she developed the Rorschach test as a clinical instrument analyzing specific dynamic factors rather than providing only a diagnosis. Her study of Van Gogh, *Van Gogh, sa vie, sa maladie et son oeuvre* (1963) confirmed her findings that the sensory type lives in the abstract and her work on childrens' drawings is set out in *De van Gogh et Seurat aux dessins d'enfants*. Mieczyslaw Minkowski (1884–), Swiss neurologist and brother of Eugene, was a research worker in the Pavlov Physiological Laboratory in St. Petersburg from 1907 to 1908 and worked in a neuropsychiatric clinic in Berlin from 1909 to 1911. In 1928 he became a professor of neurology at Zurich University and the president of the Swiss Neurological Society (1943–46). He wrote a number of neurological research papers beginning in 1925 with "Zum gegenwaertigen Stand der Lehre von den Reflexen." His work on the foetus included "Prenatal neuropathologic changes leading to neurological or mental disturbances" and his integrative views are expressed in "Neurobiologie, Moral und Religion" (1963). He was the president of the Swiss friends of the Hebrew University, Jerusalem from 1932 to 1947.

Bibliography: *Cahiers du Groupe Françoise Minkowska* (1965), 169–75; *Bulletin du Groupement Français du Rorschach* (July 1952); *Mieczyslaw Minkowski zum 70. Geburtstag* (1954), 23–33.
[Lo.M.]

MINKOWSKI, HERMANN (1864–1909), German mathematician. Minkowski, who was born in Alexoten, Lithuania, was taken to Koenigsberg, Germany, by his parents when he was eight years old. He held chairs of mathematics at Koenigsberg in 1895, Zurich in 1896, and in Goettingen

Hermann Minkowski, German mathematician. Jerusalem, J.N.U.L., Schwadron Collection.

(where a special chair was created for him) in 1902. In 1881 the Paris Academy of Science offered their prize for an investigation of the representation of integers as sums of squares. Although only a freshman, he produced a brilliant paper which went far beyond his terms of reference. The Academy overlooked his writing in German, a language not permitted by the prize regulations, and awarded him a prize. Minkowski's early work was on the theory of numbers. Apart from some work of *Eisenstein and others, Minkowski is entitled to nearly all the credit for creating the geometry of numbers. He was one of the earliest mathematicians to realize the significance of *Cantor's theory of sets at a time when this theory was not appreciated by most mathematicians. The later work of Minkowski was inspired by *Einstein's special theory of relativity which was first published in 1905. He produced the four-dimensional formulation of relativity which has given rise to the term "Minkowski space." He also made contributions to the theories of electrodynamics and hydrodynamics. The collected works of Minkowski were edited by D. Hilbert in two volumes and published in 1911 in Leipzig. The first volume contains a biographical article by Hilbert. In addition to his papers, he published the book *Diophantische Approximationen* (1907).

Bibliography: J. C. Poggendorff, *Biographisch-literarisches Handwoerterbuch . . . der exakten Wissenschaften*, 5 (1926), s.v.

[B.S.]

MINKOWSKI, PINCHAS ("Pinie"; 1859–1924), Russian cantor and composer. He was born in Belaya Tserkov, Ukraine, where his father was the town cantor. Minkowski received his basic training from his father, and joined the

Pinchas Minkowski, Odessa cantor. Jerusalem, J.N.U.L., Schwadron Collection.

choir of Nissan *Spivak ("Belzer") in Kishinev. At the age of 18, he was appointed Spivak's successor and three years later became chief cantor of the Choral Synagogue ("Chor-Schul") in Kishinev. After further study in Vienna, he sang in Kherson, Lemberg, and Odessa, and spent three years at the Kahal Adas Yeshurun Synagogue in New York, but was recalled to Odessa in 1892 as chief cantor of the Brody Synagogue, an office he held for 30 years. Minkowski had a tenor voice of natural sweetness though lacking in power. He avoided extraneous effects such as word repetition, falsetto, and needless coloraturas. A prominent member of the intellectual group which flourished in Odessa, headed by *Bialik, he lectured at the Jewish Conservatory, was chairman of the *Ha-Zamir* (The Nightingale) musical society, and published many articles on *ḥazzanut* and Jewish music, in Hebrew, Yiddish, and German. After the Russian Revolution he left for the United States, where he continued to sing and lecture.

Many of Minkowski's compositions remained in manuscript and are preserved, with his papers, in the Jewish National and University Library, Jerusalem. His setting of Bialik's poem *Shabbat ha-Malkah* ("Sabbath the Queen"), to a chorale-like melody, became a much-loved song for Friday evening in Israel and in many communities and synagogues abroad.

Bibliography: Sendrey, Music, indexes; Friedmann, Lebensbilder, 3 (1927), 55; idem, *Dem Andenken Eduard Birnbaums*, 1 (1922), 131ff.; *Di Khazonim Velt* (Dec. 1933); Jewish Ministers-Cantors Association of America and Canada, *Di Geshikhte fun Khazones* (1924), 88.

[J.L.N.]

MINNEAPOLIS-SAINT PAUL, so-called Twin Cities in *Minnesota; a metropolitan area of one and a half million inhabitants. The cities comprises the core area of the state's industry, notably milling, lumber, and electronics. Minneapolis, though younger, is about double the size of the older city and has 20,000 Jews compared to Saint Paul's 10,000. The earliest Jewish settlers of Saint Paul (incorporated in 1849) had previous American residency; later immigrants came directly from Europe, primarily from Germany. Many brought small capital with them and in time became retail and wholesale merchants of note. Jewish life was organized in the early 1850s when two fledgling congregations of south and east Germans combined into Mount Zion Hebrew Congregation (inc. 1856). Among the founders were members of the Rose family; fur trader Joseph Ullmann; and *ḥazzan* Kalman Lion. The first rabbi, Leopold Wintner, came in 1871 and soon found the congregation responsive to Reform. An Orthodox congregation was incorporated in 1875 (Sons of Jacob); among its founders were Samuel Coddon, Moses Calmenson, and Aaron Mark. To honor the last-named, the city's Conservative synagogue was later named Temple of Aaron (inc. 1912 under the leadership of Joseph Levy). East European settlers came in considerable numbers after 1881, settling on the west side of the Mississippi near the downtown area. To assist them in the process of Americanization, Sophie Wirth established Neighborhood House, later one of the nation's outstanding social-work centers. The dimunition of social divisions between eastern and western settlers after World War I made possible the creation of community-wide projects and institutions: a *talmud torah*, a home for the aged (established together with Minneapolis Jewry), a community center, and a convalescent home (Sholom Residence); a Jewish golf club was founded in the 1920s and a Jewish town club failed after a few years. In the 1950s two well-known architects built synagogues in the city: Eric Mendelsohn designed Mount Zion on Summit Avenue and

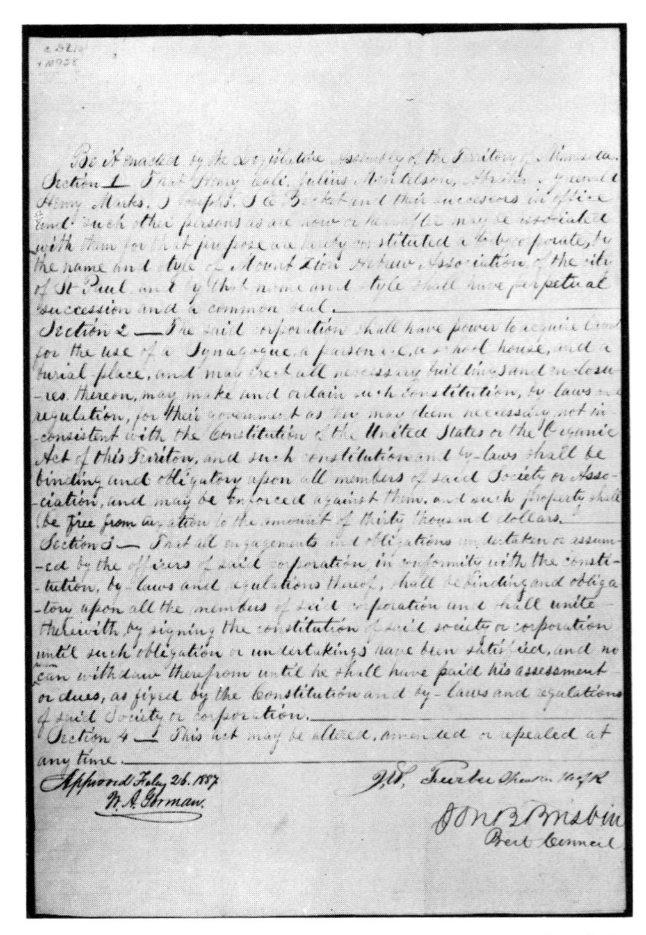

Be it enacted by the Legislative Assembly of the Territory of Minnesota.
Section 1 That Henry [illegible] Julius [illegible] [illegible] Henry Marks. Joseph [illegible] and their successors in office and such other persons as are now or hereafter may be associated with them for that purpose are hereby constituted a body corporate, by the name and style of Mount Zion Hebrew Association of the city of St Paul and by that name and style shall have perpetual succession and a common seal.
Section 2 — The said corporation shall have power to acquire land for the use of a Synagogue, a parsonage, a school house, and a burial place, and may erect all necessary buildings and enclosures thereon, may make and ordain such constitution, by-laws and regulation, for their government as they may deem necessary not inconsistent with the Constitution of the United States or the Organic Act of this Territory, and such constitution and by-laws shall be binding and obligatory upon all members of said Society or Association, and may be enforced against them, and such property shall be free from taxation to the amount of thirty thousand dollars.
Section 3 — That all engagements and obligations undertaken or assumed by the officers of said corporation, in conformity with the constitution, by-laws and regulations thereof, shall be binding and obligatory upon all the members of said corporation and shall unite therewith by signing the constitution of said society or corporation until such obligation or undertakings have been satisfied, and no can withdraw therefrom until he shall have paid his assessment or dues, as fixed by the Constitution and by-laws and regulations of said Society or corporation.
Section 4 — This act may be altered, amended or repealed at any time.
Approved Feby 26. 1857
W. A. Gorman
[illegible]
John B. Brisbin
Prest Council

Figure 1. Charter of the Mount Zion Hebrew Congregation, Saint Paul, Minnesota Territory, 1857. Courtesy Minnesota Historical Society, Saint Paul.

Percival Goodman, Temple of Aaron on Mississippi River Boulevard. The weekly *Saint Paul Jewish News* has been published since 1953.

Because Saint Paul's Jews had come to the city near the time of its first settlement, they had been readily accepted by their environment and quickly entered public life. Jacob J. Noah became secretary of the constitutional convention and Isaac M. Cardozo was for 30 years United States commissioner; he was followed in the office by Charles Bechhoefer, who later became the state's first Jewish judge of the District Court. Even in subsequent years, when social exclusion patterns were hardening all over America, Saint Paul preserved an unusual degree of flexibility, admitting Jews to town clubs and elevating them to positions of civic leadership. When Jewish immigrants left their first homes on the West Side and moved uptown, they did not at first reestablish Jewish districts but were widely scattered throughout the city, which in turn underscored their high rate of social integration. Only after World War II did Jews concentrate in Highland Park, where they formed an appreciable section of the district's upper middle-class population.

Minneapolis developed differently. The city was incorporated in 1866 and while some Jewish settlers came a few years later, Jewish community life did not begin until 1878 when Congregation Shaarai Tov (later Temple Israel) was established. Of the founding families the Edward Bernsteins were English; most of the others, like Rees, Alexander, Robitshek, and Pflaum, were German in origin. Very shortly afterward East European settlers arrived in large numbers. Their vigor matched that of the expanding city, which soon overtook the older twin across the river. Since the newly arriving Jews found social patterns in heavily Scandanavian Minneapolis already hardened, their life tended to turn inward and much energy was expanded on establishing strong Jewish institutions. The leading Orthodox synagogues were Adath Jeshurun (inc. 1884; it later became Conservative), Kenesseth Israel (inc. 1891), and Mikro Kodesh (established 1901); Beth El was founded as a Conservative congregation in 1921. Minneapolis Jews lived in two distinct areas, the near south side with its middle-class complexion and the near north side, the first gathering place of new arrivals. Religious orientations reflected economic and social diversities. Reform Jews lived on the south side, as did the more liberal Conservatives, while the Orthodox congregations, and traditionally oriented Beth El, were located on the north side. After World War II, the latter area was largely emptied of Jews, migration going into suburban areas, especially St. Louis Park and Golden Valley, where older congregations moved or new ones were established. The Minneapolis Talmud Torah achieved fame as one of the outstanding Jewish institutions in North America; its guide for many years was the physician, Dr. George Gordon. The school was later named in his honor; the building now belongs to the city, and is part of its public educational resources. Minneapolis now has a Jewish day school; there is a Hillel House at the University of Minnesota.

Mount Sinai Hospital opened in 1961, sparked by the leadership of industrialist Jay Phillips. There are two Jewish golf clubs and a town club. *The American Jewish World*, a weekly, was established in 1912 by Rabbi S. N. Deinard and Leo Frisch and has served the city and state. In the 1940s Minneapolis was called the "capital of anti-Semitism in the United States," but a conscious development toward acceptance and integration brought remarkable changes in the city's social structure, highlighted by the election of a Jew, Arthur Naftalin, as mayor in 1961. In this process the Minnesota Jewish Community Relations Council, directed

Figure 2. Interior of Temple of Aaron in Saint Paul, designed by Percival Goodman, with Ark curtain by Helen Frankenthaler. Photo Ruby Loos.

by Samuel Scheiner for most of the years since its founding in 1938, has played a significant role. On the whole, the Jewish communities in the Twin Cities now resemble one another. Neither has kept pace with the area's general increase in population. The greater economic activity of Minneapolis has given its Jewry a somewhat larger share of inner and outer dynamism, while the Saint Paul community has mirrored that city's slower development.

In both communities rabbis have generally occupied their pulpits for extended terms or even a lifetime. Among those from Minneapolis have been: Solomon M. Silber (d. 1925); orientalist Samuel N. Deinard; halakhist Solomon I. Levin; sociologist Albert I. Gordon; and Nachum Shulman; David Aronson was rabbi for 35 years at Beth El and became president of the Rabbinical Assembly; Albert G. Minda served Temple Israel for 40 years and was chosen president of the Central Conference of American Rabbis; in St. Paul, Isaac L. Rypins (d. 1951); Joseph B. Hurvitz (d. 1954); Harry S. Margolis (d. 1946); Herman M. Cohen (d. 1970); W. Gunther Plaut, who wrote the history of Minnesota Jewry and played a leading role in the state's artistic and political life; and Bernard S. Raskas, who became the first Jewish chaplain in the state's legislature. In 1948 the Minnesota Rabbinical Association, composed of members of all groups, made socio-religious history by insisting that weddings must henceforth be held in homes or synagogues to receive rabbinic participation.

Among the communal leaders who dominated Jewish institutional life during the first part of the century were Josep Schanfeld, Isaac Schulman, Jacob Dittenhofer, Lewis Paper (synagogues); Hiram D. Frankel (B'nai B'rith), Dr. Moses Barron, Jessie Calmenson (Zionism), and George Kaplan (Hebrew education). Three couples achieved special prominence in the Jewish as well as general community: Emanuel Cohen (in 1924 the Jewish Center was named after him) and his wife Nina, who was a daughter of Sabato *Morais and a founder of the National Council of Jewish Women (NCJW); Arthur and Fanny Brin (the latter became national president of the NCJW); and Milton and Irma Firestone, active in synagogue, defense, and refugee resettlement work.

Bibliography: W. G. Plaut, *The Jews in Minnesota—the First Seventy-Five Years* (1959); A. I. Gordon, *Jews in Transition* (1949); R. Danenbaum, in: *Reform Advocate* (Nov. 16, 1807, special Minnesota edition), 7–40; H. D. Frankel, *ibid.*, 41–53; E. J. Lipman and A. Vorspan, *A Tale of Ten Cities* (1962), 253–89; W. G. Plaut, *Mount Zion, 1856–1956* (1956); W. Hoffman, *Those Were the Days* (1957); J. R. Kramer and S. Leventman, *Children of the Gilded Ghetto* (1961).

[W.G.P.]

MINNESOTA, state of the U.S. in the north central tier with about 3½ million inhabitants, and a Jewish population of under 35,000. Jews went to the area before it attained statehood (1858), finding a fluid pioneer society which accepted them without reserve. Among the founders of the state and secretary of its constitutional assembly was Jacob J. Noah, son of Mordecai Manuel Noah. Prominent family names of the pioneer days were Elfelt, Austrian, Ullmann, all of them merchants. The first synagogue was Mount Zion Hebrew Congregation in Saint Paul (1856); its first rabbi, Leopold Wintner, went to the state in 1871. Most early Jewish settlers were of German origin; East Europeans arrived in large numbers after 1881. Efforts were made to settle the newcomers in agricultural colonies further west (Painted Woods and Devil's Lake, North Dakota), but the experiments failed and in time the colonies were abandoned. Immigrants began to move to all parts of the state; they were often peddlers, railroad laborers, and farmers. By 1900 every small town had acquired a few Jewish families, but sixty years later the trend to the larger centers, as well as migration away from the state, had concentrated the Jewish population in Greater *Minneapolis (20,000) and Saint Paul (10,000). Duluth had decreased to 1,600; Virginia to 175; Hibbing to 155; others like Austin, Albert Lea, and Rochester had about 100 or fewer Jews. The early division into German and Eastern Jews disappeared between the two world wars. Communal institutions were usually representative of all elements, so that federations and welfare funds achieved better than average levels of giving. Zionists established statewide groups from the beginning of the movement; volunteers from Minnesota fought in the *Jewish Legion. The Minneapolis Talmud Torah has been a

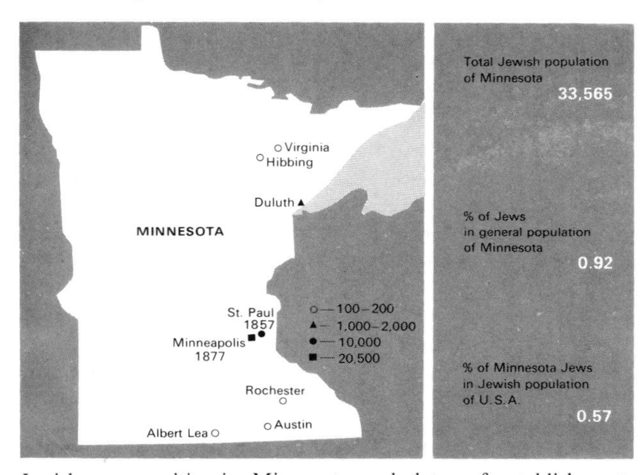

Jewish communities in Minnesota and dates of establishment. Population figures for 1968.

national model for Hebrew education. The Jewish Community Relations Council of Minnesota (est. 1938) represents the major statewide civic defense and community relations agencies. Jews have contributed to secondary levels of the judiciary and political life (mayors of various cities, members of the State legislature); they have held and hold important teaching and research positions in a number of colleges and especially at the University of Minnesota, and they have made their most significant contribution to the general community by leadership in civic work, heading drives, organizations, and institutions. At the celebration of the tercentenary of American Jewry (1954) a special section of Judaica was established by the Minnesota Historical Society. The oldest Jewish newspaper in Minnesota is *The American Jewish World,* which was established in 1912 and published in Minneapolis.

Bibliography: W. G. Plaut, *The Jews in Minnesota—The First Seventy-Five Years* (1959). [W.G.P.]

MINNITH (Heb. מִנִּית), one of the farthest limits of the area in which Jephthah smote the Ammonites (Judg. 11:33). The wheat of Minnith was traded in exchange for goods from Tyre (Ezek. 27:17). Eusebius (Onom. 132:2) locates the place at the fourth Roman mile on the road from Heshbon to Philadelphia (Rabbath-Ammon). It has accordingly been placed at Khirbat el-Ḥanūttiyya in the fertile Heshbon plain, 6 mi. (c. 9½ km.) north-northeast of Ḥisbān. The earlier identification with Umm al-Ḥanāfish has generally been abandoned.

Bibliography: C. R. Conder, *Survey of Eastern Palestine* (1889), 246ff.; Schultze, in: PJB, 28 (1932), 75; Abel, Geog, 2 (1938), 388; Glueck, in: AASOR, 18/19 (1939), 161–62; Hentschke, in: ZDPV, 76 (1960), 122; Press, Ereẓ, s.v.; EM, s.v. (incl. bibl.). [M.A.-Y.]

MINOR, OSIP S. (**Joseph**; 1861–1932), Russian revolutionary and a leader of the Social Revolutionary Party. Born in Minsk, he was the son of Rabbi S. Z. *Minor. While still a student at the University of Moscow, he joined the "People's Will" (Narodnaya Volya) Society. In 1883 he was arrested for the first time, and in 1887 he was exiled to Siberia. After participating in a rebellion of exiles in Yakutsk, he was sentenced to forced labor for life (1889). Freed in 1896, he was banned from living in European Russia. In 1900 he nevertheless returned to Russia and settled in Vilna. He resumed his revolutionary activities, traveled abroad, and was one of the organizers of the Social Revolutionary Party. In 1909 he was again arrested as a result of the intervention of the czarist agent Y. F. *Azeff and was sentenced to ten years' forced labor. He was freed at the time of the Revolution of 1917 and was briefly mayor of Moscow. Minor left Russia in 1919 after the Bolshevik victory and settled in France, where he became chairman of the Society for Assistance to Exiles and Political Prisoners in Russia. He died in Paris. His book *Eto bylo davno* ("It Was Long Ago") appeared posthumously in 1933.

Bibliography: *Sotsialisticheskiy Vestnik,* 19 (1932), 16; V. Chernov, *Yidishe Tuer in der Partey Sotsial Revolutsionern* (1948), 246–58. [Y.S.]

MINOR, SOLOMON ZALMAN (**Zalkind**; 1826–1900), writer and scholar, one of the pioneers of the Russian-Jewish intelligentsia. As a youth, he entered the newly opened government rabbinical seminary in Vilna and was one of its first two graduates—he was later a Talmud teacher in his seminary. Through the efforts of the *maskilim* he was elected **kazyonny ravvin* ("government-appointed rabbi") of the Minsk community in 1859. One of the first to preach in Russian in the synagogue, he became well known for his sermons, which were published in book form and served as models for other rabbis. Minor was active in the promotion of *Haskalah in Minsk, and in 1869 he was invited to serve as rabbi in Moscow. In the early 1890s, when the Jews of Moscow were persecuted, he interceded with the authorities on behalf of his community and was consequently expelled from Moscow on the order of the governor of the city, the Grand Duke Sergei. He then returned to Vilna and continued his literary activity there. Minor published many articles in the Russian-Jewish and the Hebrew press, for the most part under the name "Remez." He conducted a debate with anti-Semites (including the priest *Lutostansky) and was a friend of Tolstoy and directed his studies in Hebrew and the Bible. He was one of the first Jewish scholars to work in the field of the history of Russian Jewry. His son LAZAR (ELIEZER) MINOR was a professor of nervous diseases and another son, Osip *Minor, was a leader of the Social Revolutionary Party.

Bibliography: J. Slutsky in: *He-Avar*, 7 (1960), 29–48; S. Guenzburg, in: *Knizhki Voskhoda*, 2 (1901), 128–35; A. Katzenelson, in: *Yevreyskaya Starina*, 2 (1909), 175–88. [Y.S.]

MINORCA, Mediterranean island of the Balearic group. The earliest information about the Jews on the island dates from 418 C.E. when Severus, the bishop of Minorca, reports on the victory of Christianity in the island. The agitation he fomented led to the destruction of the synagogue. Many Jews, especially the women, died for their faith: a few succeeded in hiding in the forests and caves. According to Severus he gained 540 Jews for Christianity. While it existed, the community was organized as a national group under the leadership of a "defensor": the last, Theodore, acted as **archisynagogos*. There is no information available on the Jews during the Byzantine and Muslim rule. When Minorca was reconquered by the Christians during the reign of James I of Aragon, he received help from the Jews to equip the expedition. Most of the later history of the Jews of Minorca is closely connected with that of their coreligionists in *Majorca. In 1319 King Sancho I declared that they and the Jews of the nearby island of Ibiza were to be included in all the levies imposed upon them by the communal leaders of Majorca. The Jews shared the sufferings of the general population when Minorca was almost depleted of its inhabitants during the *Black Death (1348). After the disorders which swept Spain in 1391 there were apparently no Jews on the island. Nevertheless a number of Judaizers in Minorca were sentenced by the Inquisition of Majorca which maintained a commission at Mahón. A small Jewish community existed again in Minorca during the temporary English occupation in the 18th century (1720–56; 1762–81).

Bibliography: Baer, Spain, 1 (1961), 17, 174, 381, 404; P. G. Segeni, *Carta encíclica del obispo Severo* (1937); C. Roth, in: B. Schindler (ed.), *Gaster Anniversary Volume* (1936), 492–7; B. Braunstein, *Chuetas of Majorca* (1936), 118ff.; J. Parkes, *Conflict of the Church and the Synagogue* (1963), 204–5; López de Meneses, in: *Estudios de edad media de la Corona de Aragon*, 6 (1956), 353, 255, 388. [H.B.]

MINORITY BLOC (1922–30), political alliance of representatives of the national minorities in Poland created with the aim of obtaining representation in the Sejm corresponding to their numbers in the population—up to 40%. The Bloc was formed in 1922 in reaction to the election regulations issued under the pressure of the extreme nationalist bloc led by the clergymen Lutoslawski, which sought to present to the world an artificial image of a monolithic national state. In the mapping of the constituencies there was blatant discrimination between the Polish ethnographic region and the mixed regions, as well as the intentional addition of rural and urban units to the disadvantage of scattered minorities such as the Jews and the Germans. The common objective of assuring their national rights enabled the parties to overcome the wide differences which prevailed among the various ethnic sections and to establish a countrywide bloc. Its initiator was the German Hasbach, and its executor and organizer was the Zionist leader Yiẓḥak *Gruenbaum. The Ukrainians of Galicia boycotted the elections because in theory they did not yet recognize the Polish government; the Zionists of Galicia therefore presented their own national list. On the other hand, in Congress Poland and in the Belorussian border regions ("Kresy") the overwhelming majority of the Jewish public, with the exception of the *Folkspartei, the *Bund and the *Po'alei Zion, supported the Bloc. The Poles regarded this union as a hostile act because they suspected its partners of irredentist tendencies and anti-national aims. The elections brought an impressive victory for the Minority Bloc, which won 66 seats, including 17 Jewish ones. The drastic defeat of the Polish lists was most evident in the mixed border regions. In eastern Galicia 15 Jewish representatives were elected as a result of the Ukrainians' abstention and in western Galicia two, so that the "Jewish club" consisted of 34 seats in the Sejm and 12 in the Senate. During the parliamentary term of 1922–27 only loose links were maintained between the minority "clubs," because the policy of all the Polish factions was to achieve the dissolution of the Bloc either by fomenting disunion within its ranks or by promising to fulfill specific demands. In 1923 Premier Sikorski, who headed the Leftist coalition, attempted to win over the Ukrainians and the Belorussians, while in 1925 the *Grabski government endeavored to attract the Jews by means of an "agreement" which became known as the **Ugoda*. In 1926 Marshal Pilsudski came to power in the wake of the May coup d'état. The new regime adopted the slogan of "moral improvement" (*sanacja*) and attempted to form a wide public front for constructive purposes. However, the hopes which had been aroused among the national minorities rapidly melted away when the weakening of parliamentary government became apparent and the promises to fulfill national aspirations in culture and education did not materialize. With the approach of the elections of March 1928 a second Minority Bloc was organized. On this occasion it was joined by the Ukrainians of Galicia, and their representative, Dmitri Levitsky, became the active colleague of Gruenbaum and Hasbach. In the meantime, however, conditions had changed. A split, arising out of social differences, had occurred within the minorities. This prevented the affiliation of the Radicals, and the Bloc thus became an associaton of political parties instead of whole national groupings. The representation of the Jews was also reduced as a result of the departure of all the Galician Zionists, who formed their own national list, and the pro-government bloc consisting of Agudat Israel, the Folkspartei, and a faction of the organization of merchants and craftsmen. In addition to this there were Orthodox and assimilationist Jewish circles who preferred to vote directly for the government list. These differences were responsible for a sharp decrease in the number of Jewish representatives: seven in the Minority Bloc; and six in the National List of Galicia. The other lists did not obtain a single seat.

After the third Sejm was unexpectedly dissolved by the president before the end of its term, new elections were held in 1930 in an atmosphere of growing political suppression. Internal frictions rendered the establishment of a countrywide Zionist list impossible. Among the Ukrainians radical nationalistic feelings were expressed in the thesis that since they constituted a majority in their regions, it was not in their interest to maintain a union with scattered minority groups. The Zionists of Congress Poland under the leadership of Gruenbaum joined forces in six regions with the German minority of central and western Poland—a substitute for the former comprehensive Minority Bloc. The economic businessmen list of Agudat Israel, the Folkspartei, and the merchants also increased their strength. The government employed harsh measures against the candidates of the reduced Minority Bloc, who did not secure more than two seats. The Zionists of Galicia only succeeded in obtaining four seats. Thus ended the attempt to unite the minorities in a common political campaign, and in the relations between the Jews and the other minority groups there were increasing differences, estrangement, and even hostility as a result of the economic and political suffocation of the masses.

Bibliography: I. Schiper, *Żydzi w Polsce odrodzonej*, 2 (1930), 286–311; L. Halpern, *Polityka żydowska w Sejmie i Senacie Rzeczypospolitej, 1919–1933* (1933). [M.LAN.]

MINORITY RIGHTS, rights enjoyed by Jews and other ethnic minorities between the two world wars in some countries, mainly eastern and southeastern Europe, according to the provisions of the minorities treaties at the Versailles Peace Conference, 1919. In all the other states the treatment of minority nationals was regarded as an internal matter, subject only to the state's own laws and not to international law. In those states which were bound, between the two world wars, by the minorities treaties, Jews and other minority nationals were guaranteed certain minimal rights, and the *League of Nations created a machinery for supervising their implementation. These were rights granted in addition to civil, political, and religious freedoms. Whereas the *French Revolution and *Napoleon brought *emancipation of the individual in parts of Europe as an equal citizen of the state, the minority rights expanded the concept of equality to include ethnic and cultural distinctions within the territory of the state. These national rights differed from medieval *autonomy in that the latter presupposed a society that is subdivided into corporations, each of which lives according to its own distinct law. The minority rights, on the other hand, posited an egalitarian society, where the individual enjoyed individual rights plus his rights as a person belonging to an ethnic or religious minority. The proponents of the idea gave it widely differing interpretations. Minority rights tended to embrace largely secular, as opposed to religious, elements; therefore the terms cultural, national, ethnic, or linguistic are interchangeable with the term minority.

Development of the Idea. The idea originated at the beginning of the 20th century in the multi-national states of Eastern Europe where it was impossible to carve out territorial units to accommodate particular ethnic groups. Karl Renner, an Austrian socialist, published in 1902 his *Der Kampf der oesterreichischen Nationen um den Staat* in which he developed the proposition that national affiliation was primarily a personal and not a territorial matter. He therefore advocated that the state represent a federation of nationalities, without separation of state and nationality, similar to the separation of Church and state. Since the Jews represented an extraterritorial minority *par excellence* the idea that they constitute a distinct nationality and are therefore entitled to a special national existence appealed very strongly to East European Jewish intellectuals. Chaim *Zhitlowsky and Simon *Dubnow in Russia, and Nathan *Birnbaum in Austria, attracted at first only a small group of intellectuals to their ideas of national autonomy. Zhitlowsky, an emigré socialist revolutionary, sought to synthesize socialism with nationalism as early as 1883. He demanded for Jews "national equal rights with all peoples" and asserted that only through the Yiddish language could the social and national revival of the Jewish people be effected. He maintained that one could remain identified with the Jewish nationality even if abandoning the Jewish religion. He urged the Jewish masses to participate in the class struggle as a national unit. Alone among the cosmopolitan Jewish socialists he favored national socialism.

In 1897 he began publishing philosophical studies in Jewish history and a comprehensive program of action which later appeared in book form as *Pisma o starom i novom yevreystvie* ("Letters on Old and Modern Judaism," 1907). His main thesis was that national consciousness consists mainly of spiritual-cultural determinants and that these national characteristics can be maintained by the Jews in the future in the lands of their dispersion, just as they have survived the lack of territory or unity of language since the end of the second commonwealth. After emancipation of the individual the Jews as a group should be granted national self-government within the framework of the state along with other national minorities. His secularization of the national idea as opposed to those who saw the essence of Judaism in religion, and his optimistic view of the future of Judaism in the Diaspora, were the main underpinnings of his insistence on national cultural autonomy.

Popular Movement. These meager beginnings in academic speculation turned into a powerful popular movement during the 1905 revolution in Russia (1904–07), petered out from 1907 to 1914, and then gained in volume in both east and west during World War I. A number of middle-class parties and socialists tended toward "*assimilation"; i.e. they sought only civil and political rights, and shied away from nationalist identification. Before long, however, *autonomism developed into a mighty stream; most Jewish parties adopted Diaspora nationalist plans in their platforms. The *League for Equal Rights for Jews, consisting of middle-class liberals and Zionists, met illegally in 1905 and declared in favour of "civil, political, and national rights . . . the freedom of national-cultural self-determination . . . a comprehensive *kehillah* autonomy, freedom of language and of school education." This was adopted despite the wishes of the top leadership which was anti-nationalistic. The Zionists, too, at their conference in *Helsingfors, Finland, in 1906, demanded "the recognition of the Jewish nationality with the right of self-government in all affairs of Jewish life." This was achieved although large segments of political Zionists clung to the doctrine that creative Jewish living was possible in Palestine only. In 1918 the Zionist headquarters issued the "Copenhagen Manifesto," which demanded a national home in Palestine, and in all other countries full equality of rights, including "national autonomy, cultural, social, and political, for the Jewish population of countries largely settled by Jews, as well as of all other countries whose Jewish population demands it"; and admission into the "League of Free Nations."

The followers of Dubnow's Diaspora nationalism formed the *Folkspartei (People's Party) in 1906, only to remain a mere handful. The *Bund in Russia, Poland, and Lithuania was organized in 1897. Though it initially had made the class struggle paramount in its program, it soon became a major protagonist of autonomism, with especial emphasis on Yiddish as the national language. The proletarian Zionist groups, the *Jewish Socialist Workers' Party (Sejmists), the *Jewish Social Democratic Party, *Po'alei Zion, and the *Zionist Socialist Workers' Party, more or less hesitantly, also came around to demand national self-determination. Similar agitation took place in Austrian Jewry and to a lesser extent in the Ottoman Empire and the United States. Thus in the space of less than two decades national autonomy grew from a mere theory into a mass movement. During World War I activity was transferred to the west. In the United States, after several years of numerous meetings, the *American Jewish Congress was organized in 1918 to present the Jewish case for Palestine and minority rights for the Jews of Europe at the Peace Conference. They adopted a "Jewish Bill of Rights" to be presented to the conference. In addition to guarantees of equal civil, political, religious, and national rights, it proposed autonomous management of communal institutions by minorities, respect for the languages of ethnic groups, and no discrimination against Sabbath observance. Whereas in the U.S. a modicum of accommodations was arrived at between the nationalists and the members of the non-nationalist *American Jewish Committee, no such rapprochement was achieved in England or France.

At the Peace Conference. At the Versailles Conference the Jews assumed leadership in the struggle for minority rights. Delegations and petitions from Jews in many countries began to arrive in Paris. Immediately an attempt was made to form a united front, and a Committee of Jewish Delegations (*Comité des Délégations Juives) was formed. Most of the erstwhile opponents bowed to the desires of the East European Jews who were directly concerned. The French and British delegations, who refused to join the Committee of Jewish Delegations, agreed not to oppose actively the efforts of the majority to attain national rights.

Minority Treaties. After prolonged and stubborn negotiations that lasted in some cases till 1923, minorities treaties were signed by the newly created states of Poland, Czechoslovakia, Rumania, Yugoslavia, and Greece; and by the defeated states of Austria, Hungary, Bulgaria, and Turkey; declarations of willingness to abide by minority stipulations were secured from Lithuania, Latvia, Estonia, Albania, and several other localities. Iraq made its Minorities Declaration when it became independent in 1932. The Polish Minority Treaty became the model for all the rest. It had 12 articles. Some of them dealt with the basic civil, political, and religious rights of minorities. The specific rights of minority nations were dealt with in detail. Polish nationals were to have the free use "of any language in private intercourse, in commerce, in religion, in the press, or in publications of any kind, or at public meetings." Minority nationals were guaranteed "the use of their own language, either orally or in writing, before the courts." They were also authorized "to establish and control, at their own expense, charitable, educational, religious and social institutions, with the right to use their own language and to exercise their religion freely therein." Minorities were guaranteed the right to establish schools in their own language, and to obtain an equitable share of public funds for their "educational, religious, and charitable purposes." Finally, in view of the special position of the Jews in Poland, who were not concentrated in any one area in compact masses but were diffused over the entire country, and in view of Polish anti-Semitism, two special "Jewish articles" were inserted to safeguard their unique position. Article 10 read:

> Educational Committees appointed locally by the Jewish communities of Poland will, subject to the general control of the State, provide for the distribution of the proportional share of public funds allocated to Jewish schools in accordance with article 9, and for the organization and management of these schools.

Article 11 provided that: "Jews shall not be compelled to perform any act which constitutes a violation of their Sabbath," with specific reference to attendance at courts of law, and elections or registration for electoral or other purposes. Other articles dealt with enforcement. The minority obligations must be recognized as fundamental law of the country. Infractions were to be supervised by the League of Nations, and member-states of the League Council were entitled to appeal to a world court. Some of the other countries resolutely resisted the minorities provisions, but were forced to sign them. The "Jewish articles" were omitted in some treaties. There was general satisfaction among Jews with the provisions of the Minorities Treaties. Some were jubilant over the new era that had dawned to enable them to live their own lives and to develop their own culture.

Implementation of Treaty Provisions. The minorities system represented a remarkable experiment in international control that lasted some 20 years. With all its faults, substantive and procedural, it could have developed into a major force for minority protection. However, it crumbled along with the *League of Nations that sponsored it. The system helped prevent serious disturbances by providing minorities an outlet in the international provisions for resolving grievances and by serving as a brake on oppressive chauvinism. In most minority states there were provisions for national education, and protection against undesirable assimilation, and some of them experimented, on their own initiative, in autonomous minority institutions on a considerable scale. The main weakness lay in the refusal of minority states to act on their international pledges in good faith. Some of the substantive provisions of the Minority Treaties lacked precision. The procedure in hearing complaints was faulty. The League itself did not pursue recalcitrant states with proper vigor. Only the Permanent Court of International Justice at The Hague tried valiantly, in two cases brought before it, to preserve decency and public order. All this was to no avail. In 1934 the world was stunned by the declaration of Col. Józef Beck (Polish minister of foreign affairs) renouncing minority obligations. The whole structure toppled along with the League of Nations. World War II put an abrupt end to the experiment.

Treatment of Jews by Countries. The Jews had been most instrumental in the promulgation of minority rights. They set out full of hope for a new deal. They were the ones to be most disappointed. Unlike other minorities they did not constitute a threat to the state by irredentist or restoration dreams. Except for three cases, they did not resort to petitioning Geneva on their grievances, as did other minorities; they feared antagonizing their governments. Only Estonia excelled in granting its minorities, including the Jews, complete autonomy. A chair of Jewish studies was established there at the university of Dorpat (*Tartu).

LATVIA. Although Latvia by a law of 1921 narrowed the grant of rights, including minority rights, to those who could prove residence over a period of 20 years, it provided liberal allowances for minority schools until 1934. The Education Law of 1919 provided for compulsory education in the language of the family. Central and local authorities were to establish such schools and to bear the necessary expense. Such a class was to be established if at least 30 pupils were enrolled. The minority section of the ministry of education had a Jewish division, its head nominated by the Jews, subject to the approval of the Council of Ministers. The Jewish educational system thrived. This autonomy, however, was limited to schools; Latvia never enacted laws regarding cultural, religious, and welfare organizations of minorities. In 1934, with the abolition of the democratic regime, school autonomy was virtually nullified by a new law which provided that paid officials of the state administer minorities school systems, that a child be instructed in his family's language provided he could express his thoughts in that language, and that state and local subventions to minority education not exceed their ratio in the population.

LITHUANIA. In Lithuania, too, there was at first a great surge of hope when the constitution in 1922 granted to minorities autonomy and the right to levy taxes. Autonomous Jewish communities, already recognized by law in 1920, were allowed to administer their own cultural, welfare, social, and educational affairs. These communities were united into a national council with a minister of state for Jewish affairs who could levy taxes for Jewish needs and exercised some authority in school affairs. The schools were under the ministry of education. The national and municipal authorities were charged with subventing the Jewish schools. They were entitled to employ Yiddish in government offices. All this exuberant activity in national self-determination came to a halt after only two years. In 1924 both the Jewish national council and the ministry of Jewish affairs were abolished. The following year the local communal organizations were disbanded. Only a modicum of school autonomy remained.

Poland and Other Countries. In Poland anti-Semitism was rampant, especially in the economic sphere. Almost all Polish parties obstinately opposed the granting of equal minority treatment for Jews. The government did not open public schools in Hebrew or Yiddish. The school system established by the Jews themselves was subsidized very grudgingly and in diminishing manner. Jewish religious communities were permitted to deal with cultural and social matters and to organize a council of all congregations. Such a council, however, never convened. Most odious was the limitation of the numbers of Jewish students at state universities by a **numerus clausus*. Despite all these restrictions and an endemic poverty, the Jews of Poland succeeded in maintaining a vibrant cultural life and a thriving network of schools in both Yiddish and Hebrew. In Rumania the government disclaimed anti-Semitic tendencies, yet tolerated the most virulent attacks by Jew-baiting parties. The Rumanian language was forced upon Jewish children in schools; the religious sensibilities of Jewish students were violated. In the higher schools of learning a tacit *numerus clausus* prevailed. Yugoslavia respected the rights of its Jewish minority. Apart from Nazi Germany, Hungary was the only state which introduced a *numerus clausus* for Jews not only in practice but by official legislation.

In Turkey the right not to appear in court or to transact legal business on their holidays was vouchsafed the Jews. The autonomy enjoyed by Jews for many centuries was gradually narrowed by the new nationalist regime. Turkish was made the language of instruction in schools. Schools could be directed only by Turkish nationals. In 1926 Turkey renounced its minority obligations. The office of the **ḥakham bashi*, the chief rabbi, was abolished and with it the unified organization of the Jewish communities. Iraq granted to religious congregations the right to form schools in the language of their members. Jewish and Armenian minorities were granted certain autonomous rights.

In Soviet Russia. Due to unsettled conditions in Russia during the period of the Peace Conference no arrangements were made there for minorities protection. The country itself, however, experienced inordinate agitation for minority rights during the revolutions of 1917. Again the Jews were most active. Hundreds of meetings and conferences were held as if to celebrate the new-found freedom. On April 3, 1917, Alexander Kerensky, head of the Provisional Government, published a decree removing all restrictions based on "religion, sect, or nationality." All Jewish parties, middle-class or proletarian, gradually united on the question of autonomy. At the end of July 1917 a preliminary conference agreed upon a platform for a Russian Jewish congress to be convened soon. It proposed an elaboration of "the fundamentals of Jewish self-government in Russia; the determination of legal guarantees for the Jewish national minority," as well as the communal organization of Russian Jewry, and the civil and national rights of the Jews in Poland, Palestine, and Rumania. The congress never took place due to the seizure of power by the Bolsheviks. On Nov. 15, 1917, the new Soviet government issued the Declaration of the Rights of Peoples which proclaimed the principle of national self-determination, even to the point of secession. In the Ukraine the Jews were the leading spirits in a flurry of legislative plans designed to establish national-personal autonomy as a fundamental law. On Jan. 9, 1918, the Ukrainian parliament enacted into law a detailed set of articles prepared by the Jewish secretariat. It all came to naught, however, in the political turmoil that ensued with the occupation of the Ukraine by the Germans. It fell to Soviet Russia to launch an experiment in autonomy for minorities on a vast scale. The Soviet government departed from the personal principle of minority rights, namely, that they would apply to all members of a particular nationality throughout the country, and proclaimed, instead, the rights of territorial nationalities. A soviet or a region with a national majority could enjoy cultural autonomy. Since the Jews were scattered all over the country in the large cities, this privilege did not apply to them. Only in hamlets and villages or certain regions where they constituted a majority did they enjoy linguistic, judicial, and educational self-rule. Jews had 67 courts of their own where the official language was Yiddish. In the late 1930s they had five autonomous regions in the Ukraine and the Crimea and 224 local Jewish soviets. In 1931, 160,000 pupils attended Yiddish schools. The high point of this policy was reached in 1927 when *Birobidzhan, a territory in eastern Siberia, was proclaimed a Jewish autonomous region inviting Jewish settlers. None of these efforts, however, were directed at the perpetuation of Jewish identity. On the contrary, the stated purpose of the Soviet government and of the **yevsektsiya* (the Jewish sections of the ruling Communist Party) was to eradicate Judaism in favor of atheism and Communism. The Yiddish courts aimed at weaning the Jews away from their accustomed rabbinic courts. The schools proscribed all religious and traditional Jewish content. They declined rapidly before World War II and were not reopened after the war. In the last years of the Stalin era all vestiges of Jewish national life were cruelly obliterated.

In the Western world the demand for minority rights was seldom heard. There the Jews were satisfied with civil rights and the freedom to foster their own religion and culture.

After World War II. In the *United Nations, which after World War II succeeded the League of Nations, no minority rights provisions survived. Instead, emphasis was put on human rights, concerning all men, including members of the majority nation. In 1966 an International Covenant on Civil and Political Rights was drawn up, which in its 27th paragraph stipulates that "in those States in which ethnic, religious, or linguistic minorities exist, persons belonging to such minorities shall not be denied the right, in community with the other members of their group, to enjoy their own culture, to profess and practice their own religion, or to use their own language." This provision is binding on member-states of the UN which sign and ratify the Covenant.

Bibliography: O. Janowsky, *Jews and Minority Rights* (1933); J. Robinson et al., *Were the Minorities Treaties a Failure?* (1943); I. Elbogen, *A Century of Jewish Life* (1960), 502ff., 507ff., 532ff.

[I.L.]

MINOR PROPHETS, a collection of the books of 12 prophets: *Hosea, *Joel, *Amos, *Obadiah, *Jonah, *Micah, *Nahum, *Habbakuk, *Zephaniah, *Haggai, *Zechariah, and *Malachi. This collection counts as a single book (the last) of the second division—the Prophets (Heb. *Nevi'im*)—of the Palestinian Canon. In the Alexandrian Canon (according to the Septuagint), Minor Prophets, again as a single book, occurs in the fourth and last division, that of prophecy, and is the first of the ten books enumerated there, but the order of the first six of the 12 is there Hosea, Amos, Micah, Joel, Obadiah, and Jonah. The designation "Minor Prophets" alternates with the title "The Twelve" as the designation of this collection, the latter being the native Jewish one (Heb. שנים עשר; Aram. תרי עשר, BB 14b) and that of the Septuagint *(Dodekapropheton)*, while the former seems to be rooted in the Latin designation of the Vulgate *(Prophetae Minores)*. The adjective "minor" in the title "Minor Prophets" does not reflect upon the relative importance of the 12 prophets in comparison to Isaiah, Jeremiah, and Ezekiel, but rather upon their much smaller size. This is implied by the observation about Hosea in *Bava Batra* 14b. The order of the prophets within the anthology is based on a combination of Midrash, the chronological understanding current at the time of compilation, and certain word associations. For example, Hosea is first because his book opens (1:2): "When God first spoke to Hosea" (cf. BB 14b). Amos is placed third after the Book of Joel because of the occurrence of two very similar verses, one at the end of Joel (4:16) and the second at the beginning of Amos (1:2). Finally, the last three books, Haggai, Zechariah, and Malachi, were put at the very end of the anthology because they were thought to be the only prophets of the 12 who belonged chronologically to the Second Temple period. The Minor Prophets could not have been compiled as an anthology any earlier than the fourth century B.C.E., the probable date of the Book of Jonah, the latest of the 12 books. Its compilation can be no later than the time of Ben Sira (c. 180 B.C.E.), however, since the latter, in praising the Israelite heroes in chronological order, mentions all the other prophets by name, each one in his own age, while the Minor Prophets are grouped together namelessly as "the twelve prophets" (Ecclus. 44–49).

See also *Bible, Canon.

Bibliography: M. L. Margolis, *The Hebrew Scriptures in the Making* (1922), 18; M. Z. Segal, *Mevo ha-Mikra*, 4 (1964), 838; O. Eissfeldt, *The Old Testament, an Introduction* (1965), 382–4, incl. bibl.

[H.Co.]

MINOR TRACTATES. In addition to the 63 regular tractates of the Mishnah and Talmud, there are appended at the end of the fourth order, **Nezikin*, 14 smaller or minor tractates which were first published together in their present format in the Romm-Vilna edition (1886). These tractates contain a wealth of legal and aggadic material. In manuscript and published form, these uncanonical treatises may also be found under different titles, arrangements, and order. Their appellation as minor or smaller tractates does not necessarily refer to their size, but rather to the fact that they were not canonized. **Avot de-Rabbi Nathan* for instance, consists of 41 chapters. **Soferim*, *Semaḥot (Evel Rabbati)*, and *Kallah Rabbati* are also of considerable length. The other main tractates are **Kallah*, **Derekh Ereẓ Rabbah*, and *Derekh Ereẓ Zuta*. For additional details see the articles on the individual tractates. Also included in this section, however, are seven more brief treaties which were compiled to give in a methodological form the rules of topics which were not dealt with in specific tractates of the Talmud. These are *Gerim*, about proselytes; *Kutim*, about Samaritans; *Avadim*, about Hebrew slaves; *Sefer Torah*, on the writing of a Torah scroll; *Tefillin*, on the precept of **tefillin; Ẓiẓit*, on the fringes (**ẓiẓit*); and *Mezuzah*, on the **mezuzah;* and it is sometimes only to them that the term minor tractates applies (see *Shem ha-Gedolim*, II, 161 and cf. Eccles. R. 5:8,2). The time when these works were compiled remains uncertain. Some scholars assign them to the end of the geonic period, but recent scholarship favors a much earlier date. M. Higger, in the introduction to his critical edition of these seven minor tractates, judges them to be the "first post-mishnaic compendia regulating specific Jewish practices and usages." His opinion is that "most of the Minor Tractates are Palestinian in origin, but were later modified or elaborated in Babylonia." Thus it may be that the original composition of these codes was already completed by 400 C.E. Since they were of Palestinian origin, they were not included in the final redaction of the Babylonian Talmud.

The first medieval scholar to clearly cite one of these brief codes is *Naḥmanides. In his *Torat ha-Adam* (*Inyan ha-Hoẓa'ah; Kitvei Rabbenu Moshe b. Naḥman*, ed. by C. D. Chavel, 2 (1964), 100) and in his *Milḥemet ha-Shem* to Alfasi (Alfasi; MK 16a), he cites the passage in *Ẓiẓit* which discusses whether the fringes in the *tallit* in which the deceased is buried should be untied. Menahem b. Solomon *Me'iri likewise makes reference to this same passage in *Ẓiẓit* (*Beit ha-Beḥirah al Massekhet Berakhot*, ed. by S. Dikman (1965[2]), 61b). A similar passage, to be found in *Semaḥot* (ch. 12), is twice cited by *tosafot* (Pes. 40b and Av. Zar. 65b). Although a substantial portion of these tractates consists of material already in the Talmud, they occasionally contain items which are not found elsewhere, such as the above-cited text from *Ẓiẓit*. Another example of such new material is the concept that the main shortcoming of the Samaritans was that they denied the centrality of Jerusalem. *Kutim* concludes with the statement that when the Samaritans renounce Mount Gerizim and acknowledge Jerusalem and the resurrection of the dead, they will be accepted as Jews.

Gerim: *Gerim* consists of four chapters: (1) The preliminary procedure for receiving proselytes is detailed; (2) Regulations are set forth regarding the circumcision, ritual bath, and sacrifice, of converts; (3) The *ger toshav* is defined by Meir as one who has merely renounced idolatry, although according to Judah he is one who will only eat the meat of ritually slaughtered animals; (4) Jews are exhorted to maintain a friendly attitude toward proselytes.

Kutim: *Kutim* regulates the relationship between *Samaritans, Jews, and gentiles, in two chapters: (1) Sales to and intermarriage with Samaritans are prohibited since they desecrate holy objects, but it is permitted to lend them money; (2) Buying meat, wine, cheese, and bread from the Samaritans is discussed.

Avadim: *Avadim* contains three chapters: (1) The validity of the regulations concerning Hebrew slaves is limited to the period when the *Jubilee is observed, and the purchase and manumission of bondmen is detailed; (2) The relationship between the master and his slave, the slave's family's obligation to redeem him, and his status after redemption are discussed; (3) The details of the ceremony prescribed for a slave who does not wish to go free, and the acquiring of freedom by a slave when he is sold to a non-Jew or outside of Palestine are given.

Sefer Torah: *Sefer Torah* has five chapters: (1) details of the writing material that may be utilized are given; (2) the blank spaces that must be left between sections of the scroll are explained; (3) laws for the reading and respect of the Torah are given; (4) the names of God and the interdiction against erasing them are explained; (5) the method for writing God's names is laid down. These five chapters are almost identical with the first five chapters of *Soferim*.

Tefillin: *Tefillin* contains only one chapter, and it gives the rules for writing the biblical passages on the parchment of the *tefillin*, the manner and time of wearing them, and those persons who are obligated to wear them.

Ẓiẓit: *Ẓiẓit* consists of only one chapter which details the regulations of the fringes (Num. 15:38–40; Deut. 22:12). It discusses such topics as the persons who are obligated to obey this law, the garments which are exempt, the number of threads in each fringe, and the manner of dyeing the blue thread that is part of the fringes.

Mezuzah: *Mezuzah* has two chapters: (1) details are given of the parchment to be used and the types of doorposts that require a *mezuzah;* (2) the exact spot for the *mezuzah,* its case, and differences in regulations for houses within and outside of Palestine are discussed.

In the Romm edition of the Talmud, only *Gerim* has a detailed commentary, entitled *Naḥalat Ya'akov,* by R. Jacob Neuberg of Offenbach. His commentary on the first five chapters of *Soferim* also serves as a commentary to *Sefer Torah.* More recent commentaries to these tractates were published by Samuel I. Hillman of London and R. Ḥayyim Kanievsky of Bene-Berak (1963–65). These seven tractates have been twice translated into English. Michael Higger published his edited text and translation in 1930. In 1965, the Soncino Press issued a new English translation.

Bibliography: M. Higger (ed.), *Sheva Massekhtot Ketannot* (1930), introd.; idem (ed.), *Massekhet Semaḥot* (1931), introd.; J. Goldin, *The Fathers according to Rabbi Nathan* (1956), introd.; D. Zlotnick, *The Tractate Mourning* (1966), introd. [A.Ro.]

MINOW, NEWTON NORMAN (1926–), U.S. lawyer and public official. Born in Milwaukee, Minow served as law clerk to U.S. Supreme Chief Justice Fred M. Vinson (1951–52), and as administrative assistant to Governor Adlai Stevenson of Illinois (1952–53). He was a member of Stevenson's campaign staff during the latter's two attempts for the presidency (1952 and 1956), and was also a partner in two Stevenson law firms (1955–57 and 1957–61). In 1961 President John F. Kennedy appointed Minow chairman of the Federal Communications Commission. Minow caused a furor within the television industry soon after becoming chairman by describing most of its programming as a "vast wasteland." His conception that the FCC should oversee the networks and protect the public interest brought industry charges of government censorship and interference, but resulted in congressional legislation to assist educational television, the passage of the Communications Satellite Bill (1962), and an attempt to vary and enlarge the area of television progamming by enabling new channels to operate on the ultrahigh frequency band. Under his direction the FCC also attempted closely to supervise television and radio advertising. Minow resigned from the agency in 1963 to become executive vice-president and general counsel to the Encyclopaedia Britannica. Active in Jewish affairs, he was a member of B'nai B'rith and a director of the Chicago chapter of the American Jewish Committee. He wrote *Equal Time: The Private Broadcasters and the Public Interest* (1964).

Bibliography: L. J. Silver, *Profiles in Success* (1965), 303–13. [Ed.]

MINSK, capital of Belorussian S.S.R.; in *Poland-Lithuania from the beginning of the 14th century until 1793; under czarist rule, the capital of the province of Minsk; the most important commercial center of Belorussia from the 15th century. Jews first leased the customs duties of Minsk in 1489, and during the 16th century they began to settle in the town. In 1579 King Stephen Báthory granted the Jews of Minsk a charter, but in 1606 King Sigismund III prohibited Jews from opening shops there or engaging in commerce. In 1633 King Ladislaus IV confirmed these rights and permitted the Jews of Minsk to acquire real estate on the market square or anywhere else, and to buy land for a new cemetery. During the *Chmielnicki revolt and the Russian-Polish War which followed it, the Jews of Minsk were among those who suffered. In 1679 King John III Sobieski confirmed their right to the ownership of houses and shops, their synagogue and cemetery, and restated their freedom to engage in commerce and crafts and their exemption from all jurisdiction excepting that of the king. These rights were confirmed in their entirety by King Augustus II in 1722. Hence the community of Minsk prospered during the 17th and 18th centuries in spite of the opposition of the townspeople. In 1766 1,322 Jewish poll tax payers were registered in Minsk. Jews were prominent in the town's commercial life and at the fairs of nearby *Mir and Kapulia (see *Market Days and Fairs). The spiritual life of the community was also enriched. In 1685 a yeshivah was established by the local rabbi, Moses Mordecai. Among the rabbis and *rashei yeshivah* of Minsk during the 18th century were Jehiel b. Solomon *Heilprin, Aryeh Leib b. Asher *Gunzberg, and Raphael *Cohen. In the framework of the *Councils of the Lands, Minsk was subordinated to *Brest-Litovsk (Brisk) in 1623, but by 1631 Minsk and its surrounding district was considered a separate province.

During the 19th century, Minsk was one of the largest and most important communities in Russia. In 1847 the Jewish population numbered 12,976, rising to 47,562 (52.3% of the total population) in 1897, which made Minsk the fourth largest community in the *Pale of Settlement. Jewish life in the first half of the 19th century is reflected in the community records, which were published with a Russian translation by Jacob *Brafman. *Mitnaggedim* were influential in Minsk, and Ḥasidism was relatively weak. There were several yeshivot in the town, the largest of which was known as "Blumke's Kloyz." At the end of the 19th century Jeroham Judah Leib *Perelmann, who was known as "the *gadol* [the great scholar] of Minsk," officiated there as rabbi. A circle of *maskilim* also existed in the town, and in the 1840s several Jewish schools which included secular subjects in their curricula were opened there. Minsk was one of the places where the Jewish labor movement originated and developed. In the mid-1870s circles of Jewish Socialists were organized, which were very active during the 1880s and 1890s. The years 1893–94 also saw the birth of the "national opposition" to them, led by A. *Liessin. In 1895 a convention of Jewish Socialists was held in Minsk, which discussed the projected establishment of a Jewish Socialist Federation. The Jewish Socialists of Minsk sent delegates to the founding convention of the *Bund in 1897, and Minsk became one of the centers of the Bund's activities, being the first seat of the movement's central committee until 1898, when it was dispersed by the police. From 1901 to 1903, Minsk likewise became the center of the activities of the *Independent Jewish Workers' Party. Jews were predominant in the demonstrations and revolutionary meetings held in the town in 1905 and were also the principal victims of the riots directed against liberal elements in general which took place in October 1905. Groups of Ḥovevei Zion (see *Ḥibbat Zion) were first organized in Minsk in the early 1880s. In 1882 the Kibbutz Niddeḥei Israel association was founded there, and in 1890 the Agudat ha-Elef. Later, Zionism became very influential. In 1902, with the authorization of the government, the Second Convention of Russian Zionists was held in Minsk. In the communal elections of 1918, the Zionists and

The Jewish cemetery in Minsk.

*Po'alei Zion won 33 seats, the Orthodox 25 seats, the Bund 17 seats, the nonaffiliated six seats, and the *Folkspartei and the *United Jewish Socialists Workers' Party two seats each.

After the establishment of the Soviet regime, Jewish communal and religious life was silenced at Minsk as elsewhere in the Soviet Union. The suppressed religious and national institutions were replaced by institutions of Jewish culture based on the Yiddish language and Communist ideology, and Minsk became an important center of Jewish-Communist cultural activity in the Soviet Union. Yiddish schools were established, and at the Institute of Belorussian Culture, founded in 1924, a Jewish section was organized. It published several scientific works, including *Tsaytshrift* (5 vols., 1926–31) devoted to Jewish history, literature, and folklore. A Jewish department was also established (1921) within the faculty of education of the University of Minsk. These institutions, however, were closed down in the mid-1930s. Various newspapers, periodicals, and other publications in Yiddish were issued in the town. These included the daily newspaper *Der Shtern* (1918–21), *Der Veker* (1917–25; until 1921 the organ of the Bund), *Oktyabr* (1925–41), and the literary monthly *Shtern* (1925–41). In 1926, there were 53,686 Jews in Minsk (40.8% of the population).

Hebrew Printing. In 1808 Simḥah Zimel set up in Minsk a Hebrew printing press which he had brought from *Grodno. Up to 1823, he had printed at least 12 books, mostly liturgical. Another press was established in 1820 by Gerson Blaustein, who by 1837 had also printed 12 books, again mostly liturgical, though including one volume of Hebrew poetry by M. *Letteris (1832). In the 20th century a Hebrew press once more operated in Minsk, printing books and newspapers mainly for local use. After the Russian Revolution, the studies in the history of Russian Jewry and Yiddish literature which were published in Yiddish by the Jewish section of the Institute of Belorussian Culture were printed in Minsk.

The Minsk Province. In czarist Russia, the province of Minsk was one of the "western" provinces of the Pale of Settlement. In 1797 its *gubernator* presented Czar Paul I with the resolutions of the meetings of the province noblemen, who alleged that the Jews were responsible for the sorry plight of the peasants of the province and for the famine which then raged. This statement was the forerunner of the program to expel the Jews from the villages, which later took the form of the "Jewish Statute" of 1804 (see *Russia). In 1847 there were 37 Jewish *kahal* administrations, in which 87,633 Jews were registered. In 1897 the Jews of the province numbered 345,015 (16% of its population); 37.5% of them lived in the towns, the same number in the townlets, and 25% in the villages. The largest communities of the province (with the exception of Minsk itself) were then *Pinsk (21,065 Jews), *Bobruisk (20,759), *Slutsk (10,264), *Borisov (7,722), *Mozyr (5,631), *Rechitsa (5,334), *Novogrudok (5,015), *Nesvizh (4,687), and Shchedrin (4,002); 41.5% of the province's Jews earned their livelihood in crafts and as hired labor, and 28.9% from commerce. About 21,000 Jews (6.1% of all those in the province) depended on agriculture, and over 6,000 of them lived in the mostly small Jewish agricultural settlements. In Minsk oblast there were 70,713 Jews (13.1% of the total population) in 1926; in the Minsk oblast as it had been organized in 1938 (with the exception of the town of Minsk itself), there were 9,054 Jews (0.61% of the population) in 1959.

[Y.S.]

Holocaust Period. Though the 1939 census gave no details of individual Jewish communities, it is estimated that the Jewish population of Minsk at the outbreak of the German-Soviet war (June 1941) numbered about 90,000 (around 37% of the total). Some 100,000 inhabitants were left in the city when the German forces entered on June 28. The population rose to 150,000 as the front line moved farther east, and tens of thousands who had fled and had been overtaken by the speed of the German advance, turned back. About one third of these were local Jews. Their number was increased by refugees from as far west as *Bialystok, as well as by survivors of mass executions carried out by the *Einsatzkommandos* (mobile killing squads) in the vicinity, so that another 30,000 Jews were added. Later, about 8,000 German, Austrian, and Czech Jews were deported to Minsk, so that despite the fact that a large number of Minsk Jews had been murdered before the establishment of the ghetto, at least 85,000 Jews were confined in it. Their choice of Minsk as a site for a large Jewish slave labor camp was dictated by military needs and the geographical position of the city in the rear of two German army groups advancing on Leningrad and Moscow.

Immediately following the occupation of Minsk, the German city commandant ordered all males between the ages of 15 and 45 to report for registration under the penalty of death. About 40,000 reported and, in a field at Drozdy outside Minsk, were segregated in three sections: Jews, Red Army men, and non-Jewish civilians. On the fifth day the non-Jewish civilians were released. All Jewish members of the intelligentsia were ordered to step forward; the several thousand who did so were marched off to the nearby woods and machine-gunned. The remaining Jews were moved to Minsk prison and released on Aug. 20, 1941. On the same day the city commandant issued an ordinance for the establishment of a ghetto in a suburb consisting mostly of wooden cottages, and ordered every Jew to wear the yellow badge. All Jews had to be inside the ghetto by July 25, but the Judenrat managed to delay the date until the middle of August by means of bribes. As there were no Jewish communal organizations to provide the Germans with officials to carry out their orders, a group of Jews was arrested. One of them, Ilya Mushkin, who knew a little German, was appointed head of a Judenrat and ordered to select the other officials.

Once inside the ghetto, the Jews were terrorized by nightly murders and kidnappings carried out by the Germans and their local henchmen. On the nights of August 14, 25, and 31, thousands were taken away and only a few appeared in the dreaded "labor" camp on Shirokaya Street, where in addition to Jews the Germans held non-Jewish Red Army men. On Nov. 7, 1941, 12,000 Jews were seized and taken to Tuchinka, where they were machine-gunned at the side of the newly dug pits. Some of the emptied streets were used to house 1,500 German Jews, most of them from *Hamburg. By means of barbed wire fences, the ghetto was henceforth divided into three sections: the main ghetto for "unskilled" Jews; a section for "skilled" workers and Judenrat employees, including the ghetto police; and a section housing the German, Austrian, and Czech Jews. On Nov. 20, 1941, 5,000 people were removed to Tuchinka, where they were murdered. Some of the emptied streets were used to house 6,500 Jews brought from Germany, Austria, and Czechoslovakia.

At the end of February 1942, the *Gestapo asked the Judenrat to turn over 5,000 Jews not employed in Wehrmacht enterprises. The resistance leaders ordered Serebryanskiy, the chief of the ghetto police and a member of the resistance organization, to use his trustworthy policemen to warn the Jews of the impending massacre and tell them to hide. On March 1 the Germans ordered the Judenrat to dig a pit in Ratomskaya Street, an unpaved ravine in the center of the ghetto. On the following morning, after the columns of workers had left the ghetto, Nazi officials arrived and demanded the 5,000 victims.

Informed that the Judenrat had been unable to collect them, the Germans began a hunt for their victims. Dr. Chernis, the woman in charge of the ghetto orphanage, and Fleysher, the supervisor, were ordered to bring their charges in front of the Judenrat building. Unaware of what awaited their children, they led them, dressed and washed, and carrying the youngest in their arms, toward the building, but when they arrived in Ratomskaya Street they were all thrown into the pit and buried alive. When the columns of workers returned at night, several thousand were taken to *Koidanovo and murdered there. Others were forced to join the people rounded up inside the ghetto and butchered in the Ratomskaya Street ravine.

Shortly after the March 2 massacre, the Germans discovered the existence of the underground organization in the "Aryan" part of Minsk in which several Jews, such as R. M. Bromberg and M. P. Malkevich had played a prominent role, and its connection with a similar organization inside the ghetto. On the night of March 31, 1942, the Gestapo raided the ghetto and arrested several resistance leaders, but failed to capture the head of the resistance, Hersh *Smolar. The raid was followed by nightly massacres directed against relatives and neighbors of runaways, in an attempt to discourage Jews from fleeing to the forests to join the partisans. On July 28, 1942, after the labor columns left the ghetto, the Germans and their local collaborators invaded the ghetto and for three days murdered and tortured the inhabitants. Some 10,000 were murdered, including 3,500 German, Austrian, and Czech Jews, most of whom were old people, women, and children. Nine thousand Jews still survived. On Feb. 1, 1943, 1,500 Jews were rounded up and shot over open pits at Maly Trostenets. The number of survivors was systematically reduced by the shooting of smaller groups of men and the gassing of women and children in vans during the summer. To speed up the total annihilation, a transport of some 2,000 people, including a group of Jewish Red Army men held in the Shirokaya Street camp, were sent to *Sobibor on Sept. 18, 1943. This transport included Lt. Alexander *Pecherski and Shelomo Lejtman, the latter a Jewish Communist from Poland, who together led the revolt in the death camp on Oct. 14, 1943. On September 22, Generalkommissar Kube was killed by a bomb placed by his Belorussian maid, E. G. Mazanik. The assassination was organized by David Keymakh, the political commissar of the detachment commanded by G. M. Linkov, who as "Uncle Batya" became one of the most successful Soviet partisan leaders. This event speeded up the final liquidation of the ghetto, which took place on Oct. 21, 1943.

Resistance. The resistance record of the Jews imprisoned in Minsk Ghetto is unique. One Sunday in 1941, within days of finding themselves inside the ghetto, a group of local Jews and Jewish Communists from Poland met and decided that it was the duty of the Minsk Jews to take an active part in the war against the German invaders. They rejected the possibility of armed resistance inside the ghetto and decided to devote all their efforts to effecting the escape of the largest possible number of Jews into the forests in order to become partisans. Four resistance groups arose in the "Aryan" part of the city in August and September 1941. However, it was only after the November 7 massacre that Hersh Smolar, the Polish-born leader of the Jewish resistance, met Isai Pavlovich Kozinets, known as Slavek, the leader of one of the four groups, who subsequently became the leader of the entire underground movement in Minsk. It was only in 1969 that it became known that Kozinets was a Jew born at Genichesk on the Azov Sea and that his first name was Joshua. A petroleum engineer by profession, Kozinets had been in charge of the installations in Bialystok at the outbreak of the war. The underground organization inside the ghetto then became an integral part of the city underground and was known as the "Ernst Thaelmann district," in recognition of the part played by the ghetto inhabitants in the struggle against the Nazis. The Judenrat itself, under Mushkin, took orders from the city-underground committee and played a unique part in diverting much of the production from the workshops and factories manned by Jews to the needs of the partisans. The Jewish organization provided the city underground with news of what was happening in the outside world by establishing a radio monitoring station. It also supplied a printing press and printers, while the ghetto hospital provided surgical and other treatment for wounded partisans. Moreover, Jews employed in the factories working for the Wehrmacht set an example to their Belorussian fellow workers in how to sabotage production. In 1942 the ghetto resistance was better organized and more efficient than the city organization, and the Jews, who ran incomparably greater risks than their Russian and Belorussian fellow citizens, contributed greatly in the common fight against the Germans. In return, the Jewish resistance leaders asked their "Aryan" comrades to help them save the maximum number of Jews from slaughter by making possible their escape into the forests to become partisans. As their assistance proved inadequate, the Jews also had to take the initiative in developing the partisan movement. They organized the nuclei of future partisan detachments inside the ghetto, while M. Gebelev and M. Pruslin, two of the Jewish resistance leaders, helped organize similar ten-man teams in the "Aryan" part of the city. Furthermore, when most of the "Aryan" resistance leaders fell into the hands of the Germans in the spring of 1942, Gebelev and other Jews played a decisive role in rebuilding the city organization. Gebelev was actually captured when preparing the escape of a group of Russian prisoners of war to the forests. The first organized group of Jewish partisans left the ghetto in December 1941 to join Captain Sergeyev-Bystrov's detachment, which in time grew into the Stalin Brigade. Many Jews escaped with the help of the railwaymen's resistance group headed by Kuznetsov; they formed a large proportion of the Narodny Mstitel ("People's Avenger") Brigade, which Kuznetsov later commanded. The Jews of Minsk created the 406, Kutuzov, Budyonny, Dzerzhinskiy, Sergei Lazo, and Parkhomenko Detachments, as well as the 106 Family Detachment, which provided protection in the forests for over 600 Jewish women and children. Jews also formed a large percentage of the Frunze Detachment. The Kutuzov Detachment became the nucleus of the Second Minsk Brigade, while the Parkhomenko Detachment, formed mostly by Jews who had been helped to escape from the ghetto by boys and girls ranging in age from 11 to 15, served as the basis of the Chapayev Brigade. Hundreds of Minsk Jews were also active in other brigades.

Altogether some 10,000 Minsk Jews succeeded in escaping from the Minsk ghetto—a proportion without parallel in the history of the city ghettos of Poland and the occupied territories of the Soviet Union. Of those who escaped, perhaps no more than half survived the war.

[R.A.]

Contemporary Jewry. A memorial to the Jewish victims of the Holocaust was erected in Minsk immediately after World War II—the only one in the U.S.S.R.—bearing a Yiddish inscription which explicitly mentions Jewish victims. On Jan. 13, 1948, Solomon *Mikhoels, the chairman of the Jewish *Anti-Facist Committee and the director of the Jewish State Theater in Moscow, was murdered in Lodochnaya Street in Minsk while visiting the city on an official mission. Later the murder was acknowledged to have been the work of the secret police (on Stalin's orders). In the 1959 census 38,842 Jews were registered in Minsk, 5,716 of whom declared Yiddish to be their mother tongue. However, the population figure was estimated to be in fact between 50,000 and 60,000. The Great Synagogue of Minsk was closed down by the authorities in 1959, and in the same year private religious services were dispersed by the militia. A small synagogue was left, but in 1964 it was destroyed, as the site was earmarked for new apartment buildings. Eventually the Jewish congregation was allowed to open a small synagogue in a wooden house on the outskirts of the city. There is no Jewish cemetery in Minsk, but Jews are buried in a separate section in the general cemetery. *Mazzah* baking was banned for several years, and on March 23, 1964, an article in the local newspaper, *Sovetskaya Belorussiya*, condemned the sending of packages of *mazzah* to Minsk from Jewish communities abroad. Kosher poultry, however, was available. In 1968 several young Jews were arrested for Zionist activity. [ED.]

Bibliography: S. A. Bershadski, *Russko-yevreyskiy Arkhiv*, 1 (1882), nos. 20, 53, 63, 109; 3 (1903), nos. 14, 41, 52, 60; A. Subbotin, *V cherte yevreyskoy osedlosti*, 1 (1888), 4–47; B. Eisenstadt, *Rabbanei Minsk va-Hakhameha* (1898); *Regesty i nadpisi* 3 vols. (1889–1913), indexes; Khorosh, in: *Voskhod*, no. 12 (1901), 100–10); A. H. Shabad, *Toledot ha-Yamim she-Averu al ha-Hevra Kaddisha "Shivah Keru'im" u-Veit ha-Midrash ha-Gadol ba-Ir Minsk*, 2 vols. (1904–12); *Die Judenpogrome in Russland*, 2 (1909), 458–65; S. Dubnow (ed.), *Pinkas ha-Medinah* (1925), index; Alexandrov, in: Institute of Belorussian Culture, *Tsaytshrift*, 1 (1926), 239–49; 2–3 (1928), 763–78; 4 (1930), 199–224; S. Agurski, *Revolyutsionnoye dvizheniye v Belorussii* (1928), 139–43 and passim (= *Di Revolutsionere Bavegung in Vaysrusland* (1931), 168–71); Levitats, in: *Zion*, 3 (1938), 170–8; A. Liessin, *Zikhronot ve-Havayot* (1943), 1–78, 116–31; A. Yaari, in: KS, 20 (1943/44), 163–70; *Yahadut Lita*, 1 (1959), index; A. Greenbaum, *Jewish Scholarship in Soviet Russia* (1959), 22–27, 66–73, passim; J. S. Hertz (ed.), *Geshikhte fun Bund*, 3 vols. (1960–66), indexes; Goldstein, in: *He-Avar*, 14 (1967), 3–27. HOLOCAUST AND AFTER: H. Smolar, *Fun Minsker Geto* (1946); idem, *Resistance in Minsk* (1966); S. Schwarz, *Jews in the Soviet Union* (1951), index; J. Greenstein, in: *Sefer Pabianice* (1956), 349–73 (Yid.); *Sefer ha-Partizanim ha-Yehudim*, 1 (1958), 501–37; K. Loewenstein, *Minsk: im Lager der deutschen Juden* (1961).

MINSK CONFERENCE, the second conference of Russian Zionists, held publicly and with the government's permission in Minsk from Sept. 4 to Sept. 10, 1902. The number of representatives was estimated at 526. The Minsk Conference was in essence the "first all-Russian Zionist Congress," an assembly of a national minority in a state that had suppressed national minorities and denied them the right of assembly. Two organized factions were represented at the conference: *Mizrachi with 160 representatives and the *Democratic Fraction with about 60 representatives. The majority of representatives did not align with either group but organized a neutral faction. The main point of contention between Mizrachi and the Democratic Fraction was the cultural question. Mizrachi opposed the Zionist Organization's conducting cultural activities, demanding instead, practical work in Erez Israel by means of the *Jewish National Fund (JNF) and the *Jewish Colonial Trust. Jehiel *Tschlenow was elected chairman. M. *Ussishkin proposed the establishment of a "Zionist Guard" composed of young men whose task would be to deliver public speeches on the Zionist idea, organize schools, write propaganda pamphlets, etc. This call for practical efforts enthused many delegates, especially among the youth. The focal point of the conference was the delivery of reports on cultural activities by N. *Sokolow and *Ahad Ha-Am. The latter explained his outlook on the close relationship between the movement of national renaissance and cultural work; Sokolow proposed that Hebrew be the official language of the Zionist Organization. Isaac *Reines, the Mizrachi leader, expressed his objections to the Zionist Organization's conducting cultural activities. After a vehement debate, the conference's presidium summoned both Ahad Ha-Am and Reines to a consultation, in which the latter accepted the proposal to choose two educational committees—a traditional one and a progressive one. This arrangement dissolved the crisis that threatened to split the Russian Zionist Movement. After the conference, there was a marked change for the worse in the government's attitude toward the Jews in general and the Zionist Organization in particular. During Passover 1903 the *Kishinev pogrom took place, and in June of the same

Delegates to the Minsk Zionist Conference, 1902. Courtesy J.N.U.L. Photo Collection, Jerusalem.

year all Zionist activities were totally prohibited in Russia.

Bibliography: M. Nurock, *Ve'idat Ziyyonei Rusyah* (1963), includes introduction by I. Klausner; A. Boehm, *Die Zionistische Bewegung*, 1 (1935), 200, 296, 517ff.; Ch. Weizmann, *Letters and Papers*, 1 (1968), index; M. Kleinman, in: *Lu'aḥ Aḥi'asaf* (1902), 454–70; *He-Avar*, 9 (1962), 94–106; A. Raphaeli (Zenziper), in: *Kazir*, 1 (1964), 60–75; *Die Welt*, nos 37, 38, 40 (1902); S. Eisenstadt (ed.), *Yeḥi'el Tschlenow* (Heb., 1937). [I.K.]

MINSKI, NIKOLAI MAXIMOVICH (pseudonym of **N. M. Vilenkin**; 1855–1937), Russian poet and essayist. Born in Glubokoye, near Vilna, Minski studied law at St. Petersburg. For a time he was influenced by P. *Smolenskin and the rising Jewish nationalism among young, educated Russian Jews. In 1879–80 he wrote a series of essays, under the pseudonym "Nord-Vest," in which he argued that the Jewish problem in Russia could be solved by the creation of a Jewish farming class which would "cleanse Judaism of its impurities." He also claimed that all Jewish groups were opposed to socialism. Minski later became alienated from Jewish affairs, and before the turn of the century converted to Christianity. He published his first poems in 1876. His early poetry, such as *Belyye nochi* ("White Nights," 1879), deals with socialist and folk themes, but his later writing betrays his disillusionment with socialism and an attraction to mysticism and Nietzschean philosophy. During the 1905 Revolution, Minski helped to publish *Novaya zhizn* ("New Life"), the organ of the Bolshevik wing of the Social Democrats. He translated the *Internationale* into Russian, but with the failure of the Revolution he was imprisoned and thereafter he was freed and left Russia. During the 1917 Revolution he wrote anti-Bolshevik articles for the French press. Some of Minski's poetry, which Soviet critics have stigmatized as decadent, appeared in a Hebrew translation by Leah Goldberg (*Yalkut Shirat he-Ammim*, 1 (1942), 5–6).

Bibliography: M. Slonim, *Modern Russian Literature* (1953), index. [Y.MA.]

MINSK MAZOWIECKI (Pol. **Mińsk Mazowiecki**), town in E. central Poland. Minsk Mazowiecki received urban status in the first half of the 15th century, but Jewish settlement did not develop there until the close of the 18th century. From the beginning, and particularly during the second half, of the 19th century, the number of Jews increased until they were the majority in the town. In 1827 there were 260 Jews in a general population of 770, while by 1864 they numbered 620 (46.3% of the total population). In 1897 there were 3,445 Jews (55.6%). During World War I the number of Jews decreased as a result of migration to Warsaw and other large centers. In 1921 the Jewish population numbered 4,130 (39.3%). During the period between the two world wars the Polish population increased considerably, while the Jewish population grew at a slower rate. On the eve of World War II 5,845 Jews lived there.

The Jewish community was not at first independent; at the close of the 18th century the rabbi also served the Kaluszyn community. During the 19th century ḥasidic groups such as those of Gur (*Gora Kalwaria) and Parysow gained in strength, and the court of the *zaddik* of Minsk Mazowiecki was established by R. Jacob Perlov at the close of the 19th century. After World War I his successor, the *zaddik* Alter Israel Simeon, removed his seat to Warsaw. There were eight Jews among the 24 members of the municipal council elected in 1927. The Jewish population's political affiliations may be deduced from the 1931 elections to the community council, which included seven members of *Agudat Israel, four craftsmen, and one member of right *Po'alei Zion. The Jews of Minsk Mazowiecki earned their livelihood principally from small trade and crafts. During the 1930s they aroused the jealousy of

Jews of Minsk Mazowiecki being taken from their Sabbath prayers by German soldiers for factory work, 1939. Courtesy Leib Rochman, Jerusalem.

the Polish tradesmen and craftsmen, who declared an economic war on them. As a result of this struggle, severe anti-Jewish riots broke out in May 1936, which were fomented by the anti-Semitic *Endecja party and destroyed the means of livelihood of the Jews. Anti-Semitic agitation was particularly violent in the town on the eve of World War II. [SH.L.K.]

Holocaust Period. In 1940 about 2,000 Jews from Pabianice, Kalisz, and Lipno were forced to settle in Minsk Mazowiecki. In August 1940 a ghetto was established and on Aug. 21, 1942, the great *aktion* in Minsk Mazowiecki took place when about 1,000 were shot on the spot. Almost all of the rest of the Jewish population was transferred to the *Treblinka death camp and exterminated there. Only two groups of workers in the town were left: one, with about 150 men, was transferred to a camp in the Rudzki factory; and the second, with over 500 men, was placed in a camp in the Kopernik school building. Another several hundred succeeded in fleeing the town. Some of them organized small partisan units which became mixed Jewish-Russian units and operated for some time in the region. On Dec. 24, 1942, the Germans shot 218 workers from the Kopernik camp. On Jan. 10, 1943, this camp was liquidated. On the same day the Jewish prisoners offered armed resistance, during which a few Germans were killed or wounded. On June 5, 1943, the camp in the Rudzki factory was liquidated and all its inmates were shot. No Jewish community in Minsk Mazowiecki was reconstituted. [S.KR.]

Bibliography: T. Brustin-Berenstein, in: BZIH, no. 1 (1952), 83–125, passim.

MINTMASTERS AND MONEYERS. In the Middle Ages rulers tended to lease the right of minting coins to mintmasters or to grant and sell the right to their territorial vassals, who themselves employed such mintmasters. Jews carried out this prestigious and profitable enterprise mainly either as suppliers of precious metals for minting purposes or as distributors of coins; very rarely were they the actual craftsmen. In general, in the later Middle Ages, the Jewish master of the mint or purveyor was superseded by a Christian.

The Jew *Priscus was probably master of the mint for King Clotaire of the Franks and issued the royal coins at Chalon-sur-Saône around 555 C.E. Some Czech numismatists consider that Omeriz, Mizleta, and Nacub, moneyers for Duke Boleslav II in Prague toward the end of the tenth century, were Jews. This is also true of Zanta and Noc, who worked at the Vysehrad mint (near Prague).

Ladislaus II of Bohemia (1158–73) had a Jewish mintmaster in his province of Lusatia. In the 13th century a cleric complained that the Jews were still lessees of the mint and customs. For much of the 12th and 13th centuries the coinage of some Polish rulers was issued by Jewish mintmasters and often had Hebrew inscriptions on the coins. Boleslav IV (1146–73) used Jews to mint and distribute his currency. Shortly after, Casimir II (1177–94) allowed a Hebrew inscription to appear on state coins. Mieszko III (1173–77, 1195–1202) gave a life grant to the Jews to lease the state mint, and Polish currency in the last two decades of the 12th century was stamped solely in Hebrew. Most of the inscriptions were various dedications to Mieszko. Boleslav of Kujawy and Mieszko the Younger imitated their father. Boleslav permitted his own name to be stamped in Hebrew, while Mieszko the Younger allowed the names of Jewish mintmasters, such as Ben Jacob and Joseph ha-Kohen, to be inscribed; sometimes the names covered the entire face of the coin, as in the case of R. Abraham b. Isaac Nagid. Przemyslav I later continued this practice some 40 years, as did his son Przemyslav II; Menahem, Jacob, and Abraham were mintmasters whose names were stamped on coins (see illustration).

In later Polish history, Jews continued to be mintmasters, although no Hebrew appeared on their coins. In 1360 the Cracow mint was transferred to *Lewko, an important Jewish financier. Under Sigismund I, between 1509 and 1518, Abraham *Ezofowitz was minister of the exchequer and in charge of minting coins. In 1555 Sigismund II leased the mint in his Lithuanian province of Poland for three years to a Jew in Vilna. He again gave the Vilna concession to the Jews Felix and *Borodavka in 1560. Because of their prominence in the fields of money changing, moneylending, and finance, Jews participated in minting activities in Poland almost without interruption from the early stages of the kingdom until its partition. From the 17th century, the Councils of the Lands, both in Poland and Lithuania, showed much concern and great reservation about coin minting and the coin trade.

Jews leased mints in Christian Spain as early as the 11th century. Bonnom (Shem Tov) made gold coins under the authority of Count Ramón Berenguer I of Barcelona. In 1066 the count's son sold the right to mint coinage to a syndicate which included David b. Jacob ha-Ivri. *Benveniste de Porta (d. 1268) leased the mint of Barcelona from James I of Aragon. Sancho IV of Castile gave a similar concession to Abraham el Barchilon in 1287. A century later, in 1331, Alfonso XI of Castile repeated this with Samuel *ibn Waqar (Aben Huacar); Pedro IV of Aragon gave control of the royal mint to a Jewish company at about the same time.

As early as 1063 Queen Anastasia of Hungary permitted a Jew to mint his own coins at the royal mint. Hebrew appears on a coin of Andrew II in the early 13th century. Andrew's Golden Bull of 1222 excluded Jews and Muslims from the office of mintmaster, but the prohibition was disregarded, for the coins of his son Bela IV and his grandson Stephen V bear Hebrew letters, apparently standing for the initials or signs of Jewish mintmasters.

The first Jew recorded by name in Austria was *Shlom the mintmaster, massacred by crusaders in 1195. The nobility obtained a decree in 1222 specifically excluding Jews from the post, but Jews were again employed in this capacity some 40 years later. Jewish mintmasters were found in other German states and principalities, particularly in the 12th century, though their role was much less significant in the centuries that followed. In the Wetterau region, thin coins stamped on one side only, known as

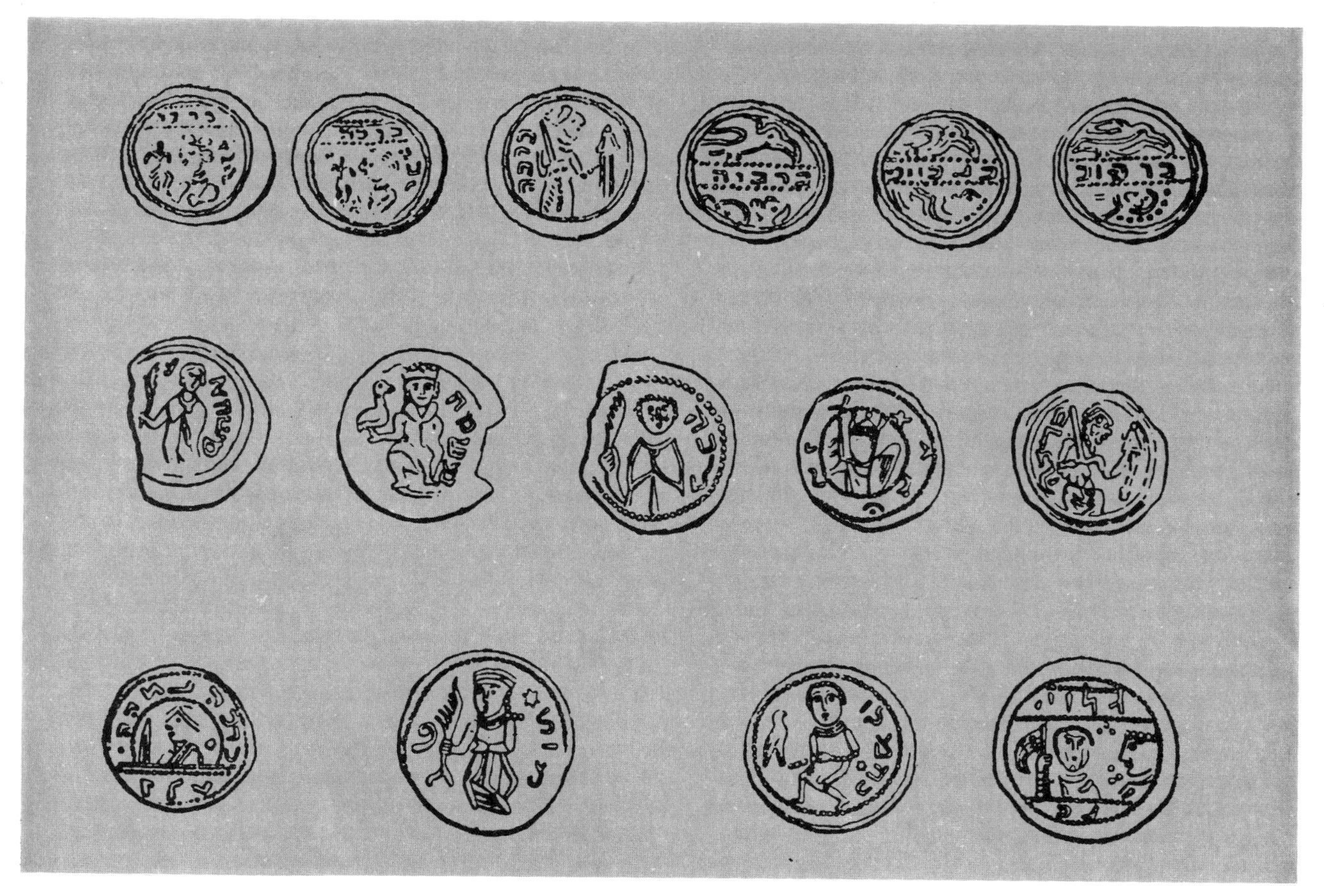

Chart of Polish coins bearing Hebrew inscriptions. The coins, which are all stamped on one side only, are of the period between 1170 and 1220, when Jews held the concession for minting Poland's coins. From I. Schiper (ed.), *Żydzi w Polsce odrodzonej,* Warsaw, vol. 2, 1934.

bracteates, were issued between 1170 and 1180, with the name David ha-Kohen imprinted in Hebrew. In this same period Otto the Rich, margrave of Meissen, employed Gershon, who also struck his name in Hebrew on bracteates. Nearby, at Lausitz and Pegau, Jews operated mints for the local nobility. Twelfth-century bracteates from Saxony, made under both Count von Mansfeld and Duke Bernhard I, show Hebrew letters. Similarly Jehiel, the name of a Jewish mintmaster at Wuerzburg in the early 13th century, is clearly marked in Hebrew on numerous bracteates. The question of whether a Jewish mintmaster might operate on the Sabbath appears twice in contemporary responsa; he might do so only if he had a Christian partner. The number of Jewish mintmasters was restricted, however, both by the appearance of Christian symbols and formulas on coins and by guild regulations.

The 16th and 17th centuries witnessed political and economic developments in central Europe which enabled Jews to play an unprecedented role in purveying. The growing independence of the many petty German states, the mercantilist theory of the supreme value of precious metals for state economy, as well as the readiness of the unprincipled rulers to issue debased coin, combined to create a need for expertise and initiative. The increased demand for currency was thwarted by the depletion of the silver mines; the metals had to be imported from the Americas or bought at the entrepôts of Amsterdam, London, and Hamburg, where Sephardi Jews were prominent in the bullion trade. In Poland, too, Jews were experts in all aspects of the coin trade. The princes and rulers of the petty and larger states of the Holy Roman Empire and elsewhere turned to them for purveying, minting, and distributing currency. This was done by means of contracts (see *contractors) between the ruler and his *Muenzjude* ("mint Jew"), who was to be found at virtually every court. The purveying of silver was conducted by a sophisticated network of contractors and subcontractors reaching down to the level of the peddler (see *peddling), entrusted with the task of buying up foreign coinage, silver and copper wares, and anything else suitable. The actual minting was supervised by Jews, contractors of the mint. The coin dies were often made by Jewish seal engravers, a profession which Jews tended to monopolize, by virtue of its being free of medieval guild restrictions. The distribution of the freshly minted, often inferior quality coinage was often entrusted to military contractors, frequently Jews. While *Muenzjuden* were active throughout the 17th and 18th centuries, their activity increased even further during the unstable periods of intensive monetary activity, especially so from 1618 to 1623, the 1670s and 1680s, from 1756 to 1763, and at all times during war and turmoil. During these crucial phases the activity of the *Muenzjuden* brought them into a disrepute that aroused anti-Jewish feelings, reaching a peak during the Seven Years' War.

Among the more prominent Jewish mintmasters of the 16th century were Phybes of Hanover, a lessee of the mint at Wunstorf, Brunswick, in 1566, and Isaac Meir (Mayer) of Prague, who administered the mint from 1546 to 1549. The most famous was *Lippold, the mintmaster of Brandenburg, who ruled the electorate's Jewry with an iron hand. In the first decades of the 17th century, a number of Jewish mintmasters and contractors achieved fame, influence, and notoriety, such as Albertus *Denis (Alvaro Diniz), Jacob *Bassevi of Treuenberg, and Israel Wolf (Auerbacher) in Vienna. In Breslau Manasseh of Hotzenplotz gained a foothold to power through his services to the mint, and the number of Jewish silver purveyors in other minting centers in Austria and southern Germany was large. In 1627 they supplied 29% of the silver to the Breslau imperial mint and 50% in 1656. The dependence of the government on such purveyors increased in the 18th century to 78% in 1704, and to 94% in 1720. In the crisis of the 1670s and 1680s Jews were less prominent, although some *Court Jews were active in the precious metals and coin trades. Among such Court Jews was Jacob Mussaphia, of the duchy of Holstein-Gottorf. Jewish mintmasters reestablished communities in Saxony, from which Jews had been expelled. The nuclei of the Jewish communities of Leipzig and Dresden was formed by the *Muenzjuden*. Gerd Levi (1659–1739) received a licence to buy and supply silver (1710) to the Leipzig mint; his son, Levi Gerd, continued in his father's footsteps.

The classical country of Jewish minting activity, however, was Prussia. Throughout most of the 17th and 18th centuries the *Muenzjuden* constituted the leadership of the Berlin community. Israel Aron, first head of the newly reconstituted (1671) community of Viennese exiles, was purveyor to the Berlin mint. His widow, Esther, married the court jeweler Jost *Liebmann and received (between 1700 and 1713) permission to mint large series of small coins as payment for the precious stones which she had supplied to the court. Levin Veit monopolized the purveying of silver in the years 1717 to 1721 and received permission to smelt and refine silver. In the 1750s two firms, that of Daniel *Itzig and members of the *Gomperz family, and that of V. H. *Ephraim and members of the *Fraenkel family, competed fiercely, one outbidding the other for the state minting contract. Frederick II's growing and urgent demands for funds during the war forced the competing firms into a partnership (in 1758), which leased all Prussian and Saxon mints. The Saxon mints of Leipzig and Dresden had been occupied by Frederick, who turned them over to his entrepreneurs, who then issued successive series of millions of more debased Saxon coins. These were known as "Ephraimiten" and gave rise to the bitter popular refrain: "Pretty on the outside, worthless within; on the outside Frederick, Ephraim within." Frederick instituted similar proceedings with the currency of Mecklenburg-Schwerin, Anhalt-Zerbst, and Anhalt-Dessau, and he was also forced to debase Prussian currency. The last Ephraim-Frederick contract was signed on Dec. 17, 1762. After the war *Muenzjuden* were employed in buying up the corrupt coinage and in supplying silver for the reconstituted currency. Ephraim and his sons were gradually overshadowed by the Itzig family, who were sole purveyors of precious metals between 1771 and 1786. One of Itzig's many agents was Joachim David *Friedlaender of Koenigsberg and his sons (David was the most talented). The last important mint entrepreneur was Liepmann Meyer Wulff of Berlin, who supplied the mint between 1799 and the Prussian debacle of 1806, after which thorough governmental reforms were introduced which abolished the need for the services of private silver and gold purveyors.

The tradition of Jewish moneyers and mintmasters in the Muslim world goes back to the Middle Ages. A certain Sumayr was die cutter and mintmaster for Abdalmalik (685–705), the Umayyad caliph at Damascus. Since the earliest Muslim coins were struck at this time, Sumayr was one of the technical founders of Islamic coinage. Jewish moneyers were known in Cairo from earliest times, possibly being successors to those previously operating in Alexandria. Japheth b. Abraham, in partnership with two other Jews, was administrator of the Fostat mint (see *Cairo) in about 1086. A brief mention is made in a document from the Cairo *Genizah* of two Jewish partners working the caliphate mint in the second half of the 12th century. The most noted Cairo mintmasters were Isaac *Sholal and Abraham Castro, who was appointed to the position after the conquest of Egypt by Sultan Selim (c. 1520). When the Egyptian viceroy, Ahmed Pasha, plotted independence, it was Castro who informed Constantinople. He was reinstated after Ahmed's defeat in 1524. In the 1660s this same position was held by the court banker Raphael Joseph, known as Chelebi. Under Murad III (1574–95) the director of the Turkish mint was a Jew, Hodja Nessimi (or Nissim). In this same period, Moses *Benveniste—known to the Turks as Hodja Moussahibi—was involved in the currency "reform" which led to a revolt of the janissaries against "Jews' Money" in 1589. Samuel b. Abraham, head of the Crimean Karaites, was moneyer to the last Tatar khan in the mid-18th century. As the treasury minister, he held the official title of Aga. His son Benjamin succeeded him in both position and title. When the Crimea was conquered by Russia in 1783, Benjamin was permitted to retain his title. Yaḥyā b. Judah *Badiḥi (1810–88) was minter for the imam of Yemen in the mid-19th century.

See also *Banking; *Court Jews; *Moneylending; *Medalists; *Numismatics; Coins and Currency.

Bibliography: Medieval Europe: P. Grierson, *Bibliographie Numismatique* (1966); S. Stern, *Court Jew* (1950), 47, 157, 162–76, 211, 218; M. Hoffmann, *Geldhandel der deutschen Juden* (1910); S. Katz, *Jews in the Visigothic and Frankish Kingdoms of France and Gaul* (1934), 122f.; d'Amecourt, in: *Annuaire de la Société française de Numismatique et d'Archéologie*, 4 (1873), 128–31; J. Cahn, in: *Zeitschrift fuer Numismatik*, 33 (1922); *Biographical Dictionary of Medalists*, 8 vols. (1902–30); Baer, Spain, 1 (1961), 146, 327, 131–2; 2 (1966), 29; Neuman, Spain, 2 (1942), 237, 245, 252; D. M. Friedenberg, in: *Numismatist*, 130 (1967), 1515–28; W. Gumowski, *Handbuch der polnischen Numismatik* (1960), 91–96; I. Schiper, *Di Virtshaft Geshikhte fun di Yidn in Poyln Beysn Mittelalter* (1929), 235ff.; A. Wolf, in: MGJV, 9 (1902), 24–25; L. Réthy and G. Probszt, *Corpus Nummorum Hungariae*, 71, 74, 77, 89. Central Europe and Modern Era: H. I. Bloom, *Economic Activities of the Jews of Amsterdam* (1933); B. Brilling, *Geschichte der Juden in Breslau 1754–1802* (1960); idem, in: JGGJC, 7 (1935), 387–98; F. Redlich, in: *Explorations in Entrepreneurial History*, 3 (1951), 161–98; H. Kellenbenz, *Sephardim an der unteren Elbe* (1958), 210–44; H. Schnee, *Hoffinanz und der Moderne Staat*, 5 vols. (1953–67); A. Pribram, *Urkunden und Akten zur Geschichte der Juden in Wien* (1918), index s.v. *Muenzjuden;* M. Koehler, *Juden in Halberstadt* (1927), 41–48; S. Stern, *Preussische Staat und die Juden*, 2 (1962), Akten: no. 46–71; no. 124–8; no. 144–69; no. 177; M. Grunwald, *Samuel Oppenheimer und sein Kreis* (1913), index. Muslim Countries: S. D. Goitein, *A Mediterranean Society*, 1 (1967), 362, 365; S. Poznański, *Babylonische Geonim* (1914), 133; S. Assaf, in: *Zion*, 1 (1937), 256f.; A. N. Pollak, *ibid.*, 24–30.

[D.M.F./H.W.]

MINTZ, MOSES BEN ISAAC (15th century), German talmudist. Moses was born in Mainz sometime between 1420 and 1430. He studied under his father, Israel *Isserlein, and Jacob *Weil. During his extensive travels, he visited various towns, investigating their customs and communal regulations. His first rabbinate was at Wuerzburg where he served for a short time, until the expulsion of the Jews from the town in 1453. He proceeded to Mainz, where he stayed until the expulsion of 1462. From there he went to Landau and in 1464 to Ulm. In 1469 he was appointed rabbi of Bamberg. Four years later he went to Nuremberg and the following year to Posen. While there he decided to emigrate to Ereẓ Israel; he had already made all final preparations when for some reason he had to abandon his plan, and it appears that he remained in Posen until the end of his life. The year of his death is unknown.

Mintz's influence spread in Germany and beyond. He was involved in communal affairs and individuals, including outstanding scholars, as well as communities turned to him with their problems and disputes. Concern for the community and its general welfare was of paramount importance to him. He directed a yeshivah and engaged in discussions with his pupils. In 1456–57 R. Seligman Bing Oppenheim and R. Menahem Bachrach convened a council in *Bingen for the purpose of enacting *takkanot* that would be binding on other communities also—a step which did not meet with the approval of the rabbis of Germany. Despite his esteem for Seligman Bing, Mintz strongly opposed them and the *takkanot* were not adopted. Similarly, when he felt that Bing had been guilty of faulty judgment, he did not hesitate to criticize him, though there was nothing personal in his criticism. In another dispute in Italy, when Liva Landa placed a ban upon the rabbis of Padua, including Mintz's cousin Isaac Mintz, Moses agreed to place Landa under a ban although he was a venerable scholar and teacher, "unless he withdraw his ban and appease the rabbis of Padua," and at the same time he appealed to the rabbis of Padua "to waive their rights and show respect for a sage." Should Landa remain obdurate, however, "then the ban on him is to remain in force." Moses concludes: "I do this neither for my own honor nor for the honor of my family, but for the sake of Heaven to prevent the increase of strife in Israel." Moses was an accomplished *ḥazzan* and conducted the services on the high holidays. His best-known pupil is *Joseph b. Moses, author of the *Leket Yosher*.

Moses Mintz's fame rests on his responsa (Cracow, 1617); the 119 published, chiefly on civil and matrimonial law, abound in references to local customs and *takkanot*, ancient and new, including those ascribed to *Gershom b. Judah of Mainz and *takkanot ShUM* (Speyer, Worms, and Mainz). The index lists 120 responsa, but the last one has been omitted from all editions. This may be because of its subject, which the author describes as: "The stern words I wrote to the seven elders of the Regensburg community. It lays down that one who has a right of settlement in a community and leaves, subsequently to return, has not lost his previous right . . . And it explains that a scholar should not take advantage of his status to act haughtily." The main source for Moses' biography is the responsa, where it is related that his wife Minlan was "crowned with the crown of the Torah and piety." They also include many local *takkanot* introduced by Mintz, some of a social character, including rulings on the vestments a reader should don when conducting the service, how a man should conduct himself during prayer, etc.

Of special value are three responsa in manuscript entitled "The Three Branches," which are an important source for the history of the yeshivot of Germany in the 15th century. They depict the woeful condition of pupil-teacher relations, which had broken down as a result of the arrogance of the teachers and their exaggerated concern for their dignity, as well as because of the pupils' desire for greater freedom of activity and the acquisition of social status. The laymen, too, did not accept the authority of the rabbis and disregarded their rulings. The responsa reflect other aspects of the life of the Jews in Germany: their economic, social, family, and religious life, study, the attitude of the Jews to gentiles, persecutions, and expulsions, etc.

Bibliography: Joseph b. Moses, *Leket Yosher*, ed. by J. Freimann, 2 (1904), 45 no. 103 (introd.); Guedemann, Gesch Erz, 3 (1888), index; M. A. Szulwas, *Die Juden in Wuerzburg* (1934), 77; Tal, in: *Sinai*, 40 (1957), 228–47, 278–92.

[Sh.T.]

MINTZ, PAUL (1870–after 1940), Latvian lawyer. Born in Dvinsk (Daugavpils), Mintz was one of the most prominent lawyers in Riga. After Latvia became an independent republic (1918), he was appointed professor of criminal law at the University of Riga. He was a member of the Latvian National Council and the Constituent Assembly, and was the only Jewish member of the Latvian government, serving as state controller. He published various legal works and was chairman of the commission preparing the Latvian code of criminal law. He was also active in Jewish affairs as founder of the Ḥevrat Mefiẓei Haskalah (*Society for the Promotion of Culture Among the Jews of Russia), in Riga, chairman of the Jewish National-Democratic Party, chairman of the commission preparing a draft for the legal framework of Jewish national autonomy, a non-Zionist member of the *Jewish Agency for Palestine, and chairman of the Jewish Lawyers' Society in Latvia. In 1940, when Latvia was occupied by the Soviet forces, Mintz was arrested together with other Jewish and non-Jewish leaders and deported to Kansk, near Krasnoyarsk, and later to a Soviet labor camp, where he died.

Bibliography: *Yahadut Latvia* (1953), index. [Jo.Ga.]

MINYAN (Heb. מִנְיָן; "number"), designation for the quorum of ten male adults, aged 13 years or over, necessary for public synagogue service and certain other religious ceremonies. The Talmud (Ber. 21b; Meg. 23b) derives this number from the term *edah* ("community"), which in the Scriptures is applied to the ten spies (Num. 14:27). Thus ten men constitute a congregation. The Talmud (Ket. 7b) also mentions Ruth 4:2 and Psalms 68:27. Some relate the rule to Abraham's plea to God to save Sodom if at least ten righteous men were found there (Gen. 18:32). On the basis of Psalms 82:1: "God standeth in the congregation of God," the Talmud explains that if ten men pray together the Divine Presence is with them (Ber. 6a). This quorum of ten adult males is necessary for the following sections of the public synagogue service: The repetition of the *Amidah* with *Kedushah*, the pentateuchal and *haftarah* reading, priestly benedictions (Meg. 4:3), and the *Kaddish*. Some also require a *minyan* for the recital of the *Barekhu* invocation; others permit this to be said even if only six or seven males are present (Sof. 10:6). The accepted custom in emergency cases is nine adults and a boy holding a Bible (based on PdRE, 8; see Tos. Ber. 48a and Sh. Ar., OḤ, 55:4). A quorum of ten is also necessary in the rites of comforting the mourners (*ma'amad u-moshav;* Meg. 4:3; Meg. 23b). The recital of the seven nuptial blessings at wedding ceremonies and the special invocation preceding grace ("Let us bless our God of whose bounty we have eaten") also require a *minyan* (*ibid.*).

Ten male adults constitute a quorum in any place, and there is no need for a synagogue building or an officiating rabbi to hold divine services. In talmudic times a community was regarded as "a city" if there were at least "ten idle men" (not occupied by work or other duties) who could come to each synagogue service to make up the *minyan* (Meg. 1:3). R. Johanan said "when God comes to a synagogue and does not find a *minyan* there, He is angry, as it is written (Isa. 50:2). 'Wherefore, when I came, was there no man? When I called, was there none to answer?' " (Ber. 6b). In traditional congregations, especially in Eastern Europe, when it was difficult to hold daily services with a *minyan*, it was customary to pay a few old or idle men to be present twice a day at the services. These people were called "*minyan* men." In the Reform ritual women are counted in the minimum quorum of ten persons to constitute a public prayer service since they have full religious equality with men (see S. Freehof, *Reform Jewish Practice*, 1 (1948[2]), 49–52).

Bibliography: Eisenstein, Dinim, 239ff.; Elbogen, Gottesdienst, 493ff.; JE, 8 (1907), 603; JL, 4 (1930), 203ff. [Ed.]

MINYAT ZIFTA, town in Lower Egypt, on the eastern tributary of the Nile. In the Fāṭimid period, there was an important Jewish community in this town. R. *Abraham b. Shabbetai, who wrote several works on *halakhah*, was rabbi (*ḥaver*) of the community at the beginning of the 12th century, and after him, his son Shabbetai held the same position for many years. In a list of contributions to a collection among the communities of Lower Egypt at the middle of the same century, Minyat Zifta is mentioned as the second largest contributor. From the *Genizah* documents it appears that the social status of the Jews was variegated; among them were craftsmen, merchants, and government officials. The Jewish population decreased over the generations and in the 19th century, Jacob *Saphir found only five families there: in 1897 there were 84 Jews, in 1907, 54, and in 1927 only 37. By 1924 the synagogue had already been sold, and in 1937 there was only one family living in the town.

Bibliography: J. Saphir, *Even Sappir* (1866), 8b; Mann, Egypt, 2 (1922), 257–9, 287, 290; Mann, Texts, 1 (1931), 446ff.; Poznański, in: REJ, 65 (1913), 43; Goitein, in: JQR, 49 (1958/59), 41; J. M. Landau, *Ha-Yehudim be-Mizrayim ba-Me'ah ha-Tesha-Esreh* (1967), 51–52. [E.A.]

MINZ, ABRAHAM BEN JUDAH HA-LEVI (d. 1525), Italian scholar and rabbi. Some time before 1509, acting on behalf of his father, Judah b. Eliezer ha-Levi *Minz of Padua, he insulted the famous rabbi, Jacob Margolis of Regensburg. Both father and son subsequently made public apology. In January 1509, after his father's death, Abraham was appointed to succeed him, but in July of the same year a decree of expulsion was issued against him by the Venetian authorities for having presented a gift in the name of the Padua community to the chief of the conquering imperial German army during the sack of Padua. The decree was appparently revoked some time thereafter, as Minz is known to have visited Padua about ten years later. After leaving Padua, Abraham spent 15 months in Ferrara, being supported there by the wealthy *parnas*, Norsa, whom he later sided with in the notorious *Finzi-Norsa controversy, at the height of which Jacob *Pollak, a partisan of Abraham Raphael Finzi, and Minz excommunicated each other. Abraham subsequently became rabbi in Mantua. His son-in-law Meir *Katzenellenbogen, occupied the Padua rabbinate.

Abraham was the author of a number of responsa, which are printed together with those of his uncle by marriage, R. Liwa of Ferrara (Venice, 1511). He was the author, too, of *Seder Gittin va-Ḥaliẓah*, printed together with the responsa of his father and his son-in-law (Venice, 1553). He died in Padua.

Bibliography: A. Marx, *Studies in Jewish history and Booklore* (1944), 107–54 (=*Abhandlungen . . . Chajes* (1933), 149–93); I. T. Eisenstadt and S. Wiener, *Da'at Kedoshim* (1897/98), 5–38, 88 (third pagination). [S.E.]

MINZ, BENJAMIN (1903–1961), leader of the *Po'alei Agudat Israel movement. Born in Lodz, Poland, Minz went to Palestine in 1925. A member of Agudat Israel from his youth, he persistently advocated cooperation with the Zionist Movement, despite the opposition of his leaders. At the Third Great Assembly of Agudat Israel (Marienbad, 1937), he was elected a member of the Central Council, and in 1938 was elected to the Po'alei Agudat Israel Executive. During World War II, he was active on the Va'ad ha-Hazzalah (rescue committee), and after the war he worked in D.P. camps in Germany (see *Displaced Persons). He initiated the founding of the World Union of Po'alei Agudat Israel at the Antwerp Conference (1946), and as its head led the movement into close cooperation with the institutions of the *yishuv*, in opposition to the policy of *Agudat Israel. Minz was a member of the Provisional State Council of Israel (1948) and later of the Knesset. He was elected deputy speaker of the Second Knesset and held the post until the Fourth Knesset. He

Benjamin Minz, Po'alei Agudat Israel leader. Courtesy Government Press Office, Tel Aviv.

overruled a decision of the Council of Torah Sages of Agudat Israel and joined the coalition government as minister of posts in 1960, thus causing a rift between his party and Agudat Israel. Minz wrote several books, mainly on ḥasidic topics. [M.Fr.]

MINZ, JUDAH BEN ELIEZER HA-LEVI (c. 1408–1506), Italian rabbi. Judah, a first cousin of Moses *Mintz, was a member of a family of scholars and bankers which derived its name from the town of Mainz, where he was probably born. It is presumed that Minz left Mainz in 1462 during the expulsion of the Jews (see Graetz, Hist, 4 (1894), 294). He settled in Padua where he became rabbi and rector of the yeshivah and where he remained until his death. In Padua he was taught by R. Asher (Israel) Enschechin, a German talmudist, who lived in the city during his latter years (Resp. Judah Minz, nos. 2, 3; *Leket Yosher*, 2 (1904), xlvii, no. 113). Minz corresponded on halakhic matters with many famous rabbis of his time, including Elijah *Mizraḥi of Turkey (who supported Minz in a quarrel with Elijah Delmedigo, the cause of which is unknown), Israel Isserlein of Wiener-Neustadt, Israel *Bruna of Regensburg and Joseph *Colon of Mantua (see *Seder ha-Get* of Abraham Minz at the end of Judah's responsa and *Leket Yosher*, 2 (1904), xxxii, no. 54). His responsa are a valuable historical source and reveal his involvement in the problems of his time (see e.g., *Leket Yosher*, nos. 5, 6, 11). Ghirondi's assertion that Judah was a student of philosophy, and, subsequently, a professor of philosophy at the University of Padua (Ghirondi-Neppi 122ff.), is now held to be unfounded. In his ritual decisions Judah leaned heavily on his German predecessors (see e.g., Resp. Judah Minz, nos. 7, 13, 15), but rather uniquely, permitted men to masquerade as women on Purim (*ibid.* no. 16). Minz's library and most of his manuscripts were destroyed in the year of his death during the sack of Padua (see introd. to *Leket Yosher*). Sixteen of his responsa were discovered by his grandson Joseph b. Abraham Minz and were published in Venice in 1553 by the husband of Judah's granddaughter, Meir *Katzenellenbogen, together with his own responsa and the *Seder Gittin va-Ḥaliẓah* of Abraham b. Judah ha-Levi *Minz. Many later editions have been published, among them one with notes and a preface by Johanan Moses Preschel (1898).

Bibliography: Benjacob, Oẓar, 557; Michael, Or, no. 1020; S. Eidelberg, *Jewish Life in Austria in the XVth Century* (1962), 86 n. 21, 103 n. 69; I. T. Eisenstadt and S. Wiener, *Da'at Kedoshim* (1898), Supplement, 63; Finkelstein, Middle Ages, 27, 306, 308; Guedemann, Gesch Erz, 3 (1888), 251 passim; Joseph b. Moses, *Leket Yosher*, ed. by J. Freimann, 2 (1904), xxxii, no. 54; Weiss, Dor, 5 (1924), 280–2; M. A. Shulwas, *Ḥayyei ha-Yehudim be-Italyah bi-Tekufat ha-Renaissance* (1955), 355, index s.v. *Yehudah Minz*; M. D. Cassuto, *Ha-Yehudim be-Firenze bi-Tekufat ha-Renaissance* (1967), 229. [S.E.]

MIR, town in Grodno oblast, Belorussian S.S.R. From 1569 until 1813 the town and the surrounding estates were the property of the Radziwill princes. Jews first settled in Mir at the beginning of the 17th century. To begin with they were under the jurisdiction of the community of *Nesvizh, but within a few years their numbers had rapidly increased and it can be assumed that they then had their own communal organizations. The Jews became an important factor in local trade and at the two annual fairs held in Mir. Many of them also earned their livelihood as carters. Jewish merchants from every part of Lithuania and Poland were attracted to the fairs of Mir, where they carried on an extensive trade in furs (exporting them especially to Leipzig), horses, oxen, spices, grain, textiles, tobacco (from 1672), and wine. In the records of the Lithuanian council (see *Councils of the Lands) Mir is mentioned for the first time in 1662. From 1673, the taxes owed by the Jews of Lithuania to state institutions and debts to other creditors were occasionally collected at the Mir fairs. In 1685 after complaints by the Jewish representatives, Catherine Sapieha of the Radziwill family instructed the administrator of the town to respect the rights of the Jews and to refrain from dispensing justice or arbitrating in their internal affairs.

During the early decades of the 18th century, the Jewish population of Mir increased considerably. The local Jewish contribution to the poll tax rose from 45 zlotys in 1673 to 1,160 zlotys in 1700 and 1,350 zlotys in 1720. During this period the merchants of Mir maintained fruitful commercial relations with *Leipzig, *Koenigsberg, *Memel, and Libau (*Liepaja). In 1697, 1702, and 1751, the community leaders of Lithuania Jewry conferred in Mir, which then acquired the status of an autonomous community. From the second half of the 18th century, the economic situation of the community declined. In 1760 the Jews of Mir paid 480 zlotys in poll tax; the census of 1765 recorded 607 Jews in the town and the vicinity who paid this tax.

Prominent rabbis officiated in Mir during the 18th century. The first *av bet din* known by name (in the late 1720s) was R. Meir b. Isaac *Eisenstadt, followed by R. Ẓevi Hirsch ha-Kohen *Rappoport; during the middle of that century, R. Solomon Zalman b. Judah Mirkish, author of *Shulḥan Shelomo* (Frankfort on the Oder, 1771), held rabbinical office for 15 years. He was succeeded by R. Ẓevi Hirsh Eisenstadt. During the rabbinate of R. Joseph David Ajzensztat (1776–1826), the famous yeshivah of Mir was founded. At the beginning of the 19th century *Ḥabad Ḥasidism acquired considerable influence in the community.

In 1806 the Mir community numbered 807, including 106 tailors, five goldsmiths, six cord-makers, and about 30 merchants. In the 65 nearby villages, there were 494 Jews in 1818. The numbers in Mir itself rose to 2,273 in 1847 and 3,319 (about 62% of the total population) in 1897. From the second half of the 19th century, with the exception of the wood, grain, horse, and textile merchants who formed the upper class, the majority of the local Jews were craftsmen such as scribes, carters, butchers, and tailors. The wooden synagogue, which had been erected in the middle of the 18th century, was burnt down in 1901. With the threat of pogroms in 1904–05, Mir Jews organized a *self-defense organization. During this period, the *Bund and *Po'alei Zion movements won many adherents in the town. The Zionist movement was organized there in 1914. In 1921 there were 2,074 Jews (c. 55% of the population) living in the town. Their difficult economic situation deteriorated even further from the late 1920s. A Yiddish elementary school and kindergarten were founded in 1917; during the 1920s they were administered by CYSHO and during the 1930s by the Shul-Kult. During the same period, *Tarbut, *Yavneh, and *Beth Jacob schools functioned in Mir. The Jewish library was founded in 1908.

The yeshivah of Mir, founded by Samuel b. Ḥayyim *Tiktinski in 1815 and directed by his son Abraham after his death, played a central role in the spiritual life of the community. From 1836 it was headed by Moses Abraham b. Joseph Ajzensztat and later by Ḥayyim Zalman *Bresler, rabbi of the town, who resigned as the result of a dispute. From then on, the offices of town rabbi and *rosh yeshivah* were separated. From the 1880s, the rabbi was Yom Tov *Lipman (R. Lipa). In 1903 he was succeeded by R. Elijah David *Rabinowitz Teomim, who served until his *aliyah* to Ereẓ Israel. The last rabbi of Mir was Abraham Ẓevi Kamai (from 1917 until the Holocaust). During World War I, the yeshivah of Mir was transferred to Poltava but returned to the town in 1921, and was then headed by R. Eliezer Judah Finkel. Mir was the birthplace of Zalman *Shazar (Rubashov). [A CY.]

Holocaust Period. Under Soviet rule (1939–41) private enterprise was gradually stifled and factories, businesses, and even large buildings were taken over by the state. The yeshivah students and rabbis, headed by R. Eliezer Judah Finkel, moved to Vilna in still independent Lithuania (Finkel managed to reach Palestine and founded the Mir Yeshivah in Jerusalem). The Germans captured Mir on June 27, 1941. They immediately executed scores of Jews on charges of Soviet collaboration. On Nov. 9, 1941, 1,500 Jews were murdered on the outskirts of the town. The surviving 850 Jews were segregated into a ghetto, and transferred in May 1942 to the ancient fortress in the city. A young Jew, Shemuel (Oswald) Rufeisen, born in the Cracow district, played a key role in the Mir resistance movement. After the removal of the Jews to the Mirski fortress, a resistance movement of 80 members was organized to offer armed resistance to the imminent *Aktion* ("action") against the Jewish population. Working in groups of five, they acquired weapons and trained themselves. Their central command was made up of Ha-Shomer ha-Ẓa'ir, Deror, Bund, and Communists.

Early in August 1942 Rufeisen informed the underground that the Germans would begin their liquidation campaign on Aug. 13, 1942. On Aug. 9, 1942, about 200 young people left for the forests on the assumption that no effective resistance action against the Germans could be taken inside the ghetto. On August 13 the liquidation action began, and all those who had remained in the ghetto were murdered in Yablonoshchina and buried in mass graves. Those who had escaped to the forests were confronted with many difficulties. Russian partisan units often refused to accept Jews into their ranks, and many of the Mir Jews who came to the forests were killed by anti-Semitic Russian partisans. Despite all these difficulties, Mir Jews managed to join Soviet partisan units, and took part in sabotage activities. Following the arrival of the Soviet army the Jewish partisans from Mir joined the Soviet forces to continue the fight against the Nazis up till the end of the war.

The student body of the yeshivah was saved during the war by escaping to *Shanghai. After the war (1947), the yeshivah was transferred to Brooklyn, New York (Mirrer Yeshivah Central Institute). Some of its scholars later joined the Mir Yeshivah in Jerusalem. [AR.W.]

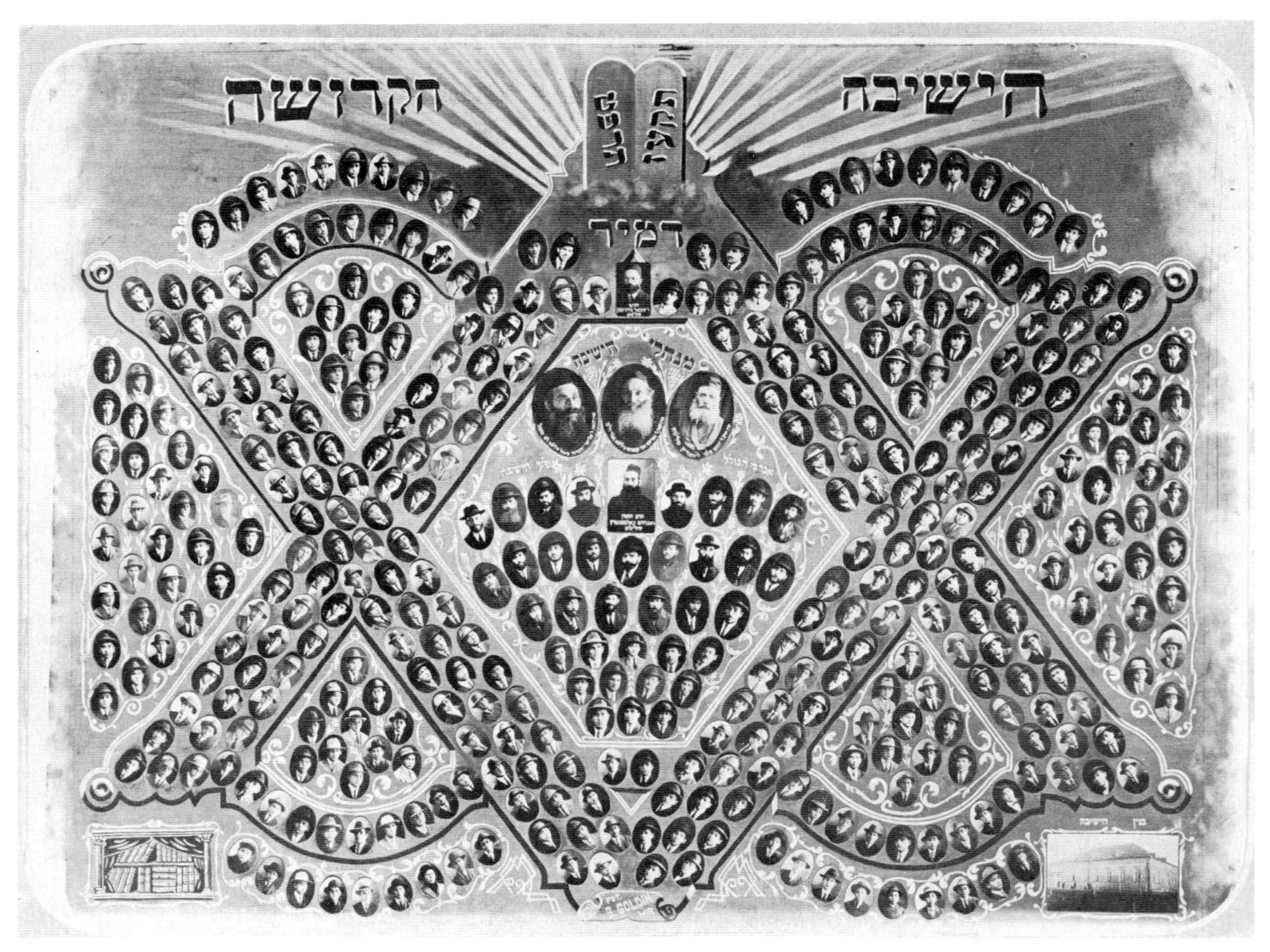

Students and teachers of the Mir Yeshivah, 1929. Jerusalem, J.N.U.L., Schwadron Collection.

Bibliography: S. Dubnow, *Pinkas Medinat Lita* (1925), 197, 240–1, 257–9; Halpern, Pinkas, index; idem, *Tosafot u-Millu'im le-"Pinkas Medinat Lita"* (1935), 31–33, 40–44, 51–52, 66–67; *Regesty i nadpisi,* 2 (1899), nos. 1184, 1232, 1235, 1596; S. Maimon, *Autobiography,* ed. by M. Hadas (1967); I. Schiper, *Dzieje handlu żydowskiego na ziemiach polskich* (1937), index; R. Markgraf, *Zur Geschichte der Juden auf den Messen in Leipzig von 1664–1839* (1894), 29–30; N. Blumenthal (ed.), *Sefer Mir* (Heb. and Yid., 1962).

°**MIRABEAU, HONORÉ GABRIEL RIQUETI, COMTE DE** (1749–91), statesman of the *French Revolution. Mirabeau became interested in the Jewish question during his visits to Holland in 1776, England in 1784, and Prussia in 1786. Influenced by the enlightened members of the Jewish communities in the capitals of these three countries, he was particularly attracted by the image of Moses *Mendelssohn. In the book resulting from this journey, *Sur Moses Mendelssohn, sur la réforme politique des Juifs* (London, 1787), he argued that the faults of the Jews were those of their circumstances. Although his main reason for admiring Mendelssohn was that "humanity and truth" seemed much clearer to him than "the dark phantoms of the talmudists," Mirabeau did not consider Judaism an immoral faith, and he defended it against attacks both old and new. In the course of his argument, he repeated *Dohm's assertion that "the Jew is more of a man than he is a Jew." Quoting from Turgot and *Rousseau in support of his pro-Jewish arguments, Mirabeau affirms that history proves that "the Jews, considered as men and as citizens, were greatly corrupted only because they were denied their rights." Like Dohm he advocated preserving some measure of Jewish autonomy, a view he developed in his memorandum to *Frederick the Great of Prussia, *De la monarchie prussienne* (1788), p.462, but he envisaged it as a transitory phenomenon; the organized Jewish community would wither away and die as the Jews entered fully into the economic and social life of the majority. Mirabeau continued to work for the emancipation of the Jews as he saw it. In the debate of Dec. 24, 1789, he denied Rewbell's assertion that "they [the Jews] do not regard themselves as citizens," and followed *Clermont-Tonnerre in stating that the very fact that the Jews were requesting equality was proof of their desire to cease being Jewish in any separatist way.

Bibliography: L. Kahn, *Les juifs de Paris pendant la révolution* (1898); H. de Jouvenel, *Stormy Life of Mirabeau* (1929); A. Hertzberg, *French Enlightenment and the Jews* (1968), index.

[E.B.]

MIRACLE. Biblical Hebrew has no word corresponding to the English "miracle." Occasionally, the Bible mentions "wonders" *(pele', nifla'ot)* meaning "miracles" (Ex. 3:20; Josh. 3:5; Ps. 78:11; etc.), but the meaning of "wonder" is much broader than "miracle." A particular class of miracles, however, can be considered as a definite biblical concept, since it is designated by terms of its own. These are the "signs" *('otot, mofetim),* i.e., extraordinary and surprising events which God brought about in order to demonstrate His power and will in particular situations, when men had to be convinced. A sign can be given as proof of prophecy. Thus the altar of Beth-El collapsed as a sign that the prophecy of its future destruction was true (I Kings 13:1–6). The more important signs occurred in Egypt: the staff turned into a serpent to show that Moses was indeed sent by God (Ex. 4:1–7); the ten plagues coerced Pharaoh to accept the divine command and let the people go. Deuteronomy 13 raises the problem of a sign given by a false prophet: it can be genuine, brought about by God to test the people, who must not obey under any circumstances a prophet summoning them to idolatry. The problem shows that "signs" as proofs of prophecy were regarded—at least among theologians—as regular (or indeed necessary) events.

Some biblical miracles are more than signs, i.e., their purpose goes beyond the mere proof of divine power. Israel was saved and Egypt's army destroyed by the parting of the Red Sea, the people were given water and food in the desert by means of miraculous acts, and so on. Both Samaria (II Kings 6:8–7:20) and Jerusalem (II Kings 19:35) miraculously escaped conquest by besieging armies. Such miracles can be viewed as direct divine intervention at critical moments of human history. Even in these incidents the element of a "sign" is never wholly absent. *Dathan and Abiram and their followers were swallowed by the earth; it was a just punishment, whose suddenness was demanded by the situation. Moses' words (Num. 16:28–30), however, designate the event clearly as a sign. It is also stated that when Israel saw the mighty deed of Egypt's destruction in the sea they believed in God and in Moses (Ex. 14:31). Evidently, the Bible makes no distinction between signs proper and miraculous divine intervention in human history. There is a third type of miracle in the Bible in which the sheer admiration of the wonder-worker seems more important than both elements discussed above. One cannot escape this impression when reading the stories about Elijah and, to an even greater degree, about Elisha. Such stories are a regular feature of popular religion of all times and in all places; in the Bible they are almost entirely confined to the figures of these two "nonliterary" prophets.

The problem of whether miracles are "natural" or "supernatural," which was of concern to scholars of later ages, does not bother Bible writers. In one case (Num. 16:30) a miracle is described as a "creation," which indicates an awareness of what moderns might call the "suspension of natural laws" (see also Ex. 34:10). On the other hand, the miracle of the descent of the quail (Num. 9:18–23) is quite plainly and clearly described as a "natural"—though unexpected—occurrence and yet is treated as a full-scale miracle. Bible writers simply do not question God's ability to do anything, by any means.

The intellectual's dislike of miracles has furnished the mainstream of Bible criticism with a yardstick: some "sources" contain more accounts of miracles than others, and are therefore deemed less "valuable." Scholars with apologetic tendencies tend to minimize the importance of Bible miracles, in their endeavor to make biblical religion less "crude" and more "pure." This case can be based on the preponderance of the "sign" concept in the Bible discussed above, but is nevertheless wrong. The Bible does not, as a rule, tell miracle stories for their own sake, but it does regard the "signs and wonders" of God as extremely important. Man has to know that God can do anything, whenever and wherever He chooses; that this has been demonstrated in history many times; and the sacred history of Israel has been shaped often enough by direct and quite evident divine intervention. Faith that can do without this notion of miracles is possible, but unthinkable in biblical terms. [J.L.]

In The Talmud. The almost universal word for a miracle in the talmudical literature is the term נֵס *(nes)* used in the Bible for a "sign" or "standard." The biblical miracles are unquestionably accepted by the sages of the Talmud. Insofar as their theological aspect is concerned, three main considerations exercised the minds of the sages: (1) the reversal of the order of creation with its corollary of an insufficiency in the act of creation; (2) the miracle as a testimony of the truth of religion; and (3) the "daily miracles" which do not involve a disturbance of the order of creation.

(1) According to the rabbis, the miracles were, so to speak, preordained and provided for in the act of creation. "R. Johanan said God made a condition with the sea that it would part before the Children of Israel . . . R. Jeremiah b. Eleazar said not with the sea alone, but with whatever God created on the six days of creation . . . God commanded heaven and earth that they should be silent before Moses; the sun and moon that they should stand still before Joshua; the ravens that they should feed Elijah; the fire that it should not harm Hananiah, Mishael, and Azariah; the lions that they injure not Daniel; the heavens that they should open to the voice of Ezekiel; and the fish that it should cast up Jonah'" (Gen. R. 5:45). Another passage emphasizes this idea even more strongly. When God commanded Moses to lift up his staff and part the Red Sea, Moses argued with God that it would involve a breach of his own act of creation, God answered him, "Thou hast not read the beginning of the Torah . . . I made a condition at the time"; and only then did Moses heed the divine behest (Ex. R. 21:6). In the same vein, the Mishnah (Avot 5:6) enumerates ten things which "were created on the eve of the Sabbath [of creation] at twilight," including the mouth of the earth which opened up to swallow Korah (Num. 16:32), the mouth of the ass of Balaam which spoke (Num. 22:28), the manna (Ex. 16:14), and the rod of Moses (Ex. 4:17). As Zangwill (quoted by J. H. Hertz, Comm. to Prayer Book) puts it the Talmud sages "discovered the reign of universal law through exceptions, the miracles that had to be created specially and were still a part of the order of the world, bound to appear in due time."

(2) That miracles are not evidence of religious truth is clearly and explicitly stated in the Bible (Deut. 13:2–4). The rabbis emphasize this in a striking incident wherein R. Eliezer b. Hyrcanus called for, and achieved, a series of miracles for the purpose of proving that his halakhic ruling was correct, but R. Joshua disdainfully rejected them, quoting "the Torah is not in heaven" and his contrary view was accepted (BM 59a).

(3) The rabbis, however, almost go out of their way to emphasize the daily miracle of life which does not express itself in violations of the laws of nature. "Come and consider how many miracles the Holy One, blessed be He, performs for man, and he is unaware of it. If a man were to swallow unmasticated bread, it would descend into his bowels and scratch him, but God created a well in the throat of man which enables it to descend safely" (Ex. R. 24:1). This thought is expressed in the formula of thanksgiving prayer (*Modim*) which forms part of the daily *Amidah*, "for Thy miracles which are daily with us, and for Thy wonders and Thy benefits, which are wrought at all times, evening, morning, and night."

In this connection is it not without interest that the formula of thanksgiving "for the miracles . . . which Thou didst wage for our fathers" is confined to the two festivals of Ḥanukkah and Purim (Sof. 20:6; the formula is found in *Seder R. Amram*). It is true that the rabbis emphasize the miraculous aspect of the Ḥannukah legend of the pure oil which was sufficient for one day only but lasted for eight until new oil could be brought (Shab. 21b), to which there is no reference in the Book of Maccabees, and that many of the regulations of the festival are enjoined "in order to publicize the miracle" (Shab. 23b), but this miracle cannot compare with the biblical miracles, and there is no *deus ex machina* miracle in the story of Purim. On the whole they belong to the class of "natural miracles." The parting of the Red Sea is regarded as the greatest ("most difficult") of the biblical miracles (Pes. 118a).

Although the Talmud is replete with stories and legends of miracles wrought for its worthies (cf. especially Ta'an. 21–25), it is generally accepted that the age of miracles (probably for the benefit of the people as a whole) has ceased, because "they were performed for those who were willing to sacrifice themselves for the sanctification of the Name, and we are not worthy of having miracles performed for us" (Ber. 20a; Ta'an. 18b; Sanh. 94b).

Nevertheless ten minor miracles happened in the time of the Temple (Avot 5:5). They include such mundane miracles as that no person was ever bitten by a snake or scorpion in Jerusalem, that there was always accommodation to be found there (during the pilgrim festivals), and that rain never extinguished the altar fire.

It is forbidden to rely upon miracles (Pes. 64b). "One should never stand in a place of danger and say 'a miracle will happen to me' since perhaps it will not happen, and if it does, it will be deducted from his merits" (Ta'an. 20b). But "the recipient of a miracle does not recognize the miracle" (Nid. 31a). When coming to a place where miracles were wrought for the Jewish people one must recite a special blessing (Ber. 9:1 and 54a). [L.I.R.]

In Medieval Jewish Philosophy. The subject of miracles was one of the most important and problematic in the writings of medieval Jewish philosophy. The medieval philosopher found it difficult to accept the biblical notion of miracles, not only because it was difficult to explain the particular miracles described in the Bible in terms of contemporary science but also because the acceptance of miracles entailed the belief in creation and divine providence—notions rejected by Greek philosophy.

The first of the medieval Jewish philosophers, *Saadiah Gaon, who, following the Mu'tazilites (see *Kalam), proved the existence of God from the temporal origin of the world (*Beliefs and Opinions* 1:2), and deduced the concept of divine omnipotence from the concept of creation (2:4), does not question the possibility of miracles. Since he accepted the concepts of creation and divine providence, it was consistent for him to maintain that God may see fit to alter His creation in order to preserve the faithful or in order to confirm His revelations to the prophets. The purpose of miracles, according to Saadiah, was to confirm the prophet as God's emissary whose word is truth (3:4, 5).

Saadiah believed that a perfect correlation exists between the content of revelation and the conclusions of rational investigation. Thus the miracle, insofar as it confirms revelation, confirms at the same time the conclusions of rational investigation—the existence of God, His unity, and the creation of the world. It might seem, therefore, that the miracle is superfluous. However, Saadiah maintained that while the intellectual verification of revealed doctrines is indeed an obligation, it is lengthy and accessible to few, and, therefore, revelation and miracles are required for the masses. Revelation and miracles are helpful even for those capable of speculation, insofar as they serve as guides in the search for the truth.

To distinguish between the true religion and a false one which lays claim to miracles, both the miraculous occurrence itself, as well as the doctrine it confirms, must be subjected to scientific scrutiny. One must examine the supposed miracle to discover whether it may not have been illusory (ch. 3), and also the tradition which reports it (introd.). Because there is a correlation between that which is revealed and that which is arrived at through rational speculation, nothing which clearly contradicts intellectual judgment may be accepted as prophecy (excluding, of course, phenomena which transcend intellectual understanding; 3:8).

Neoplatonism. Like Saadiah, the early Jewish Neoplatonists accepted the possibility of miracles without question.

While they attributed the same function to miracles as Saadiah had, their conception of the phenomenon of the miracle itself was different. The Neoplatonists no longer viewed miracles as events which contradict the natural order thus serving as evidence of God's will, but rather as the interposition of a higher supranatural order amid the natural order below it. The Neoplatonists maintained that a miracle can take place only in the presence of a person who is worthy of the suprasensual order and attracts it in the form of a particular providence, that person being the prophet. The prophet plays an active role in the manifestation of the miracle. Miracles do not merely serve to confirm the content of the revelation; they are in themselves revelations in the sense that they represent the direct appearance of the divine order in the midst of the natural order (cf. Ibn Ezra, commentary on Ex. 3:15, and 6:3).

The Challenge of Aristotelianism. The problem of miracles grew more acute as the Aristotelian influence on Jewish philosophy became stronger. According to Aristotelianism, which conceives of the natural order as deriving necessarily from the rational Being of God, all that contradicts nature is, by definition, contradictory to reason. Thus a Jewish philosopher confronted by these Aristotelian teachings had two alternatives: if he rejected Aristotelian physics and metaphysics he was challenged by the intellectual demands that physics and metaphysics make, and if he accepted them, he had to account within their framework for the existence of revelation which is the basis of the Torah.

*Judah Halevi accepted the first alternative, Maimonides, the second. Judah Halevi set out from the premise that experience takes precedence over intellectual judgment. Although the intellect might deny the possibility of the occurrence of miracles, the fact of miracles is upheld by the immediate authenticity of the event and the authenticity of the tradition which recorded it (*Kuzari*, 1:5). Rejecting the idea that intellectual judgment must confirm the substance of revelation, and perceiving that the miracle *per se* is no evidence of the validity of the prophet's utterances, Judah Halevi does not, as did Saadiah, regard the miracle as an affirmation of the content of revelation, but views the miracle as itself a direct revelation of God. God's direct communication with a person or a nation is a miracle. The deviation from the natural order for the purpose of guiding a man or a nation to their religious destiny is a miracle. Both occurrences share the fact of God's immediate presence in the lives of men. The miracle, therefore, affirms nothing more than the possibility of its occurrence (1:13–25), and revelation can be verified only as an immediate experience. The authenticity of the revelation at Sinai was established by the fact that all of Israel were granted prophecy together with Moses and could bear witness to revelation out of their own experience. This fact confirmed the revelation for all time, and any prophecy which conflicts with it must be invalid even if it is supposedly supported by miracles (1:80–90).

Maimonides. While Maimonides adopted Aristotelian physics and metaphysics, he deviated from the Aristotelian view that the world is eternal. He upheld the assumption of the temporal origin of the world, although he maintained that it can be neither proved or disproved conclusively, as the only one which allows for miracles (Guide 2:25). Miracles, according to Maimonides, are necessary in order to sustain the authority of revelation for the masses, as well as to support the biblical assumption that God guides men by giving them the Law.

In his attempt to reconcile the concept of miracles with the Aristotelianism that he accepted, Maimonides maintained that the creation of the world as well as miracles are voluntary acts of God, and that in its essence and constitution the world reflects divine reason. Thus there is no conflict between divine wisdom and divine will, both of which were impressed upon the original mould of creation (3:25). According to Maimonides, miracles are predetermined at the time of creation and thus do not indicate a change in God's will or wisdom. The difference between the act of nature and the miracle is a difference between the regular and the unique, although the unique is also governed by its own laws. Indeed, the miracle, like creation, is a unique occurrence which establishes a reality or an order. For example, the miracles of the patriarchs and Moses established the existence of a nation with a particular role to play in the order of the world. The Sinaitic revelation established an ideal legislation for human conduct. Maimonides was careful not to define the miracle as an abrogation of the laws of nature. He explained that in the miracle of the crossing of the Red Sea (Sea of Reeds), for example, the nature of the water was not changed but was affected by another natural force, the wind. A miracle, such as the revelation at Mt. Sinai, was the manifestation of a particular act of creation, and thus may be considered an addition to nature rather than an abrogation thereof.

In sum, Maimonides concurred with Aristotle's position that reality derives from divine reason and therefore not everything imaginable is necessarily possible. While he did maintain that there are things which nature disallows, he differed with Aristotle on the limitation of the possible. Aristotle maintained that only that which exists is possible, whereas Maimonides posited the possibility of singular, constitutive occurrences as equally a necessary effect of divine wisdom (3:15). In accordance with his definition of miracles as constitutive events of general significance, Maimonides elevated the miracles of Moses above all others, while he interpreted allegorically many other biblical episodes which when understood literally are miraculous (2:46, 47).

Nahmanides. Among Jewish philosophers after Maimonides there were those who repudiated the belief in the temporal origin of the world and in miracles, explaining biblical references to them as allegories. There were also renewed attempts to prove that miracles did take place, notably by Naḥmanides, who disputed Maimonides' conception of miracles from a kabbalistic viewpoint. In opposition to Maimonides' view of nature as a necessary effect of divine wisdom, Naḥmanides posited the miracle as preceding nature. The miracle is not a singular occurrence—it is an immutable supranatural reality. According to Naḥmanides, "nature and worldly order do not affect the ends of the Torah," and therefore the destiny of Israel is not natural but miraculous. However, miracles do not necessarily conflict with, or deviate from, the natural order. Naḥmanides postulated a distinction between self-evident miracles, i.e., those which deviate from the natural order thus serving to impart faith to unbelievers and the ignorant, and hidden miracles, which consist in the unusual coincidence of a number of natural events. The miraculous nature of the latter will be evident only to the believer (A. Jellinek (ed.), *Torat Adonai Temimah*, passim).

Ḥasdai Crescas. The most fully developed critique of Maimonides' position is found in Ḥasdai *Crescas' writings. Crescas held that the world was created *ex nihilo* but had no temporal beginning. The world is eternal and continually renewed by God, characterized by Crescas as infinite grace. As well as being infinitely good, God is omnipotent, and therefore miracles, which are instruments of good, are not merely within His power and in harmony with His wisdom but are a necessary effect of His being (Or Adonai, 2, proposition 3:1).

For Crescas, miracles were neither a deviation from nature nor in conflict with it, but an expression of a supranatural order. What distinguishes miracles from natural occurrences is not the fact of their deviation from the natural order, which is after all an external manifestation, but an intrinsic quality. Whereas the natural occurrence is brought about by God indirectly, expresses a limited force, occurs as part of a process, and has only a relative existence, the miracle is brought about directly by God, expresses unlimited power, is a singular event, is not part of a process, and has an absolute existence (*ibid.*, proposition 3:2). This conception of miracles fits in with Crescas' view that the world is continually recreated *ex nihilo* by the divine will: the world itself is actually a perpetual miracle which encompasses the natural order. Thus the miracle is not an aberration of nature, rather it precedes nature. The ultimate purpose of the miracle is to impart faith to unbelievers and to strengthen the faith of believers. However, he did not regard the miracle as an external verification of prophecy, but, along the lines of Judah Halevi, he believed that in every event in which the infinite power of God is revealed, God becomes present to man, and thus heresy and doubt are abolished (*ibid.*, 3, proposition 4:2). In Crescas' doctrine there is a strong universalistic orientation, although emphasis is placed on the particular supranatural providence of Israel: God's grace, being infinite, must reveal itself to everyone, and the miracle which will bring this about, the resurrection of the dead, will be superior even to the miracles performed by Moses (*ibid.*, 3, proposition 4:2).

An analysis of Crescas' doctrine illustrates the development of the concept of miracles through the confrontation with Platonism and Aristotelianism, in that it represents a critical synthesis of both. The miracle, which had been regarded as an external confirmation of revelation, came to be viewed not as a non-natural occurrence but as an immediate revelation of the truth of the Torah. In his critical synthetic doctrine Crescas also anticipated ideas which were fully developed only by modern Jewish philosophers.

[EL.S.]

In Later Jewish Thought. S. D. *Luzzatto was against the rational approach to religion, which he dubbed "Hellenism," and claimed that Judaism, based on love and mercy, was superior. Attacking the Jewish philosophers of his day for trying to assimilate Judaism to the barren "Hellenism" of Western culture, he affirmed the historicity of the miracles in the Bible, including the miracle of prophecy, and he held that miracles were proof of divine providence.

Samuel *Hirsch in his *Die Religionsphilosophie der Juden* (1842) also upheld the historicity of the miracles recorded in the Bible. However, for him it was not the miraculous incident itself that was important, but its educational value. In the biblical period, God revealed Himself to Israel by means of miracles in order to demonstrate that He was above nature and that nature was not omnipotent—an idea which the Israelites had acquired in Egypt. Once the idea of the omnipotence of nature had been uprooted, miracles were no longer necessary, and therefore, ceased to take place. According to Hirsch, however, there was one miracle that did not just take place in the past but has continued up to the present, namely, the existence of the Jewish people, which serves as an additional means of teaching the existence of God.

Moses *Mendelssohn maintained that the truth of any religion cannot be proved by appealing to miracles; it can be proved only on the basis of the rationality of its doctrine. Only after a religious faith has been upheld by reason is it possible to consider the miracles associated with that religion. While Mendelssohn did not reject the possibility of miracles, he stressed that Judaism did not appeal for belief to the authority of miracles but to that of direct revelation witnessed by the entire people.

Nachman *Krochmal felt that there were potent spiritual forces underlying the workings of nature. These forces can operate and cause events which defy the laws of nature and appear miraculous. However, not all miracles are of this type. There is another class of miracles in which God actually directly interferes in nature. However, Krochmal does not satisfactorily explain this class of miracles in terms of his general metaphysical system. [ED.]

Contemporary Views. There have been two trends in modern Jewish thought concerning miracles. The first, represented by such thinkers as F. *Rosenzweig, M. *Buber, and A. J. *Heschel, has returned to an almost biblical conception of miracles, based upon the idea that the miracle is a "sign" of God's presence. The second trend, represented by M. *Kaplan, may be said to follow the rationalistic approach of the medieval philosophers. However, it goes beyond the medievals in denying the significance of miracles qua miracles. The first trend explains away the problem of the miracle being contrary to natural law by proposing a new definition of the miracle, according to which the essence of the miracle does not lie in its being contradictory to nature, but in its having a particular significance in history. The second trend, in a sense, chooses science over miracles, denying any validity to the miracle, insofar as it supposedly goes against natural law.

Rosenzweig holds, as does Maimonides, that the miracles of the Bible were built into the scheme of things from creation, hence, they were part of the natural order. These events were miracles because they played a significant role in history. Rosenzweig attempts to connect science and miracles, or what he called objectivity (idealism) and subjectivity (personal meaning), revelation being the point at which they are joined. The man who receives and lives a revelation carries both in him. The miracle of personal revelation is genuine. It infuses meaning into a particular moment, while its impact carries over into the future (see F. Rosenzweig, *Kokhav ha-Ge'ullah* (1970), 131–48).

Buber also stressed that no miracle is contrary to nature, maintaining that the miracle and nature are two different aspects of the same phenomenon—revelation. For Buber, man's attitude is the essential element in the miracle: the miracle is "our receptivity to the eternal revelation." Buber approaches biblical miracles by asking "what human relation to real events this could have been . . . (which) grew into the written account we have read" (*Moses* (1958), 61ff.). A man today can experience the same relation to real events, the same miracle, that biblical man experienced. The attitude that a man has to events, the world, or other people is the raw material out of which experiences that are miracles arise. For a person properly attuned, any event may be considered a miracle, in terms of its meaning for him.

Heschel stresses the same points using various terms such as "the legacy of wonder" (*God in Search of Man* (1959), 43), or "radical amazement," terms that he gives to the sense of mystery and awe that he attributed to biblical figures. He writes that "What stirred their souls was neither the hidden nor the apparent, but the hidden in the apparent; not the order but the mystery of the order that prevails in the universe" (*ibid.*, 56). He also speaks of the "ineffable," and of a sudden extraordinary and meaningful moment which he calls an "event" as distinguished from "process," the usual scientific way of looking at things.

M. Kaplan conceives of the accounts of miracles in Jewish literature as reflecting the attempt "of the ancient authors to prove and illustrate God's power and goodness" (*Judaism as a Civilization* (1934), 98). Kaplan maintained that these traditions concerning miracles were in conflict with modern thought, and that the belief in miracles that contravene natural law is a "psychological impossibility for most people" (*Questions Jews Ask* (1956), 155–6). The idea of God's exercising control and direction over the workings of the world is passé after modern physics. However, while Kaplan rejects the literalness of the miracle, he sees in the concept that God performs miracles for the sake of the righteous an important idea that has value for modern man, namely, the idea of responsibility and loyalty to what is right. [M.GR.]

Bibliography: O. Procksch, *Theologie des Alten Testaments* (1950), 454–8; C. Tresmontant, *Etudes de métaphysique biblique* (1955), 223–8; S. V. McCasland, in: JBL, 76 (1957), 149–52; W. Eichrodt, *Theology of the Old Testament*, 2 (1967), 162–7; G. Quell, in: *Verbannung und Heimkehr* (1961), 253–300. IN MEDIEVAL JEWISH PHILOSOPHY: Guttmann, Philosophies, index; Husik, Philosophy, 358ff.

MIRANDA, SALOMON RODRIGUES DE (1878–1941), Dutch socialist politician. Born in Amsterdam of poor parents, Miranda became a diamond worker and joined the General Diamond Workers Trade Union (A.N.D.B.) on its establishment. Soon he became one of its leading figures. Miranda was also a prominent member of the Dutch Labor Party (S.D.A.P.) and represented the party as an Amsterdam municipal councillor after 1911. In 1919 he was made alderman for the distribution and price control of foodstuffs which were in short supply after World War I and solved the problem, against considerable opposition, by the creation of municipal food shops. Miranda was minister of housing and public works from 1929 to 1933 and 1935 to 1939. In this capacity he was responsible for the building of several workers' quarters which were remarkable for their architectural design. After the German invasion of Holland, he was arrested and taken to Amersfoort concentration camp where he met his death. [H.BO.]

MIRANDA DE EBRO, city in Castile, N. Spain. It had one of the oldest Jewish communities in Castile. The *fuero* ("municipal charter") granted to Miranda de Ebro in 1099 gave the Jews equal rights with the Christian and Moorish residents. In 1290 the community numbered 15 families who paid an annual tax of 3,312 maravedis and 744 maravedis in services. Jews from Miranda went to work in the fields of neighboring villages. In 1304 Ferdinand IV confirmed that the Jews, Moors, and Christians in Miranda had equal rights, in particular as regards financial liabilities. Ferdinand's ruling was reconfirmed by Alfonso XI in 1347 and by Pedro I in 1351. In 1360, at the beginning of the civil war between Pedro the Cruel and Henry of Trastamara, Henry's supporters in the city attacked the Jewish population and many were massacred. Pedro punished the ringleaders and the municipal authorities, but on finally gaining control of the city Henry granted a moratorium on debts owed to Jews for a year. The privileges of Jews in Miranda, as enumerated to the authorities in Burgos in 1453, included the right to own synagogues, to participate in the tax apportionment, and to work on Sundays at home or in closed workshops, as well as exemption from paying dues to the cathedral. By the system of taxation introduced by Jacob ibn Nuñez in 1474, several neighboring communities were joined with Miranda and their joint tax was fixed at 2,000 maravedis. In 1485 they had to pay a levy of 107 castellanos for the war with Granada. On the expulsion of the Jews from Spain in 1492, the synagogue of Miranda was handed over to the municipal council. The remains of the synagogue in Miranda are preserved in a house in Calle de la Fuenta (no. 18). The Jewish quarter was located in and around the present Calle de la Independencia (formerly de los Judíos).

Bibliography: Baer, Spain, 1 (1961), 423; Baer, Urkunden, index; F. Cantera, *Fuero de Miranda de Ebro* (1945); idem, *Sinagogas españolas* (1955), 246–51; idem, in: *Sefarad*, 1 (1941), 89–140; 2 (1942), 327–75; 22 (1962), 15–16; Suárez Fernández, Documentos, index. [H.B.]

MIRELMAN, family of Argentine industrialists and Jewish leaders. SIMON (1894–) was born in London, moved to Switzerland, and settled in Buenos Aires in 1914, founding a silk-weaving factory. Together with his brothers, who soon followed him to Argentina, he developed the factory into a prosperous concern. He was president of B'nai B'rith, the Committee Against Anti-Semitism (later *DAIA), the Argentine-Israel Cultural Institution, the United Jewish Appeal, and the Israel Bond Drive. He was a member of the board of directors of the Hebrew University. ROBERT (1898–) was born in Russia and followed his elder brother to Buenos Aires. He was president of the Jewish Hospital, the Libertad Street Synagogue, and one of the founders of the Beth-El Conservative Congregation. JOSEPH (1902–) was born in Russia, as was JACOB (1900–), and, before settling in Israel, Joseph was active in Zionist affairs in Buenos Aires, being one of the leading Revisionists there. LEON (1907–), born in Switzerland, became president of the United Jewish Appeal.

The Mirelman brothers were benefactors of many Jewish causes, especially those connected with Israel. They founded the Editorial Israel, which published more than 100 books of Jewish interest. They established the Arpalsa Company and its Israel counterpart, Isar, for the import of frozen meat from Argentina to Israel. [P.LI.]

MIRÈS, JULES ISAAC (1809–1871), French financier. Born in Bordeaux, Mirès moved to Paris in 1841 and, after successful stock exchange operations he acquired and established several periodicals whose news services benefited his financial projects. These included transportation, public utilities, and urban renewal. Among the last were slum clearance, port installations, and gas lighting at Marseilles. Mirès also obtained railroad concessions in Rumania and negotiated Ottoman state loans. At the peak of his power in 1861 he was convicted of fraud, but the conviction was quashed. However, his career had ended, and he died almost a pauper. Besides his defense writ *A mes juges, ma vie et mes affaires* (Paris, 1861) Mirès published numerous financial articles and polemic pamphlets. [J.O.R.]

MIRIAM (Heb. מִרְיָם; perhaps "wish"; Ar. *Marām*, or a compound of Egyptian *mer*, meaning "love"), the daughter of *Amram and Jochebed and sister of *Moses and *Aaron (Num. 26:59; I Chron. 5:29). According to tradition, Miriam is the sister, mentioned in Exodus 2:2–8, who advised Pharaoh's daughter to call a Hebrew nurse for him. However, some scholars reason that since Miriam was mentioned last in the reference to Amram's children (Num. 26:59; I Chron. 5:29), she must have been the youngest, and therefore, the sister mentioned in Exodus 2:2–8 must have been Amram's child by another wife. The critical view is that the representation of Moses, Aaron, and Miriam as "siblings" is secondary. The title "prophetess" was given to Miriam when she appeared, timbrel in hand, at the head of the singing and dancing women after the crossing of the Red Sea (Ex. 15:20–21). It was an Israelite custom for women to welcome the men with timbrels and dancing when they returned from the battlefield and at other celebrations (cf. Judg. 11:34; I Sam. 18:6–7; Ps. 68:26).

Miriam is also mentioned in the context of hers and

Illustration from the *Schocken Haggadah*, northern Italy, first quarter of the 15th century, showing Miriam dancing with a timbrel in her hand (Ex. 15:20). Jerusalem, Schocken Library, Ms. 24085. Photo Alfred Bernheim, Jerusalem.

Aaron's attempt to challenge Moses' exclusive right to speak in the name of the Lord (Num. 12). Miriam is mentioned first, and according to G. B. Gray, the verb appearing in the feminine, *va-tedabber be-* ("she spoke against"), suggests that Miriam led this revolt, or that Miriam alone rebelled and that Aaron's name was added to mitigate her offense. In any event, she alone was punished. The text suggests that the cause of the rebellion was Moses' marriage to an Ethiopian (Cushite) woman (Num. 12:1), but many scholars believe that this line was added by a later editor. Indeed, without that line the text becomes much clearer, i.e., Miriam and Aaron objected to Moses' exclusive right to prophecy in God's name (cf. Num. 11:25–30). Miriam was therefore smitten with leprosy, and was healed only after Moses interceded on her behalf and after being quarantined for seven days. Her punishment is recalled again (Deut. 24:9), as a warning against leprosy. Miriam died in Kadesh and was buried there (Num. 20:1). She is mentioned in Micah with Moses and Aaron as one of the three who led Israel out of Egypt (6:4). [E.STE.]

In the Aggadah: Miriam was so called in reference to the bitterness of the bondage of Egypt (מר, "bitter"; Ex. R. 26:1). Although she is referred to as a prophetess in the Bible (Ex. 15:20), none of her prophecies is mentioned there. The *aggadah*, however, fills the lacuna. It explains that her father *Amram, unwilling to have children who would be doomed to death, divorced his wife after Pharaoh's decree. Miriam urged him to remarry *Jochebed, rebuking him for being even more cruel than Pharaoh since the latter had decreed only against the male children, and prophesying that a child would be born from them who would be the liberator of Israel. Amram acceded and Miriam sang and danced before her parents on the occasion of the remarriage (Sot. 12a–13a; BB 120a). Miriam is identified by some rabbis with Puah (from פעה, "to open the mouth": Ex. R. 1:13; Rashi, Sot. 11b), one of the midwives (Ex. 1:15), who was so called because she comforted the mother and cooed to the child to make it open its mouth. As a reward she was destined to have illustrious descendants. She is also identified with Azubah, the wife of Caleb (I Chron. 2:18); their son, Hur (Ex. R. 1:17) was the grandfather of Bezalel, who inherited the wisdom of his great-grandmother and was the architect of the Sanctuary. Some rabbis hold that even King David was descended from her (Sif. Num. 78; Ex. R. 48:3–4).

Miriam is portrayed as fearless in her rebukes. As a child, she reprimanded Pharaoh for his cruelty, and he refrained from putting her to death only as a result of her mother's plea that she was but a child (Ex. R. 1:13). She also saw fit to rebuke *Moses when he separated from Zipporah, because she felt that he should procreate (Sif. Num. 99). Although Miriam was punished with leprosy, God honored her by Himself officiating as the kohen to declare her definitely a leper and subsequently to declare her cleansed (Zev. 102a). Because she had waited for Moses by the river, the Israelites waited for her to recover (Sot. 11a). A miraculous well, created during the twilight on the eve of the first Sabbath (Avot 5:6), accompanied the Children of Israel in the desert due to her merits (Ta'an. 9a). Like Moses and Aaron, she too died by the kiss of God since the angel of death had no power over her (BB 17a). [A.RO.]

In Islam. In his early prophecies Muhammad speaks about Miriam (Mary, Ar. Maryam) and her son Jesus, who was born of the Holy Spirit (Sura 19:20; 23:52; 66:12). It is, however, also said in Sura 19:29 that she was the sister of Aaron, while in the third Sura (3:31), known as the sura of the family of *ʿImrān, she is described as the daughter of ʿImrān. In connection with the decrees of Firʿawn (*Pharaoh), Muhammad related that the mother of Mūsā (Moses) ordered his sister to watch over the ark in which Moses had been placed (20:41–42; 28:10–12)—without mentioning her name. On another occasion (66:11–12), he mentions the wife of Pharaoh and Miriam (the mother of Jesus) among the righteous women. According to Tabarī and Thaʿlabī, Miriam was married to Caleb, while in Kisāʾī's tale about Qārūn (*Korah) it is said that Miriam was his wife and that it was from her he had learned the science of alchemy, the reason for his attainment to wealth. [H.Z.H.]

For Miriam in the Arts, see *Moses, in the Arts.

Bibliography: IN THE BIBLE: M. D. Cassuto, *Perush al Sefer Shemot* (1953²), 125–6; Haran, in: *Tarbiz*, 25 (1955), 13–14; M. Z. Segal, *Masoret u-Vikkoret* (1957), 89–90; O. Bardenhower, *Der Name Maria* (1895); Haupt, in: AJSLL, 20 (1903/4), 152; Zorell, in: *Zeitschrift fuer katholische Theologie*, 30 (1906), 356–60; G. B. Gray, *Numbers* (ICC, 1903), 120–8; H. Gressmann, *Moses und seine Zeit* (1913), 264–75, 351–52; Humbert, in: ZAW, 38 (1919–20), 86; Voelten, *ibid.*, 111–12; Noth, Personennamen, 60; Bauer, in: ZAW, 51 (1933), 87n. 2; 53 (1935), 59; Rozelaar, in: VT, 2 (1952), 226; C. H. Gordon, *Ugaritic Manual* (1955), 292, no. 1170. IN THE AGGADAH: M. Haran, in: JSS, 5 (1960), 54–55; Ginzberg, Legends, index. IN ISLAM: Ṭabarī, *Taʾrīkh*, 1 (1357 A.H.), 307; Thaʿlabī, *Qiṣaṣ* (1356 A.H.), 141, 203; Kisāʾī, *Qiṣaṣ*, ed. by Eisenberg (1922–23), 229–30; A. Geiger, *Was hat Mohammed aus dem Judenthume aufgenommen?* (1902), 154; H. Speyer, *Die biblischen Erzaehlungen im Qoran* (1931, repr. 1961), 242–3.

MIROSLAV (Ger. **Misslitz**), town in S. Moravia, Czechoslovakia. Jews apparently settled there after their expulsion from the Moravian royal cities (1454). There is a record of a community during the Turkish wars; subsequently it diminished to only three families, but later absorbed refugees from the *Chmielnicki massacres (1648). In 1666, 20 Jews were put in chains and expelled from the town. Subsequently Jews from *Vienna settled in the town, bringing the total Jewish population to 18 families. The oldest legible tombstone in the Jewish cemetery dates from 1692. The *Familiants laws allotted 119 families to Miroslav, where in 1753, 64 families lived in 18 houses. Their number had risen to 448 persons (18% of the total population) in 1801 and remained the same in 1820. In 1831 Rafael Koenig (b. 1808) became the first Jewish locksmith in the Hapsburg Empire. A synagogue in the Reform style was erected in 1845. In 1867 a political community (see *politische Gemeinden*) was established, which was incorporated in the municipality in 1924. The Jewish population reached its peak in 1857, when it numbered 1,032, subsequently declining to 424 in 1869 and then rising slightly to 528 in 1900. During World War I some 350 refugees fled to Miroslav, but few of them settled. In 1930 the community numbered 291 (6.6% of the total). The remainder of the community was deported to Nazi extermination camps in 1942 and the synagogue equipment was sent to the Central Jewish Museum in Prague. Although the community was not revived after the war, the Jewish quarter was preserved in its original plan.

Bibliography: E. Reich, in: H. Gold (ed.), *Die Juden und Judengemeinden Boehmens in Vergangenheit und Gegenwart* (1934), 387–405; D. Kaufmann, in: MWJ, 17 (1890), 289–301. [M.La.]

MIRSKY, AARON (1914–), Hebrew writer. Born in Novogrodek, Poland, he was ordained as a rabbi and emigrated to Ereẓ Israel in 1935. He was an editor at the Mosad Bialik publishing house (1950–60), and, from 1952, taught Hebrew literature at the Hebrew University (professor, 1965). He published studies on ancient and medieval Hebrew poetry and on the Hebrew language. His books include *Yalkut ha-Piyyutim* (1958), an annotated anthology of medieval Hebrew religious poetry; *Shirei Yiẓḥak Ibn Ḥalfon* (1961), with an introduction and textual variants; *Reshit ha-Piyyut* (1965); and a volume of his own poetry, *Alei Si'aḥ* (1966). [G.K.]

MIRSKY, SAMUEL KALMAN (1899–1967), rabbinic scholar, religious Zionist, and Hebraist. Born in Russia, Mirsky emigrated as a child with his parents to Palestine, where he received a thorough talmudic education and *semikhah* at 16. After teaching for some time at various yeshivot, he graduated from the Palestine Government Law School in 1924 and settled in the United States in 1926. He began teaching at Rabbi Isaac Elchanan Theological Seminary in 1936; in 1954 he became professor of rabbinics and director of the Israel Institute at Yeshiva University. In 1942 Mirsky was appointed rabbi of the Borough Park, New York, Young Israel Congregation. He took a leading part in the work of *Mizrachi and of *Histadrut Ivrit of America, serving as president of the latter in 1958 and founding its Hebrew Academy and its journal *Perakim*, which he edited (3 vols., 1957–63). He also edited the Hebrew quarterly *Talpioth* (9 vols., 1944–65), the annual of

Samuel Kalman Mirsky, rabbinic scholar. Courtesy Genazim, Tel Aviv.

the Sura Research Publishing Foundation, *Sura* (4 vols., 1953–64), which he founded, and the *Morashah* book series. Mirsky's main scholarly achievement lay in the publication of medieval critical texts, such as Aḥai Gaon's *She'iltot* (4 vols., 1959–66) and two commentaries on Alfasi, *Perush Rabbi Yehudah ben Binyamin Anav* (1955) and *Perush Rabbi Yonatan ha-Kohen mi-Lunel al-Megillah u-Mo'ed Katan* (1956). Only the first part of his new edition of the 13th-century halakhic compendium by Zedekiah b. Abraham Anau, *Shibbolei ha-Leket* (1966), with an extensive introduction, appeared. Mirsky also published collections of his own articles and edited two books of essays on the leading figures and institutions of modern Jewish scholarship, *Mosedot Torah be-Eiropah* (1957) and *Ishim u-Demuyyot be-Ḥokhmat Yisrael be-Eiropah* (1959). He contributed many articles to periodicals, some in English, some in Hebrew. Two of his originally written autobiographical articles for *Genazim* appeared in *Hadoar* (Nov. 3 and 10, 1967).

Bibliography: S. Bernstein and G. A. Churgin (eds.), *Sefer Yovel . . . Mirsky* (1958), incl. bibl.; G. Appel (ed.), *S. K. Mirsky Memorial Volume* (Heb. and Eng., 1970), incl. bibl. [El.S.]

MISES, LUDWIG EDLER VON (1881–), economist, best known for his work on monetary theory and his criticism of interventionism and central planning. Born in Lemberg, the son of an Austrian railway engineer, von Mises was educated in Vienna. As professor of economics at the University of Vienna from 1913 to 1938, he represented the Austrian economic school of thought. He served as a consultant to the Austrian Chamber of Commerce and formed the Austrian Institute for Business Cycle Research in 1926. From 1934 Von Mises taught in Geneva and from 1940 in New York. Together with Luigi Einaudi, Jacques Rueff, and Wilhelm Roepke, he founded the Mont Pélerin Society, an influential international association of free-market economists and sociologists. His writings include: *The Theory of Money and Credit* (1912); *Kritik des Interventionismus* (1929); *Die Ursachen der Wirtschaftskrise* (1931); *The Ultimate Foundation of Economic Science* (1962); *Human Action: a Treatise on Economics* (1966[3]).

Bibliography: H. Sennholz (ed.), *On Freedom and Free Enterprise* (1956). [J.O.R.]

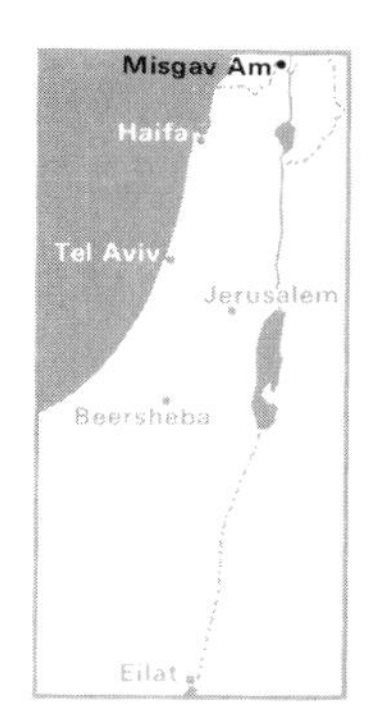

MISGAV AM (Heb. מִשְׂגַּב עָם; "Stronghold of the People"), kibbutz on the Naphtali Ridge, on the Israel-Lebanese border, affiliated with Ha-Kibbutz ha-Me'uḥad. Its establishment in 1945 by a group of Ha-No'ar ha-Oved youth 2,770 ft. (840 m.) above sea level and accessible only by steep footpaths, was a daring undertaking. In the Israel War of Independence (1948) Misgav Am was for many months completely isolated, but served eventually as a base for Israel forces in "Operation Ḥiram." In 1969 the kibbutz cultivated the hilly terrain in its vicinity, and also had fields, orchards, and carp ponds in the Ḥuleh Valley below. [E.O.]

MI SHE-BERAKH (Heb. מִי שֶׁבֵּרַךְ; "He Who Blessed"), initial words of a prayer formula said on various occasions and invoking God's blessing on the community and on individuals.

During the Sabbath morning service after the Torah reading a blessing is invoked "May He who blessed our forefathers . . . bless this holy congregation . . . " The wording of this *Mi she-Berakh* varies in the various rites, but in its essence can be found in the oldest manuscripts. In different communities there are various additional *Mi she-Berakh* prayers, e.g., for one who does not interrupt his prayers from *Barukh she-Amar* through the *Amidah*, for

נקתי · וה׳ שוכן בציון · ובכתבי הקודש נאמר
למה יאמרו הגוים איה נא אלהיהם · ירע בגוים
לעינינו · נקמת דם עבדיך השפוך : ואומר כי
דורש דמים אותם זכר לא שכח צעקת ענוים · ואומר
ידין בגוים מלא גויות · מחץ ראש על ארץ
רבה · מנחל בדרך ישתה על כן ירים ראש ❖

אבותינו אברהם יצחק ויעקב משה ואהרן
דוד ושלמה הוא יברך את כל הקהל הקדוש הזה
אותם ואת כל אשר להם בעבור שנודרים לתעניות
של שני וחמישי ושני ובשכר זה
המקום
ישמרם ויצילם מכל צרה וצוקה מכל נגע
ומכל מחלה וישלח ברכה והצלחה בכל מעשה
ידיהם עם כל ישראל אחיהם ונאמר אמן ❖

The *Mi she-Berakh* prayer from a *ḥazzan's* prayer book, Moravia(?), 18th century. Cecil Roth Collection. Photo David Harris, Jerusalem.

one who always comes on time to the synagogue, etc. In Israel there is a *Mi she-Berakh* for the soldiers of the Israel Defense Forces. A personal *Mi she-Berakh* is generally recited for every person called to the reading of the law sometimes specifying the donation being made to the synagogue. If the person called to the Torah is celebrating a special occasion, such as his bar mitzvah, forthcoming marriage, or the birth of a child, the prayer is worded so as to make reference to the event. For a female child the name is usually given in the prayer. The usual *Mi she-Berakh* starts with the words "May He who blessed our fathers Abraham, Isaac, and Jacob bless . . .," however, when the blessing is invoked for a sick female or one recovering from childbirth, the names of the matriarchs, Sarah, Rebekah, Rachel, and Leah are added to the invocation. It is also customary to recite relevant versions of the prayer at banquets celebrating events of religious importance.

Bibliography: Eisenstein, Dinim, s.v.

[Ed.]

MISHMAR HA-EMEK (Heb. מִשְׁמַר הָעֵמֶק; "Guard of the Valley"), kibbutz on the southwest rim of the *Jezreel Valley, Israel, affiliated with Kibbutz Arẓi ha-Shomer ha-Ẓa'ir. It was founded in 1926 by pioneers from Poland (joined later by immigrants from other countries) as the first Jewish settlement in the area. It soon became a center of Ha-Shomer ha-Ẓa'ir movement, particularly since the first regional school of the Kibbutz Arẓi network was set up there. In the Israel *War of Independence (1948), Mishmar ha-Emek successfully resisted the first large-scale attack of the Arab "Liberation Army," commanded by Fawzī al-Qāwuqjī, aimed at a breakthrough to Haifa. The attacking Arab forces were eventually thrown back toward *Megiddo and Jenin (April 1948). In 1969, the kibbutz, with 700 inhabitants, based its economy on intensive and diverse farming and a plastics factory for electrical appliances and household goods. The Ha-Shomer ha-Ẓa'ir Forest which was planted in the hills near the kibbutz at the end of the 1920s has become part of the Menasheh Forest, the largest in the country. The kibbutz has a local museum.

[E.O.]

MISHMAR HA-NEGEV (Heb. מִשְׁמַר הַנֶּגֶב; "Guard of the Negev"), kibbutz in S. Israel, 12 mi. (20 km.) N.W. of Beersheba, affiliated with Ha-Kibbutz ha-Me'uḥad. It was one of the 11 Jewish settlements established in one night (Oct. 6, 1946) in the South and Negev as a continuation of the "tower and stockade" principle. In the Israel *War of Independence (1948), the kibbutz constituted an important link with the isolated Negev settlements and served as a base for the Israel forces which captured Beersheba. Its members, numbering 462 in 1969, originated from Latin American countries, France, North Africa, Bulgaria, and other countries. In 1969 its economy was based on agriculture irrigated by the National Water Carrier, and on a plastics factory. The local archaeological museum displays artifacts from the vicinity where ancient *Gerar is supposed to have been located.

[E.O.]

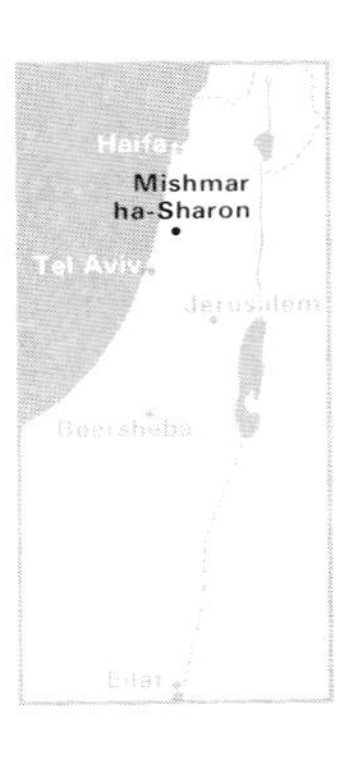

MISHMAR HA-SHARON (Heb. מִשְׁמַר הַשָּׁרוֹן; "Guard of the Sharon"), kibbutz in central Israel, in the Ḥefer Plain, affiliated with Iḥud ha-Kevuẓot ve-ha-Kibbutzim, founded in 1933. Mishmar ha-Sharon developed intensive, irrigated farming, including citrus, and dairy cattle; it pioneered in raising flowers. The kibbutz also runs a bakery. In 1969 its population was 400.

[E.O.]

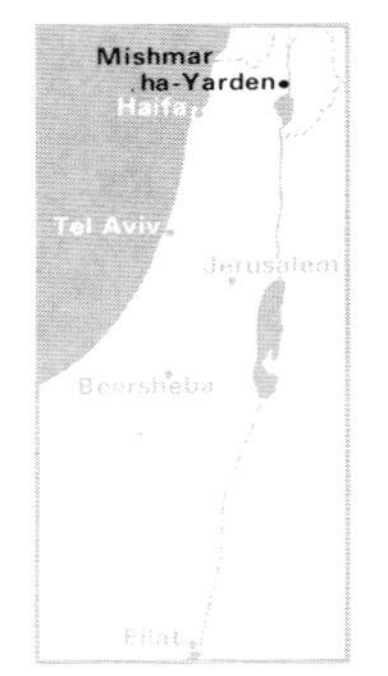

MISHMAR HA-YARDEN (Heb. מִשְׁמַר הַיַּרְדֵּן; "Guard of the Jordan"), moshav in northern Israel, near the upper Jordan River course, affiliated with the *Ḥerut Movement. In 1884 a Jew living in the United States acquired the land, to establish a farm, Shoshannat ha-Yarden, but shortly after sold his holding to a Ḥovevei Zion group from Russia which founded the moshavah of Mishmar ha-Yarden (1890). Although it received aid from Baron Edmond de *Rothschild, the village, which was based mainly on extensive grain crops, did not make much headway. It suffered from isolation and the endemic malaria. In 1946 the village, reinforced with the settlement of Irgun Wedgwood, a group of World War II veterans, intensified its farming. In the Israel *War of Independence, the Syrian army crossed the Jordan River from the *Golan over the nearby *Benot Ya'akov Bridge, and established a bridgehead at Mishmar ha-Yarden, in an attempt to cut off the Ḥuleh Valley and penetrate into Galilee (May 1948). The attempt of Israel forces to encircle the Syrians from the east in "Operation Berosh" (July 1948) was unsuccessful, but the bridgehead was contained and its area reduced. When the Syrians evacuated the area as a result of the armistice terms (1949), hardly any traces remained of the moshavah. At the end of 1949, the moshav and a kibbutz, *Gadot, were founded on the site. Until the Six-Day War (June 1967), Mishmar ha-Yarden was the frequent object of sniping and shelling from Syrian positions, just beyond the Jordan River. Most of the moshav's inhabitants originate from Morocco. Its farming was based on irrigated field and garden crops, deciduous fruit orchards, and dairy cattle. [E.O.]

MISHMAROT (Heb. מִשְׁמָרוֹת; "Guard Posts"), kibbutz in central Israel, near *Pardes Ḥannah, affiliated with Iḥud ha-Kevuzot ve-ha-Kibbutzim, founded in 1933. Mishmarot developed citrus, banana, and other fruit and dairy cattle, became a partner in a large plywood factory, and set up smaller plants for metal products and furniture parts. Its population in 1968 was 240. [E.O.]

MISHMAROT AND MA'AMADOT, priestly and levitical divisions.

Historical. According to I Chronicles 24–26 and rabbinic tradition, the priests and the Levites were organized into courses, or divisions. According to post-biblical evidence, these divisions used to serve in rotation. The term which is rendered as "course" (Heb. *mishmar, mishmarot*) is the one used in post-biblical sources (*The Scroll of the War of the Sons of Light Against the Sons of Darkness,* p. 2, 2ff.; Suk. 5:6–7; Ta'an. 2:6–7, et al.), whereas the Bible generally employs the term "division" (Heb. *maḥlakah, maḥlakot*).

According to I Chronicles 23:1ff., it was King David who divided all the priests and Levites according to their families and clans and assigned them their tasks in the *Temple. This arrangement is attributed to David also in the description of the dedication of the Temple by Solomon in II Chronicles 8:14. The text of Nehemiah 12:45–46 ascribes the assignment of tasks to the Levites and priests to both David and Solomon. There is no information about the working arrangements in the Temple anywhere else in the Bible; neither is there any allusion to courses among the detailed instructions for the priests and Levites in the Bible. It would appear that even the listing of the divisions of priests and singers and porters, as given in I Chronicles 24–26, dates from the Second Temple era, and that they reflect a Second Temple reality, a conclusion based on the comparison of the list in I Chronicles 24 with the lists of the priestly families in the Book of Ezra and Nehemiah and post-biblical sources.

In the list of returnees in Ezra 2:36–39 (Neh. 7:39–41)—apparently a record of a general census after the rebuilding of the Temple—only four priestly clans are listed: the sons of Jedaiah (of the house of Jeshua), the sons of Immer, the sons of Pashhur, and the sons of Harim. They totaled 4,289, which was a tenth of the number of returnees. This is a complete record of all the priests as of that date, and they belonged to only four families or clans. Of these four clans, three —Jedaiah, Immer, and Harim—appear again in the list of the 24 divisions of the priesthood in I Chronicles 24:7ff. Again, a detailed list of priests (as representatives of clans) leads the list of 22 names of those who signed the covenant in Nehemiah 10:2–9. Eight of these—Immer (Amariah), Malchijah, Shebaniah (Shecaniah), Harim, Abijah, Mijamin, Maaziah, and Bilgai (Bilgah)—recur in the list in I Chronicles 24. With minor differences, these names are the same as those of the priestly clans listed in Nehemiah 12:12–20, which is attributed to the time of Joiakim, the high priest and the father of the high priest Eliashib of the period of Nehemiah. Fifteen names in the latter list are identical with the names of the signers of the covenant, including the eight clans which figure in the list of divisions in Chronicles; and it includes two names which recur in the Chronicles list, including Jehoiarib (Joiarib), the division to which the Hasmoneans belonged. These two lists—of Nehemiah 10 and of Nehemiah 12—also predate the list of 24 priestly divisions in the book of Chronicles.

It would appear, then, that the author of Chronicles ascribed to David certain later arrangements of divine service, and that the priestly courses were actually not established until the Second Temple era. On the other hand, it may be argued that, although the list of courses in I Chronicles 24–26 reflects reality at the time of the author, the fact that priestly tasks were performed by established divisions serving in rotation indicates an historical tradition. Indeed, the theory that some sort of courses existed in the First Temple is supported by the parallel with the system of divisions in Egyptian temples, despite the generally dissimilar natures of the two priesthoods. The four priestly families mentioned in the list of returnees in Ezra 2:36–39 may possibly have corresponded to the four priestly divisions of the First Temple, which also served in rotation. Comparison of the list of priests in the Book of Ezra and Nehemiah and the list of the 24 priestly courses in Chronicles illustrates the relationship between all these lists, on the one hand, and the priority of the lists in the Book of Ezra and Nehemiah, on the other. The earliest among them is the list of four priestly families, mentioned in Ezra 2, from the time of the Return, which is based on the divisions in the First Temple. According to this list, the number of priests was already very large (4,289 men), and even the number of priests in one family was so great that they could not serve in the Temple simultaneously. An arrangement whereby the groups of priests would serve in rotation was necessary. The families were divided into clans, and the clans into courses (cf. rabbinic tradition: "four divisions returned from Exile—Jedaiah, Harim, Pashhur, and Immer; and the prophets in Jerusalem organized them into four-and-twenty divisions," Tosef., Ta'an. 2:1; TJ, Ta'an. 4:2, 67d, et al.). Perhaps to be included in the same framework is the account given by Josephus (Apion, 2:108) concerning four priestly tribes that rotated service in the Temple at regular intervals. Indeed, there are those who would amend the text to read "twenty-four" in this place as well (cf. Jos., Life, 2; Jos., Ant., 7:366). A tradition concerning the gradual consolidation of the 24 priestly courses appear also in Tosefta, *Ta'anit* 4:2, and TJ, *Ta'anit* 4:2, 67d.

The establishment of 24 priestly courses and the order of their service as described in I Chronicles 24 was meant to be a permanent arrangement. When this order was established and at what time the list was made is not known. In any event, it was a late development, at least one or two generations after the time of High Priest Joiakim, to which the list of priestly clans in Nehemiah 12 is attributed. Various scholars date this list at the beginning of the Hasmonean era, since Jehoiarib, the representative of the Hasmonean clan, heads the list (I Chron. 24), whereas in Nehemiah his name is 16th on the list. According to this theory, the family of Jehoiarib was primarily a provincial one, which did not achieve greatness until the Hasmonean period. However, according to I Maccabees 2:1, the house of Joiarib (Jehoiarib) was Jerusalemite; only Mattathias moved to Modin (Modi'in, presumably because of the perilous times.). Although he is mentioned 16th on the Nehemiah list, he appears before Jedaiah, whose family was important from the early days of the Return of Exiles (Neh. 12:6, 19). The date of the list of 24 priestly courses may therefore be set close to the period of Nehemiah, still during the Persian occupation. Possibly Nehemiah, who testifies that it was he himself who assigned the priests and the levites their various duties (Neh. 13:30), also established the arrangement of the 24 priestly courses, despite his failure to specify it in the account of his activities. [J. Li.]

Talmudic Data. As the priests were numerous and

scattered throughout Palestine, it was impossible for all of them to officiate at the same time. An arrangement was therefore made whereby they were divided (in the final stage) regionally into 24 *mishmarot* (lit. "guards"; Ta'an. 4:2), which served in a regular weekly rotation. The *mishmarot* were further broken up into a varying number of *battei avot* ("houses," or "families"). Each division and subdivision was presided over by a head, called *rosh mishmar* and *rosh bet av* respectively (Tosef., Hor. 2:10); there is also mention made of a *bet av* (Tam. 1:1; Mid. 1:8; cf. Yoma 1:5). The levites were similarly divided into 24 *mishmarot*, which replaced each other every week (I Chron. 25:8ff, et al.; Jos., Ant., 7:363ff.; Ta'an. 4:2). These were in turn subdivided into seven *battei avot*, and presided over by "heads." Finally, there was an analogous division of the Israelites themselves into 24 *mishmarot*, each of which had to take its turn in coming to Jerusalem for a week. They served to represent the whole body of the people while the daily (communal) offerings were sacrificed, for "how can a man's offering be offered while he does not stand by it?" (Ta'an. 4:2, et al.).

That part of the *mishmar* of priests, Levites, or Israelites actually engaged in the performance of its duty was called a *ma'amad* or *ammud* ("station") and was headed by a *rosh ma'amad* (Tam. 5:6). When the time for the service of a *mishmar* came round, all the priests and Levites belonging to it would go to Jerusalem. Not all the Israelites of that *mishmar*, however, proceeded to Jerusalem. A portion of them certainly did (Ta'an. 4:2; cf. Tosef., Ta'an. 4:3), but those who could not do so assembled in their own towns and read the story of creation, etc. Only those in Jerusalem who actually "stood by" while the sacrifice was being offered could, strictly speaking, be called a *ma'amad*, or *ammud* (see Sof. 17:5; but see Lieberman, *Tosefta ki-Feshutah* 5, 1962, 1104, who shows that according to a different opinion the *ma'amadot* were of Israelites alone).

Activities. These 24 *mishmarot* conducted the daily Temple service, each in turn officiating for one week. Every Sabbath they changed, the retiring *mishmar* offering the morning and *musaf* additional sacrifices, whereas the new *mishmar* offered the evening one, and laid the fresh shewbread on the table (Tosef., Suk. 4:24–25). On the three pilgrim festivals, all the 24 *mishmarot* officiated together (Suk. 5:7–8). Each priestly *mishmar* had in the Temple its own ring at which its members slaughtered their animals (Mid. 3:5) and its own niche in which their vestments were kept (Tam. 5:3). Bilga's niche was, however, permanently blocked up and its ring immovable (Suk. 5:8), a sign of disgrace, because one of its members had once acted shamefully (Suk. 56b). The weekly *mishmarot* of priests were broken up into between four and nine subdivisions (*battei avot*). If there were fewer than seven, some would officiate twice during the week. If, on the other hand, there were more than seven, then on some days two would have to serve together (Tosef., Ta'an. 2:2, et al.). Furthermore, as only a small part of a *bet av* was required to serve at any given time, lots were drawn to decide which individual priests should officiate each day (Yoma 2:2–4, et al.).

A number of restrictions were placed upon members of the *mishmar* and *bet av* during their week (or day) of office. Thus, members of the *mishmar* were permitted to drink wine by night but not by day, whereas those of the *bet av* could not drink wine either by day or night, as they might be called upon to assist in the Temple service at any conceivable hour. Members of the *mishmar* and of the (Israelite) *ma'amad* alike were forbidden to cut their hair or wash their clothes throughout the week—as this should have been done earlier—except on Thursday, so that due honor be accorded the Sabbath (Ta'an. 2:7). On certain communal fast days, members of the *mishmar* and the *bet av* were permitted to eat, or else to fast only partially, so as to have enough strength to carry out their Temple duties (Ta'an. 2:6). The men of the Israelite *ma'amad*, however, would fast from Monday to Thursday on their week of service, while from Sunday to Friday they read (in sections) the chapter of Creation (Gen. 1; Ta'an. 4:2–3). Members of the *mishmar* who were not engaged in actual service would pray that the sacrifices of their officiating brethren be acceptable; while those of the Israelite *ma'amad* who could not come to Jerusalem gathered in their local synagogues (or meeting places) and prayed for the welfare of sailors, wayfarers, children, pregnant women, etc. The *ma'amadot* were considered to be of such importance that it was said that without them heaven and earth could not have survived (Ta'an. 27b; cf. the reading in Sof. 17:15). The institution of the *ma'amadot*, which dates back to the beginning of the Second Temple (see sources cited below), seems to have formed the basis of what later became the synagogal system.

History. Concerning the origins of the *mishmar* system, there are three conflicting (tannaitic) traditions recorded in rabbinic literature: (1) Moses established eight (priestly) *mishmarot*, to which David and Samuel added another eight. Finally, on the return from the Babylonian Exile, 24 were established (TJ, Ta'an. 4:2, 67); (2) Moses established eight (priestly and levitical) *mishmarot;* David and Samuel increased them to 24, and on the return from the Exile 24 (Israelite) *ammudim* (*ma'amadot*) were established, parallel to the priestly and levitical *mishmarot* (Tosef., Ta'an. 4:2); (3) Moses established 16 *mishmarot*, which were later increased to 24 (Ta'an. 27a). Relative unanimity of opinion is to be found only in the account of the restoration of the *mishmar* system after the Babylonian Exile. Four *mishmarot* are said to have returned from the Exile, Jedaiah, Harim, Pashchur, and Immer. "And the prophets among them [or "in Jerusalem," according to the Tosefta; i.e., Haggai, Zechariah, and Malachi] arose and made 24 lots, and put them into an urn." Then each of the four *mishmarot* drew five lots in addition to his own, making a total of six. Finally, the *rashei mishmarot* divided them into *battei avot* (TJ, Ta'an. 4:4, 68a, et al.). It would seem (from tradition (2) above) that only at this stage were the Israelite *ma'amadot* introduced.

Thus rabbinic sources trace the first origins of the *mishmarot* via David and Samuel back to Moses. However, these accounts do not appear to have the value of independent traditions, but rather to be based upon inferences drawn from scriptural passages. Thus, "... whom David and Samuel the seer did ordain, in their set office ... " (I Chron. 9:22) is said to refer to the priestly and levitical *mishmarot* (Tosef., *ibid.;* cf. TJ, *ibid.*, citing I Chron. 2:4). Nevertheless, the resultant picture presented by rabbinic sources probably has considerable historical validity. The system remained unchanged even till Josephus' time (Jos., Ant., 7:363ff.; Life, 1:2).

Long after the destruction of the Temple, memories of the *mishmarot* lingered on. In Ereẓ Israel their names were mentioned each Sabbath in the *piyyutim*. Tablets, fragments of which have survived, were fixed on synagogue walls, engraved with a list of *mishmarot* and their geographical provenance. Karaite liturgy preserved echoes of both the *mishmarot* and the *ma'amadot*. Even as late as 1034, it was still the custom in some communities to announce on each Sabbath: "Today is the holy Sabbath, holy to the Lord. Today is [the Sabbath of] which *mishmeret?* [That of] *mishmeret* ... May the Merciful One restore the *mishmeret* to its place, speedily and in our days. Amen."

[D.S.]

Bibliography: IN THE BIBLE: Schuerer, Gesch, 1 (1901), 286–97; S. Klein, *Meḥkarim Ereẓ-Yisre'eliyyim* (1924), 3–30; idem, *Ereẓ ha-Galil* (1945, 1967²), 62–68, 177–92; A. C. Welch, *The Work of the Chronicler* (1939), 8–96; H. Kees, *Das Priestertum im aegyptischen Staat* (1953), 300–8; Jepsen, in: ZAW, 66 (1954), 87–106; W. Rudolph, *Die Chronikbuecher* (1955), 152–78; Kaufmann Y., Toledot, 4 (1956), 358–9; P. Winter, in: VT, 6 (1956), 215–7 (Eng.); J. T. Milik, in: VT, *Supplement*, 4 (1957), 24–26 (Fr.); S. Talmon, in: *Scripta Hierosolymitana*, 4 (1958), 168–76 (Eng.); Avi-Yonah, in: IEJ, 12 (1962), 137–42; L. Finkelstein, *New Light from the Prophets* (1969), 49–76, 101–22. IN THE TALMUD: M. L. Bloch, *Sha'arei Torat ha-Takkanot*, 1 (1879), 27–40, 87–94; J. Liver, *Perakim be-Toledot ha-Kehunnah ve-ha-Leviyyah* (1968), 33–52; EM, 5 (1968), 569–80.

MISHNAH (Heb. מִשְׁנָה). The term Mishnah is derived from the Hebrew verb *shanah*, meaning "to repeat." Under the influence of the Aramaic word *tanna*, however, it received the meaning of "to learn," and was applied specifically to studying the Oral Law, essentially a matter of memorizing and recapitulation (Avot 3:8: "When one, walking on the road, recapitulates (what he has learnt), and interrupts his Mishnah," i.e., "study"; Avot 3:9: "Whoever forgets one word of his Mishnah"; and see Ḥag. 9b; Er. 54b). Mishnah is contrasted with *Mikra* (from *kara*, "to read"), the Written Law, which is read (Neh. 8:8). Mishnah, as a general designation of the Oral Law, included all its aspects: Midrash, *halakhot*, and *aggadot* (Sif. Deut. 344). Although the collections and orders of the Oral Law as taught in the academies of the *tannaim were called "Mishnah," that of one *tanna* was not the same as the "Mishnah" of another, either in scope, contents, or form. As early as the middle of the second century there were divergent views on what constituted the essence of the Mishnah: "What is Mishnah? R. Meir said: *halakhot*. R. Judah said: Midrash" (Kid. 49a); R. Judah thus included the Midrash in the Mishnah. However, the word was used specifically to designate the *halakhah*, for which it became a synonym, so that while a single *halakhah* is called a Mishnah (Git. 5:6 et al.), the Mishnah as a whole is referred to as *halakhot* (TJ, Hor. 3:7, 48c). For a considerable time after its redaction the *amoraim* called the Mishnah as we know it, "our Mishnah" (Heb. *mishnatenu* or, in Aramaic, *matnitin*), to distinguish it from other collections of Mishnayot ("the Mishnah" of R. Hoshaiah, or "the Mishnah" of Bar Kappara: see TJ, *ibid.*; see also BB 154b, and Rashbam, *ibid.* 138a: "When we speak of Mishnah we also mean the *baraita*"). "Our Mishnah," which became simply the Mishnah or the Mishnayot, refers to the existing six orders of the Mishnah that were redacted, arranged, and revised about the beginning of the third century by *Judah ha-Nasi, who was also known simply as Rabbi.

The Sources of the Mishnah. From a study of several tractates of the Mishnah and sometimes even of one tractate or chapter, it is easy to discern differences in linguistic style (the *amora* Rav, in commenting on the language of the Mishnah in BK 1:1, said (BK 6b): "This *tanna* was a Jerusalemite") as well as in the presentation of statements. These differences are to be explained as due alike to the lengthy history of the *halakhah* and the varied sources of its growth, as well as to the sages' different ways of transmitting, teaching, and arranging the *halakhot*. Some were transmitted as decrees and regulations (Bik. 3:7; Shev. 4:2; Ma'as. Sh. 5:15), some as groups of local laws (BM 7:1) which were no more than local customs, and some as historical *halakhot* dictated by prevailing circumstances (Sanh. 9:6). Still others were transmitted as groups of decided *halakhot* on a particular subject, such as those on the relations between neighbors and partners (BM 10; BB 1–2), inheritance (BB 8), the procedures of *battei din* (Sanh. 4:4–5), and penalties and their execution (Sanh. 7). Parallels to many of these and similar *halakhot* can be found in the legal works both of the ancient East and of the Greek-Hellenistic world. In the days of the Hasmoneans, and even in the period preceding, these works were undoubtedly studied in the actual language of the jurists.

Antiquated expressions have been preserved mainly in the tractates dealing with *halakhot* observed only in Temple times and describing the order and ritual ceremonies of the Temple service. These *mishnayot* are distinguished by their archaic language and by an epic description of prevailing conditions. Almost the entire tractate *Tamid*, which gives an account of the morning Temple service, belongs to this type, and except for two *mishnayot* where there is a divergence of opinion (5:2, 7:2), the entire tractate was taught anonymously. A statement of the Mishnah (3:1) is quoted in the Tosefta (Yoma 1:13), which says of it: "These are the words of R. Simeon of Mizpeh." The *amora* Johanan referred to the tractate as "*Tamid* of R. Simeon of Mizpeh" (TJ, Yoma 2:3, 39d). The *amora* Jacob b. Aḥa commented: "And not all of it but only the statements required by the rabbis," meaning that the entire extant tractate had not been preserved in its original form, but that adaptations and additions had been incorporated in various places. Simeon of Mizpeh, who flourished in the days of Rabban Gamaliel the Elder (Pe'ah 2:6), was an eyewitness to the sacrifices offered in the Temple, the order of which he received from those well-versed in the subject. The phraseology and style of the Mishnah testify to the immediacy of the description, as shown, for example, by its conclusion (7:3) "The deputy high priest stood on the horn of the altar with the flags in his hand, and two priests on the table of the fat with two (silver) trumpets in their hands. They blew a *teki'ah*, a *teru'ah*, and a *teki'ah* [kinds of blast], and then went and stood by Ben Arza, the one on his right hand and the other on his left. When he bent down to make the libation the deputy high priest waved the flags, Ben Arza struck the cymbals, and the levites chanted the Psalm. When they came to a pause, a *teki'ah* was blown, and the public prostrated themselves. At every pause there was a *teki'ah* and at every *teki'ah* a prostration. This was the order of the regular daily sacrifice for the service of the house of our God."

Figure 1. Page from the Kaufmann manuscript of the Mishnah, undated, 12th–14th centuries. Budapest, Library of the Hungarian Academy of Sciences, Kaufmann Collection, Ms. A 50.

Similar to *Tamid* is the tractate *Middot* ("Measures"), which describes the Temple Mount and the Temple's shape, measurements, courts, chambers, and cells. The evidence of the *amoraim* Abbahu (TJ, Yoma 2:3, 39d) and Huna (Yoma 16a), "Who is the *tanna* of (the anonymous *mishnayot* in) *Middot?* It is R. Eliezer b. Jacob," is substantiated by statements in the Mishnah itself, such as "With regard to the southwestern (corner of the court), R. Eliezer b. Jacob said: I forget what it was used for" (Mid. 2:5), and "With regard to the wood chamber, R. Eliezer b. Jacob said: I forget what it was used for" (Mid. 5:4). The original Mishnah apparently did not mention Eliezer b. Jacob's name, which was later added by the *tanna* who taught the Mishnah. This *tanna* was probably Abba Saul, in whose name the concluding *tanna* taught: "There they stored wine and oil, and it was called the oil storage room" (Mid. 2:5). Similarly, in the statement, "R. Eliezer b. Jacob said: Once they found my mother's brother asleep, and they burnt his clothes" (Mid. 1:2), the name of its author was added to indicate whose maternal uncle it was. Asher b. Jehiel commented on this Mishnah: "From this, too, we can infer that (the author of) the anonymous *mishnayot* of *Middot* was R. Eliezer b. Jacob."

This category of *mishnayot* which describe the order and ceremonies in the Temple includes the order of the Day of Atonement contained in *Yoma* (5:7: "Every act of the Day of Atonement mentioned according to the prescribed order"), the description of the *mitzvot* of the willow branch and the joyous procession of the water libation in *Sukkah* (4:5, and 9), the order of fast days in *Ta'anit* (2:1–5), and arrangement of the *ma'amadot* (see **Mishmarot* and *Ma'amadot*) and the wood-festival (Ta'an. 4:2–5). To it likewise belongs the account of the offering of the first fruits in the days of the king Agrippa (Bik. 3:2–6, and see the description there: "The governors and chiefs and treasurers (of the Temple) went out to meet them . . . and when they reached the Temple Mount even King Agrippa would take the basket and place it on his shoulder . . . While the basket was still on his shoulder he would recite . . ."), as well as a similar account of the pentateuchal section read by the king on *yom *hakhel* (during the festival of Tabernacles immediately following the conclusion of the sabbatical year) in *Sotah* (7:8: "King Agrippa stood and received it and read standing"), and the order of preparing the ashes of the heifer, which in several respects resembles that of *Yoma* (Par. 3:1) and which lists the names of high priests who prepared the ashes of the heifer (Par. 3:5).

Certain ceremonies which according to the biblical injunction demanded a confession or some declaration are taught in the Mishnah in the midrashic method of interpreting the Bible, such as: "'I have put away the hallowed things out of my house'—this refers to the second tithe and the fruit of plants in their fourth year; 'I have given them unto the levite'—this refers to the tithe of the levites; 'and also have given them'—this refers to the heave-offering and the heave-offering of the tithe . . ." (Ma'as. Sh. 5:10–13). Interpreted in a similar manner are the remarks of the priest anointed to accompany the army to battle (Sot. 8:1–2), of the officers to the people (Sot. 8:5–7), and of the priest when examining house plagues (Neg. 12:5–7).

Many laws of levitical cleanness and uncleanness and laws pertaining to the priesthood, to the legitimacy of families, and their genealogy presumably had their source in priestly circles (see Er. 10:15; Shek. 8:1–2; Ḥag. 3:5; Sanh. 9:6). Some priestly laws relating to other spheres have also been preserved in the Mishnah (RH 1:7; Ket. 13:1–2). Similarly, the *halakhot* concerning trustworthiness with regard to the heave-offering, tithes, and degrees of uncleanness and cleanness apparently originated in groups that united for the scrupulous observance of these *halakhot* (Dem. 2:2–3; Ḥag. 2:7, 3:6–7). The rules governing the admission of new members to such groups as described in the Mishnah (and in the Tosefta) have parallels in those regulating admission to the society of the Essenes, to the sect of *yaḥad* (the Qumran community), and to similar groups among other peoples—parallels which confirm the antiquity of the formulation and phraseology of these *halakhot*.

Many *halakhot* in the Mishnah have their source in the judgments of *battei din* in cases which came before them. Established as precedents, these judgments were adopted as the *halakhah*. The number of *halakhot* in the Mishnah which have their origin in a *bet din*'s decisions is larger than would appear at first sight. Whereas in the Mishnah in the order of *Mo'ed* 24 such judgments are cited, the Tosefta of the same order has 80. Frequently, the substance of the judgment has been omitted, the Mishnah contenting itself with a testimony on the *halakhah* given in that particular case, and at times, the nature of the testimony has also been left out and only the plain *halakhah* is stated. Proofs of this development largely derive from a comparison between the *halakhot* in our *mishnayot* and the *beraitot* in the Tosefta and in the Babylonian and Jerusalem Talmuds. Sometimes, however, this can be deduced by comparing parallel *mishnayot* in different tractates. Thus it is taught in *Parah* (6:4): "If one placed one's hand or foot or vegetable leaves (under running water) in order that the water should flow into a barrel, the water is unfit. If one placed there leaves of reeds or leaves of nuts, the water is fit. This is the general rule: If (the water is conducted into the barrel by means of) anything susceptible to uncleanness, it is unfit; (by means of) anything not susceptible to uncleanness, it is fit." In the parallel Mishnah in *Mikva'ot* (5:5) this *halakhah* is worded as follows: "R. Zadok testified that if flowing water exceeds dripping water (with which it is mixed), it is fit (as flowing water). If dripping water becomes flowing water, its flow may be blocked by a stick or by a reed or even by a man or a woman who has a running issue, and then one may go down and immerse oneself in it. This is the opinion of R. Judah. R. Yose says: One may not stop the flow of water with anything susceptible to uncleanness." The first *halakhah* was taught in terms of a testimony, the second in terms of a difference of opinion between R. Judah and R. Yose. But in the Mishnah in *Eduyyot* (7:3–4) it is explained: "R. Zadok testified that flowing water, which exceeds dripping water in quantity, is fit. There was such a case at Birat Happilya, and when the case came before the sages, they declared it fit. R. Zadok testified that flowing water, which was conducted through leaves of nuts, is fit. There was such a case at Ahalaya, and when the case came before (the sages in) the Chamber of Hewn Stone they declared it fit." There is not the slightest doubt that this case is the source of the Mishnah in *Parah*, of which Ḥiyya b. Abba said in the name of R. Johanan: "This Mishnah was taught on the testimony of R. Zadok" (Zev. 25b), the original expression "leaves of nuts" used by R. Zadok having been retained in it.

There were *halakhot* which were undoubtedly decided by the *tannaim* on the basis of the expositions of biblical verses, but here various stages of a clear development are to be distinguished from the Mishnah's beginnings to the days of Hillel, and from Hillel to the destruction of the Second Temple; similarly to be distinguished are the different approaches of R. Eliezer and R. Joshua on the one hand and of Neḥunya b. ha-Kanah and Nahum of Gimzu on the other, and even of R. Tarfon and R. Ishmael on the one hand and of R. Akiva on the other. It is interesting to note the reliance placed on the exposition of a biblical verse to support a *halakhah* in: "What was done with money collected for the freewill offerings? They bought with them burnt offerings, the flesh (of which) was for God and the hides for the priests"; this was (based on) the exposition of Leviticus 5:19 expounded by Jehoiada, the high priest, which was "It is a guilt offering"—refers to the priests' share while "he is certainly guilty before the Lord"—refers to the share of "the altar" (the Lord; Shek. 6:6). Of yet another priestly exposition Rabban Johanan b. Zakkai said: "The priests expounded this verse (in this way) for their own benefit" (Shek. 1:4). Nevertheless, Shemaiah and Avtalyon, who were known as "great interpreters," also did not wish to decide, on the basis of the interpretation of a biblical verse, that the festival sacrifice *(ḥagigah)* overrides the Sabbath (Pes. 70b). Although Hillel sat and interpreted biblical verses the whole day, the sons of *Bathyra refused to accept his views until he said to them: "Thus have I received the tradition from the mouths of Shemaiah and Avtalyon" (TJ, Pes. 6:1, 33a; and see Tos. 4:1 and Pes. 66a). R. Eliezer and R. Joshua were likewise disposed to accept interpretations and deductions only insofar as these confirmed a ruling of the sages which they had received (Neg. 9:3, 11, 7; see also Sot. 5:2; Naz. 7:4). Such interpretations, at first gradually accepted as a basis of the *halakhah*, were later increasingly adopted as such, with the curtailment of internal rule and the deprivation of the Sanhedrin's authority. In keeping with his general outlook on the Oral Law, R. Akiva compared the validity of such interpretations to that of a traditional (Mosaic) law *(*halakhah le-Moshe mi-Sinai)*. Many *halakhot* in our Mishnah, their source being taught there in accordance with R. Akiva's opinion (see later), are without doubt fundamentally based on interpretations of biblical verses. At times, however, prevailing circumstances imposed and determined the approach in these interpretations. One example of this will suffice: "'And the officers shall speak further to the people...' R. Akiva says: 'Fearful and faint-hearted' is to be understood literally, that is, he is unable to stand in the battle-ranks and see a drawn sword. R. Yose ha-Gelili says: 'Fearful and faint-hearted' refers to one who is afraid because of the transgressions he has committed" (Sot. 8:5). R. Akiva, who supported the revolt of Bar Kokhba, apparently preferred the literal meaning of the verse to its homiletical exposition.

How the Mishnah was Produced and Arranged. The great diversity which has been found in the sources of the *halakhah* provides grounds for assuming that the transmission and preservation of certain *halakhot* were the monopoly of the circles in which they originated and were developed. The *halakhot* relating to the Temple and sacrifices and to uncleanness and cleanness were undoubtedly known to the priests (see the laws of Ḥanina Segan ha-Kohanim: Pes. 1:6; Shek. 4:4) and the special Temple officers (Shek. 5:1), who were not always disposed to teach them to others (Yoma 3:11). Just as *halakhot* pertaining to damages, commercial transactions, and deeds were preserved by the judges of civil law in Jerusalem (Ket. 13:1–4) and elsewhere (the judges of Sepphoris; BB 6:7), so a tradition about *halakhot* which were forgotten by leading sages was similarly preserved by ordinary people. Thus the Mishnah states: "Hillel says: A *hin*-full of drawn water renders the *mikveh* unfit... and Shammai says: Nine *kavvim*. But the sages say: It is according to the opinion neither of the one nor of the other. But when two weavers from the Dung Gate in Jerusalem came and testified in the name of Shemaiah and Avtalyon, 'Three logs of drawn water render the *mikveh* unfit,' the sages confirmed their statement" (Eduy. 1:3).

Bet Shammai and Bet Hillel often differ in the interpretation of early *mishnayot* (Pes. 1:1; Kid. 1:1; Ḥul. 11:2; Oho. 7:3), and where no decision was reached regarding these differences of opinion, they were taught in each *bet midrash* in accordance with its own particular approach. Such was also the case with the disputes between Shammai and Hillel themselves, whose pupils differed on the character of these controversies. A Mishnah, for example, declares: "Whatever one ferments, or seasons, or makes *medumma* [mixing secular] with *terumah*, with *orlah*, or with 'mixed seeds' of the vineyard, is prohibited. Bet Shammai say: It also renders unclean; Bet Hillel say: Nothing renders unclean unless there be of it (a quantity in size) 'like an egg'" (Or. 2:4). However, then came "Dostai of Yatmah... and said: I received a tradition from Shammai the Elder who said: Never does anything render unclean unless there be of it (a quantity in size) 'like an egg'" (Or. 2:5, and see 2:12). Uncertainty about the meaning of early *halakhot* led the sages transmitting them to explain what was obscure in them, and in the course of such explanations, differing views were expressed.

The multiplicity of divergent opinions was a factor in expediting the arrangement of the *mishnayot*. One of those who undoubtedly arranged *mishnayot* was Joshua b. Hananiah who is reported as having said: "I have only heard" (Par. 1:1; Nid. 1:3), "I have heard explicitly" (Pes. 9:6; Yev. 8:4); and there are transmitted statements which "R. Joshua learnt thus," that is, worded in that particular way (Ta'an. 4:4; Tosef. Ḥul. 2:9). The tractate *Kinnim* which is dialectic in character and clarifies individual cases is the Mishnah of R. Joshua, as evidenced by its conclusion: "R. Joshua said: This is what (the sages) said..." (Kin. 3:6; and see Zev. 67b–68a).

To R. Joshua's Mishnah belong the *mishnayot* of *Tevul*

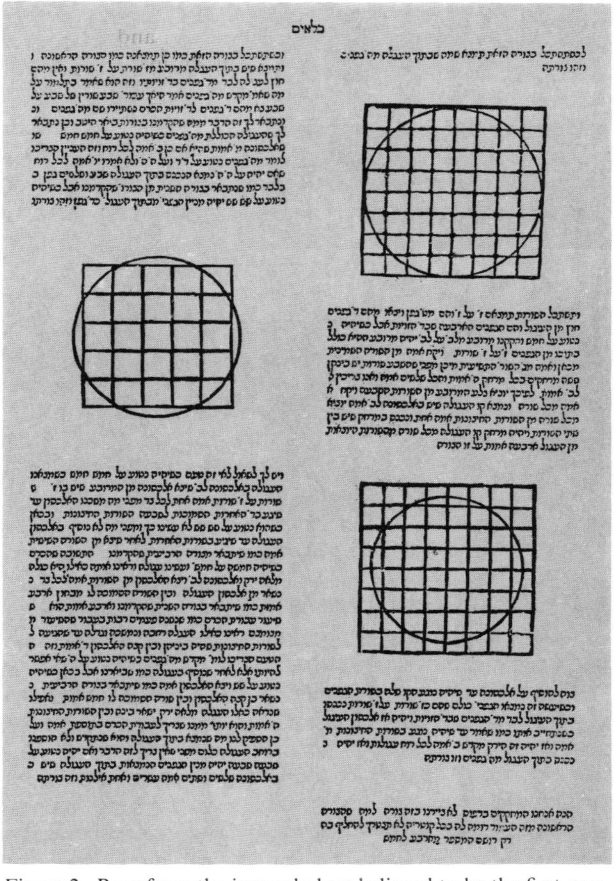

Figure 2. Page from the incunabulum believed to be the first complete printed edition of the Mishnah. Printed by Joshua Solomon Soncino, Naples, 1492. Jerusalem, J.N.U.L. Incunabula list, no. 55.

Yom 4:1–7 ("Concerning all these, R. Joshua said: This is an innovation which the scribes have introduced and I have nothing to reply"); those of *Zavim* 5:1–12 ("This was the general principle which R. Joshua formulated": 5:1; cf. Toh. 2:2: "R. Joshua says . . ."; and see Shab. 14a: "Rabbah b. Bar Ḥana said: It is R. Joshua (who holds this opinion)"); and those of *Me'ilah* 4:3–5 ("R. Joshua laid down the general rule"—4:3; cf. Yoma 8:2; and see Yoma 81a: "R. Ḥisda said: This has been taught as a difference of opinion and it accords with the view of R. Joshua"). *Niddah* 10:4 gives one of the three learned questions which the Alexandrians addressed to Joshua b. Hananiah (Nid. 69b), another being found in *Nega'im* 14:13, at the end of which it is explicitly stated: "This is what the men of Alexandria asked of R. Joshua." Reference has been made to the sophistical, theoretical questions in tractate *Kinnim*. When Eleazar Ḥisma, the pupil of R. Joshua, said "*Kinnim* and the calculations concerning the starting times of menstruants are essential ordinances" (Avot 3:19), he undoubtedly referred to R. Joshua's Mishnah on these subjects.

The arrangement of *halakhot* according to subjects is hinted at in *Ḥagigah* 1:8: "(The *halakhot* concerning) the dissolution of vows hover in the air and have no support. The *halakhot* concerning the Sabbath, festival offerings, and acts of trespass are like mountains suspended by a hair, for they have scant scriptural basis but many *halakhot*. The *halakhot* concerning civil cases and Temple services, levitical cleanness and uncleanness, and the forbidden relations have good support and are the essentials of the Torah." Besides those listed in this Mishnah, the Tosefta (Er. 11:24; Ḥag. 1:9) states that "there are, in addition to them, vows of valuation, dedications, immovable properties, and the second tithe, which have good support, many biblical verses being interpreted but few *halakhot*. Abba Yose b. Ḥanin says: These eight are the branches of the Torah, the essential *halakhot*." Abba Yose b. Ḥanin, who lived, as did R. Joshua, at the end of the Second Temple period, thus increased the number of halakhic collections mentioned in the Mishnah to eight divisions.

Like R. Joshua, Eliezer b. Hyrcanus taught and arranged the *halakhot* according to subject matter, and although his excommunication led to the supplanting of his Mishnah, remnants of it have nevertheless been preserved in our Mishnah: "R. Ilai said: I heard from R. Eliezer . . . I likewise heard from him . . ." (see Er. 2:6). *Ḥallah* 1:6 is identical with R. Ilai's statement quoting R. Eliezer (see Tosef. Ḥal. 1:6). At times, however, R. Eliezer's statements were ascribed to, and taught in the name of, R. Joshua (Sanh. 7:11: "R. Akiva said in the name of R. Joshua: Two who gather cucumbers . . .," whereas the Tosefta (Sanh. 11:5) has: "R. Akiva said: R. Eliezer interpreted three hundred *halakhot* . . . and I have learnt only two things from him . . . Two who gather cucumbers . . ."). The fact that R. Eliezer's statements were infrequently taught was responsible for numerous variants in them, but there were also deliberate changes—in that statements of his were quoted as those of R. Joshua so as to decide the *halakhah* in accordance with the latter. These substitutions increased to such an extent that it became necessary to issue a warning: "Whence do we learn that whoever substitutes R. Joshua's statements for those of R. Eliezer, and R. Eliezer's for those of R. Joshua, saying that what is clean is unclean and what is unclean is clean, violates a prohibition? From the biblical injunction (Deut. 19:14): 'Thou shalt not remove thy neighbor's landmark'" (Sif. Deut. 188; such substitutions were still made by the *amoraim:* see Pes. 27a; Shevu. 19a). Accordingly, it is not surprising that groups of *mishnayot* of R. Eliezer's Mishnah have not been preserved, an exception being the Mishnah *Parah* (1:1; 2:1; 4:1–3), which also contains many controversies between R. Eliezer and R. Joshua.

In addition to halakhic arrangements based on subject matter, there is also evidence of the study and arrangement of *halakhot* on the basis of other principles, as in the case, for example, of an entire tractate, *Eduyyot*. The following testimony has been preserved on the origin and production of this tractate: "When the sages assembled in Rabban Johanan b. Zakkai's *bet midrash* at Jabneh, they said: The time will yet come when a man will seek after one of the words of the Torah and not find it, after one of the words of scribes and not find it . . . That one of the words of the Torah shall not be like another, they said: Let us begin from Hillel and Shammai . . ." (Tosef. Eduy. 1:1). It is learnt from parallel sources that this assembly of sages at Jabneh took place in R. Joshua's old age (Tosef. Sot. 7:9–12; TJ, *ibid.* 3:4, 18d; and see ARN[1], 14, 58ff.; on the significance of the tradition that "*Eduyyot* was taught on that day," see Epstein, Tannaim, 422–5). The purpose of the tractate was to arrange, clarify, and decide on the controversies between Shammai and Hillel, Bet Shammai and Bet Hillel, and R. Eliezer and R. Joshua. The extant tractate of *Eduyyot* contains testimonies from earlier collections of *mishnayot*. Nor has it been preserved in its original form or even in a uniform version, the *halakhot* of a *tanna* also being taught in a group of *mishnayot* elsewhere, such as the decrees of Johanan the high priest (Ma'as. Sh., end; Sot. 9:10), the *halakhot* of two judges of civil law (Ket. 13:1, 3), and the regulations of Johanan b. Zakkai (RH 4:1–4).

In various tractates groups of *mishnayot* have been preserved with their arrangement based not on their contents but on their form. In *Megillah* 1:4–11 there are 13 *halakhot* on different subjects, all introduced by the formula "there is no difference between . . . and . . . save only." Since most of these *mishnayot* occur in various tractates each dealing with its own specific subject, and even the first of them ("there is no difference between the first Adar and the second Adar save only in the reading of the *megillah* . . .") is in effect taught in the first clause of that same Mishnah, it is evident that this entire group emanated from a *tanna*'s *bet midrash* in which its Mishnah was arranged not according to the contents of the *halakhot* but according to some common feature. This collection was undoubtedly more extensive, as attested by the *beraitot* in the Tosefta (Meg. 1:8–13), which, although using the same formula, have no parallel in the Mishnah. To this type of collection belong the *mishnayot* in *Arakhin:* there is no . . . less than . . . nor more than" (2:1–6), or "at times in the direction of leniency, at others in the direction of stringency" (3:1–5), and this formula is also found in various tractates in other *mishnayot* not included in *Arakhin* (Or. 2:6–7; Ned. 10:8; Me'il. 1:4) but undoubtedly once part of the same collection. In a number of *mishnayot* in Menaḥot (3:4–4:4) that have the common formula, "the (absence of) one invalidates the other," there are *halakhot* which are otherwise unknown, such as: "Of the four portions of Scripture in the *tefillin*, the (absence of) one invalidates the others" (3:7), and "the (absence of the) blue (in the fringes) does not invalidate the white" (4:1). A similar series of *mishnayot* arranged according to some external principle is contained in *Ḥullin* 1:4–7 ("what is valid for . . . is invalid for . . ."; "when there is . . . there is no . . ."), in *Me'ilah* 4:1–6 ("can combine with one another"), a collection used already by R. Joshua (*ibid.* 4:3: "R. Joshua laid down the general rule": see above, and in *Niddah* 6:2–10 ("all that . . . but there may be . . .")). Similar to these arrangements of *mishnayot* are collections which are based not only on a common stylistic formula but also on a common principle, such as *Ketubbot* 2:2–5 ("the mouth that forbade is the mouth that permitted"), *Gittin* 3:3 ("on the presumption that he is still alive"), *Gittin* 4:2–5:4 (*halakhot* instituted "as a precaution for the general good"), and *Nazir* 9:4 ("there is a basis for it").

Although, therefore, it is clear that collections of *mishnayot* arranged according to various principles existed, their extent cannot be determined. As has been seen, the work of arrangement allowed room for the continued growth of the *halakhot* in the academies of the *tannaim* both in Jabneh and elsewhere after the destruction of the Second Temple. Excelling all others in this sphere was R. Akiva, "the father of the Mishnah," of whom it was said that he systematized Midrash *(halakhah), halakhot (mishnayot),* and *aggadot* (TJ, Shek 5:1, 48c). Judah ha-Nasi said, "To whom can R. Akiva be compared? To a worker who took his basket and went forth. He found wheat which he put in it, he found barley which he put in it, he found spelt which he put in it, lentils which he put in it. When he entered to recite a blessing, he separated the wheat by itself . . . In a like manner R. Akiva arranged the entire Torah" (ARN[1] 18, p. 67; and see Rashi, Git. 67a). There is the well-known statement of R. Johanan (Sanh. 86a): "(The author of) an anonymous Mishnah is R. Meir; of an anonymous Tosefta, R. Nehemiah; of an anonymous (dictum in the) *Sifra,* R. Judah, and in the *Sifrei,* R. Simeon; and all are taught in accordance with the view of R. Akiva." This means that in his Mishnah R. Meir taught that of R. Akiva anonymously, and hence one never finds in the Mishnah "'R. Meir says in the name of R. Akiva,' since as R. Johanan declared: Everyone knows that R. Meir was the pupil of R. Akiva" (TJ, Ber. 1:14b). R. Akiva explained the earlier *halakhot* (Makhsh. 4:9: "R. Akiva says," but in the Tosef., *ibid.* 2:9: "R. Akiva explained"), and where his teachers and colleagues said, "I am unable to explain this" (Yev. 8:4; Tosef. Zev. 1:8), he amplified, defined (Pe'ah 4, 5; Tosef. Pes. 1, 7 [cf. Mishnah *ibid.* 2:1]; Shab. 1:7; Tosef., *ibid.* 1:22; Shab. 18b), and gave a ruling (Ma'as. Sh. 2:4; Suk. 3:9). By expositions of biblical verses he controverted earlier *halakhot,* and he did not always pay regard to testimonies and traditions (Nid. 6:11; Tosef., *ibid.* 6:6; Nid. 52b). But on occasion he also retracted his former view (Uk. 3:2, after his retraction; see Tosef., *ibid.* 3:2). It is explicitly said in the Talmuds of many *mishnayot:* "Whose opinion does the Mishnah represent? R. Akiva's" (Yev. 52b; Av. Zar. 51b; Bek. 32b). Groups of *mishnayot* in various tractates can, from parallel passages, be shown to be from the Mishnah of R. Akiva: *Yevamot* 10:3 occurs in the Tosefta (*ibid.* 11:6) as "the words of R. Meir in the name of R. Akiva," while the style of "some (women) are permitted . . . and forbidden . . ." (Yev. 9:1) is reminiscent of the language of *Mikva'ot* 7:1, which is the Mishnah of R. Akiva ("R. Akiva said: R. Ishmael once argued against me"). There are grounds for maintaining that other similarly formulated *mishnayot* derive from R. Akiva's Mishnah, such as: "Some bring first fruits *(bikkurim)* and recite (the declaration) . . . others bring them but do not make the declaration . . ." (Bik. 1:1), and "some women bring an offering . . . and some do not bring one" (Ker. 1:3). At times his aggadic conclusion of a tractate has been preserved, as, for example, in Yoma.

R. Akiva's pupils, who in principle accepted his method of arrangement and his Mishnah, but were divided in their views as to both its contents and the formulation of *halakhot,* introduced into their *mishnayot* collections some of the teachings of other *tannaim,* even citing their words anonymously. R. Judah did this with the Mishnah of R. Eliezer (Zev. 3:6; see Tosef., *ibid.* 2:17). R. Yose, who received the tradition from Johanan b. Nuri (Ket. 1:10; Tosef., Shev. 4:13; Meg. 2:4) and was the pupil of R. Ḥalafta, disagreed with R. Akiva (Tosef., Ma'as. Sh. 1:13; BB 2:15), and at times their Mishnah is taught anonymously in accordance with R. Ishmael's view (Ket. 5:8). Our Mishnah embodies also collections whose relation to R. Akiva's Mishnah is not clear but which in any event used earlier compilations. To this category belongs the group of Abba Saul's *mishnayot.* In *Gittin* 5:4 it is said: "A guardian who was appointed by the father of the orphans is required to take an oath (when they come of age), but if he was appointed by the *bet din* he need not take an oath. Abba Saul says that the rule is the reverse." Abba Saul did not use these words; his Mishnah had the opposite version in full, but Rabbi or some predecessor of his worded the Mishnah in this abbreviated form. In *Kiddushin* 4:1 there is the statement: "Ten genealogical classes returned to Ereẓ Israel from Babylon: priests, levites, Israelites, . . . *netinim, shetuki* (one whose father is unknown), and foundlings . . . Abba Saul called the *shetuki, 'beduki.'*" What this means is that in his Mishnah of "Ten genealogical classes" Abba Saul had the word *beduki* instead of *shetuki.* At times Abba Saul's Mishnah is distinguished not by a different version but by additions, such as in *Ketubbot* 7:6, which, after listing the women who are to be divorced without receiving their *ketubbah,* adds: "Abba Saul said: A wife who curses her husband's parents in his presence also," since this had been included in his Mishnah in addition to those previously enumerated. Accordingly, wherever it is stated in the Mishnah "So-and-so says: Also . . .," it may be assumed that the redactor of the Mishnah had before him that *tanna*'s Mishnah which contained this supplementary statement. On this basis it is possible to distinguish, for example, in *Ma'aserot* 5:8, the Mishnah which preceded R. Meir and R. Yose and which was undoubtedly that of R. Akiva, and to recognize the differences between R. Meir's Mishnah and that of R. Yose (see Lewy, *Ueber einige Fragmente aus der Mischna des Abba Saul,* 1876, see bibl.). Remnants of earlier *mishnayot* collections are also indicated, in the absence of a controversy, by the expression "So said R. So-and-so" (Shab. 12:3; Suk. 2:1), which denotes that this *tanna's* statement is a continuation of the preceding one, as was said by R. Johanan in *Demai* 3:6 (TJ, 23d): "The first part of the Mishnah, too, accords with R. Judah's opinion" (see Git. 61b; and see Epstein, Tannaim, 123). By these and similar means remnants of the *mishnayot* collections of R. Yose, R. Simeon, R. Eleazar, and others can be distinguished.

Judah ha-Nasi (=Rabbi)'s Method of Redacting the Mishnah. All that has thus far been said about the existence of various *mishnayot* collections and their incorporation in our Mishnah clearly shows that Judah ha-Nasi embodied in his Mishnah most of the *mishnayot* (BM 33b). Thus Samson of Chinon declared: "Although Rabbi [Judah ha-Nasi] systematized the *mishnayot,* they had previously been systematized, but he stated the *halakhah* both anonymously and according to the views of a score of disciples of the sages, one saying this, another this, and he this, as he deemed right. But neither the Mishnah nor the tractate was displaced, and he arranged it in its original order. There is evidence for this from the end of tractate *Kelim* where it is said: 'R. Yose observed: Blessed are you, *Kelim.* For though you entered with uncleanness, you have gone forth with cleanness.' This was said because it begins with 'fathers of uncleanness' and ends with 'a grasshopper is clean.' If Rabbi, when arranging the Mishnah, changed the order laid down by his predecessors, how could R. Yose have made this statement, seeing that he preceded Rabbi's arrangement of the Mishnah, and by what means then could he have known how it would begin and how it would end . . .

This was the method adopted by Rabbi's predecessors and he followed in their footsteps ..." (Samson of Chinon, *Sefer Keritot, "Leshon Limmudim,"* pt. 2 no. 58, S.B.D. and J. M. Sofer, ed. (1965), 267ff.).

Even as Rabbi undoubtedly embodied in his Mishnah many sources that were available to him, and did so in their original phraseology, formulation, and order, so it can likewise be shown that he not only incorporated the available *halakhot,* but changed their content, combined various sources, added to them, and also laid down authoritative rulings. This is attested by statements of *amoraim* in their argumentations, such as "the Mishnah represents an individual opinion" (Suk. 19b; *Iggeret Rav Sherira Ga'on,* ed. by B. M. Lewin (1921), 54), "I taught that as the opinion of an individual" (Ḥul. 55b, and variant readings), "all this chapter is the teaching of R. Meir except that the name of its author has been changed" (TJ, Git. 8:5, 49c). The *amoraim* saw in Rabbi's manner of stating *mishnayot* anonymously what was tantamount to a decision by him in favor of this or that *tanna.* The Mishnah in *Ḥullin* 8:1 says: "It is forbidden to cook any flesh in milk, except the flesh of fish and of locusts ... If a person vowed to abstain from flesh, he may partake of the flesh of fish and locusts." Against this the objection was raised (*ibid.* 104a) that "The first clause of the Mishnah is in accordance with the view of the rabbis, the second in accordance with that of R. Akiva." To this objection the reply was that "with regard to vows he (Rabbi) adopted the view of R. Akiva and with regard to flesh (cooked) in milk he adopted that of the rabbis." On the contradiction between the *mishnayot* in *Ḥullin* 6:2 and 8:3, Ḥiyya b. Abba said (*ibid.* 85a): "Rabbi approved R. Meir's view on the law of 'It and its young' and stated it in the Mishnah as the view of the sages, and he approved R. Simeon's view on the law of covering up the blood and stated it in our Mishnah as the view of the sages." Similarly, the *amora* R. Joseph resolved the contradictions which he found in a Mishnah by assuming that Rabbi stated it anonymously in one part in accordance with the view of one *tanna* and in another in accordance with that of another *tanna.* "The authority here is Rabbi, and he decides now in accordance with one, now in accordance with another *tanna*" (RH 7b, and parallels). These explanations of the *amoraim* were not only intended to resolve such difficulties but actually accorded with Rabbi's method of redacting the Mishnah, as a comparison of parallel sources shows. On the Mishnah in *Yevamot* (8:6): "R. Eleazar stated (for copulation) with a hermaphrodite the penalty of stoning is incurred as if he were a male," there is Rabbi's testimony (*ibid.* 84a): "When I went to learn Torah under R. Eleazar b. Shammu'a, his pupils combined against me ... and did not let me learn more than this single thing in our Mishnah ..." It is evident that Rabbi incorporated R. Eleazar's statement in the Mishnah.

Not all the *mishnayot* in which Rabbi's name occurs are additions, some of them being in fact his own Mishnah. In the Mishnayot of R. Meir, R. Judah, and R. Yose, Rabbi altered their statements "I say ... and they say" or "So-and-so said and I say" (see Tosef. Git. 1:5: "R. Eleazar said, I said to Meir ..."), substituting for them "R. Meir (or R. Judah or R. Yose) says." Similarly the *tanna* of Rabbi's *bet midrash* altered the phrase "I say" to "Rabbi says." There are *mishnayot* which were taught in accordance with Rabbi's decision, even though the expression "the words of So-and-so are acceptable in ...," indicating a ruling, is not explicitly mentioned in the Mishnah (cf. Shev. 10:1 with Tosef. *ibid.* 8:3; Shab. 8:5 with Tosef. 8:20; et al.; Ar. 8:5 seems to be an addition on the basis of Tosef., *ibid.* 4:33; it is not to be found in the Munich Ms.), but is learnt from the parallel *beraitot.* In *Ḥullin* 8:3 it is said: "If a drop of milk fell on a piece of meat (in a pot boiling on the fire) and imparted a flavor to that piece of meat, the latter is forbidden. If the pot was stirred, then it is forbidden only if (the drop of milk) imparted a flavor (to all that was) in that pot." Rabbi's decision in the Tosefta (*ibid.* 8:6) is: "If a drop of milk fell on a piece of meat, R. Judah says: (It is forbidden) if it imparted a flavor to that piece of meat; and the sages say: (It is forbidden if it imparted a flavor to all that was) in that pot. Rabbi said: The words of R. Judah are acceptable if he neither stirred nor covered the pot, and the words of the sages if he stirred or covered it." (See Shev. 10:1 and cf. Tosef., *ibid.* 8:3; Ma'as. Sh. 4:7 and cf. Kid. 6a.)

The state of the extant sources does not enable us to decide whether, in redacting the Mishnah, Rabbi applied a single, uniform, and comprehensive principle. The nature of the sources at his disposal and the extent of their circulation among the sages determined, apparently, his attitude to them, what he should accept or reject, adopt in its original phraseology and form, or emend and change. Thus on the one hand it is stated that a Mishnah "was not removed from its place" and that *mishnayot* were stated anonymously although contrary to Rabbi's view (Ber. 4:5, and see Tosef., *ibid.* 3:18; see also RH 19b; Bek. 51a). On the other hand, the statement is also found: "The *tanna* of the Mishnah is Rabbi himself, who incorporates the views of both *tannaim.* For the laws of uncleanness he gives the view of R. Ishmael, and for the laws of oaths the view of R. Akiva." In explaining this, R. Ashi said: "I repeated this statement to R. Kahana, and he said to me: Do not think that Rabbi simply incorporated in the Mishnah the view of both *tannaim* and that he did not agree with them. The fact is that Rabbi himself, for reasons of his own, agrees (with the one in the one case and with the other in the other case"; Shevu. 4a). These and similar circumstances (TJ, Sot. 3:6, 19b; and see above) leave no doubt that Rabbi, in conformity with his usual procedure, gave a ruling by deciding between conflicting sources. The Mishnah is undoubtedly not a work of judicial decisions nor merely "a collection of the Oral Law" (Ḥ. Albeck, *Mavo la-Mishnah,* (1959), 274) but rather a legal canon, not only because it contains *mishnayot* which Rabbi stated either in conformity with his decision or as anonymous *mishnayot* without quoting the divergent opinions mentioned in the *baraita,* but because, in the very act of selecting and combining extracts from the *mishnayot* collections of various academies, he apparently aimed at imparting diversity to his Mishnah and making it representative of all the known collections of *mishnayot,* so as to ensure for it universal acceptance. By doing so he decided the *halakhah.* Rabbi's collection became the Mishnah and all the rest *beraitot.* A "canon" was established—a criterion on the basis of and in relation to which all the other *mishnayot* were evaluated—and this marked the finalization of the Mishnah. Yet our Mishnah, which is that of Rabbi, has additions and changes by Rabbi himself, introduced in the course of the many years during which he redacted and arranged it. It also incorporates additional decisions by his sons (Mak. 3:15; Avot 2:2) and even by his grandson (Av. Zar. 2:6, see Tos. 36a s.v. *asher*), as well as additions based not only on *beraitot,* and indicated as such in manuscripts (see Ket. 7:6, Ms. Cambridge), but also on the Talmud, principally aggadic additions at the end of tractates and chapters. However, no material which could modify or alter its essence was now embodied in the Mishnah, as had previously been done with other *mishnayot* collections. Instead the new subject matter was incorporated in the Talmud and studied as an exposition of the Mishnah. In this way Rabbi created a legal codex which did not spell the conclusion of the *halakhah* but rather provided it with a common and stable basis. This was apparently his purpose in redacting the Mishnah.

The Question of Committing the Mishnah to Writing. This question is bound up with the problem of the writing down of the Oral Law on which there were divergent views between the *geonim* and the early authorities. Saadiah Gaon, R. Samuel b. Hophni, Rabbenu Nissim, and Maimonides held that each sage committed the Oral Law to writing for himself, as did Rabbi, too, in the case of the Mishnah. However, Rashi and those who followed his view maintained that nothing was written down in earlier times, and even the Mishnah and the Talmud were not committed to writing until the days of the *savoraim*. In the literature of the sages the prohibition against committing it to writing is explicitly mentioned (Tanḥ., Va-Yera 5; *ibid.*, Tissa 34; Tem. 14a–b). Nonetheless, evidence is not lacking that practical halakhic decisions were written down (TJ, Git. 5:3, 46d; Ket. 49b; BM 114a; Ḥul. 95b; Men. 70a). Modern scholars have sought to adduce proofs for the one or the other view from the emendations and corrections of the Mishnah found in the Talmuds, some pointing to mistakes which result from the transposition of written letters or from homoeoteleuton. Against this, however, it is argued that such mistakes could also occur in oral transmission. The Mishnah was clearly taught orally and its teachers, who are called *tannaim* (Sot. 22a), acted as its living books; but this still does not prove that there were not also written books. Nor can it be determined whether the *tanna* Isaac Ruba, of whom Judah ha-Nasi said, "every Mishnah has been critically examined by him," was not the keeper of a written copy of the Mishnah.

The Division of the Mishnah. The Mishnah is divided into six orders *(sedarim)*. The expression *shita sidrei mishnah* ("the six orders of the Mishnah") was first used by R. Ḥiyya in the Babylonian Talmud (Ket. 103b; BM 85b), the corresponding term in the Ereẓ Israel Midrashim (Song R. on 6:4, no. 2; Esth. R. 1:12) being *shishah sidrei mishnah* or *shishah erkhei mishnah*. Resh Lakish listed the sequence of the orders, which he based on the verse (Isa. 33:6): "And there shall be faith in thy times, strength, salvation, wisdom, and knowledge": "faith" refers to the order *Zera'im* ("Seeds"), "thy times" to the order *Mo'ed* ("Festivals"), "strength" to the order *Nashim* ("Women"), "salvation" to the order *Nezikin* ("Damages"), "wisdom" to the order *Kodashim* ("Holy Things"), and "knowledge" to the order *Tohorot* ("Purities"; Shab. 31a). A different sequence of the orders is given in the name of R. Tanḥuma who based it on another verse: *Nashim, Zera'im, Mo'ed, Kodashim, Tohorot,* and *Nezikin* (Mid. Ps. 19:14). There was undoubtedly no fixed sequence to the orders. Each order is divided into *massekhtot* ("tractates"), the word, signifying literally a web of woven fabric *(tractatus)*, being first mentioned by R. Ḥiyya (Shab. 3b). Whereas the number of tractates is reckoned as 63, it is given in *Song of Songs Rabbah* on 6:9, no. 2 and in parallel passages as 60, *Bava Kamma, Bava Meẓia,* and *Bava Batra* being regarded as one tractate, that of *Nezikin* ("the whole of *Nezikin* forms one tractate"; BK 102a), as were also *Sanhedrin-Makkot*. The sequence of the tractates in the various orders differed. Except for the first order, the tractates in the remaining five orders were apparently arranged according to their size and the number of their chapters. Thus, for example, in the order *Mo'ed,* the tractate of *Shabbat,* in which there are 24 chapters, comes first, while *Mo'ed Katan* and *Ḥagigah,* each with three chapters, come last. In the Munich manuscript of the Babylonian Talmud, *Berakhot* comes at the end of the order *Mo'ed,* and in the *Aggadot ha-Talmud* at the beginning of the order. In the order *Zera'im* there are differences in the Mishnah, Tosefta, and various manuscripts, in the sequence of the tractates. The chapters as well as some of their titles are mentioned in the Talmud, but the extent of a chapter was neither fixed nor identical, there being many variations and even errors in it. The division into *mishnayot* or *halakhot* was in the main known to the Jerusalem and Babylonian Talmuds. However, the length of an individual Mishnah is not identical in our Mishnah, the Babylonian Talmud, and the Jerusalem Talmud, the division in the printed editions of the Babylonian Talmud being a practical one, intended to facilitate the study of the Talmud. However, in manuscripts, in which the Mishnah is given at the beginning of each chapter, the division differs in several respects, while in early manuscripts it is not indicated by numbers but by spaces, and there are modifications and transpositions in the sequence of the *mishnayot*.

The Text of the Mishnah. The influence of the *tannaim*, teachers of the Mishnah, was considerable. They emended it in accordance with the statements of *amoraim* whose interpretation they incorporated in it, so that the later *amoraim* were at times unaware that the text of a particular Mishnah was not the original one but had been emended by those who taught it (Ber. 1:1; TJ *ibid.* 1:1, 3a; TB *ibid.* 9a). Yet even though the early *amoraim* disagreed with a Mishnah, they refrained from emending it or changing its wording (TJ, Shab. 11:1, 13a: "Rav said: Here it should not read 'exempted' but 'permitted'") or taught their view by giving the text and commenting on it (Er. 99a: "R. Johanan said: Reverse the statement"; and see Rashi, ad loc., s.v. *muḥlefet*). From the third generation of *amoraim* onward, however, emendations also increased by reason of the problems raised by this intensive study. In the Babylonian Talmud the terms used to indicate emendations are אימא *(eima)*, תני *(tani)*, איפוך *(eipukh)*, סמי מכאן *(samei mi-kan)*, אינה משנה *(einah mishnah)*, הכי קאמר *(hakhi ke-amar)*, הכי קתני *(hakhi ka-tanei)*, and in the Jerusalem Talmud אין כאן *(ein kan)*, לית כאן *(leit kan)*, כיני מתניתא *(keini matnita)*. In the course of time variants arose between Babylonia and Ereẓ Israel (BM 4:1, and see TJ 9c and TB 44a), as well as between the various academies in these two countries. The additions and emendations of the *amoraim* in one center were not taught in the other. From this derived also the considerable differences between the extant manuscripts, in some of which there are early additions such as are not found in the majority of printed versions. The most important extant manuscripts are the Kaufmann manuscript in the Library of the Hungarian Academy of Sciences in Budapest (a photographic reproduction was published in 1930); Parma manuscript 168; Cambridge manuscript 73 (published by W. H. Lowe, under the title *Matnita de-Talmuda di-Venei Ma'arava,* 1883); and Oxford manuscript 117, which also contains Maimonides' commentary, regarded as his holograph (published by R. Edelmann and S. D. Sassoon, 1956–66). Complete manuscripts of the Mishnah are also found in the Munich manuscript, the only complete one of the Babylonian Talmud (a photographic reproduction of it was published, 1912), and in a single manuscript of the Jerusalem Talmud, Leyden Scaliger 3. Manuscripts of individual orders and tractates are found on all the sections of the Talmud. The Mishnah in manuscripts of tractates of the Babylonian Talmud does not represent the authentic Babylonian version, even as that in the Jerusalem Talmud does not always reflect the Ereẓ Israel version. The reason is that, copying as they did from Mishnah texts in their possession, the copyists of the Talmuds at times placed at the beginning of a tractate of the Babylonian Talmud a Mishnah taken from a text written according to the Ereẓ Israel version, and similarly the version of a Mishnah at the beginning of a chapter in the Jerusalem Talmud does not accord with that of the Ereẓ Israel tradition. Distinguished by an unusual spelling, manuscripts of the Ereẓ Israel version of the Mishnah, such as the Kaufmann manuscript, also preserve remnants of the living language of Ereẓ Israel, whereas in the Babylonian version these features are blurred—the phraseology, style, and vocalization of the Mishnah having been given a literary quality. Great importance attaches to the many *genizah* fragments of the Mishnah and of the Talmuds dispersed in various libraries for fixing the text and the vocalization of the Mishnah.

Printed Editions of the Mishnah. The Mishnah was first printed in Spain in about 1485. But since only individual pages of this edition have been preserved, that printed at Naples in 1492 and comprising the entire Mishnah as well as Maimonides' commentary is generally regarded as the first edition. It inclines mainly to the Jerusalem text, although several of its passages were emended in accordance with that of the Babylonian, as were most of the later printed versions of the Mishnah from that of Venice 1546/7 onward. Particularly important is the edition of Yom Tov Lipmann Heller, who, availing himself of manuscripts, produced a corrected version of the Mishnah. First published with his commentary *Tosafot Yom Tov* in Prague, 1614–17, it became the basis of all subsequent editions. As yet there is no critical edition of the Mishnah which includes all the variant readings contained in manuscripts, *genizah* fragments and quotations of the Mishnah found in the Talmuds and in the works of the early authorities and their commentaries. Basic research and preparatory work for such an edition are incorporated in J. N. Epstein's *Mavo le-Nusaḥ ha-Mishnah* (see bibl.).

Commentaries on the Mishnah. The contribution made in the geonic period to explaining the Mishnah was meager, for the struggle against Karaism did not permit of the Mishnah's being separated from the Talmud and of emphasizing its individual value. Nevertheless there are evidences that the *geonim*, Saadiah Gaon and Ḥai Gaon wrote commentaries on the Mishnah, but these are no longer extant nor is their scope known. *Perush ha-Ge'onim al Seder Tohorot* (published by J. N. Epstein, 1921–24), a collection of several geonic commentaries thought to have been compiled by R. Simeon Kayyara (idem, in: *Tarbiz*, 16 (1945), 77), consists mainly of a glossary in which the words are explained on the basis of Aramaic, Arabic, Greek, and Persian analogues. In its comments the work relies not only on the Tosefta, the Talmuds, and the Targums (as well as the LXX, p. 63) but also on geonic interpretations and responsa. R. Nathan, the head of the academy, who flourished in the 11th century, wrote an Arabic commentary on the six orders of the Mishnah which is extant only in an extract made from it by a compiler, apparently in Yemen, and published in a Hebrew translation (*Mishnayot*, El Ha-Mekorot ed., 1955–58).

Maimonides, who attests that even the greatest of the *geonim*, when asked the explanation of a Mishnah, was constrained to answer, "I shall see what is said in the Talmud," restored to the Mishnah its diadem of independence by writing an Arabic commentary on the entire Mishnah which he called *Kitab al-Siraj* ("The Book of Light"). Beginning it in 1168, he spent seven years on his commentary, parts of which were translated into Hebrew by Judah al-Ḥarizi and R. Samuel ibn Tibbon, but it was only on the instructions of Solomon b. Abraham Adret that the entire commentary was translated in c. 1297 by several hands. As previously stated, the Hebrew version of the commentary was published in the first edition of the Mishnah (Naples, 1492) and has, since the Bomberg 1520–23 edition, been included in all printed editions of the Talmud. To his commentary Maimonides added an introduction on the development of the Oral Law, as well as prefaces to the orders and tractates. While Maimonides declared that for his commentary he selected the best talmudic explanations, he at times gave new interpretations, but in this respect also he had predecessors among the *geonim* (see B. M. Lewin (ed.), *Oẓar ha-Ge'onim* 8 (Ketubbot, 1939), 310; see also *Perush ha-Ge'onim al Seder Tohorot*, Makhshirin 5:9). Maimonides wrote two editions of his commentary, in the second of which he retracted several statements he had made in the first edition.

In the Middle Ages commentators paid special attention to the order *Zera'im* which has no Babylonian Talmud (except for *Berakhot*) and to the order *Tohorot* which has neither Babylonian nor Jerusalem *Gemara*. In the middle of the 12th century Isaac b. Melchizedek of Siponto in southern Italy wrote such a commentary, of which only that on *Zera'im* has been preserved (printed in the Romm, Vilna, edition of the Talmud). A comprehensive commentary on these two orders was written by the tosafist Samson of Sens at the end of the 12th century. Among the early authorities who composed commentaries on parts of the Mishnah, which are partially extant, mention should also be made of *Abraham b. David, *Elijah Menahem of London, and *Asher b. Jehiel. A complete commentary on the whole Mishnah was written only at the end of the 15th century by Obadiah *Bertinoro. First published at Venice in 1548–49, it was subsequently printed in almost all editions of the Mishnah and became the most popular and widespread commentary. Yom Tov Lipmann Heller wrote glosses to it, in which he not only supplemented his predecessor's commentary and added comments to passages that were still obscure, but chiefly contributed to laying down the correct text of the Mishnah (see above). At that time Solomon Adeni of Yemen composed at Hebron the work *Melekhet Shelomo*, which, although likewise supplementing Obadiah Bertinoro's commentary, in fact includes a large selection of the comments of his teacher Bezalel *Ashkenazi and in particular of Joseph *Ashkenazi, "the great *tanna* who always studied the *mishnayot* with a tune and corrected the entire Mishnah on the basis of various manuscripts" (published in the Romm, Vilna Mishnah). Solomon Adeni himself used manuscripts which he described as accurate or accurately written. Great popularity was enjoyed by Israel *Lipschuetz's *Tiferet Yisrael* (first published between 1810 and 1850; and afterward in the *mishnayot* printed in Warsaw and Vilna). This commentary bears witness to the influence of the Haskalah, not in its spirit but rather in its tone. Ḥayyim Naḥman Bialik began to produce a commentary on the Mishnah but succeeded in completing only the order *Zera'im* (1932). The project was taken up anew by the Bialik Institute, which published the whole Mishnah with the commentary of Ḥ. Albeck (introductions and supplements) and vocalized by H. Yalon, Jerusalem, 1957–50 (see bibl.).

Translations. The Mishnah, together with the commentaries of Maimonides and Bertinoro, was translated into Latin by Guilielmus Surenhusius (Amsterdam, 1698–1703) and into German by Johann Jacob Rabe (Onolzbach, 1760–63). Particular mention should also be made of the German translation, with a new commentary, under the editorship of David Hoffmann and with the collaboration of Edward Baneth and others (1887–1933), as also of H. Danby's English translation (1933). It was also translated into English by P. Blackman (7 vols., 1951–56).

See also *Talmud.

Bibliography: *Iggeret Rav Sherira Ga'on,* ed. by B. M. Lewin (1921); Frankel, Mishnah; J. Bruell, *Mevo ha-Mishnah* (1876–85); I. Lewy, in: *Zweiter Bericht ueber die Hochschule fuer die Wissenschaft des Judenthums in Berlin* (1876); D. Hoffmann, *Die erste Mischna und die Controversen der Tannaim* (1881); L. Ginzberg, *Studies in the Origin of the Mishna* (1920); Epstein, Mishnah; Epstein, Tanna'im, 13–240; idem, in: YMMY, 2 (1925), 5–22; Ḥ. Albeck, *Untersuchungen ueber die Redaktion der Mischna* (1923); idem, *Mavo la-Mishnah* (1959); E. E. Urbach, in: *Beḥinot,* 3 (1953), 74–80; idem, in: *Molad,* 17 (1959), 422–40; S. Lieberman, *Hellenism in Jewish Palestine* (1950), 83–99; H. Yalon, *Mavo le-Nikkud ha-Mishnah* (1964). [E.E.U.]

MISHNAT HA-MIDDOT (Heb. מִשְׁנַת הַמִּדּוֹת; "treatise of measures"), considered the earliest Hebrew geometry. *Mishnat ha-Middot* comprises various methods for determining the dimensions of various plane and solid geometric figures. Its five chapters include, among other matters, a discussion of triangles, quadrilaterals, and frusta. The Heronic formula for the area of a triangle in terms of the lengths of the sides is given. For π the value of 3 1/7 is used and this divergence from the biblical 3 is homiletically justified. One of the extant manuscripts has a sixth chapter dealing with the Tabernacle which is similar to sections of the **Baraita de-Melekhet ha-Mishkan.* In spite of the similar names, there seems to be no connection between this work and the **Baraita de-49 Middot* which is frequently cited by medieval commentators. This treatise is written in a distinctive Hebrew that combines mishnaic style with a technical terminology that has affinities with Arabic, although it stands apart from the Hebrew mathematical terminology of the Hispano-Arabic period. In content, the *Mishnat ha-Middot* belongs to the stream of oriental mathematics represented, e.g., by Heron, Greek mathematician (c. 100 C.E.) in the Hellenistic period, and al-Khwarizmi (c. 825 C.E.) in the Arabic period, to both of whose works it offers striking parallels. Some attribute it to R. *Nehemiah (c. 150 C.E.), and see it as a link between the Hellenistic and Arabic texts, while others assign it to an unknown author of the Arabic period.

Bibliography: S. Gandz (ed.), *Mishnat ha-Middot* (Eng., trans. 1932); Ẓarefati, in: *Leshonenu,* 23 (1958/59), 156–71; 24 (1959/60), 73–94. [B.WE.]

MISHPAT IVRI. This article is arranged according to the following outline:

DEFINITION AND TERMINOLOGY

The term *mishpat Ivri* (מִשְׁפָּט עִבְרִי) is now generally accepted as embracing only those matters of the **halakhah* (Jewish law) whose equivalent is customarily dealt with in other present-day legal systems, that is, matters pertaining to relations between man and man and not the precepts governing the relationship between man and his Maker. This definition diverges from the original meaning of the Hebrew term *mishpat* or *mishpatim.* Used in the sense of a system of laws—like the English term "law," or the German term *"Recht"*—the term refers not only to matters between man and man (in the sense of *jus, ius humanum*), but also to the precepts between man and his Maker (in the sense of *fas, ius divinum*). Thus for instance in Exodus 21:1 the words *ve-elleh ha-mishpatim* are stated by way of introduction to chapters 21, 22 and 23, which deal not only with matters of civil and criminal law but also with the laws of the sabbatical year, the Sabbath, first fruits, and so on.

Another Hebrew term for law is the word *dinim* (sing. *din*), used to designate matters included in the fourth mishnaic order, *Nezikin* (see Deut. 17:8; Ḥag. 1:8; *Ramban* Gen. 34:13). The term comprises two main classes of laws, namely *dinei mamonot* and *dinei nefashot.* The concept of *dinei mamonot* corresponds to but is not identical with "civil law," since it is wider than the latter in some respects (see Sanh. 2:2 and see below) and narrower in others, excluding, for instance, that part of family law dealing with what is ritually permitted and prohibited, the laws of usury, and so on. (Subject to this qualification, the term civil law will be used below and in the other articles on Jewish law as the equivalent of *dinei mamonot.*) The concept *dinei nefashot* takes in that part of the criminal law dealing with matters that call for capital and certain other forms of corporal punishment. (The term *dinei kenasot* relates to matters which are part of *dinei mamonot;* see *Obligation, Law of.) However, even the term *dinim* does not exclude matters concerning the precepts between man and God, as is evident from the concept of *dinei issur ve-hetter*—ritual prohibitions and permissions.

The reason for the absence in Hebrew sources of an accepted term describing legal norms pertaining exclusively to relations between man and man—for instance in the sense of "English law" or "Swiss law"—lies in the basic fact that both the laws applicable between man and man and the precepts concerning man and God have a single and common source, namely the *Written and the *Oral Law. This fact further asserts itself in the phenomenon that all parts of the entire halakhic system share and are subject to common modes of creation, thought and expression, as well as principles and rules (see below). This, however, constitutes no hindrance to the acceptance of the term *mishpat ivri* in the sense here described. The term first came to be used in this sense around the beginning of the 20th century, when the Jewish national awakening—which to some extent stimulated also the desire for a return to Jewish law—prompted a search for a Hebrew term to designate that part of the *halakhah* whose subject matter paralleled that which normally comprises other legal systems. What was sought was a suitable term that would circumscribe the bounds of the legal research and preparatory work to be undertaken. Thus there was accepted the term *mishpat "Ivri,"* in the same way as *safah "Ivrit"* and later also *medinah "Ivrit."* Today the term *mishpat Ivri,* as defined above, is generally accepted in all fields of practical legal life and research in the sense here described. In the Knesset legislation use is made of the term *din Torah* (authorized Eng. translation, "Jewish religious law": see, e.g., sec. 2, "Rabbinical Courts Jurisdiction (Marriage and Divorce) Law," 1953); this Hebrew term is inaccurate as far as the distinction between *de-oraita* and *de-rabbanan* (see below) is concerned.

"RELIGIOUS" HALAKHAH AND "LEGAL" HALAKHAH

Common Features. The "religious" and the "legal" norms of the *halakhah* share certain common features, a fact that finds expression in a number of ways (and accounts for our use of inverted commas since the *halakhah* does not recognize the concept of special "religious" law, which is used here in its modern sense). In the talmudic discussions the same theoretical argumentation, terminology, and modes of interpretation that are applied to a matter of civil law are applied also to matters concerning, for instance, the Sabbath, the sacrificial cult and ritual purity and impurity. Many legal principles are common to both parts of the *halakhah*. Thus for instance the laws of *agency apply in the same way to matters of **hekdesh*, **terumah*, and the slaughter of the paschal sacrifice, as they do to matters of marriage, divorce, recovery of debt, and so on. Moreover, the essential legal principle underlying the principal-agent relationship—that "a person's agent is as himself"—was derived by the scholars from the scriptural passages dealing with matters of the paschal sacrifice and *terumah* (Kid. 41b, etc.), and it is in relation to the laws of prayer that the solitary mishnaic reference to the above principle is made (Ber. 5:5). "Religious" directives are often found to be based on "legal" directives. This is illustrated in the discussions on the question of whether a person who has acquired the right to no more than the fruits of his neighbor's field, may, when bringing the first fruit, read the *Bikkurim* portion which includes the passage, "And now, behold, I have brought the first fruit of the land, which Thou, O Lord, hast given me" (Deut. 26:10), since this involves a declaration that the land is his. The answer is made dependent on the elucidation of a question of legal principle, whether acquisition of the fruits (*kinyan perot*) is as acquisition of the body (*kinyan ha-guf;* Git. 47b)—an elucidation which has important consequences in all fields of Jewish law.

To their common origin must also be attributed a mutual interaction between the two parts of the *halakhah*, with directions pertaining to the "religious" field supplementing lacunae in the "legal" field. This is illustrated in the law concerning the father's duty to maintain his children. In the *takkanah* of Usha, as finally accepted, it was laid down that the duty extended to children until the age of six years. In practice it sometimes happened that a father failed to maintain his minor children above the age of six and in such an event the court compelled the father to do so by applying two rules pertaining to the laws of charity: first, that a person who has sufficient for his own needs may be compelled to give charity if there is a poor man in need; secondly, that as regards the giving of charity, "the poor of a person's own household take precedence over the poor of his town, and the poor of his town over those of another town," and of all the poor the father's children are the nearest to him (Ket. 49b; Sh. Ar., YD 251:3, EH 71:1). Another illustration is found in the post-talmudic development regarding the establishment of an obligation by way of the promisor's vow or oath or undertaking on pain of ban to give or do according to his promise—whose fulfillment is imposed on him as a religious duty. This method was employed especially in the case of obligations which were incapable of being established in terms of the "legal" rules of the *halakhah*, such as an obligation relating to something not yet in existence (*Rema* ḤM 209:4), or one tainted with the defect of **asmakhta* (Sh. Ar., ḤM 207:19) and so on (see *Obligation, Law of).

Distinguishing Between "Religious" and "Legal" Halakhah—Ritual and Civil Law. A study of the halakhic sources reveals that the *halakhah*, notwithstanding its overall unity, distinguishes materially between the two main fields of its subject matter, between "matters of *mamon*" or "*mamona*" and "matters not of *mamon*" or "*issura*" (lit. "prohibitions," i.e., ritual law). Although the concepts of *issura* and *mamona* are not coextensive with the modern concepts of "religious" and "legal" law (see above), the material distinction made between them exerted a decisive influence on the evolutionary path taken by that large part of the *halakhah* embraced in the term *mishpat Ivri*. The first manifestations of the distinction date back to the time of Bet Shammai and Bet Hillel (Yev. 15a/b; Eduy. 1:12—"If you have permitted in a matter relating to the stringent prohibition of incest, shall you not permit in civil matters (*mamon*) which are less stringent?") and in the course of time it became entrenched in many fields of the *halakhah*, as illustrated in the following examples: As regards the freedom of stipulation, the principle was laid down that "when a person contracts out of the law contained in the Torah, a stipulation which relates to a matter of *mamon* is valid but one that relates to a matter not of *mamon* is invalid" (Tosef., Kid. 3:7–8). The explanation is that the legal order prescribed by the Torah in civil matters was not enjoined in the form of a binding obligation (i.e., *jus cogens*), but as conditional on the will of the parties (i.e., *jus dispositivum; Ramban*, Nov. BB 126b) except in cases of a stipulation inimical to personal freedom or the public weal (for details see *Contract). In case of an illegal contract the rule is that a contract whose fulfillment involves the transgression of law shall not be enforced, but transgression of a "religious" prohibition does not deprive the contract of legal validity and it will be enforced by the court; hence, "if a person sells or gives on the Sabbath, and certainly on festivals, even though he should be flogged, his act is effective" and an obligation undertaken on the Sabbath is similarly valid, "and a *kinyan* performed on the Sabbath (i.e., *kinyan sudar*, see *Acquisition) is valid, and the writing and handing over take place after the Sabbath" (Yad, Mekhirah 30:7).

The distinction between *issura* and *mamona* also has an important bearing on the question of legislative authority in Jewish law. While such authority was to some extent limited in matters of *issura*, it remained fully effective in matters of *mamona* (see **Takkanot*). So far as the legislative authority conferred on the public and its leaders was concerned, this never extended beyond matters pertaining to the civil law and criminal-police offenses (see **Takkanot ha-Kahal*). The distinction is also an important factor in the binding force of custom, particularly as regards the basic principle that "custom overrides the law," which is applicable in matters of the civil law exclusively (see **Minhag*). Similarly, different rules and principles of decision were laid down for civil and for ritual matters. A basic principle is that matters of ritual law are not to be learned from matters of civil law and vice versa, for the reason that on the one hand ritual matters are by their very nature of greater stringency than matters of the civil law, while on the other hand the rule that "the burden of proof rests on the person seeking to recover from his fellow" applies to civil but not to ritual law. Flowing therefrom are a number of rules applicable to matters of the ritual law only (for instance, that in certain circumstances "the majority is not followed in civil law matters"; BK 46b). It was likewise accepted by all scholars that the rule of **dina de-malkhuta dina* has no application to matters of ritual law (*Tashbeẓ*, 1:158, and see below), since all the reasons given for the adoption of the doctrine are relevant only to matters of the civil law. Thus the *halakhah* represents a unitary system of law with both its "religious" precepts and "legal" directions sharing a common origin and theoretical propagation as well as mutual principles and rules, the one part supplementing the other. At the same time the *halakhah*, as crystallized during its different periods, evolved a clear distinction between matters of *issura* and those of *mamona*, the latter being the counterpart of a substantial part of the subject matter of modern legal systems. This material distinction lent the legal part of the *halakhah*, which was the more sensitive and subject to the influence of changing social and economic realities, a wide flexibility and capacity for development.

LAW AND MORALS

Jewish law, like other legal systems, distinguishes between legal norms enforced by sanction of the courts and moral and ethical norms lacking such sanction. However, Jewish law also recognizes the existence of a special reciprocal tie between law and morality, a tie that stems from the common origin of both concepts in Judaic sources. The Pentateuchal commands, "Thou shalt not kill" and "Thou shalt not steal" (Ex. 20:13), are enjoined with the same finality as "Thou shalt love thy neighbor as thyself: I am the Lord" (Lev. 19:18), and the common origin of the concepts of law and morality remained a guideline for Judaism in all periods and generations (see, e.g., *Bertinoro* Avot 1:1). The stated tie finds expression in the fact that from time to time Jewish law, functioning as a legal system, itself impels recourse to a moral imperative for which there is no court sanction, and in so doing sometimes prepares the way to conversion of the moral imperative into a fully sanctioned norm. An illustration is to be found in the law of tort, where there are cases in which the tortfeasor is legally exempt from the payment of compensation—whether for lack of necessary causality between his act and the resultant damage, or because he acted with license, or for other reasons—yet with reference to many of these cases the rule was laid down that the person occasioning damage to another "is exempt according to the laws of man but liable according to the law of Heaven" (BK 6:4; BK 55b; and codes), or "he is exempt according to the law of man but his judgment is entrusted to Heaven" (Tosef., BK 6:6–17). Liability according to the law of Heaven means, according to some scholars, that although the court should not compel compliance by regular sanction it "should bring pressure to bear on him, verbally, without compulsion" (*Yam shel Shelomo*, BK 6:6); others held that the court should exercise no constraint—not even verbal—but should inform the individual: "We do not compel you, but you shall have to fulfill your duty to Heaven" (*ibid.*). Hence even the adjuration that the duty to Heaven must be fulfilled is addressed to the individual concerned by the court.

An instance of the conversion of a moral imperative into a legally sanctioned norm is to be found in the direction to act *li-fenim mi-shurat ha-din* (i.e., leniently, beyond the requirements of the law). In the Talmud this direction does not generally carry the import of a norm fortified by some form of sanction, and means only that it is fitting for the person who has a concern for his manner of conduct not to base his deeds on the strict letter of the law but to act leniently beyond the requirements of the law (as in the matter of restoring lost property or that of paying compensation for damage resulting from an erroneous opinion: BM 24b and 30b; BK 99b). As regards the talmudic matter concerning the exemption of workers from liability for damage caused by them—even though they are unable to prove the absence of negligence on their part—the *posekim* were divided on whether or not this involved an enforceable duty to act beyond the requirements of the law (*Mordekhai* and others; see *Baḥ* ḤM 12:4). In the post-talmudic era the direction to act *li-fenim mi-shurat ha-din* became, according to the majority of scholars, a full fledged legal norm enforced in certain instances by the court (for instance in the case of a wealthy litigant; *Baḥ* loc. cit. and *Rema* ḤM 12:2). See also *Law and Morality.

DE-ORAITA AND DE-RABBANAN

Jewish law, in fact the entire *halakhah*, distinguishes between two categories of law, expressed in the two Aramaic terms *de-oraita* ("of the Torah") and *de-rabbanan* ("of the scholars"). The second category is sometimes also termed *mi-divrei soferim* (a term which has an additional meaning, see Sanh. 88b, but is normally used as the equivalent of *de-rabbanan*) or *takkanat ḥakhamim*.

Distinguishing Between the Two Categories. Classification of the halakhic rules into these two categories is beset with many difficulties and has been the subject of much scholarly discussion and research (see Z. H. Ḥayyut (Chajes), *Torat ha-Nevi'im*, s.v. *"Torah she be-al peh"*; Ḥ. Albeck, *Mavo ha-Mishnah* (1959), 49–53). Certainly the rules expressly stated in the Pentateuch are *de-oraita*, while those clearly originating from the enactments or decrees of the scholars are *de-rabbanan*. More difficult is classification of the rules deriving from one of the different modes of Pentateuchal Midrash (exegesis, see *Interpretation). Maimonides held that any such rule was not to be considered *de-oraita* unless the interpretation accorded with a tradition from Moses at Sinai and the Talmud specifically lays down that the rule is *de-oraita* (*Sefer ha-Mitzvot*, rule no. 2). Naḥmanides held that such rules were *de-oraita* except when the Talmud specifically determines that the midrashic derivation of a particular rule amounts to no more than *asmakhta*, in which event the rule is *de-rabbanan* (*Hassagot ha-Ramban le-Sefer ha-Mitzvot*, ad loc.). Naḥmanides' opinion was accepted by a majority of the scholars (many of whom interpret Maimonides' view in a manner which tends to reconcile it with that of Naḥmanides). This, however, still does not constitute an adequate distinction, since there are *halakhot* which are regarded as *de-oraita* even though they are linked to particular scriptural passages by way of *asmakhta* alone, and there are also many *halakhot* which are regarded as *de-oraita* even though they do not originate from the legal source of Midrash (but from some other legal source, such as *sevarah*). Nor does classification of the *halakhah* into *de-oraita* and *de-rabbanan* necessarily have a bearing on the antiquity of a particular law, since it is possible that a law classified as *de-rabbanan* had its origin in a particularly ancient *takkanah*, whereas a later law may be classified as *de-oraita* because of its derivation from the interpretation of Pentateuchal passages. There are many institutions whose classification into one or other of the two stated categories occasioned doubt to the scholars of different periods, for instance, in the following matters: **ketubbah* (Ket. 10a; 110b); the husband's right to inherit his wife's property (Ket. 83a; Bek. 52b; and see *Succession); the husband's duty to maintain his wife (Ket. 47b; and see *Maintenance); *kinyan meshikhah* (BM 47b); and modes of acquisition deriving from trade custom (*Kesef ha-Kedoshim*, Sh. Ar., ḤM, 201:1) and other matters. There is accordingly no absolute and exhaustive classification of the *halakhah* into *de-oraita* and *de-rabbanan* and the only method of determining the class to which a particular law belongs is an examination of the Talmudic and post-talmudic literature to determine the manner in which such law was classified by the sages of the Talmud and scholars who decided and codified the *halakhah*.

Legal Consequences of the Classification. A basic divergence between the two categories of law occurs when there is doubt or dispute as to the applicability or scope of a particular rule in certain circumstances: in a *de-oraita* matter a stringent approach is required, whereas a lenient approach is indicated in a *de-rabbanan* matter (Beẓah 3b; Av. Zar. 7a). In some cases the scholars laid down alleviations of the law as regards a *de-rabbanan* legal obligation, even in the absence of any doubt as to the existence of such an obligation (for instance as regards recovery of the *ketubbah* money; Tosef., Ket. 13 (12):3 and Ket. 110b;

see also *Conflict of Laws) when special circumstances justified such leniency (Ket. 86a; *Rashbam* BB 132b). In general however the scholars "imparted to their enactments the force of rules of the Torah" (see Git. 64b–65a; Ket. 84a). When the scholars saw the need for introducing a basic legal institution into daily life, they sometimes even enforced a rule of the rabbinical law more restrictively than a rule of the Torah. For this reason it was laid down that the parties may not stipulate for the payment of a lesser **ketubbah* amount than that determined by the scholars, notwithstanding the rule of freedom of stipulation in civil matters, even those pertaining to the *de-oraita* law (Ket. 56a). The rule that a legal obligation classified as part of the rabbinical law has the same legal efficacy as a *de-oraita* obligation is of special importance in view of the fact that so many of the rules in all the different branches of Jewish law belong to the *de-rabbanan* category (particularly those concerning the modes of acquisition, and the laws of obligation and tort). Any diminished regard for the standing and validity of a rule of the rabbinical law would have entailed the possibility of a far-reaching effect on the manner of execution and enforcement of such rules (see detailed discussion in Radbaz, 1,503).

THE BASIC NORM AND THE SOURCES OF JEWISH LAW

Three Meanings of the Expression "Source of Law." Every legal system gives occasion for inquiry into the sources of its law *(fontes juris, Die Quellen des Rechts)*. The expression "source of law" has three principal meanings, which may be distinguished as literary, historical, and legal sources of law.

The literary sources of law (in German, *Die Erkenntnisquellen des Rechts*) are those sources which serve as the recognized and authentic literary repository of the various rules and directions of a particular legal system for purpose of ascertaining their content.

The historical sources are those sources which constitute the historical-factual origin of particular legal norms. Legal research is largely concerned with an investigation of the historical sources of the directions comprising a particular legal system, of the various influences of one legal system on another, and other similar questions. The historical sources of law, in the wide sense of the expression, may also include any economic, social, moral, or other factor that led to the creation of a particular legal norm and there are many instances of laws which were enacted in answer to particular economic or social needs.

The legal sources (in German *Die Entstehungsquellen des Rechts*) are the sources of law and means of creating law recognized by a legal system itself as conferring binding force on the norms of that system (see J. W. Salmond, *Jurisprudence* (1966), 109ff.).

The distinction between a legal and a historical source of law is of a material nature. The quest for the legal source of a particular norm is aimed at ascertaining the source from which the latter derives the force of law, that is, the principle within the relevent legal system which serves to confer binding validity on such a norm. Thus it is possible to ascertain that a norm has its legal source in statute or precedent and so on, without any need to be concerned with the factual background or historical origin of such a norm. Salmond states: "This is an important distinction which calls for careful consideration. In respect of its origin a rule of law is often of long descent. The immediate source of a rule of English law may be the decision of an English court of justice. But that court may have drawn the matter of its decision from the writings of some lawyer, let us say the celebrated Frenchman, Pothier; and Pothier in his turn may have taken it from the compilations of the emperor Justinian, who may have obtained it from the praetorian edict. In such a case all these things—the decision, the works of Pothier, the Corpus Juris Civilis, and the Edictum Perpetuum—are the successive material sources of the rule of English law. But there is a difference between them for the precedent is the legal source of the rule, and the others are merely its historical sources. The precedent is its source, not merely in fact, but in law also. The others are its sources in fact, but obtain no legal recognition as such" (op. cit., p. 109).

The historical sources of law play only an indirect role in the evolution of a legal system, as factors which either offer a possible course to follow by way of imitation (as in the absorption of a principle from a different legal system) or create a need for the further developement of such a legal system (as in the case of particular economic or social conditions). On the other hand, the legal sources play a direct role in the evolution of a legal system, serving as the sole means to add to, subtract from, or vary in any other way the existing norms of that system. This division of the sources of law into three classes is valid also for the Jewish legal system.

The Literary Sources of Jewish Law. VARIOUS CLASSES OF INFORMATIVE SOURCES OF LAW. The literary sources of a legal system constitute, as already mentioned, authentic sources for the ascertainment of its legal norms. Thus, for instance, the laws of a country may be ascertained from its official Statute Books. Similarly, knowledge of the law may also be gathered from what is called "the literature of the law." This includes the literature in which the law is discussed or interpreted, although that literature itself is not recognized as an authoritative and authentic source from which binding legal norms may be ascertained (e.g., legal textbooks and articles: see Salmond, op. cit. 112, n. C). From a certain standpoint even general literature may contribute greatly toward a better knowledge of a legal system. Thus, if an author gives a historical-economic description of a particular period and mentions bankruptcies and the imprisonment of debtors, it may be possible to learn from this that it was customary at that time to imprison a debtor for the nonpayment of his debt; this may be deduced from the contents of a book even though the author dealt only incidentally with the legal aspects of that subject. In this regard, both the literature of the law and general literature must be approached with caution and the degree of the author's accuracy and objectivity carefully examined in each case. These informative sources avail also in Jewish law. While its authoritative literary sources are the most important informative class, both literature of the law and general literature serve the important function of filling in the social and economic background to many legal norms. They are of added importance—subject to the above cautionary remarks—in relation to those periods when there were few authoritative literary sources, as was the position in Jewish law until the literary redactions undertaken in the tannaitic period. The different literary sources of the *halakhah* are briefly reviewed below in a general manner. (These are separately discussed elsewhere in greater detail; see, e.g., *Mishnah; *Talmud.)

FROM THE WRITTEN LAW UNTIL THE PERIOD OF THE TANNAIM. The Bible is not only the source of authority of the whole of the Jewish legal system (see below), it is also its first and foremost authoritative literary source. It contains legal directions which date from patriarchal times onward and are dispersed in specific books and chapters of the Pentateuch (Gen. 23:3–20; 31:41–43; Ex. 20–23; Lev. 5; 18–21; 24–25; 27; Num. 27:35–36; Deut. 1; 4–5; 15–17; 19–25). The next authoritative literary source is represented by the Books of the Prophets and the Hagiographa. From these information may be gained on the laws concerning the modes of acquisition (Ruth 4; Jer. 32 and see TJ, Kid. 1:5; 60c), the monarchy (I Sam. 8; I Kings 21), suretyship (Prov. 6: 1–5; 11–15, et al.), the laws confining criminal responsibility to the transgressor (II Kings 14:6), and so on. It may be noted that the Prophets and Hagiographa contain scant material of a legal nature. The attention of the prophets and chroniclers was mainly directed to the numerous internal and external wars of their times, to moral, social, and religious problems. Therefore the silence of these sources on different matters of the law cannot be interpreted as pointing to the absence of a legal order on such matters.

Much of the accumulated knowledge of Jewish law in the above period and for some time after can be found in the informative sources termed literature of the law and general literature. These include the *papyri (such as the Elephantine papyri of the fifth century B.C.E.), the *Septuagint (end of the third century B.C.E.), the writings of *Philo (first half of the first century), the writings of Josephus (the period of the Temple destruction), the *Apocrypha (from the fourth century B.C.E. until the year 200), and other works. This literature contains some *halakhot* which are identical to those quoted in talmudic literature and others which are sometimes contrary to it. This may indicate a possible development in certain norms of Jewish law or it may also be that this literature preserved *halakhot* that appeared in talmudic sources which are no longer extant. Great care is needed in deducing conclusions from this literature: sometimes it represents the viewpoint of small sects of even a single individual; sometimes it may show the influence of a surrounding legal system (as in the case of the Elephantine papyri); sometimes the particular author gathered a rule of Jewish law from a translation and not in its original form (as did Philo in making use of Greek translations); and sometimes the description of certain matters reveals a blatant tendentiousness (see, for instance, Jos., Ant. 4:279 (ed. Schalit) note 174; ed. Shor, note 3).

From the Tannaitic Period Until the Redaction of the Talmud. This period, spanning the lives of the *tannaim* and *amoraim*, gave rise to literary creations which constitute the classical sources of Jewish law and the starting point, until this day, for the study or discussion of any matter in it. Extant from tannaitic times are the following: compilations of halakhic Midrashim (see **Midreshei Halakhah* and *Interpretation); the Mishnah—compiled by Judah ha-Nasi and constituting the post-Mosaic "Corpus Juris" of Jewish law—and the *Tosefta (see *Codification of Law); other authoritative tannaitic literary sources are the **Beraitot* included in the two Talmuds, and **Megillat Ta'anit* which includes, besides descriptions of political and military events, halakhic and legal material. Authoritative amoraic literary sources are the Jerusalem Talmud and the Babylonian Talmud, which include commentaries and expositions on the Mishnah, *memrot* (new *halakhot* of the *amoraim*), *ma'asim* (i.e., cases, see **Ma'aseh*), questions and answers, *takkanot*, and *gezerot* as well as rules of decision (see *Codification of Law).

The Post-Talmudic Period. The following are the three main branches of the post-talmudic literary sources of Jewish law commencing from the geonic period:

(1) The *Perushim* and *Ḥiddushim*—commentaries and novellae—to the Mishnah and Talmud (as well as the other talmudic literary sources). The commentary literature represents the efforts of the scholars to elucidate the earlier literary sources with a view to facilitating the study and understanding of them; the classic commentary is that of *Rashi on the Babylonian Talmud (11th century). The novellae literature is a product of the study and comparison by the scholars of different sources and their reconciliation of contradictory statements within the talmudic literature, in the course of which new interpretations and *halakhot* were derived; the classic novellae are those of the *tosafists to the Babylonian Talmud (12th and 13th centuries). Of these two literary branches the commentaries represent the earlier development, which reached its peak in the 11th century (i.e., as regards commentaries on the TB; the commentaries on the TJ date from the 16th century onward), only then to be followed by the novellae, which have continued to be written until the present day.

(2) *She'elot u-Teshuvot*—the *responsa prudentium* of Jewish law. The responsa literature represents the decisions and conclusions written down by halakhic scholars in answer to written questions submitted to them. For the major part of the post-talmudic period these questions came either from *dayyanim* who sat in judgment over the litigants in their own community and found it necessary to turn to the outstanding halakhic scholars in the area for the solution to difficult problems, or they arose from disputes between the individual and the community, or between different communities, which came directly before the competent scholars of the particular area. The responsa represent legal decisions on concrete questions arising in daily life and served as the main vehicle for the creativity and evolution of Jewish law in post-talmudic times. This body of literature is the case law of the Jewish legal system, estimated to include a total of approximately 300,000 judgments and decisions (see also **Ma'aseh;* *Responsa).

(3) The Codes (see in detail under *Codification of Law). Besides these three main sources two other classes of literary sources belonging to this period may be mentioned: first, the collections of bonds and deeds (see **Shetarot*), i.e., forms of written documents in use at various times during this period and serving to order the legal relations between parties in different fields of the law—such as deeds of sale, indebtedness, lease, marriage, and *ketubbah;* secondly, the collections of *takkanot*, particularly the *takkanot* enacted by the community and its leadership, namely *takkanot ha-kahal.* In addition, there is the auxiliary literature of Jewish law consisting of various works of aid and reference, which may conveniently be classified into five categories: (1) works of introduction to the Talmud or to the *halakhah* in general (such as the *Iggeret R.* **Sherira Ga'on;* the *Sefer ha-Keritot* of *Samson b. Isaac of Chinon; et al.); (2) encyclopedias of the *halakhah* (such as *Paḥad Yiẓhak* by Isaac *Lampronti and, more recently, the *Enẓikloped-yah Talmudit*, etc.); (3) biographies of the halakhic scholars (such as the *Sefer ha-Kabbalah* of Abraham ibn Daud; first part of *Shem ha-Gedolim* of Ḥ. J. D. Azulai); (4) bibliographies of halakhic works (such as the *Oẓar ha-Sefarim* by Benjacob, the second part of *Shem ha-Gedolim* by Ḥ. J. D. Azulai); and (5) lexicons and dictionaries (such as *He-Arukh* by Nathan b. Jehiel of Rome; the *Arukh Completum* by A. Kohut; Levi's *Wörterbuch;* and Jastrow's *Aramaic Dictionary of the Talmud*). The main literary source in the post-talmudic period, however, remained the Talmud while around it and in continuation thereof there grew up a vast and profound literature in the form of all the aforementioned branches, sources, and auxiliary works.

The Historical Sources of Jewish Law. It is possible to point to the historical background of many norms of Jewish law—to the economic, social, and moral conditions leading to their creation (particularly in the case of the norms originating from *takkanot*), or to the influence of a different legal system (see below) and similar historical influences. General research on such historical sources is to be found in various works dealing with the history of the *halakhah* and some special research has been done on this subject (latterly, for instance, Y. Baer, *Yisrael ba-Ammim;* idem, in: *Zion*, 17 (1951/52), 1–55; 27 (1961/62), 117–55). Ascertaining the precise historical sources of a particular legal norm is often a formidable task which offers no assurance that the correct answer will be found. Some proffered answers lie in the realm of mere conjecture and are unacceptable without adequate further investigation and proof (see for instance the strictures of G. Alon in his *Meḥkarim*, 2 (1958), 181–247).

The Legal Sources of Jewish Law. There are six legal sources of Jewish law (as regards the Written Law see below): (1) *kabbalah* ("tradition"), based on "tradition transmitted from person to person" back to Moses from God (Avot 1:1; ARN *ibid.;* Yad, Mamrim, 1:2; Maim., Introd. to Comm. Mishnah); it is materially different from the other legal sources of Jewish law, since it is not subject to change or development but is, by its very nature, static and immutable, whereas the other legal sources are dynamic by nature and mainly serve as the means toward the continued creativity and evolution of Jewish law; (2) Midrash ("exegesis" and "interpretation"), embracing the norms derived from interpretation of the Written Law and of the *halakhah* in all periods, and to a certain extent also taking in other principles relating to interpretation of deeds, communal enactments, and so on; (3) *takkanah* and *gezerah*, representing the legislative activities of the competent halakhic authorities and public bodies in every generation; (4) *minhag*, representing the legal norms derived from custom in all its different forms; (5) *ma'aseh*, representing the legal norms derived from judicial decision or the conduct of a halakhic scholar in a particular concrete case; (6) *sevarah*, representing the legal norms originating directly from the legal-human logic of the halakhic scholars.

The last five of these are recognized in Jewish law as being capable of both solving new legal and social problems and changing existing legal norms, when this need arises from the prevailing economic, social, and moral realities. In making use of these legal sources the halakhic scholars continued to shape and develop the Jewish legal system, which gave direction to the daily realities of life while being itself directed by them. This task the halakhic scholars carried out with a constant concern for the continued creativity and evolution of the *halakhah*, tempered at the same time by the heavy responsibility of preserving its spirit, objective, and continuity. This twofold assignment is entrusted in Jewish law to the halakhic scholars in every generation: "the judge that shall be in those days" (Deut. 17:9 and Sif. Deut. 153), in accordance with the fundamental principle that "the court of Jephthah is as that of Samuel . . . for the contemporary judge is in his generation as the judge who was in earlier generations" (Eccles. R. 1:4, no. 4; Tosef., RH 2 (1):3; RH 25b). No supra-human power—such as a heavenly voice or the prophet acting as bearer of the divine vision—has ever had any authority or influence in the determination and decision of the *halakhah* (Sifra, Be-Ḥukkotai 13:7–8; BM 59b; TJ, MK 3:1, 81d; for further particulars see *Authority, Rabbinical).

The Basic Norm of Jewish Law. As already mentioned, by the legal sources of a legal system is meant those sources which that legal system itself recognizes as valid sources from which its legal norms derive their binding force. Whence do these legal sources themselves derive their authority and validity? How and by whom have they been recognized as having the efficacy to determine and introduce legal norms into the legal system concerned? Salmond (loc. cit.) states (111–2): "There must be found in every legal system certain ultimate principles, from which all others are derived, but which are themselves self-existent. Before there can be any talk of legal sources, there must be already in existence some law which establishes them and gives them their authority . . . These ultimate principles are the *Grundnorm* or basic rules of recognition of the legal system." Thus the direct legal source of a municipal bylaw is the authority of the municipality to make bylaws; the bylaw has legal validity because parliament has delegated power to the municipality to make bylaws, while there exists a further rule—the *Grundnorm*—which determines that an act of parliament has binding authority in the English legal system.

So in any legal system there is to be found a chain of delegation of power extending from the ultimate legal value—the *Grundnorm*—to lower ones. The source of authority of the ultimate legal principle must be sought beyond the concepts of law and within the confines of history, religious faith, and beliefs, and the like: "But whence comes the rule that acts of parliament have the force of law? This is legally ultimate; its source is historical only, not legal. The historians of the constitution know its origin, but lawyers must accept it as self-existent. It is the law because it is the law, and for no other reason than that it is possible for the law itself to take notice of" (Salmond, op. cit., p. 111).

In the above-mentioned sense the basic norm of the Jewish legal system is the rule that everything stated in the Written Law is of binding authority for the Jewish legal system. The basic norm of Jewish law therefore not only expresses the concept of the delegation of power, but it is actually woven into the substantive content of the Written Law, the latter constituting the eternal and immutable constitution of Jewish law. This norm is the fountain of authority and starting point for the entire halakhic system with all its changes and evolution throughout the generations, and it is this norm that delegates authority to the legal sources of Jewish law rendering them valid means toward the continuing creativity and evolution of the latter. The source of authority of this basic norm itself is the basic tenet of Judaism that the source of authority of the Torah is divine command. In considering the matter from the aspect of Judaism as a whole it has to be said that there cannot be seen in it a system of legal norms isolated from and independent of other constellations of norms. All these constellations of norms have a single and uniform ultimate value, namely divine command as expressed in the Torah given to Moses at Sinai. Hence even the pre-Mosaic laws mentioned in the Written Torah—for instance concerning circumcision and the prohibition on flesh torn from a living animal, robbery, incest and so on—have binding force "because the Holy One commanded us through Moses" (Maim. Comm. Ḥul. 7:6) and because at the time the Torah was given "Israel entered into a covenant to observe them" (*Rashbam* Gen. 26:5).

The exclusive authority to interpret the Written Law and ensure its continuing evolution was found by the halakhic scholars to be delegated, in the Written Torah itself, to the halakhic scholars of every succeeding generation. Such authority they derived from a number of Pentateuchal passages, particularly Deuteronomy 17:8–11, in which the resolution of problems and disputes arising from time to time is entrusted to the teachers and judges in every generation (see also *Authority, Rabbinical). In this and in other passages the halakhic scholars found not only their general authority to resolve problems but also the appointed means, that is the legal sources, wherewith to reach this goal (see Yad, Mamrim, 1:2; Maim., Introd. to Comm. Mishnah). Further particulars of Pentateuchal passages as a basis for the various legal sources of Jewish law are given elsewhere under the heading of each legal source.

THE DIFFERENT PERIODS OF JEWISH LAW

Jewish law has a history extending over a period of more than 3,000 years. For reasons of convenience and, to a certain extent, for historical and substantive reasons, this may be divided into two general periods, each with its own further sub-divisions; the first covering the time from the Written Law until the closing of the Talmud, the second from the post-talmudic period until the present day. This division between talmudic and post-talmudic *halakhah* has no bearing on the matter of the continuing creativity and evolution of Jewish law. Such creativity not only continued uninterruptedly after the closing of the Talmud but, as regards volume and literary output, even gathered momentum in certain fields of the law. The significance of the closing of the Talmud as a historic turning point in Jewish law finds expression in the degree of authenticity attributed to the talmudic *halakhah,* which was accepted in Judaism as the authoritative expression and rendering of the Oral Law: "All matters stated in the *Gemara* . . . must be followed . . . and have been agreed to by all Israel" (Maim., Introd. to *Mishneh Torah*). Until the redaction of the tannaitic literary sources—and to some extent even of the amoraic—the Written Law was the direct source according to which the law was applied by the *dayyan.* After the redaction of the talmudic literary sources the Written Law still remained the constitution of Jewish law, but the Mishnah, the halakhic Midrashim *(midreshei halakhah),* the two Talmuds, and the remaining talmudic literature became the direct sources according to which all matters of Jewish law were decided. The talmudic literature became the starting point for any study or discussion of Jewish law, and retained this status even after Jewish law was enriched—in the course of some 1,500 years—by many additional literary creations which, in comprehensiveness, orderly arrangement, and convenience of use, overtake the talmudic literature. The first great period of Jewish law is further distinguished by the fact that in this period Jewish law acquired its characteristic lines and forms of legal thought and expression, and the fact that in this period there were evolved and consolidated the legal sources which served as the vehicle for the creativity and development of Jewish law in this and in the post-talmudic period.

The first general period can be subdivided in six eras: (1) the biblical age (up to the time of Ezra and Nehemiah, about the middle of the fifth century B.C.E.); (2) the period from Ezra and Nehemiah until the age of the *zugot* (up to 160 B.C.E. approximately), the greater part of which is customarily described as the age of the *soferim* ("the scribes"; see N. Krochmal, *Moreh Nevukhei ha-Zeman,* ed. Rawidowicz, 56, 194), but latterly the use of the term as descriptive of the scholars of this period only has been criticized (see Kaufmann, Y., Toledot, 4 pt. 1 (1960), 481–5); (3) the age of the *zugot* ("the pairs"; from 160 B.C.E. up to the beginning of the Common Era), which takes its name from the five pairs of leading scholars who headed the *battei din* during this period. (The names of the *zugot,* of whom the last pair were Hillel and Shammai, are given in Ḥag. 2 and Avot 1); (4) the age of the *tannaim* (up to 220 C.E.) which spans the activities of six generations of *tannaim,* from *Gamaliel the Elder (grandson of Hillel) and his contemporaries to *Judah ha-Nasi (redactor of the Mishnah). The generation succeeding R. Judah (that of R. *Ḥiyya Rabbah and his contemporaries) saw the transition from the tannaitic age to that of the *amoraim.* Besides the Mishnah, there are extant from the end of this period also collections of halakhic Midrashim, the Tosefta, and other tannaitic literary sources; (5) the age of the *amoraim* embracing the activities of five generations of *amoraim* in Ereẓ Israel (until the end of the fourth century C.E.) and eight generations of *amoraim* in Babylon (up to the end of the fifth century). Extant from this period are the Jerusalem and Babylonian Talmuds; (6) the age of the *savoraim* (up to the end of the sixth century or, according to some scholars, the middle of the seventh century). This age must be regarded as the closing part of the talmudic period since the *savoraim* were mainly occupied with completing the redaction of the Babylonian Talmud and determining rules of decision (see *Codification of Law).

In the second period there are two main subdivisions, the age of the *geonim* and the rabbinic age, but the latter may be subdivided into six further categories. (1) The age of the *geonim* (from the end of the age of the *savoraim* until approximately the middle of the 11th century). The name is derived from the official title by which the heads of the academies of *Sura and *Pumbedita were known during this period. For most of this period the Babylonian academies remained the spiritual center of Jewry as a whole and most Jewish communities assigned absolute legal validity to the decisions and responsa of the *geonim.* For internal Jewish and external political reasons, the ties of the Babylonian *geonim* with the centers of learning that had arisen in North Africa and Spain became loosened towards the end of this period and, commencing from the middle of the 11th century, the phenomenon of a single spiritual center for the various centers of Jewish life came to an end and each of the latter began to rely on its leaders and teachers. This new reality was to exercise a great deal of influence on the subsequent modes of development of Jewish law, evidenced, for instance, in the proliferation of local custom and legislation (see **Takkanot;* **Takkanot ha-Kahal;* *Conflict of Laws). The *geonim* were instrumental in converting the Babylonian Talmud into the source according to which the *halakhah* was decided for all Jewry. In addition, this period saw the first flowering of the division of the post-talmudic literary sources of Jewish law into its three branches which exist until the present day—namely the commentaries and novellae, the responsa, and the codes (see above). Among the better-known *geonim* are R. Yehudai, R. Amram, R. Saadiah, R. Samuel b. Hophni, R. Sherira, and Sherira's son, R. Hai. Of the well-known figures of this period who did not officially hold the title of *gaon,* mention may be made of R. Aḥa (Aḥai) of Shabḥa, author of the *Sefer ha-She'iltot,* and R. Simeon Kayyara, author of the *Halakhot Gedolot* (see *Codification of Law). (2) The rabbinic age, which followed, was itself divided into three periods: (a) The period of the *rishonim* (the "early" scholars), from the middle of the 11th century (the time of Isaac Alfasi) until the 16th century (the time of Joseph Caro and Moses Isserles). This was the golden period of the rabbinic age in which were compiled the classic creations in all three branches of the post-talmudic literary sources of Jewish law: Rashi's commentary on the Talmud and the novellae of the tosafists; the codes of Isaac Alfasi, Maimonides, Jacob b. Asher, Joseph Caro, Moses Isserles, and others; the responsa collections of Solomon b. Abraham Adret (Rashba), Meir (Maharam) of Rothenburg, Asher b. Jehiel (Rosh), Isaac b. Sheshet Perfet (Ribash), Simeon b. Ẓemah Duran (Tashbeẓ), Joseph b. Solomon Colon (Maharik), and others. This was also the period in which the main part of the communal enactments was produced. It embraces the rise and decline of Spanish Jewry, and its close saw the initial flowering of several other Jewish centers—particularly in Ereẓ Israel and Poland-Lithuania—whose outstanding scholars were to make a great contribution to Jewish law, especially to its codification and to its responsa literature.

(b) The period of the *aḥaronim* (the "later" scholars), from the time of Joseph Caro and Moses Isserles until the coming of emancipation around the end of the 18th century. The legal creativity reflected in the three abovementioned literary sources of Jewish law was continued in this period, particularly in the field of the responsa, which reached a peak of activity. From this period there have also come down numerous collections of communal enactments (such as the *Pinkas Va'ad Arba Araẓot, Pinkas Medinat Lita, Takkanot Mehrin,* and others).

(c) The period of the abrogation of Jewish judicial autonomy. The era of emancipation, which brought in its train the abrogation of Jewish judicial autonomy, represents a turning point in the evolution of Jewish law. This period may be further subdivided: from the end of the 18th century until the beginning of the 20th century, i.e., until the period of Jewish national awakening; from the beginning of the 20th century until the establishment of the State of Israel in 1948; from the establishment of the State of Israel onward.

JEWISH LAW—A LAW OF LIFE AND PRACTICE

For the greater part of its history of over 3,000 years, Jewish law has served the Jewish people while they not only lacked political independence but were for a considerable part of this period deprived of their own homeland—Ereẓ Israel—and dispersed throughout the various countries of the Diaspora. The legal systems of other ancient peoples went into decline as soon as they lost their political sovereignty, eventually ceasing to exist except in scattered archaeological remains. Even Roman law, which has left an imprint upon—and still nourishes—many other legal systems, ceased to exist as a creative law of life and practice after having reached its peak of development in Justinian's *Corpus Juris,* in the middle of the sixth century. In the case of Jewish law, the position is otherwise. Despite loss of political independence and lack of physical tie with the homeland, the Jewish people retained judicial autonomy and Jewish law not only did not decline, but it experienced most of its creativity and structural evolution—the Babylonian Talmud and all the other post-talmudic creativity—after the exile. Two factors explain this unique phenomenon: an internal one resting on the substance and nature of Jewish law and its place in the cultural life of the Jewish people, and an external one resting on the general juridical-political outlook that was common in the political history of the nations among whom the Jews lived up to the 18th century.

The Religious and National Character of Jewish Law. Of the two above factors, the internal one is the more important, based as it is on the character of Jewish law which is both religious and national. It is a basic tenet of the Jewish faith that the source of Jewish law—like that of the entire edifice of the *halakhah*—is divine revelation; in the same way as the Jew is commanded in the Written Law to uphold the "religious" precepts—those pertaining to man's relations with the Almighty, such as the laws of the Sabbath and the festivals, the laws of *kashrut* and the like—so he is commanded in the Torah itself to uphold the "legal" precepts—those pertaining to man's relations with his fellows, for instance in matters concerning the law of labor, tort, property, and different matters of the criminal law. The Ten Commandments enjoin observance of the Sabbath and "Thou shalt not steal," or "Thou shalt not murder," equally—as it were in the same breath. Hence, just as the vitality of the "religious" life remained unaffected by the people's exile, so the "legal" life continued to have unabated validity, and questions arising in both fields were brought before the same court or halakhic scholar for decision.

In addition to its religious character Jewish law has also been the national law of the Jewish people and its entire development has been the creative invention of this people. In this regard Jewish law differs from other legal systems, such as the Canon law or Muslim law, which were created and developed by followers of the faith—Catholic or Muslim—among many different nations. Notwithstanding its dispersion, the Jewish people continued to exist as a nation—not only as a religious sect—and constantly sought recourse to Jewish law, which it regarded as a part of its national assets through which to give expression to its essential being and character in all fields of its internal social and economic life.

The Jewish Judicial System—The Scope of its Jurisdiction. A precondition for the practical application of a legal system is the existence of an effective judicial machinery to administer and carry out the law. The Pentateuchal law provides express and detailed instructions for the maintenance of a judicial system (Ex. 18:21–27; Deut. 16:18; see also **Bet Din*) and a Jewish judicial system has always existed, even in the absence of Jewish political sovereignty and in all countries of the Diaspora. The Jewish court *(bet din),* alongside the various institutions of Jewish autonomy (the exilarch, the community, inter-communal organizations), provided the mainstay of Jewish internal autonomy from the destruction of the Temple until the period of emancipation. The scope of Jewish judicial autonomy underwent change from time to time depending mainly on the attitude of the ruling power under whose protection the Jews lived.

After the destruction of the Temple, Jewish judicial autonomy was restricted for a short period in Ereẓ Israel (according to talmudic tradition jurisdiction over capital punishment *(dinei nefashot)* was abolished 40 years before the destruction (Shab. 15a; TJ, Sanh. 1:1, 18a; 7:2, 24b), but in practice the Jewish courts apparently did deal with such cases at least until the destruction). Soon, however, autonomy was fully restored and the time of R. Gamaliel, R. Akiva, and their contemporaries was one of the most creative periods in the history of Jewish law. Later, with the decrees of Hadrian and the revolt of Bar Kokhba, Jewish judicial autonomy was faced with another crisis (TJ, Sanh. 7, 2, 24b), but by the end of the second century C.E., autonomy had already been fully restored (see Alon, *Toledot,* 1 (1958[3]), 129f.). The Babylonian Jewish center enjoyed wide judicial autonomy from an early period, and one of its main institutions was the Jewish court. After the decline of the Babylonian center the Jewish courts in all other centers continued to exercise the judicial function in matters between Jews. The halakhic scholars and communal leaders sought to impose a strict internal discipline in order to insure that all disputes between Jews would be aired before the Jewish judicial institutions. At the same time, they made every effort to obtain charters of privileges from the various rulers under whom they lived in order to insure the independence of Jewish law and the grant of powers of compulsion to the Jewish courts and internal authorities (see below).

The jurisdiction of the Jewish courts extended first and foremost to most civil law matters such as property, obligations, tort, family and succession law, and also to matters concerning the administration of local Jewish government at the hands of the representative communal and intercommunal institutions—such as election to the latter bodies, tax imposition and collection, relations between the individual and the community, and the like (see below). This measure of judicial autonomy was generally extended (up to the 18th century), even in times and places of restriction of the rights of Jews. In many centers such autonomy extended even to criminal matters, varying from place to place in its scope and modes of execution. In certain places it also extended to capital offenses, particularly with reference to *informers (e.g., in Spain, see Resp. Rashba, 1:181; 5:290; Resp. Rosh, 17:1, 8; *Zikhron Yehudah*, 58 and 79; Resp. Ritba, 131; Resp. Ribash, 251; in Poland—see Resp. Maharam of Lublin, 138, etc.; see also *Capital Punishment); in other places it extended merely to religious offenses, offenses against property, and police administrative offenses.

The wide range of matters over which the Jews enjoyed autonomous jurisdiction may be gathered from a study of the responsa literature containing decisions given by the leading halakhic scholars of different periods on concrete questions arising from the daily realities. Thus, out of some 1,050 responsa of *Asher b. Jehiel—one of the leading scholars of German and Spanish Jewry in the second half of the 13th century and the beginning of the 14th—one-fifth (about 200) deal with precepts concerning man and God (such as the laws of prayer, festivals, forbidden food, and the like) and the remaining four-fifths with Jewish law (i.e., matters for the greater part included in Sh. Ar., EH and ḤM). Of the latter group, some 170 questions deal with matters of Jewish family law (marriage and divorce, parent and child, and the like) and the rest, more than 600, are concerned with all other "legal" branches of Jewish law (civil, criminal, and public-administrative; see Elon, Mafte'aḥ, introd. (Heb. and Eng.)). A similar ratio of subject matter is found to be more or less constant in all the responsa literature up to the 16th century, and slightly different in that of the 17th and 18th centuries, where the percentage of matters concerning religious law is somewhat higher. A material change can be detected in the responsa literature from the 18th century onward—following the era of emancipation, which saw the abrogation of Jewish judicial autonomy—and by far the greater part of these responsa deal with matters of religious precepts and family law, with a modest and minor place reserved for the remaining branches of Jewish law.

The Available Sanctions of the Jewish Judicial System. Within the framework of judicial autonomy described above the Jewish courts and competent authorities of the self-ruling bodies had the power to impose sanctions. These too varied from place to place and from period to period. The ordinary means of compulsion were attachment of property, monetary fines, and corporal punishment. In certain centers there were even Jewish prisons under the control of Jewish institutions and supervised by Jewish wardens (see *Imprisonment). At times the autonomous Jewish authorities had to seek the assistance of the central authorities in carrying out the sanctions imposed by the Jewish courts, especially so in case of the death sentence. A common and most effective sanction was the **ḥerem*, the quality and severity of which varied from place to place and also according to the nature of the offense and the degree of compulsion required. The use of this sanction was essential in circumstances where the Jewish authorities lacked the normal attributes of sovereignty, and it served as a most effective deterrent and means of compulsion in view of the self-centered living and residential conditions of the Jewish collectivity as an autonomous group. A person on whom the ban was pronounced was to a greater or lesser extent removed from the religious and social life of the community, and the stringent consequences of this sanction induced many halakhic scholars to refrain from its imposition except in the most difficult and serious cases.

The Prohibition on Litigation in the Gentile Courts. A striking expression of the religious and national character of Jewish law is to be found in the prohibition on litigation in the gentile courts *(arka'ot shel goyim)*, to which the halakhic scholars and communal leaders attached the utmost importance. The first mention of this prohibition was made soon after the destruction of the Temple, when Jewish judicial autonomy was for a short period restricted by the authority of Rome (see above). It was laid down that there was to be no resort to the gentile courts not only when the material law applied in the latter courts differed from Jewish law but even when their law on a particular matter was the same as that applied in the Jewish courts (Git. 88b). Resort to the gentile courts was regarded as prejudicial to the existence of Jewish judicial autonomy and the prohibition served as a protective shield insuring the uninterrupted existence of such autonomy throughout the period of Exile; any person transgressing the prohibition was "deemed to have reviled and blasphemed and rebelled against the Torah of Moses our teacher" (Yad, Sanhedrin 26:17, based on Tanḥ. *Mishpatim*, 3). Contrary to the general principle that every rule of the civil law *(mamonot)* is *jus dispositivum*, so that in respect of it a man may contract out of the law of the Torah, it was laid down by a majority of halakhic scholars that the parties to a transaction may not mutually agree to submit their dispute to the jurisdiction of a gentile court, and also that resort to the gentile courts is not justifiable on the principle of *dina de-malkhuta dina* ("the law of the land is law"; *Ramban* Ex. 21:1; Resp. Rashba, vol. 6, no. 254; Tur and Sh. Ar., ḤM 26:1, 3).

In the political and social realities of the different centers of the dispersion it was not always fully possible to enforce this prohibition. As early as the middle of the ninth century Paltoi Gaon laid down that it was permissible to institute proceedings in a gentile court against a party aggressively and obdurately refusing to appear in a Jewish court (B. M. Levin (ed.), *Oẓar ha-Ge'onim*, BK, Resp. no. 227). It was decided that in such a case the plaintiff, after first obtaining leave of the Jewish court, might prosecute his claim in the gentile court, "in order not to strengthen the hands of the powerful and violent who do not obey the law" (Yad, Sanhedrin 26:7 and *Radbaz* thereto; Tur and Sh. Ar., ḤM 16:2, 4). At times resort to the gentile courts was permitted in certain matters in which the central authorities had a special interest, such as disputes over land (Resp. *Rema*, no. 109), governmental taxes and currency (Finkelstein, bibl., pp. 361f.). Some of the halakhic scholars permitted recourse to the gentile courts when this was agreed on by both parties (Resp. Maharam of Rothenburg, ed. Cremona, no. 78; Finkelstein, op. cit., pp. 153, 156 and n. 1; *Sma* ḤM 26 n. 11 and *Taz* thereto; see also *Siftei Kohen*, ḤM 22, n. 15). In different periods there were communities and places where Jews scorned the prohibition, but in general the halakhic scholars and communal leaders firmly stood guard over the authority of the Jewish courts by enacting special *takkanot* and adopting sharp countervailing measures against those who thus undermined the autonomy of Jewish jurisdiction (see Assaf, *Battei ha-Din* ..., 11, 17–18, 24, 109–13; Elon, in: ILR 2 (1967), 524–7; as regards recourse to the gentile courts from the period of the emancipation onwards see below).

Arbitration and the Jurisdiction of Lay Jewish Tribunals. The aim of preventing recourse to the gentile courts as a means of preserving Jewish judicial autonomy induced the halakhic scholars to maintain judicial institutions composed of Jewish judges, even if the judgments of the latter were not based on Jewish law, or were based on this law in slight measure only. Institutions of this kind were arbitral bodies and lay tribunals in their various forms.

The arbitral body had its origin in the second half of the second century (R. Meir and other *tannaim*: Sanh. 3:1–3), when Jewish judicial autonomy was restricted, as we have already noted, by the decrees of Roman imperial rule following on the Bar Kokhba revolt. The courts were destroyed and those which remained were deprived of the power of compulsion. In these circumstances the scholars directed the people to the institution of *arbitration, in which *ro'ei bakar* ("herdsmen," simple folk untutored in the law) could also sit and adjudicate in accordance with their own good sense and understanding. In order to give such adjudication a Jewish form, the scholars laid down that the arbitral body should be composed of three arbitrators (Sanh. 3: 1), like the Jewish court which was always composed of at least three *dayyanim* (*ibid.* 1: 1; and see **Bet Din*) and unlike the position in Roman law where there was generally a single arbitrator. Even after the restoration of judicial autonomy, arbitration continued to fulfill an important function alongside the regular judicial institutions, and its rules and procedures were prescribed by the halakhic scholars (see also *Compromise).

Of interest is the evolution of the institution of adjudication by lay judges (*hedyotot*, i.e., persons untutored in Jewish law; the term also has the meaning of judges tutored in the *halakhah* but lacking **semikhah* ("ordination"; see, e.g., Git. 88b), a distinction that must be borne in mind). The precise origin of this institution is disputed by scholars; one opinion is that it dates from before the destruction of the Temple, while others hold that it too developed after the Bar Kokhba revolt and the withdrawal of autonomous jurisdiction from the Jewish courts (see Elon, op. cit., p. 529). Lay jurisdiction was likewise designed to ensure that the people would bring their disputes before Jewish judges—even if the latter were not versed in the law—rather than resort to the gentile courts. These tribunals were composed of three members, one of whom had to be *gamir*—i.e., to have acquired some knowledge of the *halakhah*—while the other two had to be persons fit at least to understand any matter explained to them (Sanh. 3a, *Rashi* and Nov. Ran ad loc.). The scholars bestowed on the lay tribunal authority to deal with all matters of civil law, to the exclusion of criminal matters (Sanh. 3a and *Piskei Rosh* thereto, 1) along with power to compel the appearance of the parties (*Piskei Rosh* thereto, 2; Tos. to Sanh. 5a; Tur ḤM 3:3; Sh. Ar., ḤM 3: 1). In order to prevent resort to the gentile courts at all costs in post-talmudic times the scholars laid down that in any community where not even one *gamir* was to be found, three laymen could make up the tribunal even if none of them possessed this minimal qualification, provided that they were "fit and God-fearing persons, spurning corruption and equipped with sense and understanding"; such tribunals could deal also with criminal matters, in cases of great need and after much prior forethought and consultation (Resp. Rashba, vol. 2, no. 290). The existence of tribunals composed entirely of lay judges is confirmed in other historical sources (see, e.g., the Valladolid *takkanot* of 1432, in Finkelstein, bibl., pp. 356–7), and the validity of such courts was halakhically recognized (*Rema* ḤM 8: 1).

In general, the major part of the legal hearings, in disputes between individual Jews and between the individual and the communal authorities, took place before a court composed of three *dayyanim* expert in Jewish law and deciding in accordance therewith (a court of this kind called simply, *bet din;* Resp. Rashba, vol. 1, no. 1010); however, in most Jewish centers there were also lay tribunals functioning alongside these courts as a permanent judicial institution (a court of this nature being referred to as *bet din shel hedyotot;* Rashba loc. cit.). Many factors—social, economic, standards of knowledge and education—determined the measure of resort to lay tribunals. Their judges (known by different names: *tovei ha-ir, berurei tevi'ot, berurei averot, piskei ba'alei battim, parnasim, zekenim,* etc.) generally based their decisions on communal enactments (see **Takkanot ha-Kahal*), trade usages (see **Minhag*), appraisal, justice, and equity (see e.g. Resp. Rashba, vol. 2, no. 290; vol. 3, no. 393 et al.; Resp. Maharshal, no. 93; Resp. *Rema* no. 33) and at times even upon a particular branch of a foreign legal system (*Beit ha-Beḥirah*, Sanh. 23a concerning "courts in Syria"; see also *takkanot* of the Leghorn community: S. Toaff in: *Sefunot*, 9 (1964/65), 190f.). Sometimes lay tribunals turned to halakhic scholars for their opinion and advice (*Zikhron Yehudah*, no. 58). In some places the limits of their jurisdiction were clearly defined. Mention is made of a tribunal composed of *tovei ha-ir* which dealt with tax matters (Resp. Rosh no. 7: 11). At times there was a predetermined division of matters over which the different courts were to have jurisdiction; thus a *takkanah* of the Lithuanian community prescribed that the courts of the communal leaders were to deal with matters of monopolies as well as certain tax and penal matters, and the *dayyanim* of the community with matters of civil law (*Pinkas ha-Medinah [Lita]*, no. 364); in a *takkanah* of the Leghorn community it was laid down that all matters of trade, insurance, and the like were to be dealt with by the communal leaders (*adonei ha-ma'amad*) judging in accordance with the general law as regards trade customs, but that matters of marriage and divorce, inheritance, mortgage, interest, and the like were to be dealt with according to Jewish law (Toaff, in: *Sefunot* loc. cit.).

The lay tribunals were originally and primarily instituted for the purpose of preventing resort to the gentile courts and also so as to enable certain matters of trade and the like, which were dependent on local custom, to come before a tribunal of merchants and professional experts. These tribunals tended, however, to gain in influence and to assume jurisdiction in additional matters, notwithstanding the existence of courts composed of *dayyanim* learned in the law. The halakhic scholars regarded this development as posing a threat to the ordered evolution of Jewish jurisdiction and application of Jewish law (see, e.g., Resp. Maharyu, no. 146). The fact that these tribunals tried matters according to appraisal and a subjective feel for justice, rather than according to any fixed legal rules, led the scholars to apprehend the danger of possible partiality and perversion of justice, especially since the tribunals were generally composed of the leaders and wealthy members of the community with the poorer and less influential members of society almost completely unrepresented. Strong criticism to this effect was often expressed by the scholars (see, e.g., *Keneh Ḥokhmah, Derush ha-Dayyanim*, pp. 25f.; *Derushei ha-Ẓelaḥ*, 3: 12–4). However, such criticism never challenged the basic existence and positive merits of an institution which served as a vital additional means of preventing recourse to the gentile courts. For this reason adjudication by lay tribunals was also held to "accord with the Torah," even if it had not always the same merit as adjudication by the courts of *dayyanim*, and only "the practice in a few places to turn without hesitation to the gentile courts is actually contrary to the Torah and amounts to a public profanation of the Divine Name for which those who act in this way will have to account" (*Sefer ha-Zikhronot*, 10:3). To do so was to undermine Jewish judicial autonomy. (In Sh. Ar., ḤM the matter of lay tribunals (ch. 8) is clearly distinguished from the stringent prohibition on recourse to the gentile courts (ch. 26); see also M. Elon, in: ILR, 2 (1967), 529–37.)

The Judicial-Political Position and Social-Fiscal Relations. The national-religious character of Jewish law, and the profound awareness that a zealous watch over this inalienable asset would ensure the continued existence and unity of the Jewish people, thus constituted the primary element in the application of Jewish law in the daily life of the Jewish people even when dispersed in exile. Yet it may be asked how it proved possible for the Jews to maintain judicial autonomy under the political sovereignty of the governments under whose rule they lived, and what motivated the state authorities to respond to the demand of the Jewish collectivity for its own autonomy. The answer lies in the second of the two factors mentioned above, that is the judicial-political concepts of government and jurisdiction as these were common up to the 18th century, and the fiscal and social relations between the central authorities and the different strata, including foreigners, who dwelt under their rule. The judicial system was based on the individual's adherence to one of a number of distinctive groups with different legal systems which were recognized by the state. Unlike modern centralistic states, the medieval state was corporative in nature and comprised of a series of autonomous strata and bodies, such as the nobility, the burghers, the guilds, etc. The latter frequently competed with one another and some of them with the central authority, and the Jewish community was often the object of rivalry among these different strata, bodies, and the central authority. This political-legal reality rendered possible the existence of an autonomous Jewish group with its own judicial autonomy. The central authority, as well as the different strata and bodies amidst whom the Jews lived, regarded it as their "duty" and right to impose on the Jews heavy taxes in return for the privileges of settlement and residence. The collection of such taxation from each individual involved many difficulties, especially as the Jews were counted as members of a separate and foreign national group. The authorities accordingly found it convenient to impose an aggregate tax on the Jewish collectivity as a whole and for this purpose to enable the latter to be a unitary autonomous body, functioning in such manner that its leaders would bear the responsibility of producing the total amount of the tax apportioned and collected by each community from among its individual members. The existence of an autonomous public Jewish body also made it possible to give directions and conduct negotiations on other state rights and obligations through the recognized leaders of this body. Considerations of faith and religious opinions held by the Christian rulers may also have contributed to the grant of autonomous Jewish jurisdiction (see H. H. Ben-Sasson, *Perakim be-Toledot ha-Yehudim bi-Ymei ha-Beinayim* (196), 90–91).

In this manner a zealously pursued desire of the Jewish people coincided with the existence of external historical conditions and factors to enable this people to preserve its religious and national law as a law of life and practice, faithfully served and interpreted by Jewish courts throughout the dispersion. The preservation by the Jews of their national law has been the main factor in the preservation of Jewish national existence. In the words of Y. Kaufmann *(Golah ve-Nekhar)*, "It was judicial autonomy which truly made of the Jewish nation in exile 'a state within a state' " (1 (1929), 518) and "This autonomy derived from the striving of the nation to embody in its life the ideal of the Torah to the utmost limits. It derived especially from the striving to uphold the Jewish legal system, the Law of the Torah, and to base thereon the order of internal life. For this reason the ancient autonomy was fundamentally a judicial autonomy" (*ibid.*, 2 (1930), 312).

THE EVOLUTION OF JEWISH LAW

A material feature of Jewish law is the fact of its ever-continuing evolution. This is the logical and necessary outcome of the fact of Jewish law's being a living and practical law, since constant evolution is a characteristic feature of every living thing whether it is discernible during the passage from one state to another or only clearly distinguishable in the perspective of history. It will be clear to anyone taking up the *halakhah* that he has before him one large unit in which the earlier and later, the basis and the construction, are all interwoven and arranged according to subject matter with no particular regard shown for historical-epochal distinctions. The halakhic scholars rightly considered that Jewish law was of a nature which required them to unite and integrate the various periods of the *halakhah* into a single, all-embracing epoch of unitary *halakhah*, and not to divide and differentiate between different stages and periods. This is a legitimate and accepted conception in any system of legal thought, especially in a legal system which, by its very nature, deems the existing body of laws to be the starting point for its own renewal and further development. This is also largely true, as regards, for instance, the development of most of English law. However, this conception does not in any way bar the scholar from examining each and every one of the institutions of Jewish law in historical perspective, with a view to determining the different stages of development they may have undergone. Morever, an examination of such different stages of development and of the legal sources through which these stages were integrated into the fabric of Jewish law will reveal that the halakhic scholars themselves frequently emphasized the changes and development through which one or other institution of Jewish law had passed. This is evidenced in their resort not only to *takkanah*—a means of expressly adding to or changing the existing law—but also to Midrash and the other legal sources of Jewish law (see M. Elon, *Ḥerut ha-Perat* . . . 12 (introd.), 261–4).

Submission to Jewish law and the Jewish courts brought in its wake an unending creative development of the Jewish legal system. Social realities and economic exigencies change from period to period, and among the special conditions of the Jewish people must be included the social and economic variations that marked the different centers of the dispersion. Even when the Jewish people had possessed a single political center—and later on a spiritual center—there had existed a various and widely scattered Diaspora; however, geographical dispersion really began to impress its mark more critically at the end of the tenth and the beginning of the 11th century when the one center, the Babylonian, which had until then held sway over the entire Diaspora, declined and a number of centers made their appearance side by side and successively in North Africa, in Spain and Germany, in France and Italy, in Turkey, Egypt, and the Balkan countries, in Poland-Lithuania, and elsewhere. It is certainly true that despite the geographical scattering, Jewish scholars everywhere dealt with the same talmudic and rabbinic sources and that very often contact, personal and by correspondence, was also maintained among the different centers. But the variations in the social, commercial, and economic life of the Jews in each center, their communal organization and representative institutions in each locality, their relationship with the gentile environment and the state authorities—all these from time to time gave rise to problems for some of which the existing Jewish law provided no express solution and for some of which it was necessary to find solutions which differed from those provided by the existing law. At times the influence of local conditions led to the absorption of undesirable legal principles which were contrary to the spirit of Jewish law and did not serve to advance the system of law as a whole. To the extent that such foreign principles deviated from the fundamental doctrines of Jewish law they generally came to be rejected in the course of time (see, e.g., *Imprisonment, *Imprisonment for Debt).

Thus Jewish law continued to evolve as a law of life and practice, giving direction to the daily realities while being itself directed thereby. The phenomenon of a legal system which demands that the determination of its law and its solutions to legal problems be founded on the past while answering the manifold needs of every succeeding generation is found to be true of Jewish law in all periods of its history, both in the time of Jewish political sovereignty and during the long period when this was absent but the Jewish people enjoyed judicial autonomy in Ereẓ Israel, in Babylonia, and in all the other countries of the dispersion. This demand was satisfied through the ever-continuing evolutionary development of the institutions of Jewish law and through preservation of the central concept of each institution which constituted the common factor of all the different stages and changes through which it passed. (For illustrations of such development, see *Authority, Rabbinical; *Capital Punishment; *Contract; **Ha'anakah;* **Hassagat Gevul;* *Imprisonment for Debt; *Lien; *Limitation of Actions; *Obligation, Law of; *Surety; *Taxation. See also *Interpretation; **Ma'aseh;* **Minhag;* **Sevarah;* **Takkanot;* **Takkanot ha-Kahal;* and see M. Elon, *Ḥerut ha-Perat* . . ., 12 (introd.), and 255ff.)

Since the development of Jewish law was the outcome of the practical application of the latter in daily life, it follows that in places where there was diminished submission to Jewish law and its courts system there was a corresponding falling off in the creative development of this legal system, as is evidenced, for instance, in the case of Italian Jewry in certain periods (Resp. Rambam (ed. Leipzig), pt. 1, no. 140, p. 26; *Sefer ha-Zikhronot,* 10:3). This was, however, an uncommon phenomenon until the 18th century and the era of emancipation. Thereafter, with the abrogation of Jewish judicial autonomy, Jewish law was to a far lesser extent a law of practice and this was to lead to a far-reaching diminution in the creativity of Jewish law (see below).

THE EVOLUTION OF JEWISH LAW REFLECTED IN ITS LITERARY SOURCES

Sefer ha-Zikhronot (loc. cit.) emphasizes that recourse to the Jewish courts is of importance not only for the continuance of the creative development of Jewish law itself but also for the enlargement of its literature. A study of the various matters with which halakhic literature has dealt at different times shows that the part of the *halakhah* which was of practical application came to occupy an increasingly and incomparably larger place than the part that was not of such application.

The Mishnah as compiled by Judah ha-Nasi contains six orders, each of which treats of one basic branch of the *halakhah,* and together they embrace the whole halakhic system. In the two Talmuds, the literary creations following immediately upon the Mishnah, the following phenomenon is apparent: the Babylonian Talmud, unlike the Jerusalem Talmud, contains no Talmud on the order of *Zera'im* (apart from the tractate *Berakhot* dealing with prayers and benedictions). There is no doubt that the Babylonian *amoraim,* like those of Ereẓ Israel, studied all the six orders of the Mishnah and their deliberations on *Zera'im* are largely scattered throughout the tractates of the other orders. That no Babylonian Talmud was edited for this order is due to the fact that the rules therein stated—"precepts which are dependent on the land" (these being applicable only in Ereẓ Israel), such as the laws of *shevi'it* (the Sabbatical Year) and *pe'ah* (the corner of the field)—were not of practical concern in Babylonia, whereas in Ereẓ Israel itself, where these rules were actually applied, a Talmud on this order was compiled and edited. In the post-talmudic period the overwhelming part of the halakhic literary creativity was also concentrated on the "precepts contemporaneously in use," that is on the branches of the *halakhah* which were of everyday use and not on the laws connected with the "precepts dependent on the land" with the Temple, ritual purity, and the like. It is found that sometimes even theoretical study itself was centered around the practical orders—*Mo'ed, Nashim,* and *Nezikin*—and those tractates of the other orders containing precepts in contemporaneous use—such as *Berakhot, Ḥullin* (concerning the laws of ritual slaughter and *kashrut*), and *Niddah* (concerning ritual purity of women)—were arranged together with these three orders (see *Beit ha-Beḥirah* (ed. Jerusalem, 1965[2]), Introd. to Ber., p. 32). In geonic times many monographs were written on various halakhic subjects, most of them on strictly legal topics and part on matters of ritual law, the majority of both kinds dealing exclusively with the laws of everyday use. These monographs were primarily compiled for practical use in the *battei din.*

This phenomenon recurs in two branches of the post-talmudic literature—in the responsa and in the codifications—and to a certain extent also in the third branch, the commentaries and novellae. Thus Alfasi included in his code only those laws then operative and not, for instance, the laws of the order of *Kodashim* (except the tractate *Ḥullin* in which the topics discussed remained of contemporaneous significance). The only one to deviate from this path was Maimonides in his code, *Mishneh Torah.* He sought to restore the *halakhah* to its original dimensions by including in his code even matters of faith and belief, which he formulated in legal style. However, this undertaking was unique and in all subsequent codifications, such as *Piskei Rosh, Arba'ah Turim,* and Shulḥan Arukh, the example set by Alfasi was followed and only the rules in current application were included. The responsa literature also deals overwhelmingly with practical questions of the law and not with matters of ritual purity and defilement or sacrifices. This is obviously due to the fact that problems arose, and were referred to the leading halakhic scholars for solution, only in the area of the practical day-to-day application of the law. In the commentaries and novellae alone is there found any more extensive discussion of the "theoretical" branches of the *halakhah,* but even here the greater part is devoted to practical halakhic matters. This is one explanation for the fact that commentaries and novellae to the Jerusalem Talmud were written only from the 16th century onward, following the renewal of the Jewish settlement in Ereẓ Israel in this period. (It is noteworthy that in latter times—before and since the establishment of the State of Israel—there has been greatly increased creativity in the field of the laws pertaining to the order of *Zera'im,* in all three literary branches of the *halakhah,* clearly because these laws have once more come to be of practical significance.) While it is true that at all periods Jewish law was frequently studied in purely theoretical manner, as Torah for its own sake, and an appreciable literature was created to this end, yet such study and literary creativity represent no more than embellishments of the main core, aids to the knowledge of Jewish law for everyday use in practical life.

THE DIFFERENT BRANCHES OF JEWISH LAW

Illustrations of Development and Change in the Different Branches of Jewish Law. In the different periods of its history Jewish law has comprised all the branches of law customary in other legal systems although from time to time changes of a structural nature took place. The institutions of Jewish law in all its different branches underwent, as already mentioned, an ever-continuing process of creative development. In some fields—for instance property, family and inheritance, procedure and evidence—this process was of no material consequence as regards the framework or content of a particular branch of the law, notwithstanding any changes in its principles. In other fields the process had a more material effect as regards the content and classification of an entire branch of the law.

Laws of Obligation. A change of this nature took place, for instance, in the field of the laws of obligation. The original Jewish law fundamentally and unequivocally rejected any form of enslavement of the debtor's person as a means towards realizing the creditor's rights (see *Execution, Civic). Consequently there arose the need to find a strong alternative means of ensuring the fulfillment of an obligation in the form of an encumbrance on the debtor's property, which found expression in a right of lien over the debtor's property automatically conferred on the creditor upon creation of the obligation. For this reason an obligation in Jewish law had essentially a real character because the creditor was afforded a right of a real nature in the debtor's property, and in consequence of this many rules belonging to the field of property law came to be applied also to the laws of obligation (see *Lien; *Obligation, Law of). In the course of time, the nature of the contractual obligation in Jewish law underwent a substantive change, one that found expression in a series of basic innovations introduced and given recognition in successive stages; these included the possibility, contrary to the laws of property, of establishing an obligation with regard to something not yet in existence; the possibility of establishing an obligation whether or not the property in the debtor's possession at such a time was capable of satisfying the debt, and a long series of further developments (see *Contract). Such a substantive change in the subject matter of a legal institution is an important factor in its classification or reclassification as belonging, for instance, to the field of the laws of obligation rather than the laws of property.

Administrative Law. A different phenomenon is evidenced in the field of administrative law, for the central subjects of this branch changed almost completely in consequence of the material changes in the nature of public Jewish leadership and administration in different periods. Whereas in ancient times the institutions of public law determined relations between the individual leader—the king (see *King and Kingdom), the **nasi*, the exilarch—and the people, new social realities spurred the development of a pervasive system of administrative law based on collective leadership, elected or appointed. The representative and elective institutions of local Jewish government and intercommunal organization were built up on the principles of Jewish law, and the halakhic scholars as well as the communal leaders were called upon to resolve (the latter by way of communal enactments) the numerous problems arising in the field of administrative law. These related, among others, to the determination of relations between the individual and the public authority, between the latter and its servants; to the composition of the communal institutions and the methods of election and appointment to the latter and to other public positions (see *Public Authority); to the modes of legislation of the community and to the legal administration of its institutions (see **Hekdesh*; **Takkanot ha-Kahal*); to the imposition and collection of taxes (see *Taxation), and to many additional problems concerning economic and fiscal relations in the community. This wide range of problems was dealt with in a very large number of responsa and communal enactments, in the course of which the halakhic scholars and public leaders developed a new and complete system of public law within the framework of the *halakhah*.

Conflict of Laws. In the field of the conflict of laws development came mainly in consequence of periodic migratory movements and social changes in the life of the Jewish people. The conflict of laws is not usually regarded as a distinct branch of Jewish law, because of the substantive nature of Jewish law as a personal law purporting to apply to each and every Jew wherever he may be—even beyond the territorial limits of Jewish sovereignty or autonomy. From this it naturally follows that in Jewish law no importance attaches to the fact, as such, that a contract between two Jews is scheduled to mature in a different country than that in which it was concluded—a fact that is normally the staple source of problems arising in the area of the conflict of laws. Nevertheless, the fact that for the greater part of their history, the Jews enjoyed their judicial autonomy under the political sovereignty of the foreign ruler with his own legal system, and especially the fact of the geographical dispersion of the various Jewish centers, inevitably caused the Jewish legal system to be confronted with many fundamental problems relating to the conflict of laws. There developed in Jewish law the phenomenon of a multiplicity of *takkanot* and customs relating to the same legal subject but varying in content from place to place. To some extent this phenomenon was also present in talmudic times, but it assumed significant proportions only from the tenth century onward when there ceased to be a single Jewish center exercising hegemony over the other centers of the Diaspora. The result of the rise of many centers was the proliferation of local *takkanot*, customs, and legal decisions, which brought in train the problem of the choice between different laws—not between Jewish law and any other law, but between the rules deriving from differing customs and *takkanot* within the Jewish legal system itself. Similarly, as a result of the close contact between Jewish law and the various legal systems of the nations amidst whom the Jewish collectivity lived, there evolved the principle of *dina de-malkhuta dina* and, flowing from this, various rules pertaining to the field of the conflict of laws.

Criminal Law. A different and completely opposite trend is evidenced in the field of criminal law. During those periods when the Jewish people enjoyed full judicial authority, it is possible to point to the existence of important principles and great creativity extending also to the criminal law (see *Penal Law; *Punishment). However, the scope of application of this branch of the law was already substantially narrowed around the time of the Temple destruction, and in consequence it reflects a diminished creative continuity and a smaller framework. It is true, as already mentioned, that in some places Jewish judicial jurisdiction extended even to capital offenses but in most centers the criminal jurisdiction of the Jewish courts was confined to offenses against property, administrative offenses, and the like. On the whole the lack of sovereignty deprived the Jewish people of the media required for the proper implementation of criminal jurisdiction and of suitable conditions for its organic development. All these factors therefore stunted the growth of the functional framework and content of this branch of Jewish law.

Classification of the Different Branches of Jewish Law. Like other legal systems, Jewish law has its own distinctive basic principles pertaining to each of the different branches of the system. Sometimes these principles are unique to Jewish law and characterize its approach to matters such as personal freedom and the rights of the individual, the substance and nature of legal and moral obligations, the concept of ownership of property, the essential nature of judicial jurisdiction, modes of proof, and other fundamental questions. In other cases the principles of Jewish law correspond to parallel principles in other legal systems. Such differences and similarities are dealt with elsewhere under the heading of the subject to which they pertain.

A full enumeration of the articles on Jewish law appearing in this Encyclopaedia is given below, some articles being repeated since they pertain to more than one branch of law:

THE SOURCES OF LAW: Authority, Rabbinical; Codification of Law; Interpretation; *Ma'aseh; Minhag; Mishpat Ivri; Sevarah; Takkanot; Takkanot ha-Kahal.*

GENERAL: Agency, Law of; *Asmakhta;* Conditions; *Ḥazakah* (in part); Law and Morals; Legal Person; Majority Rule; Maxims, Legal; Mistake; Noachide Laws; *Ones; Shetar;* Slavery.

THE LAWS OF PROPERTY: Acquisition; Gifts; *Ḥazakah; Hefker; Hekdesh;* Lost Property, Finder of; *Maẓranut; Ona'ah;* Ownership; Property; Sale; Servitude; Slavery; *Ye'ush.*

THE LAWS OF OBLIGATION: Antichresis; Assignment; Contract; Gifts; *Ha'anakah; Hassagat Gevul;* Labor Law; Lease and Hire; Lien; Loans; Maritime Law; *Meḥilah;* Obligation, Law of; Partnership; Pledge; Sale; *Shalish; Shi'buda de-Rabbi Nathan; Shomerim;* Surety; Unjust Enrichment; Usury.

THE LAWS OF TORT: *Avot Nezikin;* Damages; *Gerama;* Nuisance; Theft and Robbery (civil aspects); Torts.

FAMILY LAW AND INHERITANCE: Adoption; *Agunah;* Apostate (Family Law); Apotropos; Betrothal; Bigamy; Child Marriage; Civil Marriage; Concubine; Divorce; Dowry; Embryo; Firstborn; Husband and Wife; *Ketubbah;* Levirate Marriage and *Ḥaliẓah;* Maintenance; *Mamzer;* Marriage; Marriage, Prohibited; Mixed Marriage (Legal Aspects); Orphan; Parent and Child (Legal Aspects); Rape; Succession; Widow; Wills; *Yuḥasin.*

CRIMINAL LAW: Abduction; Abortion; Adultery; Assault; Blood Avenger; Bribery; Capital Punishment; City of Refuge; Compounding Offenses; Confiscation; Crucifixion; Expropriation and Forfeiture; Contempt of Court; Divine Punishment; Extraordinary Remedies; Fine; Flogging; Forgery; Fraud; Gambling; *Hafka'at She'arim; Ḥerem;* Homicide; Imprisonment; Incest; Informer (Legal Aspects); Oppression; Ordeal; Penal Law; Perjury; Police Offenses; Punishment; Rape; Rebellious Son; Sexual Offenses; Slander; Sorcery; Suicide; *Talion;* Theft and Robbery (Criminal Aspects); Usury; Weight and Measures (Criminal Aspects).

THE LAWS OF PROCEDURE AND EVIDENCE: Admission; Arbitration; Attorney; *Bet Din;* Compromise; Confession; Evidence; Execution (Civil); Extraordinary Remedies; *Ḥerem;* Imprisonment for Debt; Limitation of Actions; Oath; Pleas; Practice and Procedure (Civil and Penal Law); *Shetar;* Witness.

MERCANTILE LAW: Acquisition; Agency, Law of; Contract; *Hafka'at She'arim; Hassagat Gevul;* Imprisonment for debt; Labor Law; Lease and Hire; Legal Person; Loans; Maritime Law; *Minhag;* Obligation, Law of; *Ona'ah;* Partnership; Sale; *Shalish; Shetar; Shomerim; Takkanot; Takkanot ha-Kahal;* Taxation; Usury. (The articles enumerated above are all mentioned under other branches of the law, but are grouped together here because of the commercial elements they contain.)

PUBLIC AND ADMINISTRATIVE LAW: Confiscation; Expropriation, and Forfeiture; *Dina de-Malkhuta Dina; Hekdesh;* Public Authority; *Takkanot ha-Kahal;* Taxation.

CONFLICT OF LAWS: Conflict of Laws; *Dina de-Malkhuta Dina;* Domicile.

It may be added that classification of the subjects comprising a legal system is a task beset with difficulties, particularly so in the case of the Jewish law, and calls for the exercise of much care. Thus, for instance, certain institutions of Jewish law are classified both under the laws of property and the laws of obligation because of the close connection between these two branches of the law. This is true also as regards the classification of criminal matters, which in Jewish law do not always conform to those customarily classified in other legal systems as part of criminal law. It is questionable whether the classification of subject matter in one legal system is appropriate for another and any automatic application to Jewish law of the classification adopted in another legal system is especially liable to be misleading. To a certain extent the special legal terminology of Jewish law also influences the manner of classification of its subject matter (see for instance the definitions above of the terms *mishpat Ivri, issura, mamona,* and others). The difficulties entailed in the classification of Jewish law into defined legal branches derive in part from the fact that during the periods when the foundations of the various rules of Jewish law were laid, the system knew only a classification of a most general nature. This is reflected in the Mishnah and in the remaining halakhic literature of the tannaitic period and also in the two Talmuds. A more definitive and detailed classification of Jewish law came only with the compilation of Maimonides' code, the *Mishneh Torah,* and some of the subsequent codes. A classification of the subject matter of Jewish law in keeping with the character and spirit of this legal system is possible only after deep and careful study of its different institutions. For these reasons the above classification is not to be regarded as final and absolute.

PUBLIC JEWISH LEADERSHIP IN THE DEVELOPMENT OF JEWISH LAW

The halakhic scholars and the *battei din* filled the central role in the development of the Jewish legal system. In addition, an important creative role was filled by the public leadership and representation of the Jewish people in all the different institutional forms it assumed throughout the history of the Jews: from the kings, the *nesi'im,* and exilarchs down to the elected or appointed representatives of the community.

The King's Law. The fundamentals of the laws concerning the king and his kingdom are enjoined in the Pentateuch (Deut. 17:14–20, dealing mainly with the duties of the king and his modes of conduct), in the first Book of Samuel (ch. 8, in which the prerogatives of the king and the duties owed him by the people are defined), and in other biblical passages (see for instance I Kings 21, concerning the matter of Naboth's vineyard). The scholars also learned about the powers of the king from certain biblical statements concerning leaders of the people other than the kings (see for instance Josh. 1:18 concerning rebellion against the kingdom; cf. Sanh. 49a). The king was vested with wide powers in the legislative (see **Takkanot*), judicial, and executive fields, with authority to deviate in various matters from the rules as laid down in the *halakhah.* His authority was not confined solely to fiscal and economic matters relating directly to the rule of the kingdom, such as taxation and the mobilization of manpower or property, but extended also to the field of criminal law. In the latter field he had authority, for instance, to impose the death sentence on a murderer, despite the existence of formal defects in the evidence against him, when this was required "for the sake of good order in accordance with the needs of the hour" (Yad, Melakhim 3:10; 5:1–3 *ibid.*, Roẓe'aḥ 2:4 and Sanhedrin 14:2, 18:6).

The king's law represents the earliest determination in Jewish law of a creative factor not directly attributable to halakhic scholars, and the *halakhah* conferred similar creative authority on the various other post-monarchic institutions of central Jewish government. Thus for instance it was said of the exilarchs who headed the internal Jewish government in the Babylonian exile that "they take the place of the king" (Yad, Sanhedrin 4:13, based on Sanh. 5a and *Rashi* ad loc.) and that the king's law applies "in every generation . . . in favor of the leaders of each generation" (*Beit ha-Beḥirah,* Sanh. 52b; see also *Mishpat Kohen,* no. 144). The question of the relationship between the regular law and the king's law is often the subject of discussion in halakhic literature, particularly of the post-talmudic period.

R. *Nissim b. Reuben Gerondi explains the parallel existence of the two systems on the basis that justice administered according to law, while correct and ideal, does not always answer the social and other needs of the hour, and that this function is filled by administration of the king's law; for this reason Scripture enjoins the king to have the Torah with him always, "that his heart be not lifted up above his brethren" (Deut. 17:14–20), because inasmuch as he is not always subject to the law he must at all times, when making use of his powers, take particular care to ensure that he does not deviate from the general object of the Torah and its principles of justice and equity (*Derashot Ran*, Derush no. 11). All subsequent creative authority permitted in Jewish law to deviate, in certain cases, from the rules of the *halakhah* was subject to this above basic requirement (see *Minhag; Takkanot ha-Kahal*). In later periods different scholars found a legal basis for the authority of the king's law in the idea of an agreement between the king and the people in terms of which the latter allows the king his prerogatives in all matters falling within the king's law in return for his undertaking to guard and protect the people (see Z. H. Chajes: *Torat ha-Nevi'im*, ch. 7 "*Melekh Yisrael*"). This idea was apparently the influence of the commonly accepted medieval theory which based the validity of the king's law on a consensus of the people, a theory which different halakhic scholars also adopted as a basis for the doctrine of *dina de-malkhuta dina*.

Local Jewish Government. Creativity in the legislative field of Jewish law is also evidenced at the local governmental level. The halakhic sources relating to the early part of the Second Temple period already mention certain legislative powers entrusted to the townspeople (*Benei ha-Ir*, see Tosef., BM 11:23, BB 8b). From this modest beginning there developed, at a much later stage, a wide legislative creativity at the hands of the autonomous governmental institutions of the Jewish community and intercommunal organizations. This was expressed in the *takkanot ha-kahal*, enacted, particularly from the tenth century onward, in all fields of the civil, criminal, and administrative law. As in the case of the king's law, it was possible for these enactments to be contrary to a particular rule of the *halakhah*, and the scholars determined ways to ensure that such enactments remained an integral part of the overall Jewish legal system. One of their principal means was to check that the enactments did not conflict with the Jewish law principles of justice and equity. Another contribution to Jewish law, not directly attributable to the halakhic scholars, was that which resulted from participation of the public in some of the institutions of Jewish jurisdiction, such as arbitration and the lay tribunals (see above). Although at times these jurisdictional institutions were prejudicial to the orderly evolution of Jewish law, it may nevertheless be accepted that the generally harmonious cooperation that existed between these institutions and the halakhic scholars enabled the public leaders to make a significant contribution toward the forging of a stronger link between Jewish law and the realities and problems of everyday life. This in turn was a spur to the further development of Jewish law.

THE RELATIONSHIP BETWEEN JEWISH LAW AND FOREIGN LAW

The question of the relationship between Jewish law and foreign law has two aspects. First, the extent—if any—of reciprocal relations and influence of the one on the other in a manner leading to the integration into the one legal system of legal directives deriving from the other; secondly, the extent of the recognition—if any—given to a directive of a foreign legal system, without such recognition involving any integration of the directive into the host system. These are two separate but related aspects, for recognition by the host system of the validity of a foreign legal principle entails, in certain cases, some measure of recognition—witting or unwitting—of the correctness of the foreign principle and of the possibility that the contents of the host legal system may be influenced in a manner leading to the integration of a foreign legal principle into its own framework.

Reciprocal Influences. From the 17th century onward a great deal of research in Jewish law has been devoted to the subject of mutual influence between Jewish law and other legal systems (latterly see B. Cohen, bibl., Introd. and ch. 1). More than any other, this field of research has been particularly conducive to the adoption of an apologetic approach—in the form of both an over-emphasis on the influence of foreign law on the Jewish legal system and exaggeration of the influence of Jewish law on other legal systems. Moreover, the influence of one legal system on another is no easy matter to prove because of the possibility that similar circumstances may have led to the evolution of like institutions in different legal systems, uninfluenced by each other. However, in general it may be said that there were reciprocal relations and influences between Jewish law and the surrounding legal systems or that of the nation under whose political sovereignty Jewish law functioned in any particular period of its history. The fact that the Jewish collectivity lived its social and economic life in accordance with its own law, yet all the while was under the patronage of many different nations with their own legal systems, inevitably left the mark of Jewish law on the other legal systems. The reverse process applied equally: the halakhic scholars were familiar with the law applied in the general courts of the land and sometimes even recommended the adoption of a foreign legal practice which commended itself to them (see, e.g., Elon, Mafte'aḥ 425; *Pesakim u-Khetavim* no. 83; Resp. Israel of Bruna no. 132). In certain cases the halakhic scholars recognized the particular social efficacy of certain aspects of the foreign law (see **Derashot Ran*, Derush no. 11) and sometimes they were not even deterred from lauding the gentile administration of justice when they found this superior to that of the Jews (*Sefer ha-Ḥasidim* no. 1301). To some extent directives of the foreign law were absorbed by Jewish law by means of the legal source of custom (see **Minhag*). When absorption of a foreign principle did take place, such a principle underwent a process of internal "digestion" designed to accommodate it to the general principles and objectives of Jewish law. If in particular social circumstances a foreign principle was occasionally absorbed which conflicted with the fundamental doctrines of Jewish law, such a principle was usually rejected in the end by the Jewish legal system (see, e.g., M. Elon, *Ḥerut ha-Perat ...*, pp. 238–54; 259f.).

Recognition of Foreign Legal Rules. The much-discussed subject of the validity in Jewish law of the provisions of a foreign legal system centers around the doctrine of *dina de-malkhuta dina*, which holds that the law of the land is law and must be followed. The earliest formulation of the doctrine was made in the Babylonian Exile by the *amora* Samuel as appears from some of the legal explanations given for its entrenchment. An unqualified recognition of the provisions of the foreign law pertaining to civil matters—*dinei mamonot* (in matters of ritual law the doctrine of *dina de-malkhuta dina* never applied; *Tashbeẓ*, 1:158 and see above)—would have constituted a serious danger to the orderly evolution of the Jewish legal system and may well have rendered it of theoretical interest only. As the main means of averting this danger many halakhic scholars restricted the scope of the above doctrine—contrary to the plain meaning of some talmudic *halakhot*—by holding it applicable solely to certain matters falling within the sphere of relations between the central authorities and the public, such as taxation, expropriation of property for governmental purposes, and the like. Such restriction was expressly justified on the ground that extension of the doctrine to all matters of civil law would lead to "nullification of all the laws of Israel" (*Beit ha-Beḥirah*, BK 113b). Even the scholars who in principle extended the doctrine beyond matters concerning relations between the authorities and the public (see Resp. Rashba, vol. 1, no. 895; Nov. Ramban, BB 55a; Nov. Ran and *Nimmukei Yosef ibid.*; *Sefer ha-Terumot* 46:8, 5), did not always carry this out in practice (see Resp. Rashba, vol. 6, no. 254) and some scholars restricted the scope of the doctrine in other ways (see *Teshuvot Ḥakhmei Provinẓyah* (ed. A. Sofer), pp. 426f.; *Siftei Kohen*, ḤM 73, n. 39). The *halakhah* was decided according to the view that restricted the application of the doctrine solely to certain matters concerning relations between the authorities and the public (*Rema* ḤM 369:11).

The proliferous and ever-continuing creativity evidenced in talmudic and post-talmudic Jewish law offers eloquent proof of the fact that the doctrine of *dina de-malkhuta dina* remained only a marginal aspect of the Jewish legal system. Indeed, by their judicious use of the doctrine, the scholars rendered it a contributory factor toward the preservation of Jewish judiciai jurisdiction, since qualified recognition of certain matters of foreign law enabled the Jewish collectivity to adapt itself, in the required and necessary manner, to the conditions of the gentile environment. The attitude of Jewish law toward a different legal system is determined, first and foremost, by its basic objective of safeguarding its own continued existence and, flowing therefrom, autonomous Jewish jurisdiction with all that it entails. As long as the realization of this objective is not endangered, no obstacle presents itself in Jewish law to resorting in certain cases, as the need arises, to a rule deriving from foreign law. Even then, however, such recognition is given only to the extent that the rule of the foreign law is not in conflict with any of the fundamental Jewish law principles of justice and equity. For this reason Jewish law attributes no validity to the law of the land with regard to a directive which does not apply equally to all but discriminates between different citizens, since any directive of this nature "is robbery" (Yad, Gezelah 5:14). Similarly, Jewish law holds the imposition of a monetary fine on the whole public, on account of the transgression of a few individuals, to be "absolute robbery" because such conduct contraverts the principle which prohibits the imposition of a collective fine and vicarious criminal responsibility (Resp. Ribash Ha-Ḥadashot no. 9; in support the following references are cited: Gen. 18:25; Num. 15:22; Pes. 113b; see also Deut. 24:15 and II Kings 14:6).

THE ERA OF EMANCIPATION

Inner Spiritual and External Political Changes. On the eve of emancipation and the end of Jewish autonomy, substantial changes began to manifest themselves in Jewish law which were crucial to its development. As already indicated, two basic factors account for the survival of Jewish law as an operative law, even when it was deprived of its single territorial center and political sovereignty: the first the internal discipline of traditional Jewish society which regarded itself enjoined from a national-religious point of view to preserve Jewish law as a living force, and the second the political circumstances of the corporative medieval state. Both these elements now underwent a decisive change. At the same time as the rise of pressures for equality of rights for all, including Jews, the governments of Europe in turn deprived the Jewish community of the mandatory jurisdictional rights of the Jewish courts, even in matters of civil law; the use of the *ḥerem* as well as other means of execution were forbidden. But the main factor for the progressive ending of the living practice of Jewish law was the social-spiritual change that began to assert itself among the Jewish people. The Jewish community, which had hitherto regarded the *halakhah* as the supreme value of its existence, split into a society part of which remained traditional while part no longer regarded itself as bound to the observance of the Torah and its precepts, and this decisively weakened the internal factor of a religious imperative to order daily practical life in accordance with Jewish law. This substantive change in the spiritual outlook of the Jewish world carried with it also a disregard for the national element in Jewish law and not only did the leaders of the community not oppose the abolition of Jewish judicial autonomy but a good number of them welcomed the ending of the "separation" between the Jewish and the general public, regarding it as promising achievement of the hoped-for freedoms and equality of rights as well as organic integration into the vibrant Europe of the emancipation era.

The Abrogation of Jewish Judicial Autonomy. With the beginning of this transformation relating to the continued existence of Jewish judicial autonomy, a number of the leading halakhic scholars gave voice to their concern and warned about the religious and national dangers inherent in yielding up this autonomy. Thus R. Ezekiel *Landau railed against the frequent recourse to the gentile courts, a practice so prevalent that "all three pillars of the world are shaken: the Law, Truth and Peace" (*Derushei ha-Ẓelaḥ*, 8:14; 22:24). R. Raphael *Cohn, spiritual leader of various communities in Poland-Lithuania and Germany in the 18th century, devoted much effort in the latter years of his life toward the preservation of an autonomous Jewish legal system and all it entailed. Acknowledging the new reality of a laxity in Torah observance by a section of the Jewish public, he emphasized that the neglect of recourse to Jewish judicial jurisdiction was the most serious defect in non-observance of the laws of the Torah, and he particularly criticized those members of the Jewish public who saw the abrogation of such Jewish jurisdiction as a step toward equality of rights and duties (see *Zekher Ẓaddik*, pp. 7, 8, 20).

These political and spiritual changes, which were increasingly manifest in the course of the 19th century, left their impress upon that part of Jewry that continued to preserve the religious tradition. As regards Western and Central European Jewry, recourse to the general courts rapidly became widespread and common to all Jewish circles. Traditional Jewry of Eastern Europe still preserved for some considerable time its connection with Jewish law and brought its disputes to the rabbi and his *bet din* for *din Torah*. However, the decisions of the rabbinical courts became more and more arbitral awards and compromise settlements, lacking the semblance of judgments under a living and organic law, and in the course of time, here also, resort to the general courts grew increasingly. Even the halakhic scholars reconciled themselves with the new situation of the lack of judicial autonomy and justified it on the principle of *dina de-malkhuta dina*—quite contrary to the attitude taken by the scholars in earlier periods (see, e.g., *Kelei Ḥemdah*, Mishpatim, no. 1, and see above). The main and greater part of Jewish law in civil and criminal, administrative and public matters, came to be treated as if it were rules "not contemporaneously applied" and now studied merely theoretically. The only sphere of Jewish law that continued to be practiced was a part of family law, the arrangement of marriage and divorce in accordance therewith. In this field, involving the laws of prohibitions and permissions, a powerful internal discipline continued to govern traditional Jewry and to some extent also those who did not observe religious precepts. However, recognition by the central authorities of such marriage and divorce varied from country to country in the Diaspora.

Continuance of Judicial Autonomy in the Eastern Jewish Centers. An interesting phenomenon is the fact that to some extent Jewish law continued to develop as a living law among oriental Jewish communities in Turkey, North Africa, and elsewhere. This phenomenon is partly explained by the different political circumstances of the Ottoman Empire in the 19th and 20th centuries, but was also an outcome of the determined struggle waged by oriental Jewish communities, as in Algeria for instance, to retain their judicial independence in the face of efforts by the central authorities to impose on them the general law of the land. A demonstrative expression of this reality is the fact that even in the 19th century the responsa literature of this Jewry continued to occupy itself to a very large extent with matters of the *Ḥoshen Mishpat* arising from actual events in everyday life, while the responsa literature of European Jewry of this period is very poor in this respect and even then is more of a theoretical study than a consideration or practical problems.

Consequences of the Abrogation of Judicial Autonomy. The abrogation of Jewish judicial autonomy carried with it two far-reaching consequences with regard to the world of Jewish law. In the first place, Jewish law's dynamism as a living law of practice was greatly inhibited and its organic development suffered a marked curtailment. It was unfortunate for Jewish law that this development occurred in the course of the 19th century, a period which saw a revolution in social, economic, and industrial life that left a decisive imprint on different legal fields. The other consequence was the loss, by the greater part of the 19th-century Diaspora communities, of the former deep national and religious awareness that daily practical life, ordered in accordance with Jewish law, in all fields, became an integral part of the way of life of the Jewish people. This consequence, as was later to become apparent, carried even more fateful implications for Jewish law than those flowing from the first-mentioned consequence.

THE PERIOD OF JEWISH NATIONAL AWAKENING

Ha-Mishpat ha-Ivri Society and Mishpat ha-Shalom ha-Ivri. The Jewish national awakening and the rise of Zionism also evoked a change in the mental attitude of the Jewish people toward Jewish law. Soon after the *Balfour Declaration the Ha-Mishpat ha-Ivri Society was founded in Moscow. Its members—drawn from all sections of the Jewish public—regarded the return of Jewish society to Jewish law as an aspect of national renaissance parallel to the building of the Jewish homeland and revival of the Hebrew language. Among the goals set by the society was the preparation of suitable literature on Jewish law and the establishment in Jerusalem of an institute—within the framework of a university—for research into that law preparatory to its adoption in the future Jewish state. In the editorial introduction to the first number of the journal *Ha-Mishpat ha-Ivri* (Moscow, 1918) it is noted that "the 'legal' *halakhah* has been integrally bound up with the 'religious' *halakhah* . . . [yet] . . . over the last decades a process has begun of separating out our law from its religion and ethics, and we intend to continue this process in order to prepare our law for a secular existence." The pursuit of this object was and still is a controversial one and its desirability as well as manner of achievement remain central problems relating to the integration of Jewish law into the legal system of the State of Israel (see below).

In 1909–10, on the initiative of the head of the Palestine office of the Zionist Organization, Mishpat ha-Shalom ha-Ivri was established in Jaffa as a judicial institution for the adjudication of disputes between Jews in Ereẓ Israel. In the course of time district tribunals were established in a number of places and over them a supreme tribunal. Between the years 1918 and 1936 rules and regulations were issued containing directives as to judicial organs, procedure, evidence, and so on. The first head of Mishpat ha-Shalom ha-Ivri was Arthur *Ruppin and the writer S. Y. *Agnon served as its first secretary. Mishpat ha-Shalom ha-Ivri functioned as an arbitral body and its work was facilitated by the enactment of the Arbitration Ordinance in 1926, which recognized the submission of disputes not only to individual arbitrators but also to an existing "arbitration tribunal" (see *Arbitration). It worked alongside the official bodies, first of the Ottoman Imperial government and later of the Mandatory power, and alongside the rabbinical courts. Mishpat ha-Shalom ha-Ivri did not, however, achieve its goal. Its main activities were confined to the years 1920–30 and after this date the number of cases brought before it began to wane. All in all it cannot be said to have produced any real harvest of Jewish law in consequence of its deliberations and decisions. Some of the reasons for this were objective, such as the tribunal's lack of powers of compulsion and the fact that it provoked sharp criticism from the rabbinical courts, the leaders of national religious Jewry, and respected scholars such as S. *Assaf who were opposed to the existence of fixed judicial bodies outside the framework of the rabbinical courts and in opposition to them. Mainly, however, its lack of success was due to the fact that not only did it not assume to decide according to the existing *halakhah* as set out in the Shulḥan Arukh *Ḥoshen Mishpat* and the subsequent halakhic literature, but it possessed no system of norms, either of Jewish law or generally, upon which to act. In fact, proceedings before this tribunal were much like inquiries by laymen based on generally conceived principles of justice and equity, ethics and public good, since the judges were for the larger part persons of general education only, without any legal training or specific knowledge of law (see P. Daikan, *Toledot Mishpat ha-Shalom ha-Ivri*, and bibl. there cited; J. Yonovitz, Introd. to S. Assaf, *Ha-Onshin* . . . (1922), 5–6).

Jewish Law in the Rabbinical Courts. At the beginning of the 20th century the rabbinical courts in Ereẓ Israel displayed a total lack of central organization. With the establishment of the Chief Rabbinate in 1921, most of the rabbinical courts came to organize themselves within the framework of this institution. In matters of personal status, the rabbinical courts were assigned exclusive jurisdiction as regards marriage, divorce, and "probate" of wills, and concurrent jurisdiction as regards maintenance, succession, etc. (all other areas of the law remained within the jurisdiction of the general Mandatory courts). The task of this supreme halakhic institution was pictured by its first head, Rabbi *Kook. After outlining the important creative role played by the *battei din* in all periods, through the enactment of *takkanot*, he went on to add that "in our renewed national life in Ereẓ Israel there will certainly sometimes be great need to make important *takkanot* which, as long as they are consented to by the majority of the competent scholars and are then accepted by the community, will carry the force of a law of the Torah" (*Ha-Tor*, 1 (1921), nos. 18, 21–22). To some extent the rabbinical courts were equal to this important task in matters of procedure and personal status, but in all other areas of Jewish law almost nothing was achieved.

MATTERS OF PROCEDURE AND PERSONAL STATUS. An

important *takkanah* enacted immediately in 1921 established the Rabbinical Supreme Court of Appeal, thus introduced a regular appellate tribunal which had not previously existed in Jewish law (see *Practice and Procedure). That this *takkanah* rendered the appellate court an integral part of the Jewish legal system was made clear in a judgment of the Rabbinical High Court of Appeal of Jerusalem which rejected the contention that no right of appeal existed in Jewish law, holding that "the right of appeal has been enacted by a rabbinical *takkanah*, the force of which is as that of a rule of our Holy Torah" (OPD, p. 71).

At first the rules of procedure in the rabbinical court left much to be desired, but improvement followed upon the publication in 1943 of procedural regulations by the Chief Rabbinate Council. These included detailed provisions on the initiation of proceedings, on procedure during the hearing, rules of evidence, modes of appeal, and on other matters. A series of forms were also appended, among them statements of claim, summonses of parties and witnesses, applications for appeal and so on. In part these regulations were based on Jewish law and in part they showed the influence of existing practice in the general legal system. An innovation in Jewish law were the detailed rules laid down concerning the payment of various court fees and the adoption of children. The most radical innovation introduced by the above regulations involved an engagement by the rabbinical courts to distribute the estate of a deceased person in accordance with the provisions of the Succession Ordinance of 1923, which prescribed an order of distribution treating husband and wife and son and daughter in terms of equality. In 1944 a number of *takkanot* were enacted introducing further important changes: the customary minimum sum of the *ketubbah* was increased; the levir refusing to grant the widow of his brother *ḥaliẓah* was rendered obliged to maintain her until releasing her (see *Levirate Marriage and *Ḥaliẓah*); an important *takkanah* imposed on the father the legal duty to maintain his sons and daughters up to the age of 15 years and not merely until the age of six years in accordance with talmudic law (see *Parent and Child; M. Elon, *Ḥakikah Datit* . . ., 157ff.).

After 1944, however, creativity by way of *takkanot* ceased almost entirely, except for three additional *takkanot* enacted by the Chief Rabbinate in 1950 (the principal one involving a prohibition on the marriage of children under the age of 16 years; see *Child Marriage). This may be regarded as a matter for great regret since a number of urgent problems in the area of personal status still await solution by way of *takkanah* (such as certain cases of hardship for the **agunah*, problems relating to the joint property of the spouses, and other matters). On the other hand, there has since the 1940s been halakhic creativity in the area of personal status by means of interpretation as applied in actual cases. In this manner, for instance, there was innovated the substantive principle giving a woman, upon divorce, the right to receive over and above her *ketubbah* a certain additional sum, called "compensation." The amount thereof varies with the circumstances, one of the important considerations in its determination being the need to award the woman part of the property acquired in the course of the marriage through the joint efforts of the spouses (see M. Elon, *Ḥakikah Datit* . . ., loc. cit.).

OTHER FIELDS OF THE LAW. In fields of the law other than personal status the rabbinical courts were assigned no jurisdiction under the general law of the land, and the bearers of the *halakhah* initiated no real effort toward adaption of the Jewish legal system to the contemporary social and economic needs of Ereẓ Israel Jewry. The call to the people to submit their disputes in civil matters to the rabbinical courts by way of arbitration brought a very restricted response, even from the religious section of the community. Hence, except in a few exceptional cases, no evidence is to be found in the judgments of the rabbinical courts of any creative activity in the overwhelming part of the civil law. One notable exception is represented by a leading judgment given in 1946, in a matter concerning the laws of evidence. A marriage was entered into before two witnesses in the absence of a rabbi. As violators of the Sabbath both witnesses were incompetent (Sh. Ar., ḤM 34:2, 24) and since they were the only witnesses the marriage stood to be regarded invalid according to Jewish law. On the man's death, this was the contention raised by the remaining heirs of the deceased in opposition to the woman's claim to the widow's share in the estate of the deceased. The court, however, recognized the validity of the marriage, holding the witnesses to have been competent: "For reasons of religious transgression . . . and bearing in mind the fact . . . that libertarianism has increasingly spread for general and universal reasons, transgressions of this kind are not likely to affect the credibility of witnesses . . . who act almost unwittingly. The disqualification of transgressors as witnesses arises from the fear that their evidence will be false . . . and therefore in such cases the credibility of a witness is largely determined by reasons of time and place. If it is clear to the court that the person is not one who is likely to lie for the sake of deriving a benefit, he is to be admitted as a competent witness" (OPD, p. 137). This decision of principle was essential to the proper administration of justice under present day social realities in which a substantial part of the public is not religiously observant, and it is carried out in practice by the rabbinical courts.

Jewish Law and the Hebrew Language. It is appropriate that the quest for the restoration of Jewish law as a law of practice be compared with the struggle for the revival of Hebrew as a spoken language. From one aspect the latter represented the more difficult task. Ever since the beginning of the Diaspora, Hebrew had served almost exclusively as a literary language, not spoken in the common pursuits of everyday life, and as a result of emancipation it came to be further and further removed from life—even the spiritual and cultural—of the Jewish people. Many of the faithful followers of the Zionist movement in its early stages entertained doubt about the possibility of using Hebrew in modern conditions: "Who among us knows sufficient Hebrew to ask for a train ticket in this language?" asked Herzl, who contemplated a Jewish state without Hebrew as its commonly spoken language (*The Jewish State*, ch. 5). Yet an inner awareness that the use of Hebrew in the social, economic, and cultural life of the people was a prime requisite without which there could be no complete national revival led eventually to Hebrew becoming not merely a holy tongue, but the national language, written and spoken, of the Jewish people returning to its homeland. As a result of the untiring efforts of individuals and public bodies expressions and terms were coined and style and forms created, largely drawn from the ancient treasure houses of the language, and in this manner there flowered a modern living language based on and preserving continuity with the ancient holy tongue.

In other respects the possibility of restoring Jewish law was more limited than the revival of Hebrew, which is not so dependent on political sovereignty or assistance from the ruling authorities and is more closely connected with individual inclination and the wishes of interested bodies; legal norms encroach more on the realm of philosophy and ideological outlook than do the byways of a language and the task of restoring Jewish law demanded more comprehensive study and preparation than did the revival of

Hebrew. Yet it is conceivable that these obstacles to the restoration of Jewish law could have been overcome by a determined effort. To a large extent the political autonomy of the Jews in Ereẓ Israel in the pre-state period was similar to that enjoyed by the Jewish people in the Diaspora until emancipation, an autonomy which also allowed for judicial independence. Moreover, by far the greater part of the subject matter with which Jewish law deals—such as obligations, property, public administration, and so on—is free of fundamental religious or ideological dispute. However, emancipation had produced a weakened religious and national consciousness of the need for daily life to be ordered in accordance with Jewish law, and all sections of the population displayed an irresolute apathy toward the preparation of Jewish law for its historic task. It is true that research was undertaken and books were written by scholars such as A. *Gulak, S. *Assaf, and A. *Freimann, which were of importance for the scientific research of Jewish law. But the required auxiliary literature of the law, written in convenient form with the law phrased and classified in accordance with modern legal concepts and terminology, was not prepared, nor were possible solutions to modern legal problems for which Jewish law has no ready or adequate existing answer, although it allows for one to be found by way of *takkanah* or any other of its recognized creative legal sources.

The Legal System in Ereẓ Israel Preceding the Establishment of the State of Israel. The unique legal system in force in Ereẓ Israel under the British mandatory regime was a factor which might have served as a strong stimulus toward the integration of Jewish law into the legal system of the State about to be established. The principles which governed the mandatory legal system were set out in Article 46 of the Palestine Order in Council of 1922. In accordance with this, on the eve of the establishment of the State of Israel there was crystallized a legal system nourished by a number of legal systems: the *Mejelle*, based on Muslim religious law; various Ottoman laws embracing principles of French law and other legal systems; mandatory ordinances based on English law; law based on the English common law and doctrines of equity introduced into the mandatory legal system, in cases where the existing system provided no solutions to concrete problems. In addition, matters of personal status were to a considerable extent dealt with under the religious law of the different communities recognized by the general law. This was a legal system composed of a number of disparate elements and created a situation inviting its own replacement by a homogeneous legal system.

JEWISH LAW IN THE STATE OF ISRAEL

The Official Position Assigned to Jewish Law. On the establishment of the State of Israel, Jewish law continued to occupy the same official position in the legal structure of the state as it had done in the pre-State period. The Law and Administration Ordinance of 1948 prescribed that the law in existence on the eve of establishment of the state should remain in force (sec. 11), with the practical result that officially Jewish law was incorporated in the area of personal status only. At the same time the Hebrew language celebrated its final victory, even in a formal sense, and section 15b of the above ordinance repealed any provision in any law requiring the use of English, thus making Hebrew the language of the state, of its law, and of its everyday life.

Matters of Personal Status. The jurisdiction of the rabbinical courts was defined in a Knesset law of 1953 which, save for one or two changes, entailed no substantial departure from the existing situation. It gave the rabbinical courts exclusive jurisdiction in matters of *marriage, *divorce, and *ḥaliẓah;* as regards the wife's claim for maintenance, jurisdiction is given to the court to which the wife applies—the rabbinical or the district court. In this and in other laws there were also prescribed the circumstances in which the rabbinical courts have concurrent jurisdiction in other matters of personal status (see *Adoption; *Apotropos; *Maintenance; *Succession).

The Rabbinical Courts. Matters entrusted to the jurisdiction of the rabbinical courts are naturally dealt with in accordance with Jewish law. In the course of their activities these courts have given decisions introducing a number of important innovations in Jewish law, such as a married woman's right to the income deriving from the pursuit of her own profession, and recognition of the existence of mutual pecuniary rights between spouses married abroad in a civil ceremony only, and so on (see M. Elon, *Ḥakikah Datit ...*, 166–72). In certain matters the law prescribes that the rabbinical courts too must decide in accordance with the general law. In the Succession Ordinance of 1923 provision was made for the treatment of son and daughter, husband and wife, on terms of equality as regards the division of certain kinds of property on succession, and the Women's Equal Rights Law, 1951, extended the directive to all other property. Some of the other main provisions of this law are the following: men and women are equated as regards all legal acts; the father and mother are given natural guardianship of their children; a married woman is given full capacity of acquisition during marriage and retention of her rights to property acquired by her prior to the marriage. In addition this law allows the litigants, if they are above the age of 18 years, to consent to having their case tried according to the laws of their community. It also states that its provisions shall not affect any halakhic prohibition or permission relating to marriage or divorce. In the main its provisions accord with the position under Jewish law as it has evolved (for instance as regards equal rights on succession), a notable exception relating to the husband's right to the fruits of his wife's *melog* property (see *Husband and Wife). A law of 1955 prescribes the status and manner of appointment of rabbinical court *dayyanim* and, except for two variations, its provisions correspond closely to those laid down in the Judges Law, 1953. (As regards two variations see M. Elon, *Ḥakikah Datit ...*, 47–49.)

The General Courts. In matters of personal status concerning Jewish parties the general courts are also required to decide according to Jewish law, except when a law of the state makes express provision on the matter. As already mentioned, the general courts have jurisdiction in all matters not entrusted to the exclusive jurisdiction of the rabbinical courts. Matters of marriage and divorce may also be pronounced on by the general courts, either when the problem arises incidentally to the matter before the court (for instance in a claim by the wife for maintenance there may arise incidentally thereto the question of the validity of her marriage), or in a matter brought before the Supreme Court sitting as a High Court of Justice. Possibly a rabbinical court and a general court, even though both apply Jewish law, may arrive at entirely different conclusions. Thus, for instance, the general courts first resort to the principles of private international law before applying Jewish law and therefore may recognize a marriage entered into abroad as valid in accordance with the law of the country concerned, even when it is invalid according to Jewish law. In addition the general courts apply only substantive Jewish law and not its laws of evidence and procedure, thus for instance admitting the testimony of the parties themselves and that of their relatives.

Legislative Provisions Contrary to Jewish Law. Legislation in the area of personal status contrary to Jewish law is reflected in a number of provisions, scattered in various Knesset laws, which confer on the commonly reputed spouse ("wife" as well as "husband") numerous rights. These provisions relate to rights of a social-economic nature (pensions, tenants' protection, and so on), rights under the Succession Law, and include also the right conferred on a woman to give her child born of the man reputed to be her husband the latter's family name, even without his consent. These rights were held by the Supreme Court to extend to the commonly reputed spouse even though the latter (or even both parties) be validly married to another (except with regard the right of succession, which is only available if, upon the death of one of the parties who have lived together as husband and wife in a common household, neither is then married to another). The explanation that the above enactments were made in order to alleviate the hardship which is sometimes suffered by a couple who are unable to marry on account of Jewish law prohibition (for instance in certain cases of the *agunah*) is indeed weighty and hope may be expressed that the Chief Rabbinate will speedily find solutions to these problems. Nevertheless, it does not seem to justify the institution of the reputed spouse with its threat to the orderly existence of the family unit. This institution is the subject of controversy in Israel society and there are recent indications of a tendency by the Supreme Court to limit its scope (see M. Elon, *Ḥakikah Datit* . . ., 119–54).

"Who is a Jew?"—Answered According to Jewish Law. In March 1970 an amendment to the Law of Return of 1950 incorporated into this law a most material principle of Jewish law. This law, which ensures for every Jew the right to come to Israel as an *oleh* and automatic citizenship from the moment of his arrival, was amended to define the term "Jew" as a person born of a Jewish mother or converted to Judaism, who is not a member of a different religious faith. This definition, including the latter part, is entirely in accord with Jewish law. A Jew converted to a different faith remains a Jew as regards his personal status and all this entails—such as the need for him to grant a divorce to his Jewish wife—but he is deprived of various religio-social rights and is not numbered as a member of the Jewish community (i.e., he cannot be counted toward **minyan* and so on); for this reason he is also deprived of the rights of a Jew under the Law of Return. The stated definition applies also for purposes of registering an individual's Jewish nationality *(le'om)* in the population register and related documents, including the identity card (see also *Jew).

Legislation Conforming With Ritual Law. In addition to the already mentioned cases, Israel law is also based on the *halakhah*—in the wide sense of the term—in a number of different matters. Thus in 1948 the Provisional Council of State enacted that the supply of *kasher* food be ensured to all Jewish soldiers of the Defense Army of Israel; a law of 1962 prohibits the raising, keeping, or slaughtering of pigs in Israel except in specified areas (populated mainly by non-Jews) and for certain other limited purposes; the provisions of the Law and Administration Ordinance of 1948 (as amended) lay down that the Sabbath and the Jewish festivals shall be prescribed days of rest in the state (but do not prohibit labor on such days, such matters being ordered in certain respects in the Hours of Work and Rest Law of 1951) and allows non-Jews the right to observe their own Sabbath and festivals as days of rest.

The "Unofficial" Application of Jewish Law in the State. Independence of the Israel Legal System. As already mentioned, Jewish law is reserved no official place in the Israel legal system save in matters of personal status. The proposal (made by P. Daikan on the eve of the state's establishment and subsequently raised again by others) that Israel law be freed from its independence on the English common law and principles of equity and that Jewish law be resorted to in any case of lacuna in the law of the state (see above, Art. 46 of the Palestine Order in Council) was not accepted. Until the present time there is to be found in two Laws only, the Succession Law of 1965 and the Land Law of 1969, a provision (entitled "Autarky of this Law") which excludes the operation of the aforementioned article 46 in all matters with which the relevant law is concerned. None of the other laws so far passed by the Knesset proclaims its own independent operation. To some extent such independence has been established in the case law in consequence of decisions by the Supreme Court to the effect that the post-1948 English case law does not have binding force in Israel law as does that of the pre-1948 period, and even reliance on the pre-1948 English case law is also gradually diminishing.

Legislation Based on Jewish Law Principles. In some measure law in the State of Israel follows the principles of Jewish law even in areas where the latter system has not officially been rendered applicable. In the introduction to a draft bill for one of the early comprehensive laws there were set out the general legislative guidelines adopted for the entire area of the civil law. The legislative policy thus enunciated assigned to Jewish law the status of "the main but not the only or binding source" and enumerated the existing legal and factual position in Israel as well as the laws of other countries as additional sources (Draft Bill for a Succession Law, published by the Ministry of Justice in 1952). To some extent this policy has been adhered to in practice and some of the matters enacted in accordance with the principles of Jewish law are the following: the possibility of separate ownership of dwellings in a cooperative house (see *Ownership); the prohibition of delay in the payment of wages (see *Labor Law); the right of the dismissed employee to severance pay (see **Ha'anakah*); the legal arrangement concerning imprisonment for debt; the laws of bailment (see **Shomerim*), and so on. Particular reliance on Jewish law is to be found in the provisions of various Knesset laws in the area of family law, relating among others to the following matters: the duty of a person to maintain, besides his wife and children, also his other relatives (on the Jewish law principle of obliging a person to uphold the *mitzvah* of *ẓedakah;* see *Maintenance); in matters of guardianship that the minor's own good is the primary consideration and that "the court is the father of all orphans" and a complete departure—expressed in various provisions—from the Roman law concept of *patria potestas* (see *Apotropos); in matters of succession Jewish law is followed in the conferment of equal rights on all children of the deceased whether born in or out of wedlock, in the solution provided to the problem which arises in the case of commorientes (see *Succession), in acceptance of the Jewish law institution of a *shekhiv mera* will (see *Wills) and in the provision made for maintenance out of the estate of the deceased (see *Widow).

Legislation Contrary to Jewish Law. In contrast, there are Knesset laws containing provisions which are—without any real justification—contrary to the position taken by Jewish law. Some of the matters so enacted are the following: the right of the creditor to turn directly to the surety even without initial agreement to this effect (see *Surety); the right of a party to plead prescription of a claim along with an admission as to the existence of the debt (see *Limitation of Actions); the automatic administration of an oath to all witnesses whereas Jewish law leaves the matter to the discretion of the court (Resp. Ribash no. 170; *Tashbeẓ*, 3:15; *Rema* ḤM 28:2; for further illustrations see Elon, in: ILR, 4 (1969), 80–140).

JEWISH LAW IN THE CASE LAW OF THE GENERAL COURTS. The decisions of the courts, particularly of the Supreme Court, represent a further channel through which the influence of Jewish law is brought to bear on the Israel legal system. In numerous decisions of the Supreme Court diverse legal matters have been dealt with by way of a comparison between the position under the general law and Jewish law respectively, the two systems sometimes leading the judges to the same conclusion and sometimes otherwise. In some cases Jewish law has been quoted for the purpose of construing legal terms and definitions and on occasion Jewish law has constituted the primary legal source relied on by the Supreme Court, even in areas in which Jewish law is not expressly rendered applicable. This integration of Jewish law through the case law of the general courts is of great practical significance from the aspect of the confrontation between Jewish law and the legal problems that have arisen before the courts in the 1950s and 1960s.

JEWISH LAW IN THE CASE LAW OF THE RABBINICAL COURTS. A noteworthy phenomenon is the existence of a proliferous case law of the rabbinical courts, in diverse areas of the civil law, in matters coming before these courts as arbitral bodies. Some 30% of the judgments of these courts published since the middle of the 1960s deal with matters unrelated to personal status and concern, for instance, labor law, contracts, copyright, partnership, pledge, administrative law, and so on. These offer an instructive insight into the manner in which concrete questions of everyday life are dealt with in accordance with Jewish law and represent an important contribution to the solution of modern social and economic problems (see, e.g., *Contract; **Ha'anakah;* *Labor Law; *Public Authority).

Attitudes Toward Jewish Law in the Law of the State. Integration of Jewish law into the legal system of Israel is sometimes opposed because it entails a "secularization" of the *halakhah* since the acceptance by the state of a Jewish law principle does not stem from recognition of the binding validity of such a principle from the religious point of view, but is dictated by purely human and national interests. The argument views that by such integration the Knesset's own binding authority substitutes itself as the source of authority of any Jewish law principle it has adopted, and that neither the Knesset nor the general courts possess the necessary qualifications postulated by the halakhic system for deciding any of its rules. This view is decried by a decisive majority of religious Jewry and its spiritual leaders, who consider that the *halakhah* does not become secularized for the mere reason that the theory of the general law may hold a change to have taken place as regards the basic norm of a particular halakhic rule. It is argued that neither the Knesset nor the courts purport—nor indeed is it possible for them to do so—to decide the *halakhah* within the religious meaning of such activity; that not only is the *halakhah* not prejudiced by its integration into the legal system of the state, but the halakhic system itself commends that the legal order in the Jewish state shall, even if not based on religious faith, correspond with the substance of Jewish law and its principles of justice and equity rather than be founded on other legal systems. For some generations now this middle path has been followed by a decisive majority of religious Jewry, also with regard to other fundamental Jewish values, as with the revived use of the holy tongue in everyday secular life and with the settlement of the holy land even without observance of the religious precepts. The declared attitude of non-observant Jewry also favors the assignment of first priority to the reception of Jewish law principles when these are in keeping with present-day social and economic needs (see, e.g., the statement made in the session of Nov. 29, 1965, by Knesset members belonging to almost all political parties with reference to the Gift Law and Pledge Law Bills (*Divrei ha-Keneset*, v. 44, pp. 24–36)). It should be borne in mind that except in the area of family law the subject matter of Jewish law is generally free of fundamental public dispute of a religious or ideological nature.

The integration of Jewish law into the legal system of Israel is of importance to the former since it has a vital need to contend with the problems of practical everyday life as the only means toward the restoration of its former, almost unbroken, creative and evolutionary function, and this in its natural environment—the Jewish state and its legal system. Such an integration of Jewish law is no less important for the legal system of the State. Israel legislation is of an eclectic nature, the legislator choosing as he sees fit from many different legal systems. There is well-founded apprehension that this must necessarily result in a lack of homogeneity and lead to contradictions in Israel law due to the absence of a common axis around which the entire legal structure may revolve. A legal system so constructed moreover lacks roots and a past. If, as the revival of Hebrew proved, a people's language has to lean on history and foundations, then a priori a people's legal system requires roots and a past on which to draw for sustenance and growth. The absence of these requisites in Israel law accounts for the large number of Supreme Court decisions evidencing resort to numerous legal systems in a search for solutions to legal problems. The appointed way for the emerging legal system of the Jewish state to take root, to find the common denominator for its laws as well as the homogeneity it requires, is for it to become linked and integrated in the proper way with historical Jewish legal thinking and creativity.

Modes of Integration. Achievement of the desired integration of Jewish law with the Israel legal system demands strict observance of the rule that in all legislative activity preference be given to every principle of Jewish law which is in keeping with the existing social and economic exigencies. It is also necessary to ensure that all principles of Jewish law adopted in the laws of the state shall be construed within the spirit of the Jewish sources of law from which they were derived. Finally, it is necessary to lay down a "Jewish version" of the controversial Article 46, to the effect that the Jewish sources of law shall be resorted to in the event of any lacuna in the existing law. The decisions of the Supreme Court and of the rabbinical courts in matters involving Jewish law—not only in the area of personal status but in all its different fields—and a long series of varied research studies undertaken in recent years, point to the fact that it is within the power of Jewish law to contend successfully with the overall range of new problems that arise. In addition, Jewish law occupies a substantial part of the law faculty study curriculum at different universities in Israel and to the new generation of Israel lawyers and jurists Jewish law is no longer a remote and unfamiliar subject. Accelerated research activity in the different fields of Jewish law and the preparation of an auxiliary literature to facilitate study of and resort to the latter will be invaluable aids to the process of integrating the legal system of the State of Israel and Jewish law.

Legal Creativity. During various periods of its history Jewish law has experienced the reality of jurisdiction and legislation existing alongside the jurisdictional and legislative system of the halakhic authority itself—as illustrated by the king's law, jurisdiction of the public leadership, lay jurisdiction, and communal enactments. In numerous matters such jurisdiction and legislation of the Jewish leadership diverged from the rules of Jewish law, but the halakhic system evolved a series of rules and principles which ensured that such jurisdiction and legislation of the public leadership became an integral part of the overall system (see above *Takkanot ha-Kahal*). It is true that during all the above-mentioned periods the entire Jewish people looked upon Jewish law as the ultimate and binding value, whereas the same cannot be said of the present-day Jewish public, which, in the existing socio-cultural realities, finds itself divided on matters of religious faith and ideological outlook. Yet in this society there have developed certain cultural and social values—such as the restored language and homeland—which exist as the undisputed assets of all. Consequently the hope may be expressed that the acceptance of Jewish law principles into the legal system of Israel in a proper and consistent manner, along with the latter's formation of a tie with Jewish law for purposes of its own supplementation, will ensure that at some time in the future unity and integrity— and thereby continuity as well—will also be restored to this precious cultural and spiritual asset of the Jewish nation, that is, Jewish law.

Bibliography: Gulak, Yesodei, 1 (1922), 3–31; 4 (1922), 3–45; S. Assaf, *Ha-Onshin Aḥarei Ḥatimat ha-Talmud* (1922); idem, *Battei ha-Din ve-Sidreihem Aḥarei Ḥatimat ha-Talmud* (1924); A. H. Freimann, in: *Lu'aḥ ha-Arez* (1945/46), 110–25; Ḥ. Cohen, in: *Ha-Peraklit*, 3 (1946), 38ff.; Baron, Community; Hebrew Law and the State of Israel: a Symposium, in: *Sura*, 3 (1957/58), 457–518; Alon, Toledot[2]; Alon, Meḥkarim; M. Silberg, *Kakh Darko shel Talmud* (1961), 66ff.; Finkelstein, Middle Ages; M. Elon, *Ḥerut ha-Perat be-Darkhei Geviyyat Ḥov*... (1964), 11–14 (introd.), 255–69; idem, in: ILR, 2 (1967), 515–65; 3 (1968), 88–126; 416–57; 4 (1969), 80–140; idem, in: *Ha-Peraklit*, 25 (1968/69), 27–53; idem, *Ḥakikah Datit*... (1968); B. Cohen, *Jewish and Roman Law*, 2 vols. (1966); J. I. Englard, in: ILR, 3 (1968), 254–78.

[M.E.]

MI-SINAI NIGGUNIM (Heb.-Yidd. נִגּוּנִים, נִגּוּנֵי מִסִּינַי "Melodies from Mt. Sinai"), Hebrew term for a traditional group of cantorial melodies sung in the Ashkenazi synagogues of both East and West European rite and regarded as obligatory and for which no other melody may be substituted. Located at those points in the service where the liturgical and emotional elements join in equal force, the *Mi-Sinai* tunes may be called the heart of Ashkenazi synagogue song.

Mi-Sinai is an abbreviated form of **Halakhah le-Moshe mi-Sinai*, referring to an ordinance going back to Moses, who received it on Mt. Sinai. The term was connected with biblical chant in the 12th century (*Sefer Ḥasidim*, ed. Wistinezki-Freimann §817); its present application is due to A. Z. *Idelsohn. In cantorial circles, the *Mi-Sinai* melodies are called "Tunes of our Rabbi Maharil" (erroneously, also Maharal), or, in Eastern Europe, *skarbowe niggunim* (Polish: "official" tunes).

The family of *Mi-Sinai* tunes includes about ten solemn compositions which are associated mainly with prayers of the Penitential Days (see ex. 1–7). The exact scope cannot be determined precisely, since the tradition is not unanimous and was never codified authoritatively. The distinctive features of the melodies are as follows: they must belong to the common patrimony of the Eastern and Western Ashkenazi rites; must invariably be found in their proper liturgical place; and must exhibit a special musical structure (see below). Accordingly, ancient psalmodies such as **Akdamut Millin*, or the many melodies designated as "ancient" by the 19th century compilers, and well-known hymn melodies (e.g., **Eli Ẓiyyon*) do not belong to this category. A close examination reveals that they do not entirely comply with the conditions, and no *ḥazzan* would count them among the *Mi-Sinai* tunes. However, there still remain some border cases which are classified differently by different writers.

The usual concept of "melody" as an indivisible unit is not applicable to the *Mi-Sinai niggunim*. They are real compositions built of several sections ("movements") of individual character. These are often fitted to the divisions of the text (e.g., the **Kaddish*), but may also be constructed on an independent plan (e.g., the **Kol Nidrei* tune). In

Mi-Sinai tunes: inventory of initial motives. No. 2, cf. **Amidah;* earliest notation, 1783 (Aaron Beer). No. 3, for full version see *Music, example 30; earliest evidence, c. 1800 (Jacob Goldstein). No. 4, cf. **Aleinu le-Shabbe'aḥ;* earliest evidence, 1765 (A. Beer). No. 5, earliest notation, 1765 (A. Beer). No. 6, cf. **Avodah;* earliest notation, 1791 (A. Beer). No. 7, earliest notation, 1744 (Judah Elias of Hanover). No. 8, earliest evidence, 1782 (A. Beer). Nos. 1 and 9, conventional form notated by H. Avenary.

general, the first section is individual and characteristic of the specific tune; the following ones may include motives or entire themes of other *niggunim*, thereby creating a "family likeness" among the members of this group. Every section contains one or more "themes," which are composed of short motives (see music examples of **Aleinu*; **Avodah*). The order of these themes is usually constant, distinguishing this music clearly from the **nusaḥ* style. An important feature is the plasticity of themes and motives, which allows for their easy adaptation to a wide range of texts. Still more characteristic is the liberty granted to the performer to shape the music by himself; tradition prescribes only the approximate layout and motivic profile—an "idea" which the singer must realize in sounds. This challenge to creative improvisation recalls principles governing oriental music and exceeds by far the freedom of embellishment in older European art. Therefore one should not expect to discover the archetype of any *Mi-Sinai* tune, for there exist only numerous "realizations" of a certain mental image (cf. **Maqām*). Other oriental features are the free rhythm, which cannot be fitted to regular bars without distortion, and the rich and fluent coloratura adorning it. Tonality is modal (today with a bias to major and minor); **Shtayger* scales occur, but are not maintained rigorously (ex. 1, no. 3; see full version in *Music, ex. 30).

In East Ashkenazi tradition, the bond between music and text has been loosened: entire sections may be sung without words. Certain themes, still found in the earlier Western notated documents, have become lost, and others changed their places in the established order. As a result those themes or sections which were preserved came to be repeated in order to provide for the full text. This regressive evolution in the East was apparently caused by the early displacement of these communities from the birthplace and centers of *Mi-Sinai* song. The Western *ḥazzanim*, on the other hand, developed extensive, and elaborate compositions from the original tunes. Such "Fantasias" were in fashion from about 1750 to 1850.

That the musical ideas and outlines of the *Mi-Sinai niggunim* originated in the Middle Ages can be concluded from musical evidence, a few references in literature, and, above all, the fact that they are found in two Ashkenazi rites, which separated early in their history. It may be supposed that the sufferings during Crusader times made Ashkenazi Jewry ripe for expressing in music the deep feelings that emanate from these melodies. Their character and profound musicality also attracted gentile composers, such as Max Bruch (*Kol Nidrei*, op. 47) and Maurice Ravel (*Kaddish*, 1914); their confrontation with the idioms of contemporary music is demonstrated in A. *Schoenberg's *Kol Nidrei* (1938).

Bibliography: A. Z. Idelsohn, in: *Zeitschrift fuer Musikwissenschaft*, 8 (1926), 449–72; H. Avenary, in: *Yuval*, 1 (1968), 65–85.
[H.Av.]

MISKOLC, town in N.E. Hungary. Jews attended the Miskolc fairs at the beginning of the 18th century, and the first Jewish settlers earned their livelihood from the sale of alcoholic beverages. In 1717 the municipal council sought to expel them but reconsidered its attitude in 1728 and granted them the right to sell at the market. The number of Jews gradually increased, supplanting the Greek merchants from Macedonia. In 1765 several Jews owned houses. They enjoyed judicial independence and were authorized to impose fines and corporal punishment. Early in the 19th century there were two rabbis in the community. Many Jews acquired houses and land, but the majority engaged in commerce and crafts. When the local guild excluded Jews from membership in the unions, the Jews organized their own guild. The cemetery, dating from 1759, was still in use in 1970. The first synagogue was erected in 1765. The Great Synagogue was built in 1861; it was here that a choir, which aroused violent reactions on the part of the Orthodox, appeared for the first time. In 1870 the community joined the Neologians (see *Neology), but in 1875 a single Orthodox community was formed.

The educational institutions were among the most developed and ramified throughout the country. There were three yeshivot, an elementary school, two sub-secondary schools, and the only seminary for female teachers in Hungary. The Ḥasidim established a separate elementary school. In the course of time the percentage of Jews of the general population became the highest in Hungary (around 20%), numbering 1,096 in 1840, 3,412 in 1857; 4,117 in 1880, 10,029 in 1910, and 11,300 in 1920.

Holocaust Period and After. In 1941, when there were 10,428 Jews in the town, 500 were deported to the German-occupied part of Poland for alleged irregularities in their nationality, and were murdered in *Kamenets-Podolski. Large numbers of youths, as well as elderly people, were conscripted into labor battalions and taken to the Ukrainian front, where most of them were exterminated. After the German occupation of Hungary (March 19, 1944) the Jews of the town, about 10,000 in number, were deported to *Auschwitz; only 105 of them survived.

After the liberation Miskolc became an important transit center for those who returned from the concentration camps. The elementary school was reopened and existed until the nationalization of elementary schools (1948). The reconstituted community had 2,353 members in 1946 and 1,000 in 1970.

Bibliography: B. Halmay and A. Leszik, *Miskolc* (1929); *Miskolci zsidó élet*, 1 (1948); *Uj Élet*, 23 no. 7 (1968), 4; 24, no. 20 (1969), 1; E. László, in: R. L. Braham (ed.), *Hungarian Jewish Studies*, 2 (1969), 137–82.
[L.H.]

MISREPHOTH-MAIM (Heb. מִשְׂרְפוֹת מַיִם), one of the farthest limits of the flight of the Canaanites after defeat by the waters of Merom (Josh. 11:8) and a boundary of the Sidonians (Josh. 13:6). Some scholars suggest reading Misrefot mi-Yam ("at the sea," i.e., on the west). It may be mentioned in the Egyptian Execration texts, dating to approximately 1800 B.C.E., as *ʾisrpʾi*, which appears beside Achsaph. Abel and others identified it with Khirbat al-Mushayrifa, near Rosh ha-Nikrah. This site was partly excavated in 1951 by Miriam Tadmor and M. Prausnitz and remains dating to the early Bronze Age, including a wall of early Bronze II–III, and to middle Bronze Age I were uncovered. However, the site did not yield remains of the late Bronze Age, which corresponds to the time of the biblical descriptions. Recently, Aharoni suggested that it is not the name of a city, but a definition of the border of Sidon, which may be identified with the outlet of the Litani River.

Bibliography: Prausnitz, in: *Atiqot*, 1 (1955), 139ff.; Tadmor and Prausnitz, *ibid.*, 2 (1959), 72ff.; Abel, Géog, 2 (1938), 388; Aharoni, Land, index; M. Noth, *Das Buch Josua* (1938), 43.
[M.A.-Y.]

MISSISSIPPI, southern state of the U.S. The 1968 Jewish population of Mississippi was 4,015 out of a total of 2,315,900. Jews settled along the Gulf of Mexico from earliest times; they came via Mobile, Alabama, and New Orleans, Louisiana. There are extant records of their presence in what is now Biloxi, on the Gulf, and Natchez, on the Mississippi River. By the 1830s these communities had Jewish cemeteries. High cotton prices, cheap land, and steamboat traffic stimulated population expansion, bringing a considerable number of Jews from Germany and

Synagogue of Beth Israel Congregation in Jackson, Mississippi, consecrated in 1967. Courtesy Perry E. Nussbaum, Jackson.

Alsace who made a living as peddlers and small storekeepers. Although their total number at the beginning of the Civil War (1861) is unknown, between 200 and 300 served in the Confederate armies. The Eastern European Jewish migration of the late 1800s increased the settlement in the state, particularly in the cotton plantations of the Delta. In the 20th century their descendants have been important in its economic development. The state's reforestation program and aggressive industrialization have brought in branch operations from the North, particularly in clothing and wood products. Many have absentee Jewish ownership. The economy is still predominantly agricultural. Since the mid-1950s there has been a steady decline in the Jewish population. The mounting turmoil over school desegregation and civil rights slowed the pace of newcomers, while most Jewish youth of the state left for higher education and did not return. Chain store expansion into Mississippi has led to the disappearance of family-owned enterprises and a consequent loss in Jewish numbers. The exception is Jackson, the capital city, which is favorably located for homes of Jewish traveling salesmen. It is also the locale for the new Medical Center of the University of Mississippi, the state's Research and Development Center, and a regional U.S. Veterans Hospital and Administrative offices, all of which employ Jewish professionals.

Mississippi Jewish communities are synagogue oriented. Most of the Jews in isolated communities maintain membership in the nearest congregation. In 1936 the state's synagogues reported a total membership of 2,897, with six resident rabbis. In 1970 there were eight rabbis and 20 synagogue structures, several of the latter used spasmodically or not at all. Congregations in the state include: Adath Israel in Cleveland (79 families); B'nai Israel, Natchez (60 families, founded 1840); Beth Israel, Jackson (150 families, founded 1860); Hebrew Union, Greenville (176 families); Beth Israel, Meridian (100 families, founded 1868); Beth Israel, Clarksdale (100 families); Anshe Chesed, Vicksburg (105 families, founded 1841)—all Reform; and Ahavath Hayim, Greenwood (40 families, founded 1893)—Orthodox. Gemilluth Chessed of Port Gibson (four families, founded 1859), is the smallest affiliate of the Union of American Hebrew Congregations. B'nai Israel of Columbus, founded in 1845, has 23 families. It should be noted that many families in the state consist of one or two members in the elderly brackets. Jackson, for reasons noted above, is the exception, with 420 Jews, the majority young parents with children. There were 11 B'nai B'rith lodges and four Hadassah chapters in the state. Jackson and Vicksburg have organized Jewish Welfare Federations. Greenville has a YMHA. The Mississippi Assembly of Jewish Congregations, founded in 1955 by the Jackson rabbi, dissolved about ten years later. Fewer than five Jews have been members of the state legislature in the 20th century, and no Jew has achieved prominence in politics. The state's historic one-party (Democrat) alignment has been distinguished since World War II by revolts against the national party. Jews have held presidential offices in statewide business, professional, and welfare organizations. A noteworthy number of Jews in the smaller communities have been mayors, councilmen, school-board members, etc. Since the U.S. Supreme Court school desegregation decision in 1954, two of the state's rabbis, Charles Mantinband and Perry E. Nussbaum, achieved various degrees of prominence for their efforts on behalf of Negro and civil rights. They pioneered in the development of local and statewide organizations. The former occupied Hattiesburg's Beth Israel pulpit from 1952 to 1963, when he moved to Longview, Texas. The latter went to Jackson in 1954. He assumed the role of penitentiary "chaplain" to the "Freedom Riders" of all creeds and races, and was among the founders of the state's Committee of Concern, which raised funds to rebuild burned Negro churches. His newly dedicated fifth Synagogue edifice (the first was destroyed during the Civil War) was dynamited by terrorists in September 1967 after months of an exceptionally bigoted political campaign. Two months later his home was severely damaged by a similar device. Meridian's new synagogue was dynamited in May 1968. Jackson is the national headquarters for the White Citizens' Councils (founded after 1954) and state headquarters for the revived Ku Klux Klan and other "hate" organizations.

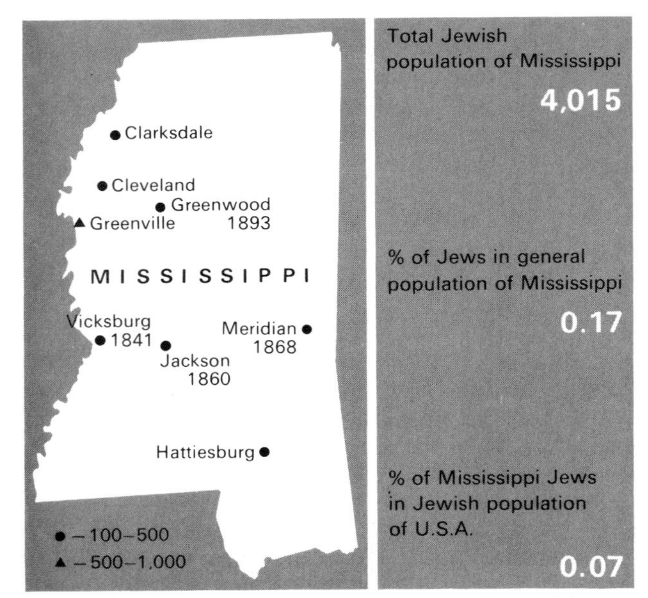

Jewish communities in Mississippi and dates of establishment. Population figures for 1968.

Bibliography: United States, Work Projects Administration, The Mississippi Historical Records Survey Project, *Inventory of the Church and Synagogue Archives of Mississippi: Jewish Congregations and Organizations* (1940), mimeographed. [P.E.N.]

MISSOURI, state located in the central part of the United States. The Jewish population of Missouri in 1968 was 80,600, with 98.1% living in the *St. Louis (57,000) and *Kansas City (22,000) metropolitan areas. About 1,600 Jews live in at least 27 smaller towns, in eight of which there are congregations. Jews were legally admitted into the area of Missouri with the Louisiana Purchase in 1803. The first known Jewish Missourian was Ezekiel Block, a slave owner who was part of a traditionally oriented family which gradually left Schwihau, Bohemia, between 1796 and 1850.

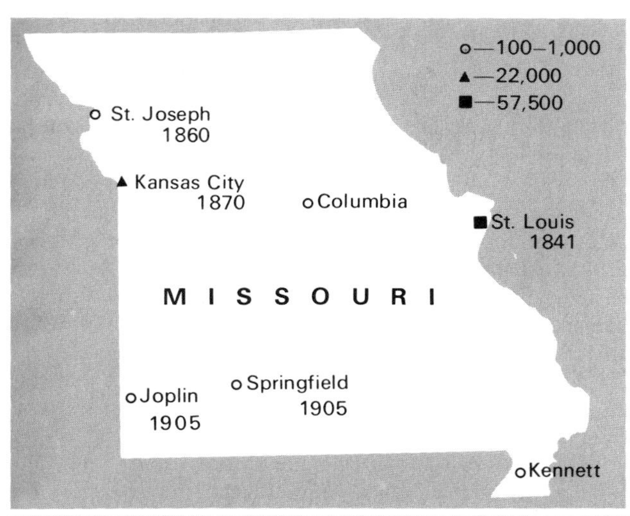

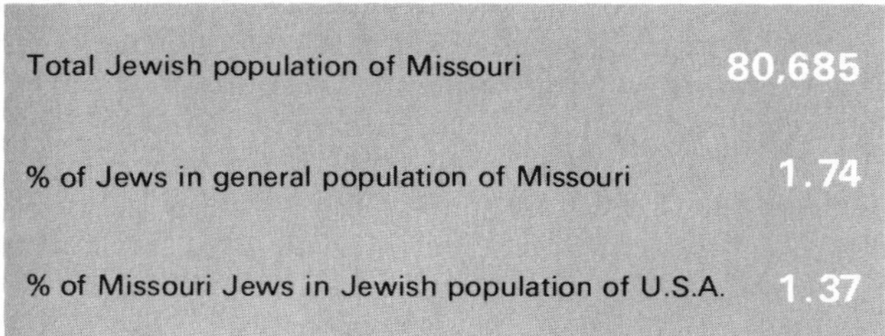

Jewish communities in Missouri and dates of establishment. Population figures for 1968.

At least 23 family members settled in Troy, Perryville, and mainly Cape Girardeau, Louisiana, and St. Louis. They engaged primarily in merchandising, but one also became a lawyer and another a mill owner and an insurance company resident. Most eventually married Christians. However, one married into the Philipson family of St. Louis, the first Jewish family in that town.

By 1837 St. Louis had a *minyan* and, although the city had less than 100 Jews, a cemetery was founded in 1840 and a congregation in 1841. By mid-century the Jewish population in St. Louis increased to between 600 and 700 due to the German immigration of 1848-53, which also led to a Jewish influx into St. Joseph and Kansas City where congregations were established in 1860 and 1870 respectively. Congregations were established in the mid-1880s in the state capital, Jefferson City, and by 1905 in both Springfield (south-central) and Joplin (southwest). By 1950 regular services were being held at Missouri University Hillel in Columbia, Fort Leonard Wood, and in Cape Girardeau (southeast). By the early 1960s the Jews of Sedalia (west-central) had organized their own congregation. Two of the most popular organizations in outstate Missouri are B'nai B'rith and B'nai B'rith Anti-Defamation League.

Bibliography: AJHSP (1914) index; D. I. Makovsky, *The Philipsons; the First Jewish Settlers in St. Louis 1807-1858* (1958); S. Bowman, *Tribute to Isidore Busch* (1920). [D.I.M.]

MISTAKE. A legal transaction requires that the "making up of the mind" (or the conclusive intention of the parties to close the bargain—*gemirat ha-da'at*) be demonstrated (see *Acquisition, Modes of). When it is apparent that one of the parties lacked such conclusive intention, the transaction may be voided, but only at the instance of that party. One of the factors showing that the required conclusive intention was missing is mistake, whether caused by the mistaken party himself or by the other party, whether willfully or unintentionally or whether relating to the subject matter of the transaction, its price, or any other aspect of the transaction. In all these cases the mistaken party is allowed to withdraw from the transaction, provided that the mistake is outwardly and objectively revealed, and not of a subjective nature only, even if it can be proved.

The contracts of *sale and *marriage exemplify the rules of mistake in Jewish law. An error as to price is generally termed *ona'ah* (overreaching), but when relating to the subject matter or any other aspect of the transaction it is termed *mikkaḥ ta'ut* (mistake). If the mistake is common to both parties the contract is voidable at the instance of either of them, otherwise it is voidable only at the instance of the mistaken party (Maim. Yad, Mekhirah 17:1–2). If however the latter consented to the transaction as actually carried out, such consent being demonstrated by him either explicitly or by his subsequent use of the subject matter of the transaction with knowledge of the mistake (*ibid.* 15:3),

Synagogue interior of the United Hebrew Congregation, St. Louis, Missouri.

he may not withdraw from the transaction, even though it does not accord with his original intention. Since the test for mistake is an objective one, the transaction will be voidable only if the majority of those of a particular place and time would consider it material, so that one would generally be expected to refuse to accept the property sold if the true position were made known (*ibid.* 15:5). Thus, if bad wheat is sold as good, i.e., a mistake as to quality, the purchaser may withdraw. Similarly the seller may withdraw if he purported to sell bad wheat, which is in fact found to be good. If the mistake concerns the nature of the object sold, e.g., when a person sells dark-colored wheat which is found to be white, or olive wood that turns out to be sycamore, both parties may withdraw since this is not what was agreed upon (*ibid.* 17:1–2). Similarly, the discovery of a defect in the property sold entitles the purchaser to void the transaction, provided that he has not waived such right by his interim use of the property (*ibid.* 15:3). The purchaser retains this right even if the seller mentioned the defect at the time the transaction was negotiated, but did so in a manner that would not normally be taken as revealing the true existence of the defect. An example of this kind of mistake would be if the seller declares, "this cow is blind, lame, given to biting and to lying down under a load" and it is found to have one or other of these latter two defects but is neither blind nor lame, since the purchaser naturally assumed that the latter defects were as nonexistent as the two former ones (*ibid.* 15:7–8).

Generally speaking, mistake is established when the subject matter of the transaction suffers from a defect rendering it unfit for the known purpose for which it is acquired. Thus the purchaser of a slave may withdraw from the transaction if the slave is found to be ill or to have committed armed robbery, but not if he merely has a scar or a bad odor, which do not interfere with his work (*ibid.* 12–13). Similarly, it is a mistake if an ox is purchased for ploughing purposes and is found to be given to goring (*ibid.* 16:5). When the mistake is discovered only through use of the subject matter, which is of such a nature that on account of such use it can no longer be returned to the seller, the seller must refund the money—an example being if seeds bought for sowing fail to grow or if an animal bought for slaughtering is found to be ritually unclean (*ibid.* 16:1, 6). So too, the seller must refund the money if the subject matter is lost on account of a latent defect, as for instance where an ox is sold and is left with the purchaser's cattle but is unable to eat and starves to death on account of defective teeth (*ibid.* 9). However, it is the purchaser's own responsibility if the subject matter is stolen or lost after the discovery of a defect therein (*ibid.* 4).

In the State of Israel, the rules of mistake are governed by English law in the field of contract, and by the Law of Sale (1968) in the field of property which follows the draft of the uniform international sale of goods law. On mistake in criminal law, see *Penal Law.

Bibliography: Gulak, Yesodei, 1 (1922), 63f.; 2 (1922), 156; Herzog, Instit, 2 (1939), 116–29. [Sh.A.]

MITHREDATH (Heb. מִתְרְדָת; LXX, **Mithradates**), a popular Persian name meaning "Given by Mithra," and borne by kings of Parthia and Pontus and a king of Armenia. The name Mithredath occurs in the Elephantine papyri (Cowley, Aramaic, 26:2, 7; E. G. Kraeling, *The Brooklyn Museum Aramaic Papyri* (1953), 3:23b) and designates two individuals in the Bible. One is the treasurer whom Cyrus ordered to deliver the Temple vessels to Sheshbazzar, for return to Jerusalem (Ezra 1:8). The other is an official who apparently wrote a letter to Artaxerxes I against Jerusalem (Ezra 4:7).

Bibliography: R. A. Bowman, in: *The Interpreter's Bible*, 3 (1954), 574, 598–9; J. M. Myers, *Ezra-Nehemiah* (1965, Anchor Bible), 9, 32ff. [B.Po.]

MITHRIDATES, FLAVIUS, sobriquet of a 15th-century humanist and orientalist (apparently Samuel b. Nissim al-Faraj) of Agrigento, Sicily. He became converted to Christianity, taking the name Guglielmo Raimondo de Moncada, and is also referred to as Guglielmus Siculus ("the Sicilian"). Mithridates taught Arabic, Hebrew, and Aramaic in Italy, France, and Germany and was one of the teachers of the humanist Giovanni *Pico della Mirandola. After his conversion he became lecturer in theology at the Sapienza in Rome. He translated works from Arabic, Hebrew, and Greek into Latin, including parts of the Koran for Federigo da Montefeltro, duke of Urbino, intending also to translate it into Hebrew and Syriac. For Pico he translated Menahem *Recanati's commentary on the Torah, *Levi b. Gershom's commentary on the Song of Songs, a treatise on resurrection by Maimonides, and kabbalistic works. Mithridates preached a sermon before the pope on the sufferings of Jesus (*Sermo de Passione Domini*, ed. by H. Wirszubski, 1963), in which he drew on the Midrash and Jewish and Muslim traditions. He took part in religious disputations with Jewish scholars in Florence.

Bibliography: Starrabba, in: *Archivio Storico Siciliano*, 2 (1878), 15–19; Secret, in: REJ, 106 (1957), 96–102; idem, *Les Kabbalistes Chrétiens de la Renaissance* (1964), index; Wirszubski, in: *Sefer Yovel . . . Y. Baer* (1960), 191–206; Cassuto, in: ZGJD, 5 (1934), 230–6; Baron, Social², 13 (1969), 174–5, 401–2. [M.E.A.]

Supposed portrait of Flavius Mithridates in the initial letter of the dedicatory preface of a Latin manuscript containing his translations from the Arabic. Rome, Vatican Library, Ms. Urban, Lat. 1384, fol. 2.

MITIN, MARK BORISOVICH (1901–), Russian ideologist. Born in Zhitomir, he joined the Communist Party in 1919. Educated in Moscow, he held executive positions at the Krupskaya Communist Academy of Pedagogical

Sciences, a training school for party theoreticians. At the same time he worked in the Institute of Philosophy of the U.S.S.R. Academy of Sciences. In 1939, he became director of the Marx-Engels-Lenin-Stalin Institute and five years later he assumed the position of chief of the philosophy department of the Central Committee's higher party school. For his services to the party, Mitin was awarded two Orders of Lenin, two Orders of the Red Banner of Labor, and the Stalin Prize in 1949. Between 1939 and 1961, he served as a member of the Party Central Committee, one of the few Jews permitted to occupy such a high party post. Never deviating from Stalinism, and taking an active part in the anti-Jewish campaign during the *doctors' plot, etc., Mitin's philosophical and historical books included *Dialekticheskiy i istoricheskiy materializm* (1934); *Istoricheskaya rol G.V.Plekhanova v russkom i mezhdunarodnom rabochem dvizhenii* (1957); *Filosofiya i sovremennost* (1960). He was coeditor of the massive five-volume *Istoriya filosofii* (1957–61), and was editor of the journal *Voprosy filosofii*. [W.K.]

MITNAGGEDIM (Heb. מִתְנַגְּדִים; sing. *Mitnagged;* lit. "opponents"), a designation for the opponents of the *Ḥasidim. The name originally arose from the bitter opposition evinced to the rise, way of life, and leadership of the ḥasidic movement founded by *Israel b. Eliezer Ba'al Shem Tov, but in the course of time lost its connotation of actual strife, and became a positive description, representative of a way of life. Since it was the personality and genius of *Elijah b. Solomon Zalman the Gaon of Vilna (1720–1797) which gave the powerful impetus to the rise of the *Mitnaggedim,* this way of life became especially characteristic of Lithuanian Jewry (except for the Lithuanian Ḥasidim, particularly the *Karlin dynasty and the Ḥabad trend). His iron will and intellectual perseverance shaped, through an elect circle of pupils, both adamant opposition to Ḥasidism, as well as the patterning of institutions, tendencies of thought and expression, and a way of life which formed a specific culture. One of its characteristics, which derived from the opposition to the charismatic miracle-working leadership of the ḥasidic rabbis, was a pronounced skepticism and a severe criticism of credulity and authoritarianism. After the death of Elijah the Gaon of Vilna the struggle between the Ḥasidim and the *Mitnaggedim* assumed even more bitter proportions than during his lifetime, with mutual recrimination, but by the second half of the 19th century the hostility began to subside. One of the causes of the cessation of hostilities was the common front which both formed against the Haskalah. The main differences between them today are in matters of rite, the Ḥasidim having adopted the prayer book of Isaac Luria (largely the Sephardi *minhag*) while the *Mitnaggedim* retained the Polish form of the Ashkenazi *minhag*, and in the greater stress laid by the *Mitnaggedim* on study of the Talmud, while the Ḥasidim emphasize the emotional side of Judaism. There are large groups of *Mitnaggedim*, most of Lithuanian origin, in the State of Israel, the United States, England, and South Africa. The term *Mitnagged*, however, is not confined to Jews of Lithuanian origin.

Bibliography: M. Wilensky, *Ḥasidim u-Mitnaggedim* (1970).

[Ed.]

MITTWOCH, EUGEN (1876–1942), German orientalist. Born in Schrimm, Germany, Mittwoch originally intended to be a rabbi and studied at the Rabbinical Seminary in Berlin. He made his first journey to the East with Moritz *Sobernheim and thus became familiar with Palestine and the culture of the Near East. He returned to the Orient with Paul *Nathan in 1907 and helped him set up the *Hilfsverein's school system in Palestine. Mittwoch himself was one of the first German Jews to speak modern Hebrew. He taught at the University of Berlin (1915–16) and at the University of Greifswald (1917) and returned to Berlin in 1919 to serve as a professor at the Seminary for Oriental Languages, of which he became director in 1920. In 1933, having been dismissed from his position by the Nazis, Mittwoch first directed the office of the Joint Distribution Committee in Berlin and in 1939 moved to England where he assisted the Ministry of Information on Arabian and Persian problems. Between 1910 and 1930 Mittwoch was active in educating young *Falashas, and was a prominent member of the Hilfsverein der deutschen Juden. He also cooperated in the Jewish World Relief Conference and was a representative at HICEM (a relief organization) from its inception. He was the last president of the council of the Gesellschaft zur Foerderung der Wissenschaft des Judentums and transferred the scholarly material from its office to England in 1938. He served on the executive of the Centralverein deutscher Staatsbuerger juedischen Glaubens.

Mittwoch's special scholarly interest was in the study of classical and modern Arabic as well as Ethiopian dialects and literature. In his *Zur Entstehungsgeschichte des islamischen Gebets und Kultus* (1913) he illustrated the influence of Jewish prayer and liturgy on Islam. He also contributed to Hebrew epigraphy as well as to that of South Arabian, Himyaritic, and Sabean inscriptions. Among his other works is *Die arabischen Lehrbuecher der Augenheilkunde* (with J. Hirschberg and J. Lippert, 1905). Mittwoch also wrote about Islamic art and modern Islamic politics. He was a coeditor of the jubilee edition of the works of Moses Mendelssohn (seven vols., 1929–38). In 1937 the Gesellschaft presented him with a *Festschrift* (see bibliography).

Bibliography: I. Elbogen, *Eugen Mittwoch, zum 60. Geburtstag* (1937), 186–93, incl. bibl. (= MGWJ, 81 (1937), 243–50).

[Ed.]

MITZVAH (Heb. מִצְוָה), a commandment, precept, or religious duty. The term is derived from the Hebrew root צוה which means "to command" or "to ordain." In common usage, *mitzvah* has taken on the meaning of a good deed. Already in the Talmud, this word was used for a meritorious act as distinct from a positive commandment. The rabbis for instance declared it "a *mitzvah* to hearken to the words of the sages" (Ḥul. 106a; cf. Git. 15a). Although many different terms such as *ḥukkah* ("statute," Ex. 27:21), *mishpat* ("ordinance," Deut. 4:5), *edut* ("testimony," Deut. 4:45), *mishmeret* ("observance," Lev. 8:35), and *torah* ("teaching," Ex. 16:28) are mentioned in the Pentateuch to indicate laws only the word *mitzvah* is generally used to include all its commandments. There are traditionally 613 biblical *Commandments which are divided into 248 positive mandates and 365 prohibitions. With the increased ritual obligations imposed by the rabbis, the *mitzvot* were also separated into two main categories: *mitzvot de-oraita*, the biblical commandments, and *mitzvot de-rabbanan*, the rabbinic commandments (Pes. 10a; Suk. 44a). There are also instances when the *mitzvot* were classified as *mitzvot kallot*, less important *mitzvot*, and *mitzvot ḥamurot*, more important *mitzvot* (e.g., Ḥul. 12:5; Yev. 47b; Av. Zar. 3a). Nevertheless, the rabbis exhorted the people to be mindful of all the *mitzvot*, both light and grave, since the reward for the fulfillment of each precept is not known to man (Avot 2:1). The *mitzvot* were further divided into *sikhliyyot* (rational) and *shimiyyot* (revealed) by medieval Jewish philosophers (see *Commandments, Reasons for). Other distinctions have also been made, such as: commandments performed with the external limbs of the body and those by the heart; commandments regulating conduct between man and his Maker and between man and his fellows; and commandments applicable only to Ereẓ Israel and those not dependent upon Ereẓ Israel. Responsibility for the *mitzvot* is formally assumed by boys at the age of 13 plus one day, and by girls at 12 plus one day (see *Bar Mitzvah, Bat Mitzvah, and *Puberty). Women are exempt from all affirmative precepts contingent upon a particular time or season although the Talmud also makes those of the Sabbath, Ḥanukkah, Purim, and Passover obligatory on them. All negative precepts, whether limited to a certain time or not, are binding upon both men and women (Kid. 1:7). The performance of most *mitzvot* is preceded by a *benediction which is usually worded: "Who has sanctified us by His commandments and commanded us to . . ." The omission of the benediction, however, does not invalidate the performance of the *mitzvah*. The opposite of *mitzvah* is **averah*, a transgression. A "precept fulfilled through a transgression" is considered as an *averah*, e.g., one does not discharge his obligation through a stolen *lulav* (Suk. 30a; see *Four Species). Although *mitzvot* were not meant to provide material enjoyment (RH 28a), and the final reward for their performance is in the hereafter (Kid. 39b), true joy and sanctity can be attained only through their observance (Shab. 30b; Sifra 9:2). Man should not anticipate any material recompense for performing the *mitzvot*, but one *mitzvah* brings another in its train (Avot 1:3; 4:2). "God desired to make Israel worthy, therefore He enlarged the Law and multiplied its *mitzvot*" (Mak. 3:16).

See also *Commandments, The 613; *Commandments, Reasons for.

Bibliography: M. Steckelmacher, in: *Festschrift . . . A. Schwartz* (1917), 259–68; J. M. Guttmann, in: *Bericht des juedisch-theologischen Seminars Fraenckel'scher Stiftung fuer das Jahr 1927* (1928); idem, *Beḥinat Kiyyum ha-Mitzvot*, in: *Bericht . . . 1930* (1931); J. Heinemann, *Ta'amei ha-Mitzvot be-Sifrut Yisrael*, 1 (1954[3]), 22–35; Alon, Meḥkarim, 2 (1958), 111–9; E. E. Urbach, *Ḥazal—Pirkei Emunot ve-De'ot* (1967), 279–347. [A.Ro.]

MIVḤAR HA-PENINIM (Heb. "A Choice of Pearls"), an ethical work consisting of a collection of epigrams, usually attributed to Solomon b. Judah ibn *Gabirol. It was believed that Gabirol made the collection in preparation for composing his small ethical work, *Tikkun Middot ha-Nefesh*. *Mivḥar ha-Peninim* (Soncino, 1484) is undoubtedly a translation from the Arabic; the material included in it was taken from Islamic ethical literature, much of it from Persian and Indian sources.

The book is divided into chapters ("Gates," *she'arim*). Some of them contain a long chain of instructions, epigrams, and parables relating to the subject of the chapter, as for example *Sha'ar ha-Ḥokhmah* ("The Gate of Wisdom"), *Sha'ar ha-Anavah* ("The Gate of Humility"), and *Sha'ar ha-Emunah* ("The Gate of Belief"). However, most of the chapters give no serious treatment of their ostensible subject and have a title for nothing but a single epigram or ethical paragraph. They deal with all aspects of religious and social life, from the unity of God (*Sha'ar ha-Yiḥud*) to the proper way to treat one's friends. One of the chapters is an ethical will—"*Sha'ar Ẓavva'at Av li-Veno*" ("Gate of the Will of a Father to his Son").

Mivḥar ha-Peninim was translated into Hebrew by Judah ibn *Tibbon, who translated most of the early Jewish works on philosophy from Arabic. It is not, however, a typical product of the genre, despite the clear influences of philosophical-ethical thinking found in it. Rather it is a popular collection of ethical epigrams and parables, collected from Arabic ethical literature. Its authorship has not been established, and there is no clear evidence that it was written by Gabirol. Some traditional editions attribute it to *Jedaiah b. Abraham Bedersi (ha-Penini), although there is no basis for this view either. The book has been very popular throughout the ages; it was used by the Ḥasidei Ashkenaz as well as by philosophers. It has been often printed and many commentaries have been written on it, even in modern times.

Bibliography: A. Marx, in: HUCA, 4 (1927), 433–48. [Y.D.]

MIXED MARRIAGE, INTERMARRIAGE. The terms intermarriage and mixed marriage are used interchangeably. Intermarriage in the present context is defined as a marriage where one partner professes a religion different from that of his spouse. Marriages in which a partner has converted to the faith of the other are not considered intermarriages. Therefore, marriages between *converts to Judaism and born Jews are not treated here.

Problems of Measurement. Formation Data Versus Status Data. Statistical data on the frequency of religious intermarriage are obtained from marriage licences on which groom and bride state their religions, and from questionnaires connected with censuses or community surveys. Questionnaires reveal the religious composition of married couples and the status of heterogamy within a population. It is of the utmost importance to distinguish between intermarriage formation and heterogamy status data.

Individual Rates Versus Couple Rates. A number of methodological problems complicate the computation of intermarriage rates. Some researchers base their rates upon the number of individuals who marry out. However, since the couple is the basic unit in the marriage relationship and since the couple is expected to be homogamous, intermarriage rates are most meaningfully computed by determining the ratio of intermarried couples to the total number of couples in which one or both partners are Jewish.

Surveys of the Organized Jewish Community Versus Comprehensive Surveys. Surveys which produce intermarriage data should indicate whether the survey was limited to the organized Jewish community or encompassed the total population of a locality. As might be expected, the former type yields a significantly lower rate of intermarriage than the latter. Surveys of the former type are sponsored by local Jewish organizations in the United States over the past 40 years yielded an intermarriage status rate of about 6%. By contrast the Greater Washington survey which sampled the total population yielded a rate of 13.2%, more than double that of the organized Jewish community.

The Extent of Jewish Intermarriage. Magnitude. The accompanying table shows some recent intermarriage rates. In contrast to the period between World Wars I and II there are no data for Eastern and Southeastern Europe. The table reveals considerable variations from country to country and even within one country, namely the United States. Status rates range from a high of 26% for Switzerland and the Netherlands to a low of 7.2% for the United States; formation rates from a high of 80.6% in West Germany to a low of 16.8% in Canada.

The Meaning of Intermarriage Rates: The Problem of Jewish Survival. There is a widespread belief that a high rate of Jewish intermarriage in a given locality leads to the disappearance of the Jewish community there. "How high is high?" The answer will be found in a comparison of what the intermarriage rate might be if random selection of partners would occur (expected random rate) with the actual (observed) intermarriage rate. A 1957 sample survey in the United States revealed that, compared to Catholics and Protestants, Jews are least likely to intermarry.

Social Factors Related to Intermarriage. Romantic Love Versus Group Cohesion. In the Western world the selection of marital partners is governed by two considera-

Table. Intermarriage Rates of Jewish Populations

Country	Year	Size of Jewish Population	% of Total Population	Intermarriage	
				Status Rate %	Formation Rate %
United States[1]	1957	5,000,000	3.00	7.2	—
District of Columbia[2]	1956	80,900	4.70	13.1	—
State of Iowa[3]	1953–59	9,100	.33	—	42.2
State of Indiana[3]	1960–63	23,300	.50	—	48.8
Canada[4]	1961–65	254,400	1.39	—	16.8
Australia[5]	1961	59,300	.56	8.3	—
West Germany[6]	1961–65	22,700	.04	—	80.8
Switzerland	1950	19,000	.40	26.0	—
Switzerland[8]	1963–67	20,000	.37	—	56.7
The Netherlands[9]	1954	24,000	.13	26.0	—

Source: [1] U.S. Bureau of the Census: Sample Survey.
[2] Jewish Community Council of Greater Washington: Communal Survey.
[3] State Department of Health, Vital Statistics.
[4] Dominion Bureau of Statistics: Vital Statistics.
[5] Commonwealth Census, 1961.
[6] West Germany, Vital Statistics.
[7] Switzerland: 1950 Census of Population.
[8] Swiss Vital Statistics.
[9] Dutch official and private statistics.

tions. One is the romantic love ideal, which tends to override considerations of race, creed, cultural origin, or social class. The other consideration is group survival, the pressure to marry a member of one's own race, religion, or cultural group. The effectiveness of this pressure is directly related to the value that adults place upon the survival of their group. Elopements can be considered an extreme case of romantic love, producing a maximum rate of intermarriage, while arranged marriages can be viewed as a most conscious effort to foster group survival generating a minimum of such marriages.

Size of the Jewish Community. DENSITY AND CONCENTRATION. It has been repeatedly observed that the rate of intermarriage is the result of density, the proportion that a subgroup constitutes of the total population in a given locality. However, density becomes relevant only when the will for group survival has been weakened or abandoned. Once group cohesion is weakened, however, the factor of density operates in the expected manner: the smaller the proportion that Jews constitute of the total population in a given locality, the larger the intermarriage rate becomes. This relationship has been observed in Canada, the United States, and Australia. For example, in the United States the intermarriage formation rate in the state of Indiana between 1960 and 1963 was 38.6% for the five large Jewish settlements and 63.5% for those counties where there was only a scattering of Jewish families. Jews are well aware of the fact that dispersal of Jewish families over a rural or urban area increases the likelihood of intermarriage. Therefore, in urban areas they have been eager to concentrate their residence in specific neighborhoods and to locate their institutions within them.

AGE OF JEWISH SETTLEMENT AND DEMOCRATIC SOCIAL PROCESSES. Jews more than any other religio-ethnic group have been involved in migrations from one country to another. As immigrants they have encountered economic, cultural, and social barriers. However, in democratic societies where equalizing processes between immigrants and older settlers and between different racial, ethnic, and religious groups are at least not discouraged and at best consciously fostered, these barriers will be lowered with increasing length of settlement. In time, then, Jews will become "acculturated," i.e., less distinguishable from older settlers and other immigrant groups.

The most significant break in cultural continuity, social distance, and personal identity occurs with the birth of each new generation. Therefore, intermarriage is likely to increase with increased length of Jewish settlement, as measured by generations, and in the absence of continued Jewish immigration. The Greater Washington survey found that intermarried families increased from 1.4% among the foreign born, the first generation, to 10.2% among the native born of foreign parentage, the second generation, to 17.9% among the native born of native parentage, the third generation. The readiness of Jewish individuals to intermarry is met by a corresponding frame of mind on the part of non-Jews, who, as members of the upper classes, are no longer conscious of previous status differentials or who, as members of other immigrant groups, have also been "acculturated." The fact that a new wave of immigrants can effectively lower earlier upward trends of intermarriage can best be demonstrated by Australia and to a lesser extent by Canada. In Australia, mainly because of the immigration of refugees from Nazi Europe, the Jewish population nearly doubled between 1933 and 1954. At the same time the percentage of intermarried families dropped drastically from a high of 29% for Jewish husbands and 16% for Jewish wives in 1921 to a low of 12% for Jewish husbands and 6% for Jewish wives in 1961.

OCCUPATION AND EMPLOYMENT STATUS. Occupation and employment status (independent owner versus employee) are factors significantly related to intermarriage. As long as occupational choice was limited by discriminatory practices, occupational homogeneity discouraged intermarriage. With virtually unlimited freedom of occupational choice in the United States, individuals who break away from traditional occupations are likely to have a higher intermarriage rate. The growth of corporate capitalism is also likely to generate a higher rate of intermarriage. Since large corporations demand from their executives considerable geographic and social mobility, local ties to the organized Jewish communities become attenuated. Surveys in the mid-50s revealed that roughly 80% of the heads of Jewish households in the United States were engaged in white-collar occupations while only 20% did blue-collar work. Within the white-collar group, managers, proprietors, and officials constituted the largest concentration, with 36% of all heads of Jewish households. It comes as no surprise, then, that the intermarriage formation rate for the latter group amounted to only 10% (for first marriages) in the state of Iowa. For the total white-collar group the rate was 27.2% and for blue-collar workers 46.8%. Thus the expectation that Jews who adhere to the traditional occupational pattern are less likely to intermarry was borne out.

SECULAR EDUCATION. Secular education in the Western world has two major functions. One is to ensure the continuity of cultural tradition and values, the acquisition of basic skills, and of occupational training. The other is to provide for cultural change, the production of new ideas, and technical innovation. Students who are oriented to or exposed to the first type of schooling should be less inclined to intermarry than students enrolled in the second type. The Greater Washington survey supports the expectation for the native-born of native parentage. The intermarriage rate of those who had enrolled in the first type was nearly one-third lower than of those who had attended the second type.

RELIGIOUS EDUCATION. There is a widespread belief that Jewish education, including a bar mitzvah ceremony, helps to keep young men from marrying outside the Jewish faith. The Greater Washington survey showed that this belief is well founded as far as the native-born of native parentage (the third and subsequent generation) is concerned. Religious education cut the intermarriage status rate in half. It was 16.4% for those husbands who had been exposed to religious school as compared to 30.2% who had not had such instruction. Since the ethnic bond—expressed in secular activities and in a common language—has been virtually dissolved in the third generation, exposure to religious instruction, which usually includes some learning of Jewish history and some identification with Israel, serves as a check to intermarriage.

SEX DISTRIBUTION AND INTERMARRIAGE. At the present time Jewish men are more likely to intermarry than are Jewish women. One reason for this differential is that men take the initiative in proposing marriage. This is especially significant in localities where Jewish families are sparsely settled. Jewish parents allow their sons more freedom in dating across religious lines. However, recent years have witnessed an increase in the proportion of Jewish women who intermarry and it is likely that the sex differential will diminish in the future. The proportion of Jewish men who intermarry varies from country to country and within a country from place to place. In Canada only 10.2% of all bridegrooms intermarried between 1955 and 1960, as compared with 26.7% in Iowa between 1953 and 1959. In the Netherlands, the percentage of such bridegrooms rose from 36.4% in 1946 to 44% in 1958. In Indiana, only about half as many Jewish bridegrooms intermarried in the five relatively large Jewish communities of the state (30% versus 55.8%). Jewish brides exhibit similar variations in their propensity to intermarry.

PREVIOUS MARITAL STATUS. Data available for the United States and the Netherlands demonstrate that the previous marital status of a person affects his decision to intermarry. Previously widowed persons, upon remarriage, have a lower intermarriage rate than persons never before married. By contrast, persons who were previously divorced have a considerably higher intermarriage rate than the never married. For example, in Indiana one group of previously divorced couples had an intermarriage formation rate of 64.9% as compared with 33.2% for the never married before and 20% for the previously widowed.

The Prevention of Intermarriage. In societies where democracy and individualism are dominant values, intermarriage is bound to occur. Empirical observations have revealed that Jewish communities are trying to keep the frequency low with the help of a "survival" formula consisting of voluntary segregation, residence in a high-status area, a modicum of Jewish education, and Jewish group consciousness in the form of Zionism which is defined as supporting the State of Israel. [ER.R.]

Legal Aspects. THE CONCEPT. A mixed marriage is a marriage of a non-Jew to a Jew, i.e., one born of Jewish parents, or whose mother alone was Jewish, or who has become a proselyte in accordance with Jewish law (see *Jew; **Yuhasin*). Conversion from the Jewish religion, both in the case of a Jew by birth and of a proselyte who reverts to his "evil" ways, has no halakhic significance in respect of the law on mixed marriages. For "an Israelite, even if he has sinned, is still an Israelite" (Sanh. 44a; Rashi thereto; see *Apostasy).

MIXED MARRIAGES ARE PROHIBITED AND INVALID. From the biblical passage (Deut. 7:3) "neither shalt thou make marriages with them: thy daughter thou shalt not give unto his son, nor his daughter shalt thou take unto thy son," the sages inferred that marriage with a non-Jew is forbidden as a negative precept by the Torah (Av. Zar. 36b; Yad, Issurei Bi'ah 12: 1–2; Sh. Ar., EH 16: 1). As the passage cited refers to the "seven nations" ("The Hittite, and the Girgashite, and the Amorite, and the Canaanite, and the Perizzite, and the Hivite, and the Jebusite," Deut. 7: 1), according to one opinion, the prohibition applies only to intermarriage with those seven nations. Others maintain, however, that the prohibition applies to all gentiles because after the prohibition "neither shalt thou make marriages" the biblical passage continues: "For he will turn away thy son from following after Me" (Deut. 7:4), which serves "to include all who would turn [their children] away" (Av. Zar. 36b; Yev. 77a; and codes). The prohibition against marrying a gentile is also explicitly stated in the period of the return to Zion: "And that we would not give our daughters unto the peoples of the land, nor take their daughters for our sons" (Neh. 10:31; see Maim. *ibid.*). It was also inferred from the passage in Deuteronomy that in a mixed marriage there is "no institution of marriage," i.e., mixed marriages are not legally valid and cause no change in personal status (Kid. 68b; Yev. 45a; and codes). Hence if the Jewish partner of such a marriage subsequently wishes to marry a Jew there is no need, according to the *halakhah*, for divorce from the previous "marriage." However, where one or even both of the parties to a marriage are apostate Jews who have married in a halakhically binding manner, neither can marry a Jew as long as the first marriage is not terminated by death or divorce, since a purported change of religion does not affect personal status (Yev. 47b; Bek. 30b; Sh. Ar., EH 44:9). Similarly if both parties (or only one of them) apostasize after a halakhically valid marriage and are then divorced by way of a civil divorce, neither party can marry a Jew until the previous marriage is terminated as above (Yad, Ishut 4: 15; Rema, EH 154:23).

MIXED MARRIAGES HAVE NO LEGAL CONSEQUENCES. Since mixed marriages are not binding, such marriages entail no legal consequences (Yad loc. cit.). Hence, the prohibitions of marriage (in respect of certain relations of the other spouse), which apply to a valid marriage, do not apply to the parties—even after the non-Jewish partner has become a proselyte (see *Marriage, Prohibited). Similarly the wife has no halakhic right to be maintained by her "husband," since this right arises only if a valid marriage exists between them. For the same reason, in a mixed marriage none of the inheritance rights that flow from a valid marriage, such as the husband's right to inherit his wife's estate (see *Succession), come into effect.

The State of Israel. It is impossible to contract a mixed marriage in the State of Israel, since according to section 2 of the Rabbinical Courts Jurisdiction (Marriage and Divorce) Law, 5713–1953, no marriages of Jews in Israel are valid unless contracted in accordance with the law of the Torah. However, the criminal code does not provide criminal punishment for contracting a mixed marriage in Israel. Where a mixed marriage is contracted in the Diaspora, proceedings regarding it cannot be brought directly before the Israel rabbinical courts inasmuch as such courts have jurisdiction only in the event of both parties being Jews. In 1969, however, a law was passed whereby such marriages can be dissolved at the discretion of the president of the Supreme Court. If a problem arises before the civil courts, such as a wife's claim for maintenance, the civil courts will act according to the general principles of private international law, and where such a marriage cannot be denied validity according to those principles, it will be sustained. The Succession Law, 5725–1965 provides that differences of religion do not affect rights of inheritance.

[B.-Z.Sch.]

Reform and Conservative Practice. Most Conservative and Reform rabbis request conversion from the non-Jewish spouse before undertaking any action as regards marriage, although a small, though growing minority of Reform rabbis are prepared to officiate at mixed marriages (N. Mirsky, in *Midstream*, 16 (Jan. 1970), 40–46). The practice of almost all Conservative rabbis is not to perform a marriage between a Jew and a non-Jew. Indeed those rabbis who do perform such marriages do so only in emergency cases. Another question which was debated by the Conservative Rabbinical Assembly was the status of an intermarried Jew as regards membership in a Conservative congregation. The practice until 1963 had been to exclude such an intermarried Jew from synagogue membership. In 1963 the law committee of the Rabbinical Assembly adopted a modified view of the former position and, while affirming their opposition to mixed marriages, allowed the Jewish partner of a non-Jewish marriage to become a member of their congregation, provided that there was a definite agreement to raise the children of the marriage as Jews. The privileges of membership did not extend to the non-Jewish spouse, and the Jewish partner was restricted from holding office in the synagogue. All restrictions were to be lifted when the non-Jewish partner accepted Judaism.

Reform practice on the other hand was to accept both members of the marriage as members of the congregation, and to urge that any children of the marriage be brought to the Jewish religious school so that they could have Jewish training. They felt that by this policy they would be able to influence the non-Jewish spouse to affiliate with Judaism.

[Ed.]

Bibliography: J. E. Mayer, *Jewish-Gentile Courtships* (1961); W. J. Cahnman (ed.), *Intermarriage and Jewish Life* (1963); JJSO, 3 (1961), 195–242; 4 (1962), 47–71; W. M. Lipman, *ibid.*, 8 (1966), 213–39; JSQS, index s.v. *Intermarriage;* E. Rosenthal, in: AJYB, 64 (1963), 3–53; idem, in: *Journal of Marriage and the Family*, 32 no. 3 (1970), 435–40; M. Sklare, in: *Commentary*, 37 (April 1964), 46–52; 49 (1970), 51–58; M. Davis, *Beit Yisrael ba-Amerikah* (1970), 276–342 (incl. bibl.); I. Ellman, in: *Dispersion and Unity*, 9 (1969), 111–42; N. Mirsky, in: *Midstream*, 16 (1970), 40–46; M. Altschuler, in: *Beḥinot*, 1 (1970), 56–58; A. Schwartz, in: AJYB, 71 (1970), 101–22. Legal Aspects: ET, 5 (1953), 286–93, 295–300; B. Shereshevsky, *Dinei Mishpaḥah* (1967²), 80–87, 349–51; M. Elon, *Ḥakikah Datit* (1968), 77–79, 85–89.

MIXED SPECIES (Heb. כִּלְאַיִם; *kilayim*), prohibition mentioned twice in the Bible. Leviticus 19:19 states: "Ye shall keep my statutes. Thou shalt not let thy cattle gender with a diverse kind; thou shalt not sow thy field with two kinds of seed; neither shall there come upon thee a garment of two kinds of stuff mingled together." Deuteronomy 22:9–11 states: "Thou shalt not sow thy vineyard with two kinds of seed; lest the fulness of the seed which thou hast sown be forfeited together with the increase of the vineyard. Thou shalt not plow with an ox and an ass together. Thou shalt not wear a mingled stuff, wool and linen together." From these two passages the sages deduced six types of mixing of species which are forbidden: the mixing of seeds; the grafting of different species of trees and vegetables; the mixing of seed in a vineyard; the hybridization of domestic and wild animals; plowing or driving with domestic or non-domestic animals of different species; and the mixing of wool and linen (**sha'atnez*).

The prohibitions against mixing species are defined in Mishnah *Kilayim* 8:1 "It is forbidden to sow diverse kinds in a vineyard or to suffer them to grow, and it is forbidden to have any benefit from them. It is forbidden to sow diverse kinds of seed or to suffer them to grow, but they may be eaten and certainly benefit may be derived from them. Mixed materials are permitted for all purposes, only the weaving of them being forbidden. Hybrid cattle may be reared and maintained; it is forbidden only to breed them." The many *halakhot* connected with the laws of mixed species are taught in the Mishnah, Tosefta, and Jerusalem Talmud of the tractate **Kilayim*. The chief problems relating to those laws are detailed below.

The Mixing of Seeds. The prohibition applies to the sowing together of two kinds of grains if they are regarded as belonging to different species (see below), or of grain and legume, as well as of other edible plants. A lenient ruling was given regarding vegetables, which were customarily sown in small beds, and it was permitted to sow five species at specified distances from one another in a bed one cubit square and with variations even 13 species (Kil. 3:1). According to most authorities, it is obligatory to separate fields sown with different species by the space of a *rova* (104 square cubits) or of three furrows (two cubits). In the opinion of some commentators, including Solomon Sirillio and Elijah Gaon of Vilna, the measures mentioned in the Mishnah (Kil. 2:6–10) refer to the size of the plot near which a different kind may be sown (and not to the space by which they must be separated), since plots of this size and larger have the appearance of separate fields, and there is no fear that they may be thought to have been planted indiscriminately, nor is there any risk that the different species will derive sustenance from one another. The prohibition of mixed seeds applies only in Ereẓ Israel, while the prohibitions of the other mixed species are of universal application (Kid. 39a).

The Mixing of Trees. This is not mentioned explicitly in the Bible but is inferred from the juxtaposition of verses (Lev. 19:19), "Thou shalt not let thy cattle gender with a diverse kind; thou shalt not sow thy field with two kinds of seed," which were interpreted to mean, "Just as the prohibition of cattle refers to mating, so does that of the field to grafting" (Kid. 39a), i.e., it is forbidden to graft two plant species in the same way as it is forbidden to mate two animal species. Some inferred the prohibition of grafting plants of different species from the beginning of the verse (Lev. 19:19): "Ye shall keep my statutes"; *Sifra, Kedoshim* (Perek 4:17) and the Jerusalem Talmud (Kil. 1:7, 27b) explain that the word *ḥukkah* ("statute"), is connected with the root *ḥakok* ("to carve"), i.e., that it is forbidden to change by grafting the original form "carved out" by the Creator at Creation. The prohibition applies to grafting a tree onto a tree, a vegetable onto a tree, and a tree onto a vegetable (Kil. 1:7). However, it is permitted to plant different trees side by side and to sow vegetables or grain among trees.

Mixing in the Vineyard. The laws of mixed species in the vineyard are stringent and complex, and almost half of the tractate *Kilayim* is devoted to them. The Bible (Deut. 22:9) rules that the resulting vines and seed become forfeit, and it is forbidden either to eat them or to benefit from them. The prohibition applies to grain but not to any trees among the vines. Concerning vegetables and other plants there are differences of opinion in the Mishnah and Talmud as to which are forbidden by biblical law and which permitted. A distance of four cubits must be allowed between a vineyard and any species forbidden to be sown there. In the case of a single vine, however, it suffices to leave a distance of three or six handbreadths (Kil. 6:1).

Mixing of Cattle. According to the Mishnah (Kil. 8:1) "they may be reared and maintained, and it is only forbidden to breed them." "To rear and maintain" means that different species of cattle may be reared together without the fear that they will crossbreed. Some explain it to mean that the product of crossbreeding (e.g., a mule) may be reared. This prohibition applies to domestic and wild animals and to birds (BK 5:7).

Plowing and Driving with Two Species. The Bible forbids only plowing with an ox and an ass. The rabbis, however, explained that "Scripture spoke what was customary," i.e., people were accustomed to plow with an ox or an ass, but the prohibition applies equally to plowing with any two other species and to riding, leading, and driving with them (Kil. 8:2).

Problems of Definition. In the discussion of the laws of mixed species the problem of defining like and unlike species arises. Although criteria for determining whether a plant or animal belongs to one species or another are laid down, an examination of the pairs enumerated in the Mishnah that do or do not constitute mixed species shows that there is no identity between the term "species" used in the law of mixed species and the term as applied by the modern system of botanical and zoological classification. Mixed species were determined by a tradition crystallized in the course of many generations (cf. Tosef., Kil. 1:3–4). Indeed two plants which are now classified as belonging to different species or even to different genera are reckoned as the same species for the law of mixed species (e.g., wheat and tares; Kil. 1:1). In contrast, however, different strains of the same species are regarded as different species (Kil. 1:6). With regard to mixed seeds an *amora* in the Jerusalem Talmud (Kil. 1:5, 27a) summarizes: "in some cases [the form of] the fruit is the determinant, and in others the leaf," while another *amora* notes: "in some cases the taste of the fruit is the determinant."

One of the assumptions in the prohibitions of mixed trees is the possibility of crossbreeding by grafting the scion of one species onto the stock of a second. Thus it is pointed out in the Jerusalem Talmud that grafting the almond onto the terebinth produces the *pistachio, a fruit similar to that of both these species but systematically very far removed from the almond. It is almost certain that a graft of such a nature will not take and it is certain that a species which has the median characteristics of the scion and the stock cannot be obtained by grafting. The early scholars saw an analogy between the grafting of plants and the crossbreeding of animals, but this latter could be compared to the cross-pollination of plants, a technique unknown to the ancients.

These views on grafting stem from the once-accepted assumption that environmental factors were liable to change the hereditary characteristics of the creature (see *Biology). The opinion that new species could be created by grafting belongs to agricultural folklore, and also to Greco-Roman "science," and from there entered into rabbinic literature. Because of the prohibition of mixed species, Jews were unable to test the truth of this notion. Many *halakhot* on the subject commence with the formula: "If a gentile grafted" species A with species B, then species C is produced. It should be stressed, however, that *halakhot* of this nature, common in the Tosefta and the Jerusalem Talmud, were not incorporated in the Mishnah (see **Kilayim*).

Reasons for the Precept of Mixed Species. Some of the reasons given for the prohibition stemmed from the above-mentioned belief that the effects of environmental factors are hereditary. To the same category belongs the reason for forbidding change in the order of Creation. Naḥmanides gives this reason in his biblical commentary (to Lev. 19:19), adding that if the crossbreeding of a horse and an ass produces a mule, which is a miserable creature that cannot beget, so too when mixed species of trees are grafted, "their fruit does not grow thereafter." Maimonides (*Guide* 3, 49) explains that the man who couples creatures of different species defies the laws of nature and of ethics, and similarly in the grafting and mixing of plants. It was part of the false beliefs of idolators that this served as a specific for fertility (*ibid.* 3, 37). That crossbreeding was unnatural was an early belief: Josephus (Ant., 4:229) explained that "nature delighteth not in the conjunction of things dissimilar." Rabbenu Nathan, *av ha-yeshivah* (Ereẓ Israel in the 11th century), gives an agricultural reason, that one species prevents the development of the adjacent one (commentary to Mishnah Kil. ch. 1). A similar reason for the prohibition of mixed seeds in the vineyard was given earlier by Philo: "since as a result of it too great a burden is put upon the earth" (Spec. 4:211). Some Greek and Roman agricultural writers laid down that summer plants which impoverish the soil should not be sown in the vineyard (Pliny, Naturalis 18, 101) and that it is forbidden to sow intermediate plantings in a vineyard (Geoponica 5, 11).

As against those who sought to rationalize the prohibition, Rashi concluded: "These statutes are a royal decree, for which there is no reason." In point of fact it is impossible to determine the reasons for the prohibition. Post factum, however, it seems that as a result of the care taken by Jews in this matter, the fields were kept free of weeds and the purity of plant species was preserved. It is also possible that it was a contributory factor to the success of Jewish agriculture in Ereẓ Israel.

At the present day, prohibitions of mixed species have raised a number of problems for farmers who adhere to these laws. Thus they are prevented from sowing vetch with grain as fodder in order to prevent the vetch from trailing on the ground. The problem was solved by the introduction of strains of vetch which do not trail. In connection with the prohibition against grafting trees of different species, experiments have taken place on stocks belonging to the same species as the scion, but so far no satisfactory solution to the matter has been found.

Bibliography: Loew, Flora, 4 (1934), 291ff.; J. Feliks, *Ha-Ḥakla'ut be-Ereẓ Yisrael bi-Tekufat ha-Midrash ve-ha-Talmud* (1963); idem, *Kilei Zera'im ve-Harkavah* (1967). [J.F.]

MIZMOR LE-DAVID (Heb. מִזְמוֹר לְדָוִד; "A Psalm to David"), a frequently occurring superscription to a number of psalms whose authorship is ascribed to King *David. Many of them form part of the traditional liturgy. Among them are (1) Psalm 29 ("Ascribe unto the Lord, O ye sons of might"), the last of the six psalms chanted at the Sabbath eve service at which the Sabbath is welcomed; and on Sabbath mornings, after the conclusion of the *Torah reading, when the Torah scroll is carried back in solemn procession to the *Ark. (2) Psalm 23 ("The Lord is my shepherd, I shall not want"), which in the Sephardi ritual is sung prior to the **Kiddush* on Sabbath morning, and in the Ashkenazi ritual, on Sabbath afternoon at the third meal

Mizraḥ

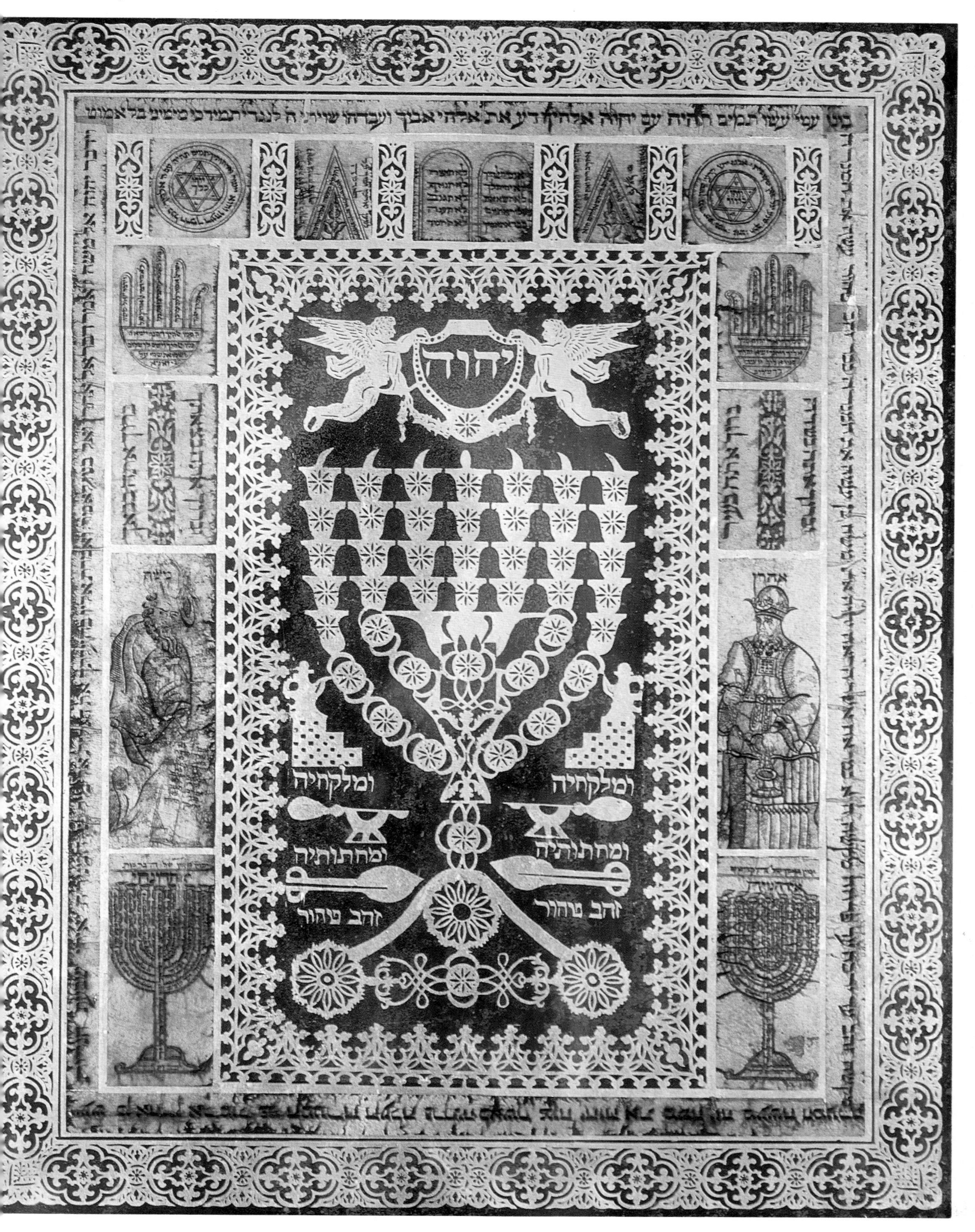

-ATE 1. *Mizraḥ,* painted glass, Italy, 17th century. The *menorah* is surrounded by ritual implements connected with its use. The decoration also cludes magical symbols, among them a *Magen David.* Jerusalem, Michael Kaufman Collection. Photo David Harris, Jerusalem.

PLATE 2. *Mizraḥ*, papercut and watercolor, Russia, 1810. Made by Ẓevi Hirsch Deliatizki for Ephraim Joseph Ginsburg. Cleveland, Joseph B. and Olyn Horwitz Judaica Collection

(*Se'udah Shelishit). According to one talmudic opinion (Pes. 118a), it was also sung as a festive hymn at the Passover *seder.

Bibliography: JE, 8 (1904), 624–5; Elbogen, Gottesdienst, index s.v. *Psalm 29*. [Ed.]

MIZMOR SHIR LE-YOM HA-SHABBAT (Heb. מִזְמוֹר שִׁיר לְיוֹם הַשַּׁבָּת; "A Psalm, a Song for the Sabbath Day"), the superscription of Psalm 92 which, according to the Talmud (Tam. 7:4, RH 31a, Sof. 18:1) was the Sabbath hymn chanted by the levites in the Temple. The Psalm forms part of the Sabbath eve service in which the Sabbath (*Kabbalat Shabbat) is welcomed. It is also part of the *Pesukei de-Zimra and the daily hymn at the conclusion of the Sabbath morning service as well as in the Sabbath *Minḥah* service in the Sephardi and some Ashkenazi rites. Some aggadic sources ascribe its authorship to Adam who pronounced it in his great joy for the gift of repentance. In the course of time, it was forgotten until Moses reintroduced it with ten other psalms (Gen. R. 22, end; Mid. Ps. 90:30).

Bibliography: JE, 8 (1904), 625–7; Eisenstein, Dinim s.v. [Ed.]

MIZPAH (Heb. מִצְפָּה; "lookout point"), moshavah in northern Israel, W. of Tiberias, founded in 1908 by *Second Aliyah pioneers from Russia, on *Jewish Colonization Association (ICA) land. The small village, based on mixed farming, has preserved its original layout of closely grouped farmsteads interconnected by a surrounding basalt wall. In 1968 its population was 39. [E.O.]

MIZPEH or **MIZPAH** (Heb. מִצְפֶּה, מִצְפָּה, הַמִּצְפָּה; "lookout point"), the name of several places mentioned in the Bible.

(1) A city belonging to the tribe of Benjamin (Josh. 18:26), the best-known place with the name of Mizpeh. The Israelites gathered there to punish the tribe of Benjamin after the outrage committed by the men of Gibeah (Judg. 20–21). Samuel assembled the people to fight against the Philistines and judged them in Mizpah (I Sam. 7:5ff.; 10:17). Asa of Judah fortified the place (I Kings 15:22; II Chron. 16:6). Gedaliah, the son of Ahikam, established the capital of Judah in Mizpah after the fall of Jerusalem and was later assassinated there (II Kings 25:22ff.; Jer. 40–41). It was a district capital in the time of Nehemiah (Neh. 3:7, 15, 19). The place of origin of Simeon of Mizpeh (Pe'ah 2:6) is uncertain.

The ancient site is identified with Tell al-Naṣbeh about 8 mi. (13 km.) north of Jerusalem, following A. Raboisson (*Les Maspeh*, 1897). It was excavated from 1926 to 1936 by W. F. Badè on behalf of the Pacific Institute of Religion in Berkeley. The first settlement there dates to the Early Bronze Age. Its main period of occupation, however, belongs to the Iron Age. The excavations uncovered the main part of the city, which contained many four-room houses typical of the period, some unusually large and built with pillars. Outstanding is a ninth-century wall and gate, evidently built by Rehoboam, which had been preceded by a tenth-century casemate wall. The mound was occupied until the Hellenistic period. A number of tombs uncovered there date from the Canaanite to the Hellenistic periods and were very rich in finds.

Hebrew seals and seal impressions were particularly abundant on the site. A seal with the inscription "Jaazaniah

Israelite gate at Mizpeh (Tell al-Naṣbeh) near Jerusalem, part of the fortifications built by King Asa, ninth century B.C.E. Courtesy Israel Department of Antiquities, Jerusalem.

servant of the king" is ascribed by some to the Jezaniah who met with Gedaliah at Mizpah (Jer. 40:8; 42:1). A special seal from the Persian period reading *mṣh* (Mozah?) is interpreted by various scholars as an abbreviation of Mizpeh (*mṣ[p]h*).

(2) The land of Mizpah (Josh. 11:3) or the valley of Mizpeh (Josh. 11:8) in the north of the country below the Hermon, an area settled by the Hivites. It was probably located in the region of Marj al-ʿAyyūn (ʿIyyon), north of Metullah.

(3) A place in Gilead which marked the boundary between the territories of Laban and Jacob (Gen. 31:49). It is perhaps identical with Ramoth-Gilead, a border stronghold between Aram and Israel in northern Gilead (I Kings 22:3).

(4) The hometown of *Jephthah, also in Gilead, but farther south than (3) above. The Israelites gathered there before setting out for battle against the Ammonites (Judg. 10–11). It is identical with Ramath-Mizpeh in the vicinity of Mahanaim of Joshua 13:26. It has been tentatively identified with Khirbat Jalʿad south of the Jabbok.

(5) A city in the territory of the tribe of Judah in the vicinity of Lachish (Josh. 15:38). Eusebius (Onom. 130:2—Masseba) describes it as a village near Eleutheropolis (Bet Guvrin).

(6) A Mizpeh of Moab (Rujm al-Mushayrifa?) is mentioned in I Samuel 22:3.

(7) A Mizpeh (Massepha) at which Judah Maccabee assembled his army against Gorgias (I Macc. 3:46) is probably identical with Nabi Samuîl northwest of Jerusalem.

Bibliography: C. C. McCown et al., *Tell en Nasbeh*, 1 (1947); J. C. Wampler, *Tell en Nasbeh*, 2 (1947); Avigad, in: IEJ, 8 (1958), 113ff.; Albright, in: AASOR, 4 (1924), 90ff.; Abel, Geog, 2 (1938), 340ff.; Aharoni, Land, index; Diringer, in: D. Winton Thomas (ed.), *Archaeology and Old Testament Study* (1967), 329ff.; EM, s.v. incl. bibl. [M.A.-Y.]

MIZPEH RAMON (Heb. מִצְפֵּה רָמוֹן), development town in S. Israel, in the Negev Hills, 54 mi. (87 km.) S. of Beersheba toward Eilat. Founded in 1954, initially as a labor camp of the workers employed in the construction of the highway, it became an "urban cooperative," and when this dispersed seven months later, it was turned into a development town. At the beginning conditions were extremely hard; water had to be brought in trucks from the north and communications were frequently cut off when the highway to the north was blocked by floods. In spite of these difficulties the town absorbed new immigrants from North Africa and Europe and in 1968 had a population of

1,470. Miẓpeh Ramon's economy is based principally on industry and mining, the most important enterprises being the Ramon gypsum mines and the Ḥarsit ve-Ḥol Zakh ceramic clay and glass-sand mines in the nearby Ramon Crater. An industrial area has been earmarked west of the town. Although servicing the central Negev, traffic has diminished since the opening of the Sedom-Eilat road. East of the town nucleus, where a sculpture garden has been laid out, a part of the municipal area has been allocated to the Israel army, and some of the inhabitants of the town are employed in servicing nearby camps. The name means "Ramon Lookout," and refers to the town's site on the rim of the Ramon Crater, which affords a remarkable view of Negev desert landscape. [S.H.]

MIZRA (Heb. מִזְרָע; "sown field"), kibbutz in northern Israel, north of Afulah, affiliated with Kibbutz Arẓi Ha-Shomer ha-Ẓa'ir. It was founded in 1923 by pioneers from Central Europe, who were later joined by others. In 1969 Mizra had 610 inhabitants. Farming is highly intensive and the kibbutz also runs a sausage factory and a plant producing hydraulic presses. [E.O.]

MIZRACHI (term coined from some of the letters of the Hebrew words *merkaz ruḥani*, spiritual center), religious Zionist movement whose aim was expressed in its motto: "The Land of Israel for the people of Israel according to the Torah of Israel" (coined by Rabbi Meir Berlin—Bar-Ilan). Mizrachi was founded in 1902 as a religious faction in the World Zionist Organization. The name was first used by Samuel *Mohilewer, an early leader of *Ḥibbat Zion, to express the idea that the Torah should be the spiritual center for Zionism.

The Beginning of Mizrachi. Many religious Jews, including famous rabbis, joined the movement of political Zionism, which worked toward the establishment of a Jewish state in the Land of Israel. Among the first to join was Rabbi Isaac *Reines, who responded to Theodor *Herzl's call and devoted his energies to spreading the idea of a national renaissance among Orthodox Jews. Reines believed that the Zionist movement must be dedicated exclusively to a political goal, and he led the fight against the inclusion of cultural activities in the Zionist program. After the Fifth Zionist Congress, however, when the strength of the "cultural" camp grew and official permission was granted to establish factions (federations) within the framework of the Zionist Organization, Reines decided to found a federation of religious Zionists. Toward this end, he convened the founding convention in Vilna on March 4–5, 1902, and it established the national-religious organization within the Zionist Organization. At the suggestion of Rabbi Abraham *Slutzky, the organization was called Mizrachi.

An outstanding participant at the founding convention was Rabbi Ze'ev *Jawitz, who was charged with composing the organization's first manifesto. Two groups clashed at the founding convention: the "political" faction, which called for the preservation of the purely political character of the Zionist movement and opposed the decision of the Fifth Zionist Congress (1901) obligating the Zionist Organization to include cultural activities in its program; and the "cultural" faction, which demanded that Mizrachi, as a "spiritual center," influence the Zionist movement and its work in the Land of Israel in its traditional-religious spirit. The Mizrachi program, which was accepted by the majority of the participants at the founding convention, stated that the Zionist Organization should not engage in activities that do not have a direct relationship to Zionism, and it was stated in the manifesto that Mizrachi should try "to gather around it all those Zionists who wish to purge practical Zionism of any alien element that is not directly related to political and practical Zionism." These decisions seem to reveal the victory of the "political" faction. Jawitz, however, who formulated the manifesto, succeeded in reflecting in it both viewpoints and thus satisfied both trends. An opening was thus created for cultural activities, albeit only in the framework of branches, "in line with local conditions and in the spirit of Orthodoxy."

A year after its establishment, Mizrachi's second conference was convened in Lida on March 22–24, 1903. During its first year, Mizrachi succeeded in building up 210 branches in Russia alone (which then included Poland, Lithuania, Courland, etc.). Mizrachi societies were also established in Galicia, Rumania, Austria, Hungary, Germany, England, and Switzerland. First attempts were made to organize Mizrachi in Ereẓ Israel, and two-and-a-half years after it was founded, its branches also became active in Western Europe and in the United States. The first world conference of Mizrachi took place, with the participation of about 100 delegates, in Pressburg, Hungary (now Bratislava, Czechoslovakia), on Aug. 21–23, 1904. The conference laid the foundation for the Mizrachi World Organization. Reines was the conference's chairman and delivered the opening address in Hebrew. Other speakers included Nehemiah *Nobel, among the great rabbis of Western Europe; Jawitz; Rabbi Nahum Grinhaus from Troki; and Rabbi Yehudah Leib Fishman (*Maimon). The movement's program was summed up at the conference as follows: (1) Mizrachi is an organization of Zionists who follow the *Basle Program and desire to work for the perpetuation of Jewish national life. Mizrachi sees the perpetuation of the Jewish people in the observance of the Torah, Jewish tradition, and the *mitzvot* and the return to the land of its forefathers. (2) Mizrachi will remain within the framework of the Zionist Organization, in which it will struggle for its opinions and views. However, it will create a special organization of its own for its religious and cultural activities. (3) The purpose of Mizrachi is to realize its goals by employing all the legal means at its disposal to explain its ideas to all Orthodox circles, by creating and distributing national-religious literature, and by educating youth in the spirit of its ideals and programs.

From Crisis to Expansion. At the Tenth Zionist Congress, which took place in Basle in 1911, the question of cultural work was again raised, and a bitter battle ensued between its advocates and opponents. In order to establish its stand on the question, Mizrachi called a meeting before the congress and decided to fight against the inclusion of cultural work in the Zionist program, but not by threatening secession. The majority at the congress, however, decided to include cultural work in the framework of the Zionist Organization's activities. Consequently, all the Mizrachi delegates walked out of the hall to demonstrate their opposition to the decision. The fifth world conference of Mizrachi was held in Berlin, immediately after the Zionist Congress, to formulate a stand on the decision of the Zionist Congress about cultural activities. The delegates from Russia and Poland were in favor of a struggle within the Zionist Organization using all possible means short of creating a split, for any schism would be a tragedy for the entire Jewish people and the national renaissance. On the other hand, representatives from the center in Frankfort and some of the Swiss and Hungarian delegates were in favor of withdrawing from the Zionist Organization. The Berlin conference finally decided against leaving the Zionist Organization while conducting the struggle within its ranks. This decision brought about a rift in the ranks of Mizrachi, and a number of its leaders, including members of the head office in Frankfort, left the organization. As a result the center of Mizrachi was moved to Altona, near Hamburg. Louis Frank was elected chairman and was later the second president of World Mizrachi.

During the term of the Hamburg executive, the central office of Mizrachi was established in the Land of Israel under the direction of Rabbi Fishman. Also during the Hamburg period, Rabbi Meir Berlin (Bar-Ilan) began working as the general secretary organizer of the Mizrachi World Organization. He left Lithuania for Berlin and there published the weekly *Ha-Ivri.* When Rabbi Berlin entered office, Mizrachi received a great impetus in its work and became a strong and influential factor both in the Zionist movement and among religious Jewry. Under his leadership, the first conference of Mizrachi to take place in the United States was convened in 1914, in Cincinnati, Ohio, and he succeeded in making the movement into an important factor in the lives of American Jewry and in the American Zionist movement. Rabbi Berlin was joined there by Rabbi Fishman, who had been expelled from Ereẓ Israel during World War I by the Turkish authorities and who added projects of his own and the atmosphere of Ereẓ Israel to the American movement. The first world conference of Mizrachi that took place after World War I (Amsterdam, Jan. 14–15, 1920) decided to transfer the seat of the world center to Jerusalem. Mizrachi was thus the first Zionist party to establish its center in Ereẓ Israel (and specifically in Jerusalem). In 1923 Rabbi Berlin,who was the leader of the movement and expanded its activities, settled in Ereẓ Israel. Some time later he was also elected president of the world organization and remained in this position until his death.

Mizrachi in Ereẓ Israel. After fundamental organizational preparation within circles of the old *yishuv* and organizational work that began in March 1918, including the foundation of branches in various areas of settlement in the country and the establishment of a "temporary center" in Jaffa, the foundations for Mizrachi were laid in Ereẓ Israel. Its first conference was held on Sept. 2, 1918, and since then Mizrachi has become a political and cultural force in the country. Among the founders of Mizrachi in Ereẓ Israel were Rabbi Ben-Zion *Ouziel, then the rabbi of Jaffa and afterward the Sephardi chief rabbi *(rishon le-Zion),* and Moshe *Ostrovsky (ha-Meiri), then the rabbi of the settlement of Ekron and afterward a member of the Va'ad Le'ummi. Rabbi Fishman participated at the second national conference (September 1919) after returning to the country from his absence during the war. Mizrachi reached the height of its development with the transfer of its world center to the country and especially after Rabbi Berlin settled there in 1923. During certain periods, Rabbi Berlin also served as the chairman of Mizrachi in the country.

As early as its first conference in Ereẓ Israel, Mizrachi raised the matter of establishing the offices of the rabbinate as one of the major points on the agenda. It subsequently devoted much effort to ensure the success of the conference to establish the chief rabbinate of Ereẓ Israel, which took place through the initiative of Rabbi Abraham Isaac *Kook in Jerusalem in February 1921. After great efforts, in December 1919 Mizrachi succeeded in acquiring the recognition of the Zionist institutions for its trend of religious education as a part of the educational system of the Zionist Organization.

With the end of World War I and the publication of the *Balfour Declaration, the Third Aliyah began to arrive in Palestine and brought with it members of Ẓe'irei Mizrachi, who strove to build up the land on the basis of pioneering labor and religious renewal. As young pioneers they called for "personal fulfillment," i.e., for religious Zionists to settle in Ereẓ Israel and build it in the spirit of the Torah. Their vision was expressed in the short motto *"Torah va-Avodah,"* which became the basis for the religious labor movement and the establishment of *Ha-Po'el ha-Mizrachi in Ereẓ Israel. The idea struck roots in the Diaspora as well and became the slogan of the mass movement, called Torah va-Avodah, throughout the world. It was an active participant in the Jewish Agency prior to 1948 and has been an active partner in Israel's government coalitions since the birth of the State with the exception of a single year. It has consistently polled about 10% of the total vote in Israel. In 1969 it had 11 representatives in the Knesset and three cabinet ministers. (See *Israel, Political Life and Parties.) The party is also active on the municipal level, and in some areas, particularly in newer sections of the country settled by North African or Yemenite Jews of Orthodox convictions, has either elected mayors or holds the balance of power. It is the main supporter of the chief rabbinate and the dominating force in most of Israel's religious councils.

Educational Work. After the crisis that overcame Russian Jewry with the outbreak of the Russo-Japanese War, the revolution, and the pogroms that followed (1905), it was practically impossible to maintain the world center of Mizrachi in Russia. It was therefore decided to transfer the seat of its executive to Frankfort, Germany. During the "Frankfort period," Mizrachi activities became more systematic.Their most important aspect was the beginning of the educational work of Mizrachi in Ereẓ Israel. The world center decided to send Rabbi Fishman to study the situation of education in Ereẓ Israel and find ways to develop educational and cultural activities there. He laid the foundation for the establishment of the Taḥkemoni School in Jaffa, the first educational institution of Mizrachi in the country, which inaugurated Mizrachi's educational system based on a synthesis of "the people of Israel, the Torah, and Zion."

In 1920 an agreement was reached in the World Zionist Organization that ensured Mizrachi autonomy in the field of religious education in Ereẓ Israel. An educational program began to be designed, followed by the establishment of a network of Mizrachi schools, which included kindergartens, elementary schools, high schools, yeshivot, vocational schools, and teachers' seminaries. The educational network of Mizrachi continued to exist as a separate trend in Israel until the establishment of the State religious school system in the 1953/54 school year (see *Israel: Education). The large majority of Mizrachi schools, which then encompassed more than 60,000 students and about 3,000 teachers, were integrated into the new framework of governmental religious education. The yeshivot have been the most outstanding achievement of Mizrachi education. In 16 high school-level yeshivot of *Benei Akiva, students receive both a yeshivah and general education; in four girls' schools the educational program is parallel to that of the yeshivot. The network includes Midrashiat No'am in Pardes Ḥannah, "Torah and Melakhah" yeshivot, the agricultural yeshivah at Kefar ha-Ro'eh, and the yeshivah for higher studies at Kerem Yavneh. At *Bar-Ilan University in Ramat Gan, which was established by Mizrachi in the United States, there were more than 7,000 students in 1970, with extensions in Safed, Ashkelon, and the Jordan Valley. After the 20th world conference of Mizrachi (1962), the educational work of the movement was administered by the

Center for Religious Education in Israel, affiliated with the world center of Mizrachi-Ha-Po'el ha-Mizrachi and the movement in Israel.

Structure of the World Movement. From 1955 the world movement of Mizrachi and Ha-Po'el ha-Mizrachi constituted one united organization. Before the merger of the two movements, however, they existed as separate world organizations—Mizrachi as the Mizrachi World Organization and Ha-Po'el ha-Mizrachi as Berit ha-Olamit shel Torah va-Avodah. The activities among women and youth had also been separate. The world center of Mizrachi and Ha-Po'el ha-Mizrachi is the highest body of the religious Zionist framework and constitutes a common executive of the two movements. It is elected by the world conference of the movement, which meets every few years. Rabbi Meir Berlin served as president of the world movement for many years. After his death (1949), Rabbi A. L. *Gellman was elected chairman of the world center. At the 21st world conference (1968), Ḥayyim Moshe *Shapira was elected president of the world center and the world movement and Rabbi Ẓemaḥ Zambrowski was elected chairman of the world center. The world movement's financial instrument is the Keren Ereẓ Israel shel Mizrachi.

When Mizrachi and Ha-Po'el ha-Mizrachi united throughout the world, a common conference of the two organizations in Israel was held in the summer of 1956 and decided to found a united party by the name of the *National Religious Party (Miflagah Datit Le'ummit, abbreviated to Mafdal). At the second conference of the N.R.P. and the 13th conference of Ha-Po'el ha-Mizrachi in Israel (1963), the responsibilities and tasks of the N.R.P. and Ha-Po'el ha-Mizrachi were divided as follows: the party will deal with matters of policy, municipal affairs, organization of the middle class, religion and rabbis, public relations and publication of the daily newspaper *Ha-Ẓofeh;* Ha-Po'el ha-Mizrachi with organization, fees, immigration and absorption, labor and vocational affairs, housing, settlement, culture, pension funds and economic affairs, matters concerning free professionals, and departments for elderly members and development towns.

Projects and Achievements. Mizrachi fought for the observance of the Sabbath in Israel and the preservation of the character of the Sabbath and Jewish holidays in the public life of the Jewish community. It initiated the establishment of the Ministry of Religions in the government of Israel and of covering the religious needs of the population from government funds and local authorities. Its efforts also led to the passage of the laws governing *kashrut* and Sabbath observance in the Israel Defense Forces, marriage and divorce, rabbinical judges, etc. Through the initiative of Rabbi Berlin, the Mifal ha-Torah Lema'an ha-Yeshivot be-Ereẓ Israel (Torah Fund for Yeshivot in the Land of Israel) was established whose publication of the Talmud and the *Encyclopedia Talmudica* is in progress. In the field of literature and journalism, the daily *Ha-Ẓofeh* and *Mosad ha-Rav Kook, established by Rabbi Fishman and constituting the largest publishing house in the world for literature on the Torah and studies of Judaism, are worthy of mention. Since its foundation, more than 1,000 books have been published by the Mosad or with its aid.

Women's and youth organizations also hold an important place in the framework of the world movement. The women in the Mizrachi movement have taken part in the activities of Histadrut Nashim Mizrachi (Omen; Women's Mizrachi Federation in Ereẓ Israel) and Mo'eẓet ha-Po'alot shel Ha-Po'el ha-Mizrachi, which integrated into one movement called the National Religious Women's Movement in Ereẓ Israel, encompassing more than 50,000 members. This movement is active in the sphere of establishing kindergartens and day nurseries, the cultural absorption of new immigrants, the organization of agricultural and vocational training for its members, etc. Among the youth organizations centered around Mizrachi is *Benei Akiva. Until the union of Mizrachi and Ha-Po'el ha-Mizrachi and the establishment of the N.R.P., the youth organization No'am (short for No'ar Mizrachi), which was founded on Ḥanukkah 1940 and established Midrashiat No'am in Pardes Ḥannah, existed separately. Other youth organizations are Ha-No'ar ha-Dati ha-Oved for working youth and Ha-Mishmeret ha-Ẓe'irah (The Young Guard), which encompassed thousands of students and army veterans. The world center of Mizrachi and Ha-Po'el ha-Mizrachi also established a special department for the young generation that centralized the activities of Ha-Mishmeret ha-Ẓe'irah around the world. Finally, there is the religious sports organization, Eliẓur.

The Mizrachi movement also established a series of financial and economic institutions including Bank ha-Mizrachi and Bank Ha-Po'el ha-Mizrachi, which united and established the United Mizrachi Bank, the fourth largest bank in the country; Mishhav, a company for construction and the establishment of religious quarters and suburbs; a center for the economic institutions and programs of the movement; the cooperative of Ha-Po'el ha-Mizrachi; pension funds; etc. [Y.Go.]

In the United States. Mizrachi of America was founded in 1911 with groups in New York and St. Louis. Rabbi D. B. Abramowitz was the first president. The organization did not become effective until 1913, when Rabbi Meir Berlin settled in New York and became the leader of the movement. Following a tour of the country by Rabbi Berlin, Mizrachi held its first annual convention in Cincinnati in 1914. The Mizrachi Palestine Fund was established in 1928, and in 1936 became part of the United Palestine Appeal. Its youth movement, Benei Akiva, was established in 1934. In 1951 Mizrachi merged with Ha-Po'el ha-Mizrachi, which had been established early in the 1920s. The combined organization and its women's affiliates claimed a membership of 60,000–70,000 and in 1969 had a budget of $220,000. It has a youth group and is the parent organization of Va'ad Hachinuch Hacharedi, which promotes Hebrew day schools. [L.Be.]

Bibliography: M. Waxman, *Mizrachi, its Aims and Purposes* (1918); P. Churgin and L. Gellman (eds.), *Mizrachi Jubilee Publication of the Mizrachi Organization of America 1911–1936* (1936); J. L. Maimon, *History of the Mizrachi Movement* (1938); S. Z. Shragai, *Vision and Realization* (1945); S. Rosenblatt, *History of the Mizrachi Movement* (1951); Y. Tirosh, *Essence of Religious Zionism* (1964); idem, *Religion and State in Israel: The Religious Zionist Standpoint* (1965); Mizrachi-Ha-Po'el ha-Mizrachi, *The Length and Breadth of the Land* (1965); B. Cohen, *Religious Zionism—a Revaluation* (1966); M. Berlin, *Mi-Volozhin ad Yerushalayim*, 2 vols. (1939–40); idem, *Bi-Shevilei ha-Teḥiyyah* (1940); idem, *Kitvei*... (1940); M. Ostrovsky, *Toledot ha-Mizrachi be-Ereẓ-Yisrael* (1944); I. Goldschlag, *Mi-Vilna ad Yerushalayim* (1954); *Mizrachi Woman* (1933–); *Mizrachi Outlook* (1936–57); *Jewish Horizon* (1957–).

MIZRAḤ (Heb. מִזְרָח; "east"), designation of the direction to be faced during prayer, of the wall of the synagogue where seats were reserved for the rabbi and other dignitaries, and of an ornamental wall plaque used to indicate the location of east. The custom of facing the Temple during prayer has biblical origins beginning with Solomon's prayer (I Kings 8:34, 44, 48; II Chron. 6:34). The Bible also relates that Daniel prayed three times daily in his chamber, the windows of which were opened toward Jerusalem (Dan. 6:11). The rule laid down in the Mishnah

(Ber. 4:5) and amplified in the Talmud, is that if one prays in the Diaspora, he shall direct himself toward Ereẓ Israel; in Ereẓ Israel, toward Jerusalem; in Jerusalem, toward the Temple; and in the Temple, toward the Holy of Holies. If a man is east of the Temple, he should turn westward; if in the west, eastward; in the south, northward; and if in the north, southward. Thus all Jews direct their prayers toward one place (Ber. 30a; T. J. Ber. 4:5 8b–c; Tosef., Ber. 3:16). The term *mizraḥ*, therefore, applies properly to the cities and countries situated west of Jerusalem. Excavations of ancient synagogues generally bear this out, as those houses of worship found in Miletus, Priene, and Aegina, all west of Ereẓ Israel, show an eastern orientation, as has been recorded of Egyptian synagogues (Jos., Apion, 2:10). Those synagogues north of Jerusalem and west of the Jordan River, as *Bet Alfa, *Capernaum, *Hammath, and *Chorazin all face southward, whereas ancient sanctuaries east of the Jordan, such as Val-Dokkī, Umm al-Qanātir, Jarash, and *Dura-Europos all face west. In the south, the synagogue excavated at *Masada faces northwest to Jerusalem. The directions frequently varied slightly due to the terrain. Exceptions have been found in the synagogues at Khirbat Summāqa, a village on Mt. Carmel, and at ʿUsifiyyā, where the orientations are not toward Jerusalem. There is no satisfactory explanation for this divergence from the norm. In the early Christian church it was also customary to pray facing toward the Holy Land. For Islam the original direction of prayer *(qibla)* was toward Jerusalem, but this was subsequently changed by Muhammad in favor of Mecca.

Excavations of ancient synagogues show that the earliest houses of worship had their entrances facing Jerusalem, and portals, therefore, indicated the sacred direction. The remains of the Dura-Europos synagogue on the Euphrates reveal that by the third century C.E. the doors were on the eastern side and the opposite wall, in which a special niche had been made to place the scrolls during worship, faced Jerusalem. This niche was too small to have been the permanent location of the ark, which was obviously still portable at that time. In Ereẓ Israel the wall facing the Temple site was changed from the side of entrance to the side of the ark in the fifth or sixth century. This change is already found in synagogues at Naaran near Jericho and Bet Alfa. Worshipers came through the portals and immediately faced both the scrolls and Jerusalem. However, in those sanctuaries found in Hammath, Yafa in Galilee, and Eshtemoa in Judea, the sacred direction is properly south in the first two cases and north in the third, while the entrance is from the eastern side. This may be in imitation of the Tent of Meeting, which had its gates on the eastern side (Num. 2:2–3; 3:38), or of Solomon's Temple, the portals of which were to the east (Ezek. 43:1–4), although the precise reason is not known. Maimonides, quoting the second passage in Numbers, states that the doors of the synagogue should face east, while the Ark should be placed "in the direction in which people pray in that city," i.e., toward Jerusalem (Yad, Tefillah, 11:2). The Shulḥan Arukh records the same rule, but to avoid the semblance of worshiping the sun by facing east, it recommends that one turn toward the southeast (Isserles OḤ 94:2; also Suk. 5:4). If a person is unable to ascertain the points of the compass, he should direct his heart toward Jerusalem. This was also the opinion of R. Tarfon and R. Sheshet, who held that, since the Divine Presence is everywhere, the essential requirement is to direct one's heart to God (BB 25a). It is customary in traditional homes to mark the eastern wall to enable a person to recite his prayers in the proper direction. Artistic wall plaques inscribed with the word *mizraḥ* and scriptural passages like "From the rising *(mi-mizraḥ)* of the sun unto the going down thereof, the Lord's name is to be praised" (Ps. 113:3), kabbalistic inscriptions, or pictures of holy places are used for this purpose.

Bibliography: Goodenough, Symbols, 1 (1953), 216; F. Landsberger, in: HUCA, 28 (1957), 181–203; L. A. Mayer, *Bibliography of Jewish Art* (1967), index; E. L. Sukenik, *The Ancient Synagogue of Beth Alpha* (1932), 11; idem, *The Ancient Synagogue of El-Ḥammeh* (1935), 78–81; idem, *Ancient Synagogues in Palestine and Greece* (1934), 27, 50–52; Y. Yadin, *Masada* (Eng., 1966), 180, 184. [ED.]

MIZRAḤI, DAVID BEN SHALOM (c. 1696–1771), one of the most prominent *halakhah* scholars in Yemen. Mizraḥi propagated Torah studies and headed the synagogue of the *nagid* Sar Shalom Irāqi (al-Usta). When the need was felt for a commentary on the Shulḥan Arukh adapted to the requirements of Yemenite Jewry and its customs, David Mizraḥi undertook this task in his work *Shetilei Zeitim* (1886–91), on *Oraḥ Ḥayyim* (1886–91; 1895). He explains the Shulḥan Arukh with brevity and clarity, quoting the customs of Yemenite Jewry which are not mentioned by R. Moses *Isserles and the commentaries of the Shulḥan Arukh. He retained all the notes of R. Moses Isserles that are in agreement with the Shulḥan Arukh and omitted everything that was in contradiction to it, including customs. Mizraḥi adopted the same style in his work *Rashei Besamim* (1895) on the *Yoreh De'ah*. His third work is *Revid ha-Zahav* (1955), responsa and novellas on the Shulḥan Arukh and R. Moses Isserles (some of which were written by his son Yiḥya). This work is the first of its kind in the responsa literature of Yemenite Jewry. [Y.R.]

MIZRAḤI, ELIJAH (c. 1450–1526), rabbinical authority, the greatest of the rabbis of the Ottoman Empire of his time. Mizraḥi was of Romaniot origin (the original Turkish Jews as distinct from the Spanish exiles) and was born and educated in Constantinople. Among his teachers he mentions Elijah ha-Levi in rabbinic studies and Mordecai Comitiano (see *Comtino) in general studies. Until the death of Moses *Capsali, Mizraḥi devoted himself to study and public instruction. As early as 1475 he is mentioned as heading a *keneset* (probably a school in addition to a synagogue) and as having students. During this period of his life he was involved in controversies with *Moses Esrim ve-Arba and Perez Colon, and despite his stormy and aggressive temperament he submitted to the intervention of Capsali in these disputes, an intervention which reveals a certain tension between them. Perhaps for this reason he took no part in the famous controversy between Capsali and Joseph Colon. After the death of Capsali in 1498 Mizraḥi became the foremost rabbinical authority in Constantinople and in fact throughout the whole Ottoman Empire. From far and near, problems of *halakhah* and procedure were addressed to him. There is reason to believe that he filled the position of head of the rabbis of Constantinople (though he did not have the title of *ḥakham bashi*, appointed by the sultan, since that office did not exist at that period). Nevertheless, it would seem that his authority derived not from any official position, but from the recognition of his personality and strength. He was considered both by his contemporaries and later generations as the greatest *posek* of his time in Turkey. He was firm and unbending in his decisions, and even the great rabbis among the Spanish exiles accepted his authority.

In his responsa (56) he gives a description of his daily routine, which reveals the strain under which he worked. Fulfilling a number of functions simultaneously, he conducted the affairs of the community, gave decisions on all matters, headed a yeshivah, and taught not only Talmud but secular subjects. At the same time he wrote commentaries on both religious and scientific works, had an inner circle of select students whom he taught the codes, and wrote responsa in answer to queries addressed to him from afar. Like Moses Capsali he was active in the problem of the absorption of the exiles from Spain and Portugal, collecting funds on their behalf, and forcing the wealthy members of the community to pay the amounts imposed on them (Resp. 66). Mizraḥi's attitude to these exiles was one of respect and high regard. He appreciated that their standards of culture and knowledge were higher than those of the native Turkish Jews, but nevertheless he came out firmly against attempts by some of them to impose their will on the old community. He resisted attempts on their part to impose customs and procedures to which they were accustomed, but which were contrary to those ruling in Turkey. Of special importance was his attitude toward the Karaites. On the one hand he exerted himself to attract them to the Rabbanites, and, in opposition to Moses Capsali, to give them instruction in both secular subjects and even in the Oral Law, and in this context firmly resisted every attempt to isolate them. On the other hand he completely rejected on halakhic grounds the permissibility of intermarriage between Karaites and Rabbanites. Mizraḥi's halakhic method is distinctive and clear. He lays down fundamental principles and raises possible objections to his own statements, so that every topic is exhaustively examined and clarified. His responsa were accepted as authoritative by his and succeeding generations, despite the fact that some of the leading contemporary scholars opposed his views.

His best-known pupils and colleagues were *Elijah ha-Levi, *Tam ibn Yaḥya, and Abraham ibn Yaish. Mizraḥi suffered greatly from ill health, financial strain, and family misfortunes. Three of his sons are known, Gershon, Israel, and Reuben, and a daughter. There are legends about his son-in-law's connections with the court of the sultan. Reuben died during his father's lifetime. Gershon was the victim of a libel that during a severe illness he had sought to be converted to Islam. He had to abandon his family and, after paying heavy bribes, escaped to Naxos, but even there he suffered persecution and strife. These two incidents, as well as the death of his wife, affected Mizraḥi greatly. His third son, Israel, published his father's Rashi commentary and *Sefer ha-Mispar*. Mizraḥi died in Constantinople and Joseph *Taitaẓak eulogized his works.

Mizraḥi's personality and multi-faceted character emerge clearly from his works. His main activity was in the writing and teaching of both *halakhah* and general knowledge, but his main fame rests upon his crowning achievement, his supercommentary to Rashi (1st ed. Venice, 1527), a fact which he himself states. In this work he exhaustively discusses almost every word in Rashi, but does not refrain from disagreeing with him on numerous occasions. On the other hand he defends Rashi against the criticism of Naḥmanides. This work has given rise to a veritable literature. Later commentators answered his criticism and justified Rashi. The two works, Rashi's commentary and Mizraḥi's supercommentary, became a main subject of study of rabbinical commentators of the Bible from the 16th century onward. The work has an added importance as a result of the quotations it gives from the Romaniot scholars of the 14th and 15th centuries for which his work is the sole source side by side with those of Ibn Ezra and the French and German scholars. Mizraḥi's responsa, published in two collections, number 140, but of them only 110 are his, although they undoubtedly represent only a fraction of his many responsa. More than 40 are still in various manuscripts. A comparison between the two reveals the many errors in the printed responsa, particularly in the Constantinople edition. An extant fragment (Resp. Const. 96) reveals the method of teaching in his yeshivah, consisting of notes made at the time by one of his pupils.

The only other rabbinic work of Mizraḥi published is his novellae on the *Sefer Mitzvot Gadol* of *Moses of Coucy (Constantinople, 1521), the only work of his published in his lifetime. His work on the *Halakhot* of Isaac Alfasi is not extant. In the field of secular knowledge his *Sefer ha-Mispar* (Constantinople, 1533) on mathematics is famous. It was highly thought of in its time and has been translated into Latin. He also wrote a commentary on Ptolemy's *Almagest* and on Euclid's *Elements*. R. Moses Almosnino possessed a commentary by Mizraḥi on the "Intentions of the Philosophers" of Al-*Ghazālī. Mizraḥi took a negative attitude toward Kabbalah, particularly against relying on it for halakhic decisions, and the introduction of kabbalistic ideas into the prayer book.

Bibliography: A. Geiger (ed.), *Melo Ḥofnayim* (1840), 12 (Heb. pt.); Conforte, Kore, index; E. Bashyazi, *Adderet Eliyahu* (1833); M. Almosnino, *Ma'amaẓ Ko'aḥ* (Venice, 1588), 138b.; *Me'ora'ot Olam* (Izmir, 1756); M. Lattes, *De Vita et Scriptis Eliae Kapsalii* (Padua, 1869); Michael, Or, nos. 161–4, 306; Rosanes, Togarmah, 1 (1930), 70–77; A. Freimann, in: *Zion*, 1 (1936), 188–91; *Ha-Segullah*, 5 no. 5 (1938); A. Ovadyah, *Ketavim Nivḥarim*, 1 (1942), 63–198; S. Assaf, *Be-Oholei Ya'akov* (1953), 145–96; Steinschneider, Uebersetzungen, 322, 508, 524. [Jos.H.]

MIẒRAYIM (Heb. מִצְרַיִם), Hebrew place-name. In the Septuagint it is rendered as Egypt (Gr. Αἴγυπτος). The Hebrew proper noun, however, has a broader range of meaning. As Aiguptos, the name of the country was derived from a name for the city of Memphis, *Ḥet-kau-ptaḥ* ("Castle of the *ka*-souls of Ptah"), so the name of Miẓrayim may have been derived from the name of a city of Lower Egypt, if not of Lower Egypt itself. This is based on the occurrences in the Bible of Miẓrayim in combination with Pathros (*pa to resy;* "the southern country," i.e., Upper Egypt), in which cases Miẓrayim seems to mean Lower Egypt (*To Mehy*). Secondarily, it came to mean both all of Egypt and Egyptians, and was—and still is—the common Hebrew word for Egypt. [AL.R.S.]

MLADA BOLESLAV (Czech **Mladá Boleslav;** Ger. **Jungbunzlau**), town in N. Bohemia, Czechoslovakia. One of the important communities in Bohemia, it is first mentioned in 1471 and is noted in a Hebrew document of 1556. Eleven families lived there in 1570, and a synagogue was recorded in 1579. The cemetery (well known mainly because of the tombstone of Jacob *Bassevi von Treuenberg) was consecrated in 1584 and still existed in 1970. The number of adult Jews in the town in 1615 was 120. In 1643 the community came under the protection of the Swedish king for a time. The community elders were forced to sign an agreement in 1661 which greatly limited their freedom of commerce. At the end of the century, Jews had a near monopoly of transportation. In 1710 a shopkeeper, David Brandeis, was accused of poisoning a Christian with plum jam; the day of his release was celebrated on the tenth of Adar as *Povidl* ("plum jam") *Purim*. After a fire in the late 17th century had destroyed part of the Jewish quarter and the synagogue, the community built a new synagogue on the model of the Meisl synagogue in Prague. It had to be demolished in 1960 because of decay. The Jewish population numbered 794 in 1834; 865 (9.1% of the total population) in 1880; 402 (2.8% of the total) in 1910; 419 in 1921; and 264 (1.3%) in 1930. In 1922 a local Jewish museum was founded; its treasures were later transferred to the Central Jewish Museum in Prague.

Cut-glass goblet of the Mlada Boleslav *ḥevra kaddisha,* with a scene of a hearse preceded by members of the burial society and followed by the family and mourners, 1838. Prague, State Jewish Museum.

In 1942 the Jews from Mlada Boleslav and the surrounding district were concentrated in the old castle. Of the 1,041 persons deported to *Theresienstadt in January 1943, only 40 were still alive in November 1944. After World War II a small congregation was reestablished, administered by the Prague community.

Among the outstanding rabbis of Mlada Boleslav were Moses Isaac Spira (until 1702), Ezekiel Glogau-Schlesinger (until 1821), and Isaac Spitz (1824–42). The house in which Sigfried *Kapper (1821–1879) lived was marked by a memorial tablet. Jewish life in Mlada Boleslav at the beginning of the 19th century is described in Leopold *Kompert's *Die Kinder des Randars* ("The Randar Children"). Mlada Boleslav was considered a kind of a Bohemian *Chelm and many tales were told of "*Bumsler Shtiklekh*" ("pranks"). The Prague scholar Meir *Fischels (Bumsla) came from Mlada Boleslav. A **seliḥah*, printed in 1854 to commemorate a conflagration, was the last literary production of this kind published in Bohemia. Benjamin Isaac (d. 1750), "Jew merchant of extensive charity" in London, came from Mlada Boleslav, and he set up a foundation in his name in his native community.

Bibliography: A. E. Goldmann and M. Gruenwald, in: H. Gold (ed.), *Juden und Judengemeinden Boehmens . . .* (1934), 204–21; M. Gruenwald, in: MWJ (1888), 192–6; idem, in: *Českožidovský kalendar,* 11 (1891/92), 138ff.; H. Volávková, *Schicksal des Juedischen Museums in Prag* (1965); R. Iltis (ed.), *Die aussaeen unter Traenen . . .* (1959), 99–101; Roth, England, 284.

[J.HER.]

MLAWA (Pol. **Mława;** Rus. **Mlava**), town in the province of Warsaw, N.E. central Poland. The earliest documented information on the Jewish community is dated 1543. It is included in a report of a case of *blood libel, which mentions the name of the *parnas* of the community—Berechiah (Pol. Bogusław). In 1569 there were 23 Jewish families living in the town and in 1578 they had increased to 34. Their main sources of livelihood were the livestock trade and crafts. A charge of desecrating the *Host in 1670, and the fires which devastated Mlawa in 1659 and 1692 caused the number of Jews gradually to decrease. On the other hand, the Jewish population of the suburb of Zabrody, which was beyond the area of municipal jurisdiction, and the surrounding villages, increased.

Until 1753, the community of Mlawa was under the jurisdiction of that of *Ciechanow. The growth of economic activity in the region during the last third of the 18th century brought an increase in the Jewish population. The 1765 census showed 70 Jewish families numbering 487 poll-tax payers in Mlawa and the neighboring villages. Fifteen houses in the town were owned by Jews. Sources of 1781 mention a Jewish population of 718. After the Prussian conquest (1793), the town was granted a *de non tolerandis Judaeis* privilege, and the Jews then moved to the suburb of Zabrody.

The Jews returned to Mlawa with the establishment of the grand duchy of Warsaw (1807). In 1808 they numbered 137, forming 15% of the population. Following restrictions on Jewish settlement, a special quarter was established in 1824, and only there (with some rare exceptions) were Jews permitted to live. In addition, the entry of Jews from other regions was almost completely prohibited, because of the location of the town in the border area. In 1827, there were 792 Jews (36% of the population) living in the town. The ghetto and the other restrictions on residence and ownership of real estate were abolished in 1862. Once the railway lines from Mlawa to Warsaw (1877) and Gdansk (1883) were opened, the trade in grain, livestock, wood, and army supplies, from which many Jews earned their livelihood, increased considerably. Between 1857 and 1897, the Jewish population of Mlawa grew from 1,650 to 4,845 (41% of the population).

The influence of Ḥasidism manifested itself among the Jews of Mlawa from the beginning of the 19th century. With the consolidation of their economic situation at the close of that century, the influence of *Mitnaggedim* circles gained in strength (in 1870, Wolf Lipszie was appointed rabbi of the town). The last rabbi of Mlawa, R. Jehiel Moses Segalowicz (appointed 1901), was known as one of the *Mitnaggedim.* In the late 1890s, a *Ḥovevei Zion circle was organized in the town. During the revolution and pogroms of 1905–06, the *Bund and the *Po'alei Zion wielded considerable influence among the Jewish workers, youth, and intelligentsia of Mlawa. The Jewish author Joseph *Opatoshu, the Hebrew author Jakir *Warshavsky, and the publicist and leader of the Bund in Poland, Victor *Alter, were born in Mlawa, where they also began their careers. Between 1921 and 1927 the Jewish population of Mlawa increased from 5,923 to 6,301. A newspaper, *Dos Mlauer Lebn,* was published; its editors included Bunim Warshavsky, Moses Lichtensztain, and Moses Laska.

Holocaust Period. At the outbreak of World War II there were about 6,500 Jews in Mlawa. At the beginning of November 1939 the Germans destroyed all the synagogues in Mlawa and the vicinity. The first deportation took place on Dec. 6, 1940, when 300 Jews were deported to *Miedzyrzec Podlaski, *Lubartow, and *Lublin; they shared the fate of the Jews there. The ghetto was established on Dec. 7–8, 1940, and liquidated two years later on Nov. 24, 1942. The last deportations took place from Nov. 10, 1942, to Dec. 10, 1942; almost all the Jews were deported to *Treblinka death camp. The Jewish community of Mlawa was not reconstituted after the war. Organizations of former residents of Mlawa are active in Israel, the United States, and Mexico.

Bibliography: Halpern, Pinkas, index; B. Wasiutyński, *Ludność żydowska w Polsce w wiekach XIX i XX* (1930), 23, 46f., 75, 78; S. Pazyra, *Geneza i rozwój miast mazowieckich* (1959), 398; Y. Trunk, *Geschikhte fun Yidn in Plotsk* (1939), 59, 62, 65; A. G. von Hoelske, *Geographie und Statistik von West- Sued- und Neu-Ostpreussen* (Berlin, 1800), 497; J. Shakky (ed.), *Pinkes Mlave* (1950); S. Zuchowski, *Odgłos processów kryminalnych na Żydach* (1700); Irgun Yoẓe'ei Mlawa be-Israel, *Yedi'on* (1967); *Pinkas Mlawa* (Yid., 1950). [A.Cy.]

MNEMONICS or **MEMORA TECHNICA** (Heb. סִימָן, *siman;* "a sign"), devices based on the principle that the mind is able to recall relatively unfamiliar ideas by connecting, as some artificial whole, parts of them which are mutually suggestive. Mnemonics are widely used in the Talmud—as in post-talmudic literature—but their use in the former was rendered imperative by the fact that the Talmud was originally transmitted orally, and even after it was committed to writing, both the scarcity of the texts, and the custom of teaching the text orally which prevailed in the geonic academies (Weiss, Dor, 3 (1904[4]), 215ff.; Halevy, Dorot, 3 (1928), 227) made it necessary for mnemonic devices to be employed. The rabbis laid great store on the efficacy of mnemonics as an aid to study. R. Ḥisda in Babylon deduced that the Torah can be acquired only by the use of mnemonics, adducing as evidence the verse "Put it in their mouth" (Deut. 31:19) reading *simona* —mnemonic for *sima* ("put"); R. Taḥlifa in Palestine explained that in Palestine they deduced the same lesson from the verse "Set thee up waymarks" (Jer. 31:21), proving that the "waymarks" refer to mnemonics (Er. 54b). The fact that the scholars of Judah retained their learning while those of Galilee forgot it was ascribed to the fact that the former employed mnemonics while the latter did not (Er. 53a). The verse in Ecclesiastes 12:9, "and besides that Koheleth . . . taught the people knowledge" was explained that he taught them by mnemonics (Er. 21b). It has been suggested that the widespread use of the alphabetical *acrostic in the Bible (e.g., Lam. 1–4; Ps. 119 and 145) had a mnemonic purpose since it reminded the person who recited it of the letter with which the succeeding verse commenced, but this form of mnemonic, though widely used in medieval poetry and even in prayers (e.g., *El Barukh* in the morning service, *Tikkanta Shabbat* in the Sabbath *Musaf*) is not at all resorted to in the Talmud.

The mnemonic devices of the Talmud can be divided into two main categories, those in which the mnemonic is an integral part of the text, forming part of its body, and those in which a passage is preceded by the mnemonic as an aid to the memory of what is to follow. The former are usually designated as *simankha*, i.e., "your mnemonic," while for the latter the simple word *siman* is given. Since the essence of the mnemonic is to call to mind the unfamiliar by use of the familiar, it naturally follows that it consists of the use of a well-known phrase. These phrases can be divided into biblical verses, since knowledge of the text of the Bible was regarded as axiomatic, well-known talmudic phrases, popular proverbs, or readily remembered catchphrases.

Biblical Mnemonics. Examples of biblical verses used for this purpose are numerous. For the six orders into which the Mishnah is divided, Isaiah 33:6 was cited: "There shall be faith in thy times, strength, salvation, wisdom, and knowledge," each of the nouns indicating a specific order (Shab. 31a). That basilicas attached to royal buildings are forbidden because of idolatry, but those of baths and storehouses permitted was to be remembered by the mnemonic "to bind [forbid] their kings with chains" (Ps. 149:8; Av. Zar. 16b). The law that if the lungs of animals are liver-colored they are permitted, but if flesh-colored forbidden had the mnemonic "and if flesh in the field, it is *terefah*" (Ex. 22:30; Ḥul. 47b). The mnemonic to remember that one should not curse one's parents in the presence of one's children is the verse (Gen. 48:5), "Ephraim and Manasseh [the grandchildren] shall be mine even as Reuben and Simeon [the children]" (Ket. 72b).

Talmudic Phrases. The bird called the moor-cock is forbidden as food, but the moor-hen permitted; the mnemonic is the rabbinic interpretation of the prohibition of an Ammonite to enter the congregation (Deut. 23:4): "An Ammonite," but not an Ammonite woman. A bird called the wine-drinker is also forbidden, and the mnemonic is "a drunkard is forbidden to officiate" (cf. Sanh. 22b). These are two examples given from a list in *Ḥullin* 62b.

Catchphrases. By their nature these are pithy statements in which the element of apparent paradox is often used. Thus the fact that a fish called the "sea ass" is permitted while one termed "the sea bull" is forbidden produces the mnemonic "the unclean is clean, the clean unclean," since the ass is forbidden and the ox permitted for consumption. To remember that meditating on sin can be worse than its actual commission, the mnemonic was devised "the odor of meat" (i.e., the odor of the meat excites the appetite more than the meat itself).

Mnemonics are used as an easy way to remember different statements in the name of one authority. Thus three statements on charity by R. Eleazar (BB 9a) provide the mnemonic "great is the sanctuary of Moses." Three statements of R. Manasseh found in different parts of the tractate *Ḥullin* (4a, 31a, 51a) are mnemonically connected by the sentence, "Inserting a blade into rams" (Ḥul. 4a). It is one of the characteristics of the methodology of the Talmud that a statement in the name of a sage which is relevant to the discussion is followed by a number of statements in the name of the same sage which have no connection with the subject under discussion. The need for mnemonics in these cases was obvious, and as far as possible they are made into a sentence. Thus three statements of Samuel b. Nahamani in the name of R. Johanan (the first has Nahamani in the texts) were to be remembered by the sentence "In truth money shall he see." An interesting example is provided in the same passage. Six anonymous popular epigrams are quoted, for all of which Samuel finds a biblical proof verse. They are combined in a mnemonic which (probably) means "Hear, Vashti, Seven Songs, (and) another" (Sanh. 7a). It is obvious, however, that any device which aided the memory was pressed into service. There was a difference of opinion between the scholars of Pumbedita and Sura as to the number of nails permitted in a shoe for walking on the Sabbath. R. Ḥiyya reported that the former said 24, the latter 22. The mnemonic was "Ḥiyya lost two nails in walking from Pumbedita to Sura" (Shab. 60b).

Popular Proverbs. The wealthy Simeon b. Judah ha-Nasi was of the opinion that a certain defect in an animal did not render the animal invalid and he ate its meat, while the poor R. Ḥiyya discarded it as invalid; they had a similar disagreement about the oil for the Temple. In both cases the mnemonic was the popular proverb, "the wealthy are parsimonious" (Ḥul. 46a; Men. 86a). Among the most frequent devisors of mnemonics are Rava, R. Papa, R. Safra, and especially R. Naḥman b. Isaac.

The second category of mnemonics (indicated by the word *siman* without the suffix) is usually merely a combination of words, each indicating a topic. Sometimes it is possible to make a sentence out of them (e.g., a mnemonic in *Ḥullin* 46b, "Date, Red, Dry Scabs" may be read as "A date, red and dry with scabs"), but sometimes this is quite impossible. These *simanim* appear to be post-talmudic and were often omitted from the text. In *Bava Batra* 113a the mnemonic has been omitted from the printed texts, but the word *siman* has been retained, giving rise to the erroneous view that it was the name of an *amora*. There was in fact a tendency to ignore the *simanim* even if they were printed, a practice of which Isaiah *Horowitz strongly disapproved, insisting that they had a mystic connotation (*Torah she-be-Al Peh, ayin, Shenei Luhot ha-Berit* (Amsterdam, 1698), 407b).

Another type of mnemonic consisted merely of the initial letters of words. The best known example is the mnemonic *DeẒaKH ADaSH BeAḤaB* for the ten plagues. The Midrash states that it was engraved on the staff of Moses and calls it a **notarikon* (Ex. R. 5:6) but in the Passover Haggadah it is referred to as *simanim*. Another example is the word *MaNẒePaKh* for the letters of the alphabet which have a final form. The Talmud makes a kind of mnemonic of this mnemonic, seeing in it a reference to the fact that "the prophets [seers] introduced them" *(ẓofim amarum)*, i.e., *MiN ẒoFayiKH* ("from thy prophets"; Meg. 2b). The medieval grammarians similarly made the mnemonic *BaGaD KeFaT* for the six letters which take a *dagesh kal*. The six things in which Shemini Aẓeret is regarded as a festival independent of Sukkot is indicated by the words *PaZeR KeSHeV*, each letter indicating one of the things. The six laws in which the opinion of Abbaye prevails over that of Rava is indicated by the mnemonic *YaAL KaGaM* (BM 22b). The difference of opinion as to the order of the festival blessings for wine *(yayin)*, *Kiddush*, the festival *(zeman)*, the candle *(ner)*, and *Havdalah* is indicated by whether it should be *YaKZaNaH* or *YaKNeHaZ* (Pes. 102b, 103a). For the order of biblical readings for the intermediate days of Passover a full sentence was used,"He dragged an ox, and sanctified it with money" (Meg. 31a).

The use of mnemonics did not end with the Talmud, and they are found in late rabbinic literature. The laws of *terefah* begin, "there are eight categories of *terefah* and their *siman* is *DaN HaNaK NeFeSH*" (YD 29:1). A remarkable calendrical mnemonic is provided by *atbash* (the cryptogram whereby the first letter of the alphabet, *alef*, is equated with the last, *tav;* the second, *bet*, with the penultimate *shin*, etc.) so as to determine the days of the week on which the festivals of a certain year fall. *Alef, bet*, etc. represent the eight days of Passover, and the rule is that *alef*=*tav* (Tishah be-Av); *bet*=*shin* (Shavuot); *gimmel*=*resh* (Rosh Ha-Shanah); *dalet*=*kaf* (*Keri'at ha-Torah*, i.e., Simḥat Torah in the Diaspora); *he*=*Ẓadi* (*Ẓom*, i.e., the Day of Atonement); *vav*=*peh* (Purim, but of the previous year). The list ends with *vav*. *Zayin*, however, corresponds to *ayin*, and the seventh day of Passover always falls on the same day of the week as Israel Independence Day. Another calendrical mnemonic is *"Lo ADU Rosh ve-lo BaDU Pesaḥ,"* i.e., (the first day of) Rosh Ha-Shanah cannot fall on the first, fourth, or sixth day of the week *(alef, dalet, vav)*, nor Passover on the second, fourth, or sixth *(bet, dalet, vav)*.

Distinct from mnemonics, although they serve the same purpose, are such mnemonic aids as are frequent in the Mishnah, whereby *mishnayot* on completely unrelated topics are grouped together because of their identical opening formula, e.g., "the only difference between A and B is" (Meg. 1), and "that which is invalid in A is valid in B" (Ḥul. 1:4–6).

See also *Abbreviations.

Bibliography: J. Bruell, *Doresh le-Ẓiyyon* (1864); Bruell, *Jahrbuecher*, 2 (1876), 58–67; B. Epstein, *Torah Temimah* to Ex. 34:27 (n. 40) and Num. 21:18 (n. 18); P. J. Kohn, *Sefer ha-Simanim ha-Shalem* (1953).

[L.I.R.]

MOAB (Heb. מוֹאָב), a land E. of the Jordan and the Dead Sea, one of Israel's neighbors in biblical times. The highland of Moab extends southward to the Zered River (Wādī al-Ḥasā'), eastward to the desert, and westward to the Dead Sea. Its northern boundary was much disputed; sometimes it was limited by the river Arnon and sometimes it extended north of the Dead Sea (cf. the "plains of Moab" in Num. 26:3). The area of Moab is mountainous in the south, with ridges up to 4,000 ft. (1,250 m.), leveling off to a plateau in the north (the biblical *mishor*, "tableland"). The decline to the desert is gradual; that to the Dead Sea steep. The area was traversed by the "King's Highway." Its economy was mainly pastoral (cf. II Kings 3:4).

The People and the Country. Archaeological surveys have established that after a period of pre-Moabite settlement in the last centuries of the third millennium, Moabite tribes settled the country in about the mid-14th century B.C.E., not long before the Exodus. They were of Semitic stock, closely akin to the Israelites. [M.A.-Y.]

According to the tradition in Genesis 19:30–38, Moab (LXX: Μωαβ) was born to Lot by his elder daughter in the vicinity of the town of Zoar, at the southeastern tip of the Dead Sea. The meaning of the name, according to Targum Jonathan and the Septuagint, is "from my father" (cf. Gen. 19:37). Other than this tradition, there is no further information on the origin of the Moabites and the process of their formation into a national kingdom in Transjordan. The story of the birth of Moab and Ammon to Lot, son of Haran, the brother of Abraham, was intended to explain, in a popular midrashic manner, the names Moab and Ammon. However, the tradition of ethnic kinship between the children of Lot and Israel, echoes of which occur elsewhere in the Bible, is not based merely on the geographical proximity of these peoples to Israel. Biblical tradition and especially the Moabite language and the conjectured time of their settlement in Transjordan suggest that the Moabites were among the tribes of the sons of Eber, who spread out from the Syrian-Arabian desert in the second millennium B.C.E., and established national kingdoms throughout the Fertile Crescent. The Moabites, like the *Ammonites and *Edomites, were not among the pre-Israelite inhabitants of the land of Canaan (Gen. 10:15–20; 15:18–21; et al.). According to Deuteronomy (2:10–11), the Emim formerly occupied the land of Moab—"a people great, and many, and tall, like the Anakim" (see *Rephaim)—but it does not indicate when and in what circumstances they were driven out by the Moabites. Egyptian lists of the Middle and New Kingdoms (until the end of the 14th century) do not mention Moab as a people, state, or territorial region. The archaeological survey of N. Glueck has revealed an interruption in the continuity of settlement in the Transjordanian plateau from the 19th until the 14th centuries B.C.E. During this period central and southern Transjordan were occupied by nomadic tribes. The mention of the sons of Seth in Transjordan (Num. 24:17) almost certainly refers to the nomadic Shutu tribes mentioned in Egyptian and Akkadian sources of the second millennium B.C.E. Only a few well-fortified settlements, such as Ader, Balūʿa, Aroer, and Khirbat al-Madayyina, near Wādī al-Thamad, southeast of *Dibon, had the strength to withstand the raids from the east, while the other settlements were destroyed. It may be assumed, following Glueck, that the renewal of permanent settlement in Transjordan at the close of the 14th century, and the appearance of a new agricultural society, is connected with the penetration of West Semitic tribes, including the Moabites, from the east. After the Moabites were in possession of Transjordan, they founded a state that embraced regions on both sides of the Arnon (Wādi al-Mawjib). North of the Arnon, Moab extended to "the tableland" (Deut. 4:43; Josh. 13:9; Jer. 48:21), to the valley of Heshbon (Wādī Ḥisbān) and to "the plains of Moab" opposite Jericho (Num. 22:1). The "tableland" is a plateau rising to approximately 2,400 ft. (800 m.) above sea level. It is rich in pasturage and fertile farmland (cf. Num. 32:1–4). South of the Arnon, the land of Moab extended over a mountainous plateau, which is suitable for cattle raising; it rises to approximately 3,750 ft. (1,250 m.) above sea level. The Zered River (Wādī al-Ḥasā') marked the border between Moab and *Edom. Moab was bounded on the west by the Dead Sea and the southernmost part of the Jordan up to the Nimrin Valley. "The mountains of Abarim" and "the slopes of Pisgah" (Num. 27:12; Deut. 3:17) refer to the steep slopes of the Moabite plateau which descend to the Dead Sea. The Moabite plateau terminates on the east in shelving slopes which descend to the desert that marked the eastern border of Moab.

Throughout the entire area of Moab, there have been discovered the remains of numerous settlements which existed from the 13th to the sixth centuries B.C.E. The capital of Moab was Kir-Hareseth or Kir of Moab (II Kings 3:25; Isa. 15:1; 16:11; Jer. 48:31, 36), modern Karak, in the heart of Moabite territory south of the Arnon. However, most of the large settlements were situated in the fertile tableland (Num. 32; Josh. 13:16–27): prominent in their importance were Aroer (Khirbat ʿArāʿir), overlooking the fords of the Arnon, Dibon (Dhībān), Ataroth (Khirbat ʿAṭṭārūs), Medeba (Mādabā), and Nebo (Muḥayyiṭ). The topographical conformation of Moab does not favor easy communications. The many wadis flowing into the Dead Sea have sawed deep ravines that make passage difficult. Only in the northern plateau region, in the territory of Medeba, was there a wide, convenient road, which connected the regions on both sides of the Jordan. Great importance was attached to the "King's Highway," the international route which connected Arabia and Egypt with Syria and Mesopotamia, and of which a section passed through the Moabite plateau.

The geographical and economic conditions of Moab made it easy for the Moabites to achieve a suitable blend of their desert heritage with the values of an urban and rural society; this is to be attributed to Moab's position on the border of the desert and to its economy, which was based, on the one hand, upon agriculture, and, on the other, upon cattle raising and trade conducted along the desert routes. Living in a border country, the Moabites, like the Edomites and Ammonites, were in need of effective defense against sudden attacks by raiders from the desert, as well as against invasion by the regular armies of neighboring countries. For this reason, the Moabites organized themselves into a national kingdom administered from a single center at the beginning of their settlement in Moab; only a permanent and strong leadership was capable of establishing a system of border fortresses, of setting up a permanent force able to match itself against external dangers, and of organizing guards for protection of the section of the "King's Highway" which passed through Moab. The archaeological survey of Moab and the excavations at Aroer and Dibon, as well as the epigraphic material, have revealed the technical skill of the Moabites in the building of strongholds, watchtowers, walled cities, and installations for collecting water. They built fortresses along the borders. On the eastern border, along the edge of the desert, strong and impressive forts have been discovered; the most prominent are Khirbat al-Madayyina, overlooking the Zered River, Maḥāy, Mudaybīʿ, al-Madyyina, overlooking one of the southern tributaries of the Arnon, Qaṣr Abu al Kharaq, and Qaṣr al-ʿĀl, overlooking the fords of the Arnon on the south. These are only some of the fortresses which guarded entry into Moab from the east. In the service of the king of Moab were garrisons stationed in fortresses and troops trained for field combat and siege. He was assisted by a staff of officers who held various positions, such as that of scribe; one of the Moabite seals carries the name of "Chemoshʿam [son of] Chemosh'el ha-sofer."

Most of the Moabite population obtained its livelihood from agriculture and cattle raising. *Mesha, king of Moab, was called a sheep-master (II Kings 3:4). In areas unsuitable for agriculture, chiefly in the easternmost part of the country, the settlers lived in temporary dwellings (huts or tents), and continued to lead a seminomadic way of life, either as shepherds or as escorts of the merchant caravans that made their way along the nearby desert routes. Moabite culture, to the extent that it is revealed by the finds, most of which are from the Middle Iron Age, was influenced by various other cultures, chiefly by Aram in the north and Arabia in the south. Despite the eclectic character of Moabite culture, the Moabites developed a style of their own, which is particularly conspicuous in the pottery. Pottery sherds defined as Moabite have been discovered in large quantities in many settlements in the land of Moab proper and in localities north of the Arnon.

Moabite religion was essentially idolatrous and was national in character. *Chemosh was the national god of Moab (I Kings 11:7, et al.), and was worshiped on high places and in temples. The god's name was used as a theophoric component in Moabite personal names. Proscription (*ḥerem*, Mesha stele, line 17), burnt offerings—either of an animal or, in special circumstances, of a human being (Num. 23:1, 14, 29; II Kings 3:27)—and circumcision (Jer. 9:24–25) were features of Moabite cultic practices. The polytheism of Moabite religion is attested by the names "ʿAshtar-Chemosh" (Mesha stele, line 17), "Beth-Baal-Peor" (cf. Num. 25), "Bamoth-Baal," and apparently also by the noun *'ari'el* ("altar hearths"; II Sam. 23:20; in Mesha stele, line 12, it is the name of an Israelite person or object), as well as by the many clay figurines found at various Moabite settlements, especially at Khirbet al-Madayyina near Wādī al-Thamad.

The language and script of the Moabites is known first and foremost from the *Mesha stele, found in Mesha's native Dibon in 1868, as well as from two stele fragments (one found at Dibon and the other at Karak), from seals, and from Moabite personal names. The language belongs to the northwest Semitic family, and is close to the northern dialect of Hebrew. The Moabite script does not differ essentially from the Canaanite-Hebrew alphabetic script, and by the middle of the ninth century B.C.E. it had already attained a fine form. The length of the Mesha inscription and its content, style, and form testify to a developed tradition of writing.

The History of Moab and its Relation with Israel. The first period of Moabite history bears the marks of Egyptian influence, as expressed in the stele found at Khirbat Balūʿa in Moab. Its estimated date is approximately 1200 B.C.E. The relief on the monument depicts a figure, perhaps of the local ruler, in the presence of a god and goddess. Above the relief can be seen traces of several lines of writing in a script as yet undeciphered. Both the relief and the inscription contain clearly Egyptian characteristics. (According to some scholars, the Balūʿa stele may be regarded as one of the earliest monuments of a Moabite tradition of writing.)

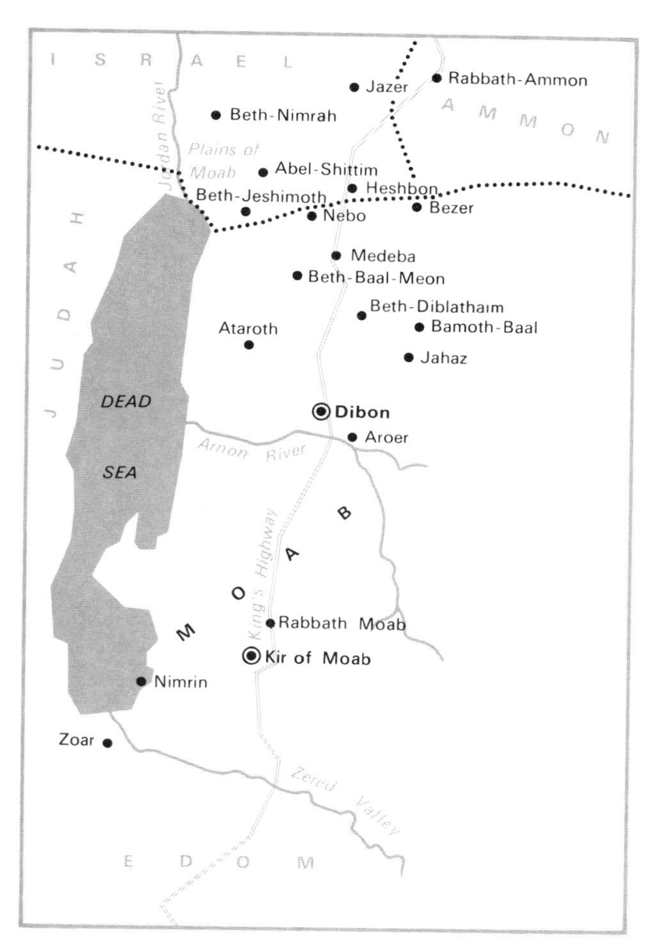

Moab in the time of Mesha (9th century B.C.E.). Based on Y. Aharoni, *Carta's Atlas of the Bible*, Jerusalem, 1964.

The land of Moab *(m-ʾ-b)* is mentioned in the geographical list of Ramses II (13th century B.C.E.). Ramses II undertook an expedition to Transjordan and captured cities in Moab, including Dibon. In the days of the first king of Moab, in the 13th century B.C.E., the Moabites were driven from the region north of the river Arnon by the Amorite king *Sihon, who ruled in Heshbon (Num. 21:27–35; cf. Isa. 15–16; Jer. 48). A short time later, Sihon's entire kingdom, from Wadi Jabbok to the Arnon, fell into the hands of the Israelites (Num. 21:13, 15, 24; 22:36; 33:44, et al.), who had reached the tableland by way of the desert east of Moab, because the king of Moab refused to allow them passage through his country. Fearing that they would now attack his land from the north, *Balak son of Zippor, the king of Moab, hired *Balaam to curse them, but on YHWH's order, so goes the tradition, Balaam blessed them instead. Their inhospitality and their spite are made the reason for a prohibition against admitting Moabites and Ammonites "into the assembly of the Lord forever" (Deut. 23:4–8; Neh. 13:1). However, the enmity between Israel and Moab, echoes of which are also found in prophecies about the nations, was not the result of a single incident, but grew out of a bitter and protracted struggle over disputed areas in Transjordan. With the conquest of the land of Sihon, the tribes of Reuben and Gad were settled in the tableland (Num. 32; Josh. 13), and the Arnon marked the border between Israel and Moab (Deut. 2:36; 3:8; Judg. 11:20; et al.). However, it is clear that a Moabite population remained north of the Arnon even after the conquest of the tableland from Sihon by the Israelites. An echo of the relations between the Moabites and Israelites in the tableland is the story of the affair of Baal-Peor in Shittim in the plains of Moab (Num. 25). The course of events following the Israelite conquest clearly shows that the Moabites did not surrender the tableland, and the region became a focus of strife between Israel and Moab as the border moved northward to the plains of Moab or southward to the Arnon, in accordance with the balance of power between Israel and Moab. The first attempt by Moab to reconquer the areas it had lost is the aforementioned incident of Balak and Balaam (Num. 22; cf. Micah 6:5). Numbers 22:6 and Joshua 24:9 suggest that Balak, with the support of the Midianites, waged war against the Israelites in an attempt to drive them from the tableland (but cf. Judg. 11:25–26). In the time of *Eglon, king of Moab (Judg. 3), the Moabites succeeded in thrusting northward across the Arnon. They imposed their rule on the tribes of Reuben and Gad, and perhaps also upon the Ammonites, and even penetrated by way of the plains of Moab and Jericho to the center of the country on the western side of the Jordan, within the bounds of the territory of Ephraim and Benjamin. The Israelites were obliged to pay tribute and to bring a gift to the king of Moab. *Ehud son of Gera of the tribe of Benjamin saved Israel from the Moabites. In the time of *Jephthah the tableland was in the possession of Israel (Judg. 11:26). The datum in Genesis 36:35, according to which Hadad son of Bedad king of Edom smote Midian in the field of Moab (c. 1100 B.C.E.), is explained by some commentators as evidence of Edomite or, more plausibly, Midianite rule over Moab.The narrative in the Book of Ruth concerning the immigration of a Judean family to Moab when a severe drought struck Judah indicates that the history of relations between Israel and Moab included periods of tranquillity and peace (cf. also I Chron. 4:22; 8:8).

The attacks by Moab on Israel at the end of the period of the Judges and in the time of Saul (Ps. 83:7, 9; I Sam. 14:47), and perhaps in the time of his son Eshbaal as well, served as a justification for David to wage war against Moab and to subdue it (II Sam. 8:2; 23:20; cf. Num. 24:17), despite the friendly ties that had developed between David, a descendant of Ruth the Moabite, and the king of Moab (I Sam. 22:3–5). The actions taken by David against Moab after he had subjugated them (II Sam. 8:2; I Chron. 18:2), although not sufficiently clarified, are indicative of the intense enmity that prevailed between Israel and Moab. David did not abolish the monarchy in Moab, but contented himself with its subjection (II Sam. 8:2; I Chron. 18:2). After the division of Solomon's kingdom, Moab came under the domination of the Northern Kingdom of Israel. As indicated by the stele of Mesha, king of Moab, it is probable that a long time before the death of Ahab, the Moabites threw off the rule of Israel and seized control over areas north of the Arnon (cf. II Kings 1:1; 3:5). The rise to power of Aram-Damascus immediately after the death of Solomon and its pressure on Israel (I Kings 15:16–20), the expedition of *Shishak against the kingdoms of Israel and Judah, and the intense struggle between the house of Jeroboam son of Nebat and the house of David, especially in the time of Baasha and Asa, presented an opportunity to throw off the domination of Israel. The Moabites seized control of the tableland up to Medeba. Since Mesha called himself "king of Moab, the Dibonite," it is possible that his father, whose name, as far as can be seen, was Chemosh-yatti (?), had already established Dibon as the royal capital. The period of Moab's independence came to an end when the political and military situation of Israel improved under the rule of Omri. Omri "took possession" of the land of Medeba, but out of political and military considerations did not conquer the region of Dibon from Moab. Instead, he imposed his authority on the king of Moab, who resided in Dibon. The subjection continued throughout the days of

Omri "and part of the days of his son," apparently Ahab. When the pressure of the Arameans on Israel in the time of Ahab increased, Mesha withheld tribute from Ahab. The king of Moab took steps to strengthen his kingdom against the expected attack by the king of Israel. Mesha first secured communications between the region of Moab south of the Arnon and the region of Dibon by fortifying Aroer and building roads along the Arnon. He strengthened his city of residence, built an acropolis in it, and prepared the city to withstand a protracted siege. Ahab did not turn his attention to Moab, but satisfied himself with fortifying Jericho (I Kings 16:34), which commanded the fords of the Jordan. Mesha, who had rebelled against Israel, chose not to participate in the joint campaign of Aram and Israel against Shalmaneser III in the year 853 B.C.E. (battle of *Karkar). Only after the death of Ahab did Mesha find the time ripe to begin the conquest of the entire tableland. He conquered Ataroth and the land of Ataroth, inhabited by the tribe of *Gad, Beth-Diblathaim, and the strong fortress of Jahaz on the border of the desert. He then continued northward, conquering Medeba and the land of Medeba, together with the large fortress of Bezer. The capture of Medeba opened the road to the plains of Moab for the Moabites; Mesha continued in a northwesterly direction to the plains of Moab by way of Wādī al-Harī, and seized control of the largest Israelite city of *Nebo, which he consecrated to ʿAshtar-Chemosh. Toward the end of the inscription, Mesha mentions an expedition to Horonaim in southern Moab, close to Zoar (cf. Isa. 15:5; Jer. 48:5, 34). Thus Mesha succeeded in restoring the borders of the Moabite kingdom from the tip of the Dead Sea in the south to the vicinity of the plains of Moab in the north. He rebuilt cities in the tableland and settled Moabites in them. Some scholars hold that the expedition of Mesha to Horonaim is connected with the narrative in II Kings 3 of the joint campaign of *Jehoram, king of Israel, *Jehoshaphat, king of Judah, and the king of *Edom. The campaign of the three kings was carried out by way of Edom in order to attack Moab from the south, since the way to Moab from the plains of Moab was held by Mesha and was well defended by Moabite garrisons. In the battle that took place on the southern border of Moab, Jehoram and his allies defeated the Moabite army (II Kings 3:20–24). Subsequently the allied armies penetrated into the heart of Moab and besieged the capital Kir-Hareseth (3:24–26). From the biblical description it appears that the armies of Israel and Judah withdrew from Moab without succeeding in conquering the capital. According to II Kings 3:27, the king of Moab, in an act of despair, sacrificed his firstborn son upon the wall as a burnt offering, an act that brought "great wrath upon Israel." Despite this, the great destruction caused to the cities of Moab in the campaign of the three kings weakened Moab and undermined Moabite rule in the tableland. Although Moabite bands were still able to make raids into Israel west of the Jordan (II Kings 13:20), almost all of the tableland returned to Israelite possession, as is suggested by II Kings 10:32–33, which is concerned with Hazael's seizure of Transjordan down to the Arnon. Still later, in the time of Jeroboam son of Jehoash, king of Israel, Israelite rule in the tableland was consolidated (II Kings 14:25; Amos 6:14), and Moab may have recognized the rule of Israel. Moab apparently never again attained full independence. Before it could benefit from the decline and fall of the kingdom of Israel, it was forced to recognize the sovereignty of the Assyrian empire.

The Moabites Under Assyrian and Babylonian Rule and the End of their Kingdom. The expedition of *Tiglath-Pileser III to Israel in 734–733 B.C.E. brought the states of Transjordan under the rule of the Assyrian Empire. In one of his inscriptions, Tiglath-Pileser III mentions Salaman the Moabite (*Sa-la-ma-nu KUR Ma-ʾ-ba-ai*) among the kings of Syria and Israel who brought him tribute, apparently in 732 B.C.E. The paying of tribute was an expression of recognition of Assyrian rule. Acceptance of Assyrian sovereignty was generally bound up with the payment of tribute at fixed times, the offering of a gift on appointed occasions, bond service, and military aid to the Assyrian king for his expeditions. The Assyrians usually appointed an inspector (*qēpu*) to work alongside the local ruler, and placed Assyrian garrison troops in fortresses and citadels, both in the provinces and in the domain of the vassal king. Aianūr of the land of Tabeel, who reported the raid of the men of Gidir into Moab to the Assyrian king, was apparently responsible to the latter for the state of affairs in Moab. An Assyrian letter from Nimrud of the last third of the eighth century B.C.E. mentions a delegation from Moab which came to the city of Calah (Nimrud) to present a gift of horses to the Assyrian king. The king of Moab did not heed the words of incitement of Iamani, king of Ashdod, to rebel against Sargon II in 713 B.C.E. When Sennacherib conducted a military campaign against Hezekiah in 701 B.C.E., Chemosh-nadab the Moabite (*Kam-mu-su-na-ad-bi KUR Ma-ʾ-ba-ai*) came to meet him, bearing many gifts. In approximately 677 B.C.E. Esarhaddon, king of Assyria, ordered "the 22 kings of Ḫatti, the sea coast, and within the sea" to drag cedar and pine beams from the mountains of Lebanon and Sirion to the capital Nineveh in order to build his palace. Included among these kings is Muṣuri, the king of Moab (*Mu-ṣur-i šar KUR Ma-ʾa-ab*). Ashurbanipal also relates that "22 kings of the seacoast, of the islands of the sea, and of the mainland, servants subject to me" brought him numerous gifts and accompanied him with their troops on his first expedition to Egypt in 667 B.C.E. It is highly probable that Muṣuri the Moabite was among these kings. An Assyrian list of tribute from the time of Esarhaddon or Ashurbanipal states that the Moabites tendered "one gold mina" as tribute to Assyria. The kings of Transjordan bore Assyrian sovereignty without attempting to throw it off, because they were aware that the Assyrian government, in the prevailing circumstances, was of greater benefit than harm. The Assyrian government usually defended loyal vassal kings from neighboring enemies. Danger to the peace of the countries of Transjordan came chiefly from the inhabitants of the desert, whose pressure on the border countries increased, beginning in the eighth century B.C.E. From the description of the wars of Ashurbanipal against the Arabs, it is clear that the Assyrians stationed garrisons along the border of the desert in order to prevent attempts by the nomadic tribes to penetrate into the cultivated areas. The Assyrians were interested in strengthening the border countries against the desert raiders, and consequently the former were included in the defense system of the empire. The defeat of Amuladi, king of Kedar, by Chemosh-halta, king of Moab (*Ka-ma-as-ḫal-ta-a šar KUR Ma-ʾa-ab*), is merely one episode in a chain of similar events that are no different from that which occurred 500 years previously, when Hadad son of Bedad the Edomite defeated the tribes of Midian in the field of Moab (Gen. 36:35). Furthermore, under the Assyrian rule, the peoples of Transjordan extended the borders of their kingdoms into areas with an Israelite population, and they enjoyed economic prosperity. The Assyrians managed the defense of the desert caravan routes that connected Egypt and Arabia with Syria and Mesopotamia. Echoes of Moab's economic prosperity and of the extent of its territory appear in the prophecies about Moab (Isa. 25:10–12; Jer. 48, chiefly verses 7 and 29; Ezek. 25:9; Zeph. 2:8).

The passage from Assyrian to Babylonian rule did not

involve a great change in the status of the kingdom of Moab. The king of Moab was apparently numbered with "all the kings of the land of Ḫeth [Ḫatti]" who brought tribute to Nebuchadnezzar when the Chaldean king campaigned against Ashkelon (c. 604/3 B.C.E.). Moabite and Ammonite troops were in the service of the king of Babylon when the revolt of Jehoiakim was crushed (II Kings 24:1–2; cf. Ezek. 25:6–8). However, a few years later a change in the policy of Moab toward Babylon is noticeable. In the fourth year of Zedekiah of Judah (594 B.C.E.), the king of Moab participated in a scheme to form a conspiracy against Babylon (Jer. 27:3). While there is no explicit information about the fate of the conspiracy, Moab apparently did not come to the aid of Zedekiah, but stood aside when the Chaldean army drew near. A Babylonian punitive expedition against the countries of Transjordan was undertaken in the fifth year of the destruction of Jerusalem, i.e., the 23rd year of Nebuchadnezzar's reign. Josephus states that in that year the Chaldean king proceeded against the army of Syria and defeated it, and that he also fought against the Ammonites and Moabites (Jos., Ant., 10:181; cf. Jer. 40:11; 48:7). Although there is no certain information that it was the Babylonian empire which brought about the end of the kingdom of Moab and turned it into a Babylonian province, the lack of information about Moab as an independent or semi-independent kingdom after the period of Babylonian rule, as well as a reference to the province of Moab (Ezra 2:6) during the first period of Persian rule in Israel, indicate that Moab was made a Babylonian province in the time of Nebuchadnezzar or a short time after his death. Glueck's archaeological survey testifies to a decline of settlement in Transjordan which ended with complete destruction in the sixth century B.C.E. The destruction was apparently a result of the collapse of the defense system on the desert front, which desert nomads broke through in order to raid Transjordan (e.g., the sons of Kedar and Nebaioth), damaging cultivated lands and destroying permanent settlements. Many Moabites were driven from the region south of the Arnon. Some of them concentrated in the region of the plateau, a region that was later known as Moabitis, and some dispersed to near and distant countries. The Moabite population remaining in Moab was assimilated among the Arabian tribes who took possession of the land. The punishment of the kingdoms of Transjordan cited by Ezekiel (25:4–10; 35:15) faithfully reflects the disaster that befell the settlements in Transjordan, and points to the settling in of nomads and shepherds from the east. The lament on the destruction of Moab in Numbers 21:27–35, which is echoed in Isaiah 15–16 and Jeremiah 48, is an old fragment of Moabite poetry. Moab achieved an additional period of prosperity in the Hellenistic-Roman period, but by then it had already been taken over by the Nabatean tribes, and was included in the Nabatean kingdom. In Hasmonean times, Alexander Yannai conquered the area, which was returned to the Nabateans by Hyrcanus II. It was later incorporated into Provincia Arabia. [B.O.]

Bibliography: H. Tristram, *The Land of Moab* (1873); A. H. Van Zyl, *The Moabites* (1960); A. Musil, *Arabia Petraea*, 1 (1907); Aharoni, Land, index; EM, s.v. (incl. bibl.); N. Glueck, in: AASOR, 14 (1934), 1–114; 15 (1935), 1–202; 18–19 (1939), 1–288; 25–28 (1951), 1–423; H. L. Ginsberg, in: *Alexander Marx Jubilee Volume* (1950), 347–68; R. E. Murphy, in: CBQ, 15 (1953), 409–17; W. L. Reed and F. V. Winnett, in: BASOR, 172 (1963), 1–9; F. V. Winnett and W. L. Reed, in: AASOR, 36–37 (1964), 1–79; W. H. Ward and M. F. Martin, in: ADAJ, 8–9 (1964), 5–29; J. Liver, in: PEQ, 99 (1967), 14–31.

MOCATTA, English family of Marrano origin. MOSES MOCATTA appears in a Bevis Marks (London) synagogue list in 1671. His granddaughter REBECCA married as her second husband Moses Lumbrozo de Mattos. Their son ABRAHAM (who added the name Mocatta and later dropped Lumbrozo de Mattos) joined with Asher Goldsmid to

Abraham Lumbrozo de Mattos Mocatta, English banker. Jerusalem, J.N.U.L., Schwadron Collection.

found Mocatta and *Goldsmid, later bullion brokers to the Bank of England. Abraham Mocatta had 11 children (including Rachel, mother of Sir Moses *Montefiore). His son MOSES (1768–1857) retired early from business to devote himself to scholarship. He published *Faith Strengthened* (1851), a translation of Isaac b. Abraham *Troki's *Ḥizzuk Emunah*, and *The Inquisition and Judaism* (1845), a translation of a Portuguese inquisitorial sermon and the reply to it. In communal life, he was specially concerned with education and the reorganization of the Sephardi schools, "Sha'arei Tikvah."

Moses' children included DAVID (1806–1882), an architect, a pupil of Sir John Soane, and best-known for his railway stations on the London to Brighton line. As architect for his cousin Sir Moses Montefiore at Ramsgate, he was the first Jew to design an English synagogue. Another son, ISAAC LINDO (1818–1879), wrote tracts on Jewish moral teachings and social questions. Nine of the 24 founders of the Reform Congregation were Mocattas, including Moses and his nephew Abraham, father of FREDERICK DAVID MOCATTA (1828–1905). Philanthropist, scholar, and communal leader, Frederick was the representative ideal of late Victorian Anglo-Jewry. Active in both the Charity Organization Society and the Jewish Board of Guardians, he campaigned for the reform of voting charities. Widely traveled, he lectured on contemporary Jewish communities and wrote on Jewish history, publishing *The Jews and the Inquisition* in 1887. A munificent patron of scholarship, he was a correspondent and supporter of *Zunz. Sympathetic to most Jewish causes (although disapproving of nascent Zionism), he was an observant Jew and member of two Orthodox synagogues as well as his family's Reform congregation. He left his library to University College, London, and the Jewish Historical Society of England.

One branch of the Mocatta family remained within the Orthodox community: a descendant of this was SIR ALAN ABRAHAM MOCATTA (1907–), a judge of the High Court from 1961, also active in Anglo-Jewish communal and historical affairs (president of the Board of Elders of the Spanish and Portuguese Synagogue, and chairman of the Council of Jews' College, 1945–62). He was the joint editor of *Scrutton on Charter Parties* (14th–17th editions).

Bibliography: J. W. Scott, in: J. M. Shaftesley (ed.), *Remember the Days* (1966), 323–31; R. P. Lehmann, *Nova Bibliotheca Anglo-Judaica* (1961), 74, 171, 207; A. M. Hyamson, *Sephardim of England* (1951), index; J. Picciotto, *Sketches of Anglo-Jewish History* (1956[2]), index; Roth, Mag Bibl, index; Roth, Art, 724, 781; V. D. Lipman, *Century of Social Service 1859–1959* (1959), index; E. Jamilly, in: JHSET, 18 (1953–55), 134. [V.D.L.]

MOCH, JULES SALVADOR (1893–), French socialist leader. Born in Paris, Moch worked as an engineer and industrial manager from 1920 to 1927. From 1928 to 1940 he sat as a socialist deputy in the National Assembly and in 1936 was made secretary-general of the prime minister's office under Leon *Blum, who held him in high esteem for his wide scientific and managerial experience. He was later under-secretary of state (1937) and minister of public works (1938).

During World War II, Moch served in the French navy; in 1940, after the fall of France, he was imprisoned for voting in the National Assembly against the granting of constitutional powers to Marshal Pétain. He escaped and joined the Free French Navy in 1943. In the following year he became a member of the Consultative Assembly and on the termination of the war a member of the National Assembly. From 1945 to 1947 Moch was minister of public works and between 1946 and 1951 he held important posts in 11 successive cabinets, serving as minister of the interior, vice-premier, and minister of defense. In 1949 he was nominated premier but failed to secure a majority. Between 1953 and 1960 he served as French representative at the Geneva disarmament conference. He returned to the Ministry of the Interior in 1958 for a short period but resigned when General De Gaulle came to power.

Moch was one of the most respected figures in the French socialist movement. As a member of the French government he gave considerable assistance to Jewish refugees as he took a keen interest in Zionism. He was an enthusiastic supporter of Israel, paying several visits, and closely following the development of the Israel labor movement. Among Moch's many publications were *Restitutions et réparations* (1921) and *La Russie des Soviets* (1925). He also wrote a number of books on financial questions including *Le Parti Socialiste et la politique financière* (1928), which were issued as handbooks by the French Socialist Party to demonstrate their ability to handle economic affairs. [M.R.]

MOCHA (Mukhā), minor seaport on the Red Sea in S.W. Yemen. Until the 19th century, Mocha was well known as a harbor for the export of coffee (Mocca). It can be concluded from the words of the poet Zechariah al-Ḍāhirī in his *Sefer ha-Musar* ("Book of Ethics") that a Jewish community existed there during the 16th century. He relates that after the cruel expulsion from *San'a in 1578, an emissary from Tiberias, Abraham b. Isaac Ashkenazi, arrived in Mocha. He propagated Torah learning and also engaged in the trade of religious books. In 1859, a few days before he left Yemen, Jacob *Saphir arrived in Mocha. He found eight Jewish families living in a derelict quarter outside the city walls in wooden and reed constructions, as was the case in many other Yemenite towns. There were not sufficient members to form a *minyan* (quorum) for the Rosh Ha-Shanah services. However, in about 1770 there had been some 400 Jewish families in the town, including some wealthy merchants, craftsmen, goldsmiths, weavers, and builders of smelting furnaces. Aaron Araki ha-Kohen (early 18th century) erected a magnificent synagogue in Mocha. He himself lived there for some years as a ruler and judge. One of the plagues, which are common in this region, caused the Jews to abandon the town and they dispersed in the mountain villages. Only about 100 families returned to Mocha. As a result of oppression and persecution—the last at the time of the Egyptian conquest in 1883—the development of Aden as a British colony, and the competition of the port of Hodeidah, the number of Jews gradually dwindled. By the 20th century no Jews remained in Mocha.

Bibliography: Zechariah al-Ḍāhiri, *Sefer ha-Musar,* ed. by Y. Ratzaby (1965), 39–40, 285, 424–6; J. Saphir, *Even Sappir,* 1 (1886), 100–1, 110b; A. Grohmann, *Suedarabien als Wirtschaftsgebiet, 1922–1933,* 1 (1922), 102–6; 2 (1933), 84, 105, 109. [H.Z.H.]

MODAI, ḤAYYIM (d. 1794), Safed scholar. In 1749 Modai journeyed to Europe as an emissary of the Safed community. Passing through Egypt he came across a manuscript of geonic responsa which he published 43 years later under the title *Sha'arei Ẓedek* (Salonika, 1792). In 1755 he was appointed a member of the *bet din* in Constantinople as well as one of the *pekidim* ("commissioners") of Safed in the town. Following the earthquake in Safed in 1760, he was again sent to Europe in 1762 as an emissary for the town by the Constantinople commissioners, who published four letters on the subject of his mission in order to give it full publicity. After visiting various Italian towns (Mantua, Turin, and Venice in 1763) he went to Holland and England (Amsterdam and London in 1765), and Germany. In 1766 he was in Prague where he had halakhic discussions with Ezekiel *Landau, who refers to him in respectful terms (responsa *Ḥayyim le-Olam,* YD no. 2; *Noda bi-Yhudah, Mahadura Kamma,* YD no. 87–88). Four years later he returned to Constantinople where he stayed until the death of Ḥayyim b. David Abulafia, when he was invited to succeed him as the rabbi of Smyrna. There he remained until 1793. At the end of his commendation to *Sha'arei Ẓedek,* Modai expresses his longing to return to Safed. His wish was fulfilled and he returned to Safed in 1793. His works include: *Tiv Gittin* (1875), containing the bills of divorce arranged by him between 1737 and 1775 with the glosses of Yom Tov Israel; and *Ḥayyim le-Olam* (1878–79), responsa in two parts, including many written while on his travels; it also contains the responsa of his grandson, Nissim Ḥayyim Modai, entitled *Meimar Ḥayyim.* His glosses on the Shulḥan Arukh, *Oraḥ Ḥayyim* and *Yoreh De'ah,* and the *Peri Ḥadash* appear in the *Berakh Moshe* (Leghorn, 1809) of Moses b. Mordecai Galante (pp. 151–69); a responsum by him in the *Ma'amar ha-Melekh* (Salonika, 1806), of Raphael Abraham Maẓli'aḥ; and an alphabetical poem on the smoking of tobacco (*toton*) at the beginning of the *Avodah Tammah* (1903) of Joshua Raphael Benveniste. From 1767 Modai was on friendly terms with Ḥ. J. D. Azulai; on one ruling—in connection with reading from an invalid *Sefer Torah*—they expressed opposing views; the correspondence between them continued until 1787.

Bibliography: S. Ḥazan, *Ha-Ma'alot li-Shelomo* (1894), 31a–32a, 39b; M. Benayahu, *R. Ḥayyim Yosef David Azulai,* 1 (Heb., 1959), 362–6; 2 (1959), 412–3; I. Ben Zvi, in: *Sefunot,* 6 (1962), 360, 381–3; S. Emmanuel, *ibid.,* 406–7, 411, 419; S. Simonsohn, *ibid.,* 334, 348–9; Yaari, Sheluḥei, 130–1, 451–5. [J.Ho.]

MODEH ANI (Heb. מוֹדֶה אֲנִי; "I give thanks"), initial words of a prayer said immediately upon waking in the morning. The short prayer ("I give thanks unto Thee, O living and eternal King, who hast restored my soul unto me in mercy; great is Thy faithfulness") does not mention any of the Divine Names and may therefore be said while still in bed and before performing the prescribed morning ablutions; hence it was preferred to the traditional *Elohai Neshamah* prayer (which was transferred to the morning benedictions).

Modeh Ani, possibly a shortened version of the *Elohai Neshamah* prayer (Ber. 60b), is of late origin and seems to have been composed about the 17th century; it was printed for the first time in the addenda to the prayer book *Seder ha-Yom* (1695). Because of its shortness and simplicity it became a favorite morning prayer for very small children before they are capable of reciting the ordinary daily morning service.

Bibliography: Hertz, Prayer, 1116ff. [ED.]

MODEL, MARX (d. 1709), *Court Jew of *Ansbach. The Model family originated in *Oettingen in the 16th century and subsequently spread throughout *Bavaria. It included a number of rabbis and Court Jews, foremost of whom was Marx Model, who in 1676 inherited his father's position as military and court purveyor at the court of the Margrave of Ansbach. One of the earliest Court Jews to engage in economic ventures, Marx acquired a number of estates and farms, a paper mill, and a workshop making roof tiles. In 1691 he was freed from custom duties and was granted the right to be sole publisher of the Talmud in Ansbach. His eldest daughter married Wolf, son of Samuel *Oppenheimer, the influential Austrian Court Jew; Model served the latter as agent and supplier of silver for the mint and aided him in revoking an expulsion order against the Jews of Rothenburg. Model maintained his own synagogue and cantor in Ansbach. His unsuccessful attempt to unite the rival Jewish communities of *Fuerth was utilized by his rival Elkan *Fraenkel, who undermined his position at court and subjected the Jews to a harsher rule. However, Fraenkel's triumph was short-lived; Model's sons inherited their father's position and intrigued to bring about the eventual fall of the Fraenkels.

Bibliography: S. Haenle, *Geschichte der Juden im ehemaligen Fuerstenthum Ansbach* (1867); L. Loewenstein, in: JJLG, 8 (1910), 131–4; L. Lamm, *ibid.*, 22 (1932), 152–9; M. Grunwald, *Samuel Oppenheimer* (1913), 305; S. Stern, *The Court Jew* (1950), 100, 193; H. Schnee, *Die Hoffinanz und der moderne Staat*, 4 (1963), 27–28; D. J. Cohen, in: *Kovez al Yad*, 6 pt. 2 (1966), 470, 514–5. [ED.]

MODENA, city in N. central Italy. The first document relating to Jews in Modena may date back to 1025, but the existence of a stable Jewish community, formed by loan-bankers who originated from *Perugia, *Rimini, and Fermo, was not recorded until 1393. For many years the Jews of Modena enjoyed the protection of the house of Este, who ruled Modena as well as Ferrara. When in 1597 the duchy of Ferrara became part of the Papal States, Modena with Reggio Emilia remained under Este rule. Because of the advantageous conditions it offered to the Jews, in the 17th and 18th centuries the duchy of Modena attracted a large Jewish settlement; over 1,000 Jews lived in the town itself. Some Sephardi immigrants maintained their own synagogue. Modena was long a principal center of scholarship of Italian Jewry and was distinguished as a seat of kabbalistic study. Among its scholars were the remarkable bibliophile Abraham Joseph Solomon *Graziani, *Aaron Berechiah of Modena, Abraham *Rovigo, and Ishmael *Cohen (in Italian, Laudadio Sacerdote). Although they were confined to the ghetto in 1638, the Jews of Modena were allowed to carry on their business activities freely. Moneylending survived officially until 1767, far longer than in most other Italian towns. In 1796 Modena was occupied by the French and became part of the Cisalpine Republic. One of the *centumviri* was a Jew, Moses Formiggini, who later became a senator of the republic. The Jews of Modena contributed effectively to the Italian Risorgimento, collaborating with the Carbonari, the secret revolutionary movement, and financing it. In periods of reaction the ghetto restrictions were renewed. With the proclamation of the Kingdom of Italy in 1861 the Jews of Modena were granted full equality with the other citizens. Yet the community, which up to the middle of the 19th century still consisted of about 1,000 Jews, then began to decline. Devotion to Ereẓ Israel was particularly strong in Modena in the ghetto period, and later on Zionism obtained an early foothold there: the monthly *L'Idea Sionista* was published in Modena from 1900 by Professor Carlo Conegliano, of the faculty of law.

The synagogue of Modena in 1873. Jerusalem, Italian Synagogue Collection.

In 1931 the community of Modena had a membership of 474 Jews. During the Holocaust at least 15 were sent to extermination camps. After the war there were 185 persons left in the community; their numbers had decreased to 150 by 1969, and the services were held irregularly.

Bibliography: Milano, Bibliotheca, index; Milano, Italia, index; Roth, Italy, index; A. Balletti, *Gli ebrei e gli estensi* (1930[2]), passim; C. Bernheimer, *Catalogo dei manuscritti orientali della Biblioteca Estense* (1960); J. Vaccari, *Villa Emma: un episodio agli albori della Resistenza modenese nel quadro delle persecuzioni razziste* (1960); Levi Minzi, in: *Israel* (Feb. 19, 1931); C. Levi, in: *Riforma sociale*, 4 (1897), 962–9; Milano, in: RMI, 11 (1936/37), 450–5; Artom, *ibid.*, 44–49. [A.To.]

MODENA, AVTALYON (da; 1529–1611), Italian scholar, and son of Mordecai (Angelo da) Modena, the eminent physician. After studying in Padua, Avtalyon settled in Ferrara, where he became noted as a talmudist and scholar; Azariah dei *Rossi mentions him with deference in his *Me'or Einayim*. He took part in the famous controversy on the ritual propriety of the *mikveh* constructed at *Rovigo. When the papal attack on Jewish literature was renewed in 1581, he went to Rome as delegate of the Italian Jewish communities and is said to have made a two-hour oration in Latin before the assembled Curia, as the result of which the edict was modified. He was known also as a writer of verse. Letters addressed to him are preserved among the correspondence of his nephew Leone *Modena.

Bibliography: L. Blau, *Leo Modenas Briefe und Schriftstuecke* ... (1905), 41, 81 (Heb.); Ghirondi-Neppi, 26–29. [C.R.]

MODENA, LEONE (Judah Aryeh; sometimes called **Leon da Modena;** 1571–1648), Italian rabbi, scholar, and writer. On the expulsion of the Jews from Bologna in 1569 his father, Isaac, son of Mordecai Modena, moved to Ferrara, but during the earthquake of 1570 took refuge in Venice, where Leone was born. Leone was, however, brought up in Ferrara where he became known as an infant prodigy, reading the prophetical portion publicly in synagogue at the age of two-and-a-half and being able to translate passages of the Pentateuch into Italian at the age of three. He had the normal education of an Italian Jewish youth of good family at the time, not only in Hebrew and rabbinic studies, but also in versification, the Italian language, and Latin. At the age of nine he was sent away to study, his teachers including the poet-grammarian Samuel *Archivolti at Padua. At 12 he translated passages from Ariosto's poem, *Orlando Furioso*, into Hebrew verse. At 13 he composed a poem which made sense whether read as Italian or as Hebrew, in memory of another teacher of his, Moses della Rocca.

When his father's economic situation deteriorated, he was obliged to begin giving private lessons in 1589. In 1593 Modena was appointed elementary teacher and preacher (not at that time a position of highest dignity) in Venice, with which city he continued to be particularly associated to the end of his life. His sermons became famous in the city and often attracted distinguished gentile audiences. His rabbinical and talmudic knowledge was extensive, and his opinion was frequently consulted by learned contemporaries. A facile and prolific versifier, Modena was responsible for the majority of the epitaphs which figure on the tombstones of the Venetian cemetery at this period. He also wrote Italian prose and verse, and on occasion Latin. He was remarkably articulate; a large number of manuscripts in his clear and characteristic hand, composed in a limpid and vivacious Hebrew, have been preserved (including scores of letters and responsa). In consequence, more information about him and the details of his private life is available than on almost any other Jew of his age.

These sources reveal a curiously contradictory type, whose learning was vitiated by serious defects of character. Modena frequented bad company and his sons were disreputable. Notwithstanding repeated vows of repentance he could not tear himself away from gambling; as a result he was perpetually on the verge of penury and had to recourse to all manner of expedients in order to earn a livelihood. In his revealing autobiography, *Ḥayyei Yehudah*, he naively lists 26 occupations to which he resorted from time to time, including brokerage, translating, writing letters and verses for others, arranging marriages, composing amulets and teaching their composition, and even writing sermons for others to deliver. He had some ability as a musician and acted as secretary and *maestro di cappella* of the musical academy which was established in the Venetian ghetto in 1632. Modena composed at least one "comedy" in Italian and acted in amateur theatrical performances. He even dabbled in alchemy, but the only practical result (notwithstanding his high hopes) was the death by lead-poisoning of his most promising son. On the other hand, he had a remarkable reputation among Christian scholars, who regarded him as the outstanding representative of Jewish learning of the day. He carried on a wide correspondence with them, and was mentioned with respect in their writings. His expert rabbinical opinions naturally reflect a liberality of outlook. He championed the introduction of the music of his friend Salomone de *Rossi into the synagogue, defended the playing of ball games in the ghetto on the Sabbath, and did not object to going about bare-headed. However, he was not consistent. At times his writings are in diametrical opposition to his practices and sometimes irreconcilably contradict themselves, as when he both condemned and defended the playing of games of chance, and both championed and attacked the Kabbalah and mysticism.

Modena as a Writer. His unstable character notwithstanding, Modena's contribution to Hebrew letters cannot be ignored. His autobiography, mentioned above, is the first frank, intimate autobiography to be written in Hebrew, and can be regarded as a classic of this genre. His sermons, collected in *Midbar Yehudah*, are also unrivalled examples of the rhetorical and homiletical art which developed in Renaissance Italy. Although not always original in content, they are consummate in form and influence later Hebrew homiletics. However Modena's main contribution to Hebrew literature was in polemics. In *Magen ve-Ẓinnah* he attacks systematically the views of Uriel da *Costa, and defends the oral tradition and talmudic literature; the *Kol Sakhal*, on the other hand, which is attributed to him, makes the most bitter and complete case against oral tradition to be written in Hebrew until the Reform movement of the 19th century, when many of the arguments were repeated. In *Ari Nohem* Modena followed the tradition of anti-kabbalistic polemic started in Italy by Elijah *Delmedigo in the 15th century, but his criticism of the Zohar and of Isaac *Luria and his school is much more systematic and complete than the writings of his predecessors. Many of his arguments refuting the authenticity of Simeon Bar Yoḥai's authorship of the Zohar serve modern scholars. His *Magen va-Ḥerev* is one of the most effective anti-Christian polemics to be written in Hebrew (even in the incomplete form in which the work has been preserved). Modena used contemporary scientific and historical critical methods, as well as traditional exegesis, to show the superficiality of the Christian interpretation of Scripture and the illogicalities in its dogma. Modena regarded his life as a failure, especially because he felt that he had lost the battle against his own shortcomings. However, his literary achievements disprove his own evaluation.

Modena's published writings, many of them embodying the word *aryeh* ("lion") or Yehudah in the title in reference to his name, include: *Beit Leḥem Yehudah*, an index to the *Ein Ya'akov* (Venice, 1625); *Bat Yehudah* (Venice, 1635, subsequently incorporated in the *Ein Ya'akov*, to which it is a supplement); *Ẓemaḥ Ẓaddik*, a translation of the Italian ethical work *Fior di Virtù* (Venice, 1600); *Galut Yehudah* (*Novo dittionario hebraico e italiano*; Venice, 1612; Padua, 1640); *Midbar Yehudah*, sermons (Venice, 1602); *Lev Aryeh*, mnemotechnical (Venice, 1612); *Sur me-Ra*, against gambling (Venice, 1595); *Ḥayyei Yehudah*, autobiography (see above; ed. A. Kahana, Zhitomir, 1911); *Historia de' riti Ebraici* (in Italian), written at the request of the English ambassador in Venice for presentation to King James I (Paris, 1637; many further editions and translations); *Magen va-Herev*, anti-Christian polemic (see above; ed. S. Simonsohn, Jerusalem, 1960); *Ziknei Yehuda*, responsa (ed. S. Simonsohn, Jerusalem, 1956); *Magen ve-Ẓinnah* (see above; ed. A. Geiger, Breslau, 1856); *Sha'agat Aryeh*, a refutation of an attack on Jewish tradition, and *Kol Sakhal* (see above, ascribed to a Spanish Jew of the 16th century—whether or not it was actually written by Modena has long been discussed (both published under the title *Beḥinat ha-Kabbalah*, by I. S. Reggio, Gorizia, 1852)). Modena's Hebrew correspondence was edited by L. Blau (Budapest, 1905–06) and his Hebrew poems by S. Bernstein (Philadelphia, 1932); the Italian letters with Christian Hebraists by C. Roth (*Jewish Studies in Memory of Israel Abrahams* (1927), 384–401; reprinted in RMI, 11 (1936–37), 409–23). A complete bibliography of his writings, both published and unpublished, may be found in S. Simonsohn's introduction to the *Ziknei Yehudah* (see above) and in Cassuto's article (in RMI, 8 (1933), 132–42).

Bibliography: E. Rivkin, *Leon da Modena and the Kol Sakhal* (1952); S. Simonsen, in *Festschrift . . . A. Berliner* (1903), 337–44; I. Sonne, in: HUCA, 21 (1948), 1–28; N. Samaja, in: RMI, 21 (1955), 73–84; C. Roth, in: JHSET, 11 (1924–27), 206–25; 17 (1951–52), 39–43; I. Rivkind, in: *Tarbiz*, 4 (1933), 366–76; idem, in: *Sefer ha-Yovel . . . L. Ginzburg* (1946), 401–23; Adler, Prat. Mus., index. [C.R.]

MODERN, JUDAH (1819–1893), Hungarian rabbi. Modern was born in Pressburg where he became one of the outstanding pupils of Moses Sofer, Meir Asch, and Moses Teitelbaum. In 1837 he married the daughter of Samuel Zanvil ha-Kohen of Sziget and remained in Sziget for the rest of his life, refusing to accept offers of rabbinic office. On the title page of his *Zikhron Shemu'el* it states: "Neither rabbi nor *av bet din*, despising honor and praise, engaged in Torah by day and by night." In Sziget he became attracted to *Ḥasidism and, to the displeasure of his teacher, Moses Sofer, paid visits to the ḥasidic rabbis. He was one of the leaders of the community which in 1886 broke with the Orthodox community of Sziget and established the separatist community which was called Ha-Kehillah ha-Sefaradit.

Modern was the author of *Zikhron Shemu'el* (1867), a detailed commentary on tractate *Gittin*, and *Peri ha-Eẓ* (1885–87), on the

Pentateuch. He published Judah Kahana's *Terumat ha-Keri* (1858), on the Tur and Shulḥan Arukh, *Ḥoshen Mishpat*, with his own glosses and novellae. Individual responsa by him have appeared in various works.

Bibliography: J. J. Greenwald, *Zikkaron la-Rishonim* (1909), 38–45; idem, *Mazzevat Kodesh* (1952), 36–39; N. Ben-Menahem, in: *Sinai*, 63 (1968), 172–6. [N.B.-M.]

MODIGLIANI, AMEDEO (1884–1920) painter. Modigliani was born in Leghorn, the son of a small businessman. One of his brothers, Vittorio Emanuele *Modigliani, was an active Socialist leader. Amedeo studied art at Florence and Venice. In 1905 he went to Paris. While there, though leading a life of dissipation, he learned a great deal from Cézanne, Gauguin, Toulouse-Lautrec, and from African sculpture. He greatly admired the last, and his own sculpture was in a similar simplified abstract style. Despite his many love affairs, his excesses of drunkenness, and frequent lapses into illness, aggravated by poverty, he managed to produce, within his relatively short career, a substantial body of work. More than 20 of his sculptures, some 500 paintings, and thousands of watercolors and drawings have survived. Modigliani usually painted single figures with backgrounds only vaguely defined. There are portraits of his fellow artists and of the two women who played leading roles in his life, the English poet Beatrice Hastings with whom he lived from 1914 to 1916 and later his wife Jeanne Hébuterne. His sitters included the streetwalkers of the Left Bank whom Modigliani never made pretty but who always evoke pity. His portraits look as if he had caught the sitter in a moment of utter fatigue, lonely and devoid of glamor or gaiety. Their energy has been drained and their hands dangle limply on their laps. Their heads are inclined and their eyes look listlessly and unseeing, as though staring from another world. His women seem to be constructed of almond shapes connected by cylindrical necks to larger ovoids formed by the rounded shoulders of the upper body.

"Portrait of the Young Girl Elvira" by Amedeo Modigliani, 1918/19. Oil on canvas, 25½×18½ in. (65×47 cm.). Geneva, Oscar Ghez Collection.

Modigliani was a superb draftsman and his color sense was fascinating. His sensuous nudes are painted in broad planes of vivid ochre, orange, and earthy hues, surrounded by strong lines. His iridescent tones are achieved by covering thin layers of color with many coats of varnish. In 1917 his only one-man show was a complete fiasco. The police ordered the five canvases of nudes to be removed and this led to a scandal. It was soon after his death that the greatness of his work was discovered and his paintings and sculpture were acquired by leading museums and collectors all over the world.

Bibliography: F. Russoli, *Modigliani* (Eng., 1959); A. Werner, *Modigliani the Sculptor* (1962, 1965); J. Modigliani, *Modigliani* (Eng., 1958). [A.W.]

MODIGLIANI, VITTORIO EMANUELE (1872–1947), Italian lawyer and politician; brother of the artist Amedeo *Modigliani. Born in Leghorn, Modigliani joined the Socialist party as a student. From 1913 to 1924 he sat as a Socialist in the Italian parliament. He opposed Italian participation in World War I and supported the formula of a peace without victor or vanquished. In 1924 Modigliani joined the rest of his party in abstaining from all parliamentary activity in protest against the new Fascist law making parliamentary opposition ineffective. He appeared for the prosecution in the Giacomo Matteotti trial in 1923–24 in which leading Fascists were accused of complicity in Matteotti's assassination. Soon afterward he left Italy in protest against the Fascist regime and lived in Austria and France where he was a virulent opponent of Fascism. Modigliani participated in the formation of a socialist pro-Palestine committee formed in Brussels. He returned to Italy in 1945 and was elected a deputy to the constituent assembly and chairman of the Italian Socialist Party. [G.R.]

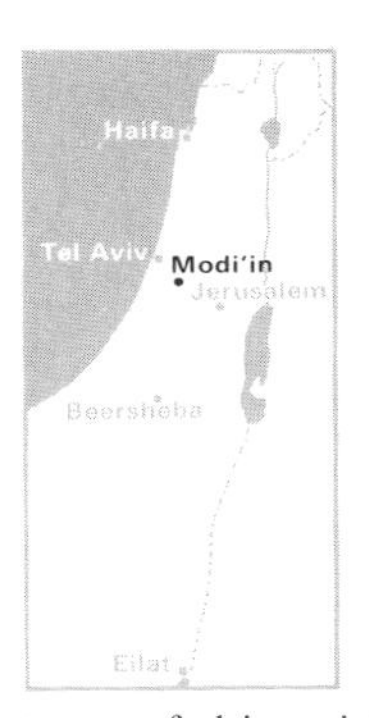

MODI'IN (or **Modi'im**; Heb. מוֹדִיעִין, מוֹדִיעִים), village in the toparchy of Lydda, the home town of Mattathias the Hasmonean and of his descendants; here the Hasmonean revolt broke out (I Macc. 2:1, 15, 23). Although the rebels were soon forced to evacuate the village, they were able to bury their dead there (I Macc. 2:70; 9:19; 13:25–30). Simeon the Hasmonean built a splendid mausoleum, which was adorned with seven pyramids and high columns with sculptures of ships visible from the sea. In the time of Jonathan, Modi'in passed into Jewish possession with the rest of the toparchy of Lydda. There Judah defeated Antiochus V (II Macc. 13:14ff.) and John and Judah, the sons of Simeon, camped before the battle of Kidron (I Macc. 16:4). In the Mishnah, it is described as a town on the border of Judah (Pes. 9:2; Ḥag. 3:5). It was the home town of R. Eleazar of Modi'in, a close relative of Bar Kokhba and perhaps identical with Eleazar the high priest, who appears on coins of the Second Jewish War. In the Onomasticon of Eusebius and on the Madaba Map it is located east of Lydda; it is now identified with the village of al-Midya, 7½ mi. (12 km.) east of Lydda. The ancient site is located at Ra's al-Midya, north of the village, where pottery from the Iron Age and later periods has been found. The tombs of the Maccabees have been tentatively located at Sheikh al-Gharbāwī, across the valley of Modi'in. Annually at Ḥanukkah, a torch is solemnly lit at the tombs and raced to Jerusalem. [M.A.-Y.]

Modi'im and Modi'im Region. In the Israel *War of Independence, the area west of the Naḥal Modi'im gorge was occupied by Israel forces in July 1948, while the village al-Midya remained beyond the 1949 armistice line in

Torch being carried from Modi'in, Ḥanukkah, 1964. Courtesy Government Press Office, Tel Aviv.

Jordanian territory. In the 1950s and 1960s, the Herzl Forest of *Ben Shemen was gradually enlarged eastward to become the Modi'im Forest, and an observation tower and amphitheater were built there. In 1964, the Modi'im region development project was started, providing for further afforestation and land reclamation; the area's northern section was set aside as an ultimate reserve for the expansion of the Tel Aviv conurbation, with plans laid out for the construction of a future city to be named Makkabit. In 1965, a *Naḥal outpost settlement, Mevo Modi'im (מְבוֹא מוֹדִיעִים), was established less than a mile (1 km.) from the armistice line by a group affiliated with *Po'alei Agudat Israel. After the *Six-Day War, these settlers moved southeastward to set up a new village in the Aijalon Valley, at the foot of the *Beth-Ḥoron ascent, while the site of Mevo Modi'im, which has poor and rocky soil, was earmarked for a village to be based on industry and a Po'alei Agudat Israel seminary. Forest planting continued after 1967 on both sides of the former armistice line, carried out in the west by Jewish laborers and in the east by Arabs. [E.O.]

Bibliography: Guérin, in: PEFQS, 2 (1870), 390; F. M. Abel, *Les Livres des Maceabées* (1949); idem, in: RB, 32 (1923), 496ff.; Beyer, in: ZDPV, 56 (1933), 223.

MODON (now **Methone**), port city in S.W. Peloponnesus, Greece. Benjamin of Tudela found a Jewish community in Modon, and it became of importance during the Venetian rule. Four travelers in the late 15th century recorded details about this Jewish community ruled by the Venetians (1206–1500). In 1481 Meshullam of Volterra found 300 Jewish families in Modon in a ghetto "on the outskirts of the city" engaged in trade and handicrafts. Jews were engaged in the silk and tanning industries as well as the maritime trade. Jews were excluded from citizenship and obliged to provide an executioner, as in other Venetian colonies. Jewish men and women had to perform forced labor. Modon fell to the Turks in 1501, whereupon many exiles from Spain settled there. Venice demanded an exorbitant sum from its Jewish population. In the assault on the town in 1531 by the Knights of Malta, Jewish captives were presumed to have been among those non-Christians carried off by the invaders. The Jewish community ceased to exist after the Venetian-Turkish war of 1646.

Bibliography: J. Starr, *Romania* (1949), 63–72. [S.Mar.]

MODZHITZ, ḥasidic dynasty in Poland (family name: Taub). Its founder was Israel of Modzhitz (d. 1921), son of Samuel Elijah of Zwole. He emphasized the value of music in Ḥasidism and is regarded as the creator of the ḥasidic melody as an art form. Israel composed hundreds of melodies, of which the best known are those to *Ezkerah Elohim ve-Ehemayah*, consisting of over 30 stanzas composed at a time of physical suffering, and to *Le-Mizmor Todah* (also called *Niggun li-Meḥusserei Bayit* ("A Tune for the Homeless"), expressing the distress of Jewish refugees during World War I. Much of his teachings are devoted to the praise of music. His son, Saul Jedidiah Eleazar (d. 1947), was *av bet din* in Rakov and Karzow. In 1929 he moved to Otwock near Warsaw and after his father's death headed the Modzhitz Ḥasidim. He combined Torah with music, and popularized the Modzhitz melodies throughout the Jewish world, composing hundreds of tunes. He edited and published his father's sermons with his own in *Divrei Yisrael* (Lublin, 1901–04; Warsaw, 1912; Warsaw, 1930; New York, 1931) and in the Passover *Haggadah, Ishei Yisrael* (Warsaw, 1938); he also edited and published the booklets *Tiferet Yisrael—Kunteres Ma'amarim* (Warsaw, 1936–38; Brooklyn, 1941–47). He died in Tel Aviv.

Bibliography: M. S. Geshuri (ed.), *La-Ḥasidim Mizmor* (1936); idem, *Neginah va-Ḥasidut be-Veit Kuzmir u-Venoteha* (1952).

[A.Ru.]

MO'ED (Heb. מוֹעֵד), the second of the six orders of the Mishnah according to the accepted order established by *Simeon b. Lakish. He interpreted the verse (Isa. 33:6), "and the stability of thy times shall be a hoard of salvation, wisdom, and knowledge..." such that "stability" refers to the order *Zera'im*, "thy times" to the order *Mo'ed*... (Shab. 31a, et al.). In the order given by R. Tanḥum, however, it is the fourth (Num. R. 13:15). *Mo'ed* treats comprehensively of the Sabbath and the festivals of the Jewish calendar, but it includes tractates **Eruvin*, which is a kind of appendix to *Shabbat*, **Shekalim*, because of the fixed appointed time for the collection of the half-*shekel* (see Shek. 1:1–3), and **Ta'anit*, dealing with congregational fasts, since to some extent its subject matter is similar to that of the festivals. *Mo'ed* comprises 12 tractates arranged, as are all the orders, in descending order according to the number of chapters. They are: (1) **Shabbat*, with 24 chapters; (2) *Eruvim*, 10; (3) **Pesaḥim*, 10; (4) *Shekalim*, 8; (5) **Yoma*, 8; (6) **Sukkah*, 5; (7) **Beẓah* or *Yom Tov*, 5; (8) **Rosh Ha-Shanah*, 4; (9) *Ta'anit*, 4; (10) **Megillah*, 4; (11) **Mo'ed Katan* or *Mashkin*, 3; (12) **Ḥagigah*, 3; in all, 88 chapters.

In the Tosefta of *Mo'ed*, *Shabbat* has 17 (or 18) chapters; *Eruvin* 8 (or 11), *Pesaḥim* 10, *Shekalim* 3, *Kippurim* 4 (or 5), *Sukkah* 4, *Yom Tov* 4, *Rosh Ha-Shanah* 2 (or 4), *Ta'aniyyot* 3 (or 4), *Megillah* 3 (or 4), *Mo'ed Katan* 2, and *Ḥagigah* 3. There is no *Gemara* to *Shekalim* in the Babylonian Talmud but there is in the Jerusalem Talmud. In contrast to all the other orders which have plural names, the name of *Mo'ed* is in the singular. The reason is apparently that the concept *Mo'ed* has two meanings, one in the sense of a festival and the other in that of a fixed time, as for example, "the season *[mo'ed]* that thou camest forth out of Egypt" (Deut. 16:6), or, "therefore will I take back My corn in the time thereof, and My wine in the season thereof *[be-mo'ado]*" (Hos. 2:11). In this sense the Bible uses the term *Mo'ed* in the singular, and this is apparently the implication of the use of the singular for the name of the order, since it treats not only of the festivals, but also of other topics that nevertheless have a fixed time, such as *Shekalim*, *Ta'anit* and the readings of the Law. It seems that the tractate *Shabbat* alone was once called *Mo'ed*.

Bibliography: Epstein, Mishnah, 980ff.; Albeck, *Shishah Sidrei Mishnah, Seder Mo'ed* (1952). [A.Ar.]

MO'ED KATAN (Heb. מוֹעֵד קָטָן: "small festival"), 11th tractate in the Mishnah order of *Mo'ed*, concerned mainly with *ḥol ha-mo'ed ("the intermediate days of the festivals of *Passover and *Sukkot"). The original name of this tractate seems to have been *Mo'ed* (TJ, MK, 2:5, 81b) and in fact throughout this tractate the intermediate days are referred to as *Mo'ed* and not as *ḥol ha-mo'ed.* To distinguish the tractate **Mo'ed* from the mishnaic order of that name, the former was sometimes referred to as *Mashkin* (Lev. R. 34:4), its opening word. The present designation, *Mo'ed Katan*, prevailed to distinguish the tractate from its order.

While the Scripture does not explicitly forbid work on *ḥol ha-mo'ed*, Leviticus 23:37, speaking of the daily festival sacrifices, includes the intermediate days of the festival in the term "holy convocation" and on account of this *ḥol ha-mo'ed* is considered as semi-festival, days on which certain kinds of work (and as a rule all unnecessary work) are forbidden. Chapter 1 of the tractate discusses a great variety of activities (e.g., agriculture, burial, marriage, sowing, repairs) which under given circumstances may be allowed on *ḥol ha-mo'ed.*

Chapter 2 speaks of further kinds of work (e.g., pressing olives, or finishing the manufacture of wine, and gathering fruits, etc.) which are allowed if they are urgent; the general rule is that no work which should have been done before the festival or could be postponed until after the festival may be done on *ḥol ha-mo'ed.* Chapter 3 speaks of the conditions under which shaving, washing clothes, drawing up of documents and other scribal activity are allowed; it then discusses the manner in which mourning customs are observed on Sabbath and festivals, including New Moon, Ḥanukkah, and Purim. The tractate ends on a note of comfort by quoting Isaiah 25:8: "He will swallow up death for ever, and the Lord will wipe away tears from all faces." The *Gemara* in Chapter 3 explains the connection between the laws of the intermediate days and those of mourning. In the context, the Babylonian *Gemara* discusses details of burial and mourning customs and records several interesting funeral orations and dirges, and deals with the laws of excommunication. There is also a *Gemara* in the Jerusalem Talmud. In the Tosefta the material of the tractate is divided into two chapters, and like the Mishnah contains many details which reflect life and conditions during the tannaitic period. An English translation and introduction by H. M. Lazarus is to be found in the Soncino Talmud translation (1938).

Engraving for the tractate *Mo'ed Katan*, showing the performance of tasks permitted on *ḥol ha-mo'ed*, from a title page of the Hebrew-Latin Mishnah illustrated by Mich. Richey, Amsterdam, 1700–04. Jerusalem, J.N.U.L.

Bibliography: H. M. Reinhold, *Tal Ḥayyim . . . al Massekhet Mo'ed Katan . . .* (Lvov, 1866); Ḥ. Albeck, *Shishah Sidrei Mishnah*, 2 (1958), 371–3.

[A.Z.E.]

MOELLIN, JACOB BEN MOSES (?1360–1427), usually referred to as **Maharil** (**M**orenu **ha-R**av **J**acob ha-**L**evi) and also as **Mahari Segal** and **Mahari Molin**), the foremost talmudist of his generation and head of the Jewish communities of Germany, Austria, and Bohemia. Born in Mainz, Jacob was taught by his father, one of its leading rabbis, and then proceeded to Austria, where he studied under Meir ha-Levi and Shalom b. Isaac, who ordained him rabbi with the title *morenu.* Summoned to Mainz while still young to succeed his father who had died in 1387, Jacob founded a yeshivah there to which many students streamed. The students lived in his house and were supported by "the means provided for him by the leaders of the country" (*Sefer Maharil*). From this yeshivah came the greatest rabbis of Germany and Austria of the next generation, among them Jacob *Weil.

Moellin became famous throughout Europe. While he was still young halakhic problems were addressed to him "since from your mouth Torah goes forth to all Israel" (Maharil, resp. no. 148). He was also regarded as the leader of the people in that troubled period. During the Hussite wars and the strengthening of Catholic reaction various communities turned to him for help. On this occasion he decreed a three-day fast upon the whole community, "even upon sucklings," and also took the matter up with the government, with successful results. His rulings, together with those of Israel *Isserlein, serve as the foundation of all the traditions which were kept in German Jewry. In his decisions Moellin took prevailing conditions into consideration, and when a matter which affected the economic position of the community came before him, he assembled the scholars and "investigated the matter until he found a favorable solution." When he felt he had been too strict, he excused himself saying, "I have been very strict with you because you are without a rabbi" (resp. no. 26). He attacked rabbis who "bought" rabbinical positions which they were unqualified to fill (Jacob Weil, *Dinim ve-Halakhot*, no. 68, Kapust ed. (1834), 59b), and protested against the neglect of Torah study and against the widespread practice of giving decisions based on abridged halakhic works. In his sermons he placed particular emphasis upon the *mitzvah* of charity, and he was keenly solicitous of the honor of the poor.

Moellin also occupied himself with astronomy and applied himself to the solution of astronomical problems with the aid of instruments, and the study of the astronomical work *Shesh Kenafayim* of Immanuel b. Jacob *Bonfils. Jacob was well-versed in the different German dialects and composed Hebrew rhymed verse (in Ms.) and *piyyutim* (Joseph b. Moses, *Leket Yosher*, ed. by J. Freimann, 1 (1903), 50). Though, like all the rabbis of Germany, he shunned philosophy, he acted with a degree of tolerance toward those who, attracted by it, had strayed in matters of belief. He declared valid the *sheḥitah* of one who "accepted resurrection only as a traditional belief, but denied that there was a biblical basis for it," even declaring that "though his sin is too great to be tolerated, he is not under suspicion of deliberately transgressing the Torah" (resp. no. 194, p. 64a–b).

Moellin was renowned as a *ḥazzan* and his activities left a lasting influence on the Ashkenazi tradition. His opinion that traditional tunes should not be changed was a constantly stabilizing factor. The so-called "*Niggunei*

Maharil," attributed to him (or at least thought to have been sanctioned by him) were in use in the Mainz community until modern times (see Idelsohn, Music, 170, 177, 206, 456, and see *Mi-Sinai melodies).

His known works are: (1) *Minhagei Maharil* (*Sefer Maharil*, first published in Sabionetta, 1556), compiled by his pupil Zalman of St. Goar who for many years noted down his halakhic statements, customs and, in particular, the explanations he heard from him. Through the efforts of various copyists, the work enjoyed wide circulation. Most of the customs noted in it were included by Moses Isserles in his glosses to the Shulḥan Arukh; (2) Responsa, some copied and arranged by Eleazar b. Jacob and published for the first time in Venice in 1549. A far more complete collection has been preserved in manuscript (Margoliouth, Cat. No. 575). The printed editions of the *Maharil* are full of errors, apparently having been published from a corrupt copy. Moellin died in Worms.

Bibliography: G. Steiman, *Custom and Survival—A Study of the Life and Work of R. Jacob Molin* (1963); G. Polak, *Halikhot Kedem* (1846), 79–86; Guedemann, Gesch Erz, 3 (1888), 17–20; D. Kaufmann, in: MGWJ, 42 (1898), 223–9; Weiss, Dor, 5 (1904[4]), 81f., 239–42; Joseph b. Moses, *Leket Yosher*, ed. by J. Freimann, 2 (1904), XXXV, 132; Finkelstein, Middle Ages, index, s.v. *Maharil;* L. Rosenthal, in: MGWJ, 71 (1927), 364–7; L. Greenwald, *Maharil u-Zemanno* (1944); M. S. Geshuri, in: *Sinai*, 13 (1943/44), 317–49; Hacohen, *ibid.*, 57 (1965), 133–7. [E.K.]

MO'EẒET HA-PO'ALOT, the General Council of Women Workers of Israel, founded in 1922 as a part of the *Histadrut (the General Federation of Labor). Its roots go back to the pioneering movement of the Second *Aliyah, when girls, as well as young men, went to build Ereẓ Israel "by the sweat of their brow." Masculine prejudices continued to exist even in an idealistic society. For women to work, especially in the open field, was considered not only unfair competition but a fall from grace. The handful of *ḥalutzot* (pioneer women) banded together, proclaiming the slogan: "Women demand the right to be partners in the revival of our People and to fulfill themselves . . . as women and as human beings." In 1968 the membership of Mo'eẓet ha-Po'alot totaled 486,000, composed of three categories: wage-earners—177,000; women members of cooperative villages (kibbutzim or moshavim)—33,000; and wives of Histadrut members, known as Immahot Ovedot (working mothers)—276,000.

Since women are now accepted as full-fledged members of the trade unions, Mo'eẓot ha-Po'alot is preoccupied mainly with social services and the special problems of working women, such as retirement age, maternity benefits, vocational training, and career advancement. Branches of Immahot Ovedot exist in every town and village, providing social services and education for housewives. Assisted by *Pioneer Women organizations in 12 countries, it maintains some 500 social and educational institutions, such as day-nurseries, children's residential homes, kindergartens, youth clubs, and summer camps, catering in 1968 to some 20,000 children. Special attention is given to children of immigrants and culturally deprived families, who are generally referred to these institutions by social workers. It also supports four residential agricultural high schools (two in cooperation with WIZO), four workshops for immigrants, several community centers (the largest of which is Bet Elisheva in Jerusalem), girls' vocational high schools (including a school for baby nurses), women's hostels, and special training courses for some 7,500 women and girls. In scores of women's clubs, immigrants are taught Hebrew, home economics, and social responsibility. Residential seminars, study days, field trips, and lectures are organized. An advisory bureau on legal and psychological problems assists widows and orphans.

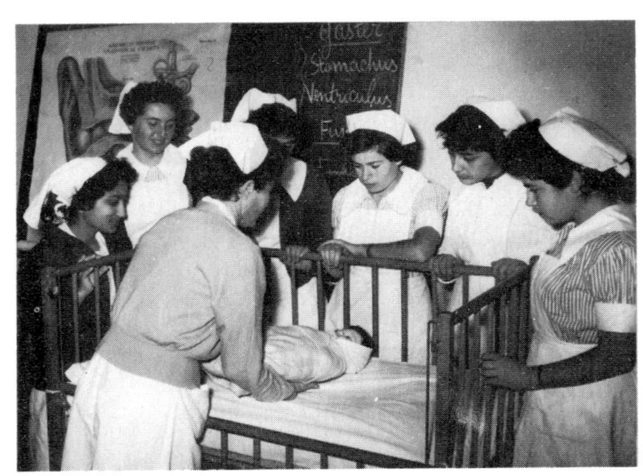

Instruction of student nurses at the Omna baby home and nurses' training school of the Mo'eẓet ha-Po'alot, Haifa. Photo Mirlin-Yaron, Tel Aviv.

The executive of Mo'eẓet ha-Po'alot is elected by general ballot every four years (simultaneously with the Histadrut elections). Mo'eẓet ha-Po'alot is affiliated with many women's international movements and, through the Histadrut, with the International Labor Office (ILO), participating particularly in committees pertaining to women workers.

Bibliography: Pioneer Women's Organization, *Pioneer Woman* (1926–); A. Maimon (Fishman), *Ḥamishim Shenot Tenu'at ha-Po'alot 1904–1954* (1955[2]); R. Katznelson-Shazar, *Im Pa'amei ha-Dor*, 2 vols. (1963). [SH.H.]

MOGADOR (Souirah), Moroccan port on the Atlantic Ocean, a kilometer distant from the island of Cerne which in antiquity was a commercial base of the Phoenicians and Carthagenians and where, under King Juba II (23 C.E.) the famous purple of Getulia was manufactured. From the Middle Ages until the 17th century there were sugarcane refineries in the vicinity of Mogador, and the sugar trade was concentrated in the hands of the Jews. The activity of Mogador, which was brought to a halt between 1650 and 1760, started anew when Sultan Muhammad ibn Abdallah decided to build a city and a port through which the greater part of the international commerce of his kingdom would be conveyed. The most important Jewish families of the country sent some of their members there. The sultan chose ten of them and conferred upon them the title of *tājir al-sulṭān* ("merchant of the king"), together with the duties and prerogatives attached to it. The most luxurious dwellings of the town were given to them and they administered funds of the treasury, outfitted ships, and were entrusted with missions to the European courts; they often represented the Christian nations and for a century and a half dominated Moroccan trade. The privileged personalities became the nucleus of a dynamic community which until a few decades ago gave the town a distinctly Jewish character. In Mogador everyone rested on the Sabbath and the Jewish festivals. The measures taken by Mulay Yazid (1790–92) against the Jews did not reach Mogador because he was assassinated in the meantime. However, the cholera epidemic in 1799 strengthened the trend to emigrate to England and the Americas. Until 1808, when it was decided to confine the Jews within a mellah, they lived among the other inhabitants. From then onward the only exceptions were the families of the "merchants of the king" and some businessmen of European origin. About 800 Jewish persons thus continued to live in the residential quarter together

Figure 1. Mogador woman in traditional holiday dress *(Kesua el Kbira)*. Jerusalem, Israel Museum Photo Collection, Department of Ethnography. Photo Shulman, 1953.

Figure 2. Jew from Mogador. Jerusalem, Israel Museum Photo Collection. Department of Ethnography. Photo Shulman, 1953.

with the Muslim and Christian officials. This distinction intensified the differences which already existed within the community. In 1844 when the town was bombarded by the French, the tribes of the surrounding area came to ransack it. In the mellah the Jews defended themselves, weapons in hand, but many of them preferred to abandon the town. They were replaced by thousands of other coreligionists. The overcrowding of the mellah was unprecedented. After passing through Mogador in 1864, Sir Moses Montefiore, together with the community leaders Abraham and Jacob *Corcos, attempted to remedy this situation by obtaining the allocation of a second quarter for the unfortunate Jews. The waves of new arrivals however continued. During the 19th century the Jewish population grew from 4,000 to 14,000. The community was led by the old established families. The spiritual leaders included such scholars as R. Abraham *Coriat, R. Abraham ibn *Attar, and R. Mas'ūd Knafo (d. 1910); the tomb of one of them, R. Ḥayyim *Pinto (d. 1835), who was renowned as a saint, was venerated. In general, the Jews of Mogador were highly educated. In Morocco their musicians were of repute. The town possessed some very beautiful synagogues, numerous *battei midrashim,* and yeshivot. In about 1800 there were two private Jewish schools in which the language of instruction was English. Two more public schools were founded in 1862 and 1864. In 1887 the Anglo-Jewish Association subsidized a school for girls. The English influence in Mogador was long predominant. The French school of the Alliance Israélite Universelle, founded in 1867, was attended by the children of the poverty-stricken classes. Under the French protectorate Mogador lost some of its economic importance and only a small community remained there (about 5,000 souls). Many of them left in the 1950s and 1960s. By 1970 most of its former members lived in Europe, America, and Israel, and only a few hundred Jews continued to live in Mogador.

Bibliography: A. Chouraqui, *Between East and West* (1968), index; Hirschberg, Afrikah, index; Miège, Maroc, passim; A. Jodin, *Les Etablissements du roi Juba II aux Iles Purpuraires (Mogador)* (1967). [D.Co.]

MOGILEV, city in Mogilev oblast, Belorussian S.S.R.; from the middle of the 14th century until 1772 Mogilev was part of Poland-Lithuania; under czarist Russia, it was the chief town of the province of Mogilev. One of the largest and most important in Belorussia, the Mogilev community was founded during the 16th century by Jews who leased the collection of customs duties; the first of these was Michael *Jozefowicz (1522). During the 1580s one of the most prominent Jewish merchants of Lithuania, Ephraim b. Jerahmeel (Afrash Rakhmaelovich) lived in Mogilev and leased the customs duties. In 1585 the Christian population requested King Stephen Báthory to prohibit the settlement of Jews in Mogilev. Although the king agreed, the order was not carried out and Jews continued to live in the town. A synagogue existed from the beginning of the 17th century. The struggle between the townspeople and the Jews of Mogilev continued throughout the 17th and 18th centuries. In 1626 King Sigismund III Vasa granted letters patent to the town (confirmed by King Ladislaus IV in 1633) in which it was stipulated that all the Jews must move into the street where the synagogue stood, beyond the city walls. On Rosh Ha-Shanah 5406 (1645) the townspeople, led by the mayor, attacked the Jews. In 1646 the municipality decided to forbid the Jews to live in lodgings rented from the townspeople or to acquire these lodgings. This too was confirmed by King Ladislaus IV. When Mogilev was occupied by the invading Russian armies in 1654, on the request of the townspeople Czar Alexis Mikhailovich ordered the expulsion of the Jews. Their houses were to be shared equally between the municipality and the Russians. The order was not immedi-

Detail of the polychromatic ceiling of the Mogilev synagogue, executed by Ḥayyim b. Isaac Segal of Slutsk in 1710. From M. and K. Piechotka, *Wooden Synagogues,* Warsaw, 1959.

ately carried out, but as the Polish army approached Mogilev in 1655, the Russian commander drove the Jews out of the town and ordered their massacre. Those Jews who remained became apostates. After the end of the war the community was renewed and most of the apostates returned to Judaism. In 1656 John II Casimir granted letters patent to the town according to which the Jews were forbidden to live within the walls of the city and to build houses or maintain shops there. There was a *blood libel in Mogilev in 1692. In 1736 King Augustus III confirmed the earlier letters patent of John II Casimir, adding further anti-Jewish restrictions. Restrictive orders on settlement and occupations were later reissued, but were not applied in practice.

In spite of opposition, the community continued to develop. By 1692 there were two synagogues. In 1748 the municipality reprimanded the townspeople because they themselves had helped the Jews to settle in the center of the town and to engage in commerce. In 1766, 642 poll tax paying Jews were registered within the community of Mogilev and the surrounding villages. In the *Councils of the Lands Mogilev was subordinated to *Brest-Litovsk. The community developed to a considerable extent after Mogilev was annexed by Russia. The Jews of the annexed region were granted judicial autonomy, and the community of Mogilev was designated as the central community of the whole province, its *bet din* being given authority to hear appeals against the legal decisions of the province's communities. The Jews played a principal role in Mogilev's extensive trade with Riga, Memel, Koenigsberg, and Danzig (*Gdansk) and later with southern Russia. In 1847 there were 7,897 Jews registered in Mogilev. The Jews were greatly influenced by *Ḥabad Ḥasidism, but by the end of the 18th century there were several *maskilim* among the wealthy merchants. In 1783 one of them, Jacob Hirsch, addressed a memorandum to the Russian government in which he suggested that the *ḥadarim* and *talmud torah* schools in both the district of Mogilev and the town itself be converted into schools where secular studies would also be taught. During the 1860s and early 1870s Pavel (Pesaḥ) *Axelrod, who had studied at the local secondary school and later spread the ideas of the Haskalah among Jewish youth, lived in Mogilev. In 1870 the *Malbim (Meir Leib b. Jehiel Michael) was invited to become rabbi of Mogilev, but was soon compelled to leave the town after the *maskilim* denounced him to the authorities as disloyal to Russia. In 1897 there were 21,539 Jews in Mogilev (about 50% of the total population). In October 1904 pogroms were initiated by soldiers mobilized for the war against Japan. Mogilev was one of the important centers of the *Bund, and of the Zionist Movement. Following World War I and the establishment of the Communist regime, the number of Jews decreased and by 1926 only 17,105 (34.1% of the population) remained. During the 1920s a violent struggle occurred between the religious circles and the Zionists on the one hand, and the *Yevsektsiya on the other, which terminated with the liquidation of Jewish communal life in the town. Mogilev was the birthplace of *Mordecai b. Hillel Hakohen, Nachman *Syrkin, and Jacob *Mazeh.

When Mogilev was occupied by the Germans during World War II (1941), those Jews who did not escape were massacred. It was estimated that there were about 7,000 to 10,000 Jews in Mogilev in 1959. The last synagogue was closed down by the authorities in 1959 and turned into a sports gymnasium. There was a Jewish cemetery.

The Province of Mogilev. Together with the province of Vitebsk, it was the first region with a large Jewish population to be annexed by Russia, later comprising the core of the *Pale of Settlement as one of the "western" provinces in which most of Russian Jewry was concentrated. The province of Mogilev was one of the two provinces where the prohibition concerning the settlement of Jews in the villages, included in the "Jewish Constitution" of 1804, was fully applied (in 1823). In 1847, 87,739 Jews were registered in the communities of the province. By 1897 the number had risen to 203,947 (12.1% of the total population), 37.9% living in the towns, 38.9% in the townlets, and 23.06% in the villages. The large communities of the province included (in addition to Mogilev): *Gomel (20,385 Jews), *Orsha (7,383 Jews), *Shklov (5,422 Jews), *Mstislavl (5,076 Jews), and *Rogachev (5,047 Jews). In 1897, 38.95% of the province's Jews earned their livelihood from commerce and 36.90% in crafts; 9,517 Jews (4.7% of the total Jewish population) depended on agriculture. There were about 70 small Jewish agricultural settlements in the province. Under the Soviet regime, most of the territory of the province was incorporated into the oblasts of Mogilev, Vitebsk, and Gomel. In 1926 there were 48,900 Jews in the oblast of Mogilev.

Bibliography: Belkind, in: *Keneset Yisrael,* 1 (1886), 699–704; Dubnow, in: *Pardes,* 3 (1896), 94–100; Darin-Drabkin, in: *Haaretz* (Dec. 6, 1963); Mstislavskiy, in: *Voskhod* (Sept. 1–10, Oct. 1–16, Dec. 1–8, 1886); P. B. Axelrod, *Perezhitoye i peredumanoye* (1923), 33–67.

[Y.S.]

MOGILEV-PODOLSKI, city in Vinnitsa oblast, Ukrainian S.S.R.; in Poland until 1795; under czarist rule it was a district town of Podolia. Mogilev-Podolski was an important station on the commercial route between Moldavia and Ukraine. Jews are first mentioned in the town in 1637, but the community is not recorded among those who were victims of the *Chmielnicki massacres of 1648–49. In 1765 there were 957 Jews in Mogilev and the vicinity. The number had grown to 5,411 in 1847, and by 1897 there were 12,344 (55.3% of the total population) Jews in the town itself. In 1808 H. Z. Stein and his father, David, transferred their Hebrew press from Slopkovicz to Mogilev and operated there until 1819 producing 24 books. In October 1905 the community suffered in the wave of pogroms. With the establishment of the Soviet regime, the Jewish communal organization and its institutions were liquidated. In 1926 the Jewish population had fallen to 9,622 (41.8% of the total). After the occupation of the town by the Germans and Rumanians during World War II (1941), Mogilev was incorporated into the region of *Transnistria. During the war years the largest concentration of Jews expelled by the Rumanians from Bessarabia and Bukovina to Transnistria was to be found in Mogilev. In September 1943 these refugees, most of whom were from Bukovina, numbered 13,184. According to the 1959 census there were about 4,700 Jews in Mogilev (22.5% of the population). The last synagogue was closed down by the authorities in the mid-1960s.

Bibliography: Berman, in: *Reshumot*, 1 (1925), 411–3; Ya'ari, in: KS, 23 (1946/47), 309–27; *Die Judenpogrome in Russland*, 2 (1909), 443–6; M. Carp, *Cartea neagră*, 3 vols. (1946–48), index; PK Romanyah (1969), 461–73. [Y.S.]

MOHÁCSI, JENŐ (1886–1944), Hungarian author and translator. Born in Mohács, Mohácsi studied law and began his writing career as a literary journalist. A man of great versatility who wrote poetry and Hungarian and German prose, he was outstanding as a translator and was instrumental in gaining a world public for Hungarian literature. His best work was a literary biography of Imre Madách (1823–64), author of the dramatic poem *Az Ember tragédiája* ("The Tragedy of Man"), of which Mohácsi also made a complete German translation (1904[4]). He translated such classics of Hungarian drama as *Bánk Bán*, a historical play by József Katona (1791–1830), and *Csongor és Tünde*, a fairy tale by Mihály Vörösmarty (1800–1855). His original works include *Hegedű és koldusbot* ("A Violin and a Beggar's Staff," 1942); *Madách* (1935), a playlet; and *Gemma, Dante Hitvese* ("Gemma, Dante's Wife," 1944). Mohácsi was secretary of the Judah Halevi Society for the dissemination of Hebrew literature and wrote a book about the poet (1941). Together with many other Jewish journalists he was arrested by the Nazis in 1944 and scheduled for deportation. His exemption certificate, signed by the regent of Hungary, Admiral Horthy, never reached him, and he died during transportation.

Bibliography: *Magyar Irodalmi Lexikon*, 2 (1965), 259.

[B.Y.]

MOHILEWER, SAMUEL (1824–1898), rabbi, early member of *Ḥovevei Zion in Russia, and a founder of religious Zionism. Born in Glebokie (now Glubokoye), Vilna district, the son of a rabbinical family, Mohilewer was ordained a rabbi by the Volozhin yeshivah (1842) and took up the post of rabbi in his native city from 1848, in Szaki from 1854, in Suwalki from 1860, and in Radom from 1868. In each place he was active in community affairs, especially during the Polish rebellion (1863), toward which he asked the Jews to maintain a neutral attitude. In his articles,

Samuel Mohilewer, a founder of religious Zionism. Courtesy Central Zionist Archives, Jerusalem.

which were published in *Ha-Levanon*, he stressed the need for cooperation with the *maskilim* for the welfare of the people and demanded that the rabbis "combine the Torah and wisdom as the time is appropriate." In 1873 he participated in the St. Petersburg gathering of rabbis and the leading moderate *maskilim* and tried to bring the two sides closer together. He was attracted to the idea of settling Ereẓ Israel even before the 1881 pogroms, but immediately after they took place he went to Brody and Lvov in order to encourage the masses of refugees who fled Russia and to influence the philanthropists and workers who came to their aid to divert the stream of migration to Ereẓ Israel. Afterward, together with two other rabbis, he appealed to the Russian rabbis to found an organization for *aliyah* to Ereẓ Israel and to settle there. Even after many rabbis withdrew their support of *Ḥibbat Zion because the movement was headed by *maskilim* and "students," Mohilewer remained faithful to the concept and supported the efforts of L. *Pinsker and M. L. *Lilienblum to organize the various Ḥovevei Zion into one organization.

Mohilewer was among those who influenced Edmond de *Rothschild to extend aid to the first settlements in Ereẓ Israel and induced him to establish a settlement for Jewish farmers coming from Russia (*Ekron). He then influenced Jews in Bialystok and its surroundings to settle in *Petaḥ Tikvah. In 1883 he was chosen as rabbi of Bialystok under an agreement with the members of the community that he be allowed to devote himself to his public activities several months a year. Mohilewer was the honorary president of the *Kattowitz Conference of Ḥovevei Zion (1884). His speech at the closing session of the conference on the "Dry Bones" (Ezek. 37) served as a foundation for the sermons of the preachers of Ḥibbat Zion and of Zionism for the following years. In 1888 he joined I. E. *Spektor, M. *Eliasberg, and others who allowed the farmers to work the fields during the *shemittah* year in the Jewish settlements in Ereẓ Israel. He chaired the Ḥovevei Zion conferences in Druskininkai (1887) and in Vilna (1889) and struggled for the influence of the Orthodox circles in the movement. Through his influence a board of rabbis was chosen to ensure that the settlement work in Ereẓ Israel was carried out in a traditional Jewish spirit.

In 1890 Mohilewer was among the first speakers at the Odessa founding assembly of The Society in Support of Jewish Farmers and Artisans in Syria and Palestine (the official name of the Odessa Committee of Ḥovevei Zion). After the meeting he headed a Ḥovevei Zion group on a tour of Ereẓ Israel, and upon his return published his open letter entitled "The Purpose of My Trip to the Holy Land," in which he called upon Ḥovevei Zion "to work physically and financially for the sake of Ereẓ Israel." At a gathering of Ḥovevei Zion in Druskininkai (1893), it was decided, at Mohilewer's initiative, to establish a Spiritual Center (Merkaz Ruḥani—*Mizrachi) for the movement to direct public relations activities and explain ideas connected with the settlement of Ereẓ Israel. It was also decided to plant a citron orchard on land adjoining Ḥaderah and to name it Gan Shemu'el, in honor of Mohilewer's 70th birthday. Mohilewer and his close associates continued in their propaganda work, especially among the Orthodox Jews, and the Mizrachi became the foundation for the development of the religious Zionist movement, which four years after Mohilewer's death became a faction in the Zionist Organization (assuming officially the name Mizrachi).

Mohilewer joined the World Zionist Organization when it was founded by *Herzl, but because of his physical weakness he was not able to participate in the First Congress in 1897. His letter was read to the delegates, however, and created a great impression upon them. He was chosen as one of the four leaders who were charged with directing the work of the Zionist Movement in Russia and as the head of its "spiritual center" which disseminated directives to the members in their work. In his last letter before his death, Mohilewer called upon the Jews of Russia to support the *Jewish Colonial Trust. The basic goals in his public relations work were the attainment of a deep attachment to the commandment to settle Ereẓ Israel, "which is the foundation of the existence of our people"; and tolerance toward the *maskilim* as a prerequisite to the unity of the Jewish people, which was necessary for the rebuilding of the Jewish homeland.

Mohilewer wrote many short works including responsa, talmudic and rabbinical novellae, homilies, and scholarly works. Most of these writings were lost in the Bialystok pogrom (1906). A part of those that survived were published under the name *Ḥikrei Halakhah u-She'elot u-Teshuvot* (1944). [Y.S.]

His grandson, JOSEF MOHILEWER (1872–1943), was a Zionist leader and educator in Russia and Ereẓ Israel. Born in Radom, Poland, he received a traditional Jewish education from his grandfather. He was active in various Zionist groups, and from 1902 was a government-appointed rabbi in Bialystok. Mohilewer was active in the fields of Jewish education and community affairs in Odessa. In 1920 he moved to Palestine, where he became deputy headmaster of the Jerusalem Teachers' Seminary and, from 1923, headmaster of the Hebrew High School in Jerusalem. He published articles in the Russian, German, and Hebrew press. [A.A.]

Bibliography: N. Sokolow, *Hibbath Zion* (Eng., 1935), index; idem, *History of Zionism*, 2 (1919), index; M. Ben-Zvi (comp.), *Rabbi Samuel Mohilewer* (Eng., 1945); I. Nissenbaum, *Ha-Rav Shemu'el Mohilewer* (1930): idem, *Ha-Dat ve-ha-Teḥiyyah ha-Le'ummit* (1920), 92–118; A. Druyanow, *Ketavim le-Toledot Ḥibbat Ẓiyyon ve-Yishuv Ereẓ-Yisrael* (1932), index; Y. L. Fishman, *Sefer Shemu'el* (1923); S. Federbush, *Ḥazon Torah ve-Ẓiyyon* (1960), 99–117; I. Trivaks and E. Steinman, *Sefer Me'ah Shanah* (1938), 365–86; Tidhar, 1 (1947), 291–2; A. Hertzberg, *Zionist Idea* (1960), 398–404; L. Jung (ed.), *Men of the Spirit* (1964), 415–35.

MOHR, ABRAHAM MENAHEM MENDEL (1815–1868), Hebrew scholar. Born in Lemberg, he was a *maskil* who wrote in Hebrew and Yiddish. His fecund literary work commenced in 1834 when he published *Magen ha-Ḥokhmah*, in which he defended science and philosophy.

Abraham Mohr, 19th-century Hebrew scholar. Jerusalem, J.N.U.L., Schwadron Collection.

Together with N. I. Fischmann, Jacob Bodek, and Jacob Mentsch he issued the two volume *Ha-Ro'eh u-Mevakker Sifrei Meḥabberei Zemannenu* (1837, 1839), in which famous scholars were harshly criticized. The book aroused the anger of his contemporaries. His publication *Yerushalayim*, which appeared for three issues (1844–45), was more moderate. In 1848–49 he published a Yiddish newspaper, *Tsaytung*, which at the time was the only Yiddish newspaper in the world. Mohr wrote about the Rothschilds (*Tiferet Yisrael*, 1843), Columbus (1846), and Napoleon III (*Ḥut ha-Meshullash*, 1853). His works also included *Mevasseret Ẓiyyon*, (1847), a geography of Palestine and its Jewish inhabitants, and his Purim parodies *Kol Bo le-Purim* (1855) and *Shulḥan Arukh Even ha-Shetiyyah* (1861). He published editions of *Mikveh Yisrael* by Manasseh Ben Israel (1847) and *La-Yesharim Tehillah* by M. Ḥ. Luzzatto (1859).

Bibliography: Zeitlin, Bibliotheca, 242–4; Kressel, Leksikon, 2 (1967), 320–2. [G.K.]

MOHR (Mohar), MEIR (1888–1967), Hebrew writer. Born in Rozwadow, Galicia, Mohr left for the U.S. in 1908, where he worked as a tailor and a part-time teacher. After returning to Galicia he taught in Jaslo. Recruited for the Austrian army during World War I, in which he served until 1918, Mohr afterward taught in Tarnow and in various German cities, including Berlin (from 1923). From 1939, when he left Berlin for Palestine, he taught Hebrew to children and to adults.

Mohr's publication, under the pen name R. Simla'i, of light, humorous verse in G. Rosenzweig's *Ha-Devorah* (1912) was followed by poems, articles, and essays in the majority of Hebrew newspapers and literary periodicals of this period. In his later years, he regularly published articles and poems in *Ha-Po'el ha-Ẓa'ir*. His books are *Ayin be-Ayin* (1950), a selection of his poetry, and *Ḥeret Enosh* (1959), a selection of his essays on poetry and prose. Mohr translated exclusively into Hebrew.

His son, JEHIEL MAR (MOHAR; 1921–1969), also a Hebrew poet, was born in Tarnow, and went to Ereẓ Israel in 1937. He was a founding member of kibbutz Dovrat. Mar published five volumes of poetry, of which the first, *Mi-Lev va-Nof*, appeared in 1951. His verse aimed at a simple conversational idiom often achieved by irony. One of Israel's most skillful writers of lyrics for popular songs, he published these lyrics under the name Mohar.

Bibliography: Y. Keshet, *Maskiyyot* (1954), 221–8; *Kol Kitvei G. Schoffmann*, 4 (1960), 250–1; 5 (1960), 166; A. Cohen, *Soferim Ivriyyim Benei Zemannenu* (1964), 247–9. [G.K.]

MOINESTI (Rum. **Moineşti**), town in Moldavia, E. central Rumania. Tombstones from 1740 and 1748 prove the existence of a Jewish settlement predating the foundation of the town (1781) and dating back to the discovery of oil in the vicinity. There were 42 Jewish taxpayers in 1820, 500 families in 1885, and 2,398 individuals in 1899 (50.6% of the total population). The community was organized in 1885 and had five prayer houses, a ritual bath, and a primary school for boys (founded in 1893) as well as one for girls (1900). The locality played a prominent role in the history of the colonization of Ereẓ Israel. Jews from Moinesti were the founders of *Rosh Pinnah. In 1881 a group of 50 families was organized which sent David *Schub as a delegate to Ereẓ Israel. He purchased the plots of land where 22 families settled in the summer of 1882, together with several families from other Moldavian cities. The Moinesti Jews addressed a call to all the Rumanian Jews; the pre-Zionist movement Yishuv Ereẓ Israel was subsequently established. Between the two world wars the number of the Jews decreased to 1,761 (26.6% of the total). After emancipation (1919) there were Jewish members on the municipal council, and in 1930 Moinesti even elected a Jew as deputy mayor. Tristan *Tzara (Sami Rosenstein), a founder of the Dadaist movement, was born in Moinesti.

In World War II the Jews of Moinesti were expelled to Botosani. About 80 families returned after the war. The Jewish population numbered 480 in 1947, 400 in 1950, and about 15 families in 1969.

Bibliography: PK Romanyah, 177–9; E. Schwarzfeld, *Impopularea, reîmpopularea si întemeierea tîrgurilor si tîrgusoarelor în Moldova* (1914), 40, 44, 85; I. Klausner, *Ḥibbat Ẓiyyon be-Rumanyah* (1958). [TH.L.]

MOÏSE, ABRAHAM (c. 1736–1809), progenitor of the Moïse family of South Carolina. Born in Strasbourg in Alsace, France, Moïse emigrated to the West Indies and was living at Cape François, Santo Domingo, when a

Negro slave insurrection broke out in 1791. He and his family were forced to flee and made their way to Charleston, South Carolina, reputedly leaving their wealth behind. Aged 56, he started anew as a small shopkeeper and later became a vendue master (auctioneer). His descendants achieved distinction in various fields.

Bibliography: H. Moïse, *The Moïse Family of South Carolina*, (1961). [T.J.T.]

MOÏSE, PENINA (1797–1880), U.S. poet, hymnist, and teacher; daughter of Abraham *Moïse. Penina Moïse left school at the age of 12—when her father died—to help support her large family, which had been left without means, by doing needlework. On her own, she continued to study and read avidly, showing a literary talent at an early age and becoming a prolific writer of verse. She frequently contributed poems to the Charleston *Courier* which were on a variety of subjects, many on current events. She also wrote for the leading papers and periodicals of her day. In 1833 she published a small volume of her poems, *Fancy's Sketch Book*. She was admired by Charleston's antebellum writers. A devout Jew, she was superintendent of Beth Elohim Congregation's Sunday school and was the author of the first American Jewish hymnal. When the congregation installed the first American synagogue organ in 1841, she composed hymns for the organ service. A book of her hymns was published by Beth Elohim; later editions were used by other Reform temples. Many are still found in the *Union Hymnal* of the Union of American Hebrew Congregations. They are notable for a spirit of submission to the will of God. In her sixties Penina Moïse gradually became blind, but, with rare courage, she continued to write, using her niece as an amanuensis. She was widely known as Charleston's "blind poetess." Reduced to poverty after the Civil War, she, her sister, and niece eked out a modest living with a small private girls' school, in which she gave oral instruction by drawing on her remarkable memory. Her warmth and sympathy made her a favorite confidante of youth. Her hymns and poetry were published, as *Secular and Religious Works* (1911). She never married.

Bibliography: B. A. Elzas, *Jews of South Carolina* (1905), 181–4; S. A. Dinkins, in: *American Jews' Annual, 5646* (1885/86), ch. 5.
[T.J.T.]

MOÏSE, THEODORE SYDNEY (1806–1883), U.S. painter; grandson of Abraham *Moïse. He received an elementary knowledge of painting from his aunt, Penina *Moïse. He worked in Charleston until 1836, advertising his service as a portrait painter, picture restorer, and ornamental draftsman. He then moved to New Orleans, where by 1842 he had become associated with the portrait and genre painter, Trevor T. Fowler. They traveled together through the South, executing paintings of the rich landowners, their families, their personnel, even their horses and dogs. It is sometimes impossible to distinguish Moïse's work from that of Fowler. Moïse's sitters included Mordecai *Cohen, General Jackson (City Hall, New Orleans), and Governor Herbert (State Library, New Orleans). The Court House of New Orleans contains many portraits of judges by Moïse, also "Life on the Metarie" (with portraits of 44 prominent turfmen), and an enormous painting with portraits of 64 members of the Volunteer Fire Brigade parading in the city's Canal Street. Moïse served with distinction in the Confederate Army in the defense of the lower Mississippi during the Civil War, and was instrumental in the employment of floating fire rafts to repel the Federal fleet. A dashing cavalier and a spendthrift, he often painted pictures in order to cancel debts.

[A.W.]

Portrait by Theodore Sydney Moïse of the American patriot, Henry Clay, 1843. Oil on canvas, $51 \times 39\frac{1}{2}$ in. (129.5×100 cm.). New York, Metropolitan Museum of Art, gift of Grace H. Dodge, 1909.

MOISEIWITSCH, BENNO (1890–1963), pianist. Born in Odessa, Moiseiwitsch won the Anton Rubinstein Prize at the Odessa Academy at the age of nine, and later studied with Theodor Leschetizky in Vienna. He was regarded by many as the finest Chopin interpreter of his time. His London debut took place in 1909. He settled in England during World War I and thereafter played frequently in Britain and on concert tours abroad. His repertoire was extremely wide, but in his later years he tended to confine his programs to the standard favorites. His daughter, TANYA MOISEIWITSCH (1914–), became a theatrical designer. She designed 50 productions in Dublin, and from 1940 worked in London, Stratford, and Edinburgh. She also designed productions at Stratford, Ontario, at the New York Metropolitan Opera, the Habimah, Tel Aviv, etc.

Bibliography: M. Moiseiwitsch, *Moiseiwitsch* (Eng., 1965); R. Newqvist, *Showcase* (1966), 277–86 (on Tanya). [D.L.S.]

MOISSAN, HENRI (1852–1907), French inorganic chemist and Nobel Prize winner. Moissan was born in Paris of a non-Jewish father and a Jewish mother. He joined the Ecole Supérieure de Pharmacie, where in 1886 he became professor of toxicology and in 1899 professor of inorganic chemistry. From 1900 he was professor of inorganic chemistry at the Sorbonne. Moissan's main work was on metal oxides and inorganic and organic fluorine compounds. He developed a laboratory electric furnace which he used to make artificial (black) diamonds. He was awarded the Nobel Prize for Chemistry in 1906 for his investigation and isolation of the element fluorine, and for the adoption in the service of science of the electric furnace called after him.

Moissan published his work in scientific journals and in his books, *Le Four Electrique* (1897) and *Le Fluor et ses composés* (1900); he also wrote an inorganic chemistry textbook in five volumes, *Traité de chimie minérale* (1904–06).

Bibliography: W.R., in: *Proceedings of the Royal Society*, A80 suppl. (1908), xxx–xxxvii; Ramsey, in: *Journal of the Chemical Society*, 101 (1912), 477–88; Lebeau, in: *Bulletin de la Société Chimique de France* (1935), 135–8; T. N. Levitan, *Laureates: Jewish Winners of the Nobel Prize* (1960), 30–33. [S.A.M.]

MOISSIS, ASHER (1899–), Greek author, translator, and Jewish communal leader. Born in Trikkala, Moissis became a lawyer, but soon began to take an active part in Jewish communal and Zionist affairs. In 1917 he founded the Zionist monthly *Israel* which he edited for the two years of its existence. In the early 1930s he began to publish books

Asher Moissis, Greek author and communal leader.

on Jewish subjects, particularly concerned with Greco-Jewish relations through the ages. Before World War II he wrote *Dheka pende imere ana tin Evraikyin Palestinin* ("Fifteen Days Across Jewish Palestine," 1933), *Isaghoyi is to Oikoyeniakon Dhikyeon ton en Elldi Israiliton* ("Introductory Study of the Civil Laws of the Jewish Family in Greece," 1934), and a translation of the *Autoemancipation* of J. L. *Pinsker (1933). He was president of the Jewish National Fund (1930–38), of the Salonika Jewish community (1934–36), and of the Greek Zionist Federation (1936–38). Following the liberation of Greece, Moissis resumed his communal and literary activities. He was president of the Central Council of Jewish Communities in Greece (1944–49) and, from 1948, honorary consul of Israel in Athens. He translated parts of the diaries of Theodor Herzl (1952) and the *History of Modern Hebrew Literature* by Joseph Klausner (1968). His postwar books include *I Filia Ellinon kye Evreon ana tous Eonas* ("The Friendship of Jews and Greeks Through the Centuries," 1953), *Elleno-ioudhaikye Melete* ("Helleno-Judaic Studies," 1958), and *Pion "Ellinismon" Katepolemisan i Makkavei* ("The Hellenism that the Maccabees Fought," 1962). After the Six-Day War of 1967 he wrote *Istoria kye Thrili yiro apo to Tikhos ton Dhakrion* ("History and Legend Concerning the Wailing Wall," 1968), which was translated into Italian and English, the latter by Rae Dalven. Moissis also translated into Greek verse the *Haggadah* (1970). Moissis was probably the most committed and prolific Jewish writer in modern Greece. [R.D.]

°**MOJECKI, PRZECLAW** (second half of 16th and early 17th century), Polish Catholic priest and anti-Semitic author. His principle work, *O zydowskich okrucieństwach, mordach y zabobonach* ("The Cruelty, Murders, and Superstitions of the Jews"), was the first outright attack on the Jews and Judaism in Polish political writings. The pamphlet, which first appeared in Cracow in 1589 and was later printed in 1598 (Cracow) and in 1636 (Lvov), was dedicated to Prince Janusz Ostrogski—a newly converted Catholic—in the hope of convincing him to support the expulsion of the Jews from Poland. The author gives 25 stories of *blood libels from various countries and nine from Poland. Mojecki complains that Jewish trade finally results in the depletion of the country's resources in waste and corruption because of the encouragement of luxury, and that the Jews are not under the jurisdiction of the authorities of the towns in which they live. Moreover, Mojecki is of the opinion that the Jews are traitors to Poland and spy for the Turks, the Tatars, and the rulers of Moscow. The author attempts to convince his readers that God rewards those who persecute and expel the Jews and commends the measures adopted by the kingdoms of France, Spain, and Germany toward the Jews. This work, which was influenced by German and Italian anti-Semitic literature, was influential in the propagation of anti-Semitic ideas in Polish literature of the 17th century.

Bibliography: K. Bartoszewicz, *Antysemityzm w literaturze polskiej XV–XVII w.* (1914), 40–50; S. Dubnow, *Divrei Yemei Am Olam*, 6 (1958[6]), 161–2. [A.Cy.]

MOK, MAURITS (1907–), Dutch poet. Born in Haarlem, the son of a small trader who was unable to give him a secondary education, Mok started work as a clerk in a diamond firm, but soon left to devote himself to writing. He translated many books, and was art critic for the daily *Algemeen Handelsblad*. Although he wrote a number of novels, including *Badseizoen* (1934) and *Figuren in het zand* (1939), he gained importance chiefly as a poet. Mok belonged to the "Amsterdam School"—a group of poets associated with the periodical *Criterium*. His early verse was of epic character but after World War II it became mainly lyrical. His central themes are the Bible, social involvement, the rising threat of Hitlerism, and, later, grief for those who never returned. His early poetry includes *Exodus* (1938), *Kaas- en Broodspel* (1938), and *Scheppingsdroom* (1940). While in hiding during World War II, he published, under the pen name of Hector Mantinga, the poem *De zeven hoofdzonden* (1942). Mok's postwar poetry—"poetry of silence," as one critic called it—deals with the fate of murdered friends and relatives. It includes *Het wankel hart* ("The Wavering Heart," 1946), *Silhouetten* (1948), and *Aan de Vermoorden uit Israël* ("To the Murdered of Israel," 1950). His later epic verse does not match the quality of his early work. In the collection *Gedenk de mens* (1957) and in *Achtergrond* (1965) mourning gives way to an acceptance of life. A selection of his verse appeared in 1967 under the title *Stadiën*.

Bibliography: E. Hoornik, *Tafelronde* (1940); A. Donker, *Hannibal over den Helicon* (1940). [G.A.-T.]

MOKADY, MOSHE (1902–), Israel painter. He was born in Tarnow and in 1914 moved with his family to Vienna where he studied art under Lazar Krestin. He also

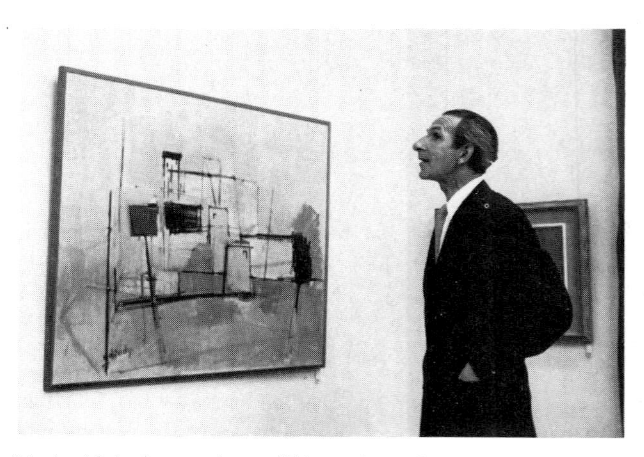

Moshe Mokady at a show of his works at the Tel Aviv Museum, 1958. Courtesy Government Press Office, Tel Aviv.

studied painting and music in Zurich from 1916 until 1920 when he emigrated to Palestine. During a five-year stay in Paris (1927–32), Mokady was influenced by the Jewish expressionism of the Paris School. His portraits in the 1930s are examples of this style. In his later work he developed an unusual treatment of colors, combining them in ways which conformed to the rhythm of the pictures. His stark landscapes led to abstract paintings based on a simplified relationship among shapes. In 1949 Mokady was appointed artistic adviser to the Ministry of Education and Culture in Jerusalem, and in 1952, director of the Avni Institute of Painting and Sculpture in Tel Aviv. [Y.Fi.]

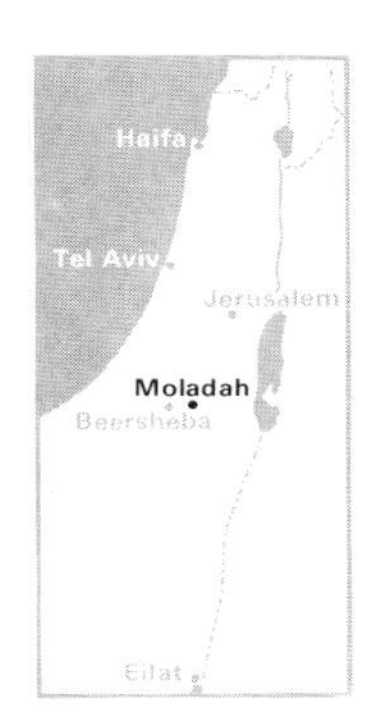

MOLADAH (Heb. מוֹלָדָה), city in the Negev of Judah, described in Joshua 19:2 and I Chronicles 4:28 as a town of the tribe of Simeon, and in Joshua 15:26 as a town of the tribe of Judah in the Negev, near Beer-Sheba. It is among the cities listed in Nehemiah 11:26, apparently settlements which endured through the Babylonian Exile. The commonly proposed identification with the Malatha of Josephus (Ant., 18:147) and the Malaatha of Eusebius (Onom. 14:3; 88:4; 108:3) is baseless. Khirbat al-Waṭan, approximately 8 mi. (13 km.) east of Beersheba, has been suggested as a possible identification. Pottery found on the site dates from the Iron Age. The Arabic name may be a translation of the Hebrew (both Ar. *waṭen* and Heb. *moladah;* "birthplace").

Bibliography: Abel, Geog, 2 (1938), 391–2; EM, s.v. (incl. bibl.); Press, Ereẓ, s.v.; Avi-Yonah, Geog, index. [M.A.-Y.]

MOLCHO, SOLOMON (c. 1500–1532), kabbalist and pseudo-messiah. Born in Lisbon of Marrano parents, he was originally called Diogo Pires. Though details on his early life are scarce, it is clear that he received a secular education, and at the age of 21 was appointed secretary to the king's council and recorder at the court of appeals. It is probable that Molcho secretly studied the Kabbalah. On meeting David *Reuveni after the latter's arrival in Portugal in 1525, he asked to be circumcised. Reuveni dissuaded him but, undeterred, Molcho circumcised himself and took a Hebrew name. While the symbolic meaning of the name is obscure, some scholarly opinion takes it as referring to Molcho's spiritual kinship with Reuveni (the name Molcho deriving from the Hebrew *melekh*="king"). Reuveni suggested to Molcho that he flee, while he himself was forced to leave Portugal because of the suspicion that he had had a part in Molcho's conversion. The details of Molcho's flight are uncertain. Reuveni later claimed that he had sent him on a mysterious diplomatic mission to Turkey; Molcho himself stated that a divine command had directed his departure. His destination is also somewhat obscure. There are those who claim that he spent some time in Italy, Jerusalem, Safed, Damascus, and even Constantinople. All authorities agree, however, that he settled for a period in Salonika where he studied Kabbalah in the *bet ha-midrash* of Joseph *Taitaẓak. There he probably met R. Joseph b. Ephraim *Caro, whose writings reflect his admiration for Molcho. In Salonika Molcho gathered disciples and students who prevailed upon him to publish a collection of his sermons which are filled with expectation of coming redemption, *Derashot* (Salonika, 1529). In later editions the work is entitled *Sefer ha-Mefo'ar*. In the sack of Rome in 1527 he saw the signs of the coming redemption, and returned to Italy in 1529 and began to preach about it in Ancona. His sermons attracted many people, including

Banner allegedly carried by Solomon Molcho on his mission to Emperor Charles V at Regensburg in 1532. Prague, State Jewish Museum.

Christians. The accusations of an informer that he was a Marrano who had reverted to Judaism caused him to flee to Pesaro and eventually to Rome. By then Molcho had become convinced that he was indeed the Messiah. In fulfillment of the talmudic legend (Sanh. 98a) that recounted the suffering of the Messiah, Molcho, dressed as a beggar, sat for 30 days, tasting no meat or wine, among the sick and the infirm on a bridge over the Tiber by the pope's palace.

Molcho succeeded in gaining the confidence of Pope *Clement VII, who granted him protection (1530). His standing was further strengthened when his prophecies of a flood in Rome (1530) and an earthquake in Portugal (January 1531) came true. He preached widely and was successful in preventing the spread of the Inquisition to Portugal. He left Rome for Venice at the end of 1530 for an unsuccessful meeting with Reuveni. Attempting to mediate in a dispute between Jacob *Mantino, the pope's physician, and Elijah *Ḥalfon, kabbalist and physician, Molcho succeeded only in arousing the enmity of Mantino. Molcho fled to Rome and a friendlier atmosphere, but Mantino, seeing danger in Molcho's activities, followed him and intrigued against him. Molcho was accused by an inquisitional court of judaizing and was condemned to be burned at the stake. He was saved by the personal intervention of the pope and another man was burned in his place. In 1532 Molcho left for northern Italy, where he again met with Reuveni. Together they went on a mission to Emperor Charles V who was then at Regensburg. Although the nature of their mission to Charles is somewhat speculative, R. *Joseph (Joselmann) of Rosheim records in his memoirs that Molcho came in order to rouse the emperor to call upon the Jews to fight against the Turks. However, Charles brought Molcho to Mantua, where he was tried and burned at the stake in late 1532 after refusing to recant and convert to Christianity. Many Jews and Marranos in Italy, however, did not accept that Molcho had died, but believed that he had been saved once more.

The influence of Molcho was considerable both during his lifetime and after his death. R. Joseph of Orly took note of Molcho in his messianic prophecies. Already in 1531 an important messianic movement had spread under his influence and had reached Poland. Some of his belongings were saved by the Jews of Prague and displayed long after his death; his influence on Shabbateanism (see *Shabbetai Ẓevi) was not insignificant. In addition to his *Sefer ha-Mefo'ar*, Molcho left a number of letters incorporated by R. Joseph ha-Kohen in his historical writings and in *Ḥayyat Kaneh* edited by Abraham Rothenberg in 1648, and some poetry. His life and that of Reuveni were the subject of much fictional writing, such as M. Brod's *Reuveni Fuerst der Juden* (1925), E. Fleg's *Le Juif du pape* (1925), and A. A. Kabak's *Shelomoh Molkho* (1928–29).

Bibliography: A. Z. Aescoly (ed.), *Ḥayyat Kaneh* (1938); idem, *Sippur David ha-Re'uveni* (1940), 27–64, 140–83; idem, *Ha-Tenu'ot ha-Meshiḥiyyot be-Yisrael* (1956), 266–78; 365–412; R. J. Z. Werblowsky, *Joseph Caro: Lawyer and Mystic* (1962), 97–99; Scholem, Shabbetai Zevi, index: R. Joseph Caro, *Maggid Yesharim* (Amsterdam, 1644); A. H. Silver, *A History of Messianic Speculation in Israel* (1927), 133–5, 147–50; D. Kaufmann, in REJ, 24 (1897), 121–7; Vogelstein-Rieger, 2 (1895), 53–58; S. Stern, *Josel of Rosheim* (1965), 133–7; J. H. Greenstone, *The Messiah Idea in Jewish History* (1906), 195–202. [J.SHO./ED.]

MOLE, rodent. The only mole found in Israel is the mole rat *(Spalax ehrenbergi)*, a small mammal belonging to the order Rodentia. It is blind, its rudimentary eyes being covered with a membrane. Inhabiting subterranean burrows which it digs, it throws up the ground in a continuous series of mounds. Sometimes it builds a nest in a small mound. Into these burrows, Isaiah prophesied (2:20) a man would cast away "his idols of silver, and his idols of gold . . . to the moles and to the bats," the biblical word here for "moles," *ḥafor perot*, denoting a burrower in Aramaic (*pina* i.e., "burrower"). According to another opinion *ḥafor perot* refers to an animal which digs up fruits in the ground. In talmudic literature the mole rat is called *eishut* which, because of the damage it causes to crops, may be hunted also on the intermediate days of a festival (MK 1:4). The word *eshet*, which occurs in Psalms (58:9) in a reference to those "that have not seen the sun," has been identified by some with *eishut*, i.e., mole rats "which do not see the sun but burrow in the ground and live there" (Mid. Ps. to 58:9). In modern Hebrew the mole rat is called *ḥoled*, mentioned among the unclean creeping things (Lev. 11:29). The biblical *ḥoled*, however, is the *rat.

The identification of *ḥafor perot* with the mole rat is most plausible. However, some scholars believe that it is a kind of bat (cf. Tur-Sinai, in: *Leshonenu*, no. 26, 77ff.), and S. Lieberman holds that it is the "flying fox" (which is not found in Israel) or the fruit bat (cf. *Leshonenu*, no. 29, 132f.).

Bibliography: Lewysohn, Zool, 101, no. 135; J. Feliks, *The Animal World of the Bible* (1962), 43; M. Dor, *Leksikon Zo'ologi* (1965), 121. [J.F.]

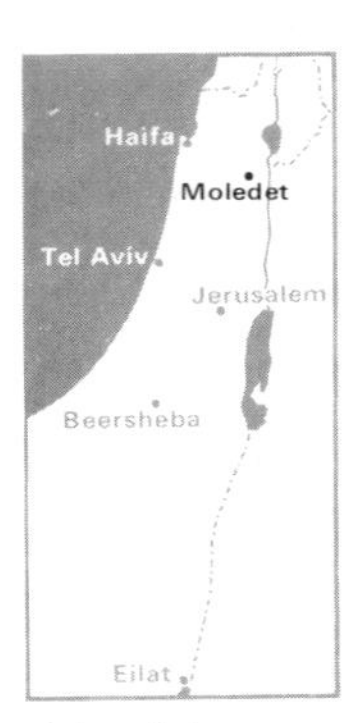

MOLEDET (B'nai B'rith; Heb. מוֹלֶדֶת (בְּנֵי בְּרִית); "Homeland"), moshav shittufi in northern Israel in S.E. Lower Galilee, affiliated with Tenu'at ha-Moshavim. Moledet was founded in 1937 by pioneers from Germany as a tower and stockade settlement, its construction being aided by the *B'nai B'rith. In its initial years Moledet had to defend itself against frequent attacks by Arabs, and in 1939 was for the most part destroyed in a conflagration. Since then, the moshav shittufi has progressed and it is based on crops, orchards, and cattle. Its population in 1968 was 340. [E.O.]

°**MOLITOR, FRANZ JOSEPH** (1779–1860), Christian philosopher and kabbalist. Born into a Catholic family at Oberursel, near Frankfort, Molitor at first studied law. Later he concentrated on research into the philosophy of history and was deeply influenced by *Schelling. His first book, *Ideen zu einer kuenftigen Dynamik der Geschichte* (Frankfort, 1805), was an evaluation of the various books of idealistic philosophy. He pursued this inquiry in his next two books, in which he established Schelling's central position although he criticized the latter's *Philosophy and Religion*. Molitor moved in liberal intellectual circles and consequently came into contact with Jews. He advocated the establishment of the Jewish school at Frankfort, later known as the Philanthropin, and was one of its first teachers. Full of enthusiasm he joined the *Freemasons and in 1808 he became a member of their "Jewish" lodge, Zur aufgehenden Morgenroethe, which he fought to have recognized. He headed this lodge in 1812, but finally succumbed to the opposition of the Masonic leaders and closed it in 1816. From the start of his activity in Jewish and Masonic circles he befriended Ephraim Joseph *Hirschfeld and was influenced by his campaign for Jewish-Christian brotherhood. Unlike Molitor's other Jewish acquaintances, who favored the *Haskalah, Hirschfeld was the first to direct Molitor's attention to *Kabbalah as a way of attaining this brotherhood. Schelling's espousal of theosophy in 1809 also influenced Molitor to explore Jewish theosophy, although he never compromised his faith in liberal Catholicism and Masonry.

Molitor's ascetic life weakened his body and he was almost completely paralyzed for over 40 years. From 1816 he concentrated on the study of Judaism and the Kabbalah but his Jewish guides, other than Hirschfeld, are unknown. He considered the Kabbalah to be that part of Jewish tradition which had preserved, in relative purity, those ultimate truths of primeval religion which tend to become more and more revealed with the progress of history. Learning Hebrew and Aramaic, he explored in depth both talmudic and kabbalistic literature. With the aim of describing kabbalistic teaching in all its depth and breadth, he devoted 40 years to this task. The four volumes of his great anonymous work, *Philosophie der Geschichte oder ueber die Tradition*, were actually intended as an introduction to the main bulk of the work, which remained uncompleted. After the appearance of the first volume (1827) he became acquainted with the philosophy of Franz von Baader, whose influence is marked in the succeeding volumes and in the second, much enlarged, edition of the first volume (part 2, 1834; part 3, 1839; part 4, 1853; part 1, in a second edition, 1857). The first volumes of his work are devoted to the principles of Judaism in the light of Kabbalah with special emphasis, in the third volume, on purity and impurity; the fourth volume emphasizes the importance of Kabbalah for Christianity.

Despite his Christian theosophic leanings, Molitor's work remains unsurpassed by any previous attempt both in speculative depth and familiarity with Jewish sources. His influence can be discerned in the work of all Christian theologians who were inspired by Baader. Molitor died in Frankfort on March 23, 1860. His admiration for the Kabbalah was ignored by Jewish researchers in the 19th century, but it may well be that the weaknesses in the historical chapters of his book led the researchers to dismiss him completely.

Bibliography: J. Katz, *Freemasons and Jews* (1970), 33–37, 58–63; R. Rocholl, *Beitraege zu einer Geschichte deutscher Theosophie mit besonderer Ruecksicht auf Molitor's Philosophie der Geschichte* (1856); C. Frankenstein, *Molitor's metaphysische Geschichtsphilosophie* (1928); G. Scholem, *Bibliographia Kabbalistica* (1927), 108–9; G. Van Rijnberk, *Episodes de la Vie Ésotérique 1780–1824* (1948), 174–91 (portrait). [G.SCH.]

MOLLER, HANS (1896–1962) and his cousin **ERICH** (1895–), textile industrialists in Ereẓ Israel. Born in Vienna and Ostrava, respectively, Hans and Erich were the fourth generation of textile industrialists. The Moller family owned the cotton-spinning mill, founded in 1865 by their great-grandfather, Simon Katzau in Babi (Bohemia). They both went to Palestine in 1933 and in 1934 founded Ata Textile Company at Kefar Ata. They finally settled in Palestine in 1938. This was the first integrated cotton, spinning, weaving, dyeing, and finishing plant in the country, manufacturing and retailing ready-to-wear clothing and supplying the Allied forces in the Middle East during World War II. Originally a family business, Ata became a public company. In 1967 it had 1,861 employees. In 1948 a subsidiary company, Kurdaneh Textile Works Ltd., was founded. Erich left Ata in 1949 to build Moller Textile Ltd., a spinning, twisting, and dyeing plant in Nahariyyah. Both plants have made major contributions to Israel export. [K.GR.]

MOLNÁR, FERENC (originally **Neumann**, 1878–1952), Hungarian playwright and novelist. Born in Budapest, Molnár's first novel, *Az éhes város* ("The Hungry City," 1900) was an historical picture of Budapest, and particularly of its Jewish quarter. The children's story, *A Pál utcai fiúk* (1907; *The Paul Street Boys*, 1927), was Molnár's outstanding work. Another of his social novels, *Andor* (1918[2]), symbolized the young Jewish intellectual destroyed by the defects of his own character. During World War I Molnár was a war correspondent, and some of his experiences appeared in his *Egy haditudósíto emlekei* ("Memoirs of a War Correspondent," 1916). In Molnár's books, which brilliantly expose contemporary Hungarian social problems, the central figure is always a weak-willed Jew who makes himself ridiculous by trying to imitate his surroundings.

It was as a dramatist that Molnár was most distinguished. His witty dialogue owes much to Oscar Wilde. His ideas are sometimes fantastic, but never ridiculous. His first play was *A doktor úr* ("The Lawyer," 1902). He achieved world fame with *Az ördög* (1907; *The Devil*, 1908); the tragicomedy *Liliom* (1909; Eng. vers., 1921), *A testőr* (1910; *The Guardsman*, 1924); and *A farkas* (1912; *The Tale of the Wolf*, 1914). All these characters deal with the problems of a changing society, and the characters are, almost without exception, Jews fighting to improve their image, sometimes turning into caricatures in the process. *The Guardsman* inspired Oscar *Strauss' musical comedy *The Chocolate Soldier*; *Liliom* became the musical *Carousel* (1945), by Richard *Rodgers and Oscar *Hammerstein. Molnár also wrote lyrical, symbolic dramas. Most of his plays have been translated into English. There are two anthologies of his stage works, *Plays* (1927) and *The Plays of Ferenc Molnár* (1929, 1937[2]); and a prose anthology, *Husbands and Lovers* (1924). During the end of the 1930s, anti-Semitism drove Molnár from Hungary and he lived in France and Switzerland, but emigrated to the U.S. in 1940. His last major work, the autobiographical *Útitárs a száműzetésben* (1958; appeared in English as *Companion in Exile*, 1950).

Ferenc Molnár, Hungarian playwright and novelist. From J. Gassner, *Masters of the Drama*, New York, 1940.

Bibliography: B. Halmi, *Molnár Ferenc*... (Hung., 1929); *Magyar Irodalmi Lexicon*, 2 (1965), 263–6; S. J. Kunitz and H. Haycroft (eds.), *Twentieth Century Authors* (1942), 970f. [B.Y.]

MOLOCH, CULT OF. Evidence concerning Moloch worship in ancient Israel is found in the legal, as well as in the historical and prophetic literature of the Bible. The testimonies of the Pentateuch, which seem to be the most ancient and therefore the most reliable ones, should be divided, according to the formulation of the law, into two groups: the laws of the *Holiness Code which speak about giving or passing children (lit. seed) to Moloch (Lev. 18:21; 20:2, 3, 4) and the law in *Deuteronomy which speaks of "passing [one's] son or daughter through fire" (18:10). The author of the Book of Kings, who was influenced ideologically and stylistically by Deuteronomy, speaks about "passing [one's] son and daughter through fire" (II Kings 16:3; 17:17; 21:6). II Kings 23:10 speaks about "passing [one's] son or daughter through fire to Moloch," which actually constitutes a conflation of the formula in Leviticus with that of Deuteronomy. In all these sources there is no mention of "burning" or "sacrificing" (slaughtering) children to Moloch. These latter terms are found, on the other hand, in the prophetic sources: Jeremiah 7:31; 19:5; Ezekiel 16:21; 20:31; 23:37, 39; and one may add here Isaiah 57:5; and Psalms 106:37–38. The difference in the presentation of the Moloch worship in the legal-historical and in the prophetic sources is significant. A legislator has to be precise in his formulation and therefore his description is more trustworthy than that of the prophet or preacher who tends to exaggerate. At any rate, the fact that the legal-historical, in contrast to the prophetic-poetic, sources do not mention real burning should serve as a warning against a hasty identification of Moloch with human sacrifice. In order to understand the true nature of Moloch worship another methodological observation has to be made. Distinction should be made between human sacrifice as a sporadic deed at a time of crisis and distress, such as the holocaust of the son of Mesha king of Moab (II Kings 3:27), or as an act which serves to express an unusual degree of religious devotion as the binding of Isaac (cf. Micah 6:7), on the one hand, and the Moloch cult which was an established institution with a fixed location (the Topheth), on the other. This observation is all the more important since it undermines the prevalent opinion about the connection between the Carthaginian child sacrifices and the Moloch institution. As the classical sources have it, the sacrifices of children at Carthage usually came after a defeat and a great disaster—a religious practice based upon an ancient mythological tradition. Thus Phoenician tradition ascribed to Sanchuniaton relates that the god Elos (= El) sacrificed his son following a war which brought disaster upon the state. There is no real connection therefore between the Phoenician-Punic child sacrifices which are sporadic and conditioned by crisis and the Moloch worship which was an institution or cult.

The Name. The accepted view since A. *Geiger is that Moloch is a tendentious misvocalization of the word *melekh*, "king," the original vowels being changed and patterned after the vocalization of *boshet*, "shame," which was often used as an intentional substitute for Baal (see *Euphemism and Dysphemism). It is true that the names Moloch (I Kings 11:7) and Milcom occur in the Bible in reference to an Ammonite god, and that deities by the name Malik/Muluk are attested to from the 18th century B.C.E. onward. However, the laws and warnings against the worship of the Moloch could hardly refer to these particular deities. It is unlikely that one particular god that is not especially famous would be singled out for mention, while other prominent gods, e.g., Baal, are not mentioned by name in the Torah even once. That the original vocalization was *melekh* may be learned from Isaiah 30:33, which undoubtedly alludes to the ceremony of the Moloch rites. The fact that the Septuagint of the Pentateuch (which was the first to be translated by the Greek translators) translates *molekh* as "king" *(archon)* seems also to indicate that at the time of the translation of the Torah the reading *molekh* instead of *melekh* was as yet unknown.

A new dimension has been added to the problem of the name Moloch since the discovery of some Latin dedicatory inscriptions in North Africa. In these inscriptions the term *molchomor*—which has been equated with מלכ אמר in the Punic inscriptions, the meaning of which was also unclear—occurs in the context of a lamb offering. The context has provided a clue to the meaning of both *molchomor* and מלכ אמר. *Molchomor* has been interpreted as *molech immer,* i.e., *molech,* "sacrifice" (see below) and *ommor,* "a lamb." This interpretation, however, is beset by difficulties. First, it is hard to explain how *immer* (Aram. and Akk. "lamb") became *ommor;* no less difficult is the interpretation of *molech* as sacrifice. O. Eissfeldt argued (on the basis of Syriac) that *molech* means "vow," but this can hardly be reconciled with the biblical text. It would be futile to translate *liznot ʾaḥare ha-molekh* (לזנות אחרי המלך) in Leviticus 20:5: "to go astray after the vow." Besides, it is methodologically unsound to explain a Hebrew word in the Bible on the sole basis of a late Aramaic word. Another expression occurring in the Punic inscriptions מלכאדם, turned out to be even more crucial for the understanding of the Hebrew *molekh.* Here again some scholars understood the term as human sacrifice. However, as in the case of מלכ אמר, no objective evidence has been found for this interpretation of מלכאדם. The most plausible explanation is, as has already been suggested, that the term means "king of mankind," and is the epithet of the god to whom the inscription is dedicated. The word "king" was indeed a common attribute of the deities in the Phoenician-Punic sphere, e.g., Melkart ("king of the city," i.e., Tyre), מלכבעל, etc. El, the head of the Canaanite pantheon, later identified with Kronos, was named Malkandros (Plutarch, *De Iside et Osiride,* 16) which means "king of man" (Greek *aner* [gen. *andros*], "man"), in other words מלכאדם. This is corroborated by evidence from the Assyrian-Aramean sphere where the epithet "King" is applied to the god Adad/Hadad, who is identified with the Canaanite-Phoenician Baal—was also called "King," cf. מלכבעל—"Baal is king." Furthermore, a series of Assyrian-Aramean documents analyzed by K. Deller showed that Adadmilki or Adadšarru ("Adad the king") was actually the god to whom children, sometimes firstborn, were burned. C. H. W. Johns, who first published these documents, contended that burning is used here in the figurative sense, meaning dedication (*Assyrian Deeds and Documents,* 3 (1923), 345–6). This has been confirmed by Deller in his investigation. The Assyrian material sheds new light on II Kings 17 where Adadmelech (to be read instead of Adrammelech) is the god to whom the Sepharvites burn/dedicate their children (verse 31). Adadmelech in this verse stands next to Anammelech who has been correctly related by scholars to Anath who bears the title "Queen of Heaven," the standard term for Ishtar in Akkadian (*šarrat šamê;* cf. Sum. *nin.anna.ak=* Inanna). The pair Adad and Ishtar, or the "king" and the "queen," are the ones to whom children are dedicated in the Assyrian-Aramean documents quoted above. Adad and ʿAshtart were actually the dominant gods in Syro-Palestine until the beginning of the common era, as may be deduced from the passage preserved by Philo of Byblos (ascribed to Sanchuniaton): "Ashtart the great and Zeus Demarus who is Hadad, the king of the gods, were enthroned on the earth" (Eusebius, *Praeparatio Evangelica* 1:10, 31; cf. O. Eissfeldt, *Kleine Schriften,* 3 (1966), 335–9). Another instructive example is the second-century B.C.E. Greek inscription, found in Acre, that is dedicated to Hadad and Atargatis (=combination of Ishtar and Anath) who listen to prayer (M. Avi-Yonah, in: IEJ, 9 (1959), 1–2). As will be shown below, the introduction of the Moloch coincided with the introduction of the worship of the "queen of the heaven," although the latter persisted after the reform of Josiah whereas the Moloch cult seems to have perished following the reform. The worship of the Moloch along with the worship of the "queen of the heaven" are therefore to be seen against the background of the widespread worship in the Assyro-Aramean culture of Adad/Hadad, the king, and Ishtar Ashtarth/Anath, the queen, that began in the ninth-eighth century B.C.E. This sheds new light on the controversial passage Amos 5:26: "... You carried the canopy [Heb. *sikkut* is a deliberate misvocalization of *sukkat* or *sukkot* to make it resemble to שִׁקּוּץ; *shikkuẓ,* "abhorrence," cf. LXX and 6QD 14–17] of your king and the *kaiwanu* [changed deliberately into *kiyyun,* as *skikkuẓ*] of your image[s] the star of your god[s] which you made for yourselves." The *kamānu/kawānu,* found in Jeremiah 7:18, and 44:19, is a cultic cake in the form of a star which is the image of Ishtar, who is called in Akkadian *kakkab šamê,* "the star of the Heaven." The image of Ishtar צלמיכם כוכב אלהיכם, is depicted here as having been carried under a canopy in a procession, a procedure attested in the Assyrian documents (cf. L. Waterman, Royal Correspondence of the Assyrian Empire, 1 (1930), no. 1212, rev. 1–10; for corrected reading see A. L. Oppenheim, in: BASOR, 107 (1947), 8, n. 4), but unrecognized until now. "Your king" in this verse is none other than her consort Adad the king, sometimes identical with the sun-god Shamash.

The Nature of the Worship. As already indicated above, the legal and historical sources speak about passing children to Moloch in fire. According to the rabbinic interpretation, this prohibition is against passing children through fire and then delivering them to the pagan priests. In other words, according to this interpretation, this refers to an initiation rite. This kind of initiation or consecration is actually attested to in various cultures (see most recently T. H. Gaster, in bibl.) and the Septuagint interprets Deuteronomy 18:10 in a similar manner. That this is not just a Midrash of the rabbis, which might have influenced the Septuagint, is indicated by the fact that this tradition also underlies the Book of Jubilees which is quite ancient and in other respects contradicts rabbinic *halakhah.* The Book of Jubilees 30:7ff. connects intermarrriage or rather the marrying off of one's children to pagans with the sin of Moloch. This tradition seems to be echoed in the dissenting opinion of R. Ishmael (cf. Meg. 4:9) in *Sifrei Deuteronomy* 18, who explains the prohibition of Moloch as the impregnation of a pagan woman, an interpretation lying behind the Syriac translation in Leviticus 18 and 20. The common denominator of all these traditions is the understanding of Moloch worship as the transfer of Jewish children to paganism either by delivering them directly to pagan priests or by procreation through intercourse with a pagan woman. This tradition, which could hardly be an invention, is now corroborated by the evidence in the Assyrian documents. In the framework of the penalty clauses of some neo-Assyrian contracts there is the threat that if one of the parties violates the contract, he will burn his son to Adad the king and give his daughter to Ishtar, or Belet-ṣēri. As indicated, the scholars dealing with these texts are of the opinion that the burning has to be taken in this case in the figurative sense. This is supported by the fact that in some cases it is explicitly specified that the offender will dedicate his sons as priests to Adad and his daughters as hierodules to Ishtar. Most of the penalties in these contracts are indeed payments and dedications in favor of the gods and their sanctuaries. From the fact that Ahaz, who opened the door to Assyria and Assyrian culture and religion (see e.g., II Kings 16:6ff.), was the first king to indulge in the worship of Moloch (II Kings 16:3) it may be deduced that this was introduced through Assyrian influence along with other practices such as the burning of incense on the roofs (II Kings 23:12), the sun chariots (23:11), and the tents for the Asherah (23:7). There is no reason to suppose that the Moloch was introduced as a result of Phoenician influence, as is commonly supposed. Were this true one would expect to find the Moloch worship in Northern Israel, which was overwhelmed by Phoenician influence, especially at the period of the Omri dynasty. No allusion, however, to this practice in the Northern Kingdom has been found. The worship of Moloch, which was practiced at a special site (outside the walls of Jerusalem in the valley of Ben-Hinnom) called Topheth, became firmly established in the time of King Manasseh, his son Amon, and at the beginning of Josiah's reign. It seems to have been completely eradicated by Josiah within the framework of his reform activities (II Kings 23:10). Jeremiah's references to this worship (7:31; 19:1ff.; 32:35) apply to the days of Manasseh and also to the time of Josiah before the reform (see Kaufmann Y., Toledot, 3 (1960), 382–90).

Bibliography: Ḥ. Albeck, *Das Buch der Jubilaeen und die Halacha* (1930), 26ff.; O. Eissfeldt, *Molk als Opferbegriff im Punischen und Hebraeischen* ... (1935), 46ff.; N. H. Tur-Sinai, *Ha-Lashon ve-ha-Sefer*, 1 (1954²). 81ff.; H. Cazelles, in: DBI Supplément, 5 (1957), 1337–46; R. de Vaux, *Studies in Old Testament Sacrifice* (1964), 52–90; M. Buber, *Malkhut Shamayim* (1965), 99–100; K. Deller, in: *Orientalia*, 34 (1965), 382–6; T. H. Gaster, *Myth, Legend and Custom in the Old Testament* (1969), 586–8. [Mo.W.]

MOLODECHNO, town in Molodechno oblast, W. Belorussian S.S.R.; during the interwar period it was within Poland. The Jewish community in Molodechno numbered 251 in 1847, increasing to 1,105 (46% of the total population) in 1897. After improvement in the economic situation resulting from the construction of a railroad in 1905 the Great Synagogue was erected in 1906. Later a prayer house was built by the Ḥasidim. A government school for Jewish boys, with a special vocational department and boarding facilities was erected, but was destroyed at the time of the Polish annexation. Under Polish rule Jewish children received their education in the Hebrew *Tarbut elementary school. The Jews were mainly engaged in trade and crafts. During World War II Molodechno was occupied by the Russians; then by the Germans, who exterminated the Jewish population, with the exception of about ten persons, who had survived by fleeing to Russia or by marriage with Christians. [Z.E.]

Orchestra of the Molodechno boy's boarding school, 1894. Photo N. Neifakh, Minsk. J.N.U.L. Photo Archives.

MOLODOWSKY, KADIA (1894–), Yiddish poet and novelist. Born in Lithuania, Molodowsky received her early education from her father. She then departed for Warsaw and Odessa to prepare for a teaching career. After the 1917 Revolution she participated in the publications of the Kiev Yiddish Group but soon returned to Warsaw to teach at Yiddish schools. For her pupils she wrote playful verses, ballads, and poetic tales, some of which were set to music and sung in Yiddish schools in many lands. In 1935 Molodowsky settled in New York. Her many volumes of verse reflect her experiences in Europe, America, and Israel. She displayed her concerns for the oppressed poor, the tragedy of war, and the Holocaust. After the establishment of the State of Israel in 1948, a new tone appeared in her

Kadia Molodowsky, Yiddish poet. Courtesy S. Liptzin, Jerusalem.

work. She wrote lyrics expressing her joy at the restoration of Zion, many of which were publicly sung and broadcast in Israel. Her drama *Nokh'n Got fun Midber* ("Toward the God of the Desert," 1949) was staged by Israel's Ohel Theater in 1956, and her novel *Baym Toyer* ("At the Gate," 1967) described the fate of new immigrants, life in the kibbutz, and the forging of a nation. Other works of fiction include a novel, *Fun Lublin biz New York* ("From Lublin to New York," 1942), and a short story collection, *A Shtub mit Zibn Fentster* ("A House with Seven Windows," 1957). Among her volumes of poetry are *Kheshvendike Nekht* (1927); *Dzike Gas* (1933), *Freydke* (1935), *Ale Fentster tsu der Zun* (1938), and *Likht fun Dornboym* (1965). Poems in English translation: S. Z. Betsky, *Onions and Cucumbers and Plums* (1958); R. Whitman, *An Anthology of Yiddish Poetry* (1966).

Bibliography: M. Ravitch, *Mayn Leksikon* (1945), 122–4; E. Auerbach, in: JBA, 24 (1966–67), 97–106; C. Madison, *Yiddish Literature* (1968), 319–20. [S.L.]

MOMBERT, ALFRED (1872–1942), German poet. The son of a prosperous Jewish physician of Karlsruhe, Mombert practiced law at Heidelberg from 1900 to 1906. Thereafter he traveled widely, absorbed many literary influences, and devoted himself entirely to poetry. He led a solitary life and associated with only a few close friends, notably Martin *Buber, the poet and novelist Hans Carossa, and his biographer, Richard Benz. Mombert was a forerunner of German expressionism, and an ecstatic lyricist who sought, not altogether successfully, to transmute mystical visions into comprehensible verbal images. When *Tag und Nacht*, his first volume of lyrics, appeared in 1894, the German poet Richard Dehmel detected in him the fervor of the ancient Hebrew prophets. Others saw in Mombert a German counterpart of William Blake. The titles of his early publications are eloquent: *Der Gluehende* (1896); *Die Schoepfung* (1897); *Die Bluete des Chaos* (1905); and *Der Sonne-Geist* (1905). His creative zenith was reached with a dramatic trilogy in free verse entitled *Aeon* (1907–11). He also published *Der Held der Erde* (1919) and *Atair* (1925). Mombert was arrested by the Gestapo in October 1940, together with the surviving Jews of Heidelberg, and transported to the Nazi concentration camp of Gurs in France. Following the intercession of non-Jewish admirers, he was allowed to leave for Switzerland after a year; but his health had been undermined and he died a few months later. Mombert's last work, *Sfaira der Alte*, was published in part in 1936; the full text appeared posthumously in 1958.

Bibliography: R. Benz, *Der Dichter Alfred Mombert* (1947); M. Buber, in: G. Krojanker (ed.), *Juden in der deutschen Literatur* (1922), 113–20. [S.L.]

MOMENT, DER, Yiddish daily newspaper in Poland. The paper was founded in Warsaw in November 1910 by Ẓevi Hirsch *Prylucki. Working with him was his son, Noah *Prylucki, and Hillel *Zeitlin. *Der Moment* became one of the most influential of the Jewish dailies of Poland, with a circulation of about 30,000, although that figure was far exceeded in times of tension: during the *Beilis blood libel proceedings, 1911–13, it reached a circulation of 150,000, and shortly before World War II it printed 60,000 copies daily.

In 1914 *Der Moment* published its first dispatches from Ereẓ Israel; its contributor was Izhak *Ben-Zvi. The Russians suspended the paper in July 1915, but 18 days later the invading Germans allowed it to continue under censorship. During the Warsaw municipal elections of 1916, the paper backed the *Folkspartei. Prominent among the paper's contributors after the war were Hirsh David *Nomberg, Julius *Schwalbe, Ignacy *Schiper and from 1925 Isaac *Schwarzbart. In 1936 the paper became a cooperative, and two years later was taken over by a syndicate which adopted a Revisionist policy. It printed Vladimir Jabotinsky's article "The Eleventh Hour" in 1938 and also his series *"Fun Mayn Tagebukh."* The publication of *Der Moment* was discontinued in September 1939 with the Nazi invasion of Poland. [A.Fi.]

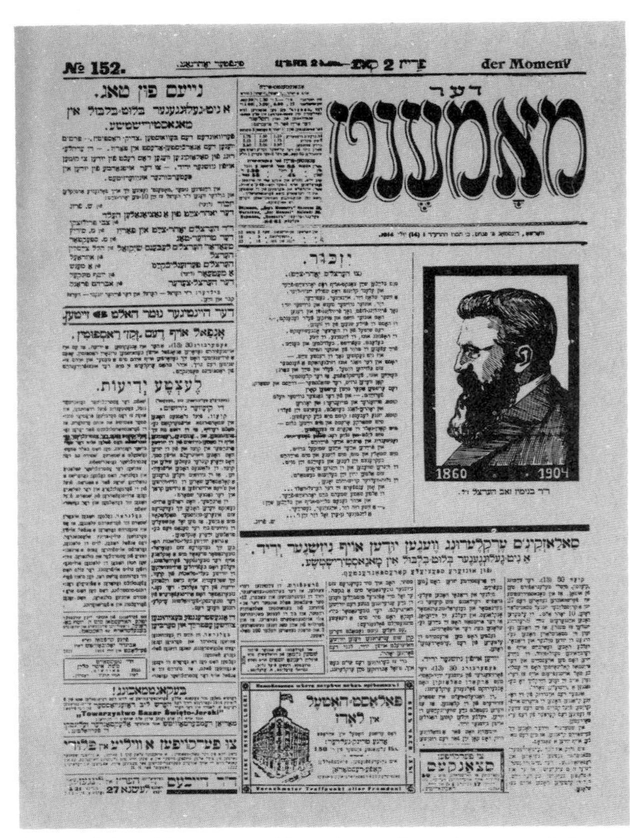
№ 152.

der Moment

דער

מאָמענט

נייעס פון טאג.

א ניט-געלונגענער בלוט-בלבול אין מאָאַסטרישטשע.

יזכור.

1860 1904

Issue of *Der Moment,* marking the tenth anniversary of Herzl's death, July 14, 1914. Jerusalem, J.N.U.L.

MOMIGLIANO, ARNALDO DANTE (1908–), historian of antiquity; born in Caraglio (Cuneo), Italy. After the Italian anti-Semitic legislation of 1938 he settled in England, where in 1951 he became professor of ancient history at University College, London. Momigliano wrote, in Italian, books on Thucydides, Claudius, Philip of Macedon, as well as works on classical historiography. His best-known English books are *Conflict Between Paganism and Christianity in the Fourth Century* (1963), and *Studies in Historiography* (1966). One of his earlier works, *Prime Linee di Storia della Tradizione Maccabaica* (1930, 3d ed. 1968), was an impressive contribution to Jewish history of the Hellenistic and Roman periods. Also notable were his *Ricerche sull' organizzazione della Giudea sotte il dominio romano* (1934, 1967) and his chapters on the Second Temple period in the *Cambridge Ancient History*. A comprehensive bibliography of Momigliano's works is included in his *Quarto contributo alia storia depli studi classici e del mondo antico* (pp. 669–719). [Be.S.]

MOMIGLIANO, ATTILIO (1883–1952), Italian literary critic and historian. Momigliano was professor of Italian literature at the universities of Catania, Pisa, and Florence. After 1938 he was forced out of academic life by Mussolini's racist legislation and settled in Florence, where he continued to write under the pen name of Giorgio Flores. He returned to his teaching post following the liberation. Momigliano has been called "an attentive and subtle impressionist of criticism." He was remarkably alive to the most delicate vibrations of poetry, reconstructing character motivation and presenting the results of his diligent reading in a calm and lucid prose. Though skillful in bringing out detail in texts ranging from Dante's *Divina Commedia* to Tasso's *Gerusalemme Liberata,* he nevertheless failed to appreciate a literary work as a whole and lacked any historicist interest. The critic Luigi Russo found in Momigliano's Jewish origin an explanation for his isolation and historical detachment. A prolific writer, Momigliano published short literary essays and textual commentaries in the Italian press, all of unusual interest. His works include *Impressioni di un lettore contemporaneo* (1925); *Introduzione ai poeti* (1946); *Studi di poesia* (1938; 1948²); and *Elzeviri* (1945). He also wrote valuable monographs such as *L'indole e il riso di L. Pulci* (1907), *Carlo Porta* (1910), and *Dante, Manzoni e Verga* (1944), but his best books were perhaps those based on his knowledge and analysis of Manzoni's works: *L'Innominato* (1913) and *La vita e le opere del Manzoni* (1933³).

Bibliography: G. Trombatore, *Saggi critici* (1950), 266–75; G. Getto, *Poeti...* (1953), 138–61; L. Russo, *La critica letteraria contemporanea* (1967), index; N. Libertini, in: *Annuario dell'Istituto tecnico-statale G. Galilei di Firenze* (1966), 3–33. [L.C.]

°**MOMMSEN, THEODOR** (1817–1903), German classical scholar and historian; a vigorous opponent of anti-Semitism. A staunch liberal member of the Prussian and German parliaments and a luminary of Berlin University, Mommsen was active on behalf of Russian Jewry and consistently opposed all anti-Semitic manifestations, from the appearance of Adolf *Stoecker, the court preacher (1878), to the electoral success of Hermann *Ahlwardt (1902). He was also a prominent member of the *Verein zur Abwehr des Antisemitismus and signed the public declaration of German notables against anti-Semitism (1880). Mommsen was the sole Christian to attack his colleague, Heinrich *Treitschke, the nationalist historian and anti-Semite. Paradoxically, a passage in his *History of Rome,* in which he described the Jews as one of the elements leading to the breakdown of the Roman state and the growth of cosmopolitanism, was repeatedly utilized by anti-Semites. Whereas Mommsen took a positive attitude to the Jewish role in furthering universalism, anti-Semites viewed the passage in a contemporary, ultra-nationalist setting. Despite his liberalism Mommsen had no sympathy with the Jews' wish to preserve their cultural inheritance and religious independence. He called upon them to abandon their separateness and assimilate in a more thorough fashion; thus he shared the theoretical assumptions and principles of some conservative German leaders.

Bibliography: H. Liebeschuetz, *Judentum im deutschen Geschichtsbild* (1967), index; idem, in: VLBI, 7 (1962), 153–82; U. Tal, in: JSOS, 26 (1964), 23–41; W. Boehlich, *Der Berliner Antisemitismusstreit* (1967); L. Wickert, in: *Historische Zeitschrift*, 205 (1967), 254–94.

[M.Gra.]

MONASH, SIR JOHN (1865–1931), Australian engineer and soldier who commanded the Australian forces in the Allied armies during World War I. Monash was born in

Sir John Monash, commander of the Australian expeditionary forces in the Allied armies in World War I. Courtesy *Herald and Weekly Times*, Melbourne.

Melbourne into an immigrant family who had been printers of Hebrew books in Vienna. He was related to Heinrich *Graetz. At the university, he displayed exceptional versatility. Besides a doctorate in engineering, he graduated in arts and law, and also studied medicine. After 1900 he specialized in reinforced concrete construction, introducing this engineering technique into Victoria, Tasmania, and South Australia. Between 1913 and 1915 he was president of the Victorian Institute of Engineers. Monash was never a professional soldier. He volunteered for the Victoria militia in 1884 and was commissioned three years later. In 1900 he won a gold medal for military articles in the *Commonwealth Journal*, and on the outbreak of World War I, he had already risen to the rank of colonel in the militia. In April 1915 Monash commanded the Fourth Infantry Brigade at Gallipoli. Although the campaign was unsuccessful, the Australian and New Zealand troops under his command distinguished themselves and "Monash Valley" there was so named in commemoration of his service. He was sent to France in the following year and in April 1917 participated with the Canadian forces in the capture of Vimy Ridge. In May 1918, as lieutenant general, he was appointed to lead the entire Australian and New Zealand Army Corps (ANZACS) on the western front, and his troops played a decisive part in breaking the German lines on the Amiens front in the summer of 1918. The Allied offensive brought about the end of World War I and gained Monash a reputation as the most resourceful leader in the British army. The British prime minister, Lloyd George, described him as the only soldier of World War I with the necessary qualities of leadership. Besides numerous military decorations he received honorary degrees from the universities of Oxford, Cambridge, and London. After the Armistice, he led his ANZACS through the streets on London, and received a tumultuous welcome. He returned to Australia and resumed his engineering practice. He replanned the electricity supply in Victoria, basing it on the exploitation of huge brown coal deposits at the open cast mine fields of Yallourn, in Victoria. He was made vice-chancellor of Melbourne University. In 1930, shortly before his death, he was made a full general, the first Jew to attain that rank in any army. He wrote of his campaigns in *Australian Victories in France in 1918* (1920). Monash remained a practicing Jew all his life. He took an active part in Jewish affairs in Australia and was president of the Zionist Federation in 1928. A village in Israel, Kefar Monash, bears his name.

Bibliography: I. A. Isaacs, *Australia's Greatest Military Genius* (1937); E. Rubin, *140 Jewish Marshals, Generals and Admirals* (1952), 41–57; J. Ben Hirsch, *Jewish General Officers*, 1 (1967), 5–7; P. H. Emden, *Jews of Britain* (1943), 453–7, index; F. M. Cutlack (ed.), *War Letters of General Monash* (1934²); *The Australian* (Oct. 17, 1931); Gordon, in: *Australian Jewish Historical Society*, 6, no. 2 (1966), 69–80.

[Ed.]

MONASTIR (Serbo-Croat, **Bitolj;** Macedonian, **Bitola**), town in Yugoslav Macedonia (since 1918), near the Greek border. Monastir was situated on one of the ancient and main trade routes of the Balkans (the Roman "Via Egnatia") which went from the Albanian port of Durazzo to Salonika and Constantinople. It is therefore not surprising that Jews lived there already in Roman times. Direct evidence of Jewish settlement in this region was discovered in 1930 by a Yugoslav archaeologist, Joso Petrovic, who found at nearby Stobi a column from a third-century C.E. synagogue donated by one Claudius Tiberius Polycharmos, *pater synagogae* ("father of the Synagogue")—the chief *parnas*. Marmorstein presumes that the ancestors of Polycharmos were freemen of the emperor Claudius who had left Rome for Macedonia around the middle of the first century.

Nothing is known about Jewish settlement in Monastir in the Byzantine period. In the 12th century there were

Part of a column from the third-century synagogue at Stobi near Monastir. The Greek inscription records the part played in the building of the synagogue by the *parnas*, Claudius Tiberius Polycharmos. Belgrade, National Museum.

Greek-speaking (*Romaniot) Jewish artisans and traders in the town. More Jews arrived after the expulsion from Hungary in the 14th century. At the end of the 15th century refugees from Asia Minor and during the first half of the 16th century many Spanish exiles who came by the coast or through Salonika settled in Monastir. Throughout the Ottoman period (1382–1913) Monastir was a lively commercial center. Trade was mainly in Jewish hands (export of liqûor, olive oil, salt and salted fish, and import of wool, silk and woven cloth, copper, etc.); many Jews were tanners, silversmiths, cheesemakers, etc. In the 16th century R. Joseph b. Lev was head of the yeshivah. In the 18th century Abraham b. Judah di Buton was a rabbi of Monastir. A fire which swept through the town in 1863 destroyed over 1,000 Jewish homes and shops. A blood libel accusation was leveled against the Jews in 1900.

In 1884 there were 4,000 Jews in Monastir and in 1910, 7,000. After World War I the economic situation deteriorated considerably and many Jews left the town, mainly for the United States and Chile, while others settled in Jerusalem. The remaining Jews were impoverished and there were many unemployed and poor people who were workers, porters, and peddlers. Between the two world wars community activity was manifold and intense with growing Zionist conscience and endeavor; the leader was Leon Kamhi. In the 1930s the central Jewish bodies became aware of the acute social problems in this community and introduced vocational training courses, encouraged *halutz* youth movements and other activities, but the time was too short. This old community with its several synagogues, diverse social and cultural institutions, as well as a rich and original Judeo-Spanish folklore with some Turkish admixtures, was wiped out during the Holocaust; the approximately 3,500 Jews were deported by the Bulgarian occupation authorities, for the most part to Treblinka on April 5, 1943. In 1952 there were only one or two Jews in the town.

Bibliography: Marmorstein, in: JQR, 27 (1936/37); Rosanes, Togarmah, 1 (1930), 152–3; 2 (1938), 41, 59; M. Luria, *Study of the Monastir Dialect of Judeo-Spanish* (1930), 1–9; *Jevrejski Kalendar za godinu 5713* (1952), 189–95.

[Z.Lo.]

MONASTYRISKA (Pol. **Monasterzyska**), city in Tarnopol oblast, Ukrainian S.S.R. Until 1772 the city was part of the Reissen province in the kingdom of Poland, and from 1772 until 1918 in eastern Galicia under Austrian rule. The Jewish community numbered 2,450 (56% of the total population) in 1890 and 2,041 (49%) in 1910. Until World War I the community had four synagogues and an elementary school administered by the *Baron de Hirsch Fund. After the war the number of Jews decreased to 1,168 (39% of the total) in 1921, and 1,488 in 1931). [Ed.]

Holocaust Period. By 1939 the number of Jews had grown again and was close to 3,000. During the period of Soviet rule (1939–41), the activities of the Jewish community were stopped. The Jewish social services were also liquidated. The Jews tried to adjust to the new conditions and some of the youth moved to the large cities. With the outbreak of war between Germany and the U.S.S.R. (June 22, 1941), the Ukrainian nationalists began to attack the Jews. These attacks intensified after the Soviets withdrew from the city at the end of June. On July 13 hundreds of Jews deported from Hungary were brought to the city. In March 1942 the Jews of Kopyczynce and Koropiec were brought to the city. At the beginning of October an *Aktion* was carried out and hundreds were sent to the *Belzec death camp. At the end of October, the Jews of Monastyriska were transported to Buczacz, where they perished together with the Jews of this city. Jewish life in the town was not revived after the war.

[Ar.W.]

Bibliography: B. Wasiutyński, *Ludność żydowska w Polsce w wiekach XIX i XX* (1930), 120, 130.

MONATSSCHRIFT FUER GESCHICHTE UND WISSENSCHAFT DES JUDENTUMS, learned monthly publication which appeared in Germany for 83 years between 1851 and 1939. The *Monatsschrift* was founded by Z. *Frankel, while he was still rabbi at Dresden, to serve as the organ of what was called the "positive-historical school" in Jewish life and scholarship, which took up a middle position between Reform as represented by A. *Geiger, and Orthodoxy as interpreted by S. R. *Hirsch and A. *Hildesheimer. This type of Judaism, conservative in its approach to Jewish observance and ritual but undogmatic in matters of scholarship and research, was taught at the Jewish Theological Seminary at Breslau, founded in 1854 with Frankel as head; the *Monatsschrift* was intimately though not formally connected with this Seminary and drew its editors and contributors mainly from the ranks of its lecturers and alumni. Frankel remained the editor of the *Monatsschrift* until his death in 1868. In the post-revolutionary years after 1848, Frankel had hoped to stem the growing indifference of the younger generation to Jewish values by spreading the scientific knowledge of the Jewish past, thus reviving Jewish consciousness and self-respect. Frankel hoped, in particular, to influence the younger generation of rabbis who had turned their back on traditional learning. In time, the *Monatsschrift* became the Jewish world's leading journal. Frankel himself wrote about a quarter of the material published under his editorship, dealing with such subjects as the Septuagint, Jewish Hellenism, history of *halakhah,* and religious disputations in antiquity; he also wrote many painstaking book reviews. In 1869 H. *Graetz took over the editorship, assisted from 1882 to 1886 by P. F. Frankl of the Berlin *Hochschule. Graetz himself wrote mainly on Jewish history, Bible, and the language of the Mishnah. In 1887, when Graetz was 70, publication ceased for five years until M. *Brann revived it in 1892, sharing the editorship with D. *Kaufmann until his death in 1899, upon which Brann continued as sole editor. In 1903 the *Monatsschrift* found a new financial backer in the *Gesellschaft zur Foerderung der Wissenschaft des Judentums. At Brann's death in 1920, I. *Heinemann took over until his immigration to Palestine in 1938. The last volume was prepared by L. *Baeck. From Frankel to the last, the *Monatsschrift* steered, more or less, an even course. Articles ranged over the entire gamut of Jewish scholarship. The editors generally tended to avoid systematic theology and purely religious problems. Most of the nearly 500 contributors were rabbis and seminary or university lecturers from Germany, Austria, and Hungary; but there were some from other European countries, the U.S., and Ereẓ Israel. The last volume (83, 1939) of the *Monatsschrift,* a tragic and heroic monument to German-Jewish scholarship in its death throes, was confiscated and destroyed by the Nazis and only a few copies were saved; it was reprinted in 1964. Previously A. Posner had published a general index for volumes 1–75 (1938, repr. 1966).

Bibliography: D. S. Loewinger, in: S. Federbush (ed.), *Ḥokhmat Yisrael be-Ma'arav Eiropah,* 1 (1959), 529ff.; K. Wilhelm, in: G. Kisch (ed.), *The Breslau Seminary* (1963), 325ff.; L. Baerwald, *ibid.,* 351ff.

[N.N.G.]

MONCALVO, small town in Piedmont, northern Italy. The first Jewish settlers in Moncalvo arrived presumably after the expulsions from France, as it was one of the only three communities following the *Apam (=*Asti, *Fossano, Moncalvo) liturgy, which was of French origin (see

*Liturgy). The first documents attesting to the presence of Jews in Moncalvo date only from the 1570s. When Moncalvo passed to the dukes of Savoy, the situation of the Jews deteriorated. They were confined to a ghetto in 1723 and forbidden to own real estate. At that time 176 Jews lived in Moncalvo. By 1836 there were 233 and in 1860 a new synagogue was dedicated, but toward the end of the 19th century the community declined. On the eve of World War II the community ceased to exist.

Bibliography: Roth, Italy, index; Milano, Italia, index; Milano, Bibliotheca, index; Foà, in: *Scritti . . . Riccardo Bacchi* (1950), 188–201; idem, in: *Israel* (May 12, 1932); Servi, in: *Corriere Israelitico*, 4 (1865/66), 315–6; Disegni, in: *Scritti . . . Sally Mayer* (1956), 78–81 (Italian section).
[D.C.]

MONCORVO (Torre de Moncorvo), town in N. Portugal, district of Braganca. Early a center of Jewish life, Moncorvo was one of the seven provincial centers with an official rabbinical seat. Its rabbi was authorized by the crown to adjudicate all civil, criminal, and religious questions concerning the Jews of the Bragança district. Once a year the **arraby moor* ("chief rabbi") visited Moncorvo to hear appeals. During the Peninsular War of 1803–13, a large number of Conversos—who were referred to simply as Jews by the Old Christians—entered Moncorvo as refugees from the neighboring town of Vila Nova de Fozcoa, where they were persecuted for alleged sympathy with the French. Mutual recriminations between the two towns eventually developed into armed battles. The descendants of these *New Christians were still in Moncorvo in 1917, when the Polish engineer Samuel *Schwarz made contact with the remnants of Portuguese Jewry. In 1927, when A. C. de *Barros Basto proselytized among the Conversos of the Bragança district, a special community was established in Moncorvo.

Bibliography: Graetz, Hist, 4 (1967), 159; R. Way, *A Geography of Spain and Portugal* (1962), 160; M. Kayserling, *Geschichte der Juden in Portugal* (1867), 13; N. Slouschz, *Ha-Anusim be-Portugal* (1932), 68–69.
[ED.]

MOND (Melchett), British family of chemists and industrialists, of German origin. LUDWIG MOND (1839–1909) was born in Cassel, Germany. In 1859, while working at a small soda works, he patented a method for the recovery of the sulfur otherwise wasted in the process. Mond went to England where he tried to sell his patent. His process was not economical under British conditions, however, and he left for Holland. In 1867 Mond returned to England where he met Ernest Solvay (1838–1922), a Belgian chemist who had devised a process for making soda based on the use of ammonia. Mond put this process into operation when he joined Sir John Brunner (1842–1919) in founding the firm of Brunner, Mond and Company in 1873. In 1884 he developed a new process for the recovery of nickel and formed the Mond Nickel Company which is still in operation. He was a noted art collector and most of his paintings were donated to the National Gallery in London. Of his two sons, the elder, SIR ROBERT LUDWIG MOND (1868–1938), a scientist in his own right, was also a notable archaeologist, associated with the discovery of the *Elephantine papyri, and treasurer of the Palestine Exploration Fund. He was vice-president of the Friends of the *Hebrew University and leader of the British Empire's anti-Nazi boycott.

The younger son, ALFRED MORITZ MOND (1868–1930), later the first Baron Melchett, entered his father's firm. During his lifetime Brunner, Mond and Co. greatly expanded and, after merging with other companies, became Imperial Chemical Industries (I.C.I.) in 1926. Mond

Alfred Mond (center with walking stick) and his daughter with Meir Dizengoff (next to her) and Chaim Weizmann (left), Tel Aviv, 1922. Courtesy Central Zionist Archives, Jerusalem.

entered Parliament as a Liberal in 1906. He was made commissioner of works in the cabinet of Lloyd George (1916–21) and later became minister of health (1921–22). In 1924 Mond opened a debate in Parliament on the respective merits of the capitalist system and socialism and his address was considered an outstanding defense of private enterprise. In 1926, in disagreement over the land policy, he transferred his allegiance to the Conservative Party. He initiated a conference between leaders of commerce and industry on the one hand, and the workers organized in the Trades Union Congress headed by Sir Ben Turner on the other (1928). Out of this conference emerged the Mond-Turner agreement for industrial relations. In the same year he was raised to the peerage, as Baron Melchett.

Alfred Mond was not brought up as a Jew. His sole connection with Judaism in the earlier stage of his public life was that he helped to support the synagogue of Swansea, his parliamentary constituency, in order to present a more favorable picture there of the Jews and Judaism. Nevertheless, he was the butt of anti-Semitic attacks, and in consequence was won over to Zionism after the Balfour Declaration. He then became a dedicated Zionist and contributor to Zionist causes. Mond was one of the founders of the enlarged *Jewish Agency in 1929 and the chairman of its council. He acquired an estate in Ereẓ Israel in Migdal overlooking the Sea of Galilee, and a township in central Israel, Tel Mond, bears his name. Alfred Mond was married to a non-Jew and his two children, EVA VIOLET (1895–), who married the second Marquis of *Reading, and HENRY (1898–1949), second Baron Melchett, were brought up in the Christian faith but converted to Judaism after the rise of Hitler. Lady Reading was an active Zionist and president of the British section of the *World Jewish Congress. Henry, also an ardent Zionist, succeeded his father as chairman of the council of the Jewish Agency and was president of the World Union of *Maccabi. Henry's son, JULIAN EDWARD ALFRED (1925–), third Baron Melchett, was appointed chairman of the nationalized steel industry in 1967.

Bibliography: H. H. Bolitho, *Alfred Mond, First Lord Melchett* (1933); J. M. Cohen, *Life of Ludwig Mond* (1956); P. Emden, *Jews of Britain* (1943), index; W. J. Reader, *Imperial Chemical Industries; A History*, vol. 1 *The Forerunners* (1970).
[M.R.]

MOND, BERNHARD STANISLAW (1887–1944), Polish general. Born in Stanislav, Galicia, he fought in the Austro-Hungarian army during World War I. In 1916 he was taken prisoner by the Russians and released in February 1918 following the peace of Brest-Litovsk. At the end of World War I Mond joined the army of newly independent Poland and fought in the defense of Lvov against the invading Ukrainian forces. In 1920 he commanded an infantry regiment against the Bolsheviks in Russia. Subsequently, Mond became commander of Vilna. At the outbreak of World War II, he commanded an army corps with the rank of major-general. After the fall of Poland Mond was taken prisoner by the Germans and died in a prisoner-of-war camp. [Ed.]

MONDAY AND THURSDAY (in Heb. *Sheni va-Ḥamishi*, "the second and fifth [day of the week]"), those days on which the liturgy of the morning service includes additional penitential and supplicatory prayers (among them the long **Taḥanun*). On these days in ancient times villagers came to town for marketing and attending law courts. Pious Jews also fast on Monday, Thursday, and again on the Monday following the first Sabbath of the new month after *Passover and *Sukkot. These three days are known as *"Behab"* (see *Fast Days, and *Shovavim Tat). Some ultra-pietists make voluntary fasts every week on these days. The morning service on Mondays and Thursdays also includes a reading from the Pentateuch. Three persons are called up to the reading, but only the first part of the weekly portion of the following Sabbath is covered in the reading (see *Torah, Reading of).

Bibliography: Elbogen, Gottesdienst, 76–77, 155–7, 207–25; Eisenstein, Dinim, 428. [Ed.]

MONDOLFO, RODOLFO (1877–), Italian historian of philosophy. Born in Senigalia, Mondolfo began teaching at Padua (1904). He was appointed professor at Turin in 1910, and at Bologna in 1913. Because of the racial laws he lost his post in 1938 (reinstated 1944), and moved to Argentina where he was professor at Córdoba (1940) and Tucumán (1948). Mondolfo's first studies were on psychology in the 17th and 18th centuries. Next he turned to studies of Hobbes, Helvétius, and Rousseau. After his work on Lassalle (*La filosofia della storia di Ferdinand Lassalle*, 1909), Engels (*Il materialisma storico di Federico Engels*, 1912), Feuerbach and Marx (*Feuerbach e Marx*, 1919), he devoted himself to the study of Marxism, emphasizing the activistic, humanistic side as opposed to the materialistic one, as in *Sulle orme di Marx* (1919, 1948[4]) and *Intorno a Gramsci e alla filosofia della prassi* (1955). After the rise of Mussolini and the suppression of his *Biblioteca di studi sociali* in 1925, he turned to Greek philosophy and made many original contributions, especially in *L'Infinito nel pensiero dei Greci* (1934), his edition of Zeller (*La filosofia dei Greci*, 2 vols, 1932–38), and *Problemi del pensiero antico* (1936, 1961[3]). In Argentina he wrote other works on Greek thought, one on Bruno, Galileo, and Campanella, and *Problemas y métodos de la investigación en historia de la filosofia* (1949).

Bibliography: G. Morra, in: *Enciclopedia filosofia*, 3 (1957), 677–8, incl. bibl.; *Enciclopedia Italiana*, appendix, 2 (1949), s.v. [R.H.P.]

MONEY CHANGERS. Money changing was very common in the Roman Near East, where there was a proliferation of currency systems and standards. In Palestine, as in Egypt, each district had its *basilikai trapezai* ("royal bank") retained from Hellenistic times (Jos., Life, 38), and probably each village had its own money changer (cf. Sif. Deut., 306).

In the period of the Second Temple vast numbers of Jews streamed to Palestine and Jerusalem "out of every nation under heaven" (Acts 2:5), taking with them considerable sums of money in foreign currencies. This is referred to in the famous instance of Jesus' driving the money changers out of the Temple (Matt. 21:12). Not only did these foreign coins have to be changed but also ordinary deposits were often handed over to the Temple authorities for safe deposit in the Temple treasury (Jos., Wars 6:281–2). Thus Jerusalem became a sort of central bourse and exchange mart, and the Temple vaults served as "safe deposits" in which every type of coin was represented (TJ, Ma'as. Sh. 1:2, 52d, and parallels). The business of money exchange was carried out by the *shulḥani* ("exchange banker"), who would change foreign coins into local currency and vice versa (Tosef., Shek. 2:13; Matt. 21:12). People coming from distant countries would bring their money in large denominations rather than in cumbersome small coins. The provision of small change was a further function of the *shulḥani* (cf. Sif. Deut., 306; Ma'as Sh., 2:9). For both of these kinds of transactions the *shulḥani* charged a small fee (agio), called in rabbinic literature a *kolbon* (a word of doubtful etymology but perhaps from the Greek *κόλλυβος* "small coin"; TJ, Shek. 1:6, 46b). This premium seems to have varied from 4% to 8% (Shek. 1:6, et al.). The *shulḥani* served also as a banker, and would receive money on deposit for investment and pay out an interest at a fixed rate (Matt. 25:27), although this was contrary to Jewish law (see below; *Moneylending).

Thus the *shulḥani* fulfilled three major functions: (a) foreign exchange (b) the changing of large denominations into small ones, and vice versa, and (c) banking. Three terms for "money-changer" are found in the New Testament: (a) *kermatistēs* (John 2:14) (b) *kollybistēs* (Matt. 21:12), and (c) *trapezitēs* (literally, *shulḥani;* Matt. 25:27, et al.). It seems probable that these three terms correspond to the three functions of the *shulḥani* outlined above. Thus *kermatistēs*, from *kermatizō*, "to cut small," is one who gives small change; *kollybistēs*, from *kollybos*, changed foreign currency; while the *trapezitēs* was a banker (from *trapeza*, "table").

The *shulḥanim* in Jerusalem used to set up their "tables" in the outer court of the Temple for the convenience of the numerous worshipers, especially those from foreign countries (Matt. 21:12–13). Excavations around the Temple walls have uncovered stores or kiosks, some of which, it has been surmised, were occupied by money changers. The Mishnah states that on the 15th of Adar, every year, "tables" were set up in the provinces (or in Jerusalem) for the collection of the statutory annual half-shekel, and on the 25th of Adar they were set up in the Temple itself (Shek. 1:3). The activity of the Jewish banker, *shulḥani*, was of a closely defined nature, as his transactions had to be in accordance with the biblical prohibition against taking interest *(ribit)*. The Talmud records much information relating to his activities. An additional and interesting feature of his business was the payment on request of sums deposited with him for that purpose (BM 9:12).

Bibliography: F. Heichelheim, in: T. Frank, *An Economic Survey of Ancient Rome*, 4 (1938), 224–7, 247–8, 256–7 (bibl.); F. Madden, in: *Numismatic Chronicle* (1876), 290–7; A. Gulak, in: *Tarbiz*, 2 (1931), 154–71. [D.S.]

MONEYLENDING.

The Religious Context. Biblical Period. Deuteronomy 23:20–21 states: "You shall not lend on interest to your brother, interest of food or money or anything on which interest can be charged. You may charge interest to a foreigner, but not to your brother that the Lord, your God, may bless you in all you put your hand to in the land into which you are going, to possess it." This text has become the subject of much discussion and controversy for nearly two millennia. Within the framework of the so-called Book of the Covenant, another law on moneylending is to be found, in Exodus 23:24: "If you lend money to my people, to the poor with you, you shall not act toward him like a creditor. You must not lay interest *[neshekh]* upon him." In this verse, *nosheh* ("creditor") is philologically and semantically equivalent to the Assyrian *rašu* ("creditor"), the professional moneylender. A third pentateuchal law on interest-bearing loans occurs in Leviticus 25:35–38, in a context usually referred to as the Holiness Code: "If your brother has become poor and cannot support himself with you, you shall assist him [as] a resident alien *[ger ve-toshav]*, and he shall live with you. You shall not give him your money on interest *[be-neshekh]*, nor give him your food for increase *[be-marbit]*. I am the Lord, your God, who brought you forth out of the land of Egypt, to give you the land of Canaan, to be your God." Usually the difference between *neshekh* and *tarbit* or *marbit* is explained as a difference between interest on capital and interest on food. The passage in Deuteronomy, however, also refers to interest on food *(neshekh okhel)* and it is possible that the two codes employ a slightly different terminology.

Many attempts have been made to answer questions on the literary form and the dates of these pentateuchal laws, but during the last decades detailed study of the various Ancient Near Eastern codes from the 19th to the 12th centuries B.C.E. has enabled scholars to substantiate their opinions on the *Sitz im Leben* of the Hebrew law collections more accurately than hitherto possible. The Book of the Covenant is generally considered the oldest of the pentateuchal codes, because of the social and economic structure it presupposes. No urban life or king is referred to, and there is no organized state or priesthood. There is, moreover, ethnological evidence of many similarly primitive units, among whom all loans of money and food were given free of interest, usually up to the time of the next harvest when they could be paid back by the debtor. Such legislation could not, of course, apply to the alien *(nokhri)*, who was not a permanent resident.

In comparison, there are some similarities but also major differences between the pentateuchal law codes and their Ancient Near Eastern antecedents. The latter mirror a society much more fully developed than that of the still half-sedentary Hebrews. Thus, the *tamkarum* appears as a professional moneylender in various sections of the Code of Hammurapi, where rates of interest are specified for food as well as for money loans. Even in relatively late strata of the Bible, it is the Canaanite rather than the Israelite or the Hebrew, who is represented as the merchant or the trader. Had the nucleus of the Hebrew Codes been compiled at the time of the monarchy, they would have reflected quite different socio-economic conditions. Their literary form is of equal importance. In his *Urspruenge des israelitischen Rechts* (1934), 69ff., A. Alt distinguishes between casuistic law, characteristic of the Ancient Near Eastern codes, and apodictic law, more frequently, although by no means exclusively, found in comparable Israelitic source material. Exodus 22:24 is a mixture of both. The casuistic beginning, "If you lend money to my people . . .," which would logically be followed by a reference to the rate of interest or to the punishment to be meted out to a defaulting debtor, concludes apodictically with: "You shall not act as a creditor."

The Holiness and the Deuteronomic Codes are normally assigned to a much later date than that of the Book of the Covenant. The problem of their editing and ultimate incorporation into the Pentateuch is a difficult one, but as far as the laws on interest are concerned, all of them have elements in common, which stress, directly or indirectly, a special covenant between God and Israel and the consequent obligations of brotherhood between the members of the community. Just as biblical history with its predominantly theological tendencies has been described as *Heilsgeschichte*, much of biblical law may be classified as *Heilsgesetz*, addressing itself to the pre-state sacred institution of the 12 tribes. Moreover, Ancient Near Eastern codes do not claim divine inspiration, while all Hebrew laws are presented as having been revealed by God to Moses, even if, as in the case of the prohibitions against taking interest from a brother, no guidance is given as to judicial procedures against ruthless exploitation of the poor. The few other passages in the Bible which refer to moneylending confirm the impression that the relevant pentateuchal ordinances were interpreted by the prophets, psalmists, wisdom-writers, and chroniclers more as moral exhortations than as laws (cf. Hab. 2:6; Ezek. 18; Ps. 15:5; Prov. 28:8; II Kings 4:1–2; and Neh. 5:1–11; for apocryphal and pseudepigraphical literature, see Ecclus. 20:15; 29 and IV Macc. 2:8). Neither indignation nor pious hopes could replace the jurisdiction of established courts.

Documentary evidence of the nonobservance of these pentateuchal admonitions comes only from the Diaspora, but affords an even clearer picture of prevailing conditions. Thus, the Aramaic Papyri show that the Jews of the military colony in Elephantine lent each other money on interest at the rate of 60% per annum in the fifth century (cf. Cowley, Aramaic nos. 10 and 11). In the Tebtunis Papyri, numbers 815, 817, and 818, loans at interest between Jews are also referred to. These documents belong to the third and second centuries respectively, and reflect typical Hellenistic usage in their formulation (cf. Tcherikover, Corpus, 1 (1957)). In the talmudic period such documents would be invalid. Aristotle had expressed contempt for the taking of interest in a well-known utterance in his *Ethics* (4:3), basing his opinion on the nature of money which is in itself not subject to physical growth. In addition, on several occasions during the last few pre-Christian centuries, popular resentment against impoverishment through usury forced Greek and Roman legislators to forbid the taking of interest altogether, although enactments of this sort did not remain in force for long. Among Jewish Hellenistic writers, Philo appears to have been the first to add his own comment to Deuteronomy 23:20, by extending the prohibition about taking interest from the brother to anyone of the same citizenship *(astos)*, or nation *(homofulos)* in *De Virtutibus*, 82. He is, however, not quite consistent and keeps himself closer to the biblical text in *De Specialibus Legibus* (II, 73ff. and 122).

The Talmudic Period. After the destruction of the Temple, halakhists and aggadists determined the development of Jewish religious law proper, at least until the 17th century. The tannaitic Midrash *Sifrei Deuteronomy* 23:20f. understands *la-nokhri tashikh* as a positive commandment; i.e., you shall lend at interest to a foreigner. Although this is possible on philological grounds, heavy oppression under Roman rule in the first part of the second century may have led to such an interpretation, particularly since R. Akiva was closely connected with the revolt of Bar Kokhba and with the editing of the *Sifrei*. The contemporary *Mekhilta of R. Ishmael* offers a different explanation on the related passage in Exodus 22:24. Interest-free money should be lent to Jews and gentiles alike, although a Jew should be given preference. In addition, one commentator states that it is only toward the poor that one should not act as a professional moneylender, but one may do so toward the rich. From the third century onward, the prohibition against taking interest had been accepted as applicable to every Jew, rich or poor. The *Mekhilta* on Exodus 22:24, ends with a homiletic statement by R. Meir: "He who lends on interest . . . has no share in Him who decreed against taking interest." Similar denunciations occur frequently in halakhic and aggadic Midrashim, in Mishnah, Tosefta, *baraita*, and the Babylonian and Jerusalem Talmuds. Transgressors against the ever growing injunctions are called robbers and murderers. They are likened to those who rear pigs, described as denying the fundamental tenets of the Jewish faith and declared to be unfit as witnesses. The frequency of such utterances implies the frequency of the offenses. It is to be stressed, however, against apologetic tendencies that still prevail in the relevant literature, that views of this kind refer to inter-Jewish transactions only, unless the gentile is explicitly included in the prohibition. The expression "even interest from a non-Jew" (*afillu ribbit de-goi*) implies that the difference between them is still clearly felt.

As to inter-Jewish transactions, discussions continue as to whether paid interest, fixed or unfixed, can be taken back for the debtor by the judges. Also proposed are the relinquishment of the principal and the rescinding of written contracts or *shetarot* on which interest was specified. The Mishnah (BM 5:6) says quite plainly that one may lend to and borrow from gentiles at interest. In the course of the debate in the *Gemara* (ad loc.) R. Naḥman transmits Rav Huna's objection to taking interest from anybody, but it is, apparently again for apologetic reasons, generally overlooked that his view is challenged by Rava on the basis of the Deuteronomic law and the Mishnah which precedes the *Gemara*. R. Ḥiyya replies that money may only be lent on interest to the non-Jew, as far as it is necessary for the sustenance of the Jew (*bi-khedei ḥayyav*). Ravina maintains that the reason for this restriction is based on religious self-protection. The lender should reduce his contact with the alien to a minimum, lest he learn from the debtor's deeds (*shema yilmad mi-ma'asav;* see also Rashi on Mak. 24a, s.v. *afillu le-akkum*). The Jewish scholar, on the other hand, is allowed to take interest from non-Jews, even where there is no economic necessity, because he would not be influenced by the practices of the latter.

There is one further aspect regarding moneylending at interest in talmudic literature which calls for attention—the regulations against the employment of a non-Jewish intermediary, a device sometimes resorted to in order to make illegal inter-Jewish loan transactions possible. A number of tannaitic traditions have a bearing on the subject (cf. BM 71bf. and TJ, BM 10c; Tos., BM 5:15). This convention has a prehistory in Roman law. Livy mentions that at the beginning of the second century B.C.E., Roman creditors had found a device (*fraus*) for collecting interest by transferring the ownership of accounts to citizens of allied states, who thus became the real or fictitious lenders without being subject to internal Roman legislation (ed. by E. T. Sage (1935), 10:18). That such evasive tactics were current among Jews of the talmudic period is evident not only from the various *halakhot*, but also from the following homiletic statement in *Bava Meẓia* 61b: "Why did the All-Merciful mention the Exodus from Egypt in connection with the law on interest? . . .The Holy One, blessed be He, answered: 'I, who distinguished between the firstborn and those who were not firstborn in Egypt, shall in future punish him who hangs his money on a gentile and lends it on interest to a Jew.'"

THE GEONIC PERIOD. This period lasted from about the seventh to the 11th centuries. During that time, the main autonomous center of Jewish life was in Babylonia, although the decisions of the *geonim* were considered binding in the remotest communities of Europe and Africa. The Jews were active as artisans, builders, merchants, and as experts in agriculture and horticulture in many parts of the new Islamic world. Yet the Koran (4:160) is the first source to accuse them of usury. Contemporary halakhic compendia offer little original material on the subject. Only one responsum of the ninth century, by Amram Gaon (*Sha'arei Ẓedek*, 1792, p. 40a), forbids any moneylending on interest, permitting only such as would come about in a credit transaction involving the exchange of money and fruit. He adds that Muslims, too, allow this according to their law. The strong anti-usury legislation of Islam as well as the almost unrestricted professional facilities then open to Jews prompted him to be stricter than the traditional rulings on Jewish-gentile money transactions. In an anonymous responsum of the tenth century, biblical and talmudic ordinances are stressed again, and it is left to the discretion of the pious to refrain from moneylending altogether.

THE EARLY RABBINIC PERIOD (c. 1000–1300). The center of Jewish life shifted toward Europe. The academies of Babylonia were gradually replaced by famous schools in France, Germany, and Spain. Monographs on the various European countries contain detailed accounts of the general and specific in their history. Two factors, however, stand out: growing anti-Jewish legislation and the development of the feudal system with its demand for a Christian oath on the acquisition of land. As a result, Jews were increasingly cut off from landownership. Yet even in countries like Spain and Italy, where Jewish urbanization took place less rapidly than in England and Germany, the Jews themselves no longer desired close contact with the soil, although they complained more and more about the shrinking opportunities to support themselves. An often quoted responsum by the French 11th-century scholar, Joseph b. Samuel Tov Elem *Bonfils, illustrates the change. Leah, the questioner, expresses dissatisfaction with the fact that taxes for which the community was responsible to the government were evenly distributed among the Jewish owners of fields and among merchants and traders. She is assessed for the ground she holds and for the crops it yields. In addition, the rulers of the land take their share from it. In contrast, money lent on interest is profitable, because the pledge remains in the hand of the creditor, and the principal increases without effort or expense. Joseph Tov Elem agrees with Leah's arguments against those who wish to assess her (cf. Responsa of Meir of Rothenburg, 1895, no. 941). Generally it must be said that early medieval rabbinic legislation cleared the path for a great variety of gentile-Jewish and inter-Jewish money transactions. Especially the authority of Jacob b. Meir Tam, Rashi's grandson, carried great weight with his contemporaries and successors. He summarizes the reasons for a number of his decisions in the following way: "Today people usually lend money on interest to gentiles . . . because we have to pay taxes to the king and princes and everything serves to sustain ourselves [*kedei ḥayyenu*]. We live among the nations and it is impossible for us to earn a living unless we deal with them. It is, therefore, no more forbidden to lend at interest because 'one might learn from their deeds' than it is to engage in any other business" (cf., e.g., Tos., BM 70b, 71b and Av. Zar. 2a).

Menahem b. Solomon Meiri, an eminent 13th-century scholar, gives an account of the position in Provence: "In our days nobody cares about refraining from business dealings with and loans to gentiles, even on their festivals—not a *gaon*, not a rabbi, not a scholar, not a pupil, not a *ḥasid* ["pious man"], and not one who pretends to be a *ḥasid*. All these laws refer only to idolators and their images, but all transactions with Christians are perfectly legal." Meiri coined a special phrase for this group: "nations who are restrained by the paths of their religion" (cf. J. Katz, in: *Zion*, 18 (1953), 18ff.). He thus differs implicitly or explicitly, with most of his predecessors, including Maimonides. Only the Ḥasidei Ashkenaz, German-Jewish pietists and some Spanish kabbalists of the beginning of the 13th century, viewed the new development with anxiety and disfavor. According to them, interest should not be charged to gentiles if a living could be made from the fields, although they no longer ventured to state this in terms of a legal prohibition. Contemporary Jewish commentators on the Bible follow the same distinctions as halakhic literature. In addition, they reflect full awareness of Christian polemics against the ever increasing number of Jewish moneylenders. David *Kimḥi of Narbonne says the following about Psalms 15:5: "...the Hebrew must not overreach or rob the alien or steal from him, but interest which he takes by full agreement [with a non-Jewish lender] is permitted...If the gentile is kind to the Jew, the Jew must certainly be kind and good to him..." He adds explicitly that his views should serve as an answer to those Christians who maintain that David did not distinguish between the Israelite and the gentile.

Meir b. Simeon's only partly edited manuscript (Parma 2749) *Milḥemet Mitzvah* ("Obligatory War") contains by far the richest source material on Jewish-gentile moneylending transactions. His attempts to defend old and established practices show greater knowledge of former privileges granted by popes, emperors, and feudal lords than that of any of his predecessors, and he makes the widest possible and often ingenious use of practically all biblical and talmudic data on the subject. One or two generations older than David Kimḥi and also from Narbonne, he had frequent discussions with the lower and higher clergy, including two archbishops, the second of whom was probably Guido Fulcodi, who later became Pope Clement IV.

It was on this occasion that Meir was confronted with the same accusations about gentile disadvantages in Jewish law as those which had been made in the famous Paris disputation in 1240 at the palace of Louis IX. No Latin record of his disputation appears to be extant, and it is doubtful whether he could have said all he wrote down in the diary of his public activities. The whole historical background of his time is unfolded in his work—anti-Jewish legislation, persecutions, expulsions, and his able and often successful efforts to counter them. His sharp criticism of the release of interest and sometimes even of the principal, owed to Jews by the Crusaders, is of special significance. Fearless defense and daring attack are often juxtaposed. Thus, Joseph b. Nathan ha-Mekanne *Official, a contemporary and fellow-citizen of Meir b. Simeon, refutes the attacks against Jewish moneylending with the by now usual arguments, and subsequently adds: "You lend money at high rates ... of 100% ... and take reward for delayed payment" (Z. Kahn, in: *Birkhat Avraham ... Berliner* (1903), 89).

Jewish moneylenders in England acted, as far as one can judge from their documents, in exactly the same way as those on the continent—i.e., in accordance with the ordinances of the sages *(ke-tikkun ḥakhamin)*, even if there are certain peculiarities which seem to be influenced by non-Jewish legal practice. Thus, *ribbit* ("interest"), unless used in connection with *ribbit al yedei goi* ("inter-Jewish interest charges, made possible through a gentile proxy"), occurs only four out of about 30 times in M. D. Davis' *Hebrew Deeds* (1888). Instead of *ribbit, shevaḥ* ("profit") is used. In some inter-gentile promissory notes, too, the expression *lucrum* ("gain") is found for *fenus* ("usury"). There is also the sudden emergence of the formula "if the stipulated time for repayment of the loan is over" *(im ya'avor zeman)* in Hebrew *shetarot* ("promissory notes" see *Shetar*) of English provenance. According to talmudic law, there is no justification for this, but contemporary regulations of civil and canon law had adopted the Roman concepts of *lucrum cessans* and *damnum emergens*. They may well have found their way into inter-Jewish transactions, although still under the proviso that creditor A allow creditor B to borrow from a gentile, to indemnify the lender against damage or loss of gain.

In Spain, too, similar practices, perhaps even without the gentile intermediary, seem to have become customary during the 13th century, as is known from a responsum by Solomon b. Abraham Adret (ed. Hanau, 1600, 172b). He declares such convention to be forbidden, but adds that, strictly speaking, we have in this case to deal with a penalty *(kenas)* and not with interest. Officially, at least, Max Weber's distinction between *Binnen-* and *Aussen-Moral* retained its validity in talmudic and rabbinic law. Similar Christian differentiations between the "brother" and the "other" can be traced back to the Church Father Ambrose of the fourth century. According to him, the Jew must be loaded with such a burden of usury that by the very punishment of the charges imposed upon him, he is compelled to move more quickly toward righteousness (*De Tobia*, 1, Migne, P. L. 14 (1845), 799; and T. P. McLaughlin, *Medieval Studies*, 1 (1939), 92, 137).

THE LATE RABBINIC PERIOD (c. 1300–1600). The Jewish analogue of this position was expressed by the 14th-century French philosopher and exegete, *Levi b. Gershom, who also holds that it is a positive commandment to lend money to an alien on interest, "if he needs it ..., because one should not benefit an idolator ... and cause him as much damage as possible without deviating from righteousness," i.e., without demanding from him exorbitant rates of interest (see his commentary on Deut. 23:21). Such sentiments are extreme, though not isolated (cf. R. Tam on BM 70b and Maimonides' uncensored comment on Av. Zar. chs. 3 and 4). Sometimes the passion of the spirit gave way to the demands of economic necessity, and periods of quasi-normal business relationships between believers and non-believers interrupted the cold or actual war between them. More often the force of faith, never quite unconnected with the relatively high proportion of Jewish moneylenders, broke through and led to their persecution and expulsion. An ultimate judgment on the priority of powers which determine political and ideological reality remains difficult, if not impossible. The situation differed from country to country, from province to province, and even from town to town. Yet an analysis of the uneven and widely dispersed Jewish and Christian source material, ranging from the 14th to the 17th centuries, reveals an astounding development from unyielding medieval thought patterns to their integration with new economic theories, and leads almost to a breakdown of denominational barriers.

In his *Ikkarim*, the Spanish philosopher Joseph *Albo declares that the "brother" in the Deuteronomic law refers to everyone who is not an idolator. Interest is, therefore, only to be taken from one who belongs to the "seven nations of old"—for instance, from an Amorite or Amalekite: "If it is permitted to take his life, surely one may take his property" (*Im gufo muttar mamono kol she-ken*; ed. Husik, 3 (1946), 237). Albo's words are an almost literal translation of Ambrose's *"ubi enim jus est belli, ibi est usurae"* (cf. also Plato's *Laws*, 10:909). In a position of defense vis-à-vis the archbishop of Narbonne, Meir b. Simeon had advanced a similar argument. Albo's statement is not part of the public disputation in Tortosa (1413) in which he was one of the Jewish spokesmen, but a record of another encounter with a Christian opponent. It is clear, however, that he did not refer to current halakhic practices, although some talmudic proof texts can be found in their support. Other Jewish writings, not concerned with interdenominational altercations, do not question the legality of charging interest from gentiles. Thus, Joseph Colon, who came from France and held a distinguished position in the Italian rabbinate during the second part of the 15th century, states casually that the Jews of both countries hardly engaged in any other business (Resp. Maharik 118, 132). Abraham b. Mordecai Farissol (1451–1526) confirms Colon's assessment of circumstances prevailing in Italy. Conditions of this kind were bound to bring about irregularities, but they were not restricted to Jews. Early propaganda of the Franciscans was, in fact, not specifically directed against the Jews. *Hebraei et Christiani usurarii* were the target of Bernardino da Feltre.

The establishment of Jewish loan banks was subject to a license of the papal administration or of the local rulers or of both. The stipulations of these *condotte* varied from time to time and from place to place. They were often changed unexpectedly, and as a result the insecurity of the Jewish moneylender increased, however much he might have profited from an occasional boom. Matters came to a climax through the propaganda for the establishment of Christian loan-banks, the *montes pietatis*, which were originally meant to work on a nonprofit basis. Particularly during the Lenten period "the friars [*ha-doreshim*] are a strap of castigation for Israel and preach every day to destroy us . . . Their hand is heavy upon us . . . and the situation reaches a point when both body and property are endangered" (Colon, ed. princeps, no. 192).

Isaac Abrabanel's view on interest-bearing loans to gentiles is laid down in his commentary on Deuteronomy 23:21, and forms part of his elaborate exegesis of the whole book, which was completed in Monopoli in 1496 and published in uncensored form in Sabbioneta in 1551. He expounded his theories "before Christian scholars and the masters of the land." The first three of his arguments offer nothing new; only the fourth is straightforward and assailable on philological and historical grounds. At the same time, it foreshadows the general development toward capitalism, so characteristic of the 16th century: "There is nothing unworthy about interest . . . because it is proper that people should make profit out of their money, wine, and corn, and if someone wants money from someone else . . . why should a farmer . . . who received wheat to sow his field not give the lender 10% if he is successful, as he usually should be? This is an ordinary business transaction and correct. . . . Interest-free loans should only be given to the coreligionist, to whom we owe special kindness." Abrabanel sums up with an assurance to his readers that what he had said in the first three paragraphs was only meant "to promote peace. What a Jew should really believe is laid down in the tradition of the sages."

Shortly before the completion of Abrabanel's commentary on Deuteronomy, Abraham b. Mordecai Farissol had a disputation in Ferrara at the famous Palace of Ercole d'Este I, again attended by many prominent people (cf. *Magen Avraham*, ch. 73, ed. by D. S. Loewinger in: HHY, 12 (1928), 290ff.). Some of Farissol's answers also represent a definite opposition to medieval economic concepts. His formulations might well be borrowed from the views of contemporary civil lawyers. In contrast to the opinion of the canonists and of Levi b. Gershom who, like Aristotle, considered money as barren metal, a distinction is now drawn between primitive and advanced society: "After society had expanded and people began to be distinguished from one another by their views . . . there followed a new Nature and another Order. The custom of giving another person something for nothing ceased unless the person was poor. Thus, the law has developed to pay rent for houses . . . and to make loans . . . All comes for a price . . . Sometimes credit is even more important than lending an animal or a house. Hence . . . it is appropriate to give some compensation for a loan. A proof for this argument is that even the *ba'alei ha-datot* [canonists] have agreed that one may pay up to 5% for the lending of money." Farissol seems to refer especially to the *montes pietatis*, which were forced to charge a small amount for the maintenance of their administration. As to the rates of interest charged, "one need not ponder over them, because they are agreed upon by the communities who require money from the Jews. They fluctuate according . . . to the availability or scarcity of silver and gold and the demand for it."

In 1588 the physician David de Pomis published his *De Medico Hebraeo Enarratio Apologetica*, in which he set himself the task of putting on record the devoted services of distinguished Jewish doctors in the past. The book, written in Latin, also contains his views on moneylending to gentiles. His effusive flattery about the relationship between Christianity and Judaism makes it unnecessary to refer to the first part of his arguments. Only in the last paragraph of the relevant section does he return to the practical aspects of the problem: "If the Jews do sometimes take interest from Christians, it can either be maintained that they abuse the law or . . ." and here his statements are almost identical with those of Farissol, ". . . their transactions represent an official agreement between the parties concerned . . . A Jew could effect the same transaction with another Jew according to recent rabbinic authorities." One form is technically called *tarsha* and the other *hetter iska* (cf. Sh. Ar., YD 167, 177). Both concessions represent developments dictated by the general change of economic conditions. In practice, de Pomis' labored defense came late. It was Calvin who challenged the Deuteronomic differentiation between the "brother" and the "alien" on principle. According to him, interest is forbidden only insofar as it is contrary to equity and charity. Otherwise, "*nous sommes frères sans aucune distinction.*" The enunciation of his program became the decisive formula for the new spirit of capitalism.

From Otherhood to Brotherhood? From the 17th century onward, the collapse of the traditional Christian exegesis of Deuteronomy 23 is apparent in Europe and in the U.S. On the Jewish side, too, responsa on the subject become less frequent; even the records of the Council of the Four Lands have relatively little to say on the matter. The *hetter iska* (see *Usury) had opened the path to a mercantilistic interpretation of talmudic law. Nevertheless, on the readmission of the Jews to England, Manasseh Ben Israel, in his *Humble Address to His Highness the Lord Protector of the Commonwealth of England*, did not deem it necessary to revoke the ancient distinction: "For to lay out the money without any profit was commanded only toward their brethren of the same nation of the Jews, but not to any other nation" (cf. B. N. Nelson, *Idea of Usury* (1949), 73–109). In spite of occasional regressions, a gradual improvement of the position of the Jews in Western Europe became noticeable. Moneylending still remained one of their main occupations, but they also traded, sometimes simultaneously, in all kinds of merchandise, or they earned their living as craftsmen and artisans. Above all, there was the ascendancy of the Court Jew who, in spite of his fluctuating fortunes, played an important part in the economic administration of the estate of many a duke and king in peace and war (cf. H. Schnee, *Die Hoffinanz und der moderne Staat*, 6 vols., 1953–67). The Age of Reason further contributed to the disappearance of barriers between the various denominations. Although Leopold I expelled the Jews from Vienna and Lower Austria in 1670,

Joseph II issued his *Toleranzpatent* only about 100 years later.

In 1807, the ecclesiastical and lay representatives of French, Italian, and German Jewry assembled in Paris to attend a meeting that had been convened by Napoleon. Bearing the proud title, "Grand Sanhedrin," it concluded a development of 2,000 years and to many of those who had come seemed to open a new era. Two of the 12 questions they were asked concerned the problem of inter-Jewish and Jewish-gentile loan transactions. Although eminent rabbinic scholars of personal integrity were present, the answers, *Décisions Doctrinales* or, in their Hebrew version, *takkanot*, reveal neither any depth of historical understanding nor sincerity on the part of those who were responsible for their formulation. *Neshekh*, for example, is defined as a rate of interest to be determined by the *Code Civil (Code Napoléon)* of France. Such interest may be charged by one Jew from another, provided that the lender share the risk of loss and the chance of gain, and that the debtor give indemnification to the creditor in the case of *damnum emergens*. Only the poor Jew must be charged no interest at all. Gentiles, particularly those living in France or Italy, are to be considered as brothers of the Jews, and there must not be any difference between them if charity is required. Those who disregard this ordinance will be called sinners and transgressors of the law of the holy Torah. All this may, to a degree, be defensible from the standpoint of the *halakhah*, but a complete renunciation of Jewish autonomy is implied. Jews have become Frenchmen of the Israelite persuasion. The law of the State *(ḥok ha-medinah)* sets the tone and the "Grand Sanhedrin" decides accordingly (*Takkanot ha-Sanhedrin shel Paris* (1958), 56–67). Ishmael b. Abraham Isaac ha-Kohen of Modena, who also received an invitation to the Paris Sanhedrin, was too old to make the journey, but gave his answers to each question in writing. Although gentle and dignified in his reply, he disassociates himself from the views expressed in the *Décisions Doctrinales:* "To deny permission to lend money on interest to gentiles is against all exegetes, against the *Gemara*, and against the literal understanding of the Bible" (cf. J. Rosenthal, in: *Talpioth*, 4 (1950), 583).

Events of the last 150 years belied the identification of the "brother" and the "other," and in all probability the reaction of the old rabbi of Modena and those who thought like him, even at the beginning of the 19th century has not disappeared from Jewish life. The full awareness of covenantal relationship between God and Israel and Jew and Jew is still strongly felt. Until this day many Jewish banks both in and outside Israel display a notice to the effect that it is understood that business and loan transactions between Jews will be conducted according to *hetter iska* regulations.

See also *Usury. [S.STE.]

The Historical Context. The biblical injunctions against usury relate neither exclusively nor mainly to moneylending on interest. Their spirit reflects a nomadic and village society where the borrowing of goods is the norm, and moneylending the exception. Yet the so-called archives of the *Murashu house discovered at Nippur show Jews in Babylonian regions engaged in extensive financial operations. The Talmud largely treats the problem of usury and interest from the point of view of product loans, though financial operations are also dealt with in this connection. There is evidence that as Jews moved in the city life of the Roman Empire, some of them gave loans on interest.

With the development of an urban economy in the caliphate of the ninth century, the financing of the ever-growing needs of trade, of crafts, and of the state, became a pressing need. Jews financed the business of their coreligionists through participating in various ways as partners, both in financing and in profits. While some of these means of participation were actual, others were formal only, devised to evade the prohibitions on usury. In the tenth century, large-scale Jewish financiers appear, like the *Netira family, who loaned large sums to the state on interest, against the collateral of state incomes. These loans were evidently the accumulated savings of middle- and small-scale Jewish merchants, deposited with Jewish state bankers for greater income and security. When (up to the 15th century) the majority of the Jewish people lived in Islamic lands and in Christian Spain, moneylending was one of the occupations of Jews, as of other city dwellers. While in Northwestern Europe Jews first came mainly as international traders, when some of them later turned to local trade (1000 C.E.), they engaged in credit operations. The impact of the First Crusade (1096–99) on the status and livelihood of the Jews in France, Germany, and England drove them out of trade through the lack of security arising from the inimical attitude of society in general; at the same time, Jewish merchants and craftsmen were denied any share in the Christian towns and *guilds which were rapidly evolving as the only social framework for trade and crafts in those countries. This crystallized at a time when European trade, agriculture, and building were expanding and in need of financing. Ready cash—which then meant precious metals—was scarce. Available means in Christian hands were channeled into credit for merchant ventures and other relatively creative loans, in which it was also easier to formulate partnerships that evaded the stigma of usury. Under such circumstances the Church found it easy to act in accordance with the agricultural ethos of its upper strata, and to insist on the prohibition of usury. There remained the field of loans for consumption—the need for which arose in cases of illness, litigation, and unforeseen expenses—for which Christian capital was not readily available and where usury was least avoidable. Deprived of its former uses, Jewish capital entered this field, as well as granting any other possible loan. Hence among the Jews of the region between the Pyrenees and Scotland, between the Atlantic and the Elbe, usury became the main source of livelihood from about the 12th to the 15th centuries. They were not the only people to lend money on interest in that region: there were also the Cahorsins of southern France, the Catalans, and the Lombards. But religious enmity, the social separateness of the Jews, and their hateful image, combined to identify Jew with usurer in the western Christian imagination. In those countries Jews sometimes lent on a debt deed only, without surety. Medieval Hebrew sources from those regions described this kind of loan as *be-emunah* ("on trust"), a practice usually reserved for established and proved clients. Most loans were given on the double surety of a written deed and a collateral (Heb. *mashkon*). Since repayment of a loan for consumption was often difficult, the needy debtor came to hate the infidel Jewish creditor who, out of his own need, had helped him. Many anti-Jewish persecutions hence acquired an economic as well as a religious character, the instigators being no less anxious to destroy incriminating bonds than to eliminate accursed infidels.

In England the extent as well as the problems of Jewish moneylending were seen at their clearest. The most common interest rate was twopence in the pound a week (43⅓ annually), though half and twice as much were also common. There were many partnerships, often between members of the same family; this form was utilized by the extremely wealthy *Aaron of Lincoln. To supervise Jewish lending, to insure maximum tax exactions from the Jewish lenders, and to make certain that debt deeds would not be lost even in times of massacres, the *Archa system was introduced. In the 13th century Jewish moneylending was conducted through tenants of the commons and of the middle class, whose bonds were bought up, on default, by the nobility and ecclesiastical institutions. This too, aroused the enmity of the commoners toward the Jews. In 1275 Edward III passed severe anti-usury laws, at the same time exacting extremely high tallages and calling in Italian moneylenders to replace the Jews. Some of the latter turned to coin-clipping, which led in part to the total expulsion in 1290.

Though in the heterogeneous Holy Roman Empire moneylending practices varied greatly according to time and place, the history of Jewish moneylending in *Regensburg may be typical of Rhenish and south German cities. Until about 1250 the municipality was the chief beneficiary of Jewish loans; until about 1400 the nobility and clergy were the main recipients; while after 1400 knights, burghers, and artisans pawned objects for short terms, and borrowed small sums at high rates of interest. This latter situation eventually became the focus of lower-class enmity toward the Jews and contributed to their expulsion in 1519.

Interest rates in Germany fluctuated greatly in practice and even in their legal norms. Frederick II of Austria fixed the Jews' maximum interest rate at 173⅓% in 1244; in the more developed cities of the Rhineland and south Germany 43⅓% was more common, though this rate did not apply in the case of foreigners or peasants; 86⅔% was also common and acceptable. An investigation in 1676, motivated by anti-Jewish feeling, in the electoral Palatinate in western Germany, showed that an interest rate of 14.5% was honored there by the Jewish moneylenders. The Christian rulers who exploited Jews as their agents for usury—and then extorted from them a large part of their usurious gains, especially when the Jews became impoverished—used to proclaim moratoriums on the individual, partial, or total debts to Jews. The respective treasuries all profited by such measures, the best known being those of Emperor Wenceslaus in 1385 and 1390, which utterly impoverished the Jews while barely alleviating the burdens of the treasury. Likewise, total and bare-faced confiscation was often resorted to, as was expulsion, which left the field open to the Jews' remaining competitors. Because of the collateral in their hands Jewish moneylenders frequently engaged in related occupations, such as the repair and upkeep of clothes, armor, and precious objects, and in their sale when pledges were not redeemed, a frequent occurrence. Hence the rudiments of certain crafts, as well as the sale of *secondhand goods, were an integral part of this occupation. Articles regulating moneylending constituted the core of all charters issued to Jews in medieval Germany from the 12th century. They determined not only the rates of interest, but also ensured the rights of the creditor to the collateral, even if it had been stolen. The moneylender had to take an oath that he had received it in good faith and in daylight whereupon the legal owner of the collateral had to repay him the amount loaned on the pledge. This right clashed with Germanic legal conceptions, which demanded the return of the object to the rightful owner without any payment; hence the misconception that the charters allowed the Jews to act as fences.

When it became apparent in Italy that the citizens had need of cash loans, the activities of Jewish moneylenders were regulated by means of the *condotta*, conditions set out in charter treaties between municipalities or rulers and Jewish moneylenders, first signed in the late 13th century in Umbria. The interest rate varied between 15% and 25% and was never to exceed the value of the pledge. The profit of the loan-banks in 15th-century Florence was approximately 4% (see also **Monti di Pietà*).

The first privilege granted to Jews in Poland in 1264 regarded them mainly as moneylenders. However, under favorable conditions, Jews soon took part in other economic activities, so that within a century moneylending became only one of their many-sided economic functions in the Polish cities and countryside. The *Arenda system, for example, stems from a change from lending to leasing. By the end of the 16th century, Jewish trade demanded more capital than the Jews themselves possessed, so that many Jewish traders became indebted to Christians. Lending on interest between Jews was explicitly initiated and legalized there, in the institution *hetter iska*, a legal device which created a formal partnership between creditor and debtor. Interest rates inside the Jewish business community in the latter half of the 17th century were between 25% and 33⅓%, whereas the Christians loaned at 6%–10%, and interest rates between Jews and Christians ranged between these two figures. Jews also developed their own system of credit bonds—the *mamran (membranum)*—used mainly at the great fairs of Poland-Lithuania. With the rise of modern *banking, Jewish moneylending of the conventional type gradually decreased in importance, though in Western Germany and in *Alsace-Lorraine it was sufficiently widespread to be detrimental to *emancipation of the Jews during the French Revolution, and later on to influence the attitude of *Napoleon Bonaparte to Jewish emancipation. It likewise was one of the causes of the anti-Jewish *Hep! Hep! disturbances of 1819, as well as 1830 and 1848.

When Jews moved to western countries in the late 19th–early 20th centuries, moneylending was a frequent occupation, especially in the first and second generation, and the Jewish moneylender became a familiar stereotype.

See also *Economic History (in supplementary articles).

[ED.]

Bibliography: S. Stein, in: *Essays . . . J. H. Hertz* (1942), 403f.; idem, in: JTS, 4 (1953), 161–70; idem, in: HJ, 17 (1955), 3–40; idem, in: JSS, 1 (1956), 141–64; 2 (1957), 94; idem, in: JJS, 10 (1959), 45–61; idem, *Jewish-Christian Disputations in 13th Century Narbonne* (Inaugural Lecture, University College, London, 1969), 1–27; D. Tama, *Transactions of the Parisian Sanhedrin* (1807); W. Sombart, *Die Juden und das Wirtschaftsleben* (1911); Roth, Italy; J. T. Noonan, Jr., *Scholastic Analysis of Usury* (1957); R. W. Emery, *Jews of Perpignan in the 13th Century* (1959); J. Katz, *Exclusiveness and Tolerance* (1961); Baer, Spain; S. Stern, *Der preussische Staat und die Juden*, 2 vols. (1962); J. Parkes, *Jew in the Medieval Community* (1938), index, s.v. *usury;* B. N. Nelson, *Idea of Usury* (1949), index, s.v. *Jews;* L. Poliakov, *Les banchieri juifs et le Saint-Siège* (1965); M. Neumann, *Geschichte des Wuchers in Deutschland* (1865), 292–347; J. E. Scherer, *Die Rechtsverhaeltnisse der Juden in den deutsch-oesterreichischen Laendern* (1901), 185–96; G. Caro, *Sozial- und Wirtschaftsgeschichte der Juden im Mittelalter*, 2 vols. (1908–20), index, s.v. *Wucher;* M. Hoffmann, *Der Geldhandel der deutschen Juden waehrend des Mittelalters* (1910); R. Straus, *Die Judengemeinde Regensburg* (1932); idem, *Regensburg und Augsburg* (1939); idem, *Die Juden in Wirtschaft und Gesellschaft* (1964); Kisch, Germany, index; M. Breger, *Zur Handelsgeschichte der Juden in Polen im 17. Jahrhundert* (1932); W. J. Fischel, *Jews in the Economic and Political Life of Medieval Islam* (1937); Z. Szajkowski, *Agricultural Credit and Napoleon's Anti-Jewish Decrees* (1953); idem, *Economic Status of the Jews in Alsace, Metz and Lorraine* (1954); H. H. Ben-Sasson, *Hagut ve-Hanhagah* (1959); idem, *Toledot Am Yisrael*, 2 (1969), 92–98; S. Simonsohn, *Toledot ha-Yehudim be-Dukkasut Mantovah*, 2 vols. (1962–64), index, s.v. *Halva'ah u-Malvim be-Ribbit;* H. G. Richardson, *English Jewry under Angevin Kings* (1960), index, s.v. *usury;* S. Grayzel, *The Church and the Jews in the XIIIth Century* (1966[2]), index; S. D. Goitein, *Mediterranean Society*, 1 (1967), index, s.v. *loans on interest;* F. R. Salter, in: *Cambridge Historical Journal*, 5 (1935–37), 193–211; P. Elman, in: *Economic History Review*, 7 (1936–37), 145–54.

MONGOLIA, region of E. central Asia. Outer Mongolia became the Mongolian People's Republic in 1924 and Inner Mongolia remained under Chinese rule. At the end of the 19th century Jewish families from Siberia traded with Mongolia and a few settled there as a result of their businesses. Between 1918 and 1920 Russian Jews, fleeing from the civil war atrocities, crossed Lake Baikal to settle in Outer Mongolia. Most of them were wiped out in 1921 by the White Russian units which were retreating before the advancing Soviet forces. In 1925–26, a Russian-Jewish journalist discovered 50 newly settled Jewish families in a deserted area of Outer Mongolia, some 200 miles from the Manchurian border. Ulan Bator (formerly Urga), the capital of the Mongolian People's Republic, had a community of 600 Russian Jews in 1926, including watchmakers, jewelers, barbers, furriers, and construction workers. The increasing Soviet influence in the area induced most of them to leave Outer Mongolia for *Manchuria and elsewhere. Those who remained were employees of state enterprises. There were also a few Jews among the Soviet specialists sent to Mongolia. Jews visited Outer Mongolia from the Manchurian town of Hailar during the 1920s only seasonally in order to buy furs and other domestic products, but they did not take up permanent residence.

Bibliography: M. Wischnitzer, *Juden in der Welt* (1935), 305–7; A. Druyanow in: *Reshumot*, 3 (1923), 549–51. [R.L.]

MONIS, JUDAH (1683–1764), Colonial American Hebraist. Monis, who was born in Algiers or Italy, was educated in Leghorn and Amsterdam. Very little is known about his career before he went to America. On Feb. 28, 1715/16, he was admitted as a freeman of New York, his occupation being that of merchant, although at a later period he was described as having been a rabbi in Jamaica and in New York. Much of his erudition may have been

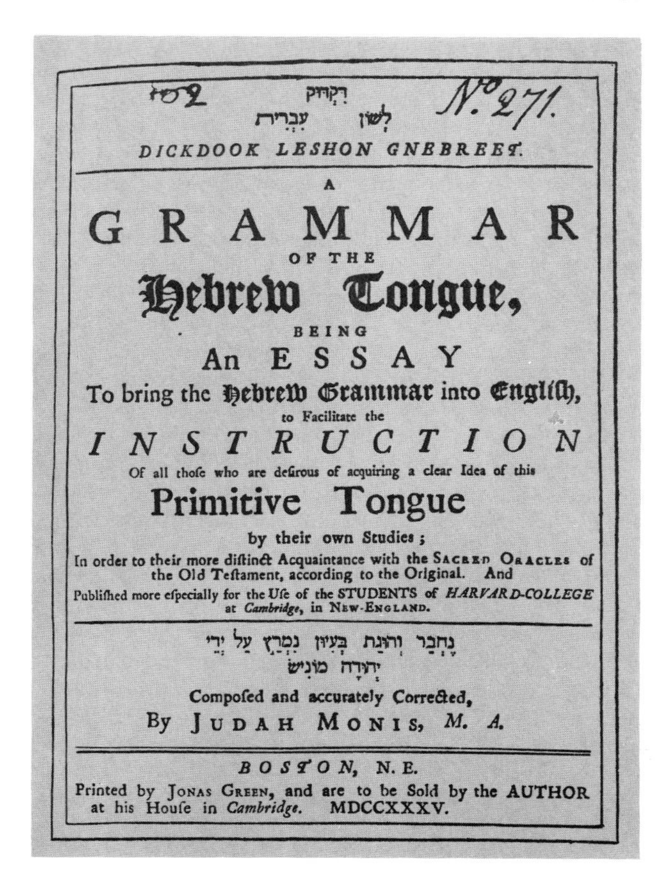
דקדוק לשון עברית

No. 271

DICKDOOK LESHON GNEBREET.

A

GRAMMAR

OF THE

Hebrew Tongue,

BEING

An ESSAY

To bring the Hebrew Grammar into English,

to Facilitate the

INSTRUCTION

Of all thofe who are defirous of acquiring a clear Idea of this

Primitive Tongue

by their own Studies;

In order to their more diftinct Acquaintance with the SACRED ORACLES of the Old Teftament, according to the Original. And Publifhed more efpecially for the Ufe of the STUDENTS of HARVARD-COLLEGE at Cambridge, in NEW-ENGLAND.

נחבר והוגה בעיון נמרץ על ידי
יהודה מוניש

Compofed and accurately Corrected,

By JUDAH MONIS, M. A.

BOSTON, N. E.

Printed by JONAS GREEN, and are to be Sold by the AUTHOR at his Houfe in Cambridge. MDCCXXXV.

Title page of the Hebrew grammar by the Harvard Hebraist, Judah Monis, Cambridge, Mass., 1735. Cecil Roth Collection.

secondhand. He appears in the Boston area in 1720, and on March 27, 1722 was publicly baptized in the College Hall at Cambridge, at which time the Reverend Benjamin Colman delivered *A Discourse . . . Before the Baptism of R. Judah Monis, to which were added Three Discourses, Written by Mr. Monis himself, The Truth, The Whole Truth, Nothing but the Truth. One of which was deliver'd by him at his Baptism* (Boston, 1722). Monis' essays are an apology and defense of his new faith, and in support of the doctrine of the Trinity drawn from "the Old Testament, and with the Authority of the Cabalistical Rabbies, Ancient and Modern." Shortly after his conversion, on April 30, 1722 he was appointed instructor of Hebrew at Harvard College, a position he held until his resignation in 1760. Monis received the degree of Master of Arts from Harvard in 1723. His instructorship, marriage, and academic degree came after his conversion to Protestant Christianity.

The study of Hebrew was a required subject at Harvard College, and Monis' Hebrew grammar, *Dickdook Leshon Gnebreet: A Grammar of the Hebrew Tongue* was published in Cambridge in 1735, sponsored by the Harvard Corporation. It was published in English:

> to Facilitate the Instruction of all those that are desirous of acquiring a clear Idea of this Primitive Tongue by their own Studies; In order to their more distinct Acquaintance with the Sacred Oracles of the Old Testament, according to the Original, And Published more especially for the Use of the Students of Harvard College.

Monis insisted on the use of the Hebrew vowel points in this grammar as being essential for the correct pronunciation of the Hebrew. Monis also owned a manuscript volume of Kabbalistic tracts and excerpts (372 pages), some transcribed by him, and some in the handwriting of others. His brother-in-law, the Rev. John Martyn, presented his books and manuscripts to Harvard College Library in 1767. Monis also left a small fund for the needy widows of Christian ministers.

Bibliography: L. M. Friedman, in: AJHSP, 22 (1914), 1–24; I. S. Meyer, *Proceedings of the Massachusetts Historical Society*, 52 (1919), I. S. Meyer, *ibid.*, 35 (1939), 145–70; G. F. Moore, in: *Proceedings of the Massachusetts Historical Society*, 52 (1919), 285–312; C. K. Shipton (ed.), *Sibley's Harvard Graduates*, 7 (1945), 380–1, 626, 639–46. [I.S.M.]

MONITOR (Heb. כֹּחַ; lit. "strength"; AV "chameleon"; JPS: "land crocodile"), reptile included in the Pentateuch among the creeping things which are prohibited as food and whose dead bodies defile by contact (Lev. 11:30–39). The reference is to the *Varanus griseus*. It is the largest reptile found in Israel, with a length, including its long tail, of up to 4 ft. (1.20 m.). Feeding on reptiles and rodents, it is frequently found in the southern coastal belt, in the Negev, and in the Arabah. Alone of the reptiles in the country it hibernates for six months in a burrow in the ground, and it is then that the Bedouin catch it, using it for medicinal purposes and eating its flesh, which the Greeks, who called it a land crocodile, believed granted immunization from poisoned arrows. It is usually hunted while in a torpid state, for when awake it is aggressive, defending itself by biting and lashing out with its powerful tail. The Septuagint and Vulgate identified the biblical *ko'aḥ* with the *chameleon.

Bibliography: Lewysohn, Zool, 223–4, no. 274; J. Feliks, *The Animal World of the Bible* (1962), 99. [J.F.]

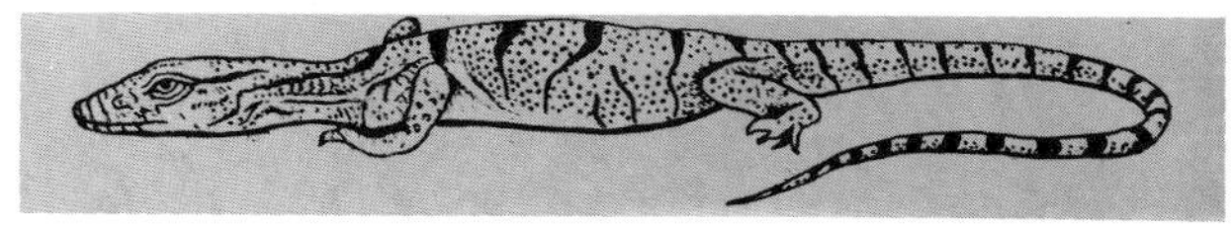

Monitor *(Varanus griseus)*, the *ko'aḥ* of the Bible. Courtesy J. Feliks, Jerusalem.

MONOBAZ I AND II, two kings of *Adiabene in the first century, C.E. Monobaz I was both brother and husband of Queen *Helena. His attitude to Judaism is unknown, but in view of the fact that his sister-wife and their son Izates both became converts to Judaism, it is highly probable that he was sympathetic to it. Monobaz I and Helena had a son, Monobaz, who was older than his brother Izates, but when Monobaz I died, Helena, in accordance with the king's testament, placed Izates upon the throne. Monobaz II was loyal to his younger brother and like him embraced Judaism. He succeeded Izates to the throne. Little is known of Monobaz II. Josephus, who is the main source, relates that he sent the remains of his mother and brother to Jerusalem for burial, and that he erected a palace in Jerusalem, which was called by his name (Wars 5:252). Many of his kinsmen took part with distinction in the war against the Romans (Wars 2:520). Though Josephus features Izates as the chief figure among the converts to Judaism of the Adiabene royal dynasty, the account of Monobaz II in the talmudic literature makes a deeper impression, highlighting his generosity to the people of Jerusalem and the Temple, his righteousness, and his wisdom. His circumcision and that of his brother are also mentioned.

Bibliography: Yoma 3:10; BB 11a; Tosef., Yoma 2:3; Gen. R. 46:10; Jos., Ant. 20:17–96; Derenbourg, Hist, 224–7; Schuerer, Gesch, 3 (1909[4]), 169–72; Klausner, Bayit Sheni, 5 (1951[2]), 44–49. [U.R.]

MONOGAMY, the custom and social or religious institution, often sanctioned by law, according to which a person can be married to only one single mate at a time. The discussion in this article is restricted to polygyny and monogyny in Jewish practice, since polyandry was absolutely forbidden by biblical law.

The Bible does not limit the right of a man to have more than one wife. Indeed, many instances are cited where a man has several wives (and *concubines)—a prevalent custom in the Ancient Near East. It seems, however, that due to economic conditions, most of the people did not practice polygamy or even bigamy. Indeed practice was more monogamous than theory. The ethos underlying the creation story (Gen. 2), and the last chapter of Proverbs, is essentially monogamous. The situation changed during the Second Temple period. In addition to the economic factors which gave justifiable grounds to monogamy—factors applicable even more than in the First Temple period—the concept of mutual fidelity between husband and wife took root. Some men refrained from taking more than one wife because of an explicit agreement they had made with their first wife. Such agreements, preserved in Babylonian and Assyrian documents, are also to be found in the *Elephantine (Yeb) documents (Cowley, Aramaic, 44ff., no. 15, line 31ff.

Bigamy and polygamy, while on the decrease, were mainly practiced among Hellenistic Jews (Joseph the *Tobiad, *Herod, the administrator of *Agrippa (Suk. 27a), but they are also mentioned in the *halakhah* (Yev. 1:1–4; Ket. 10:1–6; Git. 2:7; Kid. 2:6–7; cf. Justin Martyr, *Dialogue with Tryphon*, 134:1; 141:4), and occurred even in the families of sages (Yev. 15a). Bigamy took place sometimes because of a "*levirate marriage or the sterility of the first wife. Yet despite the rare occurrence of polygamy, its explicit prohibition in the *halakhah* of the Dead Sea Sect that saw polygamy as a Pentateuchal prohibition (Damascus Document 4:20–5:5) was a complete innovation. Christianity adopted a similar attitude, which was in conformity with Jesus' approach to marriage and to divorce (Tit. 1:6; I Tim. 3:2, 12).

But even the Mishnah and the *baraitot* clearly reflect a situation which was almost completely monogamist (Yev. 2:10; etc.). Some sages preferred **ḥaliẓah* ("levirate divorce") to *yibbum* ("levirate marriage"; Bek. 1:7); others violently condemned marriage to two wives even for the purpose of procreation (Ket. 62b). According to R. Ammi, a Palestinian *amora*, "Whoever takes a second wife in addition to his first one shall divorce the first and pay her *ketubbah*" (Yev. 65a). Such statements possibly reflect the influence of Roman custom which prohibited polygamy, especially since all the Jews of the empire became Roman citizens after 212 C.E. The Roman emperor *Theodosius issued a prohibition against the practice of bigamy and polygamy among Jews, but it did not disappear completely.

The Jews of Babylonia also practiced bigamy and polygamy, despite the Persian monogamistic background, and Rava said: "A man may marry several women in addition to his wife, on condition that he can provide for them" (Yev. 65a; cf. Ket. 80b; Pes. 113a). The sages however advised that one should not take more than four wives (and this would appear to be the source of the Muslim law which permits only four wives). Under the influence of the Muslim custom during the Babylonian geonic period, polygamous marriage became even more common (see Lewin, Oẓar, Yevamot (1936), 148–54). With the *Karaites, polygamy was a controversial issue. Bigamy was practiced among North African and Spanish Jews. There were women, however, who demanded that it be explicitly written in the document of marriage or in the *ketubbah* that the husband would not take a second wife.

In Germany and northern France polygamy was rare, mainly due to the economic conditions and to the influence of the Christian environment. It seems that at the beginning of the 12th century, the Jewish communities issued a regulation which forbade polygyny. Later, this regulation became a *ḥerem* (ban), attributed to R. *Gershom b. Judah. In the case of a levirate marriage, or the sterility of the first wife, the regulation was disregarded, while in cases where the wife had become insane (and could not therefore be divorced, see *Divorce) a regulation was introduced whereby the *ḥerem* could be lifted by 100 rabbis from three countries (or three communities). By the 13th century, however, it had already been decided that levirate marriage was to be abolished and *ḥaliẓah* performed instead. The ban on bigamous marriage however did not include a clause annulling the offender's second marriage (see Yev. 110a; BB 48b): For example, although the man had disregarded the *ḥerem*, broken the law, and married a second woman, his second marriage remained valid; but he could be compelled to divorce his second wife. The prohibition on bigamy became widespread in most countries of the Ashkenazi Diaspora, but not in Provence, Spain, North Africa, and among the oriental communities, and it was accepted only by Ashkenazi halakhic authorities. Bigamy was however not common even in those localities where it had not been prohibited, including the Islamic countries.

In the Palestinian *yishuv*, bigamy was extremely rare and in the State of Israel it is prohibited by law (the 1951 law on equal rights to women); although immigrants coming with more than one wife are allowed to maintain that status. In 1950 the Chief Rabbinate of Israel unanimously decided that *ḥaliẓah* was preferred to *yibbum* (Herzog, *Heikhal Yiẓḥak, Even ha-Ezer*, 1 (1960), 51n). See *Bigamy; *Marriage.

Bibliography: Z. Falk, *Jewish Matrimonial Law in Middle Ages* (1966), 1–34 (esp. 1 n.1, 34 n.3; exhaustive bibl.); P. Tishby, in: *Tarbiz*, 34 (1964/65), 49–55; Eidelberg, *ibid.*, 287f. [M.D.H.]

MONOTHEISM, in its literal meaning, oneness of the godhead (i.e., one God). The concept of monotheism is embedded in the domain of religious discourse, and its full and relevant significance must be derived from the connotation which it carries within this domain. Monotheism is usually attributed to biblical faith as its unique and distinct contribution to the history of religious thought. The significance of the word monotheism in its biblical context is taken to lie in the "mono," in the godhead's being one. As such, it is contrasted with paganism, the fundamental religious alternative to biblical faith, whose distinctive religious concept is taken to be polytheism, i.e., the plurality of the godhead (many gods). The difference between the biblical and pagan orientation is thus constituted here as a mere arithmetical difference, a difference between one and many gods. On this basis, biblical monotheism is seen by modern biblical scholars as emerging gradually and in a continuous line from the polytheistic thought of paganism. The mediating stage in such a development is found in monolatry, where the godhead is reduced to one only as far as worship is concerned, while ontologically there is a plurality of gods. It is a mediating stage inasmuch as the arithmetical reduction to oneness is partial. The full reduction of the godhead in all its aspects to oneness emerges from monolatry only later in biblical classical prophecy, when God is claimed not only as the one God of Israel but as the one God of universal history. Here, by drawing the arithmetical reduction to oneness in all the aspects of the godhead, biblical faith achieves ultimately its distinctive, unique character. It is observed, however, that an ontological arithmetical unity of the godhead is achieved also in paganism, even with a remarkable degree of purity (e.g., Plotinus). It must be concluded, therefore, that paganism too has a monotheistic formulation. Yet it is generally felt that a fundamental difference between biblical faith and paganism does exist, and that this difference is expressed in the respective concepts of monotheism. This difference, however, cannot be accounted for on the basis of monotheism understood as the arithmetical oneness of the godhead.

Theistic Monotheism. Consequently, it has been suggested that the difference between biblical and pagan monotheism lies in the fact that the former is theistic while the latter is pantheistic. While it is true that biblical monotheism is exclusively theistic and that pagan monotheism has a definite tendency toward pantheism, to formulate the difference between biblical and pagan monotheism on this basis is to formulate the difference with regard to a totally different aspect of the godhead from that to which the concept of monotheism refers. Monotheism refers to the being of the godhead as such, while theism and pantheism refer to the relation subsisting between the godhead and the world. Thus, while this attempt locates a difference which may follow from the fundamental difference within the concept of monotheism, it does not locate that fundamental difference itself.

Ethical Monotheism. The same point can be made regarding yet another attempt to locate the difference between biblical and pagan monotheism, according to which biblical monotheism is ethical while pagan monotheism is purely philosophical-ontological. Correlated to this is the suggestion that, while paganism arrives at the oneness of its godhead through philosophical reasoning and because of ontological-metaphysical considerations, biblical faith arrives at the oneness of its godhead because of ethical considerations and through a direct insight into the absolute character of the moral law. Thus, biblical monotheism can be distinguished from pagan monotheism in that it alone is ethical monotheism. Here again, however, the distinction is located in an aspect to which the concept of monotheism as such does not refer; the concept of monotheism as such conveys no ethical connotation. It may be that this distinction follows from the proper understanding of the difference between the meaning of monotheism in the biblical context and its use in the context of paganism, but this distinction as such does not capture this difference. In attempting to define the difference it is interesting first to note that the two formulations above have already shifted the aspect where the difference is to be located from the "mono" to the "theos" part of the concept of monotheism; the theistic-pantheistic distinction refers to the relation of the "theos" to the world while the ethical-metaphysical distinction refers to what kind of a "theos" is involved. This means that the difference between biblical faith and paganism is no longer seen as a quantitative difference, i.e., how many gods are involved, but as a qualitative difference, i.e., what kind of a god is involved. This shift is essential to a proper understanding of the difference and must form the basis of the attempted formulation.

Ultimate Being. On this basis it can be asserted that the minimal necessary connotation of the term "theos" in the concept of monotheism is that of ultimate being. As such, the arithmetical comparison between biblical monotheism and pagan polytheism is clearly seen to be illegitimate. The "theos" in pagan polytheism is not ultimate. It is superhuman, or "man writ large," but still it remains finite and non-absolute. In polytheism a plurality of ultimate beings is untenable and self-contradictory. Consequently, the "theos" in biblical monotheism and the "theos" in pagan polytheism connote two different kinds of being, for the difference between ultimate and non-ultimate being is not merely quantitative but qualitative. It is not legitimate, however, to compare quantitatively entities which belong to different orders of being. In order to locate the difference meaningfully it must be determined with reference to the same kind of entity, i.e., to the ultimate being which is connoted by the concept of monotheism. As such, however, it is not correct to speak of the development of the concept of monotheism in paganism. Paganism always had a conception of ultimate being transcending its gods and, as indicated above, ultimate being necessitates oneness. There can be no development from many to one with regard to ultimate being. Thus, if the "theos" in monotheism signifies ultimate being, paganism always had a conception of monotheism. The only development that can be pointed to is a development in its articulation, i.e., a development from the cultic-mythological to the speculative-philosophical expression. If the "theos" in monotheism, however, signifies only ultimate being, then it would not be possible to locate any difference between biblical and pagan monotheism, for then the "mono" conveys no additional information which is not already conveyed by the "theos" in itself. In order for the concept of monotheism to have a distinct meaning, the "theos" has to stand for something more than ultimate being. It is here that the real, fundamental difference between pagan and biblical monotheism becomes evident.

Personal Monotheism. In biblical monotheism the "theos" stands for a god who is personal. The "mono" connotes essentially not arithmetical oneness but oneness in the sense of uniqueness. Ultimate being is uniquely one in that it excludes the existence of any other qualitatively similar being. Thus, the authentic meaning of biblical monotheism is the assertion that the "mono," i.e., the unique, the ultimate, is "theos," i.e., a personal being, and this is the distinctive and unique feature of biblical faith and its monotheistic formulation. Paganism, while it too always had a conception of ultimate being and thus a conception of a unitary being, never asserted that ultimate being is personal. It follows from this analysis that the development of biblical monotheism from paganism cannot be envisioned as a linear, continuous development, but must be seen as a "jump" from one orbit to another, for the change that biblical monotheism introduced is qualitative and not quantitative. There is no continuous line of development either from nonpersonal to personal being or from relative being to ultimate being. This development involves a shift in perspective. While the above articulates the distinctive and essential content of the monotheistic conception of Judaism, it does not preclude or invalidate the fact that the monotheistic conception in Judaism may convey also the arithmetical oneness and the ontological uniqueness of God. Indeed, in post-biblical Judaism (and even in some biblical instances) it is these notions that come to the fore and become the main expressions of the Jewish monotheistic conception. It would seem, however, that the notion of the arithmetical unity of God arises mainly as a reaction against pluralistic formulations found in other religions, such as the *dualism of the Zoroastrian, Manichean, or Gnostic formulation and the trinitarianism of Christianity. The notion of the ontological uniqueness of the godhead arises mainly when Judaism conceives and expresses itself in the philosophical-metaphysical domain, i.e., when its God becomes the god of the philosophers.

Monotheism in Jewish Sources. Thus, Deutero-Isaiah, in response to Persian dualism, stresses the oneness of God in the sense that He alone is God, the one and only creator and ultimate cause of all phenomena: "I form light and create darkness; I make peace and create evil" (Isa. 45:7). This assertion is repeated frequently in rabbinic literature: "He who brought all things into being and who is their first cause is one" (Maimonides, *Sefer ha-Mitzvot*, positive commandment 2); "I have created all things in pairs. Heaven and earth, man and woman, . . . but my glory is one and unique" (Deut. R. 2:31). Likewise, the specific use of this assertion polemically against dualism and trinitarianism is extensive: "'I am the first' for I have no father, 'and I am the last' for I have no son, 'and beside me there is no

God' for I have no brother" (Ex. R. 29:5); "The Lord, both in His role as our God [who loves us and extends His providence to us, i.e., the second person of the trinity] and the Lord [as He is in Himself, i.e., the first person of the trinity] is one from every aspect" (Leon de Modena, *Magen va-Ḥerev*, 2:7, 31–32). Furthermore, a number of the basic tenets of Judaism follow logically from this assertion of the arithmetical oneness of God, and rabbinic literature derives them from it. Thus, all forms of idolatry are rejected: God's absolute sovereignty and glory is proclaimed; both love and judgment, mercy and justice are attributed to one and the same God; God's infinity in time as the one God in the past, present, and future is declared. Although the concept of arithmetical oneness is involved also in the assertion of God's unity, the latter is distinct in that God is here distinguished qualitatively rather than merely quantitatively. This assertion finds its expression mainly in philosophical speculation, where the uniqueness of God is understood as essentially conveying the non-composite, non-divisible nature of His being (see Attributes of *God). This is expressed by Maimonides when he says that God is "not one of a genus nor of a species and not as one human being who is a compound divisible into many unities; not a unity like the ordinary material body which is one in number but takes on endless divisions and parts" (*Guide of the Perplexed*, 1:51ff.). This means that "God is one in perfect simplicity" (Ḥasdai *Crescas, *Or Adonai*, 1:1, 1), that He is wholly other (Saadiah Gaon, *Book of Beliefs and Opinions*, 2:1), and unique (Baḥya ibn Paquda, *Ḥovot ha-Levavot*, "*Sha'ar ha-Yiḥud*"). Even in rabbinic Judaism, although the emphasis is clearly placed on the two aspects of the monotheistic idea, i.e., the arithmetical oneness and the ontological uniqueness of God, the fundamental underlying assertion is that God is first and foremost a personal being. Thus, though shifting the emphasis, rabbinic Judaism remains fully bound to that aspect of the monotheistic idea where Judaism makes its fundamental and distinctive contribution to the history of religions.

See also Conceptions of *God.

Bibliography: Y. Kaufmann, *The Religion of Israel* (1960), index; Guttmann, Philosophies, index; A. Altmann, in: *Tarbiz*, 27 (1958), 301–9; G. Vajda, in: A. Altmann (ed.), *Jewish Medieval and Renaissance Studies* (1966), 49–74. [M.H.V.]

MONSKY, HENRY (**Ẓevi;** 1890–1947), U.S. communal leader, organization executive, and lawyer. Monsky was born in Russia and taken as an infant to Omaha, Nebraska. Of Orthodox background, as a matter of principle he belonged to Reform, Conservative, and Orthodox synagogues. In 1921 he founded the Omaha Community Chest and Welfare Federation, serving as its first vice-president and later as president (1929); he was a trustee of Boys' Town, a member of the National Board of Community Chests and Council, Inc., president of the Nebraska Council of Social Work, and chairman of the Executive Committee of the National Conference of Prevention and Control of Juvenile Delinquency. Monsky was elected president of the Omaha lodge of B'nai B'rith in 1912 and eventually served as national president of the organization (1938–47). In 1941 he was invited by President Franklin D. Roosevelt to plan for the Office of Civilian Defense.

A lifelong Zionist, Monsky succeeded in enlisting the support of non-Zionists in protests against the British White Paper, Cyprus internment, and restrictions of immigration to Palestine. On Dec. 8, 1942, he led a delegation of representatives of Jewish organizations to the White House to call Roosevelt's attention to the plight of the Jews of Europe and to request firm action against the Nazis. Monsky collaborated with Zionists as the principal organizer of the all-inclusive *American Jewish Conference of 1943 in Pittsburgh, Pennsylvania, at which the U.S. Jewish community endorsed the Zionist program of a Jewish commonwealth. In April 1945, as consultant to the U.S. delegation to the United Nations Organizing Conference in San Francisco, he effectively helped influence the

Henry Monsky, president of U.S. B'nai B'rith. From *American Jewish Yearbook, 1947–48*, Philadelphia, Pa.

UN leaders to guarantee the rights of any states or peoples living under international bodies such as the Palestine British Mandate. He testified before the 1946 Anglo-American Commission of Inquiry in favor of this demand and also served as a member of U.S. attorney general Tom Clark's Juvenile Delinquency Board. Monsky's Jewish communal interests included leadership positions in the Council of Jewish Federation and Welfare Funds, the Joint Distribution Committee, the National Conference of Christians and Jews, the Jewish Welfare Board, the American Friends of the Hebrew University, and the United Palestine Appeal. A moshav in Israel, Ramat Ẓevi, is named in his memory. [BE.K.]

MONTAGU, English banking family, prominent in politics and public life. SAMUEL MONTAGU, FIRST BARON SWAYTHLING (1832–1911), banker, communal worker, and philanthropist, was born in Liverpool as Montagu Samuel, but in his boyhood the names were reversed. In 1853 he founded the merchant bankers, Samuel Montagu and Company. By securing a larger proportion of the exchange business, he helped make London the chief clearing house of the international money market. He was Liberal member of parliament for Whitechapel from 1885 to 1900, and a benefactor to its poor, Jewish and non-Jewish. An advocate of, and writer on, decimalization of the currency and adoption of the metric system, he was consulted by successive chancellors of the exchequer on financial matters and in 1894 persuaded the government to exempt from death duties works of art and gifts to universities, museums, and art galleries. In 1894 he was made a baronet and in 1907 a baron. A strictly observant Jew, he assumed leadership of the Orthodox Russo-Jewish immigrants, founding in 1887 the Federation of Synagogues to unite the small congregations. He, however, worshiped at the fashionable New West End Synagogue and was a life member of the United Synagogue Council, though because of disagreements with its president, the first Lord Rothschild, he was inactive there. A masterful personality, he traveled to Palestine, Russia, and the United States on behalf of Jewry, but vigorously opposed Zionism.

His eldest son, LOUIS SAMUEL (1869–1927), SECOND BARON SWAYTHLING, was president of the Federation of Synagogues. Also an anti-Zionist, he declared, "Judaism is to me only a religion." He married Gladys, daughter of Colonel A. E. W. *Goldsmid. Their second son, EWEN EDWARD (1901–) was president of the United Synagogue (1954–62). After wartime service in naval intelligence (later describing some of the tactics of intelligence work in the best-selling *The Man Who Never Was,* 1953), he became judge advocate of the fleet and chairman of Middlesex Quarter Sessions (a leading London judicial post). Samuel Montagu's second son, EDWIN SAMUEL (1879–1924), a Liberal politician, was elected to parliament in 1906, becoming private secretary to Herbert Asquith (later prime minister).

Figure 1. Edwin Montagu, British secretary of state for India. Jerusalem, J.N.U.L., Schwadron Collection.

As parliamentary undersecretary of state for India from 1910 to 1914, he championed Indian aspirations to independence. In 1914 he became financial secretary to the Treasury, in 1915, chancellor of the duchy of Lancaster, and in 1916, minister of munitions. Secretary of state for India in Lloyd George's administration (1917–22), he was responsible for the Government of India Act (1919), devolving wide powers of self-government. He resigned in 1922, because of his opposition to government policy which was offensive to Indian Muslims, and lost his parliamentary seat the same year. In Jewish affairs, he was best known as an uncompromising opponent of Zionism and of the Balfour Declaration, being largely responsible for the modification of the original text.

His sister LILIAN HELEN (Lily; 1873–1963), social worker and magistrate, founded the West Central Girls' Club in 1893. A pioneer of Liberal Judaism in Britain, in 1902, with Claude Goldsmid *Montefiore, she established the Jewish Religious Union which sponsored the Liberal Jewish Synagogue, and in 1926 the World Union for Progressive Judaism. She conducted Liberal Jewish services, wrote on religious subjects, and also published a biography of her father.

Bibliography: S. D. Waley, *Edwin Montagu* ... (1964); Ch. Weizmann, *Trial and Error* (1950), index; L. Stein, *Balfour Declaration* (1961), index; R. P. Lehmann, *Nova Bibliotheca Anglo-Judaica* (1961), index; Roth, Mag Bibl, index; DNB, s.v.; JC (June 17, 1927), 11–12; (Jan. 25, 1963), 1, 7, 35; *The Times* (June 6, 1927, Jan. 24, 1963).
[V.D.L.]

Figure 2. Lilian Montagu delivering a sermon at the Berlin Reform synagogue, 1928. Jerusalem, J.N.U.L., Schwadron Collection.

MONTAGU, MONTAGUE FRANCIS ASHLEY (1905–), physical and cultural anthropologist. Born in London, Montagu served as research associate in the British Museum of Natural History (1926–27) and as curator of physical anthropology at the Wellcome Historical Museum, London (1929–30). He emigrated to the U.S. and taught anatomy at New York University (1931–38) and Hahnemann Medical College and Hospital (1938–49), and was chairman of the anthropology department at Rutgers University (1945–55). An expert in physical anthropology and evolutionary theory, he served as rapporteur of the UNESCO committee of experts which formulated the 1950 UNESCO *Statement on Race* (1951, 1952^{2}), and was a member of the second UNESCO committee of experts of geneticists and physical anthropologists. Convinced that the idea of race was not only fallacious but antihuman and socially destructive, he dedicated his rhetorical and literary gifts to the production of a number of popular books on this question and on anthropological themes of large humanistic interest. Among his best known works were: *Coming into Being among the Australian Aborigines* (1937, 1938^{2}); *Man's Most Dangerous Myth* ... (1942, 1964^{4}); *Human Heredity* (1959, 1964^{2}); *Man in Process* (1961); and *The Direction of Human Evolution* (1955, 1959^{3}).

Bibliography: *Current Biography Yearbook, 1967* (1968), 294–7.
[E.FI.]

MONTANA, one of the Rocky Mountain states of the United States. In 1969 it had a Jewish population of 615 out of a total of 710,000. The principal Jewish communities were in Butte (175) and Billings (100), and they had the state's only two synagogues. Jews also lived in Helena, Anaconda, Great Falls, Bozeman, Miles City, Livingston, Missoula, and Havre. The first Jews, who arrived in 1862 during the gold rush at Bannock and Virginia City, were miners, wagon drivers, merchants, freighters, hotel and saloon keepers, lawyers, and journalists, many of whom became solid citizens in the raucous mining camps. Ben Ezekiel was chief clerk of the first territorial legislature and Jacob Feldberg was a member of Virginia City's first town council. Jews were also among the leaders of the vigilantes who suppressed outlawry. The oldest Jewish settlement dates from 1864 with the arrival of Jewish merchants in Helena. One of the pioneers was Gumpertz Goldberg, for whose wife Helena is said to have been named. The First Hebrew Benevolent Society, organized in 1865, became the nucleus for Temple Emanu-El, founded in 1887; their synagogue, the state's first synagogue, was built in 1891. When the Jewish community declined in the 1920s, the synagogue was deeded to the state, and it now houses the State Department of Public Welfare. When Butte became the biggest city in the state following the silver and gold booms around Anaconda in the 1870s, most of the early Jewish settlers and the later arrivals settled there. There was a Jewish congregation, Beth Israel, in Butte in 1877. It split over ritual in 1897 and a second one came into being, but today there is only one congregation with a synagogue dating from 1904. Long before Montana became a state in 1889, its Jewish residents were counted among its leading citizens. Henry Jacobs was Butte's first mayor in 1879, and Henry Lupin held that office from 1885 to 1889. Charles S. Cohan, editor of *The Butte Miner,* wrote the words for the state song. One of the early cattlemen was Louis Kaufman, who employed the cowboy artist Charlie Russell. Between 1873 and 1906 four Jews were grand masters of the State Masonic Grand Lodge: Sol Star, Moses Morris, H. Sol Hepner, and Henry I. Frank, a former mayor of Butte. Livingston, Great Falls, and Havre also had Jewish mayors before 1900. Among the colorful figures in the early days of the state were Daniel Bandman, a Shakespearean actor who

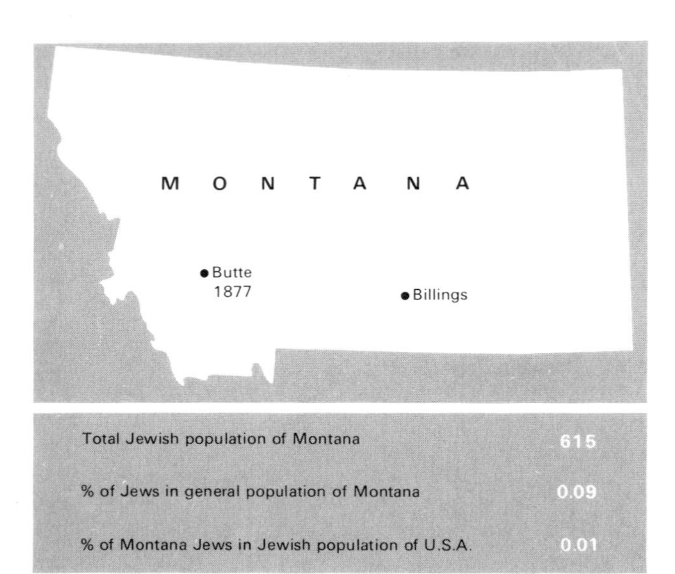

Jewish communities in Montana and dates of establishment. Population figures for 1968.

brought theater to the mining camps (Bandman's Bridge outside Missoula is named for him); Moses Solomon, a Buffalo hunter and Indian fighter; and Philip Deidesheimer, a mining superintendent, who invented the square set system of mining timbers and for whom Philipsburg is named. The Bob Marshall Wilderness Area of 950,000 acres in the Flathead National Forest is named for the son of Louis *Marshall, who was chief of the division of recreation in the U.S. Forest Service.

Bibliography: B. Kelson, *The Jews of Montana* (thesis, University of Montana, 1950); B. Postal and L. Koppman, *A Jewish Tourist's Guide to the U.S.* (1954), 281–9. [B.P.]

MONTCLUS (Heb. הר סגור, מונטקלוש, מונטקלוס), former town and fortress at the foot of the Pyrenees, in Aragon, western Spain. Jews apparently lived in the fortress of Montclus and the adjacent area from the beginning of the 11th century. The annual tax paid by the community in the 13th century was reduced by the king from 800 to 500 solidos in 1271, increased to 707 solidos and 3½ denarii in Jaca coin in 1304, and again reduced to 450 solidos in 1315. In 1298 James II ordered an investigation on the rate of interest charged by Jews on loans.

The Montclus community helped to rehabilitate Jews expelled from France in 1306. In 1307 the king authorized the community to absorb four families, including those of the physician Maestre Boninfante and Vitalis de Boulogne. However, between the end of June and the beginning of July 1320, the community was annihilated in the *Pastoureaux (Shepherds) massacres. On July 22, James II ordered that assistance should be given to the survivors, but that Jewish children who had been forcibly baptized were to remain in Christian households. In 1321 the king freed the remnant of the community from paying taxes and ordered that the walls of the fortress should be rebuilt, but by 1323 the Jews of Montclus had to pay taxes like the other Jews of the kingdom to finance the royal expedition to Sardinia. His successor, Alfonso IV, in 1335 freed the community from paying taxes, as did Pedro IV in 1341–42. Nevertheless, when disorders broke out in 1333, the commander of the fortress, Garcia Bardaxi, who did nothing to prevent the rioters from massacring the Jews, was pardoned.

With the expulsion of the Jews from Spain in 1492, Montclus began to decline. In the 17th century it was completely abandoned.

Bibliography: Baer, Studien, 149; Baer, Urkunden, 1 (1929), index; Baer, Spain, 1 (1961), 42; 2 (1966), 15; S. ibn Verga, *Shevet Yehudah*, ed. by A. Shochat (1947), 25; Miret y Sans, in: REJ, 53 (1907), 255ff.; Cardoner and Vendre, in: *Sefarad*, 7 (1947), 311, 328; Ashtor, Korot, 2 (1966), 153. [H.B.]

MONTEFIORE, CLAUDE JOSEPH GOLDSMID (1858–1938), theologian and leader of Liberal Judaism in England. Montefiore was a great-nephew of Sir Moses *Montefiore and a grandson of Isaac Lyon *Goldsmid. He studied at Balliol College, Oxford, where he came under the influence of the master of Balliol, Benjamin Jowett, the famous liberal Christian thinker. Later he studied Judaism at the *Hochschule (Lehranstalt) fuer die Wissenschaft des Judentums in Berlin, and under Solomon *Schechter whom he had taken to England as his private tutor. A man of means, Montefiore did not serve as a professional scholar or man of religion but nevertheless frequently preached eloquent sermons.

In 1888 he founded the *Jewish Quarterly Review*, which he financed and edited, with Israel *Abrahams, as coeditor, to 1908. He was the founder in England of a radical Reform movement (Jewish Religious Union, 1902), which led in 1911 to the establishment of the Liberal Jewish Synagogue; he served as its president. In 1926 Montefiore was elected president of the World Union for Progressive Judaism, an office which he held until his death. Together with the Catholic theologian Baron von Hugel, he founded the London Society for the Study of Religion, a select group of Jewish and Christian thinkers which met regularly to read and discuss papers on the philosophy of religion. A generous philanthropist, he assisted many Jewish and general good causes. He was a determined opponent of Zionism, and as president of the *Anglo-Jewish Association (1895–1921) tried to prevent the signing of the Balfour Declaration. He was president of the Jewish Religious Union and of the Jewish Historical Society of England (1899–1900). He also played a major part in the educational life of the Jewish community and beyond, and University College, Southampton, presented him with a volume of essays on his 70th birthday (*Speculum Religionis*, 1929).

Works. Montefiore was a prolific writer. In addition to numerous articles in periodicals, he wrote: *Aspects of Judaism* (1895^2), sermons, together with Israel Abrahams; *Bible for Home Reading* (2 vols., 1897–1899^2); *The Synoptic Gospels* (2 vols.; 1909; 1927^2; repr. 1968), a commentary on

Claude Montefiore, English Liberal Jewish leader and scholar.

the Gospels primarily for the Jewish reader; *Liberal Judaism* (1903); *Some Elements of the Religious Teaching of Jesus* (1910); *Outlines of Liberal Judaism* (1912, 1923^2);

Judaism and St. Paul (1914); *Liberal Judaism and Hellenism* (1918); *The Old Testament and After* (1923); *Rabbinic Literature and Gospel Teaching* (1930); and *A Short Devotional Introduction to the Hebrew Bible for the Use of Jews and Jewesses* (1936). Together with Herbert *Loewe, Montefiore published: *A Rabbinic Anthology* (1938; repr. 1960, 1963), a collection of rabbinic teachings with remarkable notes by the two editors, one Liberal and the other Orthodox. Montefiore delivered the Hibbert Lectures (1892) on *Origin and Growth of Religion as Illustrated by the Religion of the Ancient Hebrews.*

Thought. At the center of Montefiore's thought was his complete conviction of the truth of Jewish theism. He acknowledged that the Jewish conception of God and His relation to man and that of the relation of religion to morality are akin to but not identical with Christian conceptions dealing with these themes. The distinctiveness of Jewish theism lies in its insistence on both the transcendence and immanence of God. Montefiore holds that modern Biblical scholarship has demonstrated conclusively that the Pentateuchal Code is not Mosaic, homogeneous, and perfect. Yet this does not mean that the conception of law in religion should be abandoned. Man discovers the Law within him but it is also revealed to him.

Montefiore was very suspicious of Jewish nationalism because of its "narrowness" and its betrayal, in his view, of Jewish universalism. He was so much at home in England that his affinities were much closer to his native land than to the community of Israel throughout the world.

The greatest cause of offense to traditionalists was Montefiore's leaning toward Christianity. He viewed Christianity entirely sympathetically, and seemed to look forward to the religion of the future as embracing all that is good in both Judaism and Christianity as well as in other religions.

Montefiore's main contention is that in some respects but not in others the Christian ethic is more admirable than the Jewish and that there is a mystical, appealing note sounded in the Gospels not sounded in quite the same way in the Bible. Jesus, for Montefiore, was a great teacher but not divine as Christians have it. He was opposed to any attempt at placing the New Testament on a par with the Hebrew Scriptures or at having readings from the New Testament in any act of Jewish worship. He, nevertheless, felt that the time had come for Jews to read and understand the New Testament and even allow it to occupy an honored place in present-day Judaism. Soon after the publication of *The Synoptic Gospels*, Aḥad Ha-Am launched a vigorous attack against it (*Al Parashat Derakhim*, 4 (1921), 38–58). Aḥad Ha-Am argued that Jewish ethic, based on justice, is incompatible with the Christian ethic based on love, so that it is impossible for the same man to embrace both of them at the same time.

Bibliography: V. E. Reichert, in: CCARY, 38 (1928), 499–520; F. C. Burkitt, in: *Speculum Religionis* (1929), 1–17; J. Wolf, in: *La Question d'Israel (bulletin catholique)*, 17 (1939), 503–16; 561–72; L. Cohen, *Some Recollections...* (1940), incl. bibl.; W. R. Matthews, *Claude Montefiore, the Man and his Thought* (1956); F. C. Schwartz, in: JQR, 55 (1964/65), 23–52; A. Montefiore, in: *Quest*, 1 (London, 1965), 73–75; N. Bentwich, *C. M. and his Tutor in Rabbinics* (1966), incl. bibl.; W. Jacob, in: *Judaism*, 19 no. 3 (1970), 328–43.

[L.J.]

MONTEFIORE, JOSEPH BARROW (1803–1893), Australian pioneer. A cousin of Sir Moses *Montefiore, Joseph Barrow Montefiore was born in London. At the age of 23, he bought a seat on the London Stock Exchange and became one of the 12 "Jew brokers" in the city. He emigrated to Australia in 1830 with considerable means at his disposal and was granted 5,000 acres of land. In Melbourne, Sydney, and later in South Australia, he acquired extensive parcels of land and was active in sheep-farming, the wool trade, and mining. In 1838 he was invited to give evidence to the House of Lords on the state of the islands of New Zealand. He and his elder brother Jacob, who was one of the 11 commissioners appointed by King William IV to organize the administration of South Australia, helped to establish the Bank of Australasia. Montefiore, who had ultimately made his home in Adelaide, became one of its most prominent commercial and industrial figures. When in Sydney, he was South Australia's agent in New South Wales, and one of the original trustees of the State Savings Bank of South Australia. He helped to bring about the separation of Victoria from New South Wales in 1850. In 1832 Montefiore helped to organize Australia's first congregation, the Sydney Synagogue, the predecessor of the Great Synagogue, and was its first president. He was a trustee of the Jewish cemetery, for which he had secured a land grant from the government. The township of Montefiore in South Australia and Montefiore Hill in Adelaide are tributes to the pioneering work of Montefiore and his family. He spent the last years of his life in England.

[I.P.]

MONTEFIORE, JOSHUA (1762–1843), British-born lawyer and author. Montefiore, an uncle of Sir Moses *Montefiore, was born in London. He was admitted to practice as a solicitor in 1784. In 1787 he was in Jamaica, where discriminatory precedent prevented his admission as an attorney and notary. He participated in an unsuccessful expedition in 1792 to establish a British colony without slave labor off the west coast of Africa, near Sierra Leone, an adventure he described in *An Authentic Account of the Late Expedition to Bulam* (1794). He went to the United States, pursued the practice of law, and for a time edited a New York weekly political journal, *Men and Measures*, said to have been subsidized by the British government. Montefiore compiled a number of useful lay guides to commercial law which sold briskly in England and the U.S., including *Law of Copyright* (1802), *Commercial Dictionary* (1803; first U.S., ed., 1811), *Traders and Manufacturers Compendium* (1804), *American Traders Compendium* (1811), and *Commercial and Notarial Precedents* (1804). Montefiore's second wife was a Catholic, but his eight children were raised as Protestants. At his request, he was buried on the farm on the outskirts of St. Albans, Vermont, where he had settled in 1835.

Bibliography: M. J. Kohler, in: AJHSP, 19 (1910), 179–80; L. M. Friedman, *ibid.*, 40 (1950), 119–34.

[I.S.M.]

MONTEFIORE, JUDITH (1784–1862), daughter of Levi Barent *Cohen and wife of Sir Moses *Montefiore, whom she married in 1812. Her influence on her husband was profound. She left a diary of their first visit to Palestine in 1827 and described their second visit in 1838 in her *Notes from a Private Journal* (1844). She was the author, or coauthor, of the first Anglo-Jewish cookery book, the *Jewish Manual* by "A Lady" (1846). Her memory was commemorated by her husband in the foundation of the Judith Lady Montefiore College.

Bibliography: See Sir Moses *Montefiore; Lipman, in: JHSET, 21 (1962–67), 287–303.

[S.L.L.]

MONTEFIORE, SIR MOSES (1784–1885), most famous Anglo-Jew of the 19th century. Montefiore was born in Leghorn while his parents were on a visit from London, where he was brought up, being taught elementary Hebrew by his maternal uncle Moses *Mocatta. First apprenticed to a firm of wholesale grocers and tea merchants, he left to

Figure 1. Etching depicting the career of Sir Moses Montefiore, 1883. 1. Captain, Surrey Militia, 1805. 2. Carrying despatches of the Battle of Navarino, 1827. 3. First visit to the East, 1827. 4. With Mehemet Ali of Egypt. 5. With Nicholas I of Russia. 6. Traveling in the desert. Tel Aviv, Einhorn Collection. Photo David Harris, Jerusalem.

become one of the 12 "Jew brokers" in the City of London. After initial setbacks, he went into partnership with his brother Abraham and the firm acquired a high reputation. His marriage in 1812 to Judith Cohen (see Judith *Montefiore) made him brother-in-law of Nathan Mayer *Rothschild, for whom his firm acted as stockbrokers. After his retirement from regular business in 1824, though he retained various commercial directorships, he had the time and the fortune to undertake communal and civic responsibilities.

Contrary to accepted opinion, he was apparently somewhat lax in religious observance in earlier life; but from 1827, after his first visit to Ereẓ Israel, until the end of his life, he was a strictly observant Jew. Montefiore maintained his own synagogue on his estate at Ramsgate from 1833 and in later years traveled with his own *shoḥet*. His determined opposition checked the growth of the Reform movement in England. Though a patron of scholars, he had no pretensions to scholarship himself. He paid seven visits to Ereẓ Israel, the last in 1874. In 1838 his scheme for acquiring land to enable Jews in Ereẓ Israel to become self-supporting through agriculture was frustrated when Mehemet Ali, viceroy of Egypt, who had shown sympathy for the idea, was forced by the great powers to give up his conquests from the Turks. He later attempted to bring industry to the country, introducing a printing press and a textile factory, and inspired the founding of several agricultural colonies. The Yemin Moshe quarter outside the Old City of Jerusalem was due to his endeavors and named after him. In 1855, by the will of Judah *Touro, the U.S. philanthropist, he was appointed to administer a bequest of $50,000 for Jews of the Holy Land.

Montefiore was sheriff of London in 1837–38 and was knighted by Queen Victoria on her first visit to the City. He received a baronetcy in 1846 in recognition of his humanitarian efforts on behalf of his fellow Jews. Although president of the *Board of Deputies of British Jews from 1835 to 1874 (with only one brief interruption), he did not, after the early years, play a prominent part in the emancipation struggle but devoted himself to helping oppressed Jewries overseas. He has been described as the last of the **shtadlanim* who by their personal standing with their governments were able to further the cause of Jews elsewhere. He was active as such from the time of the *Damascus Affair in 1840. In 1846, he visited Russia to persuade the authorities to alleviate persecution of the Jewish population, and went to Morocco in 1863 and Rumania in 1867 for the same purpose. His intervention in the *Mortara Case in 1855, however, proved a failure. Some of his achievements appear in retrospect as transitory. Although in 1872, after representing the Board of Deputies at the bicentenary celebrations of Peter the Great, he reported that a new age had dawned for the Jews of Russia, persecution was renewed in 1881. Lover of Ereẓ Israel though he was and believer in the messianic restoration of a Jewish state, he did not conceive of large-scale, planned development of the country as a solution to the Jewish problem. This was largely because Montefiore (and his contemporaries) trusted absolutely in the inevitability of progress and with it worldwide emancipation for the Jews.

Nevertheless, both in his own lifetime and since, he enjoyed enormous prestige. Montefiore's physical presence (he was 6 ft. 3 in. tall), his commanding personality, his philanthropy, and his complete disinterestedness, made him highly respected and admired both in England and abroad. The support of the British government for his activities—consonant with British policies overseas—and the personal regard shown him by Queen Victoria added to his reputation. His 100th birthday was celebrated as a public holiday by Jewish communities the world over.

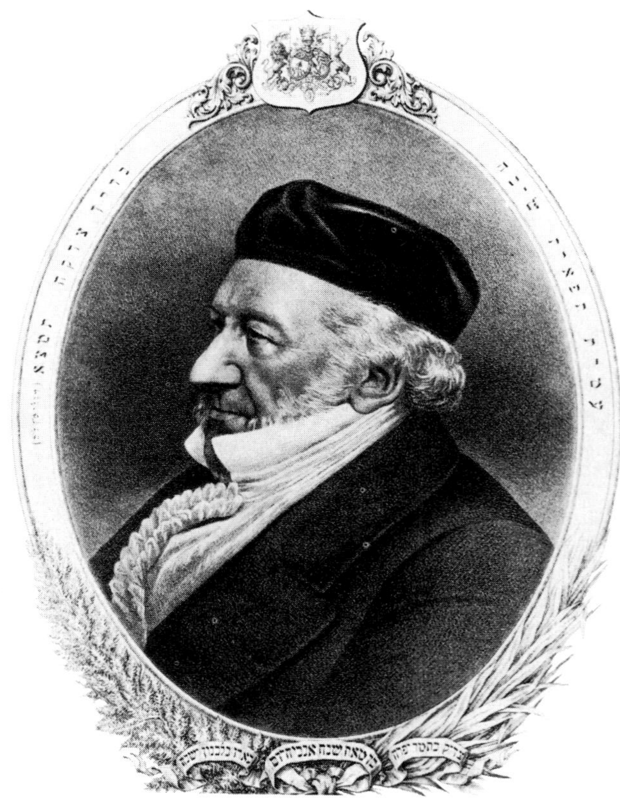

Figure 2. Portrait of Sir Moses Montefiore, on the occasion of his 100th birthday. Jerusalem, J.N.U.L., Schwadron Collection.

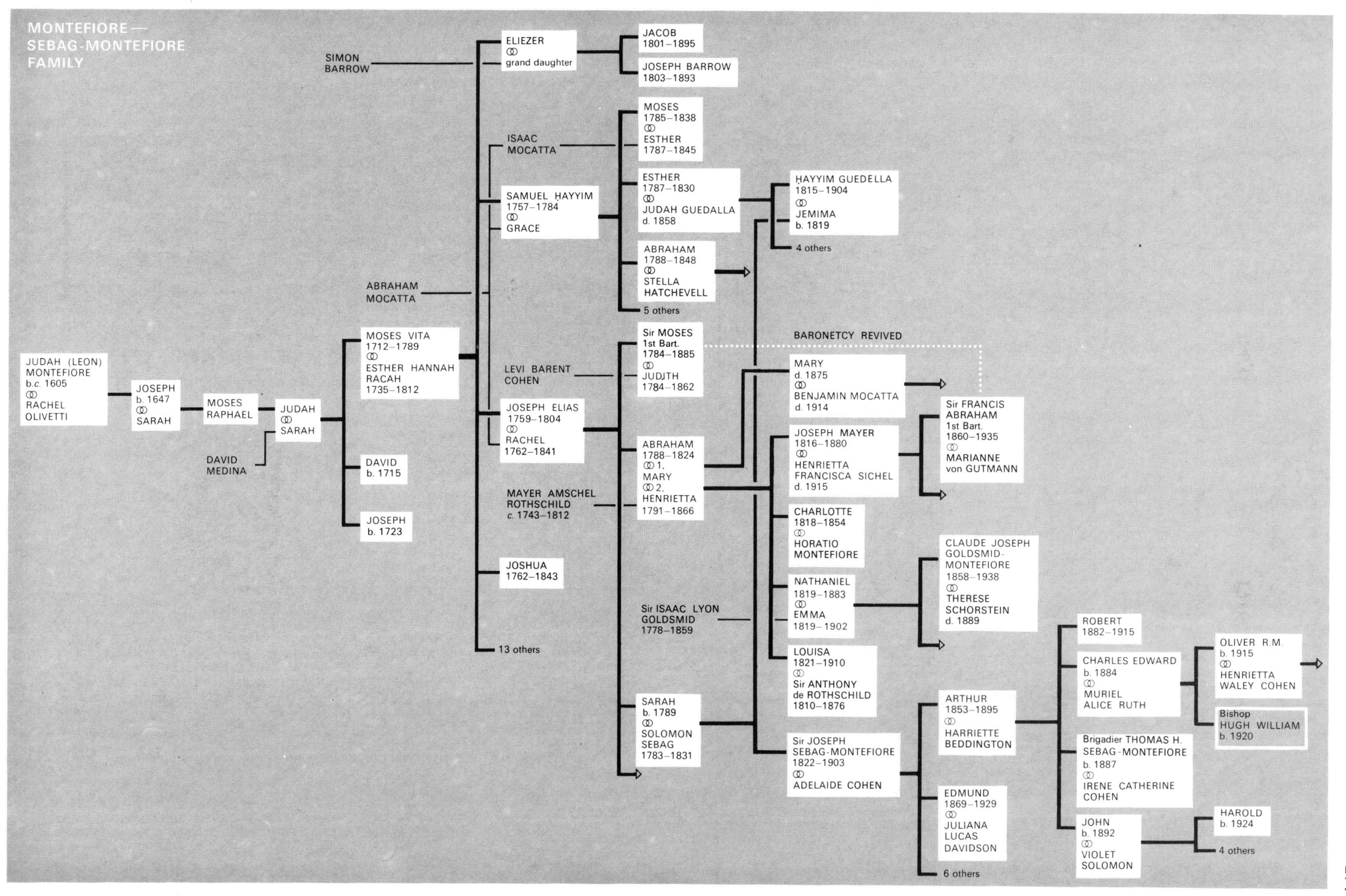
MONTEFIORE — SEBAG-MONTEFIORE FAMILY
JUDAH (LEON) MONTEFIORE b.c. 1605 ∞ RACHEL OLIVETTI
JOSEPH b. 1647 ∞ SARAH
MOSES RAPHAEL
JUDAH ∞ SARAH
DAVID MEDINA
MOSES VITA 1712–1789 ∞ ESTHER HANNAH RACAH 1735–1812
DAVID b. 1715
JOSEPH b. 1723
SIMON BARROW
ABRAHAM MOCATTA
ELIEZER ∞ grand daughter
ISAAC MOCATTA
SAMUEL ḤAYYIM 1757–1784 ∞ GRACE
LEVI BARENT COHEN
JOSEPH ELIAS 1759–1804 ∞ RACHEL 1762–1841
MAYER AMSCHEL ROTHSCHILD c. 1743–1812
JOSHUA 1762–1843
13 others
JACOB 1801–1895
JOSEPH BARROW 1803–1893
MOSES 1785–1838 ∞ ESTHER 1787–1845
ESTHER 1787–1830 ∞ JUDAH GUEDALLA d. 1858
ABRAHAM 1788–1848 ∞ STELLA HATCHEVELL
5 others
Sir MOSES 1st Bart. 1784–1885 ∞ JUDITH 1784–1862
ABRAHAM 1788–1824 ∞ 1. MARY ∞ 2. HENRIETTA 1791–1866
Sir ISAAC LYON GOLDSMID 1778–1859
SARAH b. 1789 ∞ SOLOMON SEBAG 1783–1831
ḤAYYIM GUEDELLA 1815–1904 ∞ JEMIMA b. 1819
4 others
BARONETCY REVIVED
MARY d. 1875 ∞ BENJAMIN MOCATTA d. 1914
JOSEPH MAYER 1816–1880 ∞ HENRIETTA FRANCISCA SICHEL d. 1915
CHARLOTTE 1818–1854 ∞ HORATIO MONTEFIORE
NATHANIEL 1819–1883 ∞ EMMA 1819–1902
LOUISA 1821–1910 ∞ Sir ANTHONY de ROTHSCHILD 1810–1876
Sir JOSEPH SEBAG-MONTEFIORE 1822–1903 ∞ ADELAIDE COHEN
Sir FRANCIS ABRAHAM 1st Bart. 1860–1935 ∞ MARIANNE von GUTMANN
CLAUDE JOSEPH GOLDSMID-MONTEFIORE 1858–1938 ∞ THERESE SCHORSTEIN d. 1889
ARTHUR 1853–1895 ∞ HARRIETTE BEDDINGTON
EDMUND 1869–1929 ∞ JULIANA LUCAS DAVIDSON
6 others
ROBERT 1882–1915
CHARLES EDWARD b. 1884 ∞ MURIEL ALICE RUTH
Brigadier THOMAS H. SEBAG-MONTEFIORE b. 1887 ∞ IRENE CATHERINE COHEN
JOHN b. 1892 ∞ VIOLET SOLOMON
OLIVER R.M. b. 1915 ∞ HENRIETTA WALEY COHEN
Bishop HUGH WILLIAM b. 1920
HAROLD b. 1924
4 others

Bibliography: Roth, Mag Bibl, 140–6; Lehmann, Nova Bibl, 109, 112, 117; L. Wolf, *Sir Moses Montefiore* (1885, Eng.); L. Loewe, *Diaries of Sir Moses and Lady Montefiore*, 2 vols. (1890); P. Goodman, *Moses Montefiore* (1925, Eng.); S. U. Nahon, *Sir Moses Montefiore* (Eng. 1965). [V.D.L.]

MONTEFIORE, SEBAG-MONTEFIORE, English family originating from Leghorn, Italy. The first to come to England were the brothers MOSES VITA (1712–1789), who set up successfully as an importer of Italian straw hats, and

Sir Joseph Sebag-Montefiore, British stockbroker. Jerusalem, J.N.U.L., Schwadron Collection.

JOSEPH (b. 1723). The former had 17 children who intermarried with the Anglo-Jewish families. His grandsons Joseph Barrow *Montefiore (1803–1893) and JACOB MONTEFIORE (1801–1895) were prominent in early Australian history; two other sons were Joshua *Montefiore and JOSEPH ELIAS (1759–1804) who married Rachel Mocatta and was the father of Sir Moses *Montefiore. Sir Moses' brother and business partner, ABRAHAM (1788–1824), married as his second wife Henrietta Rothschild. Their two sons were JOSEPH MAYER (1816–1880) and NATHANIEL (1819–1883), the father of Claude Goldsmid *Montefiore. Joseph Mayer succeeded Sir Moses as president of the Board of Deputies in 1874, after having been the first vice-president since 1857. Under his presidency the Board and the Anglo-Jewish Association cooperated to form the Conjoint Foreign Committee. Joseph Mayer's eldest son, Sir Francis Abraham Montefiore, succeeded to Sir Moses' baronetcy in 1886, when the title, which had become extinct, was revived in his favor. With his death the title became extinct.

Sir Moses' sister SARAH (b. 1789) married Solomon Sebag (1783–1831). Their son JOSEPH (1822–1903), a stockbroker who amassed a fortune, was the closest associate of Sir Moses in his last years and heir to his Ramsgate estate. In 1885 he added the name of Montefiore to his own by royal license, the family name henceforward being Sebag-Montefiore. He was a justice of the peace, high sheriff of Kent in 1889, and was knighted in 1896. Joseph, who had accompanied Sir Moses to Ereẓ Israel in 1866, remained concerned with the welfare of the Jews there, administering on behalf of the Spanish and Portuguese synagogue the Holy Land Trust bequeathed by Sir Moses. In the 1890s he was a vice-president of the *Ḥovevei Zion. He was president of the Board of Deputies from 1895 until his death. His grandson ROBERT (1882–1915), a leading member of the London County Council and the Anglo-Jewish community, was killed in World War I. The London County Council named an East London school in his memory.

In the mid-20th century, some members of the family remained active both in public life and in the Sephardi community: BRIGADIER T. H. SEBAG-MONTEFIORE; OLIVER SEBAG-MONTEFIORE, a president of the London Jewish Welfare Board; and HAROLD SEBAG-MONTEFIORE (b. 1924), a Conservative member of the Greater London Council and president of the Anglo-Jewish Association. However, as with many of the older and wealthier Anglo-Jewish families, there has been considerable assimilation into English society, many of the members marrying non-Jews. An example was Sir Joseph's great-grandson, HUGH WILLIAMS MONTEFIORE (1920–), converted to Christianity while still at school and entered the Anglican Church in 1949. He taught theology at Cambridge (1951–63) and was appointed bishop suffragan of Kingston upon Thames, Surrey, in 1970.

Bibliography: D. A. J. Cardozo and P. Goodman, *Think and Thank*, 2 vols. (1933); A. M. Hyamson, *Sephardim of England* (1951), index; Roth, England, index; J. Picciotto, *Sketches of Anglo-Jewish History* (1956[2]), index. [V.D.L.]

MONTÉLIMAR, town in the department of Drôme, S.E. France. The first explicit mention of the presence of Jews in Montélimar dates from 1222. The community attained considerable importance during the 14th and first half of the 15th centuries. The synagogue, remains of which still existed at the end of the 19th century, was situated in the Rue de Juiverie or the Rue Puits-Neuf; the school (or possibly another synagogue) was near the Porte Saint-Martin and the cemetery to the northwest of the present cemeteries. The community also maintained a special butcher's shop. As late as 1452, the dauphin granted the Jews of Montélimar, with Jews in several other localities of Dauphiné, some advantageous privileges; the municipal authorities, however, endeavored to render the lives of the Jews intolerable, for instance by compelling them to attend missionary sermons from 1453 onward. The same situation occurred at the end of the century: in 1476, King Louis XI had granted letters of protection to the Jews of Montélimar; however, in 1486, when only seven Jewish families remained there, the townsmen accused them of debauchery and shady practices and demanded their expulsion. From 1489, there no longer appear to have been Jews in Montélimar and the Jewish cemetery was closed. At the beginning of World War II, 150 Jewish families found refuge in Montélimar. There was no organized Jewish community in Montélimar in the 1960s.

Bibliography: Gross, Gal Jud, 319; de Coston, *Histoire de Montélimar*, 1 (1878), 516ff., 4 (1891), 521; Z. Szajkowski, *Analytical Franco-Jewish Gazetteer 1939–1945* (1966), 186. [B.BL.]

MONTEREAU (Montereau-Faut-Yonne), town in the department of Seine-et-Marne, France. A Jewish community existed in Montereau by 1228 consisting of at least 12 families. In 1251, the Jews of Montereau are mentioned in the poll tax roster of the Jews of Champagne. A new community was constituted after the return of the Jews to France in 1359. The houses of two of its members, Benion of Salins and Sannset of Baumes, were looted during the riots of 1381. The memory of the medieval community was preserved until the 18th century in the name of a quay known as the Port-aux-Juifs.

Bibliography: H. Stein, in: *Annales de la Société Historique et Archéologique du Gâtinais*, 17 (1899), 54ff.; A. Longnon, *Documents relatifs au comté de Champagne*, 2 (1904), 418; 3 (1904), 11, 299. [B.BL.]

°**MONTESQUIEU, CHARLES LOUIS DE SECONDAT, BARON DE LA BRÈDE ET DE** (1689–1755), French writer and political philosopher. Montesquieu inherited the humanistic French tradition of Jean *Bodin, with his vision of a society tolerant toward all religions, including Judaism. His earliest statement on the Jews was in the *Lettres Persanes* (1721), 50, where he described Judaism as "a mother who has given birth to two daughters [Christianity and Islam] who have struck her a thousand blows." In *L'Esprit des lois* (25:13), published in 1748, he reacted to the burning of a ten-year-old Jewish girl by the *Inquisition with an eloquent denunciation cast in the form of an argument written by a Jew: "You complain [he said to the inquisitors] that the emperor of Japan is having all the Christians in his domain burnt on a slow fire; but he could answer you: 'We treat you, who do not believe as we do, as you treat those who do not believe as you do' . . . If you do not want to be Christian, at least be human." Nevertheless, he was not entirely uncritical of the Jews. Also in the *Lettres persanes,* his traveler writes: "Know that wherever there is money there are Jews." In a passage from *Mélanges inédits,* which was published posthumously (1892), the rabbinic texts are considered to have fashioned the low taste and character of the Jews, for there was not "one among [the rabbis] of even a minor order of genius." But this private opinion of Montesquieu at his most Christian was unknown in the 18th century. His relativistic view, which ran counter to *Voltaire's absolute deism in favor of an appreciation of the Jew and Judaism as one of the many valid forms of culture and religion, was one that influenced history.

Bibliography: J. Weill, in: REJ, 49 (1904), 150ff.; R. R. Lambert, in: *Univers Israélite,* 94 (1938/39), 421ff.; R. Shackleton, *Montesquieu . . .* (Eng., 1961), 354–5; A. Ages, in: *Romanische Forschungen,* 81 (1969), 214ff.; A. Hertzberg, *French Enlightenment and the Jews* (1968), index; L. Poliakov, *Histoire de l'antisémitisime,* 3 (1968), index.

[AR.H.]

MONTEUX, PIERRE (1875–1964), conductor. Born in Paris, Monteux studied at the Paris Conservatoire where he won the first prize for violin in 1896. He played the viola in various orchestras and founded an orchestra of his own, the Concerts Berlioz. From 1911 to 1914 he conducted the Ballets Russes of Diaghilev, giving the first performances of Ravel's *Daphnis et Chloë,* Debussy's *Jeux,* and Stravinsky's *Petrouchka, Le Sacre du Printemps,* and *Le Rossignol.* He was conductor of the Metropolitan Opera in New York from 1917 to 1919 and then of the Boston Symphony Orchestra until 1924. From 1924 to 1934 he appeared as second conductor of the Concertgebouw in Amsterdam. He founded the Orchestre Symphonique de Paris (1929–38) and from 1936 to 1952 he was director of the San Francisco Symphony Orchestra. Monteux's conducting was faithful to the intentions of the composer, and combined brilliant technique with profound musical culture.

Pierre Monteux, conductor. Drawing by Dolbin, 1954. From A. Meyer, *Collection Musicale,* Paris, 1961.

Bibliography: Baker, Biog. Dict; Riemann-Gurlitt; Grove, Dict.; MGG.

[C.AB.]

MONTEVIDEO, capital of Uruguay with a population of 1,300,000, and a Jewish population of 48,000 (96% of the Jewish population of the country). The community was established before World War I by immigrants from Eastern Europe and the Middle East. Beginning in the lower echelons of commerce and handicrafts, the Jews today belong chiefly to the middle class, with a substantial proportion in industry, commerce, and the liberal professions; few still belong to the working class. The main organization is the Comité Central Israilita (Jewish Central Committee), which incorporates the four *kehillot:* Jewish community of Montevideo (Ashkenazi), the Sephardi Jewish community, the New Jewish Congregation of Montevideo (Eastern and Central Europe), and the Hungarian Jewish community, along with most of the other organizations, except those of Communist ideology and affiliations. Another central body is the Zionist Organization of Uruguay, which represents all the local Zionist organizations. Although the object of anti-Semitic propaganda during the 1930s and the victim of some attacks during the early 1960s, the Jews of Montevideo were not the target of urban terrorism launched in the 1960s by the extreme-left Tupamaru. Economic deterioration and social upheavals, however, severely affected the stability of the Jewish community. For fuller details, see *Uruguay.

[R.P.RA.]

MONTEZINOS, ANTONIO DE (**Aaron Levi;** d.c. 1650), Marrano traveler. On a trip to South America during 1641–42, Montezinos discovered a group of natives in Ecuador who could recite the *Shema* and were acquainted with other Jewish rituals. He brought this news to Amsterdam in 1644, and the congregational authorities—*Manasseh Ben Israel among them—had him repeat his account under oath. The assumption was that these natives were a remnant of the ten lost *tribes, of the tribes of Reuben and Levi according to Montezinos. He then left for Brazil where he died, reasserting on his deathbed the truth of his report. Manasseh Ben Israel dwells on Montezinos' discovery in a booklet entitled *Esperança de Israel* ("The Hope of Israel," Amsterdam, 1650), which he dedicated to the British parliament, appending it to his petition for the readmittance of Jews to England. His thesis was that Montezinos' account points to an imminent fulfillment of the messianic prophecy of the lost tribes of Israel being reunited with Judah. The Montezinos report aroused literary interest even outside Jewish circles. In 1650 Thomas Thorowgood (1595–1669) published his *Iewes in America, or Probabilities that the Americans Are of that Race.* In reply Sir Hamon L'Estrange (1583–1654) wrote *Americans no Iewes, or Improbabilities that the Americans Are of that Race* (London, 1652). Thorowgood then retorted with *Jews in America, or Probabilities that those Indians are Judaical, Made More Probable by Some Additionals to the Former Conjectures* (London, 1660).

Bibliography: C. Roth, *Life of Menasseh Ben Israel* (1934), 176–92, 330–1.

[ED.]

MONTEZINOS, DAVID (1828–1916), librarian and bibliophile in Amsterdam. His father, Raphael Montezinos, served as rabbi of the Portuguese community there from 1852 to 1866. David studied at the Ez Ḥayyim seminary where he obtained the title *maggid.* An enthusiastic bibliophile, he acquired one of the largest private libraries of the time. In 1866 he was appointed librarian of the Ez Ḥayyim library. In 1889, after the death of his wife, he donated his private collection to the library of the seminary, including 20,000 books, pamphlets, manuscripts, and illustrations. It contained extensive material relating to the Jews in Holland, and in particular to the Spanish-Portuguese community. The library was named after Montezinos and was directed by him until his death. Montezinos wrote a number of bibliographic studies, published in *Letterbode*, as well as a monograph on David *Franco-Mendes, published in 1867 in *Joodsch-letterkundige bijdragen.*

Bibliography: J.S. de Silva Rosa, *David Montezinos, de stichter der "Livraria D. Montezinos"* (1914); idem, *David Montezinos* (Dutch, 1917); idem, *Geschiedenis der Portugeesche Joden te Amsterdam* (1925), 153ff. [Ed.]

David Montezinos (left) librarian of the Ez Ḥayyim library, Amsterdam, 1866–1916, photographed with his successor, Jacob S. da Silva Rosa. Courtesy Portuguese Jewish Community, Amsterdam.

MONTI DI PIETÀ (Montes pietatis), savings and loan agencies originally formed in Italian cities in the mid-15th century; considered as the predecessors of the modern credit union. Historically, the word *mons* was used during the Middle Ages to designate funds collected for a specific purpose, *pietatis* being added to identify them as nonspeculative. The initial object of the *monti* was to provide loans at a relatively low rate of interest (4–15%) to small artisans and dealers and to the poor in general, on the pledge of various goods. The interest was used to defray administrative expenses and salaries of employees. The formation of the *monti* was the result of a combination of factors, both economic and theological. It arose from the decline of handicrafts and the ensuing impoverishment of the masses, and a scarcity of money; and from the desire to oust the Jews from the business of *moneylending, which they had successfully practiced as their principal profession. The growing prosperity of Jewish bankers aroused the wrath of the *Franciscans who, as some historians have pointed out, themselves often came from the ranks of the "new aristocracy," the merchant class.

Previously the progressive monopolization of moneylending by Jewish bankers had been justified both morally and theologically; on the one hand, it helped the poor, and on the other hand, it saved Christians from committing the sin of usury; but the founders of the *monti* advanced the argument that it was necessary to protect Christians from the voracity of Jewish usurers. The establishment of the first *monti* in *Perugia in 1462, after an earlier experiment eight years before at Ancona, came at the climax of a campaign against Jewish moneylenders waged by the Observant friars, the radical wing of the Franciscans. Its primary sponsor was Fra Michele da Milano, who protested vigorously against the arrangements then existing between the Jewish loan bankers and the city of Perugia. In subsequent years the Franciscans sought support for the expansion of the institution, preaching on its behalf throughout Italy, in opposition to the *Dominicans and the Augustinians, who condemned what they called the *"montes impietatis"* as a breach of the prohibition on usury proclaimed by Jesus (Luke 6:33). Foremost among those in favor of the institution was *Bernardino of Feltre, who bent all his charismatic talent for rabble-rousing to denouncing the Jewish moneylender. His sermons led to the establishment of the *monti* in many cities and were instrumental in the widespread persecution of Jews during the blood libel in *Trent in 1475 as well as in many other parts of the country. Pope Paul II approved (1467) the establishment of a *monte* in Perugia, despite theological opposition, and successive popes sanctioned *monti* in other Italian cities. By 1494 there were 30 *monti* in central and northern Italy. The controversy was finally settled by the papal bull, *Inter multiplicis* (May 1515), issued by *Leo X at the Fourth *Lateran Council, which declared the *monti* neither sinful nor illicit but, on the contrary, meritorious.

The institution of the *monti* did not, in itself, arouse the fears of the Jews. In some cases Jewish loan bankers, recognizing the charitable nature of the *monti,* actually gave them support. One such loan banker, Manuele da Camerino, bequeathed a considerable sum to the *monte* of Florence which had been set up by Girolamo Savonarola. At times Jewish loan bankers utilized the *monti* for their own purposes, depositing in it a pledge left with them, thereby raising capital for further operations. The *monti* were not in a position to meet the growing need for capital, and, as a result, there were times when Jewish loan bankers were allowed to reopen their *condotte* in the Italian cities, as occurred in Florence after the return of the Medici in 1512. Eventually, both *monti* and Jewish loan bankers found it possible to coexist and the first decades of the 16th century proved to be among the most prosperous for the Italian Jewish banker. By the mid-16th century it was common practice for many *monti* to make loans to businessmen (at an interest rate of from 8 to 10%) as well as to the poor. The *Monti di Pietà* remained an essentially urban feature, an outgrowth of conditions specific to Italy. The decision of the Lateran Council of 1515 to allow *urbi et orbi* the establishment of *monti* was the signal for setting up official lending institutions sponsored by governments in the Catholic countries of Europe.

Bibliography: L. Poliakov, *Les Banquiers juifs et le Saint-Siège du XIIIe au XVIIe siècle* (1965), 169–98, passim; M. Weber, *Origines des Monts-de-Piété* (1920); A. Sapori, *History of the Principal Public Banks* (1934), 373–8; G. Fabiani, *Gli Ebrei e il Monte di Pietà in Ascoli* (1942), 169–72; M. Ciardini, *I banchieri ebrei in Firenze nel secolo XV e il monte di pietà fondato da Girolamo Savonarola* (1907); N. Mengozzi, *Il Monte dei Paschi e le sue aziende* (1913); U. Cassuto, *Gli Ebrei a Firenze* (1918), 51–82; Roth, Italy, 166–77; S. Simonsohn, *Toledot ha-Yehudim be-Dukkasut Mantovah* (1963), 7–16; D. Carpi, *Ha-Yehudim be-Padovah bi-Tekufat ha-Renaissance* (1967), unpublished thesis Hebr. Univ., Jerusalem. [E.B.]

MONTIEL, town in Castile, central Spain, in the frontier district of La Mancha. The small community there had close relations with the Order of Santiago, on whose lands it was situated. In 1273 the head of the Order, Pelayo Pérez, gave Don Samuel, Don Bono, and Don Jacob, all of them Jews under the jurisdiction of the Order, the right to settle their debts out of tax farming. They not only farmed the general taxes in Montiel but also in other lands belonging to the Order. At that time tax farming produced considerable revenues. In 1290 the taxes paid to the king by the community of Montiel amounted to about 1,522 maravedis. The community probably suffered during the persecutions of 1391 when most of the La Mancha communities were destroyed. Nevertheless, a community may have existed in Montiel in the second half of the 15th century; Don Isaac Abudarham, a resident of Toledo, farmed the *alcabala* ("indirect taxes") there in 1462.

Bibliography: Baer, Urkunden, 2 (1936), 62ff., 81, 310. [H.B.]

MONTOR, HENRY (1905–), U.S. organization executive and Zionist. Montor, born in Canada, was taken to the U.S. as a boy. He was active in Zionist affairs from his youth and assistant editor of the *New Palestine* (1926–30). During his service with the United Palestine Appeal (1930–39) and as executive vice-president of the United Jewish Appeal (1939–50), Montor directed the raising of previously unparalleled amounts from overseas Jewry for Israel. As vice-president and chief executive of the American Financial and Development Corporation for Israel (1951–55), Montor established the Israel bond campaigns and supervised the sale of approximately $190 million worth of bonds for Israel. He resigned this position in 1955 to found his own brokerage firm. [Ed.]

MONTORO, ANTÓN DE (1404–1480?), Spanish Converso poet who denounced the persecution of his fellow converts. He was born in Andalusia, probably in Montoro, and because he dealt in clothes he came to be known as the "tailor of Cordoba." He flourished during the reigns of Henry IV and Ferdinand and Isabella. Montoro was a noted writer of humorous and satirical verse which won him the esteem of the court poets, but despite his success he never denied his humble origin or relinquished his trade. In a humorous poem addressed to his horse he admitted that he had children, grandchildren, parents, and a sister who had not converted. Montoro was one of the few authentic and sincere voices of the age. He protested vigorously against the treatment of the Conversos and satirized the weak efforts of Alfonso de Aguilar, the governor of Cordoba, to stop the outrages. After the sack of Carmona in 1474, Montoro implored Ferdinand and Isabella to protect his people, whose sufferings he portrayed most movingly. He concluded his poem with a ferocious joke, saying that the killing should at least be postponed until Christmas, when the fire would be more welcome. Critics have therefore accused Montoro of cynicism, not realizing that the remark represents the black humor of despair. Despite his work on behalf of the Conversos, Montoro himself was apparently sincere in his Catholic beliefs and in a poem addressed to Queen Isabella toward the end of his life lamented that in 70 years he had been unable to lose the name of "old Jewish dog," despite the fact that he went to church and ate bacon. Montoro engaged in a poetic feud with another convert, *Juan (Poeta) de Valladolid. The two men exchanged mutual insults, much to the amusement of their contemporaries. Montoro also rebuked Rodrigo de *Cota de Maguaque for his thoughtless attacks on fellow Conversos; such criticism, he claimed, might eventually rebound on its author.

Bibliography: E. Cotarelo y Mori (ed.), *Cancionero de Antón de Montoro* (1900); Roth, Marranos, 37; Baer, Spain, 2 (1966), 310ff. [K.R.S.]

MONTPELLIER, capital of the Hérault department, southern France. The first implicit evidence of the presence of Jews there is found in the will of Guilhem V, Lord of Montpellier, who forbade the investiture of a Jew as bailiff. Even though *Benjamin of Tudela, in about 1165, does not mention any figure for the Jewish population of Montpellier, its importance can be deduced from the fact that he mentions several yeshivot. Until at least the close of the 12th century the Jews of Montpellier appear to have been particularly active in commerce; they are explicitly mentioned in the trade agreement between Montpellier and *Agde; and they appear in the tariff of taxes due from the merchants of Montpellier in *Narbonne. Until the close of the 12th century they do not appear to have practiced moneylending. In times of war, particularly when the town was besieged, the Jews helped in its defense by supplying weapons, for instance 20,000 arrows, as noted in an agreement at the beginning of the 13th century. From the middle of the 13th century moneylending was regulated by the ordinances of James I, king of *Majorca, who also ruled over the duchy of Montpellier together with the bishop of Maguelonne: before any contract was drawn up, the Jewish lender was called upon to swear that it involved neither fraud nor usury. In addition, the consuls of the town prohibited loans to people under the age of 25 without the consent of their parents. James I's legislation concerning the Jews promulgated in 1267 was fairly favorable, especially the clause prohibiting their prosecution on the basis of an anonymous denunciation. Those who accused or denounced Jews were to provide two guarantors and were threatened with being condemned themselves if they could not prove their accusation; bail was to be granted to the accused Jew if he could provide a satisfactory guarantee.

During the 13th century a Jewish quarter existed on the present site of the Rue Barralerie (until the 15th century it was named Sabatarié Neuve); in the first house on this street there are still some remains of the synagogue and in particular of the *mikveh* in the cellar. Although the Jews were dispossessed of their ancient cemetery when James I gave it to the Cistercians of Valemagne in 1263, the latter were required to refund the cost of the exhumation and the transfer of the remains to the new cemetery. When the Jews were expelled from France in 1306, the king of Majorca opposed the measure. After considerable delay, the expulsion finally took place, and it was scant comfort to the Jews that the king of France was required to give to the king of Majorca two-thirds of the booty seized from his Jews and one-third of that taken from the other Jews of Montpellier.

In 1315, when the return to France was authorized, the Jews of Montpellier, like those elsewhere, were again placed under the authority of their former lords. In 1319 Sancho I, king of Majorca, permitted them to acquire a cemetery. It is not known in which quarter the Jews lived during this short stay, which lasted until 1322 (or 1323). In 1349 James III of Majorca sold his seigneury over Montpellier to Phillip VI of France. Thus when the Jews reestablished themselves there in 1359 they found themselves under the direct sovereignty of the king of France, Charles V. After their first having been assigned to the Castelmoton quarter, complaints from the Christian inhabitants compelled them to move to the Rue de la Vielle Intendance quarter, where they owned a synagogue and a school (after 1365). The Jews had to provide large financial contributions to the defense of the town, particularly in 1362 and 1363. In 1374 they were also obliged to participate in guarding the gates. The erection of a new synagogue of great beauty in 1387 gave rise to a lawsuit with the bishop of Maguelonne, to whom the Jews paid the then enormous sum of 400 livres. In Montpellier the final expulsion of the Jews from France in 1394 was preceded by violent accusations against them in the municipal council.

Scholars. Even though the town had numerous Jewish physicians—who were subjected to a probative examination from 1272—there is no valid evidence that the Jews had a part in founding and organizing the school of medicine there. Excluding those scholars who only lived temporarily in Montpellier, such as *Abraham b. David of Posquières, the foremost scholar in the town was *Solomon b. Abraham b. Samuel, who denounced the work of Maimonides to the Inquisition. One of his leading followers was his disciple, *Jonah b. Abraham Gerondi, who died in Toledo. The liturgical poet *Aryeh Judah Harari lived there during the second half of the 13th century, as did *Aaron b. Joseph ha-Levi, the opponent of Solomon b. Abraham *Adret, and Isaac b. Jacob ha-Kohen *Alfasi. From 1303 to 1306 Montpellier was again the scene of a renewed polemic between the supporters and opponents of the study of philosophy. The latter were led by Jacob b. Machir ibn *Tibbon. In the later medieval community of Montpellier, the physician and philosopher Abraham *Avigdor was particularly distinguished.

Later Centuries. In the middle of the 16th century the presence in Montpellier of *Conversos, who chiefly lived among the Protestant population, is vouched for by a Swiss traveler, a student named Platter. From the beginning of the 16th century Jews from *Comtat Venaissin traded in the town. In 1653 the attorney general of the parliament of Toulouse directed the town magistrates to expel them. Similar orders were repeated in 1679 and 1680. A special register was opened at the town record office for the Jews who made their way to Montpellier as a result of a general authorization, granted from the end of the 17th century, enabling them to trade for one month during each season. From 1714 nine Jews were allowed to settle in the town; others followed with the tacit consent of the magistrates, in spite of complaints by the Christian merchants. At the beginning of the 19th century (1805) the Jewish community consisted of 105 persons and was headed by R. Moïse Milhau, who represented the department of Vaucluse at the great *Sanhedrin. Thirteen local Jews served in the armies of the revolution and of the empire, five as volunteers. The historian and physician Joseph *Salvador was born in Montpellier of an old Spanish-Jewish family which had fled the Inquisition. At the beginning of the 20th century there were about 35 Jewish families in Montpellier.

Holocaust and Contemporary Periods. After the 1940 armistice, Montpellier, which was in the unoccupied zone, became a center for Jewish refugees from the occupied part of France. After the latter was occupied by the Germans, Montpellier became an important relaying station for the Jewish partisans. After the liberation the community was reorganized and by 1960 had 600 members. The arrival of Jews from North Africa increased the number to 2,000 in 1969, when the community had a communal center and a Sephardi synagogue with 300 seats. There were two kosher butchers and a *talmud torah*.

Bibliography: Gross, Gal Jud, 322–35; C. d'Aigrefeuille, *Histoire de la ville de Montpellier*, 2 (1875²), 348ff.; A. Germain, *Histoire du Commerce de Montpellier*, 2 vols. (1861), index s.v. *Juifs*, S. Kahn, in: REJ, 19 (1889), 259–81; 22 (1891), 264–79; 23 (1891), 265–78; 28 (1894), 118–41; 33 (1896), 283–303; G. Saige, *Les Juifs du Languedoc* (1881), index; L. H. Escuret, *Vieilles rues de Montpellier*, 2 (1964), 23ff., 28–34; Z. Szajkowski, *Franco-Judaica* (1962), index.

[B.BL.]

MONTREAL, largest city in *Canada, situated on the Island of Montreal, at the junction of the St. Lawrence and Ottawa rivers, in the province of Quebec. The population of the Jewish community in metropolitan Montreal, the oldest

Figure 1. A sermon at Shaar Hashomayim Congregation, Montreal, c. 1890. From S. Rosenberg, *The Jewish Community in Canada*, Vol. I, Montreal, 1970.

and largest in Canada, was estimated at 121,000 in 1970 out of an approximate total of $2\frac{1}{4}$ million.

Jews first went to Montreal in 1760 as officers and commissaries with the British Army under General Amherst, and after the surrender of the city to the British on Sept. 8, 1760, several Jews settled in Montreal as merchants, fur traders, exporters, and importers. They were joined by relatives and friends from England and the British colonies in North America. Among the earliest Jewish settlers in Montreal were: Lazarus and Samuel David; Andrew Hays; Uriah, Isaac, and Samuel Judah; Levy and Ezekiel Solomons; Levy and Myer Michaels; Abraham Franks, Myer Myers, Simon Levy, Barnet Lyon, and Heineman Pines.

Synagogues. The earliest Jewish settlers in Montreal had previously lived in New York, in which the only synagogue in 1760 was the Shearith Israel Congregation, founded by Jews of Spanish and Portuguese origin, which followed the Sephardi *minhag*. In December 1768, when there were sufficient permanent Jewish residents in Montreal, they formed a congregation which adopted the same name and followed the same Sephardi *minhag* as the synagogue they had attended in New York. The small congregation worshiped in a room on 86 James Street until 1777, when the first synagogue building was erected on land owned by David David at the junction of Notre Dame and St. James streets. After the death of David David in 1824, the congregation decided to move to another site. However, it was not until 1838 that another site was purchased and a new synagogue built on Chenneville and Lagauchtiere streets, and this building served the community until 1890, when following the northward and westward growth and movement of the Jewish population, the old synagogue was sold and a new synagogue built on Stanley Street. Fifty years later, a new and larger synagogue was built in the new Snowden residential area of the city.

The congregation did not receive legal and official government recognition until 1831. Then, upon the request of the Jewish citizens of Montreal, an act was passed by the Legislative Assembly of Quebec permitting the incorporation in each of the centers of Montreal, Quebec, and Trois Rivieres of a Jewish religious body empowered to hold land for the erection of a synagogue, a minister's house, and a cemetery, and authorizing the minister of the Jewish congregation to keep a register of births, marriages, and deaths. The first minister of the Shearith Israel Congregation was the Rev. Jacob Raphael Cohen, who went to Canada from England in 1778 and held that position until 1782. He was succeeded by the Rev. R. de Lara from 1782 to 1810. From 1810 to 1840 the congregation had no minister. The Rev. David Piza served the congregation from 1840 to 1846, when he returned to England. In 1847 the Rev. Abraham *de Sola, grandson of Rabbi Raphael Meldola, the *ḥakham* of the Sephardi Congregation in London, went to Montreal as spiritual leader of the Shearith Israel—Spanish and Portuguese Congregation. He held this position until his death in 1882. He was the first Sephardi rabbi to become a permanent resident in Canada, and also played a prominent role in the cultural life of the non-Jewish population of Montreal. He was appointed professor of Hebrew and oriental literature at McGill University soon after his arrival in Montreal, was for many years president of the Natural History Society of Montreal, was a prolific writer on Jewish religious and historical subjects, and was the first Jew awarded an honorary LL.D. by McGill University (in 1858). His eldest son Aaron David Meldola de Sola, born in 1853, succeeded his father on the latter's death in 1882 and officiated until his death in 1918.

In 1846 a new act of the Quebec Legislature replaced the old act of 1831 and incorporated two congregations in Montreal, the congregation of Portuguese Jews (Shearith Israel) and the congregation of German and Polish Jews. However, it was not until 1858 that Jews who preferred the Ashkenazi *minhag,* most of whom had previously been members of the Spanish and Portuguese congregations, were able to purchase a lot on De Bullion Street near Craig Street and erect a synagogue called the German and Polish Synagogue. This was subsequently renamed the Shaar Hashomayim Synagogue, and was the first Ashkenazi Orthodox synagogue erected in Canada. In 1886 the congregation sold its synagogue building and built a new synagogue on McGill College Avenue. In 1892 a new and larger synagogue was built in the residential suburb of Westmount.

The number of Jewish congregations in metropolitan Montreal increased rapidly from 1946, and there were 40 synagogues in 1970, of which 33 were Orthodox, three were Conservative, three were Reform, and one was Reconstructionist. Among the Orthodox congregations were four following the Sephardi *minhag,* which were established from 1965 on by Jewish immigrants from Morocco, Algeria, and Egypt.

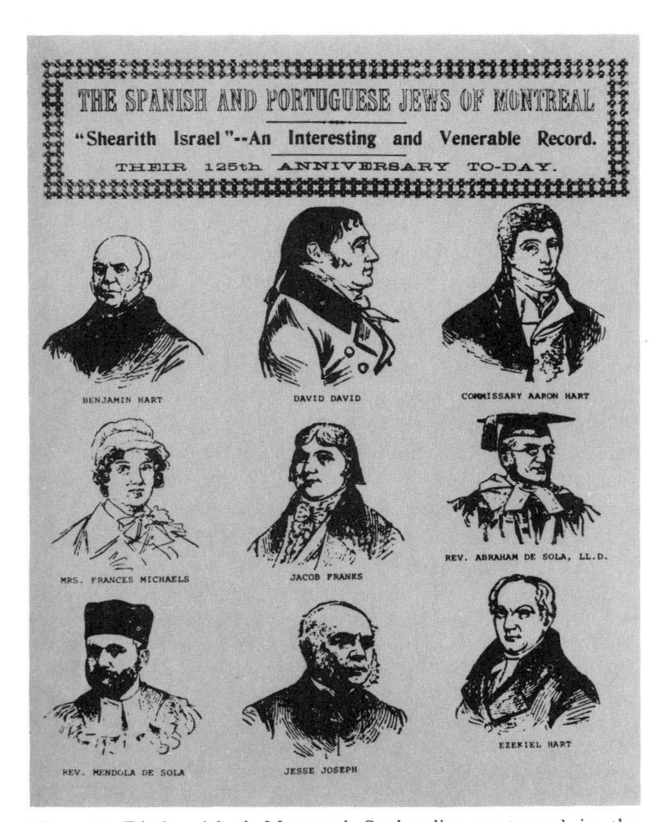

Figure 2. Distinguished Montreal Sephardim portrayed in the *Montreal Daily Star* of December 30, 1893, on the occasion of the 125th anniversary of the establishment of the community. From S. Rosenberg, *The Jewish Community in Canada.*

Education. In 1970, unlike the situation in the other provinces of Canada, there were no secular nondenominational public schools in Montreal. In accordance with the British North America Act of 1867 there were in Quebec only two types of tax-supported public schools, one Roman Catholic and the other Protestant. Members of the Protestant and Catholic Public School Boards in Montreal were not elected, but appointed, and until 1968 there were no Jewish members of the Protestant School Board of Greater Montreal. All school taxes paid by Jewish property owners went to the Protestant School Board, and in return Jewish children had the right to attend the schools of the Protestant School Board of Greater Montreal, and were exempted from Christian religious instruction upon request of their parents. From 1903 on attempts were made by the Montreal Jewish community at various times to obtain changes in legislation which would establish a secular nondenominational system of public schools or tax-supported Jewish schools parallel with and with powers equal to the existing Roman Catholic and Protestant public schools, but without success. After protracted negotiations, five Jews were appointed by the Quebec Provincial Government to the Protestant School Board of Greater Montreal in 1968 from a list recommended by the Canadian Jewish Congress. The Protestant Board agreed to accept as "associate schools" those Jewish voluntary elementary and high schools which had the same pedagogical standards and regulations pertaining to training of teaching staff, curriculum, and salaries, and to pay an annual grant of $350 per Jewish pupil attending one of the nine approved "associate" Jewish day schools, leaving Hebrew studies and religious instruction to be financed by the associate Jewish day schools themselves. In 1969 there were about 5,000 children attending the Jewish day schools in Montreal which were approved "associate schools" receiving the aforementioned per capita grant, and the Jewish children attending the Protestant elementary and high schools in 1969 numbered 17,000.

Demography. The Jewish population of Montreal increased from 403 in 1861 to 811 in 1881; 6,975 in 1901; 45,846 in 1921; 63,937 in 1941; and 102,724 in 1961, according to the Canadian government census figures. However, the Jewish population of metropolitan Montreal decreased from 6.1% in 1921 to 4.9% in 1961. Jews formed the third largest ethnic group in metropolitan Montreal during the period from 1901 to 1961, exceeded only by the population of French origin with 64.2%, and those of Anglo-Celtic origin with 17.9%. Thirty-four percent of the total Jewish population of Canada lived in Montreal. By 1961 this percentage had increased to 40.4. In 1961 there were 72 cities, towns, and villages in what is known as the suburban metropolitan Montreal census area, and Jews were resident in 64 of them. Of the total Jewish population of metropolitan Montreal in 1901, 98.2% lived within the boundaries of the city of Montreal itself, and there were only three suburban cities, Westmount, Lachine, and Verdun in which Jews were resident, and in none of these suburbs did the Jewish population exceed 65.

By 1921 the number of suburban towns and villages within the metropolitan Montreal census area in which Jews were resident had increased to nine. Their Jewish population constituted 6.6% of the total Jewish population within the metropolitan Montreal area, and two of them,

Outremont and Westmount, each had a little more than 1,000 Jewish residents. In 1941 Jews were living in ten of these suburban cities and towns, forming 20.1% of the total Jewish population of metropolitan Montreal, and the Jewish population of Outremont had increased to 10,338, while the Jewish population of Westmount had increased to 1,625. The migration of the Jewish population from the old area of settlement within the city of Montreal to the new suburban residential areas continued, and by 1961 the Jewish population of Westmount had increased to 2,322, while the Jewish population of Outremont, which was adjacent to the old area of Jewish settlement within the city of Montreal had decreased to 9,033.

In 1961 Jews living in the newer residential suburban fringe constituted 36.4% of the total Jewish population of metropolitan Montreal, and there were seven suburban cities and towns within that area, each with a Jewish population exceeding 1,000. Those residential suburbs with their Jewish population in 1961 were Outremont (9,033), Cote St. Rue (8,307), St. Laurent (7,696), Chomedy (3,493), Mount Royal (2,617), Westmount (2,222), and Hampstead (1,560).

The majority of the total Jewish population in metropolitan Montreal in 1961 was Canadian-born (56.9%), while 11.7% were born in Poland; 10.0% in Russia; 4.4% in Rumania; 3.6% in Hungary; 2.3% in the United States; 1.6% in the United Kingdom; 4.4% in other European countries; and 5.1% in all other countries. Of the total Jewish population of metropolitan Montreal in 1961, 53.8% reported English as their mother tongue and 30.2% reported Yiddish as their mother tongue; while 97.2% could speak English and 36.1% could speak both official languages, English and French. Jews engaged in commerce formed 30% of the total Jewish labor force in metropolitan Montreal in 1961, followed by 22% in industry, 16% in clerical occupations, 13% in the professions, 12% in service occupations, 2% in transport and communications, 1% in construction, and 1% in unskilled labor.

Organization. In 1970 the national headquarters of almost all Jewish communal organizations in Canada were situated in that city. These organizations included: the Canadian Jewish Congress; the Federated Zionist Organization of Canada; the Jewish Immigrant Aid Services of Canada; Labour Zionist Movement of Canada; Canadian Hadassah-Wizo; Canadian Mizrachi-ha-Po'el ha-Mizrachi; Pioneer Women of Canada; and the Keren ha-Tarbut.

The Young Men's Hebrew Benevolent Society founded in Montreal in 1863 was the first Jewish social welfare organization in Canada; its object was to assist the increasing stream of Jewish immigrants fleeing from discrimination and persecution in Eastern Europe. It changed its name to the Baron de Hirsch Institute in 1900 in recognition of the munificent grants made to it by Baroness Clara de Hirsch. As the Jewish population of Montreal increased, the Montreal Jewish community became more self-supporting and fund-raising campaigns multiplied; and in 1916 the Baron de Hirsch Institute, the Mount Sinai Sanatorium, the Herzl Dispensary, and the Jewish Home for the Aged combined to form the Federation of Jewish Community Services. During the period from 1916 to 1965 the number of Jewish social welfare and health agencies continued to multiply rapidly and the need for larger funds necessary to maintain them brought about the organization of a Combined Jewish Appeal Campaign in 1941, which in 1951 joined with the United Israel Appeal to conduct one annual fund-raising campaign.

In 1965 the need for still greater coordination, planning, fund-raising, and cooperative action in Jewish community affairs brought about the reorganization of the Montreal

Figure 3. Wedding ceremony in the Shaar Hashomayim synagogue in Montreal, the oldest Ashkenazi synagogue in Canada. Photo Forbath, Montreal.

Federation of Jewish Community Services and the Combined Jewish Appeal into a new all-embracing body named the Allied Jewish Community Services of Montreal. The constituent agencies of the Allied Jewish Community Services of Montreal included: the Baron de Hirsch Family and Child Welfare Service; the Jewish General Hospital; Mount Sinai Hospital; Jewish Hospital of Hope; Maimonides Hospital and Home for the Aged; Jewish Convalescent Hospital; Herzl Health Centre; Jewish Vocational Service; Jewish Children's Summer Camps; Jewish Immigrant Aid Services; Hillel Foundation; Jewish Public Library; institutes of Jewish Studies at McGill and Montreal universities; and the Golden Age Association. The partners in the Annual Combined Appeal in 1970 were the United Israel Appeal, the United Jewish Relief Agencies, and the Canadian Jewish Congress; the amount raised in the 1969 Combined Campaign in Montreal was $9,155,340.

Members of the Jewish community in Montreal have been prominent in the political, musical, literary, and artistic life of Canada during the past century. Lazarus Phillips, prominent Jewish lawyer active in Jewish communal life, was appointed a member of the Canadian Senate in 1969. In 1970 Victor Goldbloom, who was reelected as a member of the Quebec Provincial Legislature, became the first Jew to hold the position of a cabinet minister in the Quebec Provincial Government.

Bibliography: Jewish Immigrant Aid Society of Canada, *Studies and Documents on Immigration and Integration in Canada* (1962–70); Federation of Jewish Philanthropies in Montreal, *Annual Report* (1924–69); L. Rosenberg, *Canada's Jews, A Social and Economic Study* (1939); A. D. Hart (ed.), *The Jew in Canada* (1926); S. I. Belkin, *Through Narrow Gates; A Review of Jewish Immigration, Colonization and Immigrant Aid Work in Canada, 1840–1940* (1966); B. G. Sack, *History of the Jews in Canada* (1965); I. Medres, *Montreal fun Nechten* (1947); S. Rosenberg, *The Jewish Community in Canada* (1970). [L.Ros.]

MONZÓN (Monson, Montisson), city in Aragon, N.E. Spain. The history of three communities, Monzón, Barbastro, and Lérida, was closely interconnected. Information on Jewish settlement in Monzón, which had many connections with the local Knights Templar, dates back to the second half of the 12th century. In 1232 the Monzón community joined the communities which pronounced a counter-ban against the scholars who banned the study of *Maimonides' writings. For taxation purposes the community formed part of a *collecta* (tax administrative unit) with the neighboring communities of Albalate de Cinca, Alcoletge, Pomar, Estadilla, and Granadella. In 1271 the annual tax paid to the crown by the community of Monzón amounted to 4,000 sólidos. A ruling of Solomon b. Abraham ibn *Adret (Responsa, pt. 3, no. 242; cf. Responsa of Isaac b. Sheshet, no. 19) indicates how the tax was paid in Monzón. Anti-Jewish riots occurred in Monzón in 1260. During the persecutions at the time of the *Black Death (1348), the Jews of Monzón entrenched themselves inside their walled quarter and were thus saved. They suffered no harm during the 1391 persecutions, although a number of them subsequently became *Conversos. The community sent Don Joseph ha-Levi and R. Yom Tov Caracosa as its representatives to the disputation of *Tortosa in 1413–14, which had serious consequences for the Monzón community. In 1414 the antipope *Benedict XIII wrote to the bishop of Lérida authorizing him to turn the synagogue of Monzón into a church, since the majority of the community's members had become converted. He also ordered that property belonging to the burial society and the *talmud torah* should be given as *beneficium* to the chapel to be erected in the new church. However it seems that later the community revived. Forty-four names of Jewish householders are mentioned in the notarial records of 1465–78. No details are recorded regarding the departure of the Jews from Monzón on the expulsion of the Jews from Spain in 1492.

Bibliography: Baer, Spain, index; Baer, Studien, 149; Baer, Urkunden, 1 (1929), index; Neuman, Spain, index; Ashtor, Korot, 2 (1966), 174; F. Cantera, *Sinagogas españolas* (1955), 251–2; Vendrell Gallostra, in: *Sefarad*, 3 (1943), 124; Romano, *ibid.*, 13 (1953), 72ff.; Lopez de Meneses, *ibid.*, 14 (1954), 108; Cabezudo Astrain, *ibid.*, 23 (1963), 266f., 274, 280, 282.

[H.B.]

MONZON, ABRAHAM, the name of two scholars. (1) (d. after 1603), halakhic authority and preacher, and apparently of North African origin. During his youth he lived in Egypt, where he studied under R. Bezalel *Ashkenazi. His pupils in Egypt included R. Abraham *Iskandari. He later went to Constantinople, where he died. He wrote halakhic decisions, and homiletical interpretations; some of his responsa are scattered in various manuscripts and in the works of contemporary scholars, such as Joseph di *Trani, Samuel de *Medina, Bezalel Ashkenazi, and Solomon b. Abraham ha-Kohen. *Azulai saw in manuscript a composition of his on the work *Imrei Emet*, by Menahem de *Lonzano, criticizing the kabbalistic system of R. Ḥayyim *Vital. Azulai also saw a collection of his sermons.

(2) (18th century), rabbi and author. He was born in Tetuan, Morocco, where he engaged unsuccessfully in commerce. He therefore wandered to Algiers and Oran and in about 1732 arrived in Egypt where he was considered as one of the most prominent rabbis. His works are extant in manuscript.

Bibliography: J. Ayash, *Responsa Beit Yehudah* (Leghorn, 1746), *Ḥoshen Mishpat*, no. 4 (75a); Conforte, Kore, 39–43, 48–49; J. M. Toledano, *Ner ha-Ma'arav* (1911), 158–9, 230–1; J. Ben-Naim, *Malkhei Rabbanan* (1931), 13b; Rosanes, Togarmah, 5 (1938), 336–7; S. Assaf, *Mekorot u-Meḥkarim* (1946), 206–8; Hirschberg, Afrikah, 2 (1965), 115.

[A.D.]

MOON (Heb. usually יָרֵחַ, *yare'aḥ;* poetical form לְבָנָה, *levanah;* Isa. 24:23; 30:26; Song 6:10). A deity for ancient Israel's neighbors, the moon is for Israel "the lesser light" created on the fourth day of creation "to rule the night" (Gen. 1:16). The calendar used in ancient Israel was probably lunisolar. At any rate the month was based on the periodical recurrence of the moon's phases. (For full details, see *Calendar.) The New Moon, Rosh Ḥodesh, the beginning of a new period, was proclaimed by the Sanhedrin and marked by the blowing of trumpets and special offerings (Num. 10:10, et al.), and was a minor holiday of which liturgical traces have remained (see *New Moon). Two main festivals, Passover and Sukkot, begin at the full moon.

Cult. As a male deity, the moon (Nanna) was worshiped by the Sumerians and by the Semites in general. Known as Sin among the eastern Semites, the moon god was called Eraḥ in the "west." Sin was the patron god of Ur and Haran, which were connected with the origins of the Patriarchs. The popularity of the moon cult is attested by the frequency of theophoric names with the divine element Sin or Eraḥ. The Israelites were warned against worshiping the moon, and convicted transgressors were punished by stoning (Deut. 4:19; 17:3–5). The moon cult was, nevertheless, introduced into Judah by King Manasseh (II Kings 21:3) but was subsequently abolished by King Josiah (II Kings 23:5).

For fuller details see *Host of Heaven.

In the Aggadah. Rabbinic literature uses *levanah*, and not *yare'aḥ* for the moon. The moon and the sun were created on the 28th of Elul (PdRE 8), and were originally equal in size (both being referred to as "the two great lights"— Gen. 1:16), but jealousy between them caused dissensions, so that God decided to make one of them smaller. The moon was chosen to be degraded because it had unlawfully intruded into the sphere of the sun, and hence the difference between the sun, "the greater light," and the moon, "the lesser light" *(ibid.)*. The unlawful intrusion is based on the phenomenon that the moon is sometimes visible during the day (PdRE 6; Gen. R. 6:3). The remarkable statement is made that the he-goat offered on the New Moon is a sin-offering brought by God; according to the Midrash this was for having permitted the moon to encroach upon the domain of the sun (Gen. R. 6:3), but the Talmud says it was for diminishing its size (Ḥul. 60b). God also appeased the moon by surrounding it with stars like a viceroy encircled

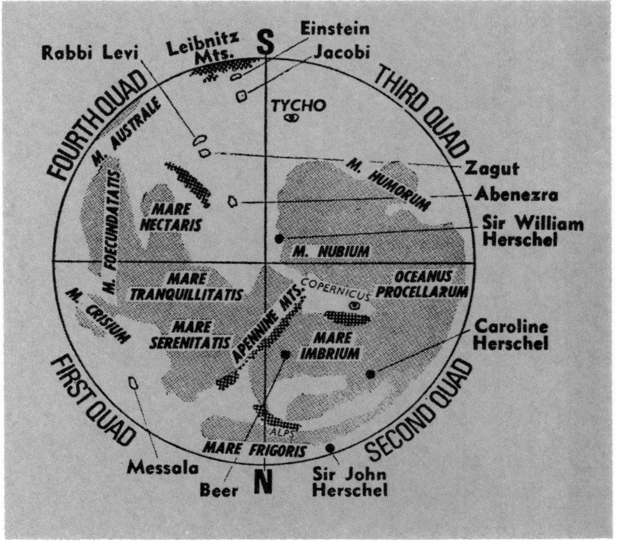

Diagram of the moon, showing areas named after Jews. From *Jewish Chronicle*, London, July 1969.

by his assistants (Gen. R. 6:4). God's original intention was that the sun alone should furnish light to the earth, but foreseeing the future idolatrous worship of the heavenly objects, He decided that it would be better to have two large celestial bodies, thus minimizing the danger of one becoming a central deity (Gen. R. 6: 1). For this reason the sun and moon stand in judgment daily before the Almighty, ashamed to go forth, and pleading, "People worship us and anger the Holy One, blessed be He!" (Mid. Ps. 19: 11).

The moon was designated as Jacob's luminary, while the sun symbolized Esau. The Jewish nation bases its calendar on the lunar year, since they have a portion in this world and the world to come, like the moon which can be seen both by day and by night (Gen. R. 6:3). An eclipse of the moon is therefore considered an evil omen for Israel, and is attributed to four different sins: forgery, false testimony breeding small cattle in Ereẓ Israel (since they damage the crops of the field), and cutting down fruit trees (Suk. 29a). The rabbis declared that the countenance of Moses was like that of the sun, while that of Joshua was like that of the moon (BB 75a). Esther, who brought light to Israel after the evil decree of Ahasuerus, is likewise compared to the moon, which enables people to rejoice and walk about when it illuminates the darkness of the night (Ex. R. 15:6). In the future, seven companies of righteous men whose faces will shine like the sun and the moon will welcome the presence of God (Lev. R. 30:2). Moses did not comprehend exactly when the New Moon was to be sanctified until God showed him the form of the moon when it was beginning its monthly cycle and said to him, "When you see it like this, sanctify it" (Mekh. Pisḥa 1).

See also *Moon, Blessing of the. [Ed.]

Bibliography: Ginzberg, Legends, index s.v. *Moon*.

MOON, BLESSING OF THE, prayer of thanksgiving recited at the periodical reappearance of the moon's crescent. In Hebrew, the prayer is known by several names: *Birkat ha-Levanah* ("the blessing of the moon") or *Kiddush Levanah* ("sanctification of the moon"). It can be recited from the third evening after the appearance of the new moon until the 15th of the lunar month; after that day, the moon begins to diminish. The prayer is recited only if the moon is clearly visible (not when it is hidden by clouds) and it should preferably be said in the open air. According to the Talmud (Sanh. 42a), "Whoever pronounces the benediction over the new moon in its due time welcomes, as it were, the presence of the *Shekhinah*" ("Divine Presence") and hence it is recommended (Sof. 20: 1) to pronounce the benediction, if possible, on the evening after the departure of the Sabbath when one is still in a festive mood and clad in one's best clothes. The blessing of the new moon in some rites is delayed in the month of Av, until after the Ninth of *Av, in Tishri, until after the *Day of Atonement, and in Tevet until after the fast of the tenth of *Tevet. A mourner does not bless the moon until after **shivah* ("the first week of mourning"); in the rainy season, however, when the moon is often hidden by clouds, he recites it whenever possible. The blessing of the moon is not recited on Sabbath and holiday eves, mainly because of the prohibition to carry prayer books outside the house or synagogue building when there is no **eruv*. The basic text of the blessing is given in *Sanhedrin* 42a and in *Soferim* 2: 1, but many addditions were subsequently made. In the present Ashkenazi ritual, the blessing is introduced by the recital of Psalms 148: 1–6 (in the Sephardi rite also Ps. 8:4–5), after which a benediction praising God as the creator and master of nature is pronounced. In the mishnaic period, the proclamation of the new month by the rabbinical court was celebrated with

The Blessing of the Moon, from Johann Bodenschatz, *Kirchliche Verfassung der heutigen Juden*, Frankfort and Leipzig, 1748. Cecil Roth Collection.

dancing and rejoicing. It is still customary to rise on the tips of the toes in the direction of the moon while reciting three times "As I dance toward thee, but cannot touch thee, so shall none of my evil-inclined enemies be able to touch me." This is followed by "Long live David, King of Israel" (also pronounced three times) and by the greeting *Shalom aleikhem* ("Peace be to you") which is extended to those standing around who respond *Aleikhem shalom* ("to you be peace"). This part of the ceremony is reminiscent of the days of *Judah ha-Nasi when the Romans abrogated the authority of the rabbinical court to consecrate the new moon which therefore had to be carried out clandestinely. "Long live David, King of Israel" served as a password between Judah ha-Nasi and his emissary R. *Ḥiyya (RH 25a). It also voiced Israel's continuous hope for redemption by the Messiah, a descendant of David whose kingdom would be "established forever as the moon" (Ps. 89:38). The ceremony concludes with the recital of several scriptural verses, a quotation from the Talmud (Sanh. 42a) "In the school of R. Ishmael it was taught: Had Israel merited no other privilege than to greet the presence of their Heavenly Father once a month, it were sufficient," the plea that God readjust the deficiency of the light of the moon caused by the moon's complaint against the sun (Ḥul. 60b), and a prayer for the fulfillment of the promise of the restoration of the Kingdom of Israel when the Jews will "seek the Lord their God, and David their King" (Hos. 3:5). The blessing of the new moon and the festive character of Rosh Ḥodesh (New Month) originated in the time of the *Second Temple. Due to the significance of the moon in the Jewish *calendar (see Ex. 12:2), it may be of much older origin; in the course of time it has, however, undergone substantial changes. The rite takes the moon as a symbol of the renewal in nature as well as of Israel's renewal and redemption. Various other elements, some of them of a superstitious nature, have become attached to the rite.

Bibliography: Hertz, Prayer, 994–5; E. Levi, *Yesodot ha-Tefillah* (1952[2]), 302–5; Idelsohn, Liturgy, 160–1; ET, s.v. *Birkat ha-Levanah;* E. Munk, *The World of Prayer,* 2 (1963), 94–101.
[M.Y.]

°**MOORE, GEORGE FOOT** (1851–1931), U.S. teacher of religion. Moore graduated from Yale in 1872 and from Union Theological Seminary in 1877, was ordained to the Presbyterian ministry in 1878, and became professor of Hebrew in Andover Theological Seminary in 1883. In 1902 he went to Harvard and was made professor of the history of religion in 1904.

Moore's work was of importance in four fields—the shaping of U.S. scholarship, the reshaping of U.S. concepts of religion, the study of the Hebrew Bible, and the study of tannaitic Judaism. For scholarship, he helped introduce the "scientific" standards and concepts developed in Germany into the U.S. His influence was exercised through his own example, teaching, committee work, editorship of the *Andover Review* (1884–93), the *Harvard Theological Review* (1908–14, 1921–31), and *Harvard Theological Studies* (1916–31), innumerable book reviews, articles, and lectures, and participation in learned societies. He was president of the American Academy of Arts and Sciences, the Massachusetts Historical Society, and the Society of Biblical Literature. Thus he also did much to shape the concept of religion as a universal human activity of which the various religions are particular instances, and the study, one of the "humanities." This conception was important for the ecumenical movement, cooperation between Christians and Jews, reorientation of missions from conversion to social work, and introduction of courses on the history of religion into college curricula. The professor of history of religion appeared as a new social type, distinct from the chaplain and the professor of theology, and Moore's works—*Metempsychosis* (1914), *The Birth and Growth of Religion* (1923), *History of Religions* (2 vols., 1913–19, 1927–28)—were used in many courses.

In the study of the Hebrew Bible Moore not only introduced German methods, standards, and conclusions, but added his own common sense and enormous learning. Beside his many articles in the *Andover Review* and Cheyne's *Encyclopaedia Biblica,* his *Critical and Exegetical Commentary on Judges* (1895) remains most valuable. Finally, his *Judaism in the First Centuries of the Christian Era: The Age of the Tannaim* (3 vols., 1927–30, 1966[2]) is an outstanding study of rabbinic Judaism. Although it too

George Foot Moore, U.S. theologian. Andover-Harvard Theological Library, Cambridge, Mass.

much neglects the mystical, magical, and apocalyptic sides of Judaism, its apology for tannaitic teaching as a reasonable, humane, and pious working out of biblical tradition is conclusive and has been of great importance not only for Christians, but also for Jewish understanding of Judaism.

Bibliography: DAB, 13 (1934), 124–5, incl. bibl.; M. Smith, in: *Harvard Library Bulletin,* 15 (1967), 169–79.
[M.Sm.]

MOPP (Max Oppenheimer; 1885–1954), painter. Born in Vienna, he studied there and in Prague, and lived in Berlin from 1926 until the rise of Hitler. He returned to Vienna,

Self-portrait by Mopp (Max Oppenheimer). New York, Leo Baeck Institute.

but left after the *Anschluss* and settled in New York. His early portraits and landscapes show the influence of his contemporary Oskar Kokoschka. In Zurich he was influenced by dadaism for a short time, appeared in the famous "Cabaret Voltaire," and contributed drawings to an exhibition. But Mopp was basically an expressionist, known primarily as a masterly portraitist, with deep psychological insight. A music-lover and an accomplished violinist, he painted many group portraits of celebrated string quartets. A large painting, "Orchestra," intended as an homage to the late Gustav Mahler, was started in 1920 but completed only in 1940. Mopp illustrated several books, among them stories by Heinrich *Heine and Gustave Flaubert, and two works by the chess master, Emanuel *Lasker. [A.W.]

MORAIS, SABATO (1823–1897), U.S. rabbi and founder of the *Jewish Theological Seminary. Morais, who was born in Leghorn, Italy, received his early Hebrew education from teachers in his community. At the age of 22, he applied for the position of assistant *ḥazzan* at the Spanish and Portuguese (Bevis Marks) congregation in London and in 1846 he became director of that congregation's orphan school. During his five years in England he learned much about Jewish life in an Anglo-Saxon environment, and established a friendship with Moses Montefiore and the Italian patriot, Mazzini. In 1851 he arrived in the U.S. to become *ḥazzan* of Mikveh Israel congregation in Philadelphia, succeeding Isaac Leeser. He served in this position until his death, 47 years later. He strove to unite the Sephardi and the Ashkenazi elements in the congregation, and later to help the Russian Jewish immigrants. Morais influenced many young men who became leaders of American Jewry, including Cyrus *Adler, Mayer *Sulzberger, and Solomon *Solis-Cohen.

He had a deep love for Jewish music and a great interest in Jewish scholarship, especially of Sephardi studies. He translated a work of S. D. Luzzatto and rendered the writings of other Italian Jewish scholars into English. He was involved in the revival of Hebrew and wrote prose and poetry and encouraged others to write in Hebrew. He published a commentary on the Book of Esther and translated Jeremiah for the Jewish Publication Society edition of the Bible. In 1887 he received an honorary LL.D. from the University of Pennsylvania, the first Jew to receive this distinction.

Sabato Morais, founder of the Jewish Theological Seminary of America. Courtesy Jewish Theological Seminary, New York.

Morais was neither an original thinker nor an incisive expositor but his earnestness and breadth of outlook enabled him to rally the forces of Conservatism in American Jewry at a time when the drift was predominantly in the direction of Reform. At one stage he showed a readiness to cooperate with I. M. Wise in the work of Hebrew Union College, but the radical nature of the Pittsburgh Platform (1885) convinced him that a separate institution to train rabbis on Conservative lines was needed. He was the prime mover in the establishment of the Jewish Theological Seminary (1887) and was president of its faculty until his death.

Bibliography: M. Davis, in: AJHSP, 37 (1947), 55–93; idem, in: *Sefer ha-Shanah li-Yhudei Amerikah* (1945), 574–92; idem, *Emergence of Conservative Judaism* (1963), index. [J.Ri.]

MORAVIA (Czech **Morava,** Ger. **Maehren,** Heb. מערהרין, מרהרן), central region of *Czechoslovakia. A political unit from around 769, it formed the nucleus of the Great Moravian Empire (first half of the ninth century until 906). From 1029 it was under Bohemian rule, then in 1182 it became a margravate and as such a direct fief of the empire. Together with *Bohemia it became part of the *Hapsburg Empire (1526–1918), and then part of Czechoslovakia, united with former Austrian Silesia after 1927. Between 1939 and 1945 it was part of the Nazi-occupied Protectorate of Bohemia-Moravia after parts had been ceded to Germany as a result of the Munich Agreement of September 1938. It has been replaced, in 1960, by the establishment of two provinces, southern and northern Moravia. Partly because of the region's location on the crossroads of Europe, throughout the centuries there was a considerable amount of reciprocal influence between Moravian Jewry and the Jewries of the surrounding countries. It had a thriving cultural life, promoted by the high degree of autonomy and communal organization it developed. Moravian Jews played a large part in the development of the communities in Vienna and northwestern Hungary.

From the Early Settlement to the 17th Century. Documentation of the first stages of Moravian Jewry is very scanty. In all probability Jews first came to Moravia as traders in the wake of the Roman legions. According to tradition some communities (e.g., *Ivanice, *Jemnice, *Pohorelice, and *Trebic) were founded in the first millennium, C.E. but such reports cannot be substantiated. Moravia is mentioned rarely in early medieval Jewish sources. However, it may well be that some authorities confused part of Bohemia with Moravia. As other authorities referred to all Slav countries as "Canaan," it is difficult to make any positive identification of a Jewish settlement in Moravia. It is likely that Jews lived in Moravia before the date of conclusive documentary evidence for their presence. In the biography of Bishop Clement of Bulgaria (d. 916) it is reported that after the death of the Byzantine missionary Methodius (885), when the Frankish Church prevailed in the Byzantine Empire, about 200 Slav priests were sold to Jewish slave traders. The Raffelstaetten toll regulations (903–906), which fixed relations between the Great Moravian and the Carolingian empires, mention Jews as slave traders, but do not say whether they resided in Moravia. According to the Bohemian chronicler Cosmas of Prague (1039?–1125), a baptized Jew built the Podivin castle in southern Moravia in 1067; Cosmas also mentions a community in *Brno (Bruenn) in 1091. *Isaac Dorbelo, a student of R. Jacob b. Meir *Tam, speaks of observing the rite of the *Olomouc (Olmuetz) community around 1146 (*Maḥzor Vitry*, Hurwitz ed. (1923), 247, 388). The first extant document explicitly mentioning Jews in Moravia is the *Jihlava (Iglau) city law of 1249. In 1254 *Premysl Ottokar II issued his charter, an adaptation of one originally issued in 1244 by Duke Frederick II of Austria (1230–46). Among other provisions it forbade forced conversion and condemned the *blood libel. A gravestone excavated in *Znojmo (Znaim), dated 1256, is the oldest known Jewish tombstone from Moravia. In 1268 Premysl Ottokar II renewed his charter; at the time the Jews of Brno were expected to contribute a quarter of the cost of strengthening the city wall. In an undated document (probably from c. 1273–78) he exempted the Brno Jews from all their dues for one year since they had become impoverished. Writing to the pope in 1273, Bishop Bruno of Olomouc complained that the Jews of his diocese employed Christian wet nurses, accepted sacred objects as pledges, and that the interest they took during one year exceeded the initial loan. The first time a Jew, Nathan, is mentioned by name is in 1278, in connection with a lawsuit about church property. Solomon b. Abraham *Adret (d. 1310), responding to a question addressed to him from Moravia, mentions the *Austerlitz (Slavkov) and *Trest (Triesch) communities. Wenceslaus II confirmed Premysl Ottokar's charter (1283 and 1305) "at the request of the Jews of Moravia."

When Moravia passed under the rule of the Luxembourg dynasty in 1311, the Jewish community of Brno, carrying their Torah Scrolls, participated in the celebrations welcoming King John of Luxembourg to the city. In 1322 John permitted the bishop of Olomouc to settle one Jew in four of his towns (*Kromeriz (Kremsier), Mohelnice, Vyskov, and Svitavy (Zwittau)), and to benefit from their tax payments. At that time Jews earned their livelihood mainly as moneylenders, but gentile moneylenders could also be found. Several Moravian communities, such as Jemnice (Jamnitz), Trebic, and Znojmo, were affected by the wave of massacres evoked by the *Pulkau *Host desecration in 1338. A toll privilege granted in 1341 to the monastery of Vilimov, which was on the main road between Moravia and Bohemia, puts Jewish merchants on a par with their gentile counterparts and mentions a great variety of merchandise in which they dealt. *Charles IV granted the cities of Brno and Jihlava the right to admit Jews in 1345, making the Jihlava community independent of that in Brno. There was an influx of Jews fleeing from Germany into Moravia during the *Black Death massacres (1348–49). In 1349 the bishop of Olomouc complained to the city authorities that Jews did not wear special Jewish hats, as they were supposed to do. Between 1362 and 1415 Jews were free to accept real estate as security on loans.

Some of the Jews expelled from Austria in 1421 (the **Wiener Gesera*) settled in Moravia. Accused of supporting the *Hussites, the Jihlava community was expelled by Albert V, duke of Austria and margrave of Moravia, in 1426. As a result of John of *Capistrano's activities, the Jews

Jewish Communities in Moravia before World War I. After Th. Haas, *Die Juden in Maehren*, 1908.

List of alternative names for places shown on map

Altstadt—Stare Mesto
Auspitz—Hustopece
Aussee—Usov
Austerlitz—Slavkov
Bajkowitz—Bojkovice
Battelau—Batelov
Bautsch—Budisov
Bielitz—Bielsko
Bisenz—Bzenec
Bistritz—Bystrice nad Pernstynem
Blansko
Boskowitz—Boskovice
Bruenn—Brno
Bruesau—Brezova
Butschowitz—Bucovice
Bystritz—Bystrice pod Hostynem
Damboritz—Damborice
Datschitz—Dacice
Eibenschitz—Ivancice
Eisgrub—Lednice
Eiwanowitz—Ivanovice na Hane
Frain—Vranov
Frankstadt—Frenstat pod Radhostem
Freiberg—Pribor
Freistadt—Karvina
Freiwaldau—Jesenik
Friedek—Frydek
Fulnek—Fulnek
Gaya—Kyjov
Gewitsch—Jevicko
Goeding—Hodonin
Gross Bitesch—Velka Bites
Gross Meseritsch—Velke Mezirici
Hof—Dvorce
Hohenstadt—Zabreh
Holleschau—Holesov
Hotzenplotz—Osoblaha
Hrottowitz—Hrotovice
Hullein—Hulin
Iglau—Jihlava
Ingrowitz—Jimramov
Jaegerndorf—Krnov
Jamnitz—Jemnice
Joslowitz—Jaroslavice
Kanitz—Dolni Kounice
Klobouk—Klobouky
Kojetein—Kojetin
Konitz—Konice
Koritschan—Korycany
Kostel—Podivin
Kosteletz—Kostelec
Kremsier—Kromeriz
Kromau—Moravsky Krumlov
Kunstadt—Kunstat
Kwassitz—Kvasice
Leipnik—Lipnik nad Becvou
Liebau—Libava
Littau—Litovel
Lomnitz—Lomnice
Loschitz—Lostice
Lundenburg—Breclav
Maehrisch Budwitz—Moravske Budejovice
Maehrisch Neustadt—Unicov
Maehrisch Ostrau—Moravska Ostrava
Maehrisch Truebau—Moravska Trebova
Misslitz—Miroslav
Mistek
Mueglitz—Mohelnice
Namest—Namest nad Oslavou
Napagedl—Napajedle
Neu Rausnitz—Rousinov
Neustadtl—Nove Mesto na Morave
Neutitschein—Novy Jicin
Nikolsburg—Mikulov
Oderberg—Bohumin
Olmuetz—Olomouc
Pirnitz—Pirnice
Plumenau—Plumlov
Pohrlitz—Pohrelice
Prerau—Prerov
Prossnitz—Prostejov
Puklitz—Puklice
Pullitz—Police
Roemerstadt—Rymarov
Roznau—Roznov pod Radhostem
Saar—Zdar
Schaffa—Safov
Schoenberg—Sumperk
Seelowitz—Zidlochovice
Shildberg—Stity
Skotschau—Skoczow
Steinitz—Zdanice
Sternberg—Sternberk
Strassnitz—Straznice
Teltsch—Telc
Teschen—Cesky Tesin
Tischnowitz—Tisnov
Tobitschau—Tovacov
Trebitsch—Trebic
Triesch—Trest
Troppau—Opava
Ungarisch Brod—Uhersky Brod
Ungarisch Hradisch—Uherske Hradiste
Ungarish Ostra—Uhersky Ostroh
Wagstadt—Bilovec
Wallachisch Klobouk—Valasske Klobouky
Wallachisch Meseritsch—Valasske Mezirici
Weisskirchen—Hranice
Wessely—Veseli nad Moravou
Wischau—Vyskov
Wisowitz—Vizovice
Witkowitz—Vitkovice
Woelking—Bolikov
Wsetin—Vsetin
Zdounek—Zdounky
Zlabings—Slavonice
Zlin—Gottwaldov
Znaim—Znojmo
Zwittau—Svitavy

Figure 1. The synagogue of the Moravian capital, Brno (Bruenn), built in 1855. Jerusalem, Israel Museum Photo Archives.

were expelled from five of the six royal cities in 1454 (Jihlava, Brno, Olomouc, Znojmo, and Neustadt; the sixth royal city, Uherske Hradiste, expelled the Jews in 1514). The royal cities remained forbidden to them until after the 1848 revolution. The Jews who were expelled settled in the villages. During the 16th century, when there was no central power in Moravia ("in every castle a king"), the Jews were settled in small towns and villages under the protection of the local lords. The latter treated them well, not only because of the part they played in the economic development of their domains, which they shared initially with the Anabaptist communes, but also because some of the lords belonged to the Bohemian Brethren (see *Hussites) or were humanists; many therefore believed in religious tolerance. The importance of the Jews in the Moravian economic life (as military purveyors and *Court Jews) increased because of the constant threat of the Turkish wars. Since several Christian sects lived side by side it became somewhat easier for the Jew to pursue his own interests without interference. When the Anabaptists were expelled (1622), and the country became depopulated during the Thirty Years' War (1618–48), the Jews took over new economic areas and were also permitted to acquire houses formerly occupied by "heretics." However, at the same time some communities suffered severely during the war (e.g., Kromeriz and *Hodonin (Goeding)). Moravia also absorbed refugees from Poland after the *Chmielnicki massacres (1648), among them scholars such as Gershon *Ashkenazi, author of *Avodat ha-Gershuni*, and Shabbetai Kohen, author of *Siftei Kohen*, the renowned commentary on the Shulḥan Arukh, who became rabbi of Holesov. Many Jews also arrived after the expulsion from Vienna (1670).

At this time an increasing number of Moravian Jews were engaged in crafts, a process that had already begun in the 16th century, and the cloth and wool merchants and tailors, who made goods to be sold at fairs, were laying the foundations of the textile and clothing industry for which Moravia was later known. In 1629 *Ferdinand II permitted the Jews to attend markets and fairs in the royal cities, on payment of a special body tax (*Leibmaut;* see **Leibzoll*); in spite of protests from the guilds and merchants, the charter was renewed in 1657, 1658, and 1723. Jews also attended fairs outside Moravia, especially those in *Krems, *Linz, *Breslau (Wroczlaw), and *Leipzig. In 1650 the Moravian Diet decided that Jews might reside only where they had been living before 1618, but the decision was not enforced. Later this was modified by the Diet of 1681 to permit Jews to dwell where they lived before 1657.

The Modern Era. On July 31, 1725, during the reign of Charles VI, an imperial order fixed the number of registered Jewish families at 5,106 and threatened any locality which accepted Jews where they had not been previously settled with a fine of 1,000 ducats. On September 20 of that year the same penalty was imposed on anyone who allowed Jews to come into possession of real estate, particularly customhouses, mills, wool-shearing sheds, and breweries. The first enactment was reinforced a year later by allowing only one son in a family to marry (see *Familiants Law); the second was never carried out as it would have deprived noblemen of lucrative revenue and most Jews of their livelihood. Under Charles VI the geographical separation of the Jews was implemented in most Moravian towns.

*Maria Theresa threatened Moravian Jewry with expulsion (Jan. 2, 1745) but rescinded her order, permitting them to remain for another ten years. In 1748, however, she raised their toleration tax (*Schutzgeld*) from a total of 8,000 florins (since 1723) to 87,700 for the next five years and 76,700 in the following five; in 1752 the tax was fixed at 90,000 florins. Two years later the empress' definitive "General Police Law and Commercial Regulations for the Jewry of the Margravate of Moravia" appeared; as its name indicates it regulated all legal, religious, and commercial aspects of Jewish life in Moravia. The authority of the **Landesrabbiner* was defined and his election regulated, as were those of the other offices of the **Landesjudenschaft*. In essence the law was based on a translation by Aloys von *Sonnenfels of the resolutions and ordinances of the old Council of Moravian Jewry. Although the earliest recorded session of the council had taken place in 1651, it was at least a century older, for a Bendit Axelrod Levi was mentioned in 1519 as being "head of all Moravian communities." The names of most Moravian rabbis were recorded from the mid-16th century.

A clearer picture of the council emerges after the Thirty Years' War (1618–48): Moravia (*medinah*) was divided into three provinces (*galil*), in each of which two heads (*rashei galil*) officiated; at the same time, each one was a member of the governing body of Moravian Jewry (*rashei ha-medinah*). The chief authority was the *Landesrabbiner* (*rav medinah*), who had jurisdiction over both secular and religious matters. His seat was in *Mikulov (Nikolsburg). His presence at council sessions was obligatory and he was the authoritative interpreter of their decisions. There were two types of council: the governing "small" council of six heads of provinces, and the "large" legislative one, which was attended by representatives of the communities and met every three years at a different community. The franchise was very limited and the council oligarchic in spirit and practice. The last "large" council, that of 1748, was attended by 61 representatives elected by 367 houseowners. Its main function was the election of small bodies of

Figure 2. The old Jewish quarter of Jemnice, southern Moravia. Prague, Czechoslovak State Archives.

electors and legislators. The authority of the council was undermined by the absolutist state, which in 1728 defined its ordinances as "temporary"; from 1754 Maria Theresa limited the independence of the communities and their central council. The main function of the council and the *Landesrabbiner* was to divide the tax load justly among the communities. When *Landesrabbiner* Menahem *Krochmal was called upon to settle a dispute between the poor and the rich over the control of the communities he claimed that the decisive voice belonged to those who contributed more to the community. Krochmal's tenure (1648–61) was vital in the formulation of the 311 ordinances *(shai takkanot)* of the Moravian council. Among his noted predecessors were R. *Judah Loew b. Bezalel (Maharal) and R. Yom Tov Lipmann *Heller. Among the more distinguished holders of the office were David *Oppenheim (from 1690 to 1704); Gabriel b. Judah Loew *Eskeles, nominated in 1690; and his son Issachar Berush (Bernard) *Eskeles, (d. 1753), who also became chief rabbi of Hungary and successfully averted the 1745 expulsion threat. His successor, R. Moses b. Aaron *Lemberger, ordained that henceforth at least 25 students should attend the Mikulov (Nikolsburg) yeshivah, and that each Moravian sub-province should support two yeshivot with ten students each. R. Gershon Pullitz and R. Gershon *Chajes (*Landesrabbiner* 1780–89) fought against the insidious influence of Shabbateanism and Frankism in Moravia: in 1773 Jacob *Frank resided in Brno, where the *Dobruschka family were among his adherents; members of the *Prostejov (Prossnitz) community were commonly called *Schebse* since so many of them were followers of Shabbetai Ẓevi.

In spite of the hostile attitude of Charles VI and Maria Theresa and the continuous curtailment of the authority of the council and the *Landesrabbiner*, there was a thriving communal life in Moravia. In the first half of the 19th century the *Landesrabbiner* Mordecai *Benet (d. 1829), Nehemiah (Menahem) Nahum *Trebitsch (d. 1842), and Samson Raphael *Hirsch (served from 1846 to 1851) wielded great influence. Besides the spiritual metropolis of Nikolsburg, there were important centers of learning in Boskowitz (*Boskovice), Ungarisch-Brod (*Uhersky Brod), Kremsier, Leipnik (*Lipnik nad Becvou), and Prossnitz.

The situation of Moravian Jews improved after Joseph II's **Toleranzpatent*, which abolished the body tax (see **Leibzoll*) and other special taxes and permitted some freedom of movement. But the limitation of the number of Jewish families remained, the number of licensed *(systematisiert)* Jewish families being kept at 5,106, later raised to 5,400. An edict of Francis II in 1798 limited their rights of settlement to an area of 52 Jewish communities *(Judengemeinden)*, mostly in places where communities had existed from early times. The six royal cities remained closed to the Jews. Like most of the local Christian communities, the Jewish communities were subject to the authority of the feudal lord. At that time the largest communities were Mikulov with 620 families, Prostejov with 328, Boskovice with 326, and Holesov with 265. The total number of registered Jews increased from 20,327 in 1754 to 28,396 in 1803 (the actual numbers might have been from 10 to 20% higher). The revolutionary year of 1848 brought the abolition of most legal and economic restrictions, the right of free movement and settlement, and freedom of worship, but also gave rise to anti-Jewish disturbances: in Prostejov a Jewish national guard, 200 men strong, was organized. These measures of freedom were enacted by the Austrian parliament which convened in Kromeriz. *Landesrabbiner* S. R. Hirsch sent two messages to parliament. The process of legal emancipation was completed in the Austrian constitution of 1867. In conformity with the new municipal laws (passed temporarily in 1849 and definitively in 1867) 27 of the 52 Jewish communities were constituted as Jewish municipalities *(*politische gemeinden)* with full municipal independence, and existed as such until the end of the Hapsburg monarchy, in striking contrast to the abolition of Jewish municipal autonomy in Prague in 1850 and in Galicia in 1866. The legalization of the Jewish religious autonomy, a longer process, was not completed until 1890, when 50 Jewish religious communities *(Kultusgemeinden)* were recognized, 39 in places where old communities existed and 11 in newly established Jewish centers.

The restrictions imposed on the Jews by Charles VI and Maria Theresa, most of which remained in force until the second half of the 19th century, led many Moravian Jews to leave the country, mainly for Hungary (Slovakia) and later for Austria. After equal rights and freedom of movement were granted new communities were established in the big cities of Brno, Olomouc, Ostrava (Maehrisch Ostrau), and Jihlava, while others were set up in small places that previously Jews had only visited on market days. At the same time many Moravian Jews left for other parts of the Hapsburg Empire, particularly Vienna, and some emigrated. As a result, the Jewish population of Moravia remained relatively static at a time when the world Jewish population was rising, and even declined slightly from 1890:

Year	Number of Jews
1830	29,462
1840	37,316
1848	37,548
1857	42,611
1869	42,644
1880	44,175
1890	45,324
1900	44,255
1910	41,255
1921	37,989

In 1787 Joseph II ordered that half of the main tax on Moravian Jewry (then 88,280 florins) be allowed to accumulate in a fund (known as *Landesmassafond*) for the payment of the *Landesrabbiner* and other officials. In 1831, when the fund was sealed, the capital was allocated for low-interest loans for needy communities. An assembly of 45 Moravian communities convened in 1862 in order to try to obtain control of the fund, which was managed by state officials. After protracted negotiations, *Francis Joseph I awarded the guardianship of the fund (almost 1,000,000 kronen) to an elected curatorium whose first chairman was Julius von Gomperz of Brno. This curatorium served in lieu of a central Jewish organization until the collapse of the Austrian regime and enabled Moravian Jewry to alleviate the lot of the declining small communities. Jews were mainly engaged in trade, but increasing numbers entered some industries and the free professions or became white-collar workers (mainly in undertakings owned by Jews). They were prominent in the wool industry of Brno, the silk industry of northern Moravia, the clothing industry in Prostejov, Boskovice, and some other towns, the leather industry, the sugar industry in central and southern Moravia, and the malt industry in Olomouc. The brothers Wilhelm and David von *Gutmann (orginally from Lipnik) developed jointly with the Rothschilds the coal mines of Ostrava and established the great iron and steel works there. The Rothschilds also built the Kaiser Ferdinand Nordbahn, a railway linking Vienna and Galicia via Moravia and Silesia. Consequently there was a substantial number of Jewish railway engineers, employees, engine drivers, licensees of railway restaurants, etc. In the late 19th

ברוך אתה ה' אמ"ה הטוב והמטיב
בא"י אמ"ה שחלק מכבודו לבשר ודם

Figure 3. Page from *Seder Birkat ha-Mazon*, a typical example of Moravian illumination, Mikulov (Nikolsburg), 1728. Copenhagen, Royal Library, Cod. Hebr. 32, fol. 11 v.

and 20th centuries Jews were also prominent in the timber industry and trade, the glass industry, hat-making, hosiery, and even in the development of water power.

The close ties between Moravian Jews and Vienna persisted until the end of the Austrian monarchy, and even increased after emancipation, since Moravia had no university under Austrian rule. Consequently, the great majority of Moravian Jews spoke German. In 1900, 77% of all Moravian Jews declared German as their mother tongue, 16% Czech, and 7% other languages (mainly foreigners), but this did not indicate any strong political assimilationist trend toward Germany or hostility toward Czech nationalism. Jews enthusiastically supported the candidacy of T. G. *Masaryk for the Austrian parliament in 1907 and 1911. Students from Moravian communities studying in Vienna were among the first followers of Theodor Herzl and many Zionist associations sprang up in Moravia, from the early days of Zionism.

After the Czechoslovak Republic had been established in 1918, Moravian Jews frequently constituted the bridge between the Jews in Bohemia on the one hand and those in Slovakia and Subcarpathian Ruthenia on the other, between traditionalists and modernists, Zionist and non-Zionists; 60% of Moravian Jews declared themselves as being of Jewish nationality. The first provincial union of Jewish communities was established in November 1918 under the leadership of Alois *Hilf from Ostrava; this union became instrumental in the emergence and consolidation of the Jewish National Council as well as in the setting up of the Supreme Council of the Jewish Religious Communities in Bohemia, Moravia, and Silesia. The Central Committee of the Zionist Oraganization in Czechoslovakia had its seat in Ostrava from 1921 to 1938, under the chairmanship of Joseph *Rufeisen; the center of *He-Halutz was also located in Ostrava and the main office of Keren Hayesod in Brno for a long time. Brno had the only Jewish high school in the western part of Czechoslovakia and Ostrava had a fully equipped vocational school. Moravian Jews were represented by a Zionist in the provincial Diet. However, the number of Jews continued to decline, from 45,306 in Moravia and Silesia in 1921 to 41,250 in 1930, almost half of whom were concentrated in the three cities Brno, Ostrava, and Olomouc. The venerable communities dwindled or even disintegrated.

When the Germans occupied Austria in March 1938, several thousand Jews escaped to Moravia, mainly to Brno. They were followed in September and October of that year by a few thousand more from the areas detached from Czechoslovakia and incorporated in Germany by the Munich Agreement. The majority of Jews in the Teschen (Tesin; Cieszyn) district, ceded to Poland, did not flee. On March 15, 1939, the remaining parts of Moravia were occupied by Nazi Germany and became part of the Protectorate of Bohemia-Moravia. Immediately after the conquest, the lot of the Jews in northeast Moravia was especially disastrous. They constituted a high percentage of those expelled to the Nisko reservate in the Lublin area. Many perished there in the first winter of the war; others returned, only to join their fellows in *Theresienstadt and various extermination camps. After the war, very few survivors returned to Moravia, and the majority of them later emigrated to Israel and other countries. In 1970 barely 2,000 Jews remained in former Moravia, the largest community being in Brno. Brno was also the seat of the chief rabbi for Moravia, Richard *Feder, who later became chief rabbi of Czechoslovakia. When he died in 1970, at the age of 95, the rabbinate remained vacant. The Jewish museum of Mikulov, established shortly before World War

Figure 4. Faience pitcher used by the *ḥevra kaddisha* of Mikulov, Moravia, 1801. Prague, State Jewish Museum.

II, was reconstituted as part of the state museum; another Jewish museum was established by the state in Holesov.

For fuller details on the contemporary period see *Czechoslovakia. For fuller details on the Holocaust period see *Protectorate of Bohemia-Moravia.

Bibliography: H. Gold (ed.), *Die Juden und Judengemeinden Maehrens in Vergangenheit und Gegenwart* (1929); Th. Haas, *Die Juden in Maehren* (1908); B. Bretholz, *Geschichte der Juden im Mittelalter, I. Teil bis zum Jahre 1350* (1934); idem, *Quellen zur Geschichte der Juden in Maehren vom XI. bis zum XV. Jahrhundert (1067–1411)* (1935); I. Halpern, *Takkanot Medinat Mehrin* (1952); Baron, Community, index; L. Loew, *Gesammelte Schriften*, 2 (1892), 165–218; W. Mueller, *Urkundliche Beitraege zur Geschichte der maehrischen Judenschaft im 17. und 18. Jahrhundert* (1903); M. Lamed, in: BLBI, 8 (1965), 32, 302–14; G. Kisch, in: *The Jews of Czechoslovakia*, 1 (1968), 1–11; H. Kohn, *ibid.*, 12–20; R. Kestenberg-Gladstein, *ibid.*, 21–71; G. Fleischmann, *ibid.*, 267–329; H. Stransky, *ibid.*, 330–58; J. C. Pick, *ibid.*, 359–438, passim; R. Kestenberg-Gladstein, *Neuere Geschichte der Juden in den boehmischen Laendern. I. Das Zeitalter der Aufklaerung 1780–1830* (1969); idem, in: *Gesher*, 2–3 (1969), 11–82; F. Weltsch, *ibid.*, 207–12; idem, in: *Prag vi-Yrushalayim* (n. d.), 23–35; N. M. Gelber, *ibid.*, 36–51; A. F. Pribram, *Urkunden und Akten* . . ., 2 vols. (1918), index; Bondy-Dworský; M. H. Friedlaender, *Kore ha-Dorot. Beitraege zur Geschichte der Juden in Maehren* (1876); idem, *Tiferet Yisrael, Schilderungen aus dem inneren Leben der Juden in Maehren in vormaerzlichen Zeiten* (1878); R. Jakobson and M. Halle, in: *For Max Weinreich* (1964), 147–72; B. Bretholz and A. Glaser, in: *Zeitschrift fuer Geschichte der Juden in der Tschechoslowakei*, 3 (1932/33), 25–34; J. Bronner, *ibid.*, 1 (1930/31), 243–7; B. Brilling, *ibid.*, 2 (1931/32), 1–20, 237–56; T. Haas, *ibid.*, 32–38; L. Moses, *ibid.*, 4 (1934), 18–24; A. Engel, in: JGGJČ, 2 (1930), 50–97; B. Heilig, *ibid.*, 3 (1931), 307–448; 4 (1932), 7–62; W. Zacek, *ibid.*, 5 (1933), 175–98; A. Freud, in: BLBI, 2 (1959), 222–9; H. H. Ben-Sasson, *Hagut ve-Hanhagah* (1959), index; Y. L. Bialer, *Min ha-Genazim*, 2 (1968/69), 33–36; H. Flesch, in: MGWJ, 71 (1927), 71, 74; 74 (1930), 197–217; M. Wischnitzer, in: JSOS, 16 (1954), 335–60; S. Simonsohn, in: *Sefer Yovel . . . N. M. Gelber* (1963), 127–64; Y. Toury, *Mehumah u-Mevukhah be-Mahpekhat 1848* (1968), index; G. Horowitz, *The Spirit of Jewish Law* (1963[2]), 86–87; Germ Jud, 1 (1963), 171–3; 2 (1968), 510–2.

[M.La./Ed.]

MORAVIA (Pincherle), ALBERTO (1907–), Italian novelist and critic. Born in Rome, Moravia took his pen name from his immigrant ancestors' country of origin. He made his reputation with works published after World War II, and in English-speaking lands was widely regarded as the outstanding Italian writer of his time. Moravia's first novel, *Gli Indifferenti* (1929; *The Indifferent Ones*, 1932; reissued as *The Time of Indifference*, 1953), was covertly critical of middle class society and its passive and cynical acceptance of the Fascist dictatorship. His violent hostility toward the bourgeoisie into which he had himself been born

Alberto Moravia, Italian novelist. Courtesy V. Bompiani, Milan.

and the relentless psychological analysis of the characters in his works came to the fore in *Le ambizioni sbagliate* (1935; *Wheel of Fortune*, 1938) and dominated many later novels. Moravia's early writings made it clear that he had set out to combine the 19th-century narrative tradition of Dostoevski and Flaubert with the aesthetic principles of the realistic or naturalistic novel. Totally estranged from Judaism, Moravia served during World War II as a foreign correspondent in Germany and the Far East. His postwar works dealt largely with themes such as adolescence and relations between the sexes, and remained outside of any established literary current.

Moravia's artistry and skillful characterization are especially evident in the novels which he published after World War II: *Agostino* (1945, Eng. trans. 1947); *La Romana* (1947; *The Woman of Rome*, 1949); *La disubbidienza* (1948; *Disobedience*, 1950); *Il Conformista* (1951; *The Conformist*, 1952); and *Il disprezzo* (1954; *A Ghost at Noon*, 1955). However, some critics were sensitive to the writer's preoccupation with sex and to his disinclination to pass judgment on the amorality of his heroes. There is a warmer, more sympathetic tone to his stories about the lower strata of society in *Racconti romani* (1954; *Roman Tales*, 1956) and in *Il Paradiso* (1970). Moravia distinguished himself as a novelist most of all, perhaps, in *La Ciociara* (1957; *Two Women*, 1958), an acute study of two characters, contrasting intellect and sensuality, which was made into a successful motion picture. His later works include *La noia* (1960; *The Empty Canvas*, 1961); *L'attenzione* (1965; Fr. trans. *L'Attention*, 1966); and a volume of short stories, *Una cosa è una cosa* (1967). Moravia also published *L'uomo come fine* (1964; *Man as an End: A Defense of Humanism*, 1966), a collection of major essays published between the years 1941 and 1962, and a book of plays, *Teatro* (1958). The variety of his interests may be gauged from three other books—*Un mese in U.R.S.S.* (1958; Fr. trans. *Un Mois en U.R.S.S.*, 1954), *Un idea dell' India* (1962), and *La rivoluzione culturale in Cina* (1967; *The Red Book and the Great Wall*, 1968).

Bibliography: A. Limentani, *Alberto Moravia tra esistenza e realtà* (1962); E. Sanguineti, *Alberto Moravia* (It. 1962); O. Del Buono, *Moravia* (Ital., 1962), incl. bibl.; M. F. Cimmino, *Lettura di Moravia* (1967); P. Pancrazi, *Scrittori italiani del Novecento* (1939[2]), index; idem, *Scrittori d'oggi*, 1 (1942), index; G. De Robertis, *Scrittori del Novecento* (1958[2]), index; E. Kanduth, *Wesenszuege der modernen italienischen Erzaehlliteratur* . . . (1968), incl. bibl.

[G.R.]

MORAVSKE BUDEJOVICE (Czech **Moravské Budějovice**; Ger. **Maehrisch-Budwitz**), small town in S. Moravia, Czechoslovakia. Its Jewish community is mentioned among those suffering from the wave of massacres following the Host desecration of *Pulkau in 1338. One Jew, Jacob, is mentioned in 1363 and in 1386 as a member of a consortium buying and selling a village. From 1528 transactions between Jews and gentiles, involving loans and the sale of houses, horses, and grain, are mentioned frequently in the town records. In 1562 the community numbered 47, and its members were not permitted to sell alcoholic beverages or to brew beer. The community was expelled in 1564. There were no Jews in the town until 1774, when a tobacco agent settled there, and in 1808 a Jew leased a distillery. Between 1794 and 1842, 120 Jewish merchants attended the local fairs. There were 19 Jews in Moravske Budejovice in 1848, 58 in 1869, 127 in 1890, and 97 in 1900. A congregation was founded in 1867 and recognized as a community in 1890. A cemetery was consecrated in 1908 and a synagogue in 1910. From 1926 the community was administered by the *Safov (Schaffa) community. Its members numbered 77 in 1930 (1.8% of the total population). In 1942 those Jews remaining after the German occupation were deported to extermination camps, and the synagogue equipment was sent to the Central Jewish Museum in Prague. No community was reestablished after World War II.

Bibliography: J. Fišer, in: H. Gold (ed.), *Juden und Judengemeinden Maehrens* (1929), 343–67; Bondy-Dworský, 1 (1906), nos. 673, 679; Germ Jud, 2 pt. 2 (1968), 512 s.v. *Maehrisch-Budwitz*. [M.LA.]

MORAVSKY KRUMLOV (Czech. **Moravský Krumlov;** Ger. **Maehrisch-Kromau;** Heb. קרומענו), town in Moravia, Czechoslovakia. The community was in existence before 1437, the presence of Jews being mentioned in 1402. A synagogue was built in 1547. The number of families allotted by the *Familiants laws was 49. In 1800, 43 houses were owned by Jews, a situation which was quite unusual in Moravia. With the 1848 Revolution and the freedom of settlement the Jewish population decreased steadily, from 356 persons in 1830, to 226 in 1869, 140 in 1880, and 116 in 1900. In 1930 it numbered only 34 persons (0.9% of the total population). The community had become a **politische Gemeinde* after 1848, but gave up this privilege in 1869. From 1915 the community was under the guidance of Heinrich *Flesch, rabbi of nearby Dolni-Kounice. The community was liquidated under the Nazi occupation.

Bibliography: H. Flesch, in: JJLG, 17 (1926), 57–84; idem, in: H. Gold (ed.), *Juden und Judengemeinden Maehrens* (1929), 369–71.

[M.LA.]

MORAWITZ, KARL RITTER VON (1846–1914), Austrian banker. Born in Iglau (now Jihlava), Moravia, he was educated in Prague and began working as a bank clerk in small banking houses in Prague and Dresden. In 1860 he joined the Banque de Paris et des Pays-Bas in Paris, an establishment of Ludwig *Bamberger with whom Morawitz became closely associated. Subsequently he entered the Paris office of the Ottoman Bank, but as a foreigner had to leave that post in 1870 after the outbreak of the Franco-Prussian War. He then worked for Baron Maurice de *Hirsch and his railway enterprises and in 1906 became president of the Anglo-Austrian Bank, which post he held until his death. Morawitz was an expert in international finance, and his experience and connections made him an influential adviser. Shortly before his death he was knighted by Emperor Franz Joseph. Morawitz frequently wrote and lectured, and his book, *Les Finances de la Turquie* (1902), is a standard work on the financial history of the Ottoman Empire. Other publications include *Aus der Werkstatt eines Bankmannes, Aus Arbeitstagen und Mussestunden* (1907), and a history of the Anglo-Austrian Bank, *50 Jahre Geschichte einer Wiener Bank* (1913). [J.O.R.]

MORDECAI (Heb. מָרְדֳּכַי, מָרְדְּכָי, hypocoristic masculine proper name containing the theophoric element Marduk), name of two Biblical figures:

1) One of the 12 leaders who returned from Babylonia to Jerusalem at the time of Zerubbabel (Ezra 2:2; Neh. 7:7).

2) A Jew who lived in Shushan (Susa), the residence of the Persian King, Ahasuerus (Xerxes I), who reigned from 486 to 465 B.C.E. Mordecai was the great-grandson of a Benjamite of Jerusalem by the name of Kish who was a member of the group that was taken into exile by King Nebuchadnezzar of Babylon together with King Jehoiachin of Judah in 597 B.C.E. Since this group consisted mainly of the upper classes (II Kings 24:14), and since the name Kish is otherwise known only as that of the father of the Benjamite king Saul, the implication is doubtless that Mordecai's great-grandfather and, hence, he himself were descended from King Saul. Mordecai was foster father to his cousin *Esther (Esth. 2:5ff.).

When Esther was chosen for the harem of King Ahasuerus as a replacement for the deposed Queen Vashti, Mordecai charged her not to reveal her ancestry or nationality. Since he "sat in the king's gate" (Esth. 2:21), i.e., was one of the king's consultants (cf. Dan. 2:49), Mordecai was able to inquire daily about her welfare (Esth. 2:10–11); and when he discovered a plot by Bigthan and Teresh to assassinate the king, he informed her, and she passed the information on to the king in Mordecai's name. The plotters were impaled; and the incident, with the part played in it by Mordecai, was recorded in the royal annals (Esth. 2:21ff.). For the time being, however, he was not rewarded, while Haman, a descendant of the Amalekite Agag, who was spared by Mordecai's ancestor Saul (I Sam. 15), was elevated by the king above all his other officials. Mordecai was the only one of these officials who refused to obey the king's command to bow down to Haman (Esth. 3:1ff.). This refusal has often been explained on religious grounds, but not only does Judaism not forbid, it actually enjoins, the showing of respect to highly placed persons, Jewish or otherwise. When Mordecai's colleagues asked him for the reason for his behavior he merely told them that he was a Jew, and the narrator evidently takes it for granted that everybody knew that there was a sacred, perpetual feud between Jews and Amalekites (Ex. 17:14ff.; Deut. 25:17ff.).

Haman for his part resolved to avenge himself not only on Mordecai but on the entire Jewish people, and persuaded the king to decree their extermination by a pogrom on a given day (Esth. 3:6ff.). Then Mordecai urged Esther to intercede on behalf of her people with Ahasuerus. Providence, he saw, had put her there for such an act. Failure to act would result in her own destruction but the Jews would still be delivered (Esth. 4). In an unexpected turn of events Mordecai was rewarded for having saved the king's life by being dressed in royal garb and promenaded around the city on a royal steed by Haman (*ibid.* 6). As a result of Esther's intervention Haman was hanged on the same gallows (7:10) he had prepared for Mordecai (5:13f.), who was further rewarded by receiving Haman's property (8:1f.) and being appointed vizier (10:3). His fame spread abroad and all Persian officials aided the Jews in destroying their enemies. Mordecai recorded all these events and he and Esther wrote to all the Jews to commemorate the days of deliverance annually (14th and 15th day of Adar; Esth. 9). In Hasmonean times the 14th of Adar was known as the "Day of Mordecai" (II Macc. 15:36).

A cuneiform tablet from the end of the reign of Darius I or the beginning of that of Xerxes (Ahasuerus) mentions an official named Marduka, whom some scholars have identified with the biblical Mordecai. It has further been suggested that the prominence of Jews in the Murashu tablets from the time of Xerxes' successors Artaxerxes I and Darius II and

Etching by Rembrandt van Rijn, 1606, showing Mordecai on the king's horse, being led through the city square by Haman (Esth. 6:11). Amsterdam, Rijksmuseum.

their absence from documents of earlier reigns accords with the statement that Mordecai "sought [and achieved] the welfare of his people" (Esth. 10:3).

See also *Esther; *Purim. [B.Po.]

In the Aggadah. The fact that Mordecai is referred to as both a Benjamite (Yemini) and a Judean (Yehudi) (Esth. 2:5) is explained in various ways: as a tribute to David, who belonged to the tribe of Judah, for saving the life of Shimei the Benjamite who is regarded as Mordecai's ancestor, or because his mother was of this tribe. His name is interpreted to mean "pure myrrh" (*mor*-myrrh, *decai*-pure) for he was as refined and noble as pure myrrh (Meg. 12a). Mordecai was a prophet and is sometimes identified with Malachi (*ibid.*). He prophesied in the second year of Darius (Meg. 15a). Mordecai fasted from the eve of Passover till its seventh day, supplicating God to mete out punishment to Ahasuerus for his desecration of the Temple vessels (Targ. Jon., Esth. 1:10).

Mordecai was appointed to the royal court at the request of Esther (Yal., Esth. 10:53). Thus it was while attending on the king that he discovered the plot of Bigthan and Teresh. They were Tarseans and spoke their native language in plotting to poison Ahasuerus, unaware that Mordecai knew 70 languages (Meg. 13b). It was on account of his ability as a linguist that he was called Bilshan (Men. 65a). When the court officials asked Mordecai why he refused to pay homage to Haman while his ancestor Jacob prostrated himself before Haman's ancestor Esau, Mordecai answered "I am a descendant of Benjamin, who was not yet born when that took place" (Targ. Sheni, Esth. 3:4). The true reason for Haman's hatred of Mordecai and the Jews was that he had once sold himself as a slave to Mordecai and whenever they met his erstwhile master used to remind him of this fact (Meg. 15b).

After the fatal decree had been signed Mordecai asked three schoolchildren to repeat to him the biblical verses they had just learned. The children recited three different biblical verses, each containing a prophecy that Israel should not fear the evil designs against them. Mordecai had been informed of the king's decree by Elijah. The prayer he and Esther prayed then unto God was the *Hallel.* The days Mordecai decided that Jews should fast were the first three days of Passover (Meg. 15a). When Mordecai saw Haman coming to him with the royal insignia he thought his last moment had come. He therefore told his pupils to flee and leave him alone to his fate, but they refused. Mordecai spent what he thought were his last moments in prayer and Haman had to wait until he had finished. Since Mordecai had been fasting and mourning for several days he refused to don the king's apparel until he had bathed and trimmed his hair. But upon a decree of Esther the baths and all the barber shops were closed on this day so that Haman had to act as valet to Mordecai. Haman had also to offer him his back to enable Mordecai to mount the horse (Meg. 16a).

While Haman conducted Mordecai through the streets, 27,000 youths from the court marched before him, bearing golden cups and beakers (Targ. Sheni, Esth. 6:11). As he rode, Mordecai and his pupils gave praise to God (Lev. R. 28:6). As soon as the procession was over Mordecai put off the royal attire and again covering himself with sackcloth, resumed his prayers and fasting (Meg. 16a). He did not stop praying until Ahasuerus charged him with the execution of Haman. In spite of Haman's pleas Mordecai insisted upon hanging him like the commonest criminal (Targ. Sheni, Esth. 7:10). Mordecai became king of the Jews (Esth. R. 10:12). As such he had coins struck which bore sackcloth and ashes on one side and a golden crown on the other (Gen. R. 39:11). However in the measure in which Mordecai gained worldly power and consideration he lost spiritually, because his high political function left him no time for study of the Torah. From first among the scholars of Israel he had dropped to seventh place among them (Meg. 16b). [Ed.]

Bibliography: S. H. Horn, in: BRE, 9 (1964), 14ff. In the Aggadah: Ginzberg, Legends, index.

MORDECAI, ALFRED (1804–1887), U.S. soldier, engineer, and ordnance expert. Born in Warrenton, North Carolina, son of Jacob *Mordecai, Alfred was educated at

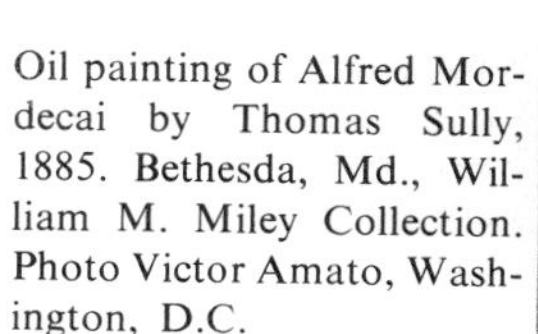

Oil painting of Alfred Mordecai by Thomas Sully, 1885. Bethesda, Md., William M. Miley Collection. Photo Victor Amato, Washington, D.C.

the West Point Military Academy, passing out first in his class. He was commissioned in the Engineers, but transferred in 1832 to the Ordnance Department, where he remained until his retirement, with the rank of major, in 1861, on the eve of the Civil War. Mordecai served from 1839 to 1860 on the U.S. Ordnance Board, where he helped to develop and systematize weapons, ammunition, and equipment. His greatest contribution to American military technology was the introduction of scientific research and development to the military art. He was twice sent to Europe to study arms systems and production methods and commanded the arsenals at Frankford, Pennsylvania, Washington, D.C., and Watervliet, New York. He wrote several military works, notably *Second Report of Experiments in Gunpowder* (1849), and *Ordnance Manual for the Use of the Officers of the United States Army* (1841, 1850). His son Alfred (1840–1920) was also an ordnance officer and rose to the rank of brigadier general.

Bibliography: S. L. Falk, *Soldier-Technologist: Major Alfred Mordecai and the Beginnings of Science in the United States Army* (1959), incl. bibl.; idem, in: AJA, 10 (1958), 125–32; A. Mordecai, in: *North Carolina Historical Review,* 22 (1945), 58–108; S. L. Falk, in: A. J. Karp (ed.), *The Jewish Experience in America,* 3 (1969), 300–22.

[S.L.F.]

MORDECAI, JACOB (1762–1838), U.S. merchant and educator. Born in Philadelphia, his early formal education was slight, but he studied at home and in the synagogue and later earned a reputation as a scholar and biblical authority. He moved to Richmond, Virginia, in 1782 and became an independent businessman. In 1784 he was in New York, where he formed a brief partnership with Haym *Salomon, but after the death of the latter in 1785, Mordecai's business failed. He returned to Virginia, attempting various commercial ventures, and finally in 1792 moved to Warrenton, North Carolina, where he became a successful merchant. In 1807 Mordecai lost heavily in tobacco speculations and was forced to give up his business. In 1809, encouraged and backed by a group of townspeople, he opened the Warrenton Female Academy, which became famous throughout the South as a school for girls. Mordecai and his family ran the Academy successfully until 1819, when he sold it and moved to a farm near Richmond. He served as president of Beth Shalome, the first synagogue in the city, which he had helped found. He lived in Richmond from 1832.

Portrait of Jacob Mordecai, U.S. merchant and educator, by Wesley Jarvis. Raleigh, North Carolina, W. G. Mordecai Collection. Photo Siddell Studio, Raleigh, N.C.

Bibliography: Mordecai, in: AJHSP, 6 (1897), 39–48; Falk, in: *North Carolina Historical Review*, 35 (1958), 281–98. [S.L.F.]

MORDECAI (MOKHI'AḤ) BEN ḤAYYIM OF EISENSTADT (1650–1729), wandering Shabbatean preacher—hence his cognomen *Mokhi'aḥ* ("reprover"). He propagated faith in *Shabbetai Ẓevi as the Messiah after the latter's conversion to Islam. An extreme ascetic, he wandered through Hungary, Moravia, Italy, and Poland spreading the doctrine, previously enunciated by *Nathan of Gaza, that for mystical reasons Shabbetai Ẓevi had to undergo conversion and that his death was merely an illusion. In three years, he insisted, the "Messiah" would reappear. Invited to Italy in 1682 by R. Issachar Behr *Perlhefter and R. Abraham *Rovigo of Modena—both secret Shabbatean adherents—he put forth the claim that while Shabbetai Ẓevi had been the Messiah b. Ephraim, he, Mordecai, was the Messiah b. David. Apocalyptic writings stemming from Rovigo's circle and probably written by Perlhefter (1678–80) portray him as the forerunner of the Messiah. In the above-mentioned document reference is made to his plan to go to Rome in order to make certain "messianic" preparations. Upon meeting him in Modena, his host, R. Perlhefter, recognizing signs of madness in him, turned against him, apparently causing Mordecai's abrupt departure from Italy some time before 1682. He thereupon traveled through Bohemia and Poland, where, thanks to his prepossessing personality and fiery preaching, he won numerous adherents. Heinrich *Graetz dubbed him a "Jewish Vicente *Ferrer."

Bibliography: Graetz, Gesch, 10 (1896), note 4, ii; J. Leveen, in: *Ignace Goldziher Memorial Volume*, 1 (1948), 393–9; G. Scholem, in: *Sefer Dinaburg* (1949), 240ff. (Heb.); I. Tishby, *Netivei Emunah u-Minut* (1964), s.v. *Eisenstadt, Mordecai.* [Th.F.]

MORDECAI BEN HILLEL HA-KOHEN (1240?–1298), author and rabbinic authority in Germany. The only biographical details known of him are that he was a descendant of *Eliezer b. Joel ha-Levi, a relative of *Asher b. Jehiel, and a brother-in-law of Meir ha-Kohen, author of the *Haggahot Maimoniyyot*, that he was an outstanding pupil of *Meir b. Baruch of Rothenburg, *Isaac b. Moses (author of *Or Zaru'a*), and *Perez b. Elijah of Corbeil. He appears to have spent some time in Goslar (Resp. Maharam of Rothenburg, ed. Lemberg, 476), from there moving to Nuremberg, where he died a martyr's death in the *Rindfleisch massacres, together with his wife and five children.

Mordecai's fame rests on the *Sefer Mordekhai*, always referred to as "the *Mordekhai*." This gigantic compendium consists of elaborations on talmudic problems in the style of the **tosafot*. However, it follows the arrangement of laws used by Isaac *Alfasi, its aim having been to spread the learning of the French and German scholars and of their predecessors, by attaching them to the work of Alfasi, which had a wide circulation; but the *Mordekhai* does not refer at all to the content of Alfasi's book. Over 300 books and authors are cited in the *Mordekhai*, including whole pages from *Or Zaru'a* and dozens of responsa of Meir of Rothenburg in full. The absence of any of the writings which Meir of Rothenburg sent to his pupils while he was in prison proves that the book was completed before 1286, the year of Meir's incarceration. On the other hand, it is clear from the many references to "my master, Rabbi Mordecai" that the book was not edited by Mordecai himself but by his sons and pupils. If the *Sefer ha-Dinim* of Judah ha-Kohen and *Sefer ha-Ḥokhmah* of Baruch b. Samuel are still known today, it is almost entirely thanks to the *Mordekhai*. The history of the spread of the *Mordekhai* and the transmigrations of its many versions in manuscript and in print is one of the most complicated in all of rabbinic literature. Because of the book's tremendous scope two main compilations of extracts, the "Austrian" and the "Rhenish," were made from it within a few decades, mainly reflecting regional laws and customs, and differing greatly from one another. The Rhenish version—which is the one extant—includes the views of many French and English scholars, and the customs of the German communities. These customs had spread eastward as far as Poland, but were not accepted west of Germany. The Austrian version reflects the *minhag* of southeastern Europe including the customs of Austria, Hungary, Bohemia, Saxony, and Moravia, and mentions many Austrian scholars. This version was in the possession of Israel *Isserlein.

In 1376 Samuel *Schlettstadt edited an abridgement of the *Mordekhai* (*Mordekhai ha-Katan*), adding glosses of his own (*Haggahot Mordekhai*). In print, these appeared independently at the end of the book, but sometimes they were confused with the text. This abridgment was based on the Rhenish version, and when Schlettstadt later obtained a copy of the Austrian version, he added some passages from it. The *Halakhot Ketannot* in the *Mordekhai* are also Schlettstadt's work. Many other abridgments have been made, both by copyists and by printers, this activity having begun, in fact, shortly after Mordecai's death. Apart from Schlettstadt's abridgment, there are extant two printed versions of the book (see below) and a larger number of versions in manuscript. Many manuscripts are extant in libraries in many parts of the world, but no two of them are identical, and all of them are different from *Mordekhai ha-Gadol* (the unabridged *Mordekhai*), also extant in manuscript, which was too long to be copied in full. In view of this situation, Judah Loew of Prague ruled that the *Mordekhai* should not be used as the basis for legal decisions. The *Mordekhai* was first printed together with the first edition of the Talmud (tractates *Berakhot* and *Beẓah*, by Soncino, 1483–84). While the amplifications on *Berakhot* are shorter than those in the regular printed editions, those on *Beẓah* are much longer. It was also published together with Alfasi's abridgment of the Talmud in Constantinople, 1508–09. The *Mordekhai* was published separately, and on the whole Talmud, in Riva di Trento, 1559–60, in an

Mordecai b. Hillel ha-Kohen's commentary on the Mishnah, transcribed by Nethanel b. Levi Trabot, Ferrara, 1457 (fol. 14). Vercelli, Italy, Seminario Vescovile.

edition containing matter not found in the standard edition, which was published later from other manuscripts. Before printing a new edition, printers would generally compare the various editions already previously published, for the purpose of reconciling them, a practice which helped confuse matters even more. Following the ruling of Judah Loew, all passages that were lenient or permissive on points not stated in the Talmud were expunged from the printed editions (but not from the Mss.), causing the accuracy of the text to deteriorate still further.

The *Mordekhai* exerted a powerful influence in Germany on the manner of arriving at halakhic rulings until the time of Moses *Isserles, mainly through Israel Isserlein, who relied on it considerably in his *Terumat ha-Deshen,* and Joseph *Colon. The book was also most influential in the world of Sephardi *halakhah*—which it reached in its abridged form—and Mordecai b. Hillel ha-Kohen is one of the few Ashkenazi authorities cited by Joseph *Caro in his *Beit Yosef.* Many scholars wrote interpretations, amplifications, glosses, or corrections to the *Mordekhai,* including: Israel *Bruna, Israel Isserlein, *Joshua Boaz b. Simeon, Moses Isserles (who inserted the page references to the tractates of the Talmud), *Menahem of Tiktin (who wrote *Ḥiddushei Anshei Shem* on it), Isaiah b. Abraham *Horowitz, and Mordecai *Benet. *Kiẓẓur Piskei ha-Mordekhai,* by Joseph *Ottolengo, which is generally published together with the *Mordekhai* also deserves mention. Up to and including the time of Moses Isserles, small groups of Jews would get together for the regular and systematic study of the work. In addition to this book, Mordecai also composed a rhymed composition on the dietary laws (Venice, c. 1550), and a poem on the rules of vocalization. He also wrote a work on the laws pertaining to the Holy Land and the laws of *ḥallah* ("the priest's share of the dough") published in Z. Bindowitz, *Ḥut ha-Meshullash* (1940). Five of his *piyyutim* are extant including the *seliḥah Mah Rav Tuvekh,* a lament for Abraham the proselyte who died a martyr's death in 1264 at Augsburg.

Bibliography: S. Cohen, in: *Sinai,* 9–16 (1942/43–1946/47), passim; I. A. Agus, *Teshuvot Ba'alei ha-Tosafot* (1954), introd.; Bialer, in: *Genazim* (1967), 19–45; Urbach, Tosafot, index; Rosenthal, in: *Shanah be-Shanah* (1967/68), 234; Zulbach, in: JJLG, 3 (1905); 5 (1907); Zunz, Lit Poesie, 364; Germ Jud, 404; Davidson, Oẓar, 4 (1933), 436.

[I.T.-S.]

MORDECAI BEN JUDAH HA-LEVI (d. 1684), *posek* and rabbinical authority in Egypt. Mordecai was the son-in-law of R. Abraham Tarikah. He served for over 40 years as rabbi, all or part of the time as *dayyan* of Cairo and of *Rosetta, and moved to Jerusalem in 1684, dying there in the same year. In 1678 a sharp dispute broke out between R. Gabriel Esperanza, one of the leading scholars of Safed, and Mordecai ha-Levi over a *halakhic* ruling. The dispute was brought before R. Moses *Galante, the leading rabbi of Jerusalem, but he refused to become involved. His only published work was a collection of responsa, *Darkhei No'am* (Venice, 1697). It is a storehouse of information on the history of 17th-century Egyptian Jewry, which contains the responsa of many scholars of Mordecai's generation. The historian R. David *Conforte was among his friends. Other works written by him which were never published include: *Avodat ha-Kodesh,* a commentary on the Torah; *Mikra'ei Kodesh,* hermeneutics; *Toledot Adam,* concerning the education of children; and *Sof Adam,* collected eulogies. His son R. *Abraham b. Mordecai ha-Levi was the author of *Ginnat Veradim.*

Bibliography: R. A. Ben-Simeon, *Tuv Miẓrayim* (1908), 24; Frumkin-Rivlin, 2 (1928), 96–98; M. Benayahu, in: *Sinai,* 43 (1958), 105–8.

[A.D.]

MORDECAI BEN NAPHTALI HIRSCH OF KREMSIER (d. c. 1670), talmudic commentator and scribe. Mordecai came from Kremsier (Kromeriz), but lived in Cracow and died there. He was the pupil and friend of Shabbetai Sheftel *Horowitz, with whom he established friendship in Posen in 1648. He was famous as a preacher and was referred to as "the chief preacher." Among his works were *Ketoret ha-Mizbe'aḥ* (Amsterdam, 1660), expositions of the *aggadot* in the tractate *Berakhot,* and a study of the destruction of the Temple and the length of the exile; *Ketoret ha-Sammim* (*ibid.,* 1671), a commentary on the *Targum Jonathan and the Palestine Targum to the Pentateuch, to which was appended a kabbalistic commentary on *Berakhot;* and the elegy *Shema Eli Kol Bekhi ve-Kinah* (Lublin?, c. 1650, according to Steinschneider; see bibliography) on the 120,000 martyrs slain in the *Chmielnicki massacres, together with his own commentary to it.

Bibliography: Steinschneider, Cat Bod, 1671f. no. 6253; Landshuth, Ammudei, 200; Gurland, in: *Oẓar ha-Sifrut,* 2 (1888), 161–3 (first pagination); Davidson, Oẓar, 3 (1930), 484 no. 1656.

[J.Ho.]

MORDECAI BEN NISAN (17th–18th centuries), Karaite scholar living in Kukizov, near Lvov (Lemberg), Poland. In answer to an inquiry by Jacob Trigland, professor at Leiden, Mordecai composed in 1699 an exposition of Karaism entitled *Dod Mordekhai* (Hamburg, 1714, with Latin translation; Hebrew text alone, Vienna, 1830, repr. 1966) in which he defends the antiquity of Karaism (reaching back into the Second Temple period) and its independence from Sadduceeism, and traces in brief the history of Karaite literature. His other works include *Ma'amar Mordekhai,* a supercommentary on the *Mivḥar* of *Aaron b. Joseph (unpublished); and *Levush Malkut,* on the differences between the Karaites and the Rabbanites (published by Neubauer; see bibliography). Some hymns by him are included in the official Karaite prayer book.

Bibliography: Fuerst, Karaeertum, 3 (1869), 87ff.; A. Neubauer,

Aus der Petersburger Bibliothek (1866), 76ff.; S. Poznański, *The Karaite Literary Opponents of Saadiah Gaon* (1908), 87; Mann, Texts, 2 (1935), index. [L.N.]

MORDECAI OF NESKHIZ (Rus. **Nesukhoyshe;** 1752–1800), ḥasidic *ẓaddik*, founder of the Neskhiz dynasty and one of the most famous "miracle-workers" of his generation. He was a disciple of *Jehiel Michael of Zloczow and became friendly with *Aryeh Leib of Shpola whom he met in Jehiel Michael's house. His name appears in the list of prominent *ẓaddikim* of 1798–1820 which mitnaggedic writers included in their works against Ḥasidism. After serving as rabbi in Leshnev (Leszniow), in the province of Brody, where a ḥasidic group flourished as early as 1772, he settled in Nesvizh, near Kovel in Volhynia, around 1790. There he became renowned as a "miracle-working" *ẓaddik* and "his miracles in heaven and earth were revealed to the world; raising the dead, healing the sick, and enabling deserted wives to remarry . . . and he became a great wonder" (*Zikkaron Tov* (1892), 99). According to another tradition "Mordecai of Neskhiz was familiar with the mysteries of creation . . . and wrought many miracles but he regretted his actions" (Uri of Strelisk, *Imrei Kodesh* (1871), 9). A wealthy man, Mordecai commissioned the scribe *Moses of Przeworsk to copy a Torah scroll for him. The work took three years and he paid him 400 zlotys. He wrote a small pamphlet, later published under the title of *Rishpei Esh* (1869).

Bibliography: Dubnow, Ḥasidut, index; M. Buber, *Tales of the Ḥasidim*, 1 (1968[4]), 164–6; L. I. Newman, *The Ḥasidic Anthology* (1963), index s.v. *Neschizer*. [Ed.]

MORDELL, LOUIS JOEL (1888–1972), British mathematician. Mordell was professor of mathematics at Manchester from 1923 to 1945 and professor at Cambridge from 1945. He was elected a Fellow of the Royal Society in 1924, and president of the London Mathematical Society from 1943 until 1945. Mordell wrote many articles on the theory of numbers and allied topics. In addition he published *Three Lectures on Fermat's Last Theorem* (1921); *A Chapter on the Theory of Numbers* (1947); *Reflections of a Mathematician* (1958); and *Diophantine Equations* (1969). [B.S.]

MORDELL, PHINEHAS (1861–1934), Hebrew grammarian and scholar. Mordell was born in Shat (Kovno province) and studied in Yelizavetgrad. In 1881, he went to the U.S. and settled in Philadelphia. During his first years there Mordell worked at various trades and was a beadle in a synagogue, at the same time industriously pursuing the study of Hebrew language and grammar. He was associated with the Wissenschaft scholars in the U.S. as well as with Hebrew writers. Finally, after achieving a wide reputation, he worked until 1903 partly as a teacher and partly as a night watchman in order to devote the day to his studies. He was among the pioneer proponents of Zionism and the Hebrew language movement in the U.S. Mordell spent much of his time on the study of Hebrew language and grammar and especially on the *Sefer *Yeẓirah* which he edited and to which he wrote a comprehensive commentary in English (1914). In 1895 he published, without commentary, the corrected text of *Sefer Yeẓirah*. He was greatly encouraged in his linguistic studies by Aḥad Ha-Am (Asher Ginsberg), who published some of Mordell's articles in *Ha-Shilo'aḥ* (vols. 3 (1898), 478–9; 5 (1899), 233–46; 10 (1902), 431–42; see *Iggerot Aḥad Ha-Am*, 2 (1957), 410–1). He continued publishing linguistic studies in *Ha-Toren*, 4 (1917/18), 8f.; *Ha-Ivri*, 9 (1919), no. 1, 3, 4, 5, 6, 9, 12, 17, 19, 21, 22, 24 (a series of articles on the reading of Hebrew which was also published separately); *Ha-Olam ha-Yehudi* (1924); and *Leshonenu*, 3 (1930). His articles were also published in English (8 articles in JQR, 1912–34) and one was published in Yiddish. Mordell left an extensive Hebrew commentary to the *Sefer Yeẓirah* and chapters on grammar (unpublished). His son was Louis Joel *Mordell, the mathematician.

Bibliography: J. Zausmer, *Be-Ikvei ha-Dor* (1957), 3–32. [G.K.]

°**MORDOVTSEV, DANIIL LUKICH** (1830–1905), Russian writer who preached the return of the Jews to Ereẓ Israel. Mordovtsev was a Ukrainian and one of the leaders of the Ukrainian nationalist movement throughout his life. Until 1866 he worked in various government offices, and afterward engaged in his historical and literary work. In his time he was one of the few liberals in Russian who openly sympathized with the Jews. In 1873 he began to publish articles refuting prevalent accusations by Russians, including liberals, against the Jews, and in particular attacked anti-Jewish instigators. In the summer of 1881 he visited Ereẓ Israel and in Jerusalem met a number of Jewish refugees who had fled from the pogrom in Odessa. In his series of stories and travel impressions he repeatedly expressed the demand that the nations of the world restore Ereẓ Israel to the Jews. His literary activity in this area increased especially after the pogroms of the early 1880s in Russia. In his historical stories, he censured the Ukrainian pogroms against the Jews. His stories on Jewish topics include *Za chto zhe?* ("Why?" 1884); *Mezhdu molotom i zakovalney* ("Between Hammer and Anvil," 1891), and *Irod* ("Herod"). These stories were translated into Hebrew and Yiddish (some by Z. *Shazar). His support for the Jewish national movement continued until his death and became especially strong from the time of the appearance of political Zionism.

Bibliography: I. Maor, in: *Shivat Ẓiyyon*, 2–3 (1951/52), 69–82; M. Ben Hillel ha-Kohen, *In Mame Loshn* (1935), 237–55. [G.K.]

°**MORDVINOV, NICOLAI SEMIONOVICH** (1754–1845), Russian statesman and admiral; president of the Department of Civil and Ecclesiastical Affairs of the Council of State. In 1802, as a member of the Council of State, he supported the proposal not to limit the commercial rights of the Jews in the *Pale of Settlement, but in the 1820s he insisted on the mass expulsion of the Jews from the villages and rural settlements. In the blood libel case at *Velizh, Mordvinov took a stand in favor of the Jewish community. Owner of an estate near Velizh and knowing many local Jews, he followed the case closely; when it reached its final stage and came to the attention of his department, he helped to establish the innocence of the Jews, settling the matter by a ukase issued in 1835.

Bibliography: Gessen, in: *Voskhod*, 4 (1903), 3–34; 5 (1903), 3–28; idem, *Velizhskaya drama* (1905); Rivkin, in: *Perezhitoye*, 3 (1911), 60–102. [Ed.]

MORENO, JACOB L. (1892–), U.S. social scientist. Born in Bucharest, he emigrated to the U.S. in 1927. He taught at New York University from 1952 to 1960 and was the founder of the Sociometric Institute and the Theater for Psychodrama. He edited the *International Journal of Sociometry, Group Psychiatry*, and *Group Psychotherapy and Sociodrama*. Moreno initiated the sociometric method in the social sciences. Sociometry assumes that societies have, besides a formal structure, an informal and emotionally based depth-structure of human relations, connecting the individual with other individuals. These relations can be made evident by appropriate methods. Among the techniques Moreno introduced for this purpose were the sociometric test, the sociogram, the interaction diagram, the locogram, and the sociomatrix. These techniques lead to group-therapeutic approaches, especially in "psychodrama" and "sociodrama." In these, the conventional doctor-patient relationship is replaced by acting in which the participants purge themselves through reliving and acting out their experience. These methods have been applied in a variety of situations, especially in schools, industries, and armies.

Major publications of Moreno, apart from a great many papers and monographs, are *Das Stegreiftheater* (1924; *The Theater of Spontaneity*, tr. by the author, 1947); *Who Shall Survive?* (1934, rev. ed. 1953); *Sociometry, Experimental Method and the Science of Society* (1951); *The First Psychodramatic Family* (1964); and *Discovery of Spontaneous Man* (1965). [W.J.C.]

MORESHET, institute in Israel for research into and knowledge of the Holocaust and Jewish heroism, dedicated to the memory of Mordecai *Anilewicz. Established in 1963 on the initiative of a group of ghetto fighters and former partisans, mainly members of *Ha-Shomer ha-Ẓa'ir, Moreshet has a comprehensive archive, research, and publishing center at *Givat Ḥavivah. The archive consists mainly of eyewitness accounts. The foundation publishes memoirs, diaries, and research on the Holocaust period and anti-Nazi resistance. Its periodical, **Yalkut Moreshet*, contains testimonies and related writings. Some of the institute's exhibits are displayed at the museum of kibbutz *Yad Mordekhai. [I.Gu.]

MORESHETH-GATH (Heb. מוֹרֶשֶׁת גַּת), town of the tribe of Judah in the Shephelah, between Lachish and Achzib. It is mentioned by the prophet Micah, who was born there (Micah 1:1, 14; Jer. 26:18). Later sources (Eusebius, Onom. 134:10: Sozomenus, *Historia Ecclesiastica* 9:17; Jerome, *In Micam* 1:10) identify it with a village, which is also called Birat Satia or Kiryat Satia, in the territory of Eleutheropolis (Bet Guvrin). The *Madaba Map indicates a village called Morasthi to the north of Eleutheropolis, near a church of St. Micah. Some scholars have identified Birat Satia with Khirbat Saʿad or Khirbat al-Baṣal and Moresheth-Gath with nearby Tell al-Judayda; others have looked for it at Tell Khirbat al-Bayḍāʾ approximately 4 mi. (6 km.) northeast of Bet Guvrin. The Gath fortified by Rehoboam (II Chron. 11:8) has also been tentatively identified with Moresheth-Gath.

Bibliography: A. Saarisalo, in: JPOS, 11 (1931), 98ff.; J. Jeremias, in: PJB, 29 (1933), 42–53; EM, 4 (1962), 741f.; Aharoni, Land, index. [M.A.-Y.]

MORGENSTERN, JULIAN (1881–), U.S. Reform rabbi, Bible scholar, and president of the *Hebrew Union College. Born in St. Francisville, Illinois, Morgenstern graduated from the University of Cincinnati in 1901 and was ordained at the Hebrew Union College in 1902. He received his doctorate at Heidelberg in 1904; his dissertation was published as *Doctrine of Sin in the Babylonian Religion* (1905). After three years as rabbi in Lafayette, Indiana, he turned to academic life, teaching biblical and Semitic languages, concentrating on biblical studies, at Hebrew Union College.

In 1921 Morgenstern became acting president of the college and in 1922 was elected president; he was the first alumnus to hold this office. During his presidency the number of students and faculty and the scope of college activity grew markedly. Departments of education, social studies, and Jewish music were established; new buildings were erected; an endowment fund was created; the college, previously a department of the Union of American Hebrew Congregations, was independently chartered, and the Hebrew Union School of Religious Education was established in New York City. *Hebrew Union College Annual*, founded in 1924, at once became one of the world's outstanding publications in Jewish scholarship. During the Hitler period, a dozen European scholars found a haven at

Julian Morgenstern, president of Hebrew Union College. Courtesy American Jewish Archives, Cincinnati, Ohio.

the college, chiefly as the result of Morgenstern's efforts. At first anti-Zionist, Morgenstern later modified his position on the creation of a Jewish state. After retiring as college president in 1947, Morgenstern continued to teach Bible. He served as president of the American Oriental Society and the Society of Biblical Literature; he was for many years recording secretary, and then honorary president, of the Central Conference of American Rabbis and one of the founders of the World Union for Progressive Judaism.

Biblical Studies. As a young professor Morgenstern immersed himself in biblical studies and published relatively little. As his views matured, the number and extent of his publications increased. Three works originally published in the *Annual* were later issued in book form: *Amos Studies* (1941); *Ark, the Aphod, and the "Tent of Meeting"* (1945); and *Message of Deutero-Isaiah* (1961). Among many other important essays in the *Annual* are "Oldest Document of the Hexateuch" (1927), which provided the first solid support for the so-called Kenite hypothesis (see *Kenites; *Pentateuch), and a series of studies on the calendars of ancient Israel (1924, 1926, 1935, 1947–48). Starting as a follower of the *Wellhausen school, Morgenstern became increasingly independent in his approach to Bible problems. In his analysis of documentary sources he relied chiefly on differences in economic, social, and political background rather than on differences of vocabulary and style. In his reconstruction of biblical history, he gave much weight to economic and social factors without minimizing the role of inspired thinkers and teachers. In his studies of the calendar, he showed that changes in the nomenclature of the months and the dating of the festivals reflected significant changes in the life of the people of Israel. He also found evidence that in the early post-Exilic period there was a strong universalist trend expressed in proselyting activity, which came to a catastrophic end when a coalition of neighboring states destroyed Jerusalem and burned the Second Temple. (The Temple of Ezra-Nehemiah, later rebuilt by Herod, was thus actually the Third Temple; see "Jerusalem—485 B.C.," in HUCA, 1956, 1957, 1960; see *Temple.) Morgenstern's continuing vigor in scholarly activity is evident in his *Fire on the Altar* (1963), *Some Significant Antecedents of Christianity* (1966), and *Rites of Birth, Marriage, Death, and Kindred Occasions Among the Semites* (1966). More popular in character are *Jewish Interpretation of Genesis* (1919), *Book of Genesis: A Jewish Interpretation* (1965^2), and a collection of lectures and papers, *As a Mighty Stream* (1949).

Views on Reform. His historical research convinced him

that what had been called "universalism" and "particularism" are not mutually antagonistic, but that both are necessary and each complements the other. Despite his official role within the Reform movement, Morgenstern was dissatisfied with the term "Reform Judaism," which he regarded as reflective of conditions in 19th-century Germany rather than in 20th-century America, and as carrying with it certain overtones of sectarian separatism. He preferred to speak (so far as the United States is concerned) of an emerging American Judaism, more pragmatic and less dogmatic than early Reform; and he envisioned an ultimate synthesis of the Reform and Conservative movements, in a pattern not yet evident.

Bibliography: M. Lieberman, in: HUCA, 32 (1961), 1–9; B. J. Bamberger, in: *CCAR Journal* (April 1957); 1–4; L. Finkelstein (ed.), *Thirteen Americans: Their Spiritual Autobiographies* (1953), 253–372. [B.J.B.]

MORGENSTERN (née **Bauer**), **LINA** (1830–1909), German educational theorist, philanthropist, and author. Born in Breslau, she founded a society for supporting poor schoolchildren when she was only 18. In 1854, she married Theodor Morgenstern, a manufacturer, and they settled in Berlin.

Lina Morgenstern, German philanthropist and writer. Jerusalem, J.N.U.L., Schwadron Collection.

From 1859 on, she devoted her life to education and philanthropy. She helped organize the first Froebel kindergartens, and in 1860 published *Das Paradies der Kindheit* (1904), a textbook based on Froebel's method. She established the first free kitchens for the needy in 1866, and in 1873 founded the *Berliner Hausfrauenverein*, a society which served to educate women and safeguard their welfare. The society conducted a cooking school, for which she wrote all the textbooks. In 1887, together with two nurses, she opened a school for nursing. In 1896, she convened the first International Women's Congress, in Berlin, where 1,800 delegates from all parts of the world heard her lectures on women's rights. She was active in peace movements, and served as vice-president of the Alliance des Femmes pour la Paix. She edited and wrote many books including storybooks for children, novels, biographies, cookbooks, periodicals for women, and books on women's problems.

Bibliography: Wininger, Biog, 4 (1925), 429–31. [S.Z.L.]

MORGENSTERN, OSKAR (1902–), U.S. economist. Born in Goerlitz (Germany), Morgenstern taught at the University of Vienna (1928–38) and served as a director of the Austrian Institute of Business Cycle Research (1931–38). From 1936 to 1938 he served concomitantly as an adviser to the Austrian Ministry of Commerce and from 1936 to 1946 as a member of the committee of statistical experts of the League of Nations. In 1938 he settled in the United States and taught at Princeton University, where he became a full professor in 1944, and in 1948 director of its econometric research program. From 1955 to 1957 he was a consultant to the U.S. Atomic Energy Commission and from 1959 to 1960 the White House consultant on atomic energy matters. In addition to general economic theory his principal interests were econometrics and business cycles. His publications include *Die Grenzen der Wirtschaftspolitik* (1934; *The Limits of Economics*, 1937); *Economic Activity Analysis* (1954); *The Question of National Defense* (1959); *International Financial Transactions and Business Cycles* (1959); and *On the Accuracy of Economic Observations* (1950, 1963[2]).

Bibliography: M. Shubik (ed.), *Essays in Mathematical Economics* (1967), incl. bibl. [J.O.R.]

MORGENTHAU, U.S. family of public officials. HENRY MORGENTHAU SR. (1856–1946), financier and diplomat, was born in Mannheim, Germany. His family emigrated to the United States in 1865, settling in New York City. He studied at the College of the City of New York and graduated from Columbia Law School in 1877. He specialized in real estate law and soon concentrated on several highly successful New York City real estate ventures. He relinquished his law practice in 1899 and served as president of the Central Realty Bond and Trust

Figure 1. Henry Morgenthau, U.S. financier and diplomat. Jerusalem, J.N.U.L., Schwadron Collection.

Company and, from 1905 to 1913, as president of Henry Morgenthau Company.

Retiring from active business affairs, Morgenthau entered national politics. He was chairman of the Democratic National Committee's finance committee during Woodrow Wilson's 1912 and 1916 presidential campaigns and served as ambassador to Turkey from 1913 to 1916. His diplomatic efforts were largely concerned with the protection of Christian missionaries, Armenians, and Jews in the Ottoman empire. He particularly helped Jews in Palestine who were suffering from food shortage. He was also in charge of the interests of all Allied states then at war with Turkey. In 1919 Morgenthau was named by Wilson to head a U.S. commission investigating the treatment of Jews in Poland (see *Morgenthau Commission). A strong advocate of the League of Nations, Morgenthau was appointed chairman of its Refugee Settlement Commission in 1923 and implemented the complicated transfer of over a million Greeks from Turkish territory to Greece and of several hundred thousand Turks from Greece to Turkey. Morgenthau was one of the organizers of the International Red Cross and Near East Relief, Inc. He was a leader of the American Red Cross and a liberal patron of musical organizations. He was also active in Jewish religious and philanthropic work; he founded Bronx House in 1911 and served on the executive committee of B'nai B'rith. He was president of the Free Synagogue of New York, but resigned in 1919 because of his opposition to Stephen S. *Wise's Zionism.

Morgenthau was the author of *Ambassador Morgenthau's Story* (1918), an autobiography; *All in a Lifetime*

(1922); *My Trip Around the World* (1928); and *I Was Sent to Athens* (1930).

His son HENRY MORGENTHAU JR. (1891–1967) was an agricultural expert and cabinet member. Henry Morgenthau Jr., who was born in New York City, studied agriculture at Cornell University. He purchased a large farm in Dutchess County, New York, modernized it, and operated it successfully. During World War I he worked to increase food production and also served as an officer in the navy. In 1922 Morgenthau purchased the *American Agriculturist* and used this journal to propagate his views on the state of American agriculture. Governor Franklin D. Roosevelt, a friend and Dutchess County neighbor, in 1928 appointed Morgenthau chairman of the Agricultural Advisory Commission and in 1930 appointed him state conservation commissioner. In response to the Depression, Morgenthau developed state work projects which were later used as models for national programs during Roosevelt's presidency.

Joining Roosevelt in Washington, Morgenthau served as head of the Federal Farm Board and the Farm Credit Administration, and in early 1934 was named secretary of the treasury. A skillful and dynamic administrator, he thoroughly reorganized the Treasury Department. U.S.

Figure 2. Henry Morgenthau, Jr., secretary of the U.S. Treasury. Jerusalem, J.N.U.L., Schwadron Collection.

national and international monetary policies instituted in the 1930s for the stabilization of the economy owed much to his initiative. In addition, he supported tax reforms emphasizing greater obligations of the wealthy. His humanitarian interests were consistently evident in his concern for relief activities. Morgenthau was one of the early champions of preparation for U.S. involvement in World War II and of support for the Allied nations early in the war; he promoted foreign purchases, industrial mobilization, and the huge wartime bond drives. In 1943 Morgenthau successfully intervened with Secretary of State Cordell Hull to obtain State Department approval of a plan of the World Jewish Congress to transfer private U.S. funds to Europe to rescue French and Rumanian Jews. It was at Morgenthau's suggestion that Roosevelt established the *War Refugee Board as a presidential executive agency in January 1944.

As the end of the war approached, Morgenthau proposed a peace plan involving the partition of Germany and its conversion into an essentially agrarian area. The Morgenthau Plan, presented in his *Germany Is Our Problem* (1945), stirred much debate and Morgenthau resigned after Roosevelt's death.

While still at the Treasury, Morgenthau worked with such Jewish organizations as Mt. Sinai Hospital, B'nai B'rith, and the Jewish Welfare Board. In 1947–50 he served as general chairman and in 1950–53 as honorary chairman of the United Jewish Appeal; the unprecedented sums raised by the appeal during these crucial years significantly aided the new State of Israel. Morgenthau also served as chairman of the board of governors of the Hebrew University (1950–51) and of the American Financial and Development Corporation for Israel, and the Israel Bond drive (1951–54).

Henry Morgenthau Jr.'s son ROBERT MORRIS MORGENTHAU (1919–) was born in New York. He served in the Navy during World War II and engaged in private legal practice in New York (1948–61). In 1961 he was appointed U.S. attorney for the southern district of New York and served with distinction until 1970, winning a reputation for integrity and efficient prosecution. He was an unsuccessful candidate for governor of New York in 1962. Among his Jewish communal affiliations were the Anti-Defamation League, the New York Federation of Jewish Philanthropies, and Brandeis University.

Bibliography: Adler, in: *Herzl Year Book*, 5 (1963), 249–81; J. M. Blum, *From the Diaries of Henry Morgenthau Jr.*, 3 vols. (1959–67); idem, *Roosevelt and Morgenthau* (1970); A. D. Morse, *While Six Million Died* (1967), index; R. N. Lebow, in: JSOS, 32 (1970), 267–85.

[Mo.Ro.]

MORGENTHAU, HANS JOACHIM (1904–), political scientist. Born in Coburg, Germany, Morgenthau qualified as a lawyer and practiced in Munich from 1927 to 1930, when he became an assistant at the University of Frankfort. He was acting president of the Frankfort Labor Court from 1931 to 1933 and was professor of international law at the Madrid Institute of International and Economic Studies from 1935 to 1937, when he emigrated to the United States. From 1943 he taught international politics at the University of Chicago; in 1968 he was also appointed professor of political science at the City College of New York. He also served as consultant to the U.S. departments of State and Defense.

Morgenthau was the predominant figure in the post-World War II effort to refocus the study of international relations on the observed regularities of human conduct, rather than on the idealistic pursuit of abstract norms. This political realism gained wide influence with the publication of his *Scientific Man vs. Power Politics* (1947), and especially *Politics among Nations* (1949), which became the leading text in the field. Morgenthau was also active as a commentator on U.S. current affairs. His writings were published as *Politics in the Twentieth Century* (3 vols., 1962) and in 1970 as *Truth and Power*. Many of Morgenthau's

Hans Morgenthau, political scientist.

writings were translated into foreign languages, and he served as editor of numerous philosophical, legal, and scientific journals.

[AL.D.]

MORGENTHAU COMMISSION (July–September 1919), U.S. commission, headed by Henry *Morgenthau Sr., to investigate the situation of the Polish Jews after the pogroms which took place in Poland at the end of World War I. The news of the pogroms set off stormy demonstrations in the important Jewish centers of the West. The representatives of the Polish National Committee in Paris were troubled by the extent of this reaction, and sought to improve their image with the public and among leading statesmen in order to strengthen their position at the forthcoming peace treaty negotiations. It was against this background that the Polish premier, Ignace Paderewski, suggested to President Wilson that an American commission be sent to Poland in order to carry out an objective investigation of the facts on the spot, and to prove that the rumors which had been circulated were maliciously exaggerated.

The mission, besides its chairman, also included lieutenant general E. Jadwin, the lawyer H. G. Johnson, and the jurist Arthur L. *Goodhart as adviser. The commission considered that its task was not only to note facts but to uncover their causes and offer proposals for improving the situation. The activities of the commission in Poland lasted two months. The public and parliamentary debates on the ratification of the Treaty of *Versailles and the Minority Treaty (see *Minority Rights) connected with it aroused exaggerated sensitivity among the Poles, some of whom were inclined to regard the commission as an expression of mistrust on the part of the Anglo-French Entente. The Morgenthau Commission met with the representatives of the various groups in Polish Jewry, paying special attention to the views of the parliament representatives and leaders of the political parties. Morgenthau did not conceal his sympathy for the assimilationists, and was impressed by the *ẓaddik* of Gur (*Gora Kalwaria) as the spokesman of the ḥasidic masses. The commission visited the large urban centers and spent some time in disputed areas such as *Lvov and *Vilna, as well as in such towns as *Pinsk and *Kielce which had been the scene of pogroms. Morgenthau spoke to a considerable number of Polish leaders of various political parties. Morgenthau treated the unconventional figure of Marshal *Pilsudski with respect, the latter making no effort to hide his dissatisfaction with the whole idea of the commission, as a slur on the honor of Poland. Because of his delicate position as a Jew, Morgenthau made a point of appearing objective, and was inclined to justify the Poles as much as possible.

The report of the commission was published in the *New York Times* on Oct. 3, 1919. It tended to minimize the outbreak of violence to a number of incidents occurring against a background of tension and hostile acts, perpetrated by the occupation armies and retreating forces. As for the future, the equality of all citizens, without any distinctions in their rights or obligations, was to be ensured. Endeavors were to be made to introduce changes in the lives of the Jews by diversifying the branches of economy in which they were engaged and by increased vocational training.

Bibliography: H. Morgenthau, *All in a Lifetime* (1922); A. L. Goodhart, *Poland and the Minority Races* (1920); AJYB, 22 (1920/21), 255; H. M. Rabinowicz, *The Legacy of Polish Jewry* (1965), 38–41.

[M.LAN.]

MORGULIS, MANASSEH (Mikhail; 1837–1912), Russian writer and lawyer. Born in Berdichev, Ukraine, Morgulis was among the first to be educated in the government schools for Jews. In 1861 he completed his studies at the government rabbinical seminary in Zhitomir, and in 1864 he entered the University of Kiev, where he helped to create a Jewish students' circle working for the education of the masses and the propagation of information on Judaism in the Russian language. At the same time he contributed to the Hebrew and Russian Jewish press, as well as to the general press. In 1869 he graduated in law and settled in Odessa. He joined the group which published the *Den*, and in his "Impressions from Abroad," he presented a comparison between the situation of the Jews in Western Europe and in Russia. Attacking anti-Semitism in numerous essays, he sought to reform Jewish life from within. One of his longest essays dealt with the history of the education of the Jews (in *Yevreyskaya Biblioteka,* vols. 1–3).

Morgulis considered that Russian Jewry should accept Russian culture while remaining loyal to the religious-national values of Judaism. He therefore supported Yiddish literature, contributed to the Jewish press, and cooperated with the moderate *Ḥovevei Zion inasmuch as they minimized their projects for "the settlement of Palestine." Although initially he was a member of the committee of the Society for the Support of Agricultural Workers and Craftsmen of Syria and Ereẓ Israel, his violent opposition to political Zionism led him to abandon such activities; he also combated attempts to strengthen the Hebrew elements in the modern Jewish schools. A committee member of the Odessa branch of the *Society for the Promotion of Culture Among the Jews of Russia, he was also actively involved in the community's educational institutions, especially the vocational school, Trud, and the *talmud torah,* which were models for all the Russian communities. Morgulis' principal essays and studies were published in his *Voprosy yevreyskoy zhizni* ("Problems of Jewish Life," 1889), and his memoirs (in *Voskhod,* 1895–97 and in *Yevreyskiy Mir,* 1911) are of historical value.

Bibliography: L. M. Bramson, *Obshchestvenno-kulturnaya deyatelnost M. G. Morgulisa* (1912).

[Y.S.]

MORHANGE, town in the department of Moselle, N.E. France. Jews are first mentioned there in 1686. As a result of complaints by the townsmen about the increase in the number of Jewish families, Duke Leopold ordered the Jews not to attract new coreligionists to Morhange. In 1734 the townsmen demanded that Jewish residence should be confined to a single street, and that the number of authorized Jewish families should again be reduced. The Jews were compelled to conform with this order, despite their attempts to circumvent it with the connivance of some of the Christian inhabitants. Only five Jewish families remained in Morhange by 1739, the rest having moved away, mainly to Metz. Their numbers increased slightly after the French Revolution. The synagogue was destroyed by the Germans during World War II. Morhange has supplied the patronymic of several families of Lorraine.

Bibliography: *Mémoires de la Société Archéologique de Lorraine,* 45 (1895), 284ff.; *Revue juive de Lorraine,* 6 (1930), 156ff.; 8 (1932), 82ff.; REJ, 49 (1904), 124; Z. Szajkowski, *Franco-Judaica* (1962), no. 727; idem, *Analytical Franco-Jewish Gazetteer* (1966), 230.

[B.BL.]

MORIAH (Heb. מוֹרִיָּה), an unidentified locality mentioned in the Bible. Abraham was ordered to offer Isaac as a burnt offering in the "land of Moriah," which was three days' distance from Beersheba and visible "[from] afar" (Gen. 22:2–4). Early tradition identifies "mount" Moriah with the place where Solomon built the Temple. Josephus also locates the sacrifice on the mountain where David [sic] later built the Temple (Ant., 1:226). Talmudic scholars explain the name Moriah as derived from the "the mountain of myrrh" (in Song 4:6; Mekh., Be-Shallaḥ 3; Gen. R. 50:7). The Septuagint, in translating "Amoria" (Amorite) for Moriah, offers another explanation. The assumption that Abraham intended to sacrifice Isaac on the threshing floor of Jebus (Jerusalem), in full view of the Canaanite city, is farfetched; nor is the Temple Mount visible from afar, as it is hidden by the higher mountains around it. It seems more probable that the biblical story left the location of Moriah deliberately vague; the importance of the sacrifice of Isaac in the series of covenants between God and Israel made it natural that at an early time this supreme act of faith was located on the site destined to become the most holy sanctuary of Israel, the Temple of Solomon, just as the Samaritans transferred the act to their holy mountain, Mt. Gerizim.

See also **Akedah*.

Bibliography: Abel, Geog, 1 (1933), 374–5; EM, 4 (1962), 741–2.

[M.A.-Y.]

MORIAH, Hebrew publishing house. In 1901 Ḥ. N. *Bialik, together with Y. H. *Rawnitzki, S. Ben-Zion, and others, founded the Moriah publishing house in Odessa, their primary intention being the printing of educational material for modern Hebrew schools. Up to 1914 they issued a large amount of such literature, including Bialik-Rawnitzki's famous anthology *Sefer ha-Aggadah.* Moriah's activities were expanded (under E. L. Lewinsky) to include the best in modern Hebrew literature, such as works by Mendele Mokher Seforim, Shalom Aleichem, I. L. Peretz, S. Asch, and D. Frischmann; poetry by Bialik, Tchernichowsky, and Z. Shneur; and scholarly works by M. L. Lilienblum, D. Neumark, and S. Krauss. Moriah became the leading house for modern Hebrew publishing, but World War I and the Russian Revolution caused the end of this remarkably successful enterprise. It was succeeded by the *Dvir publishing house, set up in Berlin after the war by some of the founders of Moriah.

Bibliography: Ḥ. N. Bialik, *Devir u-Moriyyah* (1926). [Ed.]

MORNING BENEDICTIONS (Heb. בִּרְכּוֹת הַשַּׁחַר), designation of a series of benedictions (the number and sequence varying in the different rituals), which constitute the first part of the morning prayer (**Shaharit*). After a number of preliminary hymns, the following blessings are recited: (1) for ablution; (2) for the wondrous harmony of the bodily functions; (3) the three Torah blessings (**Birkat ha-Torah*), which in some versions appear in a different place; and (4) *Elohai Neshamah* (based upon Ber. 60b) closing with the formula: "Blessed art Thou, O Lord, Who restores the souls unto the dead." (A variant reading is: "Who quickens the dead"; in some Progressive rituals: "Who heals the flesh and doest wondrously.") This is followed by a series of 15 benedictions (but this number varies in different versions) praising God who: (1) "endows the cock with the ability to distinguish between day and night"; (2) "has not made me a heathen"; (3) "has not made me a slave"; (4) "has not made me a woman"; women say: "who has made me according to Thy will"; (these last three blessings are near the end in the Sephardi rite and some ḥasidic rites and are omitted in the Progressive prayer books where the formula "Who has made me a Jew" is said instead by both men and women); (5) "enlightens the blind"; (6) "clothes the naked"; (7) "looses the bound"; (8) "raises them that are bowed down"; (9) "stretches out the earth upon the waters"; (10) "has provided me with all my necessities"; (11) "has ordained the steps of man"; (12) "girds Israel with might"; (13) "crowns Israel with glory"; (14) "gives strength to the weary" (this does not appear in all versions); and (15) "causes sleep to pass from my eyes." These blessings, most of which are mentioned in the Talmud (Ber. 60b), were recited originally at home during the various stages of a person's awakening: opening his eyes, standing up, getting dressed, etc. Maimonides opposed their recital at public worship (Yad, Tefillah, 7:9), but in the course of time they were incorporated into the morning service in the synagogue, probably because people did not remember by heart their wording or their order.

Several personal prayers of tannaitic and amoraic origin (quoted in Ber. 16b, 60b) are then recited. These are followed by the scriptural account of the **Akedah*, by the confession of R. Johanan (Yoma 87b), by the **Shema*, the order of sacrifices (*parashat ha-korbanot*), and in most rites, especially the Sephardi, *ha-ketoret Pittum*, and by talmudic sections: *Zevaḥim* (Mishnah, chapter 5) and the *baraita* of R. Ishmael (Introd. to Sifra, Leviticus). The morning service proper then begins.

Bibliography: E. Munk, *The World of Prayer*, 1 (1954), 18–56; Elbogen, Gottesdienst, s.v. *Birkhot ha-Shaḥar;* Eisenstein, Dinim, s.v. *Birkhot ha-Shaḥar;* J. Heinemann, *Ha-Tefillah bi-Tekufat ha-Tanna'im ve-ha-Amora'im* (1966²), index s.v. *Birkhot ha-Shaḥar;* Freehof, in: HUCA, 23 pt. 2 (1950–51), 339–54; Abrahams, Companion, x–xix. [Ed.]

MORNING FREIHEIT, U.S. daily Yiddish newspaper. Founded in 1922 by the Jewish section of the American Communist Party, the *Freiheit* managed for several years under the editorship of Moissay *Olgin to maintain high journalistic standards and to assemble a staff that included such first-rate writers as H. *Leivick, Moshe Leib *Halpern, David *Ignatoff, and Moshe *Katz. By the late 1920s, however, the *Freiheit* had become an unswerving Party organ, as was demonstrated by its total support for the Arabs during the 1929 Palestine riots. This position alienated many of its readers and caused its circulation to slip sharply from its peak of 14,000. Subsequently, the *Freiheit* remained loyal to the Moscow line through the Hitler-Stalin pact and the Cold War, regaining a measure of independence only in the 1950s, with the onset of de-Stalinization in Russia. In 1970 it was appearing five times a week and had an estimated 8,000 circulation.

Bibliography: M. Epstein, *Jew and Communism* (1959), index; J. L. Teller, *Strangers and Natives* (1968), index (incl. bibl.). [Ed.]

MOROCCO, westernmost country in North Africa. The first arrival of Jews in Morocco goes back to antiquity. There are numerous legends which claim that they settled in the country before the destruction of the First Temple.

Figure 1. Marrakesh interior described as "an opulent Jew's house." Lithograph by Giles from G. Beauclerk, *Journey to Morocco in 1826*. Cecil Roth Collection.

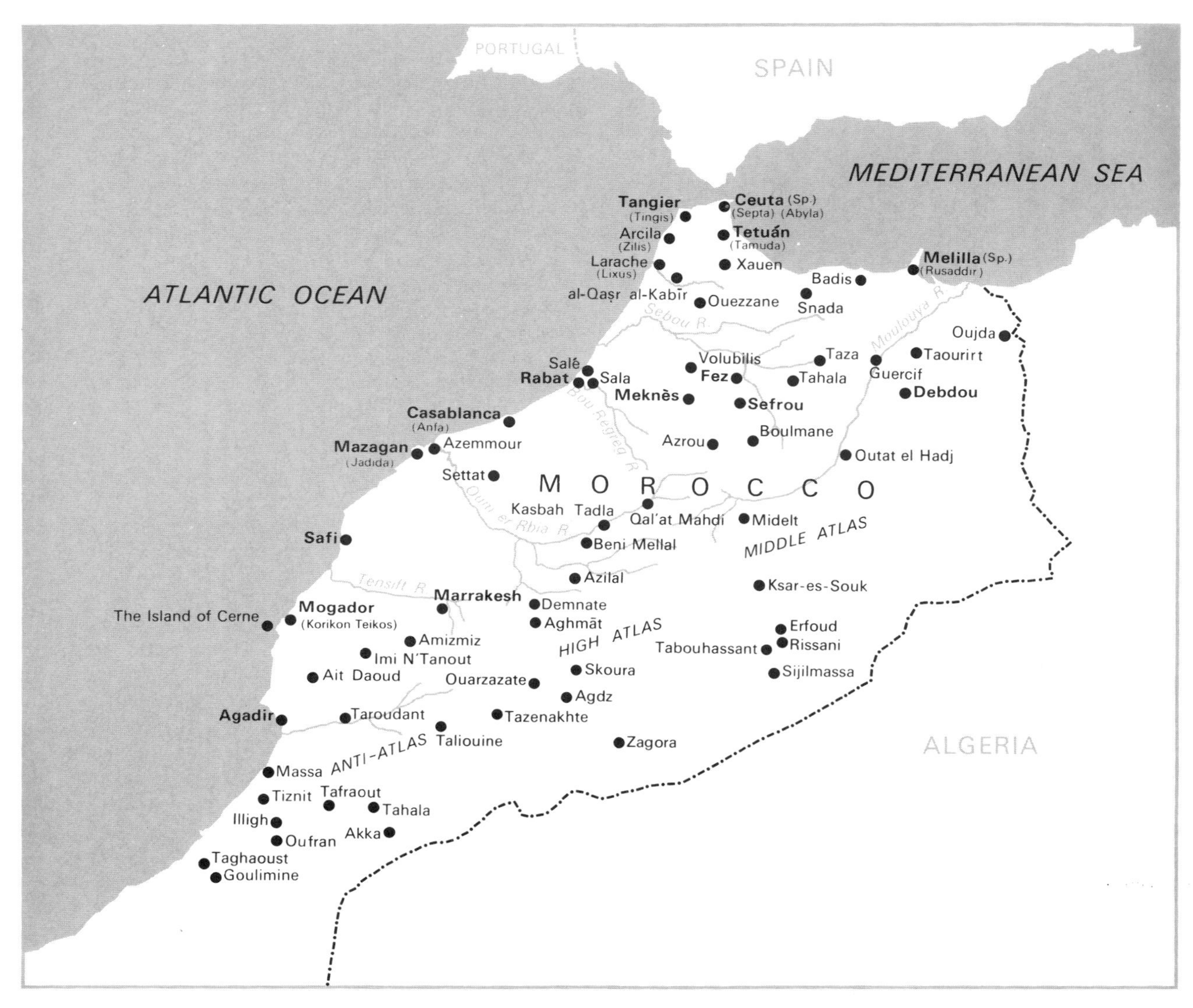

Jewish communities of Morocco. Names in boldface type indicate communities existing in 1971.

Early History. From the fifth to the third centuries B.C.E. the Carthaginian gold market was situated in Morocco. On this historical basis, an ancient legend relates that some five centuries before the Carthaginian expansion, in the days of Solomon and the Phoenicians, the Hebrews came to Sala (Chella) in the vicinity of Salé (Rabat) in order to purchase gold in large quantities. In another legend it is related that Joab was sent to Morocco to fight the Philistines, who had been driven out of Canaan; an inscription describing this expedition is said to have existed near the present-day town of Zagora. Wadi Oued Draa and the region of Oufran (Ifran of the Anti-Atlas) are said to have been the sites of important Jewish settlements before the destruction of the Second Temple. The earliest epigraphic evidence on the presence of Jews in Morocco, however, comes from the second century C.E. It consists essentially of inscriptions on tombstones found in the ruins of the Roman town of Volubilis, between Fez and Meknès, and another inscription discovered in Salé. The latter is in Greek, while one of the inscriptions of Volubilis is in Hebrew.

Morocco, like the remainder of the Maghreb, was one of the favorite territories for Jewish missionary activities. The Jews, together with those whom they succeeded in converting, appear to have originally been numerous and particularly powerful. The great Arabic historian of the 14th century, Ibn Khaldūn, names a number of large Moroccan *Berber tribes who were converted to Judaism prior to the Arab conquest. These were the Fandalâwqa, Madyūna, Bahlūla, Ghiyāta, and Bāzāz tribes. The capital of the last was also named Bāzāz or Qulʿat-Mahdī. It was completely inhabited by Jews and did not disappear until the 12th century. It was situated near the present-day town of Sefrou. Other tribes, such as the Barghwāṭa, were also heavily Judaized.

Between 581 and 693 many Jews were compelled to leave Spain as a result of the persecutions of the Visigoth kings who, while forcing them to accept baptism, also adopted draconian measures against them. According to later traditions, thousands of Spanish Jews had settled in Africa by 693. It is told that these Jews, together with their Moroccan coreligionists, plotted to conquer or deliver Spain into the hands of the more tolerant Muslims (694). Some historians maintain that there were Jews among the Berber-Muslim invaders of Spain in 711.

Arab Conquest and Rule. The Arab conquest of Morocco and its conversion to Islam did not bring about the elimination of the Jews or the Judaized Berbers. However, when Idris I seized power in 788, it was his intention to compel all the inhabitants of the country to embrace Islam. After the death of Idris I, there remained some Jewish or Judaized tribes in the area of *Fez. When Idris II (791–828) decided to establish his capital in Fez, he authorized Jews of all origins to settle there. Their dispersion in all the regions was one of the principal reasons for their economic strength at the time. The story goes that the inhabitants of Fez revolted against the ruler Yaḥya (860), who had violated the chastity of a Jewish girl. The pogrom in Fez in 1033 is to be seen as an isolated event due to the Jewish support for the Maghrawas, the rivals of the Ifrenids. At a later date, the *Almoravides prohibited the Jews to live in their capital *Marrakesh.

THE ALMORAVIDES AND THE ALMOHADS. The most brilliant period of the Jews of Morocco from the spiritual and intellectual point of view belongs to the reigns of the Idrisids and their successors. The numerous departures for Spain drained neither the strength of Moroccan Jewry nor its intellectual activity. Even after the departure of R. Isaac *Alfasi from Fez for Cordoba (1088), Judaism in Morocco retained its vigor. Under the Almoravides there was even a trend in the opposite direction. Two of the physicians of the Almoravide sovereigns, *Meir ibn Kamniel and Solomon Abūab Muʿallim in Marrakesh, were of Spanish origin, one from Seville and the other from Saragossa. Both were distinguished Torah scholars. There were also scholars in *Ceuta, the native town of Joseph ibn Aknin, the disciple of Maimonides. There was also an important center of learning in *Sijilmassa (ancient capital of Tafilalet oasis). Scholars were to be found in the Atlas region, in Aghmāt; of these, there is information on the talmudist Zechariah b. Judah Aghmati. In Fez studies were carried on continuously; it was for this reason that *Maimonides and his family settled there after leaving Spain during the persecution of the Almohads.

The doctrine of the mahdi Ibn Tūmart, which inaugurated the *Almohad movement, did not tolerate the existence of non-Muslims. At the beginning, the latter were among the victims of the Almohad soldiers, who were highlanders in search of plunder. Indeed, many of the Jews were wealthy. By the time that Abd al-Muʾmin (1128–63) had finally imposed Almohad domination in 1154, many Jews had already converted under the threat of the sword. After that, there was a short period of improvement in the situation of the Jews in Fez. Those who had been spared from the massacres and the conversions were then able to resume a relatively normal life. This situation changed with the advent of Abu Yaʿqūb Yusuf (1165–84). The recrudescence of fanaticism once more resulted in the forced conversion of Jews. The *dayyan* of Fez, R. Judah ha-Kohen ibn Shushan, who refused to submit to this, was burnt alive, and at that time Maimonides left Morocco. The situation deteriorated even further under al-Mansur (1184–99) who imposed on the Jews, including those already converted, the wearing of a distinctive sign, the *Shikla*, because he did not believe in the sincerity of their conversion. The presence of Jews was authorized once more by al-Mʾamun (1227–32), but their appearance drew the anger of the Muslims who massacred all of them in Marrakesh (1232). The Jews did not return in considerable numbers until the time of the dynasty of the *Merinids, who replaced the Almohads in 1269. During Almohad rule many Moroccan Jews had left the country for the East, above all for Christian Spain. Large numbers of them settled in the territories of the kings of Aragon, in Catalonia and Majorca, where they were favorably received.

THE MERINIDS AND THE WATTASIDS. The Merinids proved themselves particularly friendly toward the Jews. When the still-fanatic mobs attacked them in 1275, the Merinid sultan intervened personally to save them. The sovereigns of this dynasty benevolently received the Jewish ambassadors of the Christian kings of Spain and admitted Jews among their closest courtiers. Of these Jews, Khalifa b. Waqqāsa (Ruqqasa) became steward of the household of the sultan Abu Yaʿqūb and his intimate counselor. A victim of palace intrigues, he was put to death in 1302. His nephew, who was also named Khalifa, held the same office and suffered the same fate (1310). However, there were no repercussions against the Moroccan Jews as a result of the executions of their powerful coreligionists. They were the principal factors in the prosperity of the country. The Sahara gold trade, which was of primary importance, and the exchanges with the Christian countries were completely under their control. Their relatives and

Figure 2. Nineteenth-century engraving showing the sultan of Morocco receiving Sir Moses Montefiore in the courtyard of his palace. Courtesy D. Corcos, Jerusalem.

Figure 3. Painting of a Sabbath afternoon scene in a Jewish quarter in Morocco, c. 19th century. Attributed to Lecomte-Dunouy. Jerusalem, Israel Museum Photo Archives.

associates in the kingdom of Aragon financed, when necessary, the navies which defended the Moroccan ports. In addition to the *jizya (poll tax) they paid enormous sums to the treasury in customs duties for their imports and exports.

In the outlying areas, particularly in the Atlas region where there were large concentrations of Jews of early origin, the Jews wielded great influence in both the political and spiritual domains. Jewish physicians enjoyed well-deserved renown. The study of Kabbalah, as well as philosophy, was then in vogue. The last Moroccan philosopher of the Middle Ages was Judah b. Nissim ibn *Malka, who was still alive in 1365.

From 1375 the Muslim world of the West clearly entered into its period of decline. The Jews of Morocco were all the more affected by this development because, unlike in *Algeria, there was no revival due to the arrival of important Jewish personalities fleeing from the Spanish persecutions of 1391. The Jews who came to Morocco during this period were mainly of average erudition; morever, just like their native brothers, they encountered the fanaticism which had been introduced among the Muslim masses by the mystics who had then founded the Marabout movement. This movement eroded the authority of the last Merinid sovereigns, and a serious deterioration in the condition of the Jews ensued. In 1438 the Jews of Fez were enclosed within a special quarter (see *Jewish Quarters), the first Moroccan *mellah.

The political and economic situation in Morocco during the 15th century was bad. The sultan Abd al-Ḥaqq turned to the Jews in order to straighten out his finances. He chose the Jew Aaron ben Battas as his prime minister, but a short while later the Merinid dynasty was ended (1465) with the assassination of its last representative and his Jewish minister. A large number of Jews lost their lives in this revolution, and many others were forcibly converted. They were authorized, however, to return to Judaism when Muhammad al-Shaykh al-Waṭṭāsī came to power in 1471. According to local traditions, groups of Jews had in the meantime taken refuge in Spain. Among these were the family of the scholar and poet Saadiah *ibn Danan, who settled in Granada, as well as Ḥayyim *Gagin, who became the leader of the native Jews upon his return to Morocco in 1492.

The Jewish chroniclers are unanimous in their description of the welcome accorded by the sultan Muhammad al-Shaykh al-Waṭṭāsī to the Spanish and Portuguese refugees (*megorashim*) in 1492 and 1496. Bands of plunderers, however, attacked the numerous Jews on the roads to Fez, the town to which they had been attracted. Once they arrived there, they found a lack of accommodations and they camped in the surrounding fields. About 20,000 of them died as a result of disasters, famine, and diseases. Many of them returned to Spain. Under the influence of powerful religious personalities, the majority of them, both distinguished families and the common people, permanently settled in the country. Among this new population there were such eminent men as Jacob Qénizal, Abraham *Saba, Abraham of Torrutiel, Joshua *Corcos, Naḥman Sunbal, and others. There was, however, also a trend for emigration to Italy, Turkey, and Palestine. Among those who left Morocco at that time were Abraham *Zacuto, Jacob (I) *Berab, *David ibn Abi Zimra, and Judah Ḥayyat.

The newcomers were generally ill received by their native coreligionists (*toshavim*). In spite of the fact that the *megorashim* rapidly assumed the leadership in southern communities, such a possibility was for a long time withheld from them in the north. The *toshavim* feared their commercial rivalry and their technical superiority. Controversies broke out between the two elements. The former went so far as to question the faith of the *megorashim*. The latter, however, succeeded in strengthening their position and in due course dominated all the communities where they were represented. Fez became their spiritual center. Their rabbis issued a large number of *takkanot*, which were known by the name of "*takkanot* of the exiles of Castile." These dealt essentially with the laws of marriage, divorce, and inheritance and were based on Spanish tradition. For 450 years they separated themselves in this manner from the *toshavim*. The descendants of the *megorashim* jealously adhered to their ways and customs. They worshiped in their own synagogues and sometimes had their own lots in the cemeteries. In such northern communities as Tetuán and Tangier the native Jews were completely assimilated among the descendants of the *megorashim*. Oblivious to their own origin, they disdainfully referred to their brothers of the interior as *Forasteros* ("aliens," i.e., to the Castilian community). Until recently, most of these communities spoke Ḥakétia, a mixture of Spanish, Hebrew, and an Arabic dialect. The ancient Castilian language, which differs from the Ladino spoken in the Orient, was, until the 19th

Figure 4. Recreation period at the Auguste Beaumier School, Mogador, 1955.

Figure 5. Group of Jews from village in Atlas Mountains.

century, in current usage among a large number of families of Spanish origin in both the north and south of the country.

At the beginning of the 16th century Portugal occupied some of the Moroccan coast on the shores of the Atlantic. Communities of *megorashim* had settled in such ports as Azemmour and Safi. From the beginning, cordial relations were established between them and the Portuguese, who employed their members as official interpreters and negotiators. The political role of these men was of prime importance to the kings of Portugal. Indeed, the latter granted the Jews of their Moroccan bases rights which may be considered as extraordinary for that period; they loaded such families as *Benzamero, Adibe, and Dardeiro with favors. On the other hand, these Jews, as loyal subjects, did not hesitate in sacrificing their property or even their lives when this was required by Portuguese interests. The coreligionists who lived under the sharifs of Marrakesh or the Wattasids of Fez were the principal factors in arranging the peace, always unstable, between the Portuguese and the Muslims. Jacob *Rosales and Jacob *Roti, talented ministers of the Wattasids, endeavored to create a lasting reconciliation between the Christians and the Muslims. Counselors of Muslim princes such as Menahem Sananes or Abraham Cordovi pursued similar objectives. These exiles from Spain and Portugal often traveled to the Portuguese kings as Moroccan ambassadors. During their stay in the Iberian Peninsula they also induced the *Marranos to establish themselves in Morocco.

During the 16th century, Morocco became a haven for Marranos who arrived from the Iberian Peninsula, the Madeira Islands, the Azores, the Canary Islands, and even the Americas. In Tetuán, Fez, Meknès, and Marrakesh there were centers for reconversion to Judaism. Some Jews succeeded in transferring their fortunes there, while others, such as skillful craftsmen and especially the gunsmiths, found immediate employment. It was early Marranos who introduced a new process for the extracting of sugar from sugarcane. Due to their methods Morocco became the leading producer of the world's best sugar during the 16th–17th centuries.

Until recent times, the Jews of Morocco engaged in a variety of professions. In some regions there were farmers and cattle breeders among them; in general, however, they were mostly craftsmen, small tradesmen, peddlers, and, at times, moneylenders. Some industries, such as that of beeswax, and the trading of rubber and ostrich feathers were exclusively concentrated in the hands of the Jews. For religious reasons, the Muslims ceded to them the craftsmanship and trade of precious metals as well as the making of wine and its sale. Until 1912 the overwhelming majority of the maritime trade was controlled by a closed society of Jewish merchants. Wealthy and influential from father to son, some of them were court bankers or high officials. They held the title of "merchants of the sultan," obtained for themselves or their protégés monopolies over a large number of products or foodstuffs, and held a monopoly over certain ports or took them in lease; the European countries entrusted them with their interests and they represented them before the sultan, officially or semi-officially. But the majority of the Jewish population, however, suffered in helpless poverty. The droughts which preceded famine and the exorbitant and arbitrary taxes which were temporarily levied on the communities from the 16th to the middle of the 18th century were the cause of their poverty. Nevertheless, the misfortunes which struck one community did not affect the others. It was thus, for example, a common occurrence that while Jews died of hunger in Fez or were persecuted in Meknès, prosperity reigned in the mellah of Marrakesh and Jews ruled the town of *Debdou.

When there was a weakening of the central authority of the sultan, Morocco was divided up into subordinated territory (*Bled al-Makhzen*) and unsubordinated territory (*Bled al-Sibā*), the latter of which was always that of the Berbers under whom the Jews generally suffered less in their capacity of tolerated "protected subjects" (**dhimmi*). Many of them were the serfs of the Muslim lord; however, until the 19th century there were also many Jews in the High Atlas Mountains, the Sūs (Sous), and the Rif, essentially Berber regions, who carried weapons, rode horses, and did not pay the *jizya*.

Like the Berbers, the Jewish masses of Morocco were marked by their religiosity. But a sincere, profound, and intellectual piety also prevailed within Moroccan Judaism; its development was inspired by the writings of Maimonides. Over the last centuries this Judaism produced genuine scholars and a large number of authors, such as members of the families of Ibn Danān, Ibn Ḥayyim, *Abensur, *Almosnino, Assaban, Ben-Attar, *Berdugo, de *Avila, de Loya (*Delouga), *Elbaz, *Uzziel, *Serfaty, *Serero, *Toledano, and others. On given dates thousands of Jews left on regular pilgrimages (*Ziara*) through the country to the tombs of saints whose origin was at times unknown and who were venerated by both Jews and Muslims.

In many educated circles there was an inclination toward mysticism: its members devoted themselves almost exclusively to the study of Kabbalah. The Zohar, much esteemed in Morocco, was often the principal work in their

Figure 6. Jews outside the mellah of Agoin in the Atlas Mountains. Jerusalem, Israel Museum Photo Collection, Department of Ethnography. Photo Shulman, 1953.

curriculum. In several communities, particularly in Salé, Safi, and Marrakesh, teachers and disciples were grouped in closed circles from which emerged such personalities as Joseph Gikatilla, author of *Ginnat Egoz;* Abraham ha-Levi Berukhim, author of *Tikkun Shabbat;* Joseph ibn Teboul, author of *Perush al Idra Rabba;* Abraham b. Mūsā; Ḥayyim b. Moses *Attar, author of *Or ha-Ḥayyim;* Raphael Moses Elbaz, author of *Kisse Melakhim;* Joseph Corcos, author of *Yosef Ḥen;* Solomon Amar; and Abraham Azulai. Initiates of the Kabbalah have remained numerous in Morocco until the present day. Many others followed *Shabbetai Ẓevi. During the middle of the 17th century the movement of this pseudo-Messiah achieved considerable success in Morocco. In the West, an important role in checking it was played by the Moroccan rabbis Jacob *Sasportas, Daniel Toledano, and Aaron ha-*Siboni.

THE *SAʿDIS. According to a tradition, a Jewish scholar of Wadi Draa forecast to the Saʿdian sharifs that they would accede to the throne of Morocco. Encouraged by this prediction, they set out to conquer the country and took Marrakesh in 1525 and Fez in 1549. In fact, the Jewish counselors of the sharifs were not strangers to their progress. Their coreligionists—administrators, merchants, and bankers—supplied their financial requirements; other Jews, former Marranos who maintained close relations with Europe, supplied them with weapons in their capacity as armorers. When the Portuguese army was defeated by Abd al-Malik at the Battle of al-Qaṣr al-Kabīr (or Battle of the Three Kings, 1578), the Jews commemorated the event by a joyful Purim (*Purim de los Cristianos*). On the other hand, the tens of thousands of Christian prisoners taken in this battle were fortunate enough to be ransomed by the descendants of the *megorashim*, who treated them with indulgence. The liberation of these prisoners against ransom by their families and the conquest of Sudan in 1591 brought a considerable quantity of gold to Morocco. Many Jewish families, especially those in the retinue of Ahmad al-Mansur, were among the beneficiaries of this exceptional

Figure 7. Marrakesh copper craftsman. Jerusalem, Israel Museum Photo Collection, Department of Ethnography. Photo Shulman, 1953.

prosperity. Of an enterprising nature, the Jews of Morocco traveled as far as India in the conduct of their trade; they also had gained a hold in the financial world, particularly in Tuscany, in one direction, and in northwestern Europe, in the other. This activity was in concert with the politics of the young Netherlands, which sought to strangle the economic power of Spain. In 1608 Samuel *Pallache arrived in the Netherlands and in 1610 he signed the first pact of alliance between Morocco and a Christian country. The Pallache family played an active role in the political and economic interests of Morocco in Europe over a long period. The sultan Zidah (1603–1628) and his successors (1628–1659) took many other Jews into their service. As in former times, every Muslim leader had his Jewish counselor. The latter were the natural protectors of the Jewish masses. As a result, these masses generally lived in superior conditions to those of the Muslim population, which resigned itself to its fate.

"Frankish" Jewish families from Leghorn and Holland settled in Morocco. Some were attracted by the pirate traffic which operated from Salé and Tetuán. In Tangier, which was under British domination, a small community of "Frankish" Jews existed from 1661; relations with the Muslims, however, were maintained through the mediation of the Jews of Tetuán: until the evacuation of the town in 1684, the Parienté and the Falcon families played an important political role in the relations between the English and the Muslims. Moroccan Jews had also inaugurated a migratory movement a long while before.

There was a fair amount of emigration in the direction of the Holy Land, Turkey, Egypt, Italy (especially Leghorn and Venice), Amsterdam, Hamburg, England, and the countries of the two Americas. Occasionally, in their old age and once they had made their fortune, emigrants returned to their communities of origin. In Tetuán and later in Mogador this was a frequent occurrence.

THE ʿALAWIDS. The Jews played a particularly important role in the rise to power of the ʿAlawid (Alouite) dynasty of Hasanid descent, which still governed Morocco in the 1960s. This role has been distorted by a legend which relates that at the time an extremely rich Jew, Aaron Ben-Meshal, governed the region of Taza and, as a tribute, demanded a young Muslim girl from Fez every year. By deceit, Mulay al-Rashid (1660–72) succeeded in assassinating this Jew and seizing his riches; the *ṭolba* ("students") assisted him in this exploit. He was thus able to become the first sultan of the ʿAlawid dynasty. To this day, this legendary event is celebrated with much pomp by the *ṭolba* of Fez. In reality, Mulay al-Rashid, who lacked financial means, was backed by the Jews of the Taza, which was then an important commercial center and the first place which he had dominated; he employed a faithful and wise Jewish counselor and banker, Aaron Carsinet. In order to gain control of Fez, where he was enthroned, he entered the city through the mellah, where in secret he spent the night in the house of a notable named Judah Monsano. Mulay al-Rashid subsequently adopted a favorable attitude toward the Jews. His reign was a most prosperous one.

The Jews also successfully contributed to the rise to power of the brother of Mulay al-Rashid, Mulay Ismail (1672–1727), one of the most outstanding Moroccan monarchs. Mulay Ismail was *khalifa* ("viceroy") in Meknes when, through one of his Jewish friends, Joseph *Maymeran, he learned of the death of his brother in Marrakesh. The speed with which he received this precious information and the large sum of money which Maymeran lent him enabled Mulay Ismail to have himself proclaimed sultan immediately. It is also related that not wanting to be indebted to Joseph Maymeran, Mulay Ismail had him assassinated. In fact, he appointed him steward of the palace, a function of considerable importance which was later held by his son Abraham Maymeran, who had become the principal favorite of the sultan. The Toledanos, Ben-Attars, and Maymerans all enjoyed the favors of Mulay Ismail, who during various periods appointed one or the other as *shaykh al-Yahud* with authority over all the Jews of the kingdom. Moses Ben Attar signed a treaty with England in his name; Joseph and Ḥayyim Toledano were his ambassadors to the Netherlands and London. Moreover, the Jews who were close to Mulay Ismail wielded their influence over him. Thus, in spite of his cupidity, violence, and cruelty, the Jews fared better under him than the Muslim masses. The greatest part of his long reign was marked by peace and security, and the Jewish communities were able to develop in every respect. However, during the last years of his reign, years which were overshadowed by plagues and conflicts between his rival sons, the situation of the Jews began to deteriorate.

Beginnings of European Intervention. The 30 years of anarchy and plunder which followed upon the death of Mulay Ismail exhausted and impoverished the Jewish communities of the interior; they consequently transformed their social framework. The Middle Atlas region was literally drained of its Jews. The departure of the village Jews toward the urban centers changed the aspect of the mellahs of Fez and Meknès. These quarters, which had until then been well maintained, were converted into slums, with the exception of a few middle-class streets. Most of the ancient families were ruined and lost all power, only to be replaced by a few parvenus. Some Ben-Kikis and Mamans were sent on diplomatic missions to Europe; their rivalry with the former Jewish bourgeoisie caused controversies within the community; some members of the Levy-Yuly family became "confidants" of the sultans. Slowly, the towns of the interior were abandoned by their leading Jewish elements in favor of the ports, to which the new arrivals were already linked by ancient ties with the Jewish financial circles living there. Rabat, Safi, and especially Marrakesh replaced Fez and Meknès as rabbinical centers.

Mulay Muhammad b. Abdallah (1757–1790) had formally been viceroy of southern Morocco from 1745. He had established security and, with the assistance of Jewish and Christian financial circles, a prosperity unknown in the north of the country reigned there. As under the Saʿdians, Marrakesh once more became the capital and royal residence. Its Jewish community flourished but then entered a period of decline as a result of the avariciousness of the sultan in his old age. The community of Safi took over the leading place in the foreign trade of Morocco, while that of Agadir acquired the monopoly over the trading with the Sahara. These roles later became the privilege of the community of Mogador, which was founded in 1767. The condition of the Jews improved throughout the country. Jews from abroad came to settle in Morocco. Among these were the Attals and Cardosos (Cordoza), who entered the service of the sovereign. Cardoso, however, drew the jealousy of the Attals upon himself and paid for this with his life. The leading favorite of the sultan was Samuel *Sunbal, a scholar, ambassador to Denmark, and the last "sheikh" of Moroccan Jewry. Certain Jewish personalities encouraged friendship with the United States, where their relatives had emigrated and with whom they had important commercial ties. Isaac Cordoza Nuñes, an interpreter of the sultan in Marrakesh, and Isaac Pinto, a Moroccan established in the United States, were largely responsible for the signing of a treaty between Morocco and the United States in 1787, whereby the U.S. Congress paid Morocco

Figure 8. Carpet weaving in Damnate. Jerusalem, Israel Museum Photo Collection, Department of Ethnography. Photo Shulman, 1953.

for the protection of U.S. shipping interests in the Mediterranean.

Mulay Muhammad entrusted the Jews with all his negotiations with the Christian countries. Those of the community of Tetuán, whose members included some wealthy merchants and who, as in Mogador, acted as consuls, refused the rebellious son of the sultan, Mulay al-Yazid, an important loan which he had requested from them. When he came to power, Mulay al-Yazid (1790–92) wreaked cruel vengeance upon them and his hatred fell upon all the Jews of the kingdom. This was the greatest disaster which befell them after the period of the Almohads. In the first place, the community of Tetuán was handed over to the army, which plundered and perpetrated murder and rape. The communities of Larache, Arcila, al-Qaṣr al-Kabīr, Taza, Fez, and Meknès then suffered the same fate. All the Jewish personalities who had been employed by the late sultan and upon whom Mulay al-Yazid could lay his hands were hung by their feet at the gates of Meknès, where they remained for 15 days before they died. The treasurer Mordecai Chriqui, who refused to convert, was handed over to the executioner and Jacob Attal, who accepted such an offer, nevertheless died after being hanged by his heels. The notables and the Muslim masses then rose to intervene on behalf of the Jews. They hid many of them in their houses and saved a great many others. In Rabat, the governor Bargash saved the community from the worst. At the time Marrakesh had not been subordinated. Once it fell, the Jewish community was sacked, the men and children were massacred, and hundreds of women were taken into captivity. Mulay al-Yazid had the eyes of 300 Muslim notables of the town put out. Thousands of others were convened to the Great Mosque for prayers and massacred there. Shortly before he died as the result of a wound received in a battle near Marrakesh, Mulay al-Yazid ordered the drawing up of lengthy lists of Jewish and Muslim notables in Fez, Meknès, and Mogador who were to be massacred. He died before the order was carried out.

The advent of Mulay Suleiman (1792–1822) came as a certain deliverance. The new monarch was indeed opposed to violence, but he proved to be a fanatic and the Jews felt the consequences. As he sought to seal off Morocco from foreign influence, he reduced trade with Europe to a considerable extent. He also decreed the establishment of ghettos in the wealthiest communities. In 1808 the Jews of

Tetuán, Rabat, Salé, and Mogador were for the first time enclosed within mellahs. The only exceptions were a few families in Mogador who continued to live in the residential quarter of the town. Since they were economically indispensable to the country, he restored to some of them their former prerogatives, notably to the Aflalos, the Corcos, the Guedallas, the Levy-Yulys, the Macnins, and the Sebags. He chose his diplomats, his bankers, and his counselors from these families. The terrible epidemics of 1799 and 1818 depopulated Morocco and wrought havoc with its social and economic conditions. As a result, some of these families emigrated to England, where they gained a prominent place within the Jewish society of London. One of the members of the Levy-Yuly family, Moses, emigrated to the United States, where his son David *Yulee became the first senator of Jewish origin.

The reigns of Mulay Abd al-Raḥman (1822–59) and his successors Mulay Muhammad b. Abd al-Raḥman (1859–73) and Mulay al-Ḥasan (1873–94) were marked by the pressure of the Christian powers on Morocco and an increased activity of the Jews in the economic and diplomatic fields. Meyer *Macnin was appointed ambassador in London (1827); Judah *Benoliel, consul in Gibraltar, successfully negotiated several treaties; Abraham *Corcos and Moses Aflalo were entrusted with several delicate missions; many other Jews, such as the families of *Altaras, *Benchimol, and *Abensur, played important roles in Moroccan affairs. Until 1875 consular representation in the Moroccan towns was almost entirely assumed by Jewish merchants, and many of them held such functions into the 20th century. The European powers, concerned with their economic interests, granted protection to a large number of Jews. By often exploiting the defense of their protégés as a pretext, they interfered with the internal affairs of Morocco. A Jewish consular agent, Victor *Darmon, was summarily executed on a trumped-up charge (1844). This became one of the causes of the Spanish-Moroccan War of 1860, when Jews were compelled to take refuge in Gibraltar, while those of Tetuán were the victims of a pogrom. Tangier and Mogador were bombarded by the French fleet. In Mogador the Jews, assailed by the tribes who came to plunder the town, defended themselves by force of arms. In Tangier, which only suffered some material damage, the Jews celebrated with a Purim (*Purim de las bombas*). Emigration nevertheless rose and the sultan reintroduced the exit tax which was to be paid by every individual who left the country. However, those who desired to settle in the Holy Land were exempted from this tax (1858). A number of families, many of them wealthy, then established themselves in Palestine.

The Moroccan people, already fanaticized by the French conquest of Algeria, accused the Jews of being the agents of European influence in Morocco. In some of the regions populated by the Berbers, the situation of the Jews became quite precarious. Measures which even went beyond the restrictions of Muslim law were imposed against the Jewish masses of the interior, which were more vulnerable than those living along the coasts: Jews were often sentenced to bastinado for trifling reasons. This situation prompted a visit by Sir Moses Montefiore to the court of Mulay Muhammad in Marrakesh; the later promulgated a *dahir* ("royal decree"; February 1864) which was marked by extreme benevolence toward the Jews and granted them equality of rights with all Moroccans. Nevertheless, this decree was never respected by the *qāʾids* and pashas. An energetic protest was then made by the consul general of the United States and other powers intervened on behalf of the Jews. France reinforced the system of consular protection and the other nations followed in her wake.

Figure 9. Marrakesh Jewish women in festive dress. Jerusalem, Israel Museum Photo Collection, Department of Ethnology. Photo Shulman, 1953.

During the reign of Mulay al-Ḥasan and at the beginning of that of Mulay Abd al-Aziz (1894–1908), the Jews lived in tranquility. Mulay al-Ḥasan held a positive attitude toward his Jewish subjects, receiving their deepest respect in return. Upon the death of the sultan, the chamberlain (vizier) Ba Ahmad treated the Jews with justice and fairness. During the 19th century Moroccan Jewry, whose number has been variously evaluated as being between 200,000 and 400,000, produced many renowned rabbis, poets, and talmudists, as well as a number of legal authorities whose works continued to serve as the basis for the justice dispensed by Jewish tribunals under the French Protectorate. These scholars included R. Abraham *Coriat and R. Masʿūd Knafo of Mogador, R. Masʿūd Ben-Moha and R. Mordecai Serfaty of Marrakesh, R. Joseph *Elmaleh of Rabat, R. Raphael Encaoua of Salé, R. Vidal Serfaty of Fez, R. Isaac Ben-Walīd of Tetuán, and R. Mordecai Bengio of Tangier. Many of these leaders realized the importance of secular studies for the masses and they assisted the *Alliance Israélite Universelle of Paris in founding its first schools in Tetuán in 1862, in Tangier in 1865, in Mogador in 1867, and in other Moroccan towns from 1874. In contrast, other rabbis violently opposed the establishment of these schools, which they foresaw, quite correctly, would encourage an estrangement from Judaism.

Upon the death of Ba Ahmad (1900) an epidemic of plague ravaged Morocco. In the mellah of Fez alone, there were more than 3,000 victims; the country then entered a period of anarchy during which the Jewish population suffered greatly. During the entire second half of the 19th century thousands of impoverished Jews swelled the Jewish populations of the large urban centers. The overcrowding of the Jewish quarters became indescribable. This exodus went on uninterruptedly into the 20th century. *Casablanca, which underwent a tremendous expansion, was its final halting place. The misery which prevailed in the Jewish quarters and which was partly due to the inability of the ex-villagers to adapt themselves to urban life, became one of the social stains of Morocco.

The French Protectorate. Early Period. The establishment of the French Protectorate in 1912 was marked in Fez by a pogrom which claimed over 100 victims (April 18–19, 1912). However, there were no incidents in the zone assigned to Spain or in Tangier, which was declared an international town. Under the French and Spanish dominations the Jews enjoyed complete freedom in all matters pertaining to their traditions, religion, occupations, and movement. France and Spain did not interfere with the status of the Jews of Morocco, who remained subject to the sultan's protection—this proved to be advantageous for them when the anti-Jewish laws were issued by the *Vichy government. In a *dahir* of May 22, 1918, the French authorities contented themselves with granting official status to the existing organization of the Jewish communities, with a few modifications. These changes were more particularly emphasized by the *dahir* of 1931. During the 19th century a council of notables appointed by the population was responsible for the administration of the community. A *gizbar* ("treasurer"), who was elected by the leading personalities of the town, was co-opted to the council. The council and the *gizbar* were responsible for the nomination of the rabbis-judges *(dayyanim)*. After 1912 the nation which assured the protectorate, i.e., France, claimed for itself, directly or indirectly, most of the prerogatives emanating from this organization and more particularly the tutelage of the community committees, which then became mere benevolent institutions. These committees, the number of whose members varied with the numerical importance of the community, as well as their presidents, were appointed by the grand vizier, who in practice was dependent on the protectorate authorities. Moreover, the committees were supervised by a Jewish official of the government, who was chosen because of his devotion to French interests. By the maintenance of such a strict control over the Jewish elements of the country the protectorate authorities revealed their distrust. Few Jews, however, were politically hostile toward France. It was the task of the community committees to bring relief to the numerous Jews living in miserable conditions. Their budget continued to be raised from the income derived from the scale of *kasher* wine and meat, the revenues from charitable trusts *(hekdesh)* which they administered, and the often generous contributions of the upper classes and Jews from overseas. The authorities did not grant them any subsidies.

With the exception of Tangier, where there were special circumstances, and a few other rare cases, the old Jewish upper class kept its distance from these community committees. They were constituted of new elements which came from a middle class that until then had been practically nonexistent in Morocco. The members of these committees were generally all loyal to the French authorities. The children of the long-time upper class were usually sent to the French primary or secondary schools. Their religious instruction was entrusted to private teachers. Living within a traditional environment which had withstood many a trial, they were sheltered from religious estrangement and unreserved assimilation. The westernization of the new class, which was accomplished by the Alliance Israélite Universelle, was too rapid and often superficial. Many of them discarded all adherence to tradition. Their potential complete integration among the colonizers, however, was thwarted by the anti-Semitism of the middle-class Frenchmen of North Africa. A large number of Jews of this new social class amassed considerable wealth as a result of the accelerated development of the country. This new middle class formed an important section of the larger, as well as the smaller, communities. Moroccan Jewry was consequently transformed. Some Jews took up higher studies in Morocco itself or in French universities.

From 1912 Morocco attracted a large number of Jews from Algeria and Tunisia. Others arrived from Middle Eastern countries and Europe. In 1939 the Jewish population of Morocco, including the foreign Jews, was estimated at 225,000. Until then, political Zionism had won only a few adherents in Morocco. Zionism, however, was often discussed in youth movements and organizations and regular lectures on the subject were given in the Jewish circles. The philanthropist Raphael Benozérof was most active in the Zionist movement in Morocco, spreading its ideas among both the masses and the elite of the Jewish community. A periodical, *L'Avenir Illustré,* which was published in Casablanca from 1926, regarded itself as the organ of Moroccan Jewry, as well as the standard-bearer of Zionism. It aroused the opposition of those who stood for the evolution of Moroccan Jewry and its assimilation into French culture. From 1932 this faction published the *L'Union Marocaine.* In 1939 World War II interrupted the publication of these two Jewish organs. [D.Co.]

Holocaust Period. Moroccan Jews were neither despoiled nor deported by the Germans, although they suffered from incessant humiliations under the Vichy government (see *France, Holocaust Period) and from the extremist interpretation of its laws. These *lois d'exceptions,* passed on Oct. 31, 1940, caused a deterioration in the relations between Jews and Muslims, despite Sultan Muhammad V's declaration that all his subjects were equal. There were Jewish quotas in the schools; Jews received only half the food ration allotted to the Muslim population and were obliged to live in the mellah, where the overcrowding caused epidemics. Foreign Jews who sought sanctuary in Morocco were placed in labor or concentration camps, together with "undesirable" elements. Immediately after the U.S. landings, the Rabbi Eliahu Synagogue in Casablanca was desecrated and pogroms broke out all over the country. Moroccan Jewry's economic, legal, and social status was gradually restored only after June 1943, when the Gaullists came to power. [R.At.]

Contemporary Period. In 1948 about 238,000 Jews lived in French Morocco, 15,000 in Spanish Morocco, and 12,000 in the international zone of Tangier. The 1951 census in French Morocco indicated 199,156 Jews and, together with the Jewish population of Spanish Morocco, the total number of Moroccan Jews then reached about 222,000. The first census conducted in united Morocco in 1960 recorded 159,806 Jews, while in 1962 an estimated 130,000 Jews lived in the whole of Morocco, decreasing to 85,000 in 1964, and about 42,000 in 1968. The two censuses of 1951 and 1960 give valuable evidence of the demography of the Jewish population in Morocco. In 1951 over a third of the Jews lived in small towns and villages, but in 1961, as a result of the mass exodus to Israel, only about a quarter of them still lived there. The continued *aliyah* after 1960 reduced this number even further, so that the majority of Jews in the country in the late 1960s were concentrated in the major cities. Census data show that among the emigrants there were more young people than old; this is confirmed by the census conducted in Israel in 1961.

The dispersal of Moroccan Jews throughout scores of towns, townlets, and villages, which sometimes contained only a few dozen families, made it difficult to provide Jewish *education for all who wanted it, and up to the time of the mass exodus there were places in which there were no Jewish educational institutions. This is one of the reasons for the high percentage of illiteracy among Moroccan Jewry, even in 1960. In a sample of 2% of the overall Jewish

Figure 10. Ḥanukkah lamp from Morocco, brass, 17th century. Tel Aviv, I. Einhorn Collection. Photo David Harris, Jerusalem.

population aged five and over taken in Morocco in 1960, 43.2% were illiterate (i.e., could not read Arabic or French, for those who knew only Hebrew letters were counted as illiterate). However, the 10–14-age group had an illiteracy rate of only 18.1%, whereas the age group 60 years and older had a rate of 76.3%. The 52 schools of the Alliance Israélite Universelle had 21,823 pupils in 1948, and in 1956 28,702 pupils attended its 82 institutions. The number of its pupils subsequently dropped to 9,000 in 1965, of whom about 1,000 were non-Jewish. In October 1960, the Moroccan government nationalized a fourth of the schools run by the Alliance Israélite Universelle, turning them into government schools, to which hundreds of non-Jewish pupils were accepted. Apart from the Alliance Israélite Universelle institutions, there were also schools run by Oẓar ha-Torah, Em ha-Banim, and, from 1950, by the Lubavicher ḥasidic movement. *Talmud torah* schools and *ḥadarim* continued to exist, despite the fact that the opening of new *ḥadarim* was forbidden in 1953. The lack of a sufficient number of schools, along with the emigration of many educated Jews to France, resulted in a low number of university graduates in Morocco. In 1954 there were only 239 Jewish university students, of whom 151 studied abroad. According to government statistics in 1964, of the 75,000 Jews who remained in the country there were only 60 physicians, 15 dentists, 50 pharmacists, and 44 lawyers. However, in proportion to the Muslim population, the Jews were better educated, for in that year the whole country contained only 232 lawyers.

Despite the fact that a few wealthy Jews lived in Morocco, most Moroccan Jews were considered to be poor. Many of them were peddlers or artisans or lived on social assistance. Since Jews lived in poverty and poor sanitary conditions in crowded homes of the mellah, where eight to ten people sometimes dwelt in one room, many Moroccan Jews suffered from diseases, especially trachoma. In fact, among the pupils attending Alliance Israélite Universelle institutions in Casablanca 30% suffered from trachoma, and the Alliance Israélite Universelle had to open a special school for them. This was also one of the reasons for the Israel government's adoption of a policy of health selectivity toward Moroccan immigrants. The Jewish Agency for Israel and *OSE worked in cooperation with many local doctors to treat Moroccan Jews before entry to Israel.

In the mid-20th century the legal status of Moroccan Jewry improved. With the exception of a few Casablanca Jews, they did not have the right to vote in local elections. Disputes between Jews and non-Jews had to be settled in Muslim courts, which judged according to Muslim law. Jews were not allowed to elect their own representatives on the Jewish community councils, the members being appointed by the authorities. After the independence of Israel (1948) the Jews in Morocco, as in the East, suffered from severe attacks by the population. In June 1948, 43 Jews were murdered and 155 injured at Jérada (Djérada) and Oujda, after nationalists incited the population. However, the government brought scores of guilty to trial, sentencing two of them to death and others to imprisonment. Despite this, there were more pogroms at Oujda, and four Jews were killed (October 1953). On the eve of Moroccan independence in 1954, attacks on Jews were recorded in Casablanca, Rabat, and Petitjean, and a number of Jews were murdered. Much Jewish property was looted in various places throughout the country, and the Alliance Israélite Universelle schools at Boujad, Mazagan, and elsewhere were set on fire. Emigration increased. While between 1948 and 1953 about 30,000 Jews went to Israel, emigration figures in 1954–55 rose to 37,000 since the Jews feared that when Morocco gained her independence their situation would become worse.

However, when Sultan Muhammad V (1953–61) returned from exile and Morocco gained its independence in March 1956, the situation of the Jews improved. For the first time in their history they became citizens with equal rights. In 1956 the king even appointed Leon *Ben Zaqen minister of posts, and other Jews began to gain important positions in the government administration as officials and in courts of law as judges. Jews were also appointed to the advisory council, the first being David Benazareff, shortly after his appointment to the presidency of the Casablanca community council. But on May 13, 1956, an order was issued forbidding Jews to leave for Israel, and in June 1956 the offices of the Kadimah organization, which dealt with emigration, were closed. The 20 or so Israelis then living in Morocco were deported. After long negotiations with the representative of the World Jewish Congress, the government permitted the emigration of the 6,325 Jews in the Mazagan camp who were ready to leave for Israel. In fact, the government did not prevent individual Jews from leaving, and sometimes turned a blind eye to mass emigration. However, vigilance on the Moroccan frontiers increased in July 1957, after pressure from the opposition parties, and obstacles began to be placed in the way of those Jews requesting permission to travel legally for a short visit abroad. From that time on they had to show proof that they were able to support themselves abroad. Afterward (1958–59), a number of Jews were tried and sentenced for smuggling their currency, or even for possessing an obsolete calendar issued by the Jewish National Fund. In 1958 when a new government was formed, Ben Zaqen was not included, and a number of Jewish officials were dismissed. In 1959 all Zionist activity was forbidden in Morocco, and many Jewish organizations were forced to close their doors. That year, swastikas were daubed in Casablanca and Rabat. As a result of this situation and despite the illegal exit, about 47,000 Jews went from Morocco to Israel between 1956 and 1960. The process of leaving illegally involved great hardship, and there was even the case of the sinking of a small boat with 43 emigrants (1961).

After the sudden death of the king Muhammad and the accession to the throne of his son, Hassan II (1961), there was a change for the better in the government's relations with the Jews. Hassan's first step was to make emigration to Israel legal. He also ensured the security and equality of the Jews and gave important state appointments to Jews. Among others, Salomon Bensabat was appointed a High Court judge, Albert Sasson became dean of the science faculty of the University of Rabat, while in 1963 Meyer Obadiah was appointed as a member of the National Assembly, and David Amar was appointed senator. When Obadiah went to France in 1967, he was succeeded by Jacob Banon. However, during this period anti-Jewish propaganda increased in Morocco, organized mainly by the Istiqlāl Party, led by ʿAllāl al-Fasi, who at the time also served as minister of Islamic affairs. The party journal and the rest of the Moroccan press, with the exception of newspapers supported by the government party, published much incendiary material against Jews, and in 1965 the *al-Istiqlāl* newspaper published extracts from the *Protocols of the Elders of Zion*. Between 1961 and 1963, and especially in 1962, many young Jewish girls were kidnapped and forced to embrace Islam. The condition of the Jews worsened upon the outbreak of the Six-Day War (June 1967), after incitement by the Istiqlāl. The party encouraged Muslims to enforce an economic boycott of the Jews, but King Hassan adopted a firm policy so that Jews were not seriously harmed, and the economic boycott was abolished.

Mass emigration of Jews from Morocco continued, especially after June 1967. The emigrants now included wealthy and educated Jews, who no longer believed in the possibility of a peaceful life in Morocco. Among the emigrants were lawyers, engineers, and doctors. The mass exodus caused the closing of most Jewish institutions, yeshivot, schools, and many synagogues. The community in the 1960s lacked rabbis, *dayyanim*, and even readers of the Law in synagogue. The charitable organizations that functioned throughout Morocco were liquidated; Jewish newspapers were closed. One of these, *La Voix des Communautés*, published in Rabat, closed in 1956, but reappeared from February 1961 until November 1963; it was the organ of the Conseil des Communautés Israélites du Maroc. The conseil, founded by a *dahir* (royal decree) in May 1945, represented all Moroccan Jewry and was comprised of members of the community committees of the principal towns. Internal rivalries between leaders of Casablanca Jewry resulted in the dissolution of the council in 1962.

When Morocco gained its independence, a royal decree of January 1956 abolished rabbinical courts and turned them into state courts of law, with the exception of the Supreme Rabbinical Tribune in Rabat, which was abolished by government order in 1965. From 1945 the rabbinical court was headed by Chief Rabbi Shaul D. ibn Danān, who went to Israel in 1966. From 1965, the other members of the rabbinical court were appointed judges in state courts. Jews who remained in Morocco were subject to military service, according to the military service law of 1966. As a result of the mass exodus, young Jews were not drafted into the army, nor were those liable for military service prevented from leaving Morocco. In 1970, some 35,000 Jews were living in Morocco. Of those who had emigrated most lived in Israel, but a considerable number, mainly the wealthy and more highly educated, had settled in France and Canada.

[H.J.C.]

Morocco's Attitude to Israel. When Morocco achieved its independence in 1956, it joined the Arab League and adopted that body's general attitude toward the Arab-Israel conflict. In spite of its geographical distance from the scene of hostilities, it adhered verbally to Arab extremist anti-Israel policies and slogans, in order to subdue internal opposition from both the right-wing Istiqlāl party and the left-wing parties and criticism against the monarchy from the "revolutionary" Arab states. But the real policy of King Hassan II, however, was a rather cautious one. For instance Morocco did not sever relations with West Germany when Bonn established diplomatic ties with Israel in 1965. During the Six-Day War (1967), Morocco sent troops to the front, but the fighting was over before they reached Morocco's eastern border. After the war Hassan's attitude approached that of President Bourghiba, of *Tunisia, calling on the Arabs to be realistic and seek a political settlement with Israel. On the other hand, Morocco expressed dissatisfaction with the U.N. Security Council Resolution of Nov. 22, 1967 (although it supported it in the end) because of its population's particular sensitivity to the religious aspect of the Jerusalem problem.

Anti-Israel feelings in Moroccan public opinion after the Six-Day War were expressed by an attempted economic boycott of the Jewish community in Morocco and of imports from the United States and Western Europe. The authorities officially condemned this action and suppressed it. The king called upon the public to differentiate between the Jews of Morocco and "the Zionists." The secretary general of the Moroccan Trade Unions (UMT), Maḥjūb ben Ṣadīq, criticized the king's policy and was supported by the Istiqlāl party and the Muslim masses. Ben Ṣadīq was arrested and condemned to 18 months in prison—a sentence which brought strong protests from Algeria, Syria, and Egypt.

Until the beginning of 1970, King Hassan II openly criticized the acts of terror of the Palestinian organizations, especially the hijacking of airplanes. However, he changed his attitude toward the Palestine Liberation Organization when al-Fatah adopted the program of establishing a "democratic Arab Palestine where Christians, Jews, and Muslims could live in peace together." He supported this idea as the sole solution for the Middle East problem. The king held that the conflict should be resolved among the Palestinians themselves—the Jews of Palestine and the Arabs of Palestine—leaving out the great powers, whose presence in the Mediterranean region concerned Morocco. From 1970 Morocco contributed a sum of $4,000,000 annually to the P.L.O. to be collected from new indirect taxes.

[D.Co./R.Co.]

Bibliography: General: Hirschberg, Afrikah; A. Chouraqui, *From East to West* (1968); M. Nahon, *Les Israélites au Maroc* (1909); J. M. Toledano, *Ner ha-Ma'arav* (1911); M. L. Ortega, *Los Hebreos en Marruecos* (1919); M. Eisenbeth, *Les Juifs du Maroc* (1948); G. Vajda, *Un receuil de textes historiques Judeo-Marocains* (1951); I. D. Abbou, *Musulmans Andalous et Judéo-Espagnols* (1953); D. Corcos, *Les Juifs du Maroc et leurs Mellahs* (1971); D. Noy (ed.), *Moroccan Jewish Folk-Tales* (1966); SIHM, *France 1st series*, 1–3 (1905–11); *Pays-Bas*, 1–4 (1906–23); *Angleterre*, 1–3 (1918–35); *Espagne*, 1–3 (1921–63). From Antiquity to the Arab Conquest (717 c.e.): J. Goulven, in: *Hesperis* (1921), 317–36; A. Laredo, *Bérberes y Hebreos en Marruecos* (1954). Idrisids to Almohads Period (790 c.e.–1269 c.e.): C. Monteil, in: *Hesperis*, (1951), 265–95; A. Halkin, in: *Joshua Starr Memorial Volume* (1953), 102–10; D. Corcos, in: *Zion*, 32 (1967), 137–60; S. D. Goitein, *A Mediterranean Society*, 1 (1967), passim. Merinid and Wattasid Period (1269 c.e.–1550 c.e.); D. Corcos, in: JQR, 54 (1963/64), 271–87; 55 (1964/65), 53–81, 138–50; idem, in: *Sefunot*, 10 (1966), 55–101. Saʿdi Period (1550 c.e.–1659 c.e.); H. de Mendoca, *Jornada de Africa* (1607), passim; D. Corcos, in: *Zion*, 25 (1960), 122–33. Alawid Period: H. Bentov, in: *Sefunot*, 10

(1966), 414–95. FROM AḤMAD AD-DAHABI TO MULAY YAZID (1727 C.E.–1792 C.E.): J. Braithwaite, *History of the Revolutions in the Empire of Morocco* (1729), passim; L. de Chenier, *Present State of the Empire of Morocco*, 2 vols. (1788), passim; S. M. Schiller-Szinessy, *Massa be-Arav, Romanelli's Travels in Morocco* (1886). FROM MULAY SULEIMAN TO MULAY AL-ḤASAN (1792 C.E.–1894 C.E.): Miège, Maroc, passim. FROM MULAY ʿABD AL ʿAZIZ TO MULAY YUSEF (1894 C.E.–1912 C.E.): N. Leven, *Cinquante ans d'histoire*, 2 vols. (1914–20). FRENCH AND SPANISH PROTECTORATES AND CONTEMPORARY PERIOD: D. Bensimon-Donath, *Evolution du judaïsme marocain sous le protectorat français 1912–1956* (1968); S. Romanelli, *Ketavim Nivḥarim, Massa ba-Arav*, ed. by H. Schirmann (1968); N. Robinson, in: J. Freid (ed.), *Jews in the Modern World*, 1 (1962), 50–90.

MOROGOWSKI, JACOB SAMUEL ("Zaydl Rovner"; 1856–1942), *ḥazzan*, composer, and conductor. Born in Radomyshl, Ukraine, Morogowski in his youth worked as a flour merchant, at the same time serving as the "musician" of the Makarov Rabbi Twersky. His fame as a *ḥazzan* began to spread after the rabbi ordered him to officiate in the High Holy Day services of his *bet ha-midrash*. He then officiated as *ḥazzan* for five years in Kiev, where he studied music under the violinist Podhozer, and from 1881 to 1914 he officiated as *ḥazzan* in the communities of Zaslavl, Rovno (hence the name "Zaydl Rovner"), Kishinev (as the successor of Nisan *Belzer), Berdichev (as the successor of Yeruḥam ha-Katan *Blindman), London, and Lemberg, from where he returned to Rovno. In all these posts he was accompanied by a large choir, and for weekday services and festive occasions he also made use of an orchestra. His compositions enthralled his audiences and brought him worldwide fame. In 1914, Morogowski emigrated to the United States, where he remained until his death. He left a rich musical treasury of prayers for *ḥazzan*, choir and orchestra, as well as marches. All his works were characterized by a true prayer style, fervent religious feeling, and ḥasidic melody. Hundreds of *ḥazzanim* considered themselves as his disciples. Some of his published compositions are: *Halleluyah*, for choir and orchestra (1897); *Kinos* (Heb. text, 1922); *Uhawti*, for choir and orchestra (1899); and *Tisborach* (1874).

Bibliography: Sendrey, Music, nos. 3530, 5689–91; *Di Shul un Khazonim Velt*, 3 (1939); Cantors' Association of the United States and Canada, *Di Geshikhte fun Khazones* (1924), 92; A. Zaludkowski, *Kultur-Treger fun der Idisher Liturgie* (1930), 310; A. Friedmann, *Lebensbilder beruehmter Kantoren* ..., 3 (1927), 121; H. Harris, *Toledot ha-Neginah ve-ha-Ḥazzanut be-Yisrael* (1950), 433.
[J.L.N.]

MOROSINI, GIULIO (Samuel ben David Naḥmias; 1612–1683), apostate scholar, and polemicist. He was born in Salonika of a *Marrano family which had reverted to Judaism. His grandfather, Isaac, who had been a Christian in his youth, was referred to as "Paul Teshuvah" after his return to Judaism. When Morosini was a child, his family moved to Venice, where he studied under Leone *Modena. He at first engaged in commerce, traveling throughout the Ottoman Empire, and became converted to Christianity in Venice in 1649, when his family lost its fortune. In 1671 he became a clerk at the Collegium de Propaganda Fide. He completed the work, begun by the apostate Giovanni Battista Jonah, on textual variants in the Targums (Ms. Vat. Urb. 59; Ms. Oxford 2341). Morosini also engaged zealously in missionary activity among Jews, and wrote a work in three parts, *La Via della Fede* (Rome, 1683). In the first part, he attempts to show that it is the duty of the Jews to embrace Christianity. The second part contains important information on contemporary Jewish life and customs both in the home and in the synagogue. In the third part Morosini tries to demonstrate that the Jews do not observe the Ten Commandments, whereas the Christians do. A polemic against this work appears in Joshua *Segre's *Asham Talui*.

Bibliography: Wolf, Bibliotheca, 3 (1727), 1126f.; G. Bartolocci, *Bibliotheca Magna Rabbinica*, 3 (1683), 755f.; 4 (1693), 404; Neubauer, Cat, 816f. n. 2341; M. Steinschneider, in: *Vessillo Israelitico*, 30 (1882), 372f.; idem, in: MGWJ, 43 (1899), 514f.; Vogelstein-Rieger, 2 (1896), 287; D. Simonsen, in: *Festschrift* ... *A. Berliner* (1903), 337–44; C. Roth, in: RMI, 3 (1928), 156f.
[U.C./ED.]

MORPURGO, North Italian family of Austrian origin. Its earliest known member was Israel b. Pethahiah *Isserlein (1390–1460), who settled in Marburg, Styria, and became known also as R. Israel Marburg. In 1624 members of the Marburger or Marpurger family were appointed *Court Jews by Emperor Ferdinand II. About the mid-17th century they were to be found in various parts of Europe, North Africa, and the East, but mainly in northern Italy, at Trieste, Ancona, Venice, and Padua. Arriving there from Gradisca d'Isonzo (Austria), they eventually changed their name to Morpurgo, and distinguished themselves in various fields. Members include the noted talmudist Samson *Morpurgo and ELIJAH MORPURGO (1740–1830), a Hebraist. GIUSEPPE LAZZARO MORPURGO (1759–1833) was a poet and financier. He wrote verses in Hebrew and Italian, was a supporter of Napoleon, and founded the well-known insurance company Assicurazioni Generali of Trieste. He also presided over the Jewish community there. MOSÈ MORPURGO visited Ereẓ Israel, where he met Ḥayyim Joseph David *Azulai (1764). Also of the family were Rachel *Morpurgo, poet, and EMILIO MORPURGO (1822–1882), who taught economics at Padua University and was undersecretary for agriculture in 1867. ABRAHAM VITA MORPURGO, a publicist from Gorizia, founded the *Corriere Israelitico* in 1867. He made a collection of prayers in Italian for the Jews of Trieste (1855), and translated the *Haggadah* into Italian (1864). Salomone *Morpurgo was a philologist and librarian. ELIO MORPURGO (1858–1943) was born at Udine, of which he was mayor in 1908. He served as undersecretary for posts in 1906 and 1908, and was made a senator for life in 1920. He was deported by the Germans in 1943. BENEDETTO MORPURGO (1861–1944), pathologist, member of the Lincei academy, held the chair of pathology at Turin University from 1900 to 1935. Following the Fascist discriminatory laws of 1938, he took refuge in Argentina, and died in Buenos Aires. GINO MORPURGO translated the Books of Ecclesiastes and Esther into Italian (1898–1904). GIULIO MORPURGO (1865–1931), of Gorizia, taught commercial technology at Trieste University and wrote numerous monographs on commercial subjects. EDGARDO MORPURGO (1866–1942), physician and Jewish historian, wrote *Psicologia e psicopatologia degli Ebrei* (1905); *Le origini del movimento Sionista* (1905); *La Famiglia Morpurgo di Gradisca sull' Isonzo, 1585–1885* (1909). Morpurgo donated to the library of Padua University the collection of Judaica belonging to his family, the *Raccolta Morpurgo di letteratura e storia dei popoli semitici*, whose catalog he published in 1924. LUCIANO MORPURGO (b. 1886), born in Spalato, publisher, wrote *Poesia della famiglia ebraica* (1948). Giuseppe *Morpurgo was an author and educator. VITTORIO MORPURGO (b. 1890), de Janeiro. MARCO MORPURGO (1920–1948) and EDGARDO an architect, designed buildings in Rome, Tirana, and Rio URI MORPURGO (1923–1948), grandsons of the historian Edgardo Morpurgo, were Zionist pioneers. Both met their deaths during Israel's War of Independence, the first near Sedeh Eliyahu, and the second near Haifa.

Bibliography: E. Morpurgo, *La Famiglia Morpurgo di Gradisca sull' Isonzo* (1909); I. M. Molho, in: *Ozar Yehudei Sefarad*, 9 (1966), 102–3; G. Bedarida, *Ebrei d'Italia* (1950), index; M. Vardi, in: RMI, 15 (1949), 523–8; F. Luzzatto, *ibid.*, 17 (1951), 12–31; M. A. Szulwas, *Roma vi-Yrushalayim* (1944), 176. [E.B.]

MORPURGO, GIUSEPPE (1887–1967), Italian author and educator. A secondary school teacher, Morpurgo was for some time after 1938 headmaster of the Jewish school in Turin. His writings on school education retain considerable value. He also edited popular literary anthologies, his subjects including Virgil, Petrarch, and Leopardi. His fiction includes the novels *Yom ha-Kippurim* (1925) and *Beati misericordes* (1930). The first deals with the problems of Jews loyal to their religious tradition, but fascinated by humanist culture and liberal Western European society, in which they may nevertheless face suffocation. Morpurgo seems to visualize two possible outcomes of this conflict—complete assimilation through mixed marriage arising from a faulty education, or emigration to Erez Israel, the land of Jewish regeneration. The author's avowedly Zionist outlook is here quite explicit. In his second novel, Morpurgo examines a Catholic case of conscience, probing spiritual and theological questions with depth and learning. [L.C.]

MORPURGO, RACHEL (1790–1871), Italian Hebrew poet. Born in Trieste, she was a relative and close friend of S. D. *Luzzatto, who strongly influenced her and fostered her wide-ranging Hebrew education. Like Luzzatto, she hoped to revive Hebrew poetry in Italy, and wrote Hebrew poems which S. D. Luzzatto placed in *Kokhevei Yiẓhak*. They were extremely popular with Hebrew readers, and won praise and fame that exceeded their artistry. Most of her poems describe autobiographical or familial incidents; some are written in the style of Spanish Hebrew religious poetry and Italian Hebrew poetry, depicting Jewish historic values and traditions. Rachel Morpurgo had a good knowledge of Hebrew and she carried on the tradition of poetry common among Italian Jews since the Renaissance. Her poems and letters were collected and were published as an anthology entitled *Ugav Raḥel* by Vittorio (Ḥayyim Isaac) *Castiglioni (1890), new ed. by Y. Zmora, 1943.

Bibliography: N. Salaman, *Rachel Morpurgo and Contemporary Hebrew Poets in Italy* (1924), 34–52; Luzzatto, in: *Kokhevei Yiẓhak*, 35 (1868); Klausner, Sifrut, 4 (1953[2]), 38–49; S. Morais, *Italian Hebrew Literature* (1926), 199–202; J. L. Landau, *Short Lectures on Modern Hebrew Literature* (1938[2]), 160. [El.K.]

MORPURGO, SALOMONE (1860–1942), Italian philologist and librarian. While still a student Morpurgo was an active member of the Italian nationalist movement. He was arrested by the Austrian authorities in his native Trieste and received a prison sentence. He then moved to Rome, where he became coeditor of the *Archivio storico per Trieste, l'Istria e il Trentino* (1881–95), which campaigned in favor of the Irredentist claim to Italy's Austrian-controlled territories. Best known for his literary work, Morpurgo was a coeditor of the *Rivista critica della letteratura italiana* (1884–91), director of the Riccardiana library in Rome (whose *Manoscritti italiani* he carefully described), and subsequently headed the Marciana library in Venice, which he transferred to the Palazzo della Zecca (*La Biblioteca Marciana nella sua nuova sede*, 1906). From 1905 to 1923 Morpurgo directed and reorganized the National Library in Florence. He investigated the medieval Italian version of the legend of the *Wandering Jew, publishing *L'ebreo errante in Italia* (1891), and edited the Italian manuscript of the story written in Florence by Antonio di Francesco d'Andrea early in the 15th century, which predates the well-known German edition of the legend. A pupil of the eminent writer Giosuè Carducci (1835–1907), Morpurgo specialized in the study of old Italian dialects and literary sources, and prepared editions of various manuscripts, analyzing their linguistic features and their relation to the figurative arts. The outcome of this work was his *Supplemento alle opere volgari a stampa dei secoli XIII e XIV, indicate e descritte da F. Zambrini* (1929; reissued 1961). A leading authority on Dante and Petrarch, Morpurgo later taught Italian literature at the University of Bologna.

Bibliography: E. Battisti, in: *Studi Trentini*, 23 (1922), 135–6; *L'Osservatore Romano* (Feb. 18, 1942). [G.R.]

MORPURGO, SAMSON BEN JOSHUA MOSES (1681–1740), Italian rabbi and physician. Samson was born in Gradisca d'Isonzo, Friuli. While still young he was taken by his parents to neighboring Gorizia, where he studied under Jacob Hai Gentili, the rabbi of the community, and his son, Manasseh. At the age of 12 or 13 he moved to Venice and there received a thorough education in the yeshivah of Samuel Aboab as well as from his old teacher Manasseh Gentili who had meanwhile moved to Venice. After some years he went to Padua to study medicine in the university there and in 1700 received the degree of doctor of philosophy and medicine. From then on he devoted himself to the study of Talmud, traveling between Padua and Venice and between Gorizia and Mantua where he studied under the outstanding scholar Briel, who in 1709 ordained him rabbi. In that year he was appointed a member of the *bet din* of the kabbalist Joseph Fiametta (Lehavah) whose daughter Rebecca he married. On the death of his wife in 1716 he married her sister, Judith. On the death of his father-in-law in 1721 Samson succeeded him as rabbi of the community, a post he held until his death. Morpurgo had connections with all the great scholars of his generation, who turned to him for counsel on complicated cases in the field of *halakhah*, among them Isaac Lampronti, who quotes Samson's rulings in his *Paḥad Yiẓhak*, Moses Ḥagiz, and Benjamin ha-Kohen of Reggio. His skill as a doctor in Ancona, recognized by both Jews and Christians, and his profound compassion, particularly toward the suffering

Samson b. Joshua Moses Morpurgo, Italian rabbi and physician.

poor, won him the love and respect of all. In 1730 a devastating influenza plague swept Ancona, and, despite the Church ban against Jewish doctors' treating the Christian sick, Samson distinguished himself in the care he gave to all the town's inhabitants. In consequence, Cardinal Lambertini publicly presented him in 1731 with a document which expressed his gratitude and his esteem for Samson's devotion. Samson was involved in the polemics of the rabbis of the generation against Nehemiah Ḥiyya *Ḥayon, and was among those who took up a tolerant attitude toward him. There is extant correspondence between Morpurgo and Moses Ḥagiz on this subject from the end of 1711 to the beginning of 1715. The *Or Boker* (Venice, 1741) contains a prayer that was said at his grave on the anniversary of his death. The following of his works have been published: *Confutazioni alle Saette del Gionata del Benetelli* (Venice, 1703–04), a polemic against the Christian priest Luigi Maria Benetelli who wrote *Le Saette di Gionata scagliate a favor degli Ebrei* (1703), a book filled with hatred of the Jews and their religion; *Eẓ ha-Da'at* (*ibid.*, 1704), a philosophical commentary on the *Beḥinat Olam* of Jedaiah Bedersi; and *Shemesh Ẓedakah* (*ibid.*, 1743), a collection of responsa published posthumously by his son Moses Ḥayyim.

Bibliography: E. Morpurgo, *La Famiglia Morpurgo . . .* (1909), 32–34, 65–69, 77, 104; I. Sonne, in: *Kobez al Jad*, 2 (1937), 157–96; B. Cohen, in: *Sefer ha-Yovel . . . A. Marx* (1943), 56; M. Wilensky, in: KS, 23 (1946/47), 199; idem, in: *Sinai*, 25 (1949), 68–75.

[G.La.]

MORRIS, HENRY HARRIS (1878–1954), South African lawyer, for 20 years the leading defense counsel and King's Counsel at the South African criminal bar. Henry Morris was the son of Hyman Morris, president of the first synagogue in Johannesburg. Morris had a reputation for grasping the human essentials in a situation and for his acute understanding of motives. He was at his best in cross-examination, when he could be forceful and caustic, but also urbane. Morris left a book of memoirs, *The First Forty Years* (1948). [L.S.]

MORRIS, NATHAN (1890–1970), English Jewish educator. Born in Novogrudok, Russia, Morris went to England in 1909 and became a teacher in the Liverpool Hebrew Higher Grade School directed by J. S. *Fox, subsequently serving as headmaster of the institution (1912–20). Morris was founder and headmaster of the Glasgow Hebrew College, where he served from 1920 until 1929, when he was appointed education officer of the Jewish Religious Education Board of London, a post he held until 1940. When the ravages of war threatened Jewish schooling in Great Britain, he founded and directed the Joint Emergency Committee for Jewish Religious Education (1940–45), which set up classes for children in places far removed from the large population centers. At the end of the war, Morris was invited to take charge of the programs of the Central Council for Jewish Religious Education in the United Kingdom and Eire and of the London Board for Jewish Religious Education (both 1945–48).

With Israel's independence, he helped to found the Jewish Agency's Department of Education and Culture and served as its director from 1949 until 1959, when he retired and returned to London. Morris wrote various Hebrew textbooks and educational manuals, but his most important work was the three-volume study on the history of Jewish education from the tannaitic period to the present, *Toledot ha-Ḥinnukh shel Am Yisrael* (1960–64). The study is a monumental work and the first of its kind in Jewish historiography. [Ju.P.]

MORRIS, NELSON (1839–1907), U.S. meat-packing executive. Morris, who was born in the Black Forest region of Germany, was taken to the U.S. at the age of 12. In 1854 he began working in the New York stockyards and two years later, he went into the meat-packing business for himself in Chicago. At the outbreak of the Civil War, Morris received a contract to supply meat to the Union armies. He subsequently supplied all the meat for the Army of the West later in the war, and filled meat-supply contracts for the governments of England, Germany, and France. His firm of Morris & Company was one of the largest in the U.S.

His son Ira Nelson Morris (1875–1942), who was born in Chicago, was a diplomat and author. Morris early severed his active connection with his father's firm. He served as commissioner-general to Italy (1913) and as U.S. minister to Sweden (1914–23). His books include: *With the Trade Winds* (1897); and *From an American Legation* (1926). [Ed.]

MORRIS, RICHARD BRANDON (1904–), U.S. historian. Born and educated in New York, Morris taught at City College, New York, from 1927 to 1949, and became professor of history at Columbia in 1949. Among his important books are: *Studies in the History of American*

Richard B. Morris, U.S. historian. Courtesy Columbia University, New York.

Law (1930); *The Peacemakers* (1965); *Government and Labor in Early America* (1946); and *The American Revolution Reconsidered* (1967). He was coeditor of *The New American Nation* series (1953–); the *Encyclopedia of American History* (1953, 1963); and a *Documentary History of the United States* (1968– ; 12 volumes published, 30 volumes projected). He also wrote *John Jay, The Nation and the Court* (1967) and *The Emerging Nations and the American Revolution* (1970). He made noteworthy contributions in the field of archival preservation. He also served as chairman of the board of the editors of *Labor History*.

[S.I.P.]

MORSE, DAVID ABNER (1907–), U.S. labor executive and lawyer. Morse, who was born in New York, worked on the legal staff of the U.S. Department of the Interior (1933–34), as chief counsel for its Petroleum Labor Policy Board (1934–35), and as a regional attorney for the National Labor Relations Board in New York (1935–38), before entering private law practice. From 1940 to 1942 Morse was impartial chairman for the milk industry in the metropolitan New York area. After serving with the U. S. Air Force (1942–45), Morse held the position of general counsel for the National Labor Relations Board (1945–47) until appointed assistant secretary of labor. In 1948 he was elected director general of the International Labor Organization (ILO) based in Geneva, Switzerland. As ILO head,

Morse directed its establishment of international labor standards and its training programs designed to assist underdeveloped countries and particularly their workers, in raising their standards of living and bettering their job conditions. When the organization was awarded the Nobel Peace Prize in 1969, Morse accepted the award on behalf of the ILO. In 1970 he resigned as ILO director general and became the impartial chairman of the New York coat and suit industry. [ED.]

MORSE, LEOPOLD (1831–1892), U.S. congressman. Morse, who was born in Wachenheim, Bavaria, went to the U.S. in 1849. In 1850 he moved to Boston, Massachusetts, where he worked in a clothing store. In 1864 Morse and Ferdinand Strauss formed the Leopold Morse Company which specialized in the manufacture of men's clothing and soon became the largest of its kind in New England. After twice running unsuccessfully for Congress on the Democratic ticket (1870, 1872), Morse subsequently served five terms in Congress as Democratic representative from Massachusetts (1877–85, 1887–89). Morse was rumored to be a leading choice for the post of secretary of war in Grover Cleveland's cabinet, but religious prejudices were supposed to have ruled out his appointment. Active in Jewish affairs, Morse founded the Boston Home for Infirm Hebrews and Orphanage, renamed the Leopold Morse Home for Infirm Hebrews and Orphanage after his death. [ED.]

MORTARA, LODOVICO (1855–1937), Italian jurist and statesman. Born in Mantua where his father Marco *Mortara was chief rabbi, he lectured from 1886 at the universities of Pisa and Naples. He became professor of law at Naples in 1903 and at the same time a magistrate in Rome. He was promoted to membership of the Supreme Court in Rome where he held the offices of attorney general, public prosecutor, and eventually first president of the Supreme Court of Cassation. In 1919 Mortara became minister of justice and in the following year was appointed to the Senate. He was an outspoken critic of Fascism and opposed the constitutional changes introduced by Mussolini. His writings ran into many editions and strongly influenced the development of Italian jurisprudence. They include: *Lo Stato Moderno et la Giustizia* (1885); *Principii di Procedura Civile* (1922[7]); *Manuale di Procedura Civile* (1921[3]). Mortara also edited the review *La Giurisprudenza Italiana* (1891–), Italy's leading judicial publication.

Bibliography: M. Rotundi, *L. Mortara* (1937); P. Calamandrei, *L. Mortara* (1937). [G.R.]

MORTARA, MARCO (1815–1894), Italian rabbi and scholar. He attended the rabbinical seminary in Padua under Samuel David *Luzzatto, was ordained in 1836, and from 1842 officiated as rabbi of Mantua. Mortara represented the liberal trend in Judaism in Italy and argued that a distinction be made between the Jewish religion and Jewish nationality. He proposed a conference of Italian rabbis in 1866 in order to secure certain reforms in Jewish practices but his suggestion did not materialize. In the sphere of biblical study, Mortara opposed the documentary hypothesis and argued for the unity and Mosaic authorship of the Pentateuch (1843). He considered that the task of Judaism was to spread monotheism and morality throughout the world and that this was facilitated by the Dispersion. Mortara published books on the principles of Judaism and a new edition of the prayer book whose translation into Italian was based on that by S. D. Luzzatto. His most important work was in the area of bibliography and includes a catalog of the manuscripts in the library of the Mantua community (1878), and *Mazkeret Ḥakhmei Italyah* (*Indice alfabetico dei rabbini e scrittori israeliti di cose giudaiche in Italia;* 1886), a list of approximately 2,000 Jewish scholars living in Italy from the first to the 19th centuries. He was a notable bibliophile, his collection of manuscripts being purchased after his death by David *Kaufmann.

Marco Mortara, Italian rabbi and scholar. Jerusalem, J.N.U.L., Schwadron Collection.

Bibliography: *Corriere Israelitico,* 22 (1884), 227–8; *Vessillo Israelitico,* 34 (1886), 188–9; 42 (1894), 59–62; Shunami, Bibl, nos. 3987–88. [M.E.A.]

MORTARA CASE, case of the abduction of a Jewish child by Catholic conversionists. On the night of June 23–24, 1858, Edgardo Mortara, aged six years and ten months, son of a Jewish family in Bologna, Italy, was abducted by the papal police and conveyed to Rome where he was taken to the House of *Catechumens. The boy had been secretly baptized five years before in an irregular fashion by a Christian domestic servant, who thought, as she said later, that he was about to die. The parents vainly attempted to get their child back. This flagrant abduction of a minor had many precedents in Italy. The church, moreover, had always maintained that the extemporized baptism of a child who was in danger of death was valid even if it had been carried out against the parents' will. The case caused a universal outcry. Napoleon III was among those who protested against the infringement of religious freedom and parental rights. Sir Moses *Montefiore went to Rome in 1859, in the hope of obtaining the child's release. The founding of the *Alliance Israélite Universelle in 1860, in order to "defend the civil rights and religious freedom of the Jews," was due partly to this case. Pope *Pius IX, however, rejected all petitions submitted to him. In 1860,

The kidnapping of Edgardo Mortara, 1858. Drawing by Moritz Oppenheim.

after the annexation of Bologna to the Italian kingdom, the boy's parents took new steps, again in vain, for the return of the child. With the ending of the pope's secular power in 1870, Edgardo Mortara who had taken the name Pius and in the meantime was a novice in an Augustinian order—was free to return to his family and religion. However, he refused to do so. Mortara, who preached eloquently in six languages, was such an ardent conversionist that he received the title of "apostolic missionary" from Leo XIII. He became canon in Rome and professor of theology. He died at the Abbey of Bouhay near Liège in Belgium in 1940.

Bibliography: G. Volli, *Il caso Mortara nel primo centenario* (1960); idem, in: *Bolletino del Museo del Risorgimento*, 5 (1960), 1087–1152; idem, in: *Scritti . . . Federico Luzzatto* (1962), 309–20; idem, in: RMI, 26 (1960), with illustrations; A. F. Day, *The Mortara Mystery* (1930); Meisl, in: MGWJ, 77 (1933), 321–8; B. W. Korn, *American Reaction to the Mortara Case: 1858–1859* (1957); J. L. Altholz, in: JSOS, 23 (1961), 111-8. [G.R.]

MORTEIRA, SAUL LEVI (c. 1596–1660), rabbi and scholar in Amsterdam. Morteira was born in Venice, and studied there under Leone *Modena. In 1611 he accompanied the physician Elijah *Montalto to Paris, and on the latter's death in 1616 brought his body for burial to Amsterdam, where he himself subsequently settled. A few years after his arrival he was elected *ḥakham* of the Beit Ya'akov community. When three Sephardi communities merged to form the Talmud Torah congregation in 1638, Morteira was appointed one of its rabbis, taught Talmud and *tosafot* to advanced students, and preached in the synagogue three times a month. He founded the Keter Torah Yeshivah in Amsterdam and Baruch *Spinoza was among his students. Morteira was a member of the *bet din* that excommunicated Spinoza.

Morteira's works include *Givat Sha'ul* (Amsterdam, 1645), a collection of sermons arranged in the order of the weekly portions of the reading of the Law, and a work (no longer extant) on the immortality of the soul, both written in Hebrew. Only fragments of his responsa, mentioned in the introduction to his sermons, have survived. In addition, he wrote a number of apologetics for Judaism in Spanish; among them, *La Eternidad de la Ley de Mosseh* ("The Eternal Nature of the Law of Moses"); *Preguntas que hizo un clériqo de Roan a las quales respondí* ("Questions of a Priest from Rouen and My Answers to Them"); *Obstáculos y oposiciones contra la religión cristiana* ("Criticisms and Arguments Against the Christian Religion"); and a treatise against the 16th-century Italian apostate, *Sistus of Siena. Also perserved in many copies is his *Providencia de Dios con Ysrael* ("The Providence of God with Israel") which contains an account of the vicissitudes of the founders of the New Amsterdam (New York) community on their escape from Brazil. None of these works was printed. Morteira's *Discursos Académicos* is printed in Reuel *Jesurun's *Dialogo dos Montes* (completed 1624; published in Amsterdam, 1767). His apologetic works circulated widely in manuscript and had a profound influence on the Sephardi communities in Western Europe.

Bibliography: Kayserling, Bibl, 74–75; Steinschneider, Cat Bod, 2508–09; J. S. da Silva Rosa, *Geschiedenis der Portugeesche Joden te Amsterdam* (1925), index; C. Roth, *Life of Manasseh Ben Israel* (1934), index; F. Kupfer, in: *Przeglad Orientalistyczny* (1955), 97–99; A. Wiznitzer, in: HJ 20 (1958), 110ff.; I. S. Revah, *Spinoza et Juan de Prado* (1959), index. [J.KA.]

MORWITZ, EDWARD (1815–1893), U.S. physician and journalist. Morwitz, who was born in Danzig, studied oriental languages in Halle and medicine at the University of Berlin. He participated in the revolutionary upheavals of 1848, then fled to the U.S. Settling in Philadelphia, Morwitz first practiced medicine (1850) but swiftly moved to leadership in German-language journalism and publishing. He took an active role in the affairs of the Democratic Party, but supported the Union cause during the Civil War. When the German Dispensary (now Lankenau Hospital) in Philadelphia was threatened with closure during the war, Morwitz himself took charge and served as its medical director. He organized the German Press Association of Pennsylvania in 1862, and through merger and expansion ultimately controlled a large number of German-language and English newspapers. Morwitz' primary interests and contributions were in the area of German immigrant cultural and political activities, but he did maintain ties with the Jewish community through his membership in Kenesseth Israel Congregation and his ownership of the Philadelphia *Jewish Record* from 1875 to 1886.

Bibliography: DAB, 13 (1934), 271–2, incl. bibl.; H. S. Morais, *Jews of Philadelphia* (1894), 338–40; B. W. Korn, *Eventful Years and Experiences* (1954), passim. [B.W.K.]

MOSBACH, city in Baden, W. Germany. A Jewish community was in existence in Mosbach by the second half of the 13th century. In 1298 the *Rindfleisch massacres took 55 Jewish lives. Jews also suffered in 1343, when they were accused of desecrating the *Host, and during the *Black Death persecutions of 1349. By 1381 just one Jew lived in the city and the number of the Jews there remained small throughout the following centuries. They traded in livestock, salt, and wine. The municipal authorities periodically sought to restrict Jewish commercial activity. In 1722 there were eight Jewish families in the city; the number had grown to 19 by 1773. A cemetery was consecrated in 1599 but no synagogue was built until 1860, and a Jewish school was established only in 1876. From 1827 the seat of the district rabbinate was in Mosbach. Leopold *Loewenstein (1843–1924), author of works on German Jewish history, served there as a rabbi from 1887 to 1924.

The 19th century saw a significant growth in the Jewish population. There were 100 persons in 1824, and 192 in 1884. By 1900 the numbers had declined to 161, 159 in 1925, 134 in 1933, and 18 in 1939. The Jews had been active in the commercial and industrial life of the city as merchants in grain and livestock, and owners of a cigar factory, liquor distillery, and numerous other businesses which were all disrupted when the boycott of Jewish merchants began on April 1, 1933. On Nov. 10, 1938, the synagogue was burned and the cemetery desecrated. On Oct. 22, 1940, 13 Jews were deported to *Gurs, only two of whom survived the war. The rabbi, Julius Greilsheimer, fled to Holland in 1939 only to be deported from there to Auschwitz where he perished together with his family. In 1947 a grove of 100 trees were planted by the city in his memory and that of the Jewish community.

Bibliography: Germ Jud, 2 (1968), 548; Salfeld, Martyrol, 54, 61, 66, 78, 80; F. Hundsnurscher and G. Taddey, *Die juedischen Gemeinden in Baden* (1968). [A.SHA.]

MOSBACHER, EMIL JR. (1922–), U.S. yachtsman and businessman. Born in Mt. Vernon, N.Y., Mosbacher won intercollegiate sailing titles for Dartmouth College and during World War II served as an officer in the U.S. navy. He returned to sailing in 1949, and from 1950 to 1957 defeated the nation's best yachtsmen in International One-Design Class competition. Mosbacher skippered his first 12-meter class sloop, the 19-year-old *Vim*, in 1958. He was at the helm of *Weatherly* in 1962, when she successfully defended yachting's most prized trophy (the America's Cup) against the Australian challenger, *Gretel*. He defeated the Australians again in the 1967 America's Cup races. A successful businessman, Mosbacher was chosen by President Richard Nixon to serve as the State Department's chief of protocol in 1969. He was converted to the Episcopal faith.

Bibliography: *Time* (Aug. 18, 1967). [J.H.S.]

MOSCATI, SABATINO (1922–), Italian orientalist. Moscati taught Hebrew, Semitic languages, and the history of religions at the universities of Florence, Naples, and Rome. He was a member of the Accademia dei Lincei and edited the *Rivista di Studi Orientali*. His most important works deal with the origins of the Semites, the language and peoples of Palestine and Syria, and the history of the Arabs. Among them are *Le antiche civiltà semitiche* (1961; *Ancient Semitic Civilizations*, 1957); *L'epigrafia ebraica antica 1935–50* (1951); *I manoscritti ebraici del Deserto di Giuda* (1955); *I predecessori d'Israele* (1956); *Il profilo dell'Oriente mediterraneo* (1956; *The Face of the Ancient Orient*, 1960, repr. 1963); *An Introduction to the Comparative Grammar of the Semitic Languages* (1964). [A.M.R.]

MOSCATO, JUDAH BEN JOSEPH (c. 1530–c. 1593), one of the most important rabbis, authors, and preachers of the Italian Jewish Renaissance. He was forced to leave his native town Osimo when the Jews were expelled from the main places in the papal states by Pope Pius V in 1569. Moscato went to Mantua, at that time one of the great centers of Jewish culture and scholarship in Italy. It seems that not long after his arrival in the city, he became the official preacher of the Mantua community, and in 1587 was nominated to the post of chief rabbi.

Spheres of Interest. Moscato's range of learning and knowledge extended over all fields of cultural interest to Jews of the Renaissance, and he was better versed in them than most of his contemporaries. Besides being steeped in Jewish traditional culture, rabbinic literature, and *aggadah*, he was at home in Jewish medieval philosophy and was also familiar with classical philosophy; he was especially an advocate of Plato and of the medieval neoplatonists and Arab philosophies. Philosophic in his outlook, Moscato was, nevertheless, familiar with the Kabbalah which had become popular in the late 16th century and had begun to influence Italian Jewish intellectuals. His approach to a number of subjects, especially ethics and prayer, was distinctly mystical: he often quotes from the *Zohar, frequently using its ideas without mentioning the source. He also quotes Moses *Cordovero, mostly from his *Pardes Rimmonim*. Moscato's educational and cultural horizons extended to such secular sciences and disciplines as medicine, music, astronomy, and especially classical rhetoric. In all these fields, he quotes from the classical masters, as well as from medieval works. He was acquainted with a number of contemporary Italian non-Jewish writers, such as Pico della Mirandola whom he quotes in his *Nefuẓot Yehudah* (sermon 8, fol. 23c) even supporting a number of obviously christological passages. Moscato, explaining his reliance on non-Jewish sources and his frequent reference to them, states that all the great philosophers had been disciples of ancient Jewish kings and prophets; that philosophy, a Jewish science which was part of Israel's ancient culture, had been lost during the long period of exile, and was preserved only in the writings of the non-Jewish students of Jewish teachers. This idea, in vogue from the 13th century, came to explain the existence of non-Jewish philosophy in religious Jewish works. Moscato used it effectively; in his sermon on music, for instance (*Nefuẓot Yehudah*, sermon 1), he argues in detail that the fundamental concepts of Renaissance music were based on the terms and formulas found in the Psalms, and concludes that King David was the inventor and teacher of the discipline of music, even though in Moscato's times the terms and forms were known in Latin and in Italian.

Moscato's Works. The spirit of the Jewish Renaissance is reflected in Moscato's two major works, *Kol Yehudah* and *Nefuẓot Yehudah*. The former (Venice, 1594) is a commentary on *Judah Halevi's *Kuzari*, which became one of the major influences in 16th-century Jewish ideology in Italy and elsewhere. Moscato's exegesis was a motivating factor in the process, and reflected the new interest taken in this author. In his commentary, Moscato also based himself on the writings of other Jewish philosophers who were little read or studied at the time, like *Philo.

Moscato's second major work, *Nefuẓot Yehudah* (Venice, 1589), is a collection of sermons preached in Mantua on the major holidays, on the special Sabbaths, at weddings, and at funerals. The sermons, 52 in number, correspond to the number of weeks in a year, signifying a full cycle, even though the sermons were not delivered weekly. Moscato's sermons may be described as a revolutionary innovation in Hebrew homiletic literature. None before him and very few, if any, after him achieved such a high degree of aestheticism in the genre. His sermons clearly reveal the influence of the Renaissance on the dialectic method of Hebrew homiletics. His main purpose was not to teach or educate, but to give aesthetic pleasure to his listeners—the actual congregation sitting before him. His sermons were, therefore, not written to be published as a book; it is rather their oral delivery which is reflected at every point. It is possible that Moscato preached both in Hebrew and in Italian, for it is known that many non-Jewish scholars came to listen to his sermons. However, the sermons collected in *Nefuẓot Yehudah* were undoubtedly delivered in Hebrew on special occasions; the fact is sometimes referred to directly, sometimes is reflected in the contents. Moscato's great achievement in the field of rhetoric and homiletics lies in the fact that even though his primary aim was to please his listeners, he also succeeded in being instructive, and in developing some ideas, original either in content or in formulation. He drew on his vast knowledge of philosophy and of the Kabbalah in order to develop ethical ideas and to interpret them in a new way so that they might be acceptable to Jewish culture in Renaissance Italy (see *Preaching). Many of the great preachers in Italy who came after him, including Azariah *Figo (Picho) and Leone *Modena, applied Moscato's ideas and methods of preaching, creating thus a new school in homiletics.

Besides these two major works, Moscato also wrote some poetry: a prayer for rain to be recited in time of drought, composed in 1590; a dirge on the death of R. Joseph *Caro; a dirge on the death of the Duchess of Savoy; and a few other poems. Certain of his exegetical works, mentioned in his known works, have not survived.

Bibliography: I. Bettan, *Studies in Jewish Preaching* (1939), 192–225; idem, in: HUCA, 6 (1929), 297–326; A. Apfelbaum, *Toledot ha-Ga'on Rabbi Yehudah Moscato* (1900); S. Simonsohn, *Toledot ha-Yehudim be-Dukkasut Mantovah*, 2 (1964), index; C. Roth, *Jews in the Renaissance* (1959), index. [Y.D.]

MOSCHELES, IGNAZ (1794–1870), pianist and composer. Born in Prague, he studied in Vienna, but settled in London in 1826 as a concert pianist. In 1846 Felix *Mendelssohn (to whom he had given piano lessons in 1824) invited him to become piano teacher at the Leipzig Conservatory. He taught there to the end of his life. Moscheles' playing was noted for its precision and brilliance, but in comparison with Chopin and Liszt was rather classicist in attitude. He wrote many compositions in a Mendelssohnian style, the best being the "Etudes" (Op. 70). He also prepared the

Ignaz Moscheles, pianist. Jerusalem, J.N.U.L., Schwadron Collection.

piano-vocal score of Beethoven's *Fidelio*, under the composer's supervision (1814), and translated A. Schindler's biography of Beethoven into English, with additions (1841).

Bibliography: Baker, Biog Dict, s.v.; MGG, s.v.; Riemann-Gurlitt, s.v., incl. bibl.; J. Roche, in: *Musical Times* (March 1970), 264–6. [C.AB.]

MOSCOW (Rus. **Moskva**), capital of the U.S.S.R. and from the Middle Ages the political, economic, and commercial center of *Russia. Up to the end of the 18th century, Jews were forbidden to reside in Moscow although many Jewish merchants from Poland and Lithuania visited the city. In 1676 Jews who brought their wares to Moscow were expelled. Apostates and forced converts who maintained varying degrees of connection with Judaism and the Jews were to be found in Moscow during various periods. A few Jews among the prisoners brought to Moscow after the wars against Poland apostatized and settled there. A physician of Jewish origin, Daniel Gordon, was employed by the court in Moscow from 1657 to 1687; Peter Shafirov, one of the most important advisers of Czar Peter the Great, was also of Jewish origin.

With the Russian annexation of Belorussia (1772), the number of Jewish merchants living in Moscow for commercial reasons increased; they came in particular from *Shklov, then an important commercial center in Belorussia. One of these was the contractor and merchant Nathan Note *Notkin. In 1790 Moscow merchants requested that the presence and commercial activities of the Jews in the city be prohibited. A royal decree forbidding Jewish merchants to settle in the inner districts of Russia was issued in 1791. However, they were authorized to stay for temporary periods in Moscow to carry on their trade. Most of the Jews who came to Moscow lodged at the Glebovskoye podvorye, an inn which was situated in the center of the market quarter. Jewish merchants continued to play an important role in the trade between Moscow and the southern and western regions of Russia, as well as in the export of Moscow's goods, and in 1828 the turnover of this trade was estimated at 27,000,000 rubles. As a result, Russian industrialists in Moscow supported the rights of

Figure 1. Twenty-fifth anniversary meeting in Moscow of the early Zionist group, Benei Zion, 1909. The photograph includes: 1. Jehiel Joseph Levontin, 2. Jacob Mazeh, 3. Jehiel Tschlenow, 4. Pesah Marek, 5. Isaac Naiditsch, 6. Eliezer Tcherikower. Jerusalem, J.N.U.L., Schwadron Collection.

Figure 2. The Moscow Jewish State Theater in a production of *King Lear* with S. Mikhoels in the title role, 1935. Courtesy S.R.J.C., Jerusalem.

№ 69

העם

שנה ראשונה.

ארץ ישראל לעם ישראל.

הדיקלרציה של אנגליה על ארץ-ישראל.

המניפסט של המרכז הציוני אל העם העברי.

ארץ-ישראל לישראל.

Figure 3. Last issue of the Moscow Hebrew newspaper, *Ha-Am*, November 23, 1917. The lead article is on the Balfour Declaration. Jerusalem, Central Zionist Archives.

Figure 4. The Israel Embassy in Moscow, prior to June 1967.

the Jews. In 1828 Jewish merchants who were members of the first and second guilds were authorized to remain in Moscow on business for a period of one month only. They were forbidden to open shops or to engage in trade within the city boundaries. To facilitate the execution of these regulations, the Jews were compelled to lodge solely in the Glebovskoye podvorye. The inn was a charitable trust which had been handed over to the Moscow city council to use its income for the maintenance of a municipal eye clinic. Exorbitant prices were soon extorted from Jewish merchants who had to stay at the inn. After a few years, third-class merchants were also authorized to enter the town under the same conditions and the period of their stay was prolonged to six months. About 250 people made use of this right every year. As a result of these restrictions Jewish trade decreased to about 12,000,000 rubles annually during subsequent years. When Alexander II came to the throne (1855), Jewish merchants were permitted to reside temporarily in all the sections of the town.

The first Jews to settle permanently in Moscow, and the founders of the community, were *Cantonists who had finished military service, some of whom had married Jewish women from the *Pale of Settlement. In 1858 there were 340 Jewish men and 104 Jewish women in the whole of the district of Moscow. After Jewish merchants of the first guild, university graduates, and craftsmen were allowed to settle in the interior of Russia, the number of Jews increased rapidly. Some were extremely wealthy, such as Eliezer *Polyakov, one of the most important bankers in Russia and head of the community, and K. Z. *Wissotzki. From 1865 to 1884 Ḥayyim Berlin officiated as rabbi of Moscow, and in 1869 the community invited S. Z. *Minor, one of the outstanding students of the Vilna rabbinical seminary, to serve as the **kazyonny ravvin* (government-appointed rabbi). There was an estimated Jewish population of 8,000 in the city in 1871, which had grown to around 12,000 in 1882 and 35,000 (over 3% of the total population) in 1890, just before the expulsion. The governor of Moscow, Prince Dolgorukov, was known for his liberal attitude toward the Jews, and (after receiving bribes and gifts) the local administration overlooked their illegal presence (as in the case of fictive craftsmen). A considerable number of industrialists and merchants recognized the advantages deriving from Jewish presence in the city, and in a memorandum addressed to the minister of finance in 1882 they pointed out their great contribution to the city's prosperity. While anti-Jewish persecutions and decrees were gaining momentum throughout Russia after the accession of Alexander III, a period of relative ease, the legacy of the previous czar, continued in Moscow. This situation changed completely with the deposition of Prince Dolgorukov and the appointment of Grand Prince Sergei Alexandrovich as governor of the city. During the 14 years (1891–1905) of his term in office, his main aim was "to protect Moscow from Jewry."

Figure 5. Israel national basketball team at the opening in Moscow of the Eighth European Basketball Championship games, 1953. Photo Baruch Bagg, Tel Aviv.

The Expulsion. On March 28, 1891 (Passover Eve 5651), a law was issued abolishing the right of Jewish craftsmen to reside in Moscow and prohibiting their entry into the city in the future. The police immediately began to expel thousands of families, some of whom had lived in Moscow for several decades or were even born there. They were granted a period of from three months to a year to dispose of their property and many were compelled to sell out to their neighbors at derisory prices. The poor and destitute were sent to the Pale of Settlement with criminal transports. On October 15 the right of descendants of the Cantonists to live in the town was abrogated, if they were not registered with the Moscow community. The expulsion reached its climax during the cold winter days of 1892. While the police made a concerted effort to search out the Jews and drive them out of the city, generous rewards were offered for the seizure of any still in hiding. The press was not permitted to report on the details of the expulsion. An appeal to the government made by merchants and industrialists in 1892 and their warning of the economic damage that would result from the expulsion were of no avail. Police sources estimated that about 30,000 persons were expelled. About 5,000 Jews remained—families of some Cantonists, wealthy merchants and their servants, and members of the liberal professions. The Moscow expulsion came as a deep shock to Russian Jewry. A considerable number of those expelled arrived in Warsaw and Lodz and transferred their economic activities there. Decrees regulating residence in Moscow became even more severe. In 1899 the authorities ordered that no more Jewish merchants were to be registered in the first guild unless authorized by the minister of finance. At the height of the expulsion period, the authorities closed down the new synagogue, as well as nine of the 14 prayer houses. Rabbi S. Z. Minor, who requested the reopening of the synagogue, was expelled from the city. The struggle for the use of the synagogue continued for many years and it was not until 1906 that permission was granted for its reopening. In 1897 there were 8,095 Jews and 216 Karaites in Moscow (0.8% of the total population). In 1902 there were 9,339 Jews there, and half of them declared Yiddish as their mother tongue; the overwhelming majority of the others declared it to be Russian. In 1893 J. *Mazeh was elected as rabbi of Moscow, remaining its spiritual leader until his death in 1923. A considerable number of the members of the small community were wealthy merchants and intellectuals. Assimilated Jews (some of whom apostatized) held an important place in the cultural life of the city. In 1911 there were around 700 Jewish students in the higher institutions of learning in Moscow.

After the outbreak of World War I, from 1915, a stream of Jewish refugees began to arrive in Moscow from the German-occupied regions. They took part in the development of war industries in the town and some of them amassed large fortunes. In a short time, Moscow became a Jewish center. Hebrew printing presses were set up, and in the town of Bogorodsk (near Moscow) a large yeshivah was established on the pattern of the Lithuanian yeshivot. The foundations of the Hebrew theater *Habimah were then laid. Among the new rich were Zionists and nationally conscious Jews who were ready to support every cultural activity. Most outstanding of these were H. *Zlatopolsky, his son-in-law Y. Persitz, and A. J. *Stybel. Authorization was given for the publication of a Hebrew weekly, *Ha-Am*. Cultural activity increased in scope with the outbreak of the

Figure 6. Baking *mazzah* in Moscow.

Figure 7. The entrance to the Great Synagogue on a festival (1965).

February 1917 Revolution. It was symbolical that O. *Minor, the son of S. Z. Minor, a leader of the Social Revolutionary Party, was elected as chairman of the Moscow municipal council. *Ha-Am* became a daily newspaper and two large publishing houses, Ommanut (founded by Zlatopolsky and Persitz) and that of A. J. Stybel, were set up. The founding conference of the organization for Hebrew education and culture, *Tarbut, was held in Moscow in the spring of 1917. This activity also continued during the first year of the Bolshevik Revolution (three volumes of *Ha-Tekufah* were published in 1918, as well as others) but the new regime, with the assistance of its Jewish supporters, rapidly liquidated the institutions of Hebrew culture in Moscow. The Habimah theater was more fortunate; it presented An-Ski's *Dibbuk (Dybbuk)* in Moscow for the first time in January 1922 and continued to exist under the protection of several prominent members of the Russian artistic and literary world who defended it as a first-class artistic institution, until it left the Soviet Union in 1926.

When Moscow became the capital of the Soviet Union, its Jewish population rapidly increased. In 1920 there were 28,000 Jews in the city, which had become severely depopulated as a result of the civil war. By 1923 the number had increased to 86,000 and by 1926 to 131,000 (6.5% of the total population). In 1940 the Jewish population was estimated at 400,000. The headquarters of the *Yevsektsiya was situated in Moscow, and there its central newspaper *Der Emes* (1920–38) was published as well as many other Yiddish newspapers and books. The Jewish State Theater (known in Russian as GOSET from its initials), directed by S. *Mikhoels, was also situated in Moscow. For a number of years, small circles of organized Zionists continued to exist in the city, which was the central seat of the legal *He-Ḥalutz (which published its own newspaper from 1924 to 1926) and of the groups of the Left *Po'alei Zion. All these were liquidated by 1928. During World War II, the Jews shared the sufferings of the war with the city's other inhabitants. From 1943 Moscow was the seat of the Jewish *Anti-Fascist Committee which gathered together personalities of Jewish origin who were outstanding in Soviet public affairs. Founded to assist the Soviet Union in its war effort against Nazi Germany and to mobilize world Jewish opinion and aid for this purpose, it published a newspaper, *Eynikeyt*. [Y.S.]

After World War II. The Anti-Fascist Committee attempted to continue with its activities even after the war until it was brutally liquidated in 1948–49, as a first step in the total liquidation of organized Jewish life in the "black years" of Stalin's regime. Most of its leading members were arrested and executed in 1952. Because Moscow is the capital and a "window" of the Soviet Union, it has been possible for world Jewry to follow the destinies of Moscow's Jews more than those in other cities and the latter have been more able to meet with Jews from outside the Soviet Union. When Golda *Meir, the first diplomatic representative of the State of Israel, arrived in Moscow in September 1948, a spontaneous mass demonstration of Jews in her honor took place on the High Holidays near and around the Great Synagogue. The mere presence of an Israel diplomatic mission with an Israel flag in the center of Moscow was a constant stimulus to Jewish and pro-Israel sentiments among the Jews of Moscow and Jewish visitors from other parts of the Soviet Union. The Israel delegation to the Youth Festival, held in Moscow in 1957, was the first occasion of personal contacts between Jewish youth from Israel and the U.S.S.R. It is considered to have been a turning point in the revival of Jewish national feelings and their daring demonstration in public on the part of Soviet Jewish youth. Already in 1958, on *Simḥat Torah eve more than 10,000 young Jews gathered around the Great Synagogue to dance and sing Yiddish and Hebrew songs. They refused to be intimidated by the militia and to disperse. Thus these mass gatherings of young Jews, which also take place on their Jewish holidays, became a traditional feature of Jewish life in Moscow.

In 1955 some elderly Jews were tried and sentenced to several years of imprisonment in labor camps for possessing and distributing Israel newspapers and Hebrew literature and gathering in groups to read them. For similar "offenses" several Jews of the Great Synagogue congregation were punished in 1963.

In 1970 three synagogues were functioning in the city of Moscow. Apart from the Great Synagogue on Arkhipova Street, there were two small synagogues—in the suburbs of Maryina Roshcha and Cherkizovo, which were wooden buildings, more of the type of a *shtibl* than of a full-fledged synagogue. In addition to them, there was a synagogue in the nearby town of Malakhovka, practically also a suburb of Greater Moscow, which has had a sizable Jewish population from prerevolutionary times. The Great Synagogue and its rabbi (first S. *Schliefer and after his death J. L. *Levin) serve the authorities often as unofficial representatives of Soviet Jewry to the outside world. In the 1950s and 1960s the Great Synagogue was allowed to issue a Jewish calendar and to send it to other synagogues in the U.S.S.R. In 1956 Rabbi Schliefer was granted permission to print a prayer book, by photostat from old prayer books. He named it *Siddur ha-Shalom* ("peace prayer book") and deleted from it all references to wars and victories (as, e.g., in the Ḥanukkah benedictions). It was said to have been printed in 3,000 copies, but it was very rarely seen in other synagogues in the Soviet Union. (A second edition of it was printed, ostensibly in 10,000 copies, in 1968 by Rabbi

Levin, but it also was not much in use in Soviet synagogues.) In 1957 Rabbi Schliefer received permission from the authorities to open a yeshivah on the premises of the Great Synagogue. He called it "Kol Ya'akov," and for several years a small number of young and middle-aged Jews (about 12 persons a year), mostly from Georgia, were trained there, almost all of them as *shoḥatim* (ritual slaughterers), whereas the number of ordained rabbis did not exceed one or two. In 1961 the yeshivah, though officially still in existence, almost ceased to function, mainly because of the refusal of the Soviet authorities to grant permission to yeshivah students, who went for the holiday to their homes outside Moscow, to come back and register again as temporary residents of the city for the purpose of study. By 1963, 37 students had passed through the yeshivah; 25 of them were trained as *shoḥatim*. In 1965 only one student was there, and in 1966 the number was six. The unrestricted baking of *mazzah* in a rented bakery and its distribution in food stores was discontinued in Moscow, as in most areas of the Soviet Union, in 1962. However, it was partially permitted again in 1964 and definitely in 1965, but under a different system: it was done under the supervision of the synagogue board and was only for "believers" who brought their own flour and registered their names. The ritual slaughtering of poultry was allowed in the precincts of the Great Synagogue whereas kosher beef was obtainable until 1964 twice a week at a special store on the outskirts of the city. From 1961 a barrier was erected in the Great Synagogue to separate foreign visitors, including Israel diplomats, from the congregation, and the synagogue officers were responsible to the authorities for strictly enforcing the segregation.

In 1959, on Rosh Ha-Shanah eve, an anti-Jewish riot took place in Malakhovka, a suburb of Moscow. The synagogue was set afire, but quickly extinguished; the *shammash* of the Jewish cemetery was murdered by unknown persons and on the walls a typewritten anti-Semitic tract appeared, signed by "the B. Zh. S. R. Committee," the Russian initials of the prerevolutionary anti-Semitic slogan "Hit the Yids and save Russia." At first Soviet spokesmen denied the facts, but several months later admitted them to foreign visitors, assuring them that the hooligans were apprehended and severely punished. The Soviet press did not mention the incident at all. In 1960 a stir was created among Moscow Jewry when burying at the Jewish cemetery was almost discontinued and Jews were forced to bury their dead in a separate section of a general cemetery. This section was filled up in 1963 and subsequent Jewish burials had to take place alongside non-Jewish ones. Some Jews in various ways obtained the privilege of burying their dead in the remaining space of the old Jewish cemetery, others carried them to the Jewish cemetery of Malakhovka. At the same period several Jews in Moscow were accused, tried, and sentenced to the severest punishment, including execution, for "economic crimes," such as speculation, organizing illicit production and sale of consumer goods in collusion with high officials of the militia, directors of factories, etc. Their trials were accompanied by inflammatory feature articles (called "feuilletons") in the central Moscow press with pronounced anti-Semitic overtones. However, Moscow was also the center of other developments. In 1959 some Yiddish books, most of them selective works of the classics (*Shalom Aleichem, I. L. *Peretz, D. *Bergelson, etc.), were published there after a prolonged period of the complete obliteration of any printed Yiddish word. Yiddish folklore concerts took place relatively frequently in the city and drew large crowds. Even a semiprofessional theater troupe, headed by the elderly actor Benjamin Schwartzer, was established and mainly performed Shalom Aleichem plays in provincial cities. In 1961 the Yiddish journal **Sovetish Heymland*, edited by an officially appointed editor, the poet Aaron *Vergelis, began to appear as an "organ of the Soviet Writers' Union," first as a bimonthly, later as a monthly. It also served as a kind of Soviet-Jewish mouthpiece for foreign Jews and visiting Jewish intellectuals were invited to its premises to meet members of its editorial staff. In 1963 and 1965 collections of Israel Hebrew poetry and prose were published in Russian translation, as well as a Hebrew-Russian dictionary in 1965 (in 25,000 copies), which was sold out in a few weeks.

Figure 8. Chief Rabbi Levin (right) and Cantor Steinberg during a Passover service in the Moscow Great Synagogue, 1966. Courtesy D. Bar-Tov, Jerusalem.

Contacts with Israel took manifold forms. The Israel embassy invited to its receptions not only the rabbis and board members of the various synagogues, but also Jewish writers, artists, and other intellectuals. In various sport events, international scientific congresses, and international exhibitions Israel was almost always represented, and often not only Moscow Jews but also Jews from other parts of the Soviet Union, even from outlying regions, came especially to the capital "to see the Israelis." From time to time Israel popular singers (e.g., Nechama Hendel, Geulah Gil, etc.) and other artists performed in Moscow and aroused great enthusiasm, particularly among young Jews.

The Six-Day War and the rupture of diplomatic relations between the Soviet Union and Israel (June 1967) put an end to these contacts. But, on the other hand, many Moscow Jews, especially the young, began more and more openly to demonstrate their pro-Israel feelings—by continuing increasingly their mass gatherings around the Great Synagogue, by signing collective protests against the refusal to grant them exit permits to Israel, by studying Hebrew in small groups, etc. Unlike other cities, like *Riga, *Leningrad, *Kishinev, and some towns in *Georgia, there were hardly any sanctions applied in Moscow in 1970 against pro-Israel Jews.

In the census of 1959, 239,246 Jews (4.7% of the total population) were registered in the municipal area of Moscow. Of these, 132,223 were women and 107,023 were men. 20,331 of them (about 8.5%) declared Yiddish to be their mother tongue. These numbers are thought to be a gross underestimate because many tens of thousands of Jews declared at the census their "nationality" to be Russian (some opinions evaluate the number of Moscow's Jews as high as 500,000). [Ed.]

Bibliography: Ettinger, in: *Zion*, 18 (1953), 136–68; J. Mazeh, *Zikhronot*, 2 (1936); Dubnow, Divrei, 10 (1958), 94–97; Dubnow, Hist Russ, index; Marek, in: *Voskhod*, no. 2–3 (1893), 200–29; no. 6 (1893), 73–91; no. 9 (1895), 22–33; Goldovski, in: *Byloye*, 9

(1907); Katznelson, in: *Yevreyskaya Starina*, 1 (1909), 175–88; Hessen (Gessen), in: *Perezhitoye*, 1 (1908), 51–65; idem, in: *Yevreyskaya Starina*, 8 (1915), 1–19, 153–72; Eisenberg, *ibid.*, 13 (1930), 81–99.

MOSENTHAL, South African family, who, in successive generations, played a major part in the 19th-century development of the country's commerce, banking, and,

Joseph Mosenthal, South African businessman and civic leader. Courtesy Fieldhill Publishing Co., Johannesburg.

especially, agricultural export trade. The family came from Hesse-Cassel, Germany, and the first to immigrate was JOSEPH MOSENTHAL (1813–1871), who settled at the Cape in 1839. He was joined by his brothers ADOLPH (1812–1882) and JULIUS (1819–1880), and the three set up in business in Cape Town as Mosenthal Brothers. The firm continued to flourish under family control until well into the 20th century. From their main business centers in Cape Town, Port Elizabeth, and Graaff Reinet, the Mosenthals spread their activities throughout the Cape Colony, and later through the Transvaal. They established numerous trading posts in the interior and organized transport to and from the coast. Their first interest was the marketing of wool and hides, but they gradually expanded their activities to embrace gold and diamond mining, industrial enterprises, and banking. In the early years they issued their own banknotes, which were widely circulated, but which were withdrawn by the firm with the development of the colony's commercial banking system.

The Mosenthals made a special study of ostrich farming and opened up export markets for its products. They introduced merino sheep from France and Angora goats from Turkey; Adolph Mosenthal himself went to the Black Sea to arrange for the importation of the goats after earlier attempts had failed. This was the beginning of South Africa's staple mohair industry. In 1857 Julius Mosenthal was the first professing Jew to be elected to the Legislative Council of the Eastern (Cape) Province, and Joseph Mosenthal was elected to the same body in 1861. A fourth brother, Salomon Hermann *Mosenthal became well known as a Viennese dramatist. Other leading members of the family were HARRY (1850–1915) and WILLIAM (1861–1933), both sons of Adolph.

In the 19th century, the Mosenthals helped a number of German-Jewish immigrants to settle in South Africa. Joseph Mosenthal, like his brothers, was a conforming Jew, and was one of the founders of the Cape Town Hebrew Congregation in 1841. In later years the Mosenthals, like many of the other early Jewish families in South Africa, married out of the faith, and their descendants were no longer identified as Jews.

Bibliography: L. Herrman, *History of the Jews in South Africa* (1935), index; G. Saron and H. Hotz, *The Jews in South Africa* . . . (1955), 349–52; I. Abrahams, *Birth of a Community* (1955), index.

[L.S.]

MOSENTHAL, SALOMON HERMANN (1821–1877), German playwright. Mosenthal, who was born in Cassel, was a member of the *Mosenthal family. He first wrote poems (*Gedichte*, 1845), but turned to the theater and wrote a dozen melodramas. He also provided opera libretti for Flotow and Goldmark, and for Nicolai's *Merry Wives of Windsor* (1849). His most famous play was *Deborah*, which was adapted for the English stage as *Leah, the Forsaken* and this adaptation was twice made into movies (1908, 1912). Deborah, a passionate, gypsy-like Jewess, loves Joseph, the minister's son, but renounces her love for the sake of Joseph's happiness. The highly charged scenes are shot through with social criticism whose purpose is the achievement of greater tolerance. Mosenthal published a volume of stories of characteristic Jewish life, *Bilder aus dem juedischen Familienleben* (1878). He also wrote *Die Sklaven* (1847), *Caecilie von Albano* (1851), and *Die Sirene* (1875). His collected works were published posthumously in 1878. He was ennobled as Ritter von Mosenthal in 1871.

Bibliography: M. Martersteig, *Das deutsche Theater im 19. Jahrhundert* (1904), 402, 423.

[S.L.S.]

MOSER, JACOB (1839–1922), early British Zionist and a sponsor of the Herzlia High School in Tel Aviv. Born in Kappeln, Schleswig, Moser moved to England in the 1860s and settled in Bradford. He and his wife engaged in philanthropic activities there, especially the establishment of hospitals and schools for the poor. He joined the Zionist movement with the appearance of Theodor Herzl and was a member of the Zionist General Council, the board of the Jewish Colonial Trust, the Anglo-Palestine Corporation, the Jewish National Fund, and the presidium of a number of Zionist Congresses. At the Eighth Zionist Congress (1907), David *Wolffsohn announced Moser's contribution of 80,000 francs toward the establishment of the first Hebrew high school (in Jaffa) on the condition that the school bear Herzl's name. This was the largest contribution made by an individual to the Zionist Organization up to World War I. Moser visited Ereẓ Israel in 1908 and 1910 and followed the high school's early steps, adding large sums to his contribution so that the building could be complete, supplies and equipment could be purchased, etc. He also supported other projects in Ereẓ Israel (e.g., Ben-Yehuda's Hebrew dictionary, the Bezalel School of Arts and Crafts, etc.). Moser continued his philanthropic activities until his last years. In 1909 he was chosen an honorary citizen of Bradford and later became mayor of the city.

Bibliography: B. Ben-Yehuda (ed.), *Sippurah shel ha-Gimnazyah "Herẓliyyah"* (1970); Tidhar, 18 (n.d.), 5358–60 index.

[G.K.]

Jacob Moser, British patron of the Herzlia High School in Tel Aviv. He is holding a bas-relief of the building to which he contributed large sums of money. Jerusalem, J.N.U.L., Schwadron Collection.

MOSER, MOSES (1796–1838), banker and a founder of the *Verein fuer Kultur und Wissenschaft des Judentums. An employee (and eventually partner) in the firm of Moses Friedlaender (son of David *Friedlaender), he attended philosophical lectures at Berlin University although he had no formal secondary education. There he met Eduard *Gans, Leopold *Zunz, and other young Jewish intellectuals, with whom he eventually founded the Verein (Nov. 7, 1819). Moser, who exerted a stabilizing and moderating influence within the Verein, was its treasurer (1821–22) and secretary (Nov. 1819; 1822–23). He also gave five lectures and contributed three articles. After the dissolution of the Verein, Moser, the one member esteemed by all, maintained his ties with L. Zunz, E. Wohlwill, and others. However, his most valued and most famous friend was Heinrich *Heine, who in his letters expressed his affection and esteem for Moser. Despite some setbacks the friendship endured. In 1819 Moser and some colleagues joined the patrician society, Gesellschaft der Freunde (founded in 1792 by D. Friedlaender and A. *Mendelssohn), in the vain hope of subverting it from within. Moser eventually became its president (1836–38).

Bibliography: H. G. Reissner, *Eduard Gans* (Ger., 1965), index; idem, in: YLBI, 2 (1957), 189–90; A. Friedlaender, *ibid.*, 11 (1966), 269–99; N. N. Glatzer (ed.), *L. Zunz* (Ger., 1964), index; *Briefe von H. Heine an seinen Freund M. Moser* (1862). [Ed.]

MOSES (Heb. מֹשֶׁה; LXX, Μω(υ)σης; Vulg. *Moyses*), leader, prophet, and lawgiver (first half of the 13th century B.C.E.). Commissioned to take the Israelites out of Egypt, Moses led them from his 80th year to his death at 120 during their wanderings in the wilderness until their arrival at the Plains of Moab.

This article is arranged according to the following outline:

BIBLICAL VIEW

The Bible enshrines a galaxy of great men and women each of whom made a distinctive contribution to Jewish history and culture. Moses towers above them all: he is incomparable (Num. 12:6–8; Deut. 34:10). He is not only a national leader; it is he who fashioned the nation of Israel, transforming a horde of slaves into a people potentially capable of becoming "a treasured possession" and "a kingdom of priests" (Ex. 19:5–6). He was not only a prophet, but the father of the prophets; his spirit inspired later generations of godly men to preach, each in his own way, Mosaic ideals with Mosaic courage (cf. Num. 12:6–7; the story of the 70 elders is symbolic of Moses' influence on subsequent generations of leaders and prophets). He was not only Israel's first religious teacher; he gave Israel the Torah—a law of justice, holiness, and loving-kindness. He translated the divine word into the concrete realities of a rule of life that became the basis of Jewish belief, ethics, worship, and jurisprudence in all generations. Nevertheless, Scripture portrays Moses as human (Ex. 33:21ff.) and mortal (Deut. 34:5). He had faults as well as virtues, and was punished by the very God whom he taught Israel to worship. Not till the advent of Hellenism was the lawgiver described as Θεῖος ἀνήρ ("a divine man"). In the Bible he is only the "human rod" with which God performs His spiritual miracles.

Biography. The primary sources for the story of Moses' life and works are contained in Exodus, Leviticus, Numbers, and Deuteronomy. Additional references are to be found in Joshua, Judges, I Samuel, I and II Kings, Isaiah, Hosea, Micah, Malachi, Psalms, Daniel, Ezra, Nehemiah, and I and II Chronicles. The salient references will be given in the course of the article.

Early Life. Moses' father and mother—Amram and Jochebed—were both of the tribe of Levi; he had an older sister, Miriam, and an older brother, Aaron (Ex. 2:1; 6:16–20; 7:7; Num. 26:59; I Chron. 23:12–14). The future redeemer of Israel was born at the height of the Egyptian persecution of the Israelites. The Pharaoh that "knew not Joseph" (Ex. 1:8) had set taskmasters over the Children of Israel to oppress them with forced labor (Ex. 1:11). In order to reduce their numbers he had also instructed the Hebrew midwives, Shiphrah and Puah, to kill the Israelite boys at birth, but owing to the piety of these women the plan failed (Ex. 1:15ff.). Thereupon Pharaoh charged all his people to throw every newborn Hebrew boy into the Nile (Ex. 1:22). Jochebed succeeded in concealing the infant Moses for three months (Ex. 2:2). Thereafter she made a wicker basket for him, caulked with bitumen and pitch, and placed it among the reeds of the river, while his sister watched from a distance. Pharaoh's daughter, spying the basket when she came down to bathe, ordered one of her maids to fetch it. The princess took pity on the crying babe and decided to adopt him. At Miriam's suggestion Moses' own mother was given the task of nursing the child until he was old enough to be returned to Pharaoh's daughter. In this way Moses the Hebrew was, ironically, brought up as a prince in Pharaoh's own palace. The hand of providence is manifest in these events; Pharaoh's very plan of destruction became part of the divine design of redemption. The wondrous story is also intended to indicate the historic destiny awaiting the child. Possibly even his name *Moshe* is a pointer in this direction. The popular etymology (undoubtedly *Moshe* is an Egyptian name, probably meaning "son") "I drew him out of the water" (Ex. 2:10) should logically have required the form *mashui* ("one that has been drawn out"), not *moshe* ("one that draws out"). But the infant was one day to "draw out" his people from the Sea of Reeds and bondage.

Although Moses was reared and educated as an Egyptian of the highest caste, he remained conscious of his origin and sympathetic to his kindred. When he grew to manhood, he went out to his brethren and witnessed their tribulations. He was the prototype of the unassimilable Jew. But his early Egyptian training seems to have been a necessary stage in the process of fitting him for his future role as Israel's liberator. His outlook was molded by a sense of freedom that his kinsfolk could not enjoy. On the other hand, "learned in all the wisdom of the Egyptians" (Acts 7:22), his finest instincts were revolted by the Egyptian way of life; he yearned for a nobler kind of society dedicated to a conception of God unknown to the Egyptians. He was outraged by his first contact with the realities of the bondage. He saw an Egyptian beating a Hebrew slave and, overcome by an irresistible feeling of righteous indignation, he slew the Egyptian and hid him in the sand, thinking his deed would not be discovered. His second experience was even sadder: he found two Hebrews fighting. His intervention drew from the aggressor the retort: "Who made you chief and ruler over us? Do you mean to kill me as you killed the Egyptian?" To escape Pharaoh's wrath, Moses fled to Midian (Ex. 2:11–15). The episode proved two things. Though Moses was a man of high ideals and great moral courage, he still lacked the self-discipline requisite to true leadership. Uncontrolled sporadic violence was not the way to salvation. Imperial Egypt was not to be vanquished by such methods. Nor were the Children of Israel ready for redemption; they lacked unity and a true understanding of the horror of their plight. They were still slaves in spirit as well as in body.

FLIGHT TO MIDIAN AND THE MISSION. In Midian Moses, always the foe of unrighteousness irrespective of the victim's race, rose again in defense of the persecuted. He saved the daughters of the priest Reuel (also called Jethro, Jether, and Hobab),who had come to water their father's flocks, from the hands of the bullying local shepherds. As a result of the incident Moses stayed with the priest and married his daughter Zipporah, by whom he had two sons, Gershom and Eliezer (Ex. 2:15–22; 18:3–4; cf. Judg. 18:30; I Chron. 23:15–17). In the timeless desert, tending the flocks of his father-in-law, Moses' character slowly matured. The turning point in his career came when he was vouchsafed a theophany in the region of Horeb. He saw a bush aflame with a fire that did not consume it. On turning aside to investigate the marvelous sight, he heard the voice of God calling him. In the vision God bade Moses redeem Israel from Egypt, where a new king now reigned. Moses resisted the divine commission. The inner struggle of his soul finds expression in ever new excuses. The dialogue veers in different directions. Four times Moses changes the course of his argument: he feels inadequate to the task; he inquires by what name God is to be announced to the Israelites; he doubts that the Children of Israel will listen to him; he protests that he is slow of speech. Patiently God answers each objection. He would be with Moses and the fact that the Israelites, when they left Egypt, would serve the Lord at this mountain would be a sign to him that God had sent him; he was to tell his people that "I am that I am" had spoken to him; and He who gives man speech would teach him what to say. Together with the elders he was to ask Pharaoh's permission for the Israelites to go on a three-day journey into the wilderness to sacrifice to the Lord, although the request would certainly be refused. To help him convince the Israelites, the Lord gave Moses three wondrous signs (the rod becomes a snake and is restored to its former state; his hand becomes leprous and is healed; the Nile water, poured out on the ground, turns to blood). But still, without further rational argument, Moses refuses. The Lord is angered, but promises to let Aaron be Moses' spokesman, and bids him take the rod with which to perform the signs (Ex. 3:1–4:17; 7:1).

Figure 1. Illustration of Moses before the burning bush (Ex. 3), from a 13th-century Spanish *Haggadah*. Parma, Biblioteca Palatina, Ms. Parma 2411, fol. 3v.

The wonders wrought by Moses both in Egypt and in the wilderness have, superficially, a magical quality. But biblical miracles are to be distinguished from magic practices in two vital respects: they are not only different in degree (cf. "the finger of God," Ex. 8:15), but also in character and objective. Magic implies the existence of a realm of power transcending nature and the deities; Moses' "signs and portents" served as evidence of God's will, and as such formed part of the universal order (cf. Avot 5:4). Moses' "call" has no biblical parallel. Even Gideon (Judg. 6:11–24) and Jeremiah (1:4–10) in the end accepted the divine commission unconditionally. In the case of Moses the Lord actually had to make a concession (the help of Aaron). The story not only highlights Moses' humility and diffidence, but his absolute sincerity, which was devoid of all personal ambition and pride. Once, however, Moses undertook his historic mission, the negative qualities underscored in his first communion with God became positive attributes of unqualified dedication, by which alone Israel could be delivered from servitude and remolded for freedom.

THE RETURN TO EGYPT AND THE EXODUS. Moses' initial efforts were frustrating. At the very beginning of his homeward journey an obscure incident occurred that almost proved fatal to Moses; he was only saved by the timely action of Zipporah in circumcising their son (Ex. 4:24–26). Pharaoh responded to the request of Moses and Aaron by augmenting the people's burdens. Henceforth they were to provide their own straw for making the bricks. Understandably the Israelites lost confidence in their would-be redeemer, who was himself discouraged (Ex. 4:27–5:23).

Events now assume a new dynamic. In a second revelation God announced: "I am the Lord. I appeared to Abraham, Isaac, and Jacob as El Shaddai ["Almighty"], but I did not make Myself known to them by My name YHWH" (Ex. 6:2–3). The divine announcement does not mean that the Tetragrammaton was a hitherto unknown name of God. It is not only frequently mentioned in Genesis and was apparently known to the Patriarchs, but it even forms part of the theophoric name of Moses' mother (*Yokheved*, Jochebed). Names in the Bible are not merely labels but descriptive epithets. They are particularly significant when applied to God. The Patriarchs were heads of families; the divine relationship with these families was adequately reflected in the name Shaddai, expressive of God's power. But Israel was now on the threshold of national history; the nexus between the nation and its God necessitated a new understanding of Godhead. YHWH, more fully explained as "I am that I am," expressed the abiding providence that would sustain the people throughout their unfolding history (cf. Ex. 3:12).

Pharaoh's hardness of heart (for the statement "And the Lord hardened the heart of Pharaoh" see *God) called for sterner measures. By means of a series of ten devastating plagues (blood, frogs, gnats, swarm of flies, pest, boils, hail, locusts, darkness, death of the firstborn—man and beast), arranged schematically (see U. Cassuto, *Exodus* (1967), 92ff.), Pharaoh's resistance and tergiversations were gradually overcome. Before the incidence of the final and climactic plague, the Israelites were enjoined to offer up a sacrifice on the 14th of the first month (Abib=Nisan), and to daub the lintel and the two doorposts with its blood: "For when the Lord goes through to smite the Egyptians, He will see the blood . . . and will pass over the door and not let the destroyer enter or smite your home" (Ex. 12:23). The last plague brought immediate surrender. The departure of the Israelites was now speeded by the panic-stricken Egyptians with the utmost impatience, so that the people had to take their dough before it was leavened and baked unleavened cakes (Ex. 6:10–12:36).

The Israelites, accompanied by "a mixed multitude" that had clambered onto the bandwagon of the Exodus, left Egypt on the 15th of Nisan. They marched into freedom laden not only with Egyptian spoil, but enriched, above all, by a new religion. Already in Egypt they had eaten the Passover sacrifice ("because He passed over the houses of the Israelites"), instituted the Feast of Unleavened Bread ("for there was no time for the dough of our fathers to become leavened"), and promulgated the law of the consecration of the firstborn ("at the time that I smote every firstborn in the land of Egypt, I consecrated every firstborn in Israel, man and beast, to Myself"). Judaism, in its first inchoate phase, had come into being (Ex. 12–13).

Crossing the Sea of Reeds. Pharaoh, however, soon repented his liberating act. The urgency with which the Israelites were expelled from Egypt was matched by the haste with which Pharaoh sought to recapture his bondmen. The final scene was enacted by the Sea of Reeds. Hemmed in between the sea and the Egyptian cohorts, with only the pillar of cloud (of fire, by night) between the fugitives and their pursuers, the Israelites cried unto the Lord, the only power that could now save them. The end came with dramatic swiftness. Moses sundered the waters with his rod; Israel crossed the seabed dry-shod, but their would-be captors were drowned by the returning waters (Ex. 14). The ode of triumph that Moses and the Children of Israel sang after their deliverence from the Egyptians (Ex. 15) is one of the most beautiful psalms in the Bible. Characteristically it contains no mention of Moses, just as the creedal recital in connection with the first fruits has no reference to the liberator (Deut. 26:5–9). The glory and the thanksgiving are accorded solely to the Lord. The personality cult was eschewed by Moses. The crossing of the Sea of Reeds completed the first stage of the process of redemption. It was the phase marking the liberation of Israel from bondage.

Covenant at Sinai and the Desert Period. The ultimate goal lay ahead at Mount Horeb (Sinai), where in the third month after the Exodus the people were to witness the epoch-making revelation of God, hear the Decalogue issuing forth from Sinai, and declare their eternal loyalty to the Divine Law in the words, "All that the Lord has spoken we will do and obey" (Ex. 19:1ff.; 24:7). Israel entered into a covenant with the Lord (24:8), of which the Ten Words or *Decalogue, usually, but erroneously, called the Ten Commandments, formed the preamble and the Torah precepts the conditions. The covenant with YHWH was the real purpose of the Exodus. Freedom was not just the negation of servitude; it must have positive spiritual content. Even the plagues were intended not only to humble Pharaoh, but to establish the Lord's sovereignty throughout the earth (Ex. 9:29). At Sinai ethical monotheism was enthroned as Israel's faith.

But from the sublime heights of God's mountain Israel plunged into the abyss of the Golden Calf. Moses had ascended the mountain of the Lord to receive the tablets of the Decalogue and spent 40 days and nights there. Disturbed by Moses' delay in returning to the camp, the Israelites persuaded Aaron to make them a god that would go before them, since they did not know what had happened to their leader. The bovine image that Aaron produced was to serve as a surrogate for Moses, and in Aaron's view probably only represented God's visible throne. It nevertheless constituted unforgivable religious treason, for the people regarded the calf as an actual deity ("These are your gods, O Israel"), and the lawgiver, conscious of the spiritual catastrophe that had befallen Israel, shattered the tablets of the Decalogue. The covenant was broken; the calf and the Ten Words could not exist in juxtaposition.

The tragedy left a deep spiritual trauma, but was not fatal. Moses ground the idol to dust and made the Israelites drink its powdered remains. With the help of the loyal tribe of Levi he slew 3,000 of the idolators. Then, in a heartrending supplication, he interceded with the Lord for his people: "But now, if Thou wilt forgive their sin—and if not, blot me, I pray Thee, out of Thy book which Thou has written." God forgave, in accordance with His attributes (cf. Ex. 34:7). Again Moses ascended the mountain and received a new copy of the Decalogue. He was also vouchsafed deeper insight into the divine glory and

Figure 2. Moses receiving the Law, his hands covered as a sign of holiness. Page from the *Kosmas Indicopleustes*, a 12th-century Greek manuscript. Sinai Peninsula, Monastery of St. Catherine, Ms. 1186, fol. 75v. Photo Richard Cleave, Jerusalem.

character (Ex. 34:6–7). The architect of Israel's religion was also responsible for the establishment of Israel's first shrine—the *Mishkan* ("Dwelling Place"; usually called the Tabernacle). It was the sequel, as it were, of the theophany on Mount Sinai; it was the symbol of God's continuing presence. Although Moses performed certain sacerdotal functions on special occasions (Ex. 24:6; Lev. 8:6ff.), and is even called a priest in Psalm 99:6, he is never actually portrayed as such in the Torah. The Tent of Meeting, referred to in Exodus 33:7–11, is not to be identified with the Tabernacle. It was Moses' own tent, which served temporarily as a meeting place between him and God, until the time of "wrath was past." It was pitched outside the camp, which had been recently defiled by idolatry (see Rashi, Ibn Ezra, and Naḥmanides to Ex. 33:7; Cassuto, *Exodus* (1967), 429ff.).

The desert wanderings were, for understandable reasons, a period of constant tension and crisis. The people lacked food and were not content with the manna; at times they demanded meat (Ex. 16:12ff.; Num. 11:4–6; 21:5). Often they were in need of drinking water (Ex. 15:23ff.; 17:2–7; Num. 20:1–13). On one occasion, when Moses struck the rock to produce water, instead of speaking to it, he was himself condemned for lack of faith (Num. 20:7–13). Repeatedly the people murmured and even threatened to appoint a new leader to take them back to Egypt (Ex. 5:21; 14:11–12; 15:24; 16:28; 17:2–7; Num. 11:4–6; 14:1–4; 20:2–5; 21:4–5). Of the 12 spies sent to investigate the nature of the Promised Land, ten brought back an unfavorable report: the land was exceedingly fertile (as evidence they showed a huge cluster of grapes), but unconquerable; moreover it devoured its inhabitants. Caleb and Joshua, who gave an encouraging account, failed to convince the people, and in consequence the entire generation (except Joshua and Caleb) were condemned to die in the wilderness and not enter the Land (Num. 13–14). The weary people were prey to all kinds of dangers. The Levite Korah (Moses' cousin), aided by Dathan, Abiram, and On of the tribe of Reuben, accused Moses and Aaron of self-aggrandizement, and advanced a claim to the priesthood. The horror of the challenge and its implicit peril are reflected in the punishment meted out to the rebels: the earth swallowed them up and thousands of others died through plague (Num. 16–17). Even Miriam and Aaron once criticized Moses on account of the Cushite woman (Zipporah or an Ethiopian?) whom he had married (Num. 12). Only after 40 years of wandering was Israel's goal in sight. Skirting Edom (Esau's territory), which would not permit them to pass through, and warned not to seize any Ammonite territory (Deut. 2:19), the wanderers were engaged in battle by Sihon the Amorite and Og, king of Bashan. The Israelites defeated both these kings and divided their lands among the tribes of Reuben, Gad, and the half-tribe of Manasseh (Num. 21:4–35; 32:1–42). While the period of the wilderness is depicted in the Pentateuch as a turbulent age, the prophets, on the other hand, emphasize its positive aspects. In the desert the Children of Israel had, despite their backslidings, evinced an unforgettable love of the Lord (Jer. 2:1–3). The wasteland had exerted a formative, healing influence on Israel; Hosea yearned for a renewal of the experience (2:1ff.; cf. 9:10). Undoubtedly Israel's slave mentality was gradually expurgated in the wilderness. A new generation of conquerors emerged from the desert, united by a new conception of God, a new spiritual faith, a new law of life, and a new sense of common destiny.

Moses had also trained the people for democracy. The appointment of the 70 elders was more than an act of captiousness or diffidence; in declaring "Would that all the Lord's people were prophets" the nation-builder revealed his very soul (Num. 11:16–30; cf. Ex. 3:16–19; 24:9–11). While the priesthood was hereditary, Joshua, and not one of Moses' sons, was appointed by the lawgiver to be his successor. A certain rational secularism also marks Moses' organizational arrangements. He accepts Jethro's advice in reorganizing the judicial system (Ex. 18); he asks his father-in-law to act as the people's eyes in the wilderness (Num. 10:29–32). The numbering of the people (Num. 1:2ff.; 26:1ff.), the sending of emissaries to Edom (Num. 20:14) and to Sihon (21:21–22), and even the appointment of scouts to spy out the land (13:2ff.; 21:32; Deut. 1:22–23) have distinct secular overtones. The blending of faith and reason was characteristic of Moses.

THE LAST DAYS. In the Plains of Moab Moses' life began to draw to its close. Miriam and Aaron had already died (Num. 20:1, 24–29); Moses, too, was denied entry by the Lord into the land that was the lodestar of his hopes. All his pleadings were in vain (Deut. 3:25). Instead Moses was bidden to appoint Joshua as his successor (Num. 27:16–23; Deut. 1:8; 31:3, 14, 23), and on the borders of the Promised Land the aged leader delivered three hortatory addresses (Deut. 1–4; 5–28; 29–30) in which he reviewed the history of the 40-years' wandering and gave a resume of the Torah Code. After admonishing and blessing his people and viewing the land from the top of Pisgah, he died at the age of 120 by the command of the Lord, and was buried by Him in an unknown grave (Deut. 34). The tomb of Moses was not to become a cultic site. The valedictory song (*Ha'azinu*) that Moses taught the Children of Israel (Deut. 32) and the testamentary benedictions (Deut. 33) form a beautiful epilogue to the biblical account of Moses. The tribute to Moses with which the Torah concludes (Deut. 34:10–12) underscores the uniqueness of Moses' character and achievements. But a higher tribute still was paid to "the lord of the prophets" by one of the last of the prophets. When the sun of Hebrew prophecy was setting, Malachi cried, "Remember the law of My servant Moses" (3:22 [4:4]). The Jewish future was possible only on the Torah foundations laid down by Moses. His personality holds together, as it were, the entire framework of Jewish history.

[I.ABR.]

Critical Assessment.‡ No primary source of information on Moses exists outside the Bible. The Pentateuch is the main repository of the traditions regarding Moses' life and work. All other biblical allusions to Moses depend on the Pentateuch, with the exception of Hosea 12:14, perhaps Micah 6:4 and Isaiah 63:11, and genealogical notices in Judges 1:16; 4:11; 18:30; I Chronicles 23:14–15. For critical treatment, the data are collected by topics in the following paragraphs: the pentateuchal data are followed by the extra-pentateuchal, and then assessed critically. The order of appearance in the narrative is followed in the main.

BIRTH STORY. Moses was born in Egypt to Levite parents—Amram son of Kohath son of Levi, and Jochebed daughter of Levi, Amram's aunt (Ex. 6:20; Num. 26:59; I Chron. 5:29; 23:13). He was their third child, after Aaron (older by three years, Ex. 7:7) and Miriam (older still, cf. 2:4). He was placed by his mother in the Nile to protect him from Pharaoh's decree against male infants of the Hebrews. Found by Pharaoh's daughter, he was returned to his mother for nursing, but later brought back to the princess

‡Although there are certain overlaps between this section and that preceding, they have been retained so as not to impair the unity of either section (Ed.).

who adopted him and named him *Moshe*, "explaining, 'I drew him out *[meshitihu]* of the water' " (Ex. 2:1–10).

The story contains generic elements that are discounted by historians. The infant castaway who grows up to be a hero is considered a legendary motif; it appears, for example, in the birth stories of Sargon of Akkad (Pritchard, Texts, 119) and Cyrus (Herodotus 1: 107ff.); an Egyptian myth tells of the concealment of the infant god Horus by his mother among marsh reeds to protect him from Seth (Helck). On the other hand, the representation of Israel's savior as being of Egyptian provenance and rearing (though, to be sure, of Hebrew stock) is singularly unstereotypical, and is supported by the Egyptian names of other Levites—Phinehas, Merari, Hophni, and perhaps Aaron and Miriam as well (Albright). The name of Moses too is probably to be derived from the final, verbal element in such Egyptian names as Ptah-mose ("Ptah is born"), which occurs independently in names of the New Kingdom (Griffiths). Connection with Hebrew *mashah*, "draw out," like other such name interpretations, is based on assonance rather than etymology (e.g., the connection of Noah with the unrelated verb *nḥm;* Gen. 5:29); as a Hebrew name, *Moshe* is of very rare, if not unique, formation. (The derivation of the Greek form *Mōusēs* from Egyptian *môu*, "water," and *esês*, "saved," given by Josephus (Ant. 2:228; cf. Apion 1:286; Philo, I Mos. 17), has no bearing on the Hebrew (Černý in Griffiths, see bibl.)).

Moses' connection with the Levites figures in the *Golden Calf story (Ex. 32:26ff.) and in Judges 18:30, where one of his Levite descendants (see below) is said to have founded the priestly line of the Danite sanctuary (cf. also the later Levitical status of Moses' descendants, I Chron. 23: 14). His relationship to Aaron

Figure 3. Scenes from the life of Moses in the *Sarajevo Haggadah*, fol. 21, Spain, 14th century. Above, Moses with his flock by the burning bush; below, Moses watches as Aaron performs the miracle with his rod in front of Pharaoh (Ex. 5:8–12). Sarajevo, National Museum.

shares the obscurity surrounding the origins of the Aaronide priesthood. Friction between Moses and the Levites on the one hand and Aaron on the other appears in the Golden Calf story and suggests a background of rival ecclesiastical lines. But Aaron's impunity speaks for a high rank independent of Moses—in which respect he is Moses' "brother" and peer. Moses, Aaron, and Miriam are linked in Numbers 12:1–2 and with the Exodus in Micah 6:4; such a family of spiritual persons is unknown in later Israel, but has pagan analogues.

Early Manhood and Sojourn in Midian. Forced to flee Egypt because of his fatal intervention on behalf of a Hebrew slave, Moses rescues the shepherdess daughters of a Midianite priest from other shepherds who had driven them off. Invited to join the priest's family, he marries his daughter, Zipporah—who bears him two sons, Gershom and Eliezer—and tends his flocks (Ex. 2: 10–22; 18:3–4). The episodes of Moses' early manhood foreshadow his career as a savior of the oppressed; they are poetically apt but historically unverifiable. His flight to Midian recalls the story of the Egyptian official Si-nuhe who, having fallen out of favor at the court, fled to Syria, where he settled and married among Semitic tribes (Pritchard, Texts, 18ff.). The tradition of Moses' Midianite connection is unclear in details. His father-in-law is variously named Reuel (Ex. 2: 18; cf. Num. 10:29), Hobab (Judg. 4: 11; cf. Num. 10:29) and *Jethro-Jether (Ex. 3: 1; 4: 18; 18: 1ff.). A wife of Moses is called a Cushite (Num. 12: 1)—perhaps of the tribe Cushan, a synonym of Midian in Habakkuk 3:7 (cf. W. F. Albright, in: BASOR, 83 (1941) 34, n. 8), and thus identical with Zipporah, though the absence of cross-reference is remarkable. Yet the later alliance with Israel of the nomad Kenites, descendants of Hobab (Judg. 1: 16; 4: 11; I Sam. 15:6ff.), coupled with the enmity between Midian and Israel that began in the pre-settlement age and continued for generations (Num. 22:4ff.; 31: 1ff.; Judg. 6–7), supports the historicity of an early connection between Israel and a Midianite group—the Kenites, relatives of Moses.

The Commissioning and the Exodus. Once while tending the flocks deep in the wilderness at the Mountain of God, Moses was surprised by a call out of a burning bush to become God's agent in the deliverance of Israel from bondage. God's name, YHWH, was revealed and interpreted to him, and identified with the God of the Patriarchs. Returning to Egypt with (Ex. 4:20) or without (18:2) his family, Moses was rebuffed by Pharaoh, recommissioned by God, and armed with wonders to bring Pharaoh to his knees. A climactic series of plagues forced the king to release the Israelites. After executing the protective rite of the paschal sacrifice, which saved them from the final plague of the firstborn, the Israelites marched out of Egypt. Soon, however, the Egyptians set out to retake them. Overtaken at the Sea of Reeds, the Israelites escaped through the miraculously divided sea, while the pursuing Egyptians were drowned as the waters closed back on them. Thereupon the people "believed in YHWH and in Moses, his servant" and sang a triumphal hymn to God (Ex. 3–15).

The present form of the burning bush story is a composite and elaborated account of the call of the first messenger of God to Israel. Its essence—the overpowering, unavoidable command to go on God's mission—reappears in all accounts of prophetic calls; there is little reason to doubt that it was the experience of the founder of the line (cf. the succession listed in I Sam. 12:8, 11). An allusion to this story seems to be contained in the divine epithet "Bush-Dweller" found in the (tenth-century?) Blessing of Moses (Deut. 33: 16). The antiquity of the worship of YHWH and of his association with the "Mountain of God" variously named Horeb and Sinai is problematic. Pre-Mosaic worship of YHWH as a deity whose seat was in the wilderness south of Palestine is hinted at by 14th-century Egyptian references to "a land of the bedouin of YHW'" adjacent to Edom (cf. the provenance of YHWH in the old poems, Deut. 33:2; Judg. 5:4–5, and in Hab. 3:3), and the association of YHWH with Horeb-Sinai prior to Israel's coming there is suggested by Exodus 19:4 ("and brought you to me"). To be sure, Moses is depicted as ignorant of the sanctity of the place (as Jacob was of the sanctity of Beth-El, "the gate of heaven" (Gen. 18:16)) and his experience and conception of YHWH have no known antecedents, but some link with prior religious data cannot be ruled out (though the speculative association of *Kenites-Midianites with YHWH worship has little to stand on).

The new significance of YHWH with the advent of Moses is indicated by the appearance of the first names bearing an element of the tetragrammaton in connection with Moses: Jochebed and Joshua; no such element occurs in theophoric names of the patriarchal age (on which fact light is shed by Ex. 6:3: modern criticism follows the acute suggestion of the Karaite Jeshua b. Judah (cited by Ibn Ezra, ad loc.) that occurrences of the tetragrammaton in divine communications with the Patriarchs is anachronistic, cf. *Pentateuch). The conception of the messenger or agent of YHWH, sent and equipped with wondrous signs to help Israel, has its first embodiment in Moses and is a distinctive and dominant feature of Israelite religion thereafter. That a new start was made with the God YHWH and his apostle Moses is the core of the burning bush story; the discontinuity that must be postulated at the beginning of Israel's history makes it credible. Moses plays a central role in the story of the *Plagues of Egypt and the Exodus, dramatically woven out of various strands of tradition (see *Exodus, Book of). The line of song ascribed to Miriam in Exodus 15:21 appears as the opening of a triumphal hymn to God in 15:1, which can hardly be detached from it (though verses 12–18 may be a later element), and must be allowed the same antiquity. Reflexes of these traditions, assigning a primary role to Moses, appear in Hosea 12:14 and Micah 6:4 datable to the eighth century; of indeterminate pre-Exilic date are the references in Joshua 24:5 and Psalms 105:26 to the role of Moses and Aaron in the plagues, and in I Samuel 12:6, 8 and Psalms 77:21 (where an echo of Ex. 15:13 occurs) to the brothers' part in the Exodus. Moses is linked with the parting of the sea in the post-Exilic Isaiah 63:11 (where; in the received Hebrew, a pun on Moses' name may appear (*mosheh ʿammo*, "who drew his people out [of the water]"); but the Septuagint lacks these words, and various manuscripts and the Syriac version read *mosheh ʿavdo*, "his servant Moses"). M. Noth's theory eliminating Moses from the original form of these traditions does not plausibly account for his recurring presence in their present form.

LEADER OF THE WANDERINGS THROUGH THE WILDERNESS. Moses conducted the people into the wilderness, aiming for "the Mountain of God" (cf. Ex. 3:12). On the way he had to organize them under the headship of his aide-de-camp, Joshua, into a fighting force to fend off marauding Amalekites (Ex. 17:8ff.). At Sinai, the first threat to his new faith appeared in the Golden Calf apostasy; Moses met it with harsh resolution, executing the offenders with the help of his Levite kinsmen (Ex. 32). At Sinai, too, Moses established the administrative organs of the people: advised by Jethro, he appointed a hierarchy of deputies to govern and judge them (Ex. 18:13ff.; Deut. 1:9ff.), whose military titles ("officers of thousands, hundreds, fifties, tens") accord with the disposition of the people, after their census,

Figure 4. Moses, supported by Aaron and Hur, directs Joshua's battle with Amalek (Ex. 17:8–13). Detail from the *menorah* designed by Benno Elkan for the Knesset in Jerusalem. Photo Yiẓhak Amit, kibbutz Zorah.

as an army (Num. 1–2). (For the revelation at Sinai, see below.) After celebrating the second Passover (Num. 9), Israel made ready to march on to the Promised Land. Moses requested his father-in-law's service as guide along the way (Num. 10:29ff.); then, with the Ark in the lead, Moses invoked YHWH's victory over all his enemies, and set off (Num. 10:35–36). The post-Sinai part of the wilderness wanderings was filled with challenges to Moses' authority (see next section). Numbers 11:11–12, 16ff. tells of the appointment of 70 elders, inspired by God with some of Moses' spirit to enable them to share the burden of leadership with Moses (but Ex. 24:9ff. seems to suppose their presence already at Sinai). The worst crises came with the demoralizing report of the spies sent from Kadesh to reconnoiter Canaan, and the failure of the subsequent rash attempt to invade directly, made in defiance of Moses' prohibition (Num. 13–14). Frustration induced by the prolonged, forced stay in the wilderness bred the revolt of *Korah and 250 chief men against the authority of Moses and Aaron (Num. 16), which ended with their miraculous destruction. Moses had to crush a second apostasy, incited by Moabite-Midianite women (on the advice of Balaam (Num. 22:16)), at Shittim, in Transjordan (Num. 25). Moses' martial achievements came at the close of his career. His request for peaceful passage through Amorite Transjordan having been denied, Moses led successful campaigns against the kings *Sihon and *Og and, after a preliminary reconnaissance, against the region of Jazer (Num. 21:21ff.; Deut. 2:24–3:11). He allocated the land to the tribes of Reuben, Gad, and half-Manasseh after their oath to participate in the conquest of Cisjordan (Num. 32; Deut. 3:12ff.; Josh. 13:15ff.), and reserved in it three cities of refuge (Deut. 4:41ff.; but cf. Josh. 20:8, which dates this act to the time of Joshua). His last campaign was a retributive war against Midian (Num. 31). In the last year of the wanderings, Moses appointed Eleazar to succeed his father, Aaron, in the priestly duties (Num. 20:23ff.), and his aide, Joshua, to succeed him in the leadership of the people (Num. 27:15ff.; Deut. 31).

The credibility of the wilderness narratives is impaired by their inconsistency (e.g., with respect to the 70 elders; and see the next section), chronological obscurities (e.g., the events in Num. 20–21 and their relation to Deut. 1–2), apparent doublets (e.g., Num. 21:1–3 and 14:45), and divergent itineraries (especially in Num. 33:17ff., which, e.g., has no trace of a southern movement from Kadesh, contrast 14:25, and in 14:41ff. which traces a route arriving at the Plains of Moab without circling the lands of Edom and Moab; contrast Num. 21:4; Deut. 2). Moreover, the presence of Moses is not consistent throughout this material (e.g., Num. 21:1–3), so that critics have assumed that data on tribal movements other than those led by Moses have been combined in these narratives (on the supposition that the migration of the Hebrews was not the single movement into which tradition has characteristically simplified it). But having made allowance for simplification and schematization, the agreement of tradition on Moses' presence at Sinai, Kadesh, and in Transjordan implies his leadership of a band of migrants from Egypt to Palestine. To survive they must have been organized and administered; in the wild region they traversed they were exposed to attack by nomad marauders; recurrent want and rebellion against their leaders during the long journey was to be expected. Xenophon's *Anabasis* provides numerous analogies to the tribulations of the Israelites as described in the Torah. That the adventures of this miserable band became the common property of all Israel is due to their having been perceived as the saving acts of God by those who underwent them in the aura of Moses.

INTERCESSOR. The stories of Israel's trials of God during their journey fall into two groups: the pre-Sinai trials, in which God's saving power is shown after Moses cries to God, or through a wonder announced by Moses (Ex. 14:15; 15:25; 16:1ff.; 17:4, 11), and the post-Sinai trials, in which the people, though answered, are punished for their faithlessness. Moses is still instrumental in supplying the people's needs, but he now must also intercede on their behalf to assuage God's anger. Moses' first intercession was his recrimination against God for allowing Israel's suffering to increase after his first audience with Pharaoh (Ex. 5:22–23). The longest is in the Golden Calf story—Moses' dramatic plea to God to rescind His decree of annihilation, then to agree to accompany Israel in their journey to the Promised Land. Banking on his favor with God, Moses cajoles Him to reveal to him His "ways," i.e., His merciful attributes (in effect a broader definition of His name; note the similarity of Ex. 33:13, 19 to 3:13–14), upon hearing which he presses God to forgive Israel (Ex. 32–34). Only less dramatic is Moses' other great confrontation with God, wrathful over Israel's disbelief in his capacity to give them victory over the Canaanites. Once again God threatens to destroy Israel, and once again Moses intercedes mightily on Israel's behalf, invoking God's revealed attribute of mercy, and calling upon him to manifest His strength through forbearance (Num. 14:11ff.). Further intercessions occur at Taberah (Num. 11), at the time of Miriam's leprosy (Num. 12), at the rebellion of Korah ("Will one man sin and you rage at the whole community?" Num. 16:22), and at the plague of serpents—to cure which Moses made a *copper serpent (Num. 21:4ff.). Tradition coupled Moses and Samuel as the archetypal intercessors on Israel's behalf (Jer. 15:1). A striking figure, taken from Ezekiel 22:30, is applied to Moses in the post-Exilic Psalm 106:23: "He would have destroyed them, had not Moses, His chosen one, stood in the breach in front of Him, to keep His wrath from destroying them." Psalm 103:7 alludes to Moses' eliciting God's attributes, and cites a few of them. The formulas of intercession in the two major narratives of Exodus 32–34 and Numbers 14 are doubtless part of a liturgical tradition (cf. Joel 2:13) whose attribution to Moses cannot be verified. The intercessory role of later prophets is firmly established; the depiction of Moses as a master of this role accords with his status as founder of Israel's prophetic line (see below), and may well be authentic. Singular authentication is given to Moses' copper serpent: down to the eighth century a copper serpent ascribed to Moses was lodged in the Jerusalem Temple; King Hezekiah ordered it cut down because the people were making burnt offerings to it (II Kings 18:4).

MEDIATOR OF THE COVENANT AND LAWGIVER. At Sinai, Moses negotiated Israel's acceptance of God's offer of a covenant, prepared the people for the covenant theophany, led them to God for the theophany, and strengthened them to sustain the experience (Ex. 19–20). The people heard the *Decalogue directly from God; Deuteronomy 5:5, however, insinuates Moses between the parties "to tell you what God spoke." Shattered by the experience, the people asked Moses to be their intermediary with God henceforth (Ex. 20:18–21 [15–18]; Deut. 5:20–28). Moses then received detailed stipulations of the covenant ("the *Book of the Covenant," Ex. 24:7) which he related to the people, and upon securing their assent to be bound by them, wrote down and ratified them in a solemn ceremony (Ex. 24:3–11). Later he received the written form of the Decalogue on stone tablets, which he deposited in the Ark of the Covenant (Ex. 24:12; 32:15–16; 34:1, 28–29; Deut. 9:9ff.; 10:1ff.). According to Deuteronomy, Moses recited all these stipulations to the generation about to enter Canaan during his last days, in the Plains of Moab. He concluded the recitation with warnings, blessings, and curses, then committed it to writing and deposited the document—"the Book of Torah"—in the Ark, alongside the tablets (Deut. 31:9, 24ff.). In between the two covenant-makings, at the beginning and at the end of the journey through the wilderness, Moses received a host of ritual, religious, and moral injunctions, in the Tent of Meeting at Sinai and in the Plains of Moab (Lev. 1:1ff.; 26:46; 27:34; Num. 36:13). In addition to these large and small collections of injunctions, issued at the initiative of God, Moses sought and received oracular decisions in difficult cases, as need arose. This role was reserved for him in the administrative organization of the camp suggested by Jethro (Ex. 18:19–20) and its performance is illustrated in the cases of the blasphemer (Lev. 24), the Sabbath breaker (Num. 15:32ff.), and the daughters of Zelophehad (Num. 27; cf. Num. 36). The figure of Moses as the mediator of God's laws and admonitions to Israel appears in biblical literature influenced by Deuteronomy and in post-Exilic writings. Thus the deuteronomistically edited Book of Joshua is haunted by Moses, the lawgiver; indeed it reads as the record of fulfillment of Moses' admonitions (e.g., 1:1ff.; 4:10ff.; 8:31ff.; 11:15ff.; 14:6, 9; 17:4; 20:2). Material in the same spirit and style is found in Kings: I Kings 2:3; 8:53, 56; II Kings 14:6; 18:6; 21:8; 23:25. In writings of the Persian period, Moses appears exclusively as the author of the Torah and the founder of Israel's sacred institutions (Mal. 3:22; Ezra 3:2; Neh. 1:7ff.; 8:1, 14; 9:14; 10:30; I Chron. 6:34; 21:29; II Chron. 8:13; 24:6; 35:6, 12). For a critical assessment of this representation of Moses, see the end of the next section.

Cult Founder and Priest. Moses not only proclaimed the proper name of God, by which He was henceforth to be invoked in worship ("This shall be My name forever/This My appellation [*zikhri*, lit. 'call-word'] for all time," Ex. 3:15), he instructed Israel in YHWH's sacred seasons—starting with Passover and *mazzot* (Ex. 12) and the Sabbath (Ex. 16) and proceeding to the whole cultic calendar and its related prescribed sacrifices (Ex. 23:14ff.; 34:18ff.; Lev. 23; Num. 28:29; Deut. 16). The non-festival sacrificial system, too, was ordained by him (Lev. 1–7). He received the blueprint of the Tabernacle and supervised its construction (Ex. 25–31; 35–40). He inaugurated it and consecrated its clergy (Lev. 8). Moses is described as exercising specific priestly functions (e.g., handling the blood of sacrifice) both in the ceremony of covenant ratification (Ex. 24:6, 8) and during the inauguration of the Tabernacle and priesthood (Lev. 8).

Only two allusions to Moses' priestly aspect occur in extra-pentateuchal writing: Psalm 99:6 counts Moses with Aaron as a priest of YHWH (traditional exegetes refer this to his role in Lev. 8), and the priesthood of the Danite sanctuary traced their line to a descendant of Moses (Judg. 18:30—crediting the talmudic notice that the suspended *nun* of "Manasseh" is a deliberate device to obscure the derivation of this ignoble priesthood from Moses; BB 109b). According to the post-Exilic record, and in line with the Aaronide monopoly of the priesthood prescribed by the Torah, the descendants of Moses were counted as Levites, not priests (I Chron. 23:14). Criticism finds the ascription to Moses of the vast corpus of rules and admonitions in Exodus, Leviticus, Numbers, and Deuteronomy improbable. Its arguments—from inconsistency, variant repetitions, diversity in style and viewpoint, and divergent historical presuppositions—can be found in articles on the books in question and on the *Pentateuch as a whole. Yet the origin and motive of this ascription can be described, and its poetic justice defended. The constant, stable element in the history of Israel during the biblical period is the consciousness of being a religious community, bound together by a common link to YHWH. No political change or revolution broke the continuity of this element. Under tribal rule or united monarchy, in a divided kingdom or in exile, and no less under Persian rule, the idea of a primary allegiance to the will of YHWH, prior to all political forms, defined Israelite identity. From latest to earliest times this allegiance was expressed in zeal for YHWH's exclusive claim upon Israel (i.e., hostility toward foreign cults), in iconoclasm (persecution of idolatry), in peculiar religious institutions (e.g., the Sabbath), and in moral earnestness resulting from the communal responsibility to God for violations of morality (Judg. 20; II Sam. 4:11). Its symbol was the Ark of the Covenant (as early as the time of the Judges, I Sam. 4), and its exponents were agents and messengers of YHWH who admonished error and saved from distress (e.g., Jerubbaal, Judg. 6ff.). These elements, constitutive of Israel's identity and singularity from the very beginning of its occupation of Canaan, cannot be ascribed to events or persons from that time. On the contrary, since the tendency of post-occupation circumstances was centrifugal, any contemporary unity must be attributed to previously established ties that were strong enough to survive the centrifugal pulls and assimilatory temptations of life in Canaan. These ties were perforce formed, then, in the "wilderness" period, when the embryo of later Israel was wandering, unsettled, along the southern and eastern edges of Canaan. The question of their author—for elements so contrary to their environment require the assumption of a revolutionary mind for their invention—is answered by Moses in his role of covenant mediator and cult founder. The above-mentioned features of Israelite religion may, with plausibility, be ascribed to Moses, as well as their integrating framework, the idea of the covenant with YHWH. However rudimentary the terms of the Mosaic covenant may have been (some suppose no more than the Decalogue, others include parts of the Book of the Covenant; criteria for positive ascription are wanting), they were enough to serve as the constitution of the religiopolitical community of Israel; subsequent development of these terms, their ramifications, their adjustments to changing times, was regarded as part and parcel of the original. All regulations constitutive of the religious community of Israel were covenant regulations; all were issued by God and communicated to Israel by the mediator Moses. Something of the process may be glimpsed at in Nehemiah 10:30ff. and II Chronicles 30:16; 35:12, where rites are ascribed to the Torah of Moses that are not in fact to be found there.

Death and Burial. Although commissioned to bring Israel into the Promised Land (e.g., Ex. 33:1ff.), Moses died in the Plains of Moab, outside its borders. Numbers 20:2–13 accounts for this by the offense of Moses and Aaron at Kadesh, in connection with procuring water for the grumbling people—"the waters of contention" *(me merivah)*. Wherein the brothers failed to "believe" God and "sanctify him in the sight of the Israelites" (Num. 20:12) is obscure. The interpretation in Psalms 106:32–33 is ambiguous: this much seems clear, however: that Moses is blamed for speaking rashly. In Deuteronomy, on the other hand, Moses is denied entry into the Promised Land on account of the people: their display of faithlessness during the incident of the spies made God turn upon Moses as

Figure 5. Moses blessing the children of Israel before his death. Illustration from the *León Bible*, Spain, 1162. León, Archives of the Royal Collegiate Church of San Isidoro, Ms. 3, fol. 90r.

well. It was then He decreed that Moses (as well as his whole generation) would not enter the land (Deut. 1:37; 3:26; 4:21). When his time had come, Moses was commanded to ascend Mount Nebo, from which he could view the length and breadth of the Promised Land. There he died and was buried in the valley, "in the land of Moab, opposite Beth-Peor; and no man knows his burial place, to this day" (Deut. 34; cf. Num. 27:12ff.). The various theological explanations of Moses' death in Transjordan vouch for the authenticity of the fact. The surprising obliteration of his burial-place savors of a deliberate aversion toward his apotheosis, which might have grown out of veneration of his grave as a shrine. Such an apotheosis was likely in view of the singular status accorded Moses in Israelite tradition.

Unique Status. The wonders performed by Moses on behalf of Israel exceed those of any subsequent prophet (Deut. 34:11–12). He not only outdid Egypt's magicians (whose virtuosity, as displayed, e.g., in the Westcar Papyrus (A. Erman, *The Ancient Egyptians*, 36ff.), illuminates the issue of the first part of the plague narratives), he also prevailed over the mightiest forces of nature—splitting both the sea (Ex. 14) and the earth (Num. 16). That in so doing he no more than activated the power of God, and in God's own cause, is unfailingly noted; no room is left for regarding Moses as a magician, aggrandizing himself through native powers or occult arts. One superhuman trait, however, does pertain to him: the ability to endure, on more than one occasion, a fast of forty days (Ex. 24:18; 34:28; Deut. 9:9, 18; cf. Elijah's similar feat, I Kings 19:8). Miraculous features, part of the traditional image of the "man of God," are ascribed to Moses in the highest degree as befits his heroic role. No later figure is portrayed so close to God as Moses. God spoke with him "face to face" (Ex. 33:11), and allowed him such a prolonged intimacy that as a result (after Moses' intercession in the wake of the Golden Calf apostasy) Moses' face was fearsomely radiant, so that he had to wear a mask in ordinary intercourse with people (Ex. 34:19ff.). The covenant made after this apostasy, on the basis of Moses' favor with God, specifically names Moses as an equal party with the people (Ex. 34:27; cf. 34:10, and the corresponding usage in the intercession in Ex. 33:16 ("I and your people," twice)). The equation corresponds to God's substitution of Moses for all the rest of the people in Exodus 32:10 (cf. Num. 14:12) and Moses' readiness to lay down his life on their behalf (Ex. 32:32). That Moses cannot simply be subsumed under the rubric "prophet" (*navi'*) is the lesson taught to Aaron and Miriam in Numbers 12:6ff.: prophetic revelation is in the form of dream or vision; Moses, however, has the freedom of YHWH's house (i.e., may obtain audiences at will), he speaks with God "mouth to mouth," and is granted sight of YHWH (not a necessary contradiction of Ex. 33:20ff., where Moses is denied sight of God's face, but not of His back). In fact, Moses is never called a "prophet" in the Pentateuch (he is alluded to as such only in Hosea 12:14), but rather YHWH's "servant" (*'eved*)— the usual epithet in extra-pentateuchal literature as well (Num. 12:7–8; Deut. 34:5; Josh. 1:1; once he is styled God's "chosen one" (*beḥir*, Ps. 106:23), a synonym of "servant" in Isa. 42:1, 45:4; Ps. 89:4). In Deuteronomy (33:1) and later literature (Josh. 14:6; Ps. 90:1; Ezra 3:2; I Chron. 23:14; II Chron. 30:16) Moses is occasionally called "the man of God," a prophetic epithet. His spirit inspires ecstasy (Num. 11:25), just as contact with the prophet Samuel does (I Sam. 19:20ff.). Moreover, he is compared to prophets in Numbers 12, Deuteronomy 18:18, and 34:10, and in the last passage he is represented as their unequaled archetype. But the catalog of pagan analogues to the Israelite prophet in Deuteronomy 18:10–11 suggests that the term *navi'* was too restricted to oracular, divinatory, and magic-like functions to be applied to so comprehensive a figure as Moses (though, since he performed these functions, he might justly be considered a prophetic archetype). Just in those two narratives where Moses' relation to prophecy is manifest, a point is made of his meekness and forbearance. He does not share his servant's alarm at the apparently independent prophesying of *Eldad and Medad; on the contrary, he wishes the entire people were prophets (Num. 11:26ff.). Nor will he assert himself even against rival claims of his brother and sister, for he was "the meekest man on earth" (Num. 12:3). Perhaps here, too, a distinction between Moses' character and that of later prophets is intended (contrast II Kings 2:23–24).

Final Considerations. Moses is not consistently present in biblical literature. He dominates the Pentateuch and Joshua—the repository of traditions about the birth of the nation. He reappears in the revival and refounding literature of late monarchic and post-Exilic times. But references to him in the prophetic and hymnal writings (e.g., Psalms) are negligible. This is not remarkable, however, and does not imply an earlier, more authentic stage of tradition in which Moses played a negligible role in accounts of Israel's beginnings (von Rad). The prophets have a mind only for Israel's allegiance to God, which they regard as an immediate relationship. Just as their judgment of their contemporaries takes little account of the king's mediating role (in contrast to the historiography of the Book of Kings), so their allusions to the past virtually ignore intermediaries. As for hymnal literature, God is its subject, and praise or confession its mode of expression; the psalmist is too taken up with God to pay regard to another. Moses' slighting by prophets and psalmists says as little about his place in contemporary historical traditions as does his even more total omission from the Passover *Haggadah*. What better proof exists of the error of discounting the Moses tradition on the basis of hymns than the *Haggadah's* hymnic confession **Dayyeinu*, in which Israel's career from Egypt to the settlement is rehearsed in 13 stages without a reference to Moses. All innovation in the later religion of Israel is attributable to individuals known by name: the monarchy to Samuel and David; the Temple to David and Solomon; reforms in the official religion to kings Asa, Jehu, Hezekiah, Josiah, the priests Jehoiada and Hilkiah, and the prophets Elisha, Elijah, and Huldah; new moral-historical and eschatological conceptions to Amos, Hosea, Isaiah, Jeremiah—and the list is not ended. Had no founder of the worship of YHWH and the covenant institutions that characterized Israel from its beginnings been recorded in tradition, analogy would have required postulating him. The traditions of Israel point unanimously to Moses as the founder of all the constitutional elements of the religious community of Israel (excepting the monarchy). Anachronistic attribution to him of much later elaboration on these elements does not negate the Mosaic core. No single figure in later Israel plays the many roles ascribed to Moses; his image cannot therefore be interpreted as an anachronistic projection of later times. The best analogue to Moses in the history of religions, Muhammad, exhibits the very same multiplicity of roles—oracle, political-military leader, cult founder, and lawgiver. Thus internal and external analogy combine to authenticate the unusually multifaceted image of the founder of the national-religious community of Israel.

[Mo.G.]

IN HELLENISTIC LITERATURE

Inventor and Civilizer, Lawgiver and Philosopher. The Jewish-Hellenistic tendency to adopt the sages of ancient culture entailed a whole series of farfetched identifications (e.g., Isis-Eve; Serapis-Joseph; Atlas-Enoch; Bel Kronos-Nimrod; Orpheus-David; Musaeos-Moses; Zoroaster-Ezekiel) and culminated in the attribution of the most important contributions of civilization to Jewish cultural hero-figures. Thus, Moses became for Eupolemus (whose chronology placed him more than 500 years before the Trojan War) the first wise man, and the first to invent writing for the Jews (from whom it was taken over by the Phoenicians, and from the Phoenicians, by the Greeks; Eusebius, *Praeparatio Evangelica*, 9:26). According to Artapanos, Moses (who is identified with Musaeos and also with Hermes-Thot) was the teacher of Orpheus, discovered the art of writing, was the first philosopher, and invented a variety of machines for peace and war. He was also responsible for the political organization of Egypt (having divided the land into 36 nomes), and was the originator of the animal cults of the Egyptians, which were seen as the only practical means available to overcome the unstable character of the Egyptian masses (Eusebius, op. cit. 9:27). The earliest philosophical exegete of the Pentateuch, Aristobulus, claimed that Homer and Hesiod drew much of their material from the Books of Moses, which, according to him, had been translated long before the Septuagint (Eusebius, op. cit. 13:12). Philo maintains that Heraclitus snatched his theory of opposites from Moses "like a thief" (*Quaestiones et Solutiones in Genesin* 4:152). Similarly, he says that the Greek legislators "copied" various laws from the laws of Moses (Spec. 4:61). Philo even states that Moses anticipated Plato's doctrine of creation from preexistent matter, by teaching in Genesis that there was water, darkness, and chaos before the world came into being (*De Providentia*, ed. J. B. Aucher (1822), 111; cf. Justin Martyr, *Apologia*, 1:59). According to Josephus, Moses was the most ancient of all legislators in the records of the world. Indeed, he maintains that the very word "law" was unknown in ancient Greece (Jos., Apion 2:154). Moreover, "in two points in particular, Plato followed the example of our legislator [Moses]. He prescribed as the primary duty of the citizens a study of their laws, which they must all learn word for word by heart, and he took precautions to prevent foreigners from mixing with them at random" (*ibid.* 257). "Our earliest imitators," concludes Josephus, "were the Greek philosophers, who, though ostensibly observing the laws of their own countries, yet in their conduct and philosophy were Moses' disciples" (*ibid.* 281). The only analogue in the pagan world to these ascriptions of priority to Moses is the famous statement of Numenius of Apamea (second century C.E.), who introduced allegorical interpretation of the Hebrew Bible to the pagan world (fragments 19 and 32, L), that Plato was just a Moses who spoke Greek (fragment 10, L). Philo also asserts that Moses was "the best of all lawgivers in all countries," and that his laws are most excellent and truly come from God. This is proved by the fact that while other law codes have been upset for innumerable reasons, the laws of Moses have remained firm and immovable, and "we may hope that they will remain for all future ages . . . so long as the sun and moon and the whole heaven and universe exist" (II Mos. 12). Furthermore, not only Jews but almost every other people have attained enough holiness to value and honor these laws. In fact, says Philo, "it is only natural that when people are not flourishing, their belongings to some degree are under a cloud, but if a fresh start should be made to brighter prospects . . . each nation would . . . throw overboard its ancestral customs and turn to honoring our laws alone" (*ibid.* 44). In spite of the declining political fortunes of the Jews during the period of the Roman Empire, an occasional note of admiration for Moses is still found in writers like Pseudo-Longinus, who speaks glowingly of the great legislator's lofty genius (*On the Sublime* 9:9), but Numenius, Tacitus, Galen, Celsus, Porphyry, and Julian, on the other hand, are highly critical of, and even hostile to, Moses.

Anti-Semitic Attacks on Moses. The earliest Greek references to Moses were quite favorable. Hecataeus of Abdera presented Moses as the founder of the Jewish state, ascribing to him the conquest of Palestine and the building of Jerusalem and the Temple. He explained, in the Platonic manner, that Moses divided his people into 12 tribes, because 12 is a perfect number, corresponding to the number of months in the year (cf. Plato, *Laws*, 745b–d; *Republic*, 546b). He also discovered a solicitude for military training in Moses' endeavor to train the youth in moral restraint and heroic endurance (Diodorus 40:3; in: Th. Reinach, *Textes d'auteurs Grecs et Romains relatifs au Judaïsme* (1895), 14ff.). More important, he emphasized that Moses instituted no images in the worship of God, so that God should not be conceived of anthropomorphically, since the all-encompassing heavens alone (i.e., the cosmos) are to be identified as God. Posidonius of Apamea similarly emphasized that Moses worshiped no idols, and identified God with nature (Strabo 16:35). Soon, however, a reaction set in, and Moses became the butt of a venomous anti-Semitic literature. Hecataeus had earlier observed that Moses had initiated a form of life encouraging seclusion from man and a hatred of aliens. According to the Egyptian priest Manetho (third century), Moses was a rebellious priest of Heliopolis, called Osarsiph (cf. Chaeremon and Jos., Apion 1:32), who commanded the Jews to slaughter the sacred animals of Egypt, and established, with the aid of the Hyksos, a 13-year reign of cruelty over the Egyptians, until he was finally expelled by Pharaoh Amenophis (Jos., Apion 1:228ff.; Reinach, *ibid.*, 11). Lysimachus wrote that he instructed the Jews to show goodwill to no man, to always offer the worst advice, and to overthrow any temples and altars of the gods which they found (Jos., Apion 1:309; Reinach, *ibid.*, 59). Apollonius Molon accused Moses of being a charlatan and impostor, who gave the Jews bad laws. Posidonius says that upon entering the Holy of Holies, Antiochus Epiphanes saw the statue of a bearded man riding on an ass (cf. Tacitus, *Histories*, 5:3) and holding a book. This was Moses, who gave the Jews laws of hatred toward all mankind (Diodorus 34:1, 3; Reinach, *ibid.* 57–58). Finally, Nicarchus (cf. Ptolemy Chennos of Alexandria, and Helladius) writes that Moses was called *Alpha* (an honorific title for members of the Museum at Alexandria, and possibly applied to Moses in Jewish-Hellenistic literature), because he had leprous spots *(alphous)* all over his body (Reinach, *ibid.*, 122, 361–62).

The Biography of Moses. The sparse biographical details of the biblical narrative concerning Moses are considerably elaborated and expanded in the characteristic style of Jewish-Hellenistic literature. Demetrius (end of third century), in his "On the Kings in Judea," identified the Cushite woman whom Moses married (Num. 12:1) with Zipporah, by arguing that as far as one can infer from the names (the LXX lists among the sons of Dedan, Abraham's grandson from the family of Keturah, also Raguel, who, according to Demetrius, was Jethro's father), Zipporah was a sixth-generation descendant of Abraham's family. According to the Bible, Abraham sent the sons of Keturah away "eastward, to the land of the East" (Gen. 25:6), which Demetrius identified as the land of Cush. "It was on this account," concluded Demetrius, "that Aaron and Miriam declared that Moses took a Cushite woman" (Eusebius, op. cit. 9:29). The first elaborate account of Moses' life is to be found in Artapanus' "On the Jews." According to Artapanus, Pharaoh's daughter, Merris (Jos.,

Ant., 2:224 gives her name as Thermuthis), was barren, and therefore adopted a Jewish child whom she named Moshe. Merris' husband, Chenephres, king of Memphis, grew jealous of Moses, and tried to dispose of him by sending him into battle against the Ethiopians with inadequate forces. After a ten-year campaign, the Ethiopians so admired Moses that, under his influence, they adopted the rite of circumcision. Artapanus knew nothing, however, of Moses' romance with the Ethiopian king's daughter and her betrayal of the capital city to him (Jos., Ant., 2:252), and it must be assumed that, like Demetrius and Ezekiel the Poet, he identified the Cushite woman whom Moses married with Zipporah. Artapanus' version of the biblical story of Moses' slaying of the Egyptian emphasizes the latter's plotting against Moses' life. Indeed, it was in a last resort to defend his life, that Moses slew the Egyptian Chanethothes. Moses' efforts to free his people land him in jail, but the irons binding him miraculously fall off, and the jail doors open of themselves (cf. the experiences of the imprisoned god Dionysus in Euripides' *The Bacchanals*, 600ff.). Moses' rod, according to Artapanus, was found in every Egyptian temple and was similar to the *seistron* or "rattle" used in the worship of Isis. It was by means of the *seistron* that Isis raised the waters of the Nile, and thus she was called in the Isis hymns *Seistrophóros*. Artapanus mentions two traditions concerning the Red Sea, that of Memphis and that of Heliopolis. That of Heliopolis follows the Bible, while that of Memphis explains the event by saying that Moses knew the area well and waited for the ebb tide (cf. Jos., Ant. 2:341–49). Finally, the reason given for the Egyptians' pursuit of the Israelites was their desire to retrieve the property borrowed from them (cf. Philo, I Mos. 1:141). A similar explanation is given by Trogus Pompeius, who says, however, that the Jews stole the holy utensils of the Egyptians (Justin 36:2, 13). Artapanus' account closes with a description of Moses: "Moses, they say, was tall and ruddy, with long white hair, and dignified" (Eusebius, op. cit. 9:27). The 269 lines preserved from the tragedy of Ezekiel the Poet on Exodus include a long soliloquy by Moses recounting his career down to his flight to Midian; a dialogue which recounts a dream in which a royal personage enthrones Moses on a throne which reaches heavenward, whereupon Moses surveys the heavenly host who fall on their knees before him, and then pass by as he counts them; and a detailed description of a remarkable bird, apparently the phoenix, at Elim (cf. Herodotus 2:73; Pliny, *Natural History*, 10:3–5; Job. 29:18; Gen. R. 19:5; Sanh. 108b; II En. 6:6; 8:6; II Bar. 6–7; Eusebius, op. cit., 9:16–37). In his *De vita Mosis*, Philo depicts Moses in his fourfold role as king, legislator, priest, and prophet. Whereas the fame of Moses' law, writes Philo, has traveled throughout the civilized world, the man himself, as he really was, was known to few. Greek men of letters, perhaps through envy, have refused to treat him as worthy of memory. Although there is no attempt in this treatise to refute the anti-Semitic literature on Moses, Philo does refer in his *Hypothetica* (355) to the charge that Moses was "an impostor and prating mountebank." He also strangely explains the Exodus there as due partly to Jewish overpopulation in Egypt (cf. Tacitus, *Histories*, 5:4) and also to the revelations of God in dreams and visions bidding them to go forth. Moreover, he points out that the Israelites' admiration for the man who gave them their laws was so great, that anything which seemed good to him also seemed good to them. Therefore, whether what he told them came from his own reasoning or from some supernatural source, they referred it all to God (*ibid.*, 357). In the *De vita Mosis*, Philo explains how the child Moses happened to be found by Pharaoh's daughter. In a state of constant depression over not having a child who could succeed her father she finally broke down on one occasion, and, though she had hitherto always remained in her quarters, she set off with her maids to the river where Moses was exposed. Since he had been taken up from the waters, she called him Moses, *mou* being the Egyptian word for water. As he grew in beauty and nobility, she decided to claim him as her own son, having at an earlier time artificially enlarged the figure of her womb to make him pass as her real child. Teachers arrived from different parts of Egypt and even from Greece. In a short time, however, he advanced beyond their capacities. Moses thus acquired the best of both Greek and Egyptian education. In his desire to live for the soul alone and not for the body, he lived frugally, scorning all luxury. Moses' career as a shepherd served as good training and a preliminary exercise in kingship for one destined to command the herd of mankind. Since Moses abjured the accumulation of wealth, God rewarded him by placing the whole world in his hands. Therefore each element obeyed him as its master, and submitted to his command (cf. II Mos., 201; Wisd. 19:6). His partnership with God also entitled him to bear the same title: "For he was named god and the king of the whole nation, and entered into the darkness where God was, that is, into the unseen, invisible, incorporeal, and archetypal essence of existing things."

A few further details may be added from Josephus' account of Moses (Ant. 2:201ff.). Pharaoh decreed that all male infants of the Hebrews be drowned on the advice of a sacred scribe who had divined the birth of one who, if allowed to live, would abase Egypt and exalt Israel. Moses' easy birth spared his mother violent pangs and discovery by the watchful Egyptian midwives. His size and beauty enchanted princess Thermuthis, who found him on the Nile. Because he refused to take the breast of any Egyptian wet nurse, his mother was engaged to suckle him. Moses' precocity was displayed in his very games. Moreover, when the princess laid the babe in her father's arms, and the latter, to please his daughter, placed his diadem upon the child's head, Moses tore it off, flung it to the ground, and trampled it underfoot. This was taken as an ill omen, and the sacred scribe who had foretold his birth rushed forward to kill him. Thermuthis, however, was too quick for him and snatched the child away. Carried away by his Hellenistic ambience, Josephus says that, after crossing the Red Sea, Moses composed a song to God in hexameter verse.

Some last points of interest may be gleaned from Pseudo-Philo's *Liber Antiquitatum Biblicarum* (first century C.E.). According to this work, Moses was born circumcised (cf. Sot. 12a, Ex. R. 1:20). Pharaoh's daughter comes down to bathe in the Nile at this particular time because she had had a dream. Before Moses smashes the tablets, he looks upon them and sees that there is no writing on them. The reason given for his not entering the Promised Land was that he should be spared the sight of the idols that were to mislead his people. Moses dies at the hands of God, who buries him personally (cf. Deut. R. 11:10), and on the day of his death the heavenly praise of God was omitted, something which never occurred before and was never to occur again.

MOSES IN THE APOCALYPTIC TRADITION. According to the *Assumption of Moses* (c. 7–30 C.E.), Moses was prepared from before the foundation of the world to be the mediator of God's covenant with his people (1:14; 3:12). No single place was worthy to mark the site of his burial, for his sepulcher was from the rising to the setting sun (11:8). Moses' relation to Israel did not cease with his death, for he was appointed by God to be their intercessor in the spiritual world. This work also includes the debate between Michael and Satan over the burial of Moses. Satan opposes Michael's commission to bury Moses, on the ground that he is the lord of matter. To this claim Michael rejoins: "The Lord rebuke thee, for it was God's spirit that created the world and all mankind." In other words, Satan grants God Moses' soul, but claims his body as belonging to his exclusive domain. The author, speaking through Michael, rejects this gnostic dualism by insisting that God is Lord of both spirit and flesh, since he is the creator of all (R. H. Charles, Apocrypha, 2 (1897), 105–7). It may be well to allude here to the apocalyptic tradition connected with the name of Moses and also with Ezra, the "second Moses." In the *Assumption of Moses*, Moses gives Joshua secret books which are to be preserved and hidden "until the day of repentance in the visitation wherewith the Lord shall visit thee in the consummation of the end of days" (1:18). In Jubilees, too, the account is given of a secret tradition revealed to Moses on Sinai in which he is shown all the events of history both past and future (1:26). With this may be compared II Esdras 14, where Ezra, the "second Moses," receives by divine revelation the 24 books of canonical Scripture which he has to publish openly and the 70 books representing the apocalyptic tradition which he has to keep secret.

Moses as Magician. In pagan literature, Moses was, naturally enough, sometimes represented as a great magician. Numenius of Apamea, for example, presents him as a magician greater than his rivals Iannes and Iambres because his prayers were more powerful than theirs (fragments 18 and 19, L; cf. Pliny, *Natural History*, 30:1, 11; Reinach, op. cit. 282; Trogus Pompeius = Justin *Epitome* 36:2; Reinach, op. cit., 253). Moreover, in some of the magic papyri, Moses appears as the possessor of mysteries given to him by God (K. Preisendanz, *Papyri Graecae Magicae*, 2, 87f.). Finally, it may be noted that in some of the Qumran fragments, secret astrological teachings were ascribed to Moses (J. T. Milik, in: RB, 63 (1956), 61). [D.W.]

RABBINIC VIEW

A marked ambivalence is to be observed in the Jewish tradition with regard to the personality of Moses. On the one hand, Moses is the greatest of all the Jewish teachers, a powerfully numinous figure, the man with whom God speaks "face to face," the intermediary between God and man, the master of the prophets, and the recipient of God's law for mankind. On the other hand, the utmost care is taken to avoid the ascription of divine or semi-divine powers to Moses. Moses is a man, with human faults and failings. Strenuous attempts are made to reject any "personality cult," even when the personality in question is so towering as Moses. Judaism is not "Mosaism" but the religion of the Jewish people. God, not Moses, gives His Torah to His people Israel. There are to be found Jewish thinkers, evidently in response to the claims made for Jesus by Christianity and for Muhammad by Islam, who elevate the role of Moses so that the religion is made to center around him. However, the opposite tendency is equally notable. Precisely because Christianity and Islam center around a person, Jewish thinkers declared that Judaism, on the contrary, singles out no one person, not even a Moses, as belonging to the heart of the faith. The stresses in this matter vary in proportion to the particular strength of the challenge in the period during which the role of Moses is considered. The need is keenly felt to affirm the supremacy of Moses and yet, at the same time, to deny him any divine honors.

Rav and Samuel said that 50 gates of understanding were created in the world, and all but one were given to Moses, for it is said (Ps. 8:6): "For Thou hast made him [Moses] but a little lower than the angels" (Ned. 38a). All the prophets saw God as one looks into a dim glass, but Moses as one who looks through a clear glass (Yev. 49b). When Moses was born the whole house was filled with light (Sot. 12a). Moses was so kind, gentle, and considerate to his sheep when tending the flock of Jethro that God made him the shepherd of Israel (Ex. R. 2:2). For Moses such a great thing as the fear of God was very easy of attainment (Ber. 33b). R. Johanan said: "The Holy One, blessed be He, causes His Divine Presence to rest only upon him who is strong, wealthy, wise, and meek and Moses had all these qualifications" (Ned. 38a). According to one opinion, Moses did not really die but still stands and ministers to God as he did while on Mount Sinai (Sot. 13b). Moses was righteous from the beginning of his life to the end of it, as was Aaron (Meg. 11a). Here, and frequently in the rabbinic literature, the praise of Moses is coupled with that of Aaron. The humility of Moses and Aaron was greater than that of Abraham since Abraham spoke of himself as dust and ashes (Gen. 18:27) whereas Moses and Aaron declared that they were nothing at all (Ex. 16:8). The whole world exists only on account of the merit of Moses and Aaron (Ḥul. 89a). These and similar sayings are typical of the rabbinic determination to go to the utmost lengths in lauding Moses; yet sayings of a not too different nature are found lauding other biblical heroes, and in some of the passages Aaron is made to share Moses' glory.

For the rabbis generally Moses is *Moshe Rabbenu* ("Moses our master," i.e. teacher), the teacher of the Torah par excellence. Neumark (*Toledot ha-Ikkarim* (1919[2]), 85f.) has, however, conjectured that the absence of this title from the whole of the Mishnah is a conscious anti-Christian reaction in which the character of Moses is played down somewhat by avoiding the giving to him of a title given to Jesus (Acts. 2:36). It is also suggested in the Mishnah (RH 3:8) that the hands of Moses did not in themselves have any effect on the fortunes of Israel in the battle with Amalek. It was only when Israel lifted up their eyes to God in response to Moses' uplifted hands that God helped them. R. Eleazar, commenting on the verse "Go down" (Ex. 32:7), remarks: "The Holy One, blessed be He, said to Moses: 'Moses, descend from thy greatness. Have I given to thee greatness except for the sake of Israel? And now Israel have sinned; then why do I want thee?'" (Ber. 32a). R. Yose said that if Moses had not preceded him, Ezra would have been worthy of receiving the Torah for Israel (Sanh. 21b). Nor were the rabbis averse on occasion to criticizing Moses for his quick temper (Pes. 66b; Sot. 13b) and to stating that he erred, though ready to acknowledge his mistake (Zev. 101a).

In the rabbinic tradition Moses was not only given the Written Law but the Oral Law, including the "laws given to Moses at Sinai" (**Halakhah le-Moshe mi-Sinai*), and whatever new interpretation of the law is ever brought before his teacher by a keen student of the Torah was already given to Moses at Sinai (TJ, Pe'ah 2:6, 17a). The idea that new teachings were truly new and yet were implied in the Torah given to Moses is conveyed in the story of Moses being transported through time to the academy of Akiva and feeling disturbed at his inability to comprehend Akiva's teachings until he heard Akiva declare that he had received them as a tradition from Moses at Sinai (Men. 29b). The idea that the foremost Jewish teachers who produced innovations—Hillel, Johanan b. Zakkai, and Akiva—are to be identified with Moses, whose work they continued, is expressed in the statement that they, like Moses, also lived for 120 years, divided into three periods of 40 years (Sif. Deut. 327). According to one interpretation, widely accepted in the Middle Ages, the name "Moses" was, in fact, sometimes given to scholars as a title of honor (Beẓah 38b). [L.J.]

In the Aggadah. Heaven and earth were only created for the sake of Moses (Lev. R. 36:4). The account of the creation of water on the second day does not close with the customary formula "and God saw that it was good" since Moses was destined to be punished through water (Gen. R. 4:6). Noah was only rescued from the Flood because Moses was destined to descend from him (Gen. R. 26:6). The ascending and descending angels seen by Jacob in his nocturnal vision (Gen. 28:12) were in reality Moses and Aaron (Gen. R. 68:12).

His parents' house was filled with light on the day of his birth. He was born circumcised (Sot. 12a) on Adar 7th (Meg. 13b). He spoke with his parents on the day of his birth, and prophesied at the age of three (Mid. Petirat Moshe, in: Jellinek, *Beit ha-Midrash,* 1:128). Pharaoh's daughter went down to bathe since she was afflicted with leprosy, but as soon as she touched the ark of Moses she was healed. She therefore took pity upon the child and saved him, despite the protests of her maidens. When she opened the ark she saw the *Shekhinah* next to Moses, and heard his cry, which sounded like that of a mature youngster (Ex. R. 1:23, 24). Pharaoh's astrologers had previously predicted that the savior of Israel would shortly be born and that he would be punished through water. After Moses was placed in the Nile, they told Pharaoh that the redeemer had already been cast into the water, whereupon Pharaoh rescinded his decree that the male children should be put to death (Ex. R. 1:24). Not only were all the future children saved, but even the 600,000 children cast into the Nile together with Moses were also rescued (Gen. R. 97:3). Moses refused to suck at the breast of Egyptian foster-mothers because the mouth which was destined to speak with the *Shekhinah* would not take unclean milk (Sot. 12b). His unique beauty captivated the royal household and he was adopted by Pharaoh's daughter, who constantly displayed her affection for him. Even Pharaoh played with the baby, who often took his crown and placed it upon his own head. The king's advisers were frightened by this behavior and they counseled Pharaoh to put him to death. However, Jethro, who was among the royal counselors, insisted on first testing the youngster. A gold vessel and a live coal were brought before Moses, and he was about to reach for the gold when the angel Gabriel came and deflected his hand to the hot coal. The baby placed a live coal into his mouth, burning his tongue, and as a result he acquired the impediment in his speech (Ex. R. 1:26).

Figure 6. The infant Moses challenging Pharaoh and undergoing the ordeal by fire. Illustration of the midrashic tradition from a manuscript of the Judeo-Persian paraphrase of Pentateuch stories by the 13th-century poet, Maula Shahin of Shiraz. Tabriz, 1686. Jerusalem, Israel Museum.

Moses not only sympathized with the sufferings of his brethren, but he also aided them in their tasks by himself preparing the clay for the bricks. He also assigned them responsibilities in accordance with their abilities so that the strong carried greater burdens while the weak discharged lesser tasks (Ex. R. 1:27). He slew the cruel Egyptian taskmaster only after the angels decreed his death since he had previously defiled the wife of one of the Hebrew slaves in his charge and subsequently sought to slay the husband. Moses killed the Egyptian either by means of the Divine Name or by his own physical strength. After Dathan and Abiram informed on Moses to Pharaoh, he was condemned to death, but the executioner's sword had no effect on him, since his neck became like a pillar of ivory (Ex. R. 1:28–31). Moses saved the daughters of Jethro after the shepherds had cast them into the well, and he also protected them from their immoral designs. Moses drew out only one bucketful and with this watered all the flock there assembled, since the water was blessed at his hands (Ex. R. 1:32). According to one tradition, Mose could marry Zipporah only after he agreed to Jethro's condition that one of their children be raised in Jethro's faith while the rest could be trained in the Hebraic tradition. Because of this agreement, Gershom was not circumcised, and on the way to Egypt Moses almost met his death because of this neglect (Ex. 4:24–26; Mekh., Amalek), but in the opinion of other sages (Mekh. *ibid.;* TJ, Ned. 3:14, 38b) Moses could not circumcise his second son Eliezer, because he had been born just prior to his departure for Egypt, and his only fault was that he did not do so immediately on reaching the resting place.

Before God confers greatness on a man he is first tested through small matters and then promoted to importance. Moses displayed his trustworthiness by leading the sheep into the wilderness in order to keep them from despoiling the fields of others. He then showed his mercy by carrying a young kid on his shoulders after it had exhausted itself by running to a pool of water (Ex. R. 2:2–3). God appeared to him in a burning bush to illustrate that the Jews were as indestructible as the bush which was not consumed by the flames (Ex. R. 2:5). Many reasons are given for Moses' initial hesitancy in accepting the mission of redeeming his brethren: he recoiled from the honor and prestige which would accrue to him for successfully completing the task (Tanḥ. va-Yikra, 3); he feared to trespass upon the domain of his elder brother whom he felt should be the redeemer (Ex. R. 3:16); he desired the redeemer to be God Himself rather than a mortal so that the redemption would be eternal (Ex. R. 3:4); he was angry because God had already deserted the children of Israel for 210 years and permitted many pious individuals to be slain by their Egyptian taskmasters (Mekh. SbY to 6:2).

The sages likewise were perplexed by Moses' seemingly disrespectful reply to God that since he had spoken to

Pharaoh the lot of his people had not improved (Ex. 5:22–23). Various explanations are given for the tone of Moses' lament: the taunts of Dathan and Abiram regarding his lack of success provoked Moses' anger (Ex. R. 6:2); Moses mistakenly thought that the redemption would entirely come about through the attribute of mercy and would therefore be instantaneous (Ex. R. 6:3); he felt that his generation of Israelites did not deserve the severe punishment of bondage; and he did not doubt that God would ultimately redeem His people, but he was grieved for those children who were being daily immured in the new buildings and would not be redeemed. The attribute of justice sought to strike Moses, but God protected him since He knew that Moses only spoke out of his love for his brethren (Ex. R. 5:22). The elders started to accompany Moses and Aaron to Pharaoh's palace (Ex. 3:18) but gradually stole away furtively, singly or in pairs, so that by the time the palace was reached only Moses and Aaron were left (Ex. R. 5:14). Despite the harsh messages which Moses delivered to Pharaoh, he constantly accorded him the respect due to royalty (Ex. R. 5:15; Zev. 102a). Moses executed all the plagues except for those connected with water and dust, since he had been saved through water and the dust had concealed the body of the Egyptian he slew (Ex. 2:12; Ex. R. 9:10; 10:7). When Moses announced the final plague, he did not state the exact time of its incidence, saying only that "about midnight" (Ex. 11:4) because he feared that Pharaoh's astrologers might miscalculate and declare him a liar (Ber. 4a). During the Exodus, while the masses thought only of taking the gold and silver of the Egyptians, Moses went and retrieved the coffin of Joseph which subsequently accompanied the Israelites in the desert (Mekh. 2, Proem. Sot. 13a).

Moses went up to Mount Sinai, enveloped by a cloud which sanctified him for receiving the Torah (Yoma 4a). After he ascended on high, the ministering angels contested the right of "one born of woman to receive the treasures of the Torah." Encouraged by the Almighty, Moses demonstrated to the angels that only mortals were subject to the Torah's regulations and therefore it was rightfully theirs. The angels thereupon became friendly with Moses, and each one revealed its secret to him (Shab. 89a). In abstaining from food during the 40 days on Mt. Sinai Moses acted as do the angels (BM 86b). He received instruction from God by day and reviewed the teachings at night (Ex. R. 47:8). Not only were the Bible, Mishnah, Talmud, and *aggadah* taught to Moses, but all interpretations that were destined to be propounded by future students were also revealed to him (Ex. R. 47:1). Before Moses ascended the mountain, he promised to return by midday of the 41st day. On that day Satan confused the world so that to the Israelites it appeared to be afternoon when it was actually still morning. Satan told them that Moses had died and would never return, whereupon the people made the Golden Calf (Shab. 89a). Moses broke the tablets, and made it appear that the Torah had not been given, to prevent the sinners from being punished (ARN[2] 2:5–6). God approved of this action (Shab. 87a) and when Moses realized that Israel's fate depended upon him and his prayers, he began to defend them (Ber. 32a). He argued that God had not enjoined the prohibition against idolatry upon the children of Israel since the singular and not the plural is used in the command (Ex. 20:3–5), and it applied only to him (Ex. R. 47:9; for the additional justifications set forth by Moses see *Golden Calf). Moses refused God's offer to make him the ancestor of a great nation since he feared that he would be accused of seeking only his glory and not that of the people (Ber. 32a).

God would not grant Moses' wish to behold all His glory since Moses had refused to look at him through the burning bush (Ber. 7a). He was hidden in the same cave which was later occupied by Elijah (I Kings 19:9–14). If there had been an aperture even as minute as the point of a needle, Moses would have been consumed by the passing divine light (Meg. 19b). Moses received only the reflection of this light, and from its radiance his face subsequently shone (Ex. R. 47:6). During this revelation, Moses was granted profound insight into the problem of theodicy (Ber. 7a). Afterward he was known as the master of Torah, wisdom, and prophecy (Meg. 13a) since he possessed 49 of the 50 divisions of wisdom (RH 21b). He was the greatest prophet among the Israelites (Deut. 34:10) although, according to one view, Balaam was almost his equal so that the heathen nations could not attribute their wickedness to the lack of the prophetic spirit (Sif. Deut. 357; SER 26:141–2; but cf. TJ, Sot. 5:8, 20d; Lev. R. 1:12–14). Moses insisted on giving a complete account of the materials collected for the Tabernacle since he overheard scoffers claiming that he had embezzled a portion of the gold and silver (Ex. R. 51:6). During the seven days of the dedication of the sanctuary, Moses officiated as the high priest. He was also considered the king of Israel during the 40-year sojourn in the desert. When Moses requested these two offices for a permanent heritage, he was told that the priesthood was already assigned to Aaron, while royalty was designated for David (Ex. R. 2:6).

Moses insisted that his sin of striking the rock be recorded in the Torah (Num. 20:11) so that future generations would not mistakenly ascribe other transgressions or faults to him (Sif. Deut. 26; Num. R. 19:12). The impatience of the people and the jeers of the scoffers were the cause of his smiting the rock in anger (Num. R. 19:9). In reality, God had long before decreed that Moses should not enter the Promised Land and Moses' offense in Kadesh was only a pretext so that He might not appear unjust. God explained to Moses that if he were not buried in the desert with the generation that left Egypt, people would mistakenly declare that the generation of the wilderness had no share in the world to come (Num. R. 19:13). Moses immediately obeyed God's command to avenge the Israelite people on the Midianites (Num. 31:2), although he knew that after it was fulfilled he would die (Num. R. 22:22). Before his death, Moses pleaded for the appointment of a successor who would successfully cope with the dissimilar temperaments of the people (Num. R. 21:2). Moses also requested that his successor lead his people into war, and not remain behind the troops as was the customary practice of gentile kings (Sif. Num. 139). Moses pleaded that the decree against his entering the Holy Land be rescinded so that he could share in the joy of his people after experiencing their sorrow (Deut. R. 11:10). However, God refused his repeated requests since the leader of the generation should remain with his followers, and the generation of Moses was buried in the wilderness (Num. R. 19:13); and because the time had come for Joshua to exercise his leadership (Deut. R., ed. S. Lieberman, pp. 48, 124).

Moses died at the kiss of God (Deut. R. 11:10; BB 17a) on the anniversary of his birth, Adar 7th (Tosef., Sof. 11:2). God himself buried Moses (Sot. 14a) in a grave which had been prepared for him since the eve of the Sabbath of creation (Pes. 54a). His tomb is opposite Beth-Peor to atone for the sin of the Israelites in worshiping the idol Peor (Num. 25:3). Nevertheless, his grave cannot be discovered, since to a person standing in the valley it looks as though it is on a mountain peak, whereas from the mountain peak it looks as though it is in the valley (Sot. 14a).

See also *Amram; *Jochebed; *Aaron; *Miriam; *Bezalel; and *Korah.

[A.Ro.]

IN MEDIEVAL JEWISH THOUGHT

All Jewish philosophers agree that the prophetic revelation of Moses was different from, and superior to, the prophecy (see *Prophets and Prophecy) of all other prophets. *Judah Halevi writes that Moses' prophecy came directly from God: He did not receive his prophecy while asleep or in a state between sleeping and waking, nor did he arrive at it through union with the active intellect (*Kuzari*, 1:87). The term "prophet" when applied to Moses and other prophets is, according to *Maimonides, amphibolous. In his discussion of prophecy in the *Guide of the Perplexed*, Maimonides states that he will allude to the prophecy of Moses only in order to contrast it with prophecy in general (*Guide*, 2:35). He spells out four distinctions between the prophecy of Moses and that of other prophets (Yad, Yesodei ha-Torah, 7:6; Comm. on Sanh. 10, 7th principle). The revelations of all the prophets, except for Moses, took place in dreams and visions (Num. 12:6); through the medium of an angel, and hence they prophesied in riddles and symbolic language (Num. 12:18); in a trance-like state (Gen. 15:12); and at intervals of varying duration according to God's choice. Moses, by contrast, received his prophetic message while fully awake; in nonsymbolic language; directly from God, rather than through the medium of an angel; and at the time of his own choosing (Num. 12:6–8; Ex. 33:11). It seems that these differences between the prophecy of Moses and that of other prophets can be reduced to one basic difference, namely, that imaginative faculty played no role in Moses' prophetic experience, while it played a major role in the case of the other prophets, prophecy being, according to Maimonides, "an overflow from God, through the intermediation of the active intellect, toward the rational faculty in the first place, and thereafter the imaginative faculty" (*Guide*, 2:36, see Abrabanel's commentary on this passage). He writes that while other prophets "can hear only in a dream of prophecy that God has spoken to him . . . Moses . . . heard Him from above the ark cover, from between the two cherubim, without action on the part of the imaginative faculty" (*Guide*, 2:45). Moses' prophetic experience, then, seems to have been dependent on the superior development of his rational faculty, and it is probable that according to Maimonides—although he does not say so explicitly—Moses attained union with the active intellect (see S. Pines (tr.), *Guide of the Perplexed* (1963), translator's introduction, lxxvii–xcii). J. Guttmann has suggested that according to Maimonides, Moses' prophecy differed from that of the other prophets insofar as it transcended "the natural order and was wholly due to a supernatural action of God," while the prophecies of the other prophets resulted from the development of their rational and imaginative faculties. In this way, Guttmann maintains, Maimonides "safeguards the uniqueness of biblical religion which Moses transmitted against the danger inherent in a naturalistic interpretation of prophecy" (Guttmann, Philosophies, 172). S. Atlas, on the other hand, interprets Maimonides as asserting that while Moses' prophetic experience did not depend on his imaginative faculty, it did depend to a large extent on the superior development of his rational faculty, and was hence not totally dependent on the supernatural action of God. However, he too maintains that in Maimonides' view there was an important element in Moses' prophetic experience—an element not common to the experiences of the other prophets—which was the result of God's creative will, namely, the giving of laws (Atlas, in HUCA, 25 (1954), 369–400). Medieval philosophers considered Moses' qualities of courage, modesty, and justice to be prerequisites for prophetic experience (see for example *Guide*, 2:38–40).

[D.KA.]

For Judah Loew b. Bazalel (the Maharal) of Prague (*Tiferet Yisrael* (1955), 64–67), Moses is a superhuman being occupying a midway position between the supernatural beings and humans. This is why he was able to be equally at home in heaven and on earth and this is hinted at in his name since the letter *mem* of *Moshe* is the middle letter of the alphabet. Samson Raphael Hirsch (Comm. to Ex. 24:1), on the other hand, denies any qualitative superiority to Moses. Very curious is the legend recorded by Israel Lipschuetz b. Gedaliah (*Tiferet Yisrael* to Kid. end, n. 77). A certain king, having heard of Moses' fame, sent a renowned painter to portray Moses' features. On the painter's return with the portrait the king showed it to his sages, who unanimously proclaimed that the features portrayed were those of a degenerate. The astonished king journeyed to the camp of Moses and observed for himself that the portrait did not lie. Moses admitted that the sages were right and that he had been given from birth many evil traits of character but that he had held them under control and succeeded in conquering them. This, the narrative concludes, was Moses' greatness, that, in spite of his tremendous handicaps, he managed to become the man of God. Various attempts have, in fact, been made by some rabbis to ban the further publication of this legend as a denigration of Moses' character.

The biblical commentators discuss why God arranged for Moses to be brought up by the daughter of Pharaoh. Abraham ibn Ezra (Comm. to Ex. 2:3) suggests that this was first to teach Moses courage and leadership, faculties he would not have been able to achieve if he had grown up among a slave people, and, secondly, so that Moses might have the respect of his people which he would not have had if he had grown up with them from infancy. Isaac Arama (*Akedat Yiẓḥak*, 43) understands the matter to belong to God's purpose that the tyrant king be defeated through a member of his own household. Naḥmanides (Comm. to Ex. 2:11) argues that Moses was brought up in Pharaoh's palace to accustom him to being in the royal presence, since it was his destiny to stand before Pharaoh to demand the release of the Israelites.

In the Kabbalah, too, there is great elevation of the character of Moses. On the verse: "And Moses went up to

Figure 7. Moses with the Decalogue in a miniature from an illuminated Hebrew manuscript, Troyes (?), France, c. 1280. Those around him are wearing medieval Jewish hats. London, British Museum, Add. Ms. 11639, fol. 741v.

God" (Ex. 19:3), the Zohar (II, 79b) remarks: "See the difference between Moses and all other human beings. When other human beings ascend it is to wealth or honor or power, but when Moses ascends what does Scripture say? 'And Moses went up to God.' Happy is his portion." The section of the Zohar known as *Ra'aya Meheimna,* "Faithful Shepherd," is in the form of mystical discourses conveyed to Simeon b. Yaḥai by Moses in heaven. Moses and Aaron on earth are, for the Zohar, the counterparts of the **Sefirot Neẓaḥ* and *Hod* (I, 21b–22a). The high mystical state of Moses is described in the Zohar as Moses having "intercourse" with the **Shekhinah,* whose "husband" he was. Moses was a reincarnation of Abel (*Sha'ar ha-Pesukim,* Exodus, beg.). Hence, like Abel, the first shepherd, he was a shepherd (*Avodat Yisrael* by Israel of Koznice, Exodus beg.). Godly men chose the occupation of shepherd because it kept them far from the cities where men are prone to sin and because it afforded them the opportunities of communing with God (Baḥya ibn Asher, Comm. to Ex. 3:1).

MODERN INTERPRETATIONS

*Aḥad Ha-Am begins his essay on Moses (*Al Parashat Derakhim*[3] 210–21) by stating that he remains unmoved by the speculations of scholars as to whether Moses really existed since the true hero is not the historical figure but the man who is portrayed in the Jewish tradition as the embodiment of the Jewish spirit. This Moses is neither a great military strategist nor an astute politician. Nor is his role primarily that of lawgiver in the accepted sense since the laws he gives are for the future ideal state still to be realized. Moses is rather the "master of the prophets," the highest example of the prophetic ideal as expressed in a human life. The prophet is ruthless in his pursuit of justice which is, for him, a categorical imperative brooking no opposition. Moses' vision is of the perfect society, of the what ought to be rather than the what is. Moses embarks on his prophetic career with a protest against injustice and oppression and devotes the rest of his life to his ideal. He hears the voice of God speaking to him in his heart urging him to become the deliverer of his downtrodden people. This God who speaks to him and to the people is not a tribal god but the God of all men, every one of whom is created in His image. Because his vision is unqualified Moses must die without entering the Promised Land. The prophet is too uncompromising to be the leader of the people in the stark realities of the actual human situation. The leadership must pass to another more capable of coming to terms with life as it is, even though this involves a diminution of the dream. Thus Moses is the symbol of Israel's divine discontent with the present. Like Moses, Israel learned to live only in the past and the future, its life a pilgrimage from past to future. For Israel as for Moses the present, as it falls short of the ideal, has no real existence.

Sigmund *Freud's *Moses and Monotheism* (1939) is an interpretation of Moses' work and character which has been widely discussed, though the majority of scholars reject Freud's anthropology and his views on biblical scholarship. According to Freud, Moses was not an Israelite but an Egyptian. The monotheism he taught was derived from a period of pure monotheism established during the reign of Ikhnaton. Following a hint thrown out by Sellin based on an obscure passage in the Book of Hosea, Freud believed that the Israelites, unable to accept Moses' new ideas, eventually murdered him. But Moses' monotheistic teachings lived on in the racial unconscious of the Israelites to reappear hundreds of years later in the monotheism of the prophets. The slaying of Moses repeated what, for Freud, was the sin of primitive man, the slaying of the primal father by his jealous sons. Because of this, monotheistic religion is haunted by guilt feelings and the need for atonement. Freud admits the speculative nature of his theory but feels that it is in accord with his ideas on how religion began and on man's needs for a father figure.

Martin *Buber in his book *Moses* accepts the basic historicity of Moses but makes a distinction between saga and history. The saga is not history but neither is it fiction. It follows in the footsteps of the historical events and describes the impact they had. Creative memory is at work in the saga. But the saga is not simply a matter of group psychology. We can get behind it to the actual historical events which made such an impact on the people that they could only explain these events as of divine power at work in them. It is not a case of "historization of myth" but of "mythization of history." At the same time, in the Moses saga, the "mythical" element is not a myth of the gods. The human figure is not transfigured, so that the element of sober historical recording is still present. Describing the God of Moses, Buber writes: "He is the One who brings His own out, He is their leader and advance guard; prince of the people, legislator and the sender of a great message. He acts on the level of history on the peoples and between the peoples. What He aims at and cares for is a people. He makes His demand that the people shall be entirely 'His' people, a 'holy' people; that means, a people whose entire life is hallowed by justice and loyalty, a people for God and for the world . . . That Moses experiences Him in this fashion and serves Him accordingly is what has set that man apart as a living and effective force at all times; and that is what places him thus apart in our own day, which possibly requires him more than any earlier day has ever done." [L.J.]

IN CHRISTIAN TRADITION

Moses is mentioned more often than any other biblical figure in the New Testament, which emphasizes the parallel between the ministries of Moses and Jesus (Matt. 8:4; 17:1–8; Mark 7:10; 9:2–8; 10:2–9). As Israel's lawgiver and liberator, Moses—according to Christian tradition—prefigures the ministry of Jesus and prophesies the coming of the Savior and the mediator of the new covenant. Moses is an example of deep faith in God (Heb. 11:23–29), and like Jesus, he encounters the people's incomprehension and hostility (Acts 7:17–44). Jesus, however, surpasses Moses in all respects. Unlike the face of Moses, that of Jesus is unveiled and his superior glory is spiritual (II Cor. 3:6–18). Moses appears as God's faithful servant, but Jesus is God's son (Heb. 3:5–6). Moses seals the covenant with the blood of animals, but the Messiah's covenant, which for Christians definitely supercedes the Mosaic Law, is sealed by his own sacrifice (Heb. 9:11–22). In addition, the events of the Exodus appear to the Church Fathers as typological events of Jesus' life; the passage through the Red Sea is the type of Salvation through baptism; and the water gushing out of the rock that Moses struck is a symbol of the Eucharist. [Ed.]

IN ISLAM

The personality and deeds of Mūsā (Moses) occupy an important place in the Koran. The events of his life, from the moment of his birth, are related at length. Indeed Nūḥ (*Noah), Ibrāhīm (*Abraham), and Moses were the first believers, and it was Moses who prophesied the coming of Muhammad, whose faith was that of Moses (Sura 7:140, 156; 42:11). At the same time of the decree of Firʿawn (Pharaoh) and his counselors, *Hāmām and Qārūn (Korah), Moses' life was endangered when he was placed in the ark. However, Āsiya (see *Pharaoh), the wife (!) of Firʿawn, pitied Moses, saved him, and brought him up in her house (26:17; 28:6–10). Muhammad adapts the biblical tale of Jacob's labor for Laban inserting its years as those of Moses' employment by Shuʿayb (Jethro) in order to gain the hand of his daughter (28:27). He also adds details from the *aggadah:* Moses refused to suckle at the breasts of Egyptian women (28:11); one of the believers at the court of Pharaoh attempted to save Moses (40:29); Allah hung the mountain over the people of Israel like a pail in order that they would accept the Torah (2:60, 87; 7:170); on the sending of the spies (see *Joshua b. Nun = Yūshaʿ); on Korah (Qārūn) and his treasures; and many similar details. The Koran also contains themes and figures which are unknown in the ancient literature, such as the tale of al-*Sāmirī, who casts the Golden Calf, and the journey of Moses and his servant to the end of the world (18:59–81; see below). Some of the tales about Moses are also mentioned in the poetry of *Umayya ibn Abi al-Ṣalt, and are embellished by Muslim legend, and interwoven with new legends. The biblical ʿImrān (Amram), husband of Yukhābid (Jochebed) and father of Moses and Aaron, is only mentioned in post-koranic literature. ʿImrān (Amram) of the Koran is the husband of Hannah (her name is not mentioned in the Koran, but in later works) and the father of Miriam (Maryam), the mother of Jesus (Sura 3, "The House of ʿImrān"). ʿImrān, the father of Moses, was one of Pharaoh's bodyguards; after the decree against the male children was issued, he did not leave the palace and did not have marital relations with his wife. A great bird, however, brought his wife Yukhābid to him, to the bedroom of Pharaoh, without drawing the attention of the bodyguards; she became pregnant and gave birth to Moses (al-Kisāʾī, 201). The ark of Moses had marvelous healing powers from which Pharaoh's daughter benefitted. The infant Moses was saved from the fiery furnace just as Abraham had been; Pharaoh examined the child by placing a plate of coals and a plate full of gold in front of him. Moses wished to touch the gold, but an angel diverted his hand and put a burning coal in his mouth, which caused him later to stammer. The sheep of Jethro gave birth to spotted and speckled lambs. The staff of Moses came from a tree which had grown in the Garden of Eden, and which he inherited from the prophets, from Adam via Jacob. The death of Moses is described as an event unparalleled in world history, particularly in the tales of ʿUmāra (Ms., fol. 23v). The number of pages devoted to Moses in the "Legends of the Prophets" emphasizes the many legends which have been circulated.

Moses' Journey. The tale of the journey of Moses and his servant (Sura 18:59–81) is a departure from the framework of the biblical tales and legends. Moses set out to find the confluence of the two seas. On the way the servant forgot the roasted fish which was to serve as their provisions. They encountered the prophet of Allah and Moses asked him for a sign which would teach him wisdom and lead him along the proper course. The prophet consented on the condition that he would not question the meaning of the events which would occur en route. They boarded a ship and the prophet drilled a hole in it. Moses wondered about this act, forgot his promise, and asked the prophet whether it was his intention to drown them. Continuing on their way, the prophet killed a youth; and when they reached a town whose inhabitants refused them hospitality, the prophet held up a fence which was about to collapse. The prophet then explained to Moses the meaning of his surprising actions. The ship, which was the property of poor men, was about to fall into the hands of a pirate king. The youth would have caused his upright parents to sin; in his place, an upright son was born. Under the fence there was a treasure, the property of orphans, which was discovered after a while.

Since this tale does not belong to the legends of Moses which were widespread in the Orient, some of the Muslim commentators attempted to explain that it did not refer to Moses son of ʿImrān, but to another Moses. Most of the commentators, however, uphold the traditional explanation; they also explain that the servant was Yūshaʿ b. Nūn. The name of the prophet whom Moses asked for guidance is al-Khaḍir (al-Khiḍr, "the Green One"). However, other names are also mentioned. Thaʿlabī (p. 188) reports in the name of *Wahb b. Munabbih that it was Irmiyā b. Ḥilfiyā (!). The principal outlines of the tale of the journey can be found in the epic Gilgamesh (see *Flood) and in the romance of Alexander the Great, as related in the Syrian sources. It closely corresponds to the Jewish legend about R. Joshua b. Levi who set out on a journey with the prophet Elijah. The Jewish tale is found in two almost identical versions, though with a change in the order of events. One was published by A. Jellinek (*Bet ha-Midrash*, 5 (1877)) and the other in *Ḥibbur Yafeh min ha-Yeshuʿah* by R. Nissim b. Jacob. The introduction to the Jewish tale is identical to that of the Koran, except that Moses is replaced by R. Joshua b. Levi and the prophet (al-Khaḍir) by the prophet Elijah. The details of the story also differ: Elijah kills the cow of poor men who had received him and his companion with hospitality. They later stay with a wealthy man who neither pays attention to them nor gives them anything to eat. Elijah, however, prayed and rebuilt the wall of his house, which was about to collapse. Elijah and R. Joshua again came to a place of wealthy men who were indifferent toward them. Nevertheless, Elijah blessed them that they all might become leaders. When, however, they came to a place of the poor who were hospitable to them, the blessing was that they should have one leader. Elijah explained that all his actions and words had been favorable to the poor. With the exception of the story of the wall which was about to collapse, the Jewish tale differs from the Muslim account in its details. [H.Z.H.]

IN THE ARTS

Of all the major biblical figures, not excepting David, Jacob, Joseph, and Solomon, Moses has inspired the largest amount of creative endeavor in literature, art, and music. Treatment of this figure also involves several associated themes, such as the Ten Plagues, the Exodus, and the Revelation on Sinai. By far the earliest literary work on the subject was *Exagoge* ("The Exodus from Egypt"), a drama by the second-century B.C.E. Alexandrian writer *Ezekiel (Ezekielos) the Poet, preserved as a fragment by the Church Father *Eusebius of Caesarea (modern editions by E. H. Gifford, 1903; and by J. Bloch, 1929). The first play known to have been written by a Jew, this was also the first recorded biblical drama. The characters who appear in it include Moses, Zipporah, Jethro, and an invented Chum. The *Exagoge*, an interesting example of late classical Greek theater, anticipates the miracle and mystery plays of the Middle Ages. In medieval drama, Moses figures in the *Ordo Prophetarum*, the French *Mistère du Viel Testament*, and in some of the English cycles: the *Ludus Coventriae* of Lincoln (*Moses and the Two Tablets*), the Towneley plays (*Pharaoh*), and the York series (*The Departure of the Israelites from Egypt*). Interest in the theme thereafter waned for a time. In the 16th century there were only a few works of note, such as a play by Diego Sanchez (c. 1530), and the *Meistersinger* Hans Sach's *Die Kintheit Mosi* (1553). Although Moses was one of the Old Testament heroes that appealed to Protestant writers of the 17th century, most of the works about him were of Catholic inspiration: one of the English *Stonyhurst Pageants* (c. 1625); *Exodus*, a neo-Latin sacred tragedy by Balthasar Crusius (1605); *Moïse sauvé* (1653), a tedious epic by Marc-Antoine de Gérard Saint-Amant; and *Pascha, of tede verlossingte Israëls uit Egypten* (1612), a five-act play by Joost van den Vondel.

In the 18th century, treatment was at first light, but more serious attention was given by writers of the last decades, particularly with the rise of the oratorio and musical drama. *The Plagues of Egypt* (London, 1708), an anonymous English poem, was followed by Poisson's one-act comedy, *La Déroute de Pharaon* (1718), and by texts for many musical compositions; notably Joannes Theodorus' neo-Latin drama *Aaron a Moyse fratre sacerdos inauguratus* (1730); Charles Jennens' *Israel in Egypt* (c. 1738), which served as libretto for Handel's well-known oratorio; and Benjamin Stillingfleet's *Moses and Zipporah* (1765). Three works of greater significance, all written at about the same time, were Hannah More's *Moses in the Bulrushes*, one of her *Sacred Dramas* (1782); Friedrich *Schiller's youthful epic, *Die Sendung Mosis* (1783); and Naphtali (Hartwig) *Wessely's 18-canto Hebrew epic, *Shirei Tiferet* (1782–1829). Wessely's poem, an account of the Exodus culminating in the giving of the Law at Sinai, betrays the influence of F. G. Klopstock's *Der Messias* (1748–73) and, in the spirit of the *Haskalah, presents Moses as a devout philosopher battling against fanaticism and ignorance. *Shirei Tiferet* was later translated into German (*Die Moseide*, 1795) and part into French (1815).

A dramatic revival of literary interest in the theme took place from the first decade of the 19th century, possibly as a result of the political and social upheavals of the age. Among the earlier works were August Klingmann's five-act drama, *Moses* (1812); David Lyndsay's *The Plague of Darkness* and *The Last Plague* (in *Drama of the Ancient World*, 1822); and Antonio Maria Robiola's Italian verse epic, *Il Mosè* (1823). Moses was the hero of several poetic compositions by French writers, beginning with *Les bergères de Madian, ou La jeunesse de Moise* (1779–80) by Stéphanie Félicité Ducrest de Saint-Aubin, countess de Genlis, which was translated into Hebrew (1834). In Alfred de Vigny's "Moïse" (*Poèmes antiques et modernes*, 1826), the Lawgiver is a tragic, weary figure, pleading with God on Nebo for release from his consuming task. He is also the central character in three other French works: François René de Chateaubriand's verse tragedy, *Moïse* (1836); a

24-canto poem of the same title (1850) by Ambroise Anatole de Montesquiou-Fézensac; and Victor Hugo's brief poem, "Le Temple" (in *La Legende des Siecles*, 1859[1]), which is based on Exodus 31:1–6. Elsewhere, Imre Madách wrote the drama, *Mózes* (1860), where the Hebrew Exodus was reinterpreted in terms of the Hungarian struggle for liberation. During the 19th century, Jewish authors also found inspiration in the biblical and rabbinic accounts of the life of Moses. Solomon Ludwig *Steinheim wrote the story *Sinai* (1823); Isaac Candia published the Hebrew play, *Toledot Moshe* (1829); and Moritz Rappaport was the author of a German epic poem, *Mose* (1842). The U.S. dramatist Samuel B. H. *Judah wrote *The Maid of Midian*, a biblical tragedy that was never staged because of the writer's sacrilegious treatment of the slaying of the Midianite captives (Num. 31:2–18). Contrasting sharply with this approach was the reverence expressed by *Heine in his late *Gestaendnisse* ("Confessions," 1854)—"How small Sinai appears when Moses stands upon it!" According to Heine the Lawgiver was an artist on a colossal scale, who built "human pyramids and human obelisks" and fashioned "a great, holy, and eternal people" out of a poor shepherd clan that would serve as a model for all other nations.

Literary Works by 20th-Century Non-Jewish Writers. Verse inspired by the life and career of Moses includes S. D. Polevaya's Russian biblical poem *Iskhod* (1913), Rainer Maria Rilke's *Der Tod Moses*, and *Moysey* (1922; Eng. 1938), a poem in Ukrainian by Ivan Franko. The yield has been richer in fiction, especially from the years following World War I when a number of novels were written on the theme. During World War II Zora Neale Hurston published *The Man of the Mountain* (1941; U.S. ed., *Moses*) and the U.S. novelist William George Hardy produced *All the Trumpets Sounded* (1942). Among novels that appeared during the postwar era were Dorothy Clarke Wildon's *Prince of Egypt* (1949); the Polish Catholic Dobraczyński's *Pustynia* (1957; German ed. *Die Wueste*, 1957); and the Hungarian writer János Kodolányi's *Az égő csipkebokor* ("The Burning Bush," 1957). Moses was also the hero of a Danish trilogy by Poul Hoffmann: *Den braendende tornebusk* (1961; *The Burning Bush*, 1961); *Den evige ild* (1961; *The Eternal Fire*, 1962); and *Kobberslangen* (1958; *The Brazen Serpent*, 1963). There are several treatments of Moses in modern drama. Earlier plays of the 20th century include Henry R. C. Dobbs' *Korah* (1903); five-act dramas, both entitled *Moses*, by Karl Hauptmann (1906) and Viktor Hahn (1907); and Oskar Kokoschka's *Der brennende Dornbusch* (1911); the Czech author Stanislav Lom wrote the drama *Vůdce* (1916; *The Leader*, 1917). The Nietzsche-an idea of the superman which had inspired Isaac *Rosenberg's remarkable short drama *Moses* (1916) inspired first a play by Lawrence Langner (1924), who treated the story as a myth on which to develop modern theories, and later Christopher Fry's *The Firstborn* (1946), in which Moses is again divested of his biblical qualities. Fry transforms his central character into an Egyptian military hero torn between idealism and reality, who finds himself providing the impetus for the Hebrews' liberation movement.

20th-Century Jewish Writers. Some of the most powerful and significant literary treatments of Moses in the 20th century have, understandably, been written by Jews. Max Donkhin published the five-act Russian drama, *Moysey* (1901), and Israel *Zangwill's "Moses and Jesus" (in *Blind Children*, 1903) records the imaginary encounter and bitter dialogue of the protagonists. Angiolo *Orvieto's dramatic poem *Mosè* (1905) was later set to music by his fellow-Italian G. Orefice; and Naomi Nunes Carvalho wrote three dialogues involving Moses (in *Vox Humana*, 1912). Other literary treatments include the Czech play *Mojzis* (1919), by Eduard *Leda, and Markus Gottfried's Hebrew epic, *Moshe*, published in the same year. After World War I, the subject was treated by a number of eminent Jewish authors in various genres. Midrashic legends were reworked by Rudolf *Kayser (*Moses Tod*, 1921) and Edmond *Fleg (*Moise reconté par les Sages*, 1925; Eng. *The Life of Moses*, 1928); and there were narrative works in Hebrew by David *Frischmann (*"Sinai,"* in *Ba-Midbar*, 1923) and Ḥayyim *Hazaz—who showed a modern approach in *Ḥatan Damim* (1925; Eng. tr. by I. M. Lask, *Bridegroom of Blood*). Three other novels of the interwar years were Lina Eckenstein's *Tutankh-Aten; a Story of the Past* (1924), a fictionalized history; Louis *Untermeyer's *Moses* (1928); and *Fertzig Yohr in Midbor* (1934), a Yiddish work by Saul Saphire. The U.S. poet Robert Nathan's "Moses on Nebo" (in *A Winter Tide*, 1940) presented the sad vision of Israel's millennial wanderings; Károly *Pap's *Mózes* was staged by the Budapest Jewish Theater just before the author's deportation in 1944. Konrad Bercovici's *The Exodus* (1947) was probably the first postwar attempt to recreate the Bible story in U.S. fiction. It was followed by many new treatments, including *Moyshe* (1951; *Moses*, 1951), one of the best-known Yiddish novels of Sholem *Asch, and two Hebrew novels by Israel writers: Ben-Zion Firer's *Moshe* (1959) and Y. Shurun's *Ḥalom Leil Setav* ("Dream of an Autumn Night," 1960). Other works in the same genre have been written by Howard *Fast (*Moses, Prince of Egypt*, 1958) and the Dutch author Manuel van *Loggem (*Mozes, de wording van een volk*, 1947, 1960[2]).

In Art. Together with David, Jacob, and Samson, Moses is one of the most popular Old Testament figures in art. The medieval church considered him both a type of the Messiah and one of the prophets who foretold his coming. In early Christian art until the end of the Carolingian period, Moses was often represented as a beardless youth holding a rod. He was later conceived in the form in which he still lives in popular imagination: as a patriarchal figure with a flowing, double-pointed beard, clasping the Tablets of the Law. Two horns were shown protruding from his head, because the Latin (Vulgate) translation of the Bible used during the Middle Ages mistranslated the verb "sent forth beams" as "horns" (*karan*, קרן) in Exodus 34:35. There are medieval sculptures of Moses at Chartres and elsewhere, and a Renaissance figure by Donatello in the Campanile at Florence. The most striking examples are the horned figure by Claus Sluter (1406) for the Well of the Prophets (or Well of Moses) at Dijon, France, and the horned statue by Michelangelo at San Pietro in Vincoli, Rome. This work, the most famous portrayal of Moses in art, was originally intended for the mausoleum of Pope Julius II. Many art cycles relate the various episodes in the life of Moses. Among the earliest is a Jewish source, the third-century frescoes from the synagogue at *Dura-Europos.

Figure 8. "Moses" by Giovanni Pisano (c. 1250–1330), incorporating the standard Christian misinterpretation of Moses with horns. Siena, Museo dell' Opera Metropolitana.

Fuller cycles appear in Italy after the fifth century, such as the mosaics at Santa Maria Maggiore, Rome. There is a portrayal of the early life of Moses carved in ivory relief (Lipsanotheca, Brescia). A modern cycle of paintings, "Moses" (1924), was executed by the artist Uriel *Birnbaum.

Scenes from the life of Moses figure in many famous manuscripts, such as the sixth-century Vienna Genesis, the seventh-century Ashburnham Pentateuch, the ninth-century Bible of Charles the Bald, the 12th-century *Hortus Deliciarum* and Admont Bible, the 13th-century St. Louis Psalter, and the 14th-century Queen Mary Psalter. They are also found in medieval Hebrew manuscripts. Illustrations of the Exodus played a major part in the adornment of Passover **Haggadot*. There are also illuminations in German *maḥzorim* and other manuscripts. The *Haggadot* also include illustrations to a number of midrashic legends, such as the tale of the infant Moses who took Pharaoh's crown from his head and placed it on his own (Ex. R. 1:26). An episode from the same legend is treated in paintings by Giorgione (Uffizi Gallery, Florence) and Nicolas Poussin (Paris, Louvre). Other legends depicted include the petrification of Moses' neck when he was sentenced to be executed for killing the Egyptian (Ex. R. 1:28–31) and Pharaoh bathing in the blood of Israelite children as a cure for leprosy (Ex. R. 1:34). Scenes from the life of Moses also appear in mosaics at St. Mark's, Venice. Two scenes from the Exodus appear on the wings to the triptych of the Last Supper by Dirk Bouts (St. Pierre, Louvain): the paschal feast eaten by the Israelites before their departure from Egypt (a prefiguration of the Last Supper), and the gathering of the manna. The life of Moses inspired many frescoes of the Italian Renaissance. Benozzo Gozzoli dealt with the subject in frescoes at the Campo Santo, Pisa, and there are frescoes in the Sistine Chapel of the Vatican by Botticelli, Pinturicio, and Signorelli. The Exodus was also treated in the Vatican frescoes of the school of Raphael. In the Brera Gallery, Milan, there is a series of paintings by Bernardino Luini that depict scenes from the Exodus, including the crossing of the Red Sea. In his murals for the School of San Rocco, Venice, Tintoretto painted "The Rain of Manna," "Moses Striking the Rock," and "The Raising of the Serpent in the Wilderness" with his usual boldness and employment of violent contrasts of light and darkness. More than any other painter, Nicolas Poussin was haunted by the figure of Moses. He painted a larger number of canvases, forming an almost complete cycle of the lawgiver's life. Among them are "Moses and the Burning Bush" (Copenhagen Museum), "The Rain of Manna," "Moses Striking the Rock" (a subject he treated seven times), "The Spies Carrying the Cluster of Grapes" (Louvre), and "The Dance Around the Golden Calf" (National Gallery, London). In the 20th century, the figure of Moses has interested *Chagall and Ben-Zion who have both painted scenes from his life.

Figure 9. "The Finding of Moses," by Paolo Veronese, c. 1570. Oil on canvas, 23×17½ in. (57×44 cm.). Washington, D.C., National Gallery of Art.

Some individual episodes call for more detailed consideration. The finding of Moses, Moses and the burning bush, Moses striking the rock, and the giving of the Law are the subjects which have most interested artists. The finding of Moses (Ex. 2:5–10) was painted with elegance by the Venetian artist Paolo Veronese (two versions in the Hermitage and Prado). There is also a painting of this subject by *Rembrandt (Johnson Collection, Philadelphia). Jochebed, the mother of Moses, and her infant son are the subject of a tender family group by the English artist Simeon *Solomon. Moses and the burning bush (Ex. 3:1–14) occasionally appeared in early Christian art, but this subject is particularly associated with the popularity of the Marial cult in the Middle Ages. The burning bush was held to symbolize virgin birth, in that the virgin was penetrated but not consumed by the flames of the Holy Spirit. In medieval art Mary is therefore represented as rising out of the bush which burns at her feet. An example of the Marial interpretation is a major work of the 15th-century Provençal school, "The Coronation of the Virgin" by Enguerrand Charenton (Hospice of Villeneuve-les-Avignon). There is a more traditional representation of the burning bush episode in an engraving by Hans Holbein the younger. The ten plagues of Egypt (Ex. 7–12) are sometimes represented by the last plague, the slaying of the firstborn. There is a treatment of this subject by the English landscape painter J. M. W. Turner in the National Gallery, London. In one of the many illustrations to the Bible executed by Paul Gustave Doré, Pharaoh, overwhelmed by the disaster, implores Moses to lead the Israelites out of Egypt. The crossing of the Red Sea (Ex. 12–15) often appears in Byzantine manuscripts. There is a painting of this subject by the German Renaissance artist Lucas Cranach (Pinakothek, Munich), who also depicted Miriam's dance of triumph (Ex. 15:20–21; Augsburg Gallery). Moses striking the rock (Ex. 17:1–7; Num. 10:1–3) was one of the most popular subjects in early Christian art, where it is found in the murals of the catacombs, on Roman sarcophagi, and on gilded glass. Another Holbein engraving shows the Israelites gathering the manna; while Moses is seen with his hands supported by Aaron and Hur in a painting of the battle with Amalek (Ex. 17:8–16) by the English artist Sir John Millais. The giving of the Law (Ex. 20:1–18) appears on early Christian sarcophagi and in medieval art. Apart from the above-mentioned statue by Michelangelo, the most famous treatment of this episode is the painting by Rembrandt (Berlin Museum) of Moses breaking the tablets (Ex. 32:19). The raising of the serpent in the wilderness (Num. 21:6–9) was a popular subject in the Middle Ages and Renaissance, being understood as a prefiguration of the raising of the cross. The subject also lent itself to the dramatic, convoluted compositions of baroque artists. There is a painting by Rubens in the National Gallery, London, and one by his pupil, Anthony Van Dyck in the Prado. The death of Moses (Deut. 34) is depicted in a watercolor by William *Blake in accordance with a legend that, when Moses died, Satan tried to snatch his soul but was warded off by St. Michael's lance.

The lawgiver's brother Aaron is shown clad in the long robes of a high priest, a stone-studded breastplate on his chest and a turban or tiara on his head. He carries his flowering rod or censer, signifying priesthood. The revolt of Korah against Moses and Aaron (Num. 16) and the tragic fate that overtakes the rebels form the subject of an illustration by Jean Fouquet to the *Jewish Antiquities* of Josephus (Bibliothèque Nationale, Paris). The medieval Church thought of the rebels as heretics; on the other hand, the papacy associated Aaron with itself and for this reason Botticelli was commissioned to include the episode in his frescoes for the Sistine Chapel in the Vatican. [Ed.]

In Music. The story of Moses, interwoven with that of the Israelites, has also inspired many musical compositions from the Renaissance era onward, as well as Jewish and other folk songs. The following survey lists selected settings of texts and episodes from the Pentateuch, including even the relatively few which do not mention Moses himself. (1) Oratorios, Operas, Cantatas, and

Choral Works: Jachet van Berchem, *Locutus est Dominus ad Moysen; Stetit Moyses coram Pharaone* (motets, printed 1538–59); Claudio Monteverdi, *Audi coelum* (motets, added to the *Vesperae* of 1610); Giovanni Paolo Colonna, *Mosé legato di Dio e liberatore del popolo ebreo* (oratorio, 1686); Giovanni Battista Bassani, *Mosé risorto dalle acque* (oratorio, 1694); Antonio Vivaldi, *Moyses Deus Pharaonis* (oratorio, 1714; libretto only preserved); Johann Adolf Hasse (1699–1783), *Serpentes in deserto* (oratorio; the authenticity of another oratorio, *Mosé,* is doubtful); Nicolo Porpora (1686–1768), *Israel ab Aegyptiis liberatus* (oratorio); Georg Friedrich Handel, *Israel in Egypt* (oratorio)—text compiled by Charles Jennens, first performed in London at the King's Theatre, April, 4, 1739. This is one of Handel's major compositions and ranks among the outstanding works in the genre. Built mainly on the expression of the chorus, symbolizing the people of Israel, it reaches its climax with its description of the crossing of the Red Sea and in the "Song of Triumph"; Carl Philipp Emanuel Bach, *Die Israeliten in der Wueste* (oratorio, text by Schiebeler, printed by the composer in Hamburg, 1775, and first performed in Breslau, 1798); François Giroust, *Le Mont-Sinai ou Le Décalogue* (oratorio, Latin text, 1785); Johann Christoph Friedrich Bach, *Mosis Mutter und ihre Tochter* (duodrama, 1788); Giovanni Paisello (1740–1816), *Mosé in Egitto* (cantata for three voices); Konradin Kreutzer, *Die Sendung Mosis* (oratorio, 1814); Gioacchino Rossini, *Mosé in Egitto* (opera, text by Léon Tottola, premiere in Italian at Naples, 1818)—The revised version in French, *Moïse,* first performed in Paris (1827), included the famous "Prayer of Moses" which was one of the favorite subjects for fantasias, variations, and arrangements throughout the 19th century. The plot is that of a typical grand opera, with an interwoven dramatic love story not found in the biblical text; Franz Schubert, *Miriams Siegesgesang* (for soprano solo, mixed choir, and piano, opus 136; text by Franz Grillparzer, 1828); Karl Loewe, *Die eherne Schlange* (cantata for men's choir a capella, 1834); Adolf Bernhard *Marx, *Moses* (oratorio, 1841); Félicien David, *Moïse au Sinai* ("ode symphonique," i.e., oratorio, 1846); Camille Saint-Saëns, *Moïse sauvé des eaux* (cantata, text by Victor Hugo, c. 1851); Anton *Berlijn, *Moses auf Nebo* (oratorio) Anton *Rubinstein, *Moses* (oratorio, 1892); Marcus *Hast, *The Death of Moses* (oratorio, 1897); Jules Massenet, *La terre promise* (oratorio, 1900); Bernard Rogers, *The Exodus* (cantata, 1932); Arnold *Schoenberg, *Moses und Aaron* (opera, text by the composer, two acts completed in 1932; composition resumed in 1951; unfinished)—*Moses und Aaron* was first performed, in concert form, as a radio broadcast from Hamburg (first two acts, 1954); and was first staged in Zurich (June 6, 1957). In this highly philosophical work, the composer expresses the conflict between the Lawgiver, who cannot communicate his vision to the people (Moses = Schoenberg himself?), the weak and wavering people, and the glib mediator (Aaron = the critics, conventional composers?). See K. Woerner, *Gotteswort und Magie: die Oper Moses und Aron* [sic] (1959); D. Newlin, *Yuval I* (1968), 204–20; Darius Milhaud, *Opus Americanum 2,* op. 219 (orchestral suite, originally composed as a ballet, *The Man of Midian,* for the Ballet Theater (1940, not produced) and first performed as an orchestral suite, 1940); Wadi'a Sabrá (1876–1952), Lebanese Maronite composer, *Le chant de Moïse* (oratorio); Roger Vuataz, *Moïse* (oratorio for five reciters, soprano, choir, and orchestra, 1947); Jacob *Weinberg, *The Life of Moses* (oratorio, 1955); Josef Tal, *Exodus* (first version, for piano and drums, as "choreographic poem" for the dancer Deborah Bertonoff; second version ("Exodus I"), for baritone and orchestra (1945/46); third version ("Exodus II"), electronic composition, including processed human voices (1958/59); the first electronic work produced in Israel). (2) Jewish Folk Tradition. Among the musical notations made by *Obadiah the (Norman) Proselyte (11th–12th centuries) there is a setting of a *piyyut* in honor of Moses, *Mi al Har Ḥorev ha-Amidi* (see illus. in col. 1307–8). Jewish folk-song tradition contains a large number of songs about Moses, such as *Yismaḥ Moshe,* found in almost all communities; the religious Ladino songs, e.g., *Cantar vos quiero un mahase* (on the birth of Moses) and *A catorce era del mes* (on the Exodus); and the epic Aramaic songs of the Jews of *Kurdistan about Moses and Pharaoh's daughter, the battle between Israel and Amalek, and the death of Moses. Many of these songs are sung on Shavuot or Simḥat Torah. Among modern Israel folk songs are Yedidyah *Admon's *U-Moshe Hikkah al Ẓur,* and two children's songs, *Benei Yisrael Po Kullanu* (Joel *Engel, after a Yemenite

Figure 10. Moses killing the Egyptian, in a detail from a 13th-century icon, thought to be from Constantinople. Sinai Peninsula, Monastery of St. Catherine, Icon 359.

melody) and *Dumam Shatah Tevah Ketannah* (K. Y. Silman, after an East Ashkenazi melody). Yehuda *Sharett's setting of the *Haggadah ("Nusaḥ Yagur")* is both a functional "liturgy" for kibbutz use and an oratorio. (3) Other Folk-Song Traditions. While a few songs about Moses and the Exodus exist in older Christian music, the most prominent examples can be found in the Afro-American spirituals—notably the powerful *Go Down Moses* ("When Israel was in Egypt land—let my people go!"), which has become an international favorite. The Palestinian Arab tradition of mass pilgrimage to the legendary tomb of Moses on the festival of Nebi Musa has given rise to its own repertory of mass chants. One of these, *Ya ḥalili ya ḥabibi, ya ḥawaja Musa,* has become an Israel *Hora*-song. [B.B.]

Bibliography: H. Gressmann, *Mose und seine Zeit* (1913); P. Volz, *Mose und seine Werk* (1932[2]); F. James, *Personalities of the Old Testament* (1939), 1–44; M. Buber, *Moses* (Eng., 1947); Kaufmann Y., Toledot, 2 (1947); Kaufmann Y., Religion, 212–44; J. Griffiths, in JNES, 12 (1953), 225ff.; G. von Rad, *Old Testament Theology,* 1 (1962), 289ff.; E. Osswald, *Das Bild des Mose* (1962); H. H. Rowley, *Men of God* (1963), 1ff.; W. Helck, in: VT, 15 (1965), 48; H. Schmid, *Mose, Ueberlieferung und Geschichte* (1968); S. Loewenstamm, in: EM, 5 (1968), 482–95; W. F. Albright, *Yahweh and the Gods of Canaan* (1968); A. Cody, *A History of the Old Testament Priesthood* (1969), 39ff. In Hellenistic Literature: J. Freudenthal, *Hellenistische Studien,* 1–2 (1878); F. Reinach, *Textes d'auteurs grecs et romains relatifs au judaisme* (1895); I. Lévy, *La Légende de Pythagore de Grèce en Palestine* (1927), 137–53; K. Preisendanz (ed.), *Papyri Graecae Magicae,* 2 vols. (1928–31); E. R. Goodenough, *By Light, Light . . .* (1935), 181–234, 289–91; M. Braun, *History and Romance in Graeco-Oriental Literature* (1938); G. Vermés, *Moïse, L'Homme de l'Alliance* (1955); Alon, Meḥkarim, 1 (1957), 196–7; I. Guttman, *Ha-Sifrut ha-Yehudit ha-Hellenistit,* 2 vols. (1958–63); E. R. Dodds, in: *Entretiens sur l'Antiquité classique* (1966), 1–32; B. Z. Wacholder, *Nicolaus of Damascus* (1962), 57–58; R. Le Deaut, in: *Biblica,* 45 (1964), 198–219; M. Hengel, *Judentum und Hellenismus* (1969); J. G. Gayer, in: JTS, 20 (1969), 245–8; M. Stern, in: S. Safrai et al. (eds.), *Sefer . . . G. Alon* (1970), 169–91; R. Williamson, *Philo and the Epistle to the Hebrews* (1970). In the Aggadah: R. Bloch, in: *Cahiers Sioniens,* 8 (1954), 211–85; S. E. Loewenstamm, in: *Tarbiz,* 27 (1958), 142–57; G. Vermes, *Scripture and Tradition in Judaism* (1961), 178–90. Medieval Jewish Thought: Y. Levinger, in: *Fourth World Congress of Jewish Studies, Papers,* 2 (1968), 335–9 (Heb.), 20 (Eng. summ.); A. Reines, in: HUCA, 33 (1962), 221–53; 34 (1963), 195–215. In Christian Tradition: J. Daniélou, *Sacramentum futuri* (1950), 129–200; P. Demann, in: *Cahiers Sioniens,* 8 (1954), 189–244; DBI, Supplement, 5 (1957), 1335–37. In Islam: Ṭabarī, *Ta'arīkh,* 1 (1357 A. H.), 270–312; ʿUmāra, Ms. fol. 15v.–24v.; Thaʿlabī, *Qiṣaṣ* (1356 A.H.), 140–210; Kisāʾī, *Qiṣaṣ* (1356 A.H.), 194–240; H. Speyer, *Die biblischen Erzaehlungen im Qoran* (1961), 225–363; J. W. Hirschberg, *Juedische und christliche Lehren im vor- und fruehislamischen Arabien* (1939), 129–34. Moses' Journey: Ṭabarī, *Ta'arīkh,* 1 (1357 A.H.), 256–64; Ṭabarī, *Tafsīr,* 15 (1328 A.H.), 171–6, 16 (1328 A.H.), 2–7; ʿUmara Ms. fol. 3v–18v; Thaʿlabī, *Qiṣaṣ* (1356 A.H.), 183–94; Kisāʾi, *Qiṣaṣ* (1356

A.H.), 230–3; Zamakhsharī, 1 (1343 A.H.), 574–6; A. Jellinek (ed.), *Bet ha-Midrash*, 5 (1877), 133–5; J. Obermann, *Studies in Islam and Judaism* (1933), 10–13; H. Z. Hirschberg (ed. and tr.), *Ḥibbur Yafe me-ha-Yeshu'ah* (1969²), introd. 51, 61–62, tr. 6–8; EIS, s.v. *Khaḍir*. IN ARTS: M. Roston, *Biblical Drama in England* (1968), index; E. Becker, *Das Quellwunder des Moses in der altchristlichen Kunst* (1909); L. Réau, *Iconographie de l'Art chrétien*, 2 pt., 1 (1957), 175–216; R. Mellinkoff, *The Horned Moses in Medieval Art and Thought* (1971).

MOSES, ASSUMPTION OF. Title of the incomplete text of an apocryphal writing, which consists, largely, of an address, in the form of a prophecy, by Moses to his successor, Joshua. The substance of the prophecy concerns the future fate of Israel and the End of Days. Only scant attention is paid to the epochs of the Judges and Kings, the onslaught of Nebuchadnezzar and the Babylonian Exile, and to the return of the exiles. However, with discussion of the Hasmonean period the story becomes considerably more detailed.

The defiling of the altar in the temple is described in detail, i.e., blemished offerings which were presented by slaves, the offspring of slaves, rather than by priests (5:4). It is unclear whether this is a specific reference to John Hyrcanus (cf. Jos., Ant. 13:288–92). Unmistakable, however, is the allusion to the Hasmoneans in the mention of the reunion of the kingdom with the priesthood (6:1). The subsequent cruel rule of "an insolent king . . . who will not be of the race of the priests" (6:2) is depicted in detail, and its length (34 years) is specified (6:6). The prophecy continues: "And he shall beget children (who) succeeding him shall rule for shorter periods" (6:7); cohorts will assault and a powerful king of the west will conquer the country (6:8). It is at this point that the prophecy of political events ends, and 7:1 reads: "And when this is done the times shall be ended . . ." The succeeding sequence describes: the hypocrisy of the ruling class; the chaos of the persecutions (in chap. 8, which contains traces of the era of Domitian, although this may be a later interpolation); the appearance of a Levite, Taxo, who with his seven sons prefers death to active resistance (9); and a poetic representation of the intervention of God and of the victory of Israel over "the eagle" (an obvious reference to Rome). The text ends, abruptly, with the reply of Joshua (11), and with the final answer of Moses.

The work was discovered as a palimpsest in the Ambrosiana library in Milan by M. Ceriani, the Italian orientalist, and first published in 1861. The present Latin version of the text has remained untouched by Christian annotators. It is based upon a Greek original, although whether the first version was in Hebrew or in Aramaic is unknown. The contents of chapter one strongly suggest that the work originated in the first century, although some details in the following chapters may indicate another date (c. 130). It is probable that "the insolent king" referred to is Herod the Great, the length of whose reign may have corresponded to the 34 years mentioned in the text (6:6). It is difficult to agree with opinions which maintain that the passage refers to Alexander Yannai and Pompey and that the reign of 34 years was inserted later. If the Herodian interpretation is correct, then the work was composed after the campaign of *Quintilus Varus in 4 B.C.E. (perhaps referred to in 6:8), i.e., during the rule of Herod's sons. Allusions in the text which refer to events after that period are obscure. A study by J. Licht (see bibl.) proposes a Hasmonean date for the basic elements of the work, together with a reworking and adaptation by a post-Herodian editor. The present title of the manuscript is based on a tradition of the Church Fathers that a work of this name existed in ancient times. Clement of Alexandria, Didymus, and Origen, for example, claimed that the mention of the struggle between the archangel Michael and Satan for the body of Moses, in Jude 5:9, is based upon a work entitled the *Assumptio* or *Ascensio Moysis (Mosis)*. However, although the lost sections of the work probably contained descriptions of the death of Moses and his ascent to heaven, this story is not mentioned in the portion of the text quoted by Gelasius of Cyzicus in his "History of the Council of Nicaea" as being taken from the Ἀνάληψις Μωυσέως ("The Ascension of Moses"). Neither is any reference made to the ascent of Moses in the Ceriani fragment. Indeed a more appropriate title for the extant palimpsest would appear to be *The Testament of Moses* (which is also mentioned as a distinct work in ancient Church documents); especially in light of the fact that reference is made in the present text (1:10) to Deuteronomy 31:7–8. The words "*Liber Profetiae Moysis*" in the text itself (1:5) could, however, indicate that this may have been its original title. Whatever the case, the present version of the text is probably the result of an amalgamation between an original work, *Testamentum Moses* (or *Liber Profetiae Moysis*), and a later composition, the *Assumptio Moysis*.

Bibliography: E. Kautzsch, *Apokryphen und Pseudepigraphen des Alten Testaments*, 2 (1900), 311–31; Kamenetzki, in: *Ha-Shilo'aḥ*, 15 (1905), 38–50; Beer, in: Herzog-Hauck, 16 (1905); O. Holtzmann, *Neutestamentliche Zeitgeschichte* (1906²), 301–3; Schuerer, Gesch, 3 (1909⁴), 294–305; Charles, Apocrypha, 2 (1913), 407–24; Licht, in: JJS, 12 (1961), 95–105.

[W.M./ED.]

MOSES, BLESSING OF. Deuteronomy 33 is presented as Moses' blessing of the tribes of Israel shortly before his death, and it is traditionally considered a prophecy of future conditions. The critical view, however, is not that the poem is actually Mosaic, for it describes Israel after the conquest, when the tribes had settled in Canaan. It is of uncertain date. It has been dated on orthographic grounds to the 11th century B.C.E., although it may have been written down in the tenth century (Cross and Freedman). This dating also fits the political and social conditions described: Judah was oppressed by the Philistines, and Reuben, suffering from Ammonite encroachment, had practically disappeared; Simeon had vanished as an ethnic entity, and Dan had already moved north. Others date the poem later. Driver places it either shortly after the reign of Jeroboam I or in the middle of the reign of Jeroboam II. The poem is probably of northern origin, for Judah is portrayed as weak and separated from his brothers, while Joseph, who has the longest and most lavish blessing, is called *nezir 'eḥaw*—the "prince" or "distinguished one" of his brothers. The poem is divided into two parts: the framework and the body. The framework consists of (a) the exordium (verses 2–5) telling how God appeared from Sinai, gave Israel a law through Moses, and established himself as king in their midst (possibly verse 5 tells of the foundation of human kingship in Israel), and (b) the hymnic conclusion (verses 26–29) lauding God's glory and might, and celebrating Israel's happiness, prosperity, and security under God's protection. The body (verses 6–25) consists of 11 eulogistic sayings characterizing the tribes or praying for their well-being (Simeon is not mentioned). The sayings themselves may be older than the song. Each blessing after the first is introduced by the narrator, e.g., "And of Levi he said . . . " (8). The ordering principle is a combination of the age of the eponyms and the importance of the tribes. In general the poem describes Israel in its ideal condition: a tribal league with God alone as king, settled in their land and flourishing (except for Judah and Reuben) under the protection of God and the theocratic guidance of Levi. The atmosphere is one of peace and security. The language of the poem is extremely difficult because of its antiquity and epigrammatic style, and the text apparently contains many corruptions, so that much of the interpretation is necessarily problematic.

Bibliography: Commentaries on Deuteronomy; T. H. Gaster, in: JBL, 66 (1947), 53–62; F. M. Cross and D. N. Freedman, *ibid.*, 67 (1948), 191–210.

[M.Fo.]

MOSES, CHRONICLES OF (Heb. דִּבְרֵי הַיָּמִים לְמֹשֶׁה רַבֵּנוּ, *Divrei ha-Yamim le-Moshe Rabbenu*), a story on the life of Moses written in the early Middle Ages. The prophet's early life, before the Exodus from Egypt, forms the major part of the story while his later life and death are described only very briefly. The author based himself on some of the midrashic interpretations of the life of Moses as told in the Book of Exodus, but the many adventures ascribed in the work to Moses are the product of the author's fertile imagination.

According to the story, *Balaam the Magician was adviser to the king of Egypt in Moses' time; *Jethro, also one of the king's advisers, was driven away from the royal court after he tried to help the Jews in Egypt. The author also describes a number of miracles (not mentioned in the Bible) that supposedly occurred in Moses' youth and which saved him from disaster. Completely new stories were also added to Moses' biography, e.g., a very detailed tale about his becoming king of Ethiopia, after he had driven away Balaam who had seized the Ethiopian throne. In the story, Moses reigned for 40 years in the kingdom.

Divrei ha-Yamim le-Moshe Rabbenu is similar to other early medieval tales in which a biblical story is adapted in the light of conventions, mores, and concepts of the Middle Ages. The narrative element is usually emphasized in these stories. Abraham and many other sages were also the subjects of such tales which were often erroneously considered to belong to midrashic literature. Later writers in adapting biblical stories also compiled and adapted these different versions, e.g., the author of **Sefer ha-Yashar* (Venice, 1625; see *Fiction, Hebrew: The Hebrew Story in the Middle Ages). *"Midrash Petirat Moshe Rabbenu"* ("A Midrash on the Death of Moses") is another story about Moses written in the Middle Ages. The narrative aspect is not dominant but rather the midrashic elements which are ethical in content and meant to convey a moral. Moses' death is described in a mythological setting involving a confrontation between God and Samael (Satan).

Bibliography: A. Jellinek, *Beit ha-Midrash*, 1 (1938^2), xxif. (Ger.), 115–29 (Heb.); 2 (1938^2), vii–xi (Ger.), 1–11 (Heb.).

[Y.D.]

MOSES, ISAAC S. (1847–1926), U.S. Reform rabbi. Moses, who was born in Zaniemysl, Poznan, had not completed his education before he settled in the United States in the early 1870s. He was appointed to rabbinic positions in Quincy, Illinois (1876), Milwaukee (1879), and Chicago (1888). In 1901 he became rabbi of the Central Synagogue, New York, where he remained until his retirement in 1919.

In his early days in the United States, Moses was considered a radical Reformer, but later he took a more moderate position. In 1884 he introduced his own prayer book *(Tefillat Yisrael)*. Moses was a founding member of the Central Conference of American Rabbis and a member of the Reform committee charged with compiling an official prayer book. The appearance of the *Union Prayer Book* in 1894 has been credited to his personal initiative in preparing and circulating a manuscript when the committee's work seemed to be leading nowhere. Moses also published a number of sermons and textbooks for children. His *Sabbath School Hymnal*, first issued in 1894, ran into 14 editions. While in Milwaukee he edited the weekly *Der Zeitgeist* (1880-82).

Bibliography: CCARY, 37 (1927), 250; L. J. Swichkow and L. P. Gartner, *The History of the Jews in Milwaukee* (1963), passim.

[S.D.T.]

MOSES, MARCUS (Mordecai Hamburger; d. 1735), Anglo-Indian pioneer. Son of Moses Libusch, a leader of Hamburg Jewry, he married a daughter of Glueckel von *Hameln and settled in London. Here his criticism of a divorce issued by R. Aaron *Hart brought him into conflict with the established Ashkenazi community. He was excommunicated, and in consequence in 1707 set up his own synagogue (later the Hambro synagogue). Becoming impoverished in 1712 he went to Fort St. George (*Madras) in India, and was involved in the purchase for the governor of Madras, Thomas Pitt, of the famous Pitt diamond, later sold to the regent of France. In 1721 he returned to England a wealthy man and built his congregation a new synagogue. In 1731 he went back to India where he died. His eldest son, known as Moses Marcus (b. 1701), was converted to Christianity and published in 1724 an autobiographical tract (later translated into Dutch) justifying his action, as well as books on biblical study.

Bibliography: C. Roth, *The Great Synagogue, London* (1950), 35–46, 114–9; Roth, Mag Bibl, 285, 351, 408; idem, *Anglo-Jewish Letters* (1938), 97–98; H. D. Love, *Vestige of Old Madras*, 4 vols. (1913); Hart, in: *Jewish Historical Society of England, Miscellanies*, 3 (1937), 57–76.

[W.J.F.]

MOSES, MYER (1779–1833), U.S. merchant, soldier, and public official. Moses, who was born in Charleston, South Carolina, was active in the South Carolina Society for Promotion of Domestic Arts and Manufactories and was director of the Planters and Mechanics Bank. In 1809 Moses became a captain of volunteers and he later served in the War of 1812. He represented Charleston in the 1810 state legislature, and served on the Charleston public school commission in 1811 and 1823. In 1825 Moses moved to New York City.

[N.O.]

MOSES, RAPHAEL J. (1812–1893), U.S. lawyer and state legislator. Born in Charleston, South Carolina, into a family of colonial American origin, Moses attended grade school but left school at the age of 13. After an apprenticeship in business, he set himself up in Charleston as a merchant. After the 1838 fire destroyed his business, he moved to St. Joseph, Florida, then to Apalachicola, Florida, where he studied law and opened his own practice. He then moved to Columbus, Georgia, where his practice flourished and he became a leader of the bar. He also ventured into fruit growing. Before the Civil War he was the first to ship Georgia peaches to Savannah and thence by steamer to New York City. An ardent secessionist, Moses, although over military age, quickly volunteered his services at the outbreak of the Civil War. He rose to the rank of major and served as Confederate Commissary for the State of Georgia until the war's end. Moses retained his deep feeling for the "Lost Cause" to the end of his life.

Returning to Columbus, Moses resumed his law practice and was elected to the first postwar Georgia state legislature, where he was made chairman of the Judiciary Committee. In 1878, while campaigning for the U.S. Congress, Moses heard that his opponent, W. O. Tuggle, had taunted him with being a Jew. In "An Open Letter to the Hon. W. O. Tuggle," first published in the Columbus *Daily Times* (Aug. 29, 1878) and reprinted many times, he eloquently answered: " . . . I feel it an honor to be one of a race whom persecution cannot crush . . . whom prejudice has in vain endeavored to subdue . . . who . . . after nearly nineteen centuries of persecution still survive as a nation and assert their manhood and intelligence . . . Would you honor me? Call me Jew. Would you place in unenviable prominence your unchristian prejudices and narrow bigotry? Call me Jew." Moses lost the election nevertheless.

Bibliography: B. A. Elzas, *Jews of South Carolina* (1905), 199–202; C. Reznikoff and U. Z. Engelmann, *Jews of Charleston* (1950), 289–90 (reprint of letter to Tuggle). [T.I.T.]

MOSES, ROBERT (1888–), U.S. parks and highways developer. Moses was born in New Haven, Connecticut, to well-to-do Spanish-Jewish parents. He denied his Jewish affiliation. Moses' Ph.D. thesis in political science from Columbia was published as *Civil Service of Great Britain* (1914). He later wrote *Theory and Practice in Politics* (1939), *LaGuardia: A Salute and a Memoir* (1957), and *Tribute to Governor Smith* (1962).

Moses in 1919 joined the staff of Governor Alfred E. Smith and served as chief of staff of a New York State commission on administrative reorganization. He then began his long career on state parks and highways agencies as president of the New York State Council of Parks (1924–63) and chairman of the Long Island State Parks Commission (1924–63). He also served as secretary of state for New York (1927–28). In 1934 Moses was the unsuccessful Republican candidate for governor of New York.

In 1934 Moses became Mayor LaGuardia's parks commissioner, a post he held under four mayors (to 1960). As commissioner he inaugurated massive public works of the New Deal type. He was responsible, for example, for construction of the Triborough Bridge structures (dedicated 1936); Grand Central Parkway; Belt (later called Marine) Parkway; Henry Hudson Parkway, in the Bronx; Franklin D. Roosevelt Drive, in Manhattan; Fire Island state park; the Niagara power plant; and the Coliseum convention hall. Moses also served as city construction coordinator (1946–60); as chairman of the Jones Beach State Parkway Authority (1933–63); as member (1934) and then chairman (1936–46) of the Triborough Bridge Authority and of the Consolidated Triborough Bridge and City Tunnel Authority (1946–68); as sole member (1938) of the New York City Parkway Authority; as chairman of the state committee on postwar employment (1948); as chief consultant on public works to the Hoover Commission on Reorganization of the Executive Branch (1948); and as president of the 1964–65 New York World's Fair. Impatient of results, Moses was frequently embroiled in controversies in which he displayed his acerbic wit and combative style.

Bibliography: C. Rodgers, *Robert Moses: Builder for Democracy* (1952). [R.SK.]

MOSES, SIEGFRIED (1887–), German Zionist leader and Israel public official. Born in Lautenburg, Germany, Moses practiced as a lawyer from 1912 to 1937. In 1917 he was appointed food controller of the city of Danzig and in 1919 he became deputy director of the Union of German Municipalities, a post he held until 1920. From 1923 to 1929 he was manager of the Schocken Department Store Co. in Zwickau. In his student days he was active in the union of Jewish student fraternities (see *Kartell Juedischer Verbindungen) and was the editor of *Der Juedische Student*. In 1920 he was appointed a member of the board of the Jewish Workers Aid Society in Berlin and was its executive chairman from 1921 to 1923. He was a delegate to several Zionist Congresses and was the president of the Zionist Organization of Germany during the period 1933–37. Moses was also active in Jewish communal affairs as vice-chairman of the Reichsvertretung der Juden in Deutschland, 1933–37, and as a member of the Berlin Community Council. He settled in Palestine in 1937 and assumed the post of managing director of *Ha'avara (transfer of Jewish assets in Germany to Palestine). For a period of ten years (1939–49), he worked as a certified public accountant and income tax expert. He was a member of the *Jewish Agency Delegation to the United Nations in 1947 and in 1949 was appointed Israel's first State Comptroller, a post which he held until his retirement in 1961. In 1957 he was elected president of Irgun Olei Merkaz Europa ("Association of Settlers from Central Europe") and president of the Council of Jews from Germany and of the Leo Baeck Institute. He was the chairman of the Advisory Committee of the United Restitution Organization in Israel and a member of the board of Bank Leumi. Moses wrote *The Income Tax Ordinance of Palestine* (1942, 1946), *Jewish Post-War Claims* (1944), and articles on Jewish subjects and his professional work.

Siegfried Moses, German Zionist leader and Israel's first State Comptroller.

Bibliography: D. Lazar, *Rashim be-Yisrael*, 2 (1955), 132–6. [K.L.]

MOSES BEN ABRAHAM OF PONTOISE (12th century), French tosafist. Moses was a pupil of Jacob *Tam. The *Sefer ha-Yashar* of R. Tam discusses a number of problems, concerned mainly with the clarification of the plain meaning of various talmudic passages, which Moses put before his teacher (Responsa nos. 51, 52, 69–70). The theoretical nature of most of the questions and the answers, and their importance for an understanding of the relevant talmudic passages, led to their inclusion, in substance, in the standard *tosafot*, as well as in the works of such *rishonim* as *Mordecai b. Hillel, *Meir b. Baruch of Rothenburg, and others. The tosafists also mention Moses in connection with other subjects and they cite his comments in the various collections of their biblical commentaries. A short verse of two lines by Moses, coming at the end of the list of positive precepts in the **Azharot* of *Elijah ha-Zaken, together with a commentary to it, has been preserved (*Kobez al Jad*, 1 (1936), 8).

Bibliography: Urbach, Tosafot, 111–3. [I.T.-S.]

MOSES BEN DANIEL OF ROHATYN (end of 17th century), Galician author. His name suggests that he was born in Rohatyn (Rogatin), but according to the preface of his works he lived in Zolkiew, where he published his *Sugyat ha-Talmud* (1693). The work, consisting of 40 paragraphs, is a methodology of the Talmud. It deals particularly with the commentaries of Rashi and *tosafot* and the manner in which they were studied at the time according to the two dialectical methods of Talmud study known as the "Nuremberger" and the "Regensburger" (see *Yeshivot). The work was translated into Latin by H. J. van Bashuysen, and was published in the Latin translation of the *Halikhot Olam* of Joshua b. Joseph ha-Levi (Hanover, 1714 pp. 363ff.).

Bibliography: S. Buber, *Kiryah Nisgavah* (1903), 58 no. 229. [ED.]

MOSES (ben Isaac) BEN HA-NESI'AH (late 13th century), Hebrew grammarian and lexicographer; lived in

England. His mother was apparently Jewish and was known as "Countess" or "Contesse," in Hebrew *Ha-Nesi'-ah;* hence his name: Ben ha-Nesi'ah. His only extant work, *Sefer ha-Shoham* ("The Onyx Book"), is the sole source for the scanty information available on him. In the introduction, he states that in his youth he wrote a grammar book, *Leshon Limmudim* ("Language of Learning"). This work is not extant and some scholars assume that extracts of it were included in *Sefer ha-Shoham,* written later. The author chose the name שֹׁהַם (Shoham), because it is an anagram of his name מֹשֶׁה (Moses). From the work, it can be learned that the author's teacher was R. *Moses b. Yom Tov ha-Nakdan ("the Punctuator") of London (c. 1268) and that he had a knowledge of Arabic. Moses b. ha-Nesi'ah was acquainted with many of the works of his predecessors.

Sefer ha-Shoham is divided into three parts. The first is a general introduction to the Hebrew language, a study of the origin of the letters, and on the formative letters and their role, etc. In the second part, the author reviews the verbs and divides them into seven groups. His system was possibly influenced by that of Judah b. David *Ḥayyuj. He then lists the nouns, classified into 162 metric groups, according to the method of David *Kimḥi. The third part deals with the particles, adverbs, numerals, vocalization, and accents. He added also a dictionary of the Aramaic words found in the Bible. Only the introduction to *Sefer ha-Shoham* and the section dealing with the verbs have been published (1947).

Bibliography: Moses b. Isaac ha-Nesi'ah, *Sefer ha-Shoham,* ed. by B. Klar, 1 (1947), vii–viii (introd.), 5–16 (Eng. section) 16 n. 24 (additional bibliography). [N.N.]

MOSES BEN ḤANOKH (d. c. 965), Spanish rabbi. The principal source for the biographic details of this famous scholar is the story of the *Four Captives told by Abraham *ibn Daud in his *Sefer ha-Kabbalah* (*The Book of Tradition,* ed. by G. D. Cohen (1967), 63–69). This story tells how R. Moses' wife cast herself into the sea in order to escape from her captor, how he was sold as a slave at Cordoba and redeemed, and how his erudition resulted in his becoming recognized as rabbi of the community. But, according to sources which have since been discovered, this story seems to be unacceptable. It would indeed seem that R. Moses came probably from southern Italy. It is quite possible that he was indeed taken prisoner on a sea journey at the time he traveled to Spain, because a maritime war was then being waged between the Umayyad caliphate of Spain and the Fāṭimid kingdom of North Africa. In any case, it seems that R. Moses arrived in Spain during the 950s and became rabbi of Cordoba. He enjoyed the protection of the minister *Ḥisdai ibn Shaprut, who by coordinating the policies of Abd-al-Raḥmān III (912–961), the Umayyad caliph of Cordoba, sought to make the Jewish population of Spain independent of the Jewish center in Babylonia. R. Moses headed the yeshivah, which had many pupils, and also answered halakhic questions which were addressed to him from other towns. His responsa were regarded by his contemporaries as authoritative and no less valuable than the responsa of the Babylonian *geonim.* Many were included in the collections of geonic responsa, such as *Sha'arei Ẓedek* (Salonika, 1792), *Ge'onei Mizraḥ u-Ma'arav* (ed. by J. Miller, Berlin, 1888), and some were quoted by the **rishonim,* particularly by the author of *"Ha-Ittur,"* R. *Isaac b. Abba Mari of Marseilles. His responsa in a German translation were collected by J. Miller. A responsum attributed to Moses, the *gaon* of Sura, is in fact by Moses b. Ḥanokh. From the time of Moses b. Ḥanokh the practical dependence of Spanish scholars upon Babylonian scholars ceased in everything connected with *halakhah* and custom. In addition to his outstanding erudition, his great humility and exceptional modesty left a deep impression on his contemporaries. He was succeeded by his son *Ḥanokh.

Bibliography: Ashtor, Korot, 1 (1966[2]), 155–9, 289–90; G. D. Cohen, in: PAAJR, 29 (1960/61), 55–131; M. Margolioth, *Hilkhot ha-Nagid* (1962), 6–8; S. Abramson, *R. Nissim Ga'on* (Heb., 1965), 307; J. Miller, *Siebenter Bericht ueber die Lehranstalt fuer die Wissenschaft des Judenthums in Berlin* (1889), 3–4, 8–10. [E.A.]

MOSES BEN ISAIAH KATZ (end of 17th and early 18th centuries), Polish rabbi and homilist. Katz was a pupil of Solomon *Luria and was rabbi successively of Medzibezh, Brody, and Przemysl. He is the author of *Penei Moshe* (Wilhermsdorf, 1716), a commentary on the aggadic passages of 18 treatises of the Babylonian and Jerusalem Talmuds. (This work should not be confused with *Penei Moshe,* the standard commentary on the Jerusalem Talmud by Moses *Margolies.) He reveals a remarkable homiletic ingenuity in his work *Keren Or* (Zolkiew, 1721). As the title suggests, the work is a commentary on this phrase which occurs in Exodus 34:30, 35 ("the skin of his face shone"). He gives no less than 50 different explanations of the phrase. It has been suggested that Katz may be identical with Moses b. Isaiah Wengrow, the author of *Berit Matteh Moshe* (Berlin, 1701), a commentary on the Passover *Haggadah* with novellae on the tractate *Zevaḥim.*

Bibliography: Fuerst, Bibliotheca, 3 (1863), 120; Halpern, Pinkas, 279–81, 501. [Ed.]

MOSES BEN JACOB OF COUCY (13th century), French scholar and tosafist. His father Jacob is mentioned a number of times in the printed *tosafot* (Kid. 43b; et al.). Moses was the maternal grandson of the tosafist *Ḥayyim ha-Kohen and brother-in-law of *Samson of Coucy. His principal teacher was *Judah Sir Leon.

Moses of Coucy is the first example among French Jews of an itinerant preacher, wandering from town to town and from country to country to rouse the masses to draw near to God by the active observance of His precepts. He began his preaching in Spain in 1236, being motivated to do so, according to his own words, by some mystical revelation which he experienced. The nature of this revelation is not clear, although it was possibly connected with the reckoning of the Redemption, a pursuit in which Judah Sir Leon, who designated 1236 for its beginning, also engaged. His sermons excited a massive response and, in his own words, brought about the repentance of "thousands and tens of thousands," especially in respect to observance of the precepts of *tefillin, mezuzah,* and *ẓiẓit,* which in that era (as other sources also testify) had grown very lax. He called also for the curbing of sexual relations with gentile women, widespread in Spain at that time, and taught in his sermons a method of repentance close in formula to the spirit of Ḥasidei Ashkenaz, though to a much less severe degree. He stressed the value of Torah study in a regular and orderly manner, and was one of the first to call for greater equity and propriety in economic dealings with the gentile community. Thus Moses checked, at least temporarily, the decline in the observance of the positive precepts of Judaism among the masses and the scholars in Spain which had resulted from the tendency toward rationalization and to the extravagant allegorization of Scripture caused by the influence of Maimonides' philosophic writings. He later visited other countries (which, he does not specify) and in 1240 was in Paris where he took part in the well-known disputation on the Talmud with Nicholas *Donin. These activities earned him the name of Moses ha-Darshan, in consequence of which he has sometimes been confused with *Moses ha-Darshan of Narbonne.

Moses of Coucy's reputation rests on his extensive and important work, the *Sefer Mitzvot Gadol* (*SeMaG;* first published before 1480 (Rome?), and subsequently published three times by 1547, in Italy). The work is unique among the prolific rabbinic writing of the period. It includes, in effect, the essence of the Oral Law, arranged in the order of the precepts and divided into two parts: positive precepts and negative precepts. The work is based on Maimonides' *Mishneh Torah*, which is cited word by word on every page. He supplements Maimonides' words with an abundance of sources, from the Babylonian and Jerusalem Talmuds and the Midrashim, as well as from the works of French and German *rishonim*, which he possessed either in the original or in precis. Moses adapts the language of the Midrashim so closely to the style of Maimonides that one is often under the impression that he has before him an alternative reading of the halakhic Midrash. Although the book follows the arrangement of the precepts, their number and order differ from those of Maimonides, both because Moses did not know Maimonides' *Sefer ha-Mitzvot* but only the list of precepts in the introduction to the *Mishneh Torah*, and because at the end of the book he included rabbinic precepts, in keeping with the practical aim he had set himself in compiling it: to instruct the people in the way of the Lord. In pursuit of this aim, he also varied the arrangement of the precepts, separating those applicable in our time from those which are not. The *SeMaG* marks the penetration of the works of Maimonides (which Moses probably "discovered" during his stay in Spain) into the halakhic world of France. Though Maimonides was known to Moses' teacher, Judah Sir Leon, as well as to *Samson of Sens, they merely quoted him a number of times, whereas Moses made him the basis of his whole project. He seems not to have been unaware of the great paradox in the possibility that it was precisely Maimonides who contributed to the undermining of practical *halakhah* in the countries under his influence, as a result of his use of allegory in general, and of his having posited reasons for the precepts in particular. Although the period of Moses' activity began only a few years after the first controversy in Europe around the works of Maimonides, he makes no reference whatsoever to it in his work, perhaps feeling that his special relationship to Maimonides disqualified him as an impartial judge in the matter. Among works of French and German scholars frequently used and cited by Moses, sometimes by name and sometimes not, are the *tosafot* of Samson of Sens, the *Sefer ha-Terumah* of *Baruch b. Isaac of Worms, and the *Sefer Yere'im* of *Eliezer b. Samuel of Metz. His practice, in general, is to begin with a scriptural verse touching on the subject, to cite the interpretations of the verse found in the Talmuds and the halakhic Midrashim, to give the relevant talmudic discussions, the words of the commentators and *posekim*, and a summary of the *halakhah*—all this with the degree of editing and adaptation of style necessary to give greater fluency to the language, every effort being made to avoid casuistry and prolixity. Moses weaves into his words an abundance of aggadic material, quotations from the sources, or the homiletic creations of his own spirit, all marked by their wholesomeness and simplicity, with love of God and of his fellow man.

The *SeMaG* won great popularity among scholars and *posekim*. Many tens of manuscripts of the work have been preserved to the present time, an unusual phenomenon with a book of such great length. It was also one of the first Hebrew books to be printed. It has served as a standard guide to halakhic practice for scholars in all generations, notable among them being *Mordecai b. Hillel, *Meir ha-Kohen, a pupil of *Meir b. Baruch of Rothenburg, in his *Haggahot Maimuniyyot*, as well as all the pupils of *Perez of Corbeil. Quotations from it occur in the printed *tosafot*. Great scholars of all generations have written commentaries to it, among them Isaac *Stein, Joseph *Colon, Elijah *Mizrachi, Solomon *Luria, and Ḥayyim *Benveniste. Joshua *Boaz included the *SeMaG* with the Shulḥan Arukh and Maimonides' *Mishneh Torah* among the references given in his *Ein Mishpat*, an indication of the work's indispensability. The tremendous influence of the book is particularly evidenced by the fact that *Isaac of Corbeil, who in his time bore the title of "Head of the Yeshivot of France," found it necessary to compile the *Sefer Mitzvot Katan*, which is completely dependent upon the *SeMaG*, and to make it compulsory daily learning for every Jew. Perez, and his pupils after him, who wrote glosses and notes to the book of Isaac of Corbeil, all associated themselves in their rulings with the *SeMaG*, which they continually quoted. This estimate of the *SeMaG* persisted, among both Ashkenazim and Sephardim, until the time of Joseph *Caro's Shulḥan Arukh; and Moses b. Jacob of Coucy is numbered among the great *posekim* of all generations.

The *tosafot* of Moses of Coucy to *Yoma*, first published with the title *Tosafot Yeshanim* in the Amsterdam (1714–17) edition of the Talmud, have come down to us. He also wrote a commentary on the Torah (known among *rishonim* as "*Peshatei ha-Ram mi-Coucy*"), which is much quoted in the *Minḥat Yehudah* (in *Da'at Zekenim*, Leghorn, 1783) of Judah b. Eliezer. In the *SeMaG* (positive precept no. 16) Moses tells of a special prayer he composed for the benefit of those wishing to repent. Two versions of such a prayer attributed to him have lately been published from manuscripts.

Bibliography: E. E. Urbach, in: *Zion*, 12 (1946/47), 159; Urbach, Tosafot, 384–95 and index; Ch. Tchernowitz, *Toledot ha-Posekim*, 2 (1947), 87–92; Sonne, in: *Sefer ha-Yovel... A. Marx* (1950), 209–19; Gilat, in: *Tarbiz*, 28 (1958/59), 54–58. [I.T.-S.]

MOSES BEN JACOB OF KIEV (also called **Moses ha-Goleh** and **Moses of Kiev II;** 1449–c. 1520), talmudic scholar and author. Moses was born, according to various scholars, in Seduva (Shadov), Lithuania (see A. Epstein, *Kitvei*... 1 (1950), 303–7). I. Zinberg, however, is of the opinion that he was born in Tarov, Kiev region (*Toledot Sifrut Yisrael*, 3 (1958), 161–6, 354). He died in Kaffa (Feodosiya), Crimea. At that time there were no important Torah institutions in Poland and Russia, and Moses traveled to Constantinople where he became friendly with both Rabbanites and Karaites. He also studied astronomy there under the Karaite Elijah ha-Shayazi, author of *Adderet Eliyahu*. He settled in Kiev and acquired a reputation in various branches of literature. He was a biblical exegete, talmudist, *paytan*, linguist, and kabbalist. From Kiev he wrote a polemical work against *Gan Eden*, the book of precepts of the Karaite scholar Abraham b. Elijah. In 1482 the Tatars attacked Kiev. Moses' possessions, including his library, were plundered. He himself escaped, but his children were taken captive to the Crimea, and Moses journeyed to various communities to collect money for their ransom. When passing through Karaite communities he disputed with their scholars. After ransoming his children, Moses returned to Kiev. He then wrote his works *Sefer ha-Dikduk*, a Hebrew grammar, and *Yesod ha-Ibbur*, on the calendar. In 1495 the Jews of Lithuania and the Ukraine were expelled, and Moses again was forced to wander. During these wanderings he wrote *Shushan Sodot* on automatic and cryptic writing, as well as *Ozar ha-Shem* and *Sha'arei Ẓedek* on the upper **Sefirot*, which are no longer extant. In 1506, while he was staying in the Lithuanian (i.e., Belorussian) town of Lida, it was attacked by the Tatars and Moses was taken captive. He was carried off to the Crimea where he was ransomed by the Jews of the city of Salkhat. From there he removed to Kaffa in the Crimea where he settled. Here Moses filled an important cultural role as rabbi and head of the community. He succeeded in uniting the members of the community who had come from different countries, and also compiled a prayer book for them which became known as *Minhag Kaffa* and was adopted by all the communities of the Crimea. Moses also compiled special regulations for the community. He succeeded in completing there his *Oẓar Neḥmad*, a supercommentary to the Pentateuch commentary of Abraham ibn Ezra. [S.E.]

MOSES BEN JOAB (d. after 1530), Hebrew poet who lived in Florence. His *diwan* (Montefiore Collection, Ms. 366) contains a colorful variety of poems, ranging from elegy to satire, from love song to religious hymn, and from epigram to epithalamium. The collection consists of three groups: (1) satiric verses, in which the poet presents a series of persons characteristic of his time, such as Isaac of Correggio and Solomon of Poggibonsi; (2) love songs stylistically modelled on the Spanish poets and Immanuel of Rome; (3) religious poetry—artistically the most important of his work. While it contains all the flavor of the early hymnology, some well-known secular motives have also been included, without in any way detracting from the poetic form. The greater part of his religious verse is consecrated to the festivals. One of his poems describes the tragic conditions in Florence during the siege of 1529–30.

Bibliography: U. Cassuto, *Gli ebrei a Firenze nell'età del Rinascimento* (1918), 340–54; idem, in: MGWJ, 77 (1933), 365–84; Davidson, Oẓar, 4 (1933), 36, no. 204; Schirmann, Italyah, 236–40.
[Yo.D.]

MOSES BEN JOSEPH BEN MERWAN LEVI (12th century), one of the renowned scholars of Narbonne. Moses belonged to a distinguished family. His grandfather "was very pious, a man of substance and of good deeds, benefiting Israel with his wealth, and causing many evil decrees to be revoked." His uncle, under whom he studied, was Isaac b. Merwan Levi, rabbi of Narbonne. His father was also a scholar, and his brother Meir one of the scholars of Narbonne. Moses himself was head of a yeshivah and a member of the *bet din* of Narbonne headed by *Abraham b. Isaac. Most of the scholars of Narbonne were pupils of Moses, among them *Abraham b. David and *Zerahiah b. Isaac ha-Levi. A commentary which he wrote on most of the Talmud is no longer extant. The few quotations from it in the works of the scholars of Provence and Catalonia show it to have been written in the style of the early German and French scholars, with the aim of establishing the *halakhah*. It was intended (though not in the manner of a polemic) to defend the old Provencal traditions against the influence of the Spanish school in Lunel in the 12th century, the prime exponent of which was Abraham b. Isaac who follows in the steps of *Alfasi and *Judah b. Barzillai al-Bargeloni. In addition to his commentary, Moses' responsa and customs are also quoted in that literature. He exerted a great influence on the scholars of Provence and Catalonia, particularly on Zerahiah ha-Levi and *Naḥmanides, who quote him extensively.

Bibliography: Benedikt, in: *Tarbiz*, 19 (1948), 19–34; 22 (1951), 85–109; I. Twersky, *Rabad of Posquières* (1962), index. [B.Z.B.]

MOSES BEN JOSEPH HA-LEVI (13th century), philosopher. Nothing is known about Moses' life; the suggestion that he was a member of the famous Abulafia family has not been proven. He was highly regarded by Joseph b. Abraham *ibn Wakar, and is quoted by Crescas, Albo, and Isaac Abrabanel. His major work *Ma'amar Elohi* ("Metaphysical Treatise"), as well as fragments from two of his minor works (all written in Arabic), were discovered and incorporated in Ibn Wakar's *Treatise on the Harmony between Philosophy and the Revealed Law* (c. 1340). Two manuscripts of the Hebrew versions of the *Ma'amar* are extant (Bodleian and Leningrad), while a third, previously in the library of the cathedral of Pamplona, Spain, can no longer be traced. The *Ma'amar Elohi* seeks to establish the existence of the First Cause (God); to refute erroneous views concerning this subject and concerning the attributes of God; and to investigate the emanation of beings from the First Cause. Moses, disagreeing with Aristotle, Alexander of Aphrodisias, and Averroes, holds with Themistius, al-Fārābī, and Avicenna, that the "First Intellect," which emanated directly from God without an intermediary, is the Prime Mover of the celestial spheres. His doctrine of Divine attributes seeks to avoid plurality in God and therefore denies all attributes superadded to His essence. He admits, however, not only negative attributes but also attributes of essence, such as knowledge, will, and power, as well as attributes denoting action as "Creator." (Moses makes no reference whatever to Maimonides' thorough treatment of this theme.) Divine Providence, according to him, does not involve God's knowledge of individuals, but only the universal rule of God, employing the human intellect as an agent of the Active *Intellect. Of the two other fragments one deals with the problem of Divine Providence and the other with al-Ghazālī's doctrine of the "Word" *(Kalima)*. Approving of Ghazālī's doctrine, Moses establishes a metaphysical entity above the "First Intellect," the Prime Mover, and immediately below God, the First Cause. [A.Alt.]

Moses also wrote, assuming that Steinschneider's identification is correct, a work on musical harmonies, a short section of which is quoted by *Shemtov Shaprut b. Isaac of Tudela in his Hebrew commentary on Avicenna's *Canon* (Munich, Ms. Hebr. 8, fol. 330b). Moses describes the mathematical relations of musical intervals as well as some arithmetical operations carried out with them. The rather elementary contents of this text comply with Arabic musical theory. Its musical terminology is basically identical with that used in a Hebrew version of the musical chapter in Umayya ibn abī al-Ṣalt's encyclopedia (Paris, Cod. Hebr. 1037[1]); thus Moses' treatise may originally have been in Hebrew. [H.Av.]

MOSES BEN JOSHUA (Ben Mar David) OF NARBONNE (Narboni, Lat., **Maestre Vidal Bellsom [Blasom?];** d. 1362), French philosopher and physician. Moses was born in Perpignan at the end of the 13th, or beginning of the 14th century, to a family originally from Narbonne. As a youth he studied with his father and private tutors, and was introduced to the study of Maimonides at the age of 13. In addition to the Bible, rabbinic literature, and Jewish philosophy, he studied general philosophy and medicine. Moses began his literary career in Perpignan, where he remained until 1344, and continued in Spain, writing most of his works there. Although he lived in various Spanish cities—he mentions Cervera, Barcelona, Soria, Toledo, and Burgos—he never completely severed his ties with Perpignan. He expressed nostalgia for the intellectual circles there and intended to return. He probably spoke Provencal and Catalan, and it is likely that he knew Arabic and some Latin. He shows no familiarity, however, with Christian thinkers, the major philosophical influence on him being Islamic thought, particularly Averroes, whose works he read in Hebrew translation. Moses, who is known primarily for his commentary on

Maimonides' *Guide of the Perplexed* and for his espousal of Averroes' teachings, is the author of some 20 works, an impressive number for the troubled period in which he lived. An early work, *Ma'amar ba-Sekhel ha-Hiyyulani* or *Ma'amar be-Efsharut ha-Devekut*, was written in Perpignan under conditions of siege and warfare; in Spain, as a physician, he undoubtedly had to cope with the bubonic plague of 1348–50 and, as a Jew, with the anti-Semitism that followed it. In 1349 he fled Cervera with the rest of the Jewish community, leaving his possessions and books behind. Before his work on Maimonides, Moses had written a number of commentaries and supercommentaries, most of them on Islamic philosophical texts. He composed major commentaries on al-*Ghazālī's *Maqāṣid al-Falāsifa* ("Intentions of the Philosophers") and Ibn Ṭufayl's *Ḥayy ibn Yaqẓān* and a number of supercommentaries to Averroes' commentaries on Aristotle's works on logic, physics, metaphysics, astronomy, and psychology. Moses' commentary on the *Guide* (ed. by I. Euchel, and printed together with text of the *Guide*, 1791; ed. J. Goldenthal, 1852; the latter reprinted with text, 1946, and in *Sheloshah Kadmonei Mefareshei ha-Moreh*, 1961), his last work, begun in Toledo in 1355 and finished in Soria in 1362, was based on his thorough knowledge of Islamic philosophy. He opposed Maimonides' neoplatonic interpretations of Aristotle's doctrines, which Maimonides had derived from al-Fārābī and Avicenna, with Averroes' more purely Aristotelian interpretations. He criticized, in particular, Maimonides' discussion of the proofs for the existence of God, his concept of God, and his doctrine of divine attributes. In the following, more conservative centuries, critics such as Isaac *Arama, Isaac *Abrabanel, and Joseph *Delmedigo opposed his Averroistic critique of Maimonides' *Guide* and his clarification of points that Maimonides had left discreetly implicit. They also disparaged his difficult style of writing and highly eclectic, often confusing use of sources.

In *Iggeret al Shi'ur Komah* (ed. and tr. into English as *Epistle on Shiur Qomah* by A. Altmann in his *Jewish Medieval and Renaissance Studies* (1967), 225–88), one of his early works, Moses attempted a reconciliation between philosophy and Kabbalah, reflecting the influence of Joseph *ibn Waqar. He pursued a similar direction in his commentary on Ibn Ṭufayl's work (see G. Vajda, *Recherches sur la philosophie et la Kabbale* (1962), 396–403). Though more critical of kabbalistic concepts in his later years, Moses retained throughout his writings an affinity for the mystical phrase and symbol, a trait which has attracted recent scholarly attention (see Altmann's essay, *ibid.*). Averroes' doctrine of the conjunction of man's perfected intellect with the universal Agent Intellect that Moses accepted in his *Ma'amar bi-Shelemut ha-Nefesh* ("Treatise on the Perfection of the Soul," Paris, Bibliotheque Nationale, Ms. Heb., 988) resembles the mystic's experience of eternal being and loss of individuality in his relation to his creator. In his *Ma'amar bi-Shelemut ha-Nefesh*, Moses quoted almost the whole of Averroes' middle commentary on Aristotle's *De Anima*, as well as much of his "Treatise on the Possibility of Conjunction," to which he then added his own comments. Among Moses' other works are *Ha-Ma'amar bi-Veḥirah* ("Treatise on Free Will," ed. by E. Ashkenazi in *Sefer Divrei Ḥakhamim* (1849), 37–41), a polemical work written in answer to *Abner of Burgos' *Minḥat Kena'ot*, which expounds a theory of determinism; a number of medical treatises, in particular *Oraḥ Ḥayyim*, in which his reliance on classical and medieval sources is ostensibly tempered by an empirical approach; commentaries on Lamentations and Job; and four works which are no longer extant: a supercommentary on Abraham ibn Ezra's allegorical commentary on Genesis 2:2; *Pirkei Moshe*, a work containing philosophical aphorisms; a treatise on metaphysics; and a supercommentary on Averroes' commentary on Aristotle's *De Caelo et Mundo*.

Bibliography: Husik, Philosophy, index, s.v. *Moses of Narbonne;* Guttmann, Philosophies, 206–8, 225; Munk, Mélanges, 502–6; Ivry, in: JQR, 57 (1966/67), 271–97; Steinschneider, Cat. Bod, 1967–77; Steinschneider, Ueberetzungen, index s.v. *Moses Narboni;* Renan, Ecrivains, 320–35; Ch. Touti, in: *Archives d'histoire doctrinale et littéraire du moyen âge*, 21 (1954), 193–205.

[A.L.I.]

MOSES BEN LEVI (12th century), communal leader and poet in Egypt. From fragments of the Cairo *Genizah*, it has become clear that Moses was in charge of the affairs of the Jewish community of Qalyub, north of Cairo. In 1195 the heads of the Jewish community there addressed themselves to *Sar Shalom b. Moses ha-Levi, the *gaon* of the Fostat yeshivah, with a request that he confirm the appointment of Moses b. Levi as officer in charge of communal affairs after his position had been challenged. In his reply, the *gaon* praises Moses who also served in the offices of *ḥazzan*, *shoḥet*, and teacher of the community. An autobiographical *maqāma* by Moses is extant in the Kaufmann collection of the *Genizah*, which reveals details of his life before his arrival in Qalyub. At first he occupied himself with various matters, but after a time he immersed himself in Torah study alone. Two and a half years later he decided to leave his locality, the identity of which is unknown, after a quarrel with his parents. Reaching Qalyub, he was amazed at its beauty, and wrote poems in its praise. He appears to be identical with Moses b. ha-Levi from whom there remains a blank verse poem (Ar. *muwashshaḥ*).

Bibliography: Mann, Egypt, 1 (1920), 237; 2 (1922), 298; D. Z. Banet, in: *Sefer ha-Yovel . . . A. Marx* (1950), 77–79; J. H. Schirmann, *Shirim Ḥadashim min ha-Genizah* (1965), 377–84.

[A.D.]

MOSES BEN MENAHEM GRAF (also known as **Moses Praeger;** 1650–1700/1710), kabbalist born in Prague. After the conflagration in the Prague ghetto (1689), Moses moved to Nikolsburg (Mikulov), where he studied under the kabbalist Eliezer Mendel b. Mordecai. He was given lodging and support by David *Oppenheim, who, like Samson *Wertheimer of Vienna, encouraged the publication of his writings. Leaving Nikolsburg, Moses attempted to settle in various European cities, reaching Fuerth in 1696 and Dessau in 1698. It is not certain whether he died there or whether he returned to Prague in his later years. Moses' published works include: *Zera Kodesh*, a kabbalistic work with an appendix describing the exorcism of a *dibbuk* in Nikolsburg (Fuerth, 1696); a second edition, without the *dibbuk* story, was published by Simeon b. David Abiob of Hebron, together with his *Bat Melekh* (Venice, 1712; reprinted Munkacz, 1893); and *Va-Yakhel Moshe*, a kabbalistic discussion of various portions of the Zohar and of the *Adam de-Aẓilut*, with a special commentary on the latter concept entitled *Masveh Moshe*, introduced and annotated by Samuel b. Solomon Kohen, cantor in Brody (Dessau, 1699). In this last work Moses often criticizes the teachings of Moses *Cordovero and his followers.

Bibliography: J. Guenzig, *Die Wundermaenner im juedischen Volke* (1921), 102–6.

[Jo.H./Ed.]

MOSES BEN MEVORAKH (12th century), leader of Egyptian Jewry. He was the *nagid* of Egyptian Jewry from c. 1110 to before 1141, having been appointed to the position after the death of his father, the *nagid* *Mevorakh. He was assisted by his two sons, Mevorakh and Judah, who acted as "vice-*negidim*." In his time the Jews of Egypt were oppressed, and he intervened in their favor. A *kinah* on his mother's death, which appears to have been written by him, has been preserved in the Cairo *Genizah*. On her death, which made an impression on Egyptian Jewry, another *kinah* is known to have been written by Ẓedakah b. Judah. From the *kinah* of Moses, it appears that he was influenced by the poets of the Spanish school, an influence evident in

Ẓedakah's *kinah* as well. A poem written in his honor by Abraham b. Shabbetai of Minyat Zifta, Egypt, which was found among the manuscripts of the *Genizah*, has also been published by J. Mann (see bibliography).

Bibliography: Mann, Egypt, 1 (1920), 210, 213; 2 (1922), 255–59; J. H. Schirmann, *Shirim Ḥadashim min ha-Genizah* (1965), 97–102.

[ED.]

MOSES BEN SAMUEL OF DAMASCUS (14th century), Karaite poet. Moses, who was born in Safed, Ereẓ Israel, was employed in Damascus as clerk in charge of the emir's private estates. In 1354 the emir received an order requiring him to remove non-Muslims from government service. Moses was seized, charged with blasphemy against Islam, and given the choice of forfeiting his life or becoming a Muslim. He chose the latter. Some time later the emir went on a pilgrimage to Mecca, and Moses was compelled to accompany him. What he observed of the pilgrimage ritual led him to resolve to return to Judaism. The emir at first refused to release him but he fell ill and soon died. Moses then appears to have escaped to Egypt and entered the service of the royal vizier, apparently returning to his ancestral faith. His works, all in Hebrew verse, include a description of his tribulations and of his Mecca pilgrimage. His liturgical pieces display depth of feeling and an occasional lyrical inspiration.

Bibliography: Mann, Texts, 2 (1935), 213–32; L. Nemoy, *Karaite Anthology* (1952), 147–69.

[L.N.]

MOSES BEN SHEM TOV DE LEON (c. 1240–1305), a leading kabbalist, author of the bulk of the *Zohar. Moses was apparently born in Leon, near Castile—he also calls himself Moses "from the town of Leon," in his *Shekel ha-Kodesh*. Nothing is known of his teachers and early studies. Apart from religious study, he was also attracted to philosophy; Maimonides' *Guide of the Perplexed* was copied for him in 1264 (Moscow, Ms. Guenzburg 771). Moses subsequently turned to *Kabbalah, and when wandering among the communities of Castile, he became friendly with the kabbalists there. He immersed himself in the lore of the Geronese school of kabbalists and in the traditions of the Gnostic circle of *Moses of Burgos and Todros *Abulafia and in the 1270s and 80s drew particularly close to Joseph *Gikatilla. Moved by an unusual enthusiasm, combined with the urge to counteract the influence of certain rationalistic trends, Moses composed various writings toward the close of the 1270s. Presented in the guise of pseudepigraphica, they were designed to propagate the doctrine of kabbalism in the pattern in which it had crystallized in his own mind. Completed before 1286 they form the *Midrash ha-Ne'elam*, or "Mystical Midrash," and are the main substance of the Zohar. The later stratum in this composite work was written by another kabbalist. The major part of these writings is in Aramaic, but Moses also composed Hebrew pseudepigraphica on ethics and the eschatology of the soul. The "Testament of R. Eliezer the Great," also called *Orḥot Ḥayyim*, is evidence of the author's hesitations in choosing between the *tannaim* *Eliezer b. Hyrcanus and *Simeon b. Yoḥai as the hero of his pseudepigraphical construction. He also intended to compose a new Book of Enoch, parts of which he embodies in his *Mishkan ha-Edut*.

For a number of years, during the composition of the Zohar, and at least until 1291, he resided in Guadalajara, circulating from his home the first parts of the Zohar, which included a partly different version of the *Midrash ha-Ne'elam* (G. Scholem, in *Sefer ha-Yovel ... L. Ginzberg* (1946), 425–46, Heb. section). In Guadalajara he was associated with Isaac ibn *Sahulah, who is the first known to quote from the *Midrash ha-Ne'elam*. He dedicated some of his books to Joseph b. Todros Abulafia in Toledo. After 1292 Moses led a wandering life until, in later years, he settled in Ávila, and then probably devoted himself almost exclusively to the circulation of copies of the Zohar. Meeting *Isaac b. Samuel of Acre in Valladolid in 1305, he invited him to Ávila to see the ancient original manuscript of the Zohar in his home. However, on his return Moses fell ill and died in Arévalo (*Sefer Yuḥasin*, ed. H. Filipowski, 88). His widow denied the existence of such a manuscript. The Hebrew writings which bear his name are based on the same sources as those utilized in the Zohar and they frequently make veiled allusions to it without specifying it by name. These writings and the portions of the Zohar composed by Moses frequently serve to clarify one another; the former can be regarded as the authentic exegesis of the doctrine enshrined in the Zohar.

Numerous copies of several of these works were made in succeeding generations, and it seems that Moses himself circulated the texts in different versions. According to Abraham b. Solomon of Torrutiel (Neubauer, Chronicles, 1 (1887), 105) he was the author of 24 books. Those fully or partly extant are *Shoshan Edut* (1286), which Moses mentions as his first work (Cambridge, Add. Ms. 505, includes about half the work); *Sefer ha-Rimmon* (1287), an exposition of the kabbalistic reasons for the *mitzvot*, wholly constructed on Zohar homiletics (several Mss., e.g., Oxford, Bodleian, Ms. Opp. 344); *Or Zaru'a* (1288/89), on the act of *Creation (Oxford, Bodleian, Ms. Poc. 296, other parts in Ms. Vatican 428, 80–90): this was apparently extended by another kabbalist to cover the whole section *Bereshit*, Genesis 1–6 (Ms. Vatican 212); *Ha-Nefesh ha-Ḥakhamah*, written in 1290 for his pupil Jacob, whom Isaac of Acre met after Moses' death: a corrupt text was published in 1608 which contained numerous addenda from a work by a contemporary Spanish kabbalist; a lengthy titleless commentary on the ten *Sefirot* (see *Kabbalah) and penances (a large part in Munich Ms. 47); *Shekel ha-Kodesh* (1292, publ. 1912; an excellent text in Oxford, Bodleian Ms. Opp. 563); *Mishkan ha-Edut*, on the fate of the soul after death, with a commentary on the vision of Ezekiel appearing in numerous manuscripts (Berlin, Vatican, et al.) as an independent book: both here and in his introduction to *Or Zaru'a* Moses divulges the reasons for his literary activities; *Maskiyyot Kesef* (written after 1293), a commentary on the prayers, a sequel to the lost *Sefer Tappuḥei Zahav* (Ms. Adler, 1577); responsa on points of Kabbalah (ed. by Tishby, in: *Kobez al Jad*, vol. 5, 1951); a treatise on various mystical themes (Schocken Library, Ms. Kab. 14, 78–99; Ms. Vatican 428); another commentary on the ten *Sefirot*, *Sod Eser Sefirot Belimah ...* (Madrid, Escorial, Ms. G III 14). Moses also wrote: *Sefer Pardes* ("Book of Paradise"); *Sha'arei Ẓedek*, on Ecclesiastes; *Mashal ha-Kadmoni* (after the title of his friend Isaac ibn Sahula's work); responsa on questions concerning Elijah; a commentary on Song of Songs; and a polemic directed against the Sadducees (or Karaites?), mentioned by *Abner of Burgos (REJ, 18 (1889), 62). The *Sefer ha-Shem* (publ. in *Heikhal ha-Shem*, Venice, 1605) on the designations of the *Sefirot*, ascribed to him from the 15th century onward, was written by another kabbalist named Moses in the middle of the 14th century.

See also *Kabbalah.

Bibliography: Scholem, Mysticism, ch. 5; idem, in: KS, 1 (1924), 45–52; idem, in: *Madda'ei ha-Yahadut*, 1 (1926), 16–29; idem, in: MGWJ, 71 (1927), 109–23; S. D. Luzzatto, *Iggerot Shadal* (1891), 259; Steinschneider, Cat Bod, 1847–56; idem, in: HB, 10 (1870), 156–61; A. Jellinek, *Moses ben Schem Tob de Leon und sein Verhaeltnis zum Sohar* (1851); I. Tishby, *Mishnat ha-Zohar*, 2 vols.

(1949), general introd. and introds. to different *sidrot;* Y. Nadav, in: *Ozar Yehudei Sefarad,* 2 (1959), 69–76; E. Gottlieb, in: *Tarbiz,* 33 (1964), 287–313; I. Ta-Shma, *ibid.,* 39 (1969), 184–94; 40 (1970), 105–6; S. Z. Havlin, *ibid.,* 107–9. [G.Sch.]

MOSES BEN SOLOMON BEN SIMEON OF BURGOS (1230/1235–c. 1300), kabbalist in Spain; he was rabbi in Burgos from about 1260. Moses—also known as Moses Cinfa, evidently after his mother—came from a distinguished family. The pupil and spiritual heir of the kabbalists *Isaac and *Jacob b. Jacob ha-Kohen (who were brothers), and a leading kabbalist in Castile, he began to impart a knowledge of Kabbalah as soon as he assumed office in Burgos; his pupils included Isaac b. Solomon ibn *Sahula and Todros *Abulafia. Isaac *Albalag regarded him as the foremost kabbalist of his generation. Abraham *Abulafia met him and his pupil Shem Tov (b. Maor; "Major") between 1271 and 1274, and endeavored to attract him to his doctrine of prophetic kabbalism. Toward the end of his life Moses met *Isaac b. Samuel of Acre who recounts the event in his *Me'irat Einayim.* Isaac heard Moses utter the harsh epigram expressing the relationship of philosophy to Kabbalah: "The position attained by their heads reaches only the positon of our feet"—a motto of a gnostic-type statement indicating that the kabbalist has access to realms where the philosopher is unable to tread. Moses was a strict traditionalist and the value of his kabbalistic writings lies not so much in their original thought, as in the service they render as a treasury and repository of many traditions rarely mentioned by his contemporaries, but those which were generally not absorbed into the *Zohar.

Moses' works consist of: (1) a commentary on Song of Songs *in extenso,* no longer extant but available to Isaac ibn Sahula; (2) a commentary on the ten "left" *sefirot* (*Eser ha-Sefirot ha-Semaliyyot;* i.e., the impure *Sefirot*), also called *Ammud ha-Semali* ("The Left Pillar"; published by G. Scholem); (3) commentaries on the three *haftarot*—*Merkevet Yeshayahu* ("Throne and Chariot Vision of Isaiah"), *Merkevet Yeḥezkel* ("Throne and Chariot Vision of Ezekiel"), and *Mareh ha-Menorah shel Zekharyah* ("Zechariah's Vision of the Candelabrum"; fragments in Scholem); (4) a commentary on the 42-lettered Divine Name, the bulk of which was published anonymously in the collection *Likkutim me-Rav Hai Gaon* (1798), the introduction and important concluding remarks are published by Scholem; (5) an amplification of the treatise by his teacher Isaac ha-Kohen on "Emanation" (fragments published by Scholem); (6) *Sod Shelosh Esreh Middot u-Ferushan* ("The Mystery of the 13 Divine Attributes and Their Interpretation"), which is, in fact, a kabbalistic explanation of the early tract **Shi'ur Komah* ("Measure of the Body"; published by Scholem); (7) diverse mystical compositions on various subjects.

Moses had access to a variety of sources, including works affiliated to the circle centering on *Sefer ha-*Iyyun,* as well as a number of pseudepigraphica. All the traditions upon which he relied in his *Ammud ha-Semali* are in this category. The crystallization of a definitely gnostic trend in kabbalism can be clearly traced in his writings. He also enlarges on kabbalistic traditions relating to the efficacy of pronouncing the Divine Names as incantations, but emphasizes that he never attempted to translate theory into practice.

Bibliography: Scholem, in: *Tarbiz,* 3 (1931/32), 258–86; 4 (1932/33), 54–77, 207–25; 5 (1933/34), 50–60, 180–98, 305–23. [G.Sch.]

MOSES BEN YOM-TOV (d. 1268), London rabbi and grammarian, member of one of the most distinguished and wealthy families in England at that time. Moses himself was a businessman who did a great deal for the Jewish community of London. He was also known by the name of Magister Mosseus. His father, Yom-Tov, was the author of *Sefer ha-Tena'im.* Moses wrote a commentary to the Talmud and to the *halakhot* of Isaac *Alfasi, after the manner of the tosafists. Part of his commentaries were published by Urbach (see bibliography). In his commentary he quotes a great deal from the tosafist *Isaac b. Abraham. He was the first English talmudist who made much use of the rulings of Maimonides. Many of his contemporary scholars frequently mention and cite him in their writings. A responsum he wrote to his friend *Moses of Evreux is known. Among his pupils was the grammarian *Moses (b. Isaac) Ha-Nesi'ah, the author of the *Sefer ha-Shoham* (Jerusalem, 1947), who was mistakenly identified by A. Geiger with Moses ben Yom-Tov. Moses was the author of the *Darkhei ha-Nikkud ve-ha-Neginot,* principles of biblical punctuation and accentuation, first published by Jacob b. Ḥayyim ibn Adonijah in the margin of the masorah section at the end of the Daniel Bomberg edition of the Bible (Venice, 1524–25). From 1822 on this work was published separately several times. A scientific edition was published by D. S. Loewinger (see bibliography). Moses was also the author of a book on forbidden foods that was not published. He was the father of two sons, *Elijah Menahem b. Moses of London and *Benedict b. Moses of Lincoln.

Bibliography: Steinschneider, Handbuch, 95 n. 1356; H. P. Stokes, *Studies in Anglo-Jewish History* (1913), 3ff.; D. S. Loewinger, in: HḤY, 3 (1929), 267–344; C. Roth, *The Jews of Medieval Oxford* (1951), 115f.; idem, in: JHSET, 15 (1939–45), 31; Urbach, Tosafot, 401–3; E. E. Urbach, in: *Tiferet Yisrael: Essays Presented to Chief Rabbi Israel Brodie* (1960), 10, 19–44 (Heb. pt.); I. Ta-Shema, in: *Sinai,* 65 (1969), 202f. [A.D.]

MOSES ESRIM VE-ARBA (late 15th century), rabbi and emissary of Jerusalem. His unusual name ("Moses twenty-four") derives from the fact that he was born in Vierundzwanzig Hoefe ("24 courts") in the Aberndorf region of the province of Wuerttemberg in Germany. In the opinion of Alfred *Freimann (disputed by others), who identifies this Moses with the Moses Ashkenazi mentioned in various documents included in the journal of Michael *Balbo, Moses was sent in 1474 as an emissary of the Jewish community of Jerusalem to the island of Crete. There he became friendly with Michael Balbo, who frequently discussed with him philosophical and kabbalistic problems, such as the belief in metempsychosis, which Moses rejected. In 1475 he arrived in Constantinople with the intention of collecting money to rebuild a synagogue in Jerusalem destroyed by the Muslims. Elijah *Capsali wrote to Joseph *Taitaẓak that when Moses was there he was the cause of a bitter dispute between Moses *Capsali, chief rabbi of Constantinople, and Joseph *Colon, one of the important rabbis of Italy in the 15th century. Moses Capsali refused to assist Moses in collecting contributions for fear of the Turkish government, which had forbidden the transfer of money from Turkey to Ereẓ Israel, then under Mamluk rule. Infuriated, Moses joined the opponents of Capsali who endeavored to undermine his reputation and spread allegations that he had given incorrect decisions in matrimonial matters, so causing many to enter unwittingly into prohibited relations. Moses took the accusations of Capsali's opponents to Joseph Colon who, without verifying the facts, excommunicated Capsali. Moses proceeded to Italy in continuation of his mission. According to S. Z. *Shazar (Rubashow), it was Moses who compiled or copied the classical work, *Dos *Shemuel Bukh* (Augsburg, 1544), an epic in Yiddish based on the Book of Samuel. From his signature on the colophon of the manuscript, it appears that he also compiled glosses to Abraham ibn Ezra's Pentateuch commentary.

Bibliography: M. Lattes (ed.), *Likkutim Shonim mi-Sefer de-Bei Eliyahu . . . Eliyahu Capsali* (1896), 13–15; Graetz-Rabbinowitz, 6 (1898), 305–8, 433–5; Rubashow, in: *Zukunft,* 32 (1927), 428f.; Rosanes, Togarmah, 1 (1930[2]), 44f.; Al. Freimann, in: *Zion,* 1

Top right—The call of Moses (Ex. 3:1–6). Top left—Moses returning to Egypt and meeting Aaron (Ex. 4:20 and 27). Bottom right—Moses and Aaron performing the miracle before the elders of Israel (Ex. 4:30). Bottom left—Moses and Aaron before Pharaoh (Ex. 5:1–5). A full-page miniature from the *Golden Haggadah*, Barcelona, c. 1320. London, British Museum, Add. ms. 27210, fol. 10v ($9\frac{3}{4} \times 7\frac{3}{4}$ ins/24.7 × 19.5 cm.).

(1936), 188–202; Yaari, Sheluḥei, 214–7; Zinberg, Sifrut, 4 (1958), 60–66, 185f.; Gottlieb, in: *Sefunot*, 11 (1967), 45. [A.D.]

MOSES HA-DARSHAN (11th century), scholar and aggadist of Narbonne. Moses was the teacher of *Nathan b. Jehiel of Rome, who quotes him in the *Arukh*, sometimes anonymously. *Jacob Tam in *Sefer ha-Yashar* (part of responsa ed. by F. Rosenthal (1898), 189f. no. 46:4) considers him, together with his brother Levi, and Joseph *Bonfils, among the early leaders of French Jewry. Moses is chiefly renowned for his contribution to midrashic literature. Rashi in his commentaries on Scripture, especially on the Pentateuch, frequently quotes from Moses ha-Darshan's *Yesod*, which was apparently a book of scriptural expositions, consisting chiefly of the exegesis of words and midrashic sayings. It is not known whether the work also embraced the rest of the Bible. For many years the *Genesis Rabbah* by Moses ha-Darshan, frequently quoted by Raymond *Martini in his polemic work *Pugio Fidei*, constituted a unique problem. No book of that name was known to scholars in previous centuries. Isaac *Abrabanel, for one, stated in his *Yeshu'ot Meshiḥo* that he did not know of such a book and suspected it to be a forgery. Only recently has it become evident that the early authorities did indeed know a midrashic anthology by Moses ha-Darshan, or at least one emanating from his school, and that this extensive anthology was the basis of the Midrash called **Genesis Rabbati*, which was apparently adapted and abridged from the work of Moses. In this Midrash, Moses based himself entirely upon **Genesis Rabbah*, but drew upon his vast store of knowledge and remarkable creative ability to develop and enlarge the central ideas of the source by comparing them with other verses and passages, and connecting them with homilies occurring elsewhere. Moses made abundant use of the Mishnah, the Talmud (chiefly the Babylonian), the *Midrashei Rabbah* and *Tanḥuma*, the *Pesikta*, *Pirkei de-Rabbi Eliezer*, and others.

There is ground for the suggestion that the portions *Ba-Midbar* and *Naso* in **Numbers Rabbah*, as well as the midrashic anthology called *Midrash Aggadah* (ed. by S. Buber, 1894), largely emanate from the *bet-midrash* of Moses ha-Darshan. One unique characteristic of Moses' midrashic work is his use of the *aggadot* embedded in the *Apocrypha such as Jubilees, Enoch, The Testament of the Twelve Patriarchs, and others, of which he possessed an improved Hebrew text. He also drew upon the collected Midrashim of his predecessors compiled from the Apocryphal literature, particularly from *Midrash Tadshe* (see Smaller *Midrashim) which with its proem was ascribed by Moses to the *tanna*, *Phinehas b. Jair. Some wish to ascribe to Moses several other extant minor Midrashim, on the basis of their similarity to his known work. In addition to citation in Rashi and Nathan b. Jehiel, the work was extensively quoted by *Tobiah b. Eliezer in his midrashic collection, *Lekaḥ Tov;* Menaḥem b. Solomon, in his anthology, *Sekhel Tov;* and, very much later by Abraham *Saba in his *Ẓeror ha-Mor*.

Bibliography: A. Epstein, *Mi-Kadmoniyyot ha-Yehudim*, 1 (1887), i–xiv; idem, *Moshe ha-Darshan mi-Narbonah* (1891); *Kitvei R. Avraham Epstein*, 1 (1950), 215–44; S. Lieberman, *Sheki'in* (1939), 52ff.; Zunz-Albeck, Derashot, 144f.; S. Buber (ed.), *Midrash Aggadah*, 1 (1894), introd.; Ḥ. Albeck (ed.), *Bereshit Rabbati* (1940), introd. 1–36. [I.T.-S.]

MOSES HA-KOHEN OF TORDESILLAS (second half of 14th century), rabbi born in Tordesillas, Spain. Moses experienced the terrible sufferings caused during the civil war in Castile, 1366–69. He moved to Avila, and was evidently appointed rabbi of the congregation there. Moses represented the Jewish side in the religious *disputation ordered to be held in Avila in 1375. There were four sessions and Moses apparently emerged triumphant. After engaging successfully in an additional debate held with a pupil of *Abner of Burgos, he committed his arguments to writing in his still-unpublished work *Ezer ha-Emunah*.

Bibliography: J. Loeb, in: REJ, 18 (1889), 226–30; Baer, Spain, 1 (1961), 374–5; J. Rosenthal, in: *Aresheth*, 2 (1960), 147 no. 61; D. S. Loewinger and B. D. Weinryb, *Catalogue of the Hebrew Manuscripts in the Library of the Juedisch-Theologisches Seminar in Breslau* (1965), 172. [Ed.]

MOSES ḤAYYIM EPHRAIM OF SUDYLKOW (c. 1740–1800?), ḥasidic preacher and *ẓaddik*, son of *Adel, the daughter of *Israel b. Eliezer Ba'al Shem Tov. He was the eldest brother of *Baruch b. Jehiel of Medzibezh. He is praised in the well-known letter of Israel Ba'al Shem Tov to his brother-in-law, *Abraham Gershon of Kutow. Although he knew that a *ẓaddik* was a highly influential figure he did not gather many Ḥasidim round him, but lived in humility and poverty. He served as a preacher in Sudylkow and popularized Ḥasidism through his work, *Degel Maḥaneh Efrayim* (date and place of publication are unknown), a classic of Ḥasidism. The book is made up of sermons on the weekly portions from the Pentateuch. At the end of the book there is a collection of "dreams" (*ḥalomot*) from 1780 to 1785, describing mystical visions. The work, with the addition of stories and parables, is written in a pleasant and lucid manner. It contains important teachings and traditions of the Ba'al Shem Tov and his disciples, and shows also the influence of *Dov Baer of Mezhirech. It expresses social criticism of those scholars who boast of their Torah learning, in contrast with the Ḥasidim who are distinguished by their humility. He notes that in study for its own sake the letters of the Torah serve as a focus for meditation and concentration, and that the light of the **En Sof* (Infinite) shines through these letters to the student of the Torah. Because every generation interprets the Torah according to its needs, the *ẓaddik*, as the representative of the Torah, may be permitted to break a particular law when necessary. Moses Ḥayyim, however, warned Ḥasidim against superficial imitation of the *ẓaddikim*. The obligation, according to Lurianic Kabbalah, to "elevate the sparks" (*ha'ala'at ha-niẓoẓot*), is expanded by Moses Ḥayyim to everything including slaves and animals. Thus, he also advocates the elevation of undesirable thoughts (*ha'ala'at maḥashavot zarot*). Moses Ḥayyim held that man would enter the palace of truth and redemption of the soul only by constantly thinking of God. He emphasizes his admiration for his grandfather and states that redemption and the end of the Exile would occur when the teachings of the Ba'al Shem Tov were accepted. However, he states that whereas in previous generations (i.e., during the time of Israel Ba'al Shem Tov) one might have hoped for the imminent advent of the messianic age, as a result of the spiritual decline in his time, this possibility had diminished.

Bibliography: M. Gutman, *Geza Kodesh* (1951); Dubnow, Ḥasidut, 204–8; Y. Tishby, in: *Zion*... (1967), 33–34; J. Weiss, in: *I. Brodie Jubilee Volume* (1967), 167–8; R. Schatz-Uffenheimer, *Ha-Ḥasidut ke-Mistikah* (1968), 185, index. [Mo.Hal.]

MOSES ISAAC (Darshan; also known as the **Kelmer Maggid;** 1828–1899), the main preacher of the *Musar movement. Moses Isaac was born near Slonim. In his youth he already showed exceptional abilities as a preacher and delivered his first sermon in Slonim at the age of 15. Moses Isaac became a shopkeeper in a nearby town, but, failing to earn a livelihood, returned to Slonim to seek other means of subsistence. Reluctant to make a living from religious activity, he refused tempting offers to serve as a preacher, but at last accepted a position as preacher to a synagogue in Slonim, requesting the meager salary of half a ruble a week. Dissatisfied with his lack of influence, he accepted a similar position at Novaya Mysh, but there also he found no satisfaction. At the age of 21 he relinquished his position and proceeded to Kovno (Kaunas) in order to study under R. Israel *Lipkin, the founder of the Musar movement. He remained there until he had absorbed the teachings of that movement, and Lipkin, recognizing his outstanding abilities as a preacher and his potential influence, charged him with propagating its ideals. For over half a century Moses Isaac was the outstanding *maggid* of the Musar movement. He accepted positions as preacher to various communities—Kelme (1850–53; whence his name, the Kelmer Maggid), Zagare (1853–58), Oshmyany (1858–60), and Minsk (1860–63)—but essentially he was an itinerant preacher, traveling from town to town.

In his sermons Moses Isaac departed entirely from the exegetical and expository method of preaching current in his time, and applied himself solely to raising the moral and ethical standards of the communities. Wherever he came he would first pay a visit to the local rabbi in order to acquaint himself with the social evils prevalent in the community and then fearlessly denounce them. The following extract from one of his published sermons (*Tokhaḥat Ḥayyim*, no. 7) is indicative of the content of his homilies: "If a man recites Psalms from morning to night but tells lies and is guilty of slander; if he prays with devotion and recites the Grace after Meals aloud, but has no compassion for his fellowman; if with the same enthusiasm as he fulfills every precept between man and God, he vindictively persecutes anyone who has done him a wrong . . . he can be called a wicked man." He inveighed particularly against commercial malpractices, exploitation of the poor, and dishonest practices toward non-Jews. His influence was unbounded. Contemporary newspapers report how on the morrow of his sermons he would visit the local market, and shopkeepers would destroy their false weights and measures. A dishonest shopkeeper is said to have lost his reason as a result of these denunciations, while another committed suicide. He did not hesitate to name flagrant transgressors, especially unworthy communal leaders, from the pulpit. As a result, on more than one occasion he was maligned, denounced to the government, and imprisoned, but, undeterred, he continued his reproofs.

Moses Isaac used to preach in a unique singsong, sometimes bursting into song and although he was ridiculed for it, especially by the *maskilim* whom he vigorously attacked, the effect upon the masses was hypnotic. J. L. Gordon, the leader of the *maskilim*, complained (in *Allgemeine Zeitung des Judenthums*, 25 (1861), 168–70) of his "obscurantism" in establishing "Musar shtiebels" (conventicles for the study of Musar), and that he was so successful that he had established one in Mitau (Jelgava), Latvia, a center of the *maskilim*. Moses Isaac established scores of such "Musar shtiebels" throughout the country, synagogues for humble workers, arranging study courses for them, and philanthropic societies. In 1884 he visited London where the chief rabbi, Nathan Adler, and Samuel Montagu (the first Lord Swaythling), founder and head of the Federation of Synagogues, were greatly impressed by him and defrayed the expenses of his visit. In 1898 he moved to Lida to settle with his son Ben Zion Darshan, and died in the following year. His only published work is the *Tokhaḥat Ḥayyim* (Vilna, 1897), ten of his sermons which he chose as examples of his teachings.

Bibliography: D. Katz, *Tenu'at ha-Musar*, 2 (1954), 395–407.

[L.I.R.]

MOSES (Mesharshia) KAHANA BEN JACOB, *gaon* of Sura, 825–836. Moses, who succeeded Kimoi b. Rav Ashi, is identical with Mesharshia Kahana b. Mar Rav Jacob who is mentioned in the Spanish version of the "Letter of *Sherira Gaon" (ed. by B. M. Lewin (1921), 115). He is apparently not identical with Moses, *gaon* of Sura in the ninth century, who was a brother of *Zadok Gaon, the father of *Nahshon Gaon. Many of his responsa have been preserved in the works of the *geonim* and the *rishonim*. Some touching on the liturgy are quoted in the *seder* of *Amram Gaon. In many responsa he is referred to simply as Moses Gaon. In one of his responsa Hai Gaon writes that Mesharshia occupied himself with amulets and charms, stating that faith in them was characteristic of the students of Sura (*Ozar ha-Ge'onim*, B. M. Lewin, 4 (1931), Ḥagigah, 20).

Bibliography: Rapoport, in: *Bikkurei ha-Ittim*, 10 (1829), 35 no. 25; J. Mueller, *Mafte'ah li-Teshuvot ha-Ge'onim* (1891), 75–79; Cowley, in: JQR, 18 (1905/06), 402; L. Ginzberg, *Geonica*, 2 (1909), index s.v. *Moshe Gaon*.

[A.D.]

MOSES LEIB OF SASOV (1745–1807), ḥasidic rabbi. He was a pupil of Samuel Shmelke *Horowitz of Nikolsburg, *Dov Baer the Maggid of Mezhirech, and *Elimelech of Lyzhansk. He spent 13 years studying both Torah and Kabbalah under Samuel Shmelke who was then rabbi in Rychwal and Sieniawa. Moses wrote novellae on several tractates of the Talmud, part of which were published in the pamphlets *Likkutei ha-ReMaL* (1856), *Torat ha-ReMaL ha-Shalem* (1903), and *Ḥiddushei ha-ReMaL* (1921). For several years he lived in Opatov. When he moved to Sasov he attracted many followers and the town became a great ḥasidic center. His disciples included Jacob Isaac of *Przysucha (Peshiskhah), Ẓevi Hirsch of *Zhidachov, Menahem Mendel of Kosov, and others. Moses was known for his abounding love for all Jews and for his charity, on account of which he was called "father of widows and orphans." He composed many ḥasidic melodies and dances. His successor was his only son, JEKUTHIEL SHMELKE, who was seven years old when his father died. Jekuthiel grew up in the homes of *Abraham Ḥayyim of Zloczow, Menahem Mendel of Kosov, and Israel of *Ruzhin in Sadagora (Sadgora), and returned to Sasov in 1849.

Bibliography: Y. Raphael, *Sefer ha-Ḥasidut* (1956); idem, *Sasov* (1946); M. Buber, *Tales of the Ḥasidim, The Later Masters* (1966), 81–95.

[YI.R.]

MOSES (ben Nethanel) NATHAN (14th century), communal worker and poet. Moses, who lived in Tarrega, Catalonia, left a collection of moral parables in rhymed meter, entitled *Toẓe'ot Ḥayyim*, which was published in the *Shetei Yadot* (Venice, 1618, 142–50) of Menahem b. Judah de *Lonzano. It contains 58 sections with aphorisms on counsel, quickness, industry, humility, and other virtues. A short acrostic poem prefaces the proverbs, each word ending with a letter of his name. While the work contains no original ideas, it is composed in a clear and beautiful style. A manuscript of the book is extant in Paris (Bibliothèque Nationale, no. 1284). It is possible that its author is identical with the communal worker Moses Nathan who lived in the 14th century, known from Hebrew sources and also from Christian documents, where he is referred to as Moses Naçan (Nazan). In the *takkanot* issued in 1354 by the representatives of the communities of Aragon when they met in Barcelona, Moses Nathan was the first of the signatories. He may also be identical with the Mosse Açan (Azan), who wrote a poem on chess that has survived in a Castilian translation.

Bibliography: Schirmann, Sefarad, 2 (1956), 541–3, 697;

Davidson, Oẓar, 4 (1933), 449; Baer, Urkunden, 1 (1929), 306–7, 350–9. [A.D.]

MOSES OF EVREUX (**Moses b. Schne'or**), one of three brothers known as *Gedolei Evreux* ("the greatest [scholars] of Evreux") in the first half of the 13th century. Moses was the brother of *Isaac of Evreux and apparently a pupil of *Samson of Sens. Moses' individual teaching cannot always be identified since it is incorporated with that of his brothers, the whole being referred to by the *rishonim* as "the view of Evreux." He is mentioned by name, however, in the *Shitah Mekubbeẓet* to *Bava Kamma* and in late collections of *tosafot* to *Zevaḥim, Menaḥot,* and *Bekhorot.* His comments on the Pentateuch are known from the *Sefer ha-Gan* of Aaron b. Joseph ha-Kohen. The similarity of some of his ethical sayings quoted in the *Kol Bo* to Naḥmanides' "Ethical Letter" to his son led some scholars to ascribe the latter work to Moses, but there are no solid grounds for doing so. Moses' son, Samuel, is referred to as the author of a prayer book. The work *Al ha-Kol* (published in *Ha-Goren,* 7 (1908)) containing rulings, *halakhot,* and customs, was compiled by one of his pupils.

Bibliography: Weiss, in: *Ha-Goren,* 7 (1908), 76–111; Urbach, Tosafot, 395–9 and index s.v. *Moshe b. Senior me-Evreux;* Preschel, in: *Talpioth,* 8 (1961), 49–53; Y. Lipschitz (ed.), *Tosefot Evreux* (1969), 19–28. [I.T.-S.]

MOSES OF KIEV (12th century), talmudist. No biographical details about him are known. He appears to have visited Western Europe, and probably knew the tosafist Jacob *Tam personally. In Tam's *Sefer ha-Yashar* (1811 Vienna edition, no. 522) a halakhic saying occurs "that Moses of Kiev received from Rabbenu Tam." It is possible that he stayed for some time in the latter's yeshivah in Ramerupt. A. Epstein (in MGWJ, 39 (1895), 511) attempts to identify Moses of Kiev with Moses of Russia mentioned in the *Sefer ha-Shoham.* According to Epstein, Moses left Russia for France in 1124 following the expulsion of the Jews in that year from Kiev. Urbach (Tosafot, 193), however, disagrees, since in 1124 Rabbenu Tam was still very young. Moreover there is no information about an expulsion of the Jews from Kiev in 1124, though a great fire did break out there in that year. It appears that Moses arrived in France at a much later period.

Moses addressed queries to *Samuel b. Ali, head of the Babylonian academy: "Thus sent Samuel b. Ali head of the academy from Babylon to R. Moses of Kiev" (Responsa Meir of Rothenburg, ed. by R. N. Rabinowitz (1860), no. 443). The connection between Moses and Samuel b. Ali is also referred to in the *Sefer Yiḥusei Tanna'im ve-Amora'im* of Judah b. Kalonymus.

Bibliography: A. Harkavy, *Ḥadashim Gam Yeshanim,* 1 no. 7 (1895–96), 44–45; F. Kupfer and T. Lewicki, *Źródła hebrajskie do dziejów słowian* (1956). [S.E.]

MOSES OF PALERMO (c. 1275), Sicilian translator. Moses of Palermo was one of a group of Jewish translators from southern Italy who were active in Naples and Salerno at the request of Charles of Anjou (1226–85). Their work continued the tradition of Jewish translation that flourished during the reign of Frederick II and his natural son Manfred. Charles apparently paid Moses a regular stipend as an official translator. On the occasion of his journey from Salerno to Naples in 1270, Moses received payment of "an ounce of gold" at Charles' command. A document dated 1277 states that the king ordered Maestro Matteo Siciliaco to give Latin lessons to Moses of Palermo, thus enabling him to translate scientific texts from the Arabic. Moses' name is primarily linked with the translation of a "Treatise on the Healing of Horses" ascribed to Hippocrates (*Liber de curationibus infirmitatum equorum quem translavit de lingua arabica in latinam Magister Moyses de Palermo*). This was translated into Italian, together with another article on the same subject, and published in 1865 as *Trattati di mascalcia attribuiti ad Ippocrate, tradotti dall'arabo in latino da Maestro Moise da Palermo, volgarizzati nel sec. XIII* (ed. P. Delprato). One of the earliest scientific texts written in Italian, this translation played an important part in the development of scientific terminology in the Italian language. It was widely circulated both in Italy and in other countries throughout the Middle Ages. Another version of the treatise, also in Italian, was entitled *Libro della natura dei cavalli,* and this was often reprinted during the Renaissance era.

Bibliography: M. Steinschneider, in: HB, 10 (1870), 8–11; Steinschneider, Uebersetzungen, 2 (1893), 985; U. Cassuto, in: *Vessillo Israelitico,* 59 (1911), 341; Roth, *Jews in the Renaissance* (1959), 69–70. [J.B.S.]

MOSES OF PAVIA, medieval talmudist (dates unknown). Moses of Pavia is reported as being mentioned in the talmudic lexicon *Arukh* of *Nathan b. Jehiel, although his name nowhere appears in the printed editions. There are no certain details concerning the time and place of his labors. In the *Mikdash Me'at* of Moses de Rieti (15th cent.), it is noted that Moses of Pavia died a martyr's death in Lombardy, but there is no discernible historical basis for this statement. In the Parma manuscript (De'Rossi 1360) the event is pinpointed as having taken place in 1096, i.e., at the time of the First Crusade. It is possible that Moses was one of the German scholars who migrated to Germany and were murdered there in 1096. Kaufmann's conjecture (Schriften, 3 (1915), 26) is that Moses of Pavia is to be identified with a tutor of the same name who, after having been banned, went to Capua and later to Pavia.

Bibliography: Guedemann, Gesch Erz, 2 (1884), 14; Kohut, Arukh, 1 (1926[2]), xxxviii; S. J. L. Rapoport, *Toledot Rabbi Natan Ish Romi* (1913), 56 n. 41; Zunz, Gesch, 57; Zunz, Poesie, 19. [U.C./Ed.]

MOSES SHOHAM BEN DAN OF DOLINA (end of 18th century), ḥasidic author and preacher in Dolina in eastern Galicia. He was a disciple of *Israel b. Eliezer Ba'al Shem Tov, and was related by marriage to *Jehiel Michal of Zloczow. He quotes traditions and teachings of both in his works: *Divrei Moshe* (Polonnoye, 1801), commentaries on the Torah; *Imrei Shoham* (1880), on the tractates *Ketubbot, Kiddushin* and *Bava Meẓia; Seraf Peri Eẓ Ḥayyim* (1866), on the *Peri Eẓ Ḥayyim* of Ḥayyim *Vital.

Bibliography: S. Y. Agnon, *Ha-Esh ve-ha-Eẓim* (1962), 106–7; M. Kamelhar, *Ha-Ḥasidut ve-Ẓiyyon* (1963), 104–6. [Ed.]

MOSES ZE'EV (Wolf) BEN ELIEZER OF GRODNO (d. 1830), Lithuanian rabbi. Moses was born and grew up in Grodno. He was appointed *rosh yeshivah* there but left in 1813 to become the *av bet din* in Tiktin, where he stayed until 1824. He was then appointed *av bet din* in Bialystok, remaining there until his death. When Moses was first given this appointment, the people in Bialystok were concerned that he was so young, but he wittily replied that this was a fault which would improve with age. His best-known work, *Marot ha-Ẓove'ot* (Grodno, 1810) on the laws concerning *agunah,* is based upon the relevant chapter (17) of Shulḥan Arukh *Even ha-Ezer.* He also wrote *Ḥiddushei Moharmaz* (1858), on the commentary of R. Jonathan b. David Ha-Cohen of Lunel to Alfasi on tractate *Eruvin,* and three works all with the same title, *Aguddat Ezov:* (1) a collection of sermons (Bialystok, 1824) concluding with *Alon Bakhut,* nine funeral orations on great rabbis; (2) responsa (2 vols.;

1885–86); (3) novellae on the Shulḥan Arukh (1904). On the title page of the *Marot ha-Ẓove'ot* he gives his family tree in detail back to *Judah Loew b. Bezalel of Prague, stating where each of his forebears served as rabbi.

Bibliography: Fuenn, Keneset, 301f. [AN.L.L.]

MOSHAV (מוֹשָׁב) or **MOSHAV OVEDIM** (מוֹשַׁב עוֹבְדִים, "workers settlement"), cooperative smallholders' village in Ereẓ Israel combining some of the features of both cooperative and private farming. The idea was evolved during World War I in the quest for a form of settlement that would not only express national and social aspirations on the basis of collective principles like the kibbutz, but also provide scope for individual initiative and independent farm management. The idea was mooted in articles published in various periodicals and was given definite shape in a pamphlet *Yissud Moshevei Ovedim* ("The Establishment of Workers' Villages," 1919) by Eliezer *Joffe, who formulated the social and economic principles on which the moshav should be based: nationally owned land, mutual aid, cooperative purchasing and marketing, and the family as the fundamental unit. These principles were further developed in the writings of Yiẓhak Vilkanski (Elazari-*Volcani), the agronomist, who dealt with the economic structure desirable for the moshav and regarded it as the appropriate answer to the needs of mass settlement. This evaluation was fully vindicated after the establishment of the State of Israel, when tens of thousands of new immigrant families were settled on the land in hundreds of moshavim.

At first the moshav economy was based on mixed farming, which, it was expected, would supply most of the farmer's needs and give him greater stamina to withstand agricultural fluctuations and crises than the single-crop farm. It would also permit the work to be spread out evenly over the year, a point of particular importance since the settler and his family had to cultivate the farm by themselves without the aid of hired seasonal labor.

Milestones of Moshav Settlement. The first two moshavim were founded in 1921, *Nahalal in September in the northern Jezreel Valley and *Kefar Yeḥezkel in December in the eastern part. Most of the members had formerly lived in kibbutzim (Deganyah, Kinneret, Ḥuldah, and Merḥavyah). Within ten years another eight moshavim were founded, most of them in the Jezreel Valley. At the beginning of the 1930s, the movement was given a new impetus by widespread settlement in the Ḥefer Plain by the Hityashvut ha-Elef scheme, intended to settle 1,000 families on the land in the Sharon and Judea, and by the establishment of the first moshavim in the south. The landholdings were small compared with those of the first moshavim, as it was assumed that incomes would be supplemented and the farms consolidated by work outside the moshav in fruit groves and construction projects. During the Arab rebellion of 1936–39, more moshavim were established all over the country, especially in the valleys and in the south, as *Stockade and Watchtower settlements. At the end of World War II, a number of moshavim were established by demobilized soldiers from the *Jewish Brigade and other Jewish units in the British army. In 1948, when the State of Israel was established, there were 58 moshavim in the country.

Most of the new immigrants who arrived in large numbers immediately after the establishment of the state differed in many respects from the pioneers who had settled on the land after spending years in training and preparation. They consisted mainly of families with many children, elderly persons, even entire communities brought over en masse. The moshav ovedim, with its family structure, was

Kefar Yeḥezkel, one of the first two moshavim to be established in Ereẓ Israel. Courtesy Government Press Office, Tel Aviv.

felt to be the only medium of settling these immigrants on the land. Hundreds of veterans from the older moshavim came forward to recruit new immigrants for settlements, to set up moshavim, and particularly to instruct and guide the new settlers. In the period 1949–56, 250 new moshavim were established, with a population that approached 100,000 in 1970.

The Moshav Movement (Tenu'at ha-Moshavim). The moshav movement was founded in the mid-1930s to cope with the problems of the existing moshavim, to mold and preserve their social structure, and to help establish more moshavim. The movement developed a series of economic, financial, and service institutions to advance these purposes. These include: Keren ha-Moshavim, a mutual assistance fund; the Ein Ḥai Bank; Tagmulim la-Moshavim, a savings and pension fund for members; Bittu'aḥ Hadadi, a mutual insurance company; Matam (Mishkei Tenu'at ha-Moshavim—Moshav Movement Farms), which provides low-priced, high-quality products; Bank le-Mashkanta'ot (Mortgage Bank), which provides loans for private and public building in the moshavim; and regional purchasing organizations, with some 30 to 50 moshavim in each, to organize marketing and supplies. The latter have set up enterprises, in cooperation with local councils, to lower the cost of services and supplies, and improve production facilities. Examples of these enterprises are citrus-canning plants, fodder plants, slaughterhouses, fruit-packing plants, egg-sorting warehouses, and cold storage plants. The movement has departments for education, culture, social activities, internal arbitration, advice and training in farming and organization, and absorption of new settlers. It also has a youth section, and it publishes periodicals.

In 1970 there were 212 moshavim, with a total population of 75,000, affiliated to Tenu'at ha-Moshavim. Other moshav movements were: the Union of Religious Cooperative Movements of *Ha-Po'el ha-Mizrachi, with 56 moshavim and a membership of 24,000; the Farmers' Union (Ha-Iḥud ha-Ḥakla'i), with 32 villages and 10,000 people; and the cooperative Agricultural Center of the *Ḥerut Movement and *Betar, with eight moshavim and 1,500 people. There were also 13 moshavim with 4,000 people affiliated to *Ha-Oved ha-Ẓiyyoni; nine, with 2,500, to *Po'alei Agudat Israel and *Agudat Israel; six, with 1,600, to the *Farmers' Federation (Hitaḥdut ha-Ikkarim); two with 370 to *Mapam; and eight unaffiliated moshavim, with 3,400 people; making a total of 346 moshavim with a combined population of about 122,000–95,600 living in 269 moshavim founded after the establishment of the State of Israel in May 1948 and 26,500 living in 77 veteran moshavim.

Organization of the Moshav. Each moshav is organized as a cooperative society for agricultural settlement and constitutes a unit of local government administered by the management of the society. The moshav operates in accordance with the Cooperative Societies Ordinance, 1933, under the authority of the Registrar of Cooperative Societies; its accounts are audited by the audit unions for agricultural cooperation. Its activities are governed by a general set of regulations which serve as a pattern for those of the individual moshavim. At an annual assembly of members, each moshav elects its management, which comprises a managing committee, a control board, and committees for economic, social, educational, and cultural activities. Disputes between members or between a member and the management are submitted for arbitration and decision to the social committee or a judicial committee of the parent movement. The moshav helps its members to obtain credit, purchase seed, fertilizer, and fodder, and to market their produce. It maintains farming equipment and vehicles (sometimes together with neighboring moshavim), workshops, cooperative stores, etc. It provides members' children with primary and post-primary education in local or regional schools, and fosters cultural activities; members receive medical care in local clinics.

The society erects all the public buildings and installations including pumping installations, central irrigation network, supply stores, dairies, refrigeration and sorting plants, schools, clinics, and sports facilities. It finances its investments partly by direct taxation of members and partly by loans based on a general mutual guarantee by the members. The general assembly decides on the annual budget, composed of the local government budget (covered by direct taxes) and the administrative budget (covered partly by taxes and partly by levies on items of income and on various types of production outlays). In the 1960s the moshav set itself new goals: securing production rights in nationally planned branches of agriculture (dairy farming, poultry farming, orchards, etc.); the encouragement of new crops, notably for export purposes; and the protection of members' interests in taxation and social security. The expansion and social developments of the moshavim have given rise to the need for a legal basis for their life and activities. The draft Cooperative Societies Law submitted to the Knesset contains a special chapter dealing with the legal framework of the moshav. This is designed, in accordance with existing conditions, to safeguard established principles and ensure that the moshav and the moshav movement will continue to develop as an efficient and healthy unit of the national economy and society.

The Moshav as an Example to Developing Countries. In recent years the moshav and its way of life have attracted the interest of some leaders and many students from Asia, Africa, and Latin America. Thousands of them have gone to Israel to study the methods of the moshav, which they regard as a possible solution to the problems of organizing agriculture in their own countries. The moshav movement has been host to students and has organized study courses for them. It has also provided Israel's technical assistance program (see State of *Israel, Foreign Policy) with many instructors to establish and advise settlements of the moshav type in these countries. Today there are scores of such settlements in Africa, Asia, and Latin America, with moshav members from Israel as instructors. The moshav movement, together with the Israel Ministry of Foreign Affairs, has also established a volunteer movement for foreign service, and many young men from moshavim have served, and are serving, as volunteers in developing countries, living and working with the local population.

Bibliography: H. Viteles, *A History of the Cooperative Movement in Israel*, 4 (1968), incl. bibl.; I. M. Klayman, *The Moshav in Israel* (1970); D. Weintraub, M. Lissak, and Y. Azmon, *Moshava, Kibbutz and Moshav*... (1969); R. Tamsma, *De Moshav Ovdiem* (Dutch, 1966), English summary; *ibid.*, 342–91, incl. bibl.; H. Darin-Drabkin, *Patterns of Cooperative Agriculture in Israel* (1962); S. Dayan, *Man and the Soil* (1965); E. Meyer, *Der Moshav 1948–1963* (1967); E. Joffe, *Ketavim*, 2 vols. (1947); idem, *Yissud Moshevei Ovedim* (1919); A. Assaf, *Moshevei ha-Ovedim be-Yisrael* (1954); Y. Uri, *Bi-Netivei Moshav ha-Ovedim* (1950); I. Korn, *Kibbutz ha-Galuyyot be-Hitnaḥaluto* (1964); R. Weitz, *Darkenu ba-Ḥakla'ut u-va-Hityashevut* (1959); Y. Shapira (ed.), *Nahalal*... (1947); *Kefar Yeḥezkel* (Heb. anthol., 1948); E. Labes, *Handbook of the Moshav* (1959); D. Weintraub, *Immigration and Social Change* (1971).

[U.F.]

MOSHAV SHITTUFI (מוֹשָׁב שִׁתּוּפִי, collective moshav), a form of settlement combining features of the *kibbutz and the *moshav. The originators of the idea wanted to combine the advantages of both forms of settlement, while avoiding what they regarded as overemphasis on collectivism in the kibbutz and on individual farming in the moshav. They therefore separated production from consumption, adopting the productive system of the kibbutz and the preservation of the family unit in the moshav. The village's lands and installations—sometimes including industrial plants—are collectively owned and operated, as in the kibbutz, but each family has its own home and is responsible for its own cooking, domestic economy, and the care of children, as in the moshav. Mothers generally work outside the home for two or three hours a day five times a week. From the proceeds of the moshav shittufi's farming and other enterprises, each family is allotted a sum to meet its own needs, while the village as a whole provides education for the children, medical services, cultural activities, and the like.

The first two moshavim shittufiyyim—*Kefar Ḥittim in Lower Galilee and *Moledet in the Gilboa district—were founded in 1936–37, and after World War II many of the demobilized soldiers who settled on the land chose this form of settlement. In 1970 there were 22 moshavim shittufiyyim with a total population of 4,200. Eight belonged to Tenu'at ha-Moshavim, five to Ha-Oved ha-Ẓiyyoni, four to Ha-Po'el ha-Mizrachi, three to the Ḥerut movement, and one each to the Farmers' Union and Po'alei Agudat Israel. To coordinate their activities, the moshavim shittufiyyim maintain an inter-movement committee.

For bibliography, see *Moshav. [U.F.]

MOSKONI (Mashkoni), JUDAH LEON BEN MOSES (b. 1328), medieval philosopher and scholar from Ocrida in Bulgaria. As a result of disturbances caused by war Moskoni left his native town in 1360 and traveled extensively through many countries. While at Negropon he became a pupil of *Shemariah b. Elijah b. Jacob. During his travels he formed close ties with the great Jewish scholars of Egypt, Morocco, Italy, and southern France. Moskoni was well acquainted with the Hebrew and Arabic philosophic literature of his time, and stressed the importance of studying grammar for an understanding of the Bible. His main work is a supercommentary to the commentaries of Abraham ibn Ezra on the Pentateuch under the title *Even ha-Ezer* which he wrote in 1362, but he also wrote other works in the fields of Hebrew grammar, biblical exegesis, and philosophy. The year of his death is not known. Some fragments of his commentary to Genesis (1:1–2) were published by N. Ben-Menahem; and to Exodus (some chapters) by A. Berliner and D. Hoffmann (see bibliography). Special importance is attached to Moskoni because of his edition of the Hebrew *Josippon. He had at his disposal a number of versions of the book, but in the end selected the long adaptation of it, divided it into chapters, and added an interesting and detailed introduction. His edition has been preserved in two manuscripts and is the basis of the Constantinople edition of *Josippon*, where his introduction appears in an abbreviated and adapted form. All the standard editions of *Josippon* are merely reprints of this version. His introduction to *Josippon* was published by A. Berliner and D. Hoffmann.

Bibliography: Vogelstein-Rieger, 1 (1896), 186, 450; HB, 9 (1869), 16; A. Berliner and D. Hoffmann (eds.), *Oẓar Tov*, 1 (1878), 1–10, 17–25, 41–42; N. Ben-Menahem, in: *Oẓar Yehudei Sefarad*, 2 (1959), 43–54; idem, in: *Aresheth*, 3 (1961), 74. [D.FL.]

MOSKOWITZ, HENRY (1879–1936), U.S. social worker and community leader. Moskowitz, who was born in Husse, Rumania, went to the United States in his youth. He helped organize the Madison House Social Settlement. In 1907 he became active in the Ethical Culture Society and remained an associate leader of that group until 1913. From 1913 until 1917 Moskowitz served under the New York City reformist mayor, John P. Mitchell, as chairman of several city commissions. He was also an active leader of the Progressive Party under Theodore Roosevelt. In Jewish affairs Moskowitz served on the executive of the Joint Distribution Committee and as the executive chairman of American ORT and was elected in 1936 to the executive committee of its World Union. Moskowitz was closely associated with Governor Alfred E. Smith and, together with Norman Hapgood, wrote Smith's biography, *Up From City Streets* (1927). He also edited *Progressive Democracy: Speeches and State Papers of Alfred E. Smith* (1928) and wrote *Jewish Reconstruction in Russia, Poland, Romania; a report* (1925).

Moskowitz's wife BELLE LINDER ISRAELS MOSKOWITZ (1877–1933), who was born in New York City, worked on the professional staff of the Educational Alliance in New York City from 1900 to 1903 and married Henry Moskowitz in 1914. In 1908 she joined the staff of *The Survey*, remaining there for two years. She subsequently became increasingly involved in communal and political activity, and in public relations counseling. Belle Moskowitz later served on many of Governor Alfred E. Smith's state commissions and became his confidante and adviser. During the 1928 presidential campaign, when Smith was the Democratic nominee, Belle Moskowitz was the publicity chairman of the party. She also served as director of both the National Council of Jewish Women and the Women's City Club, and secretary to the Mayor's Commission of Women on National Defense. She championed such causes as public health and housing. Following Smith's defeat in the 1928 presidential race, she became the president of Publicity Associates, where she remained until her death. [ED.]

MOSLER, HENRY (1841–1920), U.S. painter. He was born in New York and studied art in Cincinnati, Duesseldorf, and Paris. He moved to Europe where he lived in Munich and Paris. The French government purchased his painting, "The Return of the Prodigal Son," for the Luxembourg Museum. Other pictures acquired by public collections include "The Birth of the Flag" (Betsy Ross and her friends stitching the first American flag) in the Corcoran Gallery in Washington, D.C., and "A Wedding Festival in Brittany" in the Metropolitan Museum of New York. Mosler was the recipient of many honors. Even if some of his compositions may appear over-elaborate and theatrical, there can be no doubt about the high quality of his portraits, executed in fresh, vigorous brushwork. [A.W.]

MOSS, JOHN (1771–1847), Philadelphia merchant, shipping magnate, and civic leader. Moss emigrated to the U.S. as a glass engraver from London in 1796. Opening a dry goods store in Philadelphia in 1807, he quickly became a major importer, ultimately owning a large number of ships. After he turned the active direction of his firm over to his brothers in 1823, Moss shifted his own concerns to banking and insurance, canal companies, and civic enterprises. In 1828 he was elected to the Common Council on the Jacksonian Democratic Party ticket, and in this role he participated in the establishment of the world-famous Wills Eye Hospital. Moss was one of the rich Philadelphia Jews who entered almost every phase of civic activity: he was a steward of the Society of Sons of St. George; a life subscriber to the Orphan Society; and a founding member of the Musical Fund Society. This status was not achieved at the sacrifice of Jewish identification; he was an active member of Mikveh Israel Congregation, a major contributor to its building fund of 1818, and, late in life, a supporter of Isaac Leeser's American Jewish Publication Society. As presiding officer at the Philadelphia *Damascus Affair protest meeting in 1840, Moss had become the representative of his community.

Bibliography: Rosenbloom, Biogr Dict; L. Moss, in: AJHSP, 2 (1894), 171–4; E. Wolf and M. Whiteman, *History of the Jews of Philadelphia* (1957), index; S. A. Moss, *Genealogy of John Moss and his Wife, Rebecca . . .* (1937). [B.W.K.]

MOSSE, family originating from the Prussian town of Maerkisch Friedland. The family's name was originally Moses but MARKUS MOSSE (1807–1865) changed his to Mosse. Born in Graetz, Posen, Markus was a well-known physician and became president of the local Jewish community. He fought on the side of the Polish nationalists during the 1848 uprising and was wounded and taken prisoner.

Markus Mosse had eight sons and six daughters. His eldest son SALOMON (1837–1903) founded the Mosse linen house in Berlin and was joined by two other sons THEODOR (1842–1916) and PAUL (1849–1920). Two other sons Albert (see below) and MAXIMUS (1857–1920) became lawyers.

ALBERT MOSSE (1846–1925) specialized in administrative law. A judge for many years, he became a state supreme court judge in Koenigsberg in 1890. He taught administrative law to Japanese diplomats in Berlin, and as adviser to the Japanese government in Tokyo prepared the Japanese constitution and advised the Japanese government on concluding treaties. He was active in Jewish affairs as a member of the board of the Jewish community in Berlin and vice-president of the Verband der deutschen Juden.

Another son of Markus, RUDOLF MOSSE (1843–1920), founded the Mosse publishing house in Berlin in 1867 (see Jews in *Publishing). Born in Graetz, Rudolf was apprenticed in the Merzbacher printing firm in Posen. He worked for printing firms in Berlin and Leipzig and bought the Leipzig newspaper *Der Telegraf* in 1864. In the following year he joined the Leipzig firm of Apitsch where he produced an advertising section for the widely read family magazine, *Die Gartenlaube*. Rudolf opened his own advertising agency in Berlin in 1867 and was joined by his brother EMIL (1854–1911) in 1870. The firm published address books and telephone directories and was associated with the publication of several German newspapers, including the *Berliner Tageblatt*, the *Deutsches Montagsblatt*, and the **Allgemeine Zeitung des Judentums*. By the turn of the century Rudolf had established branch offices all over Germany as well as in Austria and Switzerland and his publishing house was world famous.

Rudolf Mosse was noted as a philanthropist. He established a hospital in Graetz and an educational institute in Wilhelmsdorf with an endowment of several million marks. He set up a fund for his employees and made liberal contributions to literary and artistic enterprises. He was also active in the Jewish community in Berlin.

Rudolf's son-in-law HANS LACHMAN-MOSSE (1885–1944) was the last head of the Mosse publishing house. He worked in banking before entering the Mosse concern in 1910. Following the rise of Hitler, he resigned and the publishing house was seized by the Nazis. He moved to Paris in 1935 and in 1940 emigrated to the United States.

Bibliography: R. Hamburger, *Zeitungsverlag und Annoncen-Expedition Rudolf Mosse* (1928); W. E. Mosse, in: YLBI, 4 (1959), 237–59; E. Hamburger, *ibid.*, 9 (1964), 226; Wininger, Biog, 4 (1925–31), 454–6; WWWJ (1965), 683; O. Neumann, in: *Juedische Familien-Forschung*, 11 (1935), 665ff., 685ff.; *C. C. Silverman Jubilee Volume* (1969), 15–20. [S.KA.]

MOSSE, GEORGE L. (1918–), U.S. historian. Born in Berlin, Mosse taught at Iowa, Stanford, and the University of Wisconsin, where he was appointed professor of history. He was president of the American Society for Reformation Research (1961–62) and was coeditor of the *Journal of Contemporary History*.

Mosse's principal interests were in 16th-century history, cultural history, and modern Germany, with special reference to the Nazis and anti-Semitism. His books *The Reformation* (1963) and *Europe in the Sixteenth Century* (with H. G. Koenigsberger, 1968) were important contributions to early modern history, while a series of later works—*The Crisis of German Ideology* (ed., 1964), *Nazi Culture* (1966), and *Germans and Jews* (1968)—explored modern Germany, particularly the fate of German Jewry. To this latter subject he brought his expert knowledge of more than four centuries of German history and a close familiarity with the development of European culture, a subject on which he also wrote in *The Culture of Western Europe* (1961). [T.K.R.]

MOSSERI, prominent family in Egypt, said to have come there from Italy around 1750. NISSIM MOSSERI (1848–1897), with his son and his brothers, founded the banking house of J. N. Mosseri et Fils Cie. (1876). JOSEPH (1869–1934), the eldest son of Nissim, was honored with the title of *bey* for his financial services to the Egyptian government. Joseph's three brothers, Eli, Jacques, and Maurice, founded a second bank in 1904, Banque Mosseri et Cie. ELI (1879–1940) headed many companies, one of which built the King David Hotel in Jerusalem. JACQUES (1884–1934), Nissim's third son, studied languages at Cambridge and later secured permission for Solomon Schechter to investigate the Cairo **Genizah*. Jacques himself collected *genizah* fragments. A delegate of Egyptian Jewry to the 11th Zionist Congress (1913), he founded the Zionist Organization in Egypt in 1917. VICTOR MOSSERI (1873–1930), brother-in-law and cousin of the Mosseri brothers, was an agricultural engineer. He did research for the improvement of several crops, publishing some 60 monographs, and developed an important new variety of cotton. ALBERT MOSSERI (1867–1933), also a cousin, was born in Cairo. He studied medicine in Paris, where he became acquainted with *Herzl and *Nordau. He began a Zionist newspaper *Kadimah* there. Serving as a doctor with the British army in World War I, he later left his profession and began in 1919 to publish the weekly *Israel* in Cairo, originally in Hebrew, then in Arabic, and French. After his death, his wife, MAZAL MATHILDA (1894–), continued the publication until 1939. Their son MACCABEE (1914–1948) served as an officer in the Palmaḥ and was killed when bringing supplies to Jerusalem. The effort to control the supply route (May 1948) was called "Operation Maccabee" after him. [H.Y.C./J.O.R.]

MOSSINSOHN, YIGAL (1917–), Israel author and playwright. Born in Ein-Gannim, Mossinsohn was a member of kibbutz Na'an from 1938 to 1950 and served in the Palmaḥ and the Israel Defense Forces from 1943 to 1949. After six years in the United States (1959–65), he returned to Israel. Mossinsohn wrote stories, novels, plays, thrillers, and adventure books for children, and dealt with topical and historical themes. His first book, a collection of stories, *Aforim ka-Sak* ("Gray as a Sack"), was published in 1946. In 1948 the Habimah Theater staged his first play *Be-Arvot ha-Negev* ("In the Negev Desert"), which was a popular success. The theme of the play was the heroic stand of kibbutz Negbah against the invading Egyptian army during the Israel War of Independence. Mossinsohn has also written several other topical plays. A great success was his series of thrillers for children and teenagers *Ḥasambah*, starting 1950, which found a host of imitators.

Additional works include: (1) Stories and novels; *Mi Amar she-Hu Shaḥor* (1948); *Ha Derekh li-Yriḥo* (1950); *Derekh Gever* (1953); *Yehudah Ish Keriyyot* (1963, *Judas*, 1963). (2) Plays: *Tamar Eshet Er* (1947); *Im Yesh Ẓedek* (1951); *Cambyses* (Heb. 1955); *Casablan* (1958; later, the basis of a musical play); *Eldorado* (1963); *Shimshon* (1968); and others. For English translations see Goell Bibl.

Bibliography: A. Cohen, *Soferim Ivriyyim Benei Zemannenu* (1964), 73–77; Kressel, Leksikon, 2 (1967), 327. [G.AV.]

MOSSINSON, BENZION (1878–1942), Hebrew educator and Zionist leader. He was born in Andreyevka, in southern Russia. In 1904 he joined the opposition, headed by Menahem *Ussishkin, to Herzl's *Uganda Scheme and was

Benzion Mossinson, Hebrew educator and Zionist leader. Courtesy Central Zionist Archives, Jerusalem.

sent as an emissary to Ereẓ Israel to try to eradicate the leanings to the Uganda idea among certain circles in the *yishuv*. He taught at the Herzlia high school from 1907 and served as its principal from 1912 to 1941. A teacher of Bible, he introduced "Bible criticism" into Ereẓ Israel high schools. Exiled by the Turkish authorities during World War I, Mossinson went to the United States. He was a delegate to Zionist Congresses, being elected to the General Zionist Council and its presidium, and went on missions to various countries on behalf of the Zionist Movement. Mossinson was a founder of the "A faction" of the *General Zionists (which later evolved into the *Progressive Party). He edited the General Zionist weekly, *Ha-Ẓiyyoni ha-Kelali.* In 1941 he became director of the Education Department of the Va'ad Le'ummi. In addition to articles in Russian and Hebrew periodicals, Mossinson published *Ha-Ivrit be-Arẓenu* (1917), and *Ha-Nevi'im* (1919, 1944[2]). The Youth Aliyah agricultural school at Magdi'el is named after him.

Bibliography: Tidhar, 2 (1948), 645; D. Smilanski, *Im Benei Arẓi ve-Iri* (1958), 150–5. [A.A.]

MOSSNER, WALTHER VON (1846–1932), German general. Born in Berlin, Mossner, a superb cavalryman, was commissioned into the King's Hussars in 1865, as an act of personal favor by King William I, to his banker father, despite the hostility of his fellow officers who regarded the commissioning of a Jew in a cavalry regiment as an unwelcome precedent. Mossner was eventually baptized and was decorated for distinguished services in the Austro-Prussian War of 1866. In 1872 he was appointed to the German general staff and later was ennobled. He was made William II's aide-de-camp in 1892 and from 1896 to 1898 commanded the third cavalry brigade. Mossner became governor of Strasbourg in 1903 and in the following year was given command of a cavalry division with the rank of major general. He retired in 1910 and was awarded the High Order of the Black Eagle, the last Prussian general to be so honored.

Bibliography: B. Buelow, *Denkwuerdigkeiten*, 4 (1931). [Ed.]

MOST (Ger. **Bruex**), city in N.W. Bohemia, Czechoslovakia. A Jewish moneylender is recorded in Most in 1393; there was a Jewish street situated near the monastery in the 14th century. When the Jews were expelled in 1453 most of them settled in *Litomerice. One Jew was allowed to settle in Most in 1839, and after 1848 some Jews from the surrounding villages moved to the city. There were 15 Jews in 1861, when a congregation was established; the synagogue was dedicated in 1872. Some of the rabbis of Most later became eminent: Alexander *Kisch (1874–77), Joseph Samuel *Bloch (1877–79), and Gotthard *Deutsch (1884–91). In 1930 there were 662 Jews in Most (2.4% of the total population). The community owed its importance and affluence to the development of lignite mining by the *Petschek and Weimann firms. During the Sudeten crisis the community dispersed, and the synagogue was destroyed on Nov. 10, 1938. The congregation was reestablished in 1945, mainly by Jews from *Subcarpathian Ruthenia, under the administration of the *Usti nad Labem community.

Bibliography: M. Halberstam, in: H. Gold (ed.), *Die Juden und Judengemeinden Boehmens* (1934), 70–77; J. C. Pick, in: *Jews of Czechoslovakia*, 1 (1968), 374–5; R. Iltis (ed.), *Die aussaeen unter Traenen . . .* (1959), 25; G. Deutsch, *Scrolls*, 2 (1917), 321–40; Bondy-Dworský, nos. 180–1, 191, 194–5, 198, 200, 202–8, 214, 216–7, 229, 234, 236–8, 240, 246–7, 254, 266, 271, 277. [J.Her.]

MOSTEL, ZERO (Samuel Joel Mostel; 1915–), U.S. actor. Born in Brooklyn, N.Y., he first acquired the name "Zero" because of his poor marks at school. Nevertheless, he graduated from City College, then taught painting and drawing and made extra money entertaining. A successful career as comedian followed in Hollywood and on Broadway, mostly in portrayals of corpulent villains. His leftist views, however, led to his blacklisting, and it was not until 1958, when the political climate had changed, that he resumed full-scale activity. He appeared as Leopold Bloom in an off-Broadway production, *Ulysses in Nighttown* (1958), which was followed by stage successes in Ionesco's *Rhinoceros* (1961); *A Funny Thing Happened on the Way to the Forum* (1962); and *Fiddler on the Roof* (1964). He also appeared in a number of movies. [R.R.]

Zero Mostel in the role of Tevye in the original production of *Fiddler on the Roof*, New York, 1964. From *Zero by Mostel*, Horizon Press, New York, 1965. Photo Max Waldman.

MOSTISKA (Pol. **Mościska**), city in Lvov oblast, Ukrainian S.S.R.; from 1772 to 1918 in eastern Galicia, under Austrian rule. Jews first settled there in the 18th century. The community was under the jurisdiction of the Council of Reissen province (see *Councils of the Lands). In 1880 there were 2,123 Jews in Mostiska (51% of the total population) and in 1900 they numbered 2, 548 (55%). From 1919 to 1939 the city belonged to Poland. In 1921 the Jewish community numbered 2,328 (49%). Before the outbreak of World War II there were about 2,500 Jews in Mostiska. The Jewish community was liquidated on Nov. 28, 1942, when the Jews were deported to *Belzec death camp.

Bibliography: B. Wasiutyński, *Ludność żydowska w Polsce w XIX i XX wiekach* (1930), 96, 107, 116. [Ed.]

MOSUL, city in N. Iraq, on the Tigris river. Jews settled in Mosul, or rather in ancient *Nineveh (a suburb of which probably stood on the site of the present Mosul), on the left bank of the Tigris, when Shalmaneser, king of Assyria (730–712 B.C.E.), conquered Samaria.

In the middle of the seventh century C.E. there was a Jewish community in Mosul living in a special quarter called *Maḥallat al-Yahūd* ("the Jewish Quarter"; according to Ibn al-Fagīh B.G.A. v p. 129; Batādhuri, Futuḥ, 1907, p. 340). In the middle of the tenth century the Jewish philosopher Ibn Abi Saʿīd ibn Uthmān Saʿīd al-Mawṣilī lived in Mosul and through another Jew asked a contemporary Arab-Christian philosopher to settle several philosophical questions (see S. Pines, in: PAAJR, 34 (1966), 103–36). During the first half of the 12th century the Jewish community of Mosul increased when a Muslim principality was established there. It was ruled by Atabeg Zangī (1127–46) and his sons who sought to unite all the small kingdoms in the vicinity of Mosul, to expand his domain up to Syria, and later to make a joint attack on the Crusaders. Many Jews who had suffered from the Crusaders in Ereẓ Israel came to the town and placed themselves under the protection of the Muslim rulers, who did not harm them. The traveler Benjamin of Tudela, who visited Mosul before 1170, found "approximately 7,000 Jews headed by R. Zakkai (b. Azariah b. Solomon), the *nasi* who claimed to be from the Davidic line, and R. Joseph , who is called Burhan al-Falak [Ar. "Globe"] who is the [astrologer] to the king Zein al-Dīn" (Benjamin, Travels, p. 94). R. Pethahiah of Regensburg, who visited Mosul about ten years later, found more than 6,000 Jews and two *nesi'im*: David and Samuel, two cousins who were of the Davidic line. The *nesi'im* had the authority to imprison transgressors. Every Jew paid a tax, one *dinār* per year, half of which was for the authorities and half for the *nesi'im*. They had fields and vineyards.

In 1289 the head of the flourishing community was the exilarch *David b. Daniel. He, together with 11 members of the local rabbinical college, signed a letter threatening Solomon Petit of Acre, the opponent of Maimonides, with excommunication (Graetz, Gesch, 7 (c. 1900), 166).

After a brief period of prosperity at the beginning of the Il-Khan rule, at the time of the vizier *Saʿd al-Dawla in the second half of the 13th century, there followed a swift decline and harsh setbacks which impoverished the community. The savage Tamerlane, who captured the city at the end of the 14th century, caused great harm to its inhabitants. Nevertheless, there was a great yeshivah in the city at the beginning of the 16th century, which sent one of its students to the Adoni family to serve as rabbi of the Baghdad community (A. Ben-Jacob, *Kehillot Yehudei Kurdistan* (1961), 34–36).

In 1848 the traveler Benjamin II found 450 Jewish families there (Benjamin II, *Masei Yisrael* (1859), 34). In the 20th century, there was no improvement in the situation of the Jews of Mosul. They remained enclosed in their neighborhood, most of them poor and ignorant, a few of them merchants. Schools established by the Alliance Israélite Universelle in 1906 (for boys) and in 1912 (for girls) were closed at the outbreak of World War I. In about 1930 schools for boys and girls were established by the philanthropist Eliezer *Kadoorie, but there was no Jewish high school. A few children attended government schools and a very small number attained a higher education.

Probably because of their lowly position the Jews of Mosul did not arouse the envy of their neighbors and were not persecuted. Nevertheless, they lived in great fear throughout this entire period. The rabbis of the community were not highly regarded. During World War I the chief rabbi of the community was R. Elijah Barazani, and from the 1920s, his son R. Solomon Barazani (d. 1960), who remained in this position until he emigrated to Israel in 1951. In the years 1950–55 all the Jews of Mosul emigrated to Israel.

Bibliography: D. S. Sassoon, *History of the Jews in Baghdad* (1949), index; A. Ben-Jacob, *Yehudei Bavel* (1965), index; idem, *Kehillot Yehudei Kurdistan* (1961), index. [A.B.J./P.Bo./H.J.C.]

MOTAL, ABRAHAM BEN JACOB (1568–1658), rabbi and *dayyan* of Salonika. Motal was born in Salonika, where he studied under Samuel Ḥayyun and *Solomon ha-Kohen, whose works he transcribed. He served first as head of the yeshivah of the Old Lisbon community of the city, and on the death of *Ḥayyim Shabbetai in 1647 succeeded him as Salonika's chief rabbi. Among his distinguished disciples were Aaron *Lapapa, Benjamin Melamad of Smyrna, Samuel Adarbi, Abraham ibn Naḥmias, Isaac Alkabeẓ of Constantinople, Abraham *Galanti, and Levi Passariel of Salonika. Of his many works, only *Torat Nazir*, on the tractate of that name, has been published (Salonika, 1821). Appended to it is his *Kunteres Shemot ha-Gittin*. Many of his halakhic discussions appear in the works of contemporary scholars but most of his responsa have remained in manuscript.

Bibliography: Conforte, Kore, index; I. S. Emmanuel, *Maẓẓevot Saloniki*, 1 (1963), 322f., no. 736. [A.D.]

MOTH (Heb. עָשׁ, *ash* and סָס, *sas;* AV, JPS—"worm"), insect said to eat and destroy clothes (Isa. 51:8; cf. 50:9; Job 13:28). The word *ash* is also used as a synonym for disintegration and destruction (Hos. 5:12; Ps. 39:12). These names refer to the clothes-moth *Tineola*, the larva of which feeds on wool. The metamorphosing larva (caterpillar) spins a cocoon, in which it develops into a chrysalis, to be transformed later into an imago. The tottering house of the wicked is compared to a cocoon (Job 27:18). Other species of moth that damage seeds, fruit, and trees are also to be found in Israel. The Talmud speaks of the *sasa* that infests trees (TJ, Ḥag. 2:3, 78a, according to the reading of Ha-Meiri; cf. Yoma 9b: the *sas-magor* which attacks cedars). The *noses* that destroys trees (Isa. 10:18) may be the *sas*, the reference here being to the moth which bores into trees, such as the larvae of the *Zeuzera pirina*, one of the worst arboreal pests in Israel.

Bibliography: Lewysohn, Zool., 308; F. S. Bodenheimer, *Animal and Man in Bible Lands* (1960), 78, 114, 140; J. Feliks, *Animal World of the Bible* (1962), 126f. [J.F.]

MOTION PICTURES. Since the early years of motion pictures, Jews have played a major role in the development of the industry and have been prominent in all its branches. This is true not only of Hollywood, where the role played by Jews is generally known and acknowledged, but of the German film industry up to the Nazi era, Russian film production up to the time of the Stalinist purges of the 1930s, the British film industry up to the present, and contempory underground motion pictures in the United States. The motion picture was created at a time when the Jews were seeking entry into the economic and cultural life of their host countries. Their involvement with motion pictures was due to a number of factors: the film business had not developed a tradition of its own and had no vested interests to defend; participation in it required no intimate knowledge of the vernacular; and films were not yet the realm of businessmen, entrepreneurs, or professional entertainers, but rather scientists, such as Edison and Lumière, who had no idea of the economic and industrial future of their inventions. In addition, the motion picture was initially regarded as a low-grade form of entertainment—suitable only for the immigrant or the uneducated masses—rather than a valid art form, and those connected with films were held in contempt. New immigrants, therefore, found it relatively easy to enter this field, and Jewish immigrants used the opportunity to transform the media from a marginal branch of entertainment into a multi-million dollar industry.

In the United States. The early film makers in the United States were mainly scientists and technicians, few of whom were Jews. As time passed, entertainers from vaudeville and the circus, including some Jews, entered the new medium, but Jews were concentrated mostly in film distribution and exhibition, and as the industry grew, the distributor, who purchased the film from the producer and rented it to the exhibitor, became prominent. Most of the Jews connected with motion pictures at the beginning of the 20th century were the owners of shabby, little movie theaters, especially in the poor, immigrant quarters. The new form of entertainment enjoyed great popularity, as the silent-film audience did not have to contend with the difficulties of a new language. In order to ensure a steady flow of films, some of the theater owners entered the field of distribution, which, in turn, enabled them to control more theaters and eventually to acquire them outright. As owners came from the same background as their audiences, they had a sure sense for the kind of films that would be popular and they therefore prospered. Their earnings enabled them to take another step and enter the field of film production, either by founding new companies or acquiring existing companies that were in financial difficulties. Thus within a short span of time, erstwhile owners of shabby theaters became the heads of large film companies, with a turnover of millions of dollars, hundreds of employees, large studios, distributing outlets, and movie theaters all over the world.

The first Jewish producer was Max Anderson (Aronson), who was also an actor, scriptwriter, and director. He had played the lead in Edwin S. Porter's *The Great Train Robbery* (1903), the first genuine American feature film. Anderson became partner in the Essenay Co., where he worked as a writer, producer, and actor. In 1908 he initiated the "Bronco Billy" series of westerns, which was a great success, and of which 375 films were produced in a seven-year period. The first Jewish film distributors to enter the field of production were Sigmund Lubin of Philadelphia, who was the owner of a chain of movie theaters, and William Selig of Chicago; their first films came out in 1903–04. In 1909 Edison signed an agreement with most of the large film companies that led to the founding of the

Figure 1. Sarah Bernhardt in *Queen Elizabeth*, a film brought to the U.S. in 1912 by Adolph Zukor and Daniel Frohman. Courtesy Paramount Pictures Corporation, New York.

Motion Picture Patents Co. Its purpose was to end the competition then raging among the production companies, prevent the creation of new companies, and protect producers against distributors and exhibitors. The theater owners were forced to rent projectors and films only from the Motion Picture Patents Co. Selig, Lubin and the Essenay Co. were among the signatories to the agreement. Most of the independent distributors were forced out of business; two of them, however, Carl *Laemmle and William *Fox, decided to fight the Patents Co. with the backing of Marcus Loew, the owner of a large chain of theaters. They waged their battle in the press and in the courts, produced films at cut-rate prices, and finally won, when a 1915 court decision ordered the liquidation of the Patents Co. and ushered in the era of the independent production companies. Fox and Laemmle were the first to combine all aspects of the film industry—production, distribution, and exhibition—within a single company and thus became the forerunners of the huge film companies that characterized Hollywood in the 1920s.

The first large Hollywood company was Paramount, which was founded and managed by Adolph Zukor. Together with Daniel *Frohman, a theatrical agent, Zukor decided to import a prestigious European film, *Queen Elizabeth* (1912), starring Sarah *Bernhardt. The film was shown in legitimate theater halls and was reviewed in the regular press, enabling Zukor to claim that film was a legitimate art form. Under the slogan "Famous Players in Famous Plays," Zukor produced films based on literary and dramatic works with casts of well-established, legitimate actors. He also initiated the practice of advertising the "star" actors in films; the first "star" he promoted was Mary Pickford. Jesse *Lasky owned a similar production company in Hollywood, and in 1917 he and Zukor founded a joint distribution company called Paramount; two years later their production companies also merged. Paramount produced, distributed, and exhibited films through its own worldwide theater chain. Lasky also brought two of his partners, Samuel *Goldwyn (Goldfish) and Cecil B. De Mille, into the new company. As Paramount continued to grow, smaller producers were compelled either to disband or merge with one another in order to compete. Paramount's commercial power was based upon the block-booking system that forced local exhibitors to rent an outline group of Paramount's films, rather than choose only those they desired. One producer who tried to fight Paramount was Carl Laemmle. In 1912 he founded the Universal Film Manufacturing Company (which later became Universal Studios), moved the company to Hollywood, and developed it into one of the giants. William Fox, his former partner in the fight against the Patents Co., joined Twentieth Century and also made it into one of the large Hollywood companies. Louis B. *Mayer, who owned a chain of movie theaters (mainly in New England), purchased the Metro Co. in Hollywood (which had its own studios) and founded the Metro-Mayer Co. Samuel Goldfish (Goldwyn) left Paramount in 1919 and, together with the Selwyn brothers, founded the Goldwyn Co. In 1924 it merged with Metro-Mayer to form Metro-Goldwyn-Mayer (M.G.M.), which was headed by Mayer; Goldwyn himself did not join M.G.M. and instead established one of Hollywood's outstanding independent production companies.

Two other companies headed by Jews reached greatness

only with the advent of talking pictures. One was Columbia, owned and dominated by Harry *Cohn from 1929 until his death in 1958. Cohn built Columbia into a large company during the 1930s by producing a series of successful films by the clever use of stars and directors. The other company was Warner Brothers, founded by Sam, Jack, Albert, and Harry *Warner. They started out with a small exhibition hall, later became the managers of the First National Theater chain, and eventually formed their own company. In 1923 they bought out the Fitagraph Company, owners of the Vitaphone, which was a sort of record that played simultaneously with the silent film. Seeking to improve their difficult financial situation, in 1926 they developed the invention and turned out the first film with its own musical score. A year later Warner Brothers produced *The Jazz Singer*, starring Al *Jolson, containing both dialogue and singing parts. This film brought about the "sound revolution" in motion pictures and made Warner Brothers into one of the great Hollywood companies. Thus all the large Hollywood companies, with the exception of United Artists (a distributing company established by Hollywood actors who feared that the big producers would restrict their artistic freedom), were founded and controlled by Jews. In addition, the first bank to finance the film industry was the Jewish-owned Kuhn, Loeb and Co., in 1919.

Other Jews who played a leading role in the large companies were Barney *Balaban, who joined Paramount and became its president in 1936; Nicholas and Joseph M. Schenk, who became presidents of M.G.M. (while Mayer was in charge of its Hollywood operations); and Irving *Thalberg, who was production manager of M.G.M. from the end of the 1920s until his death in 1936. Thalberg, who was responsible for production at the age of 23, was the wunderkind of the film industry and became the symbol of the successful Hollywood producer. In 1951, when Mayer was dismissed from his post at M.G.M. he was replaced by Dore *Schary, who had built a career as a writer. He was given the task of raising the artistic level of the films produced by the faltering company, but was unable to maintain the position. A similar position was held by William Goetz, who was head of 20th Century-Fox and, at a later stage, of Universal International Co.

Most of the numerous Jewish producers were employed by the large companies. They included Joe Pasternak, Walter Wanger, Arthur Freed, Jerry Wald, Pandro S. Berman, and others. An even more important influence on the film industry—because of their greater control over the nature of the finished product—were the independent producers, among whom Jews were in the majority. Outstanding independents were Mike Todd, producer of *Around the World in 80 Days*, who was connected with the Todd-AO method of cinematography; and David O. *Selznick, the son of Lewis J. Selznick, one of the industry's pioneers. Next to Samuel Goldwyn, David Selznick became the most famous and successful independent producer. He was responsible for the production of *Gone With the Wind* (1939), which was one of the most profitable films in Hollywood's history, having grossed $72,000,000 through 1970. Among his other films were *David Copperfield, King Kong, Spellbound*, and *Rebecca*. Hal Roach, one of the most prolific producers of comedies, was responsible for a part of the Harold Lloyd series and for the Laurel and Hardy films during the 1920s and 1930s. Sam Spiegel, who maintained a high artistic standard, using outstanding directors and choosing serious subjects, produced such films as *The African Queen, On the Waterfront, The Bridge on the River Kwai*, and *Lawrence of Arabia*. The Mirisch Brothers, originally theater owners, established their own company in 1957. After the decline of the big studios, it became one of the most successful Hollywood enterprises, producing *West Side Story* and *The Great Escape*. Stanley *Kramer, an independent producer who was connected with Columbia, was responsible for some of the best films to come out of Hollywood after 1945. Believing that audiences wanted films that dealt with the contemporary life, he produced such films as *Home of the Brave, Champion, High Noon, Death of a Salesman*. Later on he also directed *On the Beach, Judgment at Nuremberg*, and *Ship of Fools*. Joseph E. Levine, who began as a theater owner and became an importer of cheap or erotic Italian films, then turned to the financing of outstanding European films *($8\frac{1}{2}$)*, and later produced such films as *The Carpetbaggers, Where Love Has Gone*, and *Harlow*.

A large number of Jews are found among Hollywood film directors as well. Ernst *Lubitsch, who came to the United States in 1923 after achieving fame in Germany, was best known for directing sophisticated comedies with a finesse that became known as the "Lubitsch touch." Among his films were *Ninotchka, To Be Or Not To Be*, and *Cluny Brown*. Erich von *Stroheim, an Austrian-born actor and director, became known in the 1920s for his realistic direction, especially in the film *Greed*. His acting captivated audiences for a period of 30 years. Josef von *Sternberg directed several realistic films in the United States in the 1920s; he directed *Blue Angel* in Germany in 1930 and became Marlene Dietrich's permanent director, and his style turned to the baroque and artificial, based on light effects. William *Wyler, who was born in Germany, began his career as a director in 1928; his films were based mainly on adaptations of literary works, and he was particularly successful in the direction of female stars. Billy *Wilder also began his career in Germany, together with Fred Zinne-

Figure 2. Erich von Stroheim, actor and director, in *Blind Husbands*, 1919. Courtesy Universal Pictures, New York.

mann and Robert Siodmak. For a while he worked with Lubitsch, and his films were distinguished by their sharp humor and bitter irony.

A great many other Jews directed films that earned success at the box office or brought them critical acclaim. A random list of such directors includes Jules *Dassin, Garson Kanin, Fred Zinnemann, Joseph L. Mankiewicz, Sidney Lumet, John Frankenheimer, Roman Polanski, Michael Curtiz, Mervyn Le Roy, Otto *Preminger, Richard Brooks, George Cukor, Daniel Mann, Delbért Mann, Robert Rossen. The number of scriptwriters is so vast that only a few can be mentioned here. The most famous was Ben *Hecht, who excelled in the highly realistic quality of his dialogue and in the field of suspense films; others were Samson Raphaelson, who worked with Lubitsch and Hitchcock; George Axelrod, who wrote the script for comedies and sharp satires; and Carl Forman, scriptwriter of some of Stanley Kramer's films. Among the prominent composers of musical scores are Irving *Berlin, Alfred Newman, Franz Waxman, Dmitri Tiomkin, Elmer Bernstein, and Burt Bacharach. A small sample of well-known Jewish actors and actresses includes the *Marx Brothers, Danny *Kaye, Jerry Lewis, Paul *Muni, Edward G. *Robinson, Eddie *Cantor, John Garfield, Al Jolson, Peter Lorre, Zero *Mostel, Tony Curtis, Alan Arkin, Lee J. Cobb, Kirk *Douglas, Melvyn Douglas, Rod Steiger, Dustin Hoffman, Elliot Gould, Theda Bara, Alla Nazimova, Louise Rainer, Paulette Goddard, Sylvia Sidney, Shelley Winters, Judy Holiday, and Barbra *Streisand. A number of film stars converted to Judaism including Sammy Davis Junior, Marilyn Monroe, and Elizabeth Taylor.

In Britain. Although the proportion of Jews involved in films was much smaller than in America, they made a significant contribution to the British film industry and were among its pioneers. For a long period, American competition made it impossible for the British motion picture to gain a foothold in the world market. It was a Hungarian Jew, Sir Alexander *Korda, who finally pulled the British industry out of the doldrums. Korda had been a pioneer of film making in Hungary and after World War I had worked in Austria, Germany, France, and Hollywood. In 1930 he moved to Britain and founded the London Films Company, for which he directed and produced some of the best films credited to Britain in the 1930s and the 1940s. His success was due to his fine artistic sense, his ability to build artists from different fields into a working team, and his belief that by employing great British actors and choosing the proper subjects, the British film could be adapted to suit the American market. His greatest success as a director was *The Private Life of Henry VIII* (1933), in which he punctured the formal rigidity associated with royalty; he had other successes in *The Private Life of Don Juan* and in *Rembrandt*. His greatest achievements were as the producer of such films as *The Scarlet Pimpernel, Catherine the Great, Elephant Boy, Lady Hamilton,* and *The Third Man,* which established Britain's reputation for fine films. His brother, Zoltan Korda, also worked for London Films as a successful director. Sir Michael *Balcon, who was initially in charge of Alfred Hitchcock's British films, earned his reputation after World War II managing the operations of Ealing Studios. This company created the series of comedies (known as the "Ealing Comedies") that depict the eccentric British character with subtle humor and irony (such films as *Kind Hearts and Coronets, Whisky Galore,* and *The Ladykillers*). Another outstanding producer was Harry Saltzman, a partner in the James Bond series; he later produced mainly war films and, from time to time,

Figure 3. Al Jolson in the leading role in the first talking film, *The Jazz Singer,* 1928. Courtesy Museum of Modern Art, Film Stills Archive, New York.

low-budget artistic films. Anatole de Grunwald also was a producer of note. A noted young director was John Schlesinger, who was responsible for such films as *Billy Liar, Darling,* and *Midnight Cowboy.* Among the outstanding British film actors were Leslie Howard, Elizabeth *Bergner (who moved from Germany in the 1930s, as did Anton Walbrook), Claire Bloom, Yvonne Mitchell, Laurence Harvey, and Peter *Sellers.

In France. Max Linder, a comic actor, had a large share in the creation of the film comedy, especially of the type that made Charlie Chaplin famous. In his films, dating from 1906 to 1925, Linder reveals himself as a sad clown, a great mimic, and an acrobat, expressing the same kind of pathos that later came to be associated with Chaplin. He also wrote and directed all of his films. Several other outstanding directors were Abel Gance (*La Roue, J'Accuse,* and *Napoléon*); and Jean Epstein, who directed such surrealistic films as *Fall of the House of Usher* and *Finis Terrae.* There are also Jewish producers, but in France they are far less important than the directors, since the budget at the disposal of the producers is small and the companies are created on an ad hoc basis to produce one or two films only. French directors include Claude Lelouch, known for the film *A Man and a Woman,* and Claude Berri, whose films deal with Jewish subjects (see below). The outstanding French film actors include Harry *Baur, Simone Signoret, Robert Hirsch, and Anouk Aimée.

In Germany. As in the United States, the impetus to produce films catering to popular taste in Germany came from Jewish owners of a chain of theaters. In 1913 Paul Davidson and Hermann Fellner, who had been exhibiting films since 1905, established their own production company and made films based on German folklore and legend, as well as comedies (it was for this company that Ernst Lubitsch made his early films). In 1919 Erich Pommer directed the Deutsches Eclair (Decla) film company, which some time later merged with UFA, a company that produced outstanding German films in the 1920s and the early 1930s. Pommer remained at the head of the company and determined the style and quality of the films in this period. He went in for daring artistic experiments and provided ample opportunity for talented film people to prove their mettle. As a result, the German film became the most advanced of its time; this was, in fact, the golden age of the German film industry. Lubitsch began his career with a series of comedies (some of them against a Jewish background) and then turned to the direction of light-hearted historical films. His overwhelming success resulted in his being invited to the United States. Another film produced by Pommer, *The Cabinet of Dr. Caligari,* which became a prestigious success for the German cinema, was written by Hans Janowitz and Carl Mayer. In general, Jews made a great contribution to the German cultural life in the 1920s and participated in the avant-garde artistic experimentation of this period. The painter Hans Richter produced experimental and abstract films and was a pioneer of this genre. The leading German-Jewish film director was Fritz *Lang, whose films are a marvelous portrayal of the social and cultural atmosphere prevailing in Germany at the time. They include *Der muede Tod* ("The Weary Death"), based on a medieval legend; two films based on the Nibelungen saga; two terror films; *Metropolis,* sharply critical of various aspects of industrial society; and *M,* the story of the Duesseldorf child murderer, which was Lang's last German film. When Hitler came to power, the Jews working for the German film industry were forced to flee the country. Most of them found their way to Hollywood, others to London, Paris, and Prague.

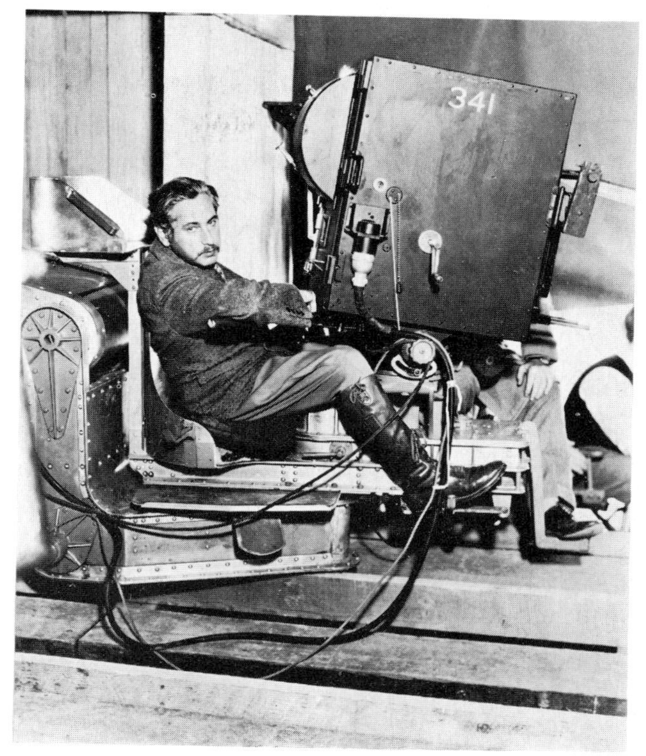

Figure 4. Josef von Sternberg on the set of *The Blue Angel,* 1930. Courtesy Museum of Modern Art, Film Stills Archive, New York.

In Poland. Before the rise of the Jewish state, Poland was the only country that offered possibilities for the development of a Jewish film industry. Attempts to create a Jewish film tradition began before World War I, when film versions were made of the plays of Jacob *Gordin. Mark Tovbin, a pioneer in the field, filmed *Mirele Efros* with Esther Rachel Kaminska (see *Kaminski) in the title role and other members of her family in the cast. Nahum Lipovski filmed Gordin's play *Hasa die Yesoeme* ("Hasa the Orphan") with Esther Lipovska as the orphan. It was not until the 1920s, however, that attempts at making films were resumed. In 1924 Leah Farber worked with Henrik Baum, as scenario writer, on producing films on Yiddish folk themes. Among them was *Tkies-Kaf* ("The Hand Contract"), based on a legend similar to that of *The Dybbuk,* directed by Zygmunt *Turkow, who also played the role of Elijah. Other roles were played by Esther Rachel Kaminska, her daughter Ida, and her granddaughter Ruth Turkow, then a child. In 1927 the same company filmed another legendary story, *Der Lamedvovnik* ("One of the Thirty-Six"), by H. Baum, starring Jonas *Turkow and directed by Henryk Shara (Shapira). In 1929 a company known as Forbert—after Leo Forbert, the first Jewish film producer after the war—filmed a version of Josef *Opatoshu's novel *In the Polish Woods,* with H. Baum as screenwriter, Jonas Turkow as director, and Dina Blumenfeld and Silver Rich in the leading roles.

The first Yiddish talking pictures were made in 1932, when Itzhak and Shaul Goskind formed a company known as Sektor and made documentaries of the Jewish communities in Warsaw, Lodz, Vilna, Lvov, Cracow, and Bialystok and then undertook popular productions with S. Dzigan and I. Szumacher. They produced *Al Khet,* with screenplay by the writer Israel Moshe *Neiman, directed by A. Marten, with Rachel Holtzer and A. Morewski in the leading roles; *Un'a Heim* ("Without a Home," by A. Kacyzne), directed by Alexander Marten, with Ida Kaminska and the Dzigan-Szumacher partnership; and *Freylikhe Kabtsonim* ("The Merry Beggars"), a story by Moshe *Broderzon, with

Zygmunt Turkow, Dzigan-Szumacher and Ruth Turkow in the cast. They also did a documentary called *Mir Kumen On* ("We're on the Way"), directed by Alexander Ford. Ford also did *Sabra* (1933).

Films of distinction were Josef Green's productions *Yidl mit'n Fidl*, lyrics by Itzik *Manger, starring Molly *Picon; *Mammele*, also starring Molly Picon; *Purim Shpiler*, with Z. Turkow, Anya Liton, L. Samberg, and Miriam Kressin (screenplays by Konrad Tam) and *A Brivele der Mammen*, written by M. Osherowitz (screenplay by A. Kacyzne) and directed by L. Tristan. This was the last Yiddish film made in Poland before the outbreak of World War II. Leo-Film did a talking version of *Tkies-Kaf* in 1937 with scenario by H. Baum, direction by Henrik Shara, and Z. Turkow as Elijah. *An-Sky's *Dybbuk* was also filmed in 1937, with a scenario by Katzisne, direction by Michal Vashiasky, and a cast including A. Morewski, Isaac Samberg, Moshe Lipman, Lili Liliana, and L. Leo Libgold. After World War II a cooperative, "Kinor," for Yiddish-speaking films was organized in Lodz by Shaul Goskind and Joseph Goldberg. From 1946 until 1950 two full-length films and about 12 shorts were produced including *Unzere Kinder*, which was made with Niusia Gold, Dzigan-Szumacher, and orphans from Alenuwek (Lodz). In 1951 "Kinor" was liquidated and the members left, mostly for Israel. The Polish State Film produced a work on the Warsaw Ghetto, *Ulica Graniczna* ("Border Street"), directed by A. Ford. Subsequently, several documentaries were made in Yiddish by American producers. Post-World War II films artists who did not specifically deal with Jewish themes were Alexander Ford (later in Israel) and Roman Polanski (who settled in the U.S. in the 1960s).

In the U.S.S.R. Jews also took a large part in the motion picture industry in the U.S.S.R. Foremost among them was Sergei *Eisenstein, the great genius of the Soviet cinema, whose contribution to the progress made by motion pictures probably exceeds that of any other single film artist. His films, including *Battleship, Strike, Alexander, Old and New, October, Potemkin, Ivan the Terrible* (1 and 2), and *Alexander Nevski*, are still regarded as high achievements of the motion picture art and are studied by scholars and artists alike. His theories on the cinematic art, published in several volumes, remain an outstanding expression of motion picture aesthetics. The formalist experiments made by Eisenstein in the 1920s provoked the ire of the Soviet authorities and caused him great hardship throughout the 1930s and 1940s; the controversy over *Ivan the Terrible* shortly preceded his death. Other Jews who

Figure 5. Paul Muni during a rehearsal for *The Last Angry Man*, a Fred Kohlman production directed by Daniel Mann, 1959.

Figure 6. Scene from *Exodus*, produced in Israel by Otto Preminger, with Paul Newman in a starring role, 1959. Courtesy United Artists Co., New York.

entered the Soviet motion picture industry in the 1920s were Friedrich Ermler, Abraham Room, Mikhail Romm, Juli Raizman, Leonid Trauberg, Esther Schub, and L. O. Arnshtam. They sought formal solutions to the artistic problems encountered, and when socialist realism became the prescribed doctrine, they were forced to compromise with the new conditions. A noted Jewish director was Dziga Vertov, a native of Poland, whose real name was Denis Kaufman and whose brother, Boris Kaufman, was a well-known American cameraman. In 1924 Vertov propounded the theory of *Kino-Glas* ("Cinema-Eye"): *Kino-Glas* films were made outside the studio without actors, set, or a script. "They are written by the camera in the purest cine-language, and are completely visual." Vertov became the father of the documentary film, and his newsreels, "*kino pravda*," were the forerunners of *cinéma-verité*.

A number of Jewish directors were also active in the 1930s, including Yosif Heifitz and Alexander Zarkhy (who worked as a team for some time), Yosef Olshanski (also a scriptwriter), Samson Samsonov, and Yakov Segal. Yiddish motion pictures flourished in the Soviet Union in the 1930s, centering around the great Yiddish actor Shlomo *Mikhoels (who was later murdered during the Stalin purges), whose outstanding films were *King Lear* and *Menahem Mendel*.

Other European Countries. In other countries of Eastern Europe Jewish motion picture directors came to the fore after World War II, when film production first entered a serious phase of development. In Czechoslovakia Jan Kádar directed *Shop on Main Street*, and Milos Forman earned his reputation with such comedies as *Peter and Pavla, Firemen's Ball*, and *Loves of a Blonde*. A Swedish director named Mauritz Stiller became famous in the 1910s and 1920s for the style, humor, and aesthetic feeling of his films. His claim to fame now rests on his discovery of Greta Garbo, whom he accompanied to the United States where he died soon after his arrival.

Films on Jewish Themes. The first known film on a Jewish theme was the Edison production of *A Dance in Jerusalem* made in Palestine in 1902 and lasting less than two minutes. Films about Jews in the early years of the century were principally caricatures such as *The Yiddisher Cowboy* (1909, 1911) or films about the Jewish life on New York's Lower East Side. Later films, however, emphasized Jewish ethnic awareness, as in *Heart of a Jewess* (1913), while in the 1920s Jewish themes portrayed the conflicts between American Jews and other minorities like the Irish. After 1930, probably as a result of the development of anti-Semitism, Jewish themes were deliberately subdued. Thus in *The Life of Emile Zola* the film barely mentions the fact that Dreyfus

Figure 7. Chaim Topol in the title role of *Sallah Shabbati*, written and directed by the Israel satirist, Ephraim Kishon, 1964. Courtesy Sallah Co., Tel Aviv.

was Jewish, while *The Great Dictator* plays down the fact that in one of the two parts Chaplin is portraying a Jew. American films about World War II feature Jews along with other minorities as stereotypes of brave Americans, and it was not until the 1960s that American films began to portray Jewish characters as people and not as caricatures or stereotypes. An example of this development was *Goodbye Columbus*, a portrayal of Jewish life in a rich urban community.

A French film, *David Golder* (1931), directed by Julien Duvivier, depicts the life of a Jewish immigrant to France (Harry Baur) who, although successful in business, does not find happiness. In this work, however, the fact that the main character is Jewish is incidental, and the film's aim is to show that material success is earned at the expense of other human values.

The first outstanding film to portray the attitude of the Nazis toward the Jews was *Professor Mamlock*, a Soviet production describing the persecution suffered by an innocent scientist because he was not an "Aryan." Not until 1940 was the plight of German Jews a subject for motion pictures. Charlie Chaplin's *The Great Dictator* was mainly an attack on the "ridiculous" *Fuehrer*, but it also showed the sufferings of the Jews and was an appeal for peace and brotherhood among the nations. The Jewish barber's speech at the end of the film is a masterpiece of persuasive oratory. In the following years, Hollywood and England dealt more and more with the theme of Nazi-occupied Europe, but the fate of the Jews is never stressed and few films related to it at all. On the other hand, Nazi Germany put out an anti-Semitic film version of *Jew Suess*, directed by Veit Harlan.

Some time after the war, when the true dimensions of the Holocaust came to light, the treatment of the Jewish problem underwent a certain change. A considerable number of European films dealing with the Holocaust were produced, while the U.S. industry was rather slow in taking up the subject. A film on Auschwitz—*The Last Stage*, by Wanda Jakubowska—was produced in Poland, followed by *Border Street* (the story of the revolt of the Warsaw Ghetto) by Alexander Ford. In Switzerland, Leopold Lindtberg produced several films dealing with the fate of European Jewry, and Hungary produced *Somewhere in Europe*, also dedicated to the theme of the Holocaust. In general, the countries that had been directly affected attempted to describe the horror by means of motion pictures. In the United States, only one picture at all related to the subject appeared at this time—*The Search*, by Fred Zinnemann—and even here the reference to the Holocaust is only incidental. Germany tried to cope with its deeds by producing films that inquired into the cause and nature of Nazi anti-Semitism: *Lang ist der Weg*, a semi-documentary dealing with the fate of the Jews; *Marriage in the Shadow*, a film based on the story of Joachim Gottschalk, a German actor who committed suicide rather than obey Goebbels' order to divorce his Jewish wife; *Der Prozess*, by G. W. Pabst, which describes a blood libel trial that took place in a Hungarian village in 1882; and *The Murderers Among Us*, which came out at a later stage. Finally, there was Kurt Hoffman's *Wir Wunderkinder*, which treated the subject in a sharply satiric manner. Italy produced *The Wandering Jew*, a general treatment of the Holocaust; *Gold of Rome*, which tells the story of the ransom the Jews of Rome were forced to pay the Nazis; and *Generale de la Rovere*, by R. Rossellini, which shows the execution of Jews in a Roman prison.

Some years later, a new type of film dealing with the Holocaust made its appearance. Whereas the films produced in the immediate postwar period were more of an outcry against the horror, later films sought to give the subject artistic expression and examine the deeper causes of the events. *Night and Fog*, a short film by Alain Resnais, investigates the mechanism that enables man to destroy his fellowman. Another French film, *L'Enclos*, by Armand Gatti, describes a man's loss of his humanity by telling the story of a life-and-death struggle between a Jewish prisoner and a German "political." *Chronique D'un Eté*, a French *cinéma-verité* film, examines the effect of the Holocaust upon a Jewish woman a decade-and-a-half after the war. An Italian film, *Kapo*, by Gilo Pontecorvo, also grapples with the problem of man losing his humanity in the concentration camps and tries to prove that the human spirit triumphs over the worst suppression. In Czechoslovakia, Klos and Kadar produced *The Shop on Main Street* (with Ida Kaminska), a story of the relationship between an elderly Jewish woman and a gentile man who is given her shop in the "Aryanization" process, against the background of the Holocaust, and there were a good number of such films in the U.S.S.R., Poland, Czechoslovakia, and Hungary. In the United States, *Judgment at Nuremberg*, directed by Stanley *Kramer, examined the German judicial system and the influence of Germany's past upon its present; and *The Pawnbroker*, directed by Sidney Lumet, inquired into the life of a survivor of the Holocaust 20 years later; George Stevens' *The Diary of Anne Frank* animated the famous journal on the screen.

The subject of anti-Semitism also came up for reexamination, but the American film industry did not acquit itself too well in this attempt. Anti-Semitism was often coupled with the race problem, and both were treated in a superficial and banal manner. At times the two subjects were

Figure 8. Roman Polanski directing Catherine Deneuve in the British film *Repulsion*, 1965. Courtesy Museum of Modern Art, Film Stills Archive, New York.

Figure 9. Anouk Aimée in the French film, *A Man and a Woman*, directed by Claude Lelouch, 1966. Courtesy United Artists Co., New York.

interchanged, and books about anti-Semitism served as the basis for films on the discrimination against Negroes, which could not but work out to the detriment of both. Two such films were *Crossfire*, by Edward Dmytryk, and *Gentleman's Agreement*, by Elia Kazan, and both were too simplistic. There were, however, a number of films in which anti-Semitism received more sensitive treatment, all of which were adapted from literary works: *Me and the Colonel*, *The Young Lions*, *Ship of Fools*, and *The Fixer*. European films dealing with anti-Semitism were, as a rule, superior to the American ones. The French film *Avant le Déluge*, by André Cayatte, affords the subject dramatic treatment, and *The Old Man and the Boy*, directed by Claude Berri (which was shown in the United States under the title *The Two of Us*) is in a humorous vein, a fact which does not detract from its seriousness. In Poland the film *Bad Luck*, by Andrzej Munk, told the story of a non-Jewish Pole who suffered all his life from his "Jewish" nose.

A number of less significant Jewish subjects were also treated in motion pictures. Most of these were derived from Jewish mysticism, the Kabbalah, and the world of magic superstition. One such subject was *The Golem* (of which at least four versions have been made); others included the Jewish vampire in Polanski's *The Fearless Vampire Killers* and the dialogue between the priest and the rabbi in *Sister Joan of the Angels*, by Jerzy Kawalerewicz. Other films dealt with the Jewish way of life in either a sympathetic or a satirical manner. Examples of such films are *Marjorie Morningstar*, *Mazel Tov (Marry Me, Marry Me)*, by Claude Berri and Peter Pearce's *Goodbye Columbus*, based on the book by Philip *Roth. Yet a third kind of Jewish film depicts the dissolution of a traditional society or the decay discovered under a mantle of wealth and prosperity. These include two Italian films: *Sandra*, by Lucchino Visconti, and *The Gardens of the Finzi-Contini* by Vittorio de Sica, based on the novel by Giorgio *Bassani. The problematic nature of treating Jewish subjects in motion pictures was best illustrated in the case of *Oliver Twist*. In the musical, Fagin appears as a lovable figure, quite untrue to the original, and no one could raise any objection. In the film (1948), however, directed by David Lean (with Alec Guinness as Fagin), he appears as Dickens created him, and the Jews regarded this characterization as an expression of anti-Semitism and demonstrated against its exhibition. The American motion picture industry continues to deal with Jewish subjects, albeit in a noncommittal manner, either in the form of comedies or the biographies of famous men. Examples of the former are *A Hole in the Head*, *Enter Laughing*, *Bye-Bye Braverman*, *The Producers*, *A Majority of One*, and *Captain Newman*. The biographical genre is represented by *Freud*, *Rhapsody in Blue*, *Funny Girl*, *Life of Benny Goodman*, and *The Last Angry Man*. There have been several films on the subject of the State of Israel. All of these films were made in Israel, and most by Israel companies (see below).

In Israel. Little of significance was filmed in Palestine before World War I although most of Sidney Olcott's famous film *From the Manger to the Cross* (1913) was filmed there. Newsreels and Zionist propaganda films were made in Ereẓ Israel especially after World War I, but they in themselves did not constitute a true film industry.

The pioneer in film making in Palestine was Natan Axelrod, who went there in 1926 from the Soviet Union, where he had worked in the film industry. With primitive means he established the country's first film company, Moledet, which concentrated mainly on newsreels, but also made feature films, the best-known of which was *Oded ha-Noded* (1933). At the end of the 1930s, Axelrod established the Carmel Films, which produced the country's first weekly newsreels. His only competitor at the time was Baruch Agadati, the artist, who produced newsreels and one full-length feature. After World War II a number of films were produced on subjects connected with the Holocaust, the rehabilitation of Jewish children in Palestine, and "illegal" immigration. They were made mostly by

Figure 10. Oded Kotler (left) and Shai Osherov in the Israel film *Three Days and a Child*, directed by Uri Zohar, 1967. Photo Miriam Vardy, Tel Aviv.

Figure 11. Fagin portrayed by Ron Moody in Lionel Bart's *Oliver*, 1968. Courtesy Columbia Pictures Corp., New York.

Americans, such as Herbert Klein (*My Father's House*, 1946, and *The Illegals*, 1947; both scripts by Meyer *Levin).

After the establishment of independence, a need was felt for the production of films, especially for propaganda abroad and educational purposes in Israel. The Geva (1950) and Herzliyyah (1951) film studios were set up and made scores of documentary films, mostly for the government information services. Some of them were on a high technical and artistic standard and even won international prizes; they also helped to prepare a cadre of trained personnel for the film industry. In contrast, the few feature films made at the time were rather primitive and failed at the box offices. Among the new immigrants were a number of film makers, especially from Poland, who raised the level of the industry. In addition, several foreign films made in Israel, especially Otto Preminger's *Exodus* (1959), *The Juggler*, and *Cast a Giant Shadow*—the last about David *Marcus— enabled the local workers to gain experience in the Hollywood type of production.

In view of the economic, educational, and cultural importance of the film industry, the Knesset passed The Encouragement of Israel Film Law (1954), which provided substantial government financial aid, up to 50% of the income earned in Israel. As a result, a film with a medium-sized production budget (the range is between IL200,000—about $57,000—for a "low-cost" film and IL 1 million for an "expensive" one) with average success at the box office could cover its production costs from the Israel market alone. This led to a gradual rise in the number of films produced and later, also, in technical and artistic standards, and a number of small producing companies were established. One of their main concerns was to provide reliable financial backing for their films. The main backers are usually studios, distributors, and others in the field, as well as general investment companies, private owners of capital, and the film producers themselves. Some of the directors are professionals, but most of them come from the theater or the entertainment field. The main weakness of the industry is the shortage of professional scriptwriters.

The subjects of the films are mostly taken from life in Israel (the various communities and the relations between them, the three wars since the establishment of the state, satires, kibbutz life, etc.), and the stories are generally written specifically for film, although there are also adaptations of literary works, plays, entertainment programs, and classic Jewish works (such as An-Ski's *Dybbuk* and works by *Goldfaden and *Shalom Aleichem). Many films are mediocre, but there have been some with an individual artistic or characteristically Israel character, as well as films that show the influence of the modern European and U.S. schools and try to make a contribution to world cinema. Israel participates with some success in the important film festivals. Professional film makers from abroad have been invited to collaborate in the making of Israel films and co-productions have been made with such countries as Italy, West Germany, Japan, and especially France.

The most active Israel producer and director was Menahem Golan, who, up to 1969, had directed nine Israel films, the best known of which were *Tevye and His Seven Daughters* and *My Love in Jerusalem*. His films are usually based on topical subjects or theatrical successes and use popular Israel stars. The humorist Ephraim *Kishon has directed five films, the first of which, *Sallah Shabbati*, was widely successful abroad and brought fame to its star, Chaim *Topol. Uri Zohar, the popular entertainer, directed films which fall into two categories: popular comedies and more ambitious undertakings, very influenced by the European cinema such as *Sheloshah Yamim ve-Yeled* ("Three Days and a Child"), whose star, Oded Kotler, won the best actor's prize at the 1967 Cannes Film Festival and *Kol Mamzer Melekh* ("Every Bastard a King"), on the Six-Day War. David Perlov was an original director with a power of expression. A number of young film makers have been working on a noncommercial basis. Their films, which are less costly to make, have been individualistic and tentative, but some of them have displayed considerable expressive power and they have slowly won recognition.

After the Six-Day War (1967) there was great interest in film making in Israel, as part of the international interest in Israel affairs in general. The introduction of television in 1968 further strengthened the industry. Studios became overloaded with work for television, which encouraged expansion and the building of new studios, as well as more intensive training of film personnel. At the beginning of 1969 the Ministry of Commerce and Industry established the Israel Film Center to deal with all matters concerned with the making of films in Israel and the marketing of them abroad.

Figure 12. Shmuel Rodensky in the title role of *Tevye and his Seven Daughters*, the Israel film produced and directed by Menaḥem Golan, 1968–69.

Figure 13. Alan Arkin in the United Artists film, *Popi*, c. 1969. Courtesy Museum of Modern Art, Film Stills Archive, New York.

Bibliography: T. Ramsaye, *A Million and One Nights, A History of the Motion Picture* (1964); E. Goodman, *The Fifty-Year Decline and Fall of Hollywood* (1961); R. Griffith and A. Mayer, *The Movies: The Sixty-Year Story of the World Hollywood and its Effects on America, from the pre-Nickelodeon Days to the Present* (1957); B. B. Hampton, *History of the Movies* (1930); Y. Harel, *Ha-Kolno'a me-Reshito ve-ad Ha-Yom* (1956), 216–40; N. Ingber, in: *Ha-Ummah*, 5 (1966), 246–61; *Omanut ha-Kolno'a*, 28 (1963), 5–15. [NA.I.]

Alphabetical List of Entries, Including Capsule Articles. The individuals whose names are marked with an asterisk in the list below form the subjects of articles in their appropriate alphabetical position in the Encyclopaedia.

AIMÉE, ANOUK (Françoise Dreyfus; 1932–), French actress. Aimée gained the attention of the French public in 1957, in the film *Les Mauvaises Rencontres*. In Federico Fellini's *La Dolce Vita* (1960), and *8½* (1963), she was cast in roles reflecting modern boredom and world-weariness. She was nominated for an Academy Award as best actress for her part in Lelouch's *A Man and A Woman* (1966).

ARKIN, ALAN W. (1934–), U.S. actor. Arkin began his career as a folk singer and later joined a group in Chicago that specialized in improvisations. He appeared in Joseph Stein's comedy *Enter Laughing* (1963), and became a star overnight. His next Broadway success was in Murray Schisgal's *Luv* (1964). He starred in the films *The Russians Are Coming* (1966), *Wait Until Dark* (1967), *The Heart is a Lonely Hunter* (1968), and *Catch 22* (1970).

AXELROD, GEORGE (1922–), U.S. comedy writer, movie director, and producer. Axelrod, who was born in New York City, began writing for radio and television. He wrote several successful plays—*Seven Year Itch* (1953), *Bus Stop* (1956), *Once More, with Feeling* (1958)—and began his film career writing the adaptations for *Seven Year Itch* and *Bus Stop*. Associated with several films as co-writer and co-producer, including *Visit to a Small Planet* (1957) and *Breakfast at Tiffany's* (1961), he wrote the screenplay for *The Manchurian Candidate* (1962), and wrote, directed, and produced *Lord Love a Duck* (1966) and *Secret Life of an American Wife* (1968).

***BALABAN, BARNEY** (1887–1971), U.S. motion picture executive.

***BALCON, SIR MICHAEL** (1896–), English film producer.

BARA, THEDA (Theodosia Goodman; 1890–1955), U.S. film actress. Born in Cincinnati, Ohio, Theda Bara was noted for her femme fatale roles. William Fox realized her potentialities and cast her in *A Fool There Was* (1915) under the name by which she came to be known as the foremost "vamp" of the screen. Among her other films were *Carmen* (1916), *Romeo and Juliet* (1917), *Camille* (1918), and *Salome* (1925).

***BAUR, HARRY** (1883–1943), French actor.

***BERGNER, ELIZABETH** (1897–), German and English stage and film actress.

BENOÎT-LÉVY, JEAN (1888–1959), French producer-director and author of books on cinema. His best-known films include: *La Maternelle* (1933) and *La Mort du Cygne* (1938).

BERMAN, PANDRO S. (1905–), U.S. film producer. Berman was responsible for the production of 85 films for RKO including the Ginger Rogers-Fred Astaire musicals. In 1940 he signed a contract with M.G.M. His *National Velvet* (1945) brought Elizabeth Taylor to public attention. His other productions included *The Seventh Cross* (1944), *Of Human Bondage* (1948), *Madam Bovary* (1949), and *The Brothers Karamazov* (1958).

***BERNSTEIN, SIDNEY LEWIS (Lord Bernstein;** 1899–), English television pioneer and publisher.

BERRI, CLAUDE (Claude Langman; 1935–), French writer-director. After the German invasion of France he was sent for safety to live with a non-Jewish, anti-Semitic peasant, an experience reflected in his *Le Vieil Homme et L'Enfant* (*The Two of Us;* 1968), which he directed and wrote. Berri's next film was *Mazel tov* (*Marry Me, Marry Me;* 1969), about a Jewish wedding, in which Berri plays the bridegroom. He also wrote and directed *Le Pistonné* (1971).

BLOOM, CLAIRE (1931–), British actress. Claire Bloom won acclaim in *The Lady's Not for Burning* (1949), and as Juliet in the 1952 Old Vic production of *Romeo and Juliet*. Later plays include *Duel of Angels* (London, 1958) and *Rashomon* (Broadway, 1959). She gained screen fame as the ballerina in Charlie Chaplin's *Limelight* (1951). Other films include *Richard III* (1956), *Alexander the Great* (1956), *The Brothers Karamazov* (1958), and *The Spy Who Came in From the Cold* (1966). Her television appearances included the 1956 production of Shaw's *Antony and Cleopatra* and, in 1967, *Dark Lovers*, a program of readings from the letters of Abelard and Heloise.

BROOKS, RICHARD (1912–), U.S. film director and writer. Serving in the Marines in World War II, Brooks was threatened with court-martial for a novel about racial discrimination in the services, *Brick Foxhole* (1945). Sinclair Lewis intervened successfully on his behalf and his direction of Lewis's *Elmer Gantry* (1960) won an Oscar. Brooks also directed *Blackboard Jungle* (1955), a film about racial tension in New York schools, *Cat on a Hot Tin Roof* (1968), *The Brothers Karamazov* (1958), and *Sweet Bird of Youth* (1962). He wrote the screenplay for his film of Truman Capote's *In Cold Blood* (1967).

BUTTONS, RED (1919–), U.S. vaudeville and television comic. Born in New York City, Buttons appeared on Broadway in plays including *The Admiral Had a Wife* (1941), *Wine, Women, and Song* (1942), and *Winged Victory* (1944), and on television in the Red

Figure 14. Zero Mostel and Harry Belafonte, in *The Angel Levine*, based on a story by Bernard Malamud, 1969.

Figure 15. Dustin Hoffman (right) and Jon Voight in *Midnight Cowboy*, directed by John Schlesinger, 1969. Courtesy Museum of Modern Art, Film Stills Archive, New York.

Buttons Show (1952–55). Among his most important films are *Winged Victory* (1944), *Sayonara* (1957) for which he won an Oscar, *The Longest Day* (1961), *A Ticklish Affair* (1963), and *They Shoot Horses, Don't They?* (1970).

***CANTOR, EDDIE** (1892–1964), U.S. stage and film comedian.

COBB, LEE J. (1911–), U.S. actor. Born in New York City, Cobb worked with the Group Theater, N.Y., during the 1930s, acting in *Waiting for Lefty, Golden Boy, The Gentle People*, and *Winged Victory*. His portrayal of Willy Loman in Arthur *Miller's *Death of a Salesman* (1949) won him awards. He appeared in many other Broadway plays and in films including *On the Waterfront* (1954) and *Exodus* (1960).

***COHN, HARRY** (1891–1956), U.S. film executive.

CUKOR, GEORGE (1899–), U.S. movie director. Born in New York City, Cukor began his theater career as an assistant stage manager, and later directed several troupes (1921–29). His directorial work, included adaptations from novels and plays (including *Dinner at Eight*, 1933), and he directed many well-known actresses, including Katherine Hepburn, in *A Bill of Divorcement* (1932), *Little Women* (1933), *Philadelphia Story* (1940), and *Holiday* (1938); Greta Garbo, in *Camille* (1937); Ingrid Bergman, in *Gaslight* (1944); Judy Holliday, in *Born Yesterday* (1950) and *It Should Happen to You* (1954); Judy Garland, in *A Star Is Born* (1954); Audrey Hepburn, in *My Fair Lady* (1964); and Marilyn Monroe, in *Let's Make Love* (1960).

CURTIS, TONY (**Bernard Schwartz**; 1925–), U.S. actor. Born in New York, Curtis began his career on the stage in a settlement house in the Bronx. He then went from summer stock companies to off-Broadway shows, and finally to Hollywood. His first major dramatic role was in *Trapeze* (1956), followed by *Sweet Smell of Success* (1957). He starred in many films including *The Defiant Ones* (1958), *Some Like it Hot* (1959), *Spartacus* (1960), *Taras Bulba* (1962), *Boeing, Boeing* (1966), *Don't Make Waves* (1967), and *The Boston Strangler* (1968).

DA SILVA (Silverblatt), HOWARD (1909–), U.S. actor. Born in Cleveland, Da Silva at first worked as a stage actor. After learning the craft he worked at the Civic Repertory Theater in New York until 1934 and later he played in many theatrical productions, and Broadway musicals including *Alice in Wonderland, Waiting for Lefty, The World of Shalom Aleichem, Oklahoma*, and *Fiorello*. He also directed plays and wrote the Broadway comedy *The Zulu and the Zayde*. Da Silva has appeared in numerous films since 1936 including *Abe Lincoln in Illinois, Nine Lives Are Not Enough, Lost Weekend, They Live by Night, David and Lisa*, and *Topkapi*.

***DASSIN, JULES** (1911–), U.S. film and stage director.

DE GRUNWALD, ANATOLE (1910–1967), British film producer and writer. Born in St. Petersburg, De Grunwald started in British films before World War II. His first big success was in his adaptation of Terence Rattigan's play *French Without Tears* (1940) and he subsequently wrote, produced, or collaborated in a score of productions. His reputation grew with *The Way to the Stars* (1945) which won the National Film Award as the best British film made during the war; *Spitfire* (1943), and *Secret Mission* (1942). He also produced *Queen of Spades* (1948), *The Winslow Boy* (1946), *The V.I.P.'s* (1963), and *The Yellow Rolls-Royce* (1965).

DIAMOND, I. A. L. (**Itek Dominici**; 1920–), U.S. film-script-writer. Born in Ughemi, Rumania, Diamond was taken to New York, where his father changed the family name. A mathematics prodigy at high school, he studied engineering at Columbia University but took up writing and added the initials I. A. L. to his name. He wrote four college musical shows, and at graduation received an offer from Paramount studios in Hollywood. He collaborated with Billy Wilder on the films *Some Like it Hot* (1959), *The Apartment* (1960), *One, Two, Three* (1961), and *Irma la Douce* (1963).

***DOUGLAS, KIRK** (1916–), U.S. stage and film actor.

DOUGLAS, MELVYN (1901–), U.S. actor. Son of Edouard Hesselberg, a musician, Douglas first appeared on the New York stage in 1928 in *A Free Soul*. He went to Hollywood in 1931 to act in a screen version of *Tonight or Never*. After his army service in World War II, Douglas' Broadway appearances included *Two Blind Mice* (1949), *Inherit the Wind* (1955), *Walz of the Toreadors* (1956), *The Best Man* (1960), and *Spofford* (1967). His films include *Counsellor-at-Law* (1933), *The Shining Hour* (1938), *Ninotchka* (1939), and *Billy Budd* (1962).

***EISENSTEIN, SERGEI MIKHAILOVICH** (1898–1948), Russian film director.

EPSTEIN, JEAN (1897–1953), French director. Epstein was born in Warsaw but lived and worked in France. As a young man the experimental cinema attracted him, and he directed his first film, *Pasteur*, when he was 25, thereafter working largely in the realistic mode, using outdoor settings and everyday scenes in such films as *La Belle Nivernaise* and *Finis Terrae* (1928), a documentary-style tale of Bannec island fishermen. In *La Chute de la Maison Usher* (1928) he created notable indoor atmospheric effects as well, introducing the use of slow motion. One of his last films was *Les Feux de*

Figure 16, Elliot Gould with Genevieve Waite in Pandro S. Berman's production of *Move*, directed by Stuart Rosenberg, 1970. Courtesy Museum of Modern Art, Film Stills Archive, New York.

la Mer (1948). His sister MARIE EPSTEIN (b. 1899) worked with him and also with Jean Benoît-Lévy, writing the screenplay for and sharing direction of the classic *La Maternelle* (1933) with Benoît-Lévy.

EPSTEIN, JULIUS J. (1909–), and **PHILIP G.** (1909–1952), U.S. screenwriters. New York-born identical twins, Julius and Philip Epstein had their first play, *And Stars Remain*, produced by the Theater Guild in 1936. After working separately for two years, they joined Warner Brothers and became the best-known screenwriting team of the 1940s. Their films included *Casablanca* (1942), *The Man Who Came to Dinner* (1942), *Arsenic and Old Lace* (1944), and *Saturday's Children* (1946). After Philip's death Julius continued to work alone, and among his screenplays were *Fanny* (1964) and *Any Wednesday* (1966).

FLEISCHER, MAX (1889–1972), cartoonist and producer. Born in Austria, Fleischer created Betty Boop, Koko, the Inkwell Series, Popeye the Sailorman, and other cartoon characters. His feature cartoons include *Gulliver's Travels* (1939) and *Mr. Bing Goes to Town* (1941).

FORD, ALEXANDER (1908–), Polish film producer. Born in Lodz, Ford worked in Palestine in 1933 with a Polish unit making a story-documentary, *Sabra*. His *Droga Młodych* ("Road of the Young," 1936), banned in Poland, was exhibited in Paris. He became the director of Film Polski in 1945. He gained recognition for *Ulica Graniczna* ("Border Street," Venice gold medal, 1948), which dealt with the Warsaw ghetto. *Młodość Chopina* ("Youth of Chopin," 1952), *Piœtka z Ulicy Barskiej* ("Five Boys of Barski Street," Cannes Festival Prize, 1954); and *Krzyzacy* ("Crusader," 1960). Prevented from making a film on Janusz *Korczak, Ford left Poland in 1968 and settled in Israel in 1970.

FOREMAN, CARL (1914–), U.S. writer, producer, and director. Born in Chicago, he saw army service during World War II after which he began movie scriptwriting and prepared the scenarios for films such as *Champion* (1948), *Home of the Brave* (1948), *High Noon* (1950), and *Bridge on the River Kwai* (1957). Called before a congressional committee during the McCarthy era he declined to testify on whether he was a member of The Communist Party on the grounds of the Fifth Amendment; in 1956 he himself chose to testify before congress, and was given what he described as "a clean bill of political health." From the early 1950s he lived and worked in London, and headed his own production company there. He wrote and produced *Guns of Navarone* (1961); wrote, produced, and directed *Victors* (1963); and produced *Born Free* (1965) and *MacKenna's Gold* (1969). He has served as president of the writers guild in England (1968), board member of the British Film Institute, and honorary president of the Screen Writers Guild of Israel, (where he conducted a course in screen-writing).

FORMAN, MILOS (1932–), Czech film director. Forman's early years were spent in a town near Prague, where his father was a teacher. In 1963 he made *Black Peter*, in 1964, *Loves of a Blonde*, a film distributed and internationally acclaimed. *The Fireman's Ball* (1968), a wry treatment of Czech bureaucracy, effected its own irony when it caused 40,000 fireman to quit after Novotny released the film. All were appeased when Forman offered his own critical interpretation (a parody in itself) of the film as broad allegory.

***FOX, WILLIAM** (1879–1952), U.S. film producer.

FRANKENHEIMER, JOHN MICHAEL (1930–), director. Born in New York City of Catholic-Jewish parentage, Frankenheimer graduated from La Salle Military Academy (1947). He was a director for CBS television (1945–49) producing, among other programs, *The Turn of the Screw*, and *Days of Wine and Roses*. Frankenheimer's films include *The Young Stranger* (1957), *The Young Savages* (1961), *The Manchurian Candidate* (1962), *The Train* (1964), *Grand Prix* (1966), *The Fixer* (1968), and *The Gypsy Moths* (1969).

FREED (originally **Grossman**), **ARTHUR** (1894–), U.S. popular lyricist and producer of motion picture musicals. Freed was born in Charleston, S.C., and grew up in Seattle, Wash. He was a piano player for the music publishers Waterman, Berlin, and Snyder (see Irving *Berlin), toured the Chicago area with the *Marx brothers for several months, and later with Gus Edwards' vaudeville circuit for a year and a half. After army service in 1917–19, Freed wrote his first popular song hit, "I Cried for You, Now It's Your Turn to Cry over Me," with music by his partner, Nacio Herb Brown. He and Brown produced revues at the Orange Grove Theater using their own songs. Freed's work in motion pictures began when he and Brown wrote the songs for Metro-Goldwyn-Mayer's and Hollywood's first musical, *Broadway Melody of 1929*. In 1939 Freed produced, for M.G.M., *Babes in Arms*, the first of about 50 musicals, including *Strike Up the Band* (1940), *Cabin in the Sky* (1943), *Meet Me in St. Louis* (1944), *On the Town* (1949), *American in Paris* (1951), and *Singin' in the Rain* (1952), the title of the last being a Freed song originally performed in M.G.M.'s second musical, *Hollywood Revue*.

***FRIENDLY, FRED W.** (1915–), U.S. television writer and director.

GARFIELD, JOHN (**Julius Garfinkle**; 1913–1952), U.S. actor. Born in New York, Garfield, deeply disturbed by the death of his mother, played truant, but was persuaded by a child psychologist to study acting. He attended drama school and later joined the Group Theater Company. He first played on Broadway in Elmer *Rice's *Counselor-at-Law* (1931) and then took the lead in Clifford *Odets' *Golden Boy* (1937). He began his film career in 1938, typed as a "tough," but he played the lover in *Saturday's Children* and Danny in Steinbeck's *Tortilla Flat* (1942). In 1948 he starred as the prize fighter in *Body and Soul* (1947) but returned to the stage in *Skipper Next to God* for the Experimental Theater (1948).

GODDARD, PAULETTE (**Marian Levee**; 1911–), U.S. film actress. Paulette Goddard was chosen by Charlie Chaplin to star opposite him as the waif in *Modern Times* (1936), and they were subsequently married. Four years later she again starred with Chaplin in his first talking film, *The Great Dictator* (1940). In 1944 she married the actor-director Burgess Meredith. They produced and starred in *Dairy of A Chambermaid* (1946). Among her other films were *The Women* (1939), *Northwest Mounted Police* (1940), and *The Unholy Four* (1954). In 1958 she married the novelist Erich Maria Remarque.

***GOLDWYN, SAMUEL** (1882–), U.S. film producer.

HAAS, HUGO (1901–1968), Czechoslovakian actor and film director. Haas was with the National Theater in Prague before World War II, and also acted in many Czech films. In 1939 he escaped from Nazi-occupied Prague and went to the United States. On Broadway, he appeared in Čapek's *R.U.R.* and in a dramatization of Tolstoy's *War and Peace*. He eventually formed his own company in Hollywood. Among his pictures were *Pick-up* (1951) and *Edge of Hell* (1956). He also played the title role in the TV series *Rabbi on Wheels*. In 1963, Haas settled in Vienna.

HARVEY, LAURENCE (1928–), British actor. Born in Lithuania, Harvey was brought up in South Africa, where the family name was Skikne. He went to England after World War II and achieved his first big success at Stratford-on-Avon in *Romeo and Juliet* (1954), which he also played on the screen. Starring roles followed in the musical *Camelot* (1964) and in many feature films. He was at his best in cynical roles of the British realistic school such as in *Room at the Top* (1959) and *Darling* (1966).

***HECHT, BEN** (1894–1964), U.S. author and screenwriter.

HOFFMANN, DUSTIN (1937–), U.S. actor. Born in Los Angeles, California, his role in *The Graduate* (1967), his first motion picture performance, was considered the year's most significant screen debut. His subsequent films included *Midnight Cowboy* (1969), *John and Mary* (1969), and *Little Big Man* (1970).

HOLLIDAY, JUDY (**Judith Tuvim**; 1923–1965), U.S. actress. Born in New York, her father, Abraham Tuvim (1894–1954) was executive director of the Foundation for the Jewish National Fund. Judy Holliday made her Broadway debut in *Kiss Them For Me* (1945), winning an award. A year later she starred in the Broadway play *Born Yesterday*, then played in the film version and won an Academy Award (Best Actress), 1950. She appeared in several other films including *The Solid Gold Cadillac* (1956), and in Broadway musicals.

HOWARD, LESLIE (**Leslie Stainer**; 1893–1943), British actor. Born in London, Howard started as a bank clerk and made his first appearance on the stage in 1918. He subsequently acted in many plays in London and New York and started film work in 1930. On the screen he came to typify British upper-class urbanity. His most famous roles were in *The Scarlet Pimpernel* (1933), *Pygmalion* (1938), *Gone With the Wind* (1939), and *Pimpernel Smith* (1941). He was killed when the plane in which he was flying from Lisbon in 1943 was shot down by the Germans.

JAFFE, SAM (1897–), U.S. actor. Jaffe, born in New York, began with the Washington Square players in 1915, and later played Jewish roles in *The God of Vengeance* (1922). *The Main Line* (1924), *Izzy* (1925). *The Jazz Singer* (1925–28), and *The Gentle People* for Group Theater (1939). His film career included parts in *Lost Horizon* (1937), *Grand Hotel* (1932), *The Asphalt Jungle*, and *Ben-Hur* (1959). He became widely known in the 1960s for his role in the U.S. television series, *Ben Casey*.

JAMES, SIDNEY (1913–), British actor. James first appeared with the Repertory Players, Johannesburg; then with army entertainment units. After World War II, he acted on the London stage as a rough-hewn character in comedy roles. Subsequently, he appeared in more than 60 film productions. Among them were *The Small Back Room* (1949), *The Lavender Hill Mob* (1951), *A King in New York* (1957), *The Story of Esther Costello* (1957), and the *Carry On* series. He was also a popular figure in many radio and television programs, particularly with Tony Hancock.

***JOLSON, AL** (1886–1950), U.S. musical and film star.

KÁDAR, JÁN (1918–), film director. Born in Budapest, Kádar was imprisoned in a Hungarian labor camp during World War II. Later he worked for the Czech state film studios, and with Elmar Klos made *Death Is Called Engelchen*, which won acclaim. He became known in the West for the film *The Shop on Main Street* (1965), which starred Ida Kaminska and won an Academy Award. Kádar was linked with the writers and artists involved in the liberal movement in Czechoslovakia in 1968. In 1969 he directed the American film of Bernard *Malamud's story, *Angel Levine*.

KAMINSKA, IDA (1899–), actress (see *Kaminski).

KANIN, GARSON (1912–), U.S. playwright and director. Kanin, born in Rochester, N.Y., became a Hollywood director for Samuel Goldwyn at 25. He directed John Barrymore in *A Great Man Votes* (1939) and Ginger Rogers in *Bachelor Mother* (1939). After Army service during World War II Kanin was co-director, with Sir Carol Reed, of *The True Story* (1945), a film on the Allied victory. Plays that he wrote include *A Gift of Time* (1962) and *Come on Strong* (1962). He wrote and directed the Broadway hit play *Born Yesterday* (1946). Together with his author-actress wife Ruth Gordon, Kanin coauthored such films as *Adam's Rib* (1949) and *The Marrying Kind* (1952). He directed and produced *A Very Rich Woman* (1965), written and acted by his wife. His book, *Remembering Mr. Maugham* (1966) is a collection of reminiscences.

KATZMAN, SAM (1901–), U.S. motion picture producer. Chiefly a producer for low-budget films, Katzman's films include: the *Jungle Jim* series, *Rock Around the Clock* (1956), *Get Yourself a College Girl* (1965), and many other serials based on comic strip and radio characters.

KAUFMAN, BORIS (1906–), motion picture cameraman. He was born in Bialystok, Poland; and after working in the film industry in France from 1928 to 1940 and serving in the French army, went to New York in 1942. He worked for American war propaganda productions and became one of America's foremost cameramen. In 1955 he won an Academy Award for *On the Waterfront*. Other films he worked in include *Twelve Angry Men* (1957), *Splendor in the Grass* (1961), *The Pawnbroker* (1964), *The Group* (1966), and *The Brotherhood* (1969).

***KAYE, DANNY** (1913–), U.S. film comedian.

***KORDA, SIR ALEXANDER** (1893–1956), English film producer.

***KRAMER, STANLEY** (1913–), U.S. film producer and director.

KRASNA, NORMAN (1909–), U.S. film producer and playwright. Krasna started as a clerk in New York and rose to earn $100,000 for writing and directing a single motion picture. Among his Broadway plays were *Dear Ruth* (1944) and *John Loves Mary* (1947). His 30 screenplays include *Richest Girl in the World* (1934), *Princess O'Rourke* which won an Academy Award in 1943, and *Sunday in New York* (1961).

KUBRICK, STANLEY (1928–), U.S. film producer. Born in New York, Kubrick made his first feature film, *Fear and Desire*, in 1953 and his first moneymaking film, *The Killing*, in 1956. He aroused much controversy with films such as *Paths of Glory* (1958), on the stupidity of war, *Spartacus* (1960), *Lolita* (1962), and *Dr. Strangelove* (1963), an anti-military establishment movie. *2001: A Space Odyssey* (1968) was widely considered to be a major work.

***LAEMMLE, CARL** (1867–1939), U.S. film producer.

***LANG, FRITZ** (1890–), Austrian film director and screenwriter.

***LASKY, JESSE L.** (1880–1958), U.S. film producer.

LEHMAN, ERNEST (1915–), U.S. film producer and screenwriter. Born in New York, Lehman went to Hollywood in 1951 and won Writers' Guild awards for his screenwriting in *Sabrina* (1954), *The King and I* (1956), *North by Northwest* (1959), *West Side Story* (1961), and *The Sound of Music* (1965). As a producer he made his debut in 1966 with *Who's Afraid of Virginia Woolf?* for which he also wrote the screenplay. He was also writer-producer for *Hello, Dolly!* (1969).

LELOUCH, CLAUDE (1937–), French film director. Born in Paris, Lelouch and his mother moved through Europe during World War II to evade the Nazis but were captured toward the end of the war and spent three months in Dachau. He made a short film at 14, and four years later a television film in the United States. In 1960 he made his first feature film, but *Un homme et une femme* ("A Man and a Woman"), winner of a 1966 Cannes Film Festival prize, put him in the front ranks of French cinema. He made *Vivre pour vivre* (1967) and *La vie, l'amour, la mort* (1968).

LE ROY, MERVYN (1900–), film producer and director. Born in San Francisco, Le Roy first worked as a cameraman, and directed his first film *No Place to Go* in 1927. A prominent Hollywood figure for over 40 years, his films include *The Wizard of Oz* (1939), *Thirty Seconds Over Tokyo* (1944), *Quo Vadis?* (1951), *Mister Roberts* (1955), and *Majority of One* (1961). He was active in Republican politics.

LESTER, RICHARD (1932–), film director. Born in the United States, Lester went to work in England. He won prominence in 1964 with *A Hard Day's Night*, a quasi-documentary in which the Beatles poked fun at the craze they themselves had started. In 1965, his comedy *The Knack* won a first prize at the Cannes Film Festival. Among his other movies are *Help* (1965), also made with the Beatles; *How I Won the War* (1967), a controversial antiwar satire; and *Petulia* (1968), a drama.

LEVINE, JOSEPH E. (1905–), U.S. motion picture producer. Born in Boston, Levine was a theater owner and movie distributor (1943) before becoming a producer. His films include *Jack the Ripper* (1959), *Hercules* (1959), *Bocaccio '70*, *Divorce Italian Style*, *Marriage Italian Style*, *Yesterday, Today, and Tomorrow*, *The Carpetbaggers* (1964), and *Harlow* (1965).

LEWIS, JERRY (Levitch, Joseph; 1926–), U.S. comedian. Born in Newark, N.J., Lewis started his career at 14 and joined Dean Martin to form a successful comedy team. Together they made 16 films and appeared extensively in nightclubs and on television. After parting from Martin in 1956, Lewis became a successful comedian on his own, and directed and appeared in many films, including *Don't Give up the Ship* (1959), *Cinderfella* (1960), *The Errand Boy* (1961), *It's Only Money* (1962), and *The Nutty Professor* (1963). He was active in philanthropic and Zionist work.

LINDER, MAX (originally **Gabriel-Maxmillien Leuvielle**; 1883–1925), French silent movie comedy star. Linder was born in Saint-Loubès to a family of vintners. His first film was *Première Sortie d'un Collegien* (1905); thereafter he turned out perhaps one film every week or so, to 1914. The character of the natty, slightly run-down, but highly-spirited Max achieved worldwide renown, inspiring Charlie Chaplin to develop a similar character early in his career. Linder fought in World War I, permanently impairing his health and affecting his emotional stability. His last film was *Roi du Cirque* (1925). Few copies of his films have been saved.

LITVAK, (Michael) ANATOLE (1902–), U.S. film producer and director. Born in Kiev, Litvak was at a Russian dramatic school until the age of 16, and then worked in Soviet film studios. After leaving the U.S.S.R. in 1924, he directed films in Europe and the United States in French, German, and English. His European films included *Dolly macht Karriere* (1930), *Mayerling* (1936), and *L'Equipage* (1935). His major American films are *The Snake Pit* (1949), *Sorry, Wrong Number* (1948), *Act of Love* (1954), *Anastasia* (1956), *The Journey* (1958), *Goodbye Again* (1961), and *The Night of the Generals* (1967).

LOEW, MARCUS (1872–1927), U.S. motion picture executive. Born in New York, Loew rose to a powerful position in the American film industry. Loew began his career in motion pictures by showing films in rented halls. In 1919 he bought Metro Pictures, Inc., and in 1924 acquired Goldwyn Pictures. With the appointment of Louis B. Mayer as vice-president, M.G.M. was formed, Loew's Inc., gaining controlling interest. At his death, he was president of Metro-Goldwyn-Mayer film studios of Hollywood and of Loew's Inc., one of the largest cinema chains in the United States.

LOM, HERBERT (1917–), actor. Born in Prague, Lom was trained in London and made his first British picture in 1940, *Mein Kampf—My Crimes.* He became known for his earthy characterizations and made his first West End appearance in 1951 in *The Seventh Veil.* His most notable success was as the king in *The King and I* (1953). Films in which he appeared include *War and Peace* (1956), *Spartacus* (1960), and *El Cid* (1961). He also starred in successful television series.

LORRE, PETER (1904–1964), film actor. Born in Hungary, Lorre joined a German theatrical troupe at 17 and for a time worked with the German dramatist Bertold Brecht. In 1931 his performance as the killer in *M.* made him famous. Lorre, a thickset man who could look both amiable and sinister, went to London for Alfred Hitchcock's *The Man Who Knew Too Much* (1934) and then to Hollywood. Among his notable films were *The Maltese Falcon* (1941), *Casablanca* (1942), *Arsenic and Old Lace* (1944), *Confidential Agent* (1945), and *20,000 Leagues under the Sea* (1954).

***LUBITSCH, ERNST** (1862–1947), German-U.S. film producer and director.

LUKAS, PAUL (1895–1971), U.S. actor, born in Budapest. After nine years at the Comedy Theater, Lukas went to the U.S. in 1927 and became prominent in films and plays. The high point of his career was his portrayal of Kurt Mueller, a German refugee, in *Watch on the Rhine,* on the stage in 1941 and on the screen in 1943. He won awards for both performances. He also appeared on Broadway in *Call Me Madam* (1950) and *Flight Into Egypt* (1952). His films include *Dodsworth* (1936), *Address Unknown* (1944), *Berlin Express* (1948), and *Four Horsemen of the Apocalypse* (1962).

LUMET, SIDNEY (1924–), U.S. theatrical and film director. Born in Philadelphia, Lumet was a child actor at the Yiddish Art Theater. He appeared on Broadway in 1935 and later directed off-Broadway shows. He joined the Columbia Broadcasting System in 1950 and gained a reputation as a director of live television dramas. The first film he directed was *Twelve Angry Men* (1957), and in 1962 he directed O'Neill's *Long Day's Journey Into Night.* His later films include *Fail Safe* (1964), *The Pawnbroker* (1965), *The Hill* (1965), *The Group* (1966), *The Deadly Affair* (1967), and *Funny Girl* (1968).

MANKIEWICZ, JOSEPH LEO (1909–), U.S. film writer and director. Born in Wilkes-Barre, Pa., Mankiewicz worked on scripts for Paramount, M.G.M., and Fox. He received Academy awards for *A Letter to Three Wives* (1948) and *All About Eve* (1950). In 1952 he formed Figaro Inc., and produced, wrote, and directed *The Barefoot Contessa* (1954), and was the producer of *The Quiet American* (1958). Films he directed include *Guys and Dolls* (1955), *Suddenly Last Summer* (1959), *Cleopatra* (1963), and *The Honey Pot* (1967).

MANN, DANIEL (1912–), U.S. director. Mann was born in New York and began his career in entertainment as a musician in resorts. He served in the army in World War II, was trained at Neighborhood Playhouse in New York, began directing television productions, and was later a director for theater and for movie adaptations of the same plays, including *Come Back, Little Sheba* (1950; 1952), and *Rose Tattoo* (1951; 1955). He also directed the movies *Teahouse of the August Moon* (1956), *Five Finger Exercise* (1962), *Our Man Flint* (1965), and *For Love of Ivy* (1967).

MANN, DELBERT (1920–), U.S. director. Born in Lawrence, Kansas, Mann served in the U.S. Air Force during World War II and entered the theater as stage manager and then director for repertory and summer playhouse productions. From 1949 to 1955 he directed a number of television dramas, including Playhouse 90 and Omnibus productions, and in 1955 directed the movie *Marty,* from a television original. He also directed the movies *Bachelor Party* (1957), *Separate Tables* (1958), *Desire Under the Elms* (1958), *Middle of the Night* (1959), *Dark at the Top of the Stairs* (1960), and *Quick Before It Melts!* (1965). He served as president of the Directors Guild of America. In 1968 he began working outside the United States, directing movies premiered on television and then shown in movie theaters, including *Heidi* (1969), *David Copperfield* (1970), and *Jane Eyre* (1971).

MARX, CHICO (1891–1961), U.S. film comedian. See *Marx Brothers.

MARX, GROUCHO (1895–), U.S. film comedian. See *Marx Brothers.

MARX, HARPO (1893–1964), U.S. film comedian. See *Marx Brothers.

MARX, ZEPPO (1901–), U.S. film theatrical agent. See *Marx Brothers.

***MAYER, LOUIS B.** (1885–1957), U.S. film executive.

MIRISCH, HAROLD (1907–), **MARVIN** (1918–), and **WALTER** (1921–), U.S. film producers. Born in New York, the Mirisch brothers became a team in 1952, when they joined Allied Artists as executives. They wished to produce high-quality films by giving a free hand to independent film-makers, but Allied dropped the plan after two productions, and in 1957 the brothers set up their own company. They scored an immediate success with their first film, Billy Wilder's *Some Like It Hot* (1959). Others included *The Apartment* (1960), *West Side Story* (1961), *The Children's Hour* (1962), and *In the Heat of the Night* (1967).

***MOSTEL, ZERO** (1915–), U.S. actor.

***MUNI, PAUL** (1895–1967), U.S. stage and film actor.

NAZIMOVA, ALLA (1879–1945), Russian-U.S. actress. Born in Yalta, Nazimova went to New York with a Russian company in 1905, making her debut in the play *The Chosen People.* She stayed in the United States, became a success on the U.S. stage, and had her first screen role in *War Brides* (1916). One of the earliest film stars, she played in *Heart of a Child* (1920), *Madonna of the Streets* (1924), *Since You Went Away* (1944), and *In our Time* (1944). She also appeared in the anti-Nazi film *Escape* (1940).

NEWMAN, PAUL (1925–), U.S. actor. Born in Cleveland, Ohio, Newman first appeared on Broadway in *Picnic* (1953); his first film was *The Silver Chalice* (1955). Among Newman's notable films are *Cat on a Hot Tin Roof* (1958), *The Long Hot Summer* (1958), *Exodus* (1960), *From the Terrace* (1960), *Sweet Bird of Youth* (1962), *Hud, The Hustler* (1961), and *Butch Cassidy and the Sundance Kid* (1969).

***NICHOLS, MIKE (Peschowsky, Michael Igor; 1931–**), U.S. actor and director.

OPHUELS, MAX (1902–1957), film director. Born in Germany, Ophuels worked at the Vienna Burgtheater and later made films in Germany until the rise of the Nazis. Early successes were *Liebelei* (1933) and *La Signora di Tutti* (1934). Other films were *Letter From an Unknown Woman* (Hollywood, 1948), the French *La Ronde* (1950), and *The Earrings of Madame de...* (1953). His expressionist film *Lola Montez* (1955) aroused controversy among film critics in the United States after the showing of its complete version there in 1969.

PASTERNAK, JOSEPH (1901–), U.S. producer. Pasternak, who was born in Szilagy-Somlyo, emigrated to the United States in 1921 and two years later began working in films. By the end of the 1920s he was a producer for Universal Pictures in Central Europe, and from 1936 he produced over 100 films in the United States, always light comedy musicals such as *Three Smart Girls* (1936) with Deanna Durbin—the first of ten she made for Pasternak; movies that starred Mario Lanza; and *It Started with Eve* (1941); *Destry Rides Again* (1939), with Marlene Dietrich; *Spinout* (1966), with Elvis Presley; and *Sweet Ride* (1968). Pasternak wrote an autobiography, *Easy the Hard Way* (1956), and a cookbook, *Cooking with Love and Paprika* (1966).

***PICON, MOLLY** (1898–), U.S. actress.

POLANSKI, ROMAN (1933–), film director, writer, and actor. Born in Paris, Polanski went to Poland with his parents at the age of three. He won awards for his film *Two Men and a Wardrobe* (1958). Among his films are *Mammals* (1961), *Knife in the Water* (1962), *Repulsion* (1965), and *Rosemary's Baby* (1968), which showed his mastery of suspense and the macabre. He also acted, most notably in *The Fearless Vampire Killers.* In the 1960s he settled in the U.S.

POMMER, ERICH (1889–1966), German producer. Pommer, after serving in the German army in World War I, by 1919 was directing the Deutsches Eclair (Decla) film company and had gathered a staff that included the director Fritz *Lang and the set and costume designers who had been associated with the avant-garde Der Sturm group, Pommer's expressionist succès de scandale. *Cabinet of Dr. Caligari* (1919) was followed by *Dr. Mabuse* (1922); *Niebelungen* (1924), produced after Decla had merged with the German colossus of the industry, UFA; *Variety* (1925); *Metropolis* (1925/26); *Blue Angel* (1930); and *Last Laugh.* The day Hitler became chancellor of Germany, Pommer left the country for Paris, where he produced *Liliom* (1934) with Lang. In the 1930s he worked in England as an independent and in the United States for Fox, producing *Jamaica Inn* (1939) with Alfred Hitchcock and adapting the Sidney Howard play *They Knew What They Wanted* (1940). He worked again in Germany as an independent producer after the war.

***PREMINGER, OTTO LUDWIG** (1906–), U.S. film and stage director and producer.

RAINER, LUISE (1912–), Austrian actress. Born in Vienna, Rainer began her career in Duesseldorf, Germany, in 1928, and later joined Reinhardt's company in Berlin and appeared in *Saint Joan* and *Six Characters in Search of an Author.* Leaving Germany in 1935, she went to Hollywood and became famous in films such as *Escapade* (1935), *The Good Earth* (1937), for which she won an Oscar, *The Great Ziegfeld* (1936), and *The Great Waltz* (1938). Her first role on the English stage was in *Behold the Bride* (London, 1939) and on the New York stage, *A Kiss for Cinderella* (1942). Clifford *Odets, the playwright, was her first husband.

***RICHTER, HANS** (1888–), German and U.S. film producer.

RITZ BROTHERS (b. **Joachim**), **AL** (1903–1965), **JIMMY** (1905–), and **HARRY** (1908–), U.S. vaudeville comedy team. Born in Newark, N.J., the Ritz Brothers began public appearances as "The Collegians." Their slapstick succeeded in several Broadway revues, and their first film was *Sing, Baby, Sing* (1936). Other films were *One in a Million* (1937), *The Goldwyn Follies* (1938), and *Pack Up Your Troubles* (1932). They all later appeared on television.

***ROBINSON, EDWARD G.** (1893–), U.S. stage and film actor.

ROSSEN, ROBERT (1908–1966), U.S. film producer. Born in New York, Rossen was a prizefighter in his early years and worked on the stage before becoming a screenwriter in 1939. He wrote the screenplay for *Roaring Twenties, Edge of Darkness,* and *Sea Wolf.* Films he directed include *Body and Soul* (1947), *All the King's Men,* which won Hollywood's Academy award for best picture of the year in 1949; *The Hustler* (1961) and *Lilith* (1964).

SALTZMAN, HARRY (1915–), film producer. Born in Saint John, N.B., Canada, Saltzman founded Lowndes Productions Ltd. in 1964. His films include *Look Back in Anger* (1959), *The Entertainer* (1960), *Saturday Night and Sunday Morning* (1961), *Dr. No* (1963), *From Russia with Love* (1964), *Goldfinger* (1964), *Thunderball* (1965), and *Battle of Britain.* His television productions include the Robert Montgomery Show and Captain Gallant of the Foreign Legion.

SASLAVSKY, LUIS (1908–), Argentine film director. Born in Santa Fé, Saslavsky was drawn into the film world as a reporter for *La Nación* in Hollywood. He returned to Argentina, and directed *Crimen a las tres* (1935), *La Fuga* (1937), and *Nace un Amor* (1938). He later sacrificed some of his intellectual quality to popular taste but continued to show some originality, as in *Historia de una Noche* (1941). During the Perón dictatorship Saslavsky lived in Europe, directing *Corona Negra* in Spain in 1952, and other films in both Spain and France. Returning to Argentina, he produced *Las Ratas* (1963).

***SCHARY, DORE** (1905–), U.S. film writer and producer.

***SCHILDKRAUT, JOSEPH** (1895–1964), U.S. stage and film actor.

SCHLESINGER, JOHN (1926–), English director. Schlesinger was born in London. He toured in repertory until 1959 and then directed BBC-TV films. His first feature film was *A Kind of Loving* (1962), followed by *Billy Liar* (1963), *Darling* (1965), and *Far from the Madding Crowd* (1967). Schlesinger directed several plays, including *Timon of Athens* for the Royal Shakespeare Company.

***SELLERS, PETER** (1925–), English actor.

SELZNICK, DAVID OLIVER (1902–1965), U.S. film producer. See *Selznick.

SELZNICK, LEWIS J. (1872–1933), U.S. film executive. See *Selznick.

SELZNICK, MYRON C. (1898–1944), U.S. press agent. See *Selznick.

SIDNEY, SYLVIA (**Sophia Koscow**; 1910–), U.S. actress. Born in New York, Sylvia Sidney first appeared there in 1927 and became internationally known after her part in the film *Street Scene* (1931). She played for the Guild Theater in *To Quito and Back* (1937) and for the Group Theater in *The Gentle People* (1939). She acted in summer theaters, played in *The Four-Poster* on Broadway in 1956, and toured in *Auntie Mame* (1958–59). Her films included *Madame Butterfly, Jennie Gerhardt, Fury, The Searching Wind* (1946), *Love from a Stranger* (1947), and *Behind the High Wall* (1956).

SIGNORET (**Kaminker**), **SIMONE** (1921–), French film actress. Born in Wiesbaden, Germany, the daughter of a French Army officer, Signoret (her mother's name) was brought up in Paris. A femme fatale role in *Macadam* (1946) started her rise to stardom in French films. In several productions she appeared with the singer and actor Yves Montand, whom she married in 1951. She achieved international stardom and an Oscar for her role in the British film *Room at the Top* (1959), and subsequently acted in other British, Italian, French, and American films, including *L'Aveu* (1970).

SPIEGEL, SAMUEL P. (1904–), U.S. motion picture producer. Born in Austria, Spiegel came to the United States in 1939. His pictures include *The Stranger* (1945), *African Queen* (1951), *On the Waterfront* (1954), *The Bridge on the River Kwai* (1957), which received the Academy Award for the best picture (1957), *Lawrence of Arabia* (1962), and *The Night of the Generals* (1966). Spiegel was also known for a time as S. P. Eagle. He was the brother of Shalom *Spiegel.

STEIGER, ROD (1925–), U.S. movie, stage, and television actor. Born in Westhampton, N.Y. Steiger served four years as a torpedoman on a destroyer during World War II. His first performance, as "Marty" in the original television play in the early 1950s, won him acclaim. His versatile talent has earned him many awards: an Oscar for his Mississippi sheriff in the film, *In the Heat of the Night* (1967); Oscar nominations for his first film, *On the Waterfront* (1954) and for *The Pawnbroker* (1965), in which he played Sol Nazerman, a Jewish pawnbroker haunted by memories of Nazi Germany. With Claire Bloom, to whom he was then married, he won an Emmy award in 1967 for *Dark Lovers,* a dramatic reading of the letters of Abelard and Heloise presented on New York's noncommercial television channel.

***STERNBERG, JOSEF VON** (1894–1969), U.S. film director.

***STREISAND, BARBRA** (1942–), U.S. actress, singer, and musical comedy star.

STRICK, JOSEPH (1923–), U.S. film director and producer. Born in Pittsburgh, Pa., Strick started his career with documentaries and later applied documentary realism to feature films. He gained a reputation with such films as *The Big Break* (1950), *The Savage Eye* (1960), and *The Balcony* (1963). The outstanding example of his method was *Ulysses* (1967), a version of the novel by James Joyce. Strick also produced *Ring of Bright Water* (1969), a film based on Gavin Maxwell's book on porpoises.

STROHEIM, ERICH VON (1885–1957), film actor and director. Born in Austria, von Stroheim, with his bullet-shaped head and his monocle, became famous for his Teutonic roles. He directed and acted in Hollywood, and his film *Greed* (1923) is still considered a masterpiece. In 1937 he went to France to play in Jean Renoir's *La Grande Illusion.* As his Jewish identity was not known he was able to work in France after the Nazi occupation and appeared in some 30 films before going back to Hollywood to act in *Five Graves to Cairo* (1943) and *Sunset Boulevard* (1950).

***THALBERG, IRVING GRANT** (1899–1936), U.S. film producer and executive.

TODD, MIKE (**Avrom Girsch Goldbogen**; 1909–1958), U.S. producer and impresario. Born in Minneapolis, Todd was the son of a Polish-born rabbi. He produced 21 shows on Broadway, largely light musicals, and was a financial promoter of two motion picture filming innovations, Cinerama and Todd-AO. In 1956 he made the $6.5 million film of Jules Verne's *Around the World in 80 Days* which, by the time of his death in a plane crash, had grossed $33 million. Of his three marriages, the second and third were to the film actresses Joan Blondell and Elizabeth Taylor.

***TOEPLITZ, JERRY** (1909–), Polish film historian and critic.

***TOPOL, CHAIM** (1935–), Israel stage and film actor.

TURKOW, JONES (1898–), Polish actor. See *Turkow.

TURKOW, ZIGMUNT (1896–1970), Polish actor and director. See *Turkow.

VERTOV, DZIGA (originally **Denis Kaufman**; 1897–1954), Russian pioneer in newsreel-documentary movie director and founder of the "cine-eye, cine-ear" theory. He edited (early 1920s) the newsreel *kino-pravda* from film taken by cameramen he dispatched throughout the U.S.S.R. After 1924 Vertov headed his own group of movie theorists and filmmakers; his brother and chief cameramen MIKHAIL KAUFMAN went with him. Among his documentaries are *One Sixth of the World* (1927), *Three Songs of Lenin* (1932), and *Lullaby* (1937).

WALBROOK, ANTON (Wohlbrück; 1900–1967), Austrian actor. Born in Vienna, Walbrook began his career under Max *Reinhardt and later starred in German films. After settling in England in 1937 he won acclaim for his stage performances in *Design for Living* (1939) and *Watch on the Rhine* (1942). His film career, spanning three decades, included roles as Arnie Albert in *Victoria The Great* (1937), *Sixty Glorious Years* (1938), *Dangerous Moonlight* (1941), *The 49th Parallel* (1941), *Colonel Blimp* (1943), *The Queen of Spades* (1948), and *I Accuse!* (1958), based on the *Dreyfus Case. He returned to Central Europe in the 1960s and died in Bavaria.

WALD, JERRY (1912–1962), U.S. screenwriter and producer. Wald was born in Brooklyn, N.Y. During 1934–41 Wald wrote or coauthored a number of scenarios, included *The Drive by Night*. Then, as an associate producer (1941) and producer (1942–50) for Warner Brothers, he turned out a number of successful films, including *Destination Tokyo, Objective, Burma,* and *Johnny Belinda*. In 1950 he formed the independent Wald-Krasna Productions with the writer Norman Krasna, an arrangement severed in 1952. Wald then became production vice president at Columbia. From 1956 he headed Jerry Wald Productions at Twentieth Century-Fox.

WARNER, ALBERT (c. 1880–), U.S. film executive. See *Warner.

WARNER, HARRY (1876–1958), U.S. film executive. See *Warner.

WARNER, JACK (1892–), U.S. film executive. See *Warner.

WARNER, SAM (1884–1927), U.S. film executive. See *Warner.

***WILDER, BILLY** (1906–), U.S. film director and writer.

WEISS, JIŘÍ (1913–), Czechoslovakian film director. Weiss made documentaries and won an international prize in 1934 at the Venice Biennale and the Czechoslovak Stage prize in 1937. During World War II, he made films for the exiled Czechoslovak government in London. He returned to Prague in 1945 and won the State film prize for the historical picture *Vstanou noví bojovníci* ("New Fighters Will Rise," 1951) a film on coalminers without professional actors. He also won the Critics prize, Berlin, for *31 ve stínu* ("31 Degrees in the Shade, 1965). His best film, *Romeo, Julie a tma* (1961) was based on an anti-Nazi novel by Jan Očenášek.

WINTERS, SHELLEY (Shirley Schrift; 1922–), U.S. actress. Born in St. Louis, Missouri, Shelley Winters appeared in the operetta *Rosalinda* (1942). *A Double Life* (1948) was her first successful film. Later she became famous for her interpretation of two prototypes—a streetgirl and a mother. In 1959 she won an Oscar for her role in *The Diary of Anne Frank*, and in 1965 she won another Academy Award for *A Patch of Blue*. Her other films include *Lolita* (1962), *The Balcony* (1963), and *The Moving Target* (1965), and her plays, *Who's Afraid of Virginia Woolf?* (1965) and *The Night of the Iguana* (1962). Shelley Winters appeared frequently at Jewish benefit rallies.

WISE, ROBERT (1914–), U.S. film producer and director. Born in Winchester, Indiana, Wise worked at RKO studios from 1933 to 1943, and edited Orson Welles' classic, *Citizen Kane* (1941). He was made a director in 1943 and became one of Hollywood's most successful film-makers. He won four Academy awards as director of *I Want to Live* (1958), director and producer of *West Side Story* (1961), and co-director of *The Sound of Music* (1965), one of the most profitable films ever made. He also directed *The Sand Pebbles* (1966) and *Star* (1968). Wise was active in the civil rights movement in Hollywood.

WOLPER, DAVID LLOYD (1928–), U.S. producer of television documentaries. Born in New York, Wolper's first commercial venture was to buy old Hollywood films and to sell them to the infant television industry. In 1958 he formed Wolper Productions. His film *The Race for Space* (1959) established his reputation as an independent documentary producer. Other notable documentaries were *The Miracle* (1959), *The Making of the President, 1960* (1963), *Biography*, a weekly TV series, *Let My People Go* (1965), the story of the creation of the State of Israel, and *The Rise and Fall of the Third Reich* (1968).

***WYLER, WILLIAM** (1902–), U.S. film director and producer.

WYNN, ED (Isaiah Edwin Leopold; 1886–1966), U.S. comedian. Born in Philadelphia of an immigrant family from Prague, Wynn was known for 60 years as "The Perfect Fool." In 1919, when earning $1,700 weekly, he joined a choristers' strike and was then blacklisted by managements. Using his savings, Wynn staged the *Ed Wynn Carnival* (1919–21), *The Perfect Fool* (1921–22), and *The Grab Bag* (1925). His films included: *Boys and Girls Together* (1940–41), *Marjorie Morningstar*, and *The Diary of Anne Frank* (1959).

WYNN, KEENAN (1916–), U.S. actor. Born in New York, the son of Ed Wynn, of whom he wrote a biography, Keenan toured in stock companies and appeared on the New York stage and on television before making his debut in films, in *See Here Private Hargrove* (1944). Subsequent films in which he acted include *The Hucksters* (1947), *Kiss Me Kate* (1953), *Don't Go Near the Water* (1957), *The Absent-Minded Professor* (1962), *The Americanization of Emily* (1964), *Finian's Rainbow* (1968), and *MacKennas Gold* (1969).

ZINNEMANN, FRED (1907–), U.S. film director and producer. Born in Vienna, Zinnemann went to Hollywood in 1929, worked as a script clerk, and in 1934 directed a full-length documentary, *The Wave*. Later he applied documentary techniques to feature films, and worked for M.G.M. until 1950, when he started on his own. Among his most important films are *The Search* (1948), *High Noon* (1952), an Academy award winner, *From Here to Eternity* (1953), *A Hatful of Rain* (1957), and *A Man for All Seasons* (1966), also an Academy award winner.

***ZUKOR, ADOLPH** (1873–), U.S. motion picture executive and producer.

MOTTL, FELIX JOSEF (1856–1911), German conductor and composer. Born near Vienna, he studied with Anton Bruckner and Joseph Hellmesberger. When he was 24, Liszt conducted his first composition, the opera *Agnes Bernauer* at Weimar. From 1881 to 1903 he was court conductor and then *Generalmusikdirektor* at Karlsruhe, acquiring a brilliant reputation. For the next four years he was conductor of the opera at Munich, making the city a center of operatic life. Mottl devoted himself to the interpretation of the works of Berlioz, Peter Cornelius, and Wagner. In 1887 he appeared at the first Wagner festival at Bayreuth, and in 1890 presented the first full production of Berlioz' *Les Troyens* at Karlsruhe. He also conducted in London and New York. Mottl's compositions include three operas, lieder, and chamber music, but he is best remembered for his orchestral arrangements of works by Lully, Rameau, Mozart, and Gluck, and for his piano reductions of Wagner's operas.

Bibliography: MGG; Grove, Dict; Riemann-Gurlitt. [J.Co.]

MOTZKIN, LEO (Aryeh Leib; 1867–1933), Zionist leader and protagonist of the struggle for Jewish rights in the Diaspora. Born in Brovary, near Kiev, Motzkin received a

Leo Motzkin, Zionist leader. Caricature by Kagan, 1933. Jerusalem, J.N.U.L., Schwadron Collection.

traditional Jewish education and witnessed in his youth the Kiev pogrom in 1881. He studied in Berlin where he was among the founders of the Russian-Jewish Scientific Society (1887), whose members were Jewish students from Russia and Galicia who supported the *Ḥibbat Zion movement.

They conducted heated debates with the majority of the Russian Jewish students, who were attracted to socialism and cosmopolitanism. When he completed his studies, Motzkin abandoned his opportunities for a scientific career and devoted himself to activities for the Jewish national cause. He was one of the strongest critics of the methods of Ḥovevei Zion and, with the appearance of Theodor *Herzl, Motzkin immediately joined the newly formed Zionist Organization at the First Zionist Congress and headed a group of delegates that demanded a clear and decisive wording of the *Basle Program. Before the Second Congress, Herzl sent him to Ereẓ Israel, and in his report to the Congress Motzkin criticized the settlement methods of Baron de *Rothschild and the Ḥovevei Zion and called for a political agreement with the Ottoman government. Despite his ideological closeness to Herzl, he joined the *Democratic Fraction, which he represented at the Fifth Zionist Congress (1901) and at the Conference of Russian Zionists in Minsk (1902). He kept aloof from the controversy over the *Uganda Scheme because of his deep attachment to Ereẓ Israel, on the one hand, and the urgent need to help the oppressed Jewish masses, on the other.

In 1905 Motzkin anonymously edited the revolutionary Russian *Russische Korrespondenz*, which was published in Berlin and provided West European newspapers with information on Russia in a radical spirit. He dedicated considerable space to the fate of the Jews and the anti-Jewish excesses. The Zionist Organization requested Motzkin to publish a book on the wave of pogroms in Russia; it was written for the most part by Motzkin himself (signed A. Linden) and was published in two parts in 1909–10 under the name *Die Judenpogrome in Russland*. The book contained thorough research into anti-Jewish violence in Russia from the beginning of the 19th century to its climax during the Russian Revolution of 1905–06, including descriptions of pogroms in various areas and towns and stressed the role of Jewish *self-defense. In 1912 Motzkin's pamphlet *The Legal Sufferings of the Jews in Russia* came out in an English translation by an anonymous author. It was also distributed in Russian among the Duma delegates in St. Petersburg. During the *Beilis trial (1911–13), Motzkin organized an information service in West European countries and Russia and spurred public figures to speak out against the blood libel. At the same time he was a leading activist in the Hebrew language movement and among the first to speak Hebrew at conferences and meetings devoted to this subject. During World War I, he was head of the Copenhagen Office of the World Zionist Organization and the liaison between the various Zionist organizations in the warring countries. At the end of 1915 he left for the United States to mobilize support for the Jewish war victims on the East European front and also for the struggle to ensure equal rights for the Jews of Russia. At the end of the war, Motzkin demanded that the Zionist Movement also concern itself with the civil rights of the Jews in the Diaspora. Thus he took a leading part in the establishment of the *Comité des Délégations Juives at the Paris Peace Conference, to which various Jewish bodies were affiliated, including the World Zionist Organization, and which later became a standing institution at the League of Nations, serving as a world Jewish representative for all affairs other than those connected with Ereẓ Israel. In the following years as well, Motzkin continued to direct the committee, which concerned itself particularly with the struggle against anti-Semitism (inter alia with the legal defense of Shalom *Schwartzbard for the assassination of Simon *Petlyura, who was held responsible for the pogroms in the Ukraine) and with the defense of Jewish rights. For this purpose he was active in the movement supporting the League of Nations and in the international Congresses of National Minorities. He did not abandon his Zionist work, however, and served as permanent chairman of the Zionist General Council and of many Zionist Congresses.

When the Nazis came to power in Germany, Motzkin headed the anti-Nazi struggle of the Jewish people and brought the oppression of German Jewry before the League of Nations. When, under pressure from the German ethnic minorities in other countries, the Congress of National Minorities refused to deliberate on the situation of German Jews under the Nazis, Motzkin withdrew from the organization. He died in the midst of feverish activity to ensure political and financial aid to German Jewry. In 1939 *Sefer Motzkin*, including a selection of his writings and speeches, was published together with a monograph on him by the editor, A. Bein.

His son THEODORE SAMUEL (1908–1970) was a mathematician and educator. Born in Berlin, from 1936 to 1948 he taught at the Hebrew University, Jerusalem. He settled in the United States in 1948, and was a research fellow of Havard University from 1948 to 1950, after which he was a professor and research mathematician at the University of California. He contributed to the subjects of inequalities, approximation, polynomials, and geometry. He wrote *Contributions to the Theory of Linear Inequalities*.

Bibliography: S. Kling, in: *Herzl Year Book*, 2 (1959), 228–50; L. Lipsky, *A Gallery of Zionist Profiles* (1956), *Ha-Olam* (Nov. 16, 1933).

[Y.S.]

MOUNTAIN JEWS (Tats), Jewish tribe in Soviet Dagestan and neighboring areas in E. Caucasus. It is supposed that the name derives from "mountain of the Jews" (*Chufut* or *Dzuhud Dag* in the Tat language), an ancient name of Dagestan, indicating its large Jewish population.

According to legend both the Mountain Jews and their neighbors, the Jews of *Georgia, arrived in the Caucasus at the time of *Nebuchadnezzar. The Talmud mentions a Jewish community in the city of Derbent as early as the third century C.E., and the *amora* R. Simeon Safra taught there (TJ, Meg. 4, 5, 75b). The Mountain Jews brought with them a north-Iranian dialect, which points to the geographical origins of the tribe. In time, through absorbing Caucasian expressions and a number of Hebrew words, it became their own particular dialect, *Judeo-Tat. The historical script is cursive Hebrew, similar to Rashi script. The period of *Khazar rule was a golden era for the Caucasian Jews, and even after the Mongol conquest their number did not greatly decline. A Dutch priest who traveled in the Caucasus in 1254 mentions the dense Jewish population in the Derbent region. In a Russian chronicle of 1346 the eastern Caucasus is called Zhidy ("land of the Jews," or popularly Chufut-Dag).

From the middle of the 16th century, the rural Jewish settlements declined. In a mountain valley near Derbent, named Chufut-Karta or Dzhuhud-Karta ("valley of the Jews"), there was a large complex of villages. Isaac Anisimov, a member of the tribe and historian of its past, told (in *Ha-Meliz*, no. 234, 1894) of a manuscript in his possession which "contains decisions, rules, and religious customs adopted by the rabbis of Chufut-Karta in the 16th and 17th centuries." In the largest village, Aba-Sava, the Jewish inhabitants defended themselves against the Muslim conquerers in 1769. About 157 warriors fell in the last battle; the survivors settled in Derbent. Until the annexation of Dagestan to Russia at the beginning of the 19th century, the Mountain Jews were completely cut off from the rest of the Jewish world. According to their own testimony they had never heard about the Jews in Europe. It was only after Jews from the European areas of Russia had settled in the Caucasus that the warrior tribe of Mountain Jews became gradually influenced by the centers of Jewish culture; they then sent their sons to study at the yeshivot of Lithuania and Poland. In spite of this, changes in the way of life and cultural level took place slowly. In his travel book *Sefer ha-Massa'ot be-Ereẓ Kavkaz* (1886) Joseph Judah *Chorny, who traveled in the Caucasus for eight years (1867–75) gives detailed information on the life and settlements (about 30 at the time) of the Mountain Jews. Another valuable source is the book of the Russian writer Nemirovich-Danchenko (*Voinstvuyushchii Izrail;* "Fighting Israel," 1886), in which he records his vivid impressions of his stay among the tribe. The Mountain Jews were then simple people, mostly illiterate, but proud, courageous, and freedom-loving. Farmers and hunters, they always carried a dagger or similar weapon in their typical Caucasian dress. The Tat Jews were prepared at any time to defend by their sword their family or their honor. Their dwellings were low mud huts, whose inside walls were hung with polished weapons. The synagogue, its exterior resembling a mosque, served as a *ḥeder* for the children. Sitting on the floor they learned the Torah by heart from the *ḥakham*. Of the Jewish festivals, Purim and Passover were especially celebrated. Their Passover **seder* had a special form differing from the traditional *seder*. During the night of *Hoshana Rabba the girls used to dance; according to Tat tradition, this is the night when a man's fate is decided. The marriage ceremony contained foreign influences, and the circumcision ceremony was generally held in the synagogue. Tat family names are mostly biblical names, to which the Russian suffix "ov" was added, e.g., Pinkhasov, Binyaminov, etc. The custom of the vendetta was practiced until recently. A common superstition was the kindling of fire next to the head of a sick person. The Tats also swore by fire, which points to their Persian origin. The European Jews who settled in Derbent and other cities tried to disseminate modern Judaism among the Tats and attracted the educated youths to Jewish public and national activities. Mountain Jews were especially receptive to the Zionist idea. An early settler in Ereẓ Israel was R. Jacob Yiẓḥaki, formerly *av bet din* of the Dagestan community and a founder of *Be'er Ya'akov, which was named after him. Young Mountain Jews like Ezekiel Nisanov were among the first members of *Ha-Shomer.

Under Soviet Rule. The Russian Revolution (1917) aroused hopes for the improvement of the economic situation and social status of the Mountain Jews. During the civil war they suffered at the hands of the anti-Semitic counterrevolutionary armies, and, true to tradition, they took up arms against them, organizing a cavalry unit which fought alongside the Red Army. Members of the tribe took an active part in the various activities of the Zionist movement in the Caucasus. The spokesman of Dagestan Zionists was Gershon Muradov, who suggested the establishment of a cavalry battalion of 5,000 Mountain Jews to join the *Jewish Legion in Palestine. Educational and cultural activities increased among the youth; some joined the Zionist organization Aḥdut. A Po'alei-Zion periodical in the Tat language, *Korsokh* ("Labor"), was published for a short time. But after the consolidation of Soviet rule, Muradov was arrested on charges of underground activities and he died in exile. In the 1920s, in addition to their catastrophic economic situation, the Dagestan Jews also had to contend with murderous anti-Jewish attacks from their Muslim neighbors, which the local authorities made no attempt to control. After complaints lodged by the Jews, a representative of the Soviet government was sent to investigate the situation. He corroborated their claims of economic discrimination and neglect in granting them social services, and stated that the Mountain Jews were deprived of their rights as a legitimate national minority. In the 1930s there was a relative improvement in the economic situation. Some Mountain Jews found employment in offices or factories, while others joined Jewish kolkhozes established on the initiative of OZET. Four economically successful kolkhozes still existed in 1970. In World War II the German armies reached the northern Caucasus and the Jews of Grozny and Nalchik suffered from Nazi persecutions; many were killed. Thousands of Mountain Jews fought in the ranks of the Soviet army and at least four were awarded the highest military decoration as Heroes of the Soviet Union.

As in the rest of the Soviet Union, in the Caucasus, too, Jews had to contend with attempts at forced assimilation. A decree of 1928 ordered the adoption of the Latin alphabet instead of the Hebrew one for the Judeo-Tat, and in 1938 this was changed again into the Russian Cyrillic alphabet. Attempts were also made to eradicate the Hebrew elements in their language and literature. The official anti-Zionist propaganda kindled the traditional hatred of the Jews among the Muslim population, culminating in 1960 in the publication of a *blood libel in an article published in the official party organ of the city of Buinaksk (Dagestan), *Kommunist*. Following Jewish protests, the paper published a "correction" two days later, but the article achieved its aim: the local synagogue was closed down. The Tat-Jewish theater and the outstanding dance group were liquidated as early as the 1930s. The attempts at forced assimilation were however, unsuccessful. There were almost no instances of mixed marriages, and almost all marriages were celebrated in religious ceremonies. All male children were circumcised. Even the younger generation, educated in joint schools, remained faithful to the Jewish people and tradition. On the Sabbath and festivals they attended religious services in the Mountain Jews' own synagogues, only four of which still remained in 1970, in the great communities of *Derbent, Makhachkala, *Nalchik, and *Baku (Azerbaijan). The framework of the large family clan *(patronymia)*, a traditional phenomenon typical of Tat society, remained intact under Soviet rule, protecting its members from assimilation and dissociation from Judaism. According to the 1959 Soviet census, 25,225 Jews declared Judeo-Tat to be their mother tongue; two-thirds of them lived in Dagestan, one-quarter in Azerbaijan, and the rest in northern Caucasus. The largest community was in Derbent, the large port city of the region.

Literature. The most important literary heritage of the Mountain Jews is the national epic in Judeo-Tat, *Shiraha* (the name probably derives from the Hebrew *shirah*, "poem"), which abounds in biblical associations and figures. One of the most beautiful poems is the "Song of the Mountain Jews," which expresses their yearning for the ancient homeland "so near, in front of your eyes, put out your hand and touch it." It also mentions the "maids of Deborah," the "brave horsemen of Samson," and the "heirs of Bar Kokhba." The epic was translated into Yiddish by the Soviet-Jewish writer M. Helmond. Mishi (Moshe) Bakhsheyev, poet, novelist, and playwright, born in Derbent in 1910, laid the foundations for the modern Tat literature, which began to develop in the 1930s. His publications include "Earth," a play dealing with life on a Jewish kolkhoz, a novel "Cluster of Grapes," and a collection of poetry. Other poets are Amrami Isakov, whose collection of children's songs has been translated into Russian, and Zion Izagayev, who has published three volumes of poems. A literary almanac, *Woton Sovetimag* ("Soviet Homeland"), the first of its kind in Judeo-Tat, edited by Hizigil (Ezekiel) Avshalomov and published in Makhachkala in 1963, assembled the works of 27 Tat writers, selecting mainly works which reflect the integration of the Mountain Jews in Soviet society. Visitors to the region reported a deep-felt longing for the State of Israel among the Mountain Jews, which became particularly strong after the 1967 Six-Day War in spite of the official anti-Israel propaganda campaign (see also *Judeo-Tat).

Bibliography: Z. Anisimov, in: *Ha-Shilo'aḥ*, 18 (1908); D. G. Maggid, *Yevrei na Kavkaze* (1918); Yu. Larin, *Yevrei i antisemitizm v SSSR* (1929); M. M. Ikhilov, in: *Sovetskaya Etnologiya*, 1 (1950); I. Ben-Zvi, *Nidḥei Yisrael* (1968); A. L. Eliav, *Between Hammer and Sickle* (1969[2]), 166–71. [Mo.N.]

MOUNT OF OLIVES (Olivet), mountain overlooking *Jerusalem from the east, beyond the *Kidron Brook. From the orographic point of view, the Mount of Olives is part of a spur projecting near Mount Scopus (Ra'ʾs al-Mushārif), from the country-long water divide which continues southward. The Mount of Olives ridge has three peaks. Upon the highest, 2,684 ft. (826 meters) above sea level, the original buildings of the *Hebrew University were constructed and opened in 1925. This area is commonly, although mistakenly, known as Mount Scopus. On the second peak, 2,645 ft. (814 meters) above the sea, is the site of Augusta Victoria Hospital. On the third, 2,652 ft. (816 meters) high, lies the Arab village of al-Ṭūr (*ha-har*, "the mountain"), an epithet whose source is in the Aramaic name of the Mount of Olives, Tura Zita. The Mount of Olives ends in this peak, though a spur of it continues to Ra'ʾs al-ʿAmūd (2,444 ft.; 752 meters), draining to the Kidron brook southward, to the village of *Shiloaḥ (Silwān). Even at its highest, the Mount of Olives is lower than the highest point in the Romemah district, which is the highest point of the water divide in Jerusalem (2,697 ft; 829 meters). However, since the Mount of Olives stands so very high (351 ft; 108 meters) in relation to the deep Kidron brook beneath it, it seems much higher than it actually is. From a geological point of view, the mountain is entirely within the Senonian region, while phytogeographically speaking, it is within the bounds of the Judean Desert.

In the Bible, the mountain is called the Ascent of the Olives (Heb. *Ma'aleh ha-Zeitim;* II Sam. 15:30), it being

Aerial view of the Jewish cemetery on the Mount of Olives, with the Intercontinental Hotel in the background. Photo Werner Braun, Jerusalem.

said of the top of the mountain (verse 32) "that this was where David was accustomed to worship God." This sanctity is apparently what prompted Solomon to build a *high place "in the mount that is before Jerusalem" (I Kings 11:7). However, according to II Kings 23:13, the high place which he built was "on the right hand [i.e., to the south] of the mount of corruption (i.e., the Mount of Olives)," that is, probably at Ra'ṣ al-ʿAmūd. Ezekiel 11:23 gives an important place to the Mount of Olives in his vision of the end of days: the glory of the Lord will arise and stand "upon the mountain which is on the east side of the city." The name Mount of Olives in its present form first appears in Zechariah 14:4: "His feet shall stand in that day upon the Mount of Olives, which is before Jerusalem on the east." Zechariah describes how in his vision the mountain is cleft in two. During the period of the Second Temple, the Mount of Olives was of great importance in Jerusalem: the *red heifer was burnt upon it; a bridge, or possibly two such bridges, connected its slopes with the Temple Mount. During the period of the Roman procurator Felix, thousands gathered upon it, there to be beguiled into believing the words of a false Egyptian prophet (Jos., Ant. 20:169; Wars 2:262). During the siege of Jerusalem, the Tenth Roman Legion encamped on it (Wars 5:70, where the location of the Mount of Olives is clearly established as being six *ris* (=3,707 ft.; 1,110 meters) east of Jerusalem, across a deep valley called Kidron). During the period of the Second Temple, at the order of the Sanhedrin, beacons would be lit on the Mount of Olives (*har ha-meshiḥah*, "Mount of Anointing"), in order to announce the sanctification of the New Moon. These flares could be seen as far away as Sartaba (RH 2:4).

The Gospels frequently refer to the Mount of Olives (by its Greek name *τὸ ὄρος Ἐλαιῶν*). Jesus and his followers encamped on one of its peaks on their way to Jerusalem. From its slopes, he wept for Jerusalem when he foresaw its coming destruction. At its foot is Gethsemane (Heb. Gat(h)-Shemanim), where he and his disciples spent the night before his arrest, and from it Jesus rose to heaven after being crucified and resurrected. For these reasons, Christianity, upon attaining supremacy, erected several churches and monasteries on the mountain. On its summit, the Church of the Ascension was erected and further down the Church of Eleona was built by the emperor Constantine. In Gethsemane a church was constructed during the Byzantine period and was refurbished by the Crusaders. According to Muslim tradition, the caliph Omar encamped on the Mount of Olives while receiving the surrender of Jerusalem (638).

Once the Jews were authorized to return to Jerusalem by the Arab conquerors, the pilgrimages to Jerusalem were also resumed. These pilgrimages generally took place during the month of Tishri. In these, the Mount of Olives held an important place, especially from the end of the eighth century, when the Jews were no longer allowed to enter the Temple Mount. On the festival of *Hoshana Rabba, they circled the Mount of Olives seven times, in song and prayer. On Hoshana Rabba, the Palestinian *rosh yeshivah* announced the "Proclamation of the Mount of Olives" concerning the new moons, the festivals, and the intercalation of years, a practice which was based on the ancient kindling of beacons on new moons on the Mount of Olives. On this same day the *rosh yeshivah* appointed members to the "Great Sanhedrin" and accorded titles of honor to those who had worked in favor of the Palestinian academy. Bans on the unobservant and on those who rebelled against authority, especially against the Karaites, were not lacking on such occasions. The clashes with the Karaites resulted in the intervention of the authorities, and they even prohibited the *rashei yeshivah* from issuing bans.

The choice of the Mount of Olives as the site of pilgrimages and gatherings was based on midrashic tradition: "The Divine Presence traveled ten journeys, from the cover of the Ark to the Cherub . . . and from the Town to the Mount of Olives" (RH 31a; Lam. R., Proem 25). In the letters of the *rashei yeshivah* the Mount of Olives is referred to as "the site of the footstool of our God." A tenth century guidebook found in the Cairo *Genizah* points out "the site of the footstool of our God" on "a stone whose length is ten cubits, its breadth two cubits, and its height two cubits." The armchair of the Palestinian *rosh yeshivah* was placed on this "stool" during the gatherings and the festive ceremonies which accompanied the pilgrimages. From this spot, the *rosh yeshivah* addressed the celebrants, and it was here that he received their contributions.

The site of the prayers and the gatherings was, according to the documents of the *Genizah*, above "Absalom's Monument," "opposite the Temple and the Gate of the Priest," which was situated along the southern third of the eastern wall of the Temple Mount. This corresponds to the open space above the slope of the Mount of Olives, which is today covered with Jewish graves, to the south of the Mount's summit. Here according to a medieval tradition, was the site "on which the priest who burnt the [Red] Heifer stood, sought out, and saw the Temple when he sprinkled the blood" (Mid. 2:6; Yoma 16a). The Arabs call this area "al-Qa'da" ("The Sitting Place"). This name might be an echo of the seat of the Palestinian *rosh yeshivah* during the pilgrimages to Jerusalem during the Arab period. [Jo.Br./M.A.-Y.]

At the foot of the mountain rock-hewn tombs can be found from the period of the First Temple (Tomb of Pharaoh's Daughter) and the Second Temple (so-called Tomb of Zechariah, Tomb of the Sons of Hezir, and the so-called Tomb of Absalom). Consequently, this spur of the Mount of Olives became, with the passage of time, a burial place for the Jews of Jerusalem. Because the *Ma'aseh Daniel* (A. Jellinek, *Bet ha-Midrash*, vol. 5, 128) states that at the end of days the Messiah will ascend the Mount and it will be there that Ezekiel shall blow his trumpet for the resurrection of the dead (Ginzberg, Legends, 6 (1959), 438), through the years the graves spread over the slopes and up to the top. At the end of the 19th century, the Russians erected the Church of Gethsemane at the foot of the mount, and at the al-Tūr summit, a monastery and tower. Kaiser William II of Germany, after visiting Jerusalem in 1898, erected a hospice for pilgrims known as Augusta Victoria on the second peak. The Englishman, Sir John Grey Hill, built a house on the third peak ("Mount Scopus"), which was later acquired by the Hebrew University for one of its buildings. During Israel's War of Independence, the university buildings remained in Israel hands even though they were surrounded by Arab held territory. This situation was frozen by the Armistice agreement, causing friction and many incidents. Israel was permitted to keep a number of policemen on the mount and these were changed every two weeks in a convoy which had to pass under UN auspices through Jordan-held territory. The Jewish cemeteries and monuments on the Mount of Olives, but outside Israeli territory, were vandalized by the Arabs. In 1953, at the site known as Dominus Flevit at the foot of the mount, many Jewish grave sites were discovered. The entire Mount was captured by Israel troops in the Six-Day War (1967) and arrangements were subsequently made for the restoration of the Jewish cemeteries, and the Hebrew University began to return to its earlier location on Mount Scopus. [Ed.]

Bibliography: J. Braslavi, in: *Eretz-Israel*, 7 (1964), 69–80; idem, in: Israel Exploration Society, *Yerushalayim le-Doroteihah* (1968),

120–44 (Eng. summ. 63); H. Z. Hirschberg, in: BJPES, 13 (1947), 156–64; Mann, Egypt, index; Mann, Texts, index s.v. *Mount Olivet;* L. H. Vincent and F. M. Abel, *Jérusalem nouvelle*, 2 (1914), 3ff.; G. H. Dalman, *Jerusalem und sein Gelaende* (1930), 25–55; F. M. Abel, *Géographie de la Palestine*, 1 (1933), 372–4; S. Assaf and L. Meir (eds.), *Sefer ha-Yishuv*, 2 (1944), index s.v. *Har Ha-Zeitim;* Press, Ereẓ, 2 (1948), 207; M. Avi-Yonah (ed.), *Sefer Yerushalayim* (1956), illust. btwn. p. 16–17.

MOURNING (Heb. אֵבֶל), the expression of grief and sorrow over the death of a close relative, friend, national leader, or in response to a national calamity. The lamentation (Heb. קִינָה *(kinah, qinah);* נְהִי, *nehi)* is the specifically literary and musical expression of such grief. The rite of mourning most frequently attested in the narrative and poetic sections of the Bible is the rending of garments. Thus Reuben rends his garments on finding Joseph missing (Gen. 37:29). Jacob does so on seeing Joseph's bloodstained cloak (Gen. 37:34). Joshua responds in this way to the defeat at Ai (Josh. 7:6), Hezekiah, to the words of the Rab-Shakeh (II Kings 19:1 = Isa. 37:1), and Mordecai, to news of the decree of genocide (Esth. 4:1). Job rends his garments on hearing of the death of his children (Job 1:20), and his friends tear their clothing to commiserate with him (2:12). The rending of garments may be simply an outlet for pent-up emotions, or it may have developed as a symbolic substitute for the mutilation of the flesh. Almost as frequent as the rending of garments is the wearing of sackcloth (e.g., II Sam. 3:31; Ps. 30:12; Lam. 2:10). Ezekiel prophesies that Tyre will mourn by the removal of embroidered garments and the donning of special mourning robes (Ezek. 26:16; cf. 7:27). The woman of Tekoa whom Joab sent to King David was likewise dressed in mourning garments (II Sam. 14:2), which may be identical with the garments of widowhood worn by Tamar the widow of Er (Gen. 38:14, 19). Micah suggests that it was not unusual for a mourner to appear naked (Micah 1:8). Other mourning practices which survived in later Judaism are the placing of dust on the head (Josh. 7:6; II Sam. 13:19; Jer. 6:26; 25:34; Ezek. 27:30; Lam. 2:10 etc.; cf. Ta'an. 15b), refraining from wearing ornaments (Ex. 33:4; cf. Sh. Ar., YD 389:3), abstaining from anointing and washing (II Sam. 12:20; cf. Ta'an. 1:6), and fasting (II Sam. 3:35; Esth. 4:3; Ezra 10:6; Neh. 1:4; cf. Ta'an. 1:4ff.). Isaiah describes mourners beating their breasts (Heb. *safad*, Isa. 32:12). The Hebrew term for beating the breast (*safad, misped;* Akk. *sipittu*) becomes a general term for "mourning" (e.g., Gen. 23:2), which takes on the sense of "wailing" (I Kings 13:30; Micah 1:8). Other rites of mourning related to the hair and beard. At the death of Nadab and Abihu, apparently, the Israelites uncovered or disheveled their hair as a sign of mourning. Aaron, Eleazar, and Ithamar, who as priests were forbidden to mourn, were thus prohibited from following this practice (Lev. 10:6). While it became obligatory in later Judaism for mourners to let their hair grow (MK 14b), the prophets (Isa. 22:12; Jer. 16:6; Ezek. 7:18; Amos 8:10) describe tonsure as a standard rite of mourning. Similarly Job shaves his head on hearing of the death of his children (Job 1:20). Deuteronomy 21:12 even prescribes the shaving of the head as a rite of mourning to be observed by the gentile maiden taken captive in war. According to Ezekiel 24:17 it was customary to remove one's turban as an expression of grief (cf. Isa. 61:10). The covering of the head may also be attested as a rite of mourning in II Samuel 15:30; Jeremiah 14:3–4 and Esther 6:12; 7:8, if the Hebrew *ḥafui* is derived from the Hebrew verb *ḥafah*, "to cover." If it is derived from the Arabic *ḥāfī*, "barefoot," which is also the root of Hebrew *yaḥef*, "barefoot," the latter references may corroborate the testimony of Ezekiel and Deutero-Isaiah. Alongside tonsure and the shaving of the beard, the prophets take for granted the practice of cutting gashes in the flesh of the hands or elsewhere (Jer. 16:6; 41:5). They seem unaware of any prohibition against these rites. Leviticus 21:5 prohibits only the priests from making incisions in the flesh, shaving the beard, and tonsure, as from all other rites of mourning, except on the occasion of the death of the priest's father, mother, son, daughter, brother, or unmarried sister. Leviticus 19:27–28 prohibits all Israel from shaving, cutting the hair, tattooing (see *tattoo), and making incisions as a rite of mourning. Deuteronomy 14:1 prohibits all Israel from making incisions in the flesh and from employing tonsure as a rite of mourning. In Leviticus 19 the prohibitions are motivated by the desire to avoid ritual impurity, while in Deuteronomy 14 they are motivated by the striving for holiness. Micah (3:7) and Ezekiel (24:17) mention the covering of the upper lip as an expression of grief. The same practice along with the uncovering (or disheveling) of the hair and the rending of garments is prescribed for lepers in Leviticus 13:45. In the Bible the typical posture for the mourner is sitting (Ezek. 26:16; Jonah 3:6; Job 2:13) or lying (II Sam. 13:31; Lam. 2:21) on the ground, as in later Judaism (Sh. Ar., YD 387:1). Placing the hands on the head (II Sam. 13:19; Jer. 2:37) and prostration (Jer. 4:28; 14:2; Ps. 35:14) are also attested. The Bible does not distinguish, as does later Judaism, between the mourning that precedes the funeral (Heb. *aninut*) and that which follows burial (cf. Ber. 17b ff.). The practices which later Judaism associates with the former are therefore referred to simply as rites of mourning in the Bible. Thus Daniel (Dan. 10:23) mourned by abstaining from meat and wine. Although the Mishnah (Ket. 4:4) prescribes the playing of flutes at funerals, the Bible associates mourning with the cessation of both dancing and instrumental music (Isa. 24:8; Jer. 31:12; Ps.

Figure 1. Two women mourning over a coffin; a detail from an illustration from the *Rothschild Miscellany*, Ferrara (?), c. 1470. Jerusalem, Israel Museum, Ms. 180/51, fol. 121v. Photo David Harris, Jerusalem.

30:12; Job 30:31; Lam. 5:15; Eccles. 3:4), as do later Jewish authorities (Sot. 48a). From the association of gift-giving with the cessation of mourning in Esther 9:22, one may surmise that the exchange of gifts was forbidden to mourners, as in later Judaism (Sh. Ar., YD 385:3). Later Judaism understood its various mourning rites both as an affirmation of the value of the deceased (Sem. 9) and as an appeal to God for mercy (Ta'an. 2:1). Each of these approaches has been advocated to the exclusion of the other by modern schools of anthropology. Most likely both lie behind many of the biblical practices. T. H. Gaster suggests that the mutilation of the body was originally intended to provide the ghost of the departed with blood to drink, while the cutting of the hair enabled the ghost to draw on the strength it embodied.

Lamentations. Lamentations are poetic compositions functionally equivalent to the modern eulogy. Composed by literary giants like David (II Sam. 1:17ff.; 3:33ff.) and Jeremiah (II Chron. 35:25), these tributes were, in accordance with the standard literary usage, chanted rather than declaimed. These eulogies were frequently composed in a special meter, which modern scholars have designated as the *qinah* meter (i.e., lamentation meter). It is characterized by the division of each verse into two unequal parts, in contrast to the usually parallel structure of biblical poetry. Jeremiah speaks of a professional class of women who composed and chanted lamentations (*mekonenot, meqonenot*, Jer. 9:16). Their art was regarded as a branch of wisdom, and thus they are called "skilled" (Heb. *ḥakhamot*). Men and women singers made lamentations and preserved them for future generations as part of the general education of the young (II Chron. 35:25). Another expression of grief was the exclamation *ho-ho* (Amos 5:16) or *hoi* (I Kings 13:30; Jer. 22:18; 34:5). A specified period of mourning is only prescribed by the Bible in connection with the captive gentile maiden (Deut. 21:13). She is required to mourn her parents for one month. The later Jewish custom of seven days of mourning is observed by Joseph on the death of Jacob (Gen. 50:10; the Egyptians mourned him for 70 (50:3)), the inhabitants of Jabesh-Gilead upon the burial of Saul and Jonathan (I Sam. 31:13 = I Chron. 10:12), and Job and his friends at the height of Job's suffering (Job 2:13). Daniel's observance of three weeks of mourning (Dan. 10:2) may reflect the author's awareness of the week as a standard period of mourning. Moses and Aaron were each mourned for 30 days (Num. 20:29; Deut. 34:8), while Jacob and Ephraim each mourned "many days" (Gen. 37:34; I Chron. 7:22) for their children. While Jeremiah (41:5) tells of contemporaries who expressed grief by bringing sacrifices to the Temple, Nehemiah (Neh. 8:9) suggests the incompatibility of religious festivities and mourning (cf. Ta'an. 2:8, 10). The comforting of mourners is accomplished by the tenderly spoken word (Isa. 40:1–2), by sitting with the mourner (Job. 2:13), by providing him with compensation for his loss (Gen. 24:67; Isa. 60:2–9), and by offering him bread and wine (II Sam. 3:35; Jer. 16:7). The bread is called "bread of agony" (*leḥem onashim*, Ezek. 24:17; cf. *leḥem ʾonim* in Hos. 9:4), and the wine, "the cup of consolation" (Jer. 16:7). The serving of such a meal has been variously explained as an affirmation of the bonds between the survivors, a reaffirmation of life itself after a period of fasting from death to burial, and as an act of conviviality with the soul of the deceased.

[M.I.G.]

Talmudic and Medieval Periods. Although the laws and customs of mourning are largely based on the biblical references, many additional ones developed out of usage and custom and as such are of rabbinical rather than biblical authority. In general, there has been a consistency in mourning practices from the biblical era, but in particular between the talmudic period and modern times. With few exceptions the rules of mourning described and laid down in the Talmud and the early sources are identical with those observed today. These laws were designed to provide both for the "dignity of the departed" and the "dignity of the living" (cf. Sanh. 46b–47a). The body, regarded as the creation of God and the dwelling place of the soul, was accorded every respect. Likewise, every attempt was made to ease the grief of the mourners and to share their sorrow. The pain of death was mitigated by viewing it as the moment of transition from the temporal world to the eternal world (Zohar No'ah, 66a). One of the rabbis interpreted the biblical verse "And, behold, it was very good" (Gen. 1:31) to refer to death (Gen. R. 9:5, 10; see *Life and Death).

It was customary "to pour out all drawn water" in the neighborhood of the house in which the person died (Sh. Ar., YD 339:5). Originally deriving from folk beliefs, this custom was subsequently explained as a method of announcing a death since Jews were always reluctant to be the bearers of evil tidings (*Siftei Kohen*, YD 339:5, n. 9). Others interpreted that this act indicated that the deceased was an important person, therefore the supply of water was lessened just as "there was no water for the congregation" (Num. 20:2) after the death of Miriam (*Be'er ha-Golah*, YD 339:5, n. 8). The dead body was not left alone, and watchers remained with the corpse until the funeral either to honor the dead or to guard the corpse against possible damage. These watchers were exempted from the performance of other positive commandments while engaged in this meritorious deed (Ber. 3:1). Before the funeral the body was ritually purified (see **Tohorah*). Professional women mourners, who clapped their hands in grief, and sang dirges and lamentations, led the public display of grief at the funeral. Dirges were recited responsively while lamentations were sung in unison (MK 3:8, 9; see **Kinah*). The prevalent rabbinic opinion was that only the first day of the mourning period was of biblical authority (Asheri to MK 3:27; 34b; Maim. Yad, Avel, 1:1), while the seven-day mourning period was instituted by Moses (TJ, Ket. 1:1, 25a). The rabbis distinguished four stages in the mourning period: **aninut*, the period between death and burial; *avelut* or *shivah*, the seven days following burial; **sheloshim*, the time until the 30th day after burial; and the first year (TJ, MK 3:7, 83c).

Aninut. During the *aninut* period, the mourner was called an *onen*. Although still obligated to abide by the negative precepts of the Torah, the *onen* was absolved from the performance of many positive religious duties such as the recital of the **Shema* and the donning of *tallit* and *tefillin* (MK 23b). He thus indicated his respect for the memory of the deceased since he was so distraught that he could not discharge his religious obligations (Sem. 10; Deut. R. 9:1). In addition, freedom from certain religious obligations enabled the *onen* to attend to the needs of the dead and his burial without distraction. The rule that "he who is engaged in a religious act is exempt from performing other religious duties" applied (Suk. 25a). It was also forbidden for the *onen* to eat meat or drink wine (Ber. 17b) or overindulge in eating (TJ, Ber. 3:1, 6a). If death occurred on the Sabbath, or if the Sabbath was part of the *aninut* period, the *onen* was obligated to discharge all his religious obligations (MK 23b), and he was even permitted to eat meat and drink wine on that day (Ber. 18a).

Shivah. Immediately after the funeral, the *shivah* ("seven") mourning period began. The bereaved family gathered in the house of the deceased and sat on overturned

Figure 2. Pewter plate for serving food to mourners, from Augsburg, Germany, 1739. The inscription specifically mentions eggs and lentils. Cleveland, Ohio, Olyn and Joseph Horowitz Collection Judaica.

couches or beds and enrobed their heads. The mourners were obligated to rend their garments and to recite the *dayyan ha-emet* ("the true Judge") blessing (see **Keri'ah*). They were also not to leave the house (MK 23a), perform manual labor, conduct business transactions, bathe, anoint the body, cut the hair, cohabit, wear leather shoes, wash clothes, greet acquaintances, and study the Torah (MK 15a–b). They were, however, permitted to study sorrowful portions of the Bible and Talmud such as Job, Lamentations, parts of Jeremiah, and the laws of mourning. The mourner's first meal after the funeral was known as *Se'uddat Havra'ah* (Meal of Consolation). The meal was provided by friends and neighbors in accordance with the talmudic injunction that "a mourner is forbidden to eat of his own bread on the first day (of mourning" (MK 27b). It was also forbidden for the mourner to don *tefillin* on the first day of the *shivah* period (Ket. 6b; Sh. Ar., YD 388:1). The rabbis considered the first three days as the most intense, declaring, "Three days for weeping and seven for lamenting" (MK 27b).

SHELOSHIM. Modified mourning continued through the *sheloshim* period when the mourner was told "not to cut the hair and wear pressed clothes" (MK 27b). During the *sheloshim* it was also forbidden for the mourner to marry, to attend places of entertainment or festive events (even when primarily of religious significance), to embark on a business journey, or to participate in social gatherings (MK 22b–23a; Yad, Avel 6:2). When mourning for parents, some of the above prohibitions remained applicable during the entire 12 months following the day of death. The mourner was not permitted to trim his hair until his companions rebuked him. He was also enjoined from entering "a house of rejoicing" during this period (MK 22b).

RELATIONSHIPS REQUIRING MOURNING. The observance of these formal rules of mourning was required for the nearest of kin corresponding to those for whom a priest was to defile himself, i.e., a wife (husband), father, mother, son, daughter, brother, and sister (Lev. 21:1–3; MK 20b), but not an infant less than 30 days old (Yad, Avel 1:6). The Talmud also relates instances when aspects of mourning were observed upon the death of teachers and scholars. Thus when R. Johanan died, R. Ammi observed the seven and the 30 days of mourning (MK 25b). In mourning for a *ḥakham* one bared the arm and shoulder on the right; for the *av bet din* on the left, and for a *nasi* on both sides (MK 22b; Sem. 9:2).

TERMINATION OF MOURNING. Although the Sabbath was included in the seven days of mourning, no outward signs of mourning were permitted on that day. Private observances such as the prohibition against washing remained in force on the Sabbath (MK 23b; Maim, Yad, Avel 10:1). If burial took place before a festival and the mourner observed the mourning rite for even a short period prior to the festival, the entire *shivah* period was annulled by the holiday. If the *shivah* had been completed, then the incoming festival canceled the entire *sheloshim* period. If, however, the funeral took place on **Ḥol ha-Mo'ed,* the *shivah* and *sheloshim* were observed after the termination of the festival. In the Diaspora, the last day of the festival counted as one of the days of the *shivah* and *sheloshim* (MK 3:5–7; Sh. Ar., YD 399, 13; 400).

Relatives and friends visited the mourner during the week of *shivah*. Discreet individuals expressed their condolences in sympathetic silence (cf. Job. 2:13). In general, visitors were advised not to speak until the mourner began the conversation (MK 28b). Upon leaving, it became customary for the visitor to approach the mourner and say: "May the Almighty comfort you among the other mourners for Zion and Jerusalem." Rabbinical literature explained the reasons for the choice of seven as the main period of mourning. Commenting on the verse "I will turn your feasts into mourning" (Amos 8:10), it was explained that just as the days of the feasts (Passover and Sukkot) are seven so the period of mourning is also for seven days (MK 20a). The Zohar gives a mystical reason: "For seven days the soul goes to and fro between the house and the grave, mourning for the body" (Zohar, *Va-Yeḥi,* 226a). The institution of *shivah* was considered even more ancient than the flood. The rabbis interpreted "And it came to pass after the seven days, that the waters of the flood were upon the earth" (Gen. 7:10) to mean that God postponed retribution until after the seven days of mourning for the righteous Methuselah (Gen. 5:27; Sanh. 108b). The rabbis discouraged excessive mourning. Jeremiah's charge, "Weep ye not for the dead, neither bemoan him" (Jer. 22:10) was interpreted to mean "weep not in excess, nor bemoan too much." Accordingly, intensive mourning ceased after the *sheloshim*. Thereafter, God declares to the one who continues to mourn "Ye are not more compassionate toward the departed than I." The rabbis stated that whoever indulged in excessive grief over his dead finally had to weep for another. It was related that a woman in the neighborhood of R. Huna ultimately lost all seven of her sons because she wept excessively for each one (MK 27b).

Modern Practice. Most of the observances described above are still practiced by traditional Jews all over the world. In most communities today there are burial societies or funeral chapels which arrange the details of the *tohorah* and the burial. The *onenim* still have the responsibility of contacting the burial society as well as obtaining death and other certificates which may be required before the funeral can be held. They must also inform relatives and friends so that proper honor and respect can be paid to the deceased. In the house of *shivah* couches and beds are no longer overturned; the mourners sitting instead on low stools. With the exception that mourners no longer muffle their heads, all the other restrictions are observed. Slippers of cloth, felt, or rubber are worn instead of leather footwear. Women also abstain from using cosmetics during the *shivah* period. A candle burns continuously in the house of mourning for the entire seven days. It has also become customary to cover mirrors or turn them to the wall. Among the explanations offered for this practice is that prayer is forbidden in front of a mirror, since the reflection distracts the attention of the worshiper. Another interpretation is that mirrors, often associated with vanity, are out of place at such a time.

Prayers in the Home and Changes in the Liturgy. By the end of the Middle Ages, praying in the house of *shivah* was a well-established custom (cf. Shab. 152a–b). Nowadays a **minyan* gathers in the house of mourning for the daily *Shaḥarit* and *Minḥah-Ma'ariv* services. For the reading of the Law during these home services a Torah Scroll may be borrowed from the communal synagogue provided that proper facilities for its care are available and that it will be read on three occasions. If it is not possible to obtain a *minyan* in the home, the mourner may attend the synagogue for services and the recitation of **Kaddish*. Generally the mourner attends the synagogue for Sabbath and festival service. In the house of mourning and in the mourner's personal prayers, the following changes in the normal order of the services are made: (1) The talmudical passage *pittum ha-ketoret* (Ker. 6a; Hertz, Prayer, 546), describing the compounding of the incenses for daily offering in the Temple, is omitted by the mourner since he is forbidden to study Torah.

(2) Likewise the mourner omits the recitation of *eizehu mekoman*, the chapter of the Mishnah which describes the appointed places for the various animal sacrifices (Zev. 5:1–8; Hertz, Prayer, 38–40).

(3) The *Priestly Blessing (Num. 6:24–26; Hertz, Prayer, 154), which concludes with the greeting of peace, is omitted in the house of mourning because the mourner may not extend greetings. In Jerusalem, however, it is recited.

(4) **Taḥanun* (Hertz, Prayer, 168–86) is omitted because its theme, "I have sinned before thee," is deemed inappropriate for a mourner.

(5) Psalm 20 (Hertz, Prayer, 200) is also omitted because it will intensify the mourner's grief during his "day of trouble" (Ps. 20:2).

(6) The verse beginning, "And as for me, this is my covenant with them, saith the Lord" is omitted from the *u-Va le-Ẓiyyon* (Hertz, Prayer, 202) because the mourner does not desire a covenant which will perpetuate his unhappy situation.

(7) Psalm 49 which declares that the injustices and inequalities of human existence are corrected in the hereafter is recited after the daily service in the house of mourning (Hertz, Prayer, 1088–90).

(8) The mourner omits the six Psalms (95–99; 29) recited before the *Ma'ariv* service on Friday night (Hertz, Prayer, 346–54). He remains in the anteroom until the conclusion of **lekhah dodi*. He then enters the synagogue and the congregation rises and greets him with the traditional greeting extended to mourners: "May the Almighty . . . " (Hertz, Prayer, 358).

(9) **Hallel* (Hertz, Prayer, 756–72) is not recited in the house of *shivah* on *Rosh Ḥodesh because it contains such verses as "The dead praise not the Lord, neither any that go down into silence" (Ps. 115:17), and "This is the day which the Lord hath made, we will rejoice and be glad in it" (Ps. 118:24). In most rites, however, it is recited when the mourners leave the room. If Rosh Ḥodesh coincides with the Sabbath, Hallel should be recited even if the services are being held in the house of mourning since no public display of mourning is permissible on the Sabbath.

(10) The mourner is not called up to the reading of the Law during the week of *shivah* even if he is the only kohen or levite in the congregation.

There are indications that it was customary for mourners to wear black throughout the *sheloshim* (Yoma 39b; Shab. 114a; Sem. 2:8). Nowadays, however, Jews are not permitted to dress in black clothing or to wear black armbands as signs of mourning since these are considered non-Jewish customs (see **Ḥukkat ha-Goi*). Similarly, the bringing of gifts to the house of *shivah* is considered an emulation of non-Jewish practice. During the *sheloshim* period it is customary for the mourner to change his synagogue seat for weekday services. When mourning for parents, a different seat is occupied during the entire 12-month period. The **Kaddish*, however, is recited by the person mourning a parent or child for 11 months. **Yahrzeit* is observed on the anniversary of the Jewish date of the person's death. There is an opinion that when three or more days elapse between death and burial, the first *Yahrzeit* is observed on the date of burial. Nevertheless, during subsequent years, *Yahrzeit* is observed on the anniversary of the date of death (*Taz, Shakh* and *Be'er Hetev*, YD 402:12). Reform Judaism has greatly modified the above laws and customs. The week of mourning is often shortened, and, frequently, only a period of three days is observed. Practices such as the rending of garments, sitting on low stools, not wearing leather shoes, and not attending places of entertainment during the period of the 30 days or first year are not generally observed by Reform Jews. Some have the religious services in the home only for the first three days, while others have them only after returning home from the funeral.

See also *Burial; *Death; **Likkut Aẓamot*.

[A.Ro.]

Figure 3. Jewish widow from Erfoud, Morocco, in white mourning attire. Jerusalem, Israel Museum Photo Collection, Department of Ethnology. Photo Shulman, 1953.

Bibliography: BIBLE: K. Budde, in: ZAW, 2 (1882), 1–52; B. Malinowski, *Magic, Science and Religion* (1925); E. Durkheim, *The Elementary Forms of the Religious Life* (1947); Kaufmann Y.,

Toledot, 2 (1960), 544–56; K. V. H. Ringgren, *Israelite Religion* (1963), 239–42; T. H. Gaster, *Myth, Legend and Custom in the Old Testament* (1969), 590–604. TALMUD AND MEDIEVAL PERIODS: Y. M. Tukazinsky, *Sefer Gesher ha-Ḥayyim* (1947: 1960²); J. J. Greenwald, *Kol-Bo al Aveilut*, 3 vols. (1947–52); C. N. Denburg, *Code of Hebrew Law*, 1 (1954); B. Yashar, *Seder ha-Aveilut ve-ha-Niḥumim* (1956); S. Spero, *Journey into Light* (1959); H. M. Rabinowicz, *Guide to Life* (1964); D. Zlotnick (ed. and tr.), *The Tractate "Mourning" (Semaḥot)* (1966); M. Lamm, *Jewish Way in Death and Mourning* (1969).

MOUSE (Heb. עַכְבָּר, *akhbar*), small rodent enumerated in the Bible with the rat and five reptiles ("creeping things"). It is so classified because as a result of its short legs its belly touches the ground as it walks. Isaiah (66:17) vehemently assails those who "eat swine's flesh, detestable things, and the mouse" at idolatrous ceremonies. The *akhbar* includes both the house mouse, *Mus musculus*, and the field mouse, *Microtus guenthri*, the latter wreaking havoc with crops. Their depredations can amount to a plague destroying substantial parts of the harvest. It was such a plague which visited the Philistines who captured the Ark of the Covenant of the Lord (I Sam. 6:4–11). They not only "marred the land" but also caused a plague of "emerods." It has been suggested that the latter reference is to a pestilence caused by the microbe, *Pasteurella pestis*, transmitted to man by rodent fleas. The symptoms are a swelling of the lymphatic glands especially in the groins, which was thought to be a form of hemorrhoids. Both house and field mice are frequently mentioned in the Mishnah and Talmud. The ancient view of the possibility of spontaneous generation finds expression in the statement that the mouse was formed from the earth (Ḥul. 9:6). A mean person was called "a mouse lying in his money" (Sanh. 29b). One who eats food which has been nibbled by mice was said to forget his learning (Hor. 13a).

Bibliography: Lewysohn, Zool, 105–7, 345; F. S. Bodenheimer, *Animal and Man in Bible Lands* (1960), 21–23, 46, 101, 110. [J.F.]

°**MOWINCKEL, SIGMUND OLAF PLYTT** (1884–1965), Norwegian biblical scholar. Mowinckel taught at the University of Oslo (then Kristiania) from 1917. His doctoral thesis (1916) was a study of the Book of Nehemiah, and one of his last books was also devoted to Nehemiah (*Studien zu dem Buche Ezra-Nehemia*, 3 vols., 1964–65). His first book on the Psalms, *The Royal Psalms in the Bible*, was also issued in 1916, and his chief work, *Psalmenstudien* (vols. 1–6) was published between 1921 and 1924. In this work, he placed the psalms in their cultic context and interpreted them in the light of this background. These *Psalmenstudien* were republished in 1961, and in 1963 an English translation of his last work on the Psalms was issued (*The Psalms in Israel's Worship*, 2 vols, 1962; Norwegian version, *Offersang og Sangoffer*, 1951). In 1964 two works on the Pentateuch were published, *Erwaegungen zur Pentateuchquellenfrage* and *Tetrateuch, Pentateuch, Hexateuch; Palestina for Israel* ("Palestine before Israel," 1965) and *Israels opphvog eldste historie* ("Israel's Origin and Oldest History," 1967) were published posthumously. Mowinckel's main ideas have been widely accepted by biblical scholars, and his influence in Europe, especially Scandinavia, has been considerable. [A.S.K.]

MOYAL, ESTHER (1873–1948), Arabic journalist and feminist. Esther Moyal, a member of the Lazari (al-Azharī) family of Beirut, began taking part in public affairs in 1893, while she was teaching for the Scottish Church mission. She took over the correspondence of the Lebanese Women's League and in the same year was sent to Chicago to represent the Lebanon at the International Women's Conference. She was active in various women's organizations such as Bākūrat Sūriya ("The Dawn of Syria") and Nahḍat al-Nisā' ("The Awakening Women"). In 1894 she married a medical student, Simon Moyal in Jaffa. After he qualified they settled in Cairo, where in 1898 Esther founded the monthly *al-ʿĀʾila* ("The Family"), which became a weekly in 1904. She also became a frequent contributor to the leading Cairo daily, *al-Ahrām* and the Egyptian literary periodical *al-Hilāl*. The Moyals moved to Jaffa in 1908 and the following year she helped establish an organization of Jewish women in the city. In 1913 she became joint editor with her husband of the Jaffa periodical, *Ṣawt al-ʿUthmāniyya* ("The Voice of the Ottoman"). Widowed in 1915, she went to live in Marseilles, returning to Jaffa in the mid-40s. Her writings include a life of Emile Zola and Arabic translations of French books. [H.J.C.]

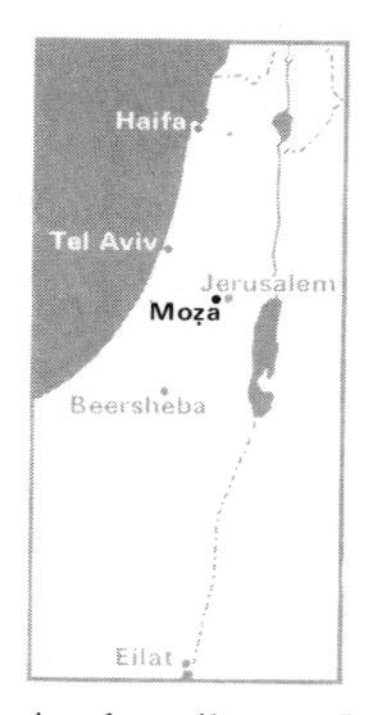

MOZA or **(Ha-) MOZAH** (Heb. מוֹצָא , הַמֹּצָה), town in Benjamin mentioned in the city list of Benjamin with Mizpeh and Chephirah (Josh. 18:26) and in the genealogy of Benjamin with Alemeth, Azmaveth, and Eleasah (I Chron. 8:36). The name also occurs in the genealogy of Caleb (I Chron. 2:46), but a connection between this Moza and the Benjamite Moza is doubtful, as another locality might be meant. According to one reading, the "*Mṣh*" seal stamps found on jar handles at Jericho and Tell ab-Naṣba and belonging to the Persian period attest the existence of an administrative center at Moza at that time. It is identified with Khirbat Beit Mizza to the west of Jerusalem and situated near a spring in a valley rich in olive groves and vineyards. It is probably identical with the Roman colony *Emmaus, established by Vespasian after the siege of Jerusalem at a distance of 30 stadia (c. 3½ mi.) from Jerusalem; he settled 800 veterans there (Jos., Wars, 7:217). A village below Jerusalem called Moẓa, where willow branches were cut for the rites at the Sukkot, is mentioned in the Mishnah (Suk. 4:5), i.e., in reference to the times before the destruction of the Second Temple. According to the Jerusalem Talmud (Suk. 4:3, 54b), the name of Moẓa was changed to Colonia and a "source of Colonia" is mentioned by Cyrillus Scythopolitanus (*Vita Sabae*, 67). The latter locality was probably at the site of the Arab village Qālūnya (see below). Remains of a Roman road station, a bath, Jewish and Roman tombs, and a Byzantine monastery were found in the area. [M.A.-Y.]

Modern Times. The land of Moẓa (moshavah), on the site of ancient Moza, was the first rural site in Ereẓ Israel acquired by Jews for farming purposes (by inhabitants of the old city of Jerusalem headed by Yehoshua *Yellin in 1859). A few families worked the land and terraced the hillsides, but did not live permanently at Moẓa. In 1894 the Jerusalem chapter of the *B'nai B'rith founded a small village on the site. One of the first industrial enterprises in the country was a tile and roof tile factory which used the local Moẓa marl as raw material. It was built by the Moẓa settlers at the beginning of the 20th century. In the 1929 Arab riots the village was largely destroyed and seven of its inhabitants were murdered, but the village was soon restored and in 1933 Moẓa Illit ("Upper Moẓa") was founded as an adjacent moshav. On the hilltop southwest of Moẓa, *Kuppat Ḥolim, the Histadrut Sick Fund, opened the Arza Convalescent Home in the 1930s, in the place where Theodor *Herzl on his 1898 visit to the country

Theodor Herzl (second from right) beside the tree he planted at Moẓa, 1898. Courtesy Central Zionist Archives, Jerusalem.

planted a cypress tree (at the time erroneously identified as the biblical cedar from which the name "Arza" was derived). The tree was felled in World War I by unknown persons. In the Israel *War of Independence (1948) Moẓa was in grave danger until the neighboring Arab village of Qālūnya fell to Jewish forces and was abandoned by its inhabitants. Although most of the inhabitants in Moẓa are employed in Jerusalem, some keep farms. From the late 1950s a garden suburb of Jerusalem developed at Moẓa.

Bibliography: EM, 4 (1962), 738; Avigad, in: IEJ, 8 (1958), 113–9. [E.O.]

MOZNAYIM (Heb. מֹאזְנַיִם), literary organ of the Hebrew Writers Association in Israel. *Moznayim* was founded in 1929, under the editorship of Y. D. *Berkowitz and F. Lachower, when the association ceased to endorse its previous organ, *Ketuvim*, edited by A. Steinman and A. *Shlonsky. Published first as a weekly in Tel Aviv, *Moznayim* became a monthly in 1933. It appeared regularly until the spring of 1947, when it ceased publication until the autumn of that year. *Moznayim* reappeared as a fortnightly only until the State of Israel was about to be established. *Moznayim*, in a new series, was published as a monthly from 1955.

The first volumes bear the stamp of *Bialik, a frequent contributor, and his contemporaries. Eventually, younger writers also left their influence upon this publication. All literary genres were encouraged: poetry, the story, the essay, criticism, the review, the scholarly study in the form of a popular lecture, publication of literary documents (e.g., letters), and translations from world literature. Hebrew writers from different generations and different parts of the world have participated. Until the Holocaust the majority of East European Hebrew writers contributed and, later, Hebrew writers in the United States and other countries were published.

In honor of the U.S. Hebrew writer, Reuben *Wallenrod, *Moznayim* annually presents an award for the most distinguished poem, story, or essay published in the periodical. An index to the first hundred issues was issued in 1944. [G.K.]

MOZYR, city in Gomel oblast, Belorussian S.S.R. After the second partition of Poland (1793), Mozyr was annexed by Russia and became a district town in the province of Minsk until the Russian Revolution. Mozyr is mentioned in a Russian document as one of the towns which fell to the soldiers of *Chmielnicki in 1648. According to the document the insurgents massacred the Poles and the Jews. In 1766 there were 896 Jews in the community of Mozyr and the surrounding villages who were registered as paying poll tax; these increased to 2,256 in 1847 and 5,631 (70% of the total population) in 1897. The Jews played an important role in the wood industry which developed in the town and its vicinity, owning several sawmills and match factories. Mozyr was one of the towns where the *Bund was active. During the Russian Civil War (1917–21) the Jews suffered at the hands of the "volunteer army" of Bulak-Balakhowic, who fought the Soviet regime. With the consolidation of the Soviet regime Jewish public institutions were liquidated. In 1926 there were 5,901 persons in the town (61.3% of the population). When Mozyr was occupied by the Germans during World War II (1941), the Jews were concentrated in a ghetto, and at the beginning of January 1942 they were shot or drowned in the Pripet River.

Bibliography: S. Agurski, *Revolyutsionnoye dvizheniye v Belorussii* (1928), 142; *Prestupleniya nemetsko—fashistskikn okkupantov v Belorussii* (1965), 310, 320. [Y.S.]

MSTISLAVL (referred to by the Jews as **Amtchislav**), city in Mogilev oblast, Belorussian S.S.R.; until 1772 in Poland-Lithuania; under czarist rule, part of Mogilev province. Jews are first mentioned as inhabitants of Mstislavl in 1590, although they had leased the taxes of the area from the mid-16th century. In 1639 there was a synagogue in Mstislavl. During the Northern War between Peter the Great and Charles XII of Sweden, Peter's troops entered Mstislavl (1708) and many Jews were injured. In 1765 there were 552 Jews registered as paying poll tax in the town and surrounding villages. As a result of their critical economic situation, 271 Jews left the town and district in 1808 for agricultural settlements in southern Russia. At the end of December 1843 a quarrel broke out between some Jews and a group of soldiers who had come to confiscate some smuggled merchandise in a Jewish shop. Magnifying the incident, the local authorities described it to the government as a Jewish rebellion against the authorities. When informed of the affair, Nicholas I ordered that every tenth Jew in the town be impressed into the army. It was only after numerous intercessions in the capital that investigators from St. Petersburg were sent to Mstislavl. The accusations of rebellion were refuted and the collective punishment revoked. Subsequently, the day the decree was rescinded (Kislev 3) was celebrated as the *Purim D'Amtchislav*. In 1847 there were 3,815 Jews registered in Mstislavl and in 1897 they numbered 5,076 (59.7% of the population). Most of them were *Mitnaggedim*, but there was also a considerable minority of *Ḥabad Ḥasidim. After World War I the Jewish population decreased, until in 1926 only 3,371 (42% of the total population) remained. When the Germans occupied the town during World War II (1941), those Jews who did not succeed in escaping were massacred. S. *Dubnow was a native of Mstislavl.

Bibliography: Dubnow, in: *He-Avar,* 1 (1918), 63–75; 8 (1961), 149–52; Lifshits, *ibid.,* 8 (1961), 81–100; Smilak, in: *Reshumot,* 4 (1926), 287–94; Dubnow, in: *YIVO Bleter,* 1 (1931), 404–7; Dubnow, in: *Voskhod,* no. 1 (1889), 176–84; no. 8 (1893), 24–28; no. 9 (1899), 33–59; Gessen, in: *Perezhitoye,* 2 (1910), 54–77; Anski, *ibid.,* 248–57.

[Y.S.]

MUBASHSHIR BEN NISSI HA-LEVI (tenth century), Babylonian scholar who lived in Baghdad; also known as **Ibn Ussāba** or **ʿUnnāba.** Mubashshir comments on the works of *Saadiah Gaon, contained in *Kitāb Istidrāk al-Sahw* ("Book of Correction of Errors"), fragments of which were found in the Cairo *Genizah* and printed. The purpose of his book is not quite clear; the introduction leads one to believe that he sought to point out Saadiah's errors rather than to correct them, and the contents of the book strengthen this impression to the extent that at times the author seems to agree with Saadiah Gaon's Karaite critics. The book had a large circulation, especially in Spain, and is mentioned by many Jewish scholars.

Bibliography: A. Harkavy, *Zikkaron la-Rishonim ve-gam la-Aḥaronim,* 1 no. 4 (1891), 68–73, 182–5; Levin Oẓar, 8 (1938), 86 (third section); Mevasser b. Nissi ha-Levi, *Hassagot Al Rav Sa'adyah Ga'on,* ed. by M. Zucker (1955); Baron, Social, 5 (1957), 390 no. 21; 7 (1958), 15–16; S. Abramson, in: *Sinai.* 57 (1965), 15–17; M. Zucker, *ibid.,* 58 (1966), 95–98; S. M. Stern, in: REJ, 126 (1967), 113–7.

[A.D.]

MUBASHSHIR BEN RAV KIMOI HA-KOHEN (d. 925), *gaon* of the Pumbedita Academy from 917 to 925, a post to which he was appointed upon the death of R. Judah Gaon (the grandfather of R. *Sherira Gaon). Mubashshir belonged to the faction which opposed the appointment of *David b. Zakkai as exilarch, apparently because of his family relationship with Mar *Ukba, the deposed exilarch. In turn, when David b. Zakkai did become exilarch, he refused to recognize Mubashshir in his post and appointed R. *Kohen Ẓedek as head of the Pumbedita Academy; the members of the Academy were split into two factions, each supporting one of the two *geonim.* A prominent supporter of Mubashshir was *Ben Meir, the *gaon* of Ereẓ Israel, who conducted an active campaign against both David b. Zakkai and R. Kohen Ẓedek. Saadiah Gaon, on the other hand, when he came to Baghdad in 921, joined Mubashshir's opponents. Mubashshir appointed R. *Aaron b. Joseph Sarjado as *rosh kallah* Pumbedita, in spite of his not being the scion of a scholarly family. In 922 David b. Zakkai made peace with Mubashshir and most of the members of the Academy accepted the latter's leadership; R. Kohen Ẓedek, and the few members who remained loyal to him, left the Academy but continued to receive their share of its income. None of Mubashshir's teachings and responsa has been preserved. On Mubashshir's death in 925 his rival R. Kohen Ẓedek succeeded him as *gaon.*

Bibliography: B. M. Lewin (ed.), *Iggeret Sherira Ga'on* (1921), 119–20; Mann, in: *Tarbiz,* 5 (1933/34), 150–8; Abramson, Merkazim, 21–23.

[A.D.]

°**MUCIANUS, CAIUS LICINIUS,** governor of Syria during the Roman War (66–70 C.E.) and a prominent supporter of Vespasian's successful attempt to assume the leadership of the Roman Empire. As governor of Syria, Mucianus is known to have supported certain privileges of the Jewish community at Antioch. In 69, together with other generals in the east, Mucianus urged Vespasian to become emperor, and subsequently was dispatched with a substantial force to Italy, to secure Rome from the supporters of Vitellius. He entered the city during the last days of 69, and prepared the way for Vespasian's triumphant arrival there in the summer of 70 C.E.

Bibliography: Kappelmacher, in: Pauly-Wissowa, 25 (1926), 436–43 no. 116a; Schuerer, Hist, 263.

[I.G.]

MUEHLHAUSEN, city in E. Germany. Though the exact date of the earliest Jewish settlement in Muehlhausen is unknown, there was certainly a Jewish settlement there c. 1300, and a synagogue is mentioned in 1311. The relationship between the town and the community (*"universitas Judaeorum"*) was regulated by the municipal council in 1311. Jurisdiction over the Jews of Muehlhausen and the income from them was contested between the municipality and the landgraves of *Thuringia, who during the *Black Death persecutions advised the burghers to massacre the Jews; this occurred on March 21, 1349. Among the martyrs was a scholar, R. Eliezer. Many of the exiles settled permanently in Erfurt and Frankfort. The property of the deceased Jews was the object of bitter contention between Charles IV and the city. In 1374 Jews were again present in Muehlhausen, and the townspeople were released from all debts owed them in 1391. In 1433 the Jews had to pay 200 florins as a coronation tax; throughout the 15th century they were taxed heavily by all governmental authorities. Regulations of 1472 ordered the Jews to stay out of the homes of Christians and to wear the yellow *badge; the women had to wear two blue stripes on their headdresses. In 1543 all Jews were expelled. Jews originating from Muehlhausen were living in Cracow, Poznan, and Lissa in the 17th century. The first **Schutzjuden* returned to Muehlhausen in 1643 and in 1692 there were four Jewish households, rising to 14 families around 1781, 144 persons in 1843, 180 in 1907, and 170 in 1932. On the eve of the Nazi rise to power the community possessed a synagogue, religious school, and three philanthropic organizations. Repressive measures resulting in emigration brought the number of Jews down to 70 in 1939. The community was annihilated during World War II.

Bibliography: *Denkschrift zu dem Entwurf einer Verordnung die Verhaeltnisse der Juden betreffend* (1847), pt. 1 B, 26; P. Wertheim, *Kalendar und Jahrbuch* (1857); A. Jaraczewski, *Geschichte der Juden in Erfurt* (1868), 2 n. 2, 25 n. 2, 72; L. Lewin, in: JJLG, 5 (1907), 109–10; MGADJ, 3 (1912), 164; 4 (1913), 179; 5 (1914), 26, 114, 188; U. Weinberg, in: JJLG, 16 (1924), 275, 278, 280, 283, 287–8, 294–6; S. Neufeld, in: MGWJ, 69 (1925), 287, 291, 293; *Handbuch der juedischen Gemeindeverwaltung* (1907), 53; (1924), 45; S. Neufeld, *Die Juden im thueringen-saechsischen Gebiet waehrend des Mittelalters* (1927) passim; FJW, 118; Germ Jud, 2 (1968), 550–2.

[ED.]

MUEHSAM, ERICH (1878–1934), German poet, playwright, and anarchist. Muehsam, born in Berlin, rejected his Jewish family background while still a student. Like his father, he at first practiced pharmacy, but soon entered politics and published a short-lived anarchist newspaper, *Der arme Teufel* (1902). Under the influence of Gustav *Landauer, Muehsam joined the "Neue Gesellschaft," a group of libertarian writers. He began to publish books of verse, notably *Die Wueste* (1904), *Der Krater* (1909), and from 1908, contributed satirical poems to the humorous magazine *Simplicissimus.* Muehsam later wrote another book of verse, *Brennende Erde* (1920) and wrote several plays, including *Judas* (1921; 1924[2]) and *Staatsraeson* (1928), a dramatization of the Sacco-Vanzetti case.

In 1911 he founded his own anarchist periodical, *Kain, Zeitschrift fuer Menschlichkeit.* This ceased publication on the outbreak of World War I, owing to its publisher's anti-militarism. Later in the war Muehsam helped to organize a strike at the Krupp works in Munich and was sent to prison in January 1918. Released in the following

November, he immediately resumed publication of *Kain* which lasted until April 1919, continued his anti-war agitation, and took an active part in the overthrow of the Bavarian monarchy. Muehsam was a prominent figure in

Erich Muehsam, German author and anarchist, detail of a portrait. Courtesy Charlotte Landau, Haifa.

Kurt *Eisner's Bavarian Soviet Republic of 1919 and was sentenced to 15 years imprisonment on its overthrow. He was released, however, after five years in jail. From 1924 until his reincarceration by the Nazis in 1933, he edited *Fanal,* the monthly organ of philosophical anarchists. His comparison of Lenin to Moses in an elegy on the death of Lenin was not appreciated by the Marxists. In spite of his fiery opinions and wild appearance, Muehsam was a kindly man. After prolonged torture in various concentration camps, Muehsam was finally murdered by the Nazis at Oranienburg on July 9, 1934.

Bibliography: K. Muehsam, *Der Leidensweg Erich Muehsams* (1935); R. Foerster, *Erich Muehsam* . . . (Ger., 1919). [S.L.]

MUELHAUSEN, YOM TOV LIPMANN (14th–15th centuries), scholar, polemist, philosopher, kabbalist, and one of the great rabbis of Bohemia in his time. His name indicates that he, or his family, probably originally came from Mulhouse in Alsace; all that is known with certainty, however, is that he was active chiefly in Prague, where he lived before 1389, that he was among those affected by the "Edict of Prague" which took place in that year, and that in 1407 he was appointed *Judex Judaeorum* ("judge of the Jews") there. Yom Tov was the pupil of the outstanding Austrian scholars, *Meir b. Baruch ha-Levi, *Sar Shalom of Neustadt, Samson b. Eleazar, and particularly of the brothers, Menahem and Avigdor Kara, serving with the last two as *dayyan* in Prague. He journeyed a great deal in Bohemia, Austria, and Poland with the aim of acquainting himself with shortcomings in the observance of *halakhah* and custom and rectifying them. There is information of his activities and his varied **takkanot* in Cracow, Lindau (German Bavaria), and Erfurt, where he introduced permanent and amended rules for the writing of Scrolls of the Law, *tefillin,* and *mezuzot,* in the making of a *shofar* and the manner in which it should be sounded, the order of granting a bill of divorce, etc. These rules were adopted in many districts of Austria and Bohemia and named after him. He also had a ramified correspondence with great contemporary talmudists, including Jacob *Moellin and Jacob b. Judah *Weil. Between 1440 and 1450 he was one of the heads of the council of the Ashkenazi communities known as Va'ad Erfurt ("The Council at Erfurt"), but its exact date and activities are not known.

Yom Tov Lipmann's activity as a polemist gave him lasting renown even among non-Jews, who over many years produced a complete and ramified literature in refutation of him known by the general name of Anti-Lipmanniana. He began these activities early in his life when he conducted polemics with the bishop of Linda, on the initiative of the bishop, and in a spirit of mutual tolerance and non-provocation. Some of the other priests of Linda disputed with him also, and part of this series of polemics was later included in his *Niẓẓaḥon* (see below). According to a Christian source, Muelhausen went to listen to the sermons of their preachers, and it is possible that he actually initiated some of his polemics at those gatherings. His best-known disputation, which had the most serious consequences, was that with the apostate Pesaḥ (Peter). It was connected with the edict of apostasy issued against the Jews of Prague in 1389, as a result of which Peter came out with a series of public attacks upon the Jews who deny and despise Christianity. A proposal was made that the Jews hold a disputation with him to justify themselves, and Muelhausen was chosen for this purpose. No details are known either of the staging or the content of this disputation, but as a result of it 80 Jews were martyred, and the remainder, including Yom Tov Lipmann, were saved by a "miracle" of unknown nature.

Except for the *Sefer ha-Niẓẓaḥon* Muelhausen's books were written after 1407, when he was *Judex Judaeorum* in Prague. He dealt chiefly with Kabbalah, *halakhah,* and philosophy, but all three topics were intertwined. His various works have become part of the contemporary Jewish heritage, as has the whole form of the *halakhah* laid down by him. They afford evidence of his great erudition in the sources of *halakhah* and *aggadah,* in the Bible and its exegesis, in Kabbalah, and particularly in philosophy—in which he attained the highest level reached until then among the Jews of that country. He is, in fact, the first known scholar of Bohemia who openly occupied himself with philosophy, having a sound knowledge of the subject. He based himself on Maimonides' *Guide of the Perplexed,* and it was he who first gave it wide publicity in Poland and the neighboring countries, just as he endeavored to establish his halakhic views in accordance with the opinion of Maimonides. Undoubtedly it was Muelhausen who influenced the great Polish rabbi, Moses *Isserles, to follow Maimonides in his study of philosophy and *halakhah.* Muelhausen was well acquainted with what was known of the teaching of Saadiah Gaon and also made frequent use of early works on Kabbalah, such as the *Sefer *Yeẓirah,* the *Heikhalot* literature (see *Merkabah mysticism), the *Sefer ha-Bahir, Sefer ha-Temurah, Ma'arekhet ha-Elohut,* etc. He also knew the works of *Baḥya ibn Paquda, Solomon ibn *Gabirol, and Abraham *ibn Ezra. One contemporary scholar whose works he frequently used was *Shemariah b. Elijah ha-Ikriti of Negropont. Muelhausen occupied himself intensively with Kabbalah, and, in addition to the above-mentioned works the influence of Naḥmanides—whose esoteric remarks, like those of Ibn Ezra, he sought to explain—is evident. In his view there is no contradiction between Kabbalah and philosophy; he maintained that Maimonides too was a kabbalist but that he merely gave a philosophical garb to his words. His writings on Kabbalah are also generally written in the accepted style of medieval Jewish philosophy, with the result that many scholars were led to the erroneous conclusion that as a philosopher, he was opposed to Kabbalah. However, the new texts published during recent decades have removed all doubts on this matter. The central problems which he discusses, namely the reasons for the precepts, the fundamentals of faith, free will, and omniscience, the suffering of the righteous, corporeality, etc.—all serve a threefold purpose: the refutation of heretics, the attainment of philosophical truth, and the establishment of the foundations of kabbalistic mysticism. His chief kabbalistic work is the *Sefer ha-Eshkol* (ed. by J. Kaufman, 1927) written in 1413, which is wholly influenced by the Spanish kabbalists of the school of *Azriel b. Menahem of Gerona, and in his *Alfa Beta* the great influence upon him of the Ḥasidei Ashkenaz is recognizable.

Muelhausen's halakhic writings reveal his complete command of all rabbinic literature up to his own time. Some of his many polemics were assembled by him in the *Sefer ha-Niẓẓaḥon* which he intended to serve as a handbook for the ordinary Jew compelled at times to wrestle with complex theological problems beyond his ability. The work was written in 1390 and was much copied in manuscript. It was first published by the priest Theodore Hackspan (Altdorf, 1644). Hackspan strove to edit it with maximum faithfulness to the source, and with the aim of enabling Christian scholars to oppose it, but he did not succeed because neither he nor the workers in his press understood either the language of the sources or their subject matter. As a result this edition is full of errors; despite this it has great value for correcting many mistakes in the subsequent editions. The first Jewish edition was published in Amsterdam in 1701. It was only rarely reprinted because of the papal decree against its publication and circulation, and there is a variety of bibliographical problems connected with the various editions of the book. Muelhausen's method was to expose the Christian lack of understanding of the Hebrew sources with their linguistic and contextual associations and to ridicule aspects of the Christian religion. His great superiority over other polemists was based on his knowledge of Latin and lay in his intimate knowledge of Christian literature—the New Testament, the Vulgate, and the leading Church Fathers, as well as the works of the late Christian scholars. Frequently his polemics are based on sound philology. His familiarity with Christian sources was, however, less than that of Isaac *Troki, and his arguments are more popular in character and not so "logical." He undoubtedly made use of early Jewish polemic material included in various collections, among them an earlier *Sefer Niẓẓaḥon* (probably by Joseph *Official) as well as of oral traditions. He selected and summarized the best of the answers, according to his understanding and according to the taste of his contemporaries, connecting them with topical questions. Among Christian scholars who applied themselves to refuting his arguments may be mentioned chiefly Bodker, Sebastian *Muenster, and J. *Buxtorf, and especially J. C. *Wagenseil, who also included short fragments both from the *Niẓẓaḥon* and from the *Niẓẓaḥon Yashan* in his book *Tela Ignea Satanae.*

Muelhausen's *Sefer Alfa Beta,* on the shape of the letters and their inner meaning, was written for the benefit of scribes of Scrolls of the Law, *tefillin,* and *mezuzot* and of those who wished to devote themselves to esoteric study. It was published in the second part of the *Barukh she-Amar* (Shklov, 1804) of Samson b. Eliezer and its identity was recognized only about a century ago (previously it had been regarded as part of the *Barukh she-Amar*). Muelhausen also wrote **haggahot* to the *Barukh she-Amar* itself, but these were incorporated in the text so that they cannot be recognized. He also wrote *Tikkun Sefer Torah,* containing the order of open and closed sections of the Torah (see **Sefer Torah*) as well as many essential scribal regulations. This work was issued by E. Kupfer and S. Loewinger (see bibl.). Other works are *Sefer ha-Eshkol* and *Sefer Kavvanot ha-Tefillah* (appended to *Sefer ha-Eshkol,* 1927), a commentary on the *Shir ha-Yiḥud* (see J. Kaufman, p. 80f.), and various prayers and *piyyutim* printed in different places. His *Sefer ha-Berit,* on the meaning of the 13 attributes, was published from a manuscript by E. Kupfer (see bibl.). Other works written by him have not been found. Muelhausen's works have important historical value, particularly regarding the status and the situation of the Jews at the time of the Hussite wars.

Bibliography: J. Kaufmann, *R. Yom Tov Lipmann Muelhausen* (Heb., 1927); B. Mark and E. Kupfer, in: *Bleter far Geshikhte,* 6 no. 4 (1953), 79–83; E. Kupfer, in: *Sinai,* 56 (1965), 330–42; idem and S. Loewinger, *ibid.,* 60 (1967), 237–68; I. Sonne, in: *Studies in Bibliography and Booklore,* 1 no. 2 (1953), 60f., 68f.; I. Ta-Shema, in: KS, 45 (1969/70), 120–2; M. M. Meshi-Zahav, *Kovez Sifrei Setam* (1970).

[I.T.-S.]

MUELLER, DAVID HEINRICH (1846–1912), orientalist. He was born in Buczacz (Galicia), which was also the hometown of his relative S. Y. *Agnon. In his youth Mueller was influenced by *Rappaport, *Zunz, *Krochmal, and *Smolenskin. He studied at the *Jewish Theological Seminary at Breslau, but his lack of talent as a preacher forced him to leave the seminary and to specialize in Semitic languages. From 1876 he taught oriental languages at Vienna University and also lectured at the Vienna Jewish Theological Seminary from its foundation in 1893. In 1889 he was elected a member of the Austro-Hungarian Academy of Sciences. Shortly before his death he was ennobled under the title of Baron Mueller von Deham.

Mueller undertook in 1877 a journey to the Orient which produced a crop of publications on South-Arabian inscriptions, on castles and palaces in that region (2 parts, 1879–81), and a detailed report on this expedition (1878). He also edited S. Langer's journal on his travels in Syria and Arabia and the inscriptions he had discovered (1883); Hamadani's Arabian geography (2 parts, 1884–91); and Tabari's annals (1888–89). Mueller also wrote comparative studies of Semitic languages (1884); on the cuneiform writings discovered at Ashrut Dargha (1886/87); and on the particular division of sibilants in the South-Arabian dialect (1888). His articles in the Vienna *Zeitschrift fuer die Kunde des Morgenlandes,* of which he was an editor, also dealt with early Semitic epigraphy. A second expedition to South Arabia led by Mueller resulted in several volumes of reports of which Mueller wrote three, dealing mainly with the linguistic and literary discoveries.

David Heinrich Mueller, orientalist. Jerusalem, J.N.U.L., Schwadron Collection.

When the Code of *Hammurapi was discovered, Mueller wrote on its relationship to the laws of the Pentateuch (1903, translating the Code into biblical Hebrew), and to those of the Syrio-Roman Lawbook (1905). In biblical studies proper (*Biblische Studien,* 5 vols., 1895–98), Mueller advanced a novel theory on the structure and rhythm of biblical poetry. Mueller, in general, adopted a conservative attitude to the Bible text and was averse to emendations.

Bibliography: G. Rosenmann, in: JJGL, 17 (1914), 145–57; Yeshayahu, in: S. Federbush (ed.), *Ḥokhmat Yisrael be-Eiropah* (1965), 401f.; *Epigraphische Denkmaeler aus Abessinien, nach Abklatschen von J. Theodore Bent, esq.* (1894); *Epigraphische Denkmaeler aus Arabien* (Wien, 1889); *Die Haggadah von Sarajevo* (1898); *Die Mehri- und Soqoṭri-Sprache* (1902–07); *Das syrisch-roemische Rechtsbuch und Ḥammurabi* (1905); G. Rosenmann, in: *Sefer ha-Zikkaron le-Beit ha-Midrash be-Vinah* (1946), 24–29.

[N.H.T.-S.]

MUELLER, ERNST (1880–c. 1947), mathematician and writer on Kabbalah and philosophy. Born at Misslitz, Moravia, Mueller taught at the Kiryat Sefer agricultural school, Jaffa (1907–09). From 1911 he worked at the Jewish community library in Vienna, and after its closure by the Nazis emigrated to England. His *Der Sohar und seine Lehre* went through three editions (1920, 1923, 1959), and he translated selections of the Zohar into German (*Sohar, das heilige Buch der Kabbalah*, 1932). Mueller wrote a *History of Jewish Mysticism* (1946). He translated a selection of Bialik's poems (*Gedichte*, 1911), as well as Abraham ibn Ezra's *Sefer ha-Eḥad* (*Buch der Einheit*, 1920), with notes and an excursus on the author as mathematician. On the occasion of the tercentenary of Spinoza's birth he published a (supplementary) bibliography of Spinoza literature (1932). He prepared a German stage version of Plato's Symposium (1932). [ED.]

°**MUELLER, HEINRICH** (1900–?), last chief of the *Gestapo. Mueller joined the Bavarian police after serving as an NCO pilot during World War I. *Heydrich retained him as an expert on communism in the Bavarian political police even though Mueller in this period was not a Nazi but a member of the Bavarian Volkspartei. Mueller in 1933 joined the *SS and the SD (secret police), but became a Nazi Party member only in 1939. When *Heydrich took charge of the Gestapo, Mueller, who had become one of his top aides, went with him to Berlin. He soon became chief of the executive of the office (Main Branch II). When the Security Police (Sipo) was organized, he was appointed chief of its political police section and in effect head of the Gestapo. The suppression of all organized opposition to the Nazi regime was, among other factors, due to Mueller's efficiency and ruthlessness, which included the application of torture on his victims. Mueller was involved in the hoax whereby "Polish" attacks on Germany served as a pretext for the outbreak of World War II. On Sept. 27, 1939, Mueller was appointed chief of Office IV of the *RSHA (Reich Security Main Office). Besides being responsible for the murder of hundreds of thousands of Soviet prisoners of war and an untold number of political prisoners, Mueller was one of the key figures of the "Final Solution" (see *Holocaust, General Survey). *Eichmann's IVB 4 Section was part of his office. Mueller participated in the *Wannsee Conference and, as the war drew to a close, opposed all efforts to spare Jews. He made every effort to remain in the background and, last seen in Hitler's bunker on April 29, 1945, he succeeded in quietly disappearing when the Third Reich collapsed.

Bibliography: H. Hoehne, *Der Orden unter dem Totenkopf* (1967); Institut fuer Zeitgeschichte, *Gutachten des Instituts fuer Zeitgeschichte*, 1 (1958), 169, 219, 232, 297; G. Reitlinger, *Final Solution* (1968²), index; IMT, *Trial of the Major War Criminals*, 24 (1949), index; R. Hilberg, *Destruction of the European Jews* (1961), index. [Y.RE.]

MUELLER, JOEL (1827–1895), rabbinical scholar and authority on geonic texts. Born at Maehrisch Ostrau, Moravia, Mueller received his early talmudic education from his father, rabbi in Maehrisch Ostrau, whom he succeeded in 1853. After a period as rabbi in Leipa, Bohemia, and as a teacher of religion in Vienna, in 1884 he began teaching at the Berlin Hochschule fuer die Wissenschaft des Judentums.

Mueller published a series of rabbinic texts, chiefly responsa, of the geonic and immediate post-geonic period, which are models of scholarly editions. The most important are the post-talmudic tractate *Massekhet *Soferim* (1878), with an introduction and copious notes in German; a post-talmudic work on ritual differences between Ereẓ Israel and Babylon, *Hilluf Minhagim* (in *Ha-Shaḥar* 7 (1876), and 8 (1877); published separately, 1878); *Teshuvot Ḥakhmei Ẓarefat ve-Loter* ("Responsa of French and Lorraine Scholars," 1881, repr. 1959, 1967); *Teshuvot Ge'onei Mizraḥ u-Ma'arav* ("Responsa of Eastern and Western Geonim,"

Joel Mueller, authority on geonic texts. Jerusalem, J.N.U.L., Schwadron Collection.

in *Bet Talmud*, 4 (1885); and 5 (1886); published separately 1888; repr. 1959, 1966); *Mafte'aḥ li-Teshuvot Ge'onim* ("Introduction to Geonic Responsa," 1891; repr. 1959); and *Halakhot Pesukot* ("Short Geonic Responsa," 1893). Mueller also edited Saadiah's "Book (on the law) of Inheritance" *Traité des Successions* . . . for J. Derenbourg's edition of Saadiah's writings (*Oeuvres Complètes*; vol. 9, 1897). For the annual reports of the Lehranstalt he published studies on responsa in the pre-geonic period (in: 4, 1886); on those of tenth-century Spanish teachers (in: 7, 1889); on Yehudai Gaon (in: 8, 1890), and on the responsa of Meshullam b. Kalonymus (in: 11, 1893); see also his *Responsa of Kalonymos of Lucca* (*Teshuvot Rabbenu Kalonymos mi-Lucca*, 1891).

Bibliography: M. Schreiner, *Gedaechtnisrede auf Joel Mueller* (1896); *Bericht ueber die Lehranstalt fuer die Wissenschaft des Judentums*, 15 (1897), 32ff.; S. Federbush, *Ḥokhmat Yisrael be-Eiropah* (1965), 402. [ED.]

MUELLER-COHEN, ANITA (1890–1962), social worker. Born in Vienna, Anita Mueller-Cohen became a social worker while still in her youth. During World War I she did relief work in the war-stricken areas of Galicia and Bukovina. She devoted herself to establishing lying-in hospitals for mothers, day nurseries and medical services for children, and institutions for the care of the aged. After the war she led the effort to help returning soldiers to readjust themselves and established milk stations for undernourished children throughout Austria. She directed the placement of orphaned children in Jewish homes in a number of West European countries and in 1920 promoted the adoption in North and South America of child victims of persecution in Eastern Europe. In that year she became a member of the Vienna City Council. Anita Mueller-Cohen settled in Tel Aviv in 1936 and continued her child welfare and other social services. [ED.]

MUENSTER, city in North Rhine Westphalia, W. Germany. Jews lived there from at least the middle of the 13th century, maintaining a synagogue, a cemetery (mentioned in 1301; a fragment of a tombstone dated 1324 has been preserved), and a *mikveh*. In the wake of the *Black Death persecutions (1349/50), the Jews were expelled or killed and their property confiscated or destroyed. Between 1350 and 1810, Jews were not allowed to reside in Muenster but were only allowed to pass through. They were, however, tolerated since the 16th century within the bishopric of Muenster. They received letters of protection from the bishop and founded several congregations. After 1650 these congregations were united in the **Landjudenschaft*. The head of this corporation was the *"Judenvorgaenger,"* the first was (1657) Nini Levi, brother of Behrend *Levi. The seat of the rabbi of the *Landjudenschaft (*Landrabbiner)* was in Warendorf (near Muenster), the largest Jewish community of the bishopric. The last *Landrabbiner* were the *Court Jew Michael Mayer Breslauer (1771–89) and his son David (1789–1815). When Muenster passed to the duchy of *Berg (1808–10) and to the French Empire (1810–13), the first Jews settled in the city; their residence there was legalized by Prussia in 1819. They officially founded a new community in 1854. The first prayer house was situated in the Loerstrasse; the cemetery was established in 1811, and the synagogue was built in 1880.

From 1816 *Landrabbiner* Abraham *Sutro lived in Muenster although he did not act as rabbi of the community, which in 1879 appointed Dr. J. Mansbach as preacher and cantor. He was succeeded by S. Kessler. The first rabbi, who took office in 1919, was Dr. Fritz Steinthal (who emigrated to South America in 1938). His successor, Dr. Julius Voos of Kamen, was deported to *Auschwitz in 1943. Among the most notable members of the community were Professor Alexander Haindorf (1782–1862), cofounder of the Marks-Haindorf Foundation for the training of elementary school teachers and for the advancement of artisans and artists among the Jews, and the first Jewish professor at Muenster Academy (university); and the poet Eli Marcus (1854–1935), cofounder of the "Zoological Evening Society," author of poems and many plays in the Low German dialect of the Muensterland.

During the Nazi era the community was reduced from 558 Jews (0.4% of the population) in 1933 to 308 (0.2%) in 1939. The synagogue was destroyed in November 1938 (see **Kristallnacht*). The first deportation from Muenster city and district (to Riga) took place in December 1941 (403 persons); in 1942 the last large-scale transport went eastward, followed by individual deportations in 1943 and 1944. After World War II a new congregation was founded, which included besides Muenster the Jews of Ahaus, Beckum, Borken, Burgsteinfurt, Coesfeld. This new community of Muenster numbered 142 members in 1970. The synagogue was built in 1961.

Bibliography: Complete bibliography by B. Brilling, in: H. C. Meyer, *Aus Geschichte und Leben der Juden in Westfalen* (1962), 251–3; idem, in: *Westfalen*, 44 (1966), 212–7; B. Brilling and H. Richtering (ed.), *Westfalia Judaica*, 1 (1967), index; idem (ed.), *Juden in Muenster 1933–1945* (1960); F. Lazarus, in: ZGJD, 7 (1937), 240–3; idem, in: MGWJ, 80 (1936), 106–17; 81 (1937), 444–5; J. Raphael, in: *Zeitschrift fuer die Geschichte der Juden*, 6 (1969), 74f.; H. Schnee, *Die Hoffinanz und der moderne Staat*, 3 (1955), 54–67; 6 (1967), 153–71; Leeser, in: AZJ, 73 (1909), 583ff.; Germ Jud, 1 (1963), 238–9; 2 (1968), 561–3. [B.Br.]

°**MUENSTER, SEBASTIAN** (**Munsterus;** 1489–1552), German Hebraist and reformer. Born in Ingelheim, Muenster entered the Franciscan order in 1505. Turning to the study of Hebrew, he became a pupil of Conrad *Pellicanus in Basle from about 1510 and of Elijah *Levita, whose major grammatical works he translated and edited from 1525. Next to Johann *Reuchlin Muenster was the outstanding Christian Hebraist of the 16th century. He taught Hebrew at Heidelberg (1524–28) and, by the time he was appointed professor of Hebrew at Basle University (1528), had become a Protestant. Unlike Pellicanus, Muenster was a prolific author and translator. He reissued Reuchlin's *De rudimentis Hebraicis* and published about 40 works, including *Epitome Hebraicae grammaticae* (1520); *Institutiones Grammaticae in Hebraeam Linguam* (Basle, 1524); *Chaldaica Grammatica* (Basle, 1527), the first Aramaic grammar by a Christian, based on the *Arukh* of *Nathan b. Jehiel of Rome; a list of the 613 Commandments (Basle, 1533) culled from the *Sefer Mitzvot Katan* of *Isaac b. Joseph of Corbeil; translations of *Josippon, and of works by David *Kimḥi and E. Levita; and a grammar of rabbinic Hebrew (Basle, 1542). His outstanding *Hebraica Biblia* (2 vols, Basle, 1534–35), which is provided with an original Latin text independent of the Vulgate, represents the first Protestant translation of the Old Testament from Hebrew into Latin. Like Paulus *Fagius, Muenster translated into Hebrew the Apocryphal Book of Tobit (Basle, 1542), which later reappeared in the London Polyglot Bible (1654–57). His Hebrew version (with annotations) of the Gospel of St. Matthew (*"Torat ha-Mashi'aḥ,"* Basle, 1537), dedicated to Henry VIII of England, was the first Hebrew translation of any portion of the New Testament. Muenster's use of Jewish polemical literature in the preparation of his Hebrew edition of Matthew outraged Guillaume *Postel, who bitterly attacked his fellow Hebraist in the concluding section of his *De orbis terrae concordia....* Muenster was also a mathematician, cosmographer, and cartographer. He annotated the Latin version of Abraham b. Ḥiyya's astronomical and geographical work, *Ẓurat ha-Areẓ* (Basle, 1546).

Bibliography: J. Perles, *Beitraege zur Geschichte der hebraeischen und aramaeischen Studien* (1884), 20–44, 154ff.; F. Secret, *Les Kabbalistes Chrétiens de la Renaissance* (1964), 141, 144f.; idem, in: *Bibliothèque d'Humanisme et Renaissance*, 22 (1960), 377–80; Baron, Social[2], 13 (1969), 233–4, 432; E. I. J. Rosenthal, in: I. Epstein (ed.), *Essays ... J. H. Hertz* (1943), 350–69. [G.E.S.]

MUENSTERBERG, HUGO (1863–1916), psychologist. Born in Danzig, baptized at the time of his appointment to Freiberg University, Muensterberg developed the first psychological laboratory there. His fields of research included such varied problems as auditory space perception, estimation of size, kinesthesis, memory, the time sense, attention, and the influence of drugs on mental work. These were published in the series *Beitraege zur experimentellen Psychologie* (1889–92). Muensterberg enjoyed a reputation as one of the most brilliant young psychologists. As the result of a quarrel in the field of work, he was prevented, on anti-Semitic grounds—in spite of his baptism—from receiving a Berlin University appointment. Other appointments were turned down on the basis of unfavorable comments on his work by his colleagues. On the other hand, his work had attracted the attention of America's preeminent psychologist, Harvard's William James. Muensterberg was given a trial period at Harvard (1892–95), which was followed by a permanent appointment. Muensterberg's contribution is not widely appreciated today, mainly because he left no disciples.

Many modern trends in psychology are traceable to Muensterberg. On the theoretical side, Muensterberg was a forerunner of the functionalist school of psychology. His principles were described in *Grundzuege der Psychologie* (1900), with a second edition published posthumously by Max *Dessoir in 1918. His English text, *Psychology, General and Applied* (1914), although not well received, shows the scope and originality of his thinking. In 1898 he served as president of the American Psychological Association and as president of the American Philosophical Association in 1908. He was undoubtedly responsible for the growth of applied psychology. His work inspired William *Stern, Otto Klemm, and Otto *Lipmann. He devised tests for the selection of motormen and developed other testing procedures. He had a hand in the invention of the so-called lie detector and he instituted some of the first attempts at psychotherapy. In his day he was the great popularizer of psychology. He also took an interest in psychic phenomena, exposing the medium Madame

Eusapia Paladino and writing, in a negative vein, on thought transference.

Muensterberg's last years were marked by increasing political activity. Although originally a marginal German,

Hugo Muensterberg, psychologist. Courtesy Harvard University, Cambridge, Mass.

he remained a superpatriotic German who never gave up his German citizenship. At the outbreak of World War I he tried by all possible means to prevent the entry of the U.S. into the war and to work for a negotiated peace. His correspondence with the German chancellor, von Bethmann-Hollweg, presenting his plans to have President Wilson act as mediator, was intercepted and aroused violent feelings. In the midst of this controversy, he died as he was lecturing to his class.

Bibliography: F. Wunderlich, *Hugo Muensterberg's Bedeutung fuer die Nationaloekonomie* (1920); W. Stern, in: *Journal of Applied Psychology*, 1(1917), 186–8; A. A. Roback *History of American Psychology* (1964²), 212–39 and index. [H.E.A.]

MUENZ, ELEAZAR (Lazar) BEN ARYEH LEIB (1837–1921), rabbi and preacher in Poland and Germany. Muenz was a grandson of Eleazar *Low, the author of *Shemen Roke'aḥ*. He was appointed to the rabbinate of Oswiecim (Auschwitz) near Cracow before 1867. In 1875 he was appointed to the rabbinate of Kempen (Kepna) district of Posen, where he remained until after 1905. From there he moved to Wuerzburg and subsequently to Nuremberg. At the end of World War I he was living in Ansbach, where he died. He was the author of *Get Mesuddar* (1932), on the law of names in bills of divorce. Among his other works, written in German, are *Die modernen Anklagen gegen das Judentum als falsch nachgewiesen* (1882); *Religioese Zeitfragen* (1887, 1909²), a collection of his homilies; *Torat Nashim* (Ger., 1905), on the laws of family purity, frequently reprinted; and *Rabbi Eleasar, genannt Schemen Rokeach* (1895), a detailed biography of his grandfather.

Bibliography: E. Muenz, *Get Mesuddar* (1932), introd. [Ed.]

MUENZ (Minz), MOSES BEN ISAAC HA-LEVI (c. 1750–1831), Hungarian rabbi. Muenz was born in Podolia or in Galicia. After serving as rabbi in Vishravitz and in Brody, he was appointed in 1789 rabbi of Alt-Ofen (Óbuda) where he remained for the rest of his life. As a result of his activity there and his great reputation, the community became renowned. He represented the community at all royal ceremonies, including the coronation of Francis I. The addresses he delivered on those occasions were published in Hebrew and German. In 1793 he was appointed by the government chief rabbi of the whole Pest region. By virtue of this appointment he was granted the right to serve as Jewish judge in all the judicial affairs of the communities in the area, and not only in religious matters. This right was limited in 1796, but it did not affect the prestige in which he was held. On his initiative, and as a result of his endeavor, a beautiful synagogue was built by the community in 1822. It is still standing and has been proclaimed by the Hungarian government as a protected historical site. The sermon he preached at its consecration, *Devir ha-Bayit*, was published that same year in Vienna. To the second edition (1931) a biography of the author was added by D. S. Loewinger.

During the period of Muenz's rabbinate, tendencies toward religious reform began to be manifested in Hungary. At the beginning Muenz was relatively tolerant toward these reforms and even maintained friendly ties with the leader of the reformers, Aaron *Chorin, but later he took a strong stand against their aspirations in general and against Chorin in particular. In 1803 Chorin's book *Emek ha-Shaveh* appeared with the commendation of Muenz, but by 1805 Muenz was presiding over the **bet din* that summoned Chorin before it and rebuked him sharply, compelling him to rescind his progressive attitudes. Although the civil government revoked the ruling of rabbis headed by Muenz it was supported by the Orthodox community. His responsa were published by his son Joseph Isaac, under the title *Sefer Maharam Minz* (Prague, 1827). He also published, with his annotations, *Peri Ya'akov* (Ofen, 1830) of Jacob ben Moses. Orthodox Jews of Budapest used to visit his grave in the cemetery of Alt-Ofen during the days of Elul and of *seliḥot*. In 1949 this cemetery was cleared by order of the government and Muenz's remains and the tombstones were transferred to another cemetery in Budapest and reinterred near the graves of those killed by the Nazis, where the custom of visiting his grave continues.

Bibliography: S. Buechler, *A zsidók története Budapesten* ... (1901), 299–320; *Magyar Zsidó Lexikon* (1929), 622; D. S. Loewinger, in: *Devir ha-Bayit* (1931), 1–6. [Y.M.]

°**MUHAMMAD** (c. 571–632), founder and prophet of *Islam. Muhammad was born into the Meccan tribe of Quraysh. As a young man, Muhammad traveled with trading caravans to Syria, acting as steward for Khadīja, a rich widow. She was perhaps 40, and he 25, when she proposed marriage. Their marriage made him financially secure and provided him with important moral support in the early stages of his prophetic career. While Khadīja was alive, he took no other wife. She bore him six children; only one, Fāṭima, gave him a lasting line of descendants. There is little information on Muhammad's activities during the next 15 years.

Muhammad in Mecca. Muhammad was given to solitude and meditation on the barren rocky hills outside Mecca, often contemplating the causes and roots of the social malaise of Meccan society. From about 610, he had visions (cf. Sura 53:1–18), and was commanded, as the messenger of God, to recite certain verses which were throbbing in his mind (Sura 96:1–5; cf. also other contemporaneous passages, 68:1–5; 74:1–2; 93:1–2). Muhammad's reaction was one of fear and anxiety. Khadīja reassured him, and her cousin Waraqa, a Christian, exclaimed that what Muhammad recited was comparable with the law revealed to Moses. This encouragement was doubly important when the revelations stopped for a period, leaving Muhammad despondent and depressed. The *Koran denies the accusation that Muhammad had a mentor teaching him the verses he recited. The originality of the verses cannot be doubted. As for stories from the Jewish and Christian scriptures which found their way into the Koran, Muhammad neither read these scriptures nor had extensive contact with people well versed in them. Yet it cannot be denied that he had much opportunity to hear biblical, as well as noncanonical stories, secondhand in his meetings with ordinary Jews and Christians in Arabia and Syria. The reason why Muhammad did not wholly attach his movement either to Christianity or Judaism can be explained partially by the political implications of these religions in Arabia. Christianity meant alignment with Byzantium; Judaism through the big Jewish center in Babylonia had associations with Persian interests. A nonaligned national religion was required to win over the Arabs. Muhammad began to preach to his friends, and soon established a small community which met in order to learn the Koran and to worship God. The koranic message at this time concentrated on God's goodness and power, the return to God and final judgment, the necessity for man to be humble and grateful toward God and to worship Him, and the obligation of generosity and respect for the rights of the poor and the defenseless. The last two injunctions, stimulated the opposition of the elite of Mecca. In addition, opposition developed from the fear that in time Muhammad's following might unseat the ruling clique. The opposition intensified when Muhammad began to attack traditional polytheism. The Arabs had subscribed to a vague monotheism, with reverence for some lesser gods whose shrines were located near Mecca. At first Muhammad was prepared to consider the latter as intercessory beings, such as angels. When he saw that this would compromise the monotheism he espoused, he declared an end to worship at the shrines. Only the Kaʿba, in Mecca (to which the Arabs made an annual pilgrimage) purified of its idols, would remain as a shrine to the one God. This proposal would not have aroused much popular resistance, since the people had little regard for the traditional gods, and those with business interests in the shrines were neither numerous nor powerful. Meccan leaders, however, seized upon Muhammad's opposition to the religion of their fathers as a point around which they could arouse the populace against him, and thus eliminate his threat to their power. Thus what might have been a minor issue was inflated beyond proportion, and consequently polemics form a major part of the Koran.

Muhammad in Medina. As the opposition increased, Muhammad sought protection and a base for his activities at al-Ṭā'if, 40 miles from Mecca, but did not succeed. He was able to reenter Mecca only by first obtaining the temporary protection of the clan of Nawfal. The turning point for Muhammad came during the pilgrimage season of 620. A delegation from *Medina, impressed by his personality and message, sought his help in mediating a conflict simmering in Medina. The delegation returned in 621, and promised to accept Muhammad as a prophet, to obey him, and not to commit certain sins. Muhammad sent an agent to Medina to instruct the people in Islam and to review the situation. In 622 pilgrims from nearly all the Arab clans of Medina renewed the pledge of the previous year with the added promise to fight on Muhammad's behalf. Medina, an oasis 250 miles north of Mecca, was the home of about 20 clans which professed Judaism, but in language, culture, and even blood were hardly distinguishable from the Arabs. They had played an important part in the development of the oasis and once ruled the area. Arab clans who settled there, however, outnumbered the Jews and gained control in the early sixth century. The raids and reprisals, practiced by Arabs in the desert, escalated into a struggle between two blocs of allied clans, Aws and most of the Khazraj. Each had clients from the Jewish tribes and nomadic clans. The struggle culminated in the battle of Buʿāth, in about 618, with heavy slaughter on both sides. Unable to solve their problems, the residents of Medina requested Muhammad's arbitration. While negotiations with Muhammad were in progress, he gave the signal for his Meccan followers to slip quietly away to Medina. Soon only Muhammad himself, Abu Bakr, ʿAlī, and some of their families remained. The Meccans became aware of what had transpired, and only by an amazing feat did Muhammad and his companions make their way to Medina, where he arrived on Sept. 22, 622. The Islamic era is dated from the beginning of the Arab year in which Muhammad's *hijra*, or emigration, took place; i.e., July 16, 622. Muhammad's position in Medina was that of religious leader and arbiter of disputes. Aside from that, his only political authority was that of head of the group of emigrants *(muhājirūn)*, which was federated with the eight major Medinan clans called the supporters *(anṣār)*. The Jews were included in the arrangement as allies of one of the eight clans. Muhammad was anxious that the Jews acknowledge that he was a prophet. He emphasized the identity and continuity of his message with that of the earlier prophets; adopted Jerusalem as the **qibla*, or direction to be faced in prayer; practiced the Jewish fast of *ʿ*ashūrā'*; and made Friday afternoon the time of weekly communal worship. The Jews, especially the three major clans, were not impressed, and from the start found fault with Muhammad's assertions.

Muhammad's order to change the *qibla* from Jerusalem to Mecca symbolized the abandoning of his attempt to win over the Jews. He claimed that Islam was true to the religion of Abraham, who was not a Jew, and that any differences between himself and the Jews and Christians stemmed from their concealment or corruption of the truth. Muhammad asserted that the Jews had erred by rejecting him just as they previously had denied other prophets. These and similar arguments were the source of polemics between the two faiths which later developed.

The Jewish Tribes. In April 624 a scuffle in the market between Muslims and Jews of the *Qaynuqāʿ tribe resulted in the deaths of one from each group. The Qaynuqāʿ, who were traders and goldsmiths of Medina, retired to their strongholds where they were besieged. They surrendered to Muhammad after 15 days, and were given three days to leave the city, without their arms and probably without their goldsmiths' tools as well. They stopped at a nearby Jewish community, and a month later moved on to Syria.

In August 625, when morale among the Muslims was low after an unsuccessful battle with the Meccans, Muhammad visited the Jewish tribe of *Naḍīr and demanded financial aid. They told him to wait while they prepared a meal. Several moments later Muhammad went home, explaining to his companions that he received a warning from God that the Jews were planning to attack him while he sat there. He immediately sent an ultimatum to the Naḍīr, demanding that if they did not leave Medina within ten days they would be put to death. If they left, however, they would continue to own their palm groves and receive part of the produce. The Naḍīr held out 15 days before surrendering to Muhammad. They had to abandon their weapons and were not entitled to their date harvest. The tribe proceeded to *Khaybar, 70 miles to the north. When the Meccans unsuccessfully besieged Medina, the *Qurayẓa, the last major clan of Jews in Medina, were neutral but engaged in clandestine negotiations with the Meccans. After the Meccans departed, Muhammad turned his forces against the strongholds of the Qurayẓa. After 25 days they asked to surrender on the same terms as the Naḍīr. However, Muhammad demanded an unconditional surrender, which they accepted. Some of the tribe of Aws allied with Qurayẓa appealed on their behalf. Muhammad met their request by appointing as judge Saʿd ibn-Muʿādh, a leader of the Aws. Saʿd decreed that all the men of Qurayẓa (about 600) should be put to death, and the women and children sold as slaves. The sentence was carried out the next day. This severe action cannot be interpreted as an attack against Jews as such, since other minor Jewish clans which had maintained neutrality were allowed to remain in Medina unmolested. The deep and underlying reasons for Muhammad's attacks on the Qaynuqāʿ and the Naḍīr lay in their criticism of the koranic revelation which aimed at undermining the ideological foundation of the entire Islamic political order. They also were giving political support to Muhammad's opponents. As long as the Jews refrained from such hostile activities they were unmolested.

The Jews' last base of opposition to Muhammad was Khaybar, where they actively conspired with neighboring Arabs to confront Muhammad in battle. In May–June 628 Muhammad conquered the oasis. The settlement with the Jews stipulated that they would continue to live there, but pay a tax on half of their produce. This was a new principle regarding the status of minorities in Muslim territories, although it was applied with less stringent conditions on other occasions.

In January 630 Muhammad set out for Mecca with 10,000 men. The city submitted without resistance, except for a skirmish between a few men. Muhammad gave a general amnesty and forbade pillage. A few people were not included in the amnesty and executed, among them several anti-Muslim propagandists. The Kaʿba was cleansed of its idols. In the same month Muhammad defeated a force of 20,000 Bedouin in the battle of Ḥunayn, near Mecca, thus demonstrating that he was the most powerful leader in Arabia. Tribes all over Arabia allied themselves to Muhammad and became Muslims. Forbidden to raid one another, they had to divert their energies and the drive to the north began, but did not reach beyond Arabia before Muhammad's death. In March 632 Muhammad led the greater pilgrimage, the hajj. Returning to Medina in poor health, he died on June 8, leaving Abu Bakr to lead the prayers in his stead, but making no other provision for succession.

See also *Islam; *Koran; *Bible: in Islam.

Bibliography: A. Guillaume, *Life of Muhammad, A Translation of Isḥāq's Sīrat Rasūl Allāh* (1955); A. Sprenger, *Das Leben und die Lehre des Mohammed,* 3 vols. (1869); L. Caetani (comp.), *Annali dell'Islam,* 10 vols. (1905–26); idem, *Studi di storia orientale,* 3 (1914); A. J. Wensinck, *Mohammed en de Joden te Medina* (1908); F. Buhl, *Das Leben Muhammeds* (1930); K. Ahrens, *Muhammed als Religionsstifter* (1935); T. Andrae, *Mohammed, The Man and His Faith* (1955[2]); W. M. Watt, *Muhammad at Mecca* (1953); idem, *Muhammad at Medina* (1956); EIS, 3 (1936), 641–59. [EH/ED.]

°**MUHAMMAD ALI** (1769–1849), ruler of Egypt from 1805 to 1849. First coming to Egypt in 1799 with the Ottoman sultan's armies, Muhammad Ali quickly rose to power there and conquered the Sudan, Palestine, and Syria. He successfully subdued the Mamluks, massacring them in 1811. By exploiting the weakness of the Ottomans and the disunity of the Great Powers, he consolidated his position by military campaigns outside Egypt and important reforms within the country. He also appointed French officers who had retired from their duties at the close of the Napoleonic Wars (see *Dembinski). Nevertheless he was unable to maintain his hold over Palestine and Syria, owing to the opposition of Britain and other European countries—with the exception of France—and finally came into conflict with the sultan in 1840. His only important achievement in his foreign policy was the commitment of the sultan to leave the governorship of Egypt in the hands of his family. His internal reforms were also largely motivated by personal interests but they partially helped in developing and rebuilding Egypt. Despite his severity and his cruel punishments, the lot of his subjects improved. The public administration and the collection of taxes became more efficient, but the reforms essentially took place in the fields of irrigation, agriculture, industry, commerce, justice, health, and education. The relative security within Egypt encouraged commerce; the members of the religious minorities, such as Christians and Jews, also played an active role. Nevertheless, as a result of his personal retention of various monopolies during most of his rule, Muhammad Ali increased his income, but slowed down the development of commerce. His experiments in reforming the system of justice ran foul of a lengthy tradition of corruption among many qadis (religious judges); in order to circumvent them, he established two new courts of justice, in Cairo and Alexandria, to which he appointed Muslim and Christian merchants as judges (in Alexandria, there was also a Jewish judge); they were to deal with affairs of business and commerce, especially between members of different religions. Muhammad Ali's generation did not complete the modernization of Egypt and some of his reforms were neglected after his death; the seeds for the Arabization of the country had however been sown. In any event, the Jews of Egypt exchanged the arbitrariness of the many rulers of the land—namely the Mamluks—for the arbitrariness of a single ruler. Though they were still oppressed, the authority of the law protected their persons and their property. When taxes were levied, they were treated in the same way as the other non-Muslims in Egypt, i.e. without discrimination. Personal and material security resulted in an increase in the Jewish population in Egypt (Jews immigrated there from Italy and Greece), and by the close of Muhammad Ali's rule there were over 7,000 Jews, including about 1,200 Karaites. Most of the Jews lived in towns and were essentially occupied in commerce, crafts, and public services. Under the influence of Sir Moses Montefiore, Muhammad Ali did not allow the *Damascus blood libel (1840) to spread to other places. The years of Muhammad Ali's rule of Palestine (1832–40) were a time of relief for the Jewish inhabitants of Ereẓ Israel and especially Jerusalem, which had been troubled by the Fellaheen revolts.

Bibliography: S. Ghorbal, *The Beginnings of the Egyptian Question and the Rise of Mehemet Ali* (1928); M. Sabry, *L'empire égyptien sous Mohamed-Ali et la question d' Orient (1811–1849)* (1930); H. Dodwell, *The Founder of Modern Egypt* (1931); M. Zeliger, *Mediniyyut Eiropit ba-Mizraḥ ha-Karov* (1941); H. A. B. Rivlin, *The Agricultural Policy of Muḥammad ʿAli in Egypt* (1961); J. M. Landau, *Jews in Nineteenth-century Egypt* (1969), index. [Y.M.L.]

MUHR, ABRAHAM (1781–1847), leader of Silesian Jewry. Muhr moved from Berlin to Pless (Pszczyna), Silesia. In 1813 he published a pamphlet, *Jerubaal,* in opposition to David *Friedlaender's *Ein Wort zu seiner Zeit,* which demanded extreme reforms in the liturgy and education in response to the Prussian emancipatory edict of 1812. Although Muhr opposed the repudiation of tradition in favor of questionable changes, nevertheless he proposed that sermons in German and choir singing be allowed, and was prepared to sacrifice various customs in order to make the services more respected and meaningful. Subsequently he became an advocate of Reform and an admirer of Abraham *Geiger. He was instrumental in the building of a synagogue in Pless (1835), where he carried out his 1813 proposals. In 1836 Muhr succeeded in having a cabinet order repealed which introduced the form of address "Jew" in official transactions. He also played a role in the partial repeal of the prohibition on the use of non-Jewish names. In 1840 he was one of the leaders in the organization of a regional body of Upper Silesian Jewry, the first modern union of Jewish communities in Germany. In 1844 he proposed establishing a Jewish agricultural colony. His brother, JOSEPH (1772–1848), was leader of the Berlin community.

Bibliography: M. Brann, *Abraham Muhr, ein Lebensbild* (1918); idem, in: *Festschrift Martin Philippson* (1916), 342–69; M. Antonov, in: BZIH, no. 21 (1957), 118–24, 177; *Zur Judenfrage in Deutschland* (1844); B. Mevorach, in: *Zion*, 34 (1969), 194f.

[H.W.]

MUKACHEVO (Czech. **Mukačevo;** Hung. **Munkács**), city in Transcarpathian oblast, Ukrainian S.S.R. Until 1919 Mukachevo belonged to Hungary, then until 1938 to Czechoslovakia, and from 1938 to 1945 again to Hungary. From the end of World War II it formed part of the Soviet Union. The modest beginnings of the community are reflected in documents early in the 18th century. In Jewish sources, such as the place-formulas in divorce bills, the town is referred to as "Minkatchov, a town situated on the banks of the Latartza River and of springs." The Jewish population rapidly increased and it became one of the largest communities in Hungary, renowned on the one hand for its extreme conservatism and pronounced inclination toward Ḥasidism, and on the other for its many undertakings in the fields of Hebrew education and Zionist activities. Many documents on the beginnings of the Jewish settlement in this town have been preserved and published. According to these, Jews settled there early in the second half of the 17th century. There is also evidence of isolated Jews living in the surrounding area prior to this period. In 1711 ownership of the town was transferred to the Schoenborn family of the nobility, who authorized the growth of the Jewish population on payment of taxes and levies. Local Jews were already engaged in commerce at that time and acted as brokers in trade between Galicia and Hungary. There were also Jewish farmers and craftsmen. The population was continuously augmented by arrivals from Galicia. In 1741 a Jewish community of 80 families was organized and a synagogue established; their numbers had doubled by 1815 (165), reached 202 in 1830, and 301 by 1842. In the 1848–49 Hungarian revolt against the Austrians, 247 Jews joined the local guard. From 1851, when there was already a large yeshivah in Mukachevo, the community maintained regular records of births, deaths, and marriages. A Hebrew press was founded in 1871 and many Hebrew books were published in Mukachevo (see *Kirjath Sepher, Index to Studies, Notes and Reviews* (1967), entries, 86, 192, 193, 473).

Jewish street in Mukachevo on the Sabbath. From R. Abramovitch (ed.), *The Vanished World*, New York, 1947.

The most prominent rabbis of the community were Solomon Shapira (grandson of R. Ẓevi who had also occupied this rabbinical seat for a few years); Zevi Shapira, who succeeded his father in 1893; and Ḥayyim Eleazar Shapira, who led the community from 1913 and became known as the leading opponent of Zionism in the ḥasidic world. After his death in 1937 he was succeeded by his son-in-law, Baruch Rabinowitz, subsequently rabbi in Ḥolon, Israel (for ḥasidic dynasty, see *Shapira family). In 1891 the community numbered 5,049 (47.9% of the total population) and two additional synagogues were erected in 1895 and 1903. The Jewish population continued to grow and numbered 7,675 in 1910 (44%); 10,012 in 1921 (48%); and 11,241 (43%) in 1930 of whom 88% registered their nationality as Jewish.

Between the two world wars Jews participated actively in the administration of Mukachevo and its general political life. Despite opposition by the masses, the Zionist party of Czechoslovakia found many supporters in the town. Four Yiddish periodicals were published. Pupils of the town and its surroundings streamed to the first Hebrew elementary school, which was founded in 1920 by the Organization of Hebrew Schools in Subcarpathian Ruthenia. A Hebrew secondary school was established in 1925. This was headed from 1929 by Ḥayyim *Kugel, who became a member of the Czechoslovak parliament in 1935, and later by Eliahu Rubin. At the time of the Holocaust there were about 30 synagogues in Mukachevo. Many of these were ḥasidic *battei-midrash* and *kloyzen*.

When Mukachevo reverted to Hungarian rule in 1938, the Jews immediately suffered heavily.

Holocaust Period and After. The Jews of Mukachevo were packed into a ghetto of a few streets with extremely poor sanitary conditions and almost no food. The able-bodied were pressed into forced labor. The Jews of the vicinity (about 15,000) were concentrated in two brick factories. In April 1944 a brutal deportation *Aktion* was initiated and by May 30 the city was pronounced **judenrein*. After the war, under Soviet rule the synagogues were confiscated; the last one was converted into a warehouse in 1959. Some Jews were imprisoned for practicing *sheḥitah*. Between 1,000 and 2,000 Jews were living in Mukachevo in the late 1960s.

Bibliography: J. L. Ha-Kohen Weingarten, *Arim ve-Immahot be-Yisrael*, 1 (1946), 345–71, incl. bibl.; MHJ, 2 (1937); 3 (1937); 5 pt. 1 (1959); 5 pt. 2 (1960); 7 (1963); 8 (1965), index locorum s.v. *Munkács;* L. R. Braham, *Hungarian Jewish Studies* (1966), 223–33; A. Sas, in: *Juedisches Archiv*, 2 nos. 1–2 (1928), 1–6; 2 nos. 3–4 (1929), 33–39; 2 nos. 5–7 (1929), 33–44.

[Y.M.]

MUKDONI, A. (pseudonym of **Alexander Kappel;** 1877–1958), Yiddish essayist and theater critic. Born in Lyakhovichi, Belorussia, he began his literary career in Warsaw in 1906, specializing in theater criticism. After World War I, he edited the Kovno Yiddish daily *Nayes*. In 1922 he emigrated to the United States where he joined the Yiddish daily *Jewish Morning Journal* as literary and theater critic, serving as drama editor in the years 1923–25. In addition to four volumes of memoirs and two volumes of stories and essays, he published his best critical essays in the volume *Teater* (1927), which, with its vivid portraits of Yiddish actors and keen observations on the Yiddish theater, has considerable cultural-historical value.

Bibliography: Rejzen, Leksikon, 2 (1927), 360–4; LNYL, 5 (1963), 547–53; S. Bickel, *Shrayber fun mayn Dor* (1958), 215–21; *Mukdoni Yoyvl-Zamlbukh* (1927). [Sh.B.]

MUKẒEH (Heb. מֻקְצֶה; "set aside," "excluded"), rabbinical term for objects which it is forbidden to handle on the Sabbath or festivals. According to one authority in the Talmud, the law of *mukẓeh* is a biblical injunction derived from Exodus 16:15 (Beẓah 2b; Pes. 47b). Maimonides explains that the law is intended to emphasize the distinction between the Sabbath and festivals, and weekdays (Yad, Shabbat, 24:12).

The Talmud (Shab. 124a) enumerates several categories of *mukẓeh*, including: (1) objects, such as money and tools, whose nature renders them unfit for use on the Sabbath or festivals because of their connection with forbidden work (Sh. Ar., OḤ 308:1). Such objects may only be handled if they are needed for an act permitted on these days, such as a hammer for opening nuts (308:3); (2) objects not normally used at all (e.g., broken property, pebbles), unless a specific use had been determined for them on the eve of the Sabbath or the festival (308:7); (3) objects which were not in existence (termed *nolad*), or were inaccessible at the commencement of the Sabbath or festival. This category includes newly laid eggs (322:1), fruit fallen from a tree on the same day (322:3), and milk obtained from an animal by a non-Jew (305:20); (4) objects which at the commencement of the holy day served as a base for others which are forbidden to be handled on that day such as candlesticks or a candle tray (309:4). An object which is *mukẓeh* can only be moved if its place is needed (311:8, 15a), and if it is moved in an unusual way, if it is kicked for instance, and not moved by hand (*Be'ur Halakhah* to 266:13). In all cases, objects which were *mukẓeh* at twilight on the eve of the holy day, remain *mukẓeh* throughout the holy day.

See General laws of *Sabbath.

Bibliography: J. J. Neuwirth, *Shemirat Shabbat ke-Hilkhetah* (1965), 128–52. [Ed.]

MULBERRY (Heb. תּוּת, *tut*). Two species of mulberry grow in Israel: the black, *Morus nigra*, and the white, *Morus alba*. The latter is a comparative newcomer to the region, the ancient sources referring only to the former. The mulberry seems to have originated in Persia from where it was transferred to the Middle East. There is evidence that it was growing in Greece in the sixth century B.C.E. In Aramaic literature it is first mentioned in the Book of *Ahikar, which was discovered among *Elephantine papyri, where it says: "My son, be not in a hurry, like the almond tree whose blossom is the first to appear, but whose fruit is the last to be eaten; but be equal and sensible, like the mulberry tree whose blossom is the last to appear, but whose fruit is the first to be eaten" (Ahikar, Syriac Version A, 2:7). According to the Talmud the fruit of the mulberry ripens 52 days after the flowering (Bek. 8a). In I Maccabees 6:34 it is related that the elephants brought by the Syrians were incited to battle with the juice of grapes and mulberries. The staining of the hands by the juice is referred to by the rabbis in their parable of the dialogue between God and Cain, who pleaded "Am I my brother's keeper?" (Gen. 4:9): "This may be compared to one who stole mulberries and, on beng caught by the owner, pleaded his innocence. The owner replied: 'But your hands are stained.' Thus said the Holy One, blessed be He, to Cain: 'Thy brother's blood crieth unto Me' " (Gen. R. 22:9). The mulberry initially is white, then reddens and finally becomes black (see Ma'as. 1:2). It is a large, long-living tree. Until a generation ago an old mulberry tree used to be shown in Jerusalem near the Pool of Siloam about which there was a legend (mentioned in a travel book of 1575) that Isaiah hid in the hollow of its trunk when pursued by Manasseh. Apparently the town Bertotha (Or. 1:4; et al.) takes its name from the mulberry. The white mulberry, the leaves of which are used for feeding silkworms, originated in China and was brought to Ereẓ Israel at a late date. Joseph *Nasi planted extensive orchards of them in Tiberias in 1565 with the intention of developing a silk industry. This venture, however, failed. Another effort was made in Petaḥ Tikvah by the Ḥovevei Zion, who in 1891 planted 576 dunams (144 acres) with mulberry trees, but this venture also failed. Nowadays the tree is grown in gardens for its beauty and for the shade it gives. There is no basis for the Authorized Version's rendering of *bekha'im* in II Samuel 5:23 and I Chronicles 14:14, as mulberry trees (see *Mastic).

Bibliography: Joseph ha-Kohen, *Emek ha-Bakha* (1852), 129; Loew, Flora, 1 (1928), 266–74; H. N. and A. L. Moldenke, *Plants of the Bible* (1952), 140f.; M. Zohary, *Olam ha-Ẓemaḥim* (1954), 192f. [J.F.]

MULDER, SAMUEL ISRAEL (1792–1862), educator and Hebrew author, born in Amsterdam. He was a pupil of David *Friedrichsfeld and, influenced by him, became a follower of *Mendelssohn and *Wessely. As a youth he signed himself "Salomon" or "Schrijver" [= "writer"]

Detail of a lithograph of Samuel Israel Mulder, Dutch communal leader and educator, by M. Calish, 1860. Amsterdam, Municipal Archives.

receiving the surname Mulder only in 1811. In 1818 he became an official court translator, and in 1826 was appointed principal of the *bet ha-midrash*, the seminary for rabbis and teachers in Amsterdam. From 1835 he served as the superintendent of all Jewish religious schools in Holland, and from 1849 was secretary of the Amsterdam community. Mulder translated into Dutch a large part of the Bible (1827–38), the Passover *Haggadah* (1837), and the liturgy. He also published a Bible for Jewish youth in 17 parts (1850–55) in Dutch, and a Hebrew-Dutch Dictionary (1831; with M. *Lemans). Some of his writings in Dutch are collected in his *Verspreide Lettervruchten* (1844). In his youth, Mulder helped to found the Tongeleth (To'elet) circle (a Haskalah society) in Amsterdam in 1815; he was also active as a writer in Hebrew. He published in 1817 the *Kiẓẓur Rishumei ha-Asefot*, a summary of the minutes of meetings held in the first year of the society's existence, and contributed to its publication.

Bibliography: Ḥ. N. Shapira, *Toledot ha-Sifrut ha-Ivrit ha-Ḥadashah*, 1 (1940), 555–64; E. B. Asscher, *Levensschets van Samuel Israël Mulder* (1863); Boas, in: *Amstelodamum*, 52 (1965), 126–35; Fuerst, Bibliotheca, 2 (1863), 404–5; Zeitlin, Bibliotheca, 246–7; I. Maarsen, *Tongeleth* (Dutch, 1925). [Y.A.K.]

MULE (Heb. פֶּרֶד), the offspring of a he-ass and a mare. Although a Jew is prohibited from producing such hybrids, their use is permitted (Tosef., Kil. 5:6 cites an individual view prohibiting it). Since there were different strains of horses and asses in Ereẓ Israel the mules were also of different strains. The mule is a powerful, submissive animal, particularly suitable for riding and transporting goods in the mountainous regions of Ereẓ Israel, and hence was commonly used. Nor was riding on it regarded as inferior to riding on a horse; Solomon, on the occasion of his proclamation as king, was made to ride "upon king David's mule" (I Kings 1:38), while Absalom met his death when riding on a mule (II Sam. 18:9). Ezekiel (27:14) speaks in praise of the mules of Togarmah (Turkey?). The Talmud mentions white mules as being dangerous and some sages were indignant with Judah ha-Nasi for harboring them (Ḥul. 7b). That the mule is sometimes dangerous, is sterile, and the female barren were regarded as proof that man is prohibited from interfering with the work of creation. Rabban *Simeon b. Gamaliel maintained that the first to cross a horse with an ass in order to produce a mule, thereby committing an unworthy act, was "Anah who discovered the *yemim*" (Gen. 36:24), which he explained as meaning mules. On the other hand, R. Yose held that on the termination of the first Sabbath after the Creation one of the two things which Adam did was "to cross two animals, and from them came forth the mule." He contended that thereby Adam performed an action "of a kind similar to that of Heaven," that is, he created something new, to become, as it were, a partner with the Creator in the work of creation (Pes. 54a; cf. TJ, Ber. 8:6, 12b). Some also crossbred a stallion and a she-ass, and the Talmud gives the characteristics of the two types of mule: if its ears are short, it is the offspring of a mare and a he-ass, if large, of a she-ass and a stallion (TJ, Kil. 7:3, 31c).

Bibliography: Lewysohn, Zool, 144–6, nos. 168, 169; S. Lieberman, *Tosefta ki-Feshutah,* 1 (1955), 99; F. S. Bodenheimer, *Animal and Man in Bible Lands* (1960), passim; J. Feliks, *Kilei Zera'im ve-Harkavah* (1967), 128–9.

[J.F.]

MULHOUSE (Muelhausen), city in *Alsace, in the Haut-Rhin department, France. The earliest documentation of the presence of Jews in Mulhouse dates from 1290, when one Salman was victim of a persecution. The existence of a synagogue is confirmed from 1311. The Jews of Mulhouse suffered during the *Armleder riots in January 1338, and again during the outbreaks accompanying the *Black Death (1349). By 1385, however, there were once more Jews living in Mulhouse. At the beginning of the 15th century, several Jews who had arrived from other places in Alsace were granted the freedom of the city. The nine families who were there in 1418 owned houses, engaged in moneylending, and traded in livestock. Although there was no expulsion, no Jews lived in the city between 1512 and 1655. At the beginning of the 18th century, when they were still insignificant in number, their trade flourished to the extent of arousing the jealousy of the Christian merchants, who demanded that their rights be restricted. In 1784 there were 23 Jewish families (94 persons) in the city. As it was free from the anti-Jewish riots which broke out throughout Alsace in 1789, Mulhouse became a refuge for many Jews from the surrounding district. The synagogue, built in 1822, soon proved to be too small and was replaced by a larger one in 1849. A cemetery was purchased in 1831, and the community established several other institutions, including a vocational school in 1842, and an almshouse-hospital in 1863. Two periodicals catering for all the Jews of Alsace and even beyond were published during the second half of the 19th century. From about 5,000 in 1900 the community declined to around 3,000 in 1921, remaining stable until just before World War II. Jacob *Kaplan, later chief rabbi of France, held office in Mulhouse in 1922. [B.BL.]

Holocaust and Contemporary Periods. Under German occupation in World War II the Jews who had not managed to escape were expelled on July 16, 1940, along with the Jews in the rest of Alsace and Moselle. The synagogue, which had been partially damaged, was saved from total destruction when the edifice was requisitioned by the municipal theater. In 1970 Mulhouse had 1,800 Jewish inhabitants and a well-organized and active Jewish community.

[G.LE.]

Bibliography: Germ Jud, 2 pt. 2 (1968), 554–5; E. Meininger, *Histoire de Mulhouse* (1923), 25–26 and passim; Z. Ginsburger, in: *Univers Israélite,* 54 (1898/99), 440–3; G. Wolf, in: ZGJD, 3 (1889), 182–4; S. Adler, *Geschichte der Juden in Muelhausen* (1914); M. Moeder, *Institutions de Mulhouse* (1951), 39; L. G. Werner, *Topographie historique* (1949), passim; Z. Szajkowski, *Analytical Franco-Jewish Gazetteer 1939–1945* (1966), 251.

MULISCH, HARRY (1927–), Dutch author. Born in Haarlem, Mulisch was of mixed descent, his father being a non-Jewish Czech banker, his mother a Dutch Jew. Widely recognized as one of Holland's most original modern writers, Mulisch published novels, short stories, and other prose works notable for their imaginative use of mythological, occult, and philosophical material to explore the existential problems of contemporary society. His earlier works include the novels *Archibald Strohalm* (1952), *De diamant* ("The Diamond," 1954), and *Het zwarte licht* ("The Black Light," 1956); and *Tanchelijn* (1960), a play about a 12th-century heretic. Two of Mulisch's later works were *Wenken voor de jongste dag* ("Suggestions for the Day of Judgment," 1967), which combined thoughts and anecdotes about death, an essay on Japan, and a dramatic account of a session of the United Nations after the Arab-Israel Six-Day War; and *Bericht aan de rattenkoning* ("Report to the King of the Rats," 1967[2]), on Amsterdam's young militant demonstrators, the "Provos." Mulisch, who was on the staff of *De Gids* and *Randstad,* visited Israel in 1961 to cover the *Eichmann trial, which inspired *De zaak 40/61* ("Case 40/61," 1961). Two other works on Jewish themes were the novel *Het stenen bruidsbed* ("The Stone Bridal Bed," 1959), and the autobiographical *Voer voor psychologen* ("Food for Psychologists," 1961). [G.A.-T.]

MULLER, HERMAN JOSEPH (1890–1967), U.S. geneticist and Nobel Prize winner. He was born in New York City, and after teaching at Columbia and the University of Texas went to Berlin (1932–33) on a Guggenheim Foundation fellowship. Having communist leanings, he moved to the Soviet Union (1933–37) where he

Hermann Joseph Muller, U.S. geneticist and Nobel Prize winner. Courtesy Israel Medical Association, Jerusalem.

served as senior geneticist at the U.S.S.R. Academy of Sciences. After breaking with communist philosophy he spent three years at Edinburgh University and then returned to the United States in 1940 to teach at Amherst College. In 1945 he moved to Indiana University, becoming Distinguished Service Professor in 1953. The central theme of his work has been the nature and significance of changes in the relatively stable gene material of the chromosome.

Muller is best known for his demonstration in 1926 that X-rays induce mutations, an achievement for which he received a Nobel Prize in Physiology and Medicine in 1946. His earlier contributions were concerned with the design of techniques for quantitatively determining the frequencies of gene mutations, and he was among the first to recognize that these mutations constitute the basis for evolutionary change in populations. His collaborative efforts with others in Thomas Hunt Morgan's laboratory at Columbia established the association between chromosome duplication and genetic defect. He speculated on the course of human evolution based upon the genetic principles which he helped to establish, with his classical work on the fruit fly, and long championed the establishment of a human sperm bank. He also called attention to the extreme danger to genetic material inherent in atomic activity.

Muller was the recipient of many honors. He published many works and was coauthor of *The Mechanism of Mendelian Heredity* (1915) and *Genetics, Medicine and Man* (1947). He also wrote *Out of the Night, a Biologist's View of the Future* (1935) and *Studies in Genetics* (1962).

Bibliography: Carlson, in: *Canadian Journal of Genetics and Cytology*, 9 (1967), 437–48, includes bibliography; T. N. Levitan, *Laureates: Jewish Winners of the Nobel Prize* (1960), 156–60; L. G. Grenfell, *Nobel Prize Winners in Medicine and Physiology, 1901–1950* (1953), 238–43. [G.H.F.]

MULT ÉS JÖVŐ (Hung. "Past and Future"), a literary and artistic monthly journal in the Hungarian language which appeared from 1911 to 1944. Its founder was the writer József *Patai, who edited it until 1939 and made it one of the foremost Jewish illustrated periodicals. It maintained a high standard in both its literary and pictorial content and attracted contributions by Jewish scholars from many parts of the world. It stimulated the Jewish revivalist movement in Hungary and established links between Hungarian and other Jewries. The journal was banned in 1944 at the time of the German invasion. [B.Y.]

MULŪK AL-ṬAWĀ'IF (Sp. **reyes de taifas;** "petty dynasties"), petty kingdoms which came to power in Spain during the 11th century after the fall of the *Umayyad caliphate in *Cordoba. With the Umayyad caliphate's disintegration, Berber, Arab, and slave dynasties took over various cities and their environs, spending much of the century in rivalry and warfare. The major dynasties and their centers were: the Banū Jawhar of Cordoba, Banū Ḥud of *Saragossa, Banū Zīrī (see *Zirids) of *Granada, and Banū ʿAbbād of *Seville.

The petty kingdoms employed Jews at their courts in various diplomatic and official positions and utilized their skills as translators and administrators. Jews were trusted in particular by Berber princes who feared Arab ambitions. Noteworthy are *Samuel ha-Nagid and his ill-fated son *Joseph (d. 1066) who served as viziers of Granada (the former as commander in chief of the army as well) under the kings Ḥabbūs and Bādis during the first half of the 11th century. Other courtiers include members of the Ibn *Muhājir, Ibn Migash, and Ibn Albalia families who served the Abbasids of Seville; Jekuthiel (d. 1039) was a high official, talmudist, and community leader in Saragossa, whose Jewish population greatly increased during this period. Saragossa and *Lucena, "the Jewish city," were major centers of scholarship. The rise of Jews to high positions resulted in the efflorescence of a genre new to Hebrew poetry, the praises of the courtiers who created the life style and ideals of Jewish society (see *Spain). The rise and fall of Jewish officials at court corresponded to that of the cultural achievements in the city where they served. As the Spanish Muslims had long ceased to obey Baghdad, the Jewish communities gradually came to rely mainly on their own leadership, slowly ending the hegemony of the Babylonian yeshivot (this process began under the Umayyads). The end of the petty kingdoms was marked by their request for Almoravide aid against the encroaching Christian reconquest at the end of the 11th century. The Almoravide ruler Yūsuf ibn Tāshifīn eventually took over Granada and other capitals of the mulūk al-ṭawā'if. The Almoravide capital was Seville. While the Almoravides at first removed some Jews from office, they were reinstated shortly afterward.

Bibliography: Ibn Daud, Tradition, xvii–xxiv, 71–103; Ashtor, Korot, 2 (1966), 14–25, 44f. and passim; P. Hitti, *History of the Arabs* (1960), 537–41; A. Prieto y Vives, *Reyes de Taifas* (1926), 1–88; EIS, s. v. [ED.]

MUNI, PAUL (**Muni Weisenfreund;** 1895–1967), U.S. actor. He started acting at the age of 12 in Chicago. Maurice *Schwartz recognized his talent and persuaded him to join his new Yiddish-speaking Jewish Art Theater in 1918. Muni got his first real opportunity in an English role on Broadway in *We Americans* in 1926 and his success was immediate. He had a rich voice, good command of mime and facial expression, and a capacity for varied characterization. He played his first gangster in *Four Walls*, went to Hollywood and was acknowledged a star for his work in *The Valiants* (1929). *Scarface* established his reputation and *I am a Fugitive from a Chain Gang* seemed to confirm him as

Paul Muni (front right) with his wife, Bella Finkle, and the mayor of Tel Aviv, Israel Rokach, 1938. Courtesy Keren Hayesod, United Israel Appeal, Jerusalem.

a player of "tough" roles. However, he resisted typecasting and starred in *The Story of Louis Pasteur* (1935), which won him a Motion Picture Academy award, *The Good Earth* (1936), *The Life of Emile Zola* (1937), and *Juarez* (1939). These roles expressed his true stature as an interpreter of heroism in spirit rather than in violence. Muni continued to appear in Broadway plays, including Elmer Rice's *Counsel-or-at-Law* (1931–33), Maxwell Anderson's *Key Largo* (1939), and in *Inherit the Wind* (1955). He also acted in the London run of *Death of a Salesman* and played his last film role in *The Last Angry Man.* [ED.]

MUNICH (sometimes called in Hebrew **עיר הכמרים**), capital of *Bavaria, S. West Germany. In 1229 a Jew called Abraham, from Munich, appeared as a witness at a Regensburg trial. In the second half of the 13th century Munich appears to have had a sizable Jewish community; the Jews lived in their own quarter and possessed a synagogue, a ritual bath, and a hospital. On Oct. 12, 1285, in the wake of a *blood libel, 180 Jews who had sought refuge in the synagogue were burnt to death; the names of 68 of the victims are listed in the Nuremberg **Memorbuch,* which dates from 1296. The Jews obtained permission to rebuild the synagogue in 1287, but for several centuries they remained few in number and suffered from various restrictions, which from time to time were further exacerbated (e.g., in 1315 and 1347). During the *Black Death (1348/49) the community was again annihilated. However, by 1369 there were Jews in the city once more and in 1375 Duke Frederick of Bavaria granted them (and the other Jews resident in Upper Bavaria) the privilege of paying customs duties at the same rate as non-Jews. Some years later the Jews planned the construction of a synagogue and a **hekdesh,* but their plans do not seem to have been realized. The remission of debts owed to Jews ordained by Emperor Wenceslaus (1378–1400) resulted in Munich Jews losing all their assets. They also suffered severely in 1413, when they were accused of desecration of the *Host. In 1416 the small community was granted some privileges, including permission to acquire a lot for a cemetery; in 1432, when Duke Albert III sought to impose a special tax on Munich Jews the results were disappointing. The clergy succeeded in having all the Jews of Upper Bavaria expelled in 1442, and eight years later they were also driven out of Lower Bavaria, where they had taken temporary refuge. Duke Albert gave the Munich synagogue (in the modern Gruftgasse) to Johann Hartlieb, a physician, and it was subsequently converted into a church. For almost three centuries Jews were excluded from Munich and Bavaria (although there may have been some periods when their residence was permitted, as may be deduced from a renewal of the ban announced in a 1553 police ordinance).

During the Austrian occupation, Jews were readmitted to Bavaria and some of them presumably found their way to Munich. At any rate, a new decree issued on March 22, 1715, again ordered them to leave the country. Some ten years later, a few Jews who had business dealings with the Bavarian count began to settle in Munich and by 1728 several Jews resided in the city. In 1729 (or 1734) the Court Jew, Wolf *Wertheimer, took up residence there and was joined by his family in 1742; in 1750 all Court Jews and Jews in possession of passes granting them freedom of movement were excepted from the general ban on Jewish entry into the city. A community was formed by Jews who maintained connections with the court. Of the 20 of them in 1750, there was only one woman and a single child, which attests to the temporary and migratory nature of the settlement. Except for these **Schutzjuden,* the only Jews permitted to reside in the city were those who had been

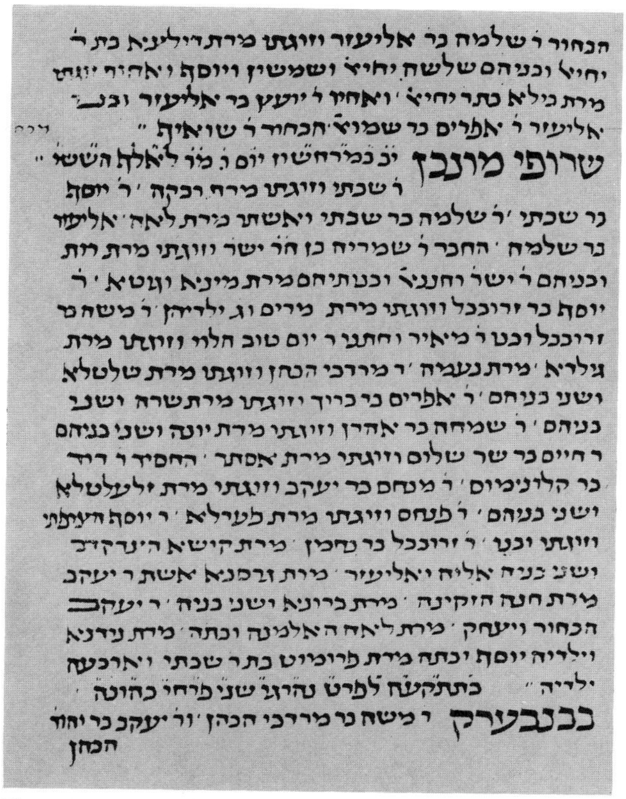
הבחור ר׳ שלמה בר אליעזר וזוגתו מרת דיליינא בת ר׳
יחיאל ובניהם שלשה יחיאל ושמשון ויוסף ואחיה זוגתו
מרת גילא בת ר׳ יחיאל ואחיו ר׳ יועץ בר אליעזר ובנו
אליעזר ר׳ אפרים בר שמואל הבחור ר׳ שואיל
שרופי מונכן י״ב במרחשון יום ו׳ מ״ו לאלף הששי
ר׳ שבתי וזוגתו מרת רבקה ר׳ יוסף
בר שבתי ר׳ שלמה בר שבתי ואשתו מרת לאה אליעזר
בר שלמה החבר ר׳ שמריה בן הר׳ ישר וזוגתו מרת רות
ובניהם ר׳ ישר וחנוך ובנותיהם מרת מינא ועטא ר׳
יוסף בר זרובבל וזוגתו מרת מרים וג׳ ילדיהן ר׳ משה בר
זרובבל ובנו ר׳ מאיר וחתנו ר׳ יום טוב הלוי וזוגתו מרת
גלריא מרת נעמיה ר׳ מרדכי הכהן וזוגתו מרת שלטלא
ושני בניהם ר׳ אפרים בר ברוך וזוגתו מרת שרה ושני
בניהם ר׳ שמחה בר אהרן וזוגתו מרת יונה ושני בניהם
ר׳ חיים בר שר שלום וזוגתו מרת אסתר החסיד ר׳ דוד
בר קלונימוס ר׳ מנחם בר יעקב וזוגתו מרת ילעלטלא
ושני בניהם ר׳ פנחס וזוגתו מרת לעריא ר׳ יוסף היעלתי
וזוגתו ובנו ר׳ זרובבל בר נחמן מרת קישא היערקידי
ושני בניה אליה ואליעזר מרת זרבנא אשת ר׳ יעקב
מרת חנה הזקינה מרת ברינא ושני בניה ר׳ יעקב
הבחור ויצחק מרת לאה האלמנה ובתה מרת עדנא
וילדיה יוסף ובתה מרת פרומיט בת ר׳ שבתי וארבעה
ילדיה כתתקעה לפרט נהרגו שני פרחי כהונה
בבנבערק ר׳ משה בר מרדכי הכהן ור׳ יעקב בר יהוד
הכהן

Figure 1. Page recording the Munich martyrs of 1285, from the Nuremberg *Memorbuch.* From H. Lamm, *Von Juden in Muenchen,* Munich, 1953.

commissioned as purveyors or who had made loans to the state; all others were permitted to stay in the city for a short while only and had to pay a substantial body tax (**Leibzoll*). This situation continued for most of the 18th century and it was not until 1794 and 1798 that the number of women and children in the city was commensurate with the number of heads of families. In 1794 there were 153 Jews, including 27 heads of families, 28 women, and 70 children; in 1798 the respective figures were 35, 33, and 98. Up to the end of the 18th century, Jewish women had to go to Kriegshaber to give birth to their children, and it was not until 1816 that Jews were permitted to bury their dead in Munich rather than transport them to Kriegshaber for burial. At this time Munich Jews gained their livelihood as *contractors for the army and the royal mint (see *mintmasters), merchants dealing in luxury wares and *livestock, moneylenders, and *peddlers. Since there was no legal basis for their residence in Munich, they did not have the right to practice their religion, and every year they had to pay a special tax to enable them to observe Sukkot. In 1805 a "Regulation for Munich Jewry" was issued (it formed the basis for the Bavarian *Judenmatrikel* of 1813); among other privileges, the Jews were permitted to inherit the right of domicile, to conduct services, and to reside in all parts of the city.

During the Napoleonic Wars, the number of Jews was augmented by immigrants, and by 1814 there were 451 Jews in the city. Two years later, the Jewish community was formally organized. In the same year the community was given permission to establish a cemetery and in 1824 a permit was issued for the construction of a synagogue (dedicated in 1827). The first Jewish religious school was founded in 1815 and a private one in 1817. The community played a leading part in Bavarian Jewry's struggle for civil rights, which lasted up to the founding of the German Reich (1871); delegates of the Bavarian communities frequently met in Munich (1819, 1821) to make common

Figure 2. The Ohel Yakob Synagogue of Munich, after its destruction on *Kristallnacht*, 1938. Courtesy Munich Municipality.

representations to the government. In the second half of the century the community grew further (from 842 in 1848 to 4,144 in 1880, and 8,739 in 1900), as a result of increased immigration from the smaller communities (especially in the last few decades of the 19th century). By 1910 20% of Bavarian Jews lived in the capital (11,000). There was also a steady immigration of Jews from Eastern Europe, mainly from Galicia, which lasted up to World War I.

Jews were prominent in the cultural life of Munich, a center of German arts, in the late 19th and 20th centuries, as well as being more equally represented in Bavarian political affairs than in other German states. After World War I a revolutionary government on the Soviet model was formed, in which Kurt *Eisner, Eugene *Levine, and Gustav *Landauer were prominent. It was routed by counterrevolutionary forces and a "White Terror" against Communists, Socialists, and Jews was instigated. In the postwar years of economic and political upheaval, Munich was a hotbed of anti-Semitic activity and the cradle of the *Nazi party; many Jews from Eastern Europe were forced to leave Munich. Sporadic anti-Semitic outbursts characterized the years till the Nazi seizure of power in 1933, when Reinhold *Heydrich and Heinrich *Himmler took control of the police; the first concentration camp, *Dachau, was erected near Munich. At the time the community numbered 10,000 persons, including an independent Orthodox community, and many cultural, social, and charitable organizations. Munich Jewry was subjected to particularly vicious and continuous acts of desecration, discrimination, terror and *boycotts, but responded with a Jewish cultural and religious revival. Between 1933 and May 15, 1938, 3,574 Jews left Munich. On July 8, 1938, the main synagogue was torn down on Hitler's express orders. During the *Kristallnacht* two synagogues were burned down, 1,000 male Jews were arrested and interned in Dachau, and one was murdered. The communal center was completely ransacked. During the war a total of 4,500 Jews were deported from Munich (3,000 of them to *Theresienstadt); only about 300 returned; 160 managed to outlive the war in Munich. A new community was founded in 1945 by former concentration camp inmates, refugees, displaced persons, and local Jews. In the following five years about 120,000 Jews, refugees, and displaced persons passed through Munich on their way to Israel. The community increased from 1,800 persons in 1952 to 3,522 in January 1970 (70% of Bavarian Jewry). In 1966 a Jewish elementary school was opened, the second in Gemany, but the postwar community was repeatedly troubled by acts of desecration and vandalism (against synagogue and cemetery). In March 1970 the Jewish home for the aged was burned down and seven people lost their lives. The Munich library contains a particularly valuable collection of Hebrew manuscripts.

Bibliography: L. Baerwald, in: *Festgabe 50 Jahre Hauptsynagoge Muenchen* (1937), 11–16; H. Lamm (ed.), *Von Juden in Muenchen* (1958); idem, in: ZGJD, 8 (1938), 99–103; Germ Jud, 1 (1963), 237f.; 2 (1968), 556–8; P. Hauke, *Zur Geschichte der Juden in Muenchen zwischen 1933 und 1945* (1968); W. J. Cahnmann, in: JSOS, 3 (1941), 283–300; idem, in: ZGJD, 7 (1937), 180–8; idem, in: HJ, 3 (1941), 7–23; A. Cohen, in: *Zeitschrift fuer Demographie und Statistik der Juden*, 15 (1919), 8–12, 121–30; idem, in: ZGJD, 2 (1931), 262–83; J. Segall, *Die Entwicklung der juedischen Bevoelkerung in Muenchen 1875–1905* (1910); P. Weiner-Odenheimer, in: *Zeitschrift fuer Demographie und Statistik der Juden*, 11 (1915), 85–96; 12 (1916), 34–43; H. Schnee, *Die Hoffinanz und der moderne Staat*, 4 (1963), 187ff.; L. Prijs, in: BLBI, 6 (1963), 67–80.
[Ed.]

MUNK, family of rabbis. Ezra (1867–1940), an Orthodox rabbi in Germany, was the son of Elias Munk, *dayyan* at Altona. He studied at the Berlin Rabbinical Seminary under his uncle Azriel (Israel) *Hildesheimer and at the Universities of Berlin and Koenigsberg. In 1897, when he was rabbi at Koenigsberg (an office he held from 1893 to 1900), his congregation seceded from the general community. In 1900 he succeeded Hildesheimer as rabbi of the Adass Yisroel congregation in Berlin. Munk acted as Orthodox adviser to the Prussian Ministry of Education and Religious Affairs, where he enjoyed great confidence. He expanded the office for **shehitah* affairs, founded by Hirsch *Hildesheimer in 1907, making it the international center for the defense of *shehitah*. Cofounder of the B.J.A. (Bund Juedischer Akademiker), the association of Orthodox students in German universities, and of the Union of Orthodox Congregations (the so-called Halberstaedter Verband), he was also chairman of the "Association of Traditional Torah-True Rabbis" and a member of the rabbinical council of the German *Agudat Israel. Among his publications are: *Gefaelschte Talmudzitate* (1924) and *Entwicklung der Verhaeltnisse der preussischen Synagogengemeinden* ... (1931). Some of his responsa (*Kahana Messayye'a Kahana*) were published by S. Z. Klein (1938). In 1938 Munk left Germany for Jerusalem, where he died. Among his sons were Eli (1899), rabbi of the Golders Green Beth Hamidrash, London, and Michael (1905), educator in the U.S., author of *Ezra ha-Sofer* (1933) and coauthor (with I. Lewin and J. Berman) of *Religious Freedom: the Right to Practice Shehitah* (1946).

Leo (1851–1917), Ezra's brother, was district rabbi at Marburg (Hesse) from 1876. He took an active part in the work of the *Deutsch-Israelitischer Gemeindebund, the *Hilfsverein der deutschen Juden, and the rabbinical associations, both general and Orthodox. Among his publications was a scholarly edition of *Targum Sheni* on Esther (1876). Elie (b. 1900), Ezra's nephew, a rabbi and writer, was district rabbi of Ansbach (Bavaria) from 1926, and from 1937 was rabbi of the Communauté Israélite de la Stricte Observance in Paris. His published works include: *Die Welt der Gebete* (2 vols. (1938); Eng., *The World of Prayer*, 2 vols., 1954–63), a commentary on the *siddur; Das Licht der Ewigkeit* (1935); *La justice sociale en Israel* (1947); *Rachel* (on the duties of Jewish women; 1951[5]); and a translation into French of Rashi's Pentateuch commentary (1957).

Bibliography: H. Seidman, in: L. Jung (ed.), *Guardians of our Heritage* (1958), 551ff.; A. Hildesheimer, in: M. Sinasohn (ed.), *Adass Jisroel Berlin* (1966), 72–83; J. Rothschild (ed.), *Leo Munk Gedenkbuch* (1918).
[Ed.]

MUNK, HERMANN (1839–1912), German physiologist; a pioneer in the field of cerebral physiology. Munk was a director of the physiological laboratory of the Veterinary School in Berlin and a member of the German Academy of Science. He studied the localization centers in the brain and his name is associated with the so-called visual sphere of the cerebrum. He also did research on the function of the thyroid gland and studied the mechanism of motion. His younger brother IMMANUEL MUNK (1852–1900), was also a physiologist. He was his brother's assistant and then taught at the Physiological Institute of Berlin University (professor from 1899).

Munk and Nathan Zuntz did research in the field of metabolism and nutrition, with particular emphasis on the function of the kidneys. He wrote *Physiologie des Menschen und der Saeugetiere* (1881) and co-edited *Zentralblatt fuer die Medizinischen Wissenschaften.*

Bibliography: S. R. Kagan, *Jewish Medicine* (1952), 163f., 168f.; *Biographisches Lexikon der hervorragenden Aerzte,* 2 (1933).

[S.M.]

°**MUNK, KAJ** (pseudonym of **Harald Leininger;** 1898–1944), Danish pastor and playwright. He showed an unusual interest in Jewish themes and his anti-Nazi writings and sermons had an incalculable effect on the Danish resistance movement during World War II. Perhaps the most influential, and certainly the most controversial, Danish playwright of his time, Munk lived—and died—for his ideals. At first he showed some sympathy for ultranationalism, betraying a certain preoccupation with the "strong men" of history. *En idealist* ("An Idealist," 1928) was a study of Herod the Great; *De udvalgte* ("The Chosen One," 1933) dealt with King David; and *Sejren* ("The Victory," 1936) was based on Mussolini's invasion of Ethiopia. Munk was, however, outraged by what he saw during a visit to Berlin in 1938, and his drama *Han sidder ved smedltediglen* (*He sits at the Melting Pot,* 1938) attacked Hitler's persecution of the Jews. Two other works by Munk which appeared in the 1930s were *Vedersø Jerusalem retur* (1934), an account of the author's journey to the Holy Land among other places; and *Os bærer den himmelske glæde* ("Heavenly Joy Bears Us," 1934), a collection of verse containing impressions of Palestine. After Denmark was overrun by the Germans, Kaj Munk came to be regarded, by Danes and Germans alike, as one of the leading spokesmen of the Danish resistance. His play *Niels Ebbesen* (1942), which deals with the Nazi occupation, was suppressed but nevertheless enjoyed a clandestine circulation. He was murdered by the Nazis.

Bibliography: R. P. Keigwin, *Kaj Munk, Playwright, Priest and Patriot* (1944); P. M. Mitchell, *History of Danish Literature* (1957), 258–62.

[ED.]

MUNK, SOLOMON (1803–1867), French orientalist. Born in Glogau, Silesia, Munk studied at the universities of Bonn and Berlin. Realizing that as a Jew he had no academic future in Germany, he left for Paris in 1828. Here he first

Solomon Munk, French orientalist. Jerusalem, J.N.U.L., Schwadron Collection.

worked as a tutor in the Rothschild family, but was soon engaged by the *Bibliothèque Nationale* and put in charge of Semitic manuscripts. His assiduous work with them led to his becoming totally blind by 1850, but it did not prevent 17 more years of fruitful scholarly activity. Before then (1840) he joined the Montefiore-Crémieux delegation to Egypt—as the latter's secretary and interpreter—which was to intervene in the *Damascus affair. When the Egyptian khedive Muhammad Ali at last agreed to issue an order to Damascus to set the falsely accused free, Munk—though some say it was L. Loewe, Montefiore's secretary—detected in the Arabic draft the word "mercy" to be granted, which at the insistence of Crémieux was changed into "freedom and peace." Crémieux and Munk used the opportunity of their visit to persuade Egyptian Jewry to modernize their school system and to bring about a rapprochement between Rabbanites and Karaites. Munk also acquired valuable manuscripts, particularly Karaitica, for the Bibliothèque Nationale. Back in Paris Munk joined the *Consistoire Central* and was elected a member of the *Académie des Inscriptions et des Belles Lettres.* In 1864 he succeeded E. *Renan as professor of Hebrew and Syriac literature at the College de France.

Munk devoted himself to the study of the Hebrew and Arabic literature of the Golden Age of Spain. It was Munk who discovered that the author of the philosophical work *Fons Vitae,* which had been preserved only in a Latin translation from the Arabic original, and whose author, called Avicebron, was believed to have been either a Muslim or an Arab Christian, was none other than the 11th-century Hebrew poet Solomon ibn *Gabirol. He discovered a manuscript of Shem Tov ibn *Falaquera's Hebrew translation of excerpts from Gabirol's original and identified this with passages in the Latin version (in his *Mélanges de philosophie juive et arabe* (1857–59; text, translation with an extensive essay on Gabirol, his writings, and philosophy). The crowning work of Munk's life was his three-volume edition of the original Arabic text (in Hebrew characters) of Maimonides' *Guide of the Perplexed* from Paris, Oxford, and Leyden manuscripts with a French translation *(Guide des Egarés)* and extensive notes (1856–66; Arabic text re-edited by B. J. Joel, 1960). All subsequent translations are based on this classic edition.

Bibliography: G. A. Kohut, *Solomon Munk* (Eng., 1902); M. Schwab, *Salomon Munk* (1900); A. Jellinek, *Salomon Munk* (Ger., 1865); H. S. Morais, *Eminent Israelites* (1880), 247–52; P. Immanuel, in: S. Federbush (ed.), *Ḥokhmat Yisrael be-Eiropah* (1965), 239–41; M. Brann, in: JJGL, 2 (1899), 148–203 (44 letters of Munk).

[ED.]

MUNKÁCSI, BERNÁT (Bernhard; 1860–1937), Hungarian philologist and ethnographer. Born in Nagyvárad (now Oradea, Rumania), into a family of rabbis, as a student in Budapest he came under the influence of several distinguished specialists in Hungarian studies (including Arminius *Vámbéry) and decided to dedicate himself to Hungarian linguistics and ethnography. He and a fellow student undertook a journey, collecting linguistic and other data on the Sereth (Siret) and Moldavo areas. Additional scientific trips were made from 1885 to study the language of the Votyak and Chuvash in the Kama and Middle Volga regions. With grants from the Hungarian Academy of Sciences and the Russian government he made ethnographic tours of the northern parts of the Urals. After 1893 he served as editor of *Ethnographia,* and in 1900 he was cofounder of a philological journal *Keleti Szemle, Revue orientale des études oural-altaïques* (1900–32), to which he contributed numerous studies on Magyar culture, linguistics, and history. During World War I he carried out linguistic research in Ossetic by interrogating Russian prisoners of war who spoke this Iranian language of the Caucasus.

From 1890 to 1930 he served as an inspector of religious instruction in the Jewish schools of Budapest. As a professional teacher he helped raise the level of existing schools, specifically the Jewish ones in Pest which he had helped to found. He prepared a program of studies for teachers, evolved a series of tests, and edited textbooks published by the Jewish community. Munkácsi's *Volksbraeuche und Volksdichtungen der Wotjaken* was edited by D. R. Fuchs and posthumously published in 1952.

Bibliography: N. Munkácsi, *Egy nagy magyar nyelvész* (1943); D. Fokos, in: *Munkácsi Bernát* ... (1930), 140–6 (incl. bibl.); UJE, 8 (1942), 39–40; *Magyar Zsidó Lexikon* (1929), 620–1. [E.F.]

MUNKÁCSI, ERNÖ (1896–1950), Hungarian jurist and art writer. Born in Páncélcseh, then Hungary, the son of Bernát *Munkácsi, he entered public service in Budapest in 1921 and was the secretary of the Neolog community. In 1923 he became legal adviser and served as chief secretary from 1942 until he went underground. During the period of the Holocaust, he proposed the idea of contacting the Hungarian anti-Nazi underground movement, and he was one of the editors of the underground manifesto which revealed to the non-Jewish community the horrors of the deportation. After the war he published documents and lists from the period of the Holocaust *Hogyan történt?* ("How Did It Happen?" 1947). As a jurist, Munkácsi devoted himself to the interpretation of the laws relating to the legal standing of the Jews. He strove for complete autonomy of the Jews in Hungary, within the framework of the laws of emancipation (1867) and repatriation (1895). He wished within this framework to educate toward an historical Jewish consciousness, and to eradicate the widespread ignorance of Jewish matters. He published many articles in Jewish journals, in particular the periodical *Mult és Jövö* ("Past and Future"), and *Libanon,* where he served as one of its editors. He later collected these articles in a volume entitled *Könyvek és kövek* ("Books and Stones," 1944). In his short book *Római napló* ("Diary from Rome," 1931), he described the relics of the Jewish past in Rome. In his comprehensive *Miniatürművészet Itália könyvtáraiban; héber kódexek* ("The Art of the Miniature in the Libraries of Italy. Hebrew Codices" 1937), he traced most of the miniature material found in the leading libraries of Italy. His German book *Der Jude von Neapel* (1939) dealt with the remants of Jewish art in southern Italy, and his English article "Ancient and Medieval Synagogues in Representations of the Fine Arts" (*Jubilee Volume Bernhard Heller,* 1941, 241–51 ed. by Munkácsi) was devoted to the representations of art in synagogues.

Bibliography: *Egyenlöség* (Nov. 1, 1930), 16; B. Munkácsi (ed.), *A nyitrai, nagyváradi és budapesti Munk család* ... *genealógiája* (1939), 17. [B.Y.]

MUQADDIM (Ar. مقدّم "leader"), Arabic word, one meaning of which designates a leader heading an army, a ship, or a community. In North African countries, this term was employed to designate a *parnas* of the Jewish community while in the Hebrew documents of Castile, Aragon, and Navarre it was employed as a synonym for **adelantados.*

Bibliography: Baer, Spain, index; Neuman, Spain, index; Hirschberg, Afrikah, index. [Ed.]

MURABBA'AT SCROLLS, manuscripts found in 1951 and 1952 in caves in Wadi Murabbaʿāt, which runs down to the Dead Sea from the west about 18 km. (11 mi.) south of Wadi Qumrān and some 25 km. (15 mi.) southeast of Jerusalem. The presence of inscribed material in this area was first suspected in October 1951 when Taʿāmra Bedouin offered some fragments of skin with Hebrew and Greek writing to the Palestine Archeological Museum, Jerusalem. The site was visited early in 1952 by a team led by G. L. Harding and Père R. de Vaux, and they explored four caves, which yielded a considerable quantity of manuscript material. In March 1955 another cave was entered by local shepherds, who found a scroll of the *Twelve Minor Prophets,* containing substantial portions of the Hebrew text of nine of the 12 books.

General. The Murabbaʿāt caves contained traces of human occupation at six distinct periods in antiquity—the Chalcolithic Age (4th millennium B.C.E.), the Middle Bronze Age (c. 2000–1500 B.C.E.), the Iron Age (more specifically the 8th and 7th centuries B.C.E.), the Hellenistic period, the Roman period, and the Arab period. From the third, fourth, fifth, and sixth of these periods written documents were discovered. From the third period, the era of the later kings of Judah, came a papyrus palimpsest inscribed in Phoenician (paleo-Hebrew) characters. The earlier writing seems to have been a letter; part of it runs: "... yahu says to you, 'I send greetings to your family. And now, do not believe every word that ... tells you....'" The original writing was washed out and replaced by four lines of script, each containing a personal name followed by numbers (perhaps listing quantities of produce to be delivered by peasants to the royal exchequer). From the Hellenistic period come two inscribed potsherds (2nd century B.C.E.). From the Arab period come some paper documents in Arabic and one or two Greek papyri. But the most numerous and by far the most interesting manuscripts come from the Roman period. These last are specially interesting because their presence at Murabbaʿāt is due to the use made of the caves as outposts of guerrilla fighters during the Bar Kokhba Revolt (132–5 C.E.). There are fragments of Genesis, Exodus, Deuteronomy, and Isaiah on skin, a few *tefillin* fragments, and a piece of a *mezuzah.* The biblical texts are uniformly of protomasoretic type. The *tefillin* are of the type which became standard from the beginning of the second century C.E. onward, unlike those found at Qumrān, which belong to an earlier type and include the Ten Commandments. There is a fragment of a liturgical document in Hebrew and fragments of some literary works in Greek. There are quite a number of contracts and deeds of sale in Hebrew, Aramaic, and Greek; of those which are intelligibly dated, the majority belong to the period preceding and during the Bar Kokhba Revolt. There are several lists of deliveries of grain and vegetables, one or two in Aramaic and/or Hebrew but mostly in Greek. Some papyrus fragments and one potsherd contain Latin writing.

The Ben Kosebah Letters. Chief interest attaches to some correspondence between Joshua b. Galgula, apparently leader of the Murabbaʿāt guerrillas, and other insurgents. One letter comes to him from the administrators of Bet Mashiko (a village in southern Judea, it appears) informing him that a certain cow has changed ownership. Another letter comes from the defenders of En-Gedi, yet another from someone at Meẓad Ḥasidin, "the fortress of the saints," perhaps meaning Khirbat Qumrān—which is shown by archaeological excavation to have been occupied by insurgents during the Bar Kokhba Revolt. Two letters come to Joshua from the leader of the revolt in person, whose name is shown to have been Simeon b. Kosebah. (It was formerly known that the name Bar Kokhba, "son of the star," had been given him by R. Akiva and other supporters on the basis of Numbers 24:17, and the name Bar Koziba, "son of falsehood," given him by his opponents. His official designation "Simeon prince of Israel" is also found on coins of the Second Revolt.) One of the letters runs: "From Simeon b. Kosebah to Joshua b. Galgula and the people of Ha-Baruk (?), greeting! I call heaven to witness against me that if any of the Galileans who are with you is ill-treated, I will put fetters on your feet as I did to Beni Aflul. Simeon b. Kosebah in [his own person]." It is not known who the luckless Beni Aflul was, or what he had done; neither is there any information that would throw light on the Galileans mentioned (there is no reason to suppose that they were Christians). The second letter (which, like the other, is in Hebrew) runs: "From Simeon to Joshua b. Galgula, greeting! Take cognizance of the fact that you must arrange for five *kors* of wheat to be sent by the [members of] my household. So prepare for each of them his lodging place. Let them stay with you over the Sabbath. See to it that the heart of each is satisfied. Be brave and keep up the courage of the people of the place. Peace! I have ordered whosoever delivers his wheat to you to bring it the day after the Sabbath." Plainly Simeon b. Kosebah was a man of peremptory temperament, a quality no doubt desirable in the leader of a revolt. With this requisition of wheat it is possible to correlate the lists of grain and vegetables discovered in the same caves. The Murabbaʿāt caves seem to have been the last redoubt of Joshua and his men and their families. The Romans pursued them there and wiped them out, as they did to their comrades in Naḥal Ḥever. Some of the manuscripts bear signs of having been violently torn up by the invaders.

Linguistic Importance. The Murabbaʿāt scrolls provide evidence that the inhabitants of Judea were trilingual at the time of the Second Revolt as they had been in the Herodian period: Hebrew, Aramaic, and Greek were used by Jews with equal facility. One Aramaic manuscript of earlier date than most (55–56 C.E.) contains the name of the Emperor Nero spelt in such a way as to yield the total 666 (NRWN QSR)—a pointer to the "number of the beast" in Revelation 13:18.

Bibliography: Benoit et al., *Discoveries in the Judaean Desert*, 2 (1961); Yaron, in: JJS, 11 (1960), 157–77. [F.F.B.]

MURASHU'S SONS, prominent banking and commercial family in the Babylonian city of Nippur, active during the reigns of Artaxerxes I and Darius II. In 1893 an expedition from the University of Pennsylvania uncovered 730 clay tablets from the family archive dating from 455 to 403 B.C.E. The texts deal with diverse undertakings such as payment of taxes on behalf of others, land management, and the granting of loans to be repaid at a high rate of interest. Some 50 of the 730 tablets contain names which were thought to be Jewish, and this led some to deduce that the Murashu family itself was Jewish. However, the conclusion is unfounded. Apart from the purely indigenous name of the firm (*muraššû* means "wildcat" in Akkadian), caution must be exercised in deciding which of the names of the clients or witnesses are characteristically Jewish and which are merely of West Semitic origin. The fact that names like Ḫanana (חנן, Hanan), Minaḫḫimmu (מנחם, Menahem), Miniamini (מנימין, Minyamin), or names compounded with *ilī* (אל, El) are attested elsewhere in Jewish contexts does not necessarily mean that their bearers at Nippur were Jews. They may have been Arameans or members of some other West Semitic group living in Babylonia. Undisputed evidence for the presence of Jews is furnished by such names as Aḫiyama (אחיה, Ahijah, Aḫiyyah), Yaḫulakim (יהולכם, Yeholakhem), Yaḫulunu (יהולינו, Yeholanu), and Yaḫunatanu (יהונתן, Jonathan, Yehonatan), which are compounded with the Tetragrammaton or some combining form of it and by such names as Shabbetai son of Haggai. The picture of the Jewish exiles in Mesopotamia which emerges after an examination of these names is one of a people engaged in a wide range of activities: they act as witnesses in documents dealing with taxes, as tenants cultivating the land of others, and as landowners on whose behalf taxes are paid. Some seem to be highly placed royal officials.

Bibliography: G. Cardascia, *Les archives des Murašû* (1951), incl. bibl. [D.B.W.]

MURCIA, capital of the former kingdom of Murcia, S.E. Spain. The kingdom was first taken from the Muslims (1243) during the reign of Ferdinand III of Castile. After the revolt of the Muslims, it was reconquered by James I, king of Aragon, who handed it over to Castile in 1265. Among those who assisted the king in his conquest of the region were Judah de la *Cavallería, who lent money for outfitting the navy in the war against the Muslims, and Astruc (or Astrug) Bonsenyor (d. 1280), father of Judah *Bonsenyor, who conducted the negotiations with the Muslims for their capitulation, and who was also translator of Arabic documents in the kingdom. Jewish officials of the kingdom of Aragon met with Jewish officials of the kingdom of Castile in the town, and in 1292 Moses ibn Turiel of Castile held important administrative positions there. *Alfonso X of Castile (1252–84), son-in-law of James I, allocated a special quarter for the Jewish community, explicitly ordering that Jews were not to live among the Christians. However, at the time of their settlement various Jews received properties in the Jewish quarter and beyond it, in the town itself. A site was also allocated for the Jewish cemetery. Once the regulations of the settlement had been stipulated, an annual tax of 30 dinars was imposed on every Jew. Jews were also compelled to hand over tithes and the first fruits of all their possessions and herds to the cathedral, as was customary in Seville. In 1307 jurisdiction over the Muslims of the kingdom of Murcia was entrusted to Don Isaac ibn Yaish, the last Jew to hold such a function.

Toward the close of the 14th century, several Jewish tax farmers were active in the kingdom and in the town, among them Solomon ibn Lop, who settled in Majorca after 1378 and who was granted the special protection of the king of Aragon. During this period, the Jews of Murcia were noted for their generosity in the redemption of prisoners and for their participation in maritime trade; this was in addition to their usual occupations in commerce, crafts, and agriculture. Although there are no details available on how the Jews of the town fared during the persecutions of 1391, the community continued to exist after that time. Some 2,000 Jews earned their livelihood in a great variety of activities. Close mutual relations were maintained with the Christian population, and two of the community elders attended the meetings of the municipal council. Throughout the 15th century Jews of Murcia were often tax farmers, both in the kingdom of Murcia and in other towns near and distant. In 1488 Samuel Abulafia was taken under the protection of the Catholic monarchs for two years in appreciation of his services to the crown during the war against Granada. Solomon b. Maimon *Zalmati printed Hebrew books in Murcia in 1490.

Details on the departure of the Jews from Murcia at the time of the expulsion are unknown but it may be assumed that they left from the port of Cartagena. After the expulsion, debts owed by Christians to the Jews were transferred to Fernando Nuñez Coronel (formerly Abraham *Seneor) and Luis de Alcalá for collection. Murcia also had Conversos, some of whom remained faithful to Judaism. Conversos even used to come there in order to return to Judaism; one such case is mentioned in the La Guardia trial (1490). At an early date, an Inquisition tribunal was established at Murcia.

Bibliography: Baer, Spain, index; Baer, Urkunden, 1 (1929), index; H. C. Lea, *A History of the Inquisition of Spain*, 1 (1906), 550; L. Piles Ros, in: *Sefarad*, 7 (1947), 357; J. Torres Fontes,

Repartimiento de Murcia (1960), passim; idem, *Los judíos murcianos en el siglo XIII* (1962); idem, *Los judíos murcianos en el reinado de Juan II* (1965); idem, *La incorporación a la caballería de los judíos murcianos en el siglo XV* (1966); Suárez Fernández, Documentos, index; J. Valdeón Baruque, *Los judíos de Castilla y la revolución Trastamara* (1968), 57, 69, 70, and passim. [H.B.]

MURMELSTEIN, BENJAMIN (1905–), rabbi, scholar, and public figure of the Holocaust period. Born in Galicia, Murmelstein studied at the Juedisch-Theologische Lehranstalt, Vienna, where he became a lecturer in 1930. From 1923 he served as rabbi of the Vienna Jewish community. He was associated with S. Krauss in preparing the supplementary volume, published in1936, to A. *Kohut's famous talmudic dictionary, *Arukh ha-Shalem*, and Murmelstein published a popular *Geschichte der Juden* and annotated selections from Josephus (both in 1938). When the Nazis occupied Austria in 1938, Murmelstein became a member of the *Judenrat appointed by them. In this capacity he wielded power, which he was accused of having used arbitrarily. Later he was deported to *Theresienstadt concentration camp; he was made deputy *Judenaeltester* (head of the Jewish council) in January 1943 and succeeded P. *Epstein as chief *Judenaeltester* in December 1943, after Epstein was murdered by the Nazis. As *Judenaeltester*—an officer whose exact and tragic powers and responsibilities are difficult to assess—Murmelstein was both hated and feared; he was described as a complex character, gifted, ambitious, cynical, and calculating. When the camp was liberated in May 1945, Murmelstein remained and held himself at the disposal of the Czech authorities. He was arrested in June and remained in custody until December 1946, when the public prosecutor withdrew the indictment because "he had been able to disprove all accusations." Murmelstein settled in Rome, where he worked first at the Papal Biblical Institute and later as a commercial agent taking no part in Jewish communal life. He published an account of events in *Terezin-Ghetto Modello di Eichmann* (1961) and in several newspaper articles (in *Neue Zuercher Zeitung* (Dec. 17, 1963), 3; Hamburg *Die Welt* (Jan. 14, 1964)).

Bibliography: H. G. Adler, *Theresienstadt* (Ger., 1960[2]), introd. and index; Z. Lederer, *Ghetto Theresienstadt* (Eng., 1953), 166–7. [Ed.]

MURVIEDRO (now **Sagunto**), city in Valencia, E. Spain, near the Mediterranean coast, built on the ruins of the Roman city Saguntum. According to a legend, a tombstone was found there bearing the inscription in Hebrew "Adoniram, treasurer of King Solomon, who came to collect the tax tribute and died." Another spurious inscription mentioned King Amaziah's military commander as having also met his death in Murviedro. Jews lived in Murviedro during Muslim rule. On capture of the city by King James I of Aragon, the Vives family was given a bakery in the city, as a reward for services rendered during the siege. Several Jews served as royal bailiffs there including Solomon Baḥye, Solomon b. Lavi de la *Cavallería (1273), and Joseph ibn Shaprut (1279–80). At the time the community numbered 50 taxpayers. The Jewish quarter was on the west side of the Roman theater, the present Calle Segovia and Calle Ramos being the main streets. In 1321 James II authorized the Jews to fortify their quarter. A large portion of the community's revenue was derived from taxes on the sale of meat and wine. Silversmiths and cobblers are specifically mentioned among the artisans obliged to pay taxes; artisans who earned less than six *denarii* a day were exempt from taxes. R. *Isaac b. Sheshet permitted indigent artisans in Murviedro to work during the intermediate days of the Jewish festivals. In 1328 the community acquired grounds for a new cemetery, tombstones from which are still preserved.

During the 1391 persecutions the Jews of Murviedro found refuge in the fortress. Hence after the massacres Murviedro became one of the most important communities of the kingdom of Aragon. In the 15th century the Jewish quarter had 120 houses and probably more than 600 residents. In 1394 the king ordered that the Jews of Murviedro should not be investigated in respect of their activities to counteract conversion or for bringing back Conversos to Judaism and assisting them to leave the country. In 1402 Queen Doña María authorized the Murviedro community to establish several societies for catering to communal needs: the *Bikkur Ḥolim society, to care for the sick; a burial society; and a *talmud torah* society. Various problems arose with the increased number of conversions. In 1416 Alfonso V dealt with the division of property of deceased Jews between the heirs who had remained Jews and those who had been converted. The Jewish silversmiths of Murviedro were celebrated for their craft; especially notable was Vidal Astori, who in 1467–69 worked for the future King Ferdinand the Catholic. In 1474 the *muqaddimūn (*adelantados)* complained to the bailiff-general about some nobles who had forbidden their vassals to trade with the Jews of Murviedro. The bailiff decided in favor of the community and proclaimed freedom of trade in the area.

The Jews of Murviedro did much to encourage their Converso brethren to return to Judaism. After the decree of expulsion was issued in March 1492, Gerica, one of the local Jews, reached an agreement with Valencia merchants to transfer 300 Jews from Murviedro to Oran, in North Africa. Other agreements dating from the end of July relate to the conveyance of Jews from Murviedro to Naples. A total of 500 Jews left the city, and the synagogue in the present Calle de la Sangre Vieja was turned into a church named Sangre de Cristo ("Blood of Jesus").

Bibliography: Baer, Spain, index; A. Chabret, *Sagunto [Murviedro], su historia y sus monumentos*, 1 (1880), 324f.; 2 (1880), 329–51, 408f., 463f.; Vendrell Gallostra, in: *Sefarad*, 3 (1943), 119, Cantera, *ibid.*, 5 (1945), 250; Piles Ros, *ibid.*, 8 (1948), 81ff., 358; 12 (1952), 119, 121; 15 (1955), 99ff.; 17 (1957), 352–73; 20 (1960), 368; F. Cantera, *Sinagogas españolas* (1955), 268–71; Cantera-Millás, Inscripciones, 293ff.; Jiménez Jiménez, in: *Actas y communiciones de IV congreso de historia de la Corona de Aragón*, 1 (1961), 251–62; Beinart, in: *Estudios*, 3 (1962), 15ff. [H.B.]

MUSAF (Heb. מוּסָף), the additional sacrifice or prayer instituted on the Sabbath and the festivals. In addition to the daily morning and afternoon sacrifices offered in the Temple, the Bible prescribed additional offerings to be brought on Sabbaths, the three *pilgrim festivals, Rosh Ha-Shanah, the Day of Atonement, and the New Moon (Num. 28–29; see *Sacrifice). These were offered after the regular morning sacrifices (Yoma 33a). An additional prayer was already recited on these days by some worshipers even when the sacrificial cult still existed (Tosef., Ber. 3:3; Suk. 53a). After the abolition of sacrifice with the destruction of the Temple, the additional prayer was formalized and took the place of these sacrifices (Ber. 26b; see *Prayer, *Liturgy). There were some *tannaim* who regarded the *Musaf* prayer service as exclusively communal, and they held that it could only be recited when one worshiped with a quorum (**minyan;* Ber. 4:7 and Ber. 30a–b). The rabbis, however, made the additional service obligatory upon every individual, both when praying alone or with a quorum, and they endowed it with the same importance as the regular morning service (Ber. 30b; Sh. Ar., OḤ 286:2).

It is customary to recite the *Musaf* service immediately

after the reading of the weekly Torah and *haftarah* portions which follow the morning prayers on Sabbaths and festivals. It is, however, permissible to recite it at any time during the day. Nevertheless, one who negligently postpones its recitation until after the seventh hour of the day is considered a "transgressor" (Ber. 4:1 and Ber. 26b, 28a).

The *Musaf* is introduced by the reader's recitation of the Half **Kaddish*. This is followed by the *Musaf* **Amidah* which, except on Rosh Ha-Shanah, consists of seven benedictions. The first three benedictions of praise and the last three benedictions of thanks are identical with those of the daily *Amidah*. The benediction *Kedushat ha-Yom* ("Sanctity of the Day") is inserted between these blessings. It consists of an introductory paragraph followed by a prayer for the restoration of the Temple service and concludes with the appropriate selection from the Torah detailing the additional sacrifice for the day. In the *Musaf* for Rosh Ha-Shanah three blessings are added in the middle: the **malkhuyyot (malkhiyyot)*, **zikhronot*, and **shofarot*. In communal prayer, the *Musaf Amidah* is generally repeated in full by the *ḥazzan* (*Rema* to Sh. Ar., OḤ 286:2). In some congregations, however, particularly among the Sephardi Jews, the *ḥazzan* chants the first three blessings aloud with the congregation. This, however, is not done on the High Holy Days, when the entire *Amidah* is always repeated by the *ḥazzan*.

The Sabbath *Musaf Amidah*, after the initial three regular blessings, consists of a composition in which the initial letters of the first 22 words follow the inverted order of the Hebrew alphabet. This prayer concludes with the description of the Sabbath *Musaf* offering from Numbers 28:9–10. A short prayer for those who observe the Sabbath follows, and the "Sanctity of the Day" concludes with the prayer beginning with the invocation "Our God and God of our fathers," common to all the *Amidot* of the Sabbath (Hertz, Prayer, 530–4).

On New Moons, the *Musaf* consists of a prayer expressing sorrow over the abolition of the sacrificial ritual and hope for its restoration. Numbers 28:11, describing the New Moon sacrifice, is quoted, and it concludes with a prayer for a blessed and happy month (*ibid.*, 778–82). When the New Moon falls on a Sabbath, the first prayer is greatly altered and is very similar to the corresponding formula for the festivals. It concludes with the quotations from Numbers for both Sabbaths and New Moon offerings (*ibid.*, 542–4).

The *Musaf Amidah* for the three festivals begins with the prayer "But on account of our sins we were exiled from our land." God is asked to gather the scattered remnant of Israel to the Holy Land and to build the Temple. The appropriate passage detailing the *Musaf* offering is then inserted, and the regular prayer for the blessings of the festival concludes this section (*ibid.*, 820–8).

The *Musaf* service for the New Year is the longest in the liturgy. It opens with the same format as the other *Amidot* of that day, followed by the prayer "But on account of our sins," and concludes with the selection from Numbers 29:1–2 describing the *Musaf* sacrifice. After this, *Aleinu* is recited, followed by the above mentioned three additional benedictions.

The *Musaf Amidah* for the Day of Atonement begins in the same way as that of the New Year. After the biblical selection in which the additional sacrifices for the day are detailed (Num. 29:7–8), a prayer for the forgiveness of sins is recited. The *Confession (see **Al Ḥet*; **Ashamnu*) forms an integral portion of this *Musaf* service just as it does in the other *Amidot* of the Day of Atonement.

It was customary to interlace the *ḥazzan's* repetition of the *Musaf Amidah* on festivals and special Sabbaths with various *piyyutim*. Except for Rosh Ha-Shanah and the Day of Atonement this is hardly done nowadays. Even on those two holidays most modern congregations recite only selections from the huge volume of *piyyutim* composed throughout the generations.

The *Musaf* services of the first day of Passover and of Shemini Aẓeret are known by special names: the former as *Tal* ("dew"), because prayers for abundant dew are recited during the repetition of the first two blessings by the cantor; the latter as *Geshem* ("rain"), because prayers for rain are recited by the cantor at the same juncture. (In Israel, the custom is to recite these two prayers before *Musaf*.)

In Reform congregations in the 19th century the *Musaf* service was either entirely abolished or modified since Reform Judaism no longer anticipated the restoration of the sacrificial cult. In the course of time, the tendency was to omit it entirely. Some Conservative congregations have rephrased references to the sacrifices so that they indicate solely past events without implying any hope for a future restoration of sacrifice.

See **Kedushah*.

Bibliography: Elbogen, Gottesdienst, 115–7 and index; Idelsohn, Liturgy, 142–4, 284; E. Levy, *Yesodot ha-Tefillah* (1952²), 45–47; J. Heinemann, *Ha-Tefillah bi-Tekufat ha-Tanna'im ve-ha-Amora'im* (1966²), 34, 172; J. J. Petuchowski, *Prayerbook Reform in Europe* (1968), 240–64, index (for Reform usage).

[A.Ro.]

MUSAR HASKEL (Heb. מוּסַר הַשְׂכֵּל; also known as **Shirei Musar Haskel** or **Sha'arei Musar Haskel**), the name of a frequently printed ethical poem of the 11th century usually attributed to *Hai b. Rav David Gaon. The poem as printed consists of 180 verses, but there is a possibility that it was not printed in full and that in some manuscripts there is more material belonging to it. It was first printed in Fano, probably in 1505, and has appeared many times since then, mostly together with the *Ka'arat Kesef* of Jehoseph b. Hanan b. Nathan *Ezobi and occasionally also with S. J. Rapoport's essay on Hai Gaon. Although there is not sufficient proof to support the traditional attribution of the work to Hai Gaon, neither is there any evidence that the attribution is impossible. The poem is written in the literary style of the Book of Proverbs and of the Wisdom of *Ben Sira. It deals with many aspects of human life, religious and social; it shows in short rhymed epigrams the ethical way of life. Among other subjects it deals with prayer, the love of God, the love of knowledge, fear of the divine judgment, the treatment of women, and the correct way to conduct business. Every couplet of the poem usually stands alone as an epigram, and only rarely is a topic dealt with in more than two lines. The work was translated into Latin by Jacob Ebert (Frankfort, 1597).

Bibliography: Benjacob, Oẓar, 307.

[Y.D.]

MUSAR MOVEMENT, movement for the education of the individual toward strict ethical behavior in the spirit of *halakhah;* it arose in the 19th century, continuing into the 20th, in the Jewish culture of the *mitnaggedim* in Lithuania, in particular becoming a trend in its yeshivot. Originally inspired by the teachings and example of the life of Joseph Sundel b. Benjamin Benish *Salanter, it began as a movement for influencing members within the community. Circumstances, however, caused a radical change in its character at an early stage and turned it from the ideal of creating a pattern for leading and exemplary members of the community to forming the personality of the young students in the yeshivot.

Israel *Lipkin (Salanter) had primarily intended to establish the movement for members of the community through their activities. About the middle of the 19th century the mitnaggedic Jewish culture was facing a severe crisis, as a result of its vulnerability to the corroding influence of Haskalah ideology. The growing poverty and congestion in the *shtetl* in the *Pale of Settlement were causing severe tension and bitterness within Jewish society. The world of the leading circles of Lithuanian Jewry was breaking up. The pupil and co-worker of Israel Lipkin, Isaac *Blaser, complained in the second half of the 19th century about the moral degeneration: "The fear of God has terribly deteriorated . . . sins are proliferating whereas formerly Torah and the fear of God went together among Jews . . . now, because of our many sins, this unity has broken up; the bonds have gone and the connection joining them has been severed. In the end, without the fear of God, the knowledge of Torah will disappear too, God forbid" (his introduction to Lipkin's *Or Yisrael* (1900)). This expressed a typical complaint of the *Mitnaggedim* of the period. Blaser was alarmed by the new phenomenon presented by the graduates of the yeshivah, who, though learned, were no longer devoted to the rigorous pattern of *halakhah*. Confronted by Ḥasidism on the one hand, and on the other by the trends in German Jewry of *Haskalah, *Reform, and *Neo-Orthodoxy, mitnaggedic Jewry was faced with the problem of how to sustain a rigorous traditional Jewish life, based mainly on learning and intellectuality. Israel Salanter at first intended to tackle the problem directly in the communities. In his first letter to the Vilna community in 1849, proposing the creation of a *musar shtibl* ("a room for moral deliberation") he wrote: "The busy man does evil wherever he turns. His business doing badly, his mind and strength become confounded and subject to the fetters of care and confusion. Therefore appoint a time on the Holy Sabbath to gather together at a fixed hour . . . the notables of the city, whom many will follow, for the study of morals. Speak quietly and deliberately without joking or irony, estimate the good traits of man and his faults, how he should be castigated to turn away from the latter and strengthen the former. Do not decide matters at a single glance, divide the good work among you—not taking up much time, not putting on too heavy a burden. Little by little, much will be gathered . . . In the quiet of reflection, in reasonable deliberation, each will strengthen his fellow and cure the foolishness of his heart and eliminate his lazy habits." His program, meant to meet the needs of busy traders, proposed their meeting for moral reflection and self improvement on the day of rest. In his third letter to the Vilna community he proposed that women join in this concern with and study of morals. In his *Iggeret ha-Musar*, Salanter particularly stressed the sin of financial fraud.

However the movement failed to attract the settled members of the community; their "laziness of habit" was too deeply ingrained. Blaser, and not Salanter, had estimated correctly: the trouble lay not so much in the area of individual morality as in the dichotomy between Torah learning and the fear of God. It may be surmised that Israel Salanter's personality—which was both admired and criticized by Orthodox and Haskalah circles—was also one of the reasons for the failure of the movement among the upper circles of mitnaggedic society.

In the later years of Israel Salanter, through the energetic drive of his devoted pupils Isaac Blaser and Simḥah Zissel *Broida, the supporters of the Musar movement turned to the education of the young, and in particular to influencing the students of the yeshivot to form early in life the alertness of moral habit which had proved so difficult to instill at a later age. Blaser founded a *kolel* at Lubcz (Lyutcha). In 1872 Simḥah Zissel founded a *musar shtibl* at Kelme. He also founded a school for youngsters at Grobina, Courland, obtaining some financial support from Orthodox circles in Germany. As the Musar movement began to penetrate the yeshivot, both through the indirect influence of its own institutions and through the direct introduction of *musar* study and methods (see below) into the yeshivot, sharp opposition arose from the traditional yeshivah leadership. Rabbis and leaders such as Aryeh Leib *Shapiro and Isaac Elhanan *Spektor of Kovno openly opposed the new educational system, but without success. Subsequently some of its opponents explicitly renounced their objection, while others ceased to speak openly against it. By the beginning of the 20th century, *musar* had become the prevailing trend in the Lithuanian yeshivot.

Methods and Goals. After its adoption by the yeshivot, and the earlier establishment of *musar shtibl* and educational institutions, the Musar movement developed an individual institutional and educational pattern. The reading of ethical works, of isolated sayings from the Midrash and Talmud, and of verses from the Bible, served as vehicles for creating a certain mood and for implanting certain feelings. The principal activity was to recite passages from these works, or a saying or verse, to a melody—taken from the repertoire of the *maggidim*—suitable for evoking a pensive atmosphere of isolation and mood of emotional receptivity toward God and His commandments, preferably in twilight or subdued lighting (from a certain aspect this resembles the "spiritual exercises" recommended by Ignatius of Loyola for the Jesuits). The reading of the intellectual matter in the text served to stimulate an emotional response, which was intended to help the student both in forming moral personality and in devotion to Talmud study.

Formally, the Musar movement was based on the study of *ethical literature, although its conception of this was highly eclectic, and its libraries included works by authors as diverse as *Jonah b. Abraham Gerondi, Moses b. Jacob *Cordovero, Moses Ḥayyim *Luzzatto (who had been excommunicated in his time), and Naphtali Hirz *Wessely (one of the leaders of Enlightenment). However, several generations of study of this variegated literature by many brilliant young men did not produce for the movement, as far as known, a single systematic commentary, either on the literature as a whole or on an individual work.

In the "minimalistic" *musar* yeshivot students devoted at least half an hour daily to studying one of these texts in unison, intoning them in the same plaintive melody. Unity was demanded only in the melody used, each student being allowed to read the book of his own choice. In these yeshivot, the *mashgi'aḥ* ("supervisor") became a second spiritual mentor of the students, equal to the *rosh yeshivah;* in the case of some personalities such as Jeroham Lebovitch at the *Mir yeshivah, he was even superior. The *mashgi'aḥ* held a *shmues* ("talk") with all the yeshivah students at least weekly, on either a general moral topic—a kind of a special yeshivah sermon—or some specific incident that had occurred in yeshivah life. Devout *musar* students often combined into a *va'ad,* several youngsters gathering together for a period to chant some *musar* saying and achieve the proper *musar* mood. Larger groups would create a *musar berzhe,* in which they would act collectively and enter collectively through a more protracted way into the same mood. In these yeshivot, commonly called "Slobodka-style" yeshivot (see also *Kovno), the student's mind was molded through this activity, through his comradeship in emotivity with fellow students, and through the influence of the *mashgi'aḥ*. In this highly charged emotional life intellectual Talmud study became encapsulated by the atmosphere created by *musar*.

The crisis in the yeshivot brought about by secularizing influences, such as the *Bund, general socialist revolutionary trends, Zionism, and Haskalah, was counteracted to a large extent by the influence of the Musar movement. Israel Salanter's original aim was also largely achieved, though indirectly, as the *"muserniks"* who entered the life of the upper circles of the *shtetl* were now imbued with the new proud and rigoristic spirit engendered by *musar* and the collective sense of identity.

There also developed a second, "maximalist," trend of *musar* yeshivot, in the so-called "Nowardok style." Its proponent, Joseph Josel, the "old man of Nowardok" (Novogrudok), applied a deeper psychological approach. This not only included many hours devoted to the study of the *musar* texts, employing if possible a more plaintive melody, with less light, but the student would also be taught to discipline himself by a series of *peules af*... ("actions to..."). Such actions were calculated to subdue his natural instincts of vanity, economic calculation, or love of material goods. A student, for example, might be ordered to go to a drug store and ask for something inappropriate, such as nails, to mingle with well-dressed people in rags, or to enter a train without a coin in his purse. By the Nowardok method, a man not only trained himself to subdue his animal and social nature, but also to check if he did so in complete emotional depth. Ḥayyim *Grade described it:

> When you ask the *Nawardoker*, 'How do you do?' the meaning is 'How is Jewishness with you? Have you advanced in spirituality?'... He who has studied *musar* will never enjoy his life further. Ḥayyim, you will remain a cripple your whole life. You write heresy... but is there any one of you really so strong that he does not desire public approval for himself? Which one of you is prepared to publish his book anonymously?... Our spiritual calm you have exchanged for passions which you will never attain, for doubts which, even after much self-torture, you will not be able to explain away. Your writing will not improve a single person, and it will make you worse

(from his "My Quarrel with Hersh Rasseyner," in: I. Howe and E. Greenberg (eds.), *Treasury of Yiddish Stories* (1954), 579–606). Even after many years the *musarnik* remembered this naked prolonged cry, "O voices of ecstasy, O hoary voices, I follow you—I follow the echo of my Elul nights seven years ago" (idem, *Mussernikes* (1969), 9).

The Musar movement is thus a civic trend which, deflected from its original aim, gradually developed an entire educational system, based on, and aiming toward, integration and subjection of the youthful emotions to a deeply instilled emotional defense system of a rigoristic Jewish life according to *halakhah*. It promoted unity through pride in this fraternity of feelings and intentions and thus served as a social bond among those who emerged from the *musar* hothouse in the yeshivot. The Slobodka and Nawardok approaches differed in their degree of extremism and the emphasis on spiritual exercise, but were based on the same principle. By 1970 the main yeshivot of the Lithuanian type were *musar* orientated, the majority of Slobodka style, and a small minority Nawardok style. Despite the system, or to some extent because of it, many left the *musar* yeshivot for more secular trends of education.

Bibliography: Ba'al Maḥshoves, in: *He-Avar*, 1 (1918), 107–16; E. Carlebach, *Mussar; Geschichte einer Bewegung* (1932; repr. from JJLG, 22 (1931/32), 293–393); D. Katz, *Tenu'at ha-Musar—Toledoteha, Ishehah ve-Shitoteha*, 5 vols. (1948–63[3]); H. H. Ben-Sasson, in: *Divrei ha-Kinnus ha-Olami le-Madda'ei ha-Yahadut*, 1 (1952), 446–9; Z. F. Ury, *Musar Movement* (1970); J. J. Weinberg, in: L. Jung (ed.), *Men of the Spirit* (1964), 213–83. [H.H.B-S.]

MUSELMANN (German for Muslim), Nazi camp slang word for prisoners on the edge of death, i.e., showing the symptoms of the last stage of hunger, disease, mental indifference, and physical exhaustion. Mostly used at *Auschwitz, the term seems to have originated from the typical deportment of the sufferers, e.g., to squat with their legs tucked away in "oriental" fashion, their faces a masklike stiffness.

Bibliography: Kowalczykowa, in: *Przegląd Lekarski*, 18 (Eng., 1962), 28–31 (incl. refs. to British medical publications). [Y.Re.]

MUSEUMS. The desire to preserve and study the material manifestations of Jewish culture within the framework of a museum is a relatively new phenomenon. It resulted from the development of scholarly research in Judaica in the great Jewish population centers of Western and Eastern Europe and the United States at the end of the 19th and beginning of the 20th centuries. During this period the first Judaica exhibitions were organized, and from them emerged the first Jewish museums which in the course of time acquired enormous collections and became storehouses of Jewish culture and *art.

The earliest approach to a Jewish museum was the collection of ritual objects bequeathed to the synagogue of the Brunswick community in the middle of the 18th century by the Court Jew Alexander David (1681–1765). Toward the end of the 19th century a number of museums had Jewish sections—for example, the Salle Hebraique at the Louvre in Paris—but these were mainly concerned with biblical and Palestinian antiquities. The first great exhibition of Jewish ritual art was held in 1878 when the collection of Joseph Strauss (1827–1870) was shown at the Universal Exhibition in the Trocadero in Paris. It was later exhibited with much additional material from English collections at the great Anglo-Jewish Historical Exhibition held at the Albert Hall in London in 1887, which for the first time gave a picture of what a Jewish Museum might comprise. The first actual Jewish museum on a small scale, with its own occasional publications, was the Juedische Museum in Vienna, opened in 1897 under the auspices of the Gesellschaft fuer Sammlung und Konservierung von Kunst- und historischen Denkmaelern des Judentums. Early in the 20th century Heinrich Frauenberger (1845–1920) established the Gesellschaft zur Erforschung juedischer Kunstdenkmaeler, whose collections formed the nucleus of the systematically developed Frankfort Jewish Museum, established in 1901, and later enriched by the collections of Sigmund Nauheim (1879–1935) and others. To the same period belongs the establishment of the Jewish museum in Prague founded by Solomon Hugo Lieben (1906). Jewish museums were established in Munich, Breslau, Mainz, Kassel, and Budapest. A tragic fate befell the Jewish Museum in Berlin, which moved into its own building on January 27, 1933, three days before Hitler came to power. Ironically, at this time it developed the most dynamic cultural and artistic activities, and became the leading Jewish museum in Europe until November 1939 when it was shut down and confiscated. During the war its collections were looted and some were taken out of Germany, while at the end of the war considerable material was taken to Eastern Europe. Similarly a part of the museum collection of the Jewish community of Berlin was found in Bavaria and was included in the Jewish Museum of the Hebrew Union College, Cincinnati. Most Jewish museums in Europe shared this fate. The entire contents of the museum of the Jewish community of Danzig (Gdansk), founded by Isser Gieldzinski in 1903, were saved at the outbreak of the war in 1939 and found their way through London to the Jewish museum in New York. An event of particular significance was the exhibition organized by Rudolf *Hallo, of a choice collection of Jewish ritual art held in 1928 in Marburg. An enthusiastic local resident, Sandor Wolf, was responsible for the maintenance of a museum to illustrate the history of the Jewish community of Eisenstadt in the Burgenland, and there was another in Nikolsburg, Moravia. A hall for the history of the Jews in Regensburg was opened in that city in 1971.

Museums in Eastern Europe. Jewish collections and museums were established in Eastern Europe as a result of the spread of the influence of Haskalah. The first Jewish museum in Poland was established in Warsaw when the Jewish historian, scholar, and collector, Matthias *Bersohn (1824–1908), donated his Judaica collection to the Jewish community of the city. The museum, named after its founder, was housed in the communal building and opened to the public in 1910. In May, 1939, the museum took over new and more spacious quarters in the communal building. The collection included ritual and secular objects in metal, wood, ceramic, embroidery, and fabric, illuminated manuscripts and inscriptions, dozens of paintings on Jewish subjects, portraits of Jewish personalities, a photo archive of Polish-Jewish antiquities, and a valuable library. During the bombardment of Warsaw in 1939, the museum building, together with its collection, was completely destroyed.

The first Jewish museum in Vilna, named for S. *An-Ski following his death in 1920, was established by the Vilna Society of Lovers of Jewish Antiquities. Housed in the Jewish communal building, it contained paintings and sculpture by Jewish artists of Vilna, a large collection of Jewish ritual and secular objects in metal, wood, and fabric, communal records and manuscripts, an archive containing thousands of documents, and a library with over 2,000 volumes. The director, Chaikal Lonsky (who had been the director of the famed Strashun library), maintained and expanded the museum. About 1930, YIVO decided to establish in Vilna a central museum for Jewish art together with an institute for the study of Jewish art. An exhibit hall, set up in the YIVO building, contained Jewish works of art, paintings, graphics, sculpture. The museum began to publish a journal in Yiddish, *Heftn far Yidisher Kunst*, on problems of Jewish art, but only one issue appeared (Nov. 1936). With the Nazi invasion of Vilna, members of the underground and the Jewish militant opposition began to hide objects from the city's two museums. When the ghetto was decimated, the museums were destroyed, but when Jewish partisans reentered Vilna with the Red Army, in July 1944, the greater part of the collection was recovered. In the summer of 1945, the remnant of the Jewish community decided to reopen a Jewish museum with the remaining collection. However, the police forbade its opening and sequestered the collection in the basement of the Vilna State Museum, where it remains.

The Lvov Museum for Jewish Art was set up as a result of the survey, collection, and restoration of Jewish folk art in eastern Galicia and Lvov. The work was undertaken by the Commission for the Preservation of Jewish Art established in 1925 by the Jewish community of Lvov. Three impressive exhibitions of Jewish folk art held in Lvov in 1894, 1913, and 1933 paved the way for the establishment in 1934 of the museum, in the building of the Jewish community. The museum was in existence until the outbreak of World War II. A collection of Jewish folk art was found in the crafts museum in Lvov; Jewish collections are presently to be found in the Museum for Ethnography and Applied Art in Lvov, now in the western Ukraine in the U.S.S.R.

The large synagogues of Cracow, the Alte Schul, the Rema Synagogue, and the Hoyche Schul contained large quantities of first-rate Jewish art. They included embroidered Ark curtains and Torah mantles; silver Torah crowns, breastplates, and pointers; old printed works, and illuminated manuscripts and documents. In 1935, with the encouragement of Meir *Balaban, a Jewish museum containing the treasures from the large synagogues was established in the Jewish community building. During World War II, the collection was completely plundered by the Nazis. In 1961, a museum was opened in the reconstructed building of the synagogue of Kazimierz, the old Jewish quarter. Named the Museum of the History and Culture of the Jews of Poland, it was made a branch of the Historical Museum of the city of Cracow.

Many Jewish collections in the U.S.S.R. have their origins in the pre-World War I activities of the Jewish Historical and Ethnographic Society, established in St. Petersburg in 1908. This group organized an ethnographic mission to gather, catalog, and organize material. The mission, headed by S. An-Ski, toured for three years, 1912–14, throughout the Ukraine, Podolia, and Volhynia, recording, collecting, and cataloging. The mission artist, Shlomo Yudubin, photographed and copied the treasures of the past. The mission's activities ended because of the war and the collection was kept in St. Petersburg. During the war An-Ski continued to tour as a member of the Red Cross, in the uniform of a Russian officer, visiting the destroyed Jewish villages on the Galician front, salvaging remains which he found in synagogues and Jewish homes plundered by the czar's cossacks.

The mission's collections formed the basis of the Jewish Ethnographic Museum which opened in 1916. The museum was closed in 1918 by the Bolshevik government, but An-Ski returned, at great personal risk, and reopened it. The Leningrad Jewish Ethnographic Museum was in existence until the 1930s. Most of the collections were then transferred to the Leningrad State Museum for the Ethnography of the Peoples of the U.S.S.R. There they have been maintained and preserved, available to scholars, but not to the general public. Part of the Jewish Ethnographic Museum collection, especially manuscripts and ancient books, was transferred to the state Saltykov-Shchedrin Public Library in Leningrad. Kiev also had a Jewish museum with an ethnographic collection. The museum was founded by the Jewish Cultural League in the early 1920s and was active for about ten years before it closed. Also founded in the 1920s were the Jewish Museum of Kiev and the All-Ukrainian Museum of Jewish Art (the "Mendele" Museum) in Odessa, with its large section devoted to Mendele Mokher Seforim. This too was closed in the 1930s. The Mendele Mokher Seforim Archive was transferred to the State Public Saltykov-Shchedrin Library in Leningrad. The Nazis plundered part of the collection remaining in Odessa, removing it to Germany, where the British forces later found it hidden in Bavaria. A number of Jewish ethnographic artifacts are exhibited in the Art Museum of the Belorussian Republic in Minsk.

After the Holocaust. Most of the Jewish museums of Europe were closed, plundered, and destroyed during the Nazi Holocaust, but the collections of a few were salvaged. After the war, the natural desire for rehabilitation caused the Jewish public to establish a number of museums to commemorate the destruction of European Jewry and its culture.

A strange fate befell the Jewish Museum of Prague when the Nazis decided to establish a "Museum of the Extinct People," with the intention of justifying their destruction of the Jewish people. Jewish ritual objects were gathered from all over Czechoslovakia and other occupied countries and placed in the Klaus Synagogue in Prague. Hence the Prague Jewish Museum found itself, at the close of the war, in possession of what is probably the greatest collection of Jewish art ever brought together, both quantitatively and qualitatively. It was assembled in seven

Figure 1. Members of the St. Petersburg Jewish Ethnographical Expedition with part of the collection, c. 1914. Second from right is the writer S. An-Ski, and extreme left, the expedition's artist, Solomon Yudovin. Courtesy Museum of Ethnography and Folklore Archives, Tel Aviv.

Figure 2. Exhibits in the Jewish Museum of Mainz, established at the beginning of the 20th century. From *Magenza—Ein Sammelheft ueber das juedische Mainz im 500 Todesjahre des Mainzer Gelehrten, Maharil,* Mainz, 1927.

Figure 3. The Jewish Museum in the "Hoyche Schul," Cracow, established after World War II.

Figure 4. The Jewish Museum, Budapest, established at the beginning of the 20th century. Courtesy Z. Efron, En-Harod.

Figure 5. The Mendele Mokher Seforim Room of the All-Ukrainian Museum of Jewish Art which existed in Odessa before World War II.

synagogue buildings and comprised over 200,000 art objects, displayed in an exhibit which constitutes a monument to an intensive Jewish life. The publications of the state-run Prague Jewish Museum are of high quality as regards both production and scientific standard. The Prague Jewish Museum opened branch museums in the towns of Bresnitze, Holešov, Mikulov-Nikolsburg, and Slavkov-Austerlitz.

The Jewish Museum of Budapest survived the Nazi period. From 1932, the museum, located in a branch of the Dohany Street Synagogue, held exhibits of Jewish life in Hungary from Roman times to the present. In 1960, the Jewish Historical Museum was opened in Belgrade. The exhibit, housed in the building of the Federation of Jewish Communities in Yugoslavia, was expanded in 1969 and reorganized into well planned and carefully laid out exhibits of Jewish life in terms of economics, religion, history, culture, tradition and folklore. The Holocaust period and the part played by Jews in the war against the Nazis and for the achieving of Jewish freedom in Yugoslavia are also emphasized. Marking the 400th anniversary of Sephardi settlement in Bosnia and Herzegovina, a museum of the history of the Jews was opened in Sarajevo's old synagogue in 1966. A small display of Judaica relating to the Jews of Bulgaria can be seen at the entrance to the Jewish community center of Sofia; likewise a number of Rumanian Jewish objects are included in the Rumanian National Historical Museum in Bucharest.

In Western Europe. The Jewish Museum in London, initially based largely on the superb English-made ritual appurtenances of the 18th century, was founded in 1932 by C. *Roth and W.S. *Samuel when the Jewish communal center at Woburn House was opened. It was enriched by choice objects purchased from the Arthur Howitt (1855–1967) collection which was auctioned that same year. Another Jewish museum in London is that of the Jewish Historical Society housed in University College, which was reconstituted about the same time by Gustave Tuck. The Ben Uri museum, established in connection with the Ben Uri Society, concentrated on modern paintings and works of art. Modest exhibits of Judaica are to be found in the British Museum and the Victoria and Albert Museum. The Strauss Collection, which was exhibited in the Trocadero in Paris in 1878 and at the Anglo-Jewish Historical Exhibition in the Albert Hall in London, 1887, was presented by Baron Nathaniel de Rothschild to the Cluny Museum in Paris, where it was, for a long time, exhibited separately. The Musée d'Art Juif in Paris developed from the Archives et Musée d'Art Populaire Juif, established in 1948. The museum concentrates on Jewish folk art from Europe and North Africa, reconstructions of eastern European synagogues, tombstones, and contemporary art by Jewish painters of the Paris school. Other Judaica collections in Paris are to be found in the Musée Carnavalet, which has documents concerning the history of the Paris community, and ancient tombstones (not exhibited); in the Musée de l'Histoire de France, which has Jewish communal charts and records; and in the Musée National des Thermes, which has a rich collection of Judaica (not exhibited). Other Judaica collections in France are found in Arles, at the Museon Arlatan, which has a small Jewish collection formerly belonging to the grandfather of the novelist, Armand Lunel; at the Musée Basque in Bayonne, which has Portuguese-Jewish secular and religious objects; at the Musée Comtadin in Carpentras, which has ritual objects, seals, and medals; at the Musée Judeo-Comtadin in Cavaillon, adjacent to the synagogue of Cavaillon, which has ritual objects, tombstones, and an ancient communal bakery; at the Musée Historique Lorrain in Nancy, which has a Jewish section mainly derived from a bequest of Rene Wiener; and at the Musée Alsacien in Strasbourg which has Jewish rooms exhibiting the collection of the Societé d'histoire des Israélites d'Alsace et de Lorraine. The rich Jewish Historical Museum in Amsterdam (Joods Historisch Museum), housed in the old Waaggebouw and forming a part of the municipal museum, primarily displays art collections of the Portuguese community of Holland. The publications and catalogs of this museum are among the most beautiful published by Jewish museums anywhere in the world.

In Denmark the Jewish Museum in Copenhagen is housed in the communal administrative building. In Sweden, the Goteborg municipal museum contains a Jewish section. The Juedisches Museum der Schweiz in Basle, established in 1966, exhibits Jewish life and customs and the history of the Jewish community in Switzerland. Although the fine Jewish museum in Leghorn, Italy, was destroyed during World War II bombardment, museums, based on the ancient treasures of the Italian community, were set up in the building of the main synagogue at Rome, in 1964, and in one of the unused synagogues of Venice, in 1957. In Spain, the ancient El Transito synagogue of Toledo, built in the 14th century by Samuel *Abulafia, was, in 1965, designated by the Spanish government a museum to illustrate the history of Sephardi Jewry. Known as the Sephardic Museum, it contains, for the most part, gravestones with Hebrew inscriptions. The Museo Arqueologico de Toledo, the Museo Historico de Barcelona, the Museo Nacional de Barcelona and many municipal and church museums in Spain and the Balearic Islands contain evidence of Jewish life in Spain up to the expulsion of 1492.

In North and South America. The history of the Jewish Museum of New York begins with the collection of Ephraim Benguiat, shown at the Columbia Exposition in Chicago in 1892–93, and cataloged by Cyrus Adler and Casanowicz. It was exhibited for some years at the Smithsonian Institute in Washington, D.C., thus conferring on the collection something of an academic status. Later it was purchased and presented by Felix M. Warburg to the Jewish Theological Seminary of America, New York, where the curator was the numismatist P. Romanoff. In 1947, the collection was transferred to the former Warburg mansion on Fifth Avenue, under the direction of Stephen S. Kayser. Here it was further enriched, especially by the munificent and discriminating donations of Harry G. Friedman, as well as by the medal and coin collections of Daniel M. Friedenberg and the collection of the Jewish Museum of Danzig. The Jewish Museum of the Hebrew Union College, Cincinnati, is almost entirely based on the font collection of Sally Kirschstein of Berlin, which was acquired in 1926. The Jewish Museum in Oakland, California, obtained a number of exhibits from Cochin (India). General museums in the United States which contain Judaica collections include the Harvard Semitic Museum, Cambridge, Mass., the Smithsonian Institution, Washington, D.C., Johns Hopkins University Museum, Baltimore, Md., and the Brooklyn Museum, Brooklyn, N.Y. After World War I and especially World War II, a number of Jewish communities and institutions have set up Jewish museums, some attached to synagogues. These include the Jewish Museum of Temple Mishkan Tefila, Boston, Mass; Hebrew Theological College Museum, Chicago, Ill.; the Maurice Spertus Museum, established in 1967, under the auspices of the Institute of Jewish Studies, Chicago, Ill.; Museum of the Temple, Cleveland, Ohio; Kol Ami Museum, Highland Park, Ill.; Sinai Temple Museum, Los Angeles, Calif.; International Synagogue Museum, Kennedy Airport, N.Y.; Temple Emanuel Museum, New York; Keneseth Israel Jewish

6

7

8

9

Figure 6. The M. Bersohn collection of the Jewish Museum of Warsaw, which existed before World War II.

Figure 7. Exhibit of Jewish guild signs in the State Jewish Museum of Prague.

Figure 8. Section of Jewish room in the Alsatian Museum, Strasbourg. Courtesy Z. Efron, En-Harod.

Figure 9. Ritual art section of the Jewish Museum, Belgrade.

10

Figure 10. The Waaggebouw, Amsterdam, which houses the Jewish Museum.

Figure 11. The Jewish Museum, Rome, in the main synagogue building.

Figure 12. The Jewish Museum, Venice, formerly a synagogue. Courtesy Z. Efron, En-Harod.

Figure 13. The Jewish Museum, London, founded in 1932 by Cecil Roth and W. S. Samuel.

11

12

13

Figure 14. Card issued by the Jewish Museum of Cape Town showing a curtain for an Ark of the Law, Germany, 1719.

Figure 15. Exhibit at the Kadman Numismatic Museum, part of the Ha-Areẓ Museum complex in Tel Aviv. Courtesy Government Press Office, Tel Aviv.

Figure 16. Jewish folk art section of the Mishkan le-Ommanut, the En-Harod Museum of Art. Courtesy Z. Efron, En-Harod.

Figure 17. The former Warburg mansion in New York, now housing the Jewish Museum.

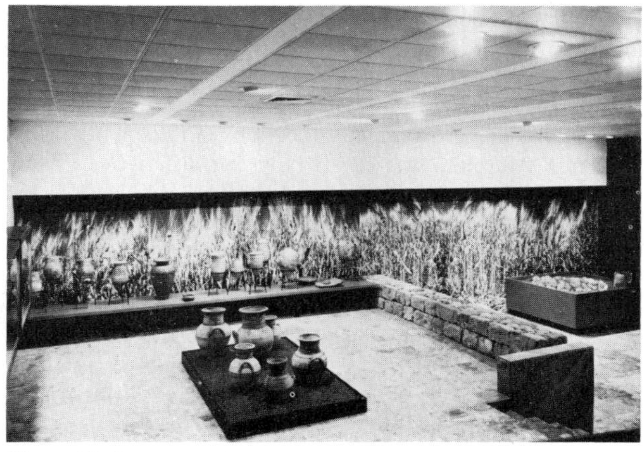

Figure 18. Pottery exhibit in the grain museum in Haifa. Courtesy Dagon, Batey Mamguroth, Ltd., Haifa. Photo Teddy Rosenthal.

Figure 19. The Masada museum, at the foot of the mountain. Courtesy Ministry of Tourism, Jerusalem. Photo Shimon Fuchs, Givatayim.

Museum, Philadelphia, Pa.; Temple Beth Israel Judaica Museum, Phoenix, Ariz.; Temple Emanuel Museum, Providence, R.I.; Rochester Jewish Museum, Rochester, N.Y.; Hebrew Theological College, Skokie, Ill.; Gallery of Jewish Art, Tulsa, Okla.; B'nai B'rith Museum, Washington, D.C.; and Jewish museums in Detroit, Mich.; Greatneck, N.Y., and Kansas City, Mo. There are also many other small Judaica collections in Conservative and Reform synagogues throughout the United States. The museums of Jewish interest in Canada include the National Museum of Congress, Montreal, Quebec, opened in 1970; the Temple Emanuel Museum, Montreal; and the Beth Tzedec Congregation Museum (the Cecil Roth Collection), Toronto.

The Jewish Historical Museum in Mexico City, D.F., has exhibits on the Jewish past in Eastern Europe, the Jewish contribution to Mexico, and the establishment of the State of Israel. A Jewish historical cultural museum is located in Willemsted, Curacao, Dutch West Indies. The Art Gallery at the YIVO Scientific Institute in Buenos Aires contains principally the works of Maurice Minkowski dealing with Eastern European Jewish life.

In South Africa, the Jewish Museum in Cape Town, established in 1958 and housed in the old synagogue, has an exhibition of Jewish ceremonial art. The Jewish Museum, Johannesburg, established in 1957, under the auspices and patronage of the South African Jewish Board of Deputies, has a collection of Jewish ceremonial art and historical documents on South African Jewry. [Z.EF.]

In Israel. The history of museums in Ereẓ Israel starts with the foundation of the Bezalel school of arts and crafts in Jerusalem by Boris *Schatz in 1906. From 1922, under the directorship of Mordechai *Narkiss, it developed into the Bezalel National Museum as the focus of knowledge on Jewish art. Bezalel owned the most important general art and Judaica collections in the country. The Tel Aviv Museum was created by the initiative of Meir *Dizengoff in 1932, and after his death was housed in his home. His collection concentrated around modern Jewish artists both in Ereẓ Israel and elsewhere. Among other museums established before the establishment of the State of Israel are the *Rockefeller Museum in Jerusalem (1927), which was established as the official archaeological museum of the Palestinian British Mandate department of archaeology. The Haifa municipal museum started with the private archaeological collection of Alexander Rosh.

Israel is a land of museums: not only do the large cities have many collections of art and archaeology but the country is dotted with some 150 museums—some large, covering many acres, and some small, in temporary sheds, but all aiming to conserve the cultural heritage of Israel and its people. Most of them are devoted to archaeology, the others being divided between art, ethnology, natural history, science and technology, and history. Archaeological objects are often found when a plow opens a furrow, a house is built, a road constructed, or a water project initiated. Often, therefore, a village museum, mainly in a kibbutz, is established through the enthusiasm and perseverance of an individual, whose accidental discovery of a shard, oil lamp, or jug recalls the distant past. Many original types of museum are improvised: they are to be found in basements, air raid shelters and attics. Art and historical museums help to preserve and display the cultural heritage of Israel's variegated communities, and to acquaint the people with the world's artistic treasures. In the large cities there are both specialized and composite museums administered by the municipalities or other public bodies.

Israel Museum. In 1964 the Bezalel National Art Museum was incorporated into the new Israel Museum. The Israel Museum, situated in the heart of modern Jerusalem, houses a collection of Jewish and world art, the archaeology of the Holy Land, and the Dead Sea Scrolls. The IL20,000,000 (about $5,730,000) complex of buildings was designed by the Israel architects Alfred Mansfeld and Dora Gad and financed by gifts from Israel, the United States, and Europe. The first IL1,500,000 (about $428,570) came from the U.S. government through its Information Media Guaranty Program, and the Israel government provided the 22-acre plot. The exhibition area totals 8,550 sq. m. (about 9,030 sq. yd.) with an additional 7,000 sq. m. (8322 sq. yd.) for stores, laboratories, workshops, a library, and offices, including those of the Israel government Department of Antiquities. The museum consists of four main divisions:

The Bezalel National Art Museum exhibits a wide range of art, with emphasis on one of the largest and most diversified collections in existence of Jewish ethnology and folk art. There are also reconstructions of two whole synagogue interiors. The collection of paintings include a cross section of Israel art, as well as Western art; 17th-century Dutch paintings, and an 18th-century French room, as well as a varied collection of 19th- and 20th-century painting, and sculpture. The graphic cabinet includes a wide collection of drawings and prints of many schools and periods. The museum holds temporary exhibitions as does its youth wing which is very active in art education.

The Samuel Bronfman Biblical and Archaeological Museum houses a collection based on that of the Israel Department of Antiquities (started in 1948). The exhibits range from an elephant tusk from about 200,000 B.C.E., Chalcolithic clay ossuaries from Azor, highly developed Canaanite pottery, and Hebrew inscriptions and other objects from the Israelite period, to representative finds from the Persian, Hellenistic, and Second Temple periods as well as the Roman, Byzantine, and Arabic civilizations. There is a selection of synagogue and church mosaics and a numismatic collection.

The Billy Rose Art Garden, designed by Isamu Noguchi, displays 19th- and 20th-century sculpture. Curved retaining walls, made of the rocks on the site, frame the exhibition space for the sculptures displayed in the open air.

The Shrine of the Book, designed by the U.S. architects Frederick J. Kiesler and Armand P. Bartos, is the repository for Israel's Dead Sea Scrolls and the Bar Kokhba letters (for details see *Dead Sea Scrolls and *Bar Kokhba).

Other Museums. The following museums are to be found in Jerusalem: the *Rockefeller Museum, which specializes in the archaeology of Ereẓ Israel; the Pontifical Biblical Institute; the Islamic Museum near the Al-Aqṣā Mosque; the Herzl Museum; the Museum of Natural History; the Museum of Religious Objects in Hechal Shlomo; and the Museum of Musical Instruments.

The Tel Aviv Museum, with its rich collections of modern paintings, sculpture, and graphic art, and its many visiting exhibits, was housed in a new building in 1971. It is an important art center in Israel. This museum, founded in 1932, expanded with the addition of the Helena Rubinstein Pavilion in 1958.

The complex Ha-Areẓ ("Homeland") Museum started with nine separate pavilions: museums for glass, ceramics, numismatics, ethnography and folklore, science and technology (including a planetarium), antiquities of Jaffa and Tel Aviv, the history of Tel Aviv, the alphabet, and Tel Qasile excavations. There are also ten other museums in Tel

Aviv, including a Museum of Man and his Work, the Haganah, and the Jabotinsky Museum.

The Haifa municipality administers museums of ancient and modern art, a maritime museum, and the "Dagon," a grain museum showing the cultivation and storage of grain through the ages.

No section of the country is without its regional and local museums, most of them created and maintained to satisfy the intense interest of the people in their past. In the north, *Beth-Shean, the ancient fortress city guarding the road from the east, displays a collection of archaeological finds and mosaics from the town and its environs; at the nearby kibbutz *Nir David is a museum of Mediterranean archaeology. The Mishkan le-Ommanut, the art museum at kibbutz *En-Harod, the first rural museum in the country, started in 1933. The object of this museum is to collect Jewish art, and it has already a rich collection of Jewish painting, sculpture, and Jewish folk art from all over the world. Beit Sturman at En-Harod exhibits the history and archaeology of the region. Wilfred Israel House, at kibbutz *Ha-Zore'a, exhibits artistic objects from the Far East and archaeological finds from the village fields; Bet Ussishkin, in kibbutz *Dan, is both a natural history museum for the Ḥuleh region and the site museum for the excavations at nearby Tel Dan. There are museums at *Ḥanitah and *Sasa in Upper Galilee, Tiberias and Nazareth in Lower Galilee, *Ayyelet ha-Shaḥar by ancient *Hazor, *Bet She'arim, close to the Jewish necropolis of the talmudic period, and *Megiddo with its imposing mound.

The coastal region is represented by municipal museums in *Acre, site museums in *Sedot Yam showing the antiquities of *Caesarea, and *Ma'agan Mikha'el showing objects found in the sea; the regional museum at Midreshet Ruppin in Ḥefer Plain exemplifies the local flora and fauna, as well as the history of the area's modern villages and their ancient sites. In the Negev, Beersheba has an archaeological museum; the kibbutzim Gevulot, Kissufim, Mishmar ha-Negev, and Nirim have their own collections; the site museums of Masadah, En-Gedi, Arad, and Avedat exhibit representative collections of the finds; *Eilat has a museum of modern art, as well as a maritime museum. [A.Bi.]

Bibliography: Mayer, Art, index s.v. *collections, exhibitions, museums;* JL, 5 (1930), 78–82, incl. bibl.; C. Roth, *The Jewish Museum* (1933); *Fuehrer durch das juedische Museum. Sammlungen der juedischen Gemeinde zu Berlin* (1935); Gesellschaft zur Erforschung juedischer Kunstdenkmaeler, *Die Sammlung Siegmund Nauheim* (1937); S. S. Kayser (ed.), *Jewish Ceremonial Art* (1959[2]); V. Benda, in: *Judaica Bohemiae,* 1 (1965), 4–8 (Ger.); *Ḥadashot Museon Yisrael* (1965–); H. Volavková, *A Story of the Jewish Museum in Prague* (1968); A. Kampf, in: *Judaism,* 17 (1968), 282–98; M. Narkiss, in: *The Jewish Quarterly,* 4 (1956–57), 24–27.

MUSHROOMS, fungus. Israel is rich in various species of mushroom which grow chiefly in the winter. A large number of them are poisonous. The poisonous ones are mainly of the genus *Amanita.* Easily recognizable among edible mushrooms are those of the genus *Boletus,* called in modern Hebrew *orniyyot* because they grow on the roots of the pine (mod. Heb. *oren*), of which most of the forests planted in Israel consist. The mushroom is not mentioned in the Bible, though some exegetes (Rashi, D. Kimḥi) identify it with the poisonous *pakku'ot* of II Kings 4:39–40. The *pakku'ot,* however, are the colocynth. In rabbinic literature the combination *kemehim u-fitriyyot* ("truffles and mushrooms") is usually found. They have in common that although they "grow in the soil" one does not recite over them the blessing for vegetables but the blessing "by whose word everything was created." The Talmud gives as the reason that unlike ordinary plants "they do not draw their nourishment from the ground but from the air" (Ber. 40b). In this way they explained the fact that they possess no true roots, being fed by other plants, and absorbing moisture from the air. Mushrooms and truffles are also exempt from tithes (see: **Ma'aser*), "because they do not grow by being sown, or, because the earth extrudes them" (TJ, Ma'as. 1:1, 48d). The latter reason refers to their quick growth, which makes it seem as if the earth is expelling them. The extensive sprouting of mushrooms after rain is reflected in the *aggadah* about *Honi ha-Ma'agel who prayed for rain after drought. After rain had fallen in abundance and the heavens were free from clouds "the people went into the fields and brought home mushrooms and truffles" (Ta'an. 23a). Truffles are found chiefly in the light soils of the Judean wilderness and in the sands of the Negev. In contrast to mushrooms, they grow under the surface. In addition to *kemehim,* truffles are called *shemarka'im* (Uk. 3:2) in the Mishnah.

Bibliography: Loew, Flora, 1 (1928), 26–44. [J.F.]

MUSIC. This article is arranged according to the following outline:

INTRODUCTION

The most workable definition of Jewish music would seem to be the functional one proposed by Curt *Sachs: "Jewish music is that music which is made by Jews, for Jews, as Jews" (in his opening lecture, to the First International Congress of Jewish Music, in Paris 1957). This defines the scope of inquiry without prejudicing its results, leaving it free to undertake the tasks of description, analysis, and whatever conclusions may be drawn.

As in all other national and ethnic cultures, the musical dimension of Jewish culture is both determined by its origins and modified by its history in proportions peculiarly its own. By dint of its origins, it kept to the same principles which obtain, in much the same way, in all the other descendants of the ancient Near Eastern "High Cultures." The music itself is created, performed, and preserved by oral tradition. Its practice is supported, and to a great extent directed, by a general body of religious and ethical doctrine and by forms of verbal art (poetry and prose), which are themselves supported and directed by this doctrine; and both of which are preserved by a written tradition.

The historical factor is that of the Diaspora. Through their dispersion, the Jews came into contact with a multiplicity of regional musical styles, practices, and ideas, some of which were more closely related to their own patrimony (as in the Near East and around the Mediterranean) and others intrinsically different (as in Europe north of the Alps and the Pyrenees). All these factors shaped the character of the mainstream of Jewish music. They have also determined the nature and location of the sources which the musicologist must explore in order to obtain his facts. The problem can be most easily understood by a comparison with the source situation of European historical musicology. There the sources of information can be ranked as follows: compositions by individuals, created and preserved by musical notation; theoretical treatises; historical documents; instrumental relics; evidence from the visual arts (iconography); and complementary evidence from the fields of religion, the verbal arts, philosophy, political history; and other complementary evidence exploited at the discretion of each scholar. Among the latter, the most important source is the folk music of the area, which survives both in tone and word by a purely oral tradition, except for a few accidental notations made in the past by curious savants, and is in itself the subject of a parallel discipline—ethnomusicology.

The source situation of Jewish music is completely different. All the factors listed above are present, but in entirely different proportions—both absolutely and for each Diaspora area and period. A particularly complicated case is that of musical notation. On the one hand, no tone script, in the European sense of the term (one sound = one symbol) was evolved in Jewish musical culture. Even European Jewry adopted the tone script of the surrounding culture only in a few communities during certain periods and only for certain sections of its total musical activity. On the other hand, the *masoretic accents serve as universal indicators of certain melodic motives for the cantillation of some of the biblical books (according to principles basically common to all Jewish communities), and their syntactical and grammatical function, which came into being at the same time as, if not earlier than, their musical one, is supported by a written tradition of doctrine and discussion. Nevertheless the melodic content of this cantillation differs in each Diaspora area and is transmitted by a purely oral tradition (cf. *Masoretic Accents, Musical Rendition).

Although this oral tradition cannot convey information of its own past, some motives (of both Ashkenazi and Sephardi tradition) have been preserved in notation from the beginning of the 16th century onward. Thus even for this single category of Jewish music, the "art" and "folk" components, the historical and ahistorical, musical and extra-musical, and the local and universal are woven together so tightly that no single strand can serve as the base for any generalization.

As in all other parts of the mainstream tradition of music in Jewish culture, the notated document is not the point of departure, but a fortunate find which may occur on the way but more often is absent. The same holds for autonomous treatises on the "art of music," whether technical or philosophical, for reasons which become clear when the history of musical thought in this culture is traced in detail. Literary sources of all kinds are the main storehouse of historical fact, and very often the only source, since it is here that Jewish life has always documented itself most fully, including its musical actions and thoughts. Yet another important source are the relics of actual musical instruments (especially for the biblical period) and the depictions of instruments and music making ranging from the dawn of history through *illuminated manuscripts to the photographs of *klezmer* ensembles in Eastern Europe before the Holocaust. The living oral traditions preserved and studied through sound recording followed by sophisticated techniques of acoustical analysis and musical transcription are equal in importance to the written, notated, and visual relic, and the application of the historical evidence can very often give them a great measure of historical dimension. Finally, there are the external sources, both historical and ethnomusical. Judicious comparisons with the musical heritage of those cultures with which the Jewish people came into contact, taking and—especially in the case of the formation of Christianity—also giving, can yield valuable insights. In addition, through still wider comparisons, even with historically unrelated cultures, Jewish music can be put into the overall perspective of the music of mankind.

The following survey of the sources is intended to give a general picture of the situation.

WRITTEN SOURCES OF DIRECT AND CIRCUMSTANTIAL EVIDENCE

Most of these do not appear as independent literary units, but as parts of larger works. Potentially, the field includes the entire written heritage of Jewish culture. Some source categories, most of which have not yet been approached by systematic musicological research, have proved to be particularly fruitful in information, such as rabbinic responsa, community registers and regulations, the literature of philosophy and the sciences, the early Midrash, and travelers' accounts. In many cases textual criticism must be applied before the source can be utilized. It must be emphasized that modern translations are only useful for a first approach; ancient and medieval translations, too, should always be considered as testimonies for their own time and place only, if the contrary cannot be proved from an independent source. The same applies to the various kinds of traditional exegesis. Manuscripts of medieval and later poetry very often contain indications that the poem is to be sung "to the tune of..." *(be-lahan, be-no'am, be-niggun);* even if the tunes themselves cannot be recovered, the existence of the repertoire itself is thus documented. When the tunes are taken from a gentile environment which uses notation—as in the German-speaking areas—even the tunes themselves can often be recovered from contemporary manuscripts or printed music. A further stage is reached by the libretti of the cantata-like works which were written mainly in Italy from the 16th century onward. The music for some of these has also survived or still waits to be recovered from the archives; but even if only the texts remain, they often contain indications such as aria, solo, and duetto. Finally, there are also a certain number of theoretical and practical treatises on music, as independent works or more often as chapters of larger treatises. Except for the "cantors' books" (such as Solomon Lipschitz' *Te'udat Shelomo,* Offenbach, 1718), the material naturally reflects the theories and practices of the surrounding culture, in the Islamic regions of Spain and the Near East or in Italy and France. Direct biographical and social evidence can be gleaned from inscriptions (including tombstones), community registers, the **Memorbuch* sources, and other archival material. A special contribution is made by extra-Jewish sources. Both non-Jewish writers and apostates from Judaism often give very detailed descriptions of musical practices in Jewish society, in works written for enlightenment or polemic, and echoes of the musical life of a Jewish community are also bound to appear in official documents of the local and state authorities. They range from a tax collector's list from Ptolemaic Egypt, mentioning "Jacob the son of Jacob, an aulos-player," to the petitions of gentile musicians to the municipality of Prague against their Jewish competitors in the 17th century.

MATERIAL RELICS AND ICONOGRAPHY

For the biblical and Second Temple periods, the written sources are complemented by literally hundreds of archaeological finds from Palestine itself. The soil conditions of Palestine are generally not favorable to the survival of instruments made of organic material, such as drums or string instruments. The archaeological finds, including metal cymbals, bells, pottery rattles, bone and ivory clappers, however, are effectively supplemented by figurines, frescoes, mosaics, pottery decorations, graffiti, images on coins, etc. External sources, such as the Phoenician ivories and bowls which reached the neighboring countries by way of commerce or booty, the decorations of synagogues in the early Diaspora (particularly important for the history of the form of the *shofar*), or the trumpets depicted in relief on the Arch of *Titus further add to the evidence. It is therefore no longer necessary to "illustrate" the story of music in ancient Israel by archaeological finds from the Egyptian or Mesopotamian cultures. Such material may still be used for purposes of comparison, but only if corroborated by a local find.

The correlation of these material relics with the textual ones, above all the Bible, is a task as difficult as it is important. In later periods, the wide choice of instruments in other cultures is limited, for Jewish society, to the *shofar* and simple noisemakers, such as decorative bells on the *rimmonim* of the synagogal scrolls or the various forms of rattling and banging devices for *Purim. The iconographical evidence, however, is to be found in many sources: illuminated manuscripts and marriage contracts, printed books (especially those written by gentiles on "Jewish customs"), synagogue decorations, embellished ritual objects, and, in later periods, even portraits.

NOTATED SOURCES

As indicated above, one cannot expect the notated sources of Jewish music to be plentiful. For the entire period before the 19th century, these notations came only from the settlements of the Ashkenazi, Italian, and European Sephardi communities (except for the earliest specimen so far discovered, the 12th-century notations of *Obadiah the Norman Proselyte, which was found in the Cairo **Genizah* and probably reflects, at least in part, a Near Eastern melodic tradition). The documents are most conveniently divided into two categories: notations reflecting oral tradition, liturgical, religious, and secular; and manuscript or printed compositions in the style of contemporary art music. The manuscripts of Obadiah contain the complete melody of a **piyyut* in praise of Moses, for Shavuot or Simḥat Torah, and two fragments: the ending of another *piyyut* and a setting of verses from Jeremiah, Proverbs, and Job in a distinctly cantillation-like style. An illuminated Bible from Spain, dating from about 1400, contains a page with the beginning of the Song of Songs, featuring a decorative band with notation.

Several German humanists of the 16th century included specimens of masoretic cantillation in their works on the Hebrew language, masorah, etc. The best known of these is the notation in Johannes *Reuchlin's *De accentibus et orthographia linguae hebraicae* (Haguenau, 1518). Some 15 other gentile writers up to the end of the 18th century feature such notations of masoretic cantillation in works on Judaistic subjects and later on also in chapters on the "Music of the Hebrews" in histories of music. As a rule, they copied and recopied the specimens from their predecessors, so that the total stock of notated documentation rises very slowly. The most prominent additions were made by Athanasius Kircher (*Musurgia Universalis,* Rome, 1650; see fig. 8), who features the German-Italian cantillation which he heard in a Roman synagogue; Daniel Jablonski, in his edition of the Hebrew Bible (Berlin, 1699), where a specimen of notated cantillation of the Pentateuch according to the tradition of the Amsterdam Sephardi community was supplied by David de Pinna (cf. *Masoretic Accents, Musical Rendition); and the 12 specimens of Ashkenazi and Sephardi cantillation, psalm intonation, and hymn tunes collected by the composer Benedetto Marcello in Venice in order to base his collection of Psalm compositions *Estro poetico-armonico* (1724–27, and subsequent editions) on "authentic Jewish tunes." They are featured in his own notation at the head of the respective settings. The musical scholar Giovanni Battista Martini gathered all the notations of his predecessors in the first volume of his *Storia Della Musica* (Bologna, 1757–81, repr. facsim. 1967), whence they were taken over (with one omission) by Johann Nikolaus Forkel in his *Allgemeine Geschichte der Musik* (Leipzig, 1788–1801, repr. facsim., 1967).

A few notations of other kinds of traditional music are found from the beginning of the 17th century onward, such as the "learning tune" of the Talmud, some of the songs of the Passover **seder,* the *Priestly Blessing, and the 13 religious folk song tunes printed by Elhanan Kirchhan (Kirchhain) in his *Simḥat ha-Nefesh,* part 2 (Fuerth, 1726/27). The earliest cantorial manual found to date is that of Judah Elias of Hanover, dated 1740, and it is followed by many others, especially toward the end of the 18th century (cf. Aaron *Beer; Isaac *Offenbach). Whether the "Jew parodies" found in the works of several Renaissance and baroque composers actually reproduce what was heard in a synagogue or played by a Jewish musician still remains to be ascertained in each case.

Art music composed in the Western European style is documented by a certain number of scores and parts of scores from Italy, southern France, and the "Portuguese" community of Amsterdam. The earliest work of this kind is Salamon de *Rossi's *Ha-Shirim Asher li-Shelomo* (Venice, 1622/23); for a more extended description of these sources see *Cantatas, Hebrew.

ORAL TRADITION

The chief treasure house of Jewish music is the living oral tradition—the many thousands of melodies and variants still current in the synagogues, schools, and homes in all Jewish communities which adhere, or at least have kept in some measure, to the ways of the past. Their systematic collection, now being made by sound recording, is an awesome and theoretically endless task. A fairly representative selection of several regional traditions was collected by A. Z. *Idelsohn in Jerusalem at the beginning of the 20th century and published in his *Thesaurus of Hebrew-Oriental Melodies* (10 vols., 1914–32): Yemen, Iraq, Persia (with some material from Bukhara and Dagestan), the "Jerusalem Sephardic" tradition, Morocco, and Eastern Europe. Earlier and contemporary collections of synagogal music (see bibliography), mainly of the Ashkenazi and European Sephardi areas, also contain varying amounts of truly traditional melodies, even if these are sometimes distorted by inadequate notation or attempts at "modernization." Much essential material still remains to be recorded. Recent events have made such undertakings more urgent than ever before, since some regional traditions were almost entirely ended by the Holocaust and others are being modified or gradually disappearing in the cultural melting pots of Israel and the remaining Diaspora "mega-centers," such as the United States. Since 1964, the National Sound Archives in the Jewish National and University Library in Jerusalem have attempted to gather all the recordings made previously by the personal initiative of scholars and collectors, beginning with those of Idelsohn, Robert *Lachmann, and Johanna *Spector and augmented them systematically by its own recording projects. By 1971, the collection numbered more than 15,000 items. Smaller collections are also to be found in some other institutions in Israel and in the important private archive of Edith *Gerson-Kiwi in Jerusalem.

HISTORY

BIBLICAL PERIOD

The Bible is the foremost and richest source for knowledge of the musical life of ancient Israel until some time after the return from the Babylonian Exile. It is complemented by several external sources: archaeological relics of musical instruments and of depictions of musical scenes; comparative material from the neighboring cultures; and post-biblical sources, such as the writings of *Philo and *Josephus, the *Apocrypha, and the *Mishnah. A truly chronological ordering of the biblical evidence on music is hardly possible, since it frequently happens that a relatively late source attributes certain occurrences to an early period, in which they could not have existed. A case in point is the chronicler's reports about the ordering of the Temple music by King David. Many details—above all the prominent status of the levitical singers, which almost overshadows that of the priests—are probably a projection back from the chronicler's own time. Some of the reports may even be nothing more than an attempt to furnish the levitical singers with a Davidic authorization in order to strengthen their position. It is therefore more prudent to draw a synthetic picture in which most of the facts can be assumed to have existed for at least a considerable part of the time.

The mythical dimension of music is represented in biblical tradition only by the story of Jubal, who was "the ancestor of all who play the *kinnor* and *ugav*" (Gen. 4:21; for names of instruments see below). Another relic of the same kind may well be found in the allusion in God's speech to Job to the day on which the creation was finished, whereupon, "the morning stars sang together and the Sons of the God[s?] raised a shout of acclamation" (Job 38:7). Most of the evidence concerns the place of music in the cult. Music is conspicuously absent in the stories of the Tabernacle in the desert wanderings. The bells (perhaps only rattling platelets, see below) on the tunic of the high priest had no musical function but an apotropaic one. The trumpets served mainly to direct the movements of the camping multitude, and their function for arousing God's "remembrance" is common to their use in the sacrifice and in war (Num 10:1–10). In the transport of the Ark to Jerusalem by David, which is accompanied by the playing of lyres, drums, rattles, and cymbals (II Sam. 6:5; I Chron. 13:8), the context is that of a popular fete, not an established cult ritual. Even the description of the inauguration of Solomon's Temple in the first chapters of I Kings lacks an explicit reference to music. Only the trumpets are mentioned in the reconstitution of the Temple services in the time of Joash (II Kings 12:14).

In Chronicles, the musical element suddenly appears as the most prominent part of the service, with detailed and repeated "duty rosters" (and genealogies) of the levitic singers and instrumentalists, as planned by David and established by Solomon. Since the lists of the returned exiles from Babylon, in Ezra and Nehemiah, include a certain number of families of Temple singers, it can be assumed that at least toward the end of the First Temple there was already some kind of organized cult music in Jerusalem. On the other hand, there are grounds to believe that the role of music in the First Temple was minimal. In the sanctuaries outside Jerusalem it was probably much more prominent: witness the "prophets' orchestra" at the high place of Gibeah (I Sam. 10:5) and Amos' fulminations against the external pomp in one of the cult centers of the northern tribes, perhaps in Shechem, "take away from me the roaring of thy songs and the playing of thy lyres will I not hear" (Amos 5:23).

After the return from Babylon, music as a sacred art and an artistic sacred act was gradually given its place in the organization of the Temple services. It seems that this did not pass without opposition. Some scholars have even tried to adduce a power struggle between the levites and the priests. Although the evidence does not mention music as a subject for quarrel, the striving of the levitic singers for prestige is implicit in the chronicler's descriptions, and may even be the reason for the insertion of the poem, or set of poems "By the waters of Babylon," in the collection of Psalms (Ps. 137). The weepers by the waters of Exile were not an abstract personification; they were the levitic singers, whom their captors would have join the other exotic court orchestras that the Assyrian and Babylonian kings kept for entertainment and took care to replenish by their expeditions of conquest. The court and temple orchestras of Mesopotamia in this period are the prototype for the Temple music established in Jerusalem after the return: a large body of stringed instruments of one or two types only (in Jerusalem *kinnor* and *nevel*); a small number, or a single pair, of cymbals; and a large choir. The trumpets of the priests constituted a separate body in every respect, with a ritual but not really musical function. In the earlier stages of religious organization, centered around inspirational-ecstatic prophecy, the role of music was understandably important (cf. I Sam. 10:5 and the story of Elisha's musically induced prophetic seizure in II Kings 3:15). David's playing and singing before Saul belongs to a related psychological aspect.

At coronations the trumpets were blown as part of the formal proclamation (II Kings 11:14), and the spontaneous and organized rejoicings after victory in war were accompanied by women who sang, drummed, and danced (a practice still current among the bedouin), cf. The Song of the *Sea, and the women's welcome of David and Saul in I Sam. 18:6–7. Music at popular feasts is described in Judges 21:19ff. Finally, the musical accompaniment at the feasts of the rich and, of course, at the king's court is also described several times, often with a note of reproach (II Sam. 19:36; Isa. 5:12; Amos 6:5; Eccles. 2:8). The musical expression of mourning is implicit in the verses of David's lament for Saul and Jonathan and explicit in the mention of the male and female mourners who repeated specially composed dirges (II Chron. 35:25). True folk music is mentioned only rarely, such as the songs and rhythmic shouts of the workers in the vineyards (probably the grape treaders) alluded to by the prophets.

The number of identifiable terms for musical instruments in the Bible comes to about 19. Some other terms, notably those appearing in the headings of the Psalms, have also been taken to represent instruments but probably mean

Figure 1a. Pair of bronze cymbals and bronze bowl (possibly a drum), from Hazor, 14th–13th century B.C.E. Cymbals, diam. c. 4 in. (10 cm.); bowl, diam. c. 8 in. (20 cm.). From Y. Yadin et al., *Hazor I*, Jerusalem, 1958.

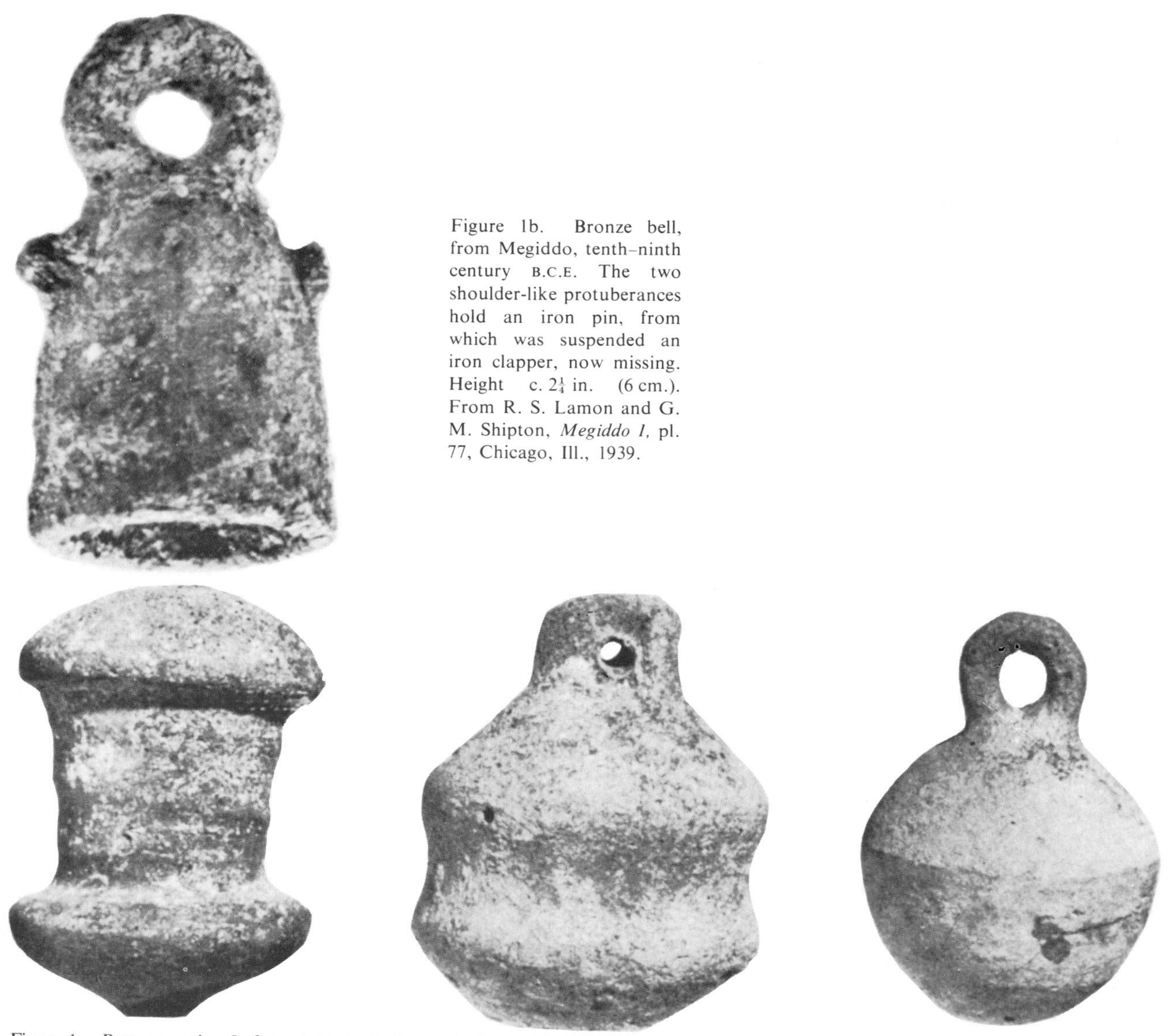

Figure 1b. Bronze bell, from Megiddo, tenth–ninth century B.C.E. The two shoulder-like protuberances hold an iron pin, from which was suspended an iron clapper, now missing. Height c. $2\frac{1}{4}$ in. (6 cm.). From R. S. Lamon and G. M. Shipton, *Megiddo I*, pl. 77, Chicago, Ill., 1939.

Figure 1c. Pottery rattles. Left to right: Beth Shemesh, first half of the first millennium B.C.E., height $3\frac{1}{2}$ in. (8.5 cm.); Gezer, first quarter of second millennium B.C.E., height 3 in. (7.5 cm.); Gezer, last quarter of second millennium B.C.E., height $4\frac{3}{4}$ in. (12 cm.). Courtesy Israel Department of Antiquities and Museums, Jerusalem.

Figure 1d. Ivory horn decorated in relief, from Ugarit, c. 14th century B.C.E. Present length 23½ in. (60 cm.), internal diameter of mouth hole ½ in. (1.5 cm.). From C. Schaeffer in *Syria 31*, Paris, 1954, p. 62.

some kind of indication of the melody. For many of the terms, a precise archaeological equivalent can already be proposed. Others still await the yield of future excavations. In the following section, the instruments will be listed and described briefly. A selection of archaeological finds can be seen in figures 1 and 2.

(1) *Asor* (עָשׂוֹר), see below, under *nevel*.

(2) *Ḥalil* (חָלִיל), double-pipe wind instrument, with the mouthpieces probably of the single-reed ("clarinet") type and probably made up of one melody pipe and one drone pipe. A folk and popular instrument, it was used for rejoicing and also in mourning ceremonies.

(3) *Ḥaẓoẓerah* (חֲצוֹצְרָה), trumpet, made of precious metal, generally silver. Blown by the priests, it was used in the sacrificial ceremony, in war, and in royal coronations.

(4) *Kaitros/Katros*, see below, under "Daniel instruments."

(5) *Keren* (קֶרֶן), Aram. *karna* (קַרְנָא), see below, under *shofar*.

(6) *Kinnor* (כִּנּוֹר). A stringed instrument of the lyre family, constituted by a body, two arms, and a yoke. The Canaanite type of the instrument, which was certainly the same as used by the Israelites, is asymmetric, with one arm shorter than the other, and its body is box shaped. The instrument was probably of an average height of 20–23 in. (50–60 cm.) and sounded in the alto range, as evinced by surviving specimens from Egypt (which took over the form and even kept the name of the instrument from the neighboring Semites). The *kinnor* is the noble string instrument of Semitic civilization, and became the chief instrument of the orchestra of the Second Temple. It was played by David and was therefore held in particular honor by the Levites. According to Josephus, it had ten strings and was sounded with a plectrum (Ant., 7:306), and according to the Mishnah its strings were made of the small intestines of sheep (Kin. 3:6).

(7) *Mashrokita* (מַשְׁרוֹקִיתָא), see below, under "Daniel instruments."

(8) *Mena'ane'im* (מְנַעַנְעִים), mentioned only in II Samuel 6:5 among the instruments played during David's transport of the Ark to Jerusalem. The parallel narrative in I Chronicles 13:8 substitutes *meẓiltayim* (cymbals). The numerous finds of pottery rattles make it highly probable, by etymological analogy (נענע "shaking"), that the term can be applied to them. After about the seventh century B.C.E., these rattles disappeared and were replaced by the newly invented metal bell (see below, under *pa'amon*).

(9) *Meẓiltayim, Ẓilẓalim, Meẓillot* (מְצִלְתַּיִם, צִלְצְלִים, מְצִילּוֹת), the first two forms probably standing for cymbals. The cymbals found in excavations were made of bronze, in the form of plates with a central hollow boss and with a metal thumb-loop. The average diameter of the finds is about 4.5 in. (12 cm.). They were played by the Levites in the Temple. The *meẓillot* of the horses, mentioned in Zechariah 14:20, are probably the same metal ball-jingles depicted on Assyrian reliefs.

(10) *Minnim* (מִנִּים), an unclear term (Ps. 150:5 and perhaps also Ps. 45:9), presumably a stringed instrument, and perhaps the lute, which was never an integral part of the Canaanite and Israelite instrumentarium.

(11) *Nevel* (נֵבֶל), a type of lyre, perhaps originating in Asia Minor, constructed differently from the *kinnor*-lyre—larger, and therefore of deeper tone. The coins of Bar Kokhba show it in a schematized form (see fig. 2e). According to Josephus it had 12 strings and was played by plucking with the fingers (Ant., 7:306). Extra-biblical sources which describe it under the name of *nabla* mention its "breathy" or "rumbling" tone. It was the second main instrument in the Temple orchestra. According to the Mishnah (Kin. 3:6), its strings were made of the large intestines of sheep. The *nevel asor* (נֵבֶל עָשׂוֹר), or, in its brief form, *asor* (Ps. 33:2; 92:4; 144:9), was perhaps a slightly smaller *nevel* with ten strings only.

(12) *Pa'amon* (פַּעֲמוֹן), mentioned only in Exodus 28:33–34 and 39:25–26 (and later by Josephus), as attached to the tunic of the High Priest alternating with the ornament called *rimmon* (pomegranate) and made of gold. The usual meaning of the term is a bell. Bells came into use in the Near East only in the seventh century B.C.E., so that the noise-making attachments to the high priest's garment in the desert Tabernacle could not have been bells proper. If the description in Exodus is not a pure projection back from the period of the First or Second Temple, the original *pa'amonim* must have been metal platelets. Later on, these were substituted by real bells. Most bells found in Palestine are small, made of bronze, and have an iron clapper.

(13–14) *Pesanterin* פְּסַנְתְּרִין and *sabbekha* (סַבְּכָא / שַׂבְּכָא), see below, under "Daniel instruments."

(15) *Shalishim* (שָׁלִשִׁים), mentioned only in I Samuel 18:6–7, as played by women. By analogy with Ugaritic *tlt*-metal (and not *tlt* and *šlš* as meaning "three"), these may be cymbals or struck metal bowls.

(16) *Shofar* (שׁוֹפָר), the horn of the ram or a wild ovine, and the only instrument to have survived in Jewish usage, probably identical with the *keren* (קֶרֶן) and *keren ha-yovel* (קֶרֶן הַיּוֹבֵל). In the Bible its function is that of a signaling instrument especially in war; its famous appearance at the siege of Jericho must be understood in this sense and not as a magical noisemaker. The *shofar*-like sound at the receiving of the Ten Commandments is also a transfer from the same domain. Only after the *shofar* was taken into the service in the Second Temple did it regain its primitive magical connotation (see also **Shofar*).

(17) *Sumponyah* (סוּמְפּוֹנְיָה), see below, under "Daniel instruments."

(18) *Tof* (תּוֹף), a shallow round frame drum, frequently played by women (cf. *Miriam), and associated with the dance.

(19) *Ugav* (עוּגָב), still unclear, but very probably not the wind instrument which medieval exegesis would have it to be. Perhaps the harp, which, like the lute *(minnim?)* was never an integral part of the Canaanite and Israelite instrumentarium.

(20) "Daniel Instruments." Daniel 3:5 describes, in Aramaic, an orchestra at the court of the Babylonian king, which includes the *karna, mashrokita, kaitros, sabbekha, pesanterin, sumponyah,* "and all kinds of instruments." *Karna* is the horn, and *kaitros, sabbekha,* and *pesanterin* are but Aramaized versions of the Greek *kithara, sambyke,* and *psalterion. Mashrokita* is a whistling or piping instrument; *sumponyah* parallels the Greek *symphoneia,* which, in itself, means only "the sounding together." It is highly probable that the term does not stand for an instrument at all, but means the concerted sound of those mentioned before. The closing of the sentence, "and all kinds of instruments," would thus be nothing but an explanatory gloss.

The forms of music can only be surmised from the forms of those parts of biblical poetry which are clearly meant to be sung. The most important of these are the Psalms, or at least a great part of the 150 poems gathered into the canon of the Psalter. Many of these open with an "invitation to music" ("Let us go and sing," "Sing to the Lord a new song"). Before the body of the Psalm itself, a shorter or longer heading formula often appears, in which at least some of the elements have a presumably musical meaning. *Mizmor* and *shir,* also combined as *mizmor-shir* and *shir-mizmor,* are clearly of this kind, but their musical difference has so far remained obscure. The term *lamenazze'aḥ* has often been thought to mean "to the choirmaster." Most tantalizing of all are the phrases prefixed by *al* ("upon"?) such as *"al-ayyelet ha-shaḥar"* (Ps. 22, literally "upon the hind [?] of the dawn"), or *"al ha-sheminit"* (Ps. 6, literally "upon the eighth"), and others which are untranslatable even literally. The most reasonable hypothesis is that these designate certain melodic types. Whether the term *selah* which appears at the end of certain verses in many psalms (and often creates a tripartite division of the psalm) has a musical meaning still remains to be proved.

The sounds themselves are lost. Although comparative studies of living Jewish and other Near Eastern traditions may be able to point to certain melodic and formal elements as "very old," their attribution to the biblical or early post-biblical period can never be confirmed by objective proof.

SECOND TEMPLE PERIOD

Only the last part of this period is documented by contemporary literature (chiefly Philo, Josephus, and the writings of the sectarians of Qumran). Much of the mishnaic narrative concerning music in the Temple service is based on eyewitness memories. The information is often very precise, such as the description of the daily morning sacrifice in Mishnah *Tamid* and the numbers of instruments in the Temple orchestra in Mishnah *Arakhin.* The figure of the Temple musician himself appears much more clearly. Thus there is Hogras ben Levi, who was prefect of the singers and would not teach his own technique of virtuoso voice production to others (Shek. 5:1; Yoma 3:11). Of the instruments mentioned in the Bible, only the Temple instruments proper appear again: *kinnor, nevel, ẓilẓal* and *meẓiltayim, ḥaẓoẓerah,* and the newly accepted *shofar.* The *ḥalil* is also mentioned as a popular instrument which was played in the Temple only on 12 days of the year (Ar. 2:3). The term *abbuv* (pipe) is used for the separate pipes of the *ḥalil.*

Other terms proposed as musical instruments by later commentaries, from the *Gemara* onward, are very probably not instruments at all, such as *niktimon, batnun, markof, iros.* Neither is the *magrefah,* a rake which was noisily thrown on the floor after the cleaning of the altar to signal to the singers in their chambers to proceed to their stations, which talmudic exegesis later turned into the equivalent of the Byzantine organ.

A separate body of musical practice and doctrine was evolved by the dissident sectarians of the period. The choral singing of the *Therapeutae in Egypt is described by Philo and Josephus and seems to be the musical base of some of the hymns found in the Dead Sea Scrolls. The sectarians seem to have eschewed the use of musical instruments, holding "the fruit of the mouth," i.e., singing, as the more pure expression of devotion. Some passages in their writings and in Ben Sira may indicate the existence of ideas which approach very closely to the sphere of musical, or rather musical-poetical theory. The catastrophe in 70 C.E. put an end to the Temple-centered music of the Jewish people and opened a new period, in which the *synagogue became the focal point of creativity in word and tone.

[B.B.]

THE EMERGENCE OF SYNAGOGUE SONG

Late Hellenistic civilization made music an all-penetrating cultural activity. The Eastern scene was dotted with theaters, arenas, and circuses where singers and virtuosos flocked together at musical contests (organized even by Herod; Jos., Ant., 15:269ff.; 16:137). Music was discussed by amateur philosophers at social gatherings of every kind. Jingling, banging, and rattling accompanied heathen cults, and the frenzying shawms of a dozen ecstatic rites intoxicated the masses. Amid this euphoric farewell feast of a dying civilization, the voices of nonconformists were emerging from places of Jewish and early Christian worship; Philo of Alexandria had already emphasized the ethical qualities of music, spurning the "effeminate" art of his gentile surroundings. Similarly, early synagogue song intentionally foregoes artistic perfection, renounces the playing of instruments, and attaches itself entirely to "the word"—the text of the Bible.

The new style of Jewish music made its appearance at a specific and fateful moment. When the destruction of the Temple in 70 C.E. demanded a complete rearrangement in the religious, liturgical, and spiritual fields, music became involved in several ways. The abolition of Temple worship also put an end to the refined instrumental art of the levites. The use of instruments in the synagogue service was prohibited (and remained so, with certain exceptions), leaving music a strictly vocal art. Needless to say, this limitation left its imprint on musical style and form. Moreover, the musical skill of the levitic singers and their tradition, accumulated over generations, were not utilized in synagogue song, and their professional teaching and rules had not survived in writing. Synagogue song was

Representation of instruments and music scenes from the biblical to the talmudic period, found in Ereẓ Israel, in the area of Canaanite culture, and in the Diaspora.

Figure 2a. Pottery incense stand, probably cultic, from Ashdod, c. 1000 B.C.E. Four of the five molded figures are playing, respectively, cymbals, a double pipe, a frame drum, and a lyre. Height 12½ in. (32 cm.) approx. Courtesy M. Dothan, Israel Department of Antiquities, Jerusalem.

Figure 2c. Alabaster relief from the palace of Sennacherib in Nineveh, end of sixth century B.C.E., showing three captive lyre players, probably from Lachish, in the charge of an Assyrian soldier. London, British Museum.

Figure 2d. Rock engraving (graffito) in the Wadi Kudeirat, northeastern Sinai, showing a row of dancers accompanied by a drummer. The leading dancer is swinging a rope or kerchief, and the scene is reminiscent of the traditional Arab *debkah* dance. Dated by Anati to the second millennium B.C.E. and by Bayer to the Hellenistic period (last centuries B.C.E.). Courtesy E. Anati, Jerusalem.

Figure 2b. Engraved panel from a small ivory casket, showing a dancer accompanied by a player on the double pipe entertaining a dignitary at a banquet. From Tel Far'ah (the ancient Sharuhen) in the Negev, c. 13th–12th century B.C.E. From W. M. Petrie, *Bet Pelet* I, pl. LV. London, 1930.

Figure 2e. Stylized representations of instruments played in the Second Temple, on coins of the Bar Kokhba Revolt, 132–35 C.E. Left to right: a pair of trumpets and two types of lyre, one probably the *kinnor,* the other the *nevel.* Jerusalem, Israel Museum, Israel Department of Antiquities Collection.

Figure 2f. A *shofar,* curved and decorated type, depicted (far right) on a fragment of a stone screen from the synagogue at Ashkelon, fifth-sixth century C.E. Courtesy Israel Department of Antiquities, Jerusalem.

Figure 2g. A *shofar,* angled and smooth type, depicted (left of *menorah*) on a relief from the synagogue of Eshtemoa, fourth century C.E. Courtesy Archaeological Survey of Israel, Jerusalem.

thus a new beginning in every respect—especially with regard to its spiritual basis.

In the new era, prayer was to take the place of sacrifice in providing atonement and grace (RH 17b). Levitical music had been an integral part of the order of sacrifices (Er. 13:2; Ar. 11a; TJ, Pes. 4:1, 30c). Its nature probably was to be as pure and flawless as the offering itself, for it was directed at the heavens and not at a human audience. It must have striven for objective and transcendental beauty and have been "art music." The task of synagogue song was a different one. The individual and the congregation both appeal to God by means of the spoken word. Prayer, regarded as "service of the heart" *(avodah she-ba-lev)*, had to express a broad scale of human feelings: joy, thanksgiving, and praise, but also supplication, consciousness of guilt, and contrition. All these emotions urge subjective expression in song and human warmth, rather than abstract beauty. The strong human element in synagogue music made itself acutely felt as soon as the professional solo singer began to appear. Before this, however, any member of a congregation could be called up to lead in prayer as a "delegate of the community" *(sheli'aḥ ẓibbur)*. The gift of a fine voice obliged a member of the community to accept the function of lay precentor (PR 25: PdRK 97a).

Among the different singing styles in which the early nonprofessional *sheliḥei ẓibbur* may have performed, are elementary ones that can be ascribed with certainty to the early synagogue. They are suited to a gathering of people assembled for singing prayer and praise and for the majority of whom artistically contrived song and complicated tunes were normally out of range. Such congregations had to be cemented together by a kind of music that was easily grasped and performed. These conditions are fulfilled by the musical forms of psalmody, chanted Bible reading, and prayer tunes bases on a simple melodic pattern. These are the archetypes of synagogue song and have been preserved by the whole range of Jewish communities over the ages.

THE ROOTS OF SYNAGOGUE SONG IN THE NEAR EASTERN COMMUNITIES (c.70–950 C.E.)

The Formation of the Basic Pattern (c. 70–500 C.E.). A strong similarity of style can be detected in the recitation of the Psalms or chapters from other biblical books by different Jewish communities. Exactly the same recitation style is to be found in the most ancient traditions of the Catholic, Orthodox, and Syrian churches. Since there was a close contact between the faiths only at a early period, the musical structure or styles of singing must have been accepted by Christianity together with the Holy Scriptures themselves. Many of its different forms, which are still employed by Jewish communities in many different parts of the world, were also described in ancient literature. The findings point to a common source of Bible song in the early synagogue.

Psalmody. The singing of Psalms occupies an important place in Jewish and in Christian worship. Both creeds share the musical pattern known as psalmody (Greek-Christian *psalmodia*). Its outlines and internal organization follow closely those of the poetic form. Each psalm may consist of a smaller or greater number of verses, without being organized in symmetrical stanzas. Accordingly, the melody of one verse may become a musical unit which is repeated as many times as there are verses in the psalm. Most of the verses are subdivided into two equal parts (hemistichs) by a caesura; similarly, the psalmodic melody is given a bipartite structure. The biblical verse is formed and characterized solely by the number of its stressed syllables, disregarding completely how many weak syllables there are between the stresses. The verse of a psalm may consequently vary widely in length, since the overall number of syllables is not constant. The tune has to be adaptable to these floating conditions; the required elasticity is provided for by a "recitation note," which may be repeated according to the particular situation.

In practice, the singer of a psalm verse reaches the "recitation note" through a short initial motion of the voice, dwells on the former for the main part of the text, and concludes the first hemistich with a medial cadence. The second hemistich is performed in the same manner, but concludes with a final cadence. Thus the basic psalmodic formula (see Mus. ex. 1) consists of:

initial motion/recitation note/medial cadence/
initial motion/recitation note/final cadence

The simple melodic material of this basic formula can be grasped and reproduced by an average audience after listening to a verse or two. In this respect, psalmody is a truly collective genre of music. Its aesthetic and psychological effect is governed by the recurrent repetition of the same

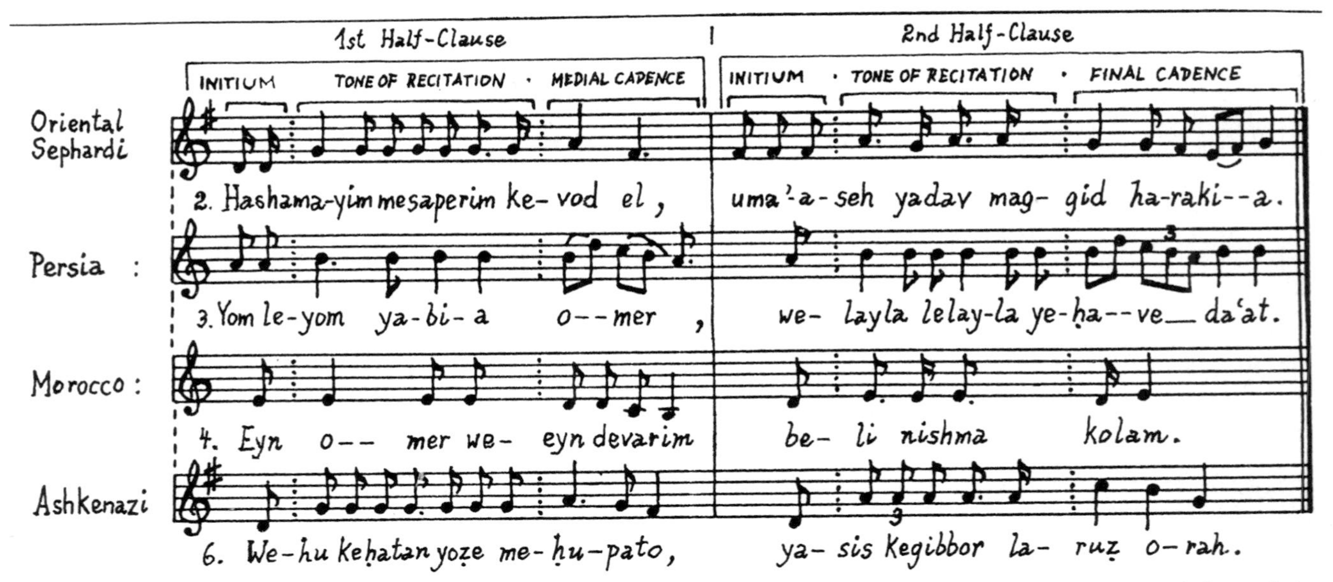

Example 1. The basic formula of psalmody. Verses of Psalm 19, as chanted in various communities. After Idelsohn, *Melodien*, vol. 4, no. 25 (Oriental Sephardi); *ibid.*, vol. 3, no. 51 (Persia); *ibid.*, vol. 5, no. 17 (Morocco); I. Lachmann, *Awaudas Yisroeil*, vol. 1, 189?, no. 154 (Western Ashkenazi).

Written evidence relevant to the history of music in Ereẓ Israel.

Figure 3a. Hexagonal clay prism of Sennacherib, containing a description of the Assyrian monarch's campaign against King Hezekiah of Judah, 701 B.C.E. This is almost identical with the copies in the British Museum and the Oriental Institute of the University of Chicago. The list of tribute paid by Hezekiah (c. II Kings, 18:14–16) includes "male and female musicians." Height 14½ in. (37 cm.). Baghdad Museum.

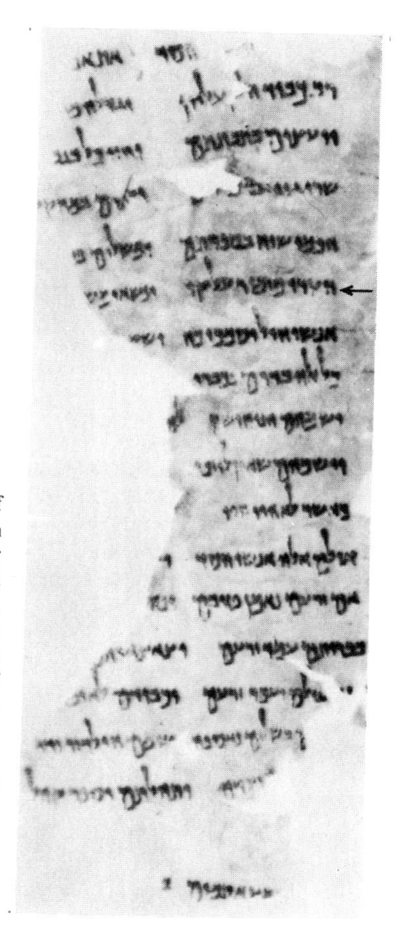

Figure 3b. The "Praise of the Fathers of Old" by Ben Sira, beginning of chapter 44, on the scroll found at Masada, first century C.E. Those praised include (fifth full line, as indicated), the *ḥokerei mizmor al kav,* of which a possible translation is, "those who study song/poetry by its rules." Jerusalem, Israel Museum, Shrine of the Book, D. Samuel and Jeane H. Gottesman Center for Biblical Manuscripts. Photo David Harris, Jerusalem.

Figure 3c. Inscription [. . . .]לבית התקיעה להכ *Le-veit ha-teki'ah lhkh* [. . . .] on a stone from a rampart or tower at the southwest corner of the Second Temple enclosure. Found on the Herodian pavement at the foot of the wall, where it had fallen when the Temple was destroyed. *Beit ha-teki'ah,* the house or place of blowing, presumably refers to the place from which a priest used to blow the trumpet at the beginning and end of the Sabbath to announce the times for the cessation and resumption of labor. Courtesy Israel Exploration Society, Jerusalem, Excavations of the Southern Wall. Photo A. B. Glik.

melodic phrase—an element of stability coupled and contrasting with the constantly changing text. The tune, after a few repetitions, loses all its interest: the attention automatically turns to the words, which continually offer something new. The accompanying vocal inflections merge and form an acoustical background which infiltrates the subconscious and creates a distinct mood, which eventually becomes associated with a certain feast or time of prayer or with grief and other emotions. The unchanging repetition of the formula throughout a psalm, which is the rule in Gregorian chant, is, in fact, seldom practiced in Jewish song. Apparently, even an unsophisticated congregation wanted to avoid dullness and to enliven the sound of the Davidic hymns (Song R. 4:4).

One line of development in psalmody led to the distribution of the performance between groups of singers. Responsorial psalmody was described as early as the Mishnah (Suk. 3:11; Sot. 5:4) and both Talmuds (Sot. 30b; Suk. 38b; TJ, Suk. 3:12, 53d). Precentor and congregation alternated in singing full verses or hemistichs (see also Mus. ex. 2b); the precentor may intone the beginning and the choir take over; or the choir may sing the concluding words. Moreover, a verse or part thereof may serve as refrain, "like an adult reading the *Hallel*, and they respond to him with the initial verse [as, e.g., in the Song of the Sea]: Moses said 'I will sing unto the Lord,' and they say 'I will sing unto the Lord'; Moses said 'for he hath triumphed gloriously,' and they say 'I will sing unto the Lord' . . ." This *baraita*, transmitted in the name of R. Akiva (d. 136 C.E.) and some of his contemporaries, treats the various forms of responsorial psalmody as old and well established. It demonstrates the transformation of the first hemistich into an actual refrain. The exclamation "Hallelujah" may be given this role when it is inserted at discretion between verses. This practice was described by Rava (c. 300 C.E.; Suk. 38b), and is found in the Christian tradition as *Psalmus alleluiatus*, and is still perpetuated by the Yemenite Jews (see Mus. ex. 2a).

Additions alien to the biblical text are very rare in Jewish tradition (Mus. ex. 2b) but have become the rule in the antiphonal psalmody of the churches. The Greek term *antiphonos* originally meant alternate singing in different pitches (e.g., by men and women or men and boys); Philo heard this performed by the sect of Therapeutae. However, worship in the synagogue, which was a congregation exclusively of men and lacked a separate clergy, was unfavorable to the formation of permanent choirs, and the embellishment of a psalm was contrary to the obligation of faithfulness to the holy text. There was no limitation, however, on the strictly musical development of psalmody, with the basic formula serving as a mere skeleton for more complex forms. The musical evolution is achieved mainly by means of variation—just as the poetic language of the Psalms draws largely upon variation within the framework of *Parallelismus membrorum*. Once again, musical composition enhances the poetry.

Jewish psalmody prefers to have hemistichs recited on different tone levels, which is very exceptional in Plainsong. Moreover, the recitation note need not remain rigid but may hover around its axis, raising stressed syllables here, marking a subdivision there, or simply adorning the tune. The initial phrases may be redoubled as well as omitted. Finally, several psalmodic formulas may be joined within the same psalm. The device of variation is capable of producing true artistic effects by a gradual escalation of its resources as, for instance, in Psalm 29 for Sabbath eve as sung in Iran (Idelsohn, *Melodien*, III (1922), no. 3): here the melody gradually gains momentum and increasingly dense texture in accord with the intensification of the poetic images. Psalmodic music may change its features according to the contents of the text to a certain extent: nevertheless, it must be content to strengthen, but never outdo, the effect of the words. The ancient pattern of psalmody is still extensively used in Jewish communities all over the world. It is worth noting that the detailed accents later added to the psalm text by the Masoretes were disregarded: the

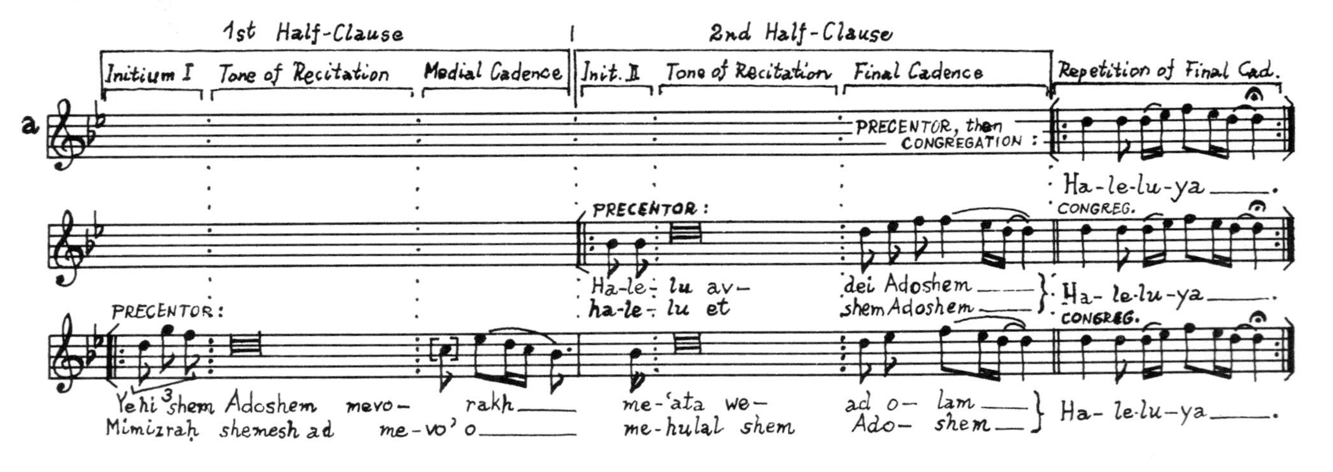

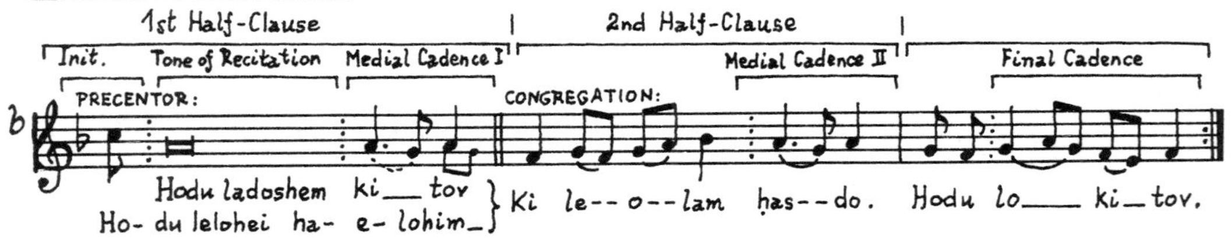

EXAMPLE 2. Responsorial psalmody. (a) *Hallel* Psalm 113, as chanted in Yemen, with a Hallelujah response by the congregation after each verse, similar to the Gregorian *Psalmus alleluiatus*. After Idelsohn, *Melodien*, vol. 1, no. 32; (b) *Hallel* Psalm 136, as chanted in Iraq, with the unwritten response, *Hodu Lo ki tov* (Praise Him for [He] is good), by the congregation after each verse. After Idelsohn, *Melodien*, vol. 2, no. 23.

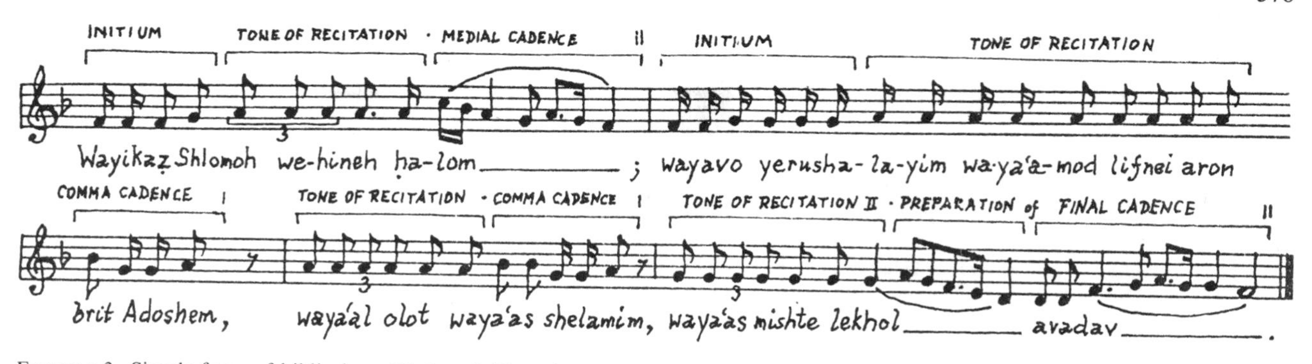

EXAMPLE 3. Simple form of biblical cantillation. I Kings 3:15, as chanted in Bukhara to a psalmodic pattern. After Idelsohn, *Melodien*, vol. 3, no. 138.

traditional manner of intoning psalms was already too deeply rooted (see also *Psalms, Musical Rendition).

BIBLE READING BY CHANT. Chapters from the Pentateuch and the Prophets are regularly read in the synagogue service, the other books of the Bible being reserved for certain feasts. It is characteristic of the synagogue that the Bible is never read like speech or declamation; it is always chanted to musical pitches and punctuated by melodic cadences attached to clauses and periods. The reading of the Bible at home or at school is performed in the same way (see also *Masoretic Accents, Musical Rendition). This custom is strange to European habits. The ancient Greeks already knew well how to distinguish between the rising and falling of the voice in rhetorical speech or stage declamation on the one hand, and true musical intervals, on the other. When the Church took over biblical chanting from the synagogue, its Roman branch retained the chant in a simple form and did not develop it any further. Eastern Christianity, however, embarked on its own development and elaboration of scriptural chanting, which took a course parallel to the developments within Judaism.

There is ample evidence of Bible chant in Jewish sources as early as the second century C.E., by which time it was an old and well-established custom. In the third century Rav interpreted the verse "And they read in the book, in the Law of God . . . and caused them to understand the reading" (Neh. 8:8) as a reference to the *piskei te'amim*, i.e., punctuation by means of melodic cadences (Meg. 3a). Still earlier, Rabbi Akiva expressed his demand for daily study—also executed in chant—by the words "Sing it every day, sing it every day" (Sanh. 99a). Finally, Johanan, head of the Tiberias Academy (d. 279), formulated the central idea of chant in this categorical manner: "Whoever reads [the Torah] without melody and the studies [Mishnah] without song, to him may be applied the verse (Ezek. 20:25): Wherefore I gave them also statutes that were not good, and ordinances whereby they should not live" (Meg. 32a). As an external witness, Jerome (c. 400 C.E., in Bethlehem) testifies that the Jews "chant off" the Torah (*decantant divina mandata:* PL 24. 561).

Talmudic sources state that the biblical verse was subdivided into clauses according to its meaning and the rhythm of speech. This division was called *pissuk te'amim* and was strictly an oral tradition, the transmission of which was incumbent upon the teachers of children. Their method of instruction was the ancient practice of chironomy—hand and finger signs that evoked the medial, final, and other cadences of Bible chant (Ned. 37b; attested by R. Akiva, Ber. 62a). Chironomy had already been used by the singers of ancient Egypt and was later also adopted by the Byzantines. It was practiced by Jews in the time of the masoretes, of Rashi (comm. on Ber. 62a), and, until recently, in Italy and Yemen. On the other hand, their absence in the sources indicates that there were no written "accents" *(te'amim)* during the talmudic period. These were gradually developed and introduced—together with vocalization—by the masoretes in the second half of the first millennium ("Although the cadential division of the verses and the reading tune were given at Mount Sinai, they were uttered according to oral tradition and not to accent marks in the book." *Maḥzor Vitry*, par. 424; 11th century). The nature of this primitive, unwritten Bible chant can be inferred from the present custom of some communities, notably the Yemenites and Bukharans, which still disregard the written accents and read the Bible in a much simpler manner, using only the well-known cadences of psalmody plus an intermediate stop (see Mus. ex. 3).

The antiquity of this modest kind of chanting is proven by its existence in the Roman Church. Like psalmody, it appears to have been accepted there as a body foreign to Western musical concepts and remained, therefore, in its primitive state.

Psalmody and melodic reading are common traits of all the "peoples of the Bible." Repeated attempts to find an archetype of it in pagan antiquity have not succeeded. Melodic enunciation has been connected with Bible recitation from the very beginning and has accompanied the Holy Scriptures through their translation into every tongue. In contrast to sensualist tendencies in art, which take the Bible text as a mere opportunity for writing a beautiful piece of music, Bible chant is the genuine expression of a spiritual concept and, as such, is opposed to the general trend of the Hellenistic period. Its restriction to a small range of notes and limited ornamentation is intentional, not "primitive," with the purpose of ensuring that the melody will never interfere with the perception of the words and the apprehension of their meaning and spiritual message. As defined by Curt *Sachs, such music making is "logogenic"—proceeding from the word and serving the word (see *Masoretic Accents, Musical Rendition).

THE EARLY STYLE OF PRAYER CHANT. During the first period of synagogue song, the precentor was normally chosen from the ranks of the congregation, and his devotion did not always have to be balanced by musical gifts and skills. Prayer tunes thus had to be simple and, simultaneously, of a plastic and variable nature in order to be fitted to longer or shorter phrases of the prose texts without difficulty. These demands are met by the "prayer modes" *(nusaḥim)* traditional and common in the Eastern and Western synagogues of today. Although it is impossible to ascribe individual tunes heard today to the early synagogue with any degree of certainty, it is legitimate to speak of the principle of chanting according to a *nusaḥ*.

Jewish prayer chant is essentially an evolution of traditional melodic patterns classifiable as "*Tefillah*-mode," "*Yoẓer*-mode," and so on. The melodic pattern of a certain *nusaḥ* consists of several motives, which are not in any fixed rhythm or meter, but are rather a melodic formula which is apt to be expanded or shortened according to the text. The motives may be repeated or omitted, they may change places and, above all, they may be subjected to variation by the singer. Melodic patterns of this kind are used in Sephardi, Ashkenazi, and Oriental communities alike. Their nature may best be recognized from their adaptation to metrical prayer texts (see Mus. ex. 4a), as well as to free recitation (Mus. ex. 4b).

The musical effect of a prayer mode rests on its "varied unity"; it establishes a common stock of motives for a whole group of prayers without imposing a rigid, unchanging framework upon it. The melodic development is stimulated by improvised variation—which has always been an important element in Jewish music (see **Nusaḥ; *Shtayger*).

THE POPULAR BACKGROUND. Psalmody, melodic reading of Bible texts, and prayer chant were made to fulfill a function in collective Jewish worship; they grew organically from a popular treasure of forms, under the guidance of basic religious ideas. The latter excluded from worship the use of the multitude of instruments which were, in fact, in the hands of Jews in Palestine and Babylonia: the frame drum *tabla* (Ar. *tabl;* Persian *tabira*) accompanied song and dance and pleased the women especially ("The sexagenarian as much as the six-year-old runs after the drum": MK 9b); the reed-pipe *abbuv* was blown; the long-necked lute *tanbura* (Ar. *tunbur*) plucked. Workmen used to sing to lighten monotonous toil such as plowing, boat towing, or weaving (Sot. 48a). Song was heard in the tavern (Sanh. 101a), and every kind of musical entertainment at the fair (Ta'an. 22a; BK 86a see Rashi) and social gatherings (Sot. 48a).

The spiritual leaders of the Babylonian Jews opposed popular music making as unsuitable for a nation in distress (relying upon Sot. 9:11 and 14). Their negative attitude ("Song in the house—destruction at the threshold," Sot. 48a) became even more entrenched when the feudal aristocracy of Sassanian Persia made music part of their hedonistic enjoyment of life, and even the exilarch Mar *Ukba I allowed himself to be attended with music at his ceremonial levee (TJ, Meg. 3:2, 74a; Git. 7a). At this time Rav *Huna issued his famous prohibition of music, which, however, had undesirable side effects and was dropped by his successor *Ḥisda (Sot. 48a). Palestine was apparently spared this unrealizable prohibition. There was never any intention to interfere with the music making at wedding festivities *(hillula);* on the contrary, this was regarded as a religious duty *(mitzvah)*.

Several legends tell of the rabbis' eagerness "to gladden the groom and bride" (Ber. 6b; TJ, Pe'ah 1:1, 15d, etc.). On these occasions, genuine responsorial singing was performed (Ber. 31a): an honored guest had to improvise a verse suitable for the company to answer with one of the current refrains (such as Ket. 16b–17a). Responsorial psalmody may have been influenced by such common customs. Antiphony, in its original meaning of alternating choirs of different pitch, was also employed at the popular level (Sot. 48a). Instrumental playing at the wedding *hillula* was officially encouraged, and this favorable attitude of the Talmud teachers became a guideline for later legal decisions.

It is not known when and why playing the flute before the bridal pair (rooted in ancient life and fertility symbolism) was abandoned; it was once a familiar and absolutely legal custom (BM 6:1). The same question arises with regard to flute playing at funerals, where this instrument symbolized life and resurrection; it was customary at the time of Josephus (Wars 3:437) and the Gospels (Matt. 9:23), and its legal aspects were still given consideration by the *tannaim* (Shab. 23:4; Ket. 4:4), but it, too, disappeared without any trace. Lamentation of the dead by wailing women could assume the form of a dirge *(*kinah, hesped)* in responsorial patterns (MK 3:8; Meg. 3b; 6a); but it often remained a short acclamation (MK 28b), probably repeated to current melodic phrases. A funeral song of the Diaspora Jews is attested in Canon 9 of the Council of Narbonne in 589 (Juster, Juifs, 1 (1914), 368, n. 3).

A relationship between synagogal and domestic singing patterns has already been noted. Since responsorial and antiphonal song is found as a frequent practice among many peoples, it may be surmised that the related forms of psalmody also derived from popular usages. As far as can be judged from the necessarily one-sided Talmudic sources, Jewish folk music remained relatively immune to the omnipresent Hellenistic influences. Near Eastern Jewry belonged to the Aramaic-speaking peoples (as evinced, for example, by the nomenclature of their musical instruments) and may have kept away from Greek theaters and circuses at the behest of its teachers (Av. Zar. 1:7; TJ, *ibid.*, 1:7, 40a; Av. Zar. 18b, etc.). In the Diaspora, however, the Jews of Miletus, Antioch, and Carthage liked the stage and the arena (Juster, Juifs, 2 (1914), 239–41). Jewish (Purim?) plays were restricted by the Codex Theodosianus of 425 (*ibid.*, 1 (1914), 360 n. 2). In any case, the lasting influence of Hellenistic musical activities in the Jewish sphere cannot be proven.

IDEAS ABOUT MUSIC. The influence of religious law *(halakhah)* on the structure of synagogue music, such as the discontinuation of instrument playing and the entire levitical tradition, has been noted above. To this should be added the rejection of the female voice from the service, exemplified by Rav's harsh statement: "The voice of a woman is indecency" (Ber. 24a, etc.). The rabbi's indifference or hostility to the sound of music changes, however, in the aggadic parts of the Talmud, where many instances of true musical feeling and appreciation of the charm of sounds are recorded. The rabbis dwelled on King David's allegoric lyre, which was sounded by the midnight wind like an "Aeolian harp" (Ber. 4a, etc.), they perceived the "song of the ears of grain" in the field (RH 8a), and let trees burst into song (TJ, Ḥag. 2:1, 77a). They fostered ideas that became universal sources of artistic inspiration: the celestial music of the angels and the righteous (Ḥag. 12b; 14a; Av. Zar. 3b; Er. 21a; Sanh. 91b; Meg. 10b, etc.; Tosef. Sot. 6:2) and the "trump of doom" (later Midrashim: *Otiyyot de-Rabbi Akiva*, letter T; Midrash Daniel, etc.). In other Midrashim (of more or less disputed date), the eternal link between mystical and musical conceptions, already extant in some of the above-quoted Talmud passages, reveals its full strength in certain peculiar hymns aimed at inducing a visionary trance. These hymns were assembled in the treatise *Heikhalot Rabbati* ("All these songs Rabbi Akiva heard when approaching the *Merkabah and understood and learned before the heavenly throne what its servants sang unto it"). They are composed in a language rich in "word-music" and vocal harmony; and one can imagine them being sung to the repetition of short melodic phrases characteristic of suggestion-inducing and spell-casting songs all over the world.

The same *Heikhalot* treatise reveals a guiding idea of sacred song in legendary form: "R. Ishmael said: Blessed is Israel—how much dearer are they to the Holy One than the servant-angels! since as soon as the servant-angels wish to proceed with their song in the heights, rivers of fire and hills of flames encircle the throne of glory, and the Holy One says: Let every angel, cherub, and seraph that I created be silenced before Me, until I have heard and listened to the voice of song and praise of Israel, my children!" Human

EXAMPLE 4. Structures of prayer modes *(nusah)*. (a) Sephardi: *Musaf* of the high holy days; *Aleinu le-Shabbe'ah*, Oriental Sephardi, after Idelsohn, *Melodien*, vol. 4, no. 249; *Ata Nigleta, ibid.*, no. 254; *Adonai Sefatai Tiftah, ibid.*, no. 233; European Sephardi (Leghorn), after F. Consolo, *Sefer Shirei Yisrael—Libro dei Canti d'Israele*, 1892, no. 335. (b) Western Ashkenazi: prayers on feast days and the new moon, blessing for Passover, after S. Naumbourg, *Zemirot Yisrael*, vol. II, 1847, no. 141.

song of praise is given preference over the pure and flawless beauty heard from the heavenly hosts, and the standards of sacred song are set by the warmth of devotion resounding from earthly voices, imperfect and human as they may be.

This concept differs from the basic idea of ecclesiastical song as laid down by Dionysius the Areopagite and repeated throughout the Middle Ages. This notion propounds that the perfect beauty of angelic song descends to the lower ranks in heaven and reaches earth as a faint echo. Church music endeavored by imitation to approach the heavenly model; it had to strive increasingly for superhuman, transcendental beauty, thus creating a perfect but cold product of art. This fundamental difference between the Jewish and Christian view of sacred music indicates what to look for in the evaluation of synagogue song. It must be judged by the perseverance of its original intention which is to be an expression of human feelings, disregarding beauty for its own sake. Whenever, during its development, appreciation of the pleasant sound as such became prominent, this attitude was most often initiated by foreign influences. As a rule, however, the basic patterns set during its first period have survived as a permanent background of Jewish music.

Evolution of the Basic Pattern and Creation of New Forms (c. 500–950). After the completion of the Talmud, c. 500 C.E., new developments began in the liturgical and musical fields. The Near Eastern communities maintained their leadership, and the innovations created there became an integral part of Jewish tradition in the entire Diaspora. During this time, as far as can be judged, Jewish music was spared serious conflict with foreign influences.

THE "LEARNED ART" OF BIBLE CHANT. According to the early, oral tradition of reading the Bible by chant, only a few main sections of a verse were distinguished by means of melodic cadences (see Mus. ex. 3 above). Although the text of the Hebrew Bible was fixed long since, every sequence of words could become meaningful only by the correct grouping of the words and a clear interrelation of clauses and subclauses. The division of a verse could become a matter of interpretation, or even ideology, and raise debates with dissenting sects or a foreign creed. It was no wonder that in epochs of insecurity a need was felt to mark the accepted infrastructure of biblical verses in an indisputable way—in writing. This was achieved by the masoretic accents which have accompanied the text ever since.

Written reading accents are a feature unknown in the Talmud (that is to say, until c. 500 C.E.). They appear to have developed from the sixth century onward. During the same period, the Syrian and Byzantine churches also introduced written reading signs. Even small groups like the Samaritans invented such signs, although the period of their origin is uncertain. No priority can be ascertained today, but the former hypothesis of a Hellenistic prototype has been finally abandoned, as has the idea of an interdependence between the different accent systems. It was a general but variously realized tendency of this era to make a new attempt at a musical script—the first one since the ancient Greeks, and completely different from their method. Greek musicians had expressed single pitches by means of graphic signs, as is done in modern European notation. This method is based on analytical thought. Writing music with accents, however, rests upon the conception of complete melodic figures or motives which are retained in the singer's memory. Their specific application in singing may be brought about by gestures of the hand (cheironomy), as documented already in the talmudic era. The motive may be given a suggestive name (*etnaḥta* "sign of rest"; *zakef* "upright," etc.); the first letter of its name may be written above the text, as was done by the Babylonian masoretes. Finally, freely invented signs could also be used, as was done by the masoretes of Tiberias.

The development of biblical accents (*ta'amei mikra*) was a prolonged process which was completed definitely only between 900 and 930 by Aaron b. Moses *Ben-Asher of Tiberias. This final and authoritative system was imposed upon the whole of Jewry. The earlier Palestinian and Babylonian accentuation fell into disuse and have only recently been recovered from rare manuscripts. The general trend of development was from simplicity to complexity. The masoretes "in good faith furnished the 24 biblical books with accents of correct judgment, with a clear manner of speech, with a sweetly enunciating palate, with beautiful oration . . . Whoever reads shall hear, whoever hears shall understand, and whoever sees shall grasp" (Moses *Ben-Asher, autograph colophon of the Cairo Codex of the Prophets, dated 895 C.E.). They proceeded from the subdivision of a sentence by accent pairs (Babylonian system) to a total accentuation of one sign, and occasionally two, on every word. Having begun with the simple indication of the traditional places of the cadences, they ultimately arrived at a "learned art" of Bible chant, prescribing how the reader was to organize his recitation.

In evaluating the musical consequences of the Tiberian "total accentuation," one basic fact should be borne in mind: an accent can seldom be regarded as a detached, self-contained unit. Not only is a disjunctive accent ("king") most often accompanied by a conjunctive one ("servant"), but several of these pairs are frequently combined to form typical groups. In music, these accent groups are matched by motive groups or melodic phrases: a chanted Bible verse is made into a continuous chain of musical motives (see Mus. ex. 5) and is clearly distinguished from the old-fashioned, psalmody-like style (cf. Mus. ex. 3 above).

EXAMPLE 5. Ashkenazi biblical chant according to the masoretic accents. I Kings 3:15, following the rendition of Joshua 1:1 in Idelsohn, *Melodien*, vol. 2, 50, no. 11.

Since the single motives are often linked by a short bridge of linear recitation (see ex. 5), this kind of chant may also be likened to a string of beads. An entire chapter read in this manner resembles a mosaic in which the same pieces are assembled in constantly varying combinations.

The translation of the masoretes' intentions into music was not accomplished smoothly. First of all, the Tiberian system of accentuation is too detailed and complex to be followed perfectly by even the most scrupulous reader. Moreover, there were Jewish communities with closer ties to the Babylonian than to the Tiberian school; they accepted the Tiberian system as a matter of book learning, but interpreted in song only part of it (the king accents) or disregarded it altogether. Writers of the 14th and 16th centuries (Simeon b. Ẓemaḥ *Duran, Elijah *Levita) explicitly attest that the Sephardim who used to obtain books and teachers from Babylonia neglected all the servant accents and some of the kings as well, and they still do so today. In Iran and Yemen there arose hybrid styles of melodic reading in which the three or four cadences of the old style are permutated arbitrarily in order to comply with the Tiberian rulings. Some remote communities, such as that of Bukhara, continue to recite simply in the old, psalmody-like style (Mus. ex. 3 above). In this way, Jewish reading practices of today form a living museum of chanting styles as they were at different stages of their development.

The Liturgical Hymn (Piyyut). Although the composition of religious poetry most certainly did not break off with the destruction of the Second Temple, the introduction of hymns as an integral part of synagogue liturgy is ascribed to the sixth century. An old tradition (first recorded by *Yehudai Gaon c. 760) connects the admission of hymns into the synagogue with an interdiction against studying the law and reciting the *Shema Yisrael*, generally linked with the hostile edict of Emperor Justinian I promulgated in 553 (Juster, Juifs, 1 (1914), 369–77). This, however, is not sufficient to explain the continuing production of hymns over the centuries, the immense creative power invested in them, the mystical touch present since the very beginning, nor the musical elaboration which they brought about. Hymn writing and singing must be regarded rather as an elementary religious force, effective in Jewry as in every other faith, and one of the main promoting forces of musical evolution.

The early designation of the genre, **ma'amad*, was soon replaced by the borrowed Greek word *piyyut*. The choice of a foreign term probably indicates the introduction of innovations, such as consequent rhyming and the division of a poem into stanzas of identical structure. In time, the stanza form became highly important to musical form: it offered the opportunity of changing the unarticulated cumulation of verses into a divisive organization of the song. This possibility, however, is hardly exploited in tunes of the older style. In present-day synagogue song, *piyyut* melodies continue the traditional usage of repeating the first line throughout the entire song. The cause is certainly the poetic rhythm, which remained as it was in biblical poetry: an equal number of stresses in the verses, occurring at unequal intervals because of the changing number of unaccentuated syllables in between. Thus, a well-known hymn of Eleazar *Kallir (early seventh century?) reads:

Ṭal ya'**asis** **ẓuf** har**im** = 3 accents, 6 syllables
ṭa'**em** bi-meod**kha** muvḥar**im** = 3 accents, 8 syllables
ḥannu**ne**kha ḥa**lez** mi-masger**im** = 3 accents, 10 syllables

A tune appropriate to such poems in "free rhythm" must be capable of extension or contraction according to the length of the text. In addition to psalmody and the principle of prayer chant, another solution to this problem was found by singing according to modal patterns, still practiced today by the Sephardim and the Eastern communities. The basic musical idea or modal pattern consists of not more than one or two tetrachords (four-tone rows); this framework is filled, in actual singing, with melodic curves, step patterns, and ornaments of every kind. A particular musical realization of the scale model will seldom be repeated, but every verse of the stanza offers a new variation of the preconceived pattern (Mus. ex. 6a).

This method of "endless variation" is characteristic of the Oriental style of Jewish song. Its Ashkenazi counterpart is more closely related to the *nusaḥ* structure of prayer chant (see above), being a plastic sequence of variable and

Example 6a. Hymn-tune constructed as a chain of variated motives. Ashkenazi melody for the *kerovah* hymns for the high holy days: (a) for *Ne'ilah* of the Day of Atonement, Bavarian version c. 1800–40 (Loew Saenger, 1781–1843), after Idelsohn, *Melodien*, vol. 7, part 3, no. 211; (b) for *Shaharit* of the New Year, Frankfort version, c. 1883, after F. Ogutsch (1845–1922), *Der Frankfurter Kantor*, 1930, no. 179; (c) for *Musaf* of the New Year, Ukrainian version, c. 1860–80, after J. Bachmann, *Schirath Jacob*, 1884, no. 90; (d) for *Musaf* of the New Year, Jerusalem version of the Lithuanian tradition as noted in 1963, after J. L. Neeman, *Nusaḥ la-Ḥazzan*, vol. 1, 1963, part 2, no. 17; (e) Psalm 65:3, chanted at *Kol Nidrei* to motives A and B of the *kerovah* melody, "Polish" version, 19th century, after A. Baer, *Baal T'fillah*, 1883[3], no. 1307.

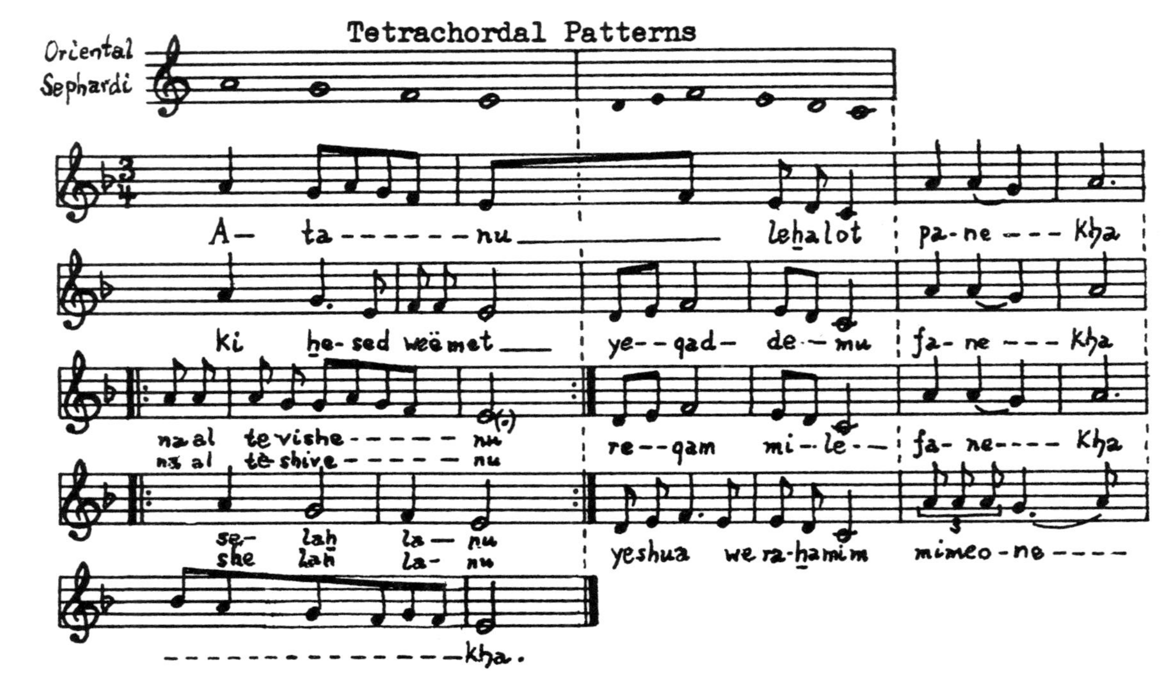

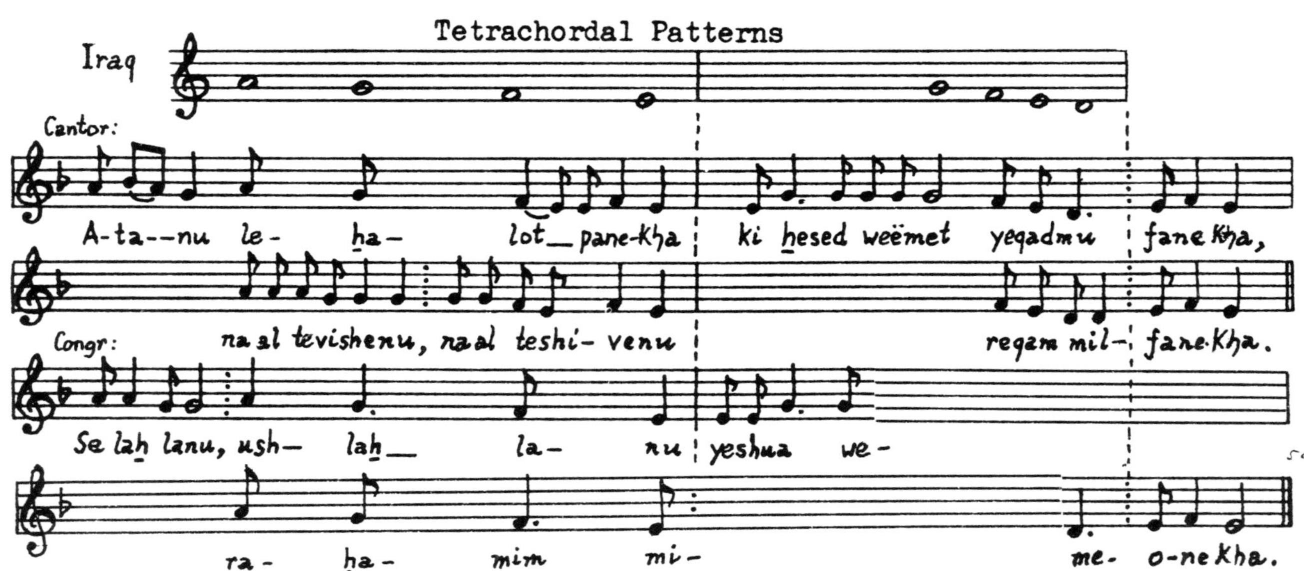

EXAMPLE 6b. Hymn-tunes constructed of variations on a modal pattern. The penitential hymn, *Atanu leḥalot,* Oriental Sephardi, after Idelsohn, *Melodien,* vol. 4, no. 95, and Iraq, *ibid.,* vol. 2, no. 45. For the same as sung in Persia to a pattern comprising one tetrachord only, cf. *ibid.,* vol. 3, no. 40.

interchangeable motives (Mus. ex. 6b). The Ashkenazi style is distinguished by the clear-cut outline of its motives and the retention of the recitation tone technique related to psalmody.

It should be understood that there is no other means of evaluating the historical forms of *piyyut* singing than by inference from present-day traditions. Tunes which show archaic features and conform neatly to the poetical form, may be regarded, as a working hypothesis, as representative of the original style. The texts of the *piyyutim* contain a considerable admixture of mystical elements recognizable, inter alia, by the exuberant accumulation of divine attributes (found as early as in the hymns of the Qumran sect and later explicitly condemned by the *tanna'im,* Ber. 33b; Meg. 18a). The exact musical consequences of these tendencies are not known, but they caused the later *geonim* (Yehudai, Nahshon) to urge the general removal of hymns from the liturgy. However, hymnal song had captivated the hearts of the people to such a degree that this proved impossible. The rabbis, therefore, looked with a certain suspicion upon the principal exponents of *piyyut* singing, the precentors who by then had already become professional ministers.

THE ḤAZZAN AND THE SYNAGOGAL SOLO STYLE. The *piyyut* as sung art-poetry demanded the expertness of a gifted soloist, especially when the singer himself was expected to compose both text and tune. A lay precentor could hardly continue to fulfill such a task. It is surmised that the early *paytanim* performed their creations themselves, having also composed or adapted the melody. It was at this period, in the last quarter of the first millennium, that the new function of the professional solo singer came into existence—presently the well-known figure of the **ḥazzan.* The title *ḥazzan* was not new. It had formerly designated an assistant of the *archisynagogus. In addition to several secular tasks, this functionary had to arrange and supervise the ceremonies in public worship. It was an honored post: the Code of Theodosius exempted its holders from taxes in 438 and Pope Gregory the Great endorsed it c. 600. It was reasonable enough also to require musical ability of applicants for the post of this synagogue master of ceremonies. The term *ḥazzanut*, derived from the title *ḥazzan*, designates either the official post or, more often, the specific melodies and musical style of the solo singer.

For the chronological determination of the *ḥazzan's* specialization in music, a *terminus ante quem* is to be found in *Nahshon's decision of about 875–880: "A *ḥazzan* who knows *piyyut* shall not be admitted to the synagogue" (B. M. Lewin, *Oẓar ha-Ge'onim*, 1 (1928), 70). The assumption of the title *ḥazzan* by the singer probably took place during the ninth century. Since the function of *ḥazzanut* soon came to be passed on from father to son, this vocation became almost a closed social class, where it was the custom for a *ḥazzan* to marry the daughter of his master or of a colleague. The ties of certain families to a musical profession are important for the growth and early training of talents and, in the long run, for the preservation of a musical tradition. There is mention, for instance, of a family of *ḥazzanim* flouishing in Baghdad in the 10th and 11th centuries: Joseph *Albaradani, the "Great *Ḥazzan*" (d. 1006), left sons and grandsons who became successive incumbents of his position, and all of them also wrote *piyyutim*.

The close connection between *ḥazzanut* and *piyyut* is demonstrated by some letters preserved in the Cairo **Genizah* (S. D. Goitein, *Sidrei Ḥinnukh* (1962), 97–102; idem, in: *Tarbiz*, 29 (1960), 357f.). The congregations in medieval Egypt were always eager to hear new hymns, and the *ḥazzanim* were compelled to exchange *piyyutim* among themselves, write them down secretly from the singing of a colleague, and engaged in correspondence as far afield as Marseilles.

It is difficult to imagine the musical character of early *ḥazzanut*. One can, however, attempt to demonstrate the common features of Oriental and European *ḥazzanim* of today with comparable gentile melodies taken as a control group. In addition, the tunes noted down by Obadiah the Norman Proselyte in the first half of the 12th century are available for comparison. With due precaution, it may be said that *ḥazzanut* implies the free evolution of a melodic line (without reference to any system of harmony). The tune therefore proceeds by seconds and other small steps, while leaping intervals are avoided. The melodic texture is dense: there are no empty intervals, no extended notes that are enlivened by a dissolution into small steps (Mus. ex. 7).

The *ḥazzan* must command a good measure of musical creativeness. He does not simple reproduce a preconceived piece of music, but must give final shape to the general outlines of a theme by an improvisation of his own. In this way, the stanza of a *piyyut* may develop in a series of variations on the traditional theme (Mus. ex. 8a).

This feature is already found in the tunes notated by Obadiah the Norman Proselyte (Mus. ex. 8b) in the 12th century. The expressive element so characteristic of *ḥazzanut* can also be discovered in Obadiah's notations. The music of a *piyyut* fragment exhibits the repetition of words, the expressive motives, and the lively "pulsation" around a single note that have remained the pride of the *ḥazzan* until today.

To sum up, musical tradition in *ḥazzanut* means a melodic pattern to be followed, the choice of a specific tetrachord or other scale which is representative of a certain mood, or a stock of motives to be arranged and rearranged in changing melodic structures. The most ancient heritage of synagogue music cannot be confined to bar lines or enclosed in a framework of symmetric phrases. Its rhythm is as free as that of the Hebrew poetry of the time. It is worth noting that melodies in free rhythm have been preserved even in European communities as a body separate from Western music.

MUSIC OF THE MEDIEVAL DIASPORA (c. 950–1500)

The close connection between musical development and changes in thought and national or social conditions is demonstrated perfectly by the changes which occurred in Jewish music as a result of the Islamic conquests, which introduced strong secular and cosmopolitan traits into the cultural life of the Near East, North Africa, and Spain. The Jewish mind does not favor revolutions in sacred music, but new and powerful elements were added to the ancient stock and gave rise to mutual reactions and interactions. In the field of secular music, however, there was a strong trend towards integration, often impeded by forced separation from the gentiles, but thrusting forward as soon as conditions allowed. This general picture is colored by the existence and interplay of different spiritual factors within Jewry itself, each of which contributed to the shaping of musical ideas and forms.

The beginning of a new period in Jewish music may be placed about the middle of the tenth century. By then, the accent systems of Bible chant had been completed; music was made a subject of philosophical reasoning; and sung poetry took on a new look by the introduction of meter and the aesthetic values connected with it. These developments in the spiritual and artistic fields went hand in hand with most important events and changes in the Near East. The conquest and unification of the Near Eastern countries by Islam brought the local Jewries into a larger world of relative liberty and openmindedness. Art and science were no longer restricted to the service of certain religious dogmas, and Jews were free to integrate themselves into the material and spiritual realms of the general culture, but the price was paid by giving up the administrative autonomy of the Jewish population, and the rapid decline of the academies and geonic authority. As a result, the hegemony of Eastern Jewry—which, until then, had supplied the Diaspora with legal decisions, books, *piyyutim*, *masorah*, rabbis, teachers, and *ḥazzanim*—came to an end. The dispersed Jewish communities were compelled to take matters into their own hands.

Integration in the Realm of Secular Music. THE SCIENCE OF MUSIC. The term *musica* did not exist in the Hebrew vocabulary until the tenth century, when it made its first appearance in the Arabized form, *mūsīkī*. It served to express the concept of the science of music (Ar. *'Ilm al-musiqi*), as *ḥokhmat ha-musikah*, later also *ḥokhmat ha-niggun*. This branch of science is reckoned as the fourth in the classical quadrivium, "the most excellent and last of the propaedeutic disciplines" (*Dunash ibn Tamim). Muslim scholars followed the ancient Greeks when analyzing acoustic and musical phenomena in the spirit of an abstract science—an idea that attracted Jewish thinkers. In

EXAMPLE 7. Ornamentation of single notes in Eastern Ashkenazi *ḥazzanut*.

EXAMPLE 8a. Improvisatory variation of a theme. Oriental Sephardi, after Idelsohn, *Melodien,* vol. 4, no. 255.

EXAMPLE 8b. Variative development. Two of the melodies notated in the 12th century by Obadiah, the Norman proselyte. Transcription by H. Avenary (cf. JJS 16, 1966, 87ff.).

the early tenth century, Isaac *Israeli and his disciple Dunash ibn Tamim held that a full command of philosophical reasoning was indispensable for religious exegesis; they actually employed musical science for their commentary on the *Sefer *Yeẓirah* (ed. by M. Grossberg (1902), 16, 40, 48). When their great contemporary *Saadiah Gaon undertook to bridge the widening gap between philosophy and religious tradition, he admitted music to the last chapter of his book on faith and knowledge *Emunot ve-De'ot* (written in 933).

Saadiah mainly follows the teachings of Al-*Kindi (d. c. 874) in describing the way in which eight types of musical rhythm affect the human temper and mood and how they should be mixed in order to lead men to the Golden Mean. This reasoning is part of the ancient doctrine of the ethical influence of music formulated by the Greek philosophers; it had been expressed earlier, however, in the biblical stories of David playing before the melancholy King Saul and of prophetic ecstasy aroused by hearing musical instruments (I Sam. 10:6; 16:16, 23; II Kings 3:15). Saadiah was following this line of thought when he selected precisely the Doctrine of "Ethos" out of the whole edifice of musical philosophy.

The historical significance of Saadiah's short chapter far exceeds that of its musical content. It demonstrates the integration of musical theory into Jewish learning. It had now become a challenge for erudite Jews in the Islamic countries to comprehend this art intellectually. Fragments of several books on music discovered in the Cairo *Genizah* were written during the 11th to 13th centuries in the Arabic language, but in Hebrew letters. Among them are extracts from the famous treatise of the Ikhwān al-Safā' and a fragment on the elements of lute playing. Contemporary book lists also provide an indication of what could be found on music in private libraries and on bookstalls, and one can imagine how much must have been lost in Cairo and in cities like Baghdad, Damascus, Kairouan, or Cordova. During the period between Saadiah Gaon and Maimonides, however, Jewish involvement in the science of music remained, in general, purely receptive, rather than creative.

The scientific approach also makes itself felt in the fields of grammar and *masorah,* thus transferring the treatment of biblical accentuation to a higher level. The system of accents itself had been completed and summed up in somewhat naïve rhymes designed to aid memorization (*Dikdukei ha-Te'amim,* ascribed to Aaron Ben-Asher himself). This old-fashioned method of teaching was continued only by the Ashkenazim (versified teachings of Rabbenu Jacob *Tam in the 12th century and of *Joseph b. Kalonymus in the 13th century). A completely different spirit governs the dry but scientific classification given to the accents by Judah *Ḥayyuj (late tenth century), *Ibn Bala'am or *Ibn Janaḥ (11th century). It is difficult to gauge the extent to which these works influenced musical performance proper, but they are witnesses to a new trend in the theoretical foundations of synagogue chant.

The classes of literature mentioned so far were addressed to a small stratum of society and never exerted as broad an influence as the books of biblical exegesis, to whose study it was everyone's moral duty to devote time and effort. Thus the exegetes and their works achieved great power in the spiritual life of the nation and inevitably played a part in forming a body of common ideas about music. It was Saadiah Gaon who won the title "head of the speakers and first of the exegetes" in the post-midrashic era. His Arabic translation of and commentary on the Book of Psalms adheres scrupulously to the principle that all instrumental music be prohibited until the Temple is rebuilt, and he even claims that instrumental music was restricted to the Temple in ancient times. Saadiah was very particular about explaining obscure musical passages in the Bible out of the biblical text alone, but, on the other hand, he rather unconcernedly translated the Hebrew words *nevel* and *kinnor* by the Arabic names of contemporary string instruments. His practice was continued by Abraham *ibn Ezra and innumerable others.

An example of an exegesis drawing on current philosophical opinions is *Baḥya b. Asher's comments on Ex. 32:19 and 15:20 (*Be'ur*, written 1291 in Spain). Relying upon the view of "the masters of musical science" that the nine musical instruments of Psalm 150 allude to the nine heavenly spheres and that seven of them derive their power from the seven planets, he explains why the *maḥol* (= Mars = evil) was the instrument played before the golden calf, while the *tof* (= Jupiter (*ẓedek*) = Justice) was beaten by Miriam, sister of the just priest Aaron. The *maḥol*, he points out, was the symbol of a sinful woman. In the course of time the opinion took shape that *maḥol* and other terms from the headings of the psalms, such as *ayyelet ha-shaḥar* and *alamot*, were musical instruments. This view recurs in literature until quite recent times. In general, the exegetical books spread an understanding and a high esteem of music; they endowed it with an image of strong spiritual power—not very different from that developed by philosophy—rather than of a self-sufficient art or a despised entertainment.

The Challenge of New Forms of Art. The philosophy and theory of music were conceived by scholars and, as an abstract science, were detached from musical composition and performance. This did not prevent leaders like Saadiah Gaon from writing hymns in the free rhythms of Kallir's school. The following generation (about 940–950), with Saadiah's disciple *Dunash b. Labrat as its leader, introduced contemporary metrics into Hebrew poetry. This was a revolutionary act of immense influence on poetry and music. Arabic poets had accepted the ancient Greek metrics based upon measured syllable durations as early as the eighth century: "Since the ancient Arabs by nature measured [their language], its very nature accorded with tonal proportions and musical composition" (*Ibn Danan, *Perek be-Ḥerez*, 15th century). The differentiation of long and short syllables is foreign to the Hebrew language; it was, rather, the intensity of enunciation that provided the poetic "weight" (*mishkal*). It may be seen, for instance, from *Yose b. Yose's *Darkekha Eloheinu le-Ha'arikh Appékha* that the singer had to utter one, two, or three syllables, as the case may be, between the accents; this precluded a regular beat and meter, and the tune had to be either psalmodic or in free rhythm. It can be said that this poetry did not include the dimension of time as an object of artistic configuration.

This old Semitic heritage was challenged by the Greco-Arab meters, which give a precise order and division to the continuum of time. The heavy pace of the old *piyyutim* was regarded as "bothersome to the public," which now preferred smoothly flowing rhythms flattering to the ear. The formal element had become autonomous, so to speak; its former dependence upon an idea (expressed in a natural flow of speech) had weakened. This process was justified by the slogan "that the beauty of Japheth should dwell in the tents of Shem." Aesthetic appreciation was clearly a new aspect in Hebrew poetry and song. Of course, it had to overcome stiff opposition, but its victory was almost complete and lasted more than half a millennium. "A pleasant musical sound" was henceforth demanded when offering a prayer (Joseph *Albo, *Ikkarim*, 4:23, 8).

In the musical field, too, a new type of melody made its appearance. Its novelty in Jewish musical tradition is signaled by the fact that there was no term to designate it, and the Arabic word *laḥan* had to be adopted for the purpose. This type of melody demanded metrical texts, and an early Muslim theoretician, Ibn Rashik, held that meter was also the foundation of melody. This idea was repeated and developed by several Jewish writers down to the 17th century (e.g., Samuel *Archivolti). Both Moses and Abraham ibn Ezra (*Ẓaḥut* (Venice, 1546), 142a, written in 1145) advocated that a poem intended to be sung should be written in equal metrical units throughout. It is understandable that mixed meters would have led to alternating duple and triple time within the melodic phrase and this seems to have been regarded as unbalanced.

Since neither Islamic nor Jewish culture record their music in writing, it is only by inference that the *laḥan* can be regarded as a "melody" according to European notions, i.e., a musical structure built of equal or corresponding sections and shaped according to a rhythmic scheme (meter). This design differs from the traditional tunes of free rhythm, as metrical poetry differs from biblical verse, and has the same advantages and drawbacks, as *Judah Halevi demonstrated (*Kuzari* 2:69).

In modern Jewish singing practice, a *laḥan* may attach itself very closely to the cyclic structure of the stanzas and may be notated with bars according to the meter of the text (Mus. ex. 9).

Example 9. Melodies shaped according to the meter of the poetry. (a) Oriental Sephardi, after Idelsohn, *Melodien*, vol. 4, no. 218; (b) basic Western Ashkenazi melody; cf. A. Baer, *Baal T'fillah*, 1883[3], no. 225.

It is evident from the examples that a "metrical" tune need not be syllabic; a series of short notes may appear on a long syllable. To judge from present practice, however, the absolute identity of poetic and musical rhythm is relatively rare. More often the tune is given its own rhythm, but even then it will be symmetrical or cyclic.

With the emergence of metrical poetry, the formal idea of the stanza became predominant; it constituted a major cycle which comprised the minor cycles of metrical units. The stanza originated in the cyclic rhythm of the dance and was therefore a popular element. Its introduction into serious songs was apt to broaden their public appeal. In the Jewish sphere, this implied the explicit invasion of musical tradition by environmental elements. This development was heralded by the extensive use of foreign strophic forms, first of all of the *shir ezor* ("girdle song," *muwāshah* in Arabic, which was probably an ancestor of both the Spanish *villancico* and the French *virelai*). This form is characterized by a certain order of rhymes and by an unchanging refrain *(pizmon)* to be performed in chorus by the audience *(Tanhum ha-Yerushalmi,* s.v. *pazzem;* see Y. Ratzhaby in: *Tazlil,* 8 (1968), 16). The melody of a *shir ezor* could be either original or taken from an earlier composition ("With the Greeks, the song was composed together with its tune; with the Arabs, every song has a tune, but not every tune has a song [exclusively associated with it]," Moses ibn Ezra, c. 1100 (Heb. transl. B. Z. Halper, *Shirat Yisrael,* 1924, 110)). The transfer of melodies from one song to another is also a common feature of Hebrew hymns from the 11th century onward ("The scribes of Spain . . . would write the tune of a well-known *piyyut* above the column of the *piyyut,*" Abraham ibn Ezra, commentary on Ps. 7:1). In a sample of about 80 hymns from the Cairo *Genizah,* published by J. H. *Schirmann in 1966 *(Piyyutim Hadashim min ha-Genizah),* the superscriptions of 32 refer the reader to the tunes of other Hebrew poems. Seventeen others, however, were written to Arabic melodies assumed to be well known in their day. This shows clearly that the acceptance of a foreign form was often accompanied by the adoption of foreign music—either by the transfer of actual melodies or as an imitation of style. Simeon Duran writes (c. 1400) of "the tunes for songs and elegies: . . . some were composed in the lands of Spain and taken by the poets from the songs of Ishmael [i.e., of the Arabs] which are very attractive: others were taken from the popular songs of the French countries and are driven to extreme melodic height and extension" (*Magen Avot,* ed. Leghorn 1785, 55b). Sometimes approved, but more often attacked, the custom of using foreign tunes remained a permanent feature in Jewish music. Later it even became an issue of mystical ideology and, in music itself, a source of hybrid forms.

The new development in poetry and music may be reduced to one common formula: both arts are given a periodic ordering, an artificial structuring of the dimension of time acquired from Greco-Arabic precedents. The mere sound of speech and song thereby becomes an experience of its own. The listener may give himself up to rhythms and sounds more harmonious and relaxed than those found in harsh reality; the words may pass before him without posing a special challenge or demand. This phenomenon was alien to the older forms of Hebrew poetry in which the "weight" of accents, like pounding hammers, drove the words into the consciousness. It is difficult to imagine that one could listen to the "beautiful flow of speech" of Isaiah or Job without being moved by its message. The impact of a sensual and aesthetic appreciation of art was a new element in Jewish music, and the first tangible sign of its progressive integration with the cultural environment.

Music at the Social and Popular Levels. After the Jews were granted relative freedom in daily life, musical elements that had no connection whatsoever with either religion or secular learning came to the fore. At the popular level, song and play had certainly never ceased to enliven festival and ordinary activities, exactly as is related of the Talmudic era (see above). An uninterrupted stream of reports and notices from the Middle Ages tell about Jewish minstrels and jugglers roaming the countries and performing before Jews and gentiles. The wandering artist had a very low status in medieval society; he was almost an outcast in Christian civilization and was regarded with the same suspicion as sometimes were the Jews. Nevertheless, minstrelsy was a very old vocation which had spread over the continent in the path of the Roman legions. When the Jews were expelled from their country, many joined the universally open class of *ludarii* (M. Jastrow, REJ, 17, 308–10), *ministrerii,* and *ioculatores.* The movement of Jews into this way of life continued during the Middle Ages and later on. Most of the Jewish communities could not offer a livelihood to all who possessed an artistic gift and felt an urge to practice it. These artists used to master not only singing and instrumental play but also the recitation of long epics and the composition of various kinds of poetry, as well as dancing, rope walking, knife throwing, etc.

This kind of "art" was acceptable not only in the villages or market places; men of high standing were also fond of hearing and seeing the minstrel and juggler, and those they liked best they would attach to their retinue. Since the roaming artist was an outsider in any case, his Jewish extraction was of no consequence in making him the court musician of a caliph or emir or of a Christian king, bishop, or knight. Some examples of the Jewish minstrels' appearance before high-class audiences may shed some light on this continuously recurring phenomenon. From Jewish tribes who settled in seventh-century Hejaz and went to war with shawm and drum came the famous singer al-Gharid al-Yahudi of Medina, said to have pleased Muhammad himself by his song. In Andalusia, *Al-Mansur al-Yahudi was appointed court musician by the caliphs of Cordoba early in the ninth century; others are known to have served the nobles of the Ibn Shaprut family, such as a certain Isaac b. Simeon (c. 1100). The Christian kings of Spain also held Jewish musicians in high esteem. Their court accounts of the 14th–16th centuries repeatedly mention Jewish *juglares* (mostly vihuela players) who received considerable remuneration and were granted pompous titles *(ministrer destroments de corda de casa de la señora reyna).* Wandering singer-poets of Jewish descent were welcome with kings and aristocrats since they added a popular flavor to the sophisticated, but sometimes dull, court atmosphere. "El Ropero," the son of a Jewish tailor, was maliciously called *malvado cohen, judío, zafío, logrero* by his rivals, but nevertheless allowed to address Isabella the Catholic with a protest song against the persecution of the Marranos in 1473. One of his contemporaries Juan (Poeta) of Valladolid, pleased the Spanish court of Naples.

The activities of Jewish singers immediately before the expulsion of their people from Spain testifies again that they were regarded as outsiders in every respect—neither Jew nor Christian. They also appear in the company of Provençal troubadours, French trouvères, or, like *Suesskind of Trimberg (c. 1220), at the seat of the bishop of Wuerzburg. The poetries of these Jewish singers, even songs on biblical subjects and those obviously written for a Jewish audience, were in the vernacular. They mastered the international repertoire to no less a degree than their gentile colleagues and added to it subjects from Bible and Midrash. One of the unexpected discoveries in the Cairo *Genizah* was the notebook of a Jewish minstrel of 1382, writing German in Hebrew letters. It contains a lengthy German epic, as well as songs on Moses, Abraham, Joseph, and a parable from the Midrash. The authors, "Eizik and Abraham the Scribes," rarely use Hebrew words (but "church" is pejoratively called *tifleh*).

The wandering singers were a class between the nations and, in general, rather estranged to their origin. They spread the works and motifs of literature over the countries and continents (e.g., Samson Pine, who interpreted the French epic of Parzival to German scribes in 1335). The tales of King Arthur were introduced to the Jewish public as well where they were transferred to the Jewish idiom or imitated, as in the *Shmuel Bukh* (15th century), the *Akedat Yiẓhak* poem, and similar compositions. Reliable sources show that such Jewish epics were sung to a fixed melodic phrase throughout the whole work like the *Chanson de Geste* and similar poems the world over. Regrettably, such tunes as the *Niggun Shmuel Bukh* were never recorded in music, but their counterparts have been preserved in the biblical ballads of the Sephardim which show that the recurrent standard phrase was varied with every repetition (Mus. ex. 10).

EXAMPLE 10. Standard phrase of epic song. In this example, the phrase is varied by alternating open and closed cadences. Ladino ballad on the sacrifice of Isaac, Morocco, after A. Larrea Palacin, *Cancionero Judío del Norte de Marruecos*, vol. 1, *Romances de Tetuan*, 1952, 123.

Minstrelsy in general holds an important share in the formation of common European melody types. Its Jewish representatives served as intermediaries between the ghettoes and their environment. They were also the bearers of an instrumental tradition, especially in the field of dance music. When conducting the elaborate musical rites of wedding ceremonies and other occasions, they transferred part of the international repertoire to the Jewish quarter (Mus. ex. 11).

It is no wonder that common European formulas of dance melodies invaded the more popular part of religious and even synagogue song (Mus. ex. 12). Although these processes belong to the popular level, their importance can hardly be overrated. It was the broad masses of the people who sang certain hymns and regulated the musical taste by giving or denying their emotional approval to the precentor. Periods when an educated musical understanding decided the forms of liturgical song remained rather isolated phenomena. One can hardly discover any influence of that art music which was so highly esteemed during the Golden Age of Andalusian Jewry, when Moses ibn Ezra gained relief from melancholy by listening to a lute player ("The sinew of my heart becomes one of his strings . . . skillful hands that feel their way and jump on a fret in just time, spread joy over the breathing souls . . . the dark doors closed, and the seat of the Most-High lies open to the initiated eyes . . .," *Shirei Ḥol*, ed. Brody, no. 72), or *Al-Ḥarizi who gave his thankful greetings to a certain Isaiah, master on the Arabic lute (he "stirs up the lute strings to sing . . . like a child in mother's lap who smiles and emits exultant shouts, not weeping . . . His playing over a dead body would awaken it, and the spirit of life would dwell upon it again . . .," *Taḥkemoni, Kuf* 463). Those beautiful and poetic words bear witness of the deep emotions felt on listening to elaborate art music. However, the conditions of the Jewish exile did not allow for a continued delight in the refined art; time and again the Jews were thrown back to the level of poor people and to the kind of music enjoyed by the same.

THE FORMATION OF CONCEPTS OF JEWISH MUSIC (12TH–14TH CENTURIES)

Since the dawn of the second millennium the impact of the musical idioms of the host cultures was felt more and more in Jewish life, religious and secular. In the face of powerful external influences, the traditional attitude to music was also revised and, eventually, rearranged. By the 13th century, three main concepts had developed that circumscribed the role of music in Jewish life in such a fundamental way as to retain their power through the ages down to the present.

The Rabbinic Attitude To Music. Wherever the Torah is applied to life in its entirety, the ethical potential of music is esteemed above its aesthetic values. Beauty of sound and formal perfection fade and are graded as a mere means of reaching a higher goal, beyond the realm of art. Rabbis did not appreciate any kind of music that was merely pleasing to hear but had no edifying objective. It goes without saying that they condemned music that was likely to stir up excessive human passion. From the time of *Hai Gaon (c. 1000) the most important Talmud commentaries and legal decisions constantly uttered warnings against listening to Arab love songs (*shi'ir al-ghazl*, *Alfasi) or the popular "girdle songs" (*muwashshah*, *Maimonides). The latter called the occupation with songbooks *(sifrei niggun)* a "waste of time in vanity" (Comm. to Sanh. 10:1). On the condition that the singer refrains from losing himself in sensual pleasure and evoking primitive instincts, however, most rabbis held music in high esteem. Song is regarded as a very desirable accompaniment to prayer. Musical perform-

EXAMPLE 11. International dance tunes in the Jewish *klezmer* repertoire. (a) Italian dance tune, *"Lamento di Tristano,"* late 14th century, after A. T. Davison and W. Apel (eds.), *Historical Anthology of Music*, vol. 1, 1950, no. 59; (b) *klezmer* tune, after Elhanan Kirchhan, *Simḥat ha-Nefesh*, part II, Fuerth, 1727, fol. 4r.

ance at public worship was naturally subject to certain prohibitions, e.g., the prohibition on playing instruments and listening to them during the Sabbath, imitating rites of foreign worship, or listening to female singing voices. Regulations of this kind impeded the introduction of the organ or the formation of mixed choirs in synagogues, for example. Another rabbinical doctrine demands that Psalm verses be enunciated by everyone in full, including the participants in responsorial chant. This gave rise to the strange "concatenated" alternation of hemistichs still practiced in several Eastern communities:

> *Solo:* The heavens declare the glory of God,
> *Choir:* and the firmament sheweth his handiwork. Day unto day uttereth speech,
> *Solo:* and the firmament sheweth his handiwork. Day unto day uttereth speech,
> *Choir:* and night unto night sheweth knowledge. There is no speech nor language,
> *Solo:* and night unto night sheweth knowledge. There is no speech nor language (Psalm 19).

Rabbi Isaiah *Horowitz, who settled in Jerusalem in the early 17th century, recommended this custom also to the West (*Kiẓẓur Shelah* (ed. 1715), fol. 66a).

The competence of the *ḥazzan* was judged by his personal respectability and good repute rather than by musical standards. This frequently expressed view was codified later in the Shulḥan Arukh (OḤ 53:4). Time and again, rabbis were inclined to reject *ḥazzanim* of a prominently artistic or virtuoso disposition, since they were suspect of aiming at public applause alone. Nevertheless, rabbis very often had to compromise or even resign themselves to the demands of the public (Solomon Luria, *Yam shel Shelomo;* Ḥul. 1:49). The guardians of law however, did not cease calling singers to order by their warnings not to disturb the balance of word and tone or sever the bond between related words by extended coloraturas: indeed, a style of singing came into existence in which vocalized coloraturas occurred only as a sort of interlude between integral word groups, instead of being sung to the syllable or a word. In the later centuries, *ḥazzanim* were often blamed by their rabbis for a "theatrical" or "operatic" mode of performance or (in unconscious conformity with Plato) for their "imitation of nature," such as when they pictured vocally the "sound of great waters" in Ps. 93:4 (Judah Leib *Zelichower, *Shirei Yehudah,* 1696, fol. 27b).

The innermost meaning of song in prayer was defined by Maimonides (or a member of his school) in the work *Pirkei Haẓlaḥah:* "Whoever says his prayer should turn his inner being entirely toward God and should never neglect to use the sweet sound of a pleasant voice: therewith he prepares his entire self for the transfer of his soul to the spiritual world, detached, as it were, from the world of matter." This statement demonstrates how a well-established tradition may be corroborated by philosophical argumentation: music is seen as cognate to the faculty of discerning the pure idea (*Guide of the Perplexed,* 3, 46), and pleasantness of sound is a precondition of its effect on the soul (*ibid.*, 3, 45).

Philosophy and Secular Education. Definitions of sacred song like that quoted above were the fruit of attempts to reconcile science and religion (cf. Saadiah Gaon, Maimonides). Music was included in the ardent debates about this problem, since it formed part of the curriculum of sciences. It remained for Maimonides' followers to establish its rightful place within Jewish education and learning. Joseph ibn *Aknin was the first to undertake this task in his book *Cure of the Souls* (*Tibb al-Nufus,* ch. 27). In Ibn Aknin's opinion the Bible itself obliges the Jewish people to learn the art of music, not only because of its association with the holy sacrifices and its high esteem in the ancient times, but because the spiritual power of music had been a source of prophecy, "guiding the mind to clear sight, to keen distinction, to the faculty of meditation." Music (which, according to Maimonides' Platonic conceptions, is located in the brain) clears the mind of all its passions and converts it into a clean vessel for receiving the spirit of holiness; therefore performed music is also one of the most powerful remedies for the suffering of the soul.

Music now penetrated education as a medium of shaping the character and developing emotional abilities. "Understanding music" (as a goal apart from practical execution) was accepted as an educational factor by the Jews of Moorish Andalusia and of Christian southern Europe, from about 1230–40. The turning point is marked by the transfer of the language of musical literature from Arabic to Hebrew. Already a century earlier *Abraham b. Ḥiyya wrote in Hebrew a comprehensive encyclopedia of the sciences of which the section on music, "On *Ḥokhmat ha-Niggun* called *musika* in Greek" is in manuscript in the Vatican library. Shemtov *Falaquera gave music its appropriate place in his educational work of 1236 *Ha-Mevakkesh* ("The Searcher"—after wisdom and happiness) and in his *Reshit Ḥokhmah* ("Beginnings of Wisdom," also translated into Latin); he also advocated Hebrew as the preferred language of studies. The latter idea guided the

EXAMPLE 12. Common European idioms in Western Ashkenazi melodies. (a) Psalm 144, Ashkenazi, as sung on Sabbath eve, notated by H. Avenary; (b) German dance song, 1556, after W. Salmen, MGG, vol. 7, 1957, col. 227; (c) Bulgarian dance melody, *ibid.,* (d) *Bergamasca,* a north Italian melody widely known since the 16th century; here in a version by Salamon de' Rossi, after P. Nettl, *Alte juedische Spielleute und Musiker,* 1923, 21; (e) Ashkenazi Passover hymn, after G. Ephros, *Cantorial Anthology,* vol. 3, 1948, 85; (f) *klezmer* tune, 1727, after E. Kirchhan, *Simḥat ha-Nefesh,* part II, fol. 2v; (g) *klezmer* tune, *ibid.,* fol. 5v; (h) European dance-music formula, descending the major scale, after W. Wiora in *Report, Sixth Congress of the International Musicological Society,* Bamberg, 1953, 1954, 170.

Figure 4. A *ḥazzan* portrayed in the *Leipzig Maḥzor,* S. Germany, c. 1320. The other figures are either *meshorerim* (singers), or two members of the congregation acting as *somekhim* ("supporters" of the *ḥazzan*). Leipzig University Library, Ms. V. 1102, vol. 1, fol. 27. Photo David Harris, Jerusalem.

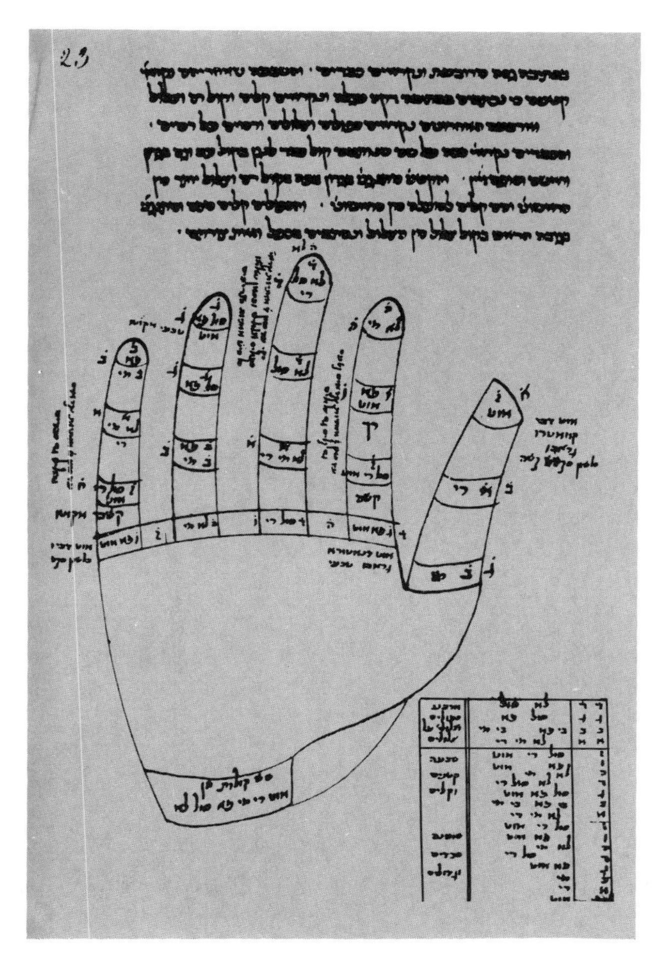

Figure 6. The Guidonian Hand for the indication of the tone-names and the table of the Hexachord, from the Hebrew music treatise compiled by Judah b. Isaac, probably in southern France, c. 13th–14th century. Paris, Bibliothèque Nationale, Ms. héb. 1037, fol. 23r.

Figure 5. Initial-word panel for the passage, "This *maẓẓah* . . ." in the *Barcelona Haggadah,* 14th century. The musicians are playing the folk and art instruments of contemporary Christian Spain, which were also used by the Jewish musicians in that country: pipe-and-tabor, fiddle, lute, bagpipes, and double hand-drums. London, British Museum, Add. Ms. 14761, fol. 61r.

Figure 7. Jewish marriage ceremony in northern Italy, mid-15th century. The ensemble partly visible in the upper right corner is the small dance orchestra of wind instruments called at that period *capella alta.* From *Vatican Arba'ah Turim,* Mantua, 1436. Rome, Vatican Library, ms. Rossiana 555.

Jews of Provence when they appointed Andalusian authors to translate science books into Hebrew. Judah ibn Tibbon had already supplied a version of Saadiah's philosophical work together with its musical appendix (see above). Judah Al-Ḥarizi translated the anecdotical *Sayings of the Philosophers* (ch. 18–20 about music). Anonymous translators contributed the extensive music treatise from the encyclopedia of *Ibn Abi al-Salt. Fragments of a musical treatise by *Moses b. Joseph ha-Levi have been preserved as a quotation.

The activities of these promoters of music education coincided—certainly not by chance—with the endeavors made in Christian Castile, Provençe, and Sicily to create a European spiritual culture independent of ecclesiastical dogma but following classical antiquity. A cosmopolitan and humanistic spirit governed the circles who fostered this movement, and the above-mentioned Abraham b. Ḥiyya served them as a translator, as did many Jews and Moors. This breath of fresh air awoke hopes for a normalization of exile conditions by transferring ingredients of secular culture into Hebrew. During these heydays of medieval civilization, Jews ornamented their books with excellent miniatures, sang the love songs of the troubadours ("a very bad custom, taken over from the surrounding peoples," Jacob *Anatoli, c. 1230) or romances (*Sefer *Ḥasidim* §142; cf. §§3; 238, c. 1200) and listened to popular tales and epics. Hebrew poets of Provence appreciated the art of famous troubadours (Abraham *Bedersi, late 13th century) but wrote exclusively in their own tongue, albeit for a limited audience ("My lyre, awaking melodies in this generation, what is it more than a forlorn song?" Abraham Bedersi).

Such tendencies received fresh impulse from the movement of the Proto-Renaissance and from new trends in French and Italian music early in the 14th century. The poet and thinker *Immanuel of Rome ("O science of music, who will understand any more the art of thy flutes and drums?" *Maḥbarot*, 21) complained: "It is a well-known fact that the science of music—a wonderful and esoteric science and art—was once thoroughly understood by our nation . . . but nowadays, none of us knows anything of it, and it is entirely in Christian hands" (Comm. Prov. 23:13). Such ideas, of whom Immanuel was only one exponent, now gave rise to a new wave of Hebrew musical literature drawn from Latin and Italian sources. The connection of its compilers with the Proto-Renaissance movement is obvious. *Kalonymus b. Kalonymus, who served King Robert II of Anjou as a science translator, also wrote a Hebrew version of Al-*Farabi's *Principles of Science* (3:5 on music), in 1314. *Levi b. Gershom, collaborating with Johannes de Muris in mathematics and astronomy, was commissioned by Philippe de Vitry to write a treatise *De numeris harmonicis* in 1343 and was thus in close touch with two outstanding figures of the *Ars Nova* in France, as was probably also that unknown music student whose Hebrew notebook refers to teachings of Jean Vaillant (c. 1400). Italian Trecento music is reflected by the memoranda of another anonymous Jew who translated into Hebrew a brief compilation of musical theory attributed to the famous Marchettus of Padua from Italian. A more comprehensive treatise of musical theory was translated from Latin by a certain *Judah b. Isaac. In his preface, the translator brings forward the favorite idea of that epoch: that Jewish occupation with musical science actually means the recovery of one's own property, lost in the turmoil of exile. Fourteenth-century Spain contributed some discussions on the role of music in medicine; they are only marginal phenomena, when compared to the strong tendency of Provençal and Italian Jewry to make the science of music a building stone of a secular culture of their own.

The endeavors of medieval Jewry to attach themselves to contemporary musical conceptions were buried under an avalanche of severe catastrophes that threatened the very existence of the Jews. These prompted the question whether the devotion to art and worldly goods was at all appropriate to a people in exile. Solomon *ibn Verga (late 15th century) expressed such opinions in a fictional discussion between King Alfonso VIII and three Jewish leaders (*Shevet Yehudah*, par. 8): "Why should you teach your children music" asks the king, "whereas you are obliged to tears and mourning all your life since the God of Heavens called you a wretched people and dispersed you for it, which he did to no other nation." The Jewish respondents cannot proffer a real answer and demonstrate a disheartened retreat from their former aims and hopes. Pushed back by the turn taken by medieval civilization, Jews had to abandon their tentative contacts with art music and musical learning. This problem was to repeat itself several times later on.

According to a pattern that became standard, rejection led to a return to traditional standards and ideas. In music, this meant a move back to the use of musical language for predominantly religious expression. By the 15th century, however, the latter had already lost its original sober purity by the adoption of metric tunes for hymnal song and by the practice of florid melodies fostered by a strong mystical movement.

Mystical Ideas and Forms. Tradition on the lines of pure *halakhah* hardly considered the innate dynamics of musical expression, but judged it by external (albeit exalted) standards. Direct and constant relations between religious experience and music are rather found in the mystical approach to faith, which needed music for communicating ideas that cannot be expressed by words and as a means of imparting visions and secret revelations. Such tendencies are already evident in the Midrashim of earlier Jewish mysticism. During the 13th century, the mystical trend gained in impetus and exerted an unprecedented power over both the contemplative and the active modes of life.

When the Kabbalah attempts to reveal the secrets of creation or of the heavens, it often has recourse to musical symbols, metaphors, and allegories. The reciprocal relation between the lower and the upper world, for exampe, is made comprehensible by analogy with musical resonance; divine love and grace are pictured by various allegories of song and dance. The Zohar gathers almost every musical allusion to mystical ideas found in the Talmud and Midrash, without adding anything really new; but it renovates and strengthens the impact of such visions as the angelical choirs (*Va-Yeẓe*, ed. Mantua, fol. 158b–159b) and their counterpart, Israel's song of praise ("so that the Holy One may be exalted from above and from below in harmony," *Shemot*, 164b; cf. *Va-Yeḥi*, 231a–b). Images of this kind had earlier been drawn in the *Heikhalot* literature (see above). Especially significant is the demand for cheerfulness in prayer, concretely expressed in song and melody: " . . . we know that the **Shekhinah* does not dwell in sad surroundings, but only amid cheerfulness. For this reason Elisha said (II Kings 3:15): 'But now bring me a minstrel; and it came to pass, when the minstrel played, that the hand of God came upon him' " (*Va-Yeshev*, 180b; cf. *Va-Yeḥi*, 216b; 249b). Contemporary and later kabbalists connect their allegories with a rather precise, almost scientific, description of musical phenomena (e.g., Abraham *Abulafia; Isaac *Arama). Mystical meditation, however, by its very nature, had to remain a privilege of the selected few. Its massive influence on music was made effective by books or commentaries in the prayer book and, more directly, by the personal example of individual mystics acting as cantors and rabbis.

Among the *Ḥasidei Ashkenaz, mystical ideas penetrated the particular mode of devout life taught by Judah he-Ḥasid and his followers. Their aim was to demonstrate the love of God and the joy in his commandments every day, and this strongly emotional element shaped a musical idiom of its own. Prayer and praise are the center of life, but they can be conducted in true perfection only by inseparable union with a tune. Singing is the natural expression of joy, and a frequent change of melodies prevents daily prayer from becoming mere routine. Absorption in song releases the abandonment of the self and the innermost concentration on the words uttered. Moreover, mystical prayer also has an active end in sight: **kavvanah*, the "intention" or concentration on the mystical union of world and creator, is to be brought about by contemplating the hidden sense behind the plain meaning of the words. These unspoken matters must be deliberated during the utterance of certain key words of the prayers. In this context, the tune has several tasks: to eliminate the diversion of mind by the surroundings, to make room for a chain of thoughts around a word, and to remind the congregation of a specific "intention." The technical term for this application of melody was *le-ha'arikh be-niggun, li-meshokh niggunim* (extending the tune), *be-orekh u-ve-meshekh niggun*, or *niggunim arukhim* (long tunes). All these terms point to the long melismas, mostly wordless coloraturas, before or within the prayer that became a distinguishing mark of mystical prayer song.

A rather simple example of melodically expressed *kavvanah* may be found in the recitation of the Book of Esther, which does not contain any explicit mention of God. When reaching chapter 6, verse 1, "On that night the king could not sleep," the same long melisma which ornaments the word "the King" during High Holiday morning prayers is intoned, symbolizing that it actually was the King of the World who intervened at this point. Other examples are the legendary association of the **Aleinu* prayer with Joshua and the walls of Jericho, which is evoked by inserted trumpet-like flourishes, or the extended tune of *Barekhu* on Sabbath night which was believed to give the souls suffering in hell an additional moment of relief. Undoubtedly a certain poetical element dwells in the "long melodies" and, at the same time, provides a challenge for the performing cantor. The latter always took pride in giving musical shape to these sometimes phantasmagorical ideas.

Along with this outlet of dynamic music making, medieval mysticism also opened the door to the intrusion of definitely popular musical elements. Just as everyone was obliged to say daily prayers, no one would be dispensed from doing so in song:

> You should never say: My voice is not agreeable . . . Speaking this way, you complain against him who did not make your voice beautiful. There is nothing that induces man to love his Creator and to enjoy his love more than the voice raised in an extended tune . . . If you are unable to add something [of your own to the prescribed text], pick out a tune that is beautiful and sweet to your ears. Offer up your prayer in such tunes, and it will be full of *kavvanah*, and your heart will be enchanted by the utterings of your mouth . . . (*Sefer Ḥasidim*, 11; 13th century).

This trend necessarily led away from every artistic or elaborate kind of music. Although the *Sefer Ḥasidim* clearly rejected "music from the tavern," the door was thrown open to a new invasion of foreign melodies, at least at the popular level of Jewish mysticism. A time was even to come when the "redemption" of a beautiful gentile tune, by its adaptation to a sacred text, was to be regarded as a great merit. The concepts of music developed by the Ḥasidei Ashkenaz deeply penetrated the communities and lasted for a long time in Central Europe. Made popular by the writings of *Eleazar b. Judah (Ha-Roke'aḥ) of Worms and numerous prayer books with commentaries of his inspiration, the musical expression of *kavvanot* became an essential task of *ḥazzanut*. It remained so as late as the 18th century, when it was replaced by the influence of East European Ḥasidism.

THE CONSOLIDATION OF REGIONAL STYLES

The spiritual developments which shaped the various concepts of sacred song were largely concluded by 1300. It fell to the 15th century to shape music itself according to the chosen ideal and to direct the accepted patterns into the channels of a continuous tradition. Differences of ideology and taste gave rise to separate musical traditions—not only of the larger groups *(Minhag Ashkenaz, Sefarad, Italyah, Romanyah)*, but even on the community level. Important but limited groups, such as the Jews of Avignon (*Carpen-

EXAMPLE 13. Old tradition of melodic extension. (a) Italian Sephardi, after F. Consolo, op. cit., Ex. 4, no. 12; Western Ashkenazi, after I. Lachmann (see Mus. ex. 1) no. 8; (b) Western Ashkenazi, notated by H. Avenary; (c) Italian, after Mordecai Ẓahalon, *Meẓiẓ u-Meliẓ*, Venice, 1715; Eastern Ashkenazi, after H. Wasserzug, *Schirei Mikdosch*, I, 1878, no. 65.

tras), Mainz, and Prague, developed a characteristic musical custom *(minhag)* of their own.

Musical Minhag. Scattered references related to the music of certain prayer or hymn texts can already be found in the earlier compendia of liturgical practice, such as *Abraham b. Nathan ha-Yarḥi's *Ha-Manhig* (c. 1205). Moreover, singing habits of venerable rabbis and *ḥazzanim* were handed down by their disciples by oral tradition. Some of the musical *minhagim* go back to the talmudic period, such as extending the melodies of *"eḥad"* in *Shema Yisrael* (Ber. 13b; 61b, see Mus. ex. 13c), of the *Amen (Ber. 47a), and of the *Priestly Blessing (Kid. 71a; see Mus. ex. 13a). The halakhic sayings treating *shofar* and *megillah* alike (Ber. 30a; Meg. 4b, etc.) are evoked by the use of an identical tune for the benedictions of both of them (Mus. ex. 13b).

The efforts to consolidate an Ashkenazi tradition of sacred song were concentrated in the school of Jacob b. Moses *Moellin, commonly called the Maharil. Although a rabbi by rank and authority, he liked to function as a *ḥazzan* (*Sefer Maharil*, ed. Lemberg, 1860, fol. 55a–b; 49b). The musical usage taught by him was, on the one hand, a continuation of existing traditions accepted from former *Ḥazzanim* (*ibid.*, 28a; 82b), but on the other, his personal choice and example became normative. As a rule, the Maharil used to acknowledge the right of local custom:

> Maharil said: Local custom should not be altered at any price, even not by unfamiliar melodies. And he told us an event in his life. Once he was *ḥazzan* during the High Holidays at the Regensburg community and sang all the prayers according to the custom of the land of Austria, which is followed there. It was difficult for him, however, so that he said the *haftorah* in the tune customary in the settlements near the Rhine.

It is remarkable how elaborate and thoughtful the musical performance of the Maharil was. His disciple, *Zalman of St. Goar, recorded many details with great care and transmitted to posterity a "score without music," so to speak, of the most important parts of the liturgy. In the service for the Ninth of Av, for instance (fol. 49b–50b), not only is the distribution of texts between congregation and cantor defined, but also what the latter had to sing in a loud, medium, and low voice, what in a mournful intonation, and where a cry of pain was to be sent up. The pauses at the end of the verses and chapters are not forgotten, nor are the extension of melodies and other discriminate implements of expression. The music of the Day of Atonement is treated in a similar way (fol. 63a; 65a).

The Maharil used to stress the importance of hymns (*Krovez*, 83b), but he wished to exclude those in the German vernacular (117a), which apparently existed then, as do such in *Ladino with the Sephardim to the present. Often the Maharil points to the identity between certain hymn tunes (28b; 74b). Unlike many other rabbis, he regarded melody as an essential element of liturgical traditon.

The "musical *minhag*" of the Maharil is also full of mystical "intentions" (*kavvanot* 40b; 55b; 56a; 66a). There are striking examples of their influence on melodical configuration: "He used to extend [the tune at] the word 'Thou' very much, obviously concentrating his mind on the faculty of 'Thou' known to all the adepts of mystics" (56a). Such musical suggestions of a hidden sense of the words were indicated by remarks in the prayer books. The *Maḥzor Hadrat Kodesh* (Venice, 1512), for instance, advises the *ḥazzan* to sing a certain chapter "to a melody" or "in a long and beautiful tune" and assigns to the prayer *Nishmat Kol Ḥai* "a beautiful melody, since all the people of Israel are given an additional soul on the Sabbath." Other books attest the use of veritable leitmotifs, in the recitation of the Book of Esther when, for instance, the drinking vessels of Ahasuerus are mentioned to the tune of the Lamentations (for they supposedly formed part of the booty from the Temple of Jerusalem). It was also an old custom to prolong the tune of *Barukh she-Amar* in the Morning Prayer (mentioned in *Ha-Manhig*, c. 1205 and in 1689 by the convert Anton *Margarita); the author *Samson b. Eliezer (14th century) relates that he used to sing it as an orphan in Prague with such a sweet voice that he was given the name *Shimshon Barukh she-Amar* (*Sefer Barukh she-Amar*, preface). Although directions for musical execution are found in the works of many authors, the Maharil was made the legendary patron of Ashkenazi *ḥazzanut* and the invention of traditional melodies was ascribed to him. In particular, the so-called **Mi-Sinai* melodies—a common heritage of Ashkenazi synagogues in both Western and Eastern Europe—were believed to go back to the authority of the Maharil (sometimes confused, by uneducated cantors, with *Judah Loew b. Bezalel, Maharal of Prague). As a matter of fact, these melodies, ascribed to an oral tradition stemming "from Mount Sinai," i.e., revealed to Moses, are common to Ashkenazi congregations all over the world. They kept their identity in Jewish settlements as distant from each other as eastern Russia and northern France, south of the Carpathians, and in Scandinavia or Britain. There is no doubt that they antedate the great migrations from Central to Eastern Europe in the 15th century or even earlier. The structural principle of the *Mi-Sinai* melodies is basically oriental, inasmuch as a cycle of certain themes or motifs is used in manifold combinations and variants according to a traditional master plan. Of course, manifestations of local taste and of "acculturation" are most often present (see *Aleinu le-Shabbe'aḥ*; **Avodah*); however, the essential identity of all the variants is undeniable. They may well have been inherited by the Ashkenazim from a still unspecified epoch in the Middle Ages.

Modal Scales in Synagogue Song. The term "modal" in music is often used (although not with scientific precision) for such sequences of tone which are different from the familiar major and minor scales, an example being the Church modes. When applying the term "modal" to Jewish music, several precautions should be borne in mind. Firstly, a modal scale need not be an octave, but may be composed of more or less than eight notes. Furthermore, it must not necessarily repeat the same intervals over the whole gamut; on the contrary, an E natural, for instance, may appear in the lower octave and an E-flat in the upper one (see Mus. ex. 14). Finally, the interval of the augmented second sometimes joins the tone and semitone as a note proper to the key. Of course, scales of vocal music will not necessarily be in the equal temperament of the piano, but may retain a certain flexibility (sharpened leading notes, neutral thirds). In oriental Jewish song, micro-intervals in the style of the region are common.

The peculiarity of Jewish modes can be recognized and evaluated best in the Ashkenazi and European-Sephardi song, since their special character stands out against the background of the music of the gentile environment. The structural framework of West and North European song consists of chains of thirds bridged by whole tones, but repressing or avoiding semitones (as does Scotch and Irish folksong still today). Oriental song, on the other hand, is built around the skeleton of a tetrachord (four consecutive notes, including a semitone or even micro-intervals). The Jewish communities of the East still rely largely upon the tetrachord or enchained tetrachords, as it may be seen from examples 4a and 6b.

As to the Jewish settlements in Europe, tunes determined

by a tetrachordal skeleton are found among the Sephardim, including the communities of Carpentras (Avignon and Comtat Venaissin), Bayonne, Rome, and the rest of Italy (the Balkans belonging to the realm of Eastern music). In Ashkenazi song, however, tetrachordal patterns have almost entirely vanished. This has preserved, instead, some features of the earliest Western, semitoneless melodics (Mus. ex. 14).

In spite of this environmental influence on Ashkenazi song, a particular "Jewish" character does prevail there in certain scale structures which are strange in the context of Western music. These are called **shtayger* (a Yiddish term equivalent to mode, manner). Actually there are more *shtaygers* than the "four synagogue modes" proposed by earlier research, but two of them outweigh the others by far: the *Ahavah Rabbah* and the *Adonai Malakh*. Their special features may be recognized from the melody-excerpts given in example 15 and accompanying analyses of their scales.

As the present Ashkenazi liturgy is an accumulation of hymns and prayers successively added in the course of time, its music also exhibits many characteristics of medieval monody. Among them are the Re- and Mi-modes (similar to the Dorian and Phrygian of plainsong), and several peculiar final clauses. A Jewish origin has often been claimed for them but may hardly be proved. An oriental or Mediterranean character is evident, however, in most of the genuine *shtaygers*, especially the *Ahavah Rabbah* and kindred scales. Its nearest parallel is the second mode of the Greek Orthodox tradition; it may also be compared with the Persian-Arab Hijjaz scale, but it has no parallel in Western art or folk music.

The Sephardi communities that settled in Italy, France, Amsterdam, and London after their expulsion from Spain, also preserve European elements in their melodies. The most remarkable of these is a strange chromaticism which imparts a certain soft and floating tonality to some of their tunes (Mus. ex. 16); it might possibly be defined as a superimposition of two different modes, or as a bi-modality, which is very remote from Western concepts of functional harmony. This kind of chromaticism is found most characteristically in examples of biblical chant notated in 1693 (Rome) and 1699 (Amsterdam), as well as during the 19th and 20th centuries. Similar "floating" phrases are found in prayers and hymns; they are a characteristic of the "sweet singing of Sepharad," whose oriental roots may at present be postulated only speculatively but cannot as yet be proved by scientific deduction.

Performance and Practice of Synagogue Song. The collaboration of a soloist (*sheli'aḥ ẓibbur* or *ḥazzan*) and the choir formed by the whole congregation represents the main feature of synagogue music. These two bodies alternate or answer each other according to a traditional division of the liturgical texts. Very old practices of responsorial performance have been preserved especially by the Sephardi communities. As indicated in the Talmud (Sot. 30b) and also adopted by the Roman Church, the cantor may intone the first words of a chapter, whereupon the choir takes over, or they may alternate and respond one to the other. Among the Sephardim the congregation is also accustomed to take up the keywords of the more important prayers from the mouth of the cantor. The division of tasks between solo and choir sometimes affects the melodical configuration. If a particular prayer is sung to a *nusaḥ* (see above), its original free rhythm may change into measured time when taken over by the congregation, and the *ḥazzan* may execute the simple pattern in elaborate coloraturas (Mus. ex. 17).

EXAMPLE 14. Old European scales in Ashkenazi melodies. Blessing formula, after Idelsohn, *Melodien*, vol. 7, part 1, no. 10; motives of masoretic cantillation, after J. Reuchlin, *De accentibus . . .*, Hagenau, 1518; Sabbath song after A. Nadel, *Die haeuslichen Sabbatgesaenge*, 1937, 14.

EXAMPLE 15. Scales and examples of two Ashkenazi *shtayger*. (a) after A. B. Birnbaum, *Ommanut ha-Ḥazzanut* 2, 1912(?), no. 35; (b) after M. Deutsch, *Vorbeterschule*, 1871, no. 409.

EXAMPLE 16. Typical Western Sephardi chromaticism. Amsterdam, 1699, as notated by David de Pinna in D. E. Jablonski, *Biblia Hebraica,* Berlin, 1699; Rome, 1955(?), after E. Gerson-Kiwi, *Bat Kol,* 1, 1955, 15; Rome, 1966, after E. Piattelli, *Canti Liturgici di rito Italiano,* 1967, 15; Leghorn, 1892, after F. Consolo, op. cit., Ex. 4, no. 335; Florence, 1956, after L. Levi, *Scritti in memoria di Sally Mayer,* 1956, 174.

EXAMPLE 17. Mutations of a *nusaḥ* pattern, Italian Sephardi, after F. Consolo, op. cit., nos. 335–6.

Many non-Ashkenazi communities provide the cantor with two assistants *(mezammerim, somekhim, maftirim)* who flank him at the prayer desk and take over at certain points of the liturgy. This custom is rooted in certain ideas about the community's representation before the Most High; here the participation of three singers does not influence the shape and manner of their music making. However, a special development in this field took place in the Ashkenazi synagogues. Their cantors also attached to themselves two assistant singers, but they did so with a view to the enrichment and beauty of their singing. According to a fixed rule, one of these assistants *(meshorerim)* had to be a boy-descant, called singer, and the other an adult, called bass. It is not known, when and why this custom was introduced; a picture in the so-called *Leipzig Maḥzor* of the 14th century may be regarded as the earliest representation of such a trio (see Fig. 4). The heyday of *ḥazzanut* with accompanying *meshorerim* was the 17th and 18th centuries, and it is only from the sources of this late period that its nature can be inferred. According to it, the assistants improvised an accompaniment of hummed chords, drones, or short figures; the singer also intoned thirds and sixths parallel to the cantilena of the *ḥazzan.* In addition, both singer and bass had their solo parts—most often extended coloraturas to be performed while the cantor paused. Famous cantors traveled, with the *meshorerim* as a part of their household, from one large center to another as guest ministers, while the less famed undertook such wanderings in search for a hoped-for permanent post. In the late baroque period, if not earlier, the traditional number of two assistants was supplemented by performers of distinctive tasks, such as the fistel singer (falsetto) and specialists in the imitation of musical instruments (*Sayt-bass, fagott-bass, fleyt-singer,* for strings, bassoon, and flute, respectively).

The use of musical instruments proper is attested in medieval Baghdad by the traveler *Pethahiah of Regensburg, between 1175 and 1190. However, this was a rare exception and restricted to the half-holidays, since the ban on instrumental music remained in force. It was only by the influence of later mystical movements that the play of instruments was employed in some 17th century Ashkenazi synagogues before the entry of the Sabbath as a token of the joy of the day of rest. Vocal performances nevertheless remained the basic characteristic of synagogue music. An incessant struggle took place in this field between older singing styles and the musical expression of spiritual tendencies that arose during the Middle Ages. This interplay of forces kept Jewish liturgical music from the petrifaction typical of many other traditions of religious chant.

MIGRATION AND BLENDING OF MUSIC STYLES (c. 1500–1750/1800)

The era of the Middle Ages is generally regarded as completed at about 1500. The Jews, however, were not yet relieved of the pressure that had built up during medieval times. For them the period between 1500 and about 1800 was a time of forced migrations, of many a spiritual crisis, of ethno-geographical regrouping, and the formation of new centers. The uprooting of large communities and their confrontation with new environments inevitably left its imprint on their music. The most conspicuous event was the migration of these exiled from Spain to the Ottoman Empire, Italy, and other countries, followed by a steadily trickling rearguard of *Marranos; the persecutions in Central Europe also directed a Jewish mass movement to the (then very spacious) Polish kingdom. The eastbound migrations of both Sephardi and Ashkenazi Jews share the fact that the emigrants preserved their original vernacular and their liturgical customs, as well as part of their music, and even imposed these on the local communities. In the long run, however, the musical atmosphere of the new lands permeated the intonation and scale structure of their song, while its melodic structure was affected to a lesser degree. The developments were not left to mere chance. New ideologies came into being and also became guiding stars for the forms and contents of musical expression.

The Mystical Movement of Safed. In the course of the Sephardi migration to the eastern countries, the small Galilean township of *Safed had become a meeting place of kabbalists and mystics. Their spiritual leader was Isaac *Luria, reverently called *ha-Ari ha-Kadosh*. The inner circle of his followers lived up to, and spread in writing, the tenets of this charismatic personality. His ideas contained a strong musical element from the very beginnings. The inner visions of the leading thinkers, and the mystical way of life accepted by the broad masses of their followers must be considered separately. The former definitely fostered the "acoustic type" of inner experience and symbolical expression. To Moses *Cordovero, for instance, the peoples on earth are "birds of varied plumage, each with its own type of music and its own song," and no sooner does the boundless power of God descend to the lower spheres "than the song of the birds is heard drawing Him through all the rooms to hear the sweet music." Their singing symbolizes the fulfillment of the divine command, and, therefore, "great skill is required for the birds to sing the song as it should be sung. Since it is part of the sage's wisdom, this skill cannot be gained unless the sage himself teaches it to the birds" (*Shi'ur Komah*, 10).

It becomes clear from the popular *Sefer ha-Yirah* ("Book of the Fear [of God]") by Eleazar *Azikri (printed in 1601) why the divine command could allegorically be called a song. There it is stated that when a man says his prayers:

> his soul should always be united with the love of God, like one who is love-sick cannot cease thinking and musing of a certain woman . . . Mightier still shall be the love of God in the heart of His followers. Now, it is the way of the affectionate—to sing; and since the love of our creator is more wonderful than the love of women, His followers shall sing unto Him from the depths of their heart.

This preponderance of love and cheerfulness expressed by song continues the trend established by the Ḥasidei Ashkenaz (see above). Like them, the mystics of Safed demand prayer song from everybody—regardless of the beauty of tunes and the agreeability of voices; only the intention and the devotion of the singer count.

In 1618, Menahem de *Lonzano, of Damascus, demanded that the pious should join the morning stars in their matutinal song of praise (cf. Job 38:7), adding: "He whose voice is bad and unpleasant, and who cannot perform hymns and songs according to their tunes and who cannot remember melodies: even to a man like him it is allotted to raise his voice." This kind of devoted singing is not measured by artistic or aesthetic standards, but according to intrinsic values beyond the realm of the audible. Consequently, a clumsy fellow may sing in his awkward manner, a fiddler may use his dance tunes, and a craftsman the melodies heard in his quarter.

The democratic tendencies in the ideology of religious song gave rise to a new wave of popular and profane tunes that infiltrated Hebrew hymnody. The Sephardim had always been very fond of singing and did not lose this predilection during the bitter days of the expulsion. This is proven by the respectable production of Hebrew hymns for extra-synagogal use, written in the popular style and connected with tunes borrowed from songs in the vernacular. An early print of *bakkashot* (Constantinople, c. 1525) attests the popularity of 13 Spanish songs with the exiles from the peninsula; six of the hymns by Solomon b. Mazal Tov (printed in 1545) were to be sung to the tune of Spanish songs, 30 to Turkish, and 29 to older Jewish ones. Solomon Mevorakh's song book of 1555 refers to only ten Turkish melodies (since it was written in Greece), and 14 taken from Jewish songs, but it quotes no less than 30 Spanish tunes that obviously were familiar to his contemporaries. Among the latter are "evergreens" of the Iberian repertoire and many pieces that have since fallen into oblivion. The natural inclination of the people to sing, both in Hebrew and in vernacular tongues, received backing from a mystical idea which suggested that every melody, even those drawn from popular or gentile sources, may become a vehicle of elated feelings.

Menahem de Lonzano preferred to compose hymns to Turkish melodies because of their ascending "to the tenth over the note *duga*" (the note D in the Persian-Arabic scale); he held that this "utmost range of the human voice," not reached by Greek, Romaniote, or Arabic tunes, was the real meaning of the Psalm verse "On the *Asor* and on the *Nevel*" (*Shetei Yadot*, fol. 141b–142a). Thus, a rabbi and mystic used his well-founded musical knowledge for imparting high flight to his hymnal song. Religious hymns designed both for the prayer house and outside (*pizmonim; bakkashot*) propagated the pious mood of Safed in the Jewish world. Among the most prominent songs of this kind are: *Asadder bi-Shevaḥin* (ascribed to Isaac Luria himself), **Lekhah Dodi* by Solomon *Alkabeẓ, *Yedid Nefesh* by Azikri, and *Yah Ribbon Olam* by Israel *Najara. The last was a very productive and inspired poet gifted with a sense for musical nuances. Many of his hymns (printed between 1587 and 1600) were written to the tunes of well-known secular songs in the Spanish or Turkish vernacular, less often in Greek and Arabic.

Najara continued an older custom of providing for a phonetic correspondence of the foreign and the Hebrew text. In this manner, the singer of a gentile song was reminded of the preferred religious alternative. The manuscript of Solomon Mevorakh (Greece, 1555), for instance, shows the replacement of the Spanish song *"Alma me llaman a mi, alma"* by the very similar sounding Hebrew *"Al Mah ke-Alman Ammi, Al Mah."* Najara substituted for the Arabic *"Ana al-samra wa-sammuni sumayra"* the words *"Anna El Shomera Nafshi mi-Levayim."* He strengthened the associative bridge still further by giving the plot of the gentile song a religious meaning. Thus the famous romance on the knight-errant Amadis becomes a tour de force of phonetic sound imitation and, at the same time, a fine allegory of Israel and God's errant glory:

(Spanish-Jewish romance)
Arbo*leda*, arbo*leda*,
Arboleda tan gen*til*,
La rais tiene d'*oro*
Y la rama de mar*fil*.

(Najara)
Ḥil yo*ledah* bi so*ledah*
Keshurah al lev bi-fe*til*
Al dod meni histir *oro*
U-me'oni me-az he'*efil*

(Mevorakh)
Ashorerah li-fe'*erah*
Azamerah na be-shi*r*

Najara fostered music in the broadest meaning by acknowledging the union of word and tone—not as an artistic game (as did later imitators), but for the pious inspiration of the common people by ways of a musical language that was their own.

The ideas of Safed, with their strong musical element, conquered communities near and far. This is indicated by the enrichment of the liturgy, especially that of the Sabbath day. The *Lekhah Dodi* was accepted all over the Diaspora, as were the six psalms of Sabbath eve, *zemirot*, and the "three repasts of the Queen" (*Shalosh Se'udot*), with the songs accompanying them. Hearty joy expressed by music had become an explicit commandment. Everywhere, both in the Sephardi and the Ashkenazi settlements, there sprouted pious brotherhoods that fostered the singing of hymns and songs at their meetings. These societies of *Shomerim la-Boker* ("Watchers of the Dawn," Italy), *Mezammerei Barukh she-Amar* ("Singers of *Barukh she-Amar*," Bohemia, Germany), *Maftirim* (Turkey) and others used to convene early in the morning or on certain festival nights for a "singing office." They were led by their own precentor and had their hymn texts published in print. The *Mezammerei Barukh she-Amar* of Prague and other large centers even played instrumental music in the synagogue on Friday afternoons in order to increase the joy and splendor of the Sabbath. Participation in these orchestras was regarded as a *mitzvah* and therefore mentioned in epitaphs (Prague, between 1632 and 1744). The traveler Abraham Levi of Amsterdam observed in 1719–24 that "the cantors also use organs, cymbals, harpsichords, and strings every Friday for greeting the Sabbath: they sing not only *Lekhah Dodi* to these instruments, but continue thereafter, singing and playing a medley of nice melodies over a whole hour." Unfortunately the nature of this evening music performed in the synagogues of Prague, Frankfort, Nikolsburg and other towns is not known. The fact that singing and playing had become a *mitzvah* and the increase of hymn production was an enormous challenge for the creation or adaptation of melodies. Since all this music was for popular consumption, it was rather free of the rules of the strictly traditional styles of synagogue songs, which may be inferred from the extant forms of such tunes.

Humanism and the Renaissance. Contemporary with the era of Safed mysticism, another encounter of East and West in the field of Jewish music was initiated by the Renaissance and Humanist movements in Italy and other parts of Europe. This was an interlude in history acted out in the circles of learned scholars and before an erudite and refined audience of art music.

The Humanistic Approach to Letters and Music. In the world of science, the traditional definitions and views of the Middle Ages were replaced by a direct dialogue with the authors of antiquity, studied in their original language. This trend extended to the Bible and later Hebrew works. Several Christian scholars studied Hebrew language and grammar, including the rules of masorah and its accentuation. After a short time, the students themselves wrote books on Hebrew grammar which contained chapters on the *te'amim*, sometimes adding the music of biblical chants. Among these were Johannes Reuchlin (*De accentibus et orthographia linguae Hebraicae*; Hagenau, 1518), Sebastian *Muenster (*Institutiones grammaticae in Hebraeam linguam*; Basel, 1524), and Johann *Boeschenstein (Munich Cod. hebr. 401). Many later writers, such as Johannes Vallensis (*Opus de prosodia Hebraeorum*; Paris, 1545) and Ercole Bottrigari (*Il Trimerone*, Ms. dated 1599) took over their notated examples. The Ashkenazi Pentateuch tunes, notated independently by several of the authors, are of very similar outlines and are based upon that same semitoneless scale which is still recognizable in the Bible chant of modern times (cf. Reuchlin's notation, Mus. ex. 14). The renewed interest in grammar and *masorah* seized Jewish circles as well. Early in the 16th century, several Hebrew authors undertook the description of contemporary practices of biblical chant. The features of the Sephardi version were described by Calo Kalonymus (Appendix to Abraham de *Balmes, *Mikneh Avram*, 1523), and compared with Ashkenazi practice by Elijah Levita (*Tuv Ta'am*, 1538).

In the field of art proper, the open-mindedness of the Renaissance period favored the reconciliation of a progressive Jewish public with art music, especially in the small town-states of upper Italy and Tuscany. A very dry historical source—the book lists delivered to the papal censor by the Jewish families of Mantua in 1559—speaks eloquently when stating that a certain Samuel Ariano had Zarlino's voluminous *Istituzioni harmoniche* in his library and that Isaac *Norzi possesed madrigal books of Cipriano de Rore, Donato, Stabile, and others. Two influential leaders of the Mantua community discussed the integration of art music in Jewish life. Judah *Moscato, rabbi of that town in 1587–94, preached a long sermon titled *Higgayon be-Khinnor* ("Meditations on the Lyre"), published in *Nefuẓot Yehudah* (Venice, 1589). He examined the subject "man and music" under the aspects of Jewish tradition from the Talmud and Midrash down to the contemporary kabbalists, as well as with reference to the Greek and Arabic philosophers. The rabbi stressed the interrelation of the harmony found in music and the harmony imagined in the soul and character of man, striving to show the legitimacy of the musical art in Judaism.

His contemporary, the physician and rabbi Abraham *Portaleone II of Mantua, wrote the book *Shiltei ha-Gibborim* ("Shields of the Heroes"; posthumously printed Venice, 1612) which may be viewed as an early attempt at biblical archaeology based on the interpretation of literary sources, in the spirit of Renaissance scholarship. The author dwells at length on levitic song and the form and nature of its musical instruments. These chapters were soon regarded as a "source" of Hebrew music by outstanding Christian writers, especially after they had been translated into Latin by Blasio *Ugolino in 1767. Disregarding its dubious informative value, this book is symptomatic of the mood governing Renaissance Jewry. Even before 1480, *Judah b. Jehiel Messer Leon of Mantua had become enthusiastic about the concordance between the Bible and ancient Greek rhetoric and other literary genres; Azariah de *Rossi took up these views, and Abraham Portaleone finally applied them to the field of music. At the time, R. Portaleone's book was likely to strengthen the consciousness of the Hebrew share in the culture of antiquity and the importance of its musical achievements.

Art Music. With the partial release of external and internal pressure, a generation of gifted Jewish musicians and composers cropped up during the 16th century. They straightway were absorbed into the fervent development of Italian music, and several Jewish composers saw their works appear in the famous printing establishments of Venice between 1575 and 1628. Outstanding talents had already begun to run the social blockade early in the Cinquecento. The convert Giovan Maria, a lute player, won great fame even beyond the Alps. He successively served the courts of Urbino (1510), Mantua (tutor of the princes, 1513–15), and finally Pope Leo X (chamber musician, 1515–21) and Clement VII (1525–26). At the Gonzaga court of Mantua the harp players Abramo (Abraham Levi) dall' *Arpa and his family were appointed before 1550. They are

Figure 8. Motives of masoretic cantillation of the German Jews in Italy (Rome?), as notated by Athanasius Kircher. From his *Musurgia Universalis*, Rome, 1650, Book 2, "Liber Philologicus," 66. Five additional motives are given on p. 67.

Figure 9. Dance of the actors at the end of a Purim play, detail from a panel in an illustrated scroll of Esther, Italy(?), 18th century. An ensemble of five musicians sits, as was customary in these plays, at the right of the improvised stage. Formerly Warsaw, Bersohn collection.

Figure 10. A Dutch synagogue, first half of 18th century, with the *ḥazzan* and *meshorerim* standing before the centrally placed *bimah*. Engraving by M. Pool Sculy. Amsterdam, Rijksmuseum, Cabinet des Estampes Inv. 16:309.

mentioned as high-ranking musicians by the art theoretician G. P. Lomazzo (1584; 1587); Daniel Levi dall'Arpa was sent to the imperial court of Vienna between 1550 and 1560. The social situation of such Jewish musicians is understood from the fact that Abramo dall' Arpa also held a license for the ritual slaughterhouse and for moneylending in his native town; his son Daniel was granted a special passport to move freely about the country.

The first Jewish composer to see his works appear in print was David *Sacerdote (Cohen) of Rovere. His first book of six-part madrigals was dedicated to the Marchese del Vasto and printed in 1575 (until now only the *Quinto* part book has been rediscovered). For the first time the designation *Hebreo* was added to the composer's name; this became the rule with all those who came after him, most probably by decree of the censor.

The most conspicuous developments took place in the duchy of Mantua, whose court harbored composers of worldwide fame such as Monteverdi. Ensembles of Jewish actors and musicians contributed to the fervent musical life of that town, including several members of the de *Rossi family ("Min-ha-Adumim"). A female singer of this family participated in the performance of one of the precursors of the opera (1608), and an Anselmo Rossi had a motet based on psalm texts printed in a collective work (1618). In 1651, Giuseppe de Rossi served the duke of Savoy at Turin. The most important musician of the family was composer Salamone de *Rossi, whose life is documented between 1586 and 1628 (see below). His works were much favored by his contemporaries, as attested by several reprints and their admission to collected editions published in Copenhagen (1605) and Antwerp (1613; 1616). He also secured a firm place in the general history of music, especially by his progressive instrumental compositions and the early application of the thorough bass. Other Jewish composers whose works have been preserved in print were Davit *Civita (1616; 1622; 1625) and Allegro Porto (1619).

Outside Italy Jewish folk musicians were very active but were not given an opportunity to gain a footing in the ranks of art music. The relative freedom prevailing in Renaissance Italy came to a sudden end with one of the usual crises of Jewish existence. When the House of Gonzaga died out and troubles seized the duchy of Mantua, the Jewish musicians had to emigrate (most went to Venice). The prosperity of that city and its large Jewish population encouraged them to found a Jewish *accademia musicale* (concert society) called "accademia degli Impediti" and later on "Compagnia dei musici." The music-loving R. Leone *Modena promoted their activities. Attempts were made to introduce instrumental play into the synagogue at the feast of Simḥat Torah; but the initiators had to yield to rabbinical objections, since the organ used by them was too reminiscent of "the foreign cult." Finally it was again a catastrophe—the plague of 1630—that cut off the manifestations of Jewish integration in art music. The last flickering of such intentions was quenched by severe rabbis about the middle of the century, but not before the first works of synagogal art music had come into existence.

EFFORTS TO ESTABLISH ART MUSIC IN THE SYNAGOGUE. From the eloquent recommendation of Judah Moscato and the delight in art music fostered in wide circles of Renaissance Judaism, it was not a far cry to welcome art music in the synagogue as well. The enthusiasm for the ancient Temple music (Abraham Portaleone, see above) suggested its reinstitution in the house of prayer. The power of conservatism and exile—conditioned humility and pessimism, however, proved hard to overcome. The power behind these progressive tendencies was Leone Modena, who, although ordained as a rabbi, was actually rather one of the errant literati and jack-of-all-trades like many a learned humanist or his younger contemporary Joseph *Delmedigo. While music was for Delmedigo a matter of science (*Sefer Elim*, Amsterdam, 1629), it was one of the 26 crafts in which Leone Modena claimed to have been engaged.

As a rabbi in his native Ferrara about 1605, he saw to the installation of a synagogue choir and to the systematical instruction of its six to eight singers in music. They performed hymns such as **Adon Olam*, **Yigdal*, *En ke-Eloheinu*, and *Aleinu le-Shabbe'aḥ* on the occasion of feasts and special Sabbaths, "in honor of God according to the order and right proportion of the voices in the art [of music]." This innovation met with the stiff resistance of a local rabbi who held that music was prohibited in exile; but Leone Modena secured a decision of four other rabbis in favor of polyphonic synagogue singing. This document was to become the main weapon for many later attempts in this direction. It was reprinted by the progressive cantor Solomon Lipschitz in 1718, as well as by Adolf *Jellinek of Vienna in 1861 (Ben Chananja 4, no. 27 suppl. as "topical for the still pending question of introducing choir singing in the sacred service of the Hungarian communities"). The most prominent place in which this decision was printed, and, at the same time, the recompense of Leone Modena's efforts, was the edition in print of Salamone de Rossi's collected synagogue compositions *Ha-Shirim Asher li-Shelomo* (Venice, 1622–23). The preface of the editor (de Modena) states that de Rossi, after his success in secular music, "dedicated his talents to God . . . and wrote down psalms, prayers and praises. As soon as one started singing [them], all the listeners were taken away by their ear-flattering beauty." The wealthy Moses Sullam and other notabilities of Jewish Venice (including the editor himself) worked hard in persuading the composer to have these liturgical works published in print.

If the flowery language of this preface can be taken at face value, de Rossi's choral works for the synagogue had already been performed from the manuscript at Mantua (possibly also at Ferrara where a Benjamin Saul Min-ha-Adumim was *ḥazzan* before 1612). The three- to eight-voiced compositions of the *Ha-Shirim Asher li-Shelomo* are not only a "first" and a solitary phenomenon in early synagogue music, they have also a particular standing within the musical work of Salamone de Rossi himself. Considering his way from the youthful freshness of the *Canzonette* (1589) down to the ripe and dramatized lyricism in his *Madrigaletti* (1628), the restraint and objectivity of his religious works becomes obvious. Rossi had no Jewish tradition of choral polyphony to start from; he could not use the idiom of church music, nor did he wish to employ his command of madrigalesque expressivity. Thus he turned to a sort of objective choral psalmody, on the one hand, and to the representative chordal columns of Gabrieli, on the other, interspersed with fine specimens of polyphonic voice weaving and a diversity of nonfunctional chords. The expressive values and musical declamation are austere, however, as compared with Rossi's secular works. They comply with Pietro Cerone's rules for psalm composition (*El Melopeo*, 1613) rather than evoking the customary conceptions of synagogue style. It should be emphasized that Rossi's compositions were intended only for particular occasions, such as "special Sabbaths and feasts," and were not designed to replace the traditional synagogue chants.

At the Crossroads of East and West. In the course of the 16th century, a rearrangement of the Jewish population in the lands of the Diaspora had taken place. The most important moves were the influx of exiles from Spain and Portugal into the Ottoman-ruled East and the immigra-

Figure 11. Intonation of the priestly blessing used in the synagogue of the Italian rite at Ferrara. From Mordecai b. Jacob Ẓahalon, *Meẓiẓ u-Meliẓ,* responsa about the quarrel over an attempt to introduce a new melody for the blessing, Venice, 1715. A 12-page appendix featuring the intonations according to the Italian, Sephardi, and Ashkenazi rites has been found only in the copy in the library of the Hebrew Union College, Cincinnati. Cincinnati, Ohio, Hebrew Union College.

Figure 12. Mural on the west wall of the wooden synagogue in Przedborz, Poland, on the theme "by the rivers of Babylon" (Ps. 137:1), painted by Judah Leib, 1760. The musical instruments, like the architecture depicted, are western. Similar scenes appear in other wooden synagogues of the period. From M. and K. Piechotka, *Wooden Synagogues,* Warsaw, 1959.

Figure 13. Marriage ceremony in Germany, 18th century. The musicians playing to the female guests include a woman performing on a hurdy-gurdy, who is probably also singing. From J. Bodenschatz, *Kirchliche Verfassung der heutigen Juden,* Frankfort and Leipzig, 1748. Cecil Roth Collection.

Figure 14. Illuminated scroll from Rome with the text of a cantata celebrating the appointment of Isaac Berechiah b. Mordecai Baraffael as *ḥatan torah* (bridegroom of the Law) on Simḥat Torah, 1766. The author is probably Rabbi Abraham ben Jacob Anav. The three singers represent wealth, honor, and life. The music has not yet been recovered. Washington, Smithsonian Institution, cat. no. 154, 634.

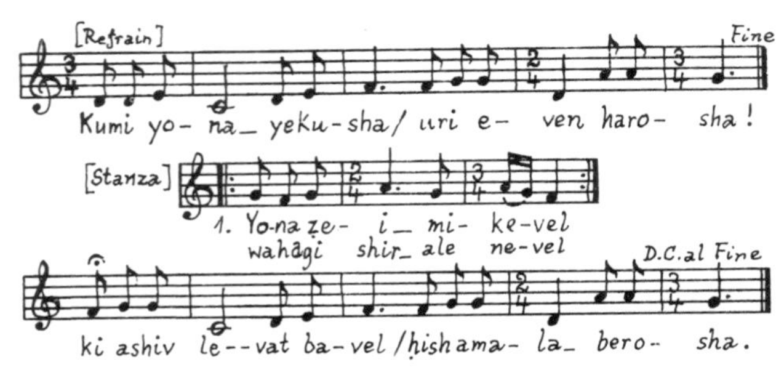

Example 18. Hymn in Spanish *Villancico* form. Poem by Israel Najara, from his *Zemirot Yisrael,* Safed, 1587; melody as sung in Iraq, beginning of 20th century, after Idelsohn, *Melodien,* vol. 2, no. 120.

tion of Ashkenazim into Poland and the rest of Eastern Europe. These mainstreams of migration led to the formation of an Oriental-Sephardi and an East-Ashkenazi branch of Jewish music each developing a special character that had not previously existed.

Consolidation of the Oriental Style of Jewish Music. The obstinacy shown by the Sephardim in their clinging to the Castilian vernacular and folk song did not prevent them from yielding to the powerful influence of oriental, especially Turkish, music. This is indicated, for instance, by the increasing use of Turkish melodies for Hebrew hymns. Musical assimilation became more spectacular when the system of **maqām* was adopted in Jewish song. Israel Najara, late in the 16th century, appears to have been the first to assign every poem to a cetain *maqām,* even when he demands a Spanish folk tune for it. His *Kumi Yonah Yekushah,* for instance, is accompanied by the instruction "Tune: *Linda era y fermosa*" but, at the same time, is classified as belonging to the *maqam Ḥusayni* (today it is sung to the *maqām Nawa;* see Mus. ex. 18). According to the Eastern custom, Najara arranged his hymns for publication in a *diwan* of 12 *maqāmāt.* The framework of *maqāmāt,* each of which also represents a certain mood or "ethos," was imposed on synagogue song in general and extended even beyond hymnody proper. The majestic *Siga* became the mode for reading the Torah and all texts referring to it; the gay *Ajam-Nawruz* was used on *Shabbat Shirah,* Simḥat Torah, and for weddings; the mournful *Ḥijjaz* expressed the mood of the Ninth of Av, funerals, and pericopes mentioning death. *Ṣabba* ("chaste love, filial affection") was reserved for texts connected with circumcisions. The most systematic adherence to the mood conventions of the *maqāmāt* was by the Aleppo community.

Poetry books dating from the 17th century onward open the section of every *maqām* with an introductory verse (*petiḥah*) in which the name of the *maqām* is echoed by a phonetically similar Hebrew word, such as for *Ḥusayni: Lazkir godlakh kedai eyni/ mi-meẓukotai hoẓieni,* or *Bitḥoni ve-koni/ ḥasini maginni;* and for *Rast: Uri Devorah, dabberi/ ki hod ve-hadar yarasht . . .* (Sephardi pronunciation: *yarast*). These short rhymes were perhaps to be sung to the rhythmically free coloraturas that are the customary introduction of every new *maqām* section. The Jews of North Africa (Maghreb) adopted oriental singing manners in accordance with the local *tubu'* ("natures," *maqāmāt*). Every group of hymns assigned to one of these modes is opened by a poem for the musical introduction called *istakhbar* ("becoming acquainted"), a parallel to the Syrian-Jewish *petiḥah* verses. A manuscript of 1745 from Morocco (Ms. Oxford, 1188) enumerates among its 24 *tubu'* also a *taba' romanze,* which obviously points to an origin in Spanish folk song.

All musical characteristics quoted up to now demonstrate the progressive orientalization of the Jews who came from the Iberian peninsula and intermingled with the veteran settlers. However, while the melodic configuration itself came to follow the ways of the East, some formal traits of European origin were retained. During the 17th century, the Eastern forms *mawwal* and *peshref* were still sparingly used (Najara, *Pizmonim* 35: "This *piyyut* is patterned after the *peshref* called Kabul Ḥasan"). The quantitative Arab meter was replaced by the syllable-counting verse known from the Romance literature. The stanzas of *piyyut* and *pizmon* were fashioned to the typical patterns of Spanish *romances* and *villancicos* (which was also a precondition for borrowing melodies from songs of these forms). Today, hymns of Najara and his followers are sung to tunes that show oriental surface features but are still tailored to the pattern of medieval *villancicos* (Mus. ex. 18): the sequence of rhymes a a / b b b a is sung to a sequence of melodic phrases A B / C C / A B (the first A B serving as a refrain).

After Najara's time, the orientalization of Eastern Sephardi music went on both at the popular and the artistic levels. The Jewish folk musicians became powerful agents in the exchange of tunes and styles; they were also fully accepted by the gentiles and their rulers. In the Maghreb, they formed well-established and sometimes famous bands. The Turkish traveler Evliya Tchelebi describes the parade of the guilds before Sultan Murad IV in 1638: 300 Jewish musicians were led by their chief, Patakoglu, together with the famous Yaco and the *tunbur*-player Karakash; later on marched the Jewish dancers, jugglers, and buffoons. The reliability of the recorded numbers is proven by Ludwig August *Frankl, who found 500 Jewish musicians of Turkish nationality in Constantinople of 1856 forming 5.6% of all the craftsmen registered by the Jewish community.

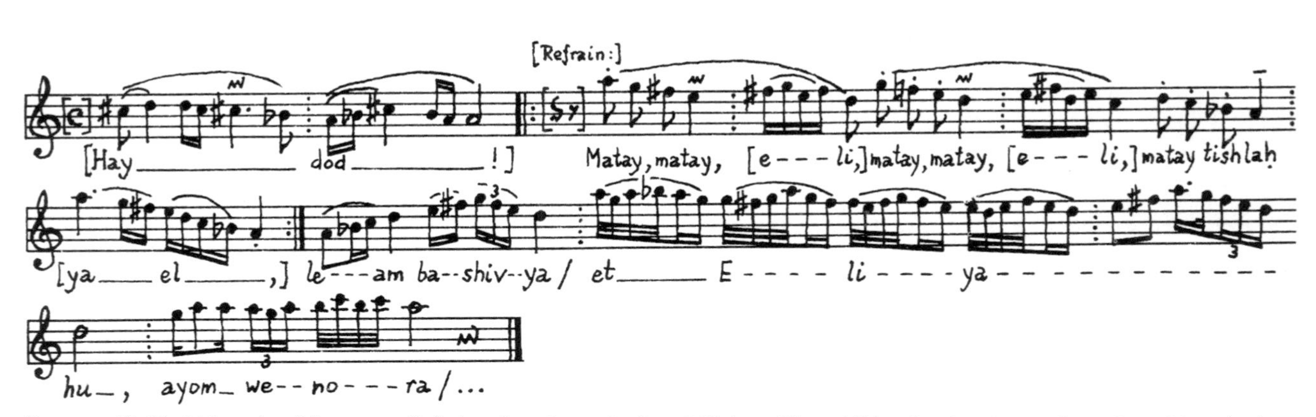

Example 19. Turkish style of *ḥazzanut.* Refrain of a *pizmon* by Israel Najara. The addition by the singer of words and interjections such as those shown in brackets is typical of this style of art music. Notated in Istanbul in 1936 and published by Th. Fuchs in *Ommanut,* Zagreb, 1, 1936–37, music supplement, 2.

The ranks of respected Turkish musician-composers were joined by Aaron Hamon (Yahudi Harun) late in the 17th century. Some of his *peshref*-suites were preserved in the so-called Harpasun notation. After him, Moses Faro ("Musi," d. 1776) and Isaac Fresco Romano ("Tanburi Issak") won great fame in the late 18th century. Turkish art music left its unmistakable imprint on the *ḥazzanut* of that country (Mus. ex. 19), as it did also in the case of the *maftirim* choirs (see above) that sometimes claim dependence on the fine melodies of the dervish orders.

As to the Sephardim settling in Italy, Amsterdam, and other parts of Christian Europe, the situation was quite different. Certainly they preserved modes and tunes of an old standing, which they held in common with their oriental brothers; there was also a steady immigration from the Eastern communities. On the other hand, the European Sephardi congregations were permanently reinforced by Marranos escaping from the peninsula—most often highly educated people with a flair for contemporary music. The writer Daniel Levi de *Barrios (born in Spain, from 1674 in Amsterdam) mentions several newcomers to the "Portuguese community" who excelled in playing the harp and *vihuela* (guitar) or flute, as well as in singing. As these returning converts were setting the fashion in cultural life, it is not surprising that the preserved music exhibits the character of contemporary art. It was in this style that Purim plays and comedies with music were performed and cantatas were composed for Simḥat Torah and other festive occasions. One of the better-known composers of this style of music was Abraham *Caceres in Amsterdam early in the 18th century. De Barrios also refers to the cantors of the Amsterdam Portuguese community, some of whom received commissions from the London, Hamburg, and other Sephardi synagogues. A musical manuscript of the *ḥazzan* Joseph de Isaac *Sarfati (mid-18th century) contains liturgical solo pieces composed in the taste of his time or directly taken over from contemporary secular works (Mus. ex. 20). It must be born in mind, however, that the *ḥazzanim* of that period used to write down only "composed" music of their own production or that of their contemporaries; there was no need to notate traditional melodies and recitations that every cantor knew by heart.

Traditional Amsterdam-Sephardi song as it is intoned or recorded today makes a deep but somewhat strange impression on the listener. One is tempted to say that this is oriental music misunderstood both by singers and notators and nevertheless performed in a naïve faithfulness. Further research may perhaps disclose that it was brought to the Netherlands by *ḥazzanim* recruited from Tunis or other Eastern areas in order to fill the vacuum of traditional song felt by the Marranos. The sound of Hebrew prayers was like a revelation to them and was faithfully preserved in spite of its displaced oriental character. But the transplantation of Eastern music to the north inevitably ended in degeneration. That this was a slow process is indicated by a tune of a *kinah* (lament) for the Ninth of Av notated in 1775 (Mus. ex. 21): the modality, the articulation of the profuse coloraturas, and especially the attack of every new phrase after a caesura still bears the unmistakable mark of Eastern origin.

The biased character of Amsterdam Portuguese music is found in the other Sephardi communities of Europe in varying degrees. London proved more "progressive" in the direction of Westernization, while the Bayonne and other Carpentras communities preserved more of the Mediterranean character (see **Avi Avi*). Leghorn and Rome retained many a non-European feature in their synagogue songs, such as tetrachord scales, free rhythm, and the variative development of modal patterns. Side by side with this conservative attitude, the Italian congregations liked to celebrate certain holidays, weddings, circumcisions, and special events (like the dedication of a new prayerhouse) by Hebrew *cantatas written in the contemporary style. Their music was of a strictly utilitarian character and significant only for the very average taste of their respective times.

THE EASTERN BRANCH OF ASHKENAZI SONG. An uninterrupted flow of Ashkenazi emigrants poured forth to the East European countries beginning in the Middle Ages and accumulated to form the most powerful Jewish community until the 20th century. The Eastern Ashkenazim preserved their old German-Jewish idiom but developed a rich religious and secular culture of their own. The special flavor of their melodies and singing habits can be distinguished from that of the Western Ashkenazim even when the tunes are identical. The material roots of this musical evolution are uncertain. The proposed influence of the *Khazars or of Byzantine Jews is only hypothetical and cannot be proven. What remains credible is the effect of country and surroundings, just as these factors imparted a Slavic tint to the song of the German settlers in the Volga region. Such influence has been proven to alter intonation and rhythm and promote the favoring of certain modal shades, as well as supply a predominantly sentimental disposition of the singer. The Eastern Ashkenazi way of singing was first discerned at its appearance in Western

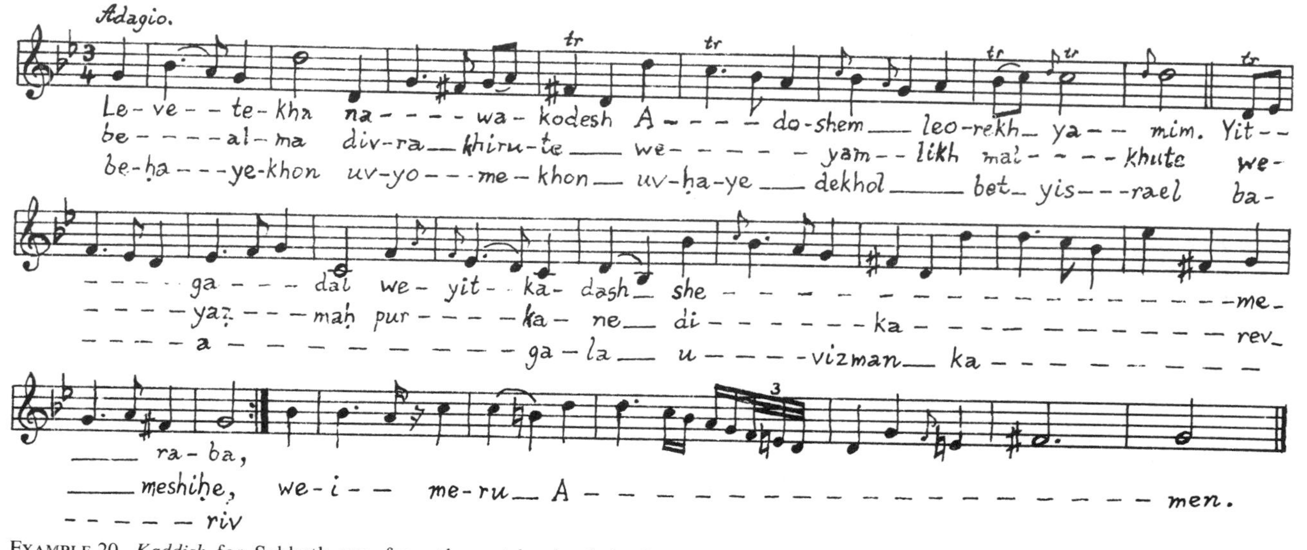

EXAMPLE 20. *Kaddish* for Sabbath eve, from the notebook of the *ḥazzan,* Joseph Sarphati, Amsterdam, middle of 18th century. The melody is adapted from the composition *Ha'Mesi'aḥ Illemim* by Abraham Caceres (fl. 1720). Jerusalem, J.N.U.L., ms. 8° Mus 2, fol. [21]v.

Example 21. Oriental singing style in the Amsterdam synagogue, 18th century. Lamentation *(kinah)* for the Ninth of Av, after H. Krieg, *Spanish Liturgical Melodies of the Portuguese Israelitisch Community, Amsterdam*, vol. 2, 1954, 2.

Europe after the renewed migration in about 1650 caused by the *Chmielnicki persecutions. A small but steady flow of rabbis, teachers, and cantors continued infiltrating the West during the 17th and 18th centuries. Thus, in 1660, Ḥayyim Selig from Lemberg was appointed *ḥazzan* at *Fuerth: Judah Leib of Zelichev served in several synagogues of western Germany and published a critical essay entitled *Shirei Yehudah* (Amsterdam, 1696); Jehiel Michal from Lublin established, in about 1700, *ḥazzanut* with assistant singers in the Amsterdam Ashkenazi synagogue; a traveling *ḥazzan* of great fame during the years 1715–25 was Jokele of Rzeszow; and Leib b. Elyakum from Gorokhov-Volhynia was made the first cantor of the new Ashkenazi prayerhouse of Amsterdam (1730). Through the activities of cantors from Poland in the most prominent places, Western Jewry was confronted with the Eastern Ashkenazi style of singing and came to like it.

Among the special features of the East Ashkenazi *ḥazzanut* was its emotional power, which was stressed in particular by the early writers. The chronicle of martyrdom *Yeven Meẓulah* (by Nathan *Hannover) tells of the surrender of four communities to the Tatars in 1648. When the *ḥazzan* Hirsh of Zywotow chanted the memorial prayer *El Male Raḥamim*, the whole congregation burst forth in tears, and even the compassion of the rough captors was stirred, until they released the Jews. A similar story was told much later of the *ḥazzan* Rasumny; his *El Male Raḥamim*, said after the *Kishinev pogrom of 1913, has been taken over by many cantors (Mus. ex. 22).

Common to the Russian and other East European peoples is the tendency to attribute to music a decisive power over human behavior and mode of action; the same is true of the Jews living among them. A highly significant characterization of East Ashkenazi *ḥazzanut* was given by Rabbi Selig Margolis in 1715 (*Ḥibburei Likkutim*, 4b–5a): a *ḥazzan* who delivers his prayers devotedly and with beautiful melodies, he holds, may stir up hearts more than any preacher. Margolis gives as an example the fact that the *ḥazzan* Baruch of Kalish moved the congregation to tears by his expressive rendition of "Perhaps the feeble and

Example 22. *El Male Raḥamim*, as sung by Shlomo Razumny, 1903. After A. Nadel, EJ, vol. 6, 1930, cols. 381–2.

Figure 15. Jehiel Michal, *ḥazzan* of the Amsterdam Ashkenazi community, 1700. Cecil Roth Collection.

miserable people may vanish" or even by the recitation of the "Thirteen Attributes of God." In particular, during the penitential days, when he chanted the prayers that had always been the domain of individual cantorial creation (*Zokhrenu le-Ḥayyim; Mekhalkel Ḥayyim; Seder ha Avodah*), "there was nobody in the synagogue whose heart was not struck and moved to repentance . . . all of them pouring out their hearts like water—the like of which does not occur in other countries that have neither melody (*niggun*) nor emotion (*hitorerut*); the *ḥazzanim* of our country, however, know well how to arouse penitence by their voices." This self-assertion stresses the emotional attitude which already distinguished Eastern Ashkenazi *ḥazzanut* in the pre-ḥasidic period. Since the late 18th century, the Jews of the West have called it "the Polish style." This designation implied, inter alia, a certain profile of rhythm shaped by syncopes and dance-like configurations. Some early examples were written down by Western cantors around 1800. It is possible that some of them reflect the practices of ḥasidic singing, such as the dance tune to the words "He redeemeth from death and releaseth from perdition" (Mus. ex. 23a); dancing is suggested here by the four-bar strains repeated with open and closed cadenzas and, especially, by the "bridge bars" between the phrases, which are also known from the *oberek* and other Slavic dances.

A minor tune of the same type (Mus. ex. 23b) embodies the full pattern of what is called "a Jewish dance." Since it is very remote from the music written by Western cantors of the 18th century, this may also be regarded as an echo of the East Ashkenazi style.

The vigor of musical life in Eastern Europe is reflected by several historical sources. It is proved by the very restrictions that the Council of the Four Lands imposed on it. As early as 1623 this board of congregations limited the

Figure 16. The entry of Jews into the concert life of Europe. Caricature by Rowlandson, 1803, on the rivalry between the singers, John Braham (right) and Charles Incledon, following the former's appearance in a successful play, *Family Quarrels*. Cecil Roth Collection.

EXAMPLE 23. Dance-like melodies from cantorial manuals of the late 18th century. (a) after Idelsohn, *Melodien*, vol. 6, part 2, no. 20; (b) *ibid.*, vol. 10, no. 245; cf. sections C and D with sections A and B of the first melody.

creative impulse of its cantors to three or four extended works on Sabbath day; the victims of the 1650 and 1655 pogroms were mourned by reducing the instrumental music of the wedding celebration to those ceremonies where it was regarded as essential ("covering" the bride and during the night after the wedding). The council also protected the *sheli'aḥ ẓibbur* and the beadle from arbitrary dismissal (1670). It controlled the livelihood of popular singers and entertainers *(marshalek, badḥan)* by obliging them to apply for a special license *(ketav badḥanut)*.

Incipient Westernization of Ashkenazi Song. It was for good reasons that the music of the Jews from Eastern Europe was appreciated in the West as a genuine and heartwarming manifestation of the true Jewish spirit in song. Whether its special character resulted from the intense "Jewishness" of life in the Eastern countries or was the outcome of a happy merger with the melos and rhythms of Slavic music, Western European Jewry has welcomed it with a sort of nostalgic feeling down to the 20th century. Apparently it was felt to be a counterpoise to the Westernization that progressively displaced national music.

This process of Westernization started and developed first at the bordering strata of Jewish society, one of which was the substratum of folk musicians *(klezmerim)* who had ever been "wanderers between two worlds" and agents of musical exchange between peoples. Their instrumental performance was accorded a definite social function, since wedding music was regarded as a sort of religious obligation, and *klezmerim* were regularly employed at the feast of Simḥat Torah and Purim, the transfer of the Torah scrolls to a new synagogue, and numerous other occasions. Even the rabbinical authorities were willing to make special legal arrangements in order to secure instrumental performance wherever it was desired.

The folk musicians of Ashkenaz used to play the lute or form small ensembles of bowed strings, preferably two violins and a gamba. They were mostly true professionals and sometimes formed trade unions or guilds (Prague, 17th century). The more important communities put their musical capacity to full display at festival processions in honor of their sovereigns (Prague in 1678, 1716, 1741; Frankfort in 1716). At the Prague festival of 1678 (described in a special Yiddish booklet) five of the usual string trios, cembalo with two fiddlers, a harpsichord with two fiddlers, a portable organ, two choirs with organ accompaniment, and a choir of *ḥazzanim* with their *meshorerim* (who "carried a sheet of music in their hands and pointed with the finger") marched in procession. The many trumpeters and drummers were probably hired from the outside, but the organs and the keyboard instruments were played by Jewish dilettante musicians.

Splendid performances of this kind did not take place every day; as a matter of fact, professional musicians seldom found a base for a decent living in their community alone. The rule was that Jewish musicians also served their Christian neighbors, and the *klezmerim* met stiff opposition from their Christian colleagues and their guilds. In 1651 the *arme Prager Juden Musicanten und Spielleuthe* had to appeal to the authorities to retain the privilege of 1640 granting them the right to play "when we are demanded by various people of rank and Christians to make music at Sundays and holidays" lest "we are bound to die miserably and to perish together with our folks" since "we poor people have to make a living of the art acquired by ourselves." Serving a broad and diversified audience called for a repertoire that pleased wide circles. The Jews in their closed quarters also obtained their share of popular songs and fashionable dance music, besides their traditional Jewish dances and tunes.

The musical features of *klezmer* music are largely unknown today, but there is some circumstancial evidence that the Jewish minstrels played in a kind of "hot style" of unusual scales and lively rhythms. This becomes obvious from Hans Newsidler's parody of a "Jews' dance" (Mus. ex. 24a) and from the scornful description by their gentile competitors (Prague, 1651) that "they keep neither time nor beat, and mockingly deprive noble and sweet music of its dignity." It appears that people nevertheless liked the exotic spices of *klezmer* music, which may perhaps be compared with the fascination exerted by gypsy tunes.

Several old *klezmer* tunes were notated by Elhanan Kirchhan of Fuerth in 1727 (*Simḥat ha-Nefesh* 2; facs.

reprod. New York, 1926). Example 24b shows a Purim song obviously composed in a humorous mood. These specimens of 1727 indicate that the general trend was already directed toward adoption of the European baroque style. A Purim *niggun* notated by cantor Judah Elias in 1744 (Mus. ex. 24c) exemplifies the inorganic linking of a traditional Jewish tune (I, G minor) through dance-like "bridge bars" (II), with a continuation in the contemporary taste (III, D minor; IV, B-flat major, modulation and *da capo*); some strains of the melody are echoed in the 1794 Purim tunes of Aaron Beer (Idelsohn, Melodien, 6, nos. 117–8) suggesting a common popular source. Songs in the vernacular followed the same direction as instrumental music. Although their foreign melodies were balanced by original invention, their constant use advanced the Westernization of music at the popular level.

Since the 17th century, the affluent classes had become accustomed to have their children, especially daughters, instructed in singing and instruments (cf. Jos. Kosman, *Noheg ka-Ẓon Yosef,* 1718, 18a; Jos. Hahn, *Yosif Omeẓ,* 1723, 890). *Glueckel of Hameln relates that her stepsister knew how to play the harpsichord well (c. 1650). During the Prague festival of 1678, the granddaughter of the community chairman played the cembalo, and Isaac Mahler's daughter the harpsichord. The tendency toward integration in music grew stronger among the upper classes during the late 18th century, when Rachel (Levin) *Varnhagen could report: "My musical instruction consisted of nothing but the music of Sebastian (Bach) and the entire school [of the period]." Heinrich *Heine's mother, Peierche van Geldern (b. 1771), had to conceal her flute ("my truly harmonious friend both in joy and grief") from her strict father. Sara Levi, daughter of the Berlin financier Daniel *Itzig, was the last and most faithful disciple of Wilhelm Friedemann Bach (d. 1784) and preserved many of his autograph works for posterity. These developments in the upper class prepared the way for the emergence of composers like Giacomo *Meyerbeer and Felix *Mendelssohn.

The trend of integration in European music finally came to affect the broad masses of the people, and the *ḥazzan,* their speaker and representative, was too dependent upon the goodwill of the public not to gratify its taste. Whereas early in the 17th century only the use of foreign melodies had been protested (by Isaiah *Horowitz and Joseph *Hahn), about 1700 and thereafter the entire style of cantorial performance was challenged by practices adopted from secular music. Violent discussions about the unstable state and reputation of cantorial art are reflected in several pamphlets. The deeper reasons for this crisis were exposed by Judah Leib Zelichover (*Shirei Yehudah,* Amsterdam, 1696). The author still clings to the medieval idea that *ḥazzanut* should be the musical expression of mystical intentions *(kavvanot)* by means of extended vocalises; he begrudges the cantors applauded by his generation for neglecting the traditional mode of singing ("saying: It's outdated and does not satisfy us") and replacing it by their own inventions or borrowings from the opera, dance bands, or street singers.

Considering the isolation of Judaism in those days and its divorce from secular art, these declarations could hardly be called overstatement. A remedy was suggested about one generation later by the cantor Solomon *Lipschitz *(Te'udat Shelomo,* Offenbach 1718, no. 30). He also censures the ambitious individualism of his colleagues ("everybody builds a stage for himself"), which mostly turned out to be imitations of the simplest forms of music, since the cantors lacked any formal musical education. Lifshuetz wishes to replace the old form of Jewish singing leaning on the lower strata of

Example 24. Characteristics of early *klezmer* music. (a) parody, *"Der Juden Tantz,"* lute piece by Hans Newsidler, 1554, after P. Nettl, *Alte juedische Spielleute und Musiker,* 64–65; (b) Purim song, after E. Kirchhan, *Simḥat ha-Nefesh,* part II, fol. 7r.; (c) *"Purim Niggun"* from the manual of Judah Elias of Hanover, 1744, no. 224, after A. Nadel, unidentified facsimile publication, Jerusalem, J.N.U.L., Jakob Michael Collection of Jewish Music, JMA 3997.

the music of the gentile environment, by more accomplished forms of art: "Making music without knowing the rules of *musica* is like a prayer without true intention *[kavvanah]*!"

The results of such ideas soon became manifest. Close to the middle of the 18th century, cantors began to use musical notation and thus began the "literary period" of Ashkenazi *ḥazzanut*. It was not the old and venerable traditions of synagogue song, however, which were put on paper, but rather the new compositions of the individual *ḥazzanim*. The earliest known document of this kind is a manuscript from 1744 written by the *Herr Musicus und Vor Saenger Juda Elias in Hannover*. After this work come the manuscripts of the most eminent cantor of his age, Aaron *Beer (1738–1821); famous as *der Bamberger Ḥazzan;* from December 1764 in Berlin). His collection contains both his own versions or new creations of synagogue melodies and those of a dozen contemporaries (published in Idelsohn, *Melodien,* 6). Other important manuscripts go back to *meshorerim* who also served their cantors as "musical secretaries" (Idelsohn, op. cit.).

The character of these cantorial works is defined, first of all, by its strict homophony, tailored to the needs of a virtuoso singer wishing to display his coloraturas *(lenaggen),* while the text is given a subordinate role. The structure of these compositions remains in the line of traditional *ḥazzanut* by developing a theme by means of variative improvisation. The resources of the basic melodies, however, are borrowed from the post-baroque music of about 1700 to 1760, often recalling the fashionable composers of that period (Monn, Wagenseil, Zach). There is little left of the strong pathos and dramatics of the true baroque, although the artistic evolution of the opening theme statement and the extensive use of sequences were imitated, as was the instrument-like treatment of the voice (Mus. ex. 25a); later in the century, some influence of the early classicists can be observed (Mus. ex. 25b).

The "new trend" of cantorial art catered to the musical taste of about 1720, but the merger of traditional and modern style was far from complete. The customary Jewish freedom of rhythm and the roving melodical line could not easily be harnessed; attempts to do so resulted in asymmetrical phrases, awkward modulation, and other flaws in conventional workmanship. Most of these cantorial compositions shared only the platitudes and the most insipid musical idioms of the period. They were the product of a superficial connection between incompatible styles—the first sign of that dualism in the West Ashkenazi musical practice that was to become the hallmark of the 19th century.

MODERN TIMES

The Nineteenth Century. By the 18th century, conditions of life had become almost unbearable in the ghettos and crowded Jewish settlements of the continent. The protracted persecutions aimed at economic, moral, and physical ruin nearly accomplished their purpose and were balanced only by the firm belief in final redemption, unbroken self-confidence, and vital energy. The growing pressure put European Jewry on two different paths of self-deliverance, as divergent from each other as the leaders Moses *Mendelssohn and *Israel b. Eliezer Ba'al Shem Tov. Assimilation, aiming at civil emancipation, was the external way toward joining the society of an enlightened Europe;

EXAMPLE 25. Cantorial compositions in 18th-century style. (a) *Hodu* for Ḥanukkah from the manual of Judah Elias of Hanover, 1744, after A. Nadel, *Der Orden Bne Briss* 9–10, 95; (b) from *Hodu* for Ḥanukkah by Moses Pan (before 1791), after Idelsohn, *Melodien,* 6, no. 55. Both compositions use the traditional melody of *Ma'oz Ẓur* as a point of departure.

*Ḥasidism, on the other hand, was entirely directed toward intrinsic values and was coupled with a certain abrogation of bitter reality. Both tendencies penetrated all aspects of life and had strong repercussions on music. A specific kind of music could demonstrate a certain ideology (e.g., use of the organ in synagogue service) or be made an essential means of spiritual exaltation (the ḥasidic *niggun*); music became a vehicle of both social integration and spiritual escapism.

The Ḥasidic Niggun. East European Jewry, suffering from increasing pauperization and the incessant menace of extermination for centuries, underwent a critical disillusionment with the failure of *Shabbetai Ẓevi and its aftereffects. At this doleful juncture, between 1730 and 1750, arose the ḥasidic movement, with its message of delivery of the soul from its detention in the body and the troubled earthly life by its ascent to spiritual, true values, thus partaking of a higher existence. As a continuation of the mystical tenets of Safed (see above), "a joyful heart and a devoted soul yearning for our Father in Heaven" were made the cornerstone of prayer, and singing became a focal point of religious experience. For the first time, music of Jewish mysticism itself becomes known and may still be heard today. Ḥasidic singing spans the entire gamut from grief and deep concern to extreme joy, from a meditative mood to ecstatic exaltation, from purposeful melodic construction to open forms or shallow banality. The intonation is rather peculiar, unconcerned with conventional beauty of sound, but always reflecting a tension of feelings and the desire for an innermost experience. Verbal expression is of minor importance; an extended tune may be evolved from a single word chosen from a sentence or sung to meaningless syllables (at the rate of a syllable per note, not as a vocalise); the singer returns, as it were, to a stammering infant language in order to express before God feelings too delicate or too intimate for a conventional verbal statement. Apparently there exist fixed patterns of syllable formation that may be connected with the pitch, duration, and sonority of the notes (Mus. ex. 26); the notators of ḥasidic tunes too often neglect them, although a true reproduction in singing is unthinkable without these particular "texts."

This kind of singing went together with the age-old mystical exercises, such as concentration, fast, contemplation of certain ideas *(kavvanah),* and rhythmical movement of the body. The ways of song came to the fore with the Ba'al Shem Tov himself, and certain melodies are still ascribed to him. After his death in 1760, his most intimate disciples settled together in the townlet of Mezhirech and developed the first flowering of the ḥasidic *niggun* during their Sabbath meetings. The foremost inventors and propagators of tunes were *Jehiel Michael of Zloczow (d. 1761, described by the Ba'al Shem Tov as having "access to the treasure-houses of heaven where he acquires the most beautiful tunes"), and *Shneour Zalman of Lyady ("Three things I have learnt at Mezhirech: what God is, what Jews are, and what a *niggun* is"). When the followers of the Ba'al Shem Tov journeyed through most of Eastern Europe founding centers of Ḥasidism, the ḥasidic *niggun* conquered the hearts of the masses, and spread even to the opponents of mysticism. Most of the leaders *(admorim)* were fond of music and even passionately addicted to it, and many created new melodies. Personalities like Levi Isaac of Berdichev and *Naḥman of Bratslav were outstanding singers.

Within the school of *Ḥabad Ḥasidism, there was also much thought devoted to the clandestine connection between music and ecstasy. Dov Ber of Lubavich (1773–1827) discussed (in his *Kunteres ha-Hitpa'alut*) three kinds of melodies: (1) tunes accompanied by words that nourish the faculty of "understanding"; (2) the wordless melody which is able to represent the psycho-physical nature of every human being; and (3) the "unsung song," the very essence of music that does not materialize in an actual tune and is found in the concentration of the mind on the divine. The reality of music thus evaporates and ends up in pure symbolism; but the wordless tune is characteristically defined as the producer of spontaneous, unintentional enthusiasm, "since the melody and the notes actually proceed from the breath of the heart in ecstasy, and yet it is entirely unconscious."

During the later days of Ḥasidism, permanent instrumental bands, singers, and "*niggun* makers" were often attached to the courts of the *admorim.* Several sub-categories of *niggun* styles developed in the course of the 19th century. The more popular specimens exhibit a marked influence of Slavic folk music; the direct use of foreign tunes is, however, generally connected with a symbolic "story" or other attempts at imparting a deeper sense to that mostly trivial stuff. The compass of *niggun* styles (see also *Ḥasidism, Musical Traditions) will be described here by one outstanding, though anonymous, example from Ḥabad tradition. This *niggun* (Mus. ex. 27) appears to reflect the mythical struggle of the entangled "divine spark" in the soul to disengage itself, rather than any static mood or condition of mind.

The tune opens with a gradual ascent from the basic pitch level to that of the fifth which is reached and finally established in section d. This initial stepping-up is characteristic of many *niggunim* and may be interpreted as symbolic of the elevation of the spirit. The peak is reached, in this example, only after repeated efforts and backslides (section a, second bar). Section e indicates a state of excitement by means of a "ḥasidic scale" descending from E' through D', C'-sharp, B-flat, A to G (well distinguished from the *Ahavah Rabbah* mode, since the final is G, and not A). However, this elevation of mind dies away, and the tune returns temporarily to the familiar regions of minor, restating part of section b in section k. A "bridge-bar" (like those customary in dance tunes, see Mus. ex. 23; 24c) forms the transition to a short episode of enthusiasm bursting forth in section m and n, then slowly calming down and returning to the repetition of section g to k. Deep and innermost experience is expressed in this particular tune by combining characteristic traits of ḥasidic singing with an unfailing sense of musical form. The masterpieces of ḥasidic song go in this or similar directions, proving the claim that

Example 26. The ḥasidic *niggun* and its filler-syllables. (a) after M. Beregowski, *Yevreyskiye narodnye pesni,* 1962, no. 99; (b) after Ch. Vinaver, *Anthology of Jewish Music,* 1955, no. 88.

EXAMPLE 27. *Niggun* of the Ḥabad Ḥasidim, for Sabbath and holy days. After Sh. Zalmanoff, *Sefer ha-Niggunim*, vol. 1, 1948, no. 74. Filler-syllables are added in singing.

singing is superior to the spoken language and is understood by God and mankind alike. Ḥasidism was also a democratic movement, and this trend is reflected by the popular elements, descending to even sheer banality that govern the bulk of extant melodies, which can duly be appreciated only in their circumstantial implication and the particular stmosphere surrounding them. The Ḥasidic song developed into a powerful stimulant of Jewish music during the 19th century and later on.

THE ABSORPTION OF THE EUROPEAN ART STYLE. While the Jews of Eastern Europe decided to overcome their miseries by a spiritual divorce from the environment, those of the West witnessed Lessing declare the equivalence of religions and the French Revolution proclaim freedom and equality for all men. This atmosphere encouraged their striving for integration in a future society of enlightened Europeans and tendencies of assimilation that ranged from slight external changes to total surrender. Music was regarded as an essential part of future integration. Therefore, both tradition and acquired practices (which could barely he kept apart) were put to a test against the taste, rules, and forms of contemporary music. The prolonged prelude of this process has already been mentioned; by the 19th century, it gained sway and momentum of decisive power. As soon as the obstacles of personal advancement were removed, musicians of Jewish birth broke away from their faith, either formally or tacitly. The Jewish community suffered from a heavy drain of talent of higher and medium caliber. This incessant process principally affected synagogue music until, in the second half of the century, it became partly dependent upon immigration of cantors from Eastern Europe—not to speak of the lack of high-ranking composers.

The extent and nature of this exodus can be gauged by a survey of Jewish-born *musicians who entered the fields of European art and were famous enough to merit entries in general encyclopedias. Among those born between 1790 and 1850, the most prominent categories were instrumentalists, especially virtuosos (28), and composers (21); next came singers and the scholars and pedagogues (11). Allegedly "typical Jewish" occupations are as yet clearly in the minority: conductors (6), publishers (2), impressarios (1), critics (0). A peak (60%) is formed by those born in the decade 1830 to 1839 who chose their profession about 1848, hopeful of being granted full civil rights. These forces were practically lost for the cultivation and development of the Jewish musical heritage. As to synagogue music, the impetus for immediate and drastic innovations came from a sudden turn at the political level. Napoleon wished to promote the social integration of his Jewish subjects by granting the superintendents of all communities with over 2,000 members an official status. Consequently, organized and binding changes in liturgy and its music could be enforced against the will of any opposition.

The Reform Movement. Napoleon also conferred his synagogue constitution upon some annexed countries, such as the Kingdom of Westphalia; among them, the Koeniglich Wuerttembergische israelitische Oberkirchenbehoerde even survived his rule. These authorities gave the official and legal framework to the already existing tendencies of correcting and amending the synagogue service. The disregard of external form, dignity, and beauty was regarded by many as an abasing stigma of exile conditions. The mystical ideas and symbols that provided so much content to *ḥazzanut* and its coloraturas were no longer understood; the congregations had changed into an audience that expected music to evoke feelings they could not find within themselves. A small but energetic circle of extremists used the communal constitution given to Westphalian Jewry to materialize its vision of a liturgy modeled after European ideas and aesthetics. Perspicaciously, they started working with the young generation, on the initiative of Israel Jacobsohn, court factor of Jerome Bonaparte and fervent champion of synagogue reform. The pupils of the Jewish mechanics school at Seesen were given formal instruction in music from 1804; they formed the choir and sang to the *organ installed in the prayer hall of their institution (1807). The music consisted of chorale-like

קינת ישרון ·

A Hebrew Dirge,

Chaunted in the Great Synagogue,

ST. JAMES'S PLACE, ALDGATE,

ON THE

Day of the Funeral of her Royal Highness

THE

PRINCESS CHARLOTTE.

BY HYMAN HURWITZ,

MASTER OF THE HEBREW ACADEMY

HIGHGATE:

WITH A TRANSLATION IN

ENGLISH VERSE, BY S. T. COLERIDGE, ESQ.

London:

Printed by H. Barnett, 2, St. James's Place, Aldgate;

AND SOLD BY T. BOOSEY, 4, OLD BROAD STREET; LACKINGTON, ALLEN, AND CO. FINSBURY SQUARE; BRIGGS AND BURTON, 156, LEADENHALL STREET; AND H. BARNETT, HEBREW BOOKSELLER, 2, ST. JAMES'S PLACE, ALDGATE.

1817.

17

בעזה״י

18

19

Figure 17. Title page of *Kinat Yeshurun*, written by Hyman Hurwitz for the memorial service held at the Great Synagogue, London, on 10th of Kislev, 1817, for Princess Charlotte, daughter of the prince regent and heiress-presumptive to the throne. The text begins *Eli Yeshurun u-vaneha*, in imitation of *Eli Ẓiyyon*, and was sung to its melody, probably by the *ḥazzan* Nathan Solomon. The English translation is by the poet Samuel Taylor Coleridge. London, 1817.

Figure 18. A *ḥazzan's* contract. This typical agreement was made between the Berdichev community and Yeroham Blindman ("Yeroham ha-Koton") in 1861. From A. Rosen (ed.), *The History of Hazanuth* . . ., 1924, 97.

Figure 19. Young members of an Eastern European synagogue choir, c. 1900. From a reproduction in the *Jewish Daily Forward*, New York.

melodies composed by their Christian music teacher to Hebrew and German texts. Soon afterward, Jacobsohn opened another Reform synagogue with organ and part singing in the Westphalian capital of Kassel. Both his institutions were forced to close, however, with the end of the kingdom in 1814. The reformer and his musical assistant went to Berlin and opened a private synagogue with an organ and a boys' choir from the free school (1815). Two years later (1817), they moved to the private synagogue established in the house of Meyerbeer's father, the banker Jacob Herz *Beer, where an organ with two manuals and pedal was put at their disposition. The bold innovations of liturgy and liturgical singing aroused disputes and quarrels with the conservatives, whereupon the government ordered the synagogue to be closed (1818).

Meanwhile, the Reform movement has spread to other communities. The Hungarian rabbi Aaron *Chorin published a book in defense of the synagogue organ (*Nogah ha-Ẓedek*, Dessau, 1818). Reform congregations had been founded at Frankfort (Philanthropin orphanage, 1816), Hamburg (1817), and during the Leipzig Fair (a synagogue opened in 1820 with tunes composed by Meyerbeer). The Hamburg synagogue was joined by many of the local Sephardim and their cantors, was very active, and existed until 1938. Its members regarded the melodic recitation of prayers and Bible reading as opposed to the spirit of the age and replaced them by plain declamation. On the other hand, some Sephardi tunes (of the "civilized" kind favored by the Marranos) were adopted. Above all, Reform congregations created German-language hymnals on the pattern of the Protestant *Gesangbuch* (first: Jos. Joelson's *Shirei Yeshurun*, Frankfort (1816)). The Hamburg hymnal (1819, many editions) contained some melodies composed by well-known musicians like A. G. Methfessel and, later, the Jewish-born Ferdinand *Hiller.

Reform congregations, however, were generally unable to recruit composers with both stature and real involvement with the task. The original tunes of their hymnals, mostly the products of music teachers, match the feebleness and absence of inspiration found in the texts. Furthermore, there existed an ideological impulse to integrate prayers with the Christian environment by adopting the tunes of well-known Protestant chorales. Banal new texts were connected with the melodies of Christological songs (*Sefer Zemirot Yisrael*, Stuttgart, 1836). After all the effort, a few jewels also took root outside Reform synagogues (*Seele, was betruebst du dich*, music by J. H. G. Stoewing; *Hoert, die Posaune toent mit Macht*, poetry by Abraham *Geiger). More important are two achievements of a general nature. First, the instruction of the youth in part singing—no longer in the old, improvised manner, but of music written according to the rules of harmony—through the schools, orphanages, and seminaries spread the understanding of European music to the less-privileged classes as well. Another innovation of lasting effect was playing the organ during the service. An object of raging and never-settled debates, the use of the organ in synagogues was made a cornerstone and symbol of later liberalism against strict observance in religious matters.

The "Improved Service" and Its Music. Attempts at radical reformation of the liturgy and its music did not go beyond a certain sector of the larger communities; in the provinces, they failed almost completely. This does not imply indifference or sluggishness on the part of the majority. In fact, a more decided and massive move toward musical "acculturation" has seldom been observed. Even where the liturgical tradition was handled with caution or left untouched, the conditions prevailing in prayer performance caused much indignation. Western Jewry strove for an improvement—for a *geordneter Gottesdienst*—and this concept included the entire field of sacred song ("orderly music of the divine service"; Sulzer).

First came the renunciation of the brilliant coloratura in the cantorial solo, once regarded as an asset in its own right. By 1800 *ḥazzanut* was hopelessly pervaded with foreign elements (mostly baroque) and had developed as a sort of half-breed that, unfortunately, demonstrated the weak spots of both its ancestors. Independent attempts at modernization were initiated by provincial cantors (Mus. ex. 28) whose abilities and taste were not up to their exaggerated aspirations. Therefore, these experimental works were discarded by the more urbanized taste.

The changed attitude toward musical performance also wished to dispose of the usual trio consisting of the cantor and two assistant singers *(meshorerim)*. The improvised accompaniment executed by the latter was to be replaced by harmonies of academic regular structure, and their solo coloraturas were to be clipped as eccentricities of an outmoded taste. Likewise, the boisterous chorus of the entire congregation lost its value as a moving acoustical experience with ancient roots and was to be silenced and substituted by well-rehearsed part singing. Such ideas and

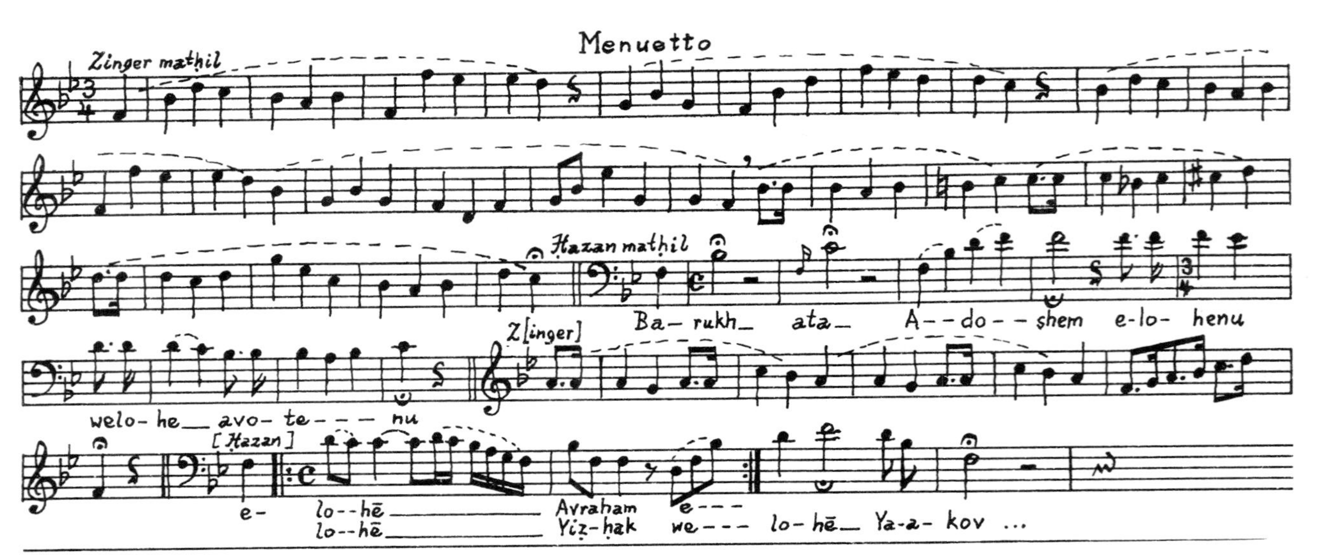

EXAMPLE 28. German provincial setting of the *Amidah* prayer for *ḥazzan* and "singer." The indications are: singer begins, *ḥazzan* begins. From an anonymous Ms., possibly Bavarian, probably early 19th century. Jerusalem, J.N.U.L., Jakob Michael Collection of Jewish Music, Ms. JMA 4249 (1), fol. 15v.

tendencies materialized during the period between the Congress of Vienna (1814–15; disappointing the hope for emancipation) and the revolutions of 1848 that led to the admission to citizenship. In the meantime, synagogue music was remodeled according to the ideas of the "Jewish European." Fortunately, a cadre of real talents remained after the great exodus of musicians to devote itself entirely to this task. All of them were proficient in synagogue song and were backed by family tradition in this vocation. Most of them were gifted with extraordinary voices, and some had already excelled as child prodigies; rich patronage had paved their way to studies of musical theory and instrumental playing. They were given the chance to realize their ideas on a large scale when they were between 19 and 30 years of age: the ardent idealism of youth contributed much to the breakthrough of the new trend.

Two forerunners had already set the first standards. Israel *Lovy, a cantor and concert singer with a phenomenal voice, established a four-part choir in the new Paris synagogue in 1822. The music he composed for this body indiscriminately combined the old *meshorerim* tradition and the choral style of the *opéra comique*. The other precursor of things to come, Maier (Meir) *Kohn of Munich, did not demonstrate Lovy's creativeness when he was commissioned to establish a choir of boys and men in 1832. He had to resort to local non-Jewish musicians for choral compositions or, at least, the harmonization of melodies arranged or composed by himself and others. Kohn's compilations, (*Vollstaendiger Jahrgang von Terzett- und Chorgesaengen der Synagoge in Muenchen . . .*) known as the *Muenchner Terzettgesaenge* (1839), became, for some decades, a vademecum for small to medium-sized communities. The compositions offered by the early proponents of the "improved service" extended to selected chapters of the liturgy and touched upon only a small part of the highly important role of the *ḥazzan*. Thoroughgoing changes of the whole extent of the musical liturgy were finally put into effect by Solomon *Sulzer in Vienna (from 1826), Hirsch *Weintraub at Koenigsberg (1838), Louis *Lewandowski in Berlin (1840), and Samuel *Naumbourg in Paris (1845). The principles guiding the various renovators of synagogue music have much in common:

> . . . We might find out the original noble forms to which we should anchor ourselves, developing them in an artistic style . . . Jewish liturgy must satisfy the musical demands while remaining Jewish; and it should not be necessary to sacrifice the Jewish characteristics to artistic forms . . . The old tunes and singing modes which became national should be improved, selected, and adjusted to the rules of art. But new musical creations should also not be avoided (Sulzer, *Denkschrift*, 1876).

The point of departure had to be a survey of the entire body of tunes and recitatives transmitted by oral tradition. For the first time in history, the complete cycle of obligatory or commonly accepted melodies was recorded in musical notation (until then, only the extraordinary, individual compositions and arrangements had been written down). In examining these invaluable documents, one should disregard the enclosure in bars of recitative and free-rhythmic tunes by which the notators paid tribute to contemporary usage; the obligation to fill the bars regularly resulted in shortening and lengthening of notes, and most of the ornamental passages do not disclose their deliberate *rubato* tempo.

The tendencies of "improvement, selection, adjustment to artistic forms" (Sulzer) enter the picture at this point. They were justified for their time, however painful to the adherents of modern historicism and folklore conservation. However, personal liberty in the aural interpretation of traditional melody patterns or "ideas" had been the characteristic procedure of Jewish music at all times; it was also the duty of the 19th-century cantor, as it had been of his predecessors. Therefore it was not a fault but their right when cantors now followed the earlier trend toward classicism with a new trend oriented toward the early romantic style in music. Consequently, their arrangements of traditional material tend toward melodies of clean-cut outlines and logical, if possible symmetric, structures. The old modes were preferably transformed to major or minor; if the specific *shtayger* scales are preserved, they are sometimes disturbed by leading notes and other dressings of modern tonality (Mus. ex. 29).

The recitatives were toned down to a rational declamation, in which melismatic figures are admitted only for scoring meaningful words or marking the clauses of the sentence.

The intended "improvement" of the cantor's part demanded a gentle touch guided by sensitivity for genuine and authentic values. A bolder approach was suited to the passages assigned to the choir. Precedents of choral performance were the *meshorerim*-accompaniment of the cantor and the largely turbulent responses of the entire congregation. The traditional singing of *meshorerim* contained elements that could be rearranged to form a choral style of genuine flavor. Attempts at this were made by Naumbourg, Sulzer, and Lewandowski. Naumbourg's arrangement of one of the *Mi-Sinai* tunes demonstrates the special features of this style (Mus. ex. 30).

The melody is given to one of the inner parts, the cantor's tenor, embedded in the chords of male voices and tender boy sopranos. The latter proceed very often in parallel thirds or sixths (both in relation to the cantor's tune and between themselves; see also Mus. ex. 32, below) and

EXAMPLE 29. A traditional melody and its 19th-century adaptations. (a) A. Baer, *Baal T'fillah*, 1883³, no. 1158; (b) Ch. Vinaver, *Anthology of Jewish Music*, 1955, no. 23; (c) S. Naumbourg, *Zemirot Yisrael*, vol. 2, 1847, no. 228; (d) L. Lewandowski, *Todah W'Simrah*, part 2, 1882, no. 179.

Cantor
ad libitum
Yit-ga-dal w'yitkadash shemē ra - - - - - ba: A- men. Be-alma divra khi-ru-te
Ten.
Basso
we-yam - - - likh malkhu - - - - te be-ḥayekhon uv-yo - - - me-khon uve-ḥa - - - - -
yē dekhol bet yisra - - - - - - - - - - el baa-ga-la uvizman kariv weïm-ru: A - - - - - - men.
Solo Soprani
pp
in tempo
Yit-ba - - - - rakh weyish-ta-baḥ weyit-pa--ar weyit-ro-mam we-yit-nas--se weyithadar weyit-a-
Sopr.
(tacet 17 bars)
leh weyit-ha - - - - lal shemē de-Kudesha : Brikh hu. Leela ul-e - - - - - -
la min kol birkha-ta we-shi-ra- ta tush - - - be-ḥa - -
ta we-ne - - ḥe-ma - - - ta daa-mi - - - - - -

Example 30. Development of the *meshorerim* style. Traditional *Musaf Kaddish* of the High Holy Days by S. Naumbourg, *Zemirot Yisrael*, vol. 2, 1847, no. 229.

produce an effect similar to certain mixture stops of an organ. The basses refrain from a steady accompaniment, entering only with hummed chords at melodic vantage points or acting like a community that joins in with the cantor's prayer. There are also solo sections provided for the bass and the soprano, frequently exhibiting an instrumental character; a sweet soprano could become a favorite of the public, and many of them later became famous cantors. The resources of this original style were tapped but not developed to any importance in West Ashkenaz, but they became preeminent in East Ashkenazi synagogue music, as shall be seen later.

The free composition of choral works in the contemporary style was challenged by still another factor—the need to give shape to the songs and responses of the congregation itself. Sulzer and Lewandowski were gifted with the inventiveness and skill for creating choir pieces of high quality. The religious element in Sulzer's music exhibits delicate feeling with a sentimental timbre, clad in simple but sweet harmonies, while Lewandowski expresses himself in a more forceful manner and avoids that common intelligibility which is apt to turn into triviality in a short while.

The first synagogue choirs were quite an experience to the congregations who had been annoyed by singing habits perpetuated by inertia alone or by barren experimentation. Sulzer's choir in the Vienna Seitenstettengassen Synagoge, was also praised by Christian visitors such as Liszt, the Abbé Mainzer, and others as both a human and musical experience. The impact of Sulzer's achievements was felt very soon by the brisk demand for his scores. Synagogue choirs were founded in Prague, Copenhagen (before 1838), Breslau, Berlin, Dresden (1840), and London (1841). Sulzer's disciples or choir singers transmitted the music of the "improved service" to the United States as well (G. M. Cohen, New York 1845; A. Kaiser, Baltimore 1866; M. Goldstein, Cincinnati 1881; E. J. Stark); their appearance antedated that of East Ashkenazi synagogue song in the Western hemisphere (New York, 1852). Cantors from the East European communities came to Vienna in order to perfect themselves with the "father of the new song in Israel" (Pinchas *Minkowski). The more important of Sulzer's Eastern disciples or followers were Osias *Abrass, Jacob *Bachmann, Nissan *Blumenthal, Wolf *Shestapol, Spitzburg ("the Russian Sulzer"), and others.

In these ways and by these men, the stage was set for musical life in the Western houses of prayer. During the second half of the century, after 1848, the liberal wing of conservative (non-Reform) synagogues added organ playing to the service order. A progressive cadre of communal leaders had decreed its admissability during the second Assembly of Rabbis held at Frankfort in 1845. It was, however, a partial vote that did not oblige or convince any sworn opponent. For instance, five years before the Berlin New Synagogue was finally furnished with an organ (1866), seven rabbis were consulted; Rabbi Michael Sachs was among the opponents, Abraham Geiger was with the advocates. In the end 74 German-Jewish communities came to have organs played at their service, according to a count made in 1933. In Russia, the first synagogue organ was installed not before 1901 (Union Temple, Odessa). Very few of the composers writing for this instrument understood its technique and spirit. Lewandowski, a pupil of E. A. Grell, was the first to produce real organ music for the synagogue.

The absorption of European standards in the musical service was paid for later in the 19th century with the weakened understanding and cultivation of the old tradition, especially of the cantor's role. The impending loss of acknowledged values was noticed in time and was averted by collecting and publishing what remained of oral tradition. Some of the related publications exhibit a remarkable sense of authenticity: outstanding is Abraham *Baer's voluminous, almost single-handed, collection, *Baal T'fillah* (1877); relatively reliable is F. *Consolo's *Libro dei canti d'Israele* (Leghorn-Sephardi tradition, 1892). Other authors who intended to create handbooks for the cantor's training imparted a little polish to the original tunes, but may still serve well for critical research (Moritz *Deutsch, *Vorbeterschule*, 1871; Meier Wodak, *Ha-Menazze'aḥ*, 1898; etc.). The Sephardi rite of Carpentras was noted by J. S. & M. Crémieu (1887), that of Paris by E. Jonas (1854), and a selection of London Portuguese melodies by the piano virtuoso E. Aguilar and D. A. de Sola (1857, unfortunately in a harmonized and metricized arrangement).

Parallel with the activities in collecting and editing, inquisitive minds strove to answer the question of the distinctive elements in Jewish music. The particular nature of the *shtayger* scales or modes, already noted by Weintraub (1854) and Naumbourg (1874), was demonstrated by the Viennese cantor and disciple of Sulzer, Josef *Singer in an attempt at systematization (1886). Outstanding in this first generation of researchers was Eduard *Birnbaum, Weintraub's successor at Koenigsberg from 1879. A sound Jewish education enabled him to place musical questions in the context of history and literature and achieve an unusually high level. His inconspicuous article (later a booklet) *Juedische Musiker am Hofe von Mantua* (1893) has become a classic in its field. An asset of lasting value is Birnbaum's collection of cantorial manuscripts and other source material (at present in the Hebrew Union College Library, Cincinnati); partly exploited by Idelsohn, it holds research tasks for generations to come.

The 19th century also witnessed the professional organization of West European cantors and the edition of periodicals in which the publication of source material and research had a place (*Der Juedische Cantor*, ed. A. Blaustein, 1879–98; *Oesterreichisch-Ungarische Cantorenzeitung*, founded by Jacob *Bauer, 1881–1902). In spite of all the activity and alertness in matters of synagogue song, the West European communities were drained more and more of its musical talents, including cantorial candidates. The gap was filled by immigrants from Eastern Europe, especially after the Russian persecutions of 1882. The Western synagogues could maintain their musical standard by recruiting the often brilliant singers originating, on a nearly equal scale, in Russia, the Baltic states, Poland, Hungary, and the neo-Prussian provinces. Finally, they outnumbered their local colleagues in the ratio of three to two. The newcomers, mostly ambitious and studious youths, learned the melodies of the Western rite with great zeal; as prescribed by Jacob Moellin (Maharil), there was no intermingling of regional traditions before 1900. Exceptions were Joseph Goldstein's enclave of Eastern virtuoso song in Vienna (1858–99), and Ḥayyim Wasserzug (Lomser), who went to London (1875) as a famous *ḥazzan*.

The Evolution of East Ashkenazi Ḥazzanut. The breakdown of inherited musical forms in the West was the work of a few decades and generally affected synagogue and Jewish communal life, albeit to varying degrees. East European Jewry remained completely immune from the advance of the times and kept its ears shut before art music, which had now become available to the middle classes throughout Europe. The developments there, however, occurred by way of a gradual and organic evolution.

The reasons for this development in Eastern Europe must be sought both in social and intellectual conditions. The Jewish population of Eastern Europe was massed in its assigned *Pale of Settlement and bound by almost medieval restrictions. Even outstanding musical talents could find an outlet only in synagogue song or, alternatively, in popular music making and entertaining. They had to contribute their sometimes considerable gifts compulsorily, to the musical life of their community, which was deeply concerned with all matters of music. Within that responsive musical microcosm, synagogue song represented the highest level of art; the interest and knowledgeability of the public was focused on the solo performance of the *ḥazzan* and subjected it to both relentless criticism and unconditional adulation. P. Minkowski, for example, commented:

> The Odessa community was not an ordinary one, but was split in two factions, accusers and defenders . . . When I had sung ancient melodies known to every listener, a dispute arose on the spot . . . as to whether my song was in the style of Abrass [Pitche] or of Bachman, and people of venerable age also conjured Zalel [Shulsinger] up from his grave in Ereẓ Israel in order to pitch my singing against Zalel's . . . (Recollections).

Ashkenazi *ḥazzanut* represented an original and self-sufficient kind of music, comparable only with certain oriental styles of song. Its most conspicuous attribute is its expressivity, the prayer of the community subsiding, as soon as the *ḥazzan's* voice is heard, and the mind completely identifies itself with the voice. Unlike the self-imposed restraint of the Western cantor, the aim is to produce an upsurge of religious feelings *(hitorerut)* and a strong and immediate response. The impressive capacities of this particular kind of song are not easily described in precise technical terms. The cantorial melody develops as a strictly monodic line, with structural points of support quite different from those of European harmony. It proceeds by many small movements, creating melodic cells which build up the body of the tune (Mus. ex. 31 and 32, units designated by letters a, b, c, etc.). Phrases composed of long-drawn single notes are nonexistent: they appear to be dissolved into flickering ornaments (Mus. ex. 32, phrase b; cf. also Abrass, Mus. ex. 1). Rhythm is not

Example 31. Eastern Ashkenazi *ḥazzanut*, c. 1800. Introductory prayer to the confession of sins on the Day of Atonement, by Solomon Weintraub (Kashtan), as notated from oral translation by D. Roitman, after G. Ephros (ed.), *Cantorial Anthology*, vol. 2, 1940, 135.

EXAMPLE 32. Eastern Ashkenazi *ḥazzanut* with "singer" soli, c. 1900. *Reẓeh,* by Aryeh Lev Schlossberg (1841–1925), after G. Ephros (ed.), *Cantorial Anthology,* vol. 4, 1953, 368–9.

confined to bars and stringent symmetry, but is as free as in the music of the oriental ancestors and relations of this style. Melodies are often shaped to *shtayger* scales; modulations are rather frequent (Mus. ex. 31) and a proof of mastery, like the oriental singers' shifting from *maqām* to *maqām*. Another archaic element is still in full vigor: the principle of variation governs both the melodic cells at every instance of recurrence and the whole structure of a piece. Often a cantorial composition contains a "double course" of the same section—first as an original statement and then as a variation of the same (Mus. ex. 31). At times, the work is composed of melodic cells arranged without any apparent order (Mus. ex. 32) exactly as the ancient *nusaḥ* style demands (see above).

One of the rules of *ḥazzanut,* however, is that there is no rule of adhering to one plan or the other: expression is the element which counts. The expressive intention is overwhelming: it dissolves the form of the underlying poetic text past recognition; single words may be repeated over and over (Mus. ex. 32), in spite of halakhic prohibition; emotional exclamations intermingle (ex. 31, cell j): and long coloraturas expand certain syllables, in particular towering above the penultima at the end of compositions. These traits may appear exaggerated to a taste accustomed to classicist restraint, but they are capable of the most suggestive presentation of sentiments, mostly in the pitiful and lachrymose mood (the expression of joy being channeled mostly through imitations of foreign song). The *ḥazzan's* voice plays on a variety of sound colors, complemented by a high falsetto (in the old contralto manner) and prefers techniques such as the gliding passage from tone to tone, slowly entering trills, and other characteristics of an advanced vocal culture.

The development of East Ashkenazi *ḥazzanut* is known only since its early 19th-century protagonists, whose exploits and compositions had been preserved in the memory of their congregations and disciples. Besides, regional schools and stylistic subdivisions, such as the Jewish-Lithuanian, Ukrainian, etc., a parting line is recognized between an older, "classical" *ḥazzanut* and a younger style influenced by Western art music.

The "classical" stage is represented in the communities of the Ukraine and Volhynia by the impressive personalities of Bezalel Shulsinger ("Ẓalel Odesser"), Yeruḥam *Blindman ("Yeruḥam ha-Koton"), Yeḥezkel of Zhitomir, and Solomon *Weintraub (Kashtan; see Mus. ex. 31). The old style was perpetuated by Israel Shkuder (1804–46) and Nissan *Spivak ("Nissi Belzer"). To judge from the small part of their music preserved, the early cantors did not indulge in the excessive coloraturas and superficial tricks preferred by the later synagogue singers. In Lithuania and Poland, the old style was upheld by Sender *Polachek of Minsk, who excelled in particular melodic formations (Sender's *shtayger*), and his disciple Baruch *Karliner, a master of spontaneous improvisation "when the spirit dwelled upon him." Galicia and Hungary had David'l Strelisker ("Dovidl *Brod"), who assumed the airs of a noble dilettante and would not give in to the modernistic tendencies of the Budapest *chor shul* of 1830.

The first waves of Sulzer's musical reform reached Eastern Europe promptly and impressed both singers and ambitious community leaders. Cantor Nissan *Blumenthal of Odessa was the first to adopt Western ways by cultivating a smooth bel canto style. Some went or were sent to Sulzer himself in Vienna (see above). Others acquired their formal education in Eastern Europe, such as Joel David Strashunsky (the "Vilner Balabess'l") with Moniuszko in Poland, and Jacob *Bachmann with Anton Rubinstein in Russia. The "Westernizing" *ḥazzanim* limited the influence of art music to choral composition, while their own solo parts were left almost untouched. In general, choral composition kept to the *meshorerim* style, touched up with more regular harmonic sequences; but showpieces of artful elaboration were also inserted indiscriminately by those who were tempted to introduce fugues or other devices of advanced academic training. In addition, their works frequently reflect the fascination exerted by Rossini and other idols of the day. The so-called choral synagogues soon brought forth specialists in choral leadership and composition, such as A. Dunajewski, Eliezer *Gerovich, and David *Nowakowski. Their creations do not lack touching moments, but are "conductors' music," incompatible with the strong and style-conscious works of their older contemporary Nissan Spivak ("Nissi Belzer").

Research in traditional Jewish music was taken up by cantor Pinchas Minkowski, one of the prominent *ḥazzanim* who left for the West. Immediately before the mass emigration of star cantors, the splendor of Ukrainian *ḥazzanut* flashed once again with Solomon *Razumny (see Mus. ex. 22).

The Twentieth Century. At the beginning of the 20th century, the specific kind of music inherited by European Jewry had no good prognosis. The spiritual and social landslides in the West had buried the characteristic features under the quicksand of fashionable tastes, leaving the original outlines barely recognizable. The traditional solo style, still fostered in the East, drifted toward brilliant but shallow display and mingled with the first attempts in formal artistry. The musical situation reflected the general conditions of European Jewry during the period. A major part of the Jewish musicians seemed to have been integrated into the gentile environment as composers and performers; nevertheless, they were looked upon as outsiders by society.

Even the most liberal individuals referred disparagingly to these Jewish musicians. *Moschles was referred to by Schuppanzigh in a letter to Beethoven in 1823 as "this Jewish boy"; H. A. Marschner in a letter to his wife referred to the "Jews' music fabrication" while Tausig is referred to as "the little Jew" (Esser to the publisher Schott, 1861). They vary from the single reference to descent (with certain overtones) to the blunt identification of Jewish musicianship with the negative elements in art (a point driven home in Richard Wagner's pamphlet *Das Judentum in der Musik* (1850) and accepted by certain composers from Pfitzner's standing downward). The keen observer Heinrich Heine held (1842) that Jewish-born artists, Mendelssohn among them, were characterized by "the complete lack of naiveté; but is there, in art, any ingenious originality without naiveté?" He obviously intended to ascribe a certain degree of mannerism to their works of art. The general validity of this sweeping statement is not easily proven; but the greatest Jewish talents did go to the extreme boundaries of stylistic means or sentiment, as if they were looking for an indefinable something that would bestow ultimate perfection upon their creations. Arnold *Schoenberg has demonstrated (*Style and Idea,* 82–84) how Gustav Mahler probed into the subconscious and unknown in his last major work of 1911 (Mus. ex. 33): "An extraordinary case, even among contemporary composers, is the melody from *Abschied,* the last movement of Mahler's *Das Lied von der Erde.* All the units vary greatly in shape, size, and content, as if they were not motivic parts of a melodic unit, but words, each of which has a purpose of its own in the sentence."

The free rhythm of this truly "talking" passage; its construction by means of addition, instead of subordination of elements; and even certain melodic idiomatics have a familiar ring to an ear trained in Jewish singing and belonging to a sphere of sound forms which includes Jewish music. A similar structural affinity is also found with the "principle of permanent variation" that governs the formation of Schoenberg's serial compositions from the early 1920s onward. It was, however, a far cry from the visionary and subconscious achievements of the great masters in the open field of pure music and the practical solutions demanded for applied music, such as synagogue song, which had to cope with tradition and habitude. But its composers also felt the need to express Jewish identity much more strongly than in the past century. The first obstacle to be overcome was their estrangement from the genuine sources of inspiration; moreover, these sources lay buried under much debris.

The Collection and Examination of the Inheritance. Gathering and transcribing the oral tradition of synagogue song had begun in the Western countries during the 19th century and was almost completed by the end of that era. This labor and the incipient research had been the work of cantors personally involved in maintaining the vocal traditions. It became the task of the present century to approach the material under broader aspects and, above all, to extend its scope to the oriental Jewish communities. The decisive step was taken by Abraham Zvi Idelsohn (1882–1938), a disciple of Eduard Birnbaum—who imbued him with the inquisitive and historical approach to tradition—educated at German conservatories and in the principles of the Leipzig school of musicology. Under the auspices of the Vienna Academy of Sciences, Idelsohn set out to collect oriental Jewish song in Jerusalem by phonograph recording (1906–21). The transcriptions fill five volumes of his monumental *Hebraeisch-orientalischer Melodienschatz* (10 vols., 1914–32). The historical and analytical prefaces afford ample background information; they were condensed and complemented later in his *Jewish Music and its Historical Development* (1929) and numerous papers.

The impact of Idelsohn's publications made itself immediately felt in general musicology, especially in Plainchant research (Peter Wagner, *Einfuehrung in die Gregorianischen Melodien* 3, 1921; frequently borrowed and repeated in later research). The reaction of specialized Jewish research came with the confrontation of European and oriental music in Israel. A wave of re-recording and extensive or intensive surveying swept over the fields of folklore, now widened beyond expectation by the "ingathering of the exiles" (from 1948). These activities form a base for present research, in addition to historical and liturgical studies by modern methods. The

Example 33. Gustav Mahler, *Das Lied von der Erde,* opening melody of the last movement, "Abschied" ("Parting"), singled out by Arnold Schoenberg for its unique melodic character (see A. Schoenberg, *Style and Idea,* 1950, 85–86). Music courtesy Universal Edition, Vienna.

integration of Jewish music in the general history of music (especially its comparative branch, foreshadowed in Curt Sachs' writings) is close to being accomplished.

Parallel to the research in Jewish oriental song went the collection of musical folklore in the European communities. At the turn of the century, songs in the Yiddish and Ladino vernacular were still sung; popular minstrelsy and instrumental playing flourished in the dense Jewish settlements of Eastern Europe and the Balkans as they had done in the past. The collection and transcription of these treasures began about 1900. It was not necessarily in the wake of Herder's ideas on folk song and national character that the Warsaw watchmaker Judah Leib *Cahan began his famous collection of folk song texts and music in 1896 (published from 1912); rather he felt the waning of his Jewish world so lovingly described in I. L. *Peretz' and *Shalom Aleichem's novels. The menace came from secularization (*Haskalah) and the attraction of the Russian big cities but it was the progressive and assimilated circles themselves that approached Jewish folk music with the methods of ethnomusicology. In 1898, the writers Saul *Ginsburg and Pesaḥ *Marek initiated a collecting campaign of folk song texts (published 1901), and the critic and composer Joel *Engel began noting down Jewish folk tunes. Their motivation sprang from the conscious acceptance of the national trend in music, already realized by the Czechs, Spaniards, and the Russians themselves. Texts alone were still published by Noah Prilutzki (1911–13); but music was the foremost issue in the phonograph recordings of "expeditions" sent to the countryside by the Petrograd Society for Jewish Folk Music and Baron *Guenzburg in 1912–14 (under the direction of S. *An-Ski). The output of Edison cylinders found its way into Soviet archives in Kiev, and the recordings were transcribed and published in part by M. *Beregovski.

After World War I, An-Ski's Jewish Historical-Ethnographical Society took over (1925–39) and published the first volume of its *Muzikalisher Pinkas* (1927, ed. A. M. Bernstein). Only a fraction of its members as well as some of their collections, reached the United States and set up the YIVO Society, New York, among others. Yiddish folk song found warm and intelligent attention there (such as the collecting activity of Ruth Rubin). Several smaller anthologies, like those of Menahem *Kipnis (Warsaw, from 1930) and Fritz Mordecai Kaufmann (Berlin, 1920) were instrumental in deepening the appreciation of Ashkenazi folkways in song.

The development was quite different as regards the Ladino folk song of the Sephardim. The first texts, published by A. Danon in 1896/97 (REJ, 32-33), aroused the interest of historians of Spanish literature. Ramon Menéndez Pidal presented his first research in this field in 1906, and the Madrid Centro de Estudios Históricos encouraged Manuel de Lara to collect tunes and texts in the Balkans and North Africa (1912, 1915). It was not until the period between the world wars and thereafter that tunes were published on a larger scale (Ortéga; Larrea Palacín). Since then, many melodies have been printed and intensive research in the *Romancero judeo-español* has been pursued in Israel and the United States (see *Ladino literature: Romancero, Musical Tradition).

The Revival of National Values in Music. The idea of imprinting a "national style" on art music of nonreligious description came late to the Jewish composers. It sprang up in Russia, but not from those composers who were linked to traditional or folk music (M. Dulitzki, D. Kabunowski, A. M. *Bernstein) and had set to music the Hebrew lyrics of the Haskalah and *Ḥibbat Zion authors. It cropped up, rather, within the thin layer of gifted

Figure 20. A children's choir at a Lag ba-Omer celebration in the Warsaw Ghetto, May 1942. The children, all orphaned or abandoned, have their heads shaved as a sanitary measure. Courtesy Yad Vashem Archives, Jerusalem.

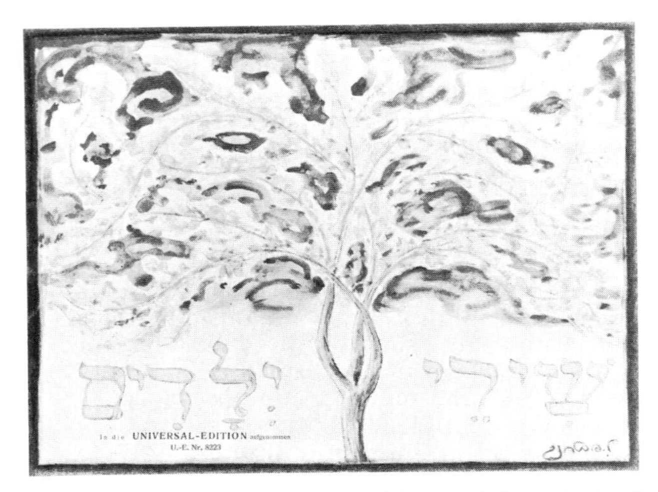

Figure 21. Cover designed by Leonid Pasternak for a book of children's songs, *Shirei Yeladim*, by Joel Engel, 1925. Jerusalem, J.N.U.L.

students paying their precious admittance to metropolitan conservatories by complete assimilation. They were either unaware of their people's special singing style or ashamed of it and did not follow the model of the national trend in Russian music, from Glinka to Mussorgsky. The impulse had to come from the outside. In St. Petersburg in about 1902, Rimsky-Korsakov used to refer all his non-Russian students to their folk music. He also urged the Jews among them to cultivate their "wonderful music which still awaits its Glinka" (according to *Saminsky). In a similar way, the young critic Yuli Dmitrevich (Joel) *Engel of Moscow was aroused to think of his cultural identity after having been asked point-blank by the mentor of the Russian national school, Vladimir Stassov: "Where is your national pride in being a Jew?" (according to Jacob *Weinberg). Many of these Jewish musicians, born between the 1870s and 1890s (the generation of Scriabin and Stravinsky), had little inner relation with living folk and traditional music (except for the few who had been disciples of cantors, such as E. Shkliar, M. Gnesin, S. *Rosowsky). Saminsky, Milner, Zhitomirsky, *Achron, Lvov, and Engel became enthusiasts of folk song collecting and arranging.

The rediscovered treasures were quickly brought before the public in unsophisticated arrangements for concert performance. Engel presented his folk song arrangements at concerts of the Moscow Ethnographical Society as early as 1901–02. The Petrograd Society for Jewish Folk Music (1908–18) had a statistically splendid record of concert performances. Its publishing house, Juwal, produced 58 works of 16 composers up to 1914, in addition to Engel's numerous songs and a collective songbook for schools. The results were sound craft-productions but not creative art. In consequence, the works of the National School did not gain ground beyond a certain sector of the Jewish audience. Talents like Joseph Achron struggled tragically for the fusion of Eastern-rooted Jewish and Western art music. The important problem of connecting self-sufficient melodic lines and modal (anti-harmonic) structures with harmonies was not solved; experiments went on in the tracks of Balakirev and Mussorgsky and later with the application of sound shading à la Debussy.

A short Russian spring after the October Revolution promised a new efflorescence of national aspirations in art. Hebrew and Yiddish *theaters (after having been banned since 1883) were founded (*Habimah, 1917; Vilna Troupe), and gave a fresh stimulus to Jewish composers. In fact, the latter's performances were at their best with incidental music such as Engel's *Dybbuk Suite* (op. 35), or A. *Krein's music to I. L. Peretz' *Night in the Old Market Place*. But very soon Jewish national art was dispersed for political reasons and its exponents went westward. After a short rallying in Berlin (about 1920–22), they made their way to the United States or Palestine. Others rode the tide and became useful members of the Soviet musical establishment (M. Gnesin, A. Krein, A. Veprik).

Those who remained in Central Europe continued the national trend. The Juwal publications of music were transferred to Vienna and carried over to the new Jibneh series (closed in 1938). This group of composers did much to foster the conscience of Jewish identity in the Western communities (J. Stutschewsky, A. Nadel, J. S. Roskin, and singers like cantor L. Gollanin); they also became closely associated with the Zionist movement.

The earlier delegates of the National School who went to Palestine left only a superficial and transitory imprint on local art development because of their inflexible views and frozen stylistic traits; but a few representatives of the old guard, such as J. Engel and J. Stutschewsky (from 1938) played important roles in musical life.

Figure 22. Advertisement of a concert in honor of Sholem Asch in Warsaw, July 5, 1930. The performers were Gershon Sirota and his daughter Helena, Menahem Kipnis, and Zimra Zeligsfeld. From I. Fater, *Yidishe Musik in Poyln . . .*, Tel Aviv, 1970, p. 169.

The massive immigration of Jewish composers and musicians to America was quickly absorbed in the well established communities of East Ashkenazi extraction with their own music theaters, choral societies, and virtuoso star cantors. Members of the National School such as Lazare Saminsky, Joseph Yasser, and others became important organizers of both sacred and secular music. They remained indebted to East Ashkenazi folk song or the styles based upon it, as can be seen, for instance, from the proceedings of the Jewish Music Forum (New York, from 1939) and similar institutions. The hope of deriving a universal Jewish style from that particular sector, with a directness bordering on imitation, is still nurtured by composers who have not experienced the pluralism of forms brought together in Israel—especially the oriental components.

The production of Jewish music in America was well appreciated within its own small province of well-disposed listeners, but it did not conquer the general and international audience of the concert halls. This was accomplished by those few Jewish composers who were gifted enough to assimilate tradition and folkways to their own language and make them part of a profound expression of musicality. They are represented by Ernest *Bloch, Darius *Milhaud, Arnold Schoenberg, and Leonard *Bernstein—each in his own, highly individual way. A new leaf in national music was turned by the generation of composers who witnessed the reestablishment of the Jewish state in Israel (for the artistic problems to be overcome and the ideas and tracks followed by them, see *Israel, Cultural Life).

New Ways in Sacred Music. The trend in art-music of Jewish orientation was from the display of an upgraded Ashkenazi idiom to a more universally understood language. This language was the common musical vernacular; it also encroached upon liturgical music, but did not altogether supersede the traditional style. The contribution of the 20th century to synagogue song must therefore be evaluated in the light of the development of East Ashkenazi *ḥazzanut* in the West. It is true that the image of this original art has been marred by virtuosity for its own sake, the search for external effects, flattering the tastes of an undiscriminating public, and by the inroads of the record industry. The field is too wide and variegated for generalizations, however, and any judgment should orient itself to the outstanding accomplishments. The development of East Ashkenazi *ḥazzanut* in the United States was initiated and furthered by immigrants from about 1880 until the end of World War II. Earlier arrivals, such as Minkowsky and Samuel *Morogowski ("Seidel Rovner"), were followed by Joseph *Rosenblatt, David Roitman, Moses (Moshe) Koussevitzky, and many others, who continued the traditional personal union of performer-composer. From the ranks of this generation, Zevulun (Zavel) *Kwartin (immigrated 1920) created and published works that can be taken as models of progressive *ḥazzanut* (Mus. ex. 34).

The most evident mark of this purely single-voice composition is the coloratura. Although it includes some recurrent patterns, these appear in no way as merely decorative adornment and avoid the brilliance for the sake of brilliance displayed by J. Rosenblatt and others. The ornament often underlines the sense and expressive contents of the text, sometimes recalling the old cantors' musical *kavvanot* (mystical "intentions"). Coloraturas are affixed to points of internal or external tension, concentrating on the essential, while the intervening, preparatory words may be passed by with a certain indifference. Kwartin claimed that he absorbed "genuine oriental formulations" during his stay in Palestine (1926–27), and took them as a model for his compositions (*Zmiroth Zebulon* 1, preface, 1928). He succeeded in combining the two related musical styles and paved the way for a revival of the venerable, but outworn, art of *ḥazzanut*.

This sphere of music, well circumscribed by tradition, barely raised the problem of harmonic accompaniment or choral harmonies; the latter was left to the usual semi-improvisatory *meshorerim* style, with the spontaneous congregational responses. However, where the service followed the Western trend of part singing and eventually came to include the organ accompaniment of choir and cantor, the problem of harmony became acute. Out of dissatisfaction with the solutions propounded during the 19th century, three specific questions—old and new—came to the fore: how to harmonize melodies of an unharmonic conception, by what means to replace romanticism in synagogue composition, and how to write choral tunes inviting the participation of the congregants. Since there was no ready-made solution, the demands of the various communities had to be met by trial and error. From the 1920s, American synagogues did much to encourage the search for solutions of this problem, by sponsoring the composition of complete services or sections, often according a great measure of freedom to the composer.

The initiative in composing new synagogue music was taken by immigrant adherents of the National School, such as Lazare Saminsky (in the U.S. from 1921) and Joseph Achron (from 1925). Previously, these had dealt with the folkloristic manifestations of sacred song, or, occasionally, with single pieces of concert appeal; now they had to adopt a modern musical language appropriate to the Jewish service or, at least, had to modernize the traditional idiom (a venture quite legitimate in the flexible ideological framework of Jewish music). They understood that they should abandon the well-trodden ways of romanticism as well as the feeble "edifying" style and obtrusive sentimentality ("to vitriol away the 'cello sentimentality' of Messrs. Bruch, etc."; A. Schoenberg on his *Kol Nidrei* version, letter to Paul Dessau, 1914). Saminsky, for instance,

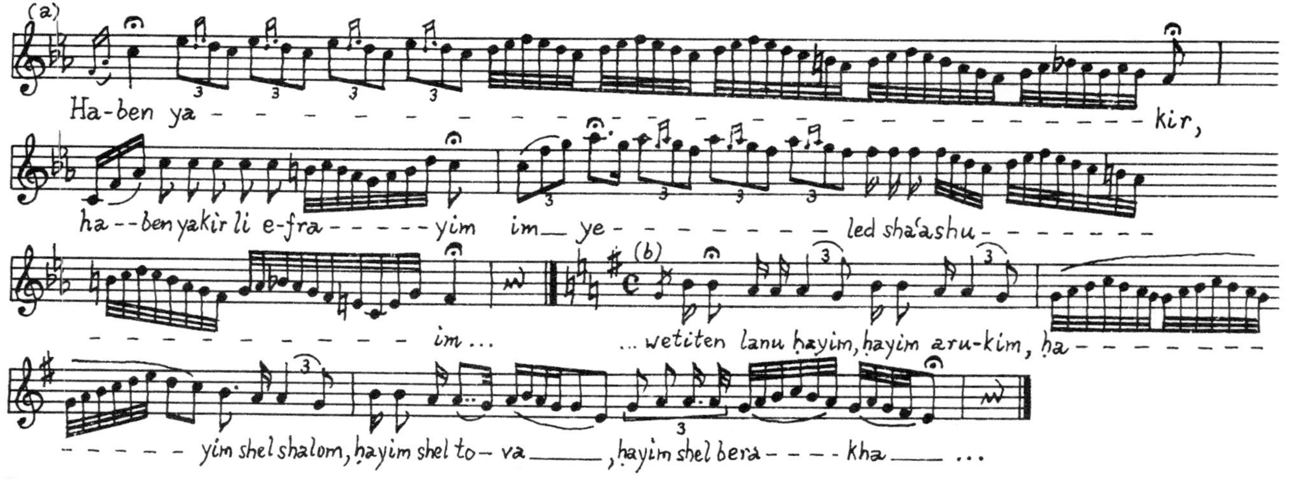

Example 34. Eastern Ashkenazi style *ḥazzanut* from the United States. Two compositions by Zawel Kwartin. After Z. Kwartin, *Zmiroth Zebulon*, vol. 1, 1928, nos. 35 and 18.

consciously renounced the plaintive *shtayger* scales in favour of what he called "the beautiful and majestic major and Aeolian minor of Hebrew melodies" (*Sabbath Evening Service*, preface, 1926). He drew much inspiration from the motive stock of Ashkenazi biblical chant and its basically pentatonic structure (*ibid.*, ch. 36). He has the Sabbath Psalm 93 sung to a tune derived from the motive-chains of Bible reading (Mus. ex. 35). The effect is an unusual relaxed expression of joy, Jewish in substance, but completely divorced from the perpetual tension of *ḥazzanut*. The composer evaded the problem of harmony by prescribing the unison of choir and organ.

Lazar *Weiner, too, relied upon pentatonics (Mus. ex. 36a), but in a more schematic way and took some of his inspiration from the earlier Israel song composers (Daniel *Sambursky, Marc *Lavry). Russian-born Isadore *Freed, educated in America and in France with Vincent d'Indy, approached the problem of harmony by employing the subtle, somewhat pallid, chords of late French romanticism (Mus. ex. 36b).

The harder line of the "expanded tonality" featured by Ernst *Toch or Hindemith, with its tonal flexibility and harsh harmonies, had a refreshing influence on modern synagogue composition: here was an antithesis to romanticism, and a certain affinity to the antiharmonic elements and heterophonic performing habits of the earlier synagogue. Heinrich Schalit applied some of these topical principles to his *Sabbath Eve Liturgy* (Munich, 1933; revised ed. New York, 1951), using several original Oriental-Sephardi tunes (e.g., the radiant ecstasy of the *Kedushah* in Idelsohn's *Melodien* 4, no. 41). A remarkable, but isolated, progress toward a synagogue choral style was made by American-born Frederick Jacobi in one of his later works (Mus. ex. 36c). The harmonies brought forth by the four-part choir have been severed from functionalism; the doubling of the voices serves rather for the acoustical strengthening and coloration as known, in principle, from *meshorerim* practice. The voices go in unison at one time and move apart at another, as in the natural heterophony of a praying congregation; there are also reminiscences of choral psalmody.

Perhaps the most prolific innovator was Hugo Chaim *Adler, cantor and disciple of Toch. When still in Germany, in Mannheim, he recoined the concept of Brecht-Hindemith's ethical cantata to the ideas of Buber's *Juedisches Lehrhaus*. After escaping to the United States in 1939, he gave a new shape to the musical service and community life of his Worcester, Massachusetts, congregation (synagogue compositions 1934–52; cantatas 1934–48). Drawing upon the same techniques as Schalit and Jacobi, Adler was more consistent in stressing the specific Jewish elements (Mus. ex. 37). Traditional features such as *shtayger* modality, and restraint to the musical essentials endow his works with character and stature.

The specimens quoted so far may demonstrate some important trends and achievements in adapting contemporary musical language to the synagogue. Among the considerable number of commissioned works are the liturgies of L. Saminsky (1926), J. Achron (1932), Darius Milhaud (op. 279; 1947), and L. *Algazi (1952). In a different category are the para-synagogal cantatas and prayer arrangements with obligatory orchestra accompaniment that are suited to concerts or meetings of religious or national celebration; this class is represented by the important works of Ernest Bloch (*Avodat ha-Kodesh*, 1930), which was commissioned for a Reform synagogue and which entered the concert repertoire, and Arnold Schoenberg (*Kol Nidrei*, 1938). Selected prayers were set to music, on the commission of prominent communities, by Leonard Bernstein (1946), Mario *Castelnuovo-Tedesco (op. 90; 1936), Lukas *Foss, Morton Gould (op. 164; 1943). Alexander *Tansmann (1946), Kurt *Weill, and others. The composers' names suggest the wide range of schools and individual styles employed but do not guarantee a degree of personal involvement and familiarity with the actual demands of the service. At any rate, the publication of new synagogue compositions, both on the traditional and the decidedly contemporary line, is growing in number, the output of the 1960s exceeding by far that of the 1950s. The impact of modern tendencies on synagogue music as a whole is checked, however, by the differences of approach to liturgy and service which form part of more comprehensive principles and ideological controversies. A new factor has been added to the question of conservativism or progress in sacred music by the meeting and clash of widely differing ritual and singing cultures in Israel. The most ancient fundamentals of Jewish song form the only common ground left for any synthesis that may be in the offing.

[H.Av.]

FOLK MUSIC

The simple division of music into folk and non-folk (art) assumes that the two kinds must be mutually exclusive, and that the one is the property of the lowest social classes while the other is that of the highest. It is doubtful whether such a division will work for more than a very small number of cultures, past or present. For the musical tradition of the Jewish people, viewed as a unit, it seems almost totally inapplicable, since most of the musical practices and forms are largely common to all social strata, and most of them are a mixture of elements which, strictly speaking, would have to be separated into folk and non-folk. Neither is the criterion of "oral tradition" decisive: it is indeed applicable as regards the music itself, but is not always applicable as regards the many texts deriving from the literary-religious heritage, which has always been considered as belonging to all.

It is only possible to arrange the various kinds of music-making in Jewish society on a continuum, at one end of which can be placed music forms which conform without doubt to all the accepted criteria of "folk," while at the other extreme will appear those in which the decisive factors come from the "non-folk" sphere. Along this continuum, each kind of music will not always differ from the preceding and following in equal measure. One example is the music of the instrumental entertainers (*klezmerim*, as they are called in Eastern Europe); it is a purely oral tradition, with its practitioners true professionals who, although of relatively low social status, are often given an important place in religious functions. Another example is masoretic cantillation, in which each male child is supposed to achieve at least a minimal proficiency. However, this is a learned practice backed by a body of complex theory and based upon written words and signs, which cannot be called folk art.

Not all musical manifestations found in the various

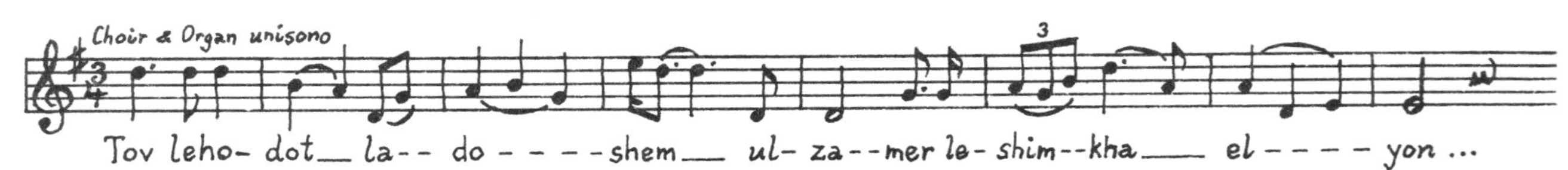

EXAMPLE 35. Choir tune developed from motives of biblical cantillation. From L. Saminsky, *Sabbath Evening Service*, op. 26, 1930.

EXAMPLE 36. Modern compositions for the synagogue. (a) Lazar Weiner, 1932, in G. Ephros (ed.), *Cantorial Anthology,* vol. 5, 1957, 64; (b) Isadore Freed, 1955, in G. Ephros, *ibid.,* 66; (c) Frederick Jacobi, 1946, in D. Putterman (ed.), *Synagogue Music by Contemporary Composers,* New York, 1951, 180–2.

Example 37. Modern psalmody for cantor and choir. Hugo Chaim Adler, *Nachlat Israel—Sabbath Eve Service*, 1952, 28–29. The organ accompaniment has been omitted here.

Jewish communities have been listed, and many which do appear are not practiced in all communities. (See also entries on various communities).

GRADATION OF FOLK AND ART ELEMENTS IN TRADITIONAL JEWISH MUSICAL CULTURE

Exlusively or Predominantly Folk Elements (musical content mostly not exclusive to Jewish society). This category includes children's play songs, work songs, cradle songs, love songs, and songs of social pastime and comment; Purim plays, epic song, dirges, and **badḥan* songs (simple); and religious group song outside the synagogue (home rituals, ḥasidic *niggun*).

Intermediate and Mixed Folk and Art Elements. To this category belong religious group song in the synagogue (prayer melodies, communally sung *piyyutim*); solo song in home rituals, cantefable narration (i.e., folktale with "built-in" song) related to the liturgical repertoire, and "learning tunes" for *ḥeder* and Talmud study; artistic group hymnody, especially with soloists (e.g., **bakkashot*), artistic *badḥanut*, and sounding the **shofar;* and instrumental and vocal entertainment music by professionals, adapted from folk and art elements of a surrounding culture.

Predominantly or Exclusively Art Elements. In this category are masoretic cantillation; virtuoso solo *ḥazzanut* and professional *paytanut;* and secular vocal and instrumental true art music by professionals and trained amateurs, taken over unchanged from a surrounding culture.

The use of the vernacular—generally a Jewish dialect-form of the local language—is almost, but not quite, congruent with the first category. The participation of women is sanctioned in most communities only for those forms and functions which appear in this category; an extreme case is observable in *Yemen where the women have a musical culture of their own. The place of instrumental folk music is difficult to evaluate at present, first, because the entire range of instrumental music as such constantly tends toward specialization, if not outright professionalism; secondly, because no Jewish community in the Diaspora has preserved any pre-Exilic folk instruments (the *shofar* may fulfill certain functions in folk rituals but is not a folk instrument) or created an instrument exclusively its own (not even the Purim noisemakers). Generalizations as to the musical and poetical forms are impossible for the exclusively or predominantly folk traditions, because they differ in each community or are commonplace characteristics of folk music as such. The only phenomenon which can possibly be singled out is that of "folk-polyphonies" in certain communities (especially Yemen), which are linked to liturgical singing. However, the "folk" designation for this practice only serves to distinguish it from European art-polyphony and is therefore apt to be misleading. As for the question whether Jewish religious music is folk or art music, it can only be said that it is, or can be, one or the other or both—according to the social and spiritual role assigned to each of its manifold forms. It may even be said that the attitude of traditional Jewish society places hardly any emphasis on the division between folk and art music, but organizes its musical experience and consciousness according to the division between secular and sacred music.

[B.B.]

MUSIC IN MODERN EREẒ ISRAEL

No real opportunities for musicians existed in Palestine until well after World War I, and even then only a very few professionals settled in the country. Early attempts to promote institutions of learning and performing were erratic and generally short-lived. In the 1920s visiting artists found interested and enthusiastic audiences in towns and settlements, but development of an organic music life did not attain appreciable proportions and standards until the 1930s, when immigration from Central Europe swelled potential audiences and brought many professional musicians—instrumentalists, teachers, and composers—who soon applied their knowledge and talents to teaching and performing. In 1936 the Palestine Orchestra (later the *Israel Philharmonic Orchestra) was established, and in the same year the Palestine Broadcasting Service was inaugurated in Jerusalem. The latter's instrumental ensemble soon grew from a few members into a full-fledged symphony orchestra, giving weekly concerts in Jerusalem, recording works of local composers, and visiting outlying locations. In the 1960s a chamber orchestra was also formed from among the orchestra's string players.

Symphonic Music. In 1927 a small symphony orchestra was founded by Fordhaus Ben-Zissi, who also dedicated his energies to an oratorio society. Other attempts eventually led to the founding of the Philharmonic Society in 1933, with conductor Michael Taube introducing subscription concerts. In 1936 the society was replaced, on a professional level, by the Palestine Orchestra (see *Israel Philharmonic Orchestra). In 1950 a City Symphony Orchestra was founded in Haifa. It performs widely in the northern part of the country. The Israel Chamber Ensemble, founded in 1965 by Gary Bertini, consists of a chamber orchestra and a small number of singers offering concerts and chamber operas. In Haifa, Ḥolon, and several smaller towns there are also string orchestras, and for many years there also existed a chamber orchestra in Ramat Gan directed by Michael *Taube. *Gadna (paramilitary youth organization) has its own large symphony orchestra, founded by Shalom Ronli-Riklis. It took first prize at the International Youth Orchestra Competition at Kerkrade, Holland, three times in succession (1958, 1962, 1966). The kibbutz movements, which at first sponsored only choral activities, developed their own symphony orchestras, bands, selected choirs and dance groups, singers and ensembles, music schools, and music teachers' seminaries.

Opera. Introduced to the country by Mordecai *Golinkin in 1923, by 1927 his Palestine Opera had presented some 20 operas in Hebrew translation. Several times revived for short periods, it eventually became the Palestine Folk Opera, and, in 1958, the Israel Opera, which under the direction of Edis de Phillippe presented the traditional repertoire. Concert versions and some stage versions of operas were presented also with international star singers and local choirs by the Israel Philharmonic Orchestra.

Chamber Music. Pioneered by cellist Thelma Yellin in the early 1920s, and by violinist Emil Hauser, founder of the first string quartet in 1933, chamber music in Israel is performed by many ensembles; outstanding among them are the New Israel String Quartet, the Tel Aviv String Quartet, the Israel Woodwind Quintet, and the Yuval Piano Trio, most of whose artists are members of the Israel Philharmonic Orchestra. The public for chamber music performances is an unusually large one, especially in the kibbutzim and villages.

Folk Music. Historical conditions precluded the organic evolution of folk music of a strongly defined, national character. From the turn of the century to the late 1920s folk music in the country passed through four phases: import of foreign songs in foreign languages, translations of these same songs into Ashkenazi Hebrew, foreign tunes set to new words reflecting the new life, and, finally, attempts to find new tunes for new lyrics, at first also greatly influenced by tunes and styles from outside Ereẓ Israel. Influences from Eastern and Western Europe, the Mediterranean countries, Arab surroundings, and the oriental Jewish communities (especially the Yemenites) mingled into heterogenous patterns. Eventually, new compositions emerged reflecting the intensification of communal life and the acceptance of modern Hebrew usage. Proper attention to accents, inflections, and other characteristics of the language gave folk music a new character. All popular music (work songs, war songs and marches, love songs, parodies, tunes celebrating harvesting and other highlights of agricultural life) had to be created without recourse to existing indigenous models, thus necessarily prolonging the evolution of prototypes through experimentation and selection. Gradually, valuable musical contributions of a constantly changing character emerged, still though perhaps too fluid to be declared definite types of Hebrew folk tunes. Some of the important pioneers of folk song creation were: Joel Engel, Emanuel Amiran, Nahum *Nardi, Yehudah *Sharett, Ephraim *Ben-Ḥaim, David Zahavi, Mordekhai *Ze'ira, Daniel Sambursky, Sara Levi-Tannai, Mattityahu *Shelem, Yedidyah *Admon, Joel Walbe, Menashe Ravina, and their successors Nira Ḥen, Emanuel Zamir, Amitai Ne'eman, and Naomi Shemer. Among composers of art music who also contributed important songs to this genre are Yiẓḥak Edel, Marc Lavry, and Alexander Uriyah *Boscovitch.

ART MUSIC STYLES. Composition has undergone a similar development. All composers coming before World War II arrived with training from foreign schools, steeped in certain traditions. Confrontation with the new society caused many different reactions: incongruent overlapping of heterogeneous styles, unwavering adherence to previous idioms or techniques, and experimentation with various folk material, such as Yemenite, Sephardi-Mediterranean, and Arabic. Before the emergence of the State of Israel, a nationalist attitude was predominant, expressed in compositions inspired by Jewish historical events, biblical personages, and geographical or other associative facts. Many of the works produced in this period belong to what was often called the "Mediterranean" style, which even in its more attractive creations was not able to free itself from a certain naiveté. The change in cultural climate in the early 1950s freed composers from their concern with specifically local values, and enabled them to experiment with new techniques, to search for new expressions, and to participate in current developments abroad, such as serialism, pointillism, and electronic devices.

Composers. Among the leading composers are Erich Walter *Sternberg, adhering to a late-Romantic, post-Wagnerian style, and almost exclusively setting Bible subjects to music; Joachim Stutschewsky, cello teacher and early collector of Eastern European Jewish musical folklore, who like Yiẓḥak Edel adhered mainly to Eastern European idioms; Paul Ben-Haim, who was among the chief exponents of the Mediterranean style which influenced many composers; Marc Lavry, Russian-inspired, a versatile and popular composer; Joseph Kaminski, combining Polish-Jewish and Israel elements; Alexander Uriyah Boscovitch, developing from Rumanian-Jewish roots to a serial-pointillistic technique; Oedoen *Partos, working from Hungarian beginnings (Kodaly), via the "Mediterranean school," to an orientalism based on *maqām* technique; Menahem *Avidom, a prolific composer of easily understood music, Mediterranean despite dodecaphonic leanings; Ḥanokh Jacoby, who adapted a technique learned from Hindemith to Israel subjects; Josef *Tal, who composed many works of importance in a personal, abstract style and in the 1960s was preoccupied with electronic techniques; Haim Alexander contributed attractive choral works; Abel Ehrlich utilized oriental forms and technique; Mordekhai *Seter mingled Yemenite and Near Eastern elements into his personal style. Among the younger generation are Ẓevi Avni (b. 1927) and Yehoshua Lakner (b 1924), who extended their writings to include electronic means; Ben

Figure 23. Recorder lesson at the Bessie Gottesfeld Children's Village in Ra'anannah. Courtesy Mizrachi Women's Organization of America, New York. Photo Leni Sonnenfeld, New York.

Zion Orgad (b. 1926) who has employed a modern technique without neglecting Israel melos; Ram Da-Oz (b. 1929), blinded in the War of Independence, who has written chamber music of expressive character; Sergiu Natra (b. 1934) and Yiẓhak Sadai (b. 1935), relative newcomers to the country, adapted themselves to their new home without foregoing a cosmopolitan, contemporary language. Among the few promising native Israelis, are No'am Sheriff (b. 1935), whose characteristics are brilliant instrumental effects, rhythmical intricacies, and colorful treatment of orchestra and smaller combinations; and Ami Ma'ayani (b. 1936), whose compositions for harp have been especially successful.

Concert Halls. Accommodating up to 3,000 people, these were built in Tel Aviv in 1957 (the Mann Auditorium, home of the Israel Philharmonic Orchestra) and in Jerusalem in 1959 (Binyenei ha-Ummah). Some kibbutzim have large concert halls in their cultural centers, and there are many smaller halls suitable for chamber music.

Light Music. Provided by many small groups, light music also takes the form of musical comedies and Broadway-type shows (in the original language or translated), which have a large share in the calendar of events. The annual competitive song festival, held on the night of Independence Day, began in 1960 with the intention of encouraging folk-style works, but developed into a venue for more internationally oriented "hits." The growing demands of the light programs of the Israel Broadcasting Authority and the radio station of the Israel Defense Forces, and later also television, created the beginning of a musical entertainment industry with all the failings common to its models in other countries. Jazz was pioneered in the 1950s by Melvin Keller, born in the United States, and continued under his inspiration by several Israel-born musicians and immigrants, especially from the United States.

Wind Bands. Although these were hardly ever set up by Jews, a police band existed in Palestine after 1921 which was staffed and conducted mainly by Jewish musicians. With the establishment of the state, military requirements necessitated the formation of brass bands. Young musicians take up wind instruments of all kinds during their army service and many continue to play them after demobilization, thus providing ample reserves for both existing and future professional orchestras. Municipalities and local councils maintain bands which, in addition to participating in popular events and national holidays, help thousands of financially deprived youngsters acquire a basic knowledge of music and provide a framework for social integration.

International Competitions and Conventions. Adding to Israel musical life, as do visiting ensembles, these have often given impetus to the formation of similar groups locally. From 1952 the triennial *Zimriyyah* ("choir festival") has brought visiting Jewish and non-Jewish choirs from many countries to Israel. These have greatly helped to raise the level of local amateur choirs. Outstanding groups are the Rinat Israel Chamber Choir, founded in 1955 by Gary Bertini; and the Tel Aviv Philharmonic Choir, founded in 1941 by Eytan Lustig, and the choir of the *Iḥud ha-Kibbutzim directed by Avner Itai and Yael Tabori. Another event is the triennial International Harp Competition in Jerusalem, inaugurated in 1959. The annual Israel Festival of music and drama, launched in 1961, adds an important international dimension to musical life in Israel.

An annual festival is also held at Kibbutz *Ein Gev, on the eastern shore of Lake Kinneret, where the ESCO Foundation (named for Ethel S. Cohen of New York) helped erect a concert hall with over 2,000 seats, providing a setting for music and dance performances during Passover week. In May of every year, from 1957 to 1970, a music festival was held in a Catholic church at *Abu Ghosh, an Arab village near Jerusalem, under the direction of Sigi Stadermann; due to external circumstances it then moved provisionally to the regional concert hall at Kibbutz Ein Hashofet. Israel has also played host to important international events: the International Society for Contemporary Music (ISCM) held its festival in Haifa in 1954; the Third International Pablo Casals Cello Competition was held in Jerusalem in 1961. The Sixteenth Conference of the International Folk Music Council, in cooperation with the International Music Council of UNESCO and local bodies

Figure 24. Ḥasidim dancing at the Western Wall in Jerusalem immediately after the Six-Day War, June 1967. Courtesy *Jerusalem Post*. Photo Weiss, Jerusalem.

was held in Jerusalem in 1963, with the theme "East and West in Music."

Music Education. Music schools were founded in Tel Aviv in 1910 and 1914, in Jerusalem in 1918, and in Haifa in 1924, but in those years their impact was negligible. The Palestine Conservatoire of Music, founded in Jerusalem in 1933 by Emil Hauser, developed over the years into the Jerusalem Music Academy and the Israel Academy of Music with two independent institutions in Tel Aviv and Jerusalem, both called the Rubin Academy of Music. The two academies prepare students for professional careers, while numerous music schools and conservatories offer instrumental instruction and general musical education. The Sharett Fund for Young Artists (sponsored by the *America-Israel Cultural Foundation) awards scholarships to music students studying to become professional musicians in Israel. Secondary schools specializing in music are attached to both academies. Three teachers' seminaries, one of them belonging to the three major kibbutz movements, in collaboration train prospective music teachers for schools. In 1965 the Hebrew University in Jerusalem set up a department of musicology within its faculty of the humanities, as did Tel Aviv University in 1966 and Bar-Ilan University in 1970.

Musicological Research. Research is carried out at two institutes at the Hebrew University, the Jewish Music Research Center and the Israel Center for Electronic Music. Founded by Israel Adler in 1965, the Jewish Music Research Center continues the work of historical and ethnomusicological research in Jewish music pioneered in the country by A. Z. Idelsohn, Robert Lachmann, Edith Gerson-Kiwi, and Ḥanoch Avenary, and collaborates in the collection of recordings by the National Sound Archives in the music department of the Jewish National and University Library. The Israel Center for Electronic Music, founded by Josef Tal in 1960, offers facilities to explore this medium and also has an ethnomusicological-analytical division. A smaller research center exists in Jerusalem at the Israel Institute for Sacred Music.

Museums. Collections of musical instruments—European, Asian, and African—exist in Jerusalem (at the Rubin Academy of Music) and in Haifa (as an independent museum and library institution).

Musical Industries. These industries include music publishing and the manufacture of instruments and records. Music publishing was pioneered by the cultural department of the *Histadrut, mainly for folk song and choral material, and by the private firm of Israel Music Publications founded in 1949 by P. E. Gradenwitz. In 1962 the Cultural Council of the Ministry of Education and Culture set up the Israel Music Institute for the publication, recording and dissemination of the works of Israel composers. Apart from recorders and percussion instruments, no modern musical instruments are as yet manufactured in Israel; an assembly plant for pianos imported from abroad was set up in 1968. From 1950 to 1970 an institution called Americans for Music Libraries in Israel (AMLI) donated musical instruments for Israel youth. Local record production was begun in 1946 by

Figure 25. A concert in the Herodian amphitheater at Caesarea during the Seventh Israel Music Festival, 1967, with Gary Bertini conducting the Israel Chamber Orchestra. Courtesy Government Press Office, Tel Aviv.

the firm Hed Arẓi, and was subsequently augmented by branches of foreign firms produced both Israel art and popular music and local pressings of foreign recordings.

Music libraries are chiefly represented by the music department of the Jewish National and University Library in Jerusalem, which possesses the largest collection of Jewish music material in the world; and by the Central Music Library in Tel Aviv; and by the Haifa Music Museum and Library. [Y.B.]

Bibliography: GENERAL: Idelsohn, Music; idem, *Toledot ha-Neginah ha-Ivrit, Mahutah, Yesodoteha ve-Hitpatteḥutah,* 1 (1924); E. Werner, in: Grove, Dict, 4 (1954[5]), 615–36; idem, *From Generation to Generation; Studies in Jewish Musical Tradition* (1968); P. Gradenwitz, *The Music of Israel; its Rise and Growth Through 5000 Years* (1949); A. Nadel, in: *Der Jude,* 7 (1923), 227–36; H. Avenary, in: MGG, 7 (1958), 226–61; E. Gerson-Kiwi, *ibid.,* 261–80; idem, in: *Madda,* 4 (1960), 26–33; idem, *The Legacy of Jewish Music Through the Ages* (1963); idem, in: *Yuval* (1968), 169–93, mus. ex. 16–25; A. M. Rothmueller, *The Music of the Jews* (1967); A. Ackermann, in: AZJ, 63 (1899), 379–82, 392–4, 414–5; A. Friedmann, *Der synagogale Gesang* (1908); idem (ed.), *Dem Andenken Eduard Birnbaums* (1922); A. Z. Idelsohn, *Phonographierte Gesaenge und Aussprache-Proben des Hebraeischen der jemenitischen, persischen und syrischen Juden* (1917); D. Milhaud, in: *Musica Hebraica,* 1–2 (1938), 18–20; M. Wohlberg, in: UJE, 8 (1942), 48–55; H. Harris, *Toledot ha-Neginah ve-ha-Ḥazzanut be-Yisrael* (1950); I. Rabinovitch, *Of Jewish Music, Ancient and Modern* (1952); E. Werner, in: *New Oxford History of Music,* 1 (1957), 313–35; A. Rechtman, *Yidishe Etnografye un Folklor* (1958); I. Adler, in: *Encyclopédie de la Musique Fasquelle,* 2 (1959), 640–54; idem, in: J. Porte (ed.), *Encyclopédie des musiques sacrées,* 1 (1968), 469–93; L. Algazi, *ibid.,* 494–9; E. Gerson-Kiwi, *ibid.,* 512–4; H. Avenary, in: R. Patai (ed.), *Studies in Biblical and Jewish Folklore* (1960), 185–98; J. Walbe, *Der Gesang Israels und seine Quellen* (1964); I. Heskes (ed.), *The Cantorial Art* (1966); Levy, Antologia; E. Piattelli, *Canti liturgici ebraici di rito italiano* (1967); C. Vinaver, *Anthology of Jewish Music* (1953); A. Herzog, *Renanot—Dappim le-Shirah u-le-Musikah Datit,* 1–10 (1958–63). THE BIBLICAL PERIOD (to c. 200 B.C.E.): Sendrey, Music, nos. 10,005–10,682; Finesinger, in: HUCA, 8–9 (1931/32), 193–228; O. R. Sellers, in: *Biblical Archaeologist,* 4 (1941), 33–47; A. Buechler, in: ZAWB, 19 (1899), 93–133, 329–44; 20 (1900), 97–135; C. Sachs, *The Rise of Music in the Ancient World—East and West* (1943); E. Werner, in: *Musical Quarterly,* 43 (1957), 21–37; idem, in: Grove, Dict, 4 (1954), 615–21; idem, in: MGG, 10 (1962), 1668–76; H. Avenary, *ibid.,* 7 (1958), 238ff. (incl. bibl.); Kraeling-Mowry, in: *New Oxford Dictionary of Music,* 1 (1957), 238ff. G. Rinaldi, in: *Biblica,* 40 (1959), 267–89; E. Gerson-Kiwi, in: *Enciclopedia de la Biblia,* 5 (1963), 364–79; O. Eissfeldt, *An Introduction to the Old Testament* (1965), 88–127, 444–54, 483–91; B. Bayer, in: EM, 5 (1967), 755–82 (incl. bibl.); idem, in: *Yuval,* 1 (1968), 89–131; idem, *The Material Relics of Music in Ancient Palestine and its Environs* (1963); S. Hoffman, *Mikra'ei Musikah* (1966); D. Wohlenberg, *Kultmusik in Israel—eine forschungsgeschichtliche Untersuchung* (1967); A. Sendrey, *Music in Ancient Israel* (1969). THE SECOND TEMPLE PERIOD (to c. 70 C.E.): H. Avenary, in: *Revue de Qumrân,* 13 (1963), 15–21; E. Werner, *The Sacred Bridge* (1959), FIRST PERIOD (c. 70 to 950 C.E.): A. Buechler, *Untersuchungen zur Entstehung und Entwicklung der hebraeischen Accente* (1891); J. Adams, *Hebrew Accentuation* (1906); S. Krauss, Tal Arch, 3 (1912), 76–99; P. Kahle, *Masoreten des Ostens* (1913); idem, *Masoreten des Westens,* 2 vols. (1927–30); A. Z. Idelsohn, in: A. M. Luncz (ed.), *Yerushalayim,* 11–12 (1916), 335–73; idem, in: *Zeitschrift fuer Musikwissenschaft,* 4 (1922), 515–24; H. Loewenstein (Avenary), *ibid.,* 12 (1930), 513–20; idem, in: *The Jewish Music Forum,* 7–8 (1946–47), 27–33; idem, in: JJS, 16 (1965), 87–104; S. Rosowsky, in: *Proceedings of the Musical Association* (1934), session 60; E. Werner, in: *Review of Religion,* 7 (1942/43), 339–52; idem, in: HUCA, 20 (1947), 407–70; 23 (1950–51), 397–432; 25 (1954), 327–45); idem, in: *Actes du Congrès de Musique Sacrée, Rome 1950* (1952), 134–48; idem, in: MGG, 10 (1962), 1668–76; A. Scheiber, in: *Sinai,* 29 (1951), 80–89; J. Kafih, *ibid.,* 29 (1951), 261–6; idem, in: *Tarbiz,* 31 (1961/62), 371–6; B. Szabolcsi, in: *Ignace Goldziher Memorial Volume,* 1 (1948); A. Shlesinger, in: *Ereẓ Yisrael . . . le-Zikhro shel M. D. Cassuto* (1954); M. Gonzalo, in: *Miscelanea de Estudios Arabes y Hebraicos,* 4 (1955), 129–41; J. L. Ne'eman, *Ẓelilei ha-Mikra* (1955); L. Levi, in: *Estratto da Scritti in Memoria di Sally Mayer* (1956), 139–93; A. W. Binder, *Biblical Chant* (1959); E. Gerson-Kiwi, in: *Festschrift Heinrich Besseler* (1962), 43–49; idem, in: *Festschrift Brunno Staeblein* (1967), 64–73; D. Weisberg, in: JQR, 56 (1965/66), 315–36; G. Engberg, in: E. Wellesz, ed., *Studies in Eastern Chant,* 1 (1966), 37–49; Y. Walbe, in: *Ethnomusicology,* 11 (1967), 54–70; A. Herzog and A. Hajdu, in: *Yuval* (1968), 194–203, mus. ex. 1–15. SECOND PERIOD, THE MUSIC OF THE MEDIEVAL DIASPORA (c. 950–1500): Y. Singer, *Die Entwicklung des synagogalen Gesanges* (1882); idem, *Die Tonarten des traditionellen Synagogengesanges (Steiger); ihr Verhaeltnis zu den Kirchentonarten und den Tonarten der Vorchristlichen Musikperiode* (1886); M. Steinschneider, in: *Beit Oẓar ha-Sifrut,* 1 (1887), 29–37; E. Kirschner, *Ueber Mittelalterliche hebraeische Poesien und ihre Singweisen* (1914); S. Krauss, *Synagogale Altertuemer* (1922), paragraphs 16.2, 16.3, 44.6; J. Schoenberg, *Die traditionellen Gesaenge des israelitischen Gottesdienstes in Deutschland* (1926); A. Z. Idelsohn, in: *Zeitschrift fuer Musikwissenschaft,* 8 (1926), 449–72; idem, in: *Reshummot,* 5 (1927), 351–61; 6 (1930), 411–22; idem, in: *Acta Musicologica,* 5 (1933), 162–8; idem, in: HUCA, 8–9 (1931–32), 495–503; 14 (1939), 559–74; H. G. Farmer, *Maimonides on Listening to Music* (1941); idem, in: *The Music Review,* 3 (1942); M. S. Geshuri, in: *Sinai,* 13 (1943–44), 317–49; 39 (1956), 298–316; B. Szabolcsi, in: *Semitic Studies in Memory of Immanuel Loew* (1947), 131–3; B. J. Cohon, in: *Journal of American Musicological Society,* 3 (1950), 17–32; H. Avenary, in: *Musica Disciplina,* 4 (1950), 51–57; 6 (1952), 27–32; idem, in: HUCA, 39 (1968), 145–62; E. Werner, in: G. Reese and R. Brandel (eds.), *The Commonwealth of Music; in Honour of Curt Sachs* (1965), 71–96; H. Wagenaar-Nolthenius, in: *Mélanges offerts à René Crozet* (1966), 881–5; Y. Ratzaby, in: *Taẓlil,* 6 (1966), 8–13; A. Shiloah, *ibid.,* 5–8; idem, in: *Fourth World Congress of Jewish Studies, Papers,* 2 (1968); idem, in: *Yuval,* 1 (1968), 221–50; I. Adler, *ibid.,* 1–47; N. Alloni, *ibid.,* 12–35; Angles, *ibid.,* 48–64; A. Heshel, in: J. Porte (ed.), *Encyclopédie des musiques sacrées,* 1 (1968), 515–20; B. Cohen, *Law and Tradition in Judaism* (1969). THIRD PERIOD, THE MIGRATION AND BLENDING OF MUSICAL STYLES (C. 1500–1800): E. Birnbaum, *Juedische Musiker am Hofe von Mantua von 1542–1628* (1893); D. Kaufmann, in: MGWJ, 39 (1895), 350–7; A. Z. Idelsohn, *ibid.,* 57 (1913), 314–25; idem, in: HUCA, 11 (1936), 569–91; P. Nettl, *Alte juedische Spielleute und Musiker* (1923); idem, in: *Musical Quarterly,* 17 (1931), 40–46; R. L. Henriques and H. M. J. Loewe, *Medieval Hebrew Minstrelsy* (1926); C. Roth, in: *Rassegna Mensile di Israel,* 3 (1927–28), 152–62; E. Werner, in: MGWJ, 45 (1937) 92–416; idem, in: *Studies in Bibliography and Booklore,* 5 (1961), 110–21; A. Nadel, in: *Musica Hebraica,* 2 (1938), 28–31; M. Vital, *Di Khazonim Velt,* 3 (1939), 2–4; E. Lifschutz, in: *YIVO Annual of Jewish Social Science,* 7 (1952), 48–83; H. Shmueli, *Higgajon Bechinnor (Betrachtung zum Leierspiel) des Jehudah . . . Moscato* (1953); J. Stutschevsky, *Ha-Klezmerim: Toledoteihem, Oraḥ-Ḥayyeihem vi-Yẓiroteihem* (1959); A. Hemsi, in: *Sefarad,* 20 (1960), 148ff.; I. Adler, *La Pratique musicale savante dans quelques communautés juives en Europe aux XVIIē et XVIIIē siècles,* 2 vols. (1966); idem, in: A. Altmann (ed.), *Jewish Medieval and Renaissance Studies* (1967), 321–64; S. Simonsohn, in: *Proceedings of the American Academy for Jewish Research,* 34 (1966), 99–110; H. Avenary, in: *Yuval* (1968), 65–85, mus. ex. 26–34; R. D. Barnett, in: JHSET, 22 (1968), 1–38; R. Katz, in: *Acta Musicologica,* 40 (1968), 65–85; M. Gorali, in: *Tatzlil,* 10 (1970), 9–28. FOURTH PERIOD, MODERN TIMES: D. Deutsch, *Die Orgel in der Synagoge* (1863); S. Sulzer, *Denkschrift an die hochgeehrte Wiener israelitische Cultus-Gemeinde, zum 50 jaehr. Jubilaeum des alten Bethauses am 1. Nissan 5636* (1876); A. Berliner, *Zur Lehr' und zur Wehr; ueber und gegen die Kirchliche Orgel im juedischen Gottesdienste* (1904); J. Lebermann, *Aus dem Kunstleben der Hessischen Residenz am Anfang des vorigen Jahrhunderts* (1904), 22–31; A. Friedmann, *Lebensbilder beruehmter Kantoren,* 3 vols. (1918–28); S. Krauss, *Zur Orgelfrage* (1919); M. Brod, in: *Musikblaetter des Anbruch,* 2 (1920); H. Berl, *Das Judentum in der Musik* (1926); A. Einstein, in: *Der Morgen,* 2 (1926), 290–602; L. L. Ssabanejew, *Die nationale juedische Schule in der Musik* (1927); M. Joseph and L. Seligman, in: JL, 4 (1930), 601–4; L. Kornitzer, in: *Juedisch-liberale Zeitung,* 11 nos. 31–33 (1931); O. Guttmann, in: *Der juedische Kantor* (1934), nos. 1–4, 6; J. Stuschevsky, *Mein Weg zur juedischen Musik* (1936); M. S. Geshuri, *La-Ḥasidim Mizmor* (1936); idem, *Neginah va-Ḥasidut* be-Veit Kuzmir u-Venoteha (1952); idem, *Ha-Niggun ve-ha-Rikkud ba-Ḥasidut*, 3 vols. (1955–59); idem, in: *Sefer ha-Besht* (1960); M. Ravina, *Mikhtavim al Musikah Yehudit me'et Yo'el Engel, M. M. Warshavsky, Shalom Aleichem* (1942); E. Werner, in: *Contemporary Jewish Record*, 6 (1943), 607–15; A. Berliner, *Ketavim Nivḥarim*, 1 (1945); R. Glanz, in: *YIVO Bleter*, 28 (1946), 394–97; M. Lewison, in: *Di Tsukunft*, 52 no. 4 (1947); W. Z. Rabinowitsch, *Ha-Ḥasidut ha-Lita'it* (1951), music appendix; H. D. Weisgal, in: *Judaism*, 3 (1954), 427–36; A. Weisser, *The Modern Renaissance of Jewish Music, Events and Figures; Eastern Europe and America* (1954); A. W. Binder, in: *The Jewish Forum*, 38 (1955), 19–21, 44–46; I. Freed, *Harmonizing the Jewish Modes* (1958); A. L. Holde, *Jews in Music* (1959); O. D. Kulka, in: BLBI, 4 (1961), 281–300; G. Krause, in: *Mitteilungen aus dem Arbeitskreis fuer Jiddistik* (1961), 36–39; A. W. Binder, *The Jewish Music Movement in America* (1963); N. Stolnitz, in: *Canadian Jewish Reference Book and Directory* (1963), 101–4; A. Tarshish, in: AJHSQ, 54 (1964), 411–49; P. Nettl, in: *Music and Letters*, 45 (1964), 337–44; D. S. Lifson, *The Yiddish Theatre in America* (1965); E. Werner, in: *Central Conference of American Rabbis Journal*, 13 (1965/66), 35–40; A. Soltes, in: I. Heskes and A. Wolfson (eds.), *The Historic Contribution of Russian Jewry to Jewish Music* (1967); A. L. Ringer, in: *Studia Musicologica*, 11 (1969), 355–70; P. E. Gradenwitz, in: *Fourth World Congress of Jewish Studies, Papers*, 2 (1968), 147–51. FOLK MUSIC: C. Seeger, "Oral Traditions in Music," in: *Funk and Wagnall's Standard Dictionary of Folklore, Mythology and Legend*, 2 (1950); G. Herzog, "Song, Folk-Song and Music of Folk-Song," in: *ibid.*; Sendrey, Music; (1951), see table of contents; Waterman, in: *Music Library Association Notes* (1950/51); *Répertoire International de Littérature Musicale (RILM)* (1967–); *The Music Index*, 1–13 (1949–); Shunami, Bibl; I. Joel, *Reshimat Ma'amarim be-Madda'ei ha-Yahadut*, 1 (1964), 49–51, 87–90; 2 (1967), 61f., 121f., 124f.; 3 (1968), 56–58, 114f., 117f.; D. Noy, in: *Meḥkerei ha-Merkaz le-Ḥeker ha-Folklor*, 1 (1970), 389–423; *Tazlil*, 10 (1970), 82–91 (index to vols. 1–10). GENERAL ARTICLES: E. Gerson-Kiwi, in: MGG, 7 (1958), 261–80 (incl. bibl.); idem, in: Grove, Dict, 3 (1954), 304–13. RECENT PARTICULAR STUDIES AND SOURCE-PUBLICATIONS: A. EUROPE, GENERAL: D. Sadan, in: *Bamah*, 9–10 (1961), 27–33; J. Stutschewsky, *Folklor Musikali shel Yehudei Mizraḥ Eiropah* (1958); W. Heiske, in: *Jahrbuch fuer Volksliedforschung*, 9 (1964), 31–44; M. Gorali et al. (eds.), *Di Goldene Pave* (1970); E. Sekuletz, *Shirei Am Yehudiyyim mi-Romanyah* (1970[2]); S. Prizament, *Di Broder Zinger* (1960); A. Rechtman, *Yidishe Etnografye un Folklor, Zikhroynes vegn der Etnografisher Ekspeditsye Angefirt fun S. An-Ski* (1958); E. Mayer, in: YLBI, 3 (1958), 202–10. See also *Ḥasidim, Music; *Society for Jewish Folk Music. B. KLEZMORIM AND BADḤANIM: J. Stutschewsky, *Ha-Kleizmerim* (1959); I. Rivkind, in: *Hadoar*, 9 (1960), 412f., 463f., 483f., 504–30, 533f., 574f.; idem, in: *Minḥah li-Yhudah* (1950), 235–57; E. Lifschutz, in: YIVOA, 7 (1952), 43–83; H. Liberman, in: *Yidishe Sprakh*, 13 (1953), 149–53; A. Yaari, in: KS, 35 (1960), 109–26; 36 (1961), 264–72. C. ASIA AND AFRICA: A. Shiloah, in: *Meḥkerei ha-Merkaz le-Ḥeker ha-Folklor*, 1 (1970), 349–68; Levi, Antologia, 5 vols. (1965–69); idem, *Chants judéo-espagnols*, 3 vols. (1959–71); A. Larrea Palacin, *Cancionero judío del Norte de Marruecos*, 2 vols. (1952–54); See also articles on musical traditions of various communities and areas, and bibliographies in articles on E. *Gerson-Kiwi, R. *Rubin, and M. S. *Geshuri. MUSIC IN MODERN ISRAEL: P. E. Gradenwitz, *The Music of Israel* (1949); idem, *Music and Musicians in Israel* (1959[2]); E. Gerson-Kiwi, in: *Acta Musicologica*, 30 (1958), 17–26; M. Smoira-Roll (Zmora), *Folk Song in Israel: An Analysis Attempted* (1963); idem (ed.), *Yesodot Mizraḥiyyim u-Ma'araviyyim ba-Musikah be-Yisrael* (1968); A. L. Ringer, in: *Musical Quarterly*, 50 (1965); idem, in: P. H. Lang and N. Broder (eds.), *Contemporary Music in Europe* (1965), 282–98; A. Shaḥar and B. Bayer, *Ha-Jazz* (1966), 149–56; B. Bayer, in: *Dukhan*, 7 (1966), 11–30, 89–98; Y. Boehm, *The Making of Music* (1966[4]); D. Harran, in: *Current Musicology*, 7 (1968), 120–7; *Tazlil*, 10 (1970), 82–91 (index to vols. 1–10); I. Miron-Michrowsky, *A Profile of Israeli Music To-day* (1964); B. Bar-Am (ed.), *Twenty Years of Israeli Music* (1968). BIBLIOGRAPHICAL WORKS: J. N. Forkel, *Allgemeine Litteratur der Music* (1792), 33–44; A. Z. Idelsohn, in: *Studies in Jewish Bibliography and Related Subjects in Memory of A. S. Freidus* (1929), 388–403; O. Kinkeldey, *ibid.*, 329–72; R. Rubin, *Jewish Book Annual*, 6 (1947), 64–70; Sendrey, Music; W. Sparger, in: *The American Hebrew* (1892), 197–9, 229, 265–6; A. Weisser, *Bibliography of Publications and Other Sources of Jewish Music* (1969); E. Werner, in: HUCA, 18 (1943/44), 397–428; idem, in: *Historia Judaica*, 6 (1944), 175–88.

MUSICIANS. Jewish musicians in the Diaspora could function, under certain conditions, not only within their own culture, but also—and sometimes even exclusively—within the culture of their host countries. Studies on the relationship between the Jewish musician and the cultural framework in which he worked have, until now, been made only from the perspective of European culture in the 19th and 20th centuries and only on composers and performers who underwent complete assimilation. Consideration of the Jewish musician's status in his own cultural milieu, however, suggests that the transfer of creative activity to the non-Jewish framework is a function of both the opportunities and limitations in the society which the musician strives to enter and the modes and status of musical activity in the society from which he departs.

The role of the musician in the traditional Diaspora Jewish community—irrespective of its location—is characterized by the two main professions of the **ḥazzan* and the **klezmer* (entertainment instrumentalist, the East European Ashkenazi term being used here as a generic one). These two professions may be considered the two extremes of a continuum to which all the other musically active members of the community and their functions can be related. The **meshorerim* (members of the synagogue choir, where such a body exists), the **shofar* blower (who may be a *ḥazzan* or a gifted amateur), the *ba'al kore* (reader of the scriptural portion), the amateur leaders of para-liturgical rituals such as the **bakkashot* or the **seder*, the ḥasidic rabbi composers and "court musicians;" and even the mourning women who exist or existed in many communities as semiprofessionals all belong to the province of *ḥazzanut*. A kind of legitimation may also be accorded to a composer or performer trained in the art music of the gentile environment when the Jewish community permits him to contribute to its liturgical or para-liturgical activities. Examples of this instance are Salamone de *Rossi, the synagogal activities of amateur musicians in the 17th and 18th centuries (see *Cantatas), and the modern or moderately modern composers who often function as musical directors in Conservative and Reform congregations in the United States.

The **badḥan*, the amateur performers of the *Purim play (and their descendants, the creators and artists of the Yiddish stage), the storyteller (whose renditions often include singing), and, by extension, the entire domain of secular domestic song belong to the province of the *klezmer*. The social status of the *klezmer* and the *ḥazzan*, however, was not truly parallel to that of their counterparts in European culture. Because of his participation in religious functions, the *klezmer* was not considered beyond the pale in the same measure as the *Spielmann;* conversely, the *ḥazzan* does not have the status of a priest or minister. The *ḥazzan's* status is higher than that of the *klezmer*, however, and is given additional prestige by the fact that a rabbi might officiate as *ḥazzan*, and that in small communities that could not afford a resident rabbi, the *ḥazzan* often fulfilled certain rabbinical functions. In the ḥasidic tradition it is even considered particularly beneficial if the *zaddik* himself officiates as *ḥazzan* on the Sabbath eve, and especially on the High Holy Days, a more powerful mediator between the people and God.

The "star" cantor is found in only two regions: the Ashkenazi, where the congregation has virtually abandoned communal singing in the service (the exception being the ḥasidic sector, where the cantor's role is significantly minimal), and the European and Near Eastern Sephardi area, in which communal participation in the singing of prayers and hymns takes place side by side with the *ḥazzan's* solo. The phenomenon of the "star" cantor may possibly be correlated with the existence of high-prestige, artistic male singers in the gentile host cultures.

From the ḥazzanic and rabbinic background come many of the singers of grand opera, conductors, theoreticians, musicologists, and music publishers.

Bandleaders and composers of popular music, along with the great string virtuosos, have inherited the *klezmer* tradition. Descendants of *klezmerim* also gravitate to membership in symphonic and entertainment orchestras, since family tradition accustoms them to the discipline of the ensemble. The symphonic composers and the great piano virtuosos, however, mostly come from a non-musical family background. When the Jewish musician transferred his activity to the gentile host culture, both the transfer and its result inevitably became dependent on the musico-social conditions obtaining in that culture. For Western Europe these include: bans on the employment of Jewish musicians; the guild system; church patronage of musical education and composition and church-dominated court patronage; limitations on Jewish participation in university and conservatoire study and teaching; the rise of the secularized, middle-class, concert and operatic culture; the supranational virtuoso and the independent composer; the problem and history of the "baptismal entrance ticket" in all its aspects; the closing or opening of entrepreneurial occupations to Jews in this field, from opera and concert management to music publishing; and, last but not least, the presence or absence of the Jewish community itself in the general concert audience.

Bibliography: P. Nettl, in: D. D. Runes (ed.), *Hebrew Impact on Western Civilization* (1951), 363–404; Sendrey, Music, 62–80, 114–25; A. Z. Idelsohn, in: *Zeitschrift fuer Musikwissenschaft*, 8 (1925/26), 449–72; H. Avenary, in: *Yuval*, 1 (1968), 65–85 (Eng.).
[B.B.]

Alphabetical List of Musicians. The individuals whose names are marked with an asterisk in the list below form the subjects of articles in their appropriate alphabetical position in the Encyclopaedia.

ABELIOVICH, LEV MOYSEYEVICH (1912–), composer. Born in Vilna, Abeliovich studied at Warsaw, and when the Nazis invaded Poland in 1939 he fled to Minsk and studied at the conservatory there until mobilization. After World War II, he devoted himself to composition and was later engaged in the study of Belorussian folk music. His compositions include three symphonies (1962, 1964, and 1967); *Symphonic Pictures* (1958); *Heroic Poem* (1957); three sonatas for piano: two sonatas for violin and piano; and chamber music and songs.

ABER, ADOLF (1893–1960), musicologist. Born in Apolda, Thuringia, Aber was assistant at the Institute of Musicology, Berlin, music critic of the *Leipziger Neueste Nachrichten* from 1918 to 1933, and also a partner in the music-publishing firm of Friedrich Hoffmeister. Settling in London in 1936, he joined the British firm of Novello. Among his many writings were *Studien zu J. S. Bachs Klavierkonzerten* (1913); *Handbuch der Musikliteratur* (1922); *Die Musik im Schauspiel* (1926); and short biographies of Bach, Beethoven, and Brahms.

ABRAHAM, OTTO (1872–1926), musicologist. Born in Berlin, Abraham became assistant to Carl Stumpf (1868–1936) at the Berlin Institute of Psychology from 1896, and collaborated with E. M. von *Hornbostel in the establishment of the "Phonogramm-archiv," one of the first of its kind and still one of the most important. Abraham's work on tone perception was one of the pioneer studies in the psychology of music. His studies, mostly with Hornbostel, on the extra-European musical traditions, put him among the founders of the modern ethnomusicological method.

***ABRASS, OSIAS (Joshua;** 1829–1883), *ḥazzan* and composer.

ACHRON, ISIDOR (1892–1948), pianist; see under *Achron, Joseph.

***ACHRON, JOSEPH** (1886–1943), composer and violinist.

***ADLER, GUIDO** (1855–1941), musicologist.

***ADLER, HUGO CHAIM** (1894–1955), *ḥazzan* and composer.

ADLER, ISRAEL (1925–), Israel musicologist and librarian. Born in Berlin. Adler was taken to Palestine in 1937 and studied at yeshivot. From 1949 to 1963 he studied in Paris. For a period he was in charge of the Hebraica-Judaica department of the Bibliothèque Nationale and published a catalog of the early Hebrew printed books in the library. On his return to Israel in 1963, he became head of the music department of the Jewish National and University Library in Jerusalem. He founded and was director of the Jewish music research center at the Hebrew University, and was chief editor of *Yuval* (1968), the record of its studies. He was editor of the music department of the *Encyclopaedia Judaica.* In 1969 Adler was appointed director of the Jewish National and University Library. His publications include *La pratique musicale savante dans quelques communautés juives en Europe aux XVIIe et XVIIIe siecles*, 2 vols. (1966).

***ADLER, LARRY** (1914–), harmonica player.

***ADMON (Gorochov), YEDIDYAH** (1894–), composer.

***AGUILAR, EMANUEL ABRAHAM** (1824–1904), pianist and composer.

***AL-BARADANI, JOSEPH** (10th century), *ḥazzan* and *paytan.*

ALEXANDER, HAIM (1915–), composer and pianist. Born in Berlin, he settled in Jerusalem in 1936 and taught at the Palestine Conservatory (which became the Rubin Academy of Music). His works, related to the "Mediterranean" style but less directly dependent on folkloristic resources, and of a neoclassical bent, include *Six Israeli Dances* (1951, versions for orchestra, piano duet, and violin and piano), *Lema'an Ẓiyyon* for choir (1955), the cantata *Jerusalem Eternal* (1967–68), and other choral, chamber, and piano works.

***ALGAZI, ISAAC** (1882–1964), *ḥazzan* and composer.

***ALGAZI, LEON (Yehudah;** 1890–1971), conductor, composer, and collector of Jewish music.

***AL-GHARID, AL-YAHUDI** (7th century), singer and composer.

***ALKAN, CHARLES HENRI-VALENTIN** (1813–1888), pianist and composer.

ALKAN, NAPOLEON (1826–1888), pianist and composer, see *Alkan, Charles Henri-Valentin.

***ALMAN, SAMUEL** (1877–1947), choral director and composer.

***AL-MANSUR AL-YAHUDI** (9th century), musician.

ALSHVANG, ARNOLD ALEKSANDROVICH (1898–1960), musicologist. Born in Kiev, Alshvang became involved in political activities and was exiled to northern Russia in 1914. On his return in 1915 he took up music and in 1917 helped in the reorganization of the Kiev Conservatory, accepting a teaching post there in 1923. In 1930 he was appointed professor at the Moscow Conservatory. Having abandoned teaching after a serious illness, he devoted himself to writing and published works on Debussy (1935), Tchaikovsky (1951 and 1959), and Beethoven (1952).

ALTER, ISRAEL (1901–), *ḥazzan;* see **Ḥazzan.*

***ALTSCHUL, JOSEPH (Yoske Slonimer;** 1840–1908), *ḥazzan.*

ALTSCHULER, MODEST (1873–1963), conductor. Born in Mogilev, Russia, Altschuler emigrated to the United States in 1896 and founded the Russian Symphony Society, New York, in 1903. He conducted it until 1925, presenting works, many of them for the first time in the United States, by Russian composers. These included world premieres of two works by Scriabin: *Poème de l'Extase* (1908) and *Prometheus* (1915), for which the "color organ," which could throw colored light on a screen as demanded by the composer, was built for the occasion. After 1925 he taught in Los Angeles.

AMAR, LICCO (1891–1959), violinist. Born in Budapest, a pupil of Henri Marteau, Amar became second violinist of the Marteau Quartet, and concertmaster of the Berlin Philharmonic Orchestra (1915–20) and of the National Theater at Mannheim (1920–23). In 1922 he organized the Amar Quartet, which included Paul Hindemith and was active until 1929 in the promotion of contemporary music. In 1935 he became professor of violin at the Conservatory of Ankara, Turkey. After 1957 he taught at the Musikhochschule in Freiburg.

AMIRAN (formerly **Pougatchov**), **EMANUEL** (1909–), composer and teacher. Born in Warsaw, Amiran went to Palestine in 1924, and after study in London, returned to teach music in schools and teachers' seminaries. He was co-founder and director of the Music Teachers Training College in Tel Aviv (1944–55), and in 1955 became supervisor of musical education in the ministry of education and culture. His songs, which are among the most important contributions to the Israel folk style, include *Emek Emek Avodah, El ha-Ma'ayan Ba Gedi Katan, Mayim Mayim, Ki mi-Ẓiyyon, Uru Aḥim ve-Na'aleh Har Ẓiyyon. Ha-Zore'im be-Dimah,* and *Halleluyah-Kumu ve-Na'aleh.* He also wrote choral, orchestral, and piano music.

***ANTHEIL, GEORGE** (1900–1959), composer and pianist.

APEL, WILLI (1893–), musicologist. Born at Konitz, Germany, Apel studied mathematics and pianoforte, but from 1925 devoted himself to musicology. In 1935 he emigrated to the United States, and in 1950 he became professor of musicology at the University of Indiana. Apel's main field of research was medieval and renaissance music. His publications include reference works such as the *Harvard Dictionary of Music* (1944; 1960[12]); *The Notation of Polyphonic Music 900–1600* (1942, 1953[5]); and *Historical Anthology of Music,* edited with A. T. Davison, two volumes (1946, 1950[5]).

APPLEBAUM, LOUIS (1918–), composer and conductor. Born in Toronto, Applebaum was a composer and conductor for the stage, radio, films, and television. He was musical director of the Canadian National Film Board and after 1961 was musical consultant for the national television network. In 1955 he established the Stratford Music Festival at Ontario, which he directed until 1960. Among his works are *Christmas Overture* (1951); *Dark of the Moon,* a ballet suite (1953); and string quartets and songs.

ARIE, RAFAEL (or **Rafaele;** 1922–), singer. Born in Sofia, Arie was a pupil of Brambaroff, the chief baritone of the Sofia Opera. He won first prize in the Geneva International Competition in 1946, and later sang leading basso roles at La Scala, Milan, and other European and American opera houses. In 1951 Igor Stravinsky chose him for the premiere in Venice of his opera *The Rake's Progress.* Arie visited Israel many times and eventually became an Israeli but continued his international concert career as one of the leading bassos of his generation.

ARLEN, HAROLD (formerly **Hyman Arluck;** 1905–), composer. Born in Buffalo, New York, Arlen was the son of a *ḥazzan.* He sang in the synagogue choir and worked as a pianist and singer in nightclubs and on river steamers. He first gained recognition as a songwriter with *Get Happy* (1928). His successes include: *Stormy Weather* (1933); the music for the film *The Wizard of Oz* (1939), including the Academy award-winning song *Over the Rainbow,* and *Star-Spangled Rhythm* (1943); *That Old Black Magic* (1944); and the music for the film *Here Come the Waves* (1944). His musicals included *Bloomer Girl* (1944), *Country Girl* (1954), *Jamaica* (1957), and *Saratoga* (1959).

ARONOVICH (AHARONOVITCH), YURI MIKHAYLOVICH (1932–), conductor. Born in Leningrad, Aronovich became conductor of the symphony orchestra in Yaroslav in 1957 and earned a reputation as an interpreter of contemporary music. After 1964 he was chief conductor of the All-Union Radio and TV Symphony Orchestra in Moscow. Many works of Soviet composers were first performed under his baton.

***ARPA, ABRAMO DALL' (Avraham Levi;** 16th century), harpist.

***ASHKENAZY, VLADIMIR DAVIDOVICH** (1937–), pianist.

***AUER, LEOPOLD** (1845–1930), violinist and teacher.

AVENARY, HANOCH (formerly **Herbert Loewenstein**; 1908–), musicologist. Born in Danzig, he went to Palestine in 1936. His musicological work, which centered on the history of Jewish music from the Middle Ages to the 19th century, was undertaken privately for a long time. After serving as a major in the research department of the Israel Air Force from 1948 to 1965, he became lecturer and research fellow at the Hebrew University and senior lecturer at Tel Aviv University. His publications include *Wort und Ton bei Oswald von Wolkenstein* (1932); *Studies in the Hebrew, Syrian and Greek Liturgical Recitative* (1963); studies in various periodicals; and articles on Jewish music in encyclopedias, including *Juedische Musik* in *MGG VII* (1957) and the section on *music (from the Middle Ages to the present) in the *Encyclopaedia Judaica.*

***AVIDOM (Mahler-Kalkstein), MENAHEM** (1908–), composer.

AVSHALOMOV, AARON (1894–1965), composer. Born in Siberia, Avshalomov lived in China for almost 20 years before settling in the United States in 1937. In his compositions he strove to create an oriental atmosphere by incorporating Chinese motifs and rhythms into European music. Among his works are two operas, *Kuan Yin* (performed in Peking in 1925), and *The Great Wall* (performed in Shanghai in 1945); a ballet, *The Soul of the Ch'in* (1933); a symphonic poem, *Peiping Hutungs* (1933); a symphony; and a piano concerto.

BACHARACH, BURT (1928–), composer. Born in Forest Hills, New York, Bacharach studied music at McGill University in Montreal and composition with Darius *Milhaud. He subsequently worked as an accompanist for several popular singers, and became especially known as accompanist and arranger for Marlene Dietrich from 1958 to 1961. He later turned to composing popular songs, achieving prominence in the field from the late 1960s onward. His compositions, which he always orchestrated himself, include the musical *Promises, Promises,* and the scores for films including *Alfie,* and *Butch Cassidy and the Sundance Kid* (with the song *Raindrops Keep Falling on my Head*).

***BACHMANN, JACOB** (1846–1905), *ḥazzan* and composer.

***BAER, ABRAHAM** (1834–1894), *ḥazzan* and editor.

***BARENBOIM, DANIEL** (1942–), pianist and conductor.

BARMAS, ISSAY (1872–1946), violinist and teacher. Born in Odessa, Barmas made his debut as soloist in Berlin in 1899 and toured Europe. He also formed his own quartet. From 1900 until 1929 he taught in Berlin, and later moved to London. Among his publications are *Die Loesung des geigentechnischen Problems* (1913), *Tonleiter-Spezialstudien, Doppelgriff-Spezialstudien,* and editions of classical works.

BARNETT, JOHN (1802–1890), composer. Barnett was born in Bedford, England. His father Bernhard Beer, a cousin of Giacomo *Meyerbeer, had changed his name to Barnett upon settling in England. John Barnett was a prolific composer for the London stage. In his opera *The Mountain Sylph* (1834) he reintroduced the composed recitative into English opera in place of the spoken dialogue. His attempt to establish an opera house at St. James's Theater was unsuccessful. In later life he settled at Cheltenham as a music teacher. He composed chamber music and songs, and published some writings on singing. His daughter, Clara Kathleen Rogers (1844–1931), became a well-known opera singer.

BARNETT, JOHN FRANCIS (1837–1916), composer. Born in London, nephew of the composer John *Barnett, he won the Queen's Scholarship at the Royal Academy of Music at the age of 12, and played Mendelssohn's piano concerto at a performance conducted by Louis Spohr. He was appointed professor at the Royal College of Music, London, in 1883. His works include piano, chamber, and orchestral music, and choral cantatas; the most successful being settings of Coleridge's *Ancient Mariner* (1867) and Keats' *Eve of St. Agnes* (1913).

***BAUER JACOB** (1852–1926), *ḥazzan.*

BAYER, BATHJA (1928–), musicologist. See Vol. 1, p. 28.

***BEER, AARON** (1738–1821), *ḥazzan* and collector.

BEIMEL, JACOB (c. 1875–1944), *ḥazzan* and writer; see **Ḥazzan.*

***BEKKER, PAUL** (1882–1937), music critic and writer.

BELLISON, SIMEON (1881–1953), clarinetist. Bellison played with the Moscow Symphony Orchestra and in 1918 organized a woodwind ensemble, Zimro, which went on tour in Asia and the U.S. In 1921 he joined the New York Philharmonic Orchestra as first clarinetist. He transcribed many Jewish compositions for his ensemble. The Bellison archives and a collection of his instruments are housed at the Rubin Academy of Music, Jerusalem.

BELY, VICTOR ARKADYEVICH (**Aronovich;** 1904–), composer and musicologist, born in Berdichev. A vocal piece *Orlyonok* ("Young Eagle," 1936) was followed by successful war songs, including a popular *Ballad of Captain Gastello.* His collection of songs won the Stalin Prize in 1952. He became a professor at the Moscow Conservatory in 1941, and was editor in chief of the Moscow journal *Muzykalnaya Zhizn.*

BELZER, NISSI (1824–1906), see *Spivak, Nissan.

***BENATZKY, RALPH** (1884–1957), composer.

BENDIX, OTTO (1845–1904), pianist. Born in Copenhagen, the brother of the conductor Victor Bendix, he studied with Niels Gade and Franz Liszt, taught piano in Copenhagen, and in 1880 went to the United States. He taught at the New England Conservatory in Boston, and in 1895 he founded his own music school in San Francisco. He also appeared as a concert pianist in the United States and Europe.

BENDIX, VICTOR EMANUEL (1851–1926), conductor and composer. Born in Copenhagen, the brother of the pianist Otto Bendix. He studied with the composer Niels Gade, and was conductor of a choral society which he founded in Copenhagen

(1872–76). From 1892 to 1893 he conducted the Volkskonzerte in Berlin. Among his compositions were *Psalm 33* for chorus and orchestra, four symphonies, and orchestral and chamber works.

***BENEDICT, SIR JULIUS (Isaac;** 1804–1885), composer and conductor.

***BEN-HAIM (Frankenburger), PAUL SHAUL** (1897–), composer.

***BEREGOVSKI, MOSES (Moshe-Aaron) YAKOVLEVICH** (1892–1961), musicologist.

BERGGRUEN, HEINRICH (1838–1889), *ḥazzan* and composer; see **Ḥazzan.*

***BERGSON, MICHAEL** (1820–1898), pianist and composer.

***BERLIJN, ANTON (Aron Wolf;** 1817–1870), composer, conductor, and *ḥazzan.*

***BERLIN (Baline), IRVING (Israel;** 1888–), composer.

BERLINSKI, HERMAN (1910–), composer. Born in Leipzig, Berlinski left Germany in 1933 and went to Paris. In 1939 he joined the French Foreign Legion, but on the fall of France emigrated to the United States. Berlinski's style combines twelve-tone techniques with traditional Hebrew cantillation. His works include a cantata *Habakkuk,* pieces for organ and piano, and liturgical Jewish compositions—*Kaddish* (1953), *Avodat Shabbat* (1957), and *Kiddush ha-Shem* (1958).

BERNSTEIN, ABRAHAM MOSES (1866–1932), *ḥazzan,* composer, and collector; see **Ḥazzan.*

***BERNSTEIN, LEONARD** (1918–), composer, conductor, and pianist.

BERTINI, GARY (1927–), conductor and composer; see under *Bertini, K. Aharon.

BIE, OSCAR (1864–1938), writer on music and the fine arts. Bie was appointed lecturer on the history of art at the Berlin Technical High School in 1890 and in 1921 teacher at the Berlin High School of Music. He was editor of the *Freie Buehne* and later of the literary review *Die neue Rundschau.* He wrote opera reviews for the *Berliner Boersenkurier,* books on piano, dance, opera, and Schubert, and *Das deutsche Lied* (1929).

***BINDER, ABRAHAM WOLFE** (1895–1966), composer and teacher.

***BIRNBAUM, ABRAHAM BAER** (1864–1922), *ḥazzan* and editor.

***BIRNBAUM, EDUARD** (1855–1920), *ḥazzan,* writer, and collector.

***BLANES, JACOB** (1877–1943), *ḥazzan.*

BLANTER, MATVEY ISAAKOVICH (1903–), songwriter. Born in Pochep, Ukraine, Blanter's pieces and music for the Leningrad Satirical Theater attracted early attention. During the period that he worked with the miniature theater "Krokodil" in Gorky, he developed an individual humorous style. He wrote for musical comedies, and his tune *Katyusha* attained popular success during World War II. His music, which made use of folk melodies, also shows urban vernacular and jazz influences.

BLAUSTEIN, ABRAHAM (1836–1914), *ḥazzan* and editor; see **Ḥazzan.*

***BLECH, LEO** (1871–1958), conductor and composer.

***BLINDMAN, YERUHAM (Yeruḥam ha-Koton;** c. 1798–1891), *ḥazzan* and composer.

***BLITZSTEIN, MARC** (1905–1964), composer.

BLOCH, ANDRÉ (1873–1960), composer. Born in Wissembourg, Alsace, Bloch studied with Guiraud and Massenet at the Paris Conservatory. After World War I he conducted the orchestra of the American Conservatory at Fontainebleau. Among his works are: the one-act *Brocéliande* (*prélude féérique,* 1925); the opera *Kaa* (1933); and *Suite Palestinienne* for cello and orchestra (1948).

***BLOCH, ERNEST** (1880–1959), composer.

BLOCH, ROSINE (1844–1891), singer. Rosine Bloch made her debut at the Paris Opera as Azucena in Verdi's *Il Trovatore* in 1865 and remained there as one of its most prominent members. Among her most notable parts was that of Fides in Meyerbeer's *Le Prophète.* She sang Amneris in the first French production of *Aida* in 1880, the year she retired.

BLOOMFIELD-ZEISLER, FANNY (1863–1927), U.S. virtuoso pianist, known for her recitals in Europe and the U.S. Born in Vienna, Fanny Bloomfield-Zeisler was taken to the U.S. in 1868. She made her debut in Chicago at eleven and then went to Vienna for further study with Theodor Leschetizky (1830–1919). She first toured Europe in 1893 and continued to appear in leading cities until World War I. She gave a special performance in Chicago in 1925, to mark the half-century of her concert career.

BLUMENFELD, FELIX MIKHAYLOVICH (1863–1931), pianist and composer. Born in Kovalovka, Kherson, Blumenfeld conducted at the Imperial Opera, 1898–1912, gave the first performance of Rimsky-Korsakov's *The Legend of the Invisible City of Kitezh* in 1906, and took Mussorgsky's *Boris Godunov* to Paris in 1908. After the Revolution, he became director of the Kiev Conservatory, and in 1922 joined the Moscow Conservatory as a piano teacher. He composed piano music, chamber music, and songs.

BLUMENTHAL, JACOB (Jacques; 1829–1908), pianist and composer. Born in Hamburg, Blumenthal settled in London during the 1848 revolution and became pianist to Queen Victoria. He was a fashionable teacher whose melodious compositions were popular in drawing rooms. His best-known piano solo was *La Source* and his best-known song, *The Message.*

***BLUMENTHAL, NISSAN** (1805–1903), *ḥazzan* and composer.

BODANZKY, ARTHUR (1877–1939), conductor. Born in Vienna, Bodanzky became assistant to Gustav *Mahler at the Vienna Opera in 1902 and subsequently conducted opera in Berlin, Prague, and Mannheim. In 1915 he was engaged by the Metropolitan Opera, New York, as conductor of their German repertory and held this position until his death. He excelled in conducting Wagner but was also a symphony conductor. He was music director of the Society of Friends of Music in New York from 1916 until 1931.

BODKY, ERWIN (1896–1958), harpsichordist. Born in Germany, from 1922 to 1933 Bodky was lecturer at various Berlin music institutions. In 1933 he emigrated to Amsterdam and in 1938 settled in the United States, where he became a lecturer at the Long School of Music, Cambridge, Massachusetts. In 1949 he was appointed professor at Brandeis University, Massachusetts. He helped to revive interest in harpsichord playing and the performance of baroque keyboard music.

BOGHEN, FELICE (1869–1945), writer, composer, and pianist. Boghen taught theory at the Instituto Reale Luigi Cherubini in Florence in 1910 and was the pianist of the Trio Florentino. He wrote an opera *Alcestis,* and piano works, and edited old Italian music. His written works include *Appunti ed esempi per l'uso dei pedali del Pianoforte* (1915), and *L'Arte di Pasquini* (1931).

***BOLAFFI, MICHELE (Michael;** 1788–1842), composer and singer.

BONAVENTURA, ARNALDO (1862–1957), musicologist; see Bonaventura, Enzo Joseph.

BOROVSKY, ALEXANDER (1889–), pianist. Borovsky studied at the St. Petersburg Conservatory from 1907 until 1912, and in the latter year won the Rubinstein Prize. From 1915 to 1920, he taught master classes at the Moscow Conservatory, and then embarked upon a successful international career as concert pianist. He settled in the United States in 1941, and was appointed professor at Boston University in 1956.

***BOSCOVICH, ALEXANDER URIYAH** (1907–1964), composer.

***BRAHAM, JOHN** (1774 or 1797–1856), singer.

BRANDON, OHEB (Oëb) ISAAC (c. 1830–1902), *ḥazzan;* see **Ḥazzan.*

BRANT, HENRY DREYFUS (1913–), composer. Born in Montreal, Brant developed a special type of composition in several media, combining theatrical presentation, the spoken word, and stereophonically directed electronic instruments. His experimental works include *5 and 10c Store* for violin, piano, and kitchenware, (1932), *Dialogue of the Jungle* for voices, whistle, sirens, and percussion (1959), and *Violin Concerto with Lights,* for violin and five electronic switches (1961). He also wrote symphonic and chamber works; an opera, *Miss O'Grady* (1936); and the score for the Palestinian film *My Father's House* (1947), which he expanded into the symphony *The Promised Land* (1948).

BRAUDO, YEVGENI MAXIMOVICH (1882–1939), musicologist. Born in Riga, Braudo was appointed professor at the Russian Institute of Art History in 1921, and later professor at Leningrad University. He contributed music criticism to *Pravda,* and was music editor of the first edition of the *Bolshaya Sovetskaya Entsiklopediya.* He wrote a history of music in three volumes (1922–27), as well as works on Bach, Wagner, Borodin, Nietzche, and E. T. A. Hoffman.

BRAUN, YEHESKIEL (1922–), composer. Born in Breslau, Braun went to Palestine in 1924 and studied at the Academy of Music in Tel Aviv, where he became a teacher. His works include *Suite for Wind Quintet* (1951), *Psalm for Strings* (1960), *Sabbath*

Eve Service (1965) for orchestra, and *Illuminations to the Book of Ruth* (1966) for orchestra.

BRECHER, GUSTAV (1879–1940), conductor, composer, and writer. Born in Eichwald, Bohemia, Brecher conducted at various operatic theaters and became music director of the Leipzig Opera (1924–33), where he presented the world premieres of Ernst Krenek's *Jonny spielt auf* (1927) and Kurt *Weill's *Mahagonny* (1930). Among his compositions was the symphonic poem *Rosmersholm*, first presented by Richard Strauss (1896). His writings were mostly concerned with operatic problems and include *Ueber Operntexte und Opernuebersetzungen* (1911). In 1940 he and his wife committed suicide on a ship intercepted by the Nazis off the Belgian coast.

BROD, DOVIDL (**David Strelisker;** 1783–1848), *ḥazzan;* see *Ḥazzan.

***BROD, MAX** (1884–1968), author, music critic, and composer.

***BRODSKY, ADOLF** (1851–1929), violinist.

BROOK, BARRY SHELLEY (1918–), musicologist. In 1945 he became professor of musicology at Queens College, New York. His special fields of research were 16th-century secular music and 18th-century instrumental music, and he was a pioneer in the application of computer technologies to various musicological and bibliographical problems. He founded the computerized *Répertoire International de Littérature Musicale*, the first journal of systematic musicological abstracts. His publications include *La Symphonie française dans la seconde moitié du XVIIIe siècle* (3 vols., 1962).

***BRUELL, IGNAZ** (1846–1907), pianist and composer.

***BRUSSILOVSKY, YEVGENI GRIGORYEVICH** (1905–), composer.

BUCHWALD, THEO (1902–), conductor. Born in Vienna, Buchwald's early conducting appointments were at Barmen-Elberfeld (Wuppertal) in 1922, the Berlin Volksoper (1923), Magdeburg (1924–26), and Munich (1927–29). He worked under Erich Kleiber at the Berlin State Opera (1929–30), and was director of symphony concerts in Halberstadt until the Nazis came to power in 1933. Reaching South America in 1935, he conducted in Chile and later moved to Peru, where he was entrusted by the government with creating the National Symphony Orchestra in Lima (1938).

BUKOFZER, MANFRED (1910–1955), musicologist. Born at Oldenburg, Germany, Bukofzer lectured at the Volkshochschule in Basle (1937–38). In 1941 he joined the faculty of the University of California at Berkeley, becoming chairman of the music department in 1954. His writings, which furnished important contributions to the study of music from the Middle Ages to the baroque, include *Geschichte des englischen Diskants und des Fauxbourdons* (1936), *Music of the Baroque Era* (1942), *Studies in Medieval and Renaissance Music* (1950), and an edition of the complete works of Dunstable (1954).

BURLE MARX, WALTER (1902–), conductor and composer. Born in São Paulo, he studied piano and conducting (with Weingartner) in Berlin from 1921 and toured in Europe until 1926, when he returned to Brazil. He formed the Philharmonic Orchestra of Rio de Janeiro in 1930, and in 1947 became director of the Rio Municipal Theater. His compositions include *Theme, Variations and Fugue* (1926), *Episodio Fantastico* (1939), and *Variações sobre o hino nacional* (1947).

***CACERES (Caseres), ABRAHAM** (18th century), composer.

CARLEBACH, SHLOMO (1926–), rabbi, composer, and singer. Born in Berlin, the son of Rabbi Hartwig Naphtali Carlebach, he went to the United States in 1939 and studied at Mesivta Tora Vo-da'ath, the Beth Midrash Gevoha of America, and Columbia University. In his songs he created a neo-ḥasidic style which blended elements of the traditional *niggun*, Israel song, and the American folk song style of the 1960s—from which he also took over the practice of singing with his own guitar accompaniment. His recordings and tours in the United States and Israel were popular both in religious and nonreligious circles. He established a "House of Love and Prayer" in California and in Jerusalem that attracted Jewish youth in the late 1960s and early 1970s.

***CASTELNUOVO-TEDESCO, MARIO** (1895–1968), composer.

CERVETTO, JACOB BASEVI (1682–1783), violoncellist and composer. Cervetto was born in Verona of a branch of the Basevi family which had as its crest the head of a stag *(cervo)*. He settled in London in 1728 or 1729 where he played in the orchestra at the Theatre Royal, Drury Lane, and later became its manager. He is credited with being the person who introduced the violoncello into England and was associated with the instrument by contemporary caricaturists. Cervetto composed several works for his instrument and chamber music. In his later years he had no connection with the Jewish community. His illegitimate son, James Cervetto (1746–1837), was also a popular cellist who composed various works.

CHAGY, BERELE (1892–1954), *ḥazzan* and composer; see *Ḥazzan.

CHASINS, ABRAHAM (1903–), pianist and writer on music. Born in New York, Chasins' romantically colored character piano pieces enjoyed considerable popularity. He wrote two piano concertos, which he performed with the Philadelphia Orchestra (1929, 1933). His *Three Chinese Pieces* for piano were played by Joseph *Lhévinne and Josef Hofmann; an orchestral version was conducted by Toscanini with the New York Philharmonic in 1931, the first work by an American composer to be included in a Toscanini program. In 1943 he joined the staff of radio station WQXR in New York as a consultant. He later became its musical director, and gave regular broadcasts of an educational nature. He published *Speaking of Pianists* (1958) and *The Appreciation of Music* (1966).

CHERNIAVSKY, family of Odessa musicians. JAN (1892–), a pianist, LEO (1890–), a violinist, and MICHAEL (1893–), a cellist, were a well-known trio. They began as infant prodigies in Russia, toured in Western Europe from 1904, went to South Africa (1908–09 and 1911), India, Australia, and New Zealand (1914), and made their New York debut in 1916. After separating, they appeared individually. Another brother, ALEXANDER (1896–), a pianist, formed a trio with his sister Marion and cousin Boris, and they toured South Africa in 1912. After World War I, he settled there as an impresario.

***CIVITA, DAVIT** (17th century), musician.

***COHEN, FRANCIS LYON** (1862–1934), rabbi and writer of Jewish liturgical music.

***COHEN, HARRIET** (1901–1967), pianist.

COLONNE, JULES EDOUARD (**Judah;** 1838–1910), conductor. Colonne studied at the Paris Conservatory, and became the leading violinist of the Paris Opera and in the Lamoureux Quartet. In 1873 he founded the Organisation du Concert National, which became the Concerts du Châtelet and finally the Concerts Colonne, which under his conductorship played an important role in fostering the performances of works by contemporary French and foreign composers. He was also the conductor of the official concerts at the Paris Exposition of 1878, and appeared as visiting conductor in Europe and New York.

CONRIED, HEINRICH ((**Cohn;** 1848–1909), impresario. Born in Austria, he reached the United States in 1878 after a career in Germany, and directed various theaters. As manager of the Metropolitan Opera (1903–08), he achieved spectacular successes by engaging such celebrities as Caruso, Chaliapin, and Scotti, and producing operas new to the American public. He presented the first production of Wagner's *Parsifal* in the U.S. in 1903, overcoming the objections of the Wagner family, and in 1907 produced Richard Strauss's *Salome*, which aroused protests on moral grounds. He returned to Europe in 1908.

CONSOLO, FEDERICO (1841–1906), violinist and composer. Born in Ancona, Italy, Consolo studied violin with Vieuxtemps and composition with Fétis and Liszt, but was forced to give up his career as a violin virtuoso in 1884 after a nerve injury. He then devoted himself to composition and musical research. His most important publication was his *Sefer Shirei Yisrael-Libro dei Canti d'Israele* (1892), an anthology of synagogue chants documenting the musical tradition of the Sephardi Jews of Italy. On the title page he called himself not only by his Italian name but also "Yehiel Nahmany Sefardi."

COOPER (Kuper), EMIL ALBERTOVICH (1877–1960), conductor. He studied violin with Hellmesberger in Vienna and composition with Taneyev in Moscow. After 1898 he conducted opera at Kiev, Moscow, and St. Petersburg, and between 1909 and 1914 conducted the Diaghilev troupe at its appearance in London and in the first Paris performance of Mussorgsky's *Khovanshchina* (1911). After the Russian Revolution he was director of the Petrograd Philharmonic Orchestra and the Mariinsky Opera Theater, and taught at the Petrograd Conservatory. In 1924 he left Russia, and worked mainly in the United States, conducting at the Chicago Civic Opera (1929) and at the Metropolitan Opera in New York (1944–50).

***COPLAND, AARON** (1900–), composer.

COWEN, SIR FREDERIC HYMEN (1852–1935), conductor and composer. Born in Jamaica, Cowen was taken to London as a child, and performed his own piano concerto there at the age of 13. He conducted the London Philharmonic Society, Halle Orchestra of Manchester, and many other orchestras. His works include four operas, four cantatas (including *The Veil*, 1910), six symphonies, orchestral and chamber works, cantatas, songs, and marches. He published an autobiography, *My Art and My Friends* (1913); a humoristic glossary of musical terms, *Music as She is Wrote* (1915); and biographies of several composers. He was knighted in 1911.

DAMARI, SHOSHANA (c. 1922–), singer. Taken to Palestine from Damar in Yemen as an infant, Damari became known in her late teens on the stage of the *Matate and Li-La-Lo theaters. Most of her songs were written by Moshe *Wilensky, in a ballad style displaying the particular character of her alto voice in the neo-Yemenite intonation which remained standard for Israel folk style singers until the end of the 1950s. From 1948 she often toured abroad, especially in the United States, and appeared in several early Israel films.

DAMROSCH, FRANK HEINO (1859–1957), conductor; see *Damrosch.

DAMROSCH, LEOPOLD (1832–1855), conductor and composer; see *Damrosch.

DAMROSCH, WALTER JOHANNES (1862–1950), conductor er; see *Damrosch.

***DA PONTE, LORENZO** (1749–1838), librettist.

DAVID, ERNEST (1825–1886), musicologist. David's works include an essay on Jewish music, *La Musique chez les Juifs* (1873). The first part deals with the instruments in the Bible, the second with the post-biblical music of the synagogue. With M. Lussy, he wrote *Histoire de la notation musicale depuis ses orgines* (1882) and published biographies of Bach (1882), Handel (1884), Mendelssohn, and Schumann (1886).

***DAVID, FERDINAND** (1810–1873), violinist and composer.

DAVID, SAMUEL (1836–1895), composer. David studied with *Halévy and obtained the Rome Prize for his cantata *Jephté* (1858). From 1872 until his death, he was musical director of the synagogues in Paris. Among his works are the operas *Absalon* and *I Macabei*, operettas, cantatas (*Le Génie de la terre*, 1859), symphonies, and synagogal works. For the synagogues of Paris, David published a collection of religious music entitled: *Po'al ḥayey adam: musique religieuse ancienne et moderne en usage dans les Temples consistoriaux israélites de Paris* (1895).

***DAVYDOV, KARL YULYEVICH** (1838–1889), cellist.

***DE PHILIPPE, EDIS** (1918–), singer and opera manager.

***DESSAU, PAUL** (1894–), composer.

***DEUTSCH, MORITZ** (1818–1892), *ḥazzan*, composer, and editor.

***DEUTSCH, OTTO ERICH** (1883–1967), musicologist.

***DIAMOND, DAVID** (1915–), composer.

DRESDEN, SEM (1881–1957), composer and teacher. Born in Amsterdam, Dresden studied there and with Pfitzner in Berlin. In 1914 he founded a choral ensemble which gave concerts of the works of the great Dutch composers and of Renaissance and modern works. He was director of the Amsterdam Conservatory (1924–37) and of the Royal Conservatory at The Hague (1937–40; 1945–49), and for a number of years president of the Society of Dutch Composers and of the Dutch section of the International Society of Contemporary Music. His compositions include *Chorus Tragicus* for choir, wind instruments, and percussion (1928, after Vondel's *Hierusalem verwoest*); Psalm 84 for choir "based on an old Hebrew prayer"; concertos for various instruments; orchestral and chamber works; and an opera, *Toto* (1945). He also wrote and edited books on music history and theory.

***DUKAS, PAUL** (1865–1935), composer.

***DUNAYEVSKI, ISAAC OSIPOVICH** (1900–1955), composer.

DUQUE, SIMON DAVID (1897–), *ḥazzan;* see **Ḥazzan.*

DYLAN, BOB (Robert Zimmerman; 1941–), singer. Born in Duluth, Minnesota, Dylan traveled throughout the country and went to New York in 1961 where he sang in the coffeehouses of Greenwich Village. He began composing shortly afterward, and immediately became a prominent figure in the folk music revival of the period and the protest song movement which arose shortly afterward. In 1965 he combined the American folk idiom with the best of rock-'n-roll, to produce "folk rock."

EBERST, ISAAC BEN JUDAH, see *Offenbach, Isaac b. Judah.

EDEL, YIẒHAK (1896–), composer and teacher. He was born in Warsaw and from 1924 to 1927 he taught music in the orphanage of Janusz *Korczak, in Warsaw. In 1929 he emigrated to Palestine where he worked as a music teacher in teachers' colleges. His works include orchestral and piano music, quartets for strings and wind instruments, songs, and cantatas. His musical style shows the influence of Eastern European Jewish tradition.

EHRLICH, ABEL (1919–), composer and teacher. Born in Crantz, Germany, Ehrlich went to Palestine in 1939. He taught theory and composition at the Oranim Teachers College and at the Rubin Academy of Music in Tel Aviv. His works, written in an uncompromising modern idiom, include chamber and choral music, and a number of comic "miniature operas." In his *Bashrav* for violin solo (1953) and *Symphonic Bashrav* for orchestra (1958), he explored the fusion of Near Eastern and Western musical elements.

EHRLICH, HERMANN (Zvi; 1815–1879), *ḥazzan*, composer, and editor; see **Ḥazzan.*

***EINSTEIN, ALFRED** (1880–1952), musicologist.

***EISLER, HANNS** (1898–1962), composer.

ELLSTEIN, ABRAHAM (Abe; 1907–1963), composer, conductor, and pianist. Born in New York, Ellstein studied with Frederick *Jacobi, Rubin *Goldmark, and Albert Stoessel, and became the accompanist for Mischa Mischakoff, Michel Piastro, Isa Kramer, and Jossele *Rosenblatt. At the age of 19 he wrote the first of his 33 scores for the Yiddish musical theater. He also wrote the scores for several Yiddish films produced in Warsaw before World War II and composed over 500 Yiddish songs. In 1957 he turned to composing works for concert, stage, and the synagogue. Among his compositions are: *Ode to the King of Kings*, a cantata in celebration of the tenth anniversary of the State of Israel; *The Thief and the Hangman*, a one-act opera; *Hora Fantasy*, for piano; *Haftorah*, for violin and string orchestra; *Negev Concerto*, for piano and orchestra; two *Sabbath Eve Services; Passover Service; The Redemption*, a Hanukkah *Oratorio* for chorus, organ, and percussion; and an opera, *The Golem* (1962).

***ELMAN, MISCHA** (1891–1967), violinist.

EMSHEIMER, ERNST (1904–), musicologist. Born in Frankfort, Germany, Emsheimer was research assistant at the Russian Academy of Sciences in Leningrad from 1932 until 1937. He accompanied a music research expedition in north Caucasia in 1936, and in 1937 joined a scientific expedition to the northwestern provinces of China. In 1949 he became curator of the Museum of Music History in Stockholm. His writings include *Musikethnographische Bibliographie der nichtslavischen Voelker in Russland* (1943); *Preliminary Remarks on Mongolian Music and Instruments* (1943); *Music of Eastern Mongolia* (1943); and *Lappischer Kultgesang* (1950). His main fields of research are the music of the northern Mongol peoples and the study of musical instruments.

***ENGEL, JOEL (Julius;** 1868–1927), composer and critic.

EPHROS, GERSHON (1890–), *ḥazzan*, editor, and composer; see **Ḥazzan.*

ERLANGER, CAMILLE (1863–1919), composer. Born in Paris of an Alsatian family, Erlanger studied at the conservatory there with Delibes and Massenet, and received the Rome Prize in 1888 for his cantata *Velléda*. He wrote nine operas—*Le Juif Polonais* (1900), based on the story by Erckman-Chatrian, remained for a long time in the operatic repertoire. He also wrote the symphonic poem *Maître et Serviteur*, based on Tolstoy's story, which remained in manuscript; *La Chasse fantastique* (1893); and many songs.

EULENBURG, ERNST (1847–1926), music publisher. The Musikverlag Eulenburg, founded by him in Leipzig in 1874, at first published mainly educational literature, but was gradually extended to include scores and especially miniature scores of orchestral and chamber music. His son KURT (b. 1879) transferred the firm to London in 1939. He enlarged the number of miniature scores and also increased the output of modern music. In 1957 the shares of the Eulenburg Edition were taken over by Schott of London.

FALL, LEO (1873–1925), composer. Born in Olomouc, Moravia, Fall, the son of a military bandmaster, was educated at the Vienna Conservatory and served as a theater conductor. His first three successful operettas, *Der fidele Bauer* (1907), *Die Dollarprinzessin* (1907), and *Die geschiedene Frau* (1908), placed him among the masters of the "second period of the operetta," with Franz Lehar and Oscar *Straus. His most popular works were *Die Rose von*

Stambul (1916) and *Madame Pompadour* (1922). Fall's music was distinguished for its charm of melody and clever orchestration.

FANO, GUIDO ALBERTO (1875–1961), composer and writer on music. Fano taught piano at the Liceo Musicale in Bologna, and became director of the conservatory in Parma (1905–11). He then taught in Naples, Palermo, and Milan. He composed an opera, *Iuturna* (1903), chamber music, piano music, and songs. Among his writings was *Le Studio del Pianoforte* (3 vols., 1923–24).

FEINBERG, SAMUEL YEVGENYEVICH (1890–1962), composer. Born in Odessa, Feinberg was appointed professor of piano at the Moscow Conservatory, and director of the piano faculty from 1936 until his death. His music was modernist and influenced by Scriabine, although it frequently contained folklore elements. Among his compositions were three piano concertos: 1931, 1944 (awarded the Stalin Prize), and 1947; 12 piano sonatas; and a sonata for violin and piano. He wrote: *Sudba muzykalnoy formy* ("The Future Musical Form," 1968) and *Pianizm kak iskusstvo* ("The Art of Piano Playing," 1968).

FEINSINGER, JOSHUA (**Shaye**; 1839–1872), *ḥazzan;* see **Ḥazzan.*

FELDMAN, GRIGORY PETROVICH (1910–1963), composer and pianist. Born in Kremenchug, Feldman studied composition under N. Miaskovsky in Moscow. His interest in Caucasian music took him to Makhachkala, the capital of the Dagestan A.S.S.R., where he taught composition (1948–49). His works include ten Jewish songs for voice and piano (1940), cello and piano concertos, symphonic works, and chamber music.

FEUERMANN, EMANUEL (1902–1942), cellist. Born in Kolomea, Galicia, and taken to Vienna at the age of seven, Feuermann gave his first public recitals in 1913. He was a teacher at Cologne Conservatory from 1918 until 1923 and became well known as a soloist. He was on the staff of the Berlin Hochschule fuer Musik (1929–33), but emigrated to the United States in 1938. There he performed as a soloist and made notable appearances in trios with Jascha *Heifetz and Artur *Rubinstein, and was acclaimed as one of the great cellists of his time.

FIEDLER, ARTHUR (1894–), conductor. Fiedler was born in Boston, where his father was a violinist with the Boston Symphony Orchestra. There had been violinists or "fiedlers" in the family for three generations. In 1925 he founded the Boston Sinfonietta, an orchestra of 22 players, and in 1930 he became permanent conductor of the Boston Pops Orchestra, renowned for its concerts of light symphonic music.

FITELBERG, GRZEGORZ (**Gregor**; 1879–1953), conductor and composer. Born in Dvinsk, Latvia, Fitelberg became conductor of the Warsaw Philharmonic Orchestra (1906–11), the Vienna Opera (1912–13), and, between 1914 and 1920, the Petrograd Musikalnya Drama Orchestra, the Moscow Bolshoi, and Diaghilev Ballet orchestras. He then returned to the Warsaw Philharmonic and formed the Polish radio's symphony orchestra. He spent World War II mainly in the U.S., and returned to the same orchestra, which he conducted until his death. Fitelberg's compositions include two symphonies (1905 and 1907), two overtures (1905 and 1906), and two orchestral rhapsodies. His son, JERZY FITELBERG (1903–1951), also a composer, was born in Warsaw and died in New York. He wrote mainly chamber and orchestral music in a neoclassical style, sometimes using Polish folk idioms.

FLESCH, CARL (1873–1944), violinist and teacher. Born in Moson, Hungary, Flesch studied in Vienna and Paris and made his debut in Vienna in 1895. After teaching at the conservatories of Bucharest (1897–1902) and Amsterdam (1903–08), he settled in Berlin, where his renown as a violin pedagogue came to equal his status as a virtuoso. From 1924 to 1928 he taught at the Curtis Institute in Philadelphia, and in 1933 left Germany, ultimately settling in Lucerne, Switzerland. He wrote the pedagogical works *Urstudien* (1910) and *Die Kunst des Violinspiels* (2 vols., 1923, 1928; Eng. trans. 1930 as well as translations into many other languages), and edited Kreutzer's and Paganini's études, the major violin concertos, and Mozart's violin sonatas (with Arthur *Schnabel). His memoirs were published posthumously by his son Carl Flesch, Jr. (Eng., 1957; Ger., 1960).

***FOSS (Fuchs), LUKAS** (1932–), composer, pianist, and conductor.

FRANKENBURGER, PAUL SHAUL, see *Ben-Haim, Paul Shaul.

FREED, ISADORE (1900–1960), composer. Born in Brest-Litovsk, Russia, Freed was taken to the United States as an infant. He studied with Ernest *Bloch in the U.S. and with Vincent d'Indy in Paris. Returning to the United States in 1934 he engaged in teaching, and was chairman of the music department of the Hart College of Music in Hartford, Connecticut, from 1944 until his death. He wrote two symphonies, violin and cello concertos, and an opera *The Princess and the Vagabond* (1948), chamber music, and choral works. His works were of a moderately modernistic idiom, with some use of American folk themes, as in his *Appalachian Symphonic Sketches* (1946). His synagogal compositions include *Sabbath Morning Service* (1950), *Ḥasidic Service* (1954), Psalm settings, and a selection from Salamon de *Rossi's *Ha-shirim asher li-Shelomo* arranged as a service for cantor, chorus, and organ (1954).

FRIEDE, SHALOM (1783–1854), *ḥazzan;* see **Ḥazzan.*

FRIEDLAENDER, MAX (1852–1934), musicologist. Born in Brieg, Silesia, Friedlaender became a noted bass singer, but after 1883 devoted himself to musicology. He accepted a teaching post at Berlin University in 1894 where he became professor. Friedlaender was an authority on German song. He discovered more than 100 lost songs by Schubert and published them in his complete edition of Schubert's songs. He also edited songs by Mozart, Beethoven, and Mendelssohn, and collections of German folk songs. His writings include the basic *Das deutsche Lied im 18. Jahrhundert* (3 vols., 1902) and *Franz Schubert: Skizze seines Lebens und Wirkens* (1928).

FRIEDMANN, ARON (1855–1936), *ḥazzan,* writer, and editor; see **Ḥazzan.*

***FRIEDMANN, MORITZ** (1823–1891), *ḥazzan* and editor.

FROMM, HERBERT (1905–), composer. Born in Kitzingen on the Main, Bavaria, Fromm studied at the Academy of Music in Munich with Paul Hindemith. After working as a theater conductor he went to the United States in 1937, became organist and director of music at Temple Beth Zion, Buffalo, and from 1941 onward at Temple Israel in Boston. His synagogue compositions include *Adath Israel,* a service for Friday evening (1952); *Song of Miriam,* for women's choir, organ, or piano (1945); *Six Madrigals* (1951), for Sabbath and festivals; *Avodat Shabbat* (1960); *Psalm Cantata,* for mixed voices, organ, trumpet, viola, flute, and timpani (1963); *Ḥemdat Yamin,* a service for Sabbath morning (1964); *Chamber Cantata* (text by Judah Halevi), for mixed voices and eight instruments (1966); *Ḥag ha-Matzot,* suite on Passover melodies for harpsichord, flute, and cello (1967); and numerous anthems and organ compositions.

GABRIELOVITCH, OSIP SOLOMONOVICH (1878–1936), pianist and conductor. Born in St. Petersburg, Gabrielovitch studied there with Anton *Rubinstein, Liadov, and Glazunov, and later with Leschetizky in Vienna. After 1896 he toured Europe and the United States as an internationally renowned concert pianist and conductor. In 1918 he was appointed conductor of the Detroit Symphony Orchestra. Ten years later he became, additionally, joint conductor of the Philadelphia Orchestra with Leopold Stokowski. He was also known for his series of historical concerts illustrating the development of keyboard music from Bach to his own day. He married the contralto Clara Clemens, the daughter of Mark Twain.

***GEBIRTIG, MORDECAI** (1877–1942), Yiddish bard and poet.

GEDALGE, ANDRÉ (1856–1926), music theorist, teacher, and composer. Born in Paris, Gedalge was professor of counterpoint and fugue at the Paris Conservatory. He became famous as a teacher, and his *Traité de la Fugue* (1901) is still considered one of the best books on the subject. He also wrote two volumes on ear training (1921–23). Gedalge composed symphonies, chamber music, and an opéra bouffe, *Pris au piège* (1895), but his main contribution to French music was through the influence which he exerted on composers such as Ravel, Milhaud, and Honegger, who were his pupils.

GEIRINGER, KARL (1899–), musicologist. Born in Vienna, Geiringer studied with Guido *Adler and Curt *Sachs, and in 1930 became custodian of the museum and library of the Gesellschaft der Musikfreunde, Vienna. In 1938 he went to London, and in 1941 was appointed professor of the history and theory of music at Boston University. Geiringer's writings include important monographs: *Musical Instruments: Their History in Western Culture,* (1943); *Haydn: a Creative Life in Music* (1946); *Brahms: his Life and Work* (1936); *The Bach Family* (1954); and *Johann Sebastian Bach: The Culmination of an Era* (1966).

GELBRUN, ARTUR (1913–), composer and conductor. Born in

Warsaw and educated in his native city and in Italy, Gelbrun settled in Israel in 1949 and became a teacher at the Rubin Academy of Music, Tel Aviv. His compositions include two symphonies, chamber music, ballets, orchestral suites, and songs with orchestra. He appeared as guest conductor of orchestras in Israel and Europe.

***GERNSHEIM, FRIEDRICH** (1839–1916), composer.

***GEROVITCH, ELIEZER** (1844–1913), *ḥazzan* and composer.

***GERSHWIN, GEORGE** (1898–1937), composer.

***GERSON-KIWI, EDITH (Esther;** 1908–), musicologist.

GESHURI, MEIR SHIMON (1897–), writer on music. Born in Myslowitz, Silesia, Geshuri went to Ereẓ Israel in 1920. He was active in the founding of the Ha-Po'el ha-Mizraḥi, but his main interest was research into Jewish music, particularly ḥasidic song. He was one of the founders of the Israel Institute for Sacred Music (1958). Geshuri was the author of numerous articles and published his main researches in *Ha-Niggun ve-ha-Rikkud ba-Ḥasidut* (3 vols., 1956–59). A bibliography of his writings was edited by B. M. Cohen in 1966.

***GILELS, EMIL GRIGOYEVICH** (1916–), pianist.

***GIOVANNI MARIA** (c. 1470–1530), lute player.

***GLANZ, LEIB** (1898–1964), *ḥazzan* and composer.

***GLIÈRE, REINHOLD MORITZEVICH** (1874–1956), composer and conductor.

***GLUCK, ALMA (Reba Fiersohn;** 1884–1938), singer.

***GNESIN, MIKHAIL FABIANOVICH** (1883–1957), composer and teacher.

***GODOWSKY, LEOPOLD** (1870–1938), pianist.

***GOLDFADEN, ABRAHAM** (1840–1908), playwright and composer.

***GOLDMAN, EDWARD FRANKO** (1878–1950), U.S. bandmaster.

***GOLDMARK, KARL** (1830–1915), composer.

GOLDMARK, RUBIN (1872–1936), U.S. musician; see *Goldmark.

GOLDSCHMIDT, HUGO (1859–1920), musicologist. Born in Breslau, Goldschmidt was co-director of the Scharwenka-Klindworth Conservatory in Berlin and subsequently professor at this conservatory until he retired because of ill health. Goldschmidt was an authority on the art of singing and on early operatic history. His writings include *Die italienische Gesangsmethode des 17. Jahrhunderts* (1890), *Handbuch der deutschen Gesangspaedagogik* (1896), *Die Musikaesthetik des 18. Jahrhunderts und ihre Beziehungen zu seinem Kunstschaffen* (1915), and *Studien zur Geschichte der italienischen Oper im 17. Jahrhundert* (2 vols., 1901–04) which has remained a basic reference work.

***GOLDSTEIN, JOSEF** (1837–1899), *ḥazzan*.

***GOLINKIN, MORDECAI** (1875–1963), opera conductor and manager.

***GOODMAN, BENNY (Benjamin David;** 1909–), clarinetist and bandleader.

GOROCHOV, YEDIDYAH, see *Admon, Yedidyah.

GOULD, MORTON (1913–), composer, conductor, pianist. Born in Richmond Hill, New York, Gould was a precocious pianist and composer. He studied at the Institute of Musical Art and worked as a pianist, arranger, and conductor with various radio orchestras and at Radio City Music Hall in New York. Later he also appeared as guest conductor with many of the major U.S. orchestras. As a composer, Gould moved freely between the domains of light and serious music, often using American folk and popular idioms, and in many works adapting jazz resources to classical forms. The following is a selection of Gould's works with the dates of their premieres: *Three American Symphonettes*, for orchestra (1933, 1935, 1937; the *Pavane* from the second symphonette became a popular light concert piece); *Spirituals*, for orchestra (1941, also played often) *Chorale and Fugue in Jazz*, for two pianos and orchestra (1936); *Latin American Symphonette*, for orchestra (1941); *Billion Dollar Baby*, a musical comedy (1945); *Lincoln Legend*, for orchestra (1942); *Interplay* (1945) and *Fall River Legend* (1948), ballets; *Of Time and the River*, for unaccompanied chorus (1946); *Concerto for Tap Dancer and Orchestra* (1952); Viola Concerto (1944); and three symphonies.

GRADENWITZ, PETER EMANUEL (1910–), musicologist and publisher. Born in Berlin, Gradenwitz settled in Palestine in 1936. He founded Israeli Music Publications, the first music publishing venture in Israel to achieve international standards and the first to publish larger works of Israel composers. Among his writings are: *Johann Stamitz* (Ger., 1936); *Toledot ha-Musikah* (1939); *Olam ha-Simfonyah* (1945, 1959[8]); *Ha-Musikah ha-Kamerit* (1948, 1953[2]); *Ha-Musikah be-Yisrael* (1949), also translated into English, German and Spanish; *Music and Musicians in Israel* (1952; rev. ed., 1959); *Olam ha-Pesanteran* (1952); and *Wege zur Musik der Gegenwart* (1963). In 1954 he organized in Haifa the first Annual Music Festival of the International Society for Contemporary Music to be held outside Europe or the United States.

GREENBERG, NOAH (1919–1966), conductor and musicologist. Born in New York, Greenberg organized the Pro Musica Antiqua group (1952) which became known for its performances of medieval liturgical music dramas, and was in effect the first U.S. "Collegium Musicum" ensemble to achieve an international reputation. He took the group to Europe in 1960 and 1963, and recorded many of its performances, including the first recording of a selection of the sacred and secular works of Salamon de *Rossi in musicologically valid versions. He also made arrangements of vocal works of the Renaissance period. The New York Pro Musica Antiqua continued its activities after his death.

***GRUENBERG, LOUIS** (1884–1964), composer.

***GUSIKOW, JOSEPH MICHAEL** (1802–1837), musician.

HAENDEL, IDA (1924–), violinist. Ida Haendel, who was born in Chelm, Poland, studied as a child prodigy with Carl *Flesch and Georges Enesco, and made her debut in London at the age of 13. She began her international concert career after World War II and came to be regarded as one of the leading soloists of her generation. In 1970 she published her autobiography, *Woman with Violin*.

HAHN, REYNALDO (1875–1947), composer and conductor. Born in Caracas, Venezuela, Hahn studied under Massenet at the Paris Conservatory. He wrote several light operas and songs which recall Massenet's melodic charm. His compositions include eight operas and light operas, incidental music to plays, pantomimes, ballets (notably *Le Dieu bleu* (1912) for the Diaghilev Ballet), two symphonic poems, chamber music, songs, an oratorio *La Reine de Sheba* (1926), and a Christmas mystery *Pastorale de Noël* (1908). From 1935 Hahn was music critic of *Le Figaro*. In 1945 he was appointed director of the Paris Opera. His book of recollections, *Thèmes variés*, appeared in 1946.

***HALÉVY, JACQUES (François) FROMENTAL ÉLIE** (1799–1862), composer.

HALEVY, LUDOVIC (1833–1908), librettist; see *Halévy.

HAMBOURG, MARK (1879–1960), pianist. Born in Russia, he settled in England in 1894 and was acclaimed as a dynamic player with a superb finger technique. He gained a world reputation.

HAMMERSTEIN, OSCAR I (1847–1919), opera manager; see *Hammerstein.

HAMMERSTEIN, OSCAR II (1895–1960), librettist; see *Hammerstein.

HASKIL, CLARA (1895–1960), pianist. Born in Bucharest, Clara Haskil studied with Cortot in Paris, where she lived from 1927 until 1940. In 1949 she acquired Swiss nationality. Her technique and capacity for poetic expression won her a great reputation. She made numerous appearances with Ysaÿe, Enesco, Casals, and Grumiaux. A Clara Haskil Prize was established at the International Music Festival in Lucerne.

HAST, MARCUS (Mordechai; 1840–1911), *ḥazzan*, editor, and composer; see **Ḥazzan*.

HAUBENSTOCK-RAMATI, ROMAN (1919–), composer. Haubenstock-Ramati was born in Cracow, where he worked as a radio conductor from 1947 until 1950. He then spent some years in Israel, heading the Central Music Library, Tel Aviv, and teaching composition at the Rubin Academy of Music there. In 1957 he settled in Vienna. Haubenstock-Ramati's compositions, orchestral and electronic, include *Blessings* (1952) for voice and nine players, and an opera *Amerika* (1962–64), based on a novel by *Kafka.

HAUSER, EMIL (1893–), violinist and teacher. Born in Budapest, Hauser became a teacher at the Hoch Conservatory, Frankfort, in 1913, and joined the Adolph Busch Quartet. In 1917 he formed the Budapest String Quartet, in which he played first violin, until emigrating to Palestine in 1932. He founded the Palestine Music Conservatory, Jerusalem, in 1933. Hauser headed the chamber music class at the Juilliard School of Music, New York, from 1947 until 1959 and Pablo Casals' master courses in Zermatt, Switzerland, for four years. His *Interpretation of Music for Ensemble* was published in 1952.

***HEIFETZ, JASCHA** (1901–), violinist.

***HELLER, STEPHEN** (1813–1888), pianist and composer.

HENDEL, NEHAMA (**Helena**; 1935–), Israel folk singer. Born in Tel Aviv, Nehama Hendel first became known when she was a member of the Baẓal Yarok troupe in the 1950s. She later formed one of the first Israel folk style duos with Ran Eliran ("Ran and Nama"), and later continued her career independently. She was the first Israel singer to evolve a soprano folk style intonation, breaking a convention established by the "Yemenite altos" such as Bracha *Zefirah and Shoshana *Damari.

***HENLE, MORITZ** (1850–1925), *ḥazzan.*

HENSCHEL, SIR GEORGE (**Isidor Georg**; 1850–1934), conductor, singer, and teacher. He was born in Breslau and was active until shortly before his death as a conductor and singer. He was successively during his career a tenor, baritone, basso, and basso profundo. Henschel was the first conductor of the Boston Symphony Orchestra (1881–84), founded the London Symphony Concerts (1886–97), conducted the Scottish Symphony Orchestra (1893–95), and taught singing at the Royal College of Music and the Institute of Musical Art in New York. He composed an opera, a requiem mass, and songs, and wrote *Personal Recollections of Johannes Brahms* (1907) and the autobiography *Musings and Memories of a Musician* (1918). He converted to Christianity in his youth. He was knighted in 1914.

***HERSCHMAN, MORDECHAI** (1888–1940), *ḥazzan.*

HERTZKA, EMIL (1869–1932), music publisher, born in Budapest. In 1901 he joined the newly founded Universal Edition in Vienna which he directed from 1907 until his death. By purchasing the rights of several older firms and actively encouraging the avant-garde composers—on whom few other publishers dared risk their resources and reputation—he became the publisher of the works of Bruckner, Mahler, and the publisher and champion of Béla Bartok, Arnold Schoenberg, Alban Berg, Kurt Weill, Jaromir Weinberger, Leos Janaček, Ernst Krenek, and others. He also founded the periodical *Musikblaetter des Anbruch.*

***HERZ, HENRI** (**Heinrich**; 1802–1883), pianist and composer.

HERZOG, GEORGE (1901–), musicologist. Born in Budapest, Herzog held academic posts at Columbia, Yale, Chicago, and Indiana universities from 1929. His main fields of research were American Indian music and the comparative study of primitive music cultures. He also recorded Yemenite and Babylonian Jewish musical traditions from among the immigrants in New York (1939–41). His writings include *Research in Primitive and Folk Music in the U.S.* (1936) and contributions to leading encyclopedias.

***HESS, DAME MYRA** (1890–1965), pianist.

***HILLER, FERDINAND** (1811–1855), composer and conductor.

HINRICHSEN, family of music publishers. In 1900 Heinrich (1868–1942) became owner of the C. F. Peters music publishing firm of Leipzig, Germany. Under his direction it developed a personal association with such famous composers as Grieg, *Mahler, *Schoenberg, Richard Strauss, and Hugo Wolf. In 1937 Heinrich's son Max (1901–) settled in London, where he established Hinrichsen Edition, Ltd. After 1949, Max and his brother Walter (1907–1969), who had emigrated to the U.S., also published under the Peters imprint.

***HORNBOSTEL, ERICH MORITZ VON** (1877–1935), musicologist.

***HOROWITZ, VLADIMIR** (1904–), pianist.

***HUBERMAN, BRONISLAW** (1882–1947), pianist.

***IDELSOHN, ABRAHAM ZVI** (1882–1938), musicologist.

JACOBI, FREDERICK (1891–1952), composer. Born in San Francisco, Jacobi studied with Rubin *Goldmark, Rafael Joseffy, Paul Juon, and Ernest *Bloch. From 1913 to 1917 he was assistant conductor at the Metropolitan Opera in New York and later taught at the Juilliard School of Music. Jacobi first attracted attention as a composer with a quartet on American Indian themes (1923). Many of his later works were on Jewish subjects or for synagogue use. *Sabbath Evening Service* (1930–31); *Six Pieces for Organ,* for use in the synagogue (1933); arrangements of Palestinian folk songs (1939–40); *Hymn* to words of Saadiah Gaon, for male choir; *Two Pieces in Sabbath Mood,* for orchestra (1946); *Ashrei ha-Ish*—arrangements of the song by Mordechai *Zeira, for mixed chorus and string orchestra (1949); and *Three Preludes,* for organ (1949).

JACOBI, GEORG (1840–1906), violinist and conductor. Born in Berlin, Jacobi worked as a violinist and conductor in Paris. In 1871 he was appointed leader of the orchestra at the Alhambra Theatre, London, where he remained for 26 years. During this period he composed or arranged the music for over 100 ballets, among them *Yolande* (1877), *The Golden Wreath,* and *Beauty and the Beast* (1898).

JACOBSTHAL, GUSTAV (1845–1912), music historian. Born in Pyritz, Pomerania, Jacobsthal was a professor at the University of Strasbourg from 1875 to 1905. He was a pioneer in the application of historical and philological research in the study of early medieval music. His chief writings are *Die Mensuralnotenschrift des 12. und 13. Jahrhunderts* (1871) and *Die chromatische Alteration im liturgischen Gesange der abendlaendischen Kirche* (1897).

JADASSOHN, SALOMON (1831–1902), music theorist. Born in Breslau, Jadassohn studied under Liszt and became a noted teacher and conductor in Leipzig. He is chiefly remembered as an exponent of orthodox musical theory. His books include *Harmonielehre* (1883, 1903[7]); *Kontrapunkt* (1884); *Kanon und Fuge* (1884); and *Die Formen in den Werken der Tonkunst* (1889). He was also a prolific composer.

JADLOWKER, HERMANN (1878–1953), tenor. Born in Riga, Jadlowker began his operatic career in Cologne in 1889. Invited to Berlin in 1901, he sang at the Berlin State Opera for five years, and in 1910 made his U.S. debut at the Metropolitan Opera, New York. Among his important roles were the Prince in the world premiere of Engelbert Humperdinck's *Koenigskinder* (1910), and Florindo in Ermanno Wolf-Ferrari's *Le Donne curiose* in its first U.S. performance in 1912. He returned to Berlin in 1913, was cantor in Riga from1929 to 1938, and then settled in Tel Aviv as a voice teacher.

JAMES, HARRY (1916–), trumpet player and band leader. Born in Albany, Georgia, James trained with his father, a circus band leader, and had his own orchestra at the age of 20. After two years with Benny *Goodman's band he started his own group, concentrating on the brass section and featuring his brilliant trumpet solos. Outstanding among his popular swing arrangements and compositions in the 1940s were *Carnival of Venice, Chiribiribin, Flight of the Bumble-Bee, Two o'Clock Jump,* and *Trumpet Rhapsody.* He married the film star Betty Grable.

***JAPHET, ISRAEL MEYER** (1818–1892), choir director and composer.

***JASSINOWSKY, PINCHAS** (1886–1954), *ḥazzan* and composer.

***JOACHIM, JOSEPH** (1831–1907), violinist.

JONAS, EMILE (1827–1905), composer. Jonas was professor of solfège at the Paris Conservatory from 1847 until 1865. His light operas, in the style of *Offenbach, enjoyed success abroad as well as in France. He was music director at the Portuguese synagogue in Paris, for which he wrote two collections of songs, *Shirot Yisrael* (1854) and *Shirei Yisrael* (1886).

***JUDAH BEN ISAAC** (14th or 15th century), music theorist.

KAHN, ERICH ITOR (1905–1956), composer and pianist. Born in Germany, Kahn spent some time in France and then settled in the United States. He was a distinguished performer of chamber music. As a composer, he was influenced by the *Schoenberg school, and made frequent use of ḥasidic material. Among his important compositions are: *Three Madrigals for Mixed Choir* (1956), *Rhapsodie Hassidique,* for mixed chorus (1938); *Ciaccona dei tempi di guerra,* for piano (1943); *Nenia Judaeis Qui Hac Aetate Perierunt,* for cello and piano (1943); and *Actus Tragicus* for ten solo instruments (1946). He died after a road accident.

KAISER, ALOIS (1840–1907), *ḥazzan;* see *Ḥazzan.*

***KALMAN, EMMERICH** (**Imre**; 1882–1953), composer.

KAMINSKI, JOSEPH, see *Kaminski.

***KARACZEWSKI, HANINA** (1877–1926), teacher and composer.

KAREL, RUDOLPH (1880–1945), composer. Born in Pilsen, Czechoslovakia, Karel was the last pupil of Dvorak. He taught for a time in Russia, and returned to Prague in 1920, where he taught at the Prague Conservatory from 1923 to 1941. In 1943 he was arrested and died at the *Theresienstadt concentration camp. His compositions include stage works, four symphonies, and chamber music.

KARLINER, BARUCH (c. 1810–1871 or 1879), *ḥazzan;* see **Ḥazzan.*

***KARNIOL, ALTER YEHIEL** (1855–1929), *ḥazzan.*

KASHTAN, SOLOMON, see *Weintraub, Solomon.

KATZ, MINDRU (1925–), concert pianist. Born in Bucharest, Katz made his debut with the Bucharest Philharmonic Orchestra, won prizes at international competitions, and went on concert tours in Eastern and Western Europe, Africa, and Australia. He settled in Israel in 1959.

KATZ, SHALOM (1919–), *ḥazzan;* see **Ḥazzan.*
***KERN, JEROME DAVID** (1885–1945), composer.
***KESTENBERG, LEO** (1882–1962), music educator.
KHERSONER, WOLF, see Shestapol, Wolf, below.
KINSKY, GEORG LUDWIG (1882–1951), musicologist. Born in Marienwerder, Kinsky, who was entirely self-taught in musicology, became curator and director of the Heyer Museum of Musical History in Cologne (1909–26) and lecturer at the University of Cologne (1921–32), where he obtained his doctorate in 1925. After 1933 he was able for some time to pursue his research privately and to lecture in the *Kulturbund, but in 1942 he was deported and worked as a slave laborer until 1945. His last years were spent in near destitution in Berlin. In his fields of research—music bibliography and the study of musical instruments—Kinsky made several major contributions to modern musicology. He prepared a bibliographical index to Beethoven's works, *Das Werk Beethovens* (completed by A. Halm and published 1955). His other publications include *Geschichte der Musik in Bildern* (1929, and several subsequent editions in German and English), an unfinished series of catalogs of the Heyer collection, and about 150 studies in periodicals.
KIPNIS, ALEXANDER (1891–), bass-baritone. Born in Zhitomir, Kipnis began his career in Germany, and was a member of the Berlin State Opera until the Nazis came to power. He performed at Bayreuth and Salzburg, at Covent Garden and Glyndebourne in England, and at the Metropolitan Opera, New York. A singer of great range and flexibility, he excelled in lieder as well as in opera and oratorio. His son Igor (1930–) was a well-known harpsichord player.
***KIPNIS, MENACHEM** (1878–1942), singer and music collector.
***KIRSCHNER, EMANUEL** (1857–1938), *ḥazzan* and composer.
***KLEMPERER, OTTO** (1885–), conductor.
KLETZKI, PAUL (1900–), conductor. Born in Lodz, Poland, Kletzki was a violinist in the Lodz Philharmonic Orchestra, took up conducting in Berlin, and in 1931 was invited by Wilhelm Furtwaengler to conduct the Berlin Philharmonic Orchestra. Compelled to leave Germany in 1933, he settled in Switzerland. After World War II, he conducted in various countries, shared the Israel Philharmonic Orchestra's 1955 European tour with Paul Paray, and in 1958 was appointed conductor of the Dallas Symphony Orchestra in Texas. He excelled in romantic music, but also promoted contemporary works.
***KOGAN, LEONID BORISSOVICH** (1924–), violinist.
***KOHN, MAIER** (1802–1875), *ḥazzan.*
KOLISCH, RUDOLF (1896–), violinist. Born in Klamm, Austria, Kolisch studied at Vienna with Otakar Ševčik (violin) and Arnold *Schoenberg (composition), and in 1922 founded the Kolisch String Quartet, which existed until 1939 and was the first such group to perform from memory. He promoted the works of modern composers, particularly those of Schoenberg and his circle. Kolisch emigrated to the United States in 1940 and in 1942 became the leader of the Pro Arte Quartet. He was one of the few left-handed concert violinists. His sister Gertrud was Schoenberg's second wife.
***KORNGOLD, ERICH WOLFGANG** (1897–1957), composer.
***KORNITZER, LEON** (1875–1947), *ḥazzan,* choral director, and editor.
KOSTELANETZ, ANDRÉ (1901–), conductor, pianist, and composer. Born in St. Petersburg, Russia, Kostelanetz gave his first piano recital at the age of five. In 1920 he became assistant conductor and choirmaster of the Petrograd Grand Opera. He left Russia for the United States in 1922, and served as an operatic coach and accompanist. Later, Kostelanetz entered commercial broadcasting, and from 1931 became renowned for his arrangements of light classical and popular compositions, performed by his own orchestra. He married the soprano Lily Pons.
***KOUSSEVITZKY, MOSHE** (1899–1966), *ḥazzan.*
***KOUSSEVITSKY, SERGE (Sergei Alexandrovich;** (1874–1951), conductor.
***KREIN, ALEXANDER ABRAMOVICH** (1883–1951), composer.
KREIN, GRIGORI (1880–1955), composer; see *Klein, Alexander.
KREIN, JULIAN (1913–), composer; son of Grigori.
KRIPS, JOSEF (1902–), conductor. Born in Vienna, Krips conducted at the Vienna State Opera, 1933–38, and from 1945. He conducted at the Salzburg Festival, and in various European countries. A visit to England in 1947 to conduct Mozart operas at Covent Garden led to his appointment as chief conductor of the London Symphony Orchestra in 1950. Later he moved to the United States.
KROSHNER, MIKHAIL YEFIMOVICH (1900–1942), composer. Born in Kiev, Kroshner became interested in Belorussian folklore while studying at Minsk and used folk tunes in his compositions. Unable to escape from Minsk before the German occupation in 1941, he perished there a year later. His major works are the ballet *The Nightingale* (1939), the cantata *The Drowned Man, Symphonic Dances,* a string quartet, songs, and arrangements of Jewish folk songs for voice and piano.
KUPER, EMIL ALBERTOVICH, see *Cooper, Emil Albertovich.
KURTH, ERNST (1886–1946), musicologist. Born in Vienna, Kurth studied there and from 1912 taught at the University of Bern. His *Grundlagen des linearen Kontrapunkts; Bach's melodische Polyphonie* (1917) established his reputation. It also influenced the younger generation of composers, and stimulated the study of Bach and the teaching of counterpoint. This work was followed by *Romantische Harmonik und ihre Krise in Wagner's Tristan* (1920), an account of romantic harmony down to Debussy. In his biographical study *Bruckner* (1925) Kurth propounded a theory of musical form. He summarized his conclusions in *Musikpsychologie* (1931).
***KWARTIN, ZAVEL (Zevulun;** 1874–1953), *ḥazzan.*
LACHMANN, ISAAK (1838–1900), *ḥazzan,* editor, and writer; see **Ḥazzan.*
***LACHMANN, ROBERT** (1892–1939), musicologist.
***LAMM, PAVEL ALEKSANDROVICH** (1882–1951), musicologist.
***LANDOWSKA, WANDA** (1877–1959), harpsichordist.
***LAVRY, MARC** (1903–1967), composer.
LEBERT (Levy), SIGMUND (1822–1884), pianist. Born in Ludwigsburg, Lebert was a noted pianoforte teacher and a founder of the Stuttgart Conservatory (1856). His *Grosse theoretisch-praktische Klavierschule* (4 vols., 1858; 1911[14]) became a classic work of pianoforte instruction and was translated into many languages.
LEIBOWITZ, RENÉ (1913–1972), composer. Born in Warsaw, Leibowitz went to France at a young age. From 1930 to 1933 he studied with *Schoenberg and Webern, and became the chief advocate of the Schoenberg school in France. He wrote a survey, *Schoenberg et son Ecole* (1947), and a treatise, *Introduction à la musique de douze sons* (1949), and promoted interest in the 12-tone principle by his work as a conductor and his own compositions for orchestra and chamber ensembles.
LEICHTENTRITT, HUGO (1874–1951), musicologist and composer. Born in Pleschen, Poland, from 1905 he taught at the Klindworth-Scharwenka Conservatory in Berlin and was also music critic for the *Vossische Zeitung.* In 1933 he left Germany and became lecturer at Harvard University. His writings include *Haendel* (Ger., 1924); *Music, History and Ideas* (1938); *Music of the Western Nations* (1956); and a widely used handbook, *Musical Form* (1911, 1952; augmented English edition, 1951). His editions of early music appeared, among others, in the *Denkmaeler deutscher Tonkunst.* Leichtentritt composed a symphony, a comic opera, chamber music, an opera *Esther* (a dramatic legend), and a cantata *The Song of Solomon.*
LEINSDORF, ERICH (1912–), conductor. Born in Vienna, Leinsdorf was assistant conductor to Bruno Walter and Toscanini at the Salzburg Festival (1934–37), and conducted in Italy, France, and Belgium. After settling in the United States in 1937, he conducted German works at the Metropolitan Opera, New York, until 1943, and then served there as musical consultant. He was appointed director of the New York City Opera in 1955 and of the Boston Symphony Orchestra in 1962, and later returned to the Metropolitan Opera.
LENDVAI, ERWIN (Loewenfeld; 1882–1949), composer. Born in Budapest, Lendvai studied there and in Milan under Puccini, and worked as choral conductor in Germany, where he did much to raise the standard of choral singing. When the Nazis came to power, he returned to Hungary, then moved to Switzerland, and later to England. He wrote a symphony (1909), an opera *Elga* (1916), and orchestral, choral, and chamber works.
LEONARD, LOTTE (1884–), soprano, born in Hamburg. Lotte Leonard received her musical training in Berlin, where she specialized in lieder and oratorio parts. She sang as soloist in the concerts of the Berlin Philharmonic Choir and at the German Bach

and Handel festivals. Leaving Germany in 1933, she became professor of singing at the International Conservatory in Paris and continued her teaching career in the United States.

***LEONI, MYER** (1740–1796), *ḥazzan* and singer.

LERT, ERNST (Ernst Josef Maria Levi; 1883–1955), conductor. Born in Vienna, Lert worked as theater director in Germany and Switzerland. From 1923 to 1929 he staged German opera at La Scala, Milan, and for the next two years was at the Metropolitan Opera in New York. He settled in the U.S. in 1938, and later directed the opera department at the Peabody Conservatory, Baltimore. He specialized in the staging of Mozart and modern operas. Lert wrote *Mozart auf dem Theater* (1918).

LEVANT, OSCAR (1906–1972), pianist and composer. Born in Pittsburgh, he studied piano with Stojowsky, and became especially known for his performances of Gershwin's *Rhapsody in Blue* and *Concerto in F.* Levant has composed chamber music in a modernistic vein, numerous piano pieces, and a piano concerto. The general public knew him mainly as a radio and television personality with a self-mocking wit. He published *A Smattering of Ignorance* (1940) and *The Memoirs of an Amnesiac* (1965). Levant also appeared in several films.

***LEVI, HERMANN** (1839–1900), conductor.

LEVI, LEO (1912–), musicologist. Born in Casale Monferrato, Italy, Levi settled in Palestine in 1935. His special fields of research were in ethnomusicology and liturgical music, especially the traditions of the Italian and Mediterranean Jewish communities, and in the comparative study of Jewish and Christian musical traditions. His extensive recordings of the various liturgical music traditions of the Italian Jewish communities, made in collaboration with the Centro Nazionale Studi di Musica Popolare in Rome, are particularly important as the greater part were obtained from the last bearers of these traditions at a time when their communities had already ceased to exist.

LEVI-TANNAI, SARAH (1911–), composer and choreographer; see *Dance.

LEVITSKY, MISCHA (1898–1941), pianist. Born in Kremenchug, Russia, Levitsky was taken by his parents to the United States in 1906. He toured widely and excelled in the interpretation of Chopin and Liszt. Among his compositions are a ballet, songs, piano pieces, and a cadenza for Beethoven's piano concerto in C minor.

LÉVY, LAZARE (1882–1964), pianist. Born in Brussels, he studied at the Paris Conservatoire. Lévy played with the principal European symphony orchestras and toured in Europe and Asia. In 1920 he succeeded Alfred Cortot as professor of piano at the Paris Conservatoire, and gained an international reputation as a pedagogue. His compositions include chamber music and pianoforte pieces.

***LEWANDOWSKI, LOUIS** (1821–1894), choral director and composer.

LEWENSOHN, JOEL DAVID, see *Loewenstein-Straschunsky, Joel David.

LHEVINNE, JOSEF (1874–1944), pianist. Born in Orel, Russia, he studied at the Moscow Conservatory, where he also taught (1902–06). In 1906 he settled in the U.S., but sojourned in Berlin from 1907 to 1919. He undertook numerous concert tours, and also gave duo-recitals with his wife, ROSINA LHEVINNE (1880–), a noted pianist in her own right. Josef Lhevinne excelled in the interpretation of the romantic composers, and was among the major concert artists of his time. Rosina Lhevinne became especially known as a piano teacher, and many of the U.S.-born pianists who rose to prominence in the 1940s and 1950s were her pupils.

LIEBERMANN, ROLF (1910–), composer. Born in Zurich, a great-nephew of Max *Liebermann, Rolf Liebermann studied law before devoting himself to music and was a pupil of Vladimir *Vogel. In 1950 he became music director of the Swiss radio and in 1959 general manager of the Hamburg State Opera, which he made one of the major music centers of the time by commissioning new operas from composers throughout the world, including Israel, and by the excellence of its production. His own operas are distinguished by fresh dramatic ideas and strict musical organization. They include *Leonore 40/45* (1952), *Penelope* (1954), and *School for Wives* (1955), based on Molière's opera. He also wrote *Concerto for Jazzband and Orchestra* (1954), the *Geigy Festival Concerto* (1958), cantatas, and songs.

LIEBERSON, GODDARD (1911–), musical executive and composer. Born in Hanley, England, Lieberson was taken to the United States as a child and studied with Bernard Rogers. In 1939 he joined the staff of Columbia Records and in 1956 was made president. In 1964 he was appointed president of the Record Industry Association of America. Lieberson edited the *Columbia Book of Musical Masterpieces* (1950). From 1966 on he sponsored the annual Lieberson prize competition for chamber works organized by the Israel League of Composers. His compositions include songs and chamber music.

***LIFSHITZ (Lifsicaite), NEHAMA** (1927–), folk singer.

LION, MEIR, see *Leoni, Myer.

LIPSCHITZ, SOLOMON BEN MOSES (1675–1758), *ḥazzan* and writer; see **Ḥazzan.*

LISSA, ZOFIA (1908–), musicologist. Born in Lvov, Zofia Lissa was cultural attaché at the Polish embassy in Moscow after World War II; she later joined the Polish Ministry of Art and Culture, and became professor of music at Warsaw University. Among her publications are: *Zarys nauki o muzyce* ("The Outlines of Musical Science," 1934, 1952[3]); *Uwagi o metodzie marksystowskiej w muzykologii* ("Remarks on the Marxist Method in Musicology," 1950); and *Historia muzyki rosyjskiej* ("History of Russian Music," 1955).

LIST, EMANUEL (1891–1967), bass. Born in Vienna, List joined the Volksoper in Vienna in 1922, the Berlin State Opera in 1923 and toured in Europe, the United States, and Australia. In 1938 he settled in the United States and sang leading Wagnerian roles at the Metropolitan Opera, New York. He also became known as a singer of German lieder.

LITINSKI, GENRIKH ILYICH (1901–), composer. Born in the Ukraine, Litinski studied at the Moscow Conservatory and joined the group Prokoll ("Productive Collective"), dedicated to composing on sociological and revolutionary subjects. From 1924 he taught at Moscow Conservatory, became professor at Gnesin Teachers Institute of Music, Moscow, in 1947, and from 1949 also held a professorship at Kazan. He organized musical activities in various Asiatic republics of the Soviet Union, and explored the folklore of the Yakut people in Siberia, which he utilized in his works. His compositions include operas, ballets, symphonies, 12 string quartets, and a string octet.

LIUZZI, FERNANDO (1884–1940), musicologist and composer. Born in Senigallia, Liuzzi studied composition and conducting in Italy and Germany. He taught composition at the major Italian conservatories and musicology at the universities of Florence, Perugia, and Rome. Liuzzi composed several stage works, some modernized versions of medieval and Renaissance musical dramas, as well as violin works and songs. His research was in the fields of aesthetics and the history of Italian music, and his major work is *La lauda e i primordi della melodia italiana* ("The Lauda and the Origins of the Italian Melodic Style," 1935).

LOESSER, FRANK (1910–1969), composer. Born in New York, Loesser wrote songs while at City College and then in the army during World War II, of which *Praise the Lord and Pass the Ammunition* became the best known. He settled in Hollywood and wrote music for films and musicals; the best known are: *Hans Christian Andersen* (film, 1952), and the musicals *Guys and Dolls* (1950), *The Most Happy Fella* (1956), and *How to Succeed in Business Without Really Trying* (1961). He was three times the recipient of the New York Drama Critics Award for the best musical score. His brother, ARTHUR LOESSER (1894–), was a pianist and writer on music, and the author of *Men, Women and Pianos: A Social History* (1954).

LOEWE, FREDERICK (1904–), composer. Born in Vienna, Loewe studied piano with Busoni and d'Albert in Berlin, and began his career as a concert pianist. He went to the United States in 1924 where he turned to composing musical comedies in partnership with the librettist Alan Jay *Lerner. Loewe's works include *Brigadoon* (1947), *Paint Your Wagon* (1951), *Camelot* (1960), and the most successful *My Fair Lady* (1956) based on Bernard Shaw's *Pygmalion.*

LOEWENSTEIN, HERBERT, see under Avenary, Hanoch.

LOMZER, ḤAYYIM, see *Wasserzug, Ḥayyim.

LOURIE, ARTHUR (Vincent; 1892–), composer, born in St. Petersburg, where he also studied and converted to Catholicism in his early 20s. Lourie became head of the music department of the Commissariat for Public Instruction after the Revolution. In 1920 he settled in Paris and emigrated to the United States in 1941. His compositions include symphonies, operas, ballets, and choral works in the avant-garde idioms of their respective periods, the later ones turning to the recreation of old forms. Lourie also wrote a biography of Serge *Koussevitzky (1931).

***LOVY, ISRAEL** (1773–1832), *ḥazzan* and composer.

LOWINSKY, EDWARD (1908–), musicologist. Born in Stuttgart, Germany, Lowinsky emigrated to the United States in 1934, and taught at the University of California at Berkeley and at the University of Chicago. He published an important investigation, *Secret Chromatic Art in the Netherlands Motet* (1946), in which he pointed out anticipations of modern practices in early Renaissance music, and also edited early music. He also contributed numerous theoretical articles to European and U.S. magazines.

LUBOSHUTZ, family of musicians. LEA LUBOSHUTZ (1887–1965), violinist, began her career as a concert violinist in Russia. She arrived in the United States in 1925 and gave violin recitals. She later became active mainly as a teacher and from 1927 was a faculty member of the Curtis Institute of Music, Philadelphia. Her son BORIS GOLDOVSKY (1908–) was a pianist, opera conductor, lecturer, and radio commentator in the United States. Her brother PIERRE LUBOSHUTZ (1894–) formed a piano duo with his wife Genia Nemenoff, and gave concerts in the United States and Europe. A sister of Lea and Pierre, Anna Luboshutz, was a cellist.

LUCCA, PAULINE (1841–1908), singer. Born in Vienna, she was the daughter of Koppelman Lucka, who had been baptized in 1834. In 1861 Giacomo *Meyerbeer recommended her for permanent engagement at the Berlin Opera, where she remained until 1872, also undertaking guest appearances. After 1872 she toured in the United States, and from 1874 to 1889 was an honorary member of the Vienna opera. She created the role of Selina in Meyerbeer's *L'Africaine,* and was considered the best Carmen of her time. A *prima donna assoluta* in the grand tradition, she had a voice range of 2½ octaves.

LYON, MYER, see *Leoni, Myer.

MACHABEY, ARMAND (1886–1966), musicologist and composer. Born in Pont-de-Roide, France, Machabey's main contributions were made in the field of medieval musicology. Among his books are *Anton Bruckner* (Fr., 1946), *Traité de la critique musicale* (1946), *Le Bel Canto* (1948), *La Notation musicale* (1952), *Girolamo Frescobaldi* (1952); and *Guillaume de Machaut: la vie et l'oeuvre musicale* (2 vols., 1955). He also composed some chamber and orchestral works.

***MAGGID, DAVID ILLARIONOVICH (Israelevich;** 1862–c. 1943), scholar and musicologist.

***MAHLER, GUSTAV** (1860–1911), composer.

MAHLER-KALKSTEIN, MENAHEM, see *Avidom, Menahem.

MAJOR, ERVIN (1901–), musicologist. Born in Budapest, the son of Julius Major (see below), he studied composition with Zoltán Kodály and Leo *Weiner and philosophy at the University of Budapest, and later became lecturer at the Budapest Conservatory. He was one of the founders of Hungarian historical musicology, specializing in the 18th and 19th centuries and in the tracing of the Hungarian influences in the works of the classical composers. He also contributed a number of central articles to the *Zenei lexikon* ("Music lexicon"; edited by B. *Szabolcsi and A. Tóth, 3 vols., 1930, 1965²).

MAJOR, JULIUS (Gyula) JACOB (1858–1925), composer, conductor, pianist, and teacher. Born in Kassa (Kosice), Major studied with Liszt, Volkmann, and Erkel. He wrote symphonies, concertos, lieder, and operas, many of which demonstrate a felicitous synthesis of the Hungarian national idiom and Western European forms. His teaching activities included founding and directing the State Music Teachers' College and the Hungarian Women's Choral Association.

MANNES, family of musicians. DAVID MANNES (1866–1959), U.S. violinist and conductor, was interested in civic betterment. In 1912 he founded the Music School Settlement for Colored People, New York. In 1916 he founded the David Mannes School of Music, with a faculty of eminent musicians. He published an autobiography, *Music is My Faith* (1938). He married CLARA DAMROSCH MANNES (1869–1948), a pianist and the daughter of conductor Leopold *Damrosch. His son, LEOPOLD MANNES (1899–1964), a pianist and teacher, succeeded his father as director of the Mannes School. He was also a research chemist, and co-invented the Kodachrome process of color photography with Leopold Godowsky, the son of the pianist Leopold *Godowsky.

MARAGOWSKY, JACOB SAMUEL, see *Morogowsky, Jacob Samuel.

***MARX, ADOLF BERNHARD** (1795–1866), musicologist.

MAYKAPAR, SAMUIL MOYSEYEVICH (1867–1938), pianist and composer. Born in Kherson, Ukraine, Maykapar was a concert pianist in Moscow, and established a music school in Tver (later Kalinin) in 1901. From 1910 he taught at St. Petersburg Conservatory, where he was appointed professor in 1917. His short piano pieces for children remain popular, especially *Biryulki ("Spillikins"), Bagatelles,* and *The Marionette Theater.* He also composed chamber music and a sonatina for violin and piano. His writings include *The Musical Ear* (1900); a study on Beethoven (1927); and *The Years of Study* (1938), an autobiography.

MEDVEDEV, MIKHAIL (Meyer Yefimovich Bernstein; 1852–1925), tenor. The son of a rabbi, he appeared as a boy *meshorer* and was encouraged by *Shalom Aleichem to study singing. While still a pupil at the Moscow Conservatory, he was chosen by Tchaikovsky and Nicolai Rubinstein for the first performance of the role of Lensky in *Eugene Onegin* (1879). He was a soloist at the Kiev Opera from 1881, at the Bolshoi Theater in Moscow from 1891 to 1892, and then at the Petersburg Imperial Opera. He toured the United States (1898–1900) and taught at Moscow, Kiev, and Saratov. Medvedev was admired both for his voice control and for his dramatic interpretations.

MENDEL, ARTHUR (1905–), musicologist, critic, and conductor. Born in Boston, Mendel was associate editor of the *Musical Quarterly,* and editor of Associated Music Publishers (1941–47). From 1937 to 1953 he conducted the Cantata Singers, a small choir performing baroque music. He became chairman of the music department at Princeton in 1952, and edited important works by Bach and Heinrich Schuetz, and, together with Hans David, *The Bach Reader* (1945).

MENDEL, HERMANN (1834–1876), music publisher and lexicographer. Born in Halle, Germany, Mendel edited a music journal, a series of operatic librettos with commentaries, and a book of folk songs. His chief work was his *Musikalisches Conversations-Lexikon* (1870–83), a music encyclopedia in 12 volumes, the last five of which were edited by August Reissmann after Mendel's death. He also published two books on *Meyerbeer (1868, 1869).

MENDELSSOHN, ARNOLD (1855–1933), composer and organist. Born in Ratibor, a collateral descendant of Felix *Mendelssohn, Mendelssohn was organist at Bonn, conductor at Bielefeld, professor at the conservatories of Cologne (1885–90), Darmstadt (1890–1912), and, from 1912, the Hoch Conservatory at Frankfort, where Paul Hindemith was his pupil. His compositions include sacred choral works, operas, symphonies, chamber music, and songs. He edited Heinrich Schuetz's oratorios, some of Monteverdi's madrigals, and wrote *Gott, Welt und Kunst* (ed. by W. Ewald, 1949).

***MENDELSSOHN, FELIX** (1809–1847), composer.

***MENUHIN, YEHUDI** (1916–), violinist.

METZGER (Metzger-Lattermann), OTTILIE (1878–1943), contralto. Born in Frankfort, she sang at the Hamburg Stadttheater (1903–14) and appeared in the Wagner operas at Bayreuth, gaining a reputation as a singer of dramatic parts. She toured in Austria and England, and the United States (1914–15), and appeared with the German Opera Company at the Manhattan Opera House, New York, in 1922–23. She died in the Theresienstadt ghetto.

MEYER, ERNST HERMANN (1905–), musicologist and composer. Born in Berlin, Meyer studied musicology in Berlin and Heidelberg, and composition with Paul Hindemith and Hanns *Eisler. He emigrated to England in 1933 and returned to Germany in 1948 to become professor of music sociology at the Humboldt University in East Berlin. An authority on the music of the 16th and 17th centuries, he wrote *English Chamber Music* (1946), *Musik im Zeitgeschehen* (1952), and *Aufsaetze ueber Musik* (1957). He composed ballet and chamber music, and a cantata, *Das Tor von Buchenwald* (1959). His teachings and compositions followed the principles of socialist ideology.

***MEYERBEER, GIACOMO (Jacob;** 1791–1864), composer.

MEZZROW, MILTON (Mezz; 1899–), clarinetist. Born in Chicago, Mezzrow became one of the outstanding representatives of the Chicago style. He was among the first white jazz musicians to perform with Negro musicians, such as Tommy Ladnier and Sidney Bechet, with whom he appeared in New York and Paris. Among his compositions are: *Really the Blues* (1938); *Royal Garden Blues* (1938); *Comin' On with the Come On* (1938); *Revolutionary Blues* (1938); *Gone Away Blues* (1945); *Out of the Gallion* (1945), and his reminiscences, *Really the Blues* (1946).

***MILHAUD, DARIUS** (1892–), composer.
***MILNER, MOSES MICHAEL** (1886–1953), composer.
***MILSTEIN, NATHAN** (1904–), violinist.
***MINKOWSKY, PINCHAS** (1859–1924), *ḥazzan*, writer, and composer.
MINSKER, SENDER, see *Polachek, Sender.
MIRON, ISSACHAR (1920–), composer. Born in Poland, Miron settled in Ereẓ Israel in 1939. He was in charge of music and art programs for the Israel Defense Forces in 1948, and from 1954 edited *Zemirot*, the Jewish Agency folk music periodical. Miron's compositions include instrumental and liturgical music, and popular songs, the best known of which is *Ẓena, Ẓena*.
***MOISEIWITSCH, BENNO** (1890–1963), pianist.
***MONTEUX, PIERRE** (1875–1964), conductor.
***MOROGOWSKY, JACOB SAMUEL (Zeidel Rovner;** 1856–1942), *ḥazzan* and composer.
***MOSCHELES, IGNAZ** (1794–1870), pianist, composer, and teacher.
MOSZKOWSKI, MORITZ (1854–1925), pianist and composer. Born in Breslau, Moszkowski taught at the Kullak Academy in Berlin until 1897 when he established his residence in Paris. He was renowned as a concert pianist, touring Europe and the United States, and also as a composer of tuneful piano pieces. Of these, *Spanish Dances* have retained a certain popularity, especially in the four-hand version. He also wrote some orchestral works and an opera *Boabdil, der letzte Maurenkoenig* (first performed in Berlin, 1892). His brother ALEXANDER MOSZKOWSKI (1851–1934), a literary critic, published two booklets of musical humor under the pseudonym Anton Notenquetscher, of which excerpts still appear in anthologies.
***MOTTL, FELIX JOSEF** (1856–1911), conductor and composer.
NACHÉZ, TIVADAR (Theodor Naschitz; 1859–1930), violinist and composer. Born in Pest, Hungary, Nachéz as a boy played with Liszt and studied under *Joachim in Berlin. In 1889, after settling in London, he embarked on his career as an internationally renowned violin virtuoso. His compositions include *Danses Tsiganes*, a violin concerto, and a string quartet. He also edited Vivaldi's violin concertos in A minor and G minor.
***NADEL, ARNO** (1878–1943), writer, composer, and music collector.
***NARDI, NAHUM** (1901–), composer.
***NATHAN, ISAAC** (1792–1864), composer.
***NAUMBOURG, SAMUEL** (1817–1880), *ḥazzan*, composer, and writer.
***NAVON, ISAAC ELIYAHU** (1859–1952), composer.
NE'EMAN, YEHOSHUA LEIB (1899–), *ḥazzan* and editor; see **Ḥazzan*.
NETTL, PAUL (1889–1972), musicologist. Born in Hohenelbe, Bohemia, Nettl was lecturer in musicology in Prague from 1919 until 1939, when he emigrated to the United States. He taught in Chicago, and at Indiana University (1946–60). His works include: *Alte juedische Spielleute und Musiker* (1923); *The Story of Dance Music* (1947); *The Book of Musical Documents* (1948); *The Other Casanova* (1950) concerning Lorenzo da Ponte; *Forgotten Musicians* (1951); *Beethoven Encyclopedia* (1956); and *Mozart and Masonry* (1957). His son BRUNO (1930–) was an ethnomusicologist, specializing in the study of American Indian music.
***NOWAKOWSKY, DAVID** (1848–1921), choral director and composer.
***OBADIAH, THE NORMAN PROSELYTE** (c. 1073–?), writer and composer.
OCHS, SIEGFRIED (1858–1929), conductor and composer. Born in Frankfort, Gemany, Ochs founded the Berlin Philharmonic Choir in 1882, revived neglected works by Bach and Handel, and promoted the music of Bruckner and Hugo Wolf. He later became professor at the Berlin Hochschule fuer Musik. He wrote a comic opera, *Im Namen des Gesetzes* (1888); an autobiographical work, *Geschehenes, Gesehenes* (1922); and *Der deutsche Gesangverein* (4 vols., 1923–28), a history of German choral singing. His humorous piano variations on the German children's song, *S'kommt ein Vogel geflogen*, imitating the style of the masters, started a trend which remained popular.
ODESSER, BEZALEL, see *Shulsinger, Bezalel.
***OFFENBACH, ISAAC BEN JUDAH** (1779–1850), *ḥazzan*.
***OFFENBACH, JACQUES** (1819–1880), composer.
***OISTRAKH, DAVID FEDOROVICH** (1908–), violinist.
OISTRAKH, IGOR (1931–), violinist, see *Oistrakh, David.

ORMANDY, EUGENE (1899–), conductor. Born in Budapest and a child prodigy, Ormandy studied the violin with Hubay and became a teacher at the Budapest Academy, later playing as first violinist with the Bluethner Orchestra in Berlin. After touring in the United States in 1921, he settled there and in 1924 began a career as conductor in New York. After conducting the New York Philharmonic and Minneapolis orchestras, among others, he became first the associate conductor of the Philadelphia Orchestra (with Leopold Stokowski; 1936–1938) and then its permanent conductor, raising it to the status of one of the major orchestras of the world. He specialized in 19th-century and modern music, and always conducted from memory.
ORNSTEIN, LEO (1895–), composer. Born in Russia, Ornstein was taken to the United States in 1907. He gave piano recitals of modern music, including his own compositions with colorful titles, which impressed audiences and critics as extreme examples of "futuristic" music. After a period of notoriety, Ornstein withdrew from the concert stage and lived in Philadelphia. At the height of his popularity, at the age of 23, he was the subject of a monograph by F. H. Martens (*Leo Ornstein: The Man, His Ideas, His Work*; 1918). Ornstein also wrote for orchestra. He was soloist with the Philadelphia Orchestra in 1925, playing his own piano concerto. He played a certain role in the early developments of new American music.
OYSHER, MOISHE (1907–1958), *ḥazzan*; see **Ḥazzan*.
***PARTOS, OEDOEN** (1909–), composer and viola player.
***PEERCE, JAN (Jacob Pincus Perelmuth;** 1904–), singer and *ḥazzan*.
***PELLEG (Pollak), FRANK** (1910–1968), harpsichordist and pianist.
PERGAMENT, MOSES (1893–), composer and music critic. Born in Helsinki, Finland, Pergament settled in Stockholm where he worked as music critic on the *Svenska Dagbladet* and later on the *Aftontidningen*. In almost all of his compositions he used motifs traceable to Jewish biblical cantillation and to folk songs of East European Jewry. Notable among his works are: *Rapsodia ebraica* for orchestra (1935); the choral symphony *Den judiska Sången* ("The Jewish Song"; 1944); the radio opera *Eli* (1959); *Dibbuk*, a fantasy for violin and orchestra (1935); *Swedish Rhapsody* for orchestra (1940); and songs.
***PIATIGORSKY, GREGOR** (1903–), cellist.
PILDERWASSER, JOSHUA, see *Weisser, Joshua.
PIMSLEUR, SALOMON (1900–1962), pianist and composer. Born in Paris, Pimsleur was taken to the United States at the age of three. He studied at Columbia University, and later became a concert pianist. He also worked on the music staff of the New York City civil service. His compositions, which include orchestral and chamber works, were in a romantic style, as often indicated by their titles, such as *Overture to Disillusionment* (1929) and *Impetuous Toccata and Fugal Fantasia* (1930). An opera, *The Diary of Anne Frank*, remained unfinished.
PINCHERLE, MARC (1888–), musicologist. Born in Constantine, Algeria, Pincherle edited the periodicals *Le Monde Musical* (1924–27) and *Musique* (1927–30) and was secretary of the Société Française de Musicologie (1932–35) and its president (1948–56). He made outstanding contributions to the study of baroque violin music on which he also lectured at the Ecole Normale de Musique. His writings include: *Les Violinistes Compositeurs et Virtuoses* (1922); *Corelli* (1933); *Antonio Vivaldi et la musique instrumentale* (2 vols., 1948); *Corelli et son temps* (1954; *Corelli, His Life, His Work*, 1956); *Vivaldi* (1955; Eng. transl. 1957), with an important thematic index; and *Histoire illustrée de la musique* (1959). He also published editions of baroque music.
PINCHIK, PIERRE (c. 1900–), *ḥazzan*; see **Ḥazzan*.
PISK, PAUL AMADEUS (1893–), musicologist and composer. Born in Vienna, Pisk studied under Arnold *Schoenberg and Guido *Adler, and attained prominence as a musical journalist. He was regarded as a spokesman for progressive German and Austrian composers. In 1936 he emigrated to the United States where he held academic posts at various universities. Pisk published a study on the masses of the 16th-century composer Jacobus Gallus (1918), which he also edited for the *Denkmaeler der Tonkunst in Oesterreich*. Among his compositions are orchestral and choral works and chamber music.
POLACHEK, SENDER (Sender Minsker; 1786–1869), *ḥazzan*; see **Ḥazzan*.

POLLACK, EGON (1879–1933), conductor. Born in Prague, Pollack was chorus master at the German Theater there and later held posts at Bremen, Leipzig, and Frankfort. From 1917 to 1932 he was principal conductor of the Hamburg Opera, which developed considerably under his direction. He conducted in Chicago (1931–32) and appeared as guest conductor in Cairo. He died in Prague of a heart attack while conducting *Fidelio*. Pollack was especially known as an interpreter of Richard Strauss. He also conducted Wagnerian opera and promoted the work of contemporaries.

POLLAK, FRANK, see *Pelleg, Frank.

POLLINI, BERNHARD (Baruch Pohl; 1838–1897), opera manager. Pollini began his career as a tenor (later baritone) in his native Cologne and while on tour with an Italian opera troupe, he became its manager. Subsequently he managed the Lemberg Theater and the Italian Opera in St. Petersburg and Moscow. Pollini directed the Hamburg City Theater from 1874 until his death. Under his leadership, it gained an international reputation both for its performances and for the many outstanding musicians, such as Gustav *Mahler, whom it first brought to public attention.

POPPER, DAVID (1843–1913), cellist and composer. Popper studied at Prague and became famous as a concert artist after his first tour of Germany in 1863. From 1868 to 1873 he was first cellist at the Vienna Opera and became a member of the Hubay Quartet. After 1896 he was professor at the Budapest Conservatory. He composed many solos which won favor among cellists, and his manual *Hohe Schule des Violoncellspiels* (c. 1901) has remained in use until today.

PORGES, HEINRICH (1837–1900), writer and conductor. Born in Prague, Porges was coeditor of the *Neue Zeitschrift fuer Musik* in Leipzig. Drawn into Richard Wagner's circle, he became a staunch champion of the composer, and after living for a while in Vienna was called to Munich by Wagner's patron, Ludwig II of Bavaria, for whom he had written a study of Wagner's *Tristan und Isolde* (publ. 1906). In 1886 he founded the Porges Choral Society which promoted the works of Berlioz and Bruckner.

POSTOLSKY, SHALOM (1893–1949), composer. Born in Siedlce, Poland, he went to Ereẓ Israel in 1920 and was among the founders of kibbutz En-Harod in 1921. Some years later he began composing songs for the needs of the kibbutz, and also arranged the *omer* and *seder* ceremonies of En-Harod. Later he settled in Bet Yiẓḥak. His songs include *Kumah Eḥa, Elef Laylah ve-Od Laylah, Ba-Ḥashai Sefinah Gosheshet (Olim), Bikkurim Peri Hillulim* (all to texts by Y. *Shenhar), *Ha-Shibbolim Penimah, Im Garin Zarata* (Levi *Ben-Amitai), and *Ein Zeh Pele* (N. *Alterman), generally corrupted to *Eizeh Pele*.

POUGATCHOV, EMANUEL, see *Amiran, Emanuel.

PRUEWER, JULIUS (1874–1943), conductor. Born in Vienna, Pruewer became a close friend of Brahms during his studies there. He worked as a conductor at Bielitz, in Cologne, and at the Breslau Municipal Theater (1896–1923), where he became director in 1920. At Breslau he gained a high reputation and produced many modern works. He later became professor at the Berlin Hochschule fuer Musik and conducted the popular concerts of the Berlin Philharmonic. In 1933 he left Germany and in 1939 settled in New York where he taught at the New York College of Music.

***PUTTERMAN, DAVID** (1901–), *ḥazzan* and editor.

***RATHAUS, KAROL** (1895–1954), composer.

RAVINA (Rabinowitz), MENASHE (1899–1968), composer and writer. Menashe Ravina was born in Pereyaslavl, Ukraine, went to Palestine in 1924, and became active as a music educator, choral organizer, music critic (for *Davar*, from 1925 until his death), and composer. He pioneered in music popularization as well as in the arranging of music and singing courses for workers. Ravina's writings include *Yo'el Engel ve-ha-Musikah ha-Yehudit* (1947); and an exercise book for solfège, *Organum and the Samaritans* (1963). His songs include *Ha-Shekediyyah Poraḥat* (text by Israel Dushman), *Alei Giv'ah* (A. Broides), and many others.

***RAVITZ, SHELOMOH** (188?–), *ḥazzan*.

***RAZUMNI, EPHRAIM ZALMAN (Solomon;** 1866–1904), *ḥazzan*.

REDLICH, HANS FERDINAND (1903–), musicologist. Born in Vienna, Redlich conducted opera in Berlin and Mainz, and after 1931 devoted himself to research and writing. In 1939 he settled in Britain, where he lectured at Cambridge University from 1942 and at Edinburgh University from 1955. He was an authority on Monteverdi and edited some of his works. His writings include *Gustav Mahler* (1919), *Claudio Monteverdi* (1949; Eng., 1952), *Bruckner and Mahler* (1955), and *Alban Berg* (1957). He composed a concerto grosso (1927) and *Hoelderlin Trilogy* for tenor and orchestra (1946).

REINER, FRITZ (1888–1963), conductor. Born in Budapest, Reiner became conductor at the Budapest People's Opera (1911–14) and musical director of the Dresden Opera (1914–21). In the United States, he was conductor in Cincinnati (1922), Pittsburgh (1938), and at the Metropolitan Opera, New York (1949–53). After 1953 he conducted the Chicago Symphony Orchestra. Reiner also appeared at Covent Garden, London, and at other opera houses. He was regarded as a "conductor's conductor," and showed great technical mastery with breadth of interpretation.

REMÉNYI (Hoffmann), EDUARD (1830–1898), violinist. Born in Heves, Hungary, Reményi studied in Vienna, became involved in the Hungarian insurrection (1848), and after its failure fled to the United States and later toured in England. Pardoned in 1860, he was appointed solo violinist to the emperor of Austria. He was noted for his brilliant technique and intensely individual style. On one of his concert tours his accompanist was the 20-year-old Brahms, and Reményi's playing of Hungarian gypsy tunes became the inspiration for Brahms' *Hungarian Dances*. Reményi made violin transcriptions of the piano works of Chopin and Field and wrote a violin concerto. He died in San Francisco while on tour.

RIETI, VITTORIO (1898–), composer. Born in Alexandria, Egypt, Rieti settled in the United States in 1939 and became instructor at various colleges. He was a prolific composer, with a light touch, and excelled in ballet music. He composed the music for Balanchine's ballets *Barabau* (1925) and *Le Bal* (1929) presented by Diaghilev. His works include other ballets, operas, oratorios, symphonies, orchestral works, chamber music, songs, and piano pieces. Among his compositions are the opera *L'Arca di Noe* (1922) and the ballet *David Triomphant* (1926).

***RIVLIN, SHELOMO ZALMAN** (1884–1962), *ḥazzan* and teacher.

ROCHBERG, GEORGE (1918–), composer. Born in Patterson, N.J., Rochberg studied with George *Szell, Leopold *Mannes, and Gian Carlo Menotti. In 1960 he became chairman of the music department of the University of Pennsylvania. His compositions include symphonies, piano works, chamber music, and songs in a moderately avant-garde idiom.

***RODGERS, RICHARD** (1902–), composer.

RODZINSKY, ARTUR (1892–1958), conductor. Born in Split, Dalmatia (Yugoslavia), Rodzinsky first conducted the Warsaw Philharmonic and Opera Orchestra, and settled in the United States in 1925. In that year he became assistant conductor to Leopold Stokowski of the Philadelphia Orchestra, and in 1937 he organized the NBC Symphony Orchestra for Toscanini. He was appointed permanent conductor of the New York Philharmonic in 1943, but resigned in 1947. He conducted the Chicago Symphony Orchestra for a year, and after 1948 lived in Rome and toured in Europe and South America.

ROGERS, BERNARD (1893–), composer. Born in New York, Rogers studied with Ernest *Bloch. His symphonic poem *To the Fallen* (1918) won him a Pulitzer traveling scholarship. He became an instructor at the Eastman School of Music, Rochester University, in 1929. Rogers wrote several operas, among them, *The Warrior* (1944), based on the story of *Samson and Delilah; choral works such as *The Exodus* (1932); an oratorio, *The Passion* (1942); and orchestral and film music. His *Art of Orchestration* appeared in 1951.

ROITMAN, DAVID (1884–1943), *ḥazzan;* see **Ḥazzan*.

ROLAND-MANUEL (Roland Alexis Manuel Levy; 1891–1966), composer and writer. Born in Paris, Roland-Manuel studied with Roussel and Ravel, and in 1947 became professor of aesthetics at the Paris Conservatory. In 1947 he was elected vice-president of the International Society for Contemporary Music, and in 1949 president of the International Music Council of UNESCO. His music is a blend of classicism and modernism, avoiding romantic tendencies. His writings include three books on Ravel, and the valuable popularization *Plaisir de la musique* (1947–55) in four volumes.

***ROMANOS MELODOS** (490?–560?), poet and composer.

***ROMBERG, SIGMUND** (1887–1951), composer.

RONALD, SIR LANDON (1873–1938), conductor and composer; see *Russell, Henry.
ROSÉ, ARNOLD JOSEF (Rosenblum; 1863–1946), violinist. Born in Jassy, Rumania, Rosé became concertmaster of the Vienna Opera and the Vienna Philharmonic at the age of 18, after conversion to Catholicism, and held these posts until 1938. In 1882 he founded the Rosé String Quartet, which won fame in Europe and in the United States. He also taught at the Vienna State Academy of Music until 1924. When the Nazis invaded Austria in 1938 he fled to England. Rosé married Gustav *Mahler's sister Justine. His brother EDWARD, a cellist, and his daughter ALMA, a violinist, died in a concentration camp.
***ROSENBLATT, JOSEF (Yossele;** 1880–1933), *ḥazzan* and composer.
ROSENTHAL, MANUEL (Emmanuel; 1904–), conductor and composer. Born in Paris, he studied under Ravel, and after conducting Parisian orchestras became leader of the National Radio Orchestra in 1934. During World War II he was a prisoner in Germany and in 1946 he went to the United States. He became instructor of composition at the College of Puget Sound in Tacoma, Washington, in 1948; he was conductor of the Seattle Symphony Orchestra from 1949 to 1951. Among his compositions are light operas and orchestral works.
ROSOWSKY, BARUCH LEIB (1814–1919), *ḥazzan;* see *Rosowsky, Solomon.
***ROSOWSKY, SOLOMON** (1878–1962), composer and musicologist.
***ROSSI, SALAMON DE** (c. 1565–c. 1630), composer.
ROTHMUELLER, AARON MARKO (1908–), baritone and composer. Born in Trnjani, Yugoslavia, Rothmueller studied composition with Alban Berg in Vienna. He sang opera in Europe. He lived in England but after World War II moved to the United States and in 1952 was appointed professor of music at the University of Indiana. His compositions include *Four Sephardic Folksongs, Three Palestinian Folksongs, Three Palestinian Love Songs,* a setting of Psalm 15, and *In Memory of C. N. Bialik* for violin, viola, and cello. He wrote *Die Musik der Juden* (1951; *The Music of the Jews,* 1953).
ROVNER, ZEIDEL, see *Morogowsky, Jacob Samuel.
***ROZSAVÖLGYI, MARK** (1789–1848), violinist, composer, and publisher.
RUBIN, RUTH (1906–), singer, folk-music collector, and author. Born in Khotin, Bessarabia, she was taken to Canada at the age of four. She published *A Treasury of Jewish Folksong* (1950), *Voices of a People* (1963), and *Jewish Folk Songs* (1965), collections in which the songs are discussed in their historical settings. The Ruth Rubin Archives of Jewish Song, in the Haifa Music Museum and Library, established in 1967, comprise the major part of her lifelong occupation with the East European Jewish folk music tradition.
***RUBINSTEIN, ANTON GRIGORYEVICH** (1829–1894), pianist and composer.
***RUBINSTEIN, ARTUR** (1886–), pianist.
RUBINSTEIN, NICOLAI GRIGORYEVICH (d. 1881), pianist and teacher; see *Rubinstein, Anton Grigoryevich.
RUDINOW, MOSHE (1891–1953), *ḥazzan.* Born in Lyubich, Ukraine, Rudinov became a *meshorer* in Chernigov and in 1905 alto soloist at the Brodski Synagogue in Kiev, under the leadership of conductor A. I. Dzimitrowski. He also appeared in Kiev as soloist in the first concert of Joel Engel's music. Rudinow became a member of the Odessa Opera and conductor of the Ha-Zamir Society in Odessa and Kherson. In 1917 he married the singer Ruth Leviash with whom he gave joint recitals in Russia and Poland (1920–25) and Palestine (1925–27). In 1927 he moved to the United States and joined the musical staff of Temple Emanuel in New York under the leadership of Lazare Saminsky. After six months as choir soloist, he was appointed cantor. Rudinow also appeared in recitals and operatic concerts with Leopold Stokowski.
***RUSSELL, HENRY** (1812–1900), composer and singer.
***SACERDOTE, DAVID** (1550–1625), composer.
***SACHS, CURT** (1881–1959), musicologist.
***SALMON, KAREL (Karl Salomon;** 1897–), composer.
SALZMAN, PNINA (1922–), pianist. Born in Tel Aviv, Pnina Salzman performed with the Israel Philharmonic Orchestra and toured other countries. She was considered the first Israel-born pianist to attain international artistic rank.
***SAMBURSKY, DANIEL** (1909–), composer.
***SAMINSKY, LAZARE** (1882–1959), composer, writer, and conductor.
SAMUEL, HAROLD (1879–1937), pianist. Born in London, Samuel studied at the Royal College of Music, where he became a professor. He appeared before the public in 1921 in a series of six brilliant recitals, given within one week, in which he played all Bach's keyboard works from memory. He became most famous as an interpreter of Bach. Samuel frequently toured in the United States and other countries.
***SANDLER, JACOB KOPPEL** (186?–1931), composer.
SCHALIT, HEINRICH (1886–), composer. Schalit was born in Vienna, and studied at the musical conservatory there. He settled in Munich, where he worked as music teacher and as organist at the Great Synagogue. In 1933 he left Germany and was appointed organist at the Great Synagogue in Rome. He later emigrated to the U.S., where he was organist for congregations in Providence, Rhode Island, and Denver, Colorado. Among his sacred compositions are his *Friday Night Liturgy,* his *Hebrew Song of Praise,* and his setting of Psalm 98. He also wrote orchestral, chamber, and piano music, as well as songs.
SCHERMAN, PINCHAS, see Szerman, Pinchas in **Ḥazzan.*
SCHILLINGER, JOSEPH (1895–1943), music teacher and composer. Born in Kharkov, Schillinger taught and conducted there and in Leningrad. In 1929 he settled in the United States, where he taught mainly at the New York School for Social Research. He believed that composition could be taught by correspondence according to mathematical principles. Many aspiring composers took lessons from him. He composed much orchestral and chamber music and published several books on his system.
SCHLESINGER, family of music publishers. ADOLF MARTIN SCHLESINGER (1768–1848) was born in Berlin, where in 1810 he founded the firm Schlesinger'sche Buch und Musikalienhandlung, which was one of Beethoven's publishers. His greatest publication was Bach's *St. Matthew Passion* (1829). His two sons were HEINRICH SCHLESINGER (1807–1879) and MORITZ (MAURICE) ADOLF SCHLESINGER (1797–1871). Heinrich maintained the Berlin firm, while in 1834 Moritz established a firm in Paris which published works by Mozart, Chopin, Berlioz, *Meyerbeer, and Donizetti, and the *Gazette* (later *Revue*) *Musicale.* The German firm passed into other hands in 1864, and the French one in 1846.
***SCHMIDT, JOSEPH** (1904–1942), singer and *ḥazzan.*
***SCHNABEL, ARTUR** (1882–1951), pianist.
SCHNEIDER, ALEXANDER (1908–), violinist. Born in Vilna, Schneider became leader of the Frankfort Symphony Orchestra. Emigrating to the United States in 1933, he joined the Budapest Quartet as second violinist until 1944 and again from 1957 and formed several other chamber music ensembles. Together with the cellist Pablo Casals he established the annual festivals held at Prades in the Pyrenees from 1950 onward and in Puerto Rico from 1957. He conducted at these festivals and also visited Israel for the summer music festivals.
***SCHOENBERG, ARNOLD** (1874–1951), composer.
***SCHORR, BARUCH** (1833–1904), *ḥazzan* and composer.
SCHORR, FRIEDRICH (1888–1953), bass-baritone. Born in Nagyvarád, Hungary, Schorr sang at Graz, Prague, and Cologne, and at the Berlin State Opera (1923–31). In 1938 he emigrated to the United States and sang at the Metropolitan Opera. One of the foremost Wagnerian singers of his time, he excelled as an interpreter of the roles of Hans Sachs and Wotan, and often appeared at the Wagner Festivals in Bayreuth.
SCHREKER, FRANZ (1878–1934), composer and conductor. Born in Monaco, after studying in Vienna Schreker became conductor of the Volksoper there (1907) and founded the Vienna Philharmonic Choir (1908). He became head of the State High School for Music, Berlin, and in 1932, professor of composition at the Prussian Academy of Arts. He was dismissed in 1933 when the Nazis rose to power. Schreker was known for his operas, which had rich Wagnerian orchestration, daring harmonies, and somewhat erotic libretti that were written by the composer. Among them were *Der ferne Klang* (1912), *Vom ewigen Leben* (1929), and *Christophorus* (1932).
SCHULHOFF, ERWIN (1894–1942), composer and pianist; see *Schulhoff, Julius.
***SCHULHOFF, JULIUS** (1825–1898), pianist and composer.
SCHULLER, GUNTHER (1925–), horn player and composer. Born in New York Schuller studied and later taught at the Manhattan School of Music. He played the horn in the Cincinnati Symphony Orchestra and at the Metropolitan Opera, New York.

In 1957 he coined the term "Third Stream" for the combination of jazz improvisations with classical musical forms, and in 1962 directed the first international jazz festival in Washington. His compositions include a *Symphony for Brass* (1950); a ballet, *Variants* (1960); a piano concerto (1962); a cello concerto (1945); and orchestral and chamber music.

***SCHUMAN, WILLIAM HOWARD** (1910–), composer.

SCHWARZ, RUDOLF (1905–), conductor. Born in Vienna, Schwarz conducted opera in Duesseldorf and Karlsruhe. When Hitler came to power he was forced to resign, and in 1936 was appointed musical director of the *Juedischer Kulturbund in Nazi Germany. In 1941 he was sent to Bergen-Belsen, and after his release settled in England. He directed the city orchestras in Bournemouth (1947–50) and Birmingham (1951–57). From 1957 to 1962 he was chief conductor of the B.B.C. Symphony Orchestra, and then became principal conductor of the Northern Sinfonia Orchestra, Newcastle.

***SECUNDA, SHOLOM** (1894–), composer.

***SEIBER, MATYAS** (1905–1960), composer.

SEIXAS, GERSHON MENDES (1745–1816), rabbi and *ḥazzan;* see *Seixas.

***SENDREY, ALFRED (Aladar Szendrei;** 1884–), conductor, writer, and composer.

SERKIN, RUDOLF (1903–), pianist. Born in Eger, Bohemia, Serkin made his first public appearance at the age of 12. He began his concert career in Berlin in 1920, and made his American debut in Washington in 1933 with the violinist Adolf Busch, whose daughter he married, and with whom he had already formed a famous duo in Europe. In 1939 he became head of the pianoforte faculty at the Curtis Institute, Philadelphia. Serkin toured Europe, the United States, and the Orient, and was recognized as one of the master performers of classical repertoire in his generation. His son PETER (1947–) was also a concert pianist.

***SETER, MORDECHAI** (1916–), composer.

SEVITZKY, FABIEN (1893–1967), conductor. Born in Vichny-Volotchok, Russia, Sevitzky adopted an abridged form of the family name so as not to seem to be imposing on the fame of his uncle, Serge *Koussevitzky. He was a double-bass player in Russian orchestras and toured Russia as a virtuoso. In 1922 he moved to Poland, and then to the United States. He played in the Philadelphia Orchestra and founded the Philadelphia String Sinfonietta in 1925. From 1935 to 1955 he was permanent conductor of the Indianapolis Symphony Orchestra which, under his direction, became one of the leading U.S. orchestras.

SHAPERO, HAROLD (1920–), composer. Born in Lynn, Massachusetts, Shapero studied composition with Ernst Krenek, Walter Piston, Paul Hindemith, and Nadia Boulanger. He was appointed professor of music at Brandeis University in 1952. Shapero wrote orchestral works, piano, and chamber music, in which traditional forms are combined with dodecaphonic techniques. His compositions include: *Symphony for Classical Orchestra* (1948); *Credo* for orchestra (1955); and a Hebrew cantata *Until Day and Night Shall Cease* (1954), commissioned by the American Jewish Tercentenary Committee.

***SHARETT, YEHUDAH** (1901–), composer.

SHAW, ARTIE (Arthur Arshawsky; 1910–), clarinetist and bandleader. Born in New York, Shaw formed a notable band, the Gramercy Five, which became one of the leading exponents of the swing style of the 1940s. During World War II he directed a naval orchestra in the Pacific and retired in Spain in later years. He published an autobiographical novel, *The Trouble with Cinderella* (1952), telling of his many marriages—among others to the film actresses Lana Turner and Ava Gardner, and to author Kathleen Winsor.

***SHELEM, MATITYAHU** (1904–), composer.

SHEMER, NAOMI (Saphir; 1933–), composer. Born at kevuẓat Kinneret, she studied at the Israel Academy of Music in Jerusalem. During her army service she wrote mainly lyrics. Her first successes, including *Shir ha-Zamar ha-Noded,* were written for the Baẓal Yarok ensemble, which she joined in 1957. In 1967, commissioned by the Israel Broadcasting Authority to write a song for the annual song festival, she wrote *Yerushalayim shel Zahav,* which immediately became popular. Sung by the soldiers at the moment of the taking of the Western Wall, it became the theme song of the Six-Day War and achieved international fame. In many Reform and other congregations in Israel and the Diaspora, the song was introduced into the liturgy for special occasions, such as Friday evening, the last *hakkafah* on *Simḥat Torah, and the synagogue service on Israel Independence Day.

SHENKER, BEN-ZION (1925–), singer and composer. Born in New York, Shenker studied music with Joshua *Weisser, with whom he sang as a *meshorer.* He became closely involved with the musical tradition of the *Modzhitz Ḥasidim as the "court musician" of the rabbi of Modzhitz, Saul Taub, who was himself a noted composer of ḥasidic songs. He made numerous performances and recordings of Modzhitz *niggunim* and of his own very popular compositions in the ḥasidic style.

SHERIFF, NOAM (1935–) composer. Born in Tel Aviv, Sheriff studied composition with Paul *Ben-Haim in Tel Aviv and with Boris Blacher in Berlin. He appeared as conductor with the Israel Philharmonic Orchestra, the Israel radio orchestras and the army orchestra, taught at the music academies in Jerusalem and Tel Aviv, and worked as an orchestrator. His compositions include *Akdamot le-Mo'ed* for the Israel Philharmonic orchestra (1957); *Song of Degrees* (1959), *Music* (1961), for woodwinds, trombone, piano, and double bass, *Ashrei* (1961), for alto, flute, two harps, and two tom-toms, and *Chaconne* for orchestra (1967).

SHERMAN, PINCHAS, see Szerman, Pinchas in *Ḥazzan.*

SHERTOK, YEHUDA, see *Sharett, Yehuda.

SHESTAPOL, WOLF (Wolf Khersoner; c. 1832–1872), *ḥazzan* and composer.

SHILOAḤ, AMNON (1928–), musicologist. Born in Argentina of a family from Syria, Shiloaḥ settled in Palestine in 1941, and studied Arabic language and literature at the Hebrew University, and musicology at the Sorbonne, where he obtained his doctorate in 1963. His fields of research are the musical history and ethnomusicology of the Arabic Near East, and the traditions of the Near Eastern and Mediterranean Jewish communities. He was senior lecturer in musicology at the University of Jerusalem and in 1969 became director of the Jewish Music Research Center at the Hebrew University. His writings include studies of medieval music treatises published in *Yuval* (vols. 1–2, 1968–71), and the article on Arab music in the *Encyclopedia Britannica.*

SHMUELI, HERZL (1920–), musicologist. Born in Turkey, Shmueli was taken to Palestine in 1933. He became director of the National Teachers' Seminary in Tel Aviv and after 1966 was assistant director of the department of musicology at Tel Aviv University. In 1951 he published, with A. U. *Boscovich, a Hebrew translation of Hindemith's *Aufgaben fuer Harmonie-Schueler.* Shmueli also wrote on musical theory, the history of the choir, and Israel folk song. He was chairman of the Israel Musicological Society (1969).

***SHULSINGER, BEZALEL (Bezalel Odesser;** c. 1790–1860), *ḥazzan.*

SILBERMANN, ALPHONS (1909–), musicologist. Born in Cologne, Silbermann was music critic of the *Nieuwe Rotterdamsche Courant* from 1933. In 1937 he emigrated to Australia and became lecturer at the State Conservatory of Music in Sydney. From 1952 he was director of sociomusical research at the French broadcasting service in Paris. In 1959 Silbermann returned to Germany as professor at the University of Cologne. His publications include *Introduction à une sociologie de la musique* (1955), *Wovon lebt die Musik?* (1957), and *Das imaginaere Tagebuch des Herrn Jacques Offenbach* (1960).

SINGER, GEORGE (1909–), conductor. Born in Prague, Singer went to Palestine in 1939 on the "illegal" immigrant ship *Tiger Hill.* He was conductor of the Palestine Opera (and later of the Israel Opera). In 1954 he conducted the premiere of Darius *Milhaud's opera *King David.* Singer often conducted the Israel Philharmonic Orchestra, the Israel Broadcasting Orchestra, and orchestras and operas in Europe and the United States, giving especially noteworthy performances of the works of Czechoslovakian and Israel composers.

SINGER, JOSEF (1841–1911), *ḥazzan* and writer.

SINGER, KURT (1885–1944), musicologist. Born in Berent in German Poland, Singer was music critic for the socialist newspaper *Vorwaerts.* In 1935 he became musical director of the *Juedischer Kulturbund. He moved to Holland in 1939 but was arrested during the German occupation and taken to the *Theresienstadt concentration camp, where he died. Singer wrote *Richard Wagner* (1913), *Bruckners Chormusik* (1924), *Berufskrankheiten des Musikers* (1927); *Diseases of the Musical Profession,* 1932), and *Heilwirkung der Musik* (1927).

SINIGAGLIA, LEONE (1868–1944), composer. Born in Turin,

Sinigaglia studied in Vienna, and in Prague with Dvořák, who interested him in folk music. His most important works are *Danze Piemontese,* for orchestra (first conducted by Toscanini, 1905) and the overture to Goldoni's play, *Le baruffe chiozzotte* (1907). He incorporated many of the tunes of his native Piedmont in his work and also published them in a collection, *Vecchie canzoni popolari del Piemonte* (6 fasc.), which appeared posthumously in 1957. Sinigaglia and his sister Alina both died of strokes on May 16, 1944, in the Ospedale Mauriziano in Turin, where they had fled from Fascist police who were rounding up Jews for deportation.

***SIPRUTINI (Sipurtini), EMANUEL** (18th century), cellist.

***SIROTA, GERSHON** (1874–1943), *ḥazzan.*

SLONIMER, YOSKE, see *Altschul, Joseph.

SLONIMSKY, NICOLAS (1894–), musicologist, composer, and conductor. Born in St. Petersburg, Slonimsky was the son of Leonid Slonimski and grandson of Ḥayyim Zelig *Slonimski. He went to the United States in 1923 and worked as opera coach at the Eastman School of Music in Rochester, New York (1925), and as secretary to Serge *Koussevitzky (1925–27). In 1928 he founded the Chamber Orchestra of Boston. Slonimsky became a champion of modern American music, which he presented on lecture tours. He edited the 4th to 7th editions of *Thompson's International Cyclopedia of Music and Musicians* (1946, 1949, 1952, 1956) and the 5th edition of *Baker's Biographical Dictionary of Musicians* (1958, re-issued with supplement in 1964). His writings include *Music since 1900* (1937), *Music of Latin America* (1945), *Thesaurus of Scales and Melodic Patterns* (1947), and *A Lexicon of Musical Invective* (1953), as well as a number of scholarly articles. He composed a number of works, some of them frankly tongue-in-cheek, such as *Moebius Strip Tease* (1965).

SOLTI, GEORG (1912–), conductor. Born in Budapest, Solti studied with Dohnanyi, Bartok, and Kodaly, and became an accomplished pianist gaining the first prize at the 1942 Geneva competition. From 1930 to 1939 he was conductor and pianist at the Budapest Opera, and later worked in Switzerland. In 1946 he went to Germany, was opera director in Munich, and then in Frankfort (1952). His international career began at this time; he became known for his wide-ranging concert and operatic repertoire, and his special competence in conducting for recordings. In 1961 Solti was appointed director of the Covent Garden Opera, London. From 1956 he frequently conducted the *Israel Philharmonic Orchestra, with which he also made several recordings.

***SPECTOR (Lichtenberg), JOHANNA** (1920–), musicologist.

SPIVACKE, HAROLD (1904–), musicologist. Born in New York, Spivacke studied at New York University, the University of Berlin, and privately with d'Albert and Hugo *Leichtentritt. In 1936 he became assistant chief and in 1937, chief of the music division of the Library of Congress, which was greatly developed under his administration. Spivacke was also a member of various directive and advisory bodies in American and international musicological organizations and president of the Music Library Association from 1951 to 1953. He published *Paganiniana* (1945) and various articles.

***SPIVAK, NISSAN (Nissi Belzer;** 1824–1906), *ḥazzan.*

STARK, EDWARD (1863–1918), composer and *ḥazzan;* see **Ḥazzan.*

STAROMINSKY, MORDECHAI, see *Seter Mordechai.

STEINBERG, MAXIMILIAN OSSEJEVICH (1883–1946), composer and teacher. Born in Vilna, Steinberg studied under Rimsky-Korsakov, whose daughter he married. He became professor of composition at the St. Petersburg Conservatory in 1908 and director in 1934. Steinberg's compositions were influenced by his master, and by his interest in Asiatic music. He wrote four symphonies, orchestral works, ballets, chamber and piano music, and edited Rimsky-Korsakov's *Foundations of Orchestration* (2 vols., 1913) and other of his works. Many prominent Soviet composers were Steinberg's pupils, including Dmitri Shostakovich and Yuri Shaporin.

STEINBERG, WILLIAM (1899–), conductor. Born in Cologne, Steinberg became assistant to Otto *Klemperer and later first conductor at the Cologne opera. He was director at the Frankfort opera (1929–33), and made it into one of the centers of progressive music. From 1933 to 1936 Steinberg was active as conductor in the *Juedischer Kulturbund, and in 1936 went to Palestine upon the invitation of Bronislaw *Huberman to organize the Palestine (later Israel Philharmonic) Orchestra for its première under Toscanini. In 1937 he became assistant conductor of the NBC Symphony Orchestra in New York, and subsequently conductor of the Buffalo Philharmonic, the Pittsburgh Symphony, and part-time conductor of the London Philharmonic orchestras.

***STERN, ISAAC** (1920–), violinist.

STERN, JULIUS (1820–1883), conductor and teacher. Born in Breslau, Stern founded the Stern'scher Gesangverein in 1847, and conducted it until 1874. The choir's performance of Mendelssohn's *Elijah* in 1847 established his reputation as a conductor. In 1850 he founded with Adolf Bernhard *Marx and Theodor Kullak the Berlin Conservatory, and was its sole director from 1856. It became one of the main centers of musical education in Germany. In 1869, he conducted the Berlin Symphony Orchestra and in 1873–75 he led the Reichshalle concerts. Stern composed an opera and works for voice, piano, and strings.

***STERNBERG, ERICH WALTER** (1891–), composer.

STEUERMANN, EDWARD (1892–1964), pianist and teacher. Born in Lemberg, Poland, Steuermann studied piano with Busoni and theory with Arnold *Schoenberg in Berlin. Later he taught at the Jewish Conservatory in Cracow, Poland. In 1936 he settled in the United States where he taught at the Philadelphia Conservatory and at the Juilliard School of Music. Steuermann devoted himself to the dissemination of modern music, particularly that of Schoenberg. He gave the first performances of all of Schoenberg's piano works and chamber works with piano accompaniment, and transcribed his orchestral works for piano.

STOLARSKY, PIOTR SOLOMOVICH, see *Stolyarsky, Peter Solomonovich.

***STOLYARSKY, PETER SOLOMONOVICH** (1871–1944), violin teacher.

STRAKOSCH, MAURICE (1825–1887), pianist and impresario. Born in Gross-Seelowitz, Moravia, Strakosch toured Europe as a pianist and emigrated to the U.S. in 1848. From 1856 he worked chiefly as an operatic impresario, managed the concerts of his sister-in-law, the celebrated soprano Adelina Patti, and toured with his company in the U.S. and Europe. Strakosch composed one opera *Giovanni di Napoli,* and pieces for piano, and wrote *Ten Commandments of Music for the Perfection of the Voice* (posthumous, 1896), and *Souvenirs d'un Impresario* (1887).

STRANSKY, JOSEF (1872–1936), conductor. Born at Humpolec, Bohemia, Stransky graduated in medicine, but turned to music and studied with Dvořák and Bruckner. He conducted at the German Theater in Prague, and later at the Stadttheater, Hamburg. In 1911 he succeeded Mahler as conductor of the New York Philharmonic Society, and in 1923 became conductor of the New York State Symphony Orchestra. He gave up conducting in 1925 to work as an art dealer.

STRASCHUNSKI, JOEL DAVID, see *Loewenstein-Straschunsky, Joel David.

***STRAUS, OSKAR** (1870–1954), composer.

STRELISKER, DAVID, see Brod, Dovidl in **Ḥazzan.*

***STUTSCHEWSKY, JOACHIM** (1891–), cellist, writer, and composer.

***SULZER, SALOMON** (1804–1890), *ḥazzan* and composer.

***SZABOLCSI, BENCE** (1899–), musicologist.

SZELL, GEORGE (1897–1970), conductor and pianist. Born in Budapest, Szell conducted in German opera houses and in Prague, and was chief conductor of the Berlin State Opera (1924–29). From 1937 he conducted the Scottish Orchestra in Glasgow, and the Residentie Orchestra of The Hague. He immigrated to the United States in 1940 and was principal conductor at the Metropolitan Opera, New York (1942–45). In 1946 he was appointed permanent conductor of the Cleveland Orchestra. Szell won repute for his extensive repertoire of modern and classical works and for his lucid interpretations of the Viennese classics.

SZENDREI, ALADAR, see *Sendrey, Alfred.

SZERMAN, PINCHAS (1887–1942), *ḥazzan;* see **Ḥazzan.*

SZERYNG, HENRYK (1918–), violinist. Born in Warsaw, Szerying studied with Karl *Flesch and Jacques Thibaud and started his career in 1933. During World War II he was liaison officer for the Polish government in exile in London, and performed for the Allied forces. In 1945 he was appointed professor of music at the National University of Mexico and went on annual tours abroad. He wrote chamber music and edited baroque violin works, especially those of Bach.

SZIGETI, JOSEPH (1892–), violinist. Born in Budapest, Szigeti studied with Hubay and made his debut at the age of seven. In 1917 he was appointed professor of violin at the Geneva Conservatory, and in 1926 settled in the United States. His playing was distinguished by ease and vigor, although his bow-arm position was very unusual—close to the body. Szigeti toured the world and participated in many festivals of modern music. He gave the first public performance of many modern works, including the violin concertos of Busoni (1912), Prokofiev (First Concerto, 1935) and Ernest *Bloch (1938). He also published numerous arrangements and a cadenza to Mozart's Third Violin Concerto. Szigeti wrote memoirs *With Strings Attached* (1947, 1967[2]), *A Violinist's Notebook* (1965), and *The Ten Beethoven Sonatas for Piano and Violin* (1965).

***TAL, JOSEF** (1910–), composer.

***TANSMAN, ALEXANDER** (1897–), composer.

TAUBE, MICHAEL (1890–1972), conductor. Born in Lodz, Poland, Taube conducted in Bonn and Cologne, in 1924 became assistant to Bruno Walter at the Berlin Opera, and in 1926 founded the Taube Chamber Concerts. In 1933 Taube was among the founders of the Juedischer Kulturbund. He emigrated to Palestine in 1934 and led a symphony orchestra in Jerusalem, which was later disbanded with the founding of the Palestine (later Israel) Philharmonic and the Palestine Broadcasting Service orchestras in 1936, which he frequently conducted. In 1956 Taube established the Ramat Gan Chamber Orchestra. He also organized the Israel Bach Society and the Israel Mozart Society which were active for several years.

TAUBER, RICHARD (Ernst Seiffert; 1892–1948), singer. Born in Linz, Austria, Tauber studied at Frankfort. In 1913 he was engaged under a five-year contract by the Dresden opera, where he sang leading tenor parts. He also sang at various other renowned opera houses in Germany and Austria, and at the Salzburg Mozart festivals. From about 1925 he turned to light opera, especially the Lehar operettas (e.g., *Land of Smiles*) in which he became internationally famous; and after 1928 also appeared in musical films. In 1938 he settled in England, where he appeared at Covent Garden. His voice charmed audiences by its tenor quality, pleasant tone, and graceful inflections. Tauber composed an operetta, *Old Chelsea* (1942) and appeared in its leading role.

TAUSIG, KARL (1841–1871), pianist. Born in Warsaw, Tausig first studied with his father, Aloys Tausig, who had been a pupil of Sigismund *Thalberg, then from the age of 14 with Liszt and became his favorite pupil. In 1865 Tausig settled in Berlin, where he opened the Schule des hoeheren Klavierspiels (School of Advanced Piano Playing). His playing was in a grand and impassioned style with remarkable tone and technique described by Liszt as "infallible." He wrote *Taegliche Studien* and also composed some virtuoso pieces and arrangements.

TEMIANKA, HENRI (1906–), violinist. Born at Greenock, Scotland, Temianka studied at the Staatliche Hochschule fuer Musik in Berlin and with Carl *Flesch at the Curtis Institute, Philadelphia. He appeared as a soloist throughout Europe and the United States and from 1946 to 1966 was leader and first violinist of the Paganini Quartet. In 1958 he founded the Temianka Chamber Symphony Orchestra, which he conducted. He was also musician-in-residence at the University of California and professor of music at California State College.

TERTIS, LIONEL (1876–), violist. Born in England, Tertis was a viola soloist. This instrument, popular in the 18th century, had been neglected, and it was due to Tertis' exceptional playing that the viola was recognized as a solo instrument. Pieces were written especially for him and he designed a viola which was widely manufactured (the Tertis model).

***THALBERG, SIGISMUND** (1812–1871), pianist.

TISCHLER, HANS (1915–), musicologist. Born in Vienna, he settled in the United States in 1938 and studied musicology at Yale University. He held positions in West Virginia at Wesleyan College (1945–47), Roosevelt University in Chicago (1947–65), and Indiana University (1965). A specialist in 13th-century music, Tischler published *Harmony in the Works of Gustav Mahler* (1937), *The Motet in 13th-Century France* (1942), *The Perceptive Musical Listener* (1955), *A Humanistic Approach to Music* (1957), and *Practical Harmony* (1964).

***TOCH, ERNST** (1887–1964), composer.

TOUREL, JENNIE (1910–), mezzo-soprano. Born in Montreal, Canada, Jennie Tourel was educated in Russia, Switzerland, and France, where she studied with Anna El-Tour, whose name she transposed to form her own stage name. In 1933 she began her career in the Opéra Comique, Paris, and in 1940 settled in the United States. She made her U.S. debut with the New York Philharmonic under Toscanini. In 1944 she joined the Metropolitan Opera. Her best-known non-operatic performance was the rendition of the vocal solo in Leonard *Bernstein's *Jeremiah* symphony at its premiere performance (1944); she also became known through appearances in concerts and for recording. She gave annual courses at the Rubin Academy of Music, Jerusalem.

***TSFASSMAN, ALEXANDER NAUMOVICH** (1906–), composer.

TUCKER, RICHARD (1914–), singer and *ḥazzan*. Born in New York, Tucker sang in a synagogue choir and studied singing under Paul Althouse. From 1939 to 1944 he was *ḥazzan* at Temple Adath Israel, Brooklyn, and also appeared in concerts and on radio. In 1944 he was engaged by the Metropolitan Opera, but continued officiating as *ḥazzan* at the Brooklyn Jewish Center until 1947. At the Metropolitan he became one of the leading lyric tenors, specializing in French and Italian operas. Tucker was distinguished for the volume and quality of his voice, and sang in the world's leading opera houses. Throughout his career Tucker continued to perform occasionally as *ḥazzan* or in cantorial recitals, and also made several cantorial recordings.

TURECK, ROSALYN (1914–), pianist. Born in Chicago, Rosalyn Tureck played with the Chicago Symphony Orchestra at the age of 11, studied at the Juilliard School of Music, and specialized in the performance of Bach's keyboard works. In 1937 she gave the first of her Bach concerts in New York, and in 1947 set out on the first of her extensive European tours. She was a faculty member of the Juilliard School of Music (1943–53), lecturer at Columbia (1953–55), and Regent's Professor at the University of California (1966). She founded the Society for the Performance of International Contemporary Music (1951–55), the Tureck Bach Players (1959), and the International Bach Society (1966). She published many Bach works in pedagogical editions.

UNGAR, BENJAMIN (1907–), *ḥazzan;* see *Ḥazzan.*

UNGER, MAX (1883–1959), musicologist. Born in Germany, Unger worked as a conductor and critic, and in 1919–20 edited the *Neue Zeitschrift fuer Musik*. In 1933 he went to Switzerland and Italy and returned to Germany after World War II. An authority on Beethoven, he published *Auf Spuren von Beethovens unsterblicher Geliebten* (1911), *Beethovens Handschrift* (1926), *Ein Faustopernplan Beethovens und Goethes* (1952), and the catalogs of two important Beethoven collections. Unger gathered material for a revised edition of Beethoven's letters and established many of their datings for the first time.

VALABREGA, CESARE (1898–1965), pianist, critic, and musicologist. Born in Pesaro, Valbrega studied the piano at the conservatory there, and literature at the University of Bologna. He toured as a concert pianist in Italy and abroad. He taught the history of music at Naples, Perugia, and Rome, where he finally settled. He published *Schumann* (1934), *Domenico Scarlatti* (1937), and *Johann Sebastian Bach* (1950), and he edited the historical anthology of 40 long-playing records, *Storia della Musica Italiana,* issued by the Italian State Sound Archives (1957).

***VEPRIK, ALEXANDER MOYSEYEVICH** (1899–1958), composer.

VILNER BALABESSL, see *Loewenstein-Straschunsky, Joel David.

***VINAVER, CHEMJO** (1900–), conductor and composer.

***VOGEL, WLADIMIR** (1896–), composer.

VOLPE, ARNOLD (1869–1940), conductor. Born at Kovno, Lithuania, Volpe emigrated to the U.S. in 1898. There he conducted the Young Men's Symphony Orchestra (1902–19), the Volpe Symphony Orchestra (1904–1914) founded by him, the Washington D.C. Opera Company (1919–22), and the University of Miami Symphony Orchestra (1926–40). He was also director of the orchestral school of the Kansas City Conservatory (1922–25). In 1918 he founded the celebrated summer concerts at the Lewisohn Stadium, New York.

WAGHALTER, IGNATZ (1882–1940), conductor and composer. Born in Warsaw, Waghalter studied in Berlin, where he became conductor of the Comic Opera. From 1912 to 1923 he was conductor and general musical director of the German Opera House in Berlin-Charlottenburg. In 1925 he visited the United States and conducted the New York State Symphony Orchestra for one season. In 1933 he moved to Prague, in 1934 to Vienna, and after 1938 he settled in New York. As a composer he was best known for his operas, particularly *Mandragola* (1914), based on

Machiavelli's comedy. He also wrote operettas, works for strings, piano works, a vaudeville, *Bibi,* songs to Yiddish texts, and piano arrangements of Yiddish songs. Waghalter wrote an autobiography, *Aus dem Ghetto in die Freiheit* (1936).

WALDMAN, LEIBELE (c. 1907–1969), *ḥazzan;* see **Ḥazzan.*

WALDTEUFEL, EMIL (1837–1915), composer. He was born in Strasbourg, where his father, Lazare Waldteufel (Wallteufel), was a piano teacher at the conservatory, and his brothers were also active as musicians. Emil Waldteufel studied at the Paris Conservatory, but left before graduating and began to write dance music. His waltzes became perennial favorites, including *Très Jolie* (op. 154), *Dolores* (op. 170), *Estudiantina* (op. 191), and especially *España* (op. 286) and the "Skaters' Waltzes" (*Les Patineurs,* op. 183). In 1865 Waldteufel was appointed chamber musician to Empress Eugénie and director of the court balls.

WALLENSTEIN, ALFRED (1898–), cellist and conductor. Born in Chigaco, Wallenstein was taken when still a child to California where he played the cello in theater orchestras and later in the San Francisco Orchestra. After studying the cello and medicine in Europe, he became first cellist of the New York Philharmonic under Toscanini (1929) and from 1931 began appearing on the radio as conductor. Two years later he formed the Wallenstein Sinfonietta, a radio orchestra which became famous for its high standard of performance and its extensive repertoire of classical and contemporary music. From 1943 to 1956 Wallenstein conducted the Los Angeles Philharmonic and after 1952 was also music director of the Hollywood Bowl.

***WALTER, BRUNO** (1876–1962), conductor.

***WASSERZUG, ḤAYYIM (Ḥayyim Lomzer;** 1822–1882), *ḥazzan* and composer.

***WEILL, KURT** (1900–1950), composer.

***WEINBERG, JACOB** (1879–1956), composer.

***WEINBERGER, JAROMIR** (1896–1967), composer.

WEINER, LAZAR (1897–), composer and conductor. Born at Cherkassy, near Kiev, Weiner emigrated to the United States at the age of 17. He settled in New York, where he conducted choral societies and the Mendelssohn Symphony Orchestra of Brooklyn. Weiner was also conductor at the Central Synagogue, New York City, on the Message of Israel radio programs, and of a Y.M.H.A. chorus. From 1952 he taught at the Hebrew Union School of Education and Sacred Music. Among his compositions are the cantatas *Legend of Toil* (1933), *Fight for Freedom* (1943), and *To Thee, America* (1944), several Friday evening services, a Saturday morning service, ballets on Jewish subjects, and choral arrangements of Jewish folk songs. His son, YEHUDI (1921–), is also known as a composer.

WEINER, LEO (1885–1960), composer and teacher. Born in Budapest, Weiner was professor at the Budapest Academy from 1908 to 1949, and gained a reputation as a teacher. As a composer, Weiner was a moderate modernist of a stature recognized beyond the borders of his country. His music, written in a Hungarian idiom, has a light and vivacious touch and shows the influence of both the French and German schools. Weiner wrote orchestral works, chamber music, piano pieces, incidental music, and music for children. He also published several books on music theory.

WEINER, MATITYAHU, see *Shelem, Matityahu.

WEINSTOCK, HERBERT (1905–1971), writer and musicologist. Born in Milwaukee, Weinstock became an executive editor at the New York publishing firm of Alfred A. Knopf. His books and articles on music include both popularizations and scholarly biographies. Weinstock's works include *Tchaikovsky* (1943), *Handel* (1946), *Chopin* (1949), *Music as an Art* (1953), and *Donizetti* (1963).

***WEINTRAUB, SOLOMON (Solomon Kashtan;** 1781–1829), *ḥazzan.*

WEINTRAUB, ZEVI HIRSCH ALTER (1811–1882), *ḥazzan;* see *Weintraub, Solomon.

***WEISGALL, HUGO** (1912–), composer.

WEISSENBERG, JULIA LAZAREVNA (1878–1942), composer. Born in Orenburg, Russia, she studied composition at the St. Petersburg Conservatory under Rimsky-Korsakov, whose son, Andrei, she married. From 1915 to 1917 she was coeditor of the periodical *Muzykalny Sovremennik.* Her compositions were often lyrical and sometimes in an exotic vein. She also wrote music for children. Among her works were operas, including *Gülnara* (1935) and *The Twelve* (1925); a cantata for chorus and orchestra; a symphonic poem, *Into the Night* (1935); and songs.

WEISSMANN, ADOLF (1873–1929), music critic and writer. Born in Rosenberg, Silesia, Weissmann settled in Berlin, and became music critic of the *Berliner Tageblatt* and the *Berliner Zeitung am Mittag.* He died in Haifa while on a lecture tour. His lively and original books include studies of Bizet, Chopin, Verdi, Puccini, *Die Musik in der Weltkrise* (1922; *The Problems of Modern Music,* 1925), *Die Musik der Sinne* (1925), and *Die Entgoetterung der Musik* (1928; *Music Come to Earth,* 1930).

***WELLESZ, EGON JOSEPH** (1885–), musicologist and composer.

WEPRIK, ALEXANDER MOISEYEVICH, see *Veprik, Alexander Moiseyevich.

***WERNER, ERIC** (1901–), musicologist.

WHITEMAN, PAUL (1890–1967), bandleader. Born in Denver, Colorado, Whiteman played the violin in the Denver Symphony Orchestra and in the San Francisco People's Symphony. After World War I he formed his own orchestra devoted to popular and light music, but which was also open to jazz influences. Whiteman, through his style of symphonic jazz, attempted to make jazz respectable by bringing it to the concert stage. He toured the United States and Europe, commissioned works from established composers, and created the annual Whiteman Awards for symphonic jazz compositions. In 1914 he premiered George *Gershwin's *Rhapsody in Blue* with the composer at the piano. He wrote *Jazz* (1926, with M. M. McBride), *How to be a Bandleader* (1941, with L. Lieber), and *Records for the Millions* (1948).

WIENER, JEAN (1896–), pianist and composer; born in Paris. Between the world wars he organized and took part in many concerts of avant-garde music, in collaboration with the French "Group of Six" (Honegger, *Milhaud, Auric, Poulenc, Tailleferre, Durey). His compositions were strongly influenced by American jazz, which he helped to popularize in France. Among his works are *Franco-American Concerto* (1922–23), piano and violin music, an operetta, and music for the cinema, theater, radio, and television.

***WIENIAWSKI, HENRI** (1835–1880), violinist and composer.

WINTERNITZ, EMANUEL (1898–), musicologist. Born in Vienna, Winternitz emigrated to the United States in 1938 and in 1942 became keeper of the collection of musical instruments at the Metropolitan Museum, New York, and its curator in 1949. He also held appointments as lecturer at Harvard, Columbia, and Yale universities. Winternitz published *Musical Autographs from Monteverdi to Hindemith* (1955); *Musical Instruments of the Western World* (1967); and various important studies on the history and iconography of musical instruments.

WITTGENSTEIN, PAUL (1887–1961), pianist. Born in Vienna, Wittgenstein studied and made his debut there in 1913. During World War I he lost his right arm at the Russian front and embarked on an extraordinary career as a one-handed pianist. He left Austria in 1930 and after 1933 settled permanently in the United States. His repertoire consisted of works he had adapted or those especially written for him, such as Ravel's *Concerto for Left Hand,* Richard Strauss' *Parergon zur Symphonia Domestica* and *Panathenaeenzug,* and many other concert and chamber works by Erich Wolfgang *Korngold, Benjamin Britten, and Hans Gál. He published a pedagogical work *Schule der linken Hand.*

WOLFF, ALBERT LOUIS (1884–), conductor and composer. Born in Paris, Wolff was associated with the Opéra Comique, becoming chorus master in 1908, conductor in 1911, and principal conductor in 1922. In 1924 he was made musical director of the Théatre des Champs Elysées, and later conducted the Concerts Lamoureux and the Concerts Pasdeloup. Famous as a conductor of French music, he toured widely in Europe and in South America (1940–45) and conducted at the New York Metropolitan Opera (1919–21). His best-known work is the opera *L'Oiseau bleu* (1919).

WOLFF, HERMANN (1845–1902), concert manager and music critic. Born in Cologne, Wolff served for some time as Anton *Rubinstein's secretary, and in 1881 founded the concert management firm in Berlin bearing his name (later known as H. Wolff and J. Sachs) which became well known throughout Europe and was associated not only with the promotion of individual artists but also with the organization of important concert series in Berlin and Hamburg. Wolff was also editor of the *Neue Berliner Musikzeitung* (1878–79) and coeditor of the *Musikwelt.*

WOLFSOHN, JULIUSZ (1880–1944), pianist, critic, and composer. Born in Warsaw, Wolfsohn studied piano at the conservatories in Warsaw, Paris, and in Vienna, where he wrote music and criticism for the *Montagblatt*. On his return to Poland in 1925 he wrote for *Muzykai Rytm* and lectured on Jewish music and musicians and on the interpretation of Chopin. Wolfsohn settled in the United States in 1933. He composed a number of works on Eastern European Jewish themes, including *Jewish Rhapsody*, *Hebrew Suite*, and *Twelve Paraphrases on Jewish Melodies*.

WOLFSTHAL, CHUNE (1851–1924), composer. Born in Tysmenitsa, Galicia, Wolfsthal was the son of a cantor. Together with his six brothers he organized the well-known Kapelle Wolfsthal ensemble in Tarnopol. It toured widely and entertained both at gentile social functions and at ḥasidic courts. After service as a military bandmaster, Wolfsthal became conductor at the Jewish Theater in Lvov but was forced to flee to Vienna in 1914, and returned to Tarnopol after the war. The operettas which he composed, *Der Teufel als Retter, R. Jehuda Halevi, Der komische Ball, Die Malke Schwo, Die Tochter Jeruschulajims, Die Drei Matunes* (from the story by I. L. Peretz), and *Bostenai* were written in the classical pattern of Johann Strauss and Suppé operettas. They were played in every Jewish theater in the world and made Wolfsthal's reputation second only to that of Abraham *Goldfaden. He also composed waltzes, marches, and dances which attained great popularity. Despite his success, Wolfsthal lived and died in poverty.

WOLPE, STEFAN (1902–1972), composer. Born in Berlin, Wolpe studied at the Berlin Academy of Music under Paul Juon and Franz Schreker. In 1933 he settled in Jerusalem where he taught at the Palestine Conservatory of Music until 1938 and greatly influenced the first generation of locally educated composers. He subsequently settled in the United States and from 1951 taught at various New York institutions. His music belongs to the Schoenberg and Webern schools and shows strong Jewish influence. Among his compositions are a ballet, *The Man from Midian* (1940); an oratorio, *Israel and his Land;* a cantata, *Jigdal;* and chamber and choral works.

WORMSER, ANDRÉ (Alphonse Toussaint; 1851–1926), composer. Born in Paris, Wormser won the Rome Prize in 1872 for the cantata *Clytemnestre*. He composed successful operas, orchestral and choral works, piano pieces, and songs. His best-known composition is the pantomine "wordless opera," *L'Enfant prodigue* (1890).

***YASSER, JOSEPH** (1893–), musicologist and choral director.

YASSINOWSKI, PINHAS, see *Jassinowski, Pinhas.

YELLIN, THELMA (1895–1959), cellist, see *Bentwich.

YERUḤAM HA-KOTON, see *Blindman, Yeruḥam.

ZALUDKOWSKI, ELIYAHU (1888–1943), *ḥazzan* and writer; see **Ḥazzan*.

***ZEFIRA, BRACHA** (c. 1915–), singer.

ZEIDEL ROVNER, see *Morogowsky, Jacob Samuel.

***ZE'IRA, MORDECHAI** (1905–), composer.

ZHITOMIRSKI, ALEXANDER MATVEYEVICH (1881–1937), composer. Born in Kherson, Crimea, Zhitomirski taught composition at the St. Petersburg Conservatory from 1914. Among his works are *Heroic Poem* for orchestra (1933); a violin concerto (1937); a string quartet (1927); *Elegy* for cello and piano; and songs to Russian, Yiddish, and French words. He was a member of the Society for Jewish Folk Music and collaborated with S. Kiselgov and P. Lvov in the publication of the Society's *Lider Zamlbukh* (1911, 1914[2]).

***ZILBERTS, ZAVEL** (1881–1949), choral director, composer, and *ḥazzan*.

°**MUSIL, ALOIS** (1868–1944), Czech orientalist, born in Rychtarov in Bohemia. He studied at the theological faculty of Olomouc and was ordained a priest in 1891; in 1895 he went to Jerusalem to join the Dominican Ecole Biblique. His field exploration began with a tr.,, to Egypt in 1896 and to Petra in 1897, when he traveled from Gaza to Damascus by way of the Negev and Transjordan. In 1898 the Vienna Academy sent him on a mission to Arabia Petrea, which he explored until 1902, discovering the desert palaces at Quṣayr ʿAmra, Ṭūba, al-Bāyir, and al-Muwaqqar. He was one of the first explorers of the ancient cities of the Negev. In addition to archaeology, he was greatly interested in mapping and in the manners and customs of the Bedouin. From 1902 to 1909 he taught at Olomouc and from 1909 to 1918 at Vienna. He explored the Syrian Desert in 1908–09, the northern Hejaz in 1910, and the Palmyrene and northern Arabia to the Hejaz in 1912–15; the last mission was semipolitical. In 1920 he began to teach at Prague University. Musil published *Ḳuṣejr ʿAmra und andere Schloesser*... (2 vols., 1902); *Arabia Petraea* (Ger., 4 vols., 1907–08), which contains the first good map of the Negev; and a four-volume series of topographical itineraries through northern Arabia, including maps of the region (1926–28). He was an exact observer, although his archaeological training was insufficient.

Bibliography: Rypka, in: *Archiv Orientální*, 10 (1938), 1ff.

[M.A.-Y.]

°**MUSOLINO, BENEDETTO** (1809–1885), Italian statesman who foretold the return of the Jews to Ereẓ Israel. Born in Pizzo (Calabria), Musolino was an exile in his youth and later joined Garibaldi's army. From 1861 he served as member of the Italian parliament and later as a senator in united Italy. He published seven books on philosophy, law, and social justice. Musolino visited Ereẓ Israel four times and wrote *Gerusalemme ed il Popolo Ebreo* (1851, first published in 1951). Based upon an analysis of the situation of the Jews in the Diaspora and their yearning to return to Ereẓ Israel, the book suggests that Britain support the establishment of a Jewish principality in Ereẓ Israel under the Turkish Crown. Musolino even formulated a complete constitution, which stipulates a prince at the head of the principality and a bicameral parliament. The official religion of the principality is Judaism and the language is Hebrew. The right to vote and to be elected would be granted only to those who read and write Hebrew. All the public offices, including jurisdiction, would be determined by the elections for one-year terms. Citizenship would automatically be granted to Jews settling there and to non-Jews who request it. Other laws include freedom of speech and assembly, the prohibition of polygamy, and compulsory education between the ages of four and sixteen. Immigration and absorption would be under the control of a domestic settlement company, and the principality would guarantee the right to work. (See also *Zionism; Utopias.)

Bibliography: M. Ishai, in: *Scritti in Memoria di Sally Mayer* (1956), 145–66 (Heb. sect.).

[Mo.I.]

MUSSAFIA, ADOLFO (1834–1905), Italian philologist. Born in Split (Spalato), Croatia, Mussafia specialized in Romance studies and taught for almost 50 years at the University of Vienna. There he became the spokesman of Austria's Italian minority. Having tried in vain to have an Italian center for higher studies established in Trieste, he eventually moved to Florence, where he spent the last years of his life. Though the son of a rabbi, Mussafia was estranged from Judaism and converted in 1860 in order to become a member of the Italian senate. A philologist of wide interests, he was one of the pioneers who took up the study of the Italian and Romance dialects, devoting his valuable and painstaking attention to early texts in Italian and the Italian dialects (*Monumenti antichi dei dialetti italiani*, 1864, and *Darstellung der romagnolischen Mundart*, 1871). Mussafia also did research in comparative literature, investigating the origins of many medieval legends about Christian saints (*Zur Katharinen-Legende*, 1874, and *Sulla leggenda del segno della Croce*, 1870), elucidating many texts, and writing critical reviews. His other major publications include *Sul testo della "Divina Commedia"* (1865); *Sul testo del "Tesoro" di Brunetto Latini* (1870); *La difesa d'un illustre* (G. Boccaccio; 1861); and the *I codici Vaticani Latini 3195 e 3196 delle "Rime" del Petrarca* (1899).

Bibliography: E. Richter, in: *Zeitschrift fuer franzoesische Sprache und Literatur*, 55 (1932), 168–93; V. Crescini, *Romanica* *fragmenta* (1932), 148–53; *Bausteine zur romanischen Philologie, Festgabe . . . A. Mussafia* (1905). [L.C.]

MUSSAFIA, BENJAMIN BEN IMMANUEL (1606–1675), rabbi, philologist, physician, and author. A descendant of Spanish Marranos, he was probably born in Spain; little is known of his early years. He received a broad philosophical education, and, apart from his great talmudic scholarship, had a sound knowledge of Latin, Greek, and Arabic. He lived in Hamburg where he distinguished himself as a physician, and gained fame in the medical profession with the publication of his books on medicine. Consequently, he was invited to act as personal physician to King Christian IV of Denmark, to whom he dedicated the scientific work *Mei ha-Yam* (Amsterdam, 1642). When the king died in 1648, Mussafia moved to Amsterdam where he became a member of the well-known *bet ha-midrash* "Keter Torah." In his old age, he acted as one of the scholars of Amsterdam, and his signature was first on the eulogy and letter of recognition of Shabbetai Ẓevi, the false messiah, which was signed by Portuguese and *bet ha-midrash* "Keter Torah" scholars. In consequence, Jacob Sasportas, a zealous fighter against the Shabbateans, attacked him in his *Oholei Ya'akov*.

Mussafia's most important work is *Musaf he-Arukh* (Amsterdam, 1655), a supplement of linguistic entries to the *Arukh* of *Nathan b. Jehiel of Rome, in which he also gave new explanations to Latin and Greek words in that work. In his research he based himself largely on *Buxtorf's lexicon. The book gave him a world reputation as a scholar, and it was published in more than 20 editions. *Zekher Rav* (Hamburg, 1638) is his first published work (subsequently in about 16 editions and many translations); written in verse, it relates the marvels of the creation. His commentary on the Jerusalem Talmud has not been published. His scientific works, written under the Latin pseudonym, Dionysius, include *Mei Zahav* (Hamburg, 1638), on the healing properties of gold; and *Mei ha-Yam* (Amsterdam, 1642), on the tidal flow.

Bibliography: Fuenn, Keneset, 169; Michael, Or, 284–5. [Y.AL.]

MUSSAFIA, ḤAYYIM ISAAC (1754–1831), rabbi. Mussafia was born in Jerusalem. In 1796, while serving as an emissary of Jerusalem to the Balkan states, he was appointed *av bet din* of Spalato in Dalmatia. His only published work is *Ḥayyim va-Ḥesed* (pt. 1, Leghorn, 1844), responsa, appended to which are the laws of blessings by Yom Tov b. Abraham *Ishbili and talmudic novellae by early Jerusalem rabbis. Isaac Badhab affirmed that part two was in his possession. Mussafia also wrote *Derekh ha-Ḥayyim ve-Tokhaḥat Musar*, and *Maskil le-Eitan*, a supercommentary on the Pentateuch commentary of Rashi and Elijah Mizraḥi (see introd. to the responsa). He was succeeded at Spalato by his son, ABRAHAM ḤAI, who was also born in Jerusalem and served as a rabbi there. Abraham founded a yeshivah in Jerusalem called Shevet Aḥim (acronym of Avraham Ḥai Isaac Mussafia), which was in existence until shortly before World War I. He composed poems and was a contributor to *Ha-Maggid*.

Bibliography: Frumkin-Rivlin, 3 (1929), 214; M. D. Gaon, *Yehudei ha-Mizraḥ be-Ereẓ Yisrael*, 1 (1928), 145; 2 (1938), 387f.; Yaari, Sheluḥei, 691. [S.MAR.]

°**MUSSERT, ANTON ADRIAAN** (1894–1946), National Socialist leader in Holland. Originally an engineer in government service, he became active in politics in 1925. He founded the National-Socialist movement (1931), which at the peak of its popularity in the 1935 election received 8% of the votes. When Holland was occupied by Nazi Germany in May 1940, he tried to conduct a national policy and resisted annexation to Germany, but eventually he became a mere tool in the hands of the Germans. After the war he was condemned to death for collaboration with the enemy. Initially Mussert did not follow an anti-Jewish policy, and even accepted Jews as members of his party. From 1935, however, Jews could not hold office in the party, and in 1940 it was decided under German pressure to expel them altogether. Mussert unsuccessfully warned against the introduction of the yellow badge. For this reason, and because he tried to save some of his Jewish comrades, the Germans regarded him as a "Jew-servant."

Bibliography: Netherlands. Rijksinstituut voor oorlogsdocumentatie, *Processen*, no. 3, "Het proces Mussert" (1948); L. de Jong, *Het Koninkrijk der Nederlanden in de Tweede Wereldoorlog*, 1 (1969), 278–385. [J.M.]

°**MUSSOLINI, BENITO** (1883–1945), Italian dictator, founder of Fascism. Mussolini's policy toward the Jews was opportunistic, while his personal view of them, although unsystematic, was not unbiased. As early as 1908, in his essay *"La filosofia della forza,"* Mussolini the socialist adopted *Nietzsche's view that Christianity, as a "reevaluation of all values," was the spiritual revenge by which the Jews in Ereẓ Israel overcame their secular enemies, the Romans. In June 1919, reflecting the line of the extreme right-wing "fasci" he had created shortly before, Mussolini attacked world Jewry in his organ *Popolo d'Italia*, defining it as "the accomplices, the soul of both Bolshevism and of capitalism." However, he reversed this stand in October 1924, saying that "Bolshevism is not, as is believed, a Jewish phenomenon," and further claiming that "Italy does not know anti-Semitism and we believe that it will never know it." At the same time he excluded Zionism, declaring that "the new Zion *[nuova Sionne]* of the Italian Jews is found here, in our beloved land, that many of them heroically defended with their blood." By its very nature, Mussolini's opportunistic maneuvering delayed a systematic anti-Jewish policy, to a greater extent than did the presence of Jews in the ranks of Fascism from its earliest phases. From 1922, when he acceded to power, to 1938, when he branded them as racially impure, Mussolini endeavored to use the Jews as an instrument of policy, especially on the international level, in conformity with his distorted view of Judaism as an "international, occult body." At the same time, he permitted a parallel undercurrent of anti-Semitism (see *Preziosi, *Farinacci) which he repudiated or encouraged in turn, whenever he saw a chance of blackmailing the Western democracies. As a rule, anti-Semitism was deemed counterproductive as a propaganda tool, as well as on the official level. In November 1923, Mussolini declared to Angelo *Sacerdoti, chief rabbi of Rome, that "the Italian government and Italian Fascism have never intended to follow nor are following an anti-Semitic policy." Concerning mixed marriage, however, Mussolini's views were strictly Catholic. In 1929, the year of the Concordat with the Vatican, he forbade his daughter Edda's projected marriage with a Jew as "a real and proper scandal."

His attitude to Zionism was similarly ambivalent. To Chaim *Weizmann he said, shortly after his accession, "You know, we could build your state *en toute pièce*." In February 1928, he personally approved and encouraged the creation of the Italy-Palestine Committee, but rebuked the Italian Zionists in November of the same year (probably in deference to the Vatican, with whom he was about to sign the concordat) charging them with disloyalty to Italy: "We therefore ask the Italian Jews: are you a religion or a nation?" (*Popolo di Roma*, Nov. 29, 1928). Subsequently he resumed his pro-Zionist policy, purely from expansionist motives, and maintained it until after the conquest of Ethiopia. As long as Mussolini kept an open window on the Western world, he was eager to present an image of Italian Fascism as "Latin" and unprejudiced, in contrast with "savage and barbarous" National Socialism. Anti-Semitism remained a "German vice" and Hitler "a fanatical idiot." Racialism was "the Aryan fallacy" (*Popolo d'Italia*, Aug. 4, 1934).

Mussolini soon reversed his position. From 1936 to all intents and purposes he dissociated himself from the Western world and drew near to his derided disciple and future master. He blamed "international Jewry" for the sanctions which castigated Italy for its Ethiopian adventure and marked the end of his rapprochement with the Western democracies. As a result, the Italian Jews had become expendable, and could finally be treated in conformity with Fascist latent intolerance toward "alien groups." Undoubtedly, Mussolini also sought to please his new German ally, but the Italian Jews were not sacrificed merely for the sake of Hitler's "brutal friendship." In search of a formula which would bind his own irresolute hands, create an unbridgeable gap between non-Jews and Jews in Italy, and enable him to be rid of all the latter in one stroke, Mussolini resorted to racialism which he now saw as politically profitable. The *Dichiarazione della Razza* of July 1938, introducing racial measures in Italy, was largely compiled and edited by himself and due entirely to his initiative; there is no evidence whatsoever that he was subjected at any moment to pressure by Hitler. His acceptance of the racial vice, deliberate and cynical, was rejected by the Italian people in their great numbers. The extent to which he was personally willing to cooperate in the physical destruction of Jews is shown by events occurring during World War II. In August 1942 the Germans asked the Italians to hand over to the German-Croatian authorities the Jews who had gone into hiding in Dalmatia, in the Italian occupation zone, and a memorandum on the subject, indicating the terrible fate in store for the Jews, was submitted to Mussolini. He scrawled in the margin: "nulla osta" ("no objection").

See also *Italy.

Bibliography: R. de Felice, *Storia degli ebrei italiani sotto il fascismo* (1961), passim; L. Salvatorelli and G. Mira, *Storia d'Italia nel periodo fascista* (1956), index; G. Bedarida, *Ebrei d'Italia* (1950), index; L. Poliakov and J. Sabille, *Jews under the Italian Occupation* (1955), 137ff.; L. Fermi, *Ebrei d'Italia* (1950), index; Ch. Weizmann, *Trial and Error* (1966), index; N. Goldmann, *Sixty Years of Jewish Life* (1970), index; E. Ludwig, *Talks with Mussolini* (1933), 69ff.; M. Michaelis, in: *Yad Vashem Studies*, 4 (1960), 7–41; Carpi, in: *Rivista di studi politici internazionali*, 28, no. 1 (1961), 35–56; idem, in: *Moreshet*, 10 (1969), 79–88. [E.B.]

MUSTAʿRAB, MUSTAʿRABS, name of the Arab-speaking, old, established Jewish communities and residents in the Middle East. The term is borrowed from the Arabic. According to Arab genealogists, the "Arab al-Mustaʿriba" were not of native Arab stock; they were naturalized, "Arabized," Arabs. In Muslim Spain the Christians who adopted Arabic and Arab customs were called "Mozarabs." The term Mustaʿrab (better: Mustaʿrib) for Arabized Jews seems a late one; it occurs from the 15th century onward and seems to have been first used by immigrants from Christian Europe for the old, established Jews in Egypt, Palestine, and Syria. The terms al-Mashāriqa ("Easterners") and Moriscos are sometimes used in the same sense.

Bibliography: Neubauer, Chronicles, 1 (1887), 146, 150; A. Yaari, *Iggerot Ereẓ Yisrael* (1943), 169; I. Ben-Zvi, *Meḥkarim u-Mekorot* (1966), 15–20. [H.Z.H.]

MUSTARD (Heb. חַרְדָּל, *ḥardal*), the name applied to two species, the common mustard (*Sinapis alba*), known in rabbinical literature as "Egyptian mustard," and the kind called simply "mustard." The latter was extracted from the seeds of a different botanical genus, *Brassica nigra*, the mustard prepared from it being darker and more pungent than the former. This species, like white mustard, grows wild in Ereẓ Israel but was also cultivated. Given favorable conditions the plant reaches a height of more than six feet. The *aggadah* relates that a man having sown "a single seed of mustard . . . would climb it as he would a fig tree" (TJ, Pe'ah 7:4, 206). The seed of this species is very small (1–1.6 mm.), and was used to indicate the smallest measure of size (Ber. 31a). The contrast between the size of plant and the seed is used in a parable in the New Testament (Matt. 13:31). Although these two species of mustard belong to different botanical genera they are very similar in appearance (except that the white mustard plant is smaller and its seed larger). Hence the rule that mustard and Egyptian mustard do not constitute *mixed species (*kilayim;* Kil. 1:2). Both have conspicuous yellow flowers (cf. Kil. 2:8–9). In Israel there are many species belonging to the family of Cruciferae which have yellow flowers and seeds with a pungent flavor. Among these the species *Sinapis arvensis* is very widespread. This is called in the Mishnah *lafsan* ("charlock") and it was laid down that "mustard and charlock, although resembling one another, do constitute *kilayim*" (Kil. 1:5).

Bibliography: Loew, Flora, 1 (1928), 516–27; H.N. and A.L. Moldenke, *Plants of the Bible* (1952), 316 (index), s.v.; J. Feliks, *Kilei Zera'im ve-Harkavah* (1967), 65–67, 256–69, 284–6; idem, *Ẓimḥiyyat ha-Mishnah*, in: *Marot ha-Mishnah, Seder Zera'im* (1967), 55f. [J.F.]

MUSZKAT, MARION (Marian, Maks; 1915–), jurist. Born in Suwalki, Muszkat served in the Polish army during World War II, rising to the rank of colonel. In 1944 he was appointed a military judge and in the following year headed the Polish military delegation at the Nuremberg war-crimes trials. In 1949 Muszkat became lecturer at the Polish Academy of Political Science and later professor of international law at the University of Warsaw. He emigrated to Israel in 1957 and lectured in international law at the Tel Aviv extension of the Hebrew University, being appointed professor when the institution became Tel Aviv University. Muszkat's works include *Interwencja—zbrodniczy oręż polityki Stanów Zjednoczonych* ("Intervention—Criminal Weapon of U.S. Policy," 1953), *Kavvei-Yesod ba-Mishpat ha-Bein-Le'ummi* (2 vols., 1959–61), and *Hitpatteḥuyyot Ḥadishot be-Mishpat u-ve-Irgunim Bein-Le'ummiyyim* (1967); and he edited *Zarys prawa międzynarodowego publicznego* ("Outlines of Public International Law," 2 vols., 1955–56) and the quarterly *Be'ayot Bein-Le'ummiyyot*.

Bibliography: Tidhar, 18 (n.d.), 5430–31. [I.I.]

MUTER, MELA (1873–1967), French painter. She was born in Warsaw and as a young woman left Poland to study in France. There she abbreviated her family name, Mutermilch, using "Muter" as her professional name. In 1937 she received a gold medal at the Paris World's Fair, and two years later she was represented in the World's Fair of New York. When the Nazis invaded France, Mela Muter was in her late sixties. Her son was killed in the war, but she managed to elude the Germans in Avignon, in southern France. There she continued to live for many years, in great poverty, until in 1965 she was rediscovered by a gallery in Cologne. Two years later, a few months before her death, her work was exhibited in New York. Crippled and no longer able to paint, she enjoyed her new fame; she used most of her earnings to aid sick children. Her "psychological portraits" were much admired. In addition to portraits, she painted mother and child groups, landscapes and still lifes, either in vigorous oils or in tender aquarelles.

Bibliography: Hahn, in: *Das Zelt*, 1 (1924), 180–2. [A.W.]

MUTNIK (Mutnikovich), ABRAHAM (pseud. **Gleb;** 1868–1930), cofounder of the *Bund. Mutnik was born in Vilkomir (Ukmerge), Russian Lithuania. In Kovno he belonged to a revolutionary circle of Narodnaya Volya (the People's Will movement) which functioned among the pupils of his school, and he was subsequently expelled from the school. In the 1880s he studied in Berlin and became acquainted with the German workers' movement. He was expelled from Germany and on returning to Russia lived in Ponevez, Lithuania, gave private lessons, and disseminated illegal revolutionary propaganda which led to his arrest. From 1894 he was a central figure among the *Jewish Social Democrats in Vilna. On its behalf he wrote a detailed report for the Congress of the Socialist International in London (1896). At the founding convention of the Bund he was elected, with V. *Kossovski and A. *Kremer, to its central committee. Mutnik drew up the first proclamation of the Bund (May 1, 1898) and represented it at the first conference of the Russian Social Democratic Workers' Party (March 1898). He was arrested in Lodz, but in 1900 he escaped abroad. In the years 1902–06 he was secretary of the Bund "committee abroad" in London and Geneva and a member of the editorial board of its organ, *Der Yidisher Arbeter*. He published an important article on the history of the Bund and its activity (in *Zhizn*, no. 2, May 1902 signed G. Ya.), he returned to Russia in 1906 and took charge of the Bund press. He then withdrew from party activities and after World War I lived in Germany. His autobiographical memoirs were published in *Zukunft* (38 (1933), 509–13, 595–6, 664–6, 718–20).

Bibliography: J. S. Hertz (ed.), *Doyres Bundistn*, 1 (1956), 122–30; J. Hertz et al. (eds.), *Geshikhte fun Bund*, 1–2 (1960–62), indexes. [M.M.]

MUYAL (Moyal), AVRAHAM (1847–1885), representative of Ḥovevei Zion in Ereẓ Israel. Born in Rabat, Morocco, Muyal went to Ereẓ Israel with his parents in 1860, becoming a wealthy merchant and banker. As a French national, he had close ties with the French consul in Jaffa. He also had considerable influence in Turkish government circles and was treated with respect by the Arab population, with whose customs and way of life he was well acquainted. Muyal did much to help Jewish settlement and obtained a permit to build houses at Ekron. He was also entrusted with financial dealings by Baron Edmond de *Rothschild concerning the settlements of Ekron and Rishon le-Zion. In 1885 Muyal was appointed as the Ḥovevei Zion representative. He built houses and established farms in Petaḥ Tikvah and put the settlement on a sounder basis. In the *Bilu settlement Gederah, where it was forbidden to build houses, he secured shelter for the settlers by rapidly erecting a structure of wooden boards and covering it with a roof. Under Turkish law, destruction was thereupon illegal.

Bibliography: I. Klausner, *Mi-Katoviẓ ad Basel*, 1 (1965), 84–89, 150–62, index; A. Druyanow, *Ketavim le-Toledot Ḥibbat Ẓiyyon ve-Yishuv Ereẓ Yisrael*, 1 (1925²), 546–9, index; S. P. Rabinowitz (ed.), *Keneset Yisrael*, 1 (1886), 934–9. [I.K.]

MYER, MORRIS (1876–1944), Yiddish editor and Zionist worker. Born in Rumania, Myer reached London in 1902 where he engaged in Yiddish journalism and was active in the Labor movement. Later an active member of the Po'alei Zion, he also became prominent in the British Zionist Federation and was delegate to several Zionist Congresses. From 1919 he was a member of the Board of Deputies of British Jews and its joint foreign committee. Through his widely circulated Yiddish daily, *Die *Zeit*, which he founded in 1913 and which existed until 1950, he was one of the chief molders of opinion among the masses of Yiddish readers in England when Whitechapel was a hub of Jewish life. He was founder of the Federation of Jewish Relief Organizations and a close follower of the London Yiddish theater in its heyday. His books in Yiddish, include *A Yidishe Utopie* (1918), *Yidish Teater in London 1902–1942* (1943), and *Dos Organizirte Yidntum in England* (1943).

Bibliography: Wininger, Biog, 4 (1929), 367–8; Rejzen, Leksikon, 2 (1930), 388–94; LNYL, 5 (1963), 602–4 (incl. bibl.). [J.Le.]

MYER, SIDNEY ("Simcha") BAERSKI (1878–1934), Australian merchant and philanthropist. Myer was born in Poland and in 1897 he migrated to Australia. After working briefly at odd jobs in Melbourne, he opened a shop in Bendigo in partnership with his brother, Elkan B. Myer. This venture failed but later Myer bought another shop in Bendigo and this time his business expanded rapidly. In 1911 Myer purchased a store in Melbourne which he called the Myer Emporium, and which became the largest business of its kind in Australia. He had also obtained control of Marshall's of Adelaide, another large department store. In the early 1930s Myer had 5,300 employees working for him in his enterprises. He provided rest houses for his workers at the seaside and in the country.

In addition to his many contributions to Jewish and general charities, Myer donated large sums for unemployment relief during the depression of the 1930s. He left sizable endowments for the promotion of free orchestral concerts and the Melbourne Symphony Orchestra and an additional large sum for the general purposes of the University of Melbourne. [Ed.]

MYERS, SIR ARTHUR MELZINER (1867–1926), New Zealand statesman. Myers became managing director of a large business concern in his native city Auckland, and from 1905 to 1909 was mayor of Auckland. He entered the New Zealand parliament in 1910 and in 1912 became a member of the cabinet as minister of finance, defense, and railways. In the National Government from 1915 to 1919 he was minister of customs, munitions, and supplies in which capacity he laid the foundations for compulsory military service. He retired from parliament in 1921. Myers was noted for his benefactions to the city of Auckland, including the Myers Park in which he built a kindergarten and a school for backward children. He lived in England from 1923 and was a member of the Royal Commission on Local Government. He was knighted in 1924. [Ed.]

MYERS, CHARLES SAMUEL (1873–1946), British psychologist. Born in London, immediately on completing his medical education he left on an anthropological expedition to Torres Strait and Borneo with W. H. R. Rivers, the founder and first director of the Cambridge Psychological Laboratory. The successful expedition returned the following year with data on hearing, smell, taste, reaction time, rhythms, and music of the local population. In 1900 he spent some time in Egypt, studying hieroglyphics, excavating, and taking anthropometric measurements in Cairo and Khartoum. On returning to Cambridge he was appointed to the psychological laboratory where, after considerable opposition, he succeeded Rivers. He published his *Text-book of Experimental Psychology* in 1909 (1925³). It was the first text to have laboratory exercises and to treat statistics for psychology students. There was also a briefer

Introduction to Experimental Psychology, which he published in 1911 (1925[3]).

During his stay in Cambridge, Myers conducted research on primitive music, synesthesia, auditory localization, and individual differences among listeners to music. He helped to found the British Journal of Psychology in 1904 and edited it from 1911 to 1924. The new psychological laboratory at Cambridge, established in 1912, was made possible by a grant which he made anonymously. He was elected secretary and then in 1920 president of the British Psychological Society.

Myers' interest in applied psychology was initiated in World War I, when he was the first to recognize shell shock as an essentially psychological condition and to treat it by psychotherapy. He had secured a commission in the Royal Army Medical Corps. In 1922 he resigned his post at Cambridge and went to London to establish the National Institute of Industrial Psychology, where work was conducted on tests of mechanical ability, manual dexterity, performance measures of general intelligence, problems of attention, and industrial fatigue. Myers became the driving force in British applied psychology and helped to gain official recognition for psychological practitioners. He was widely honored for his work. Although his desire to occupy the first chair in psychology at Cambridge was not fulfilled, he exerted considerable influence on the next generation of British psychologists through his students and his textbooks.

He also wrote: *Psychology* (1910), *Mind and Work* (1920, 1921[2]), *Industrial Psychology* (1926), *Ten years of Industrial Psychology: an Account of the First Decade of the National Institute of Industrial Psychology* (1932).

Bibliography: T. H. Pear, in: *American Journal of Psychology*, 60 (1947), 289–96. [H.E.A.]

MYERS, GUSTAVUS (1872–1942), U.S. political reformer and historian. Myers was born in Trenton, New Jersey. As a reporter for several newspapers, he belonged to the muckraking movement, attacking big business and political abuses. Myers' first exposé, *History of Public Franchises in New York City* (1900), was followed by *History of Tammany Hall* (1901, 1917[2]), and his best-known work, the *History of Great American Fortunes* (1910, 1936[3]). Among Myers' other works are: *Beyond the Borderline of Life* (1910), *History of the Supreme Court of the United States* (1912), *The History of American Idealism* (1925), *The Ending of Hereditary American Fortunes* (1939), and *History of Bigotry in the United States* (1943), in which he attacked all forms of prejudice, including anti-Semitism. Myers' reputation rests principally on his painstaking research. Highly critical of the conditions that had made abuses possible, he became convinced in later years that modern innovations were contributing toward the elimination of some economic inequalities.

Bibliography: S. J. Kunitz and H. Haycroft, *Twentieth Century Authors* (1942); J. Chamberlain, *Farewell to Reform* (1932), index; L. Filler, *Crusaders for American Liberalism* (1939), index.

[H.L.T.]

MYERS, LAWRENCE E. (Lon; 1858–1899), U.S. track athlete. Born in Richmond, Virginia, Myers began his career as a runner in 1878 and a year later became the first man to better 50 seconds for 440 yards. Between 1879 and 1884, Myers won 15 U.S., ten Canadian, and three British national titles at distances from 100 to 880 yards. He visited Great Britain in 1881, 1884, and 1885, and set the then world marks for 440 yards (48.6 seconds) and 880 yards (1:55.4). In 1881 he became the first foreign runner to win a British national title.

Myers faced his most formidable opponent, Britain's Walter George, for the first time in 1882. George won two of three races at the Polo Grounds in New York City. Racing three years later as a professional, Myers won all three races at New York's Madison Square Garden. After repeating his victory over George in Australia in 1887, Myers retired from track the following year.

Bibliography: B. Postal et al. (eds.), *Encyclopedia of Jews in Sports* (1965), 475–8. [J.H.S.]

MYERS, SIR MICHAEL (1873–1950), lawyer; chief justice of New Zealand. Born in the small township of Motueka, Myers joined the largest law firm in Wellington, acting in crown cases that were both criminal and civil. In 1922 he was appointed king's counsel and began his own practice. Six cases in which he was involved went to the Privy Council and in all of them he was successful. From 1929 to 1946, Myers was chief justice of New Zealand and his wide practical experience and keen sense of justice earned him a high reputation. In 1936 he served as justice on the Privy Council and in 1946 he represented New Zealand on the United Nations committee of jurists. Myers took an active interest in all Jewish affairs and was president of the Wellington synagogue from 1912 to 1921, a post previously held by both his father and elder brother. Myers was intensely interested in Jewish history and was patron of the Australian Jewish Historical Society. On several occasions he acted for the governor-general during the latter's absences from New Zealand. [M.S.P.]

MYERS, MORDECAI (1776–1871), U.S. merchant, army officer, and politician. Myers was born in Newport, R.I. He lived in New York State most of his life, while intermittently maintaining residence in Charleston, S.C. A member of New York City's Shearith Israel Congregation after 1792, he served as a trustee from 1800 to 1805 and donated a

Mordecai Myers, U.S. army officer and politician. Courtesy American Jewish Historical Society, Waltham, Mass.

generous sum toward the construction of a new synagogue in Greenwich Village. Subsequently he joined the army and was commissioned captain in the Third Regiment of the First Brigade Infantry (1811). He served with the Thirteenth Infantry in the War of 1812, was wounded in the battle of Chrysler's Field, and was later promoted to major. In 1814 Myers married a non-Jewish woman, and thereafter ceased to play a role in the Jewish community. He was a ranking Mason from 1823 to 1834 and was offered the office of grand master for New York State, which, however, he declined. In 1828 and from 1831 to 1834 Myers served as a Democratic assemblyman in the state legislature from New York County. Subsequently he moved to Schenectady, where he was elected mayor in 1851 and 1854. In 1860, at the age of 84, he ran unsuccessfully for a seat in the U.S. Congress. [L.He.]

MYERS, MOSES (1752–1835), U.S. merchant and civic leader. Moses Myers, the son of Haym and Rachel Louzada Myers, was born in New York City. For a time he was a junior partner in Isaac Moses & Co., a New York import-export firm, but the bankruptcy of Isaac *Moses in 1786 led Moses Myers to seek a new enterprise. With his friend Samuel *Myers, also a junior partner in the bankrupted firm, he opened a store in Norfolk, Virginia, 1787. After Samuel moved to Petersburg, Virginia (1789), Moses expanded his operations into importing and exporting. By 1812 he was the leading merchant south of the Potomac. During his early years in Norfolk, he functioned also as agent for the Philadelphia financier Stephen Girard, as superintendent of the Norfolk branch of the Bank of Richmond, and as consular agent for France and the Batavian Republic. He was elected to the city's Common Council for 1795–97 and because he polled the largest vote, served as council president. The Embargo Acts of 1807–15 and a second bankruptcy of Isaac Moses, with whom he had investments, led Moses Myers and his eldest son, John, into bankruptcy. Myers never totally recovered from this setback, despite the testimonials of 277 Norfolk and Portsmouth merchants. President John Quincy Adams later named him collector of customs, superintendent of lights, and agent for the Marine Hospital, declaring him "the first honest man in the post"; he served from 1827 to 1830.

Portrait of Moses Myers by Gilbert Stuart. Photo Longley's Studio, Cincinnati, Ohio.

In 1787, he married Eliza Judah of Montreal, widow of Detroit pioneer Chapman Abraham. Myers' handsome home, erected in 1792, remains a Norfolk landmark.

Bibliography: Stern, in: *Southern Jewish Historical Society Journal*, 1 (1958), 5–13; Rosenbloom, Biogr Dict. [S.V.]

MYERS, MYER (1723–1795), U.S. silversmith. Myers was born in New York, where his parents had migrated from Holland. He learned his trade early and at 23 set up shop on Lower Wall Street, where he not only engaged successfully in his craft but also sold tea, coffee, spices, and tobacco. By 1755 he had expanded his trade to Philadelphia. Myers was active in the general community, in Freemasonry, and in the synagogue, serving as president of Congregation Shearith Israel in New York in 1759 and again in 1770. During the American Revolution he was a patriotic stalwart, and he and his family moved from the city during the British occupation going first to Norwalk, Connecticut, and later to Philadelphia. There he used his skill to smelt down metal household goods and turn them into bullets. Myers returned to New York in 1783, and was a signatory of the address to Governor George Clinton from the "congregation of Israelites lately returned from exile." Myers was a highly skillful and versatile master craftsman, who created the first American examples of Jewish ceremonial objects, and was also distinguished for his general ornamental and functional pieces. There are many examples of his work in places of worship, museums, and private collections. For the synagogues of New York, Newport, and Philadelphia he made silver Torah bells *(rimmonim)* which are still in use. His versatility is revealed in his alms basins and baptismal bowls. His mark "myers" was most frequently stamped on his work in script in a shaped cartouche though sometimes he merely used his initials, MM. In 1786 he was elected chairman of the Gold and Silversmiths' Society of New York. He was buried in the cemetery that still exists off Chatham Square in Lower Manhattan.

Rimmonim made by Myer Myers for the Mikveh Israel Synagogue, Philadelphia, Pa. Photo Charles D. Mills and Son, Philadelphia.

Bibliography: J. W. Rosenbaum, *Myer Myers, Goldsmith* (1954), includes bibliography; G. Schoenberger, in: AJHSP, 43 (1953), 1–9. [A.W.]

MYERS, SAMUEL (1755–1836), U.S. merchant. Samuel Myers was the second child of New York silversmith Myer *Myers and his first wife, Elkaleh Myers-Cohen. As a child he worked in his father's silver shop, but soon joined his friend Moses *Myers as a junior partner in Isaac *Moses' import-export firm. A year after the firm's bankruptcy in 1786, Samuel and Moses opened a store in Norfolk, Virginia, but two years later they separated. Samuel moved to Petersburg, Virginia, the first known Jewish resident of the town. His half-brothers Moses Mears Myers and Sampson Mears Myers joined him there, all three becoming tobacco dealers. By 1798, Samuel was active in Richmond, contributing to Congregation Beth Shalome. He settled there permanently by 1803 and played an active role in business and social life as a leading Jewish citizen. Samuel's first wife, Sarah, daughter of Samuel *Judah of New York, died a year after the marriage. In 1796 Samuel and his brother Moses married daughters of the Boston merchant Moses Michael *Hays. His second son, Gustavus Adolphus Myers (1801–1869), became Richmond's leading Jew, serving for nearly three decades on the City Council and for 12 years as its president.

Samuel Myers, U.S. merchant. From *American Jewish Year Book 1923–24*, Philadelphia, Pa.

Bibliography: Rosenbloom, Biogr Dict; J. W. Rosenbaum, *Myer Myers, Goldsmith* (1954); H. T. Ezekiel and G. Lichtenstein, *History of the Jews of Richmond* (1917), index. [S.Vi.]

MYRRH (Heb. מוֹר, *mor*), one of the most important perfumes of ancient times. It is referred to 11 times in the Bible, more than any other perfume. The Hebrew, *mor*, refers to its bitter taste (*mar*, "bitter"); the root is common to the various Semitic languages, from where it was transferred to Greek Μύῤῥα and Latin *myrrha*. It is first mentioned along with the ingredients from which the holy anointing oil in the Tabernacle was prepared (Ex. 30:23–25), where it is called *mor deror*, i.e., myrrh congealed to

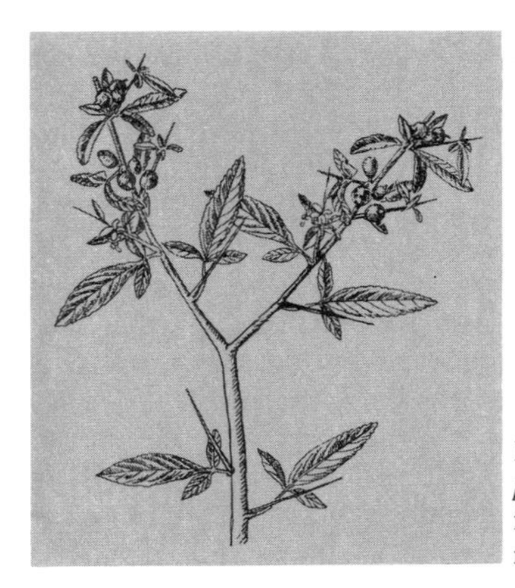

Branch of myrrh *(Commiphora abyssinica)* with fruit. Courtesy J. Feliks, Jerusalem.

form granules (*deror* from *dar*, "pearl") and then dissolved in olive oil. The king's garments were perfumed with myrrh (Ps. 45:9), and the faithless wife perfumed her couch with it when she wanted to seduce men (Prov. 7:17). The maidens were treated with it for six months before being presented to Ahasuerus (Esth. 2:12). In the Song of Songs myrrh is mentioned no less than seven times. It grew in the imaginary spice garden to which the charms of the beloved one are compared (Song 4:14; 5:1). It is upon "the mountain of myrrh" that the beloved dreams he will meet his heart's desire (4:6). The queen arrives for a meeting with the king "from the wilderness . . . perfumed with myrrh and frankincense" (3:6). The beloved one watched for her lover with her fingers dripping "flowing myrrh" (5:5), i.e., oil of myrrh, and his lips too were "dripping with flowing myrrh" (5:13). The man lying in the arms of his beloved is likened to the crystallized myrrh which the women used to wear as "a bag of myrrh" (1:13).

Myrrh is extracted from certain trees or shrubs growing in Africa or in the Arabian peninsula: *Commiphora abyssinica* and *Commiphora schimperi*. These plants contain a fragrant sap under the bark like the sap of the *acacia, from which gum arabic is prepared (Gr. κόμι; mishnaic Heb. קומוס, *kumos*). The sages warned against those who adulterated myrrh with this *kumos* (Sifra 1:12). Myrrh is variously interpreted homiletically by the rabbis as referring to Moses and Aaron or to Abraham: myrrh, the prince of spices, is Abraham who offered his son Isaac on Mt. Moriah (connecting "*mor*" with "Moriah"; Song R. 3:6, no. 2). They also connected it with Mordecai whose name was explained to mean *mor-dakhya:* "pure myrrh" (Ḥul. 139b). The *mor over*, "flowering myrrh," of the Song of Songs alludes to Israel's troubles which will pass: "Read not *mor over* but *mar over:* "passing bitterness" (cf. Shab. 30b). Saadiah Gaon, followed by Maimonides, identified "a bag of *mor*" with musk, the perfume extracted from the aromatic gland of the musk deer (see *Incense and Perfumes) but there is no basis for this.

Bibliography: Loew, Flora, 1 (1928), 249, 305–11; H. N. and A. L. Moldenke, *Plants of the Bible* (1952), 316 (index), s.v.; J. Feliks, *Olam ha-Ẓome'aḥ ha-Mikra'i* (1968²), 252–4. [J.F.]

MYRTLE (Heb. הֲדַס; *hadas*), *Myrtus communis*, a shrub, and occasionally a tree, possessing fragrant and glossy leaves. It grows wild on Mount Carmel and in Upper Galilee, and its use as a decorative shrub is widespread. The leaves usually grow in series of two and opposite each other. Some have leaves arranged in groups of three. Burning the shrubs produces a higher proportion of the latter form. The plant flowers during the summer months and later bears black berries. There are other varieties whose ripe fruit is white and whose small leaves are arranged in groups of four or more. The plant is called *asu* in Akkadian and *asa* in Aramaic. The *eẓ avot*, twice mentioned in Scripture, refers, according to rabbinical tradition, to the myrtle. It is one of the *Four Species (Lev. 23:40). The Book of Nehemiah, however, refers to both *hadas* and *eẓ avot*, in connection with the observance of the Feast of Tabernacles (Neh. 8:15). In consequence some scholars think that the name *eẓ avot* applies to any tree whose branches are closely braided together (*avotim*, "compact"). The rabbis explain that *hadas* refers to the wild myrtle branches gathered for covering the *sukkah*, while *eẓ avot* refers to the twigs of three leaved myrtles which were "with the *lulav*" (Suk. 12a). They explained that *eẓ avot* means a tree "whose branches cover its trunk . . . is shaped like a plait and resembles a chain" (Suk. 32b). The leaves of the *oleander are of similar form but were declared invalid on the grounds that it is poisonous *(ibid.)*. To satisfy the regulation concerning Tabernacles "a myrtle producing groups of three leaves from a single node" is necessary; there was a dispute concerning the validity of those varieties of myrtle, like the Egyptian myrtle, which produce many leaves from a single node (Suk. 32b–33a).

The myrtle is an evergreen (Targ. Sheni, Esth. 2:7), and the rabbis thus compared it with the good qualities of Esther whose Hebrew name was Hadassah ("myrtle"). Its aromatic branches were used for preparing the bridegroom's wreaths (Tosef., Sot. 15:8). They were used in

Buying myrtle for Sukkot at the Tel Aviv market. Courtesy Government Press Office, Tel Aviv.

festivities and betrothal celebrations, and some of the sages would juggle with myrtle branches, throwing them up and catching them (Ket. 17a). The leaves of the myrtle have the shape of the eye (Lev. R. 30:14). Its fruits, called *benot hadas* ("myrtle products"), were occasionally eaten, but are tasteless (TJ, Or. 1:1, 60c–d; Suk. 32b). Some recommended myrtle leaves as a remedy for blood pressure in the head (Git. 68b). The custom still obtains in some places of pronouncing the blessings for spices at the **Havdalah* on the termination of the Sabbath over myrtle leaves. According to *Bet Hillel the benediction over the myrtle takes precedence over the benediction over aromatic oil (Ber. 43b).

Bibliography: Loew, Flora, 2 (1924), 257–74; H. N. and A. L. Moldenke, *Plants of the Bible* (1952), 316 (index), s.v.; J. Feliks, *Olam ha-Ẓome'aḥ ha-Mikra'i* (1968[2]), 99–101.

[J.F.]

MYSH, MICHAEL (1846–?), Russian lawyer and writer; born in Korets, Volhynia. Of a poor family, Mysh attended the government Jewish school of his town. He completed his studies at the law faculty of the University of Kiev and contributed to the Russian Jewish press, devoting himself to the study of anti-Jewish legislation in Russia. He wrote commentaries, surveys, and guides on the restrictive laws against the Jews. The most important of them was *Rukovodstvo po russkim zakonam o Yevreyakh* ("Guide to the Russian Laws Concerning the Jews," 1892), which ran into four editions. He also wrote essays and books on general legal problems. His son, VLADIMIR (1873–1947), was a professor of medicine and a member of the Soviet Academy.

Bibliography: J. Frumkin (ed.), *Russian Jewry 1860–1917* (1966), 475.

[Y.S.]

MYTH, MYTHOLOGY (Gr. *μῦθος*; "word," "word content," "narrative"). A myth is a story about the universe that is considered sacred. Such a story deals with the great moments of man's life: birth, initiation, and death, referring them to events that took place in "mythical time." The myth is often recited during a dramatic representation of the event it narrates (e.g., the *Enūma eliš* was recited at the Babylonian New Year festival). Through the ritual, man becomes contemporary with the mythical event and participates in the gods' creative actions. Thus man can create, maintain, or renew fecundity, life, etc. Myths can be classified according to their subjects, as: theogonic, cosmogonic, anthropogonic, soteriological, and eschatological, myths of paradise, myths of flood, hero myths, etc.

In the Bible. The word "myth" was first applied to biblical narratives in the 18th century, when the question of the historicity of the first chapters of Genesis arose. For J. G. Eichhorn, for instance, the biblical narratives contain philosophical truth (e.g., the Garden of Eden narrative) or are based on a kernel of historical truth (the narratives concerning the Patriarchs). In the mid-19th century the term myth acquired a more precise meaning in biblical research. Biblical scholars who held that myth and polytheism were inseparable (e.g., Y. Kaufmann and H. Frankfort) denied any possibility of finding myths in the Bible, though they do not deny the existence of residues of myths or "demythologized myths" in the Bible. A number of apparent myths and mythical subjects which found their way into the Bible, have been collected and compared with extra-biblical parallels. In the prophetic and poetic books, references are made to the Lord's struggle with the primeval dragon, variously named *Tannin* ("Dragon," Isa. 27:1, 51:9; Ps. 74:13; Job 7:12), *Yam* ("Sea," Isa. 51:10; Hab. 3:8; Ps. 74:13; Job 7:12), *Nahar* ("River," Hab. 3:8; Ps. 93?), Leviathan (Isa. 27:1; Ps. 74:14), and *Rahab* (Isa. 30:7; 51:9; Ps. 89:11; Job 9:13; 26:12–13). A special parallel to this theme is found in the Ugaritic myth of Baal and his struggle against *Yam*, in which mention is made of Leviathan (*ltn;* C. H. Gordon, *Ugaritic Textbook* (1965), 67, 1:1) and *Tannin* (*tnn;* ʿ*nt, ibid.*, 3:37) as well as of *Nahar* (*nhr*). In this myth the dragon is called, as in Isaiah 27:1, *bari'aḥ* ("fleeing serpent") and ʿ*aqallaton* ("twisting serpent"; cf. Gordon, *ibid.*, 67, 1:2–3). The same theme is found in the Babylonian creation epic *Enūma eliš* (Marduk's fight with Tiamat, "Sea") and in the Hittite myth of the storm-god and the dragon Illuyankas (Pritchard, Texts, 125–6), and with variations in Sumerian, Egyptian, Phoenician, and other literatures (see also *Leviathan).

The idea that man was made out of clay (Gen. 2:7; Job 33:6) is common to the Bible and other extra-biblical literatures, especially the myth of Atraḫasis (W. G. Lambert and A. R. Millard, *Atra-Ḫasīs* (1969), 56ff.; cf. also *Enūma eliš*, 6:1–38 and the creation of Enkidu, *Gilgamesh* 1:30–40, in Pritchard, Texts, 68, 74). In Genesis 2:7, the Lord breathed into man's nostrils the breath of life; in Atraḫasis, man is the product of the mixture of clay and the flesh and blood of a slaughtered god. In the latter source, man is created to do the work the inferior gods refused to do (cf. Gen. 2:15).

The biblical story which has the most striking Mesopotamian parallel is the flood story (Gen. 6–8; *Gilgamesh*, tablet 11—in Pritchard, Texts, 93–97, cf. also Atraḫasis). In both accounts a man and his household escape the deluge thanks to divine providence; the flood hero is told to build a ship (ark); after the flood, the ship comes to rest upon a mountain (Ararat or Niṣir); birds are sent out in exploration; a much appreciated sacrifice is offered by the survivor; God (or the gods) repents of His bringing about the flood. As in other myths, the main difference between the biblical and extra-biblical version of the flood story resides in the fact that the biblical one is monotheistic. Other differences can be pointed out. For example, the fact that Noah takes with him only his family, while Utnapishtim (the Babylonian flood hero) makes a point of taking craftsmen with him, may well point to different types of society.

Residues of hero myths can be found in Genesis 5:24; 6:1–4; 10:8–9; and II Samuel 23:8ff., for example. The stories about Samson, Jephthah, Gideon, and so on have much in common with the hero myth genre.

In biblical poetry there are echoes of myths: the wind has wings (I Sam. 22:11: Hos. 4:19); thunder is the Lord's voice (II Sam. 22:14; et al.); the Lord rides the clouds (Ps. 68:5), etc. Although mythical patterns can be found in the Bible, the biblical authors are not especially interested in "extra-temporal events," but rather deal with God's intervention in history. The Bible is less interested in the cosmos than in man.

Bibliography: T. J. Meek, in: JBL, 42 (1924), 245–52; E. Norden, *Die Geburt des Kindes* (1924); Th. H. Gaster, *Thespis* (1950), idem, in: *Numen*, 1 (1964), 184ff.; Y. Kaufmann, in: JBL, 70 (1951), 179–97; H. Frankfort et al., *Before Philosophy* (1952); M. Eliade, *The Myth of the Eternal Return* (1954); idem, *Patterns in Comparative Religion* (1958); S. H. Hooke (ed.), *Myth, Ritual and Kingship* (1958); E. O. James, *Myth and Ritual in the Ancient Near East* (1958); J. Barr, in: VT, 9 (1959), 1–10; J. L. McKenzie, in: CBQ, 21 (1959), 265–82; B. S. Childs, *Myth and Reality in the Old Testament* (1960).

[ED.]

MZAB, a group of Sahara oases located in central Algeria. Descendants of the Muslim Ibāḍiyya sect, who formerly dominated Tripoli, live in Mzab. The inhabitants of Mzab came from Tahert, an ancient metropolis which was destroyed in 902, from Sedrata and from Ouargla, which was the home of a Karaite Jewish community. Mzab Jews are presumably their descendants. Until the 14th century Jews emigrated from the Ibaḍite centers of Jerba and Jebel Nafusa (Tripolitania) to Mzab. The *dayyan* of Mzab in the 16th century was Isaac Mesalati. The Jews of Mzab were chiefly goldsmiths. From the 16th to the 18th centuries many were suppliers of ostrich feathers whose export to Europe was monopolized by their coreligionists on the coast. Like all Mzabites, they were forced to seek employment as far as Tripolitania and returned only for Passover.

In the 19th century they were concentrated in Ghardaia, capital of Mzab, where they had a special quarter. They were obliged to wear black clothes and were not permitted to buy farmland. Mzab was conquered by the French in 1882. The 900 Jews in Ghardaia at that time were not granted French citizenship. In 1921 there were 1,409 Jews in the area; in 1950, 1,652; and in 1962, 500. In 1962 all the Jews left Ghardaia; most settled in France.

Bibliography: Huguet, in: *Bulletins et Mémoires de la Société d'Anthropologie de Paris,* Series 5, vol. 3 (1902), 559–73; M. Mercier, *La civilisation urbaine du Mzab* (1922); Finkel, in: JQR, 23 (1932/33), 281–3; Cohen, *ibid.*, 398; Hirschberg, in: *Sinai, Sefer Yovel* (1958), 344–55; Hirschberg, Afrikah, 2 (1965), 32–35; Casanowicz, in: *American Anthropologist* (1905), 357–9; L. C. Briggs and N. L. Suède, *No More For Ever* (1964).

[D.Co.]

The letter "N" as part of the illuminated word *In (diebus Assueri)* at the beginning of the Book of Esther in a 12th-century Latin Bible. On the right of King Ahasuerus, Haman is being hanged. The "I" frames the figure of Esther. Rheims, Bibliothèque Municipale, Ms. 23, fol. 69v.

NAAMAH (Heb. נַעֲמָה; "pleasantness"), two biblical figures. (1) Daughter of Lamech and Zillah and sister of Tubal-Cain (Gen. 4:22). (2) Ammonite wife of Solomon, mother of Rehoboam (I Kings 14:21; II Chron. 12:13).

Bibliography: EM, 5 (1968), 891–2 (incl. bibl.). [Ed.]

NAAMAN (Heb. נַעֲמָן, "pleasant"; the name occurs in Ugaritic and is an epithet of heroes in Ugaritic epics), Syrian commander, healed of leprosy by the prophet *Elisha. According to II Kings 5, Naaman, a valorous man, held by his king in great esteem but afflicted with leprosy, had a female slave from the land of Israel. From her, his wife learned that "the prophet that is in Samaria," could cure Naaman of his leprosy. Naaman departed for the land of Israel taking with him a letter from the king of Aram to the king of Israel, as well as lavish presents. The king of Israel thought that the letter asking him to cure Naaman was nothing but a trick "to seek an occasion against him." Elisha, however, asked that Naaman be brought to him. When Naaman and his escort arrived at Elisha's house, he was told by a messenger to wash seven times in the Jordan River. Offended by the prophet's brusqueness and aloofness, Naaman decided to leave the land of Israel, but on the way his servants convinced him to do what the prophet prescribed. He washed in the Jordan and was cured. Naaman then went back to Elisha convinced that "there was no God in all the earth but in Israel." In vain he entreated the prophet to accept his presents. He then asked for "two mules' burden of earth, for thy servant will henceforth offer neither burnt offering nor sacrifices unto other gods, but unto the Lord." The fact that Naaman felt it was necessary to take earth from the land of Israel to build an altar for the Lord hints at the belief that sacrifices to YHWH could only be offered on Israelite soil (cf. Josh. 22:10ff.; II Sam. 26:19). Naaman also asked forgiveness for the fact that because of his office at the court he would be obliged to perform acts that could be interpreted as idolatry. Soon after Naaman's departure, Gehazi, Elisha's servant, ran after Naaman and through deceit received from him two talents of silver and two changes of clothing. As a punishment he was cursed with Naaman's disease. That neither Naaman nor Gehazi was isolated from society (II Kings 8:4; cf. Lev. 13–14) suggests that Naaman's disease was not what is now known as leprosy (see *Leprosy).

In the Aggadah. Naaman was the archer who drew his bow at a venture and mortally wounded Ahab, King of Israel (I Kings 22:34) and thus it was that through him "the Lord had given deliverance unto Syria" (II Kings 5:1). It would therefore follow that his master, referred to in 5:18, was Ben Hadad (Mid. Ps. 90). Two reasons are given for his leprosy, one that it was a punishment for his haughtiness (Num. R. 7:5; cf. Rashi to Lev. 14:4) and the other that it was for taking an Israelite girl as maidservant to his wife (Tanḥ. Tazri'a, end). According to the *Mekhilta* (Yitro, Amalek 1) Naaman was an example of the righteous proselyte, ranking even higher than Jethro; according to the Talmud, however (Git. 57a), he became merely a *ger toshav*, a "resident alien" who accepted only the seven Noachide laws, but not all the commandments. [Ed.]

NA'AN (Heb. נַעַן), kibbutz in central Israel, E. of Reḥovot, affiliated with Ha-Kibbutz ha-Me'uḥad. It was founded in 1930 as the first village of *Ha-No'ar ha-Oved youth. The founders were later joined by immigrants from many countries. During the 1936–39 disturbances Na'an maintained friendly ties with Arab villages in the vicinity and was not attacked, but it came under siege by the British army on

"Black Saturday" June 29, 1946, when 23 settlers were wounded. In 1969 Na'an had 870 inhabitants. Its economy is based on highly intensive farming and it runs a metal plant producing irrigation and other equipment, and a mechanical laundry. The settlement's name is adapted from the Arabic name of the site, Naʿana, which in turn may be the original town of Naamah of the tribe of Judah (Josh. 15:41).

[E.O.]

NAAR, DAVID (1800–1880), U.S. politician, journalist, and public servant. Naar, who was born in St. Thomas, Danish West Indies (now Virgin Islands), was sent to Manhattanville, New York, at the age of 15 to be educated. He spent about five years there. Because of Negro insurrections in the Caribbean and the decline of trade, his family moved to New York City in 1834 and continued their tobacco importing and exporting business. In 1838 Naar purchased a farm near Elizabeth, New Jersey, became active in politics as a Democrat, and was rewarded politically with an appointment as lay judge of the Court of Common Pleas. He was appointed mayor of Elizabeth in 1849. In 1844 he was a delegate to the state constitutional convention where he vigorously and successfully advocated giving Roman Catholics the right to vote and hold office. President James K. Polk appointed him as commercial agent of the United States to St. Thomas (1845–48). Naar moved to Trenton in 1853 and bought the *Daily True American* which he edited until 1870. His nephew and son then edited the paper until 1905. The newspaper, which

David Naar, U.S. politician and newspaper editor. Portrait by E. P. Tomplinson. From *American Jewish Historical Quarterly*, Vol. 53, New York, 1964.

became a very influential factor in the Democratic Party, espoused the cause of the South, favored (at first) secession and states' rights, and was pro-slavery. Naar was attacked by his Republican opponents as "a West Indian Jew" and other epithets. Naar served as treasurer of New Jersey and a member of the Trenton Common Council. He favored free public school education, free public libraries, and was one of the founders of the Normal School for Teachers (now Trenton State College).

Bibliography: Kohn, in: AJHSQ, 53 (1964), 372–95. [S.Jo.K.]

NAARAH (Heb. נַעֲרָה), town in the Jordan Valley on the boundary between the territories of Ephraim and Benjamin (Josh. 16:7; I Chron. 7:28—Naaran). It is called Neara by Josephus who relates that Herod's son *Archelaus diverted the waters of the village to irrigate groves of palm trees (Ant., 17:340). Eusebius refers to it as Noorath and describes it as a Jewish village five miles from Jericho (Onom. 136:24). A Midrash mentions that hostile relations existed between Naarah and Jericho (Lam. R., 1:17, no. 52). The Jews living there are mentioned in late Christian sources

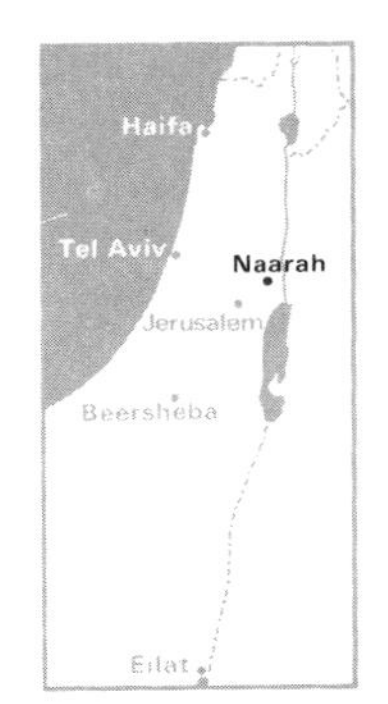

(Simeon Metaphrastes, *Life of St. Chariton* (Gr.) 7:578; Palladius, *Historia Lausiaca,* 48). Naarah is now identified with ʿAyn al-Dūk, 4½ mi. (7 km.) north of Jericho. In 1918 a mosaic pavement was accidentally uncovered there when a shell exploded; it was excavated by L. H. Vincent and B. Carrière in 1919 and 1921. The pavement was found to be part of a synagogue which consisted of a court with a pool, an L-shaped narthex, and a hall, 72×49 ft. (22×15 m.), paved with mosaics. On the pavement are depicted two gazelles at the entrance and geometric designs in the aisles. The nave is decorated with images of birds within interlocking rhombuses and circles; a zodiac with the sun in the center and the symbols of the seasons in the corners; Daniel flanked by two lions; two candelabra and ritual objects. Another candelabrum was depicted in front of the main entrance to the hall. Inscriptions in the pavement commemorate the donors: Phinehas the priest, his wife Rebekah, a certain Samuel, Benjamin the *parnas,* Marutah, Ḥalifu, etc. The images of living beings had been removed at a later date. The synagogue dates to the sixth century. The pavement (and some additional details, previously unknown) was rediscovered in 1970.

Bibliography: Vincent, in: RB, 28 (1919), 532–63; Vincent and Carrière, *ibid.,* 30 (1921), 579ff.; Vincent and Benoit, *ibid.,* 68 (1961), 163–77. [M.A.-Y.]

NABAL (Heb. נָבָל; connected with the Ar. *nabil,* "noble"), man of the town of Maon who owned much livestock near the neighboring town of Carmel, southeast of Hebron on

Episodes from the story of Nabal and Abigail (I Sam. 25) in the *Pierpont Morgan Picture Bible,* France, 13th century. Upper register, Abigail brings presents to David to assuage his anger against her husband; lower register left, Abigail confesses to Nabal; right, Nabal's death. New York, Pierpont Morgan Library, ms. 638, fol. 33v.

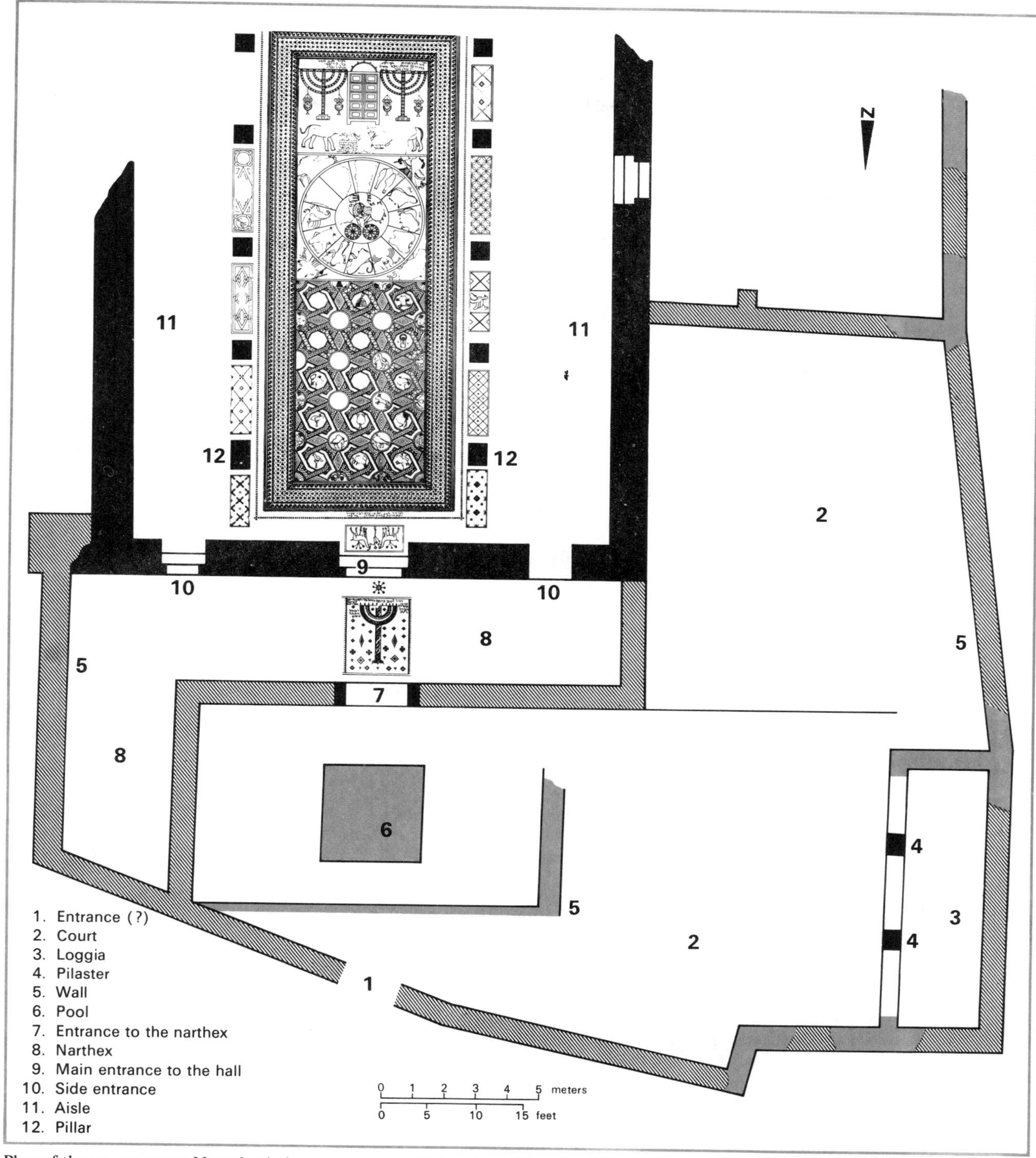

Plan of the synagogue at Naarah, sixth century C.E., with drawing of the mosaic floors in the nave and in the narthex. Based on *Encyclopaedia of Archaeological Excavation in the Holy Land*, Jerusalem, 1970.

the edge of the desert of Judah; a Calebite (I Sam. 25:3; *keri* and versions). David extended his protection to Nabal's flocks when he was camping with his men in the desert of Judah (25:14–16). Nabal refused to give him a "gift" out of his produce at the time of the sheep-shearing (25:10–11). *Abigail, Nabal's beautiful wife, appeased David and dissuaded him from taking revenge (25:18ff.). Her husband, she said, punning on his name, "as his name is, so is he; Nabal [נָבָל] is his name and outrage [נְבָלָה] is with him" (25:25). After Nabal's death by a stroke, she became David's wife (I Sam. 25:42). This tale is one of the finest narratives in the Bible and is a faithful description of the life of the prosperous cattlemen on the border of the desert of Judah. [Yo.A.]

In the Aggadah. In the Aggadah Nabal is referred to as a descendant of Caleb in order to compare his own illustrious ancestry to that of David who was descended from Ruth the Moabitess (TJ, Sanh. 2:3, 20b). He denied God, had idolatrous thoughts and was guilty of unchastity. Like *Laban, the letters of whose name are identical with those of Nabal, he was a scoundrel (Mid. Ps. 53:1). Ten days intervened between his illness and his death (I Sam. 25:38) because he had given food to each of David's ten men (I Sam. 25:5; RH 18a); or because these were the Ten Days of Penitence, when God hoped that Nabal would repent (TJ, Bik. 2:1, 64d). According to another opinion, however, Nabal was smitten more than a week after Samuel died; his death being delayed in order to avoid any confusion between the mourning for a righteous man and a wicked one (Mid. Ps. 26:7). [Ed.]

NABATEANS, a Semitic people who established a kingdom in the ancient territory of Edom in Transjordan. The Nabateans have left no written records, and knowledge of their history rests chiefly upon Greek and Latin sources, most of which are no earlier than the end of the fourth century B.C.E. and the most important of which date from the first century B.C.E. to the first century C.E. These sources regard the Nabateans as Arabs. A few scholars have essayed to connect the Nabateans with Nebaioth (Gen. 25:13; 36:3; Isa. 60:7), the firstborn of Ishmael, but it appears that on philological grounds it is impossible to establish a connection between the two words, since they are of different roots. That there is, however, a connection between the Nabateans and the Arabs is evident from the fact that many Nabatean names of people and local deities are Arabic, as well as in a few similarities in the grammar of the two languages, e.g., the definite article *al* and the plural ending *o*.

The Nabateans and the Jews in the Period of the Second Temple. The Nabateans and the Hasmoneans. The first recorded contact between the Jews and the Nabateans was in 169 B.C.E., when *Jason sought refuge with *Aretas, the Nabatean ruler. The relations between the Nabateans and the Jews became closer with the rise of the Hasmonean dynasty. At first relations between the two peoples were cordial because of their common Greek enemy (I Macc. 5:25; 9:35). When the revolt in Judea began, the Nabateans had already begun to extend their borders into Moab; at any rate Madaba was in the hands of the Nabateans when the Hasmonean brothers came to them to seek shelter for their men and possessions. Nothing is known of the history of the Nabateans during the major part of the second century B.C.E. Toward the end of the century, however, more details are forthcoming. During the third century and the first half of the second century B.C.E., the Nabatean tribes, who were partially nomadic, had established themselves in south Transjordan and in the Negev, but their tribal organization with very tenuous intertribal ties persisted. They became an organized

The Nabatean method of "runoff agriculture" used as the basis of the experimental farm established in the Negev below the remains of the ancient Nabatean city of Avedat by Michael Evenari. Photo Werner Braun, Jerusalem.

kingdom only at the end of the second century B.C.E. when the struggle between the Hellenist kingdoms of Syria and Egypt had brought about the decline of both.

Aretas I. Until this time Nabatean expansion had taken place in desert or semidesert regions, those regions being vital to the Nabateans because of the caravan routes which had developed through them. At the end of the second century B.C.E., however, the Nabateans began to expand northward, encroaching on the territory of the nations of the Near East. The expansion of the Nabatean kingdom took place at the same time as John *Hyrcanus began his conquest of Judea, and Alexander *Yannai his campaigns to extend the boundaries of his kingdom beyond the borders of Judea. Since the areas of possible expansion were severely limited, both kingdoms directed their attentions to the same areas, with the result that a clash between the Nabatean kingdom and that of Judea was inevitable. It would appear that the "Aretomos" who is stated to have undertaken raids into the Hellenist kingdoms from 110 B.C.E. onward is to be identified with Aretas who in 96 promised to help Gaza, the most important port for Nabatean commerce, in its war against Alexander Yannai; however, he arrived too late to save Gaza and the port fell to Yannai. Aretas is the first to be named "king of the Arabs" in the sources (Jos., Ant. 13:360).

*Avdat (*Obedas) I.* (Josephus calls him Ὀβέδας "Obedas, king of the Arabs," while his coins bear the legend "Avdat, king of Nabato." When Aretas I died in 96 B.C.E. Avdat I ascended the throne in Petra. With his accession, open war broke out between the Jews and Nabateans. At the beginning of Avdat's reign, Alexander Yannai undertook a succession of expeditions of conquest east of the Jordan and captured 12 towns, most of them in Moab (Jos., Ant. 13:395–7; although these had been promised to the Nabateans by Hyrcanus II). Open warfare broke out between the two kings near Gadar in Gilead (Ant. 13:372; Wars 1:90), and Yannai suffered a decisive defeat. The battle, which took place either about 93 or 90 B.C.E., checked the expansionist aims of the Judean kingdom east of the Jordan and opened the way for fresh Nabatean conquests in the south of Syria and Hauran.

Rabel I. The reign of Rabel I was exceptionally brief. After Antiochus XII Dionysus came to the throne in Damascus he decided to attack the Nabateans. For some unknown reason he did not march against them by the direct route but took a longer road by way of Judea (Ant. 13:387–91). In consequence of this he had to breach the line of fortifications erected by Yannai along the length of the Yarkon River. Antiochus finally entered the Nabatean kingdom from south of the Dead Sea. At first the Nabateans retreated, but when the Syrians had penetrated deeply into the interior of the country, "the Arab king"—whose name Josephus does not give, but whom some think to have been Aretas III (see below)—attacked them at the head of 10,000 cavalry. Antiochus fell in the battle and was decapitated (85 B.C.E.), and the remnants of the Syrian army escaped to a place called Cana. It is apparently this war that is referred to by Oranius (Stephanus Byzantinus, s.v. Μωθώ) who refers to a defeat inflicted by Rabel, king of the Nabateans, upon Antigonus the Macedonian. It appears that the Nabatean king also fell in that battle, since in the same year his brother ascended the throne.

Aretas III Philhellenos. Aretas III played the same role in his kingdom which Alexander Yannai did in Judea. Not only did he extend the borders of his kingdom northward but he also appears to have played a significant role in the situation created by the first contacts between the desert culture of the Nabateans and the urban culture of Hellenism. Already at the beginning of his reign his sway extended over Hauran and southern Syria, but in 85 B.C.E. the inhabitants of Damascus appealed to him to seize their city from their ruler Ptolemy, son of Mennaeus. Immediately afterward Aretas took arms against Alexander Yannai, defeating him in battle near Hadid in Judea. During the reign of Yannai's successor *Salome Alexandra, peace was maintained between the two kingdoms. However, when Alexandra's sons began their struggle for the succession, Aretas intervened in favor of Hyrcanus, even sending an army to Judea to besiege Aristobulus. Meanwhile, however, a new factor had arisen in the east, that of Rome, whose aim it was to fill the vacuum created by the disintegration of the Hellenistic kingdoms. In 65 B.C.E. Scaurus, the commander of Pompey's army, ordered Aretas to withdraw his army from Judea and during the withdrawal, the army suffered defeat at the hands of Aristobulus. Desirous of subjugating or at least punishing the Nabateans for their growing interference in the affairs of his area, Pompey decided to proceed on a punitive expedition against them, but the deteriorating internal situation in Judea obliged him to return as he was on his way to Petra (Ant. 14:46ff.). The turn of Petra came after the subjugation of Judea and the capture of Jerusalem. Scaurus, now governor of the newly established Roman province of Syria, set out in 62 on an expedition against the city. He plundered the vicinity of the capital to feed his hungry army, but on account of its strong natural fortifications he did not succeed in taking Petra and was obliged to withdraw in exchange for a money payment. Having thus succeeded in buying their freedom the Nabateans postponed the loss of their independence for more than 150 years. Antipater the Idumean, father of Herod, acted as intermediary between the Nabateans and the Romans.

Avdat II. Avdat II ascended the throne in 62 B.C.E. Few details of his reign are known. Some scholars think he reigned only two years, but most tend to the opinion that he ruled until 47. His existence is known chiefly from his coins. In 55 B.C.E. Gabinius, then proconsul in Syria, undertook an expedition against the Nabateans, for unknown reasons. Unfortunately, Josephus, the only historian to mention this campaign, omits to give the name of the king who ruled in Petra at the time.

The Nabateans and Herod and his House. MALCHUS I. During the reign of Malchus far-reaching changes took place in the Roman world and the Nabateans were obliged to make difficult political decisions. In the beginning of his reign, Malchus in 47 B.C.E. sent cavalry to Alexandria to assist Caesar (Caesar, *Bellum Alexandrinum* 1:1). These years coincide with Herod's attempt to seize the throne in Judea. In the year 40, when the Parthians plundered Judea, Herod approached Malchus for asylum but his request went unanswered. At that time Malchus made an enemy of Rome by involving himself with the Parthians, for which he was punished by being obliged to pay fines to *Ventidius (Dio Cassius 48:415). When Antony came to Egypt, he deprived the Nabatean kingdom of the districts bordering on the Dead Sea and presented them to Cleopatra. (Plutarch, Antony 36). In 32, Malchus sent an army to the aid of Antony in the battle of Actium (*ibid.* 61). Although Plutarch relates that Herod's army was also among those which fought on the side of Antony, it would appear that Josephus' version that Antony exempted Herod from taking part is more credible since during the battle of Actium Herod was conducting a war against the Nabateans. Finally, after a number of changes of fortune, the Nabateans were defeated.

AVDAT III. His image has become blurred by "the king's brother," the administrator or head of government, Sholi (or Syllaeus as he was known to early writers) who conducted all the business of the kingdom since the king was extremely frail. Relations between Petra and Jerusalem during this period were decidedly strained. In an endeavor to gain influence at Herod's court, Sholi sought the hand of Salome, Herod's sister, in marriage but without success. The lot of the Nabateans in their foreign policy was a sorry one. When Augustus triumphed he granted Herod rule over Bashan, Trachonitis, Hauran, and Gaulanitis, parts of which had been under Nabatean influence during most of the first century B.C.E., in recognition of his services. Shortly before the death of Avdat III the war between Herod and the Nabateans was renewed. During Herod's stay at the court of Augustus in Rome, Trachonitis rebelled against him, and the rebels were given shelter and aid by Sholi. In addition Avdat owed Herod a long-standing debt of 60,000 talents. Herod, therefore, undertook a war, in which he was victorious, to avenge himself and collect his debt. The struggle between Herod and the Nabateans moved to the court of Augustus and in 9 B.C.E. delegations of both parties appeared in Rome. It would appear that Sholi aspired to have the aged king removed in his favor. A Nabatean-Greek inscription dedicated by Sholi to the temple of Apollo in Miletus testifies to his stay in Rome during this time. While Sholi was in Rome Avdat III was poisoned, apparently by Sholi's agents. According to one tradition Avdat was deified after his death and buried in the city of Avdat (Stephanus Byzantinus, s.v. Oβoδα).

ARETAS IV. Aeneas, son of Avdat III, hastened to seize the throne without waiting for the approval of Rome (Jos., Ant. 16:293–4). His dynastic name was Aretas IV, and the honorific title granted him was *"Rehav Amah"* ("lover of his people"—i.e. Philodemos—in contrast to Aretas III, who was Philhellenos). During his long reign the economic development of the kingdom reached its peak; and in Judea Herod's reign was approaching its end and thus terminated the tension between the two kingdoms. Shortly after ascending the throne Aretas was legally confirmed as king by Augustus (Ant. 16:355). Sholi continued his activity in Rome against the new king; but the accusations of Aretas, combined with the gifts he sent, persuaded Augustus to confirm him as king, and Sholi's intrigues came to an end (Ant. 17:52ff.; Wars 1:574ff.; Strabo 16:782; C. Mueller (ed.), *Fragmenta historicum Graecorum,* vol. 3, 351). When after Herod's death disorders grew, Aretas sent a substantial military force to assist Varus, who marched against Judea at the head of two legions (Ant. 17:286ff.; Wars 2:66ff.). This event occurred in the sixth year of Aretas' reign (4 B.C.E.) and from that date, which is the period of its greatest prosperity and when its architecture, sculpture, and pottery flourished, the historical sources are silent about the Nabatean kingdom. The only item of information relating to the last years of Aretas' rule is that he divorced his wife, daughter of the tetrarch Herod Antipas, in order to be able to marry Herodias. Family quarrels and border disputes with regard to Gamala in Gaulanitis led to war between the Nabateans and Herod Antipas, who was victorious. Following complaints made by the victor to the emperor Tiberius, Vitellius, the Roman procurator, was ordered to punish Aretas. However, while on his way to Petra, Vitellius learned of the death of the emperor and turned back.

The Romans deprived the Nabateans of their political independence early in the second century C.E., but they nevertheless maintained their religion and culture which received its final blow when the Byzantines Christianized the inhabitants of their area. The Nabateans passed out of history with the advent of Islam. Their civilization has been described by Glueck as highly advanced, as scintillating as it was brief. As they emerged from the desert, simple living gave way to sophistication and their accomplishments can be traced in commerce, agriculture, engineering, architecture, and art. Their language was Aramaic and they played an important role for a time in Middle Eastern trade routes. Their religion was syncretistic. Their belief had an astral basis, and their gods, although apparently Hellenistic, remained basically oriental.

Bibliography: N. Glueck, *Deities and Dolphins* (1966; contains bibl.); J. L. Burckhart, *Travels in Syria and the Holy Land* (1822); CIS; Schuerer, Gesch, 1 (1901), 726–44; idem, Hist, 44, 98, 154; R. E. Bruennow and A. von Domaszewski, *Die Provincia Arabia,* 1 (1904); R. Dussaud, *Numismatique des Rois de Nabatène* (1904); G. H. Dalman, *Petra und seine Felsheiligtuemer* (1908); idem, *Neue Petra-Forschungen* (1912); *Publications of the Princeton University Archaeological Expeditions to Syria, in 1904–1905 and 1909* (1914); A. Jaussen and R. Savignac, *Mission Archéologique en Arabie,* 1 (1909); 2 (1914); A. Kammerer, *Petra et la Nabatène,* 2 vols. (1929–30); G. L. Robinson, *Sarcophagus of an Ancient Civilization* (1930); J. Cantineau, *Le Nabatéen* (1932); A. Schalit, in: *Eretz Israel,* 1 (1951), 104–21; A. Negev, in: IEJ, 11 (1961), 127–38; 13 (1963), 113–24; idem, in: *Elath* (1963), 118–48. [ED.]

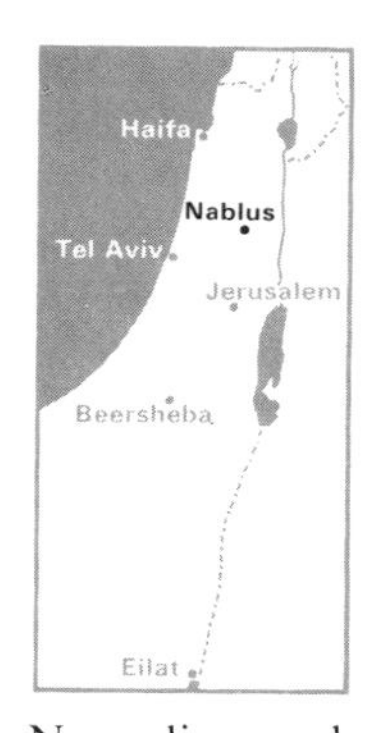

NABLUS, city in Ereẓ Israel (in later times called *Shechem in Hebrew). Nablus was founded by Vespasian in 72 C.E. as Flavia Neapolis on the site of the Samaritan village Mabartha ("the passage") situated between Mts. Ebal and Gerizim near biblical Shechem (Jos., Wars 4:449). Because of its favorable geographic position and abundance of water the city prospered; it was endowed with an extensive territory including the former Judean toparchy of Acraba. Neapolis was hostile to Septimius Severus who therefore temporarily deprived it of municipal status. In 244 Philip the Arab turned it into a Roman colony called Julia Neapolis; its coinage continued until the time of Trebonianus Gallus (251–3). Its temples included an Artemision and the city also had an agora, colonnaded streets, a stepped nymphaeum, etc. Christianity took root early in Neapolis; it was the birthplace of *Justin Martyr (c. 100) and had a bishop as early as the Council of Ancyra in 314. In Byzantine times when it was depicted on the Madaba Map as a walled town, Neapolis was a center of the *Samaritans who twice revolted and set up a "king." The city was conquered in 636 by the Arabs who retained its name in the form Nablus. It is mentioned several times in talmudic literature as Nipolis (TJ, Av. Zar. 5:4, 44d); the rabbis, as well as some early Christian authors, confused it

Figure 1. A scene in Nablus, the city established by the Romans near the site of the biblical Shechem. From S. Munk, *Palestine,* Paris, 1845.

Figure 2. Nablus as seen from Mount Gerizim, with Mount Ebal in the background. Courtesy Keren Hayesod, United Israel Appeal, Jerusalem.

with Shechem, and even with Samaria. Under Muslim rule Nablus contained a mixed population of Muslims, Persians, Samaritans, and Jews. The synagogue built in 362 by the high priest Akbon was turned into a mosque (al-Khaḍra'). From 1099 to 1187 the city was held by the crusaders who called it Naples. It was the second capital of the royal domain and contained a palace and a citadel; the city itself was unwalled at that time. In 1522 a Jewish community is mentioned in Nablus; its fortunes varied throughout the 18th and 19th centuries until it completely abandoned the city shortly after 1900. Nablus remained a center of the Samaritans, half of whom still live there. [M.A.-Y.]

Modern Period. After World War I Jews again tried to live there, but Nablus was a center of Muslim fanaticism and the 1929 Arab riots ended these attempts. The town suffered severe damage in the 1927 earthquake and was largely destroyed. The Mandatory Government aided its reconstruction along modern lines, but sought to preserve its oriental character. The Samaritan quarter lies at the foot of Mt. Gerizim; wealthier inhabitants have built their homes, mostly in the last decades, on the slopes of Mt. Ebal and Mt. Gerizim. Under the Jordanian regime (1948–67), the economy of Nablus, then the center of the largest district of the West Bank, was based mainly on administrative services and farming. In addition to its traditional industry of soapmaking (its raw material coming from the extensive olive groves of the vicinity), the first modern manufacturing enterprises made their appearance, most of them in the Sokher Valley to the east. In the *Six-Day War on June 7, 1967, Nablus was taken by an Israel column coming from the east. In the census held by Israel in the fall of 1967, Nablus had 44,000 inhabitants (as against 23,300 in 1943), of whom all were Muslim except for 370 Christians and about 250 Samaritans. When, however, the population of villages and refugee camps next to the town were added, the total number amounted to about 70,000, making Nablus the largest urban center of Samaria. [E.O.]

Bibliography: Schuerer, Gesch, 2 (1907[2]), 41ff.; Abel, Geog, 2 (1938), 396–7; idem, in: RB, 32 (1923), 120ff.

NABONIDUS (Nabû-na'id), last king of Babylon (556–539 B.C.E.), son of a governor, Nabû-balaṭsu-iqbi, and a votaress of Sin. A native of *Haran, Nabonidus was a military commander in his sixties when he ascended the throne of Babylon.

The principal cuneiform sources concerning his reign are: the Nabonidus Chronicle (Pritchard, Texts, 305–7); a basalt stela, which relates his rise to power (*ibid.*, 308–11); a memorial inscription from Haran, which tells the story of his mother (*ibid.*, 311–2); the so-called "Verse Account of Nabonidus" a libel which accuses Nabonidus of mendacity, madness, and of impiety (*ibid.*, 312–5); and foundation documents relating the rebuilding of sanctuaries.

The same period is recorded also by Herodotus, Xenophon, and Josephus. His religious activities were multiple. He restored the ziggurat of Ur, and its various temples, e.g., Esagila—the great temple of Marduk in Babylon. One of his dreams was to reconstruct the temple of Sin in Haran. This important city commanding the highways from northern Mesopotamia to Syria and Asia Minor had been in the hands of the Medes since 610. To expel the Medes, Nabonidus sought the help of the young Persian king *Cyrus. In the battle that followed, Cyrus captured the Median king Astyages—his grandfather—and annexed the Median kingdom, thus initiating the building of a great empire which was to include Babylonia as well. In the third year of his reign, Nabonidus went to Syria to raise troops for his campaign in Arabia. He took Hamath, rebuilt the temple of Sin in Haran, stayed during a brief illness in the Anti-Lebanon, and started for Arabia. He took Adummu (al-Jauf), and destroyed *Tema, which he rebuilt and made his residence for several years. His son Bêl-šar-uṣur (*Belshazzar, cf. Dan. 5) stayed in Babylon as regent during Nabonidus' long absence. His stay in Tema still puzzles historians, and various explanations have been put forward, the most accepted being that his major aim was the resurrection of the ancient moon religion of Sin.

In the fall of 539, Cyrus with the approval and perhaps even on the initiative of the priesthoods of Babylon and the other cities of southern Mesopotamia, invaded the Babylonian empire. By that time Nabonidus was back in the capital. During Cyrus' siege of Opis on the Tigris, the inhabitants revolted against Nabonidus, who massacred them. On the 15th of Tashritu (September–October), Sippar surrendered to Cyrus without battle. Nabonidus fled. The next day Babylon—whose priests, especially the priest of Marduk, opposed him—opened its gates to Cyrus and his allies (the Gutians). Nabonidus was later arrested upon his return to Babylon. On the third day of the following month Cyrus made his triumphal entrance into Babylon. "Great twigs were spread before him. The state of 'peace' was imposed on the city." Nabonidus' end is obscure; according to Josephus, however, he was treated humanely by the conqueror, who assigned Carmania (Central Iran) for his residence (Jos., Apion 1:153). Aramaic fragments from Qumran in which Nabonidus (*Nbny*) relates that while in Teman (so!) he was afflicted with an inflammation of the skin (*sheḥin*) for seven years until an unnamed Jewish soothsayer (*gazar*, a word which also appears in the Aramaic of *Daniel) advised him to pray to the God of Heaven instead of to the idols, show what sort of speculations the king's prolonged residence in remote Tema gave rise to. This suggests that the story about the seven years' lycanthropy of Nebuchadnezzar in Daniel 4 goes back ultimately to such malicious speculations about Nabonidus on the part of disaffected Babylonians.

Bibliography: S. Smith, *Babylonian Historical Texts Relating to the Capture and Downfall of Babylon* (1924), 27ff., 98ff.; R. P. Dougherty, *Nabonidus and Belshazzar* (1929); J. Lewy, in: HUCA, 19 (1946), 405–89; J. T. Milik, in: RB, 62 (1956), 407ff.; J. Roux, *Ancient Iraq* (1966), 346ff.; Pritchard, Texts, 305–15; E. Bickerman, *Four Strange Books of the Bible* (1967), 74–7.

[L.J.A.]

NABOTH (Heb. נָבוֹת), owner of a vineyard close to the palace of *Ahab king of Israel (I Kings 21:2). Naboth came from the town of Jezreel. Ahab coveted Naboth's vineyard, but Naboth refused to sell or exchange it, basing his refusal on the tradition that inherited family property cannot be

Detail from a 15th-century Dutch manuscript showing (left) Naboth being stoned as Jezebel looks on. At right, the prophet Elijah castigates King Ahab for the deed. London, British Museum, Add. Ms. 10043, fol. 184.

taken out of the family's hands: "The Lord forbid it me, that I should give the inheritance of my fathers unto thee" (21:3). In order to obtain the vineyard Ahab's wife *Jezebel fabricated an accusation against Naboth that he blasphemed God and the king (21:10). According to the custom in the Ancient East, the property of a rebel against the monarchy was confiscated and taken into the royal treasury. Evidence of this custom has also been preserved in one of the *Alalakh documents (No. 17). As a result of a staged trial Naboth's property was confiscated and he himself was stoned. Another biblical tradition states that his children were also killed. Elijah the prophet raised his voice against Ahab because of Naboth's execution and Elijah's scornful words branded Ahab a murderer and robber and foretold the doom of the royal house (I Kings 21:17–24). The story of Naboth serves as an example and symbol of the Israelite's close attachment to his inheritance and his family-tribe tradition. Furthermore, this story points to the limits of royal authority in Israel, which cannot deal arbitrarily with the lands belonging to the people. For this reason Jezebel had to represent Naboth as a rebel against the king and as blaspheming God. [H.RE.]

In the Aggadah. Naboth was Ahab's cousin, with the result that the king, by killing Naboth's sons (II Kings 9:26), could claim his vineyard by right of inheritance (Sanh. 48b). He used to make regular pilgrimages to Jerusalem, and as a great singer, many followed him. It was because he once failed to make his customary journey that his false conviction took place (PR 25, 127a). Naboth's opportunity for revenge, however, came when God asked: "Who shall entice Ahab that he may go up and fall at Ramoth-Gilead?" (I Kings 22:20–21). It was the "spirit" of Naboth which volunteered for the task (Shab. 149b). [ED.]

Bibliography: Ginzberg, Legends, 4 (1913), 187–8; 6 (1928), 311–2; I. Ḥasida, *Ishei ha-Tanakh* (1964), 329.

NACHMANOVICH (Pol. **Nachmanowicz**), wealthy family in *Lvov, Poland; its members were among the leaders of the community within the walled city of Lvov during the late 16th and early 17th centuries.

The first-known member of the family, ISAAC BEN NAḤMAN (d. 1595), is mentioned in 1565 as *dayyan* of the community, and for many years was among its leaders. As chief of the representatives of the communities of the "Land of Russia" *(Senior generalis ziem ruskich)* he participated in meetings of the Council of the Four Lands. In 1589 he was *parnas* of the Council and in 1590 he and his son Mordecai paid the first installment of a tax in its behalf. Isaac attained his high position in the community through his diversified activities as a spice merchant and tax farmer. Among other undertakings he leased an important customs station in Sniatyń, in the Lvov region, and held the rights to the lease of the state revenues in the city of Lvov and the sub-district *(starostwo)*. He was also engaged in large-scale moneylending against pledges of real estate and valuables. Through his wealth and prestige he was able to appear in the Polish law courts without having to take the Jewish *oath *(more judaico)*. Isaac also had access to the Polish kings Sigismund II Augustus and Stephen Báthory. In 1581, he was authorized to acquire a plot of municipal land where he built a magnificent synagogue in Gothic style at his own expense after the plans of an Italian architect. It became known as the "Turei Zahav" synagogue.

Isaac's elder son, NAḤMAN ISAAKOVICH (Naḥman ben Isaac; d. 1616), took over his father's affairs, including his tax farming and moneylending undertakings, and acquired the lease of the market imposts and other revenues of Lvov. He served as head of the community a number of times, and was admitted to the citizenship of Lvov, being known among Christians by the honorific "Generosus." He was also a scholar. Naḥman, who was stringent in collecting the taxes, had frequent conflicts with the local inhabitants who accused him of overcharging the customs dues, but the city council, which was dependent on his loans, rejected their complaints. From 1603 Naḥman headed a struggle to preserve the synagogue erected by his father which the Jesuits in Lvov wished to convert into a church and seminary. In 1609 a compromise was reached which left the synagogue in the ownership of the Nachmanovich family, while the Jewish community undertook to procure a suitable site for the needs of the Jesuits in the suburbs of Lvov for a sum of 20,600 zlotys. Immediately afterward, Naḥman and his brother Mordecai completed the construction of the synagogue, adding a women's gallery and magnificent religious requisites. In honor of its opening R. Isaac ha-Levi composed a "Song of Redemption" which was sung by the Jews of Lvov for many generations. The deliverance of the synagogue was preserved in the memory of the local community and gave rise to a number of legends. It was connected in folklore with Naḥman's wife Rojse ("Di gildene Rojse," as she was called by the Jews) who was renowned for her beauty and wisdom. After the death of her husband, Rojse took charge of his business affairs until her death in 1637. Her tombstone, which was preserved until the Nazi occupation, was inscribed with a Renaissance-style epitaph extolling her deeds.

The younger son of Isaac, MORDECAI (MARCUS) BEN ISAAC (d. 1635?), ranked among the elders *(seniores)* of the Lvov community, and also engaged in tax farming. In 1627 the merchants of Lvov accused him of overcharging the customs duties. He became court purveyor in 1634 to King Ladislaus IV, furnishing supplies to the Polish army in the war with Russia.

The son of Naḥman Isaakovich and Rojse, ISAAC NACHMANOVICH (Junior; b. 1595), after years of apprenticeship under the tutelage of his mother and uncle, resumed the business in his own right and on occasion acted as court banker. In 1626 he lent considerable sums of money to the royal treasury during the war with Sweden. In 1634 Isaac was given the status **servus camerae* by King Ladislaus IV, and exempted from paying all customs duties and imposts, whether levied by the crown or privately. He also expanded his commercial activities, especially the trade in textiles and supply of oxen to the army, and in partnership with others, leased the state revenues in the districts of Lvov and *Drogobych. However, by 1637 he was on the verge of bankruptcy, and in 1646 was arrested for debt. He succeeded in escaping from prison and disappeared.

Bibliography: Halpern, Pinkas, index; M. Bałaban, *Żydzi lwowscy na przelomie 16 i 17 wieku* (1906), 41–88; W. Lozinski, *Patrycjat i mieszczanstwo lwowskie w 16 i 17 wieku* (1892); J. Caro, *Geschichte der Juden in Lemberg* (1894), 34–43.
[A.Cy.]

NACHOD (Czech **Náchod**), town in N.E. Bohemia, Czechoslovakia. Its Jewish community was one of the four oldest in *Bohemia and is first mentioned in the city records of 1455. The Jewish street dates from the end of the 15th century. Jews were expelled from Nachod in 1542 and robbed on their way to Poland. They returned in 1544 and founded a school which is mentioned in 1547. The cemetery dates from 1550 and a *mikveh* from 1592. Eleven families were recorded in the town in 1570. In 1663, the Jews were accused of having caused a conflagration in which their quarter and a large part of the town was destroyed. One member of the community was executed; the whole community was attacked; and its members fled. Some founded a community in Ceska Skalice which was expelled in 1705. Soon reestablished, the Nachod community had 60 families in 1724. The synagogue was rebuilt in 1777. Jews were active in making Nachod a center of the textile industry; in 1848 Isaac Mautner founded the famous Mautner textile company. At the end of the century they were beset by anti-Semitic riots and plunder in connection with the *Hilsner case (1899). There were 150 Jewish families in Nachod in 1852; 630 persons in 1893; 463 in 1921; and 293 in 1930 (2.1% of the total population). In 1902 there were 100 Jews in 22 surrounding localities, among them formerly important communities such as Hronov, Cerveny Kostelec (Ger. Rothkosteletz), and Police nad Metuji, who were affiliated to the Nachod community. In 1934 the *Moller brothers transferred their textile factory to Palestine, founding the Ata company at *Kiryat Ata. Among the rabbis of Nachod were Heinrich (Ḥayyim) *Brody, who officiated from 1898 to 1905, and Gustav *Sicher. Under Nazi occupation in June 1939, the synagogue was desecrated, and in July the Gestapo raided Jewish homes. The cemetery—its oldest monument dating from 1648—was also destroyed. After World War II a small congregation affiliated with the *Liberec community was established, primarily by veteran soldiers from *Subcarpathian Ruthenia. Nachod was one of the important transit stations for *Beriḥah (1945–46). A monument was erected there for the victims of the Holocaust in 1958. The synagogue building was demolished in the 1960s.

Bibliography: H. Gold, *Die Juden und Judengemeinden Boehmens* (1934), 412–3; Jakobovitz, in JGGJČ, 9 (1938), 271–305; PK.
[J.Hor.]

NACHOD, JACOB (1814–1882), merchant and second president of the *Deutsch-Israelitischer Gemeindebund. An orphan, he studied at the Wolfenbuettel Samsonschule and went to Leipzig in 1830. There he founded in 1844 the Gesellschaft der Freunde, the forerunner of the Leipzig communal organization established in 1868. He cooperated with M. *Kohner in the founding of the Deutsch-Israelitischer Gemeindebund (1869) and succeeded him as its president on Kohner's death in 1877. Nachod's main contributions were in the field of education and welfare.

Bibliography: *Gedenkblaetter an J. Nachod* (1882).
[Ed.]

NADAB (Heb. נָדָב; "[God] has been generous"), eldest son of *Aaron and Elisheba daughter of Amminadab (Ex. 6:23; Num. 3:2, et al.). For details see *Abihu. (The two are always mentioned together and what applies to Abihu is also true of Nadab.) Nadab too left no sons (Num. 3:4; I Chron. 24:2).
[N.M.S.]

Nadab and Abihu in the Aggadah. Apart from the one sin which brought about their mysterious deaths, Nadab and Abihu were righteous men. As to the nature of the sin—the "strange fire" which they offered up—there are various interpretations. The most obvious explanation bases itself on the injunction against the priests' partaking of wine and strong drink before entering the sanctuary (Lev. 10:9), which immediately follows this episode. It is therefore suggested that Nadab and Abihu were in a state of intoxication when they offered up the "strange fire." A number of interpretations suggest that they neglected the various ritual requirements connected with the offerings (Lev. R. 20:8–9).

It is also suggested that their overbearing haughtiness was responsible for their deaths. They did not marry because they considered no woman good enough for themselves, saying, "Our father's brother [Moses] is a king, our mother's brother [Nahshon] is a prince, our father [Aaron] is a high priest, and we are both deputy high priests—what woman is worthy of us?" (Lev. R. 20:10). They even went so far as to wish for the death of Moses and Aaron so that they could assume the mantle of leadership (Sanh. 52a; Lev. R. 20:10). Even in the performance of the sacrifice they displayed their haughtiness by refraining from consulting with one another and by neglecting to ask Moses and Aaron whether they might offer such a sacrifice, depending instead upon their own judgment. The sages deduce from this episode that it is forbidden for a disciple to render a legal decision in the presence of his master (Lev. R. 20:7). It is, however, also suggested that their death was a vicarious punishment for their father's sin with regard to the golden calf. Moses relates: "Moreover the Lord was very angry with Aaron to have destroyed him" (Deut. 9:20), and "destruction" means extinction of offspring (Lev. R. 10:5). Moses attempted to comfort his brother by assuring him that his two remaining sons were greater than Nadab and Abihu. At Sinai, Moses was told that he would sanctify the Tabernacle through the death of a great man. He thought that the reference was to himself or Aaron, but now he realized that Nadab and Abihu were nearer to God (Lev. R. 12:2).

Their deaths were caused by "two streams of fire, ... branched off into four, and two entered into each of the

Nadab and Abihu being consumed by fire in a detail from the *menorah* by Benno Elkan, designed for the Knesset, Jerusalem. Photo Yiẓhak Amit, kibbutz Ẓorah.

nostrils of Nadab and Abihu." Their souls were burnt, although no external injury was visible (Sanh. 52a). The whole House of Israel was bidden to bewail the death of Nadab and Abihu (Lev. R. 20: 12) for "the death of a pious man is a greater misfortune to Israel than the destruction of the Temple" (Sif. Deut. 31). [A.Ro.]

Bibliography: H. Gressmann, *Mose und seine Zeit* (1913), 257–9; Noth, Personennamen, 193, 251; T. J. Meek, in: AJSLL, 45 (1929), 157; K. Moehlenbrink, in: ZAW, 52 (1934), 214–5; G. Ryckmans, *Les noms propres sud-sémitiques*, 1 (1934), 136; F. Dornseiff, in: ZAW, 53 (1935), 164; Kaufmann, Y., Toledot, 2 (1938), 264, 276; S. Feigin, *Mysteries of the Past* (1953), 430; L. A. Snijders, in: OTS, 10 (1954), 116–23; M. Haran, in: *Tarbiz*, 26 (1956/57), 116 idem, in: VT, 10 (1960), 115, 127; J. Liver, in: *Scripta Hierosolymitana*, 8 (1961), 207, 216; R. Gradwohl, in: ZAW, 75 (1963), 288ff.; U. Cassuto, *A Commentary on the Book of Exodus* (1967), 310–5. In the Aggadah: Ginzberg, Legends, index.

NADAB (Heb. נָדָב), son of Jeroboam whom he succeeded on the throne of Israel (907–906 B.C.E.). Nadab is said to have ruled for two years (I Kings 14:20; 15:25). Since it is also related that he came to the throne in the second year of Asa's reign in Judah and that he was assassinated and succeeded by *Baasha in the third year of Asa's reign (15:28), the actual period of his rule must have been less than two years. During his short reign he fought against the Philistines and laid siege to *Gibbethon. Baasha, who presumably was one of his officers, revolted against him. The usurper assassinated all the descendants of Jeroboam as predicted by Ahijah the Shilonite (15:29).

Bibliography: J. A. Montgomery, *The Book of Kings* (ICC, 1951), 279; Bright, Hist, 218–9. [Jo.S.]

NADAF (Naddaf), ABRAHAM ḤAYYIM (1866–1940), Yemenite community leader. Born in Yemen, Nadaf settled in Ereẓ Israel in 1891. At first he taught the children of the community in Jerusalem, and later proved to be an outstanding communal worker. He established several of the community's institutions and also took care of the publication of a Pentateuch and a *siddur* according to the tradition of Yemenite Jewry. He also traveled abroad as an emissary on several occasions: in 1895 to Egypt and Yemen in order to raise funds for the community's yeshivah and *talmud torah;* a second time to Yemen in 1900 as the emissary of the Yemenites and the Sephardim. In 1903, he represented the Yemenites of Jerusalem at the first assembly of Palestinian Jews, which was held in Zikhron Ya'akov at the initiative of Menaḥem *Ussishkin. Nadaf headed the separationist faction in the dispute which broke out in 1907 between the Yemenites of Jerusalem and the Sephardi *kolel* (community). He went to Constantinople and succeeded in obtaining a *firman* from the Sublime Porte, which recognized the Yemenites as an independent *kolel*. In 1908 he again went to Constantinople as the emissary of the Jews of San'a in order to request an alleviation of the poll tax. He published the first bibliography of the works of Yemenite scholars, *Seridei Teiman* ("Remnants of Yemen," 1928). Another of his works, *Anaf Ḥayyim*, consists of notes and additions to the commentary *Eẓ Ḥayyim* of R. Yiḥya Joseph Saleh on the *maḥzor* of Yemenite Jews and was published as a supplement to it (*Tikhlal Eẓ Ḥayyim*, vol. 1. 1894). [Y.R.]

NADAV, ẒEVI (1891–1959), Second Aliyah and Ha-Shomer activist, editor, and author. Born in Ein Zeitim near Safed, he was brought up in Bobruisk, Belorussia, and returned to Ereẓ Israel in 1906. Nadav was one of the founders and outstanding members of *Ha-Shomer ("Watchmen's Organization") and among the first settlers at Umm Jūnī (*Deganyah) and *Merḥavyah. In 1917, when the Nili intelligence network was uncovered, he was sentenced to forced labor in Turkey, but escaped to Russia and returned to Palestine in 1919. He was a member of *Gedud ha-Avodah ("The Labor Legion") and was active in the organization of Jewish defense in Jerusalem in 1920, in Jaffa in 1921, and in Haifa in 1929. He studied engineering and was the editor of the journal *Tekhnikah u-Madda* ("Mechanics and Science"). His memoirs, which appeared in *Kovez ha-Shomer* ("Ha-Shomer Anthology," 1937), and his books, *Mi-Ymei Shemirah ve-Haganah* ("The Days of Vigilance and Defense," 1954), and *Kakh Hithalnu* ("Thus We Began," 1958), are a source for the history of the period.

Bibliography: J. Slutzky (ed.), *Sefer Bobruisk* (1967), 572–3; Tidhar, 10 (1959), 3547–49; E. Livneh (ed.), *Nili* (Heb., 1961), index. [Y.S.]

NADEL, ARNO (1878–1943), German poet and liturgical musicologist. Born in Vilna, Lithuania, Nadel studied liturgical music under Eduard *Birnbaum in Koenigsberg. In 1895, he entered the Jewish Teachers' Institute in Berlin and spent the rest of his life in Berlin. His first book, a volume of aphorisms and verse entitled *Aus vorletzten und letzten Gruenden* (1909), betrayed the influence of Nietzschean philosophy. His later works dealt mainly with biblical and Jewish themes. They include the play "Adam," staged in Karlsruhe in 1917; *Das Jahr des Juden* (1920), a collection of 12 poems; *Rot und gluehend ist das Auge des Juden* (1920); *Der Suendenfall* (1920); and *Juedische Volkslieder* (1923). His most important verse collection, *Der Ton* (1921, enlarged 1926), constitutes his Jewish reply to the nihilism of his time. He also published a German translation of *An-Ski's drama, *Der Dybbuk* (1921), *Der weissagende Dionysos* (1934), a collection of his later poetry, was republished after World War II.

In 1916 Nadel was appointed conductor of the choir at the synagogue in the Pestalozzistrasse, and later became musical supervisor of the Berlin synagogues. He devoted much effort to the collection and study of synagogal music and East European Jewish folk song, searching for manuscripts and noting oral traditions. Many of these he published and discussed in the music supplements of the *Berlin Gemeindeblatt* and *Ost und West*, and in his articles on Jewish music in the *Juedisches Lexicon*, and the German *Encyclopaedia Judaica*. Some of the Yiddish folk songs were also published separately, as in his *Jonteff Lieder* (1919) and *Juedische Liebeslieder* (1923). Drawing on his researches,

Arno Nadel, German poet and liturgical musicologist. Jerusalem, J.N.U.L., Schwadron Collection.

Nadel restored old traditions and raised the standards of the synagogue choirs. His manuscript collection included several unique cantors' manuals, such as that of Judah Elias of Hanover (1744). All of this he planned to incorporate in a multivolume compendium of synagogal music entitled *Hallelujah*, which was to have been published under the auspices of the Berlin community. The preparation of the earlier volumes was apparently well under way before Nadel was transported to Auschwitz, where he was murdered. His papers are reported to have been hidden in time, but most have not been recovered.

Nadel was himself a composer, and wrote the incidental music for Stefan *Zweig's "Jeremias" (1918). A man of many talents, he also excelled as a graphic artist and as a painter of landscapes and portraits.

Bibliography: Stoessinger, in: *Israelitisches Wochenblatt fuer die Schweiz* (Aug. 9, 1946); A. Nadel, *Der weissagende Dionysos* (1959), ed. by F. Kemp (1959), contains a critical biography; Sendrey, Music, indexes; Baker, Biog Dict. [S.L./B.B.]

NADEL, SIEGFRED FREDERICK (1903–1956), British anthropologist. Born in Austria, Nadel studied with Moritz *Schlick and Karl *Buehler, and developed a command of contemporary philosophical and psychological theory. He then began the serious study of anthropology at the London School of Economics under B. Malinowski and C. G. Seligman. He studied the music of primitive peoples, and African linguistics with D. Westermann. He did field work in the Anglo-Egyptian Sudan and with the Nuba, from 1938 to 1940. During World War II he served with the British armed forces, and later as a lieutenant colonel with the British Military Administration, 1945–46. He successfully applied his anthropological knowledge to the administration of peoples of various origins and traditions. When a department of anthropology was established at the University of Durham in 1948 he was appointed to the chair, and in 1950 took the new chair of anthropology and sociology at the Australian National University. His ethnographic work was shown in *A Black Byzantium* (1942). In his research he investigated the deeper bases of cultures and employed new psychological techniques of investigation such as intelligence tests. Nadel's primary accomplishment, however, is in theory, which he developed in two major works, *The Foundations of Social Anthropology* (1951), and the *Theory of Social Structure* (1957). His great concern was how to unify the conceptual systems of social anthropology and sociology with a psychological framework. His *Theory of Social Structure* has been described as "one of the great theoretical teatises of twentieth century anthropology . . . which will have a lasting place in the fundamental literature of our subject" (Meyer Fortes).

Bibliography: R. Firth, in: *American Anthropologist*, 59 (1957), 117–24, incl. bibl.; M. Fortes, in: S. F. Nadel, *The Theory of Social Structure* (1957), ix–xvi; M. Janowitz, in: *Current Anthropology*, 4 no. 2 (1963), 139, 149–54; IESS, index. [E.Fi.]

NADELMAN, ELIE (1882–1946), U.S. sculptor. Nadelman, who was born in Warsaw, studied art there and in Cracow. He lived in extreme poverty in Paris for some years, but his first one-man show in 1909 was a triumph. His work at this time was mainly influenced by classical Greek art, but certain drawings and pieces of sculpture hinted at a search for a new direction. Andre Gide wrote in his *Journal* (1909): "Nadelman draws with a compass and sculpts by assembling rhombs. He has discovered that each curve of the human body is accompanied by a reciprocal curve opposite it and corresponding to it." Nadelman, who regarded himself as the father of cubism, resented his not being recognized as such. He made his way to the U.S. early in World War I, and had his first American one-man show in New York at the end of 1915. Over the years Nadelman became very successful with his fashionable, witty portrait busts. Nadelman and his wealthy wife assembled one of the finest collections of American folk art. The depression of the 1930s, however, brought a change in his fortunes and after 1932 he was virtually forgotten. He spent his last years

"Circus Woman I," bronze by Elie Nadelman, c. 1924 (this cast 1965), height 49 in. (125 cm.). New York, Private Collection. Photo Charles Uht, New York.

doing voluntary occupational therapy at the Bronx Veterans' Hospital and making sentimental little plaster figures for mass reproduction. Nadelman was rediscovered when in 1948, two years after his death, the New York Museum of Modern Art, in collaboration with the Boston Institute of Contemporary Art and the Baltimore Museum of Art, mounted a memorial exhibition of his work. This revealed him as an important sculptor, remarkable for the supple languor of his marble heads, his translations of folk art, and his comments on human foibles.

Bibliography: L. Kirstein, *Sculpture of Elie Nadelman* (1948), includes bibliography; idem, *Elie Nadelman, Drawings* (1949). [A.W.]

NAḌĪR (Ar. **Banu Naḍīr**), one of the three main Jewish tribes in ancient *Medina, the other being the Banu *Qurayẓa and the Banu *Qaynuqāʿ. The Naḍīr and the Qurayẓa tribes called themselves *kāhinan*, indicating their priestly descent. Their origin is a matter of dispute, most scholars believing that they went to Yathrib (i.e., Medina) from Judea after the Jewish rebellion against Rome (c. 70 C.E.); others hold that the Naḍīr were an Arab tribe of proselytes. The Naḍīr bore Arabic names, spoke their own dialect of Arabic, and engaged in commerce and the cultivation of dates. They were clients of the Arab tribe of the Aws of Medina. In 624, two years after his victory over the Qaynuqāʿ, Muhammad ordered the Naḍīr to leave Medina within ten days or face death because they would not accept his prophecy and were allegedly plotting against him. He stipulated, however, that they could take their movable goods and would be permitted to return for the date harvest. The Naḍīr were persuaded to remain in Medina; they were defeated and exiled by Muhammad in 626. Allowed to take all movable goods, excluding weapons, they were not permitted to return for the date harvest and their groves were burned. Their exile is recalled in Arab poetry and is the subject of Sura 59 of the Koran. Some went to Syria and others to Khaybar, where they were defeated by Muhammad in 629.

The poet *Ka'b al-Ashraf, a leading opponent of Muhammad, is believed to have been a Naḍīr or of Naḍīr descent.

Bibliography: Baron, Social[2], 3 (1957), 79f.; I. Ben-Zvi, *Niddeḥei Yisrael* (1965), 63f.; H. Z. Hirschberg, *Yisrael ba-Arav* (1946), 143–4; J. Braslavski, in: *Zion*, 1 (1936), 148, 184; W. M. Watt, *Muhammad at Medina* (1956), 217f.; De L. E. O'Leary, *Arabia Before Muhammad* (1927), 171–7; M. Ibn Isḥāq, *Life of Muhammad*, tr. by A. Guillaume (1955), index; P. K. Hitti, *History of the Arabs* (1964[8]), index; EIS, 3 pt. 2 (1936), 815. [Ed.]

NADIR, MOSHE (pseudonym of **Isaac Reis**; 1885–1943), Yiddish poet and humorist. Born in eastern Galicia, Nadir emigrated to New York at the age of 13 and at 16 began to write lyrics in which he emphasized the hardships of the immigrant generation. His later lyrics were more skeptical, and satiric. He tried to mask his sentimentalism in biting irony, which increased as he found life increasingly meaningless, and sought escape from nihilistic moodiness in jesting. He said: "When God had nothing to do, He created a world. When I have nothing to do, I destroy it." He co-edited the humorous biweekly *Der Yidishe Gazlen*, and *Der Groyser Kundes*, the most widely read Yiddish humorous periodical of his time. He participated in the literary projects of Di *Yunge and aroused interest with his volume of erotic lyrics *Vilde Royzn* (1915). Delighting readers with his paradoxes and wit, his writings served, at the same time, as a means through which he vented his anger at the world. His plays, poems, and essays were intended to shock respectable society. The fantastic is a thread often running through his stories. His major contribution to Yiddish literature, however, was his imaginative use of the language, demonstrating through his puns and coinages the plasticity of Yiddish.

Adherence to communist circles brought him release from pessimism and loneliness for a time. In 1926, on his visit to Soviet Russia, he was hailed by adoring Jewish crowds. In his articles in the communist Jewish daily *Freiheit* (1922–39), he attacked opponents of the Communist Party line. Three volumes of these articles were published in 1935–36. Disillusionment came with the Stalin-Hitler pact of 1939 and, his collection of poetry *Moyde Ani* ("I Confess"), written in 1941 and published posthumously in 1944, includes an autobiographical section in which he repudiated his former beliefs. For an English translation, see I. Howe and E. Greenberg, *A Treasury of Yiddish Stories* (1953).

Bibliography: I. C. Biletzky, *Essays on Yiddish Poetry and Prose Writers* (1969), 129–36; Rejzen, Leksikon, 2 (1927), 500–13; LNYL, 6 (1965), 126–33; S. Leshchinsky, *Literarishe Eseyen* (1955), 126–36; S. D. Singer, *Dikhter un Prozaiker* (1959), 57–66; I. Manger, *Noente Geshtaltn* (1961), 448–55; A. Tabachnik, *Dikhter un Dikhtung* (1965), 268–374; S. Liptzin, *Maturing of Yiddish Literature* (1970), 34–36. [S.L.]

°**NĀDIR SHAH,** Turkish conquerer, king of Persia, 1736–47. A religious reformer who accepted the throne of Persia only on condition that Shiʿa Islam be abolished, Nādir Shah tried to bring about a fusion of Shiʿa and Sunna Islam. He fostered the idea of a universal religion embracing Islam, Christianity, and Judaism, and his attitude toward non-Muslim minorities, markedly different from that of his predecessors, was highly tolerant. He established a Jewish community in *Meshed which, being a holy site of the Shiʿa world, had until then excluded Christians or Jews. In 1740 Nādir Shah transferred Jews from *Kazvin to Meshed, where they lived in peace and prosperity until his assassination. In the same year Nādir Shah ordered the translation into Persian of the Holy Scriptures: the Pentateuch (Tawrāt), Psalms (Zabūr), the Gospels (Ingīl), and the Koran. The work on the Pentateuch and Psalms was entrusted to a Jewish scholar in Isfahan, Bābā ibn Nuriel, who wrote his translation in Hebrew characters, later transliterated by one of the Persian scribes. Manuscripts of these Persian Bible translations with their colophons are preserved in the Vatican Library and in the Bibliothèque Nationale, Paris.

Bibliography: Margoliouth, Cat, 1 (1899, repr. 1965), 120–1, no. 159; E. Blochet, *Catalogue des manuscrits persans de la Bibliothèque Nationale*, 1 (1905), 6 no. 7; 4 (1934), 166–7, no. 2208, 168, no. 2210; W. J. Fischel, in: HTR, 45 (1952), 3–45. [W.J.F.]

NADLER, MARCUS (1895–1965), U.S. economist. Born in Austria, he joined the Austrian army in 1912. During World War I he became a Russian prisoner of war and was sent to Siberia. From there he worked his way through Manchuria to the United States, where he enrolled as a night student at Columbia University and completed his studies at George Washington University. For several years he worked for the Federal Reserve Board, and in 1927 joined the faculty of New York University as professor of finance. He also served as a consulting economist for several New York banks and research director of the Devine Institute of Finance at New York University. His publications include *The Banking Situation in New York State* (1956), *The Money Market and its Institutions* (1955), and *International Money Markets* (1935) with J. T. Madden. [J.O.R.]

NADVORNAYA (Pol. **Nadwórna**), city in Ivano-Frankovsk oblast, Ukrainian S.S.R. An organized Jewish community existed from the beginning of the 18th century. According to the 1765 census, 937 Jews paid the poll tax in Nadvornaya and the surrounding villages. During the second half of the 18th century the ḥasidic movement made its influence felt among the local Jews. Nadvornaya Jews engaged largely in agricultural trade and small crafts. In 1880 the community numbered 4,182 (64% of the total population); by 1900 the number had decreased to 3,644 (48%); and in 1921 only 2,042 Jews (34%) remained. Between the two world wars many Jews earned their livelihood from agriculture. [Ed.]

Holocaust Period. In 1941 there were about 5,000 Jews in Nadvornaya. Under Soviet rule (1939–41), community institutions and all Jewish parties ceased to function. With the outbreak of war between Germany and the U.S.S.R. (June 22, 1941), the city was occupied by the Hungarians, who were allies of the Germans. The Ukrainian population attacked the Jews, murdering many of them and looting their property. In September the Germans entered the town. On Nov. 6, 1941 an *Aktion* took place in which about 2,500 Jews were killed. In the winter of 1941/42 a number of Jews were taken to concentration camps. A ghetto was established on June 20, 1942, and in another *Aktion* in the summer of 1942, hundreds were sent to the *Belzec death camp. In September and October 1942 groups of Jews were transported to the ghetto at Stanislav and murdered there. Although at the end of 1942 the ghetto at Nadvornaya was destroyed, a few Jews succeeded in escaping and hiding in the surrounding forest; some crossed the border into Hungary. Jewish life was not reconstituted in Nadvornaya after the war. [Ar.W.]

Bibliography: R. Mahler, *Yidn in Amolikn Poyln in Likht fun Tsifern* (1958), index; B. Wasiutyński, *Ludność żydowska w Polsce w wiekach XIX i XX* (1930), 101, 123, 154, 157.

NAFTALI, PEREẒ (Fritz; 1888–1961), Israel economist, writer, and labor leader. Born in Berlin, Naftali was a leading German economist and, at an early stage of his life, became a member of the socialist movement. From 1920 to 1926 he was the economic editor of the German newspaper

Frankfurter Zeitung. He became the director of the research institute of the Deutscher Gewerkschaftsbund (German Federation of Trade Unions; 1927–33) and was a pioneer in the field of "economic democracy"; he published a book under that title which earned him considerable renown in the international labor movement.

Naftali joined the Zionist Organization in 1925, and in 1933 he settled in Palestine. For several years he was a lecturer in economics at the Haifa Technion and the Tel Aviv School of Economics and Law. From 1937 to 1949 he was director of the Bank Hapoalim. He was a member of the Tel Aviv Municipal Council, the *Histadrut Executive, and the First and Second Knesset. In the Israel government, Naftali served as minister without portfolio (1951–52), minister of agriculture (1952–55), and minister of social welfare (from January until December 1959). [W.PR.]

NAGARI (Naʿari), MOSES BEN JUDAH (14th century), philosopher. Nagari probably lived in Rome around 1300. He is the author of *Ma'amar ba-Ma'arekhet*, an index to Maimonides' *Guide of the Perplexed*, which also contains explanations of philosophical terms. This work was printed together with questions on the *Guide* addressed to Isaac *Abrabanel by Saul Cohen (Venice, 1574; reprinted in *Abrabanel, Ketavim al-Maḥashevet Yisrael*, vol. 3, 1967). Steinschneider suggested that Nagari's name should be read Naʿari and that he was a member of the Ne'arim (Adolescentoli) family. He also corrected certain mistaken notions about Nagari (Cat Bod, 1834).

Bibliography: Benjacob, Oẓar, 282 (no. 204), 355 (no. 33). [ED.]

NAGASAKI, port in S. Japan. With the opening of Japan to international relations in the mid-19th century, Nagasaki gradually grew into a center of foreign trade. In the 1860s a small number of Jews, mainly from Eastern Europe, settled in the city. In the following years they organized religious and communal activities, built a synagogue, and maintained a burial ground. In the late 19th century (when the community numbered around 100) many of them earned a livelihood by catering to the needs of Russian sailors whose ships called regularly at the port. When this business ceased with the outbreak of the Russo-Japanese War in 1904, many of the Jews moved elsewhere, and the organized Jewish community came to an end. [H.K.]

NAGEL, ERNEST (1901–), U.S. philosopher. Nagel, who was born in Nove Mesto (Moravia) emigrated to America at an early age. Though he was best known for his incisive and learned essays in the philosophy of science, Nagel's interests as a philosopher were broad. Many of his writings deal with social and political questions and with

Ernest Nagel, U.S. philosopher. Courtesy Columbia University, New York.

questions of religion. In these latter domains, influenced by his interest in the philosophy of science, his work emerges as a type of philosophical naturalism. According to Nagel, the types of explanation of the world which produce human knowledge are essentially those based on the model of explanation in the physical sciences. He argued, however, that such types of explanation must not be interpreted narrowly, as a kind of rigid scientism, but rather broadly, e.g., explanations of mental phenomena are not to be reduced to descriptions of the movement of material particles as in the physical sciences. He thus distinguished between naturalistic explanations and materialistic ones, where "materialism" is taken to mean that philosophical view which denies the existence of mind or mental qualities. In a similar vein, Nagel argued that "determinism" in physical theory is not such as to entail the denial of human freedom with regard to moral and political decisions. His analysis of morality and of human history accordingly allowed for the attribution of responsibility to human agents for their actions. Thus, he maintained that naturalism, although committed to giving a correct account of scientific knowledge, includes within its scope a place for imagination, liberal values, and human wisdom. Nagel's main contribution to the philosophy of science is to be found in *The Structure of Science* (1961). Among Nagel's other important writings are: *An Introduction to Logic and Scientific Method*, with Morris Raphael Cohen (1934); *Principles of the Theory of Probability* (1939); *Sovereign Reason* (1954); *Logic Without Metaphysics* (1956); and *Godel's Proof*, with James R. Newman (1958). He served as president of the Association of Symbolic Logic (1947–49), and as president of the Philosophy of Science Association (1960–62). [A.S.]

NAGID (pl. *negidim*, Heb. נְגִידִים, pl. נָגִיד; Ar. *ra'īs al-yahūd*), the head of the Jewish community in Islamic countries (except under *Abbasid rule where Jewry was led by the *exilarchs). In the Middle Ages, beginning with the tenth century, there were *negidim* in *Spain, *Kairouan, *Egypt, and *Yemen; in *Morocco, *Algeria, and *Tunisia there were *negidim* from the 16th to the 19th centuries.

History of the Institution of the Nagid. When the Abbasid caliphate was split up and independent kingdoms came into being, the new rulers found it necessary to appoint a leader for each non-Muslim community. ʿAbd al-Raḥmān I (751–788), founder of the Umayyad emirate in Spain, appointed a Visigoth prince to head the Christian community, and subsequent leaders of the Christians were appointed from among Christian courtiers or candidates proposed by the community. The duties of the head of the Christian community consisted of representing the community before the authorities, ensuring the payment of taxes, supervising community life, and administering the judiciary, which applied Visigoth law. In a similar manner, the heads of the Jewish community were appointed from among persons holding high rank at the court of the caliph or sultan, such as vizier, secretary, or treasurer; most, however, were physicians. Their task was to see to it that the Jewish community fulfilled the duties imposed on it (such as observing the Covenant of *Omar); they also appointed *dayyanim* and other community officials. Thus, the office of *nagid* came into being in order to serve the purposes of the Muslim state, but its existence was also in the interests of the Jews, for these *nesi'im* (see **Nasi;* the term *nagid* was first applied in the beginning of the 11th century) would intervene in their behalf to obtain better conditions or to bring about the cancellation of anti-Jewish decrees. The archetype of the institution of *nagid* was the Babylonian exilarch, with certain differences. The *negidim* did not claim Davidic descent, their appointment being based on their own achievements and their standing with the authorities, rather than their blood line, and they did

List of Negidim in Egypt

1. **Judah b. Saadiah** 1067(?)—1079(?)
2. **Mevorakh b. Saadiah** 1079(?)–1110(?)
3. **Moses b. Mevorakh** before 1115–after 1124
4. **Samuel b. Hananiah** 1141–1159
5. **Zuta** intermittently for some years after 1159
6. **Moses b. Maimon (Maimonides)**? after Zuta
7. **Abraham b. Moses Maimuni** before 1213–1237
8. **David b. Abraham Maimuni** 1237–1300
9. **Abraham b. David Maimuni** before 1291– after 1313
10. **Moses b. Abraham Maimuni**? after his father
11. **Joshua b. Abraham Maimuni** d. 1355
12. **David b. Joshua Maimuni** 1355–1374
13. **Amram** 1374– after 1384
14. **Simeon** before 1422
15. **Joseph b. Obadiah**? after 1430
16. **Abd al-Latiff b. Ibrahim b. Sams** before 1442
17. **Joseph b. Khalifah** before 1458– after 1465
18. **Solomon b. Joseph** d. 1482
19. **Nathan (Jonathan) b. Saadiah ha-Kohen Sholal** before 1484–1502
20. **Isaac ha-Kohen Sholal** 1502–1517
21. **Abraham de Castro** 1520(?)–after 1524
22. **Tajid**? second half of 16th century
23. **Jacob b. Ḥayyim Talmid**? second half of 16th century

1. Ashtor, Toledot, 1(1944), 41; S.D. Goitein, in: HUCA, 34(1963), 180.
2. S.D. Goitein, *Sidrei Ḥinnukh* (1962), 37, 128.
3–4. idem, in JQR, 53(1962/'63), 95–96.
5. E. Ashtor, in: HUCA, 27(1956), 313–5.
6. D. Neustadt, in: *Zion*, 11(1945/46), 147–8.
7. Goitein, in JQR, 53(1962/63), 96, 104.
8. *Ibid.*, 104; idem, *Sidrei Ḥinnukh*, 114.
9. idem, *Sidrei Ḥinnukh*, 114; idem, in: *Tarbiz*, 34(1965), 249–50. He served as *nagid* for several years with his father.
10. idem, in: *Tarbiz*, 34(1965), 255.
11. Ashtor, Toledot, 1(1944), 298 ff.
12. *ibid.*, 300–2; 3(1970), 88; A.H. Freimann, in: *Minḥah li-Yhudah*, dedicated to J.L. Zlotnik (1950), 175–8.
13–17. Ashtor, Toledot, 2(1951), 22–26, 84, 86–87.
18. *ibid.*, 3(1970), 154.
19. *ibid.*, 2(1951), 450–3.
20. *ibid.*, 505 ff.; A. Shoḥet, in: *Zion*, 13–14 (1948/49), 43.
21. A.N. Pollack, *ibid.*, 1(1936), 24, 28–31.
22–23. Rosanes, Togarmah, 3(1937/38)[2], 220–1.

[A.D.]

not, as a rule, derive their income from taxes imposed on the community, as did the exilarchs. The similarity of the duties of the two institutions seems to account for the legend mentioned by *David b. Solomon ibn Abi Zimra (Responsa no. 944) and Joseph b. Isaac Sambari (Neubauer, Chronicles, 1 (1887), 115–6), according to which the office of *nagid* in Egypt was created by a member of the Babylonian exilarch's family who had been invited to Egypt by the Abbasid wife of the Egyptian ruler; D. Ayalon (Neustadt, see bibliography) has shown that there is no historical truth to this legend, for there is no record of any daughter of an Abbasid caliph marrying a Fatimid caliph, and, as stated, the *negidim* did not claim Davidic descent.

Spain. Among those known to have held the office of *nagid* in Spain are *Ḥisdai ibn Shaprut, physician and statesman at the courts of ʿAbd al-Raḥmān III (ruled 912–61) and his son al-Ḥakam II (961–76). Ibn Shaprut did a great deal for the Jews in his own country, as well as for Jewish communities in other parts of the world; *Dunash b. Labrat refers to him as "judge." *Jacob ibn Jau, who succeeded Ibn Shaprut, was, according to Abraham *ibn Daud, appointed head of the Jewish community by Manṣur ibn Abi ʿAmir, the guardian of Hisham II (976–1013); the latter "issued him a document placing him in charge of all the Jewish communities from Sijilmassa to the river Duero . . . [The decree stated] that he was to adjudicate all their litigations, and that he was empowered to appoint over them whomsoever he wished and to exact from them any tax or payment to which they might be subject . . . he placed at his disposal . . . the carriage of a vicegerent. Then all the members of the community of Córdoba assembled and signed an agreement [certifying] his position as *nasi*, which stated: 'Rule thou over us, both thou, and thy son, and thy son's son also'" (Abraham ibn Daud's *The Book of Tradition*, ed. by G. D. Cohen (1967), 69). Ibn Jau was in office for only one year, and was removed by the vizier al-Manṣur. The source quoted above illustrates the duties of the office, the manner in which the appointee was chosen by the authorities, and the appointee's acceptance by the community. Both Ibn Shaprut and Ibn Jau fulfilled the duties of *nagid*, but neither bore the title. Two Spanish *negidim* who did hold the title were Samuel ibn Nagrela (*Samuel ha-Nagid; 993–1056) and his son *Jehoseph ha-Nagid. Samuel was the treasurer and secretary of King Ḥabbus of Granada; S. D. Goitein (see bibliography) assumes that the title *nagid* was awarded to him by *Hai Gaon. His son, who also served as the king's secretary, was killed in 1066; according to Goitein, he was awarded his title by *Daniel b. Azariah, *nasi* and *gaon* of Ereẓ Israel from 1051 to 1062. Both *negidim* received their titles in recognition of the aid they extended to the academies.

Kairouan. During the same period, there was a separate Jewish leadership in Kairouan, Tunisia. The first official *nagid* who was appointed by the Zirid emir was ʾAbu Isḥaq Ibrahim ibn ʿAta (Natan), who served as court physician to the emir Badis (966–1016) and his son al-Muʿizz (1016–62), the rulers of the eastern Maghreb (Tunisia and Algeria). The appointment apparently was made during the period of the madness of the Fatimid Ḥākim bi-Amr Allah (1010–12?), at which time the opportunity was grasped to free themselves from Fatimid rule. It may be assumed that even before this there was local Jewish government in Kairouan, but without formal independent status. Ibrahim, like the Spanish *negidim*, extended aid to the Babylonian academies, in addition to attending to the needs of his own community, and earned the praise of Hai Gaon, who in 1015 awarded him the honorary title of *negid ha-Golah* ("*nagid* of the Diaspora"). He died in about 1020 and was succeeded by Jacob b. Amram, who was referred to by such titles as *negid ha-Golah*, *sar ha-Segullah* ("the chosen prince"), and *pe'er ha-edah* ("pride of the community"). There is no record of his early activities and the last report about him dates from 1041. He helped the Kairouan community in times of need, sent contributions to the yeshivot in Ereẓ Israel and Babylonia, and earned the praise of the exilarch *Hezekiah b. David. He was also in contact with the Jewish community in Sicily. It is probable that there was one more *nagid* in Kairouan before the community ended in the 1160s.

Egypt. In Egypt the office of *nagid* remained in existence for over 500 years; there are extant documents which contain a wealth of details on the *negidim* and their authority and acts. Most scholars accept the view that the first *nagid* of Egyptian Jewry was *Paltiel, an Italian Jew who was brought to Egypt by al-Muʿizz, the Fatimid conqueror of Egypt (969), and was part of the ruler's officialdom. The sole source for this information is the *Ahimaaz Scroll; it stands to reason that the Shi'ite Fatimids, who decreed themselves caliphs, did not wish to depend in any way upon the Sunnite Abbasid caliphs, preferring to appoint a separate head for the Jews under their ruler rather than have them acknowledge the authority of the Babylonian exilarch, an official who was part of the Abbasid hierarchy. There are various theories concerning the true identity of Paltiel, the most recent being the one expressed by B. Lewis (see bibliography), according to which he was Musa b. Eleazar, al-Mu'izz's physician. The *Genizah* documents contain no proof of the existence of the office of *nagid* in the first half of the 11th century. The first *negidim* of whom details are found in the *Genizah* are Judah b. Saadiah, who was a court physician, held the post of *nagid* in the 1060s and the 1070s, and was referred to as "*nagid* of the People of God," and his brother *Mevorakh, who was *nagid* from about 1050 (with temporary interruptions) to 1110. Mevorakh was the physician and adviser of al-Malik al-Afdal, the acting ruler of Egypt, and was awarded no less than 14 honorary titles, some of which were typical of those used by the academies in Babylonia and Ereẓ Israel. For a while, Mevorakh was removed from office, a result of the machinations of *David b. Daniel, a member of the house of the Babylonian exilarch who had succeeded in gaining the governor's support for his claim to the leadership of Egyptian Jewry. Such competition for the office occurred on several occasions, up to the 13th century. As a rule the challenge came from members of the Babylonian exilarch's house or the Ereẓ Israel academy.

The Institution of Nagid. The *nagid* was appointed by the authorities after receiving the agreement of prominent members of the community. The choice, however, was not made in a democratic manner. Rather than the official representatives, it was the influential members of the community who recommended the candidate. Sometimes the vizier was bribed to recommend a particular person; this happened, for example, in the middle of the 12th century, in the case of *Zuta. The appointment of the *nagid* did not depend upon the consent of the exilarch or the heads of the academies, and the mention of such consent in the existing documents must be regarded as a mere formality. At times it was the son of the deceased *nagid* who was appointed in his father's place, while on some occasions preference was given to a person who had achieved a prominent position at the ruler's court. Beginning with *Abraham b. Moses b. Maimon, the son of *Maimonides, the office became hereditary, and four of his descendants served as *negidim*, the last being *David b. Joshua Maimuni. From the end of the Ayyubid dynasty and throughout the Mamluk period, the office of *nagid*, or *ra'īs al-yahūd*, had the character of a permanent institution, whose functions were defined by the authorities. Several letters of appointment from the Mamluk period are extant which contain the provision that the *ra'īs* always be a Rabbanite and that he also be in charge of the *Karaites and *Samaritans. It was his duty to appoint a prominent Karaite as leader of that community, although the head of the Samaritans received his own letter of appointment from the government. According to Qalqashandī (d. 1418), the status of *nagid* was parallel in nature to that of the Christian patriarch, and like any person of official rank wore official dress, the *khal'a*. The Arab chronicler Ibn Faḍl Allah al-'Omarī, whose work was written in 1340, tells about a *nagid*'s letter of appointment in which his authority and functions were described as follows: consolidation of the community; administration of justice to the members of the community on the basis of its religious law; responsibility for matters of personal status—betrothals, marriages, and divorces; the right of excommunication; supervision of the observance of the commandments, according to the Law of Moses and the decisions of the rabbis; the duty to ensure compliance with the Covenant of Omar, especially the prohibition of constructing new synagogues, and the order concerning the wearing of garb different from that of the Muslims; supervision of synagogues and prayer services; grading the status of the members of the community (this apparently applies to tax assessment, for there were three different rates for the poll tax, depending upon a person's economic situation); and general responsibility for the maintenance of law and order by the community. Jewish sources, primarily *Genizah* documents dating from the Fatimid period and after, give further information on the wide range of the *nagid*'s duties and activities. He protected his community from oppression by government officials and interceded with the authorities for the cancellation of unjust and severe decrees. He served as arbitrator in cases of injustice, discrimination, and unfair economic competition; attended to the needs of the weak and the suffering; and tried to retrieve lost goods, rescue Jews from prison and captivity, and raise the ransoms required for such purposes. It was he who authorized the payment of tuition fees from the communal trust fund for the education of orphans and children of the poor (five such payment orders by a single *nagid*, Abraham b. Moses b. Maimon, were found in the *Genizah*). The *nagid* was not responsible for collecting the poll tax, but it was he who ensured the payment of the tax on behalf of the poor, when the authorities did not exempt them. He had his own officials through whom he supervised *kashrut*, ritual slaughter, and marriages. Decisions made by the various communities required his confirmation, and in general he supervised the community operations by means of the *muqaddam*, his personal representative to the local community. Although he was the supreme legal authority for the community, he did not actually function as a judge, but appointed *dayyanim* who sat on his *bet din* and handled legal conflicts; the court was known as the Great *Bet Din* and it was headed by the *dayyan al-yahud*. Legal documents such as marriage writs, divorce writs, and wills were issued "by the authority" of the *nagid*. According to *Meshullam of Volterra, who visited Egypt in 1481, the *nagid's* penal powers included the right to impose capital punishment (*Massa Meshullam mi-Volterah*, ed. by A. Yaari, 1948, 57), but it is doubtful whether the authorities did in fact grant him such power. Obadiah *Bertinoro, writing in 1487–88, states that the *nagid* was empowered by the caliph "to punish, imprison, and flog" anyone who opposed his will; this seems to be a more realistic description of the *nagid's* authority. He could also use excommunication and imprisonment in those cases where the prestige of his office was not sufficient to achieve compliance with his decisions. In the Fatimid and Ayyubid periods the *negidim* did not impose taxes for the maintenance of their office; usually they were wealthy court physicians and property owners, and also received gifts from members of the community. In the Mamluk period a change seems to have taken place, and according to the testimony of David b. Solomon ibn Abi Zimra marriage and divorce proceedings became subject to a fee, out of which the *nagid* would pay the scribe, while the rest would go into his own treasury. The honors accorded to the Egyptian *nagia* were similar to those of the exilarch. Thus, the reading of the weekly portion of the Torah would be preceded by an introductory recital in honor of the *nagid*, in which he was mentioned by name. Special *Yizkor* (i.e., memorial) *piyyutim* were composed to commemorate departed *negidim*. The conquest of Ereẓ Israel by Saladin (1187) created the need for the appointment of a separate leadership for Jewish communities of Ereẓ Israel and Syria, and the office of *nagid* of Ereẓ Israel and Judah was created. The names of two such *negidim* are known, both of whom served in the 13th century: Obadiah b. ʿUlah and Hillel b. Moses. Under Mamluk rule, Ereẓ Israel had a deputy *nagid*, who was under the authority of the *nagid* of Egypt. As a rule the Egyptian *negidim* were chosen from local Jewish leaders. The last two *negidim* appointed under Mamluk rule, however, were from a family of Maghreb *ḥakhamim*: Nathan (or Jonathan) *Sholal, *nagid* from 1484 to 1502, who went from Algeria to Ereẓ Israel but then moved to Egypt, and his nephew Isaac *Sholal, who was director of the Egyptian mint. Isaac founded a yeshivah in Jerusalem and attended to the needs of the city's scholars. In 1509 he and his *bet din* enacted an ordinance exempting religious scholars from all taxes, except for the poll tax. He was deposed from his office in 1517, when Egypt was taken over by the Ottomans, and died in 1524. Under Ottoman rule, two more *negidim* were appointed in Egypt: Abraham *Castro, who was also the director of the Egyptian mint, and *Jacob b. Ḥayyim Talmid, who was sent from Istanbul (Constantinople) to Egypt in order to take up the post. According to a report by Joseph *Sambari (Neubauer, Chronicles, 1 (1887), 116–7), Jacob Talmid became involved in a controversy with Bezalel *Ashkenazi, whereupon the Egyptian governor decided to abolish the office of *nagid* in Egypt. Henceforth, it was the *ḥakham* (chief rabbi) who acted as the representative of Egyptian Jewry before the authorities.

Yemen. The existence of the office of *nagid* in Yemen may be deduced from fragmentary information contained in letters found in the *Genizah* and from inscriptions on Yemenite tombstones, both sources dating from the end of the 11th up to the beginning of the 14th centuries. The first *nagid* of whom there is knowledge was Japheth (Hasan) b. Bendar, apparently of Persian origin, who in a document dating from 1097 is referred to as a "prince of the communities." He and his descendants were residents of Aden, were clerks for merchants, and dealt in the trade with India; they exercised some measure of control over the trade routes and the price of the transit goods which passed through Yemen on their way to Egypt. Japheth's son, Maḍmun, mentioned in letters from the period 1132–51, was granted the title of "*nagid* of the Land of Yemen" by the exilarch; he also maintained contact with the gaon *Maẓli'aḥ ha-Kohen from Egypt and received an honorary title from him (in addition to six other titles of honor that he bore). In an official report of the *bet din* he is described as "appointed by the exilarchs and heads of the academies over all of Israel and acknowledged by the respective rulers in the lands of the sea and of the desert"; the latter passage seems to imply that Maḍmun had agreements with the pirate chiefs who controlled the sea routes. His son Ḥalfon inherited the title of *nagid* and served from 1152 to 1172. During his lifetime there were two other *negidim*, R. Nethanel al-*Fayyumi (d. after 1164) and his son *Jacob b. Nethanel al-Fayyumi, who was in charge of the communities in central Yemen; the latter received Maimonides' famous *Iggeret Teiman*. There are reports of another *nagid* by the name of Maḍmun (he may be identical with Shemariah b. David), who served from 1202 to 1218. Three *negidim* are known from the first half of the 13th century: Maḍmun (apparently a descendant of the first Maḍmun mentioned above) and his sons, Ḥalfon and Joshua. The title of *nagid* was also held by David b. Amram *Adani, author of *Ha-Midrash ha-Gadol*, who lived at the end of the 13th and the beginning of the 14th centuries, and may have been a descendant of the Maḍmun family.

North Africa. In the Jewish communities of the Maghreb from the 16th to the 19th centuries the office of *nagid* was held either by prominent Jewish merchants or Jews who had close contacts at the ruler's court and served as interpreters and diplomatic agents. In rabbinic literature of the time, they are referred to as *nagid me'ulleh* ("most excellent *nagid*") or *nasi*. They differed from the medieval *negidim* in that they served only a single community, rather than a whole country, and were really *rashei kahal*. Some of them, however, extended their influence beyond the confines of their own community. They were elected by the prominent members of the community and in some cases also received an appointment from the Muslim ruler. They participated in the drafting of community statutes, and were authorized to impose corporal punishment and fines and report to the Muslim authorities any person violating community regulations. The *negidim* are frequently mentioned in the "Statutes of Fez" (*Kerem Ḥemed*, 2, 1871). In the 18th century their official title in Algeria was *muqaddam*, while in Tunisia and Tripolitania it was *qā'id*.

Bibliography: SPAIN: Dinur, Golah, 3 (1961²), 128–68; H. Schirmann, in: *Zion*, 1 (1936), 261–83, 357–76; idem, in: JSS, 13 (1951), 99–126; Ashtor, Korot, 1 (1966²), 103–51, 2 (1966), 26–117. KAIROUAN: J. Mann, in: JQR, 11 (1920–21), 429–32; Hirschberg, in: *Zion*, 23–24 (1958–59), 116–73; 25 (1960), 62; Hirschberg, Afrikah, 1 (1965), 152–61; S. D. Goitein, in: *Zion*, 27 (1962), 11–13, 156–65; idem, in: *Tarbiz*, 34 (1965), 162–82. EGYPT: A. Neubauer, in: JQR, 8 (1896), 551–5; E. N. Adler, *ibid.*, 9 (1897), 712–20; D. Kaufman, *ibid.*, 10 (1898), 162–4; R. J. H. Gottheil, *ibid.*, 19 (1907), 500f., 528–32; Mann, Egypt, index; J. Mann, in: HUCA, 3 (1926), 303–5; A. N. Pollack, in: *Zion*, 1 (1936), 24–36; S. Assaf, *ibid.*, 256–7; idem, *Mekorot u-Meḥkarim* (1946), 186–99; D. Neustadt, in: *Zion*, 4 (1939), 126–49; 11 (1946), 147–8; D. Z. Baneth, in: *Sefer ha-Yovel li-Khevod . . . A. Marx* (1950), 75–87; Ashtor, Toledot, 2 (1951), 28–30, 237–58, 448–54; E. Ashtor, in: *Zion*, 30 (1965), 139–47; S. D. Goitein, *Sidrei Ḥinnukh* (1962), index; idem, in: JQR, 53 (1962–63), 93–119; idem, in: *Tarbiz*, 34 (1965), 232–56; B. Lewis, in: *Bulletin of the School of Oriental and African Studies, University of London*, 30 (1967), 177–81. YEMEN: J. Mann, in: HUCA, 3 (1926), 301–3; E. Strauss (Ashtor), in: *Zion*, 4 (1939), 217–37; Maimonides, *Iggeret Teiman*, ed. by A. S. Halkin (1952), Heb. introd., viii; Goitein, in: *Sinai*, 33 (1953), 225–37; idem, in: *Bo'i Teiman*, ed. by Y. Ratzaby (1967), 15–25. NORTH AFRICA: J. M. Toledano, *Ner ha-Ma'arav* (1911), 80, no. 25; G. Vajda, *Un recueil de textes historiques judéo-marocains* (1951), index s.v. *Nagid*; Hirschberg, Afrikah, index, s.v. *Muqaddam, Negidim, Kaid*.

[EL.B.]

NAGLER, ISADORE (1895–1959), U.S. labor leader. Born in Austria, Nagler went to the United States in 1909 and worked as a cutter, joining Local 10 of the Cutters' Union. In 1920 he was made an official of the International Ladies Garment Workers Union (ILGWU) and was a prominent anti-communist. He became vice-president of the ILGWU in 1929 and worked closely with the union president, Benjamin *Schlesinger and his successor David *Dubinsky. Nagler was general manager of the Joint Board of the Cloakmakers Union from 1928 to 1939 and was one of the founders of the American Labor Party (ALP). In 1944 he left the Labor Party with Dubinsky in protest against its pro-communist line and helped found the Liberal Party in which he was a prominent figure. He was prominent in the New York Jewish Education Committee, the Federation of Jewish Philanthropic Societies, and *ORT.

Bibliography: H. Haskel, *A Leader of the Garment Workers* (1950), incl. bibl.

[M.D.]

°**NAGYBACZONI-NAGY, VILMOS** (1884–), Hungarian general and minister of defense. In 1942 Nagybaczoni-Nagy was appointed minister of defense. At that time Jews were excluded from the Hungarian army and were drafted into the labor service. Their situation was at times intolerable, particularly at the Russian front. When Nagybaczoni-Nagy assumed office he reviewed the labor battalions at the front and immediately ordered an improvement in their conditions. Claiming that labor service was the same as military service, he abolished the discriminations against Jewish draftees and their families, then in force through anti-Jewish legislation. He ordered officers and commanders "when dealing with Jews to refrain from showing their personal feelings, and not to increase work norms and discipline by unlawful means." Nagybaczoni-Nagy expressly forbade attacking or humiliating Jews in public. He was concerned with the release of the sick and invalids, with healthy and sufficient food, a daily eight-hour rest, and with the personal cleanliness of the members of the labor battalions. As well as this, he gave his attention to the religious needs of the draftees, e.g., the keeping of the Jewish festivals as well as alloting sufficient time for donning the phylacteries. Nagybaczoni-Nagy did not hesitate to put on trial officers and commanders who behaved with cruelty.

Following repeated pressure by the Arrow Cross opposition in the Hungarian parliament, Nagybaczoni-Nagy was forced to resign. After the German occupation of Hungary (March 19, 1944) Nagybaczoni-Nagy was arrested and deported to Germany. His memoirs for the years 1939–44 were published in 1946 under the title *Végzetes esztendők* ("Crucial Years"). In 1967 Nagybaczoni-Nagy was recognized by *Yad Vashem as one of the *Righteous of the Nations.

Bibliography: E. Karsai (ed.), *Fegyvertelen álltak az aknamezőkön*, 2 vols. (1962). [B.Y.]

NAGYKANIZSA, city in S. Hungary. It is almost certain that Jews were living in Nagykanizsa in 1710, and by 1745 the community owned a synagogue. The first inscription in the register of the *ḥevra kaddisha* dates from 1782. The community was officially established in 1786 and the new *bet midrash* was erected in 1805. The community of Nagykanizsa was among the first to join the *Reform movement, although only after bitter disputes. In 1829 it adopted the ritual of the famous composer S. *Sulzer (which was identical with the traditional ritual) and introduced an ensemble of ten violinists to accompany the choir during all services except those of the New Year and the Day of Atonement. In 1845 an organ was also introduced, the first case of its kind in the service of a Hungarian Jewish community. Noteworthy Orthodox rabbis of the community were H. Torai (1776–92) and Meir Szántó (until 1831). The first rabbi belonging to the Reform movement was L. *Loew (1841–46). He was succeeded by H. B. Fassel (1851–83) and E. *Neumann (1883–1918). The latter was the only Hungarian rabbi to incorporate some of the ritual reforms suggested by A. *Geiger. The last rabbi of the community, E. Winkler (1919–44), who reintroduced the traditional ritual, accompanied his community to Auschwitz. He died in Melk (1945).

In the first Jewish school (1786–1809), opened following the reforms of Joseph II, the language of instruction was German. In 1832 Jewish education was offered in the Hungarian language. A pre-secondary school was opened in 1867, which offered courses in natural sciences as well as religious matters. In 1891–92 it was converted into a secondary commercial school (the only Jewish school of its kind in Hungary) which functioned until 1933. In addition, a general pre-secondary school was opened in 1890. The Jews of Nagykanizsa played an important role in the industrial and commercial development of the town during the first years of the 20th century. The golden era of the community lasted from 1863 to 1902 under the community

The synagogue of Nagykanizsa, built in the early 19th century. From J. Heller and Z. Vajda, *The Synagogues of Hungary*, New York, 1908.

presidents of the Guttman family who received the title Baron. The leading charitable institutions were the *ḥevra kaddisha* (founded in 1782), whose beautiful *pinkas* has been preserved in the Jewish Museum of Budapest; the Jewish Hospital (founded in 1832), and the women's organization (1843). The population rose from 500 in 1782 to 1,000 in 1830, 2,875 in 1880, 3,378 in 1910, and 3,663 in 1920. After the German occupation (March 19, 1944), 2,700 Jews were deported to Auschwitz during May of the same year. Only 300 returned in 1945. In 1970, 100 Jews were living in Nagykanizsa.

Bibliography: H. Villányi, in: L. Barbarits, *Nagykanizsa* (1929), 251–62; E. László, in: R. L. Braham (ed.), *Hungarian Jewish Studies*, 1 (1966), 61–136, incl. bibl. and notes. [J.Z.]

NAḤAL (Heb. נַחַ"ל, *Noar Ḥalutzi Loḥem;* Fighting Pioneer Youth), a regular unit of the Israel Defense Forces whose soldiers are organized in *garinim* ("groups") of pioneering youth movements in Israel and Zionist youth movements in the Diaspora that educate their members toward cooperative settlement in Israel. During their term of military service, these soldiers simultaneously participate in intensive training and social and ideological preparation toward their future as members of cooperative agricultural settlements. Naḥal has two aims: to produce first-class soldiers and to prepare *garinim* for establishing new settlements or joining existing ones. All members of such a potential group are mobilized together, form a single army unit, and together undergo training. Training consists of initial military training (at a Naḥal army camp) which is combined with ideological and social activities. There is then a period of combined agricultural and military training in a kibbutz or at a Naḥal outpost. Advanced military training in paratroop, tank, artillery, engineering, or other units follows for the men, while the girls go to live in their

Figure 1. Going on guard at the Naḥal settlement of Gerofit, in the Arabah, 1964. Courtesy Government Press Office, Tel Aviv.

destined settlement where they are later joined by the men. The group then serves for a period of *shalat* (*sherut le-lo tashlum*, "unpaid service").

The Naḥal outpost is a typical army camp with military ranks and discipline, but at the same time preparations are made for a civilian agricultural settlement. During the 20 years of its existence, Naḥal has founded 36 outposts, of which 22 have become permanent settlements. Another 18 settlements have been founded or refounded by soldiers who once served in Naḥal; in a further 70 settlements, Naḥal soldiers constitute half the membership, while in hundreds of other kibbutzim and moshavim there are smaller groups of ex-Naḥal soldiers. It has been found that four years after mobilization (i.e., a year after completing Naḥal), about a third of the soldiers remain on the land and, of these, about half (that is 15% of those who were originally members of the group), stay in their settlements after 15 and 20 years.

Figure 2. Growing tomatoes by hydroponics at the Naḥal Yam settlement in Sinai, 1967. Courtesy Government Press Office, Tel Aviv.

Naḥal is sometimes employed on special projects. For example, in 1949 it built a road to En-Gedi along the west bank of the Dead Sea. In the early 1950s it organized large-scale vegetable production. In the 1960s it employed its soldiers to teach reading and writing to both young and adult illiterates in development towns. Other countries have shown interest in Naḥal methods, and courses for Naḥal instructors have been organized in Israel for countries in Asia, Africa, and South America. Many Israelis are employed as instructors in training similar groups in developing countries.

Bibliography: G. Levitas, *Naḥal—Israel's Pioneer Fighting Youth* (1967); Ministry of Defense, Israel, *Naḥal* (1970). [Ie.Sch.]

NAHALAL or **NAHALOL** (Heb. נַהֲלָל, נַהֲלֹל), (1) town in the territory of the tribe of Zebulun, along with *Shimron and Beth-Lehem (Josh. 19:15, 21:35). The Israelites were apparently unable to dispossess the Canaanites from Nahalol (Judg. 1:30). Later, probably in the days of David, it became a levitical city belonging to the family of Merari (Josh. 21:35). In the Talmud (TJ, Meg. 1:1, 70a), it is identified with Mahalol, which corresponds to the present-day Arab village of Maʿlūl southwest of Nazareth; the remains that can be found there are of the Roman period only and include a mausoleum (Qaṣr al-Deir). The site of Nahalal proper is still in dispute. [M.A.-Y]

Nahalal, the first moshav ovedim in Ereẓ Israel. Courtesy Government Press Office, Tel Aviv.

(2) The first moshav ovedim in Ereẓ Israel. It was founded in 1921 in the western Jezreel Valley by veteran pioneers of the *Second Aliyah, some of whom had been members of the first kevuẓah, *Deganyah. The 80 settling families each received 25 acres (100 dunams) of land, and they drained the malarial swamps. (Malaria had prevented two previous attempts at settlement, one by Arabs and one by Germans.) In the 1920s, the first farm branches—field crops, cattle, and poultry—were developed and concrete stables built, while the settlers lived in wooden huts for 15 years. The village layout, devised by the architect, Richard *Kauffmann, became the pattern for many of the moshavim established before 1948; it is based on concentric circles, with the public buildings (school, administrative, and cultural buildings, cooperative shops, and warehouses) at the center, the homesteads in the innermost circle, the farm buildings in the next, and beyond it ever wider circles of gardens and fields. In 1929 a Girls' Agricultural Training Farm was established at Nahalal by *Wizo; it was headed

by Hannah Maisel-Shoḥat, wife of Eliezer *Shoḥat. In the 1940s it became a coeducational farming school of *Youth Aliyah. Nahalal is one of the principal centers of the Tenu'at ha-Moshavim. More water became available in the 1930s from the *Mekorot regional network and deep wells were drilled in the vicinity. Farming then became more intensive, fruit orchards were added, and existing branches expanded. In 1969 Nahalal, including the agricultural school, had 1,020 inhabitants. [E.O.]

Bibliography: Albright, in: AASOR, 2/3 (1923), 26; Aharoni, Land, index; EM, s.v. (incl. bibl.).

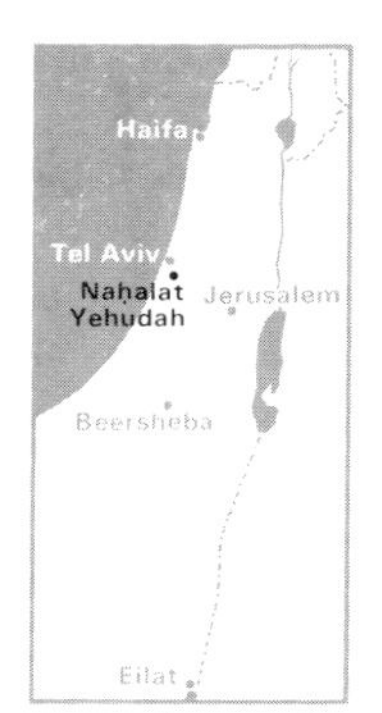

NAḤALAT YEHUDAH (Heb. נַחֲלַת יְהוּדָה), urban community with municipal council status, on the Coastal Plain of Israel near Rishon le-Zion, founded in 1914 as a moshavah by members of the Ḥibbat Zion movement of Russia. Naḥalat Yehudah was characterized by auxiliary farmsteads whose owners were employed in Rishon le-Zion or in Jaffa and Tel Aviv. After 1948 an immigrant camp (*ma'barah*) was established in Naḥalat Yehudah's municipal area, increasing its population to over 5,000. The new immigrants were later given permanent housing in other localities, so that the population decreased to 2,350 (1969). Although a number of industrial enterprises exist in Naḥalat Yehudah, many inhabitants are employed in other communities in the Tel Aviv conurbation. The name commemorates Judah Leib *Pinsker. [E.O.]

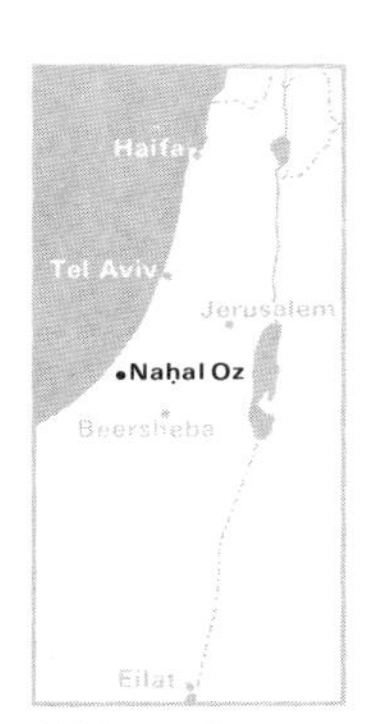

NAḤAL OZ (Heb. נַחַל עֹז), kibbutz in southern Israel, established in 1951 as a border settlement by a *Naḥal group near the Gaza Strip, affiliated with Iḥud ha-Kevuẓot ve-ha-Kibbutzim. Later, pioneers from South America and other countries joined the kibbutz. Before the *Sinai Campaign (1956), and in the days before the *Six-Day War (1967), Naḥal Oz was frequently a target for attacks and shelling from beyond the Gaza Strip border. After June 1967, a point near the kibbutz became an entrance gate to the Strip. The kibbutz economy is based on intensive farming. The name Naḥal Oz points both to the original Naḥal outpost, and to nearby Gaza (whose Hebrew name, Azzah, is derived from the same root as *oz*, meaning "strength"). [E.O.]

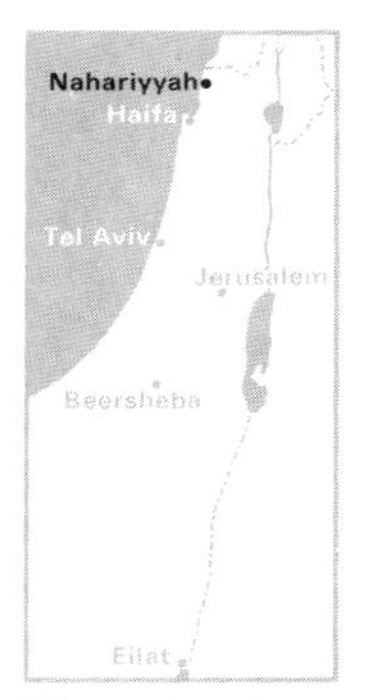

NAHARIYYAH (Heb. נַהֲרִיָּה), city in N. Israel, 6 mi. (10 km.) N. of Acre. Nahariyyah was founded in 1934 as a village (moshavah) by a group of middle-class immigrants from Germany. Their company, headed by the engineer, Yoseph Levi, bought the land, and thus gained the first Jewish foothold in the Acre Plain and Western Galilee. The settlers encountered difficulties in changing over to farming from their previous occupations in commerce and the professions. They also found themselves in an endangered and isolated position when the 1936–39 Arab riots broke out. By then beginnings were made to turn Nahariyyah into a seaside resort, in addition to developing agriculture. The population, with about 1,000 in 1941, increased to 1,400 in 1945 when manufacturing, particularly in the food branch, first began. In the years just prior to statehood, Nahariyyah served as a

The square of Nahariyyah, looking toward the municipality building. Photo Harry Dash, Nahariyyah.

landing place for "illegal" immigrant ships. In the War of Independence (1948), Nahariyyah, together with ten other Jewish settlements in Western Galilee founded in the preceding decade, was completely cut off by Arab Acre, and only intermittently were communications with Haifa maintained by means of small motor boats going to Haifa. With the capture of Acre by Israel forces, Nahariyyah was able to resume contact with the rest of the country and was included in the State of Israel. Numerous immigrants from various countries, mainly from Rumania, North Africa, and Iraq settled there. The population grew from 9,200 in 1953 to 20,700 in 1968. Nahariyyah was accorded city status. In 1969, the municipal area extended over 2,625 acres (1,050 ha.). The city's economy is based on tourism and recreation, industry, farming, trade, and services. In 1968 the city had over 30 hotels and pensions with a total capacity for 1,400 tourists. On the bathing beach a breakwater was built creating two bays, for swimming and for sailboats. There are also swimming pools. Farming continues, mostly of specialized export crops (strawberries, avocados, flowers). Local industry includes textiles, asbestos cement, metal instruments, electrical appliances, fine mechanics, paper products, agricultural machinery, etc. A new industrial zone for large enterprises was added in the north to supplement the older industrial zone near the railway station. Its commercial center is laid out along the central avenue on both sides of the Ga'aton Stream. The hotel zone stretches mainly along the beach. There is also a Malben center for the elderly. Nahariyyah has 21 public parks and ornamental gardens. Its name is derived from *nahar* ("stream") referring to the Ga'aton Stream which passes through part of the city. [E.O.]

NAHASH (Heb. נָחָשׁ; "snake"), king of the Ammonites, who enjoyed a long reign from the beginning of Saul's reign over Israel (I Sam. 11:1ff.) until some years after David was established at Jerusalem (II Sam. 10:1). Nahash is first mentioned when he encamped against Jabesh-Gilead and sought to subjugate it on most humiliating terms. The Jabeshites appealed for help to their fellow Israelites, and the crisis called forth Saul's latent capacity for leadership. He issued a call to the tribes to rally behind him and march to the relief of Jabesh-Gilead; and the force that responded inflicted a stunning defeat on the Ammonites (I Sam. 11:1ff.). Nothing more is related about Nahash until the notice of his death, where the Bible states that he had shown kindness to David (II Sam. 10:2). It is likely that he was friendly toward David because David was also an opponent of Saul. David attacked Nahash's son and successor Hanun and reduced the Ammonites to dependency. Shobi, another son of Nahash, who was one of those who befriended

David at Mahanaim during Absalom's rebellion, may later have been reigning over the Ammonites as David's vassal. Nahash, according to II Samuel 17:25, was the father of David's sister Abigail. Since David's father was Jesse, this would imply that David and his sister had only one parent in common—their mother, the tracing of their relationship through their mother being a characteristic of a beena marriage. The Nahash referred to in this verse might be Nahash king of the Ammonites, which would be an additional reason for the latter's friendliness toward David. It has been suggested, however, that there is a corruption in the text, and Nahash intruded into this verse from verse 27. According to this, "daughter of Nahash" is to be emended to read, with the Septuagint, "daughter of Jesse."

Bibliography: Noth, Personennamen 230; J. Morgenstern, in: ZAW, 47 (1929), 91–110; 49 (1931), 46–58. [Ed.]

NAH'ĀWENDĪ (Nahāwandī), BENJAMIN BEN MOSES AL- (mid-ninth century), *Karaite scholar, surnamed after the city of Nehavend (Nahavand, Nihavand), in Persia. He probably lived in Persia or Iraq, since Karaite settlement in Palestine, particularly in Jerusalem, did not begin until after Nah'āwendī's death. In the official Karaite memorial prayer he is ranked next to *Anan's son Saul, and in medieval Arabic accounts the Karaites as a group are sometimes referred to as "the followers of Anan and Benjamin." Al-*Kirkisānī, who lived a century later and whose information is usually highly reliable, states that Nah'āwendī was "learned in the lore of the Rabbanites and strong in Scripture, and served for many years as a judge." Karaite tradition regards Nah'āwendī as the person who established early Karaite teaching on a firm footing by purging it of Anan's supposedly excessive leaning toward Rabbanite doctrines. It is true that Nah'āwendī disagreed with Anan on many points of law, but at the same time he appears to have been rather tolerant; he not only had no objection to adopting Rabbanite legal ordinances, including some which have no direct support in Scripture, but is even said to have declared that every person may be guided in legal matters by his own judgment and is not obliged to submit to the decisions of commonly acknowledged authorities. On the other hand, later Karaites rejected some of Nah'āwendī's views, particularly his theory that the world was not created immediately by God, but that God created an angel who, in turn, created the world. Further, he was of the opinion that the Law was revealed by an angel, not by God, and the prophets received their prophecy from an angel. The purpose of this theory was to refer all the anthropomorphic passages in Scripture, or those which might be contrary to pure monotheism, to this angel-creator, and not to God Himself. This theory presumably represents an adaptation of a Gnostic idea, subsequently modified into the Philonic-Christian doctrine of the *logos (creative word). Nah'āwendī's borrowings from Rabbanite law seem to testify to his realization that the cry "Back to the Bible!" raised by Anan and earlier pre-Karaite schismatics, while tactically useful for their purpose of basing their laws solely on the Bible, was impractical, since biblical legislation alone could not efficiently govern the Karaites' social and economic life a thousand years later, in the vastly different conditions prevailing in the Muhammadan empire. Hence he was forced to provide guidance for his coreligionists (probably out of his own experience as a practicing judge) in such matters as identification of witnesses, loans, agency, conjugal property rights, revokable gifts, and inheritance and wills, for which Scripture supplies only vague guide rules or none at all. Unlike Anan, who wrote (so far as is known) only in Aramaic, and unlike his own successors who wrote in Arabic, Nah'āwendī wrote (again, so far as is known) in clear and fluent Hebrew, sharply distinct from the stilted Hebrew of later Karaite scholars and translators in the Byzantine Empire. His legal works comprise *Sefer Mitzvot* ("Book of Precepts") and *Sefer Dinim* ("Book of Rules"), both presumably parts of a comprehensive code of Karaite law. The *Sefer Dinim*, dealing with civil and criminal law, was published by A. Firkovich under the title *Masat Binyamin* (1835); extracts in English translation are found in L. Nemoy, *Karaite Anthology* (1952). Fragments, presumably of the *Sefer Mitzvot*, were published by A. Harkavy (*Studien und Mittheilungen*, 8 (1903), 175–84).

Nah'āwendī also wrote commentaries on some of the books of the Bible (the Pentateuch, Isaiah, Song of Songs, Ecclesiastes, Daniel), which were highly regarded even by an authority like Abraham ibn Ezra. The colophon of the *Sefer Dinim* contains the earliest-known occurrence of the term "Karaites."

Bibliography: Baron, Social², 5 (1957), 223–6; H. Wolfson, in: JQR, 51 (1960–61), 89–106; Guttmann, Philosophies, 58–59. [L.N.]

NAḤMAN BAR RAV HUNA (first half of the fifth century C.E.), Babylonian *amora*. According to the letter of Sherira Gaon (ed. by B. M. Lewin (1921), 94f.), during 452–55 Naḥman was head of the academy in Mata Meḥasya which had been revived by Ashi, succeeding Idi b. Avin, Ashi's successor. According to Halevy, the *amora* Naḥman mentioned in the Babylonian Talmud as a contemporary of Ravina and Ashi (Er. 27a; Ket. 7a; Kid. 6b; et al.) is the same person. Halevy suggests that he was the brother of the younger Ravina who completed the editing of the Babylonian Talmud, since, according to Sherira, the father of Ravina was also Huna, but this is refuted by S. and Ḥ. Albeck (see bibl.).

Bibliography: Hyman, Toledot, 940f.; Halevy, Dorot, 3 (1923), 91–93; S. Albeck, in: *Sinai—Sefer Yovel* (1958), 70f.; Ḥ. Albeck, *Mavo la-Talmudim* (1969), 434. [D.J.B.]

NAḤMAN BEN ISAAC (d. c. 356), Babylonian *amora*. Naḥman's father was not a scholar, and in consequence Naḥman showed greater honor to his friend Naḥman, son of the leading *amora* Ḥisda, than he would permit his namesake to show him (Ta'an. 21b). His mother was the sister of Aḥa b. Joseph (Shab. 140a). The Talmud relates that having been told by astrologers when she was pregnant that her son would be a thief, she watched over him from his childhood, taking care he should always go about with his head covered in order to make him conscious of the fear of Heaven. One day he was sitting and studying under a palm tree when temptation overcame him, and climbing up he bit off some of the dates. He then realized why his mother insisted on his keeping his head covered. This is one of the talmudic sources for keeping the head covered (*ibid.*; see *Head, Covering of the).

Naḥman studied under his uncle Aḥa, who because of his age leaned upon Naḥman's shoulder and was led by him (Shab. 140a). He is referred to as having waited upon a Mar Samuel (Beẓah 25b). According to R. N. Rabbinovicz however (*Dikdukei Soferim*, ad loc.), the reference is to Simeon b. Abba and the great *amora* Samuel of a previous generation. He was the head of the **kallah* in the academy of Rava where he was friendly with Adda b. Abba, with whom he attended Rava's discourses (BB 22a). He also taught in Drukeret (Shab. 94b), where he went at the invitation of Naḥman b. Ḥisda (Ta'an. 21b) and assisted him in his teaching (BB 8a), defending him several times against the criticism of Rava (Ket. 63b; Shevu. 12b; Ḥul. 88b). It is probable that he was active in Drukeret before his appointment with Rava. After Rava's death in 352 Naḥman joined the academy of Pumbedita which, since the death of

Abbaye in 338, had been combined with Rava's school in Mahoza, and held this post for the last four years of his life.

Nahman b. Isaac is frequently quoted in the Babylonian Talmud (the occurrence of his name in the Jerusalem Talmud—BK 9:1; BB 3:3; et al.—is a mistake for Nahman b. Jacob). Nahman continually stressed the need for assembling and arranging the material taught (Pes. 105a–b), and as a result paid careful attention to the correct name of the transmitters of teachings (Pes. 107a; Kid. 44a) and also made frequent use of mnemonic formulae (Shab. 60b; Ta'an. 10a; et al.). He devoted himself to biblical study and was well versed in the masorah (Shab. 28b, 55b; Yoma 75b; et al.), often using it to arrive at the correct text of the Mishnah (Shab. 77a; Bezah 35b; BK 60a). Among his colleagues were Mar son of Ravina (Shab. 61a, 108a), Papa, and Huna son of Joshua (BB 22a). He died in Pumbedita.

Bibliography: Halevy, Dorot, 2 (1923), 499–502; S. Albeck, *Mishpehot Soferim* (1903), 181ff.; Hyman, Toledot, 941–5; H. Albeck, *Mavo la-Talmudim* (1969), 371f.

[D.J.B.]

NAHMAN BEN JACOB (usually referred to without patronymic; d. c. 320 C.E.), Babylonian *amora* and a leading personality of his time. Born in Nehardea, where his father was a scribe of Samuel's *bet din* (BM 16b), Nahman sometimes quotes his father's teachings (Bezah 26a; Zev. 56a). Nahman may have studied under Samuel, since he transmits teachings in his name (Ber. 27b; Shab. 57b) and refers to him as *rabbenu* ("our master"; Ber. 38b, Er. 16b); but if so he must have then been very young, since Samuel died in 254. Nahman also transmits sayings in the names of Rav (Er. 72b; Pes. 13a), Adda b. Ahavah (BK 24a), Shila (Ber. 49b), and Isaac (Shab. 131b), with whom he was on close terms (Ta'an. 5a–6a). His main teacher, however, was Rabbah b. Avuha (Yev. 80b; Git. 72a) in whose name he frequently transmits statements (Ber. 36b; Shab. 17a). Rabbah b. Avuha wanted to give him his daughter in marriage (Yev. 80b), although it is not clear whether this occurred. It is known that Nahman ultimately married into the family of the exilarch (Hul. 124a) and in consequence was held in high esteem (Kid. 70a), and that his wife, *Yalta, had influence in the house of the exilarch (Rashi to Git. 67b). When Nehardea was destroyed in 259 by Odenathus, Nahman went to Shekanzib, but returned to Nehardea when it was rebuilt, teaching and serving as *dayyan* there (Er. 34b; Kid. 70a–b; BB 153a). There are many statements by him on both *halakhah* and *aggadah* in the Talmud, and his name is one of those most frequently mentioned in the Babylonian Talmud and also appears quite frequently in the Jerusalem Talmud. Huna held him equal to Samuel as a judge in civil law (BK 96b), and Nahman regarded himself as of sufficient standing to judge cases on his own (Sanh. 5a). In later generations it was laid down that in any dispute between Nahman and a colleague, the former's opinion was to prevail (Ket. 13a; Kid. 59b). He often visited Sura (Suk. 14b; Ket. 94a) and frequently transmitted teachings in the name of Huna, who taught there (Pes. 40a), and with whom Nahman frequently disputed (Er. 42a), referring to him as "our colleague Huna" (Git. 52b). An important contemporary was *Judah b. Ezekiel, the founder of the academy of Pumbedita; Nahman often differed with him (BK 27b) but held him in high esteem (BM 66a). On one occasion he summoned Judah to court. Judah was advised by Huna to overlook the discourtesy, and he appeared. It was only then that Nahman realized who the respondent was. Judah, however, plainly showed his irritation, whereupon Yalta advised her husband to settle the case quickly lest Judah make him appear an ignoramus (Kid. 70a–b). Other of his colleagues were Ammi (Ber. 47b) and Assi (Er. 32b), as well as Hiyya b. Abba (*ibid.*) and R. Isaac of Palestine. Once, when parting from Nahman, Isaac compared him to a rich shady fruit tree growing by the side of a stream, not lacking wealth, reputation, or honor, and said that he could only pray that each shoot taken from the parent tree should be the equal of the sire (Ta'an. 5b–6a). Among his pupils were Zera (RH 20b), Rabbah (Pes. 40a), Joseph (Yev. 66b) and Rava (Ber. 23b). Some of his aggadic sayings are: "When a woman is talking she is spinning" (a web to capture the male; Meg. 14b); "Haughtiness does not become a woman" (*ibid.*). There is definite mention of a number of his sons, Rabbah (Shab. 119a), Hon (Yev. 34b), Mar Zutra (BB 7a), and Hiyya (BB 46a). Nahman is said to have had two daughters who were taken captive. R. Elesh, taken captive with them, wanted to take them with him when he was about to escape, but did not do so, on discovering that they practiced witchcraft (Git. 45a). On his deathbed Nahman requested Rava, who was sitting by the bed, to pray to the angel of death to spare him a painful death. He later appeared to Rava in a dream and said that though his death was not painful, he would prefer not to face the fear of it again (MK 28a).

Bibliography: Hyman, Toledot, 928–39; Frankel, Mevo, 116b; Halevy, Dorot, 2 (1923), 417–21; Bacher, Bab. Amor., 79–83; H. Albeck, *Mavo la-Talmudim* (1969), 298–301; Neusner, Babylonia, 3 (1968), index.

[D.J.B.]

NAHMANIDES (Moses b. Nahman, also known as **Nahamani** and **RaMBaN**—an acronym of **R**abbi **M**oses **B**en **N**ahman; 1194–1270), Spanish rabbi and scholar and one of the leading authors of talmudic literature in the Middle Ages; philosopher, kabbalist, biblical exegete, poet, and physician. Nahmanides was born in Gerona, Catalonia, and it was after his native town that he was also referred to as Rabbenu Moses Gerondi or Yerondi. His Spanish name was Bonastrug da Porta. Nahmanides was a descendant of Isaac b. Reuben, a contemporary of Isaac b. Jacob *Alfasi. His mother was the sister of Abraham, father of Jonah b. Abraham Gerondi. His teachers included *Judah b. Yakar, a disciple of *Isaac b. Abraham of Dampierre, who established his yeshivah in Barcelona, and *Meir b. Isaac of Trinquetaille. From the first, he received the tradition of the tosafists of northern France, while from the second he learned the methods of study employed in the yeshivot of Provence. He maintained close contact with Meir b. Todros ha-Levi Abulafia of Toledo who replied to his queries, and even more so with his cousin, Jonah b. Abraham of Gerona. His colleagues also included Samuel b. Isaac *Sardi, to whom he sent the largest number of his responsa, as well as *Isaac b. Abraham of Narbonne. The responsa of Solomon b. Abraham *Adret (part 1, 120, 167) relate that Nahmanides earned his livelihood as a physician. Even though there is no information available on Nahmanides' yeshivah in Gerona, there is no doubt that it existed. His disciples included the leading halakhists of the following generation, such as Solomon b. Abraham Adret, *Aaron b. Joseph ha-Levi, David Bonafed, Jonah b. Joseph, Nahmanides' cousin, and many others. There is reason to believe that after the death of Jonah b. Abraham Gerondi in 1264, Nahmanides acted as chief rabbi of Catalonia until his emigration to Erez Israel. The Spanish rabbis of subsequent generations regarded him as their great teacher and referred to him as *ha-rav ha-ne'eman* ("the trustworthy rabbi"). In his *Nomologia*, Immanuel *Aboab states that throughout Spain it was the custom to refer to him simply as "the rabbi" or "the teacher."

When the *Maimonidean controversy broke out in *Montpellier in 1232, Nahmanides attempted to find a compromise between the opposing camps, although he

Page from an illuminated manuscript of Naḥmanides' commentary on the Pentateuch, showing the beginning of the chapter on Numbers. Florence, 1470–80. Manchester, John Rylands Library, Ms. 8., fol. 173r.

agreed with *Solomon b. Abraham of Montpellier and his followers in condemning the detrimental use which had been made of the works of Maimonides by the "philosophizers" to whom the study of secular sciences was a principal object. On the one hand, in the letters which he sent to the community leaders of Aragon, Navarre, and Castile, he sought to prevent them from taking measures against the extremists of Montpellier, while on the other hand, in his famous letter "Before I raise my voice, I err," he requested the rabbis of France that they annul the *ḥerem* which they had proclaimed against the writings of Maimonides. He argued that these were not intended for French Jewry, which was faithful to Jewish tradition, but for the Jews of the south (Provence and Spain), among whom philosophic culture had struck roots, with the objective of bringing them back to the path of the faithful. In order to avert a schism between the opposed communities and camps, he proposed a detailed program which would suit the varying conditions prevailing in France and Spain and would regulate the study of the various sciences according to the age of the students and the locality. Naḥmanides' program failed because the extremists in both camps gained the upper hand and he was isolated.

He exercised extensive influence over Jewish public life in Catalonia; even King James I (1213–1276) consulted him and in 1232, on the strength of Naḥmanides' opinion, rejected the claims of the *Alconstantini family to the position of *dayyan* over all the Jews of the kingdom. In 1263 King James coerced him into a public disputuation in Barcelona with the apostate Pablo *Christiani. The disputation, which was held in July in the presence of the king and the leaders of the *Dominicans and the *Franciscans, was a victory for Naḥmanides, the king even presenting him with 300 dinars in appreciation of the manner in which he had stated his arguments. (For further details see *Barcelona, Disputation of.) At the request of the bishop of Gerona, Naḥmanides summarized his views in a book, apparently the *Sefer ha-Vikku'aḥ*, which is still extant. The Dominicans, who had initiated the disputation, did not remain inactive, and in April 1265 they called Naḥmanides to trial for his supposed abuses against Christianity. Before the tribunal Naḥmanides stated that his words had been spoken during the disputation after the king had promised him freedom of speech, and that he had written his work at the request of the bishop. The king thereupon succeeded in extricating Naḥmanides from the complications of the trial, which was postponed for an indefinite period. Dissatisfied, the Dominicans sought the aid of Pope *Clement IV, who sent a letter to the king of Aragon requesting him to penalize Naḥmanides for writing the above work. Naḥmanides barely succeeded in escaping from Spain and during the same year emigrated to Ereẓ Israel.

A prayer in the spirit of the Psalms, which Naḥmanides composed at sea while on his way to Ereẓ Israel, has been preserved. He arrived in *Acre during the summer of 1267 and on Elul 9 of that year he went to Jerusalem. In a letter to his son Naḥman, he described the ruined state of the city seven years after the invasion of the Tatar hordes. He found few Jews, "only two brothers, dyers who bought their dye from the governor and were joined by up to ten Jews in their home on Sabbaths for prayers." On his arrival in the town he organized the remnants of the Jewish community and erected a synagogue in a derelict house; it appears that he also founded a yeshivah. Reports of his activities circulated rapidly; many Jews streamed into Jerusalem. In 1268 Naḥmanides moved to Acre, where he became the spiritual leader of the Jewish community, in succession to *Jehiel b. Joseph of Paris. From this period a sermon which he delivered in the synagogue on Rosh Ha-Shanah in 1269 has been preserved. The site of his tomb has not been ascertained; some believe that he was buried at the foot of Mount Carmel; others that he was buried in Haifa, beside the tomb of Jehiel b. Joseph of Paris; while others say that he was interred in Acre. There is also a tradition that he was buried in Jerusalem, under the slope of the montain near the village of Silwan, and another that his tomb is in Hebron.

Naḥmanides had three sons: Naḥman, to whom he sent the above-mentioned letter from Jerusalem; Solomon, who married the daughter of Jonah b. Abraham Gerondi; and Joseph, who was a favorite at the court of the king of Castile and owned an estate in *Valladolid. One of Naḥmanides' daughters married *Gershom b. Solomon, and their son was *Levi b. Gershom.

Works. About 50 of Naḥmanides' works have been preserved, in addition to many works which are doubtfully attributed to him. The majority of his works are novellae on the Talmud and *halakhah*. He also wrote books and letters connected with his public activities, including the *Sefer ha-Vikku'aḥ* already mentioned. He devoted a special work to the nature of the belief in Redemption, the *Sefer ha-Ge'ullah*, written in about 1263. He was also a gifted *paytan*, writing a number of poems and prayers, including a prayer which he composed on his entry into Jerusalem. Four of his sermons have been preserved: *Ha-Derashah la-Ḥatunnah*, dating from his youth; *Torat ha-Shem Temimah*, which he apparently delivered after the disputation of Barcelona; one on the Book of Ecclesiastes, which he delivered before his departure for Ereẓ Israel; and the sermon mentioned above, delivered in Acre on Rosh Ha-Shanah. All his works bear the imprint of his original personality, a synthesis of the culture of Spain and the piety of Germany, a talmudic education together with the teachings of Kabbalah, as well as a broad knowledge of sciences and Christian theological works. An edition of his works has been published by Ch. D. Chavel (see bibliography). [J.KA.]

As Biblical Commentator. Naḥmanides wrote his commentary on the Torah in his old age. He composed the main part in Spain, but added to it after his arrival in Ereẓ Israel. In the introduction he states the purpose of his commentary: "To appease the minds of the students, weary through exile and trouble, when they read the portion on Sabbaths and festivals." It is an extensive commentary, both on the narrative and legislative part of the Bible. Unlike his most noted predecessors, *Rashi and Abraham *ibn Ezra, who devoted themselves chiefly to the elucidation of individual words and verses, Naḥmanides, though he followed strict philological procedure when he deemed it necessary to establish the exact meaning of a work, concerns himself mainly with the sequence of the biblical passages and with the deeper meaning of the Bible's laws and narrative. He makes frequent use of the aggadic and halakhic interpretations of the talmudic and midrashic sages, but whereas Rashi quotes these without expressing his own opinions, Naḥmanides dwells on them at length, analyzes them critically, develops their ideas, and probes their compatibility with the biblical text.

The commentary of Naḥmanides is more than a mere commentary. It reflects his views on God, the Torah, Israel, and the world. The Torah is the word of God and is the source of all knowledge. The narratives of the Bible are not simple records of the past, but are portents of the future. The account of the six days of creation contains prophecies regarding the most important events of the succeeding 6,000 years, while the Sabbath foreshadows the seventh millennium which will be the Day of the Lord, and the accounts told about the patriarchs foreshadow the history of the Jewish people as a whole. Naḥmanides does not hesitate to criticize the patriarchs when their actions seem to him injustifiable. According to him (Gen. 12:11), Abraham "unintentionally committed a great sin," when, on coming to Egypt, he said out of fear for his life that his wife Sarah was his sister, for in this way he exposed her to moral corruption; rather, he should have had faith that God would save both him and his wife. Naḥmanides demonstrates great psychological insight when describing the behavior of biblical personalities. In the story of Joseph the Bible relates that "he fell on his neck and wept on his neck for a while" (Gen. 46:29). The question arises: Who wept? Jacob or Joseph? It is obvious who is more likely to weep at such a time, Naḥmanides says, the old father who finds his son alive after he had mourned for him as lost, not the son who has risen to become a king. Naḥmanides explains the laws in the light of halakhic tradition. He maintains that there is a reason for every commandment. The commandments are all for the good of man, either to keep from him something that is hurtful, to remove from him evil beliefs and habits, to teach him mercy and goodness, or to make him remember the miracles of the Lord and to know him. He explains some of the dietary laws in terms of health regulations; others he interprets as seeking to keep us from eating foods that dull the mind and harden the heart.

Naḥmanides very often quotes Rashi and Abraham ibn Ezra. Despite his great reverence for Rashi, he polemicizes with him. At times he praises Ibn Ezra, but attacks him sharply for those of his views which run counter to tradition. He holds Maimonides in high esteem, but rejects some of the reasons given in the *Guide of the Perplexed* for the commandments. He regards (Gen. 18:1) Maimonides' view that the visit of the angels to Abraham was a mere vision to contradict the Bible. Naḥmanides was the first commentator to introduce Kabbalah into his commentary.

The commentary, written in a lucid style, contains many a word of encouragement and solace to the Jewish people. At the end of the Song of *Ha'azinu* (Deut. 32), Naḥmanides writes: "And behold there is nothing conditional in this song. It is a charter testifying that we shall have to suffer heavily for our sins, but that, nevertheless, God will not destroy us, being reconciled to us (though we shall have no merits) and forgiving our sins for his name's sake alone. . . . And so our rabbis said: 'Great is the song, embracing as it does the present, the past (of Israel) and the future, this world and the world to come. . . .' And if this song were the composition of a mere astrologer we should be constrained to believe in it, considering that all its words were fulfilled. How much more have we to hope with all our hearts and to trust to the word of God, through the mouth of his prophet Moses, the faithful in all his house, like unto whom there was none, whether before him or after him." Naḥmanides' commentary became very popular and has been widely drawn upon by later commentators. Supercommentaries have been written upon it and kabbalistic treatises have been composed on its kabbalistic allusions (see below). Baḥya b. Asher and Jacob b. Asher incorporated large parts of it into their commentaries. The commentary was printed for the first time in Rome prior to 1480. A scholarly edition based on manuscripts and early printings, prepared by Ch. D. Chavel, was published in Jerusalem in 1959–60.

The commentary on Job, too, was probably written by Naḥmanides in his old age. Naḥmanides regards Job as a historical figure. He intimates that the answer to the problem of the suffering of the righteous and the prosperity of the wicked—the central theme of the book—is to be found in the belief in the transmigration of souls. The righteous are punished and the wicked rewarded for their deeds in an earlier life. Comments on other books of the Bible are found dispersed throughout Naḥmanides' writings. His *Book of Redemption (Sefer ha-Ge'ullah)* contains comments on various passages of the Book of Daniel. He also wrote a commentary on Isaiah 52:13–53:12. [T.P.]

As Halakhist. Naḥmanides' halakhic works rank among the masterpieces of rabbinic literature, and some of them have become classics. They may be divided into four categories: novellae on the Talmud, halakhic monographs, **hassagot* ("criticisms"), and responsa.

Naḥmanides' novellae, which originally covered the entire orders of *Mo'ed, Nashim,* and *Nezikin*—from early times the parts of the Talmud customarily studied in Spain—and which are for the most part extant, mark the summit of the halakhic and religious literary creativity of Spanish Jewry. They also opened a new chapter in the cultural history of that cultural community. In his novellae Naḥmanides based himself on the best of the earlier Spanish tradition and constantly availed himself of the writings of *Samuel ha-Nagid, most of which are no longer extant, of *Hananel b. Ḥushi'el, Isaac *Alfasi, *Isaac ibn Ghayyat, *Judah al-Bargeloni, Joseph *ibn Migash, and their contemporaries. Nevertheless, he mainly adopted the mode of learning characteristic of the French *tosafists, whose teachings were previously little known in Spain and whose method was not followed there. In this way Naḥmanides created a new synthesis in the method of study in Spain which was henceforward concerned with a comprehension of the talmudic argumentation for its own sake after the manner of the French scholars and not merely with elucidating *halakhah* for practical purposes, as had until then been customary among the Spanish scholars. Accordingly Naḥmanides emphasizes in his work the theoretical meaning and academic significance of the pronouncements and decisions of the leading earlier Spanish codifiers. Thus he inaugurated a new school in the method of studying the Oral Law which laid the stress on an apprehension, for its own sake, of the talmudic *sugyah* ("theme") as a whole, in point both of its inner tenor and of its relation to other relevant *sugyot* dispersed throughout the Talmud, without, however, becoming entangled in lengthy, sterile discussion. Yet there was no complete dissociation from the practical halakhic aspect. While these two trends are to be found side by side also in the *tosafot*, Naḥmanides was undoubtedly the first fully to achieve this synthesis, which pervades his novellae.

A further local "Spanish" factor which he synthesized with the French system was his constant search for ancient, critically examined, and established texts of the Talmud so as not to become involved in needless discussions to solve questions arising from corrupt readings. The tosafists, too, were aware of this problem, but not having access to enough ancient texts, they were compelled to take such versions from secondary sources, such as Hananel's glosses or the works of the *geonim*, available to them largely at second or third hand, or they made conjectural emendations of the talmudic text which led to a grave and protracted controversy among the tosafists. In this respect, Naḥmanides enjoyed an obvious advantage. Living in Spain, he had at his disposal the best talmudic texts that had been sent to that country direct from the academies of the Babylonian *geonim* 200–300 years earlier. Another factor, chiefly Spanish and conspicuous in Naḥmanides, is his extensive use of the geonic writings and the Jerusalem Talmud. This system of Naḥmanides completely superseded the earlier Spanish tradition. The greatest of his pupils, as also their pupils, having continued, developed, and improved this system, established it as the method for future generations among ever broadening circles of students of the Oral Law.

In addition to the teachings of the French scholars, of whom he speaks with profound esteem, Naḥmanides' works also contain the teachings of Provence, which he incorporated into his system of study as an inseparable part of it. The teachings of *Abraham b. Isaac of Narbonne, *Abraham b. David of Posquières, *Isaac b. Abba Mari, and many others, form an integral part of his works, the last mentioned to a large extent anonymously. Although not very apparent from a superficial reading, his associations with the teachings of Provence are even closer than with those of Spain. Besides the earlier Provençal scholars, he mentions many others from Provence, contemporaries of his, whose statements he discusses. This threefold Spanish, French, and Provençal trend is undoubtedly connected with two of his principal teachers, *Judah b. Yakar and *Nathan b. Meir of Trinquetaille, both of whom were pupils of *Isaac b. Abraham of Dampierre, the well-known tosafist. Naḥmanides' contemporary and relation, Jonah Gerondi, who likewise studied under the tosafists, also based his teachings on a similar method of study.

Naḥmanides' novellae are notable for their wealth of sources and mode of presentation, their clear, lucid style and logical structure. In his desire to arrive at the authentic literal meaning he did not hesitate to disagree even with the *geonim* and the most illustrious of the earlier authorities, such as *Hai Gaon, Isaac Alfasi, and others. He was among the first of those who in their writings developed the theoretical method, at once logical and profound, that aimed at comprehending the pivotal argument on which the *sugyah* as a whole depends. Often his novellae range far beyond the limits of the *sugyah* under discussion to a fundamental investigation of various subjects central to the *halakhah*. He also devotes much space to methodological discussions, to be found dispersed in his glosses, on the principles of the Talmud. The novellae on the Talmud were not published simultaneously, the first to appear having been those on *Bava Batra* (Venice, 1523) and the last those on *Bava Meẓia* (Jerusalem, 1929) and, in a complete edition, on *Ḥullin* (New York, ed. by S. Z. Reichmann, 1955). Most of his novellae—those on *Berakhot*, on *Mo'ed*, *Nashim*, *Nezikin*, and on *Ḥullin* and *Niddah*—were published between 1740 and 1840. His novellae to *ketubbot* go to this day under the name of Solomon b. Adret. Nearly all these were known throughout the intervening years from many manuscripts, and leading scholars, particularly among the Sephardim, quoted them in their works. His novellae were published in their entirety for the first time in 1928 in Jerusalem in two volumes. Some of his novellae on a few tractates are extant in the form of short extracts on several pages of a tractate only. He presumably composed them in this manner and was unable to complete the entire work.

Until the expulsion from Spain, Moses' novellae occupied, alongside Rashi's commentary, the place that the *tosafot* do among students of the Talmud. To such an extent were his words minutely examined and debated that methodological rules were laid down for them. In this respect, *Isaac Campanton was especially notable, declaring that Naḥmanides' statements are to be so closely studied that not a single word should appear superfluous. He even established many minute rules for extracting Naḥmanides' underlying meaning from every single passage. From the time his novellae first appeared in print their influence has become increasingly pronounced also among Ashkenazi students and yeshivot. To this day their study occupies in yeshivot of Polish-Lithuanian origin a principal place together with Rashi, the *tosafot*, and Maimonides.

The second class of Naḥmanides' halakhic literary works comprises his halakhic monographs, of which there are seven:

(1) *Dinei de-Garme* deals with a clarification of the laws regarding inconvenience to a neighbor, injury to his property, and their relation to the law of torts. Since the subject is treated in the second chapter of *Bava Batra*, this short excellent monograph was appended to his novellae on that tractate from its first appearance in print. In it Naḥmanides summarizes the principal views of the earlier authorities on the various aspects of the laws of the *assailant and his victim in general, including damage to a neighbor. In presenting the various opinions Naḥmanides treats of each with great profundity. On this subject he was, he says, forestalled by monographs of French scholars, whose names, however, he does not mention. In recent years there was published (in *Hadorom*, 23 (1966), 31–53), from a manuscript *Gerama ve-Garme* by one of the tosafists, apparently *Ephraim b. Isaac of Regensburg, and Naḥmanides may be referring to this or to a similar work. This small work of Naḥmanides was highly praised by scholars, several of whom wrote commentaries on it. A comparison between his work and that of the scholar previously mentioned clearly reveals Naḥmanides' superiority as a writer of glosses and systematizer. (2) *Mishpetei ha-Ḥerem* deals with the ways in which a ban is imposed and release obtained from it. It also treats at length of **Kol Nidrei*, said on the eve of the Day of Atonement. Although casting some doubt on its value, he nevertheless states that those accustomed to say it should not be prevented from doing so, since they rely on a custom instituted by the earlier authorities. (3–5) *Hilkhot Bekhorot* and *Hilkhot Ḥallah* written by Naḥmanides as a supplement to *Hilkhot ha-Rif* of Alfasi, from which these laws were omitted. Here Naḥmanides adopts, with great fidelity, the Aramaic used by Alfasi, as well as his particular style and mode of writing. Naḥmanides also wrote *Hilkhot Nedarim* to fill a gap in Alfasi (those printed on tractate *Nedarim* are not Alfasi's). In this work Naḥmanides included, to a much larger extent than is to be found in the writings of Alfasi, novellae and argumen-

tations in the style characteristic of his glosses on the Talmud. (6) *Torat ha-Adam* is a comprehensive and unique monograph on all the laws concerning death, starting with what is prohibited and permitted and what is a *mitzvah* as regards the sick and dying, and concluding with the laws of mourning. In point of fact this work is also in the nature of a "supplement" to *Hilkhot ha-Rif*, but in it Naḥmanides, expatiating on the subject, included many scores of talmudic and tannaitic sources as also of Sephardi and Ashkenazi views, which he compared and discussed at length in the light of the sources. Very great importance was attached to the work by the leading codifiers. *Jacob b. Asher incorporated it, in its actual order and form and with corresponding sections, in his *Tur*, as did Joseph *Caro later in his Shulḥan Arukh. Commentators on the Talmud set great store by it when dealing with the interpretation of the relevant *sugyot* in the Talmud. Of special interest on its own account is *Sha'ar ha-Gemul*, the 30th chapter of the work which, published separately some 30 years before the whole (Naples, 1490), deals with reward and punishment after death. (7) *Hilkhot Niddah* was printed in *Todat Shelamim* (Venice, 1741) of Isaiah Bassani (see *Bassano family).

The third category of Naḥmanides' halakhic writings, and the first to appear in print, comprises his works of criticism, of which there are three: (a) *hassagot* ("criticisms") of *Maimonides' *Sefer ha-Mitzvot* (Constantinople, 1510); (b) *Milḥamot Adonai* (in *Rif*, Venice, 1552) attacking *Zerahiah ha-Levi of Lunel's criticisms of *Hilkhot ha-Rif* as well as criticizing Zerahiah's *Sefer ha-Ẓava*; and (c) *Sefer ha-Zekhut*, (in *Shivah Einayim*, Leghorn, 1745) attacking Abraham b. David's criticisms of Alfasi. These three share a common feature, namely Naḥmanides' desire to vindicate the earlier authorities against the criticism of later scholars, and hence their contents do not everywhere reflect Naḥmanides' own view; thus, Maimonides having written his *Sefer ha-Mitzvot* mainly against the enumeration of the 613 commandments by the author of the *Halakhot Gedolot*, Naḥmanides took upon himself the task of defending the earlier authority against this criticism. The most important of them is *Milḥamot Adonai* which also has great intrinsic value for the comprehension of a *sugyah*, Naḥmanides devoting himself with his signal profundity and unique talents to an accurate reconstruction of the earlier views that appear to conflict with the *sugyah*. The style of the work is terse, vigorous, and not always easy to understand, calling for much concentration by the reader. In general Naḥmanides, in keeping with the basic purpose of the work, limited himself to the criticisms directed against Alfasi, but in its earlier parts the author went beyond these self-imposed limits to include in them arguments against Zerahiah ha-Levi even where the subject matter did not touch directly on Alfasi.

Naḥmanides' halakhic writings had a decisive influence on the entire history of subsequent rabbinic literature. Solomon b. Abraham Adret's glosses on the Talmud are founded on those of Naḥmanides, and Adret literally copied extracts from his work. Based principally on Naḥmanides' writings are **Sefer Ha-Ḥinnukh* (which is also based on Maimonides) and *Samuel b. Meshullam Gerondi's *Ohel Mo'ed*. A complete series of works on *Hilkhot ha-Rif* by an anonymous author, mistakenly identified as *Nissim Gerondi, are by a "pupil of Naḥmanides" and based on his teachings. *Menahem b. Solomon ha-Me'iri devoted an entire work, *Magen Avot*, to a controversy with Naḥmanides' pupils who had brought with them to Provence their teacher's customs, which were diametrically opposed to those of Provence. The very great authority enjoyed by Naḥmanides is apparent from the fact that ha-Me'iri found himself compelled to defend the views of the leading earlier authorities of Provence against those of Naḥmanides. Of his responsa only a small number are extant; a large number of them being written in reply to the questions of *Samuel b. Isaac ha-Sardi, who incorporated them in their entirety in his *Sefer ha-Terumot*. A few other responsa by him appeared in *She'elot u-Teshuvot ha-Ramban*, the vast majority of which, despite the title of the work, are by Solomon b. Abraham Adret.

It is difficult to fix the chronological order of Naḥmanides' halakhic works. It is known that he composed *Hilkhot Nedarim* in his youth, and it is clear that he wrote *Milḥamot Adonai* before most of his novellae on the Talmud. Since he composed his novellae over many years, it is impossible to determine their order. [I.T.-S.]

In Kabbalah. There is evidence that in an earlier version of his Commentary on the Pentateuch (Rome, 1480) Naḥmanides intended to discuss kabbalistic matters more explicitly, but he fell ill and was informed in a dream that he should desist. An extant fragment from an earlier version seems to indicate such a tendency. However, immediate doubts about the authenticity of the fragment were raised by Naḥmanides' students. Hints of kabbalistic references sprinkle his prolific writings, especially his commentary on the Pentateuch (Naples, 1490), commentary on the Book of Job, and the sermons. Kabbalistic concepts are woven into the eschatological discussion in the last section of his halakhic work, *Torat ha-Adam;* this section has often been printed as a separate work entitled *Sha'ar ha-Gemul*. Kabbalistic elements are readily recognizable in his liturgical poems, e.g., in *Shir ha-Neshamah*, and in the prayer on the death of R. Abraham Ḥazzan, one of the kabbalists of Gerona. Naḥmanides' single work dealing exclusively with the Kabbalah is his commentary on the first chapter of *Sefer Yeẓirah*.

Despite the paucity of his kabbalistic writings, he came to be known in his later years as an expert on the subject. Kabbalists in the late 13th and early 14th centuries made considerable literary attempts to try and solve the secrets of Naḥmanides' commentary on the Pentateuch. The most important commentaries in this vein are *Keter Shem Tov* by R. Shem Tov *ibn Gaon and *Me'irat Einayim* by R. *Isaac b. Samuel of Acre. Even as late as the beginning of the 14th century, Naḥmanides' kabbalistic writings were studied and relied upon to a far greater degree than the *Zohar itself; a definite preference for the Zohar became apparent only in about 1325.

In the course of time Naḥmanides came to be regarded as such an authority that other authors' works were wrongly attributed to him, e.g., *Ha-Emunah ve-ha-Bittaḥon* (Korets, 1485), which has been proven to be the work of R. Jacob b. Sheshet *Gerondi. G. Scholem has made intensive surveys of Naḥmanides' method in Kabbalah in his *Ursprung und Anfaenge der Kabbala* (1962) and in his series of lectures, *Ha-Kabbalah be-Geronah*, ed. by I. Ben Shlomo (1964). [E.G.]

Bibliography: General: A. Yeruham, *Ohel Raḥel* (1942); Y. Unna, *R. Moses ben Naḥman* (Heb., 1954); Hurwitz, in: *Hadorom*, 24 (1967), 39–48; I. Ta-Shma, in: KS, 43 (1968), 569–74; H. Chone, *Nachmanides* (Ger., 1930); F. Rosenthal, in: J. Guttmann (ed.), *Moses Maimonides* (vol. 1, 1908). In the Kabbalah: G. Scholem, in: KS, 6 (1930), 385–419; 21 (1044/45), 179–86; idem, *Ursprung und Anfaenge der Kabbala* (1962); idem, *Ha-Kabbalah be-Geronah*, ed. by I. Ben Shlomo (1964); Ch. D. Chavel, *Kitvei ha-Ramban* (1963); E. Gottlieb, in: J. ben Sheshet, *Meshiv Devarim Nekhoḥim*, ed. by. G. Vajda (1968), 18–20; idem, in: KS, 40 (1964/65), 1–9; idem, in: *Tarbiz*, 39 (1970), 87–89.

NAḤMAN (ben Simḥah) OF BRATSLAV (1772–1811), ḥasidic **ẓaddik* in Podolia and the Ukraine, and the center of a theological and social storm throughout most of his life. On his mother's side he was the great-grandson of *Israel b. Eliezer Ba'al Shem Tov and on his father's the grandson of *Naḥman of Horodenka (Gorodenka), a pre-ḥasidic leader prominent in the circle of the Ba'al Shem. His mother, Feige, was known as one who "possessed the holy spirit"; his father was apparently not outstanding for his scholarship. Naḥman was born in Medzibezh and was brought up in the ḥasidic atmosphere of his parents' home. He married at an early age and lived in the home of his father-in-law, a lessee of villages. After the latter's second marriage Naḥman settled in Medvedevka in the province of Kiev. Ḥasidim then gathered around him and he began to act as a *ẓaddik*.

In 1798 Naḥman went to Ereẓ Israel accompanied by his disciple and friend, Simeon. He visited Haifa, Jaffa,

Tiberias, and Safed among other places, and met *Jacob Samson of Shepetovka and *Abraham b. Alexander Katz of Kalisk who was then engaged in a controversy with *Shneur Zalman of Lyady. The two paid their respects to the great-grandson of the Ba'al Shem Tov. Since Napoleon then invaded the land, Naḥman was compelled to leave hurriedly after a stay of a few months.

In Medvedevka Naḥman joined in a local conflict, and there began to develop his theory that controversy over him was inevitable—a view which he maintained throughout his life. In the summer of 1800 he settled in Zlatopol (near Shpola), in the province of Kiev. Immediately after his arrival a dispute began between Naḥman and *Aryeh Leib, "the Grand Old Man of Shpola," the aged, popular ḥasidic leader who was highly influential in Podolia and the Ukraine. Among other accusations, Aryeh Leib averred that Naḥman's teachings seemed to contain Shabbatean and Frankist views and apparently he even took exception to Naḥman's moral conduct. The dispute becoming increasingly acrimonious, in 1802 Naḥman left Zlatopol for Bratslav. Even there (where he remained until 1810) his personality was a source of controversy among the Ḥasidim. All the *zaddikim* in the vicinity came into conflict with him, with the exception of his faithful friend *Levi Isaac of Berdichev, although even he did not come to Naḥman's defense in public. The friendly relations between Naḥman and Levi Isaac continued until the latter died one year before Naḥman's death.

Naḥman's various journeys are described in his biography, *Ḥayyei Moharan* (1875), and in *Yemei Moharan*, both by his disciple Nathan Sternhartz. In part of the latter work (vol. 2 (1904) published as *Seder ha-Nesi'ot shello le-Ereẓ Yisrael*), a mystical aim for Naḥman's trip to Ereẓ Israel is postulated, though its exact nature remains obscure. It is also stressed there that Naḥman traveled incognito. Another important journey was to Lemberg (Lvov) in 1808 which also had mystical objectives, although there is no doubt that he also intended to seek advice about his illness, then discovered to be tuberculosis. In 1810 he left Bratslav and settled in Uman with the evident intention of dying and being buried there. He died on the 18th of Tishri (on Sukkot), 1811, and was buried in Uman, where his tombstone was until recently the object of pilgrimages by the Bratslav Ḥasidim.

Naḥman as a Spiritual Figure. The extent of Shabbatean and Frankist influence on Naḥman's teachings is still not clearly known, although it undoubtedly exists in certain of his principles. However, this should not lead to the conclusion that Naḥman was a Shabbatean or a Frankist. The decisive factor in the complicated psychological problem of Naḥman is the certainty of faith. While his basic theological position was traditionally Jewish, his interest in Shabbateanism and Frankism stemmed from random thoughts or attempts at *tikkun* (restoration), which he considered to be important, more especially in view of his singular vision of himself. Apparently even during his stay in Zlatopol he had formulated a theory on the messianic status of his soul (which he held to include both Messiah the son of David and Messiah the son of Joseph), and also claimed that the Messiah was destined to be one of his descendants. His extremely radical doctrine on the *zaddik* (which always refers to himself) encompassed his role as the Messiah. Both the image of the suffering Messiah and the image of the Messiah who aids needy sinful souls through paradoxical *tikkunim* determine the structure of the messianic personality. Faith occupies a central position in the structure of values of the Bratslav ḥasidic system. The Bratslav concept of faith is paradoxical. The obligation of faith is part of the traditional Jewish religion, but first and foremost it is essential to believe in the paradoxical *zaddik*, i.e., Naḥman himself. Although questions might arise about him, his Ḥasid must believe in him wholly. These doctrines were elucidated in his teachings during his stay in Bratslav.

As in other ḥasidic trends, one of the most important institutions of Bratslav Ḥasidism was the pilgrimage to the *zaddik*. Naḥman, however, did not receive Ḥasidim on every Sabbath and festival as was customary at the courts of other *zaddikim*, but at three designated times: Rosh Ha-Shanah, the Sabbath of Ḥanukkah, and Shavuot. On Rosh Ha-Shanah in particular all Bratslav Ḥasidim were obliged to visit their *zaddik* and to pray in his company. The gathering on Rosh Ha-Shanah was renewed after Naḥman's death by Nathan in Uman and has been continued to this day; at present the Bratslav Ḥasidim meet at their center in Jerusalem.

The custom of *confession before the *zaddik*, which had previously been observed at various places under *Ḥayyim Haykel of Amdur, Shneur Zalman of Lyady, and others, became a major institution among the Bratslav Ḥasidim, possessing a twofold purpose. (1) Confession served as an initiation rite. When the Ḥasid came within the orbit of the *zaddik*, as a sign that he was becoming a Ḥasid of his master, he would enumerate his sins in the form of a confession, symbolically giving them to the *zaddik*, who prescribed suitable ways to repentance. (2) Confession was maintained as a permanent institution: the Ḥasid would confess before the *zaddik* from time to time, mainly on the eve of Rosh Ha-Shanah. The centrality of this institution gave the Bratslav Ḥasidim the name "those who confess" (Heb./Yid. *vidduiniks*). However, near the time of his death, Naḥman decided to stop hearing the confessions of his Ḥasidim.

His most important contemporary disciples were Simeon, Yudel, and Samuel Isaac. Bratslav Ḥasidism is unique, in that it embodies a kind of religious awakening which was not generally found in the Ḥasidism of that time.

Works. Almost all of the extant Bratslav literature was committed to writing by Nathan b. Naphtali Hertz Sternhartz, Naḥman's disciple, who joined his small group of Ḥasidim early in 1803. Nathan served as his scribe and literary secretary, despite the fact that he apparently was not a member of Naḥman's most intimate circle. Only after his master's death did he assume a central position in Bratslav Ḥasidism. The first volume of Naḥman's theological teachings, *Likkutei Moharan* (Ostroy, 1806), was published during his lifetime without rabbinical approbation (*haskamah*). The second volume, entitled *Likkutei Moharan Tinyana* (Mogilev, 1811), appeared posthumously. The tales which he began to relate in his last years (from 1806) are collected in *Sippurei Ma'asiyyot* (Berdichev, 1815), and constitute a special section of his work. These 13 stories were published in bilingual editions—the original Yiddish, with Nathan's Hebrew translation. S. A. Horodezky published the Hebrew version alone (Berlin, 1922). Like his teachings, the tales focus on his major concept—i.e., his own essence and his messianic soul—and there is no doubt that they should be read as allegories relating to various aspects—mainly messianic—of his soul and life. The manuscript of his most esoteric work, which is referred to in Bratslav literature by its fate, *Sefer ha-Nisraf* ("The Burned Book"), was destroyed by Naḥman's orders in 1808. Except for a few hints, its contents are unknown. Another esoteric book has apparently survived in manuscript among the Bratslav Ḥasidim and is called *Sefer ha-Ganuz* ("The Hidden Book"), for which "the Messiah will give the interpretation." Similarly, *Megillat ha-Setarim* discusses the order of the advent of the Redeemer, in which Naḥman evidently plays a major role in his two aspects, as Messiah the son of Joseph and Messiah the son of David.

Prayer was highly developed among Bratslav Ḥasidim, not only in its institutionalized form but also as spontaneous "conversations between man and his creator." Nathan Sternhartz edited a lengthy work entitled *Likkutei Tefillot* (Bratslav 1821–27) in which he transforms the teachings of his master into prayers. Bratslav Ḥasidism had little success during Naḥman's lifetime; few people joined the movement, and many left. At the time of Naḥman's death there were perhaps several hundred Ḥasidim in Podolia and the Ukraine; most were poor and some were petty tradesmen.

Bratslav Ḥasidism after Naḥman. Though the Bratslav Ḥasidim did not choose a successor to Naḥman, the reorganization of the sect after his death was the work of his disciple Nathan (1780–1845), who was outstanding not only for his literary ability but also for his extraordinary organizational talents. He gradually neglected his work as a businessman and devoted himself to the leadership of the sect, which then began to grow. Under Nathan's leadership a second dispute occurred in Bratslav Ḥasidism, initiated by the *zaddik* Moses Ẓevi of *Savran. This time, however, the ideological arguments were not clear and possibly were not the same as in the first dispute. Nathan's administration is reflected in a rich correspondence, chiefly with his son (published as *Alim li-Terufah*, 1896). After Nathan's death the leadership of the sect passed to his disciple and aide, Naḥman of Tulchin. The sect achieved notable success in the late 19th century. Between the two world wars Bratslav Ḥasidim succeeded in breaking out of their isolation from the other branches of Ḥasidism and attained considerable social recognition, especially in Poland. Bratslav Ḥasidism continued to exist in Podolia in the early years of the Soviet regime. However, it is unlikely that any sizable community existed by the 1970s.

In Ereẓ Israel most of the Bratslav Ḥasidim were concentrated in Jerusalem, especially in the Old City, and under their spiritual guide Abraham Ḥazan, they maintained extensive literary activity. After the Jordanian occupation of the Old City (1948) they moved to other parts of Jerusalem. There is also a center of Bratslav Ḥasidim in Bene-Berak which is at odds with the Jerusalem group. Bratslav Ḥasidim have been active in developing a publishing house for their literature.

[J.G.W.]

Teachings. Though Naḥman defined his teaching as based on tradition, it contains many innovations, in spite of his claim that he was the last link in the chain running from *Simeon b. Yoḥai, Isaac *Luria, and Israel b. Eliezer Ba'al Shem Tov to himself. His major ideas covered various fields. According to Naḥman, **Ein Sof* ("Infinite"), seeking to reveal Its mercy, created the world, which It rules according to Its absolute will. Divinity is inherent in everything, even in the realm of evil (*kelippot*). Thus even if a man is steeped in evil, he can easily find the Creator and repent. What can be broken can be repaired. The Lurianic doctrine of *zimzum* ("withdrawal"; see *Kabbalah) creates a paradox. On the one hand, it postulates the withdrawal and disappearance of Divinity to create a "vacuum"; on the other hand it assumes divine immanence. Naḥman holds that *zimzum* will be achieved only in the future, but he is less concerned with *zimzum* than with the space devoid of Divinity created as a result. This engenders doubts as to the existence of the Creator, and in this lies the major importance of the doctrine of *zimzum*. The formation of the "question" (*kushya*) is an important element in his doctrine and depends on the first act of the Creator in his relation to man. Thus the question has an ontological significance although its origin lies on a purely theological plane. Hence even though man may fall deep into the web of doubt, his rise is the ultimate purpose of his fall.

In addition to the question which relates to *zimzum*, there is another kind of question in connection with the "breaking of the vessels." Following the dualist motif in Lurianic Kabbalah, Naḥman asserts that the *kelippot* came into being as a result of the "breaking of the vessels" and designates a separate sphere for their destructive activity. They are also the source of secular studies, and thence of heretical questions. However, because the holy sparks (*nizozot*) fell in that sphere, it is possible and obligatory "to find salvation and leave that place" and thereby to answer heresy. The greatest questions come out of the vacuum and therefore through silence. This answer is the "holy silence" of the believer. Rational thought cannot resolve the problem of faith. Faith rises above all doubts, and in as much as it is more paradoxical and more complicated, its immanent essence is expressed to a greater degree. Rational certainty is not a matter of faith and may possibly be its worst enemy. Indeed, the faith of the believer is an expression of his free will, which is neither based on logic nor conditional on it, and can express an important religious value such as love of God. "The main purpose and perfection of man is the worship of God in naïveté and with no crafty side thoughts . . . only by faith and through the practical *mitzvot* performed according to the Torah in simplicity and naïveté, . . . because this can be done by every man, thereby achieving his ultimate objective" (*Likkutei Moharan*, pt. 1, 19). Hence R. Naḥman expresses bitter opposition to the study of philosophy, instead presenting faith as one of the highest religious values. The awareness that human logic differs fundamentally from the divine logic forms a series of paradoxes, which only the faith that recognizes the transcendent God can bridge. Faith starts where reason ends, "and where something cannot be grasped intellectually, there faith is needed" (*ibid.*, pt. 2, 8; he mentions too the stand taken by Isaac *Arama). The *galut* ("exile") continues to exist because of the lack of faith; while the meaning of redemption is that all doubts will be resolved. For this reason some scholars, such as J. Weiss, sought to define Bratslav Ḥasidism as the "Ḥasidism of faith." Others, such as I. Tishby, argue that this characterization is not sufficiently exhaustive.

Naḥman's theory of the *zaddik* is unique for it claims that there is only one true *zaddik*, Naḥman himself, who is destined to be the Messiah. The Moses-like *zaddik* gives redemptive force to the prayers of the general community. The great *zaddik's* reflection on heretical questions may bring about the spiritual elevation of those who were formerly sunk in error. Even the *niggun* (ḥasidic melody) sung by the *zaddik* has a similar influence. The biblical injunction, "I have set the Lord always before me" (Ps. 16:8) is an obligation binding on the Ḥasid's relations to the *zaddik*. It is necessary to believe in the *zaddik* in spite of doubts (which are the inevitable result of "his greatness and exaltedness"), to acknowledge that "the *zaddik* simulates his *Creator*," and that "through his teachings, the *zaddik* teaches the Holy One, Blessed be He, how to deal with us" (*Sefer ha-Middot*, 1948, "*Ẓaddik*," para. 131). It is when the *zaddik* rises above the level of *Ayin* ("Nothingness") that he is close to mankind and supervises men, as does Divine Providence. The *zaddik* lives as it were eternally, regardless of where he dwells, on earth or in the grave. A man must travel to the *zaddik* because "the main thing is what he hears from the mouth of the *zaddik*." Naḥman strongly emphasizes the obligation of confessing before the *zaddik* and advocates praising him. As the *zaddik* embodies all that is happening in the earthly and divine worlds, communication with him advances the processes of *tikkun* that Lurianic Kabbalah demands of Jews.

Naḥman's outlook on man and the world is rather

pessimistic. He believed that there were many obstacles in man's path in this world, which deserves to be called *gehinnom*. It is as if a man were suspended by a thread over a tempestuous sea. However, Nahman absolutely rejects despair. The rafts to cling to in life are faith, encouragement, joy, melody, dance, constant self-criticism, communication with the *zaddik*, and longing for direct contact with the Creator. Hence a prominent place in his teaching is occupied by prayer, which is defined as a dialogue between man and his Maker. This, however, is not limited to the content of the Jewish tradition of prayer; likewise, there is no value in the recitation of the Psalms unless there is identification with their content. The context of the "dialogue" also includes the obligation of daily isolation. Dejection, Nahman held, is one of the major reasons for man's drifting away from God, which leads to sins, the major ones being sexual. (Hence the popular treatise, *Tikkun ha-Kelali*.) Nahman effusively praises the *niggun*. According to him, there exists a complete system of *niggunim* suited to the composite range of the universe. Someone who knows how to adjust himself to musical rhythm derives great pleasure from it and achieves self-effacement. At this point, the Creator reveals himself to the one who yearns for Him, via the various stages in the order of nature. Erez Israel gives man the opportunity for spiritual elevation; there, too, he can attain faith and wisdom. This was perhaps the purpose of Nahman's voyage, and the explanation of his view that during his entire lifetime he was sustained by the wisdom-giving atmosphere of Erez Israel which raised him to the status of "the greatest of *zaddikim*" as he himself said. [Mo.Hal.]

Bibliography: G. Scholem, *Elleh Shemot Sifrei Moharan mi-Bratslav* (1928); H. Zeitlin, *R. Nahman mi-Bratslav, Hayyav ve-Torato* (1910); S. A. Horodezky, *Torat R. Nahman mi-Bratslav* (1923); idem, introduction to *Sippurei Ma'asiyyot le-R. Nahman mi-Bratslav* (1923²); Dubnow, Hasidut, index; H. Lieberman, in: *YIVO Bleter*, 29 (1947), 201–19; J. Weiss, in: *Alei-Ayin* (1952), 245–91; idem, in: *Tarbiz*, 27 (1957/58), 358–71 (= *Scholem Jubilee Volume* (Heb., 1958), 232–45); idem, in: *Erkhei ha-Yahadut* (1953), 81–90; idem, in: KS, 41 (1965/66), 557–63; 44 (1968/69), 279–97; idem, in: *Scholem Jubilee Volume* (Heb. and Eng., 1968), 101–13; idem, introduction to *Ma'gelei Si'ah* (1947); Ch. Shmeruk, in: KS, 44 (1968/69), 443; N. Z. Koenig, *Neveh Zaddikim* (1969); J. K. Miklishinsky, in: *Ha-Hasidut ve-Ziyyon* (1963), 246–56; M. Buber, *The Tales of Rabbi Nachman* (1956).

NAHMAN OF HORODENKA (Gorodenka; d. 1780), disciple of *Israel b. Eliezer Ba'al Shem Tov; his son married Feige, the granddaughter of the Ba'al Shem Tov, and their son was *Nahman of Bratslav. Little information is available on the personality of Nahman of Horodenka and his teachings. From the scattered quotations in the early hasidic literature attributed to him, it appears that he occupied himself essentially with practical questions on the method of divine worship. His encounter with the Ba'al Shem Tov became the turning point of his life, as he himself confirms: "When I was a great pietist I immersed myself every day in a *mikveh*, so cold that nobody else could bear. When I came to my house and found the place so warm that the walls were almost burning, I did not feel the warmth for almost an hour. Even so, I could not rid myself from impure thoughts until I was compelled to seek the wisdom of the Besht [Ba'al Shem Tov]" (*Shivhei ha-Besht* (1961), 112). This change of attitude expresses the complete reversal of his world outlook from ascetic to non-ascetic Hasidism. In 1764 Nahman emigrated to Erez Israel with *Menahem Mendel of Peremyshlany at the head of a group of Hasidim and settled in Tiberias.

His journey was described by Simhah b. Joshua of Zalozhtsy in *Ahavat Ziyyon* (Gorodnya, 1790; published a second time under the title *Doresh Ziyyon*, Jerusalem, 1887). Some teachings are recorded in his name by his father-in-law *Moses Hayyim Ephraim of Sudylkow in *Degel Mahaneh Efrayim*, as well as in the *Toledot Ya'akov Yosef* by *Jacob Joseph of Polonnoye.

Bibliography: A. Rubinstein, in: *Tarbiz*, 35 (1965/66) 174–91; Horodezky, Hasidut, index; *Shivhei ha-Besht* (1961), 112, 117–8, 126; Dubnow, Hasidut, 102–3, 291. [E.Z.]

NAHMAN OF KOSOV (d. 1746), kabbalist and one of the early Hasidim. A wealthy land contractor and grain dealer, he lived for a time in Ludomir (*Vladimir Volynsky) where he built a *bet midrash* with adjoining bathhouse; Nahman was associated with a group of Hasidim in Kutow (Kuty) which was active even before the appearance of *Israel b. Eliezer Ba'al Shem Tov and possibly remained independent of him even later. At first Nahman was opposed to the Ba'al Shem Tov, refusing to accept him as a religious leader. Even after recognizing the latter's authority Nahman preserved his spiritual independence, and his connections with the Ba'al Shem Tov were apparently weak. It is known that among the Kutow group "there was a condition that none of them should prophesy" (*Shivhei ha-Besht*) but Nahman did not always observe this condition. He was considered a "man of the spirit," possessing contemplative power and known for his ecstatic manner of praying; he was one of the first to introduce into public prayer the *Nosah ha-Ari* (prayer rite of Isaac *Luria).

Nahman was among the foremost teachers of devotion (**devekut*), emphasizing constant contemplation of God; *devekut*, according to him, does not contradict the requirements of social life and is not confined to moments of spiritual concentration or a propitious occasion. It is carried out by a visual technique, the letters of the Tetragrammaton and the other names of God appearing before the eyes of the person meditating (the visual method of seeing letters). Nahman recognized the importance of the dialectical fabric of a society composed of "men of matter" (the masses) and "men of form" (i.e., of the spirit), holding that man's spiritual elevation from his lowliness will take place by his association with the great and pious. Everyone should aim at progress toward perfection day by day and a gradual ascent through completeness and unity of will and intention (*kavvanah*). Nahman admitted the struggle in man's soul between the powers which are his good and evil inclinations. Life is like a "running and returning" (Ezek. 1:14), with ascents and descents; sometimes what seems to be an ascent is actually a descent, but the descents are prerequisites of the ascents and are not absolutely evil, for "intellect proceeds from instinct and spiritual desire from physical desire" (*Zafenat Pa'ne'ah*, 38a).

Nahman was suspected of Shabbateanism and since he supported Jonathan *Eybeschuetz, Jacob *Emden publicly censured him as "Nahman Kosover the ignoramus of the Shabbatean sect" (Emden, *Petah Einayim*, 14b; *Sefer Hitabbekut* (1862), 20b). However there is no real proof that Nahman was a Shabbatean. His teachings are cited in *Toledot Ya'akov Yosef* by Jacob Joseph of Polonnoye, in *Shivhei ha-Besht* (Horodezky ed. (1922), 56–57), etc.

Bibliography: A. J. Heschel, in: *H. A. Wolfson Jubilee Volume* (Heb., 1965), 113–41; J. G. Weiss, in: JJS, 8 (1957), 199–213; G. Scholem, in: *Tarbiz*, 20 (1949), 234, 239. [E.Z.]

NAHMIAS, IBN (15th–16 centuries), family of Hebrew printers from Spain. David ibn Nahmias, his brother Samuel, and David's son Samuel, left Spain in 1492 and made their way to *Constantinople. There they published *Jacob b. Asher's *Turim* in 1493 (5254). The correctness of this date, written out in words in the colophon, has been doubted by scholars such as M. *Steinschneider (*Juedische*

Typographie, 1938, 17), who assume an error of ten years. More recently, the case for the 1493 date has been strongly defended by A. K. Offenberg (see bibliography). After an interval of over ten years, the Ibn Naḥmias brothers printed a Pentateuch with Rashi, including *haftarot* with David Kimḥi's commentary and the Five Scrolls with that of Abraham ibn Ezra (1505–06). Several other books followed, among them Alfasi's *Halakhot* and Maimonides' *Code* (both 1509), and three works by Abrabanel, the only ones printed in the author's lifetime. Samuel sr. died in 1509 or 1510, and David ibn Naḥmias about a year later. David's son Samuel carried on, alone or with a partner, to 1518, when the press was leased to others. The first two works printed (*Turim* and Pentateuch) have as *printer's mark a *Magen David* surrounded by leaves and flowers.

Bibliography: A. K. Offenberg, in: *Studia Rosenthaliana,* 2 (1969), 96–112 (incl. illus. and bibl.); A. Yaari, *Ha-Defus ha-Ivri be-Kushta* (1967), 17–18, 59ff.; idem, *Diglei ha-Madpisim ha-Ivriyyim* (1944), 3, 123; A. Freimann, *Thesaurus typographiae hebraicae saeculi XV* (1924), CI, 4; Rosanes, Togarmah, 1 (1930[2]), 316–8.

[Ed.]

NAḤMIAS, JOSEPH BEN JOSEPH (first half of 14th century), biblical commentator in Toledo. Nahmias belonged to an ancient and distinguished Spanish family. Apart from the fact that he studied under *Asher b. Jehiel, little is known of his life. His reputation rests upon his biblical commentary which apparently originally encompassed most of the Bible.

The following parts have been published with introductions by M. A. Bamberger: Esther (1891), Proverbs (1912), and Jeremiah (1913). Bamberger also published Naḥmias' commentaries to *Avot* (1907) and to the *piyyut Attah Konanta* (in: JJLG, 6 (1909)), on the order of the Temple service for the Day of Atonement. His commentary to the tractate *Nedarim* has been preserved in manuscript. Naḥmias is also known to have translated many parts of Maimonides' *Guide of the Perplexed.*

Bibliography: Bamberger's introd. to his edition of the commentary to Jeremiah, Proverbs, Esther (all in German); Neubauer, in: JQR, 5 (1892/93), 709–13; Poznański, in ZHB, 1 (1896/97), 118–21.

[I.T.-S.]

NAHON, family of rabbis and community leaders of Portuguese origin, in various cities of Morocco. R. Isaac ben Joseph Nahon (mid-16th century) was a rabbi of the community of Spanish exiles (Heb. *megorashim*) in Fez and a signatory of its *takkanot* in 1545. Apparently either Benjamin (Joseph's father or brother) or Joseph was the author of *Sefer ha-Derashot* (Neubauer, Cat Bod 998). In the 17th and 18th centuries, the Nahons were international merchants in Algiers; the family originating in Tetuán. Isaac (d. 1730) was rabbi in Tetuán. During the 18th and 19th centuries the family was prominent in Marrakesh, Mogador, and particularly Tangier, where they built the Great Synagogue. They greeted Sir Moses *Montefiore on his trip to Morocco in 1864. Jonas Benasuli (b. 1888) was an architect in Tangier. Moses (Moïse; b. 1870), a distinguished educator, Francophile, and the inspector of the Alliance Israélite Universelle schools thoughout Morocco, was active in several philanthropic societies, as were the Nahon women. Other members lived in London, Gibraltar, and Leghorn, Italy.

Bibliography: J. M. Toledano, *Ner ha-Ma'arav* (1911), 61ff., 101–2; I. Laredo, *Memorias de un viejo tangerino* (1935), 120–2, 267–72; Hirschberg, Afrikah, 2 (1965), 310.

[Ed.]

NAHOR (Heb. נָחוֹר; cf. Ass. personal names **Naḫaru, Naḫiri;** Ur III, **Naḫarum**), (1) The son of Serug, the father of Terah, and the grandfather of Abraham. Of those enumerated in the genealogy of the descendants of Shem, he had the shortest life—148 years (Gen. 11:22–25; I. Chron. 1:26). (2) The son of Terah, the brother of Abraham and Haran, and the grandson of Nahor (1). His wife was *Milcah, the daughter of his brother Haran (Gen. 11:26–29).

This was a consanguineous marriage such as is common in the narratives of the Patriarchs (for example, that of Jacob with Rachel and Leah). According to E. A. Speiser, such marriages are to be seen in the light of a custom known from Horite law, whereby a girl was adopted as a daughter with the intention that the adoptive father or his son would marry her. Apparently Bethuel, the son of Nahor and Milcah, died while still young, and his children came under the protection of their grandfather Nahor. Hence Laban is called "the son of Nahor" (Gen. 29:5). However, "the son of Nahor" may constitute a clan name, as is sometimes the case in the Bible.

Abraham and Nahor are described as the progenitors of two clans which intermarried. In the ceremony marking the covenant between Jacob and Laban, the latter declared (31:53): "'May the God of Abraham and the god of Nahor'—their ancestral deities—'judge between us'"; the patriarchal god of each family would judge in any dispute between them, this being customary also in treaties in the Ancient Near East, in which each party cited his gods as witnesses to the pact.

The genealogy of Nahor states that his wife Milcah bore him eight sons and his concubine Reumah four. This represents a schematic genealogical outlook whereby 12 sons are ascribed to a progenitor, analogous to the 12 sons of Ishmael or of Jacob. B. Mazar holds that the genealogy of the sons of Nahor reflects an ancient historical reality which tallies with the expansion of the West Semitic tribes in the first half of the second millennium B.C.E. Support for this assumption is to be found in the reference to Aram as the grandson of Nahor, which indicates that the Aramean tribes were still a young and insignificant element. However, in the Table of the Nations, Aram is represented as descended from Shem himself, and Uz, the firstborn of Nahor, is represented as the firstborn of Aram (Gen. 10:22ff.). This genealogy points to a later period, when the Arameans had attained the pinnacle of their power in the Fertile Crescent. Thus the "Aramaization" of Bethuel and Laban (cf. Gen. 31:47)—and indirectly of Nahor himself which contradicts the genealogical scheme of Nahor's sons—is to be apprehended as a later anachronism engendered after the rise and expansion of the Arameans in the region of Nahor and of Aram-Naharaim at the end of the 12th and in the 11th centuries B.C.E. The ascription of Nahor's sons to a wife and to a concubine expresses a geographical and population distribution—the sons of the wife symbolizing tribes, clans, and geographical limits in the region of Aram-Naharaim and the middle Euphrates and on the borders of the Syrian desert, and the sons of the concubine, areas, tribes, and cities in the south of Syria and northern Transjordan.

(3) The city of Nahor (Ass. Naḫur, Til Naḫiri). In Genesis 24:10 it is related that the servant of Abraham went to "Aram-Naharaim, to the city of Nahor." Whether this was a place named Nahor or a city in which Nahor's family lived cannot be determined. Those holding the latter view identify the place, on the basis of Genesis 27:43 and 29:4, with *Haran. Nahor is also mentioned in Akkadian sources dating from the beginning of the second millennium to the middle of the seventh century B.C.E., as the name of a city in the Balikh valley. Nahor is first mentioned in Assyrian documents from Kanish of the 20th–19th centuries B.C.E. as an important station in the Assyrian trade with Asia Minor. Much information on the city during this period is contained in the *Mari archives, from which it is clear that Nahor was a regional capital subject to Mari and a location of its agents. From Nahor supervision was exercised over the Balikh area and the upper stretch of the Habor river; in Nahor intelligence was collected from all parts of Aram-Naharaim. Nahor was also a center for nomadic tribes which, defying all authority, endangered the caravan trade. Accordingly, the rulers of Mari were from time to time constrained to employ military means to suppress their depredations.

In the Middle Assyrian period, Nahor belonged to the kingdom of Hanigalbat, whose rulers erected a palace there. In the 13th century it was captured by the Assyrian kings Adad-Nirari I and Shalmaneser I. During this period it was the seat of a governor, as attested by Assyrian documents, from which it appears that Nahor was included in a district whose capital was Haran, near which it was apparently situated. Although the sources, as well as the archaeological survey conducted in the region of Haran, do not help to fix the exact site of Nahor, it is to be located at an important junction on the caravan route.

Bibliography: ON NAHOR AND THE SONS OF NAHOR: G. May, in: JBL, 60 (1941), 123–6; B. Meisler (Mazar), in: *Zion*, 11 (1946), 1–16; R. de Vaux, in: RB, 55 (1948), 323–4; 72 (1965), 10; N. Schneider, in: *Biblica*, 33 (1952), 519–22; J. P. Hyatt, in: VT, 5 (1955), 130–6; A. Malamat, in: BIES, 20 (1956), 71–72; idem, in: *Sefer Y. F. Baer* (1961), 1–7; idem, in: *Compte rendu, XVe Rencontre assyrienne internationale* (1966), 129ff.; idem, in: EM, 5 (1968), 805–7; K. T. Andersen, in: *Studia Theologica*, 16 (1962), 170ff.; E. A. Speiser, in: A. Altmann (ed.), *Biblical and Other Studies* (1963) 15–28; U. Cassuto, *Commentary on the Book of Exodus* (1964), 252. ON THE CITY OF NAHOR: W. F. Albright, in: BASOR, 67 (1937), 27; 78 (1940), 29–30; J. Lewy, in: *Orientalia*, 21 (1952), 272ff., 280ff.; A. Goetze, in: JCS, 7 (1953), 67; J. Bottéro and A. Finet, *Archives royales de Mari*, 5 (1954), 130, s.v. *Naḫur;* E. Weidner, in: AFO, 17 (1955–56), 45–46; M. Falkner, *ibid.*, 18 (1957), 20; F. J. Kupper, *Les nomades en Mésopotamie . . .* (1957), s.v. *Naḫur;* F. M. Tocci, *La Siria nell'età di Mari* (1960), s.v. *Naḫur;* M. Birot, in: *Archives royales de Mari*, 9 (1960), 91; G. Dossin, et al., *ibid.*, 13 (1964), 81–82, 149; A. Finet, in: *Revue d'assyriologie et d'archéologie orientale*, 60 (1966), 17ff.; A. Malamat, in: EM, 5 (1968), 807–8.

[ED.]

NAHOUM, ḤAIM (1872–1960), chief rabbi of Istanbul and Cairo. Born in Manisa, Turkey, Nahoum moved to Tiberias with his family and received his elementary education there. He then went to Smyrna, Turkey, where he was graduated from government high school, and then to Istanbul, where he studied law. Between 1893 and 1897 he studied at the rabbinical seminary in Paris, where he was ordained, and at the Higher Seminary for Semitic Languages of the Collège de France. When he returned to Istanbul, Nahoum was appointed secretary-general of the community committee and deputy director of the rabbinical seminary founded in 1898 by his father-in-law, R. Abraham Danon. At the same time, he received a government appointment as history teacher in the Turkish Military Academy. At that time, he became acquainted with the "Young Turks" who were exiled in Paris, and when they seized power in the Ottoman Empire in 1908 they appointed him chief rabbi of the Empire. In this position, Nahoum successfully intervened in favor of Jews in various localities of the Empire, especially in assuring government protection for them during World War I (it seems that it was due to him that the project of expelling the Jews from Jerusalem was averted). After the defeat of the Ottoman Empire and the removal of the "Young Turks" from power, Nahoum left Constantinople for Paris in 1920. In 1925 he was elected chief rabbi of Cairo, a post he held until his death. In June 1931 the king of Egypt appointed Nahoum a member of the Egyptian senate, and in 1933 he was appointed a member of the Arabic Language Academy in Cairo. He was also awarded many honors by the governments of Turkey, Egypt, France, Austria-Hungary, and Ethiopia. Proficient in many languages, he engaged in research on the history of Egyptian Jewry. He also published—with a French translation, notes, and a glossary of Turkish terms—a collection of 1,064 firmans (decrees by the sultan) that had been sent to the rulers of Egypt between 1597 and 1904. This work is entitled *Recueil de firmans impériaux* (1934).

Bibliography: *The Muslim World* (Hartford, Conn.), 51 (1961), 233–4; M. Fargeon, *Les Juifs en Egypte* (1938), 202–3; M. D. Gaon, *Yehudei ha-Mizraḥ be-Ereẓ Yisrael*, 2 (1938), 461, 736; H. Rabbi Abraham, in: *Haaretz* (Dec. 16, 1960), 12; Nathan in: JJSO, 6 (1964), no. 2, 172, 187; A. Galanté, *Histoire des Juifs d'Anatolie*, 2 (1939), 98.

[H.J.C.]

NAHRAI BEN NISSIM (11th century), community leader of the Iraqi Jews in Cairo. Nahrai, who was originally from *Kairouan, settled in Egypt where he became a wealthy merchant. He maintained commercial ties with several countries and specialized in the export of such precious goods as spices, pearls, and indigo to Tunisia and Sicily. However, he was also a scholar with halakhic experience and religious and legal questions were addressed to him. He was referred to as "The eminent Rabbi, the greatest of the yeshivah." He is mentioned in documents dated between 1048–95. Nearly 200 letters addressed to him were found in the *genizah* of Fostat; there are certainly only a part of his original archives.

Bibliography: Mann, Egypt, index; Starr, in: *Zion*, 1 (1935/36), 436–53; Strauss, *ibid.*, 7 (1941/42), 151–5; M. Michael, *The Archives of Nahrai b. Nissim* (1965, thesis, Hebrew University); S. D. Goitein, *Studies in Islamic History and Institutions* (1966), 287, 295, 321; idem, *A Mediterranean Society* (1967), index; idem, in: *Tarbiz*, 36 (1966/67), 59ff.

[E.A.]

NAHRAWĀN, town in Iraq, E. of Baghdad. Nahrawān was a flourishing town during the time of the Abbasid caliphs (8th and 9th centuries) because the main highway to Persia passed through the town, crossing the Nahrawān canal at this point. At this time it had a large Jewish community, some of whose members were said to have come there from Egypt. The Nahrawān community belonged to the "domain" of the exilarch. To judge by the large income that the exilarch derived from the Nahrawān community (and from Jews living in its vicinity), according to Nathan ha-Bavli the community must have been of considerable size. In the first half of the tenth century a blind scholar from Nahrawān, R. *Nissi (Nissim) al-Nahrawāni was *resh kallah* at one of the academies. He brought about a reconciliation between the exilarch David b. Zakkai and the head of the Pumbedita academy. R. Nissi subsequently became one of the exilarch's advisers. In the late Middle Ages the caravans to Persia changed their route and as a result Nahrawān fell into decay.

Bibliography: Neubauer, Chronicles, 2 (1893), 79–80, 85; A. E. Harkavy, *Zikkaron la-Rishonim ve-gam la-Aḥaronim*, 1 (1887), 141, no. 285; G. Le Strange, *The Lands of the Eastern Caliphate* (1930), 61; Mann, in: *Tarbiz*, 5 (1934), 154–5.

[E.A.]

NAHSHON (Heb. נַחְשׁוֹן; "little (?) serpent"), son of Amminadab (Ex. 6:23; Num. 2:3, et al.). Nahshon was chieftain of the tribe of Judah (Num. 2:3) which consisted of 74,600 men (Num. 2:3–4; 10:14). He assisted Moses in taking a census of the community (Num. 1:7). He was the first to present his offering at the dedication of the Tabernacle (Num. 7:12–17) and the first to proceed in the desert marches (Num. 10:14). Elisheba, his sister, married Aaron (Ex. 6:23). He was the descendant of *Perez, the son of Judah and Tamar, and his son Salmah (Ruth 4:20; Salmon, 4:21; Salma, I Chron. 2:11) was the father of Boaz. King David was thus one of his descendants. [ED.]

In the Aggadah. According to a well-known *aggadah*, Nahshon was the only one among the Israelites on reaching the Red Sea to obey the command of Moses to descend into the waters and courageously enter the waves, trusting that the promised miracle would occur and the sea be parted. The members of the tribe of Judah followed their leader's example (Mekh., Be-Shallaḥ 5; Sot. 37a). This version of the story is attributed to Tarfon (early second century).

According to an opposing version, all the tribes were eager to obey the command and competed among themselves, who was to be the first; eventually, the tribe of Benjamin jumped first into the water, but the tribe of Judah, infuriated by Benjamin's success, attacked them with stones (Mekh. loc. cit.; Sot. 36b). Benjamin's reward for being the first to descend into the sea was that the first king of Israel—Saul—was chosen from their tribe (Targum Ps. 68:28 and I Sam. 15:17), or else that the *Shekhinah* (Divine Presence) dwelt in their territory (the Temple was built in the territory of Benjamin; Mekh. and Sot., loc. cit.). According to the version which ascribes the outstanding feat of courage to Nahshon, the reward to the tribe of Judah was that kingship in Israel was accorded to them permanently. Tarfon's version was probably meant to encourage acts of rebellion—in the period of unrest preceding the Bar Kokhba Revolt—as the one and only means to reattain kingship for Judah, that is to say, to regain political independence. Various attempts to explain this *aggadah* against the background of other events remain unconvincing.

[J.HEI.]

Bibliography: Ginzberg, Legends, 3 (1947[3]), 195, 220–1; 6 (1946[3]), 75–76.

NAHSHON BAR ZADOK, *gaon* of Sura from 871–79, succeeding *Amram Gaon (who mentions him several times in his *Seder*). Nahshon's father, Zadok, had previously been *gaon* of Sura for more than 50 years, and Nahshon's son, Hai, held the office from 889–96.

Nahshon is the author of numerous responsa, in reply to queries addressed to him from various countries. Various works have been attributed to him, among them *Sefer Re'umah* (in J. Onkeneira, *Ẓafenat Pa'ne'aḥ*, Constantinople, 1566), on ritual slaughter, and he is thought by some to have been the author of *Seder Tanna'im ve-Amora'im*. Nahshon made a special study of the Jewish calendar, and is best known for his discovery that the Jewish calendar repeats itself exactly every 247 years. His writing on this phenomenon, known as the *Iggul de-R. Naḥshon*, was published under that name in the *She'erit Yosef* of *Joseph b. Shem Tov (Salonika, 1521). It is possible that it was this calendrical research which led him to take up the study of Karaite literature, since he had to familiarize himself with the works of the founder of the Karaite sect for this purpose (L. Ginzberg, *Gaonica*. 1, (1909), 158), and his interpretations of words in the Bible and Talmud may well be related to his polemics with the Karaites. Nahshon's conservative outlook led him to discourage the innovation of reciting *piyyutim* in prayer, and he disapproved of the recitation of *Kol Nidrei* on the eve of the Day of Atonement, as did his son Hai. Most of Nahshon's responsa are written in terse and difficult Aramaic, but those ascribed to him in D. Cassel's *Teshuvot Ge'onim Kadmoniyyim* (1848; see German introduction, 45) are written in a simple and fluent Hebrew. Some of his decisions conflict with the Talmud and his talmudic-aggadic interpretations do not always agree with those of former aggadists.

Bibliography: B. Z. Kahana (ed.), *Seder Tanna'im ve-Amora'im* (1935), introd. xff.; Baron, Social[2], 5 (1957), 22; 6 (1958), 124–5, 425; 7 (1958), 101; D. Cassel, *Teshuvot Ge'onim Kadmoniyyim* (1848), 9a/b; Abramson, Merkazim, 12; L. Ginzberg, *Geonica*, 1 (1909), 154–9.

[M.H.]

NAHUM (Heb. נַחוּם; a *qattūl* hypocoristic of a name like נְחֶמְיָה, "YHWH has comforted," like שָׁלוֹם for שְׁלֶמְיָה, שַׁמּוּעַ for שְׁמַעְיָה, etc.), one of the Twelve Minor Prophets. Nothing is known of the man himself other than the statement in the book's title that he was an "Elkoshite." A place called al-Qūsh, containing a grave said to be that of Nahum, is located in the neighborhood of Mosul near ancient *Nineveh, whose ruin Nahum depicts in chapters 2 and 3; this tradition connecting al-Qūsh with the prophet cannot, however, be traced beyond the 16th century. Jerome, in the prologue to his commentary on Nahum, records that the prophet was a native of a village in Galilee, which in Jerome's time was called Elcesi and is identified with el-Qauze, west of Tibnin. Some older modern scholars, such as A. W. Knobel and F. Hitzig, have suggested locating Elkosh at Capernaum ("Village of Nahum"). More credible seems to be the tradition recorded by Pseudo-Epiphanius *(De Vitis Prophetarum)*, which mentions a Judean Elkesi, "yonder," i.e., south of Eleutheropolis or Bet Guvrin, but the name Elkesi may represent Lachish, since the town of this name was situated directly south of Bet Guvrin. No definite identification of the locality denoted by the designation "Elkoshite" can therefore be made.

Nahum's literary activity took place after the capture of the Egyptian Thebes (biblical No-Amon) by Ashurbanipal in 663 B.C.E., an event which is alluded to in Nahum 3:8–10. It is not certain, however, whether he wrote before the fall of *Nineveh in August 612, when the Assyrian capital was captured and razed by the Babylonians and Medes, or shortly after its fall, when the joyful news of the oppressor's defeat was conveyed to Judah. The perfect tenses employed in chapters 2 and 3, where the event is depicted with poetic vividness and force, suggest that Nineveh had already fallen. But several passages (such as 3:11, 14–15) seem to indicate that the resistance was not yet completely crushed. It may therefore be inferred that the Book of Nahum was composed in the very year 612, shortly before Nineveh's final downfall.

The Book of Nahum. The original title of the book as a whole is probably contained in the second part of the superscription: "The book of the vision of Nahum the Elkoshite." The first part—"Oracle concerning Nineveh"—was perhaps the title of the oracle proper on Nineveh's fall; in any case, it correctly describes the main contents of the book. Chapter 1 is generally thought to form an acrostic hymn of theophany. In the opinion of several scholars the entire alphabet was represented in the original poem. The text of Nahum 1 and 2:1, 3 has accordingly been rearranged and reconstructed, mainly by G. Bickell and H. Gunkel, to form a complete alphabetic psalm of an eschatological character which they regarded as a later addition to the book. The restoration of a complete acrostic however is impossible; in fact, the poem seems to follow the alphabet only down to the letter *samekh* (1:2a, 3b–8, 9c–10a, 9ab, 2b, 10bc), with verses 9ab and 2b having been transferred to their present position by the book's last editor. One can only conjecture whether the acrostic was composed by Nahum; it is more probable that this text, like other similar ones in the Psalter, was a part of the Jerusalem liturgy. The theophany proper, employing the ancient themes of God's rule over the primordial forces of nature, is contained in verses 3b–6. It serves here as an introductory motif to a national psalm of confidence (1:7–8, 9c–10a, 9ab, 2b, 10bc), followed by an oracle addressed to Judah (1:12–13; 2:1). This liturgy actually forms the exordium to the poem on the fall of Nineveh.

The oracle addressed to the Assyrian capital was perhaps headed by the words "Oracle concerning Nineveh" (1:1). It opens with the introduction 1:11, 14, and is followed by 2:2, 4ff. and 3. The descriptions in Nahum's masterful poetry are singularly picturesque and vivid (especially 2:4–6, 11; 3:2–3, 17–19). The absence of distinctly religious motifs is remarkable, and yet P. Humbert (followed to a certain extent by E. Sellin, A. Lods, H. Lamparter, and S. J. de Vries) tried to prove that the whole Book of Nahum was a liturgy for the enthronement festival of the Lord after the fall of Nineveh in 612. Although other scholars have rejected this view, A. Bentzen (*Introduction to the Old Testament*, 2 (1958[4]), 151) considered that the book might be an "imitated" liturgy, consisting of the introductory hymn (chapter 1), the invitation to a festival (2:1), and the curse against Nineveh (chapters 2–3). A. Haldar, on the other hand, has ascribed the Book of Nahum to a cultic prophet who, in c. 614 B.C.E., foretold the approaching destruction of Nineveh by the Lord and employed the images and expressions normally used in depicting the cultic-mythical struggle of God against his foes. As these motifs are paralleled in Sumero-Akkadian and Ugaritic texts, the Book of Nahum would accordingly derive from cultic circles. S. Mowinckel early considered Nahum one of the nationalistic temple prophets of the kind attacked by Jeremiah (*Jesaja-disiplene, Profetien fra Jesaja til Jeremia* (1926), 56). Following A. Kuenen (*De Boeken des Ouden Verbonds*, 2 (1889[2]), 384), he suggested that the immediate occasion of the oracle may have been the Median attack upon Nineveh in 623 B.C.E. which, though it proved abortive and cost King Phraortes his life, may have turned the prophet's thoughts toward the city and its future destiny. Several recent commentators (such as Th. H. Robinson, K. Elliger, and M. Delcor) also consider the book an actual prophecy of doom against Nineveh uttered before its fall in 612. Nahum, however, in his extant writings, was more a nationalist poet than a prophet predicting the future. He expressed his joy over the imminent downfall of Nineveh in the forceful and vivid language of poetry, depicting the assault upon the city, the entrance effected by her foes, the scene of carnage and tumult in the streets, the flight of her inhabitants, the treasures plundered by the captors (chapter 2), and in 3:2–3 he again visualized the chariots and horsemen of the victor forcing a path through the streets. Since the Lord is against Nineveh (3:5–6), she will be as unable to avert her doom as was Thebes in Upper Egypt (3:8–11). Nineveh's fortresses have given way; her men have become as women (3:12–13); in vain she tries to endure the siege (3:14); and amid the rejoicings of all who have suffered at her hands, the proud empire of Nineveh passes away forever (3:18–19). The Book of Nahum thus indirectly depicts God's moral government of the world; He is the Avenger of wrongdoers and the sole source of security to those who trust in Him.

Bibliography: H. Gunkel, in: ZAW 13 (1893), 223–44; W. R. Arnold, *ibid.*, 21 (1901), 225–65; S. R. Driver, *The Minor Prophets...* (1906, The Century Bible); P. Haupt, in: JBL, 26 (1907), 1–53; J. M. P. Smith, *Micah, Zephaniah, Nahum, Habakkuk, Obadiah, and Joel* (ICC, 1911); W. Nowack, *Die kleinen Propheten* (1922²); G. Hirshler, in: Kahana (ed.), *Terei Asar* (1930), 51–71; Th. H. Gaster, in: JBL, 63 (1944), 51–52; A. Haldar, *Studies in the Book of Nahum* (1947); Th. Laetsch, *The Minor Prophets* (1956); Kaufmann Y., Toledot; A. George, in: DBI, s.v.; S. J. de Vries, in: VT, 16 (1966), 476–81; E. G. Kraeling, *Commentary on the Prophets* (1966); Y. Licht, in: EM, 5 (1968), s.v. [E.Li.]

NAHUM, AARON SASSON BEN ELIJAH (c. 1872–1962), educator and communal worker in Iraq. From 1920 he was chairman of the Zionist Organization in Iraq; his Zionist work was done underground because of Iraqi persecution of the Zionist movement. In 1920 he helped found a Hebrew Literary Society in Baghdad. He was the founder and, from 1924 to 1935, director of Pardes Yeladim, a school which fostered the use of Hebrew. In 1935 he settled in Palestine, where he continued to work as an educator. In 1920 he founded a Hebrew-Arab weekly in Baghdad, *Yeshurun*, of which only five numbers appeared. Under the pseudonym of "Ha-Moreh," he published a book of poems, *Sefer Shirei ha-Teḥiyyah*, containing translations and original works (2 parts, 1925; part 3 in 1931). His poems express his longing for Zion. In Palestine he also published a number of booklets, in which he appealed for religious observance.

Bibliography: H. Ben-Yoseph, in: *Ba-Ma'arakhah*, 2 (March 1963), 15; H. J. Cohen, *Ha-Pe'ilut ha-Ẓiyyonit be-Iraq* (1969), passim. [A.B.-Y.]

NAHUM, ELIEZER BEN JACOB (c. 1653–c. 1746), rabbi in Turkey and Ereẓ Israel. He served as rabbi in Adrianople, where his pupils included Solomon Shalem, later rabbi of the Sephardi community in Amsterdam. He later settled in Jerusalem and was elected *rishon le-Zion* (chief rabbi), a position he held for ten years. Among his colleagues in the *bet din* were *Meyuḥas b. Samuel, Isaac *Azulai (father of Ḥ. J. D. Azulai), and Judah *Diwan. He wrote a number of works, including a commentary on the mishnaic orders *Kodashim* and *Tohorot*, entitled *Ḥazon Naḥum* (Constantinople, 1705). The commentary on the order *Zera'im* is still in manuscript form.

Bibliography: Frumkin-Rivlin, 2 (1928), 161–3. [Sh.A.H./Ed.]

NAHUM THE MEDE (fl. second half of the first century C.E.), *tanna*. Nahum lived in Jerusalem during the period of the destruction of the Temple (Naz. 5:4). According to the *tanna* *Nathan, he was one of the judges of civil law, known as *dayyanei gezerot* (Ket. 105a; Tosef., BB 9:1). Three of Nahum's teachings have been preserved in the Mishnah (Shab. 2:1; Naz. 5:4; BB 5:2), and several more in *beraitot* (Av. Zar. 7b; Tosef., BB 9:1).

Bibliography: Bacher, Tann, 1; Hyman, Toledot, s.v. [D.J.B.]

NAHUM OF GIMZO (late first and early second century C.E.), *tanna*. As his name indicates, he probably came from *Gimzo (II Chron. 28:18) in the center of Ereẓ Israel. From the meager information preserved about his teachings and activity, it can be inferred that he was a man of considerable importance. Among his intimate pupils was *Akiva (Ber. 22a), who stayed with him for 22 years, learning from him to interpret every particle (את) of the Torah (Ḥag. 12a; cf. Pes. 22b: it is not certain whether Nahum of Gimzo is identical with Nehemiah Imsoni mentioned in the latter passage). *Ishmael, Akiva's colleague, also highly valued the teaching of Nahum, who apparently occupied himself mainly with *aggadah*. A number of legends have been preserved about him. The designation Gimzo (גמזו) was regarded as meaning "this too" (גם זו, *gam zo*), in reference to his custom of asserting of every happening, however inauspicious it seemed, "this too is for the best" (*gam zo le-tovah*), a habit elsewhere attributed to Akiva (Ber. 60b). Thus when on one occasion he was carrying a casket full of jewels as a gift to the Roman emperor and they were stolen from him at an inn and replaced by earth, he declared "this too is for the best." When he arrived at his destination and the emperor desired to put him to death for mocking him, the prophet Elijah appeared in the guise of a senator and suggested that this was possibly the legendary earth which, if thrown at the enemy in battle, is converted into deadly arrows. On being put to the test, it did indeed prove to be that earth (Ta'an. 21a). Nahum's piety is demonstrated by the story of a journey on which a poor man accosted him and asked for food. The *tanna* asked the man to wait until he had unloaded his ass, but meanwhile the hungry man died. Nahum reproached himself for not being quicker in providing help and prayed that, as a punishment, he should lose his hands, feet, and sight, and his whole body be covered with sores. Thereafter he lay in that condition in a dilapidated house on a bed with its legs immersed in water to keep away the ants, with his disciples tending him (*ibid.*).

Bibliography: Bacher, Tann, s.v.; Hyman, Toledot, 920–1. [D.J.B.]

NAIDITSCH, ISAAC ASHER (1868–1949), philanthropist and Zionist. Born in Pinsk, Naiditsch joined the Ḥibbat Zion movement in his youth. Later, he settled in Moscow and became one of Russia's greatest alcohol industrialists. He was sent by the Russian government on commercial missions several times. He carried on his Zionist work, wrote about literary subjects in Hebrew periodicals, and generously supported Hebrew writers. At the beginning of World War I he was one of the founders and directors of the Central Committee for the Relief of Jewish War Sufferers (YEKOPO). After the Russian Revolution (1917), he donated large sums of money for the purpose of promoting Hebrew culture. When the Soviet regime became established, he emigrated to France. Together with Hillel *Zlatopolsky, he suggested the idea of the *Keren Hayesod and was one of its first directors. When the Nazis occupied France, he fled to the United States, but returned to Paris in 1946. He was a close friend and adviser of Chaim *Weizmann from their youth.

Naiditsch wrote articles on Zionism and current events. Some of them were in the book *Ba-Ḥalom u-va-Ma'aseh* ("In Dream and in Practice," 1956), which also contains a collection of appreciations of his personality. He also wrote a book entitled *Edmond de Rothschild* (1945), based upon his conversations with the Baron.

Bibliography: I. Gruenbaum, *Penei ha-Dor* (1958), 333–5. [Y.S.]

NAIN, village in the Jezreel Valley, where according to the New Testament Jesus revived a dead man (Luke 7:11). It was situated on the slopes of the hill of Moreh. In the Midrash, it is located in the territory of Issachar (Gen. R.

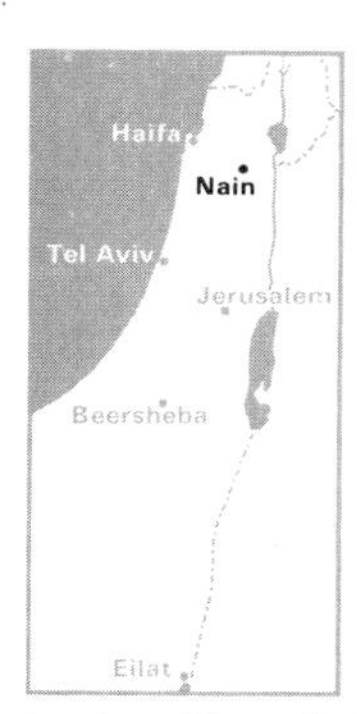

98:12). For many centuries, it was one of the villages of the district of Sepphoris. It was a large village, for it had a gate and presumably a wall. In the fourth century, Nain was made independent, remaining a separate district within Palaestina Secunda until the Arab conquest. The area of the village included the valley of Iksalo (Exaloth). The present-day village has retained the same name and is built on a slope, 5 mi. (8 km.) south-southwest of Nazareth. A spring in the village irrigates plantations of olives and figs. Rock-cut graves were found in the crags along the road leading from the village to the southwest.

Bibliography: Alt, in: PJB, 22 (1926), 60; idem, in: ZDPV, 68 (1951), 61; Schilli, in: ZDPV, 73 (1957), 141–2.

[M.A.-Y.]

NAJAR (Nadjar), prominent rabbinical family of Spanish refugees in Algeria and Tunis. R. MAIMON NAJAR (14th and early 15th century) left Majorca for Algeria in 1395. He settled in Constantine, serving as *dayyan*. Author of *Kunteres ha-Minhagot* on local practices, he corresponded with Simeon b. Ẓemaḥ *Duran on religious matters. His brother MORDECAI went to Tunis in 1391 because of persecutions in Spain; Mordecai later spent some time in Bougie, but returned to Majorca where, under duress, he had accepted Christianity. He finally settled in Algiers in 1435. NATHAN BEN MAIMON (15th century) was rabbi in Constantine and corresponded with Solomon b. Simeon Duran. JUDAH BEN JACOB (d. 1830), talmudist, author, and *dayyan* in Tunis, wrote the following works: *Limmudei ha-Shem* (Leghorn, 1787), on hermeneutics in the Talmud; *Alfei Yehudah* (Leghorn, 1794), a commentary on *Shevuot; Shevet Yehudah* (Leghorn, 1801), a commentary on the *Mekhilta; Simḥat Yehudah* (Pisa, 1816), on *Keritot, Soferim,* and *Semaḥot; Ḥayyei Yehudah* (Pisa, 1816), on *Gerim, Avadim,* and *Kuttim;* and *Oholei Yehudah* (Leghorn, 1823), on the *Sifrei*. DAVID (early 19th century) was a rabbi in Tunis and wrote *Ẓemaḥ David,* which was published posthumously with Judah Cohen *Tanudji's *Admat Yehudah* (Leghorn, 1828) and contains novellae on tractates of the Talmud and on parts of Maimonides' *Yad ha-Ḥazakah*.

Bibliography: D. Cazès, *Notes Bibliographiques . . .* (1893), s.v.; I. Epstein, *'Responsa' of . . . Rabbi Simon b. Ẓemaḥ Duran . . .* (1930, 1968²), 94–96; A. M. Hershman, *Rabbi Isaac ben Sheshet Perfet and his Times* (1943), 53, 185.

[ED.]

NAJARA, family of rabbis and kabbalists in Ereẓ Israel and Syria, originating from the town of Nájera in Spain. Apparently, the head of the family LEVI NAJARA settled in Constantinople after the expulsion from Spain (1492). His son MOSES (1) (1508?–1581), rabbi and kabbalist, lived in Damascus and in Safed. Apparently before 1546, he served as a rabbi in Damascus and corresponded with Moses di *Trani. He remained in Damascus until after 1555. He spent some time in Safed as a student of Isaac *Luria and wrote a commentary on the Torah, *Lekaḥ Tov* (Constantinople, 1571). *Sha'ar ha-Kelalim*, published in the beginning of *Eẓ Ḥayyim* of Ḥayyim *Vital, is attributed to Najara in several manuscripts. Different discourses on Lurianic Kabbalah are found in his name in manuscripts and in published works of Ḥayyim Vital. According to Shabbatean tradition, Baruchia (Russo), the head of the Shabbateans in Salonika, is reputed to have been a reincarnation of Maharam Nayar, i.e., Moses Najara. In his last years he continued to serve as rabbi in Damascus, where he died. His son was the distinguished poet Israel *Najara. The son of Israel, MOSES (2), succeeded his father as the head of the Jewish community in Gaza, according to David Conforte (*Kore ha-Dorot*, 49b), who passed through Gaza in 1645 and studied Torah with Najara. Kabbalistic sermons preserved in manuscript were attributed to him but it is possible that they were written by his grandfather, Moses Najara (1). JACOB, his son, who succeeded Moses (2), is known to have been a fervent believer in *Shabbetai Ẓevi. When Shabbetai Ẓevi reached Gaza in 1665, he stayed with Najara, whom he appointed "High Priest," although Najara was not of a priestly family *(kohen)*. In 1666 Jacob Najara sent propagandistic letters abroad supporting the messianism of Shabbetai Ẓevi and the prophecy of *Nathan of Gaza. Even after Shabbetai Ẓevi's apostasy, Najara believed in him and visited him in Adrianople in 1671 (*Sefunot*, 5 (1961), 254–61). MOSES (3), apparently a member of this family, may have been a rabbinic emissary. Between 1760 and 1790 he was one of the rabbis in Debdou, in eastern Morocco. JUDAH NAJARA, a rabbi in Constantinople, may also have been a member of this family.

Bibliography: Neubauer, Chronicles, 1 (1887), 151, 153; Rosanes, Togarmah, 3 (1938), 218–9; 4 (1935), 357; G. Scholem, *Kitvei Yad ba-Kabbalah* (1930), 127; idem, in: *Zion*, 6 (1940/41), 129; Scholem, Shabbetai Ẓevi, 1 (1967), index; J. M. Toledano, *Sarid u-Falit* (1945), 73–74; I. Ben-Zvi, *She'ar Yashuv* (1966), 378.

[A.D.]

NAJARA, ISRAEL BEN MOSES (1555?–1625?), Hebrew poet. Born apparently in Damascus, Israel served as secretary of that community in which his father, Moses Najara, was rabbi (see *Najara family). While acknowledging Israel's poetic ability, some of the rabbis of Damascus, e.g., Menahem *Lonzano and Ḥayyim *Vital, spoke disparagingly of his unconventional conduct and of his imitation of foreign poetic styles and melodies, acquired it seems, in Arab taverns. His conduct may also account for his many wanderings. In 1587 Israel published his books *Zemirot Yisrael* and *Mesaḥeket ba-Tevel* in Safed. One of his responsa is preserved in manuscript (Oxford, Mich. Add. 66). Subsequently, he served as rabbi in Gaza, where, upon his death, his son Moses succeeded him as rabbi. Though during his youth Israel also wrote secular and love poems, his chief compositions are sacred. These are distinguished by their deep religiosity, by their references to Jewish suffering, and by his yearning for redemption. He learned much from the great Jewish poets of the Spanish-Arabic period, but nevertheless frequently employed original forms and contents. His poems, numbering hundreds—the greater part still in manuscript—are outstanding in both their wealth of language and in their polished style. His poems and *piyyutim* achieved wide circulation among the various oriental communities and countries and are sung in those synagogues. The Ashkenazi communities also adopted his Sabbath song, written in Aramaic, **Yah Ribbon Olam ve-Alemayya* ("God of the world, eternity's sole Lord"). Well known, too, is his *Ketubbah le-Ḥag ha-Shavu'ot* ("Marriage Contract for Shavuot"), a poetic parody describing the wedding conditions made between Israel and God, read in many oriental communities on Shavuot. The Shabbateans and Frankists highly respected him, mistakenly regarding him as a kabbalist. They were so fond of one of his poems that they made it a hymn.

Israel's works are: *Zemirot Yisrael* (Safed, 1587), 109 poems; second edition (Salonika, 1594); third edition enlarged (Venice, 1599–1600), 346 poems and a scientific edition pointed by A. Avrunin and edited by I. Pris-Ḥorev (1946); *Mesaḥeket ba-Tevel* (Safed, 1587), moral instruction in a rhetorical style similar to that of the *Beḥinat Olam* of *Jedaiah ha-Penini Bedersi; *Meimei Yisrael*, rhetorical letters with secular and love poems, composed during his youth and appended to the third edition of his *Zemirot Yisrael; Keli Maḥazik Berakhah* (Venice, 1620), laws of grace after meals; *Shoḥatei ha-Yeladim* (Amsterdam, 1718), laws of slaughtering in an easy language comprehensible even to children; *Pizmonim* (1858), 120 poems; *She'erit Yisrael* (in Mss.), a large collection of poems, many of which have been published by various scholars; *Pizei Ohev* (Constantinople? 1597?) a commentary on the Book of Job. Some other of his works are known but not extant: *Ma'arekhot Yisrael*, a commentary to the Torah; *Mikveh Yisrael*, homilies.

Bibliography: Davidson, Oẓar, 4 (1933), 426–9; idem, *Parody in Jewish Literature* (1907), 34–36; idem, in: *Sefer ha-Yovel... S. Krauss* (1937), 193–270; idem, in: *Sefer ha-Shanah li-Yhudei Amerikah*, 4 (1939), 282–94; A. Ben-Yisrael, *Shirat ha-Ḥen* (1918), 23–58; M. D. Gaon, in: *Mizraḥ u-Ma'arav*, 5 (1930–32), 145–63; D. Yellin, in: *Jewish Studies... G. A. Kohut* (1935), 59–88 (Heb. pt.); I. Mendelson, in: *Horeb*, 9 (1946), 50–58; A. Mirsky, in: *Sefer Ish ha-Torah ve-ha-Ma'aseh .·. M. Ostrowsky* (1946), 125–32; idem, in: KS, 25 (1948/49), 39–47; idem, in: *Sefunot*, 5 (1961), 207–34; 6 (1962), 259–302; G. Scholem, in: *I. Goldziher Memorial Volume*, 1 (1948), 41–44 (Heb. pt.); idem, in: *Beḥinot*, 8 (1955), 85–86; Zinberg, Sifrut, 3 (1958), 84–100, 373–80; Waxman, Literature, 2 (1960), 93–97; H. Avenary, in: *Divrei ha-Congress ha-Olami ha-Revi'i le-Madda'ei ha-Yahadut*, 2 (1968), 383–4.

[A.D.]

NAJDORF, MIKHAIL (1910–), Argentinian chess grand master. Najdorf was born in Warsaw, and was noted as a talented player before World War II. At the outbreak of the war he was in Buenos Aires. There he adopted Argentine nationality and developed his chess prowess. Between 1943 and 1965 he won many international tournaments. He played well in Candidates' tournaments, in 1950 and 1953. Najdorf was noted for some extraordinary feats of simultaneous play. At São Paulo in 1950 he played 250 boards, winning 226 and drawing 15. His blindfold exhibitions were also impressive. At one time he held the record of 40 such games played simultaneously.

[G.A.]

NAJDUS, LEIB (1890–1918), Yiddish poet. Born in Grodno, Poland, he began publishing poems in Yiddish periodicals at the age of 17, and his first book of lyric poems (1915) revealed virtuosity in a variety of verse forms. His rhythms and rhymes display technical perfection; some of his poems were set to music. After his premature death, his friend Abraham Zak collected and edited his works in six volumes (1923–26), including two volumes of translations of European poets, primarily Russian and French.

Bibliography: Rejzen, Leksikon, 2 (1927), 552–61; LNYL, 6 (1965), 213–8; Rozansky, in: L. Najdus, *Geklibene Verk* (1958), introd.; J. Glatstein, *In Tokh Genumen* (1963), 147–54; A. Zak, *In Kinigraykh fun Yidishn Vort* (1966), 28–51; E. H. Jeshurin, *Leib Najdus Bibliography* (1962).

[M.Rav.]

NÁJERA (Najara, Nagara, Naiera), city in Castile, N. Spain. It had an old and important community which maintained relations with the Babylonian *geonim*. Letters from the community have been found in the Cairo **Genizah*. As early as the beginning of the 11th century, the community enjoyed a *fuero* ("municipal charter"), which later served as a model for similar grants of privileges to other localities. The blood price for a Jew as specified in the charter was equal to that paid for killing a knight or a member of the clergy. The charter was ratified in 1136 by Alfonso VII, and in the 13th century was included in the *fuero* of Castile. The Jewish quarter of Nájera was located near the city wall and the marketplace in the southern part of the city, and remains of the synagogue have been discovered there. The Jews of Nájera owned land and vineyards in the vicinity of the city. The importance of the community toward the end of the 13th century is shown by the tax levied upon it, which amounted in 1290 to 30,318 (according to another source 24,106) maravedis. In 1360, during the civil war between Peter the Cruel and Henry of Trastamara, Henry's supporters attacked the Jews in Nájera and many were killed. The community suffered once more at the time of Peter's victory over Henry in 1367 near Nájera. During the 15th century the position of the community in Nájera, as well as of the others in the kingdom, deteriorated, although at the beginning of the century some Jews still owned land and real estate in the old city. During the war against Granada a special levy of 18½ gold castellanos was imposed on the Jews of Nájera, San Millán de la Cogolla, and Cañas. No details are known about the fate of the community at the time of the expulsion of the Jews from Spain in 1492.

Bibliography: Baer, Spain, 1 (1961), 43, 53, 366; Baer, Urkunden, index; F. Cantera, *Sinagogas españolas* (1955), 252–3; idem, in: *Sefarad*, 2 (1942), 326; 22 (1962), 89; L. Serrano, *Cartulario de San Millán de Cogolla* (1930), 219; J. González, *El Reino de Castilla en la época de Alfonso VIII* (1960), 132; F. Cantera Orive, *Un cartulario de Santa María la Real de Nájera del año 1209* (1960); Suárez Fernández, Documentos, 69, 76, 101; Ashtor, Korot, 2 (1966), 20; Ashtor, in: *Sefarad*, 24 (1964), 44ff.

[H.B.]

NAJĪB AL-DAWLA (d. c. 1315), court physician and administrator at the court of the Il-Khāns in Persia at the end of the 13th century and beginning of the 14th century. Najīb al-Dawla was closely associated with the Jewish vizier *Saʿd al-Dawla, and with the court physician, vizier, and historian Rashīd al-Dīn (of Jewish origin, according to some sources). He seemed also to have been for some time governor of the city of Nubandagan, near Shiraz in Persia.

Bibliography: Fischel, Islam, 105; B. Spuler, *Mongolen in Iran* (1968^3), index.

[W.J.F.]

NAJRAN, chain of fertile oases and a town in N. *Yemen. A Jewish community made up of both merchants and farmers existed in Najran long before the influx in the fifth century of Christians, who were mostly Monophysites from al-*Hira. Najran became the center of Christian propaganda in southern Arabia. The persecution of the Christians of Najran by the Jewish proselyte king of *Himyar, *Yusuf Dhu Nuwas, in about 523, is recorded in Greek, Syriac, and Ethiopic Christian literature. Their martyrdom is still commemorated by the Eastern churches. The Ethiopians, aided by Justinian to some extent, wrested control of the town from Dhu Nuwas and the Himyarites. Nonetheless, Jews continued to live in Najran, maintaining their former status. Muhammad guaranteed the Christians rights in Najran, as they quickly made an agreement with him which was confirmed by his successors Abu Bakr and Omar I. Jewish communities continued to exist in Yemen and possibly in Najran.

Contemporary Period. According to Yemenite Jewish tradition, the Jews of Najran trace their origin to the Ten Tribes. They lived in the region of Najran in Saudi Arabia and were the only group of Yemenite Jews who lived outside Yemen under the rule of another kingdom. On the strength of the laws of the desert and tribal protections, they were not subjected to persecution as were the Jews of Yemen. They enjoyed the same equality of rights as the Arabs of Saudi Arabia, were not taxed, and did not pay the *jizya* (the poll tax imposed on non-Muslims in the Muslim countries "in exchange for the protection" granted them by the government). The Bedouin of Saudi Arabia, who belonged to the Sunni Islam sect, practiced religious tolerance toward them and ate meat slaughtered under their laws of *sheḥitah*. The Jews of Najran carried weapons in self-defense, as did the other inhabitants, and were renowned for their courage and strength. There was no other place in the Arabian peninsula where Jews lived in such dignity and freedom as in Najran.

By profession they were craftsmen: they worked essentially in goldsmithing and repairing arms. They earned a good livelihood and their material condition surpassed that of the Yemenite Jews. Their settlements were scattered throughout Najran in small units of two to 40 families. They lived in clay houses or in huts. Their dress, both of the men and the women, was slightly different from that of the Saudi Arabians and the Yemenite Jews. The strict barrier between men and women which was customary in social life throughout Yemen was nonexistent among them. At festivities and celebrations men and women sat together and women danced to the sound of the men's singing. Their relations with the Yemenite Jews were not very close because the two groups were under the rule of different kingdoms—Yemen and Saudi Arabia—which occasionally were at war with each other.

The life of the Jews of Najran, dispersed as they were in small settlements, did not encourage the development of Torah studies among them or the fostering of an independent spiritual culture. In matters of religion and *halakhah* they were dependent on the community of nearby Saʿda (one day away from them), and when necessary, on the *bet din* of Sanʿa. The Jews of Saʿda served as their spiritual guardians in times of need: they provided them with religious books and guided them in their religious practices. Therefore, their prayers, customs, and system of study were very closely related. In Israel they are concentrated in Kiryat Ekron, which is inhabited by the Jews of Saʿda. When the Jews of Najran immigrated to Israel in 1949, they numbered about 250.

Bibliography: S. D. Goitein, *Travels in Yemen* . . . (1941, index; De L. E. O'Leary, *Arabia before Muhammad* (1927), 143f.; A. Moberg, *Book of the Himyarite* (1924), index; H. Z. Hirschberg, *Yisrael ba-Arav* (1946), 63ff.; 80ff.; EIS, s.v.; J. Rickmans, *La Persécution des Chrétiens Himyarites au Sixième Siècle* (1956).
[Y.R.]

NAKDIMON BEN GURYON (first century C.E.), one of three celebrated wealthy men of Jerusalem during the last years of the Second Temple. Like his affluent associates *Ben Ẓiẓit ha-Kassaf and *Ben Kalba Savu'a Nakdimon studied under the rabbis and was highly regarded by *Johanan b. Zakkai (cf. PdRE 2). Legendary accounts are given of his wealth and philanthropy. On his daily journey to the house of study (the texts of that period often confuse the house of study with the Temple), he had the whole way covered with woolen carpets which he left lying there for the poor to take (Ket. 66b). Other accounts speak of his daughter's excessive use of cosmetics *(ibid.)* and his daughter-in-law's expenditure on her kitchen (Ket. 65a). He was also regarded as a wonder-worker. During a water shortage he borrowed 12 cisterns filled with water from a wealthy Roman official on condition that by a certain day he would either return the cisterns full of water or pay 12 silver talents. On the evening of the last day of the appointed time, in answer to his prayers, rain fell and filled the cisterns. When the Roman objected that the sun had already set and the appointed time had passed, Nakdimon caused the sun to shine by means of his prayer (Ta'an. 19b). During the siege of Jerusalem, he and his two associates promised to supply the city for 21 years with all necessary provisions. The Zealots, however, burned all the provisions so that need would induce the people to fight against the Romans (Git. 56a). With the fall of Jerusalem, Nakdimon lost all his wealth, and Johanan b. Zakkai met his daughter (Miriam; Lam. R. 1:16, no. 48) picking out barley corns from cattle dung (Ket. 66b; Lam.R. *ibid.*). According to a talmudic tradition his proper name was not Nakdimon but Boni (Ta'an. 20a). The *aggadot* concerning Nakdimon preserve traditions about the mode of life of the upper classes of Jerusalem society on the eve of the Jewish War and during the generation of destruction.

Bibliography: Hyman, Toledot, 948–9.
[D.J.B.]

NAME, CHANGE OF. The Bible records changing of names as symbolic of a new status or destiny e.g., Abraham (Gen. 17:5), Sarah (*ibid.* 15), Jacob (*ibid.* 32:38), and Joshua (Num. 13:16). Basing itself upon this precedent the Talmud declares that among the "four things that cancel the doom of man" is change of name (RH 16b). From this there developed in the Middle Ages the custom of changing, or more accurately giving an additional name to, the name of a person who was dangerously ill, or suffered some other misfortune, in the belief that the Angel of Death would be confused as a result of the new name. This new name was sometimes chosen by opening a Bible at random and selecting a name which occurred there, except for such names of ill repute as Esau or Korah. The most widespread custom however, which persists to the present day, was to choose auspicious names such as Ḥayyim or, among the Sephardim Ḥai (Life), Raphael (may God heal), Hezekiah (may God give strength) for males, and Ḥayyah for females. (The name Alter (old) was frequently given to a boy if several children in the family had died during infancy, this name being regarded as a good omen that he should reach old age.) In the Ashkenazi rite the change of name is effected by pronouncing a special **Mi she-Berakh* prayer which contains the following passage: "Just as his [her] name has been changed, so may the evil decree passed on him [her] be changed from justice to mercy, from death to life, from illness to a complete cure." The Sephardi rite has a different formula.

The new name given to a person is henceforth used in addition to his former name (e.g., Ḥayyim Abraham) for all religious purposes (e.g., to be called up to the Torah, in a bill of divorce, on the tombstone, etc.).

Bibliography: L. Zunz, *Namen der Juden* (1837), 51; H. E. Goldin, *Ha-Madrikh: The Rabbi's Guide* (1939), 103ff.; J. Trachtenberg, *Jewish Magic and Superstition* (1961²), 204–6.
[ED.]

NAMÉNYI, ERNEST (Ernö; 1888–1957), Hungarian art historian, economist, and writer. Born in Nagykanizsa, Naményi was the son of Rabbi Ede Neumann. He studied in Budapest and in Brussels, and after he received his doctorate in law was appointed a research associate in the Institut de Sociologie Solvay from 1911 to 1914. He specialized in banking with his uncle, P. *Philipson, the noted banker. With the outbreak of World War I he returned to Hungary, and from 1916 to 1949 served as the secretary and later the director of Országos Iparegyesület ("National Industrial Association"). He published economic and sociological articles in Hungarian and French. He also did research in Jewish art, which he felt was an educational means of striving for aesthetics and ethics in Judaism. This outlook led him to found the Jewish Liberal program movement known as "Ézsajás Vallásos Társaság" ("Isaiah Religious Society"). He was among the leaders of the Jewish Museum, and from 1942 served as its director and from 1947 as chairman, succeeding in collecting for it the best works of Jewish artists in and out of Hungary. He also worked for the central Jewish library, which included the remnants of both public and private Jewish libraries, and these collections were housed in the Rabbinical Seminary in Budapest. When the journal *Libanon* was transferred to the Jewish Museum, Naményi participated in its editing until 1944. Together with P. Gruenwald, he wrote the history of the synagogues in Budapest, *Budapesti zsinagógák* ("Synagogues of Budapest," 1949). In 1949 he emigrated to Paris, where he devoted himself to literary work exclusively in the field of Jewish art. He also published two essays on Jewish art in: C. Roth, ed., *Jewish Art* (1961), 423–54; 575–638. His last book was *L'Esprit de l'Art Juif* (1957; *The Essence of Jewish Art,* 1960).

Bibliography: *Libanon,* 8 (1943), 107–11 (Hung.). [B.Y.]

NAMES.

In the Bible. Biblical proper names, together with proper names in Old South Arabic, Canaanite (East- or Proto-Canaanite, Ugaritic, and Phoenician), Old Aramaic, Akkadian, and—with some reservations—Old Egyptian, comprise one division of the Semitic onomasticon. Within this division, the Hebrew names have particularly archaic traits. In this respect they are connected with Old South Arabic, East- or Proto-Canaanite, and Ugaritic proper names, and are distinguished from the Akkadian and Old Egyptian names, whose development led them away from the early Semitic type of naming (cf. Stamm, in *Fourth World Congress . . .,* 141–7).

The most important source for Hebrew proper names is the Bible. In addition to individual proper names found throughout the Bible, biblical genealogies from early and late times also offer numerous examples. Other sources of Hebrew names are Palestinian inscriptions (ostraca and seals), the Elephantine Papyri, and Babylonian clay tablets from the Persian period.

In Hebrew, as in old Semitic generally, two forms of proper names are to be distinguished: propositional names and epithetic names. Propositional names can be classified as either verbal or nominal sentences. A separate group is constituted by the very numerous short names, which cannot be taken into consideration here (see Noth, in bibl., p. 36ff.).

In addition to these formal criteria, another distinction, relating more to content, is that between theophoric and secular proper names.

The predicate of the (theophoric) verbal propositional names is generally in the perfect or imperfect tense. In contrast to the Akkadian, the use of the imperative mood, directed either to the divinity or to the environment, is rare. Late names such as עֲשִׂיאֵל (Asiel, "Do it, O God!") and חֲזִיאֵל (Haziel, "Look, O God!") may be considered as belonging to the former, and רְאוּבֵן (Reuben, "See, a son!"; cf. also Noth, in bibl., p. 32, and Stamm, op. cit., p. 142), as belonging to the latter.

In the perfect-tense names the "predicate-subject" type (e.g., נְתַנְאֵל, Nethanel) is, according to Hebrew syntax, on the whole more frequent than the inverse, i.e., "subject-predicate" (e.g., אֶלְנָתָן, Elnathan; cf. Noth, in bibl., pp. 20–21). The meaning of these names is expressed by the use of the past tense: they signify thanksgiving for an act of charity bestowed by the divine (e.g., "God has given").

In names formed with the imperfect tense, the "subject-predicate" type is hardly represented. This type appears only in the later monarchical and the post-Exilic periods (יְהוֹיָכִין, Jehoiachin; cf. Noth, in bibl., p. 28). On the other hand, the "predicate-subject" type is much more frequent (יְכוֹנְיָה, Jeconiah). Certain of the oldest proper names are of this type, some appearing as abridged forms not containing the word אֵל of the complete form. Examples of these are: יִצְחָק (Isaac), יַעֲקֹב (Jacob), יִשְׂרָאֵל (Israel), יוֹסֵף (Joseph), and יְרַחְמְאֵל (Jerahmeel). This type occurs more often in the periods of Moses and the Judges. It becomes scarcer during the Davidic period, almost disappearing, but regaining favor shortly before the Exile and in post-Exilic times (cf. Noth, loc. cit.).

As the Hebrew imperfect tense is both preterit and jussive in character, its meaning in proper names is disputed. Noth, probably because he believed that the perfect expresses the past tense unequivocally, preferred the jussive interpretation for the imperfect, as expressing a wish. Several proper names, which certainly contain such wishes, e.g., יְחִיָּה, יְחִיאֵל (Jehiel, Jehiah, "may he live, O God/YHWH!"), יוֹסֵף (Joseph, "may he [God] add!"), and יַחְדִּיאֵל, יֶחְדְּיָהוּ (Jahdiel, Jehdeiah, "may he rejoice, O God/YHWH!"), can be quoted in support of this theory. In opposition to it, however, there are to be found names which are vocalized not as jussive forms but as statements, such as אֶלְיָקִים (Eliakim, "God had made [the deceased] stand up again"), אֶלְיָשִׁיב (Eliashib, "God has brought back [the deceased]"), and יָעִיר (Jair, "He has protected"; for the translation of this name on the basis of the Ugaritic and Hebrew (Deut. 32:11a; Job 8:6b; root *ʿyr/ʿwr*) see Stamm, in: *Studies . . . B. Landsberger . . .,* p. 421a). It should, therefore, be taken into account that the imperfect tense should be rendered in proper names, as in general usage, sometimes as a statement, sometimes as a wish. It is not always easy to decide which of these it is, and the subject warrants further investigation. It appears that the past tense is to be preferred for the oldest names, whereas in the case of the later names the jussive is also to be considered (cf. Stamm, *ibid.,* pp. 414–5; Stamm, in: *Fourth World Congress . . .,* p. 142).

The content of theophoric propositional names is that the divinity: 1) has given, created/made, or added the child named; 2) has granted, helped, saved, and had mercy, spared, restored justice, and cured, or that it may do so. Whereas in Akkadian the content of groups 1 and 2 both refer to the child named, insofar as it is not only the object of divine gift and creation but also of mercy and salvation (cf. J. J. Stamm, *Die akkadische Namesgebung* (1939), 23ff.), this is not the case in Hebrew. Here, naturally, the content of group 1 also refers to the child; however, the content of group 2 refers to the parents. They are the ones whose prayer was granted or to whom justice was done. This is explained in the interpretation of names in the Bible (Gen. 29:31–30:24; Ex. 2:10, 22; I Sam. 1:27–28). This may well have been the case originally, while the situation in Akkadian (and in Egyptian) may represent a modernization which might have taken place under the influence of liturgical literature.

Such a modernization can also be seen in the fact that in Akkadian and Egyptian there exist propositional names with a suffix indicating the child named. Thus there are in Akkadian (for Egyptian, see J. J. Stamm, in: *Die Welt des Orients* (1955), 111–9), besides Išme-^{d}Adad ("Adad has hearkened"), the forms Ili-išmeanni ("My God has hearkened to me") and Ištar-išmēšu ("Ishtar has hearkened to him"; cf. also Stamm, in: *Fourth World Congress . . .,* 145). Hebrew, on the other hand, has nothing but נְתַנְאֵל נְתַנְיָה(וּ) (Nethanel, Nethaniah(u), "God/YHWH has given") and יִשְׁמָעֵאל, שְׁמַעְיָה(וּ) (Ishmael, Shemaiah(u), "God/YHWH has granted"). This concise, coined form dominates also in corresponding names in Old South Arabic, and with a few exceptions, also in Ugaritic-Canaanite (cf. Stamm, in: *Fourth World Congress . . .,* pp. 143–4).

In (theophoric) nominal propositional names, the first remarkable trait is that, unlike the Akkadian, those names containing a participle are scarce and of rather late origin. The only biblical examples are: מְשֵׁיזַבְאֵל (Meshezabel), מְהֵיטַבְאֵל (Mehetabel), מַהֲלַלְאֵל (Mahalalel), מְשֶׁלֶמְיָה(וּ) (Meshelemiah(u)). Very common, on the contrary, are the so-called "names of reliance," consisting of a theophoric element and an appellative, such as אֵלִיָּה(וּ) (Elijah(u), "YHWH is my God") and עֻזִּיאֵל, עֻזִּיָּה(וּ) (Uzziel, Uzziah(u), "God is my strength"). In these, the possessive "my" can refer both to the giver of the name and to its bearer. It expresses a personal utterance which the father or mother pronounces at first for the child, until the child is able to make it his own. Besides the forms containing the suffix of the first person singular there are also forms which are suffixless and, therefore, do not contain any reference to the speaker. Examples of the latter are: יוֹאָב (Joab), יוֹאָח (Joah), יוֹאֵל (Joel), יוֹעֶזֶר (Joezer); ("YHWH is father/brother/God/help"). Again, in contrast to Akkadian and Egyptian, there are no forms with a suffix of the third person singular ("YHWH is his/her father"). The suffix of the first person plural occurs only in the cry for salvation, which later became a name, עִמָּנוּאֵל (Immanuel), and in the messianic name, ה׳ צִדְקֵנוּ (Jer. 23:6).

Theophoric epithetic names are not particularly common in Hebrew, a fact which is related to the absence of the following type, common in Akkadian and Egyptian: "son/daughter of divinity X." The most popular names in this category are those constructed with עֶבֶד (*ʿeved*, "slave"), e.g., עַבְדִּיאֵל (Abdiel, "God's slave") and עֹבַדְיָה(וּ) (Obadiah(u), "[small] slave of YHWH"; cf. further Noth, in bibl., pp. 135–9).

In the above-mentioned name groups, the most frequently occurring theophoric elements are אֵל (*ʾel*) and the tetragrammaton, the latter always used in abridged form, namely, יְהוֹ (*yeho*) and יוֹ (*yo*) at the beginning, יָהוּ (*yahu*) and יָה (*yah*) at the end, of the word. The first personal name that was definitely constructed with the tetragrammaton is יְהוֹשֻׁעַ (Joshua). The name of Moses' mother, יוֹכֶבֶד (Jochebed), is more ancient, but it is extremely questionable if it really contains the biblical divine name; as for יְהוּדָה (Judah), it is certain that it does not contain the divine name. From the period of the Judges, five personal names belonging to this group, יוֹאָשׁ (Joash), יוֹתָם (Jotham), מִיכָיָה(וּ) (Micaiah(u), יְהוֹנָתָן (Jonathan), and יוֹאֵל (Joel) should be mentioned. During the monarchical period, names of this group became frequent and dominant and even retained their lasting predominance—together with those containing the theophoric אֵל (*ʾel*)—afterward. אֵל (*ʾel*) is common in personal names up to the beginning of the monarchical period, during which time it fell into almost complete disuse, reappearing again and becoming more frequent from the seventh century onward, and remaining common after the Exile (see Gray, in bibl., pp. 166ff.; Noth, in bibl., pp. 82ff.).

With other old Semitic personal names, especially South Arabic and Proto- or East-Canaanite, Hebrew names have in common the particularity that terms of kinship can take the place of the theophoric element. These are terms like אָב (*ʾav*, "father"), אָח (*ʾaḥ*, "brother"), and עַם (*ʿam*, "paternal uncle"), thus, for instance, אֲבִירָם (Abiram), אֲחִיטוּב (Ahitub), and עַמְרָם (Amram; for other examples, see Noth, in bibl., pp. 66ff.; Stamm, in: *Studies . . . B. Landsberger . . .*, pp. 416ff.). These names have their origin in the early Semitic and nomadic conceptions of tribal and clan structure, according to which deceased relatives enjoyed the divine privilege of being worshiped. In Israel, after the Conquest, this belief became extinct. If corresponding names continued to be used, this was undoubtedly based on the supposition that terms denoting kinship could be assimilated to YHWH. However, not all of these originally had a theophoric meaning. There exist those in which אָב (*ʾav*), אָח (*ʾaḥ*), and עַם (*ʿam*) designate the (deceased) father, brother, or uncle of the one named. These are the so-called substitute names (see below). (On the problem of distinguishing these secular names from the theophoric, see Stamm, in: *Studies . . . B. Landsberger . . .*, p. 418.)

Other words, some of which are very ancient, which can be used in a theophoric sense in names are: צוּר (*ẓur*, "Rock"), שַׁדַּי (*shaddai*, "the Almighty"), אָדוֹן (*ʾadon*, "Lord"), בַּעַל (*baʿal*, "Possessor/Lord"), and מֶלֶךְ (*melekh*, "king"; cf. Noth, in bibl., pp. 114ff.).

Secular epithetic names have in Hebrew, as in related languages—particularly Akkadian and Egyptian, the most diverse and disparate contents. These retain the day of birth (חַגַּי, Haggai, "he who was born on the festival"), or the origin (יְהוּדִי, Jehudi, "the Judean"), or the position within the family (בְּכוֹרַת, Becorath, "firstborn"). Other proper names give expression either to the relationship between the child and his parents, or to their joy, such as יְדִידָה (Jedidah, "the loved one") and שִׁמְשׁוֹן (Samson, "little sun"). Also frequent are names given on the basis of particularly distinctive physical traits or flaws, e.g., לָבָן/לִבְנִי (Laban/Libni, "white," probably after the color of the skin, particularly of the face), גָּדוֹל ("tall"; a proper name from Elephantine), הַקָּטָן/צוּעָר (Hakkatan/Ẓuar, "[the] small one"), בַּרְזִלַּי (Barziilai, "as hard as iron"), and קָרֵחַ/קֹרַח (Kareah/Korah, "the bald headed"; for other examples see Noth, in bibl., pp. 221ff.). In addition, names of animals and plants are not infrequent as proper names.

Two other groups of names which should be mentioned specially are substitute names, names in which expression is given, in some manner, to the view that the bearer of the name reincarnates a deceased relative, or that the latter has returned to life in, or through, the former, and women's names. This is an ancient idea which has its roots in the conception of tribal and clan structure and which does not presuppose the belief in the transmigration of souls. Parallel forms to this category of proper names can be found in many peoples; among the Semitic peoples they are particularly numerous with the Babylonians and the Egyptians.

Most groups which occur in other proper names can be found also among the substitute names. Only a few examples of each will be given here (for further illustration of the subject see Stamm, in: *Studies . . . B. Landsberger . . .*, 213–24): Verbal proposition (secular): יָשָׁבְעָם (Jashobeam, "the uncle has come back"), יָשׁוּב (Jashub, "he [the deceased] has returned"). Verbal proposition (theophoric): אֶלְיָקִים (Eliakim), אֶלְיָשִׁיב (Eliashib), and יָעִיר (Jair, see above). Nominal proposition: אֲבִירָם (Abiram), עַמְרָם (Amram; "the father/uncle is great"), and אֲבִיהוּד (Abihud), אֲחִיהוּד (Ahihud), עַמִּיהוּד (Ammihud; "my father/brother/uncle is splendor"). In these proper names the praise of the deceased simultaneously keeps his memory alive.

A form which cannot be found outside this category of substitute names is represented by those uttering, in the sense of a complaint, the quest after the deceased, thus אִיכָבוֹד (Ichabod) and אֵהוּד (Ehud; "where is the glory?"), also אִיזֶבֶל (Jezebel; "where is nobility?"), and אִיעֶזֶר (Iezer; "where is help?"). The interrogative particle *ai/e/i*, used in all these names, may also be discerned in אִיּוֹב (Job; "where is the father?").

In the epithetic names, the child either simply bears the epithet of the relative whom he replaces, thus אַחְאָב (Ahab; "father's brother"), or is named after the function which devolves to him as substitute, מְשֻׁלָּם (Meshullam, "the replaced"), מְנַחֵם (Menahem, "one that consoles"), and מְנַשֶּׁה (Manasseh, "he who makes forget").

As for women's names, the theophoric ones are relatively scarce. Much more frequent are the secular ones, i.e., designations based on the time of birth, or the origin of the bearer (of the name), on a characteristic physical or spiritual quality, or the relationship with the parents. Names of jewels, plants, and animals are also used as women's names (for details, see Stamm, in: VTS, 16, where the question as to the reasons for the relative scarceness of theophoric women's names also is raised).

[J.J.St.]

Hypocoristica, or shortened names, were common, and

were formed in various ways (see Noth, Personennamen, 36–41). Very common, especially in later times, was the formation *qattūl*, as in זַכּוּר (Zakkur) for זְכַרְיָה (Zechariah), חַשּׁוּב for חֲשַׁבְיָה, נַחוּם for נְחֶמְיָה etc. At Elephantine we even find הצול, Haẓẓūl, for הצליה and יחמול, Yaḥmūl, for יחמליה, so that the Elephantine name גדול, which was interpreted above as the adjective *gadol*, "large," is more probably to be read Gaddūl as a hypocoristicon of גְּדַלְיָה, Gedaliah. [H.L.G.]

In the Talmud. Insofar as names are concerned the talmudic literature covers a period of some 700 years, from the time of Simeon the Just (c. 200 B.C.E.) to 500 C.E. A distinction must be made between fact and homiletical propaganda. Thus, the often repeated statement giving one of the causes of the deliverance of the Children of Israel from bondage as "they did not change their names" (e.g., Lev. R. 32:5) is certainly to be viewed as a homily appealing for the retention or giving of Hebrew names, in view of the prevalent tendency of adopting foreign names. It is in this light that the interesting equivalents, Rofe (Rufus?) for Judah, Luliani (Julianus?) for Reuben, Lestim (Justus?) for Joseph, and Aleksandri for Benjamin, quoted there are to be regarded. Zunz, somewhat casuistically, suggests that these passages are to be understood as referring specifically to the change from a Hebrew name already given to a gentile name, a custom which was disapproved of as a sign of deliberate assimilation, but not to the initial granting of non-Jewish names. To be regarded in a similar light is the Targum to Amos 6:1 which renders *nekuvei reshit ha-goyim* "they give their children the same names as do gentiles." The Talmud states only that "the majority of Jews in the Diaspora have the same names as the gentiles" (Git. 11b; in Babylonia only names of idols were avoided—Git. 11a; the name Tammuza (Judah b. Tammuza; TJ, Meg. 4:5, 75b) is not evidence of the adoption of the name of the god Tammuz (= Adonis), since Tammuz had already become Hebraized as the name of the Hebrew month, cf. Dosa b. Tevet, Song R. 7:8). However, the evidence of the widespread use of non-Jewish names also in Ereẓ Israel is too obvious to be overlooked.

All the characteristics and permutations of names which are found in later generations are found among the names of the rabbis. Examples of almost every type of nomenclature can be found in the short list of the *zugot (including their fathers) as they appear in the first chapter of *Avot*. They include purely traditional biblical names, such as Simeon (see later), Joshua, and Judah; Hebrew names which are not those of biblical worthies, though they occur there, such as Hillel, Gamaliel, Johanan, and Joezer; purely Greek names such as Antigonus (in the generation immediately after Alexander the Great; cogent evidence of the rapidity of the social assimilation in nomenclature) and Avtalyon; and Aramaized forms of Hebrew names, such as Yose (twice) for Joseph, Tabbai (probably for Tobiah), and what appears to be a purely Aramaic name, Nittai. Of special interest are purely Hebrew names which do not occur in the Bible, such as Peraḥyah and (probably) Shetaḥ.

With few exceptions, all other names fall into those categories. The only forms missing are Greek names which are an obvious Grecization of Hebrew names, such as Dositheus for Nethanel or Jonathan, and purely Roman names, such as Julianus (Lulianus). There are fathers with non-Hebrew names whose sons have Hebrew names, such as Eliezer b. Hyrcanus, as there is the reverse, such as Dostai (Dositheus) b. Judah. Of interest are the names of the five sons of R. Yose b. Ḥalafta, given as Ishmael, Eleazar, Ḥalafta, Abtilus, and Menahem (Shab. 118b). Three (Ishmael, Eleazar, and Menahem;—for Ishmael see below) have purely biblical names; Ḥalafta has an Aramaic name, like his grandfather (cf. Gen. R. 37:7, where R. Yose explicitly refers to the custom of giving a child the name of "our fathers," and the eight other examples in the Talmud, of which the best known are the dynasty of Hillel, the son of Eliezer b. Hyrcanus (Men. 35a), and R. Ishmael; this custom is thought to have been derived from the Greeks—L. Loew, *Beitraege zur jued. Alterskunde*, 2, 9b); and the fifth Abtilus, has a Greek name (probably a corruption of Εὐπολεηος). Another passage (TJ, Yev. 1:1) gives the names as Ishmael, Eleazar (Lazar), Menahem, Ḥalafta, and Avdimos (Eudymos) and asks about another son of Yose called Vardimon; the Talmud explains that Vardimon is identical with Menahem, but he was so called because "his face was like *[domeh]* a rose *[vered]*." This is a homiletical interpretation similar to that which makes of Tiberias *Tovah Re'iyyatah* ("of goodly appearance"; Meg. 6a), and there is no doubt that it is a form of the Greek name Εὐρύδημος. These names raise the interesting question whether it was not the custom to have two names, one Semitic (Hebrew or Aramaic) and one Greek, as was the case with Hasmonean rulers such as John (Johanan) Hyrcanus and Salome Alexandra, and whether that is not the simple explanation of the names of the five sons of Mattathias: "Johanan called Gaddis, Simeon called Thassi, Judas called Maccabeus, Eleazar called Avarah, and Jonathan called Apphus" (I Macc. 2:2).

It is equally natural that there were names which were avoided because of their unhappy associations, and this is explicitly stated. The Talmud interprets the verse "and the name of the wicked shall rot" (Prov. 10:7) to the effect that "none name their children after them" and points to the grim example of a child being given the name of *Doeg, whose mother would every day give the increase in his weight in gold to the Temple, yet "when the enemy prevailed she slaughtered and ate him" and, because of the unfortunate choice of the name of a wicked person, "see what happened to him" (Yoma 38b). Similarly the Midrash states "Have you ever heard that a man should call his son Pharaoh, or Sisera or Sennacherib? But (one does give the name) Abraham, Isaac, Jacob, Reuben, Simeon, Levi or Judah" (Gen. R. 49:1), and in general it is stated that the name of a person determines his destiny (Ber. 7b).

In respect to this, the repeated name of Ishmael raises a difficulty. R. Yose (Gen. R. 71:3) divides names into four categories according to their beauty or ugliness as well as according to their bearers' deeds and gives Ishmael as an example of one whose "name was beautiful but his actions ugly." How then is this name so frequently found? The *tosafot* (loc. cit.) explain that it was only because, according to rabbinic tradition, he repented; and because of the bad association of the names they alter the name of Absalom, the father of Hanan the Judge (Ket. 13:1), to Avishalom (because Absalom "has no portion in the world to come" (Sanh. 103b)) and Shebna to Shechna (Tos. Yoma 38b; Ket. 104b).

By the same token, there are homilies as to the efficacy and desirability of giving names after those of biblical worthies. To the above quoted passage that fathers call their children Abraham, Isaac, Jacob, Reuben, Simeon, Levi, Judah, there is the positive injunction "One should ever examine names, to give his son a name worthy for him to become a righteous man, for sometimes the name is a contributory factor for good as for evil" (Tanḥ. Ha'azinu 7). Ephraim is praised that "the best of my sons shall be called after thee" (Lev. R. 3:2). On the contemporary plane there are quoted cases of a woman in gratitude calling her child after Nathan ha-Bavli because he had saved its life (Shab. 134a) and children called Eleazar after Eleazar b. Simeon because of a similar boon (BM 84b).

Despite that fact, however, there is one puzzling phenomenon, namely, the complete absence of names which one would expect. Not a single rabbi is known by the name of Moses (the name occurs only once in the whole talmudic literature as borne by the father-in-law of a certain scholar Huna—BB 174b, Ar. 23a), Abraham, Israel, David, or Solomon. Aaron is borne by only two *amoraim*. Of the sons of Jacob, a decided preference is given to Simeon and Judah, and among the *amoraim* to Levi and Joseph (there are no *tannaim* called Joseph and only two called Levi though, as stated, the Aramaized form Yose is common). Dan, Gad, and Asher do not occur at all, the others only rarely. (Steinschneider draws attention to a similar phenomenon among the Jews in Arabic-speaking countries.) A similar position exists with regard to the names of the prophets. Of the 15 prophets, Jeremiah, the name of one *tanna*, appears to have become popular in the amoraic period, and only one *amora* is known by the name of Ezekiel. Nahum and Jonah are of greater frequency, but the former seems to be in a class by itself, since the frequent occurrence of other names of the same root, Naḥman, Tanḥum, Tanḥuma, suggests that it was the root meaning "comfort" which decided its choice. Similarly Jonah, which occurs only among the *amoraim*, may have been influenced by the many amoraic *aggadot* (cf. Gen. R. 33:6) which identified the dove (Jonah) with Israel. Zechariah is the only name which occurs with any frequency (three *tannaim* and two *amoraim*) and Haggai (and Ḥagga). Isaiah, Hosea, Joel, Amos, Obadiah, Micah, Habakkuk, Zephaniah, and Malachi are not found at all.

It is specifically mentioned (ARN 12) that humans were not given the names of angels, and in fact such names as Raphael and Gabriel are not found.

Lastly, attention should be drawn to a passage in *Pesaḥim* 113b to the effect that Joseph of Huẓal is identical, inter alia, with Issi, the son of Gur Aryeh, who is also named Issi b. Judah. The alternatives Judah and Gur Aryeh seem to be the only example known of the custom widely prevalent in later ages to give double or alternative names on the basis of Genesis 49 and Deuteronomy 33: "Judah Aryeh," "Naphtali Zevi," "Benjamin Ze'ev," and "Joseph Bekhor Shor."

On the other hand there is clear evidence of the use of different names. In *Gittin* 34b there is a case mentioned of a woman in Babylonia known in one place as Miriam and in another as Sarah, and of a query sent from the Diaspora to Rabban Gamaliel as to the procedure to be adopted with regard to the name to be inserted on a bill of divorce in the case of a man who came from Palestine where he was known as Joseph but in Babylonia (probably) as Johanan. The fact that the "vice versa" is mentioned suggests that this case is also one of "anonymous names."

[L.I.R.]

Medieval Period and Establishment of Surnames. Variations in onomastic styles—generally a useful index of cultural diversity and change—are especially prominent in Jewish history. As the Jews moved from area to area, through many linguistic milieus, they were affected, in varying degrees, by the patterns of nomenclature in the societies around them. The tendency toward adoption of names in vogue with the non-Jewish majority—discernible throughout the Middle Ages—accelerated during the late 18th and 19th centuries with intensification of the process of emancipation. As modern Jews reaped the benefits of this emancipation, they increasingly imitated the mores of their neighbors, appellations included. Governments in some instances furthered this tendency by rewarding or even legislating the adoption of European forenames and family names. The 20th century—witness to both a deepening of the thrust toward integration of the Jews into Western society as well as repudiation of such integration—has seen rapid changes in Jewish name styles. While the Jews of the Americas and Western Europe have continued to pursue onomastic assimilation, their brethren in Israel have revived the old Hebrew nomenclature and created a new one.

Middle Ages. During the Middle Ages, Jews retained a preference for Hebrew forenames. In most cases these names were readily adaptable to the language of the surrounding society. Thus, in the Arab world, Abraham became Ibrahīm and David, Dāwud. In the Greek milieu, Joseph became Iosiph (Ἰωσηΐφ) and Shemariah, Samargia, while in the Latin West, Moses (Moshe) became Moyses and Ḥayyim, Hagin. Often Jews bore Hebrew names along with related, but not identical, non-Hebrew appellations, e.g., Eleazar-Manṣūr, Yefet-Ḥasan, Eliakim-Anastasios, Mattathia-Dieudonné, Jehiel-Vivant, Ḥayyim-Vital. Some designations popular in non-Jewish circles were taken over by Jews with no regard for Hebrew equivalence. In general, there was a greater likelihood of a non-Hebrew given name among the female members of the community. The range of non-Hebrew names adopted was broader and the percentage of women bearing such designations was higher than among the male Jewish population. Popular female forenames included Masʿūda and Sulṭāna (Arabic); Anastassu, Cali, and Zoe (Greek); Angélique, Fleurette, and Précieuse (French); Esperanza and Gracia (Spanish). Conversion into and out of the Jewish community was almost always accompanied by a symbolic change of name. The most common names for those entering the Jewish faith were Abraham and Sarah. Jews leaving their heritage took new names as well. In the Christian world, for example, designations such as Paul, Christian, and Mary were widespread, as was adoption of the names of prominent ecclesiastical or secular sponsors.

Designations appended to the given name, to identify more clearly the individual, developed already during antiquity. This tendency grew more marked throughout the Middle Ages. The most traditional of these surnames was the patronym, readily adapted from the Hebrew "ben" to the Arabic "ibn" and the French "fils." A special Arabic usage was the identification of the father by his firstborn son, the "abū" designation. In most areas a favored style of byname was that which derived from locale, in some cases the bearer's birthplace and others his adult residence. In the Arab world prominent examples are R. Isaac Alfasi and R. Saadiah al-Fayyumi. The great 13th-century leader of French Jewry was known both by the Hebrew R. Jehiel of Paris and by the French Vivant of Meaux, the latter his birthplace and the former the locus of his adult activities. Surnames derived from locale became particularly widespread in the wake of the periodic expulsions suffered by medieval Jewry. Both for ease of identification and out of nostalgia, Jews chose names that recalled their earlier homes. Thus, for example, in Turkish Jewry subsequent to 1492 surnames such as De Leon, D'Alvo, Zamora, and Toledano abounded. Another source of bynames was occupation. Medicine, printing, masonry, tailoring, dyeing, minting—all left their mark on Jewish onomastics. Physical and spiritual characteristics, such as size, age, complexion, honesty, and piety, also gave rise to series of widely used surnames. With the passage of time, in Jewish society as in general, these surnames tended to crystallize into family names, passed on from generation to generation.

There are two special types of designation, popular during the Middle Ages and early modern period, which deserve special mention. The first is the acronym. The components drawn upon for the acronym might include a title (rabbi, morenu ha-rav, ha-gaon), the given name, or the surname. Well-known examples include RaSHI (Rabbi Solomon Yiẓḥaki), RaMBaM (Rabbi Moses b. Maimon), Ha-GRA (Ha-Gaon Rabbi Elijah). The second style of designation stems from an author's *magnum opus*. In many instances, e.g., the Roke'aḥ (R. Eleazar b. Judah) and the Tur (R. Jacob b. Asher), given names and surnames were almost totally obscured by such literary appellations.

Modern Times. With the onset of emancipation there was growing imitation of forenames current in general society. Study of Berlin Jewish forenames at the beginning of the 20th century has shown a marked tendency toward appropriation of popular German designations, although some names remained peculiarly Jewish. In the U.S., the transition from immigrant-generation to first-, second-, and third-generation status has been accompanied by constantly changing given name styles. Certain names extremely popular with an earlier generation have subsequently been totally rejected, usually out of a sense that such names were excessively identified with immigrant status and with Jewishness.

Concern over the process of emancipation occasionally led governments to restrict the range of choices for Jewish given names. Such was the force, e.g., of the Austrian edict of 1787, limiting the Jews to biblical first names. The total repudiation of emancipation espoused by the Nazis expressed itself clearly in the sphere of nomenclature. On Aug. 17, 1938, a governmental decree specified 185 forenames for men and 91 for women—many with derogatory connotations—which were henceforth to be used by German Jews. Jews already bearing names other than those specified were to assume, by Jan. 1, 1939, the additional name of Israel for a male and Sarah for a female. These new appellations were to be duly registered and faithfully used in all business and legal transactions.

Along with Zionism and the revival of the Hebrew language came a new interest in Hebrew forenames. This interest was expressed in the establishment of a Commission for Hebrew Nomenclature (Va'ad Shemon Ivri) and in

PRÉFECTURE
DU DEPARTEMENT DE LA SEINE.

DÉCRET IMPÉRIAL

Concernant les Juifs qui n'ont pas de nom de famille et de prénoms fixes.

A Bayonne, le 20 juillet 1808.

NAPOLEON, EMPEREUR DES FRANÇAIS, ROI D'ITALIE ET PROTECTEUR de la Confédération du Rhin;

Sur le rapport de notre Ministre de l'Intérieur;

Notre Conseil d'Etat entendu,

Nous avons décrété et décrétons ce qui suit:

ARTICLE PREMIER.

Ceux des sujets de notre Empire qui suivent le Culte hébraïque et qui, jusqu'à présent, n'ont pas eu de nom de famille et de prénoms fixes, seront tenus d'en adopter dans les trois mois de la publication de notre présent décret, et d'en faire la déclaration pardevant l'Officier de l'Etat civil de la commune où ils sont domiciliés.

Art. II.

Les Juifs étrangers qui viendraient habiter dans l'Empire, et qui seraient dans le cas prévu par l'article premier, seront tenus de remplir la même formalité dans les trois mois qui suivront leur entrée en France.

Art. III.

Ne seront point admis comme noms de famille aucun nom tiré de l'Ancien Testament, ni aucun nom de ville. Pourront être pris comme prénoms, ceux autorisés par la loi du 11 germinal an 11.

Art. IV.

Les Consistoires, en faisant le relevé des Juifs de leur communauté, seront tenus de vérifier et de faire connaître à l'autorité s'ils ont individuellement rempli les conditions prescrites par les articles précédens. Ils seront également tenus de surveiller et de faire connaître à l'autorité ceux des Juifs de leur communauté qui auraient changé de nom sans s'être conformés aux dispositions de la susdite loi du 11 germinal an 11.

Art. V.

Seront exceptés des dispositions de notre présent décret, les Juifs de nos états, ou les Juifs étrangers qui viendraient s'y établir, lorsqu'ils auront des noms et prénoms connus et qu'ils ont constamment portés, encore que lesdits noms et prénoms soient tirés de l'Ancien Testament ou des villes qu'ils ont habitées.

Art VI.

Les Juifs mentionnés à l'article précédent, et qui voudront conserver leurs noms et prénoms, seront néanmoins tenus d'en faire la déclaration, savoir: les Juifs de nos états, pardevant la mairie de la commune où ils sont domiciliés; et les juifs étrangers, pardevant celle où ils se proposeront de fixer leur domicile: le tout dans le délai porté en l'article premier.

Art. VII.

Les Juifs qui n'auraient pas rempli les formalités prescrites par le présent décret et dans les délais y portés, seront renvoyés du territoire de l'Empire. A l'égard de ceux qui, dans quelqu'acte public ou quelque obligation privée, auraient changé de noms arbitrairement et sans s'être conformés aux dispositions de la loi du 11 germinal an 11, ils seront punis conformément aux lois, et même comme faussaires, suivant l'exigence des cas.

Art. VIII.

Notre Grand-Juge Ministre de la Justice, et nos Ministres de l'Intérieur et des cultes, sont chargés, chacun en ce qui le concerne, de l'exécution du présent décret.

Signé NAPOLÉON.

Par l'Empereur:

Le Ministre Secrétaire d'Etat, *Signé* H.-B. MARET.

Pour copie conforme:

L'Auditeur au Conseil d'Etat Secrétaire général de la Préfecture,

F. HÉLY.

AVIS.

Les Personnes domiciliées dans le département de la Seine, qui se trouvent dans le cas des dispositions du Décret impérial ci-dessus rapporté, sont prévenues que les registres sur lesquels seront reçues les déclarations prescrites par ce décret sont ouverts dans toutes les Mairies dudit département, et que ces mêmes registres seront clos le 10 novembre prochain.

Paris, le 1er. septembre 1808.

Le Conseiller d'État Préfet du Département de la Seine, *Signé* FROCHOT.

Par le Conseiller d'Etat Préfet du Département de la Seine,

L'Auditeur au Conseil d'Etat, Secrétaire général de la Préfecture, F. HÉLY.

De l'imprimerie de BALLARD, seul Imprimeur de la Préfecture du Département de la Seine, rue J.-J. Rousseau, n°. 8.

Napoleonic decree ordering the Jews of France to adopt definitive family and first names, July 20, 1808. Courtesy Bertram W. Korn, Philadelphia, Pa.

the compilation of a multivolume *Shemon Ivri*, containing both rules for Hebraization of non-Hebrew names and a wealth of information on specific Hebrew designations. Within the Jewish community of Palestine and subsequently the State of Israel there have been numerous forename styles, reflecting differences of origin and of generation. Each of the various elements that have been woven together into Israel society has retained its own traditional nomenclature. Successive generations of native-born Israelis have tended to reject older patterns and create their own—sometimes utilizing obscure biblical names, sometimes reviving prebiblical Canaanite designations, sometimes fashioning wholly new appellations. This dignified return to Hebrew forenames has been carried over, in limited measure, into the Western Jewish communities. While the predominant tendency remains westernized, a steady growth in the utilization of Hebrew names popular in Israel can be discerned in the United States and Western Europe.

As the Jews passed increasingly into the mainstream of European life, the adoption of a fixed surname became ever more important. The modes of establishing these surnames, already noted, included patronyms (Abramson, Abramowitz, Jacobson, Jacobowitz, Mendelssohn), names based on localities (Berliner, Bresslau, Poznanski, Moscowitz), vocational designations (Drucker, Schneider, Wechsler), and appellations drawn from characteristics (Alt, Klein, Schwartz). The process of altering names to suit increasingly Western tastes has been inevitable. This tendency has been obvious in the U.S. Jewish community, where the family names brought from Eastern Europe generally branded their bearers as immigrants. Cumbersome Slavic endings were dropped to form short and American-sounding names. In the earlier stages of emancipation, government edicts often had to be enacted in order to institute among the Jews the regular use of surnames. Such a step was included in the Austrian legislation of 1787. Jewish surnames were to be registered by a government commission, and where the Jews refused to select a name, this same commission was empowered to make the choice. In France, Napoleon decreed the fixing of family names for the Jews in 1808, and in Prussia in 1812 emancipation of the Jews was made contingent upon the adoption within six months of acceptable surnames. In the United States the practical necessity of registration of immigrants coupled with ignorance of English resulted in the creation of a host of new surnames for bewildered newcomers. The Zionist experience has often been associated with the Hebraization of family names. The major political figures of the first few decades of the State of Israel reflect this phenomenon: Ben-Zvi (formerly Shimshelevitz), Shazar (Rubashov), Ben-Gurion (Gruen), Sharett (Shertok), Eshkol (Shkolnik), Meir (Myerson). The most common methods of fashioning new Hebrew surnames have been the use of patronyms, the translation of the non-Hebrew name into a Hebrew equivalent, and the adoption of a Hebrew designation phonetically similar to the non-Hebrew.

The demographic upheavals and the ideological conflicts of the 19th and 20th centuries have thoroughly shattered the onomastic unity of many Jewish families. Brothers and cousins spread across the Diaspora and Israel often bear totally different family appellations—a curious testimony to the unparalleled disruptions of the past century of Jewish life.

[R.CH.]

Bibliography: IN THE BIBLE: G. B. Gray, *Studies in Hebrew Proper Names* (1896); Noth, Personennamen; J. J. Stamm, in: VTS, 7 (1960), 165–83; 16 (1967), 301–39; idem, in: *Theologische Zeitschrift*, 16 (1960), 285–97; idem, in: *Studies in Honor of D. Landsberger* (=*Assyriological Studies*, 16 (1965)), 413–24; idem, in: *Fourth World Congress of Jewish Studies*, Papers, 1 (1967),

141–7 301. In the Talmud: The two major studies of Jewish onomastics are L. Zunz, *Namen der Juden* (1837), and H. Loewe, *Geschichte der juedischen Namen* (1929). Medieval Period and Establishment of Surnames: Useful source material can often be found in onomastic excursuses or detailed indexes in descriptions of particular Jewish communities, e.g., S. Rosanes, Togarmah, 1 (1930[2]), and U. Cassuto, *Gli Ebrei a Firenze* (1918). Valuable information is also preserved in tax records, e.g., Loeb, in: REJ, 1 (1880), and Levy, *ibid.*, 19 (1889), and in funerary inscriptions, e.g., Schwab, in: *Nouvelles archives des missions scientifiques et littéraires*, 12 (1904); Kober, in: PAAJR, 14–15 (1944–45); Avneri, *ibid.*, 33 (1965); Ankori, *ibid.*, 38 (1970). Specialized studies of general interest include Steinschneider, in: JQR, 9–13 (1897–1901); Kober, in: HJ, 5 (1943); G. Kessler, *Die Familiennamen der Juden in Deutschland* (1935); Glanz, in: JSOS, 23 (1961); Friedman, in: HJ, 7 (1945).

NAMIAS, JEROME (1910–), U.S. meteorologist. Born in Bridgeport, Conn., Namias worked during the 1930s at the Blue Hill Observatory affiliated to Harvard University. In 1941 he set up the extended forecast division of the U.S. Weather Bureau in Washington, D.C., and during the years of World War II prepared the weather forecasts for the convoys crossing the Atlantic and for military maneuvers. After the war Namias was appointed assistant director of the National Meteorological Center at Suitland, Maryland. Here he developed methods for the study of weather phenomena in three dimensions. [D.Ash.]

NAMIER (Bernstein-Namierowski), SIR LEWIS (1888–1960), English historian and Zionist, pioneer of the trend in historical scholarship known as "Namierism." Born in eastern Galicia, where his parents were landowners, Namier became aware of his Jewish origin at the age of nine, upon overhearing anti-Semitic sneers at his parents' efforts to work their way into the Polish gentry. This traumatic experience turned him into a dedicated Zionist. After a spell at Vienna and Lausanne, he arrived in England in 1908. He graduated from Balliol College, Oxford, where he mixed with young men who were later to become famous, such as T. E. Lawrence and the historian Arnold J. Toynbee. Among his Jewish contemporaries were Leonard Stein and Leonard Montefiore. In 1914 Namier volunteered for the British army. He served for a time in the Foreign Office Intelligence Service and was taken to the Versailles Peace Conference to advise on problems concerning the old Hapsburg Empire, Poland, and Eastern Europe. After the war he did not turn at once to an academic career but tried his luck—unsuccessfully—in business. He needed the help of friends to complete the research for his first book and masterpiece, *The Structure of Politics at the Accession of George III* (1929). After publication of *England in the Age of the American Revolution* (1930) he was appointed professor of modern history at Manchester University (1931), holding the chair until 1953.

After his war service Namier devoted himself to the Zionist cause, although he was viewed with distrust by leaders of the Zionist movement, especially from Eastern Europe, as an outsider. Namier's Zionist creed, stemming from the outsider's need for roots and the wanderer's yearning for an anchor, found expression in 1930 in a powerful cry (in *England in the Age of the American Revolution*):

> To every man the native land is his life-giving Mother and the State raised upon the land is his law-giving Father, and the days cannot be long of a nation which fails to honor either. Only one nation has survived for two thousand years, though an orphan—my own people, the Jews. But then in the God-given Law we have enshrined the authority of a state, in the God-promised Land the idea of a Mother-Country; through the centuries from Mount Sinai we have faced Eretz Israel, our Land. Take away either, and we cease to be a nation; let both live again, and we shall be ourselves once more.

From 1927 to 1931 Namier served as political secretary to the Zionist Executive, and it was as the chief draftsman of the *Jewish Agency, with Blanche Dugdale, that Namier, with his pedantic insistence on the niceties of formulation and protocol, made his chief contribution to the Zionist cause. He played a considerable role as an intermediary in obtaining the Ramsay MacDonald Letter, which in fact canceled the Passfield *White Paper of 1930. Thanks to his friendship with Reginald Coupland, the author of the 1937 report of the Peel Commission (the first British document to bring up the idea of a Jewish state in a partitioned Palestine), Namier was able to exercise a direct impact on matters of great political importance. He served for a time as deputy to Chaim Weizmann on the Anglo-Jewish Committee for Refugees from Germany, taking up a determined stand against the "barons" of Anglo-Jewry. At the time of the St. James' Conference on Palestine, which resulted in the anti-Zionist White Paper of May 1939, Namier insisted on a forceful Zionist policy toward the British government, occasionally criticizing the line taken by Weizmann. On the outbreak of World War II he was on loan full time from Manchester University to the Jewish Agency, for which he worked until 1945. Namier kept aloof from the ideological struggles among the Zionist factions. He disliked the religious parties and had close friends in the Labor leadership. His Zionism was a romantic nationalism in the tradition of Mazzini and Pilsudski—the vision of a historic breakthrough conceived in messianic terms—but it lacked any Jewish cultural sustenance.

Namier's historical research may be classified under four headings: the social-political structure of England in the 18th century; the 1848 revolutions; the twilight of the Hapsburg monarchy; and the international crisis leading up to World War II. All four inquiries may be said to be variations on one theme: cohesion versus distintegration. His chief work, *The Structure of Politics...*, is a microscopic examination of the composition of the successive Houses of Commons under George III. His concern was with how politics are made by members of a governing elite, to the neglect of intellectual trends and social forces. Namier's biographical method was applied to the great collective *History of Parliament* (initiated by Whitehall and Westminister), of which he was coeditor. In recognition of his achievement as an historian, Namier was elected a member of the British Academy in 1944, was knighted in 1952, and was invited to give the prestigious Romanes Lecture at Oxford. These honors went some way to assuage his feelings of disappointment at having been bypassed for the Regius Professorship of Modern History at Oxford University. The rather eccentric and intensely self-centered outsider with strong and forcefully expressed likes and dislikes scared off many contemporaries. While capable of deep emotions, he lacked flexibility and was very vulnerable. After an unhappy first marriage, Namier married in church the former Julia de Beausobre, a daughter of the Russian gentry who was deeply committed to the Greek Orthodox Church and had suffered in Soviet prisons and concentration camps (described in her book *The Woman Who Could Not Die*, 1938). She played a great role in Namier's life.

Namier paid many visits to Palestine. His only visit to the State of Israel took place in 1959 in connection with the scheme for the publication of the Weizmann papers, in which he took great interest. On that occasion he gave a memorable address to the modern history seminar at the Hebrew University. It contained a kind of confession and testament and was preceded by the Hebrew incantation "If

I forget thee, O Jerusalem" tearfully spoken with a trembling voice.

Namier's publications include: *Skyscrapers* (1931); *Additions and Corrections to Sir John Fortescue's Edition of the Correspondence of King George III* (1957); *In the Margin of History* (1939); *Conflicts* (1942); *1848: The Revolution of the Intellectuals* (1946); *Facing East* (1947); *Diplomatic Prelude* (1938–39, 1948); *Europe in Decay* (1936–40, 1950); *Avenues of History* (1952); *In the Nazi Era* (1952); *Personalities and Powers* (1958); *Vanished Supremacies* (1958).

Bibliography: L. Sutherland, in: *Proceedings of the British Academy*, 48 (1962), 371–85; J. L. Talmon, in: *Commentary*, 33 (1962), 237–46; J. Namier, *Lewis Namier* (1971). [J.L.T.]

NAMIR (Nemirovsky), MORDEKHAI (1897–), Israel Labor leader, cabinet minister, and mayor of Tel-Aviv-Jaffa. Born in Bratolinbovka, Ukraine, Namir was a member of the central committee of the *Zionist Socialist Party until arrested and expelled from university. He settled in Ereẓ Israel in 1924, and held various posts in the labor movement. He became the director of the statistical section of the Histadrut from 1929 to 1935, and from 1936 to 1943 secretary-general of the Tel Aviv Workers' council. Namir was arrested by the Mandatory authorities in 1940 for organizing street demonstrations against the "White Paper" policy and was a member of the national and Tel Aviv *Haganah commands. After the establishment of the State, Namir held diplomatic posts in Bulgaria, Czechoslovakia, and Rumania and was Israel's second ambassador to the U.S.S.R. (1949–50). From 1951 he was a member of the *Knesset and held three major posts: secretary-general of the *Histadrut (1951–55), minister of labor (1956–59), and first Labor mayor of Tel Aviv (1959–69). He was responsible for extensive modernization and development schemes during his mayoralty.

Mordekhai Namir, Israel politician. Photo Erde, Tel Aviv.

Among his works in the field of economics and organizations are: *Shenatayim be-Ḥayyei ha-Histadrut, 1951–1952* (1953) and *Ha-Mazzav ha-Kalkali be-Ereẓ Yisrael be-Sof Shenat 1933* (1933).

Bibliography: D. Lazar, *Rashim be-Yisrael*, 1 (1953), 120–5. [A.A.]

NANCY, capital of Meurthe-et-Moselle department, northeastern France; former capital of the Duchy of *Lorraine. In 1286 the Jews acquired a cemetery at nearby Laxou. In 1341, and later in 1455, several Jews settled in Nancy itself only to be expelled from the Duchy in 1477. The Jews temporarily reappeared in Nancy in 1595; and Maggino Gabrieli, called "consul-general of the Hebrew and Levantine nation," attempted to establish two banks and a pawnshop in 1637–1643. In 1707 and 1712 Duke Leopold authorized three Jewish bankers from *Metz to settle in Nancy, one of whom, Samuel *Lévy, became the duke's chief tax collector in 1715. After Lévy fell into disgrace there was a hostile reaction toward the Jews. Nevertheless, in 1721 an edict authorized 70 Jewish families to remain in Lorraine, eight of them in Nancy and its surroundings. The 90 Jewish families in Nancy in 1789 (50 of whom were without authorization), included such wealthy merchants and manufacturers as the *Alcan, Goudchaux, and *Berr families from whom the trustees of the duchy's Jewish community were chosen. Herz *Cerfberr became squire of Tomblaine; and *Berr Isaac Berr became the leader of the Ashkenazi Jews in 1789. There was a house of prayer in 1745, but it was not until 1788 that a synagogue was officially erected (renovated in 1842 and 1935), eight years after the chief rabbi of Lorraine established himself in Nancy. Notable among the chief rabbis of the consistory formed in 1808 were Marchand *Ennery and Solomon *Ullmann. With the influx of people from Alsace and Moselle after 1870, the number of Jews in Nancy increased to some 4,000 by the end of the century. The prayer room of the Polish Jews was decorated by the artist *Mané-Katz. Nancy was the birthplace of the writer André *Spire and Nobel Prize winner F. *Jacob. [G.C.]

Holocaust Period. Many of Nancy's prewar Jewish population (about 3,800 in 1939) fled the city under the German occupation. Those who stayed were exposed to Nazi persecution. In three *aktionen* in 1942–43, 130 Jews of foreign origin were arrested and deported, while over 400 others were arrested and deported from the Southern Zone after it was overrun by the Germans in 1942. Only 22 survivors returned. Among the old French Jewish families, 250 victims were deported, of whom only two survived. The majority were arrested on March 2, 1944, along with 72-year-old Chief Rabbi Haguenauer, who despite his being forewarned, refused to desert the members of his community. A street in postwar Nancy bears his name. The syna-

The synagogue of Nancy, built in 1788 and renovated in 1842 and 1935. Courtesy Bernard Blumenkranz. Photo J. Roth, Paris.

gogue, as well as other buildings belonging to the Jews, were plundered by the Nazis: the synagogue interior was destroyed while the holy books were sold to a rag collector. Certain of the art works and books in the local museum and departmental archives were saved. After the war the community of Nancy was rapidly renewed, and by 1969 had about 3,000 members with a full range of Jewish communal institutions. A chair for Hebrew studies was set up at the university. [G.Le.]

Bibliography: Gross, Gal Jud, 400; C. Pfister, *Histoire de Nancy*, 1 (1902), 678–81; 3 (1908), 310–38; A. Gain et. al., in: *Revue juive de Lorraine*, 2–3 (1926–27); 9–11 (1933–35), passim; J. Godchot, in: REJ, 86 (1928), 1–35.

NANTES, city in Brittany, capital of the department of Loire-Atlantique, western France. The medieval community was apparently short-lived. The first mention of Jews there dates from 1234. In 1236 the Jews of Nantes, as in the rest of *Brittany and other provinces of western France, were victims of a persecution which accompanied the preaching of the Sixth Crusade; it was followed by their expulsion in 1240. The importance of the community is shown by the cemetery for which evidence exists from 1231. The Rue des Juifs which the community occupied still retains its name.

From the second half of the 16th century many Portuguese of *Marrano origin settled in Nantes. The Vaz, Mendez, Rodriguez, and other families found here generally became loyal Christians, whose members frequently chose an ecclesiastical career. Some Marranos whose sympathies remained with Judaism occasionally passed through Nantes but did not settle there. Thus, toward the end of the 16th century, Abraham d'Espinoza, the grandfather of Baruch *Spinoza, stayed in Nantes with a few members of his family before establishing himself in Holland. In 1636, however, several Portuguese Jews of *Bayonne, expelled from this frontier town at the time of the Franco-Spanish War, settled in the town. At the end of the 18th century a number of local merchants, in particular the old clothes dealers, instigated the prosecution of some Jewish merchants newly established in the town; however, public opinion sympathized with the Jews, as is particularly evident from the *Journal de la Correspondence de Nantes* of 1789 to 1791, and the *Feuille Nantaise* of 1795. There were 25 families in Nantes in 1808–09. In 1834 they established an organized community with a membership of 18 families. A synagogue was built in 1870, and by 1898 there were about 50 families. According to the census of 1942 carried out by the Vichy government, there were 531 Jews in Nantes. There were 53 at the beginning of September 1943. A number of Jews were arrested and imprisoned in the Caserne Richemont of Nantes but were deported in January 1944. After World War II very few Jewish families settled in Nantes and in 1960 there were only about 25. The growth of the town, and especially the arrival of Jews from North Africa, served to increase the Jewish community, so that by 1969 it had over 500 Jewish inhabitants. There was a combined synagogue and community center, religious instruction classes, and youth activities.

Bibliography: H. de Berranger, *Evocation du vieux Nantes* (1966), 15, 25; Brunschvicg, in: REJ, 14 (1887), 80ff.; 17 (1888), 123ff.; 19 (1889), 294ff.; 49 (1904), 110, 112; Z. Szajkowski, *Analytical Franco-Jewish Gazetteer 1939–1945* (1966), 213.

[B.Bl.]

NAOMI (Heb. נָעֳמִי; probably from *nuʿmay* (Ugaritic, *nʿmy*), "pleasantness"), the wife of *Elimelech the Ephrathite from Beth-Lehem in Judah who, because of famine, emigrated to Moab with his wife and his sons *Mahlon and Chilion (Ruth 1:1–2). Her husband and her two sons, who had married Moabite women, died in Moab.

Naomi (seated) receives grain from Ruth (left), and sends her out again (right). Detail from the *Pierpont Morgan Picture Bible*, France, 1250. New York, Pierpont Morgan Library, Ms. 638, fol. 18r.

When she heard that the famine in Judah had ended, Naomi returned there. Her daughters-in-law wanted to accompany her, but she tried to dissuade them from binding their destiny to hers. Chilion's widow, *Orpah, was persuaded, but Mahlon's widow, *Ruth, clung to her mother-in-law (4:10). Naomi, in return, looked after the interests of her faithful daughter-in-law so that Ruth was taken in marriage by *Boaz, a relative of the family. Naomi adopted and nursed the son born to Ruth and Boaz and so achieved a measure of consolation in her old age. [Is.A.]

In the Aggadah. Naomi was of outstanding beauty. She and Elimelech were cousins, their fathers being the sons of Nahshon son of Amminadab. From this the rabbis taught, "even the merit of one's ancestor is of no avail when one emigrates from Ereẓ Israel" (BB 91a). Naomi was so anxious to return to Ereẓ Israel that she set out on her journey barefoot and in rags. She did not even stop to rest on the Sabbath (Ruth R. 2:12). On the way she taught Ruth the laws concerning proselytes *(ibid.)*. She arrived in Beth-Lehem on the day of the funeral of Boaz's wife (BB 91a). In her youth Naomi had been a nurse to Boaz as she later became a nurse to Ruth's son, Obed (*Lekaḥ Tov* on Ruth 4:16). Proverbs 31:19 is interpreted to refer to Naomi who brought Ruth under the wings of the *Shekhinah* (Mid. Hag., Gen. 33:1). She is thus included in the 22 women of valor enumerated by the rabbis *(ibid.)*. [Ed.]

Bibliography: Ginzberg, Legends, 4 (1913), 31–32; 6 (1928), 189–92.

NAPHTALI (Heb. נַפְתָּלִי), the sixth son of Jacob and second son of Bilhah, Rachel's maid (Gen. 30:7). The name is said to derive from Rachel's words, "A fateful contest *(naftule)* I waged *(niftalti)* with my sister; yes, and I have prevailed" (Gen. 30:8). Its exact origin is uncertain. Nothing is related about Naphtali in the biblical sources except that he had four sons. He gave his name to one of the tribes of Israel.

The Tribe and its Territory. The affiliation of Naphtali to Bilhah testifies to an inferior status, at some period, among the tribes of Israel, as does its position in the listings of the sons of Jacob where it appears in the ninth (Deut. 33:23; Gen. 49:21), tenth (Gen. 35:23ff.; I Chron. 2:1), eleventh (Num. 1:15, 42), and occasionally even in last place (Gen. 46:24; Deut. 27:13). The four clans of the tribe of Naphtali are Jahzeel, Guni, Jezer, and Shillem (Gen. 46:24; Num. 26:48–50; and with some slight variants, I Chron. 7:13). These names do not seem to have any connection with settlements, a fact which testifies to their tribal, rather than territorial, origins. This would contradict the view of the German school about the formation of the Israelite tribes. (Guni may be an exception as a place name, possibly to be identified with Umm Jūnī on the east bank of the Jordan.) However, the matter is complicated because of a Gadite family with the same name (I Chron. 5:15). Naphtali's

The tribal emblem of Naphtali, "a hind let loose" (Gen. 49:21), on an Israel stamp, 1955.

territory was the sixth to be decided by lots at Shiloh in the tribal division of the land. The description in Joshua comprises border points and a list of cities (Josh. 19:32–39). The description of the boundary begins with the south, and proceeds from west to east, from the Tabor to the Jordan, with five designated border points: Heleph (apparently Khirbat ʿArbītā north of the Tabor), the Elon-Bezaanannim (apparently a geographic designation; cf. Judg. 4:11), Adami-Nekeb (apparently Khirbat Dāmiya), Jabneel (either Tell Anʿam or Khirbat Yamma), and Lakkum (apparently Khirbat el-Manṣūra close to the Jordan). The western and eastern boundaries are only alluded to by reference to the boundary of Zebulun at the south and Asher on the west. In the south, the text designates only Hukok, the point of intersection of the three tribes Naphtali, Zebulun, and Asher (Hukok is apparently the ruins of Khirbat Jumayjima to the east of Cabul). The description of the northern boundary is missing, but by reference to the northern boundary of Asher which extended to Sidon (Josh. 19:28), and relying on the fact that the northern border of David's kingdom at the time of David's census was "to Dan and from Dan they went around to Sidon" (II Sam. 24:6), it may be assumed that it followed the line Dan-Ijon-Sidon. The northern boundary of Naphtali's territory can thus be envisioned to have been to the east of this line. The list of cities is probably not complete since, according to its title, it includes only "fortified cities" (Josh. 19:35), which testifies to the character and origin of the list. Furthermore, an archaeological survey has shown that there were many populated areas in the territory of Naphtali during the period of settlement. The total number of 19 cities given at the end of the list (19:38) does not refer to the given list, and perhaps it includes also the settlements described in the list as border points.

The History of the Tribe. Information is sparse and is based only on inference. The importance of Naphtali's territory from an agricultural (Deut. 33:23) and military standpoint (Josh. 19:35, "fortified cities") and the designation of the whole of Galilee as "the land of Naphtali" (II Kings 15:29) testify to the prominent and central role of this tribe among the northern tribes during the historical period in contrast to the nomadic. At the beginning of the period of the Judges, the members of the tribe of Naphtali appear to have constituted a minority living among the Canaanites and to have been subject to them (Judg. 1:33). Only after the decisive battle between the Canaanites and the Israelite tribes during the time of Deborah did they overcome those Canaanites living within their territory. In this war, the tribe played an outstanding role. The rebellion was led by Barak the son of Abinoam from Kedesh-Naphtali (Judg. 4:6) and the men of his tribe risked their lives on the heights of the field (5:18). High praise is given to Naphtali and its territory both in the blessings of Jacob and Moses which refer to the period of the Judges. In the united kingdom of David and Solomon, Naphtali became a royal administrative district which seems to have also included the territory of Dan. (Apparently, the families of Dan were absorbed by Naphtali; cf. I Kings 7:13–14 with II Sam. 24:6; I Kings 15:20; II Chron. 2:13; 16:4.) The importance of the tribe and the districts is perhaps expressed in the appointment of the king's son-in-law as his officer there (I Kings 4:15). Apparently deriving from the same period is the list of three levitical cities in Naphtali—Kedesh, Hammoth-Dor, and Kartan (Josh. 21:32, with minor variants in I Chron. 6:61), which were religious and administrative centers set up by the

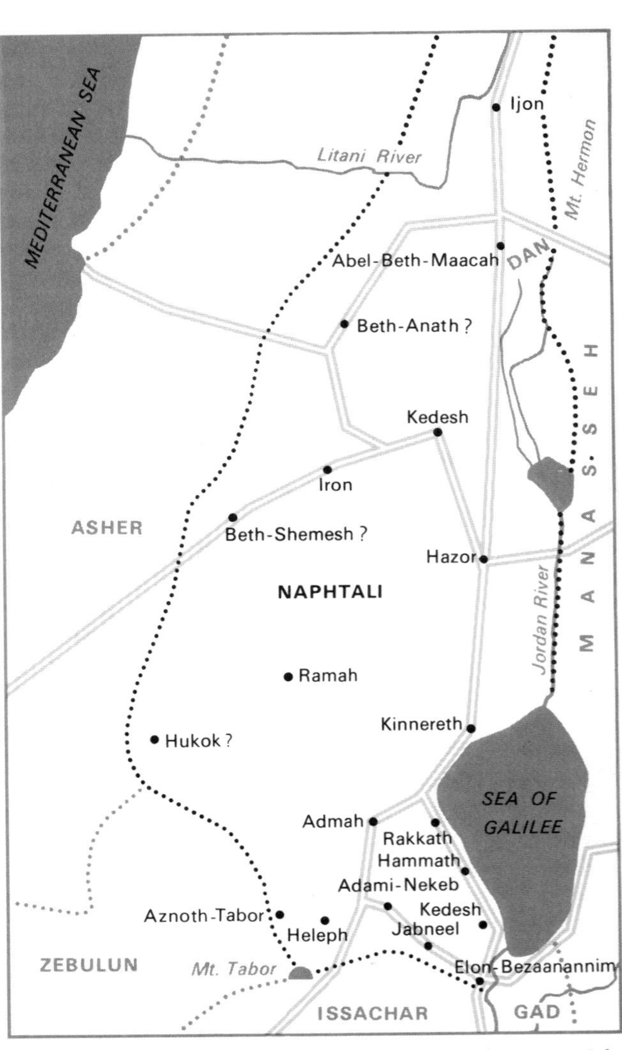

Territory of the tribe of Naphtali. After Y. Aharoni, *Lexicon Biblicum*, Dvir, Tel Aviv, 1965.

central government. One of the important fortresses established in the days of Solomon was the city of Hazor in the territory of Naphtali (I Kings 9: 15). Information about the tribe and its territory after the division of the kingdom is exceedingly scanty. From the little available it is clear that the tribe suffered from the protracted conflict between the kingdoms of Israel and Aram. In the reign of Baasha, Ben-Hadad, the king of Aram, invaded "and conquered Ijon, Dan, Abel-Beth-Maacah and all Chinneroth, with all the land of Naphtali" (I Kings 15:20) and he may possibly have annexed them to his kingdom. However, in the time of Omri and Ahab the tribe was certainly liberated. In 732 B.C.E., Tiglath-Pileser III conquered, among other places, "all the land of Naphtali and he carried the people captive to Assyria" (II Kings 15:29). It is reasonable to assume that he exiled only a section of the population, and that the territory, along with those remaining, was annexed as an Assyrian province with its center at Megiddo. In the days of Josiah, an attempt was made to reunite the northern tribes with the kingdom of the house of David, and apparently Naphtali was among them (II Chron. 34:6). However, it proved unsuccessful owing to the death of Josiah at Megiddo and the subsequent subjugation of the land.

Bibliography: A. Saarisalt, *Boundary Between Issachar and Naphtali* (1927); Abel, Georg, 2 (1938), 63–65; J. Lewy, in: HUCA, 18 (1943/44), 452, n. 122; Alt, Kl Schr, index; Y. Aharoni, *Hitnaḥalut Shivtei Yisrael ba-Galil ha-Elyon* (1957); idem, Land; Z. Kalai, *Naḥalot Shivtei Yisrael* (1967), 56–57, 191ff., 259–60, 367ff., 401ff.; *Kol Ereẓ Naphtali* (1968). [Is.A.]

NAPHTALI, TESTAMENT OF. A Hebrew fragment of a Testament of Naphtali was identified among the *Dead Sea Scrolls. It seems that this work was one of the sources of the Jewish Greek Pseudepigrapha, the Testament of the Twelve *Patriarchs. The Hebrew fragment deals with the genealogy of Bilhah and is longer than the parallel passage in the Greek text. A Testament of Naphtali in medieval Hebrew is preserved in two versions, the second, published by Wertheimer, being a secondary elaboration of the first one. The medieval Hebrew Testament, which is not identical with the text discovered in Qumran—it does not contain a genealogy of Bilhah—nor with the Greek Testament of Naphtali in the Testament of the Patriarchs, is a translation from a non-Hebrew source, probably Greek. This source was composed in the same trend as the Testament of the Patriarchs and shows clear affinities with the extant Greek Testament of Naphtali.

The ethical teaching of the medieval Hebrew Testament is based on fear of God and the golden rule (in the negative form). The stress on the importance of Levi and Judah is common to this text, the Greek Testament of the Patriarchs, and the Book of Jubilees; behind this idea lies, apparently, the Qumran concept of the two Messiahs, Messiah b. David, the anointed of Judah, and Messiah, the anointed of Aaron. In the text a dream of Naphtali is narrated which is similar to that in the Greek text (Naphtali 5: 1–3). In both versions of the dream, Levi is identified with the sun and Judah with the moon. This passage, as indeed the whole work, shows a polemical tendency against Joseph and his descendants, in sharp opposition to the very positive appreciation of Joseph in the Testament of the Patriarchs. The second dream also has a parallel in chapter 6 of the Greek Testament of Naphtali, and it also shows the same polemical attitude toward Joseph. It is an interesting fact that the text praises the Hebrew language, which is in accordance with the ideology of the whole major religious trend exemplified in the Testament of the Patriarchs and the Dead Sea Scrolls. The treatise ends with the blessing of the man "who does not defile the Holy Spirit of God which hath been put and breathed into him," a theologoumenon which has its exact parallel in the *Damascus Document.

Bibliography: T. Gaster, *Studies and Texts*, 1 (1925–28), 69–91; 3 (1925–28), 22–30; R. H. Charles, *The Greek Version of the Testament of the Twelve Patriarchs* (1908); idem, *The Testament of the Twelve Patriarchs* (1908), lxvi–lxviii, 221–7; A. J. Wertheimer, *Battei Midrashot*, 1 (1950), 193–203; Milik, *Dix ans découvertes dans le Désert de Juda* (1957), 320. [D.Fl.]

NAPLES, city and former kingdom in S. Italy. The first Jewish settlement there probably dates to the first century C.E. By the fourth century C.E. the community was of considerable size and economically important. In 536 the Jewish population helped the Goths, although unsuccessfully, to defend the city when it was besieged by the Byzantines. Eleventh- and twelfth-century documents show that the Naples community had a synagogue and a school. Jews enjoyed the right to own real estate and to dispose of it as they wished. *Benjamin of Tudela, who visited the town in c. 1159, found 500 Jews living there. From 1288, under Charles II, anti-Jewish disorders incited by Dominican preachers occurred; they reached their height in 1290 when serious outrages were committed and a synagogue was converted into a church. However, in 1330, Robert of Anjou invited Jews from the Balearic Islands to settle in Naples and in the rest of his kingdom, promising them protection against annoyance and the same taxation rights as those enjoyed by Christians. From 1442, under the rule of Aragon, conditions for the Jews in Naples and its surroundings were favorable, and attracted Jews from various parts of Europe.

At the end of 1492 and the beginning of 1493, a large influx of refugees from Sicily, Sardinia, and Spain found temporary asylum in Naples. The Spanish refugees, undernourished and sick, probably introduced the pestilence in 1492 that struck down 20,000 persons in Naples alone. Among the Spanish refugees who landed in Naples in 1492 was Don Isaac *Abrabanel, who became fiscal adviser to King Ferdinand I and Alfonso II. In 1495 the Kingdom of Naples was conquered by the Spanish and in 1496 a decree for the expulsion of the Jews was issued, although it was not implemented. The expulsion of the Jews was definitively ordered in 1510 and finally carried out: exception was made for 200 wealthy Jewish families who undertook to pay an annual tax of 300 ducats to the crown. In 1515 the *New Christians were also expelled from the kingdom. The 200 wealthy families, who had been joined by others in 1520, had increased to 600 within the following decade. Although a new decree of expulsion was issued in 1533, permission was granted to the Jews in November 1535 to reside in Naples for a further ten years against the payment of 10,000 ducats. However, the agreement was not respected by Emperor Charles V, and in 1541 he ordered the total expulsion of the Jews; this coincided with the establishment of a Christian loan bank (**Monte di Pietà*) in Naples. It was not until 1735, when the kingdom passed to the Bourbons, that Jews were readmitted into Naples and the vicinity by an edict signed by Charles IV on Feb. 3, 1740. However, following pressure by Jesuits and the Church, the few Jews who had accepted the invitation were again expelled (Sept. 18, 1746). At the beginning of the 19th century, several Jewish families were residing in Naples, among them the banker Karl Mayer von *Rothschild of Frankfort on the Main. Religious services began to be held in Naples in 1831, but a synagogue was not opened until June 1864. [A.To.]

In 1931 there were 998 Jews in the community of Naples, whose authority extended to all southern Italy. Persecutions during World War II had minor consequences as the Allied landing led to a speedy liberation of southern Italy. Nevertheless, 11 Jews were taken to extermination camps from Naples and others were killed elsewhere. After the war 534 Jews remained in the community. In 1969 there were 450 Jews in Naples. [S.D.P.]

Hebrew Printing. A Hebrew press was established in Naples not later than 1485, and in the decade which followed nearly 20 books were published, making the city one of the most important cradles of Hebrew *incunabula. Naples was then a center of general book printing and the book trade, and wealthy members of the Jewish community, including immigrants from Spain and Portugal, financed the publishing of Hebrew books. The first Jewish printer there was the German Joseph b. Jacob *Gunzenhausen, who was followed in 1490 by Joshua Solomon *Soncino. A third printer was Isaac b. Judah ibn Katorzo (of Calatayud in Spain). The first book published (in 1487) was Psalms with David Kimḥi's commentary, followed by Proverbs with a commentary by Immanuel of Rome (n.d.), and the rest of the Hagiographa in 1488. A Pentateuch (with Rashi), the Five Scrolls, and the *Antiochus Scroll appeared in 1491. The first printed edition of Abraham ibn Ezra's Pentateuch commentary came out in 1488; Naḥmanides' Pentateuch commentary was printed in 1490 by Katorzo; and that of Baḥya b. Asher in 1492. The magnificent first edition of the entire Mishnah (with Maimonides' commentary) was published in 1492. Halakhic works included Jacob Landau's *Agur* (n.d.), the first Hebrew work with approbations (**Haskamot*) and the second printed in the lifetime of the author (who was one of Gunzenhausen's typesetters); the first edition of the *Kol Bo* (n.d.); and Kimḥi's *Sefer ha-Shorashim* was published by Gunzenhausen in 1490, and by Soncino (and Katorzo?) in 1491. Baḥya b. Joseph ibn Paquda's "Duties of the Heart" (*Ḥovot ha-Levavot*) appeared in 1489, and Naḥmanides' *Sha'ar ha-Gemul* in 1490. Of particular interest are Perez Trabot's *Makre Dardekei* (1488), a 14th-century Hebrew glossary with Italian, Arabic, and also French, Provençal, and German translations; Kalonymus b. Kalonymus' satirical *Even Boḥan* (1489); a Hebrew grammar, *Petaḥ Devarai* (1492); a five-volume Hebrew translation of Avicenna's medical canon *Ha-Kanon ha-Gadol* printed for the first and only time. The fourth edition of Dante's *Divina Commedia* was published by an anonymous Jewish printer in Naples in 1477. [ED.]

Bibliography: Roth, Italy, passim; Milano, Italia, passim; E. Munkácsi, *Der Jude von Neapel* (Zurich, 1939); N. Ferorelli, *Ebrei nell'Italia meridionale*... (1915), passim; idem, in: *Vessillo Israelitico*, 54 (1906), 397–401, 466–74; 63 (1915), 146–7; Sacerdote, in: RMI, 31 (1965), 90–96; L. Poliakov, *Banquiers juifs et le Saint-Siege*... (1965), 191–5. PRINTING: J. Bloch, *Hebrew Printing in Naples* (1942) (= New York Public Library Bulletin, June 1942); D. W. Amram, *Makers of Hebrew Books in Italy*... (1909), 63ff.; Ḥ. D. Friedberg, *Toledot ha-Defus ha-Ivri be-Italyah* (1956), 49–50; Roth, Renaissance, 170–2, 176; A. M. Habermann, *Ha-Madpisim Benei Soncino* (1933), 25–30, 35–36.

°**NAPOLEON BONAPARTE** (1769–1821), emperor of the French. He proclaimed the *emancipation of the Jews in the Italian states which he had established, and the majority of the Jews in Italy hailed Napoleon as a liberator and political savior, calling him "Ḥelek Tov" (lit. "Good Part"; cf. Bona-Parte). Even by this time, however, problems had arisen from the contradictions posed by Jewish laws and communal autonomy on the one hand and the political and civic obligations of the Jews on the other. In May 1799, during Napoleon's campaign in Palestine (see below), the government newspaper *Moniteur* published the information that Napoleon had issued a manifesto in Palestine which promised the Jews their return to their country. Many European newspapers reproduced this information, although today it is questioned whether Napoleon really issued such a declaration. The news concerning the manifesto and Napoleon's Palestine campaign made little impression on the Jews in Europe. On the other hand, the campaign gave rise to millenarian hopes among certain nonconformist circles in England; for the first time, their expectation of the return of Israel to Palestine and hence to the Church was linked with realistic political projects.

Bronze medal commemorating Napoleon's Sanhedrin, dated May 30, 1806. Diam. 1½ in. (4 cm.). Jerusalem, Israel Museum. Photo David Harris, Jerusalem.

The principal influence exercised by Napoleon as emperor on Jewish history was in the years 1806 to 1808 when he convened the *Assembly of Jewish Notables and the (French) *Sanhedrin, and established the *Consistories. The programmatic documents formulated during this period and the institutions which then came into being embody the first practical expression of the demands made by a centralized modern state on the Jews who had become its citizens—"the separation of the political from the religious elements in Judaism." The news of the activities of the Jewish assemblies stirred both Jewish and gentile sectors of society in Central and Western Europe. The Austrian authorities were apprehensive that the Jews would regard Napoleon in the light of a messiah. In England, theological hopes and political projects for the "Return of Israel" intensified. On March 17, 1808, however, Napoleon issued an order restricting the economic activity and the freedom of movement of the Jews in the eastern provinces of the empire for a period of ten years, an order which became known among Jews as the "Infamous Decree."

Napoleon's victorious armies brought civic emancipation to the Jews in all the countries of Central and Western Europe where governments dependent on him were formed. The central Jewish Consistory established in the Kingdom of Westphalia was the first Jewish institution in Europe to introduce reforms into the Jewish religion. The Jews of Eastern Europe were only ephemerally influenced by Napoleon's conquests. Discussions were held among Ḥasidim as to whether support should be given to Napoleon or the Russian Czar Alexander I in order to hasten the coming of the messiah. [B.M.]

The Palestine Campaign (Feb. 8–June 1, 1799). After the conquest of Egypt in August 1798 by Napoleon's army, the defeated survivors fled to Palestine, where the pasha of *Acre, Ahmad al-Jazzār, and the Turks, attempted to organize resistance. At the beginning of February, Napoleon moved into Palestine at the head of a 13,000-man army. He took El Arish on Feb. 20 and reached Gaza on Feb. 24; the small Jewish community there fled to Hebron. On March 1 Napoleon reached Ramleh and on March 7 Jaffa surrendered after a four-day siege. The French army continued northward, crossed the southern Carmel on March 16 and 17, and reached al-Ḥāvithiyya (west of Sha'ar ha-Amakim). Haifa was captured on March 18. On March 19 the French army reached the walls of Acre; however, supported by British warships, the city withstood a protracted siege and several assaults by the French. A Jew, Ḥ. S. *Farḥi, Ahmad al-Jazzār's chief aide, played an important role in its defense. By June 1799, Napoleon's army, now plague-ridden and decimated, had moved back into Egypt.

From a political point of view, Napoleon's campaign in Palestine marked the beginning of a renewed interest of the Western Powers in Palestine as occupying an important international position. From a social-cultural point of view the importance of the campaign was much more limited. However, this was the first substantial contact made between the inhabitants of Palestine and Westerners since the destruction of Crusader Acre. [A.J.BR.]

Impact on Jewish History. The forces unleashed by Napoleon brought in their wake contradictory effects on the course of modern Jewish history. The breakup of old European feudal patterns of societal organization was eventually to open up a range of new economic and political options for the Jew. The closed societies that restricted but sheltered him were never again to be the same. On the other hand, the immediate effect of these forces was to provoke an almost total reversal in the process of civic emancipation brought about in the course of Napoleonic conquests. Nonetheless, Jewish Emancipation was to come eventually, even if its triumph was to be delayed till later in the century. Well in advance of that time the Napoleonic uprooting of the established order forced the Jewish community to contend with the many challenges posed by that process to their traditions and their lives. Already before Napoleon there were individual Jews seeking an accommodation with the world outside the ghetto. The events that surrounded the Napoleonic adventure extended the concern of the few to the preoccupation of the people as a whole. Moreover, Napoleon's insistence on a price to be paid by the Jew for his entrance into the modern world was to set the tone for much of the debate within the Jewish community during the Emancipation era. How to remain loyal to the traditions of his people and at home in the modern world was a problem with which the Jew wrestled throughout the period of his modern history; it is a problem first posed practically and seriously by the threat of Napoleonic successes. [A.SHA.]

Bibliography: R. Anchel, *Napoléon et les Juifs* (1928); E. A. Halphen (ed.), *Recueil des lois, décrets et ordonnances concernant les Israélites* (1851); Sagnac, in: *Revue de l'histoire moderne et contemporaine*, 2–3 (1901–02); P. Guedalla, *Napoleon and Palestine* (1925); Gelber, in: REJ, 83 (1927), 1–21, 113–45; F. Kobler, *The Vision was There* (1956), 42–47; F. Pietri, *Napoléon et les Israélites* (1965); B. Mevorakh, *Napoleon u-Tekufato* (1968).

NAQUET, ALFRED JOSEPH (1834–1916), French chemist and republican politician. Born at Carpentras, Vaucluse, Naquet became professor of chemistry at the Polytechnic Institute at Palermo in 1863 and later professor of medicine in Paris. He participated in the 1867 Peace Conference at Geneva, where he spoke out against the French Empire and was imprisoned for 15 months. Naquet was again imprisoned following the publication of *Réligion, Propriété, Famille* in 1869, in which he opposed religious marriage, and was also deprived of his civic rights. Following his release he went to Spain but returned to France in 1870, working for the republican government in Tours. In 1871 he was elected deputy for Vaucluse, and from 1882 was a member of the senate. Naquet represented the left wing of the Assembly and the Senate and repeatedly pressed for legislation on divorce, the laws of 1884 being known as the "loi Naquet." His support for General Boulanger in 1888 did considerable harm to his career, and following allegations of complicity in the Panama scandal, he fled to England. Although subsequently vindicated, Naquet did not take any further part in French politics. His writings include: *Principes de chimie fondés sur les théories modernes* (1865); *Le Divorce* (1877); *L'Humanité et la patrie* (1901); *La République radicale*

Caricature of Alfred Naquet, promoter of a French divorce law. Jerusalem, J.N.U.L., Schwadron Collection.

(1873); and *Socialisme collectiviste et socialisme libéral* (1890). [S.A.M.]

NARA (also **ONR: Obóz Narodowo-Radykalny:** "National-Radical Camp"), a nationalistic, anti-Semitic organization in Poland, formed on April 14, 1934. The group was organized by youth who seceded from the *Endecja (ND) Party, which was also anti-Semitic. Whereas ND was anti-German, NARA, inspired and supported by the Nazis, wanted to serve as a bridge between the anti-Semitic ideologies of both Germany and Poland. The program of NARA envisaged a fascist regime modeled on the Nazi plan. It called for the assimilation of the Slavic minorities in Poland (Ukrainians, Belorussians), and the expulsion of Jews by means of economic boycott, by seizing their sources of living, confiscating their assets, and denying them all civil rights. With such forceful economic measures against Jews, NARA aimed to win the sympathy of the masses during a critical economic period and, at the same time, form a strong movement in oppositon to *Pilsudski's regime. The membership of NARA embraced mainly city youth and university students. After widespread terrorist activities against Jews, particularly Jewish students, NARA was dissolved by the government (July 10, 1934) and its newspaper *Sztafeta*, prohibited. The group continued its illegal activities, supported and increased by various rightist groups, until it met with complete defeat in the municipal elections of December 1938.

Bibliography: S. Segal, *The New Poland and the Jews* (1938), 83; R. L. Buell, *Poland: Key to Europe* (1939); 108, 117, 187; I. Greenbaum, in: EG, 1 (1953), 113–6; *Wielka Encyklopedia Powszechna*, 8 (1966), 89–90.
[ED.]

NARBATA, Jewish district E. of Caesarea, which perhaps inherited the name of Arubboth in the third district of Solomon (I Kings 4:10); it appears in the Book of Maccabees (I Macc. 5:23) as Arbatta, a city from which Simeon evacuated Jews at the beginning of the Hasmonean

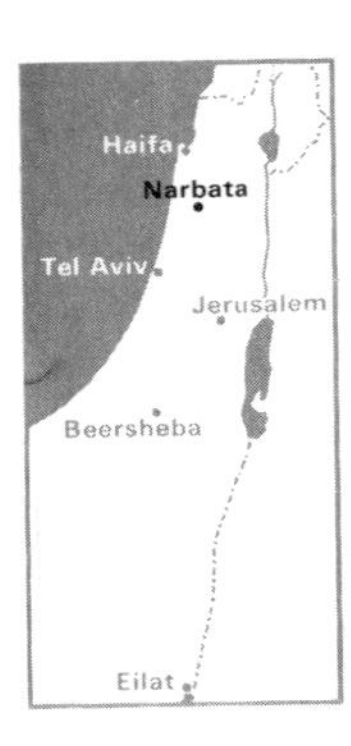

revolt. In 66 C.E., the Jews of Caesarea moved to the toparchy of Narbata because of persecution (Jos., Wars. 2:291). It is mentioned (in a different form) in the Jerusalem Talmud as the site of an inn (Ber. 6:1, 10b). The district of Narbata was inhabited by a mixture of Jews, Samaritans, and pagans. It is identified with Khirbat Baydūs, where there are remains of a town of the Roman period.

Bibliography: Avi-Yonah, Geog, 127 (incl. bibl.).

[M.A.-Y.]

NARBONI, family of French origin which established itself in Algeria toward the close of the 14th century. ALLAL BEN SIDUN BEN JOSHUA (15th century) was a wonder-working rabbi in Tlemcen. He composed a large number of *piyyutim*, some of which were included in the *maḥzor* of Tlemcen. Until recently, frequent pilgrimages were made to his grave. SHALOM (d. 1691), a financier in Algiers, was appointed *muqaddim* of the Jews of that town and played a political role in the relations with the Christian countries. MORDECAI (d. 1794) edited the work *Kol Yehudah* by Judah *Ayash of Algiers. Accused of having blasphemed Islam, he was given the alternative of conversion or death; he was beheaded in Algiers. ELIE and GEORGES, both heroes in World War I, were respectively president of the Jewish Consistory in Constantine and an army medical officer. ANDRÉ (1912–), lawyer and a leader of Algerian Jewry, participated in the defense of his coreligionists, particularly during the anti-Semitic Vichy government. A fervent Zionist, he was one of the founders of the Algerian Zionist movement. When Algeria achieved independence (1962), he settled in Israel, where he became a member of the executive of the Jewish Agency.

Bibliography: A. Cahen, *Les Juifs de l'Afrique Septentrionale* (1867), 100; M. Eisenbeth, *Le Judaisme Nord-Africain* (1931), 273; Hirschberg, Afrikah, 2 (1965), 53, 90.

[D.Co.]

NARBONNE, town in S. France, 5 mi. (8 km.) from the Mediterranean. The capital of medieval Septimania, Narbonne was ruled successively by the Visigoths (413?), the Saracens (719), and the Franks (759). About 900 it became the possession of the local viscount. In 1508 Louis XII of France annexed it to his domains. The earliest written evidence of a Jewish presence in France, from about 471, comes from Narbonne. Sidonius Apollinaris, bishop of Clermont (see *Clermont-Ferrand), entrusted a Jew by the name of Gozolas and a customer of Magnus Felix of Narbonne, with a letter for the latter. Jews are not mentioned again in Narbonne until a *Church council was held there in 589, which forbade Jews, under penalty of a heavy fine, to recite prayers aloud, even in Jewish funeral processions (canon 9, in Mansi, Collectio, IX, 1016). Soon after (597) Pope *Gregory I ordered an inquiry into a report that four captive Christian brothers had been bought by Jews of Narbonne who held them in their service. The earliest known inscription relating to the Jews of France also comes from Narbonne. It is an epitaph in Latin, including the phrase "Peace to Israel" in Hebrew, to three siblings who died either at the same time or within a short period of one another, probably victims of a plague recorded in Septimania at about the same period.

While there is no information about the Jews of Narbonne during the period of Muslim occupation, a legendary tradition of the 12th and 13th centuries tells of the election of "Jewish kings" there when the town was taken by Pépin the Short in 759. According to some sources (Philomena, *Gesta Caroli Magni ad Carcassonam; Milḥemet Mitzvah* of *Meir Simeon ha-Me'ili), Jews helped to drive out the Muslims and as a sure means of appreciation, were granted the right to be governed by a "Jewish king." Another source (the addition to the *Sefer ha-Kabbalah* of Abraham *ibn Daud) states that Charlemagne invited R. *Machir b. Judah, younger brother of *Gershom b. Judah, to become the founder of the dynasty of "Jewish kings." Although this princely dynasty is confirmed authentically only from the 11th or 12th centuries, the Jews held freehold properties by 768. Pope Stephen III in a letter addressed to Aribert, archbishop of Narbonne, was critical of the fact that Jews, by virtue of the privileges granted by the kings of France, not only owned alodial properties in both the towns and their surroundings, but also employed Christians to work in their vineyards and fields. At the close of the ninth century King Charles III the Simple (898–923) tried to dispossess the Jews of Narbonne of their estates, at first those that had been recently acquired from Christians, and later all others. These measures did not remain in force for long, and a short while later Jews again owned property, including mills which they also worked.

The partition of jurisdiction over the town between the viscount and the archbishop resulted in the emergence of two distinct groups of Jews, from the point of view of their civic administration (among themselves the Jews formed a single community). In the 11th century Archbishop Pons d'Arce nominated two Jews as toll gatherers. Between 1134 and 1143 clashes which broke out as a result of differences between Ermengarde, viscountess of Narbonne, and Alphonse Jourdain, count of Toulouse, worsened the situation of Narbonne's Jews, and many of them then emigrated to *Anjou, *Poitou, and to the kingdom of France. According to the addition to the *Sefer ha-Kabbalah*, the Jews of Narbonne numbered 2,000 around 1143; in 1161 Benjamin of Tudela mentions 300 Jews there (but since this figure probably refers to heads of families there was probably a Jewish population of some 1,500). In 1163 Jews were the objects of attacks by the Spanish crusaders but were protected by both Viscount Bérenger and Archbishop Guiffrey.

The Jewish quarter of the viscounty (known as *Grande Juiverie, Jouzaigas Majours*, etc.), which was of considerable size, situated to the north of the present Place de l'Hotel de Ville and Cours de la République, did not constitute a "closed" quarter and non-Jews and Jews lived side by side. From 1217 the Jews benefited from a very advantageous

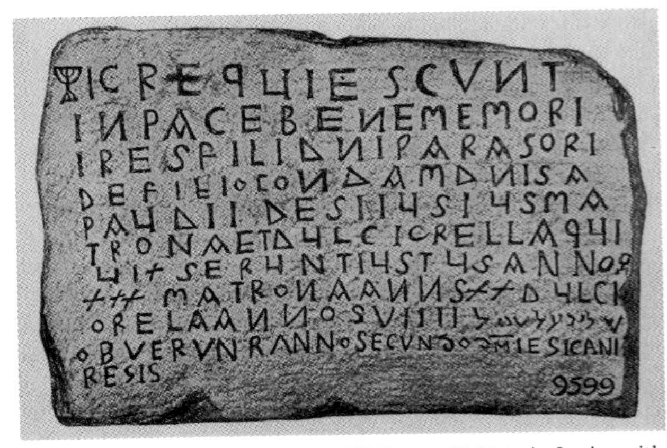

Jewish epitaph from Narbonne, 688/9 C.E. Written in Latin, with a *menorah* at the beginning and the phrase "Peace to Israel" in Hebrew toward the end, it records the burial of three children of Paragonis son of Sapandus: Justus, aged 30, Matrona, aged 20, and Dulcinorella, aged nine. Narbonne Museum.

charter granted by the viscount, in which they were represented by ten arbitrators. Although the Jewish quarter under the archbishop's jurisdiction, situated in the Belvèze quarter, did not obtain such an advantageous charter until 1284, the two Jewish sections shared all community resources. In the viscounty there were at least two synagogues, a hospital, baths, and workrooms, and in the archbishopric there was a cemetery, known as Mont judaïque (or Montjuzaic), some of whose epitaphs were found and preserved in the museum.

In 1236 a petty brawl between a Jew and a fisherman that ended in an accidental homicide set off an anti-Jewish riot which was rapidly suppressed by Viscount Aimeri IV, who ordered the restitution of all objects stolen during the pillage. The Jewish community celebrated its good fortune by a local Purim. At the end of 1246 Viscount Amauri I demonstrated his sympathy toward the Jews by attending a protest meeting against the anti-Jewish policies of King *Louis IX. It was, therefore, not surprising that the Jewish quarter of the viscounty attracted Jews from the rest of the province as well as from the archbishop's part of the town. After disputes between the two overlords of the town over the judicial status of certain Jews, both joined forces to defend themselves against the claims of the monarchy, which sought to deprive them (from the close of the 13th century) of the jurisdiction over "their" Jews. When the expulsion order was issued, however, there was no evidence of protest by either the archbishop or the viscount, and it was only with the liquidation of Jewish property that both intervened to claim their share of the profits. (Only the viscount made a satisfactory settlement with the king.) In 1306, on the eve of the expulsion, the town register indicated 165 Jewish households, or about 825 persons (less than 5% of the total population). The exiled Jews moved mainly to *Roussillon or to the Catalonian regions. A few returned in 1315 and later, in 1359, more returned. Tradition has it that three events caused the decline of the town of Narbonne: the silting of the Aude River; the expulsion of the Jews in 1306; and the *Black Death plague of 1348.

The Jews of Narbonne were engaged in both agriculture and the production of wine. With the transfer of ownership of cultivable areas Jews, nevertheless, often retained part of the harvest for themselves. Jews were also involved with salt mines and water mills. Serving as public functionaries, Narbonne's Jews also collected fees for the archbishop and acted as brokers as well as traders. A Jewish notary served to draw up contracts between Jews. There were a number of Jewish physicians in Narbonne and also some goldsmiths. Many Jews practiced moneylending, particularly from the beginning of the 13th century. (Loans were generally given against pledges, personal property, or real estate.)

In his *Sefer ha-Kabbalah,* Abraham ibn Daud mentions only two French communities which were outstanding for their learning and one of them was Narbonne. Important scholars were R. *Moses b. Joseph b. Merwan ha-Levi, R. *Abraham b. Isaac of Narbonne, and R. Meir b. Joseph (toward the middle of the 13th century), who "caused the Torah to shine forth before their disciples by the study of the Pentateuch, the Bible, the Mishnah, the Babylonian Talmud, and the Jerusalem Talmud." Benjamin of Tudela praised the town "which already has an ancient reputation for erudition. And from there, the Torah has spread throughout all countries. Scholars and men of great authority live there." Among Narbonne's most famous scholars were *Moses ha-Darshan, exegete and head of the yeshivah (toward the middle of the 11th century); Abraham b. Isaac of Narbonne, referred to as *av bet din,* the father-in-law of *Abraham b. David of Posquières and author of ritual works and talmudic commentaries (second half of the 12th century); Joseph *Kimḥi *(Maistre Petit)* and his two sons Moses *Kimḥi and David *Kimḥi (second half of the 12th and early 13th centuries); *Isaac b. Meir of Narbonne, liturgic poet (first half of the 13th century); Moses b. Joseph b. Merwan ha-Levi, teacher of (among others) Abraham b. David; Meir b. Simeon ha-Me'ili, author of *Milḥemet Mitzvah* (middle of the 13th century); and Maestro David de Caslari, physician and poet famous for his commentary on *Maimonides' *Guide;* and Moses b. Joshua b. Har David Narboni (late 13th century). There were others who stayed for a time in Narbonne or who were born there but whose activities were restricted to other places. Numerous personalities later bore the surname Narboni. The 13th-century Jewish troubadour, Bofilh, also came from Narbonne.

From the beginning of the 18th century, Jewish merchants from Avignon were authorized to visit Narbonne four times a year in order to trade there for a period of one month each time. From the close of the 18th century Jews settled in the town as permanent residents. On the eve of World War II there were hardly any Jews in Narbonne, as was still the situation in 1970.

Bibliography: Gross, Gal Jud, 401ff.; G. Saige, *Les Juifs du Languedoc* (1881), index; J. Regne, *Etude sur la condition des Juifs à Narbonne* (1912); B. Blumenkranz, *Juifs et chrétiens . . .* (1960), index; I. Levi, in: REJ, 48 (1904), 197ff.; 49 (1904), 147ff.; Frey, Corpus, no. 670; R. W. Emery, *Heresy and Inquisition in Narbonne . . .* (1941), 22; Z. Szajkowski, *Franco-Judaica* (1962), no. 309; idem, *Analytical Franco-Jewish Gazetteer* (1966), 164; Ibn Daud, Tradition, index.

[B.BL.]

NARDI (Narodietzky), NAHUM (1901–), composer. Born in Kiev, Nardi studied the piano and composition at the Kiev, Warsaw, and Vienna conservatories and went to Palestine in 1923. There he began to give piano recitals but soon turned to composing, inspired by Arab bedouin and peasant songs and the Sephardi and Yemenite melos. Many of his songs for children and adults became folk songs for which he developed an original style of piano accompaniment. Many of them were first performed at his joint recitals with the Yemenite singer, Bracha *Zefira, his first wife. For these recitals he developed an original style of piano accompaniment. In later years Nardi also promoted the careers of several other singers of Yemenite origin. Among other associations which contributed to his production and style were those with Ḥayyim Naḥman *Bialik, the poet and educator Levin *Kipnis, and the poet and composer Yiẓḥak Navon.

Nardi's songs, which have achieved folk song status, include: *Shir ha-Avodah ve-ha-Melakhah, Bein Nehar Perat, Yesh Li Gan* (Bialik), *Mi Yivneh Bayit be-Tel Aviv, Shanah Halkhah, Ani Purim* (L. Kipnis, the latter also metamorphosed by an unknown kindergarten poet into the ubiquitous *Ha-Shafan ha-Katan*); *Kakhol Yam ha-Mayim* (N. Alterman); *Hudi Ḥamudi* (M. Dafna); *Alei Givah* (Broides, the tune beginning DGFED as distinct from M. *Ravina's setting); *Pattish Masmer Nikkakh Maher* (E. Harussi); *Shetu ha-Adarim* (A. Penn); *Sisi Admat ha-Sharon* (Y. Fichmann); *Mi Yitteneni Of* (D. Shimoni), *Im Yesh Ei Sham* (Y. Karni)—both transformations of oriental Jewish folk melodies.

[B.B.]

NARESH, town situated on the bank of the Euphrates, south of the old city of Babylon and of *Sura. A canal went from near Naresh to *Nippur. The town was situated in a hilly district and extended over a very wide area (Er. 56a). As a result it was not surrounded by a wall and this constituted a danger to the safety of its inhabitants at night (Ḥul. 127a). This particularly affected the women of the city who were obliged to undergo their ritual bathing (Nid. 67b). Naresh became renowned in the talmudic era because of Rav Papa, a native of Naresh, who lived and was active there in the middle of the fourth century C.E. Rav Papa studied at *Maḥoza under Rava, and after Rava's death some of his pupils left for Naresh, where Papa served as head of the academy and Huna b. Joshua as head of the **kallah*. The Jews of Naresh engaged in agriculture (BM

68a), and among the products made by its inhabitants, thick blankets were famous (Yoma 69a). The inhabitants had a bad reputation and were known as extortioners and thieves; it was said: "If a native of Naresh kisses you, count your teeth" (Ḥul. 127a).

Bibliography: Neubauer, Geog, 365; A. Berliner, in: *Jahresbericht des Rabbiner-Seminars zu Berlin pro 5643 (1882–1883)*, 54; J. Obermeyer, *Die Landschaft Babylonien im Zeitalter des Talmuds und des Gaonates* (1929), 306–12. [M.BE.]

NARKISS, MORDECHAI (1898–1957), Israel museum curator and art historian. Narkiss was born in Skala, Poland. In 1920 he settled in Ereẓ Israel, where he continued his studies at the *Bezalel School, Jerusalem, and became assistant to the director, Boris *Schatz. Narkiss began to devote himself to amassing a collection of Jewish art and antiquities, and in 1932 became director of the *Bezalel Museum. The museum had closed down with the school after Schatz's death, but Narkiss founded the Society of Friends of the Bezalel National Museum and reopened it under the auspices of the executive of the Zionist Organization.

Mordechai Narkiss, art historian and director of the Bezalel Museum, Jerusalem. Photo A. Bernheim, Jerusalem.

Narkiss wrote on many aspects of Jewish art. Among his publications were *Matbe'ot Ereẓ Yisrael* ("Coins of Ereẓ Israel," two parts, 1936 and 1938), *The Channuka Lamp* (1939), *The Artcraft of the Yemenite Jews* (1941), and *Niello Work as a Jewish Craft* (1942). He also wrote many articles, translated books on art, and was art editor of the *Encyclopaedia Hebraica*. The sixth volume of *Eretz Israel* (1960), one of the publications of the Israel Exploration Society, was dedicated to his memory. It included a complete bibliography of his works. [ED.]

NAROL, small town in the region of Lubaczow, southeastern Poland. Founded in 1585 as the settlement of Floryjanowa, the town later received the name of Narol. Jews who settled there were active as merchants and lessees. They developed an economically flourishing community which existed until 1648/49, when the entire settlement of some 12,000 was destroyed in the *Chmielnicki pogroms. About 40,000 refugees from neighboring settlements fled to Narol in 1648 in fear of the Cossacks. When the town was captured (1649) all of them were slaughtered. Nathan Nata *Hannover, in his *Yeven Meẓulah*, described the massacre in these words: "Many were drowned in the water, many hundreds shut themselves up in the synagogue, but they broke down the doors and first slew the Jews inside it and then burnt the synagogue with the slain. There was no such slaughter in the whole of Poland ..." Documents on the history of the Jews in the town were also destroyed during the massacre. Although much wealth was lost in the Cossack plunder, a large part of it hidden under the ruins of the houses was discovered in the 19th century. Moses Kohen, rabbi of Narol, who was saved from the slaughter and later appointed rabbi of Metz in France, composed a *selihah* in which he lamented the destruction of Narol—the death of its scholars and the loss of the Torah centers in the town. The settlement never returned to its prior glory. When the *Council of Four Lands was disbanded, the town still owed sums of money on taxes and other payments to the Council. Narol was incorporated into the territory of Austria following the partition of Poland in 1772. After World War I, Narol became part of independent Poland, and in 1921 the number of Jews totaled 734 (out of 1,817). The majority of its Jews were Zionists who took an active part in the affairs of the Zionist Federation. In 1933 misfortune again overtook the town when a fire completely destroyed the houses of 23 families. No further information on the fate of the community is available. [SH.L.K.]

NAROT, JOSEPH (1913–), U.S. Reform rabbi and communal leader. Narot, who was born in Vilna, immigrated with his family to Ohio where he grew up and was educated. He was ordained by Hebrew Union College in 1940. He served first as assistant rabbi (1940–41), then as rabbi (1941–50) of Temple Beth Israel in Atlantic City, New Jersey. In 1950 he became rabbi of Temple Israel, Miami, that city's oldest Reform synagogue. In Atlantic City, Narot was active in U.J.A. drives and was founder and president of the Atlantic City Forum, composed of 60 civic organizations. He continued to divide his time between Jewish and civic concerns in Miami where he was member and chairman of the Dade County Community Board (1964–68). He was also president of the Dade County Welfare Planning Council (1961–63) and a founder of the Interfaith Agency for Social Justice. [GL.R.]

NASATIR, ABRAHAM PHINEAS (1904–), U.S. historian. Born in Santa Ana, California, Nasatir taught at the University of Iowa and then moved to San Diego State College. He was fellow of the Social Science Research Council and president of the Pacific Coast Branch of the American Historical Association.

Nasatir specialized in the history of the United States, west and southwest, and published *Before Lewis and Clark* (2 vols, 1952). He edited Etienne Derbec's *A French Journalist in the California Gold Rush* (1964). Later his interest in the southwest expanded beyond the U.S. frontier to include Hispanic America and led to a history of that area, together with Helen M. Baily, *Latin America* (1960, 1968[2]). He was active in Jewish affairs. His writings include *French Activities in California* (1945); and with G. E. Monell, *French Consuls in the United States* (1967); with N. M. Loomis, *Pedro Vial and the Roads to Santa Fé* (1967); and *Spanish War Vessels on the Mississippi, 1792–1796* (1968).

Bibliography: *Contemporary Authors*, 11–12 (1965), 287. [S.J.S.]

NASAUD (Rum. **Năsăud;** Hung. **Naszód**), town in Bistrita-Năsăud county (Transylvania), Rumania. Until 1918 and between 1940 and 1945, Nasaud was part of Hungary. While still under Hungarian rule, it was a center of the Rumanian nationalist movement. Jews settled in Nasaud after the law prohibiting their settlement was abrogated in 1848 while residence in the town itself was still barred. Jews lived in the nearby village of Jidovitza (Entredam), today named *Rebreanu. The community was Orthodox and strongly influenced by *Ḥasidism. In 1885 the government designated the community as the administrative center for the Jews of all the villages in the district. The community possessed a large synagogue, a *bet midrash*, and a *ḥeder*. Jewish children attended elementary and secondary school in which the language of instruction was Rumanian. The Jewish population in Nasaud itself declined from 859 in 1866 to 425 (12% of the total) in 1930, and 415 (12.9%) in 1940. There were 1,198 Jews living in the surrounding villages in 1930. Some 400 Jews were deported to Auschwitz in the summer of 1944. After World War II, about 110 Jews returned to Nasaud, including former residents who had survived the camps and some who had previously lived in the surrounding district. As a result of emigration to Israel and elsewhere the Jewish population dwindled and by 1971 only two families were left in the town. [Y.M.]

NASHIM (Heb. נָשִׁים; "Women"), third order of the Mishnah, according to the accepted order mentioned in the homily of *Simeon b. Lakish (Shab. 31a; according to the order given by Tanḥuma (Num. R. 13:15) it is the first). *Nashim* deals essentially with matrimonial law and with the laws governing the relations between husband and wife. It also includes the tractates **Nedarim* ("vows") and **Nazir* ("the Nazirite") respectively, since according to the Bible (Num. 30:4ff.), the vow of a wife or a girl during her minority can be annulled by the husband or father (cf. Sot. 2a). The tractates included in *Nashim* are: **Yevamot*, 16 chapters; **Ketubbot*, 13; *Nedarim*, 11; *Nazir*, 9; **Sotah*, 9; **Gittin*, 9; and **Kiddushin*, 4. As is customary, the tractates are arranged in descending order according to the number of chapters (see *Mishnah). The *mishnayot* of *Nashim* also contain incidental aggadic passages, but at the end of *Sotah* and *Kiddushin* there are more continuous aggadic passages. In the Tosefta, *Yevamot* has 14 chapters; *Ketubbot*, 12 (or 13); *Nedarim*, 7; *Nazir*, 6; *Sotah*, 15; *Gittin*, 7 (or 9); and *Kiddushin*, 5. The aggadic section is richer than that of the Mishnah, particularly in *Sotah*. Because of their practical importance for matrimonial law and sexual morality, the tractates of the order *Nashim* are stressed in rabbinic study, and the more practically relevant parts have received extensive treatment by both the medieval commentators and the later rabbinical authorities, including all the responsa literature. [D.J.B.]

NASH PAPYRUS, a second-century (c. 150) B.C.E. papyrus fragment written in square Hebrew script, containing the *Decalogue and the **Shema*. The Nash Papyrus was the oldest biblical text known before the discovery of the *Dead Sea Scrolls. A single sheet, not from a scroll, it was purchased from an Egyptian dealer by W. L. Nash, secretary of the Society of Biblical Archaeology in England and published by S. A. Cooke in 1903. The papyrus is of unknown provenance, although allegedly from Fayyum. The text of the Decalogue accords closely with the Septuagint of Exodus (20:2ff.), and must resemble the Hebrew that underlay the Septuagint translation (see table of variants in article *Decalogue). The *Shema* follows (Deut. 6:4–5), including the Septuagint's preliminary to verse 4: "And these are the statutes and the judgments that Moses (so Nash; LXX, "the Lord") commanded [the Israelites] in the wilderness when they left the land of Egypt." The papyrus breaks off after the second letter of verse 5. The combination of the Decalogue and the *Shema* indicates that the text of the papyrus represents the Torah readings included in the daily morning liturgy of Second Temple times (cf. Tam. 5:1: "they recited the Decalogue, the *Shema*, etc.").

Bibliography: S. A. Cooke, in: PSBA, 25 (1903), 34–56; F. C. Burkitt, in: JQR, 15 (1903), 392–408; J. Mann, in: HUCA, 2 (1925), 283; W. F. Albright, in: JBL, 56 (1937), 145–76; idem, in: BASOR, 115 (1949), 10–19; M. Z. (H.) Segal, in: *Leshonenu*, 15 (1947), 27–36; Birnbaum, in: BASOR, 115 (1949), 20–22; F. M. Cross, in: JBL, 74 (1955), 148 n. 3. [Mo.G.]

NASI. In biblical usage, *nasi* signifies an important person, ranging from a king to a tribal chief or the head of a large family. The *nesi'im* are the leaders of the people in the wilderness (Ex. 16:22, 34:31), and are counted by name (Num. 1:5–16); they are sent to spy out the land and are charged with its apportionment (Num. 13:1–15, 34:16ff.); they bring special gifts and sacrifices to the tabernacle (Ex. 35:27; Num. 7:10ff.). The institution reflects the tribal covenant and declines with the conquest of Canaan; it is revived by Ezekiel, who denotes by it the future ruler of the people. This prophet so names the rulers of other small nations as well, but his avoidance of the term *melekh* ("king") for the future ruler of Israel may signify disapproval of monarchical absolutism. Jewish rulers during the period of the Second Temple used the title *nasi*, thus asserting their authority while avoiding the assumption of kingship. I Maccabees 14:41 tells that Simeon the Hasmonean was declared ethnarch ("ruler of the people") by the people in 141 B.C.E., the Hebrew original of that title probably being *nasi*. Coins minted by *Bar Kokhba during the abortive revolt against Rome bear the inscription, *Shimon Nesi Yisrael*, demonstrating that the rebel leader considered himself *nasi* of the people; the title is similarly found in letters credited to Bar Kokhba.

While the rabbis understood certain biblical instances of the term to mean "king" (see Hor. 3:3), they applied the title in a more limited sense to the president of the Sanhedrin, and perhaps to the heads of other bodies and orders too. The secular head of the sect described in the *Dead Sea Scrolls also bore the title (War Scroll, ed. Yadin, p. 184; in the English edition, p. 279). Rabbinic sources call

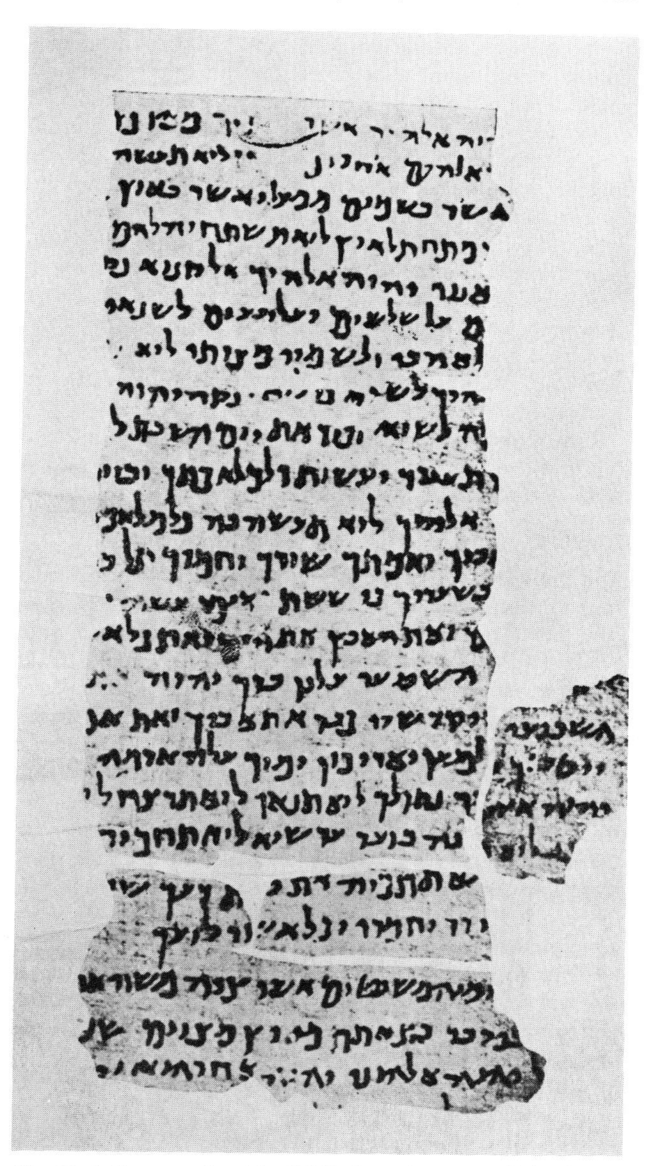

The Nash Papyrus, the oldest biblical text known until the discovery of the Dead Sea Scrolls. From E. L. Sukenik, *Megillot Genuzot*, Jerusalem, 1948.

one of the "pairs" *(zugot)*, going back to Yose b. Joezer (c. 165 B.C.E), the *nasi* (Ḥag. 2:2), and continue to use the term for the head of the court through amoraic times. Historians have long been divided on the reliability of these early sources: some claim the title is used anachronistically, its actual usage commencing only with *Judah ha-Nasi (fl. 190 C.E.); others believe it first came into use after 70 C.E., or in 30 B.C.E. at the time of Hillel the Elder; yet others accept the mishnaic testimony (the head of a Phoenician *synodos* is called *nasi* in 96 B.C.E.) and even claim that the office is pre-Maccabean. The office was held by scions of the Hillelite family, though unusual circumstances may have allowed others to hold the office for relatively short periods, and it may have been unfilled when conditions were most disturbed (such as during the Hadrianic persecutions). The last Hillelite *nasi* was Rabban Gamaliel (VI), who died in 425.

With the destruction of the Temple in 70 C.E., the office of the *nasi* becomes more significant. Onkelos performed the mourning ritual for Rabban Gamaliel II as though he were a king (see Sem. 8), and there is a strong implication that Rome extended him its recognition (see Eduy. 7:7). The Hillelite *nasi* was recognized as political head ("Patriarch") of the people by the Roman government (Cod. Theod. xvi.8), an arrangement that allowed for more effective control and administration of its Jewish subjects. From the Jewish point of view, the Patriarchate provided the people with a Roman official sympathetic to their needs, and it placed significant power in rabbinic hands. The rabbis, for their part, relaxed certain religious laws so as to allow the patriarch greater ease in Roman society. Internally, the *nasi* presided over the Sanhedrin, fixed the calendar together with the court by proclaiming the new month and intercalating the year, led public prayers for rain, and ordained scholars (the content and scope of this ordination being somewhat unclear). He kept in touch with the Jewish communities of the Diaspora, dispatching apostles to preach, teach, set up courts, and raise funds. His court possessed legislative powers, and so most *takkanot* ("enactments") were attributed to the presiding *nasi*. [G.J.B.]

Post-Geonic Period. The title *nasi* persisted for many centuries and in different lands throughout the Middle Ages, sometimes as the title of a defined head of a Jewish institution, sometimes as an honorific title only, given to important personages and to sons of illustrious families. The *nasi* as the leader of the community (see *Autonomy) is found in Jerusalem; in Fostat, Egypt; in Baghdad, Damascus, and Mosul, Syria; and in Spain under Muslim rule. Some had considerable power, similar to that of the exilarch, especially the *nesi'im* of Ereẓ Israel, Syria, and Egypt. The earliest person known in the post-geonic period to bear this title is Ẓemaḥ in Egypt or Syria, with the latest Sar Shalom b. Phinehas, who is mentioned in 1341 in Egypt and Baghdad. Most of the other twenty-odd names are from the 11th century among them *Daniel b. Azariah, *David b. Daniel, and Jedidiah b. Zakkai. One, Shem Tov, a most respected *nasi* of Jerusalem, could not prove Davidic descent and was exiled. Some *nesi'im* in Muslim Spain were appointed by the court and repesented the Jews at court, collected taxes, and acted as chief justices. The *Karaites also called their heads *nasi*, from their founder *Anan b. David through the 18th century. From early modern times the title *nasi* was also given to the heads of the **kolel* institutions of the **Ḥalukkah*. In later modern times the title "president," especially of democratic political and social bodies, was translated into Hebrew as *nasi;* as such it has been carried over into the political nomenclature of the State of Israel, being used to designate the president of the State. [I.L.]

Bibliography: R. de Vaux, Anc Isr, 8; H. Mantel, *Studies in the History of the Sanhedrin* (1961), 1–53, 175–253; idem, in: HTR, 60 (1967), 90; Alon, Meḥkarim, 2 (1958), 15–57; S. Zeitlin, *Religious and Secular Leadership* (1943), 7–15; Baron, Social[2], 2 (1952), 191–209; 5 (1957), 38–46, 314; E. A. Speiser, *Oriental and Biblical Studies* (1967), 113–26; S. Abramsky, *Bar Kokhva, Nesi Yisrael* (1961). POST-GEONIC: S. Poznański, *Babylonische Geonim im nachgaonaeischen Zeitalter* (1914); Mann, Egypt, index; Ashtor. Korot.

NASI, GRACIA (c. 1510–1569), Marrano stateswoman and patroness. A member of the first generation of Portuguese Marranos (probably of Spanish descent), her original name as a Christian in Portugal, where she was born, was Beatrice de Luna. In 1528 she married Francisco Mendes, also a Marrano, who with his brother Diogo *Mendes built up out of a business in precious stones an important banking establishment, with a branch in Antwerp (directed by Diogo) which soon outdid the main establishment in importance. In 1537, after her husband's death, the widow left Portugal with her family (including her nephew, João Micas (Miques, Miguez, later Joseph *Nasi) and went via England to the Low Countries, where she joined her brother-in-law. There she became known in aristocratic society, and assisted her brother-in-law in his efforts to aid the flight of the Marranos and to stop the activity of the Inquisition in Portugal. After Diogo's death in 1543 she fled from Flanders (1545), leaving much of her property behind, and settled in Venice. There she was denounced to the authorities as a Judaizer by her own sister Reyna, Diogo's widow. João Miques, however, secured Turkish diplomatic intervention on her behalf and she was released. She and her family then settled in Ferrara. About this time she threw off the disguise of Christianity and became known by her Jewish name of Gracia Nasi.

In Ferrara she continued her remarkable work for organizing the flight of fugitive Marranos from Portugal; this is described in Samuel *Usque's *Consolaçam as Tribulaçoens de Israel,* which (together with the Ferrara Spanish Bible of 1553) is dedicated to her in admiring terms. In 1553 Gracia Nasi settled in Constantinople, where she continued similar activity; she also patronized scholars and established academies and synagogues in Constantinople and Salonika, and perhaps elsewhere. In 1556–57, she attempted to organize a punitive boycott of the port of *Ancona in Italy, in retaliation for the burning there of 26

Gracia Nasi, Marrano leader, portrayed on a medal by Pastorino de Pastorini, 1553. Jerusalem, J.N.U.L., Schwadron Collection.

Marranos as renegades from the Christian faith; she secured the intervention of the sultan for some of the accused who were Turkish subjects, including her business agents. In 1554 she was joined in Constantinople by her nephew (henceforth Joseph Nasi), who married her only child Reyna and was now associated closely with all her enterprises, both political and commercial. In 1558 or 1559 she secured from the sultan, in return for an annual payment of 1,000 ducats, a grant of the ruined city of *Tiberias in Ereẓ Israel, where she set up a yeshivah; this grant was subsequently renewed, with a political motivation by Joseph Nasi.

Doña Gracia was certainly the outstanding Jewess of her day, and perhaps of the entire period between the fall of the Jewish state and the present. She was known as *La Senora*, or *Ha-Geveret*, and the synagogue known by this name long continued to exist in Constantinople. She was, however, inactive, perhaps because of ill-health, for some years before her death, possibly in Ereẓ Israel, in 1569.

Bibliography: C. Roth, *The House of Nasi: Dona Gracia* (1947); idem, in: *The Seventy-Fifth Anniversary Volume of the Jewish Quarterly Review* (1967), 460–72; A. Fernand-Halphen, *Une grande dame juive de la Renaissance: Gracia Mendesia Nasi* (1929); P. Grunebaum-Ballin, *Joseph Naci duc de Naxos* (1968), passim; Ginsberger, in: REJ, 83 (1930), 179–92. [C.R.]

NASI, JOSEPH (c. 1524–1579), statesman. Nasi was born as a Marrano in Portugal, perhaps descended from the ancient Spanish Jewish family of Nasi. He was the son of the Portuguese royal physician Agostinho (formerly Samuel) Micas (d. 1525), who taught medicine at the University of Lisbon. Joseph, known originally as a Christian by the name of João Micas (Miques, Míguez), accompanied his paternal aunt, Beatrice de Luna (Gracia *Nasi), when she went from Lisbon to Antwerp in 1537. After studying at the University of Louvain, he entered the banking establishment of *Mendes and was responsible for settling the family's affairs when Gracia left in 1545 for Italy. He was then in contact with Emperor *Charles V and the queen regent of the Netherlands, and is said to have been the jousting partner of their nephew, the future emperor Maximilian. Despite the dexterity of his negotiations, he was unable to save the family property from confiscation, and fled after them in about 1547. The following years he spent in France, where he became known to King Francis I, and later in Italy. He is alleged to have sought the Venetian government's concession of one of their islands as a refuge for fugitive *Marranos. Early in 1554 he joined his aunt, Gracia Nasi, in Constantinople, where he was circumcised and assumed the name of Joseph Nasi. In August he married her daughter Reyna. Henceforth, he was closely associated with his aunt in her commercial and political activities. In 1556 he joined her in organizing the blockade of the port of *Ancona to avenge the persecution of the Marranos there.

In the struggle for the succession to Sultan *Suleiman I between his sons Selim and Bajazet he supported the former, with the result that he received many favors from him, including the rank and emoluments of *muterferik* ("gentleman of the imperial retinue"). Due to his intimate knowledge of European affairs and statesmen, and his chain of agents throughout the Western world, he exercised great influence on the foreign policy of the Sublime Porte, helping Alexander Lapuseanu, the former voivode of Moldavia, to recover his throne and taking a prominent part in the peace negotiations between Poland and Turkey in 1562. In 1569 he encouraged the Netherlands' revolt against Spain and a letter of his, promising Turkish support, was read out at a meeting of the Calvinist consistory of Amsterdam. By then

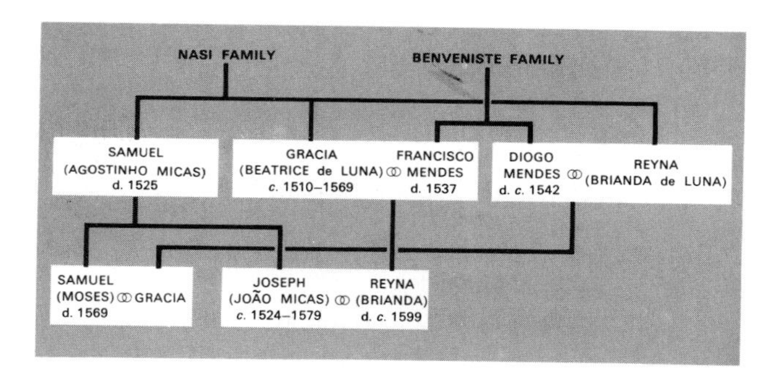

his influence at Constantinople had grown, due to the accession to the throne (1566) of his friend Sultan *Selim II, who esteemed him as his favorite. Immediately after this, he was granted a monopoly on the import of wines through the Bosporus, said to have brought him a net income of 15,000 ducats annually. In addition, he obtained important trading privileges in Poland. In order to satisfy certain claims against the king of France (who had sequestered the family property left in that country, on the pretext that Jews were not tolerated there), he obtained the sultan's firman (1568) ordering the confiscation of one-third of the merchandise on French ships docking at Alexandria. This firman was revoked in August 1569, the sultan stating that he had been misled. At this period, Nasi's influence at court seemed to wane and the French envoy, Grandchamp, launched an elaborate plot with Nasi's former physician, Daoud, in the hope of disgracing him. The plot failed and Daoud was excommunicated by the principal Jewish communities of the Turkish Empire.

Soon after Selim's accession, he appointed Nasi duke of the island of Naxos and the adjacent archipelago, whose Christian duke had recently been deposed, and eventually he also became count of Andros. He administered his duchy mainly from his palace at Belvedere near Constantinople, his local representative being Francisco Coronel or Coronello, a descendant of Abraham *Seneor, the last chief rabbi of Castile. During the War of Lepanto (1570–71) Nasi's dominions were reconquered by the Venetians for the former duke, but Nasi's authority was soon reinstated. In compensation for his loss, he is supposed to have been appointed voivode of Walachia in 1571, but the facts concerning this are obscure.

As early as 1558 or 1559, Doña Gracia obtained from the sultan various concessions in *Tiberias, then in ruins, probably with intention of founding a yeshivah there. In 1561 Joseph obtained confirmation and extension of this grant, giving him plenary authority in Tiberias and seven nearby villages in consideration of an annual payment. In the winter of 1564–65 the rebuilding of the ruined walls of Tiberias was completed, ensuring a certain degree of physical security. This was the only practical attempt to establish some sort of Jewish political center in Palestine between the fourth and 19th centuries. It is not clear, however, whether Nasi thought of it primarily as a political, a charitable, or even an economic enterprise; it is certain in any case that he never visited his domain. He attempted to develop it commercially, fostering the wool and silk industries. He also sent a circular letter to the Jewish communities of Italy inviting them to settle there, and the community of Cori in the Campania made preparations (not perhaps fulfilled) to accept his invitation *en masse*. The intrigues of the native Arabs and Christians and the jealousy of Nasi's rivals in Constantinople led him to concentrate his interest elsewhere. Nevertheless, he remained titular lord of Tiberias until his death, the concession being afterward renewed for Solomon *Abenaes.

Nasi encouraged Jewish scholarship by his patronage of various scholars, such as Moses *Almosnino who composed his "Treatise on Dreams," at Nasi's request; the physician Amatus *Lusitanus, who dedicated his fifth *Centuria* to Nasi; Isaac *Akrish, whom he supported when he was impoverished by the Constantinople fire of 1569; and Isaac *Onkeneira, his translator and director of the yeshivah and synagogue that he maintained at Belvedere. A fine library from which some manuscripts still survive adjoined these institutions. Joseph's only independent literary production, edited by the same Isaac Onkeneira, was his *Ben Porat Yosef* (Constantinople, 1577)—a polemic against astrology, which records a dispute he had with certain Christian dignitaries.

In 1569 Nasi threw his powerful influence on the side of the war party in Constantinople, and was considered to be mainly responsible for the Turkish war against Venice over Cyprus. It was reported that the sultan had promised to make him king of this island, though it would remain a Turkish fief. Some suggest that Nasi thus planned to provide a political solution to the Jewish problem of the day. Although the Turks conquered Cyprus in 1571 they suffered a naval disaster at Lepanto, in consequence of which the peace party led by Grand Vizier Mehemet Sokolli gained the ascendant. Nasi's influence henceforth waned, though he remained in possession of his dignities and privileges until his death. The balance of his achievement was disappointing, due to his inconstancy of purpose. It is difficult to decide what credence can be placed in the Spanish report that he repented of his action in abandoning Christianity and desired to return to Western Europe.

Joseph was survived by his widow, REYNA, duchess of Naxos (d. c. 1599), who maintained his library and allowed scholars access to it. In 1592 she set up a printing press in her palace at Belvedere. It was directed by Joseph b. Isaac Ashkeloni, and operated until 1594; it operated again from 1597 to 1599. Some 12 works, commemorating Reyna's generosity on the title page, were issued from the press.

Bibliography: C. Roth, *House of Nasi: The Duke of Naxos* (1948); P. Grunebaum-Ballin, *Joseph Naci, duc de Naxos* (1968); J. Reznik, *Le Duc Joseph de Naxos* (1936); A. Galanté, *Don Joseph Nasi, Duc de Naxos, d'après de nouveaux documents* (1913); idem, in: REJ, 64 (1912), 236–43; M. A. Levy, *Don Joseph Nasi, Herzog von Naxos, seine Familie, und zwei juedische Diplomaten seiner Zeit* (1859); P. Wittek, in: *Bulletin of the School of Oriental and African Studies*, 14 (1952), 381–3; Arce, in: *Sefarad*, 13 (1953), 257–86; Kaufmann, in: JQR, 2 (1889/90), 291–7; 4 (1891/92), 509–12; 13 (1900/01), 520–32; Besohn, in: MGWJ, 18 (1869), 422–4; Rahn, *ibid.*, 28 (1879), 113–21. [C.R.]

NASIELSK (Rus. **Nasyelsk**), town in Warszawa province, E. central Poland. It received its first municipal privileges in 1386. The date of the first Jewish settlement is unknown, but a wooden synagogue was erected in 1650. The community listed 1,410 Jews in 1808, 4,741 in 1910 (76% of the total population), and 2,691 in 1921. Jews were not integrated into the economic life of the town and many of them emigrated after World War I. During the period of Polish independence, there was a significant number of unemployed and poor among the Jews, a situation which deteriorated even further as a result of a boycott by Polish anti-Semites. Tension between Jews and Christians came to the fore in 1923, when the latter accused the Jews of a ritual murder. Dominant in the community was the *Agudat Israel, which in 1920, 1924, and 1931 won half of the seats of the community council. Among the educational institutions, there were the Beth Jacob schools of the Agudat Israel, the *Tarbut of the Zionists, and a Yiddish school, as well as such cultural institutions as a library and various drama circles. The wooden synagogue was rebuilt in 1880.

The wooden synogogue of Nasielsk, built in 1650 and rebuilt in 1880. Courtesy Israel Museum Photo Archives, Jerusalem.

Renowned *zaddikim*, such as R. Jacob Landa (d. 1886) and Ezekiel ha-Levi b. Meir Jehiel (d. during the Holocaust) settled in the town. [SH.L.K.]

Holocaust Period. During the Nazi occupation, Nasielsk belonged to Bezirk Zichenau, established and incorporated into East Prussia by Hitler's decree of Oct. 26, 1939. Before World War II Nasielsk had about 3,000 Jews. During the bombardment of the town, a considerable number of Jews fled eastward. After the Germans entered, the Jewish community there existed for only three months. Existing data leaves doubt whether they were deported in one mass *Aktion* (deportation) on Dec. 3, 1939, or in two deportations, beginning in September or October. Some of the victims were shut up for a day or more in the local synagogue, beaten, and herded to the station. They were loaded onto trains and dispatched to Lukow, Mezhirech, and Biala Podlaska railroad stations. There they were driven out of the train and dispersed among various towns in the Lublin region of the General Government. Some of them reached the Warsaw Ghetto, where many Jews from Nasielsk, refugees from the first days of the war, already lived. After the deportation from Nasielsk, the local Germans and soldiers seized all Jewish property. Only about 80 Jews from Nasielsk survived the Holocaust. [DE.D.]

Bibliography: *Sefer ha-Zeva'ot*, 1 (1945), 145.

NASNA (generally referred to in Hungarian Jewish historiography as **Náznánfalva**), village near Tîrgu-Mureş in Transylvania, Rumania, within Hungary to 1918 and from 1940 to 1945. With the exception of *Alba-Iulia, Nasna had the oldest Jewish community within the borders of historic Transylvania. The first reliable information about the Jews there dates from 1601. Several were members of the Turkish Sephardi community and had family or communal connections with Jews in Alba-Iulia. The curious wooden synagogue of Nasna, of which only the eastern wall was constructed of brick, was apparently built in 1747 (or according to some opinions in 1757 or 1785). The exterior resembled a granary or warehouse and the walls, ceiling, pillars, and platform were painted and ornamented in the style of the contemporary church decoration of the local Unitarians. Quotations from the Psalms and prayers were inscribed on the walls and ceiling. The synagogue was completely demolished in 1940. Some of the decorated boards which were salvaged were transferred to the Jewish Museum in Budapest. Members of the Nasna community were among the first Jews to settle in Tîrgu-Mureş from which Jews had been excluded until 1848. After the prohibition was abolished the Jewish population of Nasna dwindled. During the Holocaust the last two Jewish residents were deported to the ghetto in Tîrgu-Mures.

Bibliography: M. Avi-Shaul, in: *Reshumot*, 4 (1926), 387–90; F. Lőwy, in: *Magyar Zsidó Almanach* (1911), 144–7; G. Balázs, in: *Libanon* (Hung., 1941).

[Y.M.]

NASSAU, former duchy in W. Germany. In the Middle Ages Jews were to be found in Limburg on the Lahn, Diez, Montabaur, and other towns in the duchy. Limburg was the most important community before the *Black Death persecutions (1348), when all the Jews were annihilated. The settlement was reestablished, but there is evidence that they were again severely persecuted and expelled. After the Thirty-Years War (1618–48) *Wiesbaden emerged as the leading community. When the duchy of Nassau split up into minor principalities, Jews settled in the villages, where they engaged in peddling and livestock trading. In 1798 the French army abolished the **Leibzoll* ("body tax") in Nassau-Usingen, but it was reapplied in 1801, and only finally abolished in 1808 through the intervention of Wolf *Breidenbach, the *Court Jew of Brunswick. The authorities compensated themselves by raising the *Schutzgeld* ("protection money"; see **Schutzjuden*). Nassau-Usingen, which had 104 Jewish families, increased its territory and included about 530 Jewish families in 1805; after 1815–16, a single duchy was created. In 1836 there were 1,238 Jewish families (6,147 persons) distributed in 229 localities and conducting services in 95 *Judenschulen*. Only 11 communities in the various localities had more than 100 persons; the largest, Heddernheim, had 327, but almost all of the men were peddlers who were generally absent on their business. The capital, Wiesbaden, had 234 persons, and its rabbi, Abraham *Geiger, who served from 1832 to 1838, appealed unsuccessfully to the government to be appointed **Landrabbiner*. The Orthodox communities opposed his efforts, and Geiger left in frustration. In 1842 Reform services modeled on those of Wuerttemberg were introduced and four district rabbinates created. In 1848 full civic equality was temporarily granted, and in 1861 the Jewish *oath was abolished. In 1865, a year before it was annexed to *Prussia, as part of the province of Hesse-Nassau, there were in Nassau 7,000 Jews (1.5% of the population). Through emigration from the rural communities to the cities, in particular to Wiesbaden, their numbers subsequently decreased.

Bibliography: M. Silberstein, in: ZGJD, 5 (1892), 126–45, 335–47; A. Kober, in: *Festschrift S. Dubnow* (1930), 215–25; idem, in: *Festschrift M. Philippson* (1916), 275–301; idem, in: *Nassauische Annalen*, 66 (1955), 220–50; J. L. Frank, *Loschen Hakodesch* (1961); H. Wiener, *Abraham Geiger and Liberal Judaism* (1962), 9–17.

[ED.]

°**NASSER, GAMAL ABDUL** (1918–1970), president of the United Arab Republic (Egypt) and leader of the Pan-Arab movement. As a leading member of the revolutionary group of "free officers," in 1952 Nasser participated in overthrowing the Egyptian monarchy and establishing a republican regime. Quickly becoming the political leader of the "new" Egypt, he tried, with considerable success, not only to introduce economic and social reforms into his own country (including an agrarian reform and efforts at industrialization), but also to place Egypt and himself in the forefront of the nonaligned nations, the so-called Third World, together with Nehru's India and Tito's Yugoslavia. During this process, his extremely belligerent attitude toward Israel, as well as his interventions in the internal affairs of other Arab countries, served as the main instruments of his policy. His anti-Israel policy included the organization of an economic boycott, armed infiltration and sabotage, closing of the Suez Canal to Israel shipping, and open belligerency.

Nasser participated as an officer in Egypt's invasion of the newly established State of Israel in 1948 and was a commander of the regiment besieged at the Faluja pocket. Upon his return to Egypt, he was decisively instrumental in the bloodless military coup, led by General Mohammad Naguib, that overthrew King Farouk. By 1954 he had succeeded in ousting Naguib, assuming full power, and overcoming the opposition of the Muslim Brotherhood and remnants of the previous ruling Wafd Party and the Communists. To reinforce his leadership, he created a political framework that became the only legal party in Egypt. At that time he wrote his book *The Philosophy of the Revolution* (1955). In the first years of his rule Nasser decisively changed the political course of events in Egypt and the Middle East by several drastic steps. His arms deal with the Soviet Union (ostensibly with Czechoslovakia) overturned the delicate balance of forces between Israel and her Arab neighbors, maintained by the Western powers, and inaugurated the Israel-Egyptian arms race, which from then on dominated the Middle Eastern scene and almost evolved into a confrontation of the super powers in the late 1960s and the beginning of the 1970s. By evicting the last remnant of British forces from the Suez Canal zone and nationalizing the Suez Canal Company (1956), thus removing a barrier between Egypt and Israel, and by his deliberate policy of actively supporting the murderous *fedayeen* raids deep into Israel territory, from the Gaza Strip and from Sinai, Nasser exacerbated the situation until it exploded in the *Sinai Campaign. In spite of Egypt's total military defeat, Nasser, mainly with Soviet support, succeeded in converting it, at least in the eyes of his devoted followers, into a political victory that enhanced his prestige.

In 1956 and 1965 Nasser was the only candidate for presidential election. In the course of his reforms, Nasser nationalized the Egyptian press and removed his enemies and critics from influential positions. Over the years his anti-imperialist policy became more and more pro-Soviet, until Egypt became so dependent on the U.S.S.R. in military and economic spheres (heavy armament deliveries, military advisers, the construction of the Aswan Dam and

Gamal Abdul Nasser on a stamp issued by the United Arab Republic before the Six-Day War, 1967. Jerusalem, B. M. Ansbacher Collection.

of individual industrial plants, etc.) that in May 1967 Moscow was able to lead Nasser into the adventurous steps that provoked the *Six-Day War. After the defeat, Nasser resigned (on June 9) for a few hours, but reassumed power in response to mass demonstrations in the streets of Cairo demanding the continuation of his leadership. He tried to place the blame for the defeat on the senior military echelons, including his vice-president, Marshal Abdel Ḥakim Amar, who committed suicide. Other military leaders were convicted in show trials, and Nasser held a new election to the Arab Socialist Union.

After 1967 Nasser visited the U.S.S.R. several times. In his public pronouncements about Israel, he was careful to formulate the aim of Israel's destruction in non-explicit terms, though from time to time, particularly just before the Six-Day War, he left no doubt that this was the real aim of his policy. This again became clear at the Arab Summit Conference in Khartoum (Aug. 29–Sept. 2, 1967), when he initiated the policy of pledging the Arabs not to recognize Israel, not to negotiate with her, and not to conclude peace agreements with her. Nasser maintained that Egypt's acceptance of the Nov. 22, 1967 Security Council resolution was compatible with the "three noes" of Khartoum, but he interpreted the resolution as demanding an Israel withdrawal from all occupied territories without negotiations and a peace treaty. When his policy failed to achieve any effective pressure on Israel, he renewed military attacks along the Suez Canal zone. When this failed to achieve its aim and ultimately turned into military setbacks for Egypt, in August 1970 Nasser accepted a U.S. initiative for a limited cease-fire period and indirect negotiations with Israel, under the Security Council resolution, in exchange for an Israel acceptance of the principle of withdrawal from occupied territories. Nasser died suddenly in September 1970 before the new stage of his policy bore any fruit.

Nasser was adept at adjusting his personal image and tone to whomever he addressed, so that while in Arab eyes he was the incarnation of the fight against Israel and for Arab glory, many Western circles and media were impressed by his reasonableness and moderation. This diversity became particularly evident when, on the one hand, he gave an Indian newspaper editor a copy of the *Protocols of the *Elders of Zion* as an explanation of the Jewish "world conspiracy," while on the other, with Western people, he continuously stressed that he clearly distinguished between Jewry and Zionism.

Bibliography: P. Mansfield, *Nasser* (Eng., 1969), incl. bibl.; M. H. Kerr, *Egypt under Nasser* (1968), incl. bibl.; R. St. John, *The Boss* (1960); J. Joesten, *Nasser: The Rise to Power* (1960); W. Wynn, *Nasser of Egypt* (1959); K. Wheelock, *Nasser's New Egypt* (1960), incl. bibl.; E. Be'eri, *Army Officers in Arab Politics and Society* (1969). [ED.]

NASSY, DAVID DE ISAAC COHEN (late 18th century), Caribbean physician, Jewish community leader, and publicist. Nassy, born in Surinam into its leading Sephardi family, was a descendant of David Nassy, who had founded the Jewish community there in 1664. The younger David first appears in 1785 as a signatory to a petition for a college of letters in Surinam. Shortly thereafter he became president of the *Regenten* (board) of the local Jewish community, and in this capacity was the first signatory of a communication to the German Christian advocate of Jewish rights, Christian Wilhelm von *Dohm. At the latter's request, Nassy played a leading role in compiling *Essai historique sur la Colonie de Surinam* (2 vols., Paramaribo, 1788), a record of the Jewish role in the history of the colony. Restrictions on Jewish freedom led him to St. Thomas for a time and subsequently to Philadelphia (1792), where he was the first Jewish physician to practice in that city. An outbreak of yellow fever the following year brought him into conflict with his foremost colleague, Dr. Benjamin Rush, over diagnosis and treatment. Nassy published his findings in *Observations on the Cause, Nature, and Treatment of the Epidemic Disorder Prevalent in Philadelphia* (1793), in which he pointed out his success in losing only 19 patients (11 of whom had already received Rush's treatment) out of 117 afflicted. Nassy's scientific work earned him election to the American Philosophical Society. In 1795 he returned to Surinam, where he went into business. Three years later he published *Lettre Politico-Theologico-Morale sur les Juifs* (1798?) with a Dutch translation, supporting the emancipation of Dutch Jewry.

Bibliography: Rosenbloom, Biogr Dict; J. L. Blau and S. W. Baron (eds.), *Jews of the United States*, 2 (1963), 459–64; AJHSP, 22 (1914), 25–38; H. Bloch, in: *Journal of American Medical Association* (Feb. 10, 1969). [M.H.ST.]

NASZ PRZEGLĄD ("Our Review"), Jewish Polish-language newspaper. *Nasz Przegląd* was published in Warsaw from 1923 to 1939, and served as an informative political organ with a Zionist-nationalist orientation. It had been preceded by *Nasz Kurjer*, which first appeared in 1917 at the incentive of the journalist Jacob Appenszlak, aided financially by Joseph *Dawidsohn and Samuel Jacob *Jatzkan, editor of **Haynt*. In 1920 *Nasz Kurjer* was reorganized on a cooperative basis, and in 1923 appeared under its new name *Nasz Przegląd* as a nonparty nationalist organ. Nathan Szwalbe, Saul Wagman, Jacob Appenszlak, and Samuel Wołkowicz all served as associate editors. Its permanent contributors included noted Jewish writers and publicists, such as Samuel *Hirschhorn, Florian Sokolow, Fishel *Rotenstreich, Janusz *Korczak, the political writer Bernard Singer (who wrote under the pseudonym "Regnis"), and the historians Majer *Balaban and Emanuel *Ringelblum. Several prominent progressive Polish intellectuals worked within the framework of the newspaper, including the philologist Baudouin de Courtenay and the journalist W. Rzymowski. It had many Polish non-Jews among its readers.

Nasz Przegląd was not a campaigning newspaper and did not take a fixed ideological stand, developing a tendency to adapt to the changing political situation. The members of its staff differed in their outlooks, although the pro-Zionist trend was marked. While *Nasz Przegląd* supported the Polonization of Jewish culture, many of the Jewish intelligentsia became influenced by it toward the Zionist cause. It published installments of important works of Yiddish and modern Hebrew literature in Polish translation, including those of Joseph *Opatoshu and Singer, and J. *Klausner's *Jesus of Nazareth*. *Nasz Przegląd's* daily circulation reached 40,000 and its staff comprised some 50 writers. The newspaper owned a modern printing-house which published a children's supplement, *Mały Przegląd*, edited by Janusz Korczak, as well as a women's weekly, *Eva*, edited by Paulina Appenszlak.

Bibliography: EG, Warsaw, 1 (1953), 512–4; A. Levinson, *Toledot Yehudei Varshah* (1953), 305–6; I. Schiper et al. (eds.), *Żydzi w Polsce odrodzonej* (1932–33). [M.LAN.]

NATAL, province on the E. coast of the Republic of South Africa. The capital is Pietermaritzburg and the principal city, *Durban, is the third largest in South Africa and one of its biggest ports. At the 1960 census the Jewish population of Natal numbered 6,220 (5.4% of the Jewish population of South Africa), employed in commerce and industry, with a large proportion in professional, technical, and related occupations. Jewish associations with Natal began in 1825, when Nathaniel *Isaacs, a youth of 16, was washed ashore from a ship wrecked off the coast. He remained in the country for some years, winning the confidence of the Zulu chieftains Chaka and Dingaan, extensively exploring the interior, and trading with the tribesmen. Other Jewish pioneers were Benjamin *Norden, traveler and trader, Jonas *Bergtheil, who founded a settlement at New Germany, and Daniel de *Pass, a pioneer in the sugar-growing industry. As elsewhere in South Africa, Jews have played a prominent part in the commercial, industrial, professional, and social life of Natal. Sir Matthew *Nathan was British governor of Natal just before its entry into the Union (1910); F. C. Hollander was mayor of Durban (1910–13), a member of the Natal provincial executive, and a South African senator; and C. P. Robinson (1867–1938) sat for many years in the Natal and the Union parliaments. E. S. Henochsberg (1894–1966), J. J. Friedman (1908–), S. Miller (1916–), and R. N. Leon (1925–) were judges of the Natal Supreme Court.

A small permanent Jewish settlement in Natal began in the 1870s. In 1883 the first Hebrew congregation was constituted in Durban and the first synagogue opened there. Jewish religious services were held in Pietermaritzburg in the early 1880s and a synagogue was built in 1913, and smaller Jewish communities sprang up throughout the province from the late 19th century. In 1903 Natal was associated with the Transvaal in the formation of the first Jewish Board of Deputies in South Africa, which was amalgamated in 1912 with the Cape Board of Deputies to form the South African Board. In 1931 the Council of Natal Jewry was established to serve as the coordinating body for Jewish institutions in the province. Unlike other provincial bodies in South African Jewry, the Council is involved in the daily life of the community and is a unique structure of the national body. A Jewish Education Council (founded in 1948) cooperates with the South African Board of Jewish Education. One of the earliest Zionist societies in South Africa was formed in Durban in 1891. The University of Natal both in Pietermaritzburg and Durban had lectureships in classical and modern Hebrew.

Bibliography: L. Herrman, *History of the Jews in South Africa* (1935), 271–2; G. Saron and L. Hotz, *Jews in South Africa* (1955), index; M. Gitlin, *The Vision Amazing* (1950), index; Shrock, in: *Jewish Herald* (Rosh Ha-Shanah issue, 1959), 84–86. [L.Ho.]

NATANSON, LUDWIK (1822–1896), physician and communal worker. A member of the Jewish intellectual and assimilationist circle of Warsaw, Natanson was the son of the banker and industrialist Wolf Zelig Natanson (1795–1879). In 1847 he founded the periodical *Tygodnik Lekarski,* one of the first modern medical publications in Polish, which he edited and financed until 1872. Natanson was also one of the public health pioneers in Poland, and was active in the campaign against the cholera epidemic in Warsaw (1848–52). In 1863 he was elected to the presidency of the Polish medical society. In 1871 he became chairman of the executive of the Jewish community of Warsaw, a position he held until his death. As chairman, Natanson successfully reorganized and considerably extended the public and administrative services of the community, managing also to balance its budget. He encouraged productivity among the Jewish poverty-stricken classes and was the initiator and founder of vocational schools and a community workshop center. He supported (1878–88) the secondary school which had 1,400 Jewish pupils. On his initiative, a new school building was erected, and community organizations and the cemeteries were renovated. He was the initiator of a project to erect a modern Jewish hospital in the Czyste district, and it was also during his term of office that the magnificent synagogue of Tłomacka Street was built. In 1874 Natanson obtained authorization to establish a Jewish seminary for teachers. He was supported in his public activities by bourgeois circles and the assimilationist Jewish intelligentsia. The energy which he showed during the pogrom in Warsaw in December 1881 was of great assistance in maintaining the morale of the Jewish community.

Bibliography: J. Shatzky, *Geshikhte fun Yidn in Varshe,* 2–3 (1948–53), indexes; H. Nussbaum, *Teki weterana warszawskiej gminy Starozakonnych* (1880), 46–50; W. Konie, in: *Głos gminy żydowskiej* nos. 4–5 (1937); S. Łastik, *Z dziejów oświecenia żydowskiego* (1961), index; *Lu'aḥ Aḥi'asaf,* 5 (1897). [A.Cy.]

NATHAN (Heb. נָתָן), prophet in the days of David and Solomon. Nathan, together with Zadok the priest, anointed Solomon as king after encouraging and activating the people of the royal court to proclaim him king. Two of his prophecies are known: one about the postponement of the building of the Temple from David's time to the time of his son (II Sam. 7; I Chron. 17) and the election of David's dynasty; the second is the prophecy of rebuke to David about Bath-Sheba and the killing of Uriah (II Sam. 12:1–15). From his involvement in the life of the court and the clear connection of his prophecy to the king and the monarchy, Nathan, like the prophet Gad, may be designated as a court prophet. From the contents of his prophecies, however—not only his sharp rebuke in connection with Bath-Sheba but also his advice regarding the Temple, which was not in any way subject to the king's approval or control—there is justification for placing Nathan in the category of prophets who rebuke and advise, such as Elijah and Elisha (see *Prophets and Prophecy).

In his prophecy about the postponement of the building of the Temple to the time of Solomon, Nathan promises the House of David unconditionally that his dynasty will endure forever, and that the relationship between the Lord and each of David's successors will be like that between father and son. The reason for the postponement of the building of the Temple is not clarified. (The explanation of bloodshed in I Chron. 22:7–10 seems to have been inserted later.) On the basis of the wanderings in the wilderness, where God was present in the Tent and the Tabernacle, it would appear, however, that the monarchy was not yet firmly established, and that the time had not yet come for removing the symbols of tribal tradition—the Tent and the Tabernacle—and replacing them with a permanent house (temple) of the Lord, similar to the house (palace) of the

"Nathan Admonishing David," drawing by Rembrandt van Rijn, pen and brush with bistre, 7¼ × 10 in. (18.6×25 cm.). New York, Metropolitan Museum of Art, H. O. Havemeyer Collection.

king. The view of the monarchy in Nathan's prophecy—in which it is seen as granted to David by an act of divine grace (no reference is made to the monarchy of Saul) and as a complete and unbroken continuation of the Lord's providence and governance from the time of the Exodus from Egypt to the time of the judges—differs essentially from that of I Samuel 8–12, according to which Samuel opposed monarchy as such. The antiquity of the prophecy attributed to Nathan is attested by the description of the monarchy as a calm and secure period of respite, without any intimation of the division of the kingdom. The punishment of a king's son who transgresses will be a rebuke only "with the rod of men, and with the stripes of human beings" (II Sam. 7: 14). In the rebuke over the affair of Bath-Sheba, Nathan, by means of the parable of the poor man's lamb, traps David (even with his privilege as king) into passing judgment upon himself. This prophecy contains a harsh vision of the future of the house of David: "the sword shall never depart from your house" (II Sam. 12: 10). This prediction, which is not recalled in this way in any other passage in the Bible, and which probably does not allude to any actual event such as the division of the kingdom, stamps the rebuke with the seal of authenticity. Nathan appears not only as warning against evil and demanding expiation for murder, but also as commanding the king to establish law and justice, which is his duty as judge and is embodied in the monarchy itself, as explicitly stated in the chronicles of David's reign (II Sam. 8: 15; see *David, *Solomon). The "book of Nathan the prophet," which relates the histories of David and Solomon, is mentioned in Chronicles (I Chron. 29:9; II Chron. 9:29), in keeping with the theory of the author of Chronicles who also represents other prophets as chroniclers of the events of their days.

Bibliography: J. A. Montgomery, *The Book of Kings* (ICC, 1951), 67–79; G. Widengren, *Sakrales Koenigtum im Alten Testament* (1955), 59–61; K. H. Bernhardt, in: VT Supplement, 8 (1961), 161–3; H. W. Hertzberg, *Samuel* (1964), 282–7, 312–5.
[SH.AB.]

NATHAN, English family, distinguished in public service. The first member of the family to settle in England was MEYER (Michael) NATHAN who came from Dessau about 1790. His grandson, Jonah, married twice. SIR NATHANIEL (1843–1916), the son of Jonah's first marriage, a barrister practicing in Birmingham from 1873 to 1888, became attorney general, judge of the Supreme Court, and from 1901 to 1903 acting chief justice of Trinidad. His half brother, SIR FREDERIC LEWIS (1861–1933), explosives expert and soldier, joined the Royal Artillery in 1879 and organized explosives' manufacture before and during World War I. Later, he specialized in fuel problems and was president of the Institution of Chemical Engineers from 1925 to 1927. From 1905 to 1926 he was commandant of the Jewish Lads' Brigade. Frederic's brother SIR MATTHEW (1862–1939) joined the Royal Engineers in 1880 and served in Sudan and India. The first Jew to be a colonial governor, he was governor of the Gold Coast (1900–03), Hong Kong (1904–07), and Natal (1907–09). Secretary to the General Post Office and the Board of Inland Revenue, he was appointed undersecretary to the Lord Lieutenant of Ireland in 1914 and was in sole charge of Dublin Castle when the Easter Rising occurred in 1916. An inquiry criticized his failure to warn the British government of the danger. After serving as secretary of the Ministry of Pensions and governor of Queensland (1920–26), he retired to Somerset where he took part in local government and wrote a monumental local history. In Jewish life, he represented the New West End Synagogue on the United Synagogue Council. The fourth brother, SIR ROBERT (1866–1921), served in the Indian civil service from 1888 to 1915 and was appointed chief secretary to the governor of Eastern Bengal and Assam in 1910. In World War I he did important work in counterespionage.

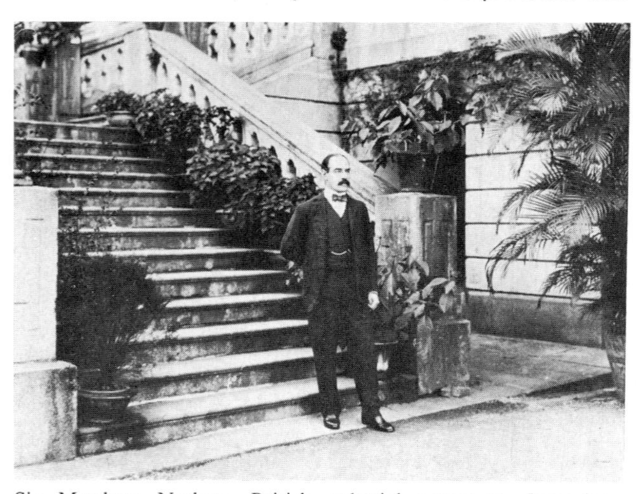
Sir Matthew Nathan, British colonial governor. Jerusalem, J.N.U.L., Schwadron Collection.

Bibliography: P. H. Emden, *Jews of Britain* (1943), index; Roth, Mag Bibl. index; DNB, s.v.
[V.D.L.]

NATHAN, U.S. family. SIMON NATHAN (1746–1822), who was born in England, went to the colonies in 1773 by way of Havana. During the Revolution, he supported the revolutionary cause and helped ship supplies to the colonists from Jamaica where he then resided. After leaving the island, he proceeded to New Orleans and from there went to Williamsburg, Virginia, in 1779. He loaned large sums of money to the Virginia state government for which he received the thanks of the then governor, Thomas Jefferson. When these loans were not repaid he suffered great financial loss, and was involved in protracted litigation with Virginia for many years. Possibly as a consequence of this litigation, he went to Philadelphia and enlisted in the militia. There, in 1780, he met and married Grace Mendes *Seixas (1752–1831), the daughter of Isaac Mendes *Seixas. Nathan became a Mason the following year, a trustee of the Congregation Mikveh Israel in 1782, and president of the congregation in the years 1782 and 1783. Soon afterward, he moved to New York, where he served as president of the Congregation Shearith Israel in 1785, 1786, 1794, and 1796. He opened a successful dry goods business with Aaron Pimental, enabling him to contribute sums of money to the synagogue.

Their son SEIXAS (Isaac Mendes) NATHAN (1785–1852) married his cousin Sara Seixas (1791–1834), daughter of Benjamin Mendes Seixas (1746–1817). They had 15 children. They and their children married into the Lazarus, Lyons, Cardozo, Gomez, and Hendricks families among others. Some of Simon Nathan's descendants include: the noted poetess EMMA *LAZARUS; her sister JOSEPHINE (1846–1910), a noted essayist; the novelist ROBERT *NATHAN; ANNIE NATHAN *MEYER, founder of Barnard College; MAUD NATHAN (1862–1946), suffragette and president of the Consumers' League for 20 years; and BENJAMIN N. *CARDOZO, member of the United States Supreme Court.

Bibliography: D. de S. Pool, *Portraits Etched in Stone* (1952).
[L.HE.]

NATHAN, ABRAHAM (d. 1745), founder of the London Ashkenazi community, also known as Reb Aberle, Aberle London, and Abraham [of] Hamburg. The son of R. Moses Nathan (Norden) of Hamburg, he was a wealthy diamond merchant and a rabbinical scholar of considerable attainment. It was through him that Ẓevi *Ashkenazi was induced to go to London in 1705 to arbitrate in the dispute then dividing the Sephardi community regarding the orthodoxy of the opinions of the haham David *Nieto. In

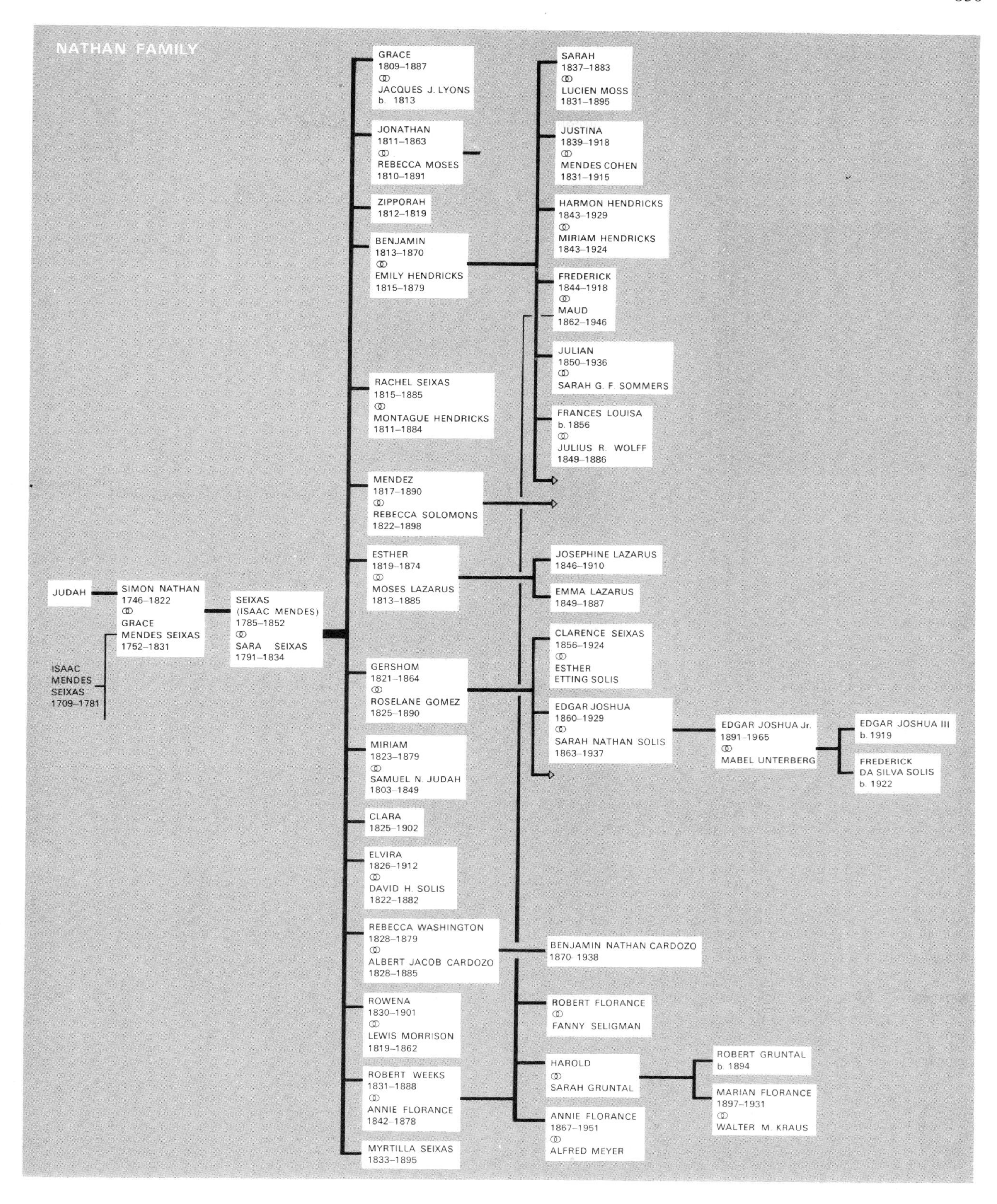

1704 Nathan was prevented by the Court of Aldermen from erecting a separate synagogue with a yeshivah attached. Later, however, he took the lead in vindictive fashion in the divorce dispute which resulted in the setting up of the Hambro' Synagogue by his rival Marcus Moses. He ultimately returned to Hamburg in reduced circumstances.

Bibliography: C. Roth, *History of the Great Synagogue* (1950), 35–45. [C.R.]

NATHAN, DAVID (1816–1886), New Zealand pioneer. Nathan arrived in Kororareka from London in 1840, trading as storekeeper. In 1841 he married Rosetta Aarons in New Zealand's first Jewish marriage. He opened a store in Auckland when it became the capital and bought 2,500 acres of land in the adjoining Manurewa. He went into auctioneering and established New Zealand's oldest and most diversified wholesale business. Sabbath and holiday services were held at his warehouse for over a decade. Through his leadership and example he unified and conciliated all groups in the congregation. A strong force in the town's financial affairs, Nathan showed particular interest in working class welfare. His two sons L. D. and N. A. Nathan successively led the congregation after his death for almost half a century.

Bibliography: L. M. Goldman, *History of the Jews in New Zealand* (1958), index. [M.S.P.]

NATHAN, ERNESTO (1845–1921), Italian statesman and the first Jewish mayor of Rome. Born in England, he came into contact with the Italian patriot Guiseppe Mazzini who was exiled to London for his radical views. Nathan was taken to Italy by his mother in 1859 and settled in Rome in 1871 soon after Rome became part of the Kingdom of Italy.

Ernesto Nathan, mayor of Rome. Jerusalem, J.N.U.L., Schwadron Collection.

He became manager of Mazzini's newspaper *Roma del Popolo* and was a passionate republican and an advocate of the secular state. Nathan became an Italian citizen in 1889 and was twice grand master of the Italian Masons. He was elected mayor of Rome in 1907 and held office until 1913. Following the Italian entry into World War I in 1915, Nathan enlisted in the army and although over 70 served at the front as a lieutenant. [ED.]

NATHAN, GEORGE JEAN (1882–1958), U.S. drama critic and editor. Born in Fort Wayne, Indiana, Nathan became the foremost American critic of his time, and took the lead in freeing the American theater of the stagey and melodramatic trappings of the *Belasco period. He was in journalism for more than 50 years, mostly linked with the world of Broadway as critic for *The Bohemian Magazine* (1906–08), *Harper's Weekly* (1908–10), *The Smart Set* (1908–23), and *The American Mercury*, which he founded with H. L. Mencken in 1924. He was also a founder—with Theodore Dreiser, Eugene O'Neill, and others—of *The American Spectator* (1932–39).

A detached, sophisticated, and cynical figure, Nathan was something of a boulevardier, not only in his personal habits but also in his writings. Nevertheless, he was a man of learning, critical insight, and courage, who paved the way for Eugene O'Neill and his type of dramatic writing. Nathan labored consistently to educate American taste to accept writers such as Sean O'Casey, Jean Giraudoux, and Ludwig Thoma. He wrote several books with Mencken, including the satirical play *Heliogabalus* (1920).

His own books, over 30 in number, include: *Mr. George Jean Nathan Presents* (1917); *The Theater, the Drama, the Girls* (1921); *Materia Critica* (1924); *Testament of a Critic* (1931); *The Theater of the Moment* (1936); *Morning After the First Night* (1938); an *Encyclopaedia of the Theater* (1940); and *The Theater of the Fifties* (1953).

Bibliography: I. Goldberg, *Theatre of George Jean Nathan* (1926); C. Angoff (ed.), *World of George Jean Nathan* (1952); S. J. Kunitz, *Twentieth Century Authors*, first suppl. (1955), incl. bibl.; *New York Times* (April 8, 1958), 1; (April 9, 1958), 36.
[C.AN.]

NATHAN, HARRY LOUIS, BARON (1889–1963), English lawyer and politician. Born in London, Nathan fought in Gallipoli, Egypt, and France during World War I. From 1929 to 1934 he was a Liberal member of Parliament and then switched and was a Labor member of Parliament from 1934 to 1935 and from 1937 to 1940. Following the outbreak of World War II Nathan became chairman of the National Defense Public Interest Committee. He was elevated to the House of Lords in 1940 as Baron Nathan of Churt and from 1946 to 1958 was minister of civil aviation in the postwar Labor government. Later he was departmental chairman of the governmental committee on the law of customs and excise and chairman of the governmental committee to investigate the law and practice of charitable trusts, which led to a new act. Lord Nathan was an active figure in Jewish communal affairs as a member of the Board of Deputies of British Jews, and president of the European Committee of the third, fourth, fifth, and sixth *Maccabiah. He was also prominent in national civic affairs as chairman of the Royal Geographical Society and of the Royal Society of Arts. Lord Nathan wrote *Medical Negligence* (1957) and *The Charities Act, 1960* (1962).

Bibliography: H. M. Hyde, *Strong for Service: the Life of Lord Nathan of Churt* (1968). [ED.]

NATHAN, HENRY (1842–1914), Canadian politician who was the first Jew to sit in the Canadian Federal Parliament. Born in London, England, Nathan emigrated to Canada in 1862, settling in Victoria, Vancouver. He was elected to the British Columbia legislature in 1870 and to the Federal Parliament in Ottawa in the following year. Nathan was instrumental in incorporating British Columbia into the Canadian Federation. In 1880 he returned to London.

Bibliography: A. D. Hart (ed.), *The Jew in Canada* (1926), 371.
[B.G.K.]

NATHAN, ISAAC (1790?–1864), composer, singer, and writer. Nathan was born at Canterbury, England, and his father was probably the local *ḥazzan*. He studied with Solomon Lyon at Cambridge to enter the rabbinate, but in about 1810 he went to London and began a career as singer, composer, and music teacher. From Domenico Corri he

Caricature of Isaac Nathan, Australian composer, by John Fairburn, London, 1820. Cecil Roth Collection. Photo David Harris, Jerusalem.

learned the classical tradition of Italian vocal culture, stemming from Corri's master, Porpora; Nathan's *Musurgia Vocalis* (1836[2]) is one of the few remaining written documentations of this method. In London he became friendly with Lord *Byron, whose *Hebrew Melodies* were written at Nathan's request and set by him to music. In the first editions of this work (from 1815 onward), which achieved great popularity, the name of John *Braham was featured on the title page as composer, in addition to that of Nathan, but Braham contributed nothing to the work except his prestige. After a financial setback, caused mainly by debts incurred while on a secret mission on behalf of King William IV, Nathan emigrated to Australia in 1841 and settled in Sydney as Australia's first resident professional composer. There he organized musical performances, published a magazine entitled *The Southern Euphrosyne*, and composed the first opera written and produced in Australia, *Don Juan of Austria* (1847). Nathan died in Sydney from injuries received while stepping off (or being run over by) a tram. His great-granddaughter Catherine Mackerras wrote his most informed biography, and her son was the conductor Charles Mackerras. His great-nephew was the pianist Harold Samuel.

Nathan's works include various operas and songs. Several traditional Jewish melodies are found in his *Musurgia Vocalis*. For some of the *Hebrew Melodies* he also used some traditional tunes, but, except for **Ma'oz Ẓur* (set to Byron's "On Jordan's Banks"), they are quite transformed by his superficial compositional initiative. In certain of the songs published in Australia, he reworked aboriginal melodies. His grandson, Harry Alfred Nathan, has been proposed as the composer of the popular Australian song "Waltzing Matilda," but the claim is a matter of dispute.

Bibliography: E. Foreman, *The Porpora Tradition* (1968); C. Mackerras, *Hebrew Melodist: A Life of Isaac Nathan* (1963); O. S. Phillips, *Isaac Nathan, Friend of Byron* (1940); C. H. Bertie, *Isaac Nathan, Australia's First Composer* (1922); R. Covell, *Australia's Music* (1967), 13–15, 59, 68–69; E. R. Dibdin, in: *Music and Letters*, 22 (1941), 85.

[B.B.]

NATHAN, JOSEPH EDWARD (1835–1912), New Zealand businessman. Born in London, Nathan prospected unsuccessfully in the Australian goldfields before arriving in Wellington in 1857. There he went into partnership with Jacob Joseph and built up the flourishing wholesale import-export business which later became Joseph Nathan and Company. He held office on the Wellington Harbor Board, the Chamber of Commerce, the Gas Company, and other enterprises, and was chief promoter and chairman of the Wellington-Manawatu railway. Glaxo Laboratories, which later became important in the manufacture of pharmaceutical products in England, developed from his cooperative farming ventures. In 1900 Nathan retired to London after having been one of the leaders of the Wellington Jewish community for over 40 years and president of its first synagogue (1870). His family remained prominent in New Zealand life.

Bibliography: L. M. Goldman, *History of the Jews in New Zealand* (1958), 148, 150, 219.

[M.S.P.]

NATHAN, MANFRED (1875–1945), South African lawyer, author, and communal leader. Born in Hanover (South Africa), the son of a German pioneer in the Cape, Nathan practiced at the Johannesburg Bar. He served for a time on the Natal Bench and became president of the South African Special Income Tax court in 1931. An assiduous writer on legal and constitutional subjects, Nathan was the author of a four-volume work, *The Common Law of South Africa* (1904–09) and the studies *The South African Commonwealth* (1919) and *Empire Government* (1928). Among his many other writings were a life of President Paul Kruger, an autobiography, *Not Heaven Itself* (1944), and several works on South African history. Nathan was active in Jewish communal life. He was a founding member of the Transvaal Jewish Board of Deputies (1903) and was president in 1905 and 1907. He was on the first executive of the South African Board of Deputies (1912) and vice-president of the South African Zionist Federation (1904–1907).

Nathan was also active in politics and was elected to municipal and provincial legislative bodies in the Transvaal, and served on the boards of educational institutions and hospitals.

Bibliography: G. Saron and L. Hotz (eds.), *The Jews in South Africa—a History* (1955), index.

[L.Ho.]

NATHAN, MORDECAI (15th cent.), French physician of Avignon, the teacher of Joseph b. Solomon *Colon. Nathan was mentioned among three "Jews and doctors of medicine" together with three "Christian doctors of medicine in Avignon" in a manuscript entitled "Thoroughly Tested Prescription for Pestilential Disease" (Bibliothèque Nationale, Ms. Français 630, fol. 54). It appears that he was also identified with M. Nadi, the mathematician (Wolf, Bibliotheca, 4 (1733), 904).

[Is.S.]

He is known by his work *Me'ir Nativ*, also called *Ya'ir Nativ* (Venice, 1523), the first Hebrew concordance of the Bible, compiled between 1437 and 1448. Nathan was familiar with Christian scholarly circles, and more than once engaged in theological polemics with them. He became convinced from these polemics of the need to prepare a Hebrew concordance of the Bible to make it easier for Hebrew-speaking Jews to reply to Christians. He arranged the books of the Bible in the order of the Vulgate (Latin translation). He explained the roots of the words in the most concise language. Verbs and nouns, however, appear in disorder, and he omitted prepositions and formative letters. He also omitted proper nouns and the Aramaic words in the Bible. Christian scholars engaged in the study of Hebrew attached great importance to the work. Mario de Calascio published the concordance a second time (Rome, 1621) together with a Latin translation, in which the defects of the Hebrew edition were remedied. Differences of opinion have arisen about the identity of the author of *Me'ir Nativ*. The inner title page gives Mordecai Nathan as the name of the author, whereas the introduction is signed by Isaac Nathan. Johannes Buxtorf concluded, therefore, that Mordecai Nathan was also known as Isaac Nathan. I. S. *Reggio concluded that the author was Isaac Nathan and that the name Mordecai on the title page was an error. A. Tauber thought that the author was Mordecai Nathan, while the Isaac, who wrote the introduction, was apparently his relative.

[A.D.]

Bibliography: I. S. Reggio, *Iggerot Yashar*, 1 (1834), 70–76; Gross, Gal Jud, 10; Gross, in: MGWJ, 29 (1880), 518–523; S. Mandelkern, *Heikhal ha-Kodesh* (1896), introd., 9–11; A. Tauber, in: KS, 2 (1925), 141–4; Renan, Rabbins, 533; E. Wickersheimer, *Dictionnaire biographique des médicins en France au Moyen-Age* (1936), 537; E. R. Malachi, *Oẓar ha-Leksikografyah ha-Ivrit* (an appendix to *Heikhal ha-Kodesh* of S. Mandelkern, 1955), 12f., 27f., 30.

NATHAN, MULLA IBRAHIM (1816–1868), British intelligence agent born in *Meshed, Persia. In about 1837 he and his brother Musa left their homeland and entered British service. They traveled throughout Afghanistan, Turkestan, and Bukhara and were connected with all the major British expeditions in Central Asia. During the first Anglo-Afghan War (1839–42), they supplied funds for British officers on remote missions, gathered intelligence and information for the military authorities, and rescued and assisted British prisoners in Afghanistan after the disaster to the British army at Kabul. They left Afghanistan in 1842, and settled in Bombay in 1844. In recognition of their services, the British government in India granted them compensation for their losses as well as a life pension. Mulla Ibrahim was offered diplomatic employment in

Meshed, but refused to return to the city in which the Jews had recently been forced to adopt Islam. In Bombay Mulla Ibrahim took an active part in the Baghdadi-Jewish

Mulla Ibrahim Nathan, British intelligence agent. From *Hebrew Union College Annual*, Vol. 29, Cincinnati, 1958.

community. Jacob *Saphir states that he was appointed as a customs official, but was exempted from duty on the Sabbath and Jewish holidays.

Bibliography: Fischel, in: HUCA, 29 (1958), 331–75. [W.J.F.]

NATHAN, PAUL (1857–1927), German politician, Jewish leader, and philanthropist. A protégé of Ludwig *Bamberger and Theodor Barth, he was associated with the Berlin liberal publication *Die Nation*, serving as its editor until 1907. Because of his influence in political circles and as founder in 1901 of the *Hilfsverein der deutschen Juden, Nathan was often regarded as the spokesman of German Jewry apart from the Zionists. He was active in almost all international Jewish conferences on emigration and relief for Jewish victims of pogroms and wars, helping to shape international political and relief campaigns to aid them. Nathan was convinced that the Jewish problem in Russia was part of the general Russian problem, to be solved only by change of regime—if necessary by revolution. He advocated economic pressure on Russia by the West, primarily through refusals to grant loans. Under Nathan's influence the Hilfsverein der deutschen Juden aided liberal and even revolutionary movements in Russia, and he was also instrumental in influencing Lucien *Wolf in England and Jacob H. *Schiff in the United States to accept its policies toward Russia. The Hilfsverein published the *Russische Korrespondenz*, which informed the press, political leaders, and other personalities of the true situation in Russia, and similar bulletins in England and Paris.

During the *Beilis trial of 1913 Nathan, with the help of Lucien Wolf in London, organized the defense of Beilis outside Russia. In Germany Nathan obtained a large number of signatures of non-Jewish personalities in favor of

Paul Nathan, German politician and Jewish leader. Jerusalem, J.N.U.L., Schwadron Collection.

Beilis and expert opinions by scientists. At the same time Nathan published the book *Der Fall Justschinski*, an account of the German pro-Beilis campaign. He was among the founders of the Comite zur Abwehr antisemitischer Angriffe in Berlin. In 1896 he published *Die Kriminalitaet der Juden* and *Die Juden als Soldaten* and *Uber das juedische rituelle Schaechtverfahren*.

Nathan was basically a sincere assimilationist who saw only in complete assimilation with the non-Jewish population, the possiblity of full emancipation in every country. Thus he strongly opposed the Zionist movement. During World War I, while German Zionists demanded autonomous rights for Jews in countries occupied by the German armed forces, Nathan gave constant help to the assimilationists of Poland. When the war broke out he helped to gain the sympathy of Jews in neutral countries for the cause of the Central Powers, his main argument being that a war against Russia, the country of barbaric pogroms, should be supported by Jews. At the beginning of the Weimar Republic Nathan officially joined the Socialist Party (S.P.D.). The German government asked him to accept the post of its ambassador to Vienna, but Nathan declined the offer because of his close association with the major Jewish organizations at a time when anti-Semitism was strong in Austria. Through his many friends abroad he tried to gain sympathy for Germany, constantly warning that the harsh conditions of the *Versailles Treaty would help bring back a totalitarian and reactionary regime in Germany from which both that nation and others would suffer. Nathan's enthusiasm for Jewish colonization in Soviet Russia led to his publishing a pamphlet in 1926 in which he favored the concentration of Soviet Jews in the far-eastern part of that country.

Bibliography: E. Feder, *Paul Nathan, ein Lebensbild* (1929); Szajkowski, in: JSOS 19 (1957), 47–50; 29 (1967), 3–26, 75–91; idem, in: PAAJR, 31 (1963), 197–218; idem, in: YLBI, 9 (1964), 131–58; idem, in: YLBI, 3 (1958), 60–80; idem, in: HJ, 14 (1952), 24–37. [Ed.]

NATHAN (Gruntal), ROBERT (1894–), U.S. novelist. Nathan was born in New York City. He wrote well over 20 short novels notable for their fantasy, light touch, and ironical style, as well as for the limited number of their characters.

Nathan's exceptional craftsmanship was revealed in his first book, *Peter Kindred* (1919). Others written over the years include *Autumn* (1921); *The Puppet Master* (1923); *The Bishop's Wife* (1928); *One More Spring* (1933), a story of the post-World War I depression; *The Enchanted Voyage* (1936); *Portrait of Jennie* (1940); *The River Journey* (1949); *Sir Henry* (1955); and *The Fair* (1964), which is set in the time of King Arthur. Nathan also wrote several novels of Jewish interest, notably *Jonah* (1925; British edition: *The Son of Amittai*); *There Is Another Heaven* (1929); *Road of Ages* (1935), an imaginative tale of Jewish exile in the Gobi Desert, partly inspired by Hitlerite persecution; and *A Star in the Wind* (1962), whose hero reaffirms his Judaism after overcoming unhappy childhood memories and encountering the spirit of a reborn Israel. Nathan's other works include two novels about refugees, *They Went On Together* (1941) and *The Sea-Gull Cry* (1942); verse collections such as *A Cedar Box* (1929), *A Winter Tide* (1940), and *The Green Leaf* (1950); and the plays, *Jezebel's Husband* and *The Sleeping Beauty* (1953).

Bibliography: S. J. Kunitz (ed.), *Twentieth Century Authors*, first suppl. (1955); D. H. Laurence, *Robert Nathan, a Bibliography* (1960); H. Breit, *Writer Observed* (1956), 119–21; R. Van Gelder, *Writers and Writing* (1946), 173–6. [J.Mer.]

NATHAN, ROBERT ROY (1908–), U.S. economist. Born in Dayton, Ohio, Nathan joined the Department of Commerce in 1933 and became prominent in President Roosevelt's reconstruction programs. During World War II he was associated with the War Production Board and the Office of War Mobilization and Reconversion. After the war he opened his own consulting firm which was active in counseling postwar rehabilitation work and economic development in many countries including France, Burma, Indonesia, Korea, Afghanistan, Ghana, Colombia, and El Salvador. During the late 1940s and the early 1950s he devoted much of his time and effort to guiding various Israel government authorities in their first official contacts with the United States government. His main professional interest was developmental economics, and his major publications include *Mobilizing for Abundance* (1944) and *Palestine—Problem and Promise* (with O. Gass and D. Creamer, 1946). [J.O.R.]

NATHAN BEN ABRAHAM I (d. c. 1053), *av bet din* of the academy of Ereẓ Israel in Jerusalem. Nathan was a scion of one of the families whose members held respected positions in the academy. Around 1011 he traveled to Kairouan to settle the estate of his father who had died there. He remained there for a number of years, studying under R. *Ḥushi'el. After the death of his maternal uncle, Rav ben Yoḥai, *av bet din* of the academy of Ereẓ Israel, Nathan claimed the position—although according to accepted custom it belonged to Tobiah, who ranked third in the academy—at the same time attempting to oust R. *Solomon b. Judah as *gaon* of the academy. In the struggle, Nathan was sponsored by Diaspora scholars, while Solomon b. Judah was supported by the local community and also favored by the Fatimid governor of *Ramleh. Nathan lived in Ramleh, attempting to assume the functions of *gaon* there, while Solomon still held his position in Jerusalem and issued a ban against Nathan. In 1042 both parties agreed that Nathan should succeed Solomon as *gaon* of the academy after the latter's death. However, when this occurred (before 1051) the office of *gaon* passed to *Daniel b. Azariah. Nothing is known of Nathan's teachings. In one of his letters of 1042 he mentions his son Abraham, whose son *Nathan II was later *av bet din* of the academy.

Bibliography: J. Mann, in: HUCA, 3 (1926), 273–6; R. Gottheil and W. H. Worrell, *Fragments from the Cairo Genizah in the Freer Collection* (1927), 197–201; S. Assaf, in: *Zion*, 2 (1927), 115f.; Mann, Texts, 1 (1931), 323–45; S. Assaf and L. A. Mayer, *Sefer ha-Yishuv*, 2 (1944), index; Shapira, in: *Yerushalayim*, 4 (1953), 118–22; Hirschberg, Afrikah, 1 (1965), 240–3; Goitein, in: *Tarbiz*, 36 (1967), 62f. [A.D.]

NATHAN BEN ABRAHAM II (d. before 1102), *av bet din* of the academy of Ereẓ Israel. Nathan was a grandson of *Nathan b. Abraham I. Few biographical details are known of him. He was appointed *av bet din* of the academy of Ereẓ Israel during the gaonate of *Abiathar in 1095, in succession to Zadok b. Josiah. Nathan compiled a short Arabic commentary to the six Orders of the Mishnah, in which he incorporated explanations of many specific words. A Yemenite scholar who lived in the 12th century copied his commentary, and added some commentaries of other scholars to it. In the opinion of some scholars, however, Nathan is himself responsible for some of the additions from the commentaries of his predecessors. It is not clear which literary sources were already used by Nathan himself and which were added by the Yemenite scholar. The scholars quoted in the commentary, except for two contemporaries, Nathan b. Jehiel of Rome and Isaac Alfasi, lived before him. Nathan, or the Yemenite scholar, frequently quotes the later *geonim*, particularly Saadiah Gaon, Samuel b. Ḥophni Gaon, Sherira Gaon, and Hai Gaon. There are few quotations from the earlier *geonim*. In general the commentary gives the meaning of words and concepts, a more extensive commentary being found only for a few tractates: *Berakhot*, *Shevu'ot*, and *Avot*. A few tractates are preceded by a short introduction explaining general concepts and essential matters necessary for an understanding of the whole tractate. R. Nathan, or the Yemenite scholar, gives a short survey of the development of the oral law down to his time in his introduction to the work. He discusses the relationship of the Tosefta to the Mishnah, taking the view that the Tosefta explains obscurities of the Mishnah. He also discusses the principles laid down by talmudic scholars for deciding *halakhah* where there are opposing opinions. The chapter divisions of the tractates in the commentary differ from the accepted form. The commentary seeems to have been widely known and it was already used by *Baruch Samuel of Aleppo.

A number of extracts were published in the original with a Hebrew translation by S. Assaf and by M. L. Sachs. The whole commentary in the Hebrew translation of J. *Kafiḥ (Kappaḥ) was published by El ha-Mekorot (Jerusalem, 1955–58) together with the Mishnah text and other commentaries.

Bibliography: Mann, Egypt, 1 (1920), 151, 193f.; 2 (1922), 229–32; S. Assaf, in: KS, 10 (1933/34), 381–8, 525–45 (= Assaf, Ge'onim, 294–332); M. L. Sachs, in: *Sinai*, 17 (1945), 167–75; S. Abramson, *Rav Nissim Ga'on* (1965), index. [A.D.]

NATHAN BEN ISAAC HA-KOHEN HA-BAVLI (i.e., the Babylonian; tenth century), chronicler who probably lived in Baghdad. The fragments of his work that have been preserved appear to be part of his book on the Jews of Baghdad, *Akhbar Baghdād*. These fragments are an important source for the study of the history of Babylonian Jewry in the tenth century. In the first fragment Nathan gives a description of the office of the exilarch, the method by which he was appointed, his duties, and his functions. The fragment also contains details of two great controversies that raged in Babylonian Jewry in the tenth century. In one, the adversaries were the exilarch *Ukba and the *gaon* of Pumbedita, *Kohen Ẓedek; it lasted from 909 to 916. In the other controversy, the adversaries were the exilarch *David b. Zakkai and *Saadiah Gaon, in about 930. From the contents of the fragment it appears that Nathan was in Babylonia at the time that the latter controversy took place. His vivid account of the ceremonial observed at the installation of an exilarch is of exceptional interest (see *Exilarch). This fragment was published (in Hebrew) in Samuel Shulam's edition of Abraham *Zacuto's *Sefer Yuḥasin* (Constantinople, 1566), and again in A. Neubauer's *Medieval Jewish Chronicles* (2 (1895), 77–88). A second fragment describes the rise of *Natira and his sons at the court of the Abbasid caliph at the end of the ninth and the beginning of the tenth century. It was published, in Arabic and in a Hebrew translation, by A. E. Harkavy (see bibliography). A third fragment, also dealing with the Ukba-Kohen Ẓedek quarrel, was published, in the original and in English translation, by I. Friedlander (see bibliography). The fragments lead to the assumption that Nathan ha-Bavli was closely associated with the circles surrounding the exilarchs and the academy heads, and that he may have been a student at one of the academies, apparently Sura. His writings contain inaccuracies and glaring omissions, e.g., he errs in the names of the *geonim* and in the chronological data. Nevertheless, he made an honest and unbiased effort to report events as he saw them happen or as they were reported to him. Some of the information contained in the fragments has been confirmed in other sources.

Bibliography: A. Harkavy, in: *Festschrift ... A. Berliner* (1903), 34–43 (Heb. part); I. Friedlander, in: JQR, 17 (1904/05), 747–61; A. Epstein, in: *Festschrift ... A. Harkavy* (1908), 169–72 (Heb. part); J. R. Marcus, *The Jew in the Medieval World* (1938), 287–92; L. Ginzberg, *Geonica*, 1 (1909), 22–37, 55–66; A. Kahana, *Sifrut ha-Historyah ha-Yisre'elit*, 1 (1922), 57–72; A. Marx, in: *Livre* *d'Hommage . . . Poznański* (1927), 76–81 (Ger.); J. Mann, in: *Tarbiz,* 5 (1933/34), 148ff.; Baron, Social², 6 (1958), 213–4; A. N. Z. Roth, in KS: 30 (1954/55), 255–6. [A.D.]

NATHAN BEN JEHIEL OF ROME (1035–c. 1110), Italian lexicographer, also called **Ba'al he-Arukh** ("the author of the *Arukh*") after the title of his lexicon. Few biographical details are known of him. Some state that he belonged to the De *Pomis or Delli Mansi family, but the view is widespread that he actually belonged to the famous *Anau (Anav) family. He was taught in his youth by his father, a *paytan* and the head of the yeshivah of Rome, and may as a young man have studied in Sicily under Maẓli'aḥ b. Elijah ibn *al-Bazak, a pupil of Hai Gaon. However, there is reason to believe that the scanty references to Maẓli'aḥ's name in Nathan's work are the addenda of an earlier copyist named Mevorakh, some of whose marginal notes, in which he also mentions that he was Al-Bazak's pupil, were later incorporated in the text of the *Arukh*. Nathan also studied under Moses ha-Darshan of Narbonne, as well as, in the view of some scholars, under Moses Kalfo of Bari and Moses of Pavia. When his father died immediately after Nathan's return to Rome about 1070, he and his two brothers Daniel and Abraham succeeded him as the heads of the yeshivah of Rome. With them he wrote responsa to halakhic questions addressed to him by various scholars, among whom was a Solomon Yiẓḥaki, identified by some as Rashi. Noted for his charitable acts, Nathan built a magnificent synagogue and a ritual bathhouse for his community. It was while serving as head of the Rome yeshivah that he wrote his classical work (which he completed in 1101) the *Arukh,* a lexicon of the Talmud and the Midrashim, containing all the talmudic terms in need of explanation; in the course of time various additions were made to it (see below). At the end of the *Arukh* there is a poem written in particularly difficult language and therefore of somewhat obscure meaning; in it the poet, lamenting his bitter lot, tells of the death of four out of his five sons during his lifetime.

In the *Arukh* Nathan gives not only the meaning but also the etymology of the words of the Talmud, including some of Aramaic, Latin, Greek, Arabic, and Persian origin. Nathan quotes many geonic interpretations and an earlier lexicon by a Ẓemaḥ of uncertain identity, as well as the comments of earlier and contemporary rabbis—among them works otherwise unknown—and halakhic decisions, although apparently irrelevant to the object of the work. He describes Jewish customs, such as that of the Babylonian Jews, who in celebrating Purim burned Haman's effigy, singing around and leaping over a bonfire (s.v. *shavvar*). The *Arukh* is important for the study of the *Midrash *Yelammedenu.* Of the other Midrashim he cites, particular note should be taken of the *Midrash Hashkem* of which only quotations have survived, and many of his citations from the Midrashim are not to be found in the extant editions. He also quotes the Palestine Targum to the Pentateuch. Words were still treated by Nathan as though they belonged to uniliteral or biliteral consonantal roots, even though the work of Judah ibn Ḥayyuj, showing that the Hebrew verb has a triliteral root, had already appeared.

The main importance of the *Arukh* lies in the extensive collection of explanations of words and subjects in the Talmud and in the profusion of the author's excellent readings, all drawn from the three chief Torah centers of that time: the teaching of the Babylonian *geonim;* the commentaries of *Hananel b. Ḥushi'el of Kairouan, which he uses extensively but in the main without acknowledgment; and the "Mainz commentaries" mentioned by him under different names ("scholars of Mainz," "pious ones of Mainz," "Mainz commentary," etc.). These explanations occur in the extant commentaries of Rabbenu Gershom without mentioning Nathan's name. Apart from these three sources he also had before him not a few of the early commentaries of Provence. Nathan frequently explains words and subjects according to the reading of Hananel b. Ḥushi'el without indicating that it is based thereon. At times he goes beyond the explanation of the word and explains the whole theme. It has now been established that these explanations are also from Hananel, given by him in other contexts. In the printed editions of the Talmud, Rashi mentions him once (Shab. 13b). The whole passage, however, is missing in some manuscripts, and it is clear that Rashi made no use of the *Arukh*. The many anonymous parallels that exist between the two works have their source in the common use made by the two scholars of "the teaching of Mainz" and of the other common exegetical traditions.

The *Arukh* achieved exceptionally wide circulation. It was apparently first published in Rome in 1469–72?, an edition that is a better version than that found in later ones printed from a different manuscript. Because of the great importance attached to the work, many supplements to and emendations of it were written. Among them is the *Agur* of Samuel b. Jacob ibn *Jama (12th century), consisting of addenda to the *Arukh* derived from the language found in geonic writings, which was published by S. Buber in *Jubelschrift . . . . H. Graetz* (1887). Menahem de *Lonzano wrote addenda, emendations, and explanations to the *Arukh* under the title of *Ha-Ma'arikh,* published in his work *Shetei Yadot* (Venice, 1618). The physician and philologist Benjamin *Mussafia, in his *Musaf he-Arukh,* which was printed in the *Arukh* (Amsterdam, 1655), corrected the Greek and Latin words. Isaiah *Berlin (18th century) wrote *Hafla'ah she-ba-Arakhin,* addenda and notes to the *Arukh* up to the letter *kaf* in the Lemberg 1857 edition of the *Arukh.* A scholarly edition, based on seven manuscripts, was published by Alexander Kohut under the title of *Arukh ha-Shalem* or *Aruch Completum* (1878–92), to which a supplement and addenda were issued by S. Krauss in his *Tosefot he-Arukh ha-Shalem* (1937). A condensed version, entitled *He-Arukh ha-Kaẓar,* by an anonymous epitomist, was first published in Constantinople.

Bibliography: S. J. L. Rapoport, in: *Bikkurei ha-Ittim* (1830), 2nd pagination, 7–79; Kohut, Arukh, 1 (1926²), introd.; Vogelstein-Rieger, 1 (1896), index; S. Krauss, *Griechische und lateinische Lehnwoerter im Talmud, Midrasch und Targum* (1898), introd. xxiv–xxxix; D. S. Blondheim, in: *Festschrift fuer A. Freimann* (1935), 24–30; idem, *Notes on the Italian Words in the Arukh Completum* (1933); S. Lieberman, in: KS, 14 (1937/38), 218–28; H. Z. Toibes, in: *Scritti in Memoria de Sally Mayer* (1956), Heb. pt. 126–41; H. J. Zimmels, in: Roth, Dark Ages, 182–4; Zunz-Albeck, Derashot, index; S. Abramson, *Rav Nissim Ga'on* (1965), index; S. Speier, in: *Leshonenu,* 31 (1967), 23–32, 189–98; 34 (1967/70), 172–9. [A.D.]

NATHAN DE-ẒUẒITA RESH GALUTA, Babylonian exilarch. According to a statement in the Talmud (Shab. 56b), he is identical with Ukban b. Nehemiah (320–340), but in the *Seder Olam Zuta* two different exilarchs are mentioned called both Ukban and Ẓuẓita: one, called Nathan Ukban (Nathan de-Ẓuẓita), lived in the third century, and the other, Mar Ukban de Ẓuẓita, a near contemporary of R. Joseph, in the fourth. Nathan seems originally to have lived a sinful life, but he later repented. The *amora* Joseph expressed the view that he must be regarded as one of the most celebrated of penitents of all time, and that he was much beloved in heaven. According to an old *aggadah* cited by Rashi (Sanh. 31b), Nathan (Masukba) was consumed by passion for a married woman and unfulfilled desire made him ill. On one occasion, in need of money, she paid him a visit of her own free will. Although he could now have had his desire, he restrained himself, and she departed untouched. From that moment his passion subsided, and a ray of light was seen to shine over his head. It is to this that the name Ẓuẓita (ray of light) refers. According to the *geonim* Ẓemaḥ and Sa'adiah, however, the name derives from the fact that in his youth Nathan used to dress and curl the fringes (*ẓiẓiot*) of his hair (B. M. Lewin, *Oẓar ha-Ge'onim* (Shab.; 1930), pt. 2 24). Rashi identified him in that passage with Mar *Ukba the *av bet din,* a contemporary of Samuel (cf. also R. Aḥai Gaon. *She'iltot,* Va-Era 42; ed. by S. K. Mirsky, 3 (1963), 43). In the manuscripts of the *She'iltot,* however, the passage, "and his name is Nathan b. Ẓuẓita" does not occur. See also *Ḥibbur Yafeh min ha-Yeshu'ah* of Nissim Gaon (ed. by H. Z. Hirschberg (1954), 73–76), from which it appears that he lived in the tannaitic period.

Bibliography: Hyman, Toledot, 956f.; J. N. Epstein, in: MGWJ, 63 (1919), 259–68; S. Abramson, *Rav Nissim Ga'on* (1965), 422f.

[D.J.B.]

NATHAN HA-BAVLI ("the Babylonian"; middle of the second century C.E.), *tanna*. Nathan came from Babylon, where his father was a leading personality. According to a geonic tradition (see *Arukh* s.v. *kamra*), he was the *exilarch. He went to Ereẓ Israel in his youth and studied under *Ishmael (Shab. 12b), *Eliezer b. Hyrcanus (Pes. 48a), *Tarfon (Zev. 97a), and *Yose ha-Gelili (Men. 38b). When the Hadrianic persecutions broke out he fled to his native Babylon. It was possibly during this period that he traveled overseas to a number of countries, including Cappadocia (Ḥul. 47b). Nathan had a great reputation in Babylon, and when *Hananiah the nephew of Joshua b. Hananiah fixed the calendar in Babylon, Nathan was one of the two scholars who were sent to remonstrate with him and succeeded in persuading him to desist (TJ, Ned. 6:13 40a; Sanh. 1:2, 19a). He took part in the convention of *Usha, and, under *Simeon b. Gamaliel, was *av bet din* at the time R. Meir was the *ḥakham* (Hor. 13b). Following a dispute with Simeon b. Gamaliel, Nathan and Meir were removed from office. Thereupon the teachings of Meir were quoted as "others say" and of Nathan as "some say." Nathan was later reinstated (Hor. 13b). Statements by Nathan are frequently quoted in *beraitot*, but his name appears only twice in the Mishnah, and even those two passages are additions which do not appear in the manuscripts. In one passage he interpreted Psalms 119:126 to mean: "They have made void the law because it was a time to work for the Lord" (Ber. 9:5). The other passage lays it down that "The surplus of money collected for burial ... is used to build a monument over the grave" (Shek. 2:5). He had a Mishnah collection of his own (Tem. 16a) and is cited as the one who transmitted the important halakhic rule that if A owes B money and B owes C, then C may claim from A (Ket. 19a; see *Shi'abuda de-Rabbi Nathan). He is said to be the author of **Avot de-Rabbi Nathan* and of the 49 hermeneutical rules of Rabbi Nathan (see *Hermeneutics). He was regarded as an authority on civil law because of his experience as a *dayyan* (BK 39a; BM 117b). It is said of Rabbi Judah ha-Nasi and Rabbi Nathan that they constituted "the conclusion of the Mishnah" (BM 86a), i.e., that they were the outstanding scholars of the close of the tannaitic period. According to the *aggadah* (Git. 70a), the prophet Elijah appeared to him and taught him. Among his aggadic sayings are: "One may modify a statement in the interest of peace" (Yev. 65b); "Do not taunt your neighbor with your own blemish" (BM 59b); and "There is no greater love than love of the Torah; there is no wisdom like the wisdom of Ereẓ Israel, and there is no beauty like the beauty of Jerusalem" (ARN, 28, 85).

Bibliography: Hyman, Toledot, 949–53; J. Bruell, *Mevo ha-Mishnah*, 1 (1876), 218–23; Frankel, Mishnah, 198–201; Bacher, Tann, 2 (1890), 437–53; Halevy, Dorot, 1 pt. 5 (1923), 817–23; A. Buechler, *Studies in Jewish History* (1956), 160–78; Neusner, Babylonia, 1 (1965), index; M. Baer, *Rashut ha-Golah be-Bavel* (1970), 29f.; A. Epstein, *Mi-Kadmoniyyot ha-Yehudim-Ketavim*, 2 (1957), 415–7.

[D.J.B.]

NATHAN OF GAZA (1643/4–1680), one of the central figures of the Shabbatean movement. His full name was Abraham Nathan b. Elisha Ḥayyim Ashkenazi, but he became famous as Nathan the Prophet of Gaza and after 1665 his admirers generally called him "the holy lamp" (*buẓina kaddisha*), the honorific given to R. *Simeon b. Yoḥai in the Zohar. His father, *Elisha Ḥayyim b. Jacob Ashkenazi, who had come from Poland or Germany, settled in Jerusalem and for many years served as an emissary of its community, visiting Poland, Germany, Italy, and (frequently) Morocco. He was a respected rabbinical scholar with kabbalistic leanings. Nathan was born in Jerusalem, probably about 1643/44. His main teacher was the famous talmudist Jacob *Ḥagiz and he seems to have been a brilliant student, quick to understand and of considerable intellectual power. Before he left Jerusalem in 1663, having married the daughter of a wealthy merchant of Gaza, Samuel Lissabonna, and settled in the latter's home town, he must have seen *Shabbetai Ẓevi, then twice his age, in the Jewish quarter of Jerusalem, where Shabbetai lived for almost the whole of 1663. It is also clear that he must have heard a great deal of talk about this strange personality and his tribulations. Strongly attracted by an ascetic way of life, Nathan took up the study of Kabbalah in 1664. The combination of great intellectual and imaginative power which was his main characteristic resulted in his having visions of angels and deceased souls after a short time. He delved deeply into Lurianic Kabbalah, following the ascetic rules laid down by Isaac *Luria. Shortly before or after Purim 1665 he had a significant ecstatic experience accompanied by a prolonged vision (he speaks of 24 hours) of the divine world revealing how its different stages were connected, a vision that differed in many significant details from the Lurianic scheme. Through this revelation he

Nathan of Gaza, kabbalist and disciple of Shabbetai Ẓevi. From Thomas Coenen, *Ydele Verwachtinge der Joden getoont in der Persoon van Sabethai Zevi*, Amsterdam, 1669.

became convinced of the messianic mission of Shabbetai Ẓevi, whose figure he saw engraved on the divine throne. (For his further intensive activities during the following year see the article on *Shabbetai Ẓevi). When the latter returned from his mission to Egypt and came to see him in Gaza, Nathan finally convinced him of his messianic destiny by producing a pseudepigraphic vision, attributed to a medieval saint, Abraham Ḥasid, who as it were foretold the birth and early history of Shabbetai Ẓevi and confirmed his superior rank.

In his ecstasy Nathan had heard a voice announcing in the name of God that Shabbetai Ẓevi was the Messiah; he therefore became the prophet of the "son of David," the mission that the biblical prophet Nathan had fulfilled for King David. As he had been vouchsafed charismatic gifts since his ecstatic awakening, many people made pilgrimages to him from Palestine, Syria, and Egypt. He showed "the roots of their souls," revealed their secret sins, and prescribed ways to penance. Since his prophetic powers were widely acknowledged as genuine, his endorsement of Shabbetai Ẓevi's messianic claim gave the decisive impetus to the mass movement which swept the Jewish people everywhere. Remaining in Gaza after Shabbetai Ẓevi left for Jerusalem and Smyrna (Izmir), he wrote letters to the Diaspora confirming that redemption was at hand and laying down elaborate kabbalistic rules of penance *(tikkunim)* to be followed by those who wished to usher in the new age. These were widely copied and the exoteric portions of the ritual were printed in many editions during 1666. It is not known why the rabbis of Jerusalem, the majority of whom (including Jacob Ḥagiz) took a stand against the messianic claims of Shabbetai Ẓevi, did nothing to interfere with Nathan's activities. The fact that the small community of Gaza, including their rabbi, Jacob *Najara, were among his followers, is insufficient explanation. In the summer of 1666, during Shabbetai's confinement in Gallipoli, Nathan composed several kabbalistic tracts of which the *Derush ha-Tanninim* has survived (published in G. Scholem, *Be-Ikkevot Mashi'aḥ*, 1944), glorifying Shabbetai's mystical state since the beginning of creation. His correspondence with Shabbetai Ẓevi during this time, however, is lost.

After receiving the news of Shabbetai's apostasy, he left Gaza early in November 1666, accompanied by a large group of supporters, including his father-in-law and his family. On Nov. 20, 1666, he wrote to Shabbetai Ẓevi from Damascus announcing that he was on his way to see him, apparently on the latter's invitation. By this time he had already begun to sign himself Nathan Benjamin, the new name Shabbetai had given him in Gaza when he appointed 12 scholars to represent the 12 tribes of Israel. Nathan's faith in his messiah never wavered and from the beginning he hinted at mystical reasons which justified the apostasy. Originally he planned to travel by sea via Alexandretta (Iskenderun) but he changed his route and went with his entourage by land, avoiding the larger Jewish communities which had been warned against him by the rabbis of Constantinople. By the end of January 1667 he arrived at Bursa (Brusa) where he was threatened with a ban unless he stayed out of the town and "kept quiet." Dispersing his group he continued with only six associates, including Samuel Gandoor, a scholar from Egypt, who became his constant companion until his death. Before leaving Bursa, he wrote a letter to Shabbetai's brothers in Smyrna, opening a long series of letters, tracts, and other pronouncements defending the apostasy and Shabbetai's continued messianic mission on kabbalistic grounds. Many of these have been preserved. On March 3, 1667, he arrived at a small village near Smyrna, then stayed until April 30 in Smyrna itself; there he met with some of the believers, but kept largely to himself. He became very reserved toward all outsiders and even repelled the delegation of three northern Italian communities who were on their way to Shabbetai Ẓevi and had been waiting to hear Nathan's explanations. The Dutch clergyman Th. Coenen has left a description of his meeting with Nathan on April 25. Nathan tried to reach Adrianople, where he would see his messiah, but he was held up in the nearby small community of Ipsala and met by a delegation from Adrianople and Constantinople. After being interrogated he was forced to sign a document (dated May 31, 1667) promising not to approach Adrianople, not to correspond with "that man" in Adrianople, and not to convene public meetings, but to keep to himself; finally he admitted that all his words would be given the lie unless the messiah appeared before September 14, a date he had fixed earlier on the strength of an additional vision. Later Nathan repudiated all these obligations, claiming that he had acted under duress. He went to see Shabbetai Ẓevi secretly then wandered with Gandoor through Thrace and Greece where sympathy with the movement was still very strong.

Early in 1668 he traveled from Janina to Corfu where he held secret conclaves with his adherents. On the initiative of Shabbetai Ẓevi himself he then undertook a journey to Italy, with the intention of carrying out a mystic ritual at the seat of the pope in Rome. His arrival in Venice around March 20 caused considerable excitement and apprehension. Under pressure from someone in the government, he was allowed to enter the ghetto where he spent approximately two weeks, being closely questioned by the rabbis but also beleaguered by a host of admirers and followers. The events of Ipsala were repeated; the rabbis published the results of their examination in a broadsheet, including a declaration in which Nathan admitted his errors; later Nathan repudiated this in statements to the believers. From Venice he and Gandoor traveled to Bologna, Florence, and Leghorn, where he stayed for some weeks strengthening the hopes of the remaining believers. He and a wealthy Italian believer, Moses Cafsuto, then proceeded to Rome, perhaps disguised as gentiles. He stayed a few days only (end of May or beginning of June) performing some secret rituals patterned on those outlined at an earlier time by Solomon *Molcho. He returned to Leghorn or, according to another source, went straight to Ancona, where he was recognized and met the rabbi, *Mahalalel Halleluyah (Alleluyah), a fervent believer, who has left a detailed account of their meeting. By that time Nathan had written an account of his mission to Rome, couched in elusive Aramaic filled with kabbalistic and apocalyptic metaphors. This was widely distributed to the groups of believers. On his return to Turkey via Ragusa and Durazzo Nathan went to stay for some time with Shabbetai Ẓevi in Adrianople. After this he spent six months in Salonika where a considerable group of scholars flocked to him to receive his new version of the Kabbalah according to Shabbatean principles. For the next ten years he remained in Macedonia and Bulgaria—apart from secret pilgrimages to Shabbetai Ẓevi after the latter's banishment to Dulcigno in Albania (1673)—staying mainly in Sofia, Adrianople, and Kastoria, and paying occasional visits to Salonika. He maintained close contacts with many other leaders of the movement who continued to consider him as a charismatic figure of the highest rank. Although Shabbetai Ẓevi never asked him to follow him into Islam, he staunchly defended not only the necessity of the messiah's apostasy, but also those "elect ones" who emulated him on his command. Many of the rabbis of the Macedonian communities stood by him, paying no heed to the excommunications and warnings emanating from Constantinople and Adrianople.

Nathan's letters reveal him as a strong personality

although the few that have been preserved from his intense correspondence with Shabbetai Ẓevi are couched in adoring and submissive terms. They contrast curiously with his obvious moral and intellectual superiority over his master. In spite of all this, there were periods of tension between the two. After Shabbetai's death Nathan withdrew even more from public contact, although he continued to preach in the synagogues of Sofia on some occasions. Refusing to admit defeat he upheld the theory that Shabbetai Ẓevi had only "disappeared" or gone into hiding in some higher sphere, whence he would return in God's own time. Israel Ḥazzan of Kastoria, who served as his secretary for about three years, took down many of his teachings and sayings after Shabbetai's death. Nathan continued to lead an ascetic life and, feeling that his end was near, left Sofia and went to Skoplje (Üsküb) where he died on Jan. 11, 1680. His grave was revered as that of a saint and over the generations many Shabbateans made pilgrimages there. His tombstone, whose inscription has been preserved, was destroyed during World War II. The many legends spread about Nathan during his lifetime increased after his death. He had two sons, of whose fate nothing is known. A sketch of Nathan drawn by a ship's mate who saw him in Gaza in the summer of 1665, which was reproduced in several contemporary broadsheets, may be authentic.

Between 1665 and 1679 Nathan embarked on a manifold literary activity. Some of his many letters are in fact theological treatises. At first, he composed kabbalistic rules and meditations for a fast of six consecutive days, *Seder Hafsakah Gedolah shel Shishah Yamim ve-Shishah Leilot*, partly printed anonymously under the title *Sefer le-Hafsakah Gedolah* (Smyrna, 1732). These were accompanied by *Tikkunei Teshuvah*, both treatises being preserved in several manuscripts. The printed edition omits all mention of Shabbetai Ẓevi's name. At about the same time he began the explanation of his new vision of the process of creation, sending several tracts on this to Raphael Joseph in Cairo. Of these only the *Derush ha-Tanninim* has been preserved. After Shabbetai's apostasy he developed his ideas in a more radical way. The most elaborate presentation of his kabbalistic system, containing constant references to the function of the Messiah and his paradoxical actions, is found in the *Sefer ha-Beri'ah*, written in 1670, in two parts. It was also known under the title *Raza de-Uvda de-Bereshit*, and in some manuscripts was accompanied by a lengthy preface which may have been conceived as a separate literary entity. The work is extant, complete or in parts, in approximately 30 manuscripts and must have enjoyed a wide distribution in Shabbatean circles up to the middle of the 18th century. A short synopsis of its ideas, from Ms. Oxford, Neubauer Cat. (Bod.) no. 2394, is included in Scholem's *Be-Ikkevot Mashi'aḥ*. During the same period Nathan composed the book *Zemir Arizim* which, as well as other kabbalistic matters, contains long disquisitions on the state of the Torah in the messianic era and a justification of Shabbetai Ẓevi's antinomian actions (complete in British Museum Or. 4536, Margoliouth, Cat, no. 856 and elsewhere). In some manuscripts it was called *Derush ha-Menorah*, and was partly included in the collection *Be-Ikkevot Mashi'aḥ*. These books were widely quoted by secret Shabbateans, sometimes even in printed works. Of his many pastoral letters, special mention must be made of the long apology for Shabbetai Ẓevi, published in *Kovez al Yad*, 6 (1966), 419–56, apparently written about 1673–74. Fragments of other writings are dispersed through several manuscripts and Shabbatean notebooks. Collections dealing with his special customs and behavior were made by his pupils in Salonika (who saw him as a reincarnation of Luria) and were distributed in Turkey and Italy, These are extant in several versions. An abridgment of Nathan's system was incorporated as the first part of the *Sha'arei Gan Eden* by *Jacob Koppel b. Moses of Mezhirech and was published as an authoritative kabbalistic text (Korets, 1803) without its heretical character being recognized.

Bibliography: G. Scholem, Shabbetai Ẓevi, passim, esp. chs. 3, 7–8; idem, *Be-Ikkevot Mashi'aḥ* (1944), a collection of Nathan's writings; idem, in: *Alei Ayin, Minḥat Devarim le-S. Z. Schocken* (1948–52), 157–211; idem, in: *H. A. Wolfson Jubilee Volume* (1965), 225–41 (Heb. sect.); C. Wirszubski, in: *Keneset, Divrei Soferim le-Zekher Ḥ. N. Bialik*, 8 (1943–44), 2nd pagination 210–46; idem, in: *Kovez Hoza'at Schocken le-Divrei Sifrut* (1941), 180–92; I. Tishby, in: *Tarbiz*, 15 (1943/44), 161–80; idem, in: KS, 21 (1945), 12–17; idem, in: *Sefunot*, 1 (1956), 80–117; idem, *Netivei Emunah ve-Minut* (1964), 30–80, 204–26, 280–95, 331–43.

[G.Sch.]

NATHANSEN, HENRI (1868–1944), Danish playwright and novelist. Born in Hjørring, Jutland, Nathansen practiced law before becoming a writer. He published some 20 works, nearly half of them plays, and in 1909 became stage director of Copenhagen's Royal Theater. Many of his plays dealt with contemporary Jewish problems. The drama *Daniel Hertz* (1908) was followed in 1912 by *Indenfor murene* ("Within the Walls") considered to be one of the finest plays in the Danish language. Nathansen here analyzes the position of the Jew in a non-Jewish environment and, in portraying the conflicts engendered by a Copenhagen Jewess' wish to marry a gentile, succeeds in airing the whole question of Jewish-Christian relations in a free society. Jewish themes also dominate Nathansen's comedy *Affaeren* (1913), the semi-autobiographical novel *Af Hugo Davids liv* (4 vols., 1917), and the last work published in his lifetime, the novel *Mendel Philipsen og Sön* (1932). His other outstanding publications include a biography of Georg *Brandes (1929) and *Portraetstudier* (1930), studies of eminent Scandinavian writers. In 1919 Nathansen issued a protest against the persecution of Polish Jewry, and in 1930 called for solidarity in the Copenhagen Jewish community to counteract the dangers of Nazi anti-Semitism. Together with the majority of Danish Jews, he fled to Sweden in October 1943. There, in a fit of depression, he took his own life.

Bibliography: *Dansk Biografisk Leksikon*, 16 (1939); *Dansk Skönlitteraert Forfatterleksikon*, 3 (1964). [T.M.]

NATHANSON, BERNHARD (Dov Baer; 1832–1916), Hebrew writer, biographer, and lexicographer. Born in Satanov, Podolia, Nathanson was a contributor to *Ha-Maggid* and *Ha-Meliz*. After the death of I. B. *Levinsohn in 1860 he was commissioned to prepare Levinsohn's manuscripts for publication, a task to which he devoted most of his literary career. He wrote a popular biography of Levinsohn, *Sefer ha-Zikhronot* (1876). Nathanson also compiled *Ma'arekhet Sifrei Kodesh* (1870), a Jewish historical lexicon, and *Sefer ha-Millim* (1880), a dictionary of foreign words.

Bibliography: N. Sokolow (ed.), *Sefer Zikkaron* (1889), 73f.; Frenk, in: *Ha-Ẓefirah* (1916), no. 45–47; Kressel, Leksikon, 2 (1967), 466. [Y.S.]

NATHANSON, JOSEPH SAUL (1810–1875), **posek*. Nathanson was born in Berezhany, the son of Aryeh Leibush Nathanson of Brody, a wealthy businessman who was also a profound talmudist. In 1825 he married Sarah Idel, the daughter of Isaac Aaron Ettinger, who was also a great scholar and a wealthy man. Nathanson, as was customary in those days, was maintained in his father-in-law's home. When his father-in-law died shortly after his marriage, his mother-in-law administered the business and took care that he would be able to live and study without financial cares, and when she died in 1841, his wife took over the responsibility. In his father-in-law's house Nathanson found a colleague in his brother-in-law, Mordecai Ze'ev *Ettinger. They studied together for several years and compiled a series of halakhic works, but they separated as a result of a difference of opinion which came to a head on the question of the permissibility of machine-baked *mazzot*. The two brothers-in-law were rival candidates for the rabbinate of Lemberg to which Nathanson was appointed in 1857. The same year his wife died, but in 1858 he married a wealthy woman and did not accept a salary.

Nathanson was the outstanding *posek* and writer of responsa of his generation. Problems reached him from all parts of the world and he corresponded with all the great contemporary scholars. In his works he is revealed principally as an instructor in practical *halakhah*. He regarded himself as responsible for the condition of *halakhah* in his time, in succession to such scholars as Akiva *Eger and Moses *Sofer. He was opposed to the method of **pilpul* for its own sake, regarding it as suitable only for youths (*Divrei Sha'ul, Aggadot,* 29b) but not for those destined to be religious teachers. He did not necessarily base his decision "upon the statements of *aḥaronim*" (*Sho'el u-Meshiv,* 2 pt. 3, no. 108), but based his rulings mainly upon the Talmud and the *rishonim*.

He tended to leniency in his rulings, and took contemporary circumstances into consideration. He was one of those who permitted machine-baked *mazzot* in opposition to the view of Solomon *Kluger. Although Kluger decided that **etrogim* from Corfu were invalid because of the fear that they were hybrids, Nathanson permitted them (*Yosef Da'at, Kilei Begadim,* no. 302). He also regarded the birds called "kibbitzer" hens as permitted according to the dietary laws although other authorities forbade them (*Sho'el u-Meshiv,* 3 pt. 2, no. 121). Although known for his permissive approach, however, he sometimes declared things forbidden simply as a precaution (*Yosef Da'at, Terefot,* 64–65). It was this which prompted Dov Berush *Meisels, rabbi of Warsaw, to say of him: "I know him of old as one who adopts a stringent and not a lenient line" (end of the pamphlet *Moda'ah le-Veit Yisrael*). Despite his leniency in halakhic ruling, he fought with all his power against the progressives in his community who wanted to introduce reforms into education. When the government sought to compel the Jews of Galicia to send their children to government schools and to bar them from the *ḥeder* until they had passed four classes of the secular schools, as well as to make the teachers pass an examination in German and pedagogy, Nathanson took the initiative in uniting the great talmudic scholars to obtain the repeal of the edict (see S. Kluger's letter of 1867 in *Toledot Shelomo* (1956), 113ff.).

On the other hand he was resolutely opposed to schism, and when Zalman Spitzer, the son-in-law of Moses Sofer, published a proclamation calling on 400 rabbis to sign a ban against the payment of taxes to communities whose leaders were progressives, he declined to sign because it would lead to discord. He also maintained harmonious relations with the preachers of the "temple" (i.e., Reform synagogue), Dr. Simeon Schwabacher and Bernhard Loewenstein.

Nathanson was completely opposed to the ḥasidic movement and its new customs. As such he upheld the Ashkenazi *minhag* opposing the custom of reciting **Hallel* in the synagogues on Passover eve (*Sho'el u-Meshiv,* 2 pt. 4, no. 135) and the custom of not donning *tefillin* during the intermediate days of the festivals (*ibid.,* 2 pt. 3, no. 87). Despite his opposition to Ḥasidism, however, he respected their leaders if they were great scholars and quoted them in his works. While still a youth in the house of his grandfather in Berezhany, he made the acquaintance of the ḥasidic rabbi Abraham David of Buczacz and wrote a commendation for his *Da'at Kedoshim* (1880). In his own works he quotes Levi Isaac of Berdichev (*Divrei Sha'ul* on the Pentateuch, passim), and among the other ḥasidic leaders he had great respect for Isaac Meir Alter, author of the *Ḥiddushei ha-Rim,* and was on friendly terms with Ḥayyim Halberstamm, the author of the *Divrei Ḥayyim*.

Although mainly occupied with *halakhah,* Nathanson devoted part of his time to biblical study, and wrote *Divrei Sha'ul,* on the Pentateuch and the Five *Scrolls. He applied himself to the study of Kabbalah, but like the other great *posekim* of his generation refrained from quoting it in support of the *halakhah* (*Sho'el u-Meshiv,* 2 pt. 3, no. 87). He was also versed in the scientific works of the Middle Ages and applied modern methods in practical halakhic rulings, such as ordering a chemical analysis to determine the presence of an admixture of forbidden matter in food (*ibid.,* 3 pt. 1, no. 377). He lectured to his students twice daily (*ibid.,* 2 pt. 3, no. 101). He did not prepare his lesson in advance, but involved his pupils in the discussions, and his lesson became a workshop for his novellae. Among his distinguished pupils were Ze'ev Wolf Salat, the publisher of his responsa, and Ẓevi Hirsch Ornstein. He supported talmudic scholars and authors, and Solomon Buber testified of him that "without exaggeration there are extant 300 commendations by him," so that he was designated *Sar ha-Maskim* ("chief approver," a pun on Gen. 40:9).

Besides the works he compiled with his brother-in-law Moses Ze'ev Ettinger, Nathanson wrote a series of works in *halakhah* and *aggadah*. His classic work in *halakhah* is his responsa *Sho'el u-Meshiv* (1865–90), in six volumes comprising 15 parts. He was also the author of *Divrei Sha'ul ve-ha-Sefer Yosef Da'at* (1878–79) on the Shulḥan Arukh, *Yoreh De'ah,* in two parts; *Yad Yosef ve-Yad Sha'ul* (1851); *Hilkhot Nedarim;* Shulḥan Arukh (YD 203–35), *Beit Sha'ul,* on the Mishnah (in the Romm Vilna edition); *Divrei Sha'ul* (1877), on the *aggadot* of the Talmud; *Divrei Sha'ul* (1875), on the Pentateuch and the five scrolls, in two parts; *Divrei Sha'ul ve-hu Sefer Ḥelek le-Shivah* (1879), on the Naḥalut *Shivah* of Samuel b. David ha-Levi; *Torat Moshe,* on the *Torat Ḥattat* of Moses Isserles (in: *Ḥamishah Sefarim Niftaḥim* (1859)); novellae glosses on the four parts of the Shulḥan Arukh; *Melekh be-Yofyo* (1866), a sermon calling to contribute to the Austrian war effort; *Avodat ha-Leviyyim* on the *Torat ha-Adam; Divrei Sha'ul ve-hu Sefer Edut bi-Yhosef* on the topics of Maimonides' *Mishneh Torah* and part of the Shulḥan Arukh; and *Ẓiyyon vi-Yrushalayim,* on the Jerusalem Talmud (in the Zhitomir edition). Many works and articles have remained unpublished.

Bibliography: *Der Israelit,* 16 (1875), 258; Fuenn, Keneset, 483f.; S. Buber, in: *Ha-Maggid,* 19 (1875), 83; *Anshei Shem* (1895), 97–99; S. M. Chones, *Toledot ha-Posekim* (1910), 277f.; A. Stern, *Meliẓei Esh al Ḥodshei Adar* (1938), 69b no. 336; M. Leiter, in: *Hadorom,* 29 (1969), 146–70; 31 (1970), 171–202; A. Bromberg, *Ha-Ga'on Rabbi Yosef Sha'ul Nathanson mi-Levov* (1960); EG, 4 (1956), 417f.; D. Halachmi, *Ḥakhmei Yisrael* (1957), 318f.; N. Herskovicz, in: *Or ha-Mizraḥ,* 20 (1970/71), 63–72. [Sh.W.]

NATHANSON, MENDEL LEVIN (1780–1868), Danish merchant and editor. Born in Altona, Nathanson went to Copenhagen at the age of 12 to join relatives. In 1798 he settled down as a wholesale draper and until 1831 was a prosperous businessman. Later on he wrote works on economics and in 1838 became editor of the *Berlingske Tidende,* making it the leading newspaper in Denmark. Nathanson was a tireless exponent of the emancipation of Danish Jews. Through his initiative the Jewish Free School for boys was founded in Copenhagen in 1805 and five years later a similar school for girls. He organized the administration of the Jewish community, favoring the religious Reform movement, and had a large share in the Danish

Mendel Levin Nathanson, Danish merchant and editor. Jerusalem, J.N.U.L., Schwadron Collection.

government's edict of March 29, 1814 which gave the Jews equal rights. His writings on economics are still studied, especially his historical and statistical presentation of Denmark's administration of public revenues up to 1836. Of special Jewish interest is his history of the Jews in Denmark, *Historisk Fremstilling af Jødernes Forhold og Stilling i Danmark* (1860). Nathanson's children all converted to Christianity.

Bibliography: G. Siesby, *Mendel Levin Nathanson: En biographisk Skizze* (1845); I. Luplan Janssen, *Mendel Levin Nathanson og hans Slaegt* (1960).

[JU.M.]

NATIONAL CONFERENCE OF JEWISH COMMUNAL SERVICE (NCJCS, organized in 1899 as the Conference of Jewish Charities), the forum and publication body for the various professional disciplines serving the American Jewish community. NCJCS membership consists of approximately 300 organizations and 2,000 practitioners in all of the fields represented by the Jewish "civil service." Its associate groups include the National Association of Jewish Center Workers, the National Council for Jewish Education, the Association of Jewish Community Relations Workers, the National Association of Jewish Homes for the Aged, and the National Association of Jewish Family, Children's and Health Services. The conference holds an annual meeting in the spring for professional examination of trends and developments in the field. It publishes the *Journal of Jewish Communal Service,* a quarterly devoted to professional writing and research.

Bibliography: National Conference of Jewish Communal Service, *Proceedings,* (1900–).

[P.D.]

NATIONAL COUNCIL OF JEWISH WOMEN, U.S. national organization founded in 1893 by Hannah Greenebaum Solomon, when she and other Jewish women from across the country gathered to participate in the Parliament of Religions at the Chicago World's Fair. The National Council of Jewish Women undertook a wide range of activities, from organizing Sabbath schools for slum children and vocational and industrial classes, to managing model tenements and offering free baths to slum dwellers. Starting with the belief that those in need required skills instead of alms, "friendly visitors" acted as pioneer social workers and family aides. Council sections sponsored free libraries, employment bureaus, kindergartens, day nurseries, and projects providing summer outings for children. They urged professionalism in religious education and sent their members to serve on religious school boards.

When Jewish immigrants began to arrive in the United States in great numbers at the turn of the century, the council met and cared for incoming single girls, becoming the first organization to serve at Ellis Island in 1904. Representatives in 250 cities and in European ports assisted the girls with immigration problems and protected them from white slavery. The girls were assisted with English classes and industrial training, and were guided to jobs, lodging, and recreation. The National Council of Jewish Women combined social action with local service. Its services were coupled with programs to help poor children with scholarship funds, penny lunches in schools, and free medical examinations in school. In 1909 the council participated in President Taft's White House Conference on Child Welfare, and in 1911 it set forth its first complete program for social legislation, including regulation of child labor, slum clearance, mothers' pensions, public health programs, and food and drug regulations. After World War I, the council helped thousands of refugees stranded in internment camps as the U.S. tightened its immigration laws. Out of the rescue work came the International Council of Jewish Women, which is today a network of Jewish women in 23 countries. During the 1920s it conducted night schools for immigrants and served Jewish people in isolated rural communities with nursing care.

When Nazism brought a new wave of refugees, the council participated in the formation of the National Coordinating Committee of Refugee Problems, which became the National Refugee Service. In the post-World War II period, it established homes for unattached girls in Paris and Athens in order to help victims of the European Holocaust. To help rebuild Jewish welfare and educational institutions, it brought more than 200 educators and welfare workers from Israel and Jewish communities abroad to the U.S. for advanced training, with the stipulation that they return home to use their new skills. Toys and educational supplies were sent to children's institutions in Europe, and to Israel, Yugoslavia, Morocco, Tunisia, and France. In Israel the council began to assist the Hebrew University's teacher education program, helping to establish its John Dewey School of Education and building a campus for the Hebrew University High School in 1963.

Cover of the periodical of the National Council of Jewish Women, *Council Woman,* April–June, 1970.

In the 1960s the National Council of Jewish Women had more than 100,000 members in communities throughout the U.S. The pioneers of the Head Start pre-school program and the first nationwide network of Golden Age Clubs, council women have also established the first halfway houses for mental patients, and many other programs. It has recruited and screened girls for the Women's Job Corps, and adopted a major national program to promote day care facilities in communities across the country. In 1968 a Council Center for Research in Education of the Disadvantaged, the first such comprehensive center in the world, was established at the Hebrew University in Jerusalem.

Bibliography: H. G. Solomon, *Fabric of My Life* (1946).

[HA.ST.]

NATIONAL FOUNDATION FOR JEWISH CULTURE, U.S. organization that supports, guides, gives information on, and initiates programs in Jewish culture. The foundation was established by the Council of Jewish Federations and Welfare Funds in 1959, following the recommendation of the council's Committee on National Jewish Cultural Services in America. Edwin Wolf II was first president and Judah J. Shapiro, secretary and executive officer. In 1965 Rabbi Daniel Jeremy Silver became president and Harry I. Barron became executive director. The foundation's information service is extended to Jewish communal bodies, institutions, and individuals. Primary among the programs initiated by the foundation are grants to students and scholars and assistance in the publication of Jewish scholarly works. From its initial grants in 1961 to 1970, the foundation awarded about 200 grants, aggregating about $395,000. [J.J.S.]

NATIONAL JEWISH COMMUNITY RELATIONS ADVISORY COUNCIL, U.S. organization, established 1944, with the object of formulating policy and coordinating the work of national and local Jewish agencies in the field of community relations in the United States. Before 1944, as organized anti-Semitic activity became a serious problem in the United States, there was much overlapping and competition among the Jewish organizations seeking to combat it. The Jewish Welfare Funds, beset with claims for support, exercised pressure for the coordination of activities, and the result was the establishment of the Council (the word "Jewish" was added to its title in 1968). It was composed initially of four national organizations and 14 local community relations councils. The purpose was to enable member agencies to exchange views and to work together voluntarily, while each member retained full autonomy.

While the Council secured a measure of coordination, competitive activity and jurisdictional conflicts remained, and in 1950, at the insistence of the larger welfare funds, the Council instituted a study of Jewish community relations work. The result was the R. M. MacIver Report under which the authority and responsibilities of the Council would have been enlarged considerably and separate spheres of activity allotted to its member agencies. The Council generally favored these proposals, but the result was the withdrawal from membership of its two most active constituents, the American Jewish Committee and the B'nai B'rith (1952). The latter returned to membership in 1965 and the Committee in the following year on terms which emphasized the autonomy of the member organizations. In 1968 the membership of the Council consisted of nine national organizations and 81 state or local community relations councils.

Bibliography: AJYB, 54 (1953), 162–77.

[ED.]

NATIONAL JEWISH HOSPITAL, a 225-bed, non-sectarian medical and research center, treating and conducting research into tuberculosis, asthma, emphysema, and other chronic respiratory diseases in Denver, Colorado. The National Jewish Hospital pioneered the development of chemotherapy for tuberculosis. Its clinical research program has produced new techniques for the diagnosis and evaluation of asthma. The hospital also conducts basic research into physio-chemical processes at the cellular level. Patients are admitted from throughout the world without regard to age, race, or creed. At the turn of the century Denver's high altitude (5,280 ft., c. 1,630 m.) and dry climate attracted thousands of "refugees from tuberculosis" seeking the "rest cure." Many, weakened by disease and unable to work, died of starvation and exposure. Denver's Jewish community, rallied by Rabbi William S. Friedman and other pioneer leaders, founded the Jewish Hospital Association of Colorado, which was incorporated on April 8, 1890. The first building, with 60 beds, was dedicated Oct. 9, 1892. Support of the new hospital crossed sectarian boundaries from the beginning, coming from private philanthropists of every creed. However, Denver alone could not support the institution. The building closed after a year. The founders appealed to B'nai B'rith, citing tuberculosis as a national health problem. The order accepted the hospital as a national project, reopened it in 1899 as a free-care tuberculosis sanatorium, and underwrote its operations during the early years. While B'nai B'rith continues to sponsor the hospital as a national project, the structure of support now consists mainly of about 250,000 Jews and non-Jews throughout the United States who contribute the bulk of the hospital's $7 million budget (1970–71). The National Jewish Hospital is formally affiliated with the University of Colorado School of Medicine.

Bibliography: S. Schaefer and E. Parsons, *A Brief History of the National Jewish Hospital at Denver* (1928); M. L. Anfenger, *The Birth of a Hospital* (1942). [R.N.B.]

NATIONAL JEWISH WELFARE BOARD (JWB), religious and welfare service organization for American Jewish military personnel, and coordinator of U.S. YMHAs and Jewish community centers.

World War I. The JWB was founded in 1917 to meet the needs of large numbers of Jews in the armed forces who required religious services. The U.S. government was known to prefer for this task a single agency representative of the Jewish community, but no single American Jewish organization was authorized to act for the entire Jewish community. In 1917 prominent Jewish leaders, notably Louis Marshall, Felix Warburg, and Cyrus Adler, took the initiative in constituting the Jewish Board for Welfare Work in the United States Army and Navy, with the YMHAs and synagogue and rabbinic bodies as the representative agencies. A reorganization added national associations such as B'nai B'rith and the National Council of Jewish Women as affiliates, and numerous local community bodies as branches of JWB.

Under the leadership of Harry Cutler as president and Cyrus Adler and Irving Lehman as heads of committees, a program of activities developed rapidly. JWB secured recognition as the official agency for Jewish religious and welfare work in military establishments. Congress was induced to authorize by law the commissioning of Jewish chaplains and the JWB enlisted the chaplains. The JWB program included both religious and general activities. The former included the organization of religious services and holiday programs, obtaining furloughs for Jewish festivals, the preparation of an abridged prayer book, a book of

Figure 1. The founders and executive committee of the National Jewish Welfare Board during World War I. Seated, left to right, are Maurice Harris, Louis Marshall, Harry Cutler, Cyrus Adler, and Charles Hartman. Standing, left to right, are Chester Teller, David de Sola Pool, Mortimer Schiff, Israel Unterberg, Henry Bernheim, and Joseph Rosenzweig.

biblical readings, etc. The general program included recreational and cultural activites. In addition, contact was established with homes of soldiers and hospital visitation was arranged.

For the JWB Board and the Chaplaincy, see *Military Service: Chaplaincy.

With the end of the war the activities of JWB were sharply reduced, and in time a broader area of function in the Jewish community was found in the Jewish center field (see below). But at the close of 1941 the new war emergency, with its vastly increased military establishment, again expanded the work of JWB.

World War II. With the basic structure of JWB at hand, the organization prepared to meet increasing needs under the leadership of Frank Weil and Louis Kraft. Through the United Service Organizations for National Defense (USO), close relationships were established with non-Jewish welfare agencies serving military personnel. As during World War I, funds were raised cooperatively, and some welfare activities were also performed jointly, advancing intercultural cooperation.

Within the Jewish community, the base of JWB was broadened. The number of organizations affiliated with the Army and Navy Committee more than doubled. The chaplaincy service was reorganized, and hundreds of local army and navy committees and a Women's Division and a Bureau of War Records was set up.

The war work of the Jewish community under JWB sponsorship was massive in scope; 311 rabbis served as chaplains in the various war theaters and on board transports and hospital ships.

Postwar Period. With the end of the war the scope of service to the military was curtailed, but unlike the period following World War I such service remained an important function of JWB. The large military establishment that remained, the armies of occupation, the North Atlantic Treaty Organization bases, and the Korean and Vietnam wars continued to command extensive services to Jewish military personnel. However, the course taken after World War I was resumed: primary attention was again devoted to the function of JWB in the Jewish centers field.

To finance its operations, JWB has relied primarily upon Jewish community funds. From the late 1920s, JWB increasingly became the beneficiary of Jewish federations and welfare funds. In 1968 allocations from welfare funds and the New York City United Jewish Appeal accounted for about 60% of the $1,870,000 budget; other important sources of income were the constituent centers, contributions from JWB associates, and income from special services. Considerable sums were also received during World War I from a joint campaign with non-Jewish welfare organizations serving the military forces, and during World War II from the USO. After the war USO allocated modest sums for USO-JWB programs.

The Jewish Center Movement. The Young Men's Hebrew Association (YMHA), or the "Jewish community center" (the term which gained currency after World War I), is an indigenous American institution. YMHAs and similar associations arose after the mid-19th century in various parts of the United States to provide educational, social, and recreational facilities for Jewish young men and women. When masses of East European Jewish immigrants arrived in the 1880s and 1890s, their "Americanization" became a primary function of these organizations. They varied in program and effectiveness, and to guide and stimulate the movement, the Council of Young Men's Hebrew and Kindred Associations (YMHA & KA) was founded in 1913 under the leadership of Cyrus Adler, Julian Mack, Louis Marshall, Felix Warburg, and others. The Council encouraged the organization of local associations and began to furnish guidance in programming, but its best energies were soon diverted to war work as an affiliate of JWB.

Development of the Movement. The leaders of the Council and of JWB were recognized elders of the community, some of whom wielded power in both organizations. A merger was effected in 1921, JWB absorbing the functions of the Council. Irving Lehman became president and Felix Warburg treasurer. The function of JWB as coordinating agency for Jewish centers was to stimulate the organization and functioning of Jewish centers and YMHAs, so as "to promote the religious, intellectual, physical, and social well-being and development of Jewish young men and women." The autonomy of the local centers and YMHAs was to be respected, JWB acting as a service organization "to assist, advise, and encourage" its constituent bodies.

The identity of the constituency was not easily established. Some 370 local associations were said to be functioning in 1921, but after amalgamation, which JWB encouraged, and disintegration, the number was reduced to 207. By 1946, 301 centers were regarded as affiliates. Affiliation, however, did not connote unity of purpose or quality of program during the 1920s and 1930s.

Functioning with a small staff and meager budget, JWB attempted to provide service for all who desired assistance and to fill needs as they became evident, for the field was relatively new. Facilities, management, personnel, and campaigns for membership and funds figured prominently in JWB work. The building service of JWB assisted in the erection of center buildings which increased from 75 in 1921 to 238 in 1939. Manuals on administration were compiled. JWB assisted in the development of a professional service, and encouraged the National Association of Jewish Center Workers, organized in 1918. By 1940, there were 223 paid executives. Organized drives increased the estimated membership of the centers from 100,000 in 1921 to 425,000 in 1940.

Program. Both a "balanced program" to serve cultural, intellectual, social, physical, and health needs and the development of the "total personality" were often professed as ideals. But in most agencies neither the human energies nor the funds for translating such ideals into functioning reality were available. However, notable progress was made. The JWB Lecture Bureau, established in 1922, encouraged lectures, forums, and classes and brought intellectual forces into intimate contact with the centers. Bulletins on program techniques and on the celebration of Jewish and civic holidays were distributed by JWB. From time to time pamphlets were prepared on Jewish historical personalities and on contemporary Jewish problems. Camping, when it became popular in the 1930s, received much attention. Also many surveys and self-studies were made, arousing local interest in the center and revealing needs.

During this period, the thinking of Mordecai M. *Kaplan had a marked influence on the field. Kaplan conceived of the Jewish community center as an all-embracing agency serving the religious, cultural, and recreational needs of the entire Jewish community—young and old, rich and poor, immigrant and native. Some individuals in the field grasped the cultural, if not the religious, implications of these ideas, but most emphasized only the values of unity and service to the entire Jewish community. A large majority of the local agencies styled themselves Jewish community centers, but program orientation was, for the most part, not materially affected.

Survey Report: Aims. World War II diverted the best efforts of JWB to the formidable task of serving the military, a task it discharged with distinction. After the war, the Jewish centers again commanded primary attention, and to clarify this JWB function a survey was undertaken, Salo Baron serving as chairman of the survey commission and Oscar Janowsky as director, conducting the survey, and presenting a comprehensive report (the "Janowsky Report").

Appraising the dual function of JWB, the report found that the record of achievement in war work far surpassed that in the centers, and attributed the difference to disparity in conceptions of purpose. The aim of war work was clear: to serve the Jewish religious and welfare needs of Jewish personnel. In regard to the centers, however, no such sharp definition of purpose had emerged. Some affiliates offered Jewish programs; others did not. A considerable body of lay and professional opinion, particularly but not exclusively in the "nonsectarian" Jewish settlements, was dogmatically opposed to any Jewish emphasis, which was disdained as "sectarianism" and condemned as a segregating influence. Not a few of the agencies, though not averse in principle to Jewish orientation were content to pay lip service to "Jewish spirit" and "Jewish ideals." In fact, the development of program material fostering Jewish orientation and suitable for group work had been neglected. Despite this diversity or lack of clarity as to basic purpose, JWB attempted to serve all affiliates, and affiliation was a mere formality. The survey report envisaged the purpose of the Jewish center in terms of a positive and affirmative Jewish position, made manifest by emphasis upon Jewish programming. It argued that a "nonsectarian Jewish center is a contradiction in terms": either the center is indeed dedicated to a Jewish purpose, and its nonsectarianism is a pose or a pretense; or, if the center is truly nonsectarian, its direction and maintenance should not be exclusively Jewish. The recommendations on the various functions of the Jewish center were formulated in the report to underscore that the program should devote primary attention to Jewish content. These recommendations, or their substance, the report proposed, should be incorporated in a "statement of principles" which should govern

Figure 2. Seder organized by the National Jewish Welfare Board for U.S. servicemen in Saigon, 1967.

affiliation. Under the leadership of Philip Klutznick, then chairman of the Jewish Center Division of JWB, of Frank Weil, and of Louis Kraft, this was done. But after a year of discussion by local boards and staffs, a modified statement of principles was adopted in 1948.

Centers in 1960s. Since 1948 the centers have grown in membership, attendance, budget, facilities, and variety of programs. There are Jewish centers in more than 180 cities and town of the United States and Canada, and the large cities maintain multiple units—New York City no less than 60. Membership is said to have increased from 425,000 in 1946 to 729,000 in 1966. Estimated aggregate attendance was 31 million in 1966, an increase of 48% over 1956. The number of trained staff rose from 900 in 1947 to over 1,600 in 1965. Local expenditures for center work, exclusive of capital outlays, increased from less than $10 million in 1947 to over $34 million in 1965. Mass migration to central cities involved new construction: from 1946 to the mid-1960s, as many as 103 new center buildings were erected and 25 enlarged at a cost in excess of $100 million.

New trends in center programs are reflected in emphasis on family membership and family participation. Nursery schools have been established, teen-age activities stressed, and service to older persons greatly increased. Camps, notably day camps, have multiplied. A World Federation of YMHAs and Jewish Community Centers was organized in 1946 under the leadership of Louis Kraft and JWB. Through this federation, United States program resources and guidance have been made available to interested groups overseas, and special efforts have aided materially in the establishment and support of the YMHA in Jerusalem. The impact of the Jewish community center is felt in Jewish communities throughout the United States. However, the fundamental question of purpose remains largely unresolved. The statement of principles, which recognized Jewish content as "fundamental to the program of the Jewish Center," has subdued overt "nonsectarianism" and silenced opposition to Jewish cultural activities on ideological grounds. Such activities, notably in the arts, have increased markedly. Israel figures prominently in many centers. The Lecture Bureau provides speakers and performers on a great variety of Jewish themes. The Jewish Book Council and Jewish Music Council (sponsored by JWB since 1944) have furnished occasions for Jewish programs during the annual Jewish Book month and Jewish Music Festival. It is difficult, however, to determine the impact or depth of influence of these activities.

There has been a notable change in attitude toward Jewish activities, especially among center workers, but potent factors have hampered the realization of emphatic and pervasive Jewish purpose in many centers. In 1948 the survey found the Jewish education of the majority of center workers grossly inadequate; it is doubtful that the situation has changed materially since then, particularly in an era of shortage of trained workers. Conferences and seminars on Jewish-content programming have been held. Some Israel educators and youth leaders have worked on center staffs. But these efforts could hardly compensate for basic deficiencies in preservice Jewish education.

Even more serious has been the tendency to give high priority to programs related to the urban crisis (programs of service to underprivileged non-Jews) and to encourage or sanction non-Jewish membership. In 1967, non-Jewish membership exceeded 25% in seven centers, and, in the country as a whole, the average non-Jewish membership was 9.5%. Where membership or clientele is mixed, the Jewish purpose of a center must inevitably become blurred. A day camp or a nursery which invites the participation of non-Jewish children cannot emphasize Jewish content.

The root problem is ambivalence on the function and purpose of the Jewish center. The rationale in center circles is that, unlike the synagogue, the center is not a religious institution. If so, and if Jewish content does not permeate the center, it is difficult to justify a sectarian institution on ethnic grounds. And once mixed membership or a mixed clientele is invited, Jewish content is inevitably affected adversely. "Nonsectarianism" has thus reappeared in a new guise.

The JWB publishes the following periodicals: *Jewish Community Center Program Aids*, quarterly (1940–); *Jewish Book Annual* (1942–); *Jewish Chaplain* (1943/44–), *JWB Circle*, seven times a year (1946–); and *JWB Year Book* (1950/51–).

Bibliography: O. I. Janowsky, *JWB Survey* (1948); O. I. Janowsky, L. Kraft, and B. Postal, *Change and Challenge: History of 50 Years of JWB* (1966); L. Kraft, *Selected Papers: Development of the Jewish Community Center* (1967); B. Rabinowitz, *Young Men's Hebrew Association, 1854–1913* (1948); Solender, in: *Journal of Jewish Community Service*, 34 (1957), 36–54; Stein, in: AJYB, 57 (1956), 3–98; Urbont, *ibid.*, 68 (1967), 29–59. [O.I.J.]

NATIONAL PARKS IN ISRAEL. The National Parks Authority was established by law in 1963 to take over the functions carried out from 1956 (with the same staff) by the Department for Landscaping and the Preservation of Historic Sites in the prime minister's office. These functions are: the preparation, laying out, and maintenance of park areas for the general public; the restoration, landscaping, and preservation of historical and archaeological sites; the construction of access roads and amenities for recreation and leisure; and, in the case of ancient sites, the provision of explanatory notice boards and pamphlets. The Authority has also established museums at several historic sites.

Israel is rich in biblical sites and the remains of post-biblical Jewish, Roman, Byzantine, Muslim, and Crusader settlements, often in surroundings of beauty, and most of the national parks have been linked with these sites. Many had suffered from centuries of neglect, since they were of little interest to the successive occupying authorities. The Authority had to clear overgrowth and thick layers of debris, undertake restoration programs where possible, and provide amenities and access for visitors, both local and from overseas. Some parks were laid out without any connection with a historic site, in order to preserve rural areas from the encroachment of urban development. Occasionally, archaeological sites were taken over for preservation and maintenance by the Authority, where the excavations had been particularly dramatic, as at *Masada; or where scholars had made spectacular finds of wide public interest, as at *Hazor, the *Bet She'arim necropolis, the

Figure 1. The national park on the Ashkelon seashore, which includes a camping site and an antiquities area. Photo A. Strajmayster, Jerusalem.

Figure 2. Gan ha-Sheloshah, the national park in the eastern Jezreel Valley formed from three natural pools. Courtesy Government Press Office, Tel Aviv.

Figure 3. The Crusader fortress of Belvoir overlooking the Jordan Valley, excavated and restored by the National Parks Authority and now called Kokhav ha-Yarden. Photo Werner Braun, Jerusalem.

ancient synagogues at *Bet Alfa, *Baram, and *Hammath (Tiberias), the Roman theater at *Caesarea, and the excavations at *Bet Yeraḥ and *Ramat Raḥel. At some sites the National Parks Authority was responsible for the excavations, undertaken by specially commissioned archaeologists, as well as for their restoration and current maintenance. Examples are: the Crusader city of Caesarea, complete with moat, walls, gates, and towers; the crypt, tunnels, and some of the walls of Crusader *Acre; the castles of *Yehi'am and *Belvoir; the Roman theater at *Beth-Shean; the Nabatean-Byzantine city of *Avedat, with its citadel, acropolis, and two churches; and the Nabatean cities of *Shivta and *Kurnub. At Masada, much of the restoration work was carried out at the same time as the excavations.

The Authority is responsible for 50 sites designated as national parks. Those already open to the public, in addition to the ones already mentioned, are: Ḥurshat Tal in Upper Galilee, with its streams, pond, lawns, and woods; the spring, bathing pool, and woodland slopes of Ma'ayan Ḥarod in the Valley of Jezreel; the three natural pools and landscaped banks of Gan ha-Sheloshah, also in Jezreel; the seashore park and antiquities of *Ashkelon; the natural pools of Ein Avedat in the northern Negev; the 25,000-acre parkland and forest of Carmel; and the Crusader remains at Aqua Bella (Ein Ḥemed) near Jerusalem. The Authority has also renovated some of the medieval synagogues of Safed, and improved the amenities at the tomb of Maimonides in Tiberias. It has carried out site-improvement work at Mount Zion in Jerusalem and at the tomb of R. *Simeon b. Yoḥai at *Meron. The Authority was one of the initiators in setting up the park at *Yad Mordekhai, which contains a reconstruction of the Egyptian attack on the kibbutz in 1948 and a small museum devoted to the defense of the southern kibbutzim during the War of Independence. Among the new parks for which plans have already been completed by the Authority is the Jerusalem national park—a green belt circling the Old City walls and covering 500 acres. The number of visitors to the national parks in 1968 exceeded 2,000,000. [Y.Y.]

NATIONALRAT (Ger. "[Jewish] National Council"), committee of Zionist groups in Austria. It was formed at the time of the collapse of Austria-Hungary in 1918, in Vienna, to advance the claims of the Jewish people as a national entity in still unsettled postwar Austria. Initially it consisted of 50 members, representing a number of Jewish organizations. The Zionist, Robert *Stricker, was one of its chairmen and its outstanding leader. Due to the segmentation of the Jewish population of old Austria, the sphere of influence of the Nationalrat was limited to the Jews of German-speaking Austria, who were too weak to demand extended minority rights. The Nationalrat was not based on elections and represented only part of the Jewish population. Its claims were opposed by the non-Zionist Jews who were satisfied with the existing legal autonomy of the Jewish religious community, and by the Social-Democratic Party, and were not accepted. Similar organizations were later established in other postwar Central European countries. The Nationalrat was instrumental in promoting modern Hebrew education by supporting the Hebrew Teachers' College (Hebraeisches Paedagogium), founded in 1917, and by establishing the Jewish Realgymnasium in 1919, a secondary school with the language of instruction partially in Hebrew. The program of the Nationalrat was later taken over by the *Juedische Volkspartei ("Jewish People's Party").

Bibliography: J. Kreppel, *Juden und Judentum von Heute* (1925), 618, 630–2; R. Weltsch, in: *Der Jude*, 3 (1918/19), 350–8; J. Fraenkel, *Robert Stricker* (Eng., 1950), 78–79; A. Boehm, *Die Zionistische Bewegung*, 2 (1937²), 685. [Hu.K.]

NATIONAL RELIGIOUS PARTY (**Mafdal,** acronym for **Miflagah Datit-Le'ummit**), Israel political party. The N.R.P. was founded in June 1956 through the merger of two religious Zionist parties, *Mizrachi and *Ha-Po'el ha-Mizrachi, which were joined by other religious circles. It constitutes a part of the world organization of Mizrachi-Ha-Po'el ha-Mizrachi and views its aim as striving toward the building of a society in Israel based on the spiritual, social, and halakhic foundations of Judaism. In addition to the aspirations it shares with other Zionist parties, the N.R.P. places emphasis on legislation based on the laws of the Torah and Jewish tradition; economic policy based on a comprehensive view of the country's needs, the need to absorb immigration, and the development of the private sector; and assuring all religious services to the public through government and public institutions. The N.R.P. views the Chief Rabbinate as the highest religious authority in the state.

With the 1956 merger, two frameworks were created for the religious Zionist movement in Israel: the National Religious Party, which is the political arm; and Histradrut Ha-Po'el ha-Mizrachi, which is the workers' and trade union organization. These two frameworks divide the following tasks between them: national and local political activities, activities for religious education and widening the network of yeshivot, culture, literature and public relations, settlement, matters of labor and labor relations, absorption of immigrants and housing, employment and cooperation, pension funds, cooperative financial and economic institutions, the National Religious Women's Movement, and youth and sports organizations.

The number of votes received by the N.R.P. grew with the increase in the number of voters in the country (see Table). On the day of the elections to the Seventh Knesset, the N.R.P. received 128,422 votes in local elections. The party, with over 100,000 dues-paying members, is the largest religious party in Israel. It advances the claim that a "state based on law" and a "state based on *halakhah*" are not contradictory notions, for it believes that in a "state based on law," the *halakhah* and Jewish traditions must serve as a basis of legislation, so that the State of Israel will be an organic continuation of the Jewish heritage. This outlook is the source of the party's struggle to integrate Jewish values in the life of the state, with emphasis on Sabbath observance, religious education,

Table. Representation of N.R.P. in Knesset

	Votes	Percent of National Vote	Representatives in Knesset
Fourth Knesset (1959)	95,581	9.9	12
Fifth Knesset (1964)	98,786	9.8	12
Sixth Knesset (1965)	107,966	8.9	11
Seventh Knesset (1969)	133,238	9.7	12

and supplying the religious needs of the community. The N.R.P. fought for the right of parents to choose religious education for their children if they wish to do so. It also worked for the continuation of the Marriage and Divorce Law, existing before the establishment of the State of Israel, which provided that divorces must be according to the religious law of the people concerned, thus insuring halakhic authority over the Jews in Israel in this sphere. (See *Israel, Legal and Judicial System.) Other achievements of the N.R.P. are in the area of Sabbath observance, the institution of *kasher* kitchens in the army and government institutions, and the supply of religious needs by the state.

The N.R.P. has usually participated in all the government coalitions, but not under all conditions. On some fundamental points of the party's outlook—such as the questions of religious education and "Who is a *Jew?"—the N.R.P. has found itself in the opposition. The party concerns itself with free economic initiative in all sectors of the economy and lessening state interference in economic life and views as a fundamental aim the establishment of a "welfare state." It also strives to make the state into a tool to realize the vision of social justice according to Jewish tradition.

The N.R.P. advanced the initiative to establish a Government of National Unity on the eve of the Six-Day War (1967) and worked after the elections to the Seventh Knesset (1969) to establish a government on the widest possible basis. Its representatives in these governments were Ḥayyim Moshe Shapira, Joseph Burg, Zerah Warhaftig, and Michael Ḥazani. The chairman of the N.R.P. faction in the Knesset in 1970 was Yiẓḥak Raphael.

After the founding convention of the N.R.P. in 1956, further conventions were held in 1963 and 1968. 97,000 members with voting rights participated in the elections to the third convention and to the councils of the local branches of the party. 633 delegates participated in the N.R.P. and Ha-Po'el ha-Mizrachi in Israel, and their composition can be broken down as follows: 550 delegates from the various urban branches; 70 from moshavim; 18 from kibbutzim. In addition, 137 members of the executive of the movement participated in an advisory capacity. Although the elections were conducted by individual ballot, two principal blocs emerged at the convention: the bloc of "unity" (*likkud;* composed of members of the former central faction, headed by Ḥayyim Moshe Shapira, together with members of the former La-Mifneh left faction, most of whom were from Ha-Kibbutz ha-Dati); and circles of the younger generation, which called for the incorporation of younger people into the leadership of the movement and the stressing of the principle of the territorial integrity of Ereẓ Israel in the political program and activities of the party. Among the policy decisions accepted at the convention the following are of note: "The National Religious Party views the political and security accomplishments that have been achieved by this generation in Ereẓ Israel, as the beginning of realization of the will of divine providence and of the processes directed toward complete salvation of the Jewish people in the land of its forefathers; the State of Israel must pursue all means at her disposal to lay the foundation for peace between her and the neighboring states and to negotiate peace treaties; in the negotiations over peace treaties, the State of Israel will be directed by three basic principles: (1) the aspiration toward enduring peace, (2) the historic religious rights over the Promised Land, and (3) assuring secure borders for the state."

See also *Mizrachi; *Ha-Po'el ha-Mizrachi; *Ha-Kibbutz ha-Dati.

Bibliography: *Ve'idat ha-Yissud shel ha-Miflagah ha-Datit Le'ummit ha-Mizrachi—ha-Po'el ha-Mizrachi* (1957); Y. Cohen, *Esrim Shanah Rishonot li-Medinat Yisrael be-Ḥayyei ha-Yahadut ha-Datit ha-Me'urgenet* (1968); P. Ferber et al. (eds), *Be-Ma'arekhot ha-Am ve-ha-Medinah* (1969); Z. Aminoah, *Bein Ve'idah li-Ve'idah* (1963); J. Salmon, *Ha-Po'el ha-Mizrachi be-Ereẓ Yisrael, Chronology and Bibliography 1920–1928* (1968). [Y.Go.]

NATIONAL SOCIALISM (for short, **Nazism**), a movement in Germany, patterned after fascism, which grew under Adolf *Hitler's leadership and ruled Germany from 1933 to 1945. The Deutsche Arbeiterpartei, founded on Jan. 5, 1919, changed its name in the summer of 1920 to Nationalsozialistische Deutsche Arbeiterpartei (NSDAP) and Hitler, who had been the seventh member of the original party, soon became its undisputed leader *(Fuehrer)*. From then on, the history of national socialism became identical with Hitler's career. As an ideology, National Socialism was a mixture of extreme nationalist, racialist ideas and a trend of populist radicalism which never formed a real unity. In its biological racialism a completely unrestrained anti-Semitism formed the main element. Thus National Socialism was between the world wars the ideology which openly promulgated the persecution and, in veiled terms, even the "elimination," i.e., physical extermination, of the Jews. During World War II, when National Socialist Germany dominated most of Europe, it succeeded in implementing its anti-Jewish extermination program to a very large extent, a process known as the Holocaust.

See *Hitler; *Holocaust, General Survey.

Bibliography: M. Broszat, *German National Socialism 1919–1945* (1966), incl. bibl.

[J.M.]

NATIONS, THE SEVENTY, a conception based on the list of the descendants of Noah given in Genesis 10, usually called "The Table of Nations." According to the table, all the nations of the earth may be classified as descended from one or another of Noah's three sons, Shem, Ham, and Japheth. The principle behind the classification is generally geographic proximity rather than ethnic or linguistic connections. Those nations descended from Japheth are *Gomer (Cimmerians), Madai (Medes), Javan (Ionians), *Ashkenaz (Scythians), *Elisha and *Kittim (Cypriots), and others (10:2–4). The lands occupied by the Japhethites bordered the Fertile Crescent in the north and penetrated the maritime regions in the west. The principal subdivisions

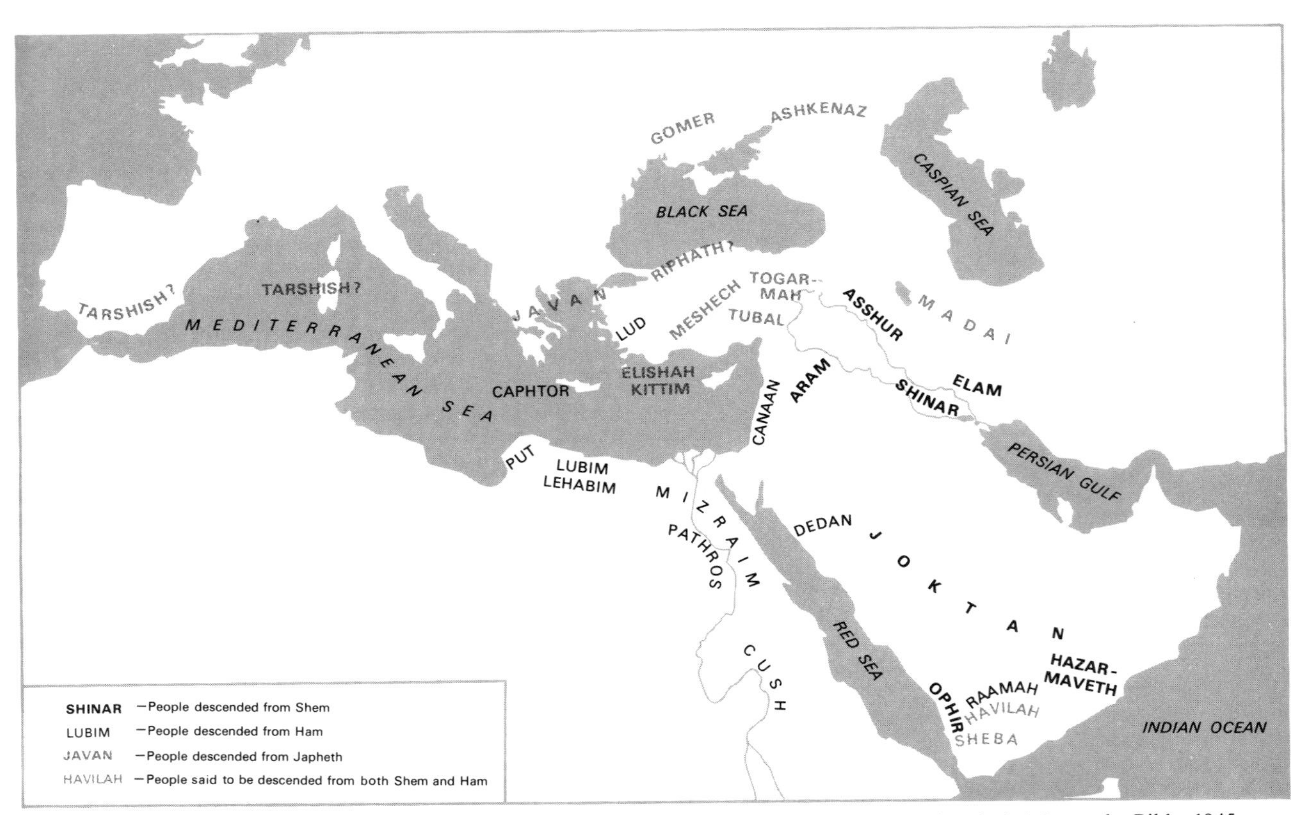

The Hebrew Table of the Nations (from Genesis 10 and related sources). After the Westminster Historical Atlas to the Bible, 1945.

of the descendants of Ham are Cush (the peoples of the southern shore of the Red Sea), Miẓraim (Egypt), Put (location uncertain, probably Cyrene), and Canaan (10:6–20). The descendants of Cush are listed in 10:7 as Seba, *Havilah, Sabtah, Raamah, and Sabtecha. According to 10:8, Cush had another son, *Nimrod, whose rule extended over all Mesopotamia. That a Mesopotamian ruler is here linked to the peoples adjacent to the Red Sea stems from the confusion caused by the fact that there were two nations known by the name Cush, one in the Nile region ("Nubia, Ethiopia") and another in Mesopotamia (the Kassites; Akk. *Kaššû*). The Bible often telescopes the two. The inclusion of the Philistines and the Cretans (Caphtorim) in the list of the descendants of the Egyptians (Miẓraim; verses 13–14) is another problem, as there is clearly no ethnic or linguistic connection between these peoples. The reason for including the Philistines in the list must, therefore, have been geographic; Crete was included because it was the original home of the Philistines. The inclusion of the Ludim, if this refers to the Lydians, in this list is also a problem. It is possible that this refers to the invasion of Egypt by the Sea Peoples. Another Lud is also mentioned as a descendant of Shem (verse 22). The classifying of Canaan in the Hamite branch of nations is again perplexing, there being no ethnic or linguistic connections between the Canaanites and the Egyptians (verse 6). The subdivision of the Canaanites is problematic too: the inclusion of Phoenicia (Sidon) among the subdivisions of the Canaanites is appropriate, since the Phoenicians referred to their country as Canaan, and the Phoenician language is close to Hebrew. However, it cannot be on ethno-linguistic grounds that the Jebusites, Hittites, Hivites, and others are listed as Canaanites (10:15–18). It seems that once again the principle behind the classification is geographic proximity. The territory of the Hamites extended from Phoenicia, through western Palestine, to northeastern Africa. The Shemites included all the "children of Eber," the eponym of the Hebrews (10:21), and hence were therefore given prominence. The Assyrians, Arameans, and numerous tribes of Arabians were classified as Shemites. It is not clear why the Elamites, whose center was southwest Persia, were considered Shemites (10:22). Perhaps they were listed with Ashur (Assyria) because they were the nearest neighbor to the east of Mesopotamia. Arpachshad, listed as the grandfather of Eber, is otherwise unknown; the name appears to be non-Semitic.

That the table does not aim at completeness is suggested by verse 5a, "From these [sons of Japheth] the maritime nations branched out"—here unnamed. Moab and Ammon, the descendants of Nahor and Keturah, the Ishmaelite tribes and Edom, and Israel itself are intentionally omitted, for they find their place at later stages of the narrative. Unexplained is the omission of Babylon. The earliest dating of the table is determined by the presence of the Cimmerians and the Scythians, who appeared in Asia Minor only in the eighth century. In general, the horizon of the table agrees remarkably (with the exception of Babylon) with that of Jeremiah (e.g., 46:9; 51:27–28) and Ezekiel (27:1ff.; 38:2ff.; 39:1), and it is likely that the table in its present form was known to these prophets. Heterogeneous and inconsistent (cf. the discrepancy between verse 7 and verses 28–29 regarding Havilah and Sheba), the table is assumed to be a combination of various sources. The material is conventionally allocated between J (verses 8–19, 25–30) and P (all the rest). Together with the story of the Tower of Babel, the table marks the end of the primeval history of mankind and the transition to the patriarchal history, which is played out against a background of a world filled with nations. Like the genealogies of 11:10–30; 25:12–18; and 36:1ff., it enables the narrative to maintain its focus on the main line of Israel's descent by summarily disposing of all collateral lines. At the same time, it shows the fulfillment of God's blessing of Noah and his sons with fertility (9:1, 7), and locates the ancestors of Israel in relation to the rest of mankind. The Jewish tradition that mankind is made up of 70 nations is based on the count in the table—although a sum is not stated in the text (cf. the itemization in *Pesikta Zutreta, No'aḥ*) and seems to underlie Deuteronomy 32:8, which speaks of God's "dividing mankind . . . in accord with the number of the sons of Israel" (namely, 70; Gen. 46:27). On the other hand, the Septuagint and the 4Q Deuteronomy fragment that read "the sons of God" (i.e., angels) instead of "the sons of Israel" reflect the notion, dated as early as the Persian period (Dan. 10:20) and possibly earlier (Ps. 82:7) that every nation has a divine patron—again, 70, in accord with Jewish tradition (Charles, Apocrypha, 2 (1913), 363 (late Hebrew Test. Patr., Naph. 9), *Pesikta Zutreta, ibid.*).

The Table of Nations served as the basis of later Jewish ethnography; for representative attempts to embrace contemporary ethno-geography under its rubrics compare Jubilees, chapters 8–9; Josephus, *Antiquities*, 1:122–147; Targum Jonathan to Genesis 10; *Genesis Rabbah*, 37; and for the late Middle Ages, Abrabanel, at the end of his commentary to Genesis 10. [ED.]

In the Midrash. In early Christian sources 72 nations and tongues were assumed (e.g., Hippolytus, 10:26; Clement of Alexandria, *Stromata* 1:26), perhaps following the Septuagint version of Genesis 10. This chapter was considered a scientific account of the division of mankind into three races—Semitic, Hamitic and Japhethic—distributed in three separate zones (Jub. 7:10ff.). There are, however, varying opinions as to how many nations belonged to each "race." The commonest system (Mid. Ps. to 9:7; et al.) ascribes to Japheth 14 nations, Ham 30, and Shem 26 (total 70), while the *Yalkut Shimoni,* Genesis 61 gives a reckoning of Japheth 15, Ham 32, and Shem 27. From this total of 74, however, subtract Shem, Arpachshad, Shelah, and Eber, who were righteous, and thus again there is a total of 70.

There is, moreover, another tradition of 60 nations, based on an exegesis of the Song of Songs 6:8 (Mid. Hag. to Gen. 10:1). *Numbers Rabbah* 14:10 speaks of 70 nations and 60 kingdoms, giving a total of 130 (cf. Num. 7:13). The tradition of 72, which is found in A. Zacuto's *Yuḥasin* (ed. Cracow (1580–81), 135) is also echoed in *Midrash Haggadah* to Genesis 10:32. It has been suggested that the 72 nations are the 70 "Noahite" nations plus

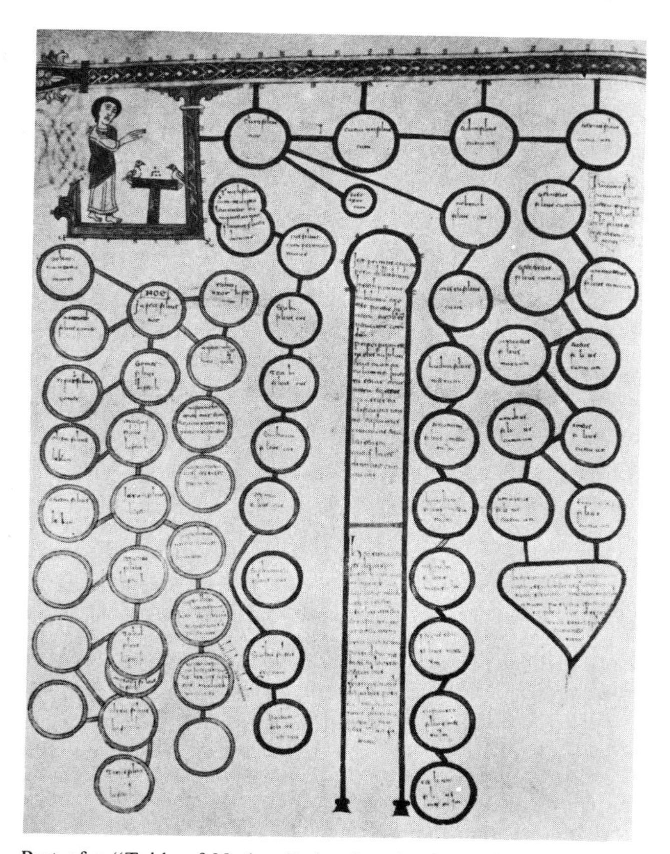

Part of a "Table of Nations" showing the descendants of Noah, from a manuscript completed in Zamora, N. Spain, 975 C.E. Noah is shown offering a sacrifice after the Flood. Gerona, Spain, Cathedral Archives, *Gerona Apocalypse,* fol. 9v.

Israel and Edom. However, Abrabanel (on Gen. 10:2) states that a straightforward reading of chapter 10 suggests 73 nations; thus 72 may have been reached by excluding the Philistines, who in Genesis 10:14 are designated as a mixed race. Just as there were 70 nations, so there were 70 languages (cf. Targ. Jon., Gen. 11:7 and Deut. 32:8). Thus the law engraved on the tablets on Mt. Ebal (Deut. 27:2ff.) was written in 70 languages (Sot. 7:5), so that all nations might read it. For the same reason, the divine voice that made itself heard at Sinai divided itself into 70 tongues (Shab. 88b et al.). However, according to *Aggadat Bereshit* 14 there are 71 languages. Perhaps the Philistines were included in that reckoning. The motif of the 70 nations is widely used in rabbinic literature (as is its derivative, the 70 tongues, e.g., *Sefer ha-Yashar,* Mi-Keẓ). Thus the 70 sacrifices offered on Tabernacles are said to atone for the 70 nations (Suk. 55b). The silver bowls, which the princes of the 12 tribes offered to the Tabernacle (Num. 7:13) weighed 70 shekels; so too did 70 nations spring from Noah (Num. R. 14:12). The 70 members of the Sanhedrin were likewise thought to correspond to the 70 nations of the world (Targ. Yer., Gen. 28:3). [D.S.]

Bibliography: S. Krauss, in: *Jewish Studies in Memory of G. A. Kohut* (1935), 379ff.; J. Simons, in: OTS, 10 (1954), 182–4; E. A. Speiser, in: IDB, 3 (1962), 235ff. (incl. bibl.); For the 4Q Deut. fragment see P. Skehan, in: BASOR, 136 (1954), 12–15; See also commentaries to Genesis. IN THE MIDRASH: Ginzberg, Legends, 5 (1925), 194f.; 7 (1938), 429; Guttmann, Mafte'aḥ, 2 (1917), 73ff.; M. Steinschneider, in: ZDMG, 4 (1850), 150ff.; 57 (1903), 476f.; S. Krauss, in: ZAW, 19 (1899), 1–14; 20 (1900), 38–43; S. Poznański, *ibid.*, 24 (1904), 301–8.

NATONEK, JOSEPH (1813–1892), rabbi, pioneer of Zionism in Hungary, and Hebrew grammarian. Born in Komlo, Hungary, Natonek, as a merchant, supplied the Hungarian revolutionary army in 1848 until its collapse. He became the principal of the Jewish school in Surany (south Slovakia), and subsequently (1861–67) rabbi in Jaszbereny and in Szekesfehervar (Stuhlweissenburg). In 1867, Natonek negotiated with the Turkish government in Constantinople to obtain a charter for the reclamation of Palestinian soil for Jewish settlement. When his endeavors proved fruitless, he returned to Budapest, where he published the magazine *Das einige Israel* ("The United Israel," 1872), in which he propagated the Zionist idea. He also produced a booklet in Hungarian, *Messiás, avagy értekezés a zsidó emancipatióról* ("The Messiah—or On the Emancipation of the Jews," 1861), in which he opposed the idea of ameliorating the Jewish situation by cultural emancipation, advocating in its place national emancipation in the spirit of Moses *Hess and modern Zionism.

Natonek's other works include the unpublished Hebrew manuscript, "On the Divine Revelation to Moses"; *Wissenschaft–Religion* (1876); and an edition of the Song of Songs (1871), published with German translation and commentary by L. Hollaender, with some additional comments of his own. He also began to prepare a dictionary of five languages, *Pentaglotte* (1861) in collaboration with Bishop Feuer of Szekesfehervar.

Bibliography: S. Weingarten, *Ha-Rav Yosef Natonek* (1942); D. B. Frenkel, *Reshit ha-Ẓiyyonut ha-Medinit ha-Modernit* (1956); Kadar, in: *Sinai,* 45 (1959), 243–52; I. Z. Zahavi, *Me-ha-Ḥatam Sofer ve-ad Herzl* (1966), 196–215. [M.Z.KA.]

NATRONAI BAR HILAI (ninth cent.), *gaon* of Sura from 853 to 858. Natronai's father Hilai, who died in 797, was also *gaon* of Sura. One of the most prolific writers of responsa among the *geonim* of the ninth century, Natronai always replied in the language in which he was addressed, whether Hebrew, Aramaic, or Arabic. He is said to have been the first to use Arabic for scholarly correspondence. He had strong ties with all parts of the Diaspora, especially Spain, and in particular Lucena, of whose Jews he was especially demanding, "since there is no non-Jew among you." His responsa deal largely with matters pertaining to liturgy, and his responsum to a query from the Lucena community as to how to fulfill the rabbinic dictum to recite 100 benedictions daily, constitutes the nucleus of the Jewish prayer book. He gave a historical explanation of Rav's statement (Shab. 24a) that it is necessary to recite the *_haftarah_ after the reading of the Pentateuch portion at the Sabbath afternoon service. According to him the Persians objected to this custom. This practice was abolished and never reinstated. He is the author of the earliest responsum regarding the geonic ordinance that debts may be collected from movable property. In another responsum, he stresses the importance of the study of the Babylonian Talmud for the unlearned since it includes both Bible and Mishnah.

Natronai did not insist that his questioners act in accordance with the customs prevailing in the two Babylonian academies. Only where he suspected Karaite influence, did his tone become authoritarian, and he declared that he who omitted the midrashic sections in the Passover _Haggadah_ should be considered a heretic and liable to excommunication. Natronai once even denounced a Palestinian law which differed from the Babylonian, maintaining, "They err and have gone astray." Natronai insisted on regular congregational recitation of the Aramaic Targum, a decision which was incorporated in R.*Amram's prayer book. He prohibited recitation from vocalized scrolls in the synagogue, a practice encouraged by the Karaites. Natronai also included in his responsa commentaries to various tractates of the Talmud. A collection of _halakhot_ similar to the *_Halakhot Keẓuvot_ which has been ascribed to him is probably a condensation from his responsa, and some of the responsa attributed to Natronai bar Hilai are probably those of Natronai bar Nehemiah, _gaon_ of Pumbedita.

Natronai was also stated to practice mysticism, through the agency of which he caused himself to be transported to Spain, where he taught the people and, just as mysteriously, to have transported himself back to Babylon. Hai Gaon denied this, suggesting that some adventurer may have impersonated Natronai in Spain. Natronai became a legendary personality and many fictitious and fanciful decisions were attributed to him, particularly in Yemenite Midrashim.

Bibliography: L. Ginzberg, _Geonica_, 2 (1909), 415; S. Assaf, _Teshuvot ha-Ge'onim_ (1928), 267; A. L. Frumkin (ed.), _Seder R. Amram_, 1 (1912), 25a–b; Lewin, _Oẓar_, 2 pt. 2 (1930), 110; 4 pt. 2 (1931), 20; H. Tykocinski, _Takkanot ha-Ge'onim_ (1959), passim; M. Havazelet, _Ha-Rambam ve-ha-Ge'onim_ (1967), 35 n. 25; S. Liebermann, _Midreshei Teiman_ (1940), 39; Baron, Social², 3 (1958), index. [M.H.]

NATRONAI BAR NEHEMIAH (also known as **Rav Yenuka**), _gaon_ of *Pumbedita, 719–730. Natronai married into the family of the exilarch. According to *Sherira Gaon he was said to have dealt so severely with the students of the academy that some of them left and went to the academy at Sura, returning only after his death. Natronai was lenient to the repentant followers of the false messiah Severus (*Serenus), though they had rejected certain talmudic ordinances, permitting them to return to the communal fold. In one responsum however, he opposed the acceptance into the community of children of certain heretical Jews, who had renounced both biblical and talmudic Judaism. Virtually nothing is known of his halakhic decisions.

Bibliography: Baron, Social², 5 (1957), 190, 193f., 207; B. M. Lewin (ed.), _Iggeret R. Sherira Ga'on_ (1921), 102f.; _Sha'arei Ẓedek_, responsa (1966²), 54–55. [M.H.]

NATRONAI BEN ḤAVIVAI (Zavinai; second half of eighth century), exilarch in Babylonia and pupil of R. *Yehudai Gaon. R.*Sherira relates in his epistle (_Iggeret Rav Sherira Ga'on_, ed. Lewin (1921), 104) that in the year 1082 of the Seleucid era (771) a conflict over the exilarchate broke out between Natronai and Zakkai b. Aḥunai, who had already occupied this position for a number of years. R. *Malkah b. R. Aḥa, the _gaon_ of Pumbedita, supported Natronai, but both yeshivot supported Zakkai b. Aḥunai. When R. Malkah died, Natronai was compelled to leave Babylonia. He then traveled to the Maghreb (or Spain). According to Spanish tradition, Natronai prepared from memory a copy of the Babylonian Talmud for the Spanish Jews. It is possible that Natronai was the grandfather of Natronai, the exilarch in Babylonia after 857.

Bibliography: L. Ginzberg, _Geonica_, 1 (1909), 17–20; B. M. Lewin, _Oẓar ha-Ge'onim_, 1 (1928), 20; S. Abrahamson (ed.), _Massekhet Avodah Zarah: Ketav Yad Beit ha-Midrash le-Rabbanim be-New York_ (1957), introd. 13. [A.D.]

NATURE. Though the Bible is full of the awareness and appreciation of nature from the creation narrative up to the Psalmist's declaration, "The heavens declare the glory of God . . ." (Ps. 19:2), it does not profess a comprehensive doctrine of nature in relation to man and God. Nature is a testimony to the work of the Creator (Isa. 40:26; Amos 5:8; Job 38–41), not a subject for speculation. As opposed to the pagan world-view which endowed natural objects with divinity, the Bible makes it quite clear that the natural world was produced by, and totally subject to, God—not in any way part of Him. This, in sum, is its doctrine of nature.

In Rabbinic Literature. A similar lack of speculative interest in nature is apparent in rabbinic literature, though to a lesser degree. Contemplation of the majesty of the heavens or the myriad creatures on earth served the rabbis as a reminder of the wondrous ways of the Creator rather than as the starting point of physical speculation. Thus when R. Akiva considered the manner in which land and sea animals were confined to, and dependent on, their respective elements he would say, "How mighty are Thy works O Lord" (Ps. 104:24; Ḥul. 127a). On the other hand, the purely aesthetic appreciation of nature was played down in preference to the more centrally religious values. This is apparent in the (generally misunderstood) passage, "He who walks by the way studying, and interrupts his studying by saying 'How pleasant is this tree, how pleasant this plowed field' . . . it is as if he were deserving of death" (Avot 3:8).

The nearest to a conceptual discussion of nature comes in rabbinic consideration of cosmogony and of miracles. The ideas that God looked into the Torah and using it as a blueprint created the natural world (Gen. R. 1:1), and that miracles were built into the natural order at the creation (Avot 5:5; Gen. R. 5:5) would seem to reflect Stoic doctrine (see *Creation and Cosmogony; *Miracles).

The teleological argument, from design in nature to the existence of a Designer, is found in rabbinic literature, albeit in a philosophically naive form. Thus it is said of Abraham that he first came to know God by pondering on the comparison between the world and a palace. Just as a palace which is illuminated must have an owner so too must the world (Gen. R. 39:1; cf. _Midrash Temurah_ 5). [ED.]

In Hellenistic and Medieval Jewish Philosophy. In their philosophy of nature, as in other branches of philosophy, Hellenistic and medieval Jewish thinkers were influenced greatly by the current general philosophical doctrines. Thus, for the most part, they adopted the view that the universe is governed by immutable laws; that all objects in the sublunar world are formed out of combinations of four basic elements—earth, air, fire, and water; that the celestial world consists of a fifth element; and that substances in the universe can be classified hierarchically as inanimate, vegetative, animate, and rational. However, the philosophical view of nature posed problems for the traditional Jewish view as expressed in the Bible and Talmud. For traditional Judaism the universe did not run according to set immutable laws. Rather God directly regulated the workings of the universe that He had created, insuring that events would lead to the specific goal He had in mind. The medieval Jewish philosopher, unable to give up this view of nature completely, sought in his philosophies of nature to reconcile the biblical and talmudic concepts of *creation and *miracles with the theories of secular philosophy. For some of them, the design and order that they observed in nature constituted the evidence for the existence of a Creator—the teleological argument.

*Philo held that the world was governed by laws which were instituted by God at the time of creation. He maintained that all objects in the universe were composed of combinations of the four elements, interpreting the wings of the seraphim in Isaiah's vision (Isa. 6) as the four elements, one pair representing earth and water, and the second pair, fire and air. The third pair he interpreted as the forces of love and opposition which initiate movement in the other four elements (*De Deo*, 9–10).

*Saadiah, too, held that all objects are composed of four basic elements (*Emunot ve-De'ot*, 10: 17; 1:3; 2:2), and that the world is governed by set laws. As a follower of the *Kalam, which accepted creation and advanced proofs for it, Saadiah had no difficulty with the doctrine of creation. Among the proofs which Saadiah advanced for creation was one based on the order existing in nature, a proof that he adopted from the Kalam. Saadiah argued that since all composite objects must be fashioned from their component parts by an intelligent being, so the world, which is itself a composite of many composites, must have been created (*ibid.*, treatise 1). *Baḥya ibn Paquda employs a similar argument in his *Ḥovot ha-Levavot* (1:6).

Neoplatonism. Adopting the neoplatonic conception of the universe as a series of descending spheres, Jewish neoplatonists sought to combine the theory of emanation with the biblical concept of creation. In attempting to do so, Isaac *Israeli, somewhat arbitrarily, maintained that the intellect, which next to God is the highest being in the world, was created by God, and that all other objects emanate from the intellect (S. Fried (ed.), *Sefer ha-Yesodot* (1900), 69). Aristotelian influences are evident in Israeli's doctrine of the elements.

Joseph ibn *Ẓaddik, although generally a neoplatonist, adopted Aristotle's philosophy of nature. However, he deviated from it in his definition of matter and form, assigning to matter the position of the one real substance and to form a status similar to that of accidents (*Sefer Olam Katan*, 1:2).

*Judah Halevi, who was generally critical of Aristotelian philosophy, criticized the Aristotelian doctrine of the four elements on the ground that it has no basis in experience, for while we do perceive the qualities of heat, cold, wetness, and dryness, we do not perceive them in their pure form as primary elements (*Kuzari*, 5: 14).

Aristotelianism. Abraham *ibn Daud, the first of the Jewish Aristotelians, in his *Emunah Ramah*, adopted the Aristotelian concepts of form and matter, substance and accident, and the categories, finding allusions to the categories in the 139th Psalm. Unable to accept the Aristotelian doctrine of the eternity of matter insofar as it conflicted with the biblical concept of creation, Ibn Daud posited the existence of a formless prime matter which was the first stage in the process of creation.

*Maimonides, while he totally accepted Aristotelian physics, differed with the Aristotelian view that the world is eternal. Maintaining that neither eternity nor creation could be proved, he chose to accept creation as the theory advanced in the Bible. He held that miracles were predetermined at the time of creation, and that they were not abrogations of natural laws, but occurred through the exertion of one natural force upon another.

*Levi b. Gershom disagreed with the Aristotelian notion that time and motion are infinite (*Milḥamot Adonai*, pt. 6, 1: 10–12). Levi proved that the world was created from the teleological character of nature. Just as every particular object in nature moves toward the realization of its own particular goal, so the universe, the sum total of all the things that exist within it, moves toward an ultimate end. He is unique among Jewish philosophers in that he rejects the idea of creation *ex nihilo*, maintaining that there existed an eternal absolutely formless matter out of which God at a particular point in time created the universe (*ibid.*, 1: 17–28). He interprets the biblical story of creation to coincide with this theory.

*Crescas criticized Aristotelian physics, especially his doctrine of space, maintaining, in opposition to Aristotle, that a vacuum was possible (*Or Adonai*, bk. 1, pt. 2, ch. 3). Crescas believed that it was inconsequential whether or not the world was eternal; what is important is that God created the world *ex nihilo*, but not necessarily at a specific moment in time. [A.I.I.]

Modern Period. Scientific philosophy entered a new phase with the doctrine of Kant that the natural world was phenomenal, being the manifestation, through the categories, of the noumenal world—the unknowable *ding an sich*. The development of this doctrine in Fichte, Hegel, and Schelling and the bifurcation of spirit and nature influenced Jewish philosophers of the school of idealism.

Solomon *Formstecher gave Schelling's doctrine of the nonconscious world soul a theistic interpretation. The world soul is the essence of the natural world though separate from, and independent of, it. Nature, in turn, is totally dependent on the world soul, being but one aspect of its manifestation. Formstecher makes a distinction between the religion of nature—in which the world soul is merely the highest principle of nature, and the religion of the spirit—in which the world soul is independent of nature and is the essence of ethics. The former is paganism, the latter Judaic religion.

In the philosophy of Samuel *Hirsch the central problem is more anthropocentric, namely, the relationship of man to nature, and the framework of his solution is Hegelian. Hirsch relates man and nature to God by regarding Him as the ideal to which man strives in asserting his freedom against nature. For in such ethical striving man is supporting spirit against nature, and spirit is the common element between man and God. Hirsch too distinguishes between the ethical religion of the spirit (Judaism), and nature religion.

Nachman *Krochmal does not, like Formstecher and Hirsch, start from the assumption of a split between spirit and nature. For him nature is merely an end point on the scale of spiritual development, which rises in degrees from primitive religion up to the Jewish world view. This leads him near to a pantheistic position in that he claims that all existence is immanent in the Absolute Spirit, God.

In the early system of Hermann *Cohen, which while accepting Kantianism rejects the unknowable *ding an sich*, the idea of God plays the role of a bridge between ethics and the natural world. It is the guarantee that ethical fulfillment is possible in nature. Since, however, God is ideal rather than real, Judaism is in essence ethics as religion. His later philosophy, however, represents a complete volte-face. There it is God who has prime ontological status, and the natural world is the vehicle of God's manifestation with no independent being of its own.

A. I. *Kook, whose philosophy has been summarized by Hugo Bergman as "mystic pantheism," believed all reality to be a manifestation of God in a myriad of individual forms which in turn have no reality without Him. The plurality of the natural world is unified in God, the source and ground of its being. Adapting a kabbalistic notion, Kook believes that holy sparks are everywhere in nature, for it is shot through with a harmonious divine force. This "life force" of nature is not, like Bergson's *élan vital*, blind, but rather purposive. Evolution of nature is interpreted to mean that all creation, striving to be reunited with God, moves toward the Divinity. Judaism is thus, for Kook, the preeminent attempt to see nature in its total harmony and to sanctify, rather than reject, the material world.

A similarly positive approach to nature is apparent in the ideology of the early Labor Zionist Movement, especially in the work of A. D. *Gordon. Here however, there are clearer heterodox tendencies toward pantheism. Life's ideal, for Gordon, is a form of cosmic harmony of the human and material worlds. This harmony has been interrupted by the unnatural urban life of the Jew in the Diaspora, and in order to reestablish it he has to return to the soil to be as near to nature as possible. Gordon's ideal of unity with nature is not simply an ethical goal but is based on the metaphysical belief that man is organically united to the cosmos, and that it is the unbalanced emphasis on the intellect rather than on man's intuition which is at the root of human alienation.

In the dialogic writings of Martin *Buber, particularly in *I and Thou*, there is an echo of the belief in the existence of "sparks" in all things. It is possible, according to Buber, to enter into an I-Thou relationship even with inanimate objects, and this relationship need not be simply passive but may be one of full mutuality. In answer to criticisms of how one can enter into what seems an essentially personal relationship with non-personal nature Buber remarks that in such a relationship the natural object reveals its being. There is a reciprocity of being between the person who addresses the object as "Thou" and the object so addressed, for the world is potentially a revelation of the divine (*I and Thou*, postscript, rev. ed. 1958). [ED.]

Bibliography: Guttmann, Philosophies, index s.v. *nature; law, natural;* and *science, natural;* Husik, Philosophy, index; I. Efros, *Philosophical Terms in the Moreh Nebukhim* (1924), 50, 134–5; H. Malter, in: *Festschrift . . . Hermann Cohen* (1912), 253–6 (Eng.); Zunz, Poesie, 634; S. H. Bergman, *Faith and Reason* (1963), 27–54, 81–97, 98–120; I. Epstein, *Judaism* (1954), index; N. Rotenstreich, *Jewish Philosophy in Modern Times* (1968), 52ff.

NATURE RESERVES IN ISRAEL. Despite its limited area, Israel has an extraordinarily varied landscape and a rich array of flora and fauna. There are some 2,500 different species of indigenous wild plants—an extremely high number in relation to the area—in its three geobotanical regions: Mediterranean, Saharo-Sindi, and Irano-Turani, as well as enclaves of tropical and European flora, the most northern and southern known. About 250 of the plants are endemic. The fauna is also varied, though it is only a remnant of the wild life of biblical times; at least 15 large mammalian species have become extinct. There are more than 20 varieties of freshwater fish, several species of amphibians and eight of reptiles, 400 varieties of birds (150 of which nest in Israel, the remainder being migratory or winter visitors), and about 70 species of mammals, mostly small rodents and bats. Gazelle, wild boar, ibex, hyena, wolf, jackal, hyrax, caracal, and lynx are still to be found.

Spring at the En-Gedi nature reserve in the Judean Desert. Photo Werner Braun, Jerusalem.

The dynamic development of modern Israel has inevitably affected plant and animal ecology. Some 500 new villages and a score of new towns, as well as the rapid expansion of existing ones, have encroached on areas of hitherto undisturbed wild life and natural vegetation. The quadrupling of the population, the rise in the standard of living, and the vast expansion of tourism, have brought large numbers of hikers and trippers to the countryside.

To protect the flora and fauna, a Nature Reserves Authority was established by the government in 1963. Some 120 areas have been selected as nature reserves in which landscape, flora, and fauna are protected in their natural condition. Some are large reserves, in which the flora and fauna maintain an equilibrium, for instance on Mt. Meron (about 70,000 dunams; 17,500 acres). There are also the smaller areas maintained for specific scientific reasons, e.g., winter pools to preserve lower crustacea and amphibians, a ridge of sandstone with its typical flora, islands on which common tern nest, and sites such as Ḥorshat Tal and Circassia as reminders of the landscape that once existed. While most of the reserves are open to the public, some are closed to preserve their scientific value. Facilities for visitors have been provided at Tel Dan, the "Tannur" near Metullah, the cave of "Pa'ar," the "Masrek" near Jerusalem, En-Gedi, etc., and the work is being extended to other places throughout the country. The Nature Reserves Authority has also undertaken to reintroduce species that have become extinct. At the *Ḥai-Bar* (wildlife) Biblical Game Reserve at Yotvata (34,500 dunams; 8,650 acres), attempts were begun in 1966 to breed some of these extinct species, with the approval of the World Wildlife Fund.

Bibliography: M. Zohary, *Geobotanikah* (Heb., 1955); Rashut Shemurot ha-Teva, *Pirsumim* (1965–). [A.Y.]

NATZWEILER-STRUTHOF, Nazi concentration camp in Alsace in existence from May 1941 to Aug. 31, 1944. The site was mainly chosen for its proximity to vast quarries where prison labor could be exploited. The camp was in the third (harshest) category of concentration camps and constituted a concentration and redistribution center for political and especially "Night and Fog" *(Nacht und Nebel)* prisoners from France and southwest Germany. The commandants were Hans Huettig, Egon Zill, Josef Kramer (the "Beast of Belsen"), and Fritz Hartjenstein, who was in charge from April 1944 until the camp inmates and staff were evacuated and sent to *Dachau at the approach of the Allies. Natzweiler-Struthof provided the Reich University at Strasbourg with inmates to be used for various pseudo-medical (including lethal) experiments. The scientists at Strasbourg experimented with combat gases and infectious diseases (hepatitis and others). In August 1943, Kramer gassed about 100 Jewish prisoners specially brought from *Auschwitz to supply August Hirt at the Reich University with specimens for his anthropological and racial skeleton collection in the anatomical institute. Among those especially brought for execution at Natzweiler were female agents of the French Resistance. Altogether 25,000 prisoners died in the camp.

Bibliography: Bibliothèque du Centre de Documentation Juive Contemporaine. For further reference see Catalogue no. 1, *La France de l'Affaire Dreyfus à nos jours* (1964), 77–78; Catalogue no. 2 (1968) 40.

[Y.RE.]

Commemorative postcard and stamp for the 20th anniversary of the liberation of the Natzweiler-Struthof concentration camp, issued by the French government Sept. 23, 1964. Jerusalem, B. M. Ansbacher Collection.

NAUHEIM (Bad Nauheim), town in Hesse, W. Germany. Jews may have lived in Nauheim as early as 1303; during the *Black Death persecutions (1348) they were expelled from the duchy of *Hanau. In 1464 three Jewish households are noted in the city; in a document of the same year they appear as imperial *Kammerknechte* ("serfs of the chamber"; see **servi camerae regis*) whose tax payments form part of a transaction between the margrave of Brandenburg and the count of Hanau. Jews are again attested as taxpayers in Nauheim in the 16th century. They were expelled once more in 1539. From the middle of the 16th century onward some **Schutzjuden* lived in Nauheim, but their number was small. Nauheim Jews began worshiping in a rented prayer room in 1830. A Jewish cemetery was consecrated in 1866, and a new one in the first years of the 20th century. The first synagogue dates from 1867; a second larger one was built in 1928. At that time the community had a religious school and a *ḥevra kaddisha*. In 1933 the Jewish population numbered 300. The synagogue survived the Nazi period and was used once more by a reestablished congregation which totaled 124 persons in 1970.

Bibliography: R. Stahl, *Geschichte der Nauheimer Juden* (1929); FJW, 395; Germ Jud, 2 (1968), 570.

[ED.]

NAUMBOURG, SAMUEL (1815–1880), *ḥazzan*, composer, and writer. Born in Dennelohe, near Ansbach (Bavaria), the descendant of almost ten generations of south German *ḥazzanim*, Naumbourg received his musical education at

Samuel Naumbourg, German *ḥazzan* and composer. From S. Naumbourg, *Zemirot Yisrael*, Paris, 1847.

Munich and sang there in Maier *Kohn's synagogue choir. After an engagement as choirmaster in Strasbourg, he came to Paris in 1843. In 1845 he was appointed first *ḥazzan* at the synagogue in the Rue Notre-Dame-de-Nazareth, under the sponsorship of Jacques Fromental *Halévy and with the government authorization to carry out his plans for a thorough reform of liturgic music (which had lapsed into disorder after the death of Israel *Lovy in 1832). In 1847 he published the first two volumes of his *Zemirot Yisrael* (vol. 1 for the Sabbath, vol. 2 for the High Holidays), with vol. 3 *Hymnes et Psaumes* added when the work was reissued in 1864 (repr. 1874, 1954). In 1874 he brought out a collection of traditional synagogue melodies, *Aguddat Shirim*, which also included some western Sephardi material, and a long preface on the history of Jewish religious music. In 1877 Naumbourg published the first modern edition of Salamon de *Rossi's *Ha-Shirim Asher li-Shelomo* (30 out of 33 pieces) and a selection of his madrigals, with the collaboration of Vincent d'Indy, under the name of *Cantiques de Salamon Rossi;* the historical importance of the undertaking is in no way diminished by its many editorial failings and liberties. Naumbourg's *Zemirot Yisrael* achieved an influence comparable to the works of his senior Solomon *Sulzer and his junior Louis *Lewandowsky. The pieces are set for *ḥazzan* and 2-to-4 part choir, with some organ accompaniments and, apart from Naumbourg's own compositions and arrangements, include some melodies by Lovy and two works by Halévy and *Meyerbeer. About half of the pieces are based on traditional material, mainly south German. The others reflect the various styles then current in the Parisian grand opera, which "gave to Naumbourg's work some international features and helped it to become widely known, and much liked and used" (Idelsohn).

Bibliography: Sendrey, Music, index; Idelsohn, Music, 262–6 and index.

[B.B.]

NAUMBURG, U.S. family of bankers and philanthropists. The founder, ELKAN NAUMBURG (1834–1924), was born in Germany, and went to the U.S. in 1850. He subsequently became a partner in the clothing firm of Naumburg, Kraus, Lauer & Company. After the firm was dissolved in 1893, Naumburg founded the banking house of E. Naumburg and Co., which specialized in advancing loans to business enterprises. A lover of music, he established and endowed the free summer concert programs at New York City's Central Park in 1905, and contributed the funds for the park's band shell. He also gave liberally to other philanthropies.

His eldest son WALTER WEHLE NAUMBURG (1867–1959), who was born in New York, entered his father's clothing business and then entered the newly established family banking business. He and his younger brother George Washington dissolved the firm in 1931 in order to devote themselves to charity. Besides continuing the Central Park concerts instituted by their father, Walter Naumburg founded the Walter W. Naumburg Musical Foundation (1926) which sponsored the debuts of talented musicians and the Musicians Foundation to care for needy musicians. He was a trustee of Mt. Sinai Hospital and a member of the Salvation Army's board.

His wife, ELSIE MARGARET BINGER NAUMBURG (1880–1953), was a well-known ornithologist who served on the staff of the American Museum of Natural History. Her monograph, *The Birds of Matto Grosso, Brazil* (1930), dealt with the ornithological finds of Theodore Roosevelt's expedition to Brazil. She established the Dr. Frank Chapman Memorial Fund to support ornithological research.

GEORGE WASHINGTON NAUMBURG (1876–1970), who was born in New York City, entered the family banking business after graduating from Harvard in 1898. During World War I, he served as assistant chief of the cotton section of the War Industries Board. In 1933, two years after his bank's dissolution, he was appointed president of the New York Guaranteed Protection Corporation. A vigorous advocate of government economy, Naumburg was treasurer of the National Economy League in the 1930s and a director and vice-president of the Citizens Budget Commission. As a philanthropist, Naumburg's principal interest lay in the area of child welfare. He was active in the National Child Welfare Association, and supported psychiatric treatment programs for children. Also active in Jewish affairs, Naumburg was a director of the Joint Distribution Committee, head of the Federation of Jewish Philanthropies' finance committee, trustee of the Jewish Board of Guardians, and president of the Baron de Hirsch Fund (1932–70).

ROBERT ELKAN NAUMBURG (1892–1953), who was born in New York, graduated from the Massachusetts Institute of Technology. A mechanical engineer and inventor, Naumburg constructed the visigraph, a machine allowing the blind to "read" electrically-embossed characters on paper. After World War II, Naumburg donated the invention to the federal government for use by sightless veterans. [ED.]

NAUMBURG, MARGARET (1890–), U.S. psychoanalyst, art therapist, and educator. Born in New York, Margaret Naumburg graduated from Barnard College, Columbia University. She then studied speech therapy with F. Matthias Alexander at the London School of Economics and child education with Maria Montessori in Rome. Influenced by Freud's theories, she maintained that the child was an individual with his own inner life and needs and that education should serve the child, and not the child, education. In 1913, she founded and conducted the first Montessori class in New York City at the Henry Settlement. A year later she launched her own school, the Walden School, based on the importance of the personal relationship between pupils and teachers. She was a pioneer in art education and in the use of art for therapeutic purposes.

Her methods were disseminated by exhibitions at meetings of the American Psychiatric Association and at international psychiatric congresses. Margaret Naumburg's many books include: *The Child and the World* (1928); *Studies of the "Free" Art Expression of Behavior Problem Children and Adolescents as a Means of Diagnosis and Therapy* (1947), *Schizophrenic Art: Its Meaning in Psychotherapy* (1950), and *Psychoneurotic Art: Its Function in Psychotherapy* (1953).

Bibliography: Walden School, *The Walden Story* (1954); Walden School, *Walden School on Its 50th Anniversary* (1964). [ER.S.]

NAUPAKTOS (Lepanto), town in W. central Greece. Benjamin of Tudela, the 12th-century traveler, reported 100 Jews in the town. The Venetians ruled there from 1407 to 1499. There was a *Romaniot community in Naupaktos and after 1492 refugees opened two synagogues, one according to the Spanish rite and the other according to the Sicilian. Jewish merchants used to send to Budapest and Turkey *lulavim* and *etrogim* which they grew in the vicinity of Naupaktos. A special "Purim of Lepanto" was celebrated on the 11th of Tevet in memory of the community's miraculous preservation following the Turkish conquest of the city (1571). In the 16th century R. Joseph Pirmon attempted to unite the three communities but was opposed by the Romaniot minority who were supported by Samuel *Medina. In the wake of the Greek uprisings against the Turks during the 18th century, the Jewish community was destroyed.

Bibliography: Rosanes, Togarmah, vols. 1 and 3, passim; S. Krauss, *Studien zur byzantinisch-juedischen Geschichte* (1914), 79. [S. MAR.]

NAVARRO, Portuguese family, prominent in the 14th and 15th centuries.

MOSES NAVARRO of Santarem (d. c. 1370), personal physician to King Pedro I and his chief tax collector, served for nearly 30 years as chief rabbi (**arraby moor*) of Portugal. The king granted Moses and his wife, Salva, the right to adopt the family name Navarro and to bequeath it to his descendants. His son, JUDAH, inherited the posts of personal physician and chief tax collector under Pedro I and continued in the latter capacity under John I. He and Solomon Negro agreed to pay some 200,000 livres annually for five years for the privilege of farming taxes. He is also known to have given the king a rich estate in Alvito, Alemtejo. Moses' grandson (or son according to Amador de los Rios), also called MOSES (d. c. 1410), was likewise chief rabbi and personal physician to the king, in this case John I. All three Navarros used their offices to benefit their fellow-Jews. Particularly noteworthy are the efforts of the younger Moses Navarro at the time of the large-scale massacres of the Spanish Jews in 1391. In that year he presented the Portuguese king with the bull decreed on July 2, 1389 by Pope Boniface IX (based on a bull of Pope *Clement VI), forbidding Christians to harm the Jews, desecrate their cemeteries, or attempt to baptize them by force. On July 17, 1392, the king ordered the promulgation of this bull throughout Portugal, reinforcing it with legislation of his own. Moses was also instrumental in acquiring the king's protection for Jewish refugees from Spain.

Bibliography: J. Amador de los Rios, *Historia social, politica y religiosa de los judios de España y Portugal*, 2 (1876), 266ff., 271, 278, 456ff.; M. Kayserling, *Geschichte der Juden in Portugal* (1867),

25, 38ff.; J. Mendes dos Remedios, *Os Judeus em Portugal*, 1 (1895), 157f., 163. [MA.C.]

NAVARRO, ABRAHAM (d. c. 1692), envoy in China and India. Navarro, a London Sephardi, was commissioned in 1682 by the East India Company to accompany the ship "Delight" to China as interpreter and linguist. In 1683 it reached Amoy, where Navarro began negotiations for opening trade relations. When these failed, Navarro returned to India, and engaged in trade. In 1689 Navarro was sent to the court of the powerful Moghul ruler Aurangzeb to negotiate a peace treaty. After a personal audience with the emperor, a firman for the British trade was obtained.

Bibliography: Fischel, in: PAAJR, 25 (1956), 39–62; 26 (1957), 25–39. [W.J.F.]

NAVEH (Heb. נָוֶה), city in Bashan, possibly mentioned in the lists of cities conquered by Thutmosis III (no. 75) and Ramses II (no. 13). Zeno visited it during his travels in 259 B.C.E. (see *Zeno Papyri). In talmudic times, it was a well-known Jewish center with its own territory (Tosef., Shev. 4:8); the *nesi'im* had extensive possessions there. Naveh and the neighboring city of Ḥalamish were at odds (Lam. R. 1:17, no. 52). Eusebius calls it a Jewish town (Onom. 136:3). The Jewish community persisted until the time of the Crusades and the city was the home town of many scholars. In Byzantine times it was part of Provincia Arabia and had a bishop. It is the present-day Arab village of Nawā, in which the legendary tomb of *Shem and the tomb of Joseph b. Saadiah (1062) are located. Jewish remains include many fragments of a synagogue built by Bar Yudan and Levi.

Bibliography: G. Schumacher, *Across the Jordan* (1866), 167ff.; Dalman, in: PJB, 8 (1913), 59–60; Mayer and Reifemberg, in: BJPES, 4 (1936), 1ff.; Braslavski, *ibid.*, 8ff.; Klein, *ibid.*, 76ff.; Amiran, in: IEJ, 6 (1956), 243–4; Avi-Yonah, Geog., 155; Press Ereẓ, 3 (1952²), 624. [M.A.-Y.]

NAVON, BENJAMIN MORDECAI BEN EPHRAIM (1788–1851), kabbalist and halakhist, one of the outstanding Jerusalem sages of his time, son of Ephraim b. Jonah Navon. Navon was called Jilibin (Çelebi, a Turkish title of honor). He was head of the kabbalists of the "Midrash Ḥasidim Kehillah Kedoshah Bet El" and head of a *bet din*. He devoted himself to a great extent to communal affairs, and assisted Israel Bak in establishing his pioneer printing press in Jerusalem in 1841. Navon wrote many responsa, some of which were published under the title *Benei Binyamin* (1876) by Jacob Saul *Elyashar, his stepson and disciple, who also included many of his sermons in his *Ish Emunim* (1885).

Bibliography: Frumkin-Rivlin, 3 (1929), 292f.; M. D. Gaon, *Yehudei ha-Mizraḥ be-Ereẓ Yisrael*, 2 (1937), 450f.; Benayahu, in: *Sinai*, 24 (1948/49), 205–14; idem, *Rabbi Ḥayyim Joseph David Azulai* (1959), 275. [A.D.]

NAVON, EPHRAIM BEN AARON (1677–1735), rabbi and halakhist. Navon was born in Constantinople, and emigrated to Jerusalem about 1700, together with his father-in-law, Judah Ergas. He returned to Turkey in 1721 as an emissary of Jerusalem. On the termination of his mission there in 1723, he was appointed a *dayyan* in the *bet din* of Judah *Rosanes in Constantinople, and later received the appointment of rabbi. While in Constantinople, he continued to concern himself with the amelioration of the material conditions of the Jewish community of Jerusalem. In 1738 his *Maḥaneh Efrayim* appeared in Constantinople, containing responsa and novellae on the Talmud and the works of early halakhic authorities. ARYEH JUDAH NAVON (1707–1761), his son, was the teacher of Yom Tov *Algazi.

Bibliography: Frumkin-Rivlin, 2 (1928), 157; Rosanes, Togarmah, 4 (1935), 207; M. D. Gaon, *Yehudei ha-Mizraḥ be-Ereẓ Yisrael*, 2 (1937), 449; Yaari, Sheluḥei, 116, 130, 361–2. [A.D.]

NAVON, ISAAC ELIYAHU (1859–1952), Israel composer and poet. Born in Adrianople (Edirne), Turkey, he taught in a Hebrew school established by his father in Constantinople and wrote for Jewish newspapers. He also helped to reorganize the Maftirim fraternity of Adrianople (most of whose members had emigrated to Constantinople), and to publish their songbook *Shirei Yisrael be-Ereẓ ha-Kedem* (1921), which contained a number of his own poems and a foreword by *Bialik. In 1929 Navon settled in Jerusalem, later in Tel Aviv, and devoted himself to spreading the Sephardi musical tradition. Some of the songs he collected or composed entered into the Israel folksong tradition, notably *"Nizzanei Shalom," "Ḥaddesh ke-Kedem Yameinu,"* and *"Gizratekh Tavnit Nogah."* He published further poems of his own in 1932.

Bibliography: M. D. Gaon, in: I. E. Navon, *Yinnon* (1932), introd.; I. Levy (ed.), *Yonah Homiyyah, Mi-Shirei Yiẓhak Eliyahu Navon* (1950), includes music; Barkai, in: *Hallel*, 1 (1930), 45–47; L. Saminsky, *Music of the Ghetto and the Bible* (1934), 159, 161; Bayer, in: *Tazlil*, 7 (1967), 149; Tidhar, 2 (1947), 728–9. [B.B.]

NAVON, JONAH BEN HANUN (1713?–1760), rabbi and author. Navon was born in Jerusalem where his father was a rabbi. He studied in the *bet ha-midrash* Bet Ya'akov Pereira under Israel Meir Mizraḥi. In 1746 he headed the *bet ha-midrash* Keneset Yisrael, founded by Ḥayyim ibn *Attar, and when the yeshivah Gedulat Mordekhai was established Navon was appointed to head it, and was at the same time one of the heads of the Yefa'er Anavim yeshivah. Among his pupils was H. J. D. *Azulai, who was the son of his brother-in-law. He traveled as an emissary of Jerusalem to North Africa in 1737, and again to Turkey and Greece during 1746–48. He was the author of responsa *Neḥpah ba-Kesef* (2 parts, Constantinople, 1748; Jerusalem, 1843), to which was added his supercommentary on Elijah *Mizraḥi's commentary to the *Sefer Mitzvot Gadol (Semag)* of *Moses of Coucy; *Get Mekushar* (Leghorn, 1785), novellae and comments on the *Get Pashut* of Moses ibn *Ḥabib. His other works have remained in manuscript. His sons were Ephraim, Benjamin, and Mordecai.

Bibliography: Frumkin-Rivlin, 3 (1929), 20–22; Yaari, Sheluḥei, 306–7; M. Benayahu, *Ha-Ḥida* (1959), 333–5. [A.D.]

NAVON, JONAH MOSES BEN BENJAMIN (d. 1841), rabbi and Jerusalem emissary. Navon, together with his cousin, Joseph Saadiah Navon, was sent to Gibraltar and to various Moroccan communities by the rabbis of Jerusalem in 1802–03 in order to mobilize financial aid for the Jerusalem community. He went on a second mission in 1804, and on his return was appointed a member of the *bet din* of Solomon Moses Suzin, whom he succeeded at the end of 1836 as *Rishon le-Zion*, a position he held until his death. Navon used his great authority to assist the Ashkenazi community of Jerusalem in acquiring the "Ḥurvah Synagogue" of Judah he-Ḥasid from the Arabs and in erecting a synagogue on the site. Navon added novellae and glosses to the *Neḥpah ba-Kesef*, vol. 2 (Jerusalem, 1843) of his grandfather, Jonah b. Hanun *Navon, and some of his own responsa appear in the *Ḥukkei Ḥayyim* (*ibid.*, 1843) of Ḥayyim *Gagin.

Bibliography: Frumkin-Rivlin, 3 (1929), 274–5; M. D. Gaon, *Yehudei ha-Mizraḥ be-Ereẓ Yisrael*, 2 (1937), 453; Benayahu, in: *Sinai*, 24 (1948/49), 25–14; Yaari, *ibid.*, 25 (1949), 320–30; Yaari, Sheluḥei, 566–7. [A.D.]

NAVON, JOSEPH (1858–1934), pioneer of Ereẓ Israel development. Navon was born into a prominent Sephardi family in Jerusalem. His father, Eliahu Navon, was the Jewish representative in the Jerusalem regional council. Joseph was educated in France, and on his return became a

Joseph Navon, pioneer of the development of Ereẓ Israel. Jerusalem, J.N.U.L., Schwadron Collection.

merchant and banker. He and his uncle Ḥayyim *Amzalak helped the settlers in Petaḥ Tikvah and Rishon le-Zion enter their lands in the land registry. With his banking partner Frontiger he pioneered in popular housing schemes in Jerusalem (including the Beit Yosef and Battei Navon quarters). He had ambitious schemes for the development of Ereẓ Israel, including railway development, the building of a port in Jaffa, and providing irrigation facilities for the citrus groves of the coastal plain. After lengthy negotiations in Constantinople, he received a concession in 1888 to construct a railway from Jaffa to Jerusalem, which he, in turn, transferred to the Société Ottomane de Chemin de Fer de Jaffa à Jerusalem et Prolongements founded by him in France in consideration of one million francs. After the opening of the line, he received the title *bey* from the Ottoman government in recognition of his services in developing Ereẓ Israel. After he lost his capital, he moved to Paris in 1894. Here he met *Herzl and tried to interest him in his plans for developing Ereẓ Israel. He died in Paris.

Bibliography: K. Grunwald, in: K. H. Manegold (ed.), *Festschrift W. Treue* (1969), 240–54 (Eng.); M. D. Gaon, *Yehudei ha-Mizraḥ be-Ereẓ Yisrael*, 2 (1937), 454–6; Tidhar, 1 (1947), 70–71. [Y.S.]

NAWI, rabbinical and philanthropic family in Iraq. Reuben ben David (end of 18th century–1821) was a prominent disciple of outstanding *ḥakhamim* in Baghdad. His main teacher, the *ḥakham* Moses b. Ḥayyim nominated him during his lifetime (1810) as his successor as *av bet din* in Baghdad, but he died prior to his master. Nawi's teachings are extant in the works of his disciples, the *dayyanim* R. Abdullah Somekh, Jacob b. Joseph b. Jawb ha-Rofe, and others. Many legends concerning his life are current among Baghdad Jews. At the end of the 19th and in the first quarter of the 20th centuries Solomon Reuben and Manasseh Solomon took an active part in the affairs of the Baghdad community, and improving the health conditions of Baghdad Jewry.

Bibliography: A. Ben Yaacov, *Yehudei Bavel* (1965), index; D. S. Sassoon, *History of the Jews in Baghdad* (1949), 136–7. [E.Hi.]

NAZARETH (Heb. נָצְרַת), town in Galilee, mentioned several times in the New Testament as the place to which Joseph returned from Egypt and where *Jesus was brought

up (Matt. 2:23; Luke 2:39, 51). Archaeological evidence has shown that the area was settled as early as the Middle Bronze Age, and tombs have been found dating from the Iron Age to Hasmonean times. According to the New Testament, Joseph and Mary lived in Nazareth before Jesus' birth, which was announced there to Mary (Luke 1:26; 2:4). When Jesus tried to preach to the people of the town, he was attacked, his assailants attempting to throw him from the Jebel Qafza, a hill 350 m. above sea level. Although he left Nazareth as a result of the incident (Luke 4:16–30; Matt. 4:13), the name Jesus of Nazareth nevertheless remained in common use both in his lifetime and among his followers, especially the apostle Peter. The early Christians were contemptuously called Nazarenes by their enemies (Matt. 21:11), and the Hebrew and Arabic terms for Christians *(Noẓeri, Nasrānī)* are derived from the town's name. Nazareth is not mentioned in non-Christian sources until the third or fourth century, when it was recorded in an inscription found at Caesarea listing the priestly courses and their seats in Galilee. According to this list (which is reproduced in the seventh-century liturgical poems of Kallir and others), the family of Happizzez (I Chron. 24:15) settled in Nazareth, a name derived in this source from the root *nṣr* (to guard). It is described by Jerome as a very small village in Galilee (Onom. 141:3). Constantine may have included it in the territory of Helenopolis, a city which he founded, but the town remained purely Jewish in the fourth century.

Excavations conducted by B. Bagatti from 1955 to 1966 on the site of the Church of the Annunciation revealed the remains of a church with a mosaic pavement dating to about 450. Below the church were pear-shaped silos,

Figure 1. Chapel in Nazareth known as "The Synagogue." Built on the site identified in the sixth century as that of the synagogue frequented by Jesus, it was transformed into a chapel by the Franciscans in the mid-18th century and now belongs to the Melkite Church. Courtesy Government Press Office, Tel Aviv.

Figure 2. The Catholic Basilica of the Annunciation (center), the largest church in the Middle East. Courtesy Government Press Office, Tel Aviv.

vaulted cellars, cisterns, and olive presses. Among the remains were about 80 partly stuccoed and inscribed stones, as well as column bases. The excavators view these finds as the remnants of a Judeo-Christian synagogue or a Constantinian church built for Jews. The first mention of a church in Nazareth was made in 570 by Antoninus Placentinus, who describes it as a converted synagogue.

In 614 the Jews in the mountains of Nazareth joined the Persians in their war against the Byzantines. Shortly before the Crusader conquest, the town was destroyed by Muslim Arabs. Tancred captured Nazareth, and the Crusaders built a church, whose finely sculptured capitals (now in the Franciscan Museum) exhibit French workmanship of the 12th century. The archbishopric of Beth-Shean was transferred to Nazareth during the Crusades. Saladin captured the town in 1187. It was again in Christian hands in 1240 and 1250, and in 1252 St. Louis of France visited there. In 1263 Baybars ordered the complete destruction of Nazareth, which remained in ruins for 400 years. The Franciscans returned to the town in 1620 by permission of the emir Fakhr al-Dīn. A new church was built under Ẓāhir al-ʿAmir in 1730. [M.A.-Y.]

Modern Nazareth and Naẓerat Illit. In April 1799 Napoleon's troops occupied Nazareth, but with his retreat it was recaptured by Aḥmad Jazzār Pasha. In 1890 the German scholar G. Schumacher estimated Nazareth's population at 7,500. Shortly before the outbreak of World War I, the German military command established its Palestinian headquarters there. The town was taken by the British in 1918; at that time there were 8,000 inhabitants, two-thirds of whom were Christian, and the rest Muslim. In the 1920s Nazareth's economy was still based largely on agriculture, as its inhabitants owned lands in the Jezreel Valley. The town remained surrounded with olive groves, which supplied it with raw materials for the manufacture of oil and soap. The Muslim element in Nazareth was strengthened when villagers from the vicinity were absorbed there. Nazareth became a market center for a wide agricultural region and a pilgrimage and tourist center, developing handicrafts, while inhabitants also found work in the Haifa industrial zone.

In July 1948, during the War of Independence, the Israel army took Nazareth from Kaukji's forces in "Operation Dekel." Its population remained and was augmented by Arabs who had abandoned other locations in Israel. It thus increased from 9,000 inhabitants in 1947 to 25,100 in 1961 and 32,900 in 1969, Muslims attaining a slight majority over Christians. Nazareth became the largest Arab center in the State of Israel (in its pre-1967 borders) and, with a number of private and public secondary schools, an important center of Arab education and culture. It has a hinterland of Arab villages both in Galilee to the north and in the southern Jezreel Valley and the Iron Hills to the south, constituting a highway junction connected with Haifa, Tiberias, Afulah, and Shefar'am. In 1970 Nazareth had 24 churches and convents of different Christian denominations, the newest being the Catholic Basilica of the Annunciation—the largest church in the Middle East—constructed between 1955 and 1968 over the Grotto of the Annunciation and the foundations of the original Byzantine church. Tourism and pilgrimages are important sources of Nazareth's economy. Other branches of its economy comprise small industries and workshops and administrative services. An increasing number of laborers have been employed in Naẓerat Illit.

In 1957 the ground was laid for the neighboring Jewish

Figure 3. Church of Jesus the Child overlooking Nazareth. Photo Ariel Berman, Haifa.

Figure 4. Alleyway in Nazareth's old quarter. Courtesy Government Press Office, Tel Aviv.

development town of Naẓerat Illit. Israel-born settlers formed the nucleus of its population, which was augmented by immigrants mainly from Europe. Its population increased from 1,000 in 1957 to 13,200 in 1969. The city has broad avenues tracing the hill contours with large apartment buildings occupying the western and central sections and industrial structures on the eastern one. The economy

Figure 5. Finished automobiles outside the Ford assembly plant in Naẓerat Illit. Courtesy Government Press Office, Tel Aviv.

of Naẓerat Illit is based on relatively large enterprises of the automobile, textile, furniture, and food industries. [S.H.]

Bibliography: C. Kopp, *Holy Places of the Gospels* (1963), 49ff.; idem, in: JPOS, 18 (1938), 181ff.; 20 (1946), 29ff.; B. Bagatti, *Excavations in Nazareth* (1969); M. J. Stiassny, *Nazareth* (Eng., 1967); Prawer, Ẓalbanim, index; M. Barash, in: *Eretz-Israel*, 7 (1964), 125–34 (Heb. section); A. Olivari, in: *La Terre Sainte* (Aug.–Sept. 1961), 201–6; M. Benvenisti, *Crusaders in the Holy Land* (1970), index; W. E. Pax, *In the Footsteps of Jesus* (1970), index.

NAZI-DEUTSCH, specific use of the German language by the National Socialists. The use of language as a tool of psychological warfare against the "enemies" of the regime occupies a special place among the instruments of persecution and extermination. Nazi-Deutsch concealed the real intentions of the governing authorities from the potential victims and lulled them into submissiveness. Unprecedented crimes were masked by the use of "innocent words." Aware that words of long-standing usage acquire frightening meanings, the National Socialists dubbed the deportation to the death camps from Central Europe "evacuation to the

East" *(Evakuierung)*, from the Netherlands "recruitment for labor in the East" *(Arbeitseinsatz)*, from Eastern Europe "resettlement" *(Umsiedlung)*. The word "shower" was used to lead the unsuspecting victims to the gas chambers. New secret words were coined with *prima facie* innocent appearance to smooth over ominous meanings. The mass destruction of the Jewish people in Europe was called the "Final Solution" *(Endloesung)*, a neologism. The actual process of physical destruction was mostly referred to as "Special Treatment" *(Sonderbehandlung)*. In the daily reports at *Auschwitz, the statistics showing the number gassed refer to numbers of "SB" (*Sonderbehandelte*—"specially treated"). The expression SB was taboo even in interoffice correspondence on the highest level. While no objection was raised by Himmler against the use of the word "Final Solution" by the inspector of statistics, Richard Korherr (author of a November 1943 top secret statistical report on the "progress of the Final Solution"), Himmler ordered that the word "special treatment" be replaced by "transporting." The Ministry of Information gave daily instructions to the press and strictly enforced the proper "use of language" *(Sprachregelung)*. Dictionaries of this language exist, and thorough research is being carried out on the subject by linguists, philologists, psychologists, sociologists, and historians.

Bibliography: Blumenthal, in: *Yad Vashem Studies*, 1 (1957), 49–66; 4 (1960), 57–96; 6 (1967), 69–82; Esh, *ibid.*, 5 (1963), 133–67, incl. bibl.; J. Robinson and P. Friedman, *Guide to Jewish History under Nazi Impact* (1960), 97; C. Berning, *Vom Abstammungsnachweis zum Zuchtwart* (1964). [J.R.]

NAZIR (נָזִיר; "Nazirite"), fourth tractate in the order *Nashim*, in the Mishnah, Tosefta, and the Babylonian and Jerusalem Talmuds. It deals, as its name indicates, with the laws of the *Nazirite (Num. 6: 1–21), and its position after the tractate **Nedarim* ("Vows") is determined by the fact that the assumption of Naziriteship was by vow. In the Babylonian Talmud it comes before *Sotah* ("The Unfaithful Wife")—although in the Bible it follows it—because "whosoever sees the degradation of an unfaithful wife will forbid himself the use of wine as leading to such behavior" (2a).

The tractate consists of nine chapters. Chapter 1 deals with the various verbal formulas used in undertaking the vow and their implications, and the duration of the three forms—the ordinary, the Samson, and the lifelong Naziriteship. Chapter 2 continues the same theme and discusses whether it is possible to limit Naziriteship to only part of its obligations. Chapter 3 deals with multiple Naziriteships, the procedure of polling the head at the end of the Naziriteship, and the intervening of ritual uncleanness terminating the Naziriteship. In Mishnah 6 of this chapter, there is the story of Queen *Helena of Adiabene who fulfilled a vow that if her son returned safely from war, she would take a Nazirite vow for seven years; this incident confirms the statement of Josephus (Wars, 2:313) that it was the custom for someone in trouble or danger to undertake a Nazirite vow. Chapter 4 deals with Naziriteship made dependent upon that of another, a stranger, husband, or wife; the consequences of annulling a Naziriteship; the father's power to impose Naziriteship upon his son; and the son's right to utilize his deceased father's Nazirite money. Chapter 5 discusses vows made in error and the situation which arose when the destruction of the Temple made the adoption of the complete Nazirite vow impossible. Chapter 6 discusses the duties of a Nazirite in greater detail, as well as the sacrifices to be brought either when the Naziriteship is interrupted by uncleanness or when it is completed in cleanness. Chapter 7 discusses on which occasions the Nazirite may defile himself for the dead, and which sources of uncleanness interrupt the Naziriteship. Chapter 8 deals with uncertain breaches of the vow. Chapter 9 discusses the fact that gentiles cannot, but women and slaves can, become Nazirites and whether the prophet Samuel was a Nazirite.

It can be demonstrated that several *mishnayot* of *Nazir* belong to the Second Temple period. Among them are 1: 1, which predates the schools of Shammai and Hillel (Tosef., Naz. 1:1 and 2:1), and *mishnayot* 7:2–3, the laws of which were disputed by the *zekenim ha-rishonim* ("the first elders," who lived during the Second Temple period; Tosef., 5: 1 and Naz. 53a). The remainder of the Mishnah of *Nazir* derives from the *Mishnayot* of Akiva's disciples, Meir, Yose, and, especially, Judah and Eleazar (Epstein, Tannaim, 386). The six chapters in the Tosefta to *Nazir* follow a different order from that of the Mishnah. Many *mishnayot* have no corresponding Tosefta and vice versa. The Tosefta includes some aggadic material. Noteworthy is the story of the high priest Simeon the Just who, though in principle opposed to people taking Nazirite vows, made an exception for a handsome youth from the south. When Simeon asked him why he had decided to cut off his flowing hair, he replied that on beholding his reflection in a pool he had become vain of his beauty and had taken a vow to "shear these locks to the glory of Heaven" (4:7).

The Babylonian Talmud to *Nazir* differs from the rest of the Talmud in language and is similar to that of the Jerusalem Talmud (cf. Pseudo-Rashi on Nazir 32a, s.v. *amar mar*). Epstein claims that it was compiled in Maḥoza and Pumbedita, where a special Aramaic dialect was used (Amoraim, 72–83), and that the anonymous discussions in the Jerusalem Talmud were taken from Rava's discussion in the Babylonian Talmud. A. Weiss, however, maintains that there is an essential difference in style, content, and the names of the rabbis quoted, and attributes the differences to the fact that the study of *Nazir* was neglected, and therefore lacks the post-amoraic embellishments given to the other tractates. The Babylonian Talmud has an important passage (23a) dealing with the importance of motive in action. It also contains the dictum (23b): "A man should always occupy himself with the Torah and its precepts even though it be for some ulterior motive, for the result will be that he will eventually do it without ulterior motive."

The rabbinic attitude to *asceticism can be seen in the dictum of Eleazar ha-Kappar (19a); that the Nazirite is called "a sinner by reason of the soul" (Num. 6: 11) because he denied himself wine: "If then one who denies himself wine only is termed a sinner, how much so then one who is

Priests cutting the hair of Nazirites after the period of vows. An engraving illustrating the tractate *Nazir* from a title page of the Hebrew-Latin edition of the Mishnah, illustrated by Mich. Richey, Amsterdam, 1700–04. Jerusalem, J.N.U.L.

an ascetic in all things!" Support for this point of view is also found in the Jerusalem Talmud (Kid. 4: 12, 66d): Man is destined to be called to account for everything (permitted) he saw (and desired) but did not partake of. After the destruction of the Temple, since it was impossible to complete Naziriteship by offering the sacrifices on its conclusion, the practice fell into disuse. Tractate *Nazir* was not studied in the academies of the *geonim*, nor were there any *halakhot* on it in the *Halakhot Pesukot, Hilkhot Re'u*, or *Halakhot Gedolot* (B. M. Lewin *Oẓar ha-Ge'onim*, 11 (1942), 8, and Epstein, Tannaim, p. 72). The commentary to *Nazir* attributed to Rashi was apparently written by his son-in-law Meir b. Samuel, who recorded the commentaries of Isaac b. Eleazar ha-Levi, Rashi's teacher. According to Epstein the *tosafot* to *Nazir* were written by the disciples of Perez of Corbeil. The talmudic tractate in the Soncino edition was translated into English by B. D. Klien (1936).

Bibliography: Halevy, Dorot, 3 (1923), 48ff.; A. Weiss, *Hithavvut ha-Talmud bi-Shelemuto* (1943), 128–57; Epstein, Tanna'im, 383–93; Epstein, Amora'im, 72–83; Ḥ. Albeck, *Shishah Sidrei Mishnah, Seder Nashim* (1954), 189–93; Z. W. Rabinowitz, *Sha'arei Torat Bavel* (1961), 299ff.; D. Halivni, *Mekorot u-Masorot* (1968), 353–433. [Ed.]

NAZIR, MOSES HA-LEVI (second half of 17th century), rabbinic author and Hebron emissary. Moses was the son-in-law of Abraham b. Hananiah, a Jerusalem scholar. He was called Nazir because of his acceptance of the ascetic practices enjoined on the *Nazirite. At the beginning of each year he would undertake the observance of such practices for that year, and the text of one of these resolutions has survived. In 1668–71 he traveled in Syria and Turkey as an emissary of Hebron and a copy of the account book of this mission is extant. It contains the names of the communities he visited, the amount received in each of them, his traveling expenses, how much was stolen during the journey, etc. While on his mission he wrote several responsa to Ḥasdai b. Samuel ha-Kohen Peraḥyah, *av bet din* of Salonika, and these too reveal Moses' fine character. He also wrote halakhic novellae on the laws of the festivals, which were published by his son Joseph, and the *Yedei Moshe* on *Ḥoshen Mishpat*, which is still in manuscript.

Moses' son Joseph (d. 1713) was born in Jerusalem, studied under Hezekiah b. David da Silva, then settled in Hebron with his father, and was apparently a Hebron emissary to Europe in 1689. From Hebron, Joseph went to Egypt and served as *av bet din* in Cairo. His responsa and novellae were published after his death by his son-in-law Joshua Zein, according to the order of the *Arba'ah Turim*, under the title *Matteh Yosef* (2 pts., Constantinople, 1717–26); the numerical value of *matteh* is 54, which is the number of responsa. In them he discussed halakhic problems with contemporary scholars, especially with Abraham Blom, rabbi of Egypt.

Bibliography: Frumkin-Rivlin, 2 (1928), 98f.; J. M. Toledano, *Sarid u-Falit* (n.d.), 39ff.; Yaari, Sheluḥei, 468–70, 480. [A.Ya.]

NAZIRITE, person who vows for a specific period to abstain from partaking of grapes or any of its products whether intoxicating or not, cutting his hair, and touching a corpse (6:3–9). Such a person is called a Nazirite (Heb. *nazir*, נָזִיר) from the root *nzr* (נזר), meaning to separate or dedicate oneself (e.g., *nifal*, Lev. 22:2; *hifil*, Lev. 15:31; Num. 6:2, 5, 12). The subject is dealt with in the Priestly Code (Num. 6:1–21) and the purpose of the law is to prescribe the proper ritual if the Nazirite period is aborted by corpse contamination (Num. 6:9–12) or if it is successfully completed (6:13–21).

In the person of the Nazirite, the layman is given a status resembling that of the priest, as he now is "holy to the Lord" (Lev. 21:6; Num. 6:8; cf. Philo, I L.A., 249). Actually, in his taboos, he approximates more the higher sanctity of the high priest in that (1) he may not contaminate himself with the dead of his immediate family (Lev. 21:11; Num. 6:7; cf. the ordinary priest, Lev. 21:1–4); (2) for him, as for the high priest, the head is the focus of sanctity (Ex. 29:7; Num. 6:11b. Note the same motive clauses, Lev. 21:12b; Num. 6:7b and compare the dedication of the ordinary priest, Ex. 29:21); (3) he abstains from intoxicants during his term (Num. 6:4)—a more stringent requirement than that of the high priest, whose abstinence, like that of his fellow priests, is limited to the time he is in the Sanctuary (Lev. 10:9).

A more instructive parallel to the Nazirite is the case of the dedication of land to the Sanctuary (Lev. 27: 16ff.). Both result from a votive dedication (Lev. 27: 16; Num. 6:2), and both dedications are for limited periods, the land reverting to its owner on the Jubilee if not redeemed earlier (implied by Lev. 27:21; Num. 6: 13). In both cases the period of dedication can be terminated earlier—the Nazirite's by contamination (Num. 6:9–12), the land's by redemption (Lev. 27:16–19). In the case of premature desanctification, a penalty is exacted: the Nazirite pays a reparation offering (*'asham*) to the Sanctuary, and the owner of the land pays an additional one-fifth of the redemption price to the Sanctuary. If the dedication period is completed, no desanctification penalty is incurred. True, the Nazirite offers up an array of sacrifices together with his hair (Num. 6: 13–20), but the sacrifices are mainly for thanksgiving, and the hair, which may not be desanctified, is consumed on the altar. Similarly, dedicated land (so the text of Lev. 27:22–24 implies) reverts to its original owner on the Jubilee without cost. In the case when the Nazirite period is interrupted by contamination, the following ritual is observed: the Nazirite must undergo sprinkling with purificatory waters on the third and seventh day (inferred from Num. 19: 14ff.); he shaves his hair on the seventh day; and on the following day three rituals are prescribed: he is purified of his contamination by a purification offering, his hair is reconsecrated and his Nazirite period begins anew, and a reparation offering is brought to expiate his desecration.

The uncut hair of the Nazirite is his distinction. (In this respect the priest differs; though forbidden to shave his hair, he is compelled to trim it; cf. Ezek. 44:20.) Its importance is indicated by the root of the term Nazirite, נזר, which refers at times to the hair (Num. 6:6, 7, 12, 18; Jer. 7:29. Note the parallelism in Gen. 49:26; Deut 33: 16). Since hair continues to grow throughout life (and apparently for a time after death), it was considered by the ancients to be the seat of man's vitality and life-force, and in ritual it often served as his substitute. A ninth-century B.C.E. bowl found in a Cypriot temple contains an inscription on its outside surface indicating that it contained the hair of the donor. It was placed there, if the reconstructed text is correct, as "a memorial" to Astarte (cf. Ex. 28:12, 29; 30:16; Num. 10:10; Zech. 6:14), i.e., as a permanent reminder to the goddess of the donor's devotion. The offering of hair is also attested in later times in Babylonia (Pritchard, Texts, 339–40), Syria (Lucian, *De dea Syra*, 55, 60), Greece (K. Meuli), and Arabia (W. R. Smith).

The narrative and prophetic literature corroborate the existence of Nazirites in Israel. Samson and Samuel were lifelong Nazirites (Judg. 13:7; I Sam. 1:21 (4Q Sam[a]), 28). Indeed, they resembled the prophets in that their dedication began not at birth but at conception (Isa. 49:1, 5; Jer. 1:5; cf. Amos 2:11). The taboos prescribed in the Torah are verified in their lives. Neither polled his hair (Judg. 13:5;

16:17; I Sam. 1:11) nor drank any wine (to judge by the prohibition to Samson's mother during her pregnancy; Judg. 13:4, 7, 14). However, the law forbidding corpse contamination was not observed (Judg. 14:9, 19; 15:8, 15; I Sam. 15:33). This divergence from the Priestly Code is implicitly reinforced by the rule set down by the angel to Samson's mother (Judg. 13:14), i.e., that she must eschew forbidden food; nothing, however, is said about contracting impurity from the dead which, according to the Priestly Code, would have automatically defiled her embryo. [J.Mi.]

In Talmud. The Mishnah and the Talmud distinguish between a lifelong Nazirite and a "Samson Nazirite" since Samson, unlike the lifelong Nazirite, was never allowed to thin his hair even when it became burdensome (Naz. 1:2). On the other hand, Samson was permitted to defile himself through contact with the dead since the angel did not enjoin him from such defilement when delineating the laws of his abstinence (Naz. 4b).

When the period of the vow was not specified, it was understood to be 30 days (Naz. 1:3). In addition to being subsumed under the general regulations governing vows, many specific formulas were developed for Nazirite commitments. "If a man says 'Let my hand be a Nazirite' or 'Let my foot be a Nazirite,' his words are of no effect. However, if he says, 'Let my head be a Nazirite' or 'Let my liver be a Nazirite' [or some other vital organ], he becomes a Nazirite" (Naz. 21b). It was customary for the wealthy to aid poor Nazirites in the purchase of their offerings (Naz. 2:5, 6), since it was felt that the most meritorious aspect of abstinence was the chance to bring a sin-offering at its conclusion (Ned. 10a). It is related that at the time of *Simeon b. Shetaḥ, 300 Nazirites came to Jerusalem. He absolved half of them of their vow, and not revealing the fact to the king Alexander Yannai, persuaded him to give what purported to be half the sacrifices needed, he "offering" to provide the other half (TJ, Ber. 7:2, 11b). The Nazirite laws applied only to Ereẓ Israel. It is related that *Helena of Adiabene took Nazirite vows for seven years. After this period she went to Ereẓ Israel where Bet Hillel ruled that she must continue for a further seven years (Naz. 3:6).

There were different reasons for taking the Nazirite vow. Some did it for the fulfillment of a wish, such as for the birth of a child (Naz. 2:7–10). One who saw the conduct of an unfaithful wife was advised to abstain completely from wine by becoming a Nazirite (Ber. 63a). Thus the passages on the wife suspected of adultery and the laws of the Nazirite are juxtaposed in the Bible (Num. 5:11–31, 6:1–21). The pious simply made a freewill vow of abstinence to afford them an opportunity to bring a sin-offering at its conclusion (Ned. 10a). The Nazirite was severely discouraged by the rabbis since *asceticism was against the spirit of Judaism (Ned. 77b; Naz. 19a; Ta'an. 11a). Their discouragement of the practice was almost certainly in protest against the excessive mourning after the destruction of the Second Temple, when large numbers of Jews became ascetics, vowing not to eat meat or to drink wine (BB 60b). The rabbis even designated the Nazirites as sinners in accordance with the verse: "And [the priest] shall make atonement for him, for that he sinned against a soul" (Num. 6:11; Ned. 10a). The high priest Simeon the Just only once in his life ate of the trespass-offering brought by a defiled Nazirite. This was when a young, handsome shepherd possessing beautiful, thick locks of hair undertook to become a Nazirite and thus had to cut his hair in order to avoid sinful thoughts (Ned. 9b; cf. the Narcissus legend in Greek mythology). The observance of the Nazirite vow may have continued for many centuries. However, it ultimately disappeared, and there is no reference to Nazirites in the Middle Ages. In modern times Nazirite practices have been observed in Jerusalem by David Cohen, a disciple of Chief Rabbi A. I. Kook. [A.Ro.]

Bibliography: W. R. Smith, *Lectures on the Religion of the Semites* (1927[3]), 323–36; K. Meuli, in: *Phyllobolia fuer Peter von der Muehl* (1946), 204–11; de Vaux, Anc Isr, 465–7; M. Haran, in: EM, 5 (1968), 795–9 (incl. bibl.); Pederson, Israel, 3–4 (1940), 263–6. In Talmud: M. Jastrow, in: JBL, 33 (1914), 266–85; H. Gevaryahu, in: *Iyyunim be-Sefer Shofetim* (1966), 522–46; Z. Weisman, in: *Tarbiz*, 36 (1967), 207–20; E. E. Urbach, *Ḥazal; Pirkei Emmunot ve-De'ot* (1969), index s.v. *nazir;* G. Scholem, *Ursprung und Anfaenge der Kabbala* (1962), 202f.

NEANDER, AUGUST (originally **David Mendel**; 1789–1850), Church historian and convert. His Orthodox father abandoned the family, complaining that his liberally educated wife was corrupting the children (four of five were eventually baptized). Though poor and sickly, David was an immediate success at the Johanneum Gymnasium in Hamburg. His honorary public address presented in Latin on the conclusion of his studies in 1805, demanding equality for the Jews in all respects but advocating the abrogation of some rites, aroused wide interest. The speech was inspired by his rationalist benefactor, who was also principal of the school. David soon fell under the varied influences of Plato, *Schleiermacher, and romanticism, and embraced Christianity at the age of 17. Neander (Gr. "new man") rapidly attained prominence in the field of Church history and became a professor at the age of 24. During the *Damascus affair (1840) he publicized his opinion that the whole ritual murder charge was a falsehood. In 1847 he opposed the admission of Jews to Berlin University, identifying them with the anti-Christian movement of the left-wing Hegelians.

Bibliography: H. Huettmann, *August Neander* (Ger., 1936); L. Schultze, *August Neander* (Ger., 1890); H. Liebeschuetz, *Das Judentum im deutschen Geschichtsbild von Hegel bis Max Weber* (1967), index.

[Ed.]

NEBAIOTH (Heb. נְבָיוֹת,נְבָית), a tribe or a group of tribes of nomads in the border deserts of Israel, identified with the Nabaiāte mentioned in the Assyrian documents from the time of Ashurbanipal. The Nebaioth are not to be connected with the *Nabateans, as some classical authors mistakenly did (cf. Jos., Ant. 1:221; 12:335, et al.; Jerome in his commentary to Gen. 25:13–18). According to Genesis 25:13 and I Chronicles 1:29, Nebaioth was the firstborn of Ishmael and according to Genesis 36:3 he was also the brother of Esau's wife Basemath, daughter of Ishmael. In Isaiah 60:6–7 Nebaioth is mentioned with Kedar, another son of Ishmael (Gen. 25:13), among the nomadic tribes on the border of Israel.

Bibliography: EM, 5 (1968), 744–6 (incl. bibl.). [Ed.]

NEBO (Heb. נְבוֹ). (1) High mountain E. of the Jordan River, opposite Jericho. It forms part of the heights of Abarim bordering the Moab plateau, where the Israelites encamped on the last stage of their journey (Deut. 32:49). The mountain is identified with Jebel Shayhān that has two peaks: Ra's al-Nibā' 2,739 ft. (835 m.) and Ra's Siyāgha 2,329 ft. (710 m.). In the Bible the peak of Mt. Nebo is called Pisgah; from there Moses beheld the Promised Land before dying. Although Ra's al-Nibā' has retained the biblical name, scholars regard the second peak as the more likely site of Pisgah, because of the magnificent view from there. Moses died on the mountain and was buried in a valley "and no one knows his burial place to this day" (Deut. 34:6). According to an apocryphal source, Jeremiah buried the Ark of the Covenant and various other objects from the Holy of Holies on the mountain (II Macc. 2:5ff.).

In Byzantine times the tomb of Moses was "rediscovered" by a shepherd (Petrus Iberus, 88) and a memorial church was erected together with a monastery on Ra's Siyāgha. The church consists of a basilica with a trefoil apse, a baptistery (dated 597), and a chapel, all paved with mosaics. Eusebius locates "Phasgo" (= Pisgah) on the way from Livias to Heshbon (Onom. 18:3). (2) Reubenite town (Num. 32:3, 38) near Mt. Nebo belonging to the family of Bela (I Chron. 5:8). It remained an Israelite possession till the revolt of the Moabite king Mesha against the house of Omri. In his stele (lines 14ff.) Mesha describes his conquest of the town, the destruction of the sanctuary of the God of Israel before the Moabite god Chemosh and the sacrifice of 7,000 men, boys, women, girls, and maidservants (see *Mesha Stele). The prophets Isaiah (15:2) and Jeremiah (48:1, 22) mention Nebo among the cities of Moab in their descriptions of the "burdens" on that land. Eusebius refers to it as a ruined town, 6 (or 8) mi. (c. 11 or 14 km.) west of Heshbon (Onom. 136:6–13).

Scholars identify Nebo either with Khirbat al-Muḥayyiṭ southeast of Ra's Siyāgha or with Khirbat ʿUyūn Mūsā ("Springs of Moses") northeast of the mountain, beside a spring of the same name. Iron Age fortresses have been discovered at both sites. (3) Town in Judah whose inhabitants were among those who returned from Babylonian Exile (Ezra 2:29; 10:43; Neh. 7:33). The place may be identical with Nob.

Bibliography: Abel, Géog, 1 (1933), 379ff.; 2 (1938), 397–8; N. Glueck, in: AASOR, 15 (1935), 109ff.; S. J. Saller, *The Memorial of Moses on Mount Nebo* (1941); S. J. Saller and B. Bagatti, *The Town of Nebo* (1949); Aharoni, Land, index; EM, 5 (1968), 685–90 (incl. bibl.). [M.A.-Y.]

NEBRASKA, state on the Great Plains located near the geographical center of continental United States. Its population in 1970 was 1,411,300, of whom approximately 8,100 are Jews.

Nebraska was organized as a territory in 1854, and within a year the stream of Jewish settlement had begun. The first Jewish settlers are believed to have been two brothers, Lewis and Henry Wessel, who went to Nebraska City from St. Louis in 1855. The next few decades brought a steady trickle of Jews who were predominantly of Central European origin (Alsace-Lorraine, Germany, Bohemia). Many had settled briefly in cities on the eastern seaboard before moving to the west, where, especially after the Civil War, the Homestead Act and railroad construction attracted new settlement. The early Jews in Nebraska were mainly merchants, such as Aaron Cahn and Meyer Hellman, who established a clothing business in Omaha to supply pioneers striking out on the Oregon Trail, and Carl Ernest Louis Golding, who was an Indian trader in Plattsmouth.

One of the most colorful figures in early Jewish life in Nebraska was Julius Meyer who settled in Omaha in 1866 and became a successful Indian trader. He mastered at least six tribal dialects, was adopted into the Pawnee tribe, and was given the name "curly-headed-white-chief-with-one-tongue." He later became a government interpreter for the

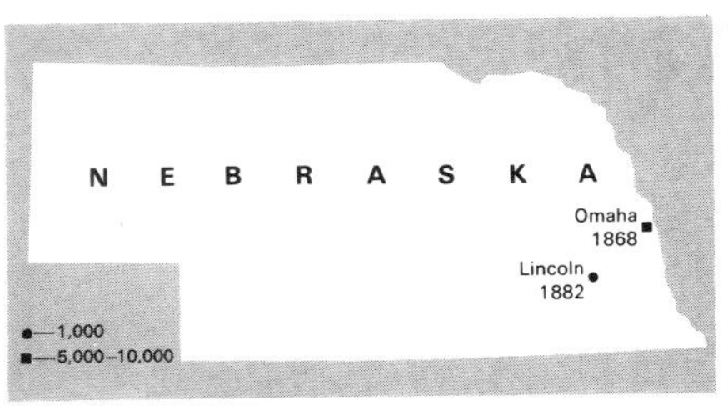

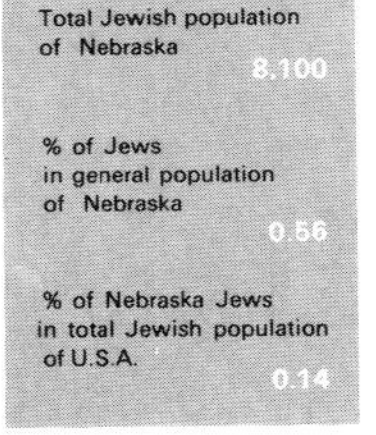

Total Jewish population of Nebraska
8,100
% of Jews in general population of Nebraska
0.56
% of Nebraska Jews in total Jewish population of U.S.A.
0.14

Jewish communities in Nebraska and dates of establishment. Population figures for 1968.

Julius Meyer, early Nebraska trader, with Indian chiefs. Courtesy American Jewish Archives, Cincinnati, Ohio.

Indians and accompanied a party of them to the Paris Exposition. Another early Indian merchant, Harris L. Levi, was less fortunate. In 1869 he joined a surveying party, all of whom were massacred by the Indians in retaliation for the slaying of two Indian youths by the surveyors.

The most important early Jewish settler was Edward *Rosewater, who went to Omaha in 1863 as manager of the Western Union, and then became active as a journalist, founding the *Omaha Evening Bee News* (1871). Rosewater was a leading and controversial figure in Republican Party affairs in the state, served as National Republican Committeeman from Nebraska, and was twice defeated for the U.S. Senate.

After 1881 Russian Jews began to arrive in large numbers, many of whom were systematically sent out west by the Industrial Removal Aid Society of New York. Some abortive attempts were made to settle the newcomers on the soil, and the Jewish Agricultural Society tried to found a colony in Cherry County in 1908, but by 1916 the experiment was abandoned.

With the exception of a handful of ranchers, the Jewish population of Nebraska, by 1970, was almost entirely concentrated in business and the professions. Scattered groups of Jews live in some of the smaller Nebraska towns (Grand Island, Norfolk, Scottsbluff, Beatrice), but only *Omaha and Lincoln sustain organized community life. Lincoln has two congregations, one Conservative and one Reform, and a Jewish Welfare Federation. The Esther K. Newman Camp, between the two cities, serves the Jewish youth of the state during the summer.

Jews have served in a wide variety of public offices in the state since its inception. Many have been mayors of their municipalities, and as early as 1863 Aaron Cahn served in the legislature. Henry *Monsky of Omaha gained national importance in the B'nai B'rith. Ben Greenberg of York was chairman of the Board of Regents of the University of Nebraska.

Bibliography: B. Postal and L. Koppman, *Jewish Tourists' Guide to the U.S.* (1954), 289–92. [SA.RA.]

NEBUCHADNEZZAR (**Nebuchadrezzar;** Heb. נְבוּכַדְנֶצַּר, נְבוּכַדְרֶאצַּר; Akk. **Nabû-kudurri-uṣur,** "O, Nabû, guard my border!"), son of Nabopolassar the Chaldean, ruler of Babylon (605–562 B.C.E.). Nebuchadnezzar succeeded to his father's throne at the time when the struggle between Babylon and Egypt for the territories that had been part of the Assyrian empire was at its height. According to the *Babylonian Chronicle,* Nebuchadnezzar waged his first war against Egypt in the region of the Euphrates, in the last year of his father's reign (605). In that year he defeated the Egyptian armies in a battle fought at *Carchemish on the

Euphrates (cf. Jer. 46:2), thereby frustrating Pharaoh-Neco's attempt to gain control of Syria and Palestine, and at the same time paving the way for the rise of Babylon as a world power. In his pursuit of the Egyptian forces Nebuchadnezzar reached the region of Hamath in central Syria, but was obliged to return to Babylon in consequence of his father's death. In the same year he returned to the land of Ḫatti, i.e., Greater Syria, and according to the *Babylonian Chronicle,* "He marched unopposed through the Ḫatti-land; in the month of Šabāṭu (Shevat) he took the heavy tribute of the Ḫatti-territory to Babylon." It would seem that Nebuchadnezzar reached Palestine and subjected Judah to his rule one or two years later. At the end of 604 he conducted a military campaign against Palestine, besieging and capturing the city of Ashkelon. In the words of the *Babylonian Chronicle,* "All the kings of the Ḫatti-land came before him and he received their heavy tribute." One of these kings was apparently *Jehoiakim of Judah.

After consolidating his rule in Palestine and Syria, Nebuchadnezzar attempted the conquest of Egypt (end of 601). The stubbornly fought encounter between the Babylonian and Egyptian armies was indecisive. Nebuchadnezzar's failure to obtain a clear-cut victory over the Egyptians may have encouraged various states in Syria and Palestine, including Judah, to revolt against Babylon. In Kislev (December) 598 Nebuchadnezzar entered Palestine, and, according to the *Babylonian Chronicle,* "he encamped against the city of Judah [i.e., Jerusalem] and on the second day of the month of Adar [i.e., March 16, 597] he seized the city and captured the king [i.e., Jehoiachin]. He appointed there a king of his own choice [i.e., Zedekiah], received its heavy tribute and sent it to Babylon" (see *Zedekiah). In the following years the Babylonian king was occupied with wars against the Elamites to the east of the Tigris, and was also obliged to suppress a revolt in the country of Akkad (695/94). His absence from Syria, and the events in Babylon and Elam, apparently encouraged the kings of Syria and Palestine to plot a further revolt against their overlord. The Egyptian rulers no doubt lent their support to uprisings against Babylon, and Zedekiah's open revolt enjoyed their active aid (Jer. 37:5ff.). In 588 the siege of Jerusalem began, and in the summer of 586 Nebuchadnezzar captured the city, laid the Temple waste, carried off a large part of the population of Judah into captivity, and put Zedekiah and other Judean nobles to death. The land of Judah was turned into a province (see *Gedaliah son of Ahikam).

Some information about the fate of the exiles in Babylon in Nebuchadnezzar's day is found in Babylonian administrative documents, in which King Jehoiachin and his sons are mentioned as receiving a regular allowance of oil from the royal treasury. On the other hand, it is hard to draw any conclusions from the Book of Daniel about this subject because of the legendary character of the stories related there. Some scholars are of the opinion that the name Nebuchadnezzar in these stories is an error for Nabonidus, since in an Aramaic text from Qumran there is a story about Nabonidus which resembles the story about Nebuchadnezzar in Daniel. Of similarly doubtful authenticity is the mention of Nebuchadnezzar in the Book of *Judith. In the years following the capture of Jerusalem, Nebuchadnezzar waged a war in Phoenicia against Tyre, most probably in 585, which, according to Josephus, lasted for 13 years (Ezek. 29:18; cf. Jos., Ant., 10:220–2; Jos., Apion, 1:154–60). Three years later (582/81) he conducted a campaign against Ammon and Moab (Jos., Ant., 10:181–2), in the course of which he also took captives from Judah (Jer. 52:30). Nebuchadnezzar must have been aware of Egypt's part in inciting the vassal states to revolt against Babylon and of its desire to establish its own power in Palestine and Syria. He therefore attacked Egypt too, but the source material dealing with this war is fragmentary and unreliable.

Despite his many foreign wars, Nebuchadnezzar did not neglect Babylon itself. From various inscriptions and archaeological finds he emerges as a dynamic and able monarch in the administrative and architectural no less than in the military field. He adorned and fortified his capital city, Babylon, with the booty and tribute that poured in from all over the Near East. He restored and renovated ancient temples in the cities of Babylonia in order to gain the support of the Babylonian priests. He also made provision for the regular irrigation of the lands of Babylonia by means of a whole network of canals connected with the Euphrates. In his reign the neo-Babylonian empire attained the pinnacle of its greatness. [B.O.]

In the Aggadah. The description of Nebuchadnezzar in the *aggadah* seems largely to be a veiled reference to Titus. He is frequently referred to as "the wicked one" (Ber. 57b; Shab. 149b; et al.) as well as "a wicked slave," and "hater and adversary" of God (Lam. R., Proem 23); Titus is depicted in similar terms (Git. 56b). The "wicked slave" charge may be connected with the notoriously humble origin of the Flavian dynasty (Suetonius, *Vespasian,* 1:1; 3:1).

Despite the relatively favorable attitude to Nebuchadnezzar in Jeremiah, Ezekiel, and Daniel, the rabbis, for the most part, depict him as a cruel, merciless conqueror who, among other things, tore the flesh off a hare and ate it while it was still alive (Ned. 65a; Lam. R. 2:10, no. 14), and forced his client kings to enter into homosexual relations with him (Shab. 149b). Several Roman emperors, including Titus (cf. Suetonius, *Divus Titus* 7:1), were said to have indulged in pederasty. Nebuchadnezzar was also reported

Figure 1. Tablet of the *Babylonian Chronicle,* on which is described Nebuchadnezzar's capture of Jerusalem in 597 B.C.E. (II Kings 24:10–17). From J. B. Pritchard, *The Ancient Near East (Supplementary Texts and Pictures Relating to the Old Testament),* Princeton, 1969.

to have cast Jehoiakim's body to the dogs (Lev. R. 19:6) and to have killed large numbers of Judean exiles in Babylonia (Sanh. 92b; PdRE 33). Likewise, he is frequently accused of having made himself into a god (Gen. R. 9:5; Ex. R. 8:2)—a transparent criticism of the Roman emperors who claimed divine honors.

Nebuchadnezzar's treatment of Zedekiah was at first favorable, and he even placed five kings under his rule; but when it seemed that they were prepared to plot against Nebuchadnezzar, Zedekiah reviled him in their presence, whereupon they betrayed Zedekiah to his suzerain (Lam. R. 2:10, no. 14). Although ostensibly based on Jeremiah 27:3, the story is remarkably similar to Josephus' account of the congress of five kings held by Agrippa I at Tiberias and rudely dispersed by the Roman governor of Syria (Ant., 19:338–41). There, too, it seems that some anti-Roman plot was being hatched, with the result that henceforth the Roman authorities became hostile to Agrippa.

Nebuchadnezzar charged the Sanhedrin with absolving Zedekiah from his vow of loyalty, and he had them punished by having their hair tied to tails of horses and being made to run from Jerusalem to Lydda (Lam. R. 2:10, no. 14). Since, according to II Kings 25:18–21, 72 leading citizens of Jerusalem—a number almost equivalent to the traditional great Sanhedrin—were executed at Riblah in Syria, the punishment mentioned in the Midrash undoubtedly alludes to some incident in the Roman period, probably to the execution of Jewish rebels at Lydda by order of Ummidius *Quadratus, governor of Syria; the dispatch from Lydda of a number of Jewish leaders to Rome where their fate was to be decided; and the subsequent beheading of a Roman tribune after being dragged round Jerusalem (Jos., Ant., 20:130–6; Jos., Wars, 2:242–6).

According to the Midrash, Nebuchadnezzar hesitated to attack Jerusalem and destroy the Temple (Lam. R. Proems 23, 30)—which is precisely what Vespasian did in 68–69 C.E., though his motives were political, not religious. Interpreting Ezekiel 21:26, the rabbis depict Nebuchadnezzar as practicing belomancy and studying various auguries before deciding whether to proceed against Jerusalem (*ibid.* 23). The same is reported in the Talmud concerning Nero (Git. 56a).

Since Nebuchadnezzar left the task of subduing Jerusalem and burning the Temple to Nebuzaradan, he is assailed mainly for trying to force image worship on the Jewish exiles. Interpreting Daniel 3:16, the Midrash depicts Shadrach, Meshach, and Abed-Nego as saying to Nebuchadnezzar, "You are our king only as regards taxes, *annonae,* fines, and poll taxes; but in this matter of which you speak to us you are just Nebuchadnezzar ... You and a dog are alike to us. O Nebuchadnezzar, bark like a dog, swell like a pitcher, chirp like a cricket"—a curse which was duly fulfilled (Lev. R. 33:6). The Roman taxes enumerated indicate an allusion to the Roman period, probably to Caligula who insisted that his statue be placed in the Temple and who was a madman just like Nebuchadnezzar (Jos., Ant., 18:261 ff.; Jos., Wars, 21:184ff.; Tacitus, *Historiae,* 5:9; Philo, *In Flaccum,* 31).

Occasionally, however, Nebuchadnezzar is viewed in a more favorable light, mainly in later rabbinic sources composed at a time when hostility to the Romans had subsided. Thus, he is said to have taken pity on the Jews after the exile of Jehoiachin, and, indeed, on Jehoiachin himself whom he provided with a wife during his long imprisonment (Lev. R. 19:6; PR 26:129). Nebuchadnezzar was one of the five persons saved from the army of Sennacherib and from that time he was inspired by the fear of God (Sanh. 95b). He was the scribe of Merodach Baladan and corrected him for writing the name of Hezekiah before that of God (Sanh. 96a). For this act he was rewarded by ruling over the whole world (Song R. 3:4, no. 2) including the world of animals and by sitting on Solomon's throne (Est. R. 1:12).

A historically significant Midrash reports that when the "exiles of Zedekiah" were brought to Babylonia by Nebuchadnezzar, they were met by the earlier deportees (of 597 B.C.E.), wearing "black underneath but white outside" and hailing Nebuchadnezzar as "conqueror of the barbarians" (Lam. R., Proem 23). This story evidently alludes to the Jews of the Hellenistic and Roman Diaspora as well as to individuals such as Josephus and Agrippa II, who had to conceal their mourning for Jerusalem and proclaim their loyalty to the Roman conquerors. [M.A.]

In Islam. In the Koran (Sura 17:4–7) it is related that the people of Israel sinned twice and were therefore punished twice. The description of these events in the Koran is very vague and the traditional Muslim commentators therefore found it difficult to present a clear and crystallized explanation of these verses. According to them the two sins were: the murder of *Isaiah or the imprisonment of *Jeremiah or the murder of *Zechariah son of Iddo; and the murder of John the Baptist. However, some elements from the *aggadah* on the murder of Zechariah have also been introduced into this story (cf. Targum Lam. 2:20). In any case, the Koran clearly hints at two destructions of the Temple.

According to Muslim legend the punishment was meted out either by *Goliath, Sennacherib, Nebuchadnezzar (Bukhtanaṣar), one of the Nabatean kings, or Persian invaders. Among the intermediaries whom Allah used to punish the people of Israel the figure of Bukhtanaṣar stands out; folklorists make frequent references to him, even adding a beautiful story about his youth to his biography. According to them, one of the people of Israel dreamed that a poor, orphaned youth would destroy the Temple and exterminate the people. He set out in search of this youth, traveled as far as Babylonia, and almost gave up the hope of finding him. Some people finally pointed out a poor orphan who carried a bundle of twigs on his head. The Israelite gave him three dirhams with which to buy meat, bread, and wine. He repeated this act the next day and for several more days. When his time came to leave, the youth was saddened by the fact that he was unable to

Figure 2. Nebuchadnezzar riding a lion, using a snake as a curb, during his seven years' exile in the ancient kingdom. Illustration of the story in the Babylonian Talmud (Shab. 150a) in the *Leipzig Maḥzor,* S. Germany, c. 1320. Leipzig, University Library, Ms. V. 1102, Vol. II, fol. 67.

repay the generosity of his Israelite benefactor. The latter told the youth that his reward would be the youth's written promise that when he ascended the throne he would spare his life and the lives of all those with him. The youth answered that his benefactor and friend was mocking him. Upon the entreaties of his mother he finally granted the request of the Israelite and gave him the written promise; a sign was even convened upon by which Bukhtanaṣar would recognize the Israelite among the great crowd. The story of Yaḥyā ibn Zakariyyā (i.e., John the Baptist) has been added to some versions of this story. The continuation of the story relates that Nebuchadnezzar destroyed the Temple as a punishment for the murder of John the Baptist and that he ordered the bodies of those who had been killed to be thrown among the ruins. Everyone who obeyed his command was exempted from the payment of the *jizya* (poll tax) for that year. The Israelite, the benefactor of Nebuchadnezzar, was not in Jerusalem on that day and was therefore unable to make use of the written promise which he had received years ago; thus, no one was saved by it. As usual, there are several versions of this story. It does not appear to have any Jewish origin, except for a weak echo of the story of the encounter between Rabban Johanan b. Zakkai and Vespasian, when Rabban Johanan announced to Vespasian that he would become king and destroy Jerusalem (Git. 56a–b). [H.Z.H.]

In the Arts. Although few of the literary, artistic, or musical works associated with Nebuchadnezzar are of the first rank, they are rather numerous; and the Babylonian king also figures in works dealing with the notable Jews who have contact with him in the Bible. Two of the earliest literary treatments were an old English play, *Nebuchadnezzar's Fierie Furnace* (reedited by M. Roesler, 1936), and an Italian miracle play in verse, *La Rapresentatione di Nabucdonosor Re di Babillonia* (c. 1530; Florence, 1558[2]). A second English play on the theme is known to have been staged in London in 1596. Nebuchadnezzar's treatment of Zedekiah and the royal house of Judah forms the subject of *Sédécie, ou les Juives* (1583), one of the most important works of the French dramatist Robert Garnier. Later, the German playwright Christian Weise added *Nebukadnezar* (1684) to his series of biblical dramas. In the 18th century, Christian Friedrich Hunold wrote a *"Singspiel," Der gestuerzte und wieder erhoehte Nebucadnezar, Koenig zu Babylon, unter dem grossen Propheten Daniel,* which was staged at Hamburg in 1728; and the Russian writer and publisher Nikolai Ivanovich Novikov published a *Komediya Navukhodonosor* (1791; in *Drevnyaya Rossiyskaya Biblioteka,* Moscow, 1788–91). Works on the subject that appeared in the 19th century include *Nabucco* (1819), a five-act verse tragedy by the Italian writer Giovanni Battista Niccolini; *Nabuco in Gerusalemme* (1829), an Italian *azione sacra* in verse; and *Nebuchodonoser* (1836), a four-act French drama by Auguste Anicet-Bourgeois written in collaboration with Francis Cornu and staged in Paris. The tragic end of the Judean monarchy also inspired Ludwig *Philippson's German dramas *Jojachin* (1858) and *Die Entthronten* (1868). On the whole, 20th-century writers have avoided the subject, an exception being the German author Heinz Welten, whose novel *Nebukadnezar: der Koenig der Koenige* appeared in 1924.

In art, the main subjects treated are the king's dreams and visions and their eventual realization. There are several works illustrating Nebuchadnezzar's dream of the metal statue with feet of clay (Dan. 2:31–35). The stone hewn without hands which topples the statue was thought by the Church Fathers and later Christian symbolists to represent the Virgin Birth (i.e., Jesus conceived without human agency). The dream is depicted in medieval manuscripts and in carvings from the Gothic cathedrals of Amiens and Laon. Nebuchadnezzar's vision of the tree (Dan. 4) appears in medieval illuminated manuscripts and on the front of Laon Cathedral, as well as in stained glass and paintings of the Middle Ages. The pitiful figure of the king reduced to grazing with the beasts (Dan. 4:32) appealed particularly to the artistic imagination of the Romanesque period (11th–12th centuries) with its feeling for the awesome and the grotesque. This scene appeared in illuminated manuscripts of the commentary on the New Testament Book of Revelations by the eighth-century Spanish monk Beatus and on the capitals of French Romanesque churches. A more recent treatment of the episode is the English visionary poet and artist William *Blake's striking depiction of the shaggy, wild-eyed monarch walking on all fours (1795). The image also occurs in Blake's prophetic work *The Marriage of Heaven and Hell*

Figure 3. "Nebuchadnezzar" by William Blake, 1795. Watercolor, $17\frac{5}{8}\times24\frac{3}{4}$ in. (44.7×63 cm.). London, Tate Gallery.

(1790) with the caption "One Law for the Lion and the Ox is Oppression." Nebuchadnezzar occasionally figures in medieval manuscript illustrations of the Three Hebrews in the Fiery Furnace (Dan. 3). In the early 15th-century *Très Riches Heures* of the Duc de Berry (Musée Condé, Chantilly), he is shown complacently stoking the furnace which encloses Shadrach, Meshach, and Abed-Nego.

Musical compositions involving Nebuchadnezzar largely deal with episodes drawn from the Book of Daniel, notably that of the Three Hebrews. They include an opera by Caldara (1731), Darius *Milhaud's *Les Miracles de la Foi* (1951), and Benjamin Britten's *The Burning Fiery Furnace* (1966). To mark the coronation of the Austrian emperor Ferdinand I as king of Lombardy and Venice, a ballet entitled *Nabucodonoser* was performed at La Scala, Milan, on September 6, 1838. The Italian composer Giuseppe Verdi was in Milan at the time and subsequently found inspiring reading in T. Solera's libretto *Nabucodnosor,* which described the Babylonian king's enslavement of the Jews and the plight of the latter in their distant exile. *Va, pensiero . . .*, the chorus of the Hebrew captives in Solera's text, fired Verdi's dormant patriotism and the opera which he wrote, *Nabucco,* had its premiere at La Scala in 1842. Its performance created widespread enthusiasm in Italy, where the Hebrew captives' prayer for deliverance was seen as a comment on the country's state of subjugation to Austria, or as the lament of exiled Italian patriots. When *Nabucco* was staged at Her Majesty's Theater, London, in 1846, it was retitled *Nino* and the biblical characters renamed, since the stage performance of biblical subjects was then still taboo in England. *Nabucco,* translated into Hebrew by Aharon *Ashman, has often been performed by the Israel Opera since its foundation in 1958.

See also *Daniel in the Arts; *Jeremiah in the Arts; *Jerusalem in the Arts. [ED.]

Bibliography: Pritchard, Texts, 307–8; D. J. Wiseman, *Chronicles of Chaldaean Kings (626–556* B.C.) . . . (1956); Freedman, in: BASOR, 145 (1951), 31–32; A. Malamat, in: IEJ, 18 (1968), 137–55; idem, in: J. Abiram (ed.), *Yerushalayim le-Doroteha* (1969), 27–48 (Eng. section, 59). IN THE AGGADAH: Ginzberg, Legends, index. IN ISLAM: Ṭabarī, 15 (1328 A.H.), 17, 22, 23; Ṭabarī, *Ta'rīk,* 1 (1357 A.H.), 385 (according to the Bible); C. Shwarzbaum, *Adam-Noah Memorial Volume for A. N. Braun* (1960), 239–63. IN THE ARTS: L. Réau, *Iconographie de l'art chrétien,* 2 (1956), 406–9; *Metropolitan Opera News* (Dec. 3, 1960); G. Martin, *Verdi, his Music, Life and Times* (1963), 97–120.

NEBUZARADAN (Heb. נְבוּזַרְאֲדָן; Akk. **Nabû-zēr-iddina;** "Nabu has given offspring"), commander of *Nebuchadnezzar's guard who was in charge of the destruction of the Temple and the deportation of the people of Judah. Acting on orders, Nebuzaradan set fire to the city of Jerusalem and leveled its walls (II Kings 25:9ff.). Certain of the ecclesiastical, military, and civil officers and leading citizens who were supporters of *Zedekiah were brought before Nebuchadnezzar at Riblah and executed (25:20), and *Gedaliah son of Ahikam was placed in charge of the remaining population.

Five years later, Nebuzaradan deported another 745 people (Jer. 52:30).

The official title of Nebuzaradan is given as *sar ha-ṭabbaḥim*, although such a designation of a court official is unknown in Mesopotamian literature. The Septuagint translates the term as "chief cook or butcher." In an inscription from the time of Nebuchadnezzar II, the chief court officer is referred to as Nabû-zēr-iddina, whose official Babylonian title is *rab nuḫatimmê* (cf., talmudic Heb. *naḥtom*, "baker"). Scholars have thus identified this officer with Nebuzaradan, and assume that the biblical title is a translation of the Babylonian one. The Aramaic translations render the term as "chief butcher" or "slaughterer," and it is probable that this official belonged to the king's guards whose duty was the infliction of capital punishment.

In the Aggadah. Nebuzaradan's loyalty to his king is praised. He attached Nebuchadnezzar's portrait to his chariot, so that he might always feel that he stood in his presence. For the same reason he accepted the assignment to conquer Jerusalem, even though he had personally witnessed Sennacherib's defeat there (Sanh. 95a–96b). His success was due to divine aid. According to one Midrash, after three and a half years he was about to abandon the task but was advised by God to measure the city walls. As soon as he did so they began to sink in the ground and ultimately disappeared (Lam. R., introd. 30). According to another account he was on the point of returning home after all the axes but the one at his disposal had been broken in the attack on Jerusalem. At that moment a voice cried out: "the time has come for the Sanctuary to be destroyed and the Temple burnt," and with his last remaining ax he destroyed one of the city gates (Sanh. 96b).

When he led the exiles captive he commanded his soldiers not to touch married women captives, lest they provoke God's wrath (Lam. R. 5:11). He forbade the captives to pray, putting to death those who did so. When, however, they had crossed the Euphrates, he desisted since they were now beyond the territory under the dominion of Israel's God (*ibid.* 5:5). Nebuzaradan is identified with Arioch (Dan. 2:14), since he roared like a lion *(ari)* at his captives. When he saw the blood of the murdered Zechariah boiling (cf. II Chron. 24:22), he put to death in revenge the scholars, young priests, and 14,000 of the people, but still the blood did not rest. In despair he exclaimed: "I have destroyed the flower of them. Do you wish me to massacre them all?" The blood immediately subsided, but so stricken was Nebuzaradan with grief, that he exclaimed: "If they who killed only one person have been so severely punished, what will be my fate?" He thereupon became a righteous proselyte (Sanh. 96b).

Bibliography: J. Montgomery, *Kings* (ICC, 1951), 562; Bright, Hist, 309; EM, 5 (1968), 732. IN THE AGGADAH: Ginzberg, Legends, index; I. Ḥasida, *Ishei ha-Tanakh* (1964), 321–2.

[ED.]

NECO (or **Necoh; Wehemibre Neko II;** c. 609–593 B.C.E.), Twenty-fifth Dynasty king of Egypt, who played a major role in the fall of Judah. Marching to aid the Assyrians after the fall of Nineveh in 612, Neco found his passage blocked at Megiddo by King *Josiah (II Kings 23:29ff.; II Chron. 35:20–24). The defeat and death of Josiah there allowed Neco to consolidate and control Syria and Palestine as far as the Euphrates. He deposed *Jehoahaz, Josiah's successor, after a three-month reign and exiled him to Egypt (II Kings 23:31–35 and Jer. 22:10–12) replacing him with *Jehoiakim as an Egyptian puppet. The Babylonian conquerors of Assyria were quick to react. In 605 *Nebuchadnezzar, the son of Nabopolassar, "crossed the river to go against the Egyptian army . . . He accomplished their defeat and beat them into non-existence" (*Babylonian Chronicle*, ed. Wiseman, 25, 67–68), and "the king of Egypt did not come again out of his land, for the king of Babylon had taken all that belonged to the king of Egypt from the brook of Egypt to the river Euphrates" (II Kings 24:7). Judah and the other Egyptian vassals gained a brief respite, for the death of Nabopolassar compelled Nebuchadnezzar to abandon his victorious advance and hasten back to Babylon to secure the throne. The respite was short, and by the end of 604 the Babylonians were in Philistia. An Aramaic letter, found in Egypt, begging the Egyptian pharaoh for aid against the Babylonian invader, probably came from Ashkelon. Jehoiakim, willingly or not, defected to the Babylonians (II Kings 24:1), but rebelled after Nebuchadnezzar was checked by Neco at the Egyptian frontier in 601. Two years later he died (was perhaps assassinated) and was replaced by his son, *Jehoiachin. Within three months Jerusalem fell, and the royal family was exiled to Babylon (II Kings 24:10–17). In 593 Neco died, but his son Psammetichus II continued to incite Zedekiah, the new ruler of Judah, against Babylon. Egypt provided no assistance, however, when Jerusalem finally fell in 587.

Bibliography: P. G. Elgood, *The Later Dynasties of Egypt* (1951); Bright, Hist, index; A. H. Gardiner, *Egypt of the Pharaohs* (1961); D. J. Wiseman, *Chronicles of the Chaldean Kings* (1956).

[AL.R.S.]

NEDARIM (Heb. נְדָרִים; "Vows"), third tractate of the order *Nashim*, though in some editions the order varies. It is based upon Numbers 30 and deals mainly with the binding quality of the spoken vow by means of which a person may forbid the use of things to himself and his own property to others. The inclusion of this topic in the order dealing with family law arises, in part, from the right of the father to annul the vows of his daughter during her minority and the right of a husband to annul most or all of his wife's vows. The Mishnah consists of 11 chapters. Chapter 1 deals with the formulas which constitute binding vows and Chapter 2 with formulas that are not binding. Chapter 3 deals with vows not binding because of lack of serious intent, constraint, and the like, as well as the interpretation of certain vow formulas; there is an incidental digression on the importance of circumcision. Chapter 4 discusses the consequences of forbidding benefit to, or being forbidden benefit from, another person. Chapter 5 continues this subject in connection with the property of partners and of members of a community or people. Chapter 6 lays down guidelines for determining what is to be included in, and what excluded from, vows appertaining to produce. Chapter 7 continues this topic in connection with places and periods of time. Chapter 8 deals with the extension in time to be given to expressions connected with recurring events, and vows made in general language arising from some specific event. Chapter 9 deals with the absolution of vows, and the grounds on which such absolution may be granted.

It includes the following moving account (Mishnah 10): It once happened that a man vowed to have nothing to do with his niece (i.e., not to marry her because of her uncomely appearance). R. Ishmael took her into his household and had her treated cosmetically ("beautified her"). He then said to the uncle: "Was it against this woman that you took the vow?" He answered in the negative, and R. Ishmael released him from his vow. Whereupon R. Ishmael wept and said: "the daughters of Israel are comely, but poverty destroys their comeliness!" When R. Ishmael died the women of Israel lamented: "Ye women of Israel, weep for R. Ishmael."

Chapter 10 deals with revocation by both father and fiancé of the vows of an affianced maiden; women whose vows cannot be revoked; the impossibility of revoking vows

Detail illustrating the tractate *Nedarim* from a title page of a Hebrew-Latin edition of the Mishnah, with illustrations by Mich. Richey. Amsterdam, 1700–04. Jerusalem, J.N.U.L.

in advance; and the period allowed for such revocation. Chapter 11 treats of the type of vow that a husband can revoke: those which affect their relations or involve self-denial; vows of women not requiring revocation; and of women whose vows are not subject to revocation. *Nedarim* is a rich source for linguistic and syntactical usages in mishnaic Hebrew and is so used by the *Gemara.* The oldest stratum of this tractate including 1:3; 2:4; 3:4; 5:5 dates from the Second Temple period. *Mishnayot* 1:1; 7:1; 9:5–6; 11:4 are apparently derived from the *mishnayot* of Akiva while the rest of Mishnah *Nedarim* originated in the *mishnayot* of his disciples, Meir, Judah, and Yose. Chapter 4 belongs to Meir; 1:1; 3:6–10; 6:1; 7:5; 8:5–7; 9:1–8 belong to R. Judah, and the passages 3:1–5, 11; chapters 5; 1:1–7 belong to Yose who actually states that Elijah the Prophet taught him the section on *Nedarim* (Songs Zuta, ed. Schachter, 44; Buber 39; Epstein, Tanna'im 140–1). *Mishnah* 11:8 to the end of the tractate consists of supplements and glosses on the laws concerning vows. *Mishnah* 1:2 mentions several terms for vows about which the *amoraim* debate whether they were borrowed from foreign languages or were coined by the rabbis (10a). One of these terms, *"konam,"* was found in the Punic inscription of Ashmanezer, king of Sidon (4:20), meaning "curse" or "vow," but it is not certain whether this Phoenician word is connected with the mishnaic term (S. Lieberman, *Greek in Jewish Palestine* (1942), 129 n. 106). Many of the laws in *Nedarim* should be seen in light of the Hellenistic practices of that period (*ibid.,* 115–43).

The Tosefta consists of only seven chapters and many of the *mishnayot* of *Nedarim* have no corresponding comments in the Tosefta, nor does the order of the laws in this Tosefta always follow that of the Mishnah. On the other hand, the Tosefta gives several laws not included in the Mishnah.

There is a *Gemara* to *Nedarim* in both the Babylonian and the Jerusalem Talmuds. The Babylonian *Gemara,* as is the case with regard to the tractate *Nazir,* is written in a peculiar dialect and various theories have been propounded to explain it. Epstein is of the opinion that it originates in the academy of Maḥoza, and since very little of the Talmud of Maḥoza reached Sura or Pumbedita, the *geonim* overlooked this tractate. In fact, during the whole of the geonic period the study of *Nedarim* was neglected in the Babylonian academies (Yehudai Gaon; B. M. Lewin, *Ozar ha-Ge'onim,* 11 (1942), 23; cf. Adler Ms. no. 2639. See A. Marmorstein, in MGWJ, 67 .(1923), 134ff.). A. Weiss maintains that the differences are due solely to its neglect in the academies in later ages, and that it therefore lacked the benefits of final polishing given to the other tractates in the post-amoraic period, though he adds that it contains a certain amount of post-amoraic material, and regards the first two discussions as entirely savoraic. The Babylonian Talmud is usually printed with the commentary of Nissim Gerondi (the Ran) in addition to one attributed to Rashi, and with *tosafot* and the commentary of Jacob b. Asher. The text is not in very good condition and the commentaries contain many variant readings.

Aggadic Material. Both Talmuds, especially the Babylonian, are rich in aggadic material as exemplified by the following sayings: "The ancestors of the arrogant never stood on Mount Sinai" (20a); "If the people of Israel had not sinned, they would have been given only the Pentateuch and the Book of Joshua" (22b); "Why have scholars very often no learned children? In order that knowledge may not be thought transmissible by inheritance and that scholars may not pride themselves on an aristocracy of mind" (81a). Biblical scholars find interest in the Talmud's remarks on the masoretic division of the Bible into verses and on the *keri* and *ketiv* which do not entirely coincide with the existing masoretic text (37b–38a). The Jerusalem Talmud tells of letters which Judah ha-Nasi addressed to Hananiah, the nephew of Joshua b. Hananiah, to dissuade him from decreeing leap years abroad. The discussion that followed ends with the saying that "a small group in Ereẓ Israel is more precious to me than a Great Sanhedrin in the Diaspora" (6:13, 40a).

The talmudic tractate was translated into English in the Soncino edition by H. Freedman (1936).

See also *Vows.

Bibliography: Ḥ. Albeck, *Shishah Sidrei Mishnah, Seder Nashim* (1954), 137–46; idem, *Mavo la-Mishnah* (1959), 266; S. Lieberman, *Greek in Jewish Palestine* (1942), 115–43; Epstein, Tanna'im, 376–82; Epstein, Amora'im, 54–71; Halevy, Dorot, 3 (1923), 48f.; A. Weiss, *Al ha-Mishnah* (1969), 155–68; idem, *Hithavvut ha-Talmud bi-Shelemuto* (1943), 57–128; D. Halivni, *Mekorot u-Masorot* (1968), 263–352; Z. W. Rabinowitz, *Sha'arei Torat Bavel* (1961), 299ff.

[Ed.]

NE'EMAN, YUVAL (1925–), Israel physicist and one of the originators of the basic strategy of the Israel army. Ne'eman was born in Tel Aviv and graduated high school at the age of 15. He joined the Haganah, was brigade

Yuval Ne'eman, Israel physicist and army strategist. Courtesy Tel Aviv University.

operations officer at the Egyptian front, and held various other appointments during the War of Independence. From 1952 to 1954, Ne'eman was director of the general staff's planning branch and strongly influenced the strategy and organization of the Israel army. From 1955 to 1957, he served as deputy director (with the rank of colonel) of the intelligence division and in 1958 he was appointed defense attaché to the U.K. and Scandinavian countries. At that time he embarked upon his second career; he completed his studies in physics at the Imperial College in London. In his thesis he proposed a symmetry scheme, known as SU(3), for the classification of the elementary particles of nature. This theory, suggested independently by M. *Gell-Mann, was a major breakthrough in elementary particle physics. During 1961–63, Ne'eman was scientific director of the Soreq Research Establishment (Israel Atomic Energy Commission) and in 1965 he became professor of physics and head of the physics department at Tel Aviv University. He published numerous works in particle physics and received several awards, among them the Israel Prize in 1969. In 1971 he was chosen to succeed George S. Wise as president of Tel Aviv University. [D.Ho.]

NEGA'IM (Heb. נְגָעִים; "Plagues"), third tractate of the order *Tohorot* in the Mishnah and Tosefta. It deals with ritual uncleanness resulting from the plague referred to in Leviticus 13 and 14, which is usually translated as "leprosy." *Nega'im* consists of 14 chapters. Chapter 1 defines the colors and shades of the various symptoms of human leprosy. Chapter 2 discusses the time these symptoms may be inspected, the posture of the sufferer when being examined, and the person qualified to make the examination. Chapter 3 details when the examination can be postponed, the procedure when the examination is made by a non-priest, and the symptoms of the plague in persons, houses, and garments. Chapter 4 contrasts the various symptoms indicating uncleanness, and the consequence of different leprous signs appearing simultaneously or in succession. Chapter 5 deals with doubtful signs of leprosy and symptoms that disappear and reappear in the same or in changed form. Chapter 6 discusses the minimum sizes of leprous signs and the parts of the body in which the appearance of the symptoms do not give rise to uncleanness. Chapter 7 deals with spots that are clean and natural or induced changes during or after the inspection. Chapter 8 discusses when the symptom covers the whole body and chapter 9 the symptoms of the plagues termed "boil" and "burning" and their relationship to one another. Chapter 10 deals with scales, chapter 11 with the leprosy of garments, and chapter 12 with the uncleanness of houses. Chapter 13 continues with the uncleanness of houses and how they and a leper pass on uncleanness. Chapter 14 deals with the procedure at the leper's cleansing and at his offering of sacrifices.

Mishnah 3:5 is an ancient one as is shown by the fact that in 10:1, where it is repeated, its contents are disputed by R. Akiva and R. Johanan b. Nuri. Similarly, the subject matter of 5:3 as in *Eduyyot* 5:6, is a matter of dispute between Akavya b. Mahalalel and the Sages. *Mishnah* 8:10 is derived from a collection of *mishnayot* which follow the same stylistic pattern; "Sometimes a person can do something to his advantage and sometimes to his disadvantage" (cf. Tosef., Yev. 4:8; Ḥul. 5:5). *Mishnayot* 12:5–7 are in the form of halakhic Midrash, the laws being connected with their biblical proof verses. Z. Frankel considers all such midrashic *mishnayot* as relics of the ancient *mishnayot* of the *soferim*, but most other scholars disagree. *Mishnayot* 10:2 and 4 are identical in content but belong to two different sources. The Mishnah from the second source was quoted because it contained an addition. The fact that the editor recopied a whole Mishnah in order to utilize some additional material is indicative of his desire to refrain from modifying the original form of the *mishnayot*. According to Albeck, the editor of the Mishnah transferred a legal description from 9:3 to 11:3.

Priests inspecting possible cases of leprosy for ritual uncleanness. Engraving illustrating the tractate *Nega'im*, from a title page of the Hebrew-Latin edition of the Mishnah published in Amsterdam, 1700–04. Jerusalem, J.N.U.L.

The Tosefta to *Nega'im* has only nine chapters and contains details not found in the Mishnah, as well as several independent groups of laws. Two groups are found in this Tosefta, the first characterized by the legal formula, "One does not" (1:11–13), and the second group by its opening word "*netek*" (i.e., a bald spot on the head or beard, 4:2–6). *Tosefta* 6:1 cites an anonymous opinion stating that the laws concerning a house defiled by leprosy have only theoretical validity because such houses never existed and never will; other rabbis, however, cite cases of such houses. *Tosefta* 6:7 claims that leprosy is a punishment for the sins of gossip and haughtiness. The laws of *Nega'im* and *Oholot* were regarded as extremely complicated and difficult, and consequently the rabbis referred to them as prototypes of deep halakhic learning. Eleazar b. Azariah, for example, told Akiva: "Why do you deal with *aggadah?* Occupy yourself with *Nega'im* and *Oholot*" (Ḥag. 14a). It is also said that King David pleaded that his Psalms, the most spiritualized form of worship, be considered before God as *Nega'im* and *Oholot* (Mid. Ps. 1:8). *Nega'im* was translated into English in the Soncino Talmud by I. W. Slotki (1948).

Bibliography: Ḥ. Albeck, *Untersuchungen ueber die Redaktion der Mischna* (1923), 49f.; idem (ed.), *Shishah Sidrei Mishnah, Seder Tohorot* (1959), 195–8. [D.J.B.]

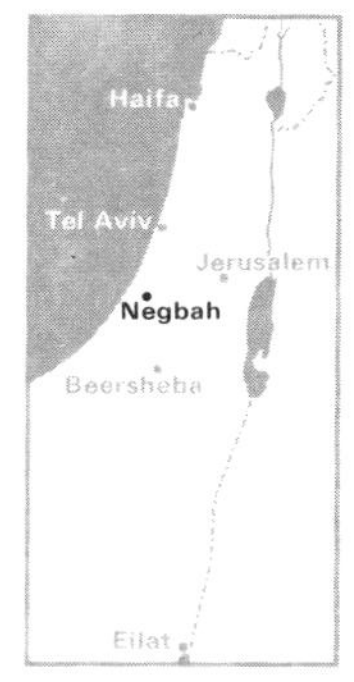

NEGBAH (Heb. נֶגְבָּה; "toward the Negev"), kibbutz in southern Israel, 6 mi. (10 km.) E. of Ashkelon, affiliated with Kibbutz Arẓi Ha-Shomer ha-Ẓa'ir. Negbah was founded by pioneers from Poland as a *stockade and watchtower settlement in the last month of the Arab riots (July 1939) and constituted the country's southernmost Jewish village at the time. As the kibbutz' name indicates, its establishment was the first of a systematic effort to gain footholds in the south and Negev. Isolated among strong Arab villages, Negbah had to repulse attacks in the first days of its existence. In the Israel *War of Independence (1948) the Egyptian army made all-out efforts to take the kibbutz. The settlers held out for six months in their entrenchments under continuous shelling, air bombardment, and tank attacks, after Egyptian forces occupied the nearby dominating Iraq Suweidān police fortress. The kibbutz was completely destroyed aboveground. The Egyptians, in violation of the local

Kibbutz Negbah on the day of its foundation as a stockade and watchtower settlement, July 1939. Courtesy J.N.F., Jerusalem.

cease-fire agreement, interfered with the passage of Israel convoys from Negbah to the Negev settlements and this led to the "Ten Plagues" Operation of the Israel army (Oct. 15, 1948); a strong Egyptian pocket continued to hold Negbah under fire until the police fortress fell on Nov. 9. The kibbutz preserved its ruined water tower in memory of the battles, and erected a monument to the defenders in its cemetery. After 1948 Negbah developed a flourishing farming economy based on intensive field and garden crops, citrus and other fruit orchards, and dairy cattle. It also established a sewing factory and a metal workshop. Its population in 1968 was 404. [E.O.]

NEGEV (Heb. נֶגֶב; from the root נגב, "dry," "parched"), an area comprising those southern parts of the Land of Israel which are characterized by a totally arid desert climate, contrasting with the semiarid Mediterranean climate of the country's center and north.

Geography. On the map describing an inverted triangle, with an apex directed to Eilat in the south, the Negev covers an area exceeding 4,600 sq. mi. (12,000 sq. km.), i.e., about half of western Palestine. Compared with other regions (Sinai excepted), distances in the Negev are considerable, exceeding 150 mi. (250 km.) from north to south, and 80 mi. (125 km.) from west to east. Whereas the Negev's northern border is a climatic one, roughly following the line of 12 in. (300 mm.) annual rainfall, the eastern border is a topographical one, sharply delineated by the Edom scarps emerging from the Arabah Valley, while in the west and southwest there is a gradual transition into Sinai. Structurally, the main partition of Cisjordan—into the Coastal Plain, the hills and the rift—continues into the Negev, with the following subregions recognizable: (1) the Negev Coastal Plain, linking up in the east with the Beersheba Basin; (2) the Negev Hills, composed of the northern and central hill regions, the Paran Plateau and the Eilat Mountains; (3) the Arabah Valley.

Geologically, most of the Negev hills resemble the hills of central and northern Israel, where folding constitutes the principal tectonic element and hard limestones and dolomites, or softer chalks with flint intercalations, are the predominant surface rock strata. Desert weathering, however, has imposed on these rocks dissimilar landscape features, which are mostly sharp and angular. The only exception are the Eilat Mountains, which, with their crystalline rocks and Nubian sandstones, form a continuation of the geological province of southern and southeastern Sinai. With the exception of the Beersheba Basin, arable soil is absent from practically all of the Negev, and wide expanses are covered with sharp flint or limestone gravel.

The Negev lies within the global subtropical desert belt of the northern hemisphere. Its climate is of the "continental" type and has two outstanding characteristics—sharp temperature differences between day and night, and summer and winter, and extremely limited amounts of precipitation, which diminish from an annual 10 in. (250 mm.) on the region's northwestern fringe to 2–4 in. (50–100 mm.) in most of its parts, and 1–2 in. (25–50 mm.) or less in the Arabah Valley and the Eilat area. Solar radiation and evaporation are strong during all seasons, and relative humidity and cloudiness remain low. Whereas the tempering influence of the Mediterranean Sea reaches inland for a score of miles at best, the Red Sea and the Eilat Gulf do not exert any such influence on the adjoining land.

The Negev's vegetation cover is universally sparse, and practically absent over large expanses. Most of the Beersheba Basin, together with the highest reaches of the central Negev Hills, falls within the Irano-Turanian semidesert zone, while the rest of the Negev belongs to the Arabian Zone, which has full desert characteristics. Similarly, the Negev has a desert fauna, including a number of indigenous species; its animal kingdom has somewhat increased in numbers due to nature-preservation measures in force since the 1950s. In the Beersheba Basin, which gradually rises eastward from 350 ft. (less than 100 m.) to 1,650 ft. (500 m.) above sea level, a thick cover of yellowish-brown loess, in sections of the west overlaid by coarse dune sands (the Ḥaluẓah, Shunrah, and Agur dunes), determines both landscape features and farming possibilities. In restricted areas, gullying by flashfloods resulted in a broken badland topography, which, however, has since the 1950s largely disappeared thanks to leveling in the framework of the soil reclamation program. Almost the entire Beersheba region belongs to the drainage basin of Naḥal Besor, which crosses it from southeast to northwest and receives three important tributaries from the east and

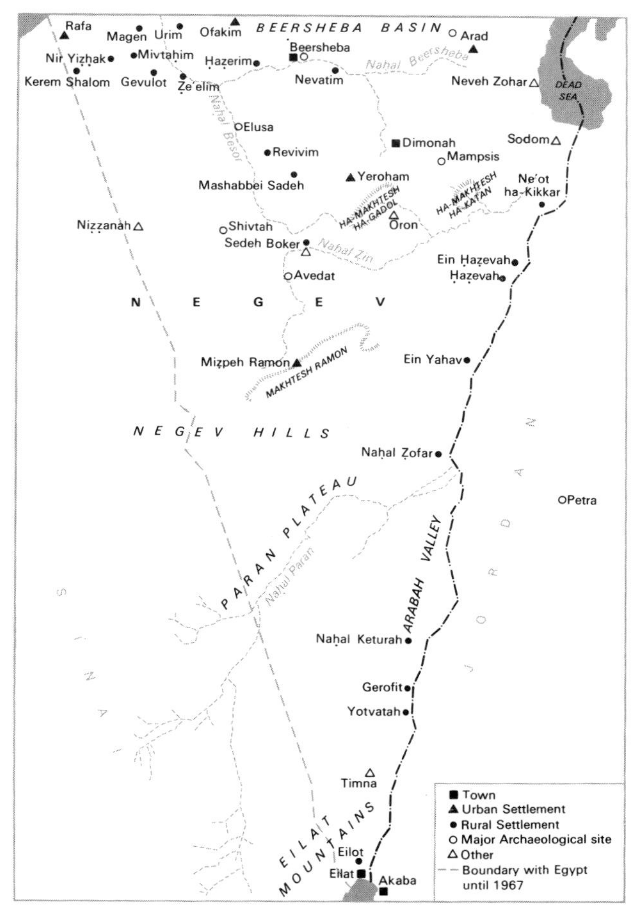

The Negev, ancient sites and modern settlements, 1971.

northeast—Naḥal Be'er Sheva, Naḥal Ḥevron, and Naḥal Gerar. The width of their beds bears no relation to the minute annual quantities of water running through them, which, at least during the last millennia, have been limited to occasional, short-lived winter floods.

Figure 1. Negev stamp issued by the Israel Post Office, 1950. Jerusalem.

In the central Negev Hills, whose folds attain heights of 3,000–3,400 ft. (900–1,035 m.) above sea level (Mt. Ramon, Mt. Sagi, Mt. Loẓ, Mt. Arif, and others), the most striking landscape feature is represented by the three huge erosional cirques (Makhtesh Ramon, Ha-Makhtesh ha-Gadol, Ha-Makhtesh ha-Katan). The wild Zin Canyon divides the hills into a northern and central section. The Paran Plateau, whose topography is more monotonous, is inclined from the southwest to the northeast, descending from 2,000 ft. (600 m.) to 330 ft. (100 m.). Naḥal Paran, the longest and most spectacular of Israel's desert wadis, runs through the plateau. Although the peaks of the Eilat Mountains attain heights of only 3,000 ft. (800–900 m.), the landscape of this area is truly mountainous and of infinite variety, with rock towers, indented and crenellated crests, between which narrow clefts cut in various directions. There is a wide range of igneous rocks (granites, diorites, quartz-porphyry, diabase, gneiss, quartzite, etc.), as well as vividly colored (ocher, yellow, rose, red, white, black and so on) Nubian sandstones, but also strongly contorted limestones and other marine sediments.

The Arabah Valley, that section of the rift extending from the Dead Sea to the Gulf of Eilat for 105 mi. (over 170 km.), is hemmed in by the continuous rock wall of Edom in the east and by the Negev Hills, of lesser height and uniformity, in the west. Its bottom ascends from 1,150 ft. (350 m.) below sea level in the Sedom salt flats over a relatively prominent step to 690 ft. (210 m.) below sea level near Ḥaẓevah, and thence continues to rise more gently to 755 ft. (230 m.), above sea level near the Sheluḥat Noẓah ridge, which protrudes into the valley 48 mi. (75 km.) north of Eilat; from that point southward, it gradually descends to the Eilat shore. The Arabah bears a cover of alluvium (sand, gravel, etc.) which obscures its rock foundations. Alluvial fans, mostly spreading in front of the Edom Mountains, obstruct the drainage of the southern Arabah and are the cause of the formation of playas (saline marshes), e.g., those of Eilat, Avronah, Yotvatah, and Sa'īdiyīn. The central and northern Arabah are drained by Naḥal ha-Aravah, which is the lower section of Naḥal Paran. Springs in the Arabah are mostly weak and brackish on the western, but stronger and sweeter on the eastern, rim. Deep well drillings in the 1960s yielded water in previously unsuspected quantities. [E.O.]

History. In the Bible, Negev refers to southern and southeastern Judah, an area split up between various groups, each of which is connected with a Negev of its own: Negev of Judah, around Beer-Sheba; Negev of Caleb, north of it; Negev of the Cherethites (Philistines), to the northwest; Negev of the Kenites, to the east; Negev of the Jerahmeelites, to the southeast. Today the name is applied to the whole southern region of Israel, extending from Beersheba to Eilat. In prehistoric times, the Negev was a well-watered and settled region, till the desiccation which accompanied the Mesolithic period. In the Chalcolithic period, a new culture developed along the dry river beds around Beer-Sheba, with pasture-bred animals, underground dwellings, and the beginning of exploitation of the Arabah copper mines for a metallurgic industry. A chain of short-lived settlements of a seminomadic, pastoral populace again appeared in various parts of the Negev in the intermediate period between the Early and Middle Bronze Ages (c. 2000 B.C.E.). The suggestion that these were situated along the main routes in the time of Abraham is refuted by most scholars. At the time of the Exodus, the Amalekites roamed in the southern part of the Negev, while the Canaanites of Arad held strongly to the north. Attempts by the Israelites to pass through the Negev on the direct route to Canaan ended in failure. The northern region is included within the boundaries of the land of Israel (Num. 34:4; Josh. 15:3). After Joshua's conquest, Simeon had a weak hold on the northern Negev centering around Beer-Sheba. Saul and David fended off the Amalekites, and Solomon and his successors set up fortresses to guard the routes to Elath and Egypt. Uzziah made the greatest effort to develop the Negev in the Israelite period, keeping up his communications with Elath through this region, and, apart from extending agriculture (II Chron. 26:10), building large fortresses at Kadesh, Arad, Ḥorvat 'Uza, and other sites.

Figure 2. Wadi al-Murrah near Sedeh Boker, in the northern Negev. Photo A. Strajmayster, Jerusalem.

Figure 3. Carved relief fragment from the Byzantine settlement at Ḥaluẓah in the northern Negev. Courtesy Israel Department of Antiquities, Jerusalem.

After the return from Babylonian exile, settlement in the area declined. Jewish connections with it in the post-biblical period are tenuous. The northern part was held by Alexander Yannai. It came under the control of the *Nabateans, who used its highways for travel from their capital Petra and from their port Aila (Elath) to Gaza and the shores of the Mediterranean. The Nabateans began to develop agriculture around certain spots in the Negev, including Avedat and Elusa, in order to provide water, as well as fodder and food, for their camels and men. Toward the end of Nabatean rule in the Negev, the area under cultivation had to be expanded in order to provide for the growing population, as is known from inscriptions around Avedat. After the annexation of Nabatea by Rome, the importance of the region declined; it revived toward the middle of the third century C.E. and entered its most prosperous era in antiquity, the late Roman and Byzantine periods. It has been estimated that at that time 40,000 dunams (10,000 acres) were under cultivation; this was mainly achieved by careful methods of dam building and distribution of rainwater by channels. Elusa, Subeita Nessana, Avedat, and Mampsis then stood in the Negev, and their ruins are still impressive. At that time, the Negev served as a transit area for those traveling to Elath and Sinai, as well as to Egypt. In the Arab period it declined and reverted to its desert state. Various biblical cities are today identified with tells in the northern Negev. [M.A.-Y.]

At the earliest stages of the modern Jewish return to the land, the Negev was visualized as a possible area of settlement by men like Z. D. *Levontin, who aimed at founding a settlement south of Gaza (1881–2). Like other Jews at the beginning of the 20th century, however, they had to abandon attempts at purchasing holdings, mainly because Bedouin vendors could not produce title deeds entered in the land registry for the tracts they offered. Attention was again directed to the Negev when Theodor *Herzl took up Davis *Trietsch's proposal of the *El-Arish Project (1903), and a daring plan for a Jewish-Bedouin alliance was also put forward. After World War I, veterans of the *Jewish Legion tried to settle on state land offered by the British authorities near the tell of Arad, but they despaired when no water was found. After the end of the 1930s, the *Jewish National Fund took over, securing and enlarging scattered holdings in the Negev which had been acquired beforehand by Jewish individuals. Thus the three "observation villages"—Gevulot, Beit Eshel, and Revivim—were set up in 1943, followed by 11 more villages established on the night of Oct. 6, 1946 and 4 more—preceding the outbreak of the War of Independence—in December 1947. All outposts were modestly supplied with water from two pipelines drawn from the Nir Am and Gevar'am wells in the southern Coastal Plain. In the 1949 Armistice Agreements with Egypt and Jordan, Israel's hold of the entire Negev was endorsed, with the single exception of the Gaza Strip. Whereas the Negev Bedouin population, of which about 15,000 remained in the Negev after 1948, increased to about 27,000 in 1969, Jewish settlement was the principal factor causing population density in the Beersheba subdistrict (whose borders are nearly identical with those of the Negev) to rise from 2.85 per sq. mi. (1.1 per sq. km.) in 1948 to 36.5 per sq. mi. (14.1 per sq. km.) in 1969; in the latter year, 180,400 inhabitants were counted, of whom 153,300 were Jews and 27,100 were Arabs.

Rural settlement quickly progressed as great efforts were invested in bringing mounting quantities of water to the Negev, first through the reconstituted pipelines from the Nir Am area in the 1950s, from the Yarkon springs ("Yarkon-Negev line"), and in the 1960s via the National Water Carrier. In the pattern of settlement comprising over 70 villages, three groups can be discerned: (1) the bulk of villages, mostly moshavim, concentrated in the northwestern Negev and arranged in regional projects (Benei Shim'on, Merḥavim, Eshkol regions); (2) security settlements, preponderantly kibbutzim, along the border of the Gaza Strip; (3) outpost settlements, of the kibbutz and moshav types (mostly in the Arabah Valley), which combine the task of border defense with pioneering new methods in desert and oasis farming. Agricultural initiative has brought citrus groves to the northwestern Negev and developed out-of-season vegetable and flower cultivation both in the western Negev (Eshkol region) and the Arabah Valley, while cotton, fodder crops, sugar beet (all irrigated), wheat, and other grain crops (the latter grown unirrigated or with auxiliary irrigation) are characteristic of the interior part of the northwestern Negev. A number of kibbutzim have also developed industrial enterprises.

Among urban settlements, the city of Beersheba has surpassed all other centers in growth and contains nearly 40% of the Negev's total population; second is Dimona on the Negev Hills; and third is Eilat. Other urban settlements have been established, in the northwest (Netivot, Ofakim) to serve as regional centers for agricultural areas and elsewhere to promote mining and industrial development (Arad, Yeroḥam, Miẓpeh Ramon). The Dead Sea minerals, as well as phosphates, copper, clay minerals, glass sand, and methane gas constitute the principal foundation for the Negev's industrial-development projects, whose important centers are the towns of Beersheba, Dimona, and Arad, the Oron and Ẓefa-Efeh phosphate mines, the factories under construction near the latter site, and the Timna Copper Works; the two latter sites, like the Sodom Dead Sea Works, however, have no resident population.

The communications network of the Negev is of great

Figure 4. Beduin children in the Negev, 1966. Courtesy J.N.F., Jerusalem.

Figure 5. Negev Brigade memorial designed by Danny Caravan, erected near Beersheba, 1968. Courtesy Government Press Office, Tel Aviv.

importance in the framework of Israel's economic infrastructure. Among highways, the Sodom-Eilat road is particularly busy. Second comes the Beersheba-Dimonah-Mizpeh Ramon-Eilat highway. The northern and western Negev has a well-developed road network. Railways link Beersheba with Kiryat Gat and Lydda in the north and with Dimonah and the Oron and Ẓefa-Efeh mines in the south; the building of a railway to Eilat is under consideration (1971). Another important economic asset is the Eilat-Ashkelon oil pipeline. Finally, the Eilat port and oilport are Israel's marine outlets to the south and east.

[E.O.]

Bibliography: C. L. Woolley and T. E. Lawrence, *The Wilderness of Zin* (1915); Y. Aharoni, in: IEJ, 8 (1958), 26ff.; 17 (1967), 1ff.; N. Glueck, *Rivers in the Desert* (1959); A. Negev, in: IEJ, 17 (1967), 46ff.; J. Braslavi (Braslavski), *Ha-Yadata et ha-Areẓ*, 2 (1947); idem, *El Eilat ve-el Yam Suf* (1952); D. H. Kallner-Amiran, in: IEJ, 1 (1950/51), 107–20; L. Picard, in: BRCI, 1 no. 1–2 (1951); 5–32; E. Loehnberg, *Ha-Negev ha-Raḥok* (1954); E. Orni and E. Efrat, *Geography of Israel* (1971[3]), ch. 2; Y. Morris, *Masters of the Desert (6000 Years in the Negev)* (1961).

NEGRO-JEWISH RELATIONS IN THE U.S. Jewish contact with blacks in the U.S. can be traced to the beginnings of the nation. Although Jews had only minimal contact with Negro slavery, some Jewish merchants in commercial centers such as *Newport were slave traders and Southern Jews owned and traded slaves. Rabbinical concern with slavery, however, did not appear until late 1860, the eve of the Civil War. Rabbi David *Einhorn of Baltimore emerged as the leading rabbinical abolitionist: he would not accept biblical slavery as a sanction for the "bestial" and dehumanizing U.S. slavery. Rabbi Morris J. *Raphall, replying, insisted that the Bible sanctioned slavery, though not its U.S. chattel variety. Rabbi Isaac Mayer *Wise was more upset with the radical abolitionists and their "warmongering" than with the slave owners. Southern rabbis, in conformity with their surroundings, supported slavery fully.

Early Defense of Civil Liberties. Not until the 20th century did U.S. Jews, who by then were much more numerous, play a substantial role in the struggle to protect the civil liberties of all U.S. citizens. In part, this was clearly

Civil rights march from Selma to Montgomery, Alabama, March 22–26, 1965. Abraham Joshua Heschel (with beard) is in the front row. To his right are Ralph Bunche, Martin Luther King, and Ralph D. Abernathy.

to protect their own rights, but it was also in defense of the values of democracy and liberalism. Up to the 1954 U.S. Supreme Court school desegregation decisions, white, and specifically Jewish, leadership played an important part in defending and helping the blacks; they were also active in the leadership of the originally radical black organization, the National Association for the Advancement of Colored People (N.A.A.C.P.). Julius *Rosenwald, an advocate of Booker T. Washington's philosophy of gradualism, underwrote 25 black YMCAs; was a trustee of Tuskegee Institute; and gave many millions for public schools and model housing for blacks. Jewish commitment to the anti-Washington wing of the N.A.A.C.P., which fought for immediate full, legal equality, is exemplified in the work of Joel E. *Spingarn and his brother Arthur B. *Spingarn, presidents, respectively, of the N.A.A.C.P. (1930–39; 1940–66). Louis *Marshall and Rabbi Stephen S. *Wise were also prominent among the early leaders. [B.Z.S.]

1954 and After. Soon after the 1954 Supreme Court decisions, the objectives of the blacks in the U.S. altered significantly and the demand for equality became more actively an effort to obtain social, economic, and political equality. This new thrust, which had its roots in the changed attitudes of the Korean War veterans who had served in the recently desegregated U.S. armed forces, became particularly significant for the Jewish community when in the early 1960s black students began a highly active civil rights movement. This movement gathered to it many young Jewish college students, who were in part led into Mississippi in the fall of 1963 by Allard K. *Lowenstein, later continuing their militancy in conjunction with the blacks in 1964–66. During this period Jewish student activism spread from involvement in Southern action with the Student Nonviolent Coordinating Committee (SNCC), the Congress of Racial Equality (CORE), and Martin Luther King's Southern Christian Leadership Conference (S.C.L.C.) to the Northern ghettos, first in concert with black organizations and later independently.

The breakdown of active Jewish participation in the civil rights movement must be attributed to more than growing black militancy and the black disillusionment with white society. After John F. *Kennedy's assassination in 1963 and Lyndon B. *Johnson's sponsorship of the civil rights and poverty legislation in 1964–66, a bitter disenchantment by both white and black students with the white establishment began to take root. The legislation, which aroused hope in the black community, failed to receive the necessary funds in the U.S. Congress, while it swept away the momentum of the civil rights movement and thus in effect bequeathed a hollow victory. Disillusioned and further alienated from white society, the black militants became more strident in their rhetoric, and a few expressed anti-Semitic opinions. Their heavy financial support from Jewish sources was forfeited. White student radicals turned to the Vietnam war as an expression of the ills of U.S. society. Jews became increasingly unwelcome as front line participants in the black civil rights organizations. By this time violence and urban destruction by blacks began to affect the urban Northern Jewish communities directly.

Relations in the Northern Urban Community. Having come into intimate urban contact with blacks after the massive black migrations which followed World War I and which brought blacks from the U.S. South to the North into what had been the Jewish districts, U.S. Jews stood near the central problem of contemporary U.S. society. While some Jews shared the prejudices of other white Americans, it was evident through 1954 that there was a strong Jewish commitment to legal equality. With the black demand for immediate integration in the large cities which focused on the public schools, "backlash," or more properly the legitimation of latent racism, emerged as a new phenomenon. Black anti-Semitism, which has historic Christian roots, began to grow. It was argued that black anti-Semitism was essentially anti-whitism, based on real situations in which a Jew often was the only white in the black neighborhood—as shop owner, landlord, social worker, teacher, Nevertheless, the U.S. urban crisis of the 1960s inextricably involved the relationship of blacks with Jews. The New York City teachers strike of 1968–69 exemplified the eruption of latent fears in both communities, as did the Jewish Defense League (J.D.L.) which began to grow from 1967. Jewish attitudes toward the blacks changed perceptibly as a result of civil disorders and the increase in violent contacts between blacks and Jews, as well as the publicity given to black anti-Semitism and the disfavor which whites (and especially Jews) found in civil rights organizations.

The Legal Battle. Jewish legal involvement in the cause for civil rights and civil liberties was particularly marked during the 1960s. Jack Greenberg of the Legal Defense Fund of the N.A.A.C.P., William Kunstler of the National Lawyers' Guild, Carl Rachlin of the Congress of Racial Equality, and other individual Jewish lawyers participated heavily in helping the civil rights movement handle its huge case load, later giving way to many black lawyers who had themselves been among the student demonstrators. Nevertheless, Jewish legal involvement was more than just a defense of black rights, and it continued to play a significant role as a bond between the black and Jewish communities. The militancy of the black community and the scare of black anti-Semitism was rejected by such black moderate leaders as Bayard Rustin, A. Phillip Randolph, and Roy Wilkins.

See also *Black Jews; *New Left. [Y.B.D.]

Bibliography: S. Katz (ed.), *Negro and Jew* (1967); B. Z. and M. L. Sobel in: *Judaism*, 15 (1966), 3–22; L. P. Gartner, in: *Conservative Judaism*, 20 no. 3 (1966), 42–49; G. T. Marx, *Protest and Prejudice* (1967); B. Korn, in AJHSP, 50 (1961), 151–201; E. Raad, in: *Commentary*, 47 (Jan., 1969), 23–33; N. Glazer, *ibid.*, 47 (April 1969), 33–39; M. Mayer, *Teachers' Strike: New York, 1968* (1969); Selected bibliography on Negro-Jewish Relations (publ. American Jewish Committee, 1966); N. Hentoff (ed.), *Black Anti-Semitism and Jewish Racism* (1969).

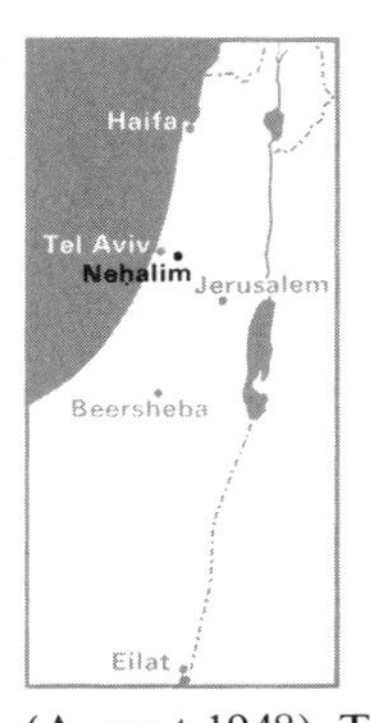

NEḤALIM (Heb. נְחָלִים; "streams"), moshav in central Israel, near Lydda (Lod) airport, affiliated with Ha-Po'el ha-Mizrachi moshavim association. Originally founded by veteran farm laborers in 1943 in the Ḥuleh Valley (where its name, referring to the Jordan River headstreams, was chosen) the moshav was largely destroyed in the Israel War of Independence and the settlers were transferred to the present site on the land of the former German colony, Wilhelma (August 1948). There, the group was joined by settlers from moshav Neveh Ya'akov, north of Jerusalem, which had to be given up in May 1948. Later, new immigrants from Hungary and Poland joined the moshav. Neḥalim had 710 inhabitants in 1969, part of them staff and pupils of a yeshivah which was opened in 1958. The village economy is based on intensive and fully irrigated farming. [E.O.]

NEHARDEA, town in Babylon, situated on the Euphrates at its junction with the Malka River, which was an important Jewish center and seat of a famous academy. Nehardea was surrounded by walls and by the Euphrates River, preventing its penetration by enemies (Jos., Ant., 18:311). The Jewish settlement of Nehardea was an early one. The first settlers were, according to tradition, those exiled in the time of Jehoiachin, king of Judah in the sixth century B.C.E. These exiles erected there a synagogue which they built with stones and earth brought from the site of the Temple. The synagogue was called Shaf ve-Yativ, i.e., "[the Divine Presence has] removed [from the Temple] and settled [in this place]" (*Iggeret Rav Sherira Ga'on,* ed. by B. M. Lewin (1921), 72 and appendices). The existence of its Jewish settlement in the century before the destruction of the Temple is attested by the fact that the Jews of Babylon concentrated in it the half-shekel offering and their donations and offerings for the Temple and dispatched them from there to Jerusalem (Jos., *ibid.*). Josephus also relates the exploits of *Anilaus and Asinaus who were natives of Nehardea. At the beginning of the second century C.E., Akiva visited Nehardea and there intercalated the year, thus testifying to the importance of the local Jewish settlements (Yev. 15:7). Nehardea was also the seat of the exilarch and his *bet din.* The town attained the zenith of its influence in the first half of the third century in the days of *Samuel, who headed its academy, and its influence was widespread (Ket. 54a). Of the scholars active there at the beginning of the amoraic period, Karna, Shila, and Abba b. Abba (Samuel's father) were noteworthy. The academy of Nehardea was destroyed in 259 by Papa b. Nezer and its scholars moved to *Pumbedita. When spiritual activity was renewed there many important scholars were active in it, including Dimi and Amemar. [Y.D.G.]

The Arab Period. There is no extant information on a Jewish settlement in Nehardea during the Arab period. Even after the town was rebuilt, the academy did not return there. Its memory was preserved in Pumbedita, however, by the fact that a group of sages who sat in one of the first three rows of the academy was referred to as "the row of Nehardea." In his responsum to R. Moses b. Meshullam of Mainz, *Elijah b. Solomon ha-Kohen refers to the academy of Sura by the name of Nehardea. In connection with a question on the custom of saying the prayer of *Ve-Hassi'enu* on Rosh Ha-Shanah and the Day of Atonement, the *gaon* replied: "Heaven forbid that there be a difference over this matter, because it is our custom in the two *metivta* (academies) in Erez Israel and Nehardea, that *Ve-Hassi'enu* is said on Rosh Ha-Shanah and the Day of Atonement." B. M. Lewin has pointed out that the reference was to Sura, where this custom prevailed, in contrast to Pumbedita, where it did not. On the other hand, for Sherira, Nehardea was synonymous with the academy of Pumbedita because it was the continuation of Nehardea. In connection with the customs of prayer he writes: "the custom is according to the established *battei midrash* of Nehardea and Sura" (B. M. Lewin (ed.), *Ginzei Kedem,* 1 (1922), 5–6). Benjamin of Tudela, who visited Iraq during the 1170s, also identifies Pumbedita with Nehardea. [EL.B.]

Bibliography: M. D. Judelevicz, *Hayyei ha-Yehudim bi-Zeman ha-Talmud, Sefer Nehardea* (1905); Funk, in: *Festschrift . . . D. Hoffmann* (1914), 97–104; J. Obermeyer, *Die Landschaft Babylonien . . .* (1929), 353 (index), s.v.; Neusner, Babylonia, indices. THE ARAB PERIOD: B. M. Lewin (ed.), *Iggeret R. Sherira Ga'on* (1921), 72–73, 100–1; Abramson, Merkazim, 44, 156; Assaf, Ge'onim, 45, 51; R. S. Weinberg, in: *Sinai,* 65 (1969), 71; Benjamin of Tudela, *Massa'ot . . .* ed. by M. N. Adler (1907, 1960), 46; Levin Ozar, 1 (1928), 34, 125; 3 (1931), 28; A. Epstein, in: MGWJ, 47 (1903), 344; Mann, Texts, 1 (1931), 89–90, 103–4; J. Mann, in: JQR, 11 (1920/21), 437.

NEHAR PEKOD, town in the district of Nehardea (Babylonia). Nehar Pekod gained note after the *tanna* R. Hananiah, the nephew of the *tanna* R. Joshua b. Hananiah, settled there following the suppression of the Bar Kokhba revolt in Erez Israel (Sanh. 32b). The town seems to have rapidly developed into a major center of Jewish life. R. Hananiah tried to establish a *bet midrash* and a Sanhedrin with the authority to continue the practice of intercalating years and fixing months, an authority which was a privilege of Erez Israel (see Ber. 63a–b; Sanh. 32b; TJ, Sanh. 1:1, 19a). The reactivated leadership in Erez Israel immediately intervened and quashed this separatist move. After the death of R. Hananiah, who was buried in Nehar Pekod, there is no further information on the town.

Bibliography: A. Berliner, *Beitraege zur Geographie und Ethnographie Babyloniens im Talmud und Midrasch,* in: *Jahres-Bericht des Rabbiner-Seminars zu Berlin pro 5643 (1882–1883),* 52; J. Obermeyer, *Die Landschaft Babylonien im Zeitalter des Talmuds und des Gaonats* (1929), 270–6; Neusner, History, 1–2 (1965–66), index. [E.HI.]

NEHAVEND (Nahavand), town in W. central Iran, in the ancient province of Media. The town is mentioned in the Talmud together with Hulvan (Halah) and *Hamadan as belonging to the "cities of Media" to which the Israelites were exiled in the time of the Assyrian kings (Kid. 72a). Nehavend gained prominence in Jewish history as a Karaite center, the birthplace of Benjamin b. Moses *Nahawendi, who is regarded as second only to *Anan. Continuing to exist throughout the centuries, the Jewish community is mentioned among those which were searched for hidden magic Hebrew books during the persecutions of *Abbas I. Its Jewish population was estimated at 500 in the 1960s. [W.J.F.]

NEHEMIAH (Heb. נְחֶמְיָה; "YHWH has comforted": fifth century B.C.E.), cupbearer of *Artaxerxes I and later governor of Judah. Nothing is known of the parentage of Nehemiah except that he was the son of Hacaliah. Two other persons of that name are mentioned in the Bible: one returned with Zerubbabel (Ezra 2:2; Neh. 7:7), and the other, a son of Azbuk, was the chief of half the district of Beth-Zur and helped in rebuilding the wall of Jerusalem (Neh. 3:16). Nehemiah the son of Hacaliah was a high official at the Persian court of Artaxerxes I, perhaps a eunuch (cf. LXX^B, Neh. 1:11, *eunochos* for *oinochoos* of LXX^A). Origen considers Nehemiah, the king's cupbearer, and his eunuch as one person. E. Weidner (see bibl.) has pointed out the importance of the cupbearer at the Assyrian court which, according to Herodotus (3:34), continued at the Persian court.

Being a trusted Jew, though a layman, Nehemiah was, at his own request, placed in charge of a very important and delicate mission—that of the governorship of Judah which involved rebuilding the walls of Jerusalem and reorganizing the Judean province. He was thus invested with great authority which he wielded with distinction and propriety. The first tasks to which he set himself with great zeal were providing protection for Judah by restoring the walls of the capital, and erecting houses for its population so that all aspects of the community could function more smoothly. Though he suffered almost continuous interference from the governor of Samaria, and perhaps from those of Ammon, Arabia, and Ashdod (6:1–9), he was sufficiently astute to avoid serious conflict, probably because he used his authority wisely and gained the confidence of his fellow Jews. Having achieved his primary objective, he next devoted himself to establishing order and justice in the community (7:1–3). Conscious of his position as a layman

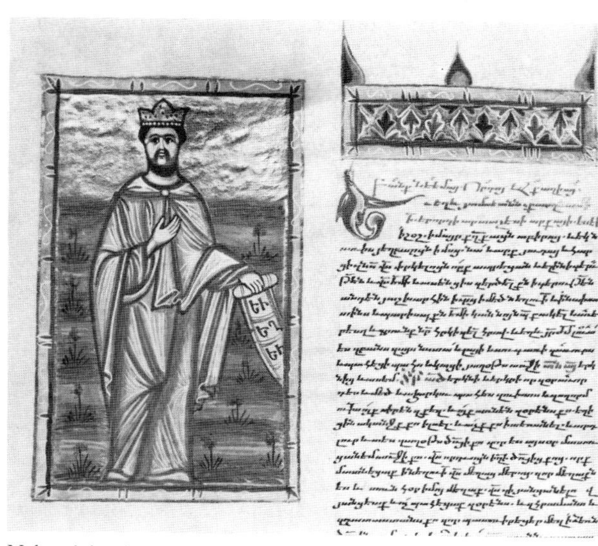
Nehemiah depicted in an Armenian manuscript Bible from Constantinople, 1649/1653. Jerusalem, Armenian Patriarchate, Ms. 1927, fol. 207b.

(and perhaps, eunuch), he submitted to the religious regulations of his time but was himself a profoundly religious man as is evident from his concern for the levites (13:10–14), his conception of the sanctity of the Temple as shown in the Tobiah affair (13:4–9), his appreciation of the Sabbath (10:32; 13:15–21), and his provision for offerings (10:33–40). It is of interest that he had drawn up his memoirs, which were doubtless placed in the Temple precincts as an inscription of his deeds and works.

Nehemiah is praised by Ben Sira (49:12b–13) and in II Maccabees 1:18, 20–36. Josephus (Ant. 11:159–74) embellished the story of Nehemiah but the Talmud and the Church Fathers were not so complimentary. The date of Nehemiah's first period of service (5:14) extended from the 20th to the 32nd year of Artaxerxes I (i.e., c. 445–433 B.C.E.). The length of his second period (13:6–7) is not stated.

See also *Exile, Babylonian; *Ezra and Nehemiah; *History. [J.M.M.]

In the Aggadah. Nehemiah is identified with *Zerubbabel, the latter name being considered as indicative of his Babylonian birth (Heb. זְרוּעַ בָּבֶל, "conceived in Babylon"; Sanh. 38a). He was called Tirshatha (Neh. 8:9) because the authorities absolved him *(hittir)* from the prohibition against gentile wine, permitting him, as cupbearer to the king, to drink *(shatah)* with him (TJ, Kid. 4:1, 65b). The strict rabbinic enactment prohibiting the handling of most vessels or utensils on the Sabbath was attributed to Nehemiah as a means of counteracting the laxity in Sabbath observance during his period (Shab. 123b; Neh. 13:15). The sages did not call the Book of Nehemiah by his name and referred to it as the second part of Ezra because Nehemiah utilized a seemingly vain expression (Neh. 5:19) and also spoke disparagingly of his predecessors, who included Daniel (Neh. 5:15; Sanh. 93b). Nehemiah completed the Book of Chronicles which was started by Ezra (BB 15a). [A.Ro.]

Bibliography: F. James, *Personalities of the Old Testament* (1943), 443–61; E. Weider, in: AFO, 17 (1956), 264–5; F. L. Moriarty, *Introducing the Old Testament* (1960), 189–201; S. Mowinckel, *Studien zu dem Buche Ezra-Nehemia*, 2 (1964), 76–83; J. M. Meyers (ed.), *Ezra-Nehemiah* (1965), 53–56, 74–77. IN THE AGGADAH: Ginzberg, Legends, 4 (1947[5]), 352; 6 (1946[3]), 438–9.

NEHEMIAH (middle of second century C.E.), *tanna*. Nehemiah was one of Akiva's outstanding disciples. The Talmud (Sanh. 86a) states that סְתָם תּוֹסֶפְתָּא ר׳ נְחֶמְיָה *(setam tosefta Rabbi Neḥemyah)*: this is generally explained as meaning that he is the author of all anonymous statements in the *Tosefta, but the explanation is doubtful. He was one of the few pupils of Akiva to outlive the Bar Kokhba revolt, and on the easing of the Hadrianic persecution took part in the activity for the renewal of the teaching of the Torah (Gen. R. 61:3; Eccles. R. 11:6). Nehemiah was one of the five ordained by Judah b. Bava at the cost of his life (Sanh. 14a). When the remaining scholars gathered at Usha to reconstruct the religious life of the people, Nehemiah was one of the speakers (Song R. 2:5, no. 3). He was also active at Bet Rimmon when the renewed calendar arrangements were made (TJ, Ḥag. 3:1), and took part in the convention of Jabneh (Ber. 63b). His name is mentioned 16 times in the Mishnah (Ma'as. 3:5; Shab. 8:4, etc.), frequently in *beraitot*, as well as both in *halakhah* (Ber. 38a; Shab. 98b) and in *aggadah* (BB 15a; Mak. 11a). The grammatical rule that the suffix ה to a noun is equivalent to the prefix ל is attributed to him (Yev 13b). He studied Merkabah mysticism (Shab. 80b), and, in the name of his father, transmitted a statement on the creation (Pes. 54a). Among his aggadic sayings are: "Beloved is suffering. For just as sacrifices bring atonement so does suffering" (Sif. Deut. 32). Another is: "A single individual is as important as the whole of creation" (ARN[1] 31, p. 46). According to the Jerusalem Talmud (Ta'an. 4:2, 88a) he was descended from the biblical Nehemiah. He lived in great poverty and on one occasion shared his pottage of lentils with a poor man, who died from eating such scant fare (Ket. 67b). He worked as a potter (TJ, BM 6:8, 11a).

Bibliography: J. Bruell, *Mevo ha-Mishnah*, 1 (1876), 198–200; Frankel, Mishnah (1923[2]), 185f., 222 n. 5, 324; Bacher, Tann; Hyman, Toledot, 924–6; Ḥ. Albeck, *Meḥkarim ba-Beraita ve-Tosefta* (1944), 63–65, 183; Epstein, Tanna'im, 241f. [ED.]

NEHEMIAH BAR KOHEN ẒEDEK (tenth century), *gaon* of the Pumbedita academy from 960 to 968; son of R. *Kohen Zedek, who also held this post. His brother R. *Hophni was the father of R. *Samuel b. Hophni. R. *Sherira Gaon tells of the controversy between R. Nehemiah and *Aaron b. Joseph ha-Kohen Sarjado which arose several years after R. Aaron Sarjado had been appointed *gaon* of Pumbedita (943); it appears that the original cause of the controversy was R. *Mubashshir b. R. Kimoi's appointment of R. Aaron as president of his *bet din*, an appointment which Kohen Ẓedek viewed with disfavor. The struggle between Nehemiah and Aaron Sarjado broke out after the death of R. *Amram, president of R. Aaron's *bet din;* Aaron wished to appoint R. *Sherira in Amram's place, while Nehemiah contended that the position was properly his. Failing to achieve his aim, Nehemiah set himself up as *gaon* in rivalry with R. Aaron. In 960, when Aaron Sarjado died, Nehemiah officially succeeded him as *gaon* of Pumbedita, and his brother Hophni was the president of his *bet din*. Sherira Gaon refused to recognize Nehemiah's appointment as *gaon*, although he did not suggest himself as *gaon* in his stead. Apparently he did not want to undermine the foundations of the gaonate. After the death of R. Hophni in 962, however, the two men agreed that Sherira Gaon would serve as Nehemiah's *av bet din*, and after the latter's death in 968, Sherira Gaon succeeded him as the *gaon* of Pumbedita. Nothing remains of Nehemiah's teachings or responsa; only a number of letters survive.

Bibliography: B. M. Lewin (ed.), *Iggeret R. Sherira Ga'on* (1921), 121, 132–4; Cowley, in: JQR, 19 (1906/07), 104–6; J. Mann, *ibid.*, 8 (1917/18), 341–7; Mann, Texts, 1 (1931), 75–83; idem, in: *Tarbiz*, 5 (1933/34), 174–6. [A.D.]

NEHEMIAH HA-KOHEN (17th century), Polish kabbalist, apparently born in Lvov. His personality remains obscure, though certain details emerge from the sometimes contradictory sources. Late in the month of Av, 1666, he arrived at the fortress in Gallipoli, Turkey, where *Shabbetai Ẓevi was imprisoned, and visited him there early in the month of Ellul. In his memoirs Loeb b. Ozer quotes information that he heard from Nehemiah concerning his disputation with Shabbetai Ẓevi, indicating that Nehemiah rejected the latter's messianic pretensions. According to Christian sources, however, Nehemiah claimed that he himself was Messiah ben Joseph and remonstrated with Shabbetai Ẓevi for announcing himself as Messiah ben David before Messiah ben Joseph had started out on his journey of tribulations. Hence for the first time Shabbetai Ẓevi found himself on the defensive before a man who, unlike all his other visitors, was not overwhelmed by him. I. Sonne questions the truth of the story about the disputation, considering it improbable that in an atmosphere of messianic tension anyone should, in the presence of the Messiah, cast doubts on the very fact of his being Messiah. After three days Nehemiah despaired of Shabbetai Ẓevi, and notified the authorities of the fortress of his own intention of converting to Islam. From there he repaired to Adrianople, where he complained to the civil authorities that Shabbetai was an impostor. Shabbetai was then brought before the sultan, in whose presence he too was converted to Islam. Having passed on his information to the Turkish authorities, Nehemiah returned at once to Lvov and to the religion of his fathers. His activities caused an uproar throughout Poland: some vindicated them, since their sole intention was to bring an end to the specious doings of Shabbetai Ẓevi, while others disapproved, since Nehemiah's activities had terminated the great messianic awakening. Nehemiah, however, was obliged to wander from place to place, ultimately leaving Poland in about 1675, excommunicated and outcast. He even changed his name to Jacob in an attempt to obscure his identity. His persecution presumably stemmed from the bitterness of the Jews of Poland and Germany, and their disillusionment with the messianic movement.

Bibliography: G. Scholem, in: *Beit Yisrael be-Polin*, 2 (1953), 44–45; idem, *Shabbetai Ẓevi*, 2 (1952), 554–64, 566–7; I. Sonne, in: *Sefunot*, 3–4 (1960), 62–66. [A.D.]

NEHER, ANDRÉ (1913–), scholar and philosopher; born in Obernai (Alsace). After having taught German in a high school before and some years after World War II, Neher spent the war years together with his father Albert Neher, his elder brother, Judge Richard Neher, and the rest of his family, dedicating his time to intensive Jewish studies. After the liberation of France, Neher emerged as a highly original and captivating thinker, and quickly became one of the spiritual leaders of the young intellectuals of the French-speaking world, preaching ideals of reasoned belief and of respect for tradition. After being appointed to the chair of Jewish Studies at the University of Strasbourg, he contributed to the development among the local Jewish community of deep feelings of responsibility toward the Jewish people in the world and toward the State of Israel in particular. Algerian Jews who came to Strasbourg found a warm welcome there, as a result of Neher's interest in them. Respected in all quarters, Neher was able to convince the local Catholic and Protestant leaders of the legitimacy of Jewish aspirations, including Zionism, and this had its repercussions at various national and international conventions.

Neher took part in various initiatives on behalf of Israel in the Diaspora. He established himself in Jerusalem,

André Neher (second from right) at a reception for Shmuel Yosef Agnon (left) at the Hebrew Institute of the University of Strasbourg, December 1966. The rector of the university, Mr. Bayen, is on the right. Courtesy J.N.U.L., Jerusalem.

dividing his time between the University of Strasbourg and academic activity in Israel (mostly at Tel Aviv University). The moving force of his philosophy is the "alliance" of God with Man, and in particular with the People of Israel. Neher found in the teachings of Judah Loew b. Bezalel (Maharal) a guide and inspiration.

His principal works include: *Transcendance et immanence* (1946; with Richard Neher); *Amos, contribution à l'étude du prophétisme* (1950); *Notes sur Qohèlèt* (1951); *L'Essence du prophétisme* (1955); *Moïse et la vocation juive* (1956); *Jerémie* (1960); *Histoire biblique du peuple d'Israël* (2 vols., 1962; with Renée Neher-Bernheim); *L'Existence juive* (1962), a collection of articles; *Le Puits de l'exil—la théologie dialectique du Maharal de Prague* (1966); *De l'hébreu au français* (1969); *Etincelles, textes rabbiniques traduits et commentés* (1970; with Abraham Epstein and Emile Sebban).

His wife RENÉE NEHER-BERNHEIM (1922–), historian, was born in Paris. She wrote *Le Judaïsme dans le monde romain* (1959), *Histoire juive de la Renaissance à nos jours* (2 vols., 1963–65), and *La Déclaration Balfour* (1969). [M.C.]

NEHORAH (Heb. נְהוֹרָה; "light"), rural center in southern Israel established in 1956 in the framework of the *Lachish regional development, to service a bloc of moshavim, comprising Nogah, Zohar, Oẓem, Shaḥar, and Nir Ḥen. Nehorah had 131 inhabitants in 1970. [E.O.]

NEHORAI (middle of second century C.E.), *tanna*. Nehorai is referred to three times in the Mishnah, once in *Nazir* 9:5, mentioning that Samuel was a Nazirite; once in *Avot* 4:14, where he says, "Exile thyself to a place of Torah; and say not it will come after thee or that thy companions will assist thee to maintain it; and lean not upon thine own understanding"; and lastly in *Kiddushin* 4:14, where he states, "I would disregard all other crafts and teach my son only Torah. For man enjoys its reward in this world, while its principal remains to him for the world to come." He is referred to further, although rarely, in *beraitot* scattered throughout the Talmud (Ber. 53b; Sanh. 20b, et al.) and in the tannaitic literature (Mekh. Pisḥa 12). Most of his statements are aggadic. Worthy of mention is his statement: "In the generation of the advent of the Messiah, young men will insult the old, and old men will rise in the presence of the young; daughters will rise against their mothers and daughters-in-law against their mothers-in-law. The face of the generation will be as the face of a dog, and a son will not be abashed in the presence of his father" (Sanh. 97a). In two places, however (Shab. 60b and Naz. 5a), he deals with *halakhah*, and in support of the second he quotes a biblical interpretation of R. Joshua. According to one tradition (Shab. 147b) his real name was either Nehemiah or Eleazar b. Arakh, but he was called Nehorai ("light") because he enlightened the eyes of his colleagues in knowledge of *halakhah*. He was a member of the synod of Usha (cf. RH 22b). The statement (Er. 13b) that Meir is the same as Nehorai must be understood as meaning that although R. Meir's real name was Nehorai, he was perhaps called Meir so as not to confuse him with this Nehorai, since he is found together with Meir in *Avot* 4:10 and in *Kiddushin* 4:14 they are both mentioned in the same Mishnah.

Bibliography: Hyman, Toledot, 918f.; Bacher, Tann, 2 (1890), 377–83.

[D.J.B.]

NEḤUNYA BEN HA-KANAH (second half of first century), *tanna*. Neḥunya was highly regarded by Johanan b. Zakkai, who was apparently his teacher (see BB 10b; but cf. Avot 2:8). He was a native of Emmaus in Judea and is therefore referred to as Neḥunya b. ha-Kanah of Emmaus by the *Tanḥuma* (Deut. to 26:13) which cites a halakhic discussion between him and Joshua b. Ḥananiah. The Tosefta (BK 7:18 and parallels in the TB) quotes a *halakhah* in his name, and he is mentioned as disputing with R. Eliezer and R. Joshua in *Ḥullin* (129b; but cf. Eduy. 6:3 and 4; it is possible that Neḥunya b. Elinathan of Kefar ha-Bavli is intended). Among his outstanding pupils was *Ishmael, who received from Neḥunya his rules for interpreting the Torah, and, like him, interpreted the whole Torah in accordance with the hermeneutical rule of *kelal u-ferat* ("general propositions and particulars"), in contrast to Akiva, who interpreted it according to the principle of *ribbui u-mi'ut* ("extension and limitation"), the method of Naḥum Ish Gimzo (Shevu. 26a; see *Hermeneutics).

Neḥunya was distinguished by his noble character, his acts of benevolence, and his relations with his fellows. When his pupils asked him by what virtue he had attained old age, he replied: "Never in my life have I sought honor through the degradation of my fellow, nor has the curse of my fellow gone up with me upon my bed [i.e., he forgave all who had vexed him before retiring to sleep], and I have been generous with my money" (Meg. 28a). The prayers he uttered on entering and leaving the house of study are revealing: "On entering what did he say? 'May it be Thy will, Oh Lord, that I become not impatient with my fellows and that they become not impatient with me, that we declare not the clean unclean nor the unclean clean . . . so that I be not put to shame both in this world and in the world to come.' On his departure what did he say? 'I give thanks to Thee, O Lord, that thou hast set my portion with those who sit in houses of study and in synagogues and not with those who sit in theaters and circuses. For I toil and they toil. I am industrious and they are industrious. I toil to possess the Garden of Eden and they toil for the pit of destruction'" (TJ, Ber. 4:2, 7d; cf. Ber. 28b for variant readings). He expressed his view of Torah study as a bulwark against the calamities and hardships of his time in his dictum: "He who takes upon himself the yoke of Torah will have the yoke of worldly care removed from him; but he who casts off the yoke of Torah will have placed upon him the yoke of the kingdom and the yoke of worldly care" (Avot 3:5). The scholars of the Kabbalah attributed to him several mystical works such as the *Sefer ha-Bahir*. The prayer **Anna be-Kho'aḥ* (based upon the Divine Name of 42 letters) is also ascribed to him.

Bibliography: Hyman, Toledot, 923; Frankel, Mishnah, 105; Bacher, Tann, 1 (1903²), index; J. Bruell, *Mevo ha-Mishnah*, 1 (1876), 94.

[Y.D.G.]

NEHUSHTAN (Heb. נְחֻשְׁתָּן), the name of the *copper serpent which King Hezekiah broke into pieces (II Kings 18:4). Since the smashing of the copper serpent parallels the shattering of the pillars and the cutting down of the Asherah *(ibid.)*, it was probably located in the Temple court in Jerusalem. It was thus one of the cultic symbols of the people who assembled in the Temple courts. Like the local shrines *(bamot)*, however, and like the two other objects named in the verse, it was illegitimate in the Deuteronomic view, in accordance with which, Hezekiah abolished the former and destroyed the latter *(ibid.)*. The Nehushtan probably stood in the Temple court, and the people believed that it had the power of curing sicknesses. In this respect the copper serpent differed from the *cherubim, whose location was in the innermost sanctum of the Temple, hidden from human sight. Some scholars hold that the copper serpent in Jerusalem was set near "the stone of Zoheleth ("the crawler's [i.e., serpent's] stone"), which is beside En-Rogel" (I Kings 1:9), that is, outside the Temple enclosure. However, there are no grounds for connecting the copper serpent with the stone of Zoheleth. At the latter, sheep and oxen were sacrificed *(ibid.)*, whereas only meal-offerings were offered to the copper serpent.

The account in Numbers 21:6–9 states that its form was that of a *saraf*, traditionally, a "fiery serpent." It probably had wings, for so *serafim* are described in the Bible (cf. Isa. 14:29; 30:6). Herodotus (2:75; 3:109) also states that in his day people told of the existence of flying serpents in the Arabian desert.

Scholars assume that the copper serpent entered the Israelite cult as a Canaanite heritage and only popular belief ascribed it to Moses. M. Noth contends that this tradition is somewhat later than the others associated with the Exodus from Egypt, since it can only have arisen after David had captured Jerusalem. H. Gressmann suggested that Moses adopted the copper serpent from the Midianites but this has been rejected by other scholars.

See also *Copper Serpent.

Bibliography: T. Noeldeke, in: ZDMG, 12 (1888), 482; H. Gressmann, *Mose und seine Zeit* (1913), 284–5; W. F. Albright, in: AJSLL, 36 (1920), 258–94; S. A. Cook, *The Religion of Ancient Palestine in the Light of Archaeology* (1930), 98ff., 117–20; M. Noth, *Ueberlieferungsgeschichte des Pentateuch* (1948), 133–4; M. Haran, in: VT, 10 (1960), 117–8.

[M.Ha.]

NEḤUTEI (**Naḥutei**; Aram. נְחוּתֵאי, נָחוֹתֵאי, sing. נְחוּתָא *Neḥuta;* "one who goes down"), rabbis who went from Ereẓ Israel academies to those of Babylonia, or vice-versa. The name was first applied to *Ulla, a native of Ereẓ Israel in the third century C.E. (TJ, Kil. 9:4, 32c). He was given this epithet because from time to time he "went down" from Ereẓ Israel to Babylonia and had discussions in Babylonia with the heads of its academies and its scholars. Rav *Ḥisda referred to Ulla as "our teacher who came down from Ereẓ Israel" (Ber. 38b; see *Dikdukei Soferim*). When he came to Babylonia, Ulla brought with him the halakhic and aggadic sayings of Johanan and Eleazar, the heads of the academy of Tiberias at that time. He also described the customs and ways of the Jews of Israel, and evoked historical memories and popular sayings current among them. He used to compare the customs current among the Jews of Babylonia with those current in Ereẓ Israel. Generally he gave preference to the customs of Ereẓ Israel, and more than once uttered caustic comments about the Jews and scholars of Babylonia (Ta'an. 9b). In the first half of the fourth century the name *neḥutei* was given to a few scholars, born apparently in Babylonia, who traveled to the academies of Ereẓ Israel and brought back with them the teachings of its scholars. The best known of them were *Dimi, Samuel b. Judah, Rabin, and *Isaac b. Joseph. The purpose of their activity was to transmit the teachings of Ereẓ Israel to Babylonia, and vice versa. Through their activity, the texts of the Mishnah and the *beraitot* and their exact meaning were established, and the halakhic and aggadic sayings of the first *amoraim* of Ereẓ Israel, such as *Ḥanina, *Johanan, *Eleazar, and *Simeon b. Lakish in Tiberias and *Abbahu in Caesarea, and of the first *amoraim* of Babylonia, such as *Rav and *Samuel, *Huna and *Ḥisda, and others, were elucidated.

By their activities the *neḥutei* contributed to the cross-fertilization of the academies of Ereẓ Israel and Babylonia. Their words were tested in the academies and compared with parallel traditions and in this way they attempted to arrive at the precise implication of the statements, their truth, and their reliability. In this way the *neḥutei* made their contribution to the formation and elucidation of many topics in the Babylonian Talmud. As a result of the connections established by the *neḥutei* between the academies of Ereẓ Israel and Babylonia the mutual knowledge of the two large Jewish communities was increased, and so the Oral Law was prevented from developing separately with the two communities becoming two nations, alien one to another. The scholars mentioned were especially active in two academies—in Tiberias in Ereẓ Israel and in Pumbedita in Babylonia. References are found at times to the *neḥutei* informing Babylonia of various *halakhot* by means of letters (Git. 9b). These scholars were active until the middle of the fourth century C.E. In the opinion of *Sherira Gaon (*Iggeret . . .*, ed. B. Lewin, p. 61) their mission ceased because of the increase of restrictive edicts in Ereẓ Israel and the decrease of Torah there. The reference is apparently to the restrictive edicts of Constantius (377–361) in the 340s and 350s and the revolt by a section of the Jews of Ereẓ Israel against Gallus in 351.

Bibliography: Halevy, Dorot, 2 (1923), 467ff.; A. Steinsaltz, in: *Talpioth*, 9 (1964), 294–306. [M.BE.]

NE'ILAH (Heb. נְעִילָה), a worship service deriving from the ritual of the Second Temple, but subsequently recited only on the Day of Atonement as its concluding rite (see Ta'an. 4:1; Ta'an. 26b and TJ, Ta'an. 4:167c; TJ, Ber. 4:1, 7b–c; Yoma 87b and TJ, Yoma 8:8, 45c). It was originally recited on all public fast days, in addition to the Day of Atonement. It also concluded the daily *Ma'amadot* (see **Mishmarot* and *Ma'amadot*), where laymen from provincial communities prayed with their priestly delegates in Jerusalem. The full name of the service is *Ne'ilat She'arim* ("Closing of the Gates"), referring to the daily closing of the Temple gates. On the Day of Atonement this literal closing *(ne'ilat sha'arei heikhal)* was associated with the symbolic closing of the heavenly gates, which remained open to prayer until sunset *(ne'ilat sha'arei shamayim)*. Throughout the year, according to the Talmud, *Ne'ilah* was recited one hour before sunset, when the Temple Gates were closed; on the Day of Atonement, because of its length, *Ne'ilah* did not begin until close to sunset. Once *Ne'ilah* was limited to the Day of Atonement, it began before twilight and ended at nightfall.

By the third century *Ne'ilah* consisted of an **Amidah* of seven benedictions, parallel to the other statutory services of the day. It likewise featured confession of sins. *Attah yode'a razei olam* ("Thou knowest the secrets of the world"), however, and **Al Ḥet* were replaced by two prayers unique to the confession in the *Ne'ilah* service: *Attah noten yad le-foshe'im* ("Thou stretchest forth Thy hand [in forgiveness] to sinners") and *Attah hivdalta enosh* ("Thou has distinguished man [from the beast]"). These recapitulate the biblical-talmudic doctrine that God eagerly forgives the truly penitent. In accordance with the rabbinic idea that the divine judgment, inscribed on *Rosh Ha-Shanah, is not sealed until the Day of Atonement ends, the word to "inscribe" (כתב, *ktv*) (in the Book of Life) is amended to "seal" (חתם, *ḥtm*). To set it off from the preceding *Minḥah* service, *Ne'ilah* is prefaced by *Ashrei* (Ps. 145) and *U-Va le-Ẓiyyon Go'el*, which ordinarily introduce *Minḥah*.

Ne'ilah was eventually embellished with sacred poetry, especially *Seliḥot*. Impressive melodies heightened the emotional impact of *Ne'ilah*. The central motif is exhortation to make a final effort to seek forgiveness before the heavenly gates close at sunset. Yet the overall tone is one of confidence, especially in the final litany. The service proper concludes with **Avinu Malkenu* and **Kaddish*. The entire ritual culminates in responsive proclamations of **Shema*, followed by *Barukh shem kevod malkhuto*, and "The Lord, He is God" (I Kings 18:39). A single *shofar* blast announces the end of the "Sabbath of Sabbaths."

Bibliography: M. Arzt, *Justice and Mercy* (1963), 271–86; L. Ginzberg, *Perushim ve-Ḥiddushim ba-Yerushalmi*, 3 (1941), 67–108; Morgenstern, in: HUCA, 6 (1929), 12–37; E. Munk, *World of Prayer*, 2 (1963), 262–7. [H.KI.]

Illuminated page of the *Ne'ilah* service from the *Leipzig Maḥzor*, Vol. II, S. Germany, c. 1320. Leipzig University Library, Ms. V 1102, fol. 176r.

NEILSON, JULIA (1868–1957), English romantic actress. Born in London, Julia was the daughter of Alexander Ritchie Neilson and Emily Davis, and was a cousin of three other well-known actresses of the Davis family, Lily Hanbury, Hilda Jacobson, and Nora Kerin. She made her first appearance in W. S. Gilbert's *Pygmalion and Galatea*, in 1888, toured with Beerbohm Tree in 1889, and acted with him at the Theatre Royal, Haymarket, for five years. In 1890 she married Fred Terry, brother of the celebrated Ellen Terry. Julia became famous for her acting in such plays as *A Woman of No Importance*, *The Prisoner of Zenda*, *Sweet Nell of Old Drury*, and *The Scarlet Pimpernel*. Her greatest success was as Rosalind in *As You Like It* (1896). She visited the U.S. in 1895 and again in 1910. In 1900, she and her husband went into management and for the next 30 years played and toured with their own company. Both their children, Dennis (1895–1932) and Phyllis (1892–), acted under the name of Neilson-Terry. Neilson's memoirs, *This for Remembrance*, were published in 1940. [Ed.]

NEISSER, HANS PHILIPP (1895–), economist. Born in Breslau, from 1922 to 1927 Neisser served on various government economic commissions and edited the economic weekly *Wirtschaft*. In 1927 he began to teach at Kiel and was at the same time director of the Institute for World Economy. Emigrating to the U.S. in 1933, he was professor of monetary theory at the University of Pennsylvania from 1933 to 1943. During the last two years of this period he headed the division of research at the U.S. Office of Price Administration in Washington. From 1943 to 1965 he was professor of economics at the New School for Social Research in New York City. His major interests were general economic theory, international economics, and monetary and banking developments. His publications include: *Der Tauschwert des Geldes* (1928); *Some International Aspects of the Business Cycle* (1936); *National Incomes and International Trade* (with F. Modigliani, 1953); and *On the Sociology of Knowledge, an Essay* (1965). [J.O.R.]

°**NEKLYUDOV, NICOLAI ADRIANOVICH** (1840–1896), Russian criminologist, counsellor to the Ministry of Justice. From 1877 Neklyudov served as member of the committee for the advancement of the economic status of the Jews. In 1880 he, together with V. D. Karpov (an official of the Ministry of Interior), submitted a memorandum to the committee refuting the charge that the Jews were engaged in unproductive activities and exploited the non-Jewish population. Neklyudov stood for the emancipation of the Jews, advocating the dissolution of the *Pale of Settlement. Such a step, he averred, would be advantageous to the non-Jewish population through the development of trade and commerce in the interior of Russia. At the same time he argued that "Reason does not justify placing a population of several millions in the same category as criminals." No action was taken on his proposal, as the committee was soon dismissed. [Ed.]

NELSON, BENJAMIN (1911–), U.S. sociologist. Born in New York, Nelson taught at the universities of Chicago and Minnesota and the State University of New York, and was professor of sociology and history at the New School for Social Research. Nelson's chief interest was in the sociological approaches to history and in the sociology of psychoanalysis and the arts. Among his numerous publications were *The Legend of the Divine Surety and the Jewish Money Lender*, *The Idea of Usury*, *From Tribal Brotherhood to Universal Otherhood* (1949); he also edited *Freud and the Twentieth Century* (1958). [W.J.C.]

NELSON, LEONHARD (1882–1927), German philosopher, a descendant of Moses Mendelssohn. Born in Berlin, he was baptized while a child. He became lecturer in philosophy in the faculty of natural sciences at Goettingen in 1909 and professor in 1919. He founded the "New Fries School," which, following J. F. Fries (1793–1873) and using psychological method, wanted to renew Kant's teaching, but on a basis entirely different from that of the Neo-Kantians. To provide a forum for this school, Nelson founded the "Discussion groups of the Fries School" (1904–08), and published many articles, the most famous of which is *"Die Unmoeglichkleit der Erkenntnistheorie"*; the English version of which appeared in the collection of his articles *Socratic Method and Critical Philosophy* (1949). His main interest was in ethics, and his own ethics are close to those of Kant but without sharing their severe pendantry. Nelson developed his ethics in *Vorlesungen ueber die Grundlagen der Ethik*, 3 vols. (1917–32). Volume 1 dealt with the bases of ethics, volume 2 with pedagogy, and volume 3 is devoted to the philosophy of law and politics. In politics Nelson was close to moderate Socialism, similar to that of Franz *Oppenheimer. The principles of society's existence cannot be surrendered to majority decisions, since this would abandon them to arbitrariness and chance, for one cannot be certain that the majority even knows what is best for it. His students issued some of his unpublished lectures, among them the great work *Fortschritte und Rueckschritte der Philosophie; von Hume und Kant bis Hegel und Fries* (1962), edited by Julius Kraft. A list of his works is to be found in *L. Nelson zum Gedaechtnis* (1953).

Bibliography: H. Falkenfeld, *Kantstudien* (1928), 247–55; *Encyclopedia of Philosophy*, 5 (1967), 463–7; B. Selchow, *L. Nelson, ein Bild seines Lebens* (1938). [Sh.H.B.]

NELSON, LOUIS (1895–1969), U.S. labor leader. Born in Kharkov, Russia, Nelson emigrated to the United States with his family as a young child. He left school at the age of 12 to work in the needle trade, joining the Raincoat Makers' Union and then the Amalgamated Clothing Workers as a tailor. A member of the Young People's Socialist League and affiliated with the left wing of the Socialist movement, he was active in opposition to the Amalgamated leadership. He was expelled from Amalgamated in the early 1920s, became a dressmaker in a dress shop and worked with the dual, Communist-controlled union, the Needle Trades Industrial Union. Later he reappraised his own position and came to believe that the small shop, which he had supported, permitted employers to avoid enforcing union conditions and that the installation of machines had in fact preserved jobs in those shops where they were installed. Nelson rejoined the International Ladies' Garment Workers' Union in 1931 and took an active part in the successful dressmakers' strike of 1933. In the following year he became manager of Local 155, the Knit Goods Workers' Union, an industrial local with a membership of under 1,000. As manager of this union for 35 years, Nelson built it up to one of the strongest and most responsible of the ILGWU locals and by 1969 it had a membership of about 14,000. In 1952 he was elected a vice-president of the ILGWU and served in that post until his death.

Long interested in Yiddish culture and education, Nelson supported the Folksbine theater and the work of YIVO. By the 1960s the membership of Local 155 was no longer primarily Jewish but Nelson continued to arrange the appearance of Jewish artists and singers before the local's members. He was prime mover in the establishment of the Jewish Labor Committee. A non-Zionist, he supported the Bund position in regard to a Jewish state. [Ed.]

NEMIROV (Pol. **Niemirów**), town in Vinnitsa oblast, Ukrainian S.S.R. It was annexed by Russia after the second

The Great Synagogue of Nemirov, erected in the early 18th century.

partition of Poland (1793), and was incorporated in the district of Podolia until the Russian Revolution. Under Polish rule it was a fortified city of considerable importance. A Jewish settlement in Nemirov is first mentioned in 1603. In the 1630s, Yom Tov Lipmann *Heller held rabbinical office there for a while. During the *Chmielnicki persecutions of 1648 thousands of Jews from other localities sought refuge in Nemirov; however, the city fell to the Cossacks, who massacred the Jews. The slaughter at Nemirov, one of the worst of that period, created a profound impression, becoming a symbol of all the terrible massacres the Jews suffered at the hands of cruel rioters. Reports and legends spread about the heroic acts of the Jews of Nemirov who chose martyrdom (see **Kiddush ha-Shem*), and rabbis and *paytanim* composed special *kinot* and *seliḥot* on the destruction of the community. At a meeting of the *Council of the Lands held in 1650, the anniversary of the massacre (20th of Sivan) was proclaimed a day of mourning and public fasting. Jews resettled in Nemirov after the town was retaken by the Poles and their situation was especially satisfactory under the Turkish rule over Podolia (1672–99). At the beginning of the 18th century the Great Synagogue was erected. Early in the 19th century, Nemirov became a center for the Ḥasidim of *Naḥman of Bratslav. In 1765, 602 Jewish poll tax payers were registered; the Jewish population increased from 4,386 in 1847 to 5,287 (59.3% of the total population) in 1897. In 1917 a democratic community headed by the Zionists was established, but with the consolidation of the Soviet régime it was liquidated. During the Russian Civil War, the Jews also suffered, but largely because of good relations with their Christian neighbors, they were spared from massacres. There were 4,176 Jews (57.2% of the population) living in Nemirov in 1926. After the German occupation during World War II (1941), the Jews of Nemirov, as well as Jewish refugees from Bessarabia, were deported for extermination in three "actions" which took place in November 1941, June 1942, and May 1943.

Bibliography: N. N. Hannover, *Yeven Meẓulah* (1966), 37–40; H. J. Gurland, *Le-Korot ha-Gezerot al Yisrael*, 1–6 (1887–89); M. N. Litinsky, *Sefer Korot Podolya ve-Kadmoniyyot ha-Yehudim Sham* (1895), 43, 45–49; Y. P. Pograbinski, in: *Reshumot*, 3 (1923), 195–214; idem, in: *Arim ve-Immahot be-Yisrael*, 2 (1948), 270–83.

[Y.S.]

NEMOY, LEON (1901–), scholar and librarian. Born in Balta, Russia, Nemoy studied classical and Slavic languages at the University of Odessa. After moving to the U.S. in 1923, he studied Semitic languages at Yale University (1924–29). He served as a librarian at the Society for the Propagation of Knowledge, Odessa, Russia (1914–21), the Academic Library of Odessa (1919–21), and the University Library of Lvov, Poland (1922–23) before assuming his duties at Yale in 1923. Rising to the post of curator of Hebrew and Arabic literature at Yale's Sterling Memorial Library, upon his retirement he became scholar-in-residence at Dropsie University, Philadelphia. Nemoy's scholarly activities were mainly devoted to research on the history of the *Karaites. His major work is his edition of the Arabic text of al-*Kirkisānī's *Kitāb al-Anwār wa-al Maraqib* (5 vols., 1939–43). He also translated a valuable collection of Karaite texts into English from Arabic, Hebrew, and Aramaic (*Karaite Anthology*, 1952), with introduction and annotations. He contributed numerous articles on Arabic philology, Karaite subjects, and the history of Jewish and Arabic medicine to various scholarly journals. He also published a catalog of the Hebrew and Yiddish books donated by Sholem *Asch to Yale (*Catalogue of Hebrew and Yiddish Manuscripts and Books from the Library of Sholem Asch*, 1945). Nemoy was one of the editors of the *Yale Judaica Series*. [M.Sch.]

NEMŢEANU, BARBU (originally **Benjamin Deutsch;** 1887–1919), Rumanian poet. Born in Galatz, Nemţeanu was the son of a teacher at the local Jewish elementary school. From 1907 onward his own verse, as well as translations of foreign poetry, appeared in Bucharest literary journals such as *Viaţa Nouă* and *Flacăra*, and the Jewish periodicals *Mântuirea* and *Lumea evree*. His collection of verses, *Stropi de soare* ("Drops of Sunshine," 1915) was warmly received by leading critics. Not a profound poet, he wrote lyrical verse about love and everyday life which was touched with light humor. He is better known for his translations from Victor Hugo, Baudelaire, Oscar Wilde, *Lessing, and, above all, *Heine, whose *Hebrew Melodies* appeared posthumously in his Rumanian translation in 1919. He also translated Yiddish works by Eliezer *Steinberg and Jacob *Groper. Nemţeanu died of tuberculosis at the age of 32.

Bibliography: E. Lovinescu, *Istoria Literaturii Române Contemporane*, 3 (1927), 223–5; G. Călinescu, *Istoria Literaturii Romîne* ... (1941), 630–1.

[A.Fe.]

NEO-ARAMAIC, general name for the various branches of spoken Aramaic, both western and eastern. Three groups of dialects are known. The first includes the dialects of Maʿlūla, a continuation of the western branch of Middle Aramaic, spoken by Christians and Muslims in three villages about 60 km. (38 mi.) north of Damascus. The second comprises the dialects spoken by Christians in the Ṭūr ʿAbdīn area in the Mardin region of southern Turkey. These dialects occupy an intermediate position between the first group and the third, the Aramaic dialects that are the continuation of the eastern branch of Middle Aramaic and are used in Kurdistan in the area on the common border of Iraq, Persia, and Turkey. Christians and Jews speak these dialects. Most of the Jews have immigrated to Israel; the Christians to the United States and Russia. The recently discovered spoken dialect of the Mandeans in Persia has a special position in the third group.

The Jewish dialects can be divided into three groups: (1) The dialects spoken in northwest Iraq (Iraqi Kurdistan). The most important settlements are Nerwa, ʿAmadiya, Zāxō, and Dehōk, to which Jezira in Turkey should be added. The dialects of this group are particularly important for historical-linguistic study, since they clearly resemble Ancient Aramaic, in pronunciation, forms, and vocabulary. (2) (Persian) Azerbaijan. The most important settlements are Salmas (Shahpur), Urmia (Rizaiyah), Naġada (Solduz), Ushnuiyeh (Šinno), to which Bašqala in Turkey should be added. (3) Persian Kurdistan. The most important settlements are Sablaġ (Mahabad), Saqqiz, Bokan, Bana, and Senna, and the Iraqi towns of Rawanduz, Irbil, Sulaymaniya (before Iraq was established as an independent political entity after World War I, it was part of the Ottoman Empire).

From the Middle Ages Jews are known to have spoken Aramaic in Kurdistan. Some scholars hold that Aramaic was not the original language of some of these Jews, but that they adopted it after their emigration (from Persia?) to the Aramaic-speaking areas. Perhaps not all the Jews from this area spoke Aramaic. The census takers did not distinguish between Jews who spoke Aramaic and those who spoke other languages. It appears that in the cities where Arabic (or Turkish) rule was strong the Jews adopted the language of their surroundings, after a period of bilingualism. Jews from places where, according to travelers, Aramaic was still spoken in the 19th century, did not bring this language with them to Israel. Immigrants from Irbil exemplify this process: both Arabic and Aramaic are the everyday language of the older generation.

When the State of Israel was established the total number of Aramaic-speaking Jews was estimated at 20,000; most of them are now in Israel, grouped largely according to their provenance. The Jews (especially from Persia and Turkey) have called their language the "language of the Targum." Other names are "the language of the Jews" and "Jabali." In Israel this language is commonly called Kurdi, even though this is the scientific name for the Iranian language of the Muslim Kurds. It seems that rabbinic scholars on rare occasions called this language Aramaic, as can be seen in two manuscripts, one from the beginning of the 18th century, the other from the beginning of the 20th. The scientific name given this language is "Eastern Neo-Aramaic" or "modern Syriac" (the latter suitable to the Christian dialects). The Christians who use this language consider Syriac the language from which their language evolved, but there is no linguistic proof for this contention.

From the historical-linguistic point of view it is assumed that the eastern dialects of Neo-Aramaic developed from a language similar to Babylonian talmudic Aramaic and Mandaic, but there are no documents extant in this language since it was not used as a literary vehicle. Similarly, the exact connection between eastern Neo-Aramaic and the Aramaic of the Babylonian Jews before they began speaking Arabic is unknown.

An idea may be obtained of some of the major features of these dialects by a description of the dialect as spoken in Zāxō, which is of particular importance for historical-linguistic study.

Phonology. The glottal stop, ʾ, parallels three consonants of Ancient Aramaic, א, ע, גֿ. ʾ from ע (or גֿ) is always retained, while the ʾ from א is liable to disappear in certain situations: *ʾurxa* ("road"), *burxa* ("on the road") as against *ʾisra* ("ten") and *bʾisra* ("by ten"). This is important in determining the etymological origin of a particular ʾ. ח is pronounced as *x* (= כֿ).

The phonemes of *b, g, d, k, p, t* which in Ancient Aramaic, as in Hebrew, had two variants each, have attained phonemic status in the modern dialects for each of their variants. The spiranted and *dageš* forms appear in all environments and are not conditioned by the accepted rules of Ancient Aramaic, for example, the ת of שתי, יתב is always given the hard pronunciation, even though it was spiranted in Ancient Aramaic under certain conditions.

The following is the transposition of *b, g, d, k, t* in Neo-Aramaic: בֿ = *w;* גֿ (through ע) = ר; כֿ = *x;* דֿ = *z;* תֿ = *s*. The different pronunciations of דֿ and תֿ in the various dialects serve as a criterion for differentiating them.

As in Eastern Syriac, the phoneme פ is always pronounced *p*. In all the Jewish dialects, however, *f* is found only in loanwords, while in most of the Christian dialects *f* is replaced by *p*.

An. Ar.	Zāxō	Dehōk	ʿAmadiya	Urmia	Irbil
ידֿא "hand"	*ʾīza*	*ʾīḏa*	*ʾīda*	*īda*	*īla*
ביתֿא "house"	*bēsa*	*bēṯa*	*bēṯa*	*bēla*	*bēla*

In loanwords the phonemes ʾ, *ḥ*, ʿ, *ġ*, *č*, *j*, *ž* are also found. The diphthongs in Ancient Aramaic have become monophthongized: *ay* > *ē* (בֵּיתָא > *bēsa*), *aw* > *ō* (יְוֹמָא > *yōma*). The same is true for diphthongs originating in Neo-Aramaic as a result of the בֿ > *w* shift: חָבְלָא *xōla*. The doubling of consonants has largely been eliminated and replaced by the lengthening of the preceding vowel, as יַמָּא > *jāma*.

Morphology. The new status constructus is formed by adding the suffix *it* to the noun base: *baxta* ("a woman"); *baxtit axōna* ("the brother's wife"). In the plural there is no differentiation of gender in adjectives, pronouns, or the verb, as: *gōra sqīla* ("A handsome man"), *baxta sqīlta* ("a beautiful woman"); *gūrē sqīlē* ("handsome men"), *baxtāsa sqīlē* ("beautiful women"). There is only one set of possessive pronouns suffixed to the nouns (both the singular and the plural).

The verb differs radically from Ancient Aramaic both in form and in content. Whereas in Ancient Aramaic the tense system has two parts (past and future), in Neo-Aramaic it is tripartite: past, present, and future. The prefixed and suffixed forms which in Ancient Aramaic were perfect and imperfect have been replaced by other forms. The form *šāqīl* (שָׁקֵל in Ancient Aramaic = active participle) is a subjunctive. It is conjugated by adding the enclitic pronouns. *Šāqil* refers to the actor and the recipient of the act is indicated by *-l-* plus pronominal suffixes, e.g., *šāqīlle* ("that he will take"). The present is formed by prefixing *g/k* to *šāqīl* (*gzamir*, "he plays"); the future by prefixing *b/p* to this form (*bzāmir*, "he will play").

Šqīl (= שְׁקִיל, the passive participle) is the basis of the past and the recipient of the action. The actor is indicated by *-l-* plus personal suffixes: *šqille* ("he took"), *šqīlāle* ("he took her"), *šqilile* ("he took them").

Neo-Aramaic has also introduced compound tenses which indicate different aspects (continuous action and perfect). The infinitive *šqāla* (*bi* usually precedes the infinitive of the first conjugation) plus the copula produce the continuous present: *bišqālā lē* ("he is taking"). The form *šqīla*, conjugated according to gender and number, with the copula, forms the present perfect: *šqīlā le* ("he has taken"), *šqīltā lā* ("she has taken"), *šqīlē lū* ("they have taken"). By adding the suffix *wa* every tense can be cast one degree into the past: *gšaqīlwa* ("he used to take"), *šqīlwālē* ("he had taken").

There are only three conjugations which parallel *qal*, *pael*, and *afel*. The reflexive conjugations that were used in Ancient Aramaic to express the passive are not found in Neo-Aramaic where the passive is formed with the passive participle plus an auxiliary verb.

Especially noteworthy is the syntax of the copula. In a sentence whose predicate is not a verb, the predicate is formed through the addition of the copula, as: *baxta sqīlta* ("a beautiful woman"), *baxta sqīlta lā* ("the woman is beautiful").

Neo-Aramaic was greatly influenced by the neighboring languages. The impact of Kurdish seems to have been especially strong in the early stages of the language and there are those who attribute the changes in the verb to it. As in all Jewish languages there are many words from

Hebrew, especially in the sphere of tradition, which were absorbed in Jewish Aramaic: סעודה (!), נשמה, מצוה, גזירה, ברכה, etc.

Writing. The Jews use the Hebrew alphabet in writing their language and they add certain diacritical signs to represent the missing consonants. In the earliest known manuscripts (17th century, north Iraq) the long vowels are indicated by *matres lectionis:* א $= \bar{a}$; 'י' $= \bar{\imath}$ or $\bar{e}$ (final $\bar{e}$ by ' or ה /יה); *waw* for short and long *u* and *o*. In later manuscripts the system was not consistently maintained, vocalization also being used for this purpose.

The use of Neo-Aramaic as a written language was limited to certain literary types intended to be read in the synagogue both during prayers and apart from it: *tafsirs* (elaborated translations) of *haftarot* and *piyyutim;* Midrashim for some of the *parashiyyot;* the midrashic Targum of Song of Songs, etc. Hebrew is used for secular purposes. It seems that the epic poems on biblical themes and the Targum in different dialects were first transcribed in Israel through the efforts of Joseph Joel *Rivlin.

Bibliography: F. Rosenthal, *Die aramaistische Forschung seit Th. Noeldeke's Veroeffentlichungen* (1939); idem (ed.), *Aramaic Handbook* (1967); R. Macuch, *Handbook of Classical and Modern Mandaic* (1965); R. Duval, *Dialectes neo-araméens de Salamas* (1883); A. J. Maclean, *Grammar of the Dialects of Vernacular Syriac* (1901); idem, *Dictionary of the Dialects of Vernacular Syriac* (1901); J. B. Segal, in: JNES, 14 (1955), 251–70; Polotzky, in: JSS, 6 (1961), 1–32; I. Garbel, *The Jewish Neo-Aramaic Dialect of Persian Azerbaijan* (1965).

[Da.C.]

NEO-FASCISM. Neo-Fascism lends itself to an exact definition even less than *Fascism, its ideological progenitor. In the postwar world all radical right-wing movements, irrespective of their doctrinal contents and differences—except those explicitly aiming at the restoration of an anti-Semitic, racialist, Nazi-type dictatorship (see *Neo-Nazism)—are commonly referred to as "neo-Fascist." They share an attitude of extreme, militant nationalism; a belief in authoritarian rather than democratic government; and a total rejection of socialist, particularly Marxist, dogma with its underlying universalist and egalitarian ethos. Inhabiting the social periphery between the middle and the working class, Neo-Fascism appeals mostly to those deprived of their former independent status (as artisans, white-collar workers, small-holders, craftsmen, etc.) by the growth of an urban, industrialized society and driven to xenophobia and hostility toward minority groups, which they believe to have either caused their social and economic decline or contributed to it. Hatreds vary according to demographic conditions. In the United States and Britain, Neo-Fascist movements have a strong anti-color bias, whereas similar French groups in the 1950s and early 1960s were anti-Algerian and in Switzerland these prejudices inspired agitation against alien workers. Anti-Semitism is almost always implicit in such attitudes and it can easily become, as in the case of the Argentinian Tacuara or the Swedish Nordiska Rikspartiet (Nordic Realm Party), an ideological focal point. In the West, the shock of the Nazi Holocaust militated after World War II against the spread of Neo-Fascist movements, particularly obsessively anti-Semitic ones; however, the Israel-Arab *Six-Day War (1967) modified this trend. Formerly disreputable anti-Semitic prejudices relabeled "anti-Zionism" became respectable again when disseminated by the Communist establishment, the *New Left, and Black Power activists. Arab anti-Israel propaganda agencies, until 1967 associated with the extreme right, have since—and without breaking their Neo-Fascist links—been courted and supported by the radical left as well.

Neo-Fascism survived best in Italy. The Movimento Sociale Italiano (MSI) obtained close to 1,500,000 votes (5.2% of the total poll) in the 1970 provincial elections, sending 32 deputies to the regional councils. However, neither occasional swastika-daubing forays into Rome's old ghetto (1958, 1960) nor parliamentary representation dating back to the early 1950s elevated the MSI to a significant position. Further to the right, the minuscule Ordine Nuovo (New Order), formed by activist dissidents from the MSI, is a terrorist, but otherwise negligible, force, cultivating links with like-minded European "New Order" movements. Prince Valerio Borghese, a former honorary MSI president, founded the militant National Front which made an abortive attempt to overthrow the government (December, 1970). In France the horrors of Nazi occupation inhibited the revival of overtly Fascist movements. Efforts by the Sidos brothers to channel resentments over the loss of empire (Indochina, North Africa) into the Neo-Fascist Jeune Nation failed, while the less clearly defined anti-establishment campaign of Pierre Poujade won 60 parliamentary seats (1956). Both his party and the anti-Gaullist extremists of the Algérie-Française OAS had Fascist and anti-Semitic overtones, but neither survived the nationalist appeal of de Gaulle's presidency. In the post-de Gaulle era, Ordre Nouveau, the successor organization to the Occident (banned 1968), gained some notoriety for militancy and street-fighting.

Neo-Fascism also failed to prosper in postwar England. Sir Oswald Mosley's once powerful British Union of Fascists, renamed British Union, had dwindled into irrelevance. A number of extremist organizations like the Empire Loyalists, the British National Party, and the Racial Preservation Society (whose street-fighting propensities gained them brief notoriety in the early 1960s), combined in 1967 to form the National Front, without, however, making any impact on national politics. In the 1970 general election the Front put up ten candidates, none of whom polled more than 1,600 votes. In the United States, the extremist right exists both inside and outside the two traditional (Republican, Democratic) parties, and is preoccupied mainly with the Negro problem and the black-white confrontation. It considers the white liberals and militant Negroes as its main enemy. Old-style primitive anti-Semitism, however, still flourishes among such movements as the Ku Klux Klan and the Christian Crusader, but the more sophisticated John Birch Society vent their anti-Jewish resentments on the "liberal establishment" represented as predominantly Jewish. The Klans, Crusaders, and Birchists are typically U.S. phenomena; lacking any party organization able to attain power, they cannot be regarded as true neo-Fascists.

Bibliography: D. Eisenberg, *The Re-emergence of Fascism* (1967).

[Er.H.]

NEOLOGY (Neologism), unofficial name of the communities in Hungary belonging to the *Reform movement. On the basis of the decisions of the General Jewish Congress (1868–69; see *Hungary), they constituted the majority and therefore called themselves the Congressionals. Reform tendencies had already appeared in the community organizations of Hungary from the beginning of the 19th century. Some were expressed in programs like that of Rabbi A. L. Rappoch (from the town of Veszprem, 1826) which called for centralization and supervision in the choice of rabbis, teachers, and communal officials. At about the same time Aaron *Chorin urged the convention of a synod of rabbis and laymen. From 1850 the Austrian government sought to assure the supervision of Jewish schools in Hungary. At that time a commission was set up to draft a constitution of 285 articles encompassing every aspect of Jewish communal life. One of the demands was for the establishment of a rabbinical seminary, which became one of the main questions of reform that led to the disputes between the communities of *Nagykanizsa, *Papa, Gyöngyös, and others.

The organizational activities of the advocates of Reform aroused the energetic but disunited opposition of *Orthodoxy, expressed particularly in the decisions of the *Michalovce Orthodox convention (1865). After the attainment of full civil rights (1867), the leaders of Pest, the most powerful Neologist community, took the initiative of preparing a memorandum on the organization of Hungarian Jewry which they submitted to the Minister of Public Instruction and Religious Affairs, Baron J. *Eötvös. They suggested that a convention of the delegates of Hungarian Jewry be held without the participation of the rabbis, in order to prevent a debate on theological questions and because the latter were liable to intervene beyond the scope of their function. This approach, which aroused the objections not only of the Orthodox but also of the Neologist Leopold *Loew, became one of the fundamental platforms in the organization of Neologist communities. Differences of opinion were already apparent at the congress's preliminary meeting, to which Orthodox delegates were not invited. In their discussions with Eötvös, the Orthodox requested permission to convene a separate congress, but Eötvös rejected any move which was liable to imply that there were two sects within Judaism. Subsequently, however, it was decided that rabbis would also be invited to the congress. The elections, which were held after extensive propaganda and not always by valid processes, assured a Neologist majority with 57.5% of the vote (the Orthodox gained 42.5%). At the end of 1868 Minister Eötvös opened the congress, whose principal theme was the organizational structure of the communities. Violent disputes broke out at once over the determination of the objectives of debates. While the Neologists tried to define the community as "a society providing for religious needs," the Orthodox insisted on the declaration that "the Jewish community of Hungary and Transylvania consists of the followers of the Mosaic-rabbinic faith and commands as they are codified in the Shulḥan Arukh." The question of the rabbinical seminary, which was to be financed by the "school fund" granted by Francis Joseph I from the fine paid by the Jews of Hungary after the 1848 Revolution was also a much disputed one. In the end, 48 of the 83 Orthodox delegates walked out and the decisions of the congress were ratified. The Orthodox, however, succeeded in organizing themselves, obtaining the authorization of the emperor. On several occasions the Neologists endeavored without success to convene another congress. Finally a meeting was held in 1935 (at which only the Neologists were represented). In 1950, on the instructions of the Communist government, a decision on the unification of Hungarian communities was passed.

The attempts of the Neologists to amalgamate with the Orthodox were to no avail. The hope of establishing this union caused the Neologists not only to refrain from introducing drastic reforms in the prayers and religious services (with the exception of the question of the organ and the pulpit, which was removed from the center of most synagogues) but also to adopt a distinctly conservative orientation, particularly in the district synagogues of the capital. There is no doubt that this preserved the unity of Hungarian Jewry in spite of the ideological split. The hoped-for ideological consolidation of the Neologist camp did not materialize either and many differences remained. As early as 1848 a circle of the younger members and even some important personalities of the Pest community sought to establish a Reform synagogue, but the community, which had already alienated itself from Orthodoxy, wished to prevent a complete split; it therefore obtained from the authorities a liquidation order against the small Reform organization (1852). In 1884 a number of individuals once more attempted to establish a Reform community. However, the national office of the Neologists intervened to deny them this right. Some stood for a liberal orientation, and for the adoption of the conservative ideology (1943). The ideological consolidation was hindered by the special organization of the communities. These contradictions were particularly evident after World War I, when the community became the sole focal point for the social activities of those who had been estranged from Judaism over a lengthy period and were attracted by communal life only because they were excluded from general society. These extreme assimilationists prevented Zionism from penetrating the communities.

During the period of Hungarian Jewry's utter isolation from the social and economic life of the country (1938–44), there was a great awakening within the Neologist communities. Their educational and charitable activities were extended until they were among the most developed in the sphere of widespread mutual assistance (where they also collaborated with the Orthodox). When the communities were reorganized after World War II, they were imbued with Zionism and a readiness to maintain relations with world Jewry, but this evolution was halted with the official prohibition of Zionist and foreign relations activities in 1949.

Bibliography: J. J. Greenwald, *Korot ha-Torah ve-ha-Emunah be-Ungarya* (1921); idem, *Le-Toledot ha-Reformaẓyah ha-Datit be-Germanyah u-ve-Ungarya* (1948); L. Loew, *Der Juedische Kongress* (1869); N. Katzburg, in: *Hungarian Jewish Studies*, 2 (1969), 1–33; idem, in: *Bar-Ilan Sefer ha-Shanah*, 2 (1964), 163–77; Weisz, in: *Libanon*, 7 (Hung., 1943), 67–72.

[B.Y.]

NEO-NAZISM, a new Nazi movement that emerged after World War II and is based on anti-Semitic doctrines similar to those propounded in Hitler's *Mein Kampf* and exemplified in the structure and aspirations of the Third Reich. Since Neo-Nazism's appeal, like that of Nazism, is specifically German, it is in Germany that one would expect the movement to flourish. However, as incitement to race hatred, as well as any attempt to resuscitate the Nazi Party, are explicitly outlawed by the Constitution and the criminal laws of the German Federal Republic (as well as in the Communist German Democratic Republic), no party overtly attempting to revive Nazism can legally exist there. Although National Socialist parties openly propagating anti-Semitism, displaying the swastika flags, and glorifying Nazi achievements sprang up under Colin Jordan in Great Britain and Lincoln Rockwell (murdered in 1967) in the United States, both have been utterly inconsequential fringe movements, of interest to the social pathologist rather than the student of politics.

Allowing for a broader definition, Neo-Nazism has come to be identified with German anti-Semitic ultranationalist, extreme right-wing movements, whether made up of old or new Nazis. Without seriously threatening the still fragile German democracy, a number of such movements gained some short-lived popularity and notoriety. The first to draw, if somewhat unwittingly, ex-Nazis into a political party was Alfred Loritz, a confused demagogue with an anti-Nazi record. His Bavarian *Economic Reconstruction Association*, founded in 1945 with U.S. consent, denounced Allied policies and articulated the widespread economic discontent of the "pre-economic-miracle" era. The "blonde Hitler," as he was sometimes called, frightened the young republic and the world at large when he gained 14.4% of the vote in his native Bavaria, winning 12 seats in the Bundestag, after the first German general election (1949). The lack of positive policies, however, coupled with internal dissensions, rent the party asunder long before it failed to gain a single seat in the following (1953) general election.

Similarly spectacular and ominous was Fritz Dorls's deliberate attempt to revive Nazism through the Socialist Reich Party (SRP). Its leadership was made up entirely of old Nazis, the most prominent of whom was the deputy chairman, Ernst Rhemer, the Wehrmacht officer who successfully thwarted the July 20, 1944, plot against Hitler. Apart from distributing anti-Semitic election leaflets, reminiscent of *Der Stuermer*, the SRP even boasted a gang organized on storm-troop lines, the so-called Reichsfront. In 1951 when the SRP gained 11% of the Lower Saxony vote, an alarmed federal government contested the party's legality before the Constitutional Court. Declared illegal as an attempt to reestablish the proscribed Nazi Party, this particular specter of resurgent Nazism disappeared. It reappeared a year later when the British arrested Dr. Naumann, one of Dr. Goebbels' top-ranking officials, whose plot to subvert the respectable Free Democratic Party by infiltrating ex-Nazis into key positions was well on the way to succeeding.

In the 1960s the spectacular and unexpected success of the NDP (National Democratic Party of Germany) aroused worldwide fears of a Nazi revival. Founded in 1965 by Adolf von Thadden to unite the hitherto splintered and ineffectual "nationalist opposition," the party shocked the German and world opinion when in the 1966–67 *Land* elections it gained admission to a number of *Land* parliaments by substantially exceeding the required 5% of the vote. Careful not to fall foul of the Constitutional Court, the NPD, run largely by ex-Nazis, appealed to exactly the same prejudices and self-assertions to which Germans responded so overwhelmingly in the Hitler era. Jews were not openly denigrated, but the State of Israel and its policies were viciously attacked. The "domination by alien big powers," reminiscent of the Nazi fiction of "Judean-Marxist world conspiracy," was denounced, as were references to Nazi crime. The party manifesto demanded "an end to the lie of Germany's exclusive guilt which serves to extort continuously thousands of millions from our people," apparently a reference to *restitution and compensation payment to Israel and individual Jews. Beset like its predecessors by internecine leadership struggles and lacking forward-looking policies, the NPD failed to gain the qualifying 5% in the 1969 general election. This failure led to a crisis of confidence, which resulted in the party losing its seats in the various *Land* parliaments after the 1970 elections. At that time it was doubtful whether Neo-Nazism still commanded a politically meaningful potential, although the phenomenon still lingered on in violently "anti-Israel" weeklies (like the *Deutsche National Zeitung*) or in the publications of ex-Reich press chief Suedermann's Druffel Verlag and similar publishing houses.

In Austria, Neo-Nazism lacked the organizational framework or a sufficiently numerous following to qualify as a politically relevant force. Among the minuscule groupings more or less openly committed to propagating Nazi ideas and extolling Nazi achievements, Theodor Soucek's Sozialorganische Bewegung Europas (SOBRE) was perhaps the most noteworthy in the early 1950s. It tried to coordinate efforts of Nazi collaborators and sympathizers in the former occupied territories to revitalize the Hitlerian "new order" in the context of the then emerging Europe. SOBRE enjoyed the support of Konrad Windisch, one of the founders of the Bund Heimattreuer Jugend (BHJ), whose initials HJ (for Hitler Jugend) proclaimed its ideological lineage and identification. Despite the insignificance of these movements, residual anti-Semitism and subliminal Nazi sympathies seemed to be more widespread in Austria than in Germany, thus the marked reluctance of Austrian authorities to prosecute and of juries to convict such war criminals and Eichmann aides as Murer, Novak, or Raiakovic and the parsimoniousness of Austrian restitution.

Argentina figured prominently in the Nazis' plans to save the movement and themselves after defeat. This tied in well with President Peron's dreams of Argentinian hegemony based on a modernized army and an independent armament industry, which the Nazi experts were to develop. Nazis headed nuclear research institutes, while World War II air aces like Rudel and Galland advised the Argentinian air force and Professor Tank, a German jet designer, started an Argentinian aircraft industry. Eichmann and his aides (Klingenfuss, Rademacher, and Dr. Mengele) found sanctuary, while Johannes von Leers, head of an anti-Jewish department in Goebbel's Propaganda Ministry, became Peron's adviser. Moreover, the Nazi gospel continued to be preached in German in *Der Weg* (Buenos Aires) and other Duerer Verlag publications. After Peron's fall (1955), some of these fugitives moved to Egypt (a Nazi sanctuary since 1945), where military needs and anti-Israel, anti-Semitic resentments offered them scope. Years later the effort of ex-Nazis to develop Egyptian jet engines, supersonic fighters, and rockets (the Messerschmidt, Brandner, and Pilz teams) caused greater international consternation than the activities of von Leers and S. S. General Bender in the Egyptian Ministry of National Guidance or of the former Gestapo chief Sellman as a police adviser on "anti-Jewish action." On the whole, however, in 1970 Neo-Nazism seemed to be declining. [ER.H.]

NEO-ORTHODOXY, name of the modernistic faction of German *Orthodoxy, first employed in a derogatory sense by its adversaries. Its forerunners were to be found among the more conservative disciples of Moses *Mendelssohn and N. H. *Wessely, like Solomon *Pappenheim and Naḥman b. Simḥah Barash. At the time of the controversy over the *Hamburg Temple (1818), the participants in the campaign against the reformers included some rabbis who adopted a stance similar to that later advocated by the Neo-Orthodox; for example those of Amsterdam, Hanau, Rawicz, and other communities, who produced the polemic, *Elleh Divrei ha-Berit* (1819). Other forerunners were the new Orthodox preacher of Hamburg, Isaac *Bernays; Jeremiah *Heinemann (1788–1855) of Berlin, the editor of *Jedidja* (1817–31); and Solomon Plessner (1797–1883) of Breslau, the author of various apologetic works.

However, the ideology of Neo-Orthodoxy crystallized later and its institutions were only established during the second half of the 19th century. In essence, the movement is connected with Samson Raphael *Hirsch and his doctrine of *Torah im derekh ereẓ* ("Torah together with the conduct of life," meaning in this context secular culture), which he expressed in his major writings. In 1851 he became rabbi of the Orthodox separatist community of Frankfort and was able to realize his ideas and plans in a suitable environment. During the second half of the 19th century, the rabbinical leadership had already suffered defeat in the campaign against reformers and assimilationists. The small groups which remained faithful to tradition referred to themselves as "remnants." At the same time, the rising tide of the Reform movement was curbed. The process of Jewish integration into general society was well advanced and was no longer conditional on their "religious" reform. Moreover, the radical line adopted by such Reform leaders as Abraham *Geiger and Samuel *Holdheim during those years had alienated important elements among the non-Orthodox (Leopold *Zunz, Zacharias *Frankel, and others).

The development of a trend combining features from both *Reform and *Orthodoxy thus became feasible. From the Reform movement it adopted the aim of integration within modern society, not only on utilitarian grounds but also through the acceptance of its scale of values, aiming at creating a symbiosis between traditional Orthodoxy and modern German-European culture; both in theory and in practice this meant the abandonment of Torah study for its own sake (as in the classical yeshivah) and adopting instead an increased concentration on practical *halakhah*. Other Reform features were the replacement of Hebrew by German as the language of Jewish culture; the acceptance of the Haskalah program in educational matters; the struggle for emancipation and the positive appreciation of the Exile; the exchange of the material idea of "Return to Zion" for that of the "Universal Mission"; German patriotism; the renouncement of a particular Jewish appearance (involving readiness to cut off the beard and the side-locks, to uncover the head when not at worship, etc.); the education of women, including their participation in religious life and their political emancipation; the abolition of the coercive powers of the community; and the acceptance of the liberal concept of freedom of conscience. From Orthodoxy the faction took: dogmatism (*emunat ḥakhamim*, "faith in the rabbis"); reservation toward the preoccupations of the Wissenschaft des Judentums and opposition to the principle of freedom of research; the acceptance of the authority of the Shulḥan Arukh and the traditions and customs of the late 18th-century German communities; acceptance of the Orthodox position on laws which came into being as a result of its campaign against the reformers, such as those against the demands for changes in synagogue usage; excessive strictness in the observation of the precepts and customs; and acquiescence in the disruption of the Jewish community and the sectarian nature of those remaining true to Orthodoxy. The second most important leader of this trend was Azriel (Israel) *Hildesheimer, who founded a rabbinical seminary (1873) and broke the monopoly of the non-Orthodox in Jewish studies. He thus made possible the integration of the intelligentsia into the neo-Orthodox circle, in contrast to Hirsch, whose system was tailored to the requirements of the ordinary community members, the so-called *ba'alei batim*. Hildesheimer was more attached to ancient rabbinic Judaism than Hirsch and his attitude to Jewish affairs in general was more positive, while his approach to general culture was less enthusiastic. As a result of this, the role Hildesheimer played in world Jewish affairs led to the creation of contacts between the German Neo-Orthodoxy, East European Jewry, and the *Ḥibbat Zion movement. In 1876 a law (the *Austrittsgesetz*) was passed which enabled individuals to secede from a church or community without changing his religious affiliation. This facilitated the secession (*Austritt*) of Orthodox minorities from communities where they considered that coexistence with the reformist leadership was impossible. In many places this situation induced the reformers to make far-reaching concessions to the Orthodox minority. German Orthodoxy thus became split over the question of whether the new law should be exploited in order that they might secede from all communities administered by reformers. To Hirsch, the *Austritt* concept became a supreme religious principle, while Seligmann Baer (or Dov Baer) *Bamberger, his Orthodox opponent, showed reserve toward both the modernism and the extremist separatism of Hirsch, and preferred to preserve the unity of the community. After some time, German Orthodoxy was again divided on another issue: the attitude toward *Zionism. One section joined the *Agudat Israel movement, while the other showed a preference for the *Mizrachi and *Ha-Po'el ha-Mizrachi and later for the *Po'alei Agudat Israel.

Bibliography: (Note: there is no critical work on the subject.) J. Wohlgemuth, in: *Festschrift . . . David Hoffmann* (1914), 435–58 (Ger. section); L. Ginzburg, *Students, Scholars and Saints* (1928), 252–62; M. Wiener, *Juedische Religion im Zeitalter der Emanzipation* (1933); O. Wolfsberg, in: *Sinai*, 4 (1939), 164–82; 14 (1944), 65–81; idem, in: Y. L. Fishman (ed), *Sefer ha-Mizrachi* (1946), 150–68 (second pagination); S. Gronemann, *Zikhronotavshel Yekke* (1946); S. Japhet, in: HJ, 10 (1948), 99–122; J. Rosenheim, *ibid.*, 135–46; H. Schwab, *History of Orthodox Jewry in Germany* (1950); I. Heinemann, *Ta'amei ha-Mitzvot be-Sifrut Yisrael*, 2 (1956), 91ff.; idem, in: HJ, 10 (1948), 123–34; 13 (1951), 29–54; J. Immanuel (ed.), *Ha-Rav Shimshon Rafa'el Hirsch, Mishnato ve-Shitato* (1962); B. Kurzweil, in: *Haaretz* (Sept. 26, 1965).

[M.Sam.]

NEOPLATONISM. The system elaborated by Plotinus and his pupil Porphyry on the basis of antecedent Middle Platonic and neo-Pythagorean developments. The system was modified by their successors, the main post-Plotinian currents and schools of late antiquity being (according to K. Praechter): the Syrian school founded by Iamblichus; the school of Pergamum (Sallust, Julian); the school of Athens (Plutarch, Syrianus, Proclus, Damascius); the school of Alexandria (Hierocles, Hermias, Ammonius and his followers: the pagans, Asclepius and Olympiodorus, and the Christians, Philoponus, Elias, David, and Stephanus); and the neoplatonists of the West (Macrobius, Chalcidius, Boethius). In the Middle Ages Neoplatonism survived in the Latin West (Johannes Scotus Erigena) and the Byzantine East (Michael Psellus) and within the Arabo-Hebraic cultural sphere, and it underwent a revival during the Renaissance (Gemistos Plethon in the Byzantine East; Marsilio Ficino, *Pico della Mirandola, and Giordano Bruno in the West).

Neoplatonism postulates the derivation by a process of emanation of a hierarchically ordered series of spheres of being, leading from an ineffable and unqualified first principle (the One) to the material world. The "descent" is associated with increasing determination and multiplicity (imperfection). Although matter at the lowest rank in the scale of being is the principle of evil, the material world, as a reflection of the intelligible, possesses goodness and beauty (cf. *Gnosticism), and by contemplation of it the human soul ascends to the spiritual world. The human soul, being spiritual and self-subsistent, is independent of the body and having descended from the supernal world, reverts to its source by means of ethical and intellectual purification (or by theurgy; e.g., Iamblichus). The stages of ascent were commonly designated (after Proclus) the *via purgativa* (purification), *via illuminativa* (illumination), and *via unitiva* (union), the highest stage, a kind of *unio mystica* (mystical union) and apotheosis, being the sole means by which the One is apprehended. Individuation and investiture of the soul with a body is devalorized; release from the fetters of the body in ecstasy or in death is equivalent to salvation, this philosophical soteriology tending toward combination with a doctrine of metempsychosis.

Neoplatonism is thus seen to be a religious movement and a doctrine of salvation as well as a philosophical system. As such, it was potentially an antagonist and an ally of the monotheistic faiths. Ancient Neoplatonism (excluding the school of Alexandria) was hostile to Christianity: Porphyry and Julian wrote refutations of Christianity; Iamblichus, Proclus, and Damascius were implacable opponents of Christianity. Indeed, Neoplatonism as a philosophical interpretation of pagan mythology (e.g., Iablichus and Proclus) represents the dying gasp of ancient paganism. The fundamental postulates of Neoplatonism conflict with those of the monotheistic faiths: an impersonal first principle, rejection of creation and revelation, the conception of man as essentially soul, and the attendant soteriology-eschatology (including metempsychosis) involving submergence of the individual soul in the universal soul. Nevertheless, for monotheistic philosophers the contradictions were not insurmountable. In fact, the method of figurative interpretation cultivated by ancient Neoplatonists (after the Pythagoreans and

Stoics) in order to identify pagan mythological themes with philosophical ideas (Proclus, for example, identified the henads of his system with the traditional gods) was employed by monotheistic philosophers in order to read their neoplatonic doctrines into the text of Scripture. The ladder of Jacob's dream was thus interpreted as a symbol of the soul's ascent (e.g., by Ibn Gabirol; see A. Altman, *Studies in Religious Philosophy and Mysticism* (1969), 54–55; and A. Nygren, *Agape and Eros* (1953²), 230, 375, 441). Creation became a metaphor for eternal procession. Revelation and prophecy were discussed in terms reminiscent of the *unio mystica*. This identification was not without some basis in ancient Neoplatonism either, if one considers the aspect of grace or divine initiative implicit in *Enneads* 5:3, 17 and 5:5, 8, or the use of the Chaldean Oracles and Orphic Hymns by Porphyry and Iamblichus. Assimilation to the divine, the goal of philosophy according to the neoplatonic introductions to Aristotle of the Alexandria school, resonated with similar ideals of the monotheistic traditions. The deep spirituality of Neoplatonism promoted the kind of synthesis with religious feeling that finds moving expression in Ibn Gabirol's poem, *Keter Malkhut*.

In order to grasp the character of Neoplatonism as it was transmitted to the medieval world of Judaism and Islam, it is necessary to understand that is was closely bound with much of the religious and pseudo-scientific heritage of late antiquity (alchemy), Hermetism (see *Hermetic Writings), magic, theurgy. Also, Neoplatonism was not simply an amplification of *Plato. Plotinus admitted into his system those aspects of Aristotelianism (also Pythagoreanism and *Stoicism) which met its requirements. Porphyry went even further and initiated the reception of *Aristotle's lecture courses into the neoplatonic curriculum. The school of Alexandria devoted much of its labors to commentaries upon Aristotle. The thesis that the views of Plato and Aristotle coincided, if properly understood, a theme traceable to Ammonius Saccas, the teacher of Plotinus, was embraced by Porphyry and influenced the course of Neoplatonism and its absorption within the Arabo-Hebraic milieu (cf. al-*Fārābī's *On the Harmony of the Opinions of the Two Sages, the Divine Plato and Aristotle*).

While reception of Neoplatonism in the medieval Latin West was mainly confined to Proclus and Pseudo-Dionysius, the Arabo-Hebraic milieu was saturated by numerous currents. Plotinus was conveyed in the guise of the *Theology of Aristotle* (a paraphrase of parts of Books 4–6 of the *Enneads*), through other paraphrases ascribed to "the Greek Sage," and a work entitled *The Divine Science* (J. van Ess, in bibl., 334ff.). The *Theology of Aristotle* is extant in a shorter (vulgate) and longer version, the latter preserved in an Arabic manuscript in Hebrew characters (in Leningrad). This longer version was translated (on the basis of a Damascus manuscript) into Hebrew and Italian by a Cypriot Jewish physician, Moses Arovas, who was also instrumental in having it rendered into Latin (S. M. Stern, in bibl., 59 n. 4, 79 n. 1).

Underlying the longer version of the *Theology of Aristotle* is another Aristotle pseudograph discovered by S. M. Stern and called by him "Ibn Ḥasdāy's Neoplatonist" (it was incorporated by *Ibn Ḥasdai in his **Ben ha-Melekh ve-ha-Nazir;* see Altmann and Stern, in bibl., 95ff.; Stern, in bibl.). (On knowledge of Porphyry's work in the medieval world of Islam, see J. van Ess, in bibl., 338; R. Walzer in *Encyclopaedia of Islam*, 2 (1965), 948–50.) Proclus' *Elements of Theology* was transmitted in the guise of the Arabic *Kitāb al-ḥayr al-maḥḍ* ("Book of the Pure Good"), known in the West as *Liber de causis* and generally understood to be a work by Aristotle, and three propositions of the *Elements of Theology* have been recovered in Arabic. Proclus' work *On the Eternity of the Universe* was also known. (For the transmission of works by Proclus, see J. van Ess, in bibl., 339ff.; H. D. Saffrey, in *Miscellanea Mediaevalia*, 2 (1963), 267ff.; and R. Walzer in *Encyclopaedia of Islam*, 1 (1960), 1340.) Another pseudo-Aristotelian work of neoplatonic character was the *Liber de pomo*, which was extremely popular and avilable in Arabic, Persian, and Hebrew (see J. Kraemer, in *Studi orientalistici in onore di Giorgio Levi della Vida*, 1 (1956), 484–506). Neoplatonic ideas are also associated with pre-Socratics (particularly Pythagoras and Empedocles) in Arabic doxographic and gnomological collections (e.g., Ṣā'id al-Andalusi's *Ṭabaqāt al-umam* and al-Shahrastānī's *al-Milal wa al-niḥal*). *Empedocles in neoplatonic dress is also preserved in *The Book of Five Substances*, of which a Hebrew translation from Arabic is extant (D. Kaufmann, *Studien ueber Salomon ibn Gabirol* (1899), 16ff.). Teachings of the school of Alexandria were transmitted mainly by Syriac-speaking Christians. The accomodation of Christian beliefs in that school (e.g., by Ammonius; see Westerink, in bibl. xii–xxv) may have served as a model for adjustment to religious belief on the part of Islamic and Jewish philosophers.

Medieval Islamic and Jewish Neoplatonism is not confined to philosophers. In both Judaism and Islam Neoplatonism entered the mystical stream. One finds such influence, for example, in the later Sufi works of al-*Ghazāli (the end of his *Mishkāt al-anwār*); it permeated Jewish kabbalistic circles in Spain and Provence, transforming an earlier gnostic tradition, and had an impact upon the German pietists (Scholem, Mysticism, 117). Israeli's *Chapter on the Elements* ("The Mantua Text"), largely based upon "Ibn Ḥasdāy's Neoplatonist," was studied by the Gerona kabbalists, attracted by the similarity between its emanationist scheme and their own system of *Sefirot*, and it was commented upon by *Azriel of Gerona (*Perush ha-Aggadot;* see Altman and Stern, in bibl., 130–2; Stern in bibl., 61).

Isaac *Israeli is the fountainhead of Jewish Neoplatonism. He defines philosophy, following the neoplatonic introductions to Aristotle, as assimilation to God according to human capacity (from Plato's *Theatetus* 176b; see Altmann and Stern, in bibl., 28ff., 197). Ascent of the human soul to the divine is described according to Proclus' three stages (*ibid.*, 185ff.), the ultimate stage depicted as becoming angelic or divine, an experience to which he applies the term *devekut*, thus anticipating its employment by later Jewish philosophers and mystics (Altmann and Stern, in bibl., 190). The famous Plotinus passage on his own ecstatic union with the One (*Enneads*, 4:8, 1) may have inspired Israeli; quoted in the *Theology of Aristotle* and in the *Rasā'il Ikhwān al-Safā'* ("Epistles of the *Brethren of Sincerity"), it is also referred to by Moses *ibn Ezra, Ibn *Gabirol, and Shem Tov ibn *Falaquera (Altmann and Stern, in bibl., 191–2). The neoplatonic doctrine concerning the unknowability of the first principle is expressed in Israeli's thesis that only God's existence (or quoddity: *anniyya, ḥaliyya*) is knowable, and not his essence (quiddity: *mahiyya*), a distinction perpetuated by *Baḥya ibn Paquda, Joseph ibn *Ẓaddik, *Judah Halevi, and Abraham *ibn Daud (Altmann and Stern, in bibl., 21–23).

The transplantation of Jewish thought to Andalusia is marked by an initial neoplatonic direction inaugurated by Ibn Gabirol. His *Mekor Ḥayyim* is unique in that it sets forth a philosophical system of neoplatonic tincture without any admixture of Jewish teaching. Significantly, the only authority named is Plato. Characteristically, the goal of human existence is the conjunction (*ittiṣāl, applicatio*) of the human soul with the supernal world through knowledge and action, i.e., intellectual and ethical purification (1:2; Arabic fragments published by S. Pines in *Tarbiz*, 27 (1958), 225–6). The fruit of the study of philosophy is said to be liberation from death and conjunction with the source of life (5:43). In the neoplatonic manner, knowledge of the First Essence is precluded because it transcends everything and is incommensurable with the intellect (1:5; Pines, *ibid.*, 224–5). Like Plotinus, Ibn Gabirol tends to rely upon concrete imagery from the world of senses in order to explain suprasensous phenomena. But the insertion of will (*irāda, voluntas*) after the First Essence and his universal hylomorphism set his system apart from that of Plotinus.

Though the impact of the *Mekor Ḥayyim* was greater upon Christian scholastic philosophy than it was in the Jewish philosophical tradition, it did exert some influence in Jewish circles. Moses ibn Ezra quoted it in his *Arugat ha-Bosem* and a Hebrew epitome was made by Falaquera. Also, Ibn Gabirol's views are quoted by Abraham *ibn Ezra in his commentaries, from which it can be seen how Ibn Gabirol bridged between his Neoplatonism and Judaism through figurative biblical interpretation.

Ibn Gabirol's successors do not evince his depth or originality. Baḥya ibn Paquda combines commonplace neoplatonic themes (e.g., God's absolute unity as distinct from the relative unity of this world) with his mystical pietism. The anonymous (Pseudo-*Baḥya) *Kitāb Maʿānī al-Nafs* treats its main theme of psychology in a neoplatonic manner. The soul is a spiritual substance whose home is the supernal world. In its descent it assimilates impressions from the celestial spheres and the zones of the elements (a gnostic-Hermetic notion), and it reascends by means of ethical and intellectual purification, whereas evil souls may be confined to the region beneath the heavens (cf. Altmann and Stern, in bibl., 114). There are also neoplatonic elements in *Abraham b. Ḥiyya's writings (his theory of emanation and doctrine of metempsychosis), and Joseph ibn Ẓaddik makes a common neoplatonic motif—that man is a microcosm—the theme of his work *(Ha-Olam ha-Katan);* but no one, aside from Ibn Gabirol, is as deeply committed to a neoplatonic world view as is Abraham ibn Ezra, even as regards such sensitive subjects as creation and prophecy. Also to be considered is Judah Halevi, whose notion of "the divine influence" *(al-Amr al-Ilāhi/ha-inyan ha-Elohi)* may be of neoplatonic origin and whose idea of the God of Abraham is said to have been "conceived metaphysically in terms of the neoplatonic idea of God" (Guttmann, Philosophies, 133).

The Aristotelian reaction in the Islamic world (*Averroes) is paralleled on the Jewish side, where in the middle of the 12th century Aristotelianism begins to displace Neoplatonism as the regnant system. However, despite Ibn Daud's strictures against Ibn Gabirol and the authoritative opinion of *Maimonides in his disesteem for Israeli, neglect of Ibn Gabirol, and contempt for popular neoplatonic works, Neoplatonism did not entirely lose its appeal for Jewish thinkers. In fact, Ibn Ḥasdai respected Israeli, as did Falaquera. Furthermore, Aristotelianism was itself thoroughly suffused with neoplatonic themes. Maimonides was far from untouched by neoplatonic influence. Words for emanation occur approximately 90 times in the first two parts of the *Guide* (D. H. Haneth, in *Tarbiz,* 23 (1952), 178). Neoplatonic traces are also discernible in his description of knowledge in terms of light and lightning metaphors (from *Avicenna or *Avempace: Pines, *Guide of the Perplexed,* civ–cv), his insistence upon denying positive attributes of God, his placing limitations upon human knowledge, and perhaps the idea of assimilation to the divine at the end of the *Guide* (3:54).

The last work in the tradition of Jewish Neoplatonism is Judah *Abrabanel's *Dialoghi di amore,* written in the atmosphere of the Renaissance revival of Neoplatonism in the manner of contemporary discussions of the *Symposium* and love treatises (see J. C. Nelson, *Renaissance Theory of Love* (1958), passim). Love is a universal unifying force. The neoplatonic One and the theory of emanation are ascribed to Plato. Divine intellect (wisdom) emanates from God as light emanates from the sun, and this intellect is the creator of the world (cf. *Enneads,* 5:9, 3), containing all essences or forms in a simple and unified way (S. Caramella (ed.), *Dialoghi d'amore* (1929), 348). Judah Abrabanel was clearly influenced by Ibn Gabirol, whom he mentions by name along with his work (*ibid.,* 246).

Bibliography: Guttmann, Philosophies, index; Husik, Philosophy, index; A. Altmann and S. M. Stern, *Isaac Israeli* (1958); J. van Ess, in: K. Flasch (ed.), *Parusia* (1965); P. Merlan, *Monopsychism, Mysticism and Metaconsciousness* (1963); idem, *From Platonism to Neoplatonism* (1960[2]); R. Klibansky, *The Continuity of the Platonic Tradition* (1953[2]); L. G. Westerink, *Anonymous Prolegomena to Platonic Philosophy* (1962); A. Altmann, in: *Tarbiz,* 27 (1958), 501–7; S. M. Stern, in: *Oriens,* 13–14 (1961), 58–120; A. H. Armstrong, *The Cambridge History of Later Greek and Early Medieval Philosophy* (1967); G. Scholem, in: *Eranos-Jahrbuch 1964,* 33 (1965), 9–50; K. Praechter, *Richtungen und Schulen im Neuplatonismus* (1910); J. Schlanger, *La philosophie de Salomon ibn Gabirol* (1968).

[J. KR.]

NE'OT MORDEKHAI (Heb. נְאוֹת מָרְדְּכַי; "Pastures of Mordecai"), kibbutz in northern Israel, 5 mi. (8 km.) S.E. of *Kiryat Shemonah. When the village was founded in 1946, Arabs launched an attack and two of the volunteers who were helping set up the first huts were killed. The founding members are from Czechoslovakia, Austria, and Germany. In 1970 the kibbutz had 625 inhabitants. Originally affiliated with Ha-Kibbutz ha-Me'uḥad, Ne'ot Mordekhai decided, after the 1951 split in that movement, to remain outside any kibbutz federation, thus becoming the only unaffiliated kibbutz. It developed highly intensive and fully irrigated farming as well as industrial enterprises—an alfalfa drying plant, a shoe factory, a factory producing cider, grape, and vegetable juices, and a sewing plant. It is named after the Argentinian Zionist Mordecai Rozovsky. [E.O.]

NEPHILIM (Heb. נְפִילִים), a race of giants said to have dwelt in pre-Israelite Canaan (Num. 13:33). Genesis 6:1–2 relates that the "sons of gods," i.e., divine or angelic beings, took mortal wives; verse 4 continues, "It was then, and later too, that the Nephilim appeared [lit., were] on earth—when the divine beings cohabited with the daughters of men, who bore them offspring. They were the heroes [Heb. *gibborim*] of old, the men of renown." This could mean that the Nephilim were contemporaneous, but not identical, with the offspring of divine beings and earthly women, who were called *gibborim* (so, e.g., Morgenstern, in HUCA 14 (1939), 85ff.). The above translation, however, follows an ancient tradition in equating the Nephilim and the *gibborim* as offspring of the union of *angels and mortals.

In apocryphal writings of the Second Temple period this fragmentary narrative was elaborated and reinterpreted. The angels were then depicted as rebels against God: lured by the charms of women, they "fell" (Heb. *nfl.* נפל), defiled their heavenly purity, and introduced all manner of sinfulness to earth. Their giant offspring were wicked and violent; the Flood was occasioned by their sinfulness. (None of these ideas is in the biblical text.) Because of their evil nature, God decreed that the Nephilim should massacre one another, although according to another view most of them perished in the Flood. One version asserts that the evil spirits originally issued from the bodies of the slain giants. These giants, or their offspring, are identified as Nephilim (See I En. 6–10, 15–16; Jub. 7:21ff.). As this dualistic myth does not appear in the apocalypses of Baruch and Esdras nor in the *aggadah* of the talmudic period, it was apparently rejected as incompatible with Jewish monotheism. The "sons of God" are explained in the Targum to Genesis 6:4 and the Midrash (Gen. R. 26:5) as young aristocrats who married the daughters of commoners. The Targum renders both *gibborim* and Nephilim by *gibbaraya;* the Midrash (Gen. R. 26:7) lists seven names applied to giants. The Babylonian Talmud mentions the names of Shamhazzai, Uzza, and Uzziel, the leaders of the fallen *angels in Enoch, but does not say that they were angels: *Yoma* 67b alludes to the sins of Uzza and Uzziel; *Niddah* 61a states that Sihon and Og were descendants of Shamhazzai. In Deuteronomy 3:11 *Og is described as a giant, and this theme was developed to a

The Nephilim shown in a page from Genesis in the *Aelfric Heptateuch,* an 11th-century manuscript from England. London, British Museum, B.M. Ms. Cotton Claudius B. IV, fol. 13.

large degree in aggadic legend. In post-talmudic literature (cf. Rashi, Yoma 67b) the long-suppressed myth came to the surface again. The Palestinian Targum gives the orthodox rendering of Genesis 6:1, but translates verse 4 as: "Shamhazzai and Uzziel fell from heaven and were on earth in those days"—identifying the Nephilim as the fallen angels rather than their children. The same identification is found in a late Midrash, which calls the fallen angels Uzza and Uzziel; another passage in the same document says the Nephilim were descendants of Cain (*Aggadat Bereshit,* ed. S. Buber, introd., p. 38). The Zohar (1:58a) also identifies the Nephilim with the fallen angels. The standard medieval Bible commentators generally followed the classical *aggadah* in rejecting the mythological interpretation and asserting that the marriages in Genesis 6 were human. Some variant opinions about the "sons of God" are offered—e.g., that their distinction was not only social, but physical and even moral, and that the offspring were called Nephilim because they "fell short" of their fathers in these respects (Nahmanides, Abrabanel; see also **Anak*).

Bibliography: U. Cassuto, in: *Sefer ha-Yovel... J. H. Hertz* (1943), 35–44; B. J. Bamberger, *Fallen Angels* (1952), 3–59; H. L. Ginsberg, in: EM, 5 (1968), 896–7 (incl. bibl.). [B.J.B.]

NEPPI, HANANEL (Grazziadio; 1759–1863), Italian rabbi and physician. Neppi was born in Ferrara and studied under Jacob Moses *Ayash and Solomon Lampronti. He was a rabbi in Ferrara, and represented his community at the *Assembly of Jewish Notables called by Napoleon in Paris (1806). In 1822 he settled in Cento, where he was rabbi until his death. (The inscription on his tombstone was engraved on a wall of the Cento synagogue.)

His works include: *Zekher Zaddikim li-Verakhah,* a biographical and bibliographical lexicon of earlier Jewish scholars, modeled on the *Shem ha-Gedolim* of H. J. D. *Azulai and printed together with the *Toledot Gedolei Yisrael* of Mordecai Samuel *Ghirondi (1853); *Livyat Hen,* a collection of responsa in six volumes, in manuscripts, some of which were printed by Yare (1908); sermons (in Mss.). An ardent student of Kabbalah, Hananel was styled "*hakham hen*" by his contemporaries. A catalog of his library was published at Lemberg in 1873.

Bibliography: Ghirondi-Neppi, 115–6; Mortara, Indice; Y. Jare, in: *Festschrift... A. Harkavy* (1908), 470. [Sh.Si.]

NERGAL-SHAREZER (Heb. נֵרְגַל שַׂר־אֶצֶר, נרגל ש(ש)ראצר Akk. ^{d}*Nergal šar-uṣur* ("Nergal protect the king!"), classical: Neriglissar), high-ranking official *(Rab Mag)* of Nebuchadnezzar (Jer. 39:3, 13). Nergal-Sharezer took part in the siege and conquest of Jerusalem in 587 B.C.E. He is probably identical with Neriglissar, a son-in-law of Nebuchadnezzar, the circumstances of whose succession to Evil-Merodach as king of Babylon are unknown, and who reigned from 560 to 556 B.C.E.

Bibliography: B. H. Langdon, *Die neubabylonischen Koenigsinschriften* (1912), 208–19; D. J. Wiseman, *Chronicles of the Chaldaean Kings* (1956), 37ff.; I. Ephal, in: EM, 5 (1968), 926–7. [Ed.]

°**NERO,** Roman emperor, 54–68 C.E. Nero reigned during a critical period in the relations between the Jews of Judea and imperial Rome. His reign saw the decline of the authority of the procurators in Judea and the outbreak of the Jewish War. He seems to have had no personal enmity against the Jews. Indeed, he supported Jewish vassal rulers and extended the borders of the kingdom of *Agrippa II to include Tiberias and a number of other towns (Jos., Ant., 20:159; Jos., Wars, 2:252). He also bestowed Armenia Minor upon *Aristobulus, son of the Jewish king of Chalcis (Ant., 20:158). In a dispute that broke out between the leaders of the high priesthood and the Jerusalem populace on the one side, and Agrippa and the procurator *Festus on the other, over the wall that had been erected to prevent Agrippa's palace from overlooking the Temple court, he decided in favor of the former (Ant., 20:195). His wife *Poppaea Sabina, who had a certain sympathy for the Jews, had a hand in this decision. Nero's persecutions after the fire in Rome affected only the Christians but not the Jews. However, a number of factors combined to damage relations between the Jews of Erez Israel and the Roman government. The excesses and extravagances of the court were reflected in monetary extortion in the provinces, including Judea. Moreover, the rise of hellenizing elements in the administration benefited the non-Jewish inhabitants of the country while damaging the interests of the Jews. The procurators of Judea in Nero's time apart from Festus (60–62 C.E.) were *Felix (52–60 C.E.), who had already been appointed by *Claudius, *Albinus (62–64 C.E.), and *Gessius Florus (64–66 C.E.). They were the worst in the history of the Roman government of the country, and their rule saw the collapse of law and order in Judea. This was particularly so during the procuratorship of *Florus, a Greek from Asia Minor, whose oppressive rule showed nothing but hatred toward the Jewish population. The situation was particularly bad in Caesarea, where, in a municipal dispute between the Jews and the Syrians, Nero decided against the Jews, annulling their privileges. Florus' conduct also caused the outbreak of disturbances in Jerusalem, which led up to the great revolt of 66. Nero, determined to crush the rebels, sent *Vespasian at the head of a large army to the country. Galilee was speedily reconquered by the Roman forces, but Jerusalem continued to hold out. According to talmudic tradition Nero became a proselyte (Git. 56a).

Bibliography: Schuerer, Hist, index; M. Radin, *The Jews Among the Greeks and Romans* (1915), 285–6, 294–8, 315–9; H. Dessau, *Geschichte der roemischen Kaiserzeit*, 2 pt. 2 (1930), 800–16; A. Momigliano, in: CAH, 10 (1934), 854–61. [M.St.]

NER TAMID (Heb. נֵר תָּמִיד; "eternal lamp"), a light which burns perpetually in front of the *ark in synagogues. It is usually placed in a receptacle suspended from the ceiling. The *ner tamid* consisted of a wick burning in olive oil and it was considered a meritorious deed and an honor to give donations for the upkeep of the *ner tamid*. Indeed, people who do so are specially mentioned in the **Mi she-Berakh* prayer recited after the Torah reading in the synagogue on Sabbath mornings. In modern times, however, the *ner tamid* is an electrical bulb. The receptacle and the chains of the *ner tamid* are usually made of precious metal.

The institution of the *ner tamid* in the synagogue is a symbolic reminder of the **menorah* which burned continually in the Temple (see Ex. 27:20; Lev. 24:2), as the synagogue is considered a spiritual replica of the Temple ("small sanctuary," Meg. 29a). Originally, therefore, the *ner tamid* was placed into a niche in the western wall of the synagogue in remembrance of the position of the *menorah* in the Temple. Later, however, it was suspended in front of the Ark. In many East European synagogues which were built of wood, the *ner tamid* was placed in special vaulted stone niches because of the possible danger of fire. The *ner tamid* has also been interpreted as being symbolic of God's presence amid Israel (Shab. 22b) or as the spiritual light which emanated from the Temple (Ex. R. 36:1).

Bibliography: Eisenstein, Dinim, 273–4; L. Yarden, *Tree of Light* (1971), index, s.v. *Eternal Light*. [Ed.]

Ner Tamid from Casablanca, Morocco, 19th century. The glass, inscribed in Hebrew, is supported by copper chains hanging from a *hamsa*, the hand-shaped talisman of the Orient. Jerusalem, Sir Isaac and Lady Wolfson Museum in Hechal Shlomo. Photo David Harris, Jerusalem.

°**NERVA** (**M. Cocceius Nerva**), Roman emperor, 96–98 C.E. He mounted the throne at the tumultuous time following the death of *Domitian and succeeded in reconciling the interests of the traditionalist senate with those of the forces of spiritual revolution, Jews, Judeophile, or Christian. He had a generous social and economic policy which attempted to alleviate the fiscal excesses and increasing pauperism in the empire. He abolished the extortionist procedure of the **Fiscus Judaicus* that had given rise to abuse under Domitian. In commemoration of this he issued coins with the inscription *Fisci Judaici Calumnia Sublata*. He exempted adherents of the Christian faith from the obligation to pay the *Fiscus Judaicus*, thus officially recognizing Christianity as a new religion and not merely a sect.

Bibliography: Stein, in: Pauly-Wissowa, 7 (1900), 133–54; R. Syme, in: *Journal of Roman Studies*, 20 (1930), 55–70; E. M. Smallwood, *Documents Illustrating the Principles of Nerva, Trajan and Hadrian* (1966); M. A. Levi, *L'impero romano*, 1 (1967); H. J. Leon, *The Jews of Ancient Rome* (1960), 36, 252; Baron, Social², 2 (1952), 83, 106. [A.M.R.]

NESHAMAH YETERAH (Heb. נְשָׁמָה יְתֵרָה, "additional soul"), a popular belief that every Jew is given an additional soul from the entrance of each Sabbath until its termination. This belief originated with the story in the Talmud (Beẓah 16a): "Resh Lakish said, 'On the eve of the Sabbath, God gives man an additional (or enlarged) soul, and at the close of the Sabbath He withdraws it from him, for it says; 'He ceased from work and rested', i.e., *va-yinnafash* (Ex. 31:17): once it (the Sabbath) ceased, the additional soul is lost.'" (וַיִּנָּפַשׁ—play on the word which could be read— וַי(ל) נֶפֶשׁ *vai (le- nefesh* "woe to the soul"). The notion of *neshamah yeterah* was richly expanded in kabbalistic literature, especially in the Zohar. One explanation for the use of spices at the **Havdalah* service is that with the departure of the *neshamah yeterah* at the end of the Sabbath, it is necessary to strengthen the faint remaining soul (Tur, OḤ 297:1). [Ed.]

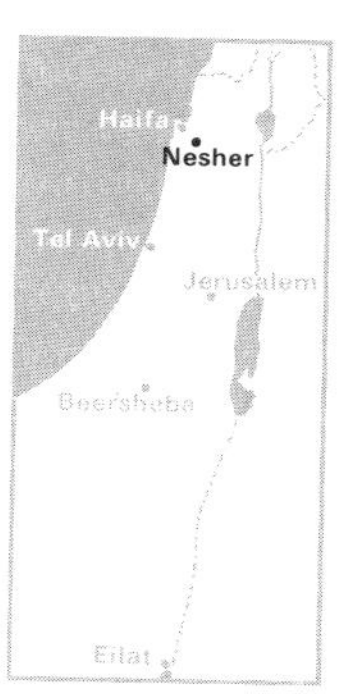

NESHER (Heb. נֶשֶׁר), urban community with municipal council status in northern Israel, 4 mi. (6 km.) S.E. of Haifa. Nesher was founded in 1925 as a workers' quarter for employees of the Nesher Cement Works. Until 1948 it consisted mainly of small wooden huts. In the *War of Independence (1948), two nearby Arab villages whose inhabitants had participated in the massacre of Jewish employees from the oil refinery were captured by Jewish forces and abandoned by their inhabitants. The villages were later taken over by new immigrants and renamed Tel Ḥanan. They were finally included in the municipal area of Nesher. Nesher's population increased from 1,500 in 1948 to 9,450 by 1968. Only 1,500 of Nesher's gainfully employed worked in 1969 in local enterprises, including the cement works, stone quarries, a motor vehicle factory, and smaller workshops. Another 3,000 commute to work in Haifa and its industrial zone. [E.O.]

NESVIZH (Pol. **Nieśwież**), town in Baranovichi oblast, Belorussian S.S.R.; formerly in Poland. Jews are mentioned in Nesvizh in the early 16th century. In 1589 the Radziwill family, who owned the town, granted the Jews certain rights, and they were subordinate to the jurisdiction of the prince. The Lithuanian Council of 1623 (see *Councils of the Lands) assigned Nesvizh to the Brest-Litovsk province but in 1634 it was made capital of its own province. Nesvizh was a center for fairs, and *dayyanim* were sent there from all Lithuanian communities. The community wielded considerable influence in the Lithuanian Council, which convened there in 1761. According to a council decision of 1634, the Nesvizh representative was one of the five men who determined the amount of funds required "to wreak vengeance for murder," referring to a blood libel against the Jews. Of the 60,000 zlotys demanded as poll tax from the whole of Lithuanian Jewry in 1721, the council fixed the share of Nesvizh and the neighboring town of Sverzhen at 1,000 zlotys, as against 1,100 zlotys imposed on Vilna. In 1811 there were 716 Jews in Nesvizh; 153 of them were craftsmen, including 91 needleworkers, 21 tanners, and 13 barbers. The community numbered 5,053 (72.7% of the total population) in 1878; 4,678 (55.4%) in 1897; 5,344 (53%) in 1914; and 3,346 (48.9%) in 1921. Besides commerce and crafts the Jews of Nesvizh engaged in horticulture and market gardening, including marketing of agricultural products. It had a textile factory, a sawmill, and a cooperative Jewish bank.

Nesvizh was known for its talmudic scholars. Among the well-known rabbis who officiated in the community at various periods were Isaac Elhanan *Spektor and Samuel Avigdor "Tosfa'ah." The last rabbi was Yitzhak Isaac Rabinovitch. Joseph Baer *Soloveichik and Pinḥas *Rozovski were natives of Nesvizh. The community had a yeshivah, a Hebrew school and kindergarten, and a Yiddish school. A branch of *Ḥovevei Zion was founded in 1871 and revived in 1888. There was considerable Zionist activity and in the 1930s *Ha-Shomer ha-Ẓa'ir maintained a training farm in Nesvizh. An association of Jewish craftsmen originally known as Po'alei Ẓedek was founded in 1908 and there was also a branch of the *Bund and Jewish members of the Communist Party.

Among the outstanding personalities who originated from Nesvizh were the philosopher Solomon *Maimon; Eliezer Dillon, who was one of two "deputies of Jewish people" sent to St. Petersburg; Moses Eleazar *Eisenstadt, the *kazyonny ravvin* in St. Petersburg; the authors and educators Nisan *Touroff and Falk *Halperin; the authors Jacob Zalman Reizin and Mordecai Ze'ev Reizin; and Nahum Meyer Shaikevich (*Shomer), the Yiddish author.
[D.R.]

Holocaust Period. In 1939 there were 6,000 Jews in Nesvizh. During the period of Soviet rule (1939–41), the community institutions were liquidated and the activity of the political parties was forbidden. Zionist youth movements, however, maintained their frameworks underground. Large economic concerns were nationalized, small-scale trade almost came to a complete stop, and artisans were organized in cooperatives. A few days after the outbreak of war between Germany and the U.S.S.R. the city was captured by the Germans. Looting and anti-Jewish incidents began. On October 19 a fine of 500,000 rubles and 2.5 kg. of gold was imposed. On October 30 all the Jews were ordered to gather in the market square and a "selection" was carried out. From among those gathered, 600 artisans were picked out and the others, about 5,000 in number, were executed near the city. The remnant of the community was concentrated in a ghetto that was surrounded by a wire fence.

At the end of December 1941, an underground organization was founded in the ghetto. It began with the acquisition of arms and the preparation of other means of self-defense. In July 1942 news of the destruction of nearby communities reached the ghetto and the underground prepared to fight. The chairman of the Judenrat, Magalif, a lawyer from Warsaw, cooperated with the underground. On July 22 the Germans surrounded the ghetto to carry out a selection. When the Germans broke through the gate, the Jews set their houses afire and defended themselves, with the few weapons they had and with knives, hatchets, and sticks. A number of Germans were injured, but the Germans and their Lithuanian collaborators overcame the inhabitants of the ghetto. A few succeeded in escaping and fled into the forests. Some organized into a partisan unit and were integrated into the Chkalov batallion of the partisans that was active in the forests of Volozhin. With the liberation of the city by the Soviets, Jewish life was not reconstituted. The survivors went to Poland, and from there some went to Ereẓ Israel and others migrated overseas.
[Ar.W.]

Bibliography: S. Dubnow (ed.), *Pinkas . . . Medinot Lita* (1925), index; H. Alexandrov, in: Vaysrusishe Visnshaft-Akademie, *Tsaytshrift*, 4 (1930), 67–73; Lita, 3 (1967); *Sefer ha-Partizanim ha-Yehudim*, 1 (1958), 545–55; *Sefer Milḥamot ha-Getta'ot* (1954), 478–80, 607.

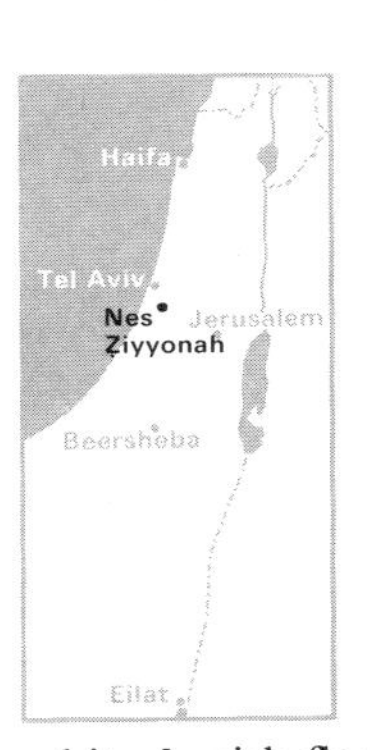

NES ẒIYYONAH (Heb. נֵס צִיּוֹנָה; "Banner toward Zion"), semiurban settlement with municipal council status in central Israel, between Rishon le-Zion and Reḥovot. Nes Ẓiyyonah was founded in 1883 in the Arab hamlet, Wadi Ḥanīn, on the initiative of a single Jewish immigrant from Russia, Reuben Lehrer. A few more Jewish families joined the founder in the first years. The moshavah was given its present name in the 1890s when, for the first time in the country, the blue and white Jewish flag was raised at its anniversary celebration. In the first decade of the 20th century, citrus groves became prominent there and attracted both immigrants of the *Second Aliyah and, in even greater numbers, Arab workers, some of whom settled there. Nes Ẓiyyonah thus became the principal stage in the struggle for the "conquest of labor." Until 1948 Nes Ẓiyyonah was the only village in the country with a mixed Arab-Jewish population—the two communities living on opposite sides of the main road and, on the whole, coexisting peacefully. In the *War of Independence (1948), the Arabs abandoned the village, which had by then 1,800 Jewish inhabitants. After 1948 Nes Ẓiyyonah quickly expanded and reached 9,500 inhabitants in 1953; its rate of growth, however, slowed down subsequently. There were 11,900 inhabitants in 1968 in a municipal area extended over 1,600 hectares—of which 1,000 were cultivated for farming. Aside from the citrus branch, Nes Ẓiyyonah is a beekeeping center, producing an annual average of 330,000 lb. (150,000 kg.) of honey. Industry is a prime factor in the local economy, employing 1,300 workers (1968) in factories for building materials, electric appliances, fiberglass, rubber, metal, and foodstuffs. A center of biological research is situated at Nes Ẓiyyonah.
[E.O.]

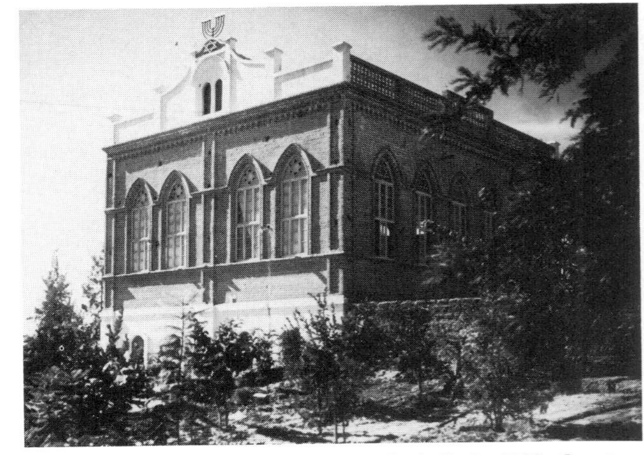

The main synagogue of Nes Ẓiyyonah, built in 1928. Courtesy Keren Hayesod, United Israel Appeal, Jerusalem.

NES ZIYYONAH, a clandestine Zionist society founded in 1885 by students of the yeshivah in Volozhin. The purpose of Nes Ẓiyyonah was to organize a group of people (rabbis, preachers, and writers) to propagate the idea of the settlement of Ereẓ Israel. The members of the society were sworn to secrecy and took it upon themselves to promote their cause orally and in print and to establish new Ḥovevei Zion societies (see *Ḥibbat Zion). The central committee of Nes Ẓiyyonah distributed circulars among its members and, when it acquired a duplicating machine, also published a *Mikhtav Itti u-Khelali* ("General Periodical") in Hebrew. It also initiated a collection of essays and asked rabbis to submit their views on the idea of settlement in Ereẓ Israel. Replies received from several outstanding rabbis served as a kind of positive "responsa" to the Ḥovevei Zion ideology. Some of the replies were published in the Hebrew press, but the book itself never came out because at the end of 1891 the police discovered the existence of the society, confiscated the duplicating machine and the archives, and put an end to Nes Ẓiyyonah's activities. Some of the rabbis' letters were included in *Shivat Ẓiyyon* (1891), a collection edited by A. J. *Slutzky. A group of former members of Nes Ẓiyyonah then founded another society with similar aims, called Neẓaḥ Israel. Among the founders was Ḥayyim Naḥman *Bialik, who was asked to formulate the aims of the new society. An article by Bialik—his first effort to appear in print— was published in **Ha-Meliẓ* 31, No. 80 (1891). The stated purpose of the society was "the settlement of our holy land in the spirit of holiness and Judaism." The society planned the establishment of a rural settlement in Ereẓ Israel with a majority of members from Nes Ẓiyyonah, which would serve as an example to all the other settlements, especially in matters of education. In 1890 societies by the name of Nes Ẓiyyonah were founded in Aleksot near Kovno and in Suwalki for the purpose of establishing a settlement in Ereẓ Israel based on religious-national ideals. Eventually the two societies merged into one and, augmented by additional members from Mariampol, laid the foundations of Ḥaderah. When the Volozhin yeshivah was closed by Russian authorities, the activities of Neẓaḥ Israel came to an end. It was reestablished at Minsk by I. Nissenbaum and was finally disbanded in 1894. [I.K.]

NETA'IM (Heb. נְטָעִים; "Plantations"), moshav in central Israel S.W. of Rishon le-Zion affiliated with Tenu'at ha-Moshavim, founded in 1932 by veteran farm laborers of the *Second Aliyah in the framework of the *Thousand Families Settlement Scheme. Citrus groves were among its intensive farming branches. In 1968 its population was 212. [E.O.]

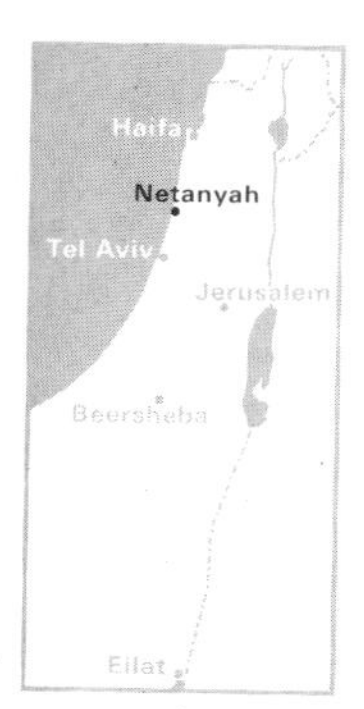

NETANYAH (Heb. נְתַנְיָה), city in central Israel, on the Sharon coast. It was founded in 1929 as a moshavah based on farming by 40 young people of the *Benei Binyamin association, led by Oved *Ben-Ami, whose parents were veteran settlers in moshavot. The village soon served as a nucleus for the settlement of the central Sharon where no Jewish villages had existed before, particularly as its founding coincided with the purchase of the *Ḥefer Plain by the *Jewish National Fund. Because it was situated between Tel Aviv and Haifa, Netanyah was able to develop as a market town for its quickly expanding rural hinterland. In the initial period citrus groves constituted Netanyah's principal economy, employing a considerable number of hired workers and thus causing an increase in population. A further growth factor was Netanyah's location at a communications center. In 1948 the population was 8,500. Later Netanyah was given city status and by 1951 its population had already mounted to 30,000, and to 60,100 by 1968, as large numbers of new immigrants were absorbed. The city economy is based mainly on tourism and industry. Netanyah is one of Israel's foremost seaside resorts and has over 60 hotels and pensions of various sizes. The foremost industrial branch is *diamond polishing, of which Netanyah became the Israel center in the 1940s, when this industry was transferred from Nazi-dominated Belgium to Palestine—although subsequently the center moved to the Tel Aviv area. Other industries include beer and citrus concentrates, pharmaceuticals and essential oils derived from plants, metals, rubber, machines, cosmetics, and fruit packing. Public institutions located at Netanyah include the Ohel Shem Culture Hall, the Malben Old People's Home, the Wingate Sports Center, and the *Ulpan Akiva. Netanyah is named after the U.S. Jewish philanthropist Nathan *Straus. [S.H.]

Netanyah, Israel city on the Mediterranean coast. Photo Werner Braun, Jerusalem.

NETANYAHU, BENZION (1910–), scholar and Zionist. Born in Warsaw, Netanyahu moved with his family to Tel Aviv in 1920. There he became active in the Zionist-Revisionist Party and its successor, the New Zionist Organization. From 1932 to 1935 he served on its executive committee and in 1934–35 as editor in chief of its daily paper *Ha-Yarden*. In 1940 he went to the United States as a member of the delegation, headed by Jabotinsky, of the World New Zionist Organization, and in the following year was appointed executive director of the New Zionist Organization of America; until 1948 he headed its press campaign and diplomatic action in the United States. From 1946 to 1948 he was a member of the American Zionist Emergency Council, under the leadership of Abba Hillel Silver.

After the establishment of the State of Israel Netanyahu turned to his numerous scholarly interests in the field of Judaica. He became the editor in chief of the *Encyclopedia Hebraica* (1948–62), general editor of *The World History of the Jewish People* (1954–64), editor in chief of the *Encyclopaedia Judaica* (1961–63), coeditor of the *Jewish Quarterly Review* (1959–60), and editor of the works of Herzl, Nordau, and Pinsker. He was a professor at Dropsie College from 1957 to 1968, serving as chairman of its

Department of Hebrew Language and Literature from 1962 to 1968. From 1968 he was professor of Hebraic studies at the University of Denver and in 1971 was appointed professor of Judaic studies and chairman of the Department of Semitic Languages at Cornell University. Netanyahu published numerous original studies in various fields of Jewish history and literature, including *Don Isaac Abravanel* (1953), 1968²) and *The Marranos of Spain* (1966).

[MA.C.]

NETHANEL BEN AL-FAYYUMI (d. about 1165), Yemenite scholar and philosopher. Nethanel appears to have been the father of Jacob b. Nethanel to whom *Maimonides addressed his *Iggeret Teiman* ("Epistle to Yemen").

Nethanel wrote the Judeo-Arabic *Bustān al-ʿUqūl* ("Garden of Intellects"), a compendium of theology published by R. Gottheil, in: *Festschrift . . . Steinschneider* (1896), 144–7; text edited and translated into English by D. Levine, 1908; translated into Hebrew under the title *Gan ha-Sekhalim* by Y. Kafaḥ, 1954. The seven chapters of the work deal with (1) divine unity, (2) man as a microcosm, (3) obedience to God, (4) repentance, (5) reliance upon God and providence, (6) the nature of the Messiah with a discussion of the Islamic concepts of the abrogation of the Torah and the prophethood of Muhammad, and (7) the future life. In his discussion of the abrogation of the Torah, Nethanel denied that the Torah would be superseded, but, at the same time, maintained that there is a certain validity in the legislation of other religions. His tolerance is evident from his contention that God sent different prophets to the various nations of the world with legislations suited to the particular temperament of each individual nation.

The *Bustān al-ʿUqūl,* a popular work, contains numerous citations from *aggadah* and from Arabic legendary and anecdotal materials. In addition to drawing upon Jewish sources, such as *Saadiah's *Book of Beliefs and Opinions* and *Baḥya's *Duties of the Heart,* Nethanel borrowed heavily from Islamic philosophy, from the Epistles of the *Brethren of Sincerity, and, as S. Pines points out, from the writings of the *Ismāʿīliya, in particular of the Fatimid branch. The Ismailian influence is particularly prominent in Nethanel's discussion of the nature of God, and the primary emanations. Pines considers the *Bustān al-ʿUqūl* an Ismailian treatise that was inspired by the theology of the Fatimids, in the same way that a work like Saadiah's *Beliefs and Opinions* was inspired by the Muʿtazilite *Kalām. Some identify the author of *Bustān* with Nethanel b. Moses ha-Levi the Gaon of Fostat or with the son of Fayyūmī b. Saadiah who sent an epistle to Maimonides.

Bibliography: EJ, 2 (1925), 260ff.; A. S. Halkin (ed.), *Iggeret Teiman (Moses Maimonides' Epistle to Yemen)* (1952), vii ff.; M. Steinschneider, in: JQR, 10 (1897/98), 522–3; idem, Arab Lit, 182; Neubauer, Cat, 2 (1906), 380; Mann, Egypt, 1 (1920), 244; 2 (1922), 315–6; S. Pines, in: *Revue de l'histoire juive en Egypte,* 1 (1947), 5–22.

[F.T.]

NETHANEL BEN ISAIAH (14th century), Yemenite scholar. Nethanel's fame rests upon his extensive midrashic anthology, *Nur al-Ẓalam* ("Light in the Darkness"). The book is a typical Yemenite Midrash: it is based upon the standard Midrashim, though with stylistic changes and adaptations, and the influence of Maimonides, with whom the author shows great familiarity, is conspicuous. Philosophical ideas from other schools as well as kabbalistic sayings are also woven into the work.

Nur al-Ẓalam contains few of the peculiarities of the other Yemenite Midrashim and is of a much higher literary standard, being comparable in this respect to the **Midrash ha-Gadol.* It was utilized by authors of later Yemenite Midrashim, among them Manẓur Aldamari, in his *Sarag al-Ekol* and Shalem *Shabazi. The Midrash was published in its entirety with a Hebrew translation accompanying the Arabic original, by Y. Kafaḥ (1957). Nethanel also wrote a commentary on Maimonides' *Mishneh Torah* which was extant until recently and subsequently lost.

Bibliography: Nathanel b. Isaiah, *Me'or ha-Afelah,* ed. by Y. Kafaḥ (1957), introd.; A. Kohut, *"Light of Shade and Lamp of Wisdom"* . . . composed by Nethanel ibn Yeshâya (= *Studies in Yemen-Hebrew Literature,* pt. 2), (bound with proceedings of the fourth Biennial Convention of the Jewish Theological Seminary Association, 1894).

[I.T.-S.]

NETHANEL BEN MESHULLAM HA-LEVI (1660/1665–1735?), Italian kabbalist. Nethanel was born in Modena and was ordained rabbi around 1685. His first rabbinical post appears to have been in his native town, during the lifetime of his father, Meshullam b. Benzion ha-Levi, a kabbalist, who was a member of the Modena rabbinate. From 1693 Nethanel was also rabbi in Lugo, Pesaro, Padua, and Cento. In 1728 he returned to Modena, apparently succeeding Ephraim Kohen of Ostrog as chief rabbi, serving in that position until his death. Some of his responsa were published in the works of his contemporaries, such as the *Paḥad Yiẓḥak* of Isaac *Lampronti and the *Shemesh Ẓedakah* (Venice, 1743) of Samson *Morpurgo. Of great importance is his responsum written in Pesaro (in *Shemesh Ẓedakah,* ḤM, no. 33), in which he discusses communal taxation and inter-community responsibility, and protests against rabbis who pass judgment on matters concerning other communities without the consent of their local rabbis. In the sphere of Kabbalah his work exhibits affinity with the thought of Moses Ḥayyim *Luzzatto. He was close to the Kabbalah circle of Abraham *Rovigo and Mordecai *Ashkenazi. His son, ẒEVI HA-LEVI, an emissary of the Holy Land, was one of the scholars of the yeshivah of Ḥayyim ibn *Attar in Jerusalem.

Bibliography: Wilensky, in: KS, 23 (1946/47), 131–9; 24 (1947/48), 160.

[A.D.]

NETHANEL BEN MOSES HA-LEVI (12th century), *gaon* and *rosh yeshivah* in Cairo. Nethanel inherited his position from his father Moses and according to documents of the Cairo *Genizah,* he held this position from 1160 to 1170. At that time, the role and the authority of the Cairo *rosh yeshivah* increased to a considerable extent because, after the death of *Samuel b. Hananiah, the position of the *nagid* was weakened as a result of the activities of *Zuta. Nethanel appointed judges and other religious officials in all the communities of Egypt and he headed the great *bet din.* He received a letter of ordination from R. *Daniel b. Ḥasdai, the exilarch in Baghdad, who thus sought to impose his authority on Egyptian Jewry; on the other hand, *Samuel b. Eli, the head of the *yeshivah* of Baghdad, supported the *geonim* of Damascus. *Benjamin of Tudela, the 12th century traveler, relates that Nethanel was in royal service. In 1171 Nethanel was succeeded by Maimonides as head of the Jews. For some unknown reason Maimonides was compelled to give way to *Sar Shalom ha-Levi, the brother of Nethanel.

Bibliography: Mann, Egypt, 1 (1920), 234–5, 237; 2 (1922), 292ff.; Mann, Texts, 1 (1931), 230–1, 257–62; Assaf, in: *Tarbiz,* 1 no. 3 (1929/30), 68; idem, *Be-Oholei Ya'akov* (1943), 91; Goitein, in: *Tarbiz,* 33 (1963/64), 184.

[E.A.]

NETHANEL OF CHINON, French tosafist of the first half of the 13th century. Nethanel is mentioned several times in the standard *tosafot* (e.g., Beẓah 3a) and is probably identical with the Nethanel and the Nethanel ha-Kadosh ("the saint"—so called because of his piety and not because of his having died a martyr's death) mentioned in *Shitah Mekubbeẓet* (BK 18a; Men. 7a). *Jehiel of Paris approached Nethanel with a problem and was directed by him to Isaac b. Todros, his older contemporary (Resp. Maharik 102). *Samuel of Evreux turned to him with halakhic problems (*Mordekhai, Ḥul.* 681). Nethanel's fellow townsman *Samson of Coucy made abundant use of his teaching in his *Sefer ha-Keritut* (Constantinople, 1516). Nethanel b. Joseph of Chinon, younger brother of Eliezer of Chinon, the author of several *piyyutim*, was probably a grandson of this Nethanel.

Bibliography: A. M. Habermann, *Shirei ha-Yiḥud ve-ha-Kavod* (1948), 73–85; Urbach, Tosafot, index s.v. *Nethanel mi-Kinon.*

[I.T.-S.]

NETHERLANDS, THE (Holland), kingdom in N. W. Europe.

In the Middle Ages. It is not known when Jews first settled in what is now the Kingdom of the Netherlands but it can be assumed that Jewish merchants followed the Roman armies into the southern regions of the country, then divided into many counties and duchies. The fact that *capitularia de Judaeis* (wrongly attributed to Charlemagne) were issued in *Nijmegen and *Aachen does not necessarily prove that Jews lived in those cities at that time (ninth century). Documentary evidence dates from the 12th century only: the earliest record is of Jewish moneylenders in Rolduc (Limburg) in 1146. More details are available from the 13th century, especially for the provinces of Brabant, Gelderland, Overijssel, and Limburg. In his will (1261) Duke Henry II ordered that all Jews be expelled from Brabant but his widow obtained a declaration from Thomas *Aquinas stating to what extent it was permissible to benefit from the Jews. In 1309 John II took a large number of Jews under his protection in his castle of Genappe (Brabant) against the mob, but in Born (Limburg) 110 Jews were murdered by the people.

In 1349 and 1350, the majority of the Jews were the victims of the *Black Death persecutions. A *platea Judeorum* existed in Maastricht (Limburg) in 1295 and in the 14th century there was a *scola Judeorum* (perhaps a synagogue), which probably disappeared in 1350. In the period from 1332 to 1349 a group of Jews originally from Germany lived in Overijssel as bankers and moneylenders, but this group too disappeared during the persecutions of 1349 and 1350. There is a great scarcity of material covering the next two centuries. Bills of the duke of Gelderland show that there were Jews living in several places in this province, and there were settlements in Limburg too. However, toward the end of the 16th century Jews were expelled from

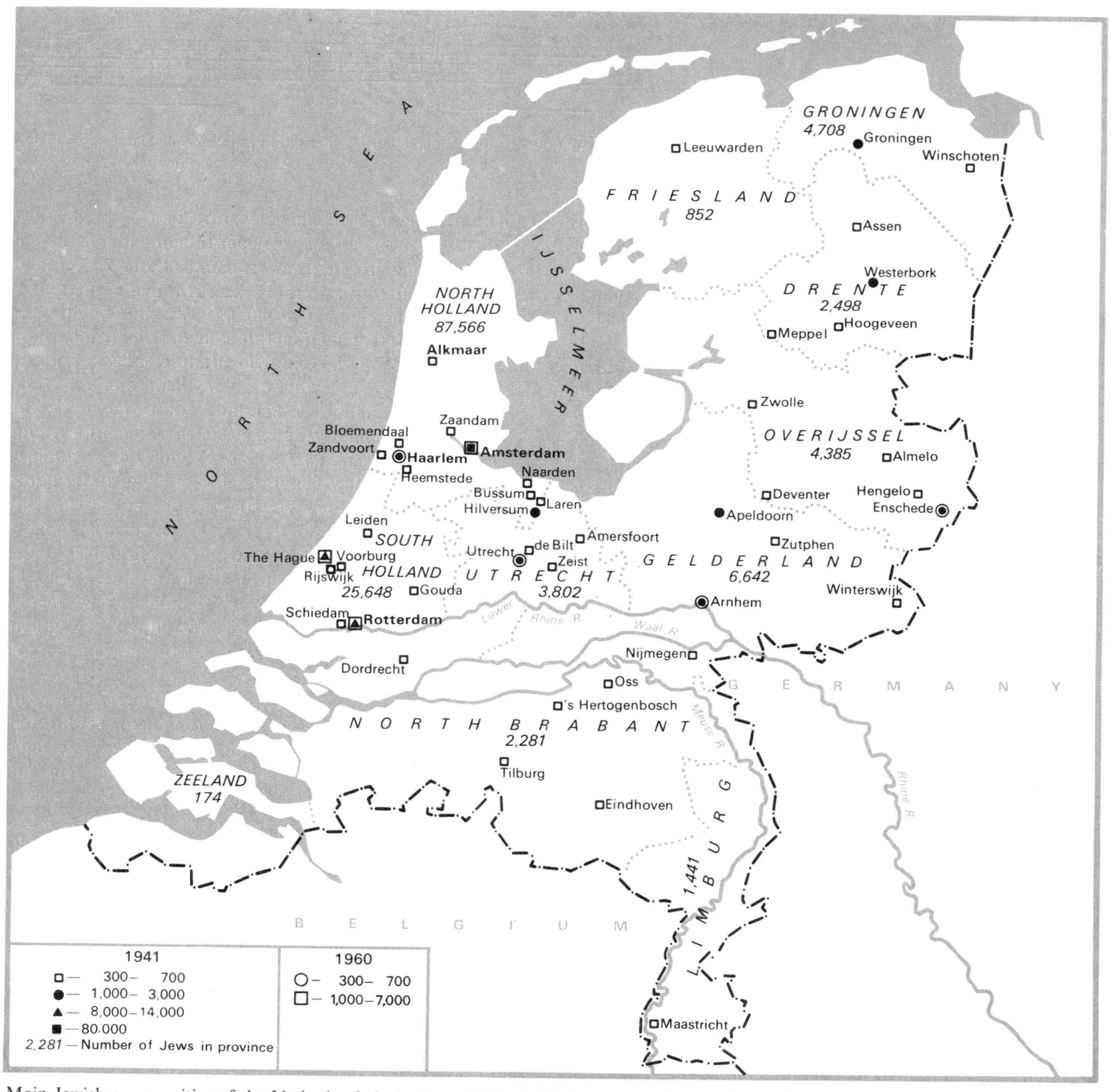

Main Jewish communities of the Netherlands in 1941 and 1960. Bold face type indicates places of Jewish settlement in the 17th century.

Figure 1. Ephraim Hezekiah Bueno, Amsterdam physician, writer, and publisher. Etching, school of Rembrandt. Amsterdam, Rijksmuseum.

Gelderland and it seems that they also disappeared from other areas when the fanatic Philip II succeeded his father Charles V (1556). As far as it is known no Jews lived in the provinces which rebelled against Spanish rule in the second half of the 17th century.

In spite of their small numbers in the country, the Jews occupy a prominent place in medieval Dutch literature: stories about Jesus and Mary are imbued with an intense hatred for the Jews, as are the legends telling of the conversions of Jews. This hatred is also expressed in the poems of the two most important poets of the Middle Ages, Jacob van Maerlant (c. 1225–c. 1291) and Jan van Boendale (1280–1365).

The Marranos and the Early Communities. Among the Portuguese merchants in the Netherlands in the 17th century many were Marranos. It is known of one of them, Marcus Perez, that he became a Calvinist and played an important role in the Netherlands' revolt against Spain. Without doubt there were many Marranos among the 20,000 merchants, industrialists, and scholars who left Antwerp in 1585 for the Republic of the United Provinces. Around 1590 the first indications of a Marrano community are to be found in *Amsterdam, but its members did not openly declare themselves as Jews. The Beth Jaäcob community was founded in secret, apparently around 1600 (in the house of Jacob *Tirado). It was discovered in 1603 and the Ashkenazi rabbi Moses Uri b. Joseph *ha-Levi, who had come from Emden the previous year, was arrested. Religious liberty was not granted in Amsterdam and therefore the Marranos who had returned to Judaism, along with newly arrived Jews from Portugal, Italy, and Turkey, tried to obtain a foothold somewhere else. In 1604 they were granted a charter in Alkmaar, and in 1605 in *Rotterdam and *Haarlem. Not only were they accorded privileges regarding military service and the Sabbath but they were also permitted to build a synagogue and open a cemetery as soon as their numbers reached 50, and to print Hebrew books. Nevertheless, only a few availed themselves of these privileges, and in spite of the difficulties most Jews settled in Amsterdam; among them was the representative of the sultan of Morocco, Don Samuel *Palache.

In 1608 a second community, Neveh Shalom, was founded by Isaac Franco and in the same year the first Sephardi rabbi, Joseph *Pardo, was appointed. As the legal status of the Jews was not clearly defined the authorities were asked by various bodies to clarify their attitude: the two lawyers, Hugo *Grotius and Adriaan Pauw, were asked to draw up special regulations for the Jews. However, in a resolution of Dec. 13, 1619, the provinces of Holland and West Friesland decided to allow each city to adopt its own policy toward the Jews. The other provinces followed this example, and this situation remained in force until 1795. For this reason the status of the Jews differed greatly in the various towns. In Amsterdam there were no restrictions on Jewish settlement, but Jews could not become burghers and were excluded from most trades; however, no such disabilities existed in several other towns. A large number of Portuguese Jews, in search of greater economic opportunities, took part in the expedition to *Brazil and in 1634 Joan Maurits van Nassau-Siegen granted the charter they had requested. When the Netherlands was compelled to cede Brazil to Portugal (1654) many Jews returned to Amsterdam. The Dutch Republic, however, demanded that its Jews be recognized as full citizens abroad and that no restrictive measure be imposed on them if they visited a foreign country, especially Spain (1657). The Ashkenazim also enjoyed the rights which the Portuguese Jews had obtained in the larger towns.

In the first half of the 18th century in the eastern part of the country also, in the area bordering Germany, small communities could be founded with complete religious liberty. Following on the activities of some Jewish robbers, however, several cities enacted measures against Jewish settlement: *Groningen (1710), *Utrecht (1713), Gouda and the province of Friesland (1712), the province of Overijssel (1724). *Amersfoort protested against one such regulation in the province of Gelderland (1726), and it was decided to introduce a certificate of good behavior, which subsequently became a requirement in most cities. Because this certificate was issued by the *parnasim*, who also had to

Figure 2. Dutch Ḥanukkah lamp, 17th century, brass, 13½×13 in. (34.5×33 cm.). Cecil Roth Collection. Photo Werner Braun, Jerusalem.

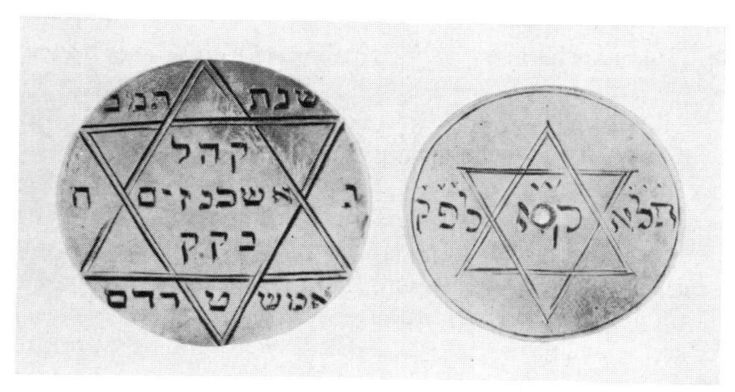

Figure 3. Silver tokens, used by the *ḥevra kaddisha* of the Amsterdam Ashkenazi community as passes for entry into the ghetto at night. The one on the left is dated 1682, the one on the right, 1671. Jerusalem, Israel Museum. Photo David Harris, Jerusalem.

guarantee the good behavior of the applicant, they acquired considerable power over the newcomers. Until *emancipation the legal position of the Jews remained unclear since it was wholly dependent on local or provincial authorities. In legal cases the Jews were subject to the laws of the land and were judged in the government courts. As they could not take the usual—Christian—oath, a special formula was introduced by the different provinces (the last in Overijssel in 1746), but this had no derogatory content. Sometimes Jews even sought the decision of Christian scholars in religious affairs. The municipal authorities intervened in the communities in the case of serious internal conflicts, as in Amsterdam in 1673 where the Polish *kehillah* was ordered to join the German one (see below) and when the authorities had to approve the regulations of the *kehillah*.

Economic Expansion. In spite of the restrictive regulations to which they were subject (which included among other things exclusion from the existing guilds), the Sephardi Jews were able to acquire some economic importance. Thanks to their knowledge of languages, administrative experience, and international relationships, they played an important part in the expanding economy of the young Republic of the Netherlands, especially from 1610 onward when Amsterdam became an established center of world trade. After 1640 there was an increase in the number of current account customers and the size of their accounts at the discount bank (Wisselbank). In the second half of the 17th century the Sephardim also occupied an important place among the shareholders of the East India Company, the most powerful Netherlands enterprise. Portuguese Jews also acquired some prominence in industry, especially in *sugar refineries, and the silk, tobacco, and *diamond industries; although the latter had been initiated by Christian polishers, in the course of time it became an exclusively Jewish industry. However they became most celebrated for *book printing; in 1626 a large number of works were produced at a high standard of printing for the day. Among the richest Portuguese Jews, who were purveyors to the army and made loans to the court, were Antonio Alvarez *Machado, the *Pereira family, Joseph de Medina and his sons, and the baron Antonio Lopez *Suasso. These and other Portuguese Jews traded in stocks and shares from the second half of the 17th century and probably constituted the majority of traders in this field (see *Stock Exchange). Such activity was centered in Amsterdam; the only other important settlements were in The *Hague, because of the proximity of the royal court, and Maarssen, a village near Utrecht (which itself did not admit Jews) which was the center of the country houses of the rich Portuguese families. From Amsterdam the Portuguese Jews took part in the economic exploration and exploitation of old and new regions, mainly in the Western hemisphere: Brazil, New Amsterdam, *Surinam, and Curaçao.

During the course of the 18th century trade declined and economic activity concentrated to a growing extent on stockjobbing. Daring speculations and successive crises led to the downfall of important families, such as the De *Pintos. The situation worsened after the economic crisis of 1772/73 and became grave during the French occupation (from 1794) when trade in goods practically came to a standstill. Government monetary measures struck especially at the rentiers, and by the end of the 18th century the once wealthy community of Amsterdam included a large number of paupers: 54% of the members had to be given financial support.

Cultural Activities of the Portuguese Community. The 17th century, the "Golden Age" of the Republic of the Netherlands, was also a time of cultural expansion for the Portuguese community. The medical profession was the most popular, and there were often several physicians in one family, as in the case of the Pharar family (Abraham "el viejo," David, and Abraham), and the *Bueno family (no less than eight, the most famous being Joseph, who in 1625 was called to the sickbed of Prince Maurits of Nassau, and whose son, Ephraim *Bueno, was painted by Rembrandt), and the De Meza, *Aboab, and De Rocamora families. The most celebrated physicians were *Zacutus Lusitanus and Isaac *Orobio de Castro. From 1655 onward there were physicians who had completed their studies in Holland,

Figure 4. Title page of *Sefer ha-Tashbeẓ*, the book of responsa by Simeon b. Ẓemaḥ Duran (1361–1444), printed in Amsterdam by Naphtali Herz Levi, 1741. The ornate decoration follows the style set by the *Amsterdam Haggadah* of 1695. Jerusalem, Israel Museum.

especially in Leiden and Utrecht. They were free to practice their profession among non-Jews also, but they were required to take a special oath. In Amsterdam, where the surgeons and pharmacists (who needed no academic training) were organized into guilds, Jews could not be officially admitted to these professions (according to the regulation of 1632). Nevertheless they set up in practice, with the result that in 1667 they were forbidden to sell medicine to non-Jews. This regulation was ignored, and so when a new regulation was issued in 1711 the restrictive clause was not included. Many Portuguese Jews were artists (notably the illuminator Shalom *Italia and engraver Jacob Gadella) and writers, mainly of poems and plays in Spanish and Portuguese; there were even two special clubs where Spanish poetry was studied. The best-known poet was Daniel Levi (Miguel) de *Barrios, the first historian of the Marrano settlement in the Netherlands.

More interesting, however, was the high level of study of Judaism and its literature from the early days of the settlement, and this in spite of the fact that large numbers of the newcomers had returned to Judaism at an advanced age. In order to teach the younger generation about Judaism the two *kehillot* in Amsterdam, Beth Jaäcob and Neveh Shalom, founded in 1616 the Talmud Torah or Ets Haim yeshivah. Through the efforts of teachers from the Sephardi Diaspora, such as Saul Levi *Morteira and Isaac Aboab da *Fonseca, the yeshivah became renowned. Among the later teachers were *Manasseh Ben Israel, Moses Raphael de *Aguilar, and Jacob *Sasportas. The facilities for printing books (see above) contributed to the high level of scholarship, and the independent production of scientific, theological, and literary works in Hebrew also developed. The most important writers were Moses *Zacuto, Solomon de *Oliveyra, Joseph *Penso de la Vega, and in the 18th century David *Franco-Mendes.

Figure 5. The Maastricht synagogue, built in 1841. Courtesy Maastricht Municipality.

The return of the Marranos to Judaism was accompanied by conflicts about the nature of their religion. In 1618 a group of strictly Orthodox Jews left Beth Jaäcob and founded the Beth Jisrael community because they did not accept the liberal leadership of the *parnas* David Pharar. Soon after, Uriel da *Costa's attack on Orthodox Judaism caused an upheaval throughout the whole *Marrano Diaspora. The most famous case was that of Baruch *Spinoza, who was banned from the *kehillah* for his heretical opinions. At this period—as among Sephardim elsewhere—Lurianic *Kabbalah had many followers in Amsterdam, which explains the enthusiasm for *Shabbetai Ẓevi that prevailed in the community in 1666. The Shabbateans maintained a strong influence for a long period and during the chief rabbinate of Solomon *Ayllon there was a serious conflict in which the Ashkenazi chief rabbi of Amsterdam Ẓevi Hirsch *Ashkenazi (Ḥakham Ẓevi) was involved (1713). The failure of the Shabbatean movement on the one hand and the power and wealth of the *kehillah* (all three congregations united in 1639) on the other led to an ever-increasing isolation from the rest of the Jewish world and to a rapprochement with Dutch society. The turning point was the founding of the famous Esnoga (synagogue), inaugurated in 1675, which subsequently dominated Sephardi community life.

The Ashkenazim. Unlike the Sephardim, the Ashkenazim spread throughout the whole Republic of the Netherlands, although their main center was also in Amsterdam. The first Ashkenazim arrived in Amsterdam around 1620, establishing their first congregation in 1635. The first emigration was from Germany but in the second half of the 17th century many Jews also came from Poland and Lithuania: they founded a separate community (1660), but in 1673, after disputes between the two, the municipal authorities ordered it to amalgamate with the German one. The community grew rapidly, outnumbering the Portuguese in the 17th century though remaining in a subservient position until the end of the 18th century. During the 17th century, the most important communities outside Amsterdam were in Rotterdam and The Hague. At that time Jews also settled in several towns in the provinces bordering Germany: Groningen, Friesland, Overijssel, and Gelderland. In spite of restrictive measures, their number increased in the 18th century, and they extended to a large number of smaller towns. There were a few very rich Ashkenazi families, such as the *Boas (The Hague), the Gomperts (Nijmegen and Amersfoort), and the Cohens (Amersfoort), but the overwhelming majority earned a meager living as peddlers, butchers, and cattle dealers. In Amsterdam the economic difficulties of the Ashkenazi Jews were even more acute and the poverty among them even greater. Apart from the diamond and book printing industries, very few trades were open to them and the majority engaged in trading in second-hand goods and foodstuffs. Foreign trade, mainly in money and shares, was concentrated in Germany and Poland. Culturally the Ashkenazi *yishuv* depended on Germany and Eastern Europe, from where most of their rabbis came. The colloquial language was Yiddish, increasingly mixed with Dutch words. Contact with the non-Jewish population was superficial, except among the very small upper class which arose in the second half of the 18th century.

Emancipation. From this group, which eventually put an end to the supremacy of the Sephardim, emerged the adherents of the so-called "patriotic trend," which was influenced by the ideas of the French Revolution. This brought them into opposition with the majority of the population and the *parnasim*, convinced adherents of the conservative Oranje Party (the party of the House of Orange). After the occupation of the Netherlands by France and the founding of the Batavian Republic (1795), the patriotic club *Felix Libertate was founded, which strove for the emancipation of the Jews and the abolition of the autonomy of the *kehillah*. After a violent controversy, the national assembly of the Batavian Republic proclaimed the complete emancipation of the Jews on Sept. 2, 1796. Nevertheless, the supporters of the emancipation were unable to obtain the leadership in the Amsterdam *kehillah;* they therefore broke away and formed a separate community (Adath Jeshurun, 1797–1808), favoring the complete integration of the Jews into Dutch society. The government, and especially King Louis Bonaparte (1806–10), supported their efforts. The king established a joint organization of all Jewish communities in the Netherlands under an Upper Consistory, and at the same time a concordat regulated relations between the "German" and "Portuguese" communities (1810). The country was divided into 11 districts where 49,973 Ashkenazim and 5,000 Sephardim lived, the latter all in Amsterdam and The Hague. The Ashkenazi community in Amsterdam numbered 31,500 members. At the same time the Jews were obliged to adopt a surname and efforts were made to spread the knowledge of the Dutch language, especially through the publication of a Dutch translation of the Bible. The annexation of the Kingdom of Holland by France (1810–13) impeded the realization of these plans. The Jewish community was severely hit economically by the war and by Napoleon's monetary measures, so that the number of paupers increased considerably.

King William I (1815–40) took an active interest in the Jewish community: he wanted to transform it into a national institution which would help the state in its task and should therefore enjoy the support of the government. His "orders in council" regulated many internal Jewish affairs; for example, the appointment of rabbis, the education of clergymen and teachers, school programs, and public worship. His decisions defined the character of the "Dutch-Israelite" and "Portuguese-Israelite" communities, as the representative Jewish bodies were called. During William's rule Jewish public education was also developed; schools for the poor were established in 1821, followed later by those for the rich, with their own inspectors, best known of whom was Dr. S. I. *Mulder. A law of 1857 made education in public schools obligatory and Jewish education was practically reduced to Sunday and evening schools. Jewish day schools were not reopened in Amsterdam until the 20th century. The government's determined battle against Yiddish and campaign for the spread of Dutch undermined the Ashkenazi community's sense of Jewish nationality.

In the 19th century the economic situation in the Netherlands as a whole remained unstable. In 1849 55% of the German and 63% of the Portuguese Jews in Amsterdam were paupers. Although no statistics are available for the rest of the country, it can be assumed that in general there too the standard of living was below the average of the rest of the population. The situation changed in the second half of the century—in Amsterdam because of the development of the diamond industry, and in the eastern region because of the rise of the cotton industry which enabled peddlers and shopkeepers to make larger profits. This gradual prosperity was accompanied by increasing urbanization; at the end of the 19th and the beginning of the 20th century many small communities ceased to exist, while in the large

NIEUWE EDITIE: 1e JAARGANG No. 1 - 11 APRIL 1941 (14 NISAN 5701)

Het Joodsche Weekblad

UITGAVE VAN DEN JOODSCHEN RAAD VOOR AMSTERDAM

JOACHIMSTHAL'S

onder verantwoordelijkheid van A. Asscher en Prof. Dr. D. Cohen

Ter inleiding

Met toestemming der Duitsche autoriteiten zal van heden af „Het Joodsche Weekblad" als uitgave van den Joodschen Raad voor Amsterdam, onder verantwoordelijkheid der ondergeteekenden, verschijnen.

Het blad zal naast mededeelingen en nieuwsberichten, artikelen bevatten, die den lezer uiteenzettingen zullen brengen omtrent Joodschen godsdienst, Joodsche wetenschap en Joodsche cultuur. Op deze wijze hoopt de redactie, die wij bereid hebben gevonden onder ons toezicht het blad samen te stellen, de lezers in te lichten omtrent alles, wat in deze dagen wetenswaardig voor hen mag worden geacht.

Wij hopen, mede door dit orgaan, den Nederlandschen Joden leiding en voorlichting te kunnen geven. Een leiding, die er naar zal streven, hunne belangen te behartigen, waar en wanneer dit mogelijk zal blijken. Een voorlichting, die hun de mogelijkheid zal bieden, officiëel en ander nieuws uit goede bron te vernemen. Daardoor zal ook het gerucht in kracht verliezen, en kan de rust behouden blijven, die voor den dagelijkschen arbeid noodzakelijk is.

Tot die gemoedsrust roepen wij allen op. Moeilijke tijden maken wij tezamen door. Wij zullen ze kunnen dragen, als wij uit het Jodendom de sterkte putten, die het ruimschoots te bieden heeft en als wij de kalmte bewaren, die ons in staat stelt, onzen plicht te doen tegenover ons zelf, ons gezin en onze omgeving.

Moge dit blad daartoe bijdragen.

A. ASSCHER
Prof. Dr. D. COHEN

OFFICIEEL

Samenstelling van den Joodschen Raad voor Amsterdam

De Beauftragte van den Rijkscommissaris voor de stad Amsterdam heeft een Joodschen Raad voor Amsterdam ingesteld, als welks voorzitters fungeeren de heeren A. Asscher en prof. dr. D. Cohen, terwijl de Raad verder bestaat uit de heeren: J. Arons, mr. N. de Beneditty, A. van den Bergh, mr. Alb. B. Gomperts, I. de Haan, A. de Hoop, mr. M. L. Kan, mr. I. Kisch, A. Krouwer, mr. H. J. van Lier, A. J. Mendes da Costa, prof. dr. J. L. Palache, mr. dr. M. I. Prins, opperrabbijn L. H. Sarlouis, dr. D. M. Sluys, A. Soep Bzn., Is. Voet en dr. I. H. J. Vos.

Figure 6. First issue of *Het Joodsche Weekblad*, the German-controlled Amsterdam Jewish weekly, April 11, 1941. On the right is reprinted the Nazi order of February 12, establishing the Amsterdam Jewish Council. Amsterdam, Jewish Historical Museum.

towns the number of Jews increased proportionally (Amsterdam: in 1849, 43% of Dutch Jewry; in 1920, 60%).

In spite of emancipation the integration of the Jews into Dutch society proceeded slowly; at first it was evident mainly among the upper classes alone, and many of these were also baptized. Lawyers in particular rose to prominent positions: Jonas Daniel *Meyer, the secretary of the commission that prepared the constitution; J. E. *Goudsmit, the first Jewish professor, was also a lawyer, as was M. H. *Godefroi, the only Jewish minister of the crown in the 19th century. The family of T. M. C. *Asser, who was awarded the Nobel Peace Prize, is another example. It was only in the second half of the 19th century, when prosperity increased and liberal ideas spread, that Jews took a larger part in public life.

After a promising beginning (including many Hebrew writers such as S. I. Mulder, M. *Lemans, and G. *Polak), cultural activities declined rapidly. Interest in the Holy Land was restricted to a small group under the leadership of the *Lehren family and A. *Prins, who founded an organization to collect money for Ereẓ Israel (1810). Efforts to establish a Reform movement in Amsterdam and Rotterdam were a complete failure. The appointment of Dr. J. H. *Duenner as rector of the Dutch Israelite Seminary (1862) and later as chief rabbi of the Ashkenazi community of Amsterdam (1874) was a turning point. Although an opponent of Reform, Duenner, who did not want to alienate nonbelieving Jews, tried to assemble a group of rabbis who had a sufficient knowledge of Judaism and a general education. In spite of his efforts, however, liberalism and socialism had an increasingly popular appeal. Liberal leaders included Samuel *Sarphati, physician and social reformer, and A. C. *Wertheim. Henry *Polak, founder of the diamond industry trade union, and other Jewish socialist leaders had considerable influence on the mass of Jews.

The Twentieth Century. In the first half of the 20th century the Jewish community in the Netherlands declined. The number of births decreased rapidly (in 1930 only 60% of the number in 1901) because of the smaller number of children born of each marriage and the increasing number of mixed marriages. The number of mixed marriages increased from 13% (in 1901) to 41% (in 1930); therefore, the percentage of Jews in relation to the total population of Holland dropped rapidly. The most important reasons for these phenomena were: (1) Jews lived mainly in towns (82% of all Jews were concentrated in seven big towns) and therefore adopted the habits of urban life; (2) after 1900 the prosperity of the Jews increased more rapidly than that of the rest of the population; and (3) the introduction of the Jews into Dutch society diminished the taboo on mixed marriages, and in this respect the Jews who considered themselves purely as a religious group followed the even stronger tendency to marry outside their religion prevalent among Catholics and Protestants. Socialist ideology also played a part in this development. Those anti-Jewish disabilities which existed (Jews were excluded from representative functions and from exclusive circles) were not strong enough to divert the general course. Nor could the Orthodox movement be a counterforce since its influence was diminishing; the secular leadership of all Jewish organizations was in the hands of non-Orthodox members while the strong Orthodox character of the *kehillot* was retained. The secular leaders neglected education and emphasized the importance of charitable institutions (Jewish hospitals, homes for invalids, the old, and mentally disturbed), which were on a high level.

Zionism obtained an early foothold in Holland but its followers remained limited to a small group of intellectuals which included J. H. *Kann, one of the first directors of the Anglo-Palestine Company; Sigmund *Seeligmann, the well-known bibliographer; and especially the chief rabbi of Amsterdam, J. H. Duenner. Until his death Duenner supported Zionism in spite of its violent rejection by all other Dutch chief rabbis, who even proscribed Zionism after the Eighth Zionist Congress at The Hague in 1907. This congress had a favorable affect on the development of the Netherlands Zionist Federation, which under the leadership of Nehemia *de Lieme, formed a small but strong organization. During World War I the many refugees who came from *Antwerp to Amsterdam and The Hague gave an impetus to greater interest in Zionism: after 1917 a national youth movement developed, a Zionist press was established, and modern Hebrew was studied. At the same time Holland became a base for the vocational training of *ḥalutzim* from Eastern Europe. Although this national-Jewish revival began during and immediately after World War I, the radical change took place under the influence of the persecutions in Germany after 1933, when a steady stream of refugees went to the Netherlands (see below). Concurrent political events strengthened the growth of the Zionist organization (at that time under the leadership of Perez *Bernstein and after his *aliyah* of A. J. Herzberg) and of the youth organizations and *He-Ḥalutz movements. Although nominally the structure of Dutch Jewry remained unchanged, in fact the emphasis was shifted from the *parnasim* to the political leadership; this had far-reaching consequences as the German occupation later proved.

In the first half of the 20th century, Jews also participated to a greater extent in Dutch society in many fields. As well as in the diamond industry, Jews were also represented in the textile industry, founding the large firms of Menko (Enschede), Spanjaard (Borne), and Kattenburg (Amsterdam), and the chain department stores of Bijenkorf and Gerzon. The margarine factory of Van den *Bergh (Unilever) developed into a worldwide firm, as did the barrel factory of Van Leer. In the professions, lawyers remained the most important: D. *Simons, J. *Oppenheim, and especially E. M. *Meyers, who compiled the new civil code for the Netherlands; but there were also many Jews in medicine, physics, philosophy, and philology. The best-known authors were the dramatist Herman Heijermans, the poet Jacob de *Haan, his sister, the prose writer Carry van *Bruggen, and the novelist Israel *Querido. There were many performing musicians among the Jews but the only composer of importance was Sem Dresden (1881–1957). Many more Jews were active in the theater: Esther de Boer van Rijk (1853–1937), Louis de Vries (1871–1940), and the noted cabaret performer Louis Davids (1883–1939). The most famous painter was Jozef *Israels; others were his son Isaac (1865–1934) and Martin Monnickendam (1874–1941). The most important sculptor was Joseph Mendes *da Costa and the best-known architect Michel *de Klerk, founder of the "Amsterdam School."

Until World War II there were four Jewish weeklies—of which the *Nieuw Israëlietisch Weekblad* (founded in 1865) and the *Joodse Wachter* (1905–) were most widely read—and also many monthlies and magazines.

Holocaust Period. On the eve of the Holocaust, there were 140,000 Jews in Holland, of whom 121,400 were members of the Ashkenazi community, 4,301 of the Sephardi community, and another 12,400 Jews were unaffiliated with the religious communities. There were also about 1,900 Christians of Jewish origin or parentage living in the Netherlands. In 1933, immediately after the Nazi rise to power, German Jews began their flight to Holland. A Comité voor Bijzondere Joodse Belangen ("Committee for Special Jewish Affairs") was established to aid the refugees on March 21, 1933, by Abraham *Asscher, president of the organization of Dutch-Jewish communities, and David *Cohen, a longtime active Zionist. The council's prime task was to facilitate absorption of refugees and aid their further emigration; to a lesser degree it also engaged in anti-Nazi propaganda. By January 1939 the committee had spent approximately 3,000,000 Dutch guilders ($780,000) for these purposes from funds collected mostly from the Jewish

Figure 7. The Jewish Quarter established by the Nazis in Amsterdam. A photograph taken in 1942. Courtesy Yad Vashem Archives, Jerusalem.

Table 1. Number of Jews in the Netherlands.

	Ashkenazim	Sephardim	Total
1780	27,000	3,000	30,000
1810[1]	49,973	3,000	53,000
1830			46,397
1849	55,412	3,214	58,626
1869	64,478	3,525	68,000
1889	78,075	5,070	83,145
1909	99,785	6,624	106,409
1930	106,723	5,194	111,917
1941[2]			139,687
1954			23,723

Table 2. Distribution over the Provinces (according to %).

	1830	1909	1930	1914	1954
Groningen	5.7	5.3	3.9	3.5	1.0
Drenthe	2.5	2.0	1.5	1.7	0.8
Overijssel	4.8	4.1	3.3	3.1	4.0
Gelderland	5.9	4.8	4.7	4.7	4.2
Utrecht	3.2	1.3	1.5	2.7	3.6
North Holland (incl. Amsterdam)	52.0	60.6	61.9	62.8	65.0
South Holland (incl. Rotterdam and The Hague)	16.3	17.6	20.1	18.3	16.6
Zeeland	1.0	0.3	0.2	0.1	0.2
North Brabant	3.1	1.7	1.5	1.6	2.6
Limburg	1.9	0.9	0.7	1.0	1.3

Table 3. Division According to Profession in 1930 (in %).

	Jews		Whole Population	
	men	women	men	women
Industry	36	39	44	22
Trade	49	35	12	14
Free professions	5	8	5	7
Rest	5	18	39	57

community in Holland. In 1939 expenses rose to approximately 3,000,000 guilders a year because of increased anti-Jewish measures in Germany. At that time there were about 30,000 German-Jewish fugitives in Holland. The Dutch government, which had continuously resisted a more liberal admission policy, decided to establish a central camp for illegal immigrants at *Westerbork, a forbidding wasteland in the northeast, not far from the German border. The financial burden fell on the committee, which was taxed 200.000 guilders yearly as of February 1939. A well-organized and extensive apparatus was needed for the committee's enormous tasks. Except for its leaders, the membership consisted almost exclusively of German Jews. The existence of this institution with its many departments (including finances, occupational rehabilitation, education, and culture) was to prove of enormous—and, according to some—fatal import for developments in Holland after the German occupation.

THE FIRST ANTI-JEWISH MEASURES. The first months following the Dutch capitulation (May 14, 1940) passed quietly. The first anti-Jewish measures taken by the German occupation authorities in September consisted of barring Jews' entrance in certain professions and residential districts. Of greater importance still was the German demand that every civil servant sign a declaration that he was an "Aryan." In November all Jewish civil servants and teachers were dismissed. A further step was compulsory registration (January 1941) and the issue of special identity cards for Jews. At the same time the Ashkenazi and Sephardi communities, in cooperation with national Jewish organizations, instituted a Committee of Coordination, which sought to formulate a unified stand in the Jewish population. The committee's president, Lodewÿk E. Visser, categorically refused to cooperate on any anti-Jewish measure. Asscher and Cohen disagreed with his stand and hoped to alleviate suffering by cooperating with the Germans. This attitude was reflected in the policy Asscher and Cohen adopted as presidents of the Jewish Council (established by German order on Feb. 12, 1941), which was made responsible for the Jews of Amsterdam. The apparatus of the Committee for Special Jewish Affairs was extended and incorporated into the Jewish Council, which increasingly supplanted the Committee of Coordination. On Oct. 27, 1941, the Germans extended the power of the Jewish Council over the whole of Holland and ordered the Committee of Coordination to suspend its activities. In every province and in Rotterdam a representative responsible to the Jewish Council was appointed. The Jewish Council developed into a huge organization, whose staff numbered approximately 17,000 at its climax. All existing Jewish institutions were incorporated into it, and a great many new departments were established to cope with problems caused by the German measures. Officially, the Jewish Council had 18 members at its inception. Its actual power, however, was in the hands of its two presidents and the senior officials. An important advantage lay in the fact that the Jewish Council had its own publication. In September 1940 all Jewish newspapers were banned by the German authorities and replaced by a single, German-controlled Jewish weekly. The issue of anti-Jewish measures in a specifically Jewish publication averted reaction by the non-Jewish population and served to further isolate the Jewish community. The *Joodsche Weekblad* first appeared on April 11, 1941. Although it initially published cultural articles and attempted to elevate the morale of the Jewish population, it ultimately became little more than a vehicle for announcements from the Jewish Council. The paper ceased publication when the presidents themselves and the last remaining officials of the council were deported (September 1943).

To isolate the Jewish population further, Jewish children were removed from public schools and an extensive network of Jewish schools was established and supervised by the Jewish Council (August 1941). At the beginning of 1942 the system provided for 1,200 children in kindergarten, 9,000 primary school children, 4,200 secondary school children, and 75 teachers-in-training in 36 cities. A total of 111 schools with 758 teachers dealt with these 14,500 students. Similar concentrations in other sectors of public life, such as hospitals, homes for the aged, youth centers, and sports clubs, took place. All the existing Jewish organizations were banned by the Germans and their funds confiscated; they were then grouped into centralized bodies functioning as departments of the Jewish Council.

The financing of the Jewish community, which was impoverished by ostracism from the economic and community life of the country, compulsory transfer of business to non-Jews, and confiscation, was a major problem. The Jewish Council levied taxes on all Jews; non-payment disqualified one from using the services of the Council. Another part of the funds came from subsidies by the bank of Lippmann, Rosenthal and Co., originally a Jewish bank that was exploited by the Germans for the pilfering of

Figure 8. Amsterdam schoolchildren wearing the yellow badge, 1942. Courtesy Yad Vashem Archives, Jerusalem.

Jewish capital. The Nazis first carried out a compulsory transfer to this bank of all Jewish property in August 1941; a sum total of 300–400,000,000 guilders (about $100,000,000) was thus extracted from the Jews of Holland. Approximately 20% of this money was spent on financing the Jewish Council and the camps at *Vught and Westerbork and income payments to the Jewish individuals involved. The rest was transferred to German institutions. There were also other ways in which the German state (or German and Dutch National-Socialists) appropriated Jewish funds. Of the 22,000 Jewish businesses, 200 "Aryanized" themselves, while 2,000 were compulsorily "Aryanized," the remainder being liquidated. This netted the Germans 75,000,000 guilders.

CONCENTRATION IN CAMPS AND IN AMSTERDAM. Before the *Wannsee Conference (Jan. 20, 1942), when many different German authorities engaged in anti-Jewish measures, one of them established labor camps in Holland whose inmates (exclusively male) endured inhuman conditions. In the course of 1942 the Jewish Council cooperated in establishing 42 of these camps all over Holland. Finally, 5,242 men from 85 towns and cities in Holland were placed in these camps to work on various development projects, some wholly superfluous. These people were ready victims at the start of the deportations for "work in the East," as they were deceptively called. In a raid *(razzia)* that took place simultaneously in all suitable locations in Holland on Friday night, Oct. 2, 1942, whole families, including 8,877 women and children, were arrested. These were transported first to Westerbork and then to *Auschwitz. The concentration of the Jews was also effected by evacuating hundreds of towns and hamlets. Non-Dutch Jews had to leave the shore region immediately at the outset of the Nazi occupation. At the end of 1941 Jews could move only to Amsterdam. Later the Jews in other parts of Holland were forced to move to Amsterdam. This activity was in the framework of making Holland *"Judenrein"* ("clean of Jews"). Finally, the Jews were forbidden to live in eight of the 11 Dutch provinces. The remaining three provinces were restricted on April 13, 1943, so that legally, with very few exceptions, Jews could only live in Amsterdam. The Nazis decreed on May 9, 1942, that the yellow badge which was meant to isolate the Jews and degrade them in the eyes of their fellow citizens, was to be worn by every Jew, and the Jewish Council was compelled to cooperate with the implementation of the order. The measure encountered much resistance from the Dutch population, even in National-Socialist circles. In protest, stars were distributed and worn by non-Jews. The Germans reported that the Jews wore their star proudly, but that they were frightened by the new anti-Jewish measures.

DEPORTATIONS. Deportations began shortly afterwards. The Germans called this operation *"Arbeitseinsatz im Osten"* ("work in the East"), but in reality it meant certain death in the extermination camps, especially Mauthausen. During the summer of 1942, the Germans systematically organized the deportation of almost all the remaining Jews. In the course of 15 months (until September 1943) the mass deportations were completed. At first, as a means of camouflaging the fate awaiting the Jews, the Nazis called young people up by mail. However, when too few people presented themselves, arrests followed. Detainees were usually transported immediately to Westerbork, which was proclaimed a *PolizeilichesDurchgangslager* ("Police-Transit Camp"; July 16, 1942). Those Jewish inmates who were originally illegal immigrants from Germany were made responsible for the internal management and organization of the camp including, almost without exception, arranging the transports to the East. The transports, sent out at intervals, comprised only part of the camp population, thus creating a "forced community" *(Zwangsgemeinschaft)* with a very complicated and widespread organization. Although living conditions were primitive, especially when the camp population suddenly swelled as a result of massive *aktionen* and deportations, life was bearable because the German administration seldom interfered in the internal life. The camp was ruled mainly by the fear of transport to the concentration camps. Approximately 100 such transports took place. Most people were sent to Auschwitz (60,000); in 1943 many transports were directed to *Sobibor (34,000 people, who were gassed upon arrival). A small minority was transported to *Theresienstadt (almost 5,000, mostly prominent personalities), and to *Bergen-Belsen (4,000 people, intended for exchange with other countries). Of the latter, 25% indeed survived the war and a number were exchanged during the war for Germans in foreign countries (222 reached Palestine; 136 entered Switzerland).

In addition to Westerbork, another camp existed for a time at Vught as part of *KL-Herzogenbusch*. Built in 1943, it seemed at first to be a work camp for a great number of Jews. When all provincial cities and towns were made *judenrein* (April–May 1943) all Jews had to move to Amsterdam. Hard labor, little food, and severe punishments made for a much more inhumane existence than in Westerbork. From June 1943 to June 1944 all 12,000 inmates of Vught were sent to Westerbork.

ATTEMPTS AT EVASION AND PROTECTION. As the Germans followed a vacillating policy toward partners of mixed marriages, some Jews did escape persecution legally. Many of these Jews were sent to labor camps, while all Jewish partners were put under pressure to have themselves sterilized; approximately 25% (of 8,610) indeed submitted to this operation. Only a very few were sent to the annihilation camps. A great number of Jews used genuine or false documents to prove that they were of Aryan descent; this attempt succeeded in more cases than could be expected, due to the cooperation of a lawyer, the German "expert" on "Aryan" extraction, Hans Callmeyer. By contrast, a petition from the Jewish Portuguese community that their members be considered as Aryans was rejected after initial approval, with fatal consequences for its members. It was extremely difficult to leave the country illegally, because two borders—the Belgian and French—

had to be crossed. A few non-Jews (Jean Weidner, Joop *Westerweel) did magnificent work by saving Jews in this way. But for the majority this escape operation was much too dangerous, too difficult, and in many instances too expensive. A better chance of surviving was offered by going into hiding with non-Jews (*"onderduiken,"* "submerging"), which was done on a large scale. According to estimates, more than 20,000 went into hiding for periods of varying duration. They were dependent on the non-Jews, who risked their lives for either financial or moral motives. A national organization came into existence to support the "hiders," more than half of whom eventually fell into German hands, mostly by betrayal. Many of the non-Jewish protectors were sent to concentration camps and tortured to death. It is estimated that approximately 10,000 Jews, among them 3,500 children, survived the war through hiding. Many of the hidden or "submerged" Jews participated in various forms of resistance against the German occupation.

See also *Amsterdam; *Bergen-Belsen; David *Cohen; Anne *Frank; Anton A. *Mussert; *Resistance; *Righteous Gentiles; *Rotterdam; Arthur *Seyss-Inquart; *Theresienstadt; *Vught; *Westerbork; *Westerweel, Joop.

Table 4. Number of Jews in Holland (according to registration in 1941).

Dutch Jews	117,999
German Jews	14,381
Jews from other countries	7,621
Total	140,001
Half Jews	15,342
Quarter Jews	6,115

Table 5. Transports to German Camps (from July 1942).

Auschwitz	± 60,000	Surviving	500
Sobibor	± 34,000	Surviving	19
Bergen-Belsen	± 4,000	Surviving	1,100
Theresienstadt	± 4,897	Surviving	1,273

Table 6. Estimated Number of Survivors.*

Camps (incl. Dutch)	± 106,000	Surviving	5,450	5%
Hiding	± 22,000	Surviving	±10,000	45%
Mixed marriage	± 10,000	Surviving	± 10,000	100%
Escaped to other countries	± 2,000	Surviving	± 2,000	100%
Total	140,000	Surviving	27,000	20%

* The numbers arrived at by the various investigations differ slightly.

Contemporary Period. DEMOGRAPHY. The population of Holland had suffered from the German occupation to a greater extent than any other country of Western Europe; approximately 500,000 laborers were deported to Germany for forced labor; the country was looted, especially during the last year of the war; and, lastly, the final phase of the war (fighting going on on Dutch soil) brought famine to most of the country, especially the cities. The Jews who emerged from their hiding places or returned from the concentration camps found a disorganized society that was neither able nor willing to compensate them for the moral deprivations and the material damage they had suffered, even though the surviving Jewish population was small. In 1946 an estimated 30,000 Jews lived in Holland, 21% of the prewar population. Of this number, 8,000 were partners of mixed marriages. By 1954 the Jewish population of Holland had decreased to 26,623. Of these, 14,068 lived in Amsterdam, 2,031 in The Hague, and 1,323 in Rotterdam. The major cause of this decrease was emigration. During eight years 4,492 Jews left Holland primarily for the United States (1,399), Israel (1,209), Canada (440), and Australia (286). The decrease in Jewish population relative to the rest of the Dutch population was even higher, due to a low birth rate and a high death rate. This situation developed as a result of the small number of young people who remained in the country.

POSTWAR RECONSTRUCTION. Economic reestablishment was at first difficult for the Jews. A long legal battle had to be fought in order for them to regain possessions, obtain recognition of life insurances, and receive a portion of the German reparation payments. When the general economic situation improved later on, satisfying settlements were obtained in all these cases, so that individuals as well as the community acquired large sums of money. The German reparation payments alone yielded 200,000,000 marks. The result was that the Jewish community, which contained a large proletariat before the war, could later be considered very wealthy. Reclaiming children who had been rescued by non-Jews became a special problem for the returning Jews. Of the 3,481 children rescued, 1,540 returned to their parents and courts immediately appointed a Jewish guardian for 472 others. The remaining 1,433 children were first placed under the guardianship of a government commission, which often chose to let the children remain with their non-Jewish rescuers. The Jewish authorities resisted their attitude, however, and engaged in many lawsuits in order to have the children placed in Jewish homes. Finally, approximately two-thirds of these children were placed under Jewish guardianship. Two cases are notorious in which the court wanted to place the children under Jewish guardianship, but the foster parents succeeded in abducting the children with the help of the Roman Catholic Church, and continued to educate them in the Roman Catholic faith.

RELIGIOUS AND SOCIAL INSTITUTIONS. No changes occurred in the organizational structure of the community after the war. The *kehillot* that existed before the war, the Dutch-Israelite, the Portuguese-Israelite, and the Liberal, were reestablished, but the relationships between them were greatly changed. The Portuguese *kehillah,* which existed only in Amsterdam, comprised only a few families; the Ashkenazi (Dutch-Israelite) *kehillah* was the largest and it comprised many small communities outside the major cities. Many of these communities were brought to an end by emigration, while others became more and more dependent on the central Jewish authorities for their religious needs and the upkeep of their synagogues. There

Figure 9. Dutch Jews about to be deported to a German concentration camp, 1942/43. Courtesy Yad Vashem Archives, Jerusalem.

Figure 10. Ark of the Law and *bimah* in the Liberal synagogue built in Amsterdam after World War II. Photo M. Ninio, Jerusalem.

were four chief rabbis: one in Amsterdam, one in The Hague, one in Rotterdam, and one traveling rabbi for the small communities. The Liberal community, which consisted almost exclusively of German refugees before the war, flourished and attracted many Jews who were estranged from Judaism. Postwar circumstances compelled the leaders of the Ashkenazi community to close many of the synagogues in the small communities; even in Amsterdam, two central synagogues in the center of the old, now depopulated and badly damaged Jewish quarter were closed. On the other hand, new synagogues were built in some communities to replace those that were destroyed during the war (e. g., in Rotterdam). The religious structure of the *kehillot* also remained unchanged after the war. There was practically no cooperation on religious affairs between the two Orthodox communities and the Liberal one, but centralization was achieved in other areas. All social institutions were concentrated under the auspices of one organization, Jewish Social Work, and money for this organization was collected by one fund, the Central Fund Raising Campaign. All fund raising for Israel was concentrated in the Collective Israel Campaign. Of the four prewar weekly newspapers, only one, the *Nieuw Israelitisch Weekblad,* remained. In addition, many local and party journals existed.

The Zionist movement, which had risen to importance immediately before the war, became the most powerful force in all Jewish organizations after the liberation. Within the Zionist movement, the Radical Faction dominated in the beginning, demanding mass *aliyah* and liquidation of the Diaspora. Indeed, practically all its leading personalities settled in Israel, leaving successors who took a more moderate position on this question. This change of view was also influenced by the disappearance of tension that existed between the Jewish and the non-Jewish population of Holland directly after the war. A general sympathy and compassion was felt for the Jews, and later for Israel. The status of the Jews in Holland in 1970 was in many respects better than it was before the war. The small Jewish community produced dozens of professors, many writers and painters, and even three cabinet ministers. In view of the unfavorable demographic prospects on the one hand and the continuing attraction of emigration, especially to Israel, on the other, it was improbable that the community would be able to maintain this status in the future. [J.M.]

Relations with Israel. A long-standing history of cooperation links the Jewish people to the Dutch, from the period of the "Golden Age" of Dutch Jewry after the expulsion of the Jews from Spain and Portugal until the demonstrations of support and acts of rescue during the Nazi occupation of the Netherlands. On Nov. 29, 1947, the Netherlands voted in favor of the UN plan to partition Palestine, and thus for the establishment of a Jewish state, and soon afterward officially recognized the new State of Israel. Formal diplomatic relations were established on the ambassadorial level, with Holland being the first country to set up its diplomatic representation in Jerusalem. The Netherlands supported Israel in the United Nations as well as in other international frameworks on a number of occasions; supported Israel against the Arab boycott and Arab aggression; and played a role in the struggle for persecuted Jews, especially Jews in the Soviet Union and the Arab countries. It was also Israel's major aid in its efforts to establish ties with the European Economic Community. When the Soviet Union severed diplomatic relations with Israel in 1953, the Netherlands represented Israel's interests in the U.S.S.R. and contributed to the resumption of diplomatic ties between the two states. It again assumed this role when the U.S.S.R. and other Communist states broke diplomatic relations with Israel after the Six-Day War (1967); subsequently Israel's interests in the U.S.S.R. and Poland were represented by Holland.

Trade relations between the two countries reached $75,-000,000 in 1966 and rose to $84,000,000 by 1968, with Dutch exports to Israel somewhat larger than Israel exports to Holland. Tourism from Holland to Israel also rose, with 7,983 tourists in 1966, 9,308 in 1967, and 14,047 in 1968. The high points in cultural exchanges were the arrangement of a Dutch art exhibit in Israel and an exhibit from the Land of the Bible and appearances of the Israel Philharmonic Orchestra in Holland. Every year an Israel delegation participated in the popular march in Nijmegen, and a Dutch delegation took part in the yearly marches that take place in Israel, which are modeled on the Dutch ones. Prime ministers, foreign ministers, and other members of the government and of parliament of the two countries carried out mutual visits. [Y.ME.]

For the musical tradition of Jews in the Netherlands see *Amsterdam.

Bibliography: GENERAL AND HISTORICAL: Brugmans-Frank; M. H. Gans, *Memorboeck* (1971); ESN; Graetz, Hist, index; S. Seeligman, *De Emancipatie der Joden in Nederland* (1918); S. van Praag, *De West-Joden en hun letterkunde* (1926); H. Poppers, *De Joden in Overijssel* (1926); E. Boekman, *Demografie van de Joden in Nederland* (1936); H. I. Bloom, *Economic Activities of the Jews of Amsterdam in the Seventeenth and Eighteenth Centuries* (1937, repr. 1969); H. Beem, *De verdwenen mediene* (1950); J. Stengers, *Les juifs dans les Pays-Bas au moyen âge* (1950); J. Melkman, *David Franco Mendes* (1951); D. Cohen, *Zwervend en dolend* (1955); M. E. Bolle, *De opheffing van de autonomie der kehilloth (Joodse gemeenten) in Nederland, 1796* (1960); L. Finkelstein (ed.), *The Jews,* 2 vols. (1960[3]), index; J. Meijer, *Het Jonas Daniël Meijerplein* (1961); idem, *Erfenis der emancipatie: het Nederlandse Jodendom in de eerste helft van de 19e eeuw* (1963); idem, *Zij lieten hun sporen* *achter* (1964); I. Lipschits, *Honderd jaar het Nieuw Israëlietisch Weekblad, 1865–1965* (1966); *Studia Rosenthaliana* (1967–); C. Reijnders, *Van "Joodsche natiën" tot Joodse Nederlanders* (1969); Shunami, Bibl, index. HOLOCAUST PERIOD: W. Warmbrunn, *The Dutch under German Occupation 1940–1945* (1963); R. Hilberg, *Destruction of the European Jews* (1961), 365–81; J. Presser, *Destruction of the Dutch Jews* (1969); idem, *Ondergang*, 2 vols. (1965); A. J. Herzberg, *Kroniek der Jodenvervolging* (1949–54); De Jong, in: *Yad Vashem Studies*, 7 (1968), 39–55; P. Mechanicus, *In Depot, Dagboek uit Westerbork* (1964); H. G. Adler, *Theresienstadt* (Ger., 1960); E. Kolb, *Bergen-Belsen* (Ger., 1962). CONTEMPORARY PERIOD: JJSO, 3 (1961), 195–242; 4 (1962), 47–71; H. Boas, *ibid.*, 5 (1963), 55–83; J. Melkman, *Geliefde vijand* (1964); M. Snijders, *Joden van Amsterdam* (1958); S. Wijnberg, *De Joden in Amsterdam* (1967); A. Vedder et al., *De Joden in Nederland na de tweede wereldoorlog* (1960).

NETHERLANDS ANTILLES (or **Dutch Antilles;** formerly **Dutch West Indies**), two groups of islands: Saba, St. Eustatius, and the southern half of St. Martin Island in the Leewards group; and Bonaire, Curaçao, and Aruba located off the coast of Venezuela; population (1969)—approximately 234,000.

Aruba. The first Jew to settle in Aruba was Moses Salomo Levy Maduro (1753). The Jewish population totaled: 19 persons in 1816; 32 in 1825; and 23 in 1867. After 1924 a number of immigrants came to the island from Holland, Surinam, and Eastern Europe. A Jewish center was established in 1942 and four years later a Jewish community was officially organized. The community's Beth Israel synagogue was dedicated in 1962. In 1970 the congregation numbered 35 families, and was served by a *hazzan*-teacher.

Curaçao. A Samuel Cohen served as an interpreter to the Dutch army which captured Curaçao from the Spaniards in 1634. Congregation Mikveh Israel was founded officially in 1651. The Jews were granted land outside the city of Willemstad, and a cemetery was opened in this quarter in 1656 and a small building rented for worship. In 1681 a second synagogue was built. Jews were living within Willemstad by 1659; a synagogue existed there by 1671, and it was enlarged in 1674 and again in 1680. This was replaced by a new structure in 1702, which, in turn, was replaced by a synagogue built in 1730–32, which was well preserved and in use in 1970. Josiau Pardo, the first *ḥakham* of the congregation, was appointed in 1674. Jacob Lopez da Fonseca, who held office from 1764 to 1815, was born in Curacao and sent to Amsterdam for his rabbinical education.

In 1744 the community was agitated by a dispute arising out of the desire of one Samuel de Leao to annul the obligations undertaken in his *ketubbah*, a dispute which eventually reached the attention of the States General at The Hague. This was followed by another quarrel concerning the Neveh Shalom synagogue in Otrabanda (the section of Willemstad lying to the west of the harbor). Members of the Jewish community had lived there since 1732, worshiping in a local synagogue which remained under the jurisdiction of the main congregation. Disputes arose in connection with the building of a new synagogue in 1745. The bitterness led to street fights. The *ḥakham* excommunicated certain parties which led to the right of burial being denied them. At one stage of the dispute, the governor had to send soldiers to every Jewish burial. The dispute was settled in 1750 by decree of Prince William of Orange-Nassau. In 1815 the engagement of a *ḥazzan* led to a secession from Mikveh Israel and the intervention of the governor. Peace was restored in 1821.

Forty years after the death of Jacob Lopez da Fonseca, the congregation appointed Aron Mendes Chumaceiro (1810–1882) as *ḥakham*. He held office until 1869. The congregation was divided by personal rivalries, and, despite his excellent work, Chumaceiro was subjected to the hostility of some of the leading members. This animosity led to a further secession from Mikveh Israel, and, on this occasion, to the establishment of a Reform congregation, Emanu-el (1864). This group opened its temple in 1866. Under Chumaceiro the older congregation introduced modifications in ritual practice, such as a mixed choir and organ music. Mikveh Israel and Emanu-el merged in 1963, and the united congregation adopted the Reconstructionist prayer book and joined the World Union for Progressive Judaism. From 1926 onward, numbers of Ashkenazi Jews, many from Rumania, settled in Curaçao. In 1932 they founded the Club Union center and in 1959 they opened the Shaarei Tzedek synagogue.

Jews were originally allowed to settle in Curaçao, on the understanding that they were to engage in agriculture. However, the arid climate and rocky soil made this condition difficult to fulfill. By 1652 Jews were engaged in trading and shipping and before long they became very prominent in the commerce of the island. Some commanded boats, armed them, and fought pirates and privateers. Jews, in common with the other settlers, bought slaves from the Dutch West India Company in Curaçao. Although the slaves were intended mainly for resale, some were for personal use. Philipe Henriquez (Jacob Senior) was one of the largest slave dealers of the 17th century. A Moses Penso owned 450 slaves at his death in 1754. Generally, the slaves of Curaçao were treated humanely by Jews and Protestants alike.

The Jews of Curaçao enjoyed excellent relations with the Dutch West India Company, which owned the island until the end of the 18th century, and with the government of Curaçao. The company protected the Jews against the few governors who were hostile to them. Most of the governors

Figure 1. Tombstone in Curaçao, Netherlands Antilles, of Mordochay Namias de Castro (d. 1716), an outstanding personality in commerce and communal life. The triumph of Mordecai from the Book of Esther is illustrated in relief. Photo J. van Essen, Curaçao.

recognized the importance of the Jewish community for the island's well-being. During the 18th century, governors often entrusted Jews with delicate missions to Venezuela and the neighboring islands. The Jews contributed liberally to the building of Curaçao's fortresses, churches, and hospitals. Three Jews attained the rank of commandant major in the civil guard. Jews were members of different councils of the island from 1830, and three became president of the Colonial Council. From 1884 a Jew was often president of the Curacao chamber of commerce. Many Curaçao Jews represented Holland as consuls in different cities in the Americas, or represented various governments in Curaçao. The Dutch government makes a substantial contribution to the salary of the rabbi of the united congregation. Many Jewish businesses were among those destroyed in rioting in 1969, although the cause of the riots was economic and not specifically directed against Jews. Some 750 Jews lived there in 1970.

St. Eustatius. In 1722 there were 21 Jews living in St. Eustatius. In 1730 they founded a community, Honen Dalim, and in 1737 built a synagogue. Differences between Ashkenazim and Sephardim in 1760 required the intervention of the island's governor to restore peace. A Rabbi Ezekiel (1775) and Jacob Robles, who died in 1790, were two of the community's *ḥazzanim*. During the American Revolutionary War, 30 Jews were deported to St. Kitts. They returned in 1781, when the island was captured by the French. The Jewish community numbered 170 people in 1790 and was very well organized. From 1795 onward, the Jewish population declined steadily until, in 1850, it consisted of three people.

St. Martin (Dutch section). Jews have lived on St. Martin from 1735. In 1783 there was an organized Jewish community recognized by the Dutch West India Company. However, by 1820 the Jewish population numbered approximately five people. In 1969 less than ten adult Jewish males lived in the Dutch section of the island.

Bibliography: I. S. and S. A. Emmanuel, *History of the Jews of the Netherlands Antilles* (1970); I. S. Emmanuel, *Precious Stones of the Jews of Curaçao, Curaçaoan Jewry, 1656–1957* (1957); idem, in: *Geschiedkundige Opstellen* (1943), 55–78; idem, in: *Lux* (1944), 143–9; idem, in: AJHSP, 44 (1955), 215–36; Cone, *ibid.*, 10 (1902), 141–57; J. M. Corcos, *A Synopsis of the History of the Jews of Curaçao from the Day of Their Settlement to the Present Time* (1897); J. L. Maduro, in: *Gedenkboek Nederland-Curaçao 1634–1934* (1934), 69–78. [I.S.E.]

Figure 2. Temple Emanu-el, Curaçao, opened in 1864.

NETHERWORLD, the abode of the dead. The peoples of the Ancient Near East had elaborate doctrines concerning the dead and their abode. The Egyptians were very optimistic concerning the afterlife. They believed that ceremonies of mummification, rituals and spells, and declarations of guiltlessness would ensure them a happy afterlife almost identical to the life they led in this world. In the afterlife they would plow, harvest, eat, and drink; in short, do all they did while they were alive (*The Book of the Dead*, 110).

For the Babylonians, on the other hand, the realm of the dead was a place to be dreaded. It was a well-organized kingdom with Ereshkigal and *Nergal as its queen and king, respectively. To enter it one had to pass through seven gates and remove one's garments. The netherworld is depicted as "... the land of no return ... the dark house ... the house which none leave who have entered it ... the road from which there is no way back ... the house wherein the entrants are bereft of light, where dust is their fare and clay their food, [where] they see no light, residing in darkness, [where] they are clothed like birds, with wings for garments, [and where] over door and bolt is spread dust" (*Descent of Ishtar to the Netherworld*, 1–11, in Pritchard, Texts, 107; cf. *Epic of Gilgamesh*, 7, 3:33–39, in Pritchard, Texts, 87). The plight of the dead could be worsened or alleviated depending on whether they were properly buried, and whether or not food and drink were brought to them. Such practices and speculations are not entirely wanting in the Bible. Deuteronomy 26:12, 14 implies that only food that has been consecrated as tithe may not be left as a gift for the dead, the practice of feeding the dead as such being permitted, while Isaiah 14:14–19 and Ezekiel 38:18ff., reflect a belief that those who are slain by the sword (and not decently buried), as also such as die uncircumcised, are assigned the lowest—and no doubt the least desirable—level of the netherworld (see Ginsberg in bibl.). On the other hand the practice of occult arts including necromancy was abhorred by the Bible (Deut. 18:11; Isa. 8:19), and there was no sacrifice to the dead (Ps. 106:28). Sacrifice to the dead means sacrifice to no-gods, such as Baal-Peor; cf. Numbers 25:2–3.

Apart from the Isaiah and Ezekiel passages referred to above, the numerous biblical references to the netherworld are vague and inspired by Ancient Near Eastern folklore. Several names are given to the abode of the dead, the most common being *She'ol*—always feminine and without the definite article—a sign of proper nouns. The term does not occur in other Semitic languages, except as a loan word from the Hebrew *She'ol*, and its etymology is obscure. Other common designations of the netherworld are: *ʾereẓ*, "earth" or "underworld" (e.g., I Sam. 28:13; Jonah 2:7; Job 10:21–22); *qever*, "grave" (Ps. 88:12); *ʿafar*, "dust" (Isa. 26:5, 19; cf. Gen. 3:19); *bor*, "pit" (e.g., Isa. 14:15; 38:18; Prov. 28:17); *shaḥat*, "pit" (Ps. 7:16); *ʾavaddon*, "Abaddon" (e.g., Job. 28:22); *dumah* (apparently = "the place of abiding"; Ps. 94:17; 115:17); *naḥale beliyyaʿal* ["the torrents of *Belial"; II Sam. 22:5); "the nether parts of the earth" (Ezek. 31:14); "the depths of the pit" (Lam. 3:55); "the land of darkness" (Job 10:21). The netherworld is located somewhere under the earth (cf. Num. 16:30ff.), or at the bottoms of the mountains (Jonah 2:7), or under the waters—the cosmic ocean (Job 26:5). It is sometimes personified as a voracious monster with a wide-open mouth (e.g., Isa. 5:14; Hab. 2:5; Prov. 1:12), Kings and commoners, nobles and paupers, masters and slaves are equal in Sheol (Job 3:13–19; Ezek. 32:18–32). For Israel's neighbors, the rule of the universe was divided among various deities, and the netherworld was the dominion of a pair of infernal gods. For Israel, however, the Lord rules over the whole universe. His sovereignty extends from heaven to Sheol (Ps. 139; Job 26:6; cf. Ps. 90:2; 102:26–28). However, there is no communication between the dead and the Lord (Ps. 88:6); no praise to the Lord comes from the netherworld (Isa. 38:18; Ps. 30:10; 88:12–13).

See also *Death, *Soul, Immortality of, *Gehinnom.

[L.J.A.]

In the Aggadah. In the *aggadah*, the name Gehenna takes the place of the biblical Sheol as the abode of the dead. The name is derived from *Gei Ben Hinnom* (Valley of the son of Hinnom, Josh. 15:8; 18:16; et al.), a valley south of Jerusalem where children were made to pass through fire to the god *Moloch (see *Gehinnom). Jeremiah prophesied that it would become "a valley of slaughter" and a place of burial (Jer. 7:32). In the course of time, the name of this accursed valley, designated for suffering, became identified with the place of retribution for the wicked after their death.

No suggestion of this later notion of Gehenna is to be found in Scripture, but in the Talmud and Midrash "Gehenna" is so used. Joshua b. Levi refers to it by seven names (Er. 19a), all of which are synonyms for the netherworld of Scripture. Later, these seven names were given to the seven divisions of Gehenna (Mid. Ps. to 11:6, Sot. 10b). Descriptions of Gehenna include foreign elements which were widespread in the Hellenistic world (through Orphic and Pythagorean sources). The punishment of "the wicked one whose tongue hangs out to lap the water of the river but is unable to reach it" (TJ, Ḥag., *ibid.*) is reminiscent of the punishment of Tantalus in Hades (Odyssey, 11:582–5). The source of this description is probably Greek, passing to Judaism, and thence to Christianity (Luke 16:24) and Islam. Most accounts of Gehenna, however, draw chiefly on the scriptural descriptions of the land of the dead. There is discernible in the *aggadot* on Gehenna a tendency to mitigate the application of strict justice, by limiting the categories of its victims (Ber. 10a; Er. 41b; et al.), and by detailing the many possibilities whereby the Jew might be delivered from its punishment (Pes. 118a; Git. 7a; et al.).

The *aggadot* about Gehenna in the Talmud and Midrash speak of its site, size, entrances, gates, divisions, and princes. A variety of motifs and partial descriptions from the Bible (sometimes self-contradictory) are combined. The *aggadah*, basing itself on verses which describe the site of the land of the dead, variously, as beneath the earth (Gen. 37:35; Deut. 32:22; et al.) and beneath the sea (Jonah 2:3–4; Job 26:5), states that Gehenna has entrances in the sea and on dry land (Er. 19a). In the school of Johanan b. Zakkai it was stated that one of its entrances is in the valley of Hinnom, near Jerusalem. There are also traditions, however, that Gehenna is in the sky (Tam. 32b), and that it is "beyond the dark mountains" (*ibid.*).

As against *aggadot* which, in the main, speak of the fire of Gehenna (Pes. 54a; BM 85a; BB 74a; et al.), there are those which describe the darkness reigning there (I Enoch, 10:4; et al.). According to Josephus, the Essenes described it as a cold and dark cave (Wars, 2:155). There are also sources combining both ideas, speaking of a fire found in Gehenna which gives no light—"fire causing darkness," or "the darkness of eternal fire." Descriptions of rivers of fire (Ḥag. 13b) in Gehenna appear also to be combinations of descriptions of its fire and of a river flowing in or near it (TJ, Ḥag. 2:2, 77d; Shab. 39a) with descriptions of the hot springs of Tiberias, whose heat is conceived as deriving from their passing the entrance to Gehenna. Extravagant accounts are given of the size of Gehenna and the power of its fire. "The world is one sixtieth of the Garden, the Garden one sixtieth of Eden, Eden one sixtieth of Gehenna—hence the world to Gehenna is as the lid to the pot. Others say Gehenna is immeasurable" (Ta'an. 10a). The account of the gates of Gehenna is followed by descriptions of the gatekeepers (Ḥag. 15b; Mid. Gan Eden, in: A. Jellinek (ed.), *Beit ha-Midrasch*, 5 (1938), 42–51) and these gatekeepers are identified with its princes (Shab. 104a).

The description of the sufferings of the wicked in Gehenna are faithful reflections of the judicial procedures during the era of their composition. The concept of "measure for measure" lies at the root of these punishments. "The suffering commences from the limb that began the transgression" (Sif. Num. 18; Tosef., Sot. 3:2). The cruel torments of Gehenna, such as hanging by different limbs of the body (TJ, Ḥag. 2:2, 77d; Mid. Gan Eden, *ibid.*; Mid. *Ke-Tappu'aḥ*), roasting by fire (excerpt from *"Ḥazon Eliyahu"* quoted by Lieberman, in *Louis Ginzberg Jubilee Volume* (1946), 249–70 (Hebrew section)) and suffocating by smoke (Mid. Gan Eden, *ibid.*), are also found in Christian books of the second, third, and fourth centuries which describe the divisions of Gehenna and the suffering of the wicked therein (e.g., "The Vision of Peter," "The Acts of Thomas," and "The Vision of Paul," the influence of the Jewish *aggadah* being easily recognizable). Undoubtedly, the cruel torments used by the Roman government in its system of punishments played their part in the envisioning of Gehenna. The punishment of the wicked in Gehenna was conceived of as parallel to the procedures for punishment in this world. Just as the lower court does not inflict punishment on the Sabbath, so in Gehenna: "During weekdays they suffer, but on the Sabbath they are given rest" (Gen. R. 11:5).

Some are characterized by severe contrast. The wicked are cast into fire, then into snow, and the process repeated (TJ, Sanh. 10:3, 29b; PdRK, 97). There is a difference of opinion between Bet Shammai and Bet Hillel as to the duration of the punishment in Gehenna (RH 16b–17a); according to the former, the thoroughly wicked remain there for everlasting disgrace; the intermediate ones (between the wicked and the good) descend to Gehenna to be purged, and ascend after purification. According to the latter, the intermediate ones do not go there at all (ARN[1] 41:15), and whereas transgressors (both Jewish and gentile) are punished in Gehenna for only 12 months, only special categories of sinners—informers, those who deny the resurrection of the dead and those who lead the masses into sin—are punished there for all time (RH *ibid.*). Rabbinic literature incorporates legends of visits to Eden and Gehenna of a type similar to that found among other peoples. Some of these are solitary visits in a dream (TJ, Ḥag. 2:2, 177d), and some escorted visits, in a dream at night. At times the visit takes place in a vision ascribed to one of the scriptural personalities, such as Moses (Mid. *Ke-Tappu'aḥ*), Isaiah (Mid. Gan Eden, *ibid.*), Daniel, Enoch, and Baruch (Apocrypha). Similar visits are attributed to *tannaim* and *amoraim* (Joshua b. Levi in Ket. 77b, of whom many *aggadot* are extant). [Ba.K.]

Bibliography: M. Jastrow, in: AJSLL, 14 (1897), 165–70; A. Lods, *La croyance a la vie future et le culte des morts dans l'antiquité israélite* (1906); P. Dhorme, in: RB, 4 (1908), 59–78; E. Ebeling, *Tod und Leben nach den Vorstellungen der Babylonier* (1931); K. Tallquist, *Sumerisch-akkadische Namen der Totenwelt* (1934); T. H. Gaster, *Thespis* (1950); H. L. Ginsberg, in: JAOS, 88 (1968), 51–52, n. 27. In the Aggadah: Ginzberg, Legends, index; Neubauer, Géogr, 36–37; P. Volz, *Die Eschatologie der juedischen Gemeinde im neutestamentlichen Zeitalter*... (1934), 328–9; Lieberman, in: *Harry Austryn Wolfson Jubilee Volume* (1965), 495–532 (Eng. section).

NETILAT YADAYIM (Heb. נְטִילַת יָדַיִם; lit. "raising the hands"), rabbinic term for the obligatory washing of the hands. The rabbis made this ritual mandatory in the following instances:

(1) upon rising from sleep (Ber. 60b; Sh. Ar., OḤ 4:1);

(2) after the excretion of bodily wastes;

(3) after the paring of nails;

(4) after the removal of shoes;

(5) after the combing of hair or touching parts of the body that are usually covered;

(6) after leaving a cemetery or participating in a funeral;

(7) after sexual intercourse (Sh. Ar., OḤ 4:18);

(8) before prayer and the recitation of the *Shema (Ber. 15a; Sh. Ar., OḤ 92:4);

(9) before eating bread (Ḥul. 105a; Sh. Ar., OḤ 158:1);

(10) before reciting Grace (Ḥul. 105a; Sh. Ar., OḤ 181:1);

Netilat Yadayim, the washing of the hands, shown in a detail of a page from the *Birds' Head Haggadah,* Germany, c. 1300. Birds' heads are used on human figures to avoid transgressing the second commandment. Jerusalem, Israel Museum, IM. 180/57, fol. 6a. Photo David Harris, Jerusalem.

(11) before eating the parsley at the Passover **seder* (Pes. 115a–6; Sh. Ar., OḤ 473:6);

(12) the levites wash the hands of the kohanim before the *Priestly Blessing (Sh. Ar., OḤ 128:6).

In all these instances the hands must be washed at least up to the third joint of the fingers, i.e., the junction of the phalanges and the metacarpus. Nevertheless, the rabbis considered it preferable to wash up to the wrist (Sh. Ar., OḤ 161:4). However, when washing before Grace, it is sufficient to wash only up to the second joint of the fingers (Sh. Ar., OḤ 181:4). A minimum of $\frac{1}{4}$ *log* (approx. $\frac{1}{2}$ pint) of water is poured over the hands from a utensil with a wide mouth, the lip of which must be undamaged (Sh. Ar., OḤ 159:1, 3; 160:13). The hands must be clean without anything adhering to them prior to the ritual washing, and no foreign object such as a ring may intervene between them and the water (Sh. Ar., OḤ 161:1–3). Upon rising from sleep, each hand must be washed three times (Sh. Ar., OḤ 4:2), but before partaking of bread, it is sufficient if they are washed once (Sh. Ar., OḤ 162:2). It is customary to hold the cup in the left hand and wash the right one first, and then to reverse the procedure (Mishnah Berurah to Sh. Ar., OḤ 158:1 n. 4). A benediction is only recited after washing the hands upon rising and before eating bread. Its text reads "... and commanded us concerning the washing of the hands." After rising, it is today recited as part of the preliminary **Shaḥarit* service, while before the meal it is recited prior to the drying of the hands (Sh. Ar., OḤ 158:11–12).

See also *Ablution; *Purity and Impurity.

Bibliography: Krauss, Tal Arch, 1 (1910), 210f., 667f.; J. Preuss, *Biblisch-talmudische Medizin* (1923[3]), 146ff.; M. Perlman, *Midrash ha-Refu'ah,* 1 (1926), 42.

[Ed.]

NETIRA (d. 916), businessman in Baghdad. Netira wielded considerable influence in the court of the caliphs and the Jewish society of Babylonia. He was at first connected with the business of his father-in-law *Joseph b. Phinehas and his partner Aaron b. Amram. With the appointment of Caliph al-Muʿtaḍiḍ in 892, he became the principal figure of Babylonian Jewry and much authority was accorded to him. He held this position until his death. During the reign of Caliph al-Muʿtaḍiḍ, Netira succeeded in frustrating the design of one of the caliph's ministers, Ibn-Abi al-Bagl, who planned to put many Jews to death. Between 909 and 916, when the controversy between the *rosh yeshivah* of Pumbedita and the exilarch *Ukva broke out, he and his father-in-law *Joseph b. Phinehas supported the *gaon.* As a result of their intervention, the exilarch Ukva was twice banished from his country. According to Nathan b. Isaac ha-Bavli, the *gaon* in question was R. *Kohen Zedek, but J. Mann has proved, on the basis of *Iggeret Rav Sherira Ga'on,* that it was R. Judah b. Samuel, the grandfather of R. *Sherira Gaon. His sons Sahl and Isaac followed their father's example and they also held important positions in Jewish society. When the dispute between the exilarch *David b. Zakkai and R. *Saadiah Gaon broke out in 930, they supported Saadiah, who was also the teacher of Sahl. It seems that his third son was Joseph b. Netira, who was one of the heads of the Fostat community in the second half of the 10th century. Apparently the sons of Netira lost their influence during the rule of Caliph al-Qâhir (932–934).

Bibliography: Neubauer, Chronicles, 2 (1895), 78–80, 83; A. E. Harkavy, in: *Birkat Avraham* (*Festschrift ... A. Berliner,* 1903), 34–43 (Heb.); S. Fraenkel, in: JQR, 17 (1905), 386–8; I. Friedlander, *ibid.,* 747–61; L. Ginzberg, *Geonica,* 2 (1909), 87–88; Fischel, Islam, 34, 36f., 40–44; J. Mann, in: *Tarbiz,* 5 (1934), 148–65; S. D. Goitein, in: *Eretz-Israel,* 7 (1964), 83–84; A. Scheiber, in: *Zion,* 30 (1965), 123–7.

[A.D.]

NETIV HA-LAMED-HE (Heb. נְתִיב הל״ה), kibbutz in the Elah Valley, central Israel, affiliated with Ha-Kibbutz ha-Me'uḥad. It was founded by a group of Israel youth in 1949, and later joined by immigrants from various countries. In the initial years Netiv ha-Lamed-He was an isolated outpost, but it progressed after the *Adullam Region development project was launched in the mid-1950s. Its farming includes field crops, fruit, etc. The kibbutz' name, "Pathway of the Thirty-Five," commemorates the *Haganah unit of 35 men who were killed by Arabs while trying to reach the besieged Eẓyon Bloc in the Israel *War of Independence (1948; see *Kefar Eẓyon). A memorial has been erected near the kibbutz.

[E.O.]

NETIVOT (Heb. נְתִיבוֹת; "Roads," from Prov. 3:17), Israel development town in N.W. Negev, 9 mi. (15 km.) S.E. of Gaza. Netivot was founded in 1956 in the framework of Israel's regional settlement and population dispersion policy. It was initially named Azzatah ("Toward Gaza"). Although placed in the center of a quickly expanding agricultural region, Netivot's progress was handicapped by the proximity of two other development towns, *Sederot and *Ofakim, and by its inability to attract schooled veteran citizens in addition to new immigrants. Netivot's growth was slow, rising from 1,231 inhabitants in 1957 to 4,830 in 1968; 95% of the immigrants originated from Tunisia and Morocco. The high percentage of children in the total population (over 40% of the inhabitants are Israel-born children) points to a large-size average family. Local industry includes textiles, wood, food processing, and diamond polishing on a small scale. [E.O.]

NETOPHAH (Heb. נְטֹפָה), Judean village, evidently near Bethlehem (I Chron. 2:54). It was the hometown of two of David's heroes (II Sam. 23:28, 29) and of a captain of Gedaliah (II Kings 25:23; Jer. 40:8). It appears after Bethlehem in the list of those returning from Babylonian exile (Ezra 2:22; Neh. 7:26). In Byzantine times, it is placed in the vicinity of Tekoa (*Life of Cyriacus*, in: PG, vol. 115, p. 929); the same source mentions a "desert of Netopha." The usual identification is with Khirbat Badd Falūḥ, about 3.4 mi. (5½ km.) south of Bethlehem, where Iron Age to Byzantine pottery was found. It has also been located at Ramat Raḥel, which, however, is identified with Beth-Cherem by its excavator.

Bibliography: Abel, Geog, 2 (1938), 399; Aharoni, Land, index; EM, 5 (1968), 829–30 (incl. bibl.). [M.A.-Y.]

NETTER, CHARLES (**Yiẓḥak**; 1826–1882), leader of the *Alliance Israélite Universelle and founder of the *Mikveh Israel Agricultural School. Born in Strasbourg, Netter went into business, first in Lille and then in Moscow and London. He moved to Paris in about 1851 and began a life-long career of public activities, establishing a Jewish vocational school in 1865, a society for safeguarding the rights of workers, and a hostel for poor artisans in 1880. A founder of the Alliance Israélite Universelle (1860), he was elected its treasurer. Various proposals submitted to the Alliance to extend its activities to Ereẓ Israel met with a favorable response on Netter's part, and the Alliance board, although opposed to the encouragement of emigration to Ereẓ Israel, was ready to help Jews already there. In 1867 Netter submitted a proposal to the Alliance to assist Jews from Persia and other Eastern countries to emigrate to Ereẓ Israel and to found agricultural settlements for them.

Charles Netter, leader of the Alliance Israélite Universelle. Jerusalem, J.N.U.L., Schwadron Collection.

The following year he visited Ereẓ Israel on behalf of the Alliance, and upon his return he recommended the creation of an agricultural school, to be followed by the founding of settlements for the school graduates. In his report Netter noted that Ereẓ Israel would provide a shelter for Jews fleeing from hostile surroundings and enable them, in the course of time, to occupy and settle the Holy Land. When his proposal was approved, he left for Constantinople in 1869, where he received the approval of the grand vizier of the Imperial State Council for the establishment of the school and the authorization of Rashid Pasha, governor of Syria, for the acquisition of 650 acres (2,600 dunams) of land for the annual rental of 1,800 francs, with a right of renewal for 25 years. A *firman* of 1870 confirmed the arrangement, whereupon he returned to Ereẓ Israel and founded the school, naming it Mikveh Israel. After a stay of four years, he fell ill and had to return to Paris, revisiting Ereẓ Israel for six months in 1873. He resumed his political activities on behalf of Jewish causes and in propaganda for the school. In 1877 he again went to Constantinople on behalf of the Alliance, and on the basis of this visit he submitted a report to the Great Powers on the situation of the Jews, especially in Rumania and Serbia. In the following year he attended the Congress of Berlin. In 1880 he was at Madrid, where an international conference was deliberating the status of Morocco, and intervened on behalf of the Jews of that country. He was disappointed with the lack of success recorded by Mikveh Israel and the general unsuitability of Ereẓ Israel for the absorption of large numbers of Jews. As a result, he opposed the *aliyah* of Russian and Rumanian Jews in the 1880s, when events in those countries created strong pressure for emigration and a movement developed to resettle Ereẓ Israel. At the end of 1881 he visited Brody, remaining there for some months, during which he arranged for the emigration of 1,200 Russian Jewish refugees to America and of a group of 28 children to Mikveh Israel. In March 1882 he even came out with a statement in the press opposing immigration to Ereẓ Israel. Similarly, a conference of Jewish organizations in Berlin, in which Netter participated, decided to support emigration to the United States and to look for other countries where Jews could find refuge, but failed to consider settlement in Ereẓ Israel. Probably under the influence of Baron Edmond de *Rothschild, who believed that an attempt should be made to turn Ereẓ Israel into a center for Jewish immigration, Netter revised his views, and in August 1882 he revisited the country. There he met Russian Jews who had settled in Rishon le-Zion and members of the *Bilu movement and offered them his help. He developed many plans for agricultural activities and the development of crafts in Ereẓ Israel, but died a month after his arrival.

Bibliography: Z. Szajkowski, in: JSOS, 4 (1942), 291–310; N. Sokolow, *Hibbath Zion* (Eng. 1935), 20, 30–34; S. Jawnieli, *Sefer ha-Ẓiyyonut*, 2 pt. 2 (1944), 16–23, 34–37; A. Druyanow, *Ketavim le-Toledot Ḥibbat Ẓiyyon ve-Yishuv Ereẓ Yisrael* (1919), index; I. Klausner, *Ḥibbat Ẓiyyon be-Rumanyah* (1958), index; idem, *Be-Hitorer Am* (1962), index; B. Dinaburg, *Mefallesei Derekh* (1946), 69–89; J. Shapiro, *Sefer Mikveh Yisrael* (1970); G. Weill, in: *Nouveaux Cahiers*, 21 (1970), 2–36; 11 (1967), 11–16; S. Hillels, *Mikveh Yisrael* (1931). [I.K.]

NETUREI KARTA, group of ultrareligious extremists, mainly in Jerusalem, who regard the establishment of a secular Jewish state in Ereẓ Israel as a sin and a denial of God, and therefore do not recognize the State of Israel. Their name, which is Aramaic for "guardians of the City," derives from a passage in the Jerusalem Talmud (Ḥag. 76:3) stating that religious scholars are the guardians and defenders of the city. Most of them come from the old *yishuv*, but they have been joined by some immigrants from Hungary, disciples of R. Joel *Teitelbaum of Satmar.

Neturei Karta broke away from *Agudat Israel in 1935, when the latter attempted to restrain extremist demands for an independent ultra-Orthodox Jerusalem community completely separate from the rest of the "Zionist" community. The group first adopted the name Ḥevrat ha-Ḥayyim, after R. Joseph Ḥayyim *Sonnenfeld. It aimed at creating "a circle free from the influence of the contemporary spirit and its fallacious opinions," and a condition of membership

Monetary scrip issued by Neturei Karta, c. 1948, to avoid the use of Israel currency. Jerusalem, B. M. Ansbacher Collection.

was "the education of sons and daughters in the traditional Jewish manner, without any change (girls' schools which teach Hebrew do not provide education in the traditional Jewish manner)." The last phrase alluded to Agudat Israel's Bet Ya'akov girls' schools, where the language of instruction is Hebrew. The name Neturei Karta was first used in 1938 by a group of youths, including members of Ḥevrat ha-Ḥayyim, who violently opposed the Jewish community's levying of the voluntary defense tax, *kofer ha-yishuv*.

During World War II, Neturei Karta came out in opposition to Agudat Israel, when it cooperated more closely with the Jewish community and the *Jewish Agency, and attacked it in *Ha-Ḥomah,* a newspaper which began to appear in 1944. In 1945, at the elections to the Orthodox Community Committee (*Va'ad ha-Edah ha-Ḥaredit*), Neturei Karta and its sympathizers gained control; one of their first acts was to exclude from membership anyone educating his daughters at a Bet Ya'akov school. During the War of Independence, Neturei Karta opposed the creation of a Jewish state and Israel's control of Jerusalem, and tried to bring about the internationalization of the city.

The most consistent members refuse to accept an Israel identity card, to recognize the competence of Israel courts, and to vote in municipal or general elections. Although they consist of only a few dozen families—concentrated in the Me'ah She'arim quarter of Jerusalem and in Bene Berak—they gained some support in wider Orthodox circles by creating periodic religious controversies, such as their demonstrations against Sabbath violation and mixed bathing. In 1966 Neturei Karta split, following the marriage of their leader R. Amram *Blau to a convert, Ruth Ben-David. Members of Neturei Karta derive their livelihood mostly from small trade and contributions from abroad, notably from disciples of the Satmar rabbi in the United States. They also have a small group of supporters in Great Britain, who publish a periodical, *Comment* (1962–).

Bibliography: Ha-Edah ha-Ḥaredit, *Keẓ ha-Ma'arakhah* (1964); Agudat Israel, *Mi Sam Keẓ la-Ma'arakhah* (1964). [M.Fr.]

NEUBAUER, ADOLF (Abraham; 1831–1907), scholar, author, librarian, and bibliographer. Born in Nagybanya, Hungary, Neubauer studied in Prague with S. J. L. *Rapaport and at the universities of Prague and Munich. In 1857 he went to Paris, where he pursued research at the Bibliothèque Nationale, and in 1864 to Jerusalem as a member of the staff of the Austro-Hungarian consulate. There, too, he sought out rare Hebrew books and manuscripts, discovering in the Karaite synagogue a manuscript of extracts from the lexicon of *David b. Abraham of Fez (15th century) which he published in the *Journal Asiatique* in 1861–62. Returning to Paris, he was befriended by the orientalists S. *Munk, J. *Derenbourg, and E. *Renan. Invited to St. Petersburg in 1864 to examine the *Firkovich collection of Karaite manuscripts, Neubauer wrote a report for the French Ministry of Education (*Rapports* . . . (1865) with S. Munk) and published *Aus der Petersburger Bibliothek, Beitraege und Dokumente zur Geschichte des Karaeerthums und der karaeischen Literatur* (1866). He presented his prize-winning essay *La Géographie du Talmud* (1868) to the Academie des Inscriptions et Belles Lettres which in spite of some criticism (J. Morgenstern, *Die franzoesische Akademie und die "Géographie des Talmuds,"* 1870[2]) has remained an important reference book. His *Notice sur la lexicographie hebraïque* . . . (1863), foreshadowing his edition of Jonah ibn *Janaḥ's *Sefer ha-Dikduk* (1875, 1968[2]), with additions and corrections by W. Bacher, and *Melekhet ha-Shir* (1865), a collection of extracts from manuscripts concerning Hebrew poetry, belong to the same period.

In 1865 Neubauer settled in England, becoming librarian at the Bodleian Library, Oxford (1868), which he enriched by judicious purchases, particularly from the Cairo **Genizah;* in 1884 he was appointed reader in rabbinic Hebrew at the university. There he produced some of his finest work, cut short in 1899 by failing eyesight. His works there include *Catalogue of the Hebrew Manuscripts in the Bodleian Library* (3 vols., 1886–1906; the second was finished by A. E. Cowley), with over 2,500 entries (some items consisting of 20–50 works); the third volume contains 40 facsimiles that illustrate Hebrew paleography of different countries and periods. He also prepared a *Catalogue of the Hebrew Manuscripts in the Jews' College* (1886).

His *The Fifty-Third Chapter of Isaiah According to the Jewish Interpreters* (vol. 1, texts, 1876; vol. 2, translations with S. R. Driver, 1877; repr. 1969) provided biblical scholarship with an anthology of Jewish reactions to christological interpretations. He

Adolf Neubauer, scholar and bibliographer. Jerusalem, J.N.U.L. Schwadron Collection.

was the first to publish original Hebrew portions of *Ben Sira as they were found in the Cairo *Genizah*, together with the text of early versions, quotations of Ben Sira in rabbinical literature, and an English translation (with A. E. Cowley, 1897). His two volumes of *Medieval Jewish Chronicles* (*Seder ha-Ḥakhamim ve-Korot ha-Yamim*, preface and notes in English, 1887–95, repr. 1967) collected texts of a number of talmudic, geonic, and medieval historiographical writings. The fruits of Neubauer's collaboration with Renan were two remarkable works of literary history: *Les rabbins français du commencement du quatorzième siècle* (1877) and *Les écrivains juifs français du* XIVe *siècle* (1893). Other editions of his include: *Vocabulaire hebraïco-français* (in: *Romanische Studien*, 2 (1875)), and *Petite Grammaire hebraïque provenant de Yemen* (Arabic, 1891), as well as *Talmudical and Rabbinical Literature* (in: *Transaction of the Philological Society*, 1875–76). In 1901 he moved to Vienna to live with his nephew A. *Buechler, and when the latter became principal of Jews' College, London, in 1906, he returned to London where he died shortly afterward.

Neubauer contributed a stream of articles, notes, and book reviews to most of the learned Jewish (and many non-Jewish) periodicals of his time.

Bibliography: S. R. Driver, in: DNB, 2nd supplement, 3 (1912), 5–7; E. Adler, in: *Studies in Jewish Bibliography . . . in Memory of A. S. Freidus* (1929), 31–54 (bibliography); B. Cohen, in: KS, 10 (1933/34), 365–71 (supplementary bibliography); H. M. J. Loewe, *Adolf Neubauer 1831–1931* (1931); A. Ben-Reshef, in: S. Federbush (ed.), *Ḥokhmat Yisrael be-Eiropah* (1965), 242–5. [Ed.]

NEUBAUER, JACOB (**Jekuthiel**; 1895–1945), halakhist and law historian; born in Leipzig. In 1917 Neubauer published *Bibelwissenschaftliche Irrungen* and in 1918 his important dissertation *Beitraege zur Geschichte des biblisch-talmudischen Eheschliessungsrechts*. When he was appointed lecturer at the Wuerzburg teachers' training school, his home became a center of Jewish intellectual life for students of all faculties. In 1933 he was chief lecturer at the rabbinical seminary in Amsterdam. Neubauer was an outstanding scholar in the history of Jewish law and in the exposition of the development of individual laws. He died in Bergen-Belsen. His *Ha-Rambam al Divrei Soferim* was published in Jerusalem in 1957.

Bibliography: B. de Vries, in: *J. J. Neubauer, Ha-Rambam al Divrei Soferim* (1957), 3–7; I. Grunfeld, *Three Generations* (1958), 65–67. [F.J.H.]

NEUBERG, GUSTAV EMBDEN CARL (1877–1956), German biochemist. Born in Hanover, Neuberg joined the Pathological Institute of the University of Berlin, becoming professor in 1919, and from 1920 directed the Kaiser Wilhelm Institute of Biochemistry, Berlin-Dahlem. The Nazis dismissed him in 1938, and he went to Amsterdam. In 1939–40 he was professor of biochemistry at the Hebrew University of Jerusalem. In 1941 he went to America, was professor at New York University until 1950, and then for a time visiting professor at Brooklyn Polytechnic. Neuberg's field of research was principally in sugars, albumen, fermentation processes, the biochemical action of light, and glycerin substitutes. He was an honorary member of ten national academies of science, the recipient of many honorary doctorates, prizes, and medals.

Bibliography: *Experimental Medicine and Surgery*, 5 (1947), 100–6, incl. bibl.; A. Auhagen, in: *Zeitschrift fuer Naturforschung*, 4 pt. B (1949), 245; *Chemical and Engineering News*, 25 (1947), 3358. [S.A.M.]

NEUBERGER, ALBERT (1908–), British biochemist. Neuberger, born in Hassfurt, Bavaria, qualified as a doctor of medicine in Wuerzburg. He then settled in England, where he undertook research first at London University and then (1939–42) at Cambridge. In 1943 he joined the Medical Research Council. After war service in India he returned to work at the University of London until 1947, when he became head of the biochemistry division of the National Institute for Medical Research. In 1955 he was appointed professor of chemical pathology at St. Mary's Hospital Medical School in London. Neuberger's main research was in the metabolism of proteins and amino acids. He was a fellow of the Royal Society, chairman of the Biochemical Society, and a governor of the Hebrew University of Jerusalem. [S.A.M.]

NEUBERGER, RICHARD LEWIS (1912–1960), U.S. senator, journalist, and author. Neuberger, born near Portland, Oregon, graduated from the University of Oregon (1935), where he edited the student newspaper. He began writing in 1928, and in 1933 *The Nation* published an article of his which realistically described the Nazi persecution of Jews and the preparation for war which he had witnessed on a visit through Germany. From 1939 to 1954 he was the *New York Times'* Northwest correspondent. Neuberger served in the Oregon House of Representatives from 1941 to 1942, when he entered the U.S. Army. An aide-de-camp to General James O'Connor during the construction of the Alaska Military Highway, he left the army a captain in 1945. In 1948 Neuberger was elected to the State Senate, and in 1955 he became the first Democratic Senator from Oregon in 40 years. An affable liberal, Neuberger was active on behalf of natural conservation, civil rights, cancer research (he was himself afflicted), housing measures, Congressional reform, and Alaska statehood. He was chairman of the Subcommittee on Indian Affairs and a member of the Interior and Public Works committees, which dealt with conservation. His books, which generally discuss politics and conservation in northern U.S., include : *An Army of the Aged* (with Kelley Loe, 1936), *Integrity—The Life of George W. Norris* (with S. B. Kahn, 1937), *Our Promised Land* (1938), *The Lewis and Clark Expedition* (1951), *Royal Canadian Mounted Police* (1953), and *Adventures in Politics* (1954).

His wife, H. Maurine (Brown) Neuberger (1907–) —who was not Jewish—worked closely with her husband completing his Senate term after his death, and in 1960 was elected to the Senate.

Bibliography: *New York Times* (March 10, Nov. 10, 1960); U.S. Congress, 86th Congress 2nd Session, *Richard Lewis Neuberger* (1960). [Ed.]

NEUBURGER, MAX (1868–1955), Austrian medical historian. Born in Vienna, Neuburger worked at the Rudolfspital and the Allegemeines Krankhaus and in 1898 went to teach at the University of Vienna. There he devoted himself more and more to medical history and was appointed professor of the history of medicine in 1904. He developed the department into a proper institute for the study of medical history and built up its library and

Medal in honor of Max Neuburger, Austrian medical historian, 1928. Jerusalem, J.N.U.L., Schwadron Collection.

museum (later described by A. Levinson, see bibl.). From 1901 to 1913 he collaborated with J. Pagel on a revised and enlarged edition of the history of medicine by his mentor, Theodor Puschmann. It appeared in three volumes, under the title *Handbuch der Geschichte der Medizin* (1902–05), a comprehensive and authoritative account of medical history. At the same time he wrote *Geschichte der Medizin* (vol. 1, 1906; vol. 2, 1911; Eng. trans. by E. Playfair 1910–25) which served at the time as the most authoritative textbook on medical history of the ancient and medieval period, and aroused much interest in its treatment of Arabic and Jewish medicine. In 1928 on the occasion of his 60th birthday, he was presented with a Festschrift by his colleagues, friends, and disciples, *Festschrift zur Feier seines 60. Geburtstages . . . Max Neuburger.*

He showed an interest in Jewish aspects of medicine, writing *Die ersten an der Wiener medizinischen Fakultaet promovierten Aerzte juedischen Stammes* (1918), and in 1936 he read a paper on Jewish doctors at the international congress for history of medicine in Jerusalem, published as *Die Stellung der juedischen Aerzte in der Geschichte der medizinischen Wissenschaften* (1936). Neuburger fled from the Nazis in 1938, settling in England, where he worked in The Wellcome Historical Medical Museum (1938–48). While in Britain he continued his research, writing *British Medicine and the Vienna School* (1943), in which he showed the reciprocal influence of both countries in medicine in the 18th and 19th centuries, and *British and German Psychiatry in the Second Half of the Early Nineteenth Century* (1945).

On his retirement in 1948 he was presented with *Festschrift zum 80. Geburtstag Max Neuburgers* in his honor (containing a bibliography). He then went to live in the U.S. until 1952, when he moved to Vienna, where he died. His other works include *Die Medizin im Flavius Josephus* (1919); *Hermann Nothnagel; Leben und Wirken* (1922); *Die Lehre von der Heilkraft der Natur im Wandel der Zeiten* (1926); and *Gomez Pereira, ein spanischer Arzt des 16. Jahrhunderts* (1936).

Bibliography: *The Times* (March 17, 1955), 8e; JC (March 25, 1955), 35; A. Levinson, *Professor Neuburger and his Institute for the History of Medicine* (1924); E. Berghoff, *Max Neuburger, Werken und Wirken* (1948), incl. bibl. [Ed.]

NEUCHÂTEL, canton and its capital city in W. Switzerland. The earliest records of Jews in the canton date from 1288, when they were accused of a blood libel and a number were put to death. During the Black Death excesses in 1348 the Jews of Neuchâtel were burned. After 1476 there are no further references to Jews living in the canton until 1767, when a few who had come from Alsace were expelled. In 1772 they arrived in the towns of *La Chaux-de-Fonds and Le Locle, but were refused permanent residence rights. By the 1780s the Jews were considered useful to the canton as they played an important part in the export of watches, though this did not prevent their expulsion in 1790. They began to return in 1812 and obtained residence rights in 1830. The Jewish population of the canton in 1844 was 144. They thrived economically during the 19th century and in 1900 numbered 1,020, declining, however, by 1969 to about 200.

Bibliography: A. Nordman, *Les Juifs dans le pays de Neuchâtel* (1923); A. Weldler-Steinberg, *Geschichte der Juden in der Schweiz* (1966), 56–57, 103. [Ed.]

NEUDA, ABRAHAM (1812–1854), rabbi in *Lostice (Loschitz), one of the first in Moravia to have a secular education. His father, Aaron Moses, was also a rabbi in Lostice from 1812 to 1831. When his father became ill, Abraham, a favorite pupil of the *Landesrabbiner* Nahum *Trebitsch of *Mikulov (Nikolsburg), substituted for him on the authorization of his teacher. After the death of Aaron Moses in 1831 the community elected Abraham rabbi, but this time Trebitsch refused his authorization because Abraham had not only preached in German but also had acquired too much secular education (albeit clandestinely) at the yeshivah. A six-year-long conflict was finally brought before the provincial authorities, who requested the advice of Loeb *Schwab on the matter. Abraham was supported by Isaac Noah *Mannheimer. The authorities compelled Trebitsch to examine Neuda before a committee of two other rabbis and a Catholic priest. In the end Trebitsch was forced to acknowledge Neuda as rabbi of Lostice. Neuda published a collection of his sermons under the title, *Massa Devar Adonai,* in 1845. In his works, he attempted to reconcile the traditional **derash* with the modern sermon. Parts of his historical account of the Jews of Moravia were published posthumously by Gerson *Wolf in **Neuzeit* (1863).

A year after Neuda's death, his wife, Fanny (1819–1894), sister of the Vienna rabbi Abraham Adolf *Schmiedl, published in his memory a prayer book in German for women, entitled, *Stunden der Andacht, ein Gebet- und Erbauungsbuch fuer Israels Frauen und Jungfrauen,* which attained great popularity among Jewish women in central Europe. It was the first prayer book of its kind to be written by a woman and took into account, besides the divine services, all the occasions in the life of a woman. Until the 1920s, 28 editions of the prayer book had been sold. In 1936 Martha Wertheimer published a revised version for the special conditions of Nazi Germany. An English translation by M. Maier, *Hours of Devotion,* was published in New York.

Bibliography: L. Loew, *Gesammelte Schriften,* 2 (1890), 203–11; B. Wachstein, in: H. Gold (ed.), *Juden und Judengemeinden Maehrens . . .* (1929), 319, includes bibliography; I. H. Weiss, *Zikhronotai* (1895), 47–49; S. W. Rosenfeld, *Stunden der Andacht* (1857), introd. [M.La.]

NEUFELD, DANIEL (1814–1874), Polish writer and educator. His name is connected with the Jewish weekly in Polish, *Jutrzenka (Ayyelet ha-Shaḥar).* Published in Warsaw from 1861 to 1863, the paper expressed Polish-Jewish solidarity during the 1863 revolution. Its goals were threefold; the diffusion of learning and culture; the promulgation of the idea of Jewish responsibility toward the Polish state; and the defense of Jews against anti-Semitism. It published serious works of scholarship on Polish Jewry and emphasized Jewish integration into the life and affairs of the general community. Such well-known personalities as Ḥayyim Zelig *Slonimski, editor of **Ha-Ẓefirah,* the historian Alexander Kraushar, and Mattias *Bersohn wrote for the journal. Publication ceased when its editor was exiled to Siberia in 1863.

Neufeld believed in a synthesis of Jewish and Polish cultures which would combine Polish patriotism and the Jewish religion. He was conservative in religious matters and progressive in his social concerns. Positively disposed toward Hebrew language and literature, Neufeld opposed Yiddish as obstructive of Jewish progress. He favored a scientific study of Jewish culture as a way of bridging past and present. Opposed to the *maskilim* of Galicia, he considered *Ḥasidism a positive force, hoping that it would encourage Polonization of the Jews. At the same time he opposed extreme assimilationist tendencies, regarding them as a break with talmudic tradition, which he saw as a nationalistic and political synthesis successful in preserving Jewish spiritual values. Presenting his ideas on education to Marquis *Wielopolski, Neufeld called for the compulsory study of religion, along with Hebrew language, Jewish history, and the geography of Ereẓ Israel. Neufeld was editor of the Jewish department of a general encyclopedia published by his friend Orgelbrand. He wrote a scholarly study of Napoleon's *Sanhedrin and a pamphlet on the establishment of a *consistory in Poland. Although he began the important task of translating the Bible into Polish, he had difficulty in obtaining permission to publish his work, the Catholic censors preferring that Jews should have to study the Bible in a Christian translation. Permission was finally granted on condition that the title page carry the notice that the translation was intended for Polish Jews. The Book of Genesis with both the Hebrew text and a Polish translation appeared in 1863, under the title *Pięcioksiąg Mojżesza dla Żydów-Polaków.*

Bibliography: J. Shatzky, *Geshikhte fun Yidn in Varshe,* 1–3 (1947–53), indices; A. Levinson, *Toledot Yehudei Varsha* (1953), 168–9; EG, 1 (1953), 245–6, 507–9.

[M.LAN.]

°**NEUGEBAUER, OTTO** (1899–), mathematician. Born in Innsbruck, Austria, Neugebauer taught at Goettingen. As editor of a scientific periodical *Mathematische Annalen* he was forbidden by the Nazis to publish contributions from Jewish scholars. He insisted on ignoring this order and then fled, first to Denmark and then to the United States.

An authority on astronomy and the history of mathematics, he contributed to the Jewish aspects of these subjects. In the 1949 issue of the Hebrew Union College Annual (22 (1949), 321–63), he published "The Astronomy of Maimonides and its Sources." In this essay he tries to clear up some difficult points and deals in one place with the practice of dividing the hour into 1,080 parts (*ḥalakim*), which is a feature of the Jewish time system and also other ancient systems. He was professor at Brown University, Providence, Rhode Island. Among his works are: an astronomical commentary to Maimonides' *Sanctification of the Moon* (*Mishneh Torah,* 3:8; 1956) and *Tafeln zur astronomischen Chronologie* (2 vols., 1912–14). He edited jointly with A. Sachs *Mathematical Cuneiform Texts* (1945).

[A.T.]

NEUGROESCHEL, MENDEL (1903–1965), Yiddish poet. Born in Nowy Sacz, Galicia, Neugroeschel practiced law in Vienna until the Anschluss. He was sent to the Dachau concentration camp, but released the following year (March 1939), and went to Brazil. Two years later he moved to New York.

In his Vienna period he was influenced by Rainer Maria Rilke and *Mani-Leib, as is evident from his first three lyric collections *In Shvartsen Malkhes* (1924), *Getseltn* (1930), and *Kaylikhdige Teg* (1935). In 1936 he published *Kleyne Antologie fun der Yidisher Lirik in Galitsie 1897–1935,* an anthology of Yiddish poetry in Galicia. In New York he felt himself a stranger and wrote sad, nostalgic lyrics about the Jewish world of his youth. His prose study, *"Di Moderne Yidishe Literatur in Galitsie"* (in *Fun Noentn Over,* 1 (1955), 267–398), affords rich insight into the Galician neo-romantic group which was influential between 1904 and 1918.

Bibliography: LNYL, 6 (1965), 212f.; Rejzen, Leksikon, 2 (1927), 552; J. Leftwich, *The Golden Peacock* (1961).

[M.RAV.]

NEUMAN, ABRAHAM AARON (1890–1970), U.S. rabbi, historian, and educator. Neuman was born in Brezan, Austria, and emigrated to the United States in 1898. He studied at the Rabbi Isaac Elhanan Yeshivah, Columbia University, and the Jewish Theological Seminary, where he was ordained in 1912. Before his ordination, he taught at the Teachers Institute of the Seminary, but the year after, he joined the faculty of *Dropsie College in Philadelphia, where he taught history until 1940. Neuman held rabbinical posts in Philadelphia at the B'nai Jeshurun congregation (1919–27) and the Sephardi congregation Mikveh Israel (1927–40). After Cyrus Adler's death in 1940 Neuman became president of Dropsie College, a post he held until his retirement in 1966. During his incumbency the college expanded its curriculum, adding departments in Middle Eastern studies, education, and philosophy. Active in the development of the Zionist movement in the United States and renowned as an orator, he was much sought after as a public speaker. He also participated actively in the work of the United Synagogue of America.

Abraham Aaron Neuman, U.S. rabbi and educator. Courtesy Dropsie College, Philadelphia, Pa.

Neuman produced a number of works of high scholarly merit, chief among them being *The Jews in Spain* (2 vols., 1942). Based primarily on the responsa of Solomon ibn *Adret (RaShBA), the work has served as a model of research in this type of Jewish source material. *Cyrus Adler, a Biography* (1942) is the evaluation of the life of an exemplary public servant during the period when American Jewry was assuming worldwide responsibilities. Neuman contributed to many scholarly periodicals, and a number of these studies appeared in *Landmarks and Goals* (1953). From 1940 to 1966 he collaborated with Solomon Zeitlin in editing the *Jewish Quarterly Review.*

Bibliography: Zeitlin, in: *Studies and Essays in Honor of A. A. Neuman* (1962), vii–xiii.

[S.G.]

NEUMANN, ALFRED (1895–1952), German novelist. Born in Lautenburg, West Prussia, Neumann studied in Munich. For several years he was literary adviser to the Munich publishing house of Georg Mueller. In 1938 he settled in Nice and from there emigrated to the U.S. in 1941. Neumann moved from Los Angeles to Florence in 1949 and died in Switzerland. Together with Heinrich Mann, Max *Brod, Alfred *Doeblin and Lion *Feuchtwanger, Neumann was responsible for the revival of the German historical novel.

Alfred Neumann, German novelist. Lithograph by Stumpp, 1927. New York, Leo Baeck Institute.

His first great work, *Der Patriot* (1925), dramatized in English as *Such Men are Dangerous,* dealt with the assassination of Czar Paul of Russia. *Der Teufel* (1926) was set during the reign of Louis XVI of France. *Rebellen* (1927) was concerned with the uprising of the Carbonari in 19th-century Italy. His other historical novels include *Koenig Haber* (1928), in which the central character is Joseph Suess *Oppenheimer ("Jew Suess"); *Koenigin Christine von*

Schweden (1936); *Neuer Caesar* (1934); *Kaiserreich* (1936); and *Die Volksfreunde* (1941). He was also the author of a successful play, *Abel* (1948).

Bibliography: F. Lennartz, *Deutsche Dichter und Schriftsteller unserer Zeit* (1959[8]), 552–5. [R.K.]

NEUMANN, EMANUEL (1893–), U.S. Zionist leader Neumann, who was born in Libau, Latvia, was taken to the U.S. shortly after his birth. Active in Zionist affairs from his youth, Neumann edited the *Young Judean* (1914–15), later served as education director of the Zionist Organization of America (1918–20). As a co-founder of the *Keren Hayesod

Emanuel Neumann, U.S. Zionist leader. Courtesy Zionist Archives, New York.

in the U.S. in 1921, he served as its director (1921–25), and was chairman of the executive committee of the United Palestine Appeal (1925–28). Neumann was also president of the Jewish National Fund in the U.S. (1929–30) and a member of the Jewish Agency in Jerusalem (1931–41). A close collaborator of Abba Hillel *Silver in influencing the Jewish community and American public opinion to the post-World War II Zionist program, Neumann served with Silver as vice-chairman of the American Zionist Emergency Council. He was the political representative of the Jewish Agency in Washington during the 1940s and instrumental in winning influential political figures to Zionism. Neumann was president of the Z.O.A. in 1947–49 and 1956–58. In 1943 Neumann organized and directed the work of the Commission on Palestine Surveys that presented an investment proposal of approximately $200 million in irrigation facilities and hydroelectric power development in the Jordan Valley. In 1947 he was a member of the Jewish Agency panel in its unsuccessful negotiations with England and a member of the agency's delegation to the UN Special Committee on Palestine which recommended that Palestine be partitioned. Although Neumann had opposed partition, he accepted the committee's recommendation as the best that the Jews would be able to obtain. After the establishment of the State, Neumann devoted himself to obtaining military and economic aid for Israel. From 1951 to 1953 he headed the Jewish Agency's economic department and its information and public relations department. He was appointed chairman of the American section of the Jewish Agency Executive in 1953. Neumann founded the Herzl Foundation (1954) and served as its first president. Although a vigorous advocate of U.S. Zionist unity, he led a majority of the World Conference of General Zionists into a new organization of the same name (1958). He served as president of this organization from 1958 to 1963 when he was elected president of the World Union of General Zionists. [Ed.]

NEUMANN, ERICH (1905–1960), Israel psychologist and psychoanalyst. Neumann, who was born in Berlin, studied analytical psychology under Carl Jung in Zurich. In 1934 he emigrated to Palestine, where he resumed his career as a psychoanalyst and therapist of the Jungian school. Later he was a frequent lecturer at the Eranos congresses in Ascona.

Neumann dealt with the inner crisis of modern man in two works, *Tiefenpsychologie und neue Ethik* (1949; *Depth Psychology and a New Ethic*, 1966) and *Krise und Erneuerung* (1961). Another major work, *Ursprungsgeschichte des Bewusstseins* (1949), first created a systematization of the human consciousness. The principal themes of his research into depth psychology were: the world of archetypes, the psychology of creative man, the psychology of the female, and the archetypal in art. Other major publications were: *Umkreisung der Mitte*, 3 vols. (1953–54); *Die Grosse Mutter* (1956; *The Great Mother*, 1955); *Der schoepferische Mensch...* (1959); *Die archetypische Welt Henry Moores* (1961; *The Archetypal World of Henry Moore*, 1959); *Das Kind* (1963); and essays in the *Eranos-Jahrbuch*, and psychological journals. [Ed.]

NEUMANN, HENRY (1882–1966), U.S. Ethical Culture leader. Neumann, who was born in New York, became leader of the newly formed Brooklyn Society for Ethical Culture in 1911, serving until his retirement in 1961. He also taught ethics in New York's Ethical Culture schools. In 1922, with his wife Julie, he founded the Brooklyn Ethical Culture School. Neumann's work reflects a combination of classic wit, moral rigor, and ethical humanism. Chief among his seven books is *Education for Moral Growth* (1923). Key figure in the American Ethical Union (Federation of Ethical Culture Societies), he was editor of *The Standard* (later the *Ethical Outlook*) and chairman of the Fraternity of Ethical Leaders (1952–61). [H.B.R.]

NEUMANN, JOHANN (Johnny) LUDWIG VON (1903–1957), U.S. mathematician. Von Neumann was born in Budapest and showed outstanding mathematical ability at an early age. He accepted a chair at Princeton University in 1931. Two years later he was appointed the first professor of mathematical physics at the newly formed Institute for Advanced Study at Princeton. In 1954 his health began to deteriorate, and he died after a prolonged and painful illness.

Von Neumann's thought processes were rapid and his associates often found it difficult to keep up with his vast flow of ideas. He was also a linguist, and could converse in seven European languages. He preferred general to special problems, and rarely worried about mathematical elegance. In connection with a long-winded but straightforward proof he is quoted as saying that he "didn't have the time to make the subject difficult." Von Neumann's interest

Johann von Neumann, mathematician. Courtesy Institute for Advanced Studies, Princeton, New Jersey. Photo Alan W. Richards, Princeton.

in quantum mechanics was aroused by his stay in Goettingen in 1926. He aimed at developing the subject as a vigorous mathematical discipline in *Mathematische Grundlagen der Quantenmechanik* (1932). This investigation led him to research in Hilbert space and the initiation of continuous geometry. In addition, Von Neumann made important contributions to measure theory, ergodic theory, continuous groups, topology, classical mechanics, hydrodynamic turbulence, and shock waves. He opened up a new branch of mathematics with his paper *"Zur Theorie der Gesellschaftsspiele,"* (in *Mathematische Annalen,* 100 (1928), 295–320) and the book *Theory of Games and Economic Behavior* (1944, 1953[3]) written in collaboration with O. Morgenstern.

Von Neumann's work in the war effort convinced him of the need for high-speed computers. He was instrumental in the development of MANIAC (the mathematical analyzer, numerical integrator, and computer) and was a member of the U.S. Atomic Energy Commission from 1955 until his death. His *Von Neumann Collected Works* were published in six volumes from 1961 to 1963.

Bibliography: *Current Biography Yearbook 1955* (1956), 624–7; Bochner, in: National Academy of Sciences, *Biographical Memoirs,* 32 (1958), 438–57; *Bulletin of the American Mathematical Society,* 64, no. 3, pt. 2 (May 1958), special issue dedicated to J. von Neumann, incl. bibl.; F. Smithies, in: *Journal of the London Mathematical Society,* 34 (1959), 373–84; S. Thomas, *Men of Space,* 1 (1960), 181–203 (incl. bibl.). [B.S.]

NEUMANN, ROBERT (1897–), novelist and satirist. Born in Vienna, the son of a mathematician and bank director, Neumann studied chemistry and literature. He became however a chocolate manufacturer. After losing his money in the inflation of the 1920s, he went to sea. His two early verse collections (1919, 1923) attracted little attention, but *Mit fremden Federn* (1927), a volume of parodies, brought him fame. Of the works that followed, the anti-Nazi novels *Sintflut* (1929) and *Die Macht* (1932; Eng. tr. *Mammon,* 1933), and *Unter falscher Flagge* (1932), another book of parodies, were particularly successful. In February 1934, less than a year after the public burning of his books by the Nazis, he moved to England. Other works of his pre-World War II period were the novels *Karriere* (1931; *On the Make,* 1932); *Sir Basil Zaharoff, der Koenig der Waffen* (1934; *Zaharoff, the Armaments King,* 1935); *Struensee* (1935; *The Queen's Doctor,* 1936); and *An den Wassern von Babylon* (written 1937–38, Ger. orig. publ. 1945; *By the Waters of Babylon,* 1939).

Neumann also began to write in English, later novels including *The Inquest* (1944; *Bibiana Santis* (Ger.), 1950); *Children of Vienna* (1946; *Kinder von Wien,* 1948); and *Blind Man's Buff* (1949). A witty and ironical writer and a gifted political and social satirist, he had a fondness for the erotic and a genius for parodying modern poets. After the war,

Robert Neumann, novelist and satirist.

when he settled in Switzerland, he wrote an autobiography, *Mein altes Haus in Kent* (1957), and then turned to somber themes relating to the Holocaust. Works of this kind are the documentaries, *Ausfluechte unseres Gewissens* (1960), on Hitler's "Final Solution"; *Hitler, Aufstieg und Untergang des Dritten Reiches* (1961); *The Pictorial History of the Third Reich* (1962); and *Der Tatbestand oder Der gute Glaube der Deutschen* (1965). Neumann also wrote plays for radio and television and another autobiography, *Vielleicht das Heitere,* was published in 1970.

Bibliography: *Robert Neumann: Stimmen der Freunde . . . Zum 60. Geburtstag . . .* (1957), incl. bibl.; H. Zohn, *Wiener Juden in der deutschen Literatur* (1964), 89–94. [S.L.]

NEUMANN, YEḤESKEL MOSHE (1893–1956), Yiddish writer. Born near Warsaw, he grew up and was educated in Lodz. He was on the staff of the *Lodzher Morgenblat,* edited booklets on literature and art, and was a founder of the Lodz writers' group "Yung Yiddish." He was on the staff of the Warsaw daily *Haynt,* whose literary editor he became in 1933, and wrote film and theater reviews. In addition to contributing to various Yiddish periodicals, he was among the pioneers of the Yiddish film and wrote scripts for *Tekias Kaf* and *Al Ḥet.* During World War II he fled to Russia, then emigrated in 1940 to Palestine, joining the editorial board of the daily *Davar.* He wrote about problems of the Yiddish and Hebrew theater, published articles in the Yiddish journal *Di Goldene Keyt,* and wrote about Jewish artists and architects. He also composed the dramatic poem *"Don Kishot in Shotn fun der Palme"* (in *Di Goldene Keyt,* 1951) and *"A Khasene in Yerusholayim"* (*ibid.,* 1953).

Bibliography: Rejzen, Leksikon, 2 (1927), 561–4; LNYL, 6 (1965), 222–6. [I.H.B.]

NEUMARK, DAVID (1866–1924), scholar and philosopher of Reform Judaism. Born in Galicia, Neumark was ordained as rabbi at the Lehranstalt fuer die Wissenschaft des Judenthums in 1897. He served as rabbi in Rakonitz (Rakovnik), Bohemia, from 1897 to 1904, and as editor in chief of the division of philosophy and *halakhah* of the proposed Hebrew encyclopedia *Oẓar ha-Yahadut* from 1904 to 1907, whose specimen volume on the principle and philosophy of Judaism he edited in 1906. He was professor of Jewish philosophy at the Veitel-Heine-Ephraimschen Lehranstalt in Berlin in 1907, and as professor of philosophy at the Hebrew Union College in Cincinnati from 1907 to 1924. In 1919 Neumark founded *The Journal of Jewish Lore and Philosophy,* which became *The Hebrew Union College Annual* in 1921.

Neumark's philosophy of Judaism is representative of the Reform Jewish position of his time, and includes the following points: Judaism is an evolving religion which has undergone change in the past and will continue to do so in the future; the vital continuing element in Judaism is ethical

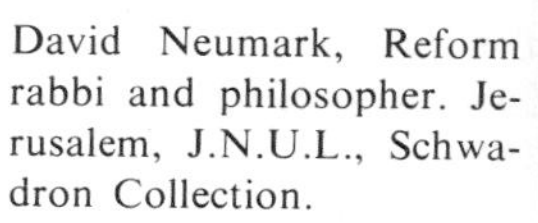

David Neumark, Reform rabbi and philosopher. Jerusalem, J.N.U.L., Schwadron Collection.

monotheism, which Jewish philosophy must defend, explicate, and refine; the Bible was written by men, and while it is a source of inspiration and instruction, it is not binding and may be disagreed with. Neumark was unusual among the Reformists of his day in that he was an ardent Zionist.

However, on the basis of his philosophy of Judaism, he insisted that Zionism must have a religious base, which for him was the only *raison d'être* for any significant Jewish enterprise.

Neumark's scholarship reflected his concept of Judaism. He attempted in his many works to show that throughout the evolution of Judaism the basic commitment of the Jew was to religion, and that the Jews remained true to Judaism through the ages only because their concepts of God and morality differed from and were superior to all other religions and philosophies of their time. Neumark's magnum opus, *Geschichte der juedischen Philosophie des Mittelalters* (1907–10; translated into Hebrew under the title *Toledot ha-Filosofyah be-Yisrael*, vol 1, 1922, vol. 2, 1929), combines considerable acumen and occasional penetrating insights with a lack of critical method and an excess of imagination. His *Essays in Jewish Philosophy* (1929) contains a bibliography of his writings, which also included "The Philosophy of Judaism" (HUCA 1925), *The Philosophy of the Bible* (1918), and *Toledot ha-Ikkarim be-Yisrael* (Odessa, 2 vols., 1912–19). [A.J.R.]

NEUMARK, EPHRAIM (1860–?), traveler and writer. Born in Eastern Europe, Neumark was taken by his parents to Ereẓ Israel. At the age of 23 he left Tiberias on a three-year journey through the Jewish communities in Syria, Kurdistan, Mesopotamia, Persia, Afghanistan, and Central Asia. The account of his travels, *Massa be-Ereẓ ha-Kedem*, is distinguished by critical observation and scholarly approach. He gives a detailed picture of every aspect of the Jewish communities in the Orient, their geographical diffusion, occupations, religious life, practices, and customs.

Bibliography: KS, 24 (1947–48), 28–29; E. Neumark, *Massa be-Ereẓ ha-Kedem*, ed. by A. Yaari (1967), with introd. and notes; idem, in: *Ha-Asif*, 5 (1889), 39–75. [W.J.F.]

NEUMEYER, KARL (1869–1941), German international lawyer. Born in Munich, Neumeyer became a lecturer at the University of Munich in 1910. He represented Germany at the sixth Hague conference on private international law in 1928. In 1929 he was made professor of international law at Munich University and in 1931 became dean of the faculty of law. Though removed from all his posts in 1933 following the Nazi rise to power, Neumeyer refused to leave Germany and continued his research until July 1941 when he and his wife committed suicide rather than be sent to a concentration camp.

Neumeyer was the author of several important works on international law, including: *Die gemeinrechtliche Entwicklung des internationalen Privat- und Strafrechts bis Bartolus* (2 vols., 1901–16), a history of international law; *Internationales Privatrecht* (1923), a detailed analysis of the sources of international law; and *Internationales Verwaltungsrecht* (4 vols., 1910–36), in which he set out his system of international administrative law.

Bibliography: *American Journal of International Law*, 35 (1941), 672. [Ed.]

NEUSNER, JACOB (1932–), U.S. scholar and historian. Neusner was born in Hartford, Connecticut, and was ordained rabbi at the Jewish Theological Seminary of America. He served on the faculties of Columbia University, the University of Wisconsin (Milwaukee), Dartmouth College, and Brown University. Neusner's five-volume *History of the Jews in Babylonia* (1965–70) was the first full-scale treatment in over half a century of the period and place that produced the Babylonian Talmud. This work reflects a "history of religions" approach and incorporates the results of modern Iranian studies. In his *Development of a Legend* (1970) and his three-volume *Rabbinic Traditions about the Pharisees* (1971) he applies the techniques of form criticism and synoptic studies to rabbinic sources. Neusner published numerous articles on a variety of topics. Collections of these shorter pieces have appeared among his other works: *Fellowship in Judaism* (1963); *History and Torah* (1965); *Judaism in a Secular Age* (1970); and *The Way of Torah* (1970). He was also active in several professional organizations and learned societies. In 1968–69 he served as president of the American Academy of Religion. [D.Go.]

NEUTRA, RICHARD JOSEPH (1892–1970), U.S. architect. Born in Vienna, after World War I Neutra worked in Switzerland as a nurseryman and landscape gardener, an experience which helped to develop his remarkable talent for his building fitting into the landscape. In 1922 he joined Erich *Mendelsohn in Berlin, and the following year they were awarded first prize for their joint design for a business center for Haifa, Palestine. Neutra emigrated to the U.S. in 1923 and studied under Frank Lloyd Wright at his architectural center at Taliesin, Wisconsin. In 1926 he settled in Los Angeles, where he entered the office of the Vienna-born architect, Rudolph Schindler. The buildings they designed and erected were among the first creations of the international style in America. Neutra was at this period concerned with town planning and architectural technology. This aspect of his work is seen in his "Rush City Reformed" (1923–30), a plan for an ideal city, in his designs for prefabricated housing units, and in his Channel Heights Housing Project, San Pedro, California (1942–44). It was for his private homes, however, that Neutra was best known. "Lovell House" (1927–29), a rambling construction in the then-modern style, established his reputation. The houses he built after World War II are often regarded as his greatest achievement. They are usually luxurious residences in which glass is extensively used to give a feeling of space; the effect of the glass is often enhanced by the use of reflecting pools of water. Neutra wrote several books, including *Survival Through Design* (1954).

Bibliography: E. McCoy, *Richard Neutra* (Eng., 1960), includes bibliography; W. Boesiger (ed.), *Richard Neutra, Buildings and Projects* (1951, 1959, 1966); A. Forsee, *Men of Modern Architecture* (1966), 131–60. [Ed.]

NEUZEIT, DIE (Ger. "Modern Times"), first Austrian Jewish weekly in German, published from 1861 to 1903. Founded in Vienna by Leopold *Kompert and Simon *Szántó in 1861, the year of the restoration of the Austrian constitution, it hailed the new era and called for the overcoming of Jewish medievalism. *Die Neuzeit* stressed the universalistic and ethical aspects of Judaism and its historic world mission as against undue emphasis on the ceremonial law. It was largely in agreement with the views of the Viennese preacher Adolf *Jellinek, who was a frequent contributor; he became editor of *Die Neuzeit* after Szántó's death in 1882. When Jellinek died in 1893, he was succeeded by D. Loewy. *Die Neuzeit* favored the efforts at Reform of Abraham *Geiger and approved the synods of Leipzig and Augsburg, presided over by Moritz *Lazarus. It was critical of the more Conservative Ludwig Philippson and the Breslau Theological Seminary, and strongly opposed the new Orthodoxy of Samson Raphael *Hirsch. Most religious controversies of the time were reflected in its pages, which carried scholarly essays as well as fiction in serialized form. *Die Neuzeit* provided information on all of Austria-Hungary, being the official organ of several Jewish organizations. It rejected both secular Jewish nationalism and Zionism.

Bibliography: *Die Neuzeit*, 1–43 (1861–1903); M. Rosenmann, *Dr. Adolf Jellinek* (Ger., 1931). [Hu.K.]

NEVADA, state located in western U.S.; Jews numbered approximately 2,380 out of a total of 440,000 in 1969. The two principal Jewish communities were in Las Vegas (2,000) and Reno (400), where the state's only two synagogues were located. Jews first went to Nevada from California in 1859 with the discovery of gold on the Comstock Lode and the silver rush around Virginia City in 1862. The gold and silver strikes brought a flood of emigrants from all corners of the country, including Jewish engineers, storekeepers, traders, lawyers, journalists, doctors, and fortune hunters. Nevada's first directory in 1862 listed 200 Jews in Virginia City, Gold Hill, Silver City, Austin, Dayton, Eureka, and Carson City. All but the latter were ghost towns by the 1960s. A congregation and B'nai B'rith lodge were organized in Virginia City in 1862. In the same year a burial society was organized there and in Eureka. Worship services were first held in Carson City in 1869. When the U.S. went on the gold standard and silver deposits gave out, Nevada's population shrank and the Jewish communities in the mining towns faded away. A short-lived community grew up at Goldfield at the turn of the century when new gold and silver discoveries were made there. In 1969 the oldest permanent Jewish community was in Reno, which became the state's principal city after the mining towns were abandoned in the 1870s.

Among the pioneer Jews was Herman Bien, a rabbi, who opened the first Jewish school at Virginia City in 1861, and served in the first territorial legislature. He was one of four Jewish members of the convention that drafted the state's first constitution in 1864. Adolph Sutro, later mayor of San Francisco, who arrived in 1860, built the Sutro tunnel that greatly aided mining operations. Albert *Michelson, the United States' first Nobel Prize winner, spent his boyhood in Virginia City, where his father was a storekeeper. Joseph Goodman was co-owner of *The Territorial Enterprise*, first printed newspaper in Nevada, which employed Samuel Clemens (Mark Twain) as a reporter. Samuel Platt, whose father came to Carson City in 1864, served as speaker of the state legislature and U.S. attorney for Nevada, and was three times Republican candidate for the U.S. Senate. Col. David Mannheim commanded troops in the Indian wars of the 1860s and Mark Strouse was the first sheriff of Carson City. Milton Badt was chief justice of the Nevada Supreme Court from 1947 to 1966, and David Zenoff was appointed to the court in 1965.

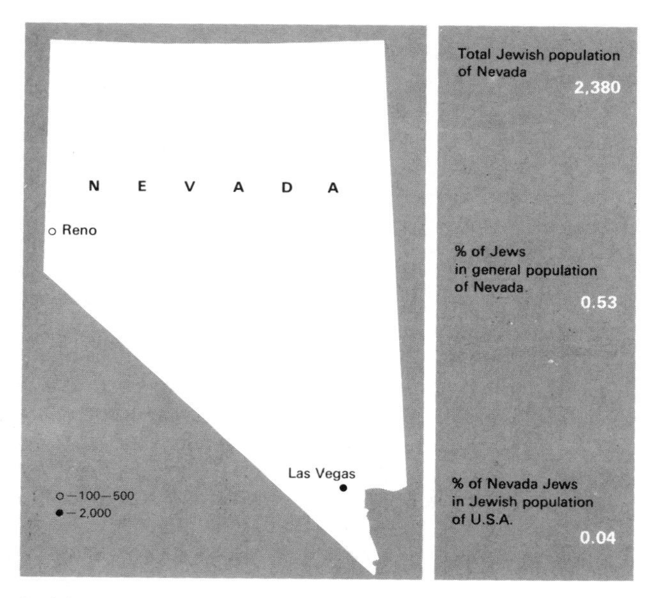

Jewish communities in Nevada. Population figures for 1968.

Many Las Vegas Jews are now employed in the gambling casinos and hotels and own various enterprises serving these establishments and their patrons. In 1970 the community supported a *talmud torah*, and the weekly *Las Vegas Israelite*, which was founded in 1965. There were many Jewish lawyers, accountants, and insurance men in Reno, attracted there by the city's role as a national center for divorce proceedings. Elko, Wells, Pioche, Carson City, Boulder City, and Winnemucca had a handful of Jews. Jewish scientists, engineers, and others resided near the Nevada Bomb Test Site at Yucca Flat, Mercury, and Nellis Air Force Base. A Jewish settlement was also growing up in the resort areas around Lake Tahoe and Lake Mead.

Bibliography: B. Postal and L. Koppman, *A Jewish Tourist's Guide to the U.S.* (1954), 293–8; R. E. and M. F. Stewart, *Adolph Sutro; A Biography* (1962), 41–58; AJA, 8 (1956), 103–5. [B.P.]

NEVAKHOVICH, JUDAH LEIB (1776–1831), one of the earliest *maskilim* in Russia. Born in Letichev, Ukraine, Nevakhovich was a teacher and a companion of Abraham *Peretz, son-in-law of the wealthy Joshua *Zeitlin of Shklov. Together with the Peretz family, Nevakhovich settled in St. Petersburg at the end of the 18th century. Having mastered German and Russian, he was employed by the Russian government as a translator of Hebrew documents, including those connected with the imprisonment of R. *Shneur Zalman of Lyady.

During the debate over legislation concerning the Jews of Russia at the beginning of the 19th century, Nevakhovich took an active part in the deliberations and wrote the pamphlet *Vopl Dushcheri iudeyskoy* (St. Petersburg, 1803; repr. in *Budushchnost*, vol. 3, 1902). The purpose of this pamphlet was to combat anti-Jewish hatred. Such hatred, Nevakhovich believed, was the cause of all the decrees and persecutions endured by his coreligionists. He called on his Russian countrymen to treat the Jews with sympathy and tolerance. He pointed out that there was no foundation to the accusations—including blood libels—brought against the Jews, and that Judaism, furthermore, was not opposed to the laws of Russia. Nevakhovich rejected the demands of Christians that the Jews be converted. Within a year of its publication, Nevakhovich's pamphlet also appeared with various changes and additions in Hebrew, under the title *Kol Shavat Bat Yehudah* ("The Voice of the Cry of the Daughter of Judah" (Shklov, 1804); repr. in *He-Avar*, vol. 2, 1918). The Hebrew version also includes a short history of Russia, followed by an essay on "the hatred of religions, truth and peace," which is in the form of a discussion between "truth" and religious hatred, with words of praise for Alexander I who convened a committee for "the reform of the situation of the Jews to their benefit and that of the country." The pamphlet, in both its Hebrew and Russian versions, marks the beginning of Haskalah literature among Russian Jewry, but it also signifies the end of his literary activity on behalf of the Jews.

In 1809 his name is present on the list of signatories to *Ha-Me'assef*, and it was about this time that Nevakhovich converted to Lutheranism. He was employed as a government official in Poland and later engaged in commerce. He also wrote dramas which were presented in St. Petersburg's theaters and translated German literature into Russia. The conversion of Nevakhovich and his companion, A. Peretz, turned many Jews away from the Haskalah movement, even in its most moderate forms. Although Nevakhovich's works appear episodic and without continuity in the literature (both Hebrew and Russian) of the Haskalah, they did, nevertheless, herald the arrival of a new period in the spiritual life of Russian Jewry. The scientist Elie *Metchnikoff was the grandson of Nevakhovich, through his daughter.

Bibliography: B. Katz, in: *Ha-Zeman*, 3 (1904), 11–15; idem, in: *He-Avar*, 2 (1958), 197–201; Klausner, Sifrut, 3 (1953), 20–24; Yu. Hessen (Gessen), *Yevrei v Rossii* (1906), 78–98, 136–9. [Y.S.]

NEVATIM (Heb. נְבָטִים; "Sprouts"), moshav in southern Israel, 5 mi. (9 km.) E. of Beersheba, affiliated with Tenu'at ha-Moshavim. It was the easternmost moshav of the 11 settlements erected in the night of Oct. 6, 1946, in the south and Negev. The founding group originated from various European countries, but immigrants from Cochin (South India) took their place after 1948. Nevatim's farming is of the oasis type, based on irrigated vegetables and field crops, fruit orchards, and poultry. In 1968 its population was 426. [E.O.]

NEVEH EITAN (Heb. נְוֵה אֵיתָן; "Habitation of the Strong"), kibbutz in central Israel in the Beth-Shean Valley, affiliated with Iḥud ha-Kevuẓot ve-ha-Kibbutzim. It was founded in 1938 as a tower and stockade settlement, after the group, which had originated from Poland, had participated in setting up neighboring *Ma'oz Ḥayyim and had lived there for several months. Farming at Neveh Eitan is intensive and irrigated, comprising field crops (e.g., cotton), dairy cattle, and carp ponds. The name is based on a passage in Jeremiah 49:19. In 1968 its population was 250. [E.O.]

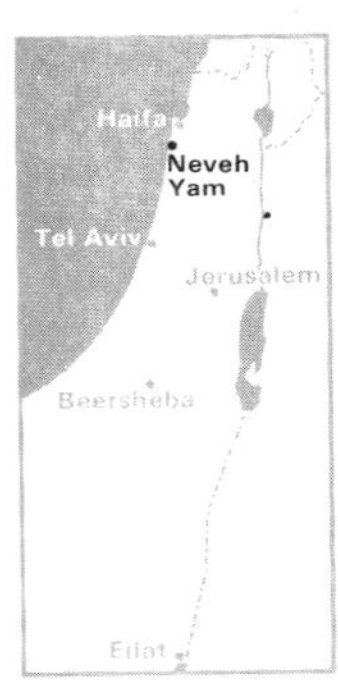

NEVEH YAM (Heb. נְוֵה יָם; "Sea Dwelling"), kibbutz in northern Israel, on the Carmel Coast near Athlit, affiliated with Iḥud ha-Kevuẓot ve-ha-Kibbutzim. Neveh Yam was founded in 1939 by a pioneer group, Ma'pilim-Gordonia, from Poland, which had received training in seafaring in the Polish port of Gdynia; they were joined by immigrants from Austria and Czechoslovakia. The kibbutz sought to develop sea fishing and aid "*illegal" immigration. Farming was at first only a sideline, but after 1948 became the mainstay of the kibbutz' economy, in addition to a guest house and a fish-canning factory. Fishing, however, was discontinued. In 1968 Neveh Yam had 130 inhabitants. [E.O.]

Kibbutz Neveh Yam, on the Carmel coast, 1947. Courtesy J.N.F., Jerusalem.

NEVELAH (Heb. נְבֵלָה; "carcass"), descriptive noun for any animal, bird, or creature which has died as a result of any process other than valid ritual slaughter (**sheḥitah*).

The Pentateuch forbids the consumption of such meat, which can be given to a resident alien, or sold to a non-Jew (Deut. 14:21; see also Pes. 21b). Punishment for eating *nevelah* applies only to "clean" animals (Meil. 16a; Maim. Yad, Ma'akhalot Asurot, 4:17) and is not added to the normal punishment for eating "unclean" animals. The *nevelah* is also one of the principal categories of ritual impurity (*tumah*), and touching or carrying it causes ritual impurity (Lev. 11:39–40; Maim. Yad, She'ar Avot ha-Tumah, 1–3).

See **Sheḥitah;* *Dietary Laws; *Purity and Impurity, Ritual; *Animals.

Bibliography: Eisenstein, Dinim, 254. [Ed.]

NEVERS, capital of the Nièvre department, central France. In 1208 Pope Innocent III protested vehemently to Hervé, count of Nevers, against the excessively advantageous conditions which he had granted the Jews of his town and county. This situation changed rapidly: in 1210 Hervé personally signed a promise that he would not retain any of the royal Jews fleeing to his lands from the king's demesne. Countess Mahaut ratified *Louis VIII's restrictive ordinance on the Jews immediately after its publication in 1224. Finally, Count Robert expelled the Jews from his county in 1294.

Bibliography: Gross, Gal Jud (1897), 387–8; R. de Lespinasse, *Le Nivernais et les Comtes de Nevers*, 2 (1911), 31f., 44, 116, 373; S. Grayzel, *The Church and the Jews in the XIIIth Century* (1966), index. [B.Bl.]

NEVU'AT HA-YELED (Heb. נְבוּאַת הַיֶּלֶד; "The Prophecy of the Child"), a medieval Hebrew short story. The body of the tale is followed by a number of occult prophecies in Aramaic. First printed at the end of *Sefer Nagid u-Meẓavveh* by Jacob *Ẓemaḥ (Constantinople, 1726) and published many times since, it was known already as early as the end of the 15th century and the beginning of the 16th when some kabbalists, among them R. *Abraham b. Eliezer ha-Levi, wrote commentaries on the prophecies in *Nevu'at ha-Yeled*. The story tells of a wonder child, Naḥman, born in the fifth century to a kabbalist; the child died very young, but immediately upon birth began to tell his mother secrets of the heavenly worlds. His father cautioned him not to reveal mysteries forbidden to man, and from then the child spoke only obscurely and enigmatically.

Modern scholars have attempted to date the story and the prophecies therein by tracing known historical events hinted at, and relating them to the text. The obscureness of the text makes this very difficult, but it seems probable that historical events in the 15th century, especially in the East, are referred to in the prophecies. However, the purpose of the story and its prophecies was to anticipate the coming of the Messiah and to describe the major political and historical events and catastrophes bringing about his final revelation. The kabbalists interpreted the prophecies as hinting at the coming of the Messiah in the early 16th century.

In literary genre, there is a great similarity between the prophecies of the Jewish child and comparable phenomena in non-Jewish literature, e.g., the cryptic prophecies of the wizard Merlin (according to legend told when he was a boy) which many medieval Christian scholars interpreted as foretelling future events. A parody on *Nevu'at ha-Yeled* was written by R. Joseph *Delmedigo in his *Maẓref le-Ḥokhmah* (Basel, 1629) about a child in Poland whose duplicity was revealed.

Bibliography: A. Z. Aešcoly, *Ha-Tenu'ot ha-Meshiḥiyyot be-Yisrael*, 1 (1956), 283–6; Scholem, in: KS, 2 (1925/26), 115–9, no. 13. [Y.D.]

NEW BEDFORD, town in Massachusetts with an estimated Jewish population of 3,100 out of a total population of 101,262 (1970). Because of its proximity to Newport, the port of New Bedford in colonial days was of importance to the group of Jewish merchants settled in Newport. In the middle of the 19th century a group of German Jews settled there, and were later joined by new arrivals. The B'nai Israel Society was established in 1857. The New Bedford Directory for 1869 contains Jewish names such as Adolphus Levi; Leon Levy, dry goods and variety store; Louis Henry, cigar maker; and Julius Simon, dry goods, fancy and retail. After 1900 East European Jews went to New Bedford in large numbers. Congregation Ahabath Achim began in 1893 with the purchase of a plot of land upon which the synagogue was built; it was inaugurated in 1899. Congregation Chesed shel Emes was incorporated in 1898 and inaugurated its synagogue in 1904. The Conservative Congregation Tifereth Israel's synagogue was dedicated in 1924. Other Jewish organizations and branches of fraternal orders also existed. A communal *talmud torah* existed until 1935. The establishment of various industrial enterprises in New Bedford in recent years has failed to arrest the decline in the Jewish population (4,520 in 1937; 3,600 in 1964; 3,100 in 1969).

[R.GL.]

NEW BRUNSWICK, U.S. industrial city on the Raritan River, in New Jersey, approximately 30 miles S.W. of New York City. In 1969 the population (est.) of the New Brunswick metropolitan area was 125,000, including a Jewish population of 15,000; the city population was 41,000, including a Jewish population of 9,000.

New Brunswick's earliest Jewish settler seems to have been Daniel Nunez, who was a justice of the peace in 1722, about 40 years after the founding of the town (1679–80). Nunez was in business in Piscataway, a small village just outside the New Brunswick city limits. Hannah Lonzoda, a widow, lived in New Brunswick from 1750 on. In 1850 some Bohemian and German Jews settled in the town, and by 1852 about 20 to 25 Jews were living there. The Jewish population grew from 90 in 1865 to 280 in 1897, slightly more than 1% of the general population. In 1888 an influx of Eastern European Jews began, and from the turn of the century on, the Jewish population of the greater New Brunswick area continued. In 1969, two Reform, five Conservative, and five Orthodox synagogues were serving the area. The oldest synagogue in New Brunswick, now Anshe Emeth Memorial Temple (Reform), was founded in 1859, probably as an Orthodox congregation; it became a Reform temple about 1890. Congregation Ahavas Achim (Orthodox) was founded in 1889. The Highland Park Conservative Temple was founded in 1930.

The Jewish Federation of Raritan Valley, launched in 1948, coordinates fund raising, social service, welfare, educational, and communal activities "calculated to enhance Jewish communal life." In 1969, 28 religious, social, and educational organizations were affiliated with the federation. A YM-YWHA was organized in 1911.

Before 1900, most New Brunswick Jews were peddlers and small shopkeepers. A few were professionals, including some Jewish teachers in the public schools in 1893, one of whom served as school principal. From 1900 to the 1930s, most of the Jewish population worked as tradesmen and artisans. In the 1960s many Jews were practicing the professions of law, medicine, accountancy, and teaching; many were engaged in business and industry. A number were serving as elected officials in municipal government. Samuel D. Hoffman (1900–1957), attorney and first president of the Jewish Federation, served as a city commissioner of New Brunswick in 1935. Harry S. Feller (1885–1954), second president of the federation and one of the organizers of the Ad Hoc Committee for United Jewish Appeal, taught in New Brunswick High School (1908–16) and served as first principal of the evening school (1912).

Among the Rutgers University Jewish community is Selman A. *Waksman, co-discoverer of streptomycin, who directed the Institute of Microbiology at Rutgers from 1949 to 1958. A B'nai B'rith Hillel Foundation was organized at Rutgers in 1943. A statewide fund-raising campaign, largely in the Jewish community and initiated by local Jewish alumni, helped set up a department of Hebraic studies at Rutgers in 1962; in 1970 the constantly growing department had 250 students.

The *Jewish Journal,* a bimonthly Anglo-Jewish newspaper published by the Jewish Federation, was founded in 1956.

[AB.H.]

NEWCASTLE-UPON-TYNE, port in Northumberland, N.E. England. Its small medieval Jewish group was expelled in 1234 at the request of the townspeople. Although there were individual Jews in the city by 1775, the organized community dates from 1831—a year after a cemetery had been acquired—by which time there were about 100 Jewish residents. A synagogue was built in 1838, but by 1868 it had become too small for the growing population and a second congregation was formed. In 1873 the two groups amalgamated and a new synagogue was opened in 1880. The community increased during the mass immigration from Eastern Europe (1881–1914) and by 1900 numbered about 2,000. The small but very Orthodox community of *Gateshead is on the opposite bank of the River Tyne from Newcastle. Newcastle itself has three Orthodox synagogues and a Reform congregation. In addition there is the normal structure of communal institutions that includes a *sheḥitah* board, a Zionist society, and a University Jewish Society. The total Jewish population for Tyneside (Newcastle, Gateshead, etc.) was 3,500 (0.38% of the total population) in 1969.

Bibliography: C. Roth, *Rise of Provincial Jewry* (1950), 84–85; Roth, England, index.

[V.D.L.]

NEW CHRISTIANS, a term applied specifically to three groups of Jewish converts to Christianity and their descendants in the Iberian Peninsula. The first group converted in the wake of the massacres in Spain in 1391 and the proselytizing fervor of the subsequent decades. The second, also in Spain, were baptized following the decree of *Ferdinand and Isabella in 1492 expelling all Jews who refused to accept Christianity. The third group, in Portugal, was converted by force and royal fiat in 1497. Like the word *Conversos, but unlike *Marranos, the term New Christian carried no intrinsic pejorative connotation, but with the increasing power of the *Inquisition and the growth of the concept of **limpieza de sangre,* the name signaled the disabilities inevitably heaped on those who bore it. In Portugal, the Marquis de Pombal officially abolished all legal distinctions between Old and New Christians in May 1773. Comparable measures were not enacted in Spain until 1860, by which time much of the distinction had been eroded by assimilation and inquisitorial repression. However, pockets of social discrimination against New Christians still continued, as, for example, against the **chuetas* of the Balearic Isles.

[MA.C.]

In Halakhic Literature. The New Christians who continued secretly to observe the precepts of Judaism as much as possible after their conversion were not regarded as voluntary apostates. The basis of this decision was the statement of Maimonides (Yad, Yesodei ha-Torah 5:3–4) that although one should allow oneself to be put to death rather than abandon one's faith in times of persecution, "nevertheless, if he transgressed and did not choose the death of a martyr, even though he has annulled the positive precept of sanctifying the Name and transgressed the injunction not to desecrate the Name, since he transgressed under duress and could not escape, he is exempted from punishment." In accordance with this *Isaac b. Sheshet ruled that those New Christians who remained in their countries because they were unable to escape and flee, if they conduct themselves in accordance with the precepts of Judaism, even if only privately, are like full Jews, their *sheḥitah* may be relied upon, their testimony in law cases is accepted, and their wine is not forbidden by touch as that of non-Jews (Resp. Ribash, no. 4). However, some authorities ruled that if the Marranos of a certain locality succeeded in fleeing to a country where they could return to Judaism, while others remained there in order to retain their material possessions, the latter were no longer presumed to have the privilege of being regarded as Jews (Ribash, *ibid.*) nor are they regarded as valid witnesses (*Tashbeẓ*, 3:47; Resp. Redakh, no. 24). Others, however, expressed more lenient views and held that no one is to be deprived of his rights as a Jew as long as he is not seen to transgress the precepts of Judaism even when there is no danger involved (*Tashbeẓ*, 1:23). Moses Isserles, too, rules that even those Marranos who are able to flee but delay because of material considerations and transgress Judaism publicly out of compulsion while remaining observant privately do not make wine forbidden by their touch (Sh. Ar., YD 124:9, and see *ibid.* 119:12).

The problem of the Marranos in *halakhah* became increasingly complex as the length of their stay and that of their descendants in their native lands wore on. Jewish religious tradition was gradually forgotten by the descendants of the Marranos in Spain and Portugal, and many of them assimilated and intermarried with the gentiles. Since for several centuries individuals and groups of descendants of Marranos continued to escape to other countries where they were absorbed in the Jewish community, doubts and differences of opinion related to the laws of marriage and personal status arose among the great talmudists about the Marranos returning to Judaism. Isaac b. Sheshet, Simeon b. Solomon Duran in Algiers, and Elijah Mizraḥi in Constantinople ruled that the children of Marranos counted as Jews in matters of marriage, divorce, levirate marriage, and **ḥaliẓah* even after several generations (*Yakhin u-Vo'az*, pt. 2, no. 38; *Mayim Amukkim*, no. 31; Maharik, Resp. no. 85 in the name of Rashi). On the other hand, some ruled that the children of Marranos born after their parents had converted and succeeding generations were to be regarded in all ways as non-Jews; their betrothal to a Jewish woman was invalid, levirate marriage did not apply to them, and even if a Marrano begot a child by a woman forbidden under penalty of **karet* the offspring does not rank as **mamzer*, and should he become a proselyte would be permitted to marry a Jew. The Marranos who had lived among gentiles for more than a century came to regard those things forbidden by the Torah as permitted and married non-Jewish women, with the result that their children were presumed to be non-Jewish unless it could be proved that their mothers were Jewish (*Keneset ha-Gedolah*, EH 4; Resp. Maharit, vol. 2, EH no. 18).

A Marrano who could have fled but did not was penalized, in that he did not inherit the property of his Jewish relatives, while every Marrano heir who hastened to return to Judaism canceled the rights of the other Marrano heirs (Resp. Reshakh, pt. 1, no. 137). According to some authority the customs of dowry and marriage allowance applying to Marranos while they lived as gentiles remain in force (Resp. Maharashdam, ḤM no. 327), but according to others the agreements made by Marranos at the time of their marriages in accordance with gentile usages had no binding force (Joseph Caro, in *Avkat Rokhel*). A testamentary disposition or the gift of a dying person made by a Marrano not in accordance with Torah law was not binding (Joseph ibn Lev in *Edut be-Ya'akov*, no. 71, 195b; *Keneset ha-Gedolah*, ḤM 161; *Torat ha-Minhagot*, no. 51).

The scholars of Safed headed by Jacob Berab imposed flagellation upon Marranos who returned to Judaism as a punishment for transgressing the prohibitions which rendered them liable to *karet* in their previous condition (*Kunteres ha-Semikhah* at the end of Resp. Maharalbaḥ) and since flagellation can be imposed only by ordained *dayyanim*, Jacob Berab and his colleagues wanted to enforce punishment when ordination was renewed (see **Semikhah*). A Marrano who escaped from his native land but was not circumcised through neglect was prevented from participating in the sacred service in the synagogue until he was circumcised (*Mayim Rabbim* of Raphael Meldola, YD nos. 51 and 52). [M.N.Z.]

See also *Marrano Diaspora.

Bibliography: Roth, Marranos, index; Baer, Spain, 2 (1966), passim; A. J. Saraiva, *Inquisição e Critãos-Novos* (1969). IN HALAKHIC LITERATURE: H. J. Zimmels, *Die Marranen in der rabbinischen Literatur* (1932); S. Assaf, *Be-Oholei Ya'akov* (1943), 145–80.

NEW HAMPSHIRE, one of the New England states, located in northeastern United States. In 1968 its population was estimated at 702,000, of which 4,260 were Jews.

The earliest reference to Jews in New Hampshire mentions William Abrams and Aaron Moses, who moved from New Castle to Sanbornton in 1693. A list of grants to settlers, dated 1770, refers to Joseph Levy, a settler near what is now Ossipee. Abraham Isaac (d. 1803), who settled at Portsmouth near the close of the American Revolution, was possibly the first Jew there. There is, however, scarcely any other reference to Jews or Jewish life in any of the state records of the early 19th century. Those mentioned were predominantly Jews from Germany.

Manchester, with a population of 1,500 Jews, has the largest Jewish community in New Hampshire. In 1967 Portsmouth had a Jewish community of approximately 300; Dover, 240; Nashua, 210; Concord, 195; Claremont, 120; Laconia and Keene, each 90; and Berlin, and other sections of northern New Hampshire, 66. The first Jewish congregations (Bney Israel in Berlin and the Conservative Temple Israel of Manchester) were founded in 1899, Temple Base Abraham, Conservative, was incorporated in Nashua; its name was modified to Temple Beth Abraham in 1959.

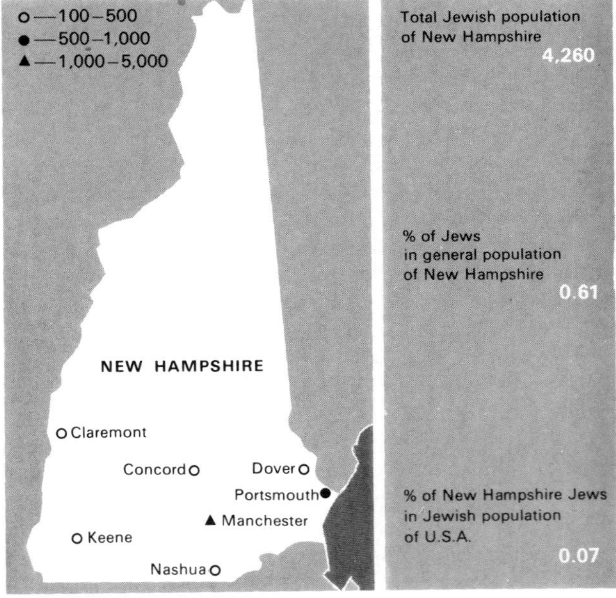

Other synagogues include: Congregation Adath Yeshurun, Reform, founded in Manchester, 1900; Temple of Israel, Conservative, Portsmouth, 1910; Congregation Beth Israel, Orthodox, Berlin, 1915; Ahavath Achim, Keene, 1916; Temple Beth Jacob, Reform, Concord, 1917, originally, Base of Jacob; Temple B'nai Israel, Laconia, about 1928; Temple of Israel, Conservative, Dover, 1938; and Temple Meyer-David, Claremont, 1949.

The Constitution of the State of New Hampshire, established October 31, 1783, required that the governor and members of the Senate and House of Representatives be Protestant; however, this requirement was stricken out in 1877. Among the Jews who have held political or appointive offices are the following: Abram M. Stahl of

Berlin, state senator, 1909–10; Arthur J. Reinhart, a Portsmouth attorney, state senator, 1941–42, 1949–50; William S. Green, a Manchester attorney, deputy attorney general, 1950–53; Morris Silver of Manchester, State Prison Board of Trustees, 1955–71; Samuel Green, a Manchester attorney, president of the state senate, 1961–63; Milton Shapiro of Concord, chairman, Department of Resources and Economic Development, and Industrial Parks Authority, 1963–68; and Saul Feldman of Manchester, a member of the state legislature, 1963 and 1965. [Lo.S./J.L.A.]

NEW HAVEN, U.S. port city in Connecticut. New Haven has a population of 135,468 (1970 est.), including 22,000 Jews. It was settled in 1638 by Puritans who envisioned it as a Wilderness Zion based on biblical law. It was 120 years later, in 1758, that the first Jews, the brothers Jacob and Solomon *Pinto, arrived. They were soon integrally involved in the city's life. With the outbreak of the Revolutionary War, the three sons of Jacob Pinto—Solomon, Abraham, and William—took up arms in the Continental army. In 1783, Jacob Pinto was a signer of the petition to Connecticut's General Assembly which brought about the incorporation of New Haven as a town.

President Ezra *Stiles of Yale College recorded in his diary the arrival of an unnamed Venetian Jewish family in the summer of 1772 who observed the Sabbath in traditional Jewish manner, "worshiping by themselves in a room in which were lights and a suspended lamp." He noted that this was purely private Jewish worship, since the Venetians were too few to constitute a synagogue quorum, "so that if thereafter there should be a synagogue in New Haven, it must not be dated from this."

A slow influx of Jewish settlers began about 1840. Families from Bavaria, their friends and kinsmen soon constituted a *minyan* which became Congregation Mishkan Israel. A burial ground was acquired in 1843. Mishkan Israel was New England's second congregation and the 14th Jewish congregation established in the United States. Soon after its founding, divergences in religious approach arose, one in the direction of Orthodoxy, the other toward Reform. In 1846 a first break occurred: a Reform group broke away, for several years conducting its own congregational service.

Until 1854 the pioneer New Haven congregation met for prayers in a variety of local halls. In 1854, Mishkan Israel Congregation, along with other U.S. congregations, received a $5,000 bequest from the estate of the philanthropist Judah *Touro. With this sum it purchased and refurbished a church as its first synagogue. By then the Reform segment of the congregation had become the majority and in 1855 the Orthodox members seceded permanently and established B'nai Sholom Congregation, which continued as a small congregation until it went out of existence in the late 1930s. Only the cemetery of this early German Orthodox congregation remains.

Mishkan Israel prospered over the decades, led by German-Jewish rabbis who maintained close ties with Rabbi Isaac M. *Wise and the growing Reform movement. In 1897 the congregation built a large synagogue in Byzantine style, in keeping with its growing affluence; the sermons, previously in German, and much of the service as well, were now in English.

The first Jewish refugees arrived from Russia in February 1882, and were followed by a steady influx of Russian-Jewish families. By 1887 the Jewish population had grown to about 3,200. In the next decade it grew to about 8,000 and the increase was greatly accelerated in the wake of the Kishinev pogrom of 1903. By the beginning of World War I, New Haven Jewry numbered about 20,000.

The first congregation organized by the immigrants from East Europe was B'nai Jacob Congregation (1882), which grew into New Haven's largest Conservative congregation. Of the 11 Orthodox congregations organized during the height of the immigration period, four remained in 1968.

The first organized charity by the Jews of New Haven was undertaken in 1881. The pioneer German Jews established the Hebrew Benevolent Society to assist the Russian-Jewish immigrants, and the latter established the Hebrew Charity Society in 1885. In 1910 the sisterhood of Mishkan Israel began to devote itself to charitable enterprise, opening a special office for the purpose. In 1919 the three charitable undertakings were formally organized into the United Jewish Charities. The Jewish Family Service, professionally staffed, came into existence in 1939.

By the mid-1920s there were in New Haven over 60 Jewish religious, charitable, fraternal, and Zionist organizations, and in addition the Young Men's and Young Women's Hebrew Association, the Jewish Home for Children, and the Jewish Home for the Aged. Community leaders, recognizing the need for coordination, in 1928 created the New Haven Jewish Community Council, to which member organizations regularly elected delegates. Out of the council's efforts there emerged the Jewish Welfare Fund and, subsequently, the Bureau of Jewish Education.

Jewish education of children has improved since the 1950s with the growth of synagogue schools, the Lubavitcher-sponsored Hebrew Day School, and the Conservative-sponsored Ezra Academy. These schools are coordinated by the Bureau of Jewish Education. A community-sponsored Hebrew High School is maintained under the bureau's supervision. Yale University has had its influence on New Haven's Jewish community, a large number of its lawyers and medical men having studied there. The number of Jewish faculty members has grown considerably. Jewish student needs are served at Yale by its own B'nai B'rith Hillel Foundation. [A.A.Ch.]

NEWHOUSE, SAMUEL IRVING (1895–), U.S. publisher. Newhouse's first venture came when, as a 16-year-old office boy in a law office, he was told by his employer to take charge of the Bayonne (N.J.) *Times*. In 1922 he acquired the floundering Staten Island (N.Y.) *Advance* for $98,000. Six years later he turned down an offer of $1,000,000 for it. His formula for success was to cut operating costs, stimulate advertising and circulation, and allow local editors complete autonomy. During the depression of the 1930s he bought five newspapers, and continued adding others, including the *Portland Oregonian* and the St. Louis *Globe-Democrat*. In 1955, in what was described as the biggest transaction in American newspaper history, he paid $18,642,000 for a package that included the Birmingham (Ala.) *News*, the Huntsville (Ala.) *Times* and four radio and television stations. In 1959, to diversify his holdings, Newhouse bought controlling interests in two important magazine publishing firms—Condé Nast (*Vogue, Glamour, House and Garden*) and Street and Smith (*Mademoiselle* and five other periodicals). He owned 15 daily newspapers, 12 national magazines, and nine radio and television stations. In 1960 he gave two million dollars to Syracuse University to establish the Newhouse Communications Center, intended to be the world's largest educational and research institute for the study of the mass media, and he made provision for its future maintenance. [I.R.]

NEW ISRAEL (Rus. **Novy Izrail**), Jewish religious sect initiated in Odessa during the 1880s. At the beginning of

1882 Jacob Priluker, a teacher at the government Jewish school of Odessa, published an article in the *Odesskiy Listok* in which he proclaimed the 15 principles of a sect to be known as New Israel, whose objective was to introduce reforms in the Jewish religion which would reconcile it with Christianity. These principles recognized the Mosaic law only, and articulated "an attitude of contempt" toward the Talmud. The day of rest was transferred from Saturday to Sunday, while circumcision and the dietary laws were abolished. The members of the sect were required to consider Russian as their national language and to observe the laws of the state. The Russian government was requested to grant civic rights to the members of the sect, to authorize them to spread their doctrine among the Jews, and to permit them to wear a special sign which would distinguish them from other Jews. Their platform was to be a breakthrough for Russian Jewry after the tribulations it had suffered through the riots and increased anti-Semitism which followed the assassination of Czar Alexander II in 1881. However, even those *maskilim* who strove for reforms within Judaism regarded Priluker's proposals with reserve. They pointed to the utilitarian nature of his reforms, which suggested that part of the Jewish heritage be abandoned in exchange for civic rights. On the other hand, Priluker was encouraged by the Russian authorities. During the same year, his book "Reform Jews" (published under the pseudonym of E. Ben-Sion) was published in St. Petersburg with government assistance. It contained a violent attack on the Talmud and traditional Judaism, thus supplying material for anti-Semitic propaganda. In 1887 Priluker traveled to Western Europe at the government's expense to establish contacts with missionaries. However, his preaching to the Jewish masses of southern Russia met with no success and the Russian government's sympathy for him declined. Indeed, his appeals for support in the publication of a Jewish newspaper which would propagate his ideas were rejected by the government. In 1891 Priluker apostatized to Protestantism and emigrated to England, and this marked the end of the attempt to establish the New Israel sect.

Bibliography: N. N. (I. L. Gordon), in: *Voskhod*, 8 pt. 2 (1882), 1–29; S. Ginsburg, *Meshumodim in Tsarishn Rusland* (1946), 90–115. [Y.S.]

Jewish communities in New Jersey and dates of establishment. Population figures for 1968.

NEW JERSEY, one of the original 13 states of the United States, total population 7,089,997 (1970), Jewish population 387,000 (1969 est.). New Jersey granted religious tolerance to its citizens as early as 1665, and the state constitution of 1844 abolished all religious qualifications for voting and holding public office.

Although the first organized Jewish communities in New Jersey were not established until the middle of the 19th century, Jewish merchants from Philadelphia and New York conducted business in the state as early as the 17th century. Among the first Jewish settlers were Aaron and Jacob Lozada, who owned a grocery and hardware store in Bound Brook as early as 1718. Daniel Nunez appears in a 1722 court record as town clerk and tax collector for Piscataway Township and justice of the peace for *Middlesex County. Perth Amboy, on the *Trenton-Philadelphia road, was a center for Jewish and other merchants from the time it became the capital of East Jersey in 1685. Among the early prominent settlers in the state was David *Naar of Elizabeth, active at the state constitutional convention in 1844, editor and mayor of Elizabeth. Nathan *Barnert was a leader in *Paterson.

German Jews settled in *Trenton, the state capital, in the 1840s, the most prominent among them being Simon Kahnweiler, a merchant and manufacturer. The Mt. Sinai Cemetery Association was incorporated in the town in 1857 and Har Sinai Congregation held its first service in 1858. The first organized Jewish community in New Jersey was in Newark (see *Essex County), where Congregation B'nai Jeshurun was incorporated in 1848. Other early communities with organized congregations included: Paterson (1847), New Brunswick (1861), Jersey City (1864), Bayonne (1878), Elizabeth (1881), *Vineland (1882), *Passaic (1899), Perth Amboy (1890), *Atlantic City (1890), Woodbine (1891), *Camden (1894), and Englewood (1896; see *Bergen County).

Demographically (1970), New Jersey was divided into two major areas of settlement—northeastern New Jersey, from Bergen County to Middlesex County, which included nearly 300,000 of the state's Jewish population, and the Camden area, near Philadelphia, which included about 18,000 Jews—as well as the northeastern shore area (Long Branch and Asbury Park), the southeastern shore (Atlantic City, 10,000 Jews), the Trenton area (10,000 Jews), and various other smaller communities throughout the state. The Jewish population of New Jersey, which was dependent upon the economic development in the northeastern sector of the state, both for employment and market outlets in nearby New York City, grew from an estimated 5,600 in

1880, to 25,000 in 1900, 40,000 in 1905, 70,000 in 1907, 258,306 in 1927, and leveled off to 259,970 in 1937. The expansion in the economy following World War II and the migration from New York City to the suburban areas during the 1950s and 1960s led to a further growth in the state's Jewish population, so that by 1969 there were 387,000 Jews in the state. Furthermore, whereas a third of the state's Jewish population resided in Newark in 1937, by the late 1960s the overwhelming majority of the Jews in the northeastern area (as was also true of the general population) lived in the suburban areas of Bergen, Essex, *Hudson, Passaic, and *Union Counties.

The economic life of New Jersey during the last half of the 19th century was largely dominated by the German Jewish community, which was small in number and engaged in small businesses and merchandising. By the end of the 1920s the waves of East European immigrants from Russia and Poland had changed the demographic nature of the northeastern part of the state: the silk industry of Paterson—largely in the hands of Polish Jews who had worked in the textile industry in Lodz and Bialystok—and the garment industry in Jersey City and Newark, as well as the woolen and worsted mills of Passaic drew heavily upon the East European and Slavic population of the area. The German Jewish population, which was occupied mainly in merchandising, and after the turn of the century in finance, real estate, and the professions began to move into the suburban areas, while the East European settlers gravitated to the city center during this period. After World War II, with the demise of the silk industry in Paterson and the disappearance of the textile and garment industries from northeastern New Jersey, Jewish life moved into the suburbs.

The Jewish colonies of Vineland, Carmel, Woodbine, Rosenhayn, and others, which were started in the late 19th century in southern New Jersey, were helped initially by the Alliance Israélite Universelle and the Baron de Hirsch Fund. Some of the communities, such as Carmel and Woodbine, found the soil generally poor and inadequate for agricultural uses, but Vineland, which had an estimated Jewish population of 2,450 in 1970, established a thriving

Figure 1. Ark of the Law of Temple B'nai Abraham, South Orange, New Jersey.

Figure 2. Temple Emanu-El, Englewood, New Jersey.

poultry industry. Arthur Goldhaft, a veterinarian, founded the Vineland Poultry Laboratories and the local poultry farmers formed the Jewish Poultry Farmers' Association. Other Jewish agricultural settlements were founded in Toms River, Lakewood, Bound Brook, Pine Brook, Perrineville, Hightstown, Flemington, Farmingdale, Point Pleasant, Englishtown, and Freehold. The total Jewish population of these settlements in 1970 was about 12,000, making them a factor in the agricultural industries of truck and poultry farming in the state. Jews have also played a significant role in the tourist industry of the shore areas of Lakewood, Long Branch, Asbury Park, and Atlantic City.

Jewish community life, which up to World War II was largely distinguished by local congregations, Hebrew schools, Jewish centers, fraternal groups, and local philanthropic organizations of an "Old World" character, quickly changed in the 1950s and 1960s with the mass migrations to the suburban areas. Center city synagogues which had formerly been organized along East European regional lines merged and took on the designations of Orthodox, Conservative, and Reform. Area-wide organizations such as the Community Council of Passaic-Clifton, which administers the United Jewish Appeal, and the Passaic-Clifton Board of Rabbis, which supervises *kashrut* in the community, arose out of the necessity to handle larger numbers of Jews who were no longer centrally located. As the majority of the Jews of Bergen and Essex counties, which had Jewish populations of about 100,000 each in 1970, was scattered throughout more than 100 suburban communities—there were 70 separate municipalities in Bergen County alone—it was found best to organize the community on a county-wide basis. Such organizations as the Bergen County Rabbinical Association (organized in 1968), Community Relations Council of Bergen County (1969), Jewish Welfare Council (1969), and others were created in the county to cope with the problem of unifying the Jewish community. Over 100 known Jewish organizations operated within Bergen County alone.

Various community newspapers have appeared in the state since the beginning of the 20th century. In 1910 Mordechai Mansky began publication of the *Newarker Wochenblat*, a Yiddish weekly which appeared until 1914. Among the early Anglo-Jewish newspapers published were: the *Jewish Chronicle* of Newark (founded in 1921), *The Jewish Post* of Paterson, and the *Jewish Review* of Jersey City. In 1947 the *Jewish News*, a weekly, was founded, and by 1969 it had a circulation of over 25,000, the largest of any community newspaper in New Jersey.

Bibliography: J. T. Cunningham, *This is New Jersey* (1953); A. M. Friedenberg, AJHSP, 17 (1909), 34–43; P. R. Goldstein, *Social Aspects of the Jewish Colonies of South Jersey* (1921); A. D. Goldhaft, *The Golden Egg* (1957); J. Brandes, *Immigrants to Freedom: Jewish Communities in Rural New Jersey since 1882* (1970); W. N. Jamison, *Religion in New Jersey* (1964); R. J. Vecoli, *The People of New Jersey* (1965).

[Y.B.-D.]

NEW LEFT, the wave of left-wing radicalism, which attracted many students and other young people in the U.S. and in Western Europe especially in the late 1960s. It had no consistent doctrine and embraced various ideologies, from the Maoist interpretation of Marxism to outright anarchism. The Jewish aspect of the movement was twofold: a disproportionate participation of Jews in the leadership and sometimes also in the ranks, and the issue of Israel and Arab anti-Israel terrorism after the Six-Day War. [ED.]

In the United States. The origins of the New Left in the United States are to be found in the late 1950s and early 1960s. It rose to considerable prominence and power by the end of the 1960s, particularly on college and university campuses, but also in the elite media and some of the mass media. The distinguishing characteristics of the New Left, until about 1966, were skepticism toward the dogmas and ideology of the "Old Left," by which was meant classical Marxism, in its various forms; a rejection of centralized control and an emphasis on participatory democracy—the direct involvement in decision making of all those affected by decisions; and a rejection of the central role of the working class in the drama of history: it was replaced by students, seen as a deprived class; by the deprived minorities—Blacks, Mexican Americans, Puerto Ricans, American Indians; and by the urban poor.

THE GROWTH OF THE NEW LEFT. The founding date of the New Left may be given as 1962, when the Port Huron statement was adopted by a group of young people who refounded the Students for a Democratic Society (S.D.S.), an organization at that time still linked to the Democratic Socialist League for Industrial Democracy. From the beginning, youth groups affiliated with one or another "Old Left" group—Socialists, Trotskyists of both major branches, Communists (both Russian and Chinese oriented)—were active within the New Left. By the end of the decade, the most radical groups dominated the New Left.

Jews have been active in the United States in all radical movements, Socialist and Communist, Old Left and New. While not particularly prominent among the founders of S.D.S. (such as Tom Hayden, Carl Oglesby, and others), they became particularly prominent in later phases of the history of the New Left. Mark Rudd, Jerry Rubin, Abby Hoffman, and others who achieved national reputation may be mentioned; in addition, on almost every major campus in which the New Left was active, Jews were prominent in the leadership. Typically, they formed between a third to more than half of the leadership and members, though a smaller percentage of the demonstrators who supported the New Left on various issues.

The first phase of New Left history emphasized organizing in northern deprived urban communities, white and black (1962 to 1964 or 1965). The second phase concentrated on massive work by students in the South in the civil rights movement, particularly in the summer of 1964 (when two of the three who were killed in Philadelphia, Mississippi, were Jewish). The third phase stressed rebellion on the campus, beginning in Berkeley, in the autumn of 1964, and continuing throughout the decade on the basis of a variety of issues: first the right to political activity on the campus, and then issues related to the Vietnam war—collaboration of university and college authorities with the draft by reporting grades, recruitment on campus by representatives of the U.S. armed forces and by U.S. corporations providing war materials, and defense and foreign-area research on the campuses. By 1967 or 1968 the original characteristics of the New Left were quite blurred: Marxist rhetoric and ideology became dominant, small groups of leaders fought for control of S.D.S. and some of them imposed a strict central rule in classic Leninist style, and some of the groups eschewed work with students on student issues in abortive efforts to organize the urban poor and some workers. In the spring of 1968, during the seizure of the buildings on the Columbia University campus, Maoist rhetoric was already strong and violence was celebrated by many elements; this tendency became stronger after the forcible suppression of student demonstrations at the Democratic Convention in Chicago in 1968. Shortly after, S.D.S. formally split, and one faction, the Weathermen, became direct advocates of violence and went underground.

JEWISH PROMINENCE. Jewish prominence in the New Left was not noted in the mass media, either because it was truly not remarked or because in the aftermath of Hitler's murderous anti-Semitism the media were reluctant to make this observation. Analysts did point out the Jewish role, however, and tried to explain it. Since Jewish students were generally affluent, and anti-Semitism had reached a very low point in the United States in the 1960s, it could not be explained by specific deprivation. One prominent theory pointed to the psychological and social characteristics of the Jewish middle-class family—rationalistic, child-centered, psychologically understanding—and argued that this produced children intolerant of rules and restrictions and insistent on the rapid achievement of an ideal society. K. Keniston, *Young Radicals* (1968), and Flacks (in: *Journal of Social Issues,* 23 (1967), 65) make this point generally for student radicals. Another theory emphasized the historical background of the Jews in America, which led them to embrace in more than average numbers Liberalism, Socialism, and Communism (N. Glazer, in: *Fortune* (Jan. 1969), 112–3, 126–9). As against many other radical movements in the past, this one did not, at least as far as the Jewish participants were concerned, involve any generation gap or break with parental values; it simply pushed these values further. This could be noted in the surprising fact that books by Jewish members of the New Left Paul Cowan, *Making of An Un-American* (1970), and Michael Myerson, *These are the Good Old Days* (1970) were dedicated to their parents.

After the Six-Day War in 1967, a crisis developed for many Jewish members of the New Left. The black militants, with whom they were allied on the home front, supported the Arabs and indulged in excessive rhetoric in denunciation of the Israelis (thus, the Black Panthers called Israelis "pigs," denounced "kosher nationalism" as "imperialism," etc.). In addition, the United States, which New Leftists opposed as the symbol of world capitalism and imperialism, provided arms to Israel and was itself the hated enemy of the Arabs, who allied themselves with the Third World and received the support of both Russian and Maoist branches of the Communist movement. This crisis led some Jewish members of the New Left to dissociate themselves from some of its manifestations. This separation began as early as September 1967, when, at the Conference for a New Politics, organized by New Left elements in Chicago, blacks insisted on the passage of a resolution denouncing the "imperialist Zionist war" in the Middle East. Many Jewish leftists were angered by this resolution; others, however, became among the most virulent enemies of "Zionist imperialism." Those Jewish New Leftists who had a more positive attitude to their people began to organize small, distinctively Jewish, New Left organizations, and these began to receive publicity in 1969, as they put pressure on established Jewish organizations to change their priorities. Among the interests of this Jewish offshoot of the New Left was support for the emigration of the Jews of Soviet Russia, more money for Jewish education, and a larger role for youth and the interests of radical youth in the activities of Jewish communal organizations.

See also *Negro-Jewish Relations in the U.S. [N.GL.]

In Western Europe. The West European New Left of the late 1960s differed in two respects from its U.S. counterpart. It lacked the reservoir of supporters among both the Negro masses and sections of the white population opposed to the war in Vietnam and it was opposed by the entrenched Socialist and Communist parties. The appeal of the European New Left thus tended to be restricted to amorphous groups on the periphery of society. However, the French students' revolt of May 1968 and similar, though less violent, demonstrations in Germany and throughout Europe, proved that under favorable conditions the New Left could act as an ideological catalyst and set into motion events of considerable consequence. Its total rejection of prevailing standards and social structures was echoed in the inarticulate, though widespread, misgivings about the values and workings of the "affluent society" and the "deadness of its culture." This applies to the well-publicized and opinion-forming sector of the New Left. There are, however, particularly in Great Britain, other, near-clandestine groupings that concentrate on disruptive industrial action, as, for example, Tariq Ali's Trotskyist International Marxist Group or the Socialist Labor League, which aim at the subversion of the trade union and have been more disruptive than the 1968 student demonstrations at the London School of Economics and other British universities.

Whereas the protagonists of the European New Left were young, its ideologues were elderly scholars, such as the French writer-philosopher Jean-Paul Sartre and Herbert *Marcuse, a German-Jewish émigré and a cofounder of the Frankfort Institute of Sociology. In his attempt to harmonize the teachings of Freud with those of Marx, Marcuse totally rejects the basic assumptions and ultimate objectives of the prevailing industrial society. Alienation in work and the repression of basic human drives could be overcome, Marcuse maintains, in a truly democratic and participatory society so organized as to serve essential human needs rather than the requirements of the socio-industrial complex. Since the service of the latter has corrupted mankind, the only hope for its future lies in the classes still untouched by the exigencies of the productive processes, which have become an obsession both under capitalism and Communism. These classes are the students of the industrialized nations and the masses of the developing Third World. From these assumptions it follows that New Left thinking on the Arab-Israel confrontation tends to sympathize with the Arabs as representatives of the oppressed Third World, while regarding the Westernized, technology-oriented Israelis with instinctive hostility. The Marxist rationalization of these feelings runs along arguments well known to Old Left Communists, that Israel and Zionism in general are only the "lackey of American imperialism," etc. Marcuse, however, disassociated himself from this attitude while on a visit to West Berlin shortly after the Six-Day War (1967).

In the Federal Republic of Germany, the New Left's most important protagonist, the SDS (Sozialistischer Deutscher Studentenbund) in 1969 repeatedly disrupted public meetings at which the Israel ambassador was to appear. Later that year New Left terrorists tried to blow up West Berlin's Jewish community hall during a service commemorating the 1938 Nazi pogroms. The revulsion aroused by these activities was criticized by their perpetrators, who, in leaflets, under the headline "Shalom and Napalm," deplored the guilt feelings of the German Left toward the Jews as "neurotic, backward-looking anti-Fascism" disregarding the "non-justifiability of the state of Israel." German New Left leaders, such as Ulrike Meinhof of the left-wing weekly *Konkret* and Dieter Kunzelmann of West Berlin's Kommune I, have joined the Palestinian *fedayeen* in Amman and inveighed against "bourgeois Germany's *Judenkomplex*." Except in the universities, the German New Left remained a negligible factor and failed to gain working-class support. Similar tendencies were at work in Italy, where such New Left organizations as Lotta Continua were militantly "anti-Zionist."

In France, in May 1968, the New Left students' revolt led to nationwide strikes, a grave government crisis, and contributed to the eventual resignation of President de Gaulle (June 1969). Among the student leaders were many Jews, such as Alain Krivine, Marc Kravetz, Alain Geismar, and Daniel Cohn-Bendit, who, as "Red Danny," became the figurehead of the uprising. Although their Jewishness did not induce them to follow an independent line on the Arab-Israel conflict, it sufficed to revive anti-Semitic resentments on either side of the political spectrum. Attacks against the German-Jew Cohn-Bendit and slogans like "France for the French" were once countered by students chanting "We are all German Jews." The French New Left succeeded temporarily in involving the workers in its struggle, but the subsequent leftist (old and new) defeat at the polls ended its role as a significant political factor. Characteristically it is the non-Jew Sartre who opposes the New Left anti-Israel slogans. It is absurd to pretend, he maintained, that "Israel is an imperialist state and that the Arabs are socialists, including their feudal states." [ER.H.]

In Israel. In Israel, the New Left remained a fringe phenomenon and those groups which actively identified with the New Left received little support, even in student circles. Maẓpen ("Compass"), which broke away from the Ha-Olam ha-Zeh group in the early 1960s, was especially vocal after the Six-Day War in calling for withdrawal from territories occupied in the war. It never had more than a handful of members and in 1970 these split into three groups.

The Semol Yisra'eli Ḥadash ("Israel New Left," known as Si'aḥ) was founded in 1969. Consisting mainly of students and members of Ha-Shomer ha-Ẓa'ir kibbutzim, it called for a more resolute peace policy on the part of the Israel government. Si'aḥ was not crystallized as a political party but stressed its nonidentification with the policies of the Rakaḥ Communist Party (see *Communism: Israel). [ED.]

Bibliography: M. S. Chertoff (ed.), *The New Left and the Jews* (1971); N. Glazer, in: JJSO, 11 (1969), 121–32; N. Glazer and L. Fein, in: *Midstream*, 17 no. 1 (1971), 32–46; Lipset, in: *Encounter*, 33 (1969), 24–35; P. Seale and M. McConville, *French Revolution 1968* (1968); W. Laqueur, in: *Commentary*, 47 no. 6 (1969), 33–41; H. Marcuse, *Protest, Demonstration, Revolt* (1968; translation of his: *Das Ende der Utopie*).

°**NEWLINSKI, PHILIPP MICHAEL** (1841–1899), *Herzl's diplomatic agent in Constantinople and the Balkan countries. The son of a Polish aristocratic family, Newlinski took up journalism. He was appointed to the staff of the Austro-Hungarian embassy in Constantinople where he became familiar with the situation in Turkey and the Balkan States, established contacts with the royal houses, and gained influence with the sultan. In 1880 he resumed his profession as a journalist, first in Paris and from 1887 in Vienna, where he founded his own newspaper, *Correspondance de l'Est*. He also published booklets on political themes. Herzl established contact with Newlinski in 1896 and persuaded him to work for the realization of Zionist aims. At first Newlinski was paid for his efforts, but under Herzl's influence he became a zealous supporter of the movement and served as Herzl's trusted adviser. He accompanied Herzl on his first visit to Constantinople and tried to arrange an audience with the sultan, but succeeded only in attaining a decoration for Herzl as a sign of the sultan's esteem. Newlinski did arrange a meeting between Herzl and Crown Prince Ferdinand of Bulgaria and himself met with the king of Serbia, obtaining the latter's support for the Zionist cause. He tried to gain the sympathy of Bismarck and the Vatican and in general was instrumental in recruiting many prominent personalities in support of Herzl's vision. Illness prevented him from attending the First Zionist Congress, but he was present at the Second Congress. His newspaper devoted a special column to Zionist affairs. In 1899 Herzl sent him to Constantinople, where he was received by the sultan. On his return from this mission Newlinski died.

Bibliography: T. Herzl, *Complete Diaries,* ed. by R. Patai, 5 (1960), index; N. M. Gelber, in: *Herzl Year Book,* 2 (1959), 113–52.

[I.K.]

NEW LONDON, city in S.E. Connecticut; its Jewish population of approximately 4,000 encompasses greater New London, Groton, and Waterford. Around 1860 Joseph Jacob Schwartz and his family, who had immigrated from Germany, were the first Jews to settle permanently in New London. Several families of similar origin settled there within the decade. Nevertheless, organized religious life did not begin until the arrival of the Jews from Eastern Europe in 1885. In 1905 there were 400 Jews in New London. In 1932 the number had increased to approximately 2,000. By 1940 the Jewish population was 2,200, augmented by a new group of Jewish refugees from Nazi Germany.

Ahavath Chesed, the first Orthodox congregation, was organized in 1892. In 1906 it elected its first rabbi, Abraham Nathan Schwartz. There are now two Orthodox congregations; a Conservative, Beth El, founded 1932; and a Reform, Temple Emanuel, 1959. The Jewish community has been represented in all fields of civic, cultural, and political life of New London. New London has had three Jewish mayors, Samuel Selleck, Moses Savin, and Harvey Mallove. Morris Lubchansky and Perry Shafner held state offices, and Abraham *Ribicoff, who settled in New London, was governor of Connecticut and senator from Connecticut. The Jewish Community Council is comprised of all of the 17 local service, fraternal, and religious organizations. All of these groups take an active part in raising funds through the Combined Jewish Appeal and participate in national and local Jewish activities. [E.Su.]

NEWMAN, ARNOLD (1919–), U.S. photographer. Born in New York, Newman specialized in portraiture, developing a style which did not necessarily flatter the subject but revealed his personality. He used as background associations and symbols connected with the life and work of the sitter. Igor Stravinsky was shown seated at the extreme left of the picture, the black and white keyboard serving to emphasize the character of the composer. Brooks Atkinson, the critic, was photographed sitting in an empty theater where the seats created a pattern of forms and highlights. Prime Minister Ben Gurion was shown with the 1948 Declaration of Independence of the State of Israel. Arnold Newman's photographs are in many of the world's major art museums. [P.P.]

NEWMAN, ISIDORE (1837–1909), U.S. banker and philanthropist. Newman, who was born in Germany, went to the U.S. in 1851. During the Civil War, he founded a bank in New Orleans. He subsequently bought and ran the Carrolton Railroad, before selling it to become main owner of New Orleans' Maison Blanche department store. Active in New Orleans' Jewish affairs, Newman was a founder of that city's B'nai B'rith lodge and a generous patron of the Jewish Children's Home (renamed for him in 1913). [Ed.]

NEWMAN, LOUIS ISRAEL (1893–1972), U.S. Reform rabbi and author. Newman, who was born in Providence, Rhode Island, was ordained by Stephen S. Wise. He served at Temple Emanu-El in San Francisco until 1930 when he was appointed rabbi of Temple Rodeph Sholom in New York. Newman was one of the leaders of the Zionist *Revisionists in the United States. His books include *Jewish Influence on Christian Reform Movements* (1924), and *Jewish People, Faith and Life* (1957). He compiled and translated the *Ḥasidic Anthology* (1934). [Ab.V.G.]

NEWMARK, Los Angeles family. Joseph Newmark (1799–1881), who was born in Neumark, West Prussia, moved to New York in 1823; he helped to found Congregation B'nai Jeshurun in that city in 1825. He lived in St. Louis from 1840 to 1845, serving there as president of the fledgling congregation. Returning to New York in 1846, Newmark helped to organize yet another congregation before he moved to the village of Los Angeles with his wife and six children in 1854. He was the first spiritual leader of the Jewish community, conducting religious services, weddings, and funerals voluntarily until a professional rabbi was engaged. He founded the Hebrew Benevolent Society in 1855 and was the founding president of Congregation B'nai Brith (today's Wilshire Boulevard Temple) in 1862. During Newmark's lifetime the congregation remained Orthodox out of respect for him.

His nephew Harris Newmark (1834–1916) went to Los Angeles in 1853 and engaged in a variety of mercantile endeavors, ultimately establishing a wholesale grocery. For more than 60 years he was intimately involved in the civic, economic, and Jewish life of the community. He was a member of the committee which brought the first railroad connection to Los Angeles and was an organizer of the Agriculture Society of the 6th district, the public library, Board of Trade, and Chamber of Commerce. He engaged in real-estate activities and was one of the developers of the town of Newmark, now Montebello.

Toward the end of his life, Newmark wrote his memoirs of early Los Angeles; published as *Sixty Years in Southern California* (1916[1], 1926[2], 1930[3]), this work stands as the classic autobiographic history of southern California.

Harris's son Marco Ross Newmark (1878–1959), like his father a businessman and civic figure, served as

Four generations of the Newmark family photographed in 1881: Joseph Newmark, first lay rabbi of Los Angeles, Rose Loeb, Estelle Newmark Loeb, and Sarah Newmark Newmark. San Marino, Calif., Henry E. Huntingdon Library and Art Gallery.

president of the Los Angeles Produce Exchange and as vice-president of the National Wholesale Grocers Association. He was ardently interested in the early history of Los Angeles and with his brother Maurice Harris (1859–1929) co-edited his father's memoirs. The two brothers also edited and published *Census of the City and County of Los Angeles, California, for the Year 1850*. His numerous articles on general and Jewish history were gathered in *Jottings in Southern California History* (1955). Newmark was a president of the Historical Society of Southern California. One of the leaders in the Jewish community, he served as president of the Federation of the Jewish Welfare Organizations, the Los Angeles Lodge of B'nai B'rith, and of the Los Angeles District of the Zionist Organization of America.

Bibliography: H. Newmark, *Sixty Years in Southern California, 1853–1913* (1916); M. Vorspan and L. P. Gartner, *History of the Jews of Los Angeles* (1970).

[M.V.]

NEW MEXICO, state in southwestern U.S., with a Jewish population of 3,700 out of a total of 1,100,000 in 1969. Most Jews lived in Albuquerque (3,000), the largest city. However, there were smaller communities in Santa Fe (150), Los Alamos (100), Roswell (100), Las Cruces (100), Taos, and Las Vegas. There were six synagogues, two in Albuquerque and one each in Las Cruces, Santa Fe, Roswell, and Los Alamos.

Luis de Carvajal y de la Cueva, a Marrano, explored a vast area of the North American continent, which included New Mexico, for Philip II of Spain in the 16th century. Bernardo Lopez de Mendizabal, the Spanish governor of New Mexico from the late 1650s to 1661, was arrested as a Judaizer and died in a Mexican prison. Modern Jewish beginnings date from 1846 with the arrival of Solomon Jacob Spiegelberg, who came as a settler with the American troops during the Mexican War and brought over his five brothers from Germany. Other relatives and landsmen brought into the territory by the Spiegelbergs as clerks in their enterprises became the nuclei of Jewish communities in Albuquerque, Las Vegas, and Roswell. One Spiegelberg employee, Benjamin Lowenstein, later was responsible for bringing 200 German Jews to New Mexico. These settlers played an extraordinary role in the economic and political life of the territory. Early Jewish merchants, in addition to the Spiegelbergs, were Sigmund, Adolph, and Bernard Seligman; Simon Nussbaum; Charles Ilfeld; and Abraham and Zadoc Staab. By 1885 the Jewish population included ranchers, mining promoters, railroad builders, irrigation experts, soldiers, and Indian traders. Among the latter were

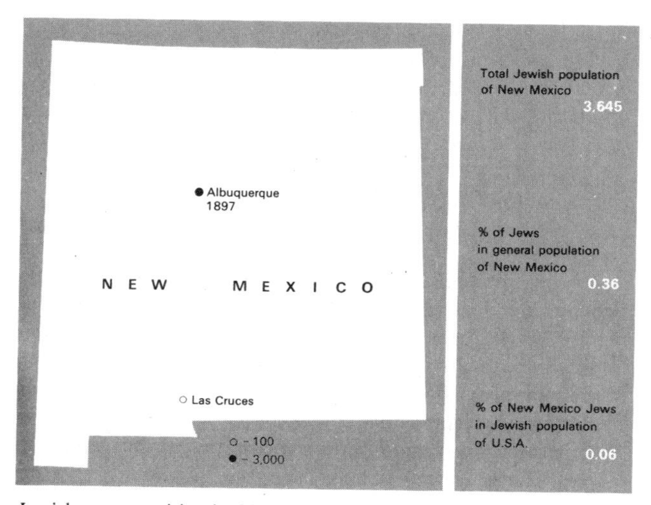

Jewish communities in New Mexico and dates of establishment. Population figures for 1968.

Figure 1. The Spiegelberg store in Santa Fe, New Mexico, built 35 years after the firm's establishment in 1846. Courtesy Museum of New Mexico, Santa Fé.

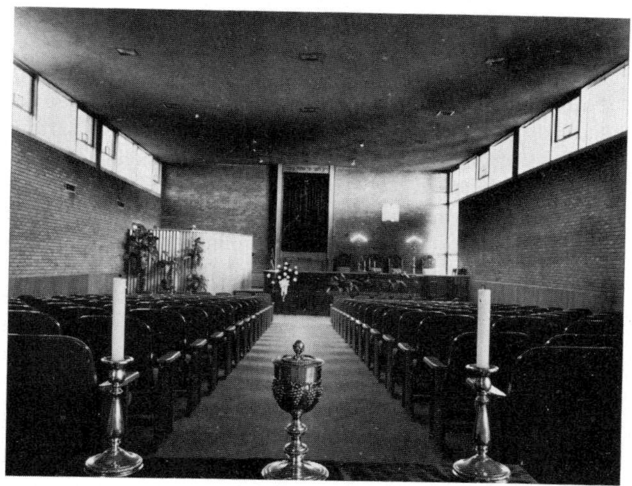

Figure 2. Congregation Albert in Albuquerque, New Mexico, designed by Max Flatow. Photo Jerry Goffe, Albuquerque, N.M.

"Navajo Sam" Dittenhoefer, who lived on an Indian reservation, and Solomon Bibo, who became an Indian chief after marrying the daughter of a chieftain from a tribe at the Accoma pueblo. The Spiegelberg wives were among the first white women in the territory.

Jews were political and cultural pioneers in New Mexico. Henry Jaffa, who came to Albuquerque in 1869, was its first mayor. Mike Mandell held that office in 1880. Nathan Jaffa was mayor of Roswell in 1882 and later served as secretary and lieutenant governor of the territory and mayor of Santa Fe. Columbus Moise Jr. was city attorney of Las Vegas in 1874 and later justice of the territorial supreme court. Almost all of the territorial legislatures from 1855 to 1900 had one or more Jewish members, and Herman Lindheim represented New Mexico Territory in the U.S. Congress in 1880. The first Jewish school was organized in the Santa Fe home of Mrs. Willi Spiegelberg. Beginning in 1860, she and her husband invited their relatives and employees from all corners of New Mexico to Rosh Ha-Shanah and Yom Kippur services in the Spiegelberg home. The territory's first Jewish organization was a B'nai B'rith lodge formed in Albuquerque in 1882. Congregation Montefiore, founded in Las Vegas in 1884, was the state's oldest. It erected the first synagogue in 1886. Sporadic services were conducted in Albuquerque beginning in 1876 and Temple Albert, established in 1886, dedicated its synagogue in 1897. There were also services in Roswell since 1890. The congregation in Santa Fe was formed in 1902.

As of 1969 New Mexico's newest Jewish community was in Los Alamos, where the first atomic bomb was made.

Composed of scientists and some businessmen, the Los Alamos Jewish community had a combined synagogue and center and also a B'nai B'rith lodge. The uranium boom of the 1950s brought a trickle of new Jewish settlers. Arthur Seligman, son of one of the pioneers and a former mayor of Santa Fe, was elected governor of the state in 1930 and 1932. Abe Zinn served as chief justice of the state supreme court from 1939 to 1941 and Irwin Stern Moises was a justice of the same court in the 1960s.

Bibliography: W. J. Parish, *The German Jew and the Commercial Revolution in Territorial New Mexico, 1850–1900* (1960); idem, *Charles Ilfeld Company: A Study in the Rise and Decline of Mercantile Capitalism in New Mexico* (1961); Fierman, in: AJHSO, 56 (1967), 371–451; B. Postal and L. Koppman, *A Jewish Tourist's Guide to the U.S.* (1954), 330–9; AJA, 8 (1956), 81–86.

[B.P.]

NEW MOON (Heb. רֹאשׁ חֹדֶשׁ, *Rosh Ḥodesh;* "head of the month"), the first day or beginning of the month. The Torah placed its celebration on a par with the observance of the festivals, declaring "Also in the day of your gladness, and in your appointed seasons, and in your new moons, ye shall blow with the trumpets over your burnt-offerings . . ." (Num. 10:10). A special *Musaf* sacrifice was ordained for the day (Num. 28:11–15). The Bible mentions various practices observed on it, including festive meals (I Sam. 20:18, and Rashi ad loc.), abstention from business transactions (Amos 8:5), and the practice of visiting the prophet (II Kings 4:23). When foretelling the chastisements that will come upon the Jewish people, Hosea says that the joys of the New Moon will cease (Hos. 2:13). The redemption is viewed as a time when "from one new moon to another, and from one Sabbath to another, shall all flesh come to worship before Me saith the Lord" (Isa. 66:23).

Originally, the New Moon was not fixed by astronomical calculations, but was solemnly proclaimed after witnesses had testified to the reappearance of the crescent of the moon. On the 30th of each month, the members of the High Court assembled in a courtyard in Jerusalem, named Beit Ya'azek, where they waited to receive the testimony of two reliable witnesses; they then sanctified the New Moon. If the moon's crescent was not seen on the 30th day, the New Moon was automatically celebrated on the 31st day. To inform the population of the beginning of the month, beacons were kindled on the Mount of Olives and thence over the entire land and in parts of the Diaspora. Later, however, the Samaritans began to light misleading beacons, and the High Court despatched messengers to far-removed communities. Those Jews who lived great distances from Jerusalem always celebrated the 30th day of the month as the New Moon. On those occasions when they were informed of its postponement to the 31st, they also observed this second consecutive day as the New Moon (RH 1:3–2:7). By the middle of the fourth century, the sages had established a permanent *calendar and the public proclamation of the New Moon was discontinued. A relic of the original practice is, however, retained in the synagogue custom of announcing the New Moon on the Sabbath preceding its celebration (see *New Moon, Announcement of).

Work is permitted on the New Moon (Shab. 24a; Ḥag. 18a; Ar. 10b), although it was customary for women to abstain from it (TJ, Ta'an. 1:6, 64c). They were allowed to observe this additional semi-festival as a reward for not having surrendered their jewelry for the creation of the golden calf (Tos. to RH 23a, s.v. *Mishum*). It later became customary for them to refrain from difficult labor, such as weaving, but to do light work such as sewing (Simon b. Ẓemaḥ Duran, *Tashbeẓ*, pt. 3 no. 244; cf. Rema, OḤ 417).

The biblical commandment of joy, so basic to festivals, (Deut. 16:14) is not explicitly prescribed in relation to the New Moon. Nevertheless, the rabbis inferred its applicability from the fact that the Bible equated the New Moon with the festivals (Num. 10:10), and from the duty to recite on it "This is the day which the Lord hath made; We will rejoice and be glad in it" (Ps. 118:24; ADPB, 770; Tur, YD, 401). It is therefore forbidden to fast on the New Moon (Ta'an. 2:10), and any funeral service is abbreviated (MK 3:9 and Sh. Ar., OḤ 420). Conversely, it is meritorious to partake of a festive repast (Sh. Ar., OḤ 419:1).

The recitation of the half-**Hallel* on the New Moon goes back to talmudic times (Ta'an. 28b). Parts of the *Hallel* were omitted since the day was not biblically sanctified by the prohibition of labor (Ar. 10b). There is a difference of opinion among the codifiers as to whether the usual blessing that "who has hallowed us by Thy commandments and has commanded us to read the *Hallel*" (ADPB, 756) should be recited on Rosh Ḥodesh. In most communities, the blessing is recited (Isserles and Sh. Ar., OḤ 422:2), but Shneur Zalman, the founder of Ḥabad Ḥasidism, ruled that only the cantor is to say the blessing, while the congregation merely responds "Amen."

On the New Moon the special prayer **Ya'aleh ve-Yavo* is inserted in the *Amidah* and in the Grace after Meals (Shab. 24a), and **Taḥanun* is not recited. The Torah reading designated for the day describes the New Moon sacrifices (Num. 28:1–15; Meg. 21b–22a). *Musaf* is also recited since an additional sacrifice was brought on this day; it begins with the words: "The beginnings of the months Thou didst assign unto Thy people for a season of atonement throughout their generations" (ADPB, 778).

The day before the New Moon has achieved importance among kabbalists, who observe it as a day of fast and repentance. It is called *Yom Kippur Katan, a minor day of atonement.

See also *Calendar; *Festivals (diagrams).

Bibliography: Elbogen, Gottesdienst, 122–6; S. J. Zevin, *Ha-Mo'adim ba-Halakhah* (1963[10]), 142–8; W. Nowack, *Lehrbuch der hebraeischen Archaeologie*, 2 (1894), 138–44. [A.Ro.]

NEW MOON, ANNOUNCEMENT OF. The Sabbath before the *New Moon, following the reading of the *haftarah*, the reader leads the congregation in announcing and blessing the coming month. This custom was introduced by the *geonim*, and its main purpose was to make a public pronouncement of the exact day(s) on which the New Moon will fall (*Maḥzor Vitry*, ed. by. S. Hurwitz (1923[2]), 173; Abudarham, *Seder Rosh Ḥodesh*, ed. Jerusalem (1959), 193). It is possible that this practice was based upon the statement of R. *Yose, that he did not pray the *Musaf* service (on the Sabbath before the New Moon) until he knew exactly when the New Moon was to occur (TJ, Sanh. 5:3, 22d; *Arukh ha-Shulḥan*, OḤ 417:8). The announcement is made after a special prayer for the house of Israel, and in the Ashkenazi rite begins: "He Who wrought miracles for our fathers, and redeemed them from slavery into freedom, may He speedily redeem us and gather our exiles from the four corners of the earth, even all Israel united in felowship; and let us say, Amen." The exact time of the *molad* (see *Calendar) is then announced and the reader proclaims the day(s) of the week on which the first day of the coming month falls; and the blessing concludes with the prayer that the New Moon be for life, peace, gladness, salvation, and consolation for the house of Israel (Hertz, Prayer, 510). Prior to the proclamation of the New Moon, the Ashkenazi ritual contains an introductory prayer, *Yehi Raẓon* which is substantially the private petition recited daily by Rav upon the completion of the *Amidah* (Ber. 16b). In order to adjust this prayer to the occasion, the sentence "to renew unto us this coming month for good and for blessing" was inserted (Hertz, Prayer, 508). This introductory prayer was first recited in the Polish ritual during the first part of the 18th century. It then gradually spread to all Ashkenazi rituals. In some rites the words *"bi-zekhut tefillat Rav"* ("by the merit of the prayer of Rav") appear at the end of the prayer. It has been suggested that this is a mistake for a marginal note which originally read *berakhot, tefillat Rav* ("blessing [see Tractate *Berakhot*] the prayer of Rav") to indicate the source and authorship of the prayer. These words were later erroneously incorporated in the liturgy, *berakhot* being changed to *bi-zekhut*. A further mistake in some rites changed *Rav* to *rabbim* making it end "by the merit of congregational prayer" (E. Munk, *The World of Prayer,* 2:49). Many Sephardi and oriental rituals contain introductory prayers for the ingathering of the exiles and the well-being of the rabbis (cf. Abudarham, loc. cit.). It became customary to recite the announcement of the New Moon while standing, in remembrance of the original sanctification of the New Moon by the *bet din* in Jerusalem, which was done when standing (*Magen Avraham* to Sh. Ar., OḤ 417:1). It is also customary for the reader to hold the Torah scroll while reciting this prayer. The Sabbath on which the New Moon is announced is popularly known as *Shabbat Mevarekhim* ("the Sabbath of the Blessing"), or the Sabbath which contains *"Rosh Ḥodesh bentshn."* A special sermon in honor of the event is preached in some communities. The New Moon of *Tishri is not blessed in advance since it is also Rosh Ha-Shanah and everyone knows when it will occur (*Mishnah Berurah, Sha'ar ha-Ẓiyyun,* 417:1, no. 2).

Bibliography: Abrahams, Companion, clxi; Elbogen, Gottesdienst, 123f.; Idelsohn, Liturgy, 141; E. Levy, *Yesodot ha-Tefillah* (1952[2]), 206.

[HA.BL.]

NEW ORLEANS, port and commercial center near the mouth of the Mississippi River in the state of *Louisiana. In 1967 the estimated population totaled 1,000,000, of which about 10,000 were Jews. It may not be assumed that Jews were among the city's first settlers when it was founded in 1718, although the "Black Code" issued by the French governor in 1724 ordered their expulsion. The first known Jewish settler after 1724 was Isaac Rodriguez Monsanto in 1759. When the city was ceded to Spain in 1762 new and more restrictive laws were promulgated.

In the early 19th century more Jews took up residence in New Orleans, which passed to the United States with the Louisiana Purchase of 1815. Judah *Touro, later a wealthy merchant and philanthropist, arrived in 1803, and Ezekiel Salomon, son of the American Revolution patriot Haym *Salomon, was governor of the United States Bank in New Orleans from 1816 to 1821. Two more Jews who later achieved high position settled in the city in 1828, Judah *Benjamin, later U.S. secretary of state, and Henry M. Hyams, later lieutenant governor of Louisiana. In the 1830s Gershom Kursheedt, who became the first communal leader, arrived in New Orleans; his brother E. Isaac Kursheedt was a colonel in the Washington Artillery, the historic New Orleans regiment.

Shaarei Chessed, the first synagogue, was chartered in 1828. In 1848 James C. Gutheim of Cincinnati was invited to serve as rabbi. The Portuguese Congregation was founded in 1846. Temple Sinai, the first Reform congregation, founded in 1870, recalled Rabbi Gutheim to New Orleans from Emanu-El in New York, to be its first rabbi. The first two congregations merged in 1878 to become the Reform Touro synagogue. Congregation Gates of Prayer, organized about 1850, was Reform by the 1940s. The Reform congregations have the largest number of members, followed by the three Orthodox congregations, Chevra Tehillim (founded in 1875), Beth Israel (1903), and Agudas Achim Anshe Sfard (1896). There is one Conservative congregation in New Orleans (1960), which represents about 150 families. The Young Jewish Society was founded in 1880 and the YMHA, in 1891. In 1910, 18 separate Jewish welfare and charity organizations merged to form the Jewish Welfare Federation.

Among some of the prominent Jews of New Orleans in the late 19th and 20th centuries were the attorney Monte M. Lemann from Louisiana; Isaac Delgado, for whom the municipal art museum was named; Martin *Behrman, who was Jewish by birth, was mayor of the city for four terms 1904–20; Samuel *Zemurray, president of the United Fruit Company; Captain Neville Levy, chairman of the Mississippi River Bridge Commission; and Percival Stern (1880–), benefactor of Tulane and Loyola universities and the Touro Infirmary, one of the South's leading medical centers. Mr. and Mrs. Edgar B. Stern provided many institutions and schools. Jews have served as presidents and board members of practically all cultural, civic, and social-welfare agencies and were charter members of some of the most exclusive social and Mardi Gras clubs, though the latter are now closed to Jews.

New Orleans received little of the Eastern European Jewish immigration to America and consequently has a high percentage of third- and fourth-generation natives among its Jewish population, which has always been well integrated into the city's general life. Approximately half of the Jewish community belongs to the three Reform synagogues. A study in 1958 showed that 25% of New Orleans' Jews were engaged in professional occupations, 40% in managerial jobs, and 18% in clerical and sales work. Relations with the non-Jewish community have traditionally been good and there was little anti-Semitism until the desegregation struggles of the 1950s and 1960s, when the anti-Negro sentiment aroused some anti-Jewish feelings as well.

Bibliography: B. W. Korn, *Early Jews of New Orleans* (1969); L. Huehner, *Life of Judah Touro* (1946); Reissman, in: JJSO, 4 (1962), 110–23; J. B. Feibelman, *Social and Economic Study of the New Orleans Jewish Community* (1941), incl. bibl.; M. Heller, *Jubilee Souvenir of Temple Sinai 1872–1922* (1922).

[J.B.F.]

Plantation home of Judah P. Benjamin at Bellechasse, near New Orleans. Courtesy Bertram W. Korn. Photo Stuart Lynn, New Orleans, 1947.

NEWPORT, seat of Newport County, Rhode Island. In 1965 its population was about 39,000, including about 1,200 Jews (3.1%).

Newport was founded in 1639, and Jewish settlement is documented there in 1677, when a number of Barbadian Jews arrived, purchasing ground for a cemetery the following year. By 1685, their right to trade had been

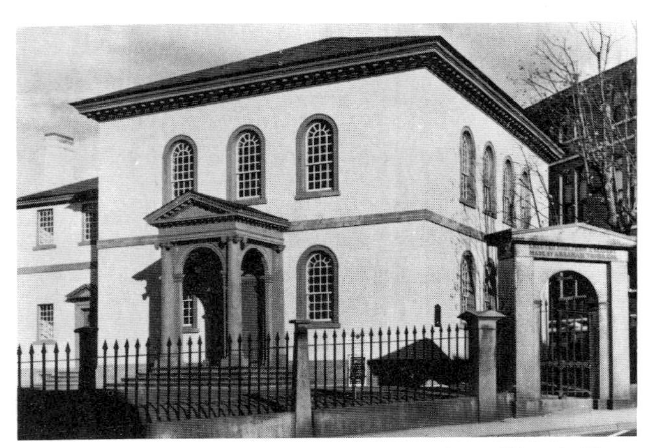

The Touro Synagogue of Congregation Yeshuat Yisrael, Newport, Rhode Island. Courtesy Society Friends Touro Synagogue National Historic Shrine, Newport, R.I.

formally recognized. Soon, however, the Jewish community disbanded, not to be revived until the 1740s when New Yorkers like the *Riveras were attracted by Newport's growing economic promise. By the mid-1750s, Congregation Nefutsé Yisrael—a few years later renamed Yeshuat Yisrael—had been organized. Isaac Touro (see Judah *Touro) arrived from Amsterdam around 1760 to become its *ḥazzan,* and in December 1763, the congregation, consisting then of perhaps 20 families, dedicated the handsome little Georgian synagogue which Peter Harrison had designed for it. (In 1946, the United States government declared this oldest extant North American synagogue a national historic site.) Between 1750 and 1776, Newport and her Jewish community enjoyed a "golden age" of mercantile prosperity. Aaron *Lopez, the town's leading merchant shipper on the eve of the Revolution, had joined his relatives there in 1752. The community was notable enough to be visited by Moses Malki, a Palestinian fund raiser, in 1759. There was even a Jewish social club, formed in 1761. By the mid-1770s, about 200 Jews—a sizable aggregation by colonial standards and an index to local economic conditions—had established themselves at Newport. Though predominantly Ashkenazi in origin, they accepted the *minhag Sefarad* as the American synagogal rite.

The Revolutionary War (1775–83) ruined Newport's trade and scattered nearly all of her most enterprising residents. On visiting Newport in 1790, President George Washington could "receive with much satisfaction" Yeshuat Yisrael's message of welcome, but the congregation was in decline. By 1822, the synagogue's Torah scrolls had been removed to the parent congregation, Shearith Israel in New York, and not a single Jew remained in Newport. Only the synagogue building and the cemetery remained, supported by funds which Isaac Touro's sons Abraham and Judah willed for that purpose. Though from 1850 on, occasional services were held there for vacationers, the synagogue was not opened for regular devotions until Abraham Pereira Mendes reconsecrated it in 1883. Ten years later the congregation formally reorganized itself, revived the name Yeshuat Yisrael, secured a charter in 1894, and set up a religious school. A separate group calling itself the Touro Congregation was chartered in 1899. Disputes as to which society had a rightful claim to the Touro bequests and to the use of the synagogue were finally settled in 1902. A ladies auxiliary began in 1903.

The reborn community was overwhelmingly Ashkenazi in descent and, by the mid-1900s, in *minhag* as well. Even Yeshuat Yisrael, now most often called the Touro Synagogue, abandoned the *minhag Sefarad* and adopted an Ashkenazi one, though in 1969 the "Sephardi" (i.e., Israeli) pronunciation, already used in the Hebrew school, was introduced into the synagogue service itself. Jewish life underwent a modest renaissance in 20th-century Newport. A *ḥevra kaddisha* burial society was founded in 1913. In 1915, the East European Orthodox Ahavas Achim Congregation was organized, followed by the Ahavas Achim Sisterhood in 1920. The United Hebrew School took shape in the late 1920s, and a Conservative congregation, Temple Shalom, was established in 1961. The Jewish Community Fund was initiated in 1941. A Y.M.H.A. had been started in Newport by 1919 and subsequently declined, but the Touro Synagogue dedicated its Jewish Community Center in the mid-1950s. Newport's preponderantly middle-class Jews have supported a variety of social, fraternal, and Zionist societies, though many of these activities have been impermanent.

Bibliography: S. F. Chyet, *Lopez of Newport* (1970); M. A. Gutstein, *Story of the Jews of Newport* (1936); idem, *To Bigotry No Sanction* (1958); E. Katz and B. Kusinitz, in: AJA, 22, no. 2 (1970); J. R. Marcus, *Colonial American Jew* (1969), index; AJHSP, 38 (1948/49), 57–76; *Rhode Island Jewish Historical Notes,* 1–4 (1954–66), indexes; A. J. Karp, *Jewish Experience in America,* 1, 2 (1969), indexes.

[S.F.C.]

NEWSPAPERS, HEBREW. This article is arranged according to the following outline:

The Spread of Hebrew Press
Main Stages of Development
  In Europe Through the Early 1880s
    Ideology of the Early Press
  In Europe Until World War I
  In Europe Between the Wars
The Duration of the Hebrew Periodicals
The Leading Periodicals and Newspapers in Europe
  The First Period: Yearbooks and Periodicals
    In Germany
    In Austro-Hungary
  The Second Period: Early Newspapers
    Linguistic and Ideological Development
  Hebrew Dailies
  The End of the Hebrew Press in Eastern Europe and Russia
The Hebrew Press in North America
Ereẓ Israel Press
  Through the Early 1880s
    Reflection of Communal Interests
  The Arrival of E. Ben-Yehuda
  The Early 1900s (Until World War I)
  The Postwar Press
The Press in the State of Israel

The term "Hebrew press" has undergone a basic metamorphosis since its early days. Originally, the term covered periodicals of varying frequency (yearbooks, monthlies, and irregular publications), the majority of which were literary and scientific in character, while only a small percentage were devoted to current affairs. News sections were almost nonexistent, and indeed would have been impractical in periodicals appearing infrequently. The first Hebrew newspaper worthy of the name, according to the concept of the time, began to appear in the mid-19th century, giving news of the Jewish and general world and containing literary, scientific, and social columns. Articles on public and current affairs, which were rare in the Hebrew periodicals of the previous 100 years, became increasingly popular in some journals. Thus a differentiation was created between the newspaper and other types of periodicals. The periodicals, too, began to modify their form and gradually devoted more attention to current affairs.

All types of periodicals, therefore, must be included

within the term "Hebrew press" in its first century (1750–1856). Following this period, a gradual differentiation set in between scholarly and literary periodicals and purely news media. This development was particularly noticeable in Ereẓ Israel where Hebrew became a living language, and periodicals began to appear, covering every field—literature, art, science, technology—while the daily newspaper grew to resemble its counterpart in European journalism.

THE SPREAD OF THE HEBREW PRESS

The Hebrew press began in Western Europe, mainly in Germany, in the second half of the 18th century. It gradually spread to Austria, and Galicia, and, a century after its initiation, appeared in czarist Russia, where there were more Hebrew readers. As the press began to flourish there, it declined in Western Europe. About the same time, a Hebrew press of an essentially Eastern European nature began to appear in Ereẓ Israel. The waves of Jewish emigration to the United States in the second half of the 19th century brought about the establishment of a Hebrew press in that country too (from the 1870s). Smaller centers of the Hebrew press were also established in England, South Africa, and, in later periods, in Latin America. Two factors determined the expansion or decline of the Hebrew press in the Diaspora: the degree of attachment to Hebrew of the Jews of a particular country, and the extent to which they acquired its native tongue. By the late 1930s the Hebrew press had almost disappeared in Eastern Europe. In Soviet Russia its decline had been deliberately encouraged, while in Poland it was brought about by competition from Polish and Yiddish. By contrast, the Hebrew press flourished in Ereẓ Israel: from modest beginnings in Jerusalem in 1863, it gradually and confidently expanded, becoming the focal point of the Hebrew press after World War I, with its center in Tel Aviv-Jaffa. Since World War II, the Hebrew press in Eastern Europe has ceased to exist; outside Israel, several periodicals are still published with varying frequency, mainly in the United States. A real Hebrew press, encompassing daily papers and periodicals covering a range of subjects, now exists only in Israel.

While, in its early years, the Hebrew press constituted only a small percentage of the total Jewish press in all languages, by the outbreak of World War II it held fourth place in the Jewish press (after English, German, and Yiddish). Today, as a result of the expansion of the Hebrew press in Israel, it holds second place (after English), and, quantitatively, accounts for more than one-quarter of the total Jewish press in all languages.

MAIN STAGES OF DEVELOPMENT

In Europe Through the Early 1880s. One of the earliest consequences of the Haskalah movement in Germany was the creation of Hebrew periodicals, such as those published in Germany and devoted to literature, philosophy, and social problems. This initial stage, which lasted almost a century (approximately 1750–1856), was inaugurated by the periodical **Kohelet Musar*, edited by Moses *Mendelssohn. The differing intervals at which the variety of periodicals at this time were published was a decisive factor in determining the contents of those periodicals: much space was given over to belles lettres, translations, world literature, and various aspects of Judaic studies while very little was devoted to news matters. In this early period Hebrew began to adapt itself to modern expression, gradually discarding its cloak of sanctity and adopting neologisms and new literary forms. During the second stage (1856–86), current affairs were gradually introduced, at first by simply citing belatedly news items from other papers. Gradually, however, the traditions of the modern press developed, ranging from reports by regular correspondents to lead articles and political commentary, simultaneously continuing the traditions of the earlier Hebrew periodicals, by devoting considerable space to all subjects. The periodical press also continued to develop as before, improving its standards and its form. The interrelation between these two areas of the press is reflected in the fact that the same writers contributed to both. The Russian censorship constituted a great hindrance to the development of journalism on public affairs, and editors consequently became adept at disguising statements in phraseology whose hidden meaning was clear to their own readers. Hebrew papers appearing outside Russia were also compelled to restrain their political commentaries, since most of their readers lived in Russia, where the papers might be banned. This accounts for the remarkable panegyrics on the czarist regime, which should not be taken at face value.

IDEOLOGY OF THE EARLY PRESS. Up to the early 1880s, the main trend was the dissemination of the Haskalah and its program for attaining equal rights. This ideology resulted in several by-products: the appeal for the creation of a productive Jewish economy by means of agricultural settlement in Russia or by engaging in crafts, and for the improvement of Jewish education by replacing the old-fashioned methods of the *ḥeder* with the teaching of secular subjects and vocational skills. After the anti-Jewish pogroms in southern Russia in the early 1880s, however, Haskalah ideology changed, and almost all the newspapers and periodicals now supported the *Ḥibbat Zion movement. Only **Ha-Maggid* had anticipated this new ideology by 20 years. Attitudes to the movement ranged from hostility (*Ivri Anokhi*) or hesitant support (**Ha-Ẓefirah*) to complete identification (*Ha-Maggid* and later **Ha-Meliẓ*).

Throughout this period, the press gradually progressed technically, nurturing several generations of writers of all types. Indeed, there is hardly a Hebrew writer who did not take his first literary steps in one of the newspapers. Some outstanding writers, such as J. L. *Gordon, also served as editors, acting as patrons to many others.

Two events, however, disturbed the peace of the press. The first, in the late 1860s and early 1870s, was the controversy regarding religious reform, sparked by its two chief advocates, Moses Leib *Lilienblum and J. L. Gordon, mainly in *Ha-Meliẓ*, and taken up by the extreme and moderate Orthodox elements in **Ha-Levanon*. The second event, less significant at the time as regards public reaction and support, but important historically, was the appearance of the socialist organs, *Ha-Emet* and **Asefat Ḥakhamim*, edited by A. S. *Liebermann, Morris *Vinchevsky, and others. These journals attracted a considerable number of writers and contributors and served as a platform for those discontented with the czarist regime on the one hand, and with the traditional Jewish way of life on the other.

In Europe Until World War I. The third stage in the Hebrew press was inaugurated by the establishment of the first Hebrew daily **Ha-Yom* edited by J. L. *Kantor (St. Petersburg)—a revolutionary event, the novelty of which is now hard to appreciate. For the first time the Hebrew press and the Hebrew language were faced with the challenge of dealing, journalistically and linguistically, with day-to-day events. *Ha-Yom* introduced many innovations and experiments. Despite the gradual disappearance of florid and involved phraseology (*meliẓah*) in all types of literature it was still used in Hebrew journalistic writing. The new paper gradually eradicated its last traces. To meet the competition, *Ha-Ẓefirah* and *Ha-Meliẓ* also became dailies in the same year (1886). All at once, a tradition of modern Hebrew journalism developed. Although almost all the Hebrew papers now shared the ideology of Ḥibbat Zion, they varied both in their local color—*Ha-Ẓefirah* being Polish and *Ha-Meliẓ* Russian—and in their particular stands within the Ḥibbat Zion movement.

The Hebrew press of Eastern Europe had now reached a peak which it was to sustain until World War I. A modern press in the true sense of the word, it attracted the best Hebrew writers of almost three generations, and Hebrew literature, in turn, flourished, as it spread to the many and varied literary publications of the day. Both *Aḥad Ha-Am and *Bialik, key figures of Hebrew literature, were nurtured by this press. Though the first Russian Revolution (1905) temporarily halted this development, it resumed shortly afterward, ending only with World War I. There was a brief but glorious and unparalleled era in the history of the Hebrew press and periodicals in Russia after the fall of the czarist regime in 1917. However, the Soviet regime soon declared the Hebrew language counterrevolutionary and suppressed all Hebrew publication.

In Europe Between the Wars. The former heights were never regained in Poland between the wars. In the 1930s, after a long struggle for survival, the only daily Hebrew paper ceased publication. It was replaced by the weekly *Ba-Derekh,* and there were years when only the pioneer youth movements maintained Hebrew newspapers in Poland. Some Hebrew journals survived within the framework of the underground movements in Nazi-occupied Poland, but ceased to exist after World War II. Through the efforts of determined individuals, the Hebrew press in other countries, such as England, survived, and appeared regularly for years (cf. Suwalski's *Ha-Yehudi*). But most of the papers and journals published outside Central Europe were short-lived, since their sole support came from emigrants from the East. As these readers acquired the language of their new country, circulation dropped, and the periodicals ceased publication. Apart from Ereẓ Israel, only in North America is there an uninterrupted tradition of Hebrew periodicals.

The one characteristic common to most Hebrew papers and periodicals over the years and throughout the world (with the exception of the extreme Orthodox and left-wing) is their strong attachment to Ḥibbat Zion, Zionism, and the State of Israel. There is an organic fusing of language and Israel content, overlapping their Jewish content. In this they are unique.

THE DURATION OF THE HEBREW PERIODICALS

Only a very small percentage of Hebrew newspapers and periodicals enjoyed longevity. The record until 1970 was held by the weekly **Ha-Po'el ha-Ẓa'ir* (63 years), the dailies **Haaretz* (57) and **Davar* (45)—all in Israel—and the weekly *Hadoar* (49) in the United States. In earlier periods the record was held by *Ha-Maggid* (47 years), *Ha-Ẓefirah* (almost 50, with short intervals), and *Ha-Meliẓ* (43). The latter two began as weeklies and later became dailies. The periodical **Ha-Shilo'aḥ* appeared in 46 volumes. Longevity is not always, however, an indication of the importance of the paper. Some short-lived papers, like the daily **Ha-Ẓofeh* at the turn of the 20th century, were of vital importance. There were also papers which appeared for decades under different names so as to evade censorship or because of licensing problems as was the case with *Ben-Yehuda's papers in Jerusalem.

THE LEADING PERIODICALS AND NEWSPAPERS IN EUROPE

The First Period: Yearbooks and Periodicals. *Kohelet Musar,* published by Mendelssohn (about 1750), was the first attempt at translating traditional ethical concepts into a modern idiom.

In Germany. Although the initial experiment was short-lived, it was revived in 1783 by a group of Mendelssohn's disciples who published *Ha-Me'assef,* the first modern Hebrew periodical. Appearing sporadically in several German towns between 1783 and 1811, it had considerable influence on the general evolvement of Hebrew Haskalah literature and, in particular, on that of the Hebrew press, both in style (as "purely" biblical as possible) and content (e.g., original and translated belles lettres, and studies of various aspects of Judaism). *Ha-Me'assef* dealt extensively with current affairs, but its main goal—the attainment of the Haskalah—was achieved at a more rapid rate than the editors and participants had ever anticipated. German Jewry, accultured to its society, no longer needed a Hebrew journal. As a result, from the first third of the 19th century, the focal point of the Hebrew Haskalah began to shift to Austria, relying mainly upon readers in Galicia, Moravia, and Italy.

In Austro-Hungary. The new periodical press in Austro-Hungary, which both culturally (i.e., Jewish culture) and geographically lay on the border between West and East, was inaugurated by the yearbooks **Bikkurei ha-Ittim,* **Kerem Ḥemed, Kokhevei Yiẓḥak,* **Oẓar Neḥmad, Bikkurim*—which appeared for over 40 years (1821–65), mainly in Vienna, but also in Prague and Berlin. Varied in content, they attracted the best of the Haskalah writers. At the same time, periodicals and literary collections began to appear at regular intervals in various parts of Galicia, serving as a nursery for modern Hebrew literature by creating the science of Judaic studies and by adapting the Hebrew language to modern belles lettres. The pioneers of Hebrew periodicals in Germany and Austria were closely attached to the German language, as is evidenced by German sections (printed in Hebrew characters) in the first volumes of *Bikkurei ha-Ittim,* and by the many translations from that language. In contrast to the above-mentioned periodicals, which allotted little or no space to current events, **Zion,* edited by I. M. *Jost and M. *Creizenach, prevailed on East European writers to participate in discussions on contemporary affairs.

An examination of the language and style of these periodicals reveals how the Hebrew language developed in liveliness and suppleness from one issue to the next. Recent studies (particularly those by Dov *Sadan) of the florid *meliẓah* style of the early *maskilim* have demonstrated that this style did not, as was formerly believed, contain biblical elements exclusively, but rather drew from the linguistic and cultural traditions of centuries of Hebrew language and literature. As a result of the intimate acquaintance which the writers of this period had with the Bible and its study over the generations, their biblical commentaries are full of valuable insights. Since, in general, the periodical press was imbued with the spirit of the moderate Haskalah, elements from all movements could contribute to it, and it managed to remain as neutral as possible, apart from sharp polemics against extreme Reform Judaism as practiced by *Geiger. This tradition of neutrality was maintained in the Hebrew press outside Ereẓ Israel as a rule, although there were periodicals that expressed more extreme views, e.g., the extreme Orthdox *Shomer Ẓiyyon ha-Ne'eman,* and the radical **He-Ḥalutz.*

The Second Period: Early Newspapers. These periodicals constituted a 100-year-long preparation for a regular journal with the form and content of a newspaper. Such a newspaper, *Ha-Maggid,* which appeared in 1856 in Lyck, eastern Prussia, on the Russian border, thus inaugurating the second period of the Hebrew press, was meant for Russian Jewry. The only periodical which Russian Jewry had hitherto produced, *Pirkei Ẓafon,* enjoyed only two issues (1841 and 1844) before it ceased publication. With *Ha-Maggid* A. L. Silbermann, the editor, created not only a new organ for Russian Jewry but also the first Hebrew newspaper that devoted considerable space to reportage and editorial comment on the news. As such, the new paper required different tools from those employed in earlier periodicals. It also introduced other innovations, e.g., a section containing translations of news items from the general press which are to be found in almost every issue; other periodicals followed suit. The Hebrew language gradually evolved into a living language, even though it retained a considerable amount of *meliẓah*. *Ha-Maggid* was also the pioneer in two other aspects: in the early 1860s it began to advocate Ḥibbat Zion and the settlement of Ereẓ Israel, while all the other newspapers remained attached to the Haskalah ideology till the early 1880s; for many years it was the only paper of general Jewish character that reflected events in all the Jewish communities, including the United States and Australia. Immediately after its establishment, four other newspapers sprang up (1860–62), which dealt primarily with events in their own geographical area: *Ha-Meliẓ* (Odessa-St. Petersburg) for Russian Jewry; **Ha-Karmel* (Vilna) for Lithuanian Jewry; *Ha-Mevasser* (Lvov) for the Jews of Galicia; and *Ha-Ẓefirah* (Warsaw and, for a short period, Berlin) for Polish Jews. (Originally devoted to science, *Ha-Ẓefirah's* later concern, under the editorship of *Sokolow, was primarily news.) All these newspapers covered current events, but likewise continued their traditions by devoting special columns to belles lettres, science, and criticism, so that even today it is difficult to envisage a Hebrew paper without such columns. These papers still constitute a rich source for Jewish scholarship; only the lack of indexes prevents their being utilized properly. The papers also stimulated additional literary forms, for which there had not been room in periodicals, and developed reportage from provincial towns and, later, from overseas. Although this reportage may contain trivia, it also constitutes an extremely rich source of information on Jewish communities throughout the world.

Linguistic and Ideological Development. A superficial comparison of a newspaper of 1856 with one of 1886 is sufficient proof of the radical development of the Hebrew press in this second stage. A new language had been created which differed greatly from that of *Ha-Me'assef* or even *Ha-Maggid* in their first years. There was also a change in the ideological content. Reality, and particularly the pogroms in southern Russia in the early 1880s, made Jews aware of the failure of the Haskalah's proposed solutions to the Jewish problem. There was, therefore, a gradual transition from the old ideals of the Haskalah and the Emancipation to the new ones of settlement of Ereẓ Israel, Zionism and, finally, political Zionism.

The distinction between the periodical press and newspapers was still obscure, since current affairs began to play a more important role in the former. Such was the case with *Smolenskin's monthly **Ha-Shaḥar,* in which an attempt was made, particularly by the editor himself, to clarify Jewish problems, both past and future, and which first arrived at the ideology of "the people of the spirit." It then took up nationalism and Zionism, strongly criticizing the Haskalah and its methods. The same is true of its rival, *Ha-Boker Or,* edited by A. B. *Gottlober, which defended Mendelssohn's school of thought. The articles on Judaica in these publications became more popular and readable as a result of the growing flexibility of the language, while their scientific basis was not impaired.

Hebrew Dailies. In the meantime, the editors were obliged to enlarge the format of their papers and to produce them at greater frequency than the original weeklies. In 1886, exactly 30 years after the publication of the first issue of *Ha-Maggid,* J. L. Kantor published *Ha-Yom,* the first Hebrew daily. To meet the competition, *Ha-Meliẓ* and *Ha-Ẓefirah* also began to be published as dailies. The letters of J. L. Gordon (then editor of *Ha-Meliẓ*), who frowned upon this new development, show the difficulties that faced Hebrew editors. Conditions, however, forced them to accept the new burden. In the daily press it was essential to eliminate florid Hebrew, since the need for rapid translations of news dispatches left no time for complicated phraseology.

From 1886, the feuilleton which had existed before the development of the daily press became an integral part of the dailies, particularly of *Ha-Yom,* to which D. Frischmann and J. L. *Katzenelson (known as Buki ben Yogli) contributed. *Ha-Meliẓ* and *Ha-Ẓefirah* continued, of necessity, to appear as dailies even after *Ha-Yom* ceased publication (1888). The oldest of the papers, *Ha-Maggid,* remained a weekly, until discontinued in 1903.

In the mid-1880s, Sokolow—a man whose grasp of the spirit of the times was almost unique in his generation of Hebrew journalism—radically changed the periodical press. In 1884 he began to publish **Ha-Asif,* weighty annuals encompassing almost all the literary forms. Enjoying unprecedented circulation, their success spurred others to issue similar annuals (e.g., *Keneset Yisrael* by S. P. *Rabinowitz, 1886). It was a new development for Hebrew periodicals to reach thousands of readers, all of them subscribers. The publication of *Ha-Asif* is therefore frequently regarded as the first literary event which created a mass Hebrew readership. Innumerable periodicals, almost all of them short-lived, appeared in the last third of the 19th century in various places in Eastern Europe, and, occasionally in the West (mainly on Judaica or as appendixes to the German Jewish press). An important contribution to the rapid adaptation of Hebrew to everyday life was made by the numerous translations in the press, periodicals, and separate books, some of which were to become classics (particularly in the field of poetry). In the early 1880s even the Orthodox *Ha-Levanon* ceased its ideological polemics with the other papers and, because of its editor, J. *Brill, joined in preaching the settlement of Ereẓ Israel and Ḥibbat Zion. Simultaneously, an Orthodox anti-Zionist press arose, e.g., *Ha-Peles, Ha-Modi'a, Ha-Kol,* which copied the modern style of the pro-Zionist press. In the 1870s the first two Hebrew socialist journals appeared, *Ha-Emet,* and *Asefat Ḥakhamim,* edited by A. S. Liebermann, M. Vinchevsky, and others. These journals, which were short-lived because of the attitude of the East and West European authorities, created a new Hebrew by introducing terms taken from socialism and communism, and by translations.

At the beginning of the present century, the two veteran papers, *Ha-Maggid* and *Ha-Meliẓ,* closed down. As if to symbolize the rise of a new and younger generation in literature and in the press, two new dailies were established in Poland and Russia: *Ha-Ẓofeh,* in Warsaw, and *Ha-Zeman,* first in St. Petersburg, later in Vilna. A new generation of writers and journalists was nurtured by these papers. *Ha-Ẓofeh* was the first paper to hold a literary competition (1903). In that competition Y. D. *Berkowitz was discovered. At the same time, *Ha-Ẓefirah* reappeared after a lengthy interval. In 1904 the weekly **Ha-Miẓpeh,* edited by S. M. Lazar, began to appear in Cracow, in place of *Ha-Maggid,* and encouraged many new writers (including S. Y. *Agnon, A. *Hameiri, U. Ẓ *Greenberg, and

Z. *Diesendruck). In none of these papers was there a clear distinction between the literary and journalistic realms. The best of the Hebrew writers of the period contributed to them (e.g., *Fichmann, *Bershadsky, *Shneour, Berkowitz).

The End of the Hebrew Press in Eastern Europe and Russia. The most outstanding of these literary periodicals was the monthly, *Ha-Shilo'aḥ,* edited by Aḥad Ha-Am and, later, by J. *Klausner; others included **Ha-Dor,* edited by Frischmann, *Ha-Zeman,* the annuals *Lu'aḥ Aḥi'asaf* and Sokolow's *Sefer ha-Shanah.* **Ha-Olam,* the official Hebrew organ of the Zionist Organization, for decades provided opportunities for Hebrew writers. It would be hard to envisage the development of the young Hebrew literature that flourished at this time—starting with Bialik—without the periodicals of the early 20th century. Although this vital period came to an abrupt end with the outbreak of World War I, its influence could be felt almost until the 1960s. The Hebrew press in Eastern Europe never recovered its former glory after World War I but gradually flickered out. In Russia, after the downfall of czarism, Hebrew literary activity flourished briefly with the appearance of the literary journals **Ha-Tekufah, Massu'ot, He-Avar, Ha-Mishpat ha-Ivri, Ereẓ,* and others, and the establishment of literary projects of formerly unknown scope (e.g., Stybel publishing house). The weekly **Ha-Am,* which later became a daily, also began to appear in this period. Soviet Russia's silencing of the Hebrew language, however, put an end to all this, a circumstance which has persisted, apart from certain isolated periodicals published in Russia, or published abroad by Russian Hebrew writers. The departure from Russia of the great majority of Hebrew writers, beginning with Bialik, marks the end of Hebrew literature and journalism in that country, and the gradual shift of its focal point to Palestine, via Berlin.

The papers and literary journals set up in Western Europe from the turn of the century till the 1930s and 1940s were a natural continuation of the Eastern European tradition. With one notable exception—*Ha-Yehudi,* edited in London from 1897 to 1913 by I. Suwalski—they were all short-lived. Another London-based journal, whose effect was in inverse ratio to its duration, was J. Ḥ *Brenner's **Ha-Me'orer* (1906–07).

While the extreme Orthodox circles, having adopted methods of the secular press, attacked Zionism, the press of the Orthodox *Mizrachi Zionist Organization, which opposed the secular movement, fought anti-Zionist Orthodox elements. It established the monthly *Ha-Mizraḥ* (1903) as well as the weeklies *Ha-Ivri* (first in Berlin and later in New York) and *Ha-Mizraḥi* in Poland after World War I.

Toward the end of the 19th century the Hebrew press in Eastern Europe began to produce more specialized journals. An educational press which lasted for decades was developed in Russia and Poland; magazines for children and youth began to appear, some of them of extremely high standard, such as *Olam Katan,* edited by S. L. *Gordon. I. H. Tawiow even put out a daily for children (*He-Ḥaver;* see *Children's Literature). Poland became the major Hebrew center in Eastern Europe between the wars after that language had been silenced in Soviet Russia. Its one Hebrew daily, however, *Ha-Ẓefirah,* could not survive in the face of the growing competition from Yiddish, on the one hand, and Polish, on the other. *Ha-Ẓefirah* closed down, was revived under another name *(Ha-Yom),* revived again under its old name, and finally discontinued in the early 1930s. For several years, it was replaced by the weekly, *Ba-Derekh,* the last Hebrew paper in Poland, which later also closed down.

A unique phenomenon, particularly in Poland between the wars, was the press of the *He-Ḥalutz and the pioneering youth movements, especially that of *Ha-Shomer ha-Ẓa'ir. At a time when Hebrew was abandoned in Poland even by the official Zionist Organization (the press of which was mainly in Yiddish and Polish), and Hebrew readers could no longer support the burden of maintaining a Hebrew paper, the youth movements safeguarded Hebrew expression (and speech) with unbounded loyalty and material sacrifice. For these young people, the Hebrew language and pioneer training were stepping stones to Zionist self-realization. Thus He-Ḥalutz issued the paper *He-Atid,* and Ha-Shomer ha-Ẓair, its organ, bearing that movement's name; other youth movements followed suit. This press was noted for its ties with Ereẓ Israel and its constant contact with the labor press there. [G.K.]

THE HEBREW PRESS IN NORTH AMERICA

Unlike the Anglo-Jewish, German-Jewish, and Yiddish presses in the United States, all of which have served large bodies of readers who often were literate in their native tongue alone, the Hebrew press was restricted from the outset to a relatively small coterie of subscribers. Nevertheless, a Hebrew periodical press has existed practically uninterruptedly in the United States ever since its inception in the last decades of the 19th century.

The first Hebrew periodical in the United States, Zvi Hirsch *Bernstein's newsletter *Ha-Ẓofeh ba-Areẓ ha-Ḥadashah* ("The Observer in a New Land") appeared in 1871, a year after the first two Yiddish journals in America, one of which was Bernstein's New York *Juedische Post.* In their early years, in fact, the two presses frequently had their fates intertwined, the same publishers, editors, and writers playing an active role in both. *Ha-Ẓofeh ba-Areẓ ha-Ḥadashah* appeared irregularly until 1876. Hebrew was also one of four languages to appear in Bernstein's *Hebrew News,* an unusual polyglot venture published for several months in 1871.

A number of Hebrew periodicals appeared briefly in New York in the 1880s and 1890s, many of them largely one-man productions. Among them were the Ḥovevei Zion organ *Ha-Le'ummi* ("The Nationalist," 1888–89), the *maskil* Ezekiel Enowitz's *Ha-Emet* ("The Truth," 1894–95) and *Eẓ ha-Da'at* ("The Tree of Knowledge," 1896), Michael *Rodkinson's *Ha-Sanegor* ("The Defender," 1890) and *Tekhunat Ru'aḥ ha-Yisre'eli* ("The Spirit of the Israelite," 1899), and Abraham *Rosenberg's *Ner ha-Ma'aravi* ("The Western Light," 1895–97). Somewhat longer lived were Zeev Wolf *Schur's *Ha-Pisgah* ("The Summit"), published irregularly in New York, Baltimore, and Chicago from 1891 to 1899, and *Ha-Ivri* ("The Hebrew," 1892–98, 1901–02), which was founded by the Yiddish publisher Kasriel *Sarasohn and edited by Gershon Rosenzweig.

The first attempt to publish a Hebrew daily in the U.S. took place in New York in 1909 with the appearance of *Ha-Yom* ("The Day") under the editorship of Moses Hacohen *Goldman, but the paper failed financially within a brief time, as did an effort to revive it in 1913. The latter year also witnessed the launching of the literary monthly *Ha-Toren* ("The Mast," weekly from 1916 to 1921), which in quality of contents and regularity of appearance far surpassed any of its predecessors. Edited originally by a staff composed of such eminent Hebraists as Max *Lipson, Daniel *Persky, Abraham *Goldberg, Y. D. Berkowitz, and Benjamin *Silkiner, *Ha-Toren* was managed from 1919 until its demise in 1925 by the author Reuben *Brainin. Contemporary with it was the literary and political Mizrachi weekly *Ha-Ivri* ("The Hebrew," New York, 1916–21), edited by Meir *Berlin, who had previously managed the same journal in Germany.

The most successful and permanent of all Hebrew periodicals in the United States, however, was the weekly *Hadoar* ("The Post"). Started as a daily in 1921 by a staff directed by Lipson and including Persky, Hirsch Leib *Gordon, Abraham Orlans, and Menachem *Ribalow, *Hadoar* was briefly discontinued in the summer of 1922 and then resumed publication as a weekly under the auspices of the *Histadruth Ivrith of America. In 1925 Menachem Ribalow became sole editor, a position he held for nearly 30 years. During this period, except for a brief hiatus in 1925, *Hadoar* appeared every week in spite of continual financial straits, publishing Hebrew authors of note from all over the world and especially numbering among its steady contributors such U.S. Hebrew writers as Hillel *Bavli, Moshe *Feinstein, Reuven *Grossman, Simon *Halkin, Ephraim *Lisitzky, Daniel Persky, Gabriel *Preil, Abraham *Regelson, Zvi *Scharfstein, Eisig *Silberschlag, Yochanan *Twersky, Meyer *Waxman, and Reuven *Wallenrod. From 1934, *Hadoar* issued a biweekly youth supplement entitled *Ha-Musaf la-Kore ha-Ẓa'ir*. Ribalow was succeeded as editor in 1953 by Moses *Maisels, who was in turn followed in 1959 by Moshe Yinon. *Hadoar's* circulation in 1970 was put at about 5,000.

In addition to *Hadoar*, the literary monthly *Bitzaron* was published in New York from 1939. Though the establishment of the State of Israel led to a broadening of interest in Hebrew among the U.S. Jewish public, the local Hebrew press has not grown as a result, in part perhaps because modern air transportation has made it possible to fly Hebrew newspapers and periodicals directly from Israel and distribute them rapidly to readers all over the United States. [H.H.]

EREẒ ISRAEL PRESS

Through the Early 1880s. In 1863—when all the East European Hebrew papers were already in existence—two papers were established in Jerusalem: *Ha-Levanon* and, later, **Ḥavaẓẓelet*. The distinguishing trait of the Ereẓ Israel Hebrew press was found in the fact that both papers advocated particular and conflicting interests within the Jerusalem community, which brought about the discontinuance of both papers after a short period. *Ha-Levanon* moved abroad and, until the early 1880s, appeared in Paris and Germany. It always retained its Ereẓ Israel background however. Only briefly, particularly when appearing in Germany as a Hebrew supplement to the German-language paper of the Orthodox community, did it serve as the mouthpiece of Orthodoxy, violently opposing the demands for religious reform of Lilienblum, J. L. Gordon, and others. *Ḥavaẓẓelet* enjoyed a different fate: revived in 1870 under the editorship of I. *Bak and, later, of his son-in-law I. D. *Frumkin, it appeared until just before World War I.

Reflection of Communal Interests. From the first, the Hebrew press in Ereẓ Israel developed along different lines from its counterparts abroad. Whereas the latter shared a love of Hebrew language and literature and were devoid of communal interests, the Ereẓ Israel press was imbued with the atmosphere of the Land of Israel and the Jerusalem Jewish community, displaying a complete absence of the tone of romantic longing for Hebrew and a Hebrew paper. Considerable space, however, was still devoted to Hebrew studies and belles lettres. Here, Hebrew was, at least in writing, the natural language of the community, as a choice of papers in other languages did not exist.

The Ereẓ Israel press is doubly important, since from the very first it aired vital problems of the Jewish community and thus developed political and topical journalism. In place of the Haskalah ideology, with which the East European press was preoccupied, these papers dealt with agricultural policy and actual problems. The conflicts between newspapers at times reached such intensity that they were banned *(ḥerem)*, a phenomenon unknown to Hebrew papers outside Ereẓ Israel. On the other hand, this press was free of censorship, and only when copies were sent to Russia, did the censor erase sections of which he disapproved. There was a sharp battle in the Jerusalem press with regard to the charitable funds *(ḥalukkah)*, touching on the basic administrative arrangements of the Jewish community. By contrast, it was typical of the editors that they were among the first to join and promote the founders of the first agricultural settlement, Petaḥ Tikvah. J. M. Salomon ceased publication of his paper, *Yehudah vi-Yrushalayim* (1878), to become one of the founders of Petaḥ Tikvah. Another editor, I. D. Frumkin, called for immigration to Ereẓ Israel upon the outbreak of the anti-Jewish pogroms in Russia in the 1880s.

The first period of the Jerusalem and Ereẓ Israel press lasted some 20 years, during which time its particular traditions were evolved. Other papers appeared, but only lasted short periods of time. In addition there were attempts to produce papers in other languages, at first Ladino (simultaneously with *Ḥavaẓẓelet;* 1870), and later, a bilingual paper in Hebrew and Yiddish, *Sha'arei Ẓiyyon* (1876), which lasted only one year, after which it appeared only in Hebrew.

Until the early 1880s, all these papers had one thing in common, despite their differences of opinion: they were rooted in the Orthodox religious tradition. Even *Ḥavaẓẓelet*, the organ of the Jerusalem Haskalah, differed in this respect from the pro-Haskalah periodicals in Europe, and its liberalism expressed itself only in its revolt against the *ḥalukkah* and its administration.

The Arrival of E. Ben-Yehuda. A new era opened for this press when Eliezer *Ben-Yehuda arrived in Ereẓ Israel in 1881, at the invitation of I. D. Frumkin, to work on *Ḥavaẓẓelet*. In 1884 he left *Ḥavaẓẓelet* to establish his own newspaper, **Ha-Ẓevi*, which revolutionized the Jerusalem press by introducing a secular tone and a modern journalistic technique. A comparison of Ben-Yehuda's paper with Frumkin's, even in the early days, clearly highlights this change. As the language employed in the Jerusalem press could not fulfill modern needs, Ben-Yehuda began to introduce linguistic innovations, particularly in areas of everyday matters. The need for innovation became more pressing when he began to translate from French literature. (Hitherto there had been only translations from German belles lettres, and sometimes from English, apparently via the German.) It was then that Ben-Yehuda conceived the idea of a Hebrew dictionary, containing simple, precise language, serving everyday needs. The use of Hebrew as a spoken language, which he initiated in his own household, was part of his Hebraist ideology, namely, that the revived national language would serve to unify all sections of the Jewish community. These innovations won Ben-Yehuda the title of "father of modern Hebrew journalism in Ereẓ Israel." The first agricultural settlements were established in the early 1880s, creating a new Hebrew community different in essence from the "old" *yishuv* in Jerusalem and other towns. In his paper, Ben-Yehuda became the spokesman of this new *yishuv*, while *Ḥavaẓẓelet* retreated from its Haskalah tendencies and became the mouthpiece of the "old" *yishuv*. Thus began the differentiation in the press of the *yishuv* which henceforth characterized the Ereẓ Israel press, and which was based on differing interests, almost unknown in the Hebrew press outside Ereẓ Israel. Licensing restrictions compelled Ben-Yehuda to change the name of his paper *(Ha-Ẓevi, Ha-Or, Hashkafah)*, and at the turn of the century, his son, Ithamar *Ben-Avi, joined him on the staff of the paper. Ben-Avi introduced further modernization, under the influence of the French press, with which he was closely acquainted. In time, weekly publication proved insufficient. Ben-Yehuda's paper began to appear several times a week and, after the Young Turks' Revolt (1908), he and his son began publishing the first Ereẓ Israel Hebrew daily, *Ha-Ẓevi* (1908, later changed to *Ha-Or*). The son introduced journalistic techniques hitherto unknown in the Hebrew press anywhere in the world: sensational headlines, reporting, generally in sweetly sentimental style, and other mannerisms which aroused opposition from the exponents of the Russian journalistic tradition. Ben-Yehuda retorted that Hebrew writers in Eastern Europe could not understand the new Ereẓ Israel community or the role of its Hebrew newspaper.

In the first two periods of the Ereẓ Israel Hebrew press there were almost no journals dealing with socio-literary matters. Considerable space, however, was devoted both to studies of Judaica and to original and translated belles lettres. A new branch of Judaica—the study of Ereẓ Israel and the history of its Jewish community—was initiated by A. M. *Luntz, who, in the early 1880s, published *Yerushalayim*, a yearbook for Ereẓ Israel studies (the first issue was published in Vienna, thereafter, in Jerusalem), and later, the popular annuals *Lu'aḥ Ereẓ Yisrael*, as well as a series of books and anthologies on these subjects. Ben-Yehuda and Luntz also encouraged the publication in Hebrew of educational journals, children's papers, and agricultural journals. On the other hand, Ereẓ Israel literature reached a critical point, as Ben-Yehuda's publications were not suitable organs for its development. As a result talented writers, such as J. Barzilai (Eisenstadt) and M. *Smilansky, published their works abroad.

The Early 1900s (Until World War I). The Second Aliyah immigrants, who began to arrive at the turn of the century, and who had more progressive political views, objected to Ben-Yehuda's journalistic style and political opinions. With meager financial resources, they established their own papers, first, *Ha-Po'el ha-Ẓa'ir* (1907 in stencil, 1908 in print), sponsored by the party of the same name, and then *Ha-Aḥdut*, sponsored by the Po'alei Zion party (1910). The new Zionism of the Second Aliyah, which advocated immigration to Ereẓ Israel and the development of Jewish manual labor, required a labor press, which was in complete contrast to Ben-Yehuda's papers. The editors of these papers—Yosef *Aharonovitch (of *Ha-Po'el ha-Ẓa'ir*), I. *Ben-Zvi, D. *Ben-Gurion, R. Yanait *Ben-Zvi, Y. *Zerubavel (editors of *Ha-Aḥdut*)—were not only journalists but the leading political figures of the new way of life. Attracting the best writers in Ereẓ Israel, these papers, and *Ha-Po'el ha-Ẓa'ir* in particular, served as a nursery for the Ereẓ Israel Hebrew literature, encouraging a whole generation of writers and thinkers, such as A. D. *Gordon, J. H. Brenner, Y. S. Rabinowitz, *Rabbi Binyamin (Radler-Feldman), and S. J. Agnon. A corresponding revolution was taking place in the same year (1907) in the field of literary periodicals, with the appearance of *Ha-Omer*.

From 1907, the press thus developed in two directions. Additional dailies began to appear later: *Ha-Ḥerut*, with Sephardi orientation (1909, at first a weekly, and, from 1912, a daily) and *Moriyyah*, of Orthodox orientation (1910). The latter was intended to replace *Ḥavaẓẓelet*, which had changed its character under Gad *Frumkin, and eventually ceased publication.

The seven years prior to World War I were decisive in the annals of the Ereẓ Israel Hebrew press. For the first time newspapers reflected the varying trends in communal life. The fact that they were written in Hebrew, which still served as a unifying factor abroad, was no longer thought of as a common denominator. Instead, the particular point of view of a specific journal now determined its readership.

The Postwar Press. World War I put an end to all these papers, and a new period opened up for the Hebrew press after the war, under the influence of the new wave of immigration (the Third Aliyah), mainly from Eastern Europe. In 1919, Hebrew writers and journalists, educated in the liberal journalistic tradition in Russia, established the daily *Haaretz* (initially *Ḥadshot ha-Areẓ*), as a continuation of the Hebrew paper initiated by the British military administration. *Haaretz* became a general Zionist progressive paper "in the Odessa style," edited by the best of the Hebrew writers, with a minority of local contributors, among them Ben-Yehuda and his son. The local journalists, however, soon found that they had little in common with the "Russian" trend, and established their own paper, **Do'ar ha-Yom* (1919), edited by Ithamar Ben-Avi. In the first issue he outlined his program in terms of the ideology of the native-born Palestinian, a concept which held the germs of the later "*Canaanite" doctrine. *Do'ar ha-Yom* introduced technical improvements into the press, which were lacking in *Haaretz*. On the other hand, *Haaretz* was distinguished by its high standard of political journalism and by a literary section which attracted the best of the writers of the time.

Both papers were published in Jerusalem. Later *Haaretz* moved to Tel Aviv (1923), under the editorship of M. *Gluecksohn. In 1937, the paper was sold to Salman *Schocken, whose son Gershom then became editor. With the transfer of *Haaretz* to Tel Aviv, this city gradually became the center of journalism. In 1925 the *Histadrut began publishing the daily *Davar* under the editorship of Berl (Be'eri) *Katznelson; following his death it was edited by Zalman *Shazar (Rubashov). Other labor newspapers appeared which reflected differences of view within the labor movement. Ha-Shomer ha-Ẓa'ir's *Mishmar* (1943) reflected that party's opposition to the majority in the Histadrut, the *yishuv*, and the Zionist movement. When *Mapai split, and the *Aḥdut Ha-Avodah party was formed (1944), the new party established a weekly, bearing its name. Again when the new party merged with Ha-Shomer ha-Ẓa'ir and Po'alei Zion to form *Mapam, the weekly was absorbed by *Mishmar*, which now changed its name to *Al ha-Mishmar* (1948). When Aḥdut Ha-Avodah broke from Mapam, it first established the weekly *Ma'avak* and then (1952–54) merged it with the daily *La-Merḥav*. This in turn merged with *Davar* in 1971.

The Revisionist party first took over *Do'ar ha-Yom* (1928–30); then it published its own newspapers, *Ha-Yarden* (1934–36) and *Ha-Mashkif* (1938–48). Following the establishment of the state, former Revisionist elements joined the *Ḥerut party and published *Ḥerut*. In 1966, when Ḥerut allied itself with the Liberal party to form *Gaḥal, a new newspaper, *Ha-Yom*, was established replacing both *Ḥerut* and the General Zionist Liberal newspaper **Ha-Boker* until 1970 when it ceased publication.

Ha-Ẓofeh, established in 1937, remains the daily organ of the Religious Zionist parties, while *Ha-Modi'a*, *Ha-Kol*, and *She'arim* express the views of the more extreme Orthodox elements. The realities of Israel politics also affected the oldest of the Hebrew papers and journals, *Ha-Po'el ha-Ẓa'ir*. It began as the organ of the Ha-Po'el ha-Ẓa'ir movement and, with the amalgamation of the latter with Aḥdut ha-Avodah to form the Mapai party (1930), became the central organ of the new party. For a short period Mapai also published *Aḥdut ha-Avodah*, a literary and social journal, edited by Z. Shazar and C. *Arlosoroff. The editors of *Ha-Po'el ha-Ẓa'ir* were

Y. Aharonovitch (till 1922), Y. *Laufbahn (until his death in 1948), and Israel *Cohen (from 1948 to 1970). When the Israel Labor Party was established, *Ha-Po'el ha-Ẓa'ir* became its weekly mouthpiece (from May 1968). In 1970, the paper ceased publication.

The struggle against the British Mandatory authorities constitutes a chapter in itself in the annals of the Hebrew press. The seizure or temporary closure of papers, particularly from the 1930s onward, was a common occurrence. Papers were often obliged to change their names and utilize unexploited licenses. This situation was at its worst in the 1940s, during the closing years of the British Mandate, when an illegal press made its appearance—consisting mainly of wall posters—which represented the underground movements (*Haganah, *Irgun Ẓeva'i Le'ummi, and *Loḥamei Ḥerut Israel (Leḥi)). The communist movement was the first to publish underground papers in Hebrew, Yiddish, and Arabic, in the 1920s. Their paper, *Kol ha-Am,* began to be circulated publicly in 1947, giving that year as the 11th year of its publication, and remains the organ of the Israel *Communist Party (Maki). In 1970 it ceased publication as a daily and began to appear as a weekly.

Many attempts have been made to publish daily Hebrew papers in cities other than Tel Aviv, but none of them has been long-lived. Until 1929 all the daily papers apart from *Do'ar ha-Yom* were, of necessity, published at noon, for technical reasons: Reuter bulletins, for example, arrived by train from Egypt. Particularly as a result of the riots of 1929, journalistic techniques improved, and the papers began to appear in the morning. The Nazi rise to power in 1933, as well as the murder of Arlosoroff in the same year, increased circulation and resulted in the establishment of afternoon papers, which appear at noon. *Haaretz, Ha-Boker* and *Davar* began to publish afternoon papers, but all these were discontinued upon the appearance of a new type of afternoon paper. The first such paper, founded by E. Carlebach, *Yedi'ot Aḥaronot,* appeared in 1939. In 1948 he left *Yedi'ot Aḥaronot,* and established *Ma'ariv,* which subsequently developed the widest circulation of any paper in Israel.

The wave of immigration from Germany, which began in 1933, confronted the Hebrew press with the problem of a readership insufficiently acquainted with the Hebrew language. The result was a new type of paper written in easy Hebrew with vowels; the more difficult words were translated (first into German, and later into other languages). Initially, these formed voweled supplements of the established press, but in 1940 the first independent voweled paper, *Hegeh* (first editor, Dov Sadan), was introduced. Many immigrant journalists from Germany took their first steps in Hebrew journalism in *Hegeh.* It ceased publication in 1946, but was renewed in 1951 as *Omer,* published, as its predecessor was, by *Davar* (editors, Dan Pines and Ẓevi Rotem). There exist several other voweled papers (not dailies), which follow the same pattern. Many journals and periodicals devoted to all aspects of life, culture, literature, science, and military affairs, for example, appear at varying intervals, ranging from weeklies to annuals, and including journals and anthologies issued irregularly. In 1968 there were more than 300 such periodicals, covering almost every conceivable subject. They are published by parties, government offices, the Israel Defense Forces, Histadrut and its various trade unions, labor settlement blocs, trade associations, scientific and technical institutions, sports organizations, teachers' associations. There is also a wide range of entertainment periodicals, satirical journals, children's papers, and journals on cinema, chess, sport, economics, and Judaica.

The labor settlement movement press, appearing in stencil or in print, constitutes a category in itself. There is almost no urban or rural settlement which does not produce a regular paper or leaflet. The labor settlement movement has been publishing papers and journals for decades, containing material of great value, both from the literary aspect and from the point of view of the history of the labor movement and its settlements.

THE PRESS IN THE STATE OF ISRAEL

There was no significant change in the number of daily papers in the first 20 years of the State of Israel but the numbers dropped from 15 to 11 between 1968 and 1971. In the latter year, there were 11 daily papers (*Haaretz, Davar, Ha-Ẓofeh, Al ha-Mishmar, She'arim, Ha-Modi'a, Omer,* two afternoon papers, *Yedi'ot Aḥaronot,* and *Ma'ariv,* a sports paper, *Hadshot ha-Sport,* and an economic journal, *Yom Yom.* The Hebrew press, from its early days, has maintained its fine traditions and has not deteriorated into "yellow" journalism. Furthermore, throughout its existence, and particularly since the 1880s, it has displayed an organic affinity with Ereẓ Israel, and its settlement, and with Zionism.

Since the establishment of the State of Israel, attention has been focused on other problems, but the ideology of the State of Israel still remains the common basis of the press. The restraints of censorship imposed by foreign rulers have been removed, except for matters of security of the state. Another relatively new phenomenon is the success of the afternoon (actually late morning) press. Basically different from all the morning and noon papers published in the country before statehood, these papers use a "lighter" style, a more graphic form with headlines and sub-headlines, a more "provocative" tone in editorials and political journalism, and more lively reportage. Other journalistic innovations have included the rise of the illustrated weekly, as a supplement of an existing paper or in its own right; the rise of the young generation in journalism, in some cases the sons and grandsons of the early journalists; the increasing role of women and reporters of Middle Eastern extraction in journalism. News from Israel war fronts and the borders was covered on the spot and often reported in special editions appearing several times each day. Journalists also participated in the wars, as military correspondents and as soldiers.

The existing newspapers maintain all the columns customary in the world press, such as art and literature, sport, and women's columns, even though these subjects are also dealt with in special weeklies and journals. Another innovation is a more outspoken attitude to sexual mores in some of the lighter journals, particularly in the illustrated press. The latter, however, are hardly differentiated from the cheap and sensational publications which have flooded the market in the second decade of statehood.

Mass immigration has led to the expansion of Israel's non-Hebrew press which has been in existence since the last third of the 19th century. In 1968, in addition to the 15 Hebrew dailies, there were also nine dailies in other languages (Yiddish, Arabic, Bulgarian, English, French, Polish, Hungarian, Rumanian, and German). The future of many of these papers is questionable, since they are likely to disappear as their readers learn Hebrew.

For a list of Hebrew newspapers see Supplementary lists in vol. 1; see also under the individual names of newspapers and periodicals.

Bibliographical Note: There is no up-to-date and detailed bibliography of the Hebrew press from its beginnings to the present day. Most of the lists enumerated in S. Shunami's *Bibliography of Jewish Bibliographies* (1965[2]), p. 94, are out-of-date. Statistics on the world Hebrew press appear in J. Fraenkel's *The Jewish Press of the*

World (1967[6]). There is a government bibliography of papers appearing in 1967 in Israel in all languages: *Newspapers and Periodicals Appearing in Israel* (1967). Generally speaking Hebrew papers that appeared outside Ereẓ Israel were better preserved. The largest collections of Hebrew papers and periodicals are to to be found in the National University Library in Jerusalem and the Zalman Pevsner press collection in Tel Aviv (now in the possession of Tel Aviv University; see, Shunami, Bibl, 633, p. 13). MONOGRAPHS. There is no comprehensive monograph on the Hebrew press throughout the world from its beginnings to the present. There are, however, monographs on individual papers and journals, mentioned in the articles on these papers. General descriptions exist only as regards Ereẓ Israel and the United States. [G.K.]

Bibliography: PRESS IN PALESTINE: G. Kressel, *Toledot ha-Ittonut ha-Ivrit be-Ereẓ Yisrael* (1964); G. Yardeni, *Ha-Ittonut ha-Ivrit be Ereẓ Yisrael bi-Shenot 1863–1904* (1969); *Sefer ha-Shanah shel ha-Ittona'im, 1941–1968* (1969); A. Barness, *The Israel Press* (1961); H. Kanaan, *Milḥamtah shel ha-Ittonut. Ma'avak ha-Ittonut ha-Ivrit be-Ereẓ Yisrael Neged ha-Shilton ha-Briti* (1969). HEBREW PRESS IN NORTH AMERICA: F. M. Brody, in: AJHSP, 33 (1934), 127–70; M. G. Brown, in: AJHSQ, 59 (1969), 139–78; D. Persky, in: M. Ribalow (ed.), *Sefer ha-Yovel shel Hadoar* (1952), 21–27; H. M. Rotblatt, in: S. Rawidowicz (ed.), *The Chicago Pinkas* (1952), 35–68; E. R. Malachi, in: *Hadoar*, 12 (1931/32), 515, 533, 548; 13 (1932/33), 44, 76, 140 (bibl. on the Hebrew press in the U.S.

NEW TESTAMENT (Gr. ἡ καινὴ διαθήκη), the Christian Holy Scriptures (other than the Hebrew Bible and the Apocrypha). The name in Greek is the translation of the Hebrew words "*Berit Ḥadashah*" in Jeremiah 31:30: "Lo, the days are coming when I will make a new covenant with the House of Israel and the House of Judah." Since Jeremiah states clearly that the "new covenant" will be made with Israel and Judah, and not with other nations, there is nothing in this passage at variance with the Jewish Holy Scriptures. The confrontation, however, of the New Testament with the Hebrew Bible—which the Christians refer to as the Old Testament—as two conflicting covenants, is already found in the Gospel of Luke (22:20) and in Paul's Epistles (e.g., I Cor. 11:25; II Cor. 3:6, 14). The New Testament, which contains 27 separate compositions, consists of two parts of different size and quality: (1) the four Gospels, Matthew, Mark, Luke, and John; (2) The Apostles (or *Apostolikon*), i.e., the Acts of the Apostles, the 13 Epistles by Paul, the Epistles to the Hebrews, two Epistles by Peter, three Epistles by John, one by James, one by Jude, and the Revelation of John (The Apocalypse).

Composition and Acceptance of the Various Writings. The works contained in the New Testament were composed by various authors at different periods. The Gospels have their source in the oral traditions which the Apostles and their disciples transmitted to the simple folk among the Jewish Nazarenes in Aramaic; to the few learned men among them, perhaps, in Hebrew; and to the gentiles in Greek. The written literature of the New Testament begins with Paul's Epistles, transcribed in numerous copies by the gentile Christian churches and read aloud in those pagan communities, which had become "messianic" ("Christian"). Educated gentile Christians also read the Epistles by themselves. The oral traditions were eventually adapted and committed to writing, as the three Synoptic Gospels (so called because of their many agreements in subject, order, and language) and, the Fourth Gospel, according to John. The first and earliest among the Synoptic Gospels is Mark (although some authorities dispute this), which was written on the eve of the destruction of the Temple (66–68 C.E.); this was followed by Matthew, approximately 80–90 C.E., and Luke, approximately 90–100 C.E. The Gospel of John followed (a point also disputed by some modern scholars) in approximately 115–125 C.E.

Not all the various writings sacred to Christianity were accepted by all the Christian Churches and canonized at the time of their composition; some were accepted only after a long struggle had been waged in their behalf. Much controversy, for instance, surrounded the Epistle to the Hebrews, which some of the Church Fathers attributed to Paul, others denying his authorship. Similar disputes arose over other early Christian writings, some of which retain a Jewish-Christian flavor (e.g., the *Didache). Still other writings— e.g., apocryphal gospels, which at one point were considered sacred and part of the canon— were completely rejected by some or all of the Christian Churches. All of the *Apocrypha and some of the Pseudepigrapha—those writings which Judaism excluded from the canon of the Bible, but which have been preserved in Greek, Ethiopian, Syriac, Armenian, or Slavic translation—were accepted by the Catholic and Orthodox Churches as a connecting link, so to speak, between the two testaments, and the Protestant Church, among its various denominations, likewise accepted some of them.

Canonization. The earliest known canon of the New Testament was compiled by Marcion, a fanatic believer in Paul and the Pauline writings, who denied the divine origin and sanctity of the Hebrew Bible. Dating to about 140 C.E., it consists of the Gospel of Luke (Paul's disciple), and the *Apostolikon*, comprising ten Epistles by Paul. (Marcion denied the authenticity of the Pastoral Epistles to Timothy and Titus, and the Epistle to the Hebrews.) The Muratorian canon (named after the Milanese librarian, Muratori, who discovered it), dating from the end of the second century, lists all the New Testament writings included in the present version, except for a few Epistles. About 160–170 C.E., Tatian, one of the Church Fathers, wrote a Gospel harmony (*Diatessaron*)—a combined version of all the four Gospels—for the eastern Syrians, which remained in use for many years. This work, however, failed to reproduce the true spirit of any one of the Gospels: it was only a "compromise," designed to eliminate the contradictions between the Synoptic Gospels and John, as well as those among the three Synoptic Gospels themselves. By 200 C.E. the New Testament contained nearly all the books which comprise it today, several of Paul's Epistles and the Revelation of John excepted. Dispute over these works persisted until about 600 C.E., in most of the Christian Churches—the Greek and the Latin, and especially the Eastern Church—but finally they were accepted among the 27 books.

The Language of the New Testament. Although the language of the New Testament, in the form that it exists today, is Greek, two earlier influences are still discernible.

(1) THE INFLUENCE OF THE ARAMAIC-HEBREW ORIGINAL. Because most of the authors were Jewish Nazarenes, they spoke, for the most part, Aramaic, and some also mishnaic Hebrew. This influence, which was detectable particularly in the original versions of Mark and Matthew, survives to some degree in their extant Greek versions and in several of the Epistles as well, including James and Jude. The rest of the works were originally written in Greek.

(2) THE SEPTUAGINT. Since this translation was used by many authors, the New Testament contains not only Aramaic words and phrases, which the disciples heard from Jesus and took care to remember out of reverence for their master (e.g. *Talitha Kumi* (Mark 5:41), *Kum, Rabboni, Eli, Eli (Elohi, Elohi) lama sabachthani* (Matt. 27:46; Mark 15:34)), but also expressions and phrases which retain their Hebrew flavor although they were transmitted through the Greek translation of the Hebrew Bible.

The Greek of the New Testament is not the literary Greek of the period in which it was composed, but primarily that spoken by the people at the time (Koine), a language known from the discoveries in Egypt in modern times of the many Greek inscriptions and papyri dealing with everyday life, from *ostraca* and from private and official letters, as well as government proclamations.

The Ethic of the New Testament. Since most of the authors of the New Testament were Jewish Christians or "God-fearing" gentiles who had converted to Christianity, the spirit of Judaism is discernible even in the compositions originally written in this popular Greek. The New Testament is still far removed from the absolute deification of Jesus, and even more so from the later idea of the Trinity. The ethic of the New Testament is a Jewish ethic, although of an extreme kind, "not of this world": Jesus, the Messiah, was crucified and ascended to Heaven, but will return to earth at the end of the days—the Parousia—and sit on the seat of judgment "at the right hand of the Almighty"; after the "pangs of the Messiah," which will precede this second and final coming, the prophet Elijah will blow the "*shofar* of the Messiah" (i.e., of the days of the Messiah) and the Kingdom of Heaven will rule upon earth. The period between the Crucifixion and the Parousia is thus a period of transition, and the ethic that ought to prevail is that of a transient world, not of an enduring one.

See also *Christianity; *Jesus; *Jewish-Christian Sects.

Bibliography: C. G. Montefiore, *Synoptic Gospels*, 2 vols. (1968[2]); I. Abrahams, *Studies in Pharisaism and the Gospels* (1967[2]); J. Klausner, *Jesus of Nazareth* (1929); idem, *From Jesus to Paul* (1946); A. Harnack, *Das Neue Testament um das Jahr 200* (1889); T. Zahn, *Geschichte des Neutestamentlichen Kanons* . . ., 1 (1888); 2 (1892); B. F. Westcott, *A General Survey of the History of the Canon of the New Testament* (1896[7]); A. Thumb, *Die griechische Sprache im Zeitalter des Hellenismus* (1901); H. Lietzmann, *Wie wurden die Buecher des Neuen Testaments Heilige Schrift?* (1907, =*Kleine Schriften*, 2 (1958), 15–98); J. Leipoldt, *Geschichte des Neutestamentlichen Kanons*, 1–2 (1907–08); H. P. V. Nunn, *The Elements of New Testament Greek* (1945[8]); A. Souter, *The Text and Canon of the New Testament* (1954[2]). [J.Kl./Ed.]

NEW YEAR. The Mishnah (RH 1:1) enumerates four separate days of the year, each of which is regarded as a New Year (Heb. Rosh Ha-Shanah, lit. "head of the year"). The fixing of those dates was essential, not only for civil and political purposes, but for the regulations concerning the procedure regarding the religious injunctions connected with agricultural produce. Since, for example, the tithe had to be given of animal produce, the fruit from the first three years of a tree's growth *(*orlah)* was forbidden, and the beginning and end of the *Sabbatical year had to be determined, it was necessary to lay down when the year began for those various calculations. With one exception (and that only according to Bet Hillel; see *Bet Hillel and Bet Shammai) all the New Years begin on the first of the month.

(1) The first of Nisan is the New Year for (Jewish) kings and for the religious calendar (for festivals). Thus if a king ascended the throne during Adar, the next month would constitute the second year of his reign, and Passover is the first festival of the year. The Talmud (RH 7a) adds that it is also the New Year for the purchase of congregational sacrifices with the shekalim (see *Shekel) collected in Adar, and for the renting of houses.

(2) The first of Elul is the New Year for the tithing of cattle (but see the first of Tishri), i.e., tithes had to be given for all cattle born between the first of Elul and the 30th of Av.

(3) The first of Tishri is the New Year for the civil calendar (including the counting of the reigns of foreign kings; see RH 3a–b and cf. Git. 8:5) for the Sabbatical and Jubilee years (plowing and planting being forbidden from that date), and for the year of planting of fruit and vegetables. The establishment of the first of Tishri as the religious New Year (see *Rosh Ha-Shanah) depends upon the statement that on that day "all the world is judged" (RH 1:2). According to R. Simeon and R. Eleazar the first of Tishri is also the New Year for the tithing of cattle and therefore there are only three New Years.

(4) The first of Shevat is the New Year for trees, according to Bet Shammai, but Bet Hillel fixed the date as the 15th of Shevat, and since the *halakhah* is established accordingly, it is this date which is celebrated today (see *Tu bi-Shevat). The reason given in the Talmud (RH 14a) is that on that date the greater part of the year's rain has fallen.

Only Rosh Ha-Shanah is fully celebrated, though in recent times a minor celebration has developed, especially in Israel, for Tu bi-Shevat. The others, as stated, are merely for calendrical computations. [Ed.]

NEW YORK CITY, foremost city of the Western Hemisphere and largest urban Jewish community in history; pop. 7,771,730 (1970), est. Jewish pop. 1,836,000 (1968); metropolitan area 11,448,480 (1970), metropolitan area Jewish (1968), 2,381,000 (including Nassau, Suffolk, Rockland, and Westchester counties).

This entry is arranged according to the following outline:

1654–1870. Dutch Colonial Period. The arrival of some 23 Sephardi (see *Sephardim in U.S.) and Ashkenazi Jews on the French privateer *St. Catherine* early in September 1654 marked the end of a tortuous journey which began earlier in the year when they left Recife, Brazil, after helping in the unsuccessful defense of the Dutch possession from Portuguese attack, rather than stay and face the Inquisition. The director general of New Netherland, Peter Stuyvesant, and the dominie Johannes Megapolensis tried to refuse haven to the penniless and tired refugees. They protested to the Dutch West India Company against the possible settlement of a "deceitful race" who professed an "abominable religion" and whose worship at the "feet of Mammon" would threaten and limit the profit of loyal subjects of the company. While Stuyvesant's plea was under consideration, other Jews including David de Ferrara and Abraham de *Lucena arrived in the spring of 1655. The population as a whole accepted the group. Instructions from the Dutch West India Company followed letters written by the Jews to their coreligionists in the company, which directed that newcomers be permitted to live, trade, and travel in New Netherland, and, in effect, to have the same privileges enjoyed in the Netherlands. Probably in deference to Stuyvesant, and due to the small size of the Jewish colony, the Jews, although permitted a burial ground, were not allowed to build a synagogue.

Despite the orders of the company the newcomers faced

Figure 1. The burial ground off Chatham Square, the oldest Jewish cemetery in New York, established in 1682.

other obstacles. The right to trade with some areas including Albany was denied as were rights to serve in the militia in lieu of paying a special tax, to own land, and to engage in retail trades such as that of baker. These restrictions were all challenges put forth by Stuyvesant. The Jews' response was twofold. The first took the form of a series of petitions drawn by Abraham de Lucena, Salvador d'Andrada, and Jacob Cohen Henriques addressed to the company in 1655 and 1656. The answers were affirmative. Burgher right, the right to conduct retail and wholesale trade in New Amsterdam, was extended to Jews in 1657, and the right to hold property was also upheld. Some Jews fought Stuyvesant on his own ground. Asser *Levy and Jacob *Barsimon (who had arrived with Solomon Pietersen in August 1654, prior to the main body of settlers) began a successful court action in November 1655 to permit Jews to serve in the militia in lieu of the payment of a special derogatory tax. Primary civil rights were thus gained within a few years of settlement.

Having secured a foothold, the first Jews began the task of sustaining themselves. While economic opportunity in the province was quite limited as compared to the opportunities available in the more stable, secure, and richer markets of Europe and the Caribbean, the average Jew managed well. In 1655 Jewish taxpayers paid 8% of the cost of the Palisade or "Waal," later the site of Wall Street, while they comprised only about 2% of the assessed population at the time. The most prominent and successful merchant was Asser Levy, whose career was as unique as it was fruitful. One of the founding group, Levy, a butcher and tanner by trade, carried on his business just outside the city's wall. He expanded his interests to real estate and trade within the city, as well as in communities along the Hudson River. Levy was one of the few pioneer Jews who remained and died in the province and whose descendants could be traced to 18th-century New York.

English Colonial Period. The surrender of New Amsterdam to the British in 1664 brought a number of changes to the Jewish settlement. Generally, civil and religious rights were widened. Jews were permitted to hold and be elected to public office and restrictions on the building of a synagogue were lifted. While there is some evidence that a synagogue existed as early as 1695, it was undoubtedly a private home used for this purpose by the Jewish community. Shearith Israel, the first congregation in New York, was probably organized in about 1706. Between 1729 and 1730 the congregation erected the first synagogue, a small building on Mill Lane—known also as Mud Lane—the site of present South William Street. This event occurred some 75 years after the original settlement and was an indication of its permanence, as well as of the acceptance by English authority of the Jewish economic and social position. Interestingly, the London and Curaçao communities, which were also founded in 1654, had built synagogues within a few years of their founding. The hesitancy of New York Jews was probably due to the smallness of their numbers, as well as to the transient nature of their status and to governmental opposition.

The roots of the colony depended upon their economic viability. During this period the Jewish merchant took a major interest in the business of overseas trade, partly because ocean traffic negated somewhat onerous local control and requirements and partly because it provided a measure of freedom which allowed him to use his special skills. Movement from place to place was its own protection—investments were widespread and thus less vulnerable. The transient, wandering Jew was an answer to the ghetto and enclosing walls, for he was more difficult to tax and to ghettoize. He carried his wealth with him, and he had knowledge of languages—Hebrew, Yiddish, German, Spanish, Portuguese, Dutch. In the Nathan Simson correspondence letters are written in three and sometimes four languages. He had a knowledge of the international market, and his kinsmen were in the Caribbean, Italy, Spain, the Near East, and India. This provided an opportunity not usually afforded the restricted Catholic or Protestant. Certain markets were specialties. When in 1699 Governor Bellomont wanted a bag of jewels which had been seized from an accused pirate appraised, he "ordered a Jew in town to be present, he understanding Jewells well."

Jews concentrated on such commodities as conditions required. They were among the first to introduce cocoa and chocolate to England and were heavily engaged in the coral, textile, and slave trades, and at times had virtual monopolies in the ginger trade. They are also said to have introduced spermaceti candles to the colonies. In 1701 Jewish merchants accounted for 12% of those engaged in overseas trade, though they represented only about 2% of the general population. In 1776 they were less than 1% of the population and less than 1% of the overseas merchants. The decline of the overseas trade indicated not only that New York Jews had become rooted but also that they had found other means of earning a living. The colonial transience gave way to permanence.

During this process Jews had struggled to obtain full citizenship, especially as it applied to trade. The Jew who wished to engage in overseas or wholesale trade had to face the question of his status, whether he was an alien or a citizen. As a citizen, except for some ambiguity with respect to his right to vote or hold office, he was allowed most rights including the right to trade. Since the English accepted Dutch citizenship equally with English, Jews who

Figure 2. David Salisbury Franks, provision agent in New York for the British army during the 17th-century French and Indian War. From *American Jewish Yearbook 1923–24*, Philadelphia, Pa.

were burghers of New Amsterdam, as well as native-born colonists, continued to be citizens under British rule. The problems facing aliens, the status of the majority of Jews, were clearly set forth in the Trade and Navigation Acts

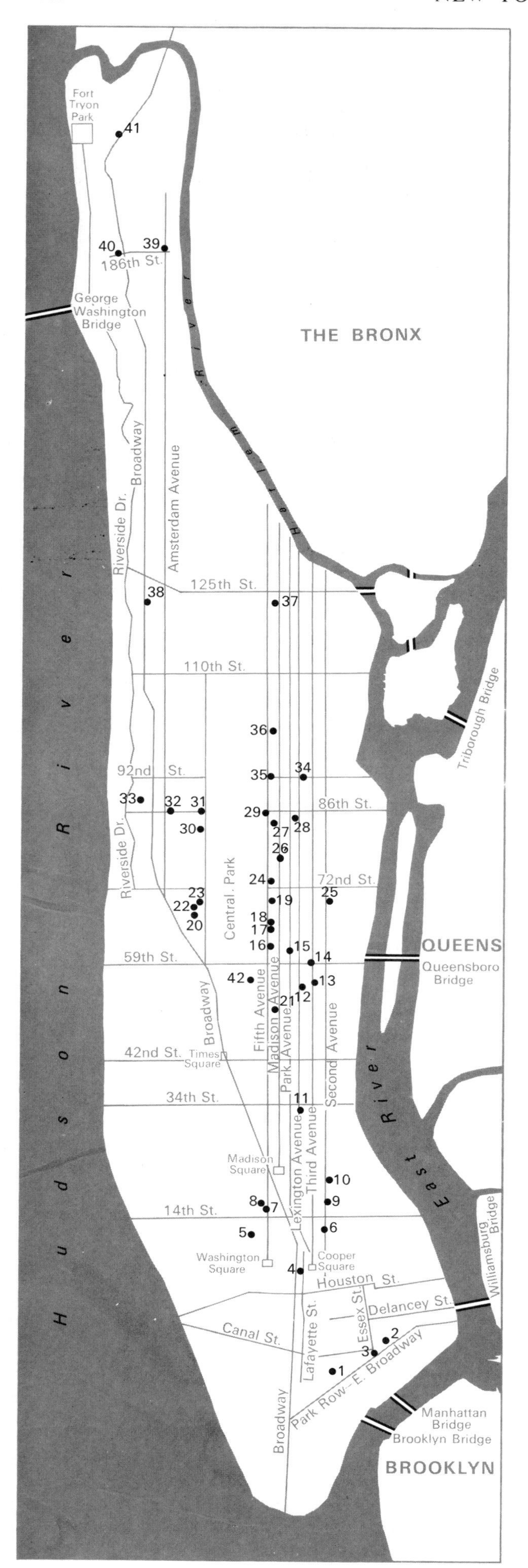

SYNAGOGUES

23 —Shearith Israel—18 W. 70th St.
33 —B'nai Jeshurun—257 W. 88th
28 —Kehilath Jeshurun—125 E. 85th
17 —Temple Emanu-El—5th Ave. and 65th St.
40 —K'hal Adath Jeshurun—85 Bennett Ave.
16 —Fifth Ave. Synagogue—5 E. 62nd St.
22 —Free Synagogue—30 W. 68th St.
30 —Rodeph Shalom—7 W. 83rd St.
32 —The Jewish Center—131 W. 86th St.
31 —S.A.J. Reconstructionist—15 W. 86th St.
12 —Central Synagogue—125 E. 55th St.

CEMETERIES

1 —Chatham Square Cemetery
5 —11th St. Cemetery—11th St. between 5th and 6th Avenues

HOSPITALS AND PHILANTHROPIC ORGANIZATIONS

36 —Mount Sinai—5th Ave.—Madison Ave; 97th St.—100th St.
41 —Jewish Memorial—Broadway and 196th St.
9 —Beth Israel—17th St. and Stuyvesant Square
37 —Joint Diseases—1919 Madison Ave.
21 —Hadassah—65 E. 52nd St.
42 —U.J.A.—1290 Ave. of the Americas
10 —United Hebrew Charities—356 2nd Ave.

YIDDISH INSTITUTIONS

6 —Yiddish Art Theater—2nd Ave., 12th St. (not in use)
3 —"Forward" Building—175 E. Broadway
29 —YIVO—1048 5th Ave.
26 —Atran Yiddish Culture House—25 E. 78th St.

ISRAEL INSTITUTIONS

19 —Israel Consulate—11 E. 70th St.
15 —Jewish Agency—515 Park Ave.

EDUCATIONAL INSTITUTIONS

2 —Educational Alliance— 197 E. Broadway St.
20 —Jewish Institute of Religion—40 W. 68th St.
38 —Jewish Theological Seminary—Broadway and 122nd St.
39 —Yeshiva University—Amsterdam Ave. and 186th St.
4 —HIAS—425 Lafayette St. (not in use)
35 —Jewish Museum—1109 5th Ave.
34 —92nd St. Young Men's Hebrew Association—Lexington Ave. and E. 92nd St.

RELIGIOUS AND COMMUNITY RELATIONS ORGANIZATIONS

13 —American Jewish Committee—165 E. 56th St.
27 —American Jewish Congress—15 E. 84th St.
24 —New York Board of Rabbis—10 E. 73th St.
8 —National Council of Young Israel—3 W. 16th St.
7 —Union of Orthodox Jewish Congregations—84 5th. Ave.
25 —United Synagogue—218 E. 70th St.
18 —Union of American Hebrew Congregations—838 5th Ave.
14 —Federation of Jewish Philanthropies—130 E. 59th St.
11 —B'nai B'rith—315 Lexington Ave.

Places of Jewish interest in Manhattan.

passed between 1650 and 1663. This central body of British law applying to the colonies was intended not only to foster mercantilism but also to prevent the encroachment upon trade by "Jews, French and other foreigners ..." Under these acts aliens could not engage in British commerce without severe penalty.

The necessity for some form of citizenship was made manifest by the Rabba Couty affair. In November 1671 Couty's ship *Trial* was condemned by the Jamaica Vice-Admiralty Court on the ground that Couty, a Jew, was by definition a foreigner. In appealing the decision in England to the Council of Trade and Plantations, Couty obtained certificates from Governor Lovelace of New York indicating that he had been a free burgher of New York for several years. On this evidence and the fact that the ship and crew were English, the council held the sentence illegal. Those Jews, therefore, who could prove native birth did not need to bother with naturalization proceedings, but the alien Jew had to become a citizen if he was to engage in foreign trade. In general, however, the Jews in New York found that the procurement of naturalization, the right to trade and hold property, and the right of inheritance were not too difficult to obtain. Merchants in England were rarely naturalized; mostly they were endenizened—i.e., they could trade, but not hold real estate. In New York, on the other hand, 46 Jews were naturalized but only six endenizened. Freemanship, the right to engage in retail trade, was also relatively easy to obtain, despite instances of prohibition. Forty-seven Jews were made freeman between 1688 and 1770.

The decline of the overseas trade brought a corresponding increase in the numbers of Jews who were local retailers and craftsmen. They engaged in the sale of a wide range of goods, such as guns (especially during war), rum, wine, ironware, glass, furs, and foodstuff. The advertisements of such merchants as Jacob Franks, Rodrigo *Pacheco, Judah *Hays, and Sampson *Simson often appeared in newspapers. They were frequently in partnership with non-Jews, such as members of the Livingston, Cuyler, or Alexander families. In some instances such partnerships developed into long friendships, as was the case of Rodrigo Pacheco with James Alexander. Myer *Myers, made freeman in 1746, became a noted silversmith and goldsmith whose work was much in demand and is displayed today in many museums. Benjamin *Etting, also a goldsmith, was made a freeman in 1769; Michael Solomon *Hays in 1769 was a watchmaker; and Abraham Isaacs in 1770, a tailor. Such occupations were not found in the period of initial settlement. Few Jews were found in the professions during this period. Dr. Elias Woolin was in the city in 1744, but there were no Jewish members of the bar, though Jews represented about 10% of the litigants in the various courts. In addition, some Jews were not successful financially. A number, including Isaac Levy, Moses Hart, and Michael Jacobs, became insolvent debtors. Some were jailed and others, such as Aaron Machado and Abraham Myers Cohen, were written off as bad debts.

During the period of British control Jewish merchants were able to hold many positions of responsibility. Jacob *Franks and his son David were provision agents for the Crown during the French and Indian War. Sampson Simson was a member of the group who received the charter for the Chamber of Commerce in 1770. Perhaps the highest position held by a Jew in colonial New York was that of colonial agent representing the colony's interests in Parliament. This post was given to Rodrigo Pacheco in 1731. Daniel and Mordecai Gomez were Spanish interpreters to the Supreme Court in New York. A number of Jews were elected to office, generally to the position of constable

Figure 3. Painting of the first synagogue in New York, the Mill Street building of Congregation Shearith Israel, erected 1729–30. From *American Jewish Historical Quarterly*, Vol. 21, New York, 1913.

or assessor. Members of the Hays family made the constabulary something of a tradition. Christian oaths necessary for office, voting, and naturalization were often modified or eliminated for the Jewish citizen. It was quite unusual for Jews to hold office in the other colonies, and the fact that they did in New York was an indication of the cosmopolitan nature of the colony and its general acceptance of the Jewish community. There was no ghetto and little overt anti-Jewish feeling in the colony. Most of the Jewish population lived in the area below Wall Street, generally in the Dock and South wards facing the East River, mixed among their Christian neighbors. Jacob Franks lived off Coenties Slip and Asser Levy resided on Stone Street, as did Jacob Acosta. The burial ground off present-day Chatham Square was also on the East Side at the end of Pearl Street, the main road through that part of town. In 1748 the Swedish naturalist Peter Kalm, then residing in the colony, wrote that Jews "enjoyed all the privileges common to the other inhabitants of the town or the province."

Exact census figures are not easily gained, but for most of the 17th and 18th centuries Jews represented between 1% and 2% of the total New York City population. In 1700 there were 17 households listed in the assessment rolls; estimating this at six per family, there were about 100 persons or 2% of the general population of 4,500. In 1722, 20 households are named or about 1½%. A peak of 31 families was recorded in 1728, about 2.3% of the general population of 8,000. This was followed by a gradual decline to 19 families in 1734, or 1.2%. In that year Jews paid 1.9% of the city's taxes; in 1722 they had paid 2%. As a group they were seemingly slightly more affluent than their neighbors. After 1734 there are no extant assessment lists for New York City, so population figures are hazardous, but it is fairly safe to rely on the 1% figure for the remaining period, although it may have been more.

Congregation Shearith Israel provided a cohesive force. Not the least of its functions was to provide a secular education, for there were no public schools. Religious subjects, as well as arithmetic and English, were taught by itinerant teachers, such as Moses Fonseca who was brought in from Curaçao to be a *ḥazzan* as well as teacher. There were strong pressures for intermarriage. Limited numbers and hostility between Sephardim and Ashkenazim, plus a basic tolerance, created a conducive atmosphere. In 1742 Phila Franks, daughter of Jacob and Abigail Franks, one of the most noted Jewish families, married Oliver Delancey, an aristocrat and an Episcopalian. A few months later her brother David married Margaret Evans of Philadelphia; their children were baptized. By the eve of the American

Revolution the pioneer Jewish citizens—the Pinheiros, De Mesquitas, Asser Levys, and their descendants—had all but disappeared from the New York scene. This was unlike the London and Curacao experience and can be explained in part by an easier social mobility and tolerance.

REVOLUTIONARY PERIOD. The advent of the American Revolution found the Jewish community divided. In the past Jews had expressed their patriotism toward the Crown by word and deed. Numbers of Jews served in the colonial wars. Samuel Myers Cohen, Jacob Franks, and others were in the militia during the King George War, Abraham Solomon died in service during the French and Indian War and others had served aboard privateers. Some, such as members of the Franks family, were commissary agents for the British government. New York Jews, however, along with many others, sensed the emancipatory action of the Revolution and the possibility of full civil and political rights. Between 1768 and 1770 some 11 Jewish merchants, including Samuel *Judah, Hayman *Levy, and Jonas *Phillips, signed Non-Importation Articles which sought repeal of the Townsend Acts. The conquest of the city by the British in 1776 caused many Jews to flee to unoccupied places, such as Philadelphia and several locations in Connecticut. One supporter of the American cause was Haym *Solomon, who for a time was imprisoned by the British as a spy. *Ḥazzan* Gershom Mendes *Seixas fled to Philadelphia and helped found Congregation Mikveh Israel in that city. Others, confident of British justice, chose to stay, and the congregation carried on services during the occupation. Among the Loyalists were Abraham Wagg, who left for England in 1779 and attempted reconciliation between the contending factions. Uriah *Hendricks, a noted merchant, remained loyal. David Franks was accused by Congress of being a Loyalist and relieved of his commissary rights with the American government. He held a similar post under the British. He also left for England, but returned after the war for a time. The majority of Jews preferred a neutral position in the conflict, partly in fear of the consequences of a wrong guess. Jews sympathetic with the British cause knew what to expect from England but did not know what their status would be under the new government. Patriotic Jews, on the other hand, looked forward to a new freedom.

Figure 4. The synagogue of Congregation Shearith Israel, on Crosby Street, occupied from 1834 to 1860. From H. Grinstein, *Rise of the Jewish Community oj New York,* Philadelphia, 1945.

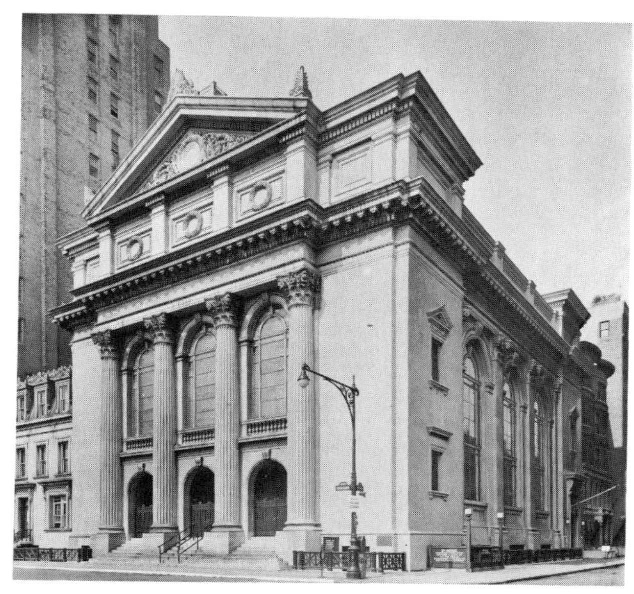

Figure 5. The present synagogue of Congregation Shearith Israel, designed by Arnold Brunner and built in 1897 at Central Park West and 70th Street. Photo Charles Kanarian, New York.

EARLY AMERICAN PERIOD. The end of the Revolution brought many distinct changes. Civil liberties, which were often a matter of governmental whim under the English, became part of the New York State constitution. Opportunities were expanded and new fields opened. Within a decade after the Revolution Judah Zuntz and Solomon *Simson were admitted to the bar. Benjamin *Seixas and Ephraim *Hart were among the founders of the New York Stock Exchange in 1792. Gershom Mendes Seixas served as a trustee of Columbia College from 1784 to 1814, and was one of 14 ministers who participated at George *Washington's first inaugural in April 1789, and Col. David M. Franks was one of the marshals in charge of the processional at the inaugural. Among the first Jewish graduates of Columbia College was Sampson Simson in 1800. Walter Judah, admitted to the college in 1795, also attended the medical school. He died while treating the sick during the yellow fever epidemic of 1798. In 1818 Governor DeWitt Clinton attended the opening of Shearith Israel when the congregation rebuilt the synagogue on the Mill Street site. No colonial governor is known to have ever shown such deference to the community.

The Revolution reduced the Jewish population to less than 1% of the population. It remained thus until the 1830s and 1840s, when an influx of German and Polish Jews caused a sudden rise to perhaps 15,000 in 1847 and to some 40,000, or approximately 4%, on the eve of the Civil War. Replacing the old and for the most part extinct pioneer generation were mostly German Jews, such as Harmon *Hendricks, son of Uriah, a mid-18th-century immigrant, who established possibly the first copper-rolling mill in the country in 1813. One of the distinctive changes in postwar New York was Jewish involvement in the political life of the community, perhaps best seen in the career of Mordecai Manuel *Noah. Born in Philadelphia in 1785, he entered into public service as consul to Tunis in 1813. He became a member of the Democratic Party and was elected high sheriff of New York in 1821, surveyor of the port from 1829 to 1833, and judge of the Court of Sessions in 1841. In 1825 he started the unsuccessful Jewish settlement of Ararat on the Niagara River. As editor of the newspaper *The Evening Star* during the 1830s, he broke with Andrew Jackson and became a founder of the Whig and Nativist parties. His espousal of Jewish causes and his involvement with politics are a distinct example of the interests of the community. His funeral in 1851 was attended with most elaborate ceremony by the Jewish settlement. The publishers Naphtali *Phillips and Naphtali *Judah were powers in the Tammany Society in the first two decades of the 19th century. Mordecai *Myers was elected to the state assembly in 1829 and 1831, while Emanuel B. *Hart was elected to the House of Representatives in 1851. He also held the posts of surveyor of the port and president of the Board of Aldermen. Greater social mobility of the Jews after the Revolution could be seen in their movement uptown from the area below Wall Street into other parts of the city. Sampson *Isaacs and Naphtali and Benjamin Judah lived in the Third Ward, the present-day Greenwich Village. The residences of Jacob b. *Seixas and Asher Marx were located on the newly burgeoning East Side. The lower midtown area was the residence of Henry Hyman, Isaac *Moses, and Hayman *Seixas. The wealthiest Jews and non-Jews resided a little below and a little above Wall Street. Harmon Hendricks, probably the richest Jew of early 19th-century New York, lived at 61 Greenwich Street. Near him, on this "quality lane," resided the almost equally wealthy Solomon J. *Isaacs, Lewis Marks, and Mrs. Isaac Moses.

The changing character of the community was also evident in the changing religious organization. In 1825 a group of Ashkenazi Jews, led by Barrow E. Cohen and Isaac B. *Kursheedt, complaining of its formality and control, broke away from the parent body, Shearith Israel, and formed the Bnai Jeshurun Congregation. In 1828 another dissenting group of Dutch, German, and Polish Jews broke from Bnai Jeshurun and formed the Congregation Anshe Chesed. In 1839 Polish members of these two groups formed Congregation Shaarey Zedek. Other German Jews formed Shaarey Hashamayim in 1839, Rodeph Shalom in 1842, and Temple Emanu-El in 1845. Dutch Jews established Bnai Israel in 1847 and French, Shaarey Brocho in 1851. The proliferation of congregational organizations and divisions of the Jewish community were due partly to the new freedom resulting from the Revolution. At first, these new congregations used a number of privately owned buildings before erecting their own synagogue buildings in what became a period of synagogue construction. The old Mill Street synagogue was sold by Shearith Israel in 1833 and a new building was erected on Crosby Street. In addition, there were five major synagogue structures in New York by 1860—Bnai Jeshurun on Greene Street, Shaarey Tefilah on Wooster, Anshe Chesed on Norfolk Street, Temple Beth El on 33rd Street, and Rodeph Shalom on Clinton Street. In the 1850s Anshe Chesed was the largest congregation in the United States. By the Civil War, Temple Emanu-El and Shearith Israel were the wealthiest and most influential of the congregations.

Religious organizations produced a number of distinguished leaders. Samuel M. *Isaacs, an English Jew who arrived in New York in 1839, was *ḥazzan* and possibly the first regular preacher in New York City. He was engaged as *ḥazzan* by Bnai Jeshurun and Shaarey Tefilah. From 1859 he edited the *Jewish Messenger*, one of the most influential Jewish periodicals. Jacques Judah *Lyons, the *ḥazzan* of Shearith Israel in the 1840s, compiled material for a proposed history of Jews in America—a task he did not complete. The first ordained rabbis arrived in the 1840s from Europe. Among them were Leo Merzbacher who ministered to Anshe Chesed and Rodeph Shalom and helped in establishing the Reform Temple Emanu-El, where he delivered sermons, attended official functions, and assisted in the education of the children. Others included Dr. Max *Lilienthal, considered the most capable preacher in German, and Dr. Morris J. *Raphall, who had a distinguished career with generally German congregations. *Ḥazzanim* with excellent singing voices who enhanced the synagogue services included Leon Sternberger of Warsaw and Ignatius Ritterman of Cracow.

The period after the Revolutionary War also saw the start of mutual-aid societies and *landsmanshaften*, which generally began as burial societies (*ḥevra kaddisha*). The Hebrah Gemilut Hasadim, organized at Shearith Israel in 1786, disbanded in 1790. As a successor Gershom Mendes Seixas founded Hebrah Hesed Vaemet in 1802, an organization still in existence. In 1826 Bnai Jeshurun formed the Hebrah Gemilut Hesed, known as the Hebrew Mutual Benefit Society, the forerunner of many such societies. The first president of this important group was Isaac B. Kursheedt. Anshe Chesed helped organize several societies, including the Montefiore Society in 1841.

There were also numerous fraternal orders founded, the most important being the Independent Order *B'nai B'rith, founded in 1843 by 12 men, including Henry Jones, Isaac Rosenberg, and R. M. Roadacher. It combined mutual aid and fraternal features to bring harmony and peace among Jews. The groups spread rapidly with lodges and memberships throughout the country. Another such society was the Hebrew Benevolent Society, established in 1822 with Daniel Jackson as its first president. He was succeeded by John I. Hart and Roland M. Mitchell. (These names are an indication of the difficulty of identifying Jews during this period.) In 1820 women of Shearith Israel had organized a Female Hebrew Benevolent Society. In 1844 the German Hebrew Benevolent Society was formed—a more narrowly based *Landsleute* group. These groups worked so well that by the eve of the Civil War few, if any, Jews had to apply to city institutions for aid. The Hebrew Benevolent Society and German Hebrew Benevolent Society united just prior to the Civil War, but other groups continued to maintain independence. Under the urging of Rev. Samuel Isaacs in the *Jewish Messenger* and Dr. Samuel *Adler of Temple Emanu-El, the Hebrew and German societies formed the Hebrew Orphan Asylum in 1859.

For years after the Revolution there were demands for a Jewish hospital. It was not until 1852, however, that Sampson Simson—with the assistance of Shearith Israel and Shaarey Tefilah and a group of native and English Jews—founded "Jews' Hospital in the City of New York."

Figure 6. Synagogue of the Ashkenazi Congregation B'nai Jeshurun, consecrated in 1827. From *American Jewish Historical Quarterly*, Vol. 27, New York, 1920.

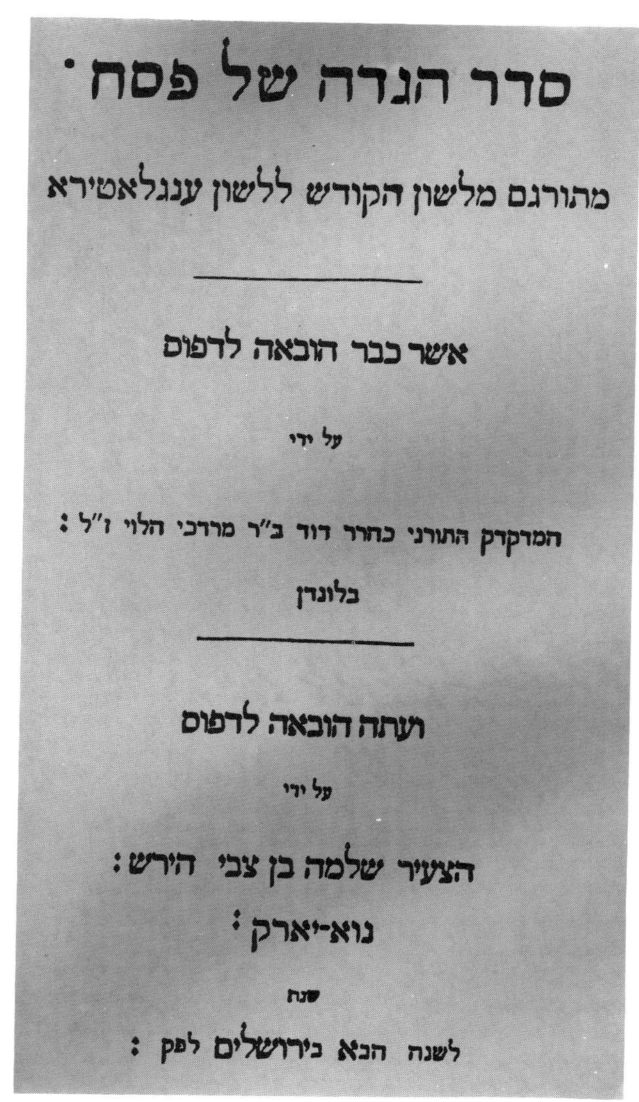
סדר הגדה של פסח ·
מתורגם מלשון הקודש ללשון ענגלאטירא
אשר כבר הובאה לדפוס
על ידי
המדקדק התורני כהרר דוד ב"ר מרדכי הלוי ז"ל :
בלונדן
ועתה הובאה לדפוס
על ידי
הצעיר שלמה בן צבי הירש :
נוא-יארק :
שנת
לשנה הבאה בירושלים לפק :

Figure 7. Hebrew title page of the first Hebrew-English *Haggadah* published in America. New York, 1837. Waltham, Mass., American Jewish Historical Society.

This became known as Mount Sinai in 1866. Contributions from Judah *Touro of New Orleans and N. K. Rosenfeld of Temple Emanu-El, among others, helped in the construction of the building in 1853. Poor patients were given free treatment. The staff, as well as patients, were Jewish and non-Jewish.

Young men's Jewish groups also became part of the social scene of 19th-century New York and reflected a universal interest in education and its dissemination, so much part of Jacksonian America. In 1852 a Hebrew Young Men's Literary Society was founded. A splinter group formed the Philodocean Society, and in 1854 another group formed the Touro Literary Institute. Other groups included the Montefiore Literary Association and the Washington Social Club. In 1858 the Young Men's and Touro groups merged to form the Hebrew Young Men's Literary Society. Jews also organized military organizations which had strong social overtones. These included Troop K, Empire Hussars, and the Young Men's Lafayette Association. Most of these social organizations, which included the Cultur Verein and Sange Verein, were formed as *landsmanshaften*, i.e., Young Men of Germany, Polish Young Men, etc. The Harmonie Club of German Jews is still in existence. Various members of these socially and culturally conscious organizations joined *B'nai B'rith prior to the Civil War and also founded the Maimonides Library Association in 1850. This was a large library, housed on Orchard Street, which was open to the public and filled a great need for such services. Elaborate balls, dinners, and charity concerts given by various organizations did much to enliven New York Jewish society. The annual ball of the Young Men's Hebrew Benevolent Society was first held in 1842, and the annual dinners of the Hebrew and German Hebrew Benevolent Societies were highlights of the social season.

The flourishing of New York Jewish society was expressed by the rise not only of community organizations but also of the press. The late 18th-century bookseller and publisher Benjamin Gomez was joined in his profession by Naphtali Phillips, publisher of the *National Advocate*, and Solomon Jackson, publisher of the first Jewish periodical in the United States, a monthly entitled *The Jew* (issued from 1823 to 1825). The first successful Jewish periodical was Robert Lyon's *The Asmonean* (1848–58), which published the debates between Jewish leaders over the necessity of a union of American Jews. In 1857 Rabbi Samuel Isaacs' *Jewish Messenger* became the voice of Orthodox Judaism and called for a union of Jewish charities, while championing a Jewish free school. There were printers skilled in the use of German type, including Henry Franks who printed a holiday prayer book, *Maḥzor mi-Kol ha-Shanah*, among other items. Isaac Bondi, rabbi of Anshe Chesed, edited the *Hebrew Leader* from 1859 to 1874. Among the works of Jewish authors published during this period were Mordecai Noah's imaginative *Book of Yashar* and Rev. Raphall's *Post-Biblical History of the Jews*. Despite an interest in literature and arts few scholarly works were produced by Jews during this time. Highly skilled Jewish artisans in the tradition of Myer Myers were few, an exception being Jacob R. *Lazarus, a painter and student of Henry Inman, whose works are today in the Metropolitan Museum of Art.

Jewish education varied little from the 18th century, except that free public schools which were Protestant in tone were available from 1805. These schools were extensively used by the Jewish population, especially after they came under governmental control in 1842, slowly gave up sectarianism, and greatly expanded, thus lessening the demand for synagogal day schools. In 1842 Rabbi Samuel Isaacs of Bnai Jeshurun converted an afternoon school to the New York Talmud Torah and Hebrew Institute. It lasted until 1847. Other congregations such as Anshe Chesed and Rodeph Shalom also started short-lived Hebrew and English schools. Jews generally objected to the teaching of Christian ethics and the use of Christian textbooks in public schools. Such objections were influential in the expansion of Hebrew schools in the 1850s. Bnai Jeshurun, Temple Emanu-El, Shaarey Zedek, and Shearith Israel all started parochial day schools combining secular and religious education. By 1854 there were seven such schools and there was great debate in the community over their necessity. As in the colonial period, the education of Jewish girls was not considered too important; they were either sent to public schools or taught by private tutors. A few unsuccessful attempts were made to establish institutions of higher education. Sampson Simson organized the Jewish Theological Seminary and Scientific Institution, but aside from this little was accomplished. Jews of New York did not support Isaac Wise's Zion Collegiate Institute in Cincinnati and little was done for Samuel M. Isaacs' Hebrew high school founded in the 1850s. Although these attempts were unsuccessful, teaching and learning took place and the interest in Jewish affairs was kept up, principally through the press.

Several world events stirred the New York Jewish community. The *Mortara case in Italy in 1859, where a

Jewish boy was converted to Christianity despite family objections, led S. M. Isaacs to form the *Board of Delegates of the American Israelites; it was intended to protect and secure civil and religious rights of Jews in the U.S. and abroad. An earlier episode, the *Damascus Affair (an accusation of ritual murder against the Jews of Damascus), led to several mass meetings in 1840 which requested President Van Buren to protest this accusation.

There was tremendous diversity to Jewish business interests during this period. Generally, however, the latter centered on small retail shops and small handicraft businesses. Some Jews held posts in civil service, generally of a minor nature, an exception being Albert *Cardozo, justice of the Supreme Court of New York. There were a few men of prominence in business. Hayman *Levy, one of the largest fur traders in the colonies, employed John Jacob Astor in his business after the Revolution. Another was Eli Hart, who was engaged in the wheat and flour business. Daniel Jackson was a noted broker and banker. Bernhard *Hart was honorary secretary of the New York Stock Exchange from 1831 to 1853. August *Belmont represented Rothschild interests in New York after he replaced Joseph L. and J. Josephs in 1836.

Civil War. The Civil War found the Jewish community, like the rest of the country, divided over the issue of slavery. New York City in many ways resembled a Southern city. Though slavery itself was prohibited after 1827, schools and theaters were segregated. Many Jews, including members of the Manumission Society of New York City, had freed their slaves, others retained them until forced to set them free. Mordecai M. Noah supported the pro-slavery position, as did Dr. Morris J. Raphall, who observed that the Ten Commandments condoned slavery. This position was attacked by Michael *Heilprin, writing in the *Tribune*, and he was joined by Rev. Samuel M. Isaacs as well as many others. With the start of the war the Jewish response was overwhelmingly in favor of the Union. On April 20, 1861, Joseph *Seligman was vice-president of a Union meeting held at Union Square. His firm, J. and J. Seligman & Co., sold federal bonds in the astonishing sum of $200,000,000. Although Jews enlisted quickly, there was strong anti-Jewish bias in the army. At first Jewish chaplains were not permitted to serve, but Samuel M. Isaacs and his son Myer were among the leaders of the successful struggle to change the restrictive terms of the law. Jewish soldiers were dispersed throughout the army, and there were few Jewish enclaves, except for Company D of the 8th, New York, National Guard.

Jews also supported the war effort by aiding the United States Sanitary Commission, and held numerous Purim balls or Feasts of Esther to help the sick and wounded. Shearith Israel, Anshe Chesed, and Temple Emanu-El were in the forefront of the effort to raise money for the war effort. The 1864 Sanitary Fair in New York, the largest held during the war, found Benjamin Nathan and Moses Lazarus on the executive committee and Moses Schloss and Lewis May on the general committee. The Jews Hospital opened its wards to the wounded and between 1862 and 1865 treated hundreds of soldiers of all faiths. Judge Albert Cardozo and Col. E. B. Hart were on the Advisory Committee of the New York State Soldiers Committee. By the end of the war the Jewish community was numerous, well-represented, and established. It had prepared the ground for future, more massive immigration. Newcomers after 1865 found a community with a history and a background of accomplishment that proved receptive to them.

[L.He.]

[CIRCULAR.]

"Jews' Hospital in New-York,"

Incorporated 5612—1852.

We send herewith the Constitution of the Society, bearing the above title, *"for the purpose of affording Surgical and Medical aid, comfort and protection in sickness to worthy and needy Israelites."* It is believed that the necessity for such an Institution, the humane object to be accomplished by well regulated and judicious management, and its importance to the Jewish community, will at once engage the attention and attachment of the whole House of Israel, and at the same time be favorably considered and responded to by the benevolent of all denominations.

For the first time in the history of this country—although frequently attempted by some of our philanthropic and benevolent co-religionists in this city—a refuge for the needy Israelite requiring surgical and medical aid, care and protection in sickness, is about to be provided; and the founders of the Institution are not without hope that, with the blessing of Providence, they are commencing a work destined hereafter to prove of incalculable benefit to the Israelites in the United States, and to relieve a vast amount of human misery and suffering.

To accomplish successfully the great and important work, will depend on the benevolence and liberality of those who favorably regard the undertaking, and have hearts "to feel another's woes,"—to such the Directors earnestly appeal for aid to further the good cause. From the mere dues of members, but an insufficient sum can be obtained; it is therefore incumbent on the Directors at once to call on those who have the ability, to enable them to carry out the objects of the Society.

It is the intention of the Directors, as early as practicable, to avail themselves of the XXXth Article of the Constitution, and to fit up a temporary hospital to accommodate as many patients as their now scanty means will afford, to be increased and enlarged as fast as the benevolence and liberality of those to whom they appeal will permit.

SAMPSON SIMSON *President*, 41 Warren-st.,
JOHN I. HART, *Vice President*, 65 Macdougal-st.,
BENJAMIN NATHAN, *Secretary*, 89 William-st.,
HENRY HENDRICKS, *Treasurer*, 77 Broad-st.

Directors:
REV. SAMUEL M. ISAACS, 669 Houston-st.,
ISAAC PHILLIPS, 602 Houston-st.,
JOHN M. DAVIES, 232 William-st.,
JOHN D. PHILLIPS, 174 Water-st.,
THEODORE J. SEIXAS, 215 Water-st.

☞ Donations, which will be gratefully acknowleged, may be addressed to any of the Officers or Directors.

$18,850.00

New York, December 31, 1851. THEO. J. SEIXAS, *Secretary.*

Figure 8. Appeal issued in December 1845 on behalf of "Jews' Hospital in New York," founded in 1852 and later called Mt. Sinai Hospital. Waltham, Mass., American Jewish Historical Society.

1870–1920. Migration and Population Growth. Beginning in the 1870s and continuing for half a century the great migration from Eastern Europe radically altered the demography, social structure, cultural life, and communal order of New York Jewry. During this period more than a million Jews settled in the city. They were overwhelmingly Yiddish-speaking and impoverished, the products of intensive Jewish group life and wretched economic conditions. Meeting the harsh problems of economic survival, social integration, and the maintenance of the ethnic heritage exacted vast physical, emotional, and intellectual efforts.

On their arrival in the city the East European Jews (Russian Jews as they were commonly called) found a Jewish settlement dominated by a group strikingly different in its cultural background, social standing, and communal outlook. By the 1870s this older settlement had become, with some important exceptions, middle class in outlook, mercantile in its economic base, and Reform Jewish in group identity. Successfully integrated in the economic life of the city and well advanced in its acculturation to the larger society, the established community drew its leadership from a socially homogenous elite of bankers, merchant princes, brokers, and manufacturers. The two groups—the prosperous and Americanized "uptown Jews" and the alien and plebeian "downtown Jews"—confronted and interacted with one another, a process which significantly shaped the course of community development during the period under review.

Two-thirds of the city's Jews in 1870 were German born or children of German-born parents. Together with the smaller subgroups—descendants of the 18th-century community, clusters of English, Dutch, and Bohemian Jews, and a growing contingent of Polish Jews (who formed a distinctive subcommunity)—the Jewish population numbered 60,000, or 4% of the inhabitants of the larger city (Manhattan and Brooklyn). By 1920 New York (all five boroughs) contained approximately 1,640,000 Jews (29% of the total population), and they comprised the most numerous ethnic group in the city. (The Italians, the second most numerous, formed 14% of the population. Their arrival in the city paralleled the Russian Jewish migration, and their initial areas of settlement adjoined the Jewish immigrant quarters.) By 1920, 45% of the Jewish population of the United States lived in New York.

As the main port of entry for immigrants, New York served as a transit point and temporary domicile for an undetermined number. The city also attracted a portion of those who entered the country through other ports, particularly Philadelphia and Baltimore, or who came to the city after having lived inland for a time. Of all immigrant groups, Jews ranked first in their preference for New York. According to S. Joseph, 1,372,189 Jews passed through the port of New York between 1881 and 1911, of whom 73% settled in the city. The table below indicates the population growth of New York and of its Jewish community. (The statistical data for New York City and Brooklyn are combined for the period prior to 1898 to permit comparison with the later period. New York City in 1870 was restricted to Manhattan Island. In 1874 it annexed three western townships in the Bronx and in 1895 annexed the eastern towns. Brooklyn remained a separate city until 1898 when it consolidated with Manhattan, the Bronx, Queens, and Richmond (Staten Island) to form the present-day city. Prior to 1900 only scattered Jews lived in the areas which later became the boroughs of Queens and Richmond.)

Population dispersion within the city accompanied this growth. In 1870 nearly two-thirds of the inhabitants of Greater New York resided in Manhattan. Fifty years later Manhattan's population had grown two and a half times, but it contained only two-fifths of the city's inhabitants. During this period Brooklyn's population multiplied fourfold, the Bronx's fifteenfold, Queens' ninefold, and Richmond's threefold. Queens and Richmond, still the most thinly inhabited areas of the city, had a density per acre of 6.1 and 3.2 persons, respectively, as compared to 27.6 for the Bronx, 39.5 for Brooklyn, and 160 for Manhattan. Thus Manhattan was the borough of highest residential density throughout the period under review. On its Lower East Side—bounded by Catherine Street, the Bowery, Third Avenue, 14th Street, and the East River—the population numbered 415,000 in 1920, a decline from a peak of 540,000 in 1910. At the height of its congestion, one-fourth of Manhattan's residents occupied one-twentieth of the island's space, an area of 1.5 sq. mi. For most of 50 years these East Side blocks, already overcrowded in 1870, were the reception center for the flood of Russian

New York City Population Growth and Jewish Population Growth: 1870–1920

Year	Total Population of Greater New York	Estimated Jewish Population	Percentage of Jews to Total Population
1870	1,362,213	60,000	4%
1880	1,912,698	80,000	4%
1890	2,507,414	225,000	9%
1900	3,437,202	580,000	11%
1910	4,766,883	1,100,000	23%
1920	5,620,048	1,643,000	29%

Jewish immigration. Only after 1900, when the immigrants themselves established new neighborhoods in areas like Harlem and Brownsville, did some newcomers come directly there bypassing the Lower East Side.

The Jews constituted the most conspicuous element in this dual phenomenon of rising congestion and rapid dispersion. In 1870 the less affluent, and those whose occupations required it, lived in the southern wards of the Lower East Side along the axis of East Broadway. Germans, Irish, and native Americans constituted a majority of the district's population. The northern tier of wards, stretching from Rivington to 14th streets, were heavily populated by Germans. Two-story frame houses were the prevailing type of residence, though many of these had already been converted to multiple-family use. By 1890 with Russian Jews pouring in, the great majority of the earlier inhabitants, including the German Jews, left the 80 square blocks of the southern wards. Ten years later they were in the process of abandoning the entire region below 14th Street to the rising tide of Jewish immigrants. The characteristic type of residency in the enlarged Jewish quarter was now the double-decker or "dumbbell" tenement. (The dumbbell shape met an 1879 municipal regulation requiring an airshaft between contiguously built tenements.) These tenements were five to eight stories in height, they occupied from 75 to 90% of a plot 25 feet wide and 100 feet deep, each floor contained four apartments—a total of 14 rooms, of which only one in each apartment received air and light from the street or from a cramped backyard. The most congested area of all was the tenth ward—the heart of the Jewish East Side. In the 46 blocks between Division, Clinton, Rivington, and Chrystie Streets which made up the ward—an area of 106 acres—there were 1,196 tenements in 1893. The population was 74,401, a density of 701.9 persons per acre.

The German Jews who left the Lower East Side in this population displacement joined their more prosperous brethren who had moved halfway up the east side of Manhattan in the years following the Civil War. They settled in the region between 50th and 90th Streets, which included the beginnings of Yorkville with its heavy concentration of Germans. Smaller contingents settled

Populations Growth by Boroughs, 1880–1920, and Jewish Population by Boroughs in 1920

	1880	1910	1920	Jewish Population 1920 (est.)	Percentage of Jews to Pop. 1920
Manhattan	1,164,673	2,331,542	2,284,103	657,101	28.8
Bronx	51,980	430,980	732,016	278,169	38.0
Brooklyn	599,495	1,643,351	2,018,356	604,380	29.9
Queens	56,559	284,041	469,042	86,194	18.4
Richmond	38,991	85,969	116,531	17,168	14.7
Total	1,912,698	4,766,883	5,620,048	1,643,012	29.2

further north in the upper-class neighborhood of Harlem, north of Central Park, and scattered numbers reached the zone of well-situated brownstone homes west of Central Park.

The relocation of synagogues and the establishment of other Jewish institutions underscored this process of removal and social differentiation: the geographical division, in short, of the Jewish populace into "uptown" and "downtown." As early as 1860 the venerable Shearith Israel moved from Crosby Street, in a rapidly declining downtown area to 19th Street near Fifth Avenue. In 1897 it moved once more to Central Park West and 70th Street, its present site. (Shaarey Tefillah, the first congregation on the Upper West Side, erected its synagogue on West 82nd Street four years earlier.) Temple Emanu-El, the leading Reform congregation in the city, moved from East 12th Street to Fifth Avenue and 43rd Street where the congregation consecrated an impressive Moorish-style edifice in 1868. Ahavath Chesed occupied its fourth site in its 26-year existence when it moved to Lexington Avenue and 55th Street in 1872 (known as the Central Synagogue, this is the oldest building in continuous use as a synagogue in New York). A year later Anshe Chesed left downtown Norfolk Street for Lexington Avenue and 63rd Street. Soon after, it consolidated with Adas Jeshurun to form Temple Beth El, which in 1891 moved to Fifth Avenue and 76th Street. Though Bnai Jeshurun, the oldest Ashkenazi congregation in the city, eventually moved to the West Side, it, too, belonged to the mainstream migration to the mid-East Side. In 1865 it occupied a newly completed house of worship, its third, on 34th Street and Broadway. It migrated further uptown to Madison Avenue and 65th Street in 1884. In 1918 the congregation moved to its present synagogue on West 88th Street near West End Avenue.

Also located in the mid-East Side area were a number of private clubs which catered to the social needs of the wealthier Jewish businessmen: Criterion, Fidelio, Freundschaft, Lotus, Progress, and the prestigious Harmonie, the club of the German-Jewish elite. Harmonie was situated in its own building on 42nd Street west of Fifth Avenue from 1867 to 1912, when it moved to 4 East 60th Street. In 1872 uptown Jews transferred one of their most esteemed philanthropic institutions, Mount Sinai Hospital, to 67th Street and Lexington Avenue. By the turn of the century additional institutions supported by the older community were operating in the area. The Baron de Hirsch Trade School on East 64th Street, the Clara de Hirsch Home for Working Girls on East 63rd Street, and the Young Men's Hebrew Association (YMHA) at Lexington and 92nd Street were the most prominent. Fourteen synagogues served the growing Yorkville settlement, half of them Reform or Conservative. They occupied spacious buildings—Beth El seated 2,400 and Emanu-El 1,600— and had annual incomes which ranged from Bnai Jeshurun's $20,000 to Emanu-El's $46,000. The Orthodox congregations mainly served a Central European element, though affluent East European Jews were moving into the area and joining them. Zichron Ephraim, organized in 1889 and located on 67th Street near Lexington Avenue, was the wealthiest. Its rabbi was New York-born and had received his university and rabbinical training in Germany and the U.S.

The Jewish settlement in Harlem developed along broadly parallel lines, though with some differences. It grew more slowly at the start. Less accessible to the center of the city—hence beyond the reach of most middle-class families—Harlem became a residential suburb for the wealthy. In 1874, when Temple Israel was established, it was the sole congregation in Harlem. Fourteen years later, when it dedicated its new synagogue on Fifth Avenue and 125th Street, three other small congregations were serving the community as well. By 1900 the number of permanent synagogues had grown to 13. Significantly, four of these had been founded by East European Jews—a sign that the movement of Russian Jews from the Lower East Side to Harlem was already well under way.

Figure 9. Lower East Side orange vendor, 1895. Courtesy Staten Island Historical Society, New York. Photo Alice Austen.

The completion of the first elevated railway in the late 1870s inaugurated a new age of transit which opened cheap, semi-rural land to intensive urban development. Along a network of expanding elevated and subway routes Russian Jewish immigrants moved out of the downtown quarter in two great streams—north to Harlem and thence to the Bronx, and southeast across the East River to Williamsburg and Brownsville. By the 1880s three elevated lines were running the length of Manhattan. In 1904 the first subway was completed. One route extended to the tip of Manhattan and opened the West Side and Washington Heights to mass settlement. A branch ran through Harlem and even before its completion brought a wave of construction to peripheral areas. The subway placed sections of the Bronx within the reach of families of modest means. In like manner the transit net spread to Brooklyn. The barrier of the East River was first breached in 1883 with the completion of the Brooklyn Bridge. The Williamsburg Bridge (1903) and the Manhattan Bridge (1909) and subway tunnels under the river vastly improved interborough transportation. A construction boom in multi-family dwellings marked the years 1904–07. In 1914 and 1915 twice as many apartment units were being built in Brooklyn as in Manhattan, a ratio that held into the 1920s, when additional subway facilities were completed.

Though transportation and moderate rents were essential for geographic mobility, rising expectations and economic progress were no less significant. The physical conditions the new immigrant encountered were tolerable while he made his initial adjustment and saved to bring the family that was left behind. With this achieved, the Jewish immigrant family looked beyond the immigrant quarter. Improved housing and environmental conditions, particularly as they might affect the young, were the predominant motives in a family's calculations (new neighborhood housing was superior because of the more stringent municipal regulations under which it was built). For the working class, moreover, the Lower East Side was losing its "walk to work" advantage. By 1910 the main employment of the Jewish immigrants—the clothing industry—was moving to the West Side between 14th and 23rd Streets (during the 1920s its center reached the Pennsylvania

Station district). This development reflected the decreasing role of the sweatshop. Once the tenement-flat sweatshop, based as it was on cheap labor drawn from the neighborhood, was restricted or eliminated, a major feature which had attracted newly arrived Jewish immigrants to the Lower East Side disappeared. The gradual elimination of the sweatshop belonged to a general improvement in labor conditions which was noticeable after 1900, when municipal housing regulations began having some effect over the worst abuses in the tenement sweatshops, and was especially marked in the 1910s due to the new militancy and effectiveness of the labor unions (see below). A shorter work week and higher wages created the margin in time and money needed to leave downtown for more congenial surroundings. In many cases the move became possible, or was hastened, when children became old enough to add to family earnings. A study of pensioned clothing workers shows that 88% of the Russian Jews left the Lower East Side after residing in the area, on the average, for 15 years. In all likelihood those who became entrepreneurs lived on the Lower East Side for a briefer time. Indeed, between 1910 and 1915 the population of the Lower East Side declined by 14% and between 1915 and 1920 by a further 11%.

The most graphic instance of the growth of a new area of settlement is the case of the Brownsville-New Lots district of Brooklyn. A small group of Jews of German origin had settled in the village of New Lots. Only in 1885, however, did they establish a synagogue, Bikur Cholim (Temple Sinai). In 1886 real-estate promoters began dividing the farmland into lots for sale and between 1890 and 1900 the Jewish population increased from less than 3,000 to more than 15,000. Five years later it had passed 49,000, and by 1916 the Brownsville-New Lots population had reached 225,490 and was served by 72 synagogues, all of which were Orthodox.

In 1920, then, the primary immigrant quarter, the Lower East Side, was continuing to lose population at a rapid pace. Other areas of settlement, some of which had assumed features of the immigrant quarter, were beginning to lose population as well. Harlem was the outstanding instance. Around 1920 it passed its peak and began its steep decline as a large and culturally important Jewish neighborhood as its Jewish residents moved to the East Bronx and Washington Heights. In the Bronx, the direction was from the East Bronx and south-central region to the upper reaches of the Grand Concourse and the Tremont-Fordham areas. A similar trend held for Brooklyn. Though Brownsville and New Lots were still growing in 1920, the more affluent Jews were moving to Eastern Parkway, Boro Park, Coney Island, and Flatbush. They were being replaced, at least in part, by a less affluent exodus from Williamsburg. A socioeconomic hierarchy of Jewish neighborhoods had come into being by 1920.

The dispersion of Jewish population and the diversification of neighborhoods were indicators and facets of the process of acculturation which is considered below.

ECONOMY. In a number of fields the Jews of New York loomed large in the economy of the city. One group of German-Jewish families played an outstanding role in revolutionizing the retail trade of the city. In the decade after the Civil War fathers and sons entered the dry goods business and transformed their establishments into great department stores, which still bear their names. Bavarian-born Benjamin *Bloomingdale and his sons Lyman and Joseph, both born in New York City, opened a dry goods store in 1872. By 1888, under the direction of the sons, Bloomingdale's employed 1,000 persons in its East Side emporium. On the West Side, the department store founded by Benjamin and Morris *Altman expanded to the point where it required the services of 1,600 employees. The giant in the field was R. H. Macy, which Isidore and Nathan *Straus joined in 1874, becoming the sole owners in 1887

Figure 10. A Purim ball in New York. From *Frank Leslie's Popular Monthly,* August 1877.

(Oscar, a third brother, had an interest in the business as well). Lazarus Straus and his three sons had migrated to New York from Georgia in 1865 and opened a pottery and glassware house which became the springboard to their association with Macys. Sterns, Gimbels, and the Brooklyn firm of Abraham and Straus were other department stores established during this time.

A significant number of German Jews entered the field of investment banking. Closely knit by ethnic, social, and family bonds, they formed a recognizable group within the business community. Membership in the same temples and clubs, common philanthropic endeavors, and frequent marriages within the social set welded the group together, a fact which was important in their business dealings and led to frequent collaboration. Possessing excellent financial ties with banking interests in Europe—and especially in Germany—they were able to tap these sources for the U.S. market. Kuhn, Loeb and Company, under the leadership of Jacob H. *Schiff, was the leading house. But J. and J. Seligman & Co., James Speyer and Company; Goldman, Sacks and Company; Lehman Brothers; Hallgarten and Company; and J. S. Bache and Company were also firms of considerable standing in the financial world.

German Jews also played a central role as entrepreneurs in the city's growing ready-made clothing industry. In 1888, of 241 such clothing manufacturers, 234 were Jewish and accounted for an annual product of $55,000,000. The needle trade was fast becoming New York's most important industry. In 1870 the city's factories and shops produced men's clothes worth $34,456,884. In 1900 the value of goods they produced reached $103,220,201, and during the same period their work force rose from 17,084 to 30,272. The growth of the women's clothing branch of the industry was more spectacular. The value of goods produced rose from $3,824,882 in 1870 to $102,711,604 in 1900. Where 3,663 workers were employed in 1870, 44,450 were employed in 1900. In 1913 the clothing industry as a whole numbered 16,552 factories and 312,245 employees.

East European Jews began streaming into the industry in the 1880s and by 1890 were the dominant element. They nearly completely displaced the German, Irish, and English craftsmen, as well as the German-Jewish manufacturers. One estimate, made in 1912, calculated that approximately 85% of the employees in the needle trades were Jewish.

The immigrant Jews entered the apparel trade in such numbers because it was close at hand, required little training, and allowed the congeniality of working with one's kind. The contracting system, which became widespread in the industry by 1890, was responsible in large measure for these conditions. Contractors—middlemen—received cut goods from the merchant or manufacturer, rented shop space (or used their own tenement flat), bought or hired sewing machines, and recruited a labor force. Generally about ten persons worked in these "outside shops" (in contrast to the larger "inside shops," where the manufacturer directly employed the work force and where working conditions were better). The minute division of labor which prevailed permitted the employment of relatively unskilled labor. In the intensely competitive conditions of the time—compounded by the seasonal nature of the industry—hard-pressed contractors recurrently raised the "task" of garments for which payment was made. Under these circumstances the notorious sweatshops developed with their cramped quarters and long hours of work. In 1890 Jacob Riis wrote:

> The homes of the Hebrew quarter are its workshops also . . . You are made fully aware of [economic conditions] before you have traveled the length of a single block in any of these East Side streets, by the whir of a thousand sewing-machines, worked at high pressure from earliest dawn till mind and muscle give out altogether. Every member of the family, from the youngest to the oldest, bears a hand, shut in the qualmy rooms, where meals are cooked and clothing washed and dried besides, the livelong day. It is not unusual to find a dozen persons—men, women, and children—at work in a single small room.

Figure 11. "Jewish Refugees from Russia passing the Statue of Liberty," engraving by C. J. Staniland, 1892. New York, Bettman Archive.

Until the turn of the century a 70-hour week was not uncommon.

With all its abuses the system of small shops which existed on the Lower East Side had its advantages for the new arrival. Old country ties often played a role in the operation of the system and softened harsh conditions with an element of familiarity. Manufacturers set up fellow townsmen, *landsleit,* as contractors; contractors hired *landsleit.* Bosses who were practicing Orthodox Jews made allowances for the religious requirements of their workers. The smaller shops of the contractors, in particular, were closed on the Sabbath. Reuben Sadowsky, a large cloak manufacturer, was not only closed on the Sabbath but encouraged weekday services in his factory. The production system with its extreme specialization also had its advantages. The new immigrants could master a subspecialty commensurate with his experience—or lack of it—and his physical stamina, and do so quickly. Finally, the very competitiveness and instability of the industry provided opportunities and hope. The ascent from worker to contractor to small manufacturer—categories not far removed from one another—beckoned to the enterprising and ambitious.

Although the needle trade was the largest single employer of East European Jews, Jewish immigrants found employment in other industries as well. Approximately 20% of the cigarmakers in the city in the early 1900s were Russian Jews. The building boom attracted Russian Jewish builders who opened the way for their countrymen to enter the field as craftsmen. At first Jewish building activity was limited primarily to renovating old tenements because of limited capital and the discriminatory practices of the craft unions. But in 1914, for example, when the Jewish painters were finally accepted into the Brotherhood of Painters and Paperhangers, 5,000 joined the union. An Inside Iron and Bronze Workers Union, organized in 1913 under the auspices of the United Hebrew Trades, had a membership of 2,000 in 1918. Branches of the food-processing industry—like baking and the slaughtering and dressing of meat—were "Jewish industries" due to the ritual requirements of *kashrut*. One of the oldest labor unions in the Jewish quarter was the bakers' union, which numbered 2,500 by 1918.

The compact Jewish settlements had a broad working-class base. A survey of the most heavily populated Jewish wards of the Lower East Side conducted by the Baron de Hirsch Fund in 1890 showed that 60% of those gainfully employed were shopworkers in the needle trades, 6.9% were shopworkers in other industries, 8.2% were artisans (mainly painters, carpenters, and tinsmiths), and 23.5% were tradesmen, nearly half of these being peddlers. Except for Hebrew teachers and musicians, no other profession was listed, and the latter group accounted for but 1.4%.

By 1920, however, the occupational and class structure had changed considerably. The change was expressed in the decrease in number of blue-collar workers, the increase in number of college students, the rise of a professional group of notable size, the growth in magnitude and income of the mercantile class, and the consolidation of a wealthy stratum composed primarily of clothing manufacturers and real-estate entrepreneurs. Lestchinsky has suggested that in 1916 nearly 40% of all gainfully employed Jews in New York City were garment workers, while the total employed in all manual work was more than 50%. By the turn of the century, a majority of the students at tuition-free City College was Jewish, and in 1918, the proportion of Jewish students was 78.7% of total enrollment. In the College of Dental and Oral Surgery, the comparable figure was 80.9%, while at the city's college for women—Hunter—the proportion was 38.7%. In 1907, 200 physicians, 115 pharmacists, and 175 dentists served downtown's Jews (the number of Jewish physicians in the borough of Manhattan rose from 450 in 1897 to 1,000 in 1907). To this group of professionals should be added the growing number of lawyers. Evening law school—generally a two-year course of study—enabled the younger generation to prepare for a professional career while being self-supporting. The careers of Morris *Hillquit and Meyer *London, labor lawyers and socialist leaders; Leo *Sanders and Aaron J. Levy, active in Tammany politics; and Isaac A. Allen and Benjamin Koeningsberg, involved in Orthodox Jewish causes, indicate some of the avenues open to the young lawyers. Especially striking was the observation of Isaac M. *Rubinow, physician, economist, and statistician. Writing in 1905 he noted the growth of "Russian Jewish fortunes in New York," many of which ranged between $25,000 and $200,000. "Almost every newly arrived Russian-Jewish laborer comes into contact with a Russian-Jewish employer, almost every Russian-Jewish tenement dweller must pay his exorbitant rent to a Russian-Jewish landlord." One could point to such wealthy clothing manufacturers as Joseph H. Cohen, Louis Borgenicht, William Fischman, and Israel Unterberg, and to real-estate developers like Harry Fischel and Nathan Lamport.

It is within this context of a "Jewish economy" that the development and impact of the Jewish labor movement in New York is best understood. Organizing the Jewish clothing workers—the primary sphere of trade-union activity—entailed treating with a constituency which considered its occupation temporary and was conservative in temper to a large degree. It meant dealing with a multitude of bosses and a host of elusive contractors. However, the fact that the trade-union struggle took place in New York and in the garment industry also made it a Jewish communal affair. This had its mitigating consequences. Clothing manufacturers like Joseph Cohen and William Fischman were also leaders of the community. Downtown social workers like Henry *Moskowitz and Lillian *Wald and their uptown sponsors Jacob Schiff and Louis *Marshall were no less concerned with the good name of the community and the social integration of the newcomers. In the 1910s this led to a stabilization of the unions, vastly improved working conditions, and a pioneering formula of labor-industry relations.

For the 20 years until the great strikes of 1909–16 the Jewish trade unions were weak and dispirited, despite occasional victories. The 1890 strike of the cloakmakers led by Joseph *Barondess was one such instance. The early success of the United Hebrew Trades was another. But ideological factionalism and seasonal apathy sapped the strength of the unions. During the 1901–09 period the groundwork was laid, however, for the emergence of an aggressive, responsible, and socially progressive Jewish labor movement. The rising curve of immigration was bringing members and adherents of the *Bund who were deeply committed to trade-union work. The socialist *Forward* was developing into the most widely read Yiddish daily and becoming a major educational medium for the Jewish working class. The Jewish socialist fraternal order, the Arbeiter Ring (*Workmen's Circle) was gaining strength. The "uprising of the twenty thousand"—a strike of the waistmakers, mostly young women—in the fall of 1909 was followed by the "great revolt" of the cloakmakers a half year later. These strikes increased the numbers and stability of the International Ladies Garment Workers Union (I.L.G.W.U.). In the summer of 1912 the furriers fought their battle for recognition. From January to March 1913 nearly 150,000 struck different branches of the apparel trades, but in particular the men's clothing industry. The strike led to the founding of the Amalgamated Clothing Workers of America (A.C.W.A.).

There were common lines to the four strikes. High emotion and a deep sense of dedication marked them all. The scene of workers pouring into the streets from their shops at the appointed hour reminded the chairman of the cloakmakers' strike of the Jews leaving Egypt. Characteristic, too, was the climate of opinion: the Jewish labor movement succeeded in mobilizing broad material and moral support for the strikers both from its own ranks and from reform circles. In all instances, moreover, prominent Jewish communal leaders intervened and mediated between Russian Jewish labor leaders and Russian Jewish manufacturers. In the best-known case, the 1910 strike, Louis *Brandeis, Louis Marshall, A. Lincoln *Filene, Henry Moskowitz, Jacob Schiff, and Meyer *Bloomfield were involved at one point or another in mediating the dispute. In the furriers' strike, Judah L. *Magnes, former rabbi of Temple Emanu-El and chairman of the New York Kehillah, was instrumental in ending the dispute. He became permanent chairman of the conference committee of the fur industry and later chairman of the council of moderators of the men's clothing industry. Finally, in all cases negotiations ended with some form of recognition for the union, a preferential or union shop, a smaller work week (generally 50 hours), a rise in wages, and arrangements for the continual arbitration of grievances. The latter provision led to the creation of joint sanitation, grievance,

Figure 12. Cover of *Leslie's Weekly*, New York, April 23, 1903, showing the corner of Orchard Street and Ludlow Street. Waltham, Mass., American Jewish Historical Society.

A SWEAT-SHOP GIRL MOVES HIS FANCY DEEPLY

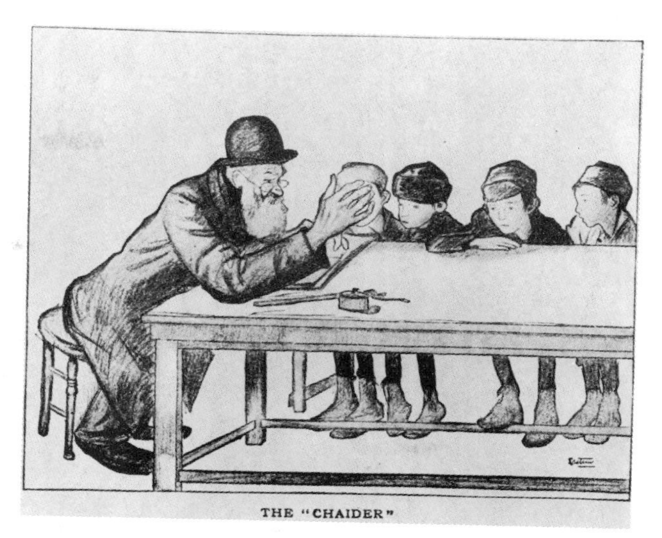

THE "CHAIDER"

THE THEATRE PRESENTS A PECULIARLY PICTURESQUE SIGHT

GOING TO THE SYNAGOGUE

WORKING GIRLS RETURNING HOME

Figures 14–18. Drawings by Jacob Epstein of Eastern European Jewish immigrants in New York, illustrating H. Hapgood, *The Spirit of the Ghetto*, New York, 1902.

Figure 13. The Central Synagogue, built in 1872, the oldest building in continuous use as a synagogue in New York. Courtesy Herbert Swartz, New York.

and arbitration committees under the chairmanship of "impartial chairmen" aided by professional staffs which supervised the enforcement of the decisions. In this there was indeed a striking innovation in labor relations which reflected a particular ethnic-economic reality and a particular Jewish group response.

COMMUNAL LIFE. In 1870 the New York Jewish community appeared to be well on its way to achieving homogeneity in form and content, directed by its Americanized element of German origin. For this group Jewish communal life expressed itself in membership in a Reform temple, and sponsorship of Jewish welfare instititions. Lay leaders of the established community found in the institutional forms a way to maintain their Jewish identity in a manner they considered compatible with American practice. Though they drew upon Jewish communal traditions, these leaders were profoundly affected by the model of American liberal Protestantism with its denominationalism, voluntarism, and moralistic rather than ritualistic emphasis.

By 1900 there were some 14 Reform synagogues in the city: nine in Manhattan, one in the Bronx, and four in Brooklyn. In 1918 there was a total of 16 Reform and 32 Conservative synagogues. (Discriminating between liberal-Conservative or Conservative-Reform was particularly difficult during the period under review.) These synagogues held services on weekends, sponsored one-day-a-week religious schools, and engaged university-trained rabbis whose most important function was delivering a weekly sermon. The leading newspapers regularly reported their discourses when reviewing the notable sermons delivered in the city's houses of worship.

Among the distinguished Reform rabbis who served in New York between 1870 and 1920 were Gustave Gottheil, Joseph Silverman, Judah L. Magnes, and Hyman G. Enelow at Emanu-El, David Einhorn, Kaufmann Kohler, and Samuel Schulman at Beth El (later amalgamated with Emanu-El), Aaron Wise, and Rudolph Grossman at Rodeph Shalom, Adolf Huebsch, Alexander Kohut, and Isaac S. Moses at Ahavath Chesed (later the Central Synagogue), and Maurice H. Harris at Temple Israel of Harlem (later on the West Side). The establishment of the Free Synagogue in 1907 as a pulpit for Stephen S. *Wise was a novel religious development, for its services were conducted on Sunday mornings at Carnegie Hall, and it also embarked upon a wide-ranging program of social service. Wise, who came to New York in 1907, and Magnes, who arrived in 1904, represented a new type of Jewish minister. American-bred and American-trained, they were young, excellent orators, and forceful—even daring—in espousing their causes and attracting large followings in the community at large. Wise became best known for his attacks on municipal corruption and industrial conditions, while Magnes' main efforts were directed toward cultural and social improvements within the Jewish community.

During the last third of the 19th century, the established community built—in addition to imposing temples—a number of large and progressive philanthropic institutions: general relief agencies, hospitals, old-age homes, orphan asylums, vocational training schools, and neighborhood centers. The outlook of these institutions reflected the receptivity of uptown's Jewish leaders to the social thought and patrician practices of the time. The emergence of scientific philanthropy, with its insistence on thorough investigation of the needy applicant, emphasis on economic and vocational rehabilitation, and espousal of the professionalization of welfare services, guided the policies of the older Jewish charities. So did the related sociological view of poverty which emphasized environmental factors, uplift, and "preventive work."

The United Hebrew Charities (U.H.C.; formed in 1874 by six philanthropic societies) was illustrative of this development. In addition to poor relief, U.H.C. operated an employment bureau and a vocational training school, granted loans to aid families launching small businesses, and maintained a work room where women were paid while they learned one of the garment trades. Its medical department employed a physician, visiting nurses, and social workers who handled home births and consumption cases. In 1911 U.H.C. opened a bureau to meet the problems of family desertion. U.H.C. expenditures rose from $46,000 in 1880, to $153,000 in 1900, to $344,000 in 1917. In 1886, 2,500 applied for assistance, and in 1900, 23,264 asked for aid. Beginning in 1901, the number of families receiving material aid decreased steadily from 8,125 to 6,014 in 1916. The vast majority were by then Russian Jewish immigrants. (As late as 1885 the largest single group of applicants were of non-East European stock.) An excerpt from a Yiddish article published in 1884 suggests the gulf which existed between the "professional methods" employed in the uptown-sponsored institutions, and the immigrant clients:

> In the philanthropic institutions of our aristocratic German Jews you see beautiful offices, desks, all decorated, but strict and angry faces. Every poor man is questioned like a criminal, is looked down upon; every unfortunate suffers self-degradation and shivers like a leaf, just as if he were standing before a Russian official.

In the field of child care two of the leading institutions in the city were the Hebrew Orphan Asylum at Amsterdam Avenue and 136th Street, which in 1917 had a capacity of 1,250 children and an annual budget of $407,130, and the Hebrew Sheltering Guardian Society. The latter moved to Pleasantville, New York in 1912, where it introduced the "cottage plan," a model program. The largest institution sponsored by the uptown Jews was Mount Sinai Hospital. In 1904 it moved to its present site, Fifth Avenue and 100th

Street. By 1916 the hospital had reached a capacity of 523 beds; its dispensary treated 243,161 patients in that year and its budget for the following year was $621,923.

These institutions were served by a distinguished group of lay and professional leaders. Lee K. Frankel and Morris D. Waldman of the United Hebrew Charities, Ludwig B. Bernstein of the Hebrew Sheltering Guardian Orphan Asylum, Solomon Lowenstein of the Hebrew Orphan Asylum, and Dr. Sigismund S. Goldwater of Mount Sinai belonged to the first rank of administrators in their respective fields. Philanthropists like Jacob H. Schiff, Irving Lehman, Isidore Straus, and George Blumenthal were intimately connected with the routine management as well as with the financing of the Montefiore Home, the 92nd Street Young Men's Hebrew Association (YMHA), the Educational Alliance, and Mount Sinai Hospital, respectively.

The notion that philanthropic institutions should be nonsectarian carried weight with the leaders of Jewish philanthropy. Nonsectarianism, however, clashed with a second approach which urged the necessity of encouraging Jewish cultural and religious activity. Supporters of the latter position differed widely in their understanding of such a program, the debate bearing upon such fundamental issues as the meaning of Americanization, the legitimacy of preserving the Old World heritage and its secular offsprings, and the nature of inter-group relationships within the New York Jewish community. These issues found their clearest institutional expression in the work of the Educational Alliance, the largest and most influential community center on the Lower East Side. In 1889 a number of uptown societies sponsoring Jewish cultural activities on the Lower East Side amalgamated and formed the Hebrew Institute. Four years later reorganization led to a change in name, emphasizing its nonsectarian stand by replacing Hebrew Institute with Educational Alliance. Its official scope was "... of an Americanizing, educational, social, and humanizing character." In 1897 the agency's president, Isidore Straus, explained that "our work may seem sectarian ... [because] we have reached chiefly Jews, but this is due to the fact that the neighborhood ... is inhabited principally by Jews." Nevertheless, the Alliance did recognize somewhat the background of its constituents. The library and reading room were well stocked with Yiddish, Hebrew, and Russian books and periodicals. A synagogue and a religious school were established as well, though they were conducted in a manner which antagonized the Orthodox. In the early 1900s the Alliance softened its attitude toward Yiddish and Yiddish culture. Zvi H. *Masliansky's discourses became a weekly event which drew large crowds, as did guest appearances by such Yiddish literary figures as Shalom Aleichem. Orthodox Jewish leaders, however, still viewed the Alliance as a bastion of Reform Judaism located in the very heart of their quarter, while to the radical intelligentsia it represented the "uptown's" use of charity and Americanization to silence social protest. Despite the opposition of these circles and the condescending approach of the lay leadership, the Jewish masses exploited the opportunities which the institution opened for them. English language classes and naturalization courses for adults, preschool instruction for newly arrived immigrant children, literary and civic clubs, music classes and a children's orchestra, drama circles and art exhibits, the Breadwinner's College inspired by Thomas Davidson, a physical education program, and the Aguilar Free Library provided a rich fare. During the first decade of the 20th century as many as 37,000 persons went weekly to the main building and to the two branch centers. Some of those who served as key members of the staff were David Blaustein, Henry Leipziger, Paul Abelson, and Belle Moskowitz. Other similar agencies of smaller scope were the Jewish Settlement House and the Temple Emanu-El Brotherhood.

Important as uptown's welfare agencies were in aiding the immigrants, they at best complemented the communal order being created by the East European Jews. Transplanted religious institutions—synagogues, *talmud torahs*, and traditional charities—constituted a major part of that order. Mutual aid associations, fraternal orders, and benevolent societies provided other avenues of group endeavor. Finally, secular ideologies spun their network of institutions adding to the heterogeneity of Jewish life and enriching it intellectually.

In organizing their synagogues—the first and most typical communal undertaking—the immigrants mostly established congregations of *landsleit*, deriving their synagogues' names mostly from the congregants' town of origin. *Landsleit* congregations proliferated. In 1887 Moses Weinberger estimated there were 130 Orthodox congregations in New York City, by far the largest number on the Lower East Side. By 1902 the number of synagogues in the downtown quarter had reached 254, and by 1917, 418. Louis Lipsky described these congregations in 1905 as "really institutional churches." A 1917 study estimated that 40% of 365 congregations located in the older sections of the Lower East Side possessed traditional adult study groups, 45% free loan associations, 33% sick benefit societies, and 91% cemetery plots. Their average seating capacity was about 180. In addition, 50 to 70 "temporary" synagogues operated for the High Holidays on the East Side alone. In 1917 only 20% of the permanent congregations owned their synagogue building.

A few older synagogues gained stature as central institutions in the downtown community. They transcended the localism of *landsmanshaft*, though they still retained a regional identity. Of this type were the Beth Hamidrash Hagadol on Norfolk Street, the Kalvarier Sons of Israel on Pike Street, the First Hungarian Congregation Ohab Zedek on Norfolk Street, and the First Roumanian Congregation Shaarei Shomayim on Rivington Street. (The Beth Hamidrash Hagadol is still located in the Norfolk Street building which it acquired in 1888.) These larger synagogues were also among the minority of congregations able to support rabbis. In 1887 there were three or four East European rabbis in New York, and in 1917 the number may not have reached more than 50. Among the most prominent were Philip H. Klein of Ohab Zedek, Moses Z. Margolis of Kehillath Jeshurun of Yorkville, Shlomo E. Jaffe of Beth Hamidrash Hagadol, Simon J. Finkelstein of Oheb Shalom in Brownsville, and Gabriel Z. Margolis of Adath Israel, and East Side mutual aid and burial society. In 1917 the number of congregations in the newer centers of Russian Jewish population was: the Bronx, 35; Williamsburg, 49; and Brownsville and East New York, 70. All of New York City contained 784 permanent and 343 temporary synagogues, in 90% of which Yiddish was the language of the sermon and of public announcements.

The plethora of small synagogues, the localism which produced them, and their constant precarious financial condition impeded their efficient operation and growth. Rivalries and vested interests compounded the situation and dogged all efforts at community collaboration in meeting the larger issues which faced the Orthodox sector. Two signal attempts at unity that failed deserve mention. In 1887 a number of Orthodox congregations federated for the purpose of creating a central religious authority to be headed by a chief rabbi. A renowned European scholar, Rabbi Jacob Joseph of Vilna, was installed as chief rabbi in 1888. The failure of the undertaking lay chiefly in the

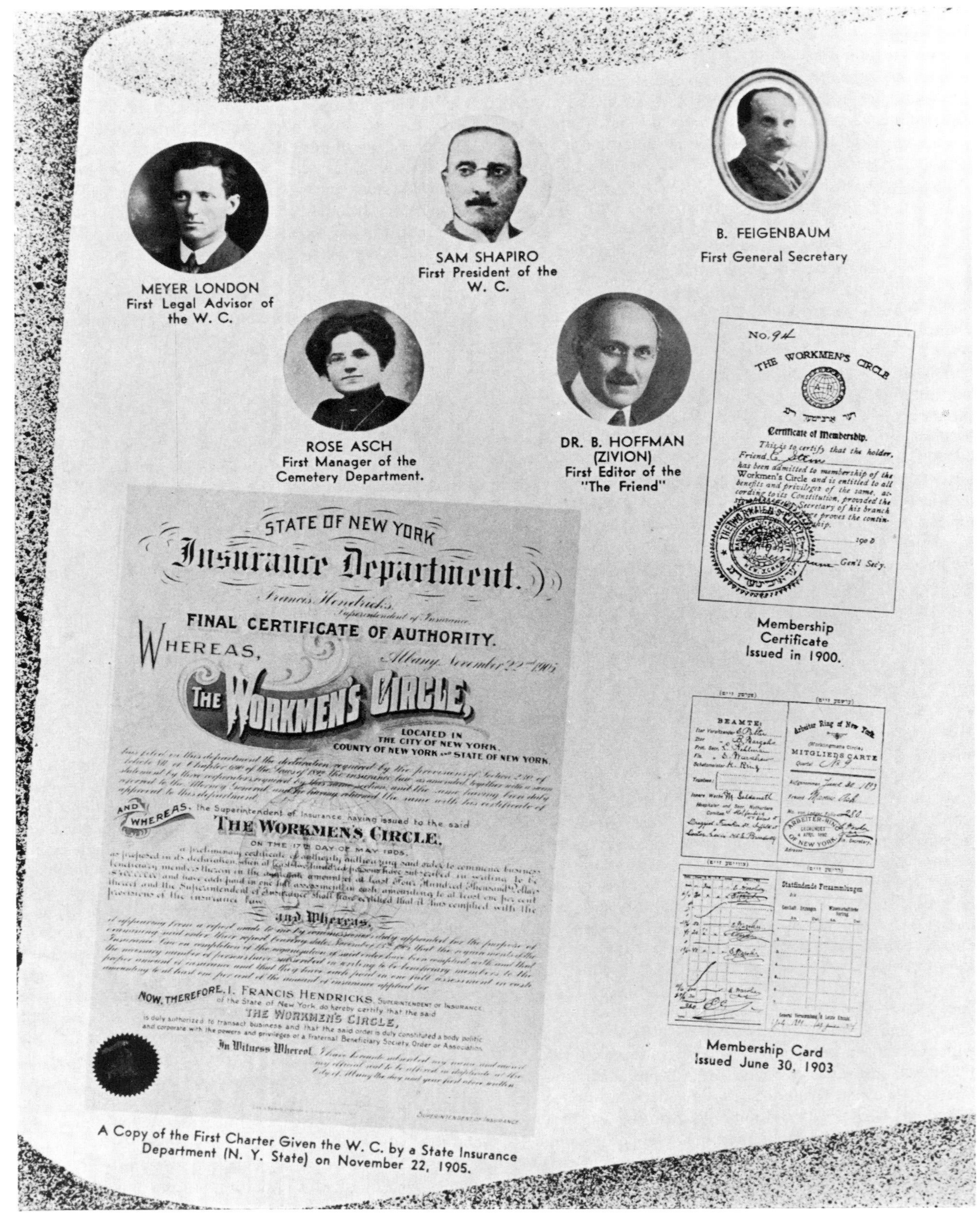

Figure 19. Montage of early leaders of the Workmen's Circle and documents of the organization, founded in 1892. From *Forty Years Workmen's Circle* (2nd ed.), New York, 1941.

inability of the chief rabbi and his supporting organization to establish communal regulation of *kashrut* and in the refusal of other rabbis to accept the chief rabbi's leadership. In 1902 Rabbi Joseph died in poverty. Under the auspices of the New York Kehillah (see below), a renewed effort was made from 1910 on to create an authoritative board of rabbis and to federate all Orthodox institutions in its support. Once again the supervision of *kashrut* was considered the key to its success. By bringing *kashrut* supervision directly under the purview of the board it was hoped that an assured income would be realized from the fees of supervision, which would then be used for financing neighborhood rabbinical courts, placing rabbis and other religious functionaries on the community's budget, and providing for Jewish religious education and other Orthodox needs. After early progress, the undertaking foundered. The community was too fragmentized; the struggle for a livelihood too consuming; and the Old World rabbis ill equipped to provide the kind of leadership required in the confusing new conditions of the U.S.

Orthodox religious education, in particular, suffered as a consequence. In 1909 the first systematic study of Jewish education revealed the grim state of affairs. Mordecai M. Kaplan, who directed the study, found that three-quarters of the Jewish children of school age received no religious education at all. Of those who did, 27% supplemented their public school sessions with attendance in 468 or more improvised, ungraded, one-room private schools, the *ḥadarim*. The level of instruction on the whole was poor; the *ḥadarim* were beyond the reach of any form of communal supervision. About 20% of those receiving Jewish instruction attended the city's 24 *talmud torahs*. Since these institutions were supported by independent associations and accepted children who could not pay the tuition fee, they were in effect communal schools to whose support over 6,000 persons contributed small sums. The eight largest schools averaged 881 students, and were generally superior to the *ḥadarim*. The most auspicious endeavor to upgrade the *talmud torahs*—by means of modern textbooks, a graded curriculum, modern pedagogical methods, improved preparation and remuneration of teachers—was sponsored by the Bureau of Education of the Kehillah beginning in 1910. Dr. Samson Benderly directed the bureau and Jacob H. Schiff and his family were its chief financial supporters. Benderly encountered considerable opposition from Orthodox circles who feared the bureau interfering with the independence of the *talmud torahs* and mistrusted it because of the religious views of its lay supporters and staff. Nevertheless, the first seven years of the Bureau's activities were auspicious ones. It recruited and trained a group of young educators, popularized the notion of communal responsibility for Jewish education, established model schools, and conducted educational research. The Bureau survived the demise of the Kehillah.

Two developments of major significance for the future course of Orthodoxy in New York took place in the 1910s. The year 1912 saw the beginning of the Young Israel movement. Immigrants' sons, concerned with the erosion of Orthodoxy, sought to combat radicalism, Reform Judaism, and indifference to the tradition by making the Orthodox service more appealing to the young. In 1915 Yeshivat Etz Chaim and the Rabbi Isaac Elchanan Theological Seminary united. The institution now offered a general high school education as well as yeshivah studies.

The comradeship of *landsleit* and the wish for protection in case of disability or death produced a vast network of mutual benefit societies, benevolent associations, and fraternal orders. Originally part of the congregations, they increasingly developed into separate organizations, offering some form of insurance, sick benefits, and interest-free loans, as well as cemetery rights. In 1917 there were about 1,000 such independent societies in New York with an aggregate membership of over 100,000, many of which found it financially advantageous to affiliate with a fraternal order. The largest order in New York City was the Independent Order Brith Abraham, which in 1917 had 90,000 members in 354 lodges. Various ideological movements recognized the attractiveness of the fraternal order and organized their own. The Arbeiter Ring (Workmen's Circle), appealing to workingmen in the name of socialism and insurance benefits, had 25,000 members in the city, and Zionists and Labor Zionists each had their own fraternal order.

Landsmanshaft societies too began to form federations. The Galician Jews were the first in 1903. The Polish *landsmanshaftn* united in 1908, while the Rumanian Jews were split into two federations. In 1911 the Federation of Oriental Jews—which reflected the increasing numbers coming from the Ottoman Empire—was established. These were loose groupings. The unifying factor was some joint effort at overseas aid and some major philanthropic undertaking. The Galicians supported the Har Moriah Hospital, the Polish Jews Beth David Hospital, and the Bessarabians the Hebrew National Orphan Home.

This concern for self-help and for one's own welfare agency also produced central institutions which came to be identified with the city's East European Jewish sub-community as a whole, of which the Hebrew Sheltering and Immigrant Aid Society (HIAS) was perhaps the most prominent. Beginning in 1909, when two older organizations merged to create it, HIAS expanded rapidly and succeeded in winning broad support in the immigrant community. Beth Israel Hospital, organized in 1890, was an instance of a downtown welfare facility whose standing in time became comparable to the older community institutions. It was founded in 1890 to provide services—such as kosher food—needed by Orthodox Jews, and places for physicians of East European origin, neither of which were available at Mount Sinai Hospital. By 1917 it had 130 beds and a budget of $155,000. One of the most respected community-wide bodies was the Hebrew Free Loan Society, established in 1892. By 1916 it had branches in the Bronx and in Brooklyn, and granted 24,330 loans, aggregating $711,940.

During the first decade of the century, influential leaders became increasingly aware of the social costs of institutional parochialism, profusion, and confusion. The sharp rise in immigration following 1903 underscored the need for more rational use of the resources and communal wealth which the community did indeed possess. Uptown Jews, willy-nilly identified with the total Jewish community, sought better ways to stem the social disorganization they sensed in the Jewish quarter and expedite the integration of the immigrants. Some downtown leaders recognized the ineffectualness of their own institutions. In both sectors of the community some viewed with alarm the alienation of the younger generation from Judaism and Jewish life.

These concerns had led to two seminal events in the communal development of New York Jews. The first was the short-lived New York Kehillah, an attempt to create a united community structure. The immediate catalyst was the accusation of police commissioner Theodore A. Bingham in 1908 that 50% of the criminals in the city were Jews. (Though the figure was exaggerated, crime in the Jewish quarter was a vexing problem.) Led by Judah *Magnes, a coalition of representative leaders established the Kehillah as a federation of Jewish organizations in 1909. Magnes served as chairman until its demise in 1922. The Kehillah created a number of bureaus—education, social morals (dealing with crime), industry (concerned with labor relations), and philanthropy. In addition, it organized a rabbinical board and a school for training communal workers. The Kehillah's productive years were, however, brief. By 1916 it had encountered financial problems which led to the separation of its bureaus. Ties to the elitist American Jewish Committee drew it into controversies over the establishment of an American Jewish congress. During World War I interest was diverted to overseas relief and international Jewish affairs, while Magnes' pacifist activity crippled his effectiveness as chairman and adversely affected the Kehillah. These factors made it impossible to overcome the fragmented state of organized Jewish life. Though a number of the activities the Kehillah initiated proved to be of lasting significance, its failure pointed to the impediments which lay on the path of community organization. No similar attempt would be made again.

Figure 20. The Lower East Side, c. 1912. From A. Schoener (ed.), *Portal to America: The Lower East Side 1879–1925*. New York, 1967. Photo Lewis W. Hine.

The establishment in 1917 of the Federation for the Support of Jewish Philanthropies—far more limited in scope than the Kehillah—proved more lasting. The federation movement to coordinate fund raising and encourage communal planning came late to New York, and from the early 1900s it encountered the opposition of the older philanthropic institutions sponsored by the German Jews who feared it might impinge upon their independence. Some, moreover, objected to a federation of Jewish charities since such a grouping cast the pall of sectarianism upon their welfare agencies. However, the proliferation of East European institutions, the failure of the Kehillah as a device of social control, and the consequent threat to their own hegemony softened their opposition to federation.

As in other cities, the New York federation encompassed the larger welfare bodies and was therefore overwhelmingly a federation of the German-Jewish philanthropies primarily interested in nonsectarian social welfare work. Of the original trustees of the federation only three were East European; of 54 constituent societies, four belonged to the East European community. A smaller Brooklyn Federation of Jewish Charities was established in 1909. Its 1917 budget was $174,000 compared to the New York federation's budget of $2,117,410.

There were signs, however, that the New York federation might develop into more than a central fund-raising agency. Soon after its establishment, under the pressure of the group which had supported the Kehillah, the federation accepted five *talmud torahs* and the Kehillah's Bureau of Jewish Education as beneficiary agencies. This implied that the federation would concern itself not only with the relief of distress but with the support of Jewish cultural endeavor. Jewish education was to become a responsibility of the Jewish community's exchequer. The federation also indicated in its first year of existence that it expected to become the spokesman of the entire community, and that it would solicit the support of the masses as well as of wealthy donors. But these statements remained little more than declarations of intention.

During the period after 1900 Zionism and Socialism played, with varying success, many-sided roles in the organizational and cultural life of the New York Jewish community. In institutional terms the Zionist achievements were minimal. The Federation of American Zionists, the Order Sons of Zion, Mizrachi, Po'alei Zion, the Jewish National Workers Alliance, Hadassah, and the Intercollegiate Zionist Association numbered in 1917 about 8,500 members who belonged to 95 loosely organized chapters. The influence of Zionism, however, went beyond membership figures. Much of the interest in Hebrew culture, Jewish education, and community planning stemmed from Zionist circles. Up to World War I the cultural Zionists who emphasized the need to revitalize Jewish cultural life in the Diaspora predominated. Judah Magnes, Israel Friedlaender, Henrietta Szold, and Mordecai Kaplan gave vigorous expression to this position from the lecture podium, in the press, and as professional and lay leaders of Jewish institutions. The socialist Po'alei Zion was similarly short on numbers and organizational success but strong on ideology and polemical talents. It constituted an intellectual force of significance at a time when the leadership of the Jewish labor movement was largely cosmopolitan and assimilationist in outlook. Following the outbreak of World War I, Zionists of all shades vastly increased their influence in the community through the Jewish congress movement. In June 1917, 125,000 participated in the election of delegates from New York City. The 100 delegates elected to represent New York's Jews were overwhelmingly of East European origin, the majority sympathizers of Zionism.

The Socialists, through the Workmen's Circle (Arbeiter Ring), possessed a stronger organizational framework than the Zionists. The order's 240 New York lodges and 25,000 members made it in 1917 the second-largest fraternal order in the city. Though the Workmen's Circle drew its membership from the Yiddish-speaking immigrant masses, it did not consciously identify itself with the Jewish community as a whole until World War I. During the war years Jewish Socialists began participating in Jewish communal affairs. The Workmen's Circle, Jewish labor unions, and the Jewish Socialist Federation (12 branches in New York) were active in the local fund-raising campaigns for overseas relief. They also joined the American Jewish congress movement, and the Workmen's Circle in a principal policy change that undertook direct support of Jewish cultural activity such as Yiddish schools.

Cultural Life. The Yiddish-speaking masses who settled in New York created a rich and varied cultural life. No less than the community's institutional structure, this life aided the newcomers in their adjustment to the great metropolis. The very size of the immigrant community, its compactness and heterogeneity, and the impact of the new condition of freedom encouraged a multiplicity of cultural undertakings. Between 1872 and 1917, for example, about 150 journals in Yiddish appeared. Ideologues, literati, artists, and entrepreneurs competed in offering guidance, information, entertainment, and psychic relief for a generation in the throes of accommodation to a strange civilization.

The Yiddish-language daily press in particular served these ends (see *Press, Jewish, in U.S.A.). By the early 1900s four stable dailies had evolved: the Orthodox and Zionist *Tageblat;* the **Jewish Morning Journal*, Orthodox, conservative on social issues, and anti-Zionist; the radical and nationalistic *Warheit;* and the socialist **Forward*. In 1914 the **Tog*, pro-Zionist and liberal, was established; it absorbed the *Warheit* in 1919. The estimated daily circulation for New York City in 1916 was: *Forward* (149,-170), *Jewish Morning Journal* (81,375), *Warheit Tageblat* (41,335). It was estimated in 1917 that nearly 600,000 persons in New York City read the Yiddish newspapers daily. Besides the staple of general and Jewish news the papers contained serialized novels, literary criticism, political essays, and a woman's page. The *Forward* created the *"Bintl Brief"* column of personal woe and editorial advice which had imitators in other papers. Editorials were slashing and polemical, frequently dealing with municipal problems and local Jewish affairs. The Yiddish press also fulfilled more mundane functions. The Orthodox found announcements and reports of the local institutions they were most interested in, while the workingmen found information concerning trade-union activities. The considerable advertising included notices of theaters, cantorial performances, books published, medicine and health aids, and, in the *Jewish Morning Journal*, want-ads. The *Forward*, in particular, sponsored communal undertakings such as theater benefits and other fund-raising activities.

Figure 21. Shop for religious articles on the Lower East Side. From K. Simon and A. Feininger (photo), *New York*, London, 1964.

The functions of the Yiddish press made its publishers and editors major communal leaders. Jacob Saphirstein of the *Jewish Morning Journal* was deeply involved in rabbinical politics. Leon Kamaiky, a proprietor of the *Tageblat*, was a vice-president of the Hebrew Sheltering and Immigrant Aid Society and a member of the American Jewish Committee and the executive committee of the Kehillah. *Forward* editor Abraham Cahan's position in the Jewish labor movement was less formal but more powerful. Indeed, the preeminent place of the Yiddish press and its editors was recognized uptown. In 1902 Louis Marshall established the *Yiddishe Velt* in an effort to assert his group's influence in the Jewish quarter. The initiative which led to the establishment of the *Tog* in 1914 came from the same circles and for the same reasons.

The role of the Yiddish press found its fullest expression in the *Forward*. Cahan was the great innovator and his paper the pacemaker of Yiddish journalism. His apprenticeship as a reporter for the New York *Commercial Advertiser* under Lincoln Steffens served him well in turning the *Forward* into the leading Yiddish daily. The simple, direct style of the paper, its humanistic, undogmatic brand of socialism and its eschewal of the Orthodox-baiting of earlier socialist journals won it great popularity. Cahan appealed to highbrow no less than lowbrow tastes, and side by side with the *"Bintl Brief"* he published virtually every Yiddish author of note. From 1912 the *Forward* occupied its own ten-story building on East Broadway, close to the Educational Alliance. The United Hebrew Trades, the Jewish Socialist Federation, and the Arbeiter Ring (Workmen's Circle) had their offices in the building. The *Forward* was the focal center of the Jewish labor movement, a powerful cultural factor in the community, and thus had become, willy-nilly, a force for Jewish group continuity.

Weeklies and monthlies filled out the broad range of ideas, movements, and professional interests of the New York community. Some, like the *Amerikaner* and the *Idishe Gazetten*, were weekly family supplements of existing newspapers. The anarchist *Freie Arbeiter Stimme*, the Zionist *Idishe Folk*, and the socialist *Zukunft* were representative of the literary and political journals sponsored by the various ideological camps. More local in their interests were such journals as the trade unions published: the *Fortschritt* of the Amalgamated Clothing Workers of America and *Naye Post* of the Joint Board of the Cloak and Skirt Makers Union. Catering to small audiences were the Hebrew journals *Ha-Ivri* and *Ha-Toren*, and the Ladino *La America* (see Hebrew *Newspapers, N. America). The Yiddish journals and dailies drew to New York and sustained a significant colony of intellectuals, writers, poets, and critics whose work was read in the press and discussed in the lecture halls and coffeehouses of the East Side.

The Yiddish theater reinforced the press. It was, Moses Rischin has written, "educator, dreammaker, chief agent of charity, social center, and recreation hub for the family."

Melodrama and romantic musical depicted historical and topical events which were drawn from the classic Jewish past, the "old home," immigrant life in the New World, and current American affairs. Nearly all weekday performances were benefits raising funds for some charity, strike fund, or literary journal. About 1900 three theaters were devoted exclusively to Yiddish drama which, together with other houses giving occasional performances, drew about 25,000 patrons a week. By 1917 the number of houses presenting Yiddish theater reached seven, of which one was located in Harlem and one in Brownsville.

Jewish immigrant life in New York inspired some of the earliest belles-lettres by Jews in English. Cahan's *Yekl* (1896) and *The Rise of David Levinsky* (1917) are the outstanding examples. For most second-generation American Jews, Yiddish literature was a closed book, and Jewish themes in the language of the land were at best of peripheral interest. The Anglo-Jewish weekly *The American Hebrew* supplied the older settlement with a resume of Jewish news and the social happenings of their circle. Its circulation was less than 10,000.

Politics and Civic Affairs. For Jews, as for all minority groups, election to public office meant, in the first place, social recognition and acceptance into the body politic of the city. Prior to the 1900s the number of Jewish officeholders was small, their posts for the most part minor, their ethnic identity an insignificant factor, and their political careers brief. Three Jewish congressmen were elected in New York City between 1870 and 1899, and all served but one term; the most prominent was Isidore Straus. Considerably more served in the state legislature. Among them was Joseph Blumenthal, who was a member of the Committee of Seventy which was responsible for the downfall of the Tweed Ring. Joseph Seligman and Simon Sterne were other members of that reform group. Blumenthal was a trustee and president of Shearith Israel and from 1886 to 1901 president of the board of trustees of the Jewish Theological Seminary. In municipal government Adolph L. Sanger, elected in 1885 as an anti-Tammany Democrat, served as president of the Board of Aldermen for one term. He, too, was active in Jewish communal affairs, serving at different times as president of the Board of Delegates of American Israelites and vice-president of the Union of American Hebrew Congregations. In the 1890s Edward Lauterbach, a specialist in railway law and a director of a number of street railways, served for three years as chairman of the Republican County Committee. Lauterbach was a director of the Hebrew Benevolent and Orphan Asylum and the Hebrew Technical Institute. Jews held minor judgeships prior to 1900, and only one, Albert Cardozo, served on the state Supreme Court. In 1871, in the wake of the Tweed scandals, Cardozo resigned to avoid impeachment (his son was Benjamin Nathan *Cardozo, on the Court of Appeals from 1914 until his elevation to the U.S. Supreme Court in 1932).

In the years following 1900 the densely populated Jewish neighborhoods and the rising political awareness of the immigrants carried increasing political weight. That a number of assembly districts and several congressional districts had Jewish majorities or pluralities was reflected in the ethnic origin of the candidates, the particular issues raised, and the language of the campaigns. The number of Jewish voters was large enough to influence the outcome of city-wide elections. Though uptown Jews denied it, a Jewish vote existed. It was not prone to act en bloc, but nevertheless responded to group interests and ethnic pride and was unafraid to demand its political due.

Jews came of age as a political force during the domination of the Tammany Hall political machine. Led by astute and, if need be, ruthless politicians, Tammany offered its constituents a host of services in return for their vote, and some of its leaders were attuned to the moods and needs of their Jewish constituents. Although a lag existed between Jewish numbers and numbers of Jewish officeholders, Tammany was sensitive to ethnic ambitions. In 1900 Henry M. Goldfogle went to Congress as representative of the Lower East Side, serving until 1921 with the exception of two terms. By 1910 Aaron J. Levy and Moritz Graubard were entrenched as East Side assemblymen, and Jews received 5 to 8% of the mayor's top appointments.

Support of Tammany was not, however, monolithic, particularly in mayoral and presidential campaigns. Anti-Tammany forces recognized this, and when mounting major reform campaigns, paid particular attention to the Jewish immigrant neighborhoods. In 1901, for example, the Fusion ticket flooded the Jewish districts with Yiddish circulars. Seth Low and William Travers Jerome were elected mayor and attorney general respectively. Jacob A. Cantor, who had fought for tenement house reform as an assemblyman in the 1880s, was elected borough president of Manhattan as a Reform Democrat. The publisher William Randolph Hearst, in his effort to defeat the Tammany candidate for mayor in 1905, carried the Jewish East Side. His *New York American* had feature stories of Russian barbarism and solicited funds for the relief of pogrom victims. Hearst even launched a Yiddish newspaper for a time. John P. Mitchel, elected mayor in 1913 on a Fusion anti-Tammany ticket, won broad support in the Jewish districts. Henry Moskowitz, head of the Madison House Settlement and a native downtown reformer, became Mitchel's commissioner of Civil Service. The downtown voters exhibited similar independence in presidential elections. From 1888 to 1912 no party carried the Eighth Assembly District, heart of the Jewish quarter, twice in succession. However, Republican Theodore Roosevelt was a particular favorite.

Among the uptown Jews a group of patrician "good-government" reformers emerged who helped finance these repeated efforts to dislodge Tammany. Among them were men like Nathan and Oscar *Straus, who belonged to the Cleveland wing of the Democratic Party, and liberal Republicans like Jacob Schiff, Isaac N. *Seligman, and Adolph *Lewisohn. They assumed a particular responsibility for wooing their downtown brethren away from the "twin evils" of Tammany and socialism by supporting the reform candidates in their East Side campaigns.

Socialism indeed had a significant political following in

Figure 22. The funeral of Shalom Aleichem in New York, 1916. Jerusalem, J.N.U.L., Schwadron Collection.

Figure 23. Students of the Shalom Aleichem Folk Institute, Bronx, New York, 1920.

the Jewish immigrant districts. On the Lower East Side the Socialists could count on a straight party vote of about 15%, and in some Jewish election districts in Brooklyn and the Bronx it may have been even higher. However, only when the party offered a candidate able and willing to appeal to the particular interest and ethnic sentiment of the East European Jew did it win at election time. In 1914 it sent Meyer London to Congress, the first socialist elected to the House of Representatives and the first elected socialist for any office from New York City. London, a lawyer for a score of Jewish labor unions, lived in the Jewish quarter, and thus spoke the language of the immigrant. He eschewed party dogma. Reelected in 1916, he won a third term in 1920 despite the fact that his party was then in complete disarray. Of special interest were the elections of 1917. Morris Hillquit, the outstanding figure in the Socialist Party, showed remarkable strength in his bid for the mayoralty. He won 22% of the vote—twice that of the Republican candidate. Ten socialist assemblymen went to Albany, seven aldermen to City Hall, and one socialist—Jacob Panken—was elected municipal court judge. The vote reflected the strong anti-war sentiment among the East European Jews as much as it did socialist sentiment.

The war years expedited the social processes that molded a variegated and fragmented Jewish public into a more homogeneous ethnic community. The same processes integrated that community into the larger polity. War brought prosperity which enabled families to leave overcrowded immigrant districts for a better, more "American" environment and so accelerated the process of acculturation. The war also confronted all Americans with the problem of their group identity, Americanized Jews of German origin no less than recently arrived East European Jews. Though it brought to the surface sharp tensions—which in a pluralistic society might be mitigated but not eliminated—the Jews of New York by 1920 could see themselves as a major group at home in the city.

[AR.G.]

1920–1970. DEMOGRAPHY. Following World War I the Jewish population of New York grew moderately to 1,765,000 in 1927 and 2,035,000 in 1937. It tapered off around 2,100,000 in 1950, and slowly decreased as Jews moved to the suburbs from the 1950s. By 1960 the Jewish population of the city had declined to 1,936,000, while that of the metropolitan area increased to 2,401,600, owing to the large growth of the Jewish population in the suburban counties (see *New York State). The city's Jewish population, which fell further to 1,836,000 by 1968, was also an aging group as younger families moved to suburbs. The move to outlying areas and suburbs by Jews and other middle-class whites in search of more comfortable residence and greener neighborhoods was intensified from the mid-1950s by negative factors which included the growing inadequacy of middle-class housing, the decline of municipal services and the public schools, and the increase of crime and racial tensions.

No less than during immigrant years, New York Jews preferred to dwell near each other. Thus, 676,000 of Brooklyn's 857,000 Jews in 1940 resided in areas where Jews formed 40% or more of the total population; and later, in 1958, 388,000 of the Bronx's 493,000 Jews were similarly concentrated. Anti-Jewish discrimination in the sale and rental of housing had been effectively quashed before 1950, except for isolated instances in opulent areas of Manhattan.

Within the city's five boroughs Jewish population centers shifted as Jews abandoned highly congested Jewish areas and moved to more widely dispersed areas further from the older, more centrally located neighborhoods. In 1918, 696,000 Jews (46% of the city's total Jewish population), lived in Manhattan. Most of them lived on the Lower East Side and uptown in Harlem. Masses of Jews left the Lower East Side as their economic improvement permitted, mainly before the Depression of 1929. While 314,200 Jews lived on the Lower East Side in 1923, by 1940 only 73,700 remained. By 1960 about 70,000 Jews lived there, mainly in cooperative housing projects sponsored by Jewish trade unions, and comprised 34% of the general population as compared to 40% in 1930. West and East Harlem, for a time the home of wealthier immigrant Jews, had about 177,000 Jews in 1923. Immediately thereafter Harlem became a Negro neighborhood; fewer than 5,000 Jews remained in 1930 and in 1940, only 2,000.

Many Jews from Manhattan and other areas moved north to the more recently settled Bronx, where in 1918 they totaled about 211,000. By 1927 about 420,000 Jews lived there, primarily in its south and south-central districts, where they comprised 40% and 70%, respectively, of the

Figure 24. Dedication ceremony for the main building of Yeshiva University in Washington Heights, 1928.

general population in 1925. By 1937 the Bronx Jewish population rose above 592,000, making that borough 44% Jewish. As new subway lines and apartment buildings were built, the movement of Jews to more northerly and less populous regions of the Bronx was facilitated. The number of Jews in the South Bronx fell from 34,200 in 1923 to less than 15,000 in 1960. Tremont, in the west-central Bronx, which had 121,000 Jews (96% of its total population) in 1925, dropped to about 44,000 before the 1960s, most of whom also quit the area during the decade that followed. However, nearby Fordham rose from 13,600 Jews in 1923 to 83,350 in 1930 and 103,000 in 1960, about 48% of the general population. The middle-class West Bronx Jewish population increased from 26,000 in 1923 to 142,886 in 1940. It declined to 121,000 in 1960, when it was still 65% of the general population, and this downward trend continued. The Jewish population of Pelham Parkway, in the northeast Bronx, rose from 3,000 in 1923 to 65,000 by 1960, or 48% of the general population, and continued to increase. Following the general trend toward the suburbs, Jews began leaving the Bronx in the 1950s, so that by 1968 only 395,000 Jews remained, with new concentrations in the outlying Van Cortlandt and Riverdale areas.

From the 1920s the borough most heavily populated by Jews was Brooklyn, where the number of Jews rose from 568,000 in 1918 to 797,000 in 1927. In contrast to Manhattan and the Bronx, Brooklyn tended to be a borough of well-defined neighborhood communities. Reputedly, Jewish religious life in Brooklyn was more active than in other boroughs. While the older Jewish neighborhoods in the northern and western regions of Brooklyn began to lose their large Jewish populations by the 1930s, Jews were moving outward to form vast new communities in the central, southern, and eastern sectors. Thus, Williamsburg, across the East River from Manhattan, a community in which Jews numbered 140,000 in 1923, had only 33,400 Jews in 1957, though even as its population declined, it attained some celebrity as the site of a large ḥasidic colony of post-World War II immigrants from Hungary and Eastern Europe. Bedford-Stuyvesant's 70,000 Jews in 1923 declined below 30,000 in 1957 and fell further in the 1960s as the area became a Negro ghetto. In 1925 about 250,000 Jews, or 82% of the population of the area, lived in East New York-New Lots-Brownsville. However, only 96,000 remained in 1957, and most of those left during the 1960s as Brownsville became predominantly black. On the other hand, in central Brooklyn the number of Jews in Boro Park increased from 46,000 in 1923 to 67,000 by 1950, in Bensonhurst from 45,000 in 1923 to 85,000 by 1950, and in Flatbush from 16,400 in 1923 to 123,000 by 1950. Sheepshead Bay in southern Brooklyn had 7,100 Jews in 1923 but 48,000, or 62% of the population, by 1950. Residential, middle-income Midwood-Marine Park grew from 3,200 Jews in 1923 to 64,000 by 1957. Jews settled early in the southern Coney Island-Manhattan Beach area, which was nearly 70% Jewish in 1940 when 53,400 Jews resided there. From the 1930s Jews also began to settle the eastern Flatlands-Canarsie area, whose Jewish population rose from 4,400 in 1923 to 28,000, or 60% of the population, in 1957.

Altogether, the Jewish population of Brooklyn began to decrease, dropping from its heights of 975,000 in 1937 and 950,000 in 1950 to 760,000 in 1968. Thus Crown Heights, close to Bedford-Stuyvesant, dropped from over 75,000 in 1950 to 58,400 by 1957, and similar drops occurred after World War II in Bensonhurst and Coney Island. The heavily Jewish East New York-New Lots area, in which 106,000 Jews lived in 1923, decreased to 74,000 Jews in 1950; it rose again, however, to 90,000 by 1957 with the construction of new housing on unoccupied land. Boro Park, in central Brooklyn, long a center of Orthodox Judaism, became strongly ḥasidic with the influx of Williamsburg Ḥasidim.

The borough of Queens saw a sustained increase in its middle- to upper-middle class Jewish population, owing to its newness, relative remoteness from the center of the city, and rapid building of large apartment-house complexes. While only 23,000 Jews lived there in 1918, the Jewish population grew to 200,000 by 1950 and 420,000 by 1968. Over 200,000 Jews moved there during the 1950s and large Jewish concentrations developed in Forest Hills-Rego Park, which had over 73,000 Jews, or 66% of the general population, by 1957; the Whitestone area, which had 24,000 Jews in 1957; Central Queens, in which 51,000 Jews lived in 1957; and Douglaston-Little Neck-Bellrose, which had 31,500 Jews in 1957. About 18,200 Jews lived in the Rockaways on the shore in 1923, and nearly 30,000 lived there by 1957.

About 5,000 Jews dwelled in the little settled, isolated borough of Richmond (Staten Island) in 1918, and that number increased moderately. In 1950 about 8,000 Jews lived there, and by 1968 their number reached about 11,000. With improved mass transportation a larger increase was anticipated.

The Jewish population of Manhattan declined from the 1920s. In 1937 there were 351,000 Jews on the island, while only 250,000 remained in 1968. Nevertheless, several neighborhoods increased. The number of Jews in well-to-do, cosmopolitan sections of the West Side rose from 21,300 in 1923 to 71,000, or 29% of the general population, by 1957. Washington Heights, the uptown residential area, had 31,500 Jews in 1923, but nearly 70,000 by 1957. It was the center for German Jewish refugees of the 1930s. Nearly all Manhattan Jewish neighborhoods apparently declined in the 1960s, however, except the expensive, rebuilt Upper East Side, where Jews increased from 22,000 in 1940 to 42,000 in 1958.

The movement to the suburbs raised the Jewish population of rapidly built Nassau County, across the city boundary from unknown but small numbers before 1940 to 329,000 in 1957 and 372,000 in 1963. Following already established city patterns, Jews tended to dwell together in such suburban centers as Great Neck, Woodmere, Laurelton, Cedarhurst, Lawrence, Roslyn, Levittown, Baldwin, and Hempstead. Beyond Nassau lay Suffolk County, in which the previously negligible Jewish population reached 12,000 in 1957 and 42,000 in 1963, with increases thereafter.

Little was known of Jewish mortality and longevity. A

Figure 25. Temple Emanu-El, founded in 1848, present building erected in 1929. Photo Fred Stein, New York.

Figure 26. The Hebrew Pen Club of New York, late 1930s. Seated left to right: A. S. Schwartz, Menahem Ribalow, Zalman Shneour, H. A. Friedland, Abraham Goldberg, Hillel Bavli; Standing: Moshe Maisels, A. Edelberg, Israel Levinthal, M. Feinstein, Abraham Spicehandler, I. Z. Frishberg, Daniel Persky. Courtesy M. Maisels, Jerusalem.

1932 survey of several neighborhoods showed Jewish infant mortality to be 40 per 1,000 compared with 57 per 1,000 of the general population. A 1953 study showed a Jewish death rate of 9.9 per 1,000 compared with 10.5 per 1,000 in general, and the average of Jews at death was 66.5, about two years above other groups.

ECONOMIC ACTIVITIES. New York Jewry formed so large a proportion of the city's population that Jewish economic habits and aptitudes broadly influenced the city's economy. Jewish labor in the garment industry, the city's foremost industry, reached its peak at about 1920. In 1921 production of men's apparel in New York City was valued at $326,832,-000, and of women's $759,628,000, in addition to such allied industries as knit goods, $83,490,000. Perhaps 200,000 Jews belonged to the trade unions of the garment industry. From this point the proportion of Jewish workers steadily declined in the clothing industry, until in the men's clothing branch it reached 39% in 1937; the new working group was largely composed of Italian women and later, Puerto Ricans. The same process operated in the ladies' garment industry. One large local of the I.L.G.W.U. was still about three-quarters Jewish in the 1940s and declined to 44% in 1958. Jews remained in the garment industry at upper levels of skill as cutters and sample makers, and as entrepreneurs and salesmen.

The Jewish labor movement in New York, after its heroic era of strike victories during the 1910s, was firmly established by 1920. The unions turned back attempts between 1920 and 1922 to reestablish the open shop. However, they were beset during the 1920s by violent factional quarrels with Communists. The latter derived support not only because of their tactical and propagandistic skill but also from post-World War I Jewish immigrants who entered the industry and felt somewhat excluded by the established union leadership and ideology. Communist tacticians "boring from within" secured control of the New York Joint Board and led it into a series of disastrous strikes culminating in 1926. The union was left in ruins and did not reestablish itself until the New Deal period. The A.C.W.A. was more fortunate, however, in maintaining its unity and power. A third garment union, the International Fur Workers' Union, succeeded in its trade-union objectives under Communist leadership, while the United Hat, Cap and Millinery Workers did likewise under liberal leaders.

During the 1920s the New York Jewish unions entered areas of activity never previously known to U.S. trade unions. They conducted large-scale adult education, health clinics, a bank, summer resorts, built model urban housing, and generously subsidized struggling trade unions in such other industries as steel, coal, and textiles. Except for their Communist wing, they became pioneers of liberal political action, thus preparing an eminent place for themselves in New Deal political and legislative affairs.

The Jewish immigrant generation was heavily represented as workers—23% "operatives and kindred" and 16% "craftsmen, foremen, and kindred" as late as 1950. The 32% who were "managers, officials, and proprietors" included a mass of shopkeepers and small businessmen. Jewish retailers were especially heavily represented in such areas as candy and stationery stores, grocery stores, hardware stores, haberdashery stores, tailor shops, and delicatessens and small restaurants. An incomplete estimate placed Jewish trade-union membership about 1928 at 134,000 of a total of 392,000 concentrated, in addition to needle and leather trades, in amusement and food preparation and distribution.

The immigrants' children, however, shifted towards sales and clerical occupations and independent business; in 1950 55% of immigrants' sons were in these groups, and only 22% remained in traditional working-class occupations. One important channel of ascent was New York's excellent public school and college system. Jews constituted 51% of enrollment in the city's academic high schools in 1931, and 49.6% of the city's college and university students in 1935. As early as 1915 they comprised 85% of the student body in the city's unique free municipal college system, a percentage which probably did not decrease before 1960; others of course attended college outside the city. This higher education launched thousands of young Jews in poor or very modest circumstances into independent business and the professions. During the 1950s about 17% of New York Jews, including the older, immigrant group, were professionally employed.

Areas of Jewish economic activity often were clearly demarcated. Thus, the port of New York, shipping and other transportation, large banks and insurance companies, and heavy industry hardly employed any Jews. Even after the removal of discriminatory employment policies in 1945, Jews remained few in these industries. Small, independent business, the garment trade and light industry employed

Figure 27. Mayor Fiorello La Guardia (center), with the actor Solomon Mikhoels (left) and the poet Itzik Feffer (right), on their visit to New York on behalf of the Soviet Anti-Fascist Committee, July 1943. From M. U. Schappes, *A Pictorial History of the Jews in the United States*, New York, 1958.

The Day
דער טאג
"THE NATIONAL JEWISH DAILY"
NEW YORK
PRICE FIVE CENTS

אידישע מלוכה

פראקלאמירט; נאמען איז „ישראל"

אידישע ארמיי פארנעמט אראבישען פארט עכו

„הגנה" פארנעמט נאך טיילען פון ירושלים

אידען שאפען אפ דאס „ווייסע פאפיר"

Figure 28. Issue of the Yiddish newspaper, *Der Tog*, May 15, 1948, reporting the establishment of the State of Israel.

masses of Jews, and Jewish entrepreneurs could be found in these fields as well as real estate, building, investment banking. Over half the city's doctors, lawyers, dentists, and public school teachers were Jews by the 1930s, notwithstanding sharp anti-Jewish discrimination. After World War II these tendencies continued as the Jews became the city's mercantile and professional ethnic group, heavily represented in academic, scientific, and civil service organizations. Reflecting their occupational changes, they formed a large part of the membership and most of the leadership in trade unions of public employees.

Political and Civic Life. As the largest single ethnic group, Jews were a highly important factor in the political life of the city, which incorporated both rivalry and understanding between the various ethnic groups. As a religious body, the Jews, who were about 27% of the city's population, were outnumbered only by the Irish-dominated Catholics, who were just over half. In no other city could Jews as a group weigh so heavily in politics, or were real or alleged Jewish political interests reckoned with so carefully. Until the 1930s the city was governed through the Manhattan organization of the Democratic Party, known as Tammany Hall, which held the support of most immigrants, including Jews. There were also Jewish Republicans, conspicuous among whom were older-stock Jews of civic reform interests, like Stanley M. Isaacs and Nathan Straus Jr., and the party's New York County leader Samuel S. Koenig. In addition Jews in East Harlem during the 1920s supported that district's dynamic U.S. Congressman, Fiorello H. *LaGuardia, a rebel Republican. The preponderant ethnic element among Socialists and Communists was also Jewish. Yet Jews generally followed the Democratic Party and some among them received the rewards of party loyalty—personal and business favors, municipal appointments, and judgeships.

The period from 1928 to 1945 witnessed far-reaching change. Jews had heavily supported Alfred E. Smith, liberal Tammany reformer of Irish stock, in his successful campaigns for the governorship of the state and unsuccessful attempt for the presidency in 1928. The coming of the Great Depression in 1929 brought New York Jewry overwhelmingly behind the New Deal and the Democratic Party; support for Franklin D. *Roosevelt during his presidential campaigns of 1932, 1936, 1940, and 1944 ran from 80% to 90%, higher than among any other group in the city. The urban liberalism of the New Deal had many of its seeds in the Jewish trade union, East Side settlement houses, and Jewish philanthropists and social workers. Jews were enthusiastic for the New Deal Jewish Democrat Herbert H. *Lehman, elected to the state governorship in 1932, 1934, 1936, and 1938, and the German immigrant New Deal Senator Robert F. Wagner. Peculiarly interesting was the election of LaGuardia as a Republican to the mayoralty of New York in 1933 by the votes of Italians, Jews mostly of middle-class reform sympathies, and upper-class good-government supporters. Of Italian stock but partially Jewish in descent and fluent in Yiddish, LaGuardia was a nominal Republican whose mastery of ethnic politics succeeded by 1937 in attracting the Jewish working class and left wing for his municipal version of the New Deal. During LaGuardia's incumbency from 1934 to 1946, Jews figured more prominently as city officials and political leaders. As fervent supporters simultaneously of the Protestant aristocrat Roosevelt, the Jewish banker Lehman, and the Italian commoner LaGuardia, New York Jews preferred liberal, reform-minded candidates and avoided Republicans unless they significantly differed from the generally conservative habits of that party. The American Labor Party (founded in 1936) and its successor the Liberal Party (organized in 1944) served their intended purpose of drawing voters of the left, especially Jews, to liberal or left-liberal candidates.

Following LaGuardia's tenure, the doctrine of "ethnic balance" became habitual in the city's politics, by which the major parties regarded it as necessary for victory on Election Day to nominate a Jew, Irishman, and Italian for the three city-wide electoral offices. The tripartite Catholic-Jew-Protestant division became accepted even in such spheres as the Board of Education, judicial nominations (where Jews may have exceeded this "quota"), and other foci of political power. Under the Democratic mayoralties from 1945 to 1966 Jews remained firmly and prominently

Figure 29. Meeting between Soviet first deputy Anastas I. Mikoyan and American Jewish Committee leaders in New York, 1959. Left to right: Mikhail Menshikov, Soviet ambassador to the U.S., Herbert Lehman, former governor of New York, Anastas Mikoyan, Irving M. Engel, and Jacob Blaustein.

Figure 30. Israel prime minister Levi Eshkol addressing an Israel Bonds dinner at the Waldorf Astoria Hotel, 1964. To the left, Avraham Harman (Israel ambassador to the U.S.) and to the right, Joseph J. Schwartz. Photo Wagner International, New York.

Democratic. During most of this period Jews were elected city-wide controllers (Lazarus Joseph, Abraham D. *Beame), presidents of various boroughs, and to the powerful position of county surrogates as well as other local judgeships. In 1965 the reigning Democrats for the first time nominated a Jew, Beame, for the mayoralty, but largely owing to a considerable Jewish defection from that party to John V. Lindsay, the Republican reformer, the latter became mayor. Readjustments of political power late in the 1960s to include Negroes and Puerto Ricans tended to reduce Jewish and other white influence, but Jews continued to be a major constituent in New York politics, sympathetic to liberal reform but protective of their status.

Since the ethnic and religious groups of New York were extensively organized, to a large extent economically distinctive, and generally resided in well-defined neighborhoods, contact between them was quite limited. Such areas as trade unionism, popular entertainment, and sports were examples of inter-ethnic relations. Throughout this period Jewish and Catholic viewpoints were in periodic friction, most frequently over the public schools. Jews strongly espoused the schools' secular, religiously neutral character, and therefore opposed governmental sponsorship of such programs as released time for religious instruction, "nonsectarian" school prayers, and official moral education as desired by Catholics. These issues were resolved by the enactment and meager subsequent results of the first, the U.S. Supreme Court's invalidation of the second, and the abandonment of the third. Also at frequent issue was Christmas observance, sometimes combined with Ḥanukkah in schools where Jewish enrollment was high. These observances were especially widespread in older suburban towns, where opposition on the part of newly arrived Jewish residents to the long-established practices of the older Christian stock brought latent local group tensions to a head in several instances during the 1950s. It gradually became the policy of leading Jewish organizations tacitly to accept these observances while trying to prevent them from becoming too pronouncedly sectarian. Most Jews in suburban towns preferred this method, particularly because they had to oppose Protestants as well as Catholics on this issue. Of much greater moment was the lengthy dispute over Catholic demands for public aid to their parochial school system, which Jews and Protestants strongly opposed. The passage of federal and state legislation in 1964 and 1965 partially granting Catholic wishes, and the break in solid Jewish opposition to state-supported religious education on the part of some religious intellectuals and Orthodox yeshivah leaders finally tended to neutralize and resolve this issue. This settlement in turn tended to bring New York into the Catholic ecumenical movement, by then well under way in most other U.S. cities.

The most damaging and widespread form of discrimination against Jews, as well as Negroes, Italians, and others, was in the hiring practices of banks, insurance companies, large corporations, law firms, and department stores, some of which were even owned by Jews. Several private universities and professional schools also imposed stringent admissions quotas against Jews and others, but the professional schools at the city's Catholic colleges enrolled a high proportion of Jews. Social discrimination against Jews, on the other hand, was so firmly fixed that the most notable Jews could not belong to many of the city's leading business and social clubs, some of which their grandparents in fact had helped to found. Long-continued pressure, primarily from New York City and led by Jews, resulted in the passage of the state's Fair Employment Practice Act in 1945 prohibiting discrimination in employment, the first such law in the U.S. By the time of its passage its direct importance to Jews had already lessened, since employment discrimination decreased from the 1940s.

Anti-Semitic organizations existed spasmodically in New York City. The Ku Klux Klan barely appeared during the 1920s. The pro-Nazi Friends of New Germany and its successor, the German-American Bund, were active from 1934 to 1941 against fierce Jewish and pro-democratic opposition. The same held true of the contemporary "Christian Front," led by Joseph E. McWilliams and Father Edward Lodge Curran, a leading propagandist, which was close to Father Charles E. Coughlin's anti-Semitic movement. It conducted anti-Semitic street meetings and fostered petty hooliganism. These groups collapsed during World War II, following which organized anti-Semitism was virtually unknown for some 20 years. From about 1965 Black militant elements, fostering and feeding upon Negro-Jewish frictions, stimulated its renewal. A climax was reached during the New York City teachers' strike of 1968, when openly anti-Semitic expressions were heard without censorious reaction by the mayor, Board of Education, and many of the city's elite, including some Jews. The inclusion of anti-Semitic material at the same time in an exhibit on Harlem at the Metropolitan Museum of Art proved highly provocative. Black militant and New Left anti-Zionism became increasingly hard to distinguish from anti-Semitism. Subsequently major efforts were begun to improve relations. At the same time Jewish militant

Figure 33. New York teachers' strike rally at City Hall, 1968. Courtesy United Federation of Teachers, New York.

elements organized the Jewish Defense League for physical self-defense in various neighborhoods (see *Negro-Jewish Relations).

COMMUNAL, RELIGIOUS, CULTURAL, AND EDUCATIONAL AFFAIRS. In the years after World War I, New York retained its unchallenged position as the center of U.S. Jewish life. Of major nationwide organizations, only B'nai B'rith did not have its headquarters there after the Union of American Hebrew Congregations moved to New York from Cincinnati in 1952. Indeed, the city became the capital of the entire Diaspora after World War II, as Zionist and other world Jewish movements established their offices there. Thus, it was habitual for New York Jews to preside over major Jewish organizations or at least to conduct their daily affairs. A probable result was the weakening of the quality of local communal leadership as many of the ablest men and women were drawn into the affairs of these national and world Jewish bodies; New York Jewry was intensely interested in worldwide Jewish affairs and mass meetings on behalf of overseas Jewry sometimes brought more than 100,000 persons.

Jacob H. Schiff's death in 1920, Judah L. Magnes' withdrawal about 1918 and his removal to Palestine in 1922 left as the most representative New York figures Louis Marshall (d. 1929), Felix M. Warburg (d. 1937), and Stephen S. Wise (d. 1949). The former two were distinctly "uptown" leaders, Marshall a lawyer and Warburg a banker-philanthropist. Wise, a Zionist and Reform rabbi, was closely linked with liberal political and religious movements and drew much of his strength as an urban populist spokesman for the mass of working and lower middle-class Jews. His personal stature and influence was the source of much of the influence of the *American Jewish Congress, which he reestablished and headed from 1930 as a politically liberal, activist, pro-Zionist counterweight to the "uptown" bodies, the *American Jewish Committee in particular. Much of the Congress' importance was lost with Wise's death and the softening of social and ideological differences after 1945. Moreover the Committee eventually broadened its communal base and retracted the anti-Zionism it had adopted during the preceding decade. Wise was thus "the rabbi" of New York to the general community, a position in which he had no successor. The ambitious attempt to coordinate communal life in the Kehillah ended by 1920, and by then New York Jewry had acculturated with such rapidity and formed so large a proportion of the city's ethnically and religiously diverse population that its minority-group consciousness was too tenuous to establish a central Jewish community. Jews who were leaders in politics, labor, business, and philanthropy, as well as rabbis, tended to exercise informally the functions of community leadership in limited spheres of New York Jewish life, and there were weak Jewish community councils founded during the 1940s in Brooklyn, Queens, and the Bronx. These characteristics explain in part the comparatively weak showing of the United Jewish Appeal, which raised only one-third to one-quarter of its funds in Greater New York, where 40% of U.S. Jewry lived.

Virtually every Jewish organization had chapters and members in the city, including *landsmanshaftn* and benefit societies, lodges, cultural bodies, charitable groups, political causes, Zionists, and synagogues, so that the total number of Jewish organizations probably exceeded 4,000 before the 1940s; with the disappearance of many lodges, benefit societies, and small immigrant synagogues there was probably a decrease thereafter. Altogether the city's Jews constituted an agglomeration of social classes, ideologies, clustered interests, and institutions, possessing Jewish identification in varying degrees of intensity.

Figure 31. "Village East," a painting by Raphael Soyer, New York, 1966. Photo W. Rosenblum, Long Island City, N.Y.

Alongside vigorous local activity on behalf of such national or worldwide causes as Zionism, fairly distinct although overlapping spheres of interest could also be discerned. There was a charitable sphere, with the Federation of Jewish Philanthropies its focal institution, which served the poor and dependent. All of the federation-affiliated hospitals and many other institutions associated with it were nonsectarian. Highly skillful direction came from social workers and executives supported by a wealthy, rather limited constituency, many of whom found fulfillment as Jews in this charitable effort alone. The federation's original 54 affiliates numbered 130 by 1968, and included hospitals, institutions for the aged and chronically ill, casework agencies, summer camps, Young Men's and Women's Hebrew Associations and neighborhood centers, and the Jewish Education Committee. Affiliates also received funds from patient and client fees, the Greater New York Fund, government assistance, and direct contributions and endowments. Service to the increasing number of aged and to troubled families (through the Jewish Family Service, successor to the United Hebrew Charities), and recreation and informal education for middle-class youth and adults slowly replaced the earlier relief services. The Jewish hospitals, some of which were rated among the world's finest, totaled about 7,000 beds in 1968. They included Mount Sinai, Montefiore, Joint Diseases (orthopedic), Brooklyn Jewish, Long Island Jewish, Jewish Hospital for Chronic Diseases, Beth El (renamed Brookdale), Beth Israel, Maimonides, Bronx-Lebanon, Hillside, and Jewish Memorial. In addition, Jacobi Hospital, a municipal hospital, was attached to Yeshiva University's Albert Einstein Medical School, and Mount Sinai Hospital opened a medical school in 1968 as a unit of the City University of New York. The federation's income rose from $2,117,000 in 1917 to the $6,000,000 level around World War II after setbacks during the 1930s, and stood at around $22,000,000 in the late 1960s. In addition, it conducted a successful $104,000,000 capital funds campaign during the late 1950s, $60,700,000 of which was devoted to hospitals and $18,100,000 to care of the aged. Except for some community centers there was little linkage with the Jewish community at large. In 1970 New York's was the sole large U.S. Jewish philanthropic federation which did not combine its campaigns with those of the

United Jewish Appeal. Early aspirations of the Federation to be New York's representative body had been given up.

Another sphere in New York Jewry was Yiddish secularist Jewish life typified by the Jewish daily *Forward*, the Workmen's Circle, Yiddish cultural societies and schools, the *Jewish Labor Committee after 1934, and the scholarly institution, *YIVO. The early associations with Jewish trade unionism lessened as Yiddish secularism became a cultural and fraternal middle-class movement. Labor Zionists in Poale Zion and the Farband-Jewish National Workers Alliance combined Yiddish with their Zionism, while Communist-oriented leftists maintained rival, parallel institutions between the late 1920s and the 1950s. Linguistic assimilation inevitably led to the decline of Yiddishism from its peak during the 1920s, and after about 1950 the Yiddish sphere included a dwindling group of veterans, a number of younger enthusiasts, and some post-World War II immigrants. A much smaller sphere was that of the Hebraists, centered in the *Histadrut Ivrith and the weekly *Hadoar*, and closely tied to Zionist and educational affairs. Composed largely of writers, Hebrew teachers, and rabbis, the Hebrew sphere shrank as the reality of Hebrew in Israel drained the vitality of Hebraic idealism in the U.S.

The religious sphere was very large and active, and was divided along lines which until the 1950s tended to be more social than theological. In several neighborhoods, particularly Boro Park, Crown Heights, Williamsburg, and sections of Flatbush in Brooklyn, as well as the Lower East Side even in its decline, Sabbaths and Jewish holidays dominated the local atmosphere as full synagogues, shut stores, and festively dressed residents were conspicuous. Large sectors of the garment industry and such kindred branches as rags and dry goods regularly closed on these days. The commerce and industry of the city as a whole came near a standstill on Rosh Ha-Shanah and Yom Kippur. The public schools were shut on those days from the 1960s because Jews, who formed a majority of the teaching staff, absented themselves.

In 1967 there were 539 Orthodox, 184 Conservative, 93 Reform, and five unclassified synagogues known in Greater New York; all but 163 of the total were within the city's boundaries. Actual synagogue affiliation tended to be low, however. A study of Brooklyn suggested that merely one-quarter of its Jews belonged to synagogues in 1945–46, a proportion which probably differed little in other boroughs. Many, however, habitually attended Orthodox synagogues without joining them, and vast numbers reserved seats on the High Holidays, the only days they attended. Quite a few of the larger Orthodox synagogues filled their seats on the High Holidays by engaging a famous cantor of the lyric, florid East European style, a practice which was at its height during the cantorial heyday of the 1920s. The suburbs, on the other hand, appear to have had higher affiliation with lower average attendance. An undetermined number of prosperous, cultured Jews formed a large part of the membership of the Community Church and the Ethical Culture Society.

Reform Judaism centered around its major temples, some of which were monumental or historic. Temple Emanu-El continued to be foremost on account of its size, wealth, and prestige, and occupied a splendid edifice at Fifth Avenue and 65th Street from 1929. Other major congregations included the Central Synagogue (whose building at Lexington Avenue and 55th Street dated to 1870), the Free Synagogue, Rodeph Shalom, Shaarey Tefilah (West End Synagogue until its transfer from the West Side to the East Side of Manhattan in 1959), Union Temple and Beth Elohim in Brooklyn, and Central Synagogue in Rockville Center (Nassau County). The older congregations did not share much in the movement within Reform toward more traditional worship. Aside from worship the primary interest of Reform Jewry was philanthropy. The Federation of Jewish Philanthropies and most leading Jewish charitable institutions were composed largely of Reform laymen, who were also prominent in general philanthropy. From the 1950s there was a gradual shift toward liberal social and political action as the major goal, but there were objections and Temple Emanu-El left the Union of American Hebrew Congregations in protest at this direction. The foremost Reform rabbi was Stephen S. Wise, who in 1922 founded the Hebraic and Zionist-oriented Jewish Institute of Religion (J.I.R.), which opened in 1925. Although the J.I.R. intended to train rabbis for all denominations, most of its graduates went to Reform. The notable early faculty included S. W. Baron, R. Marcus, H. Slonimsky, S. Spiegel, C. Tchernowitz, and others, but the school declined after its first decade. Other New York Reform rabbinic notables included Samuel Schulman, Jonah B. Wise, Louis I. Newman, Bernard J. Bamberger, Samuel H. Goldenson, Julius Mark, Charles E. Shulman, and Edward E. Klein.

New York City was the American center of Orthodox Judaism. Most of the immigrant and *landsmanshaft* synagogues of the East Side, Brownsville, and other older districts, which constituted the majority of known Orthodox synagogues, faded away in the years after World War I, although many survived as burial societies. Their successors were large, rather Anglicized neighborhood synagogues, especially in Brooklyn and the Bronx, which often sponsored afternoon Hebrew schools and sometimes Sunday schools in addition to pious study and small-scale charity. Young Israel synagogues considerably increased in number and activity. The employment of rabbis by Orthodox congregations gradually became the practice, and early incumbents of pulpits included such East European scholars as Rabbis A. D. Burack, H. Dachowitz, S. J. Finkelstein, and M. B. Tomashov. By the 1940s Orthodoxy in New York lost its intimate association with immigrant life, and tended to be divided internally between modernists oriented to the problems of Orthodox Judaism in a secular,

Figure 32. New York mayor John Lindsay presenting the key of the city to Israel prime minister, Golda Meir, September 1969. Courtesy Government Press Office, Tel Aviv.

scientific, urban society, and others indifferent or hostile to such concerns and stressing intensive piety, yeshivah study, and aloofness from non-Orthodox Judaism. The modernist trend included such congregations as Kehillath Jeshurun, The Jewish Center, Fifth Avenue Synagogue, Riverdale Jewish Center, and such rabbis as Leo Jung, Emanuel Rackman, Joseph H. Lookstein, Simon G. Kramer, Walter S. Wurzberger, and Irving Greenberg. The "pietist" group was led mainly from yeshivot and was augmented by ḥasidic immigration from the 1940s. Special Orthodox segments were the S. R. Hirsch school of German Orthodoxy, transplanted in 1938–40 to upper Manhattan under the leadership of Rabbi Joseph Breuer, and Sephardi congregations, largely in Brooklyn, composed of contemporary immigrants from Turkey, Greece, Syria, and Iraq. The venerable Shearith Israel continued under the ministry of H. P. Mendes, D. de Sola Pool, and L. C. Gerstein. The common institutional effort of Orthodox Jewry was the promotion of yeshivot, whose enrollment multiplied from below 2,000 in 1920 to approximately 5,000 in 1935, 8,000 in 1945, and 45,000 in 1968. The most striking development was that of Yeshivath Rabbi Isaac Elchanan and its high school of 1920 into Yeshiva College from 1928, under the direction of Bernard Revel. It expanded into Yeshiva University, from 1943 under the leadership of Samuel Belkin, to include several high schools, the college, graduate and professional schools, and a medical school. Its yeshivah brought notable rabbinic scholars from Europe to serve as principal *rashei yeshivah,* the first two being Rabbis S. H. Polacheck and Moses Soloveichik; Joseph B. Soloveichik, the latter's son, succeeded his father in this capacity. Other notable Orthodox yeshivah scholars and talmudists were Rabbis Joseph E. Henkin, Moses Feinstein, Jacob Kamenetsky, Moses A. Shatzkes, and Aaron Kotler. Yeshivot, rabbinic leadership of distinction, and several hundred thousand committed Orthodox Jews lent New York Jewry a tone more Orthodox than anywhere else in the U.S. The Orthodox were also the least suburbanized segment, with only 32 synagogues beyond the city limits in 1967.

The city's Conservative congregations leaned close to Orthodoxy in which most of their members and leaders, at least before 1950, had been raised. The Jewish Theological Seminary was the focal institution of the Conservatives, and exercised broad spiritual influence in the Jewish and general community. Partly owing to the influence of Mordecai M. Kaplan, Conservative synagogues also served as community centers, offering social, cultural, and recreational activities. The Jewish Center and the West Side Institutional Synagogue in Manhattan, both Orthodox although founded by Kaplan, began the trend. The Society for the Advancement of Judaism (Reconstructionist), B'nai Jeshurun, and Park Avenue Synagogue in Manhattan and the Brooklyn Jewish Center, Flatbush Jewish Center, and East Midwood Jewish Center in Brooklyn typified this trend, which was continued in many large newer synagogues in Queens and the suburbs. The Conservative growth was greatest in Queens and the new suburban towns, where 145 of their 184 synagogues were situated in 1967. Rabbinic leaders, besides Kaplan, included Israel Goldstein, Max Drob, Israel H. Levinthal, Harry Halpern, Robert Gordis, Ben Zion Bokser, Milton Steinberg, William Berkowitz, and Judah Nadich. Conservative, Orthodox, and Reform Jewry each had their local synagogue federation within their respective national bodies while the New York Board of Rabbis, under the direction of Rabbi H. H. Gordon, was an active organization of the rabbinate.

Jewish education in New York followed nationwide trends in the slow disappearance of the *ḥeder,* the rise and decline of communal *talmud torahs* and Yiddish schools in the period from 1915 to 1950, the continuance of the Sunday school, and the rapid growth of congregational schools especially after 1945 in Queens and the suburbs. Significant, distinctive local trends included the relatively smaller proportion of Jewish children who attended Sunday school and the higher proportion enrolled in yeshivot. The number of children attending a Jewish school rose from 65,000 in 1917, to 75,000 in 1935–36, and then sharply to 154,000 in 1952–53 and 202,000 in 1958, and then declined to 136,000 in 1968–69. About 23.5% of all Jewish elementary school-age children were thus enrolled in 1917, and the proportion rose to 37% in 1959. About two-thirds attended weekday schools at all periods. Yiddish education, which numbered about 6,900 pupils in 1935, declined to 3,200 in 1962. About two-thirds of yeshivah enrollment (see above) in the entire U.S. was in New York. Over 90% of it was under Orthodox auspices.

New York's Jewish libraries, institutions of Jewish learning, and serious and learned Jewish periodicals made it a major Jewish cultural center by 1920 and the principal one in the Diaspora from the onset of the Nazi era. In addition to Yeshiva University the city had numerous other yeshivot, including Torah Vadaath, Mir, Tifereth Jerusalem, Ḥafeẓ Ḥayyim, and Lubavich, to which Orthodox young men came from many parts of the U.S. and abroad. The Jewish Theological Seminary, Jewish Institute of Religion (combined with Hebrew Union College from 1948), and various divisions of Yeshiva University provided not only rabbinic training but included scholars of international standing on their faculties. Columbia was the first university in the U.S. to offer instruction in every major area of Jewish studies at the highest level. The Jewish Division of the New York Public Library and the library of the Jewish Theological Seminary (damaged by fire in 1966) were two of the six or seven leading Jewish libraries in the world, and other local institutions possessed fine collections. A Jewish museum was sponsored by the Seminary. No other city of the Diaspora offered such an abundance of Jewish scholars, books and manuscripts, and varied opportunities for study in a communal milieu which was profoundly Jewish.

CULTURE. The half-century following the end of World War I witnessed the entry of Jews in large numbers into every corner of New York artistic and cultural life. Since this period also marked the growing domination by New York City of U.S. cultural life in general, and in some areas, such as theater, music, and publishing, its virtual monopolization, New York Jews prominent in these fields found themselves automatically at the center of national attention as well. The role of New York Jews as consumers of the arts also grew immensely during these years. It is safe to say that from the 1920s on Jews formed a disproportionately high percentage of New York's theatergoers, music listeners, book purchasers, and art collectors. (One rough estimate placed Jews at 70% of the city's concert and theater audience during the 1950s.) Similarly, Jews also emerged in these years as major philanthropic patrons of the arts. After World War II, particularly, they played a prominent part in endowing and supporting local cultural and artistic institutions.

In literature many Jewish writers who had grown up in the immigrant ghetto were identified with the schools of social realism and "proletarian fiction" that were a main feature of the 1920s, and especially, of the Depression years of the 1930s. Left-wing Jewish intellectuals such as Sidney Hook, Irving Howe, Alfred Kazin, Philip Rahv, and Michael Gold clustered around such New York publications as *The Nation, The New Masses, The New Leader,* and *Partisan Review.* Some of the best descriptions ever written of New York life in the early and mid-20th century, especially of its immigrant neighborhoods, can be found in such books as Samuel Ornitz' *Haunch, Paunch and Jowl* (1925), Henry Roth's *Call It Sleep* (1934), Michael Gold's *Jews Without Money* (1930), Alfred Kazin's *On Native Grounds* (1942) and *A Walker in the City* (1951), Bernard Malamud's *The Assistant* (1957), Paul Goodman's *The Empire City* (1959), and the novels of Wallace Markfield (see *U.S. Literature, Jews in).

The poetry of Louis Zukofsky was suffused with the atmosphere of New York life, while Kenneth Koch was a leader of the school of "New York poets" in the 1960s. In the years after World War II the 92nd St. YMHA served as a center for readings of modern American poetry and for the introduction to a wide public of a number of young contemporary poets.

In the drama the Yiddish theater lost much of its vitality after the 1920s. In 1928 no less than 11 New York Yiddish theaters were giving hundreds of performances a month, a number that had shrunk to a mere occasional production by the 1960s. The golden age of the Broadway musical drama in the late 1930s, 1940s, and 1950s was dominated by Jewish composers and librettists such as George Gershwin, Jerome Kern, and the teams of Rodgers and Hammerstein, and Lerner and Loewe. Al Jolson, Eddie Cantor, Eddie Fisher, and Barbra Streisand were popular singers whose careers were associated with the New York stage. Leading Broadway playwrights of the 1930s and 1940s were Lillian Hellman, Clifford Odets, George S. Kaufman, Moss Hart, and Elmer Rice, while in the 1950s and 1960s there were Arthur Miller, Paddy Chayefsky, and Neil Simon. Paul Muni, Herschel Bernardi, Fredric March, and Ann Bancroft were nationally acclaimed actors who continually returned to the Broadway stage. Lee Strassberg's Actors Studio was an influential training ground for actors and directors after World War II, while Gene Frankel and Joseph Papp were well-known directors, and David Merrick and Herman Shumlin prominent producers. Sol Hurok, who began his career organizing local Jewish productions in Brooklyn's Brownsville, developed into the leading musical impresario in the U.S. The avant-garde, "off Broadway" theater of the 1960s was led by such groups as Julien Beck's and Judith Malina's Living Theater and Joseph Chaikin's Open Theater. Indicative of the impact of Jewish audiences on the New York theater was the fact that a number of Broadway hits of the 1950s and 1960s were on Jewish themes, the most successful of all being the musical *Fiddler on the Roof*.

The New York musical world during the period under discussion was heavily Jewish too, and Jews formed most of the instrumentalists of the New York Philharmonic Symphony Orchestra, the Metropolitan Opera Orchestra, and the National Broadcasting Company Symphony Orchestra. Among leading Jewish musical performers in

Figure 34. The Satmar Yeshivah in Williamsburg, Brooklyn. From P. Garvin, *A People Apart*, New York, 1970.

these years were the conductors Artur Rodzinski, Bruno Walter, Lukas Foss, and Leonard Bernstein; opera singers Richard Tucker, Robert Merrill, Jan Peerce, Roberta Peters, Beverly Sills, and Friedrich Schorr; instrumentalists Vladimir Horowitz and Isaac Stern; and jazz musicians Woody Herman, Stan Getz, and Zoot Sims. The New York musicians' union, Local 801, was over 70% Jewish from the 1930s on. Jews were also very active in the writing and promotion of popular music for Broadway's "Tin Pan Alley." Otto Kahn was a leading financial backer of the Metropolitan Opera in the 1920s and 1930s, while Morton Baum helped found the New York City Center for Music and Dance and was instrumental in the establishment of the Lincoln Center for the Performing Arts. Lincoln Kerstein was the chief financial benefactor of the New York City Ballet, one of whose leading choreographers was Jerome Robbins. Sophie Maslow was also a leading figure in the New York dance world.

In painting, the Soyer brothers, Raphael, Moses, and Isaac, and Chaim Gross were prominent in the social-realistic "Fourteenth Street School" that flourished in Greenwich Village in the 1920s. Ben Shahn and Jack Levine were among the many Jewish artists whose early careers were associated with the art programs of the Works Projects Administration during the Depression years. The Nazi persecution brought to New York such German expressionist painters as Lionel Feininger, Max Weber, and George Grosz. Prominent in the "New York School" of abstract expressionists that developed after World War II were Franz Klein and Mark Rothko. The Jewish Museum diverged from its tradition of exhibiting Jewish art only to sponsor a number of important avant-garde shows of sculpture and art in the 1960s. Solomon Guggenheim endowed the Guggenheim Museum of Modern Art built by Frank Lloyd Wright in 1960. Robert Lehman's world renowned collection of impressionist and post-impressionist painting was willed to the Metropolitan Museum of Art in 1969.

In WEVD, established by the *Jewish Daily Forward* in 1931, New York boasted the world's only full-time Yiddish radio station, though by 1970 much of its programming had gone over to English. Gertrude Berg, Fanny Brice, Morey Amsterdam, Walter Winchell, and Barry Gray were New York radio personalities who succeeded in becoming household names. An entire school of television comedy, deriving in the main from the comic routines of the "Borscht Belt" (see *New York State), was represented by such performers as Sam Levenson, Milton Berle, Sid Caesar, and Jerry Lewis.

From the 1920s on Jews played a prominent role in the New York publishing business, among them Horace Liveright of Liveright & Boni. B. W. Huebsch and Harold Guinzberg of Viking Press, Henry Simon and M. Lincoln Schuster of Simon & Schuster, Alfred Knopf of Alfred A. Knopf, Bennett Cerf of Random House, and Jason Epstein of Anchor Books. Many additional, smaller Jewish-owned firms appeared in the years after World War II. The German-Jewish house of Schocken Books moved to New York City in 1946. Other New York publishers who put out a largely or wholly Jewish line were Bloch Publishing Co., Thomas Yoseloff, and Abelard & Schumann.

In journalism New York's Yiddish press continued to flourish despite declining circulations in the 1920s and 1930s, but lost ground steadily in the years after World War II (see Press, Jewish in U.S.A.). Among English dailies, the internationally esteemed *New York Times*, published by Adolph Ochs and Arthur Hays Sulzberger, and the *New York Post*, published by Dorothy Schiff and J. David Stern, were Jewish-owned and were heavily read by Jews. Three

Figure 35. Members of the Jewish Defense League at a protest rally for Soviet Jewry, 1971.

New York periodicals with nation-wide audiences that were also under Jewish ownership or editorship were *The New Yorker, The Village Voice,* and the *New York Review of Books.* Among the many Jewish weeklies and monthlies published in New York in 1970 mention should be made of the influential **Commentary,* and of *Midstream, The Reconstructionist, The Jewish Spectator,* and *Congress Biweekly* (see *Press, Jewish, in U.S.A.).

Noteworthy also in the years after World War I was the growing participation of New York Jews in the area of popular sports, both as spectators and as performers. Among the better-known New York athletes of this period were boxers Benny Leonard and Barney Ross, baseball players Harry Danning, Sid Gordon, Cal Abrams, and Sandy Koufax, football quarterback Sid Luckman, and basketball star and coach Nat Holman. Mike Jacobs was a promoter of champion boxers and Hirsch Jacobs was a leading trainer of racehorses. Jews also excelled in many "minor" sports such as fencing, handball, billiards, and bowling, whose confined playing areas made them ideal for urban conditions such as those in New York.

In effect, so complete was the Jewish involvement in New York cultural life in the middle decades of the 20th century that it would be impossible to imagine practically any aspect of the latter without it. Moreover, this involvement was not at all restricted to the realms of "high" culture and the arts. On the contrary, it made itself felt most heavily in numerous areas of everyday New York life, in its impact on local speech, gestures, food, humor, and attitudes. It is doubtful indeed if anywhere else in the history of the Diaspora has a large Jewish community existed in so harmonious a symbiosis with a great metropolis without either ghettoizing itself from its surroundings or losing its own distinct sense of character and identity. Nor can the relationship be thought of as having been merely one-way. If the Jews gave to New York unstintingly of their experience, energies, and talents, they received in return an education in urbanity and a degree of cosmopolitan sophistication unknown to any other Jewish community of similar size in the past. It is little wonder that many Jews developed an attachment to New York that bordered on the devotional. Above all, when 20th-century New York Jews thought of the city they lived in, they did not simply consider it a great capital of civilization that had generously taken them in; rather, they thought of themselves—and with every justification—as joint builders of this greatness and one of its main continuing supports. Such a relationship marks a unique moment in Jewish history, and one that given current cultural and demographic trends both in the United States and the world at large is not likely to recur again. [L.P.G./H.H./E.Gr./Y.B.-D.]

Bibliography: 1654–1870: D. and T. de Sola Pool, *An Old Faith in the New World* (1955); D. de Sola Pool, *Portraits Etched in Stone* (1953); L. Hershkowitz, *Wills of Early New York Jews 1704–1799* (1967); L. Hershkowitz and I. S. Meyer, *Lee Max Friedman Collection of American Jewish Colonial Correspondence: Letters of the Franks Family 1733–1748* (1968); H. B. Grinstein, *Rise of the Jewish Community of New York 1654–1860* (1945); idem, in: HUCA, 18 (1944), 321–52; idem, in: *Jewish Review,* 2 (1944/45), 41–58, 187–203; A. M. Dushkin, *Jewish Education in New York City* (1917); R. Ernst, *Immigrant Life in New York City 1825–1863* (1949); I. J. Benjamin, *Three Years in America 1859–1862,* 1 (1956), 50–85 (trans. from the German). 1870–1920: M. Rischin, *The Promised City: New York's Jews 1870–1914* (1962), incl. bibl.; A. A. Goren, *New York Jews and the Quest for Community: The Kehillah Experiment, 1908–1922* (1970), incl. bibl.; H. Hapgood, *The Spirit of the Ghetto: Studies of the Jewish Quarter of New York* (1902); A. Cahan, *Bleter fun Mayn Lebn,* 5 vols. (1926–31; partial trans. by L. Stein, Eng., 1970); R. Sanders, *The Downtown Jews: Portraits of an Immigrant Generation* (1969); R. Lubove, *The Progressives and the Slums: Tenement House Reform in New York City* (1962); S. Birmingham, *"Our Crowd": The Great Jewish Families of New York* (1967); idem, *The Grandees* (1971); I. Markens, *The Hebrew in America* (1888); *The Jewish Communal Register of New York City, 1917–1918* (1918); J. S. Hertz, *Di Yidishe Sotsyalistishe Bavegung in Amerike* (1954); B. E. Supple, in: *Business History Review,* 31 (Summer, 1957), 143–77; L. P. Gartner, in: AJHSQ, 53 (1964), 264–81; G. Osofsky, *Harlem: The Making of a Ghetto* (1966); M. Rosenstock, *Louis Marshall: Defender of Jewish Rights* (1965); M. Dubofsky, *When Workers Organize: New York City in the Progressive Era* (1968); G. Klaperman, *The Story of Yeshiva University* (1969); N. H. Winter, *Jewish Education in a Pluralistic Society: Samson Benderly and Jewish Education in the United States* (1966); H. Berman, in: Joseph L. Blau et al. (eds.), *Essays on Jewish Life and Thought Presented in Honor of Salo Wittmayer Baron* (1959); M. Berman, in: AJHSQ, 54 (1964), 53–81; T. Levitan, *Islands of Compassion: A History of the Jewish Hospitals of New York* (1964); A. Schoener (ed.), *Portal to America: The Lower East Side 1879–1925* (1967); R. Glanz, *Studies in Judaica Americana* (1970); idem, *Jews and Italians* (1970); C. Reznikoff (ed.), *Louis Marshall: Champion of Liberty; selected papers and addresses,* 2 vols. (1957); M. Weinberger, *Ha-Yehudim ve-ha-Yahadut be-New York* (1886–87); E. Tcherikower et al., *Geshikhte fun der Yidisher Arbeter Bavegung in der Fareynikte Shtatn,* 2 vols. (1943), abbr. trans. rev. ed. A. Antonovsky, *The Early Jewish Labor Movement in the United States* (1961); L. S. Dawidowicz, in: JSOS, 25 (1963), 102–32; idem, in: *For Max Weinreich on his 70th Birthday* (1964), 31–43; Z. Szajkowszki, in: JSOS, 32 (1970), 286–306; A. Gorenstein, in: AJHSQ, 50 (1960/61), 202–38; M. Rischin, *ibid.,* 43 (1953/54), 10–36. 1920–1970: A. Mann, *LaGuardia: A Fighter Against His Times, 1882–1933* (1959); idem, *LaGuardia Comes to Power, 1933* (1965); T. J. Lowi, *At the Pleasure of the Mayor; Patronage and Power in New York City, 1898–1958* (1964); N. Glazer and D. P. Moynihan, *Beyond the Melting Pot* (1963); Federation of Jewish Philanthropies of New York, *The Golden Heritage* (1969); A. Nevins, *Herbert H. Lehman and His Era* (1963); A. F. Landesman, *Brownsville: The Birth, Development, and Passing of a Jewish Community in New York* (1969); S. S. Wise, *Challenging Years: The Autobiography of Stephen S. Wise* (1949); P. S. Foner, *The Fur and Leather Workers Union: A Story of Dramatic Struggles and Achievements* (1950); B. Z. Hoffman, *Fufzig Yor Klok-Makher Union* (1936); C. S. Liebman, in: AJYB, 66 (1965), 21–97; O. I. Janowsky (ed.), *The American Jew: A Reappraisal* (1964); J. L. Teller, *Strangers and Natives* (1968); S. Poll, *The Hasidic Community of Williamsburg; A Study of Sociology of Religion* (1962); AJYB, 31 (1929–30), 203–4; 39 (1937–38), 72; AJYB, 71 (1970), 217–28; W. Herberg, in: AJYB, 53 (1952), 3–74; M. M. Fagen, in: JSS, 1 (Jan., 1939), 73–104; J. Loft, in: JSS, 2 (Jan., 1940), 67–78; D. M. Liberson, in: JSDS, 18 no. 2 (1956), 83–117; B. Lazerwitz, in: JJSO, 3 no. 2 (1961), 254–60; S. P. Abelow, *History of Brooklyn Jewry* (1937); E. J. Lipman and A. Vorspan, *A Tale of Ten Cities* (1962); Federation of Jewish Philanthropies of New York: Demographic Study Committee (C. M. Horowitz and L. J. Kaplan), *Jewish Population of New York Area, 1900–1957* (1959).

NEW YORK STATE, an eastern state of the U.S., bounded on the north and west by the St. Lawrence Seaway, Lake Ontario, and Lake Erie, and at the southern tip by the Atlantic Ocean. Of its 17,979,712 (1970) inhabitants, about 2,522,000 are Jews. Outside New York City and its suburbs, Nassau, Suffolk, and *Westchester counties, there are about 21 Jewish communities numbering 1,000 or more, and about 150 synagogues.

After 1654, when 23 Spanish Portuguese Jews founded the first permanent Jewish settlement in North America at New Amsterdam (*New York after 1664), most Jews who settled in the area which became New York State in 1788 were of Spanish-Portuguese origin until the 19th century. Although most of these Jews lived in New York City, already in 1658 Asser *Levy dealt in real estate near Albany, and in 1678 Jacob de Lucena was trading as far north as Kingston on the Hudson River. In 1717 the successful merchants, Luis Gomez and his sons, built a trading post on the Hudson near Newburgh, and in 1732 the *Hays family settled near New Rochelle in Westchester. During the French and Indian War, Hayman *Levy, a Hanoverian, conducted a large fur trade around Lake Champlain in the north, and Lyon and Manuel *Josephson supplied goods to northern British forts. Some Jews settled on Long Island in the 1760s, while Aaron *Levy visited the Lake George region from 1805 to 1834.

Substantial German Jewish immigration began during the 1830s. Many of the immigrants settled along the upper New York State transportation routes to the Middle West: Newburgh (1848), Poughkeepsie (1848), Kingston (1853), Hudson (1867), *Albany (1838), Schenectady (1840s), Troy (1850s), Amsterdam (1874), Gloversville (1850s), *Utica (1848), Syracuse (1839), *Rochester (1848), and *Buffalo (1847) on the Hudson-Mohawk River route. Other settlements were founded in Binghamton (1885), Elmira (1850), and Olean (1882) along the southern Susquehanna River, and Plattsburg (1861) on Lake Champlain and Ogdensburg (1865) on the St. Lawrence River. By 1860 there were 20 congregations in the state and 53 by 1877. These Jews were predominantly merchants and peddlers, while some were farmers. By 1909 there were seven Jewish farmers' organizations in the state, and the first Jewish farmers' credit union was formed in 1911. Many rural Jews would join their urban brethren for High Holiday services.

An estimated 60,000–80,000 Jews lived in New York in

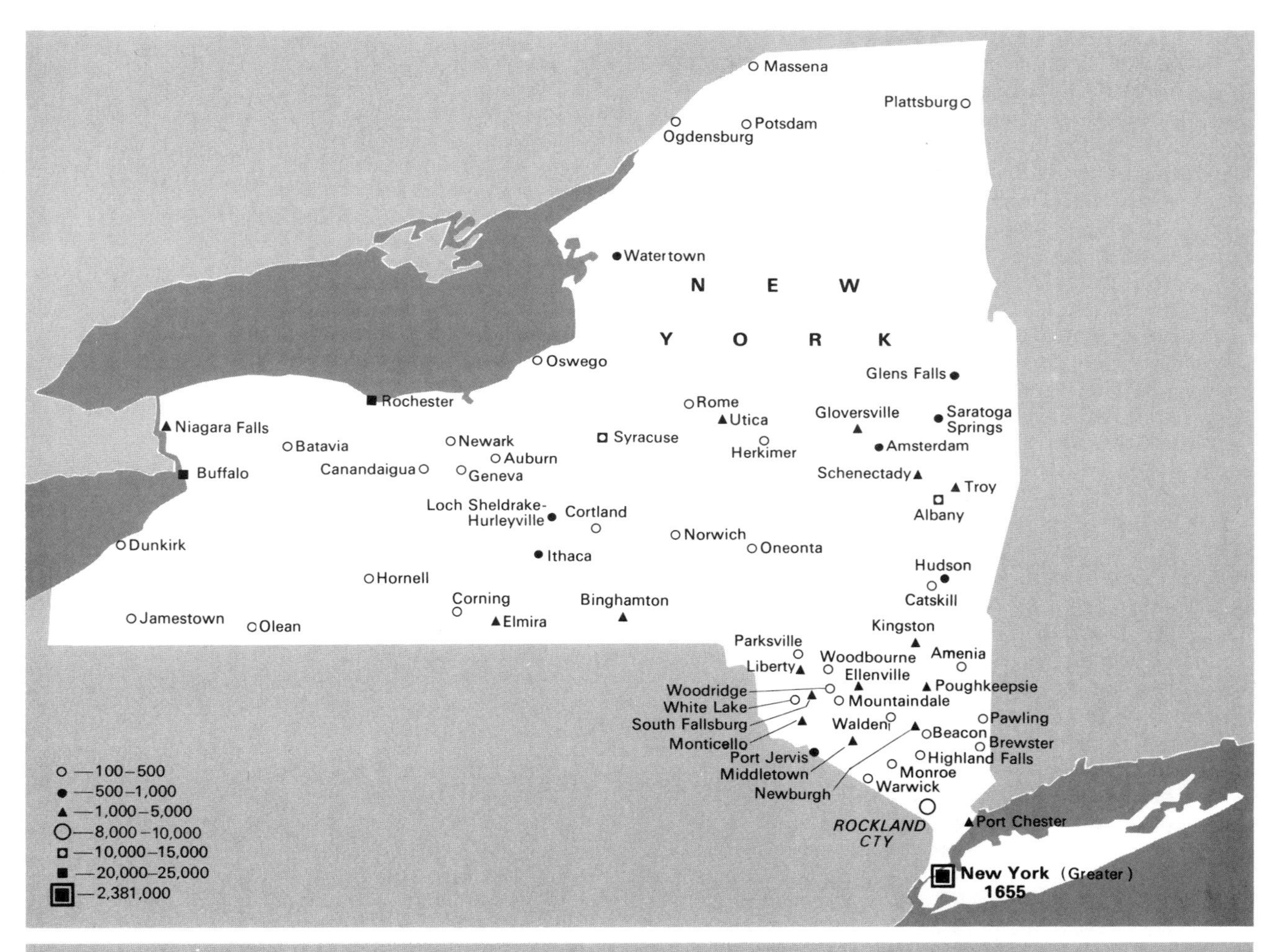

Total Jewish population of New York	2,521,755
% of Jews in general population of New York	13.95
% of New York Jews in Jewish population of U.S.A.	42.96

Jewish communities in New York. Population figures for 1968.

1880. East European immigration that occurred during the three decades following increased that number to about 900,000 by 1910. Heavy immigration continued until 1924, so that 1,835,500 Jews lived in New York in 1928. Although most of the East European Jews settled in New York City, others, encouraged to alleviate the city's congestion, settled in towns in the counties to the north of the city, such as Haverstraw (1896), Ossining (1891), Peekskill (1894), New Rochelle (1880s), Lake Placid (1903), Liberty (1880s), Spring Valley (1901), Yonkers (1860s), Mamaroneck (1890), Massena (1897), Suffern (1880s), and Tarrytown (1887), as well as Ithaca (1891) in the western part of the state. In 1940, 90% of the state's 2,206,328 (1937 figure) Jews resided in New York City. However, the next two decades saw a flow of city dwellers, including a disproportionately large number of Jews, to the suburbs. In 1940 fewer than 100,000 Jews had lived in all the suburbs, but Nassau alone had 329,000 Jews by 1956 and 372,000 in 1968; Suffolk, 20,000 by 1956 and 42,000 in 1968; and Westchester, 116,900 by 1956 and 131,000 in 1968. The number of permanent Jewish residents in the upstate resort counties of Sullivan, Ulster, and Orange did not appreciably increase from 1940. For example, Monticello in Sullivan County had 1,350 Jews in 1937 and 1,200 in 1956; Ellenville in Ulster County had 540 Jews in 1937 and 1,100 in 1968. However, during summer months these counties became swelled with city Jews, such that the area was popularly dubbed the "Borscht Belt." Several of the resort hotels, established by Jewish farmers who at first only took in boarders, became nationally famous.

Jews have attained prominence in all professions in New York, and were elected to high state and federal office. Herbert H. *Lehman was governor from 1932 to 1942, and U.S. senator, 1949–57. Jacob K. *Javits served as U.S. senator (from 1957). Among the many Jewish U.S. congressmen were Lucius N. *Littauer (1897–1907), Meyer *London (1914–18, 1920–22), Sol *Bloom (1923–49), and Emanuel *Celler (from 1923). Simon W. *Rosendale (1892–94), Nathaniel L. Goldstein (1942–54), and Louis J. Lefkowitz (from 1957) were state attorney generals, and Arthur Levitt was state controller (from 1954). Benjamin N. *Cardozo (1927–32), Irving Lehman (1940–45), and Stanley H. Fuld (from 1966) were chief justices of the Court of Appeals, the state's highest bench, while David W. Peck (1947–57) and Bernard Botein (1957–69) were presiding justices of the State Supreme Court Appellate Division. Pressure from Jewish members of the New York State Legislature led to the passage of the Fair Employment Practice Act in 1945, the first act in the U.S. prohibiting discrimination in employment practices. Party leaders in the State Senate have been Simon L. Adler (1915–26), Benjamin F. Feinberg (1944–49), and Joseph Zaretski (since 1957). Outside New York City, Jewish newspapers are published in Buffalo (since 1918), Rochester (1924), Westchester (1942), Long Island (1944), and Schenectady (1965).

Bibliography: AJYB, (1938–39, 1970); C. M. Horowitz and L. J. Kaplan, *The Estimated Jewish Population of the New York Area, 1900–1975;* J. R. Marcus, *Early American Jewry,* 1 (1961), 24–101; U. Z. Engleman, in: JSOS, 9 (April 1947), 127–74. [E.GR.]

NEW ZEALAND, member of the Commonwealth of Nations in the S. Pacific. In 1829, some 60 years after the rediscovery of New Zealand, the Sydney firm of Cooper and Levy established itself in the South Island at Port Cooper (Lyttleton) and Port Levy, a little to the north. Solomon Levy, the Jewish partner, later became a benefactor of both Jewish and Christian educational and charitable institutions. During the next decade, other Jewish traders

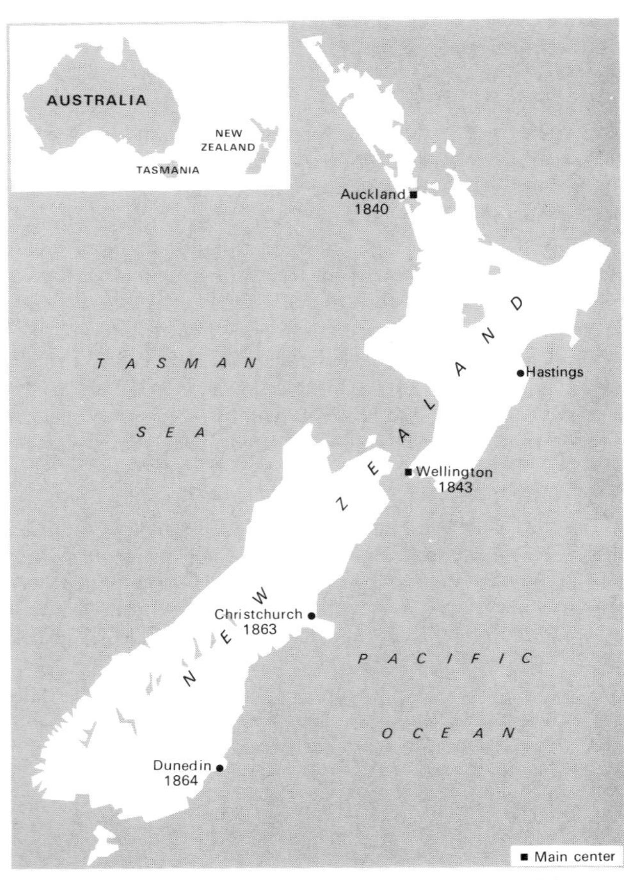

Jewish communities in New Zealand, with dates of establishment.

began to arrive. In 1830 Joseph Barrow Montefiore (a member of the English *Montefiore family) from Sydney established Montefiore Brothers, dealing largely in flax and whale oil. In 1831 Joel Samuel *Polack, author of two books on New Zealand, came first to Hokianga to trade and deal in land. He shortly transferred to Kororareka, Bay of Islands, where a cousin of J. B. Montefiore had established a trading post in 1831. Four other Jews were resident at Kororareka in 1838, but along with David *Nathan who had arrived in 1839 they moved to Auckland after it was made the capital in 1840. With a handful of other Jewish storekeepers and traders, David Nathan founded the Auckland Jewish community. Members of the congregation read the services and conducted religious functions—a pattern to be followed elsewhere in New Zealand. The first ordained minister (J. E. Myers of Auckland) was appointed to a New Zealand congregation in 1859.

In Wellington the first Jewish arrival appears to have been Abraham Hort Jr. who came in 1840 with two carpenter brothers, Solomon and Benjamin Levy. These were followed in 1843 by Abraham *Hort Sr. (1799–1869), a London Jewish communal leader who went to New Zealand with the intention of founding a community and promoting planned immigration to relieve Jewish poverty in England, through the New Zealand Company which in 1840 had begun colonizing parts of the country. Although successful in founding the Wellington community he failed to achieve his immigration plans. The discovery of gold in Otago and Westland in the 1860s led directly or indirectly to the establishment of the communities of *Dunedin and *Christchurch and to the temporary founding of those in Hokitika, Timaru, and Nelson; the Timaru synagogue still stands without a congregation. David Isaacs, formerly of the Wellington and Dunedin congregations, was appointed shortly after 1863 to Nelson and I. Zachariah of the gold-mining town of Hokitika was appointed in 1870 to the Christchurch congregation. Most of the ordained ministers came from Jews' College, England, including H. *Van Staveren (Wellington, 1877–1930) and A. Astor (Dunedin and Auckland, 1926–71). C. Pitkowsky (Wellington, 1905–30) and the brothers N. Salas (Auckland and Christchurch, 1929–58) and M. Salas (Auckland, 1934–55) came from Ereẓ Israel.

New Zealand's links with Ereẓ Israel date from the time of the Crimean War, when money was being collected in Auckland and Wellington for starving Jews in Ereẓ Israel. In 1862 Jacob *Saphir of Jerusalem visited Dunedin on a similar mission. Before New Zealand became a British colony in 1840, the Jewish population numbered less than 30. By 1861 it had risen to 326 (0.3% of the total), and six years later to 1,262 (0.6%). The gold rushes brought hundreds of Jews there, but by the 1870s their number had fallen to approximately 0.2%, above which it has never risen. The Jewish population numbered 1,611 in 1901, 2,380 in 1921, 3,470 in 1945, 4,006 (out of 2,750,000) in 1961, and just over 4,000 in 1968. The vast majority of Jews are distributed equally in Auckland and Wellington. There has always been a highly restrictive government policy on immigration except by those of British stock, and only a small number of Jewish refugees from persecution in Russia and Eastern Europe were admitted. Similarly, the numbers admitted in the wake of Nazism were inconsiderable, but these had an invigorating effect on the New Zealand community. Assimilation, principally through intermarriage, which has always been high, has accounted for the small growth of Jewish population. Today, though complemented by numerous Zionist and social organizations, the synagogues remain the hub of the communities in Auckland, Wellington, and Christchurch, where there are Orthodox ministers under the authority of the chief rabbi in London. Liberal congregations exist in Auckland (1959) and Wellington (1960). From the turn of the century, Jewish social and welfare organizations have developed. Internationally affiliated *B'nai B'rith lodges were established in Wellington (1960) and Auckland (1961). The first national monthly Jewish journal, the *New Zealand Jewish Times,* was started in the 1920s. In 1971, there was one monthly journal, the *New Zealand Jewish Chronicle.*

Interest in Zionism was rather academic until the *Balfour Declaration and the return after World War I of units from the Palestine campaign. After 1918 Louis Phillips of Auckland, who had been New Zealand's first delegate to the International Zionist Conference, led the Zionist movement. A number of young New Zealanders settled in Israel after 1948.

Free from any discriminatory disabilities, the Jews in

Figure 1. The first New Zealand synagogue, built in 1867 in Hokitika. Wellington, Alexander Turnbull Library. Photo Tait Bros., Hokitika.

Figure 2. The Nelson synagogue (center foreground) unused since 1895, photographed in 1911. Wellington, Alexander Turnbull Library, Jones Collection.

New Zealand have made valuable contributions to the country's development and progress. Sir Julius *Vogel, twice premier (1873–75 and 1876), has been called New Zealand's most far-sighted statesman, while Sir Arthur *Myers was minister of munitions in World War I. Almost every city in New Zealand has honored a Jew as its chief magistrate. There have been five Jewish mayors of Auckland; these were Philip A. Philips (1869–74) and Henry Isaacs in the 1870s, Sir Arthur Myers (1905–08), Sir Ernest David (1935–41), and Sir Dove-Myer Robinson (1959–65 and 1968–). Sir Michael *Myers of Wellington was Chief Justice from 1929 to 1946 and acted as administrator during the absence of the governor. Some noteworthy Jewish names in New Zealand journalism have been Julius Vogel, Benjamin *Farjeon the poet and novelist, Fred Pirani, Mark Cohen, and Phineas Selig, and in medicine Sir Louis Barnett (surgery), Alfred Bernstein (chest diseases), and Bernard Myers (medical services). Wolf Heinemann, the philologist of Dunedin, was the first Jew to be appointed professor in a New Zealand university (Otago, 1895). Jews have pioneered in business and farming. The oldest business in New Zealand is that of L. D. Nathan and Company. Joseph Nathan (Wellington) developed the Glaxo pharmaceutical company, now operating chiefly from England, while the establishment of New Zealand's steel mills owes much to the industrialist Sir Woolf Fisher. Jews were chiefly instrumental in developing New Zealand's brewing and hotel industries, and in the wholesale and retail clothing industries they formed early national groups. Among Jewish farmers and agriculturalists was Coleman Phillips, who formed the first cooperative dairy farm in either Australia or New Zealand. In other aspects of New Zealand life, particularly sporting, cultural, and artistic, Jews have also played their full part.

Anti-Semitism (often influenced from abroad) has appeared at times, particularly in periods of economic depression, but its manifestations have been limited.

[M.S.P.]

Relations with Israel. Friendly ties between the two countries go back to the relations established between the *yishuv* and New Zealand soldiers who served in Palestine and the Middle East during the two world wars. Israel honored the Australian and New Zealand soldiers (ANZAC) by erecting a memorial near Be'eri in southern Israel. New Zealand voted for the partition of Palestine in 1947 and accorded Israel recognition early in 1949. As it maintains only a very small foreign service, New Zealand is not represented in Israel, but Israel's ambassador to Australia is also accredited to New Zealand. New Zealand's support for Israel found expression in its votes in the U.N.

[Ed.]

Bibliography: *Journal and Proceedings of the Australian Jewish Historical Society*, 1 (1939–40), 53–55, 154–9, 293–5; 3 (1949–53), 142–51, 334–50; Hertz, in: JHSET, 10 (1921–23), 162–5; L. M. Goldman, *The History of the Jews in New Zealand* (1960).

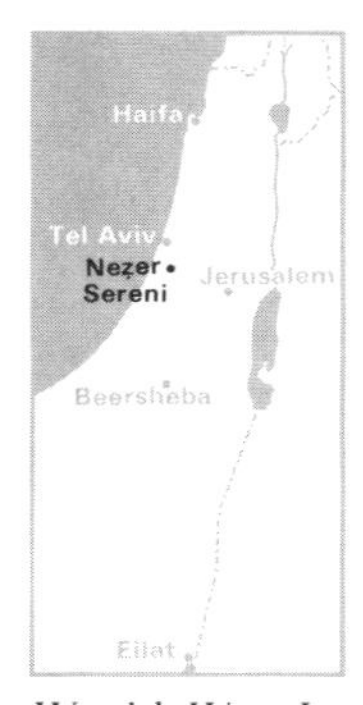

NEẒER SERENI (Heb. נֵצֶר סִירֶנִי), kibbutz in central Israel, between Nes Ẓiyyonah and Ramleh, founded on June 20, 1948, during a short cease-fire of the Israel *War of Independence, by "Kibbutz Buchenwald," composed of young survivors of the Holocaust who, while still in a displaced persons' camp, had formed a pioneering group for settlement in Palestine. The site, a German farm from the beginning of the century, was temporarily used during World War I as Gen. *Allenby's headquarters. After the 1951–52 split in *Ha-Kibbutz ha-Me'uḥad a large minority group from *Givat Brenner decided to join Kibbutz Neẓer which was affiliated with Iḥud ha-Kevuẓot ve-ha-Kibbutzim. In 1968 the kibbutz, with 510 inhabitants, engaged in intensive farming, and had three industrial plants, for foodstuffs, metal, and wood products. The name "Neẓer" ("Young Shoot") refers to Kibbutz Buchenwald's origins. After the members of Givat Brenner joined, the kibbutz was named Neẓer Sereni to commemorate the Haganah parachutist Enzo *Sereni, who had been a member of Givat Brenner. [E.O.]

The defense of kibbutz Neẓer Sereni during the Israel War of Independence, 1948. Courtesy J.N.F., Jerusalem.

NEZHIN, city in Chernigov oblast, Ukrainian S. S. R. Jews first settled in Nezhin at the beginning of the 19th century. The *ẓaddik* Dov Ber of *Lubavich, the son of *Shneur Zalman of Lyady, the "middle rabbi" of Ḥabad Ḥasidism, died and was interred in Nezhin in 1827. The town became a center for the Ḥabad Ḥasidim of the Ukraine. It was especially well known while Israel Noah Schneersohn (see *Schneersohn Family) lived there from 1867 to 1882. In 1847, 1,299 Jews were registered in the community; in 1897 there were 7,631 Jews (24% of the total population). The waves of pogroms which overtook Russian Jewry in 1881 and 1905 also affected the Jews of Nezhin. In August 1919 Nezhin's Jews were attacked by soldiers of the "volunteer army" of *Denikin. The dead included Menahem Mendel Ḥen, rabbi of Nezhin. In 1926, there were 6,131 Jews in Nezhin (16.1% of the population). During the German occupation, all Jews except those who succeeded in escaping from the town were exterminated. In 1959 there were 1,400 Jews (3% of the total population) in Nezhin. Nezhin was the birthplace of the Yiddish poet *Mani Leib.

Bibliography: S. M. Dubnow and G. I. Krasny-Agman (eds.), *Materialy dlya istorii antiyevreyskikh pogromov v Rossii*, 2 (1923), 153–4, 348–57; *Die Judenpogrome in Russland*, 2 (1909), 287–94; I. B. Shekhtman, *Pogromy Dobrovolcheskoy Armii na Ukrainie* (1932), 323–6. [Y.S.]

NEZIKIN (Heb. נְזִיקִין; "torts"), fourth order of the Mishnah according to the order given by Simeon b. Lakish (Shab. 31a), although according to another tradition (Tanḥuma in Num. R. 13:15), it is the sixth. Originally *Nezikin* was the name of the first tractate only (see below). Because of Simeon b. Lakish's homily applying to it the word *yeshu'ot* ("salvation") in Isaiah 33:6, it is so called in many rabbinic sources, including the Tosefta. *Nezikin* is devoted to civil law (except for matrimonial law, dealt with in the order **Nashim*), and the administration of justice and legal procedure, as well as penal law insofar as the subject does not appertain to some other part of the Mishnah. The tractate **Eduyyot* was included in *Nezikin* because it contains "testimonies" most of which were given before the Sanhedrin of *Jabneh after the destruction of the Temple, and is consequently connected with the tractate **Sanhedrin*. **Avodah Zarah* was placed in *Nezikin* because it deals with the *halakhot* of idolatry, some of which are given in *Sanhedrin-Makkot*, and also because it opens with prohibitions against trade with idolators, thus connecting it with the tractate *Nezikin* (**Bava Kamma*, **Bava Meẓia*, and **Bava Batra*), which gives the laws of trade in general. The inclusion of the aggadic tractate *Avot*, which deals with moral maxims, is due to the fact that it contains an exceptional number of instructions to **dayyanim*, dealt with in *Sanhedrin*.

Nezikin contains ten tractates, although at first there were only seven, the first three originally forming one tractate now divided into *Bava Kamma*, *Bava Meẓia*, and *Bava Batra* (see Av. Zar. in Mishnah Kaufmann and Cambridge, etc.). The name of the first tractate was then applied to the whole order. *Sanhedrin* and **Makkot* were also originally one tractate (and are so in the Kaufmann and Parma Mishnah, in *genizah* fragments, and elsewhere), which contained 14 chapters; they were divided into two tractates, also apparently in Babylon, for reasons that are not yet sufficiently clear. Thus in the order *Nezikin*, too, the tractates were originally arranged according to the number of chapters in descending order. *Nezikin* has the following separate tractates: *Bava Kamma*, with 10 chapters; *Bava Meẓia*, 10; *Bava Batra*, 10; *Sanhedrin*, 11; *Makkot*, 3; **Shevu'ot*, 8; *Eduyyot*, 8; *Avodah Zarah*, 5; *Avot*, 5; and **Horayot*, 3.

In the Tosefta of *Nezikin* each of the three *Bavot* has 11 chapters; *Sanhedrin*, 14; *Makkot*, 4 (or 5); *Shevu'ot*, 6; *Eduyyot*, 3; *Avodah Zarah*, 9 (or 8); and *Horayot*, 2 chapters; there is no Tosefta to *Avot*. *Eduyyot* and *Avot* have no *Gemara* in either the Jerusalem or the Babylonian Talmud. The importance of nearly all the tractates in the sphere of practical *halakhah* led to an abundant development of these spheres in rabbinic literature. Especially comprehensive is the literature on the first three tractates and on *Shevu'ot*, about which innumerable studies and commentaries have been written, which have material discussed in the responsa of all periods, and which (together with **Ketubbot* in the order *Nashim*) encompass the whole of Jewish civil law. [D.J.B.]

°NICANOR, one of the Syrian officers sent by *Lysias to fight against Judah Maccabee. He is mentioned at length in I and II Maccabees, both passages giving an account of the battle of Emmaus in which Nicanor and Gorgias were defeated by Judah. There is also mention of a Syrian commander called Nicanor who played an important role in the war against Judah in the time of Demetrius. He attempted to approach Judah peacefully or, as another version has it, to capture him by deceit. At all events he was unsuccessful. Enraged that Judah had eluded him once and later defeated him in a battle near Kefar Shalem, he threatened to wreak his vengeance on the Temple and its priests. With the arrival of reinforcements from Syria, Nicanor was once more in a position to confront Judah. In 161 B.C.E. a decisive battle was fought at Bet Horon, but Judah once again triumphed and Nicanor was slain. This was Judah's last military victory. It is uncertain whether the Nicanor who took part in the battle of Emmaus is to be identified with the Nicanor sent by Demetrius against Judah Maccabee, but it is probable that they were two separate persons. The downfall of Nicanor, who had reviled and insulted the Temple, brought joy to the people and the day of triumph, the 13th of Adar, was established as an annual festival.

Bibliography: Meg. Ta'an. 346; I Macc. 3:38; 7:27–50; II Macc. 8:9ff., 14–15; Jos., Ant., 12:402–5; Polybius, 31:14, 4; Derenbourg, Hist, 63f.; Schuerer, Hist, 31, 40ff.; F. M. Abel, *Les Livres des Maccabées* (1949), 488. [U.R.]

NICANOR'S GATE, one of the gates leading to the Temple courtyard during the period of the Second Temple. According to the Mishnah, "There were seven gates in the Temple courtyard . . . In the east there was the gate of Nicanor, which had two rooms attached, one on its right and one on its left, one the room of Phinehas the dresser and one the room of the griddle cake makers" (Mid. 1:4). This gate was one of the best known of the gifts made to the Temple and "miracles were performed in connection with the gate of Nicanor and his memory was praised" (Yoma 3:10). Of these miracles the Talmud states: "What miracles were performed by his doors? When Nicanor went to Alexandria in Egypt to bring them, on his return a huge wave threatened to engulf him. Thereupon they took one of the doors and cast it into the sea but still the sea continued to rage. When they prepared to cast the other one into the sea, Nicanor rose and clung to it, saying 'cast me in with it.'" The sea immediately became calm. He was, however, deeply grieved about the other door. As they reached the harbor of Acre it broke the surface and appeared from under the sides of the boat. Others say a sea monster swallowed it and ejected it out onto dry land. Subsequently all the gates of the Sanctuary were changed for golden ones, but the Nicanor gates, which were of bronze, were left because of the miracles wrought with them. But some say

Figure 1. Ossuary found in the "Cave of Nicanor" on Mt. Scopus, Jerusalem, first century C.E., with a Greek inscription reading: "the remains of the children of Nicanor of Alexandria who made tesy Holyland Corporation, Holyland Hotel Jerusalem. Photo Zev Radovan, Jerusalem.

Figure 2. Detail from Michael Avi-Yonah's model of Jerusalem in the time of the Second Temple, showing Nicanor's Gate (1) between the Court of Women (2) and the Temple proper (3). Courtesy Holyland Corporation, Holyland Hotel Jerusalem. Photo Zev Radovan, Jerusalem.

that they were retained because the bronze of which they were made had a golden hue. R. Eliezer b. Jacob said, "It was Corinthian copper which shone like gold" (Yoma 38a).

Scholars disagree over where the gates stood. Some claim that they were on the western side of the Court of Women which was to the east of the Court of Israelites; others maintain that they were on the eastern side of the Court of Women. The basis of this conflict is in the interpretation of a passage in Josephus (Wars, 5:204). The most recent discussion of the problem is by Schalit, who concludes that the words of Josephus are to be explained as meaning that the gates of Nicanor were "beyond" the entrance to the Sanctuary and facing "the gate that was larger," i.e., that it was on the eastern side of the Court of Women. The gates were undoubtedly made after the time of Herod (the most reasonable date being about the middle of the first century, a generation before the destruction) and were the work of an Alexandrian craftsman. Nicanor is also recorded in an inscription on a sarcophagus in a cave on Mt. Scopus in Jerusalem ("the Cave of Nicanor"). The inscription reads: "the remains of the children of Nicanor of Alexandria who made the doors." Nicanor's gift was so well known that no additional explanation was necessary. Nicanor was an Alexandrian though he may have gone to live in Jerusalem. It seems more likely, however, that his remains were brought from Alexandria to Jerusalem where he had a family tomb.

Bibliography: H. Graetz, in: MGWJ, 25 (1876), 434f.; A. Buechler, in: JQR, 11 (1898/99), 46–63; W. Dittenberger, *Orientis Graeci Inscriptiones Selectae,* 2 (1905), 295f., no. 519; E. Schuerer, in: ZNW, 7 (1906), 54ff.; O. Holtzmann, *ibid.,* 9 (1908), 71–74; idem (ed.), *Die Mischna Middot* (1913); H. Vincent and F. M. Abel, *Jérusalem,* 2 (1914), 45ff.; S. Klein, *Juedisch-palaestinisches Corpus Inscriptionum* (1920), 17f., no. 9; *Supplementum*

Epigraphicum Graecum, 8 (1937), 30, no. 200; Frey, Corpus, 2 (1952), 261f., no. 1256; M. Avi-Yonah, *Sefer Yerushalayim*, 1 (1956), 412; E. Wiesenberg, in: JJS, 3 (1952), 14–29; E. Bammel, *ibid.*, 7 (1956), 77–78; A. Schalit, *Koenig Herodes*, 1 (1969), 389ff.
[U.R.]

NICARAGUA, Central American republic. Although some Jews settled in Nicaragua in the 19th century, the present community was founded by Jews who arrived from Eastern Europe after 1929. They established the Congregación Israelita de Nicaragua, the most important Jewish association in the country. The majority of the Jews live in Managua and engage in commerce, industry, and agriculture; the few who live in the interior also engage in agriculture and commercial representation. The congregation has maintained close ties with Jewish institutions abroad. All the women in the community belong to *WIZO, which has been active in the country since 1941. Since 1935 the congregation has had its own cemetery and, since 1964, its own synagogue in Managua. Services are held on the Sabbath and on all festivals, and rabbis from abroad are invited to officiate. In 1968, 126 Jews lived in Nicaragua. [LE.HE.]

Relations with Israel. Since the establishment of the State of Israel, very cordial relations have existed between the two countries. Israel is represented in Managua by a nonresident ambassador residing in Costa Rica, and Nicaragua is represented in Israel by a nonresident ambassador residing in Rome. Israel enjoys Nicaragua's wholehearted support in the international arena, and Nicaragua has repeatedly taken steps to counteract anti-Israel moves in the United Nations. Israel has developed a ramified program in the area of technical aid. Nicaraguan trainees participated in courses in Israel, mainly in the fields of agriculture and community organization. Israel experts were active in Nicaragua in the field of agricultural settlement and conduct a mobile course in agricultural cooperation. In 1969 the scope of trade reached $100,000 in Israel exports to Nicaragua, mainly in synthetic fibers. [M.A.]

Bibliography: J. Beller, *Jews in Latin America* (1969), 145–48.

NICE (Heb. ניצה), capital of the Alpes-Maritimes department, on the Mediterranean coast of France. The Statutes of Nice, enacted in 1342 while the town belonged to Provence, compelled the Jews to wear the distinguishing *badge; this is the first specific mention of the presence of Jews in Nice. By 1406, when Nice belonged to Savoy, the community had a bailiff. In 1408 it owned a cemetery, and at least from 1428, a synagogue. An edict issued by the duke of Savoy in 1430 (also intended for the Jews of Turin), while protecting the Jews from forced baptism, enumerated a series of prohibitions (on moneylending, on interest, etc.)

Embossed leather fragment from the old synagogue of Nice, depicting the matriarch Rachel. Nice, Musée Masséna. Photo Michel de Lorenzo, Nice.

and irksome obligations (confining Jewish residence to a separate quarter, the *Giudaria*, etc.). However, in 1449, a Jew was authorized to settle there and charge a rate of 20% interest. In 1499, Jews expelled from the island of Rhodes were permitted to settle in Nice. From 1551, the Jews were placed under the jurisdiction of a *Conservator* (except in cases of crimes and offenses committed against the Catholic religion) and were authorized to engage freely in moneylending. Jews in Nice then also engaged in commerce. They could practice medicine freely. From 1648 many newcomers of "Portuguese" origin (Marranos) from Italy and Holland joined the "old Nissards," attracted by the free port edict, which expressly favored the Jews with advantageous privileges. From 1669, many Jews arrived from Oran (Algeria) and were even able to bring their slaves. The newcomers, who settled outside the ghetto, were accorded full rights in the existing community institutions without having to participate in the expenses. The Jewish community of Nice, which had been affiliated to that of Turin, became separated from it from the beginning of the 17th century. The internal fusion of the diverse groups of Jews was achieved slowly; at the same time, the authorities allowed the legal differences which governed them to become obsolete. Thus, in particular from 1732, all of them were compelled to reenter the compulsory Jewish quarter, the Rue Giudaria (the present Rue Benoît Brunice). The community, known as *Università*, was led by *massari-parnassim*, deputies, councillors, and a treasurer. The Jews of Nice conversed in Judéo-Niçois, a mixture of the local dialect and Hebrew terms. The temporary reunion of Nice with France from 1792 to 1814 brought emancipation to the Jews, but they lost it with the restoration of Sardinian administration. Thus, in 1828, the Jews were ordered to return to the ghetto, and it was only in 1848 that real emancipation was granted. The annexation of Nice by France in 1860 did not result in further changes in the social and economic situation of the Jews. The number of Jews there was approximately 300 in 1808 and 500 in 1909 (out of a total population of 95,000) and did not substantially change up to World War II. [B.BL.]

Holocaust Period. During World War II Nice came under Italian occupation which was far less severe than the German. Therefore thousands of Jews took refuge there. For a while the city became an important center for various Jewish organizations, especially after the landing of the Allies in North Africa (November 1942). However, when the Italians signed the armistice with the Allies, German troops invaded the former Italian zone (Sept. 8, 1943) and initiated brutal raids. Brunner, the SS official for Jewish affairs, was placed at the head of units formed to search out Jews. Within five months, 5,000 Jews were caught and deported. A great number of others were martyred in Nice itself. The courage displayed by the resistance and Jewish youth movements, however, along with the sympathy of the vast majority of the population and clergy, helped save thousands who were either hidden or helped to escape.

After the liberation several hundred Jews, including original inhabitants of Nice and refugees, reestablished the community. With the influx of Jews from North Africa in the 1960s, the Jewish population in Nice and the vicinity increased from 2,000 to 20,000 by 1969. [G.LE.]

Bibliography: Gross, Gal Jud, 393f.; H. Meiss, *A travers le ghetto . . . Nice* (1923); Gallois-Montbrun, in: *Annales de la Societé de Lettres . . . des Alpes-Maritimes*, 3 (1875), 242ff.; Giordan, *ibid.*, 46 (1955), 103ff.; Scialtiel, in: REJ, 67 (1914), 118ff.; Bauer, *ibid.*, 63 (1912), 269ff.; V. Emmanuel, *Les Juifs à Nice* (1902); J. Decourcelle, *La Condition des Juifs de Nice . . .* (1923), includes bibliography; L. Poliakov, *The Jews under the Italian Occupation* (1955), passim; Z. Szajkowski, *Analytical Franco-Jewish Gazetteer 1939–1945* (1966), 156.

°**NICHOLAS,** name of five popes. NICHOLAS III (Giovanni Gaetano Orsini), pope 1277–80. During his brief reign Nicholas displayed a considerable zeal for the conversion of the Jews. His bull *Vineam sorce* encouraged conversion through "sermons and other means." Copies of the document were sent (1278–79) to the *Franciscans and provincial priors of the *Dominicans in various provinces. Concurrently, however, he renewed the decisions of his predecessors forbidding the forcible baptism of Jews and protecting them from attacks by Christians. Nevertheless, several *Church councils and synods legislated against the free intercourse of Jews and Christians. It is not clear whether it was the supposed hostility of Nicholas or his mildness toward the Jews which prompted Abraham b. Samuel *Abulafia to announce his intention of visiting the pope to demand the release of captive Jews. (When he arrived, however, the pope was already on his deathbed.)

NICHOLAS IV (Girolamo Masci), pope 1288–92. Like many medieval popes, Nicholas IV displayed a mixed attitude toward the Jews. On the one hand, he issued various instructions (1288) to the inquisitors to proceed against *Conversos and he renewed earlier legislation concerning the Jews in Portugal, compelling them to wear a *badge. On the other hand, he specifically protected the Jews of Rome from being molested by Christians (January 1291). He wrote to Emperor *Rudolph (Aug. 29, 1288) requesting the release of Meir b. Baruch of *Rothenburg from prison. There is a belief that he enlisted the services of the Jewish physician and scholar Isaac b. Mordecai Maestro Gaio, who also attended Boniface VIII and who was the first of the Italian Jewish papal physicians.

NICHOLAS V (Tommaso Parentucelli), pope 1447–55. The attitude toward the Jews of this otherwise enlightened pontiff might be characterized as cruelty tempered by a certain moderation. Soon after his election, under the malign influence of John of *Capistrano, he revived the persecutory legislation of his predecessor, *Eugenius IV. Originally framed for Castile and Leon, this legislation was applied en bloc to Italy. Several subsequent edicts, based generally on those of Eugenius, imposed very severe restrictions on Jewish life. Nevertheless, while urging strong measures against Crypto-Jews, Nicholas insisted on the complete equality of New and Old Christians. After a protest by Emperor Frederick III, Nicholas reversed anti-Jewish legislation adopted by various German synods, and he also granted Borso, duke of *Ferrara, complete freedom to allow Jews to reside in his states and operate banks (1451).

Bibliography: E. A. Synan, *Popes and Jews in the Middle Ages* (1965), 119ff., 122f., 138f.; I. Loeb, in: REJ, 1 (1880), 115ff.; U. Robert, *ibid.*, 3 (1881), 219f.; 4 (1882), 94f.; D. Kaufmann, *ibid.*, 20 (1890), 35f., 48ff.; S. Grayzel, *The Church and the Jews in the XIIIth Century* (1966), index.

[N.DE-L.]

°**NICHOLAS,** name of two Russian czars.

NICHOLAS I, czar of Russia from 1825 to 1855. His reign was marked by a general reaction, the persecution of liberal elements in the country, and the oppression of religious and national minorites. Nicholas I regarded the Jews as a harmful alien group whose unity should be destroyed so that it would become completely assimilated within the Russian people. To achieve this, he adopted many measures. The first, which left its imprint on the whole of his Jewish policy, was the introduction of compulsory military service for the Jews (1827). This was accompanied by the seizure of Jewish children, who were to be educated in the schools for soldiers' children in the spirit of the Christian religion (see *Cantonists). The area of the *Pale of Settlement was reduced and the Jews were expelled from *Kiev, *Sevastopol, and *Nikolayev. There was also a suggestion that they be expelled from within 50 versts of the border. On the other hand, the government encouraged renewed agricultural settlement of the Jews in southern Russia and around their townlets, exempting the settlers from military service. The government of Nicholas I supported the *maskilim* in their struggle against Orthodoxy. Under the influence of the *maskilim*, a severe censorship was imposed on Jewish books, their publication being authorized at two presses only, in *Vilna and *Zhitomir. During the 1840s the government set out to develop the network of Jewish government schools, particularly the rabbinical seminaries of Vilna and Zhitomir, which offered a general education in addition to a Jewish education in the spirit of the *Haskalah. At the end of the 1840s, the Jews were forbidden to wear their traditional garb.

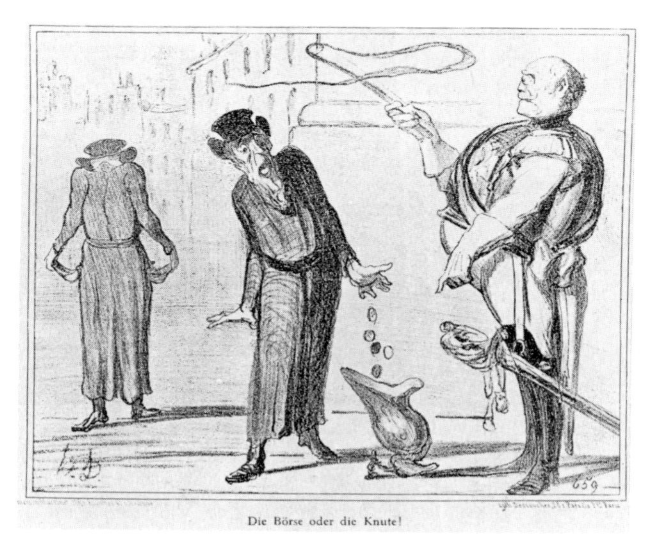
Die Börse oder die Knute!

A Daumier cartoon showing Czar Nicholas I extracting money from the Jews of Russia, c. 1855. From E. Fuchs, *Die Juden in der Karikatur*, Munich, 1921.

Toward the close of Nicholas' reign the "classification" *(razbor)* of the Jews into "useful" (merchants, craftsmen, agricultural workers) and "non-useful" persons was proposed. Severe repressive measures were to be adopted against the "non-useful"—principally the intensification of conscription. This project was interrupted by the death of Nicholas I, which also resulted in the abolition of the special conscription of Jews and in other alleviations. Of the hundreds of anti-Jewish laws which were passed during his reign, the most important for the Jews were the Jewish statutes of 1835 and 1844 (which officially abolished the Jewish communities and introduced the status of **kazyonny ravvin*). In the memory of the Jewish people, the reign of Nicholas I is regarded, especially because of the Cantonists decree, as one of the darkest periods in the history of the Jews in czarist Russia.

NICHOLAS II, Russian czar from 1894 to 1917. His reign was marked by a violent struggle against the revolutionary movement, the war against Japan (1904), which was followed by the first Russian Revolution (1905–06), and Russia's participation (1914–17) in World War I, which culminated in the Revolution of the spring of 1917 and the removal of Nicholas II from the throne. At the outset of his reign the Jews, like other Russian circles, hoped that the new czar would change the extreme reactionary and anti-Semitic policy of his father *Alexander III. This hope was, however, soon disappointed. The czar, whose education at the hands of Constantine *Pobedonostsev had made him an indubitable Jew-hater, regarded the Jews as the principal factor in the Russian revolutionary movement. He favored anti-Semitic statesmen, rejected any attempt to change the anti-Jewish laws in spite of the advice of some of the leading statesmen of his court (such as S. *Witte and P. Stolypin), and took under his aegis the violent anti-Semitic movement, "*Union of Russian People" (popularly known as the "Black Hundreds"), and other organizations formed in reaction to the liberal and revolutionary organizations. The pogroms against the Jews, which were at first due to the free hand given to anti-Jewish incitement and the rioters, were later directly perpetrated by the police and the army, as part of the campaign against the revolution. The *Beilis blood libel trial at Kiev, which was designed to set off renewed persecutions of the Jews, was inspired by the czar. Although no new anti-Jewish laws were passed during the reign of Nicholas II, the administrative pressure which accompanied the pogroms encouraged hundreds of thousands of Jews to emigrate to the U.S. and elsewhere.

Bibliography: Nicholas I: Dubnow, Divrei, 9 (1958[2]), 95–118, 208–11; Dubnow, Hist Russ, index; R. Mahler, *Divrei Yemei Yisrael, Dorot Aḥaronim,* 2 bk 1 (1970), 13–240. Nicholas II: Dubnow, Divrei, 10 (1958[2]), 102–8, 189–207, 218–24, 262–4; Dubnow, Hist Russ, index; Elbogen, Century, 371–404, 453–7; I. Ma'or, *She'elat ha-Yehudim ba-Tenu'ah ha-Liberalit ve-ha-Mahpekhanit be-Rusyah* (1964); *Die Judenpogrome in Russland* (1909); S. W. Baron, *Russian Jews under Tsars and Soviets* (1964). [Y.S.]

°**NICHOLAS, EDWARD,** author of a famous 17th-century plea in favor of the resettlement of the Jews in England. Entitled *An Apology for the Honourable Nation of the Jews, and all the Sons of Israel,* and published in London in 1648, it was translated into Spanish, perhaps by *Manasseh Ben Israel, and made a profound impression. However, since the author is otherwise unknown, there is reason to believe that the publication was inspired or even written by a Jew. Its theme was that England should make amends for her former maltreatment of the Jews by readmitting them to the country.

Bibliography: Roth, England, 153, 286; Roth, in: V. D. Lipman (ed.), *The Centuries of Anglo-Jewish History* (1961), 3. [V.D.L.]

°**NICHOLAS DE LYRE** (incorrectly **Lyra;** c. 1270– (not before) 1349), Bible commentator and theologian. A 15th-century allegation of his Jewish extraction lacks all basis. Born at Lyre, near Evreux, Normandy, Nicholas joined the Franciscan Order at Verneuil (c. 1291) and subsequently studied at Paris. He held the position of professor of theology at the Sorbonne until he was appointed Franciscan provincial of Burgundy in 1325. He wrote controversial studies against Judaism (e.g., *De Messia . . . ad Judaei argumenta, De diversis contra Judaeos . . .*) and produced a commentary on Peter Lombard's *Sentences,* which, together with the Bible, constituted the basis of Western theological studies. His importance, however, lies in *Postillae Perpetuae,* which he composed from 1322 to 1330 (published in Rome, 1471–72).

These works form a continuous commentary on the entire Bible, with priority accorded to the literal meaning, while other senses (*"moralitates"*) are relegated to 35 substantial appendixes. The *Postillae* constitute the first Christian Bible commentary to be printed. The literalist approach led Nicholas to *Rashi, whom he often cites by name (Salomo). In this he had been anticipated by the Victorine scholars, especially by *Andrew of Saint Victor whom he quotes (G. Calandra, *De . . . Andreae Victorini . . . in Ecclesiasten* (1948), 83–85). However, Nicholas, who records his perusal of a controversial tract *hebraice scriptus* ("written in Hebrew"; see Hailperin in bibl., p. 140), used Rashi directly as well. In addition he read some rabbinic material in Raymond *Martini's *Pugio Fidei.* Soon after his death, Nicholas' *Postillae* were available in virtually every library in western Christendom. Nicholas had abiding influence (Hailperin, p. 282f.). Wycliffe acknowledged his indebtedness to Nicholas in his (later) English version of the Bible (c. 1388). *Luther was particularly dependent on him, especially on Genesis. In his commentary to Daniel, Abrabanel controverts Nicholas' christological exegesis.

Bibliography: L. Wadding, *Scriptores Ordinis Minorum* (1967), 178–9; R. Bellarmin, *De Scriptoribus Ecclesiasticis* (1613), 213 (list of works); *Catholic Encylopedia,* 11 (1913), 63 (incl. bibl.); JE, 8 (1904), 231; EJ, 10 (1934), 1263; B. Smalley, *The Study of the Bible in the Middle Ages* (1952[2]), 185, 355; G. W. H. Lampe (ed.), *The History of the Bible in the West,* 2 (1969), 219; H. Hailperin, *Rashi and the Christian Scholars* (1963), passim. [Ra.L.]

°**NICHOLAS OF DAMASCUS** (b. c. 64 B.C.E.), Greek historian, peripatetic philosopher, orator, dramatist, and statesman. Nicholas came from a distinguished family in Damascus, where his father, Antipater, occupied a prominent position and was proud of his origin. For a time he was in the service of Antony and Cleopatra, acting as their children's instructor. Later he joined the court of *Herod whose confidant he became, instructing him also in philosophy and rhetoric. It was at Herod's instigation that he wrote his Universal History (see below). Nicholas' fame as a writer and an intellectual, his outstanding talents as an orator, and his connections with leading Romans equipped him to undertake delicate diplomatic tasks. He acted as Herod's representative to Marcus *Agrippa in 14 B.C.E., when the Jews of Asia Minor submitted their complaints against the inhabitants of the Greek cities (Jos., Ant., 16:29–58). He also interceded with *Augustus on behalf of Herod when the latter had lost favor in Rome due to his aggressive action against the Arabs in 8 B.C.E. (*ibid.,* 16:335–55). Nicholas exercised great influence on Herod's internal policy. According to his own testimony, he was a consistent opponent of *Antipater, Herod's eldest son, and helped to get rid of him (*ibid.,* 17:106–21). Even after Herod's death, Nicholas remained loyal to him: he traveled to Rome in 4 B.C.E., with *Archelaus, Herod's son, to obtain Augustus' confirmation of Herod's will and to defend the name of the dead king and the interests of Archelaus against the charges brought by representatives of the Jewish nation (*ibid.,* 240–8). At the same time Nicholas persuaded Archelaus not to oppose the granting of independence to the Hellenistic cities on the borders of Herod's former kingdom. On this occasion, too, Nicholas' efforts were successful, and Augustus confirmed Herod's will in broad outline. This was Nicholas' last active intervention in the affairs of Judea. He apparently stayed on in Rome.

The most famous of Nicholas' many writings was his *Historia Universalis* in 144 books, in which events are described in greater detail the nearer they approach the days of the author. Those in which he was personally involved are given special treatment. Nicholas' intervention on behalf of the Jews of Asia Minor is described in books 123 and 124 (Jos., Ant., 12:126–7). He also wrote an autobiography, the contents of which correspond to some extent to the last books of the history, as well as a biography of Augustus. Nicholas used to provide Augustus with a choice variety of dates from his estate, which Augustus called after him (Athenaeus 14:652). They are possibly the dates referred to in rabbinical literature (Av. Zar. 146; Num. R. 3:1) as "Nikolaos." Nicholas' history is no longer extant, except for lengthy excerpts, particularly those dealing with most ancient times, preserved in the compilations of Constantine Porphyrogenitus, the 10th-century Byzantine emperor. Shorter extracts have been preserved in the works of Josephus, Athenaeus, Stephanus of Byzantium, and others.

Nicholas' connections with Herod, his acquaintance with the Jews, and his defense of them on several occasions precluded him from adopting a contemptuous attitude toward the ancient Jewish tradition, as did most Greek and Roman writers. Thus he reveals a tendency to combine the Damascene-Syrian with the biblical-Jewish traditions. In the fourth book of his history he deals sympathetically with the personality of Abraham (Jos., Ant., 1·159), whom he depicts as a foreigner who came at the head of an army from the land of the Chaldees to Damascus, where he reigned as king and from which he later migrated with his people to the land of Canaan. The name of Abram, says Nicholas, is still honored in the region of Damascus. In the same book of his history he refers to the biblical account of the wars between Israel and Aram in the days of David as well as after the division of the kingdom (*ibid.*, 7:101–3). Among pre-Christian Greek writers, Nicholas is the only one to mention David. He recalls the biblical tradition when referring, in the 96th book of his history, to the Flood, and mentions that "Moses, the Jewish legislator, wrote" (*ibid.*, 1:95). To judge from these fragments, Nicholas' interest in Jewish history is due chiefly to Jewish connections with his native city, Damascus; it seems unlikely that he was a major source for the early books of Josephus' *Antiquities* which parallel the Bible.

As regards Jewish history in the period of the Second Temple, he describes the actions of *Antiochus Epiphanes against the Jews (Jos., Apion, 2:83–84) and is quoted by Josephus a number of times verbatim. Josephus was perhaps naturally attracted to the work of a man who, like himself, had written an autobiography defending himself against charges of time-serving. Nicholas' *Universal History* provided the basis of Josephus' description of Herod's kingdom in *The Jewish War* (book 1) and *Antiquities* (books 15–17). As is to be expected from a courtier and collaborator in the policy of the king, Nicholas' books about Herod are a panegyric upon him. Marked by their dramatic tension and replete with pathetic descriptions, these books are written in a spirit of open hostility toward Antipater, the son of Herod and Nicholas' mortal enemy. These characteristics are also notable in Josephus' account, except that in the *Antiquities* Josephus makes a conscious effort to free himself from the panegyrical approach of Nicholas. Josephus' dependence on Nicholas is further shown by a comparison between his account and the excerpts preserved in Nicholas' autobiography, and by the fact that for the period no longer covered by Nicholas' work (after 4 B.C.E.) Josephus' narrative is meager. The description, too, of the Hasmonean kingdom in Josephus' two works is chiefly derived from Nicholas' history, a conclusion that necessarily follows from the non-Jewish viewpoint that generally characterizes this description.

Bibliography: G. Hoelscher, *Die Quellen des Josephus* . . . (1904), 17ff.; Schuerer, Hist, index; F. Jacoby (ed.), *Die Fragmente der griechischen Historiker*, 2B Texts (1926), 324–430; 2A Commentary (1926), 29–91; R. J. H. Shutt, *Studies in Josephus* (1961), 79–92; B. Z. Wacholder, *Nicholas of Damascus* (1962). [M.St.]

NICHOLS, MIKE (Michael Igor Peschlowsky; 1932–), U.S. comedian and director. Born in Berlin and educated at the University of Chicago, Nichols joined The Compass, an off-campus theater group. He toured in cabaret with Elaine May (see *Theater) from 1954, and in 1960 they presented *An Evening with Mike Nichols and Elaine May* on Broadway. In 1961 Nichols turned to acting on his own, and then directed a series of successful plays on Broadway. Among them were *Barefoot in the Park* (1963), *The Knack* (1964), *Luv* (1964), *The Odd Couple* (1965), and *The Apple Tree* (1966). Turning to movies, he directed the film version of *Who's Afraid of Virginia Woolf?* (1966), *The Graduate* (1967), and *Catch-22* (1969). [Le.H.]

NIDDAH (Heb. נִדָּה "menstruous woman"). According to Jewish law, a woman is forbidden to maintain sexual relations with her husband during and for some time both before and after (see below) her menses.

The laws relating to the menstruous woman comprise some of the most fundamental principles of the halakhic system, while a scrupulous observance of their minutiae has been one of the distinguishing signs of an exemplary traditional Jewish family life. Among the most difficult and intricate in the entire range of the *halakhah*, these laws are elucidated in a lengthy and detailed tractate of the same name devoted to the subject (see **Niddah*, tractate). The historical development of the relevant *halakhot* through the centuries is likewise extremely complicated. To decide a law relating to a menstruous woman demands, besides a profound knowledge of the *halakhah*, experience in various medical matters, and at times also the ability to assume the grave responsibility of disqualifying a woman from pursuing a normal married life and of—at times—separating her forever from her husband. In every generation and in every place there have generally been men, referred to in the Talmud simply as "sages," who specialized in the subject, as did eminent *tannaim* and *amoraim*, to whom particularly difficult questions were sent, even from remote places, together with specimens of blood (Nid. 20b). In brief, the *halakhah* as at present codified is that sexual intercourse (and any other intimacies which may lead to it) is forbidden from the time the woman expects her menses until seven clean days (i.e., days on which no blood whatsoever is seen) have elapsed. For this purpose a minimum of five days is fixed for the menses themselves. Thus the minimum period of separation is 12 days. In the evening of the seventh day without sign of blood the woman immerses herself in a **mikveh* and normal marital relations are resumed until the next menses are expected. Any bleeding is considered as menstrual and requires a waiting period of seven clean days (see below). The laws of *niddah* are codified in the Shulḥan Arukh, *Yoreh De'ah*, 183–200.

In the Bible. A detailed discussion is devoted to the menstruous woman as part of the general "law of him that hath an issue" (Lev. 15:19–32), within the framework of the many laws of ritual *purity and impurity whose main purpose was to preserve the purity of the sanctuary and its precincts. To this aspect the Bible adds a further prohibition against sexual intercourse with a menstruous woman, the punishment for which is **karet* for both the man and the woman (*ibid.* 20:18). While this prohibition at present constitutes the main feature of the *niddah*, in the Bible it is the former context that is the decisive factor. According to the literal meaning of the biblical passages, most of which are, however, unclear, the law is thus: A woman who discerns blood within and up to a period of seven days is "impure" (*ṭeme'ah*) for those seven days from the time the blood first appears. On the eighth day—if she sees no further blood—she is "pure" (*tehorah*). Whoever touches her or anything she sits or lies on during the week of her uncleanness is "unclean until the evening," and must bathe himself in water and wash his clothes. One who has sexual intercourse with a menstruous woman is unclean for seven days, since she transfers her condition of uncleanness to him ("and her impurity is upon him"). If, however, a woman sees blood for more than seven days, she becomes a *zavah* ("one who has a discharge") and is unclean until her discharge of blood ceases. All the laws of uncleanness previously mentioned apply to her. Unlike the menstruous woman, however, the *zavah* does not revert to her cleanness immediately after her discharge of blood stops but has to wait a further seven "clean" days, reckoned from the day she has ceased to see blood. At the conclusion of this period she brings "two turtle-doves, or two young pigeons" as a sacrifice. Although not specifically mentioned in the Bible, the purification of the menstruous woman of both the first and second types was undoubtedly associated with immersion in a ritual bath, this being clearly stated in the Bible with respect to others rendered levitically unclean by reason of a discharge. The Bible does not lay down the normal length of time between one menses and another.

In the Talmud. On the basis of the tradition of the Oral Law, the sages gave the biblical passages a different interpretation. Their basic assumption is that there is a fixed cycle of 18 days, comprising seven days of *niddut* (the state of being a *niddah*) and 11 days between one menses and another, this being, in the view of the sages, the "allotted" interval. This cycle of 18 days is counted consecutively from the appearance for the first time of blood in a female at the age of puberty and in rare instances even earlier. A woman who sees blood on one or all of the 7 days is unclean for these seven days and becomes clean again on the eighth day on condition that she immerses herself in a *mikveh ("ritual bath"; see also *Ablution) and that no further blood has appeared before her immersion. If blood reappears on the eighth day, she is unclean on that day, immerses herself on the following morning, and waits until the evening. If no more blood is seen she is clean; if it is seen, she has to adopt the same procedure on the next day. If after the conclusion of the seventh day blood is discerned on three consecutive or non-consecutive days during the 11 days between one menses and another, the woman becomes a *zavah* and has to count seven "clean" days, as stated above. If, however, she passes the 11 or at least nine of the days between one menses and another in cleanness, she reverts to the beginning of a new cycle and any blood that she may see during the subsequent seven days is menstruous and does not necessitate seven "clean" days. These 11 days are a traditional law ascribed to Moses (*"Halakhah le-Moshe mi-Sinai"*). Any blood appearing during the interval between one menses and another—on the conclusion of the above-mentioned cycle of 7+11 days—is due to a discharge that requires seven "clean" days. This cycle commences from the day blood appeared for the first time and no longer depends on the appearance or nonappearance of blood: the seven days are "appropriate" for blood of menstruation, the 11 days for blood of a discharge, and only childbirth interrupts this automatic reckoning (see below). Such is the basic law; however, as early as the end of the tannaitic period Jewish women were accustomed to observe seven "clean" days for any spot of blood as large as a mustard seed which they saw (see below).

The problem that arises if a woman does not examine herself during the days of her cleanness and suddenly sees blood, is dependent on the tannaitic controversy whether the laws of fixed menses are of biblical authority or rabbinical. In the former instance the woman automatically reverts to her uncleanness retrospectively from the beginning of her fixed menses unless she has examined herself and found herself clean, whereas in the latter case she is clean until she physically feels the movement of, or sees, blood. In any event it is halakhically of great importance that a woman knows the dates of her menses since she has to refrain from sexual intercourse near their onset, so that they should not come on during coition. In the tractate *Niddah* the various types of menses, the way in which they are fixed, and their halakhic significance form the subject of numerous talmudic themes on which many and diverse views are expressed.

The sages distinguished between several types of blood, some clean, others unclean, that issue from a woman, the distinction being based on the different sources of the blood in the womb, but since modern knowledge of a woman's anatomy and physiology does not accord with the sages' assumptions, their statements are not clear. Various scholars have unsuccessfully tried to harmonize the statements of the sages on this subject with existing anatomical knowledge. But although the sages have given indications for distinguishing between one blood and another, either by its appearance or by various examinations made in a woman's body, already in talmudic times a thorough knowledge of the subject was limited to experts, so that in effect the *halakhah* was laid down that, since we are not adept in the matter, all blood renders a woman unclean. A very difficult and painful question concerns instances of a discharge of blood which is due to an external cause, as for example, an internal wound, but cannot definitely be identified as such. This problem was particularly formidable so long as its solution depended on halakhic discussions among the sages and not on a clear, objective medical examination. A more general distinction is made between a woman's blood and her other discharges which are not blood and hence are not unclean. In this instance, too, the sages have given several indications, based mainly on the intensity of the reddishness of the discharge. Here it has similarly been laid down that we no longer possess the knowledge requisite to make a precise distinction and hence any discharge, unless it is white or green (in their various shades), causes uncleanness. Whereas nowadays doubt can be easily and definitely resolved, previously this problem, like the former one, was often one of paramount human significance and an obstacle to married life for not a few women. Accordingly, the works of the codifiers in all periods contain hundreds of responsa dealing with the subject out of a manifest desire to alleviate this hardship, though with a very scant possibility of doing so.

Another problem in this category, much rarer but devoid of any practical solution, concerns a woman who changes her menses during the act of sexual intercourse. This blood is clearly menstruous, and its regular appearance at such a time prevents any possibility, according to the *halakhah*, of a married life between the couple, since after several recurrences it is considered a permanent feature, and hence coition is prohibited from the outset. In this case the couple have to be divorced, particularly if the husband has not yet fulfilled the *mitzvah* of procreation. Virginal blood forms a special halakhic subject, being in principle ritually pure, for, since its source is an external one, it is in every respect identical with blood that has issued from a wound. This was the earlier *halakhah*. Later a stricter view was taken in the matter, particularly in Babylonia, for fear that such blood might be mingled with a menstruous blood discharged due to sexual excitement, and hence the couple had to keep apart from each other immediately after the first coition. In Ereẓ Israel only individuals adopted this stricter view. In geonic times this restriction received, in Babylonia, the force of absolute law, but from the many questions addressed to the *geonim*, it is evident that in fact the prohibition did not extend throughout that country. The subject was still included as a section in *Sefer ha-Ḥillukim she-Bein Benei Bavel u-Venei Ereẓ Yisrael*, compiled in the middle of the geonic period. With the spread of the influence of the Babylonian Talmud this prohibition was generally observed among almost all Jewish communities and was laid down as a *halakhah* in the Shulḥan Arukh (EH, 193).

An essential change in the entire laws of the menstruous woman, which since talmudic times likewise became the accepted law throughout Jewry, relates to the "clear" days. This change took place due to a twofold difficulty arising from the earlier procedure: first, the lack of a reasonable and practical possibility of keeping a methodical, precise, and consecutive count of the days of menstruation and of discharge, as described above, from the first day of the appearance of blood until the end of the period of the menses; and secondly, the recognition that there is no real possibility of distinguishing with any certainty between clean and unclean blood, thus making the actual counting impracticable. In the days of Judah ha-Nasi the first regulations in this connection were issued, and in the middle of the amoraic period it was already accepted as axiomatic that seven "clear" days were to be counted for any blood seen (Nid. 66a; et al.). The essence of the regulation was that the days of menstruation were henceforth equated with those of a discharge, thus eliminating the former from the practical *halakhah*. To this regulation a further restriction was added, according to which a single spot of blood is treated as a regular flow also with regard to the necessity of counting seven "clear" days. It is evident from the sources that during the seven "clear" days only sexual intercourse was at first prohibited, as against the prohibition of all physical contact during the original days of menstruation (see below). In the course of time, however, this latter prohibition was extended to cover also the "clear" days which thus became in effect days of uncleanness (Shab. 13a).

Although trangressing the prohibition with regard to a menstruous woman is punishable with *karet*, a marriage with one is binding, and her offspring is entirely legitimate, fit even for the priesthood and suffering only from a "taint" which is unattended by any halakhic consequences. The marriage ceremony of a bride who has become menstruous shortly before is not postponed, even though, generally speaking, a marriage should be capable of immediate consummation. Nevertheless, the people observed many restrictions and minutiae with regard to the prohibition relating to the menstruous woman. In ancient times a menstruous woman was completely segregated, particularly in Ereẓ Israel where the laws of purity were still in vogue from the time when the Temple existed. Excluded from her home, the menstruous woman stayed in a special house known as "a house for uncleanness" (Nid. 7:4), she was called *galmudah* ("segregated," RH 26a), and was not allowed to adorn herself until R. Akiva permitted her to do so, that she might not be repulsive to her husband (Sifra, Meẓora, 9:12). No food was eaten with a menstruous woman (Tosef., Shab. 1:14) nor did she attend to her household duties, until the stage was reached in which "during all the days of her menstruation she is to be segregated" (ARN[1] 1, 4). The origin of this segregation lies in the custom, prevalent in Ereẓ Israel long after the destruction of the Second Temple, of eating ordinary meals prepared according to the levitical rules originally prescribed for sacred food. This custom did not obtain prevalence in Babylonia where there was neither any reason for, nor any halakhic possibility of, observing absolute purity, and where accordingly all these expressions of the menstruous woman's segregation were not practiced. Thus, in Babylonia, she attended to all the needs of her household, with the exception of filling her husband's cup of wine, making his bed, and washing him (Ket. 61a). In the latter half of the geonic period the *geonim* of Babylonia, adopting an increasingly stricter view with regard to the uncleanness of the menstruous woman, accepted the restrictions of the earlier scholars of Ereẓ Israel. Related to the spread of the Muslim religion which was particularly strict in matters associated with cleanness and uncleanness, this process reflects the strong desire of the *geonim* not to be inferior in their "cleanliness" to their neighbors. Nevertheless Maimonides at a later stage maintained that the restriction imposed on the menstruous woman to refrain from cooking, touching a garment, and so on, was devoid of any significance and might even savor of *Karaism. These restrictions were generally not adopted in Europe where the two factors that led to their introduction in Ereẓ Israel and Babylonia were lacking, as well as because of the high status enjoyed there by the Jewish woman in managing the affairs of her home.

Yet it was mainly in Europe that a strange and unusual circumstance occurred, as a result of which new and astonishing limitations and prohibitions, specifically in the religious and not in the social sphere, were imposed on the menstruous woman and on the members of her family. These measures are all contained in a small work entitled **Baraita de-Niddah* (1890) which is so strange that some scholars contended that it originated in an heretical Jewish sect. Where and when it was written has, up to the present, not been determined, although it has generally been assigned to the end of the geonic period. The special limitations mentioned in the work include the following: The menstruous woman is prohibited from entering synagogue, as is also her husband if he has been rendered unclean by her in any way (by her spittle, the dust under her feet, and so on). She is likewise prohibited from kindling the Sabbath lights. One is not allowed to enquire after her welfare or to recite a benediction in her presence. A priest whose wife, mother, or daughter is menstruous may not recite the priestly benediction in synagogue. No benefit may be derived from the work of a menstruous woman, whose very utterances defile. From the beginning of the Rabbanite period the influence of this work on codifiers has been particularly marked, and although it is generally admitted that its statements have no halakhic validity, they adopted its stringent measures. This is especially notable with regard to prohibiting a menstruous woman from entering a synagogue, which gave rise to a not insignificant literature among the early scholars of Germany.

This affair is to be understood against the background of the various superstitions current among the Jews, some of which derived from the non-Jewish environment. These superstitions held that the breath of a menstruous woman's mouth causes harm, that her glance "is disreputable and creates a bad impression," that a menstruous woman's blood proves fatal to anyone drinking it, and if mingled with the bloodstream produces pustules and boils in the newly born child. If a menstruous woman looks for a long time in a mirror, red drops resembling blood appear on it. She pollutes the air in her proximity, is regarded as sick and even as afflicted with plague, despite the fact that menstruation is natural to a woman (Naḥmanides, Gen. 31:35; Lev. 12:4, 18:19). A menstruous woman who passes between two men, if she is at the beginning of her menses, causes one of them to be killed, and produces strife between them, if she is at the end of it (Pes. 111a).

A Woman After Childbirth. The law relating to the woman who has given birth to a child is stated in Leviticus 12:1–8. According to the literal meaning of the passage, her discharge of blood is in the same category as the blood of her menstruation and hence she is unclean, like a menstruous woman, for seven days if she bears a boy and for 14 days if she has a girl. In addition to this, a further period of 33 days in the former instance and 66 in the latter is laid down, these being "the days of her purification" and the blood seen during them "the blood of purification." During this period she is permitted to her husband but may not enter the sanctuary until the days of her purification have ended and on their conclusion has brought the prescribed sacrifices. The law of the woman after childbirth was preserved in this form by the sages, who, however, added that any blood seen during the days of her purification, although not making her menstruous, is nevertheless unclean in itself and renders her unclean, requiring of her to take a ritual bath immediately that she may become clean. In the view of the sages, childbirth and the counting of the days associated therewith annuls that of the above-mentioned 11 days and a new cycle of menses begins. In the geonic period the regulation in respect of the "clear" days, previously referred to, was extended to include "the days of her purification," and consequently the custom obtained in Babylonia, Ereẓ Israel, Spain, and North African countries that a woman who had given birth to a child observed seven "clear" days for any spot of blood seen during the days of her purification. This extended regulation, which is wholly incompatible with the essential character of the days of purification in that they are not subject even to the uncleanness of menstruation, was not accepted in France and Germany, where sexual intercourse was permitted after a discharge of "blood of purification" (see Yad, Issurei Bi'ah, 11:6–7). The *baraita* in tractate *Niddah*, quoted above, mentions a yet more stringent custom according to which a woman is prohibited as a menstruous woman for all the 40 and 80 days after the birth of a son and a daughter respectively, even though she has seen no blood during the entire period of her purification. This custom was regarded by Maimonides (Yad, *ibid.*, 11:15) as "the way of heretics," and is indeed practiced by the Karaites (Anan, *Sefer ha-Mitzvot*, 19)—as also by the Falashas—and represents, according to Geiger, the view of the Sadducees.

In seeking to explain the reason and stringency, and to encourage the observance, of the prohibitions associated with menstruation, the sages dilated upon the subject in the *aggadah*. The *mitzvah* of keeping the laws relating to menstruation, one of the few applicable specifically to women, is among the three for transgressing which women die in childbirth (Shab. 2:6). Considered theoretically the most loathsome impurity, the uncleanness of the menstruous woman was metaphorically equated with the defilement imparted by carrying an idol (Shab. 9:1). This idea was prevalent already in the Bible, where the uncleanness of the menstruous woman occurs as a noun and as a metaphor for the height of defilement (Ezek. 7:19–20; Lam. 1:17; Ezra 9:11; II Chron. 29:5). Although the laws relating to the menstruous woman and their details are extremely numerous and difficult, they are considered *gufei Torah* ("essential laws"; Avot 3:18). Of those who are unable to wait until their wives' purification, it was said that "the law concerning young trees (whose fruit is forbidden for the first three years—Lev. 19:23) cuts off the feet of those who have sexual intercourse with menstruous women" (that is, should teach them patience). Such men were regarded by the sages as the worst type of transgressor. The reason for the laws of menstruation was explained by the sages as a punishment for the sin of Eve who brought about the death of Adam, and because "she shed his blood" she was punished through her blood (Gen. R. 17:13). In their homilies the sages highly praised notable women of Israel who in all ages scrupulously prevented themselves and their husbands from transgressing this prohibition, among such being Sarah (*ibid.*, 48:15), Esther (Meg. 13b), and others. The sages also stressed the psychological importance of sustaining enchantment in a married couple's sexual relations through their obligatory abstinence from intercourse while the wife is unclean (Nid. 31b). Mentioned in the Talmud among the Roman decrees intended to undermine the very existence of the Jewish faith is one that Jews were to have intercourse with menstruous women (Me'il. 17a).

Non-Jewesses. A non-Jewish menstruous woman does not impart uncleanness (Sif. Tazri'a) but there are scholars who hold that in ancient times this was not so—a state of affairs which explains Bet Hillel's statement in the Mishnah (Nid. 4:3). Furthermore, it is held that it was precisely this ancient *halakhah* that led to the decree that heathens, in general, were unclean, since as a result of their having intercourse with their menstruous wives they were considered unclean. Most scholars, however, hold the opposite view, contending that Bet Hillel's statement refers merely to the uncleanness of a menstruous woman's blood, which is like other unclean objects, and that it did not refer to the actual menstrous woman herself. It was rather the *Hasmonean *bet din* which first "decreed that a Jew who had intercourse with a heathen woman is liable on account of her being menstruous . . ." (Av. Zar. 36b), and that this decree was a general restriction intended to alienate the Jews from the heathens.

*Reform Judaism has consistently held that the observance of the laws of Niddah is not necessary in modern times.

Bibliography: C. M. Horowitz (ed.), *Tosefta Attikata*, pts. 4–5 (1890); J. Preuss, *Biblisch-talmudische Medizin* (1923[3]), 128–46; S. Baumberg, *Golden Chain* (1929); M. Margulies, *Ha-Ḥillukim she-Bein Anshei Mizraḥ u-Venei Ereẓ Yisrael* (1938), 99–102, 114–8; S. Lieberman, *Sheki'in* (1939), 22; idem, in: B. M. Levin (ed.), *Metivot* (1934), 115–8; M. Rabinowitz (ed.), *Daughter of Israel* (Eng. and Yid., 1949); Alon, Meḥkarim, 1 (1957), 121–31, 135–6, 171–2; N. Lamm, *Hedge of Roses* (1966). [I.T.-S.]

NIDDAH (Heb. נִדָּה; "menstruous woman"), seventh tractate of the order *Tohorot* in the Mishnah and in the Babylonian Talmud—the only tractate of the order with *Gemara*. The tractate deals with the ritual uncleanness of a woman which is caused by menstruation or other fluxes, and is based chiefly upon Leviticus chapters 12 and 15: 19ff.

The Mishnah consists of ten chapters. Chapter 1 discusses the determining of the onset and duration of menstruation in those with regular and irregular menses. Chapter 2 continues that topic and deals with the source and colors of the blood causing uncleanness. Chapter 3 discusses the uncleanness of a woman following miscarriage, abortion, and childbirth. Chapter 4 deals with the untrustworthiness of Samaritans and Sadducees with regard to menstruation; menstruation in the case of heathens and after childbirth; difficult confinements; and menstrual regularity. Chapter 5 deals with caesarean births; the moment that uncleanness commences; and the different ages and stages in the development of a male and female child. Chapter 6 continues this theme; deals incidentally with a list of cases in which the presence of one factor presupposes another although the reverse is not true; and deals with doubts about the source of bloodstains. Chapter 7 discusses the uncleanness of the blood itself; cases where its origin is uncertain; sources of uncleanness that have dried out; and, once again, with the untrustworthiness of Samaritans in regard to uncleanness. Chapters 8 and 9 continue the subject of doubtful stains or flows of blood. Chapter 10 continues this theme and deals with the duration of menstruation and borderline cases.

It is possible to discern several strata in the Mishnah. Thus 2:6 predates the schools of Shammai and Hillel, and Akavya b. Mahalalel. Moreover, several earlier *mishnayot* are interpreted in later *mishnayot*: thus Mishnah 1:1 is explained in 1:2, 1:3 in 1:4–6, and 2:2 in 2:3. *Mishnayot* 5:3–6 form a distinct group, which gives the various ages, from one day to 20 years, at which laws become applicable for males and females. These laws are irrelevant to the subjects of *Niddah* and were incorporated because

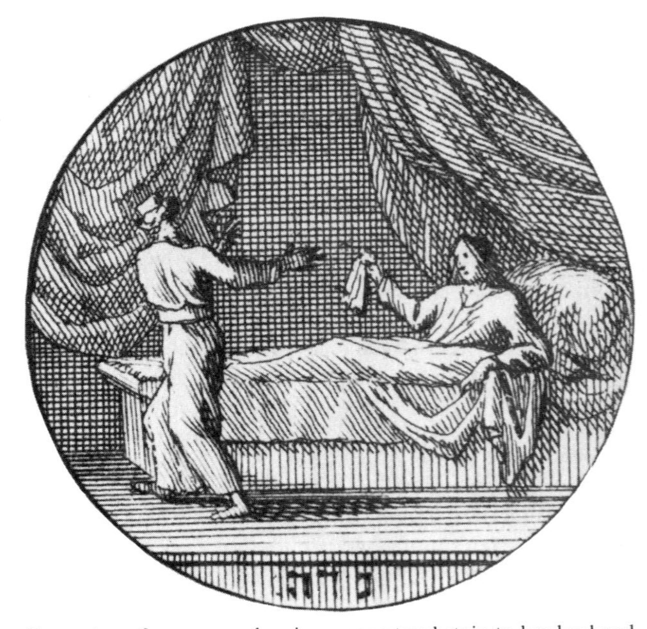

Engraving of a woman showing a menstrual stain to her husband representing the tractate *Niddah*. From a title page of the Hebrew-Latin Mishnah illustrated by Mich. Richey, Amsterdam, 1700–04. Jerusalem, J.N.U.L.

the first Mishnah states that a female child has the potential of becoming a *niddah* from the age of one day. Similarly *mishnayot* 6:2–10 consists of various laws which have as their common theme that wherever A occurs B will be found, but not the reverse. These follow 6:1, where the formula occurs with regard to the *niddah*. A. Weiss claims that most of these grouped *mishnayot* are of ancient origin, and that the editor collected and condensed most of them from older mishnaic sources (*Al ha-Mishnah* (1969), 31). The end of *Niddah* contains supplements to various *mishnayot* in the tractate; for example, *mishnayot* 9:8–10 are supplements to 1:2; *mishnayot* 9:1 and 10:1 supplement 1:7; and *mishnayot* 10:2–3 supplement 4:7 (see further Ḥ. Albeck, *Shishah Sidrei Mishnah, Seder Tohorot* (1959), 377f.).

In the Tosefta, *Niddah*, containing nine chapters, is the fifth tractate in the order *Tohorot*. It includes original legal and aggadic passages, such as a section on birth control which is debated in 2:6. Another passage sounds like a version of the Jonah story and tells about a ship that was caught in a storm; the passengers prayed to their own gods, but a little boy reproached them: "How long will you delude yourselves? Pray to the Creator of the ocean," i.e., to the God of Israel (5:17). Another group of *beraitot* tells of several reforms of existing customs, some of which were instituted for the dignity of the poor and women (9:16–18), such as the decision to give the same simple burial to both rich and poor alike. It is placed after *Nezikin* and contains very little aggadic material. In the Babylonian Talmud there is *Gemara* on the whole tractate. Because of its practical importance the tractate is much studied and much space is devoted to it both in the various codes and in the responsa literature. It contains aggadic material, one noteworthy view being (16b) that while a man's physical qualities are preordained, his moral character and spiritual outlook are left to his free choice.

Only three chapters (and a fragment of a fourth) of the Jerusalem Talmud to *Niddah* are extant, although the tosafists possessed it in its entirety. There is also a vivid description of the wonderful life of learning and joy that the embryo enjoys in his mother's womb. Before birth he is made to take the oath: "Be righteous and not wicked, and if all the world tells you 'you are righteous' consider yourself wicked" (30b). Another passage reports 12 questions and answers on law and *aggadah* that the Alexandrians asked Joshua b. Hananiah (69b–71a). The Talmud was translated into English in the Soncino edition by I. W. Slotki (1948).

Bibliography: Ḥ. Albeck, *Shishah Sidrei Mishnah, Seder Tohorot* (1959), 375–8; A. Weiss, *Al ha-Mishnah* (1969), 31, 57.

[ED.]

°NIEBUHR, KARSTEN (1733–1815), Danish orientalist. From 1761 to 1767 he traveled in Syria, Palestine, Arabia, and Persia, visiting Jerusalem in 1766. *Reisebeschreibung nach Arabien und andern umliegenden Laendern* (2 vols., 1774–78) is his account of these travels; a third volume, *Reisen durch Syrien und Palaestina*, was published by J. Olshausen in 1837. After his return to Germany, Niebuhr entered the Hanoverian civil service and at the time of his death was a councillor of state. [M.A.-Y.]

°NIEBUHR, REINHOLD (1892–1971), U.S. Protestant theologian who spent most of his teaching career at New York's Union Theological Seminary. Niebuhr brought to this position a social conscience formed during a pastorate in Detroit, Michigan, in the 1920s. Active in many public causes, gifted as a journalist, he fashioned his ethical approach in countless articles and a number of books, the most famous being the Gifford Lectures, *The Nature and Destiny of Man* (1941–43). Niebuhr frequently acknowledged that his social passion had been born at the side of activist Jews, even as his prophetic realism was nurtured by a reading of the Hebrew prophets. His own preaching reproduces something of their cadences and much of their concern for justice. "I have as a Christian theologian sought to strengthen the Hebraic-prophetic content of the Christian tradition." His conception of Judaism and blatant opposition to Christian missionary activity among Jews are expressed in Chapter 7 of his book *Pious and Secular America* (1958; publ. in England under the title: *The Godly and the Ungodly* (1958)). By 1941 Niebuhr had begun publicly to advocate a Jewish homeland, particularly for European refugees, though he also wanted to welcome refugees to America. Though consistently arguing that Palestine should be that homeland, he had a reputation for fair-mindedness in Middle Eastern affairs and was not identified with ideological Zionism. He was awarded an honorary doctorate by the Hebrew University of Jerusalem in 1967.

Bibliography: S. C. Guthrie, *The Theological Character of Reinhold Niebuhr's Social Ethic* (1959); G. Harland, *The Thought of Reinhold Niebuhr* (1960), includes bibliography; N. A. Scott, *Reinhold Niebuhr* (Eng., 1963), includes bibliography.

[M.E.M.]

NIEDERSTETTEN, city in Wuerttemberg, W. Germany. Jews were mentioned there as victims of the *Rindfleisch massacre of 1298. There is no further trace of them in the city throughout the Middle Ages until their settlement in 1675. By 1714 the community had acquired a prayer room; in 1737 a cemetery was consecrated in which Jews from Archshofen, Creglingen, Gerabronn, and Mulfingen were also buried. In that same period a *ḥevra kaddisha* was also founded. The Jews earned their livelihood mainly from trade in livestock, wine, and wool. By 1744 a synagogue was built and by 1807 the community numbered 138 Jews. The number rose to 171 in 1824, and in 1832 the community was included in the rabbinate of *Mergentheim. A religious school was also founded in the 1830s. The community numbered 215 in 1854, decreased to 163 in 1900, and to 81 in 1933. In the 20th century Jews were active as wholesale merchants in leather and wine, and as shopkeepers. They also engaged in textile manufacturing and banking. They were active in the political and cultural life of the town, and one Jew was a member of the municipal council during the Weimar Republic. In 1933 Jewish merchants were subject to the Nazi *boycott and some leaders of the community were physically assaulted. This resulted in large-scale Jewish emigration. During the general destruction on *Kristallnacht* in 1938, the synagogue itself was preserved, but eight Jewish men were sent to concentration camps. Between 1941 and 1942, 42 Jews were deported to extermination camps, never to return. In early 1945 the synagogue was destroyed as a result of the war. The ritual objects of the community were saved, however, and turned over to a U.S. army chaplain when the war ended. All that was left in 1970 of a once active community in Niederstetten was the Jewish cemetery.

Bibliography: P. Sauer, *Die juedischen Gemeinden in Wuerttemberg und Hohenzollern* (1966), 134–6, incl. bibl.

[A.SHA.]

NIEGO, JOSEPH (1863–1950), teacher and social worker. Niego was born in Adrianople into a rabbinical family. In about 1899 he was appointed director of the *Mikveh Israel Agricultural School (near Tel Aviv). He served in this post for 18 years, and during that time he went to Kurdistan on behalf of the Alliance Israélite Universelle. On his return he presented an interesting report about the Kurdish Jews which was published in French and in a Hebrew translation. Later he was nominated as inspector of the Jewish Colonization Association agricultural settlements in oriental and European countries, including its colonies in Palestine (Gederah, Be'er-Toviyyah, Sejera, Ḥaderah, etc.). He remained at this post for 20 years. His headquarters were in Istanbul, but he was also very active in agricultural research in Anatolia. In 1923 he became the manager of a loan association in Istanbul which was established by the American Jewish Joint Distribution Committee. Niego took part in the social life of the Jews in the city and was president of the B'nai B'rith Grand Orient Lodge. A jubilee book was published on his 70th birthday which was dedicated to his activities and includes some of his lectures and articles (see bibl.).

Bibliography: *Cinquante Années de Travail dans les Oeuvres Juives... Bulletin Publié à l'Occasion du sixante-dixième Anniversaire... J. Niego* (1933); M. D. Gaon, *Yehudei ha-Mizraḥ be-Ereẓ Yisrael*, 2 (1938), 468f.; M. Benayahu, *Massa Bavel* (1955), 43.

[E.Hı.]

NIEMIROWER, JACOB ISAAC (1872–1939), chief rabbi of Rumania. Niemirower was born in Lemberg. In 1897 he was appointed rabbi of Jassy and in 1911 rabbi of the Sephardi community of Bucharest. In 1921 he was appointed rabbi of the main synagogue of Bucharest and

Jacob Isaac Niemirower, chief rabbi of Rumania and first Jewish member of the Rumanian senate. Courtesy Yad Vashem Archives, Jerusalem.

shortly after, chief rabbi of Rumania. He succeeded in uniting the Jewish communities of Rumania under his leadership. As chief rabbi he was elected in 1926 to the Rumanian senate — the first Jew to receive such an appointment — and was recognized by the government as the representative of all Rumanian Jewry. He fought against the humiliating wording of the Rumanian oath, *more judaico*, and succeeded in having it annulled. By force of his intellect and personality he became the chief figure in the religious as well as in the general communal life of Rumanian Jewry. Although his election was largely due to the progressive element which dominated Jewish communal life there. Niemirower's authority was accepted by all circles, including the Orthodox, and his influence was decisive. He did much in the sphere of Jewish education—founding Jewish schools and establishing a theological seminary, a society for Jewish education called Sharon, a society for Jewish studies, etc. He was president of the order of B'nai B'rith in Rumania. He was an active Zionist and took part in the First Zionist Congress. In 1936 a Rumanian nationalist made an attempt on his life and Niemirower was slightly wounded. He published many works in Rumanian, German, and French on various Jewish topics. Between 1918 and 1932 his complete works were issued entitled *Scrieri Complete* (4 vols.). The fourth and fifth volumes of the journal *Sinai* (1932–33) were dedicated to him in honor of his 60th birthday.

Bibliography: Wininger, Biog, 4 (n.d.), 530f.; S. K. Mirsky (ed.), *Ishim u-Demuyyot be-Ḥokhmat Yisrael be-Eiropah ha-Mizraḥit Lifnei Sheki'atah* (1959), 393–403; A. Shraga (ed.), *Al Yehudei Romanyah—be Ereẓ Galutam u-va-Moledet* (n.d.), 21, 43f.; *Ha-Rav Dr. Niemirower* (1970).

[I.AL.]

NIEROP, VAN, family of Dutch jurists and economists.

NIEROP, AHASVERUS SAMUEL, VAN (1813–1878), jurist, politician, and communal leader. Born at Hoorn, Holland, Van Nierop became one of the leading attorneys in Holland. He published numerous articles on commercial law in the law journals, *Themis* and the *Weekblad voor het Recht*, and sat in the second chamber of parliament from 1851 to 1853 and from 1864 to 1866. Van Nierop played an important part in the reorganization of Jewish communal bodies which led to the establishment of the Nederlands Israelitisch Kerkgenootschap of which he was chairman of the executive (1870–71). His son, FREDERIK VAN NIEROP (1844–1925), banker, was born in Amsterdam, and graduated in law from the University of Leiden. For some years he practiced law in Amsterdam. In 1871 he became a director (later president-director) of the Amsterdamsche Bank. Van Nierop played an important part in expanding its operations. A liberal, he was an Amsterdam municipal councillor (1879–99), a member of the North Holland Provincial Council (1883–99), and sat in the Dutch senate (1899–1925). He was a governor of the Netherlands Economic Academy in Rotterdam and of many other economic and cultural institutions. Though an assimilated Jew, he was president of the Nederlands Israelitisch Kerkgenootschap. His son, HENDRIK ABRAHAM VAN NIEROP (1881–), who succeeded him as a director of the Amsterdamsche Bank in 1920, played no part in the community.

[H.BO.]

NIETO, DAVID (1654–1728), philosopher and haham of the Spanish and Portuguese Synagogue in London (1701–28). Having studied medicine at the University of Padua, Nieto functioned as *dayyan*, preacher, and physician in Leghorn before going to London. He was proficient in languages and an astronomer of some repute. His calendar (1717) served the London community until the 19th century as a guide for the Sabbath and festivals. His works indicate that he was fully aware of the religious currents and crosscurrents of his time, including *Spinozism, Deism (see conceptions of *God), and Shabbateanism. *Matteh Dan* (1714), his *magnum opus*, devoted to a defense of the Oral Law against the attacks of ex-Marranos to whom the rabbinic tradition was both novel and unacceptable, has frequently been reprinted as a defense of rabbinic Judaism (last edition: Jerusalem, 1958). *Esh Dat* (1715) was directed against the Shabbatean heresiarch, Nehemiah Ḥiyya Ḥayon. Previously, Nieto had published *Pascalogia* (1702), dealing with the date of the Christian Easter in relation to that of the Jewish Passover, and *De La Divina Providencia* (1704). The latter was an elaboration of a sermon Nieto had delivered to combat the deistic notion of a "Nature" apart from God. Nieto identified Nature with God; and,

Detail of an engraving of David Nieto, London, 1705. New York, Library of Jewish Theological Seminary of America.

although he made it clear that he had *natura naturans*, and not *natura naturata* (see *Spinoza) in mind, he was accused of Spinozistic leanings. Nevertheless, "Ḥakham Ẓevi" Ashkenazi (cf. his responsum no. 18) ruled in his favor. Nieto's *Reply to the Archbishop of Cranganor*, published posthumously in 1729, controverts the christological interpretation of the Bible. In his writings, Nieto gives evidence of wide reading in science and the humanities. He argues for the compatability of Judaism and scientific investigations. Nieto is also one of the very few Jewish theologians who used the argument *de consensu gentium* to establish the dogmas of God's existence and of retribution.

Bibliography: I. Solomons, *David Nieto and Some of his Contemporaries* (1931); A. M. Hyamson, *Sephardim of England* (1950), index; J. J. Petuchowski, *Theology of Haham David Nieto* (1954; 1970²); D. Nieto, *Ha-Kuzari ha-Sheni* (1958), introd. by J. L. Maimon, 5–20, biography by C. Roth, 261–75. [J.J.P.]

NIETO, ISAAC (1687–1773), English rabbi. Born in Leghorn, Nieto was taken to London when his father David *Nieto became haham in 1701. He was appointed to succeed him in 1732, after an interregnum of four years. Nieto seems to have had a difficult character however, and held office only until 1741, when he went abroad. Returning to England, he was admitted as a public notary and built up a considerable practice. On the death of Moses Gomes de *Mesquita (1688–1751), who had been haham since 1744, Nieto was appointed *av bet din* (in effect, acting rabbi) of the community, but resigned in 1757 in protest against the appointment to the *bet din* of Moses Cohen d'*Azevedo (1720–1784, haham from 1761). During the controversy over ritual slaughter in London, which began in 1761 through the captious criticisms of Jacob Kimḥi, Nieto attacked the *bet din* so vigorously that the *Mahamad ordered that his decisions in matters of Jewish law should thereafter be disregarded. Nieto published a number of sermons in Spanish and Portuguese, of which one appeared also in English (London, 1756) on the occasion of the earthquake of 1756; this was the first Jewish sermon to be published in English. His translations into Spanish of the liturgy for Rosh Ha-Shanah and the Day of Atonement (*ibid.*, 1740) and of the daily prayers (*ibid.*, 1771) were highly regarded for their style. Following his father's example, he also published a series of calendars.

His son Phinehas Nieto (1739–1812) carried on the family tradition by publishing a "New Calendar" (London, 1791), and his remoter descendant Abraham Ḥayyim Nieto published "Nieto's Jewish Almanac for One Hundred Years 5663–1902 to 5763–2002" (1902).

Bibliography: I. Solomons, in: JHSET, 12 (1931), 78–83; E. R. Samuel, *ibid.*, 17 (1953), 123–5; Roth, Mag Bibl, index. [C.R.]

°**NIETZSCHE, FRIEDRICH WILHELM** (1844–1900), German philosopher. In the late 19th and early 20th century Nietzsche's highly enigmatic philosophy was adopted by circles which later had a powerful influence on Fascism, Nazism, and related movements. Using barely understood slogans from his works like "the Will to Power," "the Superman," and "Transvaluation of Values," they gave their own racist and anti-Semitic twist to the philosopher's conceptions. The Nazis hailed Nietzsche as one of the spiritual progenitors of Nazism, along with H. S. *Chamberlain and R. *Wagner. His letters and writings do indeed contain anti-Semitic remarks, and his nihilistic critique of liberalism, democracy, and modern culture contributed to the rise of irrational political movements. The claim that he was anti-Semitic was reinforced by Nietzsche's sister Elizabeth (the wife of Bernhard Foerster, a rabid professional anti-Semite), his literary executor; she forged, emended, and selectively edited his writings to bring them into line with the desired image. As with regard to many other phenomena, Nietzsche's attitude to Jews is full of contradictions and obscured by his specific style and symbolism. His works contain many remarks against Jews and Judaism. However, his main reproach against Judaism was that, when deprived of freedom and filled with resentment against the Roman world, it had given birth to Christianity, the religion of humility, weakness, and slavery, whose inverted and unnatural morality had caused immeasurable harm to the Western world. Nietzsche expressed admiration for the Old Testament, its moral style, majesty, and uncompromising commandments. He accorded more praise to modern Jews than modern Germans; the Jews were a healthy and strong race; their tenacity, adaptivity, and creativity showed that they possessed the ability to carry out a "transvaluation of values." Designating anti-Semites as *Schlechtweggekommene* ("misfits"), he became an inveterate foe of anti-Semitism, which for him was the beastliest aspect of the modern slave revolts exemplified by nationalism and socialism.

Nietzsche extolled H. *Heine's mastery of the German language and rated his works highly. *Meyerbeer, *Offenbach and *Mendelssohn-Bartholdy were praised as against Wagner. Nietzsche associated with the philosopher Paul *Ree and was enamored of Lou Andreas-Salomé. His first acclaim came from Georg *Brandes, the Danish literary historian and critic. Dr. Oscar Levy was the first to translate Nietzsche into English, further helping to spread his ideas. Nietzsche also exerted a considerable influence upon modern Hebrew writers, namely M. J. *Berdyczewski, J. Ḥ. *Brenner, and S. *Tchernichowsky. He also influenced certain activist elements within the nascent Zionist movement, an influence severely criticized by *Aḥad Ha-Am. The reassessment of Nietzsche after World War II was largely the work of Walter *Kaufmann and J. L. *Talmon.

Bibliography: M. Rabinowitz, in: *Ha-Shilo'aḥ*, 9 (1902), 376–82; M. Reiche, in: REJ, 52 (1906), xxv–liii; O. Baumgartner, in: *Wissen und Leben*, 5 (1912), 526–31; L. Simon (ed. and tr.), *Selected Essays by Ahad Ha-Am* (1912, repr. 1962), 217–41; H. Berl, in: *Menorah*, 10 (1932), 59–69 (Ger.); L. Hirsch, in: *Der Morgen*, 10 (1934), 187–90; C. von Westernhagen, *Nietzsche, Juden, Antijuden* (1936); E. Lewin, *Studien zur juedischen Geschichtsphilosophie* (1938); A. Coutinho, in: *Review of Religion*, 2 (1938/39), 161–6; R. M. Lonsbach, *Friedrich Nietzsche und die Juden* (1939); A. Stern, in: *Contemporary Jewish Record*, 8 (1945), 31–42; W. A. Kaufmann, *Nietzsche* (Eng., 1968²); E. Sandvoss, *Hitler and Nietzsche* (1969); W. Greuzmann, in: *The Third Reich* (1955), 203–42. [H.W.]

NIFOCI (Nafusi), ISAAC (late 14th century), physician-astronomer and scholar of *Majorca. In 1359 King Pedro IV of Aragon invited Nifoci to Barcelona to construct clocks and astrolabes. Three years later, he was appointed palace astronomer (*maestre astralabre de casa del senyor rey*) and also received the sinecure of ritual slaughterer and inspector (*shoḥet u-vodek*) of the community of Majorca, an office he was empowered to pass on to his son Joseph. In 1380 he entered the service of the infante John as manufacturer of astrolabes (*maestre de fer stralaus*). During the persecutions of 1391 he was forcibly converted to Christianity. However, shortly afterward he took refuge in Bugia (Bougie), North Africa, where he returned to Judaism, then emigrated to Ereẓ Israel. From Bugia, Nifoci addressed a question to Simon b. Ẓemaḥ *Duran and *Isaac b. Sheshet, on whether it was permissible "to set out on a caravan journey to Palestine, on a Friday" (cf. Duran's responsa, vol. 1, no. 21).

Bibliography: Baer, Spain, index, s.v. *Isaac Nifoci*; Pons, in: *Hispania*, 16 (1956), 249–51; A. L. Isaacs, *Jews of Majorca* (1936), 93–95; I. Epstein, *Responsa of Rabbi Simon B. Zemah Duran* (1930), 101. [Ed.]

NIGER, SAMUEL (pseudonym of **Samuel Charney;** 1883–1955), Yiddish literary critic. Born in Russia, Niger was the youngest of five brothers, among whom were the

Yiddish poet Daniel *Charney, and the Bund leader and Yiddish writer Baruch Charney *Vladeck.

In his youth at a yeshivah, Niger came under the influence of the religious movement of Ḥabad Ḥasidism and for a time considered becoming a rabbi. However, when he reached Minsk and came in contact with the Zionist ideas of *Aḥad Ha-Am and the socialist doctrines of Russian revolutionists, he joined the newly founded *Zionist-Socialist Workers Party, and participated in its often illegal propaganda activities. Though repeatedly arrested and tortured in Russian prisons, he continued to write revolutionary proclamations and articles, anonymously or under pseudonyms.

Niger's first literary efforts were in Russian and Hebrew; after the 1905 Revolution he wrote mainly in Yiddish. A major essay on Sholem *Asch (1907) attracted wide attention and initiated his career as a literary critic. The following year, together with the Bundist dramatist A. *Veiter and the Zionist essayist S. *Gorelik, he founded the *Literarishe Monatshriften* in Vilna. This magazine became an influential organ of the Yiddish literary upsurge after the *Czernowitz Yiddish Conference. As Niger's reputation grew, Russian, Hebrew, and Yiddish periodicals eagerly sought his critical contributions, and his fame soon equaled, and later eclipsed that of *Ba'al-Makhshoves, the father of Yiddish literary criticism. In 1909 Niger left for Berlin and soon after for the University of Berne, Switzerland, in order to extend his knowledge of philosophy and world literature. In 1912 he returned to Vilna to edit a new monthly, *Di Yidishe Velt*, which rapidly became the authoritative organ of Yiddish belles lettres. Assisted by D. B. *Borochov, he edited *Der Pinkes* (1913), a volume devoted to the history of Yiddish literature, language, folklore, criticism, and bibliography. He also edited Zalman Rejzen's first *Leksikon fun der Yidisher Literatur un Prese* (1914).

During World War I, when the modernists clamored for new themes and new moods that would reflect the rapidly changing scene, he opposed their slogans on the ground that the concern of literature was not with ephemeral issues and fashionable innovations but with the problems of the human spirit. He stated that he would continue to judge new books and new writers on the basis of criteria derived from the great classics of world literature. His best essays of the war decade were included in the volume *Shmuesn vegn Bikher* (1922).

After the 1917 Revolution he edited the Moscow weekly *Kultur un Bildung* (1918), and the Vilna monthly *Di Naye Velt* (1919). In April 1919, Polish legionnaires stormed Vilna, broke into an apartment Niger was sharing with A. Veiter and Leib *Jaffe, shot Veiter, and threw the others into prison. After his release, Niger left for the U.S. In 1920, he joined the staff of the New York Yiddish daily *Der Tog*, and for 35 years wrote weekly reviews of books and articles on literary trends, becoming the most revered and feared Yiddish critic of his generation. His praise or censure often made or destroyed reputations. His participation in the literary monthly *Di Zukunft*, which he co-edited from 1941 to 1947, helped to maintain its high quality and enduring influence.

Niger was a pillar of the *YIVO Institute for Jewish Research from its very beginning, contributing studies to its important publications. He was also active in CYCO (Central Yiddish Culture Organization), editing its complete edition of the works of I. L. *Peretz, on whom he wrote a definitive study (1952). Niger was the chief adviser of the Louis LaMed Foundation for the Advancement of Hebrew and Yiddish Literature and, under its auspices, published his study *Di Tsveyshprakhikeyt fun Undzer Literatur* (1941). In this study, he emphasized that bilingualism had been a Jewish tradition since biblical days and that in the modern era both Hebrew and Yiddish were necessary pillars sustaining the Jewish structure. In 1948, Niger helped to found the *Congress for Jewish Culture. In 1954, he undertook to co-edit its *Leksikon fun der Nayer Yidisher Literatur*. He died while the first volume was in press. A number of his works were published posthumously: *Yidishe Shrayber in Sovet-Rusland* (1958); *Bleter Geshikhte fun der Yidisher Literatur* (1959); *Kritik un Kritiker* (1959); *Sholem Asch* (1960). Niger held that a critic must be objective, fearless, and sympathetic to every variety of genuine creative expression. He therefore sought to immerse himself in the essence of each literary personality he surveyed. He defined a literary critic as a seeker after beauty, an artist who gives expression to thoughts, feelings, and visions aroused in him by a literary work, an interpreter and elucidator of the basic meaning and structure of imaginative works. Literary history, psychology, and sociology he regarded merely as aids to the critic's main purpose—illuminating the uniqueness of a creative literary personality.

Samuel Niger, Yiddish critic. Courtesy M. Charney, Montclair, New Jersey.

Bibliography: Rejzen, Leksikon, 2 (1927), 539–51; LNYL, 6 (1965), 190–210; *Shmuel Niger-Bukh* (1958); S. Bickel, *Shrayber fun Mayn Dor* (1958), 256–93; S. D. Singer, *Dikhter un Prozaiker* (1959), 263–78; J. Glatstein, *Mit Mayne Fartogbikher* (1963), 466–85; H. Leivick, *Eseyn un Redes* (1963), 174–87; S. Liptzin, *Maturing of Yiddish Literature* (1970), 77–81. [S.L.]

NIGER OF PEREA (d. 68 C.E.), patriot leader of Perea, Transjordan. After distinguishing himself in the attack on Cestius at the outset of the revolt against the Romans in the autumn of 66, Niger apparently took charge of operations against them in Idumea, in due course becoming for a short time deputy governor of this province. Later in the same year he was placed in command of the disastrous expedition against *Ashkelon, together with *John the Essene and *Silas the Babylonian. He was the only one of the three to survive, leading another attack later on with no greater success from his base in Idumea. During the reign of terror in Jerusalem after the triumph of the Zealot extremists, he was among the moderates who were executed, apparently on suspicion of wishing to come to terms with the Romans (Jos., Wars, 2:520, 566; 3:11–27; 4:359–63).

Bibliography: Graetz, Hist, 2 (1893), 264, 296. [C.R.]

NIGHTINGALE (mod. Heb. זָמִיר, *zamir*), a name applied to singing birds of the genus *Luscinia*, of which three species are found in Israel. The most outstanding for its song is the *Luscinia megarhynchos* which hatches its eggs in the thickets of the Jordan. It is a small brown bird, common in Western Europe. The Hebrew word is mentioned only once in the Bible in a description of spring in Ereẓ Israel: "The time of the *zamir* is come, and the voice of the turtle dove is heard in our land" (Song 2:12). The parallelism between *zamir* and turtledove indicates that the reference here is to a bird and, according to the meaning of the Hebrew root, to a singing one. Apparently the nightingale is not specifically meant but rather all singing birds that in spring and during the breeding season fill the air with their melodious song. Some, however, maintain that *zamir* is derived from the root signifying "fruit-picking," since in the *Gezer Calendar there occurs the expression *yarḥo zamor* denoting the fruit-picking months in summer. But as the Song of Songs speaks of spring, this interpretation is improbable.

Bibliography: N. H. Tur-Sinai, *Ha-Lashon ve-ha-Sefer*, 1 (1954[2]), 51; J. Feliks, *Animal World of the Bible* (1962), 87. [J.F.]

NIGHT PRAYER (Heb. קְרִיאַת שְׁמַע עַל הַמִּטָּה, *Keri'at Shema al ha-Mittah;* "the reading of the *Shema on retiring," lit. "on the bed"), a prayer recited before retiring for the night. The custom to pray before going to sleep reflects man's need for protection in a state of suspended consciousness and vulnerability, especially since sleep was held in ancient times to be similar to death. Possibly practiced earlier, the Night Prayer in which one commends one's soul to God for the night became obligatory only in mishnaic times. It was incorporated into the prayer book of nearly all Jewish communities in an almost identical form (but see below): When **Arvit* became established as a community prayer to be recited in the early evening, the Night Prayer became the individual concluding prayer of the day. The name *Keri'at Shema al ha-Mittah* refers to the central part of the prayer which is the first paragraph of the *Shema*. The Talmud states that he who wishes to go to sleep should say the *Shema* until the words *Ve-hayah im shamo'a* and recite the prayer *Ha-Mappil* to God "Who causes the bands of sleep to fall upon my eyes..." (Ber. 60b). Some codifiers demand the recitation of the first two sections of the *Shema* (see R. Asher to Ber. 9 no. 23); the majority, however, require the first one only (Maim. Yad, Tefillah, 7:1–2; Tur and Sh. Ar., OḤ 239:1), to be preceded by *Ha-Mappil* (Maim. loc. cit., but see Tur and Sh. Ar., loc. cit.). The order of these two portions of the Night Prayer is widely accepted and is probably derived from the talmudic view that "man ought to recite the *Shema* and repeat it until sleep overcomes him" (TJ, Ber. 1:1, 2d). The rabbinic concept of sleep being a state of minor death is in consonance with this outlook; just as one is obliged in the last hour of life to recite the *Shema* and bless the unity of God, so one should recite the *Shema* at night and commend one's spirit to God before succumbing to sleep. The reversed order, in which the *Shema* is recited first and is followed by *Ha-Mappil*, is given by *Amram Gaon, but is less common. In Amram's order, the *Shema* is prefaced by blessing "the Lord Who has sanctified us with His commandments and commanded us to recite the *Shema*," and concludes (as in the Italian rite) with blessing "the Lord Who guards His people Israel forever." The *Ha-Mappil* benediction underwent a number of changes and considerable curtailment compared with the original talmudic version (see Yad, Tefillah 7:1, R. Asher to Ber. 9 no. 23; Tur, OḤ 239).

The significance of the Night Prayer is prophylactic: the *Shema* and *Ha-Mappil* are invocations of divine protection against the various dangers that might befall man at night and during sleep, and especially against sin. The latter idea derives from Psalm 4:51: "Tremble, and sin not, commune with your heart upon your bed, and be still." Consequently, some scholars held (Ber. 5a–b) that for a man whose sole occupation was the study of the Torah no Night Prayer was necessary or one short supplicatory text was sufficient, e.g., "I commend my spirit into Thine hand" (Ps. 31:6). According to the Mishnah (Ber. 2:5), a bridegroom on the night of his wedding was exempted from the obligation of reciting the *Shema* at night because, excited over his nuptials, he would not be able to muster the necessary concentration (Ber. 16a–b; Maim. Yad, Keri'at Shema, 4:1). In later times, however, this exemption was abolished since proper spiritual concentration at prayer was rare anyway (Tur, OḤ 70).

Subsequently more prayers and scriptural texts were added to the Night Prayer by the talmudists and later authorities: e.g., Psalm 91 (also known as *Shir shel Pegga'im;* "Song against Untoward Happenings"), Psalm 3, and certain sections from *Arvit* (e.g., *Hashkivenu* and *Barukh Adonai ba-Yom*). Further additions were made under kabbalistic influence, the latter strengthening earlier angelological elements (e.g., Gen. 48:16) in the Night Prayer.

It is customary not to recite these additional prayers and texts on the first night of Passover; as this is a "night of watching unto the Lord" (Ex. 12:42) God Himself guards the Jews from the dangers of this night (Sh. Ar., OḤ 481:2).

Bibliography: Idelsohn, Liturgy, 126–7; Abrahams, Companion, ccxiii–ccxv; E. Levi, *Yesodot ha-Tefillah* (1952[2]), 205–8; E. Munk, *The World of Prayer*, 1 (1961) 223–8. [HA.BL.]

NIGRI (Niger), PETRUS (Peter Schwarz; 1434–1483), Hebraist and polemist. Born in Bohemia, Nigri entered the Dominican Order and studied Hebrew, perfecting his knowledge in Spain, where he apparently acquired or compiled anti-Jewish polemical material subsequently exploited in his writings. On his return to Germany, he launched a conversionist campaign in several Jewish communities and ingratiated himself with the anti-Semitic bishop of Regensburg by arranging a week-long religious disputation there in 1474. In the following year, Nigri published his *Tractatus contra perfidos Judaeos de conditionibus veri Messiae*... (Esslingen, 1475), the first incunabulum to contain printed Hebrew characters, which was later consulted by Conrad *Pellicanus. It was followed by a treatise in German, *Der Stern Maschiach* (Esslingen, 1477), another early document of the Christian Kabbalah. Both works contained appended guides to the study of Hebrew and were venomously anti-Jewish and anti-talmudic. Their author characteristically identified the Trinity in the second word of the Hebrew Bible, *bara* ("created"), being said to represent the initials of *Ben* ("Son"), *Ru'aḥ* ("Spirit"), and *Av* ("Father"). Nigri, who also wrote a commentary on the Psalms, is said by Yom Tov Lipmann Heller (*Sefer Niẓẓaḥon* 1644 p. 191) to have been a Jewish apostate.

Bibliography: B. Walde, *Christliche Hebraisten Deutschlands am Ausgang des Mittelalters* (1916), 70–152; F. Secret, *Les Kabbalistes Chrétiens de la Renaissance* (1964), 18; ADB, 33 (1891), 247f.; L. M. Friedman, in: HUCA, 23, 2 (1950–51), 443–46; P. Bowe, *Judenmission im Mittelalter und die Paepste* (1942), index. [ED.]

NIJMEGEN, town in Gelderland province, E. Netherlands. Following the outbreak of the *Black Death in 1349, the Jews were accused of poisoning the wells, and the medieval community was consequently dispersed. Several Jews settled there in 1386, some receiving citizenship of the town. In the 15th century there existed a prosperous Jewish community which was not confined to a ghetto. Toward the end of that century the community declined, and when Emperor *Charles V issued his anti-Jewish laws it had already ceased to exist. A settlement was mentioned again in 1683. In the 18th century the dominant personality was Benedict Levi *Gomperz who erected a synagogue with a *bet ha-midrash*. In 1847 there were 270 Jews, and the community increased steadily throughout the 19th century. In 1872–73 a new school was built beside the synagogue, in the Moorish style, one of the first of its kind in the Netherlands. A new synagogue designed by architect Oscar Leeuw was constructed in 1912–13 in a more suitable part of the town.

Holocaust Period. In 1938 there were 450 Jews living in Nijmegen. By 1941 there were 537, 101 of them German-Jewish refugees and 33 refugees of other foreign nationalities. They arrived when the western districts were "cleared" of foreign Jews. Practically the entire Jewish population of Nijmegen was sent via *Westerbork to death camps. In 1946, 76 Jews resided in Nijmegen, only a handful being survivors of the camps.

Contemporary Period. In 1969 the number of Jews in Nijmegen, including the surrounding area, was 100, out of a total population of 150,000. The congregation remained without a resident rabbi. Only the beautiful 18th-century *menorah* has survived the demolition of the synagogue interior by the Germans as a reminder of the past.

Bibliography: J. J. F. W. van Agt, in: *Studia Rosenthaliana*, 3 (1969), 168–92 (Dutch and Summary in Eng.). [Ed.]

NIKEL, LEA (1918–), Israel painter. Lea Nikel was born in Zhitomir, Ukraine, and was brought to Palestine at the age of two. She studied painting under Avigdor *Stematsky and Yehezkiel *Streichman and became a member of the "Group of Ten." From 1950 to 1961, she worked in Paris, traveling and exhibiting in Holland and Italy. She returned to Israel in 1961 and settled ultimately in Safed. Lea Nikel was considered one of the outstanding artists after the "New Horizons" generation, and was a typical representative of the second phase of abstract art in Israel. Her work, like that of her teachers, is essentially an abstraction, in which color is liberated from all formal restraint. However, her work differs from theirs by being less lyrical, more expressive, and occasionally even violent.

Bibliography: Venice, 32nd Biennale d'Arte, *Israele (Aroch, Nikel, Tumarkin)* (1964). [Y.Fi.]

NIKITIN, VICTOR (1839–1908), writer and scholar. Nikitin's special field was the history of Jewish agricultural settlement in Russia. At the age of nine, he was kidnapped and sent to the *Cantonist regiment in Nizhni Novgorod. There he was forced to convert to Christianity, and his Jewish name (not known) was changed. Because of his excellent handwriting he was assigned to office work in the army. While in the army, he studied on his own, and after completing his military service (1869), he served as a high official in the Ministry of Agriculture. Nikitin described the life of kidnapped children and the Jewish Cantonists in "*Vek perezhit—ne pole pereyti*" (in *Yevreyskaya Biblioteka*, 4 (1876), 164–213), and in *Mnogostradalnye* ("Those who Suffer"). The latter was banned by the censors but later appeared in two editions (1872, 1896). There is a great deal of material of historical importance in his *Yevrei Zemledeltsy* ("Jewish Tillers of the Soil"), published in *Voskhod* (1881–86) and later in 1887 as a separate work, and in *Yevreyskiye poseleniya severnykh i yugo-zapadnykh guberniy* ("Jewish Settlements in Northern and Southwestern Provinces," 1894), which was written on the basis of archival material.

Bibliography: S. Ginzburg, in: *Forwards* (N.Y., Nov. 3, 1935); V. E. Rudakov, in: *Istoricheskiy Vestnik*, 5 (1908), 587–98. [Y.S.]

NIKOLAYEV, port on the Black Sea coast, Nikolayev oblast, Ukrainian S.S.R. The town was founded in 1789 and Jews settled there from its earliest days, engaging in commerce and crafts. Many of them moved there from Galicia. In 1830, among the inhabitants of the town were 24

A Nikolayev Hebrew drama circle calling itself "Habimah," 1919. Courtesy A. Rafaeli-Zenziper, Archive for Russian Zionism, Tel Aviv.

Jewish families of merchants, 691 families of townsmen, and 424 individual Jews. In 1829 a government order prohibited the residence of Jews (with the exception of those serving in the army) in Nikolayev and *Sevastopol, using the existence of naval bases in the two towns as a pretext. The Jews were allowed two years to arrange their departure. The local authorities opposed the decree, arguing that the expulsion of the Jews would harm the development of the town; the expulsion was therefore postponed until 1834. At the beginning of the reign of Alexander II the right of residence in the town was granted to Jewish merchants and industrialists (1857), and later also to craftsmen (1861). Many Jews lived in the villages and estates in the vicinity of Nikolayev, where they conducted their commerce. In 1866 all restrictions were lifted and the Jewish community of Nikolayev developed rapidly. In 1880 there were 8,325 Jews in Nikolayev, and in 1897 the number rose to 20,109 (21.8% of the total population). A native of the town, Moshe Katz, described Nikolayev in the early 20th century in his memoirs, *A Dor Vos Hot Farloren di Moyre* (1956). In October 1905 pogroms claimed several victims. During the Civil War (1919–20) the Jews of neighboring towns suffered severely. In 1926 there were 21,786 Jews (about 20.8% of the total population) in Nikolayev. Under the German occupation (August 1941), all the Jews who had not succeeded in leaving the city were murdered. With the liberation of Nikolayev (March 1944), Jews began to return to the city. According to the 1959 census, there were 15,800 Jews (7% of the population) in Nikolayev, but the actual number was probably closer to 20,000. The last synagogue was closed down by the authorities in 1962. [Y.S.]

NIKOPOL (Nicopolis), small city in the Plevna district of Bulgaria. A Byzantine Jewish community existed in Nikopol during the tenth century. Jewish refugees arrived in Nikopol after their expulsion from Hungary in 1376 and also from Bavaria after expulsion in 1470. Jews expelled from Spain also sought refuge there. During the 16th century there were six synagogues in Nikopol—a Rumanian, Hungarian, Wallachian, and Ashkenazi synagogue and two Sephardi synagogues. From 1523 to 1536 R. Joseph *Caro lived in Nikopol where he founded a famous yeshivah and continued the writing of his *Beit Yosef*. The synagogue that bears his name, Maran Beit Yosef, was destroyed several times and rebuilt in 1895. Some of the Jews expelled from Italy in 1569 by decree of Pope Pius V went to Nikopol. Those Jews who did not succeed in escaping at the approach of Michael the Brave of Wallachia, during the Turkish-Wallachian wars from 1595 to 1599, were taken to Wallachia and executed. After the

Maran Beit Yosef Synagogue in Nikopol, Bulgaria, used by the Nazis as a warehouse and stable. Courtesy Institut Scientifique Juif, Sofia.

wars R. Isaac *Beja (d. before 1630), author of *Bayit Ne-'eman,* was the rabbi of the city. In 1688 the Jewish population increased with the arrival of war refugees from Smederevo (Semendria; Serbia) following the German invasion.

During the Russian-Turkish War of 1877 the Jews of Nikopol fled to Plevna (Pleven), and Adrianople, returning after the peace treaty of 1878. The economic situation, which deteriorated after the war, induced many Jews to settle in other Bulgarian towns. In 1904 there were still 210 Jews in Nikopol, but in 1926 only 12 Jewish families remained. During World War II the city received refugees from Germany and other European countries. The Nazis converted Maran Beit Yosef synagogue into a warehouse and stable. In 1948 there were 28 Jews in Nikopol.

Bibliography: Rosanes, Togarmah, 1 (1930²), 7–8, 206, 213–4, 221, 252, and passim; idem, in *Yevreyska Tribuna,* 1 (1926), 28–37, 172–80; *Bulletin de l'Alliance Israélite Universelle,* 29 (1904), 170; S. Markus, in: *Ha-Ẓofeh* (Dec. 10, 1948).

[S.MAR.]

NILE, river in N. E. Africa. The Nile is the life stream of the civilizations flourishing in the valley bordering it. If the river is too high or too low in one year, disaster and famine follow in the next. Indeed, the ancient Egyptians saw in the yearly inundation the annual renewal of the first act of creation, the rising of the primeval mound out of the primordial ocean. From the correct observation of this yearly flooding, which enriched the fields of the lower Nile Valley with the fertile black alluvial soil, developed much of the later civilization of the pharaohs, and particularly the 365-day calendar. Unquestionably, the Egypt of the pharaohs was "the gift of the Nile." The Hebrew word for the Nile, יְאוֹר, is a loan word from the Egyptian *'itrw* ("river") which by the period of the Middle Kingdom came to designate the Nile as the river par excellence.

Although the name Nile is not explicitly mentioned in the Bible, it is alluded to as "the river" (Gen. 41:1; Ex. 2:3), the "river of Egypt" (Gen. 15:8), the "flood of Egypt" (Amos 8:8), Shihor (Josh. 13:3), brook of Egypt (according to some, but see *Egypt, Brook of), river of Cush, and many more. The Nile plays a prominent part in the early stories of the Exodus (Moses, Ex. 2:3; the ten plagues, 7:15, 20; et al.), and is used by the prophets as the symbol of Egypt (Amos 8:8; 9:5; Jer. 46:8). [AL.R.S.]

NILES (Neyhus), DAVID K. (1890–1952), U.S. presidential aide. Born in Boston to immigrant Russian parents, Niles went to work in a local department store. He regularly frequented Ford Hall's Sunday forum of public lectures and discussions, and caught the eye of the forum's director, George W. Coleman, who eventually made him his assistant. During World War I, when Coleman went to Washington as an official in the Labor Department, Niles accompanied him as an aide. After the war he continued his association with Ford Hall, of which he was appointed associate director in 1924. Through his work there he became acquainted with numerous political figures, as a result of which he took part in La Follette's 1924 presidential campaign on the Progressive ticket. In subsequent elections, he was active in the Democratic Party, working for Smith in 1928 and Roosevelt in 1932. In 1935 he returned to Washington as labor assistant to Harry Hopkins, director of the Works Progress Administration and an intimate of President Roosevelt. He remained with Hopkins when the latter was made secretary of commerce in 1938. By then a member of the White House's inner circle, Niles helped to engineer the third-term "draft" of President Roosevelt in 1940 and was appointed assistant to the president in 1942. In this capacity, he performed the functions of a political trouble-shooter, an unofficial dispenser of patronage, and a liaison man with organized labor and various racial and religious minority groups. He remained in the post when President *Truman took office in 1945 and is said to have been instrumental in helping to shape Truman's ultimately positive stand on the partition of Palestine, which led to swift U.S. recognition of the State of Israel in May 1948. With his characteristic aversion to publicity, however, which often caused him to be labeled by the press as a political "mystery man," Niles publicly referred to his interest in Israel only once in the course of his career. That was in his letter of resignation from office in 1951, in which he gave his desire to visit Israel as a private citizen as one of the reasons for his retirement.

Bibliography: Steinberg, in: *Saturday Evening Post* (Dec. 24, 1949), 24, 69–70; *New York Times* (May 22, 1951), 20.

[B.ST.]

NILI, secret pro-British spying organization, that operated under Turkish rule in Syria and Palestine during World War I, from 1915 to 1917, under the leadership of Aaron *Aaronsohn, Avshalom *Feinberg, Sarah *Aaronsohn, and Yosef *Lishansky. Its name consists of the initial letters of the Hebrew verse "*Neẓaḥ Yisrael Lo Yeshakker*" נֵצַח יִשְׂרָאֵל לֹא יְשַׁקֵּר—"the Strength of Israel will not lie" (I Sam. 15:29), which served as its password. In British official documents it is named the "A. Organization." Nili was founded by a number of Jews in the moshavot (Jewish agricultural villages), most of whom were born in the country. Their disappointment with the Turkish authorities' treatment of the Jewish population and fear of a fate similar to that of the Armenians led them to the conclusion that the future of the Jews depended on Palestine being taken over by Britain. In January 1915, Avshalom Feinberg, who worked in Aaronsohn's agricultural experimental station at Athlit, was arrested with a group of young men in Ḥaderah who were falsely accused of having contact with British boats off the coast. After his release, Feinberg presented to his teacher and friend, Aaronsohn, a plan for a Jewish revolt with the aid of the British army stationed in Egypt. Aaronsohn, who held an important position in locust control under the Turkish authorities, rejected the plan as impractical, but accepted Feinberg's basic assumption that the British army should be aided by espionage.

Establishing contact with the British headquarters in Egypt was quite difficult. The first messenger, Aaronsohn's brother Alexander, met with the disapproval of the British Arab Bureau in Cairo and went to the United States, where he conducted propaganda against Turkey and Germany. The second, Feinberg, was promised in August that contact with the group would be maintained, but the British did not keep their word; he was caught by the Turks and released only after strenuous efforts by Aaronsohn. Feinberg's trip to Turkey in February 1916, with a view to contacting British agents in neutral Rumania, did not bear fruit either. In the meantime the group was joined by Sarah Aaronsohn, Aaron's sister; Yosef Lishansky, head of a watchmen organization in the southern villages; and others, most of them from Zikhron Ya'akov, Ḥaderah, and Rishon le-Zion. Some of the recruits were enlisted in Aaronsohn's locust control staff, thus being able to move all over the country and enter military camps. Military, political, and economic information was collected in the experimental station in Athlit, but there was no way of transmitting it to the British.

To contact the British, Aaronsohn went on a fictional Turkish mission to Germany, in the summer of 1916; then to neutral Denmark, where he contacted British agents; and finally to London. There he met statesmen and soldiers, and, having gained their confidence, was sent to Cairo, where he served as intelligence adviser and helped in the planning of the British offensive against Palestine. In January 1917 Feinberg and Lishansky, disguised as Bedouin, tried to get to Egypt by land to renew contact with Aaronsohn. They were attacked by Bedouin and Feinberg was killed near the British front in Sinai. Lishansky was wounded but found his way to the British lines and joined Aaronsohn. In February 1917 contact was first established between the espionage center at Athlit and British intelligence in Egypt through Lishansky, who was brought to the coast by a British boat. The connections were maintained by sea for several months and the British received useful information collected by the group, supplemented by Aaronsohn's extensive knowledge of the geographical conditions and the personnel of the Turkish command.

The group also sought to help the Jewish population, many of whom were expelled from Jaffa and Tel Aviv by the Turks during the spring of 1917. Aaronsohn devoted much publicity to this persecution, which was later stopped. Other members helped transfer financial support to the *yishuv*, a difficult task after the United States broke off relations with Turkey in April 1917. Aaronsohn founded an assistance committee corresponding to the one in Egypt, which was set up by exiles from Palestine at the beginning of the war. Sarah Aaronsohn and Lishansky went to see Aaronsohn in Egypt and brought back £2,000 in gold coins, which they handed over to the political committee of the *yishuv*. This helped change the attitude of the Jewish

Figure 1. Home in Zikhron Ya'akov of the Aaronsohn family, leaders of Nili. On the wall is a photo of Avshalom Feinberg. Courtesy Government Press Office, Tel Aviv.

Figure 2. The Royal Navy Yacht *Managem*, used to transmit information from Nili headquarters in Palestine to British headquarters in Egypt, 1917. Courtesy Haganah Historical Archives, Tel Aviv.

population and its leaders, who were afraid of the consequences if Nili's activities were discovered by the Turks. The group was asked to arrange for two representatives of the *yishuv* to meet Aaronsohn and Zionist leaders abroad, to show that the latter approved of Nili's operations. Aaronsohn met Chaim *Weizmann and his colleagues in London in September 1917 and succeeded in convincing them of the importance of Nili's work as part of the political and military work of the section of the Zionist movement that had called for an alliance with Britain from the beginning of the war. It seemed that Nili was trying to become a political factor in Palestine and the Zionist movement; it made approaches to *Ha-Shomer and other groups.

In September 1917 the Turks caught a carrier pigeon sent from Athlit to Egypt that provided clear proof of espionage within the Jewish population, and the leadership again dissociated itself from Nili's actions. Internal conflicts weakened the organization, and there were grave suspicions over the circumstances of Feinberg's death. One of the group, Na'aman Belkind, was captured by the Turks while trying to get to Egypt and gave his interrogators information on the organization and its operations. On Oct. 1, 1917, Turkish soldiers surrounded Zikhron Ya'akov and arrested numerous people, including Sarah Aaronsohn, who committed suicide after four days' interrogation and torture. Lishansky managed to escape. The authorities hunted after suspects in other villages as well. The prisoners were taken to the Khan al-Pasha prison in Damascus. Zikhron Ya'akov was given an ultimatum: if Lishansky was not handed over, the village would be destroyed. The Jewish leaders decided to hand over the suspects and wash their hands of responsibility for them.

Lishansky took shelter among his former friends in Ha-Shomer and was taken from one village to another. As it was impossible to go on like that for a long period, the Ha-Shomer committee decided that he must die in case he fell into the hands of the Turks and brought disaster to the whole *yishuv*. Emissaries of Ha-Shomer set out to assassinate Lishansky, but succeeded only in wounding him, and he managed to escape. On his way to Egypt he was caught by Bedouin near Rishon le-Zion and handed over to the Turks. Following his interrogation in Damascus, more people were arrested. Due to the intensive endeavors of Jewish leaders and the secret intervention of German representatives, most of the prisoners were released, but 12 were sentenced to periods of one to three years in prison and 30 were conscripted into the army. Lishansky and Belkind were sentenced to death and were executed on Dec. 16, 1917. The remaining members of the organization went on with their spying activities. Aaronsohn, who was sent by Weizmann on a political and propaganda mission to the U.S., returned to Palestine in the spring of 1918 with the Zionist Commission. With his death in an air accident on May 15, 1919, the group finally broke up.

From a sociological and historical point of view, Nili was an attempt by young people born in the moshavot, under Aaronsohn's leadership, to form an independent political movement that would win the support of the entire *yishuv*. However, it was unable to appeal to a broad social stratum; hence its rapid dissolution after its leader's death. Its aid in the conquest of Palestine by the British, which was well appreciated, was part of the efforts of the pro-British section of the Zionist movement that was active in 1914–18 and determined policies in the subsequent 20 years.

Bibliography: E. Livneh (ed.), *Nili, Toledoteha shel He'azah Medinit* (1961); idem, *Aaron Aaronsohn, ha-Ish u-Zemanno* (1969); Dinur, Haganah, 1, pt. 1 (1954), 353–68; *Yoman Aaron Aaronsohn 1916–1919* (1970); A. Engle, *Nili Spies* (1959). [Y.S.]

NÎMES, capital of Gard department, S. France. Although a number of Jews took part in the revolt led by Hilderic, governor of Nîmes, against the Visigothic king Wamba in 673, there is no direct evidence that Jews were then living in the town itself. However, a community was established during the second half of the tenth century at the latest, and from 1009 there is documentary evidence of the existence of a synagogue. From the middle of the 11th century, the name Poium Judaicum was used to designate one of the seven hills enclosed within the wall of Nîmes (later Puech Juzieu, etc.; in 1970 the promenade of Mont-Duplan); the Jewish cemetery was situated there. Toward the close of the 11th century, an entire quarter of the town was known as Burgus Judaicus (later Bourg-Jézieu). At the beginning of the 13th century, the community appears to have consisted of about 100 families. Although a church synod held in Nîmes in about 1284 decreed severe measures against the Jews, the bishop of Nîmes, who had authority over the Jews of the town, was nevertheless able to protect them, even from King *Philip IV the Fair who had ordered the imprisonment of several Jews. But the bishop could not prevail against the royal expulsion order of 1306 which, in Nîmes as elsewhere, was accompanied by the confiscation of all their belongings. When the Jews returned to France in 1359, the Nîmes municipal council allocated them the Rue de Corrégerie Vieille (the modern Rue de l'Etoile). After being harassed by the Christians there, they obtained a new quarter in the Rue Caguensol (part of the Rue Guizot) and the Rue de la Jésutarie or Juiverie (Rue Fresque). Shortly afterward they moved yet again, to the Garrigues quarter. There the 1367 census recorded the only three houses in the town (out of a total of 1,400) that were owned by Jews. This community ceased to exist in 1394, after the general expulsion of the Jews from France.

In a letter to *Abraham b. David of Posquières—who lived in Nîmes long enough to be sometimes named after that town—Moses b. Judah of Béziers stressed the superiority of the yeshivah of Nîmes over all the others in southern France, comparing it to "the interior of the Temple, the seat of the Sanhedrin, from where knowledge goes forth to Israel." Other than Abraham b. David, the only scholar of the town who is known is his uncle, Judah b. Abraham. The municipal library of Nîmes possesses a rich collection of medieval Hebrew manuscripts, several of French origin, in the French provinces; all these volumes were obtained from the Carthusians of Villeneuve-lès-Avignon.

From the 17th century, some Jews of *Comtat Venaissin went to trade in Nîmes and a few of them attempted to settle there; the *parlement* of *Toulouse ordered them to leave in 1653 and again in 1679. From the end of the 17th century, the Jews obtained the right to buy and sell in Nîmes for three weeks or a month in every season. Even though this concession was abolished in 1745 and 1754, some Jews succeeded in settling in the town during the second half of the 18th century. The community of 30–40 families appointed a rabbi, Elie Espir from *Carpentras, and set up a small synagogue in a private house. After a split in the community in 1794, a new synagogue (which has been in use ever since) was built in the Rue Roussy, completed in 1796. During the Reign of Terror, three Jews of Nîmes were imprisoned; one of them was subsequently executed. In 1808, when the *consistories were established, the community was affiliated to the consistory of *Marseilles, and there were then 371 Jews in the town, with the surprising number of eight rabbis. Among the rabbis of Nîmes was Solomon Kahn (1854–1931), historian of the Jews of southern France. Other notable personalities who originated from there include Adolph *Crémieux and *Bernard Lazare. From the close of the 19th century, the community diminished steadily in number. Although 40 families were recorded in 1941, some of these were refugees from the interior of France. In 1970 the community of 1,200 persons, mainly of North African origin, possessed a synagogue and a community center.

Bibliography: Gross, Gal Jud, 395–9; J. Simon, in: REJ, 3 (1881), 225–37; idem, in: *Nemausa*, 2 (1884/85), 97–124; S. Kahn, *Notice sur les Israélites de Nîmes* (1901); idem, in: REJ, 67 (1914), 225–61; J. Vieilleville, *Nîmes...* (1941); H. Noël, in: *Revue du Midi*, 11 (1897), 182–91; B. Blumenkranz, *Juifs et chrétiens...* (1960), index; Z. Szajkowski, *Analytical Franco-Jewish Gazetteer* (1966), 190. [B.BL.]

NIMROD (Heb. נִמְרוֹד, נִמְרֹד), son of *Cush and grandson of *Ham son of *Noah (Gen. 10:8–12; I Chron. 1:10). He is described in the Table of Nations as "a mighty hunter by the grace of the Lord" (Gen. 10:9) whose exploits as a hero of the chase became proverbial. He was also "the first man of might on earth" (Gen. 10:8), i.e., the first to found a great empire after the *flood. He is said to have ruled over the famous capitals of southern Mesopotamia, Babylon, Uruk (Erech), and Akkad as well as, apparently, over the great cities of Calah and Nineveh in the land of Assyria. The term "land of Nimrod" appears as a synonymous variant of Assyria in Micah 5:5. The etymology of the name is uncertain as is also the identification of Nimrod with an historical personality. E. A. Speiser connects him with Tukulti-Ninurta I (13th century B.C.E.), who was the

Detail of illumination from a *Haggadah*, Spain, 14th century, showing the enthroned Nimrod ordering Abraham to be cast into a fiery furnace. London, British Museum, Ms. Or. 2884, fol. 3r.

first Mesopotamian ruler effectively to have combined Babylon and Assyria under a single authority. However, the association of Nimrod with Cush son of Ham presents a difficulty if Cush refers to the area south of Egypt. Another possibility is to connect it with the Kassites who conquered Babylon in the second millennium (cf. Gen. 2:13), in which case a confusion of genealogical traditions is to be presumed. The extraordinary notice about Nimrod in the Table of Nations indicates the existence of a well-known and widespread narrative about him. U. Cassuto has postulated that the five verses in Genesis 10 derive from an ancient epic devoted to his heroic exploits. [N.M.S.]

In the Aggadah. Nimrod is the prototype of rebellion against the Almighty (Ḥag. 13a), his name being interpreted as "he who made all the people rebel against God" (Pes. 94b). As the first hunter, he was the first to eat meat and to make war on other peoples (Mid. Ag. to Gen. 10:8), and he eventually became a king (PdRE 24). His physical prowess came from his coats of skin, which God had made for Adam and Eve (Gen. 3:21) and which Noah had preserved in the Ark. When the animals saw Nimrod wearing these coats, they knelt before him. He became the first man to rule the whole world and he appointed Terah, Abraham's father, his minister (PdRE 24). Elated by his glory, he became an idolator (*Sefer ha-Yashar*, Noah 9a, 1870). He built the Tower of Babel (which is called by the rabbis, "the house of Nimrod") for idol worship (Av. Zar. 53b) and he had the whole world pay divine homage to him (Mid. Hag. to Gen. 11:28). When informed of Abraham's birth, Nimrod ordered all male children to be killed (*Ma'aseh Avraham*, in: A. Jellinek, *Beit ha-Midrash*, 2 (1938², 118f.) and he later had Abraham cast into a fiery furnace because he refused to worship fire (Gen. R. 38:13).

Nimrod (identified with *Amraphel) became a vassal of his rebellious general Chedorlaomer, and was later defeated by Abraham (see Gen. 14; *Sefer ha-Yashar*, loc. cit.). He was slain by Esau who was jealous of his success as a hunter and who coveted his magic garments (PdRE 24). In messianic times Nimrod will testify before the whole world that Abraham never worshiped idols (Av. Zar. 3a). [ED.]

In Islam. Namrūd (Namrūdh) b. Kūsh (Cush), or b. Kanʿān (Canaan), is not mentioned by name in the Koran. The commentators are justified, however, in their contention that Suras 21:69; 29:23; and 37:95, in which it is said that the courtiers and the people of Abraham suggested that he be thrown into the fiery furnace, refer to Namrūd. In the discussion between the ruler of the land and Abraham (Sura 2:260), another allusion is made to Namrūd. The allusions to the Jewish *aggadot* about Abraham in the fiery furnace are sufficiently evident. At a later period Nimrod b. Cush (Gen. 10:9), or b. Canaan, is mentioned by name. The theme of Abraham, who worships God and is persecuted by the ruler, recurs in various popular literary works. In a fragment of the *qaṣīda* (poem) attributed to Samawʾal al-Quarẓī, found in the Cairo *Genizah*, the following stanza appears: "It was only in the case of one man [among our ancestors] that the fire which encircled him was changed into fragrant and bowing garden plants." The influence of Muslim legend is most clearly evident in late Jewish legend. These same descriptions are again to be found in the writings of later commentators on the Koran: Zamakhsharī (p. 888; 12th century) and Baydāwī (vol. 1, p. 620; 13th century). [H.Z.H.]

Bibliography: A. Falkenstein, in: ZA, 45 (1939), 36; E. Dhorme, *Les Religions de Babylonie et d'Assyrie* (1945), 102, 128–31; E. A. Speiser, in: Eretz Israel, 5 (1958), 32–36; U. Cassuto, *A Commentary on the Book of Genesis* (1964), 200ff.; D. O. Edzard, in: H. W. Haussig (ed.), *Woerterbuch der Mythologie*, 1 (1965), 114–5; E. Lipinski, in: RB, 73 (1966), 77, 93. IN THE AGGADAH: Ginzberg, Legends, 1 (1909), 175–9, and index. IN ISLAM: Ṭabarī, *Taʾrīkh*, 1 (1357, A.H.), 142, 201; Thaʿlabī, *Qiṣaṣ* (1356 A.H.), 80–81; J. W. Hirschberg (ed.), *Der Diwan des as-Samauʾal ibn Adijā*... (1931), 33, 63–64.

NIMZOVITCH, AARON (1886–1935), chess master. Nimzovitch, who was born in Riga, won important tournaments in the 1920s but was particularly important as a theoretician. He was responsible, together with Tartakover, Réti, and Alekhine, for the general departure from the dogmatism of *Tarrasch's "strong center" theory. Two of his openings, the Nimzovitch Defense and the Nimzo-Indian, which remained popular long after their inventor's death, carried "hyper-modern" theory into actuality. His book, *Mein System* (1925; Eng. tr., 1930), a collection of important aperçus on points of technique, is still of great value. [G.A.]

Aaron Nimzovitch, chess master. Jerusalem, J.N.U.L., Schwadron Collection.

NINE DAYS, period of mourning from the first of *Av until noon after the fast of the Ninth of *Av commemorating the destruction of the *Temple. The period is also called *Bein ha-Meẓarim* ("In Stress") and actually starts previously with the fast of *Tammuz (see *Three Weeks, The). However, from the first of Av onward, the mourning becomes more severe, and strictly observant Jews, especially in the Ashkenazi rite; (1) abstain from meat and wine except on the Sabbath; (2) recite special dirges of lamentation (*kinot*), as well as Psalm 137 ("By the rivers of Babylon") and Psalm 79 (also recited during **Tikkun Ḥaẓot*) every noon and midnight; and (3) refrain from wearing new or festive clothing. Even on the Sabbath some wear ordinary weekday clothes. Others, especially Sephardim, observe these rules of mourning only during the week in which the Ninth of Av falls (See: Maim. Yad, Ta'an. 5:6). This is in accordance with the Mishnah which ordains that during that week one should not cut one's hair or wash clothes (except on the Thursday in honor of the coming Sabbath; Ta'an. 4:7).

Bibliography: Sh. Ar, OḤ 551:1–18; 552:1–12; J. T. Lewinski (ed.), *Sefer ha-Mo'adim*, 7 (1957), 268–361; Eisenstein, Dinim, 1, 38–39. [ED.]

NINEVEH (Heb. נִינְוֵה; Akk. **Ninua, Ninâ;** in Mari **Ninuwa;** Ar. **Ninawa**), the capital of the Assyrian empire, from Sennacherib's time on, situated about 1 mi. (about $1\frac{1}{2}$ km.) E. of the Tigris, opposite modern Mosul. Since the cuneiform for Nineveh (*Ninâ*) is a fish within a house, it has been suggested that the name of the city was derived from that of a goddess associated with fish, but it seems that it is of Hurrian origin. From the Akkadian period on, the city was dedicated to the "Ishtar of Nineveh."

The ancient citadel of Nineveh was situated on a hill known today as Quyunjiq ("Little Lamb") and located near the center of the western region of the city. On the hill there were also the Assyrian royal palaces and the temples. South of this citadel is a smaller tell, called Nebi Yūnis ("The

Figure 1. Relief from Nineveh depicting King Ashurbanipal and his queen feasting in their garden, attended by servants and musicians, seventh century B.C.E. London, British Museum.

Prophet Jonah"), where, according to Islamic tradition, the prophet Jonah is buried, and on which is a large mosque. The city, however, extended over a much larger area.

Archaeological excavations were conducted in the city for about a century, mainly by the British (beginning in 1842). The excavations of 1932 (by M. E. L. Mallowan) laid the foundations for the study of the prehistory of northern Mesopotamia, the city thus becoming a key site for a knowledge and understanding of the prehistoric period.

History. The investigation made during the 1932 excavations of Quyunjiq down to its virgin soil uncovered the tell's earliest stratum, which contains remnants of the Hassuna culture and has been assigned to about 5000–4500 B.C.E.

One of the earliest written evidences is an inscription of Narâm-Sin of the Akkadian dynasty (2291–2255 B.C.E.). Hammurapi king of Babylonia mentions the city in the introduction to his code of laws as the site of a temple of Ishtar. At the beginning of the 14th century B.C.E. Nineveh belonged to Mitanni. Tushratta king of Mitanni sent the image of "Ishtar of Nineveh" (identified with the Hurrian goddess Šauška) twice to Egypt to heal Amenophis III, his ally and in-law. Subsequently, Nineveh reverted to Assyrian rule, since the Assyrian king Ashur-uballiṭ (1364–1329 B.C.E.) stated that he rebuilt the temple of Ishtar which, according to indications, was renovated a number of times between the 13th and the ninth centuries B.C.E. Individual bricks, inscribed with the builders' names and with dedicatory inscriptions that have been brought to light, attest to the existence of several palaces built during these centuries. The earliest palace of which actual remains have been uncovered is that of Ashurnaṣirpal II (883–859 B.C.E.).

Figure 2. "Jonah beside the Walls of Nineveh," ink drawing by Rembrandt van Rijn. Vienna, Graphische Sammlung Albertina. Photo Alpenland, Vienna.

The city reached its zenith toward the end of the eighth century B.C.E., when it was in effect reconstructed during the reign of Sennacherib (705–681 B.C.E.) and became the capital of the Assyrian empire. Near the city—and in fact within its limits—Sennacherib planted a botanical garden with trees from all parts of the empire, among them vines and fruit-bearing trees. Magnificent spacious palaces were erected in the city. In the southwestern corner of the site, Sennacherib built a new palace to replace the earlier smaller one that had been there, and called it "the palace which has no equal." Today it is known as "the southwestern palace." On most of the walls of the halls, reliefs have been found depicting scenes from the building of the palace as well as war scenes, including the siege of *Lachish (found in Hall xxxvi). In the disorders that broke out upon the death of Sennacherib, part of his palace was apparently burned down and left in ruins for about 40 years. On the smaller tell (Nebi Yūnis), Esarhaddon (681–669 B.C.E.) built himself a palace. Ashurbanipal (668–627 B.C.E.) reestablished his residence on the main tell (Quyunjiq). Not content with merely renovating and embellishing the palace of Sennacherib his grandfather, he built his own palace at the extremity of the tell. It was explored in the course of the excavation of Quyunjik, 1853–54, and reliefs portraying scenes from various battles and representing Assyrian art at its zenith were uncovered. Ashurbanipal's greatest achievement was the establishment of a vast royal library in the city, containing several thousand cuneiform documents in the fields of literature and ritual, science and mythology, lexicography, astronomy, and history, as well as economic documents, letters, and state contracts.

At the end of Ashurbanipal's reign, the royal residence was apparently transferred from Nineveh and established, according to one view, in Harran. Nineveh was captured, plundered, and destroyed in the summer of 612 B.C.E. by the forces of the Median and Babylonian empires, and became a desolate heap. The site itself was later occupied again until the Mongol invasion of the 14th century.

In the Bible. According to the Table of the Nations, Nineveh was established—together with other principal centers in Mesopotamia—in the days of *Nimrod (Gen. 10:10–12). In the Book of Jonah (3:3) it is referred to as "an exceedingly great city, three days' journey" (from one end to the other). A subsequent verse

(4:11) tells that its infant population alone numbered "more than a hundred and twenty thousand persons." Even if this is somewhat exaggerated, it is probable that the number of Nineveh's inhabitants at the pinnacle of its greatness in the seventh century B.C.E. was indeed extremely large (see *Jonah).

In II Kings 19:36–37 (and in the parallel passage in Isa. 37:37–38), Nineveh is mentioned as the city to which Sennacherib returned after his failure to capture Jerusalem, and in which he was murdered by his sons.

Two contemporary prophets, *Zephaniah (2:13ff.) and *Nahum, prophesied the destruction of Nineveh. [Y.K.]

In the Aggadah. Nineveh was a huge city, covering 40 square parasangs and containing a million and a half persons. The "six score thousand persons" alluded to in Jonah 4:11 refer to the population of only one of the 12 districts into which the city was divided. The voice of the prophet Jonah was so stentorian that it reached every corner of the city and all who heard his words resolved to turn aside from their ungodly ways (Mid. Jonah, 99–100, in A. Jellinek, *Beit ha-Midrash*, 1 (1938[2])). Under the leadership of their king, the people of Nineveh justly compelled God's mercy to descend upon them. The king of Nineveh was the pharaoh of the Exodus, who had been installed by the angel Gabriel. Seized with fear and terror he covered himself with sackcloth and ashes and with his own mouth made proclamation and published this decree through Nineveh: "Let neither man nor beast, herd nor flock taste anything, let them not feed nor drink water, for know that there is no God beside Him in all the world; all His words are truth, and all His judgments are true and faithful" (Yal. Ex. 176). The repentance of the people of Nineveh was sincere. They held their infants heavenward, crying, "For the sake of these innocent babes hear our prayers." They separated the young of their cattle from their dams and both began to bellow. Then the Ninevites cried, "If Thou wilt not have mercy on us, we will not have mercy upon these beasts" (Ta'an. 16a; Mid. Jonah 100–2). The penitence of the people of Nineveh manifested itself not only in fasting and praying, but also in deeds. If a man had usurped another's property, he would return it, even at the cost of leveling his castle in order to restore a stolen beam to its owner (Ta'an. 16a). Others publicly confessed their secret sins and declared themselves willing to submit to their punishment. According to the Palestinian *amoraim*, however, the repentance of the Ninevites was not sincere (TJ, Ta'an. 2:1, 65b). After 40 days they departed again from the path of piety and became more sinful than ever. Then the punishment foretold by Jonah overtook them and they were swallowed by the earth (PdRE 43). The attitude of the Palestinian aggadists in their evaluation of the repentance of the Ninevites may have been a reaction to Christian criticism of the Jews for their stubbornness in not following the example set by the people of Nineveh.

See also *Church Fathers and the *Aggadah*. [Ed.]

Bibliography: A. H. Layard, *Nineveh and its Remains* (1849); idem, *Nineveh and Babylon* (1967); H. Rassam, *Ashur and the Land of Nimrod* (1897); R. Buka, *Die Topographie Ninewes* (1915); Luckenbill, Records, 2 (1926), 417–22; R. C. Thompson and R. W. Hutchinson, *A Century of Excavation at Nineveh* (1929); R. Dhorme, in: RHR, 110 (1934), 140–56; C. J. Gadd, *The Stones of Assyria* (1936); A. Parrot, *Nineveh et l'Ancien Testament* (1955); R. W. Ehrich, *Chronologies in Old World Archaeology* (1965), index. In the Aggadah: Ginzberg, Legends, 4 (1913), 250–3; 6 (1928), 350–2; E. Urbach, in: *Tarbiz*, 20 (1950), 118–22.

NINGPO, city in Chekiang province, E. China. The presence of Jewish settlers there in 1461 is recorded on the *Kaifeng stele inscriptions, which state that when the Kaifeng synagogue was destroyed by floods in that year and the sacred scriptures were lost, the Jews of Ningpo presented emissaries of the Kaifeng community with a Torah scroll. No other evidence recording the presence of Jews in Ningpo has been preserved.

Bibliography: W. C. White, *Chinese Jews*, pt. 2 (1966[2]), 13, 27, 98.
[R.L.]

NINGSIA (now **Yinchwan**), city formerly in the predominantly Muslim Kansu province of N.W. China. Members of the Jewish Chin family from *Kaifeng settled there, but remained in touch with the religious life of the Kaifeng Jewish community. Their donations and active participation are recorded in the Kaifeng stele inscriptions of 1489 and 1512.

Bibliography: W. C. White, *Chinese Jews*, pt. 2 (1966[2]), index.
[R.L.]

NIR (Rafalkes), NAHUM (1884–1968), labor leader and second speaker of the *Knesset. Born in Warsaw, Nir qualified as a lawyer and practiced in St. Petersburg. He joined *Po'alei Zion in 1905 and represented it in 1917 during the revolution before the All-Russian Soviet of Workers' and Soldiers' Deputies. In 1918 he moved to Warsaw and was elected to its city council. After Po'alei Zion split in 1920, he became secretary of the World Union of Left Po'alei Zion, retaining the post till 1935. In 1925 he settled in

Nahum Nir, Israel labor leader and second speaker of the Knesset. Courtesy Government Press Office, Tel Aviv.

Palestine, where he practiced law and represented his party in the *Histadrut and the Va'ad Le'ummi. After Left Po'alei Zion merged with *Aḥdut ha-Avodah and, with it, joined *Mapam, he became a member of the pre-state People's Council and its deputy chairman. He was a member of the Knesset until 1965, serving as deputy speaker. On the death of Joseph *Sprinzak in 1959, he was elected speaker by an ad hoc coalition of all parties except *Mapai, and served in that capacity until the general election later that year. He wrote many articles in Russian, Yiddish, and Hebrew and published a number of books, including his memoirs, *Pirkei Ḥayyim* (1958). [A.A.]

NIR AM (Heb. נִיר עָם; "The People's Plowed Field"), kibbutz in southern Israel, 6 mi. (10 km.) N.E. of *Gaza, affiliated with Iḥud ha-Kevuẓot ve-ha-Kibbutzim. Its founding in 1943 by immigrants from Central and Eastern Europe, most of them *Youth Aliyah graduates, constituted a step in the expansion of Jewish settlement toward the Negev. Abundant groundwater reserves were discovered soon after, and in 1947 the first pipeline leading to the Negev outposts was laid from the Nir Am—*Gevar'am area. In the Israel *War of Independence (1948), the kibbutz became the headquarters, hospital, and supply center for the settlements in the south and Negev, cut off for several months from the rest of Israel. The kibbutz economy is based on intensive field crops, orchards, and dairy cattle, as well as a factory for fine cutlery. [E.O.]

NIR DAVID (Heb. נִיר דָּוִד; *nir*—"Plowed Field"), kibbutz in central Israel, at the foot of Mt. Gilboa, affiliated with Kibbutz Arẓi ha-Shomer ha-Ẓa'ir, founded in 1936 as the first *stockade and watchtower outpost in the Beth-Shean Valley. The settlers, Israel-born youth and pioneers from Poland, set up camp on the site a year earlier but after the outbreak of the Arab riots had to live temporarily at neighboring

*Bet Alfa while continuing to cultivate their land. Nir David repelled Arab attacks and soon became a model farming community, pioneering in carp breeding in ponds and in growing crops adapted to its hot climate. It opened a farming equipment metal factory and a plant producing plastic tubes. Nir David has a local museum. Its name commemorates the Zionist leader David *Wolffsohn. Its population in 1970 was 555. [E.O.]

Nir David, the first tower and stockade kibbutz in the Beth-Shean Valley, 1936. Courtesy Keren Hayesod, United Israel Appeal, Jerusalem.

NIRENBERG, MARSHALL WARREN (1927–), U.S. biochemist and Nobel Prize winner. Nirenberg was born in New York. He did research at the National Institute of Health in Bethesda, Maryland, and joined the staff in 1960, becoming chief of the laboratory of biochemical genetics of the National Heart Institute in 1962.

In a series of brilliant investigations, Nirenberg and his co-workers laid the groundwork for the solution of the genetic code: the way in which the sequence of nucleic acid (DNA) units in the gene, through the mediation of ribonucleic acid (RNA), specifies the sequence of amino acid units forming the proteins. In 1961 Nirenberg and H. J. Matthaei made a cell-free extract from the bacterium *E. coli* which, when supplied with amino acids, was stimulated to synthesize protein out of the constituent amino acids upon the addition of RNA. When a synthetic RNA-like molecule consisting only of uridylic acid—one of the four normal nucleotide components of RNA—was used, a "protein" formed of a chain of only one amino acid (phenylalanine) was formed. This was the first discovery of a code equivalence between a nucleic acid component and an amino acid. For this accomplishment, Nirenberg was co-recipient of the Nobel Prize for Physiology and Medicine in 1968. He was made a member of the U.S. National Academy of Sciences in 1967. [M.L.G.]

Marshall Warren Nirenberg, U.S. biochemist and Nobel Prize winner.

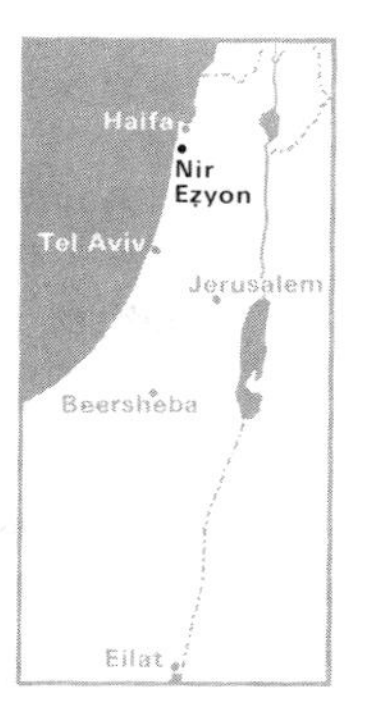

NIR EẒYON (Heb. נִיר עֶצְיוֹן), moshav shittufi in N. Israel, on Mt. Carmel, affiliated with Ha-Po'el ha-Mizrachi Moshavim Association. It was founded in 1950, initially as a kibbutz, by the surviving defenders of *Kefar Eẓyon in the Israel *War of Independence (1948), who were joined by other members of their movement. The economy is based on intensive farming. The moshav opened a resort run on strictly Orthodox-Jewish precepts. Nir Eẓyon includes the *Youth Aliyah village, Yemin Orde, which is named for Orde Charles *Wingate. Its total population in 1970 was 450. [E.O.]

Ceremony marking the founding of Nir Eẓyon, 1950. Courtesy J.N.F., Jerusalem.

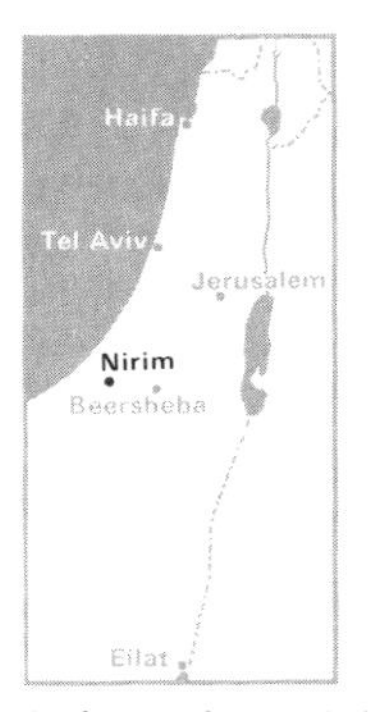

NIRIM (נִירִים; "Plowed Fields"), kibbutz in southern Israel, in the "Eshkol Region" of the western Negev, affiliated with Kibbutz Arẓi Ha-Shomer ha-Ẓa'ir. Originally established as one of the 11 villages founded in the Negev on the night of Oct. 6, 1946, it was, until 1948, the westernmost Jewish settlement in the country and the closest to Egyptian-held Sinai. The founders, Israel-born youth, were joined by pioneers from Hungary and Rumania. In the Israel *War of Independence Nirim was the first Jewish village exposed to a concentrated attack of the invading Egyptian army (May 1948). Although the kibbutz was entirely leveled, Nirim's members held their ground, compelling the enemy to change tactics and advance exclusively through Arab-inhabited terrain while leaving most of the Jewish settlements to the rear intact. After the cessation of hostilities in April 1949, the kibbutz was transferred to a site further northwest on the Gaza Strip border, while the former site was taken over by Nir Yiẓḥak, another kibbutz of Ha-Shomer ha-Ẓa'ir. Besides partly intensive farming (field crops and dairy cattle), Nirim set up an electronics factory mainly to produce farming aids. A beautiful mosaic synagogue floor, dating from the Byzantine period, was unearthed in the Nirim fields. [E.O.]

Monument at Buban, Yugoslavia, where the Jews of Nis were shot by the Nazis. Courtesy Jewish Historical Museum, Belgrade.

NIS (Serb. **Nish,** Croat. **Niš**), town in Serbia, Yugoslavia. Jews lived in Nis during the 16th century. In 1903 the town's Jewish population numbered 800, although prior to the settlement of many families in Turkey, it had been larger. The Jews were engaged mainly in the textile trade and in money changing, while a few were manual laborers. In 1925 there were 430 Jews in the town. In October 1941 the Jewish men were imprisoned in the "Red Cross" camp in Nis. In February 1942 several inmates escaped from the camp after attacking the guards, and in retaliation several hundred prisoners, most of them Jews, were shot. Two days later, more than 1,000 Jews were shot. In spring 1942 all women and children were arrested and after a few days in "Red Cross" they were sent to *Sajmiste. In 1952 there were 25 Jews in the city.

Bibliography: *Bulletin de l'Alliance Israélite Universelle,* 28 (1963), 147–8; *Zločini fašističkih okupatora . . . u Jugoslaviji* (1952), 38–40. [S.MAR.]

NISAN (Heb. נִיסָן), the post-Exilic name of the first month of the Jewish year. Its pentateuchal name is *ḥodesh ha-aviv* (lit. "month of spring," Ex. 13:4 and parallels) and it is also referred to as the month of the ripening ears of barley (*ibid.* 9:31). The post-Exilic name, occurring in the biblical and apocryphal records (Esth. 3:7, Neh. 2:1; I Esd. 5:6, Add. Esth. 1:1) and frequently in Josephus and rabbinic literature (e.g., **Megillat Ta'anit*), is linked with the Babylonian first month, Nisannu (derived from *nesa,* Heb., *nasa* "to start"). The Mishnah calls the first of Nisan the "new year for kings and festivals" (RH 1:1). Reigns of monarchs in biblical times were reckoned from that time, but later it was made the seventh month of the civil year (RH loc. cit.). The zodiacal sign of this month is *Aries.* In the present fixed Jewish calendar it invariably consists of 30 days, and the 1st of Nisan never falls on a Monday, Wednesday, or Friday (see *Calendar). In the 20th century Nisan, in its earliest occurrence, extends from March 13 to April 11, and in its latest from April 11 to May 10. According to R. Joshua, this is the month during which the world was created and the Patriarchs were born (RH 11a). It was in Nisan that God spoke to Moses from the burning bush. In this month redemption will occur in the time to come *(ibid.).* The tabernacle was erected in Nisan (Ex. 40:17), and the princes brought their offerings then (Num. 7:1–2). Because the 12 princes offered their gifts to the tabernacle every day beginning with the first of Nisan, each day was considered a festival. All public mourning is prohibited in Nisan. **Taḥanun* and **Ẓidduk ha-Din* are not recited, nor are eulogies allowed (Sh. Ar., OḤ 429:2). As "the greater part of the month was thus sanctified, the entire month is deemed holy" (*ibid.,* comm. of ***Magen** Avraham,* 3).

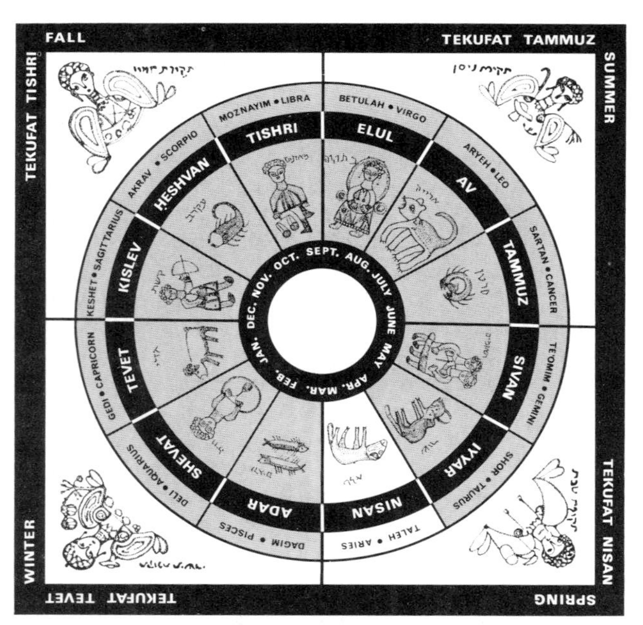

The month of Nisan in the wheel of the zodiac with the sign Aries. The signs are copied from the sixth-century mosaic floor of the synagogue at Bet Alfa, Israel.

Memorable days of Nisan include the Passover period: the 14th of Nisan, the eve of the biblical feast of *Passover when all leaven is cleared from Jewish households, and in Temple times, the *Paschal lamb was sacrificed (Ex. 12 and parallels); and the festival of Passover from the 15th to the 21st (in the Diaspora, the 22nd) of Nisan. The 15th and 21st of Nisan (in the Diaspora 15th–16th and 21st–22nd), the first and last days of Passover, respectively, are full holidays; 16th–20th of Nisan (in the Diaspora 17th–20th) are the intervening days of the festival, **ḥol ha-mo'ed.* The 16th of Nisan is the controversial "morrow of the Sabbath" (see Lev. 23:11, 15, 16) when an *omer* of barley was offered in the Temple and marked the commencement of the counting of the *omer.* Other traditional dates in this month are 1st–7th of Nisan, the defeat by the Pharisees of the Sadducees' claim that the *tamid* (Ex. 29:38–42, Num. 28:1–8) was to be defrayed by private donations (Meg. Ta'an. 1); 8th–21st of Nisan, a Pharisaic victory over the Sadducees in a dispute concerning "the morrow of the Sabbath" and the day of the month on which Shavuot falls (Meg. Ta'an. 1); 1st (or 8th), 10th, and 26th of Nisan, the respective anniversaries of the death of *Nadab and Abihu, of *Miriam, and of *Joshua, once observed as fasts (Meg. Ta'an. 13).

Bibliography: Eisenstein, Dinim, 267, s.v. [E.J.W.]

NISHAPUR, town in Khurasan, N.E. Persia. Jewish settlement here allegedly dates from the time of the early Diaspora. According to the 12th-century Jewish traveler *Benjamin of Tudela, the district of Nishapur was inhabited by descendants of the Jewish tribes Dan, Zebulun, Naphtali, and Asher. They were united under a Jewish prince named R. Joseph Amarkala ha-Levi, and were engaged in agriculture and warfare in alliance with the "infidel Turks." There were some scholars among them. In 11th-century fragments from the Cairo **Genizah,* mention is made of an Isaac Nishapuri, an Egyptian silk merchant who settled in Alexandria.

Bibliography: A. Asher (ed. and tr.), *Itinerary of R. Benjamin of Tudela* (1840), 83, 85. [W.J.F.]

NISHMAT KOL ḤAI (Heb. נִשְׁמַת כָּל חַי; "The soul of every living being"), the initial words and name of a prayer recited at Sabbath and festival morning services at the conclusion of the **Pesukei de-Zimra* introductory biblical hymns. This prayer expresses the gratitude men owe to God for His mercies in sustaining them. In talmudic literature it is called *Birkat ha-Shir* ("Benediction of the Song," Pes.

The beginning of *Nishmat Kol Ḥai*, introduced by an initial word panel with animal decorations, in the *Rothschild Miscellany*, Ferrara (?), Italy, c. 1470. Jerusalem, Israel Museum, 180/51.

10:7, and 117b–118a). Based upon the opinion of R. *Johanan, *Nishmat* also became part of the Passover **Haggadah*.

Nishmat consists of three main sections. The first contains an avowal of God's unity: "Besides Thee we have no King. Deliverer, Savior, Redeemer . . . We have no King but Thee." Some scholars believed that this passage was composed by the apostle Peter as a protest against concepts foreign to pure monotheism (A. Jellinek, *Beit ha-Midrash*, 6 (1938²), 12; *Maḥzor Vitry*, ed. by S. Hurwitz (1923²), 282; Hertz, 416). The second section starting with the words: "If our mouths were full of song as the sea . . . " originated in the tannaitic period. It is similar to the formula of thanksgiving for abundant rain recited in that period. The passage: "If our eyes were shining like the sun and the moon . . . we could not thank God for the . . . myriads of benefits He has wrought for us" especially, is thought to substantiate this ascription to the tannaitic period since it reflects the opinion of Rav Judah that God has to be praised for each drop of rain (Ber. 59b; Ta'an. 6b; Maim. Yad, Berakhot, 10:5). The third section, starting with the words: "From Egypt Thou hast redeemed us," is believed to have originated in the geonic period (c. tenth century C.E.). There is considerable disagreement among scholars about the original version of the *Nishmat*. There is, however, a general consensus that there existed an ancient but shorter version, called *Birkat ha-Shir*, which was later amplified and enlarged. This view is supported by the fact that the *Nishmat* in the Ashkenazi and in the Sephardi ritual, respectively, differ only in the wording of two or three sentences (compare *Seder R. *Amram Ga'on*, 27b and *Maḥzor Vitry* (1923), 148–54). In most prayer books the words *ha-Melekh, Shokhen ad* and *ha-El* are printed in large type, since the *ḥazzan* starts the central part of the morning service at these places, on High Holy Days, Sabbath, and festivals respectively. In the section *Be-fi yesharim* ("By the mouth of the upright") some prayer books mark an acrostic of the names Isaac and Rebekah, which was not customary in Jewish liturgical poetry prior to the Middle Ages. Some scholars consider it a later addition, but it could be also coincidental.

Bibliography: Eisenstein, Dinim, s.v.; Elbogen, Gottesdienst, 113–4; Davidson, Oẓar, 3 (1930), 231–2; E. Levy, *Yesodot ha-Tefillah* (1952²), 134–5, 228; E. D. Goldschmidt, *Haggadah shel Pesaḥ, Mekoroteha ve-Toledoteha* (1960), 66–68, 107–8; E. Munk, *The World of Prayer*, 2 (1963), 29–32; J. Heinemann, *Ha-Tefillah bi-Tekufat ha-Tanna'im ve-ha-Amora'im* (1966²), 41–45, 152; idem, in: *Tarbiz*, 30 (1960/61), 409–10.

[ED.]

NISIBIS (Neṣibin, Neẓibin), the modern townlet Nesib in S. Anatolia. Over a long period (under the Roman rule, until 363; and under the rule of Persia and the Arabs) Nisibis was a flourishing trading station on the commercial route from the Far East to the western countries. During the 13th century, as a result of the Mongol conquests, the town was destroyed; the Maghrebian traveler Ibn Baṭṭūṭa, who visited it during the first half of the 14th century, relates that most of the town was in ruins.

The first evidence of a Jewish settlement in the town was related by Josephus during the first century C.E.; he says that in Nisibis and Nehardea the Jews of Babylonia consecrated their half shekels and their vows and donations to the Temple in Jerusalem; they traveled from Nisibis to the Holy City. The community appears to have been well founded because it also absorbed the Jews of Seleucia and Ctesipon who fled the vengeance of their neighbors as a result of the acts of *Anilaeus and Asinaeus (see *Nehardea). The town is known to have been a Torah center during the second century, when Judah b. Bathyra II attracted students from as far away as Palestine. During the third century, as a result of the rising influence of the Christians, which surpassed that of their Jewish neighbors, there was a cooling down of Nisibis' relations with Palestine and its scholars.

During the period of Islamic rule the Jewish settlement in the town prospered. At the time of the great emigration of the Jews of Babylonia to the lands which bordered on the Mediterranean Sea during the tenth century, however, Jews also left Nisibis. In a document of 989, for example, Netira b. Tobiah ha-Kohen of Nisibis is mentioned as an inhabitant of the town Damietta in Egypt. During the second half of the 12th century the traveler Benjamin of Tudela nevertheless found about 1,000 Jews there; his contemporary Pethahiah of Regensburg mentions a large community, the synagogue of the *tanna* R. Judah b. Bathyra II, and two synagogues which were built, according to tradition, by Ezra the Scribe. After the campaigns of the Mongols the Jewish settlement of the town was also impoverished. R. Moses Basola, who visited the Oriental countries between 1521 and 1523, met a Jew in Beirut from the environs of Nisibis who told him of the pillar of cloud which appears on the 18th of Sivan and at Pentecost over the tomb of the *tanna* Ben Bathyra in Nisibis and also that pilgrimages to his tomb took place from the surrounding areas. Under Turkish rule the decline of the community continued and its members even turned to the Jews of Cochin with requests for support (D. S. Sassoon, *Ohel David*, 2 (1931), 995). At the close of the 19th century, according to Obermayer, there were approximately 200 miserable clay houses in the town, half of which belonged to Jews.

Bibliography: Neubauer, Géogr, 350; Jos., Ant., 18:312; J. Obermayer, *Landschaft Babylonien* . . . (1929), 128–30; J. B. Segal, in: J. M. Grintz and J. Liver (eds.), *Sefer . . . M. H. Segal* (1964), 38–39; Neusner, Babylonia, 3 (1968), index.

[E.A./M.BE.]

NISSAN (Katznelson), AVRAHAM (1888–1956), labor politician in Palestine and Israel diplomat, brother of Reuben *Katznelson. Born in Bobruisk, Belorussia, he was a medical officer in the Russian army during World War I. In 1917, between the two revolutions, he headed the Organization of Jewish Soldiers in the Russian army on the Caucasus front (10,000 men) and was attracted to Joseph *Trumpeldor's plan to set up Jewish battalions of 200,000 soldiers and volunteers and transport them to the front in Palestine to fight together with the British army for the liberation of Ereẓ Israel from the Turks. In 1919–20 he was the head of the Palestine Office of the Zionist Executive in Constantinople. In 1921–23 Nissan was active at the central office of Hitaḥdut (the union of *Ha-Po'el ha-Ẓa'ir and *Ẓe'irei Zion) in Vienna and Berlin. He settled in Palestine in 1924, served as the director of the health department of the Zionist Executive and as a member of the Va'ad Le'ummi (1931–48). He was also a member of the central committee of the Ha-Po'el ha-Ẓa'ir Party and of Mapai. From 1950 until his death, he was Israel's minister to the Scandinavian countries in Stockholm. [A.A.]

NISSELOVICH, LEOPOLD (Eliezer; 1856–1914), delegate to the Third *Duma in Russia. He was born in Bauska Courland (Russia). After graduating from the law faculty of the University of St. Petersburg (1880), he was employed in the Ministry of Finance. In connection with his work he wrote several studies on economic legislation and on the economic and financial institutions of Russia. In 1882 he left his government post to practice law. In the elections to the Third Duma (1907), he was chosen as representative for Courland province. He joined the Cadet Party (the Russian liberals) on the explicit condition that he would not have to follow the party line in matters concerning Jews. Together with his colleague, N. Friedmann, he represented the Russian Jews at this Duma, and both were frequently the target of attacks by rightist members. Nisselovich was responsible for the bill proposing the abolition of the *Pale of Settlement, presented to the Duma on May 31, 1910, with the signatures of 166 members. The bill was transferred for consideration to the Duma commission on personal freedom but did not reach the full session for debate and vote. Nisselovich died in Geneva.

Bibliography: Y. Maor, in: *He-Avar*, 7 (1960), 65–84. [Y.S.]

Leopold Nisselovich, delegate to the Third Duma in Russia. Jerusalem, J.N.U.L., Schwadron Collection.

NISSENBAUM, ISAAC (1868–1942), rabbi, Hebrew writer, and religious Zionist in Poland. Born in Bobruisk, Belorussia, Nissenbaum was ordained as a rabbi. He settled in Minsk, where he began his Zionist activity. When the yeshivah of *Volozhin was closed in 1892, he became head of the secret nationalistic association of that yeshivah, Neẓaḥ Israel, an office which he held until 1894, when he moved to Bialystok. There he became Samuel *Mohilever's secretary. From then on he was a central figure in the Zionist movement, particularly among the Orthodox Jews. After Mohilever's death, Nissenbaum served as a Zionist preacher, traversing towns and townlets in Russia, Poland, Latvia,

Isaac Nissenbaum, Polish rabbi and Mizrachi leader. Jerusalem, J.N.U.L., Schwadron Collection.

and Lithuania. He used midrashic elements in his Zionist preachings and had a considerable influence on Orthodox Jews. In 1900 he settled in Warsaw and became a regular preacher in synagogues and other places. He was an active member of Mizrachi from its beginning, a member of the executive of the Polish Zionist Organization, and one of the heads of the Jewish National Fund.

Beginning in 1889, Nissenbaum wrote many essays on current events, Zionism, and religious Zionism, as well as personal memories and several exegetical books. He was one of the editors of *Ha-Ẓefirah*, and after World War I, editor of Mizrachi's weekly in Poland. He edited a series of republished classical books in Jewish studies. The first explanatory pamphlet concerning the Jewish National Fund was written by him (1902). During World War II he remained in the Warsaw ghetto and was murdered there.

Among his homilies are *Derushim ve-Ḥomer li-Derush* (1903); *Derashot le-Khol Shabbatot ha-Shanah ve-ha-Mo'adim* (1908, 1923²); *Hagut Lev* (1911, 1925²); and *Imrei Derush* (1926). In the field of religious Zionism he wrote *Ha-Dat ve-ha-Teḥiyyah ha-Le'ummit* (1920), *Ha-Yahadut ha-Le'ummit* (1920), and a monograph on Samuel Mohilever (1930). He also published an autobiography entitled *Alei Ḥeldi* (1929, 1969²). In 1948 a selection of his writings was published in Israel under the editorship of E. M. Genichovsky, and in 1956 a selection of his letters was edited and published by I. Shapira.

Bibliography: I. Shapira, *Ha-Rav Yiẓḥak Nissenbaum* (1951). [G.K.]

NISSENSON, AARON (1898–1964), U.S. Yiddish poet. Born in Belorussia, he was taken to the U.S. at the age of 13. He graduated as a pharmacist but preferred a literary and journalistic career. In 1918 he co-edited the literary monthly *Der Onheyb*. He was business manager of the New York Yiddish daily, *Jewish Morning Journal*, for 30 years. In his last years he was press representative of the *American Jewish Joint Distribution Committee.

His first volume *Hundert Lider* ("One Hundred Songs," 1920) was followed by six other books of lyric and dramatic poems. The central hero of his dramatic poem *Der Veg tsum Mentsh* ("The Road to Man," 1934) was the American socialist leader Eugene V. Debs, symbol for him of the pure-hearted man. In the dramatic poem *Dos Tsugezogte Land* ("The Promised Land," 1937), Nissenson portrayed the struggle between good and evil as embodied in opposing personalities, beginning with Moses and Pharaoh and continuing throughout history. The poet expressed faith in science as the ultimate redeemer, leading man ever closer to moral perfection. This faith remained with him during World War II, when he composed the poems of *Dos Lebn Zingt Afile in Toyt* ("Life Sings Even in Death," 1943). In his last poems, *In Tsadiks*

Trit ("In the Footsteps of the Righteous," 1950), he continued to sing of compassionate, just human beings who would evolve from imperfect contemporary man. Shortly before his death, Nissenson published an English novel, *Song of Man* (1964), whose central character was again Eugene V. Debs.

Bibliography: Rejzen, Leksikon, 2 (1927), 571ff.; LNYL, 6 (1965), 242–5; E. Brownstone, *Ineynem un Bazunder* (1960), 54–57.

[S.L.]

NISSI (Nissim) BEN BERECHIAH AL-NAHRAWANI (late ninth–early tenth century), head of the **kallah* and poet in Babylon. Nissi appears to have come from Nahrawan in Persia. *Nathan ha-Bavli relates (Neubauer, Chronicles 2 (1895), 29–80) that when the Exilarch *David b. Zakkai was embroiled with the head of the Pumbedita Academy Rav *Kohen Ẓedek—in fact, the person involved was *Mubashir b. Rav Kimoi ha-Kohen and not Rav Kohen Ẓedek— it was Nissi, *Resh Kallah* in the Sura Academy, who succeeded in 922 in making peace between the disputants. Nathan ha-Bavli relates there that Nissi was *noda be-nissim* (i.e., a doer of miraculous deeds). In 928 when the question of appointing a *gaon* in the Sura Academy came up, this post was offered to him by *David b. Zakkai, but he refused it because of his blindness. Zemaḥ ibn Shahin and *Saadiah b. Josef Alfayumi competed for this post and despite the recommendation of Nissi that Ẓemaḥ ibn Shahin be appointed, the Exilarch appointed Saadiah to the gaonate. Nissi was one of the most important and fruitful of the *paytanim* of his country. In the Cairo *Genizah,* and also in other sources, poems and *piyyutim* by him were preserved, of which only a few have been published. Well known is his confession for the Day of Atonement, beginning: "Lord of the Universe, before all else, I have no mouth to answer," which has been adopted into many rites and republished hundreds of times. However, only with the discovery of the *Genizah* the true identity of its author became clear.

Bibliography: B. Halper, in: *Ha-Tekufah,* 20 (1923), 272–4; Davidson, Oẓar, 4 (1933), 452; J. Mann, in: *Tarbiz,* 5 (1934), 154f., 160; S. Bernstein, in: *Bitzaron,* 36 (1957), 156–64; J. Schirmann, *Shirim Ḥadashim min ha-Genizah* (1965), 23–28; A. M. Habermann, *Toledot ha-Piyyut ve-ha-Shirah* (1920), 100–4.

[A.D.]

NISSI (Nissim) BEN NOAH (11th century), Karaite writer who lived in Persia. Nissi was formerly thought to be a contemporary of *Anan b. David (c. 800), but on the basis of his use of David *Alfasi's Hebrew dictionary and Judah *Hadassi's apparent knowledge of him, Harkavy placed him in the 11th century. Nissi advocated that Karaites should study rabbinic literature and the Talmud. Two works have been attributed to him, *Sefer Aseret ha-Devarim* (Firkovich Ms. 610), a commentary on the Ten Commandments, and *Bitan ha-Maskilim* (now lost), a treatise on the precepts of Jewish Law.

Bibliography: S. Poznánski, in: JQR, 11 (1920/21), 249–50; Graetz, Gesch, 5 (1895), 199–201, 443–5; Mann, Texts, 2 (1935), 1350; Z. Ankori, *Karaites in Byzantium* (1959), 241; L. Nemoy, *Karaite Anthology* (1952), 250, 381.

[Ed.]

NISSIM, ABRAHAM ḤAYYIM (1878–1952), Iraqi government official and member of parliament; born in Baghdad. Nissim served as an employee in the administration of the sultan's estates; he later became a senior officer of the German railways in Iraq. After the British conquest he was appointed assistant to the Hilla District political officer and in the 1920s held a senior post in the Ministry of Finance. From 1930 to 1948 he represented Baghdad Jewry in the house of representatives. During most of this period he was a member of the budget committee, serving as its draftsman. He settled in Israel in 1951 and died in Ramat Gan.

[H.J.C.]

NISSIM, ISAAC (1896–), chief rabbi of Israel and *rishon le-Zion.* Nissim was born in Baghdad. His father was a merchant and also a scholar. Nissim early attained a reputation as a scholar and, although he occupied no rabbinic office, his opinion was sought in religious matters. His method of study approximated closely to that of the Lithuanian rabbis and he engaged in halakhic discusssion with them and with heads of yeshivot. He had ties with eminent rabbis of Ereẓ Israel as well as with scholars of Germany and Poland. In 1925 he settled in Jerusalem, where he was closely associated with Solomon Eliezer *Alfandari whose lectures he attended. In 1926 he published *Ẓedakah u-Mishpat,* the responsa of Ẓedakah *Ḥozin, an 18th century Baghdad scholar, together with an introduction and notes from a manuscript in his large library. Nissim wrote responsa on a variety of halakhic topics, some of them being published in his *Yein ha-Tov* (1947). In 1955 he was elected to the office of *rishon le-Zion* and chief rabbi of Israel. He displayed his independence in various fields of activity and strove for understanding and the creation of amicable relations between all sectors of the population, visiting for example, left-wing kibbutzim, which were regarded as closed to rabbis. He took a strong stand in the halakhic recognition of the Bene Israel of India and refused to meet Pope Paul VI when the latter visited Israel in January 1964. After the 1967 Six-Day War he transferred the supreme *bet din* to a building opposite the southern Wall of the Temple near the site of the Chamber of Hewn Stone, which was the ancient seat of the Sanhedrin.

Bibliography: Ṣhin, in: *Ha-Ẓofeh,* (March 27, 1964), 3; D. Lazar, *Rashim be-Yisrael,* 2 (1955), 114–8.

[Y.Go.]

Isaac Nissim, Israel chief rabbi and *rishon le-Zion,* in the traditional garb of the *ḥakham bashi.* Photo K. Weiss, Jerusalem.

NISSIM BEN JACOB BEN NISSIM IBN SHAHIN (c. 990–1062), together with *Hananel b. Ḥushi'el, the outstanding leader and talmudist of North Africa. His father headed a *bet ha-midrash* in Kairouan and was the representative of the academies of *Sura and *Pumbedita for the whole of North Africa. Little is known of Nissim's personal history. It is known that he, too, was head of an academy in Kairouan and maintained close ties with the academy of Pumbedita. After the death of Hananel, he was appointed by the Babylonian academies *Rosh bei-Rabbanan* ("Head of the College") in his stead. There were close ties between Nissim and *Samuel ha-Nagid. Samuel supported Nissim financially and Nissim served as the principal channel for Samuel's knowledge of Babylonian teachings, particularly those of Hai Gaon. When one of Nissim's sons died in childhood, Samuel composed a poem in consolation for the bereaved father. Nissim's daughter married *Joseph b. Samuel ha-Nagid, Samuel's son, and on that occasion Nissim visited Granada and taught there. According to *Abraham ibn Daud, *Solomon ibn Gabirol was among those who heard his lectures. Nissim's teachers were his father, *Ḥushi'el, and possibly also the latter's son Hananel, whose teachings reveal a close affinity with that of Nissim. Nissim obtained a great part of his halakhic tradition from Hai Gaon, with whom he corresponded. Noteworthy among his pupils is Ibn Gasom, the author of a book on the laws of prayer (see Assaf. bibl.).

Nissim was a prolific and versatile writer. Five works of great length and value are known to have been written by him: (1) *Sefer Mafte'aḥ Manulei ha-Talmud* (Vienna, 1847) on the tractates *Berakhot, Shabbat,* and *Eruvin* was first published from an early Hebrew translation and then included in the Romm (Vilna) editions of the Talmud. Subsequently, many fragments of the Arabic original were published. It is a reference book for quotations encountered in the course of talmudic study. It also gives the sources of the *beraitot* and *mishnayot* quoted in the Talmud as well as parallels in the Talmud and Midrashim and includes extensive commentaries on many talmudic themes. Only the sections on the orders *Zera'im (Berakhot), Mo'ed,* and *Nashim* are extant but it is probable that the original scope of the work was greater. (2) Commentaries on a few tractates of the Talmud, apparently written in Hebrew. Only a few fragments from several tractates are extant. (3) Halakhic rulings. A few fragments of what was evidently a comprehensive work are extant. (4) *Megillat Setarim* (completed in 1051 at the latest). This work was very well known among the **rishonim,* Sephardim as well as Ashkenazim. It was written for the most part in scholarly terms. The book contains many variegated, unrelated topics on all subjects coming within the range of interest of the scholars of the generation—beliefs and opinions, scriptural exegesis, religious polemics, explanations of passages in the Talmud and Midrashim in *halakhah* and *aggadah,* responsa on various subjects, customs and their sources, and other matters. This characteristic aspect of the book, as well as its bilingual construction (Hebrew and Arabic), which resulted in its division into two works even during the author's lifetime, led copyists in different places to arrange it in different orders according to their needs and interest, and in consequence to vary the numeration of its passages. Various compilations were made of the work, which were occasionally drawn upon by other authors such as Jacob *Tam whose *Sefer ha-Yashar* includes a number of rulings from it. The halakhic compendium *Sefer ha-Pardes* (written by *Rashi's school) may also have drawn upon it. Although the work is no longer extant, the discovery in the **Genizah* of a subject index contained in the indexer's copy (published by S. Assaf, *Tarbiz,* 11 (1940), 229–59) has made

Title page of a volume of responsa by the 14th-century Spanish talmudist, Nissim b. Reuben Gerondi, Rome, 1546.

knowledge of its contents far more precise. The book exercised a great influence upon the major halakhists of subsequent generations, including Isaac *Alfasi, *Maimonides, *Nathan b. Jehiel of Rome, *Abraham b. Nathan ha-Yarḥi, and *Isaac b. Abba Mari. (5) *Ḥibbur me-ha-Yeshu'ah* (Ferrara, 1557), Nissim's best-known work, is a collection of Hebrew stories and folktales taken from early sources. It is designed to strengthen belief, faith, and morality among the people and to raise their spirit. This work, possibly the first prose storybook in medieval Hebrew literature, paved the way for Hebrew belletristic literature as a literary genre. Tradition has it that Nissim dedicated the book to his father-in-law, Dunash, who is otherwise unknown, to console him in his mourning. The first printed edition was published from an early Hebrew translation, and the Arabic text was published by J. Obermann (see bibl.). The Hebrew version has been frequently republished, not always according to the same translation. A new Hebrew translation, together with critical annotations by H. Z. Hirschberg, was published in 1954. Additional Arabic texts have been published by S. Abramson (see bibl.). The work circulated widely even before its first printing, and had a great influence on similar story collections. *Ma'asiyyot she-ba-Talmud* (Constantinople, 1519) was based upon it, and the *Ḥibbur ha-Ma'asiyyot* (*ibid.,* 1519) is an anthology of its stories. Many of the stories included by Gaster in his *The Exempla of the Rabbis* (1924; 1968[2]) were taken from it.

Although some other works have been ascribed to Nissim on the basis of various quotations, it may be assumed that all these are from the works already referred to. This may not apply to his many responsa, which are recorded in the works of *rishonim,* though these too may have been included in his *Megillat Setarim.* Most of Nissim's works found in the *genizah* are undergoing the process of identification and publication. S. Abramson devoted the labors of a lifetime to the collection of Nissim's work from the *genizah,* from manuscripts, and from printed works, and published a monumental work.

Bibliography: Rapoport, in: *Bikkurei ha-Ittim,* 12 (1831), 56–83; S. Poznański, in: *Festschrift . . . A. Harkavy* (1908), 211–8 (Heb. sect.); Mann, Texts, index; J. Obermann (ed.), *The Arabic Original of Ibn Shahin's Book of Comfort* (1933); A. Aptowitzer, in: *Sinai,* 12 (1943), 118f.; Zunz-Albeck, Derashot, index; S. Lieberman (ed.), *Hilkhot ha-Yerushalmi le-Rabbi Moshe b. Maimon* (1947), 14f.; Assaf, in: KS, 28 (1952/53), 101ff.; S. Abramson, *Rav Nissim Ga'on* (1965); idem, in: KS, 41 (1965/66), 529–32; idem, in: *Sinai,* 60 (1967), 12–16. [I.T.-S.]

NISSIM BEN MOSES OF MARSEILLES (14th century), philosophical exegete. The dates of Nissim's birth and death are unknown. He was the author of a commentary on the Bible, extant in a number of manuscripts, entitled, variously, *Ma'aseh Nissim, Sefer ha-Nissim,* and *Ikkarei ha-Dat* (Bodleian Library, Nich. 546; Paris, Bibliothèque Nationale, cod. héb. 720; Catalog of the Laurentiana Library, Florence (1757), 139–41, no. 50). Containing allegorical and rationalistic interpretations of many biblical narratives and talmudic *aggadot,* this work reflects the influence of *Maimonides, and is typical of the exegesis of other philosophers of the 13th and early 14th centuries. Moses ibn *Tibbon is the latest of the many philosophical exegetes mentioned in the work. Internal references suggest that Nissim composed his commentary during the period of the anti-philosophical controversies which took place between 1302 and 1305 (see *Maimonidean Controversy). In addition to the chapters devoted to exegesis, the work contains an introduction of 14 chapters, devoted to a discussion of prophecy. M. Schorr believes that Nissim also wrote a philosophical homily on Ruth.

Bibliography: M. Schorr, in: *He-Ḥalutz,* 7 (1865), 102–44; Renan, Rabbins, 547–50; Gross, Gal Jud, 378. [Ed.]

NISSIM BEN REUBEN GERONDI (known from the acronym of Rabbenu Nissim as the **RaN;** ?1310–?1375), one of the most important Spanish talmudists. Nissim's family originated in Cordova and settled first in Gerona, where he is thought to have been born, and then in Barcelona, which became his permanent place of residence. Few biographical details are known of him. He never held any official rabbinical post, even though in fact he fulfilled all the functions of a rabbi and *dayyan* in his community. Furthermore, many *takkanot* enacted in Spain originated with him, and his reputation as an authoritative *posek* was such that he received queries from as far as Ereẓ Israel and Syria. He is also known to have served as a physician in the royal palace. Because of a calumny, the date and causes of which are not certain, he was imprisoned for some time. It is also known that in 1336 he wrote a *Sefer Torah* for his own use, which became well known and served as a model. This *Sefer Torah* was moved from place to place until it reached Tiberias, where it was preserved until recently. Nissim's main teacher, apart from his father, was *Perez ha-Kohen, with whom he was in close correspondence; Nissim even assisted him to become accepted as rabbi of Barcelona (after 1349). It seems that Nissim's main activity in his community was as head of the Barcelona yeshivah. Among his chief pupils were *Isaac b. Sheshet Perfet, who frequently quotes him, mostly anonymously, Ḥasdai *Crescas, Joseph *Ḥabiba, and Abraham *Tamakh.

Nissim's renown rests chiefly on his halakhic works. His method and system were solidly founded in accordance with the tradition of learning acquired from the school of Naḥmanides, Solomon b. Abraham Adret, Aaron ha-Levi of Barcelona, and their contemporaries, and though his works contain many sayings of these scholars without naming them, he adapted their words, crystallized them, and added much of his own so that his works are among the best produced by this school of learning. One of his main works is a commentary on the *halakhot* of Isaac *Alfasi to the Talmud. It seems that all the parts of this work have been preserved, and all have been published on the margin of Alfasi's commentary beginning with its first printed editions down to the present day.

This commentary comprises the tractates *Shabbat, Pesaḥim, Beẓah, Rosh Ha-Shanah, Yoma, Ta'anit, Megillah, Sukkah, Ketubbot, Gittin, Kiddushin, Shevu'ot, Avodah Zarah, Ḥullin,* and *Niddah.* He also wrote novellae to the Talmud, of which up to the present the following have been published: *Gittin* (Constantinople, 1711), *Niddah* (Venice, 1741), *Ḥullin* to the end of chapter 8 (in: *Ḥamishah Shitot,* Sulzbach, 1762), *Bava Meẓia* (Dyhrenfurth, 1823), *Shevu'ot* (Venice, 1608, at the end of the responsa of Moses *Galante), *Rosh Ha-Shanah* (1871), *Avodah Zarah* (1888), *Mo'ed Katan* (1937), *Bava Batra* (1963), *Eruvin* (1969), and *Pesaḥim* (1970).

His commentary to the tractate *Nedarim,* which is his best-known work, is published in all the usual editions of the Talmud and serves as the standard commentary to this tractate instead of that of Rashi. Some of his novellae to the Talmud still remain in manuscript, but most of them have been repeatedly republished, since they are among the works most acceptable to scholars of all countries and times. His commentaries to Alfasi differ from those to the Talmud in that they aim at giving the halakhic ruling, and in fact they have no real literary connection with Alfasi, with whom he frequently disagrees. The novellae to tractates *Megillah, Shabbat, Ketubbot,* and *Sanhedrin* published under Nissim's name are not by him. They represent one of the most difficult problems connected with the study of Nissim's works and teachings, as it is definite that a generation and more before him there lived in Barcelona another scholar with the same acronym—RaN (whose personal name is not certain), and whose works to several talmudic tractates have been recently published. Only 77 of Nissim's responsa are extant (Rome, 1545; and Constantinople, 1548[2] from a different Ms. and thereafter in many editions); also a book of 12 sermons (Constantinople 1533[1] and frequently), of a decidedly anti-philosophical character though written in the style of philosophical literature; and a commentary on the Pentateuch of which the section on Genesis has been published (1968). The publication of the commentary to the Pentateuch has removed the few doubts that remained among some scholars as to whether Nissim is the RaN of the book of sermons ascribed to him or whether they were perhaps written by the other scholar of the same name. Discernible in both these works is Nissim's strong desire to prove the superiority of prophecy and Bible over philosophy, and thereby to strengthen the people's faith and their spiritual ability to bear up during the difficult periods of persecution and polemics of those times. He also wrote *piyyutim* and poems, some of which have been preserved and published.

Bibliography: S. Assaf, *Mekorot u-Meḥkarim be-Toledot Yisrael* (1950), 173–81; A. M. Hershman, *Rabbi Isaac ben Sheshet Perfet and his Times* (1943), 192–6 and index; Baer, Spain, 2 (1966), index; S. H. Kook, *Iyyunim u-Meḥkarim,* 2 (1963), 321–4; L. A. Feldman (ed.), *Shitah la-RaN . . . al Massekhet Ketubbot* (1966) introd.; idem, in: *Koveẓ al Yad,* 7 (17; 1968), 125–60; idem (ed.), in: Nissim b. Reuven Gerondi, *Perush al ha-Torah* (1968), introd.; E. Hurwitz, in: *Hadorom,* 24 (1967), 39–87. [Le.F.]

NITRA (Hung. **Nyitra;** Ger. **Neutra**), town in S.W. Slovakia, Czechoslovakia. The Jewish community dates from the middle of the 18th century, and most of its members were then purveyors to the army. During the 1848 revolution an angry mob rioted in the town on hearing a rumor that the Jews would be granted civil rights. In the middle of the 19th century about 2,500 Jews lived in Nitra, and its yeshivah attracted 200 pupils from all over Europe due to the fame of its head, R. Ezekiel *Baneth. The community split into two, Orthodox and Neolog. An elementary school was founded in 1855, and in 1914 the Neolog community built a large synagogue. In 1921, 3,901 Jews lived in Nitra and there were 3,809 in 1930. There were then two synagogues, a Jewish hospital, and an orphanage.

Immediately after Slovakia became independent (1939), anti-Semitic terrorist acts began. The Jewish population of Nitra numbered 4,358 in 1942. Deportations began in May

The synagogue built by the Neolog community of Nitra, Slovakia, in 1914 and adapted in 1957 for Orthodox use. From R. Iltis (ed.), *Die juedischen Gemeinden in der tschechoslovakischen Republik nach dem Zweiten Weltkrieg*, Prague, 1959.

of that year, when the aged, sick, and babies were taken. Further transports followed in October and then in the summer of 1944. As a result of the intervention of R. Michael Dov *Weissmandel, the "independent" Slovakian authorities authorized the existence of the yeshivah (the only one recognized in Slovakia) and many Jews succeeded in finding shelter there until 1944. Others went into hiding in the territory held by the partisans.

Jewish life was revived in Nitra immediately after the war; both communities amalgamated and in 1947 Elias Katz was appointed rabbi. Both cemeteries, which had been desecrated under Fascist rule, were restored, and in 1951 a memorial to the victims of the Holocaust was dedicated. In 1957 the Neolog synagogue was adapted to Orthodox requirements and a *kasher* soup kitchen was added. The community with all its institutions was still active in 1970.

Bibliography: R. Iltis (ed.), *Die aussaeen unter Traenen...* (1959), 169–78; PK Germanyah. [M.La.]

NITTAI OF ARBELA (=*Arbel in Lower Galilee; second half of second century B.C.E.), one of the **zugot;* a colleague of *Joshua b. Peraḥyah. He was a pupil of *Yose b. Joezer of *Zeradah and *Yose b. Johanan of Jerusalem, the first of the *zugot*, whom he and Joshua succeeded with Nittai serving as *av bet din* (Ḥag. 2:2; Avot 1:6). All that is known of his teaching is that he took part in the only halakhic dispute of his time: whether the placing of the hands upon a sacrifice *(semikhah)* during a festival is permitted. Nittai held that it was permitted, in contrast to Joshua b. Peraḥyah who forbade it (Ḥag. 2:2). His saying preserved in Avot is: Keep at a distance from an evil neighbor; do not make yourself an associate of a wicked man; do not abandon faith in [divine] retribution (Avot 1:7).

Bibliography: Hyman, Toledot, s.v. [D.J.B.]

NIZER, LOUIS (1902–), U.S. lawyer and author. Nizer, who was born in London, was taken to the United States in 1903. An expert in areas of law related to the arts, including copyright and plagiarism, Nizer attracted clients from the theatrical and motion picture fields. He rapidly gained the confidence of the movie industry, and in 1928 was appointed attorney and executive secretary of the industry's trade association. He became well known as a magnetic courtroom lawyer, and a play about his career, *The Case of Libel*, written by Henry Denker, was produced in New York in 1963.

Nizer was active in the United Jewish Appeal and the Federation of Jewish Philanthropies. His books include: *New Courts of Industry* (1935); *What to do with Germany* (1944), in which he advocated war crimes trials for Nazis, reversion of Nazi-appropriated property to the owners, a new educational system for Germany, and the temporary loss of German sovereignty; and two widely read autobiographical volumes, *My Life in Court* (1961); and *The Jury Returns* (1966). [Ed.]

NIẒẒANAH (Heb. נִצָּנָה; Gr. **Nessana**), a ruined town in the Negev identified with ʿAwjā al-Ḥafīr on the Ismailiya road, 50 mi. (80 km.) S.W. of Beersheba. Nessana was the ancient name of the site as revealed in the papyri found there. It was founded in the second or first century B.C.E. by the Nabateans, who built a small fort with round towers (two of which were found in the excavations there) on a small hill dominating the wide and fertile Wadi Ḥafīr. Hasmonean coins found there indicate that the place had commercial relations with Judea. The site was abandoned after the Roman occupation of Petra, the Nabatean capital, in 106 C.E., but was rebuilt as a frontier post by the emperor Theodosius I (379–95). The soldiers of the garrison received plots of land in the valley and a town was built beneath the fortress (now called Hospice of St. George). Niẓẓanah was connected by a road with Elusa, the capital of the Byzantine Negev, with Elath and with Sinai. The Byzantine town included two churches with mosaic floors (one dated 435) and a large cemetery with tombstones (dated 430–64). It prospered during this period, serving merchants bound for Egypt, pilgrims traveling to Mt. Sinai, and anchorites living in the desert. The town survived the Persian and Arab conquests; papyri discovered by the Colt Expedition in 1936 show that a mixed Arab-Greek administration persisted until approximately 750 C.E. The settlement declined and was eventually abandoned until its reoccupation by the Turks as a police post in 1908. Under the British Mandate a central headquarters for the border police was located there. In May 1948, during the Israel *War of Independence, the Egyptian invasion started from this point. Israel forces took the area in December, and it was declared a demilitarized zone in the Israel-Egypt Armistice Agreement. It was also the site for the Israel-Egyptian *Mixed Armistice Commission meetings.

Bibliography: H. D. Colt et al., *Excavations at Nessana*, 3 vols. (1958). [M.A.-Y.]

NIẒẒANIM (Heb. נִצָּנִים; "sprouts"), kibbutz and youth village in southern Israel, 5 mi. (8 km.) N. of Ashkelon, affiliated with Ha-No'ar ha-Ẓiyyoni. Niẓẓanim was founded in 1943 by pioneers from Rumania, when efforts were made to expand Jewish settlement in the south and Negev. In the early stages of the Israel *War of Independence (1948), Niẓẓanim was subjected to concentrated attack by the advancing Egyptian army and suffered utter destruction. After five days of resistance, Niẓẓanim was given up on June 8, 1948, and most of its surviving defenders fell prisoner. The site was recovered in October 1948, and the kibbutz was rebuilt by the remnants of the group about 2 mi. (3 km.) further south. In 1949 a farming school, belonging to *Youth Aliyah, was opened on the original site by Niẓẓanim. In 1969 the combined population of the kibbutz and youth village was 594 persons. Niẓẓanim's economy is based on citrus groves and dairy cattle. [E.O.]

NOACHIDE LAWS, the seven laws considered by rabbinic tradition as the minimal moral duties enjoined by the Bible on all men (Sanh. 56–60; Yad, Melakhim, 8:10, 10:12). Jews are obligated to observe the whole Torah, while every non-Jew is a "son of the covenant of Noah" (see Gen. 9), and he who accepts its obligations is a *ger-toshav* ("resident-stranger" or even "semi-convert"; see Av. Zar. 64b; Maim. Yad, Melakhim 8:10). Maimonides equates the "righteous man *(ḥasid)* of the [gentile] nations" who has a share in the world to come even without becoming a Jew with the gentile who keeps these laws. Such a man is entitled to full material support from the Jewish community (see ET, 6 (1954), col. 289 s.v. *ger toshav*) and to the highest earthly honors (*Sefer Ḥasidim* (1957), 358). The seven Noachide laws as traditionally enumerated are: the prohibitions of idolatry, blasphemy, bloodshed, sexual sins, theft, and eating from a living animal, as well as the injunction to establish a legal system (Tosef., Av. Zar. 8:4; Sanh. 56a). Except for the last, all are negative, and the last itself is usually interpreted as commanding the enforcement of the others (Maim. Yad, Melakhim, 9:1). They are derived exegetically from divine demands addressed to Adam (Gen. 2:16) and Noah (see Gen. R. 34; Sanh. 59b), i.e., the progenitors of all mankind, and are thus regarded as universal. The prohibition of idolatry provides that, to ensure social stability and personal salvation, the non-Jew does not have to "know God" but must abjure false gods (Meg. 13a; Kid. 40a; Maim. Yad, Melakhim, 10:2ff.). This law refers only to actual idolatrous acts, and not to theoretical principles and, unlike Jews, Noachides are not required to suffer martyrdom rather than break this law (Sanh. 74a; TJ, Shev. 4:2). They are, however, required to choose martyrdom rather than shed human blood (Pes. 25b and Rashi). In view of the strict monotheism of Islam, Muslims were considered as Noachides (cf. ET, loc. cit., col. 291, n. 17), whereas the status of Christians was a matter of debate. Since the later Middle Ages, however, Christianity too has come to be regarded as Noachide, on the ground that *shittuf* ("associationism"—this was the Jewish interpretation of Trinitarianism) is not forbidden to non-Jews (see YD 151). Under the prohibitions of blasphemy, murder, and theft Noachides are subject to greater legal restrictions than Jews because non-Jewish society is held to be more prone to these sins (Rashi to Sanh. 57a). The prohibition of theft covers many types of acts, e.g., military conquest (*ibid.*, 59a) and dishonesty in economic life (*ibid.*, 57a; Yad, Melakhim, 9:9). A number of other Noachide prescriptions are listed in the sources (see Sanh. 57b; Mid. Ps. 21; Yad, Melakhim, 10:6), e.g., prohibitions of sorcery, castration, mixed seeds, blemished sacrifices, injunctions to practice charity, procreate, and to honor the Torah (Ḥul. 92a). These are best understood as subheadings of "the seven laws." Noachides may also freely choose to practice certain other Jewish commandments (Yad, Melakhim, 10:9–10). Jews are obligated to try to establish the Noachide Code wherever they can (*ibid.*, 8:10). Maimonides held that Noachides must not only accept "the seven laws" on their own merit, but they must accept them as divinely revealed. This follows from the thesis that all ethics are not ultimately "natural," but require a theological framework (see Schwarzschild, in: JQR, 52 (1962), 302; Fauer, in: *Tarbiz*, 38 (1968), 43–53). The Noachide covenant plays an important part in both Jewish history and historiography. Modern Jewish thinkers like Moses *Mendelssohn and Hermann *Cohen emphasized the Noachide conception as the common rational, ethical ground of Israel and mankind (see H. Cohen, *Religion der Vernunft* (1929), 135–48, 381–8), and see Noah as the symbol of the unity and perpetuity of mankind (*ibid.*, 293). Views differ as to whether the ultimate stage of humanity will comprise both Judaism and Noachidism, or whether Noachidism is only the penultimate level before the universalization of all of the Torah (see TJ, Av. Zar. 2:1). Aimé *Pallière, at the suggestion of his teacher Rabbi E. *Benamozegh, adopted the Noachide Laws and never formally converted to Judaism. [St.Sch.]

In Jewish Law. While in the amoraic period the above-mentioned list of seven precepts is clearly accepted as the framework of the Noachide Laws, a variety of tannaitic sources indicate lack of complete agreement as to the number of such laws, as well as to the specific norms to be included. The Tosefta (Av. Zar. 8:6) records four possible additional prohibitions against (1) drinking the blood of a living animal; (2) emasculation; (3) sorcery; and (4) all magical practices listed in Deuteronomy 18:10–11. The Talmud records a position which would add prohibitions against crossbreeding of animals of different species, and grafting trees of different kinds (Sanh. 56b). Nonrabbinic sources of the tannaitic period indicate even greater divergence. The Book of Jubilees (7:20ff.) records a substantially different list of six commandments given by Noah to his sons: (1) to observe righteousness (2) to cover the shame of their flesh; (3) to bless their creator; (4) to honor parents; (5) to love their neighbor; and (6) to guard against fornication, uncleanness, and all iniquity (see L. Finkelstein, bibl.). Acts (15:20) refers to four commandments addressed to non-Jews, "... that they abstain from pollutions of idols, from fornication, from things strangled, and from blood." This latter list is the only one that bears any systematic relationship to the set of religious laws which the Pentateuch makes obligatory upon resident aliens (the *ger ha-gar* and *ezraḥ*).

Nature and Purpose. There are indications that even during the talmudic period itself there was divergence of opinion as to whether the Noachide Laws constituted a formulation of natural law or were intended solely to govern the behavior of the non-Jewish resident living under Jewish jurisdiction. The natural law position is expressed most clearly by the assertion, as to five of the seven laws, that they would have been made mandatory even had they not been revealed (Yoma 67b; Sifra *Aḥarei Mot*, 13:10). Similarly, the rabbinic insistence that six of the seven Noachide Laws were actually revealed to Adam partakes of a clearly universalistic thrust (Gen. R. 16:6, 24:5). The seventh law, against the eating of flesh torn from a living animal, could have been revealed at the earliest to Noah, since prior to the flood the eating of flesh was prohibited altogether. The very fact that these laws were denominated as the "seven laws of the sons of Noah" constitutes further indication of this trend since the term "sons of Noah" is, in rabbinic usage, a technical term including all human beings except those whom Jewish law defines as being Jews. Nor was there a lack of technical terminology available specifically to describe the resident alien. On the other hand, the entire context of the talmudic discussion of the Noachide Laws is that of actual enforcement by rabbinic courts. To that end, not only is the punishment for each crime enumerated, but standards of procedure and evidence are discussed as well (Sanh. 56a–59a). This presumption of the jurisdiction of Jewish courts is most comprehensible if the laws themselves are intended to apply to non-Jews resident in areas of Jewish sovereignty. Of a similar nature is the position of Yose that the parameters of the proscription against magical practices by Noachides is the verse in Deuteronomy (18:10) which begins, "There shall not be found among you ..." (Sanh. 56b). The attempt of Finkelstein (op. cit.) to date the formulation of the seven Noachide commandments during the Hasmonean era would also suggest a rabbinic concern with the actual legal status of the non-Jew in a sovereign Jewish state. It might even be the case that the substitution by the *tanna* of the school of Manasseh of emasculation and forbidden mixtures of plants for the establishment of a judicial system and blasphemy (Sanh. 56b) itself reflects a concern with the regulation of the life of the resident alien already under the jurisdiction of Jewish courts. Of course, the seven commandments themselves are subject to either interpretation; e.g., the establishment of courts of justice can mean either an independent non-Jewish judiciary and legal system or can simply bring the non-Jew under the rubric of Jewish civil law and its judicial system.

THE BASIS OF AUTHORITY. A question related to the above is that of the basis of authority of these laws over the non-Jew. Talmudic texts seem constantly to alternate between two terms, reflecting contradictory assumptions as to the basis of authority, namely seven precepts "which were commanded" *(she-niẓtavvu)* to the Noachides, and seven precepts "which the Noachides accepted upon themselves" (*she-kibbelu aleihem;* BK 38a; TJ, Av. Zar. 2:1; Ḥul. 92ab; Hor. 8b; Sanh. 56b). This disparity between authority based on revelation as opposed to consent reaches a climax when Maimonides asserts that the only proper basis for acceptance of the Noachide laws by a non-Jew is divine authority and revelation to Moses, and that "... if he observed them due to intellectual conviction [i.e., consent] such a one is not a resident alien, nor of the righteous of the nations of the world, nor of their wise men" (Yad, Melakhim 8:11; the possibility that the final *"ve-lo"* ("nor") is a scribal error for *"ella"* ("but rather") while very appealing, is not borne out by any manuscript evidence). Of course, this same conflict between revelation and consent as basis of authority appears with regard to the binding authority of Torah over the Jew, in the form of "we will do and obey" (Ex. 24:7) as opposed to "He (God) suspended the mountain upon them like a cask, and said to them, 'If ye accept the Torah, 'tis well; if not, there shall be your burial'" (Shab. 88a).

NOACHIDE LAWS AND PRE-SINAITIC LAWS. The *amoraim,* having received a clear tradition of seven Noachide Laws, had difficulty in explaining why other pre-Sinaitic laws were not included, such as procreation, circumcision, and the law of the sinew. They propounded two somewhat strained principles to explain the anomalies. The absence of circumcision and the sinew is explained through the assertion that any pre-Sinaitic law which was not repeated at Sinai was thenceforth applicable solely to Israelites (Sanh. 59a), whence procreation, while indeed obligatory on non-Jews according to Johanan (Yev. 62a) would nevertheless not to be listed (cf. Tos. to Yev. 62a s.v. *benei;* Tos. to Ḥag. 2b s.v. *lo*).

LIABILITY FOR VIOLATION OF THE LAWS. While committed to the principle that "There is nothing permitted to an Israelite yet forbidden to a heathen" (Sanh. 59a), the seven Noachide Laws were not as extensive as the parallel prohibitions applicable to Jews, and there are indeed situations in which a non-Jew would be liable for committing an act for which a Jew would not be liable. As to the latter point, as a general rule, the Noachide is criminally liable for violation of any of his seven laws even though technical definitional limitations would prevent liability by a Jew performing the same act. Thus a non-Jew is liable for blasphemy—even if only with one of the divine attributes; murder—even of a foetus (see *Embryo); robbery—even of less than a *perutah;* and the eating of flesh torn from a living animal — even of a quantity less than the size of an olive. In all these cases a Jew would not be liable (Sanh. 56a–59b; Yad, Melakhim, ch. 9, 10). One additional element of greater severity is that violation of any one of the seven laws subjects the Noachide to capital punishment by decapitation (Sanh. 57a). [SA.B.]

Bibliography: S. Krauss, in: REJ, 47 (1903), 32–40; L. Finkelstein, in: JBL, 49 (1930), 21–25; L. Blau, in: *Abhandlungen ... Chajes* (1933), 6–21; P. L. Biberfeld, *Das noachidische Urrecht* (1937); ET, 3 (1951), 348–62; R. Loewe, in: *Studies in Memory of Leon Roth* (1966), 125–31, 136–44.

NOAH (Heb. נֹחַ), son of Lamech, father of Shem, Ham, and Japheth (Gen. 5:28–29; 6:10; I Chron. 1:4). Noah is described as a righteous and blameless man who walked with God (Gen. 6:9) and whom God decided to save from a universal *Flood to become the progenitor of a new human race. He was given instructions to build an ark (see *Ark of Noah), to provision it, and to take aboard members of his

Figure 1. Noah supervising the building of the ark. Detail of a full-page miniature in the *Sarajevo Haggadah,* Spain, 14th century. Sarajevo, National Museum, fol. 4.

family and representatives of the animal and bird kingdoms. After surviving the Flood, Noah disembarked and offered sacrifices to God, who, in turn, blessed Noah and his sons and made a covenant with them. He also laid upon them certain injunctions relative to the eating of fish and the taking of life (6:9–9:17).

In the genealogical lists of the biblical Patriarchs given in Genesis 5 and 11, Noah occupies a position midway between Adam and Abraham. He is also tenth in the line of antediluvian Patriarchs. This tradition is doubtless dependent upon a Mesopotamian source. It is especially reminiscent of a notation in the writings of Berossus (third century B.C.E.) according to which the hero of the great flood was Babylonia's tenth antediluvian king. In the biblical material dealing with the Patriarchs there is an extension of the use of the number ten, or numbers based on ten, not found in the cognate Mesopotamian notices. For instance, ten generations separate Noah from Abraham, and Noah's age is reckoned by tens and multiples of ten. Noah had reached the age of 500 at the birth of his three sons (5:32) and another period of 100 years elapsed before the onset of the deluge (7:11). However, the biblical treatment differs importantly from its Mesopotamian antecedents, for in the latter, the reigns of the antediluvian kings range from 18,600 to nearly 65,000 years. There is no denying that the lifespans of the corresponding biblical personages, including Noah's 950 years (9:28), have been considerably compressed and fall far short of the briefest reign mentioned in the related Mesopotamian texts.

Another discrepancy between the biblical and Mesopotamian traditions lies in the name of the hero. The earliest Mesopotamian flood account, written in the Sumerian language, calls the deluge hero Ziusudra, which is thought to carry the connotation "he who laid hold on life of distant days." The Sumerian name obviously has in view the immortality granted the hero after the Flood. It is this name which is reflected in the later version set down in writing by Berossus. In the ancient Babylonian versions there is likewise clearly an indebtedness to the prior Sumerian account (see *Flood). In one of these versions the hero bears the name Atra(m)ḫasis, meaning "the exceedingly wise." This name apparently is in the nature of an epithet. Woven into the famous Epic of Gilgamesh is another version, in which the man who survived the flood is known as Utnapishtim, signifying "he saw life." This is patently a loose rendering of the Sumerian Ziusudra, which symbolizes the status attained by the hero. The name Noah, by contrast, cannot be related to any of these on the basis of present knowledge.

The foregoing factors strongly suggest that in the transmission of the Babylonian antediluvian lists to biblical chroniclers an intermediate agent was active. The people most likely to have fulfilled this role are the Hurrians, whose territory included the city of Haran, where the Patriarch Abraham had his roots. The Hurrians inherited the Flood story from Babylonia. Unfortunately, their version exists in an extremely fragmentary condition, so that nothing positive can be said one way or the other on the matter. There is preserved, however, a personal name which invites comparison with the name of Noah. It is spelled syllabically: *Na-aḫ-ma-su-le-el*. It is possible, but by no means certain, that Noah is a shortened form of this name.

The Bible itself attempts to interpret the name: "This one will provide us relief from our work and from the toil of our hands" (5:29). This explanation links Noah with the Hebrew *niḥam*, "to comfort," but this is popular etymologizing and not based on linguistic principles. The true significance of the name was probably unknown to those speakers of Hebrew who inherited the Flood narrative. The interpretation of the name seems to refer to Noah's invention of wine. It is possible, however, that it reflects a lost tradition connecting Noah with the invention of the plow. The biblical statement that Noah was the first to plant a vineyard (9:20–21) seems to reflect an ancient attitude that grape culture and the making of wine were essential to civilization. The account also takes for granted that grapes were properly utilized by turning the juice into a fermented drink. Furthermore, Noah's drunkenness is presented in a matter-of-fact manner and not as reprehensible behavior. It is clear that intoxication is not at issue here, but rather that Noah's venture into viticulture provides the setting for the castigation of Israel's Canaanite neighbors. It is related that *Ham, to whom the descent of the Canaanites is traced, committed an offense when he entered the tent and viewed his father's nakedness. The offender is specifically identified as the father of *Canaan (9:22), and Noah's curse, uttered upon his awakening, is strangely aimed at Canaan rather than the disrespectful Ham. In any event, the inspiration for the scene is clearly not Mesopotamian in origin, as is the case with the greater part of the material in the first 11 chapters of Genesis.

Noah as a personality is again mentioned in the Bible only by the prophet Ezekiel (14:14, 20) who refers to him as one of three righteous men of antiquity, although Isaiah (54:9) does describe the Flood as "the waters of Noah."

[D.Y.]

In the Aggadah. Although the Bible says of Noah that he was (Gen. 6:9) "in his generations a man righteous and wholehearted," and hence was saved, not a single action is mentioned there to illustrate his righteousness. Philo, too, asks (LA 3:77): "why did he [Moses] say 'Noah found grace in the eyes of the Lord' (Gen. 6:8), when previously he had, as far as our information goes, done nothing good?" Filling in details lacking in the Bible, the *aggadah* tells of Noah's righteousness before and during the building of the ark and while he was in it. Noah's first good deed was to "introduce plows, sickles, axes, and all kinds of tools to his contemporaries," thus freeing them from doing everything with their hands (Tanḥ. Gen. 11). He was what the Greeks would call εὐεργέτης, one whose inventions benefit mankind and cause him to be particularly beloved of the gods. Noah's uprightness and love of his fellowmen are further exemplified in what he did to save his contemporaries. Instead of hurrying to build the ark, he delayed it for many years waiting until the cedars which he had planted for it had grown (Tanḥ. No'aḥ 5). Finding it difficult to disregard God's command, yet dreading the destruction of the human species, he waited for 120 years in the hope that his contemporaries would depart from their evil ways.

Noah also admonished and warned his contemporaries, and called upon them to repent. A similar motif is found also in Josephus (Ant. 1:74) and the Apostolic Fathers (Clement, 1, 7, 6).

Figure 2. Picture of Noah's ark, fashioned from Kufic script—a form of Arabic calligraphy—and signed by the Turkish artist, Hāfiz ʾOthmān (d. 1699). Boston, Mass., Museum of Fine Arts, Ross collection.

Noah's reproof of the men of his generation is derived from a reference to him as a righteous man (Gen. 6:9); the *aggadah*, states that "wherever it says 'a righteous man'—the reference is to one who forewarns others" Gen. R. 30:7), only such a one being worthy of the designation "righteous." In the Bible, Noah figures as a man wholeheartedly righteous and reticent; in the *aggadah*, a prophet, a truthful man, a monitor of his generation, a herald persecuted for his rebukes and honesty.

Noah's righteousness was also shown in his devoted attention to the animals in the ark. Because of the great care taken by Noah and his sons to provide each animal with its usual diet at its usual mealtime, they slept neither by day nor by night (Sanh. 108b; Tanḥ B. 58:2). Noah regarded himself as responsible for the preservation of all the animal species. Philo, too, stresses the fact that when God brought a flood on earth, He wished that all the species He had created should be preserved (Mos. 2:61). Plato, in one of his myths (*Protagoras*, 321), attributes a similar desire to the gods. In spite of these testimonials to Noah's high-mindedness, R. Johanan interpreted the biblical statement, "thee have I seen righteous before Me in this generation" (Gen. 7:1) as indicating Noah's righteousness only in relation to his own generation and not in relation to others (Sanh. 108a). Philo (Abr. 36) concurred, stating that Noah would not have been regarded as upright in relation to the Patriarchs: he affirmed his greatness in opposing the tendencies of his generation (*ibid.* 38). [E.E.H.]

In Christianity. In Christian symbolism Noah is one of the most important typological figures. The New Testament describes him as a symbol of the just (II Pet. 2:5), and as an example, in a sinful world, of faith in and submission to God (Heb. 11:7; Luke 17:26–27; I Pet. 3:20). As a type and prefiguration of Jesus, Noah exhorts to repentance and announces the inevitable judgment. Being spared from the universal catastrophe, he appears as a redeemer through whom humanity is saved from complete destruction and is reconciled with God.

The Flood, the ark, and the dove also serve as Christian prefigurations. Just as Noah triumphs over drowning to death in the waters of the flood, so Jesus and the Christians vanquish Satan and death through the water of baptism which initiates them into a new world (I Pet. 3:18–21). In later Christian tradition Noah's ark symbolizes the Church outside of which no salvation is possible. The dove sent out by Noah prefigures the Holy Spirit moving upon the baptismal waters, symbolizing divine reconciliation. [Ed.]

In Islam. Nūḥ (Noah) is one of Muhammad's favorite biblical characters. He devotes a complete sura to Noah (71) considering Noah's life as a prototype of his own. Noah is the reprover who attempts to make his people repent (7:57–61), but the elders scorn and do not heed him. Following the *aggadah* (Sanh. 108a and other Midrashim) Noah relates that it has been revealed to him that he must build the ark (11:29, 34, 38–39). When Noah and the members of his family entered the ark on Allah's command, one son stood at the side of the Ark and was drowned in the waters of the *Flood because he refused to enter when Noah called (11:43). According to some commentators, this son was *Canaan; hence, the belief that Noah had four sons, and not three as recorded in the Bible. Noah's wife may also have been among those who drowned in the Flood (see Tabarī, below), because as the wife of *Lot, she was not a believer (66:10–11). The Ark settled on Mount Jūdī (11:46). The poets al-Nābigha, al-Aʿshā, ʿAdī b. Zayd, and especially, Umayya ibn Abī al-Ṣalt, who were contemporaries of Muhammad, describe the ark, its construction, and the salvation of Noah. As usual, the commentators on the Koran add many legendary details and embellishments and are familiar with the names of the sons of Noah (see below). The number of those who were saved varies. One source mentions 80 survivors: Noah, his three sons, their wives, and 73 believers, the descendants of *Seth (Shīth; Tabarī 129). According to others, only eight survived: Noah and his wife (!), his three sons, and their wives.

The three sons of Noah are not mentioned by name in the Koran. Tabarī (vol. 1, pp. 132–3) presents a list stating how the land was partitioned among them, and later (pp. 140–9) includes the genealogies of all the nations which existed in his time. Sām (Shem) was the progenitor of the Arabs, the Persians, and the Rūm (Byzantines) who are considered good nations. Yāfath (Japheth) was the ancestor of the Turks and the Slavs, Yājūj and Mājūj (*Gog and Magog), all of whom possess no good qualities (p. 145), and are not noble. Hām (Ham) gave birth to the Copts, the "Blacks," and the Berbers. His sins were having carnal relations with his wife in the Ark and acting disrespectfully toward his father. [H.Z.H.]

Figure 3. Engraving of Noah seen naked by his son Ham (Gen. 9:22–24). From Conrad Lauterbach's German translation of Josephus' *Jewish Antiquities*, Strasbourg, 1574. Jerusalem, A. Bargiora Collection.

In the Arts. The dramatic aspects of the biblical story of the Flood have ensured Noah's continued popularity as a subject for treatment by writers and artists. During the Middle Ages, Noah as seen as a prefiguration of Jesus (see above) and christological interpretations were also placed on his drunkenness, which was believed to foreshadow the bitter drink of the Passion. At the same time, however, some of the English mystery plays showed Noah and his wife in a comic light, their ribald dialogue appealing to unsophisticated audiences. The English medieval cycles, which used a prefabricated stage setting of the ark, include those of Chester ("The Deluge"), Coventry ("Noah's Flood"), Towneley, and York ("The Building of the Ark" and "Noah and his Wife"). Some of these plays were presented by trade guilds, such as the Newcastle shipwrights (*Noah's Ark, or the Shipwrights' Ancient Play or Dirge*). The theme inspired the Norman poet Olivier Basselin's *"Eloge de Noé"*—a drinking song with the refrain *"O le bon vin!"* Toward the end of the 15th century, the Italian Annius of Viterbo published a book of spurious *Antiquities* (Rome, 1498) containing the "Pseudo-Berosus," a legendary account of Noah and his descendants which especially linked the Japhethites with some of the European nations. The 16th-century epic treatment of the Deluge theme was written by the Polish poet Jan Kochanowski (1558). The subject still retained some popular appeal in 17th-century England, with "Noah's Flood," a musical presentation licensed in 1662; a Bartholomew Fair "droll" entitled *The Creation of the World;* and Edward Ecclestone's opera, *Noah's Flood; or The Destruction of the World* (1679). The Dutch Catholic Joost van den Vondel's five-act drama, *Noah, of ondergang der eerste weerelt* (1667), was on a higher level than all of these.

The only major writer of the 18th century to show interest in the theme was the Swiss poet and dramatist Johann Jacob Bodmer, who devoted two separate epics to the Bible story: *Noah ein Heldengedicht* (1750, 1752[2]; published as *Die Noachide*, 1765) and *Die Synd-Flut* (1751, 1753[2]). Twentieth-century interpretations have included *Die Suendflut* (1924), a drama by the German anti-Nazi author and artist Ernst Barlach; a poem by the U.S. writer Robert *Nathan (in "A Cedar Box," 1929); *Noé* (1931; *Noah*, 1935), one of the great successes of the French dramatist André Obey; and *Noah and the Waters* (1936), a poem by the Anglo-Irish author Cecil Day Lewis. Two treatments of the post-World War II period were *The Flowering Peach* (1954) by the U.S. playwright Clifford *Odets, who transferred the Noah story to a modern setting; and Hugo Loetscher's *Noah* (1970), a satire on the affluent society, which used the biblical theme to point a contemporary moral.

In art, the main subjects treated are the Flood (Gen. 7, 8) and the drunkenness of Noah (Gen. 9). The subject matter of catacomb art is often drawn from the prayers of the *Commendatio Animae*. Like Isaac and Daniel, Noah is a popular subject in the art of the catacombs because he figures in the prayers as a symbol of the

Figure 4. Noah's ark after the flood, a page from the *Ashburnham Pentateuch*, a seventh-century illuminated manuscript of uncertain origin. Paris, Bibliothèque Nationale; Nouv. Acq. Lat. 2334, fol. 10v.

redeemed soul. Notable representations are those in the second-century murals from the catacomb of Priscilla and the fourth-century murals from that of Domitillus. In early Christian Art, the ark is represented as a small floating cask in which Noah stands alone, his arms upraised in an attitude of supplication. Later it became a floating house or three-tiered basilica, differing from a ship in that it had no oars or sails. A representation of Noah's ark is found on a mosaic from the ancient synagogue in Gerasa, Jordan, and scenes from the story of Noah are depicted in the 12th-century mosaics of Palermo and Monreale, and in the 13th-century mosaics from St. Mark's Cathedral, Venice. The theme also occurs in sculpture, frescoes, manuscript illuminations, and stained glass. There are carvings of the subject in the Gothic cathedrals of Bourges, Wells, and Salisbury, and in 12th-century wall paintings from St. Savin, France. It is illustrated in the sixth-century *Vienna Genesis* (National Library, Vienna), the seventh-century *Ashburnham Pentateuch* (Bibliothèque Nationale, Paris), the 13th-century *St. Louis Psalter*, and in a number of Hebrew manuscripts, including the French 13th-century *British Museum Miscellany* (Add. 11:639) and the 14th-century *Sarajevo Haggadah*. In the 13th-century Hispano-Provençal Farḥi Bible (formerly in the Sassoon Collection, Letchworth) there is a plan of the ark.

During the Renaissance, Lorenzo Ghiberti executed a bas-relief of the story of Noah after the Flood on his bronze gates to the Florence Baptistery, and Paolo Uccello painted a fresco of the Deluge in the Church of Santa Maria Novella in Florence. One of the most dramatic representations of the Flood is that by Michelangelo (Sistine Chapel, Vatican), who also depicted the sacrifice and the drunkenness of Noah, and Shem and Japheth covering his nakedness. In this, as in other Renaissance paintings of the subject, the sons are themselves oddly depicted in the nude. The story of Noah also figures in the Raphael frescoes in the Vatican. There are paintings of Noah entering and leaving the Ark by Jacopo Bassano in the Prado, and a painting of Noah leaving the ark by Hieronymos Bosch is in the Bojmans Museum, Rotterdam. In the 17th century, Nicolas Poussin painted the Flood as an image of winter in a series of four paintings representing the four seasons (Louvre). Poussin's painting of the sacrifice of Noah is in the Prado. Among modern artists, Lesser *Ury painted the Flood, and a painting of Noah's Ark by Marc *Chagall is in the Louvre.

In music, there were two 19th-century oratorios on the theme of the Flood, one by Johann Christian Friedrich Schmerder (1823); and *Le Déluge* (1876; première at Boston, U.S., 1880) by Camille Saint-Saëns. In 1970 *Two by Two*, a musical on the theme based on Clifford Odets' above-mentioned play and with Danny Kaye in the star role, was staged on Broadway. [Ed.]

Bibliography: A. Heidel, *The Gilgamesh Epic and Old Testament Parallels* (1946); S. N. Kramer, *History Begins at Sumer* (1959), 214–9; E. A. Speiser, in: J. J. Finkelstein and M. Greenberg (eds.), *Oriental and Biblical Studies* (1967), 244–69; N. M. Sarna, *Understanding Genesis* (1967), 37–62. In the Aggadah: Ginzberg, Legends, index. In Christianity: J. Daniélou, *Sacramentum futuri* (1950), 60ff. In Islam: Tabarī, *Ta'rīkh*, 1 (1357, A.H.), 122–33, 139–49; Tha'labī, *Qiṣaṣ* (1356, A.H.), 45–51; Kisā'ī, *Qiṣaṣ* (1356, A. H.), 85–103; J. W. Hirschberg, *Juedische und christliche Lehren im vor- und fruehislamischen Arabien* (1939), 53–58, 114–22; H. Speyer, *Die biblischen Erzaehlungen im Qoran* (1931, repr. 1961), 89–115. In the Arts: D. C. Allen, *Legend of Noah; Renaissance Rationalism in Art, Science, and Letters* (1949); D. P. Walker, in: *Journal of the Warburg and Courtauld Institutes*, 17 (1954), 204–59; J. Fink, *Noe der Gerechte in der fruehchristlichen Kunst* (1955); M. Roston, *Biblical Drama in England* (1968), index.

NOAH, BOOKS OF. Although a Book of Noah is not referred to in the Christian canon lists, there is a good deal of evidence that such a work or works existed. In Jubilee 10:1–15 reference is made to a medical and anti-demonic work transmitted by Noah to his descendants after the Flood, when, in spite of Noah's intercession, a tenth of the demons were left on earth, causing trouble and affliction. What appears to be another form of this passage is to be found in the opening paragraphs of the medieval medical treatise *Sefer Asaf ha-Rofe*. Some scholars, such as Charles, would also attribute Jubilees 7:20–39 to a Book of Noah. A second body of Noah material is that discerned by Charles in I Enoch. The chapters which appear assuredly to be drawn from a Noah book are I Enoch 6–11, 60, 65–69, 106–7. Material closely associated with I Enoch 6–11 and 106–7 appears in 1Q19, the so-called "Book of Noah" from Qumran. This text does not appear to be simply the Hebrew original of the I Enoch Noah material, but to be closely associated with it. Yet another group of Noah texts associated with ritual instructions of a priestly character is referred to in Jubilees 21:10, there as part of Abraham's instructions to Isaac. This tradition was also known to the author of the Greek "Fragments of the Testament of Levi," undoubtedly a very ancient text, again directly attributed to Noah and included in Abraham's instructions to Isaac (Greek fragment 57), and in a brief form, without the attribution to Noah, in the Testament of the Twelve Patriarchs, Levi 9:11. The Jewish magical book *Sefer ha-*Razim* is also ascribed to Noah.

Bibliography: Charles, Apocrypha, 2 (1913), 168; M. R. James, *Lost Apocrypha of the Old Testament* (1920), 11f.; Barthélemy-Milik, 84–86; M. Margalioth (ed.), *Sefer ha-Razim* (1966). [M.E.S.]

NOAH, MORDECAI MANUEL (1785–1851), U.S. editor, politician, and playwright. Noah, who was probably the most influential Jew in the United States in the early 19th century, was born in Philadelphia. His father, Manuel Noah (c. 1755–1822), was a bankrupt itinerant merchant, and Mordecai Noah was raised by his maternal grandfather, Jonas *Phillips. After apprenticeship as a gilder and carver, Noah became a clerk in the U.S. Treasury through the assistance of Robert Morris (1734–1806), the financier and senator.

Noah began his political career in Philadelphia in 1808 when he, along with other "Democratic Young Men," supported the Republican candidate, James Madison, for president. A year later Noah went to Charleston, where he edited the *City Gazette*. A war "hawk," he strongly supported the War of 1812. In 1813 he was appointed consul at Tunis, but was recalled two years later after he was accused of misappropriation of funds, though the charges were never proved. On his return to the United States, Noah established himself permanently in New York with the help of his uncle Naphtali Phillips, publisher of the *National Advocate*, which ardently supported the Democratic Party of New York County. Noah became the editor of the newspaper in 1817, giving him access to the Tammany Society. He was appointed high sheriff in 1822 and two years later was elected grand sachem of Tammany.

Portrait of Mordecai Manuel Noah by John Wesley Jarvis. New York, Congregation Shearith Israel. Courtesy Frick Art Reference Library, New York.

When Phillips sold the *National Advocate* in 1824, Noah became the publisher of the *New York National Advocate*. He broke with Tammany over its opposition to De Witt Clinton, then commissioner of canals, and in 1825 supported Clinton for governor. Noah continued to oppose Tammany in the paper he established, the *New York Enquirer*, published 1826–29. Critical of Andrew Jackson, particularly of his attack on the U.S. Bank, he associated himself with the newly created Whig Party in 1834, and as publisher and editor of the *Evening Star*, a Whig paper, demonstrated anti-immigrant and anti-Catholic bias. When the Native American Party of 1835–36, the forerunner of the Know-Nothing Party, was created, he was one of its chief supporters. He also supported the Texas revolt of 1836 against Mexico and angrily attacked the abolitionist cause. In 1841, he became a judge of the Court of Sessions.

Noah was a prolific playwright; many of his plays reflected his patriotic fervor. His first play, *Fortress of Sorrento* (written 1808), was followed by, among others, *She Would Be a Soldier* (1819); *Siege of Tripoli* (1820), also produced as *Yuseff Caramalli;* and *Marion, or the Hero of St. George* (1822).

Noah's interest in Jewish affairs drew him into activities on behalf of the congregations of Mikveh Israel in Philadelphia and Shearith Israel in New York. Long taken by the idea of a Jewish territorial restoration, Noah, in 1825, helped purchase a tract of land on Grand Island in the Niagara River near Buffalo, which he named Ararat and envisioned as a Jewish colony. Though the proposal elicited much discussion, the attempt was not a success and Noah's pretensions as ruler were ridiculed. After the failure of the Ararat experience, Noah turned more strongly to the idea of Palestine as a national home for Jews. As the best-known American Jew of his time, Noah in 1840 delivered the principal address at a meeting at B'nai Jeshurun in New York protesting the *Damascus Affair.

Bibliography: I. Goldberg, *Major Noah: American Jewish Pioneer* (1937); L. M. Friedman, *Pilgrims in a New Land* (1948), 221–32; DAB, s.v.; S. J. Kohn, in: AJHSQ, 59 (1969), 210–4; B. D. Weinryb, in: *The Jewish Experience in America*, 2 (1969), 136–57; R. Gordis, *ibid.*, 110–35; I. M. Fein, *ibid.*, 82–101. [L.He.]

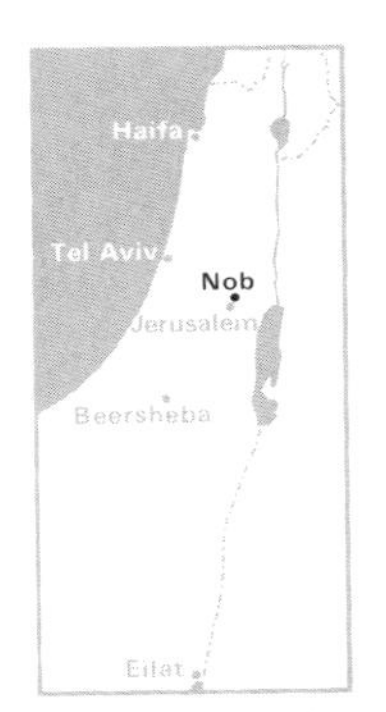

NOB (Heb. נֹב), priestly town in the territory of Benjamin, near Jerusalem. When David fled from Saul's court, he traveled by way of Nob (I Sam. 21ff.). Pretending to be on a royal mission, he obtained from the chief priest Ahimelech hallowed bread and the sword of Goliath from the local sanctuary for himself and his men. Doeg the Edomite, Saul's chief herdsman, denounced the priest to the king (I Sam. 22:9ff.); on Saul's order, he slew 85 priests and also "men and women, children and sucklings, and oxen and asses and sheep" (I Sam. 22:19). Abiathar son of Ahimelech escaped and later became high priest to David. Nob was the last stopping point, after Anathoth, of Sennacherib's northern army before their assault on Jerusalem (Isa. 10:32). It was one of the cities settled by Jews returning from Babylonian Exile. In the Mishnah, the question of the permissibility of high places at Nob is discussed (Zev. 14:7; Tosef., Zev. 13:5). The ancient city is identified with an Iron Age site near the village of ʿIsawiyya on Mt. Scopus, near the modern campus of the Hebrew University.

Bibliography: Voigt, in: JPOS, 3 (1923), 79–87; W. F. Albright, in: AASOR, 4 (1924), 139; A. Alt, in: PJB, 21 (1925), 12ff.
[M.A.-Y.]

NOBEL, NEHEMIAH ANTON (1871–1922), German Orthodox rabbi and religious leader. Born in Nagymed (Hungary), he was the son of Joseph Nobel (1840–1917), author of a number of exegetical and homiletical works (*Ḥermon*, 1919³; *Levanon*, 1911; *Tavor*, 1899; and others). After being brought up in Halberstadt, where his father was *Klausrabbinner*, Nehemiah Nobel studied at the Berlin *Rabbinerseminar. He served in the rabbinate of Cologne from 1896 to 1899, and then for several months in Koenigsberg. From there he went to the University of Marburg to study under Hermann *Cohen, who had a great influence upon him, although they did not agree about Zionism. Nobel's activity in the Zionist Movement began in Cologne. He was on close terms with Theodor *Herzl and David *Wolffsohn and was one of the original founders of the Zionist Federation in Germany. He also took part in the founding convention of the *Mizrachi movement in Pressburg (1904). Nobel's Zionist activity, motivated by his conviction that religion and nationhood are organically connected in Judaism, stood out in contrast to the united anti-Zionist front of Orthodox and liberal rabbis in Germany at the time. From 1901 he served in the rabbinate of Leipzig, from 1906 in the rabbinate of Hamburg, and finally, from 1910, in the rabbinate of Frankfort, where he succeeded Marcus *Horowitz. There he prompted closer contacts with Judaism and Zionism in circles that had been drifting away from Judaism. His sermons and preachings, in which he was extraordinarily impressive, tackled topical problems. He influenced such Jewish thinkers as Ernst

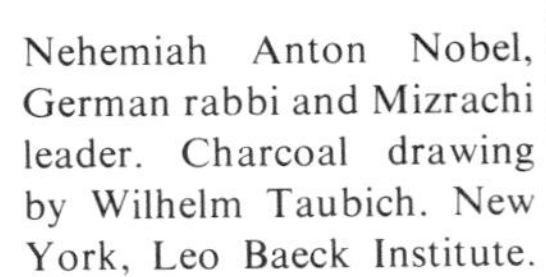

Nehemiah Anton Nobel, German rabbi and Mizrachi leader. Charcoal drawing by Wilhelm Taubich. New York, Leo Baeck Institute.

*Simon, Oscar Wolfsberg (Y. *Aviad), F. *Rosenzweig, and M. *Buber. The last two helped to publish the jubilee book for his 50th birthday (1921). In 1919 he was elected chairman of the Union of German Rabbis and was head of the Akademie fuer die Wissenschaft des Judentums. He died a short time after having been appointed professor of religion and ethics at the University of Frankfort. A number of his sermons as well as scholarly and halakhic articles, which first appeared in *Festschriften,* have been published in Hebrew as *Hagut ve-Halakhah* (1969). Nobel's younger brother, Israel (1878–1962), rabbi in Schneidemuehl and Berlin, published *Offenbarung und Tradition* (1908) and a Passover *Haggadah* with German translation and notes (1927).

Bibliography: E. E. Mayer, in: L. Jung (ed.), *Guardians of our Heritage* (1958), 563–79; *Nachrufe auf Rabbiner N. A. Nobel* (1923); O. Wolfberg, *Nehemiah Anton Nobel 1871–1922* (Ger., 1929); idem, *Ha-Rav Neḥemyah Ẓevi Nobel* (Heb., 1944); N. A. Nobel, *Hagut ve-Halakhah* (1969), with biography by Y. Aviad.

[G.K.]

NOBEL PRIZES, awarded annually to men and women who have "rendered the greatest service to mankind." Since the inception of the prize in 1899 it has been awarded to the following Jews or people of Jewish descent (all of whom have entries in the Encyclopaedia):

World Peace
1911 Alfred Fried
1911 Tobias Michael Carel Asser
1968 René Cassin

Literature
1910 Paul Johann Ludwig Heyse
1927 Henri Bergson
1958 Boris Pasternak
1966 Shmuel Yosef Agnon
1966 Nelly Sachs

Physiology and Medicine
1908 Elie Metchnikoff
1908 Paul Ehrlich
1914 Robert Bárány
1922 Otto Meyerhof
1930 Karl Landsteiner
1931 Otto Warburg
1936 Otto Loewi
1944 Joseph Erlanger
1944 Herbert Spencer Gasser
1945 Ernst Boris Chain
1946 Hermann Joseph Muller
1950 Tadeus Reichstein
1952 Selman Abraham Waksman
1953 Hans Krebs
1953 Fritz Albert Lipmann
1958 Joshua Lederberg
1959 Arthur Kornberg
1964 Konrad Bloch
1965 François Jacob
1965 Andre Lwoff
1967 George Wald
1968 Marshall W. Nirenberg
1969 Salvador Luria
1970 Julius Axelrod
1970 Sir Bernard Katz

Chemistry
1905 Adolph Von Baeyer
1906 Henri Moissan
1910 Otto Wallach
1915 Richard Willstaetter
1918 Fritz Haber
1943 George Charles de Hevesy
1961 Melvin Calvin
1962 Max Ferdinand Perutz

Physics
1907 Albert Abraham Michelson
1908 Gabriel Lippmann
1921 Albert Einstein
1922 Niels Bohr
1925 James Franck
1925 Gustav Hertz
1943 Otto Stern
1944 Isidor Isaac Rabi
1952 Felix Bloch
1954 Max Born
1959 Emilio Segrè
1960 Donald A. Glaser
1961 Robert Hofstadter
1962 Lev Davidovich Landau
1965 Richard Phillips Feynman
1965 Julian Schwinger
1967 Hans Albrecht Bethe
1969 Murray Gell-Mann

Economics
1970 Paul Anthony Samuelson

Bibliography: T. Levitan, *The Laureates: Jewish Winners of the Nobel Prize* (1960), incl. ext. bibl.; E. Feuerstein, *Ḥatnei Peras Nobel le-Safrut* (1961); E. Farber, *Nobel Prize Winners in Chemistry 1901–1961* (1963); T. L. Sourkes, *Nobel Prize Winners in Medicine and Physiology, 1901–1965* (1967[2]).

[Ed.]

°**NOELDEKE, THEODOR** (1836–1930), German orientalist. Born in Harburg, near Hamburg, Noeldeke taught from 1872 until 1906. Best known for his prizewinning *Geschichte des Qorâns* (1860), he was an acknowledged expert on the comparative philology of the Semitic languages and published grammars of New Syriac (1869), Mandaean Aramaic (1874), and Syriac (1880). His expertise in this field was fully revealed in his *Beitraege zur semitischen Sprachwissenschaft* (1904) and its supplement (1910).

Noeldeke was also a distinguished scholar in the biblical and rabbinic fields. Among his works in this sphere are *Ueber die Amalekiter und einige andere Nachbarvoelker der Israeliten* (1864); "Die Geschichte der Juden in Arabien" (in *Beitraege zur Kenntnis der Poesie der alten Araber,* 1864); *Die alttestamentliche Literatur* (1868), a French edition of which, by H. Derenbourg and J. Soury, appeared in 1873; and *Untersuchungen zur Kritik des Alten Testaments* (1869). Noeldeke, whose pupils included Louis *Ginzberg, was a prolific writer on Islamic history and Arabic and Persian culture, his general works including *Orientalische Skizzen* (1892; *Sketches from Eastern History,* 1892). He also published *Die Inschrift des Koenigs Mesa* (1870), an explanatory work on the Mesha Stele; an essay on the Aramaic papyri of Assuan (1907); and various introductions and annotations to books by other scholars, for example, Friedrich Schulthess' *Grammatik des christlich-palaestinischen Aramaeisch* (1924). [Ed.]

NOERDLINGEN, city in Bavaria, W. Germany. Jews were to be found in Noerdlingen from the 12th century, but the sources reflect an organized community only in the 13th century. Eight Jews were martyred there during the *Rindfleisch persecutions (1928), but community life was renewed soon afterward. In 1331 Emperor Louis IV granted four "honorable" Jewish elders the extraordinary privilege of jurisdiction over foreign Jews. There were about 20 Jewish houses in the Judengasse (which was also inhabited by Christians), and the community possessed a synagogue and a cemetery; the Jews made their living as moneylenders. During the *Black Death persecutions of 1348 many Jews were killed or imprisoned; their property and promissory notes were confiscated by the city. Emperor *Charles IV pardoned the burghers and cancelled their debts to the Jews. In 1348 Charles IV acceded to the city's request to readmit Jews. A synagogue was mentioned in 1357, and in 1378 the community consecrated a cemetery. However, during fresh riots in 1348 about 200 Jews were murdered and the community ceased to exist. After Jews were again admitted into the city in 1401, a new and prosperous community came into being; a new cemetery, which also

Stamps issued in honor of Jewish Nobel Prize winners. 1. Albert Einstein, Poland. 2. Adolf Von Baeyer (with Philipp Lenard), Sweden. 3. Elie Metchnikoff, U.S.S.R. 4. Paul Ehrlich (with Emil Behring), West Germany. 5. Karl Landsteiner, Austria. 6. Henri Moissan (with Camillo Golgi and S. Ramon Y Cajal), Sweden. 7. Gabriel Lippmann (with R. C. Eucken), Sweden. 8. Niels Bohr, Denmark. 9. Albert Abraham Michelson (with Eduard Buchner), Sweden. Jerusalem, B. M. Ansbacher Stamp Collection.

Hochfürstlich und Hochgräflich
Oettingisch Gleit
Nördlinger Meß
auf fußgehende Juden.
15. Kr.
den No. 17
Abb. 64. Fürstl. Oettingscher Judengeleitschein zur Nördlinger Messe.
18. Jahrhundert. Nürnberg, Germanisches Museum.

Special permit enabling a Jew to attend the Noerdlingen fair upon payment of 15 kreuzer, 18th century. Nuremberg, Germanisches Nationalmuseum.

served the neighboring communities, was put into use in 1415. Taxes were heavy: five *Schutzjuden* ("protected Jews") provided three-eighths of the amount paid by the whole 34-member city council. In 1437 Jews were forbidden to hire Christian servants and ordered to wear the Jewish *badge—though this order does not seem to have been strictly enforced. The Hussite wars resulted in temporary banishment between 1454 and 1459, and hostile agitation by the clergy led to the expulsion of the Jews in 1507. The synagogue was sold in 1517, but refugees who had settled nearby attended Noerdlingen's annual fairs. A community, with 25 families, was organized in 1870, dedicated a new synagogue in 1885, and founded a *ḥevra kaddisha* in 1898. It numbered 489 persons in 1899, and 314 (3.8% of the total) in 1913. By June 16, 1933, only 186 remained; 145 of them left before 1942, when the remnants of the Jewish community were deported. The mayor of the city prevented the destruction of the synagogue in 1938, and in 1952 it was sold to a Protestant group as a community center.

Bibliography: L. Mueller, *Aus fuenf Jahrhunderten* (1899); K. O. Mueller, *Noerdlingens Stadtrechte des Mittelalters* (1930), index s.v. *Juden;* K. Puchner and G. Wulz (eds.), *Urkunden der Stadt Noerdlingen 1233–1399*, 2 (1956), 111, no. 529; *Jahrbuch des historischen Vereins fuer Noerdlingen*, 2 (1913), 135; Baron, Social, 11 (1967[2]), 71; Germ Jud, 1 (1963), 247–8; 2 (1968), 593–7; *Gemeinde-Verzeichnis fuer das Koenigreich Bayern, Volkszaehlung 1890* (1892), 244; *Statistisches Jahrbuch des deutsch-israelitischen Gemeindebundes* (1905), 93; *Handbuch der juedischen Gemeindeverwaltung* (1913), 156; *Fuehrer durch die juedische Gemeindeverwaltung . . . in Deutschland* (1932/33), 315; T. Oelsner, in: *Transactions of the American Philosophical Society*, 60 (1970); R. Wischnitzer, in: *Chicago Jewish Forum*, 4, no. 1 (1945), 49f.; PK Bavaryah.

[ED.]

NOETHER, family of mathematicians in Germany. MAX NOETHER (1844–1921), born in Erlangen, was professor of mathematics for nearly 50 years. He made important contributions to geometry and was the foremost authority of the algebraic-geometric school in Germany. He wrote many papers on the geometry of hyperspace, Abelian and Theta functions. His son FRITZ NOETHER (1884–) became professor of applied mathematics at the Technische Hochschule, Breslau. EMMY (AMALIE) NOETHER (1882–1935), Max's daughter, was born and educated in Erlangen. She went to Goettingen in 1916, but because of the prevailing anti-feminine bias she was unable to obtain an official post. Conditions changed under the Weimar Republic and after much opposition she was appointed "unofficial extraordinary professor" in 1922. She derived an income from a lectureship in algebra. The advent of the Hitler regime forced her to emigrate to the U.S. where she was appointed professor at Bryn Mawr College, Pennsylvania. She was a pioneer in the general theory of idea, and from 1926 onward initiated advances in non-commutative algebra. A creative mathematician of high caliber, her influence on contemporary mathematics cannot be judged solely by her published work, as she exerted great influence through her students and many of her ideas were developed by them.

Bibliography: Weyl, in: *Scripta mathematica*, 3 (1935), 201–20; Van der Waerden, in: *Mathematische Annalen*, 111 (1935), 469–76.

[B.S.]

NOLA, ELIJAH BEN MENAHEM DA (baptismal name; **Giovanni Paolo Eustachio;** c. 1530–c. 1602), Italian Hebraist and apostate. One of the leading rabbis in Rome during the late 16th century, Da Nola was also a renowned physician and philosopher. When Moses *Alatino was commissioned to translate Hebrew texts into Latin, he received valuable assistance from Da Nola. While acting as a Hebrew tutor to Tommaso Aldobrandini, brother of Pope Clement VIII, Da Nola was induced to convert to Catholicism in 1568, and eventually became a *scrittore* at the Vatican library. He copied Hebrew manuscripts for Cardinal Federigo Borromeo, archbishop of Milan, many such works in his hand being preserved in the Vatican.

Da Nola later published *Sacro Settenario raccolto dalle sacre Scritture . . .* (Naples, 1579), on the symbolism of the figure 7 in the Old and New Testaments. A collection of sermons, *Salutari discorsi . . . aggiuntavi un modo utilissimo de la vita che denno tenere i Neophiti* (Naples, 1582), dedicated to Pope Gregory XII, contained an apologia for his apostasy which, the author claimed, had been based on knowledge and conviction, rather than on fear or greed. Like many others who converted during the Renaissance era, Da Nola endeavored to prove the superiority of Christianity over Judaism by judicious manipulation of kabbalistic books, particularly in regard to the significance of the Trinity and the numerical value of selected Hebrew terms.

Bibliography: C. Roth, *Jews in the Renaissance* (1959), 84, 149–50, 154; F. Secret, *Les Kabbalistes Chrétiens de la Renaissance* (1964), 247–8; U. Cassuto, *I Manoscritti Palatini Ebraici della Biblioteca Vaticana* (1935), index.

[G.E.S.]

NOMADISM, a socioeconomic mode of life based on intensive domestication of livestock which requires a regular movement of the community in an annual cycle in order to sustain the communal ecological system.

Definition. The defining feature of pastoral nomadism is movement, which is neither aimless nor boundless, from pasture to pasture and from watering point to watering point, along well-defined routes, at fixed periods, in rhythm with the rainy and dry seasons, and in greater or lesser comity with adjoining nomadic and settled groups. Little or no agriculture is practiced. Nomads necessarily rely upon trade with or raids upon agriculturalists for food and other necessities or occasional luxuries not supplied by their herds. Pastoral nomads often supply settled peoples with transport services by providing animals and serving as caravaneers. Occasionally, control of routes and specialization in trade lead to settlement of nomad elites in commercial centers such as Palmyra in Syria and Petra in Edom. Ethnographers are generally agreed that pastoral nomadism arose later than the emergence of neolithic agriculture in the Middle East. At first it involved herders of sheep and goats who adapted themselves to the spartan conditions of life on the steppe but who were unable to venture more than one or two days' journey from water. Full nomadism emerged only in about 1500–1000 B.C.E. with the domestication of camels which can go as long as 17 days without water. Introduction of the horse at a somewhat later date allowed for still more flexibility of movement and agility in warfare. Full nomadism never replaced seminomadism altogether and agriculturalists learned how to specialize on the side in pastoralism through a form of nomadism known as transhumance. Actual nomadic groups are extremely varied according to environmental conditions, types of animals bred, communal forms for establishing kinship, wealth, and status, historical fortunes of the group, and relations to surrounding nomadic and settled peoples.

In Ancient Israel. Ancient Israel was in contact with peoples who practiced pastoral nomadism. Some segments of Israel proper were pastoral nomads for varying periods of time in the arid and semiarid zones of Sinai and the Negev, Transjordan, and the rain shadow regions of Canaan, i.e., mostly on the eastern slopes of the central highlands. Excluded from consideration is animal husbandry, which is frequent in agricultural communities in which a few animals raised by farmers are allowed to forage in the human settlement and to graze on farmland stubble and fallow land. The animals referred to in the early Israelite Book of the Covenant (e.g., Ex. 21:28–37; 22:3–4, 9–12; 23:4–5, 12) reveal that the laws applied to resident farmers for whom animal husbandry was a secondary activity and among whom vast pasturage as a special ecological aspect shaping the entire socioeconomic life was absent. Also, we omit all consideration of non-pastoral nomadism, e.g., wild species moving on their own through an annual cycle and nomadic human communities of hunters, fishers, and gatherers. Full or classic pastoral nomadism entailed maximum independence through human symbiosis with the camel and, to a lesser degree, with the horse. It allowed the nomad to keep a safe distance from the settled lands but, when required to trade or raid, he could do so from a position of considerable strength. The occasional camels mentioned in early Israel, if not an outright anachronism, were for transport and were too few in number and insufficiently domesticated to have become the basis for an entire economy. The only full nomadism directly attested in the Bible is non-Israelite, e.g., a caravan of Ishmaelite-Midianite merchants who bought Joseph from his brothers (Gen. 37:25–28); Midianites, Amalekites, and people of the east who carried out camel razzias against Israel in the time of Gideon (Judg. 6:1–5); and Amalekites who raided southern Judah on a smaller scale in the time of Saul (I Sam. 30).

SEMINOMADISM. Seminomadism or partial nomadism (also known as ass nomadism to distinguish the ass from the camel as the chief form of transport) is a mode of pastoral nomadism loosely applied to peoples who are often conceived as midway in the process of settling down after an earlier fully nomadic life. This is misleading in some instances and erroneous in others. In its origins pastoral nomadism was a specific adaptation of animal domestication to desert conditions after it was first developed among agriculturalists. There are of course instances of full nomads reverting to seminomadism and finally to agricultural settlement. But there are also cases of agriculturalists who are "depressed" into seminomadism by geopolitical circumstances. Sometimes this depression is permanent, while in other cases it is temporary. There is some reason to believe that the Israelite groups in the wilderness between Egypt and Canaan were thrown temporarily into a more fully nomadic life than they had known either in Egypt or prior to their entrance into Egypt and, furthermore, that they were consciously seeking a return to a more stable and perhaps even largely agricultural existence. More precisely, seminomadism indicates the relative dependence of herders of sheep, goats, and asses on the settled peoples or on full nomads for the sharing of water rights and for permission to graze. It also refers to their relative military weakness, lacking as they do a striking force of camels or horses. The concomitant of this reality is the high probability that the seminomad will engage in some form of limited agriculture. He is often sedentary for part of the year; fields and pasture are often interspersed; and the herd sizes relative to the human population are much smaller than in full nomadism. Accordingly, the seminomad will often appear to be an incipient peasant who has not yet attained his goal or a decadent farmer who has lapsed into a less secure life. In many cases, however, the seminomad regards his way of life as more satisfying than the softer and more politically fettered existence of the peasant. Traits of seminomadism appear frequently in the patriarchal stories concerning Abraham and Lot (Gen. 12:16; 13:2–12; 18:1–8; 20:14–15; 21:25–26), Isaac (Gen. 26:12–22), Jacob and Esau (Gen. 30:43; 31:17–18; 32:13–15; 33:18–20; 36:6–8), and Joseph (Gen. 37:2, 7; 42:1–5; 43:11; 46:31–34; 47:6). The precise nature of this type (or these types) of seminomadism is difficult to assess in that the movements are not strictly described as regular but are explained largely with reference to famine, intermarriage, religious pilgrimage, and conflicts within and between groups. The Israelites in Egypt are pictured as small stock breeders who also cultivate vegetable gardens (Ex. 10:24–26; 12:1–13, 31–34, 37–39; Num. 11:4–6). Living close to the Egyptian frontier with Sinai (Ex. 1:11; 9:26; 12:37), the holy place of their deity is located a three-day journey away in the desert (Ex. 3:18; 5:3; 8:24). Their relatively self-contained economy was threatened by the recent imperial policy which forced them to work on state building projects and in state-owned fields. One tradition has it that, as they departed Egypt with their flocks, the Israelites despoiled the Egyptians of jewelry and clothing in the manner of a nomadic razzia (Ex. 3:21–22; 12:35–36). In the wilderness the Israelites present a confused picture of a seminomadic people thrust suddenly into conditions where only well-provisioned travel parties or full nomads with camels might normally survive. The Israelites adjusted to this crisis by retaining their flocks for dairy products, wool, and hides. Occasional sacrifice of their animals provided some meat but food staples were supplied by improvising with quail and wild plant products ("manna"). Water was available from oasis to oasis. Even so they seem to have survived only because the Midianites, into whom Moses is said to have married, supplied them with knowledge of the terrain and with basic survival skills; at least some of these Midianites accompanied certain of the Israelite groups into Canaan (Ex. 2:15b–22; 3:1; 18:1ff.; Num. 10:29–32; Judg. 1:16; 4:11). Although unreported, it is reasonable to suppose that the Israelites cultivated small vegetable plots during the time they spent at the oases in the vicinity of Kadesh. All available evidence points to the fact that the component groups in the larger Israelite confederation in Canaan were predominantly agricultural and engaged in supplementary animal husbandry (cf. the laws of the Covenant Code, Ex. 20:24 (19)–23:9 and the descriptions of tribal life in Gen. 49 and Deut. 33). This type of economy characterized a large majority of the population in the highlands of Galilee, Gilead, Samaria, and Judah—the heartland of ancient Israel. However, a significant minority of Israelites, who lived in the semiarid regions to the east and south, sustained a seminomadic economy. A diminishing frequency of references to such seminomadic life in later biblical books suggests that the percentage of seminomadic Israelites relative to the total population steadily declined. Given the marginal rainfall of the land, however, and the abiding attraction of the steppe for certain individuals and groups, seminomadism never ceased in biblical times. In fact, the *Rechabites were one group who made a sectarian virtue of their seminomadism, identifying it with the pure form of Yahwism and refusing adamantly to build houses or to engage in viticulture or grain-growing (Jer. 35). According to one tradition these Rechabites were actual descendants of the Midianite-Kenite group into which Moses married (I Chron. 2:55). A more individualistic version of the tendency to equate holiness with seminomadic culture was the "consecration" of a person as a nazirite, perhaps originally associated with the spontaneous leadership of a war chieftain (Num. 6:1–21; Judg. 13:5, 7; 16:17). While such primitivist equations of Yahwism with seminomadism were not central to biblical traditions, it is nonetheless striking that many of the features of the early religion of Israel, although developed by a predominantly agricultural people, were powerfully indebted to nomadic influences, e.g., the belief that the original home of YHWH was in the wilderness and the decided preference for a mobile shrine over that of a fixed shrine.

CUSTOMS AND WAY OF LIFE. As a congeries of ethnically, geographically, economically, socially, and politically diverse people formed Israel in Canaan, they adopted a framework for their socioeconomic life which drew on the norms, institutions, and practices of pastoral nomadism, with suitable modifications to settled conditions. Among these abiding influences were the practice of blood revenge (Gen. 9:5–6; Num. 35:19; Judg. 8:18–21; II Sam. 3:30; 14:4–7; 21:1–14); protection of the integrity of the patriarchal family (Ex. 20:12, 14, 17; 21:15, 17; 22:15–16, 21; Lev. 18:6–18; Deut. 25:5–10); the institutions of the *ger*—the protected resident alien (e.g., Ex. 22:20; Deut. 10:19); and the asylum (Ex. 21:13–14; Num. 35; Deut. 19), related to the nomad law of hospitality and asylum. Instead of a primitivist attempt to construct seminomadism in Canaan, early Israel was a synthetic socioeconomic formation of loosely federated seminomadic and peasant populations arranged in a socially fictitious kinship network and cemented by a common cult of YHWH. The complex transformation and adaptation of the seminomadic elements in the Israelite confederation are reflected in the ambivalent biblical attitude toward the desert, which is sometimes idealized as the setting for an originally pure Yahwism but which is more often pictured as a place of rebellion and division, in itself a region of waste and horror, the quintessence of death and danger.

Yet another form of pastoral nomadism is transhumance which occurs in communities with developed agricultural specialization where herds are moved to select pastures for a part of the year by herders who specialize in their tasks. A common form of transhumance is to take the herds into mountain ranges for summer upland pasturage after the snows have melted. In Canaan transhumance took at least two forms. Immediately following the winter rains, herds were taken some distance into the steppes to feed on the temporary spring growth. As the summer wore on, and pasturage withered, they were taken to the better watered seaward-facing plains and mountain slopes. There are some biblical data which may be read as evidence for the practice of transhumance nomadism among the Israelites. Joseph and his brothers care for the flocks near Shechem and Dothan while Jacob remains at Hebron (Gen. 37:12–17). Nabal is a man of wealth in Maon whose hired men or slaves care for his large flocks at Carmel (I Sam. 25). Wealthy landowners in Transjordan provision the exiled David with agricultural and pastoral products (II Sam. 17:27–29; 19:31–32). The Job of the prose framework (Job. 1:1ff.; 42:12–17) is a wealthy farmer who also has thousands of domesticated animals cared for by his servants. The region of Bashan in northern Transjordan was well known as a prime cattle-breeding area, to which wealthy Israelites appear to have sent their flocks and herds (Ezek. 39:18; Amos 4:1; Ps. 22:13). Israelite kings capitalized on this process by appointing stewards over royal herds and flocks which were permanently located in the most attractive pastoral regions (II Sam. 13:23; I Chron. 27:28–30; II Chron. 26:10; 32:27–29).

In order to achieve a more exact socioeconomic characterization of early Israel, scholars will increasingly require expertise both in biblical studies and in ethnography and the social sciences. It is evident that the assumption that Arab Bedouin nomadism supplies the nearest surviving approximation to Israel's nomadism, while broadly apt, lacks all exactitude unless care is taken to distinguish among the various sub-forms and historical constellations of Bedouin existence.

It is necessary to reject the vague notion that full nomadism in the Arabian peninsula was the temporally original base for Middle Eastern socioeconomic evolutionary development. Far from full nomadism having been some simple state from which seminomadism and agriculture grew, almost precisely the opposite occurred in the Middle East over millennia of time as agriculture-originated animal domestication was introduced into the sparse conditions of the desert and was elaborated through the eventual introduction of the camel and the horse. Identification of the mutually illuminating affinities between Arab and Israelite nomadism must not obscure the complex web of cultural and historical factors at work in the two different contexts from age to age and from subregion to subregion.

Bibliography: K. Budde, *The New World,* 4 (1895), 726–45; M. de Goeje, in: EI, 1 (1913), 372–7; J. Flight, in: JBL, 42 (1923), 158–226; L. Febvre, *A Geographical Introduction to History* (1925), 261–94; A. Musil, *The Manners and Customs of the Rwala Bedouins* (1930); M. von Oppenheim, *Die Beduinen,* 1–3 (1939–53); S. Nystroem, *Beduinentum und Jahwismus* (1946); C. S. Coon et al., in: EI², 1 (1960), 872–92; de Vaux, Anc Isr, 3–15; A. Jeffery, in: IDB, 1 (1962), 181–4; C. Wolf, *ibid.,* 3 (1962), 558–60; D. Amiran and Y. Ben-Arieh, in: IEJ, 13 (1963), 161–81; S. Talmon, in: A. Altmann (ed.), *Biblical Motifs* (1966), 31–63; L. Krader, in: IESS, 11 (1968), 453–61; M. Sahlins, *Tribesmen* (1968), 32–39.

[N.K.G.]

NOMBERG, HERSH DAVID (1876–1927), Yiddish essayist and short story writer. Nomberg was born into a family of rabbis and Ḥasidim, in Mszczonow, a small town near Warsaw. Though he traveled widely, Nomberg was always associated with the Polish capital. After acquiring a thorough Jewish education at yeshivot and general knowledge through self-education, he joined the circle of I. L. *Peretz, to which Abraham *Reisen and Sholem *Asch also belonged, and remained an ardent and loyal disciple of Peretz, and one of the best interpreters of his works and philosophy. It was Peretz who persuaded Nomberg to write in Yiddish and his first poem in this language appeared in 1900. Nomberg wrote for the Warsaw Hebrew paper *Ha-Ẓofeh* (1903–05) and was, for a time, its editor. His first collection of Hebrew stories appeared in 1905, followed by five collections in Yiddish. It was under his influence and that of Peretz that the struggle between Hebraists and Yiddishists at the *Czernowitz Yiddish Conference in 1908 was resolved and a compromise resolution was adopted which proclaimed Yiddish as "a" (not "the") national language of the Jews.

The anonymous hero of his masterful, psychoanalytical tale *"Fligelman"* (1908) served as a symbol for the entire generation of this crucial period. Indeed, most of Nomberg's heroes can be characterized as "Fligel" (lit. "winged man").

Hersh David Nomberg, Yiddish writer. Jerusalem, J.N.U.L., Schwadron Collection.

After 1910 Nomberg almost entirely gave up belles-lettres for politics and journalism. In 1916, he was one of the founders of the Folkspartei ("People's Party") which advocated concentration on Jewish autonomous rights in Poland, though not opposing emigration to Ereẓ Israel. He served in 1919–20 as a member of the Polish Sejm.

Nomberg helped to provide a home for Jewish writers in Warsaw. He was the driving force behind the Society for Jewish Writers and Journalists and for many years its president. This society came to be better known as "Tlomatske 13," after the address of its building, a famed center of Yiddish cultural activity until its liquidation by the Nazis. Jewish audiences followed his perceptive articles, especially in the Warsaw Yiddish daily *Der Moment,* with which he was connected for a decade. When he died in 1927, tens of thousands of his readers accompanied him to his grave near that of his friend and preceptor Peretz. His was one of the few tombstones which survived Nazi destruction.

Bibliography: Rejzen, Leksikon, 2 (1929), 523–33; LNYL, 6 (1965), 160–8; S. Lestchinsky, *Literarishe Eseyen* (1938), 58–63; M. Ravitch, *Mayn Leksikon* (1945), 141–3; S. Mendelson, *Leben un Shafen* (1949), 169–76; J. J. Trunk, *Tsvishn Viln un Onmekhtikeyt* (1930); Jeshurin, in: *Oysgeklibene Shriftn* (1956), 236–52; Kressel, Leksikon, 2 (1967), 443.

[M.Rav.]

NONES, BENJAMIN (1757–1826), U.S. patriot and soldier during the American Revolution. Nones, who was born in Bordeaux, France, served as aide-de-camp to his former schoolmate, Marquis de Lafayette (1777), fought in Count Casimir Pulaski's legion during the defense of Charleston and was cited for bravery (1779), and served as aide to General Washington, holding the rank of major. After the Revolution, Nones settled in Philadelphia where he was variously employed as a broker and factor, a notary public, and as government interpreter for French, Spanish, and Portuguese. He was active in Republican politics and, in keeping with his abolitionist sympathies, freed his slaves after the Revolution. Nones served as president of Congregation Mikveh Israel in Philadelphia.

His son JOSEPH B. NONES (1797–1887) was wounded while serving as a midshipman in a battle against Algerian pirates in 1815. At the age of 70, he wrote a colorful account of his adventures in the Navy. He was a pioneer in processing concentrated foods, and in 1829 he proposed a program to combat scurvy in the Navy. In later life, he was an importer in Philadelphia.

Bibliography: Biogr Dict (1960), 135; AJHSP, 1 (1893), 111–5.

[AB.V.G.]

NORDAU, MAX (Simon Maximilian Suedfeld; 1849–1923), co-founder of the World Zionist Organization, philosopher, writer, orator, and physician. Born in Pest, the son of Rabbi Gabriel Suedfeld, Nordau received a traditional Jewish education and remained an observant Jew until his eighteenth year, when he became a militant naturalist and evolutionist. In 1875 he earned an M.D. degree at the University of Pest, and he settled in Paris in 1880 as a practicing physician. Nordau's career in journalism dates back to his childhood. In 1867 he joined the staff of the *Pester Lloyd*, and in time he became a correspondent for leading newspapers in the Western world, including the *Vossische Zeitung* in Berlin, the *Neue Freie Presse* in Vienna, and *La Nación* in Buenos Aires, Argentina.

Nordau achieved fame as a thinker and social critic with the publication of *Die Conventionellen Luegen der Kulturmenschheit* (1883; *The Conventional Lies of Our Civilization*, 1884). He sharply criticized "the religious lie," the corruption and oppression of monarchical and aristocratic regimes, the deceptions of political and economic establishments, and the hypocritical adherence to outworn sex mores. As an alternative he set forth what has been called his "philosophy of human solidarity." Nordau's "solidaritarianism" signifies the unity of mind and love. It insists on the intimate connection between free institutions and free inquiry in all areas of human concern. The *Lies* was translated into fifteen languages, including Chinese and Japanese. It raised a storm of controversy and was banned in Austria and Russia. It was followed by *Paradoxe der Conventionellen Luegen* (1885[3]; *Paradoxes*, 1896), which

Max Nordau, philosopher and Zionist. Courtesy Keren Hayesod, United Israel Appeal, Jerusalem.

discussed such topics as optimism and pessimism, passion and prejudice, social pressure and the power of love, sham and genuine success. This work also went through several editions and translations.

Even more controversial was *Entartung* (1892; *Degeneration*, 1895), in which Nordau subjected major figures and trends in European art and literature to scathing denunciation. Applying Cesare Lombroso's term "degeneracy" to the works of such men as Nietzsche, Tolstoy, Wagner, Zola, Ibsen, and such phenomena as symbolism, spiritualism, egomania, mysticism, Parnassianism, and diabolism, Nordau predicted the coming of a human catastrophe of unprecedented proportions. An entire literature developed over *Degeneration*, including a rebuttal in book form by George Bernard Shaw. More than 60 years after its first publication, *Degeneration* continued to be the subject of doctoral dissertations accepted by American universities; the book was republished in New York in 1968. Three other works merit perhaps even greater attention than the *Lies* and *Degeneration*. The first is *Der Sinn der Geschichte* (1909; *The Interpretation of History*, 1910), which examines man's advance from parasitism through supernaturalist illusion to knowledge and human solidarity. To Nordau, the purpose of man's history was to achieve a lessening of human suffering and to actualize "the ideal of goodness and selfless love." The second, *Biologie der Ethik* (1921; *Morals and the Evolution of Man*, 1922), is a treatise on the natural roots of ethics, the relations between the legal and the moral, and the meaning of "scientific ethics," which aims at the improvement of human life through the cultivation of the twin "solidaritarian" powers of intelligence and compassion. The third, *Der Sinn der Gesittung*; "The Essence of Civilization" (written in 1920), was published in 1932 in an unsatisfactory Spanish version. In this last, fragmentary work, Nordau advocated "the elevation of the independent local community, the free city-republic, to the general type of community" as the best means of redeeming the individual from his bondage. Nordau argued the case of "solidaritarian socialism," which assigns to private property its proper limits without, however, abolishing it. Nordau regarded Communism as entirely unacceptable and, in its Bolshevik form, as "socialism gone mad."

In the field of belles lettres, Nordau's major works are *Der Krieg der Millionen* (1882), *Die Krankheit des Jahrhunderts* (1888; *The Malady of the Century*, 1896), *Seelenanalysen* (1892), *Das Recht zu Lieben* (1894; *The Right to Love*, 1895), *Drohnenschlacht* (1898; *The Drones Must Die*, 1899); *Doktor Kohn* (1899; *A Question of Honor*, 1907); *Morganatisch* (1904; *Morganatic*, 1904), *The Dwarf's Spectacles, and Other Fairy Tales* (1905), and an unpublished biblical tragedy in four acts, *Rahab* (c. 1922).

The Jewish problem was never foreign to Nordau's thoughts. His revulsion against anti-Semitism is reflected in his essay on Jacques Offenbach entitled "The Political Hep! Hep!" included in *Aus dem wahren Milliardenlande* (an abridged translation entitled *Paris Sketches* appeared in 1884). In the *Lies* Nordau condemned hatred of the Jew as a symptom of the malady of the age. Nordau's upbringing, his piety toward his Orthodox parents (his observant mother lived in his house in Paris until her death in 1900), and the references to Jewish destiny in his general writings all show that the frequent charge of Nordau's alienation from Judaism in his pre-Zionist period is exaggerated.

Nordau met Theodor *Herzl in 1892. As Paris correspondents for German-language newspapers, they witnessed the manifestations of anti-Semitism in the French capital. In November 1895 Herzl discussed his idea of a Jewish state with Nordau, after Emil Schiff, a friend concerned over his mental condition, advised him to see a psychiatrist. Far from declaring Herzl insane, however, Nordau concluded the consultation by saying: "If you are insane, we are insane together. Count on me!" To Nordau, the idea of a Jewish state appeared as a most welcome means for the implementation of his "solidaritarian" philosophy by Jews in the land of the Jews.

At the First Zionist Congress (1897), Nordau drafted the famed *Basle Program. He served as vice-president of the First to the Sixth Zionist Congresses and as president of the

Seventh to the Tenth Congresses. In his famed addresses to these Congresses he surveyed the Jewish situation in the world and described and analyzed the physical and material plight of the Jews in Eastern Europe, as well as the moral plight of the emancipated and assimilated Western Jew, who had lost his contact with his fellow-Jews and faced political and social anti-Semitism, which excluded him from non-Jewish society. These addresses, together with his other Zionist pronouncements, became classics of Zionist literature. At the Congress of 1911 he warned that if current political trends persisted, six million Jews, i.e., those living in the Russian Empire and other East-European countries, were doomed to perish. He was convinced that only political Zionism could forestall the tragedy. Nordau passionately defended Herzl's political Zionism against *Aḥad Ha-Am's cultural Zionism, which he regarded as being pre-Zionist. He believed that his opponent's idea of a "spiritual center" would only obstruct the Zionist effort to rescue large masses of Jews in Ereẓ Israel. Citing a statement of the "cultural Zionists"—that "we are not concerned with Jews but with Judaism"—Nordau told the Sixth Zionist Congress, "'Judaism without Jews'—we know you, beautiful mask! Go with this phrase and join a meeting of spiritualists!"

In loyalty to Herzl, Nordau supported the *Uganda Scheme and coined the phrase *Nachtasyl* (night asylum) to stress the temporary nature of the proposal. He himself was convinced that the idea of a charter for Uganda was a grave error, because Jews who could not go to Palestine would prefer America or Australia. An assassination attempt in Paris, by a young anti-Ugandist, Chaim Selig Luban, who held Nordau responsible for the scheme, failed. Nordau himself defended Luban before the investigating judge.

In his last conversation with Nissan *Katzenelson, Herzl stated that Nordau should be his successor as president of the Zionist Organization, adding, "I can assure you that he will lead the cause at least as well as I did or better." Nordau, however, declined to serve as president when he was offered the post after Herzl's death; he chose to remain outside the organizational hierarchy. His opposition to the cultural Zionism espoused by Aḥad Ha-Am was only matched by his opposition to the practical Zionists led by Chaim *Weizmann. Nordau believed in political action rather than in small-scale, gradual agricultural colonization.

Nordau spent World War I in exile and in relative isolation in neutral Spain. He favored Vladimir *Jabotinsky's idea of a *Jewish Legion, but felt that the Zionist movement should remain neutral, since Zionists lived in countries on both sides of the international conflict. In 1920 he delivered his celebrated Albert Hall address in London, in which he told British statesmen and Zionist leaders that if the *Balfour Declaration of 1917 was to have meaning, that meaning must be made manifest by the swift creation of a Jewish majority and ensuing Jewish political independence in Palestine. In 1919, when a wave of pogroms swept the Ukraine and other parts of Russia, he began advocating the speedy transfer of 600,000 Jews to Palestine within a matter of months. The Zionist leadership rejected his proposal as unrealistic, and in 1921 Nordau retired from active Zionist work. He died in Paris in 1923 and was interred in the Old Cemetery in Tel Aviv in 1926. In the late 1930s, Jabotinsky was to name his own program for the speedy creation of a Jewish majority in Palestine by the mass transfer of Jews from the Diaspora "The Max Nordau Plan." [M.B.-H.]

His daughter MAXA NORDAU (1897–) was a French painter. She was born in Paris, where she studied under Jules Adler. In 1937 she painted mural decorations in the Palestine pavilion at the Paris international exhibition, and during World War II lived in the U.S. A conservative representational artist, her subjects included Israel landscapes, urban scenes, workyards, nudes, and portraits. Among her portraits are *Max Nordau*, *The Young David*, and *The Pioneers*. She illustrated books, including *Contes pour Maxa* by her father, and collaborated with her mother in writing *Max Nordau, a Biography* (1943). [ED.]

Bibliography: N. Sokolow, *History of Zionism*, 2 vols. (1919), index; A. and M. Nordau, *Max Nordau* (Eng., 1943); S. Schwartz, *Max Nordau be-Iggerotav* (1944); Ch. Weizmann, *Trial and Error*, (1949), index; M. P. Foster, *Reception of Max Nordau's 'Degeneration' in England and America* (Ph.D. diss., University of Michigan, 1954); M. Ben Horin, *Max Nordau, Philosopher of Human Solidarity* (1956); idem, *Common Faith—Uncommon People* (1970); M. Gold, *Nordau on Degeneration; A Study of the Book and its Cultural Significance* (Ph.D. diss., Columbia University, 1957); T. Herzl, *Complete Diaries*, ed. and tr. by R. Patai, 5 (1960), index; M. Heyman, *The Minutes of the Zionist Council, The Uganda Controversy*, 1 (1970).

NORDEN, family of South African pioneers (mid-19th century), consisting of five brothers—Benjamin, Joshua Davis, Marcus, Samuel, and Harry. They were among the 18 Jewish members of the party of settlers sent out by the British government in 1820 to the turbulent frontier of the eastern Cape Colony. The 1820 settlers endured great privations in a wild country exposed to depredations by African tribesmen. After some years many of them, including the Nordens, settled the small towns which had sprung up. BENJAMIN NORDEN (1798–1875), a man of adventurous nature, traveled into the interior, engaged in the ivory trade, and had dealings with the Zulu king, Dingaan. He was a friend of the Boer voortrekker leader, Piet Retief. Norden was interested in plans for the development of Delagoa Bay and Port Elizabeth and joined in a gold prospecting venture. In 1840 he moved from Grahamstown, where he had a trading store with his brother MARCUS, to Cape Town and was associated with the De Pass family in exploiting the guano deposits on the west coast. In Cape Town he was active in civic affairs and was one of the municipal commissioners. He took the lead in forming Cape Town's first Hebrew congregation, Tikvath Israel (1841). When the first synagogue was built in 1849 Norden was president, holding the office until 1857 when he returned to England. JOSHUA DAVIS NORDEN (1803–1846) settled in Grahamstown as an auctioneer after leaving his frontier farm. Like his brother, he served as a municipal commissioner and was leader of the Jewish community. To defend the town from attacks by tribesmen he raised and captained the Grahamstown Yeomanry, which bore his name. In 1846 he was killed at the head of his men in a skirmish during the War of the Axe, one of a long series of "Kaffir wars." As a tribute to his "intrepidity and bravery," his former comrades erected a plaque to his memory on a wall of St. George's Cathedral, Grahamstown. A third Norden brother, SAMUEL, was killed while leading a charge in the Basuto War (1858).

Bibliography: L. Herrman, *History of the Jews in South Africa* (1935), index; G. Saron and L. Hotz, *Jews in South Africa* (1955), index; JC (July 24, 1846), repr. in: *Jewish Affairs* (March, 1953), 23–25; Mendelssohn, in: JHSET, 7 (1915), 192–4; Rosenthal, in: *Zionist Record* (South African, Sept. 30, 1932). [L.Ho.]

NORDHAUSEN, city in Thuringia, E. Germany. The earliest documentary evidence for the presence of Jews in Nordhausen dates from 1290, and by 1300 a Jewish community had come into being. Shortly thereafter a *Judenstrasse*, *mikveh*, and synagogue were established. A Jewish well is noted in records dating from 1322 and a cemetery is mentioned in 1334. During the course of a disturbance in 1324, the community's synagogue was destroyed. The Jews of the period made their living primarily through moneylending, and their sound economic position brought more Jewish immigrants into the city. In 1333 the municipal council agreed to the adjudication of all disputes between Jews by the rabbinic court. During the course of the *Black Death persecutions of 1349, however, a number of Jews suffered martyrdom. Frederick the Brave was partly responsible for deaths of Jews during this period. (A legendary account published in a Worms prayer book indicates that the entire Jewish community went dancing to its death, willingly submitting to the funeral pyre.) Although refugees from the persecutions fled to *Erfurt and *Frankfort, by 1350 at least one Jew had already returned to resettle in Nordhausen. Abandoned Jewish property was transferred by King *Charles VI to Count Henry von Hohlstein. Despite the upheaval and loss of life and property, by the end of the century a small Jewish community had reestablished itself in Nordhausen, holding its religious services in a private house. In 1391 King *Wenceslaus released the burghers from their debts to the Jews on payment of a fee to the royal chamber.

A small number of Jews continued to live in Nordhausen during the 15th century. In the 16th century they were subject to increasingly restrictive legislation and they were finally expelled in 1559. They settled in the surrounding towns, however, and continued to trade; the right to trade in Nordhausen itself was granted in 1619. By 1630 there were four **Schutzjuden* ("protected Jews") in the city; in the 18th century, however, no Jews were left. A modern community came into being only in 1808, after Nordhausen was annexed by *Westphalia. By 1817 there were 74 Jews in the city; in 1822 there were 100; in 1840 the number was 210; and in 1880, 494. A new cemetery was consecrated in 1827 and enlarged in 1854. The first rabbi in Nordhausen was Nathan Meyer, who assumed his post in 1817. A synagogue was dedicated in 1845 and the community was officially recognized in 1847. Among the prominent members of the community in the 19th century was the banker and philanthropist Jacob Plaut (1816–1901). From 1908 until 1925 the community was served with distinction by Rabbi Alfred Sepp. In 1925 the community numbered 438, in 1933 it had 394 members, five cultural and philanthropic organizations, and a religious school. In 1939, under the pressure of Nazi persecution and consequent emigration, the number of Jews declined to 128, and the community came to an end during World War II.

Bibliography: Germ Jud, 1 (1963), 247; 2 (1968), 590–3; H. Stern, *Geschichte der Juden in Nordhausen* (1927); S. Neufeld, *Die Juden im thueringisch-saechsischen Gebiet waehrend des Mittelalters* (1917), passim; E. Carmoly, in: *Der Israelit*, nos. 4–8 (1866); *Der Orient*, 9 (1848), 48, 80; AZJ, 37 (1873), 127–8; A. Lewinsky, in: MGWJ, 49 (1905), 746–51; FJW, 118–9. [A.Sha.]

NORFOLK, maritime metropolis of S.E. Virginia with a Jewish population of 8,500. The first-known Jewish settler in Norfolk, Moses Myers (1752–1835), arrived in 1787 and erected a handsome home, today a leading point of interest. An 1820 cemetery was abandoned when mid-century German immigration led to the purchase of a Hebrew cemetery. The original congregation, founded in 1848, subsequently subdivided as Ohev Sholom (1876), Reform, and Beth El (1870), Conservative. East European immigration produced a number of Orthodox congregations, now united as B'nai Israel. Post-World War II population growth from the North created Conservative Temple Israel. Norfolk society, both within and outside Jewry, remained highly stratified until the 1950s. Social anti-Semitism was strong. As a consequence, few Jews took public office, preferring to demonstrate leadership in nonsectarian charities.

The Moses Myers Mansion, home of the first Jewish settler in Norfolk, Virginia. Courtesy American Jewish Archives, Cincinnati, Ohio. Photo Craftsman, Inc., Norfolk.

Norfolk's Jews evolved slowly from predominantly mercantile occupations to those in the professions and services catering to the city's huge naval base. During World War II Norfolk was overwhelmed by the influx of armed-forces population. The Jewish community met this challenge with a successful service club at Brith Sholom Center, now continued at the expanding Jewish Community Center. Outstanding in Norfolk's economic growth have been David Lowenberg (1839–1909), a real estate and civic promoter, and Charles L. Kaufman (1896–), attorney and developer of community rehabilitation, the hospital, and the college. Since 1960 most exclusive clubs have disappeared, and Jewish community life is flourishing with enlarged synagogue and center facilities, as well as extensive support for Jewish philanthropies. Jews are also playing an expanding role in encouraging cultural endeavors.

Bibliography: M. H. Stern, in: *Journal of the Southern Jewish Historical Society* (Nov. 1958), 5–13; (Nov. 1963), 12ff. [M.H.St.]

NORMAN, EDWARD ALBERT (1900–1955), U.S. financier and philanthropist. Norman, who was born in Chicago, attended the U.S. Military Academy at West Point before transferring to Harvard. He worked for *The Survey* (1924–25) and as a research secretary for the Cooperative League of the U.S. (1925–28) before assuming the management of his family's various financial interests. Although a non-Zionist, Norman was extremely interested in the welfare of Palestine and its people and he urged a roof organization to coordinate and funnel the American Jewish aid for Palestinian educational, cultural, and social service institutions. The result was the founding of the American Fund for Israel Institutions (1939), of which Norman was president at his death (see *American-Israel Cultural Foundation).

His other posts in Jewish organizational and communal life included president of the American Economic Commission for Palestine (1939–43); national secretary for the American Jewish Committee (1946–55); non-Zionist member of the Jewish Agency's Executive Council; governor of the Hebrew University (1949–55); and director of the Joint Distribution Committee (1936–55). Norman was also president of the Group Farming Research Institute (1940–55), founded for the purpose of studying cooperative systems throughout the world; treasurer of the Urban League (1928–38); and chairman of the finance commission of the Association of American Indian Affairs. [Ed.]

NORONHA (Loronha), FERNÃO DE (?1470–?1540), New Christian explorer and colonizer of Brazil. Noronha was head of the first of the Portuguese *donatários*, associations formed to lease land for development in Brazil, and his association was composed of *New Christians. Arriving in Brazil in 1503 with six ships, troops, and supplies, he discovered an island near the north coast of the country which he named São João, although it was generally known by his name. Following the terms of his contract, he explored and colonized large areas of Brazil, exploiting them for the benefit of his company. In return for his services, King Manuel I named him Knight of the Crown in 1504 and granted him the captaincy for life of the island he discovered. According to a report of 1505 by the Venetian Lunardo Chá Masser, Noronha acted as the Lisbon agent for the senate of Venice and was a pioneer in the import and export of timber, receiving a monopoly on dyewood from the crown. His contract, originally for three years, was apparently extended to 1512 or 1515. Noronha appears to have been a wealthy Jew, close to the court, who had converted to Christianity prior to 1497. He took his surname from his godfather, a nobleman descended from the royal house of Castile.

Bibliography: A. Wiznitzer, *Jews in Colonial Brazil* (1960), 5–8; S. Leite, *Os judeus no Brasil* (1923).

[MA.C.]

NORTHAMPTON, town in central England. Its Jewish community, first mentioned in the 12th century, was one of the most important in medieval England. In 1194 representatives of Anglo-Jewry were summoned there to apportion among themselves a levy of 5,000 marks for ransoming Richard I from captivity (The Northampton Donum). Northampton had its own *archa. Though expelled from Northamptonshire in 1237, Jews were allowed to remain in Northampton itself. In 1263 they were attacked by the baronial rebels and took refuge in the castle. A ritual murder accusation occurred apparently in 1277, the repercussions and consequences of which were much exaggerated by historians. Several local Jews were executed in London in 1278 for coin-clipping. The community continued in existence until the expulsion of 1290. R. *Isaac b. Perez of Northampton was one of the most distinguished medieval Anglo-Jewish scholars. A small community was established at the end of the 19th century and in 1969 numbered approximately 300.

Bibliography: B. L. Abrahams, in: JHSET, 2 (1894–95), 85, 98; I. Abrahams, in: JHSEM, 1 (1925), lix lxxiv; A. J. Collins, in: JHSET, 15 (1946), 151–64; Roth, England, index; E. E. Urbach, in: *Essays ... Israel Brodie* (1967), 11, 15f. (Hebrew section); J. Ḥazzan, *Eẓ Ḥayyim*, ed. by I. Brodie, 1 (1962), 150, 163; 2 (1964), 203.

[C.R.]

NORTH CAROLINA, state in S.E. U.S. Its population in 1970 was 6,000,000, of which there was an estimated Jewish population (1970) of 10,000.

Early History. North Carolina was among the first of the 13 colonies explicitly to welcome Jewish settlement. In the *Fundamental Constitutions* for the Carolinas, composed by the philosopher John Locke in 1668, it was expressly stated that the colony was to be open to settlement by "Jews, heathens, and other dissenters," and that "any seven or more persons agreeing in any religion shall constitute a church or profession." The earliest Jews to establish residence in North Carolina came from the Barbados and were of Spanish-Portuguese origin.

Since early Jewish settlers established the indigo trade in America, in which North Carolina was active, it seems fair to assume that many of these traders and exporters were established along the North Carolina seacoast by the late 17th century. The earliest Jewish name of record, however, is that of Aaron Moses, who appears as a witness to a will in

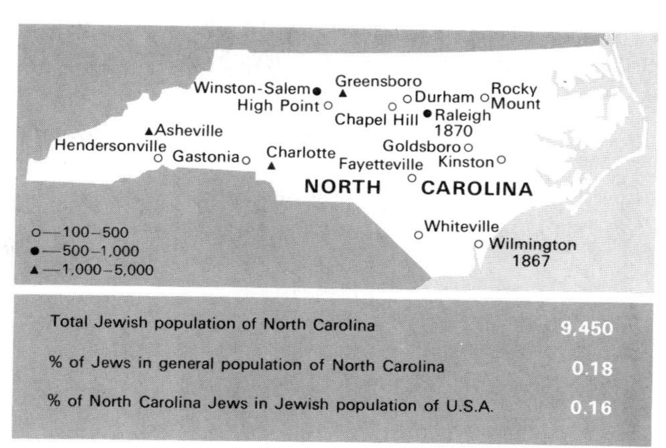

Jewish communities in North Carolina and dates of establishment. Population figures for 1968.

1740. In 1750 David David petitioned for a grant of 180 acres of land at New Hanover. The petition was granted, and in 1752 David appears on the muster roll of the New Hanover county militia. During the Revolutionary War the volunteers for Washington's army from North Carolina include the names of Aaron Cohen of Albemarle, J. Nathan of Charlotte, and Sigmund Freudenthal of New Hanover, as well as of several other probable Jews. Records of political and commercial activities at the beginning of the 19th century reveal names of North Carolina Jews. Jacob *Mordecai established the first private school for girls in the South at Warrenton, in 1809. One of his sons, George Washington Mordecai, was the first president of the Bank of North Carolina and was instrumental in building the Raleigh and Gaston Railroad. Among North Carolina Jews to serve in the Civil War were the six Cohen brothers who fought in the 40th Infantry. The first Jew to be killed in the Confederate ranks was Albert Lurie Moses of Charlotte, who died heroically at the Battle of Seven Pines. A monument stands over his grave in Columbus, Georgia. Paradoxically, despite its early adoption of religious toleration, North Carolina was one of the last states in the Union to admit Jews legally to public office. A constitutional provision forbidding officials who denied "the truth of the Protestant religion, or the divine authority of either the Old or New Testament" remained in effect until the second half of the 19th century. In actual practice, however, Catholics, Jews, Quakers, and Deists held offices of a public nature long before the article's repeal. One of the earliest test cases involved a Jew, Jacob *Henry, who was elected to the state legislature in 1808. A year later Henry's seat was challenged by an opponent as violating the state constitution; after an eloquent defense in his own behalf, he was allowed to keep his seat on a technicality. In the end, the disability clause was formally repealed under the constitutional influence of Great Britain. Catholics were admitted to the British House of Commons in 1828, Jews in 1858, and atheists in 1884, and North Carolina followed these precedents in almost perfect chronological order.

Jewish Immigration. The Jews who came to North Carolina in the second half of the 19th century, like those in all other sections of the eastern seaboard, were mostly immigrants from Germany who turned in large numbers to the one profession universally open to them: peddling. The Cherokee Indians of North Carolina commonly referred to such Jews as "egg-eaters," the reason perhaps being that many of these peddlers adhered to the Jewish dietary laws and avoided meat of any kind until they returned to their "home base" on Friday evening in time to observe the Sabbath. For Virginia and the Carolinas, the main source of merchandise supply for these peddlers was in Baltimore,

Temple Emanuel, Winston-Salem, North Carolina. Courtesy Union of American Hebrew Congregations, Cincinnati, Ohio.

but within each state peddlers had "way stations" where they stored small stocks and which they called "home for the Sabbath." In North Carolina these stations were at Wilmington, Albemarle, and Yanceyville. Often these way stations turned into permanent homes. An 1860 issue of the New York *Hebrew Leader* included the advertisement: "Wanted by the Israelites of Wilmington, North Carolina, Hazan, Schocket, Mohel [cantor, ritual slaughterer, and circumciser]."

Eventually, North Carolina's first congregation was established in Wilmington in 1867 and formally incorporated as The Temple of Israel in 1873. Other "way stations" followed. In time many Jewish peddlers became storeowners and merchants, and a considerable number acquired great wealth and distinction, such as Joseph *Fels, founder of the Fels Naphtha Company. The most spectacular of such success stories was that of the *Cone brothers, Moses Henry and Caesar, who built one of the South's greatest textile complexes in Greensboro. The Cones were the first in the cotton industry to organize worldwide distribution, and were also pioneers in the establishment of a comprehensive welfare program for their employees. After 1880 a smattering of East-European Jews began to settle in North Carolina and the number increased in the first decade of the 20th century when the rolling mills and textile plants were at their most prosperous. Jewish merchants established retail businesses in practically every city and town in the state. One of the reasons for their success was their more liberal attitude toward Negro customers, who preferred to buy in their shops. By 1910 there were five Jewish congregations in the state and a YMHA in Asheville. In 1927 there were 8,100 Jews in the state out of a total population of 3,100,000; by 1970 the non-Jewish population had doubled while the number of Jews had increased by less than 25 percent, a figure in accordance with the general reluctance of Jews in more recent decades to settle in predominantly rural areas.

Contemporary Jewry. In 1970 there were 27 synagogues in the state, 20 with full-time rabbis in Asheville, Charlotte, Durham, Fayetteville, Gastonia, Goldsboro, Greensboro, Hendersonville, Hickory, High Point, Jacksonville, Lumberton, New Bern, Raleigh, Rocky Mount, Salisbury, Weldon, Whiteville, Wilmington, and Winston-Salem. North Carolina was also the only state in the U.S. to maintain a "circuit-rider," a Jewish lay leader entrusted with visiting scattered communites unable to maintain a synagogue or rabbi of their own. The state's largest Jewish community, numbering 1,750, was in Greensboro, followed by Asheville, Charlotte, and Winston-Salem. Charlotte, Greensboro, and High Point maintained Jewish federation and welfare funds, and there was a Jewish community center in Asheville. A number of Jews have played prominent roles in 20th-century North Carolina civic and commercial life. In politics, there have been Jewish mayors in Greensboro, Durham, Fayetteville, and Gastonia, and several Jewish judges and state legislators. Moses Richter (d. 1969) amassed great wealth in the textile industry and

A pictorial record of one of the attempts to establish a Jewish settlement in North Dakota at the end of the 19th century. It shows prospective settlers at the Missouri River, some established homesteads, and a list of 40 settlers. From M. Schappes, *A Pictorial History of the Jews in the United States,* 1958.

the peach trade, much of which he gave to philanthropic causes. The author and journalist Harry *Golden published the *Carolina Israelite* which for many years was one of the most outspoken liberal organs in the South and a consistent, if often locally unpopular, champion of desegregation and civil rights. [H.Go.]

NORTH DAKOTA, state located in the upper Midwestern part of U.S. The total population (1968) of 652,000 includes 1,200 Jewish residents. In 1882, seven years before statehood, Baron de Hirsch's Jewish Colonization Association organized the area's first Jewish settlement on the shore of the Missouri River, northwest of the present capital at Bismarck. Although reports differ as to the number of families who settled in this agricultural colony, it is probable that the total did not exceed 25. Poor weather conditions and a large prairie fire caused crop failures in 1883 and 1885. By 1901 only three families remained. Outside help and the continued need to settle immigrants increased the number of families to 42 by 1906 and 250 by 1912. Another colony, fifteen miles north of Devil's Lake, failed to attract many settlers.

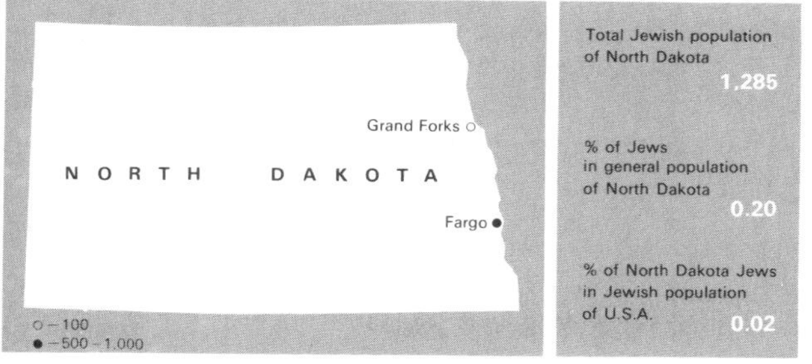

Jewish communities in North Dakota. Population figures for 1968.

By 1889 the country's growing railroad industry lured people to the eastern community of Grand Forks. A permanent congregation was established in 1892. It was from the pulpit of Bnai Israel Synagogue that President Willian McKinley urged the Jews to participate in the war with Spain. The city of Fargo also grew near the turn of the century and by 1896 a synagogue was chartered there. In the 1960s Fargo, the state's largest city, claimed a Jewish population of 500 people. One Reform congregation serves most of the families. The Jews of North Dakota are engaged mainly in retailing. A few, such as Fargo Mayor Herschel Lashkowitz, and Federal Judge Myron Bright, distinguished themselves in politics. [R.M.B.]

NORWALK, U.S. town in southwest Connecticut on Long Island Sound. In 1968 of an estimated total population of 73,000, the Jewish community comprised 5,200–5,400. As early as 1760 there was a small Jewish community in Norwalk. Michael Judah is mentioned in the Connecticut historical annals of that period, and David Judah was a soldier in the Connecticut Line in 1776. In 1776 Norwalk received an influx of Jews from New York, mainly from Congregation Shearith Israel, who were fleeing the British. In 1777 Jews were among the signatories to a petition asking for a patrol vessel for the Norwalk shore. The early community came to an end when Norwalk was burned down by the British in 1779. It was rebuilt in the 1870s by Eastern European immigrants, who were merchants and storekeepers. After 1925 more Jewish families from New York moved to Norwalk, and after World War II many more Jewish families moved to Norwalk in the general move to suburbia and in response to the development of Norwalk as an electronics and engineering center.

Beth Israel Congregation, Orthodox, founded in 1906, was the first synagogue in Norwalk and remained the only one until 1934, when Temple Beth El, Conservative, was organized. The Reform Temple Shalom was formed in 1957. Shortly after World War I, a Young Men's Hebrew Association was founded; it later became the Jewish Community Center. Norwalk has a communal Hebrew school. The United Jewish Appeal drives are sponsored by the Jewish Community Council, formed shortly after World War II to coordinate the efforts of local organizations and fund-raising campaigns.

Participation in community life is extensive. About two-thirds of the Jewish families of Norwalk are affiliated with at least one synagogue; almost 40 percent of the Jewish families belong to the Norwalk Jewish Center; and two-thirds of the adult Jews of Norwalk contribute to the Federated United Appeal Drive. Small Jewish populations in Wilton, Weston, Darien, and Georgetown also participate in Norwalk's Jewish communal life.

Prominent members of the Norwalk Jewish community have included Harry Becker, who was superintendent of schools 1952–70; Malcolm Tarlov, the 1967 national president of the Jewish War Veterans; Charles Salesky, who was president of the Hat Corporation of America; and Jack Rudolph, state senator in 1970. Several chairmen of the Board of Education have been Jewish as well. Employment appears free of anti-Jewish discrimination, but there is discrimination in upper-class social clubs. [ED.]

NORWAY, kingdom in N. Europe. Throughout the 17th and 18th centuries, when Norway and *Denmark were united, most general regulations concerning the Jews of Denmark also applied in Norway. However, according to the Norwegian Legal Code promulgated by King Christian V in 1687 the Jews were barred from admission to Norway without a letter of safe-conduct; lacking this a Jew risked arrest, fines, and deportation. As a result of this measure the special regulations allowing free access to the so-called

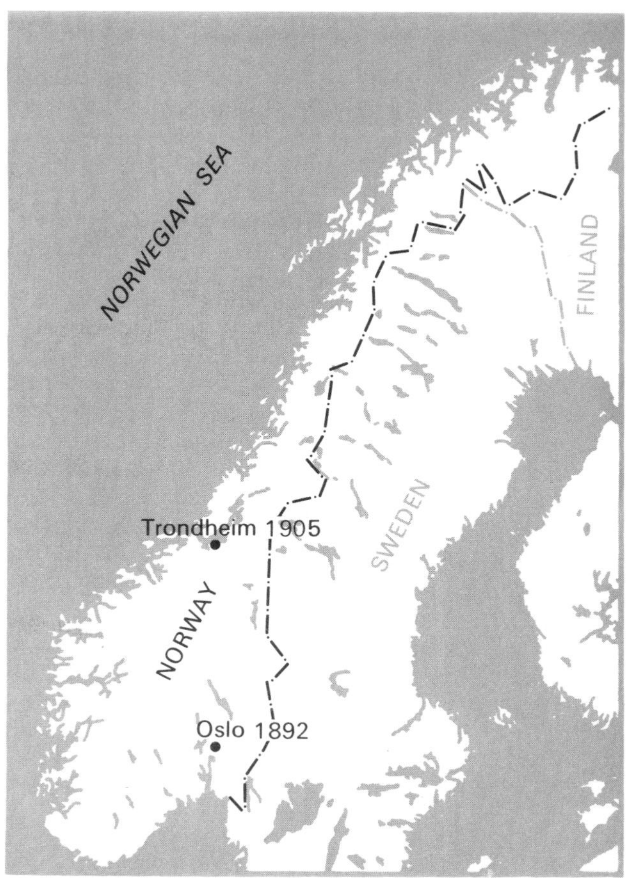

Jewish communities in Norway and dates of establishment.

The synagogue of Trondheim, Norway, the northernmost synagogue in the world. The building was originally a railroad station Courtesy F. Mendelsohn, Trondheim.

"Portuguese" Jews (issued by the Danish crown in 1657, renewed in 1670, 1684, and 1750) were not consistently adhered to by the Norwegian authorities. An incident which took place in 1734 became notorious: three Dutch "Portuguese" Jews were arrested on their arrival in the country and spent two months in prison. In the 17th and 18th centuries, few Jews stayed in Norway, usually only temporarily, though some Jews in other countries had business connections there, such as Manuel *Teixeira from Hamburg who was co-owner of Norwegian mines. Despite the liberal tenor of the Norwegian constitution of 1814, Article Two—stating that Lutheran Protestantism is the official state religion in which all Lutheran children must be brought up—confirmed the exclusion of Jews from Norway; this was strictly enforced. In 1817 a shipwrecked Jew was thrown into jail and then deported. In the 1830s, however, a more liberal spirit gradually became apparent. The government issued letters of safe conduct from time to time; one was given to Heinrich *Heine's uncle, Solomon *Heine, who was instrumental in the granting of a loan to the Norwegian state by the Copenhagen banking house of Hambro and Son. In 1844 the Ministry of Justice confirmed the free immigration rights of "Portuguese" Jews.

The repeal of the ban on Jewish settlement was largely the result of the efforts of the writer Henrik *Wergeland. In 1839 he submitted his first proposal to the Storting, the Norwegian parliament, accompanying his proposal by a lengthy memorandum and publishing his essay on the Jewish question, *Indlaeg i Jødensagen* (1841). This was followed by numerous articles in the press, several of them by Wergeland himself. In 1842 a committee on the constitution dealing with the problem made a notable proposal in which it was stated that the right to free immigration was an international one. The motion to give the Jews free access received a simple majority, i.e., more than 50% of the vote, in 1842, 1845, and 1848, but did not obtain the requisite two-thirds majority until 1851. In that year 93 votes were cast in favor of admitting the Jews with full civil rights, with ten votes against.

The First Communities. The first Jew settled in the country the following year, but few followed him for many years; in 1875 only 25 Jews had their permanent residence in Norway. After 1880 immigration increased considerably, and Eastern European Jews gradually became most numerous. In 1890 there were 214 Jews in Norway; ten years later there were 642, most of them in *Oslo, the capital, and in Trondheim, where a community developed in the 1890s. The oldest communities, called "The Mosaic Congregation," were founded in Oslo in 1892 and in Trondheim in 1905; both congregations are still in existence. Land for a cemetery was bought in Oslo as early as 1869, and the first burial took place in 1885. For some years there were several other congregations in the capital. In the years before and during World War I, young people's associations, women's groups, Zionist associations, and charitable societies were established in Oslo and Trondheim. A *B'nai B'rith lodge was founded in Oslo in 1952. The two synagogues in Oslo and Trondheim still in use today were consecrated in 1920 and 1925 respectively. A second synagogue in Oslo, dedicated in 1921, has not been in use since World War II. The highest number of Jewish inhabitants, 1,457, was recorded by the census of 1920. For many years most Norwegian Jews engaged in trade; gradually they also went into industry and some entered the professions. Between 1930 and 1940 immigration was comparatively slight. [O.M.]

Holocaust Period. The Jews of Norway, whose number in 1940 was estimated at 1,700–1,800, were hard hit during the German occupation in World War II (April 1940–May 1945). They included only a few refugees from central European countries, some 200 in number, since Norway restricted the entry of Jewish refugees even more than Denmark and Sweden. Already in October 1940 Jews were prohibited to exercise academic and other professions. In some regions the actual persecution of the Jews began in 1941, but only in the fall of 1942 did it become countrywide. In two raids, on October 25 for all men over 16 and on November 25 for women and children, 770 Jews were seized and shipped via Stettin to *Auschwitz. About 930 Jewish inhabitants succeeded in fleeing to Sweden, while about 60 others were interned in Norway proper. Very few Jews remained in hiding, in hospitals, sanatoria, or in the Jewish old-age home. Victims of the war, 60% of whom were men (two-thirds of whom were citizens of Norway), totalled 760. Twenty persons perished either through acts of war or were shot in Norway. Of those deported 740 were killed in extermination camps and only 12 returned. The Germans inflicted heavy damage on the synagogue in Trondheim, and planned to obliterate the Jewish cemetery there. The physical persecution of the Jews by the Germans was facilitated by orders given by *Quisling's government for the forced registration of all Jews (June 1942) and the confiscation of all Jewish property (October 1942). The bishops of Norway sent a letter on Nov. 11, 1942, in protest to Quisling. It was also signed by the other Protestant churches of Norway. The letter, in denunciation of the illegal acts, states: "God does not differentiate among people . . . Since the Lutheran religion is the state religion, the state cannot enact any law or decree which is in conflict with the Christian faith or the Church's confession." The letter was read on Dec. 6 and 13, 1942, from the pulpit and was quoted in the 1943 New Year message. The Norwegian people, with the guidance of its underground, to the best of their capability helped Jews to escape to Sweden, often at the risk of their own lives. [L.Y.]

Contemporary Period. Most of the survivors of the Holocaust, about 800 in number, returned to Norway from Sweden after the war. The Norwegian government was eager to demonstrate the sympathy of the Norwegian people toward the suffering Jewish people. A 1946 offer to grant asylum to unaccompanied Jewish children from the *Displaced Persons camps in Germany was turned down by the central committee of the DPs, which insisted that the surviving children be raised in Ereẓ Israel. Another offer to grant residence to about 1,000 Jewish DPs, and thus make up for the loss in Jewish population caused by the deportations, met with a more positive response. About 400 Jewish DPs came to Norway in 1947, but many left after some time for North America or Israel. With the abolition of the DP camps in Germany in the 1950s, Norway accepted several scores of "hardcore" cases. By the mid-1950s the Jewish population reached close to 1,000 souls, of whom over 700 resided in Oslo, about 150 in Trondheim, and the rest were scattered over the country.

The communities in Oslo and Trondheim were reconstituted: Orthodox services were conducted in the synagogues; social work, supported by the *American Jewish Joint Distribution Committee and the *Conference on Jewish Material Claims, was expanded; a community center was opened in Oslo in 1960; a home for the aged exists in Oslo; the small community participates in all activities for Israel; 80 school-age children receive regular religious instruction in Oslo and Trondheim; and a *B'nai B'rith lodge was established in Oslo in 1952.

The Norwegian government, the church, and all political parties have been actively engaged in eradicating anti-Semitism. Pro-Israel sentiments are very strong and found their expression in many deeds. At the beginning of 1949, the Norwegian Relief Organization brought 200 Jewish children, destined for *Youth Aliyah, from North Africa to Norway for a rehabilitation period of eight months. All but one in a second group of 29 children from Tunisia perished in an airplane crash on Nov. 25, 1949. A village of immigrants from North Africa, Yanuv, was established in the Sharon Plain in Israel in their memory; the Norwegian public contributed one million kroner (about $150,000) toward the establishment of the village. Staunch supporters of Israel in Norway included Trygve Lie, first secretary-general of the United Nations; the late leader of the Conservative Party, Carl Joachim Hambro; Odd Nansen (the son of Fridtjof Nansen), who continued the humanitarian work of his father in many fields; the leaders of the Labor Party, Einar Gerhardsen, Trygve Brattelli, Jens Christian Hange, Halvard Lange, Haaron Lie, Aase Lionaes, Finn Moe, and Martin Tranmachl; the outstanding scholars Francis Bull (literature), S. Mowinckel (Bible), Gunnar Randers (physics); and many others. Leading Norwegian personalities have also repeatedly intervened on behalf of Soviet Jewry, as well as on behalf of persecuted Jews in Arab countries.

Relations with Israel. Norway voted for the establishment of a Jewish state in 1947, and Trygve Lie, as secretary-general of the United Nations, used all his diplomatic skill to remove obstacles to the adoption of the resolution. Diplomatic relations between Norway and Israel were soon established, first through nonresident ministers, with the Israel envoy in Stockholm and the Norwegian envoy in Athens serving in that capacity, and since 1961 on the level of resident ambassadors. At the United Nations, Norway frequently came out in suppòrt of Israel. The friendly relations found expression in great celebrations of Israel's tenth anniversary and in official visits by prime ministers, foreign ministers, and of other public figures. The Norwegian General Odd Bull served as highly respected Chief of the United Nations Truce Supervision Organization from 1963 to 1970. A cultural agreement between the two countries, signed in 1956, has been instrumental in fostering scientific cooperation and cultural and artistic exchange. Tourism between Norway and Israel expanded considerably. Trade also developed satisfactorily, with Israel exporting $3,000,000–$3,500,000 annually, mainly in citrus fruit and products, yarn, tires, and fertilizers. Norwegian exports to Israel in normal years amount to a similar scope in fish, aluminum, and pulp, but in some years, 1968 for example, reached over $28,000,000 in refrigerator boats. [CH.Y]

See Israel, *Foreign Policy.

Bibliography: H. M. Koritzinsky, *Jødernes historie i Norge* (1927); O. Mendelsohn, *Jødernes historie i Norge* (1969). HOLOCAUST PERIOD: H. Valentin, in: YIVOA, 8 (1953), 224–34, passim; B. Höye and T. M. Ager, *The Fight of the Norwegian Church Against Nazism* (1943); *Eduyyot Ha-Yo'eẓ ha-Mishpati la-Memshalah Neged Adolf Eichmann* (1963), 475–80; J. M. Snoek, in: *The Grey Book* (1969), 116–9.

NORWICH, county town of Norfolk, E. England. The medieval Jewish community is first mentioned in 1144, when the discovery of the body of a boy, William of Norwich, in a wood near the town gave rise to the first recorded *blood libel in Europe. Although this apparently had no immediate effect on the community, there were attacks by citizens on the Jews in the 1230s, the one in 1234 following an accusation that the Jews had kidnapped and circumcised a Christian child. The descendants of *Jurnet of Norwich, who were financiers, patrons of learning, and scholars, dominated the community from 1160 to 1260: the lower part of their stone house still stands in King Street (as part of the "Music House"). The 13th-century community (numbering about 100 to 150) seems, from the considerable documentary evidence surviving, mainly to have consisted of financiers who lent to local traders and the rural gentry and villagers. The community suffered from the "coin-clipping" charges of 1279 and the execution for blasphemy of the local magnate, Abraham fil'Deulecresse; by the time of the general expulsion from England in 1290, it numbered only 50 souls. The poems of *Meir b. Elijah of Norwich (c. 1244) have survived, mainly in a Vatican manuscript.

Individual Jews settled in Norwich in the first half of the 18th century and there was an organized community by

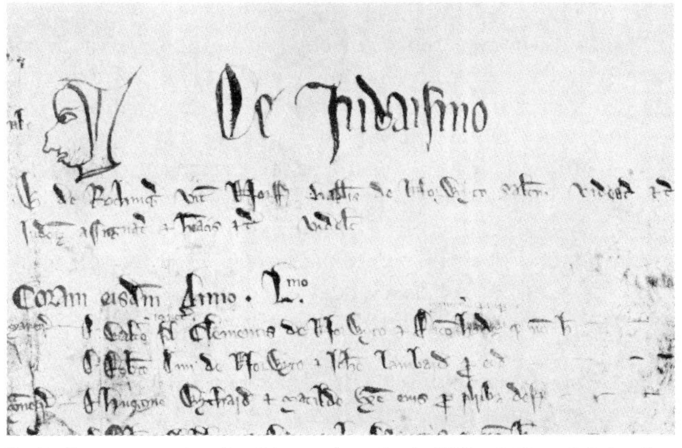

Part of an account roll addressed to the bailiffs of Norwich by the sheriff of Norfolk, c. 1289, ordering the collection of debts due from Jews of the city, including fines for the offense of clipping coins. The caricature of a Jew is labelled "Hake" (Isaac). The roll is on four skins of vellum, 57×7¾ in. (145×20 cm.). Cecil Roth Collection.

1754 when a quarrel in the synagogue attracted much attention in the press. Continuous communal activity dates from the purchase of a burial ground in 1813 and the opening of a new synagogue in 1828. Local 19th-century families included those of Samuel (father of the first Lord *Mancroft), Haldinstein, and Soman (founder of the *Norwich Argus* newspaper). The community was especially known for shoe manufacture, antique dealing, and the press and printing. The synagogue, which was destroyed by bombing in World War II, was rebuilt in 1948; the community's numbers have remained between 100 and 200 (1% of the total population) for about a century.

Bibliography: V. D. Lipman, *Jews of Medieval Norwich* (1967); C. Roth, *Rise of Provincial Jewry* (1950), 85–87; Roth, England, index; Roth, Mag Bibl, 92, 93, 170; H. Levine, *Norwich Hebrew Congregation 1840–1960* (1960?); *Jackson's Oxford Journal* (June 8, 1756).

[V.D.L.]

NORZI, Italian family whose name derives from the Umbrian city of Norcia (where Jews were living from the third century C.E.). The more common forms of the name are: de Nursia, da Norcia, da Norsa, Norsa, Norzi. A certain NATHAN (d. 1369) is considered the founder of the family. Many documents attest the presence of members of the family in Ferrara, in Bondeno, and under the House of Este in the 15th century, mainly in connection with banking activities. Although others lived in Modena, Reggio, Brescia, Verona, and Padua, the *Mantua branch was the wealthiest and most important. According to De Rossi, they came from the regions of Bologna and Turin. The Norzi family played an important part in the life of the community of Mantua. The former synagogue of the family, destroyed when the ghetto was demolished, has been entirely reconstructed on the present community premises, in Via Govi, and is now the only synagogue in Mantua. Many members of the family, pupils of Joseph Colon and Judah b. Jehiel Messer Leon, became rabbis celebrated for their learning beyond Italy.

MANUELE DA NORCIA moved from Rimini to Mantua in 1428 and obtained permission to open a loan bank (*condotta*). LEONE DE NURSIA and others were authorized in 1482 to trade in wool and silk cloths. In 1493 DANIELE DE NURSIA settled in Mantua, where he bought a house which had a painting representing the Virgin on its façade; its erasure by Daniele, although authorized by the bishop, caused a general uproar. Nursia first had to pay 1,100 gold ducats to the painter Andrea Mantegna for a painting of the Madonna, now at the Louvre; he was subsequently evicted, and the house was demolished by order of Marquis Giovanni Francesco II Gonzaga, the ruler of Mantua, who ordered that a church should be built on its premises dedicated to Santa Maria della Vittoria to commemorate his victory over the French at Fornovo. Another work by an unknown painter, now at the Basilica of S. Andrea in Mantua, depicts the ceremony of dedication, with four members of the Norzi family wearing the Jewish *badge; the words *Debellata hebraeorum temeritate* appear at the top of the painting. In 1504 ISAAC BEN DANIEL NORZI was authorized by Gonzaga to engage in moneylending. BENJAMIN BEN IMMANUEL NORZI wrote *Sod La'asot Lu'aḥ* (1477; in Ms.), a study of the Jewish calendar, and commentaries on rulings by R. Isaac Tiburino, and on the Talmud tractates *Pesaḥim, Yoma, Sukkah, Yom Tov, Rosh Ha-Shanah,* and *Megillah* (Wolff, Bibliotheca, 1 (1715), 252).

RAPHAEL BEN GABRIEL (1520–1583?), rabbi at Ferrara and Mantua, was author of various works on rational ethics in religious questions: *Se'ah Solet* (Mantua, 1561); *Marpe la-Nefesh* (Mantua, 1561; Venice, 1571); and *Oraḥ Ḥayyim* (Venice, 1549; Amsterdam, 1557). He exchanged polemics

Coat of arms of the Norzi, or Norsa, family, 1493. Cecil Roth Collection. Photo David Harris, Jerusalem.

with the rabbi of Ferrara. A *kinah* was published on the occasion of his death (Zunz, Lit, Poesie, 128, 254; C. Bernheimer, *Catalogue des manuscrits et livres rares hébraïques de la bibliothèque du Talmud Tora de Livourne* (1915), no. 27 (1)). ELIEZER BEN DAVID NORZI (16th century), son of a banker from Mantua, cousin of Raphael b. Gabriel, wrote a commentary on Abraham ibn Ezra's *Sefer ha-Shem* (1834, ch. 6), dealing with the significance of letters and of the Holy Name. The geometrical diagrams in the commentary indicate that he had knowledge of mathematics (Mortara, Indice 45; M. Steinschneider, *Die Mathematik bei den Juden* (1901), 198; S. Simonsohn, *Toledot ha-Yehudim be-Dukkasut Mantovah* (1964), 458, 474, 528). MOSES BEN JEDIDIAH SOLOMON (d. 1590) was rabbi at Mantua and author of a commentary to tractate *Middot* (Mortara, Indice; Simonsohn, *ibid.*, index). SOLOMON BEN SAMUEL, 16th-century scholar, wrote responsa (Mantua, 1588).

JEHIEL VIDAL BEN JEDIDIAH SOLOMON (d. 1665)—son of the rabbi and scholar Jedidiah Solomon Raphael ben Abraham *Norzi—was appointed rabbi of Mantua in 1628 shortly before the expulsion of the Jews from the town, when he led the exiles to San Martino. They resettled in Mantua in 1630 and he devoted himself to the community until his death. He was often at variance with his community. His responsa are scattered in the archives of the community and in works by contemporary authors (Mortara, in: *Corriere Israelitico*, 2–3 (1863–65), 56, 71; S. Wiener, *Mazkerot Rabbanei Italyah* (1898), 40, 66; S. Simonsohn, *ibid.*, index). MOSES BEN JEDIDIAH SOLOMON, rabbi in Mantua in the 17th century, brother of Jehiel, corresponded with Samuel *Aboab (S. Simonsohn, *ibid.*, index). Jedidiah Solomon ben Abraham *Norzi (1560–1616) was a rabbi and biblical scholar. ḤAYYIM BEN JEHIEL (d. c. 1698), who sat in the rabbinicial tribunal of Mantua in 1665, was a *sofer* in 1677, and became rabbi of the community with the assent of Moses *Zacuto in 1685. With Zacuto and other rabbis he drew up the statutes of the community in 1677, and issued moral precepts for the Jews of Mantua. Some of his responsa were recorded by Zacuto and other *posekim* of that time. He is often confused with another rabbi of the same name of the 16th century (Mortara, Indice, 45; P. Norsa, *I Norsa*, 2 (1959), 122; S. Simonsohn, *ibid.*, 528 and index).

Isaac ben Moses Norsa was rabbi in Ferrara in the 18th century, and author of a ruling on *sheḥitah* as part of a talmudic discussion held at Ferrara and presided over by Isaac Lampronti (*Ittur Bikkurei Kaẓir*, Venice, 1715; Steinschneider, Cat Bod, 140; Fuerst, Bibliotheca Judaica, 3 (1863). Umberto Norsa (1866–1943), scholar, translator from various languages into Italian, including the Psalms (1926, not published), was president of the community of Mantua (G. Bedarida, *Ebrei d'Italia* (1950), index). Paolo Norsa wrote a history of the Norsa family in the 14th to 16th centuries (*I Norsa*, 2 vols.; 1953–59).

Bibliography: V. Colorni, in: RMI, 9 (1934/35), 217ff.; P. Norsa, *I Norsa (1350–1950), Contributo alla Storia di una Famiglia di Banchieri*, 2 vols. (1953–59); E. Castelli, *I Banchi Feneratizi Ebraici nel Mantovano (1386–1808)* (1959); S. Simonsohn, *Toledot ha-Yehudim be-Dukkasut Mantovah* (1964); A. Portioli, *Atti e memorie R. Accademia Virgiliana Mantua* (1882), 55–79; Roth, Italy, index; Milano, Italia, index; Milano, Bibliotheca, index; G. Bedarida, *Ebrei d'Italia* (1950), index. [A.M.R.]

NORZI, JEDIDIAH SOLOMON RAPHAEL BEN ABRAHAM (1560–1616), Italian rabbi, biblical and masoretic scholar. Born in Mantua in a well-known family (see *Norzi), he was a pupil of his uncle Moses Cases, and was later appointed a member of the rabbinate of that town. He achieved a great reputation through his critical masoretic commentary on the Bible, a work to which he devoted the greater part of his life. In his researches he not only consulted published works, but undertook journeys to many countries to compare various manuscripts. He succeeded in gaining access to the manuscript of Toledo written in 1277 (known as the Codex de Rossi, no. 782). He consulted his friend R. Menahem *Lonzano, the midrashic and talmudic scholar.

Norzi's work, called *Goder Pereẓ*, was completed in 1626. It is in two parts; the first on the Pentateuch and the five Scrolls, and the second on the remaining books of the Bible together with some grammatical treatises. The work was published under the title *Minḥat Shai* (Mantua, 1742–44). The second edition (without the grammatical treatises) was published in Vienna (1816). *Minḥat Shai* is also printed in the rabbinical Bible *Mikra'ot Gedolot*. Norzi's introduction was published in 1819, and in 1876 by A. Jellinek. A commentary to the *Minḥat Shai* called *Or ha-Ḥayyim* (Vilna, 1867) was written by Ḥayyim Ze'ev Bender of Bobruisk.

Bibliography: Michael, Or, no. 951; S. Simonsohn, *Toledot ha-Yehudim be-Dukkasut Mantovah* (1964), 450, and notes 63, 64; C. Roth, *The Jews in the Renaissance* (1959), 313f. [H.J.Z.]

NOSSIG, ALFRED (1864–1943), writer, sculptor, and musician; one of the first supporters of the Jewish national movements and of Zionism. Born in Lemberg, Nossig's diversified talents found expression in literature (poems, plays, essays in literary criticism), music (a monograph on the life of Paderewski and libretto for his opera), sculpture (his works were exhibited in a number of world exhibitions and achieved considerable recognition). In addition, Nossig engaged in various public and social activities. Yet all of his life he was a kind of outsider, despite the wide veneration he enjoyed. In his youth he belonged to the assimilationist Polish Jews, and was one of the editors of their Polish-language journal. Later he abandoned them and in 1887 published the first Zionist work in Polish "An Attempt to Solve the Jewish Problem" (*Próba rozwiązania kwestji żydowskiej*, 1887), in which he proposed the establishment of a Jewish state in Palestine and adjacent countries. This book had a great impact on the Jewish intelligentsia, especially in Galicia. From that time, Nossig was active in the area of political Zionism. During that period he published books and essays on Jewish national problems and critical writings on socialism.

Nossig participated in the first Zionist Congresses but he soon ran into conflict with *Herzl, for his individualistic character prevented his cooperating with other people. From time to time, however, Nossig raised new suggestions and plans for the founding of Jewish and general societies to solve the world's problems in general, and those of the Jews in particular. Thus in 1908 he founded a Jewish colonization organization (Allgemeine Juedische Kolonisations Organization—AIKO), which, like other plans of his,

Alfred Nossig, sculptor, musician, and writer on political Zionism. Jerusalem, J.N.U.L., Schwadron Collection.

was not implemented. In his works on Jewish statistics (1887, 1903), he laid the basis for the Jewish Statistical and Demographic Institute and thus was among the founders of the scientific study of Jewish statistics. His most famous pieces of sculpture were "Wandering Jew," "Judas Maccabaeus," "Nordau," and "King Solomon." Nossig lived in Berlin until the Nazi rise to power, when he was expelled to Poland. There he continued his diversified activities, among other things, in the design of a monumental piece of statue called "The Holy Mountain" to be placed on Mount Carmel as a symbol of world peace and the establishment of a national home for the Jews in Palestine. After the Nazi occupation of Poland and the establishment of the Warsaw Ghetto, he drew up plans for Jewish emigration and submitted several memoranda to the German authorities. Upon order of the Nazi authorities, the chairman of the Warsaw *Judenrat*, Adam *Czerniakow, nominated him as a member of the *Judenrat* and head of its Department for Art, which actually existed only on paper. Early in 1943 the Jewish Fighting Organization became convinced that Nossig was collaborating with the Nazis. He was sentenced to death by the Jewish underground and shot on Feb. 22, 1943, by members of the Jewish Fighting Organization.

Bibliography: J. Friedman, in: JSOS, 21 (1965), 155–8; H. Seidman, *Yoman Getto Varshah* (1947), 204–10; A. Czerniakow, *Yoman Getto Varshah* (1969), index; A. Boehm, *Die zionistische Bewegung*, 1 (1935), index; M. Zylberberg, in: *Wiener Library Bulletin*, 23 (1969), 41–45. [G.K.]

NOSTRADAMUS, also known as **Michel de Nostre-Dame** (1503–1566), French astrologer and physician. Both of his grandfathers, Jean de Saint-Rémy and Pierre de Nostra-Donna, were professing Jews but, when Provence became a French possession in 1488, Charles VIII's anti-Jewish policy induced them to convert to Christianity. Consequently Nostradamus was born and raised as a Catholic. In 1529 he graduated from the University of Montpellier as a doctor of medicine. The unorthodox but successful methods of combating the plague which Nostradamus later described in his *Remède très-utile contre la peste* (Paris, 1561) nevertheless failed to save his own wife and children in 1538. For some years thereafter he led a

Nostradamus, French astrologer and physician. From a reprint of the 1611 edition of *Les Prophéties de M. Michel Nostradamus*, Troyes, 1740.

wanderer's existence and, while in Italy, is reputed to have sought out Jews, especially kabbalists.

On his return to France, Nostradamus turned to the occult sciences and, from 1550 onward, published a number of astrological works. The most famous of these, *Les Prophéties de Maistre Michel Nostradamus* (Lyons, 1555), consisted of some 350 quatrains couched in obscure French. The quatrains were arranged in groups of 100, and the work thus acquired its alternative title, *Les Centuries.* Among the many calamities predicted in it was the French king's death in a duel, and the astrologer's fame was assured when Henri II was accidentally killed at a royal tournament in 1559. In 1564 Nostradamus was appointed physician and counsellor to Charles IX. The first complete text of the *Centuries* appeared in 1610 and ran to countless editions, not only in French but also in many other languages. Nostradamus uncannily predicts the English and French revolutions and even the rise and fall of a German dictator (whom he calls Hister). The most celebrated astrologer of all time, Nostradamus remains one of the most fascinating and enigmatic figures of the Renaissance.

Bibliography: J. Boulenger, *Nostradamus* (Fr., 1933); R. Busquet, *Nostradamus, sa famille, son secret* (1950); J. Laver, *Nostradamus* (Eng., 1952); E. Leoni, *Nostradamus, Life and Literature* (1961).

[G.E.S.]

NOTARIKON (Gr. *νοταρικόν*; Lat. **notaricum,** from *notarius,* "shorthand-writer"), a system of abbreviations by either shortening the words or by writing only one letter of each word. This method is used in interpreting the Pentateuch and is the 30th of the 32 hermeneutical rules of the **Baraita of 32 Rules.* The word is derived from the system of stenographic shorthand used by the *notarii* in recording the proceedings in the Roman courts of justice (Kohut, Arukh, 5 (1926), 336). The word *notarikon* occurs only once in the Mishnah (Shab. 12:5). Although there is an opinion that the hermeneutic law of *notarikon* has biblical authority (Shab. 105a), the Talmud does not use it for halakhic interpretations. It is only employed in *aggadah* and **asmakhta* (support for the *halakhah*). Nevertheless, there were rabbis who objected to the excessive use of *notarikon* even in *aggadah* (Sif. Deut. 1).

The *notarikon* can be divided into two categories. One kind interprets every letter in a particular word as the abbreviation of a whole word, since "the words of the Torah are written as *notarikon*" (Mekh. Ba-Ḥodesh, 8). Thus the word נִמְרֶצֶת (*nimreẓet,* "grievous"; I Kings 2:8) stands for נוֹאֵף , מוֹאָבִי, רוֹצֵחַ, צוֹרֵר , תּוֹעֵבָה (*No'ef, Mo'avi, Roẓe'ah, Ẓorer, To'evah;* "adulterer, Moabite, murderer, oppressor, despised") and the first word of the Ten Commandments, אָנֹכִי (*Anokhi,* "I") was interpreted to mean אָנָא נַפְשִׁי כְּתָבִית יַהֲבִית (*Anna Nafshi Ketavit Yahavit;* "I Myself wrote (and) gave [them]" (Shab. 105a).

A second and later application of *notarikon* consists of breaking up a word into various components. Through this method the name רְאוּבֵן (*Re'uven,* "Reuben"; Gen. 29:32) becomes רְאוּ בֵן (*re'u ven,* "see (the) son"; PdRE 36) and the word אַבְרֵךְ (*avrekh,* "senior adviser"; Gen. 41:43) changes into אָב בְּחָכְמָה ר׳ךְ׳ בְּשָׁנִים (*Av Be-ḥokhmah, RaKH be-Shanim,* "father in wisdom (though) tender in years"; Sif. Deut. 1). Sometimes, one-syllable words are transposed. An example of this is when the noun כַּרְמֶל (*karmel,* "fresh corn"; Lev. 2:14) is taken to mean רַךְ מֶל (*rakh mel,* "tender and easily crushed"; Men. 66b). At other times, a word is even transposed although the abbreviation for one of the derived words is missing: מְצוֹרָע (*meẓora,* "leper"; Lev. 14:2), is therefore taken to mean מוֹצִיא שֵׁם רַע (*moẓi shem ra,* "slanderer"), although there is no letter *shin* in the original word (Tanḥ. Meẓora, 4). Conversely, a letter may not be used at all. Words were interpreted through the principle of *notarikon* even when the words derived from the original did not necessarily correspond to it. Thus *nazuf* ("under divine censure") is connected with *Nezem Zahav be-aF ḥazir* ("a ring of gold in the snout of a pig"; Avot 6:2). The rabbis made extensive use of the *notarikon* and the anagram in the interpretation of dreams (e.g., Ber. 57a), and many analogous usages of them can also be found in Hellenistic writings of the period (S. Lieberman, see bibl.). The use of the *notarikon* was also widespread in medieval homiletical and kabbalistic writings (e.g., *Ba'al ha-Turim* by Jacob b. Asher). Through such methods of interpretation many words in the Bible became *notarikonim.* An example of such kabbalistic interpretation is the taking of the word בְּרֵאשִׁית (*bereshit,* "in the beginning") to refer to the cosmogenic order בָּרָא רָקִיעַ אֶרֶץ שָׁמַיִם יָם תְּהוֹם (*Bara Raki'a Ereẓ SHamayim Yam Tehom;* "He created the firmament, the earth, the heavens, the sea, and the abyss"). Another example is to interpret *bereshit* to mean בָּרָא שִׁית ("created in six primordial days"; Zohar, Gen. Prologue, 3b). According to the Mishnah, Queen *Helena of Adiabene had a golden tablet made for the Temple on which the portion of the *sotah* (see *Ordeal) was written in an abbreviated *notarikon* manner (Yoma 3:10; 37b).

Bibliography: I. I. Einhorn (ed.), *Midrash Tanna'im,* 2 (1838), 34cff.; Frankel, Mishnah, index; W. Bacher, *Erkhei Midrash* (1923), 86f., 233; S. Krauss, in: *Byzantinische Zeitschrift,* 2 (1893), 512ff.; M. Halperin, *Notarikon, Simanim, Kinnuyim* (1912); S. Lieberman, *Hellenism in Jewish Palestine* (1950), 69ff.; M. D. Gross, *Oẓar ha-Aggadah,* 2 (1961), 796f. (a list of *notarikonim*).

[ED.]

°**NOTH, MARTIN** (1902–1968), German Bible scholar, disciple of Albrecht *Alt, to whose ideas Noth was deeply indebted. Noth was born in Dresden and served as professor at Koenigsberg (1930–1945) and Bonn (1945–1965). He edited *Zeitschrift des deutschen Palaestina-Vereins* from 1929 to 1964 and was director of the Deutsches Evangelische Institut in Jerusalem from 1965 until his death. Noth brought his extensive topographical studies, mainly published in *Palaestinajahrbuch* and *Zeitschrift des deutschen Palaestina-Vereins,* linguistic research (in particular, *Die israelitischen Personennamen,* 1928), and form-criticism studies to bear on problems of Israelite history. Of primary importance was his thesis that from the time of the settlement, Israel was organized into a 12-tribe confederation, similar to the Greek amphictyony (in his *Das System der zwoelf Staemme Israels,* 1930). He felt that virtually nothing can be known about pre-settlement history.

Noth was one of the foremost representatives of the form-critical approach, and his studies of pentateuchal traditions, *Ueberlieferungsgeschichte des Pentateuchs* (1948, 1960[2]), and Deuteronomy (*Ueberlieferungsgeschichtliche Studien,* 1 (1943, 1957[2])), had widespread influence on biblical research. In the former work he examined the themes of the pentateuchal narrative and the history of its traditions and presented the idea that both J and E go back to a common source, G *(Grundlage).* In the latter he originated the idea of the Deuteronomic history work, a unified history extending from Deuteronomy to II Kings (minus insertions), in which previously independent units were joined and unified by a distinctive theology and philosophy of history. In *Die Gesetze im Pentateuch* (1940), he linked Hebrew law to the religious confederation, rather than to the monarchy. He wrote commentaries to individual books of the Bible: Exodus (1959[2], Eng. tr. 1962), Leviticus (1962, Eng. tr. 1965), Numbers (1966), Joshua (1953[2]), and I Kings 1–16 (1964). He also wrote *Geschichte Israels* (1954[2], 1961[5]; *The History of Israel,* 1960[2]); and *Die Welt des Alten Testaments* (1946, 1957[3]). Some of his articles were collected in his *Gesammelte Studien* (1957, 1960[2]). *The Laws in the Pentateuch and Other Studies* (1966) is an English translation of some of his works. [M.Fo.]

NOTKIN, NATA (Nathan Note of Shklov, also **Nathan Shklover;** d. 1804), Russian merchant and army contractor. Notkin was a champion of the improvement of the status of Jews in Russia at the beginning of the 19th century. Born in Shklov, he lived in Mogilev and later in Moscow and St. Petersburg. He was introduced by General Zorich, the squire of Shklov, to Count Kurakin, and used this opportunity to act in behalf of his fellow Jews. He presented the count with a project for the establishment of large-scale agricultural colonies for the Jews of "New Russia," as well as plans for industrial plants near the ports of the Black Sea, which he hoped would direct the Jews to productive labor. Toward the end of 1802 he was invited by G. R. *Derzhavin to be a member at the Committee for the Betterment of the Jews. In all of his writings and projects Notkin tried to demonstrate to the government ways to improve the condition of the Jews, e.g., the gradual removal of Jews from the liquor business, the establishment of Jewish schools, and the direction of Jews toward productive labor. Notkin was one of the founders of the St. Petersburg Jewish community. [EJ]

NOTOVICH, OSIP KONSTANTINOVICH (1849–1914), journalist and playwright. Notovich was a graduate of the University of St. Petersburg. In his youth he converted to the Greek Orthodox Church. Acquiring the small daily *Novosti* in 1876, in time he developed it into an important political journal. Although Notovich published facts about the persecution of Jews, he did not come to their defense for fear of losing his Russian readers. Notovich wrote several philosophical works and plays, some of which were performed on the stages of the imperial theaters of Moscow and St. Petersburg. His translation of H. T. Buckle's *History of Civilization in England* (1890) was especially popular. In 1905 Notovich published a revolutionary appeal for a trade union. As a result, his newspaper was confiscated and he was summoned to court. Subsequently, he fled the country and died abroad.

Bibliography: S. Ginsburg, *Historishe Verk,* 2 (1946), 203–4.
[Ed.]

NOTTINGHAM, industrial city in the E. Midlands, England. In the 13th century Nottingham was one of the 27 centers in which an *archa* was established for the registration of Jewish debts. An attack was made on the Nottingham Jews during the Barons' Revolt in 1264. From the resettlement until the 19th century only individual Jews settled in the city. By 1805 there was a small, organized community; a cemetery was acquired in 1822; and by 1880 there were about 50 Jewish residents, though a synagogue was not built until 1890. The Nottingham lace-curtain industry was founded by a Jewish immigrant from Germany, Lewis Heymann. By 1939, the community had increased to 180, but World War II brought an influx of new residents. In addition to an Orthodox synagogue there was a Progressive congregation; communal institution included a Zionist Association and a University Jewish Society. In 1969 the community numbered 1,500 (out of a total population of 310,000).

Bibliography: C. Roth, *The Rise of Provincial Jewry* (1950), 27–89; J. Spungin, *A Short History of the Jews of Nottingham* (1951).
[V.D.L.]

NOVAYA USHITSA, town in Chmielnicki (Kamenets-Podolski oblast till 1954), Ukrainian S.S.R. The Jewish community in Novaya Ushitsa and its environs dates from the beginning of the 18th century. From 1838 to 1840, 80 Jews of the Novaya Ushitsa region, including rabbis and community leaders, were tried in what became known as the Oyshits Incident. They were accused by the governor of Kiev, General Gurayev, of the murder of two Jews who had informed on "absconders" (unregistered persons who had avoided paying taxes and doing military service) to the authorities. Most of the accused were sentenced by a military court to flogging and exile to Siberia.

The 1847 census records 725 Jews living in Novaya Ushitsa, with 1,235 in the communities of the district. The Jewish population numbered 2,213 in 1897 (34.5% of the total). After the Bolshevik Revolution and the civil war, their sources of livelihood were drastically curtailed. In 1926 there were 1,844 Jews in the town (28.4% of the total). After the *Holocaust the community ceased to exist.

Bibliography: *Perezhitoye,* 1, pt. 2 (1908), 1–7; M. Kiper, *Dos Yidishe Shtetl in Ukraine* (1929); S. Ginzburg, *Historishe Verk,* 3 (1937), 178–9; *Yidn in Ukraine,* 1 (1961), 164–78; V. B. Antonovich (comp.), *Arkhiv yugo-zapadnoy Rossii,* 2, pt. 5 (1890).
[A.Cy.]

NOVE MESTO NAD VAHOM (Slovak, **Nové Mesto nad Váhom;** Hung, **Vágújhely**), town in Czechoslovakia. Jewish settlement began in 1689 when 11 refugee families arrived in Nove Mesto from Uhersky Brod. The numbers were augmented by immigrants from Bohemia and Moravia and by 1735 the community totaled 372 persons. In 1780 the first synagogue was built; at that time the community was the second largest in Slovakia (2,320 in 1785, 43.7% of the total population). David Deutsch, author of *Ohel David* (Vienna, 1819) and associate of Moses *Sofer, was rabbi in Nove Mesto from 1810 to 1831. In the 1848 Revolution Jewish homes and institutions were attacked by Slovakian rebels. Though the community buildings were destroyed by fire eight years later, the community recovered and from the 1880s prospered in relatively quiet circumstances. There were 1,309 Jews in the town in 1930 and about 1,500 when

Slovakia became independent in 1938. R. Armin *Frieder (d. 1946) was leader of the community during the Fascist persecutions. He succeeded, through his connections with government circles, in hiding many Jews who were in danger of deportation. In March and April 1942 some 1,300 people were deported from Nove Mesto and district; only two of these returned after World War II. In October 1944 about 700 people were deported to Auschwitz; about 100 of them survived. During the war years the synagogue was destroyed. In 1965, 20–30 Jews lived in Nove Mesto.

Bibliography: J. J. Greenwald, *Mekorot le-Todedot Yisrael* (1934), 53–72; L. Rothkirchen, in: Yad Vashem, *Pinkas ha-Kehillot* (1963), 35–39; Y. Toury, *Mehumah u-Mevukhah be-Mahpekhat 1848* (1968), index. [ED.]

NOVE ZAMKY (Slovak. **Nové Zámky;** Hung. **Érsekújvár**), town in S. Slovakia, Czechoslovakia. Before the 1848 Revolution Jews were permitted to be in Nove Zamky for the duration of the fairs only. A synagogue was consecrated in the 1860s and a school opened ten years later. The community split in 1870 into a Neolog and an Orthodox congregation, which built their own synagogues in 1880 and 1883 respectively. The most eminent rabbi was Samuel *Klein, who left in 1926 and became professor of geography at the Hebrew University of Jerusalem. In 1927 a Jewish high school was opened. There were 2,535 Jews in Nove Zamky in 1930. The Jewish Credit Society had 648 deposits (totaling more than 3,000,000 kronen) in 1937. In November 1938 Nove Zamky was ceded to Hungary. During World War II most Jews were deported and very few returned after the liberation, when Czechoslovakian rule was reestablished. In August 1946 Jews sitting in a café were attacked and seven were wounded. Nevertheless, communal life was revived: a synagogue and a *mikveh* were opened, as well as a communal center and a home for the aged. In 1970 the synagogue was restored.

Bibliography: R. Iltis (ed.), *Die aussaeen unter Traenen mit Jubel werden sie ernten* (1959). [ED.]

NOVGOROD-SEVERSK, city in Chernigov oblast, Ukrainian S.S.R. During the 14th century, Novgorod-Seversk was conquered by the princes of Lithuania; in the 16th and 17th centuries it was alternately in the hands of the Poles and the Russians; and in 1667 it was definitively annexed by Russia. A Jewish settlement is mentioned for the first time in a residence permit granted to the townspeople by King *Sigismund III Vasa (1587–1632) of Poland. According to the permit Jews were forbidden to sell meat in the town, except in the courtyard of the synagogue. Also included were several tax levies which Jews were ordered to pay. During the *Chmielnicki persecutions of 1648 many Jews in Novgorod-Seversk were massacred by the Cossacks. The community was renewed only in the 19th century. In 1847 1,336 Jews were registered in the community; by 1897 the number had risen to 1,956 (32% of the total population). The community suffered in the wave of pogroms which swept over Russia in 1905. On April 6, 1918, units of the Red Army retreating before the German army savagely attacked the Jews of Novgorod-Seversk and about 90 Jews (including the author A. J. *Slutzky) lost their lives. In 1926 there were 2,089 Jews (22.8% of the total population) in the town. After the German occupation in 1941, all those Jews who did not manage to escape were killed. There is no information on a Jewish community after World War II.

Bibliography: *Die Judenpogrome in Russland,* 2 (1910), 295–300; E. Tcherikower, *Yehudim be-Ittot Mahpekhah* (1957), 529–31. [Y.S.]

NOVI SAD (Hung. **Újvidék;** Ger. **Neusatz**), city on the Danube in Vojvodina, Yugoslavia. Some Jews from Belgrade seem to have settled at the foot of the later Petroraradin fortress in the 16th century. Under Ottoman rule (16th–17th centuries) they were treated well and engaged in trade on the Danube. During the Austro-Turkish war of 1683–99, Ashkenazi Jews were among the *contractors to the Austrian army. When the region passed under Austrian rule in 1699, it was devastated and depopulated. Jews were therefore exceptionally authorized to settle in the new town of Neusatz opposite the fortress but were not allowed to form a recognized community. Austrian archives mention Salomon Hirschl, probably the first *rosh kehillah* of Novi Sad. At the beginning of the 18th century three Jewish families are known to have lived in Novi Sad; however, there were probably more, as only owners of real estate were registered. Most Jews came from Nikolsburg in Moravia. All Jews had to pay the Jewish tax (until the end of the 18th century). They were subject to limitations, such as the interdiction of acquiring real estate; as only the eldest son of each family could marry in the same town (see *Familiants Laws), others had to leave and settle elsewhere. The *ḥevra kaddisha* was founded in 1729 as a "Holy Welfare Society." Under Joseph II the teaching of German or Hungarian became obligatory, and in order to open a business or marry, Jews had to have some formal education. A Jewish school was built in Novi Sad in 1802 and a synagogue in 1829. During the Hungarian revolution of 1848–49 all Jewish property was destroyed, but in 1851 the synagogue was rebuilt, and a new, monumental one was built in 1901 (still standing in the 1970s). Previously all Vojvodina belonged to Hungary (within Austria-Hungary); however, in 1918, when Vojvodina became a part of the new Yugoslav kingdom, it formed a province closely linked with Serbia. [ED.]

Between the two world wars communal life was intensive and diversified. There was a Jewish school, a home for the aged, a modern community center, widespread Zionist activities, and Jewish newspapers were published (*Juedisches Volksblatt,* later *Juedische Zeitung Jevreyske Novine*).

Until the Holocaust, in 1941, there were 4,000 Jews in Novi Sad, out of a total population of 80,000. The extermination of the Jews of Novi Sad was carried out in successive waves, initially under the Hungarian occupation and later by German troops. It began with individual arrests, torture, and murders. On Jan. 21–23, 1942, a small rebellion near Novi Sad served as a pretext for the so-called "*razzia,*" when total curfew was ordered and Jewish homes were searched and plundered while their occupants were

Monument in the Jewish cemetery of Novi Sad. The inscription (left) reads: "To the memory of the 4,000 Jews of Novi Sad who fell as victims of Fascism 1941–45. May God remember them, together with all the righteous of the world." Courtesy Z. Efron, En-Harod.

murdered in the streets. On January 23 more than 1,400 Jews were marched to the Danube and lined up in four rows. The ice in the frozen river was broken and throughout the day Jews, including women and children, were shot in the back, disappearing in the waters, which carried corpses down to Belgrade and beyond for weeks. Among the victims were also some 400–500 Serbs. The *"razzia"* caused an upheaval even in Hungarian circles, and cabled orders arrived from Budapest to stop the massacre on the evening of January 23. Several hundred survivors, half frozen and frightened to death, were released. The extermination policy continued, however. During 1942 all male Jews between the ages of 18 and 45 were gathered into "labor battalions," maltreated, and starved (first in Hungary), and then sent to the Ukrainian front, where they perished. The last phase came with the German occupation in March 1944. With the aid of Hungarians, the Germans sought out all remaining Jews and transported them to Auschwitz in May 1944. Jewish property was plundered completely, except for personal and worthless items, which were gathered into the synagogue. About 200 Jews lived in Novi Sad in 1970, most of them survivors of P.O.W. camps. [Z.Lo.]

Bibliography: I. Radó and J. Major, *A noviszádi zsidók története* (1930); *Magyar Zsidó Lexikon* (1929), s.v. *Ujvidék; Zločini fašističkih okupatora i njihovih pomagača protiv Jevreja u Jugolaviji* (1952), ch. 5; J. Buzási, *Az ujvidéki "razzia"* (1963).

NOVOGRUDOK (Pol. **Nowogródek;** also referred to by Jews as **Novaredok**), city in Grodno oblast, Belorussian S.S.R. Novogrudok was within Poland-Lithuania until the third partition of Poland (1795), when it passed to Russia, from 1842, and a district capital in the province of Minsk. It reverted to Poland in 1921, but passed to the Soviet Union in 1939. The Jewish community of Novogrudok, one of the oldest in Lithuania, is first mentioned in documents in 1529. In 1563, at the request of the townspeople, King *Sigismund II Augustus ordered that the Jews were to move to one of two streets at a distance from the center, where space had been allocated to them for building houses. In 1576 King Stephan *Báthory confirmed all the former rights of the Jews of Novogrudok and of the other Jews in Lithuania. According to a decision of the Council of the Province of Lithuania (see *Councils of the Lands) of 1623, Novogrudok Jews were subject to the jurisdiction of the *Brest community. There were 893 poll-tax payers in the community and surrounding villages attached to it in 1765. There were 2,756 persons in 1847 and 5,105 in 1897 (63.5% of the total population). In the 19th century two of Russia's leading rabbis, Jehiel Michael *Epstein and Isaac Elhanan *Spektor, officiated in Novogrudok. At the end of the 19th century the city became one of the centers of the *Musar movement after a *yeshivah and **kolel* had been founded there in 1896 by Joseph Hurwitz, one of the most prominent disciples of Israel *Salanter and a leader of the Musar movement. During World War I the yeshivah was transferred to *Gomel. The community decreased considerably after that war, numbering 3,405 (53.4% of the total) in 1921. [Y.S.]

Holocaust Period. In 1939 there were about 6,000 Jews in Novogrudok, and after the outbreak of the war (September 1939) refugees from western Poland joined them. During the period of Soviet rule (1939–41), the institutions of the Jewish community were destroyed, enterprises were nationalized, small trade was drastically reduced, and artisans were organized in cooperatives. There were arrests among the "bourgeois" Jews. With the outbreak of the war between Germany and the U.S.S.R. on June 22, 1941, groups of Jews attempted to reach Soviet territory but the Soviet guards prevented them from crossing the border and they returned to the city. Germans entered the city on July 3, and as early as July 10 they had murdered about 50 men. On December 7 the Jews were ordered to assemble in the courtyard of the district courthouse. A "selection" was carried out and over 400 Jews were taken to the trenches near the village of Skrydlewo and were killed. The survivors concentrated in the ghetto that was set up in the suburb of Peresieka immediately after this *Aktion*. The first chairman of the Judenrat was the lawyer Ciechanowski, and the second was Chaim Ajzykowicz. Jews from the surrounding communities were also brought into the ghetto; they came from Weielub, Korelicze, Iwieniec, Rubiezewicze, Lubcz, and Naliboki.

Ark of the Law in the synagogue of Novogrudok. Courtesy Yad Vashem Archives, Jerusalem.

The second *Aktion* was carried out on Aug. 7, 1942, and most of the Jews perished in it. Only a few hundred artisans survived. They were concentrated in two places: construction workers in Peresieka and the others in a camp that was set up in the district courthouse. In October 1942 a group of about 50 Jews succeeded in escaping to the forests. Contact was made with a partisan unit headed by a Jew, Tuvyha Belski. On Feb. 6, 1943, the Germans liquidated the camp of construction workers. In another *Aktion* on May 7, about 370 people were killed including the last of the women and children. At the beginning of 1943 a resistance group was created by Berko Joselewicz, Abraham Raruwski, Yasha Kantorowiez, and others. They decided to break out of the camp in which they were imprisoned and join the partisans. They dug a tunnel, and about 100 Jews escaped. Many of them took part in the fighting against the Nazis, Belorussian collaborators, and others. After the war about 1,200 Jews returned to Novogrudok from hiding in the forests. In 1970 the Jewish population was estimated at about 75 (15 families). [Ar.W.]

Bibliography: S. A. Bershadski (ed.), *Russko-Yevreyskiy arkhiv*, 2 (1882), 183, 202; *Nedelnaya Khronika Voskhoda*, no. 47 (1887); *Ha-Ẓefirah*, 280 (1887); *Regesty i Nadpisi*, 1–2 (1899–1910), indexes; M. Z. H. Walbrinski and S. Z. Markovitz, *Le-Korot Ir Novohredak ve-Rabbaneha* (1913); A. Harkavy, *Novoredak* (1921); idem, *Perakim me-Ḥayyai* (1938), 4–18; J. Żmigródski, *Nowogródek i okolice* (1927); M. Schalit (ed.), *Oyf di Khurbons fun Milkhomes un Mehumes* (1913), 393–411, 1093–101; A. Gumener (ed.), *15 Yor Kinder-Heym in Novogrudek* (1933); *Yahadut Lita*, 1 (1959), index; *Sefer Novorodek* (1963). HOLOCAUST PERIOD: T. and Z. Belski, *Yehudei Ya'ar* (1946); B. Ajzensztajn, *Ruch podziemny w gettach i obozach* (1946), 182–3; Y. Jaffe, *Partizanim* (1951); M. Zuckerman and M. Bassok (eds.), *Milḥamot ha-Getta'ot* (1954), 63, 492–3; M. Kahanowitz, *Milḥemet ha-Partizanim ha-Yehudim be-Mizraḥ Eiropah* (1954), index; *Sefer ha-Partizanim ha-Yehudim*, 1 (1958), 415–6.

NOVOMEYSKY, MOSHE (1873–1961), industrial pioneer in Ereẓ Israel. Born in Barguzin, a village on Lake Baikal in Siberia, Novomeysky attended a secondary school in Irkutsk, graduated as a mining engineer in Germany, and engaged in gold mining in Siberia. He

Moshe Novomeysky, founder of the Palestine Potash Company. Courtesy Dead Sea Works, Ltd., Beersheba. Photo Shimon Fuchs, Givatayim.

received a Jewish upbringing and became involved in Zionism, although the Russian revolutionary movement also attracted him and he spent some time in prison. While in Germany in 1906, he became interested in a study of the potentialities of the Dead Sea as a source of valuable chemicals for industrial use. He visited Ereẓ Israel before World War I and participated in the establishment of the Palestine Industrial Syndicate in Berlin. During the war and the Russian Revolution, he was active in Jewish affairs in Siberia and became head of the National Council of Siberian Jews and of the regional Zionist Organization. When the Bolsheviks came to power he left Siberia and settled in Palestine in 1920, where he took first steps toward the realization of his plans for the exploitation of the Dead Sea. It took some ten years to obtain the necessary concession in face of opposition in the British Parliament; but eventually his Palestine Potash Company became the most important enterprise of its kind in the Middle East. During the Israel *War of Independence (1948), the Potash Works on the north of the Dead Sea were evacuated and totally destroyed by the Arab forces, and only the plant erected in the south, near Sedom, survived. After the establishment of the State of Israel, the Potash Company, registered in Britain, was replaced by an Israel company under government control. Novomeysky was also a founder of Fertilizers and Chemicals, another large chemical enterprise in Haifa.

Apart from his intensive work in the economic field, Novomeysky devoted much time to public affairs. For a time after he settled in Palestine, he acted as treasurer of the *Haganah. He was a founder of the Palestine Economic Society for the study of the country's economic problems. Deeply interested in the Arab question, he succeeded in establishing good relations with the Trans-Jordanian authorities and the hundreds of Arabs employed by his company. In later years he devoted his time to writing his reminiscences, *My Siberian Life* (1956), and the story of the Dead Sea concession, *Given to Salt* (1958). He died in Paris and was buried in Tel Aviv. [Mo.M.]

NOVOSELITSA (Rum. **Nouă Sulița** or **Sulița**), town in Ukrainian S.S.R., in the region of Bessarabia. As a result of the large emigration of Jews to Bessarabia, Novoselitsa developed in the first half of the 19th century from a rural into an urban community. There were 3,898 Jews living there (66% of the total population) in 1897 and 4,152 (86.2%) in 1930. Among the 875 members registered in the loan fund in 1925, were 461 merchants, 213 craftsmen, and 65 farmers. Prior to World War II, community institutions included a *talmud torah*, a kindergarten, and a school, all belonging to the *Tarbut network, and an old-age home. [El.F.]

Holocaust Period. The town was captured by Rumanian forces on July 2, 1941. On the same day, 800 Jews were murdered on the pretext that Jews had shot at the Rumanian troops. Sixty Jews were arrested and taken to the local spirits factory, where they were shot to death. The surviving Jews, as well as others gathered from the entire district, were rounded up and put into the factory. On July 5, the old men, the women, and children were forced into a ghetto in the town. On July 20, all the Jews were put on the road to *Transnistria. En route they were exposed to constant brutality, and the old and weak among them were put to death. They reached *Ataki, on the banks of the Dniester on August 6, by which time the Germans had closed the Ukrainian border, and the deportees were sent back to *Secureni. In a report by the gendarmerie commander at Cernauti, dated August 11, 2,800 Jews from Novoselitsa are mentioned among the prisoners of the Secureni camp. Their fate was the same as that of the other Jews in that camp; many were killed and others buried alive. Only 200 returned from Transnistria after the war. In 1959 the authorities closed down the community's two synagogues, one of them being converted into a club. In 1970 the Jewish population was estimated at about 1,000. [J.An.]

Bibliography: M. Carp, *Cartea Neagrà*, 3 (1947), index; N. Kahn in: *Eynikayt* (Sept. 11, 1945); BJCE.

°**NOVOSILTSEV, NICOLAI NIKOLAYEVICH** (1761–1836), Russian politician. As the czar's adviser in the Polish kingdom (1815), he took charge of Jewish questions. He recommended that the Polish government should gather material on the conditions of the Jews in the kingdom so that the czar could decide how to improve their situation and "make them more useful to the country." He was the author of a project which forbade the Jews to manufacture or trade in alcohol, but at the same time proposed granting them self-government, with the aim of modernizing Jewish life and promoting science and the arts, so that ultimately they would be awarded political rights. However Novosiltsev, head of the secret police, was implacably opposed to Polish nationalism, and the true purpose of this project was to sow dissension between the Jews and the Poles.

Bibliography: *Perezhitoye*, 1 (1910), 164–221; 2 (1910), 78–93; YE, 11 (c. 1912), 765–6; *Bolshaya Sovetskaya Entsiklopediya*, 30 (1954), 104; R. Mahler, *Ḥasidut ve-Haskalah* (1961), index; *Wielka Encyklopedia Powszechna*, 8 (1966), 55. [Ed.]

NOVOZYBKOV, town in S.W. Bryansk oblast, Russian S.F.S.R. Before the 1917 Revolution, Novozybkov was a district town in the province of Chernigov in the *Pale of Settlement. Although the town was founded at the beginning of the 19th century, it was not until the middle of that century that Jews were permitted to live there. In 1897 there were 3,836 Jewish residents (about 25% of the total population) and in October 1905 the town was subjected to pogroms. In 1926, 4,825 Jews (22.4% of the total) lived there. When the Germans occupied the town, in 1941, those Jews who had not succeeded in leaving were murdered. There is no subsequent information on any Jewish life in the town. [Y.S.]

NOVY, JIM (1896–1971), U.S. business executive. Novy, who was born in Knyszyn, Poland, went to the U.S. in 1913 and settled in Austin, Texas, where he played a leading role in the metal industry. A member of many Jewish organizations, he was especially active on behalf of the State of Israel. In December 1963 his long-time friend President Lyndon B. *Johnson took part in the dedication of the newly-erected synagogue of Novy's congregation, Agudas Achim in Austin, Texas, the first time a United States president ever helped dedicate a Jewish place of worship. [Ed.]

NOVY BOHUMIN (Czech **Nový Bohumín;** Ger. **Neuoderberg**), town in N.E. Moravia, Czechoslovakia. In 655 the local lord permitted a Jewish soap-maker and a Jewish distiller to settle under his jurisdiction. In 1751 six Jewish families lived in various localities of the Oderberg domain. Jews settled in the town early in the 19th century, attracted primarily by the fact that Novy Bohumin, a border town, was one of the important railway-crossings in central Europe, and was later the site of an oil refinery. The Jews there first came under the administration of the *Teschen and later of the *Ostrava community. A synagogue was built in 1900; an independent community established in 1911; and a Jewish center opened in 1924. In 1933 a large Maccabiah (sports festival) was held in Novy Bohumin. The Jewish community numbered 722 (6.6% of the total population) in 1931. During the German occupation the Jews were put to work rebuilding a bridge blown up by the Poles. The synagogue was burned on Rosh Ha-Shanah 1939. Later that year most of the Jews were deported to Nisko. The community was not revived after the Holocaust.

Bibliography: *Dr. Bloch's Oesterreichische Wochenschrift,* 28 (1911), 157; G. Wolf, in: ZGJD, 4 (1890), 193–4; B. Brilling, in: *Judaica Bohemiae,* 4 (1968), 101–18 passim, *Jews of Czechoslovakia,* 1 (1968), 199, 240–2. [M.La.]

NOVY BYDZOV (Czech **Nový Bydžov;** Ger. **Neubitschow**), town in N.E. Bohemia, Czechoslovakia. Jews are first mentioned in town records of 1514; they acquired a cemetery in 1520, the oldest tombstones dating from the mid-17th century. A synagogue was mentioned in 1559 (renovated in 1660 and 1838) and ten Jewish families were recorded in 1570. Between 1656 and 1670 Jews sold salt. After a case of plague, the community was temporarily expelled, some of its members founding communities in surrounding villages. There were 90 Jewish families in Novy Bydzov in 1724. Three years later they were segregated from Christians in a special quarter. Expellees from Prague in 1744 reinforced the community. In 1750 Mendel of Novy Bydzov was burnt at the stake in connection with the emergence of the sect of the *Abrahamites. There were 37 Jewish houses in 1786. A new cemetery was consecrated in 1885 (still in existence). Some of the 838 members of the community in 1893 lived in the 35 surrounding villages. The old Jewish quarter burned down in 1903. In 1930 the community numbered 148 (2.1% of the total population). During the Holocaust 98 Jews were deported to *Theresienstadt and from there to the death camps in 1942; one only returned. Synagogue equipment and documents were transferred to the Central Jewish Museum in Prague (see *Museums, Jewish). No congregation was reestablished after the Holocaust.

Bibliography: J. Koudelka, in: H. Gold (ed.), *Juden und Judengemeinden Boehmens* (1934), 416–9; J. Prokeš, in: JGGJČ, 8 (1936), 147–308; J. Hráský, *ibid.,* 9 (1938), 246, 259; AZDJ, 2 (1838), 562, 600; Bondy-Dworský, 299. [J.Her.]

NOVY DVOR (Rus. **Novyi Dvor),** small town in Grodno oblast, Belorussian S.S.R. The first Jews settled there during the first half of the 16th century. During the second half of the 16th century there was an organized Jewish community with a synagogue and cemetery. In 1561 12 houses and a number of orchards were owned by Jews. During the following decades Jews from Grodno joined the local community and, according to the decisions of the Council of Provinces of Lithuania (*Councils of the Lands; 1623), the community of Novy Dvor was subordinated to that of Grodno. In 1648 Jewish refugees from Ukraine arrived in Novy Dvor. A few years later local Jews suffered the onslaught of the Russian and Swedish armies. In 1766 there were 294 poll tax paying Jews in Novy Dvor and the surrounding villages. During the 19th century the sources of livelihood of the Jews of Novy Dvor were cut off and a period of economic stagnation ensued. In 1847 there were 394 Jews and in 1897, 490 (38% of the total population). In 1900 a new synagogue was erected, and during the first weeks of the Polish rule (1918) a Jewish self-defense organization was active. In 1921 there were 402 Jews (33% of the population) in Novy Dvor. From 1925 there was a *Tarbut school. The last rabbi of the community was Isaac Kamieniecki, who perished in the Holocaust.

Holocaust Period. At the end of June 1941, a few days after the Nazis entered the town, 50 Jewish men were deported to concentration camps. In October 1941 the Jews of Novy Dvor were sent to the ghetto at Ostryna, from there to Grodno (April 1942), and finally to the extermination camp of Auschwitz. Only six Jews of the community survived, three of them having joined the partisan movement. No Jews returned to Novy Dvor after World War II.

Bibliography: *Dokumenty i regesty k istorii utovskikh yevreyev,* 1 (1882), nos. 235, 236, 241, 243; Dubnow, Pinkas, 17; B. Wasiutyński, *Ludność żydowska w Polsce . . .* (1930), 83; S. A. Bershadski, *Litouskiye yevrei* (1883), 331, 347; *Sefer Zikkaron li-Kehillot Sczuczyn, Wasiliszki, Ostryna, Novy Dvor, Różana* (n.d.), 379–434. [A.Cy.]

NOVY JICIN (Czech, **Nový Jičín;** Ger. **Neutitschein**), town in Moravia, Czechoslovakia. Jews are recorded in Novy Jicin in the middle of the 14th century as owners of houses, and as cloth merchants. The Jewish lane *(Judengasse),* which in 1581 contained 46 houses, was situated next to the castle, but Jews resided in other streets as well. When the community was expelled in 1562, its leaders sold the synagogue to the mayor and presented the city with the cemetery, requesting that it should not be damaged. The expellees settled in the neighboring villages. In the late 18th and early 19th centuries Jews returned to the vicinity of the town, and by 1828 a few privileged families were again residing in it. Full freedom of settlement was granted only in 1848, and in July 1850 the authorities quelled an attempt to organize anti-Jewish riots. In 1868 the statutes of a *Kultusverein were confirmed, and by 1892 it was acknowledged as a community. The cemetery dates from 1875 and the synagogue from 1908. The Jews of Novy Jicin were active in the local textile industry and in trade. The community numbered 14 in 1847, 155 in 1868, 275 in 1880, 253 in 1900, and 206 (1.4% of the total population) in 1930.

Novy Jicin was the site of the first *hakhsharah* farm in Czechoslovakia, organized in 1921. At the time of the Sudeten crisis in 1938, the community dispersed, and it was not revived after World War II.

Bibliography: S. Mandl, in: H. Gold (ed.), *Juden und Judengemeinden Maehrens* . . . (1929), 404–16; P. Ziegler, *Zur Geschichte der Juden in Neu-Titschein* (1939); Bondy-Dworský, no. 649; Ch. D'Elvert, *Zur Geschichte der Juden in Maehren* . . . (1895), 110–3.

[ED.]

NOVY OLEKSINIEC, small town in Kremenets (Krzemieniec) district, Volhynia, Ukrainian S.S.R., noted for leather products. In 1765 203 Jewish taxpayers were registered in Oleksiniec and its suburb (Oleksiniec Stary). The printing press established there in 1760 was one of the first Hebrew presses in Russia. H. Margolis, active between 1766 and 1776, printed some 18 rabbinical works there. Noteworthy is *Zemir Arizim ve-Ḥarvot Ẓurim* (1772), a collection of anti-ḥasidic proclamations. Rabbis of Oleksiniec include Mordecai ha-Kohen Rappoport, son of Shabbetai, author of *Imrei No'am* (Oleksiniec, 1767), and Jacob Joseph ha-Levi Horovitz of Brody, installed in 1790.

Bibliography: *Yalkut Vohlin*, 1 (1945), 9; B. Friedberg, *Toledot ha-Defus ha-Ivri be-Polanyah* (1950[2]).

[ED.]

°**NOWACK, WILHELM GUSTAV HERMANN** (1850–1928), German Bible critic. Nowack was professor at Halle, and from 1881, of biblical exegesis and Hebrew in Strasbourg.

Among his writings, the *Lehrbuch der hebraeischen Archaeologie* (2 vols., 1894) represents a classical armchair approach to Palestinian archaeology in its description of ancient Israelite realia. He prepared the second edition of E. Bertheau and F. *Hitzig's commentaries on Ecclesiastes for the *Kurzgefasstes exegetisches Handbuch zum Alten Testament* (1883[2]) and the third edition of H. *Hupfeld's commentary on Psalms (2 vols., 1888). He also wrote commentaries on Amos and Hosea for the *Religionsgeschichtliche Volksbuecher* (vol. 9, 1908). From 1892 to 1903 he served as editor of *Goettinger Handkommentar zum Alten Testament*, to which he contributed the sections on the Minor Prophets (1897; 1922[3]); Judges (1902); Ruth (1902); and Samuel (1902). He also wrote on the religious development of ancient Israel (*Die sozialen Probleme in Israel und deren Bedeutung fuer die religioese Entwicklung dieses Volkes*, 1892), and on Israel's role against the background of the Assyrian Near East (*Die Zukunftshoffnungen Israels in der assyrischen Zeit*, 1902). His other studies on the Bible are: *Die Bedeutung des Hieronymus fuer alttestamentliche Textkritik* (1875); *Die assyrisch-babylonischen Keil-Inscripten und das Alte Testament* (1878); and *Der Prophet Hosea erklaert* (1880). He also prepared the masoretic text of the Minor Prophets for R. *Kittel's *Biblia Hebraica* (1906).

[Z.G.]

NOWAKOWSKI, DAVID (1848–1921), Russian choirmaster and cantor. Born in Malin near Kiev, Nowakowski went to Odessa at the age of 21. There he was choirmaster and assistant to Chief Cantor Nissan *Blumenthal in the Brody Synagogue; and then to Blumenthal's successor, Pinḥas *Minkowski. He trained the Brody Synagogue choir, long noted for its quality, and the 30 years during which he worked with Minkowski became a brilliant period in the development of synagogue music. He left printed works and hundreds of compositions in manuscript which continued to be sung by many cantors and choirs. Two volumes of his work, *Shirei David*, were published during his lifetime: *Sabbath Eve and Evening Services* (1901) and *Ne'ilah* for the Day of Atonement (1895). He employed to a large extent the traditional chants of the cantors, integrating them into the choral sections.

Bibliography: Friedmann, Lebensbilder, 3 (1927), 41–43; Sendrey, Music, index.

[J.L.N.]

NOWY DWOR MAZOWIECKI, town in Warszawa province, central Poland. The Jewish settlement appears to have been founded at the close of the 17th century. From the beginning of the 18th century there was an organized Jewish community owning a synagogue and a cemetery (which until 1780 was also used by the Jews of Praga, a suburb of Warsaw). In 1768–69, a number of Jews fleeing from the *Haidamack massacres in Podolia found refuge in Nowy Dwor, bringing the ḥasidic teachings with them. During that period the Jews earned their livelihood primarily from innkeeping and by trading in wood. A woolen cloth factory established in the 1780s by the Poniatowski family (owners of the town) was to a considerable extent dependent on Jewish merchants for its financing, for supplying its raw materials, and for taking on the bulk of its orders. Jewish craftsmen and merchants earned their livelihood from tailoring, shoemaking, carpentry, construction, innkeeping, and the supply of building materials and food to the military units stationed in the district. In 1808, 183 Jews formed 25% of the town's population; in 1827 there were 334 Jews (28% of the total population), increasing to 1,305 (49%) in 1857. A German editor, J. A. Krieger, had taken over a Hebrew printing privilege from the Warsaw printer and bookseller Du Four, so that between 1781 and 1816 Nowy Dwor had one of the most active Hebrew presses in Eastern Europe, issuing well over 100 works. The driving powers behind the business were Eliezer b. Isaac of Krotoszyn and his son-in-law, Jonathan b. Moses Jacob of Wielowicz, who had also acted as proofreader and later as manager of Krieger's bookshop in Warsaw. An ambitious project of a Talmud edition did not proceed beyond the publication of the first two volumes in 1784, and subsequently the Napoleonic wars put an end to Krueger's enterprise.

During the middle of the 19th century Jews of Lithuanian origin, who were principally employed as purveyors to the Russian authorities, settled in the town. As a result of their powerful economic status they rapidly gained control of most of the community's institutions. During the last third of the 19th century the rabbinical office was held by Jacob Moses Teomim (see *Teomim family) and until 1904 by R. Menahem Mendel Ḥayyim Landau, a leader of Agudat Israel, later a rabbi in Detroit, U.S. Landau was succeeded by Moses Aaron Taub, and between the two world wars Judah Reuben Neufeld served as the last rabbi of the town.

Industralization, the departure of Jews from regions suffering pogroms, and the expulsion of Jews from Moscow (1891) caused a rapid increase in the Jewish population of Nowy Dwor. In 1897 there were 4,735 Jews (c. 65% of the population) in the town. In 1905/06 Jewish trade unions gained in strength under the influence of the *Bund and the *Po'alei Zion. In addition to retail trade, the Jews of Nowy Dwor engaged in shoemaking, millinery, carpentry, locksmithing, tailoring, and portage; about 300 Jewish women were employed in embroidery workshops. A general conflagration in 1907, in which more than half the town's houses were destroyed, led many Jews to move to Warsaw or to emigrate to the United States. In 1920, during the war in Soviet Russia, the Polish army expelled hundreds of Jews from the town and desecrated its synagogue. In 1921 there were 3,916 Jews (50% of the population) in Nowy Dwor and 3,961 (42%) in 1931. In the municipal elections of 1927, four Jewish delegates won seats in the town's administration and the delegate of the Bund was appointed vice-mayor. For a number of years the CYSHO (*Central Yiddish School Organization) and *Tarbut schools as well as the Shalom Aleichem Library were subsidized by municipal funds. In the early 1930s Jewish haulage workers organized a self-defense movement against anti-Semitic rioters. [A.Cy.]

Holocaust Period. At the outbreak of World War II there were about 4,000 Jews in Nowy Dwor. The German army entered the town on Sept. 30, 1939. The ghetto was established at the beginning of 1941. In May 1941, 3,250 Jews were deported to Pomiechowek camp, where most of them perished. In November 1942 two deportations to *Auschwitz took place. The ghetto was liquidated on Dec. 12, 1942, when 2,000 Jews from Nowy Dwor and nearby Czerwinsk were sent to Auschwitz. After the war the Jewish community of Nowy Dwor was not reconstituted. [Ed.]

Bibliography: Warsaw, Archiwum Glówne Akt Dawnych, KRSWiD 6651 (=C.A.H.J.P., HM/3652); B. Wasiutyński, *Ludność żydowska w Pólsce w wiekach XIX i XX* (1930), 23; I. Schiper (ed.), *Dzieje handlu żydowskiego na ziemiach polskich* (1937), index; J. Shatzky, *Geshikhte fun Yidn in Varshe,* 1 (1947), 134, 137, 234; I. Ringelblum, in: *Kapitlen Geshikhte fun Amolikn Yidishn Lebn in Poyln* (1953); *Pinkas Nowy Dwor* (1965). Printing: Weinryb, in: MGWJ, 77 (1933), 214ff.; Yaari, in: KS, 9 (1933), 436ff.; 10 (1933/34), 372ff.; 19 (1942/43), 204, 216f.; B. Friedberg, *Toledot ha-Defus ha-Ivri be-Polanyah* (1950²), 75ff.

NOWY DZIENNIK ("The New Daily"), first Zionist Polish-language journal. It appeared daily in Cracow from the end of 1918. The paper was representative of the climate of linguistic assimilation current in certain nationalist Zionist circles in the region. Its founding was to some extent the result of the murder of a Jew: since, to the dismay of the Jewish community, the incident was glossed over by the Polish press, a need was felt for some independent means of expression. For technical reasons and because of censorship, the early editions of *Nowy Dziennik* were published in Moravska-Ostrava. However, by the beginning of 1919, the paper had its own building and presses in Cracow. Dr. Wilhelm Berkelhammer, who served as editor for many years, not only set an example of polished newspaper style but fought numerous and continuous battles against anti-Semitism. Other noted editors were Isaac Ignacy *Schwarzbart, Elijah Tisch, and David Lazar, the last serving until the paper's demise during the Holocaust. Among the regular contributors were Osias (Joshua) *Thon, who set the tone of the paper and gave it its political direction, and Moses Kanfer, literary and artistic critic, who was particularly devoted to the Yiddish theater. Other such well-known personalities as Isaac *Deutscher, Hersch *Lauterpacht, and Ezriel *Carlebach also contributed to the paper. Particularly noted for his essays on anti-Semitism was Matthias *Mieses. One important role played by the journal was its publication from time to time of a list compiled by the community leaders of Jews who had converted to Christianity but who sought to keep this secret from the Jewish community. Despite governmental interference and the bombing of its building by Polish nationalist extremists in 1923, the paper prospered. Carefully organized and efficiently run by Sigmund Hochwald, it grew from its initial four to a format of 32 pages. While ideologically the journal served as an organ of the Zionist Movement, its scope was quite wide, serving the general Cracow community as well as the region of western Galicia and Silesia.

Bibliography: I. Schwarzbart, *Tsishn beyde Velt Milkhomes* (1958), 128–42. [M.Lan.]

NOWY SACZ (Pol. **Nowy Sącz;** Ger. **Neu Sandec;** in Jewish sources **Zanz, Naysants**), city in the province of Cracow, S. Poland. Jewish settlement is mentioned in a document of 1469; in 1503 a Jewish eye doctor, Abraham, practiced in Nowy Sacz. The Jews participated in the reconstruction of the town after the invasion of the Swedes. The royal privilege of 1676 (ratified in 1682 by King John III Sobieski) accorded them the right of building their houses on the town's empty lots and of engaging in commerce (mainly with Hungary) and weaving. The Great Synagogue, renowned for its beautiful frescos, was completed in 1746. In 1765 there were 609 Jews (154 families) in Nowy Sacz, paying the poll tax and owning 70 houses (595 additional Jewish poll tax payers lived in 103 surrounding villages). At the beginning of the 19th century Austrian authorities compelled the Jews to live in a special quarter. During the first half of the 19th century the ḥasidic dynasty of the Zanzer Ḥasidim was established (see *Halberstam). In 1880 there were 5,163 Jews (46% of the total population) living in the town, earning their livelihoods from the sale of wood, agricultural produce, and clothing, or engaging in such trades as tailoring, carpentry, shoemaking, and engraving. By 1890 the number of Jews had decreased to 4,120 (32%); to rise again to 7,990 (32%) in 1910. Between 1900 and 1914 a Jewish school was established by the *Baron de Hirsch fund, which in 1907 was attended by 204 pupils. In 1921 the Jewish community numbered 9,009 (34%). *Tarbut and Beth Jacob schools, a yeshivah, and sport clubs were supported by the community. Over 10,000 Jews lived in Nowy Sacz before the outbreak of World War II, with another 5,000 living in smaller towns of the county. [A.Cy.]

Holocaust Period. The German army entered the town on Sept. 5, 1939, and the anti-Jewish terror began. In March 1940 about 700 Jews from Lodz were forced to settle there; in August 1941 a ghetto was established. Two forced labor camps for Jews were built by the Germans near the town: one, in Roznow, existed from the spring of 1940 until December 1942, and the second, in Lipie, from the autumn of 1942 until July 1943. Over 1,000 Jewish prisoners perished in these camps. In April 1942 a few score members of the underground *Po'alei Zion organization fell into German hands and were executed on the site of the town's Jewish cemetery. In Aug. 24–28, 1942, the entire Jewish population was deported to the *Belzec death camp and killed there. [S.Kr.]

Bibliography: R. Mahler, *Yidn in Amolikn Poyln in Likht fun Tsifern* (1958), index; B. Wasiutyński, *Ludność żydowska w Pólsce w wiekach XIX i XX* (1930), 112, 146, 150, 156; J. Sygański, *Historya Nowego Sącza,* 3 vols. (1901–02); I. Schiper, *Studya nad stosunkami gospodarczymi Żydów w Polsce podczas średniowiecza* (1911), index; idem (ed.), *Dzieje handlu żydowskiego na ziemiach polskich* (1937), index; R. Mahler, *Sefer Zanz* (1970). Holocaust: E. Podhorizer-Sandel, in: BZIH, 30 (1959), 87–109.

The former Jewish hospital of Nowy Sacz, photographed in 1964. Courtesy Yad Vashem Archives, Jerusalem.

NUISANCE. The owner or person in possession of land is not at liberty to use it as he pleases. Land, even if unencumbered, may not be used in such manner as to harm or disturb one's neighbors. Any neighbor can require the offending landowner to abate the nuisance or to have the cause thereof removed from their common boundary.

Among the restraints imposed on the use of land, the Mishnah (BB 2) makes mention of the following: A person may not dig a cistern near to his neighbor's cistern or wall, since they would thus be damaged, and he must remove lime from the vicinity of his neighbor's wall; he may not open a bakery or stable under his neighbor's barn, nor a shop on residential premises where the customers will disturb the neighbors; he may not build a wall so close to his neighbor's windows as to darken them; he must not keep his ladder near his neighbor's dovecote since it will enable a weasel to climb it and devour the pigeons; his threshing floor must not be too near a town or his neighbor's field lest the chaff harm the vegetation. There are further instances of the potentially harmful use of land enumerated in the Talmud.

The *tanna*, R. Yose, is of the opinion that the person creating a nuisance cannot be obliged to abate it and is free to act as he pleases and the injured party must keep his distance if he wishes to avoid suffering harm. The *halakhah* of the Talmud was decided in accordance with R. Yose's view, but the latter was interpreted as admitting that the tort-feasor must abate a nuisance if the interference with his neighbor's use of his property arises from his own harmful act (i.e., an act of his own body, as if he had "shot arrows" into his neighbor's domain; BB 22b). The scope of this qualification is not clear and some scholars hold that most of the injuries enumerated in the Mishnah (above) are of the kind qualified by R. Yose, which the latter concedes must be abated by the tort-feasor. Other scholars hold that R. Yose disagrees with the above-mentioned *mishnayot* and obliges the tort-feasor to abate a nuisance only when damage is actually (and directly) caused by his own act (see Rashi and Tos. *ibid.*). In fact, in the post-talmudic period, the instances in which R. Yose was considered to have conceded the existence of tort-feasor's obligation to abate a nuisance were extended as far as possible (see Asher b. Jehiel (Rosh), quoted in Tur, ḤM 155:20–23). The Talmud (BB 17b) also records the dispute over the question whether the obligation—when it exists—of abating a nuisance applies even if the offender's particular use of his land preceded that of his neighbor—the latter suffering no damage until the time of such conflicting use by him—or whether prior use takes precedence. Thus if the injured party's particular use of his land preceded his neighbor's conflicting use of his land, the latter must curtail his use, but if the other way round the obligation rests upon the injured party. There is an opinion (Tos. *ibid.*, 18b), which holds that the rule of precedence by virtue of prior use is universally accepted and that there is no dispute save with regard to a single case, that of digging a cistern in the vicinity of a common boundary with a neighbor.

Which Nuisance Must Be Abated. An analysis of the cases of nuisance referred to in talmudic literature and the reasoning behind them suggests that all cases of nuisance may be divided into four categories: (1) An interference arising when land is used in a manner usual for that particular place and time, but the neighbor suffers injury in an unusual manner, either because of the unusual use of his own land or because he is uncommonly sensitive to the disturbance. It is unanimously agreed that in this event the alleged tort-feasor is at no time obliged to abate the so-called nuisance. (2) The tort-feasor uses his land in an unusual manner for that particular place and time, while the injured neighbor uses his land in the usual manner, in the same way as other people do, and is neither more sensitive nor anxious than most people. In this event all agree that the tort-feasor must always abate the nuisance he has created. (3) Both parties use their land in the usual manner and the injured party is not uncommonly sensitive. (4) The tort-feasor uses his land in an unusual manner, and the injured party does so too or is uncommonly sensitive. The latter two categories are the subject of the dispute mentioned above between R. Yose and the sages, as to whether the party causing the nuisance is obliged to abate it or whether it must be suffered by the injured neighbor; and of the dispute whether the injuring party must always abate the nuisance or whether it is a matter of prior use taking precedence. Most acts of nuisance referred to in the Talmud fall into the third of these categories (see Albeck, bibliography).

The Rules of Nuisance as Part of the Law of Property. The prohibition against using land in a manner interfering with a neighbor's enjoyment of his own property is inherent in the proprietary rights over that immovable property, and the right to the undisturbed use of one's property may be sold like any other proprietary right. A person may sell or transfer part (or all) of his right to the undisturbed enjoyment of his property by agreeing to a particular use of his neighbor's property, whereupon the neighbor may make such use of his land regardless of any nuisance thereby caused to the former. Thus, for instance, a person may become entitled to erect a dovecote alongside this common boundary and may transfer this right, together with the land itself, to a new owner. Furthermore this right is retained by the owner of the disturbing property even when the adjacent land is sold to a new owner (see Sh. Ar., ḤM 155:24). A nuisance which is continued for a period of three years (or even from the outset, according to some scholars), if supported by a plea that the right was granted to him by the injured neighbor (or even without such a plea, according to some scholars), constitutes evidence of such right of user. However, these rules apply only when the nuisance is not so severe as to be insufferable (*ibid.*, 155:35–36.

See also *Servitudes; **Ḥazakah*.

Relationship of Nuisance to the Laws of Tort. A person suffering a nuisance may oblige his neighbor to abate the nuisance and if physical damage results from the nuisance which itself was the result of the neighbor's negligence, he is also entitled to be compensated for such damage (BB 20b). If the nuisance is of a kind which the law does not require the tort-feasor to abate, the neighbor cannot oblige the tort-feasor to do so, nor, according to some scholars, can he recover compensation for damage of a physical nature even when caused by negligence, because he, in turn, is expected to take precautions. Other scholars, however, hold the tort-feasor liable for resulting damage. If a person's use of his land is such that it may cause his neighbor damage for which compensation is payable but it is not likely that such damage will result, the neighbor cannot demand the abatement of the nuisance because people are not normally afraid of or disturbed by an unlikely risk; but if in fact the damage does result from the landowner's negligence he is obliged to compensate his neighbor. If such use of the land habitually causes damage for which compensation is payable, people will usually be disturbed thereby and the neighbor can require the abatement thereof. If the damage is of a kind which is foreseeable, the landowner will be deemed negligent, but if the damage was unforeseeable, he is exempt from liability. The law of the State of Israel (Civil Wrongs Ordinance, 1947) defines private nuisance as any conduct which causes a material interference with the reasonable use and enjoyment of another's immovable property. The injured party is entitled to compensation and the court may order the abatement of the nuisance.

Bibliography: Gulak, Yesodei, 1 (1922), 134, 146f.; ET, 8 (1957), 659–702; 10 (1961), 628–96; S. Albeck, in: *Sinai*, 60 (1967), 97–123.
[Sh.A.]

NUMBERS, BOOK OF (Heb. בְּמִדְבַּר; "in the wilderness"), the fourth book of the Pentateuch. Like the other books of the Pentateuch its name in Hebrew, *Be-Midbar* is taken from the first significant word in the book (in popular usage the book is referred to by the transliteration *Ba-Midbar*). It is the only book of the Pentateuch, however, which has a specific name in the Talmud, *Ḥummash ha-Pekudim*, which corresponds to its name in Engish, derived, through the Vulgate, from the title given in the Septuagint.

Contents and Sequence. Numbers has a broad outline, with the main thread leading from preparations for the departure from Sinai and ending with the stay in Shittim in Moab opposite Jericho, in three major sections: (1) 1:1–10:10. Continued stay at Sinai, a period of 19 days. (2) 10:11–22:1. From Sinai to the plains of Moab, which is reached in the 40th year of the Exodus (by subtraction, 38 years). (3) 22:2–36:13. In the plains of Moab, less than five months. The book is usually viewed as a congeries of materials, without theme or structure, but although the placement of every section cannot be meaningfully explained, clear patterns emerge. Numbers provides the available traditional material on the experience of the Israelites en route from the site of revelation to the site of incipient occupation. The first ten chapters conclude the bloc of priestly material dealing with the portable sanctuary, given in the previous books. Where Exodus (25–31 and 35–40) gives the details of the preparation of a portable sanctuary, and Leviticus the consecration of the officiating clergy and the sacrificial ritual, Numbers 1–10 concentrates on the movement of the sanctuary. The functionaries featured are Levites, who lend logistical support to the priests.

(1) At Sinai (1:1–10:10). The first chapters of the book concentrate on preparations, practical and cultic, for the desert marches and encampments. In chapters 1–4 the subject is the group service (צָבָא, *ẓava'*, usually military service, but not exclusively; cf. Akk. *ṣābu*, and see Naḥmanides to Num. 1:2). The laic tribes must prepare to engage in battle; the Levites carry the components of the portable sanctuary. The numbers of the able-bodied males are given; and the order in which they camped and marched with the 12 tribes ranged around the sanctuary, three on each side. This census, oriented to military preparedness as well as procedures for the march, has the same total as Exodus 38:26, namely 603, 550 (Num. 2:32). The numbers are not easy to interpret in detail, but they reflect an effort to clothe the schematic number 600,000 (see *Exodus) with the details of a tribal breakdown.

The procedures for the *Nazirite follow (6:1–21). As seen here in its aspect of supererogatory piety, the institution offers an outlet to the zealous Israelite; he may take on, for a limited time, additional personal restrictions. This part of the book, concentrating on the protection of the Tabernacle, culminates with the Priestly Blessing (6:22–27). Chapter 7, which describes the presents offered by the tribal leaders for the service of the Tabernacle, jointly (six wagons and 12 oxen) and individually, is the longest chapter in the Torah. Each tribal leader is assigned a day for his presentation, and the formula is scrupulously repeated without variation. The order of the tribes follows that of chapter 2. In final readiness for the march, two silver trumpets are fashioned (10:1–10), and instructions are provided for their use, in battle and on festive occasions. The date of departure is given (20th of Nisan, year 2 of the Exodus), and the pattern of breaking camp and forming the march. A fragment containing an interchange between Moses and his father-in-law is followed by the formulas recited at the departure of the Ark and its return to rest (10:29–36).

(2) From Sinai to the Plains of Moab (10:11–22:1). All these preparations for the imminent entry into the Promised Land came to naught as a result of the moral degeneration of the people, which is described in a series of rebellious acts which form the main subject of the second section, chapters 11–25. It results in the decree that all those who were 20 years old and more when they left Egypt, with the sole exception of Joshua and Caleb, are to die in the wilderness. The "murmuring" which runs throughout this part of the book is probably a technical term for disloyalty, in the terminology of a treaty between suzerain and vassal (see *Covenant). The first fragment gives an occasion of murmuring linked to a place-name. It is followed by a long account (11:4–35) in which the staple food, manna, is augmented by the delicacy of quail meat (as in Ex. 16). Woven into this story is the initiation of 70 elders to share the burden of the people of Israel, the prerequisite for such service being an experience of prophetic ecstasy occasioned by the presence of Moses in the vicinity of the Tent. Probably the original number was 72, six from each tribe; the failure of *Eldad and Medad to report to the Tent resulted in the installation of only 70. The cause of the disaffection, which began among the non-Israelites (11:4), was the monotony of the diet. The hunger for substantial food is satisfied, but the people gorge themselves, and a plague results. The account may have a natural basis: the sudden appearance of a flock of quails, whose flesh the Israelites consumed after it had gone bad. The next account treats the loss of faith of Miriam and Aaron (chapter 12). The occasion is Moses' marriage to a Kushite, although the laconic account gives no indication of whether the pigmentation of the woman is an issue. The affliction of Miriam with leprosy, which turns her skin white, may be a poetic judgment because she slurred a black woman. The nadir in the loss of faith is the story of the refusal to invade Canaan from the south (chapters 13–14). Twelve men, eminent representatives of each tribe, reconnoiter the land that has been promised to the Israelites. It is this incident which brings the decree of the death of that generation in the wilderness. The story is of major importance in Israelite tradition. It is similar in many points to the other great act of treason, the episode of the Golden Calf (Ex. 32–34). It has a military context, which is central to the wilderness experience and the conquest of the Promised Land. Chapter 15 is an aggregate of prescriptions, which are apparently placed here as a pause in the drama. It begins with cultic ordinances for Canaan, which serve as a placebo after the dire punishment. Then come prescriptions relating to errant behavior, climaxed by the execution of the man who gathered firewood on the Sabbath. The final section ordains the use of a garment fringe with an azure thread, to serve as a reminder of the Covenant. In pre-Israelite times the fringe had an apotropaic function, the warding off of demonic harm, and was regarded as an extension of the person. As with the *phylacteries, the fringe was transvalued by the Bible, to serve as a reminder to the Israelite that he is part of a Covenant community. This is a fitting epilogue to the account of the treason in chapters 13–14, as well as to the ordinances of errancy attached to it. The rebellion of Korah (chapters 16–17) blends two (or three) attacks on the authority of YHWH as vested in Moses and Aaron. One reflects the dissatisfaction of a group of laymen from the tribe of Reuben. Another shows the dissatisfaction of a Levite, from the most important family (Kohath) of the Levites with the assignment of Levites to the subordinate service of supporting the priests, who alone are authorized

End of the Book of Numbers in the *Coburg Pentateuch*, Germany, 1395. London, British Museum, Add. Ms. 19776, fol. 96r.

to officiate in the Tent. Through divine intervention both parties are punished. The subsequent murmuring of the Israelites against Moses and Aaron leads to punishment by plague, which is stopped when Aaron carries a pan with burning incense into the midst of the dying. In this way, the authority of Aaron is brought home strikingly, and is underscored by the contest of the staves. This is followed by a restatement of the relationship between the priests and the Levites (chapter 18), including the perquisites due to each group (*terumah* and *tithe).

Then comes the prescription of the *red heifer (chapter 19), the ashes of which serve to decontaminate those in a state of ritual pollution; the ashes also contaminate the uncontaminated. This double nature of sanctuary taboo reflects the attitude toward a superhuman power source, which can electrify or electrocute, dramatized in the Korah story. This may explain the location of chapter 19. The death of the leadership is the theme of chapter 20, which opens with the death of Miriam and ends with the death of Aaron. The cause of the death of Aaron and the doom of Moses is reported in the laconic account of water from the rock (cf. Ex. 17:1–7): they demonstrate loss of faith, which fits into the catalog of acts of disobedience.

The narrative now moves to the end of the 40 years in the wilderness. The generation of the Exodus is coming to an end. It is here that the Israelites anticipate the move into the area of Transjordan, and they ask for peaceful passage through the southern state of Edom, but permission is refused (20:14–21). They gain a victory over the Canaanite king of Arad (21:1–3), and turn south, to avoid Edom. Another incident of dissatisfaction is recorded, which is met by God with venomous snakes, followed by an antidote. Reports of their itinerary are interspersed with two fragments of poetry. Then follows the victory of Israel over the Amorite king Sihon, which results in the first acquisition of territory. This is followed by a brief account of a second victory, over Og king of Bashan. With this the Israelites have occupied the land to the north of the Transjordan states, and the narrative of the march ends.

(3) In the Plains of Moab (22:2–36:13). Chapters 22–24 is the story of *Balaam, who is hired to curse the Israelites. (The technique of poetic damnation prior to a battle is familiar from later Arabic history.) The expert is summoned in desperation by Balak, king of Moab, with the concurrence of his Midianite overlords. Repeatedly Balaam tries to curse the Israelites; he is able only to bless them, and is expelled angrily by Balak. This section demonstrates the invincibility of Israel under the protection of YHWH, impervious to the greatest outside powers, human or magical. It leads, however, to another act of treason. The people are enticed by Moabite women, and are attracted to their cultic worship; a (Simeonite) tribal leader is beguiled by a Midianite woman of high position and the two parade their liaison in the presence of the whole camp. Phinehas kills them, earning for his descendants the right of perpetual priesthood (25:1–15). The Israelites are enjoined to assail the Midianites (25:16ff.). Here the catalog of treacherous acts ends. The census of chapter 26 follows the pattern of chapter 1, with a slightly lower total, reflecting the losses resulting from punishment, which offset the natural increase. The census also serves to introduce the theme of the remainder of the book and the preparation for the conquest of Canaan.

The latter part of the book deals with the claim of the daughters of *Zelophehad, who had no sons, for a share in the future allotment. Their claim is allowed (27:1–11), with the stipulation that they marry within their own tribe, so as not to disturb the tribal divisions (chapter 36). The separation of this unit of material, and its location, is perhaps the clearest example of redactional arrangement in the Torah. The promise of the land is the subject of the remaining material. Into this outline is set, first, the ceremony of succession, so that the people have Joshua to command them during the conquest. Again the narrative is suspended, by the insertion of prescriptions concerning festival sacrifices (chapters 28–29). There is no clear reason for the placement of these cultic regulations here, except that they are part of the testamentary matter that preceded the death of Moses, as the subscription (30:1) indicates. The same is true for chapter 30, the regulations governing the validity of vows made by a woman. The defeat of Midian is recorded in chapter 31. Chapter 32 records the approval of the request of two and a half tribes to settle in the territory of the Amorites. Chapter 33 contains a list of the stations in the wilderness trek, most of which are unidentified, and many of which are not mentioned elsewhere. It is followed by the command to conquer Canaan and distribute the land among the tribes. There follows an outline of the ideal borders of the territory designated for Israelite settlement, and then the names of the men who will effect the division of the land by lot (chapter 34). Chapter 35 calls for the assignment of cities for special inhabitants: for the Levites, who have no share in the land allotment, and for the unwitting manslayer, to find refuge from the blood-avenger (cf. Ex. 21:12–14). The book ends with the resumption of the subject of Zelophehad's daughters.

Critical View. The problems of the composition of Numbers must be viewed in the broader framework of *Bible criticism. The composition of the Pentateuch from earlier sources seems beyond challenge. The main source of Numbers is P (see *Pentateuch). The argument that the priestly material is preponderantly post-Exilic because of its wordiness is belied by the discovery of numerous pre-Mosaic cultic texts from the Ancient Near East which display the same characteristics of the repetition of formulas and scrupulous detail. The argument from exaggerated and schematic numbers is similarly neutralized; earliest texts, such as the Sumerian Kings List, have exactly these features. The prodigious cultic requirements found in the priestly material are found in other early cultures, notably in Hittite sources. The theory that P's legislation reflects the post-Exilic theocracy is still widely held, but has been challenged (by Y. Kaufmann). Regarding the narrative material apart from P, it has been recognized that Numbers independently would not permit us to assign it to consistent sources; only the association with the J and E of Genesis and Exodus suggests such analysis (M. Noth). The assignment of dates is extremely hazardous. One may recognize various narrative traditions, not necessarily consistent throughout the book (or the Torah), combined with priestly material, narrative and cultic, which is of diverse dates and origins.

The attempt to descry principles and patterns of arrangement is as early as the rabbis of the Talmud. They pursued the question of juxtaposition (or sequence), and it was they who implied an order other than the simple chronological thread: "There is no earlier and later in the Torah" (see Rashi on Num. 9:1).

The *census must be compared with similar materials from *Mari (18th–17th centuries B.C.E.), where the enrollment is related to both military service and the assignment of land. The terms for the census enrollment there, *ṣābam paqādu* (or *šatāru*), and the Hebrew terms *ẓava'* and *paqad,* indicate the cognate nature of the materials. The census in Numbers has two separate contexts. In chapter 1, the military implication sets the tone for chapters 1–25, namely the trek. The census in chapter 26 closes off this section, and looks forward to the possession of Canaan by the Israelites, and the allotment of the land. The second portion of the book (chapters 27–36) is also marked off by inclusion. The subject matter is less unified, and there is the suggestion of a series of appendices following the main narrative (cf. II Sam. 21–24).

Dating and Historical Value. An indication of the historical value of Numbers is the treatment of the Midianites. O. Eissfeldt has argued cogently that in the 13th century B.C.E. the Midianites had a far-flung empire without a territorial state. They operated as overlords of nations with resident overseers. The parade example of their suzerainty is in Moab, where "the elders of Midian" are as alarmed as the Moabites over the propinquity of the militant Israelites (22:2–4). The five Midianite nobles killed in the Amorite territory of Sihon (Josh. 13:21) must have been resident overseers of Midian in Heshbon.

Eissfeldt's thesis adds dimension to the references to Midian throughout the book. As the camp at Sinai breaks up, the Midianite dignitary Hobab, related to Moses by marriage, is exhorted to accompany the Israelites. Not only would he know the wilderness areas very well, but he would be a guarantor of safe passage through the extensive areas under Midianite control. If the Kushite woman (Num. 12) is Midianite (in Hab. 3:7 Kushan is parallel to Midian), she is the daughter of Hobab. Representatives of Midian accompany the Moabite ambassadors to enlist the aid of Balaam (Num. 22:7). It is possible that the Midianites initiate the demoralization of Israel (25:6–9, 14–19). The order is given to assail Midian (not Moab), and it is carried out (chapter 31). After the second millennium B.C.E., Midianites were such a rare sight in Israel that a writer might help his readers by telling them that the Midianites were a variety of Ishmaelites (Judg. 8:24).

According to the critical view it is virtually certain that the Book of Numbers as we now have it is considerably later than Moses, but the current tendency to minimize the historic value of its contents will probably be reserved.

Religious Values. The treatment of the traditions from the wilderness experience in Numbers has many points of contact with the wilderness journey in Exodus (especially 16–17). Abrabanel has shown that the two collections are sharply distinguished: in Exodus, prior to Sinai, the Israelite failure of faith was not punished; in Numbers, after the revelation, it was punished. It seems that the Israelite traditions of the wilderness experience were largely used in duplicate, to convey the implications of the Covenant. Numbers 1–26 stresses the failure of faith even after the elaborate sanctuary ritual is instituted. The peroration comes in Deuteronomy 31:16ff. This reveals the (or a) Torah view regarding man: he is constitutionally capable of rising above the realities of everyday life, but he does not. Confronted with circumstances, the theoretical supports of religious experience desert him, and he reacts to human situations with human behavior, which is not the standard set by the deity.

On the whole, this is a depressing message. But while individuals and communities fail, the people survives, always to find another chance to live up to the Covenant standards of God. This hopeful note of recurrent opportunity is muted but audible in the latter section of Numbers. The failures of the wilderness experience are tied off: Israel is ensconced in the territory east of the Jordan. Perhaps in the land of the Covenant, the people of the Covenant will fulfill the terms of the Covenant.

Bibliography: COMMENTARIES: H. L. Strack (Ger., 1894); B. Baentsch (Ger., 1903); G. B. Gray (Eng., ICC, 1903, 1955); H. Holzinger (Ger., 1903); A. H. McNeile (Eng., 1911); H. Gressmann (Ger., 1922[2]); L. E. Elliott-Binns (Eng., 1927); P. Heinisch (Ger., 1936); J. G. Greenstone (Eng., 1948); H. Schneider (Ger., 1952); J. Marsh (Eng., 1953); M. Noth (Eng., 1966). STUDIES: M. H. Segal, in: *Eretz-Israel,* 3 (1954), 73–83; E. A. Speiser, in: BASOR, 149 (1958), 17–25; R. C. Dentan, in: IDB, 3 (1962), 567–71; B. A. Levine, in: JAOS, 85 (1965), 307–18; O. Eissfeldt, in: JBL, 87 (1968), 383–93; W. F. Albright, *Yahweh and the Gods of Canaan* (1968). [I.CA.]

NUMBERS, TYPICAL AND IMPORTANT. Biblical numbers are primarily based on the decimal system, which is of Hamito-Egyptian origin. The sexagesimal system, however, which ultimately derives from Sumerian usage, also plays an important role in Scripture, and since 60 is divisible by ten and five, the two methods of reckoning easily coalesce. The numbers in the Bible range from one (Gen. 1:5) to 100,000,000 (Dan. 7:10), though the latter figure is to be regarded as a hyperbole rather than a literal numerical expression. The largest number to be understood literally is that given in I Chronicles 21:5 in connection with David's census: 1,100,000 men from Israel plus 470,000 from Judah that drew the sword (but cf. the smaller figures in II Sam. 24:9). The idea of infinity in the mathematical sense (in contrast to the theological concept of God's unlimited powers) is not found in the Bible. However, it is recognized that there are limits to the human ability to count (Gen. 13:16; 41:49).

Biblical Arithmetic. The Israelites in biblical times did not take a special interest in mathematics. Their knowledge was confined, it seems, to their essential needs, and was based on Egyptian and Babylonian methods of calculation. The four basic arithmetical operations are represented in the Bible, but only the results—not the method of calculating—are given. Thus there are examples of simple addition (Num. 11:26), subtraction (Gen. 18:28–33), multiplication (Lev. 25:8; Num. 7:84–86), and division (Num. 31:27). More complicated operations, involving "the rule of three," are exemplified in Leviticus 25:50ff.; 27:18, 23. The Hebrews also had an elementary control of fractions, but they seem to have avoided, as did other peoples of antiquity, the problem of converting mixed fractions to a common denominator. The biblical use of complementary fractions (i.e., fractions in which the numerator is one less than the denominator, e.g., $\frac{2}{3}$, II Kings 11:7; $\frac{4}{5}$, Gen. 47:24; $\frac{9}{10}$, Neh. 11:1) shows Egyptian and Mesopotamian influence. Of particular interest is the use of certain parts of the body to express fractions or multiplication, e.g., *yad,* "hand" (fractions: *ibid.;* multiplication: Gen. 43:34); *regel,* "foot" or "times" (multiplication: Num. 22:28); *pi,* "mouth" (fraction: Zech. 13:8; multiplication: Deut. 21:17, according to many exegetes). The term *pi shenayim* originally meant two-thirds but subsequently came to signify "twice as much" (II Kings 2:9). The latter is the meaning it always has in the Mishnah and Talmud. In Deuteronomy 21:17 the sense is uncertain: the expression could mean either two-thirds of the inheritance or a double portion. *Rosh* "head," frequently occurs in the sense of "sum, total" (Ex. 30:12; Num. 1:2), or "capital" (Lev. 5:24). The curious psychological approach that enables *yad,* for example, to serve both for division and multiplication is also reflected in the use of certain denominative verbs (in the *pi'el*) derived from numbers. Thus *shillesh* denotes "to divide into three" (Deut. 19:3) and "to repeat an action three times" (I Kings 18:34). The value of π was taken to be 3 (I Kings 7:23). Even the Mishnah in *Eruvin* 1:5 retains this approximate value, but *Mishnat ha-Middot* (second century) estimates π as $\frac{22}{7}$.

Method of Expression. Biblical numbers are expressed by words denoting units, tens, 100, 200, 1,000, 2,000, 10,000, 20,000, and by combinations of these. There is no real evidence of the use of arithmetical symbols either in Scripture, or in monumental inscriptions of the biblical period, like the *Siloam Inscription (c. 700); cf. also the *Mesha Stele of the ninth century. However, the use of figures in everyday documents, chiefly for small numbers, is demonstrated by the *Samaria ostraca (eighth century), where both words and figures are employed for numerals. The *Lachish Letters (sixth century) likewise contain numerical symbols. But, whereas these figures appear to be based on Egyptian models, other Samarian inscriptions displays symbols that correspond to the Phoenician-Aramaic tradition. The *Elephantine papyri (fifth century) also use arithmetical signs (chiefly vertical strokes for units and horizontal lines for tens). In later times (the Hasmonean period and throughout the talmudic age), following the Greek example, the letters of the alphabet were given numerical values. The letters *alef* to *tet* represent the digits one to nine; *yod* to *ẓade,* the tens to 90; and *kaf* to *tav* 100 to 400; thousands are expressed by the letters for units with two dots above. The system eventually gave rise to the numerological method called **gematria,* which R. Eliezer b. R. Yose made the 29th of his 32 hermeneutical rules, and examples of which are to be found already in the New Testament (Rev. 13:18), as well as in the Talmud and Midrash; while the kabbalists went to fantastic lengths in the application of this exegetical device. In modern times, G. R. Driver has revived the idea that even in the Bible, numbers are occasionally indicated by the first letter of their name (acrophonic system) or by the numerical value of letters of the alphabet. Thus the number 318 in Genesis 14:14 represents **אליעזר** (Eliezer) (cf. Gen. R. 43:2, and the *Epistle of Barnabas*).

Symbolic and Rhetorical Use. Biblical numbers are not always intended to be taken at their face value. They are often used indefinitely—as round figures—or rhetorically, for emphasis or in a hyperbolic sense. At times the rhetorical effect is achieved through a latent number, i.e., certain words or names occur a given number of times, although the actual figure is not specified. Many numbers are noteworthy for their symbolic nuances. Hebrew literature is not altogether unique in this regard; analogues are to be found in Egyptian, Sumerian, Akkadian, Canaanite, and Hittite writings. Ugaritic, in particular, provides many examples of the rhetorical and symbolic use of numbers. Especially significant is the biblical use of sacred numbers, which play an important religious role. There is, in addition, a distinct tendency in Scripture to achieve numerical harmony or symmetry. This aspect has been worked out in considerable detail for Genesis, notably its early chapters, by U. Cassuto (see bibliography).

ONE. One is sometimes used as the indefinite article (I Sam. 24:14), and often as an indefinite pronoun, "someone, anyone, a certain man" (II Kings 4:39). Though a cardinal number, it is also used as an ordinal (Gen. 1:5; 8:5, 13; Ruth 1:4). It also signifies uniqueness and indivisibility. Hence it is expressive of the unity of marriage (Gen. 2:24) and of the doctrine of monotheism (Deut. 6:4).

TWO. The fact that various organs and limbs of the body occur in pairs (eyes, hands, etc.) invested the number two with a certain importance. The animals entered the ark in pairs; the Decalogue was inscribed on two tablets of stone. Often two sacrifices were ordained (Lev. 14:22). The fraction one-half is also common in the Bible: the half-tribe of Manasseh (Num. 32:33) and the half-shekel (Ex. 30:13). The Hebrew preference for the concrete to the abstract finds expression, inter alia, in the idiomatic use of two for "a few" (Num. 9:22; I Kings 17:12). Sometimes "three" is added to emphasize the approximate character of the number (II Kings 9:32; Job 33:29; Isa. 17:6). Mention may also be made here of the idiom *temol shilshom,* "hitherto" (literally: 'yesterday, the third day back'). A not uncommon device for achieving emphasis is the repetition (latent two) of a word or phrase (I Kings 13:2; Isa. 43:25).

THREE. Three is a very common biblical number. At times it is difficult to tell whether it is used with precision, or as a small round number (Gen. 30:36; Ex. 2:2); but the addition of the next high number establishes its approximate character (Ex. 20:5; Jer. 36:23). Of special importance is its use in sacred contexts. It conveys the idea of completeness, having a beginning, middle, and end. Even in remote antiquity the pagan peoples worshiped triads of gods (in Babylonia: Anu, Bel, and Ea; in Egypt: Isis, Osiris, and Horus). The universe was divided into heaven, earth, and the abyss (or the netherworld), which the three deities represented. The family group of father, mother, and child, without doubt, also contributed to the significance of the number. In the Bible three has various religious associations: a three-year old (or third-born) sacrifice in Genesis 15:9; three feasts (Ex. 23:14); for three years the fruit of a newly planted tree was forbidden (Lev. 19:23); ritual purification on the third day (Num. 19:12; 31:19); Daniel kneeled and prayed three times a day (Dan. 6:11). The following occurrences of three are also of interest: In Genesis 40, three has symbolic significance. It exercises a mystic power in the story of Elijah's revival of the child (I Kings 17:21). Three cities of refuge are mentioned in Deuteronomy 19:7, 9. Three daughters (plus seven sons) seems to be an ideal number (Job 1:2; 42:13). Three is latent in a number of passages where it expresses a complete and perfect number, or is used for emphasis. The expression "and God blessed" occurs, for example, three times in Genesis 1:22, 28; 2:3. The Sanctuary has three divisions: a court, a holy place, and a Holy of Holies (Ex. 26:33; 27:9; I Kings 6:16–17). In Aaron's benediction (Num. 6:24–26) the Tetragrammaton occurs thrice, and three pairs of blessings are pronounced. On the other hand, the trisagion in Isaiah 6:3 is a form of superlative (in the Qumran scroll, 1QIsa, "holy" is found only twice); while the occurrence of "temple of the Lord" three times in Jeremiah 7:4 merely lends emphasis to the prophet's mocking rebuke.

FOUR. The importance of the number four is probably derived from the four cardinal points of the compass (some scholars point to the square). It is regarded as sacred in various parts of the world, and signifies completeness and sufficiency. Four rivers issued from the Garden of Eden (Gen. 2:10). Jephthah's daughter was lamented annually for four days (Judg. 11:40). In Jeremiah 15:2 the people is divided into four groups, each subjected to a different type of disaster; in the next verse the category of "the sword" is itself divided into four phases. There are four winds; four quarters of heaven (Jer. 49:36); four sore judgments (Ezek. 14:21); and four horns that scatter Judah (Zech. 2:1 [1:18]). The number four frequently occurs in the measurements of the furniture of the Tabernacle (Ex. 25ff.; 36ff.) and of the Temple (I Kings 7). The bearers of God's throne are four (Ezek. 1, 10), and four chariots issue from two mountains (Zech. 6:1–8). Multiples of four are discernible in the length of the Tabernacle curtains—28 cubits (Ex. 26:2); in the large round number 400 (Gen. 15:13; Judg. 21:12), and in the still larger figure of 400,000 (Judg. 20:2, 17; II Chron. 13:3).

FIVE. Five probably means simply "a few" in II Kings 7:13, perhaps also in Genesis 43:34; 47:2 (cf. Er. 6:6, 8). Five as a basic number goes back to remote antiquity. There was a primitive Hamitic system based on the number five before the decimal system. It is obviously derived from the fingers of the hand used by early man in his simple calculations. In the Bible, five is related to both the decimal and sexagesimal systems. It is a feature of sacred architecture (I Kings 7:39, 49). It is also found in connection with penalties (Ex. 21:37), redemption (Num. 3:47; 18:16), and gifts (Gen. 43:34; 45:22). The fraction one-fifth is likewise common (Lev. 5:16; 22:14). It is often used as a small round number (Lev. 26:8; I Sam. 17:40; Isa. 19:18). For the multiple 50 see below. Other multiples up to 500,000 occur frequently (Gen. 5:32; Ex. 30:23–24; II Chron. 13:17, et al.).

SIX. Six is part of the sexagesimal system, but has little symbolic value. Examples of its occurrence are: the working days of the week (Ex. 20:9); the maximum years of servitude for a Hebrew slave (Ex. 21:2); the steps of Solomon's throne (I Kings 10:19–20); the wings of the seraphim (Isa. 6:2); the six-cubit measuring reed of Ezekiel's vision (Ezek. 40:5; 41:8).

SEVEN. Seven played an exceptionally important role in antiquity. It was sacred to Semitic and other peoples, including the Egyptians, Assyrians, Persians, and the Vedic folk in India. Its importance is often derived from the worship of the seven heavenly bodies: the sun, moon, and the five planets. It is also pointed out that the seven-day week was approximately a quarter of the lunar month (29½ days), and that the Pleiades (Amos 5:8) were thought to comprise seven stars. Others see the origin of the number's prominence in the fact that it is composed of the sacred numbers three and four, or in the "unrelated" character of seven in the series one to ten. Like the Sumerians, the biblical writers often add seven to a large number to indicate a very big figure. U. Cassuto writes: "It clearly follows that the chronology of the Book of Genesis as a whole is also founded on the dual principle of the sexagesimal system and the addition of seven" (*From Adam to Noah*, in bibl., 259). In the Bible the number seven is connected with every aspect of religious life in every period: e.g., the clean beasts in the ark (Gen. 7:2ff.); Abraham's covenant with Abimelech (Gen. 21:28–30); cleansing from leprosy (Lev. 14); the festivals (Lev. 23; Deut. 16:9); Balaam's altars (Num. 23); the induction of the priests and the consecration of the altars (Ex. 29:35–37); sacrifices (Gen. 8:20; Num. 28:11; Job 42:8; I Chron. 15:26); the Temple furnishings (I Kings 7:17); the *menorah* (Ex. 25:31–37; Zech. 4:2); the Temple steps (Ezek. 40:22); the width of the Temple entrance (Ezek. 41:3); the sprinkling of blood (Lev. 4:6, 17;16:14; Num. 19:4) and the like. The innate, mystic power of seven is exemplified in Joshua 6:4, 8, 13 (Jericho); Judges 16:13, 19 (Samson); and II Kings 5:10 (Naaman). It also occurs in connection with punishment (Gen. 4:24; Lev. 26:18; Deut. 28:7, 25; II Sam. 21:6; Prov. 6:31; Dan. 4:13, 20, 29; 9:27). In relation to time, seven represents a fitting (or sacred) period (Gen. 1:3ff.; 8:12; 50:10; Ex. 7:25; Lev. 8:33; Josh. 6). More generally it indicates a complete or round number of moderate size (Isa. 4:1; 11:15; Micah 5:4; Ps. 12:7 [6]; Prov. 26:16, 25; Job 1:2; Esth. 1:10; 2:9). In Deuteronomy 7:1 it is equated with "many." Other interesting references are: Genesis 29:20, 27, 30 and Judges 14:12, 17 (marriage); Ezekiel 9:2 (angels); II Kings 4:35 (sneezes of revival); Genesis 41; II Kings 8:1 (famine and plenty); Genesis 33:3 (prostrations; parallels are found in the Tell El-Amarna Letters and in Ugaritic writings). Multiples of seven bear the same character with added emphasis (Lev. 12:5; Num. 29:13; I Kings 8:65). For 70 see below. The half of seven, three and a half, also has special significance. "Times, time, and half a time" occurs in Daniel 7:25 and 12:7. "Half of the week" in Daniel 9:27 is explained by C. H. Cornill to mean 3½ years and to have its origin in the 3½ years of Antiochus' persecution. H. Gunkel, however, traces the expression to Babylonia (half Kislev, Tevet, Shevat, and Adar), the references being to the 3½ months between the winter solstice and the festival of Marduk, i.e., the period of the supremacy of Tiamat.

EIGHT AND NINE. The numbers eight and nine do not appear to have any intrinsic symbolic import. Their significance seems to be related to seven and ten respectively. The eighth day of circumcision (Gen. 17:12), of the consecration of firstborn beasts (Ex. 22:29), of the sacrifices of the defiled Nazirite (Num. 6:10), and of the holy convocation (Lev. 23:36) is simply the day after the important period of seven days. Noteworthy, however, is Ezekiel's predilection for the number eight in the Temple structure (Ezek. 40:9, 31, 34, 37). Nine is at times significant insofar as it is one less than the important number ten (Neh. 11:1).

TEN. Like five, ten is clearly derived from the use of the fingers in counting (the Sefirot, it may be noted, emanate from the fingers according to *Sefer Yeẓirah*), and is the basis of the numeral system chiefly, though not solely, used in the Bible. It expresses completeness and perfection (Gen. 24:10, 22; Josh. 22:14; Judg. 17:10; II Kings 20:9–11; Jer. 41:8; Job 19:3). Its sacred character, which may derive from the fact that it is the product of three and seven (both sacred numbers), is exemplified in the Decalogue (Ex. 20:2ff.), where it may also serve as a mnemonic; the tithes (Gen. 14:20; Num. 18:21, 26; Deut. 26:12); the Tabernacle and Temple furnishings, including multiples of ten (Ex. 26; I Kings 6–7; Ezek. 45; II Chron. 4); and the minimum number of righteous men required to save Sodom. It also occurs in latent form: e.g., there are ten patriarchs from Adam to Noah (Gen. 5), and ten from Noah to Abraham (Gen. 11:10–27). It is stated that the Israelites put the Lord to test ten times (Num. 14:22). In ritual observances the fraction one-tenth occurs frequently (Num. 28).

TWELVE. The number 12 may have derived its importance from the division of the lunar year into 12 months, and from the 12 signs of the Zodiac. It should also be noted that it can be broken down into the significant numbers five (+) seven or three (×) four. But undoubtedly its divisibility and its role in the Sumerian sexagesimal system gave it a special status. In the Bible the fact that the tribes numbered 12 (Gen. 35:22; 42:13, 32; 49:28; Num. 1:44) endowed the number with special religious significance (cf. the Greek amphictyonies). To maintain the number 12, Ephraim and Manasseh were counted as two tribes when Levi was omitted. The tribes of Ishmael likewise numbered 12 (Gen. 17:20). Representative persons and objects often correspond to the number of the tribes (Ex. 24:4; 28:21; Lev. 24:5; Num. 7:3; 17:17, 21; Josh. 4:2; I Kings 10:20; 18:31; Ezek. 48:31ff.; Ezra 6:17; 8:35). Multiples of 12 are found in the 24 classes of priests and Levites (I Chron. 24:4; 25:31); the 48 levitical cities (Num. 35:7); the 24,000 men in the monthly courses that served King David (I Chron. 27:1–15). The male descendants of Adam listed in Genesis 4:1–26 numbered 12, and the verb *yalad* ("to bear") occurs there 12 times.

TWENTY. Twenty marks a distinctive period in human life. Isaac's sons were born 20 years after marriage (Gen. 25:20, 26). Also, the age for army service was 20 (Num. 1:3).

FORTY. Forty is an important round number, indicating a fairly long period. The length of a generation is approximately 40 years. A man reaches full adulthood at 40 (cf. Josh. 14:7; II Sam. 2:10). Isaac and Esau married at 40 (Gen. 25:20; 26:34). The complete span of human life is thrice 40 (Gen. 6:3; Deut. 34:7), while twice 40 represents advanced old age (II Sam. 19:33–36; Ps. 90:10). The Israelites wandered 40 years in the wilderness (Ex. 16:35; Deut. 2:7), in which time an entire generation died out (Num. 14:33; 32:13). In I Kings 6:1 (cf. I Chron. 5:29–36 [6:3–10]) 480 years represents 12 generations. At various periods the land had rest for 40 years (Judg. 3:11; 8:28; I Sam. 4:18; 80 years in Judg. 3:30 is the equivalent of two generations) and David, Solomon, and Joash reigned for 40 years (II Sam. 5:4; I Kings 2:11; 11:42; II Chron. 24:1). This was a sign of divine grace. It is noteworthy that according to the Mesha Stele Israel oppressed Moab for 40 years. Periods of special significance often consist of 40 days (Gen. 7:4, 12; 8:6; Ex. 24:18; 34:28; Num. 13:25; Deut. 9:9ff.; 10:10; I Sam. 17:16; I Kings 19:8; Ezek. 4:6; 29:11–13; Jonah 3:4). Other interesting examples of the occurrence of 40 are: 40 lashes (Deut. 25:3); sons (Judg. 12:14); camel loads (II Kings 8:9); shekels (Neh. 5:15); Temple measurements (Ezek. 41:2; 46:22). Forty thousand indicates a very large number (Josh. 4:13; Judg. 5:8; II Sam. 10:18; I Chron. 12:37).

FIFTY. Fifty, a multiple of ten, occurs in measurements (Gen. 6:15; Ezek. 40:15); in compensation (Deut. 22:29); and in civil and military organization (Ex. 18:21; Deut. 1:15). Other multiples of ten, up to 500,000, are frequently encountered (Gen. 5:32; Ex. 30:23–24; II Chron. 13:17).

SIXTY. Sixty, the basis of the sexagesimal system, is a heritage from the Sumerians, whose method of calculation has left its mark on the civilized world to this day. The division of the circle into 360 degrees, of an hour into 60 minutes, the minute into 60 seconds, and counting by the dozen and the gross are derived from this ancient people. The system originated, it is suggested, "in a mythical addition of zenith and nadir to the four points of the compass" (McGee). Although the biblical method of reckoning is based mainly on the decimal system, many scriptural (and likewise talmudic and midrashic) numbers show a sexagesimal structure. Thus the total ages of the patriarchs from Adam to Noah and their ages at the birth of the first son are either exact multiples of five or of five with the addition of seven (see Seven above), in accordance with a stylistic Sumerian usage. All the ages in Genesis 5 are to be analysed in the same way, as U. Cassuto has shown in his commentaries to Genesis (see bibl.). The sexagesimal method of calculation applies to other parts of the Bible, too.

SEVENTY. Seventy (the product of two sacred numbers, seven times ten) is used as a round figure, with symbolic or sacred nuances. It occurs in various contexts; it is the number of the family of Jacob that went down to Egypt (Ex. 1:5; Deut. 10:22); of the palm trees at Elim; of the elders that went up with Moses, Aaron, Nadab, and Abihu (Ex. 24:9); of the elders set round about the Tent (Num. 11:24); of the years that the nations will serve the king of Babylon (Jer. 25:11ff.); and of the weeks mentioned in Daniel 9:24ff. The nations enumerated in Genesis 10 total 70 (or 71, or 72, according to others); cf. also the 77-fold of Lamech's vengeance (Gen. 4:24). In Ugaritic literature 70 funerary offerings for Baal are mentioned, and the gods are referred to as "the 70 children of Asherah."

A THOUSAND. A thousand and its multiples are frequently used in the Bible as round numbers indicating a large amount. Etymologically the Hebrew word *elef* ("thousand") denotes "a crowd," and hence at times has the sense of "tribe," "clan," or designates a military unit, which does not necessarily comprise 1,000 (Ex. 18:21; Deut. 33:17; Judg. 6:15). Flinders Petrie *(Researches in Sinai)*, interpreting *elef* to mean a family or tent, reduced the figure for the first census to 5,500, and to 5,730 for the second. Multiples of 1,000 are often hyperbolic expressions (Lev. 26:8; Deut. 32:30; I Sam. 18:7; Ps. 3:7[6]; Song 5:10). Seventy thousand (II Sam. 24:15) and 1,000,000 (Dan. 7:10; I Chron. 21:5; 22:14; II Chron. 14:8) are globular figures indicative of a vast number, while "thousands of ten thousands" (Gen. 24:60) and "ten thousand times ten thousand" (Dan. 7:10) are imaginative numerical ultimates. Similarly high figures are found in Ugaritic literature.

Accuracy. The question of the accuracy of biblical numbers is an exegetical problem. There are actual contradictions within the Bible itself (cf. II Sam. 24:9 with I Chron. 21:5). The correctness of other figures is doubted on other grounds. Unquestionably, some excessively large numbers must be regarded as symbolic or hyperbolic figures. In certain cases critics suppose that estimates—especially of enemy forces—are only rough, and possibly exaggerated, guesses. However, errors in transmission and copying must be taken into account. Manuscripts generally show that they are particularly prone to corruption where numbers are concerned. In Hebrew a single letter could change five to 50, for example. It is interesting to note that one Hebrew Ms. of the Bible (no. 9 of Kennicott) reads in Numbers 1:23, 1,050 for 59,300 (MT); Numbers 2:6, 50 for 54,400; and in Numbers 2:16, 100 for 151,450. There are also considerable divergences between the Masoretic Text, the Septuagint, and the Samaritan versions. For example, the years between the creation and the flood are 1,656 in the Hebrew Bible, 2,262 in the Septuagint, and 1,307 in the Samaritan recension.

Ascending and Descending Numbers. The manner in which large numbers are arranged is subject to interesting variations: sometimes they are arranged in ascending order (Gen. 5:17), at other times, in descending order (Gen. 23:1; Ex. 38:26), and occasionally a combination of both (Num. 3:43). The conventional explanation is that J, E, and D prefer the descending order, while P favors the ascending order. Cassuto, however, has argued that not a documentary criterion but a linguistic principle is operative here: "When the Bible gives us technical or statistical data and the like, it frequently prefers the ascending order, since the tendency to exactness in these instances causes the smaller numbers to be given precedence and prominence. On the other hand, when a solitary number occurs in a narrative passage or in a poem or in a speech and so forth, the numbers are invariably arranged, save in a few cases where special circumstances operate, according to the more natural and spontaneous order, to wit, the descending order" (*The Documentary Hypothesis*, in bibl., 52).

Numerical Harmony. Another question to which Cassuto has given special attention is that of numerical harmony. He demonstrates, for instance, that heptads repeatedly occur in Genesis 1:1–2:3, leaving no doubt that these literary variations on the theme of seven were carefully designed so as to achieve a harmony of numbers. "This numerical symmetry," he writes, "is, as it were, the golden thread that binds together all the parts of the section and serves as a convincing proof of its unity" (*From Adam to Noah*, in bibl., 15).

Graded Numbers. Another interesting feature of biblical style is the use of graded numbers. This consists of the collocation of two consecutive numbers for rhetorical purposes. The usage may be divided into three categories: (a) In prose it expresses approximation and, as a rule, fewness, and has a colloquial character (II Kings 9:32; 13:19). (b) In poetry the two numbers form a parallelism and also express inexactness (Micah 5:4; Job 5:19). A similar usage is found in Sumerian and Akkadian, and, especially, in Ugaritic epic poetry. Since numbers are involved, the parallelism cannot be expressed through synonyms, and consecutive numbers are the only alternative (cf. the parallelism between 1,000 and 10,000 in Ps. 91:17). A combination of the idiom for fewness and poetic parallelism is seen in Isaiah 17:6. (c) In proverbial sayings a schematic device is employed in which two successive numbers are given of things that share a common characteristic, and the actual items subsequently enumerated conform to the second, i.e., the higher, number (Prov. 30:15–31). The use of numbers in Proverbs (including single numbers as in Prov. 30:15a) is intended as an aid to memory. In Amos 1:3–2:6, where three and four are repeatedly mentioned, but only one example is cited, the prophet apparently uses surprise as a rhetorical factor. Reviewing the facts adumbrated above, it appears that numbers are used in the Bible not solely for statistical or arithmetical purposes. They are also employed as stylistic devices to express symbolically the idea of completeness and perfection, to convey the concept of sanctity, to provide mnemonics, and are often arranged so as to give numerical symmetry or harmony to a passage. They are used both expressly and latently to emphasize the leading thought of a text, and thus often establish its intrinsic unity. The rhetorical uses of numbers in Scripture unquestionably constitute a highly valuable aid to biblical exegesis. Furthermore, the biblical approach to numbers strongly influenced the thinking of later ages. Philo and other Hellenistic writers, the Apocryphal literature, the New Testament, the Talmud and Midrash, and especially the kabbalistic writers laid great stress on numerology in various forms. In this way, numbers became an integral part of both literature and theology.

For later periods, see **Gematria;* *Kabbalah; *Mathematics.

The full-page frontispiece to the Book of Numbers from the *Duke of Sussex Pentateuch*. It contains the initial-word *va-yedabber* and illustrations of knights holding banners with the emblems of the four leading tribes of Israel as they camped around the Tabernacle (Num. 2). The emblems are: a lion for Judah (Gen. 49 :9), an eagle for Reuben (midrash, Gen. 49 :3), a bull for Ephraim (Deut. 33 :17), and a serpent for Dan (Gen. 49 :17). Written by Ḥayyim the Scribe in South Germany, about 1300. London, British Museum, Add. ms. 15282, fol. 179v (9 × $6\frac{3}{8}$ ins / 22.8 × 16.2 cm.).

Bibliography: D. Curtis, *A Dissertation upon Odd Numbers* (1909); H. and J. Lewy, in: HUCA, 17 (1943), 1–52; U. Cassuto, *From Adam to Noah* (1961); idem, *From Noah to Abraham* (1964); idem, *The Documentary Hypothesis* (1964); idem, *Exodus* (1967).

[I.ABR.]

NUMBERS RABBAH, aggadic Midrash to the Book of Numbers, also called *Va-Yedabber Rabbah* in medieval literature. (For the name "Rabbah" see *Ruth Rabbah.*)

Structure. The book is divided into 23 sections. The Midrash on chapters 1–8 of the book of Numbers, which are the first two weekly portions as read today—*Ba-Midbar* and *Naso*—is two-and-a-half times longer than the remaining Midrash on chapters 9–36, which cover the eight remaining portions. This disproportion—five-sevenths of the Midrash applying to one-fifth of the book of Numbers—is in itself sufficient indication that there are here two different midrashim: *Numbers Rabbah I,* consisting of sections 1–14, and *Numbers Rabbah II,* consisting of sections 15–23.

Numbers Rabbah I. This appears at first sight to be an exegetical Midrash, since (with certain omissions) it forms a kind of a consecutive interpretation to Numbers 1–8, chapter by chapter and verse by verse. Nevertheless, many of its long expositions deal with one single theme and are typical of homiletic Midrashim. The division into sections is at times determined by the open and closed sections of the Torah (see *Masorah) and at times by the weekly division of the reading of the law according to the triennial cycle once customary in Ereẓ Israel. In general each section begins with an anonymous proem, either an imitation (not always successful) of the classical proem typical of the amoraic Midrashim (see *Midrash; *Homiletics), or of the type combining *halakhah* and *aggadah* common in the **Tanḥuma Yelammedenu* Midrashim. Some sections have epilogues of consolation or of future destiny. The language of the Midrash is Hebrew, in part mishnaic and in part of the early medieval period. It contains a little Galilean and also Babylonian Aramaic and a few Greek words.

In the light of the many parallels between *Numbers Rabbah I* on the one hand, and **Genesis Rabbati* and *Midrash Aggadah* (see Smaller *Midrashim) which are of the school of Moses ha-Darshan, the 11th-century scholar of Narbonne, on the other, it seems that *Numbers Rabbah I* is also based on Moses ha-Darshan's Midrash to the Pentateuch, of which it preserved not only the contents but even the terminology. This conclusion follows also from the fact that quotations by medieval scholars from the work of Moses ha-Darshan are found in *Numbers Rabbah I.* Since, however, the parallel part of *Midrash Aggadah* (to Num. 1–8) contains many homilies not in *Numbers Rabbah I,* it is obvious that *Numbers Rabbah I* is not an actual part of the work of Moses ha-Darshan, but his book served as the main source for its editor and compiler. The basis of *Numbers Rabbah I* was a Midrash of the *Tanḥuma Yelammedenu* type (which is the reason for the many parallels to these Midrashim and for the homilies which mix *halakhah* with *aggadah*), but the late compiler broke down and reconstructed its homilies, changing its character by greatly enlarging it (particularly in the case of the homilies to *Naso,* sections 6–14, which themselves constitute four-sevenths of the whole Midrash *Numbers Rabbah*), adding to it from various sources, especially from the work of Moses ha-Darshan. That work was a combination of biblical commentary, *aggadot* and homilies, and halakhic topics, and included old and new sources (the greater part of which had been revised), together with original novellae. Among the works utilized by Moses ha-Darshan were the *Apocrypha and *Pseudepigrapha of the Second Temple period, especially those of the *Enoch circle (see also

פרשה א סדר במדבר פרשה א קלה

במדבר

וידבר

Opening page of *Numbers Rabbah,* printed by Daniel Bomberg in Venice, 1545. Jerusalem, J.N.U.L.

*Jubilees; The *Testaments of the Twelve Patriarchs), of which he seems still to have had Hebrew versions. He used all the tannaitic literature, the Jerusalem Talmud, the early amoraic Midrashim, the *Tanḥuma Yelammedenu,* Midrashim (including **Pesikta Rabbati*), **Seder Eliyahu Rabbah* and *Seder Eliyahu Zuta,* the Babylonian Talmud, and even late Midrashim like the *Midrash Tadshe;* his work also contains pseudepigraphic material. *Numbers Rabbah I* also makes use of the *piyyutim* of *Kallir and of *Sefer *Yeẓirah,* and contains topics of esoteric lore, mysticism, and combinations of numbers and calculations. Hence its comparatively late Hebrew is understandable. As the compiler was apparently acquainted with the Midrash **Lekaḥ Tov,* which like the work of Moses ha-Darshan dates from the end of the 11th century, the middle of the 12th century seems to be indicated as the earliest possible date for the compiling of *Numbers Rabbah I.* It is of interest that the Paris manuscript (no. 149) of 1291 only includes sections 1–5 of *Numbers Rabbah* (on the reading of the law for Numbers), while the Munich manuscript (97, 2) of 1418 includes the whole of *Numbers Rabbah I* but not *Numbers Rabbah II.*

Numbers Rabbah II. This homiletical Midrash of the *Tanḥuma Yelammedenu* type is identical in all respects with the part parallel to it in the printed *Tanḥuma* and in Buber's edition of the *Tanḥuma.* Moreover a much better version has at times been preserved in *Numbers Rabbah II* than in the parallel passages of both the above-mentioned *Tanḥuma* Midrashim. Thus, for example, it has not the Babylonian *She'ilta,* added to the *Tanḥuma* Midrashim *Ḥukkat,* 2. Instead of the expression *Yelammedenu Rabbenu* ("teach us, our master") found in the *Tanḥuma,* it has *halakhah* (in the manuscripts, however, *Numbers Rabbah II* too has *Yelammedenu Rabbenu*). Many of the halakhic proems found in the *Tanḥuma* have been abridged in *Numbers Rabbah II,* as for example the first. However, they are found in full in the manuscripts. The division of *Numbers Rabbah II* into sections, not found in the manuscripts, is, as in the

Tanḥuma, almost identical with the division of the triennial cycle. The view accepted by the majority of critical scholars is that *Numbers Rabbah II*, which is apparently the second half of a complete Midrash whose first half, which served as the original basis, was lost, was compiled in the ninth century, like most of the *Tanḥuma Yelammedenu* Midrashim. It has, however, also some late additional interpolations from the book of Moses ha-Darshan (18:15–18; 20:5–6, lacking in the *Tanḥuma;* and 18:29 found also in the printed *Tanḥuma*).

The union of *Numbers* Midrashim *Rabbah I* and *Rabbah II* is the work of a copyist of the beginning of the 13th century. The complete Midrash was not yet known to the author of the *Yalkut Shimoni;* it seems that the first to cite it was Naḥmanides. The earliest manuscripts of the whole of *Numbers Rabbah* date only from the 15th century, but they are nevertheless much better than the printed versions.

Bibliography: Zunz-Albeck, Derashot, 125–7, 397–400.

[M.D.H.]

NUMENIUS, son of Antiochus, Jewish envoy sent by the high priest *Jonathan to renew the Hasmonean pact with Rome. Numenius, together with *Antipater the son of Jason, was instructed at the same time to deliver a pledge of friendship to the Spartans, who, according to Josephus, "received the envoys in a friendly manner" and reciprocated with a decree of their own "concerning a friendly alliance with the Jews" (Ant., 13:169–70). It appears that both envoys were used in a similar capacity by Jonathan's successor, *Simeon, and the Spartan reply to Simeon is quoted in I Maccabees 14:20ff. It has been suggested, however, that the two representatives were in fact sent to Rome and Sparta by Jonathan, who died during their mission, and therefore the Spartan correspondence is addressed to Simeon. In any event, Numenius was subsequently sent again to Rome by Simeon, taking with him on this occasion a golden shield in honor of the renewed pact. Numenius participated in yet another mission to Rome, for a similar purpose, during the early years of *John Hyrcanus. The document to this effect, however, was erroneously inserted by Josephus into the priesthood of Hyrcanus II (Jos., Ant., 14:143ff.).

Bibliography: Schuerer, Hist, 53, 63; Klausner, Bayit Sheni, 3 (1950²), 62, 76f.; M. Stern, *Ha-Te'udot le-Mered ha-Ḥashmona'im* (1965), 111, 113, 127–9, 147f., 157.

[I.G.]

NUMERUS CLAUSUS ("closed number"), amount fixed as maximal number in the admission of persons (or certain groups of persons) to specific professions (in particular the liberal professions), institutions of higher learning, professional associations, positions of public office, etc.; frequently applied to Jews. The numerus clausus on the admission of Jews to institutions of higher learning was applied in the 19th century, and extended in the 20th century, in particular in the countries of Eastern Europe, but also in others. It assumed its most characteristic form in czarist Russia (see below) as the *protsentnaya norma* where the restrictions and limitations on the admission of Jews were established by special legislation. In countries such as Poland and Rumania (see below) the numerus clausus was introduced as a quasi-legal means, or was applied in practice, as part of an anti-Semitic policy. However, in democratic countries the numerus clausus was also tacitly applied, at least in some institutions of higher learning, for social or prestige reasons. A numerus clausus of this type was applied not only to students but also (sometimes principally) to teaching staff in the universities or in admission to the civil or public services where higher professional qualifications were required. It was also applied in admission to positions which carried a special status, as in the higher ranks of the civil service, the diplomatic service, army, etc. [Ed.]

In Czarist Russia. During the first half of the 19th century, the policy of the Russian government toward the Jews, as formulated in the statutes concerning the Jews (*"polozheniya"*) of 1804, 1835, and 1844, was to attract the Jewish youth to Russian schools. This ambition encountered strong opposition from the Jewish masses who regarded education in these schools as a step toward the alienation of Jewish youth from its people and its religion. They also viewed the network of Jewish state schools established by the government to promote general education among the Jews with suspicion. In 1853 there were 159 Jewish pupils in all the secondary schools of Russia (1.3% of the total student roll), while in the universities there were a few dozen. On the other hand, the *maskilim* advocated education in the Russian schools as a means of rapprochement with the Russian people.

During the reign of Alexander II, a radical change occurred in the attitude of the Jews, especially those of the middle and upper classes, toward the Russian schools. This was due to the privileges granted to educated Jews (extension of the right of residence in 1865; important concessions with regard to military service in 1874). In 1880 the number of Jewish pupils in the secondary schools rose to 8,000 (11.5% of the total) and in the universities to 556 (6.8% of the total). These numbers increased yearly. In the educational region of Odessa (which included southern Russia) the proportion of Jewish students rose to 35.2%, and in the region of Vilna (Lithuania) to 26.7%. A Russian-Jewish stratum of intelligentsia rapidly became prominent. As service in the government and administration was closed to them, this intelligentsia concentrated in the liberal professions—medicine, law, and journalism. The members of these professions soon became aware of growing competition from Jews. A propaganda campaign was instigated against the admission of Jews into the class of the intelligentsia; this was sparked off in 1880 by a letter to the editor entitled *Zhid Idyot* ("The Jew is Coming") which was published in the widely influential newspaper *Novoye Vremya*.

Of their own initiative, higher and secondary schools in various parts of the country began to restrict the admission of Jews within their precincts. This coincided with the general policy of the government of Alexander III which sought to prevent the admission of children of the poorer classes into the higher and secondary schools. It was claimed that the Jewish students introduced a spirit of rebellion and revolution into the schools and thus had a deleterious influence over their Christian fellow students. In July 1887 the Ministry of Education decided that the proportion of Jews in all secondary schools and higher institutions subject to its jurisdiction was not to surpass 10% in the towns of the *Pale of Settlement, 5% in the towns outside it, and only 3% in the capitals of St. Petersburg and Moscow. Many schools were completely closed to Jews. In time, this regulation also spread to schools which were under the supervision of other government ministries (ministry of communications, ministry of finance, etc.). There were individual cases, after the Revolution of 1905, where the restrictions and admission prohibitions were also applied to converted Jews.

These restrictions were introduced during a period when masses of Jewish youth were besieging the Russian schools, and had severe repercussions on Jewish life. Only those who had obtained the highest marks and distinctions were likely to be admitted to Russian secondary and high schools. There were naturally instances of bribery and corruption, or parents who baptized their children so that they could enter the schools. Secondary school graduates began to convert for this end, and during the years 1907 to 1914 this became commonplace. The Lutheran clergyman Piro of Finland became known for selling baptismal certificates at a low price to all those who desired them (*"pirovtsy"*). The Jewish national and Zionist movements fought this phenomenon. These regulations also resulted in the emigration of thousands of Jewish youths to study at the universities of Western Europe (Switzerland, Germany, France, etc.). Jewish students formed the majority of the "Russian" colonies in the university towns of the West. In 1892 the number of Jewish pupils in the secondary schools had decreased to 5,394 (7% of the pupils).

Jewish youths took advantage of the possibility of completing their studies by means of external examinations. In Jewish society, the "extern" made his appearance, who studied under the guidance of private teachers and then sat for the state examinations. The anti-Semitic examiners were severe and failed many of them. In 1911 it was decided that the numerus clausus would also apply to external students, and since the number of non-Jewish external students was very limited this system was brought to an end. During the period of the Russian Revolution of 1905, when autonomy was granted to the institutions of higher learning, the numerus clausus was abolished, but immediately upon the repression of the Revolution the practice was restored. The proportion, however, was increased (to 15% in the Pale of Settlement, 10% beyond it, and 5% in the capital cities). Accordingly, the number of Jewish pupils in the secondary schools rose to 17,538 (9.1% of the pupils), and of Jewish students at the universities to 3,602 (9.4%). In the overwhelming majority of secondary schools for girls, the numerus clausus was not introduced. In 1911 about 35,000 Jewish girls studied at Russian secondary schools (13.5% of the pupils). In the educational region of Vilna (Lithuania) the proportion of Jewish girl pupils rose to 49%, in the region of Warsaw to 42.7% and in the regions of Kiev and Odessa to 33.3% (these four educational regions encompassed the whole of the Pale of Settlement). The numerus clausus served as an impetus for the establishment of private Jewish secondary schools, several of which evolved the beginnings of a national Jewish education.

All restrictions on the admission of Jews to the secondary schools and institutions of higher learning were abolished with the Revolution of February 1917. In 1919, during the brief period when the armies of *Denikin (the "White Army") gained control of large regions of southern Russia, the numerus clausus was temporarily reinstated in many towns under their control. [Y.S.]

In the Soviet Union. There are no indications of any official or unofficial numerus clausus existing in the Soviet Union until the last "Black Years" of Stalin's rule (1948–53). Even then discrimination against Jews seeking admission to Soviet universities seems to have been related to the general atmosphere of distrust and enmity, engendered by the anti-Jewish trend of official policy, rather than the result of a regulated system of limited percentages. Though legally and openly there has never been a numerus clausus for Jews in the U.S.S.R., young Jews seeking admission to certain prestige universities, or to studies leading to positions entailing use of classified information or representative status in the state or on its behalf, increasingly encountered unexpected artificial difficulties in the 1950s and 1960s. Many young Jews complained of having been rejected despite brilliant achievements in the entrance examinations in favor of non-Jews with fewer scholastic qualifications. A number of statements were made by Prime Minister Nikita Khrushchev (for instance to a French socialist delegation in 1957; see *Réalités*, May 1957) or by the minister of culture, Yekaterina Furtseva (to a correspondent of the pro-Communist American magazine, *National Guardian*, June 25, 1956) confirming the existence of a general policy to regulate cadres according to nationality—particularly and explicitly by reducing the proportion of Jews in the intelligentsia and in government departments. These statements seemed to validate the assumption of many Soviet citizens as well as of scholars abroad that, as W. Korey affirms in his study on the legal position of Soviet Jewry (1970), "unpublished governmental regulations appear to have been issued, whether in written or oral form, which establish quotas limiting educational or employment opportunities for Jews." In 1959 the minister for higher education, U. P. Yelyutin, vehemently denied the existence of such quotas, and in 1962 the U.S.S.R. ratified the UNESCO Convention against Discrimination in Education. However, some evidence to the contrary was found in 1963 in Soviet journals such as *Kommunist* and, particularly, the "Bulletin of Higher Education," which acknowledged the existence of "annually planned preferential admission quotas." An American specialist on Soviet education, N. de Witt, reached the conclusion in 1961 that a quota system existed "to the severe disadvantage of the Jewish population." According to de Witt the principle applied makes "the representation of any national or ethnic grouping in overall higher education enrolment" proportional to its size in the total Soviet population. He presented statistical data which showed that between 1935 and 1958 "the index of representation (in higher education) rose for most nationalities, but fell for Georgians and all national minorities, with a very drastic decline for the Jews."

The official statistics on the number of Jewish students, which apparently contradicted this assertion, were misleading (as some scholars, like Alec Nove and J. A. Newth, have found after a meticulous analysis, published in 1970), mainly because these overall numbers included not only students in every kind of "institute" and field of study, but also external (i.e., correspondence) students. The question whether Jews were "able to get into universities of their choice on equal terms with competitors of other nationalities" remained open. The percentage of Jewish students (including evening and correspondence students) fell from 14.4% in 1928–29 to 3.2% in 1960–61. Though the official percentage of Jews in the total population was in 1960–61 approximately 1.1% and in the urban population 2.2%, the above-mentioned percentage of Jewish students should be considered, according to A. Nove and J. A. Newth, to be proportionately low.

The majority of the Jewish proletariat perished during the German invasion in World War II, and there seems to be no doubt that, as a purely urban element consisting of white-collar workers, professional men, engineers, scientists, and people occupied in retail trade "a much larger proportion of Jews than of other nationalities endeavors to obtain higher education. It is this fact that may well give rise to discrimination. Some officials may feel that it is wrong for Jews to be so overwhelmingly non-proletarian in their composition. Others, particularly in the national republics, are concerned to provide special educational advantages for the relatively backward peoples of their own nationality." This conclusion of A. Nove and J. A. Newth seems to be borne out by a large number of case histories related by Soviet Jews themselves. [B.E.]

In Poland. The numerus clausus was one of the manifestations of the widespread anti-Semitism in Poland between the two world wars. The Polish government made use of the numerus clausus as a quasi-legal means to limit the number of Jewish students in the institutions of higher education to the minimum. The total number of students in Poland increased continuously between 1920 and 1935. From 34,266 students in 1921–22, it rose to 47,200 in 1935–36. In the same period both the number of Jewish students and their proportion in the total declined. In 1920–21 there were 8,526 Jewish students in Poland; in 1923–24 their number reached its peak figure of 9,579; but in 1935–36 their number dropped to 6,200, i.e., a decrease of about 35%. The proportion of Jewish students in the total number of students was 24.6% in 1921–22, 20% in 1928–29, and only 13.2% in 1935–36.

The results of the numerus clausus are especially instructive if the fluctuations in the number of Jewish students in the various faculties are noted. The most striking instance is the faculty of medicine. In 1923–24 there were still 1,402 Jewish medical students, forming 30.2% of the total. In 1926–27 their number dropped to 698 (18.6%), and in 1935–36 Jewish medical students formed only 13.8% of the total number. In the faculty of law their percentage in 1923–24 was 24.6%, while in 1935–36 it was only 12.5%. In the humanities the numbers for the corresponding years were 35.4% and 18.3%, and in the faculty of chemistry 25% and 12%. This tendency to a continuous decrease in the number of Jewish students in all faculties, especially in the professions of medicine, law, and engineering, was an outcome of the numerus clausus policy. It hindered the admission of Jewish students to the institutions of higher education, although the number of Jewish applicants increased in Poland and a growing number of Jewish youths wished to enter academic professions.

In Poland up to World War II there were 14 state institutions of higher education, and nine nongovernmental (e.g., the Catholic University in Lublin; commercial colleges in Warsaw, Cracow, Lvov, Lodz, etc.). Almost all of these institutions applied the numerus clausus as the leading criterion in admitting new students, though some applied it more strictly than others. In the University of Lvov, for instance, the Jewish students comprised 46.6% of the total number of students in 1921–22, while in 1930–31 (there are no statistical data for later years) they comprised only 31.9%; in the University of Warsaw the figures for the corresponding years were 31.4% and 23.8%; in the Warsaw Polytechnic 15.5% and 10.2%; in the Veterinary College in Lvov 13% and 5.4%; and in the Institute of Dentistry, 70.4% and 19.7%.

The proportion of females among Jewish students throughout this period was higher than that among non-Jewish students. The percentage of Jewish females was 33.3% in 1923–24 and 39% in 1930–31, while the numbers among non-Jews for these years were 15% and 26%. The authorities of the academic institutions were more willing to admit Jewish female students than Jewish males, since many left the universities before graduating. Another reason for not strictly applying the numerus clausus toward Jewish women was that the majority studied in the faculty of humanities (philosophy, history, literature), instead of the more demanding professions. Thus, for instance, in 1930–31, 50% of the male students studied law; 11% medicine; 16.4% philosophy; and 14.6% sciences, while 11% of the female students studied law; 3.4% medicine; 63.2% philosophy; and 1.7% sciences. In the last few years preceding World War II the authorities took even stronger discriminatory measures against the Jewish students. They introduced the system of "Jewish benches," which allocated special benches at the back of the auditoriums and classrooms to be used only by Jews. The Jewish students revolted against these regulations and refused to sit there. This frequently led to serious clashes in the universities, resulting in bloodshed and tragedy. [SHA.L.]

In Rumania. In Rumania in 1922 a numerus clausus of the admission of Jewish students was advocated by Rumanian students in the University of *Cluj. These were members of the Association of Christian Students, founded by adherents of A. C. *Cuza in Jassy earlier that year. It was adopted also by the students in the universites of Jassy, Bucharest, and Cernauti (Chernovtsy). December 10, the day of its announcement by the students in Cluj, was declared a holiday throughout Rumania by the students, who every year took the opportunity to attack Jewish students on that day. The numerus clausus in Rumania was not introduced by law. However, in practice the Christian students, by using force, prevented the Jewish students from regular studies. The position of the science and medical students was especially serious since they were prevented from using the laboratories, taking part in autopsies, etc. In the late 1920s Jewish students in this sphere were forced to go abroad, especially to France and Italy, in order to complete their studies.

At first the majority of teachers in the universities were opposed to the students' anti-Semitic activities, but with the rise of National Socialism in Germany many professors supported the numerus clausus movement. In 1933 special entrance examinations were introduced and Jewish candidates were deliberately failed. The few who were accepted were prevented by the Christian students from taking part in the studies, and in some faculties there were no Jewish students at all. Thus the numerus clausus became a numerus nullus. The Association of Christian Students was subsidized by all ministers of the interior throughout this period.

In 1935 the Rumanian statesmen A. Vaida-Voevod declared a "numerus valahicus," (a "Walachian numerus"), a disguised form of the numerus clausus. The head of the Orthodox Church in Rumania, the patriarch Miron Cristea, declared his support of the numerus valahicus in the Rumanian senate.

A law on the employment of Rumanian employees was passed in 1934, which fixed a proportion of 80% for Rumanian workers in every place of employment, and 50% for Rumanians in their management. This law was felt especially in the textile industry, banking, and commerce, where a large number of Jews was employed. Professional and trade unions, such as the lawyers', accountants', clerical workers', etc., began to evict the Jews from their membership and refused to accept new Jewish members.

At the beginning of the pro-Nazi regime of Ion Antonescu in 1940, all Jewish students were officially expelled from the schools and universities. This was also the fate of the Jewish workers in the private economic sector. [TH.L.]

In Hungary. Restrictions affecting the admission of Jewish students into the institutions of higher learning in Hungary were passed as a law in 1920. This laid down that no new students should be accepted in the universities unless they were "loyal from the national and moral standpoint," and that "the proportion of members of the various ethnic and national groups in the total number of students should amount to the proportion of such ethnic and national groups in the total population." According to the official ground for this enactment, the law was intended to prevent a surplus of persons in the liberal professions, which the dismembered country was unable to integrate. But it was clear that the law was directed against the Jews only.

The leaders of the *Neologists in Hungarian Jewry who considered the law a severe blow to Jewish equal rights, as well as the liberal opposition and especially its Jewish representatives, attempted to combat the law, but without success. Jewish students who were not admitted to institutions of higher learning were forced to go abroad to study in Germany, Austria, Czechoslovakia, Italy, France, and Belgium. The Jewish students who were admitted despite the restrictions were often insulted and sometimes beaten up by the non-Jewish students, whose "ideal" was to achieve a "numerus nullus."

Outside Hungary a number of Jewish organizations initiated a struggle against the law on the international level in 1921, basing their claims on the peace treaty of Trianon, in which Hungary had guaranteed that all its citizens should "be equal before the law . . . without distinction of race, language, or religion." The Jewish organizations sent a petition based on these lines to the *League of Nations. However, the official leadership of Hungarian Jewry refrained from cooperating with these Jewish organizations. Nevertheless the international Jewish organizations received support from Jews in Hungary as well as from the Hungarian Jewish students studying abroad.

The Hungarian government, when asked by the League of Nations to supply information concerning this question, avoided the issue by providing statistical data showing that the Jews were not discriminated against by this law. In 1925 the Joint Foreign Committee and the Alliance Israélite Universelle, fearing that other countries would adopt the numerus clausus, appealed to the Permanent Court of International Justice. This time Hungary was compelled to give a relevant answer. The Hungarian minister of education claimed in 1927 that the law was merely temporary, arising from Hungary's difficult situation, and undertook that the law would shortly be amended. When the amendment was not forthcoming Hungary was asked to hasten the procedure, and in 1928 the bill was submittd to the Hungarian parliament. According to this amendment racial criteria in admitting new students were removed and replaced by social criteria. Five categories were set up: civil servants, war veterans and army officers, small landowners and artisans, industrialists, and the merchant classes. The result was much the same. According to the new socioeconomic criteria the Jews had approximately the same status as before. The theoretically nonracial character of the amended law was a temptation to convert to Christianity. Indeed many Jews did so, like their predecessors of an earlier period, for the sake of office. The numerus clausus remained in force despite the protests of Jews and liberals.

By the second anti-Jewish law passed in 1939 the admission of new students was again put on a racial and not a confessional basis. Students of the rabbinical seminary were exempted from the law's application, since according to the government regulations of this institution its students required a doctorate in philosophy in order to obtain their rabbinical diploma, and were restricted in their choice of subject to oriental studies and philosophy. The Hungarian constituent national assembly which convened in Debrecen in December 1944 abolished the numerus clausus among the rest of the discriminatory racial legislation. [B.Y.]

In the United States. In the United States mass immigration after 1881 resulted in the partial exclusion of Jews from many of the professions. There were very few Jews in the teaching profession before 1930. In 1920 there were 214 Jewish students in the medical schools of the State of New York; by 1940 there were only 108 in the same schools. In its Annual Report in 1932, the American Jewish Committee was willing to accept the proposition that this exclusion was not entirely due to anti-Semitism but that there was "overcrowding in an already overcrowded profession" and that Jews needed to be redirected to other pursuits. This was a vain hope in an era when the opportunities for Jews in the professions were constantly decreasing, so that, for example, the proportion of Jews in veterinary medicine decreased from almost 12% to less than 2% between 1935 and 1946. The situation was somewhat better in dentistry, where by the mid-1930s about one-fifth of the students in the dental schools were Jews, but even here the leaders of the profession tried to keep Jews out.

This trend of exclusion during most of the first half of the 20th century reached down into the undergraduate schools. There was a famous incident in 1923 when President Lowell of Harvard advised that the enrollment of Jews should be limited at his school, in order to preserve the representative character of the leading academic institution of the United States. The committee that he appointed at Harvard was unanimous in opposing him and in insisting that places be given to applicants solely on the basis of merit. Lowell was denounced by the American Federation of Labor, the Boston city council, and the legislature of the State of Massachusetts, which body threatened to remove the tax exemptions that Harvard enjoyed if a discriminatory policy were followed. Despite the storm an unofficial numerus clausus continued until after World War II in most of the major American colleges and universities. In 1931 Rutgers College admitted that it was limiting the number of Jews in order "to equalize the proportion" and to prevent the university from becoming denominational. In the spring of the following year the college authorities withdrew from this position, which had been vehemently attacked by local and national Jewish agencies. Nonetheless, at the end of a generation of struggle a B'nai B'rith survey in 1946 found that Jews indeed formed about 9% of a U.S. college population that was then slightly over two million, but that they were concentrated (77%) in 50 of the largest schools, and the best smaller schools were still discriminating against them. The proportion of Jews in the professional schools was only 7%, thus indicating that discrimination was still high.

The turning point came that year. Rabbi Stephen S. *Wise mounted an attack on Columbia University for practicing unofficial discrimination against Jews by petitioning the city council of the City of New York to withdraw its tax exemption. Columbia had no choice but to announce that the question of religion would no longer figure on any of its application forms. For the flood of soldiers returning from World War II the national government was providing the funds with which to complete their education and the colleges and universities boomed in the next decade. Discrimination against Jews was hard to practice in an era when the educational institutions were seeking the maximum of government funds. In the post-World War II era, faculties were doubling and redoubling, and place was therefore available for Jews. The new postwar industries, especially electronics, required a whole new corps of technicians, and these jobs were staffed without regard to earlier exclusions. By 1968 some opinions were being expressed that the marked presence of Jews everywhere in the professions and the academic world was "arousing some resentment, envy and discontent among less successful non-Jewish faculty members."

It was estimated that by 1971 Jews formed at least 10% of the faculties of all American institutions of higher learning, and that the more highly regarded a school the more nearly likely would it have a Jewish proportion in its faculty reaching 25–50%, the Harvard faculty being probably one third Jewish. Attacks on Jews in academic life and in the professions were mounted largely from within the Negro community, which was demanding place for itself consonant with its proportion in the total population (about 10%), regardless of the results of tests or other screening devices. In this demand Negroes have come into conflict with Jews who have found what contemporary sociologists have called the "meritocracy" useful and convenient. Blacks have succeeded in obtaining a quota of their own, perhaps to some extent at the expense of Jews, in many of the best colleges. [Ar.H.]

Bibliography: Czarist Russia: Dubnow, Hist Russ, index; L. Greenberg, *Jews in Russia: The Struggle for Emancipation* (1965); S. Baron, *Russian Jews under Tsars and Soviets* (1964); J. Kreppel, *Juden und Judentum von heute* (1925), para. 77, 501–4. Soviet Union: W. Korey, in: L. Kochan (ed.), *The Jews in Soviet Russia since 1917* (1970), 90, 94–95; A. Nove and J. A. Newth, *ibid.*, 145, 154–6. Poland: S. Langnas, *Żydzi a studja akademickie w Polsce* (1933); M. Mirkin, in: *Yidishe Ekonomik*, 2 (1938), 272–6; *Polscki Rocznik statystyczny* (1921–38). Hungary: N. Katzburg, in: *Sefer ha-Shanah shel Universitat Bar Ilan*, 4–5 (1956–65), 270–88 (with an English summary); *The Jewish Minority in Hungary. Report by the Secretary and Special Delegate of the Joint Foreign Committee ...* (1926). United States: AJYB, passim; O. and M. F. Handlin, in: AJYB (1955), 75–77.

NUMISMATICS. Interest in Jewish coins arose already in the late Middle Ages, e.g., with *Maimonides and *Estori ha-Parḥi. Special studies, however, were carried out only considerably later. For geographical reasons and due to the fact that Jewish coins bear partly Greek legends, these have been generally classified as Greek coins. Among the earliest studies is one by F. Perez Bayer (*De numis hebraeo-samaritanis*, 1781). Bible research gave Jewish numismatics a special interest. One of the first in the field was the English scholar J. Y. Akerman ("Numismatic Illustration of the Narrative of Portions of the New Testament," in: *Numismatic Chronicle*, 1846/47). Another important work was written by the Italian C. Cavedoni (*Numismatica Biblica*, 1850), followed by F. de Saulcy's *Recherches sur la Numismatique Judaïque* (1854). The first work that may claim scientific value was published by F. W. Madden (*History of Jewish Coinage* ..., 1864; repr. with introd. by M. Avi-Yonah, 1967). *Coins of the Jews* (1881) was the second edition of the former. Though the research on Jewish numismatics has since greatly advanced Madden's study remains of basic value even today. T. Reinach's noteworthy book, *Jewish Coins*, appeared in 1903. In 1914 G. F. Hill published his *Catalogue of the Greek Coins of Palestine in the British Museum*. It is an excellent summary of the material then known, based on the almost complete collection of the British Museum. Hill's own critical observations add to the value of this catalog, which is indispensable for the student of Jewish numismatics. In Ereẓ Israel numismatic interest has developed in the 20th century. The first book on Jewish coins was S. Raffaeli's *Matbe'ot ha-Yehudim* (1913). This was followed by M. Narkiss' *Matbe'ot Ereẓ Yisrael* (3 vols., 1936–39). In 1940 A. Reifenberg published his *Ancient Jewish Coins* (Heb. ed., *Matbe'ot ha-Yehudim*, 1947, 1963[2]). In 1945 the Israel Numismatic Society was founded, and since then its members have contributed to the progress of numismatic research. Foremost among them was its second president, L. Kadman, who founded the Israel Numismatic Research Fund and published himself four volumes of the *Corpus Nummorum Palestinensium* (1956–61; Aelia Capitolina, Caesarea Maritima, Jewish-Roman War, and Akko-Ptolemais). Kadman was also the sponsor of the Kadman Numismatic Museum in Tel Aviv, which was inaugurated in 1962, and houses the largest numismatic library in Israel. The *Publications of the Israel Numismatic Society* have appeared since 1954. L. Kadman published in co-authorship with A. Kindler a numismatic handbook (Heb., 1963). The latter published, besides many articles on special subjects, the *Oẓar Matbe'ot Ereẓ Yisrael* (with an English summary, 1958); *The Coins of Tiberias* (Heb. and Eng., 1962);and a catalog of the collection of Jewish coins of the Bank of Israel (1969). Y. Meshorer published his corpus of *Jewish Coins of the Second Temple Period* in 1967 (Heb., 1966) with an almost up-to-date listing of all types of Jewish coins known to date.

In 1963 an International Numismatic Convention was held in Jerusalem, and its proceedings were published by the Israel Numismatic Society. The latter holds monthly meetings and seminaries, and annual conventions for its membership of 250. It also publishes a quarterly, *Israel Numismatic Journal*. Numismatic research is, however, not confined to books. Hundreds of articles and minor monographs have been written by various scholars. L. A. Mayer published a Bibliography of Jewish Numismatics which counts 882 items until 1963. In the framework of archaeological research in the Hebrew University and in the Museum of Jewish Antiquities, E. L. *Sukenik built up an extremely important collection of Palestinian coins. He was the first to identify the earliest Jewish coins by correctly reading the legend *Yehud* on them. Other important numismatic collections in Israel are in the Department of Antiquities of the Hebrew University, in the Jewish Museum, in the Bank of Israel, in the Franciscan Biblical School, and in the Pontifical Biblical Institute, all in Jerusalem. Private collections of importance are those of the late A. Reifenberg, Jerusalem, on loan to the Israel Museum; of A. Spaer, Jerusalem; of R. Hecht, Haifa; of J. Meyshan and of J. Willinger, Tel Aviv. Outside Israel the collections of the American Numismatic Society as well as the private ones of A. Klaksbald, Paris, D. Littman, Geneva, and W. Wirgin, New York, are of importance.

See *Coins and Currency.

Bibliography: L. A. Mayer, *Bibliography of Jewish Numismatics* (1966). [A.Ki.]

NUN (Heb. נ; נוּן), the 14th letter of the Hebrew alphabet; its numerical value is 50. The earliest representation of this letter is a pictograph of a serpent, which developed into the early Phoenician. The later variants are: Hebrew (Samaritan), Phoenician, and Aramaic. During the late fifth century B.C.E. and after, in Aramaic cursive in the medial position the downstroke bent leftward. Thus the Jewish medial נ and final ן *nun* forms developed. The Nabatean cursive medial *nun* became more and more similar to medial *bet*, *yod*, and *taw*; in Arabic diacritic marks distinguish *nun* ن from *ba* (ب), *ya* (ي) and *ta* (ت). The ancestor of the Latin N, the Archaic Greek developed from the early Phoenician *nun*. [Jo.Na.]

See *Alphabet.

NUNBERG, HERMAN (1884–1970), U.S. psychiatrist. Born in a Polish Jewish townlet, Nunberg studied psychiatry with Eugen Bleuler and in 1914 joined the Vienna group of psychoanalysts. At the Psychoanalytic Congress in Budapest (1918) Nunberg maintained the necessity for personal analysis in the training of its practitioners. In 1932 he went to the United States. Nunberg's earliest writings were concerned with psychoanalytic interpretation of psychotic conditions. In 1932 his first book *Allgemeine Neurosenlehre auf Psychoanalytischer Grundlage* appeared. In his preface Sigmund *Freud considered it the most accurate presentation at that time of the psychoanalytic theory of neurotic processes.

In 1949 Nunberg published his monograph, *Problems of Bisexuality as Reflected in Circumcision*, in which he collated psychoanalytic experience, especially with the dreams of a patient who had undergone circumcision after infancy, with mythological and anthropological knowledge. Freud and T. *Reik had recognized the interrelation between circumcision and castration. According to Nunberg circumcision stimulates the feminine as well as the masculine strivings of the boy. Some Jewish tradition states that Adam was created both male and female and that the creator separated his female half. This belief is reminiscent of myths and infantile speculation on the origin of the two sexes. The female is made by castrating (circumcising) the male. An afterthought in this book dwells on the "question of German guilt." The Germans submitted unconditionally to their Fuehrer. By licensing murder the Fuehrer relieved the Germans of their sense of guilt for their inability to restrict their aggression. His book *Curiosity* (1961) was based on a lecture given at the New York Academy of Medicine. He served as a member of the Committee for the Study of Suicides. In later years he was noted for his psychoanalytic elucidation of dreams. As a teacher, researcher, and clinician Nunberg was recognized for the integration of theoretical contributions and clinical observations.

Bibliography: P. Neubauer et al. (eds.), *Herman Nunberg: Memoirs* (1969). [Lo.M.]

NUNES VAIS (Nunez-Vaez), rabbinical family of Marrano extraction in Leghorn (Italy). Isaac Joseph Nunes Vais (d. 1768) was one of the rabbis of the community and colleague of *Malachi b. Jacob ha-Kohen. His *Si'aḥ Yiẓḥak* (Leghorn, 1766; 2nd vol. 1768) comprised glossaries on the talmudic tractates *Shevu'ot*, *Yoma*, and *Ḥagigah* (forming the acrostic of *Si'aḥ*). His son Jacob (d. 1814) became chief rabbi of the consistory established at Leghorn during the period of French occupation, and taught what was termed "practical theology" in the Talmud Torah when it was reorganized in 1812. He edited *Da'at Zekenim* (Leghorn, 1783) comprising amplifications of the tosafists on Rashi's pentateuchal commentaries, and *Amar Neke* (Pisa, 1810), comprising the glosses of Obadiah of *Bertinoro on Rashi. To the same family belonged ABRAHAM JOSEPH NUNES VAIS (1811–1898), physician to the bey of Tunis, and the former's son, the painter ITALO NUNES-VAIS (1860–1932) of Florence.

Bibliography: A. Lattes and A. S. Toaff, *Gli studi ebraici a Livorno* (1909), 14; M. Monteverdi, *Italo Nunes-Vais* (1969); M. Benayahu, *Rabbi Ḥayyim Yosef David Azulai* (1959), index.

[C.R.]

NUÑEZ (Nuñes), family name of Portuguese Marranos, prominent in the Sephardi Diaspora, particularly in the American colonies. PEDRO NUÑEZ (1492–1577) was a geographer with a strong attachment to Judaism. Born at Alcarcer do Sal, Portugal, he was professor of mathematics at Coimbra University, and in 1529 was appointed cosmographer to the crown. Credited with being the father of modern cartography for his treatise on the sphere (1537), he was also author of *De crepusculi* (1542) and *De arte atque ratione navigandi* (1546). His complete works were published in 1592 at Basle. HENRIQUE NŨNEZ (d. 1524), who was born at Barba, was baptized in Castile. Enlisted by King John III of Portugal to inform on the *New Christian Judaizers, he provided the monarch with a list of persons secretly conforming to Judaism, even denouncing his own younger brother. When the *Marranos discovered that Henrique was the informer in their midst, they dispatched two men, André Dias and Diego Vaz, to assassinate him. Disguised in Franciscan habit, the two succeeded in stabbing Henrique to death, but were apprehended, tortured into confessing, and executed. Henrique was then declared a martyr of the church and dubbed Firme Fé. Another HENRIQUE NUÑEZ, a physician by profession, headed a tiny Marrano group that found respite at *Bristol, England, from at least 1553 to 1555, at which time the new religious policies of Queen Mary Tudor forced him to seek refuge in France. HECTOR *NUÑEZ (1521–1591) was lay head of London's Marrano community during the reign of Elizabeth; through his business agents on the continent he was a source of intelligence for the queen.

BEATRICE NUÑEZ (c. 1568–1632) was martyred at the *auto-da-fé held in Madrid on July 4, 1632. Burned at the same time was ISABEL NUÑEZ ALVAREZ of Viseu, Portugal, who married Miguel Rodriguez of Madrid, and held title to one of Madrid's synagogues. On the same occasion, HELEN and VIOLANTE NŨNEZ both received sentences of life imprisonment. That year saw the death of still another member of the family, CLARA, at an auto-da-fé in Seville, Spain. More fortunate was the beautiful MARIA NUÑEZ (b. 1575 or 1579) who, together with a group of fellow-Marranos, escaped from Portugal in about 1593 aboard a ship bound for Holland. While at sea they were captured by a British vessel and diverted to London. En route, the British captain became infatuated with Maria and proposed marriage. A contemporaneous account tells of how Queen Elizabeth's curiosity was aroused and how Maria was presented to the queen, who then accompanied Maria on a tour of London. Maria insisted on rejoining her Jewish comrades, who went on to Amsterdam to found a community which was to become the major Marrano haven. Communal records of that period in Amsterdam list the marriage of a Maria Nuñez, aged 19, in August 1598, and the marriage of another Maria Nuñez, aged 23, in November 1598. Living in Amsterdam some time around 1700 was DAVID NUÑEZ-TORRES (1728), talmudist and a director of the Abi Yetomim orphanage. He was called to the Hague as *ḥakham* of the Spanish and Portuguese community. Actively engaged in publishing Jewish classics, he also prepared two editions of the Bible and coedited the 1697 edition of the Shulḥan Arukh as well as the 1702 edition of Maimonides' code. A catalog of his extensive personal library was published after his death.

The name Nuñez was also prominent in colonial America. J. R. Rosenbloom in his *Biographical Dictionary of Early American Jews* (1960) lists 19 members of the Nunes (Nuñez) family, mostly relatives and descendants of the Marrano SAMUEL RIBEIRO NUÑEZ, who was born in Lisbon where he became a doctor of renown and was appointed to serve the crown. Neither this appointment, however, nor his wealth guaranteed him safety from the menacing surveillance of the Inquisition. In 1732/33 he escaped on a chartered English vessel which he and his family secretly boarded while a lavish dinner party was being held at the Nuñez family mansion. Samuel was able to take some of his wealth with him to London, where he joined a group of Jews embarking for the new settlement of *Savannah, Georgia. There Governor Oglethorpe took note of the man's eminence and went on record as acknowledging that upon landing Dr. Nuñez had saved the colony from a raging epidemic. Accordingly, Oglethorpe suggested to the colonial directors that the usual Jewish disabilities might be waived in this case. With Samuel in Georgia were his mother, ZIPPORAH (b. c. 1680), his sons DANIEL (1704–1789) and MOSES (1705–1787), and his daughter ZIPPORAH (1714–1799). Families of some of the original Jewish settlers continue to live in Savannah. Elsewhere in the Americas, the Nuñez family included ROBERT NUÑEZ (1820–1889), born in *Jamaica, a leading figure there in both business and politics and founder of the journal *The Political Eagle* in 1850. Active in matters of finance, from 1863 until his death he filled a variety of government posts, ranging from member of the Jamaica House of Assembly to magistrate. He also had diplomatic contacts with the United States, Spain, Norway, and Sweden.

Bibliography: Roth, Marranos, index; J. R. Marcus, *Early American Jewry 1655–1790*, 2 (1955), index; idem, *Memoirs of American Jews 1775–1865*, 1 (1955), index; Rosenbloom, Biogr Dict, s.v.; M. Kayserling, *Geschichte der Juden in Portugal* (1867), 171–2.

[A.LI.]

NUÑEZ, HECTOR (1521–91), leader of the Marrano community in England. A distinguished physician and successful merchant, Nuñez was born in Portugal and arrived in London about 1550; he was admitted a Fellow of the Royal College of Physicians and of the Royal College of Surgeons in 1554. His large-scale trading activities in the Mediterranean enabled him to provide information for the government and it was he who brought Sir Francis Walsingham, whose friendship he enjoyed, the first news of the arrival of the Spanish Armada at Lisbon. His wife, Leonara Freire, subscribed to the upkeep of the secret synagogue in Antwerp.

Bibliography: Roth, England, 140ff., 283; idem, *Anglo-Jewish Letters* (1938), 23–26; Wolf, in: JHSET, 11 (1924–27), 6f., 23f., 37–48, 50–55.

[V.D.L.]

NUREMBERG (Ger. **Nuernberg**), city in Bavaria, S.W. Germany. A report of 1146 records that many Jews from Rhenish towns fled to Nuremberg, but Jews are first mentioned in the city in 1182. By the 13th century a large number of Jews were resident there. In reply to an enquiry from Weissenburg in 1288, the mayor and council of Nuremberg pointed out the laws then governing Jewish moneylending in the city. The **memorbuch* ascribed to

Der „Judenstain"
ein Wahrzeichen aus den Tagen vor der
Vertreibung der Juden aus Nürnberg
1499.
Von der Israelitischen Kultusgemeinde
erworben und aufgestellt
1909.
Eine Zeit kommt, da Steine verworfen
und wieder eine Zeit, da Steine
gesammelt werden. Pred. 3. 5.

Figure 1. Above, a Nuremberg *"Judenstain,"* which, before the expulsion of the Jews in 1499, formed part of the Ark in the synagogue. Below, a plaque recording the acquisition of the "Jewish stone" by the Jewish community in 1909, with the quotation, "A time to cast away stones and a time to gather stones together" (Eccl. 3:5). The stone and plaque, recovered from the ruins of one of Nuremberg's synagogues after World War II, is now in the yard of the city's Altstadtmuseum. Courtesy Stadtarchiv, Nuremberg.

Nuremberg by S. *Salfeld (see bibl.) would prove that a synagogue was consecrated there in 1296. Two years later 728 Jews were victims of the **Rindfleisch* persecutions, among them *Mordecai b. Hillel, author of the *Mordekhai.* Jews are mentioned in Nuremberg again in 1303. In 1313 Henry VII allowed the *Schultheiss* ("mayor") to admit more Jews and granted him their protection dues. However, two years later King Louis IV of Bavaria (1314–47) allowed the council to demolish the houses that the Jews had rebuilt. In 1322 the Jews of Nuremberg, and their taxes, were pledged to the burgrave Frederick IV. Although King Louis promised in 1331 to protect the Jews against oppression and demanded an annual payment of 400 florins for three years in lieu of all taxes, he allowed the council to increase this sum according to the Jews' ability to pay. The council exerted strong pressure on the Jews and many of them fled the town. Two years later, the king declared himself willing to readmit them: a list of 1338 shows that 212 authorized Jewish families (indicating a total of about 2,000 persons) were resident in the city. In 1342 Nuremberg Jews were compelled to pay the *gueldener *Opferpfennig* tax. The council continued to fight an increase in Jewish ownership of houses and in 1344 Louis IV was obliged to promise that the Jews would no longer be permitted to purchase houses owned by Christians. In the *Black Death massacres 560 Jews were burnt to death on Dec. 5, 1349; the rest fled or were expelled. *Charles IV (1346–76) exonerated the town council: promising the property of the Jews to the burgrave of Nuremberg and the bishop of Bamberg, he allowed the majority of Jewish houses to be demolished to make room for the markets; the St. Mary Church (the Frauenkirche) was built on the site of the synagogue.

However, soon afterward, growing short of money, the city authorities were anxious to attract the Jews back, and in 1351 Charles IV permitted the burgrave to admit them and ordered the officials and knights to assist them. The Jewish community in Nuremberg increased rapidly. A contract concluded in 1352 between the city council and the Jews obliged the latter to live in a special quarter (the present *Judenstrasse*) and all debts of the citizens were cancelled. A tax list of 1382 indicates that the Jewish population then numbered more than 500.

In 1310 King Henry VII had restricted their commerce in the market and established a fixed interest rate. In the 14th–15th centuries the right to live in Nuremburg could be acquired only by the head of a family, on payment to the council of a fee which was probably assessed according to the financial situation of the applicant. In addition, he had to provide guarantors and take an oath of loyalty. If a Jew wished to leave the city, he had to notify the council, pay all taxes and dues for the following year, hand over his pledges to a Jew of Nuremberg, and sell his property only to a citizen. Foreign Jews, with the exception of yeshivah

Figure 2. Nuremberg Jewish costume illustrated in an 18th-century etching. Below the picture of the synagogue are shown, left to right: top row, a leader of the community in street costume, and a man and woman dressed for synagogue; bottom row, a man leaving synagogue, a woman in house dress, and a man carrying wine for the Sabbath. From Andreas Wuerfel, *Historische Nachrichten v.d. Judengemeinde zu Nuernberg,* 1755.

Figure 3. Nuremberg Jewish hawker, c. 1790. Etching by A. Gabler, Nuremberg, Germanisches Nationalmuseum.

students, could not be given accommodation in any house. If a Nuremberg Jewish couple married they were allowed to stay four weeks only and during that period had to apply for admittance. Jews and Christians were forbidden to use each others' bathhouses. *Moneylending by Jews was regulated in substantially the same fashion as throughout Germany. Trading was forbidden to Jews in the 13th to 14th centuries except in horses and meat. The latter had to be sold at special stalls, separated from those of the Christians, who were not allowed to buy meat slaughtered by Jews. Jews were also forbidden to sell wine, beer, and some other foodstuffs to non-Jews.

As in other towns in Germany, the protection of the Jews (a profitable source of income) became a bone of contention between the municipality and the king. In 1352 the king granted the city council the right to admit Jews and promised not to pledge or to cede to anyone else the taxes payable by the Jews. However, by 1360 Charles IV admitted Jews to Nuremberg on his own accord and obtained one third of the receipts for the transference of their protection dues to the municipality; in 1371 he demanded a further 400 florins for 20 years. In 1382 King Wenceslaus IV (1378–1419) again ceded to the city the protection of the Jews and their taxes for 19 years, against an annual payment of 400 florins. Nuremberg shared with Emperor Wenceslaus in the gains from the cancellation of debts to Jews (1385). Jews in Nuremberg were arrested and released only after handing over the pledges they held and promising the city council still larger sums. The council appointed a special commission to collect the debts (without interest in the case of recent debts and with a deduction of one quarter in the case of old ones). The commission kept special accounts of "the Jews' money." Total extortion from the Jews approximated 95,000 florins at that time and a similar sum in 1390. In 1412 King Sigismund (1411–37) handed over to the burgrave in Nuremberg his share of the Jewish taxes. However, in 1414 he forced the Jews to contribute 12,000 florins to the Church Council of Constance, and in 1416 obtained an annual payment of 10% of their movable assets for three years against a promise of leaving their other assets untouched and renouncing new taxes. At times the city council prevented the king from extorting large sums (Frederick III, in 1442, had to content himself with 7,000 florins) since they wanted to retain for themselves the income from the Jews. When the Synod of Bamberg prohibited the Jews from engaging in moneylending, the council intervened to have the decree revoked. The council also saw to it that the regulation requiring Jews to wear a distinguishing *badge and headdress was not strictly enforced; only foreign Jews were obliged to wear *Gugeln*, i.e., tall white caps.

With their increasing indebtedness to them, the common citizens' hatred of the Jews also grew. The position of the Jews was aggravated by the appearance in Nuremberg of John of *Capistrano in 1454; the Jews were compelled to attend his conversionist sermons (as they were in 1478 the sermons of Peter *Schwarz). In 1467 18 Jews were burnt to death, accused of having killed four Christians. In 1470 the Jews obtained permission from Frederick III to continue moneylending for six years; three years later the council began to agitate for their expulsion. A new municipal code of 1479 forbade them to charge interest and enforced a humiliating Jewish *oath. The Jews refused to obey the council's regulations and relations between the townspeople and the Jews worsened. Around 1499 the city obtained a legal opinion from the synod that lending on interest to Christians was forbidden to Jews according to the Torah and Canon Law (W. Pirckheimer, *Briefwechsel*, 1, no. 89 (1940), 295–6). In 1498 Maximilian I (1485–1519) at last approved the expulsion of the Jews from Nuremberg for ever. In March 1499 they left the city, some settling in the surrounding villages. Their houses and the synagogue were confiscated by the mayor in favor of the emperor and then purchased by the town for 8,000 florins. The cemetery was

Figure 4. The Nuremberg Reform synagogue on Hans Sachs Square, consecrated in 1874 and demolished by the Nazis in August 1938. Courtesy Hauptamt fuer Hochbauwesen, Nuremberg. Photo Ferd. Schmidt.

destroyed and the tombstones used for building purposes; one of these stones is located in the spiral staircase of the St. Lorenzkirche.

Jewish communal *autonomy in Nuremberg was active and in the main respected. Internal Jewish matters, particularly of taxation, were decided by the rabbi (*Judenmeister*) and the council of the Jews (Judenrat); the five members of the latter were appointed every year by the town jurors. Attempts by the Jews to select their own council members were frustrated by the town authorities. The Judenrat apportioned the taxes payable by the community and administered its assets. Several noted personalities taught at the yeshivah in the city and were the community's rabbis: Mordecai b. Hillel, Jacob ha-Levi, Jacob *Margolioth, Jacob *Weil (1430–50), and Jacob *Pollack (from 1470). During Weil's period of office a synod of rabbis was convened in Nuremberg. *Meir b. Baruch of Rothenburg is said to have been rabbi of Nuremberg. Some Hebrew was printed in Nuremberg (by non-Jews) during the 16th century, first on an engraved bookplate designed by Albrecht Duerer in 1503, and in J. Boeschenstein's *Vil gutter Ermanungen* (1525) and W. Fugger's *Ein nutzlich und wolgegrundt Formular* (1553). Between 1599 and 1602 large parts of a polyglot Bible were issued by Elijah Hutter; J. L. Muehlhausen's *Sefer Nizzaḥon* (with a Latin translation) appeared in 1644, printed by W. Endler.

Return and Settlement. It was not until the end of the 17th century that Jews were allowed to enter Nuremberg to purchase goods on payment of a body tax (*Leibzoll*); but they were not allowed to remain there. In the first half of the 19th century individual Jews occasionally succeeded in staying for shorter or longer periods. At the end of the 1840s, a few Jews were living there, but it was only in 1850 that a Jew (Josef Kohn) was accepted as a citizen by the town council. A community began to form in 1857, subject to the rabbi of Fuerth. In 1859 the *Israelitischer Religionsverein* ("Jewish Religious Association") was formed, legalized as the *Kultusgemeinde* five years later. In the same year the cemetery was opened and ten years later (1874) the synagogue was consecrated. In 1875 the Orthodox members founded the Adass Israel community which opened its own synagogue in 1902 and a primary school in 1921. The Jewish population of Nuremberg increased from 11 in 1825, to 219 in 1858, and 3,032 in 1880. It continued to rise from 5,956 in 1900 to 8,603 in 1915, and 9,000 in 1933, making it the second largest community in Bavaria.

The Nazi Period. Between the two world wars Nuremberg became the center of the Nazi Party; the molesting of Jews in the streets became an everyday occurrence. Julius *Streicher established one of the first branches of the nascent Nazi Party there in 1922 and edited the notorious anti-Semitic paper *Der *Stuermer*. Between 1922 and 1933 about 200 instances of cemetery desecration were reported in and around Nuremberg. While the Nazi Party annual rallies were in progress in the city, the Jews lived in fear of humiliation and attack. The reign of terror began in 1933 when Streicher was made *Gauleiter* of Franconia. On July 30, 400 wealthy and distinguished Jewish citizens were arrested and publicly maltreated; some were forced to trim grass with their teeth. In succeeding years, boycotts and excesses continued without abating. On Aug. 10, 1938, the synagogue and communal center were demolished. Exactly three months later, a systematically organized pogrom broke out. The two remaining synagogues and numerous shops were burned to the ground. Of the 91 Jews in Germany who met their deaths on *Kristallnacht*, 26 (including ten suicides) were in Nuremberg. Immediately afterward between 2,000 and 3,000 Jews left the city. In

Figure 5. Drawing of the Orthodox synagogue on Essenwein Street, completed in 1902 and burned to the ground on *Kristallnacht*, 1938. London, Wiener Library.

1939 only 2,611 Jews remained. A total of 1,601 were deported during the war (Dr. Benno Martin, head of the police, rescued many Jews from death and alleviated the suffering of others); the three main transports were 512 to *Riga on Nov. 29, 1941 (16 survived), 426 to *Izbica on March 25, 1942 (none survived), and 533 to *Theresienstadt on Sept. 10, 1942 (27 survived).

About 65 of the former inhabitants returned after the war and a community was reorganized, which numbered 181 in 1952 and 290 in 1970.

Bibliography: A. Mueller, *Geschichte der Juden in Nuernberg* (1968). MEDIEVAL PERIOD: M. Wiener, *Regesten zur Geschichte der Juden in Deutschland waehrend des Mittelalters* (1862); O. Stabbe, *Die Juden in Deutschland* (1866), 49–66, 135–41, 211, 221, passim; H. C. B. Briegleb, in: J. Kobak's *Jeschurun*, 6 (1868), 1–28, 190–201; S. Taussig, *Geschichte der Juden in Bayern* (1874), 12, 23–24, 27, 32; M. Stern, *Die israelitische Bevoelkerung der deutschen Staedte*, 3 (1896); Salfeld, Martyrol; Aronius, Regesten; A. Suessmann, *Die Judenschuldentilgungen unter Koenig Wenzel* (1907); G. Caro, *Sozial- und Wirtschaftsgeschichte der Juden*, 2 vols. (1908–20), index; I. Schiper, *Yidisher Geshikhte*, 2 (1930); G. Kisch, in: HJ, 2 (1940), 23–24; A. Kober, in: PAAJR, 15 (1945), 65–67; Z. Avneri, in: *Zion*, 25 (1960), 57–61; Germ Jud, 1 (1963); 2 (1968); G. Michelfelder, in: *Beitraege zur Wirtschaftsgeschichte Nuernberg* (1967), 236–60. MODERN PERIOD: H. Barbeck, *Geschichte der Juden in Nuernberg und Fuerth* (1878); B. Ziemlich, *Die israelitische Kultusgemeinde in Nuernberg* (1900); R. Wassermann, in: *Zeitschrift fuer Demographie und Statistik der Juden*, 3 (1907), 77; M. Freudenthal, *Die israelitische Kultusgemeinde Nuernberg 1874–1924* (1925); ZGJD, 2 (1930), 114, 125; J. Podro, *Nuremberg, the Unholy City* (1937); Nuernberger Stadtarchiv und Volksbuecherei, *Schicksal juedischer Mitbuerger in Nuernberg 1850–1945* (1965); E. N. Peterson, *The Limits of Hitler's Power* (1969), 224–94; Yad Vashem Archives. HEBREW PRINTING: L. Loewenstein, in: JJLG, 10 (1912), 53, 168–70; A. Marx, *Jewish History and Booklore* (1944), 318; A. Freimann, *Gazetteer of Hebrew Printing* (1946), 54–55. [ED.]

NUREMBERG LAWS, two anti-Jewish statutes that were accepted on Sept. 15, 1935, during the National Socialist National Convention in Nuremberg. Following orders given by *Hitler, two laws were placed before this convention. The first, the Reich Citizenship Law, discriminated between a subject of the state and a citizen of the Reich. Article 2 of the law stated: "A citizen of the Reich is only that subject who is of German or cognate blood and who, through his conduct, shows that he is both desirous and fit to serve faithfully the German people and Reich." The law therefore negated citizenship to Jews. The second statute was the Law for the Protection of the German Blood and of the German Honor. Among other things, this law set down that "Marriages between Jews and citizens of German [or] cognate blood are forbidden; extramarital relations between Jews and citizens of German and cognate blood are forbidden; Jews may not employ female citizens of German and cognate blood under 45 years in their households; Jews are forbidden to hoist the Reich and national flag and to display the colors of the Reich. The display of Jewish colors is permissible under state protection." Because the law did not define who was a Jew, the first Regulation to the Reich Citizenship Law, dated Nov. 14, 1935, filled this omission. It established types of Jews and people of partial Jewish origin (*Mischlinge*). The concept "non-Aryan" was first used in this regulation.

In total, no less than 13 regulations were published following the Nuremberg Laws, and Jews were barred from almost all positions and professions. The regulations also stipulated, inter alia, that the movements of Jews was to be limited and the letter "J" was to be printed on their identity cards. These laws, however, were not the final delineation of Jewish status, as had been declared upon their acceptance in Nuremberg, but rather the beginning of cruel repression sanctioned by means of the law.

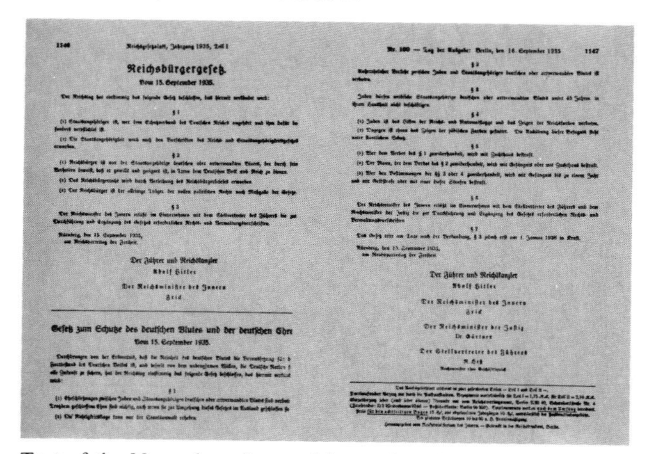

Reichsbürgergesetz.
Vom 15. September 1935.

Der Führer und Reichskanzler
Adolf Hitler
Der Reichsminister des Innern
Frick

Gesetz zum Schutze des deutschen Blutes und der deutschen Ehre
Vom 15. September 1935.

Der Führer und Reichskanzler
Adolf Hitler
Der Reichsminister des Innern
Frick
Der Reichsminister der Justiz
Dr. Gürtner
Der Stellvertreter des Führers
R. Heß

Text of the Nuremberg Laws of September 15, 1939, published in the *Reichsgesetzblatt*, Berlin, September 16, 1939.

Bibliography: Germany, Ministry of Interior, *Reichsgesetzblatt*, 1 (1935); *Deutsche Juristenzeitung* (Oct. 1935); W. Stuckart and R. Schiedmair, *Rassen- und Erbpflege in der Gesetzgebung des Reiches* (1944); H. Dawid, *Rechtsstellung der Juden und der juedischen Mischlinge in Deutschland* (1936); G. Wagner, *Die Nuernberger Judengesetze, Nationalsozialistische Rassen- und Bevoelkerungspolitik, mit Erlaeuterungen zu den Nuernberger Gesetzen* (1939); H. Thomas—Chevalier, *La Protection légale de la race. Essai sur les lois de Nuremberg* (1942); Nuremberg Trials, *Affidavit by Dr. B. Loesener* (Feb. 24, 1948, Doc. NG—1944—A); B. Loesener, in: *Vierteljahreshefte fuer Zeitgeschichte*, 9 (1961), 264–313; B. Blau, *Ausnahmerecht fuer die Juden in Deutschland, 1933–1945* (1954²); F. Muellerheim, *Die Gesetzlichen und aussergesetzlichen Massnahmen zur wirtschaftlichen Vernichtung der Juden in Deutschland 1933–1945* (1952); R. Hilberg, *Destruction of the European Jews* (1961), index; W. Scheffler, *Judenverfolgung im Dritten Reich* (1964), 120f.

[B.M.A.]

NUROCK, MORDECHAI (1879–1962), religious Zionist leader; born in Tukums, Courland. His father, R. Ẓevi Hirsh Nurock was rabbi in Courland's capital Mitau (Jelgava). In 1902 Nurock attended the Russian Zionist conference in Minsk as a delegate from Courland. In 1903 he participated in the Sixth Zionist Congress, at which he took a stand against the *Uganda Scheme. At the same time he was instrumental in gaining an important concession from the czarist government which made possible the settlement of more Jews in Courland and in Riga, though these areas were outside the *Pale of Settlement. Nurock succeeded his father as the official government-appointed rabbi of Mitau (1913). In 1915, when the Russian military command expelled the Jews from Courland, as "German spies," Nurock was invited to remain in Mitau as a military censor, but he declined and left for St. Petersburg and Moscow. He eventually settled in Moscow, where he lived until 1921, becoming the deputy chairman of the Moscow Jewish community. He was particularly active in 1917, between the February and the October Revolution, in the preparations for the All-Russian Jewish Congress, which eventually did not materialize because the new Bolshevik regime opposed it. Toward this congress Nurock established a united religious front of Zionists and non-Zionists called Masoret ve-Ḥerut ("Tradition and Freedom").

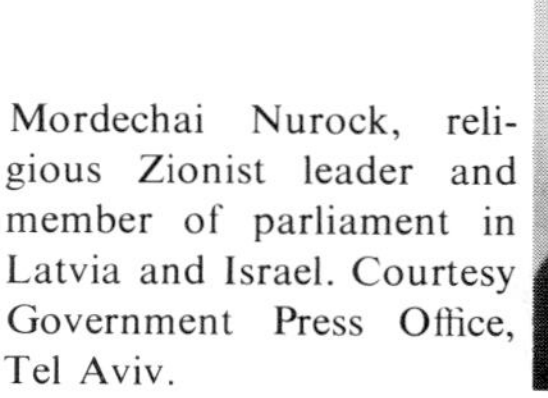

Mordechai Nurock, religious Zionist leader and member of parliament in Latvia and Israel. Courtesy Government Press Office, Tel Aviv.

In 1921 Nurock left the Soviet Union and settled in Riga where he was elected to all Latvian parliaments on the religious Zionist ticket. Five years later, as head of the Minorities' Bloc (Jews, Germans, Russians) in the Latvian parliament, Nurock was formally entrusted to form the government, whereupon he used his good offices to establish a left-of-center cabinet without participating in it personally. He was an active defender of the rights of national minorities both at interparliamentary congresses and at meetings of the Congress of National Minorities. He was one of the creators of the *World Jewish Congress and a delegate to most Zionist Congresses, at which he traditionally served as chairman of the closing session. In addition to his activity in the world leadership of the *Mizrachi movement, Nurock was a member of the Zionist General Council, the world council of HICEM, and other Jewish bodies.

After the outbreak of World War II, when Latvia was incorporated into the U.S.S.R., Nurock was arrested (1941) for his Zionist activities, but was released 14 months later. His wife and two sons, who remained in Riga, perished there in a Nazi camp. In 1945 Nurock left the Soviet Union, visited Scandinavia where he was received by King Haakon, and went to New York. In 1948 he settled in Israel and was a member of the Knesset until the end of his life, one of the very few Diaspora parliamentarians to serve in the Knesset; he also represented it at interparliamentary congresses. Nurock strongly opposed the establishment of any kind of relations between Israel and Germany, often voting independently from his faction on this issue. In 1952 he was minister of posts and a candidate for the presidency of the State.

His German booklet about the Minsk Zionist conference also appeared in Hebrew, translated, prefaced, and annotated by I. Klausner (1962).

Bibliography: A. Tartakower (ed.), *Zekher Mordekhai* (1967); D. Lazar, *Rashim be-Yisrael*, 1 (1953), 87–92; Tidhar, 4 (1950), 1566–69. [M.Bo.]

NUSAḤ (Nosaḥ; Heb. נֻסָּח , נוּסָח , נֹסַח), musical term (for its use in liturgy, see *Liturgy). The common meaning of the Hebrew noun *nusaḥ* is adapted to musical contexts both in a more general and in a very specific way. Expressions like "biblical chant *nusaḥ Sefarad*" (the Sephardi version of melodical Bible-reading; see *Liturgy), or "this cantor has a good *nusaḥ*" (he executes the traditional tunes in good taste) are easily understood as an application of the term in its normal meaning. The word *nusaḥ*, however, is also used as a technical term of synagogue music. In combinations such as *Nusaḥ ha-Tefillah, Nusaḥ Yamim Nora'im, Nusaḥ Shabbat* it denotes the specific musical mode to which a certain part of the liturgy is sung. The musical characteristics of these modes are defined by the following elements: (1) each is based upon a particular series of notes which may simply be a tetrachord, more often a combination of several overlapping tetrachords, or another scale of less or more than eight notes; (2) each contains a stock of characteristic motives which undergo constant variation; (3) each combines these motives in a completely free order, forming an "irrational" pattern; (4) the association of each *nusaḥ*, as defined by the above-mentioned three elements, is with a particular section of a specific holiday liturgy as, for instance, the *Musaf* prayer of the Penitential Feasts, the Morning Prayer on weekdays, and so on.

The music example demonstrates the very simple *Nusaḥ ha-Tefillah* used by the community of Rome in the Sabbath Morning Prayer. It moves within the descending tetrachord from D to A (with a *subtonium* added). The variability of the four motives, their irregular order, and their nonfunctional nature are evident. Other examples of *nusaḥ* patterns are given in the article *Music.

The musical definition of a *nusaḥ* and its close connection with a certain time and occasion exhibit a strong resemblance to the characteristics which are ascribed to the oriental **maqām*, the Indian *raga*, and to certain ancient parts of Roman plainsong and Byzantine hymnody (where it is defined by research as "migrating motives" or "a mosaic of motives"). It is worth noting that the *nusaḥ*-principle is known to European as well as to Eastern Jewish communities and may be regarded, therefore, as a very old musical trait in synagogue song.

Other Musical Meanings of Nusaḥ. The plural form *nusaḥim* denotes the particular tunes to which some prominent chapters of the Pentateuch are read, such as Genesis 1, the Song of the Sea (Ex. 15), or the Decalogue. The *nusaḥim* of these chapters are florid variants of the common mode of reading. Furthermore, the Aramaic plural form *nusḥa'ot* ("formulas") is sometimes used by Ashkenazi cantors for denoting a vocal "prelude" without words which introduces important prayers. [H.Av.]

NUSINOV, ISAAC (Yitzḥak; 1889–1952), Russian literary critic and historian. Born in Chernikhov, Volhynia, he studied at universities in Switzerland and Italy, returning in 1917 to Russia, where he became active in cultural life. From 1925 he taught literature at the University of Moscow and at the Yiddish department of the Western University, Moscow, and participated in the work of the Institute for Jewish Proletarian Culture of the Ukrainian Academy of Sciences, Kiev. Nusinov published many studies, essays, and papers in Yiddish journals; he also contributed to the *Bolshaya Sovetskaya Entsiklopediya* ("Great Soviet Encyclopedia") and to the *Literaturnaya Entsiklopediya* ("Literary Encyclopedia"). His books include *Teories* (1926), articles of literary criticism; *Problemen fun der Proletarisher Literatur* (1932); and *A History of Yiddish Literature*, scheduled for publication in 1927 but never published, though the manuscript was completed. Nusinov was arrested in 1948 and executed in August 1952.

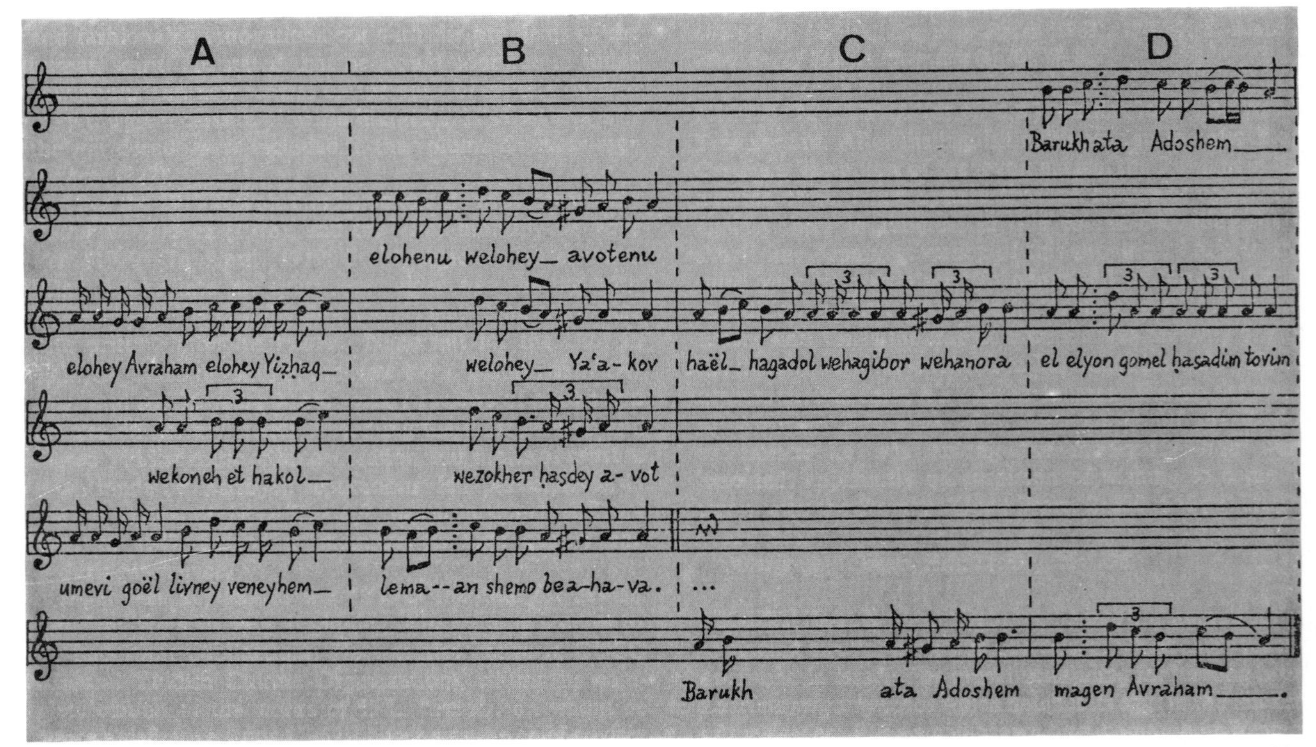

Nusaḥ of the Sabbath morning prayer. Motivic analysis of the version in E. Piattelli, *Canti liturgici ebraici di rito italiano* (1967), p. 20. Copyright: Edizioni De Santis, Rome.

Bibliography: Rejzen, Leksikon, 2 (1927), 537–9; LNYL, 6 (1965), 183; E. I. Simmons, *Through the Glass of Soviet Literature* (1953), 146. [E.Sch.]

NUSSBAUM, ARTHUR (1877–1964), professor of law. Born in Berlin, Nussbaum published *Der Polnaer Ritualmordprozess* (1906), an attack on the procedure of the prosecution at the trial of Leopold *Hilsner, the man tried after the Polna blood libel. The book led to renewed efforts on Hilsner's behalf and gained Nussbaum considerable distinction as a lawyer. In 1914 he became a lecturer at the University of Berlin and was made professor of law in 1921. Following the advent of Hitler, Nussbaum was forced to relinquish his post and he emigrated to the United States. He was research professor of public law at Columbia University from 1934.

A prolific writer in German and English, Nussbaum was an authority on commercial and private international law and his works were translated into several languages. His principle writings include: *Das Geld in Theorie und Praxis des deutschen und auslaendischen Rechts* (1925; republished as *Money in the Law*, 1939); *Deutsches internationales Privatrecht* (1932); *Principles of Private International Law* (1943); *A Concise History of the Law of Nations* (1947, 1954[2]); and *A History of the Dollar* (1957). He also contributed to numerous legal journals and was editor of the *Internationales Jahrbuch fuer Schiedsgerichtswesen in Zivil- und Handelssachen* (1926–34).

Bibliography: *Kuerschner's Deutscher Gelehrten-Kalender* (1966), s.v., incl. bibl.; *New York Times* (Nov. 23, 1964). [Ed.]

NUSSBAUM, HILARY (Hillel; 1820–1895), Polish historian, educator, and communal worker. Born in Warsaw, he was educated in the rabbinical seminary there and as a young man was active in communal affairs. He became a member *("dozor")* of the community council, and was instrumental in building the progressive synagogue of Warsaw. Nussbaum may be considered a moderate assimilationist, influenced by the positivist tendencies in the Polish society of his time.

A prolific writer, Nussbaum contributed to the Polish-Jewish periodical *Izraelita. He was also a writer of apologetics. He published a German translation of a Hebrew treatise by his father-in-law, the Hebrew *maskil* Moses Tenenboim, under the title *Der Talmud in seiner Wichtigkeit* (1880), which was a refutation of *Der Talmud in seiner Nichtigkeit* by a radical assimilationist Abraham *Buchner, an associate of the anti-Semitic Catholic priest L. *Chiarini. Nussbaum is, however, remembered mostly as an author of popular historical works, namely *Szkice historyczne z życia Żydów w Warszawie* ("Historical Sketches from the Life of Jews in Warsaw," 1881); *Historya żydow od Mojżesza do epoki obecnej* ("History of the Jews from Moses to the Present," 5 vols., 1888–90). The works of Nussbaum, although outdated, still have some value for the history of the Jews in Poland. He attempted to stress their great antiquity and their glorious past. Nussbaum, who knew Hebrew well, also published poems and articles in that language.

Bibliography: J. Shatzky, *Yidishe Bildungspolitik in Poyln fun 1806 biz 1866* (1943), index; idem, *Geshikhte fun Yidn in Varshe*, vols. 2–3 (1948–53), indexes. [J.M.R.]

NUSSBAUM, MAX (1910–), U.S. rabbi and organizational leader. Nussbaum, who was born in Suczawa (Succava), Bukovina, was ordained in 1933 by the Breslau Seminary. He served as rabbi in Berlin until 1940, when he went to the United States. He was appointed rabbi of Temple Israel in Hollywood, California, in 1942. Nussbaum served as president of the Zionist Organization of America, chairman of the American section of the World Jewish Congress, vice-president of the American Jewish Congress, and board member of the National Conference of Christians and Jews. [Ed.]

NUSSENBLATH, TULO (1895–1943), researcher into Herzl's life. Born in Stryj, Galicia, Nussenblath was an officer in the Austrian army in World War I. After the war he studied law in Vienna, but instead of working as a lawyer he engaged in historical study, concentrating in particular on the life of Herzl. He published his findings in three books: *Zeitgenossen ueber Herzl* (1929), a collection of contemporary records; *Ein Volk unterwegs zum Frieden* (1933), about the endeavors to found a peace movement, which includes Herzl's correspondence with the Zionist sympathizer Berta von Suttner; and *Herzl Jahrbuch* (1937), which was intended to become a regular annual for researches concerning Herzl's life and era, based primarily on documents not yet published. After the German occupation of Austria in 1938, Nussenblath was expelled to Poland, and when it too was conquered by the Germans, he lived in the Warsaw Ghetto, working there as a communal leader. In the spring of 1943 he was taken to a concentration camp, where he was murdered.

Bibliography: N. Eck (Eckron), *Ha-To'im be-Darkhei ha-Mavet* (1960), 228–33; N. Kudish et al., *Sefer Stryj* (1962), 120–1. [G.K.]

NUT (Heb. אֱגוֹז), in the Bible and Talmud—the walnut, *Juglans regia*, which grows wild in Greece, Asia Minor, and Central Asia. It is mentioned once only in the Bible, but frequently in rabbinic literature. Song of Songs (6:11) refers to "a garden of nuts" where also grew the vine and pomegranates. The verse was regarded as an allegory referring to the Jewish people and the many interpretations afford much information about the growth of the tree, its characteristics, and its fruits: just as regular pruning of this tree assists its development, so does the pruning of the wealth of the Jews by giving charity to those who labor in the Torah (Song R. 6:11); when the walnut tree is smitten with disease its roots should be exposed, so when Israel suffers it must examine itself from the foundation (Yal. Song 6:cf. Song R. 6:11); it is a tall tree with a smooth trunk so that a careless person is liable to fall from it and be killed, such too is the fate of a leader of Israel who is not careful *(ibid.)*; the walnut has species with shells of varying thickness, so too in Israel some have a soft charitable heart, some are average and some are hard *(ibid.)*; the walnut has "four compartments and a central carina" like the camp of Israel in the wilderness which had "four camps with the tent of meeting in the center" (*ibid.*; see Num. 2); just as if one nut is taken from a heap all the rest roll, so if one Israelite is smitten all feel it.

Walnut trees were abundant in Ereẓ Israel in the talmudic period, but because of the great demand for the nuts they were also imported (Tosef., Dem. 1:9). It flourishes mainly in the cooler regions of Israel. Josephus stresses the exceptional fertility of the valley of Gennesareth which produces trees needing heat like palms, but also walnuts that require a cool climate (Jos., Wars, 3:517). As its wood is highly combustible it was used for the altar fire in the Temple (Tam. 2:3). Because of the excellence of the timber it was used to make objets d'art (BB 89b). Its green outer skin supplied material for dyeing (Shab. 9:5) and writing (Tosef., Shab. 11:8). The fruit was regarded as of high nutritional value (Er. 29a). It was particularly beloved by children who played games with the shells. Women too used to play with them (Er. 104a) and walnut shells were also thrown in front of the bride and groom (Ber. 50b). Nowadays walnuts are chiefly to be found in Israel in the gardens of Arabs, very few walnuts being planted in Jewish settlements. The tree is sensitive to pests, but there are giant trees which produce fine crops (like the old walnut tree near the Byzantine church in Abu Gosh).

Bibliography: Loew, Flora, 2 (1924), 29–59; H.N. and A.L. Moldenke, *Plants of the Bible* (1952), index, s.v.; J. Feliks, *Olam ha-Ẓome'aḥ ha-Mikra'i* (1968²), 71–73. [J.F.]

NUZI, ancient city in N.E. Iraq at the present site of Yoghlan Tepe, about 5 mi. (8 km.) S.W. of Arrapkha, modern Kirkuk, near the foothills of southern Kurdistan. Excavations were begun in Nuzi in 1925 by E. Chiera and were continued through 1931 under the joint auspices of the American School of Oriental Research, Harvard University, and the University Museum of Pennsylvania. The earliest occupation of the site can be traced to prehistoric times. During the middle of the third millennium B.C.E. the place was called Gasur and was occupied by an ethnic group called the Subarians. The city reached the height of its importance during the 15th–14th centuries B.C.E., when it was called Nuzi and was part of the *Hurrian Mitanni Empire. It was destroyed by the Assyrians in the 14th century B.C.E. The name of the city always appears in the genitive case; its form in the nominative has been assumed by some to be *Nuzi* (e.g., E. A. Speiser), and by others, *Nuzu* (e.g., C. H. Gordon); the original name was presumably ‡*Nūz*. The written documents from the private and public archives of Nuzi and nearby Arrapkha consist of more than 4,000 tablets and are housed in the Oriental Institute of the University of Chicago and the Harvard Semitic Museum. The documents at the Oriental Institute, numbering about 1,000, have been published in the series of the Joint Expedition with the Iraq Museum at Nuzi (E. Chiera, et al., *American School of Oriental Research, Joint Expedition with the Iraq Museum at Nuzi*, 6 vols., 1927–39), and those of the public archives, numbering over 3,000, in the *Harvard Semitic Series* (ed. by E. Chiera, vols. 5, 9, 10, 13–16, 19 (1929–62, continuing)).

Analogues to Patriarchal Narratives. These tablets shed light on the lives and customs of the Hurrians, and are of importance for biblical studies, particularly for the patriarchal period. The Patriarchs and Matriarchs lived in the region of *Haran in the middle Euphrates valley, and maintained contact with this city (Gen. 11:31–12:4; 24:2–10; 27:43; 28:10; 29:4), which was one of the most important political and religious centers of the Hurrians. Since Nuzi on the east and Haran on the west were part of an integrated ethnic and cultural area, it is assumed that the socio-legal features of the former were also current in the latter, even at a somewhat earlier period. A study of the Nuzi tablets sheds light on the archaic nature of the society, reflected in the narratives about the Patriarchs, and confirms the accuracy of the early traditions embodied in these narratives.

(1) In the Hurrian society there were two types of heirs: direct, i.e., natural-born sons, and indirect, i.e., outsiders adopted by a man who had no sons. The adopted son had to respect his parents by caring for their physical needs, namely, food and clothing, and by seeing that they received a proper burial. In return, he became the sole heir to the family estate. A similar situation is reflected in Genesis 15:2–3, where Abram says that since he lacks an offspring, the one in charge of his household would be his heir. (The institution of *adoption is unknown in Mosaic law.)

(2) According to Hurrian law, the adopted son is the principal heir unless a natural son is subsequently born; the latter then becomes the principal heir and receives a double share, as in the following document: "The tablet of adoption, belonging to E., son of P., who adopted Z., son of A. Accordingly, all my lands, my buildings, my earnings, my domestics . . . I have given to Z. In case E. has sons [of his own], they shall receive a double portion and Z. shall be second. If E. has no sons, then Z. shall be (principal) heir . . . As long as E. is alive, Z. shall serve him; he shall provide him with garments." This then is the import of God's response to Abram, Genesis 15:4 "That one [your steward] shall not be your heir; none but your very own issue shall be your heir."

(3) In addition to the institution of adoption, the Hurrians also practiced the custom of concubinage, whereby the wife, if childless, had to provide her husband with a handmaid in order to bear children: "G. has been given in marriage to S. . . . If G. does not bear children, G. shall acquire a woman of the land of Lulu [i.e., a slave girl] as wife for S." (Although concubinage is also known from the code of Hammurapi, 146, it applies only to certain priestesses; this restriction is not found at Nuzi.) Thus, Genesis 16:1ff. is in perfect conformity with such customary law: "Sarai, Abram's wife, had borne him no children. She had an Egyptian maidservant whose name was Hagar. And Sarai said to Abram, 'See, the Lord has kept me from bearing. Consort with my maid; perhaps I shall have a son through her . . .' So Sarai, Abram's wife, took her maid . . . and gave her to her husband Abram as concubine." The same custom is reflected once again in the time of Rachel, who, being without child, presented her maid Bilhah to Jacob for the purpose of bearing children (Gen. 30:3). The Nuzi tablet just cited goes on to say, "G. herself shall have authority over the offspring." If this is the correct translation of the text—not absolutely certain because of a small break in the tablet before the verb "to have authority"—the wife would have legal authority over the child of the maidservant. Hence, Abram is actually citing the customary law when he says (Gen. 16:6), "Your maid is in your hands. Deal with her as you think right" (cf. Gen. 21:10). It should be noted, also, that another stipulation in this tablet states that if G. does not have sons, then her daughter inherits (cf. Num. 27:3ff.).

(4) Another custom reflected in the Nuzi tablets provides the legal background for the thrice-repeated tale of a Patriarch introducing his wife as a sister (Gen. 12:10–20; 20:1–18; 26:6–16). In the Hurrian society a wife enjoyed both greater protection and a superior position when she had the juridical status of a sister. In such a case two separate documents were drawn up: one for marriage and the other for sistership. (This is not related to the Egyptian custom of pharaohs' marrying their actual sisters. Among the Hurrians the woman was an adopted sister, not a consanguineous one.) The penalty clauses of such documents indicate that any violation of such a marriage was punished with much greater severity than a breach of a regular marriage. This custom probably reflects an underlying fratriarchal system. Moreover, the text of Genesis 24:30ff. has many points in common with such marriage documents. Of particular significance is the fact that Rebekah, who is given in marriage by her brother, is consulted (24:57) and willingly agrees to the marriage proposal (24:58). Similarly, at Nuzi in a marriage of this type the girl would often make a declaration such as, "I do this of my own free will."

(5) The sale or transference of a birthright (Gen. 25:31–34) is only possible in a society that does not consider chronological priority the sole criterion for determining inheritance. One document of Nuzi tells of a man who transferred his inheritance rights to his brother in exchange for three sheep.

(6) Since in Hurrian society the rules of primogeniture were at times subject to the discretion of the father, he could alter them at will, e.g., "As regards my son Z., I first annulled 'his relationship,' but now I have restored him to

sonship. He is the elder son and shall receive a double share." Compare Genesis 48:13–20, where Jacob favors Ephraim over Manasseh, and Genesis 49:3–4 (I Chron. 5:1), where Reuben is deprived of his birthright (cf. I Chron. 26:10). This practice is prohibited in later law (Deut. 21:15–27).

(7) At Nuzi, an oral will made to a son by a dying father had legal validity and could be upheld in court. One such "last will and testament" concerning the oral allocation of a testator's property begins with the formula, "Now that I have grown old." Genesis 27:2 has a similar introduction to a paternal "deathbed blessing."

(8) A gift of a handmaid to a new bride is written into a wedding document at Nuzi: "Morever Y. [slave girl] is herewith assigned to G. [bride] as her maid." This practice is reflected in Genesis 29:24, 29, where the handmaids Zilpah and Bilhah are presented to Leah and Rachel.

(9) Rachel's theft of her father Laban's household gods (Gen. 31:19) is partially clarified in light of the apparent Hurrian custom that possession of household gods, in addition to its religious importance, could, at times, signify a legal title to the paternal estate. This interpretation (strongly doubted by M. Greenberg) is based on the following tablet: "Tablet of adoption belonging to N., the son of A.; he adopted W., the son of P. As long as N. is alive, W. shall provide him with food and clothing. When N. dies, W. shall become the heir. Should N. have a son of his own, the latter shall divide [the estate] equally with W., but only the son of N. shall take the gods of N. However, if N. does not have a son, then W. shall take N.'s gods. Furthermore, he gave his daughter N. in marriage to W. If W. takes another wife, he shall forfeit the lands and buildings of N. [his father]." It is further possible that Jacob was the adopted son of Laban who, in accordance with the Nuzi practice just mentioned, gave him his daughter in marriage. The last clause of this tablet would also clarify the legal significance of Laban's statement, "If you ill-treat my daughters or take other wives besides my daughters . . ." (Gen. 31:50). Moreover, the complaint of both Leah and Rachel, "Have we still a share in the inheritance of our father's house? Are we not reckoned as outsiders? For he has sold us and then used up our purchase price" (Gen. 31:14–15), may be understood in the light of the Nuzi texts, which provide evidence of the favored status of native women and the inferior status of outsiders. In addition, part of the bride payment was usually reserved for the woman as her dowry. This, they say, was also used up by their father.

Analogues to the Book of the Covenant. The earliest collection of biblical law, the *Book of the Covenant, also provides one or two reflexes of laws current in the Hurrian society at Nuzi. Exodus 21:2–6, the law pertaining to the Hebrew slave, has been compared to Nuzi *Ḫabiru documents. The Ḫabiru at Nuzi were self-enslaved individuals who, occasionally with their families, served their patrons for food and raiment. No time limit was placed upon their service. If the agreement was broken, they had either to make a payment of silver or gold to their patron, incur a severe penalty, or provide a substitute in their stead. In Exodus 21:2 there is a question whether the Hebrew word *ʿIvri*, "Hebrew," is to be interpreted as a gentilic, i.e., referring to a fellow Israelite (cf. Deut. 15:12ff.; Jer. 34:8ff.), or as an appellative, i.e., referring to a slave of the Ḫabiru-type status. However, the many correlations between the legal terminology and stipulations of this section in Exodus and of the Ḫabiru documents tend to favor those who understand the word as an appellative. Though several important reforms are introduced in biblical law, e.g., the time limit of six years placed on the slave's service, after which he is freed without having to pay for his release or provide a replacement, both the *ʿIvri* in Exodus and the Ḫabiru at Nuzi are called "slaves." An exact parallel to Exodus 21:4 is found in one document where a Ḫabiru slave who was given a wife by his master is not permitted to take her or his offspring with him when he terminates his period of servitude. The formal oral declaration of Exodus 21:5 that a slave must make when he changes his status from temporary to permanent bondage is analogous to an oral declaration found in a Nuzi document on loans and debts. The ceremony marking permanent bondage takes place before God, "then his master shall bring him unto God, and shall bring him to the door, or unto the doorpost . . ." (Ex. 21:6). At Nuzi similar ceremonies took place before the *ilāni* (Akk.), "gods," who as house gods were protectors of the family estate with a quasi-juridical function. For their employment in communal law, see Exodus 22:7–10, where a deposition before a supernatural authority *(ha-ʾelohim)* is analogous to the oath ordeal before the *ilāni* at Nuzi, which was resorted to when judges did not have sufficient evidence to render a decision in a legal case. The next section, Exodus 21:7–11, has been compared by some to the Nuzi "documents of daughtership and daughter-in-lawship." The usual stipulations in the Nuzi tablets allow the purchaser upon adopting the girl to marry her himself or give her in marriage to one of his sons or slaves. The girl remains under the jurisdiction of her designated husband for life unless the agreement is broken and settlement made. Although there are several major differences in the biblical version, the law in Exodus nevertheless resembles that of Nuzi, since both pertain to the sale of a young girl by her father to a man who must assure a marital status for her.

Analogues to Laws in Leviticus. Several further examples of laws that can be traced to Hurrian influence, and which are reflected in the tablets of Nuzi, have been discovered in Leviticus (Speiser): (1) Leviticus 5:15ff. pertains to an offense for which the guilty party must bring a ram without blemish, "convertible into payment in silver by the sanctuary weight as a guilt offering," as his penalty. At Nuzi there was a type of payment listed in terms of animals rather than metal currency, which, at times, could be commuted into metal currency, but only by recording the substitution by the amount offered for each animal. (2) Leviticus 25:35–54, which lists the various stages and consequences of indebtedness and includes an injunction against exacting interest, has analogues in the Nuzi documents of loans without new interest charges. (3) In the laws pertaining to the exchange of animals (Lev. 27:9–13), there is the following stipulation: "Whether high or low [literally, "good or bad"], whatever assessment set by the priest, so shall it be" (27:12). This has been compared to a similar declaration found in Nuzi documents of exchange transactions, in this case, of fields, in which the official valuation "whether small or large" had to be regarded as final. This, according to Speiser, is an authentic reflex of a well-established economic procedure applied to a religious practice.

Analogues to Deuteronomy and Prophetic Literature. A Nuzi tablet also provides an interesting analogue to the case of the disloyal and defiant son in Deuteronomy (21:18–21). If he does not obey his mother and father, he is brought before the elders of his town for judgment. Similarly, at Nuzi, "In case S. [in this case, an adopted son] fails to obey A. and T. [his parents], if he causes them to appear before the judges, if for a second and a third time he causes them to appear . . . " his relationship is annulled. The custom of expelling an unfaithful wife naked is attested at Nuzi (as well as at Hana and on Aramaic magic bowls). It is also reflected in prophetic literature, Ezekiel 16:37–39; 23:26 and Hosea 2:4–5. In the Hosea passage, however, the emphasis is not so much on the disgrace of the guilty "woman" (alluding to Israel), as on her destitution.

Bibliography: E. A. Speiser, in: AASOR, 10 (1930), 1–73; E. A. Speiser and R. H. Pfeiffer, *ibid.*, 16 (1935/36); E. A. Speiser, in: JBL, 74 (1955), 252–6; idem, in: *Yehezkel Kaufmann Jubilee Volume* (1960), 29–45; idem, in: A. Altmann (ed.), *Biblical and Other Studies* (1963), 15–28; idem, *Genesis* (1964, Anchor Bible); C. H. Gordon, in: BA, 3 (1940), no. 1, 1–12; M. Greenberg, in: JBL, 81 (1962), 239–48; S. M. Paul, *Studies in the Book of the Covenant in the Light of Cuneiform and Biblical Law* (1971).
[SH.M.P.]

NYIREGYHAZA (Hung. **Nyiregyháza**), town in N.E. Hungary. Jews were living in the district in the 18th century, but were excluded fromNyiregyhaza itself until 1840, when they were authorized to settle in the towns. By 1848–49, 71 Jews lived in the town. In 1865 they became affiliated to the community of Nagykallo. After the general Jewish congress of 1868–69 (see *Hungary) the community remained within the framework of the **status quo ante* communities. In 1904 the Orthodox members formed a separate community. The first synagogue of the congregation was built in 1880, when the Orthodox also built their own synagogue. A Jewish elementary school serving the whole community was established in 1868 and existed until the Holocaust. Rabbis of the community included Jacob K. Friedman (officiated 1856–1905), who participated in the congress of 1868–69 as representative of the whole district; and the historian, Bela *Bernstein (1900–1944), who was deported with his congregation in the Holocaust. The court hearings of the *Tiszaeszlar blood libel case were held in Nyiregyhaza. The Jewish population numbered 60 in 1850; 1,128 in 1869; 2,097 in 1880; 2,159 in 1890; 3,008 in 1900; 5,066 in 1920; 5,134 in 1936; and 4,993 in 1941. Their economic position was favorable.

The synagogue in Nyiregyhaza. From J. Heller and X. Vajda, *The Synagogues of Hungary*, New York, 1968.

Holocaust Period and After. When World War II broke out, refugees from Poland arrived in Nyiregyhaza and were assisted by a special communal committee organized for that purpose. The community also supported refugee children from Slovakia. After the imposition by the Hungarian authorities of anti-Jewish laws and forced labor from 1938 to 1944, the Germans occupied the town on March 19, 1944. During Passover (April 17, 1944) S.S. units herded the Jews of the town and from 36 surrounding villages, totaling 17,850, into the ghetto. At the end of May and beginning of June, more than 5,000 Jews were deported in the most inhumane conditions in closed cattle wagons. Some days later the synagogue was blown up.

The two congregations in Nyiregyhaza reorganized after the war and opened a yeshivah. The number of the Jewish population decreased from 1,210 in 1946 to 180 in 1970.

Bibliography: *Zsidó Világkongresszus Magyarországi Képviselete Statisztikai Osztátyanak Közleményei*, 4 (1947), 8–9 (1948), 13–14 (1949); S. Gervai, *Nyiregyháza zsidósága élete* (1963); B. Bernstein, in: *Semitic Studies in Memory of Immanuel Loew* (1947), 57–62.
[L.H.]

NYONS, town in *Dauphiné, in the department of Drôme, S.E. France. Like the other Jews of Dauphiné, those of Nyons were not affected by the expulsions of the Jews from the Kingdom of France in 1306 and 1322. During the latter year, a number of Jews expelled from *Comtat Venaissin joined the Jews already established in Nyons. Their situation was quite satisfactory; a Jew held public office in Nyons and another was in the service of the dauphin. At the time of the *Black Death in 1348, the community suffered violent persecution. It was reconstituted about 1364 and then occupied the present Rue Juiverie. The synagogue, whose dilapidated building still existed toward the end of the 19th century, appears to have belonged to this second community. There were no Jews in Nyons by the end of the 15th century. Known among the scholars of Nyons are Isaac b. Mordecai *Kimḥi, named Petit, a liturgical author, and Ḥayyim of Vienne. At the beginning of World War II about 50 Jewish families, many of them from the Saar, lived in Nyons. In 1971 Nyons had no organized community.

Bibliography: Gross, Gal Jud, 384ff.; C. Brechet, *Pages d'histoire nyonsaise* (1927), 90ff.; Z. Szajkowski, *Analytical Franco-Jewish Gazetteer 1939–1945* (1966), 186.
[B.BL.]

Initial letter "O" of the word *Ozias* at the beginning of the prologue to the Book of Amos in a Latin Bible, France, 13th century. The illumination shows Amaziah, the priest of Beth-El (Amos 7:10–17) waving an incense burner. Lyons, Bibliothèque Nationale, Ms. 411, fol. 160v.

OAK (Heb. אַלּוֹן), the main trees of Israel's natural groves and forests. The three species which grow there have in common their strong and hard wood and all attain a great height and reach a very old age. The Hebrew name, *allon*, means strong (Amos 2:9). Extensive oak forests still exist in Bashan, and these, together with the cedars of Lebanon, symbolized pride and loftiness (Isa. 2:13; Zech. 11:2). The people of Tyre made the oars for their ships from the oaks of Bashan (Ezek. 27:6). Some oaks served as sites for idol worship (Hos. 4:13), and burial took place under them (Gen. 35:8). The oak is long-lived and when it grows old or is cut down it has the ability to renew itself, putting out new shoots from the stump or roots that in time develop into a strong tree. In his prophecy describing the fate of the Jewish people, for whom it was decreed that they should suffer great losses, the prophet Isaiah uses the image of the old oak (together with an *elah*, *terebinth) standing near the gate Shallekhet in Jerusalem that frequently had its branches and trunk cut down, only its stump remaining; yet no sooner was it felled, than the stump put forth "holy seed," sprouting new shoots (Isa. 6:13). Possibly Isaiah 11:1: "And there shall come forth a shoot out of the stock of Jesse, and a twig shall grow forth out of his roots" is a continuation of this chapter.

Evidence of this phenomenon can be seen in many oaks in Israel today. The most famous, and apparently the oldest of them, is "the oak of Abraham" in Hebron. This oak, or one of its ancestors, is mentioned in the Apocrypha—Jubilees and Tobit—as the tree under which Abraham received the kings. Josephus (Ant., 1:186; cf. Wars, 4:533) also speaks of it. *Jerome notes that Titus sold 10,000 Judean captives under this tree. Since the third century many Jewish and Christian pilgrims have mentioned that this tree is considered sacred. It is an evergreen of the species *Quercus calliprinos*, which constitutes most of the groves in the hills of Judea and Galilee. Most of them look like shrubs as a result of continuous felling and of being gnawed by goats. Some giant trees still survive (as for example at Aqua Bella, now called Ein Ḥemed). The other two species of oak growing in Israel are deciduous. On the hills of Lower Galilee (in the vicinity of Tivon and Allonim) there exist groves of the Tabor oak *(Quercus ithaburensis)*. This tree is also to be seen in the Ḥurshat Tal in the Ḥuleh valley where there are about 200 giant trees (50 ft. high with trunks of 16 ft. or more in circumference). The third species is the *Quercus infectoria (Quercus boissier)*, called in Hebrew by the corresponding name *tola* oak because of the *crimson worm *(tola)* which lives off its branches (as it does off the Tabor oak). This tree, which has a tall straight trunk, is called in the Mishnah *milah* or *milast* (Mid. 3:7).

Bibliography: Loew, Flora, 1 (1928), 621–34; Feliks, in: *Sinai*, 38 (1956/57), 85–102; idem, *Olam ha-Ẓome'aḥ ha-Mikra'i* (1968[2]), 107–9; H. N. and A. L. Moldenke, *Plants of the Bible* (1952), index.

[J.F.]

OAKLAND, city located on the east shore of San Francisco Bay, California. The 1969 metropolitan Jewish population (including Alameda and Contra Costa Counties) of Oakland was 18,000. The first Jewish organization was the Oakland Hebrew Benevolent Society (1862), which owned a cemetery and served the religious and cultural needs of the Jewish community until the founding of the First Hebrew Congregation (now Temple Sinai) in 1875. These two organizations merged in 1881. The Oakland lodge of B'nai B'rith was founded in 1875 and many local relief societies followed. The Jewish population of the city in 1880 was 227, with 68 in the suburbs. Congregation Beth Jacob, Orthodox, was founded by Eastern Europeans in 1887 and Temple Beth Abraham, Conservative, by Hungarians in 1907. The Jewish Welfare Federation of Alameda and Contra Costa Counties was organized in 1918 and the present Oakland Jewish Center was built in 1958. Metropolitan Oakland is an active Jewish community with three synagogues in the city and 11 in the suburbs. All the congregations maintain religious schools and there is a Jewish Education Council to coordinate their activities.The community maintains a *mikveh*, a kosher butcher shop, an Anglo-Jewish newspaper, a synagogue council of the East Bay, a home for the aged, a Hebrew day school, and local chapters of every national Jewish organization. Most of the Jews are in the professions or in mercantile activity. They participate in the social and cultural life of the city and are especially active in the affairs of the Oakland Symphony Orchestra. Seymour Rose is a member of the Oakland Board of Education and there are three Jewish judges in the metropolitan area (Martin Rothenberg, Joseph Genser, and Herman Mintz). To the north of Oakland is Berkeley, containing the main campus of the University of California, which has a Hillel Foundation and many distinguished Jews on the faculty, several belonging to the Jewish faculty group. Also in Berkeley is the Judah L. Magnes Memorial Museum, which was organized in 1961. The museum preserves memorabilia concerning Judah *Magnes, restores the gold-rush era Jewish cemeteries in the West, and maintains the Rabbi Morris Goldstein Library.

Bibliography: *Statistics of the Jews of the United States* (1880), 48; M. A. Meyer, *Western Jewry . . .* (1916); AJYB, 66 (1965), 537.

[R.E.L.]

OATH.

IN THE BIBLE

Definition and Form. The truth or inviolability of one's words was commonly attested in ancient Israel by oath —a self-curse made in conditional form that went into effect if the condition was fulfilled; e.g., "May harm befall me if I do so and so" (cf. Eng. "I'll be damned if I will!"). The full form, including the curse, is only rarely found, as, e.g., in the adjuration of the suspected adulteress: "'If no man has lain with you . . . be immune to harm from this water of bitterness that induces the spell. But if you have gone astray while married to your husband . . . may YHWH make you a curse and an imprecation among your people as YHWH causes your thigh to sag and your belly to distend' . . . and the woman shall say, 'Amen, amen' " (Num. 5:19–22). The oath might be accompanied by a gesture expressive of the curse: "Then I called the priests and made them take an oath to act on their word. I also shook out the bosom of my garment and said, 'So may God shake out every man from his house and from the fruit of his labor who does not fulfill his word. So may he be shaken out and emptied!' And all the assembly said, 'Amen' " (Neh. 5:12–13). As a rule, the condition alone appears in oath statements, the self-curse being omitted for superstitious reasons. Thus a negative oath normally is framed as an affirmative conditional statement with aposiopesis: "Swear to me by God, if you will kill me or if you will deliver me to my master [. . .]" (=that you will not kill or deliver me to my master; I Sam. 30:15); "By YHWH's life! if guilt shall come upon you for this [. . .]" (=no guilt shall; *ibid.* 28:10). Less often the self-curse is couched in vague terms (perhaps accompanied by a meaningful gesture): "May God do thus to me and more so, if before sunset I taste bread or anything else!" (II Sam. 3:35). So essential was the curse that the oath might be cited in the form of a curse: "The Israelites had sworn, 'Cursed be him who provides a wife for the Benjamites' " (Judg. 21:18); "Your father adjured the army, 'Cursed be the man who eats bread today' " (I Sam. 14:28). Moreover, the term "curse" (*ʾalah*) freely interchanges with "oath" (*shevuʿah*): cf. Genesis 24:8 with 24:41; the exchange of the related verbs in I Samuel 14:23 and 14:28; and the pair yoked in Numbers 5:21; Daniel 9:11; and Nehemiah 10:30. That too is the basis of the contrast in Isaiah 65:16, between "one who invokes a blessing on himself" (*mitbarekh*) and "one who swears" (i.e., one who invokes a curse upon himself). A strong malediction consisted of condemning someone to such exemplary misfortune as would make him citable in an oath: "You shall leave your name for my chosen ones to use in oaths" (Isa. 65:15; cf. Num. 5:21; Ps. 102:9). The close link between oath and curse lends color to the suggested derivation of the terms *hishbiʿa*, "adjure," *nishbaʿ*, "swear," and *shevuʿah*, "oath," from *shevaʿ*, "seven"—based on the use of seven in maledictions: e.g., Leviticus 26:18, 21, 24, etc.; Deuteronomy 28:7; II Samuel 24:13; Job 5:19; cf. too the repeated sevens in the curses of the Sfire treaty (eighth century B.C.E., Pritchard, Texts[3], 659–60). The original sense might have been "to lay [curses in] sevens on someone" or "to take [curses in] sevens on oneself." (Sevens are also associated with oaths and maledictions in Gen. 21:27–31 and Num. 23; but neither these nor the aforementioned texts support the theory that seven animals were slaughtered at oath-taking, the taker accepting their fate for himself if he broke his word (Lehmann). Biblical and extrabiblical evidence of the symbolic killing of animals at treaty ceremonies never shows so many as seven animals: Gen. 15; Jer. 34:18; Pritchard, Texts [3], 482 no. c, 532.)

Oaths were associated with an invocation of God, or some sacred and powerful equivalent, as the king (Gen. 42:15; both in II Sam. 15:21), either as witness (I Sam. 20:12 [?], 42, cf. Targ.) or in order to convict the perjurer of sacrilege —desecration of the divine name (Lev. 19:12). The terms for such invocation were *nasaʾ shem/nefesh* YHWH, "take up, utter the name/life of YHWH" (Ex. 20:7; Ps. 16:4; 24:4; 50:16) or simply *hizkir be-[shem] ʾelohim*, "mention [the name of] God" (Josh. 23:7; Isa. 48:1). The commonest formula or invocation is *ḥai YHWH* (Judg. 8:19; I Sam. 14:39), a problematic phrase whose most likely meaning is "[By] the life of YHWH!" (Greenberg). Additions to the repertoire of invocations may be gleaned from oaths ascribed to God. His swearing "by Himself" (Gen. 22:16), "by His great name" (Jer. 44:26), "His life" (Amos 6:8), "His holiness" (Amos 4:2; Ps. 89:36), "the pride of Jacob" (Amos 8:7 [=Himself? cf. Ibn Ezra]) presumably echo man's language. His oath "by His right hand and His mighty arm" (Isa. 62:8) recall later Hebrew formulas where the swearer stakes something precious (e.g., "the life of my head" [Sanh. 3:2]) as a guarantee of his word. The unique adjuration "by gazelles and hinds of the field" (Song 2:7; 3:5) suggests that these animals symbolized love or beauty (cf. Prov. 5:19). "Raising the hand to YHWH" (Gen. 14:22) was an oath-gesture (another time it is "lifting the right and left hands to heaven" [Dan. 12:7]). Of God too it is said that he "lifts His hand [to heaven]" (Ex. 6:8, Num. 14:30; Deut. 32:40; Ezek. 20:5)—meaning that He swears. The origin of the gesture is obscure, as is that of the twice-recorded patriarchal oath-gesture of the swearer's placing his hand under the thigh of his adjurer (Gen. 24:2–3, 9; 47:29). The latter was understood by the rabbis as an oath by circumcision (Gen. R. 59:8).

The Use of Oaths in Ancient Israel. Oath-taking was very common, occasions for oath-taking ranging from the personal and the trivial to the most solemn public undertakings: e.g., Judges 21:1; I Samuel 14:28; 17:55; 20:3; II Samuel 14:19; I Kings 17:1; II Kings 2:2; and Nehemiah 13:25. Personal (Gen. 21:23; I Sam. 20:42) and state or communal (Josh. 9:18; II Sam. 21:2; Ezek. 17 [cf. II Chron. 36:13]) alliances were solemnized by oaths—the parties being termed *baʿale shevuʿah*, "oath-partners" (Neh. 6:18). Israel's covenant with God involved the people in oath-like sanctions (e.g., Lev. 26; Deut. 27–28); however, the covenant sanction is only seldom expressly called an oath (of allegiance) to God, as in II Chronicles 15:12–15, which in turn evokes Nehemiah 10:30. Eschatological acceptance of God by non-Israelites is also expressed through an oath of allegiance to Him (Isa. 19:18; 45:23). The laws of the Torah reckon with the following kinds of oaths:

(a) The exculpatory oath, exacted by the plaintiff from the defendant to back the latter's plea of innocence when no witness to the facts was available; the oath was taken at the Sanctuary (Ex. 22:7, 10; the procedure is described in I Kings 8:31). If the defendant took the oath, the suit was decided in his favor (Ex. 22:10; cf. the effect of the exculpatory oath in the Old Babylonian lawsuits in Pritchard, Texts[3], 218 [E, 1], 545 [no. 10]). On the other hand, if he refused to swear, his plea was automatically rebutted and he lost the suit (cf. Pritchard, Texts[3], 545 [no. 11]). Such a self-convicted liar is referred to in Ecclesiastes 9:2 as "he who is afraid of the oath" (note esp. his position as the second, pejorative member of his pair, paralleling "the wicked," "the impure," etc. of the preceding pairs). A perjurer who repents and wishes to clear himself before God and man must follow the prescription of Leviticus 5:20–26. A special case of exculpatory oath is that of the suspected adulteress; its curse is effected through the ordeal of the "bitter waters that induce the spell" (Num. 5). See *Ordeal of jealousy.

(b) The adjuration to give testimony or information—uttered by the party interested in the testimony and directed to the community at large or against a particular party (Lev. 5:1; Judg. 17:1–3 [an example of its effectiveness]; I Kings 18:10; Prov. 29:24). One who defied the adjuration and withheld information and later wished to expiate his guilt must follow the prescription of Leviticus 5:6–13.

(c) The voluntary obligatory oath, binding the taker to do or not to do something (Lev. 5:4). The standard of righteousness was to fulfill such oaths even when they resulted in harm to the taker (Ps. 15:4). How to expiate unwitting violations of these oaths is the subject of Leviticus 5:6–13. The oath of self-denial (closely related to the vow) discussed in Numbers 30 belongs to this class. The chief concern of the law is to subject such an oath taken by a woman to the approval of her father or husband. The oath is nicely illustrated in Psalms 132:2–5. Prohibitions against taking false oaths occur in Exodus 20:7 (Deut. 5:11) and Leviticus 19:12.

Sanctions. The Bible provides no external legal sanctions for oaths; punishment for false oaths is in the hands of God "who will not hold guiltless one who swears falsely by His name" (Ex. 20:7). The perjurer "desecrates" the name of God (Lev. 19:12); he may not have access to God's holy place and its blessings (Ps. 24:4). How the divine sanction was thought to operate may be illustrated from the failure of the oracle due to Jonathan's violation of Saul's adjuration (I Sam. 14:36ff.); from the famine ascribed to Saul's violation of the oath made to the Gibeonites (II Sam. 21:1–2); and from the death of Hiel's sons ascribed to his defiance of Joshua's adjuration not to rebuild Jericho (I Kings 16:34; cf. Josh. 6:26). The divine sanctions of the oath were personified almost as demons: upon the man who was disloyal to God the curses of the covenant would "couch" (Deut. 29:19). Zechariah 5:2–4 speaks of a visionary flying scroll bearing a curse that will destroy perjurers (among others); and Daniel 9:11 speaks of the oath-curses of the Torah "pouring down" upon sinful Israel.

Appreciation of Oaths. The estimate of the biblical period that there was nothing amiss in oaths is manifest in the frequency with which God is represented as swearing. Indeed, the invocation of God in oaths was highly appreciated for its confessional value: "You must revere YHWH your God: Him shall you worship, to Him shall you hold fast, by His name shall you swear" (Deut. 10:20; cf. 6:13). So much was this so that swearing by YHWH could be used as a synonym of adhering to Him: Psalms 63:12; Isaiah 19:18 (cf. Targ. and Radak); 48:1; Jeremiah 44:26; Zephaniah 1:5 (cf. Targ.). Contrariwise, apostasy is expressed through swearing by other gods: Joshua 23:7 (cf. Ex. 23:13); Amos 8:14; Jeremiah 5:7; 12:16. Ibn Ezra's comment to Hosea 4:15 illuminates the sentiment: "Adhering to God carries with it the obligation to make mention of Him in all one's affairs, and to swear by His name, so that all who listen may perceive that he adheres lovingly to God, the name and mention of Him being always on his lips." The only offense recognized in connection with oaths by YHWH was, "Though they may swear, 'By the life of YHWH,' yet they swear falsely" (Jer. 5:2). Ecclesiastes is the only biblical writer who is wary of oaths. In 8:2–3a, he cites a proverb, "Do not rush into uttering an oath by God" (cf. a parallel wariness of vows in 5:1–6). From here it is but a step to Ben Sira's warning against addiction to oaths (23:9ff.), and Philo's recommendation to avoid them entirely (Decal. 84). [Mo.G.]

TALMUDIC LAW

General Rules.

(1) The oath, as here understood, is a mode of judicial proof. It is applicable only in civil and not in criminal cases. (For non-judicial oaths, see *Vows.)

(2) The oath is a residuary proof only: it is admitted only where no sufficient evidence is available (Shev. 45a, 48b). Where an oath had been taken and judgment pronounced, and then witnesses came forward and testified that the oath had been false, the judgment is quashed and any money recovered thereon restituted (BK 106a; Yad To'en ve-Nitan 2:11).

(3) The oath is a party oath, originally administered as purgatory oath to the defendant, but later admitted in special cases also as confirmatory oath of the plaintiff (Shevu. 7:1). (For witnesses' oaths, see below under Post-Talmudical Law.)

(4) The oath is admissible to deny, or confirm, a liquidated and valid claim only: where (or insofar as) the claim does not disclose a cause of action and could be dismissed *in limine,* no oath may be administered (BM 4b–5a; Yad, loc. cit. 1:15). An exception to this rule is made in respect of unliquidated claims for accounts against trustees, partners, and agents (Shevu. 7:8).

(5) The oath need not be confined to one particular cause of action: once the oath is administered to a defendant, he may be required to incorporate in it any number of additional claims in respect of other debts allegedly due from him to the same plaintiff (*"Gilgul Shevu'ah"*; Shevu. 7:8; Kid. 28a; Yad, loc. cit., 1:13; Sh. Ar., ḤM 94, passim).

(6) No oath is administered to suspected liars, such as gamblers, gamesters, usurers, and the like, or to people who have once perjured themselves (Shevu. 7:4; Yad, loc. cit., 2:1–2; ḤM 92:2–3), or who are otherwise disqualified as *witnesses for their wickedness (Yad, loc. cit.; ḤM 92:3).

(7) Not only is no oath administered to minors, or to the deaf and dumb, or insane persons (Yad, loc. cit., 5:12; ḤM 96:5), but originally none would be administered even to rebut the claim of any such person (Shevu. 6:4; Yad, loc. cit., 5:9; ḤM 96:1), until the law was reformed to allow such claims to be presented and require them to be rebutted an oath (Yad, loc. cit., 5:10; ḤM 96:2).

(8) Originally, oaths were admitted to rebut, or confirm, claims in respect of movable property only, excluding lands, slaves, and written deeds (Shevu. 6:5; BM 56b); but the law was later extended to allow, and require, the administration of oaths also in claims for immovables and deeds (Yad, loc. cit., 5:1; ḤM 95:1).

(9) The right to have an oath administered to one's debtor is enforceable in a separate action (BM 17a; Yad, loc. cit., 7:5). The right may, however, be contracted out

(Ket. 9:5). Opinions are divided whether this right devolves to one's heirs (Shev. 48a; Yad, Sheluhin, 9:3). Like all other enforceable debts, the liability to take an oath lapses in the seventh year of remission (Deut. 15:1; Shevu. 7:8).

(10) The duty to take an oath is personal and does not devolve on the debtor's heirs: if the debtor died after the death of the creditor, the creditor's heirs inherit the chose in action and may recover on taking the oath that the claim is still unsatisfied; but where the creditor died after the debtor's death, the claim is extinguished if it cannot be enforced otherwise than by tendering the oath (Sh. Ar., ḤM 108:11).

Classes of Oaths. The Talmud classifies the judicial oaths chronologically, the classes varying in sanctity and gravity in descending order—the earlier the severer.

The Pentateuchal Oath (Shevu'at ha-Torah).

(1) The oath of bailees: where property was entrusted to the defendant for bailment, safekeeping, or other custody, and the defendant claimed that it was lost or stolen, or that it depreciated without his fault, the oath is imposed on him to verify his defense (Shevu. 5 and 8, BK 107b; BM 93a; Yad, Shevu'ot 11:5 and She'elah u-Fikkadon, 4:1; Sh. Ar., ḤM 87:7; see also **Shomerim*).

(2) Where the defendant admits part of the claim, he will be adjudicated to pay the amount admitted and to take an oath that he does not owe more (Shevu. 6:1; BM 3a; Yad, Shevu'ot 11:5, and To'en ve-Nitan, 1:1; Sh. Ar., ḤM 87:1; see also *Admission).

(3) Where the defendant denies the claim in whole, and the plaintiff could adduce only one witness to prove his claim (for the two-witnesses-rule, see *Witness), the defendant will have to take the oath that he owes nothing (Shevu. 40a; Yad, Shevu'ot 11:5, To'en ve-Nitan, 1:1 and 3:6; Sh. Ar., ḤM 87:1 and 7).

The Mishnaic Oath (Shevu'ah mi-Divrei Soferim). The following are plaintiff's oaths ("they swear and take"):

(1) The laborer's oath: On a claim for wages, the plaintiff is entitled to judgment on taking the oath as to the amount due to him (Shevu. 7:1), provided the contract of employment is uncontested or has first been duly proved, and provided the claim is made promptly (Shev. 45b; Yad, Seḥirut, 11:6; Sh. Ar., ḤM 89:1–3). See also *Labor Law.

(2) The shopkeeper's oath: Where the plaintiff claims to have advanced money or goods to a third party upon the defendant's request, and the request is uncontested or has first been duly proved, the plaintiff may recover on taking the oath as to the amount so advanced and due to him (Shevu. 7:5; Yad, Malveh ve-Loveh, 16:5; Sh. Ar., ḤM 91:1). The fact that a debt was entered in the shopkeeper's books was not originally sufficient in itself to entitle him to recover even on taking the oath (Yad, loc. cit., 16:6); later the rule was established that where a merchant kept regular books on account, his oath would be accepted to verify his books (Rosh, Resp. nos. 86:1–2 and 103:2; Sh. Ar., ḤM 91:4–5).

(3) The landlord's oath: Where it was duly proved, or admitted, that the defendant entered the plaintiff's house empty-handed and left it with chattels in his hands, the plaintiff may recover upon his oath as to what it was the defendant had taken away (Shevu. 7:2; Shev. 46a; Yad, Gezelah va-Avedah, 4:1–2; Sh. Ar., ḤM 90:1). In the absence of the landlord himself, his wife or any other person in charge of the premises could take the oath (Shev. 46b; Yad, loc. cit., 4:6; Sh. Ar., ḤM 90:4; *Sefer Teshuvot ha-Rashba ha-Meyuḥasot le-ha-Ramban*, no. 89). The oath was later extended to all cases where it was proved, or admitted, that some monetary damage had been caused by the defendant, for instance, where he had been seen to throw the plaintiff's purse into the water or into fire: the plaintiff would be entitled to recover damages on taking the oath as to what had been the contents of the purse, provided the claim did not exceed what would normally be kept in a purse (BK 62a; Yad, Ḥovel u-Mazzik, 7:17; Sh. Ar., ḤM 388:1).

(4) The injured's oath: Where it was duly proved, or admitted, that the plaintiff had been whole and sound when encountering the defendant, and when he left him he was found injured, the plaintiff is entitled to recover damages on taking the oath that it was the defendant who had injured him (Shevu. 7:3; Yad, loc. cit., 5:4; Sh. Ar., ḤM 90:16). Where the injury could have been neither self-inflicted nor caused by a third party, however, the plaintiff was allowed to recover without taking the oath (Shev. 46b; Yad, loc. cit., 5:5; Sh. Ar., ḤM 90:16; see also *Damages).

(5) The billholder's oath: While a bill duly proved to have been made by the defendant is normally sufficient evidence of the debt (see **Shetar*), where the plaintiff "detracts" from the bill by admitting to have received part of the debt evidenced by it, he has to take the oath that the balance is still due to him (Tosef., Shevu. 6:5; Shev. 41a; Yad, Malveh ve-Loveh, 14:1; Sh. Ar., ḤM 84:1). The same rule applies to the widow's claim on her **ketubbah* (Ket. 9:7); but the widow's oath was later required even where she did not expressly admit any part payment, so as to establish that she had not received anything on account of her *ketubbah* during her husband's lifetime (Git. 4:3; Sh. Ar., EH 96:1).

(6) The shifted oath: Where the defendant is a suspected liar and cannot therefore be sworn (see above), the oath is shifted to the plaintiff to verify his claim (Shev. 7:4; Yad, To'en ve-Nitan, 2:4; Sh. Ar., ḤM 92:7). If the plaintiff is a suspected liar, too, the liability to take the oath reverts to the defendant, but as he will not be allowed to take it, judgment will anyhow be entered against him (*ibid.*). This highly unsatisfactory result was sought to be avoided by applying the general rule that the burden of proving his claim always rested on the plaintiff (see *Evidence), and as the plaintiff would not be allowed to take the shifted oath, his claim ought to be dismissed (cf. *Rema* Sh. Ar., ḤM 92:7), the more so where the plaintiff had known that the defendant was a suspected liar and ought therefore to have abstained from doing business with him (Rosh, Resp. no. 11:1).

The following is a defendant's oath ("they swear and do not pay"): (7) The Pentateuchal oath of the bailees was in the Mishnah extended to partners, tenant farmers, guardians, married women (in their capacity as agents of their husbands), and self-appointed administrators of estates (Shevu. 7:8; Yad, Sheluḥin ve-Shuttafin, 9:1; ḤM 93:1). The same oath is imposed by the husband on his wife in respect of any business carried on by her (Ket. 9:4).

The Post-Mishnaic Oath (Shevu'at Hesset). The presumption has been raised that plaintiffs will not put forward unfounded and vexatious claims; and the rule evolved (in the third century) that a plaintiff who could not otherwise prove his claim, was entitled to have an oath administered to the defendant that he did not owe anything (Shevu. 40b; Yad. To'en ve-Nitan, 1:3; Sh. Ar., ḤM 87:1). A defendant unwilling to take this oath but still persisting in his denial of indebtedness, had the right to shift the oath to the plaintiff who, upon taking it, would be entitled to recover (Shevu. 41a; Yad, loc. cit., 1:6; Sh. Ar., ḤM 87:11); but the Pentateuchal and mishnaic oaths could not be so shifted except as set out above (see the shifted oath). In the event of the plaintiff's refusing to take the shifted oath, the claim will be dismissed (Sh. Ar., ḤM 87:12).

Administration of Oaths. The Pentateuchal and mishnaic oaths are taken by holding the Scroll of the Torah in one's hand and swearing by God (Shevu. 38b; Yad, Shevu'ot, 11:8; ḤM 87:15). God need not be mentioned by name but may be described by one of His attributes. The oath is taken standing up (Shevu. 4:13; Sh. Ar., ḤM 87:16, 17). The post-mishnaic oath is taken without holding the Scroll and without mentioning God (Sh. Ar., ḤM 87:18; a contrary rule is given by Yad, Shevu'ot, 11:13, to the effect that the Scroll should at least be held out to the deponent so as to instill fear into him). The oath is pronounced either by the person taking it or by the court administering it; in the latter case, the deponent responds with "Amen" (Shevu 9:11; Yad, Shevu'ot 11:10). There was a rule to the effect that oaths must always be taken in Hebrew (Yad, Shevu'ot 11:8), but it was later mitigated so as to allow the oath to be taken in the language best understood by the deponent (*ibid.*, 11:14; Sh. Ar., ḤM 87:20).

Before administering the oath, the court warns the deponent of the gravity of the oath and the inescapability of divine punishment for any false oath. This warning is not required for the post-mishnaic oath (Shevu. 39a; Yad, Shevu'ot 11:16; Sh. Ar., ḤM 87:20–21). The court also warns the party at whose instance the oath is administered, that he should abstain if his case was wrong so as not to have the oath administered unnecessarily, whereupon that party has to say "Amen" to confirm his own good faith (Yad, To'en ve-Nitan, 1:11; Sh. Ar., ḤM 87:22).

Sanctions. (1) Where a defendant was by law required to take the Pentateuchal oath and refused, judgment would be entered against him and execution be levied against his property forthwith (Shevu. 41a; Yad, loc. cit., 1:4; Sh. Ar., ḤM 87:9).

(2) Where a plaintiff was by law allowed to take the mishnaic oath and obtain judgment, he could forego his privilege and have the post-mishnaic oath administered to the defendant (Yad, loc. cit., 1:4; Sh. Ar., ḤM 87:12). However, the defendant would then shift the post-mishnaic oath back to the plaintiff (see above), and if the plaintiff still refused to take the oath, his claim would be dismissed (Sh. Ar., ḤM 87:12); but it must be borne in mind that the refusal or reticence to take the much severer mishnaic oath did not necessarily entail such refusal or reticence in respect of the much lighter post-mishnaic oath.

(3) Where a defendant refused to take the mishnaic or post-mishnaic oath, a *ḥerem (ban) lasting 30 days would be pronounced against him (Yad, loc. cit., 1:5; Sh. Ar., ḤM 87:9); for refusal to take the oath, he would also be liable to *flogging (Yad, loc. cit., 1:5); but judgment would not be entered against him so as to authorize execution upon his goods or lands (Shevu. 41a; Yad, loc. cit.; Sh. Ar., ḤM 87:9).

POST-TALMUDIC LAW

To the classes another class was added at a much later period (as from the 14th century), namely, the testimonial oath. Originally, potential witnesses could be sworn only to the effect that they were, or were not, able to testify on a given matter (Shevu. 4:3)—the purpose of such "oath of the witnesses" was solely to avoid suppression of testimony. It was an innovation to have witnesses, who were prepared and about to give evidence, swear first that they would testify to the truth; but the swearing in of witnesses became a widespread practice (Ribash, Resp. no. 170; Tashbeẓ 3:15; Resp. Joseph ibn Lev 4:1), though not a binding rule of law (*Ḥatam Sofer*, Resp. ḤM no. 207). It is not practiced in the rabbinical courts of today. The rule appears to be that it is in the free discretion of each particular court to administer the testimonial oath whenever in its opinion circumstances so require (cf. *Beit Yosef* ḤM 28:1; *Rema* Sh. Ar., ḤM 28:2; *Urim ve-Tummim* ḤM 28:2; and *Sma*, Sh. Ar., ḤM 28 n. 16); but it has been said justifiably that a witness who cannot be believed without being first sworn, cannot be believed at all (Tos. to Kid. 43b s.v. *Hashta*).

JURAMENTUM JUDAEORUM OR MORE JUDAICO (THE JEWRY OATH)

As from the fifth century and throughout the Middle Ages, Jews testifying in non-Jewish (Christian) courts were required to take an oath which was invariably so formulated as to be binding upon them under Jewish law. Its essential elements were the solemn invocation of God; the enumeration of certain miraculous events from biblical history in which God's omnipotence was especially manifest; and curses to discourage perjury (Kisch, Germany, 275). Most medieval lawbooks and statutes contain elaborate provisions and formulae for the Jewry Oath. Many provided for concomitant degradations and insults, such as having Jews take their oaths while standing on a pigskin (*ibid.*, 278 et al.).

See *Oath *More Judaico;* *Vows and vowing. [H.H.C.]

Bibliography: In the Bible: J. Pedersen, *Der Eid bei den Semiten* (1914); M. H. Segal, in: *Leshonenu*, 1 (1929), 215–27; S. Blank, in: HUCA, 23 (1950/51), 73–95; N. H. Tur-Sinai, *Ha-Lashon ve-ha-Sefer*, 3 (1957), 177–86; M. Greenberg, in: JBL, 76 (1957), 34–39; H. Silving, in: *Yale Law Journal*, 68 (1959), 1329–48; M. R. Lehman, in: ZAW, 81 (1969), 74–91. Post-biblical: J. Seldenus, *Dissertatio de Juramentis (Excerptio ex eius libro secundo de Synedriis)* (1618); K. F. Goeschel, *Der Eid...* (1837); Z. Frankel, *Die Eidesleistung der Juden in theologischer und historischer Beziehung* (1847[2]); L. Zunz, *Die Vorschriften ueber Eidesleistung der Juden* (1859); L. Loew, in: *Ben Chananja*, 9 (1866), suppl., 17–25, reprinted in his *Gesammelte Schriften*, 3 (1893), 335–45; T. Tonelis Handl, *Die Zulaessigkeit zur Zeugenaussage und zur Eidesablegung nach mosaisch-rabbinischem Rechte* (1866; Ger., and Heb. *Edut le-Yisrael*); J. Blumenstein, *Die verschiedenen Eidesarten nach mosaisch-talmudischem Rechte und die Faelle ihrer Anwendung* (1883); R. Hirzel, *Der Eid* (1902); F. Thudichum, *Geschichte des Eides* (1911); D. Hoffmann, in: *Jeschurun*, 1 (1914), 186–97 (Ger.); J. Pedersen, *Der Eid bei den Semiten* (1914); Gulak, Yesodei, 4 (1922), 129–49; H. Tykocinsky, *Die gaonaeischen Verordnungen* (1929), 67–99; T. Bernfeld, *Eid und Geluebde nach Talmud und Schulchan Aruch* (1930[3]); S. Rosenblatt, in: PAAJR, 7 (1935/36), 229–43; Herzog, Instit, 1 (1936), 11–13; Kisch, Germany, 275–87, 506–15; idem, in: HUCA, 14 (1939), 431–56 (Ger.); Z. Warhaftig, in: *Yavneh*, 3 (1949), 147–51; ET, 1 (1951[3]), 267f.; 5 (1953), 522–4, 528; 6 (1954), 37–61; 8 (1957), 741–3; B. Cohen, in: HJ, 7 (1945), 51–74, reprinted in his *Jewish and Roman Law*, 2 (1966), 710–33, and addenda 797–800; idem, in: *Goldziher Memorial Volume*, 2 (1958), 50–70, reprinted op. cit., 734–54 and addenda 801; Elon, Mafte'aḥ, 310–26; idem, in: ILR, 4 (1969), 106–8.

OATH MORE JUDAICO or **JURAMENTUM JUDAEORUM**, the form of oath which Jews in the Middle Ages were compelled to take in lawsuits with non-Jews. Both the text of the oath and the symbolic ritual involved in taking it were intended to give it the explicit character of a self-imposed curse, entailing detailed punishment if it were falsely taken. The ceremonial and symbolism were intended to strengthen and make vivid the curse as well as to stress the distrust of the Jew and the wish to humiliate him that

Figure 1. Woodcut showing a Jew taking the special Jewish oath, *more judaico*. From Tengler, *Laienspiegel*, Augsburg, 1509. Cecil Roth Collection.

were at the root of this special oath ritual. In various formulas, an oath of this kind was the rule in Europe from the early Middle Ages until the 18th century and in some places persisted even later. One such formula is found in a capitulary ascribed to Charlemagne, though it may have been composed at a somewhat later date. The Byzantine emperor Constantine VII (913–959) promulgated such an oath, which was probably patterned after earlier rulings on the subject. Jewish oath formulas written in German are preserved in 12th-century manuscripts from Erfurt and Goerlitz. The oath was taken on the Hebrew Bible. The text of the German *Schwabenspiegel* (c. 1275) exemplifies most of its main characteristics.

> About the goods for which this man sues against thee, that thou dost not know of them nor have them, nor hast taken them into thy possession, neither thyself nor thy servants . . .
> So help thee God, who created heaven and earth, valleys and mountains, wood, foliage, and grass, that was not before;
> So help thee the Law that God wrote with His hand and gave to Moses on Mount Sinai; . . . And that so [if] thou eatest something, thou will become defiled all over, as did the King of Babylon; And that sulphur and pitch rain upon thy neck, as it rained upon Sodom and Gomorrah;
> . . . And that the earth swallow thee as it did Dathan and Abiram; . . . So art thou true and right.
> And so help thee Adonai; thou art true in what thou has sworn.
> And so that thou wouldst become leprous like Naaman: it is true.
> . . . And so that the blood and the curse ever remain upon thee which thy kindred wrought upon themselves when they tortured Jesus Christ and spake thus:
> His blood be upon us and upon our children: it is true.
> So help thee God, who appeared to Moses in a burning bush.
> It is true the oath thou hast sworn:
> By the soul which on doomsday thou must bring to judgment.
> Per deum Abraham, per deum Isaac, per deum Jacob it is true.
> So help thee God and the oath which thou hast sworn.
> Amen.

Not all formulas were as detailed or as harsh; most made no reference to the Jews as Christ-killers, yet all were intended to frighten the Jewish deponent in one way or another and to demonstrate visibly his inferior status.

The ceremonies attached to taking the oath were often even more degrading than the text. While Magdeburg jurors simply required that the deponent place his hand on the Pentateuch during the ceremony, many others insisted on ceremonials calculated to humiliate by their ludicrous and fantastic elements. According to old German custom the plaintiff or the judge held out a staff to be touched by the Jewish defendant while the oath was administered. One ritual made the Jew stand on a sow's skin, and in another he was obliged to stand on a hide of an animal that had brought forth young during the preceding fortnight: "The skin shall be cut open along the back and spread on [displaying] the teats; on it the Jew shall stand barefoot and wearing nothing but nether garment and a haircloth about his body." In yet another ceremonial the Jew had to stand on a stool, wearing his cloak and "Jew's hat" and facing the rising sun. The oath was administered either within or outside the synagogue or, less frequently, in the Christian courtroom. Yet in spite of these extravagant aspects of both ceremonial and formula, fundamentally the oath *more judaico* was patterned after Jewish religious law.

See also *Autonomy, Judicial; *Oaths.

Bibliography: Baron, Community, 3 (1942), index; Kisch, Germany, 275–87; J. R. Marcus, *Jew in the Medieval World* (1938), 49f.; J. E. Scherer, *Die Rechtsverhaeltnisse der Juden in den deutsch-oesterreichischen Laendern*, 1 (1901); O. Stobbe, *Die Juden in Deutschland waehrend des Mittelalters in politischer, sozialer und rechtlicher Beziehung* (1923[3]), 7, 153–9, 262–5. [I.L.]

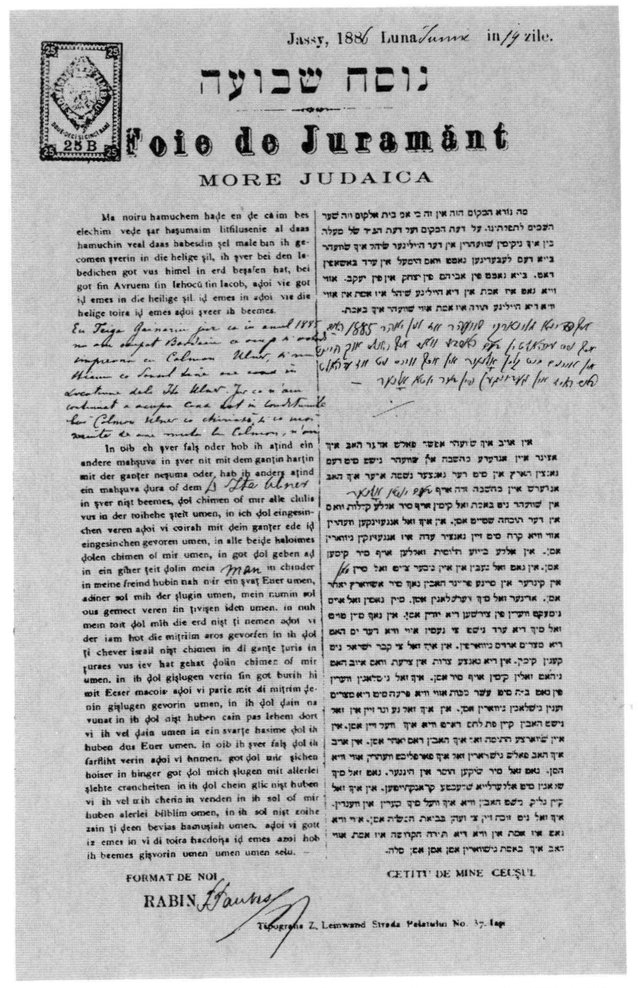

Jassy, 1886 Luna Iunie in 14 zile.

נוסח שבועה

Foie de Juramânt

MORE JUDAICA

Ma noiru hamuchem haḑe en ḑe caim bes elechim veḑe ţar haşumaim litfilusenie al daas hamuchin veal daas habesdin şel male bin ih gecomen şverin in die helige şil, ih şver bei den lebedichen got vus himel in erd beşafen hat, bei got fin Avruem fin Iehocú fin Iacob, aḑoi vie got iḑ emes in die heilige şil. iḑ emes in aḑoi vie die helige toira iḑ emes aḑoi şveer ih beemes.

FORMAT DE NOI RABIN

CETITU DE MINE CEUŞUL

Tipografia Z. Lemwand Strada Pelatului No. 17. Iaşi

Figure 2. A *more judaico* sworn in Jassy, Rumania, in 1886. The Yiddish oath, printed in Hebrew and Latin characters, preserves the main characteristics of the formulas used in Europe from the Middle Ages onward. The details of the particular case are handwritten in Rumanian and Yiddish, and the oath is witnessed by Rabbi J. Taubes. Jerusalem, J.N.U.L.

OBADIAH, king of the Khazars, a descendant of Būlān, and collateral ancestor of *Joseph according to the *Reply of Joseph* (see *Khazars). Obadiah is mentioned in the correspondence as a reformer in Khazaria who "renewed the state, established the [Jewish] religion, built synagogues and colleges, sent for many of the wise men of Israel and gave them much silver and gold, and they explained to him the books of the Bible, Mishnah and Talmud, and the whole liturgy" (*Reply*, short version). This reform probably took place in about 800 C.E., i.e., about the time when, according to Masʿūdī (*Murūj al-Dhahab*, vol. 2, 8–9), the Khazar king accepted Judaism (see *Būlān).

Bibliography: D. M. Dunlop, *History of the Jewish Khazars* (1954), 144, 148; M. I. Artamonov, *Istoriya Khazar* (1962), 278–80. [D.M.D.]

OBADIAH, BOOK OF (Heb. עֹבַדְיָה; "Servant of the Lord"). Obadiah, author of the shortest book in the Bible, is the fourth of the Minor Prophets. The same name is not necessarily a later pseudonymous designation of the book, for other persons in biblical times also had this name. The Rabbis identified Obadiah with the man of the same name who lived during Ahab's reign (I Kings 18:3–4), and they considered him an Edomite proselyte (Sanh. 39b). However, it should be noted that there is a clear similarity between Jeremiah 49:7–22 and Obadiah 1–11 (cf. Obad. 1–4, 5–6, 8 with Jer. 49:14–16, 9–10a, 7). A careful comparison of the two recensions seems to indicate that the common elements have been derived from an older source. It may therefore be inferred that in his oracle on Edom the author of Jeremiah 49:7–22 incorporated passages from an anonymous source, which was still later included in the Book of Obadiah. This view, however, does not preclude the Obadian authorship of the second part of the book. Indeed, though its 21 verses are concerned almost entirely with Edom, its unity is disputed quite independently from its relationship with Jeremiah 49.

Some scholars (e.g., A. Condamin, C. von Orelli, S. O. Isopescul, J. Theis, A. H. Edelkoort, G. C. Aalders, M. Bič, and J. Scharbert) regard the book as one single prophetic speech. J. Scharbert takes it as a prophetic liturgy composed by a cultic prophet after the fall of Jerusalem in 587 B.C.E. (verses 1–18), whereas M. Bič interprets it as an expanded oracle for the enthronement festival of the Lord. J. A. Bewer and R. Augé assume that there are two sections, verses 1–14, 15b, and 15a, 16–21, both belonging to the same prophet. This literary division of the text corrects somewhat the view of J. Wellhausen who ascribed verses 1–14 to the prophet Obadiah and considered verses 15–21 as a later addition. G. Wildeboer and J. A. Thompson assume that verses 1–9 constitute a pre-Exilic oracle, and verses 10–21 are a post-Exilic complement. Other scholars divide the book into three (C. Steuernagel, W. Rudolph, D. Deden, M. Vellas, O. Eissfeldt), four (E. Sellin), five (C. -A. Keller), six (G. Fohrer), seven (W. O. E. Oesterley), or eight (T. H. Robinson) sections. There are some formal and stylistic reasons for a division into six oracles. The first is an oracle of woe against Edom (Obad. 1b–4), paralleled in Jeremiah 49:14–16, where, in some passages, more of the original text seems to have been preserved. It mentions the Edomite fortress of Sela ("Rock"; Obad. 3) captured by King Amaziah of Judah c. 800 B.C.E. (II Kings 14:7). The second oracle of woe (Obad. 5–7) is paralleled in Jeremiah 49:8–10a, where the beginning of the poem (Jer. 49:8) is also preserved. It announces that the invader will this time penetrate the dwellings of Edom, identified there with Esau (Obad. 6), and that her allies will abandon her. In the third oracle (Obad. 8–11) the prophet first declares that YHWH has deprived Edom of her proverbial wisdom so that she is unable to prevent the ruin awaiting her (Obad. 8–9). Verses 10–11 state the reason for the curse, namely, the violence and outrage of which Edom had been guilty during Jerusalem's calamity in 587 B.C.E. Elements from the beginning (Obad. 8) of this poem are employed as an introduction to the oracles on Edom in Jeremiah 49:7–22. Another curse against Edom, related to the same events, is found in Obadiah 12–14, 15b. (Most scholars now think that verse 15a belongs to the following oracle, and verse 15b to the foregoing one.) In a series of eight imperative prohibitions the prophet summons Edom to desist from her inhuman delight at Judah's ruin and he concludes with a threat expressed in the form of a law of retaliation.

The first four sections (Obad. 1–14, 15b) address Edom in the second person plural, proclaiming the "Day of the Lord" and announcing salvation on Zion (cf. Joel 3:5) and judgment on the nations, especially on Edom (Obad. 18). The clear mention of Edom, "the House of Esau" which will be extermined on that Day, reveals that this oracle too reflects the situation after 587 B.C.E. The aid which the Edomites gave the Babylonians against Jerusalem in 587, and which is alluded to in an ostracon found in Arad, could not be forgiven. The Edomites not only exulted at the humiliation of the Judahites, but actively assisted their foes, and sought to intercept and cut off the fugitives. The remembrance of these events inspires the fifth section as well as the preceding ones, and also Isaiah 34; Jeremiah 49:7–22; Ezekiel 25:12–14; 35; Malachi 1:2–5; Psalms 137:7; Lamentations 4:21–22. These texts all seem to refer to the same events; their dominant thought is that at last Edom will receive its due punishment at the hand of the Lord. The actual disaster that befell Edom was most likely its invasion by the neighboring Arab tribes, which seem to have entirely taken over the land of Edom toward the end of the sixth century B.C.E. so that Edom remained without settled population throughout the Persian period. If so, the oracles of Obadiah 8–18, and 1–7 as well, which are not explicitly motivated by Edom's violence against Judah, may be assumed to belong to the end of the sixth century B.C.E. The opinion of scholars such as E. Sellin and J. Theis, who assign Obadiah 1–10, and especially 1–7, to the time of King Amaziah, about 800 B.C.E. (II Kings 14:7; cf. II Kings 8:20–22; Ps. 60:11–14), is based upon the fact that these verses contain no allusions to the special circumstances of 587 B.C.E. But the invitation addressed to "the nations" in Obadiah 1, the image of "robbers" in verse 5, and the probable allusion to the Babylonian allies of Edom in verse 7, may also suggest a connection between verses 1–7 and the Arab incursion of the sixth century. However, since the author of Jeremiah 49:7–22 seems to have known only Obadiah 1b–11, these verses may have been composed somewhat earlier than verses 12–18. The date and the composition of the last section (verses 19–21) is not known. Many scholars regard it as a later appendix, in which the fate of Edom is reduced to an episode of the eschatological triumph of the Jews: the territory of Judah is to be enlarged on all sides, with the inhabitants of the Negev possessing Edom, and Benjamin overflowing into Gilead. The victorious Israelites (read *nosha'im*) will ascend Mount Zion to judge the Mountain of Esau, and the Lord's kingdom will be established.

Bibliography: W. Nowack *Die Kleinen Propheten* (1922³); J. Wellhausen, *Die Kleinen Propheten* (1898³); A. Cohen, *The Twelve Prophets* (1948); J. Trinquet, in: *La Sainte Bible*. . .*de l'Ecole Biblique de Jérusalem* (1960³); Th. Laetsch, *The Minor Prophets* (1956); J. A. Thompson, in: *The Interpreter's Bible*, 6 (1956); G. C. Morgan, *The Minor Prophets. The Men and their Message* (1960); E. G. Kraeling, *Commentary on the Prophets*, 2 (1966). SPECIAL STUDIES: W. W. Cannon, in: *Theology*, 15 (1927), 129–40; 191–200; W. Rudolph, in: ZAW, 49 (1931), 222–31; S. Loewinger, in: REJ, 111 (1951), 93–94; M. Bič, in: VT Suppl., 1 (1953), 11–25; J. Gray, in: ZAW, 65 (1953), 53–59; W. Kornfeld, in: *Mélanges bibliques rédigés en l'honneur d'André Robert* (1957), 180–6; Kaufmann Y., Toledot, 4 (1967⁵), 363–5.

[E.Li.]

OBADIAH, THE NORMAN PROSELYTE (third quarter 11th century—first half 12th century). Catholic priest who converted to Judaism. Obadiah later wrote religious works and became a prominent figure in the Near Eastern Jewish communities. He was born in Oppido Lucano (Italy) as Johannes, the son of a Norman aristocrat named Dreux (Dreu, Drogo, Droco); his twin Roger was destined for knighthood. As a youth he was influenced by the conversion of Andreas, archbishop of Bari, who adopted Judaism in Constantinople and subsequently departed for Egypt. Obadiah's conversion (c. 1102) was inspired by a dream shortly after he took priestly vows, and was influenced by the study of the Bible and the persecutions of Jews in Europe by precursors of the Crusaders. He left for Constantinople, where he probably began his studies, and was wounded by Crusaders. Obadiah subsequently moved to Baghdad, where he lived in a *hekdesh* ("poorhouse") in the synagogue and studied Hebrew, the Pentateuch, and the Prophets. There he became acquainted with the poverty and the desperate circumstances of Baghdad Jewry and the tragic end of two recent pseudo-messianic movements. In 1113 he left for Aleppo, where he received a letter of recommendation from R. Baruch b. Isaac, head of the yeshivah, verifying the details of his conversion. Later he traveled to northern Palestine and met the Karaite Solomon ha-Kohen, a false messiah, in Banias (Dan) in 1121. The latter invited him to Jerusalem. Obadiah, however, departed for Egypt by way of Tyre and settled in Fostat. The main source of information concerning Obadiah is his autobiography, the so-called "Obadiah Scroll," written in biblical Hebrew. All writings related to him have been found in the Cairo *Genizah*. Only the following fragments are extant: (1) a chronicle (seven leaves); (2) a prayer book (one leaf); (3) music notes (three leaves); (4) religious poems (one leaf); and (5) the letter of recommendation by Baruch b. Isaac, part of it in Obadiah's handwriting (one leaf).

Chronological Annotated Bibliography: The record of the discovery of Obadiah's existence and works dates from the early 20th century. The beginning of the letter by Baruch b. Isaac was published by S. A. Wertheimer in *Ginzei Yerushalayim* (2 (1901), 16a–17a) and the first page of Obadiah's diary was printed by E. N. Adler (REJ, 69 (1919), 129–34). Two fragments discovered in Cambridge and a page of a prayer book written by Obadiah, found in Cincinnati, were presented by J. Mann (REJ, 89 (1930), 245–59). S. D. Goitein published another fragment containing Obadiah's original name, Johannes (JJS, 4 (1953), 74–84) and A. Scheiber, a piece of Obadiah's diary (KS, 30 (1954/55), 93–98). A *piyyut* with musical notation in Obadiah's handwriting is included in the Adler collection. Its discovery was made independently by A. Scheiber (*Tarbiz*, 34 (1964/65), 366–71) and by N. Golb (JR, 45 (1965), 153–6). The continuation of the booklet of music notes was published by N. Allony in *Sinai* (57 (1965), nos. 1–2, 43–55). A. Scheiber also published a *piyyut*, an acrostic of the name Obadiah (*Tarbiz*, 35 (1965/66), 269–73), and the original of a Hebrew fragment (HUCA, 39 (1968), 168–75, Ger.). See also: Prawer, Ẓalbanim, 1 (1963), 423–5 and J. Mann, in: *Ha-Tekufah*, 24 (1928), 335–58. [AL.SCH./ED.]

As Musician. Obadiah's main importance for Jewish studies are his notations of synagogal chant, which are the oldest discovered to date. Two chants and the terminal fragment of a third have been preserved: (1) Ms. N.Y., J.T.S., Adler collection, no. 4096b, one leaf recto-verso, contains a **piyyut*, *Mi al Har Horev*, together with its melody written in neumes; the text is a eulogy on Moses, intended for *Shavuot or *Simḥat Torah, and its acrostic reveals the name of the author, a certain 'Amr. (2) Ms. Cambridge, Univ. Libr. T. S. K5/41, one leaf containing two chants, also in neumatic notation; the recto, beginning with the words *Va-eda mah*, contains the final fragment of a non-identified *piyyut;* the verso, beginning with the words *Barukh ha-gever*, contains five biblical verses from Jeremiah, Proverbs, and Job. The chants notated in manuscript 1 and on the recto of manuscript 2 are a composition of unknown authorship in the style of the Western monodic chant of the Middle Ages. The chant on the verso of manuscript 2 is not a contemporary composition but a faithful transcription of a traditional synagogal cantillation, which Obadiah must have learned in one of the oriental communities in which he lived after his conversion. The same cantillation style is preserved up to modern days in the oral tradition of several Jewish communities in the Near East and Mediterranean areas. [I.A.]

Bibliography: For studies until 1965 see I. Adler, *Revue de musicologie*, 51 (1965), 19–51; H. Avenary, in: JJS, 16 (1966), 87–104; N. Golb, *ibid.*, 18 (1967), 43–63; A. Scheiber, in: HUCA, 39 (1968), 163–75.

OBED (Heb. עוֹבֵד ; "worshiper"; perhaps shortened from עֹבַדְיָה), son of Boaz and Ruth; father of Jesse; grandfather of King David (Ruth 4:17, 21–22; I Chron. 2:12). [ED.]

°**OBEDAS**, the name of two Arabian kings.

OBEDAS I, Arabian king during the reign of Alexander Yannai (103–76 B.C.E.). Alexander's expansionist tendencies brought him into armed conflict with a number of neighboring rulers, including Obedas. The latter, however, successfully laid an ambush for the Judean king in the Gaulan. Alexander, falling into the trap, lost an entire army which, according to Josephus, "was cooped into a deep ravine and crushed under a multitude of camels." Alexander barely escaped with his life, and his overwhelming defeat rekindled the Jewish nation's hatred toward its monarch (Jos., Wars, 1:90; Ant., 13:375).

OBEDAS II (d. c. 9 B.C.E.), Arabian king during the reign of Herod the Great. Josephus describes Obedas as "inactive and sluggish by nature; for the most part his realm was governed by Syllaeus," who at one time had been on the

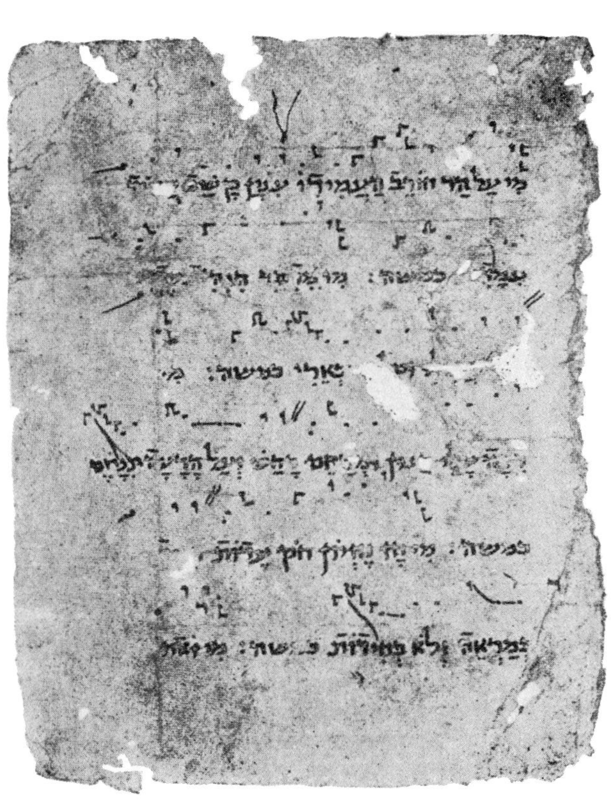

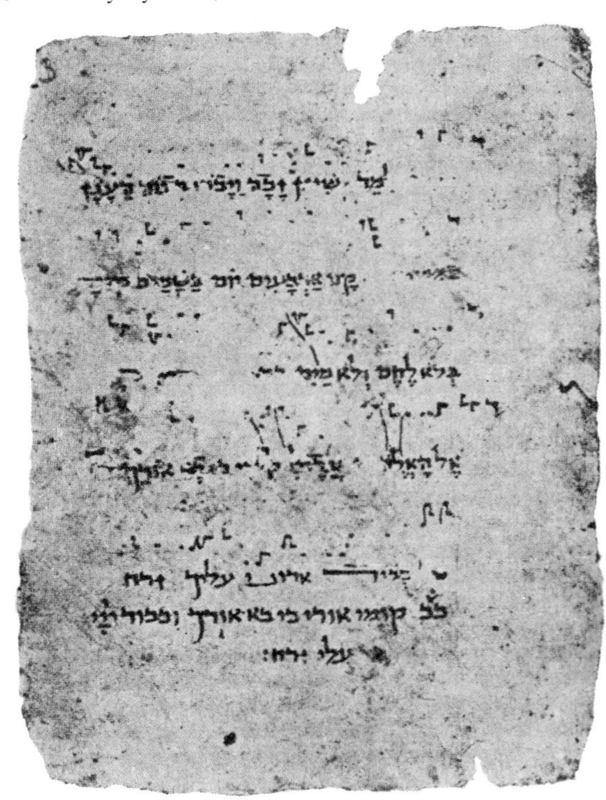

The *piyyut Mi al Har Ḥorev* with its melody notated in neumes by Obadiah the Proselyte, written from right to left to correspond to the Hebrew text. New York, Jewish Theological Seminary, Elkan N. Adler Collection, ms. 4096/b, r and v.

point of marrying Herod's sister, Salome. Syllaeus eventually became a bitter enemy of Herod. This aroused the Judean king to demand immediate repayment of 60 talents loaned to Obedas, through Syllaeus, with the claim that the time limit on the loan had expired. It is evident, however, that the feeble Obedas had little to say in the matter, and Syllaeus refused. With the death of Obedas his successor Aretas sent a letter to the Roman emperor Augustus, accusing Syllaeus of poisoning the king. This claim was probably correct, and it subsequently became known that most of Obedas' friends perished together with him (Jos., Wars, 1:487; Ant., 16:220, 279ff., 337). See *Nabateans.

Bibliography: OBEDAS I: Schuerer, Hist, 86f.; Klausner, Bayit Sheni, 3 (1950²), 150, 153. OBEDAS II: Schuerer, Hist, 154; Klausner, Bayit Sheni, 4 (1950²), 38; A. Schalit, *Koenig Herodes* (1969), 253, 599, 614f. [I.G.]

OBED-EDOM (עֹבֵד אֱדוֹם; "the servant of *Adam [the deity?]"), the name of two biblical figures. (1) The Gittite to whose house the *Ark of the Lord was transferred after the death of Uzzah (II Sam. 6: 10ff.; I Chron. 13:13–14). Uzzah had died after touching the Ark while it was being brought by David to Jerusalem. In order to prevent further calamities, the Ark was brought to the house of Obed-Edom, which was apparently situated between Kiriath-Jearim and Jerusalem. When it was reported to David three months later that the Lord had blessed Obed-Edom and his house, David brought the Ark up to Jerusalem with rejoicing. As a temple gatekeeper for the Ark, Obed-Edom is mentioned several times among the Levites (I Chron. 15:18, 21, 24; 16:5, 38), as are his descendants (I Chron. 26:8, 15). (2) A descendant of Obed-Edom the Gittite, who was in charge of the gold, the silver, and all the vessels in the Temple in Jerusalem in the days of Amaziah king of Judah (798–769 B.C.E.; II Chron. 25:24).

Bibliography: M. Dahood, in: CBQ, 35 (1963), 123–4; W. F. Albright, in: *Biblica*, 44 (1963), 292; idem, *Yahweh and the Gods of Canaan* (1968), 122. [ED.]

OBERMANN, JULIAN JOËL (1888–1956), orientalist. Born in Warsaw, Obermann taught Semitic languages at the University of Hamburg from 1919 to 1922, achieving recognition with the publication of his work on the philosophy of Al-Ghazālī in 1921. He subsequently became professor of Semitic philology at the Jewish Institute of Religion in New York, where he taught from 1923 to 1931. From 1933 to 1935 Obermann was visiting professor of Semitic languages at Yale University; he became professor in 1935. He served as coeditor of the *Journal of Biblical Literature* (1933–36). In 1944 Obermann became director of Judaic research and editor of the Yale Judaica Series, in which capacity he served until his retirement.

In the course of his career, Obermann made contributions in Semitic philology and epigraphy, Old Testament and Ugaritic studies, Islamic culture, and Arabic philosophy. His works include: *Das Problem der Kausalitaet bei den Arabern* (1916); *Der philosophische und religioese Subjektivismus Ghazalis* (1921); *The Arabic Original of Ibn Shahin's Book of Comfort* (1933); and *Ugaritic Mythology* (1948). He also edited H. Gressman's *Tower of Babel* (1928) and Gandz's translation of Maimonides' *Sanctification of the New Moon* (1956) after the death of the authors.

Bibliography: *New York Times* (Oct. 18, 1956); JAOS, 77 (1957), [R.P.S.]

OBERMEYER, JACOB (1845–1935), traveler, scholar, and teacher. Obermeyer was born in Steinhardt, Bavaria. He toured North Africa from Morocco to Egypt in 1868, proceeded to Palestine, and from there traveled to Damascus and Baghdad. He taught French at the Baghdad school of the Alliance Israélite Universelle during 1869–72, and from 1872 to 1881 he was the teacher of Prince Naib Alsultana, contender to the throne of Persia, who had been compelled to flee his native country. With his student, Obermeyer toured the whole of Mesopotamia and then accompanied the prince when he signed a peace treaty with his brother the king and returned to Persia. Obermeyer's *Die Landschaft Babylonien*... (1929) is a standard work which includes his personal observations during his years of travel as well as the works of medieval Arab geographers and various Hebrew sources. From 1884 to 1915 Obermeyer taught Arabic and Persian in Vienna.

Bibliography: S. Assaf, in: KS, 7 (1930), 60–62; Sassoon, *History of the Jews of Baghdad* (1949), 153–6. [Z.AV.]

OBERNAI (Ger. **Oberehnheim**), town in the department of Bas-Rhin, E. France. The first evidence for the presence of Jews in Obernai dates from 1215. In 1349 a Jewish woman who had been sentenced to death for coin clipping accused the Jews of propagating the *Black Death, whereupon all the Jews of Obernai were burned at the stake. Jews were recorded as living in Obernai again between 1437 and 1477 and from 1498 to 1507. Subsequently Jews were rarely even allowed to travel through Obernai or permitted to visit the local market. Only in 1647, when the town passed under French rule, where Jews again permitted to settle there. In 1784 the number of Jews in Obernai was 196. Many more were recorded as living there on the eve of World War II. About 60 lived there in 1970.

Bibliography: J. Gyss, *Histoire ... d'Obernai* (1866); Germ Jud, 1 (1937), 93f.; 2 pt. 2 (1968), 614f. [B.BL.]

OBERNIK, JUDAH (d. c. 1520), talmudist, rabbi of Mestre. Judah was a pupil of Israel Isserlein whose rulings and expositions, both heard directly and reported by others, he entered in his notebook, along with rulings of Jozman Katz, responsa of Sar Shalom of Vienna, expositions of Jacob *Moellin, glosses on the *Tashbaẓ* (Cremona, 1556) by *Perez b. Elijah of Corbeil and other material. *Joseph b. Moses, Judah Obernik's pupil, made abundant use of this notebook in his work *Leket Yosher* (ed. by J. Freimann, 2 vols., 1903–4), which he quotes at length. He conducted a halakhic correspondence with Isserlein and engaged in learned discussions with Judah *Muenz and Joseph *Colon. He was also the author of ***Seder Pesaḥ***.

Bibliography: Joseph b. Moses, *Leket Yosher*, ed. by J. Freimann, 2 (1904), xxx–xxxi. [SH.A.H./ED.]

OBLIGATIONS, LAW OF. This law is concerned with the rights of one person as against another *(jus in personam)*, as distinguished from the law of property, which is concerned with a person's rights in a chattel or other property as against the world at large *(jus in rem)*. Unlike Roman law, in Jewish law the mere existence of the obligation automatically creates in favor of the creditor a *lien *(shi'bud)* over his debtor's property, a real right attaching to the obligation, which for a very long time was regarded as stronger than the personal right afforded by the obligation. The term *ḥiyyuv* originates in the word *ḥov*, meaning both the obligation which is imposed on the debtor (e.g., BB 10:6) and the right to which the creditor is entitled (Bik. 3:12; Git. 8:3). However, *ḥov* generally refers to a pecuniary obligation only, whereas *ḥiyyuv* has come to be used in a wider sense to include also the duty to perform an act, etc., comparable to the Roman law concept of *obligatio*.

The two parties to an obligation are the debtor (*ḥayyav*, BM 12b)—on whom the duty of fulfilling the obligation is imposed—and the creditor *(ba'al ḥov)*—who has the right to claim that the obligation be fulfilled. The term *ba'al ḥov* is sometimes used in the sources to describe the debtor as well (see Elon, bibl., 1), which makes it necessary to exercise care in the use of these terms. It may be noted, too, that in Jewish law the term *malveh* ("lender") and *loveh* ("borrower") are not invariably used to denote an obligation arising from the transaction of a loan, but also to describe the parties to an obligation arising from any other transaction. This follows from the tendency in Jewish law to express a plain legal norm in concrete terms (e.g., *keren, shen, bor,* etc.; see **Avot Nezikin;* **Mishpat Ivri*), and thus the transaction of loan *(halva'ah)* is used as a concrete illustration of a clear and common obligation (e.g., sections 97–107 of Sh. Ar., ḤM are grouped under the heading *Hilkhot Geviyyat Milveh,* even though they are not confined exclusively to the recovery of debts originating from loan).

Creation of the Obligation. As in other legal systems, Jewish law recognizes the creation of obligations in two principal ways: (1) arising from *contract, whereby one party acquires a claim of right against another which the latter is obliged to honor; and (2) arising from an act of *tort (*nezek;* see *Torts), whereby the conduct of one party causes another to suffer damage, so that the latter acquires a claim of right against the tortfeasor for indemnification in respect of the damage, which the law obliges the tortfeasor to honor. The first talmudic tractate of the order of **Nezikin,* namely *Bava Kamma,* deals mainly with the laws of obligations arising from tort, i.e., harm inflicted by one man on another's person (e.g., *assault) or property (e.g., *theft and robbery), as well as harm inflicted by means of one man s property *(mamon)* on the person or property of another. In this case the owner of the property is obliged to compensate the injured party for the damage suffered through his negligence in preventing harm arising by means of his property. The other two tractates, *Bava Mezia* and *Bava Batra,* deal largely with obligations arising from contract. Jewish law distinguishes between the obligations arising from these two different sources, particularly from the point of view of the manner of recovery of the debt on the debtor's failure to make due payment of it in cash or chattels. Thus obligations arising from tort are recoverable from the best of the land *(idit),* whereas contractual obligations are recoverable only from land of average quality *(beinonit),* and the **ketubbah* obligation from the worst (*zibburit;* Git. 5:1; see also *Execution, Civil). Roman law in addition to a similar distinction between *obligationes ex contractu* and *obligationes ex delicto,* further subdivides the obligations into those which are quasi-delict and quasi-contract. Although Jewish law also recognizes quasi-contractual obligations, it does not employ the legal fiction of regarding these as arising, as it were, from a contract between the parties (as, e.g., in the case of the *negotiorum gestio*); the degree of liability imposed on the owner of a field toward one who "goes down to his field" and plants there without permission extends to the latter's expenses and, at most, to the value of the improvement from which the field has benefited (Tosef., Ket. 8:8; BK 10:3; Ket. 80a).

Fines (kenasot). In the case of obligations arising from both contract and tort, the degree of liability is coextensive with the respective objective value of the contractual transaction or with the extent of the loss sustained as a result of the damage inflicted; this liability is called *mamon.* When the measure of liability does not correspond to the value or loss it is called *kenas* ("a fine"; e.g., BK 15 a–b and see *Fines). Liability for such a fine may exist: (1) by the consent of the parties, i.e., their agreement to pay a certain liquidated sum upon breach of the contract; or (2) by operation of law, i.e., when the law provides for a measure of compensation that does not correspond to the actual loss caused by the act of tort (BK 15a–b). Such a fine by operation of law can take three possible forms: (1) the liability exceeds the actual damage (e.g., a thief being liable to pay double and four- or fivefold compensation: see *Theft and Robbery); (2) the liability is less than the actual damage (e.g., where only half-damages are payable for a *shor tam* that has gored: see **Avot Nezikin);* and (3) the liability is for a fixed and predetermined amount (e.g., in the case of defamation of a virgin: Deut. 22:19 and see also 29).

Imperfect (i.e., Unenforceable) Obligations. Jewish law recognizes the existence of two kinds of imperfect obligations. In the first category a legal obligation exists but the court will provide no remedy for the party seeking its enforcement. Thus in the case of fixed (direct) interest (*ribbit kezuzah;* e.g., 100 are lent so that 120 shall be repaid), which is prohibited by pentateuchal law, the lender is obliged to return the interest paid and it may even be reclaimed by the borrower through the court; if, however, the interest is indirect (*avak ribbit,* lit. "dust of interest"), which is forbidden by rabbinical law only, the borrower cannot reclaim the interest in court (BM 61b; Yad, Malveh 6:1; Sh. Ar., YD 161; and see *Usury). Similarly, in all cases which are regarded as robbery according to rabbinical law only—e.g., when a person wins money in a game of chance (which is regarded as unjustified even if the loser consents)—the loser cannot reclaim the money in court (Sanh. 25b; Yad, Gezelah 6:6–16, and other *posekim*). The second category of imperfect obligations derives from tort; regarding this it was prescribed that "the offender is exempt from the judgments of man but liable to the laws of heaven" (BK 55b), as for example, in the case of a man who bends his neighbor's standing grain toward a fire in such a way that the grain will catch fire if the wind changes or strengthens unexpectedly, although there is no such danger as long as the wind does not alter (BK 55b and codes; see further *Law and Morals for obligations carrying a moral or religious sanction only).

The Personal and Proprietary Aspects of Obligation in Jewish Law. Many ancient systems of law (e.g., Babylonian law, Assyrian law, the laws of Eshnunna) provided for the creditor's being able to secure repayment of his debt by enslaving the debtor or the members of his family (see Elon, bibl., 3–8). According to the early Roman "XII Tables" and by means of the *legis actio per manus injectionem,* the creditor was even afforded the right, after certain preliminary procedures, of putting the defaulting debtor to death and taking his proportionate share of the body if there were several creditors. This "right" was abrogated by the *Lex Poetelia* and replaced by the possibility of imprisoning the debtor (see *Imprisonment for Debt on the position in Jewish law).

On the other hand, Jewish law did not recognize any form of enslavement of the debtor's person (the bondsmanship referred to in the Bible is confined to two cases: one of the thief who lacks the means to make restitution (Ex. 22:2); the other of a person who voluntarily sells himself on account of utter poverty (Lev. 25:39)). The creditor is strongly adjured to act mercifully toward the borrower and not to take in pledge the latter's basic essentials nor to enter his house for the purpose of seizing a pledge (Ex. 22:24–26; Deut. 24:6, 10–13). If in practice the law was not always strictly observed and there were cases—due to the influence of surrounding legal customs—of enslavement for debt (II Kings 4:1; Isa. 50:1, etc), such cases were roundly condemned by the prophets (Amos 2:6; 8:4–6) and it appears that after the sharp reaction of Nehemiah (Neh. 5:1–13) enslavement for debt was abolished in practice as well (Elon, bibl., 8–10).

The uncertain personal nature of an obligation in Jewish

law led, in the second half of the fourth century, to fundamental differences of opinion on the substance of the borrower's personal liability to repay money to the lender. In the opinion of all scholars, restitution in the case of bailment or robbery constituted a clear legal obligation—since the bailor or the person robbed had a proprietory right in the property concerned. In the case of a loan of money, however, given in the first instance so that it could be used and expended by the borrower, in the opinion of R. Papa, the liability to repay the debt was no more than a religious duty (i.e., it was a *mitzvah* for a person to fulfill his promise and give effect to his statements (Rashi Ket. 86a)) and not a legal obligation. R. Huna, however, expressed the opinion—which was shared by the majority of the scholars and according to which the *halakhah* was decided—that the duty of repaying a debt was also a legal obligation. This personal aspect of the obligation is termed *shi'bud nafsheih* in the Talmud (i.e., pledging personal responsibility; see, e.g., Git. 13b, 49b; BK 40b; BM 94a; BB 173b). From the 11th century onward it seems, it was referred to as *shi'bud ha-guf* ("servitude of the person"), a term apparently mentioned for the first time in the statements of Alfasi (quoted in the Resp. Maharam of Rothenburg, ed. Cremona, no.146 and in greater detail in the statements of Jacob *Tam cited in the commentary of Nissim Gerondi on Rif, to Ket. 85b; see also *Contract).

The impossibility of securing repayment of a debt by enslaving the debtor created a need for the establishment of an adequate security, i.e., by charging the debtor's assets: land was well suited for this purpose since it could not be carried away and was not subject to loss or extinction. Hence the rule that, immediately a debt was created, the creditor acquired a lien over all the real estate possessed by the debtor in such a manner that the debt afforded the creditor not only a personal right of action against the debtor but also a right in the form of a lien over all his land. Land was accordingly termed "assets bearing responsibility" (*nekhasim she-yesh lahem aḥarayut;* i.e., guaranteeing the obligation of the debtor; Kid. 1:5; BM 1:6; BB 174a) and recovery therefrom was based on the creditor's charge and not on his right of recourse against the debtor personally. On the other hand, the debtor's chattels, being subject to loss and depreciation, were incapable of "bearing responsibility" for his obligation and were so termed (*nekhasim she-ein lahem aḥarayut;* Kid. 1:5), and the right of recovery from such assets was based on the creditor's personal right of recourse against the debtor (BK 11b; see also *Lien). The demands of developing commerce resulted in a substantive change in the concept of the contractual obligation in post-talmudic times; from an essentially real or property obligation it became an essentially personal one, with the property aspect subordinate to the personal.

Recovering Payment out of "Encumbered and Alienated" Assets (i.e., in the hands of a third party). The creditor's above-mentioned lien over his debtor's property did not preclude the debtor from transferring the encumbered assets to a third party, except that any such transfer could be subject to the creditor's right to seize the assets from the transferee when seeking to enforce payment of the debt. At first this right did not extend to the debtor's chattels, since the creditor had no property right in them and his right of recovery from them derived merely from the debtor's personal obligation (see *Beit ha-Beḥirah,* BB 175b); thus they were beyond the creditor's reach once they had been transferred from the debtor's ownership (Ket. 92a). However, in the course of time and with the changes in the economic circumstances of Jewish life, this distinction between land and chattels underwent substantial changes. Similarly, the general lien on the debtor's assets gave rise to many problems, concerning both the need to protect trade (*takkanot ha-shuk*) and the rights of third party purchasers, as well as the question of securing debts for the benefit of creditors, concerning which various **takkanot* were enacted at different times (see *Lien).

Verbal and Written Obligations. Jewish law distinguishes between a verbal and a written obligation, termed in the Talmud a *milveh be-al peh* and a *milveh bi-shetar* respectively (BB 175a; see also Sh. Ar., ḤM 39:1, et al.). Although phrased in the language of loan, these terms are intended to embrace all obligations of whatever origin (see above). The distinction between the two forms of obligation relates to the weight of consequence accorded each one rather than to the substance of the obligation. This finds expression in two main respects: (1) a written obligation entitles the creditor to recover payment out of the debtor's encumbered assets which are in the hands of a third party, a right unavailable in the case of a mere verbal obligation, since here the obligation or debt has no *kol* ("voice") and does not provide notice that will put prospective purchasers on their guard; (2) in the case of a written obligation, a plea by the debtor that he has repaid the debt is not accepted without proof, whereas a plea of this kind is accepted without proof in the case of a verbal obligation (Shevu. 41b; Yad, Malveh 11:1, 15:1; Sh. Ar., ḤM 70:1, 82:1; see also *Pleas).

The distinction between the two is not characterized by the mere fact of writing or its absence, and the fact that an obligation is recorded in a document does not of itself ensure the application of the special consequences attaching to a *milveh bi-shetar.* Thus, for example, an undertaking even in the debtor's own handwriting but not signed by witnesses will be treated as a *milveh be-al peh,* since only a properly written, witnessed, and signed obligation carries a "voice" and constitutes notice (BB 175b and codes). Similarly, since a written obligation affects the rights of the parties, it is not considered as such unless it has been drawn up and signed in accordance with the instructions of the parties (BB 40a and codes) and with the prior intention of constituting it a *milveh bi-shetar* and not simply an aide-memoire (Sh. Ar., ḤM 61:10). Contrariwise, it is possible that a wholly verbal obligation can be treated as a written one, as in the case of sale of land before witnesses when the purchaser from whom the land is seized may in turn exact the seller's responsibility to him out of encumbered and alienated assets sold by the latter (BB 41b). So too all verbal obligations claimed through, and upheld by, judgment of the court are treated as obligations by deed (BM 15a) which may be recovered out of encumbered and alienated assets, since in these circumstances they have a "voice" and constitute notice even if they are not evidenced in writing.

The Parties to an Obligation. On the capacity of the parties to an obligation see *Legal Capacity; *Embryo; *Legal Person.

From various scriptural sources it may be inferred that it is possible that an obligation may subsist toward a person unknown at the time (Josh. 15:16; I Sam. 17:25). This principle is also illustrated in this way: "he who says 'whoever shall bring me the tidings that my wife gave birth to a male child shall receive two hundred; that she gave birth to a female child a *maneh';* [then] if she gives birth to a male he shall receive two hundred and if to a female child, he shall receive a *maneh*" (Tosef., BB 9:5; BB 141b). It was also followed in practice in the case of a deed granted by the community in respect of the right to collect a tax, in which the name of the grantee was not specified at the time of signature, it being provided that certain communal officials would determine the person to acquire the right (Resp. Rosh no. 13:20).

Plurality of Creditors and Debtors. Both possibilities are allowed for in Jewish law. Most sources indicate that each of the co-debtors is responsible for his proportionate share only; e.g., if they borrow in a common deed (Tosef., BM 1:21), or guarantee a single debt (Tosef., BB 11:15; but cf. Yad, Malveh 25:10 and Sh. Ar., ḤM 77:3 and commentators). In the same way a judgment of the court against one of the debtors does not of itself render the others liable (Rema, ḤM 176:25). Some scholars sought to infer from another source that each of the debtors is liable for the whole amount of the debt (R. Yose, TJ, Shevu. 5:1, 136a; *Piskei ha-Rosh,* ad loc., 2); but most of the *posekim* interpreted this source as prescribing that each of the debtors, in addition to the principal obligation for his proportionate share, is also liable as surety for the remainder of the debt upon default of the other debtors (Yad, Malveh 25:9; Tur and Sh. Ar., ḤM 77:1 and see also commentators); the *halakhah* was decided accordingly.

A similar rule prevails with regard to liability for damage jointly caused by several tortfeasors, namely the apportionment of liability according to the degree of participation of each (BK 10b and codes). Opinions are divided in the codes on the question of whether each of the tortfeasors is also liable as surety for the shares of the others (Tur, ḤM, 410:29 and Sh. Ar., ḤM 410:37). Similarly, when a debt is owed to a number of creditors jointly, each of them is entitled to his proportionate share. Any one of them may claim payment of the whole amount in circumstances where it can be presumed that he is acting as an agent for his fellow creditors with regard to their shares (Ket. 94a and codes). Where there is no room for this presumption and one creditor wishes to claim recovery of his share alone, two possibilities exist: if the share of each of the creditors is known, each may separately claim his own share, e.g., in the case where a creditor is survived by a number of heirs, each claiming his known share; if the proportionate share owing to each creditor is unknown, none may separately claim recovery but must be joined in his claim by the remaining creditors (Sh. Ar., ḤM 77:9–10 and *Siftei Kohen* ad loc., n. 25; Sh. Ar., ḤM 176:25). This is also the law when the debt derives from tort.

Extinction of Obligation. An obligation is extinguished when it is fulfilled by the debtor, whether voluntarily or under compulsion by way of civil execution. (For the consequences of nonfulfillment of an obligation deriving from tort or contract see *Damages; *Tort; and *Contract.) An obligation also becomes extinguished, even if unfulfilled, when a release is granted by the creditor to the debtor (see **Meḥilah*). According to pentateuchal law, a *Jubilee year terminates certain obligations. *Hillel the Elder and his court instituted the prosbul, whereby the obligation continues to exist and is not wiped out in the seventh year (see also *Loans).

In the State of Israel. The law of obligations in the State of Israel is derived from numerous different sources: Ottoman and mandatory laws as well as Israel legislation. English common law and equity is a further source of the Israel law of obligation whenever there is a "lacuna" in the existing law (s. 46, Palestine Order in Council, 1922–47). In recent years there has been increasing legislation in this field, showing to a certain extent the influence of Jewish law. (See also State of *Israel, Jewish Law in.)

See further: *Admission, *Assignment; *Gift; *Labor Law; *Lease and Hire; *Maritime Law; *Partnership; *Sale; *Servitudes; **Shetar;* **Shomerim;* *Suretyship.

Bibliography: L. Auerbach, *Das juedische Obligationsrecht,* 1 (1870), 159ff.; I. S. Zuri, *Mishpat ha-Talmud,* 5 (1921); Gulak, Yesodei, 2 (1922), 3–30, 83–88, 105–18; idem, in: *Madda'ei ha-Yahadut,* 1 (1925/26), 46–48; idem, *Toledot ha-Mishpat be-Yisrael bi-Tekufat ha-Talmud,* 1 (*Ha-Ḥiyyuv ve-Shibudav,* 1939), 1–2, 15–52, 88–96; Herzog, Instit, 2 (1939); M. Silberg, *Kakh Darko shel Talmud* (1961), 71–75; M. Elon, *Ḥerut ha-Perat be-Darkhei Geviyyat Ḥov* (1964), 1–23. [M.E.]

OCAÑA, town in central Spain, in New Castile. Its community maintained close relations with the city of *Toledo. The *Fuero Juzgo* laws on the settlement of debts owed by Christians to Jews did not apply to Ocaña and King Ferdinand IV prohibited their enforcement in the town (1296). In 1313 King Alfonso XI granted the income from the taxes of the Jews of Ocaña to the commander of the Order of Santiago for life; previously they had paid their taxes together with the community of Toledo. A similar income, amounting to 4,000 maravedis benefiting this order, was ratified in 1386 by King John I. The community of Ocaña suffered during the riots of 1391, but it recovered soon after. Subsequently, there was also a group of Conversos which maintained close links with the local Jews. Some of the Jews who were expelled from Andalusia in 1483 found refuge in Ocaña. Among the refugees was Judah ibn Verga, one of the last Jewish tax-farmers, who lived in Ocaña from 1488 to 1491. He may have been identical with the Rabbi Judah ibn Verga portrayed by Solomon *ibn Verga in his *Shevet Yehudah.* The rabbi of Ocaña at that time was Isaac de *Leon, one of the last distinguished Spanish rabbis. It was he who maintained relations with Don Alfonso de la *Cavallería, when the latter stayed in the town from 1488 to 1489 along with the king's retinue. Information is available on ten Inquisition trials held in Ocaña at the close of the 15th century and the beginning of the 16th; from this, close contact between the Jews of the town and the Conversos from the pre-Expulsion period can be inferred. Ocaña also attracted Conversos during the 16th and 17th centuries.

Bibliography: A. Jellinek, *Philosophie und Kabbala* (1854), 15; Baer, Urkunden, index; Baer, Spain, index; Suárez Fernández, Documentos, index. [H.B.]

OCHBERG, ISAAC (1879–1938), South African philanthropist and Zionist. Ochberg was born in the Ukraine and went to South Africa in 1894. A successful Cape Town businessman, he was best known for his humanitarian project in bringing some 200 Jewish pogrom orphans from the Ukraine and Poland to South Africa after World War I. In 1921 he traveled to Russia on his own initiative, personally selected the children and organized their transportation to South Africa, where they were cared for by the Jewish orphanages in Cape Town and Johannesburg and the South African Jewish War Victims Fund. He returned to Russia the following year and distributed food, clothing, and medicines to the starving people in the war-afflicted areas. Ochberg served on the Cape executive of the South African Jewish Board of Deputies and other communal bodies. Among his benefactions were bequests to the Isaac Ochberg Fund for bursaries and to the Hebrew University for extensions and scholarships. In Israel the kibbutz Galed was also called Even Yiẓḥak in his honor, and his estate was used to purchase the land of kibbutz Daliyyah, where a monument to him was erected. [L.Ho.]

OCHRIDA. town in Macedonia, southern Yugoslavia. There were Jews living in Ochrida during the Middle Ages. The scholar Judah Leon *Mosconi lived in Ochrida. In Constantinople there was a Romaniot synagogue named after Ochrida. The Jews of Ochrida engaged in the preparation of furs and those of them who settled in

*Kastoria developed the same profession there. There is no information on the Jews of Ochrida in recent times.

Bibliography: Perles, in: *Byzantinische Zeitschrift*, 2 (1893), 569–84. [S.MAR.]

OCHS, U.S. family of newspaper publishers. JULIUS OCHS (1826–1888), founder of the family, was an immigrant from Bavaria who went into business in Louisville, Kentucky, and then in Knoxville, Tennessee. He became a communal leader and served as volunteer rabbi to the Jewish community for 25 years. His three sons rose to prominence as publishers and editors. ADOLPH SIMON OCHS (1858–1935) was the eldest and most distinguished. His career began at the age of 11, when he left school to become an office boy for the *Knoxville Chronicle*. At 17 he became a compositor for the *Louisville Courier-Journal*, and three years later he gained control of the decrepit *Chattanooga Times* for $250. He soon put it on its feet and made it one of the leading papers in the South. In 1896 he went to New York to take over the declining *New York Times*. He revitalized it and in his 39 years as its publisher he strengthened it all round; before he died he saw its circulation rise from 9,000 to 466,000 daily and 730,000 on Sunday. When he went to New York "yellow journalism" was at its height; he adopted the slogan "All the News That's Fit to Print" and appealed to intelligent readers with trustworthy and comprehensive coverage. He raised the standards of printing and advertising, and brought responsible journalism to a high level. In 1902 he bought *The Times* and *The Ledger* of Philadelphia, amalgamated them and installed his brother, GEORGE WASHINGTON OCHS (1861–1931) as editor. When the company was sold in 1913, George Ochs stayed on for two more years and then became editor of *Current History*, a monthly magazine published by the *New York Times*. He

1

2

3

4

The founder of the Ochs family of newspaper publishers and his three sons. 1. Julius Ochs. Jerusalem, J.N.U.L., Schwadron Collection. 2. Adolf Simom Ochs. 3. George Washington Ochs. 4. Milton Barlow Ochs. 2, 3, 4, Photo *New York Times* Studio.

continued in that post until his death. During World War I he anglicized his germanic-sounding family name Ochs to Ochs-Oakes. His son, JOHN B. OAKES (1913–), who worked as a political reporter for the *Washington Post*, took charge of the editorial page of the *New York Times* in 1961. MILTON B. OCHS (1864–1955), youngest brother, served with his brothers in high executive positions in Chattanooga and Philadelphia, and finally became vice-president of the New York Times Publishing Company. [I.R.]

OCTOBRISTS, constitutional-monarchist party in czarist Russia founded after the issue of the Manifesto of *Nicholas II of Oct. 30, 1905. The goal of the Octobrists was to attain certain limited freedoms, i.e., the freedom of speech, of assembly, and organization. The party also demanded the right to a legislative assembly (*Duma), elected democratically as had been promised to the Russian people in the Manifesto. In the First Imperial Duma (1906), composed mostly of constitutional-democratic factions, the Octobrists did not occupy a significant place, having only 16 seats out of a total of 500. In the Second Duma (1907) they had 44 representatives. The strength and influence of the party rose in the Third Duma (1907–1910) which was elected after electoral reforms had been introduced, conferring preferential rights on the aristocracy and restricting the electoral rights of the broader levels of the social strata. The Octobrists drew close to the reactionary right wing of the Duma which unreservedly supported the czar and his government; the leader of the faction, A. Guchkov, was elected as chairman of the Duma.

On the Jewish question the Octobrists from the very outset adopted an evasive policy. When compelled to take a clear stand they supported the retention of restrictions on Jewish rights, and did not refrain from open anti-Semitic attacks. In connection with the bill permitting greater freedom of residence outside the *Pale of Settlement (1908) the Octobrists supported the restricting amendment introduced by the reactionary majority of the Duma, which sought to intensify the restrictions. In military affairs the Octobrists demanded that the Jews be withdrawn from army service, since in their opinion the loyalty of Jews could not be relied upon in the event of war. Their opposition to the appointment of Jews as justices of the peace was rationalized on the ground that to place a Jew in such a position was contrary to the principles of a Christian state (1909). By agreement with the reactionary representatives of the Polish faction in the Third Imperial Duma, the Jews were deprived of their municipal rights in the cities of Poland. A slight relaxation in the stand taken by the Octobrists on the Jewish question was evidenced when 26 of its members in the Duma signed a bill submitted by the opposition to abolish the Pale of Settlement (1910). [S.K.]

°ODENATHUS AND ZENOBIA. Odenathus ("little ear") Septimius (258–67 C.E.) was a Palmyrene vassal of Rome; Zenobia Julia Aurelia Septimia, his wife, succeeded him as regent for their minor son Vaballathus (267–71 C.E.). Odenathus maintained at least a nominal loyalty to Rome, slaying Callistus and Quietus, the rival pretenders to the throne of the emperor Gallienus and warring against the Persians who had invaded the Roman east. Palmyra reached the zenith of her affluence when Gallienus conferred the title *corrector totius orientis* upon Odenathus, legitimizing him as the virtual viceroy of Rome over the east. His assassination left Zenobia, famous for her beauty and political acumen, the ruler of Palmyra, since their son Vaballathus was still a minor. Zenobia, controlling Syria, Egypt, and Palestine, aimed at political independence from Rome and in 271 openly assumed the title of Augusta. In the ensuing war the Roman emperor Aurelian reconquered all her territory and took her prisoner. According to Zosimus, *Historiae* (1:59, 3), Zenobia perished while crossing the Bosphorus, but most scholars accept the account of Flavius Vopiscus (Aurelian 34, 3) and Trebellius Pollio (The Thirty Pretenders 30, 24, 6) that after being exhibited in Aurelian's march of triumph, she ended her life as a Roman matron on an estate in Tibur (Tivoli).

Graetz was the first to identify Odenathus as the Ben Naẓer of the Talmud, which regards him as half king, half robber (Ket. 51b).

Funk, on the other hand, identifies him with "Adi the Arab" (Av. Zar. 33a; Men. 69b). According to the Midrash (Gen. R. 76:6), he succeeded (the pretenders) Macrianus, Carinus, and Quietus (or Cyriades) and was merely an agent of Rome, the "little horn" predicted by Daniel 7:8. If Odenathus is identical with Ben Naẓer, who according to Sherira Gaon (*Iggeret*, p. 82, ed. Lewin) destroyed Nehardea, it becomes clear why the daughters of Samuel who were captured there could be taken to Palestine to be redeemed (Ket. 23a). Zenobia is reported to have pardoned a Jewish prisoner, probably political, when shown the bloody sword with which the prisoner's brother was killed by Ben Naẓer (TJ, Ter. 8:10, 46b; Funk takes this story as a confirmation of Zenobia's collaboration in Odenathus' assassination).

Athanasius (298–373) states that Zenobia was Jewish (*Historia Arianorum ad Monachus* 71, PG 25, 777b). Though this statement is repeated by Theoredet (386–457) and Photius (820–891), scholars (S. Brady, J. Fevrière, etc.) give little credence to it. Her patronizing of Paul of Samosata, a Christian-Jewish thinker, has erroneously been given religious significance. However, recently discovered inscriptions, containing dedications such as "*levarekh shemah le-alma alma*" ("to the One whose name is blessed forever," etc.) as well as expressions from the Psalms, do testify to the penetration of Jewish ideas into the syncretistic religion of the Palmyrene population. Zenobia herself rebuilt a synagogue in Egypt. Both Odenathus and Zenobia figure in Arab legends, which may contain kernels of truth (see T. Noeldeke,).

Bibliography: T. Noeldeke, *Geschichte der Perser und Araber ... des Tabari* (1879), 22f., 25 n. 1; S. Funk, *Die Juden in Babylonien* (1902) 75–78; G. Bardy, *Paul de Samosate* (1923), 172–4; J. G. Février, *Essai sur l'historie politique et économique de Palmyre* (1931), 79–141; idem, *La religion des Palmyréniens* (1931); Lieberman, in: JQR, 37 (1946/47), 32–38; M. Avi-Yonah, *Bi-Ymei Roma u-Bizantiyyon* (1952), 81–83; E. Kornemann, *Grosse Frauen des Altertums* (1952[4]), 288–313; Baron, Social[2], 3 (1957), 62f.; Alon, Toledot, 2 (1961[2]), 168–78; Neusner, Babylonia, 2 (1966), 48–52 (which questions Sherira's date for the destruction of Nehardea in the year 258 and contains further bibliography).

[H.M.]

ODESSA, capital of Odessa oblast, Ukrainian S.S.R. In the 19th century it became the industrial and commercial center for southern Russia. In 1865 a university was founded. Odessa was an important center of the Russian revolutionary movement. Under the Soviet regime it lost some of its importance. In October 1941 Odessa was occupied by the German and Rumanian armies and was under Rumanian military rule until its liberation in April 1944.

From the 1880s until the 1920s the Jewish community of Odessa was the second largest in the whole of Russia (after *Warsaw, the capital of Poland, then within czarist Russia) and it had considerable influence on the Jews of the country. The principal characteristics of this community, and responsible for its particular importance, were the rapid and constant growth of the Jewish population and its extensive participation in the economic development of the town, the outstanding "Western" character of its cultural life and numerous communal institutions, especially educational and economic institutions, the social and political activity of the Jewish public, the mood of tension and struggle which was impressed on its history, and the Hebrew literary center which emerged there.

Beginnings of the Community. The Russians found six Jews when they took the fortress of Khadzhi-Bei in 1789; the oldest Jewish tombstone in the cemetery dates from 1793. Five Jews were among those who in 1794 received plots for the erection of houses and shops and the planting of gardens. The Gemilut Ḥesed Shel Emet society (*ḥevra kaddisha*) was founded in 1795. In 1796 Jews participated in the administration of the town. The *kahal* (community administration) was already in existence in 1798, when the first synagogue was built; the first rabbi to hold office, in 1809, was Isaac Rabinovich of Bendery.

Figure 1. Tombstone in Odessa of Isaac Babel's father (d. 1924), with "1966" painted on it to indicate to the authorities that the grave was visited during that year. Stones on graves in the U.S.S.R. not visited for over a year are normally removed and sold.

Growth of the Jewish Population. According to estimates of that period, the Jews formed approximately 10% of the total population in 1795; c. 20% (12,000 persons) during the 1840s, c. 25% (75,000 persons) in 1887, and 34.4% (165,000) upon the eve of World War I. Official statistics on the Jewish population are available from the 1850s. According to an official assessment of 1855, there were 17,000 Jews (21.7%) in the town; and according to the general censuses there were 139,984 Jews (34.65% of the population) in 1897; 153,194 Jews (36.4%) in 1926; 180,000 (29.8%) in 1939; and 106,700 Jews (c. 16%) in 1959.

Economic Status. From the start, the Jews of Odessa engaged in retail trade and crafts. Their representation in these occupations remained important. In 1910 56% of the small shops were still owned by Jews; they also constituted 63% of the town's craftsmen. Jewish economy in Odessa was distinguished by the role played by Jews in the export of grain via the harbor, in wholesale trade, banking and industry, the large numbers of Jews engaged in the liberal professions, and the existence of a large Jewish proletariat in variegated employment.

During the first half of the 19th century, the participation of the Jews in the grain export trade was limited to the purchase of grain in the villages and estates, and to brokerage and mediation in the capacity of subagents for the large export companies, which were Greek, Italian, and French. By 1838 Jews were well represented among the officials of the exchange, and as classifiers, sorters, weighers, and even loaders of grain. From the 1860s, however, Jewish enterprises won a predominant place in the grain export and succeeded in supplanting the export companies of foreign merchants from their monopolist positions. During the early 1870s, the greater part of the grain exports was handled by Jews, and by 1910 over 80% of grain export companies were Jewish owned, while Jews were responsible for almost 90% (89.2%) of grain exports. This success in Jewish trade was not only due to greater efficiency in the organization of purchases and rapidity in their expedition, but was also connected with the constant rise of grain prices and the decline of commercial profit rates, which resulted in a tremendous increase of the grain exports which passed through the port of Odessa.

Jews also held an important share of the wholesale trade; about one-half of the wholesale enterprises were owned by Jews in 1910. During the 1840s most of the bankers and moneychangers were Jews, and at the beginning of the 20th century 70% of the banks of Odessa were administered by them. Among the industrialists, Jews formed 43%, but their manufactured products amounted only to 39%. In 1910 70% of those engaged in medicine were Jews; c. 56% of those engaged in law, and c. 27% of those engaged in technical professions (engineers, architects, chemists, etc.). About two-thirds of the Jewish population were engaged in crafts and industry, in transportation and services, and in other categories of labor. More than one-half of these (about one-third of the Jewish population) belonged, from the social point of view, to the proletariat—industrial workers, apprentices in workshops, and ordinary laborers. During the 1880s these formed a considerable part of the Jewish proletariat (about one-third), and their standard of living, as that of the poorer classes, was very low. With the progress of industrialization in Odessa, many of them were integrated in new enterprises and the number of unskilled workers decreased.

The October Revolution of 1917 brought a decline in the commercial status of Odessa as well as the process of socialization. While this affected the means of livelihood of the majority of Jews, much of their experience and skills were utilized in the new social and economic structure under different designations. In 1926 Jews formed the overwhelming majority of the commercial clerks (in government stores and cooperatives), c. 90% of the members of the tailors' union, 67% of the members of the printing workers' union, c. 53% of those employed in the timber industries, c. 48% of the municipal workers (which also included drivers, electricians, etc.), and c. 40% of the members of the free professionals' union. Thousands of Jewish workers found employment in heavy industry (metal industry, sugar refineries, ship building), in which Jews had formerly been absent, and of which only 27% were members of the trade unions; during the same year, the Jews formed up to 64% of those engaged in the smaller private industries

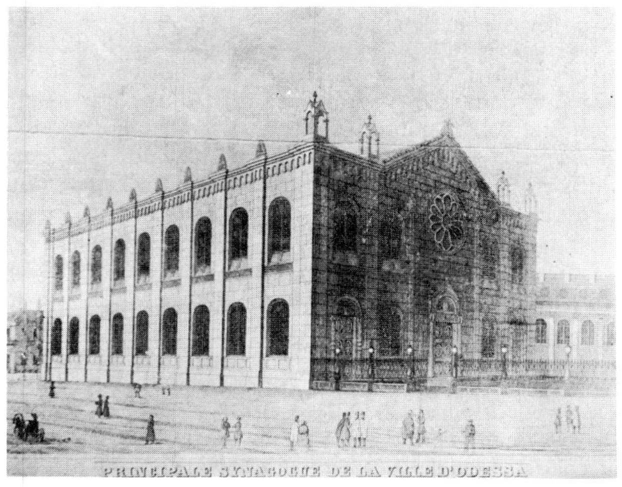

Figure 2. Drawing of the main synagogue of Odessa, built in 1840. Courtesy J.N.U.L. Photo Archives, Jerusalem.

which occupied some of those thousands who had remained unemployed and had not been successfully integrated within the new economic regime.

Cultural Trends. From the cultural aspect the Odessa community was the most "Western" in character in the *Pale of Settlement. Its population was gathered from all the regions of Russia and even from abroad (particularly from *Brody in Galicia and from Germany, during the 1820s–30s), and the throwing off of tradition became a quite familiar occurrence. This situation was expressed by a popular Jewish saying: "The fire of Hell burns around Odessa up to a distance of ten parasangs." The low standard of Torah learning within the community and the general ignorance and apathy of the Odessa Jews in their attitude to Judaism were depicted in popular witticisms, as well as in literature (Y. T. *Lewinsky). Linguistic and cultural Russian assimilation encompassed widespread classes and thus formed a social basis for the community's role as an active and organized center for the spread of Russian education among the Jews of southern Russia. The social and economic position of the *maskilim* of Odessa (the "Brodyists") drew them closer to the authorities and enabled them to gain considerable influence within the community and the shaping of its institutions. Odessa was thus the first community in Russia to be directed by *maskilim,* who retained their control over its administration throughout its existence: the "Council of the Wealthy and Permanently Appointed Jews" and later the "Commission of the Twenty" (which also included the delegates of the synagogue officials), which was organized as an opposition to the leadership of the community after 1905.

Educational and Communal Institutions. The cultural character of the community was reflected in its educational institutions. At the beginning of the 20th century, there were still about 200 *ḥadarim,* attended by about 5,000 pupils, in Odessa; 97% of these pupils came from the masses of the poor, and the *ḥadarim* were generally not of high standing. At the same time, about 6,500 pupils (boys and girls) attended 40 Jewish elementary schools (of which three were *talmudei torah* and 13 of the *Society for the Promotion of Culture among the Jews of Russia) of public, governmental, or semipublic categories. The language of instruction in these schools was Russian, whilst Jewish subjects held an insignificant place or were hardly studied at all. Many Jewish pupils studied at the government municipal schools (in 1886, over 200 pupils—8%) and government secondary schools (about 50% of the male and female pupils in 1910), about 2,500 pupils in private secondary schools, and about 700 pupils in Jewish vocational schools (for boys and girls); there were also many hundreds of Jewish students at the university (the maximum figure in 1906 was 746). In addition, Jews studied at the governmental college for music and arts (60%) and the advanced private professional colleges (for dentistry, midwifery, etc). There were also numerous evening classes and courses for adults. Of the Jewish schools, noteworthy was the vocational school Trud ("Labor") which was founded in 1864 and was the best of its class, and the yeshivah (founded 1866) which after 1906, when it was headed by Rav Ẓa'ir (Ḥayyim *Tchernowitz) and its teachers included Ḥ. N. *Bialik and J. *Klausner, attracted excellent pupils and achieved fame.

The educational institutions of Odessa became examples and models for other communities from the foundation of the first Jewish public school (in 1826), in which an attempt was made to provide a general and modern Hebrew education (with modern literature as a subject of study) under the direction of Bezalel *Stern; it had considerable influence within the Haskalah movement of Russia. Other institutions which also served as models included the synagogue of the "Brodyists," where a choir and modern singing were introduced during the 1840s, and in 1901, an organ; orphanages; agricultural training farms; summer camps for invalid children; and a large and well-equipped hospital.

Social and Political Activities. The prominent social and political activities of the Jews of Odessa had considerable influence on the rest of Russian Jewry. The community leaders and *maskilim* showed considerable initiative and made frequent representations to the authorities to obtain improvements in the condition of the Jews and their legal equality with the other inhabitants during the 1840s, 1850s, and 1870s, and called for the punishment of those who took part in the pogroms of 1871, 1881, and 1905 (see below). They were the first in Russia to adopt the system of publicly and courageously defending the Jews in the Russian-Jewish press which they had established (**Razsvet* (1860), of Joachim H. *Tarnopol and O. A. *Rabinovich; **Zion* of E. Soloveichik and L. *Pinsker; *Den* (1869), of S. *Ornstein with the permanent collaboration of I. G. *Orshanski and M. *Morgulis), while the criticisms they published of internal Jewish matters were also sharp and violent in tone. The Hebrew and Yiddish Haskalah press (**Ha-Meliz*, 1860; **Kol Mevasser*, 1863) which had been born in Odessa (under the editorship of A. *Zederbaum) also adopted this "radical" attitude to some extent. Jews of Odessa contributed largely to the local press, where they also discussed Jewish affairs. At the beginning of the 20th century, a style of Jewish awareness became apparent in discussions of Russian-speaking and Russian-educated Jews (V. *Jabotinsky and his circle) which was widely echoed within the Jewish public, particularly in southern Russia. The social and political awakening of the Jewish masses was also widespread in Odessa. Odessa Jews played an extensive and even prominent part in all trends of the Russian liberation movement. The Zionist movement also attracted masses of people.

The Pogroms. This social and political awakening of the masses arose in the atmosphere of strain and struggle surrounding the life of the community. Anti-Jewish outbreaks occurred on five occasions (1821, 1859, 1871, 1881, 1905) in Odessa, as well as many attempted attacks or unsuccessful efforts to provoke them. Intensive anti-Jewish agitation shadowed and accompanied the growth of the Jewish population and its economic and cultural achievements. Almost every sector of the Christian population contributed to the agitation and took part in the pogroms: the monopolists of the grain export (especially the Greeks in 1821; 1859; 1871) in an attempt to strike at their Jewish rivals, wealthy Russian merchants, nationalist Ukrainian intellectuals, and Christian members of the liberal professions who regarded the respected economic position of the Jews, who were "deprived of rights" in the other towns of the country, and their Russian acculturation as "the exploitation of Christians and masters at the hands of heretics and foreigners" (1871; 1881). The government administration and its supporters favored the *pogroms as a means for punishing the Jews for their participation in the revolutionary movement; pogroms were also an effective medium for diverting the anger of the discontented masses from opposition to the government to hatred of the Jews (1881, 1905); the masses, the "barefoot," the destitute, the unemployed, and the embittered of the large port city were always ready to take part in robbery and looting.

The severest pogroms occurred in 1905, and the collaboration of the authorities in their organization was evident. In this outbreak, over 300 Jews lost their lives, whilst thousands of families were injured. Among the victims were over 50 members of the Jewish *self-defense movement. Attempts to organize the movement had already been made at the time of the pogroms of the 1880s, but in this city inhabited by Jewish masses it had formed part of their existence before then and on many occasions had deterred attempted pogroms. After the Revolution, during 1917–19, the Association of Jewish Combatants was formed by ex-officers and soldiers of the Russian army. It was due to the existence of this association that no pogroms occurred in Odessa throughout the Civil War period.

Figure 3. The former synagogue of Odessa, converted to a sports club. Photo, 1969.

Zionist and Literary Center. From the inception of the *Ḥibbat Zion movement, Odessa served as its chief center. From here issued the first calls of M. L. *Lilienblum ("The revival of Israel on the land of its ancestors") and L. Pinsker ("Auto-Emancipation") which gave rise to the movement, worked for its unity ("Zerubbavel," 1883), and headed the leadership which was established after the *Kattowitz Conference ("Mazkeret Moshe," 1885–89). The *Benei Moshe society (founded by *Aḥad Ha-Am in 1889), which attempted to organize the intellectuals and activists of the movement, was established in Odessa. Odessa was also chosen as the seat of the settlement committee (the *Odessa Committee, called officially The Society for the Support of Agricultural Workers and Craftsmen in Syria and Palestine), the only legally authorized institution of the movement in Russia (1890–1917). Several other economic institutions for practical activities in Palestine (Geulah, the Carmel branch, etc.) were associated with it. Jewish emigration from Russia to Ereẓ Israel also passed through Odessa, which became the "Gateway to Zion."

The social awakening of the masses gave rise to the popular character of the Zionist movement in Odessa. It succeeded in establishing an influential and ramified organization, attracting a stream of intellectual and energetic youth from the townlets of the Pale of Settlement to Odessa—the center of culture and site of numerous schools—and provided the Jewish national movement with powerful propagandists, especially from among the ranks of those devoted to Hebrew literature. The group of authors and activists which rallied around the Zionist movement and actively participated in the work of its institutions included M. L. Lilienblum and Aḥad Ha-Am, M. M. *Ussishkin, who headed the Odessa Committee during its last decade of existence, and M. *Dizengoff, Zalman *Epstein and Y. T. Lewinsky, M. *Ben-Ammi and H. *Rawnitzky, Ḥ. N. Bialik and J. *Klausner, A. *Druyanow and A. M. Berakhyahu (Borochov), Ḥ. *Tchernowitz, S. Pen, M. *Gluecksohn and V. Jabotinsky. These had great influence on this youth, who were not only initiated into Jewish national activity, but were enriched in Jewish culture and broadened in general education. Important literary forums were established in Odessa (*Kavveret*, 1890; *Pardes*, 1891–

95; *Ha-Shilo'ah, 1897–1902; 1907–17; *Haolam, 1912–17); their editors (Aḥad Ha-Am, Y. H. Rawnitzky, Ḥ. N. Bialik, J. Klausner, A. Druyanow, and M. Gluecksohn) not only succeeded in raising them to a high literary standard but also won considerable influence among the public through the ideological integrity of their publications. The publishing houses established in Odessa (Rawnitzky, Moriah; Ḥ. N. Bialik and Y. H. Rawnitzky, S. *Ben-Zion and Y. T. Lewinsky, *Devir, founded by Bialik and his circle, from 1919) were also systematic in their standards and consistently loyal to their ideology. A Hebrew literary center and "Hebrew climate" was created in Odessa. It united the Hebrew writers by an internal bond more closely than in any other place; it attracted toward Hebrew literature authors who had become estranged from it or who had never approached it (Mendele Mokher Seforim, S. *Dubnow, Ben-David, M. Ben-Ammi, S. S. *Frug, V. Jabotinsky); it produced new authors who were to play an important and valuable role in literature (S. *Tchernichowsky, J. Klausner, N. *Slouschz, etc.); it attracted talented young authors (S. Ben-Zion, Y. *Berkowitz, J. *Fichmann, Z. *Shneour, A. A. *Kabak, E. *Steinman, and many others) who sought the benefit of this congenial literary meeting place refecting the spirit of its distinguished founders (Aḥad Ha-Am and Ḥ. N. Bialik). The arguments between the leaders of the national movement (Aḥad Ha-Am and S. Dubnow, M. M. Ussishkin and V. Jabotinsky) and its opponents, grouped around the local branch of the Society for Promotion of Culture among the Jews of Russia who stood for "striking civic roots, linguistic-cultural assimilation, and general ideals" (M. Morgulis, J. *Bikerman, etc.), were published at length and grew in severity from year to year, their influence penetrating far beyond Odessa. With the advent of the Soviet regime, Odessa ceased to be the Jewish cultural center in southern Russia. The symbol of the destruction of Hebrew culture was the departure from Odessa for Constantinople in June 1921 of a group of Hebrew authors led by Bialik. The *Yevsektsiya chose *Kharkov and *Kiev as centers for its activities among the Jews of the Ukraine. Russian-oriented assimilation prevailed among the Jews of Odessa in the 1920s (though the city belonged to the Ukraine). Over 77% of the Jewish pupils attended Russian schools in 1926 and only 22% Yiddish schools. At the University, where up to 40% of the student role was Jewish, a faculty of Yiddish existed for several years which also engaged in research of the history of Jews in southern Russia. The renowned Jewish libraries of the city were amalgamated into a single library named after Mendele Mokher Seforim. In the later 1930s, as in the rest of Russia, Jewish cultural activity ceased in Odessa and was eventually completely eradicated. The rich Jewish life in Odessa found vivid expression in Russian-Jewish fiction, as, e.g., in the novels of *Yushkevich, in Jabotinsky's autobiographical stories and his novel *Piatero* ("They Were Five," 1936) and particularly in the colorful *Odessa Tales* by Isaac *Babel, which covered both the pre-revolutionary and the revolutionary period and described the Jewish proletariat and underworld of the city. [B.D.]

Holocaust Period. After June 21, 1941, many Jews from Bukovina, Bessarabia, and western Ukraine fled from German and Rumanian rule to Odessa. Some Jews in Odessa were called up to the Red Army, and many others left during the two months' siege of the city. When Odessa was occupied on Oct. 16, 1941, by General Ciupercă's Fourth Rumanian Army assisted by German units, 80,000–90,000 Jews remained in Odessa. Two special commando groups, known as Sonderkommando 11B, which belonged to the Einsatzgruppe D headed by Otto Ohlendorf and the Rumanian Operative Echelon, were assigned to the army. These groups killed about 8,000 Jews on the first day of the occupation. The entire population had to submit to a census. Special centers for the census were created for registering Jews, and all those who reported (about 3,000–4,000 Jews) were shot on the pretext that they were "communist agents." On Oct. 22, 1941, an explosion wrecked a part of the building of the Rumanian military general headquarters (the former headquarters of the Soviet secret police). General Glogojeanu, the city's military commander, and many Rumanian and German officers and soldiers were killed. In the first reprisals carried out the following day, 5,000 persons, most of them Jews, were killed. Many of them were hanged at crossings and in the public squares. Ion *Antonescu ordered the execution of 200 Communists for every officer who had been killed, and 100 for every soldier, and ordered that one member of every Jewish family be taken hostage. Nineteen thousand Jews were arrested and brought to the square at the harbor, doused with gasoline, and burned. Another 16,000 were taken the following day to the outskirts, where all of them were massacred. Some of them, bound 40 or 50 side by side, were thrown in an antitank ditch and shot. All the others were crowded into four stores in three of which the Jews were killed by machinegun fire. The fourth store was blown up on October 25, at the hour when the headquarters had been blown up three days earlier. The other three stores were set on fire to prevent possible escape by the wounded. The massacres were commanded by Rumanian officers, but organized by Sonderkommando 11 specialists.

Another 5,000 Jews were subsequently arrested, and soon after the massacres, deported to camps set up in Bogdanovka, Domanevka, Krivoye Ozero, and other villages, where about 70,000 Jews, all from southern *Transnistria, were concentrated. During December 1941 and January 1942, almost all of them were killed by special troups of Sonderkommando (Russia) aided by Rumanian police soldiers, Ukrainian militia, and, especially, by the *SS units, made up of former German colonists in the region ("VoMi" = Volksdeutsche Mittelstelle). The burning of corpses lasted for two months. Approximately 30,000 Jews still lived in Odessa and were segregated in two ghettos set up at Slobodka and Dalnik on the outskirts. Only a small number could find accommodation in the few houses there, while the vast majority were forced to live outside in the snow and storm. Most of them froze within a few days. Typhus accounted for hundreds of victims daily. Official records dating from that period show the attempts of Jews to save themselves by falsifying documents on ethnic origin, by giving children to Christian families, or by marrying their children to Christians, while many Jews found shelter with non-Jewish friends or in the catacombs.

On Dec. 7, 1941, Odessa became the capital of Transnistria. The governor, G. Alexianu, and all the administrative institutions transferred their headquarters from Tiraspol to Odessa. Subsequently, steps were taken to make Odessa **judenrein*. First, an order was issued on Jan. 7, 1942, forcing the Jews to turn over all the gold, jewels, and objects of value in their possession. The transfer of Jews to camps in the Berezovka and Golta regions began on Jan. 12, 1942. By February 23, 19,582 Jews were dispatched in 43 overcrowded convoys by cattle truck and then by train from Odessa to Berezovka. The bodies of 50 to 60 people who died in each transport were burned near the arrival platform in the sight of their families. From Berĕzovka, the Jews, divided into groups, were sent by a forced march to the camps in the districts of Berezovka and Golta. Most of those sent to the Golta died from frost, starvation, or disease in the stables where they were quartered. The survivors, with Jewish deportees from Rumania, were sent to work on local Rumanian farms. Those who managed to receive the aid sent from the Jewish Relief Committee in Bucharest survived. The Domanevka ghetto inhabitants survived, with the deportees from Rumania, due to their superior self-organization. The people sent to the camps in the vicinity of the German colonies in the district of Berezovka were all killed by SS commando units consisting entirely of local Germans.

After the last convoy left on Feb. 23, 1942, Odessa was proclaimed *judenrein*. The local inhabitants and the occupying forces looted Jewish property. The old Jewish cemetery was desecrated and hundreds of granite and marble tombstones were shipped to Rumania and sold. The gravestone of the poet Simon Frug was recovered and after the war laid in the Jewish cemetery of Bucharest. The Mendele Mokher Seforim Library was sacked and the building demolished. In August 1942 Alexianu and SS-Brigadefuehrer Hoffmeyer—head of Sonderkommando R—signed an agreement transferring to the 7,500 Volksdeutsche living in Odessa all the local Jewish-owned apartments, including the furniture. The Jewish Theater became the Deutsches Haus for entertaining the German troops in Odessa. In the summer of 1942 the Rumanian authorities organized various handicraft workshops for their employees' service for which they brought 50 of the best Jewish artisans from the Transnistrian ghettos (deportees from Rumania). They were segregated in ghetto-like quarters in a building on Adolf Hitler Street (formerly Yekaterinovskaya Street). A delegation of the Relief Committee from Bucharest, authorized by the government to visit the ghettos of Transnistria, succeeded in January 1943 in sending them some funds.

Soviet troops under General Malinovsky returned to Odessa on April 10, 1944. It is estimated that at the time of liberation, a few thousand Jews were living in Odessa, some of them under false documents or in hiding in the catacombs. Others were given shelter by non-Jewish families. There had been numerous informers among the local Russians and Ukrainians but also persons who risked their liberty and even their lives to save Jews.

In the report of the "Soviet Extraordinary Commission for the estimation of the losses of Odessa's inhabitants" (June 14, 1944), it is not mentioned that the greatest number of victims were Jews. On the other hand, two well-known Rumanian writers (George Călinescu and Aurel *Baranga) wrote on the Holocaust of the Jews in Odessa. [D.L.]

Contemporary Period. After the Jewish survivors returned, Odessa became one of the largest Jewish centers of the Soviet Union. However there was no manifestation of communal or cultural life. Until 1956 Israel vessels visited the port of Odessa for loading and unloading, and Israel sailors visited the harbor club and were seen in the city's streets. In 1962 private prayer groups were dispersed by the authorities and religious articles found among them were confiscated. A denunciation of the Jewish religious congregation and its employees appeared in the local paper in 1964. *Maẓẓah* baking by the Jewish congregation was practically prohibited during 1959–65. It was again allowed in 1966. In 1968 the synagogue burned down, but was later rebuilt. While it was still in ruins, thousands of Jews, many of them youngsters, came to the site on Simḥat Torah eve to dance and sing. In the 1959 census 102,200 Jews were registered in Odessa, but the actual number has been estimated at about 180,000 (14–15% of the total population). There remained only one synagogue in Odessa, on the outskirts of the city, whose rabbi, Israil Schwarzblatt, was the sole rabbi ordained in the Moscow Yeshivah (founded by Rabbi *Schliefer). The old Jewish cemeteries were in disrepair. From 1968 several Jewish families were allowed to emigrate to Israel, following the increased demand for exit permits of Soviet Jews in the wake of the Six-Day War (1967). [ED.]

Bibliography: *Eshkol, Enẓiklopedyah Yisre'elit*, 1 (1929), 809–26; B. Shohetman, in: *Arim ve-Immahot be-Yisrael*, 2 (1948), 58–108 (incl. bibl.); J. Lestschinsky, *Dos Sovetishe ydntum* (1941; Heb. tr. *Ha-Yehudim be-Rusyah ha-Sovyetit*, 1943); A. P. Subbotin, *V cherte yevreyskoy osedlosti*, 2 (1888); J. J. Lerner, *Yevrei v Novorossiyskom kraye–istoricheskiye ocherki* (1901); A. Dallin, *Odessa 1941–1944* . . . (1957); Litani, in: *Yedi'ot Yad Vashem*, no. 23–24 (1960), 24–26; idem, in: *Yad Vashem Studies* (1967), 135–54; A. Werth, *Russia at War, 1941–1945* (1964), 813–26; S. Schwarz, *Jews in the Soviet Union* (1951), index, I. Ehrenburg et al. (eds.), *Cartea Neagră* . . ., 1 (1946), 92–107; M. Carp (ed.), *Cartea Neagră* . . . 2 (1948); 3 (1947), indexes; *Procesul Marii Trădări Nationale* (1946), index; PK Romanyah (1969), 390–4.

ODESSA COMMITTEE, shortened name for the Society for the Support of Jewish Farmers and Artisans in Syria and Palestine, the legalized framework of the *Ḥibbat Zion movement. It was founded in Odessa in 1890, with the permission of the Russian government and continued the work of Ḥovevei Zion in Russia until 1919. Its official aim was to help Jews who settled in "Palestine and Syria" to earn their living by productive work, especially agriculture. Leon *Pinsker, Abraham *Gruenberg (from 1891), and Menaḥem *Ussishkin (from 1906) served successively as chairman of the committee. It had an executive committee in Jaffa. When Jewish immigration to Ereẓ Israel increased, as a result of the worsening conditions of Russian Jewry, particularly after the expulsion of Jews from Moscow, the committee assisted settlement societies in the purchase of lands. Vladimir *Tiomkin, chairman of its executive committee in Jaffa, was active in organizing and planning the purchase of lands. When immigration from Russia was forbidden by the Turkish authorities, the purchases were discontinued and the Jaffa committee went bankrupt. The Russian Jews were discouraged and the income of the Odessa Committee decreased, but it gradually increased again, particularly when *Herzl began his activities and the Odessa Committe became the only legal Zionist body in Russia. The committee also received donations for special projects, such as supporting the Hebrew school in Jaffa and the workers' fund. In 1900, after the transfer by Baron Edmond de *Rothschild of the management of the supported settlements to the *Jewish Colonization Association (ICA), the Odessa Committee sent *Aḥad Ha-Am and the agronomist Abraham Sussman to investigate the situation. Their reports spoke of the harm caused by the paternalistic methods of the Baron's bureaucracy. A year later Aḥad Ha-Am took part in a delegation to the Baron, but his reply was not satisfactory.

Following the suggestions of the agronomist Akiva *Ettinger, whom the Committee sent to Ereẓ Israel in 1902, it ceased its support of individuals, encouraging private and public initiative instead. In 1903 a delegation led by Ussishkin was sent by the committee to Ereẓ Israel in order to organize the new *yishuv*. The settlers' delegates held several meetings in Zikhron Ya'akov and laid the foundations for an "Organization of the Jews in Ereẓ Israel" and the Teachers' Association. The former failed, but the latter developed.

The Odessa Committee maintained a network of information bureaus for immigrants in Odessa, Constantinople, Beirut, Jaffa, Jerusalem, and Haifa. It established moshavot and small-holdings for agricultural workers (*Be'er Ya'akov in 1908, *Ein Gannim near Petaḥ Tikvah,

האספה הכללית הראשונה בארעססא
לחברת תמיכת בני ישראל עובדי אדמה ובעלי מלאכה בסוריא ובארץ הקדושה

The first convention of the Odessa Committee, April 1904. Heads are covered out of respect for Rabbi Samuel Mohilever (1). Among others in the photograph are J. L. Pinsker (2), Abraham Gruenberg (3), Samuel Barbash (6), Aḥad Ha-Am (8), M. Ben-Ammi (11), Sholem Aleichem (18), Moses Leib Lilienblum (20), Alexander Zederbaum (21), Jacob Bernstein-Kogan (23), Abraham Elijah Lubarsky (24), Eliahu Lewin-Epstein (33), Mordecai ben Hillel Ha-Kohen (39), Vasili Bermann (40), Shlomo Berliand (42), Vladimir Tiomkin (47). Courtesy J.N.U.L. Photo Archives, Jerusalem.

and *Naḥalat Yehudah near Rishon le-Zion). It aided in the establishment of the Carmel winegrowers cooperative and Geulah company for land purchase and supported schools, book publishing, and periodicals in Ereẓ Israel. It gave the first donation for purchasing a plot for the Hebrew University in Jerusalem.

Bibliography: I. Klausner, *Mi-Kattowitz ad Basel,* 2 vols. (1965), index; *Reports of the Odessa Committee* (Heb. and Rus., 1890–1919). [I.K.]

ODETS, CLIFFORD (1906–1963), U.S. playwright. Born in Philadelphia and raised in the Bronx, New York, Odets became an actor at the age of 15. He was a cofounder of the Group Theater, where his one-act play, *Waiting for Lefty* (1935), based on the New York taxi strike of 1934, brought him early success. Two more plays were staged in the same year: *Awake and Sing!,* a drama about poor New York Jews, marked an important turning point in the portrayal of the Jew on the American stage; and *Till the Day I Die* dealt with left-wing German opposition to the Nazis. These brought Odets to the fore as the most promising playwright of the new generation. He expressed perhaps better than any dramatist of his time the hardships of the great depression of the 1930s, and while his works have lost some of their original appeal, they were in their day of considerable social significance. Their impact owed much to their vivid dialogue and characterization. Probably the finest example of the latter quality is *Golden Boy* (1937), the story of a musician turned prizefighter, which was made

Clifford Odets, U.S. playwright. Photo Ruth Sondak, Keystone Pictures, Hollywood, Calif.

into a musical in 1964. Odets also wrote *Rocket to the Moon* (1938), and *Clash by Night* (1941). After spending many years as a screenwriter in Hollywood, he returned to

Broadway with *The Big Knife* (1949), a play dealing with the corrupting influence of the film colony. Two later plays were *The Country Girl* (1950) and *The Flowering Peach* (1954), a new version of the biblical story of Noah in terms of Jewish family life.

Bibliography: E. Murray, *Clifford Odets: The Thirties and After* (1968); R. B. Shuman, *Clifford Odets* (1962); J. Gould, *Modern American Playwrights* (1966), 186–203; S. J. Kunitz (ed), *Twentieth Century Authors,* first suppl. (1955), incl. bibl. [J.MER.]

°**ODO OF CAMBRAI** (d. 1113), bishop and theologian. Among Odo's works was the polemic text *Disputatio contra Judaeum Leonem de adventu Christi,* which he claimed was an account of a disputation held in *Senlis during the Christmas season of 1106 between himself and a Jew named Léon. The disputation deals mainly with the virginal birth and the incarnation, and in some places it is clear that Odo borrowed from *Anselm of Canterbury. Odo dedicated this text to a certain Acardus, a monk from the abbey of Fémy, near Cambrai, in commemoration of his visit to this abbey, where he had already expounded the subjects covered by the *Disputatio.*

Bibliography: P. Browe, *Judenmission im Mittelalter* (1942), 63, 101, 115; F. Cayre, *Patrologie* . . ., 2 (1945[3]), 386; J. de Ghellinck, *L'essor de la littérature latine,* 1 (1946), 164; PL, 160 (1880), 1103–12. [B.BL.]

°**ODO (Eudes) OF CHÂTEAUROUX** (d. 1273), chancellor of the University of Paris from 1238. Odo was probably one of the judges at the public trial of the Talmud in 1240. Appointed cardinal bishop of Tusculum (Frascati) in 1244, he returned as papal legate to France in 1245 to preach the Crusade. A violent opponent of the Talmud, Odo was incensed by a letter from Pope Innocent IV (1247) instructing him to give back to the Jews any copies which had survived the *auto-da-fé* of 1242 (see *Talmud, Burning of). Adopting a high moral tone in his reply, Odo reproached the pope with having been duped by the wiles of the Jews, and repeated the verdict of Gregory IX that the Talmud prevented Jews from becoming Christians. It would be disgraceful, he said, for books which had been solemnly and justly burned in public to be returned to the Jews at the instance of the pope. On May 15, 1248, he issued a formal condemnation of the Talmud, forbidding copies to be returned.

Bibliography: S. Grayzel, *Church and Jews in the XIIIth Century* (1966[2]), index; idem, in: W. Jacob et al. (eds.), *Essays in Honor of Solomon B. Freehof* (1964), 220–45. [N.D.L.]

°**ODO (Eudes) OF SULLY** (c. 1160–1208), bishop of Paris from 1196. In several paragraphs of his synodal statutes (par. 15, 37–38, 60, and addenda 1–3), Odo of Sully attempted to restrict relations between Jews and Christians. Particular decrees prohibited priests from standing security for a Jew or giving him church vessels or books in pledge, and forbade Christians to use the skins of grapes which had been pressed by Jews, except as food for pigs or as fertilizer. Here, for the first time, laymen were forbidden—on pain of excommunication—to debate articles of Christian faith with the Jews. These decrees are thought to have been drawn up around 1200, but they were probably issued after July 15, 1205, the date of the letter from Pope *Innocent III to Odo calling for greater severity toward the Jews.

Bibliography: S. Grayzel, *Church and the Jews in the XIIIth Century* (1966[2]), 114f., 300f.; T. de Morembert, in: *Dictionnaire d'histoire et de géographie ecclésiastique,* 15 (1963), 1330f. [B.BL.]

°**OENOMAUS OF GADARA,** pagan philosopher of the school of younger Cynics, who lived during the reign of Hadrian (117–38). He composed a number of works, only little of which has survived. His most famous Γοήτων Φώρα (*Kata Chresterion*), fragments of which are preserved in Eusebius (Praeparatio Evangelica 1:7ff.), was a lively attack on the belief in oracles. The argument was based on the belief in free will, and it seems to have had some measure of success, because Julian, in the middle of the fourth century, upbraids him for destroying reverence for the gods (*Orationes* 7:209, also 6:199). Oenomaus aimed at a cynicism which did not slavishly follow either Antisthenes or Diogenes, defining it as "a sort of despair, a life not human but brutish, a disposition of the soul that reckons with nothing noble or virtuous or good." Oenomaus is generally identified with Avnimos ha-Gardi, who appears in rabbinic literature as a philosopher friendly toward the rabbis. He once asked them how the world was first created. Declaring themselves not versed in such matters, they referred him to Joseph the builder, who satisfied him with his reply (Ex. R. 13:1).

He was particularly friendly with R. Meir and once asked him; "Does all wool rise that is placed in the dyeing-pot?" Meir replied, "What was clean upon the body of the mother rises, what was unclean upon the body of the mother does not rise" (Ḥag. 15b). This enigmatic dialogue probably refers to the fact of Meir's teacher, *Elisha b. Avuyah, having become an apostate, and the dangers involved in Meir's learning from him (see TJ, Ḥag. 2:1, 77b). Avnimos' question is indicative of an intimate understanding of Jewish problems. This positive attitude is reflected in an episode according to which the pagans asked him whether they could overcome the Jews, and he replied that if they heard the chirping (i.e., studying) of children in the synagogues and academies, they would be unable to overcome the Jews (Gen. R. 65:20). He had some knowledge of the Bible (Ruth R. 2:13), but it is most significant that the rabbis regarded him as the greatest heathen philosopher of all ages (with Balaam, Gen. R. 65:20). This is due to his gibes at the gods and oracles, coupled with his sympathy and closeness to rabbinic circles, but also indicates the measure of their unfamiliarity with Greek philosophy (see S. Lieberman, in *Biblical and other Studies,* ed. by A. Altmann (1963), 129–30).

Bibliography: Hyman, Toledot, 946; 261; Pauly-Wissowa, 17 (1937), 2249–51. [D.S.]

°**OESTERLEY, WILLIAM OSCAR EMIL** (1866–1950), English Semitics scholar. Oesterley, who was born in Calcutta, was ordained a clergyman and taught Hebrew and Old Testament exegesis at King's College, London, from 1926. In his work he endeavored to demonstrate talmudic influence on New Testament form and content.

Among his published writings are: *The Jewish Background of Christian Liturgy* (1925); (with T. H. Robinson) *A History of Israel* (vol. 2; *From 586 B.C.E. to A.D. 135;* 1932 and many reprints); *Introduction to the Books of the Old Testament* (with T. H. Robinson, 1934) and *An Introduction to the Books of the Apocrypha* (1935); *The Jews and Judaism During the Greek Period* (1941). Oesterley also wrote commentaries to Psalms (1939; repr. 1962) and Proverbs (1929), *A Fresh Approach to the Psalms* (1937) and a metric translation of the Song of Songs, *Ancient Hebrew Poems* (1938). Together with G. H. Box he wrote an outline of Jewish literature (*A Short Survey of the Literature of Rabbinical and Mediaeval Judaism,* 1920).

OESTERREICHISCHE NATIONALBIBLIOTHEK, Austrian government library in Vienna, court library of the Austro-Hungarian Empire until 1918. The Oesterreichische Nationalbibliothek is a major European library founded in 1526.

It possesses 224 Hebrew manuscripts dating from the 13th through the 18th centuries, of which 41 are illustrated. It also has a considerable number of Hebrew incunabula, mostly Bibles, including the first complete Hebrew Bible, printed by the Soncino family in 1488. The library's papyrus collection contains 191 Hebrew texts written on papyri, parchment, and paper. Also among its holdings are a few fragments from the Cairo *Genizah*, including some written in Judeo-Arabic. The library contains an unusually complete collection of rabbinic literature from Galicia and the other eastern portions of the Austro-Hungarian Empire, since a copy of every work published under the empire had to be deposited at the Nationalbibliothek.

The printed volumes of Judaica in the library are part of the Orientalia collection, estimated at about 5% of the library's total holdings. Of the library's Judaica, in 1970 only the incunabula were catalogued separately.

Bibliography: A. Z. Schwarz, *Hebraeische Handschriften der Nationalbibliothek in Wien* (1925); F. Unterkircher, *Inventar der illuminierten Handschriften . . .*, 2 (1959). [M.A.M.]

OESTERREICHISCHES CENTRAL-ORGAN FUER GLAUBENSFREIHEIT, CULTUR, GESCHICHTE UND LITERATUR DER JUDEN, German-language Jewish weekly published in Vienna immediately after freedom of the press was granted at the beginning of the 1848 revolution. Its 49 issues appeared from April 4, 1848 to Oct. 25, 1848. The publisher and editor was Isidor *Busch, and Max (Meir) *Letteris also contributed to the first four issues. A Hebrew supplement, *Meged Geresh Yeraḥim*, edited by Isaac Samuel *Reggio, appeared once (Nisan 5408/1848). Leopold Kompert and Simon Szanto were among its contributors and Busch had many correspondents throughout the Hapsburg monarchy. At first the *Central-Organ* enthusiastically supported the revolution, taking it for granted that Jewish rights would be secured within the framework of general civic rights. Dealing at length with the legal status of the Jews in various countries, the paper was also sensitive to the social discrepancies within Jewish society and attacked leading Jewish capitalists, Rothschild in particular. The outbreak of the anti-Jewish riots in Hungary, Bohemia, Posen, and Alsace brought about a sharp change in its position. After Kompert had published his article *Auf nach Amerika!* (May 6, 1848, No. 6), the *Central-Organ* energetically campaigned for Jewish emigration to the United States, where the Jews were assured of civic equality. Emigration, organization of groups of emigrants, and information for families who intended to emigrate became one of the central themes of the newspaper. The last issue of the newspaper appeared on Oct. 25, 1848, and it probably came to an end as the result of the capture of the city six days later, following the failure of the revolution. Busch himself emigrated to the U.S.

Bibliography: G. Kisch, *In Search of Freedom* (1949), index; idem, in: AJHSP, 38 (1948/49), 185–234; J. A. Helfert, *Die Wiener Journalistik im Jahre 1848* (1877), index, s.v. *Central-Organ, oesterreichisches*. [Av.F.]

OETTINGEN, town in *Bavaria, W. Germany. Jews were to be found in Oettingen from the second half of the 13th century. The Jewish settlement suffered in 1298 during the **Rindfleisch* persecutions, and during the *Black Death persecutions of 1348 almost all the Jews were massacred. Emperor *Charles IV then transferred their property to Duke Albrecht of Oettingen. A new Jewish community, consisting mainly of moneylenders maintaining strong commercial and familial ties with *Noerdlingen, was soon reorganized. Privileges were issued for 1383–88, and a *Judenstrasse* was mentioned in 1457. The community absorbed an influx of refugees after clerical agitation resulted in the expulsion of the Jews from Noerdlingen and other Bavarian cities in 1507. Oettingen was the capital of the rival duchies of Oettingen-Spielberg and Oettingen-Wallerstein and had two synagogues (a "Catholic" and a "Lutheran" one, so named after the two branches of the Oettingen ruling house) and separate district rabbinates and communal organizations. There were many rural Jewish communities in the villages and towns of the duchies of considerable economic importance; their members were engaged in livestock dealing, peddling, and even farming. The duchies were incorporated into *Bavaria in 1806.

In the 17th and 18th centuries, the Oettingen communities benefited from the patronage of several influential *Court Jews, including Hirsch Neumark, David Oppenheim, and the *Model family, who originated in Oettingen. A pogrom resulting from a *blood libel was narrowly averted in 1690 when the murderer of a young child was discovered to be a Christian; the event was commemorated by a fast day each year thereafter on the 17th of Iyyar. The most distinguished rabbi of Oettingen-Wallerstein was Asher Loew (1789–1809), later rabbi of Metz, who opposed Moses *Mendelssohn's proposal to use a burial hall in the cemetery in order to comply with government regulations requiring corpses to be buried three days after death. Of comparable distinction in Oettingen-Spielberg was Jacob Phinehas Katzenellenbogen (1764–95). The Jewish community of Oettingen numbered about 300 in the 18th century (about 10% of the total population). A cemetery was opened in 1850 and a new synagogue built in 1853. The rural community declined from 430 persons (13.4%) in 1837 to 102 in 1910 and only 66 in 1933. On Nov. 10, 1938, Jewish homes and shops were demolished and the synagogue sacked. The rabbi was beaten and hospitalized and all Jewish men deported to *Dachau. Ten of the 11 Jews still living in Oettingen in 1942 were deported.

Bibliography: Germ Jud, 2 (1968), 633–5; L. Lamm, in: JJLG, 22 (1931–32), 147–59; J. Mann, in: ZGJD, 6 (1935), 32–39; L. Mueller, *Aus fuenf Jahrhunderten* (1900); S. Stern, *The Court Jew* (1950), index; PK, Bavaria. [H.W.]

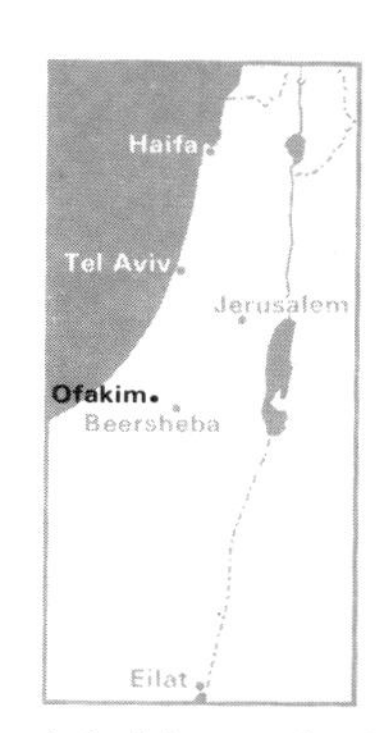

OFAKIM (Heb. אֳפָקִים; "Horizons"), development town, with municipal council status in southern Israel, 15 mi. (25 km.) N.W. of Beersheba. Ofakim was founded in 1955 as a regional center for the "Merḥavim" development region. The new immigrants who settled there suffered in the initial years from unemployment, low cultural standards, and severe social problems. The population, numbering 631 in the first year, grew to 9,200 by 1970. The majority (71%) of the inhabitants in 1965 were from Morocco and Tunisia; 5% came from India, 9% from Persia, 5% from Egypt, and the rest were from Europe or Israel-born. Families were large and the median age low, with 57.2% of the population below 20 years of age. With the opening of industrial enterprises in the 1960s (textiles, diamond polishing, bakery, basketmaking) Ofakim's economic situation improved and a manpower shortage developed. [E.O.]

OFEK, URIEL (1926–), Hebrew writer. Born in Tel Aviv, Ofek served in the Palmaḥ (1944–48). From 1951, he was co-editor, and from 1971 editor of the children's weekly *Davar li-Yladim*. His poems, stories, articles, and studies on children's literature appeared in various publications, and his plays were staged in children's theaters. He published many books for children, stories, verse, and anthologies of world children's literature. He also translated many children's books and folksongs into Hebrew. He edited memorial volumes to the soldiers who fell in Israel's War of Independence: *Benei Kiryat Ḥayyim be-Milḥemet ha-Shiḥ-*

rur (1950), and *Le-Vaneinu* (1952) His encyclopedia on children's literature, *Olam Ẓa'ir*, appeared in 1970.

Bibliography: Kressel, Leksikon, 1 (1965), 48. [G.K.]

OFFENBACH, city in Hesse, W. Germany. The Jewish community of Offenbach is mentioned in the list of communities whose members were martyred at the time of the *Black Death persecutions (1348). Individual Jews only lived in Offenbach until after the expulsion of the Jews from *Frankfort on the Main (1614); fleeing to Offenbach, they founded a small community, which in time developed and grew in strength. In 1702 one of the town's streets was called the *Judenstrasse*. The community was officially constituted in 1707; in the community regulations of that year and in the letters of privileges granted by the authorities in 1708, the organization of the synagogue and all matters of taxation, commerce, and labor were regulated. In 1708 a second *Judenstrasse* was set aside.

From 1788 to 1791 Jacob *Frank lived in the town, and his daughter Eva until 1817. During those years, thousands of Frank's adherents came to Offenbach in order to express their devotion to him and his daughter. Between 1803 and 1806 Wolf *Breidenbach of Offenbach endeavored to obtain the abolition of the body tax *(*Leibzoll)* in several of the German states. The Jewish community remained numerically stable at about 1,000 persons throughout the 19th century, while its proportion in the total population declined from about 10% to 3%. It attained a peak of 2,361 in 1910 and totaled 1,434 (1.8%) in 1933. In October 1936 large numbers of Polish Jews were expelled, and on Nov. 10, 1938, the synagogue, built in 1913–16, was burned down. The last rabbi of the community, Dr. Max *Dienemann (served 1918–39), was attacked by the mob and imprisoned. Of 554 Jews who remained on May 17, 1939, 205 were deported in October 1942 and the rest soon after. Seven former inhabitants returned after the war and with the aid of refugees rebuilt the community. In June 1956 a new synagogue was consecrated, although in that month 70 tombstones were desecrated. In January 1970 662 Jews were living in Offenbach. [Z.Av.]

Hebrew Printing. The Frankfort bookseller Seligmann Reiss and his son Herz set up a Hebrew press in Offenbach, and issued a variety of Hebrew and Judeo-German books between 1714 and 1721, among them *Beit Yisrael* by Alexander b. Moses Ethausen (1719); *Historie vom Ritter Siegmund* (1714); and similar medieval tales. Israel b. Moses Halle printed Hebrew books in Offenbach with interruptions from 1718 to at least 1738. In 1767 Hirsch Spitz of Pressburg (Bratislava) set up a Hebrew printing press in Offenbach; the press continued to operate until 1832, when competition from *Roedelheim became too strong. The well-known Amsterdam printer Abraham *Proops published Nathan Maz's *Binyan Shelomo* in Offenbach in 1784. [Ed.]

The former synagogue of Offenbach, Germany, converted into a theater after World War II. Courtesy Offenbach Municipality.

Bibliography: Silberstein, in: ZGJD, 5 (1892), 126–45; *Zeitschrift fuer Demographie und Statistik der Juden*, 4 (1908), 92; MGADJ, 1 (1909), 49–66; Z. Rubashov, *Al Tillei Beit Frank* (1923); S. Guggenheim, *Aus der Vergangenheit der israelitischen Gemeinde zu Offenbach* (1915); M. Dienemann-Hirsch, *Max Dienemann, ein Gedenkbuch* (1946); *Mitteilungen des Gesamtarchivs der deutschen Juden*, 1 (1909), 49–64; P. Arnsberg, *Von Podolien nach Offenbach* (1965); Germ Jud, 2 (1968), 625; Ḥ. D. Friedberg, *Toledot ha-Defus ha-Ivri . . . be-Eiropah* (1937), 101–4; M. Steinschneider and D. Cassel, *Juedische Typographie* (1938), 261 (repr. from Ersch und Gruber, *Allgemeine Encyclopaedie* . . ., 28, 1851).

OFFENBACH, ISAAC (1779–1850), *ḥazzan*. Isaac ben Judah, surnamed Eberst, was born in Offenbach near Frankfort. After he left his native town in 1799 to become a wandering *ḥazzan* and musician, he began to be called, "der Offenbacher," which soon became his official family name. In 1802 he settled in Deutz as a tavern musician, and in 1816 moved to Cologne, where he became a music teacher and in about 1826 the town *ḥazzan*, a post he held until shortly before his death. The seventh of his nine children, Jacob, was the composer Jacques *Offenbach.

Isaac Offenbach was a versatile musician, a prolific composer (mainly of synagogal works), and a writer and translator of merit. His historical importance stems from the fact that the documentation of his life and work has survived almost in full.

His publications are: a *Haggadah* with German translation and six appended melodies, some traditional and some composed by him (1838); a Hebrew-German youth prayer book (1839); and a number of guitar pieces. His manuscripts were given by his granddaughters to the Jewish Institute of Religion in New York, and some items also reached the Birnbaum Collection at the Hebrew Union College, Cincinnati, and the Jewish National and University Library, Jerusalem. The material includes reminiscences by his daughter, and about 20 fascicles and folders of cantorial compositions and notations of traditional melodies. Over and above their value as "cantorial" antecedents of his famous son's work, these manuscripts provide both a treasure trove of the "great tradition" of Ashkenazi *ḥazzanut* and an instructive picture of the development of a *ḥazzan* at the beginning of the Emancipation.

Bibliography: B. Bayer, in: *Proceedings of the World Conference of Jewish Studies* (Heb., 1971); A. Henseler, *Jakob Offenbach* (Ger., 1930), 16–31 and passim; P. Nettl, *Forgotten Musicians* (1951), 41–46; H. Kristeller, *Der Aufstieg des Koelners Jacques Offenbach . . . in Bildern* (1931), plates 7–11; A. W. Binder, in: *Jewish Music Journal*, 2 no. 1 (1935), 4–6 (augmented in YLBI, 16, 1971); Sendrey, Music, index. [B.B.]

OFFENBACH, JACQUES (1819–1880), French composer of comic operas and operettas. Born in Cologne, Offenbach was the son of Isaac *Offenbach. At the age of 14 young Jacob, as he was then called, was sent to study the cello at the Paris Conservatoire, but after a year, poverty compelled him to earn his living as a cellist in theater orchestras. He received basic instruction in the art of composition from the composer, Jacques *Halévy, and in 1835 took to writing short, sentimental pieces. He attracted attention more because of his eccentric behavior than the quality of his music and his first theatrical works met with little success. They were followed by years of hardship and struggle for recognition. For a time he was a conductor at the Théâtre Français, and gradually built a reputation with works such as *Pépito* (1853) and *Oyayayie ou la Reine des Iles* (1855). It

Engraving of Jacques Offenbach, by Weger. New York, Leo Baeck Institute.

was the Paris World Fair of 1855 that proved a turning point in Offenbach's career. He obtained the lease of a small theater in the Champs-Elysées, and opened it in time for the Fair under the name of *Les Bouffes Parisiens*. Its success surpassed his expectations. He took Paris by storm with musical plays such as *Les Deux Aveugles* and *Le Violoneux* and had to move to a larger theater in the Passage Choiseul. During the ensuing years he wrote about 100 stage works, many of them of enduring brilliance. Among them were *Orphée aux Enfers* (1858), *La Belle Hélène* (1864), *La Vie Parisienne* (1866), *La Grande-Duchesse de Gérolstein* (1867), *La Périchole* (1868), *Madame l'Archiduc* (1874), and finally his grand opera, *Contes d'Hoffmann*, which was first performed in 1881.

Rossini called Offenbach "our little Mozart of the Champs-Elysées"; others summed him up as "the entertainer *[amuseur]* of the Second Empire." All Europe sang his melodies and danced to his rhythms. He was not as happy, however, in his business dealings. In spite of profitable tours to Berlin, Prague, Vienna, London, and New York, he was frequently in debt and had to face harassing lawsuits. After the fall of the Empire in 1870, Offenbach's reputation declined, and during the last few years of his life he was a sick man. He did not live to see his *Contes d'Hoffmann* on the stage; when he died it existed only in an annotated piano score, on the basis of which E. Guirard made the orchestration. Together with his librettists, particularly Ludovic *Halévy and Henri Meilhac, Offenbach created a world of fantasy and joy in which, as the critic Karl *Kraus expressed it, "causality is abolished and everybody lives happily under the laws of chaos. . ."

Bibliography: J. Brindejont-Offenbach, *Offenbach, mon grand-père* (1940); S. Kracauer, *Orpheus in Paris: Offenbach and the Paris of his Time* (1938); A. Decaux, *Offenbach, roi du Second Empire* (1958); A. Moss and E. Marvel, *Cancan and Barcarolle: the Life and Times of Jacques Offenbach* (1954). [F.P.]

OFFENBURG, town in Baden, W. Germany. It appears that there were Jews in Offenburg during the 13th century. A *Judenbad (mikveh)*, 39 ft. (12 m.) deep, dating from this period was discovered in 1857. At the time of the *Black Death (1348–49), three Jews "confessed" under torture that they had poisoned the wells. Although the well was later examined and no signs of poison were found, the Jews were expelled. The town gates were not reopened to Jews until 1862. A community was formally established in 1866. The number of Jews increased from 37 in 1863 to 337 in 1900. An inn was transformed into a synagogue in 1875 and renovated in 1922. Offenburg was the seat of the district rabbinate serving dozens of rural localities, the last rabbi being Siegfried (Sinai) *Ucko. On 9/10 Nov., 1938, the interior of the synagogue was demolished, and 91 Jews were deported to *Gurs on Oct. 22, 1941. In 1967 there were four Jews in Offenburg.

Bibliography: Germ Jud, 2 (1968), 625–6; F. Hundsnurscher and G. Taddey, *Die juedischen Gemeinden in Baden* (1968), passim; FJW, 351–2; O. Kaehni, in: *Veroeffentlichungen des historischen Vereins fuer Mittelbaden*, 49 (1969). [Z.Av.]

OFFICIAL, NATHAN BEN JOSEPH and **JOSEPH,** leading polemicists of Franco-German Jewry of the 13th century. Both were in the service of the archbishop of Sens as financial agents, and hence the name Official. Joseph, the son of Nathan, is also known as Joseph the Zealot (Joseph ha-Mekanne), because he was zealous in the defense of Judaism and compiled a book under this name. Nathan came from a long line of scholars and communal leaders, many of whom were known for their passionate and indefatigable activities in defense of Judaism. Nathan conducted frequent debates with dignitaries of the Church and also with fanatical converts to Christianity. He was an eloquent debater. Joseph calls his father "the chief spokesman in everything." Among his challengers were a cardinal, archbishops, bishops, priests, monks of various orders, and zealous and fanatical converts. The debates are fully described by his son in his *Yosef ha-Mekanne*. Joseph was a pupil of *Jehiel b. Joseph of Paris and was the author of the Hebrew report of the historic disputation of 1240. Joseph, like his father, was an "Official" and continued the tradition of the family as a defender of Judaism. His book *Yosef ha-Mekanne* is a polemical commentary on the Bible, and contains a large collection of Christological passages which were discussed and refuted by Jewish exegetes and polemicists, most of them members of the Official family. Its purpose was to refute the Christological interpretation of the Bible, verse by verse, as a ready handbook of Jewish answers to the challenge of the Church. At the end of the book Joseph added a short criticism of the life of Jesus according to the Gospels, which contains a Jewish challenge to Christianity. Over 40 Jewish disputants, including some proselytes, and ten Christian disputants, including some converts, are mentioned in the book. Noteworthy is the high degree of freedom in the debates and the courage of the Jewish disputants, who accepted all challenges. This fact is especially surprising since the activities of the Officials fall in the period after the Fourth Lateran Council of 1215 with its severe anti-Jewish resolutions. The close familiarity of the Officials with Christian rites and liturgy is also remarkable. The book sheds light on Jewish-Christian relations in day-to-day life in 13th-century France and Germany, reflecting an atmosphere of relative tolerance, in which the Jew is able to accept the challenge and counter with his own challenge. The book is also important for the history of Hebrew translations of the New Testament. *Yosef ha-Mekanne* was also known under the name of *Sefer ha-Nizzaḥon* ("Book of Disputation").

It influenced similar polemical works of collections of Christologies and their refutations according to biblical order, the best known being the *Sefer ha-Nizzaḥon* of Yom Tov Lipmann *Muelhausen.

Bibliography: Z. Kahn, in: REJ, 1 (1880), 222–46, 3 (1881), 1–38; *Mi-Mizraḥ u-mi-Ma'arav*, 4 (1899), 17–25; idem, in: *Festschrift . . . A. Berliner* (1903), Heb. pt., 80–90; E. E. Urbach, in: REJ, 100 (1935), 49–77; Joseph Official, *Yosef ha-Mekanne*, ed. by J. Rosenthal (1970), introd. [J.M.R.]

OFNER, JULIUS (1845–1924), Austrian lawyer and politician. Born in Horshenz, Bohemia, Ofner qualified as a lawyer in Vienna and acquired a considerable reputation as a jurist through his writings on law and philosophy. These included *Der Servitutenbegriff nach roemischem und oesterreichischem Recht* (1884) and *Der Urentwurf und die Beratungsprotokolle des oesterreichischen Allgemeinen Buergerlichen Gesetzbuches* (1887–88). He was elected to the Lower Austrian Diet in 1896 and to the Reichsrat in 1901. Later he joined the Austrian Liberal Party and fought for comprehensive social legislation, including the extension of women's rights and the granting of suspended sentences in criminal cases. He also initiated a law preventing criminal prosecution for petty larceny known as the *Lex Ofner*.

In 1913 Ofner was appointed to the Austrian Supreme Court (*Reichsgericht*) and in 1919 was made permanent referee of its successor, the constitutional court (*Verfassungsgerichtshof*). Ofner was instrumental in obtaining the release of Leopold *Hilsner. He advocated the abolition of ecclesiastical jurisdiction in matters of marriage and divorce, and thereby aroused the hostility of the Roman Catholic majority in Vienna. The Catholics particularly resented the fact that it was a Jew who pressed for this measure, and the Jews were afraid that the intervention of a Jew in Christian affairs would lead to anti-Semitism. In the 1919 elections to the Constituent Assembly, Ofner was defeated but the seat went to another Jew, the Zionist candidate, Robert *Stricker.

Jewish woman and child of Ofran in holiday dress. The child is wearing a complete set of the necklaces peculiar to this community. Jerusalem, Israel Museum Photo Collection, Department of Ethnography. Photo Shulman, 1953.

Memorial in Vienna to Julius Ofner, inscribed with the quotation from Terence: "I am a man; nothing human is foreign to me." Jerusalem, J.N.U.L., Schwadron Collection.

Bibliography: *Julius Ofner zum 70sten Geburtstage* (1915), includes a list of his books; W. Herz, in: *Neue Oesterreichische Biographie*, 13 (1959), 104–11. [J.J.L.]

OFRAN (Ifran), place in the Anti-Atlas region of S.W. Morocco. According to Judeo-African tradition Ofran is regarded as the first site of Jewish settlement in Morocco. Many legends have been created about the ancient community of Ofran, whose first members are said to have arrived from Ereẓ Israel before the destruction of the First Temple in Jerusalem. A Jewish kingdom was set up there which was governed by the Afriat family—then named Efrati. The Jews of this kingdom are said to have belonged to the tribe of Ephraim—one of the lost Ten Tribes of Israel. Indeed, in the modern era the Afriat family administered the affairs of the community of Ofran and of all the communities of the region.

The Jewish cemetery of Ofran is very old, and there are many tombstone inscriptions dating from the Middle Ages. Local tradition ascribes some of them to the first century B.C.E. Pilgrimages were made from every part of Morocco to this cemetery, which contains the remains of revered rabbis and martyrs.

According to local traditions there was a terrible persecution following the destruction of the community by the Byzantine Christians (sic). Other persecutions have been historically proven, the last of which took place in 1792 when the pretender Bou-Hallais, who sought to be proclaimed sultan, arrived in Ofran. He seized 50 Jewish notables and gave them the alternative of converting to

Islam or death by fire. Under the guidance of their leader, Judah Afriat, they jumped one after the other into the huge furnace which had been lit for the occasion. Judah Afriat remained to the end in order to encourage those who faltered. The remains of these martyrs, known as the *Nisrafim* ("Burnt Ones"), were piously gathered and interred in the cemetery of Ofran. The account of their martyrdom was copied on parchment and circulated throughout the country. A popular etymology explains the name Ofran as a combination of *efer* ("the ashes of") and the letter *nun* (=50). Their descendants were greatly esteemed and to the present day they commemorate the anniversary of the event (the 17th of Tishri) by refraining from lighting fires in their homes.

The community of Ofran was prominent and wealthy and a large part of the trans-Sahara trade passed through its hands. After 1792 its members dispersed. They played an important role in the community of *Mogador, especially the members of the Afriat family, and during the 19th century they established a commercial house in London. For more than 50 years the Afriat house was the most important family in Anglo-Moroccan trade. The community of Ofran was reorganized in the 19th century by a few Jewish families of the region (58 families in 1820, 34 in 1883, 122 persons in 1936, and 141 persons in 1951). The community never regained its former prosperity but its members nevertheless lived in security until 1955, when they all emigrated to Israel.

Bibliography: J. M. Toledano, *Ner ha-Ma'arav* (1911), 3–5, 95, 219; J. Ben-Naim, *Malkhei Rabbanan* (1931), s.v. *Judah Afriat;* V. Monteil, in: *Hesperis,* 35 (1948), 151–62; A. I. Laredo, *Berberes y Hebreos en Marruecos* (1954), 126–44.

[D.Co.]

OG (Heb. עֹג, עוֹג), ruler of *Bashan, one of the Amorite kings in the Transjordan area during the time of Moses. The Bible remembers Og as belonging to the race of giants "who was left of the remaining Rephaim," and special attention is paid to the description of his huge iron bedstead (Deut. 3:11). The kingdom of Og comprised Bashan and the Hermon region, and extended to the Jordan river to the west (Josh. 12:4–5). Three or four of the cities of his kingdom are mentioned in the Bible—*Ashtaroth, which was apparently his capital and known as the capital of the realm (Tell el-Amarna letters, no. 197, possibly also Karnaim, cf. Gen. 14:5); Salcah (Josh. 12:5; 13:11, et al.); and *Edrei (Num. 21:33; Josh. 13:12, 31). From this it would appear that his kingdom was one of the remaining *Hyksos kingdoms whose cities at that time were scattered in Palestine. It is also possible that this kingdom was established by Amorites who invaded the area in the time of the Egyptian-Hittite struggle during the reign of Ramses II (13th century). Og was defeated by the Israelites when the eastern side of the Jordan was conquered by those who left Egypt (Num. 21:33, 35; Deut. 3:1ff.). Half of the tribe of Manasseh took Og's land as their inheritance (Josh. 13:31). This victory greatly strengthened the spirit of the people. "Sixty towns . . . fortified with high walls, gates, and bars" were then conquered (Deut. 3:4–5). Echos of this victory, which was of exceptional importance, are also encountered in later passages (Josh. 13:12; Ps. 135:11; 136:20; Neh. 9:22).

[Jo.S.]

Og and Sihon in the Aggadah. Sihon and Og were the sons of Ahijah, whose father was the fallen angel Shamḥazai (Nid. 61a), and of Ham's wife (Yal. Reub. on Gen. 7:7). Og was born before the Flood and was saved from it by Noah on the promise that he and his descendants would serve Noah as slaves in perpetuity (PdRE 23). Sihon and Og were giants, their foot alone measuring 18 cubits (Deut. R. 1:25). Og is identified with Eliezer, the servant of Abraham, who received him as a gift from Nimrod. So that he could not claim reward in the world to come for his services to his master, God paid him in this world by making him a king (Sof. 21:9; ed. M. Higger (1937) 366 and PdRE 16). During his reign he founded 60 cities, which he surrounded with high walls, the lowest of which was not less than 60 miles in height (Sof. *ibid.*). When Og, who was present at the feast Abraham made on the occasion of Isaac's weaning, was teased by all the great men assembled there for having called Abraham a sterile mule, he pointed contemptuously at Isaac, saying, "I can crush him by putting my finger on him," whereupon God said to him, "Thou makest mock of the gift given to Abraham—by thy life thou shalt look upon myriads of his descendants, and thy fate shall be to fall into their hands" (Gen. R. 53:10). Sihon, appointed by the other kings as guardian of Ereẓ Israel, extracted tribute from them (Num. R. 19:29). Sihon and Og were even greater enemies of Israel than was Pharaoh (Mid. Ps. 136:11). When Moses was about to attack them, God assured him that he had nothing to fear, for He had put their guardian angels in chains (*ibid.* and Deut. R. 1:22). Though Moses was undaunted by Sihon, he did fear Og, because he had been circumcised by Abraham (Zohar, Num. 184a) and because of the possibility that the latter's merit might stand him in good stead for having been the "one who escaped and told Abraham" (Gen. 11:13; Nid. 61a). Moses' fears were unfounded, however, in that Og's real motive had been to bring about the death of Abraham so that he could marry Sarah (Deut. R. 1:25).

Sihon was left to his own resources by Og, who was confident of his brother's ability to conquer Israel unaided (Song R. 4:8). Og himself met his death when a mountain three parasangs long, which he had uprooted to cast upon the camp of Israel, was invaded by ants dispatched by God as he carried it upon his head toward his destination. The perforated mountain slipped from Og's head to his neck, whereupon Moses struck him upon the ankle with an ax and killed him (Ber. 54a–b). Though the victory over Sihon and Og was as important as the crossing of the Red Sea, Israel did not sing a song of praise to God upon it as they had upon Pharaoh's destruction, the omission not being made good until the time of David (Mid. Ps. 136:11).

[Ed.]

Bibliography: Aharoni, Land, 191; Noth, Hist Isr, 159–60; idem, in: BBLA, 1 (1949), 1ff.; Bergman (Biran), in: JPOS, 16 (1936), 224–54; Y. Kaufmann, *Sefer Yehoshu'a* (1959), 166. In the Aggadah: Ginzberg, Legends, index.

OHEL (Heb. אֹהֶל; "Tent"), Israel theater company, originally known as the Workers' Theater of Palestine, founded in 1925 by Moshe *Halevy. It was the company's original intention to create a socialist theater whose members combined work in the theater with agricultural and industrial labor. After about two years, however, it became clear that to reach a high level of accomplishment actors must devote themselves fully to their profession. Furthermore, from the outset Ohel found it difficult to procure ideologically suitable plays. The theater's inaugural production was an adaptation of stories by I. L. *Peretz (1926) that was received with great enthusiasm, especially in the rural settlements for which Ohel's work was primarily intended. This was followed by *Dayyagim* ("Fishermen," 1927), a socialist play about the exploitation of fishermen by entrepreneurs. Thereafter, the company turned to biblical plays and the standard international repertoire.

In 1934 Ohel had reached the climax of its development. The early years of the 1930s witnessed its struggle between being a "proletarian" theater and a "national" one. It sometimes even presented "proletarian" plays that were criticized for being incongruent with the actual social and labor situation in Palestine. On its highly successful European tour in 1934, however, Ohel staged mainly biblical and national plays. Upon its return to Palestine, it produced some of its greatest successes, including ("The Good Soldier Schweik," 1935), mostly due to the talents of Meir Margalit, a comedy actor. Two years later it also staged *Yoshe Kalb,* adapted from a novel by the Yiddish author I. J. Singer and directed by Maurice *Schwartz.

The theater progressed until 1958, when it faced a crisis over being suddenly divorced from the Histadrut (General

Meir Margalit as Shimele Soroker in the Ohel production of Shalom Aleichem's play, *Ammekha*, 1964. Photo Mula and Haramaty, Tel Aviv.

Federation of Labor), which had been its parent body. The motivating factor behind the split was the theater's decline in both quality and audience-drawing power. The decline continued until 1961, when Ephraim *Kishon brought his comedy *Ha-Ketubbah* ("The Marriage Contract") to the Ohel. With Margalit in the lead, the play proved to be such a success that it revived the theater for three seasons. Under the new artistic director, Peter Frye, the theater experienced another major hit, Shalom Aleichem's *Ammekha* (1964), and proceeded to produce works by Ionesco, Brecht, and young British playwrights, using actors from outside the repertory company and the aid of foreign directors. The period of revival was short-lived, however, and the theater closed in 1969.

Bibliography: M. Kohansky, *The Hebrew Theatre* (1969), 96–106 and index; M. Halevy, *Darki alei Bamot* (1955). [M.K.]

OHEV BEN MEIR HA-NASI (late 11th–early 12th century), liturgical poet in Spain. Abraham *ibn Daud mentions him in his *Sefer ha-Kabbalah* (ed. G. D. Cohen (1967), 73, 102) together with the poet Moses *ibn Ezra, and refers to him by his Arabic name Ibn Shortmeqas.

Three of Ohev's *piyyutim* were published in *Ḥizzunim* (Constantinople, 1585), a collection of *piyyutim* which were recited in the rite of the "Westerners" who lived in Sicily. One of these, the *ofan "Erelim ve-Hashmalim"* (i.e., various kinds of angels) resembles in several details the famous *piyyut "Malakhim mamlikhim"* ("The Angels Enthrone") of Moses ibn Ezra. One of his *piyyutim* on the Ten Commandments was discovered in the Cairo *Genizah* and published by J. Schirmann.

Bibliography: J. Schirmann, in: YMḤSI, 4 (1938), 277–82; 6 (1945), 332–6; Schirmann, Sefarad, 1 (1961²), 327f.; Davidson, Oẓar, 4 (1933), 360; M. Zulay, in: *Sinai*, 25 (1949), 47–49. [Ed.]

OHIO, state in E. central U.S. Ohio was the first section of the Northwest Territory to become a state (1803). Ohio had a general population of 10,542,000 (1970), of whom an estimated 160,715 were Jews. Ohio's economy is based on manufacturing. The state ranks third in the nation in industrial production.

Joseph Jonas, a watchmaker, was the first Jew permanently to settle in the state (Cincinnati, 1817). By 1824 there were sufficient Jewish families in *Cincinnati to organize the Bene Israel congregation. The "Queen City" remained the preeminent Jewish settlement during most of the 19th century and unexpectedly played a significant role in national Jewish life, largely through the energetic organizational efforts of Rabbi Isaac Mayer *Wise. Wise, in 1854, founded the first Anglo-Jewish periodical to be published west of the Allegheny Mountains (*The Israelite*). In 1873 he organized the *Union of American Hebrew Congregations (U.A.H.C.), the first major American conference of congregations. The U.A.H.C. retained its national headquarters in Cincinnati until 1952. In 1875 Wise founded in Cincinnati, the U.S.'s first rabbinical seminary, *Hebrew Union College.

Daniel L. M. Peixotto was appointed professor at the Willoughby Medical College in 1836. His assignment marked the beginning of Jewish settlement in northern Ohio. By 1839 *Cleveland had its first congregation, the Israelite Society. Other small early settlements took place in Columbus (1838), Dayton (1842), Akron (1850), Hamilton (1855), Piqua (1858), and Portsmouth (1858). The Jewish population of Ohio grew steadily from these early years through the 1920s and has remained rather constant since. Major Jewish settlements are in Cleveland, 85,000; Cincinnati, 28,000; Columbus, 10,000; Dayton, 7,200; Toledo, 7,000; Akron, 6,500; and Youngstown, 4,850. During the 1960s there was some movement of Jews from the smaller towns to the larger cities and a great movement from the center cities to their suburbs. By 1967 less than 1%

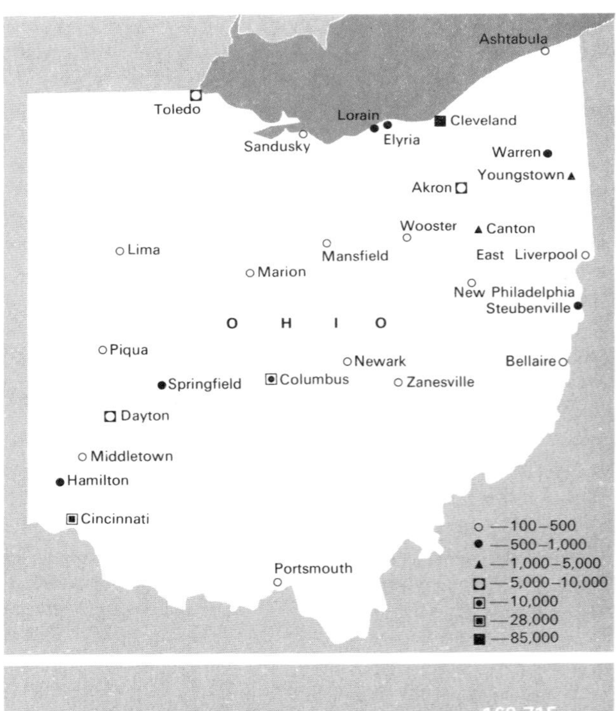

Jewish communities in Ohio. Population figures for 1968.

The Isaac Mayer Wise Temple, also known as the Plum Street Temple, Cincinnati, Ohio. Courtesy American Jewish Archives, Cincinnati.

of Cleveland's Jewish population lived in the municipality.

Ohio's Jewish population has developed a vigorous organizational life. Eleven communities have a central institutional structure, generally known as the Jewish Community Federation (Akron, Canton, Cincinnati, Cleveland, Columbus, Dayton, Lima, Steubenville, Toledo, Warren, and Youngstown). In the late 19th and early 20th centuries social welfare was the sole responsibility of voluntary organizations. In those years, and subsequently, Ohio's Jewish communities established eight community centers, 12 family service agencies, three vocational counseling services, four hospitals, and seven homes for the aged. These institutions were sponsored by and continue under Jewish auspices, although generally they are nonsectarian in sevice. Bellefaire, in Cleveland, is a regional center for the residential care of disturbed adolescents under Jewish auspices.

In 1970 there were more than 100 synagogues in the state. It is estimated that nearly three in four Jewish families maintain membership, and an estimated 20,000 children are enrolled in congregational schools; seven day schools exist in the state. The Hebrew Academy in Cleveland is the largest Jewish parochial school outside New York City. There are Bureaus of Jewish Education in Cleveland, Dayton, and Cincinnati and a College of Jewish Studies in Cleveland. Telshe Yeshiva, uprooted from Lithuania in World War II, has reestablished itself in Wickliffe, near Cleveland, where it has an enrollment of 400 students. Five Anglo-Jewish newspapers are published in Ohio: *The American Israelite* (Cincinnati), *The Cleveland Jewish News, The Ohio Jewish Chronicle* (Columbus), *The Toledo Jewish News,* and *The Youngstown Jewish Times.* The *American Jewish Archives, located on the Hebrew Union College campus, Cincinnati, is a major depository of documents dealing with U.S. Jewish history. The Hebrew Union College and the Temple in Cleveland maintain museums of Jewish ritual art.

Bibliography: D. Philipson, in: AJHSP, 8 (1900), 43–58.

[DA.J.S.]

OHOLIAB (Heb. אָהֳלִיאָב ; "the [divine] father is a [or "my"] tent," or, "tent of the father"), son of Ahisamach; of the tribe of Dan. Oholiab was appointed, together with *Bezalel, to construct the Tent of Meeting and its furnishings (Ex. 31:6; 35:34; 36:1–2; 38:23). He is said to have been a "carver and designer, and embroiderer in blue, purple, and crimson yarns, and in fine linen" (Ex. 35:35; 38:23).

Bibliography: Noth, Personennamen, 158–9.

[ED.]

OHOLOT (Heb. אָהֳלוֹת ; "tents"), the second tractate in the Mishnah order of **Tohorot*. It deals with the ritual impurity conveyed by a corpse (or parts of it) either through physical contact, or through being under a common roof. There are 18 chapters both in the Mishnah and the Tosefta. The original name of the tractate was *Ahilot* (literally, "overtenting"), by which name it is called both in the Tosefta and when it is mentioned in the *Gemara.* It also occurs in several manuscripts of the Mishnah. The name *Oholot* is a popularization attributable to the influence of the passage in Numbers 19:14: "Whoever dies in a tent." There is no *Gemara* to this tractate either in the Palestinian or Babylonian Talmud. Nevertheless, the great amount of commentary on it scattered in both Talmuds is reflected in the fact that G. Leiner published a large "synthetic" *Gemara* on the tractate by assembling and arranging all this material in an orderly manner. The Talmud (Ḥag. 11a) itself notes that the biblical treatment of the subject, consisting as it does of only four verses (Num. 19:11, 14, 16, 22), is very meager, yet rabbinic exposition has made *Oholot* one of the larger tractates of the Mishnah. The ritual uncleanness conveyed by a corpse is of the severest degree (lasting seven days) and requires sprinkling with water mixed with the ashes of the Red *Heifer (see **Parah*) as part of the purification procedure. With the destruction of the Temple, this type of ritual purification became impossible to observe and it lapsed a century or so later. The laws of the tractate, however, retained their relevance for those of priestly descent, who, except in the case of close relatives, must avoid contact with the dead.

Like most tractates of the Mishnah, *Oholot* is composed of several layers. The basic layer (although not the earliest) reflects the teaching of R. Akiva, primarily as taught by his disciple R. Meir. Other sections reflect the interpretation of R. Akiva's teachings by other pupils: Judah, Simeon, and Yose. Because the greater part of the first tractate, *Kelim,* in this same Mishnah order is rightly attributed to R. Yose, several scholars were formerly of the opinion that *Oholot* was also largely written by him. It has been recently demonstrated, however, that the role of R. Yose in this tractate is even less than of his colleagues. English translations were published by H. Danby (1939) and P. Blackman (1955) in their translations of the Mishnah.

Bibliography: G. Leiner, *Sidrei Tohorot,* 2 (1903); H. L. Strack, *Introduction to the Talmud and Midrash* (1945), 60f.; A. Goldberg (ed), *Massekhet Oholot* (1955).

[A.G.]

OHRBACH, family of U.S. department store founders and owners. NATHAN M. OHRBACH (1885–1972) was born in Vienna and taken to the United States at the age of two. He went into the retail dry goods business, and opened his own store in 1911. He established his first department store in New York City in 1923 and another in Newark in 1930. In 1935 he published his memoirs, *Getting Ahead in Retailing.* After his retirement in 1940, his son JEROME KANE OHRBACH (1907–), who was born in Brooklyn, became the head of the firm and its affiliates. In 1948 he added the Los Angeles store to the two his father had founded. Both father and son were prominent in numerous general and Jewish public organizations, including New York's Federation of Jewish

Philanthropies, the American Jewish Committee, Boy Scouts, and the City University of New York.

Bibliography: T. Mahoney and L. Sloane, *Great Merchants* (1966), 310–23. [J.O.R.]

OIL OF LIFE. There appears to have been a tradition in certain circles according to which the tree of life in the Garden of Eden was an olive tree (a tradition which is not found in Talmud or Midrash, cf. Ber. 40a; Gen. R. 15:7). As a result there emerged the belief that immortality is gained by anointing with oil. According to *Apocalypsis Mosis* 9:3, 13:1–2, when Adam fell ill Seth went to the garden to request "the oil of mercy" with which to anoint Adam and restore his health. His entreaty was refused, but the angel Michael promised that oil would be granted to the righteous at the end of days. In the parallel passage in the Latin *Vitae Adae* the oil is referred to as "the tree of mercy from which the oil of life flows" (ch. 36, cf. 40, 41). The same tradition is to be found in the Acts of Pilate (Gospel of Nicodemus III (XIX). This oil is perhaps to be identified with the heavenly oil with which Enoch is anointed and which transforms him into a heavenly being. Called "the good oil," it is shining and fragrant (II En.9=22:8–9, cf. 14=56:2). A further reference to the tree of life in the Garden of Eden as an oil-yielding tree may be found in IV Ezra 2:12—"*lignum vitae erit in illis in odorem unguenti*"—and this idea is also perhaps to be discerned in the Acts of Thomas §157. The furthest circulation of this concept is to be observed in Pseudo-Clement, *Recognitiones* 1:45 which again refers explicitly to the oil of the tree of life. The legend of Seth's quest for the oil had various later developments and acquired considerable importance in Christian legend and art.

Bibliography: Ginzberg, Legends, 5 (1925), 119; E. M. C. Quinn, *Quest of Seth for the Oil of Life* (1962). [M.E.S.]

OILS (Heb. שֶׁמֶן; יִצְהָר, "new oil"; תַּמְרוּק, מֶרְקָחָה, "ointment"), unctuous, inflammable substances, usually liquid, obtained from animal, vegetable, or mineral matter. In Job 29:6 and Deuteronomy 32:13, the references to oil flowing from rocks are hyperboles for fertility or prosperity.

Regarded as one of the characteristic products of the Land of Israel (II Kings 18:32; Jer. 40:10), oil served as an element in food (I Kings 17:12), as a cosmetic (Eccles. 9:7–8), as a fuel for lamps (Ex. 25:6), as a medicine (Isa. 1:6), and as a principal export in foreign trade (I Kings 5:25). As oil was apparently applied to leather shields to keep them supple, the expression "to oil a shield" (*mashaḥ magen*) came to be an idiom for "to make war" (Isa. 21:5). As an extension of its use in the preparation of food, oil occupied a place in sacrifices. As an extension of its cosmetic function, it played a role in various investiture proceedings.

The olives were beaten down from the tree with poles (Isa. 17:6) and were pounded into pulp in mortars or by the feet (Micah 6:15). The pulp was placed in wicker baskets from which the lightest and finest oil could easily run off. This grade of oil, known as beaten oil (Heb. *shemen katit*), is mentioned five times in the Bible. It served as fuel for the lamp in the Tabernacle (Ex. 27:20; Lev. 24:2) and as an element in the obligatory daily meal offerings (Ex. 29:40; Num. 28:5). King Solomon traded this type of oil with Hiram of Tyre in exchange for cedar and cypress wood (I Kings 5:25). After the removal of the beaten oil, a second grade was produced by heating and further pressing the pulp (for the method of extraction in the talmudic period see Mishnah Men. 8:4–5 and *Olive). Ointments were made by boiling aromatic substances in oil (Job. 41:23).

Oil was one of the three staples of life. Thus while Jacob prayed for bread to eat and clothing to wear (Gen. 28:20), Hosea described Israel's basic needs as bread and water, wool and flax, oil and drink (Hos. 2:7). As a typical product of Palestine and as a necessity, oil is listed, particularly in Deuteronomy, among the three blessings of the land in time of God's favor—grain, wine, and oil (Deut. 11:14, etc.) The same three shall be consumed by the nation that will rise against Israel from afar if Israel should lose God's favor through disobedience to His laws (Deut. 28:38–40, 51). S. M. Paul calls attention to the triad of basic needs—food, clothing, and oil—mentioned throughout the Mesopotamian legal tradition, and supports that the three necessities with which a master must provide a slave-girl, referred to in Exodus 21:7–11 are meat, clothing, and oil.

Figure 1. Oil lamp, pottery, with reliefs of a *menorah* on the handle and fruit basket near the spout. Nazareth, third/fourth century C.E. Jerusalem, Reifenberg Collection.

In addition, anointing with oil provided protection from the sun. As an element in baking (Num. 11:8; I Kings 7:12), oil played a role also in sacrifices, which are called God's bread (Heb. *leḥem 'Elohim,* Lev. 21:6). The obligatory daily morning and evening burnt offerings included a tenth of a measure of choice flour mixed with a quarter *hin* of beaten oil (Ex. 29:40; Num. 28:5). An individual's voluntary meal offering could be of five types, all of which included oil. These were 1) raw flour on which oil and frankincense were poured; 2) unleavened cakes mixed with oil; 3) unleavened wafers spread with oil; 4) broken griddle cakes on which oil was poured; and 5) choice flour fried in oil (Lev. 21:1–7).

The amount of oil and flour for the personal offering was determined in proportion to the size of the accompanying animal sacrifice according to the following scale: sheep, a

Figure 2. Oil lamp, bronze, with handle in the form of a *menorah*, supported by a *lulav*, an *etrog*, and a *shofar*. Thought to be from Alexandria fourth/fifth century C.E. Jerusalem, Israel Museum (on loan from M. Shaar Schloessinger, New York).

tenth of a measure of fine flour and a quarter *hin* of oil; ram, two-tenths of a measure of flour and one-third of a *hin* of oil; ox, three-tenths of a measure of flour and a half *hin* of oil.

Oil was regarded as a symbol of honor (Judg. 9:9), joy (Ps. 45:8), and favor (Deut. 33:24; Ps. 23:5). Therefore, oil was to be withheld from offerings associated with disgrace, sorrow, and disfavor, just as it was withheld from the body in time of mourning (II Sam. 12:20; Dan. 10:3; see *Mourning). Thus it is stated with reference to the special sacrifice offered when a man suspects his wife of adultery: "No oil shall be poured upon it and no frankincense should be laid on it, for it is a meal offering of remembrance which recalls wrong doing" (Num. 5:15). Likewise the choice flour of a sin offering is to be free of both oil and frankincense (Lev. 5:11).

In the ritual purification of a person who has recovered from leprosy oil plays a major role. The sacrifice offered on the eighth day of the procedure includes an offering of choice flour mixed with oil and the presentation of a *log* of oil—the largest measure of oil called for in any biblical rite. Some of the oil is sprinkled "before the Lord" seven times, as was blood. Some is placed on the right ear, right thumb, and right big toe of the recovered leper, where blood has already been placed; that which is left over is poured on his head. These rites symbolize the restoration of God's favor and the return of honor and joy to a man who had previously been disgraced and who had observed rites characteristic of mourning (Lev. 13:45). From the association of oil with vigor and fertility (Ps. 36:9), as, for example, in the term "son of oil" (Heb. *ben shemen*) for "fertile" (Isa. 5:1), it may be surmised that the sprinkling of the leper with oil is also symbolic of his restoration to life since the Talmud regards the leper as "a dead person" (Ned. 64b).

Virtue is frequently likened to fragrant oil (Ps. 133:2; Song 1:3; Eccles. 7:1) because both are so costly to obtain. Thus wisdom writers warn against extravagant use of oil (Prov. 21:17, 20), while the historical books of the Bible testify to its having been guarded as were silver and gold (I Chron. 9:29; 27:28). Perfumed oil was among the treasures which Hezekiah revealed to Merodach-Baladan (II Kings 20:13; Isa. 39:2). As a symbol of affluence, Isaiah (28:1, 4) associates oil with arrogance.

As an element in the normal grooming of all classes of people in the Ancient Near East, anointing with oil, like the washing that preceded and the dressing that followed it (Ezek. 16:9–10; Ruth 3:3), was symbolic of a change in status throughout the Ancient Near East. The practice of anointing in legal and cultic proceedings is to be understood in the light of the role of ablutions and the changing of garments. The Bible speaks frequently of donning victory (e.g., Isa. 59:7), honor (Ps. 104:1), disgrace (Job 8:22), etc. Likewise, it prescribes washing as the key to ritual purity (Ex. 30:20; Lev. 22:6, etc.). It is not surprising, therefore, that the consecration of Aaron to the priesthood included washing (Lev. 8:6), donning special garments (Lev. 8:7–9), and anointing his head with oil (Lev. 8:12). The consecration of Aaron's sons as priests also included these three elements (Lev. 8:6, 13, 30).

Akkadian documents from Ugarit mention the anointing of manumitted slave girls, while the Middle Assyrian laws (sections 42–43; Pritchard, Texts, 183–4) prescribe the anointing of the bride prior to marriage. In the Bible, God instructs Elijah to appoint Elisha a prophet by anointing him with oil (I Kings 19:16). Similarly, the spirit of the Lord is said to have come upon King David from the time he was anointed (I Sam. 16:13). Both in Ugarit (V AB, B 31ff.; Pritchard, Texts, 136) and in the Bible (Lev. 8:10–11), anointing with oil is associated with the dedication of temples as well as of people. Thus Jacob dedicates an altar at Beth-El by anointing it with oil (Gen. 28:18).

The anointing of kings, attested among peoples of the Ancient Near East only in Israel and among the Hittites, is mentioned in the Bible in connection with Saul (I Sam. 10:1), David (I Sam. 16:1), Solomon (I Kings 1:39), Absalom (II Sam. 19:11), Jehoash (II Kings 11:12), Jehoahaz (II Kings 23:30), and Hazael of Aram and Jehu son of Nimshi of Israel (I Kings 19:15–16). While Saul, David, Hazael, and Jehu were anointed by prophets, Solomon and Jehoash were anointed by priests. Of Absalom and Jehoahaz it is simply stated that "they anointed him." This last expression may be simply an idiom meaning "they made him king." It is certainly in this sense that Jotham employs the phrase in Judges 9:8 "the trees went to anoint (Heb. *limsho'aḥ*) over them a king." Likewise the noun "anointed one" (Heb. *mashi'aḥ*) is employed as a poetic synonym for "king" (Heb. *melekh;* II Sam. 22:51). Deutero-Isaiah thus calls Cyrus the Lord's "anointed" (Isa. 45:1), while he refers to the rulers who the Lord will subdue for Cyrus simply as "kings." Psalm 2:2 similarly contrasts the Lord's "anointed," the Davidic king of Zion, with the "kings of the earth." It is understandable, therefore, that "anointed" should eventually be the term for the human instrumentality of eschatological redemption (see *Messiah and *Anointing).

As a typical product of the land of Israel with so many diverse uses, oil played an important part in Israel's relations with her neighbors. Thus King Solomon traded 1,000 *kor* of wheat and 20 *kor* of beaten oil annually in exchange for a steady supply of cedar and cypress wood from Sidon (I Kings 5:24–25; II Chron. 2:14–15). Likewise, the same trade was revived in the sixth century by those who returned in the days of Zerubabbel and Jeshua (Ezra 3:7). Hosea 12:2 mentions sending oil to Egypt. D. J.

McCarthy notes that the expression "oil is sent to . . ." in that context appears to be a synonym for "conclude a treaty." If so, the idiom is typical of treaty terminology like "to dissect a calf" (Jer. 34:18), "covenant of salt" (Num. 8:19) and the Greek σπονδη "treaty," "libations"—all examples of synechdoche. See also *Olive, *Incense and Perfumes, *Cosmetics. [M.I.G.]

In the Talmud. Although, as stated above, the only oil employed to any extent in biblical times was *olive oil, in the period of the Talmud, many other oils (and fats) were in common use. Those oils and fats were animal, mineral, and especially vegetable. The first two Mishnayot of the second chapter of tractate *Shabbat* give a comprehensive list: pitch, wax, *kik*-oil, tail fat, tallow, both melted and solid, sesame oil, nut oil, fish oil, colocynth oil, tar, and naphtha. The wax was the residue from honey. There is a controversy as to the identity of *kik*. The identification accepted today is that it is identical with the *kikayon* of Jonah 4:6, i.e., castor oil which is mentioned in the Talmud (Shab. 21a), but two alternative suggestions are made: one that it is produced from a fish of that name (despite the fact that fish oil is specifically mentioned in the next Mishnah) while another opinion is that it is cottonseed oil. In the Jerusalem Talmud (Shab. 2:1, 4c) it is also regarded as of animal origin, but derived from a bird and it is even identified with the *ka'at* (JPS "pelican") of Leviticus 11:18. Symmachus declares that the only animal oil which may be used for the Sabbath lamp is fish oil and there is no doubt that other oils of animal origin were known and used for secular purposes (Shab. 25b).

An account of the availability of various oils is given in a protest against the opinion of Tarfon that only olive oil may be used for the Sabbath lamp: "What shall the Babylonians then do, who have only sesame oil, or the people of Medea who have only nut oil, or the Alexandrians who have only radish oil, or the people of Cappadocia who have none of these, but only naphtha?" (Shab. 26a). Sesame oil was, as is suggested in this passage, the most common oil in Babylonia, as olive oil was in Ereẓ Israel. As a result, if a man took a vow to abstain from oil without specifying which, in Ereẓ Israel it was taken to refer to olive oil, but in Babylonia to sesame (Ned. 53a). They fulfilled the same needs, for fuel, light, and food. Although extensively cultivated (BB 106a, Git. 73a), they were comparatively expensive and stated to be dearer than wheat, dates, or pomegranates (BM 21a, 104b). Oil presses are mentioned in Nehardea and Pumbedita (BK 27b).

To a different category belong balsam oil and rose oil, which were used as unguents. The former was too volatile and inflammable to be used as fuel, and a case is actually cited of a mother-in-law planning and carrying out the murder of her daughter-in-law by telling her to adorn herself with it and then light the lamp (Shab. 26a). Rose oil was so expensive in Ereẓ Israel that its use was limited to "princes"; in Sura in Babylonia, however, it was in plentiful supply and therefore used by all (Shab. 111b). [L.I.R.]

Figure 3. Marginal illumination showing Samuel anointing David with oil (center), with a Madonna and child above. From the Theodore Psalter, executed in the monastery of Studion, Constantinople, 1066. London, British Museum, Add. Ms. 19352, fol. 106.

Bibliography: E. Kutsch, *Die Salbung als Rechtsakt im Alten Testament und im alten Orient* (ZAWB, 87, 1963); D. J. McCarthy, in: VT, 14 (1964), 215–21; J. S. Licht, in: EM, 5 (1968), 526–31; S. M. Paul, in: JNES, 28 (1969), 48–53; Krauss, Tal Arch, 1 (1910), 234–7; 2 (1911), 211–27; J. Newman, *Agriculture Life of the Jews in Babylonia* (1932), 101–4.

OISTRAKH, DAVID FEDOROVICH (1908–), Russian violin virtuoso. Born in Odessa, Oistrakh studied the violin from the age of five with *Stoljarsky, made his first public appearance in 1914, and attended the Institute of Music and Drama in Odessa, 1923–26. After winning other prizes he gained international attention when he won the first prize at the Queen Elizabeth competition in Brussels in 1937. Attached to the Moscow Conservatory, he became professor in 1939 and head of the violin department in 1950. On his subsequent world tours he performed in Paris and London in 1953, in the U.S. in 1955, and was acknowledged everywhere as a master. From 1961 he also appeared as a conductor. Foremost Soviet composers (Prokofiev, Miaskovsky, Shostakovich, Khachaturian) wrote violin works for him, and he received many Soviet awards. His son IGOR OISTRAKH, (1931–), also a violinist, studied with his father at the Moscow Conservatory (1949–55). Winner of the International Festival of Democratic Youth in Budapest (1949) and the Wieniawski International Contest in 1952, he became a teacher of violin at Moscow Conservatory in 1958, and often appeared in duets with his father.

David Oistrakh. Courtesy Israel Philharmonic Orchestra. Tel Aviv. Photo Isaac Berez, Tel Aviv.

Bibliography: Baker, Biog Dict; MGG; Riemann-Gurlitt; V. Bronin, *David Oystrakh* (Rus., 1954); D. Oistrakh, in: *Sovetskaya Muzyka*, 22 no. 9 (1958), 98–105. [M.Go.]

OKHLAH VE-OKHLAH (Heb. אָכְלָה וְאָכְלָה), early collection of masoretic notes to the Bible text, arranged partly alphabetically and partly in the order of the books of the Bible. Its date and author are unknown but it was mentioned for the first time by Jonah ibn Janāḥ in the tenth century (Abu al-Walīd Marwān ibn Janāḥ, cf. חלך), by whom it was considered the most important book on the subject. Originally called *Ha-Masoret ha-Gedolah* by Rashi and R. Jacob Tam, its present name, first mentioned by R. David Kimḥi (*Sefer Shorashim*, ed. Biesenthal (1864), 334 cf. קרב), derives from the opening words of the first section, which is an alphabetic list of pairs of words occurring only twice in the Bible (once with *waw* and once without), i.e., *okhlah* (I Sam. 1:9) and *ve-okhlah* (Gen. 27:19). Jacob b. Ḥayyim gained most of his information for the *masora finalis* (list of masoretic notes found at the end of a Bible, as opposed to the *masora marginalis* written on the sides of its pages) from *Okhlah ve-Okhlah* for his Bomberg edition of the Bible (Venice, 1524/5).

After lying in obscurity for over 300 years it was rediscovered and published by S. Frensdorff (*Das Buch Ochlah W'ochlah*, 1864), and shortly afterwards a second manuscript was discovered by H. Hupfeld. Hupfeld's manuscript contains 120 citations more than Frensdorff, and it is concluded that the book was expanded over the centuries (see Graetz, bibl.).

For full discussion of the subject see *Masorah (Supplementary Entries).

Bibliography: E. Wuerthwein, *The Text of the Old Testament* (1957), 21–22; S. Frensdorff, *Das Buch Ochlah W'ochlah* (1864), introd.; H. Hupfeld, in: ZDMG, 21 (1867), 201–20; Graetz, in: MGWJ 36 (1887), 1–34.
[Ed.]

OKLAHOMA, state in S. central United States. The Jewish population in 1967 was between c. 5,000 and 6,000 out of 2,500,000. The vast majority resided in Tulsa and Oklahoma City, the two large metropolitan areas of the state. Extensive white settlement began with the famous "run" of April 22, 1889. Jews began coming to Oklahoma and Indian Territory as early as 1875. There were also Jews in the "run" of 1889. Leo Meyer of Tulsa was active in state political offices in the early territorial and statehood days. In 1890 High Holiday services were conducted in Oklahoma City. In Ardmore there were 50 Jewish people in 1890 and about 100 in 1907 when a Reform congregation, Temple Emeth, was organized. In the 1890s Jake Katz went to Stillwater and prospered. In Perry a Jew named Kretsch arrived in 1892 from his native Bohemia. Subsequently he served as mayor of the town for three or four terms. Seymor C. Heyman arrived in Oklahoma City in 1901, eventually served as president of the local Chamber of Commerce, and later became president of the school board, the only Jew to hold these offices in Oklahoma. Sam and Dave Daube of Ardmore and the Sondheimer family of Muskogee were famed for their philanthropy. Dave Schonwald, a Hungarian immigrant, came to Oklahoma Territory before the turn of the 20th century, served as a penniless section hand on the Santa Fe Railroad in Guthrie, and subsequently became president of a gas and oil company and a bank in Blackwell, ending his days as a prominent Oklahoma City businessman and Jewish leader.

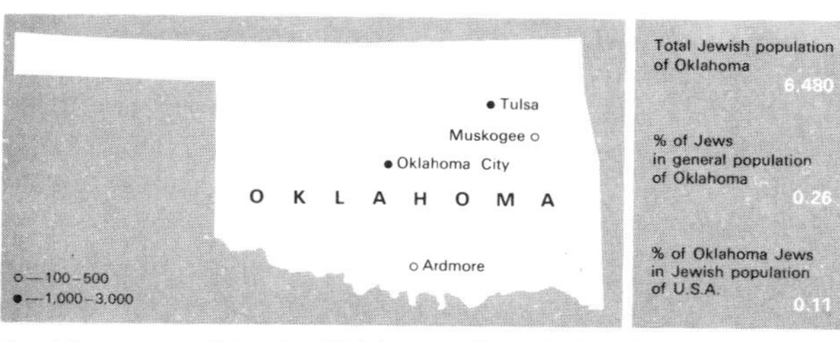

Jewish communities in Oklahoma. Population figures for 1968.

The *bimah* of Temple B'nai Israel, the Reform congregation of Oklahoma City, Okla. Courtesy Union of American Hebrew Congregations, New York. Photo John W. Gough, Tulsa.

Enid Jewish history began with the Cherokee Strip opening in 1885 when Marius Gottschalk made the "run." In Tecumseh the Krouch brothers, German immigrants, came from Kansas and Colorado to establish a business in the early 1890s. A new elementary school building stands as a memorial to the philanthropy of Max Krouch, while his brother, Julius, who was elected county Commissioner in Pottawatomie County in 1916, and sister Erna, who survived Max, continued to contribute lavishly to Jewish and non-Jewish causes. Julius Krouch was delegate to the Democratic Convention in Denver in 1908 which nominated William Jennings Bryan for president. Max Krouch was chairman of the Excise Board in Pottawatomie County under three governors (Bill Murray, Phillips, and Kerr), until he died in 1948. He also was chairman of the Draft Board in Pottawatomie County during World War II.

In Oklahoma City a Reform congregation, Temple B'nai Israel, was chartered in 1903. Gus Paul, who came from Evansville, Indiana, was a moving figure in the life of the congregation for many years. He was a prominent civic leader and served the municipal government as city attorney. The first ordained rabbi to serve a congregation in Oklahoma was Joseph Blatt. He came in 1906 to minister to the 35 families of Temple B'nai Israel. The Jewish population did not expand in proportion to the growth of the general population. In 1967 the temple's membership numbered 325 families, representing about half of the Jewish population of the city. In 1904 Emanuel Synagogue was organized as an Orthodox congregation. It is now affiliated with the Conservative movement and also embraces about half of the Jewish population of Oklahoma City in its membership. A Jewish community council was organized in 1941 to serve as a fund raising and social service agency.

In Tulsa Temple Israel, Reform, was organized in 1914. Its first rabbi came in 1917. Orthodox congregation B'nai Emunah has its origins in a *minyan* begun by Latvian immigrants in 1903. The Jewish community council of Tulsa was founded in 1938 to raise funds for national and overseas relief. Early Tulsa Jewish life sponsored the Federation of Jewish Charities—taken over by the Tulsa Community Fund—a Mutual Aid Bank, and a Hebrew Free Loan Society.

Muskogee Jewish history began with the arrival of Joseph Sondheimer in 1881. Alexander, the former's son, was the first court reporter in Oklahoma in 1891. Temple Beth Ahabah, the Reform congregation, was founded in 1905 and was heavily supported and endowed by the Sondheimer family. Eight congregations, four of which are staffed by full-time rabbis, serve the religious life of Oklahoma Jewry. Oklahoma Jewry, small though it has been, has participated significantly in the development of every aspect of the state's life. Jews were representatives in the first territorial legislature. There were also Jews in the convention which decided that Indian Territory and Oklahoma Territory should enter the Union as a single state. A number of Jews served in the state legislature through the years. Some have been elected judges and county commissioners, and have held important state and municipal appointive positions.

Bibliography: C. I. Cooper, in: *Oklahoma Jewish Chronicle* (Dec. 1929 and March 1930). [Jo.Le.]

OKO, ADOLPH S. (1883–1944), librarian and expert on Spinoza. Born near Kharkov, Russia, Oko received his education in Germany and went to the United States (1902), where he worked in the Astor Library, New York. In 1906 he was appointed librarian of Hebrew Union College, Cincinnati, retaining the position until 1933 when he resigned. Under his administration the college library was transformed. A new building, designed to hold 40,000 volumes, was opened in 1913, but so great was the rate of expansion that a second building was needed in 1931. In 1911 he began a collection of Spinozana, which he brought to unusual completeness. He also began the development of the college museum. Shortly after World War I Oko visited Europe and purchased 18,000 items, including the Edward Birnbaum music collection as well as manuscripts and printed books. Throughout his life Oko was a devoted student of Spinoza. He was a trustee of the Domus Spinozana at The Hague and a founder and U.S. secretary of the Societas Spinoza. From 1933 to 1938 he devoted himself to research on Spinoza in England, resulting in *The Spinoza Bibliography* (1964). In addition he wrote several bibliographies, among them: *Solomon Schechter, a Bibliography* (1938) and *Bibliography of . . . Kaufman Kohler* (1913). He also wrote many articles in *Menorah-Journal*, of which he was associate editor for many years. After returning to the United States he joined the staff of the American Jewish Committee and was associate editor of the *Contemporary Jewish Record* in 1943/44. [Ed.]

OLAM HA-BA (Heb. עוֹלָם הַבָּא). The term *olam ha-ba* (literally, "the coming world") in contrast to *olam ha-zeh* (literally "this world") refers to the hereafter, which begins with the termination of man's earthly life. This meaning of the expression is clearly implied in the statement of R. Jacob, quoted in *Avot* (4:17): "One moment of repentance and good deeds in this world is better than the entire life of the world to come." The earliest source in which the phrase occurs is Enoch 71:15, which is dated by R. H. Charles (Charles, Apocrypha, 2 (1913), 164), between 105 and 64 B.C.E. A synonym frequently used in place of "the world to come" is *atid lavo* ("What is to come" or "the future") as in Tosefta *Arakhin* 2:7. Often also "the days of the Messiah" are contrasted with the life of this world. An example is the comment by the colleagues of Ben Zoma (1:5) on the phrase "all the days of thy life" (Deut. 16:3) that it includes in addition to this world the era of the Messiah.

Strictly speaking the period referred to by the phrase *olam ha-ba* or its equivalent *atid lavo*, between which and the present order of things comes the age of the Messiah (cf. Zev. 118b; Tosef. Ar. 2:7; also Ar. 13b), is the final order of things beginning with the general resurrection and the last judgment. According to the Palestinian *amora* R. Johanan the golden age of the future pictured by the prophets concerned only the days of the Messiah. As for the world to come, it is said of it, "Eye hath not seen" (Isa. 64:3). His older contemporary, the Babylonian *amora* Samuel, however, held the view that the only difference between the present time and the Messianic era lay in the fact that Israel's current subjection to the rule of alien empires would cease. The new order of things would, therefore, according to him, first commence after the age of the Messiah was over (cf. Sanh. 99a; Ber. 34b).

A cardinal eschatological doctrine of rabbinic Judaism connected with the world to come was that of the restoration to life of the dead. It is listed as a dogma at the beginning of tenth chapter of Sanhedrin. "Whoever says that the revivification of the dead is not proved from the Torah," so it is remarked there, "has no portion in the world to come." The matter was, according to Josephus (Wars, 2:8, 14 and Ant. 18:1, 4), one of the chief points of difference between the Pharisees and the Sadducees, the latter asserting that the soul died together with the body. I *Maccabees, which records events down to the time of John Hyrcanus, whose reign began in the year 135 B.C.E., contains no allusion to it. The first definite historical reference to the Pharisees is that which speaks of the rift which took place between them and the aforementioned John Hyrcanus toward the end of his rule (Jos. Ant. 8:10). The Talmud (Kid. 66a) attributes the incident to his son Alexander Yannai. In the canonical Scriptures the first allusion to a return of the dead to life is made in Isaiah 26:19. However, the Sadducees contended (Sanh. 90b) that the statement "Thy dead shall live, my dead bodies shall stand up" might have referred to the dead whom Ezekiel (37:5ff.) had brought back to life in his vision, not to the general resurrection. An unequivocal reference to resurrection is contained in the last chapter of Daniel (7:2), where it is stated: "And many of those that sleep in the dust will wake, these to eternal life, and those to ignominy and eternal abhorrence." The 11th chapter of the Book of Daniel (21ff.), however, describes events that took place during the rule of Antiochus IV of Syria.

So far as the older books of the Hebrew Scriptures are concerned, man's sojourn on earth is followed by a descent to *Sheol*, which is equivelent to the grave. The patriarch Jacob, upon hearing that his favorite son Joseph had been torn to pieces by a wild beast, moaned that he "would go down in grief to his son in Sheol" (Gen. 37:35). Isaiah (14:3–21) and Ezekiel (31:15–18; 32:17–32) picture it as a dreary, gloomy place, a land of the shades (Isa. 26:19). In the Book of Job (17:13–16) it is portrayed as an abode of worms and decay. This was also, according to Akavyah b. Mahalalel (Avot 3:1), man's destiny after the termination of his life on earth. "The dead do not praise the Lord," said the Psalmist (115:17), "nor those that go down to the silence [of the grave]." Job entertained no hope of revivification. "But when man lieth down," he remarked gloomily, "he does not rise. Till the heavens be no more they will not awake nor be roused out of their sleep" (14:12).

The rewards and punishment promised in the Hebrew Scriptures as requital for man's actions, as for example in Deuteronomy 13ff. and Jeremiah 3:10ff. were, as *Saadiah Gaon already noted (*Book of Beliefs and Opinions*, 9:2), all of this world. It was in order to reconcile the sufferings of the righteous with divine justice that R. Jacob remarked (Kid. 39b) that "there was no reward for virtue in this world" and that R. Tarfon assured those who would occupy themselves with the study of the Torah that the (full) reward of the righteous would be meted out in the hereafter (Avot. 2:16). As for the nature of man's existence in the world to come the Babylonian *amora* Rav, who lived at the beginning of the third century B.C.E., was of the opinion that it was quite unlike life in this world. "There is there," he said, "neither eating, nor drinking, nor any begetting of children, no bargaining or jealousy or hatred or strife. All that the righteous do is to sit with their crowns on their heads and enjoy the effulgence of the [divine] Presence" (Ber. 17a). However, no tannaitic parallel to Rav's conception of the world to come has been found; most of his contemporaries and followers believed in the restoration of the souls into the bodies of the resurrected and their rising from their graves fully clothed (Ket. 111b). Even so bold a thinker as Saadiah Gaon, who lived centuries after the redaction of the Talmud, accepted the dogma of physical resurrection. Moses Maimonides included the bodily revivification of the dead among the Thirteen Articles of the Faith in his commentary on the tenth chapter of Mishnah Sanhedrin, though in his *Guide of the Perplexed* he speaks only of the immortality of the soul, which is an incorporated state, and passes over physical resurrection in silence. The traditional Jewish book of prayers includes a praise of God as the revivifier of the dead. The Reformist prayer book omits it completely. As it is expressed in the tenth chapter of the Mishnah of Sanhedrin, all Israelites, with certain notable exceptions, had, in the view of the *tannaim*, a share in world to come. In the opinion of R. Joshua b. Hananiah the righteous among the gentiles were also to be included (Tos. 13:2). Moses Maimonides incorporated his pronouncement in his code, which states: "The pious of the nations of the world have a portion in the world to come" (Yad, Teshuvah 3:5). It is futile to attempt to systematize the Jewish notions of the hereafter. Since its conception belonged to the realm of *aggadah*, great latitude was allowed the individual imagination. It is on this account that there exists considerable ambiguity about the meaning of the phrase *olam ha-ba*. Did it refer to the final state of man or to the one intermediate between the life of this world and the disposition of his soul in either the Garden of *Eden, which is the eternal abode, after the last judgment, of the righteous, or the *gehinnom* (gehenna), the miserable dwelling place of the wicked (Ber. 28b). The question was also asked where the souls of human beings were kept between the time of their death and the resurrection, which is supposed to take place prior to the last judgment. The answer given by R. Yose ha-Gelili was that there were special store-chambers where the souls of the righteous were deposited, as it is stated (I Sam. 25:29): "The souls of the wicked, on the other hand, would, as the verse goes on to say, "be slung away in the hollow of the sling" (Shab. 152b).

See also *Afterlife; *Messiah; *Beatitude; *Reward and Punishment; *Soul, Immortality of; *Resurrection of the Dead.

Bibliography: G. F. Moore, *Judaism in the first Centuries of the Christian Era*, 2 (1946), 377–95; Saadiah Gaon, *The Book of Beliefs and Opinions*, tr. by S. Rosenblatt (1948), 323–56; Moses Maimonides, *The Guide of the Perplexed*, tr. by S. Pines (1963), passim; C. Montefiore and H. Loewe, *Rabbinic Anthology* (1938), ch. 31 and index, s.v. *World to Come;* A. Cohen, *Everyman's Talmud* (1932), ch. 11 and index, s.v. *World to Come;* M. Kadushin, *The Rabbinic Mind* (1952), index, s.v. *Olam ha-Ba; World to Come*.

[S.R.]

OLBRACHT, IVAN (pseudonym of **Kamil Zeman;** 1882–1952), Czech author. His mother was Jewish; his father, a non-Jewish writer. Olbracht's early works, *O zlých samotářích* ("Of Evil Lonely Men," 1913), *Žalář nejtemnější* ("Darkest Prison," 1918), and *Podivné přátelství herce Jesenia* ("The Strange Friendship of the Actor Jesenius," 1919), were psychological masterpieces. He became a communist after a visit to the U.S.S.R. which inspired his *Obrazy ze současného Ruska* ("Pictures from Contemporary Russia," 1920). Later he concentrated on social themes, without, however, embracing "socialist realism."

His *Anna proletářka* ("Anne the Proletarian," 1928) is both a psychological and a social novel, while *Nikola Šuhaj loupežník* ("The Bandit Nikola Šuhaj," 1933) remains, despite its social-revolutionary tendency, a delightful ballad about a "Robin Hood" hero from sub-Carpathian Ruthenia. This poor, eastern region of Czechoslovakia also provides the setting for three more works by Olbracht: *Země beze jména* ("Land Without a Name, 1932), *Hory a staletí* ("Mountains and Centuries," 1935), and *Golet v údolí* ("*Galut* in the Valley," 1937), the last serving as a literary memorial to ḥasidic life in the sub-Carpathian region. One of his children's books, *Biblické příběhy* ("Bible Tales," 1939), is a modern treatment of Old Testament stories. Olbracht also translated Marx and Engels' *Communist Manifesto* into Czech. He was for some years a member of the Czechoslovak parliament.

Bibliography: P. Váša and A. Gregor, *Katechismus dějin české literatury* (1925); B. Václavek, *Česká literatura XX. století* (1935); J. Kunc, *Slovník českých spisovatelů beletristů* (1957).

[Av.D.]

OLDENBURG, city and former state in Lower Saxony, W. Germany. Jews lived in the city of Oldenburg in the early 14th century. In 1334 the municipal council decided to cease issuing letters of protection *(Schutzbriefe)* to Jews; however, they continued to reside there under the protection of the duke of Oldenburg, who agreed that they be allowed to deal only in money lending. The community ceased during the *Black Death persecutions (1348). Jews must have returned soon after for a privilege of 1365 granted them the same rate of interest as had been accorded the Jews of Bremen. Between 1667 and 1773 Oldenburg belonged to Denmark. In this period the dukes made use of the services of Sephardi *Court Jews and financiers from

The Oldenburg synagogue, built in 1835 and destroyed during *Kristallnacht*, 1938. From L. Trepp, *Die Landesgemeinde der Juden in Oldenburg*, 1965.

Hamburg, such as Jacob Mussaphia and his sons. A few Jews from Oldenburg attended the Leipzig fairs. Three Jewish families lived in Vechta, in the duchy of Oldenburg, in the middle 18th century. Their number increased during French occupation after 1810. A law of Aug. 25, 1827, organized communal affairs, made German names and language compulsory, regulated the conditions of their inferior civil status, and ordered a *Landrabbiner* to be appointed for Oldenburg. The first to hold this office was Nathan Marcus *Adler, who took office in 1829 and moved to Hanover in 1831. Samson Raphael *Hirsch succeeded him until1841 and there he wrote his *Choreb*. His successor was Bernhard Wechsler (d. 1874) who consecrated the new synagogue in the city in 1835. In 1859 Jewish affairs were reorganized by a new comprehensive law. The Jews of the duchy numbered 1,359 in 1900; by 1925 their number had declined to 1,015 (out of which 250 lived in the city of Oldenburg). Sizable communities existed in the towns of Delmenhorst, Jever, Varel, Vechta, and Wildeshausen; and in the region of Birkenfeld, Bosen, Hoppstaedten, Oberstein, Idar, and Soetern. The synagogue of Oldenburg was destroyed on Nov. 9/10, 1938, and the last *Landrabbiner*, Leo Trepp, was deported to *Sachsenhausen. The community was annihilated during the war. In 1959, 35 Jews were again living in Oldenburg and in 1967 a memorial was erected on the site of the synagogue.

Bibliography: L. Trepp, *Die Landesgemeinde der Juden in Oldenburg* (1965); idem, *Eternal Faith, Eternal People* (1962), 294–7; D. Mannheimer, *Gesetzessammlung betreffend die Juden im Herzogtum Oldenburg* (1918); Germ Jud, 2 (1968), 627–8; FJW (1932/33), 410–4; H. Schnee, *Die Hoffinanz und der moderne Staat*, 3 (1955), 124–7; *Zeitschrift fuer Demographie und Statistik der Juden*, 4 (1908), 14. [EJ/Z.Av.]

OLEANDER (mishnaic Heb. הַרְדּוּף *(harduf)* or הִרְדּוּפְנִי *(hirdufeni)*), the evergreen shrub with rose-colored flowers that grows wild in Israel on the banks of rivers. Cultivated varieties having flowers of various colors are also grown. Its leaves are arranged at the nodes of the stalk in groups of three. In this respect it resembles the three-leaved *myrtle. The Talmud (Suk. 32b) raises the possibility that by *eẓ avot* ("plaited tree"), one of the four species taken on the Feast of Tabernacles (Lev. 23:40), the oleander may be intended, but the suggestion is rejected on the grounds that the Bible would not have required a plant containing a dangerous poison to be taken (see Rashi, Suk. 32b). A fowl that has eaten oleander "is forbidden because of danger to life" (Ḥul. 3:5). It is, in fact, very poisonous and its ground leaves are sometimes used as mouse poison. One *tanna* held that it was because of its bitterness that this tree was used by Moses to sweeten the bitter waters (Ex. 15:25) "for God heals with that with which he wounds" (Ex. R. 50:3). The Talmud (Pes. 39a) mentions a bitter plant called *hardufenin* which is not poisonous and was eaten as a salad. The reference is apparently to the *Scorzonera*, to which the name *hardufenin* is given in modern Hebrew.

Bibliography: Loew, Flora, 1 (1924), 206–12; H.N. and A.L. Moldenke, *Plants of the Bible* (1952), index; J. Feliks, *Ẓimḥiyyat ha-Mishnah*, in: *Marot ha-Mishnah, Seder Zera'im* (1967), 38. [J.F.]

OLESKO, small town in Ukrainian S.S.R. (E. Galicia). Twelve buildings in Olesko were owned by Jews in 1628. The provincial council of *Bratslav (see *Councils of Lands) convened here in the 18th century. In 1765, 771 Jewish taxpayers were registered in Olesko and its "boroughs." The Jewish population numbered 636 in 1920 (10.7% of the total population). Noted rabbis who lived in Olesko include Ze'ev (Wolf) b. Samuel, author of *Hiddushei ha-Razah* (Zolkiew, 1771). *Ḥasidism had a following in Olesko which was the residence of *ẓaddikim;* one of them opposed the establishment of a modern Jewish school there by the Israelitische *Allianz of Vienna; it was eventually opened in 1910 after a fierce struggle. [N.M.G./Ed.]

In 1931 some 600 Jews lived in Olesko. Soon after the outbreak of World War II and until June–July 1941 the whole of the district of Tarnopol, in which Olesko was situated, was under Soviet administration. After the Nazi occupation the town belonged to the "District Galizien" created in August 1941 by the German authorities and incorporated into the General Government. The majority of the 472 Jews remaining in Olesko were deported to *Belzec concentration camp on Aug. 29, 1942. A Jewish labor camp, where "selected" men were employed by the Nazis, was situated in the town or in its vicinity; it was liquidated in June 1943. [De.D.]

Bibliography: T. Brustin-Bernstein, in: *Bleter far Geshikhte*, 6, no. 3 (1953), passim.

OLESNICA (Ger. **Oels**), town in Silesia, Poland. The first mention of a synagogue dates from 1417. Five members of the local community were accused of desecration of the *Host in *Breslau in 1453. The Jews were expelled in 1492, but by 1521 seven families were again resident. Hebrew printing in Olesnica is mainly connected with the well-known 16th-century Jewish printer, Ḥayyim *Schwarz, who, in 1530, produced the first Hebrew book printed by a Jew in Germany, a handsome Pentateuch (with the Five Scrolls and *haftarot*), of which only two copies have been preserved. In 1535 a violent storm destroyed the press bringing financial ruin to Schwarz's successors—Samuel Ester and Eliakim Herliz—and to the many members of the community who were employed by them. In the same year the community also tried in vain to intercede on behalf of their persecuted brethren in Jaegerndorf. With the destruction of the press, the community gradually dispersed and the synagogue was converted to a church (consecrated in 1695). In 1758 24 Jews were again living in the town. A synagogue served 121 persons when it was consecrated in 1840 and 330 in 1880. By 1933 144 remained, but by 1939 the number had fallen as a result of Nazi persecution.

Bibliography: M. Brann, *Geschichte der Juden in Schlesien* (1917), 205, n. 8, passim; A. Grotte, *"Synagogen," Kirchen in Schlesien* (1930), 3–12; idem, *Synagogenspuren in schlesischen Kirchen*, 1 (1937), 12–20; FJW, 95; M. Brann, in: *Jahresbericht des juedisch-theologischen Seminars* (Breslau; 1910), 167–73; A. M. Habermann, in: KS, 33 (1957/8), 509. [Ed.]

°**OLEŚNICKI, ZBIGNIEW** (1389–1455), bishop of Cracow. During the reign of Ladislau II Jagello of Poland, Oleśnicki was the power behind the throne of Wladislaw Warnenczyk and the spiritual agitator of contemporary hatred of the Jews. He was also the patron of Jan *Dlugosz, the anti-Jewish Polish chronicler. Oleśnicki invited John of *Capistrano to Poland in 1453, and his arrival coincided with the Jews' endeavor to have their general privileges agreed upon by the king. In the resulting riots of Cracow many Jews fled and a few converted to Christianity. Oleśnicki personally took care of some of the converts. He charged Casimir IV Jagello with favoring the Jews, stating that their privileges included articles which were against Christian religious principles. In a letter addressed to the Sejm at Leczyca he called these privileges "disgusting and abject." He demanded the introduction of the Jewish *badge in Poland. After the Polish armies had been defeated by the Teutonic Order at Chojnice, Oleśnicki increased his pressure on the king. At the congress of Great

Poland's nobility at Cerekwica in 1454, the king agreed to issue anti-Jewish laws. The knights, facing a new military expedition, forced the king to keep his promise, and in the same year Casimir IV Jagello issued the Nieszawa statutes which canceled the general privileges accorded to the Polish Jews and reinstated the Warta statute of 1423 making moneylending by Jews to Christians more difficult.

Bibliography: M. Balaban, *Historia Żydów w Krakowie i na kazimierzu 1304–1868*, 1 (1931); E. Maleczynska, *Społoczeństwo polskie pierwszej połowy XV wieku wobec zachodnich agadnień* (1947).

[J.Go.]

OLEVSKI, BUZI (1908–1941), Soviet Yiddish writer. Born in Volhynia, Olevski was raised in Russia and published his first poems in *Minsker Shtern* at the age of 18, eliciting the favorable reaction of critics. He published stories and poems in various Soviet periodicals and anthologies.

His stories contain depictions of people in the Civil War, in the air force, the destruction of the Jewish *shtetl*, and the heroism of the Red Army. He also wrote children's literature. Among his books are *In Vuks* (1930), *Shakhtes* (1933), *Alts Hekher un Hekher* (1933), *Kinder fun Mayn Elter* (1935), *Af Birobidzhaner Erd* (1938), *Onheyb Lebn* (1939), and *Far der Bine* (1929) of which he was an editor.

Bibliography: LNYL, 1 (1956), 103–4. [I.H.B.]

OLGIN, MOSHE J. (adopted name of **Moses Joseph Novomisky**; 1878–1939), writer, editor, and translator. Born near Kiev, Olgin studied there. He joined a student revolutionary group which developed in the Kiev branch of the Jewish Labor Bund. After leaving Kiev University in 1904, he lived in Vilna where he joined the editorial board of the Bundist *Arbeter Shtime* and the legal publication *Der Veker*. At the end of 1906, Olgin left Russia and settled in Germany, where he studied at the University of Heidelberg. He returned to Russia in 1909 and became active as a teacher and lecturer. In 1913 Olgin moved to Vienna and became the coeditor of the Bundist weekly *Di Tsayt* which was published in St. Petersburg. In 1914 he went to New York, and became a staff member of the *Jewish Daily Forward*. After the split in the Jewish Socialist Federation in 1921, he joined the Workers' Party. He was one of the founders of the Communist Yiddish Daily *Freiheit* (later *Morning Freiheit*) and remained its editor until his death. He was also the editor of the monthly *Der Hamer* (1926) and from 1932, New York correspondent of the Moscow *Pravda*. A prolific writer, he followed the Communist party line and justified Arab riots and pogroms in Palestine. Olgin wrote about political affairs, literature, and the theater.

His books include: *Mayn Shtetl in der Ukrain* (1921); *Fun Mayn Togbukh* (1926); and a posthumous collection of essays *Kultur un Folk* (1949). His books in English include: *The Soul of the Russian Revolution* (1917); *A Guide to Russian Literature* (1920); and *Gorki, Writer and Revolutionist* (1933). Olgin translated Lenin into Yiddish as well as Jack London's *The Call of the Wild* (1919) and John Reid's *Ten Days that Shook the World* (1920).

Bibliography: Rejzen, Leksikon, 1 (1926), 92–97; *Tsum Ondenk fun M. Olgin* (1939); LNYL, 1 (1956), 88–91. [E.Sch.]

OLGOPOL, townlet in Vinnitsa oblast, Ukrainian S.S.R. Before the 1917 Revolution, Olgopol was a district town in the province of Podolia. The Jewish population in 1847 was 247; by 1897 the number had increased to 2,473 (30% of the total population). Olgopol suffered heavily in 1919 at the hands of the Ukrainian bands which were active in the surroundings. Jews were also attacked by the armies of *Denikin. In 1926 the Jewish population numbered 1,660 (76.4% of the total). At the time of the German-Rumanian occupation (July 1941) most of the Jews fled from the townlet, which was incorporated into the zone annexed by the Rumanians (*Transnistria). The Jews who remained were concentrated into a ghetto together with about 600 Jews who had been expelled from *Bessarabia and *Bukovina, all of them being submitted to forced labor in the vicinity. There was no information on the presence of Jews in Olgopol in 1971. [Y.S.]

°**OLIPHANT, LAURENCE** (1829–1888), English writer and traveler, Christian mystic, and active supporter of the return of the Jewish people to Ereẓ Israel. Born of a Scotch family in the Cape of Good Hope, Oliphant traveled in many countries and wrote impressive travel books. From 1865 to 1867 he was a member of parliament. During the Russo-Turkish War (1878) he began to take an interest in the Holy Land and Jewish settlement there, in a blending of political, economical, and religious-mystic considerations. He supported Turkey and thought that the best way to revive it was by improving the condition of its Asian regions, first and foremost Palestine. He decided to submit to the sultan a plan for large-scale Jewish settlement in Palestine, supported by resources from abroad. With letters of recommendation from Lord Beaconsfield and Lord Salisbury, who approved his plan and a letter from the French minister of foreign affairs, William Henry Waddington, he went to Palestine in 1879. He investigated the country and arrived at the conclusion that the best place to start Jewish settlement was the Gilead region in Transjordan. Consequently, he negotiated with the authorities in Constantinople concerning tenancy rights and a concession for settlement. The Turkish cabinet approved the proposal, but the sultan Abdul Ḥamid rejected it for fear that it was a British intrigue. The pogroms of 1881 in Russia moved Oliphant to new undertakings. He established a group of influential Christians in London for the purpose of bringing them closer to his idea. In the same year he provided assistance to Russian Jewish refugees in Galicia by means of the mayor of London's Mansion House Relief fund. In opposition to the representatives of the Alliance Israélite Universelle who directed the emigration to the United States, he advised the Jews to go to Palestine and tried to persuade Alliance spokesmen to do the same. He also decided to renew his negotiations in Constantinople. The Turkish foreign minister, Said Pasha, regarded his plan as practical and wanted to connect it with the project of constructing a railroad in Palestine. But the negotiation could go no further, especially when the Turkish-British relations deteriorated because of Egypt, and Oliphant's efforts came to nothing. He settled in Haifa and engaged in religious and mystic contemplation. Yet he always remained attached to the Zionist idea and provided advice and assistance to the first Jewish settlers in Ereẓ Israel. His Hebrew secretary in Haifa was the poet, N. H. *Imber.

Laurence Oliphant, 19th-century English supporter of Zionism. Jerusalem, J.N.U.L., Schwadron Collection.

Oliphant was the most important Christian figure of his time supporting the idea of the Jewish Return to Zion. The *Bilu'im and Ḥovevei Zion had great hopes for his negotiations in Constantinople, and his firm position on their behalf was encouraging, even though his political undertakings failed. His writings included the programmatic book *Land of Gilead* (1880; Heb. trans. by Nahum *Sokolow as *Ereẓ Ḥemdah,* 1886) and *Haifa, or Life in Modern Palestine* (1887).

Bibliography: M. O. W. Oliphant, *Memoir on the Life of Laurence Oliphant . . .,* 2 vols. (1891); P. Henderson, *The Life of Laurence Oliphant* (1956); DNB, 14 (1921–22), 1027–31; N. Sokolow, *Hibbath Zion* (1935), 275–9 and index; idem, *History of Zionism,* 2 (1919), index; S. Jawnieli, *Sefer ha-Ẓiyyonut,* 2 pt. 1 (1942), 9–11, 90–95; I. Klausner, *Be-Hitorer Am* (1962), 72–78, 199–202, and index; G. Yardeni, *Ha-Ittonut ha-Ivrit be-Ereẓ Yisrael* (1969), index. [A.B./N.M.G.]

OLITZKI, ARYEH LEO (1898–), Israel bacteriologist. Born in Allenstein (E. Prussia), he was an assistant in the Institute of Hygiene of the University of Breslau before moving to Palestine in 1924. He continued his serological research at Hadassah Hospital, Jerusalem, and for some

Aryeh Leo Olitzki, Israel bacteriologist. Courtesy Hebrew University, Jerusalem.

years headed the bacteriology laboratories at the Hadassah hospitals in Jerusalem and Safed. He taught at the Hebrew University from 1928, becoming professor in 1949 and dean of the Medical School from 1961 to 1965. In the course of investigating problems of serology and immunology, especially in relation to infectious diseases peculiar to Israel, he discovered a method of inoculating humans against Brucellosa infection from sheep and cattle. His major breakthrough was the laboratory cultivation (with Zipporah Gershon) of the Lepra bacillus, thus paving the way toward early diagnosis of the disease and the possibility of more effective treatment. Olitzki published many scientific papers and coauthored (with N. Grossowicz) a Hebrew textbook on microbiology and immunology *(Yesodot Torat ha-Ḥaidakkim ve-ha-Ḥasinut,* 2 vols., 1964–68). He was awarded the Israel Prize in Medicine in 1967. [L.HA.]

OLITZKY, family of three brothers, all Yiddish authors. LEIB (1897–), poet and short-story writer. He taught in Yiddish schools in his native Trisk and in Warsaw until 1939. Fleeing eastward from the German invaders, he spent the war years in Soviet Russia, but returned to Poland in 1946. In 1959 he settled in Israel. His first stories and his first novel, *In a Okupirt Shtetl* ("In an Occupied Village," 1924) dealt with Jewish life under the German occupation of World War I and during the early years of the Polish Republic. There followed juvenilia, books of parables, short stories, and poems. During his years in Russia and in Communist Poland, he translated Pushkin and Krylov, wrote conformist poetry, and edited the lyrics of his brother Baruch Olitzky, who had perished under the Nazis. Four collections of Leib's lyrics were published in Israel (1960, 1962, 1964, 1967) as well as a volume of his and his brother Mattes' poems, *Lider tsu a Bruder* ("Songs to a Brother," 1964), a volume of tributes to Baruch Olitzky, some of whose lyrics were also included. Some of his poems and fables have been translated into Polish, Hebrew, and English. BARUCH (1907–1941), poet. Born in Poland, he became a teacher in the Yiddish schools of Volhynia. He made his literary debut in *Literarishe Bleter* in 1925, and subsequently published poems in various newspapers in Poland and Soviet Russia. His brother Leib edited a posthumous volume of his poetry, *Mayn Blut iz Oysgemisht* ("My Blood is Mixed," 1951). He perished during the Nazi Holocaust in Poland. MATTES (1915–) published his first book of poems, *In Fremdn Land* ("In Alien Land," 1948), while still in a postwar refugee camp in Germany. His second book, *Freylikhe Teg* ("Happy Days," 1962), the outcome of his experiences as a teacher of Jewish children in New York, consisted mainly of songs which aimed at bringing life and immediacy to Bible stories, and the joys of the Sabbath and Holy Days which he was teaching his pupils, but also included poems recalling Jewish children whom the Nazis summoned from classrooms to death-marches. He joined his brother Leib Olitzky in *Lider tsu a Bruder. Geklibene Lider* ("Selected Poems," 1967) covered a wide range of scenes and experiences, from a golden childhood in Poland, through tragic war years, to a calm existence in New York.

Bibliography: LNYL, 1 (1956), 104–6. [S.L.]

OLIVE (Heb. זַיִת), the *Olea europaea* tree and its fruit. The wild olive grows in the groves of Upper Galilee and Carmel. It is a prickly shrub producing small fruits. There are many varieties of cultivated olives, some being suitable for oil, and some for food as preserved olives. Its foliage is dense and when it becomes old, the fairly tall trunk acquires a unique pattern of twists and protuberances on its bark. There are trees in Israel estimated to be 1,000 years old that still produce fruit. In old age the tree becomes hollow but the trunk continues to grow thicker, at times achieving a circumference of 20 ft. (6 m.). The olive tree blossoms at the beginning of summer and its fruit ripens about the time of the early rains in October. The fruit, which is rich in oil, is first green, but later becomes black. Olive trees have always been the most extensively distributed and the most conspicuous in the landscape of Israel. The olive is numbered among the seven species with which Ereẓ Israel is blessed (Deut. 8:8). The Rab-Shakeh, who besieged Jerusalem, also made use of a similar description for Ereẓ Israel when promising the inhabitants of Jerusalem that he would exile them to a country of like fertility (II Kings 18:32). The bounty of Israel is frequently described by "corn, wine, and oil" (Deut. 7:13, et al.); grain, vines, and olives, which formed the basis of Israel's economy. The olive flourishes throughout the country. Its cultivation dates from early times. When the Israelites conquered the land they found extensive olive plantations (Deut. 6:11). Western Galilee, the territory of Asher, was especially rich in olives (33:24), as it is today. They flourish in mountainous areas, even among the rocks, thus producing "oil out of the flinty rock" (32:13). "The Mount of Olives" (Zech. 14:4) near Jerusalem is Har ha-Mishḥah, "the mount of Oil" of the Mishnah (Par. 3:6). The olive also develops well in the *Shephelah Lowland, where it grows near *sycamores, and David appointed a special overseer over these plantations (I Chron. 27:28).

The olive was the first to be chosen by the trees when they went "to anoint a king over themselves" in Jotham's parable (Judg. 9:8–9). The tree is full of beauty, especially when laden with fruit: "a leafy olive-tree, fair with goodly fruit" (Jer. 11:16). It is an evergreen, and the righteous who take refuge in the protection of God are compared to it (Ps.

52:10). The "olive plants" of Psalm 128:3 are the shoots that sprout from its roots and protect the trunk and, if it is cut down, they ensure its continued existence. This is the simile referred to in the words "thy children like olive saplings round about thy table." The wood is very hard and beautifully grained, making it suitable for the manufacture of small articles and ornaments, the hollow trunk of the adult tree, however, rendering it unsuitable for pieces of furniture. The olive cannot therefore be the *eẓ shemen* from which the doors of the Temple were made (I Kings 6:31).

In spring the olive tree is covered with thousands of small whitish flowers, most of which fall off before the fruit forms (cf. Job 15:33). After the fruit is formed the tree may be attacked by the olive fly, causing the fruit to rot and fall off (Deut. 28:40). The fruits are arranged upon the thin branches in parallel rows like ears of corn (Zech. 4:12). Two such olive branches at the side of the candelabrum symbolize the State of Israel, because "an olive leaf" symbolizes peace (cf. Gen. 8:11). After ripening, the fruit is harvested in two different ways, by beating the branches with sticks or by hand picking. The former way is quicker but many branches fall off and this diminishes successive harvests. This method was used in biblical times, the Bible commanding that the fruit on the fallen branches are to be a gift to the poor (Deut. 24:20). The second method was the more usual in mishnaic times and was termed *masik* ("harvesting olives"), the fingers being drawn down the branches in a milking motion so that the olives fall into the hand. By this method the "harvested" olives remained whole, whereas the "beaten" olives were bruised by the beating (Ḥal. 3:9). The best species for preserving are called *kelofsin* (Tosef., Ter. 4:3) or *keloska* olives (Av. Zar. 2:7). Though there were olives of different varieties and different sizes, the olive was designated as a standard size for many *halakhot*, and the expression "land of olive trees" was interpreted as "a land whose main standard of measurement is the olive" (Ber. 41b). Rabbinic literature contains innumerable details about the oil, its types and methods of extraction; the Midrash (Ex. R. 36:1) summing it up as follows: "The olive is left to fully ripen while it is yet on the tree after which it is brought down from the tree and beaten, . . . it is then brought up to the vat and placed in a grinding mill, where it is ground and then tied up with ropes [through which the oil is filtered], and then stones are brought [which press upon the olives] and then at last it yields its oil." [J.F.]

In Israel. Limited Jewish attempts to grow olives date back to the small Jewish settlements established during the First Aliyah. The planting of olive groves on a wider scope began at the Ben Shemen farm in 1905–06, and from then on grew steadily. From the establishment of the State of Israel (1948) there was a decline in the area covered by olives: in 1948/49 there were 137,000 dunams (34,000 acres); in 1959/60, 123,000 dunams; and in 1968/69, 107,000 dunams, of which 82,000 were on non-Jewish farms, especially in Arab villages in the Galilee. The scope of olive produce fluctuates substantially, despite the fact that the area of land under cultivation has remained fairly steady. In the most productive year, produce reached a climax of 24,500 tons (1966/67), and in the low years it reached the level of 3,800 tons (1949/50) and 2,800 tons (1954/55). In the climax year of 1966/67, 18,950 tons of olives went for food processing and another 5,550 tons yielded 3,000 tons of olive oil. In the same year the value of the olives produced and processed came to IL 17,998,000. A survey carried out by the Ministry of Agriculture after the Six-Day War (1967/68) revealed 477,600 dunams of land under olive cultivation in Judea and Samaria and 3,000 dunams in the Gaza Strip. Within the borders set by the 1949 Armistice Agreements, the Galilee and the area around Lydda were the main centers of olive cultivation. After the Six-Day War, however, the mountains of Samaria and northern Judea took the lead in olive production within the cease-fire lines. [Ed.]

Bibliography: F. Goldmann, *Der Oelbau in Palaestina zur Zeit der Mišnâh* (1907); Krauss, Tal Arch, 2 (1911), 214–26; Loew, Flora, 2 (1924), 287–95; G. Dalman, *Arbeit und Sitte in Palaestina* 4 (1935), 153–290; H. N. and A. L. Moldenke, *Plants of the Bible* (1952), 317 (index), s.v.; J. Feliks, *Ẓimḥiyyat ha-Mishnah*, in: *Marot ha-Mishnah, Seder Zera'im* (1967), 41; idem, *Kilei Zera'im ve-Harkavah* (1967), 155f.; idem, *Olam ha-Ẓome'aḥ ha-Mikra'i* (1968[2]), 25–32.

OLIVER Y FULLANA, NICOLÁS DE (fl. c. 1670), Marrano soldier and writer. Born in Majorca, he pursued a military career, rising from sergeant major in the Spanish army in Catalonia to the rank of colonel in Flanders, where he distinguished himself in action against the French. It was probably while in the Low Countries that Oliver y Fullana became a Jew and took the name of Daniel Judah. Nevertheless, he still maintained friendly relations with the Spanish military establishment in Brussels in the 1670s. His second wife, Isabel de *Correa, was a poet in Amsterdam. Oliver y Fullana, who wrote in three languages, exchanged laudatory verses with Miguel de *Barrios. He completed a part of the *Atlas Mayor* (1641) of Jan Blaeu and was cosmographer-royal to the king of Spain.

Bibliography: Kayserling, Bibl, 79; Scholberg, in: JQR, 53 (1962), 145; I. Da Costa, *Noble Families among the Sephardic Jews* (1936), 94. [K.R.S.]

OLIVETTI, Italian family of industrialists of Piedmont. Camillo Olivetti (1868–1943), who founded the firm, started a small industry in his native Ivrea for the production of instruments of electrical measurement, the first of its kind in Italy (subsequently the C.G.S. of Milan). In 1909 he introduced the production of typewriters in Italy, founded the "Ing. C. Olivetti and Co." at Ivrea and invented the typewriter bearing his name. A patriarchal figure, he strove to make his firm one of the most advanced in Europe, both technically and socially, caring especially for the welfare and education of the workers. His son Adriano (1901–1960), like his father an outspoken anti-Fascist, was responsible for a radical transformation of the Ivrea plant leading to notable production increases. In 1933, as the general director of the firm, Adriano Olivetti started production on a world scale at Ivrea, Turin, and Pozzuoli, of metal furniture, typing and calculating machines, and telescriptors. He initiated a huge housing scheme at Ivrea and built free holiday resorts. Dedicated to advanced urbanism he initiated the "Movimento di Communità," on behalf of which he sat in the Italian parliament in 1958. In 1959 he took world-wide control over the Underwood Corporation. He wrote *L'ordine politico della Communità* (1946), *Società stato communità* (1948), and *Città dell' Uomo* (1960), which set out his aspirations for social renewal through decentralized economy based on a system of communal cooperatives each autonomous with its own government, industries, and educational and cultural institutions.

Bibliography: N. Ginzburg, *Lessico famigliare* (1963), passim; E. Mann Borgese, in: *Il Ponte*, 6 (1960), 244–8; Edizioni di Communità, *Ricordo di Adriano Olivetti* (1960); B. Hirschman, in: *South African Jewish Times* (Nov. 28, 1969), 31–32. [Ed.]

OLIVEYRA, SOLOMON BEN DAVID DE (d. 1708), rabbi, philologist, and poet. Oliveyra was born in Lisbon, but lived in Amsterdam where he served as teacher of the Keter Torah association and as a member of the rabbinical council, over which he presided after the death of Jacob *Sasportas (1698).

He wrote a number of works in Hebrew and Portuguese, including grammatical treatises, lexicons and translations, of which the following may be noted: *Sharshot Gavlut* (Amsterdam, 1665), consisting of a dictionary of rhymes with chapters on meter; *Ayyelet Ahavim* (*ibid.*, 1665), an account of Abraham and the sacrifice of Isaac in prose and poetry; *Darkhei No'am* (*ibid.*, 1688–89), a guide to the study of the Talmud.

Bibliography: M. Hartmann, *Die hebraeische Verskunst* (1894), 75–79; M. B. Amzalak, in: *Revista de Estudos Hebráicos*, 1 (1928), 96–118; Kayserling, Bibl. 79–81. [ED.]

OLKUSZ (Heb. עלקוש), town in Krakow province, Poland. There was a Jewish settlement in Olkusz by the time of Casimir the Great (1333–70) who expropriated the gold and silver mines in Olkusz belonging to his Jewish banker *Levko. In 1374, however, Olkusz obtained the "privilege" *de non tolerandis Judaeis;* Jews were debarred from residing there and left for Cracow. During the reign of John Casimir (1648–69), a Jew, Marek Nekel, was granted the first concession to quarry in the hills and was allowed to trade in metals (1658). An agreement between the Jews and the municipality concluded in 1682 granted Jews domiciliary and trading rights on condition that they helped to defray the town debts; they were accordingly granted the customary privileges by John Sobieski (Dec. 3, 1682) to enable their settlement. The Olkusz community came under the jurisdiction of the Cracow *kehillah*, but in 1692, the community of Olkusz and other towns in the district seceded from Cracow, a decision endorsed by the *Council of the Four Lands. In 1764 there were 423 Jews living in Olkusz. The economic position of the town deteriorated in the 18th century after copper mines in the district had been ruined by the Swedish invasion. A *blood libel involving the Jews in Olkusz in 1787 was the last such case to occur in Poland before its partition. The principal Jew accused, a tailor, was sentenced to death, but the leaders of the community managed to obtain the intervention of King Stanislas Poniatowski and secure a reprieve. Under Austrian rule (1796–1809), the number of Jews living in Olkusz diminished, and when it was annexed to Russia the prohibition on Jewish settlement in border districts applied. However, there were 746 Jews living in Olkusz in 1856 (83.4% of the total population), 1,840 in 1897 (53.9%), 3,249 in 1909 (53%), 2,703 in 1921 (40.6%), and in 1939 about 3,000. [N.M.G.]

Holocaust Period. The Germans entered the town on Sept. 5, 1939 and subjected the Jews to beating and tormenting, plundering of property, kidnapping in the streets for hard labor, and religious persecution. The Judenrat, created in October 1939, had to take care particularly of 800 deportees who came from other localities in Upper Silesia. Transports of men to labor camps in the Reich commenced in October 1940 with the dispatch of 140 Jews. A second transport with 130 Jews left Olkusz in January 1941; the third, composed of 300 women, left in August 1941. In the spring of 1942, shortly before the liquidation of the community, the number of transports increased. In March 1942 150 women were shipped out, followed on April 20, 1942 by 140 men. One month later during Shavuot (May 21–23, 1942) about 1,000 Jews, including women, were sent out. The victims of these transports were mainly the poor, particularly refugees and deportees; those with means could temporarily avoid such transports. In the latter half of 1941 a ghetto was established in a suburb. It was open and probably not fenced off, but leaving the ghetto was forbidden and the entrances were watched by German and Jewish police. There were, together with the new arrivals, about 3,000 Jews interned in the ghetto. In the last few months prior to the liquidation, transports to labor camps increased, and the German police on March 6, 1942, publicly hanged three Jews for illegally leaving the ghetto and smuggling food.

Jews of Olkusz forced to pose for humiliating photographs with German soldiers, 1941. Courtesy Yad Vashem Archives, Jerusalem.

Local Jews were forced to build the gallows and carry out the hanging. The final liquidation took place in June 1942. A *Selektion* ("selection") was carried out to separate the most able-bodied men for labor camps from the rest of the inhabitants, among them the local rabbi; the latter were all sent to *Auschwitz. A group of some 20 Jews was left to clear up the ghetto; they were afterward deported and exterminated. The community was not reconstituted after the war. [DE.D.]

Bibliography: K. Leszczyński, in: *Biuletyn Głównej Komisji Badania Zbrodni Hitlerowskich w Polsce*, 9 (1957), 157; Balaban, in: *Yevreyskaya Starina*, 7 (1914), 163–81, 318–27.

OLLENDORFF, FRANZ (1900–), Israel engineer. Born in Berlin, Ollendorff in 1924 joined the Siemens research department in Berlin, working under Reinhold Ruedenberg. From 1928 he taught in the engineering faculty of the Berlin Technische Hochschule. After being dismissed from his post by the Nazis in 1933, he joined the teaching staff of the Jewish public school in Berlin, moving to Jerusalem when the school and staff transferred there in 1934. Ollendorff returned to Germany in the following year to organize the transfer of Jewish children to Ereẓ Israel within the framework of the newly established *Youth Aliyah. In 1937 he was finally expelled by the Gestapo and, on his return to Palestine, joined the staff of the Haifa Technion. Ollendorff was a professor there from 1939. He became research professor in the faculty of electrical engineering and worked in the field of biomedical electronics and physics. He was a member of the Israel Academy of Science and was awarded the Israel Prize for his research in magnetic fields (1954). He was elected a fellow of the American Institute of Electrical Engineers in 1963 and served as the Institute's vice-president. His interest in the education of teenagers made him a keen supporter of the Technion's vocational high school. Ollendorff wrote books and papers on electronics, physics, mathematics, accoustics, medical electronics, technical education, and other specialized fields. His publications include *Die Grundlagen der Hochfrequenztechnik* (1926); *Erdstroeme* (1928); *Die Welt der Vektoren* (1950); and *Innere Elektronik* (1955). [C.AP.]

OLLENDORFF, FRIEDRICH (1889–1951), German social welfare expert. Born in Breslau, Germany, Ollendorff studied law. After service in the German army in World War I, he was appointed legal adviser to one of the district municipalities of Berlin. He later turned to social welfare work and was one of the highest officials in the youth welfare and welfare administration of the Berlin municipality. He played an active role in preparing modern welfare legislation in Germany. In 1924 he left his post to become director of the "Zentralwohlfahrtsstelle der deutschen Juden" (Central Office for Social Welfare of German Jewry) and coeditor with Max Kreuzberger of the Collection of Welfare Legislation. Ollendorff introduced many new ideas and practices in Jewish welfare work in Germany. In 1934 he migrated to Palestine and together with his wife, Fanny, a trained social worker, became adviser to Henrietta *Szold, then director of the social welfare department of the Vaad Leummi (General Council of Palestine Jewry). He introduced the *Kartis ha-Kaḥol* (the blue contribution card) as a means of collecting regular contributions for social welfare. He became the first honorary secretary of the Jerusalem social welfare council, which was composed of the director of social welfare of the Palestine government and representatives of Jewish, Christian, and Moslem welfare institutions. He was also one of the initiators of the International Conference of Jewish Social Work, which held its first meeting in 1928 in Paris. [G.Lo.]

OLMEDO, small town near Medina del Campo, in Old Castile, N. central Spain. The date when Jews first settled there is unknown. The town was captured by Alfonso VI a short while before 1085. In 1095 it was again inhabited and was granted a *fuero* (charter). The community grew particularly during the 13th century. No information is available on Olmedo Jewry throughout the 14th century. In 1458 King John II granted the community an exemption from payment of certain taxes and levies.

Olmedo was the scene of a severe battle fought between the brothers Henry IV and the infante Alfonso in 1467. Although there is no detailed information about the community it presumably suffered as a result of the war. In 1474 the community taxes amounted to 500 maravedis while in 1491, immediately before the expulsion from Spain, they increased to 108,500 maravedis, the number of the community having probably increased by refugees from the south. In 1480 the Catholic Monarchs ordered an inquiry into the complaint made by the community concerning the closure of the street between the Jewish quarter and the town square. This indicates that the attempts to apply restrictions against the Jews in other Spanish towns were also enforced in Olmedo. After the expulsion of the Jews from Spain in March 1492, Luis de Alcalá and Fernań Núñez Coronel (Abraham *Seneor) were authorized to collect the outstanding debts owed by the Christian population to the Jews who had left because of the expulsion.

Bibliography: Baer, Urkunden, 2 (1936), 81, 135f., 325; Baer, Toledot, 396; D. de Valera, *Memorial de diversas hazañas,* ed. by J. de M. Carriazo (1941), 123ff.; Suárez Fernández, Documentos, index; P. León Tello, *Los judíos de Palencia* (1967), 193. [H.B.]

OLMO, JACOB DANIEL BEN ABRAHAM (c. 1690–1757), Italian rabbi and poet. Born in Ancona, his family moved to Ferrara, where he became a student of Isaac *Lampronti. He served as a teacher and later as head of the yeshivah of Ferrara and as rabbi of the Ashkenazi synagogue there. A student of the Kabbalah, he founded a society of *Shomerim la-Boker* ("Morning Watchers") to pray for the return to Zion. With the death of Lampronti, he became head of the local rabbinical court.

Some of Olmo's legal decisions are included in Lampronti's *Paḥad Yiẓḥak*. A collection of his decisions, entitled *Pi Ẓaddik,* is still in manuscript. His *Eden Arukh* is a poetic drama of 274 stanzas which both in form and content is a continuation and imitation of Moses *Zacuto's *Tofteh Arukh;* the two works were published in one volume (Venice, 1743). *Eden Arukh* is based on talmudic, midrashic, and kabbalistic literature. It was translated into German and into Italian by Cesare Foa (1904). He compiled a work on the sages of the Ashkenazi synagogue of Ferrara and wrote occasional poems and hymns included in various Italian liturgical works. One of his poems, in honor of the wedding of a pupil, consisted of 35 stanzas in Hebrew with Italian words echoing the last Hebrew word at the end of each stanza.

Bibliography: C. Roth, in: *Melilah,* 3–4 (1951), 204–23; U. Cassuto, in: *Eshkol-Enẓiklopedyah Yisre'elit,* 1 (1929), 890–1; F. Delitzsch, *Zur Geschichte der juedischen Poesie* . . . (1836), 73, s.v. *Ulamo;* Rhine, in: JQR, 2 (1911/12), 39–42. [Yo.D.]

OLOMOUC (Ger. **Olmuetz**), city in Moravia, Czechoslovakia. Jews are first mentioned there by *Isaac b. Dorbelo (c. 1140; a 1060 reference by a later chronicler is unreliable). In 1273 the bishop reported disapprovingly to Pope *Gregory X on the Jews of Olomouc. In 1278 Rudolph I of Hapsburg decreed that the Jews must participate in all payments to the city on the same footing as all other citizens. A 1413–20 register of the Jews *(liber fatalis)* and their transactions is extant. There was a *platea Judaeorum* (*Jewish quarter), but the Jewish community was expelled in 1454 and their property ceded to the municipality, which had to assume the taxes previously paid by the Jews. Some individual Jews, however, continued to be tolerated in the town on weekdays. The Jewish community was reconstituted in 1848 and Jews from *Prostejov (Prossnitz) and *Kromeriz transacted business there. The first Jew permitted to resettle was seized by a mob and transported out of the town on a hearse. In 1863 a congregation (*Kultusverein) was founded, in 1867 a cemetery was established, and in 1891 the community was approved. In 1897 a magnificent synagogue was dedicated and in the same year the first Zionist convention of Austria met at Olomouc. In 1900 part of the new municipal cemetery was allotted to the community. Olomouc absorbed many World War I refugees. Jews were instrumental in its economic development, mainly that of the malt industry. In 1903 there were 2,198 Jews (3.3% of the total population). With the German occupation, the synagogue was burned down (on March 15, 1939). Jews from the surroundings were concentrated in the city, and of the 3,498 deported to the extermination camps through *Theresienstadt in June–July 1942, there were 128 survivors on Nov. 7, 1944. After World War II a small community was reestablished. In 1949 a memorial to the victims of the Holocaust was dedicated in the cemetery and in 1955 a synagogue was established. In 1959 the community numbered 450, and was guided by the district rabbi of *Brno. It remained an active community. Olomouc was well-known among East European Jewry as a center for the *livestock trade.

Bibliography: B. Oppenheim, in: H. Gold (ed.), *Die Juden und Judengemeinden Maehrens* . . . (1929), 451–6; B. Bretholz, *Quellen zur Geschichte der Juden in Maehren* . . . *(1067–1411)* (1935), index; idem, *Geschichte der Juden in Maehren im Mittelalter* (1934), index; Germ Jud, 1 (1963), 254–5; 2 pt. 2 (1968), 628; R. Iltis (ed.), *Die aussaeen unter Traenen, mit Jubel werden sie ernten* (1959), 66ff.; K. Hudeczek, *Die Juden in Olmuetz* (1897); W. Haage, *Olmuetz und die Juden* (a Nazi publication, 1944); W. Mueller (ed.), *Urkundliche Beitraege zur Geschichte der maehrischen Judenschaft im 17. und 18. Jahrhundert* (1903); A. Engel, in: JGGJČ, 2 (1930), 58–59. [M.La.]

OLSCHWANGER, ISAAC WOLF (1825–1896), one of the first rabbis in Russia to join the Ḥibbat Zion movement. Born in Plunge, Lithuania, he was ordained as rabbi in 1845 and held an office in the rabbinate of Taurage (Lithuania). From 1876 until his death he served as rabbi in St. Petersburg. Throughout his life he took part in various public activities and sympathized with the moderate Haskalah movement. At the outset of the Ḥibbat Zion movement in the 1880s, he enthusiastically accepted its tenet of restoring the Jewish people to its homeland and became actively engaged in the movement's undertakings in St. Petersburg, when it still had only a few followers. Later, when the majority of rabbis expressed their opposition to the movement, Olschwanger criticized those rabbis who did not actively strive to bring about the redemption, waiting instead for a divine miracle. Unlike many rabbis, he permitted work on the land in the sabbatical year, when the issue arose for the first time in the settlements in Ereẓ Israel (1889).

Bibliography: EẒD, 1 (1958), 58–59; N. Sokolow, *Hibbath Zion* (1935), 230–1. [G.K.]

OLSHAN, ISAAC (1895–), Israel jurist. Born in Kovno, Lithuania, Olshan immigrated to Ereẓ Israel in 1912. He studied at the University of London and served in the Jewish Legion during World War I. From 1927 to 1948 he worked as a lawyer in private practice in Palestine, and after the creation of the State of Israel was one of the original five

Isaac Olshan, Israel jurist. Government Press Office, Tel Aviv.

justices appointed to the Supreme Court. Olshan became president of the Supreme Court in 1953 and served until his retirement in 1965. During his tenure of office he repeatedly emphasized that the state was as much bound by the rule of law as the individual and that respect for the rule of law was one of the foundations of a democratic society.

Bibliography: *Ha-Peraklit*, 21 (1965), 381–8. [Ed.]

°OLSHAUSEN, JUSTUS (1800–1882), German orientalist, theologian, and Bible scholar. He was born in Schleswig-Holstein and from 1830 to 1852 was professor of Oriental languages at the University of Kiel, and from 1853 professor at the University of Koenigsberg. From 1858, he was adviser to the Prussian Ministry of Religion and Culture. Olshausen was one of the first scholars who used modern philological and comparative linguistic methods in explanation of obscure passages in the Bible. He also applied modern studies in Assyriology to Bible research, and pioneered in the "Arabian School" which employs Arabic as a key to the elucidation of the Bible and the understanding of the Hebrew language and its radicals (in opposition to Ewald's system). In 1826, Olshausen published *Emendationen zum Alten Testament*, giving grammatical and historical explanations to the Old Testament. His theses on the geography, people, and culture of Mesopotamia were confirmed by the findings of later Assyriologists.

Other published works are: *Observationes criticae ad Vetus Testamentum* (1836); *Ueber das Vocalsystem der hebraeischen Sprache nach der sogenannten assyrischen Punktuation* (1865); and *Beitraege zur Kritik des ueberlieferten Textes im Buche Genesis* (1870). His critical method is explained in the second edition of Hirzel's commentary on Job which Olshausen edited (1852), and in his commentary on Psalms (1853), where he stated that most of the psalms were composed in the Maccabean period; this assertion was sharply criticized. His *Zur Topographie des alten Jerusalem* (1833) has been superseded by later discoveries; but *Ueber den Ursprung des Alphabetes und ueber die Vocalbezeichnung im Alten Testamente* (1841), a study on the origin of the Hebrew alphabet and its vocalization, is still important. *Lehrbuch der Hebraeischen Sprache* (1861) is probably his major work. It is a Hebrew grammar; the third volume, devoted to Hebrew syntax, was, however, not published.

Bibliography: Kamphausen, in: J. Herzog and A. Hauck (eds.), *Realencyklopaedie fuer protestantische Theologie und Kirche*, 14 (1904[3]), 368–71; ADB, 24 (1887), 328–30. [Ed.]

OLSVANGER, IMMANUEL (1888–1961), folklorist and Hebrew translator. Born in Poland, he was active in the Zionist movement and was a founder of the student Zionist organization He-Ḥaver. He emigrated to Ereẓ Israel in 1933.

Bein Adam le-Kono, his book of verse, was published in 1943. Olsvanger was among the first to translate Far Eastern literary texts (especially Sanskrit and Japanese) from the original into Hebrew; he also translated poems by Goethe, Dante's *Divine Comedy* (*Ha-Komedyah ha-Elohit*, 3 vols., 1944–56) to which

Immanuel Olsvanger, folklore collector and Hebrew translator. Photo Alisa Holz, Jerusalem.

he added notes and wrote an introduction, and Boccaccio's *Decameron* (1947). The two collections of Yiddish proverbs and anecdotes he edited were printed in Latin characters, *Rőyte pomerantsen* (1947) and *L'chayim!* (1949).

Bibliography: D. Lazar, *Rashim be-Yisrael*, 2 (1955), 267–71. [G.K.]

OLYKA, town in Volhynia, Ukrainian S.S.R., formerly in Poland-Lithuania. The Jewish community in Olyka is one of the oldest in Volhynia. According to one tradition it was established in 1655 by Ukrainian Jews fleeing from the *Chmielnicki massacres of 1648–49, but probably Jews had been living in Olyka before. The Olyka community was the leading member of a form of district council whose three-yearly sessions were held in the town. It thus counted as one of the principal communities of the council for the province of Volhynia (see *Councils of the Lands), with the right of veto in taxation deliberations. In 1703 the Olyka community protested that these rights had been violated by the leaders of the Volhynian council. In 1765 there were 645

The wooden synagogue of Olyka, 17th/18th century. From M. and K. Piechotka, *Wooden Synagogues*, Warsaw, 1959.

poll tax payers in the Olyka congregation; the Jewish population numbered 2,381 in 1847; 2,606 in 1897 (62% of the total population); 2,086 in 1921 (48.1%); and according to figures of the Jewish Colonization Association, 2,500 in 1924. From this date on no further information can be procured. [M.W.]

OLYMPIC GAMES. Between 1896 and 1968, 131 Jews from 17 nations won 236 medals (101 gold, 68 silver, 67 bronze) in Olympic competition. (See Tables; individual medalists are listed with their particular sport.)

In addition, Alfred Hajos (Guttmann) of Hungary, a winner of Olympic swimming medals, was awarded a silver medal in architecture in 1924, and Ferenc Mezo (1885–1961) of Hungary received a 1928 gold medal in literature. As the official historian of the Olympic Games, Mezo wrote numerous articles and books on the subject. He served as a member of the International Olympic Committee and president of the Hungarian Olympic Committee. [J.H.S.]

OMAHA, city in the state of Nebraska. A few Jews went to Omaha along with Christian pioneers when the city was first settled in the mid-1850s. The first two Jews to become permanent residents were Aaron Cahn and his brother-in-law Meyer Hellman, who opened a clothing store and eventually became well-known merchants and citizens. Another early arrival, and perhaps the most prominent early Omaha Jew, was Edward Rosewater, founder and editor of the newspaper the *Omaha Bee*. Another pioneer was Julius Meyer who arrived in 1866 and became friendly with the Ponca Indian chief Standing Bear; he learned to speak six Indian dialects and was adopted by the tribe. The Meyer family was interested in music and was instrumental in establishing the first opera house (1885). The Jewish population of Omaha remained small until after the Civil War. The year 1882 marked the arrival of the first contingent of Jewish refugees from Russia, and from that time until World War I the population increased markedly. Omaha Jews have been particularly active in the retail field.

Synagogue of Congregation Beth Israel, Omaha, Nebraska. Courtesy Union of American Hebrew Congregations, New York.

Table 1. Distribution of Olympic medals among Jews by country and sport, 1896–1968

	Austria	Belgium	Brazil	Canada	Denmark	Finland	France	Germany	Great Britain	Hungary	Italy	Poland	Rumania	South Africa	Uruguay	U.S.A.	U.S.S.R.
Basketball			1												1	2	
Boxing				1										1		5	
Canoeing										4			3				1
Cycling	3																
Fencing	2	8			1		10		4	31						2	13
Gymnastics								6		14						2	3
Ice Hockey								1									
Ice Skating-Figure	2						1									2	
Ice Skating-Speed																2	2
Judo																1	
Rowing																1	
Shooting																	2
Soccer					1					2							1
Swimming	9	1								6						6	2
Tennis											1						
Track and Field				2		2			4	3		7				15	
Water Polo		5								13							2
Weightlifting	2															4	1
Wrestling	2				1				1	3						4	2
Yachting																1	1

Table 2. Jewish Olympic medal winners

G = Gold S = Silver B = Bronze

	G	S	B
1896			
Alfred Flatow, Germany, gymnastics	3		
Felix Flatow, Germany, gymnastics	2		
Alfred Hajos-Guttmann, Hungary, swimming	2		
Dr. Paul Neumann, Austria, swimming	1		
Alfred Flatow, Germany, gymnastics		1	
Otto Herschmann, Austria, swimming			1
1900			
Myer Prinstein, USA, track	1		
Myer Prinstein, USA, track		1	
Otto Wahle, Austria, swimming		2	
Siegfried Flesch, Austria, fencing			1
1904			
Myer Prinstein, USA, track	2		
Samuel Berger, USA, boxing	1		
Daniel Frank, USA, track		1	
Otto Wahle, Austria, swimming			1
1906			
Otto Scheff, Austria, swimming	1		
Henrik Hajos-Guttmann, Hungary, swimming	1		
Myer Prinstein, USA, track	1		
Edgar Seligman, Great Britain, fencing		1	
Hugo Friend, USA, track			1
Otto Scheff, Austria, swimming			1
1908			
Dr. Jeno Fuchs, Hungary, fencing	2		
Dr. Oszkar Gerde, Hungary, fencing	1		
Lajos Werkner, Hungary, fencing	1		
Alexandre Lippmann, France, fencing	1		
Richard Weisz, Hungary, wrestling	1		
Jean Stern, France, fencing	1		
Alexander Lippmann, France, fencing		1	
Edgar Seligman, Great Britain, fencing		1	
Odon Bodor, Hungary, track			1
Otto Scheff, Austria, swimming			1
Clair S. Jacobs, USA, track			1
Paul Anspach, Belgium, fencing			1
1912			
Dr. Jeno Fuchs, Hungary, fencing	2		
Dr. Oszkar Gerde, Hungary, fencing	1		
Lajos Werkner, Hungary, fencing	1		
Paul Anspach, Belgium, fencing	2		
Henry Anspach, Belgium, fencing	1		
Gaston Salmon, Belgium, fencing	1		
Jacques Ochs, Belgium, fencing	1		
Zoltan Schenker, Hungary, fencing	1		
Edgar Seligman, Great Britain, fencing		1	
Dr. Otto Herschmann, Austria, fencing		1	
Abel Kiviat, USA, track		1	
Alvah T. Meyer, USA, track		1	
Ivan Osiier, Denmark, fencing		1	
Imre Gellert, Hungary, gymnastics		1	
Margarete Adler, Austria, swimming			1
Klara Milch, Austria, swimming			1
Josephine Sticker, Austria, swimming			1
Mor Kovacs (Koczan), Hungary, track			1
1920			
Samuel Mosberg, USA, boxing	1		
Alexandre Lippmann, France, fencing		1	
Paul Anspach, Belgium, fencing		1	
Samuel Gerson, USA, wrestling		1	
Gerard Blitz, Belgium, waterpolo		1	
Maurice Blitz, Belgium, waterpolo		1	
Fred Meyer, USA, wrestling			1
Montgomery "Moe" Herzowitch, Canada, boxing			1
Gerard Blitz, Belgium, swimming			1
Alexandre Lippmann, France, fencing			1
1924			
Harold Abrahams, Great Britain, track	1		
Elias Katz, Finland, track	1		
Alexandre Lippmann, France, fencing	1		
Louis A. Clarke, USA, track	1		
Jackie Fields, USA, boxing	1		
Janos Garai, Hungary, fencing		1	
Harold Abrahams, Great Britain, track		1	
Elias Katz, Finland, track		1	
Gerard Blitz, Belgium, waterpolo		1	
Maurice Blitz, Belgium, waterpolo		1	
Zoltan Schenker, Hungary, fencing		1	
Paul Anspach, Belgium, fencing		1	
Alfred Hajos-Guttmann, Hungary, architecture		1	
Baron H. L. De Morpurgo, Italy, tennis			1
Janos Garai, Hungary, fencing			1
Zoltan Schenker, Hungary, fencing			1
Sydney Jelinek, USA, crew			1
1928			
Fanny Rosenfeld, Canada, track	1		
Attila Petschauer, Hungary, fencing	1		
Hans Haas, Austria, weightlifting	1		
Helene Mayer, Germany, fencing	1		
Dr. Sandor Gombos, Hungary, fencing	1		
Janos Garai, Hungary, fencing	1		
Dr. Ferenc Mezo, Hungary, literature	1		
Fanny Rosenfeld, Canada, track		1	
Attlia Petschauer, Hungary, fencing		1	
Lillian Copeland, USA, track		1	
Fritzie Burger, Austria, figure skating		1	
Istvan Barta, Hungary, waterpolo		1	
Ellis R. Smouha, Great Britain, track			1
Harry Devine, USA, boxing			1
Harry Isaacs, South Africa, boxing			1
S. Rabin, Great Britain, wrestling			1
1932			
Attila Petschauer, Hungary, fencing	1		
Istvan Barta, Hungary, waterpolo	1		
Endre Kabos, Hungary, fencing	1		
Gyorgy Brody, Hungary, waterpolo	1		
Irving Jaffee, USA, speed-skating	2		
Lillian Copeland, USA, track	1		
George Gulack, USA, gymnastics	1		
Hans Haas, Austria, weightlifting		1	
Karoly Karpati, Hungary, wrestling		1	
Abraham Kurland, Denmark, wrestling		1	
Dr. Philip Erenberg, USA, gymnastics		1	
Fritzie Burger, Austria, figure skating		1	
Rudolf Ball, Germany, ice hockey			1
Endre Kabos, Hungary, fencing			1
Nikolaus Hirschl, Austria, wrestling			2
Paul Winter, France, track			1
Albert Schwartz, USA, swimming			1
Jadwiga Wajsowna (Weiss), Poland, track			1
1936			
Gyorgy Brody, Hungary, waterpolo	1		
Ilona Schacherer-Elek, Hungary, fencing	1		
Karoly Karpati, Hungary, wrestling	1		
Endre Kabos, Hungary, fencing	2		
Samuel Balter, USA, basketball	1		
Ibolya K. Csak, Hungary, track	1		
Helene Mayer, Germany, fencing		1	
Jadwiga Wajsowna (Weiss), Poland, track		1	
Gerard Blitz, Belgium, waterpolo			1
1948			
Frank Spellman, USA, weightlifting	1		
Ilona Schacherer-Elek, Hungary, fencing	1		
Henry Wittenberg, USA, wrestling	1		
Agnes Keleti, Hungary, gymnastics		1	
Dr. Steve Seymour, USA, track		1	
Dezso Gyarmati, Hungary, waterpolo		1	
James Fuchs, USA, track			1
Norman C. Armitage, USA, fencing			1
1952			
Boris Gurevich, USSR, wrestling	1		
Mikhail Perelman, USSR, gymnastics	1		
Agnes Keleti, Hungary, gymnastics	1		
Dezso Gyarmati, Hungary, waterpolo	1		
Judit Temes, Hungary, swimming	1		
Eva Szekely, Hungary, swimming	1		
Claude Netter, France, fencing	1		
Dr. Gyorgy Karpati, Hungary, waterpolo	1		
Sandor Geller, Hungary, soccer	1		
Grigori Novak, USSR, weightlifting		1	
Agnes Keleti, Hungary, gymnastics		1	
Ilona Schacherer-Elek, Hungary, fencing		1	
Henry Wittenberg, USA, wrestling		1	

	G	S	B
Lev Vainshtein, USSR, shooting			1
Agnes Keleti, Hungary, gymnastics			2
Judit Temes, Hungary, swimming			1
James Fuchs, USA, track			1
1956			
Alice Kertesz, Hungary, gymnastics	1		
Leon Rottman, Rumania, canoeing	2		
Laszlo Fabian, Hungary, canoeing	1		
Isaac Berger, USA, weightlifting	1		
Agnes Keleti, Hungary, gymnastics	4		
Dezso Gyarmati, Hungary, waterpolo	1		
Dr. Gyorgy Karpati, Hungary, waterpolo	1		
Boris Razinsky, USSR, soccer	1		
Alice Kertesz, Hungary, gymnastics		1	
Agnes Keleti, Hungary, gymnastics		2	
Allan Erdman, USSR, shooting		1	
Eva Szekely, Hungary, swimming		1	
Rafael Grach, USSR, speed-skating		1	
Andre Mouyal, France, fencing			1
Yves Dreyfus, France, fencing			1
David Tyshler, USSR, fencing			1
Yakov Rylsky, USSR, fencing			1
Imre Farkas, Hungary, canoeing			1
Boris Goikhman, USSR, waterpolo			1
1960			
Vera Krepkina, USSR, track	1		
Mark Midler, USSR, fencing	1		
Allan Jay, Great Britain, fencing		2	
Vladimir Portnoi, USSR, gymnastics		1	
Isaac Berger, USA, weightlifting		1	
Boris Goikhman, USSR, waterpolo		1	
Ildiko Uslaky-Rejto, Hungary, fencing		1	
Klara Fried, Hungary, canoeing			1
Moses Blass, Brazil, basketball			1
Albert Axelrod, USA, fencing			1
Vladimir Portnoi, USSR, gymnastics			1
Dezso Gyarmati, Hungary, waterpolo			1
David Segal, Great Britain, track			1
Robert Halperin, USA, yachting			1
Rafael Grach, USSR, speed-skating			1
Leon Rottman, Rumania, canoeing			1
Imre Farkas, Hungary, canoeing			1
Dr. Gyorgy Karpati, Hungary, waterpolo			1
1964			
Lawrence Brown, USA, basketball	1		
Gerald Ashworth, USA, track	1		
Rudolf Plyukfelder, USSR, weightlifting	1		
Dezso Gyarmati, Hungary, waterpolo	1		
Dr. Gyorgy Karpati, Hungary, waterpolo	1		
Tamas Gabor, Hungary, fencing	1		
Mark Midler, USSR, fencing	1		
Arpad Orban, Hungary, soccer	1		
Ildiko Uslaky-Rejto, Hungary, fencing	2		
Irena Kirszenstein, Poland, track	1		
Yakov Rylsky, USSR, fencing	1		
Irena Kirszenstein, Poland, track		2	
Marilyn Ramenofsky, USA, swimming		1	
Isaac Berger, USA, weightlifting		1	
James Bregman, USA, judo			1
Yves Dreyfus, France, fencing			1
1968			
Irena Kirszenstein-Szewinska, Poland, track	1		
Mark Spitz, USA, swimming	2		
Boris Gurevich, USSR, wrestling	1		
Valentin Mankin, USSR, yachting	1		
Mark Rakita, USSR, fencing	1		
Eduard Vinokurov, USSR, fencing	1		
Mark Spitz, USA, swimming		1	
Mark Rakita, USSR, fencing		1	
Grigory Kriss, USSR, fencing		2	
Josef Vitebsky, USSR, fencing		1	
Semyon Belits-Geiman, USSR, swimming		1	
Ildiko Uslaky-Rejto, Hungary, fencing		1	
Irena Kirszenstein-Szewinska, Poland, track			1
Mark Spitz, USA, swimming			1
Semyon Belits-Gieman, USSR, swimming			1
Naum Prokupets, USSR, canoeing			1
Ildiko Uslaky-Rejto, Hungary, fencing			1

Jonas L. Brandeis, who came to Omaha in 1881, founded the state's largest department store, and a number of other large retail establishments were founded by Jews. Omaha has had two Jewish mayors, Harry Zimman, who served temporary terms in 1904 and 1906, and John Rosenblatt, mayor from 1954 to 1961. Also active politically was Harry Trustin, who served many terms on the city council and was one of the drafters of the present city charter. Jews as a group have been politically influential since the 1890s.

The earliest recorded Jewish services were held in 1867; the Congregation of Israel was formally organized in 1871. Traditional services were held in the 1880s and a Conservative congregation was begun in 1929. The Associated Jewish Charities was established in 1903 and the Jewish community was federated in 1914. Aleph Zadek Aleph, international junior B'nai B'rith lodge, originated in Omaha in 1924; Henry *Monsky, an Omaha citizen and civic leader, served as national president of B'nai B'rith. Omaha Jewry, generally influential in the community as a whole, has been characterized by a large degree of cohesion and cooperation since shortly after the turn of the century, when Orthodox and Reform Jews joined together to work for their common welfare. 7,000 Jews lived there in 1968.

Bibliography: N. Bernstein, in: *Reform Advocate*, 35 (May 2, 1908), 10–52.

[Ca.G.]

OMAR, COVENANT OF (Ar. *Shurūt* or *'Uhūd;* "covenant"), the series of discriminatory regulations of Islam applied to the *dhimmi, the protected Christians and Jews; they are attributed to the second caliph, Omar (634–644). In various versions it is said that when the Christians of Syria sought their security from Omar, they accepted these conditions. M. J. de Goeje and Caetani have pointed out that this in unlikely because Omar was known for his tolerant and friendly attitude toward the protected subjects who subordinated themselves to him. During the first 50 years of the rule of the Umayyad Dynasty the protected subjects did not complain of any restrictions, and some of them attained high positions in the administration. Churches were built with the protection of the caliphs.

The first caliph to issue discriminatory regulations was Omar ibn 'Abdal 'Azīz (717–720), a religious fanatic who ordered the governor of Khurassan not to authorize the erection of synagogues and churches, to compel "them [Christians and Jews?] to wear special hats and mantles which would distinguish them from the Muslims, and to prohibit them from using a saddle, and from employing a Muslim in their service. These conditions, in addition to the obligation of paying the poll tax, expressed the degradation of the protected subjects according to the principle defined in the Koran (Sura 9:29). Their objective was to protect the ruling faith from the ancient religions and publicly separate Muslims and the members of other religions (*ghiyār*, "segregation"). Several of the details are identical with the anti-Jewish laws of the Byzantine emperors.

The conditions of the covenant are not uniform but consist of a collection of regulations and administrative restrictions which were issued by caliphs and sultans over the generations—from Omar II until the middle of the 14th century when they assumed their final form—whenever religious fanaticism or envy of the status of the protected subjects was in the ascendant. There are various versions of these conditions, ranging from the *kitāb al-'Umm* of Muhammad ibn Idrīs al-Shāfi'ī (767–820), the founder of the Shāfi'ī school, to the writings of the chroniclers of the Abbasid and especially the Mamluk periods, including that of Ibn Khaldūn (1322–1406) and those of two other versions, a short one and a lengthy one brought by

Qalqashaudī of the 15th century in Egypt. There is also a Hebrew version in the *Divrei Yosef* of Joseph b. Isaac *Sambari who lived in Egypt (1640–1703).

The following points may be summarized from the various versions: (a) The erection of churches and synagogues which did not exist during the pre-Muslim period was prohibited. (b) The Koran was not to be taught to protected subjects and a Muslim was not to be employed to instruct them. (c) Protected subjects were not to shelter spies. (d) They were not to buy a Muslim slave or maidservant, nor such as were formerly owned by a Muslim. (e) They were not to sell intoxicating liquors to Muslims, nor carcasses of animals not ritually slaughtered, or pork. (f) They were not to employ a Muslim in their service. (g) Protected subjects were to honor the Muslims and stand in their presence. They could not deceive or strike them. (h) They were to accommodate Muslim travelers for three days. (i) They were not to prevent anyone from converting to Islam. (j) They were not to resemble Muslims in their clothing or hairdressing. The Jews were to wear yellow clothes, girdles, and hats, the Christians, blue. The girdles were not to be of silk. The color of their shoes was to differ from that of the Muslims. (k) They were not to be called by Muslim names or appellations. (l) Entry into bathhouses was only to be authorized when a special sign was worn on the neck which would distinguish them from Muslims. Special bathhouses were to be built for women so that they would not bathe together with Muslim women. (m) They were forbidden to carry arms. (n) They were not to ride on horses or mules but only on asses, and then on packsaddles without any ornaments, and not on saddles. They were to ride sidesaddle. (o) Their houses were not to be higher than those of the Muslims. (p) Their tombs were not to be higher than those of the Muslims. (q) They were not to raise their voices in their churches or be seen in public with crosses. (r) They were not to be employed as governmental officials or in any position which would grant them authority over Muslims. (s) The property of the deceased was to belong to the authorities until the heirs prove their right to it according to Islamic law. If there was no heir, the property would be transferred to the authorities.

The head of the religious community was responsible for the enforcement of these conditions. Ibn al-Jawzī (d. 1200) relates that in 1031 the Christian catholicos and the Jewish exilarch were ordered to supervise the members of their communities and ensure that they wore the special garb which had been imposed on the protected subjects. Other sources mention that it was the duty of the *ra'īs* (the *nagid*) "to protect the Muslims from the Jews" by assuming responsibility for the execution of these conditions. The rights which stemmed from the upholding of the Covenant of Omar were security of life and property, freedom of religion, and internal autonomy. Anyone transgressing the covenant forfeited his right to security, especially in the case of one of the following conditions: failure to pay the poll tax; refusal to accept a Muslim legal decision; the murder of a Muslim by a protected subject; immoral relations with a Muslim woman; spying on behalf of the enemy; and cursing the Prophet in public, which was punishable by death.

The fact that instructions for upholding the covenant were repeatedly issued during various periods, and sometimes at short intervals, shows that most of the conditions were not respected. The Abbasid caliphs also issued discriminatory laws against the Christians and Jews, e.g., Harun al-Rashīd (786–809), Ma'mūn (813–833), al-Mutawakkil (847–861), who was the most extreme and published a series of restrictions in 850 and 854, and finally al-Muqtadir (908–932). The rulers required the services of physicians, clerks, specialists in minting coins, and other professionals who served them faithfully. They explained that these people were even authorized to serve as viziers upon the condition that their function consisted merely of the execution of orders *(tanfīdh)* and that they were not empowered with any personal initiative *(tafwīd)*. During periods of religious fanaticism, churches and synagogues were destroyed under the pretext that it had been forbidden to build them (see above, regulation (a)). The most outstanding example was the act of the Fatimid caliph al-Ḥākim bi-Amr Allah (996–1021) who, as the result of extreme religious fanaticism, ordered—in Egypt from 1004 and in other countries from 1008—the destruction of all churches, including that of the Holy Sepulcher in Jerusalem, and of all the synagogues throughout the Fatimid empire, in addition to a series of restrictions, which also included the choice between forced conversion to Islam or departure from the country. But this was exceptional during the period of Fatimid rule, which was generally characterized by tolerance and during which Jews and Christians rose to important positions.

The Decrees of the Almohads. Under the rule of the fanatical Almohads in Spain and Northern Africa during the 12th century, the alternative was placed before the Jews of conversion to Islam or leaving the country, and restrictions in the spirit of the Covenant of Omar were also imposed on the converts to Islam, who were suspected of only having converted outwardly. They were prohibited from possessing slaves and were disqualified from acting as guardians of orphans; the latter were removed from their families and handed over to Muslims. They were also forbidden to engage in commerce. The purpose of these restrictions was also to separate them from the Muslims by special dress. They were not allowed to wear the *'imāma* and *iḥrām* (kinds of headgear). Instead, they were requested to cover their heads with a kind of cap known as a *galansuwa*. They were ordered to wear black clothes with particularly wide hems. These restrictions were in force until the reign of Abdallah ibn Manṣūr (1199–1214). Even after the decrees of the Almohads were abolished from the 13th century onward, the *ghiyār* decrees governing dress were not completely annulled, but were not as strict as previously.

Religious fanaticism intensified during the period of the wars against the crusaders; this was evident from the campaign of incitement and pressure for the application of the Covenant of Omar, and even harsher restrictions during the *Mamluk period (1250–1516). This situation was connected with the fact that the foreign ruling class desired to appear as the protector of Islam and thus came under the influence of religious fanatics. It is known that the regulations concerning distinctive dress and the prohibition of riding horses were enforced with more severity than the other restrictions. The Mamluk rulers, nevertheless, could not dispense with the employment of the protected subjects as officials, among them some of whom attained respected positions. This fact and their obvious economic success occasionally gave rise to waves of jealousy and hatred which resulted in the publication of decrees concerning the enforcement of the laws, especially the exclusion of Jews as public officials. This was the case in 1290, when a decree in this spirit was issued by Sultan Ṣalāḥ al-Dīn Khalīl ibn Qalā'ūn. In 1301 synagogues throughout the empire were closed down for nine years. There was even a tendency to destroy them, and this was only averted after it was "proved," with the support of bribery, that they had been erected during the pre-Muslim period. During the middle of the 14th century there was a renewed wave of fanaticism which brought about very severe legislation in 1354, not only including the previous restrictions of the Covenant of Omar but also the addition of new restrictions which also affected converts to Islam, e.g., the prohibition of their employment as officials and physicians, the severance of all relations with their nonconverted relatives, and their obligatory presence five times a day at the mosque.

In the Ottoman Empire the Covenant of Omar was in force until the middle of the 19th century. The authorities imposed special dress, and Jews and Christians were forbidden to acquire slaves. There was a prohibition on the construction of synagogues and churches, which could only be circumvented by bribery and special authorization. During the 17th century synagogues and churches in the empire were destroyed on a number of occasions. The *jizya* (poll tax) was also paid, except for those connected with the royal court, e.g., court physicians, who were exempted and who were the only Jews authorized to ride on horses and wear clothing in keeping with their status.

In the 19th century, under the pressure of European countries, especially Britain, France, and Austria, firmans were issued which abolished the discriminatory measures against the Christians. The first of these abolished the poll tax (1839). It was not enforced, and under further pressure an additional firman was issued in 1855, and again in 1856 when the prohibition on the carrying of arms by non-Muslims was also abolished and they were exempted from military service. As an alternative to military service a ransom tax known as *bedel askeri*, which in practice replaced the poll tax, was imposed. This tax was not abolished until the revolution of the Young Turks in 1909, when non-Muslims were also obligated to serve actively in the army.

In the countries of the Maghreb, the Covenant of Omar remained in effect until more recently. The *jizya* was taken into consideration in the Tunisian Constitution of 1857. In the *capitulation treaties between Morocco and the European countries in the second half of the 19th century certain persons are mentioned who were exempted from this tax.

Even though in principle the Covenant of Omar applied equally to Christians and Jews, the position of the former within society was generally more favorable as a result of the backing they received from the European countries. Thus, in 1664 all the European Christians in Egypt were exempted from the poll tax. Similarly, in the emirate of Bukhara only the Jews paid this tax.

It may be said that in principle protected subjects were bound by the Covenant of Omar, but that its enforcement was conditioned by internal factors of the Muslim countries; it was dependent on the internal struggles and the conflicts between religious and economic interests, on the one hand, and the influence and the status of the protected subjects themselves and their ability to lessen the severity of the decree, on the other. The execution of the restrictions was dependent on the will of the ruler, who generally gave preference to economic interests over religious law.

Bibliography: M. Steinschneider, *Polemische und apologetische Literatur in arabischer Sprache* . . . (1877), 165–87; M. J. de Goeje, *Mémoires d'histoire . . .*, 2 (1886), 143; R. Gottheil, in: *Old Testament and Semitic Studies in Memory of W. R. Harper*, 2 (1908), 353–414; idem, in: JAOS, 41 (1921), 383–457; L. Caetani (ed.), *Annali dell' Islam*, 3 (1911), 957; A. Tritton, *Caliphs and their Non-Muslim Subjects* (1930); L. A. Mayer, in: *Sefer Magnes* (1938), 161–7 (English summary); W. J. Fischel, *Jews in the Economic and Political Life of Mediaeval Islam* (1969[2]); idem, in: *Zion*, 5 (1940), 209–13; Ashtor, Toledot, 1 (1944), 305–7; idem, in: *Sefer Zikkaron . . . G. Hirschler* (1940), 73–94; A. S. Halkin, in: *Joshua Starr Memorial Volume* (1953), 101–10 (Hebrew); Dinur, Golah, 1 pt. 1 (1958[2]), 60–70; M. Khadduri, *War and Peace in the Law of Islam* (1955), 175–201; A. Fattal, *Le Statut légal des non-Musulmans en pays d'Islam* (1958); B. Lewis, *Emergence of Modern Turkey* (1966), 114, 331; H. Z. Hirschberg, in: A. J. Arberry (ed.), *Religion in the Middle East*, 1 (1969), 150–60.

[EL.B.]

°**OMAR IBN AL-KHATTĀB,** second caliph (634–644), conqueror of Ereẓ Israel, Syria, Iraq, Persia, and Egypt. Omar organized the Muslim empire, established the rules assuring the conquerors of their special status (in spite of their numerical inferiority), fixed the calendar on the basis of the Hegira, and laid the foundations of the legal system. The administrative practices that he introduced were based on Persian and Byzantine models. A man of simple manners and approach, he adopted a humane attitude to non-Muslims as well, and earned the epithet of al-Fārūq ("he who can distinguish truth from falsehood"); according to one tradition, the Jews gave him that name. Balādhurī (d. 862) reports that the Jews of Khaybar, the last Jewish community in the Hejaz, who had been permitted by Muhammad to remain on their land in exchange for one half of their yearly crop, were expelled to Tayma and Jericho by Omar; Ibn al-Athīr (Mosul, 1160–1233) adds that Omar reimbursed them with one half the value of their land. According to Jewish sources, Omar, after the conquest of Persia, gave the Persian king's daughter to *Bustanai in marriage and appointed him to the office of exilarch. A Jewish convert to Islam, *Kaʿb al-Aḥbār, who was a member of Omar's entourage at the time of the conquest of *Jerusalem, is said to have pointed out to Omar the site of the "*Sakhra*," the "**Even Shetiyyah*" ("world's cornerstone") on the Temple Mount; Omar ordered the clearing of the Rock and the site served as a place of prayer until the time of ʿAbd al-Malik (685–705), who built the Dome of the Rock (which became popularly known as the "Mosque of Omar") on this spot. Some Christian and Arab sources report that one of the conditions set by the Christian residents of Jerusalem for their surrender to Omar was a prohibition on the residence of Jews in Jerusalem; the truth of these reports seems doubtful, since Jews did in fact live in Jerusalem during the Arab period. Omar permitted the Jews to reestablish their presence in Jerusalem— after a lapse of 500 years—and also seems to have allotted them a place for prayers on the Temple Mount (from which they were driven out at a later date). Jewish tradition regards Omar as a benevolent ruler and the Midrash (*Nistarot de-Rav Shimon bar Yoḥai*) refers to him as a "friend of Israel." According to Ṭabarī, a Jewish sage told Omar that he was destined to become the ruler of the Holy Land. Omar has been described as the author of the rules discriminating against minorities in Muslim lands (see *Omar, Covenant of), but this allegation does not stand up to scientific investigation.

Bibliography: G. Weil, *Geschichte der Chalifen* (1846), 54–148; A. Kremer, *Culturgeschichte des Orients unter den Chalifen*, 1 (1875), 14–16, 65–71, 99–105; W. Muir, *Annals of the Early Caliphate* (1883), 125–285; Ch. Tykocinski, in: *Devir*, 1 (1923), 145–79; Assaf, Mekorot, 12–22; S. D. Goitein, in: *Melilah*, 3–4 (1950), 156–65; Dinur, Golah, 1 pt. 1 (1959), 31–42; B. Zoltak, in: H. Lazarus Yafeh (ed.), *Perakim be-Toledot ha-Aravim ve-ha-Islam* (1968[2]), 105–17; H. Z. Hirschberg, *ibid.*, 269–70; A. Fattal, *Le Statut légal des non-Musulmans en pays d'Islam* (1958), 60–68.

[EL.B.]

OMER (Heb. עֹמֶר; lit. "sheaf"), an offering brought to the Temple on the 16th of Nisan and thus the name of the period between Passover and Shavuot.

The Bible (Lev. 23:9ff.) prescribes that "when you enter the land which I am giving to you and reap its harvest, you shall bring the first sheaf of your harvest to the priest . . . the priest shall wave it on the day after the sabbath." After

Figure 1. Parchment scroll indicating the counting of the *omer*, made before 1730. New York, Congregation Shearith Israel, The Spanish and Portuguese Synagogue.

the waving, a burnt offering together with a meal offering and a libation were made at the altar and after that had been done it was permissible to eat of the new harvest: "Until that very day, until you have brought the offering of your God, you shall eat no bread or parched grain or fresh ears." The exact meaning of "the day after the sabbath" in the biblical passage was a major point of controversy between the rabbis and the *Boethusians (Men. 65a–b) and, later, the *Karaites. The latter argued that the ceremony was to be performed on the day after the Sabbath immediately following the first day of Passover whereas the rabbis argued that in this context the word "sabbath" was to be understood not as the weekly Sabbath but as a "holy day" and meant the first day of Passover itself. Since the passage quoted continues with the law "And from the day on which you bring the sheaf of wave offering—the day after the sabbath—you shall count seven weeks" and the fiftieth day is Shavuot it follows that according to the sectarians the festival of Shavuot always fell on a Sunday. It has been suggested (L. Finkelstein, *The Pharisees* (1962[3]), 2, 641ff.) that this was a major factor in the dissidents' view, as having the festival always on a Sunday was far more convenient for the Temple cult.

The rabbis, in the light of Exodus 16:36—"The *Omer* is a tenth of an *ephah*"—interpreted the word as a measure of grain and also ruled that it was to be brought of barley only. The *ephah* was three *se'ot* and thus on the 16th of Nisan three *se'ot* of barley were reaped, brought to the Temple, ground and sifted, and of this, one tenth (the *omer*) was "waved" by the priest. The Mishnah (Men. 10) describes the ritual in detail. It was celebrated with a great deal of ceremony and festivity in order to stress the opinion of the rabbis that the 16th of Nisan was the correct date. The ceremony, including the reaping, took place even if the 16th of Nisan was a Sabbath; one opinion has it that on a weekday five *se'ot* were reaped since after sifting only three would remain but that on a Sabbath only three were reaped so as to avoid unnecessary work (Men. 10:1). If the barley was ripe it was taken from the vicinity of Jerusalem; otherwise it could be brought from anywhere in Israel. It was reaped by three men, each with his own scythe and basket. The grain was then brought to the Temple where it was winnowed, parched, and ground into coarse flour. It was then sifted through 13 sieves and one tenth was given to the priest who mixed it with oil and frankincense for "a pleasing odor to the Lord" and "waved" it "before the Lord." This was done by the priest taking the offering on his outstretched hands and moving it from side to side and up and down. This ceremony was interpreted as a prayer to God to protect the harvest from injurious winds and other calamities (Men. 62a). After the waving ceremony a handful was burnt on the altar and the rest was eaten by the priests.

Counting the Omer (Heb. **סְפִירַת הָעֹמֶר** , *Sefirat ha-Omer*). The injunction to count the 49 days from the 16th of Nisan until Shavuot is considered to be of Pentateuchal authority as long as the *omer* itself was offered; thus at present time it is of rabbinic authority only. The 49 days themselves are commonly known as the *sefirah*.

The counting is preceded by a special benediction "... concerning the counting of the *Omer*." Since the Bible states that "You shall count off seven weeks. They must be complete" and "You must count ... fifty days," the counting must mention both the number of days and the number of weeks (Men. 65b–66a). Hence the standard formula runs as follows: on the first day, "Today is the first day of the *Omer*"; on the eighth day, "Today is the eighth day, making one week and one day of the *Omer*, " and so on. The time for the counting, which is to be done standing, is after the evening service, that is, when the new day begins (Sh. Ar., OḤ 489:1). One who forgets to count in the evening may count during the following day, without however reciting the blessing. He may then count again the same evening, using the blessing. But if he fails to count for one complete day, he is not permitted to resume the utterance of the blessing for the whole duration of the *Omer* (Sh. Ar., OḤ 489:7–8). And since the sole stipulation of the commandment is that the number of the particular day of the *Omer* is to be spoken aloud, one should avoid uttering it inadvertently once the time for counting has arrived; for example, if one has not yet counted and is asked what the number of the day is, one should reply by giving the number of the previous day (Sh. Ar., OḤ 489:4).

The kabbalists used the 49 days (7×7) to form permutations of various *sefirot* denoting the ascent out of the 49 "gates" of impurity of the Egyptian bondage to the purity of the revelation at Sinai. In many prayer books these combinations are printed at the side of each day listed. Because the days counted "must be complete" it has become customary not to recite the evening service for

Figure 2. Pages from a booklet for counting the *Omer*, Verona, 1826. Cecil Roth Collection.

Figure 3. Chart for counting the *Omer*, Europe, 1823. The blessing is contained in the rectangle at the top, and the 49 days are specified in the chain of alternating squares and circles. The floral design in the outer border is composed of micrographic writing. Haifa, Ethnological Museum and Folklore Archives. Photo Keren-Or, Haifa.

Shavuot until after nightfall of the 49th day, whereas for other festivals it is permissible to start some time before nightfall (see *Day and Night).

In order not to forget the count of the day it was fairly common practice to have an "*omer* calendar" in the home with movable numbers on it. These "calendars" even developed into an art form and several early specimens show intricate work and lettering. [Ed.]

A Time of Mourning. From an unknown date during the talmudic period, the days of the *Omer* began to take on a character of semi-mourning; the solemnization of marriages was prohibited, then haircutting, and, later still, the use of musical instruments was banned. The mourning is normally associated with a plague said to have decimated the disciples of Rabbi Akiva, who died "because they did not treat each other with respect" (Yev. 62b; cf. Sh. Ar., OḤ 493:1). But this reason for the mourning is among the many uncertainties connected with the *Omer* period and with *Lag ba-Omer, the minor festival celebrated on its 33rd day. The Talmud alludes to the plague, but makes no mention of any commemorative mourning. This is first recorded in the eighth century, when Natronai Gaon issued a responsum confirming both the practice of mourning and the accepted reason for it (Levin, Oẓar, Yevamot, 141). Subsequent codes and compilations of custom up to and including the Shulḥan Arukh (OḤ 493) cite this reference; and most, although not all (e.g., *Toledot Adam ve-Ḥavvah*, 5, 4; *Abudraham ha-Shalem* (1959), 245), presume that the custom did in fact originate with the death of Akiva's disciples. On the other hand, Maimonides' *Mishneh Torah* and the Ashkenazi *Maḥzor Vitry* appear unaware of its very existence.

Lag ba-Omer. The origin of Lag ba-Omer is likewise shrouded in mystery. It is not explicitly mentioned any earlier than the 13th century, when Meiri in his commentary to *Yevamot* (*Beit ha-Beḥirah*, Yev. 62b) described it as the day when, "according to a tradition of the *geonim*," the "plague" surceased. Moreover there are differences of opinion as to how the date of Lag ba-Omer is to be calculated. Fundamentally, there are two approaches to the question, which in turn account for the different periods of time (according to various rites) when the mourning restrictions are held to be in force.

One school of thought sees the 33rd day of the *Omer* as the anniversary of the termination of the plague. The authority for this view derives from a Midrash, no longer extant, which was handed down by Joshua ibn Shu'aib in the 14th century, or possibly based on an unknown "Spanish manuscript" cited by Zerahiah b. Isaac ha-Levi of the 12th century (see Tur, OḤ 493). In place of reading "they died from Passover to Shavuot," this Midrash adds the word *"pros,"* i.e., "they died from Passover until before *(ad pros)* Shavuot." *"Pros"* is taken to mean 15 days before; and thus implies that the plague terminated a fortnight before Shavuot, and Lag ba-Omer is the anniversary of that day. Strictly speaking, however, 15 days before Shavuot would be the 34th day of the *Omer*, as indeed the Shulḥan Arukh concedes.

The present custom, then, must be attributed to a different calculation which is given by Isserles in his gloss to the Shulḥan Arukh. The explanation stems from a *tosafot*, also no longer extant, cited by Ibn Shu'aib and most fully elaborated on by Jacob b. Moses Moellin in the 15th century in his *Sefer Maharil* (1873), 21b. In this work, Lag ba-Omer appears not as an anniversary at all but as a symbol of the 33 weekdays that occur during the course of the 49 days of the *Omer*. After subtracting the days of Passover, and those of the Sabbath and of Rosh Ḥodesh, only 33 are left from the 49 in which mourning is permissible; this fact is symbolically observed by constituting the 33rd day as a minor festival. This second mode of interpretation gave rise to three divergent customs regarding the mourning period. Some communities observed it for the 33 days from Passover to Shavuot omitting the special days, others for the 33 between Passover and Lag ba-Omer, and others for the 33 from after Rosh Ḥodesh Iyyar to Shavuot excluding Lag ba-Omer itself. The kabbalists took an entirely different approach to the matter. As to *sefirah* days, they stressed the idea of spiritual preparation for Shavuot, the anniversary of the revelation on Mt. Sinai (*Ḥemdat Yamim*, 3, 41d). Lag ba-Omer itself marked the *hillula—the *yahrzeit* of *Simeon b. Yoḥai, by tradition the author of the Zohar. It was either the day on which he was ordained by Rabbi Akiva, or when he emerged from the cave in Meron where he had been hiding from the Romans (Shab. 33b), or the day on which he died; and it is observed as a *hillula*—a festivity or a "wedding between heaven and earth." Hence the grand celebrations which take place at Meron (*Zohar Idra Zutra*, end of *Ha'azinu*). However, although the Zohar does speak of Simeon's death as a *hillula*, there is no recorded reference to its date earlier than that in *Peri Eẓ Ḥayyim* by Ḥayyim b. Joseph Vital (16/17th century; *Sha'ar Sefirat ha-Omer*, ch. 7).

While the celebrations at Meron excited enthusiasm among all sections of Jewish society and particularly from the kabbalists, they also provoked severe criticism. R. Moses *Sofer of Pressburg (d. 1839), after opposing the popular observance of lighting bonfires and questioning all of the reasons given above for the observance of Lag ba-Omer, offered his own explanation for the holiday. Lag ba-Omer is the day when manna began to fall in the wilderness (*Resp. Ḥatam Sofer*, YD 236). Since, however, the Talmud (Shab. 87b) and the *Sefer Olam* calculate that this happened two days earlier, there is, in the last resort, no unassailable determination of what actually took place on Lag ba-Omer; the only definite tradition is that the day is a holiday.

It has for a long time been considered—Nachman Krochmal (d. 1840) being the most notable to express this view—that the cryptic reference in the Talmud to the disciples of R. Akiva and their mysterious death is in fact a veiled report of the defeat of "Akiva's soldiers" in the war with Rome (cf. Maimonides, *Yad Melakhim* 11:3; probably based on TJ, Ta'an. 4:5). As a result, a variety of new theories have arisen among modern writers as to the origin of Lag ba-Omer. R. Isaac Nissenbaum of Warsaw, author of several books on religious Zionism, suggested that Lag ba-Omer is the anniversary of some great but brief triumph by the Judeans in their forlorn war with the Romans—possibly the recapture of Jerusalem, for which special coins were struck (*Hagut Lev* (1911), 181). Y. T. Levinsky, in *Sefer ha-Mo'adim* (1955), 340–2, pursues this line further; he cites Josephus (Wars 2:402ff.) as authority for the fact that a Judean uprising commenced in 66 C.E. in the days of the procurator Florus. At the same time he concurs with the tradition associating the victory on Lag ba-Omer with Bar Kokhba 70 years later, as well as with the story that Julius Serverus' campaign against the insurrectionist Judeans was most severe during the period between Passover and Shavuot.

Eliezer Levi (*Yesodot ha-Tefillah* (1952), 232) advanced a hypothesis endeavoring to resolve another problem sensed by earlier writers; namely why we should mourn for the disciples of Rabbi Akiva, since they died as a punishment for their unseemly conduct? In view of the veiled references to the war with the Romans, he suggests, the judgment of the Talmud is to be understood not as condemning Akiva's disciples and their lack of respect for one another, but on the contrary as praising their dedication and teamwork. On the other hand, it may be that the phrases in the Talmud are to be understood in their literal sense: "Akiva's soldiers" were defeated due to a lack of coordination and unified command (see *Panim el Panim*, no. 574, May 22, 1970). The earlier traditions surrounding Bar Yoḥai's connection with Lag ba-Omer are entirely in accord with these theories, and one might then draw up a summary or composite theory in the following vein: Bar Kokhba's (i.e., Akiva's) men suffered an overwhelming defeat during the weeks between Passover and Shavuot; on the 33rd day of the *Omer* they enjoyed an important, though brief, change of fortune; and on this day Bar Yoḥai, one of the leading fighters in the uprising either emerged from hiding in Meron, or lost his life in securing the victory.

Other Explanations. Extra-rabbinic sources do not help to clarify the matter. Some students of folklore trace the mournful nature of the days of the *sefirah* to the Roman superstition against marriages in May. The fullest statement of this theory was made in the 19th century by Julius Landsberger of Darmstadt (see bibl.). The author cites Ovid (Fast 5:419ff.), who explains that the Romans did not solemnize marriages in May due to the fact that this was the month of the *Lemuria* when the souls of the departed returned to wander over the earth and disturb the peace of the living. Funeral rites *(Lemuria)* were held to appease the spirits, and no Roman maiden would jeopardize her happiness by marrying during a month associated with funeral ceremonies. According to Landsberger, the Roman superstition was adopted by the Jews, who subsequently lost all recollection of its origin and found a new rationale for it in the tragedy of Akiva's disciples. Landsberger's theory leaves many questions unanswered. It does not explain why there is a ban on haircutting during the *Omer* as well as on marriage, or why the custom prevailed in geonic countries. But it does, however, offer an ingenious explanation of the origin of Lag ba-Omer. Among the Romans, the period of superstitious fear lasted for 32 days starting from Walpurgis Night (the last night of April) and continuing throughout the 31 days of May. In commemoration of this period of 32 days, its conclusion on the 33rd day was celebrated as a festival.

Theodor H. Gaster (*Festivals of the Jewish Year* (1953), 52) suggests that Lag ba-Omer, especially with its custom of children going forth with bows and arrows, is a Jewish version of the English and German custom of shooting arrows at demons on May day, i.e., the day after Walpurgis Night. In the view of Joseph Naphtali Derenbourg (in REJ, 29 (1894), 149), Lag ba-Omer is a day in the middle of the *sefirah* period when mourning is to be relaxed, comparable to *mi-carême* observed midway during Lent. There were 34 (twice 17) bad days during the *sefirah;* a respite was needed and the first day of the second half was chosen. J. Morgenstern (in: HUCA, 39 (1968), 81–90) points out that the date of Lag ba-Omer is the approximate midpoint of the 49-day period for those dissidents who begin their *Omer* offering the day after Passover. L. H. Silberman (see bibl.) following H. Grimme, regards the day as commemorating an anniversary celebrated in honor of Marduk; and Gustav Dalman conjectured that it may have marked the first day of summer between the 13th and 25th of May, which was distinguished by the early rising of the Pleiades (cf. RH 11b).

Later Events During the Omer. If the origins of the mourning during the *sefirah* period remain obscure, more identifiable subsequent events add justification for its observance today. According to 13th-century authorities, the melancholy of the season was in remembrance of the victims of the Crusades in the Rhineland in 1096 and 1146 *(Sefer Minhag Tov, Sefer Asufot)*. These Crusades are recollected in *piyyutim* of lament during the sabbaths of the *sefirah,* together with mention of another series of massacres that took place in the springtime, i.e., those perpetrated in 1648–49 by the Cossacks and the Poles. Later and modern sources, such as the *siddur* of Jacob Emden and the *Arukh ha-Shulḥan* (OḤ 493:1) include these together with the earlier events. And in J. Vainstein's *Cycle of the Jewish Year* (1953), 131–2, the revolt of the ghettos against the Nazis in the month of Nisan is included in the discussion of the *sefirah* and mention is made of the Knesset's decision to fix the 27th of that month as a memorial day for the victims. On the other hand, Israel Independence Day (5th of Iyyar) has the status of a half-holiday, and has been included among the days on which mourning restrictions are suspended (Resp. *Kol Mevasser* pt. 1, no. 21). See also *Lag ba-Omer. [D.M.FE.]

Bibliography: S. Goren, *Torat ha-Mo'adim* (1964), 346–58; J. Landsberger, in: JZWL, 7 (1869), 81–96; L. H. Silberman, in: HUCA, 22 (1949), 221–37; J. Morgenstern, in: HUCA, 39 (1968), 81–90; D. M. Feldman, in: *Proceedings of the Rabbinical Assembly* (1962), 201–24; E. Munk, *World of Prayer,* 2 (1963), 137–42; S. Y. Zevin, *Ha-Mo'adim ba-Halakhah* (1963[10]), 292–304.

OMER (AYIN), HILLEL (1926–), Hebrew writer and poet. Born and educated in the kibbutz of *Mishmar ha-Emek, Hillel fought in the *Palmaḥ during the Israel War of Independence. After the war he studied horticulture in Paris. His first poems were published when he was 18, and his first collection, *Ereẓ ha-Ẓohorayim,* appeared in 1950. His books of stories and verse for children include *Boker Tov* (1961) and *Dodi Simḥah* (1964). In 1968, he was appointed director of the Department of Landscape and Gardening of the Tel Aviv municipality.

Bibliography: M. Shamir, *Be-Kulmos Mahir* (1960), 148–52; M. Avishai, *Bein Olamot* (1962), 174–84; S. Burnshaw et al. (eds.), *The Modern Hebrew Poem Itself* (1965), 174–7. [G.K.]

OMNAM KEN (Heb. אָמְנָם כֵּן ; "Yes, it is true"), initial words and name of a penitential *piyyut* for the *Kol Nidrei* service on the eve of the Day of Atonement, known only in the Ashkenazi (German and Polish) ritual. This *piyyut,* of an alphabetical acrostic pattern, was composed by R. *Yom Tov of Joigny, who died as a martyr in the York massacre in 1190. The *piyyut* emphasizes the sinfulness of man who fails because of his evil inclinations, and pleads for God's forgiveness and mercy. Each of its 11 stanzas ends with *salaḥti* ("I have pardoned"), derived from Numbers 14:20.

Text and English translation printed in: *High Holiday Prayerbook,* ed. by Morris Silverman (1954[2]), 233; *Service of the Synagogue, Day of Atonement,* 1 (1955), 38.

Bibliography: Davidson, Oẓar, 1 (1924), 263, no. 5764. [ED.]

OMRI (Heb. עָמְרִי), king of Israel (c. 882–871 B.C.E., I Kings 16:16–28), contemporary of King Asa of Judah. Omri's father's name is not mentioned in sources. According to II Kings 16:23, Omri reigned over the Kingdom of Israel for 12 years, six of them in Tirzah. But according to the synchronism with the king of Judah, it would seem that he reigned only eight years (I Kings 16:23, 29). The background of Omri's ascent to the throne at Tirzah was the extinction of *Baasha's dynasty and struggle for power among the high officers of the army, When the report was received that *Zimri had liquidated *Elah, son of Baasha, "all Israel" made Omri "the captain of the host," king of Israel. At that time Omri was on the field of battle, fighting the Philistines at the border town of Gibbethon (I Kings 16:15, 17; cf. 15:27). Omri and "all Israel" with him turned north to Tirzah, which they besieged and captured. After Zimri's death, the struggle for the throne continued between Omri and *Tibni son of Ginath (I Kings 16:21–22), each respectively having the support of "half of the people," and ended with the latter's death.

Of all Omri's deeds after he became king of Israel, only one item is mentioned in the Bible, which concerns his founding of the city of *Samaria. Omri left Tirzah, which had been the royal capital since the reign of *Jeroboam the son of Nebat (14:17), and built himself a new capital on land which he bought from Shemer, "the owner of the hill Samaria" (16:24). Samaria remained the capital of the Kingdom of Israel for the rest of its existence. The name Omri became an established term to indicate the Israelite kings (in the Assyrian documents *Bît Ḫumri*) even after the death of Omri and his descendants. According to archaeological evidence the building of the Samarian acropolis and the royal palace within, begun in Omri's reign, was only completed in the time of his son *Ahab. The removal of the capital from Tirzah to Samaria marks a new chapter in the history of the Israelite kingdom. Omri achieved stability in internal affairs, after a prolonged period of riots and tumult in the court, and founded a dynasty which remained in power for nearly 50 years. The stabilization of the central government brought in its wake a general improvement in Israel's military and political standing. In the stele of *Mesha king of Moab, it is related that Omri gained possession of Madaba in the northern section of the plain north of the Arnon. Omri's successes in southern Transjordan were the result of a policy of mending quarrels and establishing peaceful relations with neighbors in the north and in the south. In Omri's time the prolonged war between

Judah and Israel was discontinued. The Davidids accepted (at least temporarily) the existence of the northern kingdom and the two royal houses made a pact (see: *Ahab, *Jehoshaphat). Israel enjoyed great economic prosperity in the time of Omri as a result of the treaty with Ethbaal king of Sidon, which was sealed by the marriage between Jezebel, Ethbaal's daughter, and Ahab, apparently while Omri was still alive (cf. Amos 1:9, "the brotherly covenant"). The triple alliance between Israel, Judah, and Phoenicia served at the same time as a counterweight to the threat of Aram-Damascus, whose aim was to gain possession of the northern part of Ereẓ Israel and to establish hegemony in Syria and Ereẓ Israel (see: *Ben-Hadad). The triple alliance countered the Aramean threat but could not reduce it entirely. From I Kings 20:34 it becomes apparent that Aram-Damascus had some advantage over the Samarian kingdom. There were "bazaars" in Samaria belonging to Damascus already in Omri's time, and Israel was forced to grant special privileges to Aramean merchants in Samaria. In spite of the relative stability which Omri achieved in internal affairs and his improvement of Israel's political status externally, the biblical historiographer finds fault with Omri (I Kings 16:25–26). This negative assessment stems from the religious and social viewpoint and is in accordance with the Deuteronomic school. Indeed Omri did not abolish the worship of the golden calves which Jeroboam the son of Nebat had introduced. Moreover, the politico-economic alliance with Phoenicia had far-reaching results in cultural, religious, and social spheres—the cult of the Tyrian Baal took root among the royal courtiers, royal officers, and the urban population. The economic prosperity was not felt equally by all groups of the population, and thus the economic rift in Israelite society was widened. The increasing sway of the foreign cults on the one hand, and the social oppression (cf. "the statutes of Omri" in Micah 6:16) on the other, caused the formation of a strong opposition movement to Omri and his house, at the head of which stood the prophets, such as *Elijah and *Elisha, and those who had remained faithful to the Lord.

Bibliography: Bright, Hist, 219ff.; J. Gray, *A History of Israel* (1960), 220–3; A. Parrot, *Samaria, the Capital of the Kingdom of Israel* (1958); Morgenstern, in: HUCA, 15 (1940), 134–66; Whitley, in: VT, 2 (1952), 137–52; H. L. Ginsberg, in: *Fourth World Congress of Jewish Studies*, 1 (1967), 91–93. [B.O.]

OMSK, town in S.W. Siberia, Russian S.F.S.R. The first Jewish settlers in Omsk were exiles to Siberia. During 1828–56 Jewish children who had been seized for military service were sent to the *Cantonist regiment in Omsk. The community was formed by the exiles and ex-servicemen of the Russian army. In 1855 the first synagogue was founded and a second in 1873. The Jewish population numbered 1,138 Jews (3% of the population) in 1897. There were 4,389 Jews in the province of Omsk in 1926 and 9,175 Jews in 1959. In 1970 the Jewish population was estimated at about 10,000. There was no information available on organized Jewish life in Omsk and at that time no synagogue existed in the town. [Y.S.]

ONA'AH (Heb. אוֹנָאָה; "overreaching"), the act of wronging another by selling him an article for more than its real worth or by purchasing from him an article for less than its real worth.

Origin and Nature of the Prohibition. The prohibition against *ona'ah* has its origin in the Pentateuch, "And if thou sell aught unto thy neighbor, or buy of thy neighbor's hand, ye shall not wrong one another" (Lev. 25:14). The passage was construed by the scholars as relating to overreaching in monetary matters and they distinguished three degrees of this, according to whether the discrepancy amounts to one-sixth, less than one-sixth, or more than one-sixth of the value of the article (see below). The law of *ona'ah* applies to undercharging as well as overcharging (Sh. Ar., ḤM) 227:2). The prohibition against *ona'ah* is a separate one but is also embraced within the wider prohibition against robbery. Despite the express enjoinder of the prohibition as a negative command, transgression is not punished by *flogging since the overreaching is remediable by restitution, and the person who has overreached—whether wittingly or unwittingly—is obligated to make good the discrepancy (Yad, Mekhirah 12:1; Sh. Ar., ḤM 227:2).

Three Degrees of Ona'ah. In the case where a person has overreached by one-sixth, the transaction is valid but he must make good the discrepancy to the injured party (BM 50b). The discrepancy of one-sixth is calculated on the market value. If the discrepancy amounts to less than one-sixth, the transaction is valid and the difference need not be made good (Yad, loc. cit. 12:3). As regards sales and purchases transacted by minors the scholars, having noted that their transactions shall be valid for the sake of insuring their vital needs, also laid down that even though minors have no legal capacity to waive their rights, their mistake shall nonetheless be treated in the same way as the mistake of an adult (Sh. Ar., ḤM 235:3) and they must be deemed to waive their right in repect of overreaching amounting to less than one-sixth (see *Legal Capacity). If the discrepancy amounts to more than one-sixth the transaction is void but the injured party may waive his right in respect of the overreaching and uphold the transaction (Yad, loc. cit. 12:4). Some scholars held that the party who has overreached may insist on voiding the transaction even though the injured party is willing to waive his rights in the matter (Tos. to BM 50b).

Contracting out of the Law of Overreaching. A stipulation between the parties stating, "on condition that there is no overreaching therein" (i.e., in the transaction), or "on condition that you have no claim of overreaching against me," is invalid (Sh. Ar., ḤM 227:21), since the language used implies a stipulation contrary to a prohibition laid down in the Torah and one may not stipulate to set aside the Pentateuchal law; however, when the amounts involved in the transaction are specified, a stipulation of this nature is valid, since the injured party knows the precise amount of the overreaching to which he waives his right, and all stipulations in monetary matters are valid (*ibid. (mamon)* see also *Contract). If the parties agreed that the purchase price be determined by the valuation of a third party the parties to the transaction will have a claim against each other for overreaching if it is later found that the valuer erred in his valuation (Sh. Ar., ḤM 227:25).

Property not Subject to the Law of Overreaching. Four items are not subject to the law of overreaching: land, slaves, deeds, and consecrated property (*hekdesh;* BM 56b). "Even though it is a decree of the Torah, yet the matter must to some extent be amplified by logical reasoning. For a person sometimes buys land for more than its worth and the scholars called land something that is always worth the money paid for it and, contrariwise, when a person is in need of money but finds no purchaser he sells it (land) for much less than its worth since it is impossible to carry land from place to place. Similarly, slaves are sometimes the source of trouble, yet a person who is in need of a slave may be prepared to pay a high price for him. As regards deeds which are due for payment, these are sometimes subject to depreciation because of the financial position of the debtor or his aggressiveness. Concerning consecrated property in the Temple period, it was decided that 'if *hekdesh* worth a *maneh* had been redeemed for the equivalent of a *perutah*, the redemption was valid'—hence, in the sale of consecrated property also there is no law of overreaching, even though the Temple treasury be wronged, so that the buyer cannot retract since 'a verbal undertaking in favor of the Temple treasury is as a delivery to the common man'" (*Arukh ha-Shulḥan*, ḤM 227:34).

LAND. The law of overreaching applies neither to the sale nor the leasing of land (Yad, Mekhirah 13:14). Anything which is attached to the land is subject to the same law as the land itself, provided that it is dependent on that land itself (Sh. Ar., ḤM 193). An opinion was also expressed that the same law applies to both, even when the article attached to the land is not dependent on that land itself (*Rema*, ad loc.). A very early opinion that land outside Ereẓ Israel is considered as movable property and subject to the law of overreaching, was rejected (Tur., ḤM, 95:4).

SLAVES. There is no overreaching as regards slaves, since the law of slaves is analogous to the law of land (BM 56b. See *Slavery). Hence it was laid down as *halakhah* that the law of overreaching does not apply to the hire of laborers because it is as if the employer buys the laborer for a limited time and the latter's position is assimilated to that of a slave required for a limited period (Yad, Mekhirah, 13:15). The opinion that the law of overreaching applies to a contractor (*kabbelan;* Yad, loc. cit. 13; 18), is disagreed with by certain scholars (Nov. Ramban, BM 55a; Maggid Mishneh, Mekhirah 13:15). A minority opinion that the hire of a laborer is subject to the law of overreaching was rejected (Resp. Maharam of Rothenburg, ed. Prague, no. 749; see also *Labor Law). There is no law of overreaching as regards a Hebrew slave (*Minḥat Ḥinnukh*, no. 337).

DEEDS. There is no overreaching as regards bonds, but money bills issued in different countries at the instance of the government are treated as money in all respects since they are officially issued and are taken in payment; however, shares and the like which are not officially issued are apparently like deeds and not subject to the law of overreaching (*Pitḥei Teshuvah*, YD 305, n. 7 and ḤM 95, n. 1).

The scholars expressed differing opinions on the question of whether enormous overreaching gives ground for invalidating a transaction relating to land, slaves, or deeds; one view is that the transaction may be invalidated when the overreaching exceeds one-sixth of the price (*Halakhot*, Rif, BM 57a); another is that this may be done if the overreaching reaches one-half of the purchase price (Rif, loc. cit.); and a third is that the sale is only invalidated when the limit of one-half has been exceeded (*Rema*, ḤM 227:29; *Sma, Siftei Kohen* and *Ha-Gra*, ad loc.). However, the accepted opinion is that with regard to land, slaves, and deeds the law of overreaching never applies nor does it ever serve to invalidate the transaction (Sh. Ar., ḤM 227:29; *Siftei Kohen*, ḤM 66, n. 122).

CONSECRATED PROPERTY. In the Temple period the law of overreaching did not apply to consecrated property (BM 56b; Yad, Mekhirah 13:8) but "in these times" the law of overreaching does apply in respect of consecrated property and property dedicated to the poor (ḤM 227, n. 48; see *Hekdesh). Although it was enjoined, "if you shall sell" the law of overreaching applies to coins (BM 51b) despite the fact that a coin is not something that is sold (ḤM 227, n. 26).

Further Cases of Exclusion from the Law of Overreaching. BARTER. The accepted opinion is that the law of overreaching does not operate in a transaction of barter (see *Acquisition, Yad, Mekhirah, 13:1; Sh. Ar., ḤM 227:20). In the opinion of some scholars, utensils and animals that are stock in trade are subject to the law of overreaching even when bartered, and the rule excluding overreaching in barter was laid down solely in respect of property traded by a layman (Resp. Radbaz, no. 1340, and see below).

"ONE WHO TRADES ON TRUST." There is no overreaching as regards "one who trades on trust" (BM 51b). "How so? If the seller said to the purchaser 'I purchased this article for so and so much and I wish to earn thereon so and so much,' the purchaser will have no claim against him for overreaching" (Arukh ha-Shulḥan 227:28), "even if the overreaching amounts to more than one-sixth" (Yad, Mekhirah 14:1). On the other hand, the scholars laid down that raising the prices of commodities beyond the accepted level, or beyond those fixed by the competent authority, amounts to a transgression of the prohibition against profiteering.

PERSONAL APPAREL. The law of overreaching does not apply to the sale of apparel because the owner would not sell such articles except if he received the price he demanded (BM 51a), and this is so even when he is known to have sold these items on account of financial hardship (Resp. Rosh, no. 105:3). The scholars differed as to whether or not the "layman" has a claim in respect of overreaching (*Shitah Mekubbeẓet* loc. cit.; *Maggid Mishneh*, Mekhirah 13:2). It was held that if he has sold articles which are normally traded, he will have a claim in respect of overreaching (*Ḥananel*, BM 51a).

AGENCY. The law of *ona'ah* does not operate in respect of property sold through an agent. If the agent is overreached in any manner the sale is void since his principal may say, "I delegated you to act to my advantage and not to my detriment" (Kid. 42b; Yad, Mekhirah 13:9). If the purchaser is the injured party some scholars hold that the sale is void, as it is in the reverse case, but the accepted opinion is that in this case the law applies as if the agent were acting independently and the purchaser waives a discrepency of less than one-sixth (Rosh, loc. cit.; Sh. Ar., EH 104:6). When the fact that a party was acting as an agent remained undisclosed, the sale will be valid as long as the overreaching did not reach the stipulated measure (Yad, Sheluḥin, 2:4). The principal has the right to retract on account of overreaching even in matters which are not otherwise subject to the law of overreaching (Sh. Ar., ḤM, 227:30). He has the right either to void the sale or to uphold it but the purchaser is not entitled to seek its invalidation (*Netivot ha-Mishpat, Mishpat ha-Urim* 185, n. 8).

The law of overreaching is the same for a guardian (see *Apotropos) as it is for a principal (Sh. Ar., ḤM 227:30), even when the former is appointed by the court (Mekhirah 13:9). A partner who has bought or sold is subject to the same law as a person who has bought or sold his own property, since this is not a case in which it may properly be said, "I have delegated you to act to my advantage and not to my detriment" (*Siftei Kohen*, ḤM 77, 19). A broker who has an interest in the property sold is held by some scholars to be in the same position as an agent (*Netivot ha-Mishpat, Mishpat ha-Urim*, 222, n. 16), while another opinion is that his position is equated with that of a partner (ḤM 227, n. 42; see also **Shalish*). The law of overreaching does not apply to transactions negotiated by the "seven senior citizens" (i.e., public representatives) on behalf of the community (Ran on Rif, Meg. 8a; *Rema*, OḤ 153:7; *Taz*, thereto, n. 8).

Division of Property by Brothers or Partners. The law of overreaching applies to the division of inherited property by brothers or partners, since their position is assimilated to that of purchasers. This rule applies to partners in respect of the partnership property only and not to a mere profit-sharing or business partnership (*Arukh ha-Shulḥan*, ḤM 8, 227:338; see also *Ownership).

Claim for Restitution or Invalidation of a Transaction. A purchaser who wishes to claim restitution or to invalidate a transaction on the grounds of overreaching must do so within the time it would take for him to show the article to a merchant or other person from whom he may ascertain its market price (Sh. Ar., ḤM 227:7). Longer delay entails forfeiture of his right, but he need not pay the price if he has not yet done so (*Siftei Kohen*, thereto). If the injured party is the seller he may retract at any time since he no longer holds the article and cannot show it to a merchant (BM 50b; Yad, Mekhirah 12:6; Sh. Ar., ḤM 227:8). However, if the seller should ascertain the value of the article and thereafter fail to claim restitution of the amount of the overreaching or invalidation of the sale, he will forfeit his right to do so (Yad and Sh. Ar., loc. cit.), but another opinion is that the seller retains this right at all times (*Maggid Mishneh*, Mekhirah 12:6).

Bibliography: J. S. Zuri, *Mishpat ha-Talmud*, 5 (1921), 70–76; Gulak, Yesodei, 1 (1922), 64–66; 2 (1922), 153–60; P. Dickstein, in: *Ha-Mishpat ha-Ivri*, 1 (1925/26), 15–55; Herzog, Instit, 1 (1936), 112–7; 2 (1939), 121–4; E. Z. Melamed, in: *Yavneh*, 3 (1942), 35–56; ET, 1 (1951[3]), 153–60; B. Rabinowitz-Teomim, *Ḥukkat Mishpat* (1957), 113–40, Elon, Mafte'aḥ, 1f. [SH.SH.]

ONAGER (**Wild Ass;** Biblical פֶּרֶא, Job 39:5, also עָרוֹד). Two subspecies of the wild ass, the *Equus hemionus hemihippus*, the Syrian onager, and the *Equus hemionus onager*, the Arabian onager, existed in the Syrian desert up to the present century. The onager is described as loving freedom (Jer. 2:24) and fearless (Job 39:5–8). Its habitat is in waste places (Isa. 32:44 and Job 39:6), and Ishmael who was to dwell in the desert is called a wild ass of a man (Gen. 16:12). It appears that from time to time efforts were made to domesticate the wild ass. An ancient Sumerian picture shows it harnessed to a wagon, and the Tosefta (Kil. 5:5) forbids the yoking of an ass with an onager. It was sometimes employed for turning millstones (Av. Zar. 16b). It would appear that the wild ass flourished in the talmudic period, and its flesh was used to feed animals in the arena (Men. 103b). In Babylon fields were fenced in to prevent the onagers from doing damage (BB 36a).

Bibliography: Y. Aharoni, *Torat ha-Ḥai*, 1 (1923), 99–101; Lewysohn, Zool, 143; J. Feliks, *Animal World of the Bible* (1962), 29–30. [J.F.]

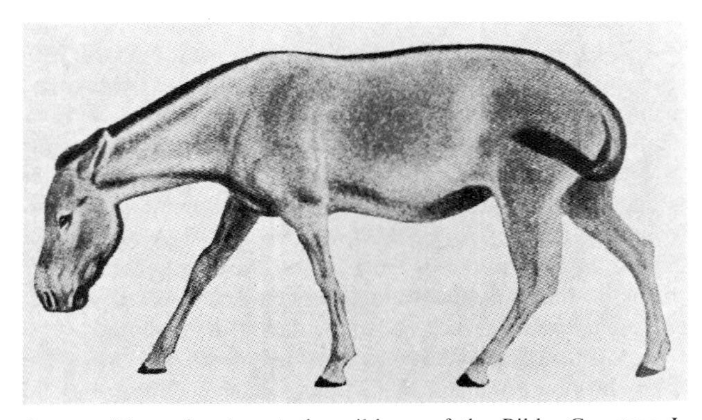

Onager *(Equus hemionus)*, the wild ass of the Bible. Courtesy J. Feliks, Jerusalem.

ONAN (Heb. אוֹנָן; "power," "wealth"), second son of Judah and Shua (Gen. 38:2–4; 46:12; Num. 26:19). After the death of his elder brother Er, Onan was instructed by his father to contract a levirate marriage with his childless sister-in-law Tamar (Gen. 38:7–8). Onan refused to fulfill his fraternal duty, and whenever he had relations with Tamar he would let the semen go to waste (presumably by *coitus interruptus*, although the term *onanism can be actually applied to masturbation), thereby avoiding effective consummation of the marriage (38:9). Onan's offensive conduct was motivated by the fact that the son born of a levirate marriage was accounted to the dead brother (Deut. 25:5–6). His uncharitableness was displeasing to the Lord who took his life (Gen. 38:10). The Judahite genealogy in I Chronicles 2:3 does not mention the death of Onan.

This story may possibly contain an historical nucleus reflecting the extinction of two clans of the tribe of Judah.

Bibliography: EM, 1 (1955), 155 (incl. bibl.); D. M. Feldman, *Birth Control in Jewish Law* (1968), 111–2. [ED.]

ONANISM, term derived from the biblical narrative of Onan, son of Judah (Gen. 38, 7–10) who "spilled" his seed "on the ground." Onanism refers to the thwarting of the sexual process in one of several ways. In Hebrew, it is called more fully, *ma'aseh Er ve-Onan* "the act of Er and Onan" and is taken by the Midrash (Gen. R. 85:5; and by Rashi to the Pentateuch) to mean *coitus interruptus* and by the Talmud (Yev. 34b) to refer either to unnatural intercourse or (cf. Nid. 13a) to masturbation. The Zohar (*Va-Yeshev*, p. 188a; *Va-Yeḥi*, p. 219b) expatiates on the evil of onanism in the last sense, which condemnation then entered the Shulḥan Arukh (EH, 23:2) to underscore the gravity of the sin of *hashḥatat zera* ("improper emission of seed"). Halakhically, there is a question whether the prohibition against onanism, in any sense, is a prohibition of biblical or of rabbinic force. A 16th-century legal work by R. Moses Trani, *Kiryat Sefer* (on Yad, Issurei Bi'ah, 21), whose express purpose is to determine which of the commandments are biblical and which rabbinic, did not reach a decision about onanism. The Onan narrative in the Bible is pre-Sinai, and the context makes it sufficiently doubtful whether Onan's sin is his contraceptive act or his frustration of the purpose of levirate marriage, i.e., to establish progeny for his brother. Other biblical bases for onanism or *hashḥatat zera* (Gen. 1:28; 6:12; Ex. 20:13; Lev. 18:6; Isa. 1:15; 57:5) are variously regarded as deductive, or "intimations" *(remez)*, from the standpoint of their biblical derivation, though the prohibition is nonetheless clear. The question is of more than academic interest, as evidenced by the circumstances under which onanism is condoned. *Coitus interruptus*, for example, is actually recommended by R. Eliezer in the Talmud (Yev. 34b) as a contraceptive procedure to prevent dilution of the mother's milk during nursing, but is rejected by the other sages and is forbidden by all the law codes, beginning with that of Maimonides (Yad, Issurei Bi'ah 21:18). Yet the factors of intent and constancy (as was indeed the case with Onan) are considered, and the responsa would permit, for example, the continuance of marital relations where interrupted coitus is unintentional or irregular. On the other hand, the deviations of "unnatural" coitus *(she-lo ke-darkah)* are objected to on moral grounds (Maim. Comm. to Sanh. 7:4), though legally permitted (Ned. 20b; Sanh. 58b). R. Isaac in *tosafot* (Yev. 34b) reconciled the leniency of the sages in law with what they condemned in Er and Onan, by distinguishing between the corrupt intent of Onan and legitimate heterosexual intent in ordinary marital relations. The responsa, too, ruled in accordance with the latter interpretation—despite the reaction that set in against this point of view after the Zohar appeared, leading R. Joseph Caro to claim that R. Isaac would not have ruled so permissively had he seen what the Zohar says on the subject (*Bedek ha-Bayit* to *Beit Yosef*, EH, 25). Other medieval mystical works sided with the Zohar in this matter, but the legal tradition affirmed the permissibility of *she-lo kedarkah* in marital relations. A post-medieval mystic, R. Jacob Emden (d. 1776), addressed himself to the difference between the talmudic and zoharic attitudes toward onanism in the sense of masturbation, which has consequences for the question of birth control. He prefers the attitude of the Talmud, and calls that of the Zohar "exaggeration" (*Mitpaḥat Sefarim* (Altona, 1768), 1:20). More important, he emphasizes a doctrine, articulated by earlier legal authorities, that the prohibition against onanism in method is not applicable to marital contraception; that when contraception is necessary and abstinence would be the alternative, then possible onanism in the use of a contraceptive device is neutralized by the positive *mitzvah* of marital sex. In the voluminous responsa literature on birth control, the dominant tendency is to rule in this manner; namely, that Onan's marriage to his brother's widow, ordinarily prohibited, was exceptionally permitted in order to produce progeny—a purpose his act frustrated. But in ordinary marriages, the sexual relation without procreative possibility is allowable; and, where contraception must be practiced, the use of a device which smacks of Onan's method but is free of his intent (*Tosefot RiD* to Yev. 12b) is preferable to abstinence, so that the *mitzvah* of marital sex can be continued. For reasons such as this, an oral contraceptive—such as the pill, or its talmudic prototype, the *kos shel ikkarin* ("cup of barrenness")—is preferable to other contraceptive devices, for an oral contraceptive is onanistic neither in intent nor in method. Because of the objectionable methods of contraception available, rabbinic responsa by and large allowed contraception only for medical reasons. However, where oral contraception is possible, the responsa would be more permissive—but only in a way consistent with the overriding *mitzvah* of procreation.

Bibliography: D. M. Feldman, *Birth Control in Jewish Law* (1968, 1970).

[D.M.Fe.]

ONDERWIJZER, ABRAHAM BEN SAMSON HA-KOHEN (1862–1934), Dutch rabbi. Born in Muiden, near Amsterdam, Onderwijzer studied at the rabbinical seminary of Amsterdam under Rabbi J. *Duenner. In 1888 he was appointed rabbi of the Ashkenazi community in Amsterdam and in 1917, chief rabbi of the town and of the province of North Holland. Onderwijzer translated the Pentateuch with Rashi's commentary into Dutch and added his own explanations (1895–1901). In 1895 he founded Bezalel, an organization of Jewish workers, for the amelioration of the religious and economic conditions of the Jewish workers in Amsterdam, most of whom worked in the diamond industry. Bezalel acted in conjunction with the general diamond workers' trade union (A.N.D.B.B.) in Holland.

Bibliography: *Orde van den Dienst ter Gelegenheid van de plechtige Bevestiging . . . A. S. Onderwijzer* (1917), S. Seeligmann, *Opperabbijn A. S. Onderwijzer* (1935).

[Y.Ho.]

ONES (Heb. אֹנֶס), either (1) compelling a person to act against his will, or (2) the occurrence of an unavoidable event that prevents or obstructs the performance of certain acts, or causes them to occur. Both categories of *ones* are derived exegetically from the verse in the Pentateuch dealing with *ones* in the sense of compulsion. With regard to the rape of a betrothed maiden, it states (Deut. 22:26): "But unto the damsel thou shalt do nothing." From this the sages inferred that in all cases of "*ones* the merciful [Torah] exempts" (Ned. 27a; BK 28b).

Compelling a Person to Act Against his Will. Categories of Ones of Compulsion. *Ones* of compulsion comprises three categories: the threat of death; physical torture; and financial loss. Compulsion by threat of death or as a result of physical torture is adjudged as *ones* in all cases (Ket. 33b; see Tos. ad loc.). Financial pressure is not considered as *ones* in cases of transgression or **issur* (acts forbidden by the Torah), but as regards money matters, divorce, or an oath the authorities differ (see below). The threat of duress *(le'enos)* counts as *ones* if the threatener possesses the power to execute the threat himself or through the agency of others (Sh. Ar., ḤM 205:7), but some scholars do not permit the extension of *ones* to such a threat (*Rema* ad loc). If the threat is made to a kinsman, for example, it is generally counted as *ones* of compulsion (Resp. Rashbash no. 339; *Haggahot Mordekhai* Git. no. 467; Resp. Bezalel Ashkenazi no. 15), but other scholars differ (*Tashbeẓ* 1:1; *Rema,* EH 134:5).

In Compulsion to Wrongdoing. Anyone who commits a transgression through *ones* is exempt (Tos. to Yev. 54a; Yad, Yesodei ha-Torah 5:4) even from the judgment of heaven (Resp. Ribash 4 and 11). Even though a person commits one of the three transgressions of which it is said that he should choose death rather than commit them, he will not be punished if he acted under duress. He is obliged, however, to expend money to enable himself to escape from a situation where otherwise he would be forced to transgress (Resp. Ribash 387; and see *Penal Law).

In Kiddushin. If a man was compelled under duress to betroth a woman, some authorities hold that the *kiddushin* (see *Marriage) is valid (Yad, Ishut 4:1 and *Maggid Mishnah* ad loc. in the name of Rashba), but others maintain that it is of no effect (Sh. Ar., EH 42:1). Those who hold that the *kiddushin* is valid base their opinion on the fact that a man can *divorce his wife without her consent (*Maggid Mishneh* loc. cit.; *Beit Shemu'el* 42, n. 1)—even after the ban of Rabbenu Gershom prohibiting divorce against the woman's will—should he have been compelled to betroth her under duress (*Beit Shemu'el* loc. cit.). If a woman is compelled under duress to be betrothed, the *kiddushin* is as valid as if she had acted willingly (BB 48b), but nevertheless the rabbis nullified it because of her partner's improper behavior (*ibid.;* see *Marriage).

In Divorce. A husband divorcing his wife must act freely (Yad, Gerushin 1:1–2), and a divorce given by the husband against his will is divorce under duress and therefore invalid. There are, however, cases in which the court may compel the husband to grant a divorce and in such cases it is valid (Git. 9:2; see *Divorce). Some authorities are of the opinion that in such cases the husband must say, "I am willing" (*Netivot ha-Mishpat, Mishpat ha-Urim* 205, n. 1), but others say that if he gives the divorce without making any remark then this is tantamount to saying, "I am willing" (*Ḥavvot Ya'ir* nos. 55 and 56). Various explanations are given for the validity of this divorce despite its being given under duress. Some explain that just as in a *sale under duress the sale is valid because of the assumption that in the end the seller made up his mind to sell (under certain conditions; see below), this is also the case in a divorce given under duress when compulsion is legally permitted (Tos. to BB 48a); others say that as it is a religious precept to obey the sages, the husband is reconciled to divorce (*Rashbam* BB 48a); while others hold that the laws of *ones* are not applicable to one legally bound to act in a particular way, even though his act results from compulsion (Yad, Gerushin 2:20). Financial duress counts as *ones* with regard to compulsion to divorce (Resp. Rashba vol. 4 no. 40; Nov. Ritba Kid. 49b s.v. *ve-ha*), but some authorities disagree and do not regard it as *ones* (*Toledot Adam ve-Ḥavvah,* Ḥavvah 24:1).

In Sale. If a purchaser snatches the property of the seller through giving him the purchase price against his will then this is an invalid sale. In this case the purchaser is treated as a predator, and he is obliged to restore the article he took as if he were a robber (BK 62a; Yad, Gezelah 1:9; see *Theft and Robbery). In certain circumstances, however, though the seller sells under duress, it is assumed that in the end he agreed to the sale for he accepted money in consideration of the transferred property. Therefore if he was given the monetary value of the property for sale and took it into his hands, the sale stands (Sh. Ar., ḤM 205:1). Some hold the sale to be valid only if he took the money at the time of the actual transaction (Yad, Mekhirah 10:1, see *Mishneh le-Melekh*), while others hold it to be valid even if the money was taken afterward *(ibid.)*. If he was compelled to reduce the price, the sale is void (Sh. Ar., ḤM 205:4), but some scholars disagree (Resp. Maharik 185). If a man is compelled to purchase, the transaction is void and the purchaser may withdraw (*Rema* ḤM 205:12), but here too there are dissident opinions (*Ha-Gra ibid.*, n. 32). In the event of the purchaser's becoming reconciled to the sale, the seller is unable to withdraw (*Netivot ha-Mishpat*, Mishpat ha-Urim 205, n. 18). In the case of a business transaction that resembles sale, such as a compromise when it is uncertain where the legal right lies, if the compromise is agreed upon under duress then the same ruling applies as for sale and the compromise prevails (*Beit Yosef* ḤM 205:16).

In Gifts. If a man is compelled to assign a *gift, the gift is void (*Rashbam* BB 47b). A transaction that resembles a gift, such as a compromise when the litigant would have succeeded at law but was forced to compromise, counts as a gift and the compromise is void (*Beit Yosef* loc. cit.). Similarly, an obligation undertaken through an acknowledgement of liability where none exists rates as a gift in regard to *ones* and the obligation cannot be enforced *(Beit Yosef loc. cit.)*.

Moda'ah ("Notification"). If the person under duress discloses in advance that the transaction he is about to acquiesce to will be effected against his will and that he has no intention of executing it, the subsequent transaction is void through lack of intent. Such a declaration to witnesses is termed *mesirat moda'ah* ("making a notification"). The witnesses usually wrote a deed of *moda'ah*, but this was not imperative (BB 40a–b; ḤM 205). If the seller makes a *moda'ah* the sale is void even though he accepts the purchase price (ḤM 205:1). A *moda'ah* made before a single witness is ineffective even if the compeller admits the duress, for since the person under duress knows that he cannot prove that he made a *moda'ah* he acquiesces in the transaction (*Sha'ar Mishpat* 46, n. 21). If, however, he made the *moda'ah* in the presence of two witnesses separately, it is effective (*Keneset ha-Gedolah*, ḤM 46, Tur no. 36). Where the sale is void because a *moda'ah* has been made, the purchaser too has the right to withdraw on becoming aware that the seller made a *moda'ah* prior to the sale (*Ḥavvot Ya'ir* no. 40).

A deed of *moda'ah* may not be written in the first instance unless the witnesses know the duress (Sh. Ar., ḤM 205:5), and the witnesses must write "we the witnesses know the *ones*" (Sh. Ar., ḤM 205:1). If they write that the person concerned made a *moda'ah* in their presence, although they were unaware of the duress, the transaction will be void if he subsequently proves that there was *ones*. If witnesses testify to, or write, the *moda'ah* without knowing the *ones*, and other witnesses testify to the *ones*, these are combined and the transaction is void *(ibid.)*. In a case where there is duress but the man under it is not able to make the *moda'ah*, if witnesses know of the *ones*, this has the same effect as a *moda'ah* (*Tashbeẓ* 2:169; *Matteh Shimon* 205, Tur no. 39). The deed of *moda'ah* may be written before or after the transaction, providing the one under duress makes the notification before the transaction (*Netivot ha-Mishpat*, Mishpat ha-Urim 205 n. 6; *Keẓot ha-Ḥoshen* 205, n. 1; *Haggahot Maimuniyyot*, Mekhirah 10:2). If the deed of *moda'ah* is undated and it is not known whether notification was made before or after the transaction because the witnesses are not available, it is valid and the transaction is void (*Rema* ḤM 205:9), for since the witnesses knew of the *ones* it is to be assumed, unless there is evidence to the contrary, that the notification was made beforehand *(ibid.)*. In the case of gifts and similar dealings, such as *remission of debt, the witnesses may write the *moda'ah* without knowing the *ones;* the *moda'ah* will then testify to lack of intent (Tur ḤM 205:12 and *Beit Yosef* thereto). The authorities differ as to why this should be so, some holding that the *moda'ah* is effective as regards a gift even without the witnesses' knowledge of the *ones*, because if there is no *ones*, why should anyone confer a gift and make a *moda'ah*? It is therefore assumed that there must be *ones*. Accordingly if it is known with certainty that there is no *ones*, the *moda'ah* may not be written. Others hold, however, that in the case of a gift manifestation of lack of proper intent is effective even without *ones* (see Gulak, Yesodei, 1 (1922), 61).

If after making the *moda'ah* the one under duress decides to effect the transaction and cancels his *moda'ah*, the transaction prevails (Sh. Ar., ḤM 205:11 and *Sma* thereto). It is possible, however, to make a *moda'ah* cancelling ab initio such a *moda'ah* and declaring that the cancellation all the time of the transaction will result from *ones* and lack of intent. Such a notification, called *"moda'ah de-moda'ah,"* cancels the transaction. To make certain that an action was not voided through a *moda'ah*, it became customary at the time of the transaction to cancel every *moda'ah* and every *moda'ah* canceling a *moda'ah ad infinitum*, or alternatively for the party involved to disqualify the witnesses before whom he made any *moda'ah* with regard to the transaction at hand, thus making them unfit to testify on his behalf. By these methods the previous *moda'ot* are voided and the act subsists (*ibid.; Beit Yosef* ḤM 205:15).

Acts Counting as Ones. A man who performs an act under an erroneous impression of the facts is described as "forced by his heart"; since his understanding of the case was in error it is included in *ones*. This *halakhah* occurs especially in connection with an oath pledged under a mistaken impression. The one who swore the oath is delivered from it and exempted from offering a sacrifice, since he swore in error (Shevu. 26a; Ned. 25b; Maim. Yad, Shevuot 1:10; see *Mistake). Forgetting rates as *ones* (BK 26b and *Nimmukei Yosef* ad loc.), as does an act performed as the result of an overpowering impulse. Hence, for example, a woman who is forced to have sexual intercourse is regarded as having been raped even though she yielded willingly during the final stages of the act, since she had not the power to resist to the end because her natural impulse compelled her desire (Yad, Sanhedrin 20:3, Issurei Bi'ah 1:9; Resp. Ḥatam Sofer, EH pt. 1, no. 18). A minor girl who commits *adultery, even willingly, is regarded as acting under duress since "the seduction of a minor is deemed *ones*" because she has no will of her own (Yev. 33b, 61b; TJ, Sot. 1:2, 16c). Some hold that a deranged woman who commits adultery also counts as *ones* (*Mishneh le-Melekh*, Ishut 11: 8), but others are doubtful about this (see *Rape).

Acts Counting as Voluntary. A man compelled to incestuous or adulterous intercourse (see *Incest) is guilty of a capital offense, since "an erection can only take place voluntarily" (Yad, Issurei Bi'ah 1:9), but some hold that he is not liable for the death penalty (*Maggid Mishneh* ad loc.). Duress arising from the person's own situation, as in the case of a man who sells his property because of financial distress, does not count as *ones* (Sh. Ar., ḤM 205:12). Similarly, if the duress was related to some other action and he was compelled to act as a cause of this—e.g., if he was compelled to give money and because he did not have it was compelled to sell—this is not *ones (ibid.)*.

Unavoidable Causes. Categories of Causes Counting as Ones. The scholars developed a threefold division of the types of *ones*, a classification which was made especially in connection with the laws of divorce; a somewhat similar one was made in connection with the law of *obligation, particularly with reference to *torts. The three categories relating to divorce (see below) are: (1) an *ones* of common occurrence; (2) an *ones* neither common nor uncommon; and (3) an uncommon *ones*. The classical examples of these are: (1) if a man returning home was delayed because the ferry was on the opposite bank of the river and so he could not cross it; (2) illness; and (3) if a man was killed when a house collapsed, or he was bitten by a snake, or devoured by a lion (Tos., *Piskei ha-Rosh* and *Mordekhai* to Ket. 2b and 3a and to Git. 73a; Sh. Ar., EH 144:1). A general *ones* not arising from human agency is termed *makkat medinah* ("regional mishap"; BM 9:6). As regards liability in the laws of obligation the division is made between an absolute *ones* and one which is relative. In the words of *rishonim* the distinction is between an *ones* "like theft" and one "like loss." The Talmud (BM 94b) has a dictum that "loss is close to negligence" while "theft is near to *ones*" (Tos. to BK 27b and to BM 82b).

Nonfulfillment of Obligation Resulting from Ones. A man bears no liability for the nonfulfillment of his obligations if he is prevented from doing so by *ones* (BK 28b; Ned. 28a), with the exception of the borrower (BM 93a; see *Bailees). It is possible that a tortfeasor too is excluded from this rule, since "man is always liable, whether acting inadvertently or willingly, whether awake or asleep" (BK 2:6), or in another version "whether acting inadvertently or willingly, accidently or deliberately" (Sanh. 72a). It has, however, been ruled that there are kinds of *ones* which exempt even tortfeasors (Tos. to Sanh. 76b). A man accepting liability for every *ones* is not liable for an uncommon one (Resp. Ribash no. 250; Resp. Moharik no. 7; Sh. Ar., ḤM 225:4).

Nonfulfillment of Obligation by Reason of Ones. If a man was to execute an act on certain conditions and his nonfulfillment of these conditions was due to *ones*, the *amoraim* differ as to whether the act counts as not having been executed because the condition was not fulfilled although the nonfulfillment was caused by *ones*, or whether the act stands since it was *ones* that prevented fulfillment of the condition (TJ, Git. 7:6, 49c; see *Beit Yosef* and *Baḥ* ḤM 21; *Siftei Kohen* ḤM 21). Some explain the former opinion as follows: The rule is that "the merciful [Torah] exempts in cases of *ones*" and not that "in cases of *ones* the merciful [Torah] obligates" the other person. For in what way is he concerned with the *ones* of the other? His obligation was dependent on the other's fulfillment of the condition, which in fact was not done (*Siftei Kohen* loc. cit.; Resp. Ḥatam Sofer, ḤM no. 1; for other explanations see the ḤM and *Malbushei Yom Tov*, Kuntres Mishpetei ha-Tanna'im 2). The *halakhah* follows the first view (*Avnei Millu'im*, EH 38:1).

Ones in Divorce. Contrary to the principle: "the merciful [Torah] exempts in cases of *ones*" the rabbinic regulation lays down "accident is no plea in divorce." Hence, if a man says to his wife: 'This is your bill of divorce if I do not return by such a date," and he does not come back in time because of *ones*, the divorce is effective and he is unable to have it set aside on the plea that he was delayed by *ones*. There were two considerations behind this regulation. If the divorce was regarded as ineffective in a case of *ones*, a chaste woman, when her husband did not arrive on the stated day, would always consider that an accident might have befallen him, even when his absence was deliberate, and thus would remain unable to remarry. A loose woman, on the other hand, would always claim that her husband's failure to return was not due to *ones* and would contract a second marriage; then when subsequently his nonreturn was found to be due to *ones*, the divorce would be invalid and her children **mamzerim*. As a result the rabbis enacted that the divorce must always take effect, even though the husband's failure to return is due to *ones*, and even though he stands on the other bank of the river and cries aloud, "See I have returned and am not responsible because of *ones*" (Ket. 2b–3a; Tos. to Ket. 3a; Sh. Ar., EH 144:1). The *rishonim* ruled that this *halakhah* applies to *ones* of common occurrence and to *ones* neither common nor uncommon, but not at all to uncommon *ones* (Tos., *Piskei ha-Rosh*, and *Mordekhai* to Ket. 2b–3a and to Git. 73a and codes).

Ones on the Due Date. A man who was obliged to perform an action within a certain period of time and relied on the fact that he still had the time to do it until the end of the period, who was then overtaken by *ones* at the very end of the period, is regarded as subject to *ones* (Sh. Ar., OḤ 108:8 and *Magen Avraham* thereto n. 11), but others do not consider this *ones* (*Rema* YD 232:12).

Bibliography: Gulak, Yesodei, 1 (1922), 57–62; 2 (1922), 70f.; M. Higger, *Intention in Talmudic Law* (1927); Herzog, Instit, 1 (1936), 101–7; 2 (1939), 130–2, 240–3, 248–75; ET, 1 (1951[3]), 162–72; 5 (1953), 698–707; Z. Karl, in: *Mazkeret Levi . . . Freund* (1953), 29, 45f.; B. Rabinovitz-Teomim, *Ḥukkat Mishpat* (1957), 182–91; B. Lipkin, in: *Sinai—Sefer Yovel* (1958), 394–402; S. Albeck, *Pesher Dinei ha-Nezikin ba-Talmud* (1965), 175–82; Elon, Mafte'aḥ, 2–4; Sh. Warhaftig, *Dinei Avodah ba-Mishpat ha-Ivri*, 2 (1969), 721–96, 829–66.

[Sh.Sh.]

ONIAS, the name of four high priests of the Second Temple period (corresponding to the Hebrew חוֹנִיו).

Onias I lived at the end of the fourth century B.C.E. I Maccabees 12:20–23 relates that Areios, king of Sparta, sent a letter to the high priest Onias, claiming that the Spartans and the Jews were brethren being descended from Abraham. Although most scholars consider the high priest referred to was Onias I, and the king, Areios I, who reigned 309–265 B.C.E., they regard the letter itself as unhistorical. There is no sufficient reason, however, to cast doubt upon the essential veracity of the incident, and it is probable that the Areios referred to is Areios I, since Areios II came to the throne about 255 B.C.E. and died while still a child. On the other hand, Onias II was not contemporary with any Areios. According to Josephus (Ant. 12:226–7), the letter was sent to Onias III, the grandson of Onias II, but this is clearly erroneous, since there is no knowledge of a Spartan king named Areios at this time.

Onias II, son of *Simeon the Just and grandson of Onias I, lived in the second half of the third century B.C.E. According to Josephus (Ant. 12:44) he was a minor when his father died, and his uncle Eleazar officiated for him during his minority. When Eleazar died, another uncle, Manasseh, took his place until Onias was old enough to assume the high priesthood. In his account of Joseph b. Tobiah (*ibid.*, 12:158), Josephus depicts Onias as miserly and foolish, and careless of the dignity of his rank, thereby allowing the rise of Joseph the tax collector. The truth would appear to be otherwise. Onias was involved in the political events connected with the war between Ptolemy III (Euergetes I) and Queen Laodice, the wife and murderess of Antiochus II Theos. Wishing to throw off the yoke of Ptolemaic Egypt, he conspired with the enemies of Ptolemy and refused to pay taxes. Ptolemy threatened to drive the Jews from their land if the tax was not paid. It would appear that Onias was high priest until the close of the second century B.C.E.

ONIAS III, a son of Simeon II and grandson of Onias II, knew how to preserve both the religious and secular authority of the house of Onias. This is demonstrated in the quarrel he had with Simeon, the head of the Temple (II Macc. 3:4). Simeon, an important official in the administration of the Temple, demanded from Onias the post of market commissioner *(Agoranomos)* which Onias refused because the *Agoranomos,* by virtue of his control over such things as the market, the price of goods, and employment, in effect exercised all real authority in the city. When his demand was rejected, Simeon turned to *Apollonius, the commander of the Syrian army, and told him that vast treasures belonging to the king were preserved in the Temple vaults. Apollonius informed Seleucus who sent his chancellor, *Heliodorus to remove the treasure. Heliodorus, however, failed to do so, and having thus lost face, had to leave Jerusalem. Thereafter Onias was hated by the Seleucid ruler who suspected him of having brought about the failure of the mission. When Antiochus IV ascended the throne (175 B.C.E.), Onias was summoned to Antioch, and his brother *Jason was appointed high priest in his place, having apparently promised a large sum of money for the appointment. After three years Jason was displaced by *Menelaus, who obtained the appointment by offering a larger sum. Menelaus, an extreme Hellenizer, brought about a rebellion in Jerusalem by the contempt with which he treated the sacrifices of the people. He went to Antioch, apparently in an attempt to restore his standing. He feared the influence of Onias who was living in Daphne, near Antioch, and persuaded Andronicus, a favorite of Antiochus, to murder the exiled high priest. There seems to be a reference to the death of Onias III in Daniel 9:26.

ONIAS IV, son of Onias III, was a candidate for the high priesthood after his father's death, but was ousted by *Alcimus. For this reason and because of the edicts of Antiochus, he left Judea, and went to Egypt. The works of Josephus present contradictory traditions (cf. Wars, 1:33; 7:423–4, and Ant., 12:387–8; 13:62). According to *The Jewish War,* it was Onias III who fled to Egypt because of the persecutions of *Antiochus Epiphanes, whereas according to the *Antiquities,* it was Onias IV, in the time of Antiochus V Eupator. In about 145 B.C.E., Ptolemy VI Philometer granted Onias authority to build a temple in Leontopolis, the Temple of Onias. The view of Tcherikover that the erection of the temple was a political act, of interest to both Onias and Ptolemy, and that it was intended merely as a local center of worship for the Jewish military settlement is a plausible one. This emerges from the fact that the temple fulfilled no religious function in the Jewish community of Egypt whose loyalties were solely to the Temple in Jerusalem. The Mishnah (Men. 13:10) mentions "the Temple of Onias," emphasizing that it had not the same religious status as the Temple in Jerusalem. Josephus regarded Onias' deed as an act of desecration. The priests of Jerusalem regarded the sacrifices in the Temple of Onias as invalid and refused to recognize the priests and levites who ministered there (Jos., Ant., 13:73; Wars, 7:431). Many Jewish soldiers came to Egypt together with Onias, and, as military settlers, were given land between Memphis and Pelusium by Philometor. This region was known from that time as "the land of Onias." Hilkiah and Hananiah, the sons of Onias, served as commanders in the army of Cleopatra III, and participated in the queen's military campaign in Israel and Syria against Ptolemy Lathyrus. They influenced Cleopatra to such an extent that she desisted from annexing Judea to Egypt (Jos., Ant., 13:284–7, 349, 354–5). In the struggle between Cleopatra and Ptolemy Physcon, after the death of Ptolemy Philometor, Onias and his sons supported the queen (Jos., Apion, 2:50). During the reign of Hyrcanus II the Jews of Onias still retained a certain military importance (Jos., Ant., 14:131–2, and Wars, 1:189 state that Pelusium was taken by force from the garrison army). The Temple of Onias was closed in 73 C.E. by order of *Vespasian.

Bibliography: II Macc. 3:1–4; 5:32–35; A. Buechler, *Die Tobiaden und die Oniaden* (1899), 74ff.; Schuerer, Hist, 24f., 54, 274; Schuerer, Gesch, 3 (1909[4]), 42, 131, 144–7; Klausner, Bayit Sheni, index, s.v. *Ḥonyo;* F.-M. Abel, *Histoire de la Palestine,* 1 (1952), 105ff.; A. Tcherikover, *Hellenistic Civilization and the Jews* (1959), 138f., 156ff., 172–4, 276ff., 389f. [ED.]

ONIAS, TEMPLE OF. A temple for the worship of God established by *Onias IV at *Leontopolis in Egypt in the middle of the second century B.C.E. Various suggestions have been put forward to explain the reason why it was erected. It has been suggested that Onias regarded the Temple in Jerusalem as having lost its sanctity as a result of its desecration by *Antiochus Epiphanes and *Menelaus; another view was that he denied the religious fitness of the Hasmonean high priesthood. The most probable assumption, however, is that he wanted to build a religious center specifically for the Jewish *Diaspora in Egypt. The temple of Onias was constructed according to the structure of the *Temple in Jerusalem, but did not resemble it in all its details. It was built in the form of a tower and was surrounded by a wall, and Onias and his sons—who continued the dynasty of Zadok—served there. The altar and its vessels were similar to those in Jerusalem save that a hanging candelabrum took the place of the standing **menorah* of the Temple in Jerusalem. The Jews of Egypt offered sacrifices there, but it seems that they did not consider the temple to be the equal to the one in Jerusalem—much less its substitute—and their attachment to the Jerusalem Temple was not weakened. Philo makes no reference to the temple of Onias.

The status of the temple of Onias from the point of view of *halakhah* is not clear. In the talmudic account (Men. 109a–110b), which combines both historical and aggadic elements, its being built is attributed to a dispute between the two sons of Simeon the Just over the high priesthood and to Onias' jealousy of his brother Simeon. Some say that Onias "offered sacrifice to an idol," but others say that "it was to heaven." Apparently, the latter view prevailed, since the *halakhah* (Men. 13:10) does not consider sacrifices in the temple of Onias as idolatry, although it disqualifies its priests from serving in Jerusalem. The verses (Isa. 19:18–19), "In that day there shall be five cities in the land of Egypt that swear to the Lord of Hosts; one shall be called the city of *heres* [JPS "destruction"]. On that day there shall be an altar to the Lord in the midst of the land of Egypt" were interpreted as referring to this temple. *Heres* ("sun") was homiletically applied to Heliopolis ("the city of sun") near Leontopolis.

The temple of Onias continued to exist after the destruction of the Temple in Jerusalem but was closed in 73 by order of Vespasian. According to Josephus 343 years passed from its foundation until its abolition. The number seems reasonable, not as a chronographic number but taken from an artificial cyclic chronology based upon a theological notion. The number 343 represents 49 sabbatical periods ($7 \times 7 \times 7$), i.e., the term of the existence of the temple of Onias was calculated in accordance with a theological chronological concept, in the manner of the concept connected with the destruction of the Temple in Jerusalem. However, if one converts 343 to Jubilees, it follows that the temple of Onias existed for six jubilees and 43 years according to this cyclic calculation. If, however, the principle of the *baraita* in *Arakhin* (see *Sabbatical Year and Jubilee) that the 50th year also counts as the first year of the next sabbatical period is accepted, six years must be added so that the period becomes six Jubilees and 49 years. According to this reckoning the temple of Onias was abolished on the eve of the seventh Jubilee of its existence.

Bibliography: A. Buechler, *Tobiaden und Oniaden* (1899); S. A. Hirsch, in: *Jews' College Jubilee Volume* (1906), 39–80; E. Meyer, *Ursprung und Anfaenge des Christentums,* 22 (1921[1-3]); H. Tchernowitz, in: *Louis Ginzberg Jubilee Volume* (1946), Heb. pt. 223–47; Klausner, Bayit Sheni, 2 (1951[2]), 140f.; 3 (1950[2]) 39, 246; V. Tcherikover, *Hellenistic Civilization and the Jews* (1959), 275–81, 392–4; idem, in: *Corpus,* 1 (1957), 17, 44–46, 52, 80. [A.SCH.]

ONION (Heb. בָּצָל), the *Allium cepa,* one of the earliest cultivated plants. It is mentioned only once in the Bible as one of the vegetables eaten in Egypt for which the Israelites longed when they were in the wilderness (Num. 11:5). Onion growing was widespread in Egypt and drawings of it are found on the pyramids. The onion, with its concentric skins, symbolized in Egypt the stellar and planetary system, and was an object of idol worship, some swearing by its name (Pliny, *Historia naturalis,* 19:101). The word appears in family names. Among the Nethinim (see *Gibeonites and Nethinim) who went from Babylon to Ereẓ Israel, a family of the children of Bazluth is mentioned (Ezra 2:52), and the Jerusalem Talmud (Ḥag. 2:2; 77d) mentions a Miriam bat Alei Beẓalim ("onion leaves") which may be a reference to Miriam the mother of Jesus.

The onion is frequently mentioned in rabbinic literature. R. Judah used to say "Eat *baẓal* [onions] and sit *ba-ẓel* [in the shade], and do not eat geese and fowl" (Pes. 114a), i.e., do not desire luxuries but be content with little. They made a distinction between "rural onions" (TJ, Shev. 2:9, 34a) and "urban onions which were the food of city folk" (Ter. 2:5). A species very near to the onion was called *beẓalẓul* (Kil. 1:3), which is possibly the shallot, the Ashkelon onion, and therefore sometimes called "scallion" which was praised by Theophrastus, Strabo, and Pliny. The onion was usually pulled up before it flowered and some of the plants were left to flower and produce seed (Pe'ah 3:3 and TJ, Pe'ah 17c). Many species of *Allium* of the same genus as the onion grow wild in Israel, where the climate and soil are very suitable for onion plants. To the Liliaceae family of onion belong some of the most beautiful of Israel's flowers (see *Flowers of the Bible).

Bibliography: Loew, Flora, 2 (1924), 125–31; H. N. and A. L. Moldenke, *Plants of the Bible* (1952), index; J. Feliks, *Olam ha-Ẓome'aḥ ha-Mikra'i* (1968[2]), 169–71. [J.F.]

ONKELOS AND AQUILA (second century C.E.), two translators of the Bible, the one into Aramaic and the other into Greek, both of whom were proselytes. Although there is no doubt of their separate existence, the translation of Onkelos being preserved in its entirety, and that of Aquila in fragments (see *Aramaic (Middle Aramaic) and *Bible, Translations), the similarity of the names has caused considerable confusion. Similar or identical incidents are given in the Babylonian Talmud and the Tosefta as applying to Onkelos, and in the Jerusalem Talmud and the Palestinian Midrashim, to Aquila (Akilas). It is therefore convenient to treat of them primarily as one, while indicating where possible where they can be distinguished from one another. Fact and legend are inextricably interwoven.

According to Epiphanius, Aquila was a native of Pontus and a relative of the emperor *Hadrian, who in about 128 appointed him to an office connected with the rebuilding of Jerusalem as Aelia Capitolina. The Midrash (Tanḥ. 41a, Mishpatim 3) also refers to him as the son of the sister of Hadrian, although the Babylonian Talmud refers to him as "Onkelos the son of Kalonikus [v. Kalonymus] the son of the sister of Titus." He became converted to Judaism, but before doing so he raised the spirits of Titus, Balaam, and Jesus (this last was expurged by the censor from the printed editions) all of whom confirmed that the people of Israel is held in the highest repute in the world to come (Git. 56b, 57a). According to the Tanḥuma, when he formed the intention of converting to Judaism, fearing the anger and opposition of Hadrian, he informed him that he wished to travel (to Ereẓ Israel) on business, and Hadrian offered him all the money he needed to remain in Rome. In any case he must have been a person of wealth, and this lends point to the comment of the Midrash (Gen. R. 70:5), to the effect that he asked R. Eliezer b. Hyrcanus whether there was no greater reward for the proselyte than that stated in the Bible, that God "loveth the stranger [*ger,* in mishnaic Hebrew a proselyte] in giving him food and raiment" (Deut. 10:18), pointing out that he was short of neither of these things. Eliezer's brusque reply might have discouraged him, but he went to R. Joshua with the same question and Joshua replied that it refers to spiritual benefits. His conversion met with the vigorous opposition of the emperor. According to the Tanḥuma he "smote him on the cheek"; according to the Talmud (Av. Zar. 11a) he sent four successive contingents of soldiers to arrest him but he succeeded in converting them all to Judaism. Onkelos was a contemporary of Rabban Gamaliel of Jabneh, and a colleague and pupil of Eliezer b. Hyrcanus and Joshua b. Hananiah (cf., above). His relationship with Gamaliel was a close one, and when Gamaliel died Onkelos arranged a costly funeral for him, such as was usually reserved for royalty (Tosef., Shab. 7 (8):18; Av. Zar. 11a). He conducted himself with the utmost piety and was particularly meticulous in adhering to the laws of ritual purity, surpassing in this respect even Rabban Gamaliel, applying to ordinary food the rules enjoined for partaking of sacrifices (Tosef., Ḥag. 3:2 and 3). On one occasion he refused to bathe in the ritual baths of Ashkelon (since he regarded it as heathen territory) and made his ablutions in the sea, while Gamaliel (according to one opinion) was not so particular (Tosef., Mik. 6:3). There is one talmudic statement attributed to him (BB 99a) that the faces of the *cherubim were turned sideways "as a pupil taking leave of his master."

The two translators are differentiated from one another in two passages of the Talmud. Where the Babylonian Talmud (Meg. 3a) states that Onkelos the Proselyte translated the Pentateuch into Aramaic (Targum) under the guidance of R. Eliezer and R. Joshua, the parallel passage in the Jerusalem Talmud (*ibid.* 1:11, 71c) clearly refers to the translation of Aquila the Proselyte into Greek, and there are some quotations in the Talmud which clearly refer to a translation into Greek (e.g., *hadar* in Lev. 23:40 is rendered as *ὕδωρ*, water). Since Azariah de *Rossi, attempts have been made to disentangle the confusion between the Aramaic translator Onkelos and the Greek translator Aquila. The prevalent opinion tends to ascribe the talmudic passages to Aquila, but when, in Babylonian sources, the name was corrupted to Onkelos, the existing anonymous translation of the Pentateuch into Aramaic was ascribed to "Onkelos the Proselyte."

Bibliography: A. Silverstone, *Aquila and Onkelos* (1931); Zunz-Albeck, Derashot; Kohut, Arukh, 1 (1926), 158, and note. For further bibliography see *Bible, Translations. [L.I.R.]

ONO (Heb. אוֹנוֹ), town in Judea, first mentioned in Thutmosis III's list of conquered towns in Canaan (No. 65). It was apparently settled originally by descendants of Benjamin (I Chron. 8:12). It appears with Lod and Hadid in the list of places resettled after the return from Babylonian

Exile (Ezra 2:33; Neh. 7:37). It was situated near the border of Samaria, for Sanballat offered to meet Nehemiah in one of the villages of the Plain of Ono as on neutral ground (Neh. 6:2). According to Nehemiah 11:35, it was located in the Ge-Harashim ("valley of craftsmen"). Ono is frequently mentioned in talmudic sources. According to the Mishnah (Arak. 9:6), it had been fortified "from the days of Joshua"; the Babylonian Talmud locates it 3 mi. (c. 5 km.) from Lod, but relations between the two towns were unfriendly (Lam. R. 1:17, no. 52). Sometime in the third century, it was made an independent municipality: a councilor of Ono is mentioned in a papyrus from Oxyrrhynchus dated 297 (no. 1205). It appears as an independent town in Byzantine town lists of the fifth and sixth centuries (Hierocles Synecdemus 719:4; Georgius Cyprius 1006). The former Arab village of Kafr ʿAnā occupied the spot until 1948. An urban settlement called *Kiryat Ono now exists nearby.

Bibliography: S. Klein, *Ereẓ Yehudah* (1939), 7–8, 20; Mazar, in: BJPES, 8 (1941), 106; Noth, in: ZDPV, 61 (1938), 46; EM, s.v. (incl. bibl.). [M.A.-Y.]

°ÓNODY, GÉZA (1848–?), Hungarian anti-Semitic leader born in Tiszaeszlar. A member of the gentry, he was elected to the lower house of parliament as a delegate of the opposition Independence Party in 1881. At first, Ónody's anti-Semitic activities were connected with the blood libel of 1882 in *Tiszaeszlar where he owned an estate. Raising the matter in parliament in May 1882, he opened the public campaign around the libel. From that time, he was one of the leading spokesmen of the group responsible for the anti-Jewish agitation which followed in the wake of the libel. In his work, *Tiszaeszlar in der Vergangenheit und Gegenwart* (1883, orig. in Hung.), Ónody sought to "prove" the authenticity of the blood libel against a historic background. When the anti-Semitic party was organized in Hungary in 1883, he became one of its leaders, together with Istóczy *Cyőző. Because of his activity in the blood libel affair and his work on the subject, he also became renowned among anti-Semites abroad, especially in Germany. He was among the leaders of anti-Semitic unions which convened the First International Anti-Jewish Congress (Dresden, 1882) and one of its most prominent participants. In 1884 he was reelected to parliament, this time on an anti-Semitic platform, and became one of the leaders of the anti-Semitic faction.

Bibliography: *Istóczy und Ónody* (1882); Z. Bosnyák, *A magyar fajvédelem uttörői* (1942), 63–102; N. Katzburg, *Antishemiyyut be-Hungariyah 1867–1914* (1969). [N.K.]

ONTARIO, Canadian province linking Manitoba (to the east) and Quebec (to the west), the Great Lakes forming much of the southern boundary. Ontario's population is (est. 1970) 7,707,000, much of it concentrated in the south; the Jewish population is 125,000, over 40% of Canada's total Jewish population. Jews were drawn to this English-speaking area, first called Upper Canada and from 1841 to 1867 termed Canada West, by its economic growth. Ontario soon had a larger total Jewish population than *Quebec province. Ontario has about 30 Jewish communities, each with some form of structured organization, be it synagogue, Hebrew school, or a more complex community council. Five communities maintain centers with professional staff: *Toronto, *Ottawa, *Hamilton, *Winsdor, and London.

Development in the South. Immigration to the southeastern counties began in the mid-19th century. Kingston was settled early by Jewish immigrants in the 1840s, notable residents being the Nordheimer brothers, who later moved to Toronto. A community was not organized until the 1890s. The Jewish population (1970) is 300. Early settlers in the eastern section were linked in the main with *Montreal, where for the first few years they travelled for High Holiday services. In 1858 and 1860 the Vinebergs (Alexander, Chananya, and Hiram), went to Cornwall, and somewhat later Noah Friedman and H. Kellert went to Lancaster. They were joined in 1864 by William Jacobs, whose son S. W. *Jacobs later was a member of Parliament (MP) and president of the Canadian Jewish Congress. These early settlers were mainly from Suwalki (Poland) and Lithuania. A number of other Jewish citizens of southeastern Ontario have followed political careers. Nathan Phillips, of Cornwall, served eight years as mayor of Toronto. Aaron Horovitz, a native of Rumania, was mayor of Cornwall for 16 years (1930–34 inclusive, in 1936, 1944–46 inclusive, and from 1949 to 1956 inclusive), and other Jews have served as aldermen in that city.

Jews went to the Niagara Peninsula in the 1880s, their numbers increasing at the time of the Russo-Japanese War. In St. Catharines a building was purchased for a synagogue in 1917; in Welland, in 1914. In 1970 there were about 200 Jews in Niagara Falls, 130 in Welland, and 600 in St. Catharines. Port Colborne, despite its tiny community (13 families), until the 1960s maintained its own Hebrew school. After World War II a community of Jewish farmers grew up in the Niagara area, aided by the Jewish Colonization Association. They maintain a synagogue in Smithville named after Baron de *Hirsch.

Belleville was settled by Jews from 1904; its Jewish population is 128. Kitchener-Waterloo (Jewish population 768), Guelph (250), Brantford (300), and Galt-Preston (85) each maintain a synagogue and rabbi-teacher. Waterloo had a Jewish mayor (Harold Paikin), as did Brantford (Max Sherman). Harold Daufman of Kitchener was Ontario's first Crown attorney. In many of these and other cities Jews have served as aldermen and school trustees. In a number of small centers where no Jewish communities exist, Jews have been elected mayor (Palmerston, Listowel, Alexandria, Engelhart, Petrolia). Other Jewish communities are Oshawa, an industrial city 30 miles east of Toronto, with 370 Jews, Chatham (130); Owen Sound; Pembroke; Peterborough (243); Stratford; and North Bay.

Northern Centers. Sault Ste. Marie (Jewish population, 1970, 100) is somewhat isolated geographically from other Jewish centers. About 400 miles west is Thunder Bay, formerly Fort Arthur-Port William (Jewish population 250), a rail and air center closely linked with Winnipeg; Thunder Bay's mayor was Saul Laskin. Timmins and Kirkland Lake had substantial Jewish communities that declined sharply with the drop in gold mining. Sudbury has about 200 Jews. Two Sudbury lawyers, Harry and Carl Waisberg, were judges in Toronto.

Political Leaders. Among Jews who have served in the provincial and federal legislatures (see *Canada) are Allan Grossman, minister of correctional services in the Ontario cabinet (1970) and Vernon Singer, deputy leader of the Liberal Party in the provincial legislature, Stephen Lewis, a member of the provincial parliament (MPP) was leader of the New Democratic Party of Ontario, and Dr. Morton Shulaman a New Democratic MPP and an author. Earlier MPPs include Conservative, E. F. Singer (1929–34); Liberal, John Glass (1934–43); Labor Progressive, J. B. Salsberg (1943–55); and Liberal, Joseph Gould, elected 1959 (d. 1965).

Bibliography: B. G. Sack, *History of the Jews in Canada* (1965); S. Rosenberg, *The Jewish Community in Canada* (1970). [B.G.K.]

ONYCHA (Heb. שְׁחֵלֶת), aromatic substance. According to the ancient translations, the *sheḥelet* included among the ingredients of the incense (Ex. 30:34) is onycha. An early *baraita* dating from Temple times has צִפֹּרֶן ("fingernail") instead of *sheḥelet* (Ker. 6a). The reference to the shell of a mollusk, the *Unguis odoratus* (shaped like a fingernail and hence its name) which is found in the Indian Ocean, and, like several other mollusks found in the Red Sea, emits a pleasant smell when burned. Ben Sira 24:15 also includes onycha (in Greek ὄνυξ as one of the ingredients of the incense in the Temple, while in Ugaritic writings it is mentioned among several spices and foods.

Bibliography: Loew, Flora, 1 (1928), 313; H.L. Ginsberg, *Kitvei Ugarit* (1936), 103; H.N. and A.L. Moldenke, *Plants of the Bible* (1952), 223f., no. 209. [J.F.]

OPATOSHU, JOSEPH (formerly **Joseph Meyer Opatovsky**; 1886–1954), Yiddish novelist and short-story writer. Born near the Polish town of Mlave, Opatoshu went to the U.S. in 1907, where he studied engineering at Cooper Union at night, and supported himself by working in a shoe factory, selling newspapers, and teaching in Hebrew

Caricature of Joseph Opatoshu, Yiddish novelist, by Henryk Berlewi, 1922. *Rimon*, no. 4, Berlin, 1923.

schools. In 1914 he graduated as a civil engineer, but soon found literature a more congenial profession. From 1910 he contributed stories to periodicals and anthologies, and in 1914 edited an anthology of his own, *Di Naye Heym* ("The New Home"), which included his story of American Jewish life, *"Fun New Yorker Geto."* When the New York Yiddish daily *Der Tog* was founded (1914), he joined its staff and for 40 years contributed stories, sketches, and serials, most of which were later reprinted in book form.

Opatoshu's early work was naturalistic, depicting scenes from contemporary life. Thus his *A Roman fun a Ferd Ganev* ("A Story of a Horse Thief," 1912), his first novel to attract wide attention, was based on his boyhood acquaintance with an unusual Jewish thief who made a living by smuggling horses across the border from Poland to Germany and who was killed while defending fellow Jews against their hostile neighbors. Opatoshu expressed his reaction to romanticism by creating thieves, smugglers, and drunkards who were a distinct contrast to the figures in the writings of *Shalom Aleichem or *Peretz. Opatoshu was one of the first Yiddish writers to depict American Jewish experience in his works. After reading some of his American stories, Shalom Aleichem encouraged Opatoshu to continue writing about Jews in the New World. Opatoshu heeded this suggestion and gave literary expression to the conflicts created by the Americanization of the Jewish immigrant in such works as *Hebrew* (or *Farloyrene Mentshn;* 1919), a naturalistic novel that deals with the problems of Jewish education in New York; *Di Tentserin* (1929) portrays declining Ḥasidism in New York; *Arum Grand Street* (1929) focuses on the immigrant Jews in the Lower East Side; and *Rase* (1923), a short-story collection that portrayed the conflict between varying ethnic and religious groups. In his novel *In Poylishe Velder* (1921; *In Polish Woods*, 1938, the first volume of a trilogy), Opatoshu described the decay of the hasidic court of Kotzk during the post-Napoleonic generation and presented a rich panorama of Polish-Jewish interrelations up to the Revolt of 1863. Often reprinted and translated into eight languages, it established Opatoshu's fame internationally, though its sequel, *1863*, made less of an impact; the last volume of the trilogy, *Aleyn* ("Alone") was the first to be published (1919). Fascinated by the Jewish past, he sought to revivify segments of it in historical novels. In his Falstaffian narrative, *A Tog in Regensburg* (*A Day in Regensburg*, 1968), as well as in *Elye Bokher* (dealing with the author of the Yiddish romance, the **Bove Buch*), both published in 1933, Opatoshu portrays the vanished world of 16th-century Jewish patricians and Yiddish minstrels in a stylized language that utilized older layers of Yiddish. In his final historical epic, *Der Letster Oyfshtand* (2 vols. 1948–52; *The Last Revolt*, 1952), Opatoshu attempted an imaginative reconstruction of daily life in second-century Judea, when the last desperate revolt of the Jews against Roman rule flared up and was crushed.

His son DAVID (1914–) was an actor. He worked with the Yiddish theater before serving in the U.S. army from 1942 to 1946. He played character roles with the Group Theater and appeared on Broadway and in Hollywood movies. He published short stories and television scripts.

Bibliography: *Opatoshu Bibliografie*, 1 (1937); 2 (1947), incl. articles written on him; LYNL, 1 (1956), 145–9; B. Rivkin, *Joseph Opatoshu's Gang* (1948); I. Freilich, *Opatoshus Shafungsveg* (1951); J. Glatstein, *In Tokh Genumen* (1956), 145–56; S. Bickel, *Shrayber fun Mayn Dor* (1958), 304–16; C. Madison, *Yiddish Literature* (1968), 326–47; N. Mayzel, *Yosef Opatoshu* (Yid., 1937), incl. bibl.; S. Liptzin, *Maturing of Yiddish Literature* (1970), 10–18. [S.L.]

OPATOW (Pol. **Opatów;** Yid. **Apta,** אַפּטאָ), town in Kielce province, E. Poland. A Jewish settlement existed in Opatow from the 16th century. In 1634 the town was divided into two sectors, the Christian and the Jewish, the latter known as the "Street of the Jews." According to Samuel Feivish in *Tit ha-Yaven* (Venice, 1670) over 200 Jewish families perished there during the Swedish invasion of Poland in 1656. Conditions became so difficult that in 1687 the *Council of the Four Lands issued an ordinance prohibiting other Jews from settling in Opatow without obtaining express permission from the community board *(kahal)*. The community in Opatow was efficiently organized at this period, and its diverse activities, including collection for the needy of Ereẓ Israel, were administered by various officers (*ne'emanim* and *gabba'im*). In the 18th century its economic position deteriorated and it became dependent on the whims of the overlords of the town and the governor. The minute book *(pinkas)* of the Opatow community was an important source of information for the history of Polish Jewry; a copy was preserved in the communal archives in Warsaw up to 1939.

The Jewish population in Opatow increased in the 19th century, numbering 2,517 in 1856 (out of a total population of 3,845), and 4,138 in 1897. Among the noted personalities who lived in Opatow the best known is the ḥasidic *ẓaddik*, *Abraham Joshua Heshel, "the rabbi of Apta."

Holocaust Period. Before World War II 5,200 Jews lived in Opatow. The town came under the Radom District of the General-Government during the Nazi occupation. Many Jews fled before the Germans entered, young Jewish men in particular escaping to Soviet-occupied territory. After the capitulation of the town, the Germans set fire to the market place where mainly Jews lived. Over the next days 200 men, Poles and Jews, were deported and never returned. A "contribution" (fine) of 60,000 marks was exacted, and Jews were evicted from the better residences which were handed over to German officers. A ghetto was officially established in the spring of 1941. It was open and without fence or guard, but Jews were forbidden to leave it on pain of death. Food, however, was available illegally in the open ghetto for high prices, so that Jews with means did not suffer from hunger. The poor (among them deportees and refugees from other places), who had no property or could not get work or were not hardy enough to get on in these difficult conditions, suffered misery and hunger, being left only with the meager, official food rations. Among the poor an epidemic of typhus broke out and a hospital was set up in the synagogue, which also served the surrounding Jewish towns. Jews engaged in hard labor in the vicinity of Opatow, on road construction and in quarries.

The number of Jews in Opatow grew continually because of the influx of refugees from surrounding townlets and villages, as well as from distant towns—*Konin, *Lodz, and *Warsaw. In September 1940 there were 5,800 Jews, 600 of them newcomers; by September 1942 there were about 7,000 Jews, 1,800 of them deportees. Shortly before the liquidation a number of Jews from Silesia settled in Opatow Ghetto, which from June 1, 1942, was one of the 17 ghettos officially left in the country.

In July 1941 the German police began abducting young men for labor camps. Raids were carried out by German police with the help of Jewish police. Jews found in hiding were often executed. Until the liquidation of the ghetto, about 1,900–2,100 Jews were sent to the labor camps. A group of youth planning armed resistance bought weapons from Poles and stored them in the garret of the synagogue. The German police, who were informed, seized the weapons and shot a group of girls who were found there. The Judenrat was composed of well-known persons, mainly Zionists. The president, Mordekhai Weissblum, is reported to have taken care of the Jewish population, organized Jewish life, and alleviated German persecution and repression by personal diplomacy and bribery. But the Judenrat was also reproached for having prepared lists of candidates for labor camps, although it also sent parcels with food and clothing to the camp inmates.

The liquidation of the ghetto took place on Oct. 20–22, 1942. German police and Ukrainians surrounded the ghetto and carried out a mass *Selektion* in the square. Six thousand Jews were driven on foot to the Jasice station near Ostrow, loaded onto wagons, and taken to *Treblinka. Another 500 to 600 Jews were taken to a labor camp in Sandomierz. During the three-day *Aktion* several hundred Jews were killed in the town. The Germans left a few score Jews in Opatow to clear the terrain and sort out Jewish property. After the work was completed the Jews were shot at the Jewish cemetery, with the exception of a few individuals, among them the president of the Judenrat, who reached labor camps in Sandomierz. The community was not reconstituted after the war. [DE.D.]

Bibliography: *Apt (Opatov), Sefer Zikkaron* . . . (Heb. and Yid., 1966); A Rutkowski, in: BZIH, no. 15–16 (1955), 75–182 passim; Yad Vashem Archives.

OPAVA (Ger. **Troppau**), city in N. Silesia, Czechoslovakia. A tale about 27 Jews being executed for well-poisoning in Opava in 1163 is probably unreliable. A Jewish community is first mentioned in 1281. Although their expulsion is not documented it is recorded that in 1501 Jews were permitted to return and buy back their houses. Jews from *Osoblaha (Hotzenplotz) traded in Opava. In 1737 20 Jewish families lived in the duchy. Several Jewish families lived in Opava at the beginning of the 19th century, and their number increased after the 1848 Revolution. At the end of the 19th century Opava became a center of the *Schoenerer brand of German nationalism, and the community suffered from anti-Semitic attacks. The community developed, inspired by its rabbi, Simon Friedmann, an ardent Zionist from his student days. In 1923 a progressive community statute was introduced. On the outskirts of Opava in the 1920s the training farm, Komorau, was a center of the He-Ḥalutz movement. The community numbered 134 in 1867, 1,127 in 1921, and in 1931, 971 (2.6% of the total population), 502 of whom declared their nationality as Jewish. At the time of the Sudeten crisis the community dispersed. The synagogue was set on fire by the Nazis. After the war the community was revived, mainly by Jews from Subcarpathian Ruthenia. In 1959 it was affiliated with the Ostrava community and it was still active in 1970 as a synagogue congregation.

The synagogue of Opava, Czechoslovakia, being burned by the Nazis in 1939. Courtesy B. M. Ansbacher, Jerusalem.

Bibliography: Germ Jud, 1 (1963), 387–8; 2 (1968), 834; Bondy-Dworský, nos. 305, 309, 1110; A. Engel, in: JGGJČ, 2 (1930), 59, 84; A. Cassuto, in: *Zeitschrift fuer Geschichte der Juden in der Tschechoslowakei*, 1 (1930), 81–90; J. Nirtl, *ibid.*, 4 (1934), 41–43; B. Brilling, in: *Judaica Bohemiae*, 4 (1968), 101–18, passim; B. Bretholz, *Quellen zur Geschichte der Juden in Maehren* (1935), index; Yad Vashem Archives. [M.LA.]

OPFERPFENNIG, a poll tax introduced in 1342 by Emperor Louis IV the Bavarian, who ordered all Jews above the age of 12 and possessing 20 gulden to pay one gulden annually so that he would be better able to protect them. The original name was *Guldenpfennig*, changed in later generations to *Opferpfennig*. The practice was motivated by sheer economic necessity and justified by Christian chroniclers on the grounds that the German emperor, as the legal successor of the Roman emperors, was the rightful recipient of the traditional Temple tax which Jews paid after the destruction of the Second Temple. The *Opferpfennig* (called *donatio* by the exchequer) was collected on Christmas day, giving the levy the ignominy of a degrading poll tax. By 1346 the emperor was already disposing of the *Opferpfennig* of *Frankfort, *Friedberg, *Gelnhausen, and *Wetzlar. *Charles IV ordered the income of the 1348 tax to be delivered to the archbishop of Triers. The *Opferpfennig*, like other taxes, was a readily transferable source of income but never grew to sizeable proportions. This poll tax was sometimes replaced by an overall fixed communal tax. Rich and powerful Jews often succeeded in buying or obtaining exemption from the tax, a symbol of servitude.

Bibliography: T. Roesel, in: MGWJ, 54 (1910), 208+10; Kisch, Germany, 167–8; Baron, Social², 9 (1965), 156. [Ed.]

OPHEL, rocky protuberance north of the city of David in Jerusalem. Its wall is mentioned in the time of Jotham (II Chron. 27:3), Manasseh (II Chron. 33:14), and Nehemiah (3:27); it formed part of the eastern fortifications of Jerusalem. In the time of Nehemiah, the Temple servants (Nethinim) lived there. According to Nehemiah 3:27, the Ophel was situated between the "tower that standeth out" of the royal palace and the water gate. The name Ophel in a general sense was applied to a city hill in Micah 4:8 and Isaiah 32:14, and specifically to a hill in Samaria (II Kings 5:24). In modern times, the name Ophel has been extended to the whole eastern hill of Old Jerusalem, including David's City. Excavations in this area were begun by Ch. Warren in 1867 and continued by C. Schick (1880, 1886), H. Guthe (1881), F. J. Bliss and A. C. Dickie (1894–97), M. Parker (1909), R. Weill (1913–24), F. J. Macalister (1923–25) and J. W. Crowfoot (1927–28). For their results, see *Jerusalem. [M.A.-Y.]

View of the Ophel from the South with the Temple Mount behind it. Photo D. Eisenberg, Jerusalem.

OPHIR (Heb. אוֹפִר, אוֹפִיר), a country in the biblical period, well known for its gold. Trade between Palestine and Ophir was possible by sea from the port of Ezion-Geber, but only in the time of Solomon was an attempt made to reach Ophir and take gold, precious stones, and sandalwood from there (I Kings 9:28; 10:11; II Chron. 8:18; 9:10). An attempt made during the reign of Jehoshaphat to reach Ophir did not succeed, as the ships prepared for this undertaking in Ezion-Geber broke on the rocks (I Kings 22:49). Sailing to Ophir apparently required much preparation, and could not be accomplished without outside help. In the days of Solomon the voyage was undertaken with the assistance of Tyrian sailors. Even in the days of Jehoshaphat, lengthy negotiations had been carried on between Jehoshaphat and Ahaziah king of Israel for the purpose of preparing the journey to Ophir, and still it did not succeed. The author of II Chronicles (20:35–37) mistakenly indicates Tarshish as the goal of Jehoshaphat's voyage. However, the evidence recorded in the book is indeed correct, namely, that the negotiations between Jehoshaphat and Ahaziah aroused bitter opposition in Judah, no doubt because of the rights Jehoshaphat granted Ahaziah—as payment for his help in preparing the trip to Ophir—in the region of Ezion-Geber, which was located within the area of Judah's sovereignty. These negotiations also testify not only that the region of Ophir was distant from Palestine and that the voyage involved much preparation and special technical, professional training in navigation, but also that the mining of gold entailed many difficulties that the Kingdom of Judah could not overcome itself. According to information preserved in the Bible, Solomon's fleet sailed to Ophir only once. The plentiful information concerning the value of the gold of Ophir which was found in Palestine corroborates the assumption that this gold reached Palestine by way of gold markets which existed throughout the world at that time. The fact that the port of Ezion-Geber served as a point of departure for ships sailing to Ophir indicates that it was also possible to reach Ophir from the coastal regions of the Red Sea; and consequently, it is reasonable to suppose that Palestine served as a channel for the transportation of gold from Ophir to Syria, Babylonia, and Asia Minor. The use of the gold of Ophir in Palestine is attested to in the inscription: [ז]הב אפר לבית חרן ("Gold of Ophir for Beth-Horon") which was found on an earthern vessel, discovered in the excavations at Tell Qasile.

There are many assumptions concerning the location of Ophir. Eupolemus was of the opinion that Ophir is an island in the Red Sea (in Eusebius, *Praeparatio Evangelica*, 9:30, 7). Josephus (Ant., 1:147; 8:164; cf. Eusebius, Onom. 176:13) locates Ophir in India—in the regions between one of the tributaries of the Indus River and China. It has also been suggested that Ophir should be located along the coast of the Arabian Peninsula, since the location of Ophir the son of Joktan the son of Eber was between Sheba and Havilah (Gen. 10:28–29), which were also famous in the biblical period for their gold (Gen. 2:11; Isa. 60:6; Ezek. 27:22; Ps. 72:15). The most likely location of Ophir to have been suggested so far is the region of Somaliland on the East African Coast, possibly extending to the neighboring coast of South Arabia. The products of Ophir are characteristically African and are similar to those of Punt, which suggests that Ophir and Punt were located in the same region. It is certain that Punt was in the area of Somaliland, and it is thus likely that Ophir was situated there as well.

Bibliography: K. Peters, *Ofir nach den neuen Entdeckungen* (1908); Pauly-Wissowa, s.v. *Saba;* B. Moritz, *Arabien* (1923), 63ff.; J. A. Montgomery, *Arabia and the Bible* (1934), 38ff.; J. Eitan, in: HUCA, 12–13 (1937–38), 61; G. W. Van Beek, in: JAOS, 78 (1958), 141–52; R. D. Barnett, *A Catalogue of the Nimrud Ivories* (1957), 59ff., 168. [Y.G.]

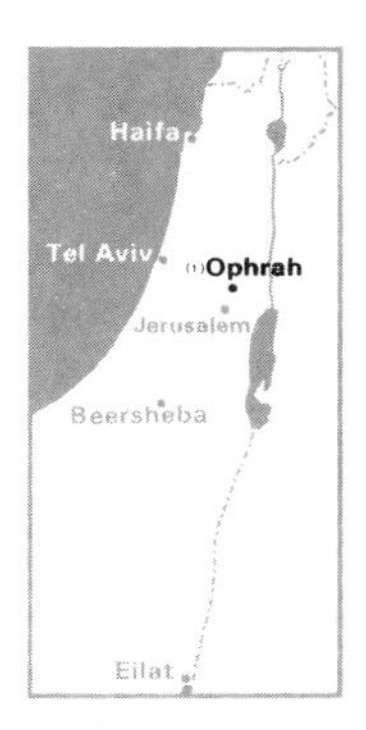

OPHRAH (Heb. עָפְרָה), name of two places mentioned in the Bible. (1) A locality in the northern part of the territory of the tribe of Benjamin near Beth-El (Josh. 18:23). Ophrah was one of the places attacked by Philistine "spoilers" shortly before the battle of Michmas (I Sam. 13:17). Abijah of Judah captured it together with Beth-El (II Chron. 13:19 as Ephrain). It was the capital of a district ceded by Samaria to Judea in 145 B.C.E., when it was called Aphaerema (I Macc. 11:34). It appears as Ephraim in the New Testament (John 11:54) and as Ephron in Eusebius (Onom. 28:4; 90:19) and on the Madaba Map. Ophrah is identified with al-Ṭayyiba, 4 mi. (6.4 km.) northeast of Beth-El. (2) Gideon's home town, which belonged to the Manassite clan of Abiezer (Judg. 6:11, 24; 8:27, 32; 9:5). Here God called on Gideon to fight the Midianites and here he ruled, died, and was buried. The identification of the place is uncertain. Most scholars locate it in the vicinity of Mt. Tabor (cf. Judg. 8:18) and the Jezreel Valley, the site of Gideon's encounter with the Midianites. Suggested sites in this region are either al-Ṭayyiba to the northeast of the hill of Moreh (the Crusader Effraon or Forbelet which is, however, also considered for Hapharaim of Issachar (Josh. 19:19)) or the tell of Affuleh which has traces of the Canaanite and Israelite periods.

Bibliography: (1) Abel, Geog, 2 (1938), 402; Aharoni, Land, index. (2) Abel, in: JPOS, 17 (1937), 31ff.; Press, Ereẓ, 4 (1955), 746; Aharoni, Land, index. [M.A.-Y.]

OPLER, MARVIN KAUFMANN (1914–), U.S. anthropologist and social psychiatrist; brother of Morris Edward *Opler. Opler was born in Buffalo, New York. After teaching anthropology, sociology, and social psychiatry at various American universities, Opler was appointed professor of social psychiatry at the University of Buffalo School of Medicine in 1958. He also served as professor of sociology and anthropology at the Graduate School of the State University of New York in Buffalo. Opler was, with Thomas A. C. Rennie, a principal investigator in the Midtown Manhattan Mental Health Research Study, 1952–60. He was an associate editor of the *International Journal of Social Psychiatry* from 1958 and associate editor of *American Anthropologist* from 1962.

His principal interests were social theory, world areas research, psychoanalytic techniques in social analysis, and social psychiatry. Opler researched groups extending from the Ute Indians to modern social groups. He pioneered research on psychotic disorders among different ethnic groups to illuminate cross-cultural perspectives in mental disease and to establish the need for the collaboration of psychiatry and anthropology in defining contexts and differentials of mental disease. This is exemplified by his book *Culture and Social Psychiatry* (1967); originally *Culture, Psychiatry, and Human Values* (1956). [E.Fi.]

OPLER, MORRIS EDWARD (1907–), U.S. anthropologist and brother of Marvin Kaufmann *Opler. Born in Buffalo, New York, Opler in 1948 was appointed to Cornell University as professor of anthropology and Asian studies, and director of its South Asia Program, 1948–66, and the India Program 1952–66. He served as president of the American Anthropological Association (1962–63).

His primary research interests were the ethnology of the Apache tribes, the cultural history of the Southwest, and the culture of India, as set out in *An Apache Way of Life* (1941). He was also author of *Social Aspects of Technical Assistance in Operation* (UNESCO, 1954). In later years he, like his brother, became interested in the relation between psychiatry and anthropology, and disturbed behavior and treatment in primitive and modern cultures. [E.Fi.]

OPOCZNO, town in central Poland. Opoczno was the birthplace of *Esterka, according to legend the mistress of Casimir the Great (1333–70). In 1588 the Polish sovereign authorized the town to expel the Jews living there, but a Jewish community had resettled in the environs by 1646. The settlement was not permanent: a judgment of the supreme tribunal in 1714 again prohibited Jews from living in the town. According to the census of 1765, however, there were 1,349 Jews in Opoczno and the vicinity (excluding infants under one). They owned 12 plots of land outside the town and 41 houses within it. A number of crafts were exclusively pursued by Jews. Judah Leib, son of Eliezer b. Solomon *Lipschuetz, author of responsa *Dammesek Eliezer,* officiated as rabbi of Opoczno at the end of the 18th century. The community numbered 1,469 in 1856, 2,425 in 1897, and 4,025 in 1909 (compared with 2,387 Christians). The 1921 census shows a marked decrease to 3,135 Jews (46.9% of the total population). [N.M.G.]

Holocaust Period. In 1939 there were about 3,000 Jews in Opoczno. The German army entered the town on Sept. 6, 1939. In November 1940 a ghetto was established and the town's Jewish population was crowded into 115 small houses. In June 1942 about 1,200 Jews from nearby villages were deported to Opoczno Ghetto which grew to over 4,200. In July 1942 about 400 men were deported to the "Hasag" slave-labor camp in Skarzysko-Kamienna and on Oct. 27, 1942, the ghetto was liquidated and all its inmates deported to *Treblinka death camp. Only 120 men were left until Jan. 3, 1943, and then exterminated. At the time of the mass deportation in October 1942, scores of Jews fled to the forests and organized partisan units there. The best-known unit, "Lions," under the command of Julian Ajzenman-Kaniewski, conducted a number of successful guerilla actions against Nazi forces and the Opoczno-Konskie railway line. After the war, the Jewish community of Opoczno was not reconstituted. [S.Kr.]

Bibliography: BZIH, no. 15–16 (1955), 82, and no. 65–66 (1968), 55–57.

OPOLE LUBELSKIE, small town in Lublin province, S. E. Poland. A silver merchant named Manasseh is known to have resided in Opole in 1626 and carried on business there. The administration of the Opole community came under the jurisdiction of the Lublin *kahal* (see *Councils of the Lands). There were 487 Jews living in Opole in 1765. The community increased substantially during the 19th century, numbering 1,799 in 1856 (nearly twice the number of gentiles), and 3,323 in 1897 (60.1% of the total). The Jewish population numbered 3,766 in 1921 (66.7%). [EJ/Ed.]

Holocaust Period. About 4,000 Jews were living in Opole Lubelskie on the eve of World War II. The number was more than doubled when about 2,500 Jews from Pulawy and over 2,000 Jews from Vienna were deported there in December 1939 and February 1941, respectively. In May 1942 an additional few hundred Jews from nearby smaller places and Slovakia were brought to the town. Jews were deported from Opole to death camps on three occasions: on March 31, 1942, to Belzec, and in May and October 1942 to Sobibor. The community was not revived after the war. [S.Kr.]

Bibliography: T. Brustin-Bernstein, in: *Bleter far Geshikhte,* 3 no. 1–2 (1950), 51–78, passim; Yad Vashem Archives.

Postmark from the Opole ghetto, 1942. From *The Holy Land Philatelist,* vol. 2, no. 23, September 1956.

OPORTO, port city in northern Portugal, on Douro River. Oporto had a vibrant Jewish community before the establishment of the Portuguese kingdom in 1143. One of its three Jewish neighborhoods was called Monte dos Judeus (Jews' Hill). The ancient synagogue structure—approved by King John in 1388—was confiscated in 1554 for use by the Order of Santa Clara. Stairs adjoining the ruins are still known as *Escadas de Esnoga* ("the Synagogue Steps") and an inscription unearthed in 1875 reveals that the synagogue had been dedicated by Don Judah. With the expulsion of the Jews from Spain in 1492, Oporto received an influx of Spanish Jews, including some 30 families who arrived as a group under the illustrious rabbi Isaac *Aboab. When Portugal ousted its Jews in 1497, Jewish communal life in Oporto was reduced to underground *Marrano activities. The Inquisition was active in the city and an

Ark of the Law of the Kadoorie Synagogue in Oporto, Portugal, erected in 1929.

auto-da-fé took place on Feb. 11, 1543. Local public opinion was so adverse, however, that no additional inquisitorial spectacles were permitted. In 1920 when Arturo Carlos de *Barros Basto set out to revive Judaism among the Marranos, Oporto became the center of his activities. The congregation Mekor Ḥayyim was organized there in 1927. In 1929 the imposing Kadoorie Synagogue was erected, housing both the congregation and an affiliated seminary for religious studies. In 1970 the Jewish community of Oporto numbered about 100 persons.

Bibliography: N. Slouschz, *Ha-Anusim be-Portugal* (1932), index; Pinho Leal, *Portugal, antigo e moderno* 12 vols. (1873–90); L. Piles Ros, in: *Sefarad*, 6 (1946), 139; 7 (1947), 357; H. Beinart, in: *Sefunot*, 5 (1961), 75–134. [A.LI.]

OPPENHEIM, town in W. Germany. Jews are first mentioned there in the tax register of 1241, according to which they were obliged to pay the emperor an annual tax of 15 marks. The Jews of the town, legally the property of the emperor, were placed under the protection of the officers in charge of the local fortress, to whom they paid their taxes. They also paid a house tax to the archbishop of Mainz. *Rudolph of Hapsburg and other kings gave letters of credit to various noblemen which were to be defrayed from the taxes paid by the Jews of Oppenheim; at times, they also leased these taxes. The burden of their taxes appears to have caused several Jews of Oppenheim to join the group which fled from the Rhineland and under the leadership of *Meir b. Baruch of Rothenburg attempted to emigrate to Ereẓ Israel (1285). At the end of July 1349, during the persecutions which followed the *Black Death, most of the Jews of Oppenheim were murdered, while others chose martyrdom (**kiddush ha-Shem*) and burned themselves to death in order to escape forced conversion at the hands of the mob. Among the martyrs was the rabbi Joel ha-Kohen.

Some time later the community was reestablished. After 1400 the right of residence was made renewable at the end of every six years, and the amount of taxes to be paid was fixed. In 1422 a plot by two Christians to kill the Jews of the town was frustrated by the municipal council. Certain protection fees and "gifts" which the Jews of Oppenheim were compelled to pay weighed upon them so heavily that despite the additional support of such communities as Worms, Mainz, and Frankfort, Oppenheim Jewry could not meet their payments and were therefore penalized (1444). In 1456, R. Seligmann Bing (or R. Seligmann Oppenheim) attempted to establish a union of the communities of the Upper Rhine, but because of community opposition and that of R. Israel Isserlein (c. 1390–1460), the project was abandoned.

The community suffered during the wars of Louis XIV, and by 1674 only three families remained in the town. By 1722 the number had grown to eight. Many Oppenheim Jews settled in Frankfort and other south German cities where they were known as "Oppenheim" or "Oppenheimer," and the name became widespread. The community numbered 20 families in 1807, 257 in 1872, 189 in 1880, and 56 in 1933. Of the 17 Jews who remained during World War II, 16 were deported. In 1970 no Jews lived in Oppenheim.

Bibliography: FJW, 405; P. Lazarus, in: ZGJD, 5 (1934), 200–4; Germ Jud, 1 (1963), 255–6; 2 (1968), 629–32; E. L. Rapp and O. Boecher, in: *Festschrift 1200 Jahre Oppenheim* (1965), 91–105.

[P.LA./Z.AV.]

OPPENHEIM, name of a German family derived from the Rhenish town of that name. In Hebrew works the members of the family are always called Oppenheim. Later some of them, especially the Vienna branch, were called Oppenheimer. Another branch of the family settled in Heidelberg and assumed the name of that town. The earliest known mention of the name is that of R. Isaac Oppenheim and R. Joel Oppenheim, both mentioned in the responsa of R. Meir of Rothenburg (d. 1293). In Worms the family early achieved distinction, providing the community with a long line of leaders and representatives, while its members were also to become founders of the Vienna Oppenheimer branch. In 1531 this family appeared in Frankfort, where they had come from Heidelberg. After the expulsion of the Jews from Frankfort in 1614, part of the family again settled in Heidelberg. In Frankfort, too, it was one of the most prominent families, many of its members serving the community as *parnasim* and *shtadlanim*, and producing many rabbis, financiers, and successful merchants. More than 200 tombstones bearing this family name are to be found in the old Jewish cemetery in Frankfort. [H.FL.]

OPPENHEIM, family of German bankers, originally from Frankfort, and later from Bonn, where in 1789 SOLOMON OPPENHEIM, JR. (1772–1828) established a commission and forwarding business. From 1798 Cologne was the headquarters of the banking house of Sal Oppenheim Jr. & Cie. Proximity both to West European financial centers and to the Rhine-Ruhr industry determined its rise after World War II to the position of Federal Germany's second largest private banking concern. The firm promoted railroad construction, river transportation, insurance, and corporate banks in Germany and abroad, participated in syndicates for the public sector, and supplied industrial credit. Solomon Oppenheim Jr. helped to establish the Paris bank of B. L. Fould et Fould-Oppenheim (now Heine & Co.). His daughter Helene married the banker Bénoît *Fould. Solomon Oppenheim Jr.'s sons, SIMON (1803–1880) and ABRAHAM (1804–1878) were ennobled and their descendants converted. Simon's great-grandsons WALDEMAR (1894–1952) and FRIEDRICH CARL (1900–), "quarter-Jews" by Nazi reckoning, had to change the firm's name to Pferdmenges (a non-family partner) & Co. in 1938. Friedrich Carl Oppenheim was imprisoned in 1944, following the abortive attempt on Hitler's life. After World War II, the bank resumed its original name and Oppenheim partnership interests. Two descendants of Solomon Oppenheim Jr. were active in public affairs: Simon's brother DAGOBERT (David; 1809–1899), who converted to Christianity, was a cofounder and codirector of the progressive daily *Rheinische Zeitung* (1841–43). Simon's baptized grandson MAX OPPENHEIM (1860–1946), a German career diplomat and orientalist, founded the Deutsches Orient Institut.

Bibliography: K. Grunwald, in: YLBI, 12 (1967), 201–2, 207; W. Treue, in: *Rheinisch-Westfaelische Wirtschaftsbiographien*, 8 (1962); idem, in: *Tradition, Zeitschrift fuer Firmen-Geschichte und Unternehmerbiographie*, 9 (1964). [H.G.R.]

OPPENHEIM, BEER BEN ISAAC (1760–1849), German rabbi and scholar. In his early youth Oppenheim studied at the yeshivah of Fuerth and then proceeded to Berlin where he apparently made contact with the followers of the Haskalah movement. His contributions to **Bikkurei ha-Ittim* are written in an attractive Hebrew style, and he carried on correspondence with Moses Israel *Landau, Isaac Samuel *Reggio, and Solomon Judah Loeb *Rapoport. He later settled in Pressburg (Bratislava), living there in favorable financial circumstances and engaging mainly in talmudic studies. In 1829 he published *Mei-Be'er*, a collection of his responsa to Moses *Muenz, Samuel b. Ezekiel *Landau, Solomon Margolis, Baruch b. Josiah *Jeiteles, his brother Ḥayyim, and other contemporary scholars. It appeared with an appendum entitled *Palgei Mayim*, containing a number of his talmudic novellae.

Bibliography: Oppenheim, in: MGWJ, 1 (1874), 63; Loewenstein, in: *Gedenkbuch... D. Kaufmann* (1900), 551; H. N. Dembitzer, *Kelilat Yofi*, 2 (1893), 58b; J. K. Duschinsky, *Toledot ha-Ga'on R. David Oppenheimer* (1922), 83f. [H.FL.]

OPPENHEIM, DAVID (1816–1876), Hebrew scholar. Born in Leipnik, Moravia, he was a rabbi in his native land and in Hungary. He published articles and studies in Hebrew and other languages, which encompassed a broad range of Hebrew literature and culture. A zealot for the Hebrew language, he fought the movement to eliminate Hebrew in the synagogue. His Hebrew studies were published in the periodicals *Bet ha-Midrash* and *Yeshurun*, and especially in *Ha-Maggid*, to which he contributed critiques of Judaica.

Bibliography: Zeitlin, Bibliotheca, 256. [G.K.]

OPPENHEIM (Oppenheimer), DAVID BEN ABRAHAM (1664–1736), rabbi. Born in Worms, his teachers were Gershon *Ashkenazi of Metz, Jacob *Ashkenazi, Benjamin Wolf Epstein of Friedberg, and *Isaac Benjamin Wolf b. Eliezer Lipman of Landsberg. While he was still a boy, he maintained a scholarly correspondence with Jair Ḥayyim *Bacharach. At the age of 17 he married Genendel, daughter of the Hanoverian Court Jew Leffman *Behrends. A nephew of Samuel *Oppenheimer, he inherited a fortune from him. At the age of 20 Oppenheim was ordained rabbi by his teachers in Metz and Landsberg, as well as by the rabbi of Worms, Aaron b. Moses *Teomim. While his noble descent, his wealth, and the influence of his family may have helped him, as a scholar of repute he was entitled to recognition in his own right. When 25 he was called to the rabbinate of the

David ben Abraham Oppenheimer, *Landrabbiner* of Moravia. Engraving by Baltzer after Kleinhard. Cecil Roth Collection.

highly respected community of Nikolsburg (*Mikulov), thus becoming **Landrabbiner* of Moravia. There he gathered many students around him, founding a *bet midrash* which he endowed with large funds to ensure its continued existence for many years. In 1698 he received a call from the community of Brest-Litovsk and, although he declined, from this time he called himself rabbi of Brest. He also declined the call to become *Landrabbiner* of the Palatinate (1702). The community of Jerusalem honored him with the title "rabbi of the Holy City," which explains the use of the title "rabbi of Israel and of many communities and districts of the Diaspora" in the heading of his introduction to the Pentateuch (Berlin, 1705). Appointed *nasi Ereẓ Israel* by Samson *Wertheimer, Oppenheim became responsible for the collection and transference of sums collected throughout Europe for the benefit of Jews in Jerusalem (see *Hierosolymitanische Stiftung, **Ḥalukkah*). Many communities turned to him for help in regularizing their internal affairs; he prepared the statutes of the community of *Hildesheim, which were partially accepted. After 12 years of successful activity in Nikolsburg, Oppenheim became rabbi of Prague, a community rich in talmudic scholarship. His munificence and liberality attracted many scholars. His wife Genendel died in 1712, and in her memory he donated a valuable Ark curtain to the Altneu synagogue. In 1713 he was appointed *Landrabbiner* of half of Bohemia, while the other half remained under the leadership of Benjamin Wolf Spira, whose daughter Shifrah, widow of Isaac b. Solomon Zalman Bondi of Prague, became Oppenheim's second wife. When Benjamin Wolf Spira died in 1715, he also became *Landrabbiner* of the other half of Bohemia.

Regarded as a man who was familiar with all branches of rabbinical and halakhic literature, Oppenheim also had a reputation as a mathematician, and many rabbis of the day turned to him with difficult questions of religious law. Many demands for his approbations (*Haskamot) were made; Loewenstein has traced more than 70 of these. Oppenheim was reluctantly drawn into contemporary quarrels. Judah Leib *Prossnitz vilified his name in an unprecedented manner—with his agreement, the rabbinate of Prossnitz (*Prostejov) had excommunicated Judah Leib—but on the other hand he was accused by Ẓevi Ashkenazi of having given material and moral support to Nehemiah *Ḥayon. It would appear that he had approved one of Ḥayon's works but that Ḥayon had printed the approbation in another. Oppenheim also had serious differences with Jonathan *Eybeshuetz, who also worked in Prague. When Eybeshuetz's students slandered him in a most vulgar fashion, serious disturbances arose between the students of their respective yeshivot, prompting the authorities to intervene. In a decree of June 16, 1722, Emperor Charles VI ordered that the students responsible for the upheaval were not to remain in Prague and that "in future, Jewish studies be under the control of the said chief rabbi Oppenheim," and that no other Prague rabbi might maintain a house of study.

From his early youth a lover of books, Oppenheim undertook long journeys in order to obtain rare manuscripts or prints. He visited the fairs at Leipzig, was in close touch with printers and book dealers, and published lists of works he sought, in order to obtain books from all lands. He used his wealth (inherited and received from his wives) to establish a library. J. C. Wolf, who obtained most of the material for his Bibliotheca Hebraea from Oppenheim's library, estimated that it contained 7,000 volumes, including 1,000 manuscripts. An incomplete catalog of Oppenheim's library appeared in 1764, a second, by Israel Bresslau, was published in Hamburg in 1782, and a third, entitled *Kohelet David,* by Isaac Metz appeared in Hamburg/Altona in 1826 with a Latin translation by Lazarus Emden. A supplement to the latter was issued by J. *Goldenthal in Leipzig in 1845. Because of censorship problems, the library was kept in Hanover; on Oppenheim's death it was inherited by his only son, Joseph, who married a daughter of Samson *Wertheimer. After Joseph's death it passed to his nephew Isaac Seligman Cohen. One of Oppenheim's grandchildren, the widow of R. Hirsch Oppenheim of Hildesheim, put the library up for sale. M. *Mendelssohn valued it at between 50 and 60,000 thaler, and it was later taxed for 150,000 thaler, but in 1829 it was finally sold for the ridiculously low sum of 9,000 thaler to Oxford, where it forms the substantial part of the Hebrew section of the *Bodleian Library. Oppenheim was a patron of Jewish scholarship and gave many editors and publishers of talmudic and halakhic works grants toward publishing costs. He willingly put manuscripts that he had obtained at great expense at the disposal of publishers, in order to make them available to the wider public. Although Oppenheim himself wrote a great deal, the greatest part of his works lies unpublished in Oxford and other libraries. His responsa were published in the collections of responsa of Jair Ḥayyim Bacharach, Jacob b. Joseph *Reicher-Backofen, Ezekiel *Katzenellenbogen, *Eliakim Goetz b. Meir, and Eliezer Lipschuetz.

Bibliography: M. Grunwald, in: MGWJ, 40 (1896), 425–8; D. Kaufmann, *ibid.*, 42 (1898), 322–5; M. Freudenthal, *ibid.*, 262–74; L. Lowenstein, in: *Gedenkbuch ... David Kaufmann* (1900), 538–59; M. Freudenthal, in: MGWJ, 46 (1902), 262–74; C. Duschinsky, in: *Ha-Ẓofeh le-Ḥokhmat Yisrael,* 5 (1921), 30–45, 145–55; 6 (1922), 26–37, 160–5, 205–56; *Soncino-Blaetter,* 2 (1927), 59–80; 3 (1929/30), 63–66; J. Rivkind, in: *Reshummot,* 4 (1929), 321–4; A. Marx, in: *Mélanges ... Israel Lévi* (1926), 451–60 (Eng.); S. H. Lieben, in: JJLG, 19 (1928), 1–38; C. Duschinsky, in: JQR, 20 (1929/30), 217–47; S. H. Lieben, in: JGGJC, 7 (1935), 437–83; D. Feuchtwang, in: *Gedenkbuch ... [des Juedischen Museums in Nikolsburg]* (1936), 51–58; A. Marx, *Studies in Jewish History and Booklore* (1944), 213–9, 238–55; D. Brilling, in: *Zion,* 12 (1946/47), 89–96; Y. Z. Cahana, in: *Sinai,* 21 (1947), 327–34; idem, in: *Arim ve-Immahot be-Yisrael,* 4 (1950), 268–72; Yaari, Sheluḥei, index; M. Benayahu, in: *Yerushalayim,* 3 (1951), 108–29; idem, in: *Sefunot,* 2 (1957/58), 131; 3–4 (1959/61), index; M. Friedmann, *ibid.,* 10 (1966/67), 496–8; B. Nosek and V. Sadek, in: *Bohemia Judaicae,* 6 (1970), 5–27.

[H.Fl./Ed.]

OPPENHEIM, ḤAYYIM (1832–1891), Hebrew scholar. Born in Moravia, a brother of David *Oppenheim, he received his academic degree as well as a teaching certificate in Vienna in 1857. He also served as rabbi in various communities. His studies and articles encompassed the entire range of talmudic, religious, and philosophic literature of the Middle Ages. Most of his studies were written in Hebrew and appeared in scholarly publications during the latter half of the 19th century. He was among the first to introduce into Hebrew scholarship the early findings of Assyriology. He also contributed to German scholarly periodicals devoted to Judaic studies.

Bibliography: Kressel, Leksikon, 1 (1965), 46.

[G.K.]

OPPENHEIM, HERMANN (1858–1919), German neurologist and researcher of the nervous system. Oppenheim, born in Warburg, published many studies on the anatomy and pathology of the brain, the spinal cord, and the peripheral nerves. He improved the methods for examining patients with nervous disorders, and introduced many important innovations in diagnostic and therapeutic procedures, especially in the diagnosis of brain tumors and their localization, as well as in meningitis aphasia. A congenital disease of the brain stem and spinal cord in infants is named after him. The fruits of his rich experiments were assembled in his work, *Lehrbuch der Nervenkrankheiten fuer Aerzte und Studierende,* which was published in seven editions (first in 1894) and translated into many languages. It became the textbook for neurologists throughout the world for decades. Oppenheim was the founder and organizer of the German Neurological Association and its chairman for many years. Despite his international reputation and a unanimous recommendation by the medical faculty of Berlin University that he be appointed to the chair in neurology, the Prussian government refused to sanction this unless he be converted to Christianity, which Oppenheim resolutely refused.

Bibliography: A. Stern, *In bewegter Zeit* (1968), 55–60.

[J.Pr.]

OPPENHEIM, JACQUES (1849–1924), Dutch jurist. Oppenheim was born in Groningen, where he became secretary of the municipality in 1873. In 1885 he was appointed professor of constitutional and administrative law at Groningen and became professor of public and international law at the University of Leiden in 1893. He was an important figure in several state commissions. He was a member of the Netherlands Royal Academy of Sciences and curator of Leiden University. Of his many books, *Het Nederlandsche Gemeenterecht* (2 vols., 1895) is still a standard textbook on Dutch municipal law. Active in Jewish affairs, Oppenheim served as governor of the Ashkenazi rabbinical seminary in Amsterdam and as chairman of the Jewish Association in Holland. During World War I he was also president of the European committee of the *American Jewish Joint Distribution Committee.

[H.Bo.]

OPPENHEIM, JOACHIM (Ḥayyim; 1832–1891), Austrian rabbi. Oppenheim was born in Eibenschitz (Moravia) where his father, Dov Baer, was a rabbi. He took over his brother David's position in the rabbinate at Jamnitz and after the death of his father (1859) he became rabbi in Eibenschitz (1860). From 1868 until his death, he served as rabbi of Thron. Oppenheim was a prolific scholar.

He had a profound knowledge of biblical, talmudic, and midrashic literature. The results of his studies in these areas were published, mostly in Hebrew, in the learned periodicals of the time. His *Toledot ha-Mishnah* (1882), an introduction to the Mishnah, was originally published in *Beit Talmud,* edited by his brother-in-law, I. H. *Weiss. Two of his sermons were published under the title *Das Tal-Gebet* (1862).

Bibliography: N. Sokolow, *Sefer Sokolow* (1943), 126–7; idem, in: *Ha-Asif,* 6 (1894), 143f. (1st pagination); C. D. Lippe, *Bibliographisches Lexicon . . .,* 1 (1881), 354f. [Ed.]

OPPENHEIM, LASSA FRANCIS LAWRENCE (1858–1919), international lawyer. Oppenheim, one of the greatest authorities in his field, was born in Windekken, Germany. In 1886 he was appointed lecturer at the University of Freiburg, but because he was Jewish was precluded from advancing in the academic field. He therefore left Germany and went to Switzerland, where he lectured at Basle University, and then to England. From 1898 to 1908 Oppenheim taught at the London School of Economics, and in 1909 became professor of international law at Cambridge. He was an adviser to the British government on questions of international law and collaborated on the British Army manual, *Land Warfare* (1912). He also prepared memoranda for the British delegates at the Paris Peace Conference in 1919. Oppenheim's authoritative treatise, *International Law,* 2 vols. (1905–06), subsequently edited by Hersch *Lauterpacht, was accepted as the principal textbook for English-speaking countries. He became leader of the positive school in international law and a supporter of the League of Nations concept.

Bibliography: Whittuck, in: *British Year Book of International Law,* 1 (1920–21), 1–10; DNB, 1912–21 (1927). [G.T.]

OPPENHEIM, MORITZ DANIEL (1799–1882), German painter. Oppenheim was born in Hanau and, after studying art at Frankfort and Munich, he went to Paris and in 1821 to Rome, where he stayed four years. There he came under the influence of the Nazarenes, a group of fervently Christian artists who painted New Testament scenes. In 1825 Oppenheim returned to Frankfort. His paintings of Old and New Testament scenes were soon widely appreciated. His most loyal patrons were the Rothschilds and he was known as "painter of the Rothschilds" and—on account of his financial success—as "the Rothschild of the painters." He earned praise from Goethe to whom he sent two drawings based on Goethe's *Hermann und Dorothea.* Goethe, whom Oppenheim visited in Weimar and whose portrait he painted, persuaded the grand duke of Weimar to bestow upon the painter the title of honorary professor. In 1833 a picture with the narrative title "Return of a Jewish Volunteer from the Wars of Liberation to his Family Still Living According to the Old Tradition" brought the artist further renown. Encouraged by its wide success, Oppenheim painted 19 other canvases on Jewish motifs. These were eventually published in an album, *Bilder aus dem altjuedischen Familienleben* (1865) which appeared in the United States as *Family Scenes from Jewish Life of Former Days* (1866). These genre scenes, realistic yet tinged with romanticism, were much appreciated. They show excellent composition, and real skill in the grouping of the *dramatis personae.* They have been frequently reproduced to illustrate books on Jewish topics. He produced a series of large pictures on confrontations between Jews and Christians, e.g., Moses Mendelssohn and Lavater, Mendelssohn and Frederick the Great. Undoubtedly, Oppenheim's best works are his numerous portraits, pencil sketches as well as oils, including portraits of Ferdinand Hiller and Gabriel Riesser. He illustrated works by Berthold Auerbach and Solomon Hermann von Mosenthal. The city of Frankfort

Self-portrait by Moritz Oppenheim in pencil, ink, and sepia, before 1820. Jerusalem, Israel Museum. Photo David Harris, Jerusalem.

commissioned him to paint portraits of past emperors for the Kaisersaal (Emperor's Hall) in the Roemer, the medieval town hall. Admirers came from all parts of Europe to visit his studio in Frankfort. He continued to paint in his skillful, charmingly naive manner until a few days before his death, unconcerned with the changes in art and taste since his student days in Rome. His autobiography was published posthumously: *Erinnerungen,* ed. by A. Oppenheim (1924).

Bibliography: L. A. Mayer, *Bibliography of Jewish Art* (1967), index; Roth, Art, 544, 522–5. [A.W.]

OPPENHEIM, PAUL LEO (1863–1934), German geologist and paleontologist. Oppenheim worked as a private scientist in Berlin, only occasionally cooperating with academic or governmental scientific institutions. In 1907 the Prussian Ministry of Education awarded him the title of "professor" in appreciation of his outstanding achievements.

During nearly 50 years of research, Oppenheim published several monographs and many papers in various fields of geology and paleontology. He was particularly interested in the study of tertiary fossils, especially those of Italy and other countries of southern Europe, as well as of the Levant regions, of Turkey, Syria, Palestine, the former German colonies of East and West Africa, and Egypt. He was internationally known as an expert of almost all groups of fossil invertebrates, but his special interest was directed to nummulites, echinoids and mollusks, and particularly to corals. Oppenheim bequeathed his unique collection of fossils and his comprehensive library to the Geology Department of the Hebrew University of Jerusalem. His numerous works advanced the stratigraphy of the Tertiary and Cretaceous formations. His longer monographs on the "Niemitzer Schichten" of Bohemia (1924) and on the "Anthozoae der Gosauschichten" of the Alps are outstanding paleontological presentations of text and illustrations. [M.A.A.]

OPPENHEIMER, CARL (1874–1941), German biochemist. Born in Berlin, Oppenheimer was the second son of a reform rabbi, and brother of the economist Franz Oppenheimer. In 1902 he joined the Berlin Agricultural Academy, and was professor there from 1908 until dismissed by the Nazis in 1936. In 1938 he went to Holland as head of the agricultural department of a company in The Hague. He died in Zeist, Holland, probably murdered by the Nazis.

As a young man Oppenheimer wrote textbooks which were translated into many languages and became the most popular chemical books for medical students all over the world: *Grundriss der organischen Chemie* (1895, 1930[14]); *Grundriss der anorganischen Chemie* (1898; 1934[14-15]). His *Die Fermente und ihre Wirkungen* (1900; 4 vols.,

1925–30[5], suppl. 2 vols., 1935–38) gave enzymology its form and structure, and was followed by *Toxine und Antitoxine* (1904). Oppenheimer held that the study of living matter needed a knowledge of both the medical and the exact sciences. From 1909 to 1936 he published numerous basic texts in biochemistry as well as founding and editing the journals *Zentralblatt fuer Biochemie und Biophysik* (1910–21) and *Enzymologia* (1936–41). [S.A.M.]

OPPENHEIMER, SIR ERNEST (1880–1957), South African financier. Born in Friedberg, Germany, he went to London at the age of 16 to work for a firm of diamond merchants, which in 1902 sent him to represent them in Kimberley. He was very successful in the diamond business and in 1917 founded the Anglo-American Corporation. He gained control of several other companies, and in 1929 became chairman of the great diamond firm of De Beers and thus the acknowledged head of the industry. During the 1930s Oppenheimer steered the diamond trade through the difficulties of the great depression, and ultimately established control of world marketing through the Diamond Corporation. His foresight also contributed to the discoveries which extended the Rand goldfields after World War II. Mayor of Kimberley from 1912 to 1915, he helped to

Sir Ernest Oppenheimer, South African financier. Courtesy Anglo-American Corporation of South Africa, Johannesburg.

raise the 2nd Battalion, the Kimberley Regiment, in World War I and was knighted in 1921. He represented Kimberley in Parliament as a supporter of Smuts from 1924 to 1938. He and his first wife, née Mary Lina Pollak, were liberal supporters of Jewish charities and interested themselves in Jewish communal affairs. After her death in 1934, he married a Catholic and converted to Christianity. In the development of the Orange Free State goldfields, Ernest Oppenheimer set high standards of town-planning and did much to promote better hospital and recreation services and housing for the Africans there and on the Witwatersrand. He was a gracious patron of the arts and sciences.

His son HARRY FREDERICK OPPENHEIMER (1908–) succeeded his father as head of the diamond industry and of more than 150 mining, manufacturing, and investment companies. His birth in Kimberley was recorded in the Jewish communal records, but later he became a member of the Anglican Church. He entered the Anglo-American Corporation, eventually succeeding his uncle, Leslie Pollak, as manager. During World War II, he saw service as an intelligence officer in the Western Desert. After the war he helped his father develop the new Orange Free State goldfields. In 1948 he entered Parliament, winning his father's former Kimberley constituency for the United Party. At the end of 1958 he retired from politics to devote himself entirely to his business interests. Harry Oppenheimer assisted materially in the development of the diamond industry in Israel.

Bibliography: T. E. Gregory, *Ernest Oppenheimer and the Economic Development of South Africa* (1962); A. P. Cartwright, *Golden Age* (1968); Oppenheimer, in: *Optima* (Sept. 1967); J. M. White, *The Land God Made in Anger* (1969). [L.S.]

OPPENHEIMER, FRANZ (1864–1943), German sociologist and economist, an initiator of cooperative agriculture in Ereẓ Israel. The son of a reform rabbi, Oppenheimer was born in Berlin and studied medicine in Freiburg and Berlin. He started his career as a practicing physician, but after graduating in economics at the University of Kiel (1908), he became *Privatdozent* at the University of Berlin in 1909 and professor at the University of Frankfort in 1917, where he occupied a newly established chair of sociology from 1919 to 1929. After Hitler's advent to power in 1933, Oppenheimer lectured in Berlin at the Hochschule fuer die Wissenschaft des Judentums. He left Germany for the U.S. in 1938 and died in Los Angeles.

Oppenheimer's sociology is developmental in character, combining in an independent way elements from the theories of Marx, Spencer, Gumplowicz, and also from the instinct theory of McDougall; to these is added a melioristic intention. Oppenheimer considered accumulation of wealth and power, and hence gross inequality among men, as originating from social conflict, exemplified in earliest times chiefly by the subjugation of peaceful farmers, craftsmen, and traders by conquering nomads and pirates. The "economic means" of accumulation through one's own work is thereby replaced by "political means," i.e., force of arms, starting with payment of tribute, then leading to serfdom, feudalism, and finally to the development of antagonistic classes under capitalism. The central evil is the monopolization of land, which forces rural populations into urban areas, and creates what Marx had defined as the "industrial reserve army." Consequently, if the monopolization of land were replaced by an agrarian cooperative system of independent farmers, free competition could be restored and a "liberal socialism" established. Oppenheimer's belief that the removal of evil institutions would do away with the domination of man by man and lead to social harmony has a dogmatic ring.

Oppenheimer's interest in Zionism and Jewish affairs dated from 1902, when Oskar *Marmorek and Johann *Kremenetzky introduced him to Theodor *Herzl. Herzl asked Oppenheimer to elaborate the economic and agricul-

Stamp commemorating Franz Oppenheimer, issued by the West German government in 1964, the centenary of his birth. Jerusalem, B. M. Ansbacher Collection.

tural parts of the Zionist program, which he did in 1903 at the Sixth Zionist Congress in Basle. In 1911 the Palestine Office of the Zionist Organization in Jaffa established at *Merḥavyah a cooperative settlement based on Oppenheimer's ideas. Although it did not prove successful and had to be reorganized, the Merḥavyah experiment laid the foundation for cooperative agricultural settlement in Ereẓ Israel.

As an opponent of nationalism, Oppenheimer became alienated from the Zionist movement, and in 1913 he withdrew from any official participation. Nevertheless, he maintained his interest in the development of Ereẓ Israel and in Jewish social problems. During World War I he became aware of the misery of the Jewish population in Eastern Europe. In 1934–35 Oppenheimer visited Palestine and explained his concepts to Jewish labor leaders, but his ideas were not enthusiatically received.

On the 100th anniversary of Oppenheimer's birth Ludwig Erhard, chancellor of the German Federal Republic and Oppenheimer's former student, eulogized him, stressing the adoption of his teacher's ideas in his own concept of "social liberalism."

His most important works are *Der Staat* (1907; *The State*, 1914) and *System der Soziologie* (4 vols., 1922–35). Some of his articles on the Merḥavyah experiment were included in the books *Genossenschaftliche Kolonisation in Palaestina* (1915); *Merchavia* (1914); and *Wege zur Gemeinschaft* (1924). He also published an autobiography, *Erlebtes, Erstrebtes, Erreichtes* (1913).

Bibliography: K. Werner, *Oppenheimers System des liberalen Sozialismus* (1928); Fuss, in: *American Journal of Economics and Sociology*, 6 (1946), 95–112; 7 (1947), 107–17; H. E. Barnes (ed.), *Introduction to the History of Sociology* (1948); J. H. Bilski (ed.), *Means and Ways Towards a Realm of Justice* (1958); Bein, *Return to the Soil* (1952), index; A. Granott, *Ishim be-Yisrael* (1956), 79–109.

[J.O.R./W.J.C./ED.]

OPPENHEIMER, FRITZ E. (1898–1968), U.S. international lawyer and diplomat. Born in Berlin, Oppenheimer served in the German Army in World War I and was wounded three times. He practiced as a lawyer in Berlin until 1936, when he was forced to leave Germany and went to London. There he acted as an adviser to the attorney general and the British Treasury and was admitted to the English bar. In 1940, Oppenheimer went to the United States where for two years he worked in a private law firm. In 1942 he enlisted in the U.S. Army and rose to become a lieutenant colonel. At the headquarters of the Supreme Allied Command, he was in charge of the reform of the German law and court system after the war. He also helped to prepare the documents relating to Germany's surrender and to draft military government and control council legislation.

On his return to the United States, Oppenheimer became special assistant to the State Department for German and Austrian affairs and adviser to the secretary of state at the meetings of the Council of Foreign Ministers (1947 and 1948). He played an important part in Germany's rehabilitation in the 1950s, helping to reorganize the German coal, iron, and steel industries, and to draft the U.S.-German treaty for the validation of German dollar bonds.

Bibliography: *New York Times* (Feb. 6, 1968), 43.

[ED.]

OPPENHEIMER, HILLEL (Heinz) REINHARD (1899–1971), Israel plant physiologist. Born in Berlin, son of the sociologist and economist Franz *Oppenheimer, Hillel Oppenheimer became assistant in plant physiology at the Geisenheim experimental station in 1923. After a year's work in Berlin he went to Palestine in 1926 as keeper of the Aaron Aaronsohn Herbarium at Zikhron Ya'akov, where he arranged and cataloged the famed botanical collection. He was head of the plant physiology section at the Hebrew University of Jerusalem in 1931–32, and in 1933 established the horticultural, physiological, and genetics station at the Jewish Agency's Agricultural Experiment Station at Reḥovot, which he directed for twenty years. From 1952 until his retirement in 1967, he was professor of horticulture and of plant physiology at the Hebrew University, and dean of its agricultural faculty, 1952–54. In 1959 he was awarded the Israel Prize in Agriculture.

Oppenheimer contributed notably to the knowledge of the theory of irrigation, plant-water relations, and the mineral and irrigation requirements of plantation crops, especially citrus, which was his special interest and on which he was a world authority. His research encompassed germination inhibitors in fruits, the osmotic and elastic properties of plant cells, and drought tolerance of plant cells; and citricultural physiology, including timing of irrigation, foliar analysis, root-stock selection, response to pruning and fruit production. He was also concerned with forestry and tree physiology, including water relations in semiarid surroundings, root structure and growth, and the action of the cambium. His work helped to bridge the gap between plant-physiology and plant-geography. Oppenheimer's books include *Giddul Aẓei Hadar* ("Citrus Growing," 1957). In 1935 he founded *The Palestine Journal of Botany*, which he edited until 1953.

Bibliography: I. Reichert, in: BRCI, section D Botany, 8D (April 1960), i–vi (includes biography, portrait, and list of publications); A. Halevy, in: *Madda*, 14 (1969), 193 (Heb.).

[J.L.M.]

OPPENHEIMER, JOSEPH BEN ISSACHAR SUESSKIND (also known as **Joseph Suess** or **"Jud [Jew] Suess"**; 1698 or 1699–1738), Court Jew and confidential financial adviser to the duke of *Wuerttemberg. His father was a prominent merchant in Heidelberg and collector of taxes from the Jews of the Palatinate. In his youth, Oppenheimer was sent to Frankfort, Amsterdam, Prague, and Vienna, where he became familiar with business methods within the circle of his wealthy relatives, the family of Samuel *Oppenheimer. He later engaged in commerce in Mannheim and Frankfort. In 1732 he became the court factor of the Prince of Wuerttemberg, Charles Alexander, and a year later he was also appointed court factor to the ruler of Hesse-Darmstadt, the elector of Cologne, as well as tax collector of the elector of the Palatinate. When Charles Alexander, who in 1733 became duke of Wuerttemberg, decided to introduce an absolute and mercantile form of government within the territory under his control, Oppenheimer was appointed state counsellor and was made responsible for the direction of financial affairs. In order to free the duke from his dependence on the allocations of the states he endeavored to establish new economic foundations for the state income. He leased enterprises and properties to Christians and Jews, at the same time authorizing Jews to settle in the country. Through his supervision of the division of private property in cases of marriage or inheritance and his control over the appointment of government officials, Oppenheimer sought to enrich the state treasury and concentrate governmental power in the hands of the duke. Exercising his authority in an autocratic fashion, he imitated the life of a contemporary nobleman, dwelling in luxury and splendor; accusations of licentiousness seem to have had some foundation. With the support of the duke, he even made two unsuccessful applications for noble status to the emperor. His efforts to establish an absolute rule based on a system of mercantile economy aroused the fierce opposition of the conservative elements in the country, an opposition that was fanned by the fact that the duke was a Catholic while the country was Protestant, and that the change in the

Portrait of Joseph Suess Oppenheimer, showing the cage in which his body was exhibited after his execution. Artist unknown, 1738. Nuremberg, Germanisches Museum.

system of government had been assisted by the Jesuits and the army.

On March 19, 1737, the duke died suddenly before his projects could be executed. On the same day Oppenheimer was arrested and charged principally with having endangered the rights of the country and embezzled the incomes of the state. Although the charges were not adequately substantiated, his property was confiscated and he was condemned to death. After the German Jewish communities had vainly attempted to obtain his release against a ransom, Oppenheimer was hanged on April 2, 1738, and his remains were publicly exhibited in an iron cage. While he was in prison, Oppenheimer, who during the period of his greatness had treated his religion with scant respect, became a pious and sincere Jew: he prayed, requested *kasher* food, and rejected the offers of the clergy to save his life if he would accept baptism, proclaiming his intention of dying as a martyr. He died reciting the *Shema.* In the year after his death, the German Jewish communities lit memorial candles for him.

Contemporary legal authorities considered that Oppenheimer's death was an act of murder. Historians, too, have viewed it as judicial murder, the result of the conflict between various interests during the transition period from medieval to modern forms of government, in which Oppenheimer played a significant part. Traditional hatred of the Jews also served to bring about the downfall of a man who rose to considerable power in a Christian state at a time when the very idea of civic emancipation for the Jews was far distant. Joseph Suess Oppenheimer was the subject of a story by M. *Lehmann, and a novel, *Jud Suess,* by L. *Feuchtwanger, both of which were translated into several languages, including English.

Bibliography: H. Schnee, *Die Hoffinanz und der moderne Staat,* 4 (1963), 109ff., 251–4; 6 (1967), 57ff.; S. Stern, *Jud Suess* (1929); idem, *The Court Jew* (1950), index; F. Baer, in: KS, 7 (1930/31), 390–3; D. Kahana, in: *Ha-Shilo'aḥ,* 4 (1898), 134–42, 239–46; H. Pardo, *Jud Suess; Historisches und juristisches Material zum Fall Veit Harlan* (1949).

[Z.Av.]

OPPENHEIMER, J. ROBERT (1904–1967), U.S. physicist. Oppenheimer was in charge of the construction of the first atomic bomb as director of the laboratories at Los Alamos, New Mexico. Born in New York City, Oppenheimer was the son of a cultured and successful businessman, who had immigrated to the U.S. from Germany. His mother, a painter and teacher, died when he was nine years old. He was a child prodigy and at the age of five was collecting geological specimens. At Harvard University, he studied physics and chemistry, Greek and Latin. He worked under the world-famous scientist Ernest Rutherford at Cambridge, England (1925–26), and went to Goettingen at the invitation of Max *Born in 1927. On his return to America he became professor simultaneously at the California Institute of Technology at Pasadena and at the University of California at Berkeley (1929–47). He was a brilliant teacher, intense and dedicated—reading no newspaper, owning no radio, and learning Sanskrit as a diversion. He became director at Los Alamos in 1943 and during World War II was hailed as a world figure for the creation of "the bomb." In October 1945 he resigned as director at Los Alamos, and in 1947 became director of the Institute of Advanced Study at Princeton (1947–66). As chairman of the General Advisory Committee of the Atomic Energy Commission he continued to influence policy. He was greatly concerned with international control of atomic weapons. He was involved in the great debate

J. Robert Oppenheimer (center) with Samuel Sambursky (left) and Chaim Pekeris, Jerusalem, 1958. Courtesy Hebrew University, Jerusalem.

with scientist Edward *Teller and the chairman of the Atomic Energy Commission Lewis *Strauss on the construction of the thermonuclear bomb. In 1954, his security clearance was cancelled because of his early association with communists in the late 1930s and his opposition to the H-Bomb (the subject of a play *In the Matter of J. Robert Oppenheimer* based on the documents by H. Kipphardt, and translated by R. Speirs, 1954). After a hearing before a special board he was declared "a loyal citizen but not a good security risk." In 1963, as a sign of restored confidence, he was given the Fermi Award for his contribution to nuclear research by the Atomic Energy Commission.

Bibliography: J. Alsop and S. Alsop, *We Accuse* (1954); J. Boskin, *The Oppenheimer Affair* (1968); H. M. Chevalier, *Oppenheimer: The Story of a Friendship* (1966); C. P. Curtis, *The Oppenheimer Case* (1955); M. Rouzé, *Robert Oppenheimer; the Man and His Theories* (1964); J. L. C. Vilar, *Le dossier Oppenheimer* (1965); N. P. Davis, *Lawrence and Oppenheimer* (1968); R. Serber et al., *Oppenheimer* (Eng., 1969); I. L. Rabi et al., *Oppenheimer* (Eng., 1969); P. Michelmore, *The Swift Years, Robert Oppenheimer's Story* (1969); J. R. Soyer, *The Oppenheimer Case: Security on Trial* (1969).

[J.E.H.]

OPPENHEIMER, KARL (1864–1926), pioneer of infant and child welfare in Germany. Born at Bruchsal in Baden, he settled in Munich in 1890 and became a leading pediatrician. During more than 30 years of practice, he personally financed an extremely successful child welfare clinic. Oppenheimer considered the main purpose of this extensive free advisory service to be an attempt to achieve a decrease in the infant mortality rate, by educating and instructing indigent mothers. Largely on his initiative, the payment of maternity benefits and the training and recruitment of welfare workers were introduced. Oppenheimer was also responsible for the realization of a school meal service and the founding of the Jewish Country Home in Wolfratshausen. Oppenheimer published numerous articles on infant feeding; his proposals and improvements in regard to the composition and preparation of artificial infant food were vigorously contested at first, but met with increasing acceptance.

Bibliography: Wininger, Biog, s.v.

[Ed.]

OPPENHEIMER, SAMUEL (1630–1703), Austrian *Court Jew and military contractor. He began his career in Heidelberg as purveyor to the elector, Karl Ludwig, and tax collector of *Palatinate Jewry. Subsequently he moved to *Vienna where he received the right of unlimited residence and extraordinary trade privileges. Like other Jews he was affected by the 1670 expulsion from Vienna but from 1672 he was in the business of supplying the Austrian army. Officially allowed to settle in 1676, he was the first Jew to be granted such a privilege after the 1670 expulsion and his entourage became the core of the reestablished Jewish community. Although his request to open a synagogue was turned down by the authorities, services were held in his home. At the time of his resettlement he was given the title of Imperial War Purveyor. During the 1673–79 war against France he organized a consortium to supply Austrian armies in the west. After the Peace of Nijmegen (1679), the treasury refused to honor a 200,000 florin debt to him and it was only through a personal appeal to the emperor that he even received partial payment. Shortly thereafter he and his entourage were imprisoned for allegedly defrauding the state, although a subsequent investigation proved the accusations to be groundless. The outbreak of the Austrian-Turkish War (1682), however, forced the state to release him and to come to terms with his pecuniary demands, which were surprisingly lenient, and it further decided to

Samuel Oppenheimer, Austrian Court Jew. Jerusalem, J.N.U.L., Schwadron Collection.

put to the test his boast of being able to supply the Austrian armies single-handedly. The emperor approved the contract just before he fled Vienna to escape from the advancing Turkish armies; nevertheless he declared that it was dangerous to give so important a position to a Jew. Oppenheimer fulfilled the contract during the desperate siege of Vienna in 1683 and, thereafter, took on all the logistic problems raised by the war: the supply of uniforms, food, and salaries for the troops, livestock for the cavalry and artillery and fodder for the beasts, as well as seeing to supplies for hospitals for the wounded. Conducting business throughout the empire, his coup was building the Danube fleet of rafts for the relief of besieged Ofen (see *Budapest).

Oppenheimer's success may be attributed to his business acumen and persistence despite the many difficulties which beset his enterprises, and especially to his organizational talents. He set up a network of contractors and subcontractors throughout central Europe, many of whom were Court Jews in their own right and some of whom established themselves by their business connections with him. A good part of his success was due to his family and its far-flung business connections. His wife, Sandela Carcassone, daughter of a Sephardi Jew of Mannheim, bore him nine children. His son Wolf married a daughter of Leffmann *Behrens, a business associate. Oppenheimer also had an entourage of secretaries and agents whom he placed in all the financial and commercial centers of Europe. One of them was his nephew and future competitor, Samson *Wertheimer. Oppenheimer raised money from many sources, not only from his fellow Jews but also from Christian merchants and bankers.

The Turkish menace was barely repulsed when *Louis XIV invaded the Palatinate in 1688 and Oppenheimer was at once called upon for assistance. Although the field commanders, *Eugen of Savoy and Margrave Louis of Baden, both praised his efficiency and contributions in the country's dilemma, the court in Vienna, and particularly

Bishop *Kollonitsch, viewed his monopolistic position with misgivings, pointing out that not only was he Austria's sole military purveyor but that a disproportionate part of the state income was being earmarked solely for him as payment for his services. All attempts to dispose of his services failed, however, for few others were in possession of sufficient capital to assume his place and none was prepared to extend credit to the state with its chronically empty treasury. The state's debts to Oppenheimer grew from 52,600 florins in 1685 to 700,000 in 1692, and to 3,000,000 in 1694, at which point it remained stable for a few years until it increased during the War of the Spanish Succession.

Bishop Kollonitsch, appointed head of the treasury in 1692, frustrated by his unsuccessful attempts to dispense with Oppenheimer's services, tried to undermine Oppenheimer by falsely accusing him of attempting to murder Samson Wertheimer. As a consequence Oppenheimer was forced to buy his freedom and establish his innocence with the sum of 500,000 florins. In 1700 when his sumptuous home was stormed and plundered by a mob, order was reluctantly restored by the authorities and the two instigators hanged. It has been suggested that the cause of the attack was Oppenheimer's intervention in suppressing an anti-Jewish book of *Eisenmenger.

When Oppenheimer died the state refused to honor its debts to his heir Emanuel and had his firm declared bankrupt. His death brought deep financial crisis to the state; it experienced great difficulty in securing the credit necessary to meet its needs. Emanuel appealed to European rulers to whom the state owed money and who intervened on his behalf. After deliberate procrastination the state refused Emanuel's demand for 6 million florins and instead demanded 4 million florins from him. This amount was based on a sum which (with compound interest), according to the state, Oppenheimer had allegedly obtained by fraud at the beginning of his career. Emanuel died in 1721 and the Oppenheimer estate was auctioned in 1763.

Although Oppenheimer was not himself learned, he was a benefactor on a scale hitherto unknown, building many synagogues and yeshivot and supporting their scholars. He also paid ransom for the return of Jews captured during the Turkish wars and supported as well R. Judah he-Ḥasid's voyage to Ereẓ Israel in 1700. Known as *"Judenkaiser"* by his contemporaries, he was a man whose complex personality, a mixture of pride and reserve, defied historical analysis. Twenty years after his death it was estimated that more than 100 persons held residence in Vienna by virtue of their being included in Oppenheimer's privileges.

Bibliography: M. Grunwald, *Samuel Oppenheimer und sein Kreis* (1913); idem, *Vienna* (1936), index; S. Stern, *Court Jew* (1950), index; H. Schnee, *Die Hoffinanz und der moderne Staat*, 3 (1955), 239–45; MHJ, 2 (1937); 5 (1960); 9 (1966); 10 (1967), indexes.

[H.W.]

OPPER, FREDERICK BURR (1857–1937), U.S. political cartoonist; an originator of the comic strip. Opper left Madison, Ohio, for New York, where he worked for 18 years on the weekly *Puck*. He joined Hearst's *New York Journal* in 1899, and his work was then syndicated through the *International News*. Opper depicted suburban types which became familiar to almost every American household. He also became Hearst's leading political caricaturist, lampooning the eccentricities of public figures, particularly during election campaigns.

A volume of his political drawings, *Willie and his Papa*, was published in 1901. His cartoons on England, *John Bull*, appeared in 1903. Other collections were *Alphabet of Joyous Trusts* (1902), *Our Antediluvian Ancestors* (1903), two volumes of his character *Happy Hooligan* (1902–07) and *Maud and the Matchless* (1907). Opper also illustrated the work of some of his contemporary humorists, including Mark Twain, Peter Finley Dunne, Bill Nye, and George V. Hobart.

Bibliography: DAB, 23 (1958), 504f. (incl. bibl.).

[Ed.]

OPPERT, GUSTAV SALOMON (1836–1908), German orientalist and Indologist. Born in Hamburg, younger brother of the archaeologist Jules *Oppert and of Ernst Jacob Oppert, the traveler, Oppert studied the lore of India, its languages, literature, and history and was appointed assistant librarian at the Bodleian Library, Oxford, and at Queen Victoria's Library in Windsor. In 1872 he was appointed professor of Sanskrit at the Presidency College in Madras, India where from 1878 to 1882 he also served as editor of the *Madras Journal of Literature and Science*. After traveling through India, the Far East, and the U.S. he accepted a teaching post at Berlin University in Dravidian languages.

He also produced a number of works in folklore, general philology, ancient Hindu culture, epigraphical studies of South Indian inscriptions; travel accounts, and editions of various classics of Sanskrit culture in the areas of philosophy, poetry and philology.

Like his brother Jules, Gustav Oppert devoted himself to various Jewish causes. He was a trustee of the Hochschule fuer die Wissenschaft des Judentums and bequeathed his estate to this organization.

Bibliography: JC (March 20, 1908), obituary; Wininger, Biog.

[E.Fi.]

OPPERT, JULES JULIUS (1825–1905), French philologist, orientalist, and archaeologist. Born in Hamburg, he studied law but changed to Oriental languages. He migrated to France where he continued his research on Old Persian and Assyrian and became a recognized authority in his field. In 1851 he was invited to join a sponsored expedition to explore Mesopotamia. The results of this expedition contained Opper's definite identification of the site of ancient Babylon, and appeared in a two-volume report, *Expédition Scientifique en Mesopotamie* (1859–63), which received a prize for the most significant discovery of the year. In 1869 Oppert joined the Collège de France, first as instructor in Assyriology, and then in 1874 as professor of Assyrian philology and archaeology.

Jules Julius Oppert, Assyriologist. Jerusalem, J.N.U.L., Schwadron Collection.

His studies in various branches of Oriental learning included Indo-Iranian, Sumerian, Elamitic, and Assyriology, in which he became a founder and preeminent authority. He discovered and deciphered numerous historical, astronomical and religious inscriptions, juridical documents, contract tablets, and collected material for his history of the Chaldean and Assyrian civilizations.

He made decisive contributions to the decipherment of cuneiform inscriptions and together with E. Hinds, H. Rawlinson, and F. Talbot was one of the pioneers in the recovery of Babylonian cuneiform. His profound knowledge of Assyriology was signified by his participation together with the scholars mentioned above in the historic experiment arranged by the Royal Asiatic Society in 1857 when a separate decipherment made by them of one identical Assyrian Royal Inscription proved the sound basis of Assyriology. Oppert continued to be most active in the field and participated in the lively dispute on the origins of the Sumerian language (see also *Mesopotamia, Assyriology). He also interpreted Assyrian, Median, and Persian history and mythology. He was one of the founders and an editor of the *Revue d'Assyriologie et d'Archéologie Orientale* (1884–) and one of the contributing editors of the *Zeitschrift fuer Assyriologie* on its establishment in 1886. Among the honors that came to him was election to the Académie des Inscriptions et Belles-Lettres in 1881, and later to the presidency of this body.

Both he and his younger brother Gustav Salomon *Oppert, philologist and Indologist, had a strong interest in Jewish affairs. Jules *Oppert was a member of the administrative executive committee of the Société des Etudes Juives and contributed to its journal, the *Revue des Etudes Juives*. He was also involved in the activities of the *Alliance Israélite Universelle and the Jewish Central Consistory. He was interested in biblical scholarship and wrote studies on the Book of Esther and Judith and the chronology of Genesis (1877).

Bibliography: Muss-Arnolt, in: *Beitraege zur Assyriologie und semitischen Sprachwissenschaft*, 2 (1894), 523–56, incl. bibl. to 1891; K. Bezold, in: ZA, 19 (1905), 169–73. [E.Fi.]

OPPRESSION (Heb. עֹשֶׁק), an offense against property, standing midway between *theft and robbery and *fraud and often overlapping with either of them. The injunction, rendered in English as "Thou shalt not oppress thy neighbor" (Lev. 19:13), really means (like the injunction immediately following: "nor rob him") that you must not try to enrich yourself by, or derive any material benefit from, any violation of your neighbor's rights. The exact dividing line between oppression (coercion) and robbery gave rise to a discussion among talmudic scholars: where a man failed to restore property to its lawful owner, some held that it was oppression if he admitted the other's ownership, and robbery if he denied it; others held it to be oppression if he asserted that he had already returned it, and robbery if he refused to return it; a third opinion was that it was oppression if he denied that he had ever received the property, and robbery if he asserted that he had already returned it; a fourth scholar held that oppression and robbery were essentially identical terms (BM 111a). The proximity in the Bible of the offenses of stealing, deceit, perjury, oppression, and robbery (Lev. 19:11–13) led an ancient authority to observe that he who steals will eventually commit deceit, perjury, oppression, and robbery (Sifra 3:2); and it is in reliance on the same authority that oppression per se has been held by some to be limited to the crime of withholding a laborer's wages (*ibid.* 3:2; cf. Rashi to Lev. 19:13). The particular oppression of laborers, in withholding their wages, is the subject of a special prohibition, accompanied by a mandatory injunction that the payment of such wages may not be delayed even for one night (Deut. 24:14–15; see *Labor Law). The definition of oppression, as it eventually emerged, is given by Maimonides in the following terms: "Oppression is the forceful withholding and not restoring of money which had been received with the owner's consent, as, for instance, where a man had taken a loan or hired a house and, on being asked to return the same, is so violent and hard that nothing can be got out of him" (Yad, Gezelah va-Avedah 1:4; and cf. ḤM 359:8). Although it is in the nature of a criminal offense, no punishment can be inflicted for such oppression, as the proper remedy is an order for the payment of the money due, and civil and criminal sanctions are mutually exclusive (see *Flogging). But the guilt before God subsists even after payment, hence a sacrificial penalty is imposed on the oppressor (Lev. 5:23–26). Oppressors are also regarded as criminals so as to disqualify them as witnesses before the court (Sanh. 25b; Yad, Edut 10:4). As against strangers, the prohibition of oppression is extended to cover also intimidations and importunities (Ex. 22:20; 23:9), even where no violation of monetary rights is involved (BM 59b and Rashi *ibid.*). Monetary oppression has frequently been denounced as one of the most reprehensible of offenses (Jer. 21:12; 22:17; Ezek. 22:29; Zech. 7:10; Mal. 3:5; Ps. 62:11; 72: 4–5; et al.), and its elimination as one of the conditions precedent to national and religious survival (Jer. 7:6).

In the State of Israel, the offense consists of taking advantage of the distress, the physical or mental weakness, or the inexperience or lightheadedness of another person in order to obtain something not legally due, or profiteering from services rendered or commodities sold (Sect. 13, Penal Law Amendment (Deceit, Blackmail and Extortion) Law, 5723–1963). [H.H.C.]

ORABUENA, noted family of Navarre in the 13th and 14th centuries. Ishmael Orabuena and his son Joseph are mentioned as important personalities in the kingdom of Navarre in 1265. Members of the family were among the signatories of the *takkanot* of Tudela (1305). The Orabuena family maintained close relations with the foremost Jewish families of the Iberian peninsula. Joseph, grandson of the above-mentioned Joseph, leased the tax collection for Tudela in 1367. He was the physician to King Charles III of Navarre, accompanied him on several journeys to France, and advised him in political matters of importance. He was chief rabbi of Navarre Jewry and it was to him that Solomon ha-Levi (Pablo de *Santa María), rabbi of Burgos, wrote announcing his intention of converting to Christianity. Joseph was still active in 1399, granting loans to the crown and providing medical services to the king.

Bibliography: M. Kayserling, *Juden in Navarra* (1861), index; Baer, Urkunden, 1 (1929), index; Baer, Spain, index. [H.B.]

ORACH (Heb. מַלּוּחַ, *mallu'aḥ*), the species *Atriplex halimus*. This shrub grows wild in the saline soil of the lower Jordan valley, in the Negev, and in the Arabah; it is also found in the sandy lands of the Sharon and in the beds of rivers. There is a concentration of the shrub at Abu-Tor in Jerusalem, close to the remains of a Byzantine church, where it may possibly have been cultivated formerly. Some Bedouin eat the leaves cooked or as salad, and they have a popular saying that "were it not for the orach the Bedouin would suffer from sores," and in fact it is rich in the vitamins which prevent skin disease. The Hebrew name *mallu'aḥ* is derived from its salty taste (*melaḥ*, "salt"). The shrub can grow in soil with a 20% salt concentration; some of the salt is excreted by the leaves and the granules cover them with a silvery layer. The massed plants in various parts of the Arabah give it its silvery gray landscape. Job (30:4) describes the food of the wretched people living in the wilderness "who pluck *mallu'aḥ* with wormwood," i.e., who feed on the leaves of the orach which they eat directly from the shrub without first preparing them (see *Wormwood). According to an ancient tradition the children of Israel ate the orach when traveling in the wilderness, and after Alexander *Yannai was victorious in the wilderness he ordered this tradition to be respected, "and they served orach on golden tables and ate it" (Kid. 66a). In talmudic times the cultivated species, *Atriplex hortensis,* which was named *kerosalkinon,* was grown and thought to be a hybrid of beet and amarynth (TJ, Kil. 1:4, 27a; Rome Ms.).

Bibliography: Loew, Fora, 1 (1924), 345–6; J. Feliks, *Kilei Zera'im ve-Harkavah* (1967), 108–9; idem, *Olam ha-Ẓome'aḥ ha-Mikra'i* (1968²), 186–7. [J.F.]

ORADEA (formerly **Oradea Mare;** Hung. **Nagyvárad,** also **Várad**; Ger. **Grosswardein**; in Hebrew and Yiddish texts the German name was used), city in Transylvania, W. Rumania; until 1918 and between 1940 and 1944 in Hungary. Although documents dating from 1407 and 1489 mention several Jews in connection with the city, the only reliable evidence of Jews residing there dates from the early 18th century. In 1722 four Jews are listed as residents. A *ḥevra kaddisha* was formed in 1731. Ten Jewish families were registered in 1736, including one *ḥazzan.* The Jewish residents in Oradea were immigrants from Moravia, Bohemia, and Poland. As the fort of Oradea lost its strategic importance after the end of the Turkish wars (1692), the Jews were later permitted to live in the adjacent Váralja quarter. In 1787 the Jews were permitted to build a synagogue; a second synagogue was built in 1812. The whole city, including the Jewish population, expanded rapidly from the end of the 18th century. The number of Jews increased from 104 taxpayers in 1830 to 1,600 persons in 1840; 10,115 (26.2% of the total population) in 1891; 12,294 (24%) in 1900; 15,115 (23.6%) in 1910; 20,587 (21%) in 1930; and 21,337 (22.9%) in 1941.

The synagogue of Oradea Mare. Courtesy C.A.H.J.P., Jerusalem.

The Jews of Oradea adopted the Hungarian language and culture earlier than any other Jewish community in Hungary. The Reform congregation, organized in 1847, was disbanded in 1848. During the Hungarian revolution in that year the Jews supported the rebels and some served in their ranks. Austrian oppression during the following decade weighed heavily on the Jews.

Conflicts between Orthodox and Reform elements within the Oradea community characterized the latter half of the 19th century. After the schism following the Hungarian Jewish Congress (see *Hungary), the Oradea community divided in 1870 into *Orthodox and *Neolog congregations, each developing separate institutions which remained active until after World War II. A Neolog temple, with an organ, was built in 1878, and an Orthodox synagogue in 1891. In both congregations well-known rabbis officiated, including the Orthodox rabbis Aaron Isaac Landsberg (1853–79), and Moses Ẓevi *Fuchs and his son Benjamin (1915–36). Rabbis of the Neolog congregation included Alexander *Kohut (1880–84), Lipót *Kecskeméti (1897–1936), the most influential, and István Vajda (1939–44), the last Neolog rabbi, who perished in *Auschwitz with the rest of his community. During World War I several ḥasidic rabbis from Bukovina and Galicia of the *Vizhnitsa and *Zhidachov dynasties found refuge in Oradea and attracted Ḥasidim from the district.

Jewish institutions in Oradea included a hospital. Jewish public schools were opened early in the 19th century. An Orthodox high school with four classes, founded in 1888, remained open until the Holocaust. A Neolog high school, founded in 1920, also continued until the Holocaust.

In the cultural and economic spheres Oradea Jewry was the most active of all the communities in Hungary or Rumania. Jews were prominent in Hungarian journalism. Hebrew printing houses operated in the city. The leading Jewish newspaper was the religious Zionist weekly *Népünk* ("Our People"; 1929–40). Branches of the Zionist movement were active in Oradea between the world wars. The National Jewish Party had supporters in Oradea, although some Jews supported the party of the Hungarian nationalists. Jews joined the Communist party and were even elected as city councillors. In 1927 several student leaders organized anti-Jewish riots in which several Jews were killed and synagogues were despoiled.

Holocaust and Contemporary Periods. The community came to an end in the summer of 1944 when the German-Hungarian administration established a ghetto and removed its occupants to death camps. A total of 25,000 Jews were deported from Oradea and its district. After the end of the war, in 1947, the Jewish population numbered 8,000, including survivors from the camps and Jews who had arrived there from other areas. Their number decreased through emigration to Israel and other countries, falling to 2,000 in 1971. The only Jewish institutions still functioning then were the three synagogues, which held services on the Sabbath and holidays. There was a *kasher* restaurant in the city.

Bibliography: L. Lakos, *A váradi zsidóság története* (1912); MHJ, 3 (1937); 5 pt. 1 (1959); 7 (1960), index. s.v. *Nagyvárad, Várad:* P. Adorján, *A halott város* (1941); B. Katona, *Várad a viharban* (1946); S. Yitzhaki, *Battei Sefer Yehudiyyim bi-Transylvanyah Bein Shetei Milḥamot Olam* (1970), 102–77. [Y.M.]

OR AKIVA (Heb. אוֹר עֲקִיבָא ; "Light of R. Akiva"), immigrant development town with municipal council status in the northern Sharon, 1½ mi. E. of *Caesarea. Construction of the town began in 1951 with the aim of providing permanent housing for the inhabitants of the Caesarea *ma'barah.* In 1968, the municipal area of Or Akiva ex-

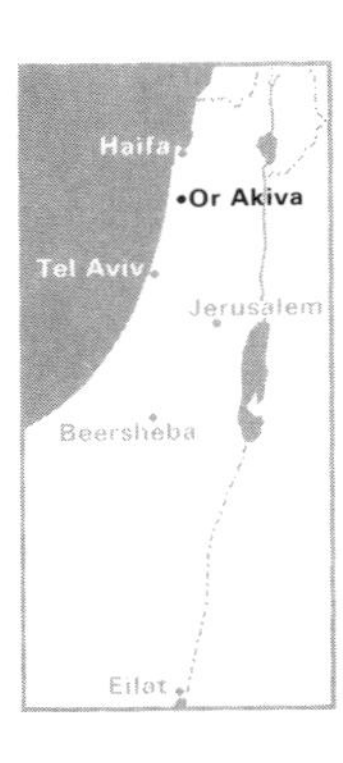

tended over 2,600 dunams (650 acres), and it had 6,000 inhabitants, as compared with 3,208 in 1961. The town's economy is based mainly on medium-size industrial enterprises (carpet weaving, silk weaving, fur coats, rubber mattresses, etc.). Further employment is provided by the tourist enterprises of Caesarea.

[S.H.]

ORAL LAW (Heb. תּוֹרָה שֶׁבְּעַל־פֶּה), the authoritative interpretation of the Written Law (*Torah, which is the text of the *Pentateuch) which was regarded as given to Moses on Sinai, and therefore coexistent with the Written Law. This view of the Oral Law was a fundamental principle of the rabbis. The Written and Oral Laws constitute together "two that are one." "It is related that a certain man stood before Shammai and said 'Rabbi, How many Torahs have you?' The rabbi replied 'Two—one written and one oral' " (ARN[1] 15, 61; cf. Sif. Deut. 351). There is a strong and close bond between the Written Law and the Oral Law, and neither can exist without the other—both from the dogmatic point of view and from that of historical reality. The Oral Law depends upon the Written Law, but at the same time, say the rabbis, it is clear that there can be no real existence for the Written Law without the Oral. The need for the positing of the existence of the Oral Law is inherent in the very character and nature of the Torah. The statutes of the Written Law could not have been fulfilled literally even in the generation in which they were given, since "that which is plain in the Torah is obscure, all the more that which is obscure" (Judah Halevi, *Kuzari*, 3, 35; cf. Moses of Coucy in *Semag*, introduction: "For the verses contradict and refute each other," and "the statements in the Written Law are vague"). Even those statutes of the Torah that appear to be clearly formulated and detailed contain more that is obscure and requires explanation than what is manifest and understandable. The reasons given for this are many and various. The Written Law contains contradictions (cf., e.g., Deut. 16:3–4 with 16:8), and there is a lack of clarity and definition: The law, "he shall surely be put to death" (Ex. 21:12 et al.), does not state whether by stoning, burning, or some other method not mentioned in the Torah. "And ye shall afflict your souls" (Lev. 16:31) does not indicate whether it means by mortification of the body through ascetic practices, by fasting, or in some other manner. The prohibition against doing work on the Sabbath does not specify the nature of work (see below). "And if men strive together and hurt a woman with child so that her fruit depart and yet no harm follow . . . But if any harm follow . . ." (Ex. 21:22–23) does not make it clear whether the "harm" refers to the woman or her embryo. Dimensions and quantities are not given, e.g., in the precepts of **leket*, *shikhhah*, and *pe'ah*, or **terumah* (the priestly portion), etc. Individual laws are given without any indication of whether the law is confined to that particular case or whether it is to be regarded merely as an example of a category of laws, e.g., the law that a slave goes free if his master destroys his eye or his tooth (Ex. 21:26–27).

There are lacunae, and laws which are not explicitly stated but to which mere passing reference is made (thus the only reference to the laws of sale and acquisition is the prohibition against overreaching—**ona'ah*); there is no reference to the laws of marriage, while the law of divorce is mentioned only incidentally in connection with the injunction that a man may not remarry his divorced wife after she has remarried and become divorced again (Deut. 24:1–4); the Torah enjoins that one sentenced to be flogged may not have more than the fixed number of lashes inflicted (Deut. 25:1–3), but nowhere does it specify which transgressions involve the punishment of a flogging. From the above it seems clear that it was impossible for life to be regulated solely in accordance with the Written Law ("and I should like someone to adjudicate between two litigants on the basis of the weekly portions, *Mishpatim* [Ex. 21–24] and *Ki Teze* [Deut. 21:10–25:19]"—Judah Halevi, *Kuzari*, 3:35). It may even be inferred from the Written Law itself that immediately after it was given there already was difficulty in understanding it. Thus, e.g., it is apparent that until he heard it explicity from God, Moses did not know what the penalty was for the transgression of gathering wood on the Sabbath (Num. 15:32–35; cf. Sif. Zut. 15:34: "Eliezar b. Simeon says: Moses did not know that he was liable to death, nor did he know how he should be executed, as can be inferred from the reply given: 'And the Lord said unto Moses: the man shall be put to death,' i.e., he is liable to death; how shall he put to death? He [God] replied: by stoning"; cf. also the case of the blasphemer in Lev. 24:10–23). As stated above, there is no definition in the Pentateuch of what constitutes work in connection with the Sabbath (or the Day of Atonement), only some of the things forbidden being explicitly mentioned (plowing, reaping, kindling fire). Furthermore, in connection with the desecration of the Sabbath, in one and the same verse (Ex. 31:14) two different punishments—death and **karet*—are given. From the point of view of its judicial literary form, the Written Law is in fact no different from other early oriental statutes which never exhausted or aimed at exhausting all the details of the laws given.

If, therefore, the statutes of the Torah could not be properly understood in the generation in which it was given, how much less could it be understood by later generations? In addition to this consideration, it was a fundamental doctrine of the rabbis that the Torah was given by God for all time, that it would never be exchanged for another Torah and certainly never rescinded, and that it provided for all possible circumstances which might arise at any time in the future. Nevertheless, in practice, changing conditions—social, economic, etc.—raised many new problems, as well as the question of their solution in accordance with the Torah. The new situations and spheres of human activity which arose, for which the Written Law did not provide, could not be ignored. In fact, from the beginning the Written Law was the basis of authority of the Oral Law for the future (Deut. 17:8–11 and see below). It can thus be regarded as a historical fact that the Oral Law existed not merely from the moment the Written Law was given (and in this sense it is correct to say that the Written and Oral Laws were given together to Moses at Sinai), but it may even be maintained that the Oral Law anticipated the Written Law, as the Written Law not only assumes the observance of the Oral Law in the future, but is in effect based on its previous existence. Since the written law relies—by allusion or by its silence—on statutes, customs, and basic laws not explicitly mentioned in it (marriage, divorce, business; see above), theses statues are ipso facto converted into a part of the Oral Law.

The impossibility of the Written Law existing without an Oral Law can also be demonstrated from Jewish history. The development of the Oral Law can be traced throughout the books of the Bible, especially in the prophets and the hagiographa, in the Jewish literature of the time of the Second Temple (Apocrypha and pseudepigrapha, in Jewish *Hellenistic literature, and in the early Targums of the Bible), the talmudic literature and the rabbinical literature throughout the generations (see *Halakhah*). Even the dissenting sects outside normative Judaism, as long as they did not abandon Judaism completely, did not maintain the Written Law without an Oral Law: the *Sadducees possessed a "Book of Decrees—who were to be stoned, who burnt, who beheaded, and who strangled" (the scholium to **Megillat Ta'anit*); the Judean desert sect developed, especially by means of biblical exegesis, a most ramified *halakhah* which has survived in its works (in particular in the Damascus Covenant, the Manual of Discipline and other works; see *Dead Sea Scrolls); and a most ramified *halakhah* also developed among the *Karaites. In the relationship of the Written to the Oral Law there exists a kind of paradox, both interesting and characteristic. From the dogmatic point of view the Oral Law has its basis in, and derives its validity from, explicit verses in the Written Law, but at the same time the Written Law itself obtains its full validity and its authority for practical *halakhah* from the Oral Law. The Written Law in fact establishes the authority of the Oral Law by laying down that "if there arise a matter too hard for thee, thou shalt turn unto the judge that shall be in those days," and "according to the tenor of the sentence which they shall declare unto thee from that place . . . According to the law which they shall teach thee, and according to the judgment which they shall tell thee shalt thou do; thou shalt not turn aside from the sentence which they shall declare unto thee, neither to the right hand, nor to the left" (Deut. 17:8–11). Yet it follows precisely from those very verses themselves that it is the Oral Law itself which determines what the *halakhah* of the Written Law is in practice, including the true meanings (as distinct from the theoretical philological meanings) of those very verses (Deut. 17:8–11) themselves.

Furthermore the Oral Law lays down explicitly that from the moment of the giving of the Written Law—"from Heaven," at Sinai, but in the language of men and to men—it is handed over absolutely to the judgment of the human intelligence of the scholars of the Oral Law, who accept the "yoke of the kingdom of Heaven" but give halakhic ruling according to their understanding ("henceforth no prophet can innovate anything"—Sifra, *Be-Ḥukkotai*, 13:7; cf. Shab. 104a), since "it is not in Heaven" (TJ, MK 3:1, 81d; BM 59b—based upon Deut. 30:12). Though indeed this rule was not accepted without protest, yet those who objected belonged to the fringes of Judaism, and it was not they who determined the *halakhah*. The Oral Law is able to circumvent the Written Law (see TJ, Kid. 1:2, 59d). In consequence of this provision, Maimonides, following the talmudic sages, ruled that "in an emergency any *bet din* may cancel even the words of the (written) Torah . . . in order to strengthen religion and to prevent people from transgressing the Torah. They may order flagellation and punish for breach of law, but such a ruling may not be effected permanently. Similarly, if they see a temporary need to set aside a positive precept, or to transgress an injunction in order to bring many back to religion, or in order to save many Israelites from grief in other matters, they may act in accordance with the needs of the time; just as the physician amputates a hand or a leg in order to preserve the life, so the *bet din* may rule at some particular time that some precept of the Torah may be transgressed temporarily in order that it may be preserved" (Yad, Mamrim 2:4). Then the sages rightly maintained that the Oral Law is the major and the main part (i.e., both in quantity and quality) of the Torah. "The Holy One made a covenant with Israel only for the sake of that transmitted orally" (Git. 60b; cf. TJ, Pe'ah 2:6, 17a: those given orally are beloved"). The Oral Law, which is well-nigh sovereign in relation to the Written Law, is the "mystery" (μυστήριον) of the Holy One (Tanḥ. Ki Tissa 34, et al.; though the sources speak of the *Mishnah, it is certain that the whole oral law is intended) because of the essential nature of its being given orally. It is this nature of the Oral Law—that it was given orally—that determines its vitality and organic development; it is not immutable and fossilized but alive and evolving. This vitality, however, could only be preserved in words not fixed in writing and in a binding and unchangeable form, but in words developing continually and unceasingly. As mentioned the Sadducees had a book of decrees in writing which was their "Oral Law" (the scholium to Meg. Ta'an.), and therefore according to their outlook the whole of the Torah too was "prepared in writing" (Kid. 66a—according to early printed versions and *Haggadot ha-Talmud*, Constantinople, 1511, 56d), i.e., the written word obligates. The Pharisees, however, claimed that the distinguishing feature and authority of the Oral Law is embedded in the fundamental rule (Deut. 31:19), "put it in their mouths" (the scholium to Meg. Ta'an.). The Oral Law was handed over to the sages, by means of whose words it is fixed and evolves from generation to generation. It is this nature and this sovereignty that are the real will of the Written Law, which was given on the basis that it be explained by means of the Oral Law. This, apparently, is the reason that although there is a disciple who expounds "more than was spoken to Moses at Sinai" (ARN[2] 13, 32), yet "even what a distinguished disciple will rule in the presence of his teacher was already conveyed to Moses at Sinai" (TJ, Pe'ah 2:6, 17a; cf. Meg. 19b and SEZ 2:171 "Surely both the Bible and Mishnah were communicated by the Almighty"). The meaning of all these and of similar sources is that from the point of view of its functional essence the whole of the Oral Law was given to Moses at Sinai, since "the Torah itself gave the sages a mind to interpret and to declare" (Sif. Num. 134; cf. "matters not revealed to Moses were revealed to Akiva"—(Tanḥ. B. Num. 117; for its true meaning cf. Men. 29b—the *aggadah* of Moses entering the yeshivah of *Akiva—"and he did not know what they were saying," not even a detail of a *halakhah* given to Moses at Sinai). Even the Holy One repeats, as it were, a *halakhah* as spoken by the sages (PdRK, ed. by D. Mandelbaum (1962), 73, et al.).

See also *Authority, Rabbinical. [M.D.H.]

Attitude of Reform Judaism. In the approximate century and a half of *Reform Judaism's existence, the development of its attitude toward the Oral Law has undergone three fairly distinct phases. In the initial stage, in the early 19th century, most Reform rabbis invoked the Oral Law itself in calling for change in halakhic practice and usage. Thus Aaron *Chorin justified the changes in the liturgy of the Reform congregation of Hamburg (established 1818) by extensive citation of the Talmud and codes. Abraham *Geiger expressed the spirit of the leaders of Reform Judaism of his time in the opening article of the first issue of his publication (*Wissenschaftliche Zeitschrift fuer juedische Theologie*, 1835) when he wrote: "Salvation lies not in the violent and reckless excision of everything which has descended to us from the past, but in the careful search into its deeper meaning, and in the aim to continue to develop historically from that which has grown historically . . . much which is now believed and observed is not tradition . . . but is a product of a certain age, and therefore can be removed by time." Geiger frequently quoted rabbinic sources to justify the abolition of rituals which he deemed a hindrance to "true" religion. This qualified appeal to talmudic tradition is reflected in Michael Creizenach's statement that the unanimous decisions of the Talmud are to be regarded as binding. In a case of divided opinion, "we follow the less strict version so long as it does not contradict our own conviction." The Breslau Synod of Reform Rabbis (1846) centered on the question of modifying Sabbath observance in the light of changed social and economic conditions. The participants buttressed their views by frequent citations from the Talmud and the standard rabbinic codes. The attitude finds expression in the declaration of David *Einhorn, which reflected the position of the majority of Reform rabbis of his age (1839): "We address the Talmud in these words, 'Israel believes thee, but not in thee; thou art a medium through which the divine may be reached but thou art not the divine.'"

This trend of introducing changes in current religious practice on the basis of halakhic precedent interpreted in liberal fashion met with strong dissent within the ranks of early Reform Judaism itself in the person of Samuel *Holdheim, one of the dominant personalities of the movement. He may be said to have spiritually fathered the anti-halakhic stance that marked the second phase of the development of Reform Judaism. His views were set forth in his book *Das Ceremonialgesetz in Messiasreich* (1845). Acdording to Holdheim, the basic purpose of the ritual law was to safeguard the holiness of the people of Israel in a pagan world. As paganism vanishes, the ritual laws are needed less and less, and with the arrival of the messianic age they will become totally superfluous. "The time has to come when one feels strong enough vis-à-vis the Talmud to oppose it, in the knowledge of having gone beyond it." Accordingly, Holdheim advocated the abolition of circumcision and changing the Sabbath to Sunday. David Einhorn, deeply influenced by Holdheim, limited the authority of the Talmud to those aspects which were attributable to the Men of the Great Assembly.

The anti-halakhic mood of Reform Judaism, a minor strain in the incipient stage of the movement, gained increasing ascendancy as the 19th century progressed and the major scene of the Reform movement's activity shifted to the United States. Bernard Felsenthal summed up the dominant mood of most of his colleagues toward the *halakhah:* "There is but one class of laws biblical or post-biblical which have eternal validity and these are the moral laws engraved by the finger of God with ineradicable letters in the spirit and nature of man" (*Kol Kore Be-Midbar,* no. 11, 1858). The official attitude of 19th-century American Reform Judaism found expression in the platform adopted in 1885 by the Conference of Reform Rabbis in Pittsburgh. The fourth paragraph of the platform reads in part: "We hold that all such Mosaic and rabbinical laws as regulate diet, priestly purity and dress originated in ages and under the influence of ideas entirely foreign to our present mental and spiritual state . . . their observance in our day is apt rather to obstruct than to further modern spiritual elevation." In this spirit, the annual meeting of the Central Conference of American Rabbis (CCAR) in 1892 declared that no initiatory rite (circumcision, ritual immersion) was required for admission into Judaism. In his work *Jewish Theology* (1928) Kaufman *Kohler formulated the position of this second phase of Reform Judaism in these words: "To them (the prophets) and to us the real Torah is the unwritten moral law which underlies the precepts of both the written law and its moral interpretation" (p. 45). "It [the Oral Law] fostered hair-splitting casuistry and caused the petrifaction of religion in the codified Halakhah" (p. 47).

In the past few decades, Reform Judaism has displayed a sharp veering away from the anti-halakhic spirit described above. The depreciation of the Shulḥan Arukh and other legal works characteristic of discussions on the subject as reported in the early *Annuals of the CCAR* have been replaced by regret that Reform Judaism lacks the sense of *halakhah* (Introd. to *Current Reform Responsa,* Solomon B. Freehof, 1969). Repeatedly, in the recent past, the demand for a specific code of practice has been raised. Though opposed to the formulation of a binding code for Reform religious practice, Solomon B. Freehof has been active, as chairman of the Responsa Committee of the CCAR, in responding to questions relating to Reform religious practice. While written in the style of traditional responsa, citing the recognized codes and legal authorities, the answers given are intended, with a few exceptions, to be merely advisory in nature. The turn toward traditional practice in Reform congregations is to be seen in the reintroduction of the bar mitzvah, calling to the Torah *(aufrufen), Havdalah,* etc. The revision of the anti-halakhic attitude of classic Reform Judaism is a process whose outcome can hardly be anticipated at this writing, but that it is one of the major concerns of contemporary Reform Judaism is evidenced by the prominent place it occupies in Reform thought and writing.

Attitude of Conservative Judaism. Zacharias *Frankel's demonstrative withdrawal from the Synod of Reform Rabbis (Frankfort, 1845) and his enunciation of Positive-Historical Judaism are regarded as the point of departure for the subsequent founding of the distinct trend in modern Judaism commonly known as *Conservative. The doctrine of Positive-Historical Judaism received considerable elaboration by Solomon *Schechter, who regarded himself as a disciple of Frankel, Leopold Zunz, and Heinrich Graetz when he wrote: "It is neither Scripture nor primitive Judaism but general custom which forms the real rule of practice . . . Liberty was always given to the great teachers of every generation to make modifications and innovations in harmony with the spirit of existing institutions. The norm as well as the sanction of Judaism is the practice actually in vogue. Its consecration is the consecration of general use or, in other words, of Catholic Israel" (*Studies in Judaism,* 1 (1896), 17–19). While the ideological leaders of Reform Judaism interpreted the thesis of the Oral Law's historical conditioning as implying its dispensability, for Schechter and his disciples the thesis, originally propounded by the *Wissenschaft Des Judentums served as one of the touchstones of the authority of the Oral Law. The divergence in viewpoint is to be attributed to the preponderant weight ascribed to tradition by the spokesmen of Conservative Judaism. In contrast to Orthodoxy, the divine origin of the Oral Law as the basis of its authority is interpreted in Conservative circles in non-literalistic fashion (see Robert Gordis, in *Tradition and Change,* ed. by Mordecai Waxman (1958), 377ff.). The frequent appeals for loyalty to the Oral Law to be found in the writings of Schechter ("It—Judaism—insists upon the observance both of the spirit and the letter . . . Judaism is absolutely incompatible with the abandonment of the Torah" (*Seminary Addresses and Other Papers* (1915), 21–22).) find their final validation in the fact that Jewish religious usage had won acceptance from the religious conscience of the overwhelming majority of the Jewish people (the concept of Catholic Israel).

Louis *Ginzberg viewed *halakhah* as constituting the mainstream of Judaism. Through his teaching and writings, he made the *halakhah* one of the central concerns of Conservative Judaism, always insisting, however, that the *halakhah* of the Talmud constituted an organic growth that retained its vitality by reason of its responsiveness to changing locale, and social and economic conditions. Yet, with a single exception—a responsum on the permissibility of the use of grape juice for sacramental purposes during the prohibition era in America—he proved reluctant to apply his theoretical understanding of the *halakhah* to the exigent problems of Jewish life in the 20th century. (For the responsum in English translation, see AJYB, 25 (1923–24), 401–25.)

The practical implications of this approach to the *halakhah* underlay the work of the Committee on Jewish Law of the Rabbinical Assembly. Established in 1927, it has issued a large number of halakhic decisions recorded in brief or in detail in the annual Proceedings of the Rabbinical Assembly. Prior to 1948, none of these decisions reflected any significant departure from traditional Orthodox practice. In 1948, the annual convention of the Rabbinical Assembly rejected a proposal that its Committee on Jewish Law "shall be instructed to hold itself bound by the authority of Jewish law and within the frame of Jewish law to labor toward progress and growth of the law to the end of adjusting it to present-day religious needs and orientation, whether it be on the side of severity or leniency." The defeat of the proposal was motivated by a desire on the part of the majority to reckon with non-halakhic factors, such as contemporary social realities and moral standards, in determining the point of view of Conservative Judaism on any specific question. Hence, in 1949 the concept was formally accepted that "decisions of the Law Committee shall be presented in the form of a traditional responsum indicating its relationship to relevant halakhic and other material."

To reflect this change in basic position, the name of the committee was changed to Committee on Jewish Law and Standards. It was reorganized and increased to 23 members, so as to offer representation for the diversity of viewpoint to be found among members of the Rabbinical Assembly. A rule of procedure was adopted whereby a member of the Rabbinical Assembly could accept either the majority or minority view of the committee. In instances where decisions were unanimous, such decisions were to be regarded as binding. Two responsa were published by the committee on Sabbath observance, in the course of which divergent views were expressed on the permissibility of riding to attend synagogue service on the Sabbath in instances where one lived beyond reasonable walking distance and the use of electricity on the Sabbath for purposes of illumination (for the responsa in question, see *Tradition and Change*, ed. by M. Waxman (1958), 349–409). To obviate the problem of the **agunah*, a woman who though divorced civilly cannot obtain a *get* (writ of divorcement), the Joint Law Conference of the Rabbinical Assembly and the Jewish Theological Seminary adopted in 1954 a *takkanah* (enactment) to be inserted in the *ketubbah* (marriage document). Latterly, the committee has adopted and in specific instances exercised, the long-dormant halakhic principle of *hafka'at kiddushin* (annullment) where, for one or another circumstance, the writing of the traditional *get* is impossible. Another halakhic decision of far-reaching consequence is that of rendering the observance of *Yom Tov Sheni* (the second days of the three festivals) a matter of option to be exercised by the rabbi of the local congregation (some members of the committee vigorously dissented on the decision; see *Conservative Judaism*, 24, no. 2 (1970), 21–59). Various responsa by the committee are to be found in the annual *Proceedings of the Rabbinical Assembly* and deal with such matters as the use of the organ on Sabbaths and festivals, the use of gentile wine *(yayin nesekh)*, the donation after death of the cornea of the eyes for purposes of transplant, ritual circumcision by a Jewish physician, cremation, synagogue membership for a Jew who has intermarried, etc. [TH.F.]

Bibliography: N. Krochmal, *Moreh Nevukhei ha-Zeman*, in: S. Rawidowicz, *Kitvei Rabbi Naḥman Krochmal* (1924), 189–93; W. Bacher, *Die exegetische Terminologie der juedischen Traditionsliteratur*, 1 (1889), 89f., 197; S. Kaatz, *Die muendliche Lehre und ihr Dogma* (1922–23); J. Heinemann, in: HUCA, 4 (1927), 149–72; Y. Kaufmann, *Golah ve-Nekhar* (1929–32), index s.v. *Torah;* H. Tchernowitz, *Toledot ha-Halakkah*, 1 (1934), 1–10, 67–136, 197–324; E. E. Urbach, in: *Tarbiz*, 17 (1945/46), 1–11; 18 (1946/47), 1–27; 27 (1957/58), 166–82; idem, Ḥazal, *Pirkei Emunot ve-De'ot* (1969), 254–78; G. F. Moore, *Judaism*, 1 (1927), 251–80; 3 (1930), 73–88; Z. H. Chajes, *Kol Sifrei . . . Ḥayyot*, 1 (1958), 1–176, 283–91; Ḥ. Albeck, *Mavo la-Mishnah* (1959), 3f.; B. De Vries, *Hoofdlijnen en Motieven in de Ontwikkeling der Halachah* (1959); M. D. Herr, in: J. Eisner (ed.), *Hagut ve-Halakhah* (1968), 131–44. ATTITUDE OF REFORM JUDAISM: D. Philipson, *Reform Movement in Judaism* (1928); W. G. Plaut, *Rise of Reform Judaism* (1963); idem, *Growth of Reform Judaism* (1965); idem, in: *Contemporary Jewish Thought*, ed. by B. Martin (1968); J. Petuchowski, *ibid.;* S. B. Freehof, *Current Reform Responsa* (1968); E. Mihaly, in: CCAR Annual, 44 (1954), 214–26; A. Guttman, *ibid.*, 48 (1958), 246–55. ATTITUDE OF CONSERVATIVE JUDAISM: B. Cohen, *Law and Tradition in Judaism* (1959); M. Davis, *Emergence of Conservative Judaism* (1963); H. Parzen, *Architects of Conservative Judaism* (1964); S. Dresner, in: *Conservative Judaism*, 16 no. 1 (1961), 1–27; S. Greenberg, *ibid.*, 19 no. 1 (1964), 36–50; D. Aronson, *ibid.*, 26 no. 1 (1969), 34–48.

ORAN, Algerian port on the Mediterranean. The Spanish refugees who arrived there in 1391 found an ancient Jewish community which had been influenced by Muslim customs. One of the newcomers, R. Amram Merovas Efrati, tried to eradicate them, but R. *Isaac b. Sheshet warned him that his efforts would not succeed. The newcomers, few in number, established connections with their former homeland and were reinforced by the Jews expelled from Spain in 1492. They all had to flee when Cardinal Ximenez occupied the town in 1509 and pillaged the Jews' property. The community was reestablished around the Cansino, Saportas, Stora, Vaez (Vais), and Mayques families who had been allowed to return and who served as dragomans and agents for the Spanish. They had a small synagogue and their religious leaders, the Cansinos and Saportas, were in contact with the Jerusalem community. The whole community (466 persons) was expelled in 1669. They sailed for *Nice, Villa-Franca (Ville Franche), and Leghorn. Only one Jew apostatized. The Jewish quarter was pillaged. The town soon fell into decay, was captured by the Moslems in 1708, and again reoccupied by the Spanish in 1732. They once again expelled the Jews who had resettled in Oran, but abandoned the town for good in 1792. The Turks attracted the Jews, selling them estates and granting them the land for a cemetery. Mordecai Darmon, from Mascara, the treasurer to the bey, constructed the great synagogue at his own expense. There was great prosperity with the arrival of the great merchants of Algiers (Aboulker, Levy-Bram), Morocco, and Gibraltar. These families had their business associates in Leghorn, Minorca, and, as a special exception to existing practice, in the Spanish ports. The bey's representatives to the European nations were Aaron Nuñez *Cardoso and Solomon Pacifico of Gibraltar. Nevertheless, the community suffered the aftereffects of the palace tragedies. In 1813 the bey's favorite, a Jewess, and her son were burned alive and some families were exiled. In 1830 the Jews were accused by the Arab tribes of collaboration with the French invaders and narrowly escaped extermination before the French troops arrived. A special Purim was instituted in memory of the event. The Jewish population of 2,000 was augmented by the arrival of Moroccan coreligionists, mostly from Tetuán, and grew steadily. Relations were strained between the two elements. The Jews left Oran when *Algeria gained its independence in 1962; a small minority settled in Israel and the others in France.

Bibliography: Bloch, in: REJ, 13 (1886), 85–104; R. Lesprès, *Oran, étude de géographie et d'histoire urbaines* (1938); Hirschberg, Afrikah, 2 (1965), 96–117; Attal, in: *Sefunot*, 5 (1961), 508 (index).
[D.Co.]

ORANGE, previously a principality and later a town in Vaucluse department, S.E. France. The earliest evidence of the presence of Jews in Orange dates from 1282 and in the locality of Courthézon from 1328, at the latest. In 1353 Raymond V, prince of Orange, granted the Jews of his principality a charter which in effect constituted a series of privileges which were remarkable, indeed almost exceptional, for the 14th century. Even before Raymond's time, however, some precedent had been set in this direction by other princes of Orange, who had, for example, already employed Jews as toll collectors. Because of these favorable conditions, a constant stream of Jews came from *Comtat Venaissin to Orange, among them the physician Durand de Cavaillon who arrived there in 1387. This situation lasted until the latter half of the 15th century. In 1477 the municipal council sought to remove Jews from the grain trade in which they were engaged in addition to moneylending (Jews frequently acted as brokers for the wealthy burghers of Orange or for Italian financiers). When the council demanded the expulsion of the Jews in 1484, the prince of Orange refused unless the town could indemnify him for the taxes that would be lost by such an action. Jewish houses were openly attacked in 1490 and the expulsion was carried out in 1505.

On several occasions during the first half of the 17th century the parliament of Orange renewed the expulsion decree. Despite this, by 1643 several Jewish families had "clandestinely" resettled in Orange. Their numbers slowly increased, until by 1731 there were 21 families (16 in Orange, 4 in Courthézon, 1 in Jonquières). The new expulsion orders were only partially applied, and from 1774 on there was a massive influx of Jews from Comtat Venaissin. With the onset of the French Revolution, however, the departure of the Jews was almost as rapid. Using their newly acquired liberties, they left Orange for more important towns. In 1808 only 36 Jews remained in Orange and almost all of them bore the name Mossé. The Jewish community rapidly dissolved and was never reconstituted.

Several eminent scholars, particularly *Levi b. Gershom, lived in Orange for varying lengths of time. Another such scholar was Mordecai, also named En Crescas, or Ezobi, of Orange, who settled in Carcassonne toward the close of the 13th century. The surname Ezobi, borne by a large number of other scholars, points to a more or less distant origin in Orange. An anonymous scholar and translator of the late 12th century and one Gershon b. Hezekiah, author of medical books in the first half of the 15th century, are intimately connected with the town of Orange.

Bibliography: Gross, Gal Jud, 18ff.; I. Loeb, in: REJ, 1 (1880), 72ff.; J. Bauer, *ibid.*, 32 (1896), 236ff.; D. Wolfson, *ibid.*, 57 (1909), 93ff.; H. Chabaut, *ibid.*, 100 (1936), 62ff.; L. Barthélemy, *Inventaire . . . Maison de Baux* (1882), index. [B.BL.]

ORANGE FREE STATE, province of the Republic of South Africa, formerly (1854–1902) an independent republic. A reputed Jew of Belgian or Portuguese origin, Adolph Coqui, helped to draft the constitution of 1854. Among the earliest settlers in *Bloemfontein were Jews, mainly from Germany. The city was laid out according to the design of Gustav Baumann, a member of the oldest Jewish family and the first Orange Free State surveyor-general. Jewish communities sprang up in many villages throughout the province, at first in the farming districts in the south. From the beginning, good relations existed with the rest of the population, predominantly Afrikaans-speaking, and Jews fought on the Boer side in the 1899–1902 war. The Jewish population reached 5,753 in 1926, but 20 years later it had dropped to 3,333, as the people left the rural areas for the large towns. Many of the smaller communities became defunct. Apart from Bloemfontein (1,260), in 1969 sizable

The communal hall adjoining the new synagogue in Bloemfontein, Orange Free State, built in 1965. Courtesy Fieldhill Publishing Co., Johannesburg.

Jewish communities existed in Kroonstad (354), Parys (105), Bethlehem (150), and in the mining town of Welkom (240). Most of these had Hebrew congregations with ministers, as well as Zionist and other Jewish societies. In 1960 the Orange Free State had a Jewish population of 3,197 (mainly concentrated in Bloemfontein), only 2.8% of the South African Jewish total. The Jewish contribution to the province's social, cultural, and professional life and to its economic development has been considerable. In many towns there have been Jewish municipal councillors and mayors, and a leading Jewish personality, Wolf Ehrlich of Bloemfontein (d. 1924), was a member of the South African Senate.

Bibliography: G. Saron and L. Hotz, *Jews in South Africa* (1955), index; M. Gitlin, *The Vision Amazing* (1950), index. [L.Ho.]

ORDEAL, the generic term for the various ways and means by which divine judgment would be ascertained. The most common form of ordeal, which survived long into the Middle Ages and beyond, was entirely unknown to biblical as well as to later Jewish law: namely, the exposing of an accused person to physical dangers which were supposed to be harmless to him if he were innocent but which were considered conclusive proof of divine condemnation if he suffered harm. The only remnant of this kind of ordeal may be found in the *Ordeal of Jealousy. It is an early talmudic tradition (Sot. 9:9) that these "waters of bitterness" ceased to be effective when adulterers proliferated. Traces of a similar ordeal by water may be found in the water that Moses made the Israelites drink after he had sprinkled it with powder ground from the golden calf (Ex. 32:20), the talmudic tradition being that this was the method used to

The high priest administering the ordeal of the "waters of bitterness" to a woman suspected of adultery. Engraving from Jacques Basnage, *République des Hébreux,* Amsterdam, 1713. Jerusalem, J.N.U.L.

detect the guilty. Another widespread method of ascertaining God's judgment was the curse. A written curse had first to be erased into the "water of bitterness" to be swallowed by the woman suspected of adultery (Num. 5:23), so that either the curse or the water or both could be instrumental in the ordeal. The curse is interchangeable with, and a forerunner of, the *oath: he who takes the oath before God (cf. Ex. 22:7–8, 10) brings God's curse on himself if he perjures himself (cf. I Kings 8:31–32; II Chron. 6:22–23). On hearing the oath sworn at His altar, God judges—condemning the wicked and justifying the righteous (see also Zech. 5:3–4; et al.). There is a statement that when atonement was made for general sinfulness (Lev. 16:21–22), God would, by changing red into white, reveal His forgiveness, or by not changing the color indicate unforgiveness (Yoma 6:8; 67a). In many instances, God's judgment was, of course, executed directly, manifesting itself in the very act of divine punishment (e.g., Num. 16:5–7, 31–35; Deut. 11:6; I Kings 18:38).

See also *Urim and Thummim.

Bibliography: J. Kohler, in: *Zeitschrift fuer vergleichende Rechtswissenschaft,* 5 (1884), 368–76; J. G. Frazer, *Folklore in the Old Testament,* 3 (1919), 304–414; J. Morgenstern, in: *HUCA Jubilee Volume 1875–1925* (1925), 113–43; R. Press, in: ZAW, 51 (1933), 121–40, 227–55; ET (1951³), 182–5; EM, 1 (1950), 179–83; 5 (1968), 1003f. [H.H.C.]

ORDEAL OF JEALOUSY. According to Numbers 5:11–31, a woman suspected of adultery that cannot be legally proved is to be brought by her husband to the priest for an ordeal of jealousy. The priest takes "holy water" (according to Sot. 2:2, from the laver) and mixes into it some earth from the floor of the Tabernacle. He then assures the woman that if she is innocent she will be immune to harm from the water, but warns her that if guilty her "belly shall distend" from the potion and "her thigh sag" (the exact sense is unknown). After this adjuration, he writes down the oath, dissolves the writing in the water, and makes the woman drink of it. Accordingly, the water is called *mayim me'arerim,* "the water that induces the spell." The ordeal has to be accompanied by a meal offering of a specific type. It is composed of barley without oil and frankincense (cf. Lev. 5:11) and is called "an offering of remembrance which recalls wrongdoing (Num. 5:15).

Critical View. The law in its present form contains repetitions (16b = 18a, 19a = 21a, 21b = 22a, 24a = 26b = 27a), which appear to be redundant, and seeming inconsistencies. Thus verse 21, inserted between the protasis and apodosis, disrupts the adjuration, while verse 24, which prescribes giving the drink before offering the meal (5:25), contradicts the express order of verse 26. These inconsistencies are reflected in the Mishnah. Whether the meal offering precedes drinking the water, as stated in verse 26, or the drinking comes before the meal offering, as in verses 24–25, is a matter of dispute (Sot. 3:2). Moreover, the interpolation in verse 21a gave rise to a disagreement over the extent of the written oath (Sot. 2:3). According to R. Judah, the priest had to write down only the oath appearing in verses 21–22; according to R. Yose, all of verses 19–22 had to be written; the prevailing opinion, however, is that the priest wrote down the adjuration of verses 19, 20, and 22 and the oath in verse 21 without the introductory directions concerning the priest *(we-hishbia' ha-kohen 'et ha-'ishah)* and the woman (*we-'amerah ha-'ishah 'amen,* 22).

These textual difficulties suggest that two literary strands have been interwoven in this chapter. One strand prescribed only an oral conditional adjuration (5:19–20, 22), whereas the other prescribed the recital of a curse and its writing, and the dissolving of the written curse in the water (5:21, 23). The latter strand also prescribed the offering of the meal (5:15, 25–26). The beginning of verse 27 is an editorial resumption *(Wiederaufnahme)* of verse 24, necessitated by the interpolation of verses 25–26. There is no way of deciding which of the two strands is original or earlier. It may be that the author had both before him when he composed the law. Yet the strand prescribing the writing of the curse shows signs of more advanced religious conceptions. God is made responsible for the curse (5:21), whereas according to the other source the water itself induces it (5:22). Furthermore, the word of God is made the agency of the curse, in the form of the writing dissolved in the water.

An ancient water ordeal consisting of an oral adjuration but no written oath is attested in a Mari text (Archives Royales de Mari, X, no. 9, lines 9–15). A heavenly scene is described in which a command is given to dissolve some earth from the gate in water and give it to drink to the (minor) gods who take an oath not to harm (or betray) Mari and its commissioner. Another analogue is found in the so-called "Hittite instructions for the temple officials." Somebody suspected of having used up the firstlings before giving them to the gods has to "drink the horn of the god of life"; if he is found guilty he will perish together with his family (Sturtevant-Bechtel in bibl., 164–165, no. 18, 4:52–53). In Mesopotamia a water ordeal consisted of being thrown into the river: the guilty sank, the innocent floated (cf. Code of Hammurapi; in Pritchard, Texts, 166, law 2). A similar procedure is attested in a letter from Mari where two suspected persons are to be submitted to the ordeal by river (see Dossin in bibl.). The river ordeal is actually applied in Mesopotamia to the case of jealousy. Thus the Code of Hammurapi (Pritchard, Texts, 171, law 132) states that "if a finger has been pointed at a married woman with regard to another man and she is not caught lying with the other man she shall leap into the river for her husband." The specification of "not being caught lying with the other man" is instructive for the understanding of the Hebrew clause: *we-hi' lo' nitpasah* (Num. 5:13b). The Babylonian parallel inclines the balance in favor of the rendering "she had not been caught in the act" (cf. Ibn Ezra to 5:13b) rather than "she had not been forced" (cf. Rashi to 5:13b).

See also *Ordeal.

Bibliography: R. Press, in: ZAW, 51 (1933), 122–6; E. H. Sturtevant and G. Bechtel, *A Hittite Chrestomathy* (1935), 164–5; G. R. Driver and J. Miles, *The Babylonian Laws,* 1 (1952), 63–65, 284; G. Dossin, in: *Comptes rendus . . . Académie des Inscriptions et Belles-Lettres* (1958), 387ff.; W. L. Moran, in: *Biblica,* 50 (1969), 50–52. [Mo.W.]

ORDZHONIKIDZE (until 1932 **Vladikavkaz;** 1944–54 **Dzaudzhikau**), capital of the N. Ossetian A.S.S.R., N. Caucasus. In 1784 the Russian government erected a fortress which dominated the road crossing the Caucasus; from the 1830s there were always some Jewish soldiers in the fortress and it was, in fact, demobilized soldiers who founded the community. A prayer room was erected in 1865, and about 20 years later authorization for the construction of a synagogue was obtained. A community of Subbotniki (*Judaizers) also existed in the town. During the 1890s the administration began to oppress the Jews. There were 1,214 Jews (about 2.8% of the total population) in 1897 and in 1926 about 1,000 (1.3% of the population). When the Germans invaded the Soviet Union, they were brought to a halt on the outskirts of the town and so the Jewish inhabitants were saved. In 1959 about 2,000 Jews lived in the town. [Y.S.]

OREB AND ZEEB (Heb. עוֹרֵב, עֹרֵב, "raven"; זְאֵב, "wolf"), two Midianite princes captured by the Ephraimites during a battle led by Gideon the judge (Judg. 7:25; 8:1–3). To commemorate the event, the places where the capture occurred were called "The Rock of Oreb" (Ẓur Orev) and "The Winepress of Zeeb" (Yekev Ze'ev). Their exact location is uncertain. The narrative relates that the two princes were decapitated and their heads brought across the Jordan to Gideon, apparently as testimony to the great valor and glory of the Ephraimites (7:25; 8:2–3). The defeat and execution of Oreb and Zeeb became proverbial as a paradigm for the annihilation of the enemies of Israel (Isa. 10:26; Ps. 83:11).

Bibliography: Y. Kaufmann, in: *Tarbiz,* 30 (1960/61), 139–47 (Heb.), 45 (Eng. summary); A. Malamat, in: PEQ, 85 (1953), 61–65; C. F. Whitley, in: VT, 7 (1957), 157–64. [N.Sch.]

OREGON, Pacific N.W. state of the U.S. with some 9,000 Jews in 1968 (out of a total of 2,008,000). Jewish settlement began in Oregon during the Western gold rushes. The first arrivals, general merchants, sold clothing, merchandise, and tools to farmers who raised food for the gold discovery regions. The largest community is Portland. German Jews founded Congregation Beth Israel in 1858. Later immigrants founded congregations along national and ideological lines. Congregation Ahavai Sholom (1869) was Polish; Congregation Shaarei Torah (1905) was Russian and East European. Oregon's Jewish population in 1861 was 250, with 100 in Portland. In 1880 it was 868, with 625 in Portland. For almost a century Jews in Oregon were general merchandise and clothing merchants. In the 1960s they were also in the professions; several taught at public and private universities, especially University of Oregon Medical School in Portland. There are almost no patterns of discrimination in the state and Jews participate in many social and cultural activities, notably in the cultural ones.

Synagogue on Park St., Portland, Oregon, built in 1905. Courtesy Oregon Historical Society, Portland.

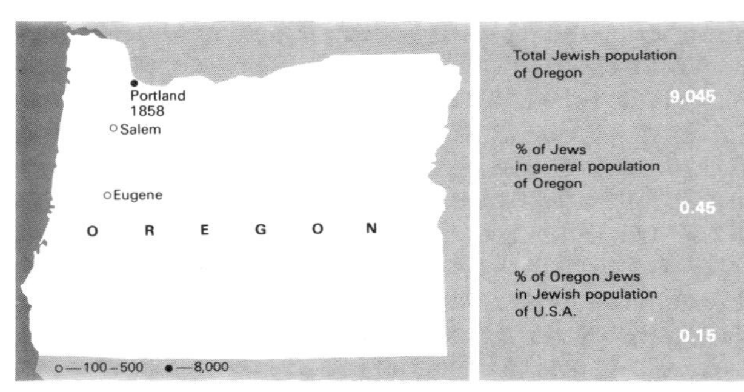

Jewish communities in Oregon, with date of establishment.

Many prominent Jews are associated with Oregon: Solomon *Hirsch, minister to Turkey; Joseph *Simon and Richard *Neuberger, U.S. senators; Julius *Meier, governor; Henry Heppner, founded the town Heppner; Samson Friendly, regent of the university; Joseph Shemanski, philanthropist; Aaron Frank, Ben Selling, and Harold Wendel, Portland's "first citizens"; and numerous mayors, judges, and state legislators. In 1970 Portland had six synagogues, a community center, welfare federation, Hebrew school, and Hillel academy. There were congregations in Salem and Eugene and Hillel counselorships at the state universities (Eugene and Corvallis) and Portland State University.

Bibliography: J. J. Nodel, *The Ties Between* (1959); AJYB (1967), index; I. J. Benjamin, *Three Years in America 1859–1862*, 2 vols. (1956); *The Jewish Chronicle Travel Guide* (1967); *Statistics of the Jews of the United States* (1880); AJYB (1965). [R.E.L.]

OREL, city in Orel oblast, Russian S.F.S.R. Orel lay outside the *Pale of Settlement. A small Jewish community was founded there during the second half of the 19th century; in 1876 it was authorized to build a synagogue. In 1897 the Jews of Orel numbered 1,750 (2.5% of the total population). Anti-Jewish riots broke out on Oct. 18, 1905, but later, during World War I, many refugees from the battle areas came to the town. In 1926 there were 3,597 Jews (4.6% of the total population); on the eve of World War II their numbers were estimated at about 6,000. With the German occupation in 1941 the Jews were concentrated in the central prison. Initially put to forced labor, they were gradually deported to extermination camps. In May 1942 all the Jews remaining in the town were massacred.

Bibliography: B. West (ed.), *Be-Ḥevlei Kelayah* (1963), 52–54. [Y.S.]

ORENSE, city in Galicia, N.W. Spain. Jews had apparently settled there by the 11th century, and in 1044 were living in the nearby fortress. Until the 1460s, no further information is available on the community which during that period probably consisted of some 30 to 40 families. In 1474, its annual tax, together with that paid by the Jews of Rivadabia, Monforte, and Allariz, amounted to 2,000 maravedis. This decreased to 1,000 maravedis in 1482, and rose to 13,500 maravedis in 1491, apparently because of the obligation to contribute to the expenses of the war against Granada. In 1489 a writ of protection was granted to the community of Orense against the attempts of several knights to attack the Jews of the town; the governor of Galicia was ordered by the Catholic monarchs to protect them. The Jewish quarter, which until 1488 bordered upon the Rua Nova, was then transferred to another site next to the Fuente del Obizpo, and the local Jews were given a period of grace to settle there. A fine of 3,000 maravedis was to be imposed on those who refrained from obeying this order. The quarter remained on that site until the expulsion in 1492.

Bibliography: F. Fita, in: *Boletín de la Academia de la Historia, Madrid*, 22 (1893), 171; Baer, Urkunden, 2 (1936), 307, 387; Suárez Fernández, Documentos, index. [H.B.]

ORENSTEIN, ALEXANDER JEREMIAH (1879–), South African medical scientist. Of Jewish origin, Orenstein was one of the teams of experts who, under W. C. Gorgas, cleared the Panama Canal Zone of yellow fever and malaria (1905–12). His experience of tropical and subtropical diseases led to his appointment in 1913 in the health services of German East Africa. In 1914 he was taken to South Africa by a Rand mining company to help reduce the incidence of pneumonia and tuberculosis which were taking a heavy toll among miners in the goldfields. Over the years, spectacular results were achieved in reducing the death rate, especially among African mine workers. Orenstein was director of the pneumoconiosis research unit of the South African Council for Scientific and Industrial Research when he retired in 1959. He had an international reputation and often represented South Africa at world health and labor conferences. Orenstein was director-general of medical services in the South African defense forces in both world wars, with the rank of brigadier (later major-general).

Bibliography: A. P. Cartwright, *Golden Age* (1968); *South Africa's Hall of Fame* (1960). [L.Ho.]

ORGAN.

Antiquity. In its conventional form, an organ is basically a set of pipes activated by compressed air, under the control of a keyboard. It is thought to have been invented in Hellenistic Alexandria around the beginning of the second century C.E., and was called *hydraulos* (ὑδραυλός—water pipe) since the air was compressed by a water-pressure mechanism. During the first centuries C.E. this mechanism came to be replaced by bellows, but the name *hydraulos* or *hydraulis* remained. The instrument spread through the Roman and Byzantine Empires as a crude but effective accompaniment to games and ceremonies in the circus and at court. Byzantine influence brought the organ both to the Persian court and to Europe in the eighth or ninth centuries.

It was the late Roman and Byzantine organ, with its multiplicity of pipes and—for that time—astounding tone-volume, that gave rise to the late talmudic identification of the *magrefah* ("rake") as an organ supposed to have been used in the Second Temple. The development of the legend, for such it is, can easily be traced. The Mishnah (Tam. 2:1; 3:8, and 5:6) states that a *magrefah* was among the implements used for cleaning the altar in the morning before the new daily sacrifice; and that the noise of its being thrown on the floor was one of several "noise-cues" which the priests used to ensure the smooth running of the ceremony (cf. *The Letter of Aristeas* 92; 94–96) in the absence of perceptible orders during the service. A hyperbole states that all these noises were audible "unto Jericho" (Tam. 3:8). The equating of *magrefah* with *hydraulis* must have occurred in the time of the *Tosefta, since Tosefta Arakhin 1:13–14 quotes R. Simeon b. Gamaliel as saying: "There was no *hydraulis* [הדראוליס] in the Temple since it confuses the voice and spoils the tune." The Jerusalem Talmud (Suk. 5:6, 55c–d) quotes R. Simeon b. Gamaliel, and then goes on to identify the biblical *ugav* with *ardablis*, and states that the *magrefah* had ten holes (or pipes) each emitting a hundred tones, or a hundred holes (or pipes) each emitting ten tones. Finally, in *Arakhin* 10b the identification *magrefah-hydraulis* appears as a categorical statement. Henceforth the identification of *magrefah* with organ remained practically unquestioned by most commentators and musicologists, although there is Rashi's compromise-exegesis to *Arakhin* 10b: "but it seems that there were two *magrefot*, one for [raking] the altar-remnants and one for song/music." [B.B.]

The Organ in the Synagogue Before the 19th Century. Little is known about the use of the organ in the synagogue before its introduction by Reform Judaism in the 19th century. The earliest evidence of its use is in Italy in the 17th century. Giulio *Morosini (Samuel Nahmias, Leone *Modena's pupil, who converted to Christianity) tells in his *Via della Fede* (Rome, 1683, p. 793) about the performance of the Jewish Academy of Music *(Accademia degli impediti)* in the Spanish synagogue of Venice, about 1628. On one occasion (Simḥat Torah) there was an organ among the instruments used but the Venetian rabbis disapproved of it because of its close association with Christian worship. But another Italian source of the 17th century indicates that the organ was not frowned upon by some Italian rabbis of this period. Abraham Joseph Solomon *Graziano, rabbi of Modena (d. 1683) observed in glosses on the Shulḥan Arukh (OḤ 560:3): "... Jewish musicians should not be prevented from playing on the organ [to accompany] songs and praises performed [in honor of] God ..." He went on to suggest that the argument of *ḥukkot ha-goyim* ("customs of the gentiles") was not relevant: no competent rabbinic authority would forbid organ playing; only ignorant people would oppose it.

The existence of a synagogue organ in Prague in the late 17th and 18th centuries is indicated by several writers. The use of the organ seems to have been linked mainly with the musical "inauguration of the Sabbath." The earliest mention is by Shabbetai *Bass, who uses the term *ugav* in the prayer book printed as a supplement to his Hebrew bibliography, *Siftei Yeshenim* (Amsterdam, 1680, 21b:3). Two later sources are J. J. *Schudt, (1664–1722) and Abraham Levi b. Menahem Tall (early 18th century). The broadsheet *Naye Tsaytung un Yudisher Oyftsug* (1716) reveals the name of the Jewish builder of the "new organ" (Meir Mahler) employed during the celebrations of the Jewish community of Prague in honor of the birth of Prince Leopold, son of the German emperor, Charles VI. [I.A.]

In the 19th and 20th Centuries. The organ was introduced by *Reform Judaism into the synagogue services as part of its stress on the aesthetic aspects of Jewish worship. The controversies surrounding the use of the organ began when Israel *Jacobson placed an organ into the temple he opened for his boys' school in Seesen, in 1810. He also employed the organ in the services which were held in private homes in Berlin from 1815 on. The Hamburg Temple, which opened in 1818, held services with organ accompaniment. From that time, this became the distinguishing feature of all Reform congregations. Of all the liturgical reforms introduced in the 19th century, none has proved to be as divisive as the introduction of the organ. The introduction of an organ into a synagogue was usually followed by an exodus of the more traditionalist members who organized services for themselves without organ accompaniment. As the shibboleth of Reform, the organ figured primarily in Germany and, in the 19th century, in America. French and Italian synagogues, not otherwise departing from traditional usage, introduced the organ without giving rise to controversy. For wedding ceremonies, the organ is played in some modern Orthodox synagogues. Many American Conservative synagogues also play it on the Sabbath. To justify their innovation, the Reformers published a collection of responsa, entitled *Nogah ha-Ẓedek* ("The Splendor of Justice," 1818). The Orthodox replied with a responsa collection of their own, *Elleh Divrei ha-Berit* ("These are the words of the Covenant," 1819). Since then, a vast literature has accumulated around the subject, consisting mainly of restatements and reformulations of the arguments used in 1818 and 1819.

Basically, three halakhic objections have been raised: (1) Playing the organ on the Sabbath, even by a non-Jew, is prohibited "work"—if not biblically forbidden, at least falling into the rabbinic category of *shevut* (occupations forbidden on Sabbaths and festivals); (2) as a sign of mourning for the destruction of the Temple, music in general is prohibited; (3) the organ is so closely associated with worship in the Christian churches that it would be a case of the prohibited "imitation of gentile customs" *(ḥukkot ha-goyim)* to play it in the synagogue. The Reform justification has taken the following form: (1) the Shulḥan Arukh (OḤ 338:2) permits the playing of music by a non-Jew on the Sabbath for the purpose of entertaining a wedding party. What is permitted for a wedding party should be permitted all the more for the enhancement of worship. Moreover, just as the rules of *shevut* did not apply to the Temple, so they should not apply to the synagogues which have taken its place; (2) the prohibition of music as a sign of mourning for the destruction of Jerusalem includes vocal no less than instrumental music. Yet tradition has obviously accepted vocal music for religious purposes (Sh. Ar., OḤ 560:3). Reform is merely extending the compromise to instrumental music as well. Beside, instrumental music was used in some pre-modern synagogues, although not on the Sabbath; a synagogue in Prague even had an organ; (3) the organ is not universal in Christian worship. Since there can be Christian worship without an organ, it follows that the instrument is by no means "essential" to that worship. Joel *Sirkes, in his responsum (Resp. Baḥ Yeshanot, no. 127) made a distinction between melodies which are an integral part of Christian worship and those which are not. The Reformers extended that distinction to musical instruments as well. In addition, they claimed instrumental music in the church is itself a borrowing from the Temple, in which there was an organ-like instrument, called *magrefah* (Ar. 10b–11a). While the use of the organ, particularly when played by non-Jewish musicians, has frequently led to the introduction of melodies akin to the traditional Jewish worship, it has likewise led both to a renaissance of modern synagogue music and to a revival of old Jewish modes. Hermann Heymann *Steinthal said: "The organ has restored to us the old *ḥazzanut*. It will preserve it, and transmit it to our children" (*Ueber Juden und Judentum*, 272). But Leopold *Zunz, a friend of the organ, cautioned: "Unity is the sweetest harmony. It is, therefore, better to refrain from the use of the organ . . ., if that should be the sole cause for a serious split in the congregation" (Zunz-Albeck, Derashot, 219). [J.J.P.]

Bibliography: ANTIQUITY: Idelsohn, Music, 14, 19, 242–4, 496; J. Yasser, in: *Journal of the American Musicological Society*, 13 (1960), 24–42; J. Perrot, *L'orgue, de ses origines hellénistiques à la fin du XIIIe siècle* (1965), 14–19; H. Avenary, in: *Tazlil*, 2 (1961), 66; C. Sachs, *The History of Musical Instruments* (1940), 124. MODERN TIMES: Sendrey, Music, nos. 2537–86; Adler, Prat Mus, 28–30, 65, 74, 112, 263; A. Berliner, *Zur Lehr' und zur Wehr, ueber und gegen die kirchliche Orgel im juedischen Gottesdienste* (1904); S. Krauss, *Zur Orgelfrage* (1919), incl. bibl.

ORGELBRAND, SAMUEL (1810–1868), Polish publisher. A graduate of the rabbinical seminary of his native Warsaw, he taught for a few years, and in 1836 he opened a shop specializing in the sale of manuscripts and old and rare books. Exploiting the demand for Jewish books because of the restrictions on their publication in Russia, he opened a publishing house for both Hebrew and Polish books. In 1844 he acquired the publishing firm of Jozef Krasinski, which he expanded and improved, becoming the most important publisher in Warsaw. For a while he was in partnership with Henryk Natanson. In 1860 he appointed the conservative *maskil* Daniel *Neufeld to head the department for Hebrew books. In 30 active years, Orgelbrand published over 250 works in 520 volumes, of which about 100 volumes were Hebrew works, sold mostly to subscribers. Between 1860 and 1864 he published the Babylonian Talmud in 20 volumes. Despite the competition of the *Romm edition of Vilna and the Zusman Javetz edition of Berlin, 12,000 copies of this edition were sold. Orgelbrand also published fine editions of the Pentateuch with commentaries, *Ein Ya'akov*, prayer books, *Ẓe'enah u-Re'enah* (1867), and other works. Between 1842 and 1850 he financed the weekly *Kmiotek* ("Peasant"), the first Polish periodical for the masses. Between 1858 and 1868 he published the first Polish general encyclopedia *(Encyklopedja Powszechna)*, in 28 volumes, which he financed from the profits of the Talmud. A large section on Judaica, edited by Daniel Neufeld and Fabian Streuch (1820–1884), was included in the encyclopedia. Orgelbrand also published a series of works by Polish authors as well as Polish translations of classical works. During the 1860s he was a member of the executive board of the Warsaw community.

His sons, HIPOLIT (1843–1920) and MIECZYSLAW (1857–1903), took over the publishing house, keeping the Polish department in operation but discontinuing the Hebrew department in 1901. Both brothers belonged to extreme assimilationist circles and converted to Christianity during the 1890s. Before closing down the Hebrew department, they invited their brother-in-law, the learned *maskil* and author Hershel Rundo, to be their partner in the publication of Hebrew works.

Samuel's brother, MAURYCY (Moses; 1826–1904), was also a publisher, active in assimilationist circles in both Warsaw and Vilna. In Vilna he published a practical dictionary of the Polish language in two volumes, *Słownik języka polskiego do podręcznego użytku* (1861). Ordered to leave Vilna in 1865 by the Russian governor, Muravyov, he returned to Warsaw in 1873, establishing a publishing house in partnership with Gebethner and Wolff, and Michael Gluecksberg. From 1878 to 1885 he was the publisher and editor of the popular Polish weekly, *Tygodnik Powszechny*.

Bibliography: B. Prus, in: *Kurier Warszawski*, 97 (1833); B. Weinryb, in: MGWJ, 77 (1933), 273–300; S. Rosencweig, in: *Nasz Przegląd* (Nov. 7–13, 1937); Z. Kobryński, in: *Miesięcznik graficzny*, 1 (1938); J. Bartosiewicz, in: *Tygodnik Ilustrowany*, 51 (1922); J. Shatzky, *Geshikhte fun Yidn in Varshe*, 3 (1953), index.
[A.CY.]

ORGEYEV (Rum. **Orhei**), city in Bessarabia, central Moldavian S.S.R. Jews are first mentioned in Orgeyev in 1741. The community developed after the Russian annexation of Bessarabia in 1812 when many Jews emigrated to the region. There were 3,102 Jews registered in 1864 and 7,144 (57.9% of the total population) in 1897. They established educational and welfare institutions, and in 1865 a *talmud torah* was opened where secular studies were also taught; in 1877 a hospital and an old age home were founded. The Jews of Orgeyev were mostly businessmen and craftsmen, but some were viniculturists on the outskirts of the town. In the late 1890s an agricultural training farm was founded and it was supported by the Jewish Colonization Association (ICA). Among the 1,480 members registered in the loan fund in 1925 there were 286 farmers. In 1930 there were 6,408 Jews (41.9% of the total population). [EL.F.]

Holocaust Period and After. When war broke out (June 1941) the Soviet army, which had been in Orgeyev from the previous June, helped Jews to escape. Some got to Kryulyany (Criuleni) and wandered from there. One group roamed through southern Russia on foot; of these, some were killed in German air raids, while others succumbed to the cold or died from starvation and disease. The survivors eventually reached Stalingrad, where the authorities dispersed them among the kolkhozes. When the front drew near, they were sent on to the Ural Mountains, central Asia, and Uzbekistan. One large group of Orgeyev Jews was located at Tashkent and the surrounding area. Those Jews who remained in Orgeyev came to a bitter end. When the German-Rumanian forces entered on July 8–10, a Jewish delegation presented itself before them to welcome them with bread and salt, but all its members were murdered on the spot. The Jewish population was enclosed in a ghetto, where it lived under extremely crowded conditions and was exposed to constant maltreatment and daily murders. On

The agricultural training farm at Orgeyev, Bessarabia, established in 1898 and closed in 1905. From *Orhiyov be-Vinyanah u-ve-Ḥurbanah*, Tel Aviv, 1959.

August 6, about 200 Jews were murdered by the 25th Rumanian regiment and their bodies were thrown into the Dniester. In 1942 all the survivors were deported to the concentration camp at Tiraspol, Transnistria; their exit from the city was accompanied by the music of a gypsy band and the old people were forced to dance in the streets. When the transport reached a nearby forest, the young men among the deportees were taken to an open field where they underwent torture and where many were shot to death by the soldiers. Others died on the way to Tiraspol and others in the Transnistrian camps. Only a few lived to see the end of the war.

There was little Jewish life after the war. The only synagogue in Orgeyev was closed down by the authorities in 1960, after they had organized a "petition" claiming that its presence was disturbing the neighbors. The Jewish population in 1970 was estimated at about 3,000. [J.AN.]

Bibliography: *Orhiyov be-Vinyanah u-ve-Ḥurbanah* (1959); M. Mircu, *Pogromurile din Basarabia* . . . (1947), 9–10.

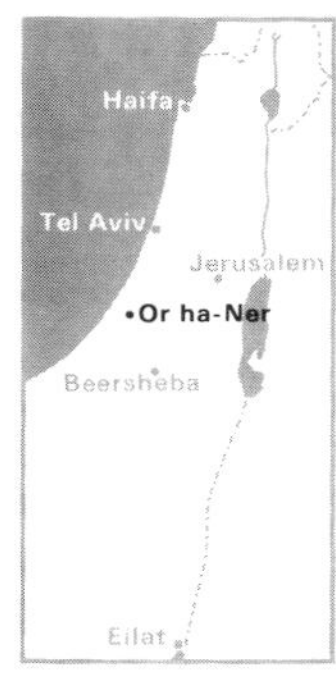

OR HA-NER (Heb. אוֹר הַנֵּר), kibbutz in the southern Coastal Plain of Israel, north of Sederot, affiliated with Iḥud ha-Kevuẓot ve-ha-Kibbutzim. Or ha-Ner was founded initially as an administered farm of the "Yiẓẓur u-Fittu'aḥ" company belonging to Iḥud ha-Kevuẓot ve-ha-Kibbutzim, in 1955. It was taken over in 1957 by the kibbutz which had previously settled in Givot Zaid near *Kiryat Tivon. Pioneers from Brazil, Mexico, Chile, and Uruguay, made up the majority of the 284 inhabitants in 1970. Or ha-Ner engages in intensive farming with irrigated field and garden crops and dairy cattle, and runs a vegetable dehydrating plant, mostly for export. The name, "Light of the Candle," referring to nearby Beror Ḥayil, is taken from Sanhedrin 32b (see *Beror Ḥayil). [E.O.]

ORḤOT ḤAYYIM (Heb. אָרְחוֹת חַיִּים; "Ways of Life"), or **Ẓavva'at Rabbi Eliezer** (Heb. צַוָּאַת רַבִּי אֱלִיעֶזֶר; "The Ethical Will of Rabbi Eliezer"), one of the most popular and best-known short treatises upon ethics and moralistic behavior in medieval Hebrew literature. *Orḥot Ḥayyim* is arranged in the form of an ethical will (*Wills, Ethical), and owing to the fact that it begins with the talmudic story about the illness of Rabbi *Eliezer b. Hyrcanus, was conventionally attributed to him. However, as early as the Middle Ages, doubts arose as to whether he was in fact the author, and Menahem b. Judah de *Lonzano and other scholars after him ascribed the work to *Eliezer b. Isaac Ashkenazi of the 11th century. *Orḥot Ḥayyim* was first printed, together with other works, in Venice in 1544; and it has been reprinted many times. There are two commentaries to it—one by Abraham Mordecai Virnikowski (1888), and one by Gershon Hanoch Leiner of Radzyn (1891).

There are several bibliographical problems in connection with *Orḥot Ḥayyim* which have been studied by Israel Abrahams and Gershom Scholem. The work consists of two parts: the first is the ethical will, comprising short paragraphs of moralistic advice given by a father to his son; and the second, called *"Seder Gan Eden,"* is a treatise on the structure of and the different palaces *(heikhalot)* in the garden of Eden. The two parts were printed as a single entity and are found together in early manuscripts; Scholem noted that the work as a whole usually appears in manuscript collections of kabbalistic material, often in close proximity to works written by *Moses b. Shem Tov de Leon, the reputed author of the Zohar.

There is virtually no doubt about the date of the second part of *Orḥot Ḥayyim;* its descriptions of the *heikhalot* of the garden of Eden bear a close resemblance to the descriptions found in the Zohar, and various other motifs are common to both works. Scholem has suggested that if the author of the Zohar had written his work in Hebrew, the result would have been very similar in style to the *"Seder Gan Eden."* Hence it must have been written by a member of the kabbalistic circles of the end of the 13th century, very probably by Moses de Leon himself.

The problem is whether the same can be said about the first part of *Orḥot Ḥayyim,* the ethical will attributed to Rabbi Eliezer. Scholem believes that it is impossible to make any distinction between the two parts; nonetheless, there are great differences in style between them, and it is difficult to discover any hint of mystical speculation in the first part. It is possible that the first part is in fact an Ashkenazi work dating from the 11th century or later, whereas the second part was added at a later period. However, the question must be regarded as an open one.

Bibliography: I. Abrahams, *Hebrew Ethical Wills,* 1 (1926), 30–49; A. Jellinek, *Beit ha-Midrash,* 3 (1938[2]), xxvi–xxviii, 131–40; G. Scholem, in: *Le-Agnon Shai* (1959), 293ff. [Y.D.]

ORḤOT ẒADDIKIM (Heb. אוֹרְחוֹת צַדִּיקִים "The Ways of the Righteous"), an anonymous work in Hebrew probably written in Germany in the 15th century. *Orḥot Ẓaddikim,* one of the most important works in Hebrew ethical literature, has always been published anonymously and though an attempt was made to identify the author with the 15th-century moralist and polemical writer, Yom Tov Lipmann Muelhausen, the hypothesis seems to be without foundation. The only historical fact cited in the work is the expulsion of the Jews from France in the 14th century. Since *Orḥot Ẓaddikim* follows the teachings of the *Ḥasidei Ashkenaz in many ways, it is possible that the author, in keeping with the admonishment of *Judah b. Samuel he-Ḥasid of Regensburg in *Sefer *Ḥasidim* (also published anonymously) for writers not to identify their work so that their descendants might not pride themselves with the accomplishments of their fathers, purposely kept the book anonymous. Despite its anonymity *Orḥot Ẓaddikim* became one of the most popular works in traditional Hebrew literature and since the 16th century nearly 80 editions, including abridged versions and translations, have been

ספר
אורחות צדיקים
אורחות צדיקים
החיבור הקטן הזה מעט הכמות ורב
האיכות הוא ספר אורחות צדיקים
ומידות הנפש
המיוסד להורות ולהשכיל את לב האבן
והנפש ולהוציאו מדרך טיט ורפש
ולהוליכו בדרך הטוב אשר הוא בלא כשלון
ולא יהיה תארם להטאת לבזוי ולקלון
נדפס פה ק"ק פראג המפורסם תחת ממשלת אדונינו הקיסר
רודלפוס יר"ה והדרו

Title page of the first complete Hebrew edition of *Orḥot Ẓaddikim,* an anonymous work on ethics. Prague, 1581.

published. The first was a shortened version in Yiddish (Isny, 1542); the full Hebrew text appeared for the first time in Prague some years later (1581, latest publication 1969).

The original title is probably not *Orḥot Ẓaddikim*, apparently given to it by the copyists and publishers. The Isny edition (1542) is called *Sefer ha-Middot* ("The Book of Ethical Qualities"), a name traditionally bestowed on Hebrew ethical works. In the introduction the author refers to the book as *Sefer ha-Middot* and in the concluding paragraph of the introduction he states "this *Sefer ha-Middot* was written and sealed with the seal of wisdom." The title is also appropriate to the structure of the work since it enumerates ethical qualities and their characteristics.

Orḥot Ẓaddikim, to a large extent a compendium of earlier Hebrew ethical thought, is based on philosophical and ethical works written in Spain, and on Ashkenazi ethical writings. The author also drew on some works written in Italy which he copied verbatim. The language and style though mainly patterned after the philosophical-ethical literature of Spain is also fused with stylistic and structural elements of the Ashkenazi ethical school. *Ḥovot ha-Levavot* by Baḥya ibn Paquda, the classical work of Jewish ethics, is one of the main sources of *Orḥot Ẓaddikim* both in its basic ideas and the many proverbs and parables which the author culled from it. *Orḥot Ẓaddikim*, more than any other medieval Hebrew ethical treatise, used proverbs and parables for elucidation. The structure of the work seems to have been influenced by Solomon ibn *Gabirol's *Tikkun Middot ha-Nefesh* which sets up pairs of ethical qualities (usually conflicting) and by *Mivḥar ha-Peninnim*, a work also attributed to Ibn Gabirol. The last chapter of *Orḥot Ẓaddikim* draws extensively on *Saadiah b. Joseph Gaon's concept of the desired harmony between the various ethical qualities in *Emunot ve-De'ot*. The influence of the ethical works of Maimonides is also marked and the author sometimes quotes whole passages verbatim. He also copied sections from *Ma'alot ha-Middot*, an ethical work by Jehiel b. Jekuthiel *Anav of Rome.

Despite the major influence that the above works had on the ideas, style, and structure of *Orḥot Ẓaddikim*, in its ethical outlook and approach the book follows the teachings of the Ḥasidei Ashkenaz, *Sefer Ḥasidim* and *Sefer ha-Roke'aḥ* by *Eleazar b. Judah of Worms, and is mainly interested in the practical and immediate meaning of the ethical qualities. Though the author also deals in generalizations and often divides every subject into sections and subsections, following the structure of medieval philosophical works, primary significance is given to practical behavior. The last chapter describes how a full religious life may be realized. This realization is not seen in the achievement of wisdom, or the unity with God through love, as is common in philosophical-ethical literature, but in the awe of and obedience to heaven, the supreme quality posited by the Ḥasidei Ashkenaz.

In the introduction, the author gives a theoretical and anthropological basis for his theory of ethics; the book is divided into *she'arim* (portals, i.e., sections), most of which are short, each devoted to a discussion of the ethical merits and demerits of a specific moral quality. The author apparently tried to arrange the chapters into pairs of contradictory qualities, but this was not followed through. Some of the major sections are devoted to pride, modesty, love (not exclusively the love of God, but all aspects of love in human life), hatred, compassion or mercy *(raḥamim)*, cruelty, joy (including a long discussion on faith in God, to which, strangely enough, a special portal was not devoted). The author discusses the negative characteristics of non-religious joy, and extols the joy found in the love of God and obedience to him. Other sections treat worry, anger, envy, zeal and laziness, truth and falsehood, flattery, gossip, and repentance. (The section on repentance is the longest and most detailed section in the work.) The last two chapters are on the Bible and the study of Torah, discussing problems of religious knowledge and wisdom, and the awe of heaven, which, to the author, is the most important quality. Awe of heaven expresses itself in man's attitude toward God in everyday life.

Orḥot Ẓaddikim greatly influenced later Hebrew ethical works. The Hebrew moralists in Safed, though kabbalists and though there is no kabbalistic element in *Orḥot Ẓaddikim*, drew on its teachings. The work also influenced ethical writers of Eastern Europe. It is even possible that the manner in which the merits and demerits of every quality are enumerated influenced Moses Ḥayyim *Luzzatto in his *Mesillat Yesharim*.

Bibliography: S. J. Cohen, *The Ways of the Righteous* (1969); Guedemann, Gesch Erz, 3 (1888), 223ff.; J. Kaufmann (Even Shemuel), *Rabbi Yom Tov Lipmann Muhlhausen* (Heb., 1927).

[Ed.]

ORIA, small town near Brindisi in Apulia, S. Italy, formerly of great importance. The Jewish settlement probably went back to classical times and Jewish sepulchral inscriptions have been found there. During the period of Byzantine rule, from the eighth century, the community was one of the most important in southern Italy, and a great deal is known about it because of the wealth of information contained in the chronicle of *Ahimaaz. This deals largely with the family of the synagogue poet *Amittai of Oria and his son *Shephatiah, who was inducted into practical mysticism in Oria by *Aaron of Baghdad. Shephatiah went on a mission to Constantinople in 873–74 to obtain the cancellation, at least so far as Oria was concerned, of the edict of conversion issued by the emperor *Basil I. In 925 the city was attacked by Arab marauders; some Jews were killed and many were enslaved, including the young Shabbetai *Donnolo. Other attacks followed during the same century. The Jewish community remained important until the 15th century, but thereafter it declined. The *Porta degli Ebrei ("Jew's Gate") still stands at the entrance of the Jewish quarter (now Piazza Donnolo).

Bibliography: Roth, Dark Ages, index; Milano, Bibliotheca, index; idem, in: RMI, 32 (1966), 414ff.; P. B. Marsella, *Da Oria viene la parola di Dio, saggio storico-critico . . .* (1952); Marcus, in: PAAJR, 5 (1933/34), 85–94. [C.R.]

ORIENTALISTS. Orientalism is the study of the languages, history, and civilization of the peoples of Asia and, due to the expansion of Islam, the northern parts of Africa. As Islam, almost from its beginning, widely influenced Jewish thought, Jewish religious and philosophical literature from the 8th century C.E. onward displays a more or less intimate knowledge of Islamic theology, philosophy, and even religious law, not to speak of the subtleties of Arabic language and literature, which did not fail to leave their mark on the corresponding Hebrew and Jewish scholarly productions. The works of men such as *Saadiah, *Judah Halevi, *Maimonides, Abraham *ibn Ezra, *Baḥya ibn Paquda, Shem Tov b. Joseph *Falaquera, and many others on the above-mentioned subjects, as well as on biblical exegesis and Hebrew grammar and lexicography, were inconceivable without their knowledge, either receptive or polemical, of Arabic and Islam. *Ibn Kammuna even wrote a kind of history of the religions—Judaism, Christianity, and Islam—in which he betrays detailed knowledge of the internal controversies of Christianity and Islam respectively. Jewish scholars occupied themselves with comparative Semitic linguistics long before Christian scholars did. The translators of Arabic works by Jews and of an immense number of books by Muslim authors on Islamic and scientific subjects still await adequate evaluation as orientalists. Noteworthy were the achievements of the Ibn *Tibbon family and Judah *Al-Ḥarizi. Apart from their own translations, Jews served as mediators between Arabic and Latin from the time that Christian scholars began to study Islamic science. The assessment of the Jewish share in these studies has been enormously facilitated by the bibliographical studies of Moritz *Steinschneider and later scholars, not only as a consequence of many newly discovered literary texts, but especially of the investigation of the thousands of documents of all kinds found in the Cairo *Genizah*.

Along with the rise of the *"Wissenschaft des Judentums"* in the last two centuries, an ever increasing number of Jews studied orientalia at the universities not only as training for the rabbinate, but also as secular historians, philosophers, and philologists. The pioneers in this field were Abraham *Geiger, Moritz *Steinschneider, Simon *Eppenstein, Samuel *Poznanski, Solomon *Munk, Adolf *Neubauer, Leopold *Dukes, and Alexander *Harkavy. Among their followers were Joseph and Hartwig *Derenburg, Wilhelm *Bacher, David *Kaufmann, Israel *Friedlaender, Samuel *Landauer, Z. *Fraenkel, Hartwig and Leo *Hirschfeld, Ignaz *Goldziher, Herman *Reckendorf, Jakob *Barth, Gotthold *Weil, Martin *Schreiner, Friedrich Kern, A. S. *Yahuda, Jacob *Mann, Daniel *Chwolson, Eugen *Mittwoch, Saul *Horovitz, Joseph *Horovitz, S. M. *Stern, Kurt Levy. Joseph *Halévi and Eduard *Glaser were among the pioneers of the search for South Arabian inscriptions. Unparalleled in his mastery of the whole field of oriental studies was Giorgio Levi della Vida. J. Blau, C. Rabin, and M. Goshen-Gottstein have all made important contributions to the study of Semitic languages. Julian Joel *Obermann III, Max Meyerhof, Immanuel *Loew, Paul *Kraus, Franz *Rosenthal, Georges *Vajda, Richard *Walzer and H. Kroner who edited many of the medical works of Maimonides in their original Arabic, deserve special mention as historians of Arabic literature, philosophy, and sciences. The investigation of Islamic arts owes many of its most valuable achievements to Ernst *Herzfeld, Leo Ary *Mayer, and R. Ettinghausen. The history of early Islam was based on new foundations by the Jerusalem Arabist M. J. Kister. Bernard *Lewis and David *Ayalon excel in the field of later Islamic history.

During the 19th century, when the deciphering of the hieroglyphs and the cuneiform scriptures enlarged the field of "Bible Lands," Jewish scholars also turned to these philologies. Morris *Jastrow and Heinrich Zimmern were among the leading Assyriologists, and the unrivaled master of this field was Benno *Landsberger. Other important contributions were made by Herman *Pick and Julius and Hildegard *Lewy.

Among the leading Egyptologists rank Georg Ebers, Georg Steindorff, Ludwig *Borchardt, A. *Ember, and H. J. *Polotsky, who also played an important part in the interpretation of the Coptic Manichaic texts discovered in Egypt. Knowledge of the Mandaic religious literature is due almost entirely to Mark *Lidzbarski, who also was the main cultivator of Semitic epigraphics. The investigation of the Ugaritic texts was greatly furthered by H. L. *Ginsberg and Umberto *Cassuto. Aramaic studies in general were cultivated by Alexander Sperber, and E. Y. *Kutscher. Noted Iranists were James *Darmesteter, Isidor *Scheftelowitz, Alexander *Kohut, and Sir Marc Aurel *Stein. Gotthold *Weil and Uriel *Heyd excelled in Turkish philology and history. Some of the leading Indologists were G. S. *Oppert and Moritz *Winternitz. Far Eastern languages were studied by B. Laufer and Arthur *Waley.

[M.PL.]

ORIENTAL LITERATURE. In the vast area between Morocco and the Pacific, Jewish writers were mainly active in Islamic culture and this survey is thus mainly concerned with the Near East.

Writers in the Arab World. Few Jewish writers gained a place in the history of Arabic literature from the pre-Islamic period until modern times, yet the number of Jewish authors in the Islamic world greatly exceeds that mentioned by Arab historians. Jews gained fame mainly in the pre-Islamic period (the *Jāhiliyya*); during the period of Islamic rule in Baghdad and Spain; and in the 19th and 20th centuries. In the pre-Islamic period Jewish poets were prominent in Arabia, notably the warrior-poet *Samuel ibn Adiyā, "The Faithful," and members of his family, and the Jewish poetess Sārā al-Qurayẓiyya, who was famous for her elegy over the dead of her tribe, which was betrayed by its Arab allies. After the rise of Islam, and because of the animosity between Muhammad and the Jewish communities and tribes of his day, Jewish poets and writers—with the notable exception of *Marḥab al-Yahūdī, the Arabian warrior poet—ceased to be mentioned, although Arabic-speaking Jews are known to have been prominent in science. It was only during the period of Islamic rule in Spain that Jewish writers reappeared in the accounts of Arab historians. Outstanding among these was the Spanish poet *Ibrāhīm ibn Sahl. Jewish scientists who wrote in Arabic gained fame at this time in Spain, North Africa, and Baghdad. Jews rarely distinguished themselves in Arabic poetry of the period, since they did not usually show great interest in the study of Arabic grammar, literature, and rhetoric. Blau (*The Emergence and Linguistic Background of Judaeo-Arabic*, 1965) has shown that Jews shunned Arabic poetry because of the difficulties involved in the study of Arabic literature and language, and mostly preferred to compose Hebrew verse. Muslim historians explain the emergence of Ibn Sahl and his fellow Jewish poets by claiming that Spanish Jews began to study Arabic grammar and literature. In the 19th and 20th centuries Jews were active in Arabic culture. Many won praise from their Muslim colleagues and some were considered by Arab literary historians to be leading pioneers of modern Arabic literature. The cultural and social revival of Arabic-speaking Jewry resulted from a number of factors. These include growing commercial prosperity, the equality in civil rights granted to ethnic minorities in the Ottoman Empire, and the competition between the European powers to gain a political and economic foothold in the region. Other factors were the demand for a multilingual intelligentsia and an efficient governmental administration, the awakening of East European Jewry and its interest in the Jewish communities of the East, the opening of Jewish schools by the *Alliance Israélite Universelle, and the intensification of Zionist activity. With the termination of Ottoman rule in the Arab lands, the establishment of the French and British mandates and the institution of Arabic as the official language of the newly emergent Arab states brought about a revolutionary revival of Arabic. Active Jewish participation in the revival of Arabic literature during the second half of the 19th century was spurred by the wish to safeguard Jewish rights in the newly liberated Arabic-speaking countries. In fact, the use of literary Arabic by Jews in the 19th century was confined mainly to the lands of the Fertile Crescent. Jews actually lagged behind other religious minorities in these countries, notably the Christians, who had adopted Arabic for liturgical and literary purposes in the 18th century. In North Africa, Yemen, and Aden, Jews preferred to use either Hebrew and their own *Judeo-Arabic dialect, or else the language of the ruling power. The prevailing attitude of Jewish writers in the Muslim countries toward Arabic was therefore utilitarian and didactic. Jews were also activated by apologetic considerations, defending the position of their people and religion against false accusations. With the rise of Zionism, the level of Jewish-Arabic cultural life was greatly enhanced. Zionism brought new vitality to the Jewish communities of the Arab lands, developing their national pride, sense of security, and consciousness of progress. Jewish writers began to demand an improvement of existing educational facilities and the furtherance of, and an increased respect for, their national uniqueness and autonomy. These trends were supported by the British and French mandatory administrations, which favored the autonomy of national and religious minorities in the area. It is thus not surprising that most of the Arabic-Jewish press was usually pro-Zionist. Any survey of Jewish literary activity in Muslim lands during the 19th–20th centuries faces a number of serious handicaps. The most serious of these are: (1) the fact that Arab writers mainly overlooked their Jewish colleagues; (2) the lack of any systematic collection of Jewish literary works in Arabic, mainly due to the low regard in which the Jews themselves held the study of Arabic language and literature (in many Jewish schools Hebrew and foreign languages entirely replaced Arabic in the curriculum); and (3) the immense difficulty involved in obtaining the necessary source material as a result of the Middle East conflict. Jewish writers were first attracted to the theater and journalism, since the former offered virtually unlimited scope for education, and the latter scope for apologetics, despite the danger of clashes with government authorites and other pressure groups.

PLAYWRIGHTS. The theater was a most effective mass medium for the purpose of education, enlightenment, and social criticism, since its aim could easily be concealed behind the camouflage of entertainment. Among the first Jewish journalists and writers to enter the field was the versatile Yaʿqūb *Sanūʿ, known also as Abu Naẓẓāra ("The Bespectacled"). An outstanding pioneer actor, stage producer, playwright, and journalist, he established his first theater in one of Cairo's large cafés. Ṣanūʿ was much influenced by Molière, Sheridan, and Goldoni, but his Arabic operettas were more to the taste of his public, which preferred lighter entertainment. One of the first stage producers in the Arab countries to employ actresses, he wrote 32 plays (mainly short comedies) and translated many others. Ṣanūʿ's criticism of the khedive Ismāʿīl and his ministers in the Egyptian paper *Abu Naẓẓāra Zarqā* ("The Man with the Blue Spectacles") led to the closing down of his paper and his deportation to France in 1878.

While the Arab national theater flourished in Egypt, enjoying government support and the visits of Syrian and Lebanese stage companies, the Jewish theater was mainly confined to amateur activity in Jewish schools. Nevertheless, premiers, ministers of education, and even the khedive Ismāʿīl and King Fayṣal I of Iraq attended its performances. Jewish amateur theater also flourished in Lebanon. The plays of Salīm Zakī Kūhīn, the son of Rabbi Zakī Kūhīn of Beirut, were staged in 1894–95. In Iraq, the Jewish schools of Baghdad and the Baghdad Jewish Literary Association promoted Arabic-Jewish theater. Original works by Jewish playwrights were also staged. In Egypt Raḥamīm Kūhīn wrote and translated many plays performed on the stage during the 1930s. His *al-Malik Dāʾūd* ("King David") was published in the Cairo Arabic-Jewish weekly *al-Shams* ("The Sun") in 1944.

JEWISH RELIGIOUS LITERATURE IN ARABIC. With the rise of the Zionist movement, Arabic-speaking Jewry experienced a cultural revival. This led both to the establishment of new Hebrew periodicals and publishing houses and to the intensive translation into Arabic of Hebrew books, including many religious works. Selections of the Babylonian Talmud were translated into Arabic under an English title by Shimon Joseph Moyal (*The Talmud, Its Origins and Its Morals*, 1909) and Hillel *Farḥi published Hebrew-Arabic liturgical works, including the high holiday *maḥzor*, prayer books, and Passover *Haggadot*. Farḥi also wrote religious tales in both languages. The Karaite scholar Murād *Faraj published an Arabic commentary on the Pentateuch and other works, including translations of Proverbs and Job. Such activity encouraged the compilation of Hebrew-Arabic lexicons, notably the Hebrew-Arabic dictionary of Murād Faraj (1925), the Hebrew-Arabic-English dictionary of Hillel Farḥi, and the pocket Hebrew-Arabic dictionary of Nissim Mallul.

NOVELISTS AND PROSE WRITERS. Very few Jewish writers in the Islamic world produced original novels, although many engaged in the translation of novels from various European languages. Outstanding in this field was Esther Azharī *Moyal, who translated nearly a dozen novels by European writers. With the exception of Najīb Ashaʿyā, who wrote in Egypt, all the Jewish writers of Arabic novels were Iraqis who emigrated to Israel during the 1950s. Ezra Menasheh ʿAbid, an editor, wrote the novel *al-Alam al-Saīd* ("The Happy World," c. 1952); and Ezra *Ḥaddad, who translated from English and Hebrew, wrote *Fuṣūl min al-Kitāb al-Muqaddas bi-Uslūb Qaṣasī* ("Chapters from the Holy Bible in Narrative Form," 1947). The outstanding Jewish novelist in Arabic was Ibrāhīm Mūsā Ibrāhīm, whose works include *Asmahān* (1961) and who joined the editorial staff of the Mapam Arabic paper *al-Mirṣād*. Greater distinction was gained in the field of the short story. Saʿd Litto Malkī, an Egyptian pioneer of the genre, published some of his work in *al-Shams*. His first collection of short stories, *Yarāi al-Awwal* ("My First Pen," 1936), contained one piece about Egyptian Jewish life, on anti-Semitism in Muslim schools. The Jewish role in this genre was more significant in Iraq, where the Arabic short story was virtually created by the Jews. Those who published fiction of this type include Meer Baṣrī; Yaʿqūb Bilbūl, who was author of *al-Jamra al Ūlā* ("The First Ember," 1937); Shalom Darwīsh; and the versatile Anwar Shaul, whose works called for social reform. Shimon (Balāṣ) Ballas (1930–), who eventually switched to Hebrew, published the novel *Ha-Maʿbarah* ("The Transit Camp," 1964) and a collection of short stories, *Mul ha-Ḥomah* ("Opposite the Wall," 1969). Esperance Cohen (1930–) published stories in the semiofficial paper *al-Anbāʾ* and in the Histadrut daily *al-Yawm*, later joining the editorial boards of the Histadrut journals. Most of these writers emigrated to Israel in the 1950s, two exceptions being Meer Baṣrī and Anwar Shaul, both anti-Zionists and Iraqi nationalists.

POETS. Modern Arabic poetry by Jews is again an almost exclusively Iraqi preserve. However, there were two notable exceptions to this rule—the Egyptian Karaite Murād Faraj and the Palestinian ʿAbdallah Nadīm Moyal. The latter belonged to a distinguished Sephardi family which settled in Ereẓ Israel. Moyal mainly wrote love poems, his lyrical collection *Ḥanīn al-Nadīm* ("The Yearning of Nadīm," 1934) being published in Beirut. At one stage of his career Moyal wrote narrative verse, producing a poetic biography of Maimonides. Iraqi Jews have played an important part in the development of modern Arabic poetry. In style, form, and idea they have tended to follow the Christian Lebanese poets active in the North American Lebanese diaspora. Those Iraqi Jewish poets of note include Anwar Shaul, Murad Mīkhā'īl, Ya'qūb Bilbūl, Abraham Obadya, Salīm Sha'shū', Shalom Katav, Shmuel Moreh, Benjamin Aaron Zakkay, David Semah, and Sasson Somekh. Bilbūl's highly introverted poems, which bear the imprint of French writing, include a sonnet collection, and Shalom Katav (1931–) wrote prose poems collected in *Mawākib al-Ḥirmān* ("The Convoys of Frustration," 1949) and *Washwashāt al-Fajr* ("Dawn's Whispering," 1958). David Semah's leftist verse appeared first in Iraqi and later in Israel periodicals. The first part of his collection *Ḥattā Yajī'u al-Rabī'* ("Till Spring Comes," 1959) contained tender love poems, while the second expressed the author's support for the Algerian war of liberation against the French and the 1959 anti-royalist coup in Iraq. Sasson Somekh (1933–), another leftist poet, also began his career as poet and translator in the Iraqi press, later writing for the Israel Communist monthly *al-Jadīd*. Like most of these Iraqi poets who settled in Israel, Somekh eventually wrote mainly in Hebrew.

Jewish Writers in Other Oriental Cultures. Though technically part of the Islamic world, some Jewish writers actually belonged to separate cultural traditions. Thus the Tunisian author *Ryvel, who wrote sensitive tales about his life in the Tunisian *ḥāra* (ghetto), chose French as his literary medium. This was also true of the Tunisian-born French novelist Albert *Memmi, the Egyptian-born novelist Élian-J. Finbert, and the Egyptian-born poet Édmond Jabès. Elsewhere in the Near East, Jews contributed to Turkish literature, notably the poetess Matilde Alçeh, the poet Jozef Ḥabib *Gerez, and the poets Ibrahim Nom and Robert Sezer. Further to the east, Jewish writers made their appearance in India, one of the earliest being Sarmad the Jew, a 17th-century poet of Hyderabad, who converted to Islam. Indian Jews of Baghdadi origin wrote in Hebrew, Arabic, or English, only Bene-Israel authors using native languages, such as Marathi. Most of the works by Bene Israel writers were liturgical, historical, or didactic; but a few produced original works of fiction. These include Bahais Joseph Talker's short novel *Gul ani Sanobar* ("Gul and Sanobar," 1867), the first of its kind in Marathi, and *Jagha che Chamatkar* ("Wonders of the World," 1869); Moses Daniel Talker's novels *Bago-Bahar* ("A Beautiful Garden," 1869) and *Premal Shushila* ("Lovely Sushila," 1872) and his Hindi play *Chhel Batao Mohana Rani* ("Stage Your Play, Mohana Rani," 1872); and S. R. Bunderker's drama *Ayushache Chitre* ("Life Picture," 1956). Other Indian authors were the prolific poet and prose writer Benjamin Samson Ashtamker, who wrote over 30 works from 1868 onward; the Baghdadi novelist Judah Aaron; and the Baghdadi poet Nissim Ezekiel, who was also a journalist. In the Far East, Chinese verse on Jewish themes was composed by three members of the *Kaifeng-Fu community during the 17th century—Ai-Shih-Tê, Chao Ying-Tou, and Shên Chu'üan.

Alphabetical List of Entries Including Capsule Articles. The individuals whose names are marked with an asterisk in the list below, form the subjects of articles in their appropriate alphabetical position in the Encyclopaedia.

ALÇEH, MATILDE (1923–1967), Turkish poet. Born in Istanbul, she contributed poems to various periodicals, including the daily *Cumhuriyet*, and also published some translations. The collection *Mart* ("The Gull," 1953) contained some of her characteristic lyrical verse. The only Turkish woman poet of Jewish birth, she married a Muslim and died in a car accident in Yugoslavia.

BAṢRI, MEER (1911–), Iraqi author and economist. Active in Baghdad commercial life, he published a volume of essays on economics (1948) and two collections of short stories, notably *Rijāl wa-Ẓilāl* ("Men and Shadows," 1955). Unlike most of Iraq's Jewish writers. Baṣrī did not emigrate to Israel and made no mention of Jews or Judaism in his works of fiction.

DARWĪSH, SHALOM (1913–), Iraqi author. A lawyer by profession, Darwīsh was secretary of the Baghdad Jewish communal council (1931–44). His first volume of Arabic short stories dealt with the life of Iraq's masses and was followed by a second collection, *Ba'd al-Nās* ("One of the People," 1948). He emigrated to Israel in 1951 and settled in Haifa.

EZEKIEL, NISSIM (1924–), Indian author and editor. Born in Bombay, he worked on *The Illustrated Weekly of India* (1952–54) and later headed the English department of the Bombay College of Arts (1961–). Ezekiel published literary reviews and wrote verse collections, including *A Time to Change and Other Poems* (1957), *The Third* (1958), and *The Unfinished Man* (1960). Some of his verse appeared in British poetry journals.

***FARAJ, MURĀD** (1866–1956), Egyptian Karaite author and theologian.

***FARḤI, HILLEL BEN JACOB** (1868–1940), Egyptian poet, translator, and physician.

***GEREZ, JOSEPH ḤABIB** (1928–), Turkish poet, artist, and communal official.

***MANSURAH, SA'ADIAH BEN JUDAH** (d. c. 1880), Yemenite poet.

MĪKHĀ'ĪL, MURAD (1906–), Iraqi poet and educator. A Baghdad lawyer, he was headmaster of the Shammāsh Jewish high school in Baghdad (1941–47). Some of his Arabic verse appeared in the Jewish press and a collection of love poems was published in 1931. Mīkhā'īl also wrote prose works in favor of women's rights and the peasants, and attacking superstition. After emigrating to Israel in 1949, he specialized in Arab education and wrote several textbooks.

MOREH, SHMUEL (1933–), Iraqi poet. Moreh, who was born in Baghdad, emigrated to Israel in 1951. He taught at the Hebrew University and wrote for the Jerusalem Arabic paper *al-Anbā'*, sometimes under a pen name. In 1968 he published an anthology of modern Arabic criticism and poetry.

***MOYAL, ESTHER** (1873–1948), Lebanese author and journalist.

NAEH, BARUKH BEN MENAHEM (1880–1943), Turkish translator and legal writer. Active in Adrianople (Edirne) public affairs, he was a Turkish infantry officer during World War I and emigrated to Palestine in 1923. Naeh's translations include works by Yehuda Burla, A. S. Friedberg, and Sholem Asch, as well as part of the Ottoman *Majalla* legal code. He also compiled a volume of guarantees and laws governing loans and debts (1937).

NOM, IBRAHIM (Avram Naon, 1870–1947), Turkish poet and lawyer. A successful Istanbul attorney, he was prominent in Turkish literary life, publishing a review and writing for leading periodicals. A collection of his verse, *Kalbi Sikeste* ("Broken Heart"), appeared in 1901. Other poems, some of which inspired popular Turkish songs, were published from 1938 until 1947 in the Ladino paper *La Boz de Türkiye*. Nom is said to have pioneered the use of the acrostic in Turkish poetry.

OBADYA, ABRAHAM (1923–), Iraqi poet. His verse collections, published in Baghdad and Cairo, include *Wabīl wa-Tal* ("Shower and Dew," 1949) and *Fī Sukūn al-Layl* ("In the Stillness of the Night," 1947), both dedicated to King Faisal II. He emigrated to Israel in 1951.

***RYVEL** (1898–), Tunisian author and educator.

***SANŪ', YA'QŪB** (1834–1912), Egyptian playwright and journalist.

SHAMOSH, YIZḤAK (1912–1968), Syrian author and translator. He practiced law in Aleppo and Damascus, edited *Le Commerce du Levant*, and contributed to literary periodicals in Egypt and the Levant. After settling in Palestine in 1937, he taught Arabic at the Hebrew University and held high posts in Israel's Broadcasting Authority and Ministry of Justice. He was an expert on the modern Arabic short story and the literature of the Arabic diaspora in the U.S.

SHA'SHU', SALIM (1926–), Iraqi poet and journalist. A Baghdad lawyer and teacher, he emigrated to Israel in 1951 and edited the Arabic weekly *al-Manār*, also working for the Arabic section of the Israel Broadcasting Authority. He hailed Israel's military achievements in his nationalist poems. His verse collection *Fī Alam al-Nūr* ("In the World of Light," 1959) was dedicated to President Ben-Zvi.

***SHAUL (Shaool), ANWAR** (1904–), Iraqi poet, author, and journalist.

Bibliography: Y. ben-Ḥanania, in: *Hed ha-Mizraḥ* (Sept. 29, 1943), 12; (Oct. 13, 1943), 6–7; (Oct. 29, 1943), 7; (Nov. 12, 1943), 6–7; idem, in: *Yad la-Koré*, 4 (1958), 14–21, 119–27; E. Marmorstein, in: JJSO, 1 (1959), 187–200; S. Moreh, in: *Middle Eastern Studies*, 3 (April 1967), 283–94; idem, in: *Ha-Mizraḥ he-Ḥadash*, 14, no. 2–3 (1964), 296–309; Ezekiel, *History and Culture of the Bene-Israel in India* (1948), 76–82; D. Salloum, *Change of Thought and Style in Iraqi Literature in the 19th and 20th Centuries* (Ar., 1959); S. Idris, in: *al-Ādāb* (Feb., March, April, Dec., 1953). [SH.M.]

°**ORIGEN** (184–253 C.E.), *Church Father and theologian. Born in Alexandria, Origen was the first Christian scholar to study Hebrew, much of which he learned from Jews. He visited Ereẓ Israel a number of times and came into contact with leading Jewish scholars there. His most influential work was the *Hexapla* (on which he worked from 230 to 240). This was an edition of the Old Testament in six parallel columns. It consisted of: (1) the Hebrew text in Hebrew letters; (2) Hebrew text in a Greek transliteration; four Greek translations: (3) Aquila's literal rendering; (4) Symmachus' precise but idiomatic rendering; (5) the freer translation of the Septuagint (as edited by Origen); and (6) Theodotion's revision of the Septuagint. Origen also wrote a *Tetrapla* (Gr. *τέταρτος* "four") containing the above Greek translations alone. Using the diacritical notations of the Alexandrian scholars Origen marked out passages of the Greek texts which were not in the Hebrew, or which should be excised, and also marked the places where a translation of the Hebrew had been omitted. Origen's purpose in collating these texts was to provide Christian scholars, who referred only to the Greek, with the means to reply to Jews, who used the Hebrew text. Neither the *Hexapla* nor the *Tetrapla* survive in entirety. Origen's work was very influential in the revision of the Septuagint text and in leading toward the unification of the canon of Church and Synagogue by clearly showing which books had and which had not been accepted into the Jewish canon.

Bibliography: E. Wuerthein, *The Text of the Old Testament* (1957), 38–41; R. M. Grant, in: A. J. Toynbee (ed.), *The Crucible of Christianity* (1969), 328–30; E. R. Bevan (ed.), *The Legacy of Israel* (1927), index. [ED.]

ORIHUELA, city in Valencia, E. Spain. When it was captured during the Christian Reconquest by Alfonso X of Castile, the Jew, Jacob ibn Dino, was taken captive by a Christian knight. Abraham ibn Baḥya collected the taxes in Orihuela and nearby Elche between 1381 and 1384. The Jews in Orihuela were evidently baptized during the persecutions of 1391. The movement led by Inés, "the Maiden of *Herrera," in 1500 found adherents among the *Conversos in Orihuela.

Bibliography: Baer, Spain, 1 (1961), 114; Baer, Urkunden, 2 (1936), 536; García Serrano, in: *Boletín de la Academia de la Historia, Madrid*, 104 (1934), 216; López de Meneses, in: *Sefarad*, 14 (1954), 111; Bellot, in: F. Torres Fontes (ed.), *Anales de Orihuela* (1954). [H.B.]

ORLAH (Heb. עָרְלָה; "uncircumcised"), tenth tractate in the order *Zera'im* in the Mishnah, Tosefta, and Jerusalem Talmud. It deals with the law prohibiting the fruit of trees during the first three years after their planting (Lev. 19:23–25). The subject matter of *orlah* being scanty, the tractate includes in its discussions the laws concerning the admixture of many other forbidden products.

The tractate has three chapters. Chapter 1 deals with intention affecting the application of the law; the kind of trees subject to the law; when a tree counts as replanted; if an unidentifiable *orlah* tree grows among other trees; edible parts of a tree not counting as fruit; and the planting or grafting of *orlah* shoots. Chapter 2 discusses the effect on produce of an admixture of *orlah*, *terumah*, etc., both as regards eating and uncleanness. Chapter 3 deals with garments dyed with the shells of *orlah* fruit; when threads of such dyed fabric are woven into a garment; the effect on ovens and food if *orlah* shells are used for fuel; difference between Ereẓ Israel, Syria, and other lands with regard to doubtful *orlah*. Mishnah 2:4 is an early one, apparently predating Shammai since he disagrees about its interpretation (*ibid.* 5), and 2:12 contains a comment by Joezer Ish ha-Birah, who lived during the period of the Second Temple. In the Tosefta *Orlah* consists of a single chapter which corresponds to *mishnayot* 1:1–5, and 3:1, 3, 5, 9. Nevertheless, the *mishnayot* 1:7, 13–15; 2:6; and 3:8 are complemented by Tosefta *Terumot* 5:9–10; 6:5–11; and 8:3, 15ff. Despite this, 17 *mishnayot* in *Orlah* remain without corresponding Tosefta (1:6–8; 2:2–6, 8–12, 17; 3:2, 4, 6). The Jerusalem Talmud deals only with the halakhic aspect of *orlah*. It contains no aggadic material. It was translated into English by H. Danby, in his *The Mishnah* (1933).

Illustration for the tractate *Orlah*, which deals with the prohibition on eating the fruit of a young tree. Engraving by Mich. Richey from a title page of the Hebrew-Latin Mishnah, Amsterdam, 1700–04. Jerusalem, J.N.U.L.

Bibliography: H. Albeck, *Shishah Sidrei Mishnah, Seder Zera'im* (1958²), 291f. [D.J.B.]

ORLAN, ḤAYYIM (1911–), Hebrew journalist and teacher. Born in Poland, Orlan immigrated to Ereẓ Israel in 1931. In 1946 he moved to Cleveland, Ohio, where he taught Hebrew and was active in the Jewish community. Orlan published stories and poems in the Hebrew newspapers of Poland, Israel, and the United States, but his main *genre* was learned articles on modern Hebrew literature, political discourses, and book reviews. He translated into Hebrew the protocol of the First Zionist Congress in Basle (1946) and, together with Isaac Fein, the three-act play of Alexandre Dumas fils, *La Femme de Claude* (*Hadoar*, Feb. 7, 1969, and subsequent issues). Orlan also edited, with an introduction, *Shirei Am* (1963), the folk songs of Abraham Hyman *Friedland.

Bibliography: Kressel, Leksikon, 1 (1965), 52–53. [EI.S.]

ORLAND, HERSHL (1896–1946), Soviet Yiddish writer. Born near Kiev, Orland moved to the city at the age of 22, and began his literary career with the publication of his first short stories, on the life of workers, in the Kiev newspaper, *Komunistishe Fon*. He was a dedicated Communist writer, whose narrative talent was fully appreciated. He wholeheartedly immersed himself in the reconstruction of the socioeconomic framework of Jewish life, the main theme of his work. Orland also edited the Kharkov paper, *Shtern*, and the journal, *Sovetishe Literatur*. When the Jewish *Anti-Fascist Committee was founded, Orland was one of its most active writers. His books include *Grobers* (1930), *Hreblies* (1931), and *Aglomerat* (1935), the last dealing with workers' life in a foundry.

Bibliography: LNYL, 1 (1958), 174–5. [I.M.B.]

ORLAND, YAAKOV (1914–), Hebrew writer. Born in the Ukraine, Orland was taken to Ereẓ Israel in 1921. In 1933 he began publishing poems, critical articles, and translations from English, German, and Yiddish. Several of his plays, both original and translations, were performed in Israel's theaters, including *Hershele Ostropoler* (1966). He also wrote lyrics for songs and was an editor of the periodicals *Ashmoret* and *Sifrut Ẓe'irah*. His books of poetry include *Ilan ba-Ru'aḥ* (1939), *Shirim al Ayit ve-al Yonah* (1946), and *Shirim me-Ereẓ Uẓ* (1963). He translated works by Byron, Oscar Wilde, E. A. Poe, A. A. Milne, Bernard Shaw, John Galsworthy, and Erich Maria Remarque. Several of his poems have appeared in English translation (for a complete list see Goell, Bibliography, index).

Bibliography: Kressel, Leksikon, 1 (1965), 53. [G.K.]

ORLÉANS, town in France, S. of Paris. A Jewish community was established in Orléans before 585. During that year, the Jews of Orléans participated in the welcome which was given to King Gontran and appealed to him to be allowed to rebuild the synagogue, which had previously

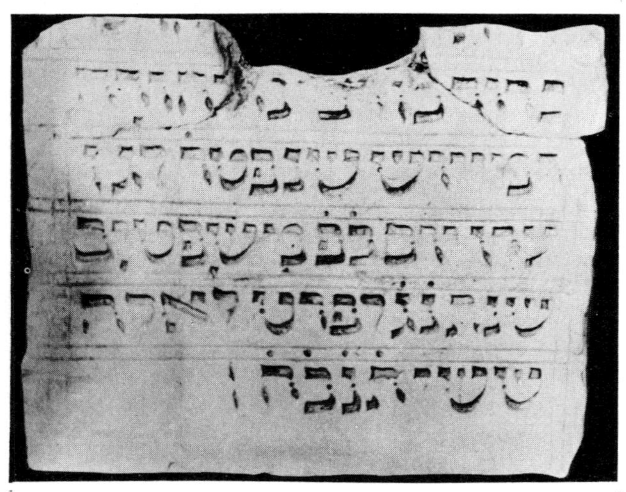

Hebrew epitaph on a tombstone from Orléans, 1293. Orléans, Museum of History and Archaeology.

been destroyed. The community may well have existed earlier, for the second, third, and fourth Councils of Orléans, held in 533, 538, and 541 respectively, had already passed legislation concerning the Jews. During the tenth century, an apostate Orléans Jew, Gautier (Walterius), owned houses in the town. At the beginning of the 11th century, the Jewish community, then quite numerous, was accused of having established relations with Caliph El Ḥakim in order to instigate persecutions of Christians in Jerusalem. The ensuing general persecution of the French Jews struck first in Orléans, from which Jews were expelled for several years. The importance of the Orléans Jewish community is again attested when in 1171 it attempted to succor the *Blois Jewish community at the time of the blood libel. After the expulsion of Jews from the French kingdom in 1182, the synagogue of Orléans was transformed into the St. Sauveur Chapel. The community was reconstituted after Jews were permitted to return to France in 1198; among the Jewish notables imprisoned in the Châtelet of Paris in 1204 were two from Orléans. The Jewish cemetery of Orléans was also used by the small surrounding communities.

The large taxes paid by the Jews of Orléans point to the numerical and economic importance of the community (although the customers for their loans were essentially drawn from among the common people), as well as to the size of the Jewish quarter (Grande Juiverie during the 13th century) and its numerous institutions, especially its two synagogues. After the expulsion of 1306, a new, smaller, community was formed between 1315 and 1322 (or 1323) and again in 1359. As a result of the complaints of the Christian inhabitants, the Jews were confined to a narrow quarter. As was the case in several other cities, notably Paris, the Jews of Orléans were the victims of a popular uprising in February 1382, later crushed by King *Charles VI. It was, however, this same king who in 1394 refused to prolong the residence of Jews in France, thus ending the medieval Jewish community of Orléans. Early in its history Orléans became an important center of Jewish learning. Isaac b. Menahem, second half of the 11th century, was cited by *Rashi for his talmudic commentaries, and was also known as a legal authority. The hymnologist Meir b. Isaac, late 11th century, was, most probably, his son; the latter's son was the biblical commentator Eleazar b. Meir b. Isaac. The most renowned scholar of Orléans was Joseph b. Isaac *Bekhor-Shor. After 1171 the tosafist *Jacob of Orléans emigrated to London, where he became one of the victims of the massacre of 1189. A Jewish community was again established at the beginning of the 19th century; it possessed a small synagogue and, by the close of the century, had about 40 members.

Contemporary Period. In 1971 there were about 500 Jews in Orléans with a synagogue-community center. In May 1969, the Jewish owners of fashion shops in Orléans suddenly found themselves in the midst of a turmoil of strange gossip, which claimed that Christian women who had been trying on dresses had been drugged and spirited away to exotic brothels. The police had absolutely no knowledge of the alleged kidnapping of any female citizen in Orléans, and yet the rumor spread like wildfire that they had been abducted from six shops, all of which were owned by Jews. Schoolgirls were warned by their teachers not to enter the suspect places and husbands would not allow their wives to go into such shops unaccompanied. The rumor persisted for several weeks, dying out only when a full-scale campaign was organized by the national press, and after conferences held by leading personalities both within and outside of Orléans.

Bibliography: Gross, Gal Jud, 30ff.; B. Blumenkranz, *Juifs et chrétiens*... (1960), index; E. Morin, *Rumour in Orleans* (1971). [B.BL./ED.]

ORLIK, EMIL (1870–1932), German painter and graphic designer. Orlik was born in Prague, son of a highly assimilated German Jewish family, and baptized in his youth. He studied in Munich and traveled widely in three continents. From 1903 until his death he was a teacher at the Arts and Crafts Academy in Berlin. Though he made

Self-portrait by Emil Orlik, 1910. Etching and mezzotint, 9½×11½ in. (24×30 cm.). New York, Leo Baeck Institute. Photo Hans R. Lippman, New York.

numerous paintings, he was primarily a master draftsman, and an accomplished printmaker, who excelled in woodcuts, etchings, and lithographs. Orlik was particularly successful in his portraits of celebrated contemporaries. A prolific and indefatigable worker, he left hundreds of prints and thousands of drawings. After his death, the *Kunstverein* in Cologne honored him with a memorial exhibition, despite the fact that the Nazi era had already begun. Orlik's estate might have been destroyed had not his brother-in-law, a banker of Prague, managed to transfer the works to Czechoslovakia, where they were hidden in a house in the woods near Prague for many years. His better-known graphic works are collected in *95 Koepfe von Orlik* (1920), *Handzeichnungen* (1924), and *Kleine Aufsaetze* (1924).

Bibliography: M. Osborn, *Emil Orlik* (Ger., 1920). [A.W.]

ORLIKOW, DAVID (1918–), Canadian politician. Born in Winnipeg, he worked as a pharmacist and served as a school trustee and alderman in Winnipeg from 1945 to 1958. From 1958 to 1962 he was a member of the Manitoba legislature and in 1962 he was elected to the Canadian parliament as a member of the New Democratic Party. Orlikow was a champion of human rights and social welfare. He advocated a comprehensive social security system, including medicare, and adequate pensions, and devoted attention to the imprisoned and mentally ill. He was executive director of the Jewish Labor Committee of Canada. [B.G.K.]

ORLINSKY, HARRY MEYER (1908–), U.S. biblical scholar and philologist. Orlinsky was born in Owen Sound, Ontario, Canada and went to the U.S. in 1931, later becoming a fellow at Dropsie College (1931–35) and Johns Hopkins University (1936–41). He was professor of Bible at the Hebrew Union College-Jewish Institute of Religion in New York City from 1943, chairman of the Society for Biblical Literature (president 1969–70), and chairman of the American Friends of the Israel Exploration Society from 1954.

Harry Meyer Orlinsky, U.S. biblical scholar. Courtesy Hebrew Union College, New York.

Orlinsky was co-translator of a five-volume English translation of Rashi's commentary on the Pentateuch, 1949–50; the only Jewish consultant of the Protestant Revised Standard Version (Old Testament, 1952); and editor of the *Library of Biblical Studies* published by Ktav Publishing House. He was editor in chief of the Jewish Publication Society's new translation of the Pentateuch (1962), to which he wrote a companion volume, *Notes on the New Translation of the Torah* (1969). His other works include *Ancient Israel* (1954; 1969[2]) and *The So-called "Servant of the Lord" and "Suffering Servant" in Second Isaiah 53* (1964), in which he argues that a servant of YHWH, originally innocent of sin and who dies for the punishment of others, is unknown in Jewish thought until the first century. His textual studies of the scrolls from the Judean Desert argue that the St. Mark's Isaiah Scroll (1QIsa[a]) was copied from memory and is not to be given independent value. [Z.G.]

ORLOFF, CHANA (1888–1968), French sculptor. Born in Staro-Konstantinov, Ukraine, Orloff left her native country at the age of 16 for Palestine, but six years later moved to Paris where she remained. She studied at the Ecole des Arts Décoratifs, and her work was exhibited, for the first time, at the Salon d'Automne of 1910. *Modigliani made a portrait

"War and Peace," bronze by Chana Orloff, French sculptor. Mount Kisco, New York, Mr. and Mrs. Leon L. Gildesgame Collection.

of her in 1912. Chana Orloff visited the United States in 1929 and 1938 and exhibited there at the Marie Sterner Gallery, New York, and at the School of the Museum of Fine Arts, Boston. She managed to survive in France during the Nazi occupation although her studio was raided and most of her works there were stolen or destroyed. After the war, she paid several visits to Israel where she made two public monuments: a bronze statue in Ramat Gan depicting the struggle of the Jewish underground and a stone group in Ein Gev. In 1961, the museums in Tel Aviv, Jerusalem, Haifa, and En-Harod honored her with a retrospective exhibition, covering 50 years.

She made many portraits in bronze of well-known contemporaries, such as David Ben-Gurion, Sholem Asch, Shmarya Levin, the actress Hanna Rovina, and the painter Reuven Rubin. She also carved subjects in wood. These include female nudes, mothers with children, men and women sitting or standing, and a variety of birds. Though a contemporary of the cubists, she did not eliminate realistic detail. Her work was realistic and heavily stylized. A mild swing toward abstraction was noticeable in the bronzes she did in the 1950s and 1960s. She could be tenderly lyrical, but also very ironic, especially in her portrait busts. She created for herself an entirely individual mode of expression.

Bibliography: L. Werth, *Chana Orloff* (Fr., 1927); H. Gamzu, *Chana Orloff* (Heb., 1949); G. Talpir, *Chana Orloff* (Heb., 1950). [A.W.]

ORNITZ, SAMUEL BADISCH (1890–1957), U.S. author. Born in New York City, Ornitz was a social worker from 1908 to 1920, and was also employed by the New York Prison Association. In 1919 he wrote a one-act play, *The Sock*, under a pseudonym, but his name became familiar with the success of his novel *Haunch, Paunch, and Jowl* (1923), one of the best-known works produced by the left-wing "proletarian" literary movement in the United States. Its anti-hero, Meyer Hirsch, is an East Sider who rises from poverty to become a shady lawyer, crooked politician, and corrupt judge. Ornitz, a professed atheist, saw no virtues in Jewish immigrant life and wished to end Jewish isolation by a policy of outright assimilation. He defied Jewish opinion with his violently hostile portrayals of Jewish types, notably the money-chasing "allrightniks" detested by contemporary leftists and anti-Semites. Ornitz also depicted the Jewish immigrant generation of the 1880–1914 era in other novels. His books include *Round the World with Jocko the Great* (1925), *A Yankee Passional* (1927), and *Bride of the Sabbath* (1951). In later life Ornitz went to Hollywood, where he wrote scripts for motion pictures.

Bibliography: S. Liptzin, *The Jew in American Literature* (1966), 131–3. [M.H.H.]

ORNSTEIN, ABRAHAM FREDERICK (1836–1895), London-born pioneer minister in Australia and South Africa. After serving the Melbourne Hebrew congregation (1866–75) and being principal of Aria College for training Jewish ministers in Portsmouth, England, Ornstein went to Cape Town in 1882 and headed the congregation there for 13 years. He was particularly interested in education. His efforts to establish a Jewish public school in Cape Town did not meet with enough support, so in 1884 he started a private "Collegiate School" for Jewish boys, which provided both Jewish and general education. Its boarding house also accepted girls from other schools in town. Ornstein ran the school successfully. It closed down after his death. Despite his abilities and sense of dedication, his ministry was marred by a number of controversies resulting from his somewhat inflexible personality, and especially from the clash between his "English" outlook and that of the Eastern European immigrants who were arriving at the Cape in increasing numbers.

Bibliography: L. Herrman, *History of the Jews in South Africa* (1935), 234, 257–66, 269; G. Saron and L. Hotz, *The Jews in South Africa* (1955), 23–26, 28–31, 124; I. Abrahams, *The Birth of a Community* (1955), index. [L.S.]

ORNSTEIN, JACOB MESHULLAM BEN MORDECAI ZE'EV (1775–1839), Galician rabbi and halakhist, son of Mordecai Ze'ev b. Moses *Ornstein. Ornstein, as a young man, married the daughter of Ẓevi Hirsch Wahl of Jaroslaw, who contributed greatly toward his material needs. After Wahl's death Ornstein was proposed as his successor, but because of the violent conflict that the suggestion aroused, he refused to accept the appointment. In 1801 he moved to Zolkiew, where he was appointed rabbi of the town and district. In 1805 he was appointed rabbi of Lemberg (Lvov) and remained there until his death. During his lifetime the Haskalah movement began to spread in Galicia. On the other hand, the ḥasidic movement also gained strength as a result of the establishment of new ḥasidic centers. Although Ornstein, who found himself at the center of these two opposing trends, did not incline to Ḥasidism and was regarded as a *Mitnagged,* he was at the same time opposed to the Haskalah movement and conducted a resolute campaign against it. He was supported in this struggle by his only son, Mordecai Ze'ev, an extremist who was regarded as the driving force in the war against the *maskilim.* Ornstein distrusted the circle of *maskilim* that was formed in Lemberg around Solomon Judah *Rapoport which included N. Krochmal, I. Erter, F. Mieses, and M. Letteris. As a result of the mounting tension between the two sides caused by Rapoport's sharp criticism of Ornstein's *Yeshu'ot Ya'akov* (see below), a ban of excommunication against Rapoport and the leaders of the *maskilim* in Lemberg was issued in 1816. It has been assumed that Ornstein's son Mordecai Ze'ev was its author but that it had his father's approval. The text of the ban refers to the "sins" of the *maskilim* in studying German and studying the Bible with Mendelssohn's commentary. The *maskilim* who ridiculed Ornstein by referring to him as "the Great Inquisitor of Galicia" translated the ban into German and complained to the government that it was illegal, since it had been forbidden to issue such bans in Austria from the time of Emperor Joseph II. As a result Ornstein was compelled publicly to rescind the ban. Rapoport and the *maskilim* reacted to Ornstein's persecution with scathing articles and satires.

Ornstein was regarded as one of the great halakhists of his era, but his main fame rests on his *Yeshu'ot Ya'akov,* novellae and talmudic disquisitions on the whole of the Shulḥan Arukh (OḤ, Zolkiew (1828); YD, *ibid.* (1809); EH, *ibid.* (1809–10)). The four parts of the work, with additions from the author's manuscript and the glosses of his grandson Ẓevi Hirsch, were published in Lemberg (1863). The work is divided into a long and a short commentary; in the latter he merely gives explanations of the Shulḥan Arukh, but in the former he summarizes the views and arguments of the *posekim* while resolving the difficulties of the different novellae by casuistic arguments. Ornstein also wrote, under the same title (which he also used for his Bible commentary), responsa on the four parts of the Shulḥan Arukh (Pietrkov, 1906). Among the questioners and respondents mentioned in it are Moses Sofer (YD, 33; EH, 2) and Aryeh Leib *Horowitz (EH, 20, 26, 29, 30). Ornstein's commentary on the Pentateuch was published in 1907.

His son MORDECAI ZE'EV refused to accept a rabbinical post for many years. He finally accepted an invitation from the Przemysl community to become its rabbi, but died in 1837, before he was able to take up his post. His responsa and novellae are to be found in his father's *Yeshu'ot Ya'akov.*

Mordecai Ze'ev's son, ẒEVI HIRSCH was appointed *av bet din* of Brest-Litovsk, and remained there until 1874, when he had to leave by order of the Russian government on the grounds that he was a foreign national. He was then appointed *av bet din* of Rzeszow. On the death of Joseph Saul *Nathanson in Lemberg, Ẓevi Hirsch was appointed to succeed him and remained there until his death in 1888. Apart from being an outstanding talmudist he also had a wide general education. He treated the *maskilim* and progressives tolerantly and succeeded in attracting them. On the other hand, he was disliked by the Ḥasidim. At the great rabbinical convention of 1882 in Lemberg, he opposed the demands of the extremists (instigated by Simeon Sofer of Cracow) to confirm the text of a statute that would rescind the right of anyone to be elected to the committee of the community if he transgressed the laws of the Shulḥan Arukh, and as a result the proposed statute was rejected. He attempted to explain to Orthodox circles in 1884 that since the Austrian government was about to introduce compulsory general education, it was desirable to organize religious schools. Because of the extremist opposition to any change in the method of the *ḥeder* and its organization, however, the previous educational structure remained in force. Some of his novellae and responsa were published in the second edition of *Yeshu'ot Ya'akov* on the Shulḥan Arukh. After his death, his son-in-law Aryeh Leib Broda published a collection of his responsa under the title *Birkat* ReZeH (Lemberg, 1889; Jerusalem, 1965[2]), together with his own additions and glosses, *Milḥamot Aryeh,* and containing his responsa from the years 1864–79.

Bibliography: Ḥ. N. Dembitzer, *Kelilat Yofi,* 1 (1888), 1506–56a; S. Buber, *Anshei Shem* (1895), 111f., 151, 199; idem, *Kiryah Nisgavah* (1903), 39; M. Weissberg, in: MGWJ, 57 (1913), 519–22; S. M. Chones, *Toledot ha-Posekim* (1910), 286f.; Z. Horowitz, in: *Oẓar ha-Ḥayyim,* 5 (1929), 207f.; M. Balaban, in: *Sefer* *ha-Yovel . . . M. Z. Brode* (1931), 29–32; A. Kamelhar, *Dor De'ah* (1935), 188–96; M. Z. Brode, in: *Keneset . . . le-Zekher Ḥ. N. Bialik*, 8 (1943–44) 104f., 109; Z. Karl, in: *Arim ve-Immahot be-Yisrael*, 1 (1950), 332f., 336; R. Margalioth, in: *Sinai*, 27 (1950), 357–60; 29 (1951), 220; EG, 4 (1956), 217–19, 221, 249, 257, 314–17, 416–18; Klausner, Sifrut, 2 (1952²), index; Zinberg, Sifrut, 6 (1960), index. [J. Ho.]

ORNSTEIN, LEONARD SALOMON (1880–1941), Dutch Zionist and physicist. Born in Nÿmegen, Ornstein became in 1915 professor of mathematical physics and in 1925 of experimental physics at Utrecht University and in 1921 director of the Utrecht Physical Laboratory. In 1929 he was made a member of the Netherlands Academy of Sciences, and in 1939 a knight in the Order of the Netherlands Lion. He was for several years a member and in 1918–1922 chairman of the Executive of the Netherlands Zionist Organization. During the same period he was also a member of the Zionist General Council. From 1925 to 1940 Ornstein was a member of the Board of Governors of the Hebrew University, and in 1933 the first chairman of *Youth Aliyah in Holland. [H.Bo.]

ORNSTEIN, MORDECAI ZE'EV BEN MOSES (d. 1787), Polish rabbi and kabbalist. His father, Moses b. Joske (d. 1764), known as "Rabbi Moses b. Rabbi Joskes," was a member of the community council of Zolkiew. Previously rabbi of Satinov, Kamenka, and Yampol, Podolia, Ornstein was appointed rabbi of Lvov in succession to Solomon b. Moses of Chelm, the author of *Mirkevet ha-Mishneh* (Frankfurt on the Oder, 1851), who moved to Ereẓ Israel. According to Ornstein's tombstone, he had been appointed rabbi of Fuerth just before he died (1787). Ornstein applied himself to the study of Kabbalah and was close in spirit to Ḥasidism, and so was referred to as "the kabbalist and Ḥasid." He is reputed to have studied for a while under Rabbi Dov Baer of Mezhirech. He was known in Lemberg as "The Great Rabbi Mordecai Ze'ev" to distinguish him from his grandson, Mordecai Ze'ev Ornstein. Ornstein did not publish any halakhic works, but his novellae are quoted by his descendants. He gave approbations to many of the works of his contemporaries, and he is referred to in terms of the greatest reverence. Of his sons, the best known are Jacob Meshullam *Ornstein, author of *Yeshu'ot Ya'akov* (1828), and Moses Joshua Hoeschel, rabbi of Taringrad and author of *Yam ha-Talmud* (Lemberg, 1825). Two of his sons-in-law are well known, Aaron ha-Levi Ittinga (the first) and Dov Berish Halperin of Berzan (Brezhany). For over a century, except for a brief gap, all the incumbents of the rabbinate of Lvov were his descendants.

Bibliography: Ḥ. N. Dembitzer, *Kelilat Yofi*, 1 (1888), 144b–146a; S. Buber, *Anshei Shem* (1895), 149–51; idem, *Kiryah Nisgavah* (1903), 59f.; M. Balaban, in: *Sefer ha-Yovel . . . M. Z. Brode* (1931), 25; Z. Karl, in: *Arim ve-Immahot be-Yisrael*, 1 (1950), 329; EG, 4 (1956), 413f. [Y.Al.]

OROBIO DE CASTRO, ISAAC (Balthazar; 1620–1687), philosopher and physician, born in Braganza, Portugal, of Marrano parentage. After studying medicine and philosophy, Orobio became a leading physician and professor of metaphysics at Salamanca. He was subsequently arrested by the Inquisition and charged with secretly practicing Judaism. Orobio was incarcerated for three years, tortured, and finally confessed. Upon his release, he fled to France, where he became professor of pharmacy at Toulouse. In 1662 he moved to Amsterdam where he joined the Jewish community, changed his name to Isaac, and practiced medicine. Orobio, who soon became one of the leading intellectual figures among the Spanish and Portuguese

Isaac Orobio de Castro, a posthumous portrait by Jacobus Groenwolt, Amsterdam, 1727. Amsterdam, Portuguese Jewish community.

refugees, wrote poetry and philosophical treatises in defense of Judaism.

His first important work consists of letters against the rationalistic defense of Judaism in answer to Alonso de Cepeda of Brussels. Among his best-known works is *Certamen philosophicum propugnatae veritatis divinae ac naturalis* (1684), a rationalistic and scholastic attempt to refute the philosophy of *Spinoza, and like Spinoza's *Ethics* written in a series of theorems. The work was also published in Fénelon's *Refutation des erreurs de Benoît de Spinosa* (1731). Orobio became acquainted with the Dutch Protestant liberal preacher, Philip van Limborch, in Amsterdam, who, impressed by Orobio's accounts of how the Spanish Inquisition functioned, used them as the chief case history in his Latin history of the Inquisition. Limborch, however, was disturbed by Orobio's anti-Christian arguments. They held a debate in the presence of John Locke which was published in 1687 *(Pauli a Limborch de Veritate Religionis Christianae, amica collatio cum erudito Judaeo)* along with the first issue of Uriel da *Costa's autobiography. Locke wrote a long review of the debate for the *Bibliothèque universelle* (vol. 7). Orobio's major anti-Christian work is *Prevenciones divinas contra la vana idolatria de las Gentes;* portions of this were published by Baron d'Holbach in French, as part of his anti-religious campaign, under the title *Israel vengé* (London, 1770). A greatly toned-down version, translated by Grace *Aguilar, was printed in English in 1842 as *Israel Defended.*

Most of Orobio's works were not published, but circulated in manuscript among the European Jewish communities. The largest collection exists in the Biblioteek Ets Ḥayyim in Amsterdam; others are in the Rosenthaliana collection in Amsterdam, in Paris, London, Oxford, and New York. An acute metaphysician, Orobio de Castro utilized materials from the Spanish scholastics of the 16th and 17th centuries to defend Judaism against freethinkers like Juan de *Prado and Spinoza, against orthodox Christians, and against religious liberals like Limborch. Certain of Orobio's arguments against Christian theology are very close to some of Spinoza's against the plurality of substance. He made interesting efforts to provide a philosophical justification for Judaism in 17th-century terms, and, in contrast to Spinoza, to show the compatibility of reason with the traditional faith.

Bibliography: Kayserling, Bibl, 81–83; Graetz, in: MGWJ, 16 (1867), 321–30; Orobio de Castro, *La Observancia de la Divina Ley de Mosseh,* ed. by M. B. Amzalak (1925), xviii–xxxix; J. de Carvalho, *Oróbio de Castro e o espinosismo* (1937); I. S. Revah, *Spinoza et le Dr. Juan de Prado* (1959), 84–153; Roth, Marranos, index.

[R.H.P.]

°**OROSIUS, PAULUS** (b. c. 385), Christian author of *Historiarum adversum paganos libri septem* ("Seven Books of Histories Against the Pagans"), a history of the world from the Creation to 417, written at the suggestion of St. Augustine as a supplement to the latter's *De civitate Dei* (book 3). It attempted to prove that the Roman Empire had suffered as many calamities before the rise of Christianity as it did afterward.

Among details concerning the Jews which he mentions are: the reasons given by Pompeius Trogus and Tacitus for the expulsion of the Jews from Egypt; the establishment of a sizable Jewish community in Hyrcania near the Caspian Sea in the fourth century B.C.E.; the capture of Jerusalem by Pompey; the plundering of the Temple by Crassus Licinius; the embassy to Caligula led by Philo; the relief of a famine (of Christians, surprisingly) in Jerusalem by Helena, queen of Adiabene (who, according to Orosius, was a Christian convert); the expulsion of the Jews from Rome by Claudius; the Jewish revolt against the Romans in 66–73 (Orosius, in common with Sulpicius Severus and in opposition to Josephus, claims that Titus gave the order to set fire to the Temple); Domitian's persecution of the Jews; the Jewish revolt against Trajan (important for confirming and supplementing Eusebius' account and now verified by inscriptions and papyri); the Bar Kokhba rebellion (in connection with which it is stated that the Jews tortured the Christians because they would not join the revolt); and the suppression of a Jewish, Samaritan, and Adiabenian revolt by Septimius Severus. Orosius' aim is essentially apologetic and his work is superficial and fragmentary. It is heavily indebted to others, especially Livy, Pompeius Trogus, Josephus, Tacitus, Eusebius, and Eutropius. His history is of limited value, except for contemporaneous events or where, as in the case of a large part of Livy, his sources are lost.

The following are the English translations of his writings: I. W. Raymond, *Seven Books of History against the Pagans* (1936); R. J. Deferrari, *Seven Books of History against the Pagans* (1964).

Bibliography: Reinach, Textes, 325, n. 1; Pauly-Wissowa, 35 (1939), 1185–95.

[L.H.FE.]

OROT (Heb. אוֹרוֹת; "Lights"), moshav in southern Israel near Kiryat Malakhi, affiliated with Tenu'at ha-Moshavim. Founded in 1952 by members of Ha-Ikkar ha-Oved Organization from the United States, the moshav cultivates irrigated field and garden crops and dairy cattle. In 1970 it had 240 inhabitants.

[E.O.]

ORPAH (Heb. עָרְפָּה), Moabite woman. Elimelech and Naomi, driven by famine from Beth-Lehem in Judah, settled in Moab. After Elimelech's death, their two sons, *Mahlon and Chilion, married Orpah and *Ruth. After her two sons died, Naomi set out for home and tried to persuade her daughters-in-law to remain behind in Moab, their native land. Orpah obeyed, while Ruth insisted on accompanying her mother-in-law (Ruth 1:4–14).

[N.M.S.]

In the Aggadah. Orpah was a daughter of Eglon, king of Moab (Ruth R. 2:9). She was called Orpah because she turned her back (*oref,* "nape of the neck") on her mother-in-law (Ruth R. 2:9). She is identified with Harafu, the mother of four Philistinian giants of whom Goliath was one (II Sam. 21:18). They were vouchsafed to her because she shed four tears for Naomi but all of them were slain by David (Sotah 42b). Goliath's punishment was delayed for 40 days (I Sam. 17:16), as a reward for Orpah accompanying Naomi on the way for 40 paces (Ruth R. 2:20).

Orpah was killed by David's general, Abishai, when she attempted to prevent him reaching her son Ishbibenob (Sanh. 95a).

[ED.]

Bibliography: Ginsberg, Legends, index; I. Ḥasida, *Ishei ha-Tanakh* (1964), 353.

ORPHAN. The meaning of the word *yatom* ("orphan") as found in the traditional literature varies in accordance with the context in which it is found. If reference is being made to the social treatment of the orphan—the tragedy of his plight and his emotional vulnerability—no distinction is made whether the child has been orphaned of his father or of his mother (Maim. Yad, De'ot 6:10). If, however, reference is being made to the special privileges accorded the orphan by the civil code, then only the fatherless child is meant (Resp. Mahayashdam, nos. 196, 454).

Social Background. The Bible is particularly concerned with the helplessness of the orphan. The command to render him justice and the prohibition against oppressing him are reiterated constantly. The great solicitude for his defenselessness is reflected in God's role as his protector: "A father of the fatherless, and a judge of the widows, is God in His holy habitation" (Ps. 68:6; cf. 10:14). In conjunction with the levite, the resident alien, and the widow, the orphan is frequently cited as the object of charity and the subject of social legislation (e.g., Deut. 16:11 and 14; 24:19–21; 26:12–13). The biblical admonitions with regard to the orphan and their specific modes of implementation as found throughout talmudic literature have been summarized by Maimonides as follows (Maim. Yad, De'ot 6:10):

> A man ought to be especially heedful of his behavior toward widows and orphans, for their souls are exceedingly depressed and their spirits low. Even if they are wealthy, even if they are the widow and orphans of a king, we are specifically enjoined concerning them, as it is said, "Ye shall not afflict any widow or orphan" (Ex. 22:21). How are we to conduct ourselves toward them? One may not speak to them otherwise than tenderly. One must show them unvarying courtesy; not hurt them physically with hard toil, nor wound their feelings with hard speech. One must take greater care of their property than of one's own. Whoever irritates them, provokes them to anger, pains them, tyrannizes over them, or causes them loss of money, is guilty of a transgression, and all the more so if one beats them or curses them. Though no stripes are inflicted for this transgression, its punishment is explicitly set forth in the Torah [in the following terms], "My wrath shall wax hot, and I will slay you with the sword" (Ex. 22:23). He Who created the world by His word made a covenant with widows and orphans that, when they will cry out because of violence, they will be answered; as it is said, "If thou afflict them in any wise—for if they cry at all unto Me, I will surely hear their cry" (Ex. 22:22). The above only applies to cases where a person afflicts them for his own ends. But if a teacher punishes orphan children in order to teach them Torah or a trade, or lead them in the right way—this is permissible. And yet he should not treat them like others, but make a distinction in their favor. He should guide them gently, with the utmost tenderness and courtesy, as it is said, "For the Lord will plead their cause" (Prov. 22:23). [In all of these rules] there is no distinction between an orphan bereft of a father or one bereft of a mother. To what age are they to be regarded in these respects as orphans? Till they reach the age when they no

longer need an adult on whom they depend to train them and care for them, and when each of them can provide for all his wants, like other grown-up persons.

Bringing Up. Taking an orphan into one's home and raising him are regarded in the Talmud as most praiseworthy: "Whoever brings up an orphan in his home, Scripture ascribes it to him as though he had begotten him" (Sanh. 19b). Such acts constitute uninterrupted *ẓedakah* ("charity"). "Happy are they that keep justice, that do righteousness at all times [Ps. 106:3]—Is it possible to do righteousness at all times? . . . This refers to a man who brings up an orphan boy or orphan girl in his house and enables them to marry" (Ket. 50a). For more particulars on this aspect see *Adoption.

Maintenance and Succession. The Talmud shows great concern for the claims of minor children to support from their father's estate. Unlike Persian authorities, the rabbis recognized no legal differences between children of "privileged" or "secondary" wives, and extended protection even to a man's proved illegitimate offspring (see *Maintenance, *Parent and Child, **Yuḥasin*). They also extended the legal protection of orphan girls by seeing to it that each **ketubbah* should specifically pledge the bridegroom's estate for the support of his surviving minor daughters (*ketubbat benan nokevan*), and, in the absence of his pledge, by construing the omission as an error. Ultimately, the right of female orphans to support came to overshadow the claims of all other heirs, and, if need be, the entire estate was used for this purpose (Ket. 4:11; 13:3; TJ, Git. 5:3–4; and commentaries; see *Succession.). In the case of impoverished orphan children whose father left little or no property, the Talmud holds the community responsible for their support, for marrying them off, and for providing them with the means to live economically independent lives. Communal funds were to be used to rent and furnish a house for a young man and to fit out a girl with clothing and a minimum dowry. If the communal funds were low, the orphan girl was given priority over the boy. If the community chest could afford to do so, the provisions provided for the orphan were made in accordance with his social position and the former manner of life to which he had been accustomed (Ket. 6:5 and 67b).

Guardianship. "The court is the father of orphans"; if a man died without appointing a guardian for his minor children, the court must do so (Yad, Naḥalot 10:5; cf. BK 37a). For more particulars see *Apotropos.

Exemptions from some Laws. Minor orphans and their property are exempt from the ordinary laws of overreaching (**ona'ah;* Sh. Ar., ḤM 109:4–5), *usury (*ribbit de-Rabbanan;* YD 160:18), the seventh-year recession of debts (*prosbul; ḤM 67:28), communal taxation for the charity fund (*ẓedakah*, with specified exceptions; BB 8a and Sh. Ar., YD 248:3). For further particulars see *Taxation.

Procedure and Litigation. Whenever orphans of any age are involved in litigation regarding their father's property or transactions, judicial practice is to enter on their behalf all pleas and all arguments that their father could have entered (BB 23a). See *Pleas; *Practice and Procedure.

See also *Child Marriage; *Execution (Civil Law); *Legal Capacity.

Bibliography: M. Cohn, in: *Zeitschrift fuer vergleichende Rechtswissenschaft*, 37 (1919–20), 417–45; Gulak, Yesodei, 1 (1922), 37, 154 n. 11; 3 (1922), 147ff.; 4 (1922), 43, 140; L. M. Epstein, *The Jewish Marriage Contract* (1927), 121–43, 175–92; Herzog, Instit, 1 (1936), 173f.; Baron, Social², 2 (1952), 253, 271; 5 (1957), 321 n. 81. [A.KIR.]

ORSHA, city in Vitebsk oblast, Belorussian S.S.R. Already in existence during the 16th century, the community of Orsha was subordinated to that of *Brest-Litovsk. In 1643 Isaiah Nahumowicz of Orsha was mentioned among the tax lessees of Lithuania. In the charter of privileges granted by King John II Casimir to the Jews (1649), Orsha is numbered among the large communities of the country. In 1765, 368 Jews in Orsha paid poll tax. There were 1,662 Jews in 1847 and 7,383 (56% of the total population) in 1897. In October 1905 over 30 Jews in the town lost their lives in a pogrom. Although in 1910 there were 9,842 Jews in Orsha, the community began to decline under the Soviet regime. In 1926 there were 6,780 Jews (30% of the total population). The Germans occupied Orsha in the middle of July 1941. At the end of 1941 thousands of Jews were shot in the Jewish cemetery. The Jewish population was estimated at about 1,000 in 1970, but there was no organized religious life.

Bibliography: *Delo o pogrome v Orshe* (1908); *Die Judenpogrome in Russland*, 2 (1909), 467–87. [Y.S.]

ORSHANSKI, ILYA (Elijah) GRIGORYEVICH (1846–1875), journalist, jurist, and historian in Russia. Orshanski, who was born in Yekaterinoslav (now Dnepropetrovsk), received both a traditional Jewish and a general education. He completed law studies at the University of Odessa in 1868, and was subsequently offered a professorship there on condition that he embrace Christianity, a condition which he unhesitatingly rejected. Orshanski's first literary endeavors appeared in the Hebrew newspapers **Ha-Meliẓ* and **Ha-Karmel*. From 1869 to 1871 he served as assistant editor of the Russian-Jewish newspaper *Den*, which was closed down in 1871 by government decree because of an article Orshanski wrote on the pogroms in Odessa of that year. In his article he openly accused the government of responsibility for the pogroms and urged the Jews to demand legal satisfaction and compensation for injuries sustained.

Ilya Grigoryevich Orshanski, Russian legal historian, Jerusalem, J.N.U.L., Schwadron Collection.

Before the newspaper was closed down, Orshanski published in it a series of articles on the legal status of the Russian Jews and their economic and social condition. These essays, among others, were published in two volumes entitled *Yevrei v Rossii* ("The Jews in Russia," 1872, 1877²) and *Russkoye zakonodatelstvo o yevreyakh* ("Russian Legislation Affecting the Jews," 1877). Despite their contemporary propagandist objectives, these studies are among the most noteworthy contributions to the history of the Jews in Russia. When discussing the economic structure of the Jews in Russia, Orshanski was the first to refrain from indulging in the defense, apology, and criticism customarily leveled by authors of the Enlightenment (*Haskalah) at Russian Jewry. His impartial, scientific analysis clarified the economic foundations of Jewish life in Russia and enabled him to determine from a historical point of view the place of the Jew in the national economy, while his keen legal mind enabled him to examine the Russian legislation affecting Jews, to trace its origins and motivations, and to demonstrate its medieval character and spirit. His "Russian Legislation Affecting the Jews" not only contains a vast amount of legal information but is also a first attempt to describe systematically the historical development of Russian legislation.

Orshanski also wrote a comprehensive, if critical essay, "*Mysli o khasidizme*" ("Reflections on Ḥasidism," in his *Yevrei v Rossii* (1877[2]), 311–46, and also in *Yevreyskaya Biblioteka*, vol.1, 1871), examining the growth and development of Ḥasidism against the economic and social background of the Jews in Ukraine in the 18th century.

In the last years of his life, Orshanski devoted his time and his pen to research and writing on general Russian law. The resultant studies, published posthumously in three volumes, gained a high reputation in the field of Russian jurisprudence, and are still considered among the finest examples of Russian juridical literature of the time. Because of his failing health Orshanski went to Germany, where he spent several years before he returned to Russia in the spring of 1875.

Bibliography: M. G. Morgulis, *Ilya Grigoryevich Orshanski i yego literaturnaya deyatelnost* (1904); E. M. Morgulis, *I. Orshanski, 1846–1875: Yego zhizn i literaturnaya deyatelnost* (1898). [S.K.]

ORSOVA (Rum. **Orşova**), town in Severin province, S.W. Rumania; until 1918 part of Hungary. Since Orsova was a border town between Hungary and Rumania, settlement of Jews was prohibited until the first half of the 19th century. After the prohibition was lifted, Jewish merchants and craftsmen, mainly from western Hungary, began to settle there. A community was founded in the old town in 1876, affiliated with the organization of Neologist communities. A synagogue was erected in 1878. The oldest tombstone in the Jewish cemetery dates from 1879. Between the world wars the community was prosperous, its members including merchants, craftsmen, physicians, and lawyers. This period saw the development of ramified Zionist activity. Activities were guided by the local rabbi, K. Löwenkopf, who held office from 1928 until 1945, when he emigrated to Palestine. In September 1942 Jewish property was confiscated by the Fascist regime, and many of the men were conscripted for forced labor, while others were expelled to *Transnistria. The Jewish population, 192 in 1930, fell to 135 in 1942 and 10 in 1947. By 1970 emigration to Israel and other places had reduced it to 20.

Bibliography: E. Deutsch, in: *Almanahul Evreesc*, 3 (1938), 141–52 (Ger.); K. Löwenkopf, in: *Uj Kelet* (Feb. 17, 1967).

[Y.M.]

ORT (initials of Rus. **Obshchestvo Rasprostraneniya Truda sredi Yevreyev,** originally meaning "Society for Manual [and Agricultural] Work [among Jews]," and later—from 1921—"Society for Spreading [Artisan and Agricultural] Work [among Jews]"), organization for the promotion and development by vocational training of skilled trades and agriculture among Jews. It was initiated by a "private letter" sent out in April 1880 to the Jews of the towns of Russia, signed by S. S. *Poliakov, Baron Horace *Guenzberg, A. J. Zak, L. M. *Rosenthal, and M. F. *Friedland, concerning the permission granted by Czar Alexander II "to collect a fund for a philanthropic purpose . . ." The Jewish population in all parts of the country was called upon to contribute to the fund which was intended "to support and develop the existing vocational schools for Jews, to help open new schools, to help the Jewish agricultural colonies, model farms, and agricultural schools." Response to the letter was widespread. A capital of 204,000 rubles was quickly collected. Over 25 years (1880–1905), ORT raised the sum of one million rubles. The interest from this sum and the dues paid by its wealthy members supported ORT in that period. The sum was lost in the 1917 Revolution. During this initial period ORT's legal status was uncertain. It was not until 1906 that it received regular legal authorization.

Figure 1. ORT school in Kaunas, Lithuania, before World War II. Courtesy Yad Vashem, Y. Kamson Collection, Jerusalem.

The 90-year history of ORT can be divided into four (principal) periods:

1880–1920. At first ORT functioned in Russia only, on a small scale. One of its aims in this period was to assist craftsmen by transferring them from the *Pale of Settlement to the Russian interior. The committee of ORT decided upon the establishment of small workshops for trades such as tailoring, shoemaking, or carpentry within a *talmud torah* or orphanage, or settled requests from needy persons. A large-scale campaign "Help Through Work" was launched between 1914 and 1916, helping needy Jews who had been driven out of their homes in wartime to find employment in the new places where they settled.

1920–1945. In 1921 ORT was established in Berlin as an international organization with the name World ORT Union. From a purely philanthropic organization it increasingly became a basic social movement in Jewish life. Subsequently ORT was active in the areas formerly within the Russian Empire—Poland, Lithuania, Latvia, and Bessarabia—as well as in Germany, France, Bulgaria, Hungary, and Rumania. This work by ORT had a considerable influence not only on the masses most directly involved, but also on Jewish communities of the so-called

Figure 2. ORT school in São Paulo, Brazil, 1947. Courtesy S. P. Link, Ḥavaẓẓelet ha-Sharon. Photo L. Liberman, São Paulo.

Figure 3. ORT Central Institute for Teacher and Technician Training, Geneva.

"helping countries," which had been invited to join the ORT movement, to support it financially, and to help it expand and consolidate its activities. Between the two wars, ORT's global work was directed by an international committee headed by Leon *Bramson, former member of the *Duma, with the help of David *Lvovich and Aaron *Syngalowski. The latter inspired the ideology of ORT and spread the idea of manual work among Jews, stressing the need for a change in the economic structure of Jewish life. The committee established ORT organizations in the United States, South Africa, Canada, South America, and many other places.

Until 1938, the Soviet Union was also an important area of ORT activity. ORT was the first organization in the Soviet Union to assist (from 1922) in the rehabilitation of Jewish farmers in the Ukraine, who had suffered severe losses, both in lives and to their farms, during World War I and the Civil War. ORT then cooperated with Komzet (see *Russia, under the Soviet regime). It assisted in the transference of many Jews in Belorussia to occupation in agriculture. Assistance to Jewish settlers was provided in Bessarabia, where ORT's activities in 1928 extended to 604 families in 37 agricultural settlements. By this year ORT had aided a total of 141 settlements with 4,737 families (c. 20,000 persons) cultivating agricultural land amounting to approximately 40,000 dessiatine (c. 108,000 acres), as shown by the following table:

Country	Number of Settlements	Number of Families	Agricultural Land (in dessiatines)
Soviet Union	86	3,222	32,232
Poland	18	911	3,100
Bessarabia	37	604	3,631
Total	141	4,737	38,963 (105,200 acres)

A report of 1934 shows that in the Soviet Union ORT operated 67 agricultural colonies, with 3,100 families or almost 10,000 persons, 47 factories and cooperatives in cities and kolkhozes, employing more than 5,000 persons, as well as many adult courses and workshops. In Poland there were 49 schools for adolescents and adult courses with over 2,000 students in addition to 12 agricultural colonies. There was also an ORT network in Rumania, Lithuania, Latvia, Hungary, Bulgaria, France, and Germany.

One of the problems which ORT tackled was to help working Jewish youth and craftsmen to integrate into the industrialization especially affecting the Eastern European countries after World War I. ORT also undertook to provide specialist training for certain professions in which, under the legislation approved by the countries of Eastern Europe (as in Poland in 1927), it was necessary to pass an examination. In the Soviet Union assistance was given to Jews who, as a result of the changed Soviet economic structure, were deprived of their occupational status (*lishentsi*), and were compelled to turn to new sources of livelihood, especially crafts.

An important sphere of ORT activity was to provide Jewish craftsmen with necessary implements. In 1920–23 ORT established a central buying agency for providing implements and machines to craftsmen who had lost them during and after World War I, as well as new materials. In 1924 a similar institution to replace the buying agency was opened in London named the ORT Tool Supply Corporation, with branches in Warsaw, Kovno (Kaunas), Riga, and Czernowitz (Chernovtsy), and in the Soviet Union.

1945–1960. The programmatic and, in particular, the geographical changes which ORT experienced during these 15 years were a result of the constantly changing economic and political situation, and especially the migration affecting the Jewish communities in various countries. In accompanying the masses of Jewish refugees and emigrants to the countries where they found new homes, ORT entered into yet more Jewish communities in Europe, Africa, Asia, and the Americas.

IN ISRAEL. Israel was the only country where the ORT idea of manual work did not need to be propagated, as it was deeply rooted there by the pioneers of the First and Second Aliyah, as well as by the *ḥalutzim* who arrived in Ereẓ Israel between the two wars. The establishment of ORT in Israel followed rapidly after the creation of the state, but former students of ORT had been settling in Palestine from the 1920s. In 1949, shortly after starting activity, ORT opened vocational courses for new

Figure 4. Student at an ORT school in France. Courtesy Joint Distribution Committee.

immigrants in Pardes Ḥannah, manual-training workshops in the children's village of *Ben Shemen, and the first vocational school sections in Jerusalem, Tel Aviv, Reḥovot, Ramleh, Jaffa, and in the yeshivah in Kefar Avraham. By 1970 ORT Israel was by far ORT's most important network. Since its establishment, ORT Israel has trained more than 70,000 skilled workers, technicians, and other specialists. In 1970 ORT covered some 40% of the secondary vocational training in Israel, working in close partnership with the Ministries of Education and Labor, and with many municipalities.

From 1960. ORT had resumed work in Poland in 1957, having interrupted its activity in 1949. More than 16,000 people were trained in the decade between 1957 and 1967, when its work was again suspended.

The basic idea and aims of ORT had remained unchanged in the years between the 1920s and the 1950s. Minor changes occurred in form and work methods, varying with the standard of living and technical development in the countries of operation and, to an even larger extent, with the economic condition and mentality of the Jewish communities there. In those years ORT carried out an important educational task. It spread its principles of work among the Jews of Algeria, Morocco, Tunisia, Iran, and India, helping to convince them that learning a trade was the surest means to acquire economic independence. ORT's work of enlightenment, and the ever improving situation of the qualified tradesman, as well as the good reputation achieved by ORT schools, made vocational training for youth accepted even in the most distant Jewish communities. By the mid-1950s there were so many applications for admission to ORT vocational schools that there were not enough vacancies. After 1960 ORT increasingly emphasized technical rather than vocational training and new skills including automation and computers.

During its 90 years of existence, over 1,000,000 people have benefited from ORT schools. ORT national organizations existed in more than 30 countries. In addition to the training programs for Jews, programs of technical assistance to developing countries in Africa, Asia, and South America have been undertaken at the request and with the help of several governments, including those of the United States, Israel, Switzerland, and the Scandinavian countries. The World ORT Union headquarters are in Geneva. In 1970 William Haber (U.S.) was president of its central board and Daniel *Mayer (France) was chairman of the executive committee; M. A. Braude (U.S.) was director general, and Vladimir Halperin (France) was director.

Figure 5. Auto mechanics class at the ORT vocational high school, Ḥolon, Israel.

Bibliography: *80 Years of ORT*, Historical Materials, Documents and Reports (1960); J. Rader, *By the Skill of their Hands, the Story of ORT* (1970). [V.Ha./Ed.]

ORTA, GARCIA DE (c. 1500–1568), Portuguese Marrano scientist and physician. Born in Castelo de Vide, he studied medicine at Salamanca and Alcalá and taught at Lisbon University. Garcia de Orta left for India in 1534. During his long stay in Goa, he served as physician to the Portuguese viceroys and leading Christian dignitaries, as well as the Muslim ruler Burhān al-Dīn Niẓām al-Mulk. In recognition of his services, the Portuguese viceroy bestowed on him, probably in 1548, the island of *Bombay, then a small fishing village.

Garcia de Orta's great work, *Coloquios dos Simples e drogas he Cousas Medicinais da India* (Goa, 1563; "Colloquies on the Simples and Drugs of India" 1913), made him "the first European writer on tropical medicine and a pioneer in pharmacology." This work, written in Portuguese in the form of a dialogue, was approved by the Inquisition and recommended by the official physician of the viceroy, Luiz de Camões. It was hailed as one of the chief cultural achievements of the 16th century, a work which brought the greatest honor to the author's country, Portugal. Garcia de Orta was long believed to be Christian, but the *Acts of the Inquisition*, published in 1934, made it clear that he was a militant Converso who had lived a dual religious life throughout his 30 years in Goa and had possibly gone there in the hope of escaping the Inquisition. He was posthumously condemned by the Inquisition in 1580, and his remains exhumed and cast into the sea.

Bibliography: W. J. Fischel, *Garcia de Orta and the Exodus of Jews from Spain and Portugal to India* (1970); Carvalho, in: *Revista da Universidade de Coimbra*, 12 (1934), 61–246; Revah, *ibid.* (1960); H. Friedenwald, *The Jews and Medicine* (1944), index; C. R. Boxer, *Two Pioneers of Tropical Medicine* (1963). [W. J. F./J. O. L.]

ORTEN, JIŘI, pseudonym of Jiří Ohrenstein (1919–1941), Czech poet. His first poems, published in literary reviews before 1939, attracted immediate attention because of their novel existentialist approach and surprisingly mature form. Orten went into hiding after the Nazi invasion, and his later works were written under constant fear of discovery. Within two years, he managed to complete four books of poetry: *Čítanka jaro* ("Primer of Spring," 1939), *Cesta k mrazu* ("The Road to the Frost," 1940), *Ohnice* (1941), and *Jeremiášův pláč* ("Jeremiah's Lament," 1941). Orten's friends arranged their publication, ascribing their authorship to "Karel Jílek" or "Jiří Jakub." He was run over and killed by a German army car on a Prague street. Two other volumes of Orten's poetry, *Zcestí* ("The Wrong Way") and *Elegie*, appeared in the definitive edition of his verse after World War II.

Bibliography: V. Černý, in: *Dilo Jiřího Ortena*, 1 (1947), 443–7; J. Kunc, *Slovník českých spisovatelů beletristu* (1957); Eisner, in: *Věstník židovské náboženské obce v Praze* (1948), 236. [Av.D.]

ORTHODOXY. The term "Orthodoxy" first appeared in respect of Judaism in 1795, and became widely used from the beginning of the 19th century in contradistinction to the *Reform movement in Judaism. In later times other terms, such as "Torah-true," became popular. Yet, in general, Orthodox came to designate those who accept as divinely inspired the totality of the historical religion of the Jewish people as it is recorded in the Written and Oral Laws and codified in the Shulḥan Arukh and its commentaries until recent times, and as it is observed in practice according to the teachings and unchanging principles of the *halakhah*. Orthodoxy as a well-defined and separate phenomenon within Jewry crystallized in response to the challenge of the changes which occurred in Jewish society in Western and Central Europe in the first half of the 19th century: Reform, the *Haskalah, and trends toward secularization. Those who opposed change and innovation felt it necessary to emphasize their stand as guardians of the Torah and its commandments under altered conditions and to find ways to safeguard their particular way of life. [N.K.]

Orthodox Judaism considers itself the authentic bearer of the religious Jewish tradition which, until *Emancipation, held sway over almost the entire Jewish community. The term Orthodoxy is actually a misnomer for a religious orientation which stresses not so much the profession of a strictly defined set of dogmas, as submission to the authority of *halakhah*. Orthodoxy's need for self-definition arose only when the mold into which Jewish life had been cast during the period of self-sufficient existence of Jewish society had been completely shattered. Orthodoxy looks upon attempts to adjust Judaism to the "spirit of the time" as utterly incompatible with the entire thrust of normative Judaism which holds that the revealed will of God rather than the values of any given age are the ultimate standard.

At the very dawn of Emancipation, many Orthodox leaders foresaw the perils which the breakdown of the ghetto walls incurred for Jewish survival. Some of them were so apprehensive about the newly available political, social, and economic opportunities, which they felt would make it almost impossible for the Jew to maintain his distinctive national and spiritual identity, that they went so far as to urge the Jewish communities to reject the privileges offered by Emancipation. Others, while willing to accept the benefits of political emancipation, were adamant in their insistence that there be no change in the policy of complete segregation from the social and cultural life of the non-Jewish environment. R. Ezekiel *Landau was so fearful that exposure to the culture of the modern world might ultimately result in total assimilation of the Jew that he proclaimed a ban on the reading of Moses *Mendelssohn's translation of the Pentateuch, even though Mendelssohn had advocated strict observance of the *halakhah*. Fear of assimilation was intensified by a number of developments, seen as alarming, ranging from numerous instances of outright conversion to Christianity to the efforts on the part of the Reform movement to transform radically the character of Judaism in order to facilitate the total integration of the Jew within modern society.

The Orthodox leadership believed that the aesthetic innovations which characterized the first phase of the Reform movement were motivated by the desire to model the synagogue on the pattern of the Protestant Church—a move that was regarded by its advocates as indispensable for gaining for the Jew full acceptance by his Christian neighbors. The claim that the introduction of organ music or the substitution of prayers in the vernacular for those in Hebrew did not violate talmudic law was refuted by 18 leading rabbinic authorities who joined in writing the book *Elleh Divrei ha-Berit* (Altona, 1819). The Orthodox community, intuitively realizing that liturgical reforms were only the beginning of a long-range process designed to change the tenets and practices of Judaism so as to remove all barriers against full immersion in the majority culture, reacted with an all-out effort to preserve the status quo. The slightest tampering with tradition was condemned.

Orthodoxy in this sense first developed in Germany and in Hungary (see Samson Raphael *Hirsch; *Neo-Orthodoxy). As its religious and political ideology crystallized, it emphasized both its opposition to those who advocated religious reform and the essential differences in its outlook and way of life from that of the reformers. At the same time, it refused to countenance any possibility of cooperation with those advocating different viewpoints. Herein lay Orthodoxy's main impetus toward organizational separation, a trend epitomized in Germany after 1876 when separation from the established community became legal, thus permitting the formation of the "separatist Orthodoxy" (*Trennungsorthodoxie*). This trend was opposed by R. Isaac Dov *Bamberger, one of the outstanding German Orthodox rabbis of his day. Underlying the opposition to secession was the reluctance to jeopardize the unity of the Jewish people. Historically, membership in the Jewish community was never regarded merely as a matter of voluntary identification with a religious denomination. One's status as a Jew was not acquired through the profession of a particular creed. With the exception of converts, the privileges and responsibilities devolving upon a member of the people of the Covenant derive from the fact that he was born a Jew. To this day Orthodoxy has not been able to resolve the dilemma that a considerable section of Jewry today no longer obey the *halakhah*. There are those who lean toward a policy of withdrawal, lest they be responsible for the implicit "recognition" of the legitimacy of non-Orthodox ideologies. Others, so concerned with preserving the unity of the Jewish people, advocate involvement of Orthodoxy in the non-Orthodox Jewish community even at the risk that their policies might be misconstrued as a willingness to condone non-Orthodox approaches. It was, ironically, the issue of separation that precipitated most of the internal conflict that has plagued Orthodoxy. In its early history, *Agudat Israel was torn asunder by the controversy over whether Orthodox Jews should be permitted to take a leading part in the organization if they, at the same time, also belonged to groups in which non-Orthodox Jews were allowed to play a prominent role. The influence of the Hungarian element finally swayed Agudat Israel to adopt a resolution barring its members from participation in non-Orthodox movements. Isaac *Breuer, a grandson of Samson Raphael Hirsch and one of the leading Agudat Israel ideologists, formulated in his *Der neue Kuzari* a philosophy of Judaism in which refusal to espouse the cause of separation was interpreted as being equivalent to the rejection of the absolute sovereignty of God.

*Mizrachi on the other hand espoused a policy of cooperation with non-Orthodox and secular elements. It is also noteworthy that in Eastern Europe most Agudat Israel circles frowned upon secular learning, while Mizrachi, as a general rule, adopted a far more sympathetic attitude toward worldly culture. In Central and Western Europe, however, Agudat Israel circles were guided not only by Hirsch's separationist policy toward the non-Orthodox community, but also subscribed to his philosophy of *Torah im derekh ereẓ* (Torah with secular education), and espoused the synthesis of Torah with modern culture. In Israel, the split between the two approaches is especially noticeable. Mizrachi and Ha-Po'el ha-Mizrachi have favored full participation in the political life of the *yishuv* and subsequently in the sovereign State of Israel. Agudat Israel circles, however, refrained from joining the Keneset Yisrael (the recognized community of the Jews in Palestine) and refused to recognize the official rabbinate appointed by that body. After the establishment of the State of Israel, Agudat Israel participated in elections to the Knesset and for some time even participated in a coalition government. A far more extreme position was adopted by *Neturei Karta. They have categorically refused to recognize the authority of a secular Jewish state which, in their opinion, came into being only through the betrayal of the religious values of Jewish tradition.

Although the followers of the *Torah im derekh ereẓ* approach advocated openness to modern culture and discouraged the insulation of the Jew from the intellectual currents of his time, they nonetheless unequivocally rejected any doctrine which in the slightest manner would jeopardize the binding characer and validity of the *halakhah*. They were unbending in their insistence that the traditional belief in *Torah min ha-Shamayim* entailed: that the Masoretic text represents an authentic record of divine communication of content; and that the Oral Torah represents in essence the application and extension of teachings and methods that are ultimately grounded in direct divine revelation (see *Oral Law). This view not only clashed with Abraham *Geiger's radical doctrine of "progressive revelation," according to which even the Bible was the product of the religious genius of the Jewish people, but also with the more moderate theory of "continuous revelation" as formulated by the positivist historical school. According to Zacharias *Frankel (considered by some to be the spiritual father of Conservative Judaism), the original Sinaitic revelation was supplemented by another kind of revelation—the ongoing revelation manifesting itself throughout history in the spirit of the Jewish people. Orthodoxy balked at Frankel's thesis that the entire structure of rabbinic Judaism was the creation of the scribes and subsequently of the *tannaim* and the *amoraim* who allegedly sought to adapt biblical Judaism to a new era by inventing the notion of an Oral Torah. From the Orthodox point of view, rabbinic Judaism represents not a radical break with the past, but rather the ingenious application and development of teachings which ultimately derive their sanction from the Sinaitic revelation. Whereas for the positivist historical school, the religious consciousness of the Jewish people provided the supreme religious authority, the Orthodox position rested upon the belief in the supernatural origin of the Law which was addressed to a "*Chosen People."

[W.S.W.]

German Orthodoxy exerted a significant influence upon Jews in Western lands, especially Holland (to which Reform had not yet spread) and Switzerland. Hungary became the center of a specific type of Orthodox development. The spread of Haskalah there and the reforms in education and synagogue worship led to tension within the communities, especially from the 1840s on (see Aaron *Chorin). Orthodoxy became very much aware of its distinctive character, especially under the influence of R. Moses *Sofer and his school. Later the call for independent organization became more pronounced. Preparations for a nationwide congress of Hungarian Jews at the end of the 1860s gave this trend an organizational and political expression in the formation of the Shomrei Hadass Society (*Glaubenswaechter*, "Guardians of the Faith"), founded in 1867 to protect and further the interest of Orthodoxy, thus becoming the first modern Orthodox political party. In a congress held from December 1868 to February 1869 the Orthodox and Reform camps split; afterward the Orthodox withdrew, announcing that the decisions of the congress were not binding on them. Independent Orthodox communities were set up in those areas where the established communal leadership had passed to the Reform camp and a countrywide organization of these separate communities was set up. Orthodox autonomy was confirmed by the government in 1871. Approximately half Hungarian Jewry joined the Orthodox communities.

Within Hungarian Orthodoxy, two strands can be discerned: (1) traditional Orthodoxy, encompassing the ḥasidic masses in the northeastern districts; and (2) non-ḥasidic Orthodoxy, which contained a segment that bore the marks of modern Orthodoxy—a measure of adaptation to its environment, general education (without the ideology of *Torah im derekh ereẓ*), and use of the language of the country. Non-ḥasidic Orthodoxy was shaped by the school of R. Moses Sofer.

In Eastern Europe until World War I, Orthodoxy preserved without a break its traditional ways of life and the time-honored educational framework. In general, the mainstream of Jewish life was identified with Orthodoxy while Haskalah and secularization were regarded as deviations. Hence there was no ground wherein a Western type of Orthodoxy could take root. Modern political Orthodox activity first appeared in Eastern Europe at the beginning of the 20th century with Agudat Israel. Orthodoxy's political activity was especially noticeable in Poland. During the period of German conquest at the time of World War I, an Orthodox political party was organized (with the aid of some German rabbis), the Shelomei Emunei Israel. In the communal and political life of the Jews in the Polish republic, Orthodoxy was most influential in the townlets, and was supported by the ḥasidic masses. The central political aim of Orthodoxy was to guarantee its autonomy in all religious matters. After World War I, a definite shift may be detected in Orthodoxy in Poland toward basic general education to a limited degree. Agudat Israel established an educational network, with Horeb schools for boys and Beth Jacob schools for girls.

European Orthodoxy, in the 19th and the beginning of the 20th centuries, was significantly influenced by the move from small settlements to urban centers (within the same country) as well as by emigration. Within the small German communities there was a kind of popular Orthodoxy, deeply attached to tradition and to local customs, and when it moved to the large cities this element brought with it a vitality and rootedness to Jewish tradition. From the end of the 19th century, countries in Western Europe absorbed newcomers from the East, who either constituted an important addition to the existing Orthodox congregations or set up new communities. After World War I, scholars from Eastern Europe (among them the rabbis Abraham Elijah Kaplan and Jehiel Jacob *Weinberg) went to Germany and other Western countries. They exerted a perceptible influence on Western Orthodoxy, providing it with a direction in scholarship and drawing it closer to the world of talmudic learning. In the interwar period, young Orthodox students from the West went to the yeshivot of Poland and Lithuania, and yeshivot of the traditional type were later established in Western Orthodox centers.

In the United States, Orthodoxy constituted one of the mainstreams of life and thought within Jewry. Different varieties of Orthodoxy coexisted. In 1898 the *Union of Orthodox Jewish Congregations of America was founded. Its declared aims were to accept "the authoritative interpretation of our rabbis as contained in the Talmud and codes." Among the leaders and teachers prominent in American Orthodoxy were the rabbis Bernard *Revel, Joseph D. *Soloveichik, and Joseph H. *Lookstein. One of the influential Orthodox centers in the United States, *Yeshiva University, inspired the establishment of many other schools offering instruction in both Jewish and secular subjects on the elementary and high school levels. This trend of U.S. Orthodoxy published the periodicals *Jewish Life*, *Jewish Forum*, *Tradition*, and *Intercom* (publication of the Association of Orthodox Jewish Societies). The differences within American Orthodoxy were evidenced by the establishment of different rabbinic bodies there. Rabbis from Eastern Europe, representing traditional Orthodoxy, make up the *Union of Orthodox Rabbis of the United States and Canada (founded in 1902), while rabbis educated in America united to form the *Rabbinical Council of America (in 1923; reorg. 1935). Ḥasidic groups, who became influential chiefly after Would War II, constitute a separate division within American Orthodoxy. Especially well known are those associated with Menahem Mendel *Shneersohn of Lubavich and Joel *Teitelbaum of Satmar. Rabbis, scholars, and the heads of yeshivot who came after World War II and built yeshivot according to the Lithuanian tradition added their special quality to American Orthodoxy. Most prominent among them was Rabbi Aaron *Kotler.

The senior central organization of the Jews of England, the *United Synagogue, is an Orthodox body in its constitution and rabbinic leadership. However, the lay leaders and congregants are not necessarily all observant in the light of the accepted Orthodox standard. Those who were dissatisfied with the degree of observance and religious spirit prevailing in the United Synagogue founded separate congregational organizations. The Federation of Synagogues, which in composition was more suited to the spirit of those who came from Eastern Europe, was founded in 1887, and its numbers multiplied with the extensive Jewish emigration to England. In 1891 the society known as Machzike Hadath ("The Upholders of the Faith"), was formed, and immigrants from Western Europe founded the congregations known as Adath Yisroel in the spirit of German Orthodoxy. In 1926 R. Victor Shonfeld established the Union of Orthodox Hebrew Congregations which attempted to unite the various branches of Western traditional Orthodoxy. [N.K.]

Trends Within Modern Orthodoxy. In spite of the new impetus given to Orthodoxy by the success of the day school and improved methods of organization and communication, evidence of grave dangers cannot be ignored. The rapid polarization within the Orthodox camp seriously threatens to split the movement completely. While much of the controversy seems to revolve around the question of membership in religious bodies containing non-Orthodox representation, the real issue goes far deeper. The so-called "modern Orthodox" element is under severe attack for allegedly condoning deviations from halakhic standards in order to attract non-observant Jews. On the other hand, there constantly come to the fore mounting restlessness and impatience on the part of significant elements that are dismayed over the slowness with which Orthodoxy has responded to the upheavals of Emancipation, the Enlightenment, and the establishment of the State of Israel. The charge has been made that instead of coming to grips with these events which have confronted the Jew with entirely new historic realities, Orthodoxy has been satisfied with voicing its disapproval of those who have reacted to them.

Some of the more "radical" thinkers regard the Hirsch type of synthesis between Torah and culture as an invaluable first step, but it must be developed much further if it is to meet contemporary needs. They look askance at the feature of "timelessness" which in Hirsch's system constitutes a hallmark of Torah and which, in their opinion, ignores the dynamic character inherent in the processes of the Oral Torah. They contend that as long as the domain of Torah remains completely insulated from the culture of a given age, the authorities or the *halakhah* cannot creatively apply teachings of Torah to ever-changing historic realities. What, therefore, is needed is not merely the coexistence but the mutual interaction of the two domains. This view, of course, runs counter to the basic tenets of "right-wing" Orthodoxy, which frowns upon the intrusion of elements derived from secular culture as a distortion of the authentic teachings of the Torah. The exponents of the more radical positions of "modern Orthodoxy" are frequently charged with cloaking under the mantle of Orthodoxy what essentially amounts to a Conservative position. This argument, however, is countered by the claim that no modifications of the *halakhah* are condoned unless they are sanctioned by the methods governing the process of halakhic development. There is no thought of "updating" the *halakhah* in order to adjust it to the spirit of the time. What is advocated is only that its meaning be explicated in the light of ever-changing historic conditions. The contention is that as long as halakhic opinion is evolved in conformity with the proper procedures of halakhic reasoning, its legitimacy as a halakhic datum is assured.

To bolster their case, the proponents of this "left wing" frequently claim to derive the basic elements of their position from the teachings of Rabbi *Kook, as well as from the philosophy of the most influential contemporary Orthodox thinker, R. Joseph B. Soloveichik. Neither of these two seminal thinkers has in any way identified himself with the views advanced by the more "progressive" wing. But Kook's readiness to attribute religious value to modern secular movements, as well as his positive stance toward cultural and scientific developments, provide a key element to a philosophy that seeks to integrate the positive contributions of the world within the fabric of Judaism. Similarly, Soloveichik's characterization of the man of faith in terms of the dialectical tension between a commitment to an eternal "covenantal community" and the responsibilities to fulfill socio-ethical tasks in a world of change is widely hailed as an endorsement of the thesis that the Jewish religious ideal does not call for withdrawal from the world but for the confrontation between human culture and the norms and values of the Torah.

Obviously, such a conception of the nature of the commitment of the Jewish faith completely disposes of the charge of "moral isolationism" that time and again has been hurled at Orthodoxy because its alleged preoccupation with the minutiae of the Law renders it insensitive to areas which do not come within the purview of formal halakhic regulation. Actually, the covenantal relationship between man and God embraces all aspects of life and cannot be confined to a mere adherence to a set of legal rules. The observance of the *halakhah,* far from exhausting the religious task of the Jew, is designed to make him more sensitive and "open" to social and moral concerns.

The Dilemma of Orthodoxy in the Modern World. Although many segments of Orthodoxy have veered away from the course of "splendid isolation" which has been espoused by the "right wing," they have not as yet been able to formulate a systematic theology capable of integrating the findings of modern science and historic scholarship. For that matter, there has not yet been developed a theory of revelation which would satisfy the demands of modern categories of thought. There are some isolated voices clamoring for less "fundamentalist" or "mechanical" approaches to revelation which would utilize some of Martin *Buber's notions and assign a large role to man's subjective response to the encounter with the Divine. But it remains to be seen whether such a solution is feasible within the framework of Orthodoxy. At any rate, some of the widely recognized Orthodox authorities unequivocally reject any approach which compromises in the slightest with the doctrine that divine revelation represents direct supernatural communication of content from God to man.

Even more serious is the problem of the increasing resistance to the Orthodox emphasis on the authoritative nature of the *halakhah.* This runs counter to the prevailing cultural emphasis upon pluralism and the individual's free subjective commitment, a freedom which challenges acceptance of objective religious values or norms imposed upon the individual from without. What renders the problem even more acute is the paradox that the Orthodox community, which places so much emphasis upon the authority of the rabbis to interpret the revealed word of God is the one that has been plagued most by conflicting claims of competing authorities. Characteristically, all efforts to establish some central authority have failed dismally. The proposal to revive the Sanhedrin, far from promoting cohesiveness, has actually precipitated considerable disharmony within the Orthodox camp. The latter, so far, has not even succeeded in evolving a loose organizational structure which would be representative of the various ideological shadings within the movement. [W.S.W.]

Bibliography: E. Schwarzschild, *Die Gruendung der israelitischen Religionsgesellschaft zu Frankfurt am Main* (1896); J. Wohlgemuth, in: *Festschrift . . . David Hoffmann* (1914), 435–53; S. Japhet, in: HJ, 10 (1948), 99–122; I. Heinemann, *ibid.*, 123–34; J. Rosenheim, *ibid.*, 135–46; H. Schwab, *History of Orthodox Jewry in Germany* (1950); B. Homa, *A Fortress in Anglo-Jewry; the Story of the Machzike Hadath* (1953); E. Rackman, in: *Judaism*, 3 (1954), 302–9; 18 (1969), 143–58; Y. Wolfsberg, in: YLBI, 1 (1956), 237–54; S. Federbush (ed.), *Ḥokhmat Yisrael be-Ma'arav Eiropah*, 3 vols. (1958–65); S. K. Mirsky (ed.), *Ishim u-Demuyyot be-Ḥokhmat Yisrael be-Eiropah ha-Mizraḥit Lifnei Sheki'atah* (1959); I. Grunfeld, *Three Generations: The Influence of Samson Raphael Hirsch on Jewish Life and Thought* (1959); S. Poll, *The Hasidic Community of Williamsburg* (1962); C. S. Liebman, in: AJYB, 66 (1965), 21–97; D. Rudavsky, *Emancipation and Adjustment* (1967); N. Lamm, in: *Jewish Life* (May–June, 1969), 5–6; N. Katzburg, in: R. Braham (ed.), *Hungarian Jewish Studies*, 2 (1969); S. Belkin, *Essays in Traditional Jewish Thought* (1956); M. Davis, in: L. Finkelstein (ed.), *The Jews, their History, Culture and Religion*, 1 (1960[3]), 488–587; I. Epstein, *The Faith of Judaism* (1954); I. Grunfeld, *Judaism Eternal* (1956); S. R. Hirsch, *The Nineteen Letters on Judaism* (1960, 1969); N. Lamm and W. S. Wurzburger (eds.), *A Treasury of Tradition* (1967).

ORVIETO, town in Umbria, central Italy. Jewish loan bankers appeared there as early as 1297, being given citizenship rights and permitted to carry weapons. In 1334 one of them was sent as envoy to a neighboring town. The prosperity of the Jewish community induced many families from outside to settle there, as did a group of Jews from Viterbo in 1396. The anti-Jewish sermons of the *Franciscan friars later caused the position of Jews to deteriorate. However, Jewish moneylending activities continued until a **monte di pietà* was established in 1464. After Orvieto came under the rule of the Church in the second half of the 16th century, anti-Jewish legislation was strictly enforced. When in 1569 *Pius V decreed the expulsion of the Jews from the Papal States, the Jewish community effectively ceased to exist, although some families came back for a short time under *Sixtus V (1585–90). The name of the church of St. Gregorio nella Sinagoga in Orvieto still commemorates the former Jewish settlement.

Bibliography: Roth, in: RMI, 17 (1951), 430ff.; Milano, Italia, index. [A.To.]

ORVIETO, ANGIOLO (1869–1967), Italian author and editor. A nephew of Alberto *Cantoni, Orvieto was a member of an old, traditionalist family. He was born and educated in Florence and, during the years preceding World War I, took an active part in the cultural life and literary disputes of the city, which was then the main center of Italian intellectual activity. With his brother Adolfo, he founded the literary review *Il Marzocco* (1896–1932), giving it a classical trend in keeping with the formalism of Italian style. At the same time, Orvieto sought the collaboration of famous writers such as Luigi Pirandello and his friends Giovanni Pascoli and Gabriele D'Annunzio. Orvieto and his journal became the center of an intellectual circle consisting of the major Italian writers. He also initiated many cultural associations, including the *Società dei papiri greci e latini* and the *Società Leonardo da Vinci;* founded the reviews *Vita Nuova* and *Nazione Letteraria;* and was for many years superintendent of the *Instituto di studi superiori* in Florence.

As a poet, Orvieto tried to give new life to the traditional Italian sonnet, but much of his verse lacks authenticity and real poetic experience. His collections of verse include *La sposa mistica* (1893), *Il velo di Maia* (1898), *Verso l'Oriente* (1912), *Le sette leggende* (1912), *Primavera della cornamusa* (1925), and *Il gonfalòn selvaggio* (1934). He was more successful with *Il Vento di Siòn* (1928), a book written after a spiritual crisis and a return to Jewish tradition, in which he achieved a more personal tone and true sincerity of expression. In this Orvieto pretends to be a 16th-century Florentine Jewish poet who tries in vain to reconcile his love for Zion with his equally sincere love for Renaissance Florence. His *Canti dell' escluso*, written during and after the Nazi persecutions and published in a single volume with *Il Vento de Siòn* in 1961, is similar in tone. He also wrote impressions of his travels, a collection of translations of English poetry, and three librettos set to music by the Jewish composer G. Orefice: *Chopin* (1901), *Elena alle porte Scee* (1904), and *Mosè* (1905). After 1928 Orvieto was active in Jewish communal life and in extreme old age became deeply observant of religious tradition. His wife, Laura Cantoni Orvieto (1876–1953), was well known as a writer of storybooks and history books for children, among which were *Leo e Lia* (1908) and *Storie di bambini molto antichi* (1951).

Bibliography: G. L. Luzzatto, in: RMI, 27 (1961), 454–61; 28 (1962), 32–39, 83–88; A. Bobbio, *Le reviste fiorentine del principio del secolo, 1903–1916* (1936). [G.R.]

OR YEHUDAH (Heb. אוֹר יְהוּדָה), Israel urban community with municipal council status, 8 mi. (13 km.) E. of Tel Aviv. Or Yehudah comprises the site of biblical *Ono. Prior to the Israel *War of Independence, two Arab villages existed on its area, Sākiyya (Sāqiyya) and Kafr 'Ānā, which were abandoned by their inhabitants before being taken by Israel forces in June 1948. In 1949, immigrants from Libya and Turkey settled there under primitive conditions. In 1950 and 1951, two large *ma'barot* (tent and hut camps) were set up, mainly for newcomers from Iraq and Rumania. Living conditions continued to be difficult until 1958, when permanent housing projects were started. The population declined from its maximum figure in 1958 (12,500) to 10,100 in 1963, and rose to 12,300 in 1970 when more than half of the total population were immigrants (over half from Iraq, and one-third from other Middle Eastern and North African countries). Or Yehudah had a large average family size and a low average age of population (52% are below 20 years of age). Out of 3,230 gainfully employed adults in 1968, 1,500 worked in industry, 300 in agriculture, and 500 in construction. Or Yehudah had 11 factories, the largest of which was a weaving factory for export. Other local enterprises engaged in metal, diamonds, and food processing. The name "Light of Judah" commemorates Rabbi Judah *Alkalai. [E.O.]

°**ORZESZKOWA (Orzeszko), ELIZA** (1841–1910), Polish novelist. Born in Grodno, Eliza Orzeszkowa was a member of the Polish landed gentry. A leading prose writer of the late 19th century, she was an advocate of social reform and endeavored to destroy the barriers separating the Poles and the Jews. Of all Polish writers, she took the greatest interest in the Jews, studying their history and even learning Hebrew and Yiddish (in spite of which there are in her writings some serious mistakes, as regards Jewish customs, etc.). An opponent of anti-Semitism, Orzeszkowa nevertheless attacked Jewish religious separatism and Zionism in the hope that Polish Jewry might ultimately be assimilated into the mainstream of Polish culture and diverted from any identification with the Germans or Russians. These ideas were propagated in her novels and short stories and in the pamphlet *"O żydach i kwestyi żydowskiej"* ("On the Jews and the Jewish Question," 1882), published after the Warsaw pogrom of December 1881. Her opposition to Zionism was expressed in an article *"O nacyonali żmie żydowskim"* (1911; published posthumously in *Kuryer Warszawski*, 1911).

One of her early novels, *Pan Graba* ("Mr. Graba," 3 vols., 1872) sympathetically described a Jewish moneylender who amasses his wealth with the sole intention of building schools for the Jews in Jerusalem; while *Eli Makower* (2 vols., 1875), shows how another Jew assists a decent Polish landowner and works for mutual understanding between their two peoples. *Meir Ezofowicz* (1878; Eng. trans. 1898), Orzeszkowa's most important Jewish work, describes a young Jew's struggle for enlightenment and human brotherhood in face of Jewish narrowness and fanaticism. This novel is remarkable for its understanding of Orthodox motivation and for its censure of those Jews, who, touched by shallow assimilation, try to imitate some of the customs of the gentiles. In *Mirtala* (1886), a historical novel set in Rome two years after the destruction of Jerusalem (i.e., 72 C.E.), the novelist portrays the life of the Jewish exiles and their relations with the gentiles. Her short stories—notably *"Silny Samson"* ("The Strong Samson," 1878); *"Gedali"* (1884), and *Rotszyldówna* ("The Rothschild Girl," written before 1891, publ. 1921)—contain sympathetic descriptions of poverty-stricken Jews. In 1905 Orzeszkowa edited an anthology of 16 short stories about Jews by ten Polish writers, entitled *Z jednego strumienia* ("From One Source").

Bibliography: I. Butkiewiczówna, *Powieści nowele żydowskie Elizy Orzeszkowej* (1937), incl. bibl. [Y.A.K.]

OSCHINSKY, LAWRENCE (1921–1965), U.S. physical anthropologist. Born in New York, he taught physical anthropology at the University of Pennsylvania graduate school of medicine, and from 1956 at Howard University Medical School. His special interest was in the anatomy of the nervous system, the races of Africa and Asia, and human evolution and the physical anthropology of the Eskimos of Siberia and Canada. His books include: *Most Ancient Eskimos* (1964) and *Racial Affinities of the Baganda and Other Bantu Tribes of British East Africa* (1954). [E.Fi.]

OSHAIAH (Hoshaiah) RABBAH (first half of the second century C.E.), Palestinian *amora*. Oshaiah was born in southern Palestine (TJ, Nid. 3:2), where he studied under *Bar Kappara (MK 24a) and *Ḥiyya (TJ, Shab. 3:1), eventually becoming the latter's assistant. His father, *Ḥama, left the family when Oshaiah was a child in order to study. When after several years Ḥama finally returned, he found that the young stranger with whom he had discussed *halakhah* on the way was his own son (Ket. 62b). When father and son subsequently disputed a particular issue, Oshaiah's grandfather, Bisa, ruled in his grandson's favor (BB 59a). Oshaiah was apparently a member of *Judah Ha-Nasi's council in Sepphoris and was entrusted with examining the witnesses of the new moon (TJ, Ned. 6:8). After Judah Ha-Nasi's death, he founded his own academy at Caesarea (TJ, Ter. 10:2). He was famed for his collection of *baraitot*, called *Mishnayot Gedolot* ("Great *Mishnayot*"; TJ, Hor. 3:5) and for the ability with which he explained them. As a result he was called *Av ha-Mishnah* ("Father of the Mishnah"; TJ, BK, 4:6). The collection was respected in Babylon, too, and *Ze'eira remarked, "Every *baraita* that was not taught in the school of Ḥiyya and Oshaiah is not authentic" (Ḥul. 141a–b).

Oshaiah was particularly strict in requiring from a prospective proselyte both circumcision and immersion in the presence of three rabbis (Yev. 46b), a decision probably prompted by his opposition to the widespread conversion of gentiles by Christian Jews. R. T. Herford (*Christianity in Talmud and Midrash* (1903), 247ff.) suggests that Oshaiah's maxim, "The Almighty dwelt kindly with Israel in scattering them" (Pes. 87b), was also directed against them. Bacher (JQR, 3 (1891), 357–60) maintains that Oshaiah had certainly heard of Origen, if not read his works, and associates the latter with "the philosopher" who asked Oshaiah, "Why was not man created circumcised?" Oshaiah replied, "Man, together with all creations, needs perfecting, and circumcision brings perfection" (Gen. R. 11:6). He was also the author of the phrase, "Custom overrides law" (TJ, BM 7:1). According to one reading, Oshaiah was poor (Meg. 7a). His kindness and consideration for his fellow men is illustrated by his apology to his son's blind teacher, whom he had not invited to a particular meal for fear that he would be embarrassed by other guests (TJ, Pe'ah 8:9, 21b). His son, Merenos, was a scholar (TJ, Git. 4:6). Among his pupils were Ammi (TJ, Shab. 3:7) and *Johanan b. Nappaḥa (TJ, Ter. 10:2). The latter continued to visit Oshaiah even when he himself became a great scholar (TJ, Sanh. 11:6, 30b). He once said, "Oshaiah in his generation is like *Meir was in his" (Er. 53a).

Bibliography: Hyman, Toledot, 110–6; Bacher, Pal Amor; Ḥ. Albeck, *Mavo la-Talmudim* (1969), 163f. [Ed.]

OSHEROWITCH, MENDL (pseudonyms; **A. Glan, M. Glebovitch, Menakhem Podolyer, M. Ovodovski;** 1888–1965), Yiddish journalist and author. Born in Trostyanets, Podolia, Ukraine, Osherowitch emigrated to the U.S. in 1909 and from 1914 on was a staff member of the New York *Jewish Daily Forward.*

His profuse writings include stories, plays, historical novels, biographies, popular history, travel impressions, theater history, criticism, and autobiography. He also translated widely from Russian and English. Much of his work appeared in the *Jewish Daily Forward,* of which he also wrote a history. His book on David *Kessler and Paul *Muni, *Dovid Kesler un Muni Vayzenfraynd* (1930), his memoirs, and his studies of Ukrainian Jewish towns are of great interest.

Bibliography: Rejzen, Leksikon, 1 (1926), 186–8; Z. Zylbercweig (ed.), *Leksikon fun Yidishn Teater* (1931), 113–4; LNYL, 1 (1956), 195–6. [L.P.]

OSHMYANY (Pol. **Oszmiana**), city in Grodno oblast, Belorussian S.S.R. Oshmyany, one of the oldest settlements in Lithuania, was granted municipal status in 1537. A Jewish community developed there at the beginning of the 18th century. In 1765 there were 376 Jewish poll-tax payers

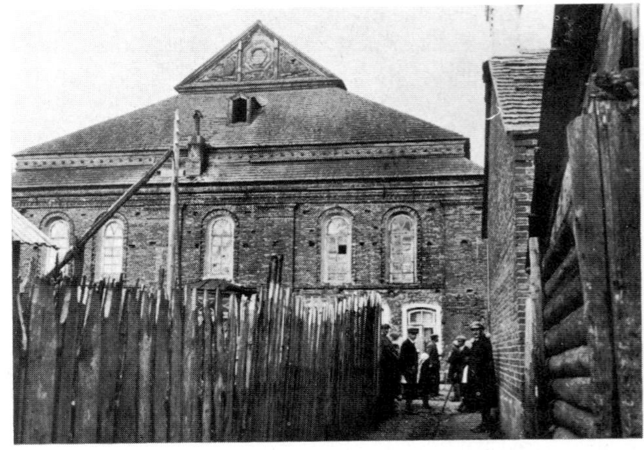

The Great Synagogue of Oshmyany, Poland, erected in 1902. Courtesy Yad Vashem Archives, Jerusalem.

in Oshmyany and the surrounding villages. In 1831, after a battle against Polish rebels, Russian soldiers set fire to Oshmyany and killed many of the town's inhabitants, including many Jews. In 1847 the community numbered 1,460, and by 1897 the number had increased to 3,808 (about 53% of the population). Jews earned their livelihood from small trade and crafts, essentially from tanning, shoemaking, tailoring, and carpentry. At the beginning of the 20th century most of the Jewish workers organized themselves into a trade union. There were seven synagogues in the town, three of them belonging to the unions of the tanners, shoemakers, and tailors. Prominent rabbis served the community during the 19th and the beginning of the 20th centuries, among them R. Meir Michael Kahana (1883), R. Mordecai b. Menahem *Rosenblatt (author of *Aleh Ḥavaẓẓelet*, 1891–1906), and R. Judah Leib Fein 1906–14).

The Great Synagogue of Oshmyana was erected in 1902. In the battles between the Red Army and the Polish Army in 1920, many Jews fell victim to the fighting. Between the two world wars (under Polish rule) the office of vice mayor was held by a Jewish delegate. During this period branches of all the Jewish parties were active in the town. The leading educational and cultural institutions were the Tarbut and Yavneh Hebrew schools, the CYSHO Yiddish school, a Hebrew library, and a drama circle. Between the years 1922 and 1925 a Jewish agricultural cooperative with 30 members functioned in the surroundings of Oshmyany. [A.CY.]

Holocaust Period and After. On June 25, 1941, three days after the outbreak of the German-Soviet War, the Germans invaded Oshmyany. On July 25 they ordered all male Jews to assemble in the square. The assembled, who numbered about 700, were taken to Bartel and murdered. In October 1941 a ghetto was established, which became overcrowded as Jews from the neighboring towns of Olshan, Smorgon, and Krawo were brought in, and disease and hunger took many lives. On June 16, 1942, about 350 youths were transferred to a camp in Miligany. In October the Germans announced that too many Jews were still living in the ghetto and that the population must be decreased, which meant extermination for some of its occupants. Receiving the information, the *Judenrat in Vilna claimed that if it performed the *Aktion* the number of victims would be reduced. Headed by Salek Dresler, members of the Vilna Jewish police participated in the *Aktion* on Oct. 27, 1942, making their *Selektion* and kidnapping more than 500 Jews, who were taken in the direction of Oglyovo, about 4 mi. (7 km.) from Oshmyana, and murdered there.

This episode roused the Jews against both the Judenrat and the Vilna Jewish police. Jacob Gens, head of the Judenrat in Vilna, took full responsibility for the *Aktion*, claiming that by sacrificing part of the Jewish population there was a chance to save the rest. Early in 1943 an underground organization was established in the ghetto, and its members left for the forests to join the partisans. On April 28, 1943, the ghetto was liquidated. Some of its 2,500 inhabitants were transferred to the Vilna ghetto, some were deported to labor camps in the vicinity, and others were killed at Ponary. After World War II Jewish life in Oshmyany did not fully revive. In 1965 there were some 25 Jewish families living there, most of whom had not previously been residents of the city. A monument to Jewish martyrs murdered by the Nazis, erected outside the city, was repeatedly desecrated. In 1970 some 300 families from Oshmyany lived in Ereẓ Israel. [AR.W.]

Bibliography: B. Wasiutyński, *Ludność żydowska w Polsce w wiekach XIX i XX* (1930), 82; *Żydzi a powstanie styczniowe, materiały osijek i dokumenty* (1963), index; *Sefer Zikkaron li-Kehillat Oshminah* (Heb., Yid., and some Eng., 1969).

°OSIANDER, ANDREAS (1498–1552), German theologian, religious reformer, and Hebraist. Osiander was a Hebrew tutor at Nuremberg and continued his studies with a Jew, Woelfflein of Schnaittach, who was given the extraordinary privilege, for the time, of visiting Nuremberg for that purpose. In the wake of the *Pezinok blood libel of 1529, Osiander published an anonymous refutation of the ritual murder charge. Although Osiander became a Protestant, in a private letter to Elijah *Levita he vehemently denounced Martin *Luther's anti-Jewish *Vom Schem Hamphoras* (1544). Osiander was made professor of Hebrew at the then newly founded University of Koenigsberg.

Bibliography: M. Stern, *Andreas Osianders Schrift ueber die Blutbeschuldigung* (1893); Baron, Social[2], 13 (1969), 228, 232f., 431f. [Y.AM.]

OSIJEK (Hung. **Eszék**, Ger. **Esseg**), town in E. Croatia, Yugoslavia; until 1918 in Austria-Hungary. Jews were first mentioned in Osijek after the Austrian conquest of Belgrade in 1688, when some 500 Jewish prisoners were taken to Osijek where they had to wait until they were ransomed by European Jewish communities (Moses Sofer, *Et Sofer*, Fuerth, 1691). Jews from the Austrian Empire began settling in Osijek under difficult conditions in the middle of the 18th century. They had no official right of residence until 1792. Religious services were held in the town from 1830, and the community was founded in 1845; it had 40 members in 1849. The congregation school and *ḥevra kaddisha* were founded in 1857; a synagogue was built in 1867. When emancipation was granted to Jews in Croatia in 1873, the community prospered and was the largest one in Croatia until 1890. In 1900 there were 1,600 Jews in Osijek. In the 20th century Osijek had two communities—one in the upper and another one in the lower town—and communal life was intensive. In 1940 there were 2,584 Jews in the two communities.

Holocaust Period. After the German conquest of Yugoslavia in April 1941, Croatia became the "Independent Croatian State" under A. *Pavelić. On April 13 Germans, *Volkdeutsche* (very numerous in this region), and Pavelić's *ustaše* (paramilitary collaborators) looted Jewish property, imposed a contribution of 20,000,000 dinars, and made all economic activity impossible for Jews; Jewish families were evicted from the center of town. On April 13 a mob of Germans, *Volkdeutsche*, and *ustaše* burned the main synagogue and destroyed the Jewish cemetery, but mass persecution did not start until June 1942. In December 1941 a camp for 2,000 Jewish women and children was established in an old mill in Djakovo, near Osijek. In February 1942 approximately 1,200 women and children from the Stara Gradiška camp were transferred to Djakovo until, because of an epidemic, the camp was liquidated and its inmates sent for extermination to Jasenovac. In June 1942 the community was ordered to build a settlement on the road to Tenje, a nearby village, where the Jews would be left unmolested. The leaders of the community were hoodwinked into building the settlement and organizing the life in it. Three thousand Jews from Osijek, and later from other places in the region, were confined there; by August 1942 they had all been sent either to Jasenovac or Auschwitz. Only Jews married to gentiles and a few who were in hiding remained in Osijek; ten managed to return from the death camps.

Contemporary Period. In 1947 there were 610 Jews in the community, including the surrounding area, and in 1949 after the immigration to Israel, 220. In 1965 a monument to Jewish fighters and victims of Nazism from Osijek and Slavonia was dedicated in a square in Osijek; it was created by Oscar Nemon of London, a native of Osijek.

Bibliography: Schwarz, in: *Jevrejski almanah*, 3 (1927/28), 193–6. [Ed.]

OSIPOVICH, NAHUM (1870–?), Russian writer. While preparing for the entrance requirements of the University of Odessa he joined the Narodnaya Volya (the "People's Will" movement) circles, was arrested by the czarist authorities, and spent 18 years in prisons and in exile. Osipovich started his literary activity in 1902. On the recommendation of the *Society for the Promotion of Culture among the Jews of Russia, he studied the educational problem of the Jews in *Bessarabia (in *Voskhod*, no. 12, 1902). His short story *"Za chto?"* ("Why?") was refused publication by the censors. Osipovich wrote many short stories devoted mainly to Jewish types and Jewish life. His works are filled with love for nature, humanity, and the Jewish people in particular. His short story *"U vody"* ("At the Water") shows his devotion to the Jewish Black Sea fishermen whom he knew so well. Soviet critics consider him representative of the Jewish petit-bourgeois intelligentsia who were unable to adapt to the new Soviet reality.

Bibliography: YE, 13 (c. 1910), 144–5; *Literaturnaya Entsiklopediya*, 8 (1949), 340. [Ed.]

OSIRIS, DANIEL ILLFA (1825–1908), French philanthropist and art patron, member of a Sephardi family of Bordeaux. He gave large sums for the promotion of technology (radio, telegraphy) and medicine (Institut Pasteur) and bequeathed his valuable art collection to the Louvre. He bought La Malmaison and part of the field of Waterloo and gave them to the French nation. He also built several synagogues. [Ed.]

Daniel Illfa Osiris, French philanthropist and art patron. Jerusalem, J.N.U.L., Schwadron Collection

OSLO, capital of Norway. When the law of 1814 prohibiting the admission of Jews to Norway was revoked in 1851, a Jewish community began to develop in Oslo; it acquired land for a cemetery in 1869 and was officially established in 1892 with 29 dues-paying members. In 1917, the community split up, and two synagogues were opened in 1920. In 1909, a "Jewish Youth Society" *(Israelitisk Ungdoms Forening)* was formed, which published a monthly journal, *Israelitin* (1909–12). A Zionist Association was formed in 1910 and from 1929 published a monthly, *Ha-Tikvah*. There were 852 Jews in Oslo in 1930, mainly engaged in commerce and industry. During World War II, some of the Jews in Oslo managed to escape to Sweden. The rest perished in Nazi concentration camps. The refugees who returned united into a single community. They were joined by several hundred displaced persons whom the Norwegian government had brought to Oslo, most of whom later emigrated to Israel or the United States. A B'nai Brith Lodge was established in 1952 and a new

Obverse and reverse of a coupon given as a receipt for a ten-kroner donation toward the building of the Kristiania (Oslo) synagogue, 1892. The sum was supposed to purchase one brick. Jerusalem, Ezra P. Gorodetsky Collection.

communal center in 1960. In 1968, there were 650 Jews in Oslo, a synagogue, and two cemeteries.

See *Norway, Holocaust period.

Bibliography: H. M. H. Koritzinsky, *Jødernes Historie i Norge* (1922), passim. [Ed.]

OSNABRUECK, city in Lower Saxony, W. Germany. Jews are mentioned as living in Osnabrueck during the 13th century and the formula of the Jewish *oath from this period is extant. From a letter of Bishop Engelbert II to the municipal council in favor of the Jews (1309), it appears that there were then ten or 13 Jewish families in Osnabrueck. As in the other towns of Germany, here too the Jews engaged in moneylending. In 1312 the bishop issued a regulation fixing the rate of interest at 36.1/9%. All offenders against this regulation had to pay a fine to the bishop and the municipal council, suggesting that at this time the Jews were dependent on the benevolence of both the bishop and the townsmen. In 1327, however, the 15 Jewish families were placed under the protection of the bishop. In 1337 Emperor Louis the Bavarian submitted the Jews to the authority of Baron Henry von Valdeck. At the time of the *Black Death (1350), the Jews of Osnabrueck

The Rolandstrasse synagogue in Osnabrueck, consecrated in 1906 and destroyed during *Kristallnacht*, 1938. From Z. Asaria, *Zur Geschichte der Juden in Osnabrueck*, Osnabrueck, 1969.

were all martyred and their property confiscated. After a few years, eight Jewish families only were permitted to settle in exchange for an annual payment of 30 marks. As was customary in other localities, this privilege was valid for only six years. They were authorized to purchase a tract of land for a cemetery in 1386 (an "old" cemetery had been mentioned in 1343). By 1424, there were only two families who were able to pay the annual tax of seven to eight guilders. The remaining Jews were expelled, and Osnabrueck received the privilege of *"non tolerandis Judaeis"* which remained in force, with the exception of three families, until the French Revolution. The townsmen were, however, jealous of the income of even these few Jews, and in 1716 a law forbade them to engage in commerce without the authorization of the municipal council. The number of Jews increased under French occupation. In 1825 there were five families and a teacher, affiliated to the Emden rabbinate. The community subsequently grew from 138 in 1871 to 379 in 1880 and 450 in 1925. A large synagogue was consecrated for the community of wealthy merchants in 1906. Anti-Semitic movements flourished in Osnabrueck, and in 1927 the synagogue and cemetery were desecrated. Between 1933 and 1938 about 350 Jews emigrated; on May 17, 1939, only 119 remained. On **Kristallnacht* the synagogue was set on fire and shops and homes were looted. During the Holocaust 102 former citizens of Osnabrueck lost their lives. During the war 400 Jewish Yugoslav officers were placed in a special P.O.W. camp in Osnabrueck. In August 1945 services were renewed in a prayer room. In 1969 a synagogue and community center for the community of 69 persons were consecrated.

Bibliography: M. Wiener, in: *Ben Chananja*, 5 (1862), 325–7; FJW, 136; Germ Jud, 2 (1968), 634–6; Z. Asaria, *Zur Geschichte der Juden in Osnabrueck* (1969).

[Az.S.]

OSOBLAHA (Ger. **Hotzenplotz**), village in Silesia, Czechoslovakia. Osoblaha was the seat of an important Jewish community during the Middle Ages, under the protection of the bishopric of *Olomouc (Olmuetz), and had its own municipal administration (see **Politische Gemeinden*) until 1849. In 1415 a decree of the bishop urged the town to treat the Jews fairly. In order to revive the town, which had been devastated by the *Hussites, in 1514 land lots were sold to Jews of Leobschuetz (Glubczyce). Twelve families from Prudnik (now Poland) settled in Osoblaha in 1570, and the community then numbered 132 families in 22 houses. They traded in Silesia and Poland and the community as such leased the distillery. A few years before the Thirty Years' War (1618–48), the *Council of the Lands succeeded in averting the community's threatened expulsion. In 1670 the Jewish community of Osoblaha absorbed several Jews expelled from Vienna. It suffered during the Seven Years' War (1756–63) and many left. There were 596 Jews living in 30 houses in 1788. The *Familiants Law of 1798 limited the community to 135 families, but in 1802 there were 153 families (845 persons); the number had fallen to 589 persons in 1830 when the Jewish quarter was destroyed by fire. It had a German-language elementary school (1803–70). During the Middle Ages important rabbis held office in Osoblaha, among them the future Moravian chief rabbi, Gershon Ḥayyot Manasse of Hotzenplotz (see *Mintmasters), who was the first purveyor to the Silesian mint (1622–24). The community declined quickly during the 19th century when most of its members moved to nearby Krnov (Jaegernodorf). In 1921 there were 37 Jews in Osoblaha and only one in 1934. The dilapidated synagogue was demolished in 1933, and the records and ritual objects were transferred to Krnov. The cemetery, damaged during World War II, was renovated by a grant from the Czechoslovak government in the 1950s.

Bibliography: E. Richter and A. Schmidt, in: *Mitteilungen zur juedischen Volkskunde*, 14 (1911), 29–36; Marmorstein, *ibid.*, 81; B. Brilling, in: *Zeitung fuer die Geschichte der Juden*, 2 (1965), 53–57; idem, in: JGGJC, 7 (1935), 387–98; R. Iltis (ed.), *Die aussaeen unter Traenen* ... (1959), 80–81; S. Rubaschow, in: *Ost und West*, 16 (1916), 199ff.

[M.La.]

OSROENE (**Osrhoene**), district within the Seleucid Empire, occupying the N.W. portion of Mesopotamia. The capital city of the district, Edessa (modern Urfa), became a Greek *polis* under Seleucus I Nicator, but during the reign of Antiochus VII Sidetes (c. 136 B.C.E.) the area was conquered by Arab tribesmen, sons of Orhai (Osroes). Thereafter the capital and the state were known as Orhai or Urhai (Orrhoene being the form given by Pliny the Elder). Situated between the Roman and Parthian Empires, the Arab kingdom tended to support the latter, and thus during the temporary Roman conquest of Mesopotamia under Trajan (116 C.E.) the reigning monarch, Abgar VII, was deposed. Although the king was eventually returned under Hadrian, total autonomy was short-lived, and in 216 the area became a Roman colony. Jews probably resided in Osroene from the late Persian and early Hellenistic periods. By the end of the Second Temple period their influence carried over to the neighboring kingdom of *Adiabene, whose royal family converted to Judaism. Christianity was also introduced into Osroene by means of the local Jewish community, and according to one legend the Jew Hananiah supposedly conveyed a letter from Jesus to King Abgar V. By the end of the second century Christianity was officially recognized in Osroene, and thereafter the office of bishop of Edessa was considered of utmost importance for Eastern Christianity.

Bibliography: A. von Gutschmid, in: *Mémoires de l'Académie de St. Petersbourg*, 35 (1887); J. Neusner, *History of the Jews in Babylonia*, 1 (1965), 166–9. [I.G.]

OSSOWETZKY, O. YEHOSHUA (1858–1929), a senior official in Baron Edmond de *Rothschild's administration in Ereẓ Israel. Born in Kiev, in 1883 Ossowetzky was appointed chief administrator in *Rishon le-Zion by Baron de Rothschild. There he induced the farmers to plant vines and doubled the settlement's land area. The "free" farmers not subsidized by the Baron clashed with Ossowetzky; their leaders were forced to leave Rishon le-Zion after the "free" farmers' revolt, while Ossowetzky was replaced by an even harsher official. In 1887 he bought 7,000 dunams (1,750 acres) of land in Kastina (later *Be'er Toviyyah), and two years later he was appointed chief official of the Baron de Rothschild in Galilee and moved to *Rosh Pinnah. There he gained great influence in Turkish circles with the aid of bribes and gifts. He used to ride in a carriage, preceded by armed Jewish horsemen. Ossowetzky extended the area of Rosh Pinnah and tried to base its economy on plantations and the silk industry. He also established the settlement of *Metullah on land he had purchased. In the 1890s Ossowetzky purchased large tracts of land in the Golan and other areas east of the Jordan River and also began purchasing land in Lower Galilee (*Sejera). When the management of the settlements was handed over to the *Jewish Colonization Association (ICA) in 1900, Ossowetzky left the country and lived in Paris till his death.

Bibliography: M. Smilansky, *Mishpaḥat ha-Adamah*, 2 (1944), 120–5; Tidhar, 3 (1949), 1318–9. [Y.S.]

OSSUARIES and SARCOPHAGI. Ossuaries, small chests in which the bones of the dead were placed after the flesh had decayed, first appear in Ereẓ Israel in the Chalcolithic period. Pottery ossuaries have been found at Ḥaderah, Bene-Berak, and Azor. Some are shaped like a four-legged receptacle with a vaulted roof, a door with a bolt in the facade, and windows in the rear. The ossuaries have painted decorations and their facades are often given the appearance of a human face.

Pottery anthropoid sarcophagi (stone coffins) dating to the transitional period between the Bronze and Iron periods, which imitate the shape of Egyptian mummies, have been found at Beth-Shean. They have been associated with the Philistines. In the Israelite period (Iron Age), sarcophagi were apparently not used. They reappear in Ereẓ Israel under the Herodian dynasty; elongated sarcophagi decorated with plant motifs have been uncovered in Herod's family tomb and in the tombs of the kings of the Adiabene dynasty in Jerusalem, and also in a large tomb on the Mount of Olives. Especially remarkable is the ornamentation of the vaulted lid of a sarcophagus from the "Tombs of the Kings," which is carved with plants common to the country, vine and olive branches, etc. A wooden coffin inlaid with bone was found at En-Gedi. In the Roman period, many carved sarcophagi were introduced into the country from abroad and imitated. A sarcophagus discovered near Caesarea portrays a battle between Greeks and Amazons, another from Turmus Aiya is carved with representations of the seasons, and among a number of sarcophagi found at Samaria (in a third-century C.E. tomb), one depicts peasants taking their produce to market. A sarcophagus with mythological scenes (Achilles among the daughters of Lycomedes; Leda) was found in the Bet She'arim cemetery (in secondary use?). Lead coffins which were cast in Tyre, Ashkelon, and Jerusalem were common in the third–fourth centuries; molds were employed for their decorations. Early Christian sarcophagi bear reliefs

Figure 1. Terra cotta ossuaries found at Ḥaderah, Azor, and Bene-Berak, dating from the Chalcolithic period (4000–3150 B.C.E.). Jerusalem, Israel Museum, Israel Department of Antiquities Collection.

Figure 2. Ossuaries *in situ* in burial caves on the Mount of Olives, dating from the Second Temple period. Photo Zev Radovan, Jerusalem.

Figure 3. Sarcophagus from Caesarea, Roman period (first–third century C.E.), with carved relief of a battle between Greeks and Amazons. Jerusalem, Rockefeller Museum, Israel Department of Antiquities. Photo Hillel Burger, Jerusalem.

Figure 4. Sarcophagus with incised decoration from a tomb on Mt. Scopus, Jerusalem, first century C.E. London, British Museum.

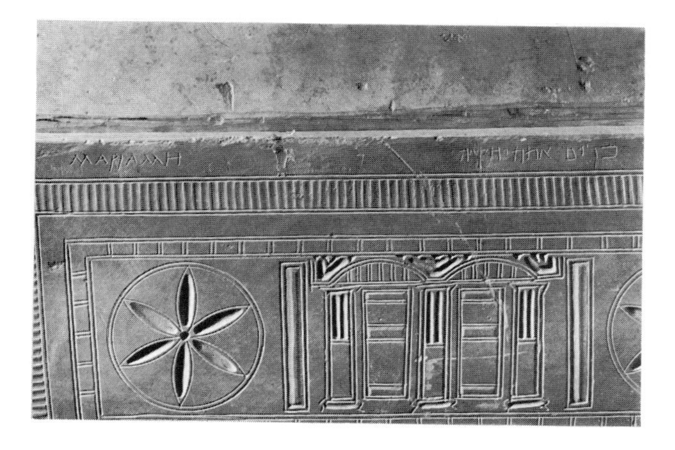

Figure 5. Detail from a Jewish sarcophagus from Jerusalem, first century C.E., with an inscription, "Miriam sister of Jehezkiah," in Hebrew, and "Mariame" in Greek. Jerusalem, Israel Museum, Israel Department of Antiquities Collection. Photo Hillel Burger, Jerusalem.

Figure 6. Sarcophagus from a third-century C.E. tomb at Samaria, with a relief of two peasants carrying produce. Courtesy Israel Department of Antiquities, Jerusalem.

depicting scenes from the Bible and the Gospels. In the Byzantine period, the use of sarcophagi died out.

Decorated stone ossuaries reappear in the first century B.C.E. and first century C.E. mainly in Jewish tombs in the vicinity of Jerusalem. Isolated examples have also been uncovered in the Sharon, Shephelah, and Galilee. These chests are associated with the custom of secondary interment in which the bones of the deceased were collected about a year after burial and placed in chests. The ossuaries are approximately 16–28 in. (40–70 cm.) long, 12–20 in. (30–50 cm.) wide, and 10–16 in. (25–40 cm.) high. The ossuaries taper slightly toward the bottom; some stand on four low legs; they are made of soft limestone with flat or vaulted lids. Many contain inscriptions on their sides in Hebrew, Aramaic, or Greek, or in two languages. In most cases only the name of the deceased or his family status is given, e.g., "Mother"; some inscriptions, however, are longer, e.g., "Dostos our father—do not open," or "The bones of the sons of Nicanor, who made the doors" (i.e., those of the Nicanor gate in the Second Temple). In rare cases (mostly in the burial of small children) one ossuary served for more than one body. The chests sometimes have a red painted decoration but the usual decoration is incised in a special technique derived from wooden prototypes. The surface of the ossuary was generally divided into two fields by square frames formed by a wavy line between two straight ones. The squares were filled with a rosette motif, usually with six leaves, but there are considerable variations in its form as well as in the decoration of the surrounding surface by the use of dots, wreaths, etc. Some contain representations of plants, buildings, or parts of them (columns, capitals), gates, and also crosshatchings (erroneously regarded by some scholars as symbols of Christianity). The ornamentation of ossuaries serves as one of the most important sources of Jewish folk art at the end of the Second Temple period.

Bibliography: Y. Brand, *Kelei ha-Ḥeres be-Sifrut ha-Talmud* (1953), ch. 12, 20; Clermont-Ganneau, Arch, 1 (1899), 381ff.; R. Schutz, in: MGWJ, 75 (1931), 286ff.; L. H. Vincent, in: RB. 43 (1934), 564ff.; Watzinger, Denkmaeler, 2 (1935); Galling, Reallexikon, s.v. *Sarkophag, Ossuar;* Frey, Corpus, 2 (1952), 245ff.; A. G. Barrois, *Manual d'archéologie biblique,* 2 (1953), 308ff.; Goodenough, Symbols, 1 (1953), 110ff.; 3 (1953), nos. 105–230; Perrot, in: *Atiqot,* 3 (1961), 1ff. [M.A.-Y.]

OSTIA, city in central Italy, near the mouth of the River Tiber, which was the port of Rome, and became at the end of the republic, and an important commercial center. At the end of the 19th century the site was excavated and a few epitaphs in Greek and Latin were discovered, which seemed to indicate the presence of a Jewish community *(universitas Judaeorum).* In 1961 the remains of a synagogue found near Ostia provided definite proof that a Jewish community had existed there. The excavations have shown that part of the building was constructed at the end of the first century, underwent alterations and enlargements during the second and third, and was considerably enlarged and partly rebuilt at the beginning of the fourth. As a result of the diminished population of the city, the synagogue fell into ruins at the end of the fourth or during the fifth centuries. The building, which is of the basilica type, stands between the ancient seashore and the coastal road *(Via Severiana),* and faces east-southeast, in the direction of Jerusalem. It has three entrance doors, recalling the synagogues of Galilee. From the door in the center a step leads down to the synagogue proper, a large rectangular hall about 81.6×41.0 ft. (24.9 ×12.5 m.). This is divided into three aisles with marble columns surmounted by finely worked capitals. It has been suggested that the lateral sections, which are divided by stone balustrades, were reserved for women. The wall at the

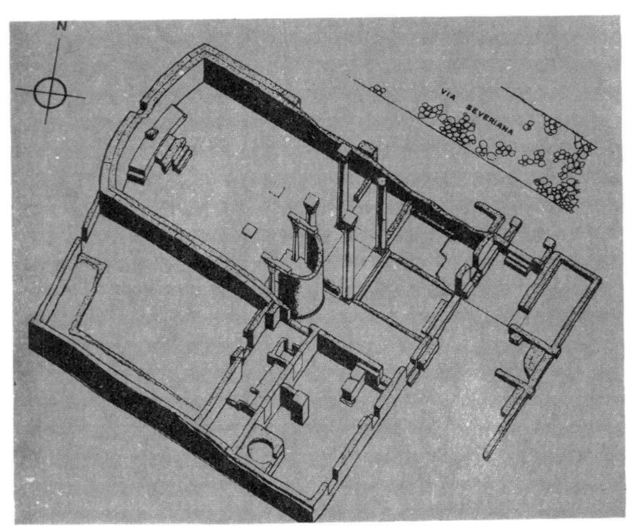

Figure 1. Axonometric projection of the ancient synagogue of Ostia, uncovered in the excavations of 1961–62. All illustrations courtesy Superintendent of Antiquities, Ostia, through U. Nahon, Jerusalem.

Figure 2. The Ostia synagogue after the first season of excavation, 1961.

Figure 3. Stone relief from an architrave of the Ostia synagogue, with a *menorah, shofar, lulav,* and *etrog*.

Figure 4. Partially reconstructed synagogue with back of Torah niche (left).

Figure 5. Room with mosaic floor adjoining the synagogue. The oven (upper right) is thought to have been used for baking *mazzot*.

back is slightly curved. In the oldest hall the seats were of stone, set against the walls. An inscription of the second–third century, partly in Latin, partly in Hebrew, refers expressly to the ark: "For the Emperor's health Mindis Faustos constructed and made at his own expense and placed the Ark for the Sacred Law . . ." In the later building the Tabernacle for the Ark rises behind the pulpit in the left aisle along its entire length, a few steps leading to it. Carved into the Tabernacle are Jewish symbols that can be found also in other synagogues of that period: a seven-branched *menorah*, a *shofar*, and a *lulav* and *etrog*. The floor is covered with mosaic. It is thought that a stove for baking *mazzot* can be identified in one of the surrounding rooms, as well as a *mikveh*, and a spacious hall which served for religious instruction or as a resting place for pilgrims. The community must have numbered several hundred Jews with a fairly high social and economic standard. The synagogue of Ostia is the first ancient synagogue known in Italy and Western Europe.

Bibliography: G. Calza, in: Pauly-Wissowa, 36 (1942), 1654–64; P. L. Zovatto, in: *Memorie storiche forogiuliesi*, 49 (1960); F. Squarciapino, in: Ministero della publica istruzione, *Bolletino d'arte* (1961), 326–37; idem, in: *Studi Romani*, 11 (1963), 129–41; idem, in: *Archaeology*, 16 (1963), 194–203. [A.M.R.]

OSTRACA (Gr. ὄστρακον, plural ὄστρακα), ancient inscribed potsherds. Ostraca were common writing materials in antiquity which were used mainly for writing receipts, temporary records, lists of names, etc., but some letters written on potsherds have also been found. Ostraca from the Middle Bronze Age II (c. 1788–1550 B.C.E.) have been found in Ereẓ Israel; the earliest one comes from the pile of debris left by *Macalister after his excavations at Gezer. It appears to represent a transitional stage between the proto-Sinaitic script and Hebrew-Phoenician alphabetic writing and has been deciphered as *klb* ("Caleb"). A later example of this transitional stage of writing appears on an ostracon from Tell el-Ḥesi discovered in the stratum attributed to the beginning of the Late Bronze Age II (c. 1400–1200 B.C.E.) which Sayce proposed reading *bla*.

Figure 1. Ostracon from the royal storehouse of the Israelite kings at Samaria, eighth century B.C.E. Jerusalem, Rockefeller Museum, Israel Department of Antiquities.

Figure 2. The "Ophel Ostracon," from Jerusalem, seventh century B.C.E. Courtesy Israel Department of Antiquities, Jerusalem.

Three inscribed potsherds from Lachish, probably dedicatory inscriptions, and one from Tell al-ʿAjjūl, are dated to the 13th century B.C.E. An ostracon found at Beth-Shemesh belongs to the transitional period between the Middle and Late Bronze Age but since it is written in ink, the potsherd and the inscription cannot be definitely dated to the same period. It seems to date to the beginning of the 12th century B.C.E. and apparently contains a list of names of workers, the number of their work days, and names of the employers. It is the first ostracon found in Ereẓ Israel which contains numerals. The latest ostracon from Ereẓ Israel was found at Tell a-Ṣarim in the Beth-Shean Valley and probably dates to the beginning of the first century B.C.E.

These ostraca are most valuable for tracing the development of the alphabet. Ostraca from the Israelite period have been found in the royal storehouse of the Israelite kings at *Samaria. These sherds, written in ink, are receipts for taxes and contain the year of payment, the name and provenance of the payer, the kind of tax (wine or oil), and some also have the name of the tax collector or the official in charge of the storehouse. These ostraca seem to date from the time of the Israelite king Jehoahaz, son of Jehu (c. 817–800 B.C.E.). Near the wall outside the city several other inscribed potsherds were found which were incised, and not written in ink. The "Ophel Ostracon" found in the City of David is assigned to the end of the period of the kingdom of Judah. It apparently contains the names of persons and their provenances. From the same period is a group of potsherds written in ink from Lachish (Tell al-Duwayr); 18 were found in the city gate and three in the latest Israelite stratum inside the city near the inner wall. In the excavations at Arad ostraca were found written in Hebrew and Aramaic and one in Egyptian. They are assigned to the end of the kingdom of Judah and early Persian period and are mostly orders to the official in charge of the fortress to provide supplies to the soldiers of the Judean kings. Several fragmentary ostraca from the Persian period were discovered in the upper stratum (sixth–fifth century B.C.E.) at Tell al-Khalayfa (cf. *Ezion-Geber, *Elath) on the coast of the Gulf of Akaba. They are written in Aramaic and are apparently receipts for wine.

Ostraca were commonly used in Egypt; those found at Elephantine are written in Aramaic in a script similiar to that appearing on the ostraca from Tell al-Khalayfa. The Egyptian ostraca, mostly tax receipts, are an important source of information on the economic history of the Ptolemaic and Roman periods in Egypt, and include records of the taxes levied on the Jews from the time of Vespasian onward.

Bibliography: S. Yeivin, *Toledot ha-Ketav ha-Ivri* (1939); R. B. Kallner, in: *Kedem*, 2 (1945), 11ff.; E. L. Sukenik, *ibid.*, 15; idem, in: PEFQS, 65 (1933), 152ff.; Y. Sukenik (Yadin), *Yedi'ot ha-Ḥevrah la-Ḥakirat Ereẓ Yisrael ve-Attikoteha*, 13 (1947), 115ff.; N. H. Torczyner, *Te'udot Lakhish* (1940); B. Maisler, in: JPOS, 21 (1948), 117ff.; U. Wilcken, *Griechische Ostraka*, 2 vols. (1899); P. Jouguet, in: *Bulletin de l'Institut Français d'Archéologie Orientale*, 2 (1902), 91ff.; E. Sachau, *Aramaeische Papyrus und Ostraka...*, 2 vols. (1911); D. Diringer, *L'alfabeto nella storia della civiltà* (1931); Diringer, Iscr, 21–79; Moscati, Epig, 27–39, 44–46, 111–3; Y. Aharoni, in: IEJ, 16 (1966), 1–17; Tcherikover, Corpus, 2 (1960), 108–76. [EH]

OSTRAVA (until 1929 **Moravska Ostrava**; Ger. **Maehrisch-Ostrau**), city in N. Moravia, Czechoslovakia; after Prague and Brno the third largest Jewish community in Czechoslovakia between the two world wars. The town was prohibited to Jews in the Middle Ages. In 1508 the local lord permitted one Jew to settle, against the wishes of the town. He was followed by others, resulting in an expulsion order of 1531, although it was only partly carried out. Jews mainly from *Osoblaha (Hotzenplotz) later did business in Ostrava. In 1786 the municipality leased its distillery to a Jew. Other Jews subsequently arrived and in 1832 a *minyan* was organized. When in 1837 the city council was in session deciding on whether to grant a Jew right of sojourn, the mob rioted and the council did not dare to decide in the affirmative. A *Kultusverein was organized in 1860 under the guidance of the *Teschen community. A cemetery was consecrated in 1872 and a community authorized in 1875; it then numbered 58 persons. The Jewish population was divided between the different parts of the city; Polnisch-Ostrau (after 1918, Slezska Ostrava), which was then under Silesian administration, and Maehrisch-Ostrau, which was under Moravian administration. After a prolonged conflict over where the community's institutions would be located, Maehrisch-Ostrau became the center.

With the rapid development of the city, caused by the development of mines and the founding of the Vitkovice steelworks by the *Gutmann brothers, the community thrived, absorbing Jews from older Moravian communities and many from Galicia. In 1879 the main synagogue was consecrated. About 3,000 Jews lived in Ostrava in the 1890s. Alois *Hilf was president of the community. Additonal synagogues were opened in the suburbs of Privoz (1904), Vitkovice (1911), Hrusov (1914), and Zabreh, among others. In 1912 the community built a vacation home for Jewish children. After 1918 Ostrava became a main center of Jewish life, where the regional offices of the Zionist Organization and of *He-Ḥalutz were located. A Jewish technical school was founded in 1919. The communal statute adopted in 1921, based on universal, proportional, and direct suffrage for men and women without regard to their citizenship, served as an example for many other communities. Among the new communal institutions opened in the 1920s were the Kedma, a home for Jewish apprentices (1924), and a new Orthodox synagogue (1926). In the community's elementary school, teaching was in German in the lower grades and in Czech in the upper grades. The community increased from 4,969 in 1921 to 6.865 in 1931 (5.4% of the total population). There were some very active communities on the outskirts and in the vicinity of Ostrava, e.g., Frystat (Ger. Freistadt; 322 in 1930), Karvinna (172 in 1930), Orlova (Ger. Orlau; 394 in 1930), and Frydek (Ger. Friedeck; 237 in 1930), Mistek (195 in 1930), Hrusov (Ger. Hruschau; 219 in 1930). Jewish life in Ostrava was depicted in the writings of Joseph *Wechsberg, a native of the town who later emigrated to the United States.

Holocaust Period. Immediately after the German occupation, the Jewish old-age home was confiscated and most of the synagogues in the city and in the suburbs of Vitk, Privoz, Hrusov and Zabreh were set on fire. On Oct. 17, 1939, about 1,200 Jews were transferred to Zarzecze, where a forced-labor camp, Nisko nad Lanem, was erected; the Ostrava community was forced to supply the materials for the building of this camp, which was known as *Zentralstelle fuer juedische Umsiedlung* ("central office for Jewish resettlement"). The Nisko camp was part of a projected plan to create a Jewish reservation in Poland, but it was soon abandoned. In March 1940, 600 Jews were driven over the border into Poland; another 500 were returned to Ostrava. Many of those driven east survived the war while those who remained were subjected to deportations. About 8,000 Jews from Ostrava and the surrounding district lost their lives in the Holocaust: about 200 were deported in four transports between Sept. 17 and Sept. 29, 1942; the residents of the old-age home were deported on June 23, 1943; and a further 3,442 Jews were deported to *Theresienstadt between Sept. 8 and Sept. 30, 1943.

Bibliography: H. Gold (ed.), *Juden und Judengemeinden Maehrens...* (1929), index s.v. *Maehrisch-Ostrau;* R. Iltis (ed.), *Die aussaeen unter Traenen...* (1959), 77–82; M. Kreutzberger (ed.), *Bibliothek und Archiv*, 1 (1970), 173. [M.La./H.W.]

OSTRICH, the largest of the birds. The ostrich, in its habits and bodily structure, has features similar to those of a camel (its Latin name is *Strutio camelus*). It was formerly commonly found in eastern Transjordan but by reason of being intensively hunted has disappeared almost entirely from the Middle East region; individual ostriches are only seldom found in eastern Transjordan, to which they apparently come from the Arabian deserts where the ostrich has also become rare. In the Bible the ostrich is called *ya'en* (יָעֵן) and *kenaf-rananim* (כְּנַף רְנָנִים; AV, JPS "the wing of the ostrich"). The former name occurs once, in Lamentations (4:3): "The daughter of my people is become cruel, like the ostriches in the wilderness." Its description as cruel is apparently connected with the fact that when in danger it is liable in its flight to hurt its chicks and also to the fact that the female often hatches only some of the eggs, the rest being abandoned and used as food for the newly hatched chicks. Job (39:13–18) contains an extensive description of the ostrich, there called *kenaf-renanim*, that is, "the wing that delights the eye with its beauty." There an account is given of the way it hatches its eggs on the ground (*ibid.*, 14–15); of the male who confuses the chicks of other females and is their leader (*ibid.*, 16); of the ostrich's meager understanding; "Because God hath deprived her of wisdom, neither hath He imparted to her understanding" (*ibid.*, 17; cf. the expression *Vogelstrausspolitik*); of its ability to escape from hunters mounted on horses (*ibid.*, 18). The translations have identified the *bat-ya'anah* (בַּת יַעֲנָה), included among the unclean birds and mentioned several times as inhabiting desolate places (Isa. 13:21; Micah 1:8; et al.), with the *ya'en*. The *bat-ya'anah* was originally a species of *owl but the name is used for ostrich in modern Hebrew. In the Mishnah the ostrich is called *na'amit* (נַעֲמִית; in Ar.: *na'ama*); in mishnaic and talmudic times the ostrich was well known. Vessels were made from its eggshells (Kel. 17:14), while some people bred it as an ornamental bird (Shab. 128a). Its ability to swallow anything was exploited; fed pieces of gold covered with dough, it evacuated them after the action of its gastric juice had refined the gold (TJ, Yoma 4:4, 41d).

Bibliography: Lewysohn, Zool, 188f., no. 240; I. Aharoni, *Zikhronot Zo'olog Ivri*, 1 (1943), 20, 33; F. S. Bodenheimer, *Animal and Man in Bible Lands* (1960), 59f.; J. Feliks, *Animal World of the Bible* (1962), 91. [J.F.]

OSTROG (Heb. אוסטרא ,אוסטרהא), city in Volhynia, Ukrainian S.S.R.; formerly in Poland. Evidence of the beginnings of Jewish settlement in Ostrog dates from the 15th century; inscriptions on two Jewish tombstones in the ancient cemetery date from 1445, and the archives of Lvov contain documents of 1447 relating to Ostrog Jewry. In 1495 the Jews were expelled from Ostrog, during the general expulsion of Jews from the grand duchy of Lithuania, but they were able to return after a short interval. Their trading activities were opposed by the burghers who in 1502 complained to the Polish king that the Ostrog Jews were depriving them of their profits from the transit trade through Lvov to Podolia and Russia. Sigismund I adjudicated a case relating to customs dues in which Ostrog Jews were involved in 1536. The growth of the Ostrog community was linked to the expansion of trade with Walachia, Walachian cattle being exchanged for cloth and other goods which the Ostrog Jews sold in Poland. They also exported timber, wax, potash, leather and leather goods via the Bug River to Danzig. The Ostrog community was one of the four original leading communities in Volhynia represented on the *Council of the Four Lands. The community perished during the Cossack uprising under *Chmielnicki in 1648–49 when 1,500 families (about 7,000 persons) were massacred. In 1661 there were only five Jewish families in the town. Later the community revived, to regain its former leading position in Volhynia, with jurisdiction over a number of communities in the vicinity. The Jews of Ostrog were miraculously saved during the *Haidamack raids in the middle of the 18th century, with the help of their Tatar neighbors. They also emerged unscathed when Russian troops in 1792 attacked the synagogue of Ostrog, believing it to be a fortress, in the fighting that preceded the second partition of Poland. In commemoration of their deliverance the Ostrog Jews instituted a "Purim of Ostrog," and the *Megillat Tammuz* was read in the synagogue on the 7th of Tammuz. At the end of the 18th century the Jewish population numbered under 2,000 and in 1830 2,206. By 1847 it had increased to 7,300, a similar figure to that in the period preceding the 1648 massacres, an influx evidently following the decree of *Nicholas I of 1843 ordering the expulsion of Jews from western border settlements (see *Russia). In 1897 the Jews numbered 9,208 out of a total population of 14,749; and in 1921 7,991 (out of 12,975). By 1939 nearly 10,500 Jews were living there.

Ostrog was one of the most important centers of Jewish religious learning in Poland, its name being interpreted in Hebrew as *Os Torah* ("the letter of the Law"). Some of Poland's most eminent scholars served as rabbis and principals of the Ostrog yeshivah, which was already in existence by the beginning of the 16th century. The first-known rabbi of the congregation and principal of the yeshivah was Kalonymus Kalman Haberkasten. Among his notable successors were Solomon *Luria (Maharshal), Isaiah *Horowitz, author of *Shenei Luḥot ha-Berit* (first quarter of the 17th century), Samuel *Edels (Maharsha), and *David b. Samuel ha-Levi (Taz). According to the last, the Ostrog yeshivah was probably the greatest in Poland: "Never have I seen so important a yeshivah as this." Ostrog was the "great town of scholars and writers" according to Nathan Nata *Hannover. The yeshivah was restored soon after the Cossack destruction through the efforts of Samuel Shmelke, who loaned a large sum to the Council of the Four Lands for its reestablishment and the maintenance of students. Its rabbis included many distinguished scholars and its graduates provided rabbis, principals of yeshivot, *dayyanim*, and *maggidim* for numerous communities. Ostrog also became celebrated as a center of *Ḥasidism which was disseminated there by several disciples of *Israel b. Eliezer (the Ba'al Shem Tov). A number of benevolent societies and foundations functioned in Ostrog, the most important being the burial society. [Az.S.]

Holocaust Period. Under Soviet rule (1939–41), the Jewish communal bodies were disbanded. A number of Zionist youth left for Vilna in the hope of reaching Palestine from there. In the summer of 1940 some Jewish families were sent into exile to the Soviet interior. When war broke out between Germany and Russia on June 22, 1941, groups of Jewish youth left the town with the retreating Soviet army. About 1,000 Jews from Ostrog reached the Soviet Union, leaving about 9,500 Jews in Ostrog itself. German forces entered Ostrog in early July 1941, and immediately embarked upon a campaign of murder and plunder among the Jewish population. On Aug. 4 3,000 Jews were rounded up and murdered in the woods in the New City, followed on September 1 by a similar action against 2,500 more victims. The members of the first *Judenrat headed by Rabbi Ginzburg, were murdered in the first murder *Aktion* in August. A second Judenrat was set up, headed by Avraham Komedant and including Chaim Dawidson, Yakov Gurewitz, and Yakov Kaplan. The third and final *Aktion* came on Oct. 15, 1942, in which 3,000 persons were taken and murdered on the outskirts of the town. About 800 Jews escaped to the forest, but few of them survived, as they were often attacked or betrayed by the Ukrainian peasants, or were murdered by gangs of the Bandera Ukrainian nationalists. Some of the escapees organized partisan units operating in the vicinity. Among the outstanding partisans were Yakov Kaplan, Mendel Treiberman, and Pesach Eisenstein. When the Soviet forces returned to Ostrog on Feb. 4, 1944, about 30 Jews emerged from the partisan ranks. Approximately another 30 came out of hiding. Later on, former Jewish inhabitants who had fled to the Soviet Union also returned, but the vast majority left Ostrog for Poland, on their way to Ereẓ Israel or other countries abroad. A society of former inhabitants of Ostrog functions in Israel. The community was not reconstituted after World War II. [Ar.W.]

Bibliography: M. M. Biber, *Mazkeret li-Gedolei Ostraha* (1908); *Arim ve-Immahot be-Yisrael*, 1 (1946), 5–40; Halpern, Pinkas; *Pinkas Ostrah: Sefer Zikkaron li-Kehillat Ostraha* (1960).

OSTROGORSKI, MOSES (1854–1917), scholar of political law and community leader. Born in Grodno, Belorussia, Ostrogorski finished his studies at the University of St. Petersburg and worked in the Ministry of Justice. In 1882 he was appointed head of the legislation department, but when the czarist reaction increased its power he was forced to resign and leave the country. His book, *La femme au point de vue du public*, published in 1892, was awarded a prize from the law faculty in Paris and was translated into English, German, and Polish. His most important book, *La démocratie et l'organisation des partis politiques* (translated into English in 1903), severely criticized the democratic regimes of England and the United States, whose main fault was that the power of the political parties suppresses individual freedom. On the basis of this book Ostrogorski became renowned among American and Western European thinkers. In 1904 he returned to Russia, where he was elected to the first *Duma in 1906 by the Jewish voters as the representative of the Grodno district. He was one of those who determined the Duma's work procedures. He also served as a member of the committee for equal rights, and with M. *Vinaver presented the case of the Jews. He was one of a six-member delegation sent by the Duma to visit the British Parliament. Although he did not formally join any political party, he always took the side of the Constitutional Democrats. As a member of the Jewish Popular Group, founded by Vinaver and *Sliozberg, he vehemently objected to the establishment of an organized group of Jewish representatives to the Duma which was demanded by the Zionists and *Dubnow. [E.M.]

OSTROLEKA (Pol. **Ostrołęka;** also **Ostrolenka**), town in Warsaw province, Poland. A permanent Jewish settlement in Ostroleka is not recorded before the 19th century, although Jews are mentioned in connection with the town in a document of 1622. An ordinance of 1826 prescribed certain areas for Jewish residence, only those with special privileges being permitted to live outside. The restriction was removed in 1862. The community, which numbered approximately 560 in 1827 (16.3% of the total population), increased to 1,129 (36.8%) in 1856; 4,832 (37.2%) in 1897; and 6,219 (53.5%) in 1909; decreasing to 3,352 (36.6%) in 1921. The 708 members of the loan society (founded in 1909) of the Ostroleka community in 1924 comprised 359 artisans, 259 small traders, 11 agriculturalists, and 79 members of other professions. [N.M.G.]

The *bet midrash* of Ostroleka, rebuilt after World War I, and turned into a bus garage by the Nazis. From *Sefer Kehillat Ostrolenka*, Tel Aviv, 1963.

Holocaust Period. Ostroleka was occupied by the Germans in September 1939. Jews were physically attacked and Jewish property confiscated. On Simḥat Torah all Jews were ordered to cross into the Soviet sector within three days. During the expulsion many were killed and their property stolen. The Jews of Ostroleka were scattered throughout the Soviet sector and found temporary asylum in Bialystok, Slonim, Lomza, and other cities. Administrative restrictions were placed upon them, and in 1940 many families were deported to the Soviet interior. Those who remained in the Soviet-occupied sector of Poland fell into the hands of the Germans after the outbreak of the German-Soviet war (June 22, 1941) and suffered the same persecutions as the local Jews—forced labor, starvation, diseases and, finally, extermination. Jews from Ostroleka were active in the resistance movements in the Vilna and Baranovichi ghettoes. Some also joined the partisans and fought in the Puszcza Naliboki and the surrounding area. [AR.W.]

Bibliography: *Sefer Kehillat Ostrolenka* (Heb. and Yid., 1963).

OSTROLENK, BERNHARD (1887–1944), U.S. economist. Ostrolenk, who was born in Warsaw, received his early schooling in Berlin, and was taken to the United States in 1897. After holding several teaching posts, he became professor of economics at the School of Business and Civic Administration at the City College of New York where he taught until his death. He also wrote for many magazines including *Current History* and *Business Week*. His major publications include: *Economic Geography* (1941); *The Surplus Farmer* (1932); and *The Economics of Branch Banking* (1930). His main interests were scientific farming and the economic problems of agriculture. During World War II, he became interested in immigration problems and the Zionist movement. [J.O.R.]

OSTROPOLER, HERSHELE (late 18th century), Yiddish jester. Although biographical facts concerning him are based on oral tradition intermingled with folklore, he was probably born in Balta, Podolia, and lived and died at Medzibezh. He derived his name from the townlet of Ostropol, Poland, where he served as *shoḥet* ("ritual slaughterer"), until his satiric wit offended the communal leaders. He then wandered through Podolia townlets becoming a familiar figure in the inns of the district. His poverty was proverbial. According to a folk legend, he was called to the ḥasidic court of Medzibezh to cure the *Ba'al Shem Tov's grandson, Reb Baruch Tulchiner, of his fits of depression by serving as his jester. His satiric barbs shocked the rich and delighted the simple folk. Booklets recording his tales, anecdotes, and witticisms appeared posthumously and were widely disseminated until the mid-20th century. He was the subject of lyrics by Ephraim *Auerbach and Itzik *Manger, a novel by I. J. *Trunk, a comedy by M. Livshitz performed by the *Vilna Troupe in 1930, a comedy by Jacob Gershenson, and a folkplay by Jacob Zonshein.

Bibliography: D. Sfard, *Shtudyes un Skitzen* (1955), 176–9; A. Holdes, *Mayses, Vitsn un Shpitslekh fun Hershele Ostropolier* (1960); Several stories of Hershele Ostropoler in English appear in I. Howe and E. Greenberg, *A Treasury of Yiddish Stories* (1953), 614–20; E. Sherman, *Hirshele Ostropoler* (Heb., 1931) includes bibliography. [S.L.]

OSTROPOLER, SAMSON BEN PESAḤ (d. 1648), kabbalist. No details are known about Ostropoler's life except those few that can be deduced from his own writings. During his lifetime, in the second quarter of the 17th century, he became widely known throughout Poland as the greatest kabbalist in the country, and the tradition about his outstanding rank lived on for several generations after his death. Considered one of the principal proponents of Lurianic Kabbalah in Poland, he corresponded with many kabbalists of his day. While serving as preacher and *maggid* in Polonnoye (Volhynia), he died a martyr's death at the head of the Jewish community (July 22, 1648) during the *Chmielnicki massacres. None of his writings was published during his lifetime and it is not until the following generation that scattered quotations in his name are found in various kabbalistic books. In 1653 Ẓevi Horowitz (or Hurwitz) ha-Levi copied in Grodno a collection of Ostropoler's kabbalistic notes (preserved in Ms. Oxford Neubauer Cat. Bod. no. 1793). His grandson incorporated this collection into his commentary on the Zohar, *Aspaklarya Me'irah* (Fuerth, 1776), dispersing it throughout many passages; only some portions were omitted. Moses Meinsters from Vienna published (Amsterdam, 1687) a small pamphlet containing *Ketavim* by Ostropoler. In 1709 the latter's nephew published in Zolkiew the book *Karnayim* with Ostropoler's commentary, *Dan Yadin*, and another batch of collectanea *(likkutim)* from his papers which also contained some of his letters on kabbalistic matters. *Karnayim*, attributed by Ostropoler to an unknown Aaron from the unknown city of Kardina, consists mainly of extremely obscure hints which are so cleverly expounded in the commentary that during the 18th century it was suggested that the book and the commentary were written by the same man. An analysis of all Ostropoler's remaining writings makes this virtually certain.

Ostropoler lived in a world of numerological mysticism and was deeply concerned with demonology, on which his writings abound in the most extraordinary statements. In the main his frequent references to Lurianic writings have no basis in Ḥayyim *Vital's texts and are only loosely connected with Israel *Sarug's brand of Lurianism. Many other quotations are equally fictitious, imitating Moses *Botarel's methods in his commentary on *Sefer Yeẓirah*. Ostropoler was apparently closely connected with two of his kabbalistic contemporaries, Nathan Shapira in Cracow and Aryeh Loew Prilik, who had similar interests but did not employ pseudepigraphy. Whereas the Lurianic writings speak of the power of evil, the *kelippot*, at great length but in a general, impersonal manner, Ostropoler liked to give each and every one special and previously unknown names, many of them obviously constructed on numerological principles. There is no doubt that he presents a psychological enigma. Anti-Christian and elaborate messianic hints appear in his writings. His main work, which is often referred to, was a commentary to the Zohar, *Maḥaneh Dan*, but no trace of this has been found. The unique character of Ostropoler's writings led to their being widely quoted in later kabbalistic literature, and they were reprinted several times. Two other commentaries on *Karnayim* were published, one by Eliezer Fischel from Stryzow (Zhitomir, 1805) denouncing those who suspected Ostropoler of being the author, and one by Samuel Samama of Tunis (Leghorn, 1825).

Bibliography: Nathan Hanover, *Yeven Meẓulah* (Venice, 1653), 7a; N. Bruell, in: *Oẓar ha-Sifrut*, 4 (1888), 468–72; G. Scholem, in: *Revue de l'Histoire des Religions*, 143 (1953), 37–39. [G.Sch.]

OSTROWIEC (also **Ostrowiec Swietokrzyski**), town in Kielce province, Poland. In 1755, the rabbi of Ostrowiec, Ezekiel b. Avigdor, took part in an assembly of the *Council of the Four Lands. Previously Eliezer b. Solomon Zalman Lipschuetz, author of responsa *Heshiv R. Eliezer ve-Si'aḥ ha-Sadeh* (Neuwied, 1749), had served as rabbi there. The community increased from 1,064 in 1827 to 2,736 in 1856 (80% of the total population) and 6,146 in 1897 (62.8%). In 1921 it numbered 10,095 (51%). Most of the Jews in Ostrowiec lived in conditions of extreme poverty. A pogrom was instigated there by factory workers in 1904. The Jewish loan fund in Ostrowiec had a membership of 474 in 1924, of whom 344 were storekeepers, tradesmen or peddlers, 97 artisans, and 33 in miscellaneous professions. [N.M.G.]

Holocaust Period. At the outbreak of World War II there were about 8,000 Jews in Ostrowiec. The first *Aktion* took place on Oct. 11–12, 1942, when 11,000 Jews from Ostrowiec and the vicinity were deported to the *Treblinka death camp. In October 1942 a forced-labor camp for Jews was established in Ostrowiec. On Jan. 16, 1943, 1,000 Jews were deported to the *Sandomierz forced-labor camp. The Jewish community was liquidated on June 10, 1943, when the remaining 2,000 Jews were transferred to Ostrowiec forced-labor camp, which was itself liquidated on Aug. 3, 1944, when the inmates were deported to *Auschwitz. An underground organization, headed by the brothers Kopel and Moshe Stein, and David Kempinski was active in Ostrowiec. They established contact with the leaders of the Jewish Fighting Organization in *Warsaw. A few groups of prisoners escaped and started guerrilla activities in the vicinity. Those who fled in July 1944 conducted guerrilla activities until the liberation of the region in July 1945. After the war the Jewish community of Ostrowiec was not reconstituted. [Ed.]

Bibliography: S. Krakowski, in: BZIH, no. 65–66 (1968), 66–68; Yad Vashem Archives; BJCE; PK.

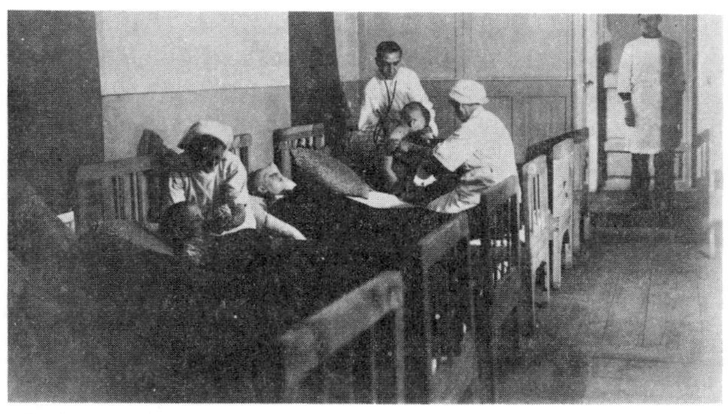

Children's ward in the Jewish Hospital of Ostrowiec. Courtesy Yad Vashem Archives, Jerusalem.

OSTROW MAZOWIECKA (Pol. **Ostrów Mazowiecka**, Russ. **Ostrov Lomzinsky**), town in the province of Warszawa, N.E. Central Poland. The intolerant attitude of the authorities of Masovia prevented the settlement of Jews for several centuries, and it was only during the 18th century that Jews succeeded in establishing themselves there permanently. In 1765 there were 68 Jews (20 families) paying the poll tax and owning 15 houses in the town, and another 45 Jews in six surrounding villages. Seven heads of families earned their livelihood from crafts; the remainder engaged in retail trade or held leases. In 1789 a Polish tribunal issued a restriction against Jewish settlement in the town, which remained in force until 1862. Jews who succeeded in settling in Ostrow Mazowiecka came mostly from central Poland and Lithuania, developing a special Yiddish dialect which combined the Yiddish language features of both areas. In spite of prohibitions there were 382 Jews living in Ostrow Mazowiecka in 1808 (34% of the total population). In 1827 they numbered 809 (39%). Jews engaged essentially in retail trade, peddling, haulage, and tailoring. In 1857 the community numbered 2,412 (61% of the population). A few wealthy families traded in wood and grain, and worked flour and saw mills. From 1850 the community supported a yeshivah. During the second half of the 19th century (somewhat later than in most other places) a dispute broke out between the Ḥasidim and the **Mitnaggedim* in the community. Rabbis of the two factions officiated alternately, notably David Solomon Margolioth, Judah Leib *Gordon, and the *ẓaddik* Gershon Ḥanokh of Radzyn. The majority of the local Ḥasidim belonged to the Gur (*Gora Kalwaria) and *Warka dynasties. In 1897 the Jewish community numbered 5,910 (60% of the population). Although at the beginning of the 20th century religious and secular Jewish educational institutions were established, it was not until the end of World War I that the community's institutions were organized to their fullest extent. In 1921, 6,812 Jews (51% of the total) made up the community's population. In 1934 the Jews of Komorowo were incorporated into the community of Ostrow Mazowiecka, and the yeshivah Beit Yosef was transferred to the town in 1922. [A.Cy.]

Holocaust Period. In 1939 over 7,000 Jews lived in Ostrow Mazowiecka. The German army entered on Sept. 8, 1939, and two days later initiated a pogrom, killing 30 Jews. At the end of September 1939 the German army withdrew for a few days and the Soviet army reached the town's suburbs since, according to the Soviet-German agreement, Ostrow Mazowiecka became a frontier town on the German side. Almost all the Jews crossed over to the Soviet side. On Nov. 11, 1939, the Germans assembled the remaining 560 Jews, drove them to a forest outside the town, and murdered them. Most of the Jewish refugees from the town settled in Bialystok but many did not succeed in leaving when the Germans invaded the Soviet Union (June 1941), and they shared the tragic plight of the Jews in Bialystok. After the war the Jewish community in Ostrow Mazowiecka was not rebuilt. Organizations of former residents of Ostrow Mazowiecka are active in Israel, the U.S., and France. [S.Kr.]

Bibliography: R. Mahler, *Yidn in Amolikn Poyln in Likht fun Tsifern* (1958), index; B. Wasiutyński, *Ludność żydowska w Polsce w wiekach XIX i XX* (1930), 36, 66, 72, 77, 79; I. Schiper (ed.), *Dzieje handlu żydowskiego na ziemiach polskich* (1937), index; *Sefer ha-Zikkaron li-Kehillat Ostrów Mazowieck* (Heb. and Yid., 1960); *Ostrow Mazowieck* (1966), a memorial book publ. in Heb.

OSTRYNA (in Jewish sources אוֹסְטְרִין), town in Grodno oblast, Belorussian S.S.R. Jews are first mentioned in Ostryna some time before 1569 as contractors of customs and taxes. In 1623 the Lithuanian Council (see *Councils of the Lands) placed Ostryna under the jurisdiction of the Grodno community. The number of Jewish poll tax payers in the town and surrounding communities was 436 in 1765. There were 405 Jews in Ostryna in 1847, 1,440 (59% of the total population) in 1897, and 1,067 (67.3%) in 1921. The Jews engaged mainly in trading, forestry, crafts, peddling, and agriculture; in the early 1920s there were 60 Jewish farmers in Ostryna. When the Germans evacuated Ostryna in 1919 the Jewish youth and military veterans established a Jewish police force to guard against peasant attacks. For the sake of Polonization of the region, the government of independent Poland moved Polish clerks, teachers, and settlers into the town. A Jewish self-defense group, which was organized in 1934, acted effectively against peasants who, incited by Polish students, were attempting to loot Jewish shops. A Jewish savings and loan fund was established in 1912 with 214 members; it was dissolved in World War I and later renewed as a cooperative bank which had 168 members in 1921.

A Hebrew school, in which the "direct method" *(Ivrit be-Ivrit)* was used to teach Hebrew, was established by the Zionist M. Gornilki. The first coeducational school was founded in 1913. In 1921 the CYSHO (*Central Yiddish School Organization) established a Yiddish school which operated a club to promote cultural activities in the spirit of the *Bund. From the earliest days of the movement Zionists were active in Ostryna. In 1923 they opened a *Tarbut school. There was a Jewish public library in the town. In 1923 a branch of *He-Ḥalutz was organized and in 1928 of He-Ḥalutz ha-Ẓa'ir. An attempt was made to establish a training center *(hakhsharah)*, based on forestry in the area. A training center of *Ha-Shomer ha-Ẓa'ir was established in 1927. Many ḥalutzim from Ostryna emigrated to Ereẓ Israel and some of them settled in kibbutzim. Among Ostryna's rabbis were Jacob Ẓevi Shapiro, author of *Tiferet Ya'akov* on the Mishnah; Jacob Tabszunsky, who during World War I gathered a group of students around him; and S. Gerszonowicz, the last rabbi, who was murdered along with his congregation by the Nazis. Harry Austryn *Wolfson was a native of Ostryna.

Holocaust Period. During World War II, when the Germans entered Ostryna on June 25, 1941, all the Jews were ordered to wear the yellow badge, and shortly after a Judenrat was established. The week after the invasion, the first Jews were killed. In October 1941 the Jews of Ostryna, together with those of Nowy-Dwor, numbering 1,200, were concentrated in two small ghettos. On Nov. 2, 1942, all the Jews from the Ostryna ghetto were deported to the Kelbasin forced-labor camp near Grodno, and at the end of the month were deported to *Auschwitz. A few young people succeeded in escaping from the trains going to Auschwitz and joined partisan units.

Bibliography: S. Dubnow (ed.), *Pinkas ... Medinat Lita* (1935), 17, 96; *Sefer Zikkaron li-Kehillot ... Ostrin* (1966); *Unzer Hilf* (1921–23); *"Ort"-Barikht* (Berlin, 1923). [D.R.]

OSWIECIM (Ger. **Auschwitz**), town in S. Poland and site of the notorious death camp. In the Middle Ages it was the capital of the duchy of that name, which in 1457 was purchased by Poland. Fairs, which attracted widespread interest, were held there in the 16th century. That Jews were living in Oswiecim as early as 1563 is attested by a charter of privileges granted by King Sigismund II Augustus which denied them residence rights near the marketplace or in the main streets and barred new Jewish settlers from the city. In 1564, when the Oswiecim regional council was undergoing reorganization, the Jews declared to the authorities concerned that the city had been inhabited by Jews since its foundation. In 1588 the community built a synagogue on grounds acquired from a burgher and established a cemetery. The transaction was confirmed by the royal chancellery. The Jews in Oswiecim suffered severely during the war between Sweden and Poland, 1656–58. Twenty houses are recorded in Jewish ownership in 1666, the number being equally small in the 18th century. According to a census of 1765 there were 133 Jewish residents. The community *(kahal)* of Oswiecim, whose jurisdiction extended over all the Jewish population in the area of the former duchy, had a membership of 862. In matters of Jewish communal administration it was subordinate to the *kahal* of Cracow. In 1773 Oswiecim came under Austrian rule. The tax levied on the community was so high that for a considerable time it was unable to meet its obligations. Two synagogues in Oswiecim, among other buildings, were destroyed by a fire in 1863. The last Austrian census in 1910 records 3,000 Jews residing in Oswiecim. The number had increased to 4,950 in 1921 (40.3% of the total population). The community was destroyed in World War II. For details of that period, see *Auschwitz.

Bibliography: M. Berson, *Dyplomataryusz* (1910), 69; M. Balinski and T. Lipinski, *Starożytna Polska,* 2 (1843); S. A. Bershadski, *Russko-Yevreyskiy Arkhiv,* 3 (1903), 228–30; M. Balaban, *Dzieje żydów w Galicji* (1914), index. [M.W.]

OTHNIEL (Heb. עָתְנִיאֵל), son of Kenaz, the first judge of Israel. He is first mentioned as a hero of the tribe of Judah during the period of the conquest of the land. As a reward for capturing Debir, he received in marriage Achsah, the daughter of *Caleb. At his wife's request Othniel also obtained from Caleb springs of water (Josh. 15:15–19; Judg. 1:11–15). As a motif, this narrative is reminiscent of the action of *Saul in promising his daughter to the one who would defeat Goliath (I Sam. 17:25). Historically, it presents a difficulty in that the capture of Debir is earlier attributed to Joshua himself (Josh. 10:38–39). The next reference to Othniel is as a divinely sent national hero who delivered Israel from the eight-year oppression of Cushan-Rishathaim, king of Aram-Naharaim, and so enabled the land to enjoy a respite from its enemies for a whole generation (Judg. 3:8–11). He was the only judge to come from a southern tribe. Othniel is described as being "the son of Kenaz, Caleb's [younger] brother" (Josh. 15:17; Judg. 1:13; 3:9). The ambiguity in the relationship is most likely to be resolved, on the basis of the genealogy of I Chronicles 4:11–15, in favor of his being Caleb's nephew. However, the problem of Othniel's identity is complicated by the fact that Kenaz is also the name of a clan. Caleb is a Kenizzite (Num. 32:12; Josh. 14:6, 14) and Kenaz is also the name of an Edomite tribe (Gen. 36:11, 15, 42; I Chron. 1:36, 53). Many scholars believe that Caleb and Othniel were respectively the eponymous ancestors of older and younger clans of the tribe of Kenaz that became absorbed within Judah. The importance of the clan of Othniel is indicated by the fact that one of David's divisional commanders in charge of the 12 monthly relays was "Heldai the Netophathite of Othniel" (I Chron. 27:15; cf. 11:30; II Sam. 23:28–29). [N.M.S.]

In the Aggadah. Othniel is identified with Jabez (I Chron. 2:55), and was so called because he counseled (Heb. *ya'az;* יעץ) and fostered the study of Torah in Israel. He restored the knowledge of the Torah, particularly the Oral Law, which had been forgotten in the period of mourning for Moses (Tem. 16a). He assumed the leadership of the people of Israel while Joshua was still alive (Gen. R. 58:2), and judged Israel for 40 years (SOR 12). According to the Alphabet of Ben Sira (II, 29a and 36a), he was one of those who was vouchsafed to enter Paradise alive. [Ed.]

Bibliography: E. Taeubler, in: HUCA, 20 (1947), 137–42; A. Malamat, in: JNES, 13 (1954), 231–42; Noth, Hist Isr, 56ff.; S. Yeivin, in: *Atiqot*, 3 (1961), 176–80; E. Danelius, in: JNES, 22 (1963), 191–3. For further bibl. see *Cushan Rishathaim. In the Aggadah: Ginzberg, Legends, index; I. Ḥasida, *Ishei ha-Tanakh* (1964), 359–60.

OTRANTO, town in Apulia, S. Italy. Tombstone inscriptions dating from the third century onward are proof of the existence of an early Jewish settlement in Otranto. The *Josippon chronicle (10th century) states that Titus settled a number of Jewish prisoners from Ereẓ Israel in the town. In the Middle Ages Otranto became one of the most prosperous Jewish centers in southern Italy. At the time of the forced conversion under the Byzantine emperor *Romanus I Lecapenus, one communal leader committed suicide, one was strangled, and one died in prison. When *Benjamin of Tudela visited Otranto in about 1159, he found about 500 Jews there. It was considered one of the most important rabbinical centers in Europe. In the *Sefer ha-Yashar*, Jacob *Tam (12th century) quotes an old saying parodying Isaiah 2:3: "For out of Bari shall go forth the Law and the word of the Lord from Otranto." When the Turks besieged Otranto in 1481, the Jews contributed 3,000 ducats for the defense of the town. In 1510, with their expulsion from the kingdom of *Naples, the Jews had to leave Otranto. A number of them settled in Salonika where they founded their own synagogue.

Bibliography: Roth, Dark Ages, index; Frey, Corpus, 1 (1936), no. 632; Milano, Bibliotheca, index; Milano, Italia, index; N. Ferorelli, *Ebrei nell' Italia meridionale . . .* (1915); Cassuto, in: *Giornale della società asiatica italiana*, 29 (1921), 97ff. [A.To.]

OTTAWA, capital of Canada, and third largest city (290,741 in 1966; in 1971 the estimated Jewish population was between 6,500 and 7,000) in the province of Ontario. Moses Bilsky first went to Ottawa in 1858 when it was still known as Bytown. He traveled to California and returned to Ottawa in 1869. Another early settler was German-born Aaron Rosenthal who went to Ottawa in 1879. In 1861 the census showed four Jews as residing within the confines of Ottawa; for 1871 none is shown and by 1881 there were 20. In 1891 the figure had more than doubled to 46. There was an almost tenfold increase to 398 by the year 1901, increasing to 1,776 in 1911 and 2,799 in 1921. The 1931 population of about 3,316 rose in the depression years to 3,809 in 1941, rising again to 4,484 in 1951 and 5,036 in 1961.

In 1892 Moses Bilsky and John Dover helped found the Adath Jeshurun synagogue. In 1904 a new building was erected. Its first religious functionary was the Rev. Jacob Mirsky, and a long-time president, A. J. *Freiman, served from 1904 to 1930. In 1902 the Agudath Achim synagogue was founded and its new building was erected in 1912. These two institutions, both Orthodox and both located in the same area, were merged in 1956 to form the Beth Shalom. Simon Eckstein, who went to Ottawa in 1952, served as rabbi of the united synagogue from 1957. The Machzikei Hadath congregation, commonly called the Murray Street Shul, follows the *nusaḥ Sefarad* (ḥasidic). Bnai Jacob synagogue was started in 1911 for Jews living in what was then the west end of the city. The Agudath Israel synagogue (founded in 1938) is affiliated with the Conservative movement: Rabbi J. Benjamin Friedberg was its spiritual leader. In the 1960s the Reform congregation Temple Israel was initiated and its rabbi from 1967 was David Powell. A later institution representing committed personal Orthodoxy is Young Israel. There are six synagogues in the city, and historically Ottawa's Jewish religious coloration has been strongly traditional.

Ottawa has contributed a number of national leaders to the Jewish scene in Canada: A. J. Freiman, who was national president of the Zionist Organization of Canada from 1920 to his death in 1944; his wife, Lillian *Freiman, who was a leader of Canadian Hadassah; their son Lawrence Freiman, who served several terms as president of the Zionist Organization of Canada; Hyman Bessin, who was head of the Canadian Mizrachi movement and from 1970 president of the Federated Zionist Organization of Canada. Ottawa is the only Jewish community in Ontario outside of Toronto to have its own home for the aged (Hillel Lodge). The Va'ad ha-Ir (Jewish Community Council) acts as a *kehillah*, conducts a Jewish center, and coordinates the community, community relations, and fund raising activity on the local level. In addition to the communal *talmud torah* and Jewish day school there is an Ottawa Modern Jewish School with a secular orientation. Samuel Rosenthal was alderman from 1902 to 1909 and in 1921; Dr. Murray Heit was an alderman (1959–64) and controller (1965–69); Lorry Greenberg was elected alderman in December 1969; Sam Berger, Q.C., was a member of the Board of Control (1956–59); Sol Max was trustee of the Ottawa Public School Board (1963–68); Jules Loeb, who later was president of the Ottawa Va'ad ha-Ir, served as mayor of South Hull, Quebec, a suburb across the Ottawa River in Quebec.

Bibliography: M. Bookman, in: *Canadian Jewish Reference Book and Director* (1963); A. D. Hart (ed.), *The Jew in Canada* (1926); M. H. Arnoni, in: *Canadian Jewish Year Book*, 2 (1940/41); B. G. Sack, *History of the Jews in Canada* (1965); S. E. Rosenberg, *Jewish Community in Canada*, 1 (1970).

[B.G.K.]

OTTENSOSSER, DAVID (1784–1858), Hebrew scholar. Born in Germany, he was a teacher at Fuerth yeshivah. Ottensosser devoted himself mainly to the study of Maimonides, upon whose works he drew in his Bible commentaries. His editions of Maimonides' works are among the best of his volumes of ancient texts, and he published Maimonides' letters with a German translation (*Iggerot ha-Moreh*, 1846) and an anthology of his teachings (*Imrei Da'at Rambam*, 1848). His explication and translation into German of Isaiah (1807) was his first effort in this field. He published a corrected edition of Mendelssohn's Bible, in which he improved upon the Pentateuch translation. He also edited Abraham Bedersi's *Olelot ha-Boḥen*, Jedaiah Bedersi's *Beḥinot Olam*, and the travelogue of Pethahiah of Regensburg, *Sibbuv ha-Olam* (with a German translation, 1854), as well as a German version (with Hebrew commentary) of the liturgy (1811).

Bibliography: Zeitlin, Bibliotheca, 258–60; Kressel, Leksikon, 1 (1965), 36.

[G.K.]

OTTINGER, ALBERT (1878–1938), U.S. lawyer, politician, and communal leader. Ottinger, who was born in New York City, was admitted to the bar in 1900. Active in

Republican politics, he became Republican leader of Manhattan's 15th Assembly District (1912), was elected to the New York State Senate (1916), and was appointed assistant U.S. attorney general by President Harding (1921). Twice elected New York State attorney general (1924,1926), Ottinger vigorously prosecuted food profiteers, loan sharks, and stock swindlers, and earned the Republican nomination for governor in 1928. He lost that election to Franklin Delano Roosevelt by 25,000 votes. A staunch opponent of Tammany Hall, he urged the probe into the Tammany activities that became known as the Seabury investigation. Active in Jewish affairs, Ottinger was chairman of New York City's Joint Distribution Committee drive (1931), and was associated with the Hebrew Orphan Asylum and the Young Men's Hebrew Association. [Ed.]

°**OTTO, RUDOLPH** (1869–1937), German Protestant theologian and historian of religion. Otto's major contribution to the study of comparative religion was his emphasis on, and analysis of, the notion of the "holy" as the specific and characteristic feature of religious experience. The "holy" is not identical with the true, the beautiful, or the moral. It is "awesome" in its grandeur and mysterious majesty. It is "wholly other" and causes ambivalent reactions, inspiring love as well as fear and producing confidence and joy as well as trembling. To express the range of meaning of the idea of the holy, Otto coined the term "numinous" (from Lat. *numen* "divine power"). While Otto's analysis may not apply to all religions, it well describes the religious consciousness of biblical religion and the religions influenced by it. The various aspects of the "numinous" as described by Otto correspond to the complementary categories of "love of God" and "fear of God" in Jewish thought, and more especially to the feelings evoked and emphasized by the liturgy of Rosh Hashanah and the Day of Atonement (the "Days of Awe"). In fact, Otto illustrated his argument by quoting not only from the Bible but also from the *piyyutim* in the prayer book for the High Holidays. Among Otto's important works are *West-oestliche Mystik* (1926; *Mysticism, East and West*, 1932) and *Reich Gottes und Menschensohn* (1934; *The Kingdom of God and the Son of Man*, 1938), but his best-known work is *Das Heilige* (1917; *The Idea of the Holy*, 1923). [R.J.Z.W.]

OTTOLENGHI (Ottolengo), Italian family of Piedmont, apparently originating in Germany, the name being an Italian form of Ettlingen. Its prominent members include: Joseph b. Nathan *Ottolenghi (d. 1570), rabbi of Cremona; Samuel David b. Jehiel *Ottolengo (d. 1718), scholar and kabbalist, born in Casale Monferrato. Abraham Azariah (Bonaiuto) Ottolenghi (1776–1851), rabbinical scholar born in *Acqui. When the French revolutionary army entered Acqui in 1796, he gave a public address on the significance of the tree of liberty erected in Acqui, as everywhere else, as a symbol of the new era. With the defeat of the French following the battle of Novi in 1799, Abraham had to flee to Genoa. After the return of the French in 1800, he returned to Acqui, and was appointed rabbi of the community, which position he held until his death. He wrote *Shir li-Khevod ha-Torah* (Leghorn, 1808). Nathan (Donato) Ottolenghi (1820–1883), the last outstanding member of the once-famous community of Acqui. On friendly terms with noted political figures of the period, including *Massimo d'Azeglio, Vincenzo Gioberti, and Cesare Balbo, he did much to better the position of both Jews and non-Jews and to improve the condition of the poor. Eleazar (Lazzaro) Ottolenghi (1820–1890), rabbi, born in Acqui. He held rabbinical office in Turin, Moncalvo, and Acqui, settling in Rome a year before his death. Author of a number of *piyyutim*, he also wrote a comedy, *Matrimonio misto* (1870), and *Dialoghi religioso-morali* (1873). In his youth, he also wrote several tragedies, one of which, *Etelwige*, was presented in Acqui in 1852. Emilio Ottolenghi (1830–1908), philanthropist, born in Acqui. In 1848 he moved to Alessandria and was elected member of the municipal council in 1882. He served as president of the community for a long period and was made a count by King Humbert I in 1883. Giuseppe *Ottolenghi (1838–1904), was an Italian general, minister of war in 1902–03, veteran of the Italian War of Liberation. Moses Jacob *Ottolenghi (1840–1901) was a writer and educator. Joshua (Salvatore) Ottolenghi (1861–1934), physician. He studied in Turin, was assistant of Cesare *Lombroso, and taught at Rome University. A pioneer in modern criminology, Ottolenghi founded (1902) the Scuola di Polizia Scientifica in Rome, the first of the kind in Italy. Donato Ottolenghi (1874–?1940) was professor of general pathology and hygiene at the universities of Pisa, Cagliari, and Bologna. Adolfo Ottolenghi (?1880–1943) served as rabbi in Venice from 1919 to 1943. During the Holocaust he was arrested by the Nazis and deported to Germany, where he perished. He was remembered in his community for his sincerity and his devotion to their needs. He wrote several historical essays, including *Leon da Modena e spunti di vita ebraica del ghetto nel sec. XVII* (1929) and *Abraham Lattes nei suoi rapporti colla republica di Daniele Manin* (1930). Raffaele Ottolenghi (?1887–1917), lawyer and publicist, devoted to the Jewish cause and to Zionism. He wrote *Voci d'Oriente* (2 vols.), a study of oriental influences in literature and of Hebrew proselytism. Mario Ottolenghi (1904–), economist and secretary of the Italian Zionist Federation (1933–39), settled in Israel in 1938. His son Michael (1934–) was professor of physical chemistry at the Hebrew University of Jerusalem.

Bibliography: Mortara, Indice, 46; E. Foa, in: *Il Vessillo Israelitico*, 31 (1883), 327–9, 343ff.; F. Servi, *ibid.*, 38 (1890), 137–9; Ghirondi-Neppi, 330, 332; Roth, Italy, index; Milano, Italia, index. [Ed.]

OTTOLENGHI, GIUSEPPE (1838–1904), Italian general and minister of war. Born in Sabionetta, Lombardy, Ottolenghi studied at the Turin military academy and fought with the Italian army in the war against Austria in

General Giuseppe Ottolenghi, Italian minister of war. Jerusalem, J.N.U.L., Schwadron Collection.

1859. In the following year he was transferred to the general staff, the first Jew to serve in that capacity in Italy. Ottolenghi was promoted to captain in 1863 and lectured on military tactics at the Modena military academy. During the Franco-Prussian War of 1870–71 he was Italian military attache in France and in 1878 was a member of the international commission to fix the boundary between Turkey and Montenegro. In 1902 he became commander of the 4th army corps with the rank of lieutenant general. In the same year he was made minister of war and a member of the senate. Ottolenghi was the recipient of many honors including the silver medal for military valor and the Cross of Savoy. He remained a loyal Jew all his life.

Bibliography: E. Rubin, *140 Jewish Marshals, Generals and Admirals* (1952), 160–2. [Mo.K.]

OTTOLENGHI, JOSEPH BEN NATHAN (d. 1570), rabbi of *Cremona, Italy. As head of the yeshivah, he made Cremona famous as a center of talmudic learning. Between 1558 and 1562 Ottolenghi published about 20 Hebrew works at the celebrated Riva di Trento press. He wrote novellae on the code of Isaac *Alfasi and compiled an index to the *Mordekhai* (the code of *Mordecai b. Hillel). Some of his contemporaries (among them the historian *Joseph ha-Kohen) considered that the burning of the Talmud and Hebrew legal works in *Cremona in 1559, when over 10,000 volumes were destroyed, was the consequence of a dispute between Ottolenghi and a certain Joshua de Cantori, aggravated by the interference of the apostate Vittorio Eliano.

Bibliography: Roth, Italy, 221, 303; Milano, Italia, 265, 620; J. Bloch, *Hebrew Printing in Riva di Trento* (1933), 3; I. Sonne, *Expurgation of Hebrew Books—the Work of Jewish Scholars* (1943), 21–38. [G.R.]

OTTOLENGHI, MOSES JACOB (1840–1901), Italian Hebrew writer and educator and pupil of Elijah *Benamozegh. He was born in Leghorn and died in Salonika. His works include *Degel ha-Torah* (an entertainment in seven acts, to be played on commencement day in houses of learning for the sons of Israel) printed in Hebrew and Ladino (Salonika, 1885), and *Ẓemaḥ David*, a collection of poems (1887). He also translated into Hebrew an Italian Jewish religious catechism, *Mishpat le-Ya'akov* (1892–95). [G.K.]

OTTOLENGO, SAMUEL DAVID BEN JEHIEL (d. 1718), Italian rabbi, kabbalist, and poet. Samuel was born in Casale Monferrato and studied under Moses *Zacuto and Benjamin Cohen. He served as chief rabbi of Padua and later of Venice.

His published works are: *Kiryati Ne'emanah* (Venice, 1715?), a digest of *Ma'avar Yabbok* of Aaron Berechiah of Modena; and *Me'il Shemu'el* (*ibid.*, 1705), an abridgement and index to the *Shenei Luḥot ha-Berit* of Isaiah *Horowitz. He also wrote a supplement to the *Tikkun Shovavim* (the initial letters of the first six weekly portions of the Book of Exodus) of Moses Zacuto that was published (*ibid.*, 1708) with the text. He founded a "Malbish Arumim" Society to assist the needy during those six weeks. Responsa, novellae, *piyyutim*, and kabbalistic articles by Ottolengo have remained in manuscript.

Bibliography: Ghirondi-Neppi, 330–2, 335; Steinschneider, Cat Bod, 2473, no. 7065. [Ed.]

OTTOMAN EMPIRE. See Supplementary Entries.

OTWOCK, town and health resort near Warsaw, Poland. It became popular among middle-class Jews from central Poland as a fashionable resort. A ḥasidic dynasty derives its name from this town. There were 2,356 Jews living in Otwock in 1908 (20.9% of the total population), and 5,408 in 1921. The 357 members of the Jewish loan society of Otwock in 1924 comprised 162 artisans, 156 merchants, and 39 members of other professions. [EJ]

Holocaust Period. On the outbreak of World War II there were 14,200 Jews in Otwock. In October 1939, one month after the occupation of the town, the Nazis burned all the synagogues there. In the summer of 1940 a few hundred young men were deported to the forced-labor camp at Tyszowce. A closed ghetto was established in January 1941. A year later, 150 young men were deported to the newly opened *Treblinka death camp, where they were among the first victims. In April 1942, 400 Jews were deported to the nearby forced-labor camp in Karczew. The great deportation to the Treblinka death camp began in August 1942. About 7,000 Jews were deported and exterminated in Treblinka, while 3,000 others, who offered passive resistance and hid themselves, were found, and most were killed on the spot. Another 700 Jews who succeeded in fleeing into the surrounding forests were killed by German armed groups searching the woods. The forced-labor camp in Karczew was liquidated on Dec. 1, 1942. After the war about 400 Jews settled in the town, but eventually all of them left Poland. A home for Jewish children and a Jewish sanatorium were active during the first postwar years. [S.Kr.]

Bibliography: *Sefer Yizkor—Otwock, Karczew* (Heb. and Yid., 1968); Yad Vashem Archives.

OUDTSHOORN, town in the Cape midlands of the Republic of South Africa. For many years Oudtshoorn was the center of the ostrich-feather industry, and Jewish immigrants played an outstanding part in its development. Arriving in the area about 1880, approximately 30 years after the town was founded, Jewish traders mainly from Lithuania mastered the methods of ostrich-farming and helped to develop world-wide markets for the feathers. Among the pioneers and recognized experts in the industry were men like the Rose brothers, and the eldest, Max, who came from Lithuania in 1890, was known as the "ostrich feather king." When the market collapsed shortly before World War I, the Roses fought hard to save the industry from ruin. At the height of the ostrich boom, Oudtshoorn had the largest Jewish population in rural South Africa, numbering 1,500 in 1913. Because of the intense communal and religious life of the Oudtshoorn community, it was sometimes called the Jerusalem of Africa. A Hebrew congregation was formed in 1883; the first synagogue was built in 1888 and another in 1896; one of these is now disused. Other communal institutions, including Zionist and philanthropic societies, and a Hebrew day school were established. The Jewish community produced many professional men and business leaders, and Jews were also prominent in the civic and cultural life of the town, in several cases serving as councillors and mayors. After the decline of the ostrich-feather industry, the Jewish population was considerably reduced. In 1968 they numbered about 300.

Bibliography: G. Saron and L. Hotz, *Jews in South Africa* (1955), index; L. Feldman, *Oudtshoorn—Yerushalayim d'Afrike* (Yid., 1940); M. Gitlin, *The Vision Amazing* (1950), index; I. Abrahams, *Birth of a Community* (1955). [L.Ho.]

OULIF, CHARLES NARCISSE (1794–1867), French lawyer and community leader, born in Metz. Oulif supported the revolution of July 1830 and was a tireless promoter of equality for the Jews. He secured the abolition in the court of Metz of the humiliating Jewish *oath (*more Judaico*) and of the term "Jew" in documents within its jurisdiction. Also in Metz, Oulif established a school for

Jewish youths and was among the founders of a society for the encouragement of technical education for Jews. Both institutions served as models for similar ones in other cities.

Bibliography: AI, 28 (1867), 265–9. [Ed.]

OUZIEL, BEN-ZION MEIR ḤAI (1880–1953), chief rabbi of Israel, *rishon le-Zion.* Ouziel was born in Jerusalem, where his father, Joseph Raphael, was the *av bet din* of the Sephardi community of Jerusalem, as well as president of the community council. At the age of 20 he became a yeshivah teacher and also founded a yeshivah called Maḥazikei Torah for Sephardi young men. In 1911, he was appointed *ḥakham bashi* of Jaffa and the district. Immediately upon his arrival in Jaffa he began to work vigorously

Ben-Zion Meir Ḥai Ouziel, Sephardi chief rabbi of Israel 1939–53. Photo K. Weiss, Jerusalem.

to raise the status of the oriental congregations there. In spirit and ideas he was close to the Ashkenazi rabbi of the Jaffa community, A. I. Kook, and their affinity helped to bring about more harmonious relations than previously existed between the two communities. During World War I he was active as leader and communal worker. His intercession with the Turkish government on behalf of persecuted Jews finally led to his exile to Damascus but he was permitted to return to Ereẓ Israel, arriving in Jerusalem before the entry of the British army. In 1921 he was appointed chief rabbi of Salonika, accepting this office with the consent of the Jaffa-Tel Aviv community for a period of three years. He returned to become chief rabbi of Tel Aviv in 1923, and in 1939 was appointed chief rabbi of Ereẓ Israel. Ouziel was a member of the temporary committee of Jews in Ereẓ Israel, a member of the Va'ad Le'ummi, and a representative at the meeting which founded the Jewish Agency. He appeared before the Mandatory government as a representative of the Jewish community and on missions in its behalf, and impressed all with his dignity and bearing. He was also founder of the yeshivah Sha'ar Zion in Jerusalem. He contributed extensively to newspapers and periodicals on religious, communal, and national topics as well as Torah novellae and Jewish philosophy.

He was the author of: *Mishpetei Ouziel,* responsa (1st ed., 3 vols., 1935–60; 2nd ed., 4 vols., 1947–64); *Sha'arei Ouziel* (1944–46), consisting of *halakhah,* general topics, and a selection of his addresses, letters, and other writings; *Mikhmannei Ouziel* (1939); *Hegyonei Ouziel* (1953–54), and still other works in manuscript. He made "Love, truth, and peace" the motto of his life. This verse (Zechariah 8:19) hung framed above his desk and was inscribed on his note paper. Two days before his death he dictated his testament. It said, inter alia, "I have kept in the forefront of my thoughts the following aims: to disseminate Torah among students, to love the Torah and its precepts, Ereẓ Israel and its sanctity; I have emphasized love for every man and woman of Israel and for the Jewish people as a whole, love for the Lord God of Israel, the bringing of peace between every man and woman of Israel—in body, in spirit, in speech, and in deed, in thought and in meditation, in intent and in act, at home and in the street, in village and in town; to bring genuine peace into the home of the Jew, into the whole assembly of Israel in all its classes and divisions, and between Israel and its Father in Heaven."

Bibliography: Tidhar, 2 (1947), 796f.; S. Don-Yaḥya, *Ha-Rav Ben-Ẓiyyon Meir Ḥai Ouziel* (1955); *Or ha-Me'ir, Mukdash le-Yovelo ha-Shivim shel . . . B. M. Ḥ. Ouziel . . .* (1950), 1–26 (Heb. pagination). [Y.Go.]

OVCHINSKI, LEVI (d. 1941?), rabbi, scholar, and historian. Born in Daugieliszki (Vilna province), Lithuania, Ovchinski studied at the yeshivah in Lida. After living for a time in Swinciany, in 1897 he was appointed rabbi in Alt-Autz, Courland, and afterward rabbi of Mittau (Jelgava). Rabbi Ovchinski and his two sons-in-law perished during the Holocaust.

Ovchinski wrote several reference works: *Naḥalat Avot* (1894), a biographical lexicon of Jewish scholars who were omitted from or only briefly mentioned in Ḥ.J.D. *Azulai's *Shem ha-Gedolim,* and A. Walden's *Shem ha-Gedolim he-Ḥadash.* In a similar category is Ovchinski's *Hadrat Ẓevi* (1914) containing the biographies of the rabbis Naḥman Idl Margolies and Ẓevi Hirsch Nurock (father of Mordechai *Nurock). His main work was *Toledot ha-Yehudim be-Kurland* (1908, 1911[2]; a Yiddish translation was published in Riga in 1928 entitled *Di Geschikhte fun di Yidn in Letland fun Yor 1561–1923),* the historical section of this book being based principally on R. *Wunderbar's volume on the same subject. The second section dealing with the history of the communities of Latvia and their rabbis is Ovchinski's most important contribution to the historiography of Latvian Jewry, based on and utilizing the minute books of the communities and burial societies, as well as other sources.

Bibliography: *Yahadut Latvia* (1953), 368–9; M. Bobe, *Perakim be-Toledot Yahadut Latvia* (1965), 205–6. [Jo.Ga.]

OVED, MOSHE (Good, Edward; 1885–1958), Yiddish writer, artist, sculptor, and gem expert. Oved left Poland in 1903, and settled in the East End of London, where he worked as a watchmaker. He began to trade in antique watches and cameo brooches and founded "Cameo Corner," a shop for antique jewelry. The royal family and

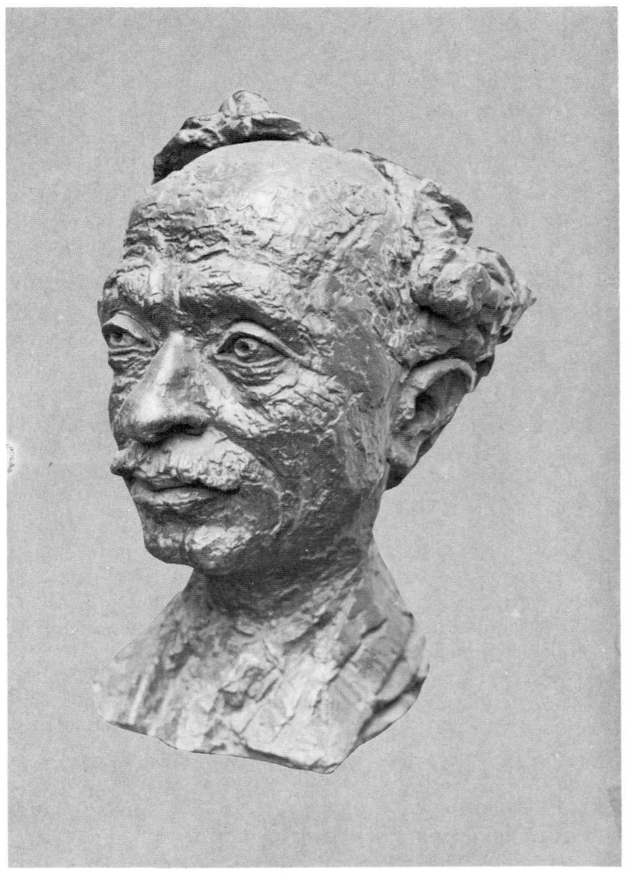

Bust of Moshe Oved, Yiddish writer and antique jeweler, by Jacob Epstein, 1946. Courtesy Ben Uri Art Gallery, London.

members of fashionable society patronized his shop. His first book in Yiddish, *Aroys fun Khaos* (1917; *Out of Chaos*, 1918), was followed by *Lebns Lider* (1924). In *Visions and Jewels* (1925), a collection of 124 autobiographical stories and short tales, he wrote about Nahum *Sokolow, Max *Nordau, Sholem *Asch, Jacob *Epstein, and others. *The Book of Affinity*, 1933, was a deluxe production with original color lithographs by Jacob *Epstein. At the age of 60 he began to produce sculpture, which reflected the classical philosophy he had expressed in his writing and poetry. Among his sculptural works are "Ram with Candelabra" and "Community of Israel," lamenting the six million Jews who died in the Holocaust.

Bibliography: Rejzen, Leksikon, 2 (1927), 721–2; LYNL, 6 (1965), 570–1. [Ch.S.S.]

OVRUCH, city in Zhitomir oblast, Ukrainian S.S.R. The first information on the Jews, in a document of 1629, mentions three families in the town. Until 1750 the community was dependent on the taxation imposed on the community of *Chernobyl. A court ordered that Ovruch be separated from Lithuania and annexed to the province of Volhynia. According to the census of 1765, there were 607 Jews in Ovruch and its environs who paid the poll tax. There were 1,773 Jews in 1847 and 3,445 (46.5% of the total population) in 1897. The end of the 18th century witnessed the spread of Ḥasidism in Ovruch and its environs. *Abraham Dov Baer, a student of Mordecai of Chernobyl, served as *av bet din*. In the second half of the 19th century, two members of the *Shneersohn family served as rabbis.

During the Russian Revolution the Jews of Ovruch were attacked several times. At the end of 1918 the Ukrainian hetman, Kozyz-Zyrko entered the town and in the course of 17 days plundered all the Jewish homes, killing 80 people. With the introduction of Soviet rule the religious and communal life of the Jews was paralyzed. In 1926 there were 3,400 Jews in Ovruch (53% of the total population). The town fell to the Nazis in the summer of 1941, and the Jews who did not manage to escape were exterminated.

In 1963, on the eve of the High Holidays, the militia broke into privately held services in Ovruch, arresting five Jews; each member attending the services was fined. In the late 1960s the Jewish population was estimated at about 2,000. No synagogue existed at that time.

Bibliography: Committee of Jewish Delegations, *The Pogroms in the Ukraine*... (1927), 134–40; L. Chasanowich, *Der Yidisher Khurbn in Ukraine* (1920), 3–20. [Y.S.]

OVSAY, JOSHUA (1883 or 1885–1957), Hebrew literary critic. Born in Russia, he lived in the U.S. from 1918 to 1955, when he immigrated to Israel.

His first publication in Hebrew appeared in *Ha-Meliẓ* and he subsequently contributed essays and articles on literature to the Hebrew (and occasionally the Yiddish) press. Some of his essays on writers and books were collected in *Ma'amarim u-Reshimot* (1947). He edited the writings of Moses Halevy (with Hillel *Bavli) and the literary anthology *Koveẓ Sippurim mi-Mendele ad Bialik* (1942). He also translated Dickens' *Old Curiosity Shop* (1924).

Bibliography: Waxman, Literature, 5 (1960²), 206f.; Kressel, Leksikon, 1 (1965), 35. [G.K.]

OWL, bird belonging to the family Strigidae. Because of the strange appearance of species of the owl, some of their conspecies were called *kippuf*, that is, resembling a *kof* ("ape"). It was also said that "their eyes are directed forward like those of human beings" and that "they have jaws like those of human beings" (Nid. 23a). They were regarded as an evil omen, so that although "all kinds of birds are a good sign in a dream," species of owls are not (Ber. 57b). Most of them utter a hooting cry like a groan, and as they inhabit ruins, they sound as though mourning over the devastation, and hence symbolize in the Bible destruction and desolation. The majority of them are included in the Pentateuch among the birds prohibited as food, and even those not mentioned there are unclean according to the principle that a bird "is unclean if (when perched on a cord stretched for it) it divides its toes evenly, two on each side" (Ḥul. 65a; cf. Ḥul. 3:6). The owl's toes, divided into two in front and two behind, assist it in seizing its prey.

Four types of owl (Strigidae). 1. little owl *(Athene noctuo glaux)*; 2. barn screech owl *(Tyto alba)*; 3. eagle owl *(Bubo bubo aharonii)*; 4. tawny owl *(Strix aluco)*, ancient Egyptian drawing. Courtesy J. Feliks, Jerusalem.

The Bible contains at least 11 names of owls. Of these the *tinshemet, ka'at, kos, yanshuf, shalakh,* and *bat ya'anah* are mentioned in the lists of unclean birds in Leviticus and Deuteronomy. For the biblical names of owls the following identifications have been suggested.

(1) The *tinshemet* (Lev. 11:18; Deut. 14:16; JPS, "horned owl"; AV, "swan") is the barn screech owl *(Tyto alba)*, its Hebrew name (which occurs also in Lev. 11:30 as that of an unclean creeping thing, but there refers to the *chameleon) being derived from נשם ("to breathe") on account of its heavy breathing. Because of its odd appearance it was regarded as "the strangest (or "the most repulsive") of birds" (Ḥul. 63a).

(2) The *ka'at* (Lev. 11:18; Deut. 14:17; JPS, AV, "pelican") is mentioned among the birds that inhabit ruined places (Isa. 34:11; Zech. 2:14). Referring to his sighing and emaciated body by reason of his suffering, the psalmist (Ps. 102:6–7) compares himself to "a *ka'at* of the wilderness." Its Hebrew name denotes vomiting *(meki)* in a reference apparently to the fact that, as do other owls, it regurgitates the bones of its prey. In desert regions there occurs a species of owl—the *Athene noctua saharae* owl—that fits in with the biblical descriptions of the *ka'at*.

(3) The *kos* (Lev. 11:17; Deut. 14:16; JPS, AV, "little owl"), that occurs together with *ka'at*, of which it is a conspecies, in Psalms (102:7), is probably the little owl *(Athene noctua glaux)*, its

Hebrew name being onomatopoeic. It has no "ears," that is, no crest of feathers. Symbolizing, as it did, wisdom to the ancient Greeks because of its large wide-open eyes, it appeared on the coins of Athens.

(4) The *yanshuf* (Lev. 11:17; Deut. 14:16; JPS, AV, "great owl"), depicted by Isaiah (34:11) as inhabiting devastated Edom together with the *ka'at*, has been identified with the long-eared owl (*Asio otus*), its Hebrew name being connected with *neshef* ("night") or with *neshifah* ("hooting"). It is found in winter in the north of Israel.

(5) The *shalakh* (Lev. 11:17; Deut. 14:17; JPS, AV, "cormorant") which, according to the Talmud, "catches fish out of the sea" (Ḥul. 63a), has been identified with the fish owl (*Ketupa zeylonensis*), the only owl in Israel that feeds on fish. It is found near Lake Kinneret.

(6) The *bat ya'anah* (Lev. 11:16; Deut. 14:15; JPS, "ostrich," AV, "owl") is, according to the ancient translations, the *ostrich, which however lives in the open desert and which rarely utters a cry, whereas the *bat ya'anah* is described as inhabiting desolate places (Isa. 34:13) and as emitting a mournful cry (Micah 1:8). For these reasons it has been identified with one of the species of owl that utters a cry when calling to one other (*ya'anah* is apparently derived from *anah* (ענה), "to answer"), this being characteristic of three strains of the species *Bubo bubo*, one of which, the dark desert eagle owl (*Bubo b. ascalaphus*), has been identified with the biblical *bat ya'anah*.

(7) The *tannim* has been identified with the second, light-colored strain of the previous species—with the *Bubo b. desertorum*. It lives in the desert and in ruins and emits a sighing cry, the name *tannim* being derived from *tanah* (תנה; "to weep"). Since it occurs together with the *bat ya'anah* among birds in the above passages, it is difficult to accept the customary modern identification of *tannim* as *jackal.

(8) The *o'aḥ* (JPS, "ferret"; AV, "doleful creature"), mentioned with the *bat ya'anah* as inhabiting ruined places (Isa. 13:21), has been identified with the third strain of the above species—the Palestinian eagle owl (*Bubo b. aharonii*), its name being onomatopoeic. The largest of the owls, it is found in the Jordan Valley, and feeds on hares and rats, reptiles and birds.

(9) The *kippod* (JPS, AV, "bittern") and the *kippoz* (JPS, "arrowsnake," AV, "great owl") are mentioned in the account of the destruction of Edom, where various birds lived and nested (Isa. 34:11, 15). Associated as its name is with the meaning of rolling oneself up into a ball, the *kippod* has been identified with the short-eared owl (*Asio flamneus*) which adopts a rotund posture and lives near swamps and in ruined places, and hence Isaiah (14:23) prophesies that Babylonia would be made into "a possession for the *kippod* and pools of water." The hedgehog is also called *kippod* or *koppad* in the Mishnah (Shab. 5:4), because it rolls itself up into a ball.

(10) The *lilit* (JPS, "night monster," AV, "screech owl"), which also occurs in Isaiah's prophecy about Edom (34:14), refers to a species of bird (cf. Nid. 24b), the word, connected with *laylah* ("night"), denoting a nocturnal bird, perhaps the tawny owl (*Strix aluco*). In the *aggadah* it is the name of a night-demon (see *Lilith).

The *sa'ir*, mentioned alongside the *lilit*, is apparently also a species of owl. This word is now applied to the smallest of the owls, the *Otus scopus*. Another view holds that it refers to a species of demon (cf. Lev. 17; II Chron. 11:15).

Bibliography: Lewysohn, Zool, 162ff.; R. Meinertzhagen, *Birds of Arabia* (1954), 318f.; J. Margolin, *Zo'ologyah*, 2 (1959), 275; F.S. Bodenheimer, *Animal and Man in Bible Lands* (1960), 54, 117f., 128; J. Feliks, *The Animal World of the Bible* (1962), 72–81; M. Dor, *Leksikon Zoologi* (1965), Eng. index. [J.F.]

OWNERSHIP (Heb. בַּעֲלוּת, *ba'alut*). As a proprietary right, ownership is the most important of all rights in property, all other rights being inferior to it. The distinction between ownership and other proprietary rights is apparent not only in matters of civil law but is especially significant in other halakhic matters. Thus, the *etrog* ("citron") and other three species prescribed for the festival of Sukkot must be one's own property and not borrowed or stolen (Sh. Ar., OḤ 649:1–2). This principle of ownership applies also to the first fruits of one's own field which have to be brought to the Temple and over which the scriptural recital (Deut. 26:1–11) is to be made (Bik. 1:1–2; Git. 47b).

The Talmud indicates that a person is the owner of property if it is in his possession for an unlimited period, or if possession thereof is due to revert to him for an unlimited period after he has temporarily parted with the property in question. At first glance, the distinctive feature of ownership appears to be the fact that a person is free to deal as he pleases with the property he owns, a power not available to the holder of any other proprietary right. It will be seen, however, that this feature is not in itself sufficient to define ownership, since it does not always apply. For instance, an owner must not use his land in a manner that interferes with a neighbor's use of his land (see *Nuisance) nor may he use his property in such manner as to commit an offense. Furthermore, a person who has agreed to encumber or submit to any restraint whatsoever on the use of his land nevertheless remains the owner. A person who lets his property, for instance, even for a long-term period continues to be the owner. It is therefore apparent that the rights of ownership may adhere even to those who are not free to deal as they please with their property. Nor does the suggestion that ownership is characterized by a person's right to sell or alienate his property prove to be sufficiently distinctive. Thus the usufructuary may also transfer his right to another (Maim. Yad, Mekhirah, 23:8) and the borrower or lessee may also do so—with the owner's permission—yet these parties do not become owners of the property to which their rights extend. On the other hand, at the time when the laws of the jubilee year were operative, the owner could not sell his land forever, yet he was its owner. Moreover, sometimes a right in property other than ownership exceeds the owner's rights therein, such as the case of a tenant who holds a 100-year lease.

Possession (reshut). The distinctive quality of ownership is closely connected with the concept of *reshut* ("possession"); so much so that the commentators do not always discriminate between the two and sometimes use the term *reshut* to denote ownership. *Reshut* (see also *acquisition) is a person's control over property, established by the existence of three requirements: (1) his ability and (2) intention to use the property (3) at any time he may wish to do so—even if only for a period of limited duration. All three requirements must be satisfied and operate simultaneously for the possession to be effective; hence coins which are in a place that cannot be reached are not in a person's *reshut*, even if they are his own (Tosef. Ma'as. Sh. 1:6). If such place is accessible to him, however, because "the way is open" and caravans pass there, the coins are said to be in his *reshut*, but not otherwise (TJ, Ma'as. Sh. 1:2, 52d). Similarly, chattels which have been stolen are in the *reshut* of the thief, since the latter is able to use the property at his pleasure and the owner is unable to prevent him from doing so or to use the property himself. Land cannot be stolen and is therefore always in possession of its owner, and since it cannot be carried away or hidden the owner can always have it restored to his use through the mediation of the court. He therefore remains free to use the land whenever he pleases, unlike a purported robber. Similarly, an object which is deposited remains in the *reshut* of its owner, not that of the bailee, from whom the owner can demand its return at any time. If, however, the bailee should refuse to return the property and denies the existence of a bailment, he will be deemed a robber and the property will thus be in his *reshut* (BM 7a and Alfasi ad loc.). Property on hire or loan for a fixed period, which the owner may not revoke, is in the *reshut* of the hirer or borrower for the duration of the stated period. In the same way, when a person sells the usufruct of his field, the field will be in the *reshut* of the usufructuary (BB 8:7), since the latter, not the owner, may use the field at his pleasure (Maim. Yad, Mekhirah, 23:7).

For the same reason, an object which is found on premises which are kept or reserved for the owner is in the latter's possession. This is so even if the premises are kept for him because people keep away from there of their own accord and not because of his own ability and power to guard his field (BM 102a); if however he is unable to use a thing which is on his premises, for instance when it is hidden and nobody expects to find it there, it will not be in his *reshut*. Property which is on a person's premises when they are not kept for him will not be in his *reshut*, as it is deemed certain to be lost or taken by others and is therefore not freely at his disposal (see *Acquisition, Modes of).

Ownership and Possession. These are by no means identical concepts. The *amora*, R. Johanan, states that stolen property is in the *reshut* of the thief, but the person robbed remains the owner (BM 7a). The same may be said with regard to hired property. *Reshut* nevertheless appears to be an essential element in the determination of ownership, for, as indicated, a person is held to be the owner if the property is permanently in his possession for an unlimited period—even if it passes out of his *reshut* for a limited period but is due to revert to him permanently (cf. Ran, Ned. 29a). Thus the law that a swarm of bees and doves of a dovecote may be owned has rabbinic authority only—for the sake of keeping the peace (BK 114b; Ḥul. 141b)—as in strict law these cannot be owned because they cannot be permanently kept in a person's *reshut*. Similarly, geese and fowl which have escaped are ownerless because they cannot be restored to the owner's *reshut* (Tos. to Ḥul. 139a). This is also the case in respect of *lost property which the owner has despaired of finding and having restored to his *reshut* (see **Ye'ush*).

Permanent *reshut* is not the only requirement of ownership, however. Ownership may cease when a person makes up his mind that the property is to pass permanently out of his *reshut*, or that it shall not return permanently into his *reshut*, as by way of *ye'ush*, or when he renounces the property (see **Hefker*), or when he conveys it to another. Consequently a deafmute, idiot, or minor, none of whom has legal understanding, cannot lose ownership in any of these ways (BM 22b; Git. 59a). Hence it may be said that the right of ownership is characterized by two basic attributes: a positive one, that the property is in the *reshut* of the claimant for a period of unlimited duration; and a negative one, that such person shall not have resolved to remove the property permanently from his *reshut*.

Ownership of Limited Duration. Despite the general principles outlined above, it is possible for ownership to be limited in point of time. The outstanding example of this is a returnable gift, which, in the opinion of Rava, is a proper gift making the donee the owner as long as the gift is with him (Suk. 41b). The comment of the *rishonim* (Asheri *ibid.* 30; Ritba, Nov. Git. 83a; Kid. 6b) is that such a gift is a complete and full conveyance, and the return of the gift requires a fresh conveyance. Since it is a condition of the gift that it must be returned to the original donor, such a gift in fact only confers title for a limited period (cf. *Kezot ha-Ḥoshen*, ḤM 241:4). Another example of ownership of limited duration is that cited by R. Isaac of the creditor acquiring a pledge for a debt (BM 82a). In this case it may also be said that this is a complete and full acquisition and the return of the pledge to the debtor requires an assignment thereof by the creditor. The Talmud discusses the question of such an assignment being involved even in the case of hire (Av. Zar. 15a).

The most important example of ownership for a limited period is to be found in the sale of land at the time that the jubilee year was customary, for in the jubilee year land reverted to the vendor. This is also the case when land is sold for any period of limited duration. In this case the acquisition is called *kinyan perot* (i.e., usufruct) in the Babylonian Talmud (Git. 47b) and *kinyan nekhasim* in the Jerusalem Talmud (Git. 4:9, 46b). It is stated in the latter that the purchaser may not dig any wells while the field is in his possession (*Mishneh la-Melekh*, to Maim. Shemittah, 11:1). According to the Babylonian Talmud (*ibid*), *kinyan perot*—before the occurrence of the first jubilee—was like an acquisition of the land itself, since people had not yet been accustomed to the restoration of the land and looked upon a sale as leading to a permanent and irrevocable acquisition. However, in the opinion of Simeon b. Lakish, from the second jubilee onward *kinyan perot* was not like the acquisition of the land itself and the seller remained the owner because at the end of the stipulated period the land would revert permanently to his possession. R. Johanan is of the opinion that *kinyan perot* is like a *kinyan* of the land itself and that the Pentateuch provided for the termination of such ownership in the jubilee year and the restoration thereof to the owner of the land. The dispute also extends to land which is sold for a fixed period. The *halakhah* was decided in accordance with the view of Simeon b. Lakish.

Because of the element of possession in the concept of ownership, it is possible for a person to own only part of a thing, provided that it is possible for such part to be in his separate possession. Thus, it can sometimes happen that one person may own land and another the trees on it (BB 37a–b), or one person may own a house and another the top story (BM 117b).

In the State of Israel, the Cooperative Houses Law, 5713–1952, in keeping with Jewish Law and contrary to the law in force until then, makes provision for the separate ownership of each apartment in a cooperative house.

See also *Acquisition.

Bibliography: Gulak, Yesodei, 1 (1922), 131–4; Herzog, Instit, 1 (1936), 69–75; S. Albeck, in: *Sefer Bar-Ilan*, 7–8 (1970), 85–94.

[Sh.A.]

OXFORD, English university town. The presence of Jews is first recorded in 1141, when they were despoiled by both claimants to the throne during the civil war. The Jewry was in the center of the town (the present St. Aldate's Street). Oxford Jews suffered greatly from the confiscatory tallage imposed in 1210. An ecclesiastical synod of the Province of Canterbury held there (1222) renewed the anti-Jewish regulations of the Fourth *Lateran Council and condemned to death a deacon who had converted to Judaism. In the 13th century Oxford possessed an **archa*. The Jewish population was, however, at all times small, probably never exceeding 150. Besides acting as moneylenders, the Jews were notorious as university landlords, which was one reason for the student riot against them in 1244, after which relations with university members were regulated. The wealthiest Oxford Jew of the period was David of Oxford (d. 1244), remarkable details of whose private life are extant. Oxford was the place of residence of R. Yom Tov and R. Moses Yom Tov of London whose son Jacob of Oxford (d. 1276/1277) was a leading member of the community. *Berechiah Natronai ha-Nakdan, author of the *Fox Fables*, is perhaps identical with Benedict le Puncteur of Oxford (c. 1200). In 1268 Oxford Jewry was heavily fined for an alleged outrage on a crucifix and in 1278–79 several Jews were arrested and some executed on charges of clipping the coinage.

From the 17th century onward Jewish-born teachers of Hebrew, mostly converts, found their way to Oxford. Permanent settlement began after the mid-18th century but

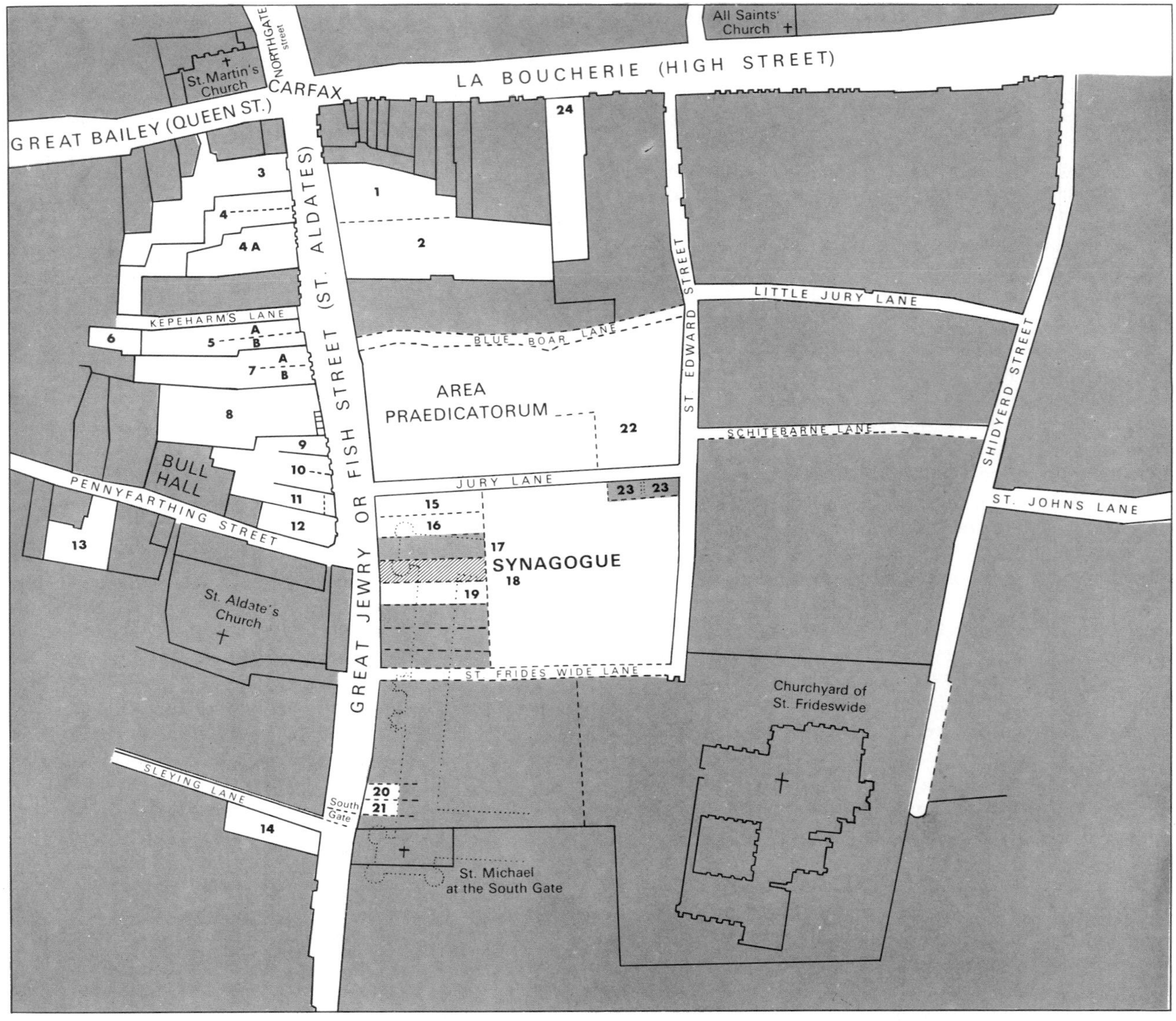

The medieval Jewry of Oxford and house owners recorded in the town registers. After C. Roth, *Jews of Medieval Oxford*, 1951.

1. Isaac b. Moses; Alberic Convers (Joscepin); Moses b. Isaac; Gildhall 1229.
2. Isaac b. Moses; Alberic Convers; David of Oxford; Domus Conversorum; Lower Gildhall.
3. Jacob b. Mag. Moses ('Jacob's Hall').
4. Moses b. Diaie; Bassena; Elekin b. Bassena.

4A. Aaron de la Rye?

5. Moses of Wallingford (?); Bonefey b. Moses; Reyna; Floria la Vedue (a).
6. Chera.
7. (a) Milo b. Deudone (b) Chera [or Vivo].
8. Josce of Colchester; Moses of Oxford; Josce b. Moses; Jacob le Eveske; Benedict le Eveske; Sarah widow of Benedict; Ducklington's Inn.
9. Samuel of Berkhamsted.
10. —father of Pya; Benedict de Caus; Pya.
11. Benedict of Winchester; Vives b. Benedict; Avegay b. Benedict.
12. Meir; Benedict de la Cornere.
13. Lumbard of Cricklade; Moyses Hall.
14. Mildegod; Vives le Lung (Keresy's Place).
15. [Simeon b. Moses?] Aaron Canis.
16. [Mag. Moses b. Simeon?]; Bonamy b. Jacob; Vives of Gloucester; Margalicia.
17. Copin of Worcester; Moses b. Jacob and Issac le Eveske.
18. Moses of Bristol and Deudone; Copin of Worcester; The Synagogue.
19. [Benjamin?]; Copin of Oxford; Mildegod; Jacob Mildegod.
20. Copin of Worcester.
21. Copin of Worcester.
22. David of Oxford; Muriel.
23. Jacob and Cresse ff. Mag. Moses.
24. Jacob and Cresse ff. Mag. Moses.

a community was organized only in 1841. Jews were first admitted to the university in 1854. By the end of the century the undergraduate element was large enough to reinforce the shrinking town community—a student society was established in 1904. Samuel *Alexander became a Fellow of Lincoln College in 1882 and James Joseph *Sylvester professor of geometry in 1883. However, such appointments became frequent only in the second quarter of the 20th century. Several distinguished German Jewish refugees arrived after 1933 and during World War II the community was enormously swollen by evacuees from London. In 1967 the Jewish population was approximately 400, in addition to approximately 200 undergraduates. However regular synagogue services are held only on the High Holidays and in termtime.

In the 16th century Hebrew studies began systematically to be pursued in the university. A regius professorship of Hebrew was established in 1546. Its incumbents included Edward *Pococke (from 1648 to 1691), E. B. Pusey (1828–1882), S. R. *Driver (1883–1914), and Herbert *Danby (1936–1953). The acquisition of the library of David *Oppenheim in 1817 made the Hebrew collection of the *Bodleian Library outstanding. H. M. J. *Loewe was lecturer in oriental languages (1914–1931). A readership in Jewish studies was established in 1939, its first incumbent being C. *Roth.

Bibliography: C. Roth, *Jews of Medieval Oxford* (1951); idem, in: *Oxford Magazine* (March 7, 1963); idem, in: *Oxoniensia*, 15 (1950), 63–80; idem, in: M. Praz (ed.), *English Miscellany*, 9 (1958), 163–71; Neubauer, in: *Collectanea of the Oxford Historical Society*, 2 (1890), 277–316; Cohen, in: JHSET, 13 (1936), 293–322.

[C.R.]

OZAR HATORAH, society for the religious education of Jewish youth in the Middle East and North Africa. Ozar Hatorah was founded in 1945 as a nonprofit organization by Isaac Shalom of New York City, Joseph Shamah of Jerusalem, and Ezra Teubal of Buenos Aires. Its founders were concerned about a result of the secularization of Jewish national life: Jewish spiritual decline and intellectual impoverishment. They hoped to rectify this by establishing schools, teaching both religious and secular subjects, throughout the Middle East and North Africa. The society, following the receipt of funds from private individuals, local communities, and the *American Jewish Joint Distribution Committee, began its work with an investigation of Jewish communities in Morocco, Algeria, Tripolitania, Cyrenaica, Egypt, Syria, Iraq, and Israel (then Palestine). With the aims of providing good teaching, facilities, food, and medical care, by 1970 Ozar Hatorah was running 23 schools and a summer camp in Morocco, 41 schools and a summer camp in Iran, two elementary schools in Syria, and an elementary school in Lyons, France, and a total of 13,610 students had been enrolled in its schools. [ED.]

OZE or **OSE**, a worldwide organization for child care, health, and hygiene among Jews, with headquarters in Paris. Launched in czarist Russia in 1912, its name is an acronym of three Russian words, *O*bshchestvo *Z*dravookhraneniya *Y*evreyev, which mean "Society for the Protection of the Health of the Jews." As the work of OZE, outlawed in Russia in 1919, spread to other countries and continents, the three initials were fitted with new words: *O*euvre de *S*ecour aux *E*nfants in France; Irgun Sanitari Ivri in Palestine; and *O*rganización para la *S*alud y *E*nseñanza in Latin America. Whatever the language, the general meaning of the name and its purpose remained the same. It signified the effort to cure or prevent sickness among Jewish people everywhere, restore and guard the health of children in OSE institutions, combat epidemics, and create living conditions under which neither individual sickness nor widespread diseases could gain new footholds.

Figure 1. Warsaw children at an OSE summer camp in Lithuania, 1925. Courtesy Joint Distribution Committee, New York.

Figure 2. An OSE nursing course in Kaunas (Kovno), Lithuania. From R. Abramovitch (ed.), *The Vanished World*, New York, 1947.

The systematic work of OSE which began in 1912 was interrupted by World War I which called for special relief measures on behalf of the war victims and hundreds of thousands of refugees and deportees from the war-stricken areas. By the end of the war, in 1917, 34 branches of OSE were already in operation in Russia. They maintained 60 dispensaries, 12 hospitals, 125 nurseries, 40 feeding centers for school children, 13 summer camps, four sanatoriums for tuberculosis patients, and other medical and child-care institutions. After the end of the war, branches of OSE spread to the new states such as Poland, Lithuania, Latvia, and Rumania as well as to Central and Western Europe, where they became very active and built a wide network of medical institutions. At that time, the headquarters of the organization were transferred to Berlin. In Poland, the branches united in 1921 under the Polish name TOZ (*T*owarzystwo *O*chrony *Z*drowia) which meant the same as OSE and had the same program of activities. Before the outbreak of World War II, TOZ maintained 368 medical and public health institutions in 72 localities where 15,443 members carried on the activities of the organization.

In the interval between the two world wars, the OSE in Poland, Rumania, Lithuania, and Latvia had under its supervision and guidance hundreds of institutions for all kinds of medical aid and child care. The results of this work was that child mortality among Jews in the countries of Eastern Europe was reduced considerably, the favus disease was eradicated, the spread of tuberculosis arrested, and general health and sanitary conditions among Jews improved. The yearly budget of all the institutions amounted to over two million dollars, about 75% acquired from local sources and about 25% from grants from the American Jewish Joint Distribution Committee and from Jewish communities all over the world. The outbreak of World War II and the Nazi Holocaust put an end to the flourishing activities and growth of the OSE. The institutions of OSE were closed, their property confiscated and looted, and their inmates and personnel sent to concentration camps and gas chambers.

After the war, OSE shifted its activities to new countries in North Africa and Latin America and to Israel, where it adjusted its program to the new conditions of life of Jews in these countries. In the postwar years, OSE carried out its relief and rehabilitation work in ten countries of Europe, nine in the Western Hemisphere, four in Africa, and in Israel, maintaining 91 medical and child-care institutions with about 85,000 children and adults under their care. The basic program of work there was the protection of mother and child, fighting epidemic diseases, school medicine and hygiene, dissemination of knowledge about preventive medicine and public health, medical research, and scholarships to physicians and nurses for professional specialization and studies. The OSE is accredited with consultative status at the United Nations Economic and Social Council, UNICEF, and the World Health Organization as a nongovernmental organization specializing in public health and child-care work among Jews.

Bibliography: J. Lestschinsky, *Ose; 40 Years of Activities and Achievements* (1952); *OSE-Rundschau*, 1–8 (1926–33); continued as: *Revue "Ose,"* 9–15 (1934–50); *Folks-gezunt*, 1–15 (1923–38); L. Gurvich, *Twenty Five Years OSE 1912–1937* (1937); L. Wulman, *Fifteen Years of Jewish Health Activities in Poland* (1937); idem, *Between Two Wars* (1941); *American OSE Review*, 1–7 (1942–50); *OSE Mail*, 1–7 (1948–54). [L.Wu.]

OZERY (Pol. **Jeziory**, Yid. **Ozhor**), town in Grodno oblast, Belorussian S. S. R. Formerly one of the royal estates where the *Magdeburg Law applied, the town was later the property of Polish nobles. Jews are mentioned in Ozery in 1667 in the *pinkas* of the Lithuanian Council (see *Councils of the Lands), in connection with a "revenge of murder" during an "assembly" in the town. In that century a wooden synagogue, widely known for its beauty, was built. In 1826 a *siddur—Tefillat Nehora ha-Shalem* —was printed at the press of Zimel Nochumowicz (of the *Romm family of printers). From 552 in 1847 the Jewish population grew to 1,892 (42.4% of the total population) in 1897, then declined to 867 (49.4%) in 1921. Ozery was known as a place for Torah study, attracting young men from the surrounding district. The main sources of Jewish livelihood were sawmills, lake fishing, tanning and other crafts, and trade. In 1937 about 89% of the 73 shops in the town were owned by Jews. Among the economic associations organized by Ozery Jews were a committee for Jewish crafts, an association of retail traders, a cooperative bank, and a free loan fund (Gemilut Ḥasadim), which had 170 members in 1924. In the mid-1920s an elementary school belonging to the CYSHO (Central Yiddish School Organization) functioned. Zionist activity started at the beginning of the century, and groups supporting the labor parties in Ereẓ Israel were active before World War II; Ozery had a center for training *ḥalutẓim*, and there was also some emigration to Ereẓ Israel. Jews from the town were among the pioneers of Jewish colonization in the Argentine.

Holocaust Period. During World War II, when the Germans occupied Ozery, the Jews were brutally treated: they were conscripted into forced labor and their property confiscated. A ghetto was soon established, enclosed by barbed wire and guarded by Jewish police and Belorussians. A Judenrat was also established. The inmates of the ghetto were taken to work in the forests and tobacco plantations,

Model of the 17th-century wooden synagogue of Ozery, Lithuania. Paris, Musée d'Art Juif. Photo Arye, Paris.

for a daily wage of one mark, half of which was deducted as "Jewish tax." Jews from nearby towns such as Eisiskes, Vasilishki, Nowy Dwor, and Porechye, were also concentrated in the ghetto of Ozery. On Nov. 11, 1942, all the Jews (1,370 according to a Nazi document) were transferred to the Kelbasin forced-labor camp near Grodno, and a few weeks later all were deported to death camps.

Bibliography: S. Dubnow (ed.) *Pinkas Medinat Lita* (1925); Institut far Vaysruslendisher Kultur, *Tsaytshrift*, 2–3 (1928), 370; KS, 8 (1931/32), 237; *Grodner Opklangen* (1950), 6. [D.R.]

OZON: Obóz Zjednoczenia Narodowego (Pol. "Camp of National Unity"), a paramilitary, anti-Semitic organization created in Poland on Oct. 2, 1937 by Colonel Adam Koc, under the auspices of President Moscicki and the minister of defense, Rydz-Smigły. Its program called for the protection of peasant ownership, the improvement of small holdings, and the control of population by encouraging peasants to migrate to the cities. By camouflaging its anti-Semitism with problems of national self-defense, OZON hoped to compete with other rightist Fascist organizations such as ONR and win over the masses. Based on nationalism, Catholicism, and anti-Semitism, OZON hoped to divert the attention of workers and peasants from the real issues of the day, such as unemployment and poverty. It encouraged disorder and lawlessness, advocated segregation in the universities, and made assaults on Jewish rights. No Jew—not even one who had fought for Poland's independence in *Pilsudski's Legion—was eligible to join OZON. Many arbitrary and even brutal anti-Jewish policies and acts, such as restricting the right of **sheḥitah*, insisting that "Aryan" principles should prevail in professional organizations, establishing economic boycotts, destroying Jewish property, and encouraging pogroms in *Radom, *Częstochowa, *Brest-Litovsk, and *Vilna, were carried out under the aegis of OZON. In December 1938 Koc, whose totalitarian tendencies were becoming too apparent, was forced to give up his leadership of OZON and was replaced by General Skwarczynski. The anti-Semitic activities of OZON continued, however, under new leadership, and Skwarczynski asked the Polish *Sejm to take energetic measures to reduce the number of Jews in Poland, for national defense reasons. As a result the Polish government opposed the British mandatory restrictions on the admission of Jews to Palestine and sent a delegation to *Madagascar to study the possibilities of Jewish immigration there. OZON continued its activities until the defeat of Poland in September 1939.

Bibliography: S. Segal, *The New Poland and the Jews* (1938), 68–75; R. L. Buell, *Poland: Key to Europe* (1939), index; I. Gruenbaum, in: EG, 1 (1953), 113–6; *Wielka Encyklopedia Powszechna*, 8 (1966), 90. [Ed.]

OZORKOW, town in Lodz province, Poland. Founded in 1811, the settlement expanded rapidly and was granted urban status in 1816. Its Jewish population grew in size because it was dependent on the development of the textile industry in Lodz. In 1860 there were 1,978 Jews (38% of the total population) and on the eve of the Holocaust in 1939 they numbered about 5,000 (33% of the total population). During the 19th century Jews established workshops for weaving. Jewish tailors were also employed by industrial enterprises in Lodz on a contractual basis. The first democratic elections to the community council were held in 1922 when 12 members were elected representing the Zionist parties, *Mizrachi, *Agudat Israel, *Bund, and *Po'alei Zion-Left. On the eve of World War II Solomon Winter, the delegate of the Zionists, was president of the community. There was a ramified network of schools in

Ozorkow established at the initiative of the Zionists (Yavneh) and Agudat Israel (Yesodei ha-Torah). The public libraries established by the Zionist Organization and Po'alei Zion stimulated cultural activities such as drama circles, evening schools, and the sports societies: *Maccabi and Ha-Kokhav (Gwiazda). In addition to the two large synagogues, the "Great Synagogue" and the "Bet ha-Midrash," there were ḥasidic houses of prayer. The last rabbi of the community was R. David Behr. The Jews were also represented on the municipal council and their delegates held the position of vice-mayor. [SH.L.K.]

Holocaust Period. At the outbreak of World War II there were several battles around Ozorkow, and immediately after occupying the city on Sept. 5, 1939, the Germans seized and shot 24 Jews in the street. The beautiful synagogue and the *bet ha-midrash* were burned and the Jews were forced to demolish the walls. Frequent raids took place for slave labor in addition to the regular supply of labor contingents from the *Judenrat. Toward the end of 1939 many Jewish families were evicted from their homes and the ghetto gradually established. The liquidation of the community took place during the spring and summer of 1942 in a series of *aktionen* the first of which was the selection of 500 Jews who were sent in an unknown direction, probably to the *Chelmno death camp. In April the Germans carried out a public hanging of eight Jews to "punish" the community for the escape of a woman from the ghetto. The largest *aktion* took place on May 21–23, 1942, when 2,000 Jews were sent to Chelmno and 800 of the able-bodied to *Lodz ghetto. All children below the age of ten were seized and deported. The final deportation took place on Aug. 21, 1942, when about 1,200 craftsmen and artisans were transferred to Lodz ghetto. A memorial book, *Ozorkov,* was published in Hebrew in 1967. [DE.D.]

Bibliography: Dabrowska, in: BZIH, no. 13–14 (1955).

Come ye and let us go up to the mountain of the Lo
of His ways and we will walk in His paths for out o
Jeru